Key to World Map Pages

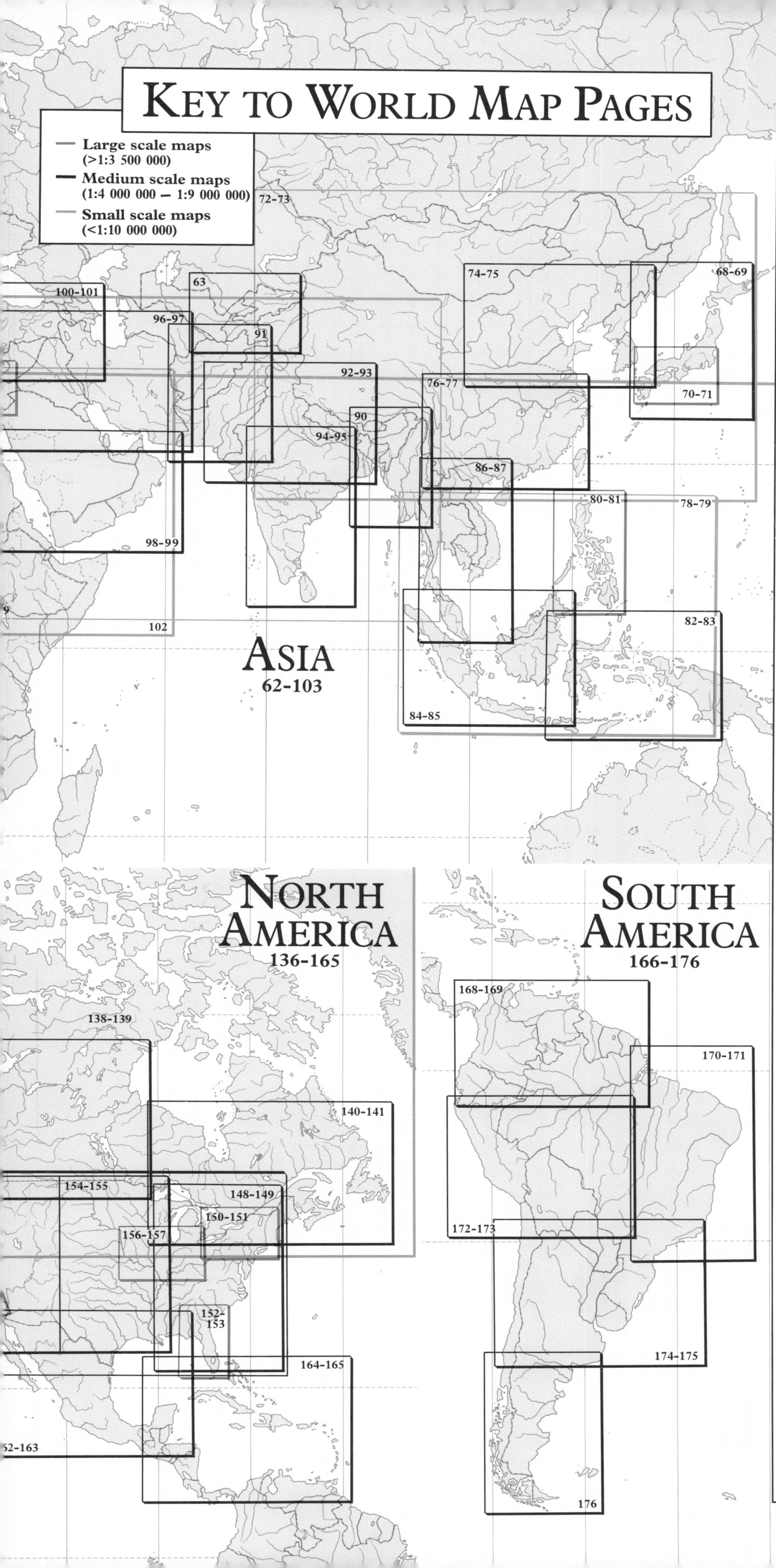

Large scale maps (>1:3 500 000)
Medium scale maps (1:4 000 000 – 1:9 000 000)
Small scale maps (<1:10 000 000)
ASIA 62-103
NORTH AMERICA 136-165
SOUTH AMERICA 166-176
72-73
100-101
63
96-97
91
92-93
90
94-95
98-99
102
74-75
68-69
70-71
76-77
86-87
80-81
78-79
82-83
84-85
138-139
140-141
154-155
148-149
150-151
156-157
152-153
164-165
162-163
168-169
170-171
172-173
174-175
176

Country Index

ATLAS
OF THE
WORLD

OXFORD

ATLAS OF THE WORLD

SEVENTH EDITION

Specialist Geography Consultants

The editors are grateful to the following people for acting as specialist geography consultants on the "*Introduction to World Geography*" front section:

Professor D. Brunsden, Kings College, University of London, UK

Dr C. Clarke, Oxford University, UK

Professor P. Haggett, University of Bristol, UK

Professor M-L. Hsu, University of Minnesota, Minnesota, USA

Professor K. McLachlan, Geopolitical and International Boundaries Research Centre, School of Oriental and African Studies, University of London, UK

Professor M. Monmonier, Syracuse University, New York, USA

Professor M. J. Tooley, University of St Andrews, UK

Dr T. Unwin, Royal Holloway, University of London, UK

The editors would also like to thank:

Keith Lye

Robin Scagell

Dr I. S. Evans, Durham University, UK

Introduction to World Geography
Picture Acknowledgements
Courtesy of NPA Group, Edenbridge, UK 48
Science Photo Library /BP/NRSC 9, /Earth Satellite Corporation 20, /NOAA 22 bottom left and bottom right

Illustrations
Stefan Chabluk
William Donohoe
Bernard Thornton Artists /Steve Seymour

Star charts
John Cox and Richard Monkhouse

Cartography by Philip's

Foreword

An authoritative and serious reference work, the Oxford *Atlas of the World* is one of the finest atlases available anywhere in the world. The atlas incorporates computer-derived maps which have been produced using the very latest in digital cartographic techniques.

The Oxford *Atlas of the World* has been revised and updated with the help of a panel of specialist geography consultants from the United Kingdom and the United States, whose specialties range from the history of cartography, urban and social geography, epidemiology and the European Union to biogeography and applied geomorphology. The result of their valuable input can be seen in the wealth of up-to-date maps and data contained in the "*Introduction to World Geography*" section of this atlas.

How to use the Atlas
The atlas is divided into a number of sections which are explained below.

World Statistics
Six pages of world statistics on topics such as area and population for every country in the world, city populations for the largest cities, climate statistics and physical dimensions – including the largest islands, lakes and seas, the highest mountains and the longest rivers, by continent. Also included in this section is a selection of detailed, up-to-date maps highlighting regions around the world that are currently in the news, such as the former Yugoslavia and Kosovo, the Near East, Iraq's "no-fly zone," Congo and its neighbors, and the "euroland" countries.

Introduction to World Geography
A richly informative section comprising 48 pages of up-to-date maps, charts, graphs and clear diagrams which explain key themes about the world in which we live. The topics covered include the Solar System, oceans, climate, the environment, cities, energy and trade. Introductory text on each spread describes and explains the patterns shown by the data.

City Maps
A detailed selection of maps for 66 urban areas around the world. These are useful for planning trips abroad as well as for comparative studies of cities worldwide. Also included is a 16-page index to the city maps.

World Maps
An outstanding collection of 176 pages of distinctive Philip's cartography. The highly acclaimed physical world maps combine relief shading with layer-colored contours to give a striking visual picture of the Earth's surface. Roads, railroads, canals, and airports are accurately depicted on the maps, and towns and cities are clearly marked. The maps show the recent place name changes in the countries of the former USSR. More information on the key features employed in the construction and presentation of the maps is given on the facing page.

Index
The 75,000-name index to the world maps includes geographical features as well as towns and cities, with both latitude/longitude and letter/figure grid references.

World Maps

The reference maps which form the main body of this atlas have been prepared in accordance with the highest standards of international cartography to provide an accurate and detailed representation of the Earth. The scales and projections used have been carefully chosen to give balanced coverage of the world, while emphasizing the most densely populated and economically significant regions. A hallmark of Philip's mapping is the use of hill shading and relief coloring to create a graphic impression of landforms: this makes the maps exceptionally easy to read. However, knowledge of the key features employed in the construction and presentation of the maps will enable the reader to derive the fullest benefit from the atlas.

Map Sequence

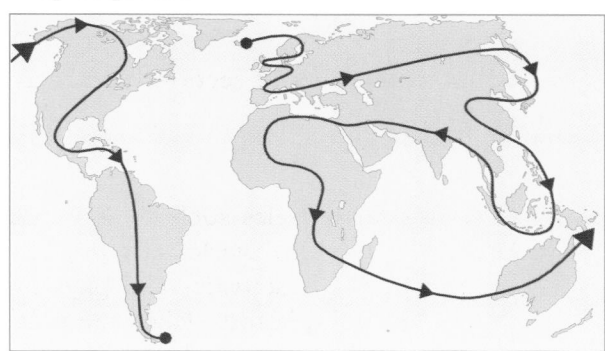

The atlas covers the Earth continent by continent: first Europe; then its land neighbor Asia (mapped north before south, in a clockwise sequence), then Africa, Australia and Oceania, North America and South America. This is the classic arrangement adopted by most cartographers since the 16th century. For each continent, there are maps at a variety of scales. First, physical relief and political maps of the whole continent; then a series of larger-scale maps of the regions within the continent, each followed, where required, by still larger-scale maps of the most important or densely populated areas. The governing principle is that by turning the pages of the atlas, the reader moves steadily from north to south through each continent, with each map overlapping its neighbors. A key map showing this sequence, and the area covered by each map, can be found on the endpapers of the atlas.

Map Presentation

With very few exceptions (e.g. for the Arctic and Antarctic), the maps are drawn with north at the top, regardless of whether they are presented upright or sideways on the page. In the borders will be found the map title; a locator diagram showing the area covered and the page numbers for maps of adjacent areas; the scale; the projection used; the degrees of latitude and longitude; and the letters and figures used in the index for locating place names and geographical features. Physical relief maps also have a height reference panel identifying the colors used for each layer of contouring.

Map Symbols

Each map contains a vast amount of detail which can only be conveyed clearly and accurately by the use of symbols. Points and circles of varying sizes locate and identify the relative importance of towns and cities; different styles of type are employed for administrative, geographical and regional place names to aid identification. A variety of pictorial symbols denote landforms such as glaciers, marshes and coral reefs, and man-made structures including roads, railroads, airports and canals. International borders are shown by red lines. Where neighboring countries are in dispute, for example in parts of the Middle East, the maps show the *de facto* boundary between nations, regardless of the legal or historical situation. The symbols are explained on the first page of the World Maps section of the atlas.

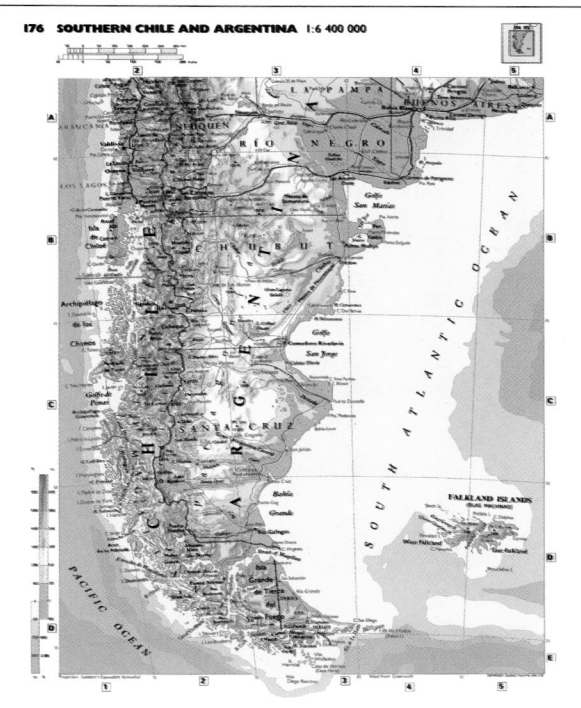

Map Scales

1:16 000 000
1 inch = 252 statute miles

The scale of each map is given in the numerical form known as the "representative fraction." The first figure is always one, signifying one unit of distance on the map; the second figure, usually in millions, is the number by which the map unit must be multiplied to give the equivalent distance on the Earth's surface. Calculations can easily be made in centimeters and kilometers, by dividing the Earth units figure by 100 000 (i.e. deleting the last five 0s). Thus 1:1 000 000 means 1 cm = 10 km. The calculation for inches and miles is more laborious, but 1 000 000 divided by 63 360 (the number of inches in a mile) shows that 1:1 000 000 means approximately 1 inch = 16 miles. The table below provides distance equivalents for scales down to 1:50 000 000.

LARGE SCALE		
1:1 000 000	1 cm = 10 km	1 inch = 16 miles
1:2 500 000	1 cm = 25 km	1 inch = 39.5 miles
1:5 000 000	1 cm = 50 km	1 inch = 79 miles
1:6 000 000	1 cm = 60 km	1 inch = 95 miles
1:8 000 000	1 cm = 80 km	1 inch = 126 miles
1:10 000 000	1 cm = 100 km	1 inch = 158 miles
1:15 000 000	1 cm = 150 km	1 inch = 237 miles
1:20 000 000	1 cm = 200 km	1 inch = 316 miles
1:50 000 000	1 cm = 500 km	1 inch = 790 miles
SMALL SCALE		

Measuring Distances

Although each map is accompanied by a scale bar, distances cannot always be measured with confidence because of the distortions involved in portraying the curved surface of the Earth on a flat page. As a general rule, the larger the map scale, the more accurate and reliable will be the distance measured. On small-scale maps such as those of the world and of entire continents, measurement may only be accurate along the "standard parallels," or central axes, and should not be attempted without considering the map projection.

Map Projections

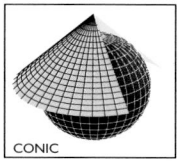  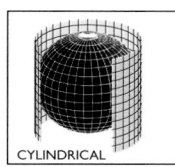

Unlike a globe, no flat map can give a true scale representation of the world in terms of area, shape and position of every region. Each of the numerous systems that have been devised for projecting the curved surface of the Earth on to a flat page involves the sacrifice of accuracy in one or more of these elements. The variations in shape and position of land masses such as Alaska, Greenland and Australia, for example, can be quite dramatic when different projections are compared.

For this atlas, the guiding principle has been to select projections that involve the least distortion of size and distance. The projection used for each map is noted in the border. Most fall into one of three categories – conic, cylindrical or azimuthal – whose basic concepts are shown above. Each involves plotting the forms of the Earth's surface on a grid of latitude and longitude lines, which may be shown as parallels, curves or radiating spokes.

Latitude and Longitude

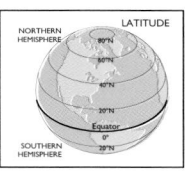 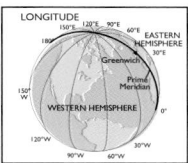 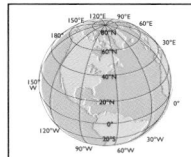

Accurate positioning of individual points on the Earth's surface is made possible by reference to the geometrical system of latitude and longitude. Latitude parallels are drawn west–east around the Earth and numbered by degrees north and south of the Equator, which is designated 0° of latitude. Longitude meridians are drawn north–south and numbered by degrees east and west of the prime meridian, 0° of longitude, which passes through Greenwich in England. By referring to these coordinates and their subdivisions of minutes (1/60th of a degree) and seconds (1/60th of a minute), any place on Earth can be located to within a few hundred yards. Latitude and longitude are indicated by blue lines on the maps; they are straight or curved according to the projection employed. Reference to these lines is the easiest way of determining the relative positions of places on different maps, and for plotting compass directions.

Name Forms

For ease of reference, both English and local name forms appear in the atlas. Oceans, seas and countries are shown in English throughout the atlas; country names may be abbreviated to their commonly accepted form (e.g. Germany, not The Federal Republic of Germany). Conventional English forms are also used for place names on the smaller-scale maps of the continents. However, local name forms are used on all large-scale and regional maps, with the English form given in brackets only for important cities – the large-scale map of Russia and Central Asia thus shows Moskva (Moscow). For countries which do not use a Roman script, place names have been transcribed according to the systems adopted by the British and US Geographic Names Authorities. For China, the Pin Yin system has been used, with some more widely known forms appearing in brackets, as with Beijing (Peking). Both English and local names appear in the index, the English form being cross-referenced to the local form.

Contents

World Statistics

Introduction to World Geography

City Maps
1–32

(Scale 1:200 000)

Index to City Maps
33–48

World Maps
1–176

The World

Europe

Scandinavia
1:4 000 000
Norway, Sweden, *Finland*

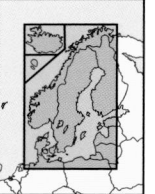

14–15

Denmark and Southern Sweden
1:2 000 000
Denmark, *Norway*, *Sweden*

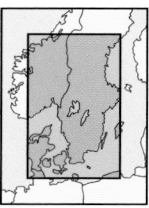

16–17

South Norway
1:2 000 000

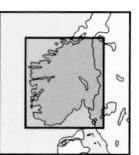

18

British Isles and North Sea
1:4 000 000

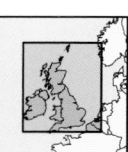

19

NOTE
The titles to the World Maps list the main countries, states and provinces covered by each map. A name given in *italics* indicates that only part of the country is shown on the map.

England and Wales
1:1 600 000
Isle of Man, Channel Islands

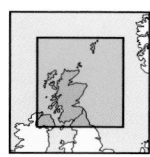

Scotland
1:1 600 000

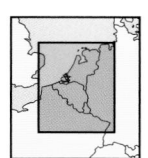

Ireland
1:1 600 000
Irish Republic, Northern Ireland

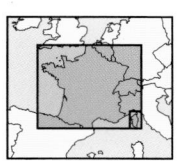

Netherlands, Belgium and Luxembourg
1:2 000 000

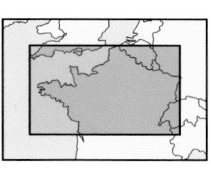

France
1:4 000 000

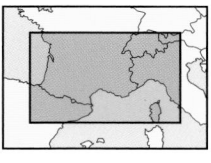

Northern France
1:2 000 000

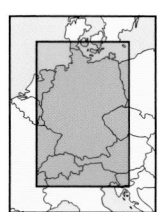

Southern France
1:2 000 000
Monaco

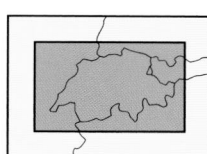

Germany
1:2 000 000

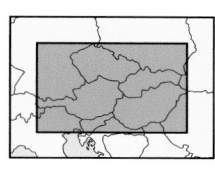

Switzerland
1:800 000
Liechtenstein

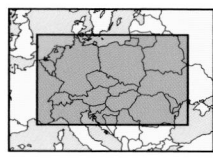

Austria, Czech Republic and Slovak Republic
1:2 000 000

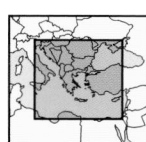

Central Europe
1:4 000 000

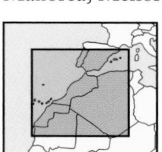

Malta, Crete, Corfu, Rhodes and Cyprus
1:800 000 / 1:1 040 000

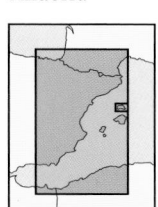

Balearics, Canaries and Madeira
1:800 000 / 1:1 600 000
Mallorca, Menorca, Ibiza

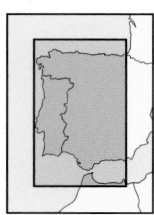

Eastern Spain
1:2 000 000
Andorra

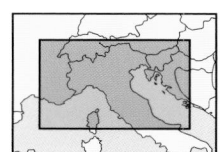

Western Spain and Portugal
1:2 000 000

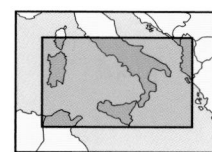

Northern Italy, Slovenia and Croatia
1:2 000 000

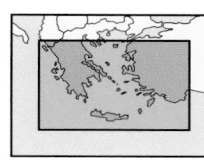

Southern Italy
1:2 000 000

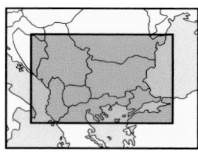

Southern Greece
1:2 000 000
Turkey

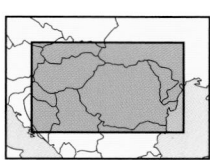

Northern Greece, Bulgaria and Yugoslavia
1:2 000 000
Macedonia

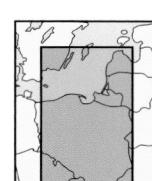

Hungary, Romania and the Lower Danube
1:2 000 000
Moldova

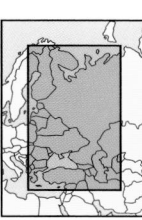

Poland and the Southern Baltic
1:2 000 000
Latvia, Lithuania

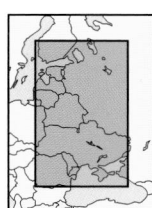

Eastern Europe and Turkey
1:8 000 000

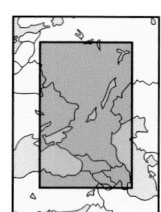

Baltic States, Belarus and Ukraine
1:4 000 000
Russia, Estonia, Latvia, Lithuania, Belarus, *Ukraine*

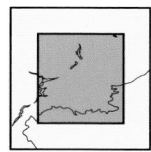

Volga Basin and the Caucasus
1:4 000 000
Russia, Georgia, Armenia, Azerbaijan

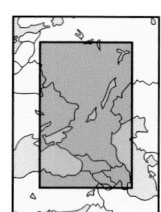

Asia

Southern Urals
1:4 000 000
Russia

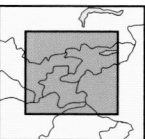

Central Asia
1:4 000 000
Kazakstan, *Kyrgyzstan*, Tajikistan, *Uzbekistan*

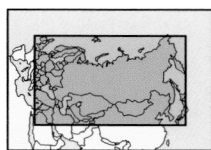

Russia and Central Asia
1:16 000 000
Russia, Kazakstan, Turkmenistan, Uzbekistan

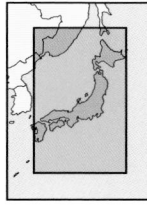

Asia: Physical
1:40 000 000

Asia: Political
1:40 000 000

Japan
1:4 000 000
Ryukyu Islands

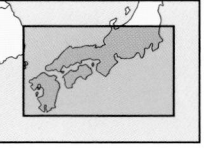

Southern Japan
1:2 000 000

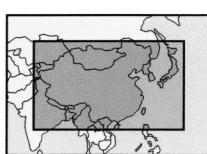
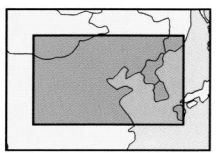
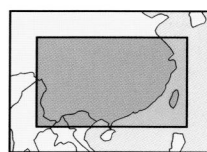
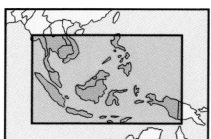
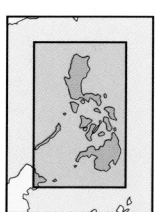
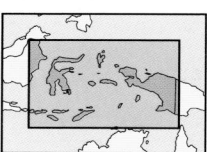
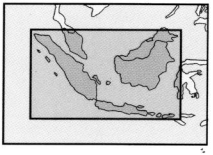
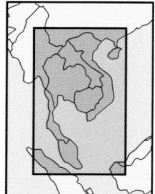
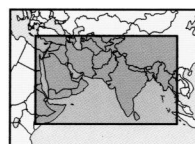
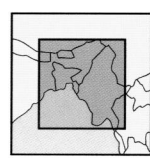

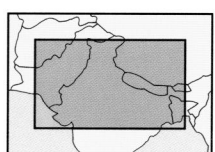
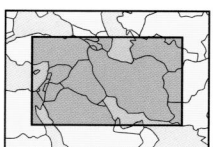
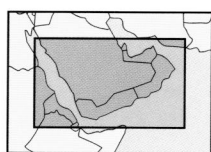
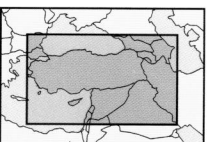
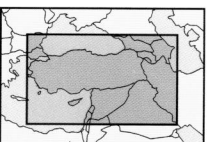
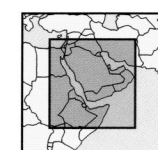
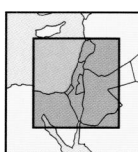
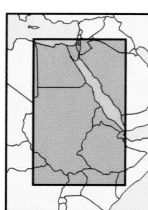
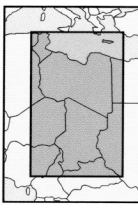
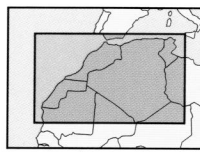
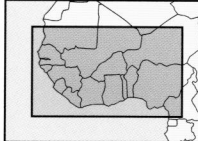
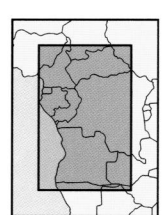
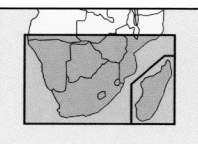
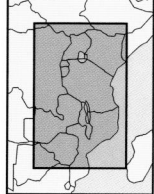
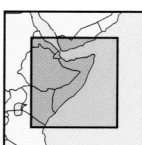

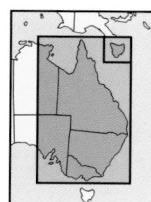
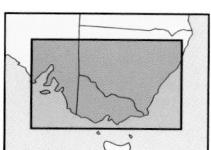
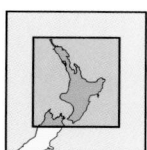

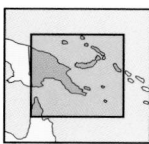
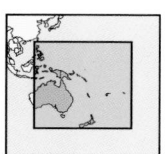
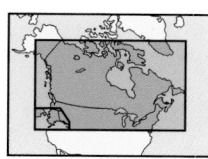
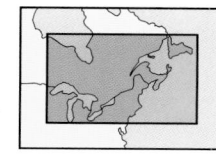
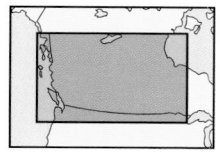

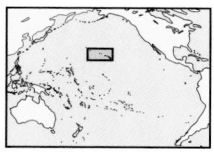
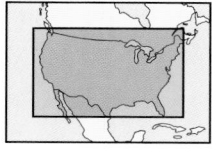
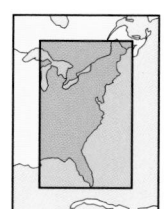
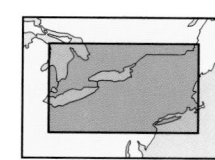

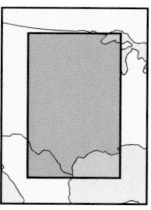
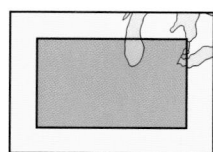
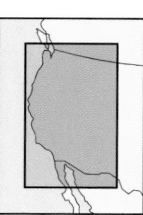
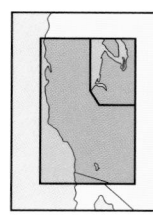
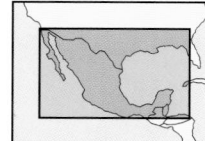
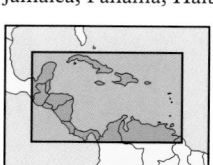
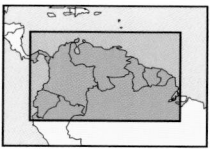

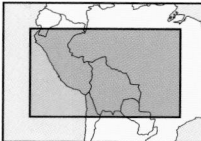
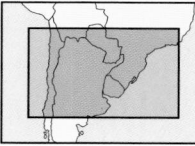
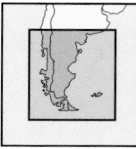

World Statistics: Countries

This alphabetical list includes all the countries and territories of the world. If a territory is not completely independent, then the country it is associated with is named. The area figures give the total area of land, inland water and ice. Units for areas and populations are thousands. The population figures are 1998 estimates. The annual income is the Gross National Product per capita in US dollars. The figures are the latest available, usually 1997.

Country/Territory	Area km² Thousands	Area miles² Thousands	Population Thousands	Capital	Annual Income US $
Adélie Land (France)	432	167	0.03	–	–
Afghanistan	652	252	24,792	Kabul	600
Albania	28.8	11.1	3,331	Tirana	750
Algeria	2,382	920	30,481	Algiers	1,490
American Samoa (US)	0.20	0.08	62	Pago Pago	2,600
Amsterdam Is. (France)	0.05	0.02	0.03	–	–
Andorra	0.45	0.17	75	Andorra La Vella	16,200
Angola	1,247	481	11,200	Luanda	340
Anguilla (UK)	0.1	0.04	11	The Valley	6,800
Antigua & Barbuda	0.44	0.17	64	St John's	7,330
Argentina	2,767	1,068	36,265	Buenos Aires	8,750
Armenia	29.8	11.5	3,422	Yerevan	530
Aruba (Netherlands)	0.19	0.07	69	Oranjestad	15,890
Ascension Is. (UK)	0.09	0.03	1.5	Georgetown	–
Australia	7,687	2,968	18,613	Canberra	20,540
Australian Antarctic Terr. (Aus.)	6,120	2,363	0	–	–
Austria	83.9	32.4	8,134	Vienna	27,980
Azerbaijan	86.6	33.4	7,856	Baku	510
Azores (Portugal)	2.2	0.87	238	Ponta Delgada	–
Bahamas	13.9	5.4	280	Nassau	11,940
Bahrain	0.68	0.26	616	Manama	7,840
Bangladesh	144	56	125,000	Dhaka	270
Barbados	0.43	0.17	259	Bridgetown	6,560
Belarus	207.6	80.1	10,409	Minsk	2,150
Belgium	30.5	11.8	10,175	Brussels	26,420
Belize	23	8.9	230	Belmopan	2,700
Benin	113	43	6,101	Porto-Novo	380
Bermuda (UK)	0.05	0.02	62	Hamilton	31,870
Bhutan	47	18.1	1,908	Thimphu	390
Bolivia	1,099	424	7,826	La Paz/Sucre	950
Bosnia-Herzegovina	51	20	3,366	Sarajevo	300
Botswana	582	225	1,448	Gaborone	4,381
Bouvet Is. (Norway)	0.05	0.02	0.02	–	–
Brazil	8,512	3,286	170,000	Brasília	4,720
British Antarctic Terr. (UK)	1,709	660	0.3	–	–
British Indian Ocean Terr. (UK)	0.08	0.03	0	–	–
Brunei	5.8	2.2	315	Bandar Seri Begawan	15,800
Bulgaria	111	43	8,240	Sofia	1,140
Burkina Faso	274	106	11,266	Ouagadougou	240
Burma (= Myanmar)	677	261	47,305	Rangoon	1,790
Burundi	27.8	10.7	5,531	Bujumbura	180
Cambodia	181	70	11,340	Phnom Penh	300
Cameroon	475	184	15,029	Yaoundé	650
Canada	9,976	3,852	30,675	Ottawa	19,290
Canary Is. (Spain)	7.3	2.8	1,494	Las Palmas/Santa Cruz	–
Cape Verde Is.	4	1.6	399	Praia	1,010
Cayman Is. (UK)	0.26	0.10	35	George Town	20,000
Central African Republic	623	241	3,376	Bangui	320
Chad	1,284	496	7,360	Ndjaména	240
Chatham Is. (NZ)	0.96	0.37	0.05	Waitangi	–
Chile	757	292	14,788	Santiago	5,020
China	9,597	3,705	1,236,915	Beijing	860
Christmas Is. (Australia)	0.14	0.05	2	The Settlement	–
Cocos (Keeling) Is. (Australia)	0.01	0.005	1	West Island	–
Colombia	1,139	440	38,581	Bogotá	2,280
Comoros	2.2	0.86	545	Moroni	450
Congo	342	132	2,658	Brazzaville	660
Congo (= Zaïre)	2,345	905	49,001	Kinshasa	110
Cook Is. (NZ)	0.24	0.09	20	Avarua	900
Costa Rica	51.1	19.7	3,605	San José	2,640
Croatia	56.5	21.8	4,672	Zagreb	4,610
Crozet Is. (France)	0.51	0.19	35	–	–
Cuba	111	43	11,051	Havana	1,300
Cyprus	9.3	3.6	749	Nicosia	13,420
Czech Republic	78.9	30.4	10,286	Prague	5,200
Denmark	43.1	16.6	5,334	Copenhagen	32,500
Djibouti	23.2	9	650	Djibouti	850
Dominica	0.75	0.29	78	Roseau	3,090
Dominican Republic	48.7	18.8	7,999	Santo Domingo	1,670
Ecuador	284	109	12,337	Quito	1,590
Egypt	1,001	387	66,050	Cairo	1,180
El Salvador	21	8.1	5,752	San Salvador	1,810
Equatorial Guinea	28.1	10.8	454	Malabo	530
Eritrea	94	36	3,842	Asmara	570
Estonia	44.7	17.3	1,421	Tallinn	3,330
Ethiopia	1,128	436	58,390	Addis Ababa	110
Falkland Is. (UK)	12.2	4.7	2	Stanley	–
Faroe Is. (Denmark)	1.4	0.54	41	Tórshavn	23,660
Fiji	18.3	7.1	802	Suva	2,470
Finland	338	131	5,149	Helsinki	24,080
France	552	213	58,805	Paris	26,050
French Guiana (France)	90	34.7	162	Cayenne	10,580
French Polynesia (France)	4	1.5	237	Papeete	7,500
Gabon	268	103	1,208	Libreville	4,230
Gambia, The	11.3	4.4	1,292	Banjul	320
Georgia	69.7	26.9	5,109	Tbilisi	840
Germany	357	138	82,079	Berlin/Bonn	28,260
Ghana	239	92	18,497	Accra	370
Gibraltar (UK)	0.007	0.003	29	Gibraltar Town	5,000
Greece	132	51	10,662	Athens	12,010
Greenland (Denmark)	2,176	840	59	Nuuk (Godthåb)	15,500
Grenada	0.34	0.13	96	St George's	2,880
Guadeloupe (France)	1.7	0.66	416	Basse-Terre	9,200
Guam (US)	0.55	0.21	149	Agana	6,000
Guatemala	109	42	12,008	Guatemala City	1,500
Guinea	246	95	7,477	Conakry	570
Guinea-Bissau	36.1	13.9	1,206	Bissau	240
Guyana	215	83	820	Georgetown	690
Haiti	27.8	10.7	6,781	Port-au-Prince	330
Honduras	112	43	5,862	Tegucigalpa	700
Hong Kong (China)	1.1	0.40	6,707	–	22,990
Hungary	93	35.9	10,208	Budapest	4,430
Iceland	103	40	271	Reykjavik	26,580
India	3,288	1,269	984,000	New Delhi	390
Indonesia	1,905	735	212,942	Jakarta	1,110
Iran	1,648	636	64,411	Tehran	4,700
Iraq	438	169	21,722	Baghdad	2,000
Ireland	70.3	27.1	3,619	Dublin	18,280
Israel	27	10.3	5,644	Jerusalem	15,810
Italy	301	116	56,783	Rome	20,120
Ivory Coast (Côte d'Ivoire)	322	125	15,446	Yamoussoukro	690
Jamaica	11	4.2	2,635	Kingston	1,560
Jan Mayen Is. (Norway)	0.38	0.15	1	–	–
Japan	378	146	125,932	Tokyo	37,850
Johnston Is. (US)	0.002	0.0009	1	–	–
Jordan	89.2	34.4	4,435	Amman	1,570
Kazakstan	2,717	1,049	16,847	Astana	1,340
Kenya	580	224	28,337	Nairobi	330
Kerguelen Is. (France)	7.2	2.8	0.7	–	–
Kermadec Is. (NZ)	0.03	0.01	0.1	–	–
Kiribati	0.72	0.28	85	Tarawa	920
Korea, North	121	47	21,234	Pyŏngyang	1,000
Korea, South	99	38.2	46,417	Seoul	10,550
Kuwait	17.8	6.9	1,913	Kuwait City	17,390
Kyrgyzstan	198.5	76.6	4,522	Bishkek	440
Laos	237	91	5,261	Vientiane	400
Latvia	65	25	2,385	Riga	2,430
Lebanon	10.4	4	3,506	Beirut	3,350
Lesotho	30.4	11.7	2,090	Maseru	670
Liberia	111	43	2,772	Monrovia	770
Libya	1,760	679	4,875	Tripoli	6,510
Liechtenstein	0.16	0.06	32	Vaduz	33,000
Lithuania	65.2	25.2	3,600	Vilnius	2,230
Luxembourg	2.6	1	425	Luxembourg	45,360
Macau (China)	0.02	0.006	429	Macau	7,500
Macedonia	25.7	9.9	2,009	Skopje	1,090
Madagascar	587	227	14,463	Antananarivo	250
Madeira (Portugal)	0.81	0.31	253	Funchal	–
Malawi	118	46	9,840	Lilongwe	220
Malaysia	330	127	20,993	Kuala Lumpur	4,680
Maldives	0.30	0.12	290	Malé	1,080
Mali	1,240	479	10,109	Bamako	260
Malta	0.32	0.12	379	Valletta	12,000
Marshall Is.	0.18	0.07	63	Dalap-Uliga-Darrit	1,890
Martinique (France)	1.1	0.42	407	Fort-de-France	10,000
Mauritania	1,030	412	2,511	Nouakchott	450
Mauritius	2.0	0.72	1,168	Port Louis	3,800
Mayotte (France)	0.37	0.14	141	Mamoundzou	1,430
Mexico	1,958	756	98,553	Mexico City	3,680
Micronesia, Fed. States of	0.70	0.27	127	Palikir	2,070
Midway Is. (US)	0.005	0.002	2	–	–
Moldova	33.7	13	4,458	Chişinău	540
Monaco	0.002	0.0001	32	Monaco	25,000
Mongolia	1,567	605	2,579	Ulan Bator	390
Montserrat (UK)	0.10	0.04	12	Plymouth	4,500
Morocco	447	172	29,114	Rabat	1,250
Mozambique	802	309	18,641	Maputo	90
Namibia	825	318	1,622	Windhoek	2,220
Nauru	0.02	0.008	12	Yaren District	10,000
Nepal	141	54	23,698	Katmandu	210
Netherlands	41.5	16	15,731	Amsterdam/The Hague	25,820
Netherlands Antilles (Neths)	0.99	0.38	210	Willemstad	10,400
New Caledonia (France)	18.6	7.2	192	Nouméa	8,000
New Zealand	269	104	3,625	Wellington	16,480
Nicaragua	130	50	4,583	Managua	410
Niger	1,267	489	9,672	Niamey	200
Nigeria	924	357	110,532	Abuja	260
Niue (NZ)	0.26	0.10	2	Alofi	–
Norfolk Is. (Australia)	0.03	0.01	2	Kingston	–
Northern Mariana Is. (US)	0.48	0.18	50	Saipan	11,500
Norway	324	125	4,420	Oslo	36,090
Oman	212	82	2,364	Muscat	4,950
Pakistan	796	307	135,135	Islamabad	490
Palau	0.46	0.18	18	Koror	5,000
Panama	77.1	29.8	2,736	Panama City	3,080
Papua New Guinea	463	179	4,600	Port Moresby	940
Paraguay	407	157	5,291	Asunción	2,010
Peru	1,285	496	26,111	Lima	2,460
Peter 1st Is. (Norway)	0.18	0.07	0	–	–
Philippines	300	116	77,736	Manila	1,220
Pitcairn Is. (UK)	0.03	0.01	0.05	Adamstown	–
Poland	313	121	38,607	Warsaw	3,590
Portugal	92.4	35.7	9,928	Lisbon	10,450
Puerto Rico (US)	9	3.5	3,860	San Juan	7,800
Qatar	11	4.2	697	Doha	11,600
Queen Maud Land (Norway)	2,800	1,081	0	–	–
Réunion (France)	2.5	0.97	705	Saint-Denis	4,500
Romania	238	92	22,396	Bucharest	1,420
Ross Dependency (NZ)	435	168	0	–	–
Russia	17,075	6,592	146,861	Moscow	2,740
Rwanda	26.3	10.2	7,956	Kigali	210
St Helena (UK)	0.12	0.05	7	Jamestown	–
St Kitts & Nevis	0.36	0.14	42	Basseterre	5,870
St Lucia	0.62	0.24	150	Castries	3,500
St Paul Is. (France)	0.007	0.003	0	–	–
St Pierre & Miquelon (France)	0.24	0.09	7	Saint Pierre	–
St Vincent & Grenadines	0.39	0.15	120	Kingstown	2,370
San Marino	0.06	0.02	25	San Marino	20,000
São Tomé & Príncipe	0.96	0.37	150	São Tomé	330
Saudi Arabia	2,150	830	20,786	Riyadh	6,790
Senegal	197	76	9,723	Dakar	550
Seychelles	0.46	0.18	79	Victoria	6,850
Sierra Leone	71.7	27.7	5,080	Freetown	200
Singapore	0.62	0.24	3,490	Singapore	32,940
Slovak Republic	49	18.9	5,393	Bratislava	3,700
Slovenia	20.3	7.8	1,972	Ljubljana	9,680
Solomon Is.	28.9	11.2	441	Honiara	900
Somalia	638	246	6,842	Mogadishu	500
South Africa	1,220	471	42,835	C. Town/Pretoria/Bloemfontein	3,400
South Georgia (UK)	3.8	1.4	0.05	–	–
South Sandwich Is. (UK)	0.38	0.15	0	–	–
Spain	505	195	39,134	Madrid	14,510
Sri Lanka	65.6	25.3	18,934	Colombo	800
Sudan	2,506	967	33,551	Khartoum	800
Surinam	163	63	427	Paramaribo	1,000
Svalbard (Norway)	62.9	24.3	4	Longyearbyen	–
Swaziland	17.4	6.7	966	Mbabane	1,210
Sweden	450	174	8,887	Stockholm	26,220
Switzerland	41.3	15.9	7,260	Bern	44,220
Syria	185	71	16,673	Damascus	1,150
Taiwan	36	13.9	21,908	Taipei	12,400
Tajikistan	143.1	55.2	6,020	Dushanbe	330
Tanzania	945	365	30,609	Dodoma	210
Thailand	513	198	60,037	Bangkok	2,800
Togo	56.8	21.9	4,906	Lomé	330
Tokelau (NZ)	0.01	0.005	2	Nukunonu	–
Tonga	0.75	0.29	107	Nuku'alofa	1,790
Trinidad & Tobago	5.1	2	1,117	Port of Spain	4,230
Tristan da Cunha (UK)	0.11	0.04	0.33	Edinburgh	–
Tunisia	164	63	9,380	Tunis	2,090
Turkey	779	301	64,568	Ankara	3,130
Turkmenistan	488.1	188.5	4,298	Ashkhabad	630
Turks & Caicos Is. (UK)	0.43	0.17	16	Cockburn Town	5,000
Tuvalu	0.03	0.01	10	Fongafale	600
Uganda	236	91	22,167	Kampala	320
Ukraine	603.7	233.1	50,125	Kiev	1,040
United Arab Emirates	83.6	32.3	2,303	Abu Dhabi	17,360
United Kingdom	243.3	94	58,970	London	20,710
United States of America	9,373	3,619	270,290	Washington, DC	28,740
Uruguay	177	68	3,285	Montevideo	6,020
Uzbekistan	447.4	172.7	23,784	Tashkent	1,010
Vanuatu	12.2	4.7	185	Port-Vila	1,290
Vatican City	0.0004	0.0002	1	–	–
Venezuela	912	352	22,803	Caracas	3,450
Vietnam	332	127	76,236	Hanoi	320
Virgin Is. (UK)	0.15	0.06	13	Road Town	–
Virgin Is. (US)	0.34	0.13	118	Charlotte Amalie	12,000
Wake Is.	0.008	0.003	0.3	–	–
Wallis & Futuna Is. (France)	0.20	0.08	15	Mata-Utu	–
Western Sahara	266	103	280	El Aaiún	300
Western Samoa	2.8	1.1	224	Apia	1,170
Yemen	528	204	16,388	Sana	270
Yugoslavia	102.3	39.5	10,500	Belgrade	2,000
Zambia	753	291	9,461	Lusaka	380
Zimbabwe	391	151	11,044	Harare	750

World Statistics: Cities

This list shows the principal cities with more than 500,000 inhabitants (only cities with more than 700,000 inhabitants are included for China and India). The figures are taken from the most recent census or estimate available, and as far as possible are the population of the metropolitan area, e.g. greater New York, Mexico or Paris. All the figures are in thousands. Local name forms have been used for the smaller cities (e.g. Kraków).

Afghanistan
Kabul 1,565
Algeria
Algiers 2,168
Oran 916
Angola
Luanda 2,418
Argentina
Buenos Aires 11,256
Córdoba 1,208
Rosario 1,118
Mendoza 773
La Plata 642
San Miguel de Tucumán 622
Mar del Plata 512
Armenia
Yerevan 1,248
Australia
Sydney 3,770
Melbourne 3,217
Brisbane 1,489
Perth 1,262
Adelaide 1,080
Austria
Vienna 1,595
Azerbaijan
Baku 1,720
Bangladesh
Dhaka 6,105
Chittagong 2,041
Khulna 877
Rajshahi 517
Belarus
Minsk 1,700
Homyel 512
Belgium
Brussels 948
Benin
Cotonou 537
Bolivia
La Paz 1,126
Santa Cruz 767
Bosnia-Herzegovina
Sarajevo 526
Brazil
São Paulo 16,417
Rio de Janeiro 9,888
Salvador 2,211
Belo Horizonte 2,091
Fortaleza 1,965
Brasília 1,821
Curitiba 1,476
Recife 1,346
Pôrto Alegre 1,288
Manaus 1,157
Belém 1,144
Goiânia 1,004
Guarulhos 972
Campinas 908
São Gonçalo 833
Nova Iguaçu 826
São Luís 780
Maceió 723
Duque de Caxias 715
São Bernardo de Campo 660
Natal 656
Teresina 655
Santo André 625
Osasco 623
Campo Grande 600
João Pessoa 549
Jaboatão 529
Bulgaria
Sofia 1,116
Burkina Faso
Ouagadougou 690
Burma (Myanmar)
Rangoon 2,513
Mandalay 533
Cambodia
Phnom Penh 920
Cameroon
Douala 1,200
Yaoundé 800
Canada
Toronto 4,344
Montréal 3,337
Vancouver 1,831
Ottawa–Hull 1,022
Edmonton 885
Calgary 831
Québec 693
Winnipeg 677
Hamilton 643
Central African Rep.
Bangui 553

Chad
Ndjaména 530
Chile
Santiago 5,067
China
Shanghai 15,082
Beijing 12,362
Tianjin 10,687
Hong Kong (SAR)* 6,502
Chongqing 3,870
Shenyang 3,860
Wuhan 3,520
Guangzhou 3,114
Harbin 2,505
Nanjing 2,211
Xi'an 2,115
Chengdu 1,933
Dalian 1,855
Changchun 1,810
Jinan 1,660
Taiyuan 1,642
Qingdao 1,584
Fuzhou, Fujian 1,380
Zibo 1,346
Zhengzhou 1,324
Lanzhou 1,296
Anshan 1,252
Fushun 1,246
Kunming 1,242
Changsha 1,198
Hangzhou 1,185
Nanchang 1,169
Shijiazhuang 1,159
Guiyang 1,131
Ürümqi 1,130
Jilin 1,118
Tangshan 1,110
Qiqihar 1,104
Baotou 1,033
Hefei 1,000
Xuzhou, Jiangsu 937
Handan 894
Wuxi 863
Luoyang 863
Datong 845
Nanning 829
Benxi 805
Yichun, Heilongjiang 800
Yantai 791
Huainan 769
Suzhou, Jiangsu 766
Daqing 753
Jixi 736
Shantou 719
Colombia
Bogotá 6,004
Cali 1,985
Medellin 1,970
Barranquilla 1,157
Cartagena 812
Congo
Brazzaville 937
Pointe-Noire 576
Congo (Zaïre)
Kinshasa 1,655
Lubumbashi 851
Mbuji-Mayi 806
Costa Rica
San José 1,220
Croatia
Zagreb 931
Cuba
Havana 2,241
Czech Republic
Prague 1,209
Denmark
Copenhagen 1,362
Dominican Republic
Santo Domingo 2,135
Santiago 691
Ecuador
Guayaquil 1,973
Quito 1,487
Egypt
Cairo 9,900
Alexandria 3,431
El Gîza 2,144
Shubra el Kheima 834
El Salvador
San Salvador 1,522
Ethiopia
Addis Ababa 2,112
Finland
Helsinki 532
France
Paris 9,319
Lyon 1,262
Marseille 1,087

Lille 959
Bordeaux 696
Toulouse 650
Nice 516
Georgia
Tbilisi 1,300
Germany
Berlin 3,470
Hamburg 1,706
Munich 1,240
Cologne 964
Frankfurt 651
Essen 616
Dortmund 600
Stuttgart 587
Düsseldorf 571
Bremen 549
Duisburg 535
Hanover 524
Ghana
Accra 949
Greece
Athens 3,097
Guatemala
Guatemala 1,167
Guinea
Conakry 1,508
Haiti
Port-au-Prince 1,255
Honduras
Tegucigalpa 813
Hungary
Budapest 1,885
India
Bombay (Mumbai) 12,572
Calcutta 10,916
Delhi 7,207
Madras (Chennai) 5,361
Hyderabad 4,280
Bangalore 4,087
Ahmadabad 3,298
Pune 2,485
Kanpur 2,111
Nagpur 1,661
Lucknow 1,642
Surat 1,517
Jaipur 1,514
Coimbatore 1,136
Vadodara 1,115
Indore 1,104
Patna 1,099
Madurai 1,094
Bhopal 1,064
Vishakhapatnam 1,052
Varanasi 1,026
Ludhiana 1,012
Agra 956
Jabalpur 887
Allahabad 858
Meerut 847
Vijayawada 845
Jamshedpur 834
Trivandrum 826
Dhanbad 818
Thane 797
Asansol 764
Nasik 722
Gwalior 720
Tiruchchirappalli 711
Amritsar 709
Indonesia
Jakarta 11,500
Surabaya 2,701
Bandung 2,368
Medan 1,910
Semarang 1,366
Palembang 1,352
Tangerang 1,198
Ujung Pandang 1,092
Bandar Lampung 832
Malang 763
Padang 721
Pakanbaru 558
Samarinda 536
Banjarmasin 535
Surakarta 516
Iran
Tehran 6,750
Mashhad 1,964
Esfahan 1,221
Tabriz 1,166
Shiraz 1,043
Ahvaz 828
Qom 780
Bakhtaran 666
Karaj 588
Iraq
Baghdad 3,841

Diyala 961
As Sulaymaniyah 952
Arbil 770
Al Mawsil 664
Kadhimain 521
Ireland
Dublin 952
Israel
Tel Aviv-Yafo 1,502
Jerusalem 591
Italy
Rome 2,775
Milan 1,369
Naples 1,067
Turin 962
Palermo 698
Genoa 678
Ivory Coast
Abidjan 2,500
Jamaica
Kingston 644
Japan
Tokyo–Yokohama 26,836
Osaka 10,601
Nagoya 2,152
Sapporo 1,757
Kyoto 1,464
Kobe 1,424
Fukuoka 1,285
Kawasaki 1,203
Hiroshima 1,109
Kitakyushu 1,020
Sendai 971
Chiba 857
Sakai 803
Kumamoto 650
Okayama 616
Sagamihara 571
Hamamatsu 562
Kagoshima 546
Funabashi 541
Higashiosaka 517
Hachioji 503
Jordan
Amman 1,300
Az-Zarqā 609
Kazakstan
Almaty 1,150
Qaraghandy 573
Kenya
Nairobi 2,000
Mombasa 600
Korea, North
Pyŏngyang 2,639
Hamhung 775
Chŏngjin 754
Chinnampo 691
Sinŭiju 500
Korea, South
Seoul 11,641
Pusan 3,814
Taegu 2,449
Inchon 2,308
Taejŏn 1,272
Kwangju 1,258
Ulsan 967
Sŏngnam 869
Puch'on 779
Suwŏn 756
Anyang 590
Chŏnju 563
Chŏngju 531
Ansan 510
P'ohang 509
Kyrgyzstan
Bishkek 584
Latvia
Riga 846
Lebanon
Beirut 1,900
Tripoli 500
Libya
Tripoli 1,083
Lithuania
Vilnius 580
Macedonia
Skopje 541
Madagascar
Antananarivo 1,053
Malaysia
Kuala Lumpur 1,145
Mali
Bamako 800
Mauritania
Nouakchott 735
Mexico
Mexico City 15,048
Guadalajara 2,847

Monterrey 2,522
Puebla 1,055
León 872
Ciudad Juárez 798
Tijuana 743
Culiacán Rosales 602
Mexicali 602
Acapulco de Juárez 592
Mérida 557
Chihuahua 530
San Luis Potosí 526
Aguascalientés 506
Moldova
Chişinău 700
Mongolia
Ulan Bator 627
Morocco
Casablanca 3,079
Rabat-Salé 1,344
Fès 735
Marrakesh 621
Mozambique
Maputo 2,000
Nepal
Katmandu 535
Netherlands
Amsterdam 1,101
Rotterdam 1,076
The Hague 694
Utrecht 548
New Zealand
Auckland 997
Nicaragua
Managua 864
Nigeria
Lagos 10,287
Ibadan 1,365
Ogbomosho 712
Kano 657
Norway
Oslo 714
Pakistan
Karachi 9,863
Lahore 5,085
Faisalabad 1,875
Peshawar 1,676
Gujranwala 1,663
Rawalpindi 1,290
Multan 1,257
Hyderabad 1,107
Paraguay
Asunción 945
Peru
Lima–Callao 6,601
Callao 638
Arequipa 620
Trujillo 509
Philippines
Manila 9,280
Quezon City 1,989
Davao 1,191
Caloocan 1,023
Cebu 662
Zamboanga 511
Poland
Warsaw 1,638
Lódz 825
Kraków 745
Wroclaw 642
Poznań 581
Portugal
Lisbon 2,561
Oporto 1,174
Romania
Bucharest 2,060
Russia
Moscow 9,233
St Petersburg 4,883
Nizhniy Novgorod 1,425
Novosibirsk 1,400
Yekaterinburg 1,300
Samara 1,200
Omsk 1,200
Chelyabinsk 1,100
Kazan 1,100
Ufa 1,100
Volgograd 1,003
Perm 1,000
Rostov 1,000
Voronezh 908
Saratov 895
Krasnoyarsk 869
Togliatti 689
Simbirsk 678
Izhevsk 654
Krasnodar 645
Vladivostok 632
Yaroslavl 629

Khabarovsk 618
Barnaul 596
Irkutsk 585
Novokuznetsk 572
Ryazan 536
Penza 534
Orenburg 532
Tula 532
Naberezhnyye-Chelny 526
Kemerovo 503
Saudi Arabia
Riyadh 1,800
Jedda 1,500
Mecca 630
Senegal
Dakar 1,571
Sierra Leone
Freetown 505
Singapore
Singapore 3,104
Somalia
Mogadishu 1,000
South Africa
Cape Town 2,350
East Rand 1,379
Johannesburg 1,196
Durban 1,137
Pretoria 1,080
West Rand 870
Port Elizabeth 853
Vanderbijlpark–Vereeniging 774
Soweto 597
Sasolburg 540
Spain
Madrid 3,029
Barcelona 1,614
Valencia 763
Sevilla 719
Zaragoza 607
Málaga 532
Sri Lanka
Colombo 1,863
Sudan
Nyala 1,267
Khartoum 925
Sharg el Nil 879
Sweden
Stockholm 1,744
Göteburg 775
Switzerland
Zürich 1,175
Bern 942
Syria
Aleppo 1,591
Damascus 1,549
Homs 644
Taiwan
Taipei 2,653
Kaohsiung 1,405
Taichung 817
Tainan 700
Panchiao 544
Tajikistan
Dushanbe 524
Tanzania
Dar-es-Salaam 1,361
Thailand
Bangkok 5,572
Togo
Lomé 590
Tunisia
Tunis 1,827
Turkey
Istanbul 7,490
Ankara 3,028
Izmir 2,333
Adana 1,472
Bursa 1,317
Konya 1,040
Gaziantep 930
Icel 908
Antalya 734
Diyarbakir 677
Kocaeli 661
Urfa 649
Kayseri 648
Manisa 641
Hatay 561
Samsun 557
Eskisehir 508
Balikesir 501
Turkmenistan
Ashkhabad 536
Uganda
Kampala 773
Ukraine
Kiev 2,630

Kharkiv 1,555
Dnipropetrovsk 1,147
Donetsk 1,088
Odesa 1,046
Zaporizhzhya 887
Lviv 802
Kryvyy Rih 720
Mariupol 510
Mykolayiv 508
United Kingdom
London 8,089
Birmingham 2,373
Manchester 2,353
Liverpool 852
Glasgow 832
Sheffield 661
Nottingham 649
Newcastle 617
Bristol 552
Leeds 529
United States
New York 16,329
Los Angeles 12,410
Chicago 7,668
Philadelphia 4,949
Washington, DC 4,466
Detroit 4,307
Houston 3,653
Atlanta 3,331
Boston 3,240
Dallas 2,898
Minneapolis–St Paul 2,688
San Diego 2,632
St Louis 2,536
Phoenix 2,473
Baltimore 2,458
Pittsburgh 2,402
Cleveland 2,222
San Francisco 2,182
Seattle 2,180
Tampa 2,157
Miami 2,025
Newark 1,934
Denver 1,796
Portland (Or.) 1,676
Kansas City (Mo.) 1,647
Cincinnati 1,581
San Jose 1,557
Norfolk 1,529
Indianapolis 1,462
Milwaukee 1,456
Sacramento 1,441
San Antonio 1,437
Columbus (Oh.) 1,423
New Orleans 1,309
Charlotte 1,260
Buffalo 1,189
Salt Lake City 1,178
Hartford 1,151
Oklahoma 1,007
Jacksonville (Fl.) 665
Omaha 663
Memphis 614
El Paso 579
Austin 514
Nashville 505
Uruguay
Montevideo 1,378
Uzbekistan
Tashkent 2,107
Venezuela
Caracas 2,784
Maracaibo 1,364
Valencia 1,032
Maracay 800
Barquisimeto 745
Ciudad Guayana 524
Vietnam
Ho Chi Minh City 4,322
Hanoi 3,056
Haiphong 783
Yemen
Sana 972
Aden 562
Yugoslavia
Belgrade 1,137
Zambia
Lusaka 982
Zimbabwe
Harare 1,189
Bulawayo 622

* SAR = Special Administrative Region of China

World Statistics: Distances

The table shows air distances in miles and kilometers between 30 major cities. Known as "Great Circle" distances, these measure the shortest routes between the cities, which aircraft use wherever possible. The maps show the world centered on six cities, and illustrate, for example, why direct flights from Japan to northern America and Europe are across the Arctic regions. The maps have been constructed on an Azimuthal Equidistant projection, on which all distances measured through the center point are true to scale. The red lines are drawn at 5,000, 10,000 and 15,000 km from the central city.

Distances below the diagonal are in Kms; distances above the diagonal are in Miles.

	Beijing	Bombay	Buenos Aires	Cairo	Calcutta	Caracas	Chicago	Hong Kong	Honolulu	Johannesburg	Lagos	London	Los Angeles	Mexico City	Moscow	Nairobi	New York	Paris	Rio de Janeiro	Rome	Singapore	Sydney	Tokyo	Wellington
Beijing	Beijing	2956	11972	4688	2031	8947	6588	1220	5070	7276	7119	5057	6251	7742	3600	5727	6828	5106	10773	5049	2783	5561	1304	6700
Bombay	4757	Bombay	9275	2706	1034	9024	8048	2683	8024	4334	4730	4467	8700	9728	3126	2816	7793	4356	8332	3837	2432	6313	4189	7686
Buenos Aires	19268	14925	Buenos Aires	7341	10268	3167	5599	11481	7558	5025	4919	6917	6122	4591	8374	6463	5298	6867	1214	6929	9867	7332	11410	6202
Cairo	7544	4355	11814	Cairo	3541	6340	6127	5064	8838	3894	2432	2180	7580	7687	1803	2197	5605	1994	6149	1325	5137	8959	5947	10268
Calcutta	3269	1664	16524	5699	Calcutta	9609	7978	1653	7048	5256	5727	4946	8152	9494	3438	3839	7921	4883	9366	4486	1800	5678	3195	7055
Caracas	14399	14522	5096	10203	15464	Caracas	2502	10166	6009	6847	4810	4664	3612	2228	6175	7173	2131	4738	2825	5196	11407	9534	8801	8154
Chicago	10603	12953	9011	3206	12839	4027	Chicago	7783	4247	8689	5973	3949	1742	1694	4971	8005	711	4132	5311	4809	9369	9243	6299	8358
Hong Kong	1963	4317	18478	8150	2659	16360	12526	Hong Kong	5543	6669	7360	5980	7232	8775	4439	5453	8047	5984	11001	5769	1615	4582	1786	5857
Honolulu	8160	12914	12164	14223	11343	9670	6836	8921	Honolulu	11934	10133	7228	2558	3781	7036	10739	4958	7437	8290	8026	6721	5075	3854	4669
Johannesburg	11710	6974	8088	6267	8459	11019	13984	10732	19206	Johannesburg	2799	5637	10362	9063	5692	1818	7979	5426	4420	4811	5381	6860	8418	7308
Lagos	11457	7612	7916	3915	9216	7741	9612	11845	16308	4505	Lagos	3118	7713	6879	3886	2366	5268	2929	3750	2510	6925	9643	8376	9973
London	8138	7190	11131	3508	7961	7507	6356	9623	11632	9071	5017	London	5442	5552	1552	4237	3463	212	5778	889	6743	10558	5942	11691
Los Angeles	10060	14000	9852	12200	13120	5812	2804	11639	4117	16676	12414	8758	Los Angeles	1549	6070	9659	2446	5645	6310	6331	8776	7502	5475	6719
Mexico City	12460	15656	7389	12372	15280	3586	2726	14122	6085	14585	11071	8936	2493	Mexico City	6664	9207	2090	5717	4780	6365	10321	8058	7024	6897
Moscow	5794	5031	13477	2902	5534	9938	8000	7144	11323	9161	6254	2498	9769	10724	Moscow	3942	4666	1545	7184	1477	5237	9008	4651	10283
Nairobi	9216	4532	10402	3536	6179	11544	12883	8776	17282	2927	3807	6819	15544	14818	6344	Nairobi	7358	4029	5548	3350	4635	7552	6996	8490
New York	10988	12541	8526	9020	12747	3430	1145	12950	7980	12841	8477	5572	3936	3264	7510	11842	New York	3626	4832	4280	9531	9935	6741	8951
Paris	8217	7010	11051	3210	7858	7625	6650	9630	11968	8732	4714	342	9085	9200	2486	6485	5836	Paris	5708	687	6671	10539	6038	11798
Rio de Janeiro	17338	13409	1953	9896	15073	4546	8547	17704	13342	7113	6035	9299	10155	7693	11562	8928	7777	9187	Rio de Janeiro	5725	9763	8389	11551	7367
Rome	8126	6175	11151	2133	7219	8363	7739	9284	12916	7743	4039	1431	10188	10243	2376	5391	6888	1105	9214	Rome	6229	10143	6127	11523
Singapore	4478	3914	15879	8267	2897	18359	15078	2599	10816	8660	11145	10852	14123	16610	8428	7460	15339	10737	15712	10025	Singapore	3915	3306	5298
Sydney	8949	10160	11800	14418	9138	15343	14875	7374	8168	11040	15519	16992	12073	12969	14497	12153	15989	16962	13501	16324	6300	Sydney	4861	1383
Tokyo	2099	6742	18362	9571	5141	14164	10137	2874	6202	13547	13480	9562	8811	11304	7485	11260	10849	9718	18589	9861	5321	7823	Tokyo	5762
Wellington	10782	12370	9981	16524	11354	13122	13451	9427	7513	11761	16050	18814	10814	11100	16549	13664	14405	18987	11855	18545	8526	2226	9273	Wellington

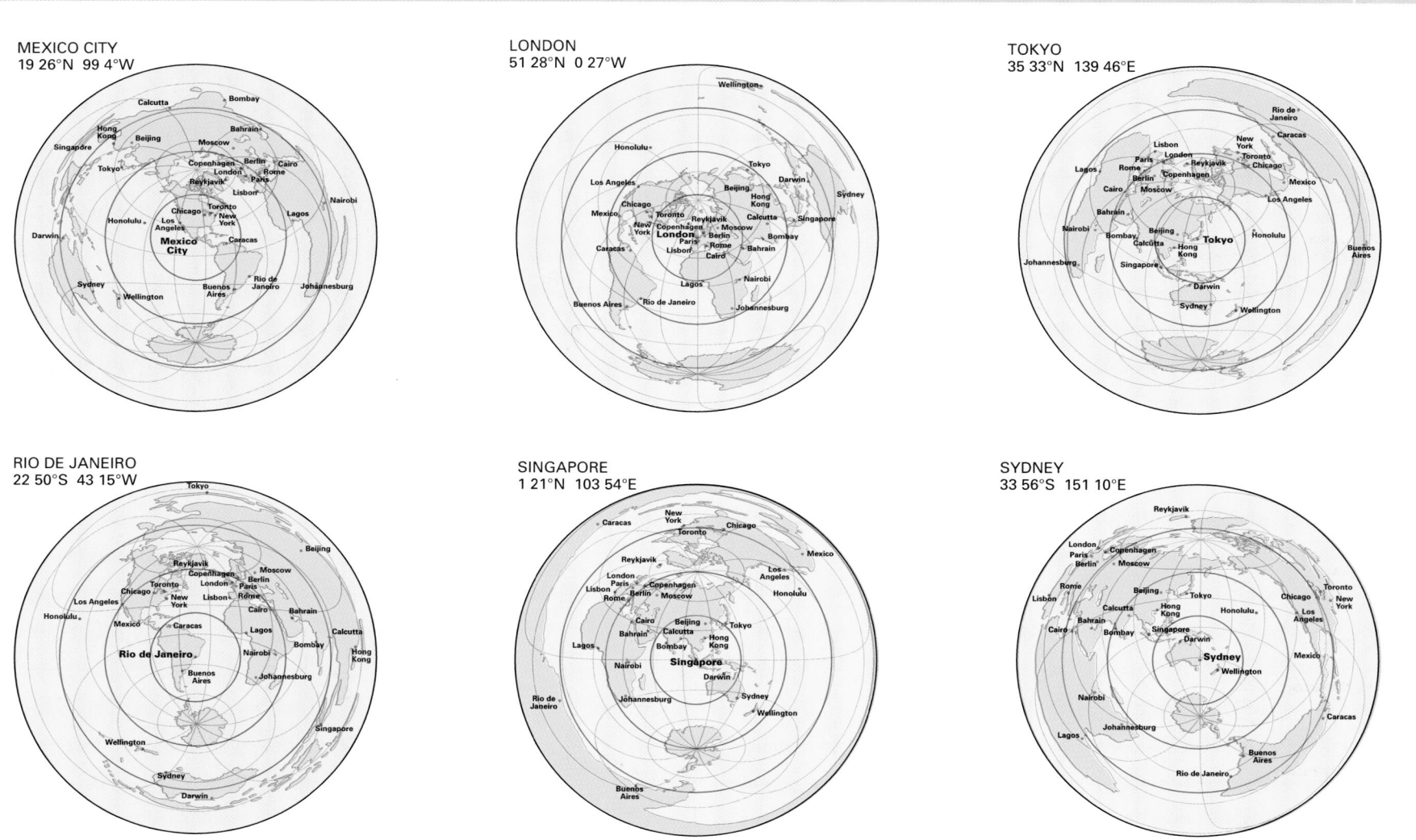

MEXICO CITY
19 26°N 99 4°W

LONDON
51 28°N 0 27°W

TOKYO
35 33°N 139 46°E

RIO DE JANEIRO
22 50°S 43 15°W

SINGAPORE
1 21°N 103 54°E

SYDNEY
33 56°S 151 10°E

World Statistics: Climate

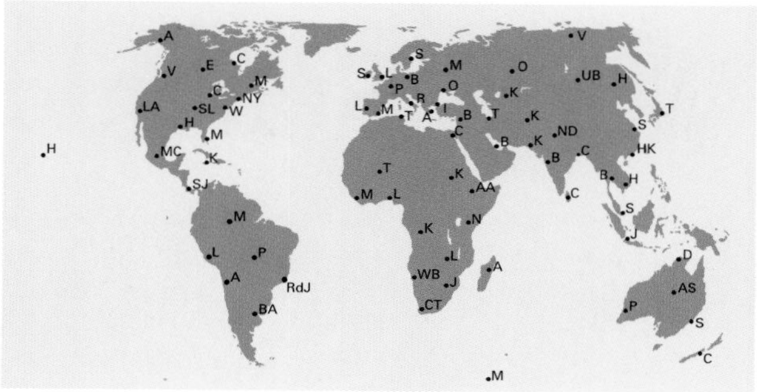

Rainfall and temperature figures are provided for more than 70 cities around the world. As climate is affected by altitude, the height of each city is shown in feet beneath its name. For each month, the figures in blue show the total rainfall or snow in inches, and in red the average temperature in degrees Fahrenheit; the total annual rainfall and average annual temperature are at the end of the rows.

EUROPE	*Jan.*	*Feb.*	*Mar.*	*Apr.*	*May*	*June*	*July*	*Aug.*	*Sept.*	*Oct.*	*Nov.*	*Dec.*	*Year*
Athens, Greece	62	37	37	23	23	14	6	7	15	51	56	71	402
351 ft	10	10	12	16	20	25	28	28	24	20	15	11	18
Berlin, Germany	46	40	33	42	49	65	73	69	48	49	46	43	603
180 ft	–1	0	4	9	14	17	19	18	15	9	5	1	9
Istanbul, Turkey	109	92	72	46	38	34	34	30	58	81	103	119	816
374 ft	5	6	7	11	16	20	23	23	20	16	12	8	14
Lisbon, Portugal	111	76	109	54	44	16	3	4	33	62	93	103	708
253 ft	11	12	14	16	17	20	22	23	21	18	14	12	17
London, UK	54	40	37	37	46	45	57	59	49	57	64	48	593
16 ft	4	5	7	9	12	16	18	17	15	11	8	5	11
Málaga, Spain	61	51	62	46	26	5	1	3	29	64	64	62	474
108 ft	12	13	16	17	19	29	25	26	23	20	16	13	18
Moscow, Russia	39	38	36	37	53	58	88	71	58	45	47	54	624
512 ft	–13	–10	–4	6	13	16	18	17	12	6	–1	–7	4
Odesa, Ukraine	57	62	30	21	34	34	42	37	37	13	35	71	473
210 ft	–3	–1	2	9	15	20	22	22	18	12	9	1	10
Paris, France	56	46	35	42	57	54	59	64	55	50	51	50	619
246 ft	3	4	8	11	15	18	20	19	17	12	7	4	12
Rome, Italy	71	62	57	51	46	37	15	21	63	99	129	93	744
56 ft	8	9	11	14	18	22	25	25	22	17	13	10	16
Shannon, Irish Republic	94	67	56	53	61	57	77	79	86	86	96	117	929
7 ft	5	5	7	9	12	14	16	16	14	11	8	6	10
Stockholm, Sweden	43	30	25	31	34	45	61	76	60	48	53	48	554
144 ft	–3	–3	–1	5	10	15	18	17	12	7	3	0	7

ASIA	*Jan.*	*Feb.*	*Mar.*	*Apr.*	*May*	*June*	*July*	*Aug.*	*Sept.*	*Oct.*	*Nov.*	*Dec.*	*Year*
Bahrain	8	18	13	8	<3	0	0	0	0	0	18	18	81
16 ft	17	18	21	25	29	32	33	34	31	28	24	19	26
Bangkok, Thailand	8	20	36	58	198	160	160	175	305	206	66	5	1,397
7 ft	26	28	29	30	29	29	28	28	28	28	26	25	28
Beirut, Lebanon	191	158	94	53	18	3	<3	<3	5	51	132	185	892
112 ft	14	14	16	18	22	24	27	28	26	24	19	16	21
Bombay, India	3	3	3	<3	18	485	617	340	264	64	13	3	1,809
36 ft	24	24	26	28	30	29	27	27	27	28	27	26	27
Calcutta, India	10	31	36	43	140	297	325	328	252	114	20	5	1,600
20 ft	20	22	27	30	30	30	29	29	29	28	23	19	26
Colombo, Sri Lanka	89	69	147	231	371	224	135	109	160	348	315	147	2,365
23 ft	26	26	27	28	28	27	27	27	27	27	26	26	27
Harbin, China	6	5	10	23	43	94	112	104	46	33	8	5	488
525 ft	–18	–15	–5	6	13	19	22	21	14	4	–6	–16	3
Ho Chi Minh, Vietnam	15	3	13	43	221	330	315	269	335	269	114	56	1,984
30 ft	26	27	29	30	29	28	28	28	27	27	27	26	28
Hong Kong, China	33	46	74	137	292	394	381	361	257	114	43	31	2,162
108 ft	16	15	18	22	26	28	28	28	27	25	21	18	23
Jakarta, Indonesia	300	300	211	147	114	97	64	43	66	112	142	203	1,798
26 ft	26	26	27	27	27	27	27	27	27	27	27	26	27
Kabul, Afghanistan	31	36	94	102	20	5	3	3	<3	15	20	10	338
5,953 ft	–3	–1	6	13	18	22	25	24	20	14	7	3	12
Karachi, Pakistan	13	10	8	3	3	18	81	41	13	<3	3	5	196
13 ft	19	20	24	28	30	31	30	29	28	28	24	20	26
Kazalinsk, Kazakstan	10	10	13	13	15	5	5	8	8	10	13	15	125
207 ft	–12	–11	–3	6	18	23	25	23	16	8	–1	–7	7
New Delhi, India	23	18	13	8	13	74	180	172	117	10	3	10	640
715 ft	14	17	23	28	33	34	31	30	29	26	20	15	25
Omsk, Russia	15	8	8	13	31	51	51	51	28	25	18	20	318
279 ft	–22	–19	–12	–1	10	16	18	16	10	1	–11	–18	–1
Shanghai, China	48	58	84	94	94	180	147	142	130	71	51	36	1,135
23 ft	4	5	9	14	20	24	28	28	23	19	12	7	16
Singapore	252	173	193	188	173	173	170	196	178	208	254	257	2,413
33 ft	26	27	28	28	28	28	28	27	27	27	27	27	27
Tehran, Iran	46	38	46	36	13	3	3	3	3	8	20	31	246
4,002 ft	2	5	9	16	21	26	30	29	25	18	12	6	17
Tokyo, Japan	48	74	107	135	147	165	142	152	234	208	97	56	1,565
20 ft	3	4	7	13	17	21	25	26	23	17	11	6	14
Ulan Bator, Mongolia	<3	<3	3	5	10	28	76	51	23	5	5	3	208
4,346 ft	–26	–21	–13	–1	6	14	16	14	8	–1	–13	–22	–3
Verkhoyansk, Russia	5	5	3	5	8	23	28	25	13	8	8	5	134
328 ft	–50	–45	–32	–15	0	12	14	9	2	–15	–38	–48	–17

AFRICA	*Jan.*	*Feb.*	*Mar.*	*Apr.*	*May*	*June*	*July*	*Aug.*	*Sept.*	*Oct.*	*Nov.*	*Dec.*	*Year*
Addis Ababa, Ethiopia	<3	3	25	135	213	201	206	239	102	28	<3	0	1,151
8,036 ft	19	20	20	20	19	18	18	19	21	22	21	20	20
Antananarivo, Madagas.	300	279	178	53	18	8	8	10	18	61	135	287	1,356
4,500 ft	21	21	21	19	18	15	14	15	17	19	21	21	19
Cairo, Egypt	5	5	5	3	3	<3	0	0	<3	<3	3	5	28
380 ft	13	15	18	21	25	28	28	28	26	24	20	15	22
Cape Town, South Africa	15	8	18	48	79	84	89	66	43	31	18	10	508
56 ft	21	21	20	17	14	13	12	13	14	16	18	19	17
Johannesburg, S. Africa	114	109	89	38	25	8	8	8	23	56	107	125	709
5,461 ft	20	20	18	16	13	10	11	13	16	18	19	20	16
Khartoum, Sudan	<3	<3	<3	<3	3	8	53	71	18	5	<3	0	158
1,279 ft	24	25	28	31	33	34	32	31	32	32	28	25	29
Kinshasa, Congo (Zaïre)	135	145	196	196	158	8	3	3	31	119	221	142	1,354
1,066 ft	26	26	27	27	26	24	23	24	25	26	26	26	25
Lagos, Nigeria	28	46	102	150	269	460	279	64	140	206	69	25	1,836
10 ft	27	28	29	28	28	26	26	25	26	26	28	28	27
Lusaka, Zambia	231	191	142	18	3	<3	<3	0	<3	10	91	150	836
4,189 ft	21	22	21	21	19	16	16	18	22	24	23	22	21
Monrovia, Liberia	31	56	97	216	516	973	996	373	744	772	236	130	5,138
75 ft	26	26	27	27	26	25	24	25	25	25	26	26	26
Nairobi, Kenya	38	64	125	211	158	46	15	23	31	53	109	86	958
5,970 ft	19	19	19	19	18	16	16	16	18	19	18	18	18
Timbuktu, Mali	<3	<3	3	<3	5	23	79	81	38	3	<3	<3	231
987 ft	22	24	28	32	34	35	32	30	32	31	28	23	29
Tunis, Tunisia	64	51	41	36	18	8	3	8	33	51	48	61	419
216 ft	10	11	13	16	19	23	26	27	25	20	16	11	18
Walvis Bay, Namibia	<3	5	8	3	3	<3	<3	3	<3	<3	<3	<3	23
23 ft	19	19	19	18	17	16	15	14	14	15	17	18	18

AUSTRALIA, NEW ZEALAND AND ANTARCTICA	*Jan.*	*Feb.*	*Mar.*	*Apr.*	*May*	*June*	*July*	*Aug.*	*Sept.*	*Oct.*	*Nov.*	*Dec.*	*Year*
Alice Springs, Australia	43	33	28	10	15	13	8	8	8	18	31	38	252
1,899 ft	29	28	25	20	15	12	12	14	18	23	26	28	21
Christchurch, N. Zealand	56	43	48	48	66	66	69	48	46	43	48	56	638
33 ft	16	16	14	12	9	6	6	7	9	12	14	16	11
Darwin, Australia	386	312	254	97	15	3	<3	3	13	51	119	239	1,491
98 ft	29	29	29	29	28	26	25	26	28	29	30	29	28
Mawson, Antarctica	11	30	20	10	44	180	4	40	3	20	0	0	362
46 ft	0	–5	–10	–14	–15	–16	–18	–18	–19	–13	–5	–1	–11
Perth, Australia	8	10	20	43	130	180	170	149	86	56	20	13	881
197 ft	23	23	22	19	16	14	13	13	15	16	19	22	18
Sydney, Australia	89	102	127	135	127	117	117	76	73	71	73	73	1,181
138 ft	22	22	21	18	15	13	12	13	15	18	19	21	17

NORTH AMERICA	*Jan.*	*Feb.*	*Mar.*	*Apr.*	*May*	*June*	*July*	*Aug.*	*Sept.*	*Oct.*	*Nov.*	*Dec.*	*Year*
Anchorage, Alaska, USA	20	18	15	10	13	18	41	66	66	56	25	23	371
131 ft	–11	–8	–5	2	7	12	14	13	9	2	–5	–11	2
Chicago, Illinois, USA	51	51	66	71	86	89	84	81	79	66	61	51	836
823 ft	–4	–3	2	9	14	20	23	22	19	12	5	–1	10
Churchill, Man., Canada	15	13	18	23	32	44	46	58	51	43	39	21	402
43 ft	–28	–26	–20	–10	–2	6	12	11	5	–2	–12	–22	–7
Edmonton, Alta., Canada	25	19	19	22	43	77	89	78	39	17	16	25	466
2,217 ft	–15	–10	–5	4	11	15	17	16	11	6	–4	–10	3
Honolulu, Hawaii, USA	104	66	79	48	25	18	23	28	36	48	64	104	643
39 ft	23	18	19	20	22	24	25	26	26	24	22	19	22
Houston, Texas, USA	89	76	84	91	119	117	99	99	104	94	89	109	1,171
39 ft	12	13	17	21	24	27	28	29	26	22	16	12	21
Kingston, Jamaica	23	15	23	31	102	89	38	91	99	180	74	36	800
112 ft	25	25	25	26	26	28	28	28	27	27	26	26	26
Los Angeles, Calif., USA	79	76	71	25	10	3	<3	<3	5	15	31	66	381
312 ft	13	14	14	16	17	19	21	22	21	18	16	14	17
Mexico City, Mexico	13	5	10	20	53	119	170	152	130	51	18	8	747
7,574 ft	12	13	16	18	19	19	17	18	18	16	14	13	16
Miami, Florida, USA	71	53	64	81	173	178	155	160	203	234	71	51	1,516
26 ft	20	20	22	23	25	27	28	28	27	25	22	21	24
Montréal, Que., Canada	72	65	74	74	66	82	90	92	88	76	81	87	946
187 ft	–10	–9	–3	–6	13	18	21	20	15	9	2	–7	6
New York City, N.Y., USA	94	97	91	81	81	84	107	109	86	89	76	91	1,092
315 ft	–1	–1	3	10	16	20	23	23	21	15	7	2	11
St Louis, Mo., USA	58	64	89	97	114	114	89	86	81	74	71	64	1,001
567 ft	0	1	7	13	19	24	26	26	22	15	8	2	14
San José, Costa Rica	15	5	20	46	229	241	211	241	305	300	145	41	1,798
3,759 ft	19	19	21	21	22	21	21	21	21	20	20	19	20
Vancouver, B.C., Canada	154	115	101	60	52	45	32	41	67	114	150	182	1,113
46 ft	3	5	6	9	12	15	17	17	14	10	6	4	10
Washington, D.C., USA	86	76	91	84	94	99	112	109	94	74	66	79	1,064
72 ft	1	2	7	12	18	23	25	24	20	14	8	3	13

SOUTH AMERICA	*Jan.*	*Feb.*	*Mar.*	*Apr.*	*May*	*June*	*July*	*Aug.*	*Sept.*	*Oct.*	*Nov.*	*Dec.*	*Year*
Antofagasta, Chile	0	0	0	<3	<3	3	5	3	<3	3	<3	0	13
308 ft	21	21	20	18	16	15	14	14	15	16	18	19	17
Buenos Aires, Argentina	79	71	109	89	76	61	56	61	79	86	84	99	950
89 ft	23	23	21	17	13	9	10	11	13	15	19	22	16
Lima, Peru	3	<3	<3	<3	5	5	8	8	8	3	3	<3	41
394 ft	23	24	24	22	19	17	17	16	17	18	19	21	20
Manaus, Brazil	249	231	262	221	170	84	58	38	46	107	142	203	1,811
144 ft	28	28	28	27	28	28	28	28	29	29	29	28	28
Paraná, Brazil	287	236	239	102	13	<3	3	5	28	127	231	310	1,582
853 ft	23	23	23	23	23	21	21	22	24	24	24	23	23
Rio de Janeiro, Brazil	125	122	130	107	79	53	41	43	66	79	104	137	1,082
200 ft	26	26	25	24	22	21	21	21	21	22	23	25	23

World Statistics: Physical Dimensions

E ach topic list is divided into continents and within a continent the items are listed in order of size. The order of the continents is as in the atlas, Europe through to South America. Certain lists down to this mark > are complete; below they are selective. The world top ten are shown in square brackets; in the case of mountains this has not been done because the world top 30 are all in Asia. The figures are rounded as appropriate.

World, Continents, Oceans

	km²	miles²	%
The World	509,450,000	196,672,000	–
Land	149,450,000	57,688,000	29.3
Water	360,000,000	138,984,000	70.7
Asia	44,500,000	17,177,000	29.8
Africa	30,302,000	11,697,000	20.3
North America	24,241,000	9,357,000	16.2
South America	17,793,000	6,868,000	11.9
Antarctica	14,100,000	5,443,000	9.4
Europe	9,957,000	3,843,000	6.7
Australia & Oceania	8,557,000	3,303,000	5.7
Pacific Ocean	179,679,000	69,356,000	49.9
Atlantic Ocean	92,373,000	35,657,000	25.7
Indian Ocean	73,917,000	28,532,000	20.5
Arctic Ocean	14,090,000	5,439,000	3.9

Seas

Pacific

	km²	miles²
South China Sea	2,974,600	1,148,500
Bering Sea	2,268,000	875,000
Sea of Okhotsk	1,528,000	590,000
East China & Yellow	1,249,000	482,000
Sea of Japan	1,008,000	389,000
Gulf of California	162,000	62,500
Bass Strait	75,000	29,000

Atlantic

	km²	miles²
Caribbean Sea	2,766,000	1,068,000
Mediterranean Sea	2,516,000	971,000
Gulf of Mexico	1,543,000	596,000
Hudson Bay	1,232,000	476,000
North Sea	575,000	223,000
Black Sea	462,000	178,000
Baltic Sea	422,170	163,000
Gulf of St Lawrence	238,000	92,000

Indian

	km²	miles²
Red Sea	438,000	169,000
The Gulf	239,000	92,000

Mountains

Europe

		m	ft
Elbrus	Russia	5,642	18,510
Mont Blanc	France/Italy	4,807	15,771
Monte Rosa	Italy/Switzerland	4,634	15,203
Dom	Switzerland	4,545	14,911
Liskamm	Switzerland	4,527	14,852
Weisshorn	Switzerland	4,505	14,780
Taschorn	Switzerland	4,490	14,730
Matterhorn/Cervino	Italy/Switzerland	4,478	14,691
Mont Maudit	France/Italy	4,465	14,649
> Dent Blanche	Switzerland	4,356	14,291
Nadelhorn	Switzerland	4,327	14,196
Grandes Jorasses	France/Italy	4,208	13,806
Jungfrau	Switzerland	4,158	13,642
Barre des Ecrins	France	4,103	13,461
Gran Paradiso	Italy	4,061	13,323
Piz Bernina	Italy/Switzerland	4,049	13,284
Eiger	Switzerland	3,970	13,025
Monte Viso	Italy	3,841	12,602
Grossglockner	Austria	3,797	12,457
Wildspitze	Austria	3,772	12,382
Monte Disgrazia	Italy	3,678	12,066
Mulhacén	Spain	3,478	11,411
Pico de Aneto	Spain	3,404	11,168
Marmolada	Italy	3,342	10,964
Etna	Italy	3,340	10,958
Punta del'Argentera	Italy	3,297	10,817
Zugspitze	Germany	2,962	9,718
Musala	Bulgaria	2,925	9,596
Olympus	Greece	2,917	9,570
Triglav	Slovenia	2,863	9,393
Monte Cinto	France (Corsica)	2,710	8,891
Gerlachovka	Slovak Republic	2,655	8,711
Torre de Cerrado	Spain	2,648	8,688
Galdhöpiggen	Norway	2,468	8,100
Hvannadalshnúkur	Iceland	2,119	6,952
Kebnekaise	Sweden	2,117	6,946
Ben Nevis	UK	1,343	4,406

Asia

		m	ft
Everest	China/Nepal	8,848	29,029
K2 (Godwin Austen)	China/Kashmir	8,611	28,251
Kanchenjunga	India/Nepal	8,598	28,208
Lhotse	China/Nepal	8,516	27,939
Makalu	China/Nepal	8,481	27,824
Cho Oyu	China/Nepal	8,201	26,906
Dhaulagiri	Nepal	8,172	26,811
Manaslu	Nepal	8,156	26,758
Nanga Parbat	Kashmir	8,126	26,660
Annapurna	Nepal	8,078	26,502
Gasherbrum	China/Kashmir	8,068	26,469
Broad Peak	China/Kashmir	8,051	26,414
Xixabangma	China	8,012	26,286
Kangbachen	India/Nepal	7,902	25,925
Jannu	India/Nepal	7,902	25,925
Gayachung Kang	Nepal	7,897	25,909
Himalchuli	Nepal	7,893	25,896
Disteghil Sar	Kashmir	7,885	25,869
Nuptse	Nepal	7,879	25,849
Khunyang Chhish	Kashmir	7,852	25,761
Masherbrum	Kashmir	7,821	25,659
Nanda Devi	India	7,817	25,646
Rakaposhi	Kashmir	7,788	25,551
Batura	Kashmir	7,785	25,541
Namche Barwa	China	7,756	25,446
Kamet	India	7,756	25,446
Soltoro Kangri	Kashmir	7,742	25,400
Gurla Mandhata	China	7,728	25,354
> Trivor	Pakistan	7,720	25,328
Kongur Shan	China	7,719	25,324
Tirich Mir	Pakistan	7,690	25,229
K'ula Shan	Bhutan/China	7,543	24,747
Pik Kommunizma	Tajikistan	7,495	24,590
Demavend	Iran	5,604	18,386
Ararat	Turkey	5,165	16,945
Gunong Kinabalu	Malaysia (Borneo)	4,101	13,455
Yu Shan	Taiwan	3,997	13,113
Fuji-San	Japan	3,776	12,388

Africa

		m	ft
Kilimanjaro	Tanzania	5,895	19,340
Mt Kenya	Kenya	5,199	17,057
Ruwenzori (Margherita)	Uganda/Congo (Z.)	5,109	16,762
Ras Dashan	Ethiopia	4,620	15,157
Meru	Tanzania	4,565	14,977
Karisimbi	Rwanda/Congo (Z.)	4,507	14,787
Mt Elgon	Kenya/Uganda	4,321	14,176
Batu	Ethiopia	4,307	14,130
Guna	Ethiopia	4,231	13,882
Toubkal	Morocco	4,165	13,665
Irhil Mgoun	Morocco	4,071	13,356
Mt Cameroon	Cameroon	4,070	13,353
Amba Ferit	Ethiopia	3,875	13,042
Pico del Teide	Spain (Tenerife)	3,718	12,198
Thabana Ntlenyana	Lesotho	3,482	11,424
Emi Koussi	Chad	3,415	11,204
> Mt aux Sources	Lesotho/S. Africa	3,282	10,768
Mt Piton	Réunion	3,069	10,069

Oceania

		m	ft
Puncak Jaya	Indonesia	5,029	16,499
Puncak Trikora	Indonesia	4,750	15,584
Puncak Mandala	Indonesia	4,702	15,427
Mt Wilhelm	Papua New Guinea	4,508	14,790
> Mauna Kea	USA (Hawaii)	4,205	13,796
Mauna Loa	USA (Hawaii)	4,170	13,681
Mt Cook (Aoraki)	New Zealand	3,753	12,313
Mt Balbi	Solomon Is.	2,439	8,002
Orohena	Tahiti	2,241	7,352
Mt Kosciuszko	Australia	2,237	7,339

North America

		m	ft
Mt McKinley (Denali)	USA (Alaska)	6,194	20,321
Mt Logan	Canada	5,959	19,551
Citlaltepetl	Mexico	5,700	18,701
Mt St Elias	USA/Canada	5,489	18,008
Popocatepetl	Mexico	5,452	17,887
Mt Foraker	USA (Alaska)	5,304	17,401
Ixtaccihuatl	Mexico	5,286	17,342
Lucania	Canada	5,227	17,149
Mt Steele	Canada	5,073	16,644
Mt Bona	USA (Alaska)	5,005	16,420
Mt Blackburn	USA (Alaska)	4,996	16,391
Mt Sanford	USA (Alaska)	4,940	16,207
Mt Wood	Canada	4,848	15,905
Nevado de Toluca	Mexico	4,670	15,321
Mt Fairweather	USA (Alaska)	4,663	15,298
Mt Hunter	USA (Alaska)	4,442	14,573

		m	ft
Mt Whitney	USA	4,418	14,495
Mt Elbert	USA	4,399	14,432
Mt Harvard	USA	4,395	14,419
Mt Rainier	USA	4,392	14,409
> Blanca Peak	USA	4,372	14,344
Longs Peak	USA	4,345	14,255
Tajumulco	Guatemala	4,220	13,845
Grand Teton	USA	4,197	13,770
Mt Waddington	Canada	3,994	13,104
Mt Robson	Canada	3,954	12,972
Chirripó Grande	Costa Rica	3,837	12,589
Mt Assiniboine	Canada	3,619	11,873
Pico Duarte	Dominican Rep.	3,175	10,417

South America

		m	ft
Aconcagua	Argentina	6,960	22,834
Bonete	Argentina	6,872	22,546
Ojos del Salado	Argentina/Chile	6,863	22,516
Pissis	Argentina	6,779	22,241
Mercedario	Argentina/Chile	6,770	22,211
Huascaran	Peru	6,768	22,204
Llullaillaco	Argentina/Chile	6,723	22,057
Nudo de Cachi	Argentina	6,720	22,047
Yerupaja	Peru	6,632	21,758
N. de Tres Cruces	Argentina/Chile	6,620	21,719
Incahuasi	Argentina/Chile	6,601	21,654
Cerro Galan	Argentina	6,600	21,654
Tupungato	Argentina/Chile	6,570	21,555
> Sajama	Bolivia	6,542	21,463
Illimani	Bolivia	6,485	21,276
Coropuna	Peru	6,425	21,079
Ausangate	Peru	6,384	20,945
Cerro del Toro	Argentina	6,380	20,932
Siula Grande	Peru	6,356	20,853
Chimborazo	Ecuador	6,267	20,561
Alpamayo	Peru	5,947	19,511
Cotapaxi	Ecuador	5,896	19,344
Pico Colon	Colombia	5,800	19,029
Pico Bolivar	Venezuela	5,007	16,427

Antarctica

	m	ft
Vinson Massif	4,897	16,066
Mt Kirkpatrick	4,528	14,855
Mt Markham	4,349	14,268

Ocean Depths

Atlantic Ocean

	m	ft	
Puerto Rico (Milwaukee) Deep	9,220	30,249	[7]
Cayman Trench	7,680	25,197	
Gulf of Mexico	5,203	17,070	
Mediterranean Sea	5,121	16,801	
Black Sea	2,211	7,254	
North Sea	660	2,165	
Baltic Sea	463	1,519	

Indian Ocean

	m	ft
Java Trench	7,450	24,442
Red Sea	2,635	8,454
Persian Gulf	73	239

Pacific Ocean

	m	ft	
Mariana Trench	11,022	36,161	[1]
Tonga Trench	10,882	35,702	[2]
Japan Trench	10,554	34,626	[3]
Kuril Trench	10,542	34,587	[4]
Mindanao Trench	10,497	34,439	[5]
Kermadec Trench	10,047	32,962	[6]
New Guinea Trench	9,140	29,987	[8]
Peru–Chile Trench	8,050	26,410	[9]
Aleutian Trench	7,822	25,662	[10]
Middle American Trench	6,662	21,857	

Arctic Ocean

	m	ft
Molloy Deep	5,608	18,399

Land Lows

		m	ft
Dead Sea	Asia	–403	–1,322
Lake Assal	Africa	–156	–512
Death Valley	N. America	–86	–282
Valdés Peninsula	S. America	–40	–131
Caspian Sea	Europe	–28	–92
Lake Eyre North	Oceania	–16	–52

Rivers

Europe

		km	miles
Volga	Caspian Sea	3,700	2,300
Danube	Black Sea	2,850	1,770
Ural	Caspian Sea	2,535	1,575
Dnepr (Dnipro)	Black Sea	2,285	1,420
Kama	Volga	2,030	1,260
Don	Black Sea	1,990	1,240
Petchora	Arctic Ocean	1,790	1,110
Oka	Volga	1,480	920
Belaya	Kama	1,420	880
Dnister (Dniester)	Black Sea	1,400	870
Vyatka	Kama	1,370	850
Rhine	North Sea	1,320	820
N. Dvina	Arctic Ocean	1,290	800
Desna	Dnepr (Dnipro)	1,190	740
Elbe	North Sea	1,145	710
Wisla	Baltic Sea	1,090	675
Loire	Atlantic Ocean	1,020	635
W. Dvina	Baltic Sea	1,019	633

Asia

		km	miles
Yangtze	Pacific Ocean	6,380	3,960 [3]
Yenisey–Angara	Arctic Ocean	5,550	3,445 [5]
Huang He	Pacific Ocean	5,464	3,395 [6]
Ob–Irtysh	Arctic Ocean	5,410	3,360 [7]
Mekong	Pacific Ocean	4,500	2,795 [9]
Amur	Pacific Ocean	4,400	2,730 [10]
Lena	Arctic Ocean	4,400	2,730
Irtysh	Ob	4,250	2,640
Yenisey	Arctic Ocean	4,090	2,540
Ob	Arctic Ocean	3,680	2,285
Indus	Indian Ocean	3,100	1,925
Brahmaputra	Indian Ocean	2,900	1,800
Syrdarya	Aral Sea	2,860	1,775
Salween	Indian Ocean	2,800	1,740
Euphrates	Indian Ocean	2,700	1,675
Vilyuy	Lena	2,650	1,645
Kolyma	Arctic Ocean	2,600	1,615
Amudarya	Aral Sea	2,540	1,575
Ural	Caspian Sea	2,535	1,575
Ganges	Indian Ocean	2,510	1,560
Si Kiang	Pacific Ocean	2,100	1,305
Irrawaddy	Indian Ocean	2,010	1,250
Tarim–Yarkand	Lop Nor	2,000	1,240
Tigris	Indian Ocean	1,900	1,180
Angara	Yenisey	1,830	1,135
Godavari	Indian Ocean	1,470	915
Sutlej	Indian Ocean	1,450	900
Yamuna	Indian Ocean	1,400	870

Africa

		km	miles
Nile	Mediterranean	6,670	4,140 [1]
Congo	Atlantic Ocean	4,670	2,900 [8]
Niger	Atlantic Ocean	4,180	2,595
Zambezi	Indian Ocean	3,540	2,200
Oubangi/Uele	Congo (Zaïre)	2,250	1,400
Kasai	Congo (Zaïre)	1,950	1,210
Shaballe	Indian Ocean	1,930	1,200
Orange	Atlantic Ocean	1,860	1,155
Cubango	Okavango Swamps	1,800	1,120
Limpopo	Indian Ocean	1,600	995
Senegal	Atlantic Ocean	1,600	995
Volta	Atlantic Ocean	1,500	930
Benue	Niger	1,350	840

Australia

		km	miles
Murray–Darling	Indian Ocean	3,750	2,330
Darling	Murray	3,070	1,905
Murray	Indian Ocean	2,575	1,600
Murrumbidgee	Murray	1,690	1,050

North America

		km	miles
Mississippi–Missouri	Gulf of Mexico	6,020	3,740 [4]
Mackenzie	Arctic Ocean	4,240	2,630
Mississippi	Gulf of Mexico	3,780	2,350
Missouri	Mississippi	3,780	2,350
Yukon	Pacific Ocean	3,185	1,980
Rio Grande	Gulf of Mexico	3,030	1,880
Arkansas	Mississippi	2,340	1,450
Colorado	Pacific Ocean	2,330	1,445
Red	Mississippi	2,040	1,270
Columbia	Pacific Ocean	1,950	1,210
Saskatchewan	Lake Winnipeg	1,940	1,205
Snake	Columbia	1,670	1,040
Churchill	Hudson Bay	1,600	990
Ohio	Mississippi	1,580	980
Brazos	Gulf of Mexico	1,400	870
St Lawrence	Atlantic Ocean	1,170	730

South America

		km	miles
Amazon	Atlantic Ocean	6,450	4,010 [2]
Paraná–Plate	Atlantic Ocean	4,500	2,800
Purus	Amazon	3,350	2,080
Madeira	Amazon	3,200	1,990
São Francisco	Atlantic Ocean	2,900	1,800
Paraná	Plate	2,800	1,740
Tocantins	Atlantic Ocean	2,750	1,710
Paraguay	Paraná	2,550	1,580
Orinoco	Atlantic Ocean	2,500	1,550
Pilcomayo	Paraná	2,500	1,550
Araguaia	Tocantins	2,250	1,400
Juruá	Amazon	2,000	1,240
Xingu	Amazon	1,980	1,230
Ucayali	Amazon	1,900	1,180
Marañón	Amazon	1,600	990
Uruguay	Plate	1,600	990
Magdalena	Caribbean Sea	1,540	960

Lakes

Europe

		km²	miles²
Lake Ladoga	Russia	17,700	6,800
Lake Onega	Russia	9,700	3,700
Saimaa system	Finland	8,000	3,100
Vänern	Sweden	5,500	2,100
Rybinskoye Res.	Russia	4,700	1,800

Asia

		km²	miles²
Caspian Sea	Asia	371,800	143,550 [1]
Lake Baykal	Russia	30,500	11,780 [8]
Aral Sea	Kazak./Uzbek.	28,687	11,086 [10]
Tonlé Sap	Cambodia	20,000	7,700
Lake Balqash	Kazakstan	18,500	7,100
Lake Dongting	China	12,000	4,600
Lake Ysyk	Kyrgyzstan	6,200	2,400
Lake Orumiyeh	Iran	5,900	2,300
Lake Koko	China	5,700	2,200
Lake Poyang	China	5,000	1,900
Lake Khanka	China/Russia	4,400	1,700
Lake Van	Turkey	3,500	1,400
Lake Ubsa	China	3,400	1,300

Africa

		km²	miles²
Lake Victoria	E. Africa	68,000	26,000 [3]
Lake Tanganyika	C. Africa	33,000	13,000 [6]
Lake Malawi/Nyasa	E. Africa	29,600	11,430 [9]
Lake Chad	C. Africa	25,000	9,700
Lake Turkana	Ethiopia/Kenya	8,500	3,300
Lake Volta	Ghana	8,500	3,300
Lake Bangweulu	Zambia	8,000	3,100
Lake Rukwa	Tanzania	7,000	2,700
Lake Mai-Ndombe	Congo (Zaïre)	6,500	2,500
Lake Kariba	Zambia/Zimbabwe	5,300	2,000
Lake Albert	Uganda/Congo (Z.)	5,300	2,000
Lake Nasser	Egypt/Sudan	5,200	2,000
Lake Mweru	Zambia/Congo (Z.)	4,900	1,900
Lake Cabora Bassa	Mozambique	4,500	1,700
Lake Kyoga	Uganda	4,400	1,700
Lake Tana	Ethiopia	3,630	1,400
Lake Kivu	Rwanda/Congo (Z.)	2,650	1,000
Lake Edward	Uganda/Congo (Z.)	2,200	850

Australia

		km²	miles²
Lake Eyre	Australia	8,900	3,400
Lake Torrens	Australia	5,800	2,200
Lake Gairdner	Australia	4,800	1,900

North America

		km²	miles²
Lake Superior	Canada/USA	82,350	31,800 [2]
Lake Huron	Canada/USA	59,600	23,010 [4]
Lake Michigan	USA	58,000	22,400 [5]
Great Bear Lake	Canada	31,800	12,280 [7]
Great Slave Lake	Canada	28,500	11,000
Lake Erie	Canada/USA	25,700	9,900
Lake Winnipeg	Canada	24,400	9,400
Lake Ontario	Canada/USA	19,500	7,500
Lake Nicaragua	Nicaragua	8,200	3,200
Lake Athabasca	Canada	8,100	3,100
Smallwood Res.	Canada	6,530	2,520
Reindeer Lake	Canada	6,400	2,500
Nettilling Lake	Canada	5,500	2,100
Lake Winnipegosis	Canada	5,400	2,100
Lake Nipigon	Canada	4,850	1,900
Lake Manitoba	Canada	4,700	1,800

South America

		km²	miles²
Lake Titicaca	Bolivia/Peru	8,300	3,200
Lake Poopo	Peru	2,800	1,100

Islands

Europe

		km²	miles²
Great Britain	UK	229,880	88,700 [8]
Iceland	Atlantic Ocean	103,000	39,800
Ireland	Ireland/UK	84,400	32,600
Novaya Zemlya (N.)	Russia	48,200	18,600
W. Spitzbergen	Norway	39,000	15,100
Novaya Zemlya (S.)	Russia	33,200	12,800
Sicily	Italy	25,500	9,800
Sardinia	Italy	24,000	9,300
N.E. Spitzbergen	Norway	15,000	5,600
Corsica	France	8,700	3,400
Crete	Greece	8,350	3,200
Zealand	Denmark	6,850	2,600

Asia

		km²	miles²
Borneo	S. E. Asia	744,360	287,400 [3]
Sumatra	Indonesia	473,600	182,860 [6]
Honshu	Japan	230,500	88,980 [7]
Sulawesi (Celebes)	Indonesia	189,000	73,000
Java	Indonesia	126,700	48,900
Luzon	Philippines	104,700	40,400
Mindanao	Philippines	101,500	39,200
Hokkaido	Japan	78,400	30,300
Sakhalin	Russia	74,060	28,600
Sri Lanka	Indian Ocean	65,600	25,300
Taiwan	Pacific Ocean	36,000	13,900
Kyushu	Japan	35,700	13,800
Hainan	China	34,000	13,100
Timor	Indonesia	33,600	13,000
Shikoku	Japan	18,800	7,300
Halmahera	Indonesia	18,000	6,900
Ceram	Indonesia	17,150	6,600
Sumbawa	Indonesia	15,450	6,000
Flores	Indonesia	15,200	5,900
Samar	Philippines	13,100	5,100
Negros	Philippines	12,700	4,900
Bangka	Indonesia	12,000	4,600
Palawan	Philippines	12,000	4,600
Panay	Philippines	11,500	4,400
Sumba	Indonesia	11,100	4,300
Mindoro	Philippines	9,750	3,800
Buru	Indonesia	9,500	3,700
Bali	Indonesia	5,600	2,200
Cyprus	Mediterranean	3,570	1,400

Africa

		km²	miles²
Madagascar	Indian Ocean	587,040	226,660 [4]
Socotra	Indian Ocean	3,600	1,400
Réunion	Indian Ocean	2,500	965
Tenerife	Atlantic Ocean	2,350	900
Mauritius	Indian Ocean	1,865	720

Oceania

		km²	miles²
New Guinea	Indon./Pap. NG	821,030	317,000 [2]
New Zealand (S.)	Pacific Ocean	150,500	58,100
New Zealand (N.)	Pacific Ocean	114,700	44,300
Tasmania	Australia	67,800	26,200
New Britain	Papua NG	37,800	14,600
New Caledonia	Pacific Ocean	19,100	7,400
Viti Levu	Fiji	10,500	4,100
Hawaii	Pacific Ocean	10,450	4,000
Bougainville	Papua NG	9,600	3,700
Guadalcanal	Solomon Is.	6,500	2,500
Vanua Levu	Fiji	5,550	2,100
New Ireland	Papua NG	3,200	1,200

North America

		km²	miles²
Greenland	Atlantic Ocean	2,175,600	839,800 [1]
Baffin Is.	Canada	508,000	196,100 [5]
Victoria Is.	Canada	212,200	81,900 [9]
Ellesmere Is.	Canada	212,000	81,800 [10]
Cuba	Caribbean Sea	110,860	42,800
Newfoundland	Canada	110,680	42,700
Hispaniola	Dom. Rep./Haiti	76,200	29,400
Banks Is.	Canada	67,000	25,900
Devon Is.	Canada	54,500	21,000
Melville Is.	Canada	42,400	16,400
Vancouver Is.	Canada	32,150	12,400
Somerset Is.	Canada	24,300	9,400
Jamaica	Caribbean Sea	11,400	4,400
Puerto Rico	Atlantic Ocean	8,900	3,400
Cape Breton Is.	Canada	4,000	1,500

South America

		km²	miles²
Tierra del Fuego	Argentina/Chile	47,000	18,100
Falkland Is. (E.)	Atlantic Ocean	6,800	2,600
South Georgia	Atlantic Ocean	4,200	1,600
Galapagos (Isabela)	Pacific Ocean	2,250	870

World: Regions in the News

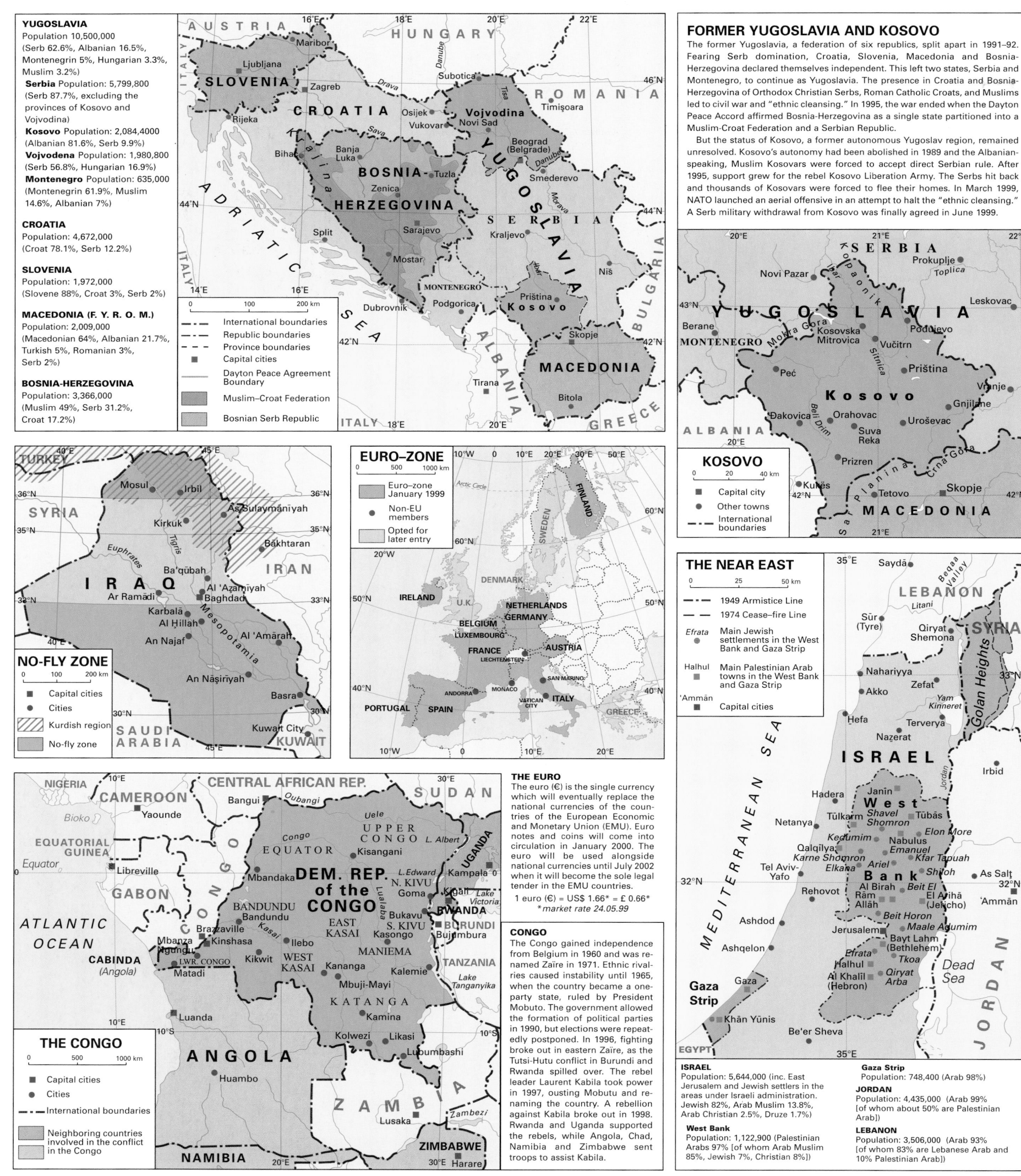

YUGOSLAVIA
Population 10,500,000
(Serb 62.6%, Albanian 16.5%,
Montenegrin 5%, Hungarian 3.3%,
Muslim 3.2%)
Serbia Population: 5,799,800
(Serb 87.7%, excluding the
provinces of Kosovo and
Vojvodina)
Kosovo Population: 2,084,4000
(Albanian 81.6%, Serb 9.9%)
Vojvodena Population: 1,980,800
(Serb 56.8%, Hungarian 16.9%)
Montenegro Population: 635,000
(Montenegrin 61.9%, Muslim
14.6%, Albanian 7%)

CROATIA
Population: 4,672,000
(Croat 78.1%, Serb 12.2%)

SLOVENIA
Population: 1,972,000
(Slovene 88%, Croat 3%, Serb 2%)

MACEDONIA (F. Y. R. O. M.)
Population: 2,009,000
(Macedonian 64%, Albanian 21.7%,
Turkish 5%, Romanian 3%,
Serb 2%)

BOSNIA-HERZEGOVINA
Population: 3,366,000
(Muslim 49%, Serb 31.2%,
Croat 17.2%)

International boundaries
Republic boundaries
Province boundaries
Capital cities
Dayton Peace Agreement Boundary
Muslim–Croat Federation
Bosnian Serb Republic

FORMER YUGOSLAVIA AND KOSOVO

The former Yugoslavia, a federation of six republics, split apart in 1991–92. Fearing Serb domination, Croatia, Slovenia, Macedonia and Bosnia-Herzegovina declared themselves independent. This left two states, Serbia and Montenegro, to continue as Yugoslavia. The presence in Croatia and Bosnia-Herzegovina of Orthodox Christian Serbs, Roman Catholic Croats, and Muslims led to civil war and "ethnic cleansing." In 1995, the war ended when the Dayton Peace Accord affirmed Bosnia-Herzegovina as a single state partitioned into a Muslim-Croat Federation and a Serbian Republic.

But the status of Kosovo, a former autonomous Yugoslav region, remained unresolved. Kosovo's autonomy had been abolished in 1989 and the Albanian-speaking, Muslim Kosovars were forced to accept direct Serbian rule. After 1995, support grew for the rebel Kosovo Liberation Army. The Serbs hit back and thousands of Kosovars were forced to flee their homes. In March 1999, NATO launched an aerial offensive in an attempt to halt the "ethnic cleansing." A Serb military withdrawal from Kosovo was finally agreed in June 1999.

KOSOVO
Capital city
Other towns
International boundaries

NO-FLY ZONE
Capital cities
Cities
Kurdish region
No-fly zone

EURO–ZONE
Euro-zone January 1999
Non-EU members
Opted for later entry

THE EURO
The euro (€) is the single currency which will eventually replace the national currencies of the countries of the European Economic and Monetary Union (EMU). Euro notes and coins will come into circulation in January 2000. The euro will be used alongside national currencies until July 2002 when it will become the sole legal tender in the EMU countries.

1 euro (€) = US$ 1.66* = £ 0.66*
*market rate 24.05.99

THE NEAR EAST
1949 Armistice Line
1974 Cease-fire Line
Efrata Main Jewish settlements in the West Bank and Gaza Strip
Halhul Main Palestinian Arab towns in the West Bank and Gaza Strip
Capital cities

THE CONGO
Capital cities
Cities
International boundaries
Neighboring countries involved in the conflict in the Congo

CONGO
The Congo gained independence from Belgium in 1960 and was re-named Zaïre in 1971. Ethnic rivalries caused instability until 1965, when the country became a one-party state, ruled by President Mobuto. The government allowed the formation of political parties in 1990, but elections were repeatedly postponed. In 1996, fighting broke out in eastern Zaire, as the Tutsi-Hutu conflict in Burundi and Rwanda spilled over. The rebel leader Laurent Kabila took power in 1997, ousting Mobutu and re-naming the country. A rebellion against Kabila broke out in 1998. Rwanda and Uganda supported the rebels, while Angola, Chad, Namibia and Zimbabwe sent troops to assist Kabila.

ISRAEL
Population: 5,644,000 (inc. East Jerusalem and Jewish settlers in the areas under Israeli administration. Jewish 82%, Arab Muslim 13.8%, Arab Christian 2.5%, Druze 1.7%)

West Bank
Population: 1,122,900 (Palestinian Arabs 97% [of whom Arab Muslim 85%, Jewish 7%, Christian 8%])

Gaza Strip
Population: 748,400 (Arab 98%)

JORDAN
Population: 4,435,000 (Arab 99% [of whom about 50% are Palestinian Arab])

LEBANON
Population: 3,506,000 (Arab 93% [of whom 83% are Lebanese Arab and 10% Palestinian Arab])

INTRODUCTION TO WORLD GEOGRAPHY

The Universe

About 15 billion years ago, time and space began with the most colossal explosion in cosmic history: the so-called "Big Bang" that is believed to have initiated the universe. According to current theory, in the first millionth of a second of its existence it expanded from a dimensionless point of infinite mass and density into a fireball about 19 billion miles across; and it has been expanding ever since.

It took almost a million years for the primal fireball to cool enough for atoms to form. They were mostly hydrogen, still the most abundant material in the universe. But the new matter was not evenly distributed around the young universe, and a few billion years later atoms in relatively dense regions began to cling together under the influence of gravity, forming distinct masses of gas separated by vast expanses of empty space. To begin with, these first proto-galaxies were dark places: the universe had cooled. But gravitational attraction continued, condensing matter into coherent lumps inside the galactic gas clouds. About three billion years later, some of these masses had contracted so much that internal pressure produced the high temperatures necessary to bring about nuclear fusion: the first stars were born.

There were several generations of stars, each feeding on the wreckage of its extinct predecessors as well as the original galactic gas swirls. With each new generation, progressively larger atoms were forged in stellar furnaces and the galaxy's range of elements, once restricted to hydrogen, grew larger. About 10 billion years after the Big Bang, a star formed on the outskirts of our galaxy with enough matter left over to create a retinue of planets. Nearly five billion years after that human beings evolved.

The Sun is one of more than 100 billion stars in the home galaxy alone. Our galaxy, in turn, forms part of a local group of approximately 30 similar structures, some much larger than our own; there are at least 100 billion other galaxies in the universe as a whole. The most distant ever observed, a highly energetic galactic core known only as quasar PC 1247 +3406, lies about 12 billion light-years away.

Life of a Star

For most of its existence, a star produces energy by the nuclear fusion of hydrogen into helium at its core. The duration of this hydrogen-burning period – known as the main sequence – depends on the star's mass; the greater the mass, the higher the core temperatures and the sooner the star's supply of hydrogen is exhausted. Dim, dwarf stars consume their hydrogen slowly, eking it out over 1,000 billion years or more. The Sun, like other stars of its mass, should spend about 10 billion years on the main sequence; since it was formed less than five billion years ago, it still has half its life left.

Once all a star's core hydrogen has been fused into helium, nuclear activity moves outward into layers of unconsumed hydrogen. For a time, energy production sharply increases: the star grows hotter and expands enormously, turning into a so-called red giant. Its energy output will increase a thousandfold, and it will swell to a hundred times its present diameter.

After a few hundred million years, helium in the core will become sufficiently compressed to initiate a new cycle of nuclear fusion: from helium to carbon. The star will contract somewhat, before beginning its last expansion, in the Sun's case engulfing the Earth and perhaps Mars. In this bloated condition, the Sun's outer layers will break off into space, leaving a tiny inner core, mainly of carbon, that shrinks progressively under the force of its own gravity: dwarf stars can attain a density more than 10,000 times that of normal matter, with crushing surface gravities to match. Gradually, the nuclear fires will die down, and the Sun will reach its terminal stage: a black dwarf, emitting insignificant amounts of energy.

However, stars more massive than the Sun may undergo another transformation. The additional mass allows gravitational collapse to continue indefinitely: eventually, all the star's remaining matter shrinks to a point, and its density approaches infinity – a state that will not permit even subatomic structures to survive.

The star has become a black hole: an anomalous "singularity" in the fabric of space and time. Although vast coruscations of radiation will be emitted by any matter falling into its grasp, the singularity itself has an escape velocity that exceeds the speed of light, and nothing can ever be released from it. Within the boundaries of the black hole, the laws of physics are suspended, but no physicist can ever observe the extraordinary events that may occur.

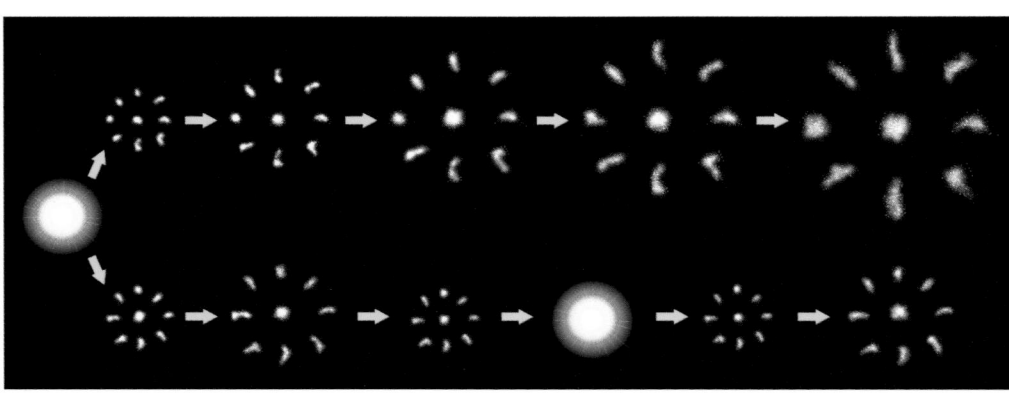

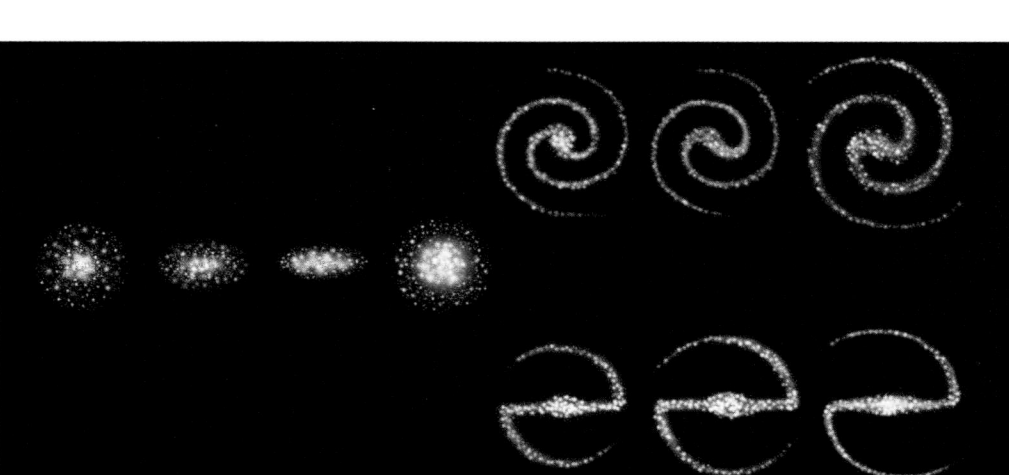

The End of the Universe

The likely fate of the universe is disputed. One theory (top left) dictates that the expansion begun at the time of the Big Bang will continue "indefinitely," with ageing galaxies moving further and further apart in an immense, dark graveyard. Alternatively, gravity may overcome the expansion (bottom left). Galaxies will fall back together until everything is again concentrated at a single point, followed by a new Big Bang and a new expansion, in an endlessly repeated cycle.

The first theory is supported by the amount of visible matter in the universe; the second assumes there is enough dark material to bring about the gravitational collapse.

Galactic Structures

Many of the universe's 100 billion galaxies show clear structural patterns, originally classified by the American astronomer Edwin Hubble in 1925. Spiral galaxies like our own (top row) have a central, almost spherical bulge and a surrounding disk composed of spiral arms. Barred spirals (bottom row) have a central bar of stars across the nucleus, with spiral arms trailing from the ends of the bar. Elliptical galaxies (far left) have a uniform appearance, ranging from a flattened disk to a near sphere. So-called SO galaxies (left row, right) have a central bulge, but no spiral arms. Most galaxies, however, have no obvious structure at all.

Galaxies also vary enormously in size, from dwarfs only 2,000 light-years across to great assemblies of stars 80 or more times larger.

The Home Galaxy

The Sun and its planets are located in one of the spiral arms, a little less than 28,000 light-years from the galactic center and orbiting around it in a period of 200 million years. The center is invisible from the Earth, masked by vast, light-absorbing clouds of interstellar dust. The galaxy is probably around 12 billion years old and, like other spiral galaxies, has three distinct regions. The central bulge is about 30,000 light-years in diameter. The disk in which the Sun is located is not much more than 1,000 light-years thick but 100,000 light-years from end to end. Around the galaxy is the halo, a spherical zone 300,000 light-years across, studded with globular star-clusters and sprinkled with individual suns.

Globular clusters

Bulge

Disk

Solar System

Star Charts

Star charts are drawn as projections of a vast, hollow sphere with the observer in the middle. Each circle below represents slightly more than one hemisphere, centered on the north and south celestial poles respectively – projections of the Earth's poles in the heavens. At the present era, the north pole is marked by the star Polaris; the south pole has no such convenient reference point.

Astronomical coordinates are normally given in terms of "Right Ascension" for longitude and "Declination" for latitude or altitude. Since the stars appear to rotate around the Earth once every 24 hours, Right Ascension is measured eastward – counterclockwise – in hours and minutes and is marked around the edge of the map. One hour is equivalent to 15 angular degrees; zero on the scale is the point at which the Sun crosses the celestial equator at the spring equinox, known to astronomers as the First Point in Aries. Unlike the Sun, stars always rise and set at the same point on the horizon. Declination measures (in degrees) a star's angular distance above or below the celestial equator and is marked on the vertical line.

To use the maps, first choose the one for your hemisphere and hold it with the month at the bottom. The stars in the lower part of the map are then due south (or north, in the southern hemisphere) at about 1 AM local time, not allowing for summer or daylight saving time. Their exact position above the horizon depends on your latitude. The closer to the Equator you live, the higher in the sky these stars will appear. Some additional stars from the map for the other hemisphere will be visible in the lower sky.

Stars near the top of the map will be below the opposite horizon at this date and time but will be visible at other times of the night and year. The sky appears to move counterclockwise around the celestial pole during the course of the day (clockwise in the southern hemisphere), so the same stars will be visible at 11 PM a month earlier.

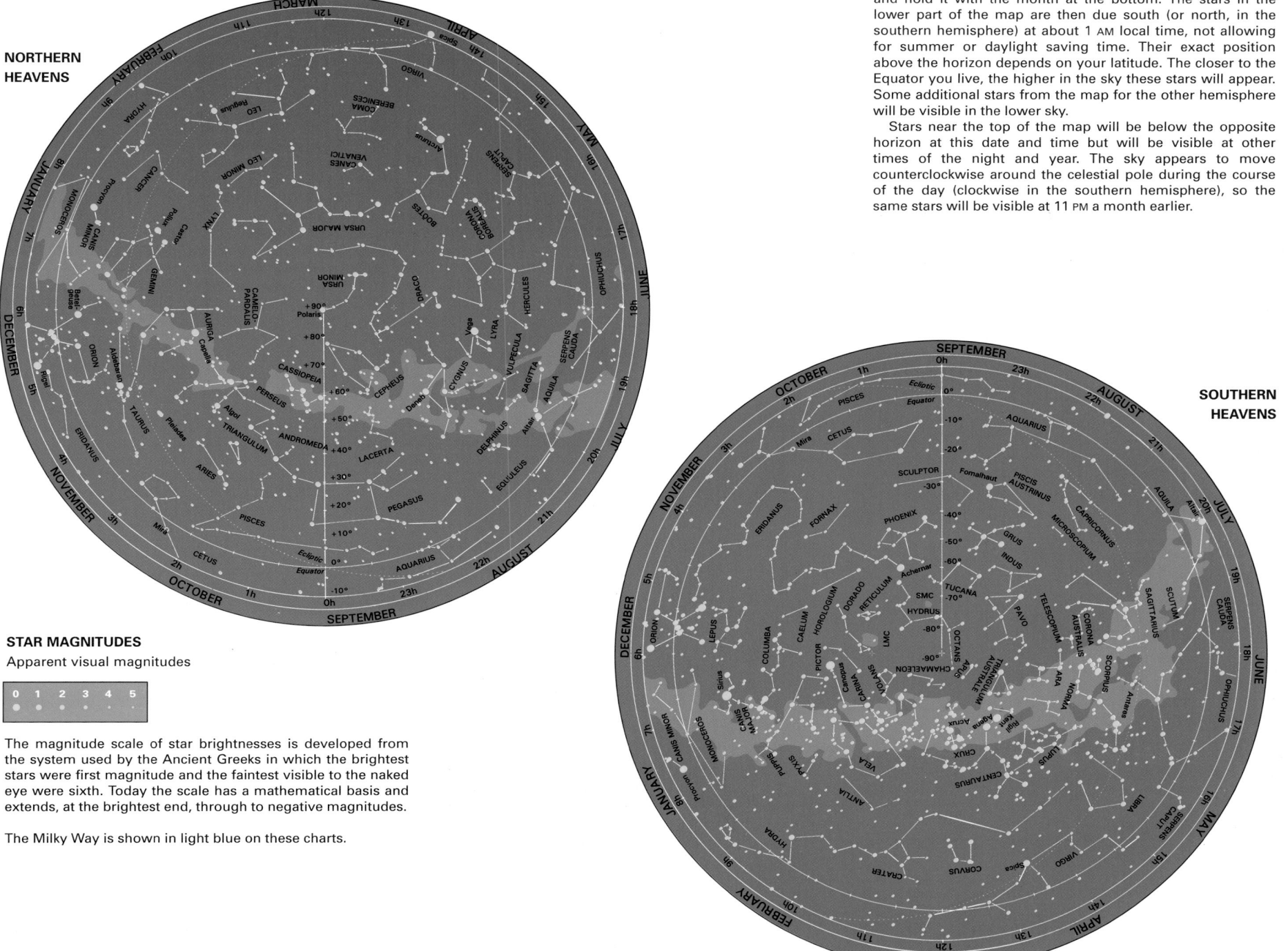

NORTHERN HEAVENS

SOUTHERN HEAVENS

STAR MAGNITUDES

Apparent visual magnitudes

| 0 | 1 | 2 | 3 | 4 | 5 |

The magnitude scale of star brightnesses is developed from the system used by the Ancient Greeks in which the brightest stars were first magnitude and the faintest visible to the naked eye were sixth. Today the scale has a mathematical basis and extends, at the brightest end, through to negative magnitudes.

The Milky Way is shown in light blue on these charts.

THE NEAREST STARS

The 20 nearest stars, excluding the Sun, with their distance from Earth in light-years*

Proxima Centauri	4.25	Many of the nearest stars, like
Alpha Centauri A	4.3	Alpha Centauri A and B, are
Alpha Centauri B	4.3	doubles, orbiting about the
Barnard's Star	6.0	common center of gravity
Wolf 359	7.8	and to all intents and
Lalande 21185	8.3	purposes equidistant from
Sirius A	8.7	Earth. Many of them are dim
Sirius B	8.7	objects, with no name other
UV Ceti A	8.7	than the designation given
UV Ceti B	8.7	by the astronomers who
Ross 154	9.4	investigated them. However,
Ross 248	10.3	they include Sirius, the
Epsilon Eridani	10.7	brightest star in the sky,
Ross 128	10.9	and Procyon, the seventh
61 Cygni A	11.1	brightest. Both are far larger
61 Cygni B	11.1	than the Sun; of the nearest
Epsilon Indi	11.2	stars, only Epsilon Eridani is
Groombridge 34A	11.2	similar in size and luminosity.
Groombridge 34B	11.2	
L789-6	11.2	* A light-year equals approx.
Procyon A	11.4	5,900 billion miles
Procyon B	11.4	

THE CONSTELLATIONS

The constellations and their English names

Andromeda	Andromeda	Circinus	Compasses	Lacerta	Lizard	Piscis Austrinus	Southern Fish
Antlia	Air Pump	Columba	Dove	Leo	Lion	Puppis	Ship's Stern
Apus	Bird of Paradise	Coma Berenices	Berenice's Hair	Leo Minor	Little Lion	Pyxis	Mariner's Compass
Aquarius	Water Carrier	Corona Australis	Southern Crown	Lepus	Hare	Reticulum	Net
Aquila	Eagle	Corona Borealis	Northern Crown	Libra	Scales	Sagitta	Arrow
Ara	Altar	Corvus	Crow	Lupus	Wolf	Sagittarius	Archer
Aries	Ram	Crater	Cup	Lynx	Lynx	Scorpius	Scorpion
Auriga	Charioteer	Crux	Southern Cross	Lyra	Lyre	Sculptor	Sculptor
Boötes	Herdsman	Cygnus	Swan	Mensa	Table	Scutum	Shield
Caelum	Chisel	Delphinus	Dolphin	Microscopium	Microscope	Serpens	Serpent
Camelopardalis	Giraffe	Dorado	Swordfish	Monoceros	Unicorn	Sextans	Sextant
Cancer	Crab	Draco	Dragon	Musca	Fly	Taurus	Bull
Canes Venatici	Hunting Dogs	Equuleus	Little Horse	Norma	Level	Telescopium	Telescope
Canis Major	Great Dog	Eridanus	Eridanus	Octans	Octant	Triangulum	Triangle
Canis Minor	Little Dog	Fornax	Furnace	Ophiuchus	Serpent Bearer	Triangulum Australe	Southern Triangle
Capricornus	Goat	Gemini	Twins	Orion	Orion	Tucana	Toucan
Carina	Keel	Grus	Crane	Pavo	Peacock	Ursa Major	Great Bear
Cassiopeia	Cassiopeia	Hercules	Hercules	Pegasus	Winged Horse	Ursa Minor	Little Bear
Centaurus	Centaur	Horologium	Clock	Perseus	Perseus	Vela	Sails
Cepheus	Cepheus	Hydra	Water Snake	Phoenix	Phoenix	Virgo	Virgin
Cetus	Whale	Hydrus	Sea Serpent	Pictor	Easel	Volans	Flying Fish
Chamaeleon	Chameleon	Indus	Indian	Pisces	Fishes	Vulpecula	Fox

The Solar System

Lying 28,000 light-years from the center of one of billions of galaxies that comprise the observable universe, our Solar System contains nine planets and their moons, innumerable asteroids and comets, and a miscellany of dust and gas, all tethered by the immense gravitational field of the Sun, the middling-sized star whose thermonuclear furnaces provide them all with heat and light. The Solar System was formed about 4.6 billion years ago, when a spinning cloud of gas, mostly hydrogen but seeded with other, heavier elements, condensed enough to ignite a nuclear reaction and create a star. The Sun still accounts for almost 99.9% of the system's total mass; one planet, Jupiter, contains most of the remainder.

By composition as well as distance, the planetary array divides quite neatly in two: an inner system of four small, solid planets, including the Earth, and an outer system, from Jupiter to Neptune, of four much larger planets composed of lighter materials, such as gas, liquid and ice. Between the two groups lies a scattering of rocky asteroids, perhaps as many as 400,000. They may be debris left over from the inner solar system's formation. The outermost planet, Pluto, may simply be the largest of a number of bodies composed of rock and ice orbiting beyond Neptune, similarly left over from the formation of the outer solar system.

By the 1990s, however, the Solar System also included some newer anomalies: several thousand spacecraft. Most were in orbit around the Earth, but some had probed far and wide around the system. The valuable information beamed back by these robotic investigators has transformed our knowledge of our celestial environment.

Much of the early history of science is the story of people trying to make sense of the errant points of light that were all they knew of the planets. Now, men have themselves stood on the Earth's Moon; probes have landed on Mars and Venus, and orbiting radars have mapped far distant landscapes with astonishing accuracy. In the 1980s, the US *Voyagers* skimmed all four major planets of the outer system, bringing new revelations with each close approach. Only Pluto, inscrutably distant in an orbit that takes it 50 times the Earth's distance from the Sun, remains unvisited by our messengers.

Orbits of the Planets

The solar planets and their orbits, showing the relative position of each planet at the vernal equinox of 1992.

Orbits are drawn to exact scale, but with the Sun and planets greatly enlarged for clarity. The Solar System is shown from the viewpoint of an observer a few light-hours distant in the direction of the constellation Hercules. Seen from such a position, above the plane of the ecliptic, all the planets revolve about the Sun in a counterclockwise direction. The perspective view exaggerates the elliptical form of all the planetary orbits: only Pluto and Mercury follow paths that deviate noticeably from circularity. Near perihelion – its closest approach to the Sun – Pluto actually passes inside the orbit of Neptune, an event that last occurred in 1983. Pluto did not regain its station as the Sun's outermost planet until February 1999.

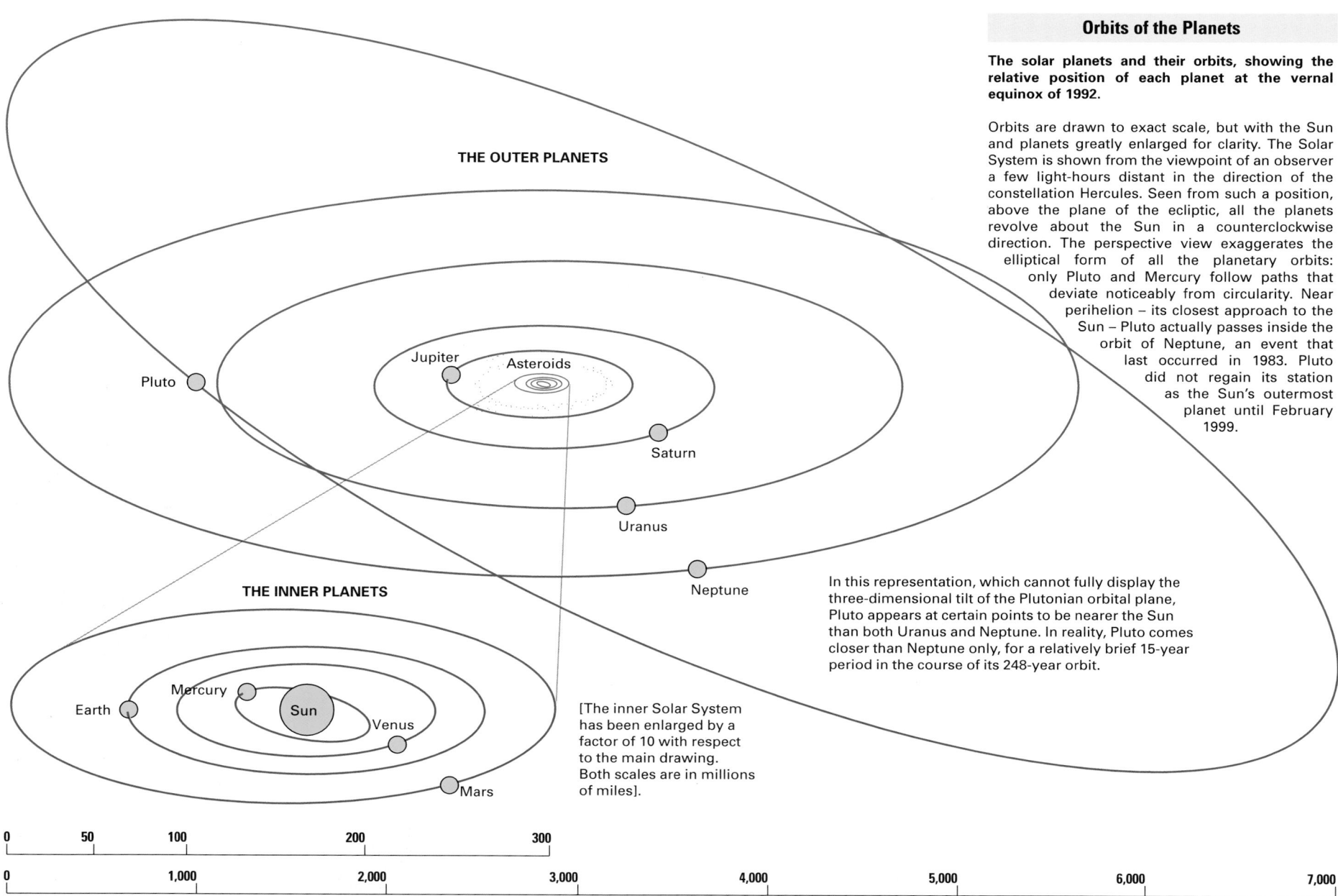

THE OUTER PLANETS

Pluto

Jupiter   Asteroids

Saturn

Uranus

Neptune

THE INNER PLANETS

Mercury

Earth

Sun

Venus

Mars

[The inner Solar System has been enlarged by a factor of 10 with respect to the main drawing. Both scales are in millions of miles].

In this representation, which cannot fully display the three-dimensional tilt of the Plutonian orbital plane, Pluto appears at certain points to be nearer the Sun than both Uranus and Neptune. In reality, Pluto comes closer than Neptune only, for a relatively brief 15-year period in the course of its 248-year orbit.

0	50	100	200	300

0	1,000	2,000	3,000	4,000	5,000	6,000	7,000

Planetary Data

	Mean distance from Sun (million miles)	Mass (Earth = 1)	Period of orbit (Earth years)	Period of rotation (Earth days)	Equatorial diameter (miles)	Average density (water = 1)	Surface gravity (Earth = 1)	Escape velocity (miles/sec)	Number of known satellites
Sun	–	332,946	–	25.38	870,000	1.41	27.9	383.7	–
Mercury	36.0	0.06	0.241	58.67	3,031	5.43	0.38	2.64	0
Venus	67.2	0.8	0.615	243.00	7,519	5.24	0.90	6.44	0
Earth	93.0	1.0	1.00	1.00	7,926	5.52	1.00	6.95	1
Mars	141.6	0.1	1.88	1.02	4,222	3.93	0.38	3.13	2
Jupiter	483.6	317.8	11.86	0.41	88,732	1.33	2.69	37.03	16
Saturn	886.0	95.2	29.46	0.42	74,500	0.706	1.16	22.12	18
Uranus	1,783.0	14.5	84.01	0.45	32,600	1.25	0.93	13.11	15
Neptune	2,793.9	17.1	164.79	0.71	30,100	1.77	1.21	15.29	8
Pluto	3,666.2	0.002	247.7	6.39	1,519	1.40	0.05	0.75	1

Planetary days are given in sidereal time – that is, with respect to the stars rather than the Sun. Most of the information in the table was confirmed by spacecraft and often obtained from photographs and other data transmitted back to the Earth. In the case of Pluto, however, only earthbound observations have been made, and no spacecraft will encounter it until well into the 21st century. Given the planet's small size and great distance, figures for its diameter and rotation period have only recently been confirmed.

Pluto is not massive enough to account for the perturbations in the orbits of Uranus and Neptune that led to its 1930 discovery, but it is now widely believed that these perturbations can be explained away as observational errors made by the earlier observers.

The Planets

Mercury is the closest planet to the Sun and hence the fastest-moving. It is very hot with a cratered, wrinkled surface very similar to that of Earth's Moon. It is small and has no gravity, hence there is no significant atmosphere.

Venus has much the same physical dimensions as Earth. Its dense atmosphere is composed of 97% CO_2 resulting in a runaway greenhouse effect that makes the Venusian surface, at 890°F, the hottest of all the planets in the Solar System. Radar mapping shows relatively level land with volcanic regions whose sulfurous discharges explain the sulfuric acid rains reported by soft-landing space probes before they succumbed to Venus' fierce climate.

Earth seen from space is easily the most beautiful of the inner planets; it is also, and more objectively, the largest, as well as the only home of known life. Living things are the main reason why the Earth is able to retain a substantial proportion of corrosive and highly reactive oxygen in its atmosphere, a state of affairs that contradicts the laws of chemical equilibrium; the oxygen in turn supports the life that constantly regenerates it.

Mars, smaller and cooler than the Earth, is nevertheless the most likely planet other than Earth where life may have formed. Vast water channels show that it was once warmer and wetter; there may still be traces of former simple life forms, though whether life could thrive in its current cold, dry and thin atmosphere is doubtful. The ice caps are mainly frozen carbon dioxide, and whatever oxygen the planet once possessed is now locked up in the iron-bearing rock that covers its cratered surface and gives it its characteristic red hue. Mars is a dustbowl with occasional storms whirling the dust high into the air.

Jupiter masses almost three times as much as all the other planets combined; had it scooped up rather more matter during its formation, it might have evolved into a small companion star for the Sun. The planet is mostly gas, under intense pressure in the lower atmosphere above a core of fiercely compressed hydrogen and helium. The upper layers form strikingly-colored rotating belts, the outward sign of the intense storms created by Jupiter's rapid diurnal rotation. Close approaches by spacecraft have shown an orbiting ring system and discovered several previously unknown moons: Jupiter has at least 16 moons.

Saturn is structurally similar to Jupiter, rotating fast enough to produce an obvious bulge at its equator. It is composed of 89% hydrogen and 11% helium, and has wind velocities in the outer atmosphere of 1,600 feet per second. Ever since the invention of the telescope, however, Saturn's rings have been the feature that has attracted most observers. *Voyager* probes in 1980 and 1981 sent back detailed pictures that showed them to be composed of thousands of separate ringlets, each in turn made up of tiny icy particles.

Uranus was unknown to the ancients. Although it is faintly visible to the naked eye, it was not discovered until 1781. Its interior is largely water, with an atmosphere of hydrogen, helium and some methane, which gives the planet its blue-green color. Observations in 1977 suggested the presence of a faint ring system, amply confirmed when *Voyager 2* swung past the planet in 1986.

Neptune is always more than 2.5 billion miles from Earth, and despite its diameter of almost 30,000 miles, it can only be seen by telescope. Its 1846 discovery was the result of mathematical predictions by astronomers seeking to explain irregularities in the orbit of Uranus, but until *Voyager 2* closed with the planet in 1989, little was known of it. Like Uranus, it has a ring system; *Voyager*'s photographs revealed a total of eight moons.

Pluto is the most mysterious of the solar planets, if only because even the most powerful telescopes can scarcely resolve it from a point of light to a disk. It was discovered as recently as 1930, like Neptune as the result of perturbations in the orbits of the two then outermost planets. Its small size, as well as its eccentric and highly tilted orbit, has led to suggestions that it is a former satellite of Neptune, somehow liberated from its primary. In 1978 Pluto was found to have a moon of its own, Charon, apparently half the size of Pluto itself.

Mean distance from the Sun in million miles (not to scale)

Planet	Distance
Mercury	36.0
Venus	67.2
Earth	93.0
Mars	141.6
Jupiter	483.6
Saturn	886.6
Uranus	1,783.0
Neptune	2,793.9
Pluto	3,666.2

Diagram not drawn to scale

Time and Motion

The basic unit of time measurement is the day, that is, one rotation of the Earth on its axis. Our present calendar is based on the solar year of 365.24 days, the time taken by the Earth to orbit the Sun.

Calendars based on the movements of the Sun and Moon have been used since ancient times. The average length of the year, according to the Julian Calendar introduced by Julius Caesar, was about 11 minutes too long. The cumulative error was rectified in 1582 by the Gregorian Calendar, when Pope Gregory XIII decreed that the day following 4 October was 15 October, and in that century years did not count as leap years unless they were divisible by 400. England finally adopted the reformed calendar in 1752, when it was 11 days behind the European mainland.

The rotation of the Earth on its axis causes day and night. Because the Earth rotates through 360° every 24 hours, the world is divided into 24 time zones centered on lines of longitude at 15° longitude.

The tilt of the Earth's axis, also called the obliquity of the ecliptic, accounts for the seasons which are so familiar in the middle latitudes. But geological evidence shows that, over long periods of time, climates change and the advances and retreats of the ice during the Pleistocene Ice Age may have been caused by regular variations in the Earth's tilt, its orbit around the Sun, and changes in the season when it is closest to the Sun (perihelion).

Earth Data

Aphelion (maximum distance from Sun): 94,452,780 miles

Perihelion (minimum distance from Sun): 91,342,080 miles

Angle of tilt (obliquity of the ecliptic): 23° 27' 08"

Length of year – solar tropical (equinox to equinox): 365.24 days

Length of year: 365 days, 5 hours, 48 minutes, 46 seconds of mean solar time

Superficial area: 197,000,000 sq mi

Land surface: 57,500,000 sq mi (29.2%)

Water surface: 139,500,000 sq mi (70.8%)

Equatorial circumference: 24,903 mi

Polar circumference: 24,860 mi

Equatorial diameter: 7,926.7 mi

Polar diameter: 7,900.0 mi

Equatorial radius: 3,963.4 mi

Polar radius: 3,950.0 mi

Volume of the Earth: 260,000 x 10⁶ cu mi

Mass of the Earth: 6.5 x 10²¹ tons

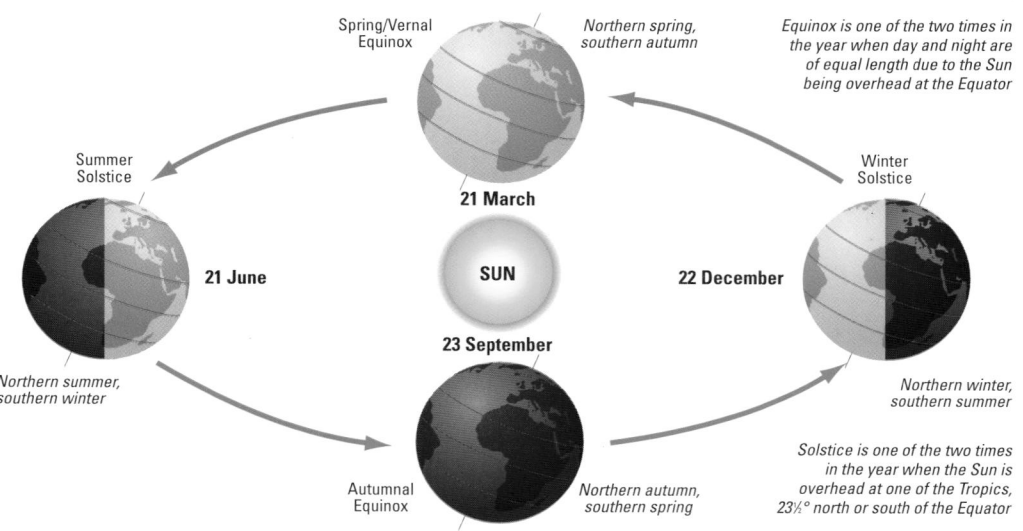

The Seasons

Seasons occur because the Earth's axis is tilted at a constant angle of 23½°. When the northern hemisphere is tilted to a maximum extent toward the Sun, on 21 June, the Sun is overhead at the Tropic of Cancer (latitude 23½° North). This is midsummer, or the summer solstice, in the northern hemisphere.

On 22 or 23 September, the Sun is overhead at the Equator, and day and night are of equal length throughout the world. This is the autumn equinox in the northern hemisphere. On 21 or 22 December, the Sun is overhead at the Tropic of Capricorn (23½° South), the winter solstice in the northern hemisphere. The overhead Sun then tracks north until, on 21 March, it is overhead at the Equator. This is the spring (vernal) equinox in the northern hemisphere.

In the southern hemisphere, the seasons are the reverse of those in the north.

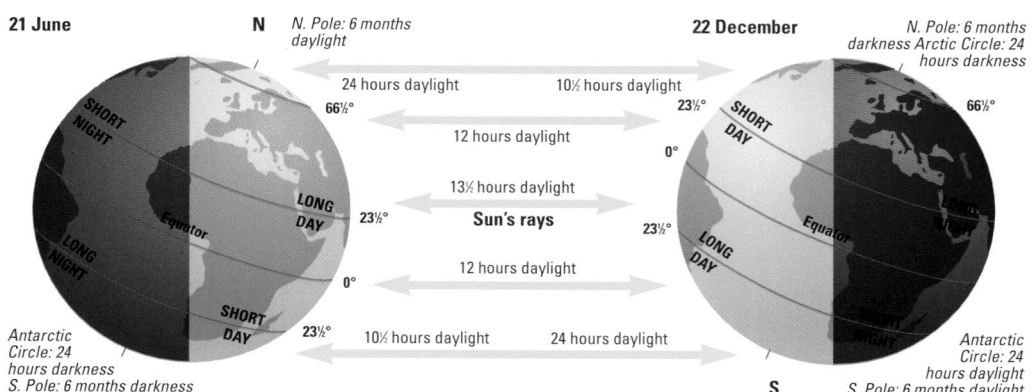

Day and Night

The Sun appears to rise in the east, reach its highest point at noon, and then set in the west, to be followed by night. In reality, it is not the Sun that is moving but the Earth rotating from west to east. The moment when the Sun's upper limb first appears above the horizon is termed sunrise; the moment when the Sun's upper limb disappears below the horizon is sunset.

At the summer solstice in the northern hemisphere (21 June), the Arctic has total daylight and the Antarctic total darkness. The opposite occurs at the winter solstice (21 or 22 December). At the Equator, the length of day and night are almost equal all year.

The Sun's Path

The diagrams on the right illustrate the apparent path of the Sun at (A) the Equator, (B) in midlatitude (45°), (C) at the Arctic Circle (66½°), and (D) at the North Pole, where there are six months of continuous daylight and six months of continuous night.

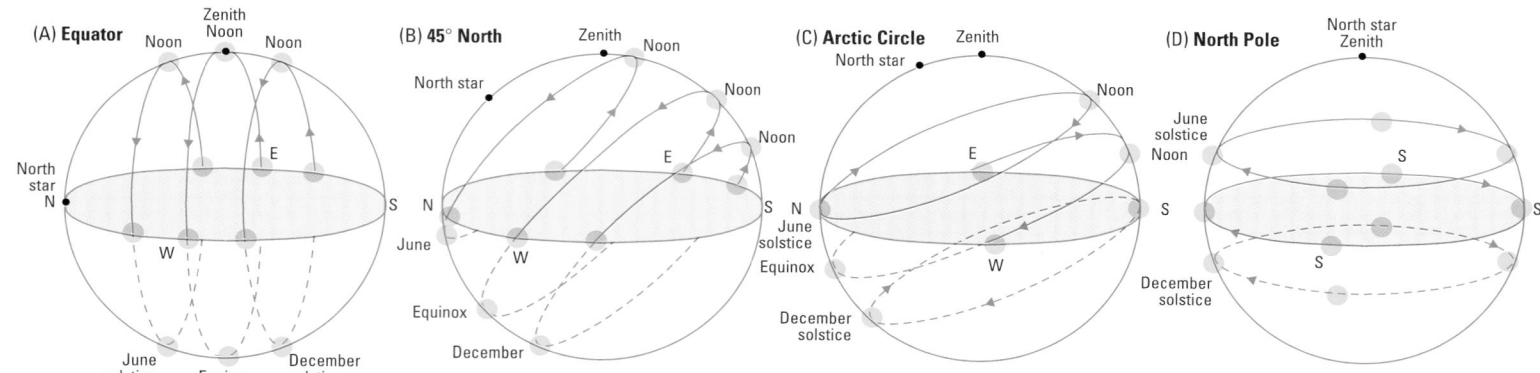

Sunrise and Sunset

The term equinox comes from two Latin words meaning "equal night." At the spring and autumn equinoxes, the Sun is vertically overhead at the Equator and all places on Earth have 12 hours of darkness and 12 of daylight. The graphs showing sunrise and sunset show that these occasions occur on 21 March and on 22 or 23 September. The graphs also show that, because the Sun remains high in the sky throughout the year, the length of the day and night at the Equator remain roughly the same throughout the year, with sunrise occurring around 6 AM and sunset at around 6 PM. The further north or south one travels, the greater the difference between the number of hours of daylight and darkness. For example, the graph, right, shows that at latitude 60°N, sunrise varies from just after 9 AM in midwinter (on 22 or 23 December) to about 2.30 AM in midsummer (around the summer solstice on 21 June). By contrast, the second graph, far right, shows that sunset at latitude 60°N occurs at about 2.45 PM in midwinter and 9.20 PM in midsummer.

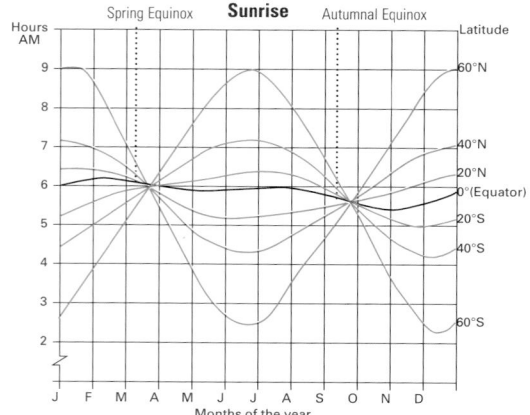

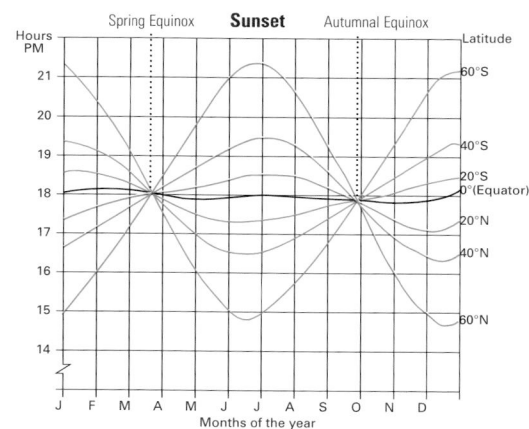

The Moon

The Moon rotates more slowly than the Earth, making one complete turn on its axis in just over 27 days. Since this corresponds to its period of revolution around the Earth, the Moon always presents the same hemisphere or face to us, and we never see "the dark side." The interval between one full Moon and the next (and between new Moons) is about 29½ days – a lunar month. The apparent changes in the shape of the Moon are caused by its changing position in relation to the Earth; like the planets, it produces no light of its own and shines only by reflecting the rays of the Sun.

Phases of the Moon

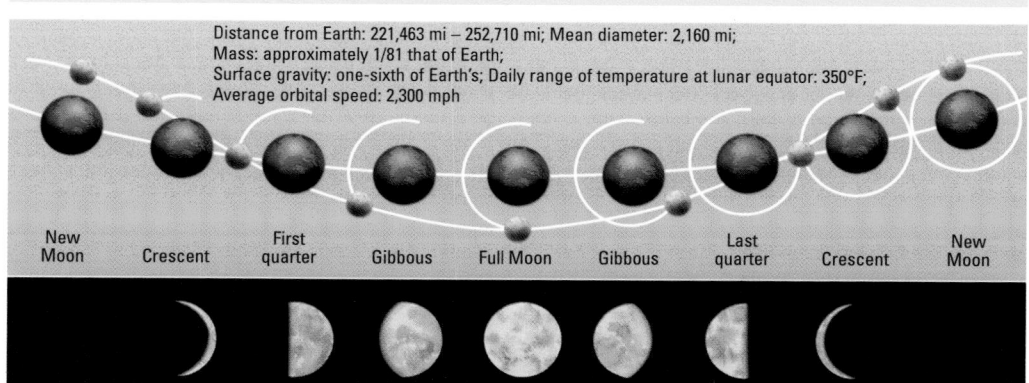

Distance from Earth: 221,463 mi – 252,710 mi; Mean diameter: 2,160 mi;
Mass: approximately 1/81 that of Earth;
Surface gravity: one-sixth of Earth's; Daily range of temperature at lunar equator: 350°F;
Average orbital speed: 2,300 mph

New Moon | Crescent | First quarter | Gibbous | Full Moon | Gibbous | Last quarter | Crescent | New Moon

Moon Data

Distance from Earth
The Moon orbits at a mean distance of 238,731 mi, at an average speed of 2,289 mph in relation to the Earth.

Size and mass
The average diameter of the Moon is 2,159.3 mi. It is 400 times smaller than the Sun but is about 400 times closer to the Earth, so we see them as the same size. The Moon has a mass of 7,975 x 10^{19} tons, with a density 3.344 times that of water.

Visibility
Only 59% of the Moon's surface is directly visible from Earth. Reflected light takes 1.25 seconds to reach Earth – compared to 8 minutes 27.3 seconds for light to reach us from the Sun.

Temperature
With the Sun overhead, the temperature on the lunar equator can reach 243°F. At night it can sink to −261°F.

Eclipses

When the Moon passes between the Sun and the Earth it causes a partial eclipse of the Sun (1) if the Earth passes through the Moon's outer shadow (P), or a total eclipse (2) if the inner cone shadow crosses the Earth's surface. In a lunar eclipse, the Earth's shadow crosses the Moon and, again, provides either a partial or total eclipse.

Eclipses of the Sun and the Moon do not occur every month because of the 5° difference between the plane of the Moon's orbit and the plane in which the Earth moves. In the 1990s only 14 lunar eclipses are possible, for example, seven partial and seven total; each is visible only from certain, and variable, parts of the world. The same period witnesses 13 solar eclipses – six partial (or annular) and seven total.

Partial eclipse (1)

P P P

Solar eclipse

Lunar eclipse

Total eclipse (2)

Tides

The daily rise and fall of the ocean's tides are the result of the gravitational pull of the Moon and that of the Sun, though the effect of the latter is only 46.6% as strong as that of the Moon. This effect is greatest on the hemisphere facing the Moon and causes a tidal "bulge." When the Sun, Earth and Moon are in line, tide-raising forces are at a maximum and Spring tides occur: high tide reaches the highest values, and low tide falls to low levels. When lunar and solar forces are least coincidental with the Sun and Moon at an angle (near the Moon's first and third quarters), Neap tides occur, which have a small tidal range.

Spring tide

Neap tide

Spring tide

Last quarter

New Moon

Full Moon

Neap tide

Gravitational pull by the Sun

First quarter

Time Zones

The Earth rotates through 360° in 24 hours, and so moves 15° every hour. The world is divided into 24 standard time zones, each centered on lines of longitude at 15° intervals. At the center of the first zone is the Prime meridian or Greenwich meridian. All places to the west of Greenwich are one hour behind for every 15° of longitude; places to the east are ahead by one hour for every 15°. When it is 12 noon at the Greenwich meridian, 180° east it is midnight of the same day – while 180° west the day is just beginning. To overcome this, the International Date Line was established, approximately following the 180° meridian. Thus, if you traveled eastward from Japan (140° East) to Samoa (170° West), you would pass from Sunday night into Sunday morning.

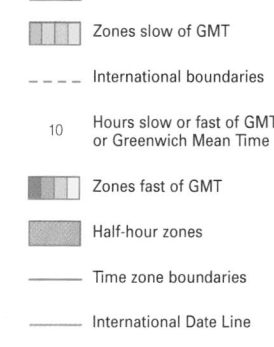

Zones using GMT

Zones slow of GMT

- - - - - International boundaries

10   Hours slow or fast of GMT or Greenwich Mean Time

Zones fast of GMT

Half-hour zones

Time zone boundaries

International Date Line

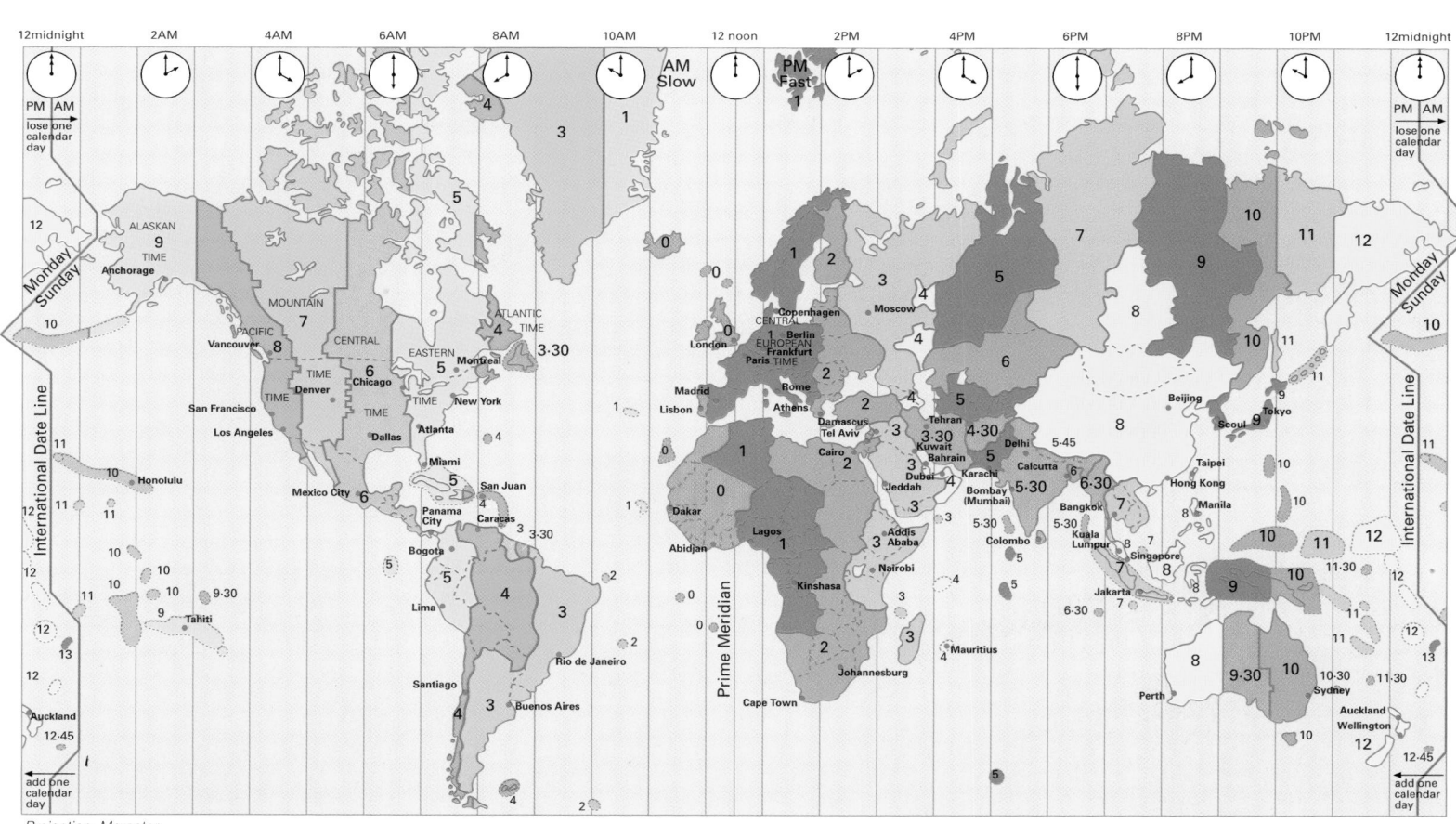

Projection: Mercator

Oceans

The last 40 years have been described as the "Space Age," but another exciting and perhaps even more important area of discovery, proceeding at the same time, has been the exploration of "inner space," namely the oceans which cover more than 70% of our planet. The study of the ocean floor and oceanic islands has revealed features that help to explain how continents move, and how the movements are related to earthquakes and volcanic activity.

Manned submersibles have established that life exists even in the deepest trenches, where the pressure reaches 1,000 atmospheres, the equivalent of the force of six and a half tons bearing down on every square inch. Further exploration in the pitch-black environment of the ocean ridges has revealed strange forms of marine life around scalding hot vents. The creatures include giant tubeworms, blind shrimps, and bacteria, some of which are genetically very different from any other known life forms. In 1996, an analysis of one micro-organism revealed that at least half of its 1,700 or so genes were hitherto unknown. This environment, which is based on chemicals, not sunlight, may resemble the places where life on Earth first began.

Another vital area of contemporary research concerns the interactions between the oceans and the atmosphere, as exemplified in the El Niño–Southern Oscillation (ENSO), and the bearing that these have on climatic change.

Most geographers divide the world's ocean waters into four areas: the Pacific, Atlantic, Indian and Arctic oceans. The most active zone in the oceans is the sun-lit upper layer, where the water is moved around by wind-blown currents. It is the home of most sea life and acts as a membrane through which the ocean breathes,

Seawater

The chemical composition of the sea, by percentage, excluding the elements of water itself

Chloride (Cl)	55.04%
Sodium (Na)	30.61%
Sulfate (SO₄)	7.69%
Magnesium (Mg)	3.69%
Calcium (Ca)	1.16%
Potassium (K)	1.10%
Bicarbonate (HCO₃)	0.41%
Bromide (Br)	0.19%
Boric Acid (H₃BO₃)	0.07%
Strontium (Sr)	0.04%
Fluoride (Fl)	0.003%
Lithium (Li)	trace
Rubidium (Rb)	trace
Phosphorus (P)	trace
Iodine (I)	trace
Barium (Ba)	trace
Arsenic (As)	trace
Cesium (Cs)	trace

Eleven constituents account for over 99% of the salt content of seawater, but seawater also contains virtually every other element. In natural conditions, its composition is broadly consistent across the world's seas and oceans; but in coastal areas especially, variations are sometimes substantial. The oceans are about 35 parts water to one part salt.

Atoll Building

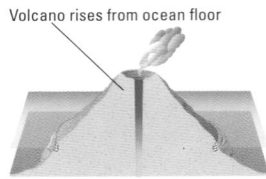

Volcano rises from ocean floor

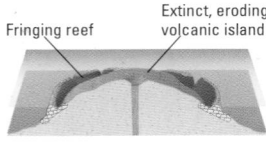

Fringing reef — Extinct, eroding volcanic island

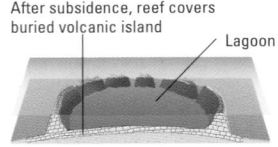

After subsidence, reef covers buried volcanic island — Lagoon

A coral atoll usually begins existence as a bare volcanic peak, thrusting above the surface of the ocean. A colony of coral – organisms with calcium carbonate skeletons – forms itself in the shallow water around the peak. The volcano is eroded and slowly sinks, leaving the coral forming a ring of hard limestone around its remnant. In time, the barrier reef of an atoll is all that remains.

Life in the Oceans

An imaginary profile of the typical coastal and oceanic zones is shown, with a selection of the life forms that might occur in the water off the Pacific Coast of Central America. The animals illustrated are not drawn to scale as the range of sizes is too great. Most marine life is confined to the first 650 feet, the upper sunlit (photic) zone, where sunlight can still penetrate. Plant and animal plankton, the basis of life in the ocean, occur in great quantities in all zones.

In the pelagic environment (open sea), vertical gradients, including those of light, temperature and salinity, determine the distribution of organisms. From the tidal zone at the coastline, the continental shelf, geologically still part of the continental landmass, drops gently to about 650 feet – the sunlit zone. At the end of the shelf, the seabed falls away in the steeper angle of the continental slope. The subsequent descent to the deep ocean floor, known as the continental rise, is more gentle, with gradients between 1 in 100 and 1 in 700 until the abyssal plains and hills between 8,000 and 19,500 feet below the surface.

The deep sea floor contains seamounts, some of which are capped by coral reefs, ocean ridges, the longest mountain chains on Earth, and deep ocean trenches, especially in the Pacific Ocean where six trenches reach depths of more than 33,000 feet, including the Mariana Trench at 36,000 feet deep.

Each of these zones contains a distinctive community of species adapted to the different conditions of salinity, temperature and light intensity. Indeed, a few organisms have been found even in the abyssal darkness of the great ocean trenches.

absorbing great quantities of carbon dioxide and partly exchanging it for oxygen.

As the depth increases, so light fades and temperatures fall until just before 3,000 feet where there is a marked temperature change at the thermocline, the boundary between the warm surface zone and the cold deep zone. Below the thermocline, slow currents are caused by density differences between bodies of water with varying temperatures and salinity.

The El Niño Phenomenon

The importance of the ocean–atmosphere interaction is nowhere more dramatically demonstrated than the El Niño phenomenon in the southern Pacific Ocean.

Under normal conditions, shown in the diagram, top right, surface water flows eastward from South America under the influence of trade winds while, near the coast, cold, nutrient-rich water (dark blue) rises to the surface and spreads westward. In the western Pacific, sea surface temperatures reach 82°F or more and warm air rises, creating a low pressure air system and causing heavy rains. The rising warm air spreads out and some of it descends over South America and the eastern Pacific creating a high pressure air system from which winds blow westward. This rotating system is called a Walker Circulation Cell.

An El Niño event, also called an El Niño–Southern Oscillation cycle, or ENSO cycle, is characterized by a reversal of currents whereby the eastward-moving South Equatorial Current extends much further eastward and the trade winds weaken. The upwelling of cold water off South America is greatly reduced and surface water temperatures rise, causing a drastic reduction in fish life. The heaviest rainfall is over the eastern Pacific, while Southeast Asia is much drier than usual. Warm air rises in the east and spreads out, descending in the western Pacific, which then becomes a high pressure area, as shown in the second diagram, below right.

During an intense El Niño, such as in 1982–83 when sea temperatures in the eastern Pacific rose by 11°F, the effects of the current and wind reversals affect the weather around the world. In Australia and Southeast Asia, the monsoon rainfall is reduced, while, in 1983–84, a severe drought occurred in the Sahel, south of the Sahara, and also in southern Africa. The south-east coast of the United States also suffered storms and heavy rainfall, and even Europe experienced changes in weather patterns, possibly as a result of consequent changes in the course of the jet stream.

Scientists have found evidence that the frequency of the El Niño event, which normally occurs every two to seven years, may have increased in recent years with warm conditions persisting in the eastern Pacific from 1990 until mid-1995, an unprecedented length of time during the 114 years for which data exist. Another intense El Niño occurred in 1997–98, with resultant freak weather conditions across the entire Pacific region. Scientists do not know the causes of the El Niño event, though some researchers are investigating possible connections between major volcanic eruptions in the tropical Pacific region, the ENSO cycle and atmospheric circulation.

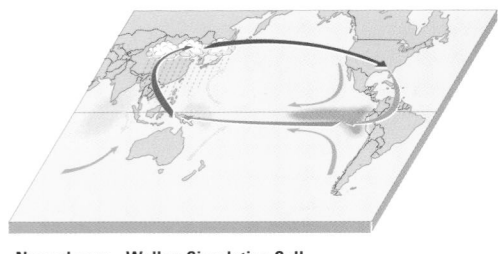

Normal year – Walker Circulation Cell

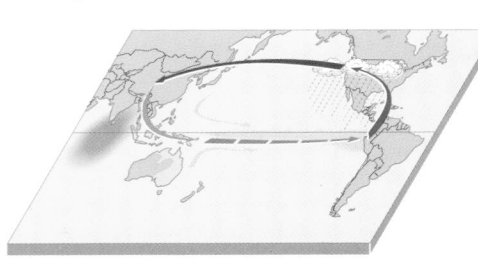

El Niño event

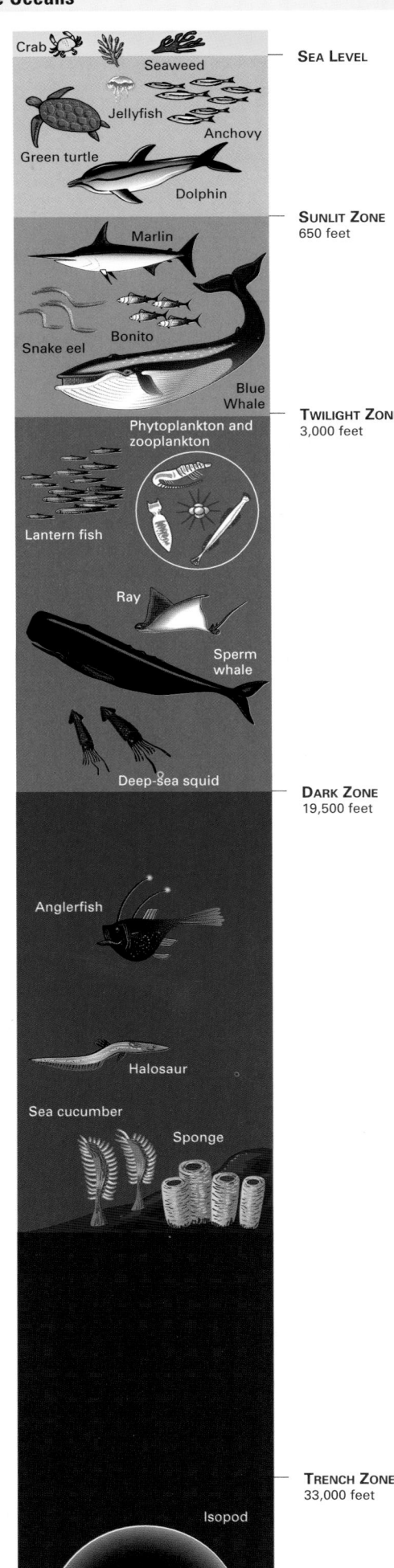

Crab · Seaweed · Jellyfish · Anchovy · Green turtle · Dolphin — **SEA LEVEL**

Marlin · Bonito · Snake eel · Blue Whale — **SUNLIT ZONE** 650 feet

Phytoplankton and zooplankton · Lantern fish · Ray · Sperm whale — **TWILIGHT ZONE** 3,000 feet

Deep-sea squid — **DARK ZONE** 19,500 feet

Anglerfish · Halosaur · Sea cucumber · Sponge

Isopod — **TRENCH ZONE** 33,000 feet

Ocean Currents

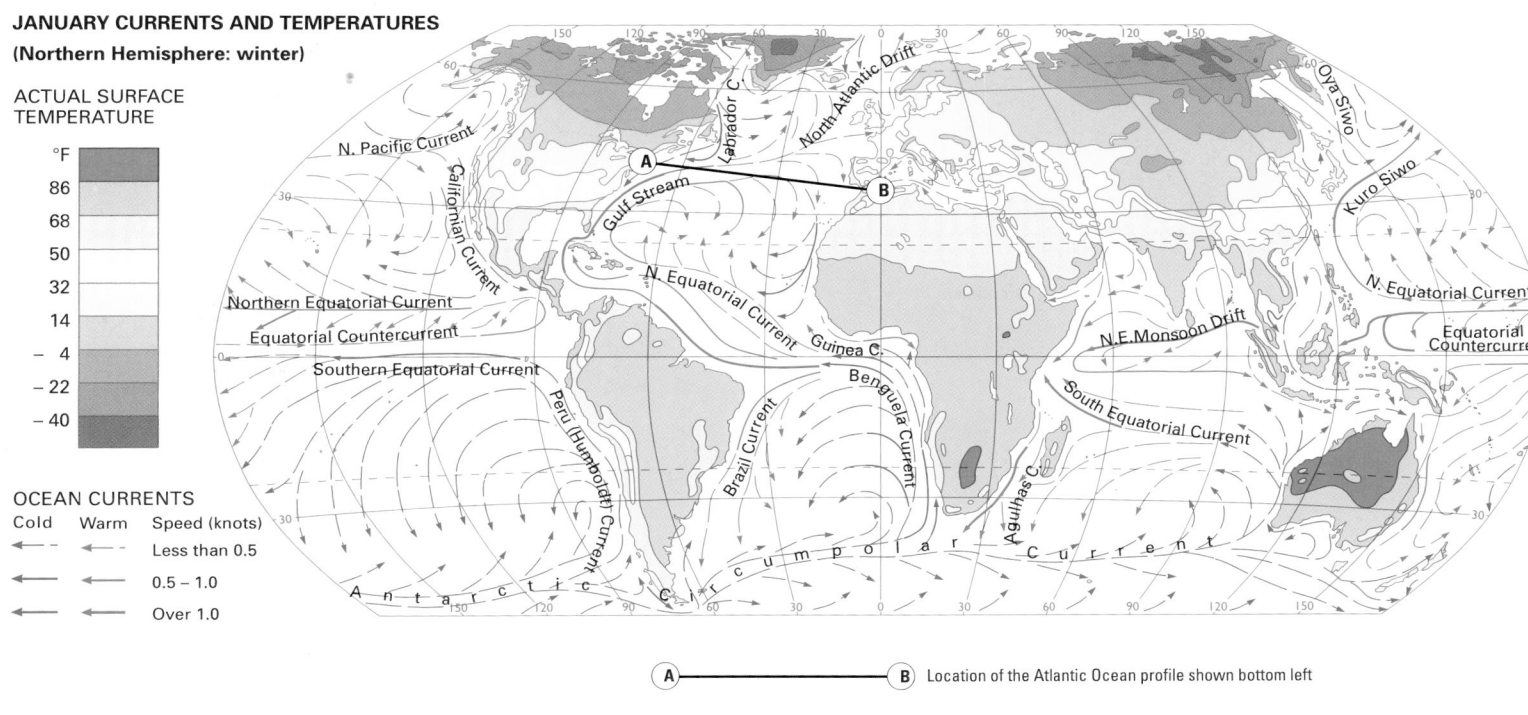

JANUARY CURRENTS AND TEMPERATURES
(Northern Hemisphere: winter)

ACTUAL SURFACE TEMPERATURE

°F	
86	
68	
50	
32	
14	
− 4	
− 22	
− 40	

OCEAN CURRENTS

Cold	Warm	Speed (knots)
←---	←---	Less than 0.5
←—	←—	0.5 – 1.0
←—	←—	Over 1.0

Ⓐ ———————————— Ⓑ Location of the Atlantic Ocean profile shown bottom left

JULY CURRENTS AND TEMPERATURES
(Northern Hemisphere: summer)

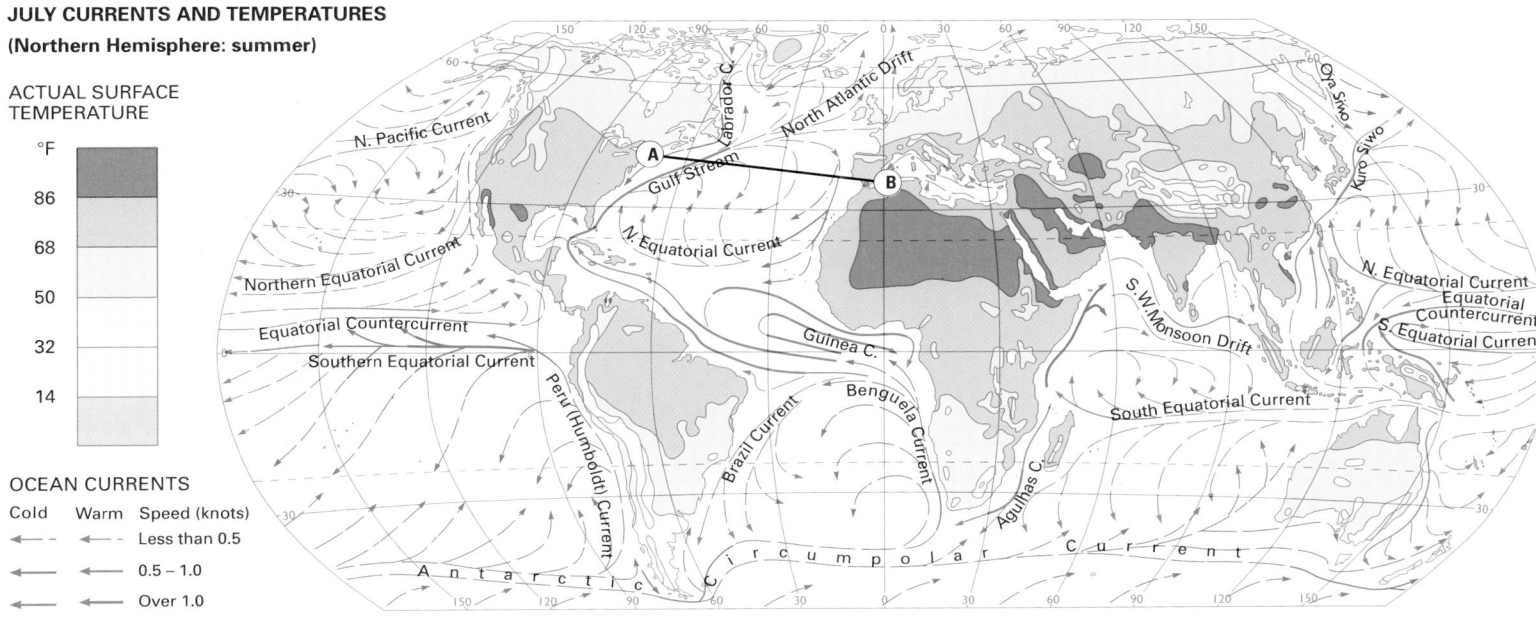

ACTUAL SURFACE TEMPERATURE

°F	
86	
68	
50	
32	
14	

OCEAN CURRENTS

Cold	Warm	Speed (knots)
←---	←---	Less than 0.5
←—	←—	0.5 – 1.0
←—	←—	Over 1.0

Moving immense quantities of energy as well as billions of tons of water every hour, the ocean currents are a vital part of the great heat engine that drives the Earth's climate. They themselves are produced by a twofold mechanism. At the surface, winds push huge masses of water before them; in the deep ocean, below an abrupt temperature gradient that separates the churning surface waters from the still depths, density variations cause slow vertical movements.

The pattern of circulation of the great surface currents is determined by the displacement known as the Coriolis effect. As the Earth turns beneath a moving object – whether it is a tennis ball or a vast mass of water – it appears to be deflected to one side. The deflection is most obvious near the Equator, where the Earth's surface is spinning eastward at 1,000 mph; currents moving poleward are curved clockwise in the northern hemisphere and counterclockwise in the southern.

The result is a system of spinning circles known as gyres. Warm currents move constantly from the Equator toward the poles, while cold water moves in the reverse direction. In this way, ocean currents act like a thermostat, helping to regulate temperatures around the world.

Depending on the annual movements of the prevailing wind belts, some currents on or near the Equator may reverse their direction in the course of the year, a variation on which Asia's monsoon rains depend and whose occasional failure has brought disaster to millions of people.

Topography of the Ocean Floor

Profile of the Atlantic Ocean

The deep ocean floor was once believed to be flat, but maps compiled from readings made by sonar equipment show that it is no more uniform than the surface of the continents. The profile, below, shows some of the features on the Atlantic Ocean floor between Massachusetts in North America and Gibraltar (for location of profile, see maps above). Around the continents are shallow continental shelves composed of rocks which are less dense than the underlying oceanic crust. The continents end at the top of the steep continental slope, which descends to the abyss via the continental rise, made up of sediments washed down from the continental shelves. The abyss contains large plains overlain by oozes but the plains are broken by volcanic seamounts and guyots (flat-topped seamounts), a few of which reach the surface as islands. The other main feature is the Mid-Atlantic Ridge, through which runs a rift valley where new crustal rock is being formed as the plates on either side move apart.

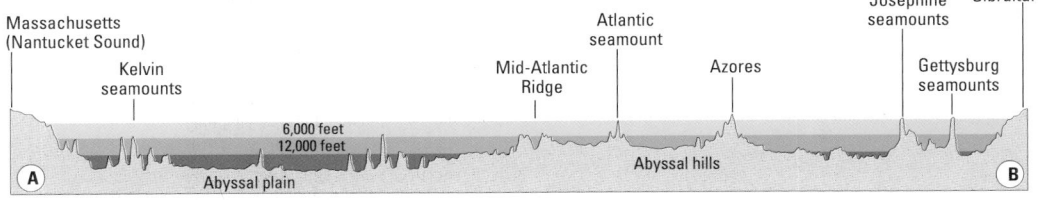

Topography of the ocean floor around Australia

In the image on the right, land areas are shown in gray, with shaded relief. The colors represent sea depth, with red representing the shallowest areas, through yellow and green to dark blue (the deepest). The data for the sea topography are from the Seasat radar satellite. The deep blue area in the upper left is the Java Trench which forms the boundary between the Indo-Australian plate and the Eurasian plate. In the top right, the New Guinea trench, which has a maximum depth of 29,865 feet, forms the border of the Indo-Australian and Pacific plates. Alongside the trenches are volcanic islands formed from magma, created as the edge of the Indo-Australian plate is subducted and melted.

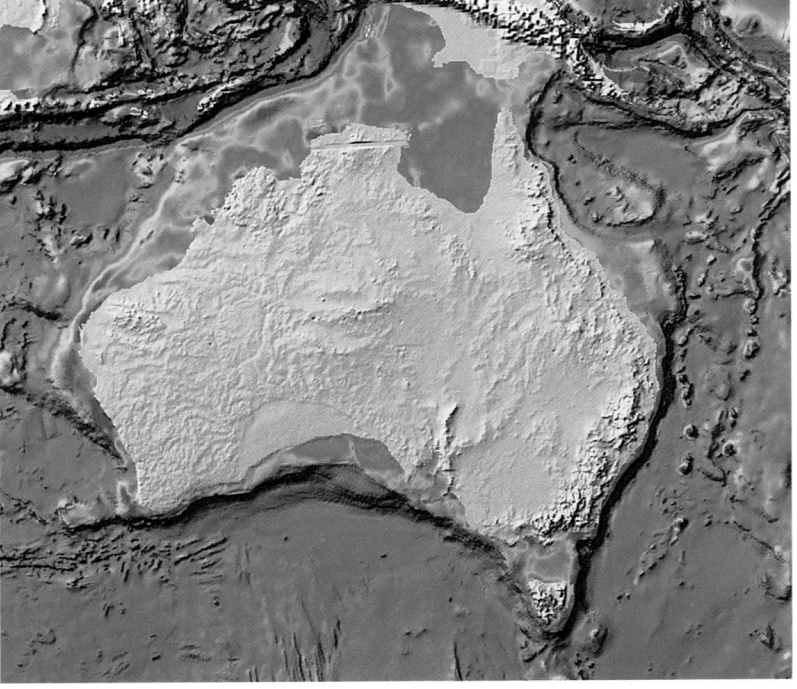

CARTOGRAPHY BY PHILIP'S. COPYRIGHT GEORGE PHILIP LTD

Geology of the Earth

Every year, earthquakes and volcanic eruptions cause much destruction throughout the world. Such phenomena were once thought to be unconnected but since the late 1960s, scientists have understood that these events are surface manifestations of the tremendous forces operating in the Earth's interior that are slowly but constantly changing the face of our planet.

The Earth is divided into three zones. The crust, a brittle, low-density zone, overlies the dense mantle. Separating the crust from the mantle is a distinct boundary called the Mohorovičić (or Moho) discontinuity. Enclosed by the mantle is the Earth's core, which consists mainly of iron and nickel.

Temperatures inside the Earth range from about 1,600°F in the upper mantle to perhaps 9,000°F in the core. Heat creates convection currents in a semimolten part of the mantle called the asthenosphere. Above the asthenosphere is the lithosphere, a solid layer about 40 miles thick, consisting of the crust and part of the mantle. The lithosphere is divided into rigid plates, moved around by the currents in the asthenosphere, a process named plate tectonics.

The Earth was formed around 4.6 billion years ago. Lighter elements floated toward the surface, where they formed crustal rocks. The oldest rocks so far discovered are nearly 4 billion years old, while the oldest fossils occur in rocks formed around 3.5 billion years ago. An explosion of life occurred at the start of the Cambrian period, 570 million years ago. The fossil record since the start of the Cambrian has enabled scientists to piece together the story of life on Earth.

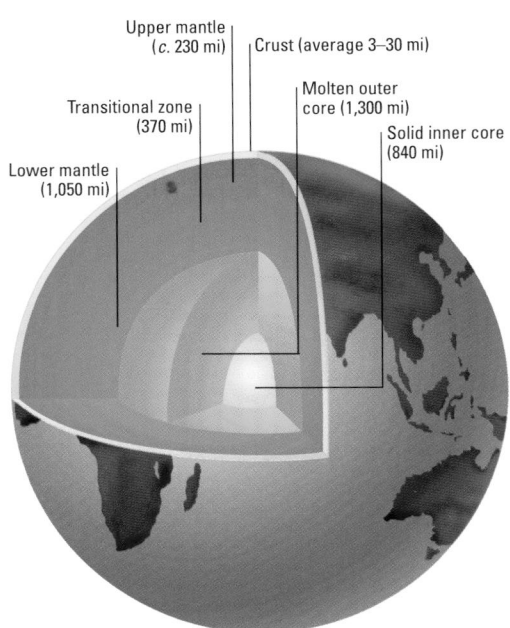

Upper mantle (c. 230 mi)
Crust (average 3–30 mi)
Transitional zone (370 mi)
Molten outer core (1,300 mi)
Lower mantle (1,050 mi)
Solid inner core (840 mi)

Plate Tectonics

In the early 20th century, the German scientist Alfred Wegener and others noticed similarities between the shapes of the continents. From a study of rocks and fossils in widely separated continents, they suggested that the continents had once been joined together and that somehow they had drifted apart. But no one knew of a mechanism that might cause continents to drift. However, in the 1950s and 1960s, evidence from studies of the ocean floor suggested that the low-density continents rest on huge slow-moving plates.

Seafloor spreading in the Indian Ocean and continental plate collision

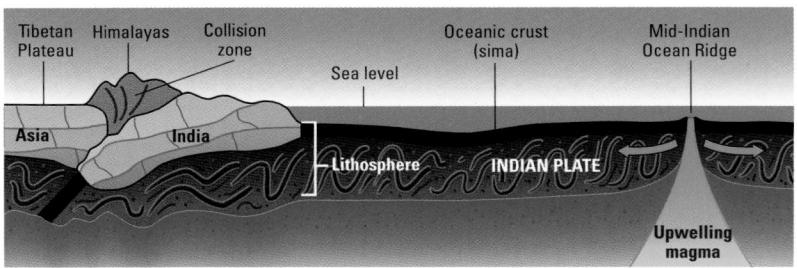

Tibetan Plateau | Himalayas | Collision zone | Sea level | Oceanic crust (sima) | Mid-Indian Ocean Ridge
Asia | India | Lithosphere | INDIAN PLATE | Upwelling magma

Seafloor spreading in the Atlantic Ocean and plate collision

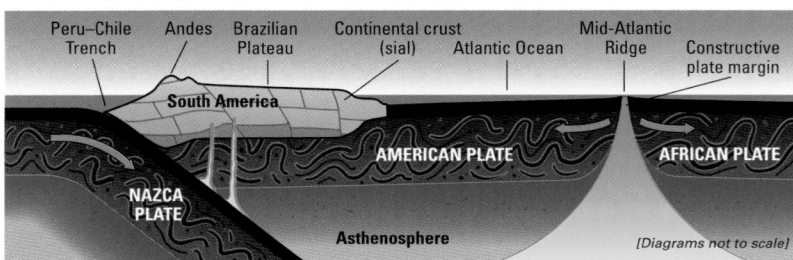

Peru–Chile Trench | Andes | Brazilian Plateau | Continental crust (sial) | Atlantic Ocean | Mid-Atlantic Ridge | Constructive plate margin
South America | AMERICAN PLATE | AFRICAN PLATE
NAZCA PLATE | Asthenosphere | [Diagrams not to scale]

The huge ridges that run through the oceans represent boundaries between plates. Here plates are diverging at rates of 20–41 mm a year. Molten magma from the mantle rises along a central rift valley to form new crustal rock. These ocean ridges, which are active zones where earthquakes and volcanic eruptions are common, are called constructive plate margins. Destructive plate margins, which occur when two plates converge, are marked by deep ocean trenches as one plate is forced under the other. The descending plate is melted to produce the magma that fuels volcanoes alongside the trenches. Movements of descending plates are often sudden and violent, triggering earthquakes in overlying continental areas. Where two continents collide, their margins are buckled up to form fold mountain ranges. A third type of plate margin, the transform fault, is not illustrated above. Along these plate margins, such as California's San Andreas fault, plates are moving parallel to each other.

The debate about plate tectonics is not over. Questions still arise as to why some active volcanoes lie far from plate margins, and why major earthquakes occur in midplate areas.

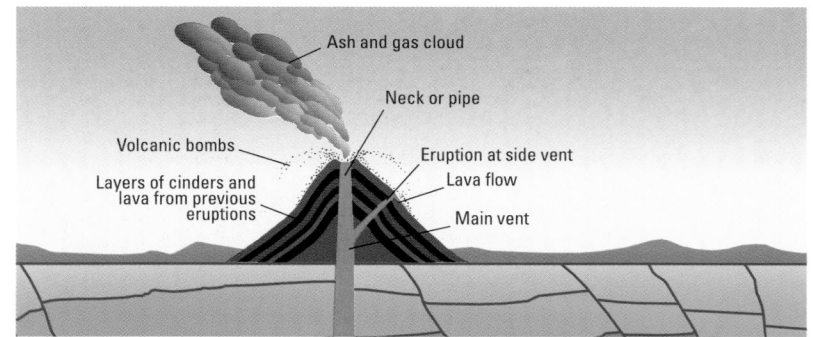

Ash and gas cloud
Neck or pipe
Volcanic bombs
Eruption at side vent
Layers of cinders and lava from previous eruptions
Lava flow
Main vent

Continental Drift

In 1915, Alfred Wegener produced a series of world maps proposing that, around 200 million years ago, the continents had been joined together in a supercontinent which he called Pangaea. This land mass started to break up about 180 million years ago and the parts drifted to their present positions. The arrows on the present day world map shows that the continents are still on the move.

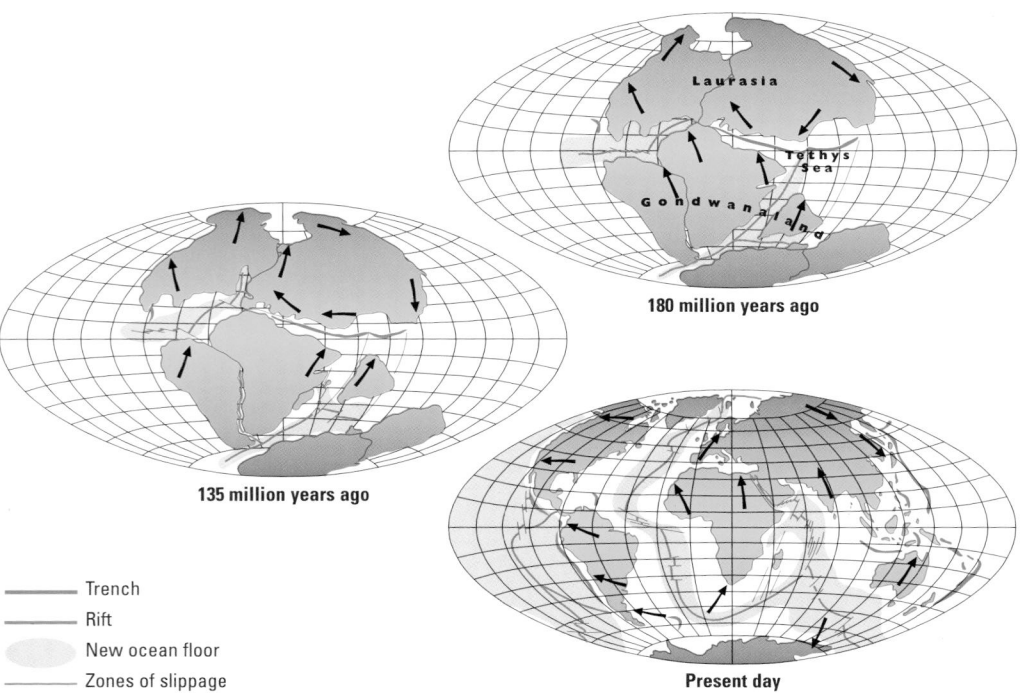

Laurasia
Tethys Sea
Gondwanaland

180 million years ago

135 million years ago

Present day

Trench
Rift
New ocean floor
Zones of slippage

Distribution of Volcanoes

Volcanoes occur when hot liquefied rock beneath the Earth's crust is pushed up by pressure to the surface as molten lava. There are some 550 known active volcanoes, around 20 of which are erupting at any one time.

▲ Land volcanoes active since 1700
↗ Direction of movement
⌒ Boundaries of tectonic plates
• Submarine volcanoes
♦ Geysers

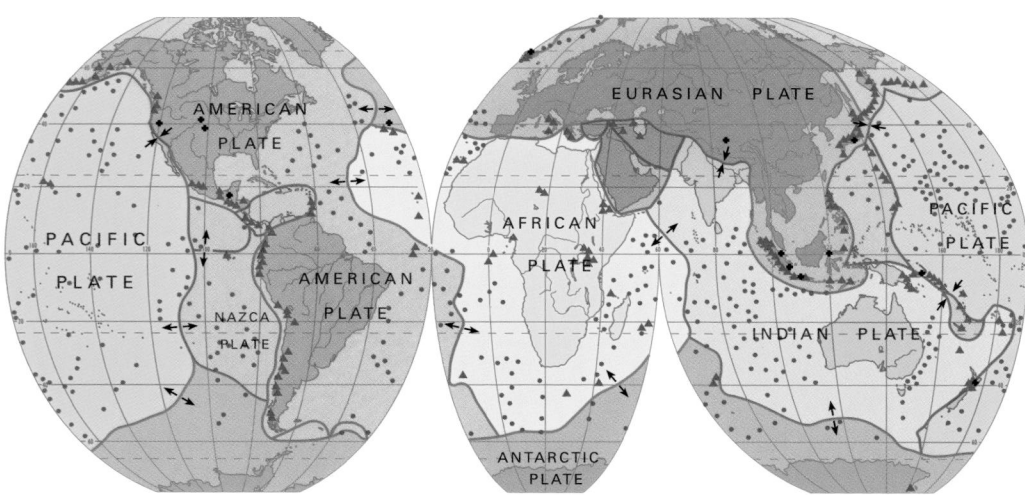

AMERICAN PLATE
EURASIAN PLATE
PACIFIC PLATE
AFRICAN PLATE
PACIFIC PLATE
NAZCA PLATE
AMERICAN PLATE
INDIAN PLATE
ANTARCTIC PLATE

Geological Time

4600

Time, in millions of years before the present, is shown on a sliding scale, greatly compressed in the distant past.

Geological time chart (left):

ERA	PERIOD	EPOCH
PRE-CAMBRIAN		
PALEOZOIC	Cambrian (570–500)	
	Ordovician (500–430)	
	Silurian (430–395)	
	Devonian (395–345)	
	Carboniferous (345–280)	
	Permian (280–225)	
MESOZOIC	Triassic (225–190)	
	Jurassic (190–135)	
	Cretaceous (135–65)	
CENOZOIC	Tertiary	Paleocene (65–53)
		Eocene (53–37)
		Oligocene (37–26)
		Miocene (26–12)
		Pliocene (12–2)
	Quaternary	Pleistocene (2–)
		Holocene 10,000 BP to present

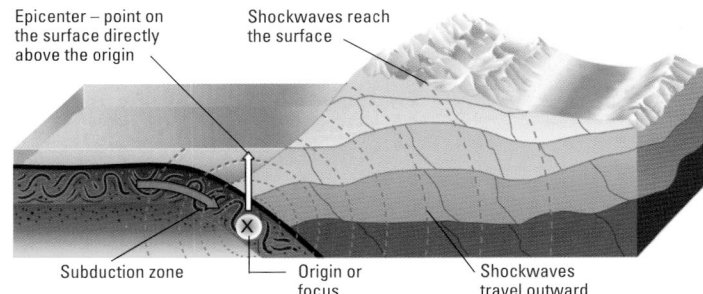

Geologists devised their timescale on the basis of relative, not calendar, ages. Accurate dating was impossible and estimates were often bitterly disputed, but the order in which the rocks were formed could be deduced from careful observation. The advent of radioactive dating – culminating in the 1950s with the development of a mass spectrometer capable of accurately measuring tiny quantities of isotopes – appears to have settled the arguments. The Earth is far older than geologists first imagined, but their painstakingly-created structure of geological time has withstood the advent of high technology.

The 4.6 billion (4,600 million) years since the formation of the Earth are divided into four great eras, further split into periods and, in the case of the most recent era, epochs. The present era is the Cenozoic ("new life"), extending backward through "middle life" and "ancient life" to the Pre-Cambrian, named after the Latin word for Wales, the location of some of the earliest known fossils. Most of the Earth's geological history is encompassed by the Pre-Cambrian: though traces of ancient life have since been found, it was largely the proliferation of fossils from the beginning of the Paleozoic era onward, some 570 million years ago, which first allowed precise subdivisions to be made.

Like the Cambrian, most are named after regions exemplifying a period's geology. Others – such as the Carboniferous ("coal-bearing") or the Cretaceous ("chalk-bearing") – are more directly descriptive.

Map legend:

- Pre-Cambrian shields
- Sedimentary cover on Pre-Cambrian shields
- Paleozoic (Caledonian and Hercynian) folding
- Sedimentary cover on Paleozoic folding
- Mesozoic folding
- Sedimentary cover on Mesozoic folding
- Cenozoic (Alpine) folding
- Sedimentary cover on Cenozoic folding
- Intensive Mesozoic and Cenozoic vulcanism
- Principal faults
- Oceanic marginal troughs
- Mid-oceanic ridges
- Overthrust faults

Earthquakes

Earthquake magnitude is usually rated according to either the Richter or the Modified Mercalli scale, both devised by seismologists in the 1930s. The Richter scale measures absolute earthquake power with mathematical precision: each step upward represents a tenfold increase in the amplitude of the shockwave. Theoretically, there is no upper limit, but the largest earthquakes measured have been rated at between 8.8 and 8.9. The 12-point Mercalli scale, based on observed effects, is often more meaningful, ranging from I (earthquakes noticed only by seismographs) to XII (total destruction); intermediate points include V (people awakened at night; unstable objects overturned), VII (collapse of ordinary buildings; chimneys and monuments fall) and IX (conspicuous cracks in ground; serious damage to reservoirs).

Earthquakes are a series of rapid vibrations originating from the slipping or faulting of parts of the Earth's crust when stresses within build up to breaking point. They usually happen at depths varying from 8 km to 30 km. Severe earthquakes cause extensive damage when they take place in populated areas, destroying structures and severing communications. Most initial loss of life occurs due to secondary causes such as falling masonry, fires and flooding.

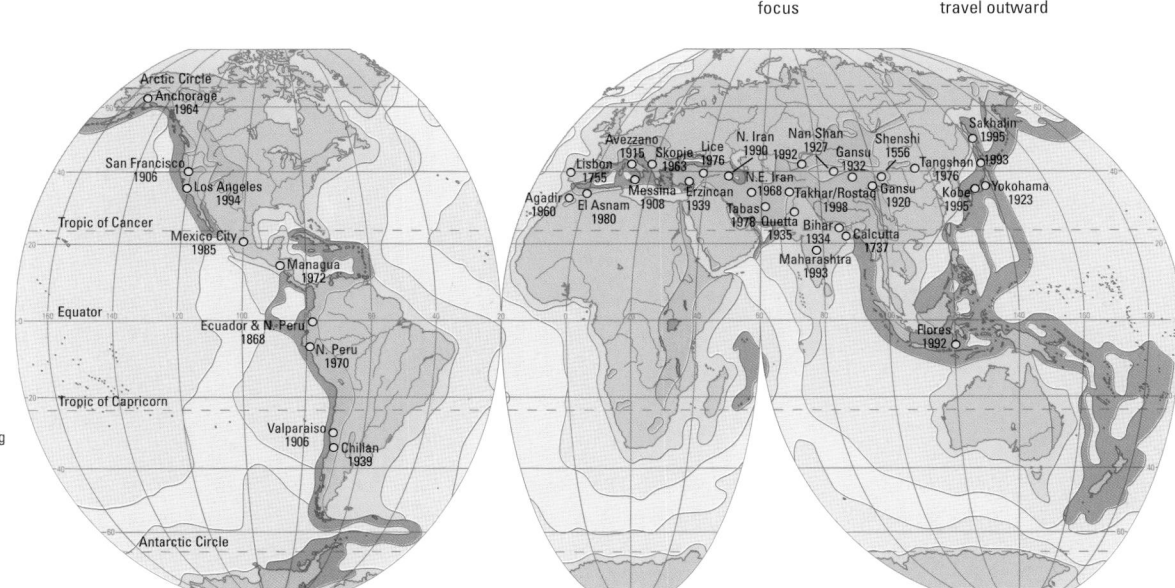

Earthquake diagram labels: Epicenter – point on the surface directly above the origin; Shockwaves reach the surface; Subduction zone; Origin or focus; Shockwaves travel outward.

Map legend:
- Mobile land areas
- Submarine zones of mobile land areas
- Stable land platforms
- Submarine extensions of land platforms
- Mid-oceanic volcanic ridges
- Oceanic platforms
- 1976 Principal earthquakes and dates

Notable Earthquakes Since 1900

Year	Location	Mag.	Deaths
1906	San Francisco, USA	8.3	503
1906	Valparaiso, Chile	8.6	22,000
1908	Messina, Italy	7.5	83,000
1915	Avezzano, Italy	7.5	30,000
1920	Gansu (Kansu), China	8.6	180,000
1923	Yokohama, Japan	8.3	143,000
1927	Nan Shan, China	8.3	200,000
1932	Gansu (Kansu), China	7.6	70,000
1933	Sanriku, Japan	8.9	2,990
1934	Bihar, India/Nepal	8.4	10,700
1935	Quetta, India*	7.5	60,000
1939	Chillan, Chile	8.3	28,000
1939	Erzincan, Turkey	7.9	30,000
1960	Agadir, Morocco	5.8	12,000
1962	Khorasan, Iran	7.1	12,230
1968	N.E. Iran	7.4	12,000
1970	N. Peru	7.7	66,794
1972	Managua, Nicaragua	6.2	5,000
1974	N. Pakistan	6.3	5,200
1976	Guatemala	7.5	22,778
1976	Tangshan, China	8.2	255,000
1978	Tabas, Iran	7.7	25,000
1980	El Asnam, Algeria	7.3	20,000
1980	S. Italy	7.2	4,800
1985	Mexico City, Mexico	8.1	4,200
1988	N.W. Armenia	6.8	55,000
1990	N. Iran	7.7	36,000
1992	Flores, Indonesia	6.8	1,895
1993	Maharashtra, India	6.4	30,000
1994	Los Angeles, USA	6.6	51
1995	Kobe, Japan	7.2	5,000
1995	Sakhalin Is., Russia	7.5	2,000
1996	Yunnan, China	7.0	240
1997	N.E. Iran	7.1	2,400
1998	Takhar, Afghanistan	6.1	4,200
1998	Rostaq, Afghanistan	7.0	5,000

The highest magnitude recorded on the Richter scale is 8.9, in Japan on 2 March 1933 (2,990 deaths). The most devastating quake ever was at Shaanxi (Shenshi) province, central China, on 3 January 1556, when an estimated 830,000 people were killed.

* now Pakistan

Landforms

The theory of plate tectonics has offered new insights as to how the Earth works, elucidating mysteries concerning continental drift, volcanic eruptions and earthquakes. It has also contributed to our understanding of how plate collisions can squeeze up layers of sediments on seabeds into fold mountain ranges, such as the Himalayas.

Yet even as mountains rise, natural forces are wearing them away. In hot, dry climates, mechanical weathering, a result of rapid temperature changes, causes the outer layers of rocks to peel away, while, in cold mountain regions, boulders are prised apart when water freezes in cracks in rocks. Chemical weathering is responsible for hollowing out limestone caves and decomposing granites.

Climatic conditions have a great bearing on the principle agent of erosion in any particular area. Running water is most important in moist temperate regions. In cold regions, ice is the major agent of erosion, and in many mountain ranges, U-shaped valleys are evidence of the erosive power of valley glaciers. Ice sheets moulded much of the Earth's surface during the Ice Ages, the most recent of which, in the northern hemisphere, ended only 10,000 years ago. Polar climates also shape the scenery of the periglacial areas that border bodies of ice. Such areas are subject to constant freeze-thaw action, which creates such features as pingos (domed mounds).

Climatic change has also affected many of the landforms in hot deserts, which were shaped by running water at a time when the deserts enjoyed much wetter climates. However, the major agent of erosion in deserts today is wind-blown sand which erodes rock strata to form mushroom-shaped rocks and caves.

The surface of the Earth is under constant assault from tectonic processes and the agents of erosion. The products of erosion, fragments of rock such as sand, are deposited to form sedimentary rocks. Metamorphic rocks are created when igneous or sedimentary rocks are buried and metamorphosed by heat and pressure. Eventually the rocks are recycled to form magma, which rises upward to start the rock cycle all over again.

The Rock Cycle

James Hutton first proposed the rock cycle in the late 1700s after he observed the slow but steady effects of erosion.

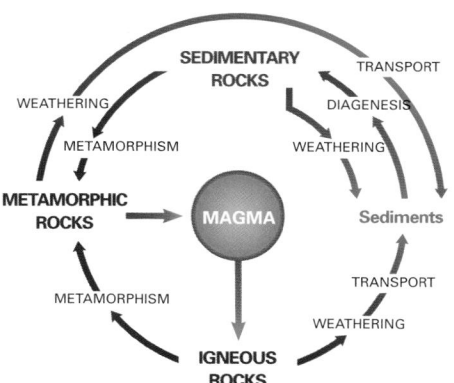

Rocks are divided into three types, according to the way in which they are formed:

Igneous rocks, including granite and basalt, are formed by the cooling of magma from within the Earth's crust.

Metamorphic rocks, such as slate, marble and quartzite, are formed below the Earth's surface by the compression or baking of existing rocks.

Sedimentary rocks, like sandstone and limestone, are formed on the surface of the Earth from the remains of living organisms and eroded fragments of older rocks.

Mountain Building

Mountains are formed when pressures on the Earth's crust caused by continental drift become so intense that the surface buckles or cracks. This happens where oceanic crust is subducted by continental crust or, more dramatically, where two tectonic plates collide: the Rockies, Andes, Alps, Urals and Himalayas resulted from such impacts. These are all known as fold mountains because they were formed by the compression of the rocks, forcing the surface to bend and fold like a crumpled rug. The Himalayas are formed from the folded former sediments of the Tethys Sea which was trapped in the collision zone between the Indian and Eurasian plates.

The other main mountain-building process occurs when the crust fractures to create faults, allowing rock to be forced upward in large blocks; or when the pressure of magma within the crust forces the surface to bulge into a dome, or erupts to form a volcano. Large mountain ranges may reveal a combination of those features; the Alps, for example, have been compressed so violently that the folds are fragmented by numerous faults and intrusions of molten igneous rock.

Over millions of years, even the greatest mountain ranges can be reduced by the agents of erosion (especially rivers) to a low rugged landscape known as a peneplain.

Types of faults: Faults occur where the crust is being stretched or compressed so violently that the rock strata break in a horizontal or vertical movement. They are classified by the direction in which the blocks of rock have moved. A normal fault results when a vertical movement causes the surface to break apart; compression causes a reverse fault. Horizontal movement causes shearing, known as a strike-slip fault. When the rock breaks in two places, the central block may be pushed up in a horst fault, or sink (creating a rift valley) in a graben fault.

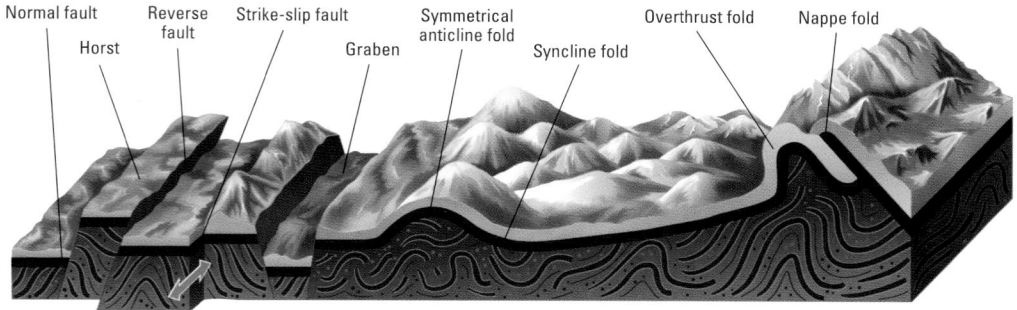

Types of fold: Folds occur when rock strata are squeezed and compressed. They are common, therefore, at destructive plate margins and where plates have collided, forcing the rocks to buckle into mountain ranges. Geographers give different names to the degrees of fold that result from continuing pressure on the rock. A simple fold may be symmetric, with even slopes on either side, but as the pressure builds up, one slope becomes steeper and the fold becomes asymmetric. Later, the ridge or "anticline" at the top of the fold may slide over the lower ground or "syncline" to form a recumbent fold. Eventually, the rock strata may break under the pressure to form an overthrust and finally a nappe fold.

Continental Glaciation

The mass balance is defined as the difference between glacier accumulation and ablation (melting), and is expressed as water equivalent in millimeters. A minus indicates a reduction in the depth or length of a glacier. As can be seen from this geographically diverse selection, glaciers are retreating in many areas worldwide. The most dramatic and serious example of this phenomenon is the continuing distintegration of several large Antarctic ice shelves.

The extent to which glacial retreat is due to global warming, or to longer term climatic fluctuations, remains a matter for debate.

Many landforms in the northern hemisphere were shaped by ice sheets and meltwater during the Pleistocene Ice Age, which began about two million years ago. During the Ice Age, the ice sheets periodically advanced and retreated. The first map shows the ice cover at its greatest extent about 200,000 years BP (before the present), when it covered about 30% of the land surface, as compared with 10% today. About 18,000 years BP, the ice covered most of Canada and as far south as the Bristol Channel in England. Around the ice sheets, land areas experienced periglacial conditions.

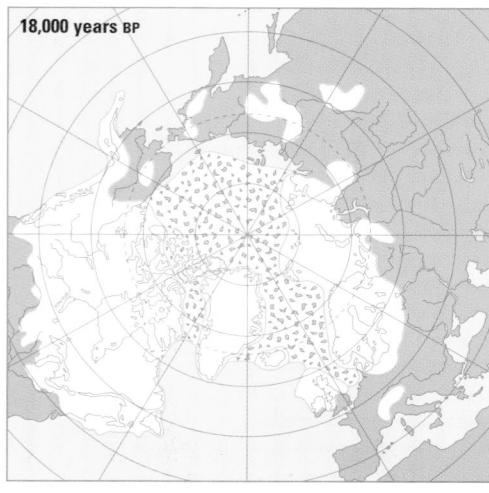

200,000 years BP

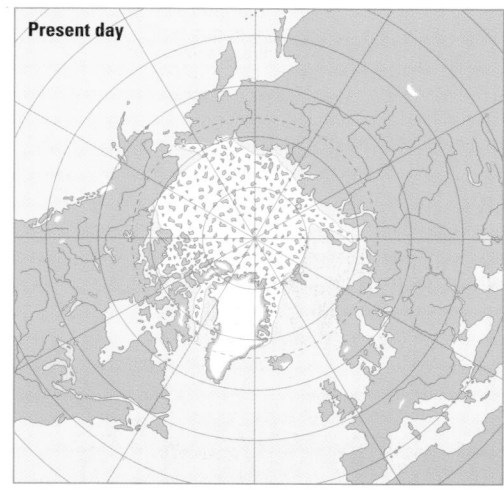

18,000 years BP

Present day

Natural Landforms

Natural landforms reflect the influence of plate tectonics through mountain-building and the generation of new rocks from the interior, together with the agents of erosion: running water, ice, winds and coastal waves. Over millions of years, mountains are gradually eroded, producing landforms that reflect the major forces that have been at work, as well as the underlying geology, the climatic conditions, which often vary over time, and the vegetation cover. The stylized diagram, below, shows some major natural landforms found in the midlatitudes.

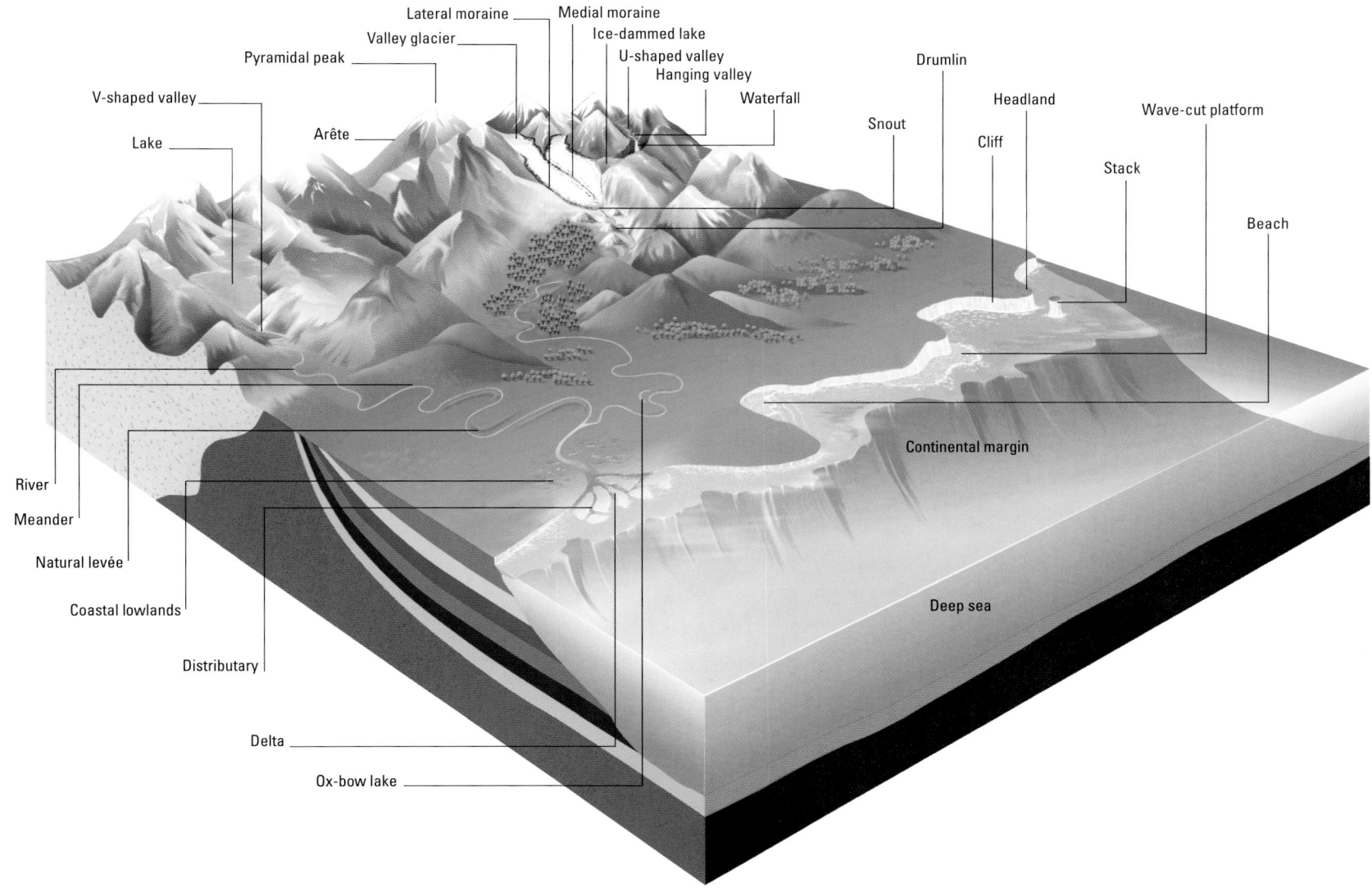

Labels: Lateral moraine, Medial moraine, Valley glacier, Ice-dammed lake, Pyramidal peak, U-shaped valley, Hanging valley, Drumlin, V-shaped valley, Waterfall, Headland, Wave-cut platform, Lake, Arête, Snout, Cliff, Stack, Beach, River, Meander, Natural levée, Coastal lowlands, Continental margin, Distributary, Deep sea, Delta, Ox-bow lake

Desert Landforms

Deserts are defined as places with an average annual precipitation of 250 mm per year, though places with a higher rainfall and a high evaporation rate may also qualify as deserts. The three types of desert landforms are known by their Arabic names, a reflection of the fact that the Sahara in North Africa is the world's largest desert. Sand desert, called erg, covers about one-fifth of the world's deserts. The rest is divided between hammada (areas of bare rock) and reg (broad plains covered by loose gravel or pebbles).

The shapes of dunes in sand deserts reflect the character of local winds. Where winds are constant in direction, the sand often piles up in crescent-shaped dunes, called barchans. Barchans are constantly on the move and their forward march, unless halted by vegetation, may overwhelm settlements at oases. Seif dunes, named after the Arabic word for sword, are long ridges of sand which lie parallel to the direction of the wind, but where winds are variable, the sand sheets are often featureless.

Wind-blown sand is an effective agent of erosion but because of the weight of sand grains, this type of erosion is confined to within 7 feet of the land surface, creating caves and mushroom-shaped rocks.

In assessing desert landforms, it is important to remember that other processes were at work in the past when the climate was very different from today. For example, cave paintings suggest that the Sahara had a much wetter climate after the end of the Ice Age and only began to dry up after about 5000 BC. However, human action, including overgrazing and the cutting down of trees for firewood, can turn a grassland region into desert – a process known as desertification.

Erg

Hammada

Reg

Surface Processes

Catastrophic changes to landforms are periodically caused by such phenomena as avalanches, landslides and volcanic eruptions, but most of the processes that shape the Earth's surface operate extremely slowly in human terms. One estimate, based on a study of landforms in the United States, suggests that, on average, just over 3 feet of land is removed from the entire surface of the country every 29,500 years. However, the terrain and the climate have a great effect on the erosion rate. For example, on cold plains, such as the Hudson Bay lowlands, the rate drops to around 3 feet for every 154,200 years, while in wet, tropical mountain areas, the rate may reach one metre for every 1,300 years.

Chemical weathering is at its greatest in warm, humid regions, while mechanical weathering, or the physical breakup of rocks, predominates in cold mountain or hot desert regions. The most familiar type of chemical weathering is caused by the reaction of rainwater containing dissolved carbon dioxide on limestone. This leads to the creation of labyrinthine cave networks dissolved by groundwater. Mechanical weathering includes frost action, while in hot deserts, rapid temperature changes cause the outer layers of rocks to expand and contract until they crack and peel away, a process called exfoliation.

The most important product of weathering is soil, which consists of rock fragments and humus, the decayed remains of plants and animals, together with living organisms, including vast numbers of micro-organisms. Soils vary in character according to the climate, ranging from the heavily leached, red laterite soils of wet tropical areas to the fertile, brown soils of dry grasslands. Soils are important because they support plants, which in turn anchor the soil and act as a protection against erosion. Soil erosion is greatest on sloping land because the steeper the slope, the greater the tendency for the soil to creep or flow downhill. The degree of movement of soil and rock downhill under the influence of gravity, called mass wasting, depends on a slope's stability. The stability may be disturbed by earthquakes or by heavy rain (water acts as a lubricant and increases the weight of the overlying material) which may trigger flows, slides or large falls of rock.

Running water is probably the world's leading agent of erosion and transportation. The energy of a river depends on several factors, including its velocity and volume, and its erosive power is at its peak when it is in full flood, sweeping soil, pebbles and even boulders along its course, cutting downward into the bedrock or widening its valley. Sea waves also exert tremendous erosive power during storms when they hurl pebbles and large rocks against the shore, undercutting cliffs and hollowing out caves. Headlands are often attacked on both sides, forming caves, then a natural arch and eventually an isolated stack.

Glacier ice forms in mountain hollows, called cirques, and spills out to form valley glaciers, which transport rocks shattered by frost action. As a glacier moves, rocks embedded in the base and sides scrape away bedrock, eroding steep-sided, flat-bottomed, U-shaped valleys. Evidence of past glaciation in mountain regions includes cirques, knife-edged ridges, or arêtes, and pyramidal peaks, or horns.

Geologists once considered that landforms evolved from "young," newly uplifted mountainous areas, through a "mature" hilly stage, to an "old age" stage when the land was reduced to an almost flat plain, or peneplain. This theory, called the "cycle of erosion," fell into disuse when it became evident that so many factors, including the effects of plate tectonics and climatic change, constantly interrupt the cycle, which takes no account of the highly complex interactions that shape the surface of our planet.

The Atmosphere

The atmosphere is a meteor shield, a radiation deflector, a thermal blanket and a source of chemical energy for the Earth's diverse life forms. Five-sixths of its mass is in the lowest layer, the troposphere which ranges in thickness from 18 to 10 km between the Equator and the poles. Powered by the Sun, the air is always on the move, flowing generally from high- to low-pressure areas. The troposphere is the layer where virtually all weather phenomena, including clouds, precipitation and winds, occur. Above the troposphere is the stratosphere, which contains the important ozone layer and extends to about 30 miles above the Earth's surface. Beyond 60 miles, atmospheric density is lower than most laboratory vacuums.

Circulation of the Air

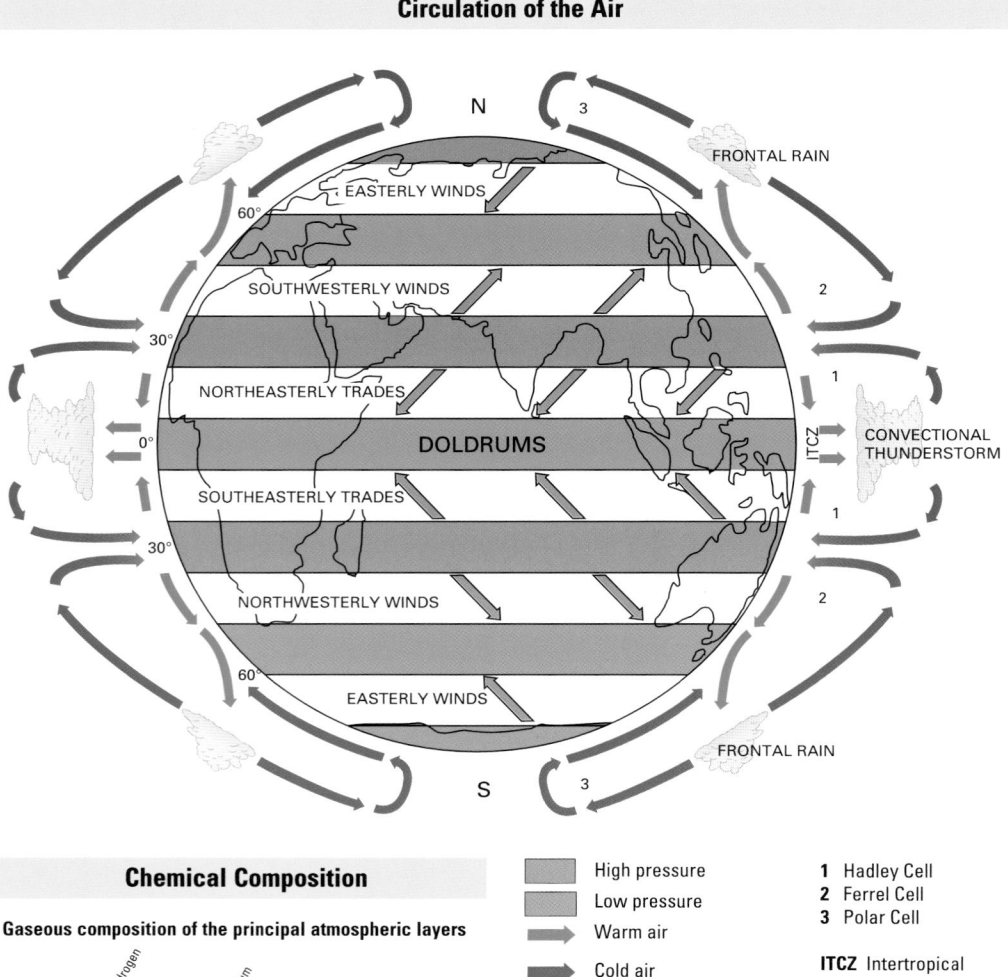

High pressure
Low pressure
Warm air
Cold air
Surface winds
Clouds

1 Hadley Cell
2 Ferrel Cell
3 Polar Cell

ITCZ Intertropical convergence zone

Structure of the Atmosphere

HUBBLE SPACE TELESCOPE
370 miles
Pressure
10^{-35} mb

350 mi

EXOSPHERE
10^{-22} mb

MIR SPACE STATION
200 miles — 200 mi
10^{-16} mb

SPACE SHUTTLE
170 miles

150 mi

THERMOSPHERE
10^{-10} mb

VOSTOCK MANNED CAPSULE
(first manned space flight, 1961)
110 miles

100 mi

AURORAE

METEOR TRAILS   60 mi
MESOSPHERE
10^{-3} mb

OZONE LAYER   30 mi
STRATOSPHERE

CONCORDE
MOUNT EVEREST
29,029 ft
6 mi
TROPOSPHERE
10^3 mb

Chemical Composition

Gaseous composition of the principal atmospheric layers

50–100% hydrogen   25–50% helium
Exosphere
Helium vanishes with increasing altitude. Above 1,500 miles the exosphere is almost entirely composed of hydrogen.

70% nitrogen   15% oxygen   15% helium
Mesosphere
The high energy of mesospheric gas gives it a notional temperature of more than 3,600°F, although its density is negligible.

80% nitrogen   18% oxygen   1% argon   1% ozone
Stratosphere
Stratospheric air contains enough ozone to make it poisonous, although it is in any case too rarified to breathe.

78% nitrogen   21% oxygen   1% argon
Troposphere
The narrowest of all the layers, this thin region contains about 85% of the atmosphere's total mass and almost all of its water vapor. It is also the realm of the Earth's weather.

Frontal Systems

Depressions, or cyclones, form along the polar front where dense polar easterlies meet warm subtropical westerlies. Depressions occur when warm air flows into waves in the polar front, while cold air flows in behind it, creating rotating air systems that bring changeable weather. Along the warm front (the boundary on the ground between the warm and cold air), the warm air flows upward over the cold air, producing a sequence of clouds which help forecasters to predict a depression's advance. Along the cold front, the advancing cold air forces warm air to rise steeply. Towering cumulonimbus clouds form in the rising air. When the cold front overtakes the warm front, the warm air is pushed above ground level to form an occluded front. Cloud and rain persist along occlusions until temperatures equalize, the air mixes, and the depression dies out.

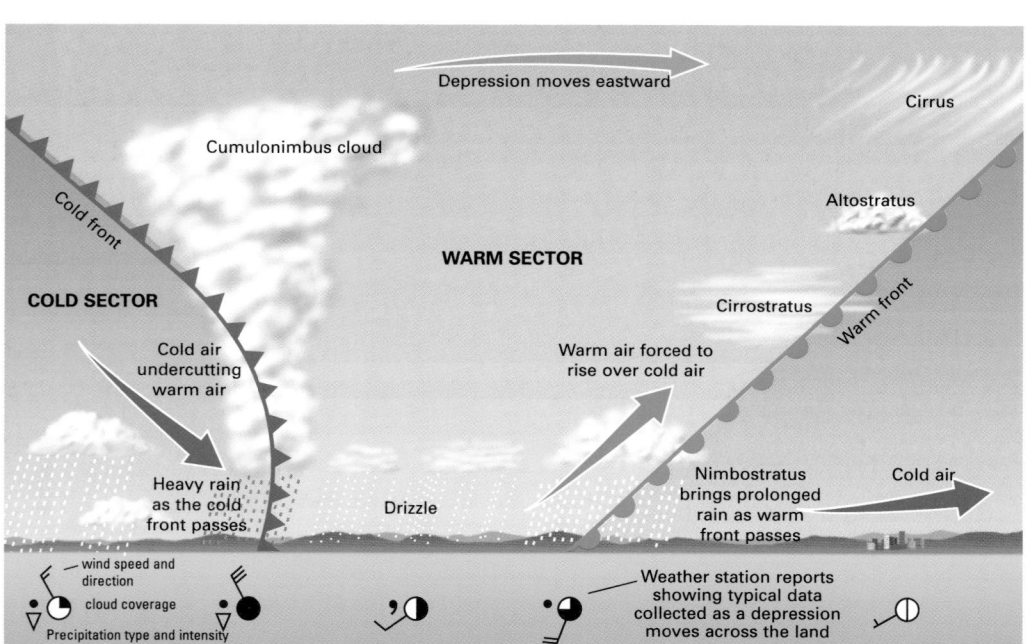

Air Masses

Air masses are bodies of air whose characteristics are broadly the same over a large area. Around the Equator, where the Sun's heat creates relatively high surface temperatures, warm air rises to create a zone of low pressure called the doldrums. The air cools and finally spreads out toward the poles. Around latitudes 30° north and south, the air sinks back to the surface, becoming warmer as it descends and creating zones of high pressure called the horse latitudes.

The high- and low-pressure zones are both areas of comparative calm, but between them lie the prevailing trade wind belts. Air also flows north and south from the high-pressure horse latitudes and these air flows meet up with cold, dense air flowing from the poles along the polar front. This basic circulatory system is complicated by the Coriolis effect, brought about by the spinning Earth. Because of the Coriolis effect, the prevailing winds do not flow directly north–south but are deflected to the right in the northern hemisphere and to the left in the southern. Along the polar front, depressions form where the polar easterlies meet the westerlies.

The first classification of clouds was developed by a London chemist, Luke Howard, in 1803, and it was later modified by the World Meteorological Organization. The main types are divided into three groups according to their altitude, and into subgroups according to their shape, which vary from hairlike filaments (cirrus), heaps or piles (cumulus), and layers (stratus). Each cloud carries some kind of message, though not always a clear one, to weather forecasters.

Classification of Clouds

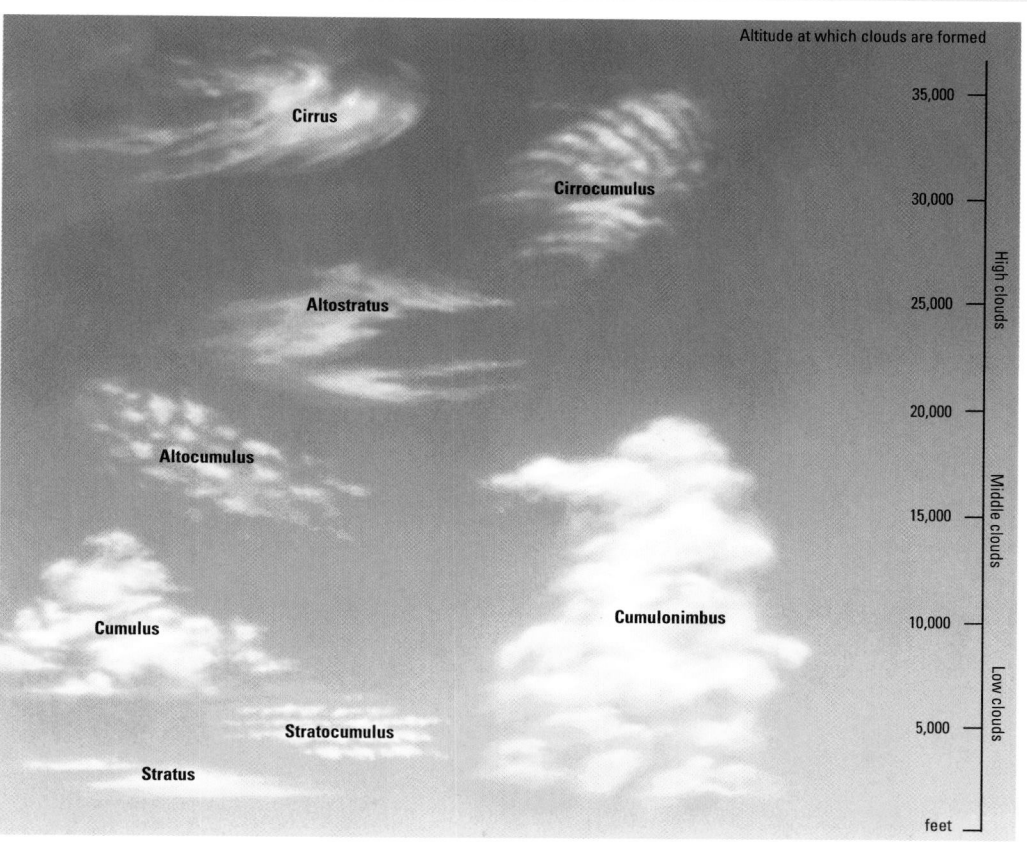

Altitude at which clouds are formed

Clouds form when damp, usually rising, air is cooled. Thus they form when a wind rises to cross hills or mountains; when a mass of air rises over, or is pushed up by, another mass of denser air; or when local heating of the ground causes convection currents.

The types of clouds are classified according to altitude as high, middle or low. The high ones, composed of ice crystals, are cirrus, cirrostratus and cirrocumulus. The middle clouds are altostratus, a gray or bluish striated, fibrous or uniform sheet producing light drizzle, and altocumulus, a thicker and fluffier version of cirrocumulus.

Low clouds include nimbostratus, a dark grey layer that brings rain or snow; cumulus, a detached heap, dark at the base; stratus, which forms dull, overcast skies at low levels; and stratocumulus, which consists of fluffy grayish-white layers.

Cumulonimbus, associated with storms and rains, heavy and dense with a flat base and a high, fluffy outline, can be tall enough to occupy middle as well as low altitudes.

Pressure and Surface Winds

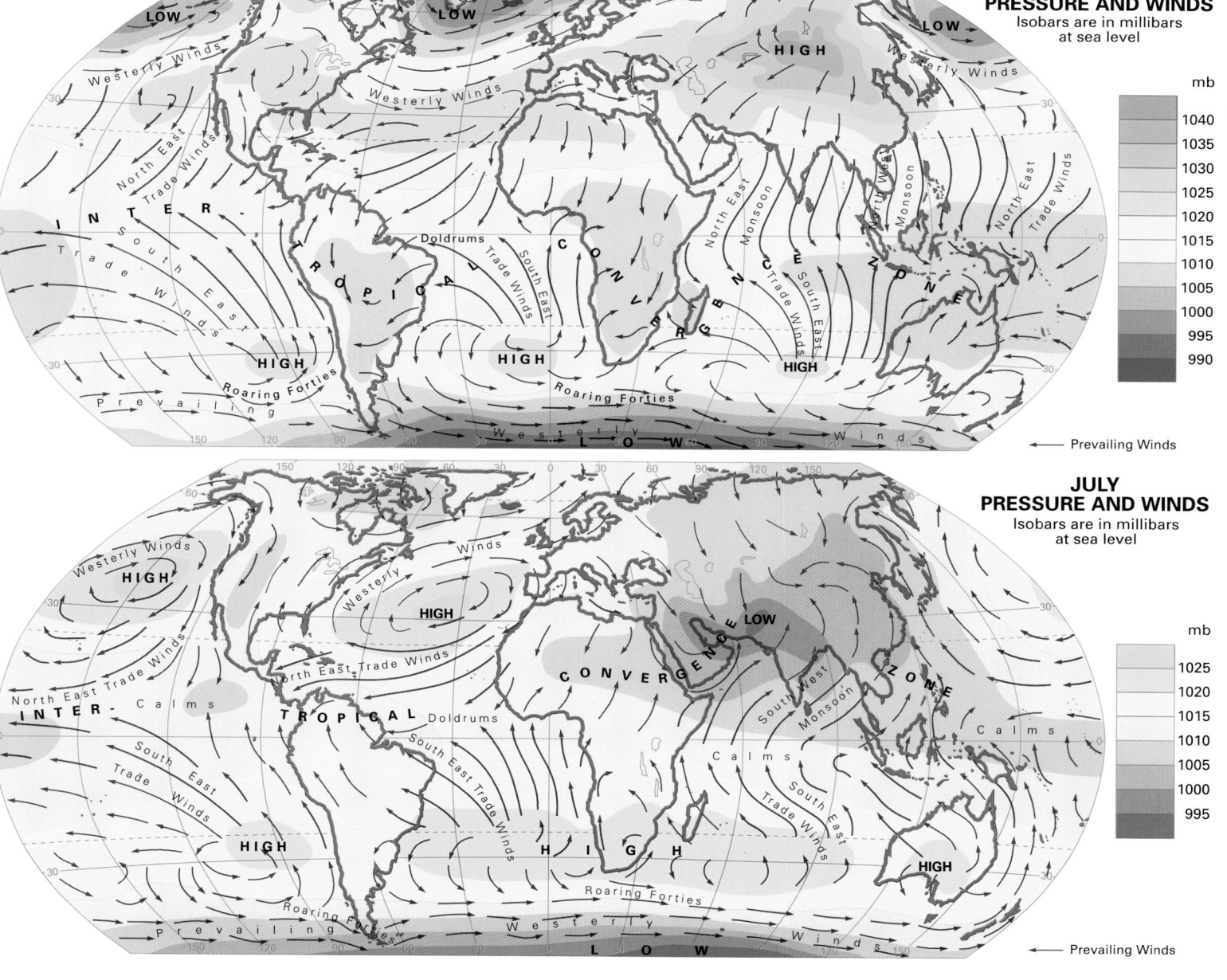

JANUARY PRESSURE AND WINDS
Isobars are in millibars at sea level

mb
1040
1035
1030
1025
1020
1015
1010
1005
1000
995
990

⟵ Prevailing Winds

JULY PRESSURE AND WINDS
Isobars are in millibars at sea level

mb
1025
1020
1015
1010
1005
1000
995

⟵ Prevailing Winds

Climate Records

Pressure and winds

Highest barometric pressure: Agata, Siberia, 1,083.8 mb at altitude 862 ft [262 m], December 31, 1968.

Lowest barometric pressure: Typhoon Tip, 300 miles [480 km] west of Guam, Pacific Ocean, 870 mb, October 12, 1979.

Highest recorded wind speed: Mt Washington, New Hampshire, USA, 231 mph [371 km/h], April 12, 1934. This is three times as strong as hurricane force on the Beaufort Scale.

Windiest place: Commonwealth Bay, George V Coast, Antarctica, where gales frequently reach over 200 mph [320 km/h].

Worst recorded storm: Bangladesh (then East Pakistan) cyclone*, November 13, 1970 – over 300,000 dead or missing. The 1991 cyclone, Bangladesh's and the world's second worst in terms of loss of life, killed an estimated 138,000 people.

Worst recorded tornado: Missouri/Illinois/Indiana, USA, March 18, 1925 – 792 deaths. The tornado was only 900 ft [275 m] wide.

Tropical cyclones are known as hurricanes in Central and North America, as typhoons in the Far East, and as willy-willies in northern Australia.

Climate

Weather is the day-to-day or hour-to-hour condition of the air, while climate is weather in the long term, the seasonal pattern of hot and cold, wet and dry, averaged over a long period. Most classifications of climate are based on a system developed by a Russian meteorologist, Vladimir Köppen, in the early 19th century. Using a code based on letters and a classification centered on two main features, temperature and precipitation, he identified five main climatic types: tropical (A), dry (B), warm temperate (C), cold temperate (D), and polar (E). A highland mountain climate (H), was added later to account for the variety of altitudinal climatic zones on high mountains. Each of these main regions was then further subdivided.

Latitude is a major factor in determining climate, but other factors add to the complexity. They include the differential heating of land and sea, the distance from the sea, the effect of mountains on winds, and the influence of ocean currents. For example, New York City, Naples and the Gobi Desert share almost the same latitude, but their climates are very different.

Climates are not indefinitely stable. During the last Ice Age, the Earth underwent alternating cold periods, called glacials, separated by warm interglacials. The Milankovich theory suggests such cycles may be caused by variations in the Earth's path around the Sun, changing from almost circular to elliptical every 95,000 years, and variations in the Earth's tilt from 21.5° to 24.5° every 42,000 years. Another factor is that the Earth is now closest to the Sun in the middle of winter in the northern hemisphere and furthest away in summer. But 12,000 years ago, at the height of the last glacial period, the northern winter fell with the Sun at its most distant.

Studies of these cycles suggest that we are now in an interglacial with a new glacial period on the way. However, many scientists believe that global warming, largely a result of burning fossil fuels and deforestation, may be occurring much faster than the great, slow cycles of the Solar System.

Tropical rainy climates
All mean monthly temperatures above 64°F.

Af	Rain forest climate
Am	Monsoon climate
Aw	Savanna climate

Dry climates
Low rainfall combined with a wide range of temperatures

| BS | Steppe climate |
| BW | Desert climate |

Warm temperate rainy climates
The mean temperature is below 64°F but above 26°F and that of the warmest month is over 50°F.

Cw	Dry winter climate
Cs	Dry summer climate
Cf	Climate with no dry season

Cold temperate rainy climates
The mean temperature of the coldest month is below 37°F but that of the warmest month is still over 50°F.

| Dw | Dry winter climate |
| Df | Climate with no dry season |

Polar climates
The mean temperature of the warmest month is below 50°F, giving permanently frozen subsoil.

| ET | Tundra climate |

The mean temperature of the warmest month is below 32°F, giving permanent ice and snow.

| EF | Polar climate |

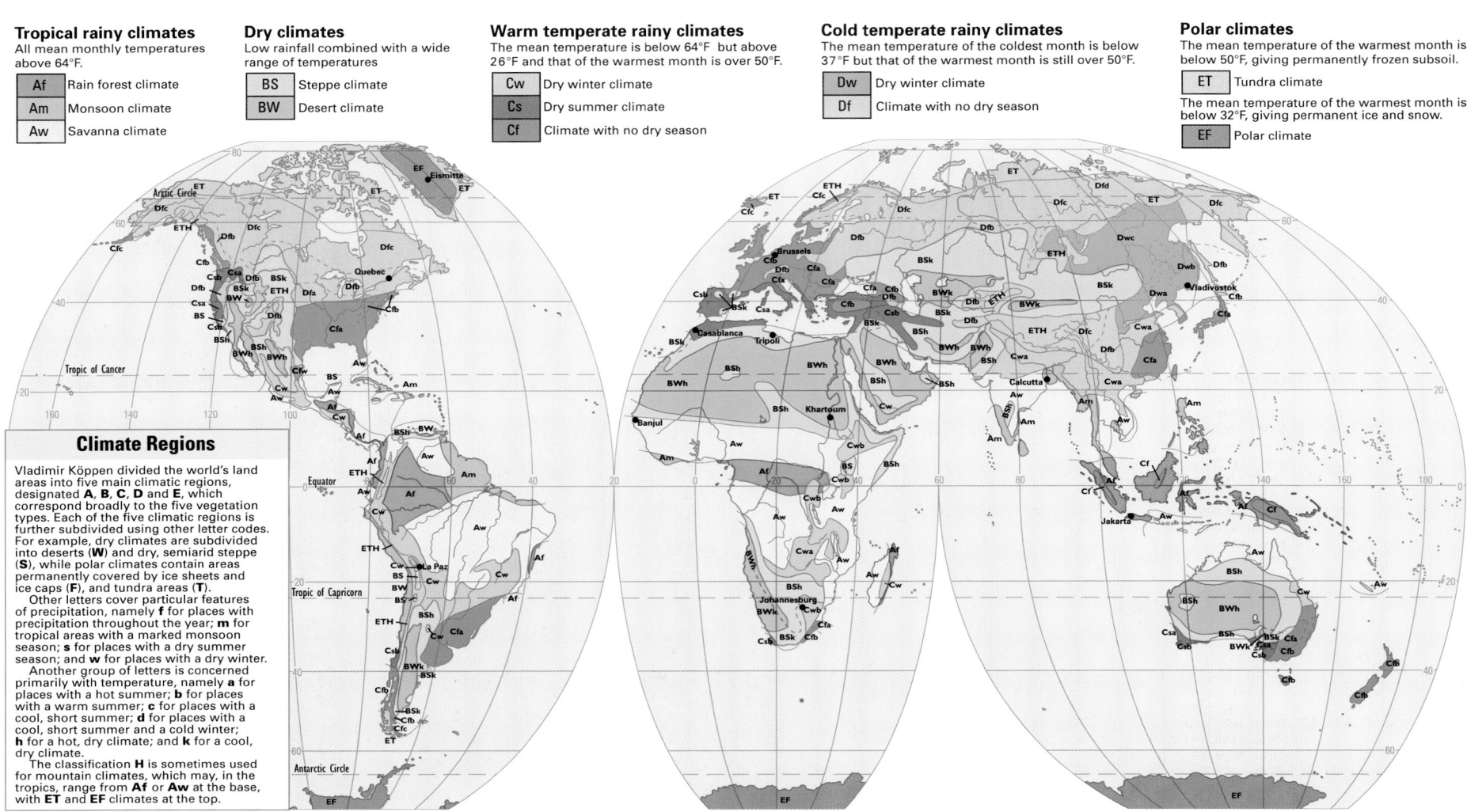

Climate Regions

Vladimir Köppen divided the world's land areas into five main climatic regions, designated **A, B, C, D** and **E**, which correspond broadly to the five vegetation types. Each of the five climatic regions is further subdivided using other letter codes. For example, dry climates are subdivided into deserts (**W**) and dry, semiarid steppe (**S**), while polar climates contain areas permanently covered by ice sheets and ice caps (**F**), and tundra areas (**T**).

Other letters cover particular features of precipitation, namely **f** for places with precipitation throughout the year; **m** for tropical areas with a marked monsoon season; **s** for places with a dry summer season; and **w** for places with a dry winter.

Another group of letters is concerned primarily with temperature, namely **a** for places with a hot summer; **b** for places with a warm summer; **c** for places with a cool, short summer; **d** for places with a cool, short summer and a cold winter; **h** for a hot, dry climate; and **k** for a cool, dry climate.

The classification **H** is sometimes used for mountain climates, which may, in the tropics, range from **Af** or **Aw** at the base, with **ET** and **EF** climates at the top.

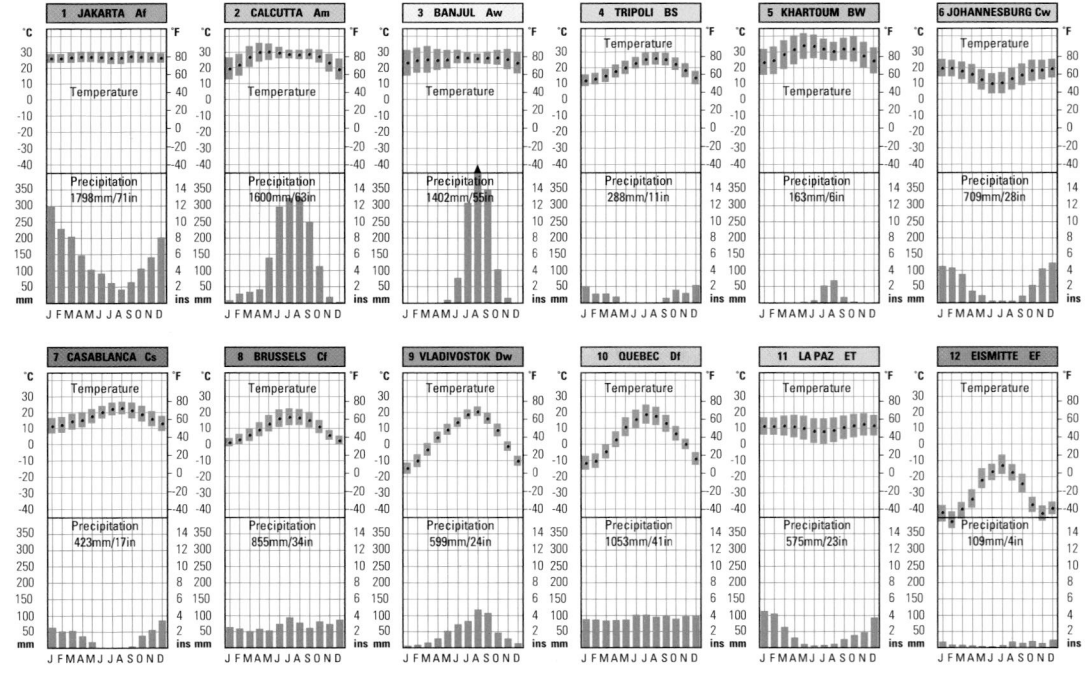

Climate and Weather Terms

Anticyclone: area of high pressure with light winds and generally quiet weather.
Absolute humidity: amount of water vapor contained in a given volume of air.
Cloud cover: amount of cloud in the sky; measured in oktas (from 1 – 8), with 0 clear, and 8 total cover.
Condensation: the conversion of water vapor, or moisture in the air, into liquid.
Cyclone: violent storm resulting from counterclockwise rotation of winds in the northern hemisphere and clockwise in the southern: called hurricane in N. America, typhoon in the Far East.
Depression: area of low pressure. The pressure gradient is toward the center.
Dew: water droplets condensed out of the air after the ground has cooled at night.
Dew point: temperature at which air becomes saturated (reaches a relative humidity of 100%) at a constant pressure.
Drizzle: precipitation where drops are less than 0.02 in [0.5 mm] in diameter.
Evaporation: conversion of water from liquid into vapor, or moisture in the air.
Front: the dividing line between two air masses.
Frost: dew that has frozen when the air temperature falls below freezing point.
Hail: frozen rain; small balls of ice, often falling during thunderstorms.
Hoar frost: formed on objects when the dew point is below freezing point.
Humidity: amount of moisture in the air.
Isobar: cartographic line connecting places of equal atmospheric pressure.
Isotherm: cartographic line connecting places of equal temperature.
Lightning: massive electrical discharge released in thunderstorm from cloud to cloud or cloud to ground, the result of the tip becoming positively charged and the bottom negatively charged.
Precipitation: measurable rain, snow, sleet or hail.
Prevailing wind: most common direction of wind at a given location.
Rain: precipitation of liquid particles with diameter larger than 0.02 in (0.5 mm].
Relative humidity: amount of water vapor contained in a given volume of air at a given temperature.
Snow: formed when water vapor condenses below freezing point.
Thunder: sound produced by the rapid expansion of air heated by lightning.
Tornado: severe funnel-shaped storm that twists as hot air spins vertically (waterspout at sea).
Whirlwind: rapidly rotating column of air, only a few feet across, made visible by dust.

Climate Change

Human factors, such as the emission of greenhouse gases through the burning of fossil fuels and deforestation, have contributed to global warming. The histogram, below, shows in blue the average global temperatures from 1860 (when sufficient observations became available for global averages to be calculated) to 1996. The red line is a 10-year running average. Overall, there is an upward trend, particularly so since the 1970s, when global warming became a matter of concern in scientific circles. The large year-to-year changes indicate the Earth's natural climatic variability and the influence of such factors as major volcanic eruptions.

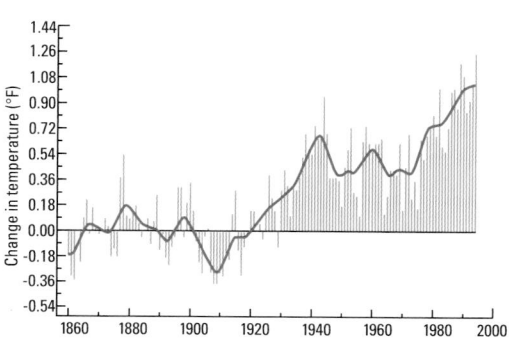

Data from the Hadley Centre for Climate Research and Prediction

Beaufort Wind Scale

Named after the 19th-century British naval officer who devised it, Admiral Beaufort, the Beaufort Scale assesses wind speed according to its effects. It was originally designed as an aid for sailors, but has since been adapted for use on the land. It is used internationally.

Scale	Wind speed km/h	mph	Effect
0	0–1	0–1	**Calm** Smoke rises vertically
1	1–5	1–3	**Light air** Wind direction shown only by smoke drift
2	6–11	4–7	**Light breeze** Wind felt on face; leaves rustle; vanes moved by wind
3	12–19	8–12	**Gentle breeze** Leaves and small twigs in constant motion; wind extends small flag
4	20–28	13–18	**Moderate** Raises dust and loose paper; small branches move
5	29–38	19–24	**Fresh** Small trees in leaf sway; crested wavelets on inland waters
6	39–49	25–31	**Strong** Large branches move; difficult to use umbrellas; overhead wires whistle
7	50–61	32–38	**Near gale** Whole trees in motion; difficult to walk against wind
8	62–74	39–46	**Gale** Twigs break from trees; walking very difficult
9	75–88	47–54	**Strong gale** Slight structural damage
10	89–102	55–63	**Storm** Trees uprooted; serious structural damage
11	103–117	64–72	**Violent storm** Widespread damage
12	118+	73+	**Hurricane**

The Monsoon

Monsoon is the term given to the seasonal reversal of wind direction, most noticeably in Southeast Asia. It results from a combination of factors: the extreme heating and cooling of large land masses in relation to the less marked changes in temperature of the adjacent seas; the northward movement of the Intertropical Convergence Zone (ITCZ); and the effect of the Himalayas on the circulation of the air.

In early March, which normally marks the end of the subcontinent's cool season and the start of the hot season, winds blow outward from the mainland. But as the overhead Sun and the ITCZ move northward, the land is intensely heated, and a low-pressure system develops. The southeast trade winds, which are drawn across the Equator, change direction and are sucked into the interior to become southwesterly winds, bringing heavy rain. By November, the overhead Sun and the ITCZ have again moved southward and the wind directions are again reversed. Cool winds blow from the Asian interior to the sea, losing any moisture on the Himalayas before descending to the coast.

Temperature

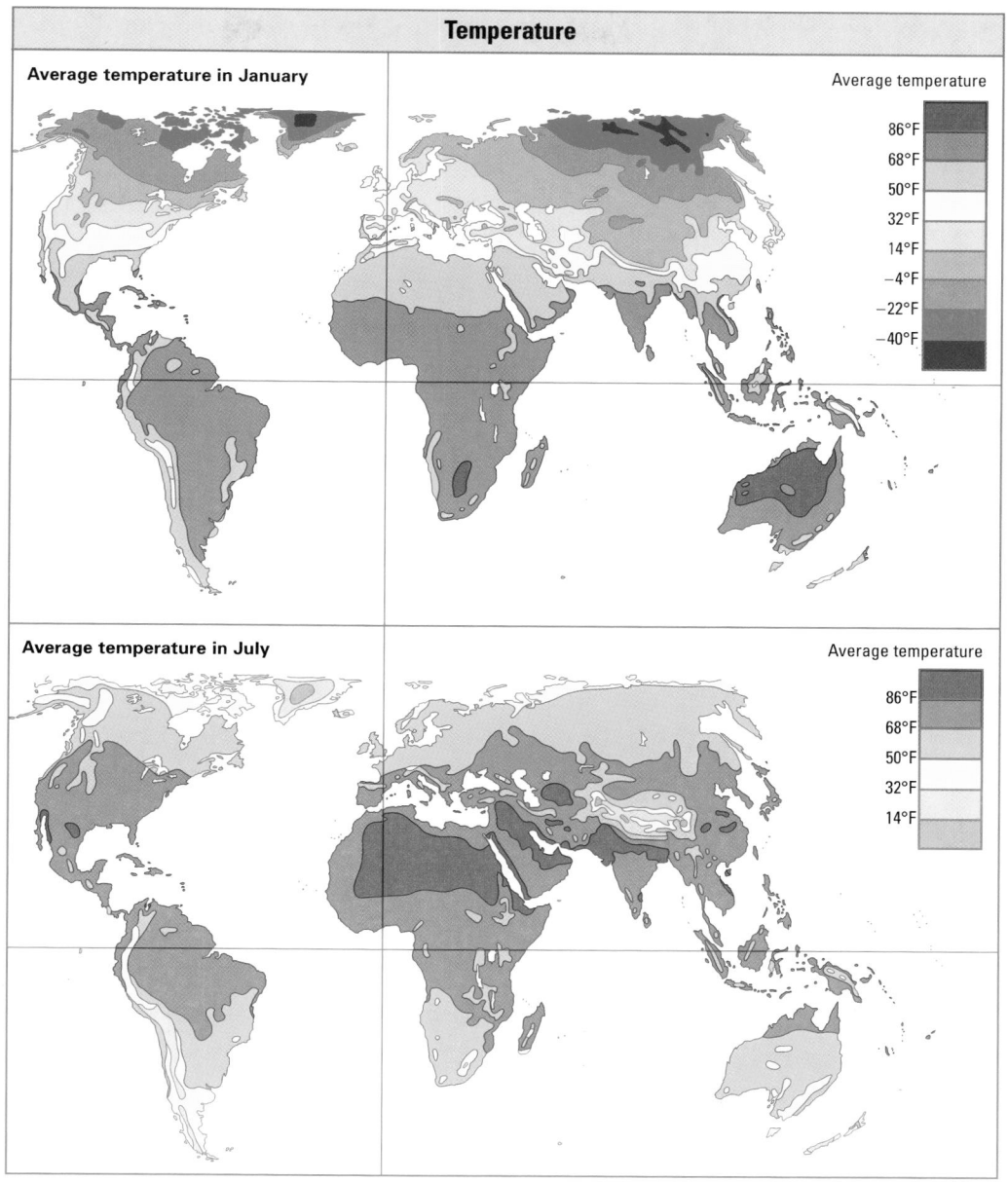

Average temperature in January

Average temperature

86°F
68°F
50°F
32°F
14°F
−4°F
−22°F
−40°F

Average temperature in July

Average temperature

86°F
68°F
50°F
32°F
14°F

Precipitation

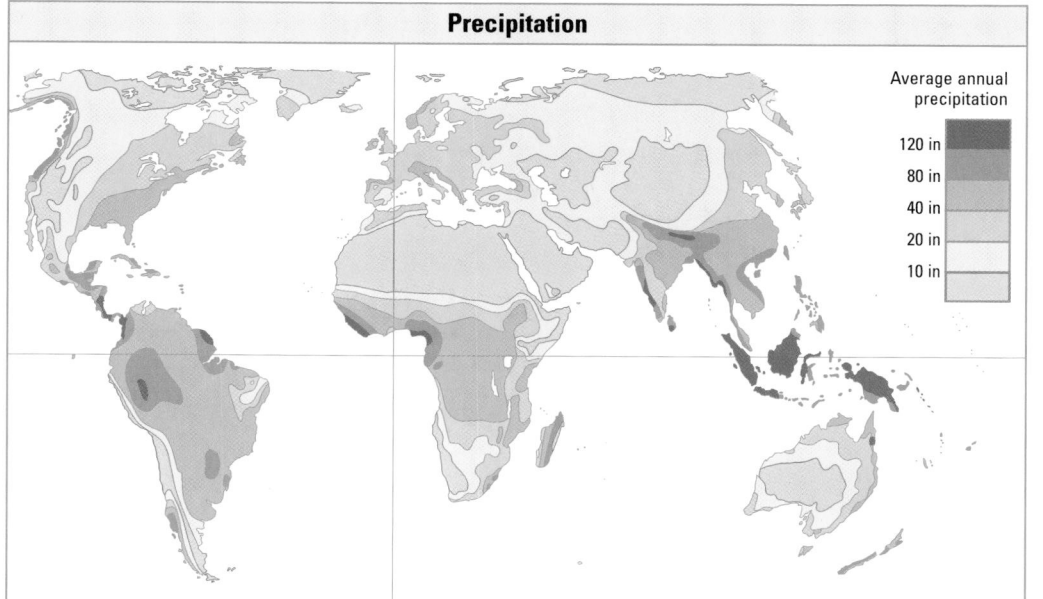

Average annual precipitation

120 in
80 in
40 in
20 in
10 in

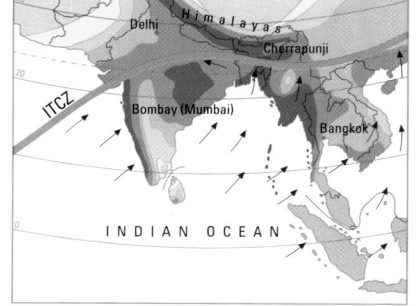

March – Start of the hot, dry season. The ITCZ is over the southern Indian Ocean.

July – The rainy season. The ITCZ has migrated northward; winds blow onshore.

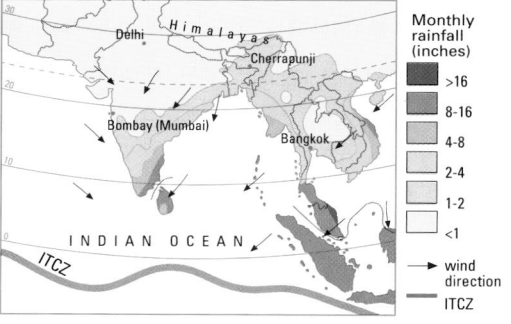

November – The ITCZ has returned south. The offshore winds are cool and dry.

Monthly rainfall (inches)

>16
8–16
4–8
2–4
1–2
<1

→ wind direction
ITCZ

Climate Records

Temperature

Highest recorded temperature: Al Aziziyah, Libya, 136.4°F [58°C], September 13, 1922.

Highest mean annual temperature: Dallol, Ethiopia, 94°F [34.4°C], 1960–66.

Longest heatwave: Marble Bar, W. Australia, 162 days over 100°F [38°C], October 23, 1923, to April 7, 1924.

Lowest recorded temperature (outside poles): Verkhoyansk, Siberia, –90°F [–68°C], February 6, 1933. Verkhoyansk also registered the greatest annual range of temperature: –94°F to 98°F [–70°C to 37°C].

Lowest mean annual temperature: Polus Nedostupnosti, Pole of Cold, Antarctica, –72°F [–57.8°C].

Precipitation

Driest place: Calama, N. Chile: no recorded rainfall in 400 years to 1971.

Wettest place (average): Tututendo, Colombia: mean annual rainfall 463.4 in [11,770 mm].

Wettest place (12 months): Cherrapunji, Meghalaya, N.E. India, 1,040 in [26,470 mm], August 1860 to August 1861. Cherrapunji also holds the record for rainfall in one month: 115 in [2,930 mm], July 1861. (See maps below.)

Wettest place (24 hours): Cilaos, Réunion, Indian Ocean, 73.6 in [1,870 mm], March 15–16, 1952.

Heaviest hailstones: Gopalganj, Bangladesh, up to 2.25 lb [1.02 kg], April 14, 1986 (killed 92 people).

Heaviest snowfall (continuous): Bessans, Savoie, France, 68 in [1,730 mm] in 19 hours, April 5–6, 1969.

Heaviest snowfall (season/year): Paradise Ranger Station, Mt Rainier, Washington, USA, 1,224.5 in [31,102 mm], February 19, 1971, to February 18, 1972.

Water and Vegetation

Without the hydrological cycle, whereby water is constantly recycled between the oceans, the atmosphere and the land, the continents would be barren. Precipitation enables plants to grow and soils to form, creating the world's natural vegetation regions and the ecosystems that support animal life. Running water also plays a major role in shaping landforms. Yet in many parts of the world, people do not have safe water to drink and suffer from diseases caused by water-borne organisms or pollution. In addition, the limited water supplies have to be shared with agriculture and industry.

In 1996, UN experts argued that the demand for water is increasing at about twice the rate of population growth. They predict that, by 2025, two-thirds of the world's population will face water shortages. This could lead to conflict and even boundary wars, especially because 300 major rivers cross national frontiers and access to their water is likely to be disputed.

The Hydrological Cycle

The world's water balance is regulated by the constant recycling of water between the oceans, atmosphere and land. The movement of water between these three reservoirs is known as the hydrological cycle. The oceans play a vital role in the hydrological cycle: 74% of the total precipitation falls over the oceans and 84% of the total evaporation comes from the oceans. Water vapor in the atmosphere circulates around the planet, transporting energy as well as the water itself. When the vapor cools, it falls as rain or snow. The whole cycle is driven by the Sun.

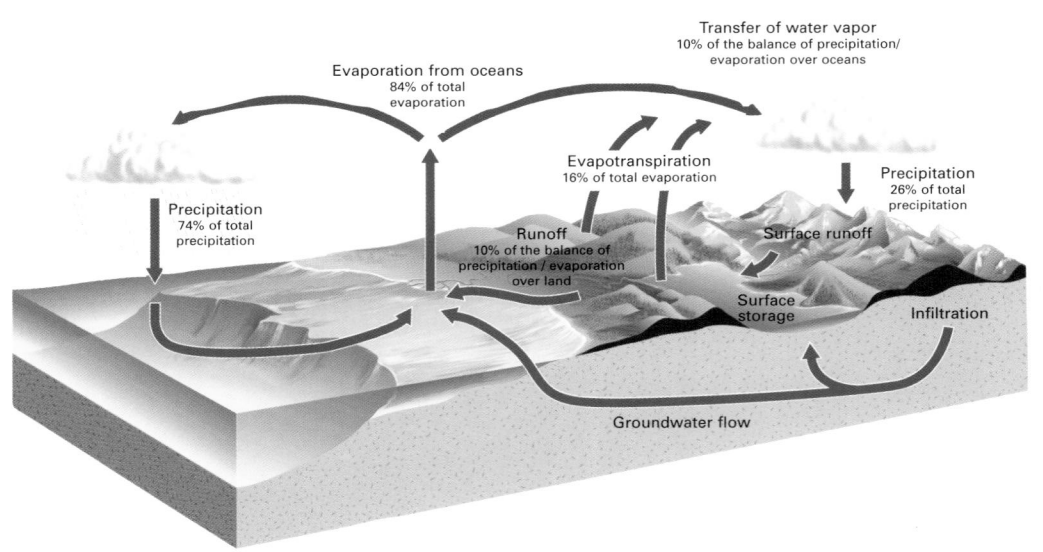

Water Distribution

The distribution of planetary water, by percentage. Oceans and ice caps together account for more than 99% of the total; the breakdown of the remainder is estimated.

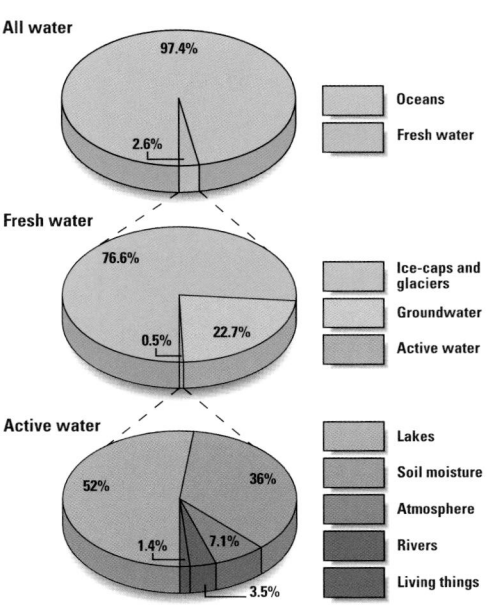

All water
- Oceans
- Fresh water

Fresh water
- Ice-caps and glaciers
- Groundwater
- Active water

Active water
- Lakes
- Soil moisture
- Atmosphere
- Rivers
- Living things

Almost all the world's water is 3 billion years old, and all of it cycles endlessly through the hydrosphere, though at different rates. Water vapor circulates over days, even hours; deep ocean water circulates over millennia; and ice-cap water remains solid for millions of years.

Water Utilization

The percentage breakdown of water usage by sector, selected countries (1996)

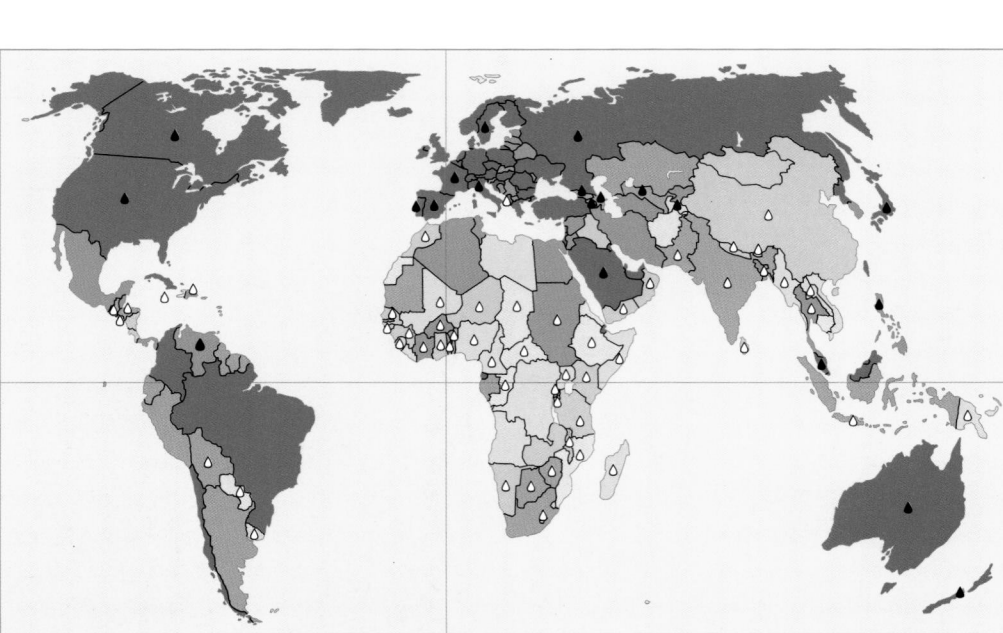

Domestic
Industrial
Agriculture

Algeria
Australia
Russian Fed.
Egypt
France
Ghana
India
Mexico
Poland
Saudi Arabia
UK
USA

Water Runoff

Annual freshwater runoff by continent in cubic miles

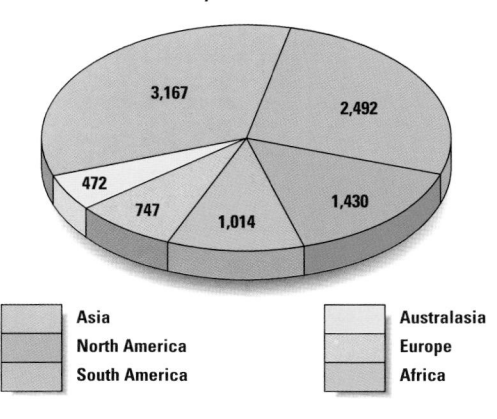

- Asia — 3,167
- North America — 2,492
- South America — 1,430
- Australasia — 472
- Europe — 747
- Africa — 1,014

Water Supply

Percentage of total population with access to safe drinking water (1995)

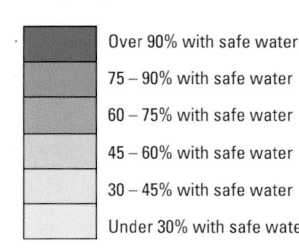

- Over 90% with safe water
- 75 – 90% with safe water
- 60 – 75% with safe water
- 45 – 60% with safe water
- 30 – 45% with safe water
- Under 30% with safe water

△ Under 80 liters average per capita daily water consumption

▲ Over 320 liters average per capita daily water consumption

Least well-provided countries

Paraguay	8%	Central Afr. Rep.	18%
Afghanistan	10%	Bhutan	21%
Cambodia	13%	Congo (D. Rep.)	25%

Watersheds

The world's major rivers; the rank of the world's 20 longest is shown in square brackets, led by the Nile and the Amazon.

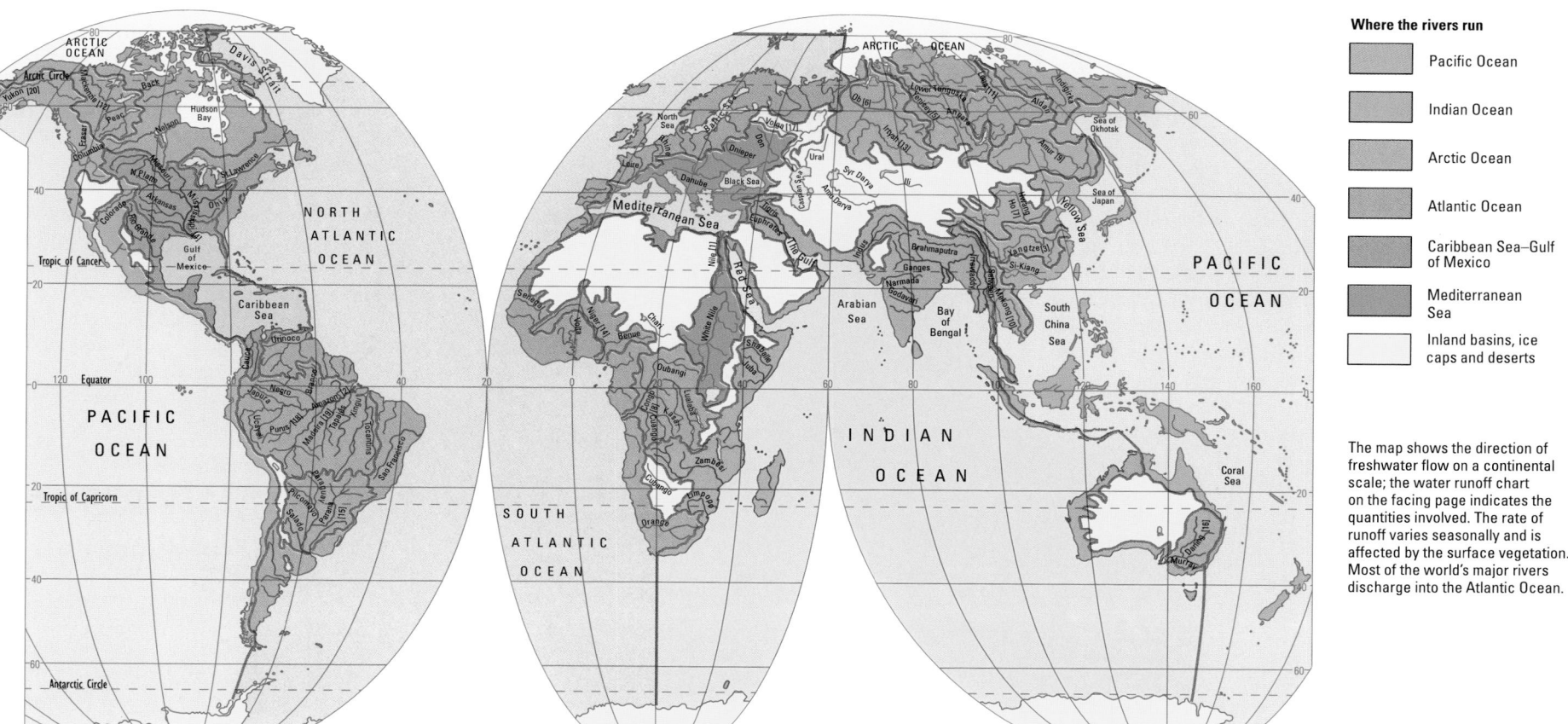

Where the rivers run

- Pacific Ocean
- Indian Ocean
- Arctic Ocean
- Atlantic Ocean
- Caribbean Sea–Gulf of Mexico
- Mediterranean Sea
- Inland basins, ice caps and deserts

The map shows the direction of freshwater flow on a continental scale; the water runoff chart on the facing page indicates the quantities involved. The rate of runoff varies seasonally and is affected by the surface vegetation. Most of the world's major rivers discharge into the Atlantic Ocean.

Annual Sediment Yield

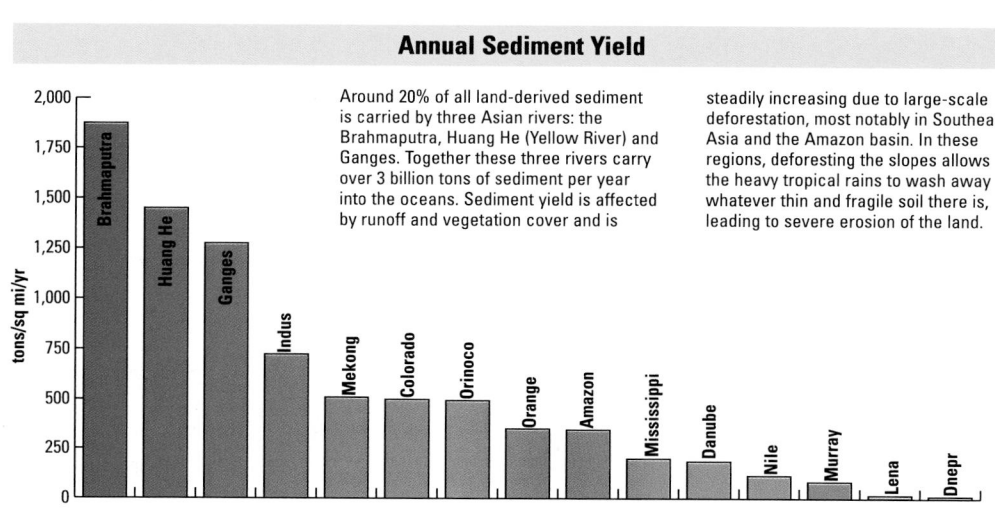

Around 20% of all land-derived sediment is carried by three Asian rivers: the Brahmaputra, Huang He (Yellow River) and Ganges. Together these three rivers carry over 3 billion tons of sediment per year into the oceans. Sediment yield is affected by runoff and vegetation cover and is steadily increasing due to large-scale deforestation, most notably in Southeast Asia and the Amazon basin. In these regions, deforesting the slopes allows the heavy tropical rains to wash away whatever thin and fragile soil there is, leading to severe erosion of the land.

Land Use by Continent

The proportion of productive land has reached its upper limit in Europe, and in Asia more than 80% of potential cropland is already under cultivation.

- Forest
- Permanent pasture and rough grazing
- Permanent crops and plantations
- Arable
- Non-productive

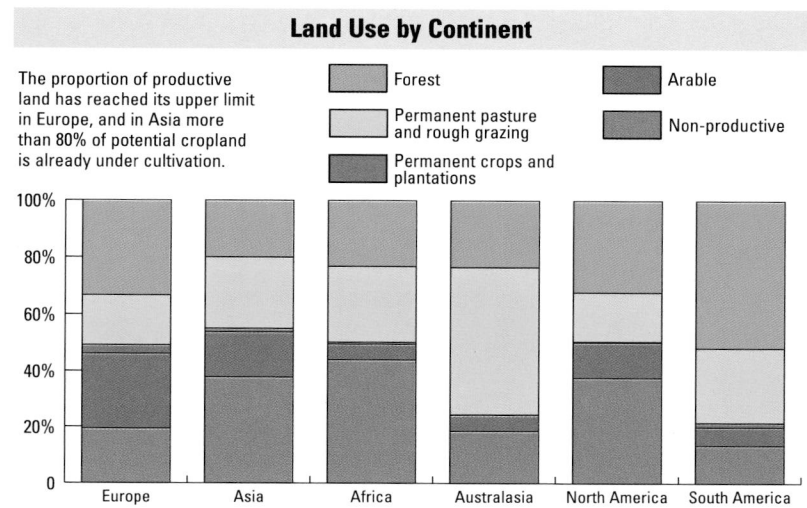

Natural Vegetation

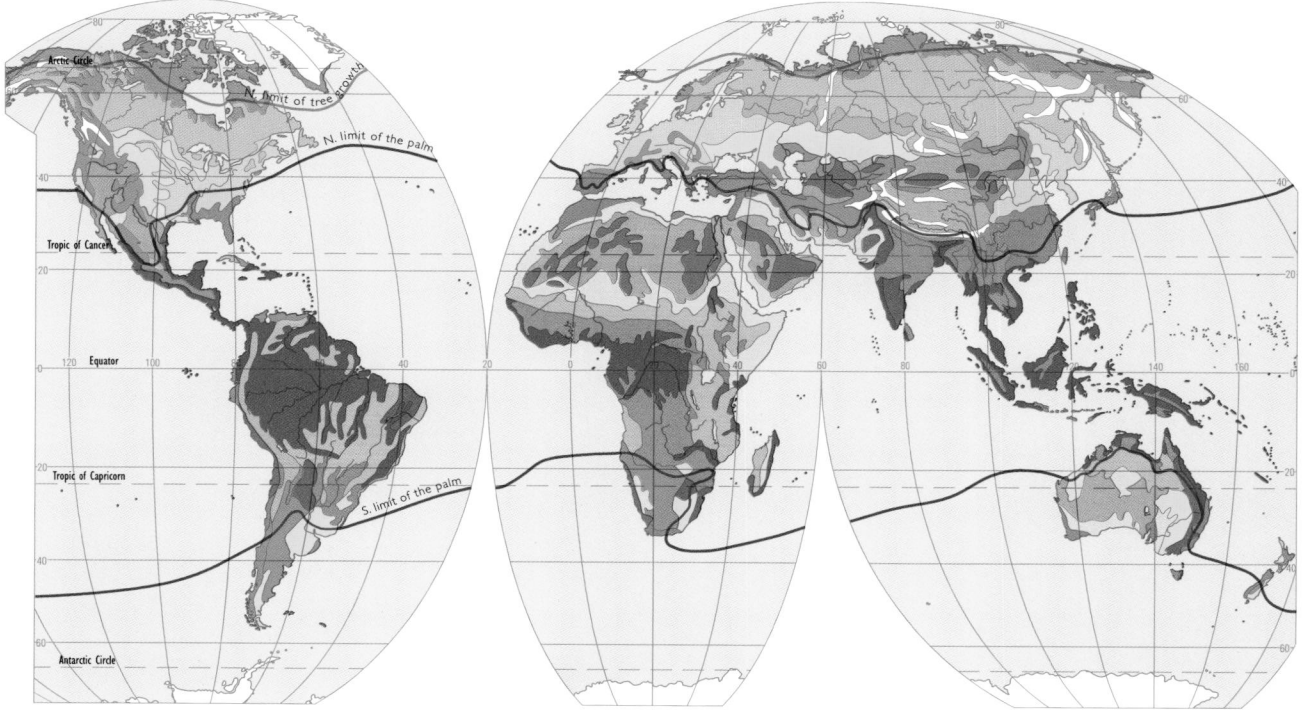

- Tropical rain forest
- Subtropical and temperate rain forest
- Monsoon woodland and open jungle
- Subtropical and temperate woodland, scrub and bush
- Tropical savanna, with low trees and bush
- Tropical savanna and grasslands
- Dry semidesert, with shrub and grass
- Desert shrub
- Desert
- Dry steppe and shrub
- Temperate grasslands, prairie and steppe
- Mediterranean hardwood forest and scrub
- Temperate deciduous forest and meadow
- Temperate deciduous and coniferous forest
- Northern coniferous forest (taiga)
- Mountainous forest, mainly coniferous
- High plateau steppe and tundra
- Arctic tundra
- Polar and mountainous ice desert

The map illustrates the natural "climax vegetation" of a region, as dictated by its climate and topography. In most cases, human agricultural activity has drastically altered the vegetation pattern. Western Europe, for example, lost most of its broadleaf forest many centuries ago, while elsewhere irrigation has turned some natural semidesert into productive land. The various vegetation regions support different kinds of animals and, in an undisturbed state, they are highly developed biological communities, or biomes.

The blue line on the map represents the northern limit of tree growth, and the red lines indicate the northern and southern limits of palm growth.

The Natural Environment

Recent discoveries of life forms in some of the world's most hostile environments, such as around the black smokers along the ocean ridges, prepared the way for the announcement by NASA scientists in 1996 that they had found microfossils in a Martian meteorite. But other scientists were sceptical, believing them to be natural mineral structures and not evidence of extraterrestrial life.

Until further evidence is available, the Earth remains the only planet where we know for sure that life exists. According to the fossil record, life on Earth appeared at least 3.5 billion years ago. Since then, it has evolved from its primitive beginnings to its modern biodiversity, including millions of plants, animals and micro-organisms. Living organisms have not only adapted to the environ-

ment but they have also changed their environment to suit themselves. For example, the Earth's early atmosphere contained little oxygen but the emergence of multicelled, oxygen-producing algae, around 2 billion years ago, led to the creation of an oxygen-rich atmosphere. This enabled land animals to populate the ancient continents.

The amount of the greenhouse gas carbon dioxide in the atmosphere would steadily increase from its present 0.03% were it not for plants. Without them, the Earth's atmosphere would, in a few million years, be similar to that of Venus, where surface temperatures reach 885°F. The Earth has evolved into a complex control system, sensing and reacting to changes and tending always to maintain the balance it has achieved.

Much discussion has centered on how that balance changes. Only recently, scientists were suggesting that we may be living in an interglacial stage of the Pleistocene Ice Age. From the 1980s, however, predictions of future climates have concentrated more on global warming, caused by pollution which has led to an increase in greenhouse gases in the atmosphere. Interference in the natural cycles that control the environment may have consequences that are hard to predict.

Furthermore, we are currently experiencing a period of mass extinction of species, causing a rapid reduction in our planet's biodiversity. A report by the World Conservation Union in 1996 stated that, of the 4,327 known mammal species, 1,096 were at risk and 169 "critically endangered."

Biodiversity in California

The photograph, left, is a false color satellite image of central California in the southwestern United States. The large inlet of the Pacific Ocean is San Francisco Bay. San Francisco lies just below the entrance to the bay, with Oakland on the far side and San Jose to the southeast. California, nicknamed the Golden State, is the third largest state in the United States and the most populous.

Because of its varied terrain and climate, California has a wide range of diverse habitats within a relatively small area. East of the forested Coast Ranges (the gray and red areas just inland from the bay) lies the fertile Central Valley, which appears as a red and blue checkerboard. The Sierra Nevada is the red area in the top right corner. In the northwest and southwest of the state, not shown here, lie parts of the Basin and Range region, much of which is desert. It includes Death Valley, which contains the country's lowest point on land at 86 m below sea level.

Forests cover about 40% of California and they include bristlecone pines, thought to be the oldest living things on Earth, together with coastal redwoods, the world's tallest trees. Wildlife is still abundant, though some species, such as the rare California condor, are on the endangered list.

The state has achieved much to protect its biodiversity. It contains eight of the 54 national parks in the United States. Two of them, Death Valley and Joshua Tree, were designated national parks as recently as 1994, as part of a conservation measure, including the protection of large areas of wilderness in the deserts.

California has vast resources and, were it a separate nation, it would rank among the world's ten most productive in terms of the total value of its goods and services. This means that, like the United States as a whole, it has resources, which many developing countries lack, to finance conservation measures. For example, the World Conservation Union reported in 1996 that 8% of mammals were threatened in the United States, as compared with 32% in the Philippines and 44% in Madagascar, two countries where habitat destruction has been on a large scale.

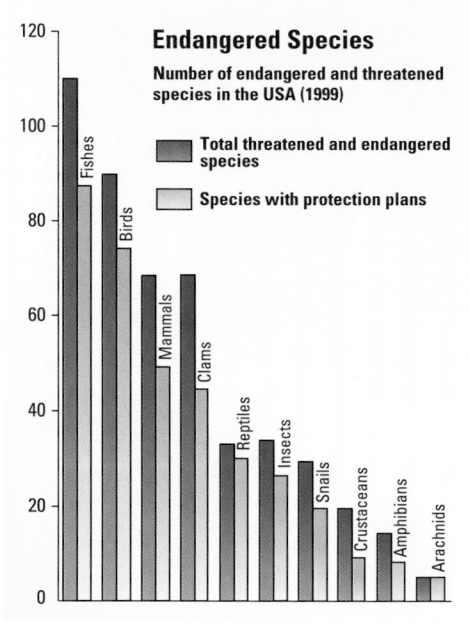

Endangered Species

Number of endangered and threatened species in the USA (1999)

- Total threatened and endangered species
- Species with protection plans

Fishes, Birds, Mammals, Clams, Reptiles, Insects, Snails, Crustaceans, Amphibians, Arachnids

Threatened Mammals

Percentage of mammal species classified as threatened (1996). Many scientists believe we are currently experiencing a period of mass extinction of species rivaling five other periods in the past half a billion years. Among the most threatened mammals are elephants, primates and rhinoceroses.

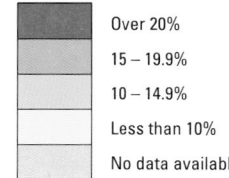

- Over 20%
- 15 – 19.9%
- 10 – 14.9%
- Less than 10%
- No data available

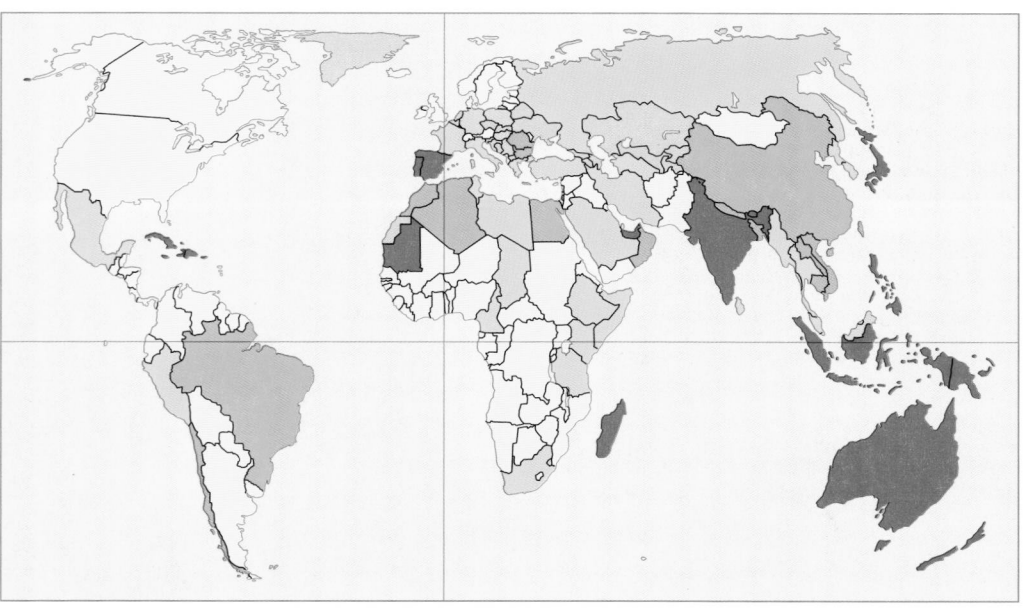

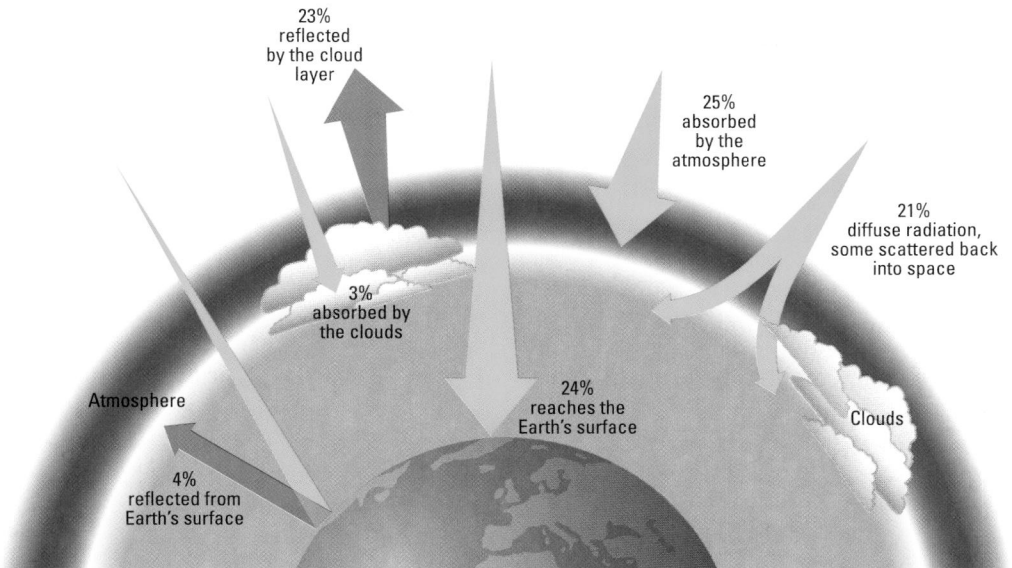

23%
reflected
by the cloud
layer

25%
absorbed
by the
atmosphere

21%
diffuse radiation,
some scattered back
into space

3%
absorbed by
the clouds

24%
reaches the
Earth's surface

Atmosphere

Clouds

4%
reflected from
Earth's surface

The Earth's Energy Balance

Apart from a modest quantity of internal heat from its molten core, the Earth receives all of its energy from the Sun. If the planet is to remain at a constant temperature, it must reradiate exactly as much energy as it receives. Even a minute surplus would lead to a warmer Earth, a deficit to a cooler one. The temperature at which thermal equilibrium is reached depends on a multitude of interconnected factors. Two of the most important are the relative brightness of the Earth – its index of reflectivity, called the "albedo" – and the heat-trapping capacity of the atmosphere – the celebrated "greenhouse effect" (see below).

Because the Sun is very hot, most of its energy arrives in the form of relatively short-wave radiation: the shorter the waves, the more energy they carry. Some of the incoming energy is reflected straight back into space, exactly as it arrived; some is absorbed by the atmosphere on its way toward the surface; some is absorbed by the Earth itself. Absorbed energy heats the Earth and its atmosphere alike. But since its temperature is very much lower than that of the Sun, the outgoing energy is emitted at much longer infra-red wavelengths. Some of the outgoing radiation escapes directly into outer space; some of it is reabsorbed by the atmosphere. Atmospheric energy eventually finds its way back into space, too, after a complex series of interactions. These include the air movements we call the weather and, almost incidentally, the maintenance of life on Earth.

This diagram does not attempt to illustrate the actual mechanisms of heat exchange, but gives a reasonable account (in percentages) of what happens to 100 energy "units." Short-wave radiation is shown in yellow, long-wave in orange.

The Carbon Cycle

Most of the constituents of the atmosphere are kept in constant balance by complex cycles in which life plays an essential and indeed a dominant part. The control of carbon dioxide, which if left to its own devices would be the dominant atmospheric gas, is possibly the most important, although since all the Earth's biological and geophysical cycles interact and interlock, it is hard to separate them even in theory and quite impossible in practice.

The Earth has a huge supply of carbon, only a small quantity of which is in the form of carbon dioxide. Of that, around 98% is dissolved in the sea; the fraction circulating in the air amounts to only 340 parts per million of the atmosphere, where its capacity as a greenhouse gas is the key regulator of the planetary temperature. In turn, life regulates the regulator, keeping carbon dioxide concentrations below danger level.

If all life were to vanish from the Earth tomorrow, the atmosphere would begin the process of change immediately, although it might take several million years to achieve a new, inorganic stability. First, the oxygen content would begin to fall away; with no more assistance than a little solar radiation, a few electrical storms and its own high chemical potential, oxygen would steadily combine with atmospheric nitrogen and volcanic outgassing. In doing so, it would yield sufficient acid to react with carbonaceous rocks such as limestone, releasing carbon dioxide. Once carbon dioxide levels exceeded about 1%, its greenhouse power would increase disproportionately. Rising temperatures – well above the boiling point of water – would speed chemical reactions; in time, the Earth's atmosphere would consist of little more than carbon dioxide and superheated water vapor.

Living things, however, circulate carbon. They do so first by simply existing: after all, the carbon atom is the basic building block of living matter.

During life, plants absorb carbon dioxide from the atmosphere and, along with various chemicals, as soluble salts from the soil, incorporating the carbon into their structure – leaves and trunks in the case of land plants, shells in the case of plankton and the tiny creatures that feed on it. The oxygen thereby freed is added to the atmosphere, at least for a time. The carbon is returned to circulation when the plants die or is passed up the food chain to the herbivores and then the carnivores that feed on them. As organisms at each of these trophic levels die, they decay, releasing the carbon which then combines once more with the oxygen released during life. However, a small proportion of carbon, about one part in 1,000, is removed almost permanently, buried beneath mud on land or at sea, sinking as dead matter to the ocean floor. In time, it is slowly compressed into sedimentary rocks such as limestone and chalk.

But in the evolution of the Earth, nothing is quite permanent. On an even longer timescale, the planet's crustal movements force new rock upward in mid-ocean ridges. Limestone deposits are moved, and sea levels change; ancient carboniferous rocks are exposed to weathering, and a little of their carbon is released to be fixed in turn by the current generation of plants.

The carbon cycle has continued quietly for an immensely long time, and without gross disturbance there is no reason why it would not continue almost indefinitely in the future. However, human beings have found a way to release fixed carbon at a rate far faster than existing global systems can recirculate it. The fossil fuels, coal, oil, gas and peat deposits, represent the work of millions of years of carbon accumulation; but it has taken only a few human generations of high-energy scavenging to endanger the entire complex regulatory cycle.

pool of CO$_2$
in atmosphere

combustion   photosynthesis

respiration   respiration   respiration

CO$_2$

CO$_2$

decay
organisms

death

respiration

carbonification,
gradual production
of fossil fuels

death

peat

coal

oil and gas

decay
organisms

The Greenhouse Effect

Constituting less than 1% of the atmosphere, the natural greenhouse gases (water vapor, carbon dioxide, methane, nitrous oxide and ozone) have a hugely disproportionate effect on the Earth's climate and even its habitability. Like the glass panes in a greenhouse, the gases are transparent to most incoming short-wave radiation, which passes freely to heat the planet beneath. But when the warmed Earth retransmits that energy, in the form of longer-wave infra-red radiation, the gases function as an opaque shield preventing some of it from escaping, so that the planetary surface (like the interior of a greenhouse) stays relatively hot.

Over the last 150 years, there has been a gradual increase in the levels of greenhouse gases (with the exception of water vapor which remains a constant in the system). These increases are causing alarm – global warming associated with a runaway greenhouse effect could bring disaster – and what is more, predictions suggest that there could be a further rise of 2.5–8°F by the year 2100. A serious reduction in the greenhouse gases would be just as damaging; a total absence of CO$_2$, for example, would leave the planet with a temperature roughly 60°F colder than at present.

N.B. The thickness of the Earth's atmosphere is proportionately much thinner than the peel of an apple.

Sun

Less heat escapes
into space

Outgoing long-
wave radiation
(infa-red) is radiated
back into space

Increased greenhouse
gases means that more long-
wave radiation is reflected
back to Earth

Atmosphere

The atmosphere of the
Earth gets hotter as
more heat is trapped

Increased
greenhouse gases
act as a shield to
long-wave radiation

Incoming short-wave
radiation (ultraviolet)
reaches the surface
of the Earth

People and the Environment

In 1996, the Intergovernmental Panel on Climate Change issued a report stating that "The balance of evidence suggests a discernible human influence on global climate through emissions of carbon dioxide and other greenhouse gases." The report acknowledged that average global temperatures have risen by about 0.9°F since the mid-19th century, but there were still reasons for caution, such as discrepancies between measurements of temperatures around the world. Furthermore, our knowledge about how climates change of their own accord is incomplete, as is our understanding of human interference, how this varies in different parts of the world and how it differs from natural climatic variability.

Human interference with nature is nothing new, at least since people turned from hunting and gathering to agriculture more than 10,000 years ago. At first, human actions seemed to have no ill effects because the systems that regulate the global environment were able to absorb damage. But from the late 18th century, the Industrial Revolution and the population explosion have caused pollution on a scale that threatens to overwhelm the Earth's ability to cope.

The 20th century witnessed many disasters, including the dumping of industrial wastes in rivers and seas, accidents at nuclear power stations, and the creation of acid rain through the release of sulphur dioxides and nitrous oxides by the burning of fossil fuels. The release of greenhouse gases are held to be the main reason for global warming, while CFCs (chlorofluoro-carbons) have damaged the ozone layer in the stratosphere, the planet's screen against ultraviolet radiation.

Global warming will lead to melting ice sheets and the flooding of fertile coastal plains. Computer models suggest that it might affect ocean currents so that northwestern Europe, which owes its mild climate to the Gulf Stream, could expect bitterly cold winters. Some models have suggested that cloud cover could increase, reflecting more solar energy back into space and so start a new Ice Age.

In many tropical areas, deforestation is making productive land barren, while in the dry grasslands bordering deserts, the removal of plant cover is causing desertification. But human ingenuity can respond to this crisis in planet management.

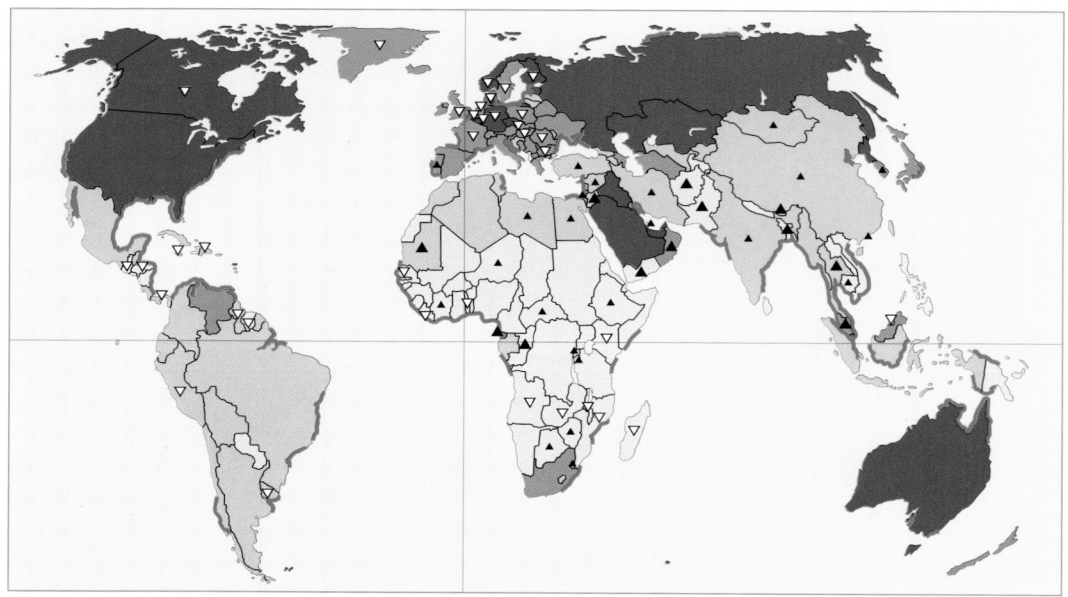

Global Warming

Carbon dioxide emissions in tons per person per year (1995)

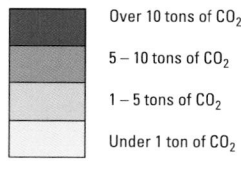

- Over 10 tons of CO_2
- 5 – 10 tons of CO_2
- 1 – 5 tons of CO_2
- Under 1 ton of CO_2

Changes in CO_2 emissions 1980–90

- ▲ Over 100% increase
- ▲ 50–100% increase
- ▽ Reduction
- ▬ Coasts in danger of flooding from rising sea levels

Records of global mean surface temperatures from 1860 to the present show that 1995 was the warmest year and that nine of the ten warmest years have occurred since 1983. This evidence of global warming is attributed mainly to the Greenhouse Effect, caused by the emission of certain gases, notably carbon dioxide (CO_2), into the atmosphere since the start of the Industrial Revolution. At first, much of the CO_2 was absorbed by the oceans. However, the vast increase in fuel combustion since 1950 has led CO_2 content in the atmosphere to increase gradually from 280 parts per million to more than 350 parts per million. Despite international action to control the emissions of some greenhouse gases, CO_2 levels are still rising.

Greenhouse Power

Relative contributions to the Greenhouse Effect by the major heat-absorbing gases in the atmosphere

The chart combines greenhouse potency and volume. Carbon dioxide has a greenhouse potential of only 1, but its concentration of 350 parts per million makes it predominate. CFC 12, with 25,000 times the absorption capacity of CO_2, is present only as 0.00044 ppm.

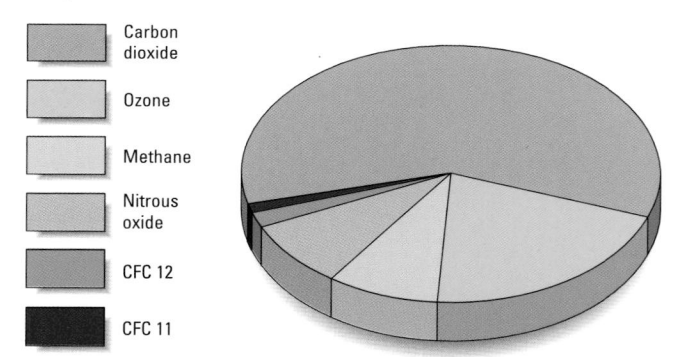

- Carbon dioxide
- Ozone
- Methane
- Nitrous oxide
- CFC 12
- CFC 11

Carbon Dioxide

Carbon dioxide released in millions of tons (latest available year)

USA 4,932; Former USSR 3,581; China 2,543; Japan; Germany; India; UK; Iraq; Canada; Italy; France; Mexico

Temperature Rise

The rise in average temperatures caused by carbon dioxide and other greenhouse gases (1960–2020)

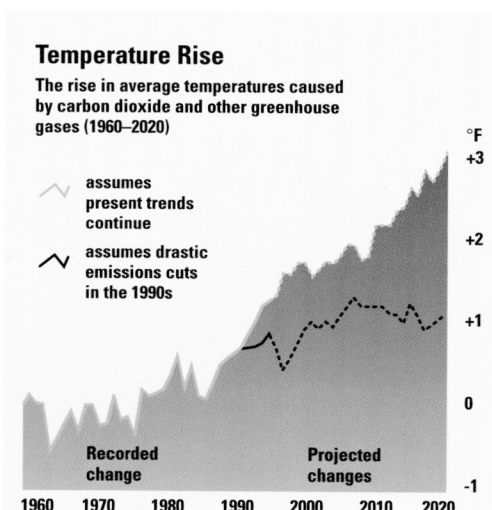

- ∿ assumes present trends continue
- ∿ assumes drastic emissions cuts in the 1990s

Recorded change — Projected changes

1960 1970 1980 1990 2000 2010 2020

The Thinning Ozone Layer

Total atmospheric ozone concentration in the southern and northern hemispheres (Dobson units, 1995)

In 1985, scientists working in Antarctica discovered a thinning of the ozone layer, commonly known as an "ozone hole." This caused immediate alarm because the ozone layer absorbs most of the Sun's dangerous ultraviolet radiation, which is believed to cause an increase in skin cancer, cataracts and damage to the immune system. Since 1985, ozone depletion has increased and, by 1996, the ozone hole over the South Pole was estimated to be as large as North America. The false color images, right, show the total atmospheric ozone concentration in the southern hemisphere (in October 1995) and the northern hemisphere (in March 1995) with the ozone hole clearly identifiable at the center. The data are from the Tiros Ozone Vertical Sounder, an instrument on the American TIROS weather satellite. The colors represent the ozone concentration in Dobson Units (DU). Normal healthy values are around 280 DU but the lowest value in the northern hemisphere reached 98 DU. Scientists agree that ozone depletion is caused by CFCs, a group of manufactured chemicals used in air conditioning systems and refrigerators. In a 1987 treaty most industrial nations agreed to phase out CFCs and a complete ban on most CFCs was agreed after the end of 1995. However, scientists believe that the chemicals will remain in the atmosphere for 50 to 100 years. As a result, ozone depletion will continue for many years.

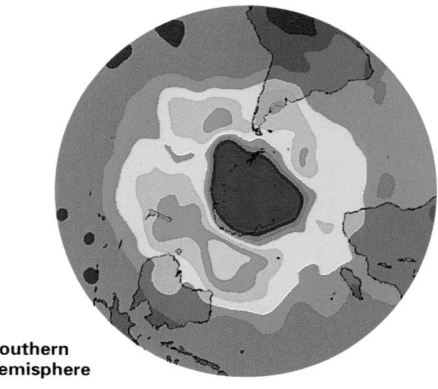

Southern hemisphere

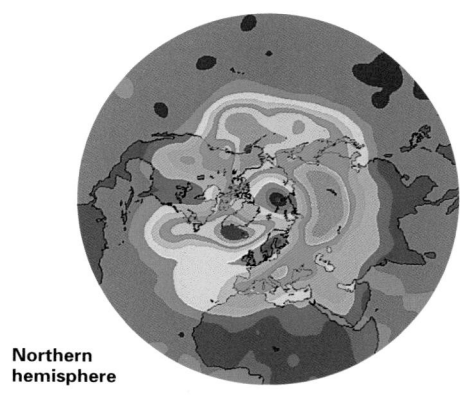

Northern hemisphere

World Pollution

Acid rain and sources of acidic emissions (latest available year)

Acid rain is caused by high levels of sulfur and nitrogen in the atmosphere. They combine with water vapor and oxygen to form acids (H_2SO_4 and HNO_3) which fall as precipitation.

 Regions where sulfur and nitrogen oxides are released in high concentrations, mainly from fossil fuel combustion

• Major cities with high levels of air pollution (including nitrogen and sulfur emissions)

Areas of heavy acid deposition

pH numbers indicate acidity, decreasing from a neutral 7. Normal rain, slightly acid from dissolved carbon dioxide, never exceeds a pH of 5.6.

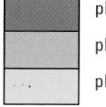

pH less than 4.0 (most acidic)

pH 4.0 to 4.5

pH 4.5 to 5.0

- - - - Areas where acid rain is a potential problem

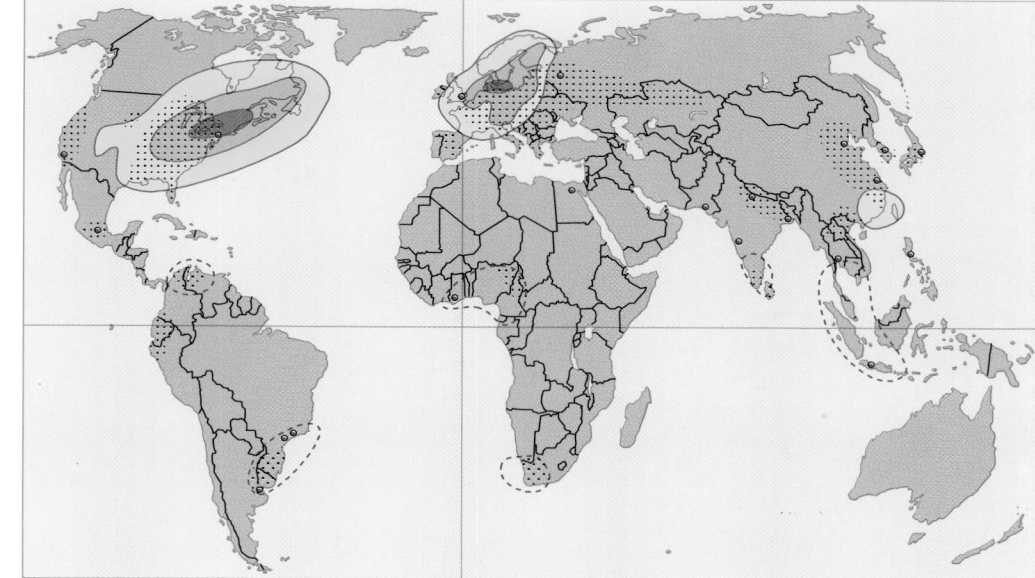

Desertification

Existing deserts

Areas with a high risk of desertification

Areas with a moderate risk of desertification

Former areas of rain forest

Existing rain forest

Deforestation

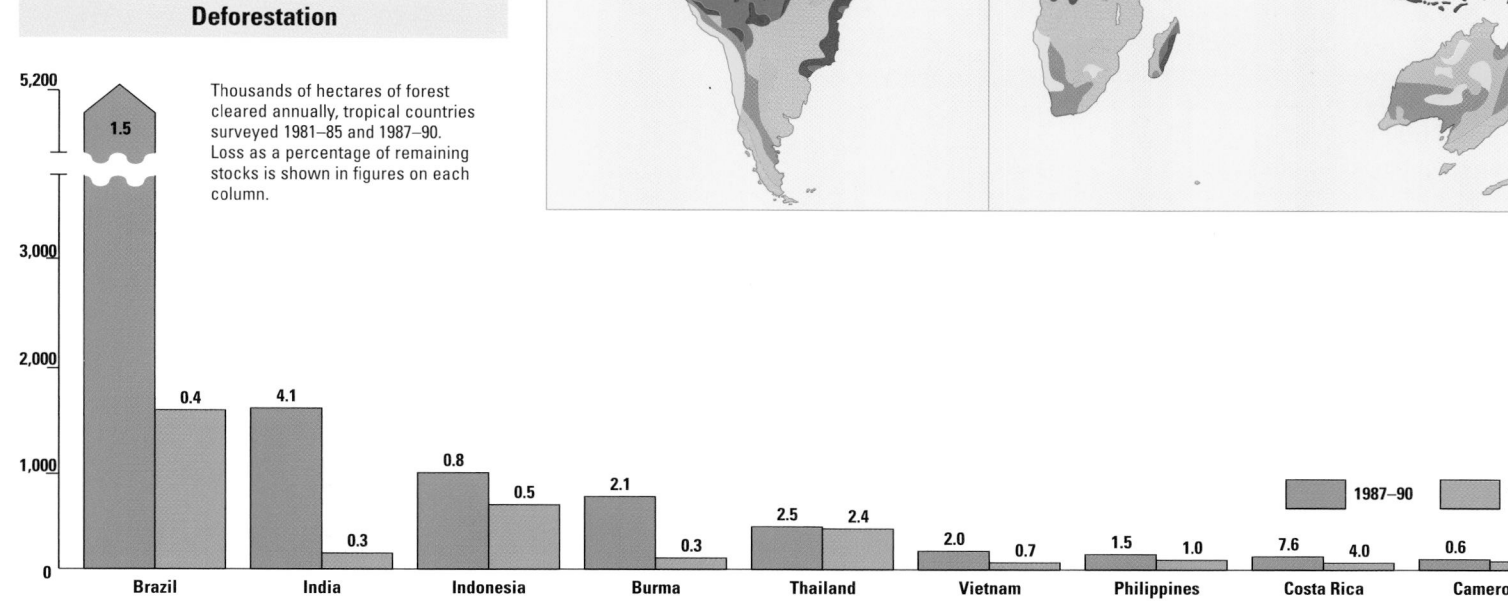

Thousands of hectares of forest cleared annually, tropical countries surveyed 1981–85 and 1987–90. Loss as a percentage of remaining stocks is shown in figures on each column.

	Brazil	India	Indonesia	Burma	Thailand	Vietnam	Philippines	Costa Rica	Cameroon
1987–90	1.5	4.1	0.8	2.1	2.5	2.0	1.5	7.6	0.6
1981–85	0.4	0.3	0.5	0.3	2.4	0.7	1.0	4.0	0.4

Water Pollution

 Severely polluted sea areas and lakes

 Polluted sea areas and lakes

 Areas of frequent oil pollution by shipping

▶ Major oil tanker spills

▲ Major oil rig blow outs

▼ Offshore dumpsites for industrial and municipal waste

——— Severely polluted rivers and estuaries

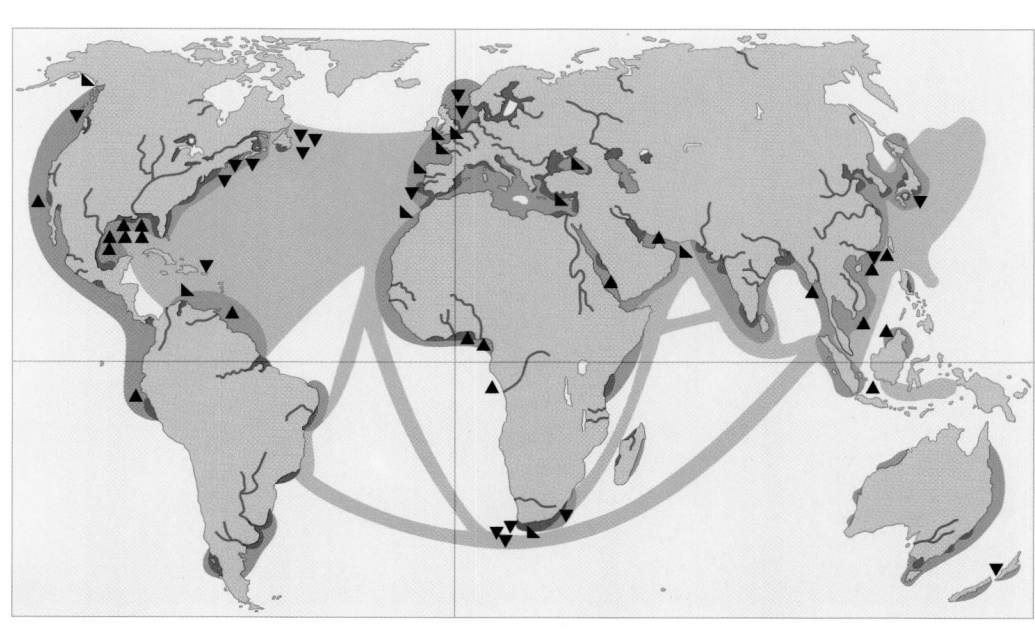

Antarctica

The vast Antarctic ice sheet, containing some 70% of the Earth's fresh water, plays a crucial role in the circulation of the atmosphere and oceans, and hence in determining the planetary climate. The frozen southern continent is also the last remaining wilderness – the largest area to remain free from human colonization.

Ever since Amundsen and Scott raced for the South Pole in 1911, various countries have pressed territorial claims over sections of Antarctica, spurred in recent years by its known and suspected mineral wealth: enough iron ore to supply the world at present levels for 200 years, large oil reserves and, probably, the biggest coal deposits on Earth.

However, the 1961 Antarctic Treaty set aside the area for peaceful uses only, guaranteeing freedom of scientific investigation, banning waste disposal and nuclear testing, and suspending the issue of territorial rights. By 1990, the original 12 signatories had grown to 25, with a further 15 nations granted observer status in subsequent deliberations. However, the Treaty itself was threatened by wrangles between different countries, government agencies and international pressure groups.

Finally, in July 1991, the belated agreement of the UK and the USA assured unanimity on a new accord to ban all mineral exploration for a further 50 years. The ban can only be rescinded if all the present signatories, plus a majority of any future adherents, agree. While the treaty has always lacked a formal mechanism for enforcement, it is firmly underwritten by public concern generated by the efforts of environmental pressure groups such as Greenpeace, which has been foremost in the campaign to have Antarctica declared a "World Park."

However, from the mid-1990s, the continent appeared to be under threat from global warming, which some scientists believe was the cause of the breakup of ice shelves along the Antarctic peninsula. Rising temperatures have also disturbed the breeding patterns of Adelie penguins.

Poisoned rivers, domestic sewage and oil spillage have combined in recent years to reduce the world's oceans to a sorry state of contamination, notably near the crowded coasts of industrialized nations. Shipping routes, too, are constantly affected by tanker discharges. Oil spills of all kinds, however, declined significantly during the 1980s, from a peak of 750,000 tons in 1979 to under 50,000 tons in 1990. The most notorious tanker spill of that period – when the *Exxon Valdez* (94,999 grt) ran aground in Prince William Sound, Alaska, in March 1989 – released only 267,000 barrels, a relatively small amount compared to the results of blow outs and war damage. Over 2,500,000 barrels were spilled during the Gulf War of 1991. The worst tanker accident in history occurred in July 1979, when the *Atlantic Empress* and the Aegean Captain collided off Trinidad, polluting the Caribbean with 1,890,000 barrels of crude oil.

Population

In 8000 BC, following the development of agriculture, the world had an estimated population of 8 million and by AD 1000 it was about 300 million. The onset of the Industrial Revolution in the late 18th century led to a population explosion. The 1 billion mark was passed by 1850, it doubled by the 1920s and doubled again to 4 billion by 1975.

Most demographers agree that the world's population, which passed the 6 billion mark in October 1999, will reach 8.9 billion by 2050. It is not expected to level out until 2200, when it will peak at around 11 billion. After 2200, it is expected to level out or even decline a little. Rapid population growth is concentrated in the developing world; the populations of some developed countries, such as Belgium and Germany, are static or have even started to decline.

The developing world includes what the World Bank describes as low-income economies, with an average per capita GNP of US $380, and middle-income economies, with a per capita GNP of $2,520. Most developing countries are in Africa, Asia and Latin America. The developed world, made up of high-income, industrialized economies with an average per capita GNP of $23,420, contains Australasia, most of Europe and North America, and Japan in Asia.

In the poorer developing countries, a high proportion of the population is young, and they face high levels of expenditure on education and health until population growth rates start to decline. In developed countries, where the population pyramids are becoming increasingly top-heavy, expenditure on pensions and healthcare for the elderly is becoming a major social problem.

Largest Nations

The world's most populous nations, in millions (1998 est.)

1.	China	1,237
2.	India	984
3.	USA	270
4.	Indonesia	213
5.	Brazil	170
6.	Russia	147
7.	Pakistan	135
8.	Japan	126
9.	Bangladesh	125
10.	Nigeria	111
11.	Mexico	99
12.	Germany	82
13.	Philippines	78
14.	Vietnam	76
15.	Egypt	66
16.	Turkey	65
17.	Iran	64
18.	Thailand	60
19.	France	59
20.	UK	59
21.	Ethiopia	58
22.	Italy	57
23.	Ukraine	50
24.	Congo (= Zaïre)	49

Crowded Nations

Population per square mile (1997), excluding nations of less than 1 million

1.	Singapore	13,587
2.	Bangladesh	2,468
3.	Taiwan	1,562
4.	Mauritius	1,474
5.	Netherlands	1,215
6.	South Korea	1,207
7.	Puerto Rico	1,119
8.	Belgium	868
9.	Japan	865
10.	India	855
11.	Lebanon	811
12.	Sri Lanka	749
13.	El Salvador	743
14.	Israel	741
15.	Rwanda	736
16.	Haiti	697
17.	Trinidad & Tobago	655
18.	Philippines	640
19.	UK	629
20.	Jamaica	622

Population Density

Inhabitants per square mile

- Over 500
- 250 – 500
- 125 – 250
- 65 – 125
- 15 – 65
- 8 – 16
- 3 – 8
- Under 3

Urban population

- ■ Over 10,000,000
- ● 5,000,000 – 10,000,000
- • 1,000,000 – 5,000,000

Places marked are conurbations, not city limits; San Francisco itself, for example, has an official population of less than a million.

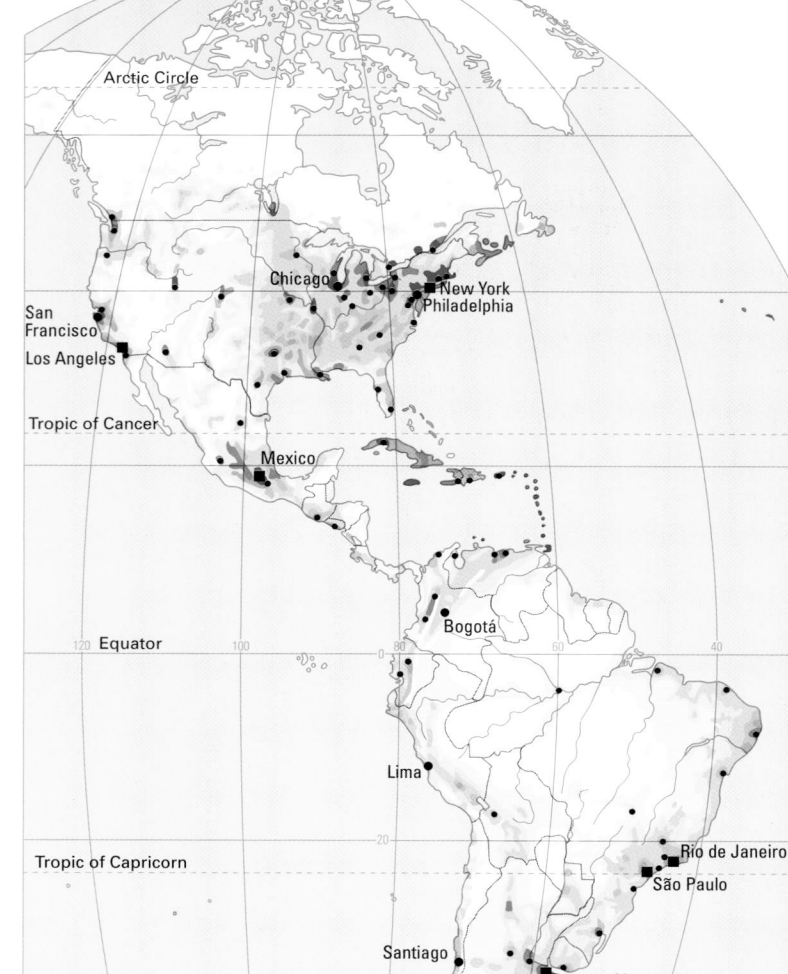

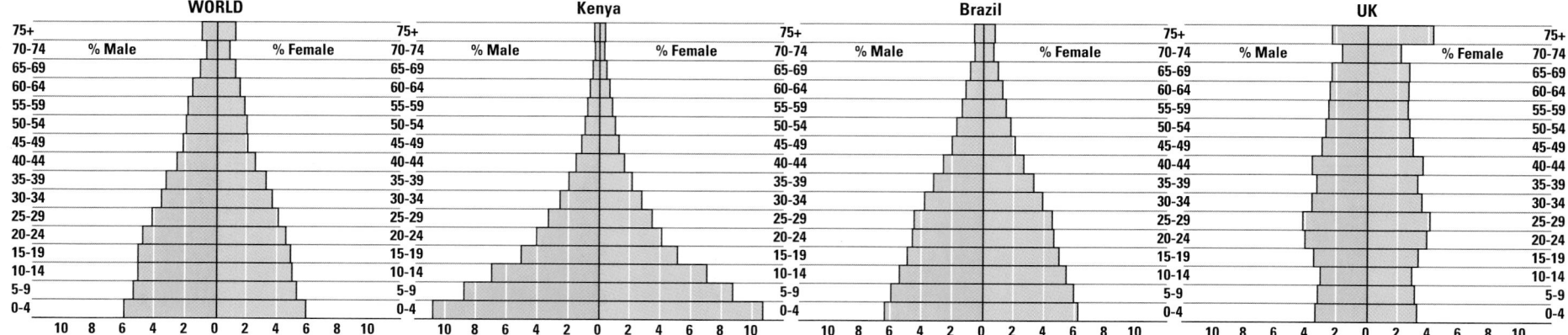

WORLD · Kenya · Brazil · UK

Rates of Growth

The world population doubled between 1950 and 1990. Small rates of population growth led to dramatic increases over two or three generations. The table below translates annual percentage growth into the number of years required to double a population.

% change	Doubling time
0.5	139.0
1.0	69.7
1.5	46.6
2.0	35.0
2.5	28.1
3.0	23.4
3.5	20.1
4.0	17.7

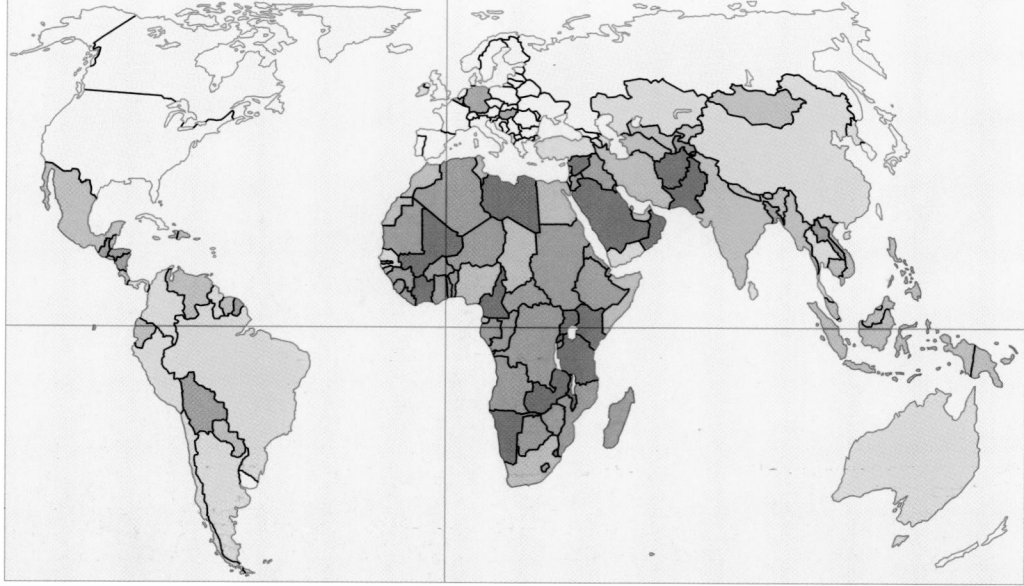

Population Change 1990–2000

The predicted population change for the years 1990–2000

- Over 40% population gain
- 30 – 40% population gain
- 20 – 30% population gain
- 10 – 20% population gain
- 0 – 10% population gain
- No change or population loss

Top 5 countries		Bottom 5 countries	
Kuwait	+75.9%	Belgium	–0.1%
Namibia	+62.5%	Hungary	–0.2%
Afghanistan	+60.1%	Grenada	–2.4%
Mali	+55.5%	Germany	–3.2%
Tanzania	+54.6%	Tonga	–3.2%

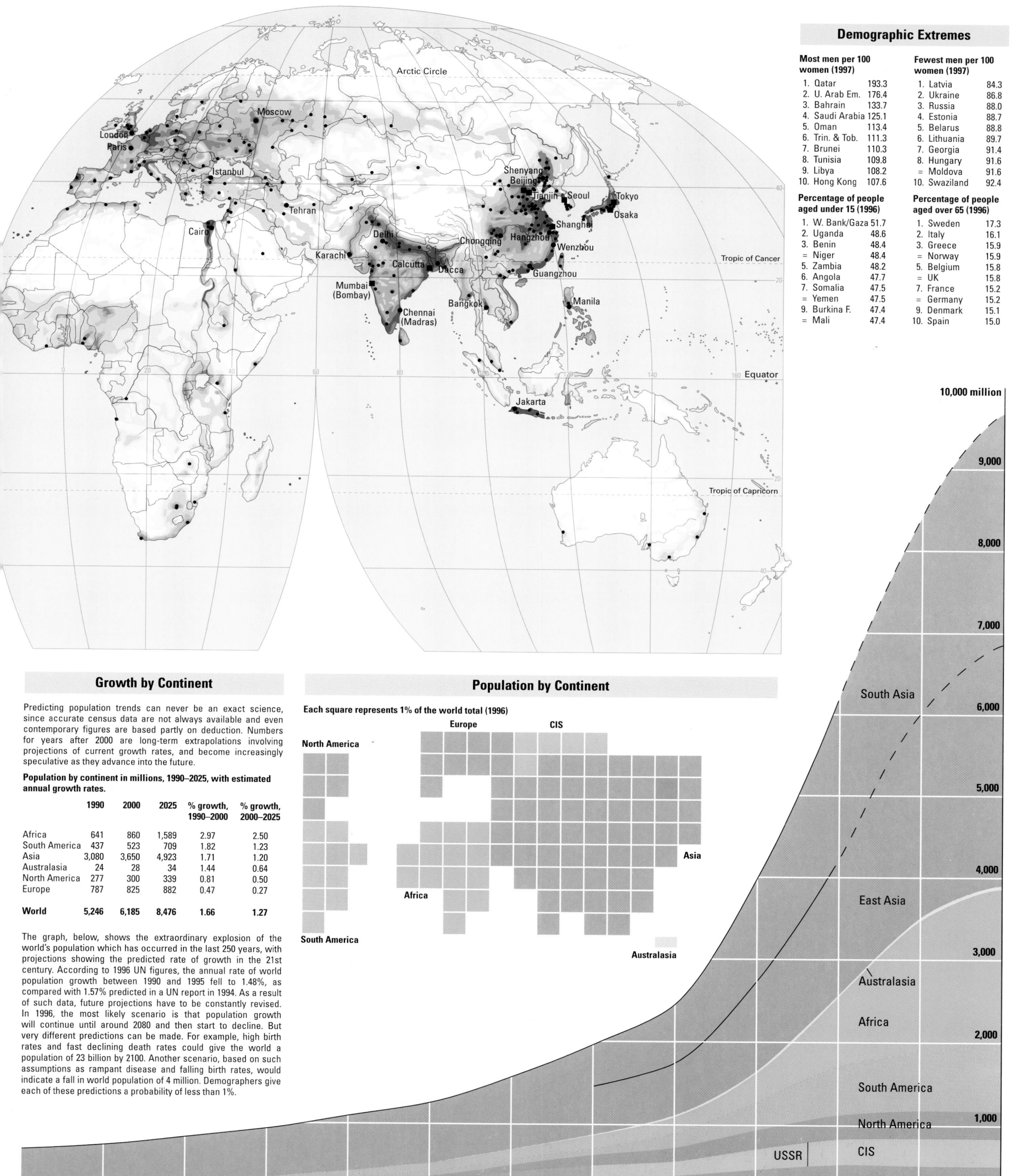

Demographic Extremes

Most men per 100 women (1997)		Fewest men per 100 women (1997)	
1. Qatar	193.3	1. Latvia	84.3
2. U. Arab Em.	176.4	2. Ukraine	86.8
3. Bahrain	133.7	3. Russia	88.0
4. Saudi Arabia	125.1	4. Estonia	88.7
5. Oman	113.4	5. Belarus	88.8
6. Trin. & Tob.	111.3	6. Lithuania	89.7
7. Brunei	110.3	7. Georgia	91.4
8. Tunisia	109.8	8. Hungary	91.6
9. Libya	108.2	= Moldova	91.6
10. Hong Kong	107.6	10. Swaziland	92.4

Percentage of people aged under 15 (1996)		Percentage of people aged over 65 (1996)	
1. W. Bank/Gaza	51.7	1. Sweden	17.3
2. Uganda	48.6	2. Italy	16.1
3. Benin	48.4	3. Greece	15.9
= Niger	48.4	= Norway	15.9
5. Zambia	48.2	5. Belgium	15.8
6. Angola	47.7	= UK	15.8
7. Somalia	47.5	7. France	15.2
= Yemen	47.5	= Germany	15.2
9. Burkina F.	47.4	9. Denmark	15.1
= Mali	47.4	10. Spain	15.0

Growth by Continent

Predicting population trends can never be an exact science, since accurate census data are not always available and even contemporary figures are based partly on deduction. Numbers for years after 2000 are long-term extrapolations involving projections of current growth rates, and become increasingly speculative as they advance into the future.

Population by continent in millions, 1990–2025, with estimated annual growth rates.

	1990	2000	2025	% growth, 1990–2000	% growth, 2000–2025
Africa	641	860	1,589	2.97	2.50
South America	437	523	709	1.82	1.23
Asia	3,080	3,650	4,923	1.71	1.20
Australasia	24	28	34	1.44	0.64
North America	277	300	339	0.81	0.50
Europe	787	825	882	0.47	0.27
World	**5,246**	**6,185**	**8,476**	**1.66**	**1.27**

The graph, below, shows the extraordinary explosion of the world's population which has occurred in the last 250 years, with projections showing the predicted rate of growth in the 21st century. According to 1996 UN figures, the annual rate of world population growth between 1990 and 1995 fell to 1.48%, as compared with 1.57% predicted in a UN report in 1994. As a result of such data, future projections have to be constantly revised. In 1996, the most likely scenario is that population growth will continue until around 2080 and then start to decline. But very different predictions can be made. For example, high birth rates and fast declining death rates could give the world a population of 23 billion by 2100. Another scenario, based on such assumptions as rampant disease and falling birth rates, would indicate a fall in world population of 4 million. Demographers give each of these predictions a probability of less than 1%.

Population by Continent

Each square represents 1% of the world total (1996)

Cities

Following the development of agriculture more than 10,000 years ago, people began to live in farming villages. Around 5,500 years ago, the world's first cities appeared in the lower Tigris and Euphrates valleys in Mesopotamia. Cities were founded in Ancient Egypt around 5,000 years ago and in China around 3,600 years ago. By contrast with the villages, most people in the early cities were not engaged in farming. Instead, they worked in craft industries, in government services, in religion and in trade. The cities became centers of early civilizations and, through trade, their influence spread far and wide. However, they were dependent on the surrounding farming communities for their food and other materials.

In 1750, prior to the start of the Industrial Revolution, barely 3% of the world's population lived in urban areas. By 1850, London and Paris had more than a million people, and, by 1900, 14% of the world's population lived in cities. By 1950, the world had 83 cities with more than a million people, and

by 1996, there were 280. By 2015, experts predict that there will be more than 500. New York City was the only city with a population in excess of 10 million in 1950; by 2015 the experts predict 27 such cities worldwide, the majority located in the developing world.

By the end of the 20th century, more than half of the world's population was living in urban areas. Despite the rapid growth of cities in developing countries, urbanization is highest in industrialized countries. For example, 78% of the people in the United States live in urban areas, with the European Union not far behind with 77%. But in countries with low-income economies, which contained nearly 60% of the world's total population in 1996, only 28% lived in urban areas.

The rapid rate of urbanization has created problems, especially in cities which have not been able to provide enough jobs and services for the expanding population. Most new city dwellers are people from rural areas and because many of them are young there is a consequent acceleration in the rate of city

population growth. In developed countries, with highly mechanized agriculture, it is population pressure that drives many people into urban areas. In developing countries, the grinding poverty of rural life and the lack of services leads to migration to urban areas.

A typical city in a developing country contains millions of people living, often illegally, in shanty towns (or "informal settlements" in politically correct parlance), while thousands live on the streets. Yet many of these shanty towns are healthier than the industrial cities of 19th-century Europe and North America. Indeed, surveys have shown that the migrants to the cities in developing countries are less likely to face poverty than they are in rural areas, while benefiting from greater access to healthcare services and education.

Modern cities face many problems, including pollution, crime and unemployment. Yet, given competent central and local government, they are capable of generating the wealth they need to solve them, as well as making a major contribution to the economy.

The Urbanization of the Earth

City-building, 1850–2000; each white spot represents a city of at least 1 million inhabitants.

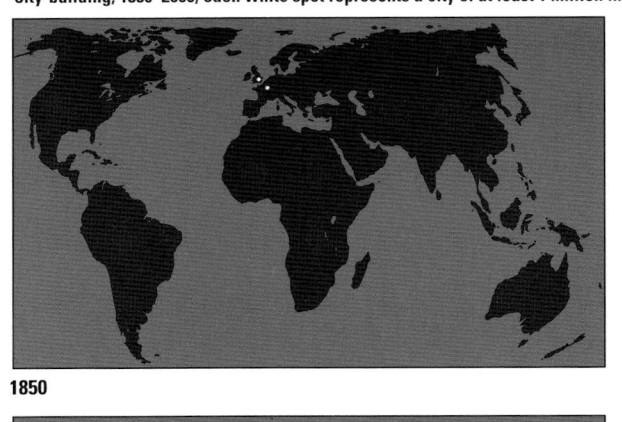

1850

1900

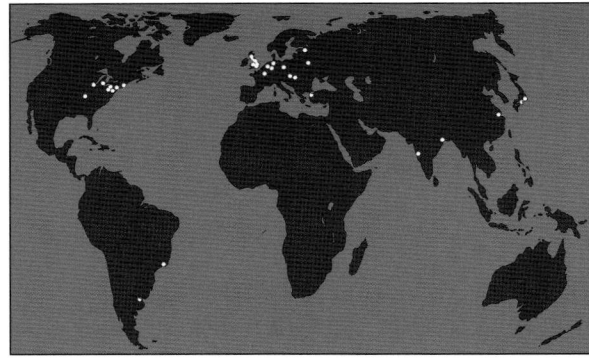

1925

1950

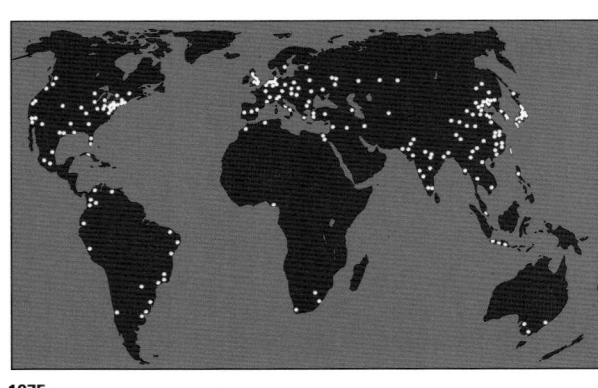

1975

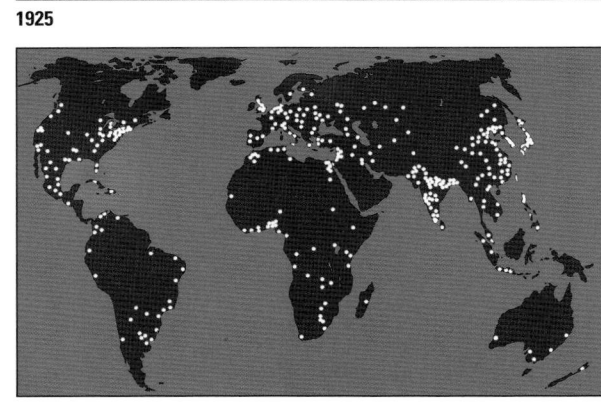

2000

Urban Population

Percentage of total population living in towns and cities (1997)

Most urbanized

Singapore	100%	Over 75%
Belgium	97%	50 – 75%
Israel	91%	25 – 50%
Uruguay	91%	10 – 25%
Netherlands	89%	Under 10%

[UK 89%]

Least urbanized

Rwanda	6%
Bhutan	8%
Burundi	8%
Nepal	11%
Swaziland	12%

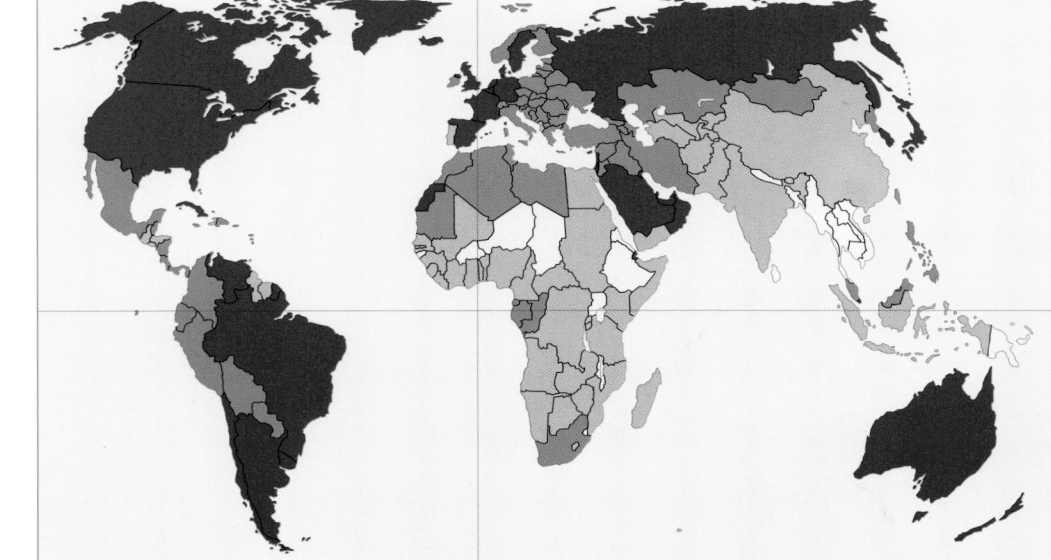

Expanding Cities

The growth of some of the world's largest cities in millions, 1950–2015.
Comparisons of city populations over time are problematic due to changes in the definition of the city limits. These figures attempt to take such changes into consideration. The figure for London is the metropolitan region.

■ 1950   ■ 2015

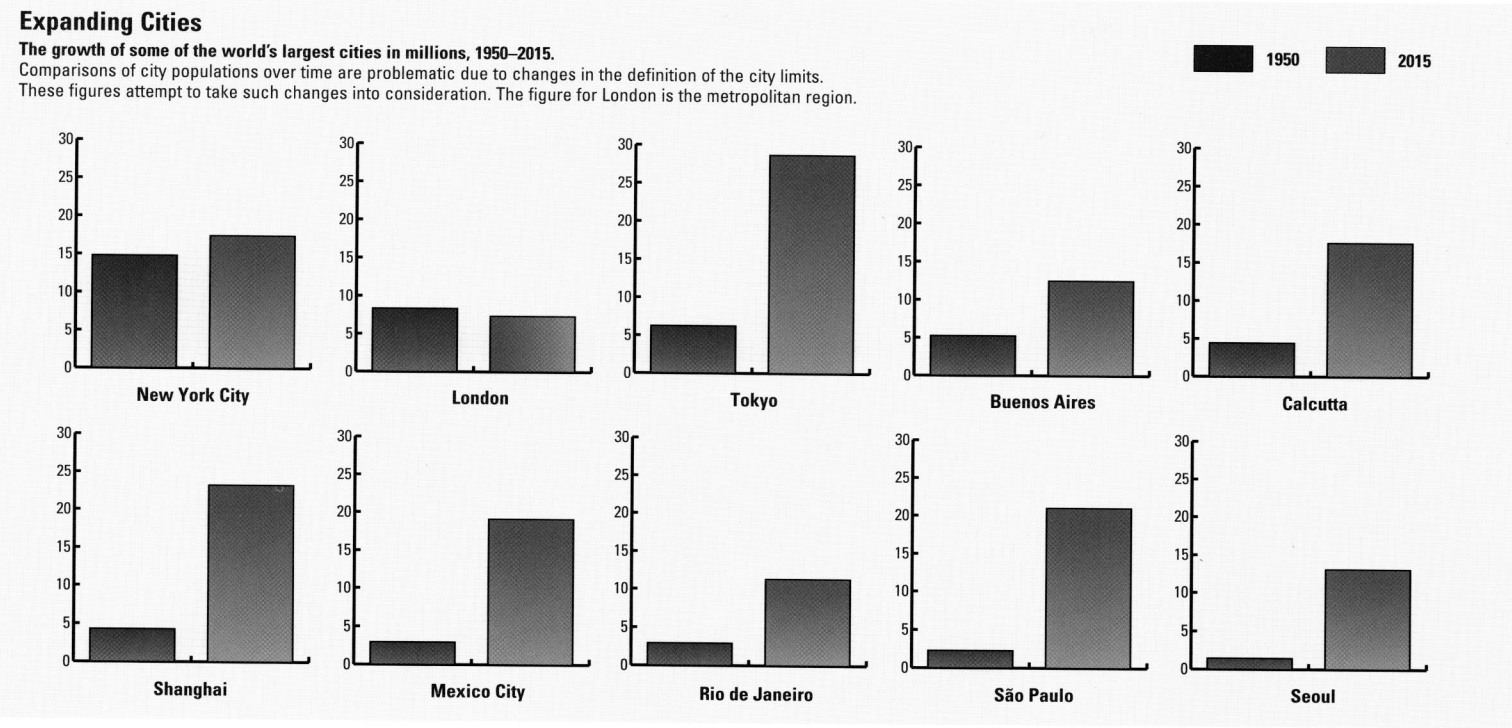

The graphs show the projected growth of megacities between 1950 and 2015. New York City, the world's largest city in 1950, reached a peak in 1970, but it has experienced periods of negative growth. London's population also declined between 1970 and 1985, before resuming a modest rate of increase. In both cases, the divergence from world trends is explained in part by counting methods. Each lies at the center of a great agglomeration, and definitions of the "city limits" may vary over time. Also, in developing countries, many areas around the megacities which are counted as urban, are rural in character. The rates of city population growth in developing countries have also often been over-estimated. For example, it was once predicted that Calcutta would have a population of 40 million by the late 1990s. The reason why many estimates have proven incorrect is partly explained by a new trend, namely that rapid urban growth is now greatest, in some regions, in the smaller cities. For example, the main expansion in West Bengal is no longer in Calcutta, but in a rash of small cities across the state.

Cities in Danger

As the decade of the 1980s advanced, most industrial countries, alarmed by acid rain and urban smog, took significant steps to limit air pollution. Well into the 1990s, however, these controls proved expensive to install and difficult to enforce, and clean air remains a luxury most developed as well as developing cities must live without.

Those taking part in the United Nations' Global Environment Monitoring System (see right) frequently show dangerous levels of pollutants ranging from soot to sulfur dioxide and photo-chemical smog; air in the majority of cities without such sampling equipment is likely to be at least as bad. Traffic, a major source of air pollution worldwide, loses Thailand's work force 44 working days each year.

Urban Air Pollution

The world's most polluted cities: number of days each year when sulfur dioxide levels exceeded the WHO threshold of 150 micrograms per cubic meter (averaged over 4 to 15 years, 1970s – 1980s)

Sulfur dioxide is the main pollutant associated with industrial cities. According to the World Health Organization, more than seven days in a year above 150 µg per cubic meter bring a serious risk of respiratory disease: at least 600 million people live in urban areas where SO_2 concentrations regularly reach damaging levels.

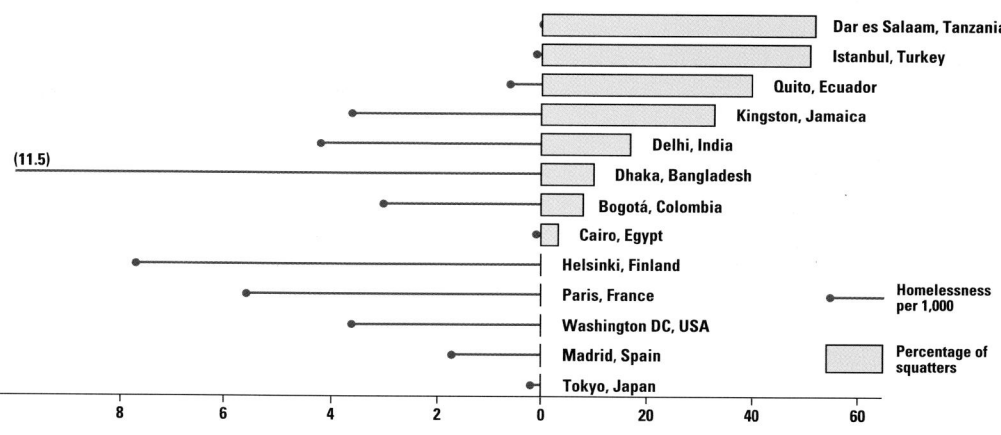

Urban Housing Needs

Proportion of the population living in squatter settlements and the number of homeless per thousand, for selected cities (1993)

Urbanization in most developing countries has been proceeding so rapidly that local governments have been unable to provide the necessary services and housing. In some cities, many people find their homes in squatter settlements, frequently without power, water and sanitation. Yet these communities are often a dynamic part of the city's economy, while their inhabitants sometimes take all kinds of initiatives, including the setting up of their own local government and self-help associations. Some of the world's richest cities also have a homeless underclass, although calculating the numbers of people involved is problematic. Yet it is the case that homelessness and unemployment are currently affecting an increasing number of people in the developed world.

Largest Cities

Early in the 21st century for the first time in history, the majority of the world's population will live in cities. Below is a list of all the cities with more than 10 million inhabitants, based on estimates for the year 2015.*

1.	Tokyo–Yokohama	28.7
2.	Bombay	27.4
3.	Lagos	24.1
4.	Shanghai	23.2
5.	Jakarta	21.5
6.	São Paulo	21.0
7.	Karachi	20.6
8.	Beijing	19.6
9.	Dhaka	19.2
10.	Mexico City	19.1
11.	Calcutta	17.6
12.	Delhi	17.5
13.	New York City	17.4
14.	Tianjin	17.1
15.	Manila	14.9
16.	Cairo	14.7
17.	Los Angeles	14.5
18.	Seoul	13.1
19.	Buenos Aires	12.5
20.	Istanbul	12.1
21.	Rio de Janeiro	11.3
22.	Lahore	10.9
23.	Hyderabad	10.6
24.	Bangkok	10.4
25.	Osaka	10.2
26.	Lima	10.1
27.	Tehran	10.0

City populations are based on urban agglomerations rather than legal city limits. In some cases where two adjacent cities have merged into one concentration, such as Tokyo–Yokohama, they have been regarded as a single unit.

* For a list of current city estimates, see page XI.

Urban Advantages

Despite overcrowding and poor housing, living standards in the developing world's cities are almost invariably better than in the surrounding countryside. Resources – financial, material and administrative – are concentrated in the towns, which are usually also the centres of political activity and pressure. Governments – frequently unstable, and rarely established on a solid democratic base – are usually more responsive to urban discontent than rural misery.

In many countries, especially in Africa, food prices are kept artificially low, appeasing underemployed urban masses at the expense of agricultural development. The imbalance encourages further cityward migration, helping to account for the astonishing rate of post-1950 urbanization and putting great strain on the ability of many nations to provide even modest improvements for their people.

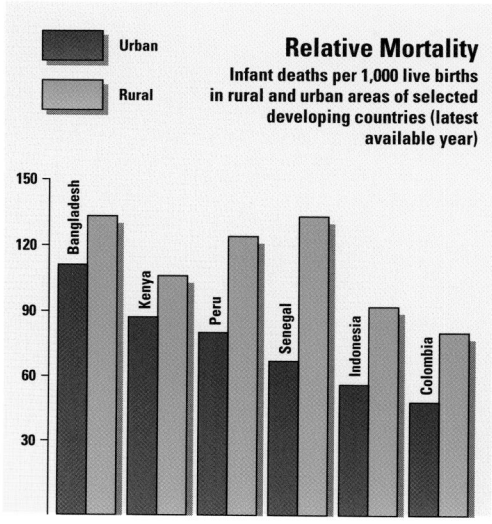

■ Urban
■ Rural

Relative Mortality
Infant deaths per 1,000 live births in rural and urban areas of selected developing countries (latest available year)

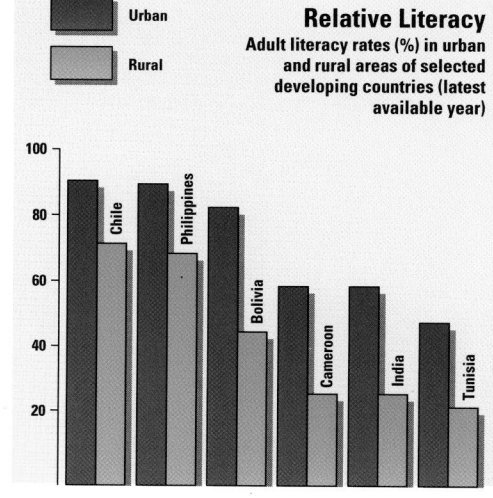

■ Urban
■ Rural

Relative Literacy
Adult literacy rates (%) in urban and rural areas of selected developing countries (latest available year)

The Human Family

For more information:
24 Population density
30 The world's refugees
    War since 1945
31 United Nations
    International
    organizations

Racial, language and religious differences have led to appalling acts of inhumanity throughout history. Yet strictly speaking, all human beings belong to one species, *Homo sapiens*, which has no subspecies. The differences between the three racial types which most people identify – namely Caucasoid, Mongoloid and Negroid – reflect not so much evolutionary differences as long periods of separation.

Migration has recently mingled the various groups to an unprecedented extent, and most nations now have some degree of racial mixing. For example, the United States has often been called a melting pot, because of the large numbers of people from various geographical locations which make up the population. The country has

no official language but, until recently, English was spoken by the vast majority of the people. But in recent years, some of the immigrants from Mexico, Cuba and other parts of Latin America have not learned English and speak only Spanish. This development disturbs those Americans who believe that the use of English binds the nation together, and several states have passed laws stating that English is their only official language.

Language is fundamental to human culture and any particular language is almost the definition of that particular culture. Because definitions of languages vary, estimates of the total number range from 3,000 to 6,000, although most are spoken by only a few people. The world's languages

are grouped into families, the largest of which are the Indo-European and Sino-Tibetan. Chinese, a Sino-Tibetan language, is spoken by more people as a first language than any other. English, an Indo-European tongue, ranks second, but it is the leading international language, because so many people speak it as their second tongue.

Like language, religion encourages cohesion in single human groups and it satisfies a deep human need by assigning people a place in a divinely ordered world. Religion is a way in which a culture can express its individuality. For example, the rise of Islamic fundamentalism in the late 20th century was partly an expression of resentment that secular Western values are being imposed on Muslims.

World Migration

The greatest voluntary migration was the colonization of North America by 30–35 million European settlers during the 19th century. The greatest forced migration involved 9–11 million Africans taken as slaves to America between 1550 and 1860. The migrations shown on the map below are mostly international, as population movements within borders are not usually recorded. Many of the statistics are necessarily estimates as so many refugees and migrant workers enter countries illegally and unrecorded. Emigrants may have a variety of motives for leaving, thus making it difficult to distinguish between voluntary and involuntary migrations.

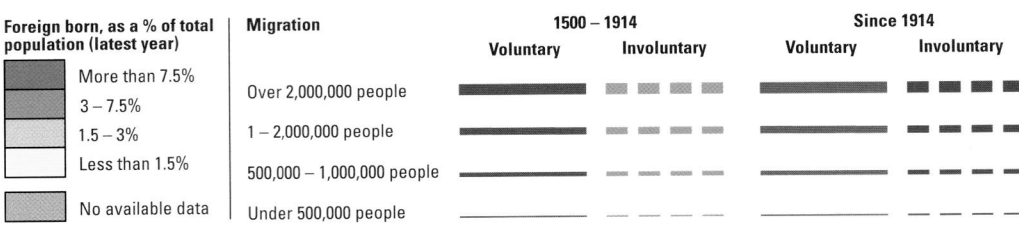

Foreign born, as a % of total population (latest year)
- More than 7.5%
- 3 – 7.5%
- 1.5 – 3%
- Less than 1.5%
- No available data

Migration
- Over 2,000,000 people
- 1 – 2,000,000 people
- 500,000 – 1,000,000 people
- Under 500,000 people

	1500 – 1914		Since 1914	
Migration	Voluntary	Involuntary	Voluntary	Involuntary

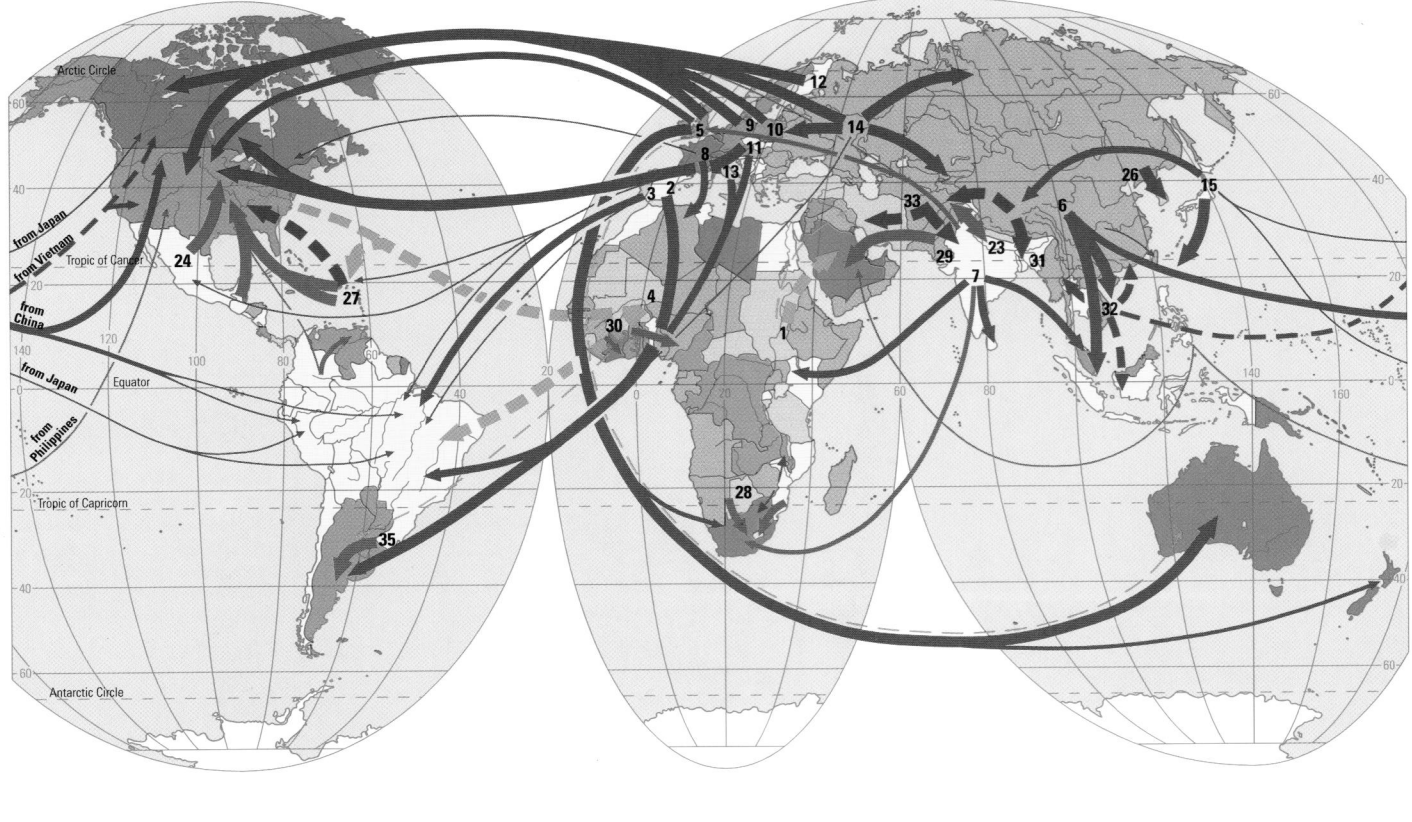

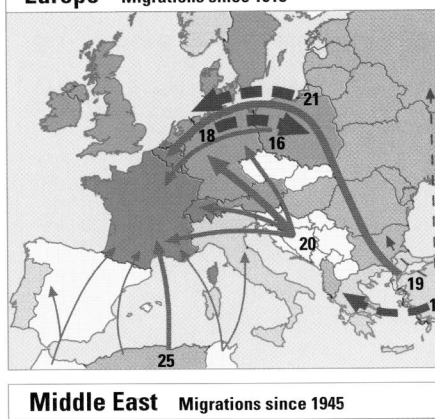

Europe Migrations since 1918

Middle East Migrations since 1945

Building the USA

US Immigration 1820–1990

"Give me your tired, your poor / Your huddled masses yearning to breathe free...."

So starts Emma Lazarus's poem "The New Colossus," inscribed on the Statue of Liberty. For decades the USA was the magnet that attracted millions of immigrants, notably from Central and Eastern Europe, the flow peaking in the early years of the 20th century. By the mid-1990s the proportion of immigrants had increased again to pre-World War II rates. In 1993/4, net immigration accounted for 30% of US population growth. Of the 904,000 immigrants, 40% were from Asia and 31% were from Central America and the Caribbean.

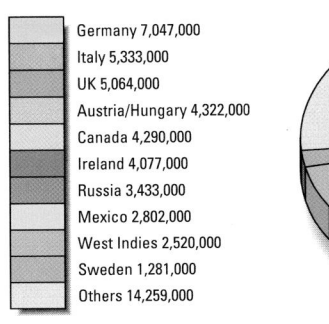

Germany 7,047,000
Italy 5,333,000
UK 5,064,000
Austria/Hungary 4,322,000
Canada 4,290,000
Ireland 4,077,000
Russia 3,433,000
Mexico 2,802,000
West Indies 2,520,000
Sweden 1,281,000
Others 14,259,000

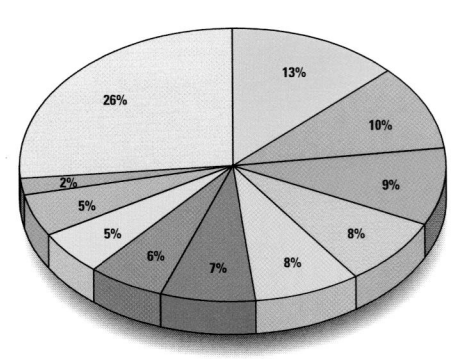

Major world migrations since 1500 (over 1,000,000 people)

1. North and East African slaves to Arabia (4.3m) 1500–1900
2. Spanish to South and Central America (2.3m) 1530–1914
3. Portuguese to Brazil (1.4m) 1530–1914
4. West African slaves to South America (4.6m) 1550–1860
      to Caribbean (4m) 1580–1860
      to North/Central America (1m) 1650–1820
5. British and Irish to North America (13.5m) 1620–1914
      to Australasia and
      South Africa (3m) 1790–1914
6. Chinese to South-east Asia (22m) 1820–1914
      to North America (1m) 1880–1914
7. Indian migrant workers (3m) 1850–1914
8. French to North Africa (1.5m) 1850–1914
9. Germans to North America (5m) 1850–1914
10. Poles to North America (3.6m) 1850–1914
11. Austro-Hungarians to North America (3.2m) 1850–1914
      to Western Europe (3.4m) 1850–1914
      to South America (1.8m) 1850–1914
12. Scandinavians to North America (2.7m) 1850–1914
13. Italians to North America (5m) 1860–1914
      to South America (3.7m) 1860–1914
14. Russians to North America (2.2m) 1880–1914
      to Western Europe (2.2m) 1880–1914
      to Siberia (6m) 1880–1914
      to Central Asia (4m) 1880–1914
15. Japanese to Eastern Asia, Southeast Asia
      and America (8m) 1900–1914
16. Poles to Western Europe (1m) 1920–1940
17. Greeks and Armenians from Turkey (1.6m) 1922–1923
18. European Jews to extermination camps (5m) 1940–1944
19. Turks to Western Europe (1.9m) 1940–
20. Yugoslavs to Western Europe (2m) 1940–
21. Germans to Western Europe (9.8m) 1945–1947
22. Palestinian refugees (2m) 1947–
23. Indian and Pakistani refugees (15m) 1947
24. Mexicans to North America (9m) 1950–
25. North Africans to Western Europe (1.1m) 1950–
26. Korean refugees (5m) 1950–1954
27. Latin Americans and West Indians to
      North America (4.7m) 1960–
28. Migrant workers to South Africa (1.5m) 1960–
29. Indians and Pakistanis to The Gulf (2.4m) 1970–
30. Migrant workers to Nigeria and Ivory Coast (3m) 1970–
31. Bangladeshi and Pakistani refugees (2m) 1972
32. Vietnamese and Cambodian refugees (1.5m) 1975–
33. Afghan refugees (6.1m) 1979–
34. Egyptians to The Gulf and Libya (2.9m) 1980–
35. Migrant workers to Argentina (2m) 1980–
36. Mozambique refugees (1.7m) 1985–
37. Yugoslav/Balkan refugees (1.7m) 1992–
38. Rwanda/Burundi refugees (2.6m) 1994–

Predominant Languages

INDO-EUROPEAN FAMILY	**AFRO-ASIATIC FAMILY**	**ALTAIC FAMILY**	**AUSTRO-ASIATIC FAMILY**	
1 Balto-Slavic group (incl. Russian, Ukrainian)	11 Semitic group (incl. Arabic)	18 Turkic group	25 Mon-Khmer group	
2 Germanic group (incl. English, German)	12 Kushitic group	19 Mongolian group	26 Munda group	
3 Celtic group	13 Berber group	20 Tungus-Manchu group	27 Vietnamese	
4 Greek		21 Japanese and Korean		
5 Albanian	14 **KHOISAN FAMILY**		28 **DRAVIDIAN FAMILY** (incl. Telugu, Tamil)	
6 Iranian group		**SINO-TIBETAN FAMILY**		
7 Armenian	15 **NIGER-CONGO FAMILY**	22 Sinitic (Chinese) languages	29 **AUSTRONESIAN FAMILY** (incl. Malay-Indonesian)	
8 Romance group (incl. Spanish, Portuguese, French, Italian)	16 **NILO-SAHARAN FAMILY**	23 Tibetic-Burmic languages		
9 Indo-Aryan group (incl. Hindi, Bengali, Urdu, Punjabi, Marathi)	17 **URALIC FAMILY**	24 **TAI FAMILY**	30 **OTHER LANGUAGES**	
10 **CAUCASIAN FAMILY**				

Official Languages

Language	Total population	World %
English	1,400m	27.0%
Chinese	1,070m	19.1%
Hindi	700m	13.5%
Spanish	280m	5.4%
Russian	270m	5.2%
French	220m	4.2%
Arabic	170m	3.3%
Portuguese	160m	3.0%
Malay	160m	3.0%
Bengali	150m	2.9%
Japanese	120m	2.3%

Languages form a kind of tree of development, splitting from a few ancient proto-tongues into branches that have grown apart and further divided with the passage of time. English and Hindi, for example, both belong to the great Indo-European family, although the relationship is only apparent after much analysis and comparison with non-Indo-European languages such as Chinese or Arabic; Hindi is part of the Indo-Aryan subgroup, whereas English is a member of Indo-European's Germanic branch; French, another Indo-European tongue, traces its descent through the Latin, or Romance, branch. A few languages – Basque is one example – have no apparent links with any other, living or dead. Most modern languages, of course, have acquired enormous quantities of vocabulary from each other.

Distribution of Living Languages

The figures refer to the number of languages currently in use in the regions shown.

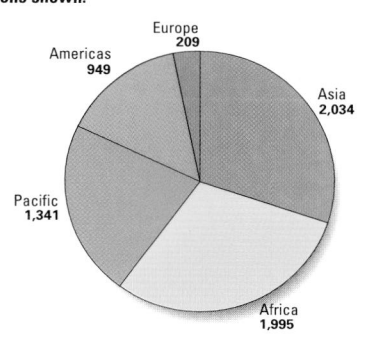

Europe 209
Americas 949
Asia 2,034
Pacific 1,341
Africa 1,995

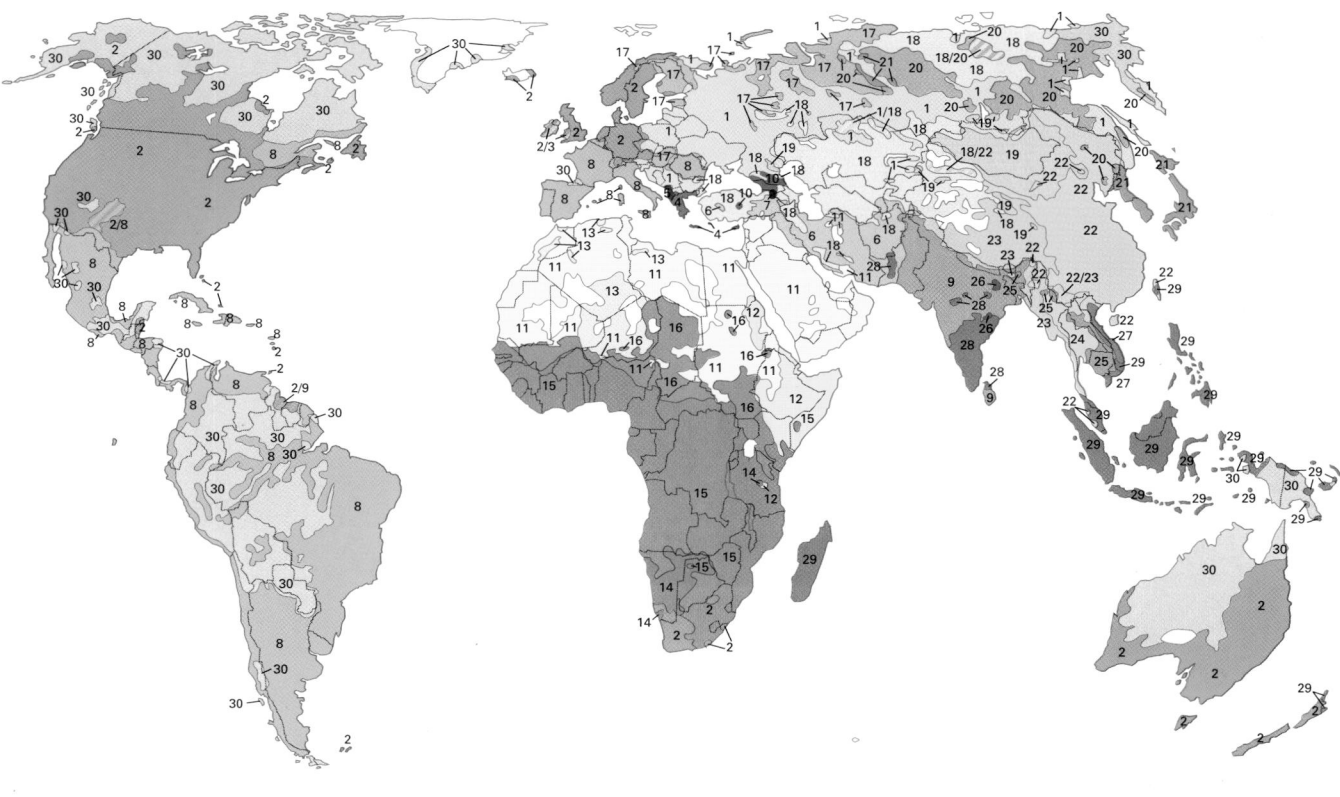

Predominant Religions

- ▲ Roman Catholicism
- Orthodox and other Eastern Churches
- • Protestantism
- Sunni Islam
- Shia Islam
- Buddhism
- Hinduism
- Confucianism
- ✶ Judaism
- Shintoism
- Tribal Religions

Religions are not as easily mapped as the physical contours of the land. Divisions are often blurred and frequently overlapping: most nations include people of many different faiths – or no faith at all. Some religions, like Islam and Christianity, have proselytes worldwide; others, like Hinduism and Confucianism, are restricted to a particular area, though modern migrations have taken some Indians and Chinese very far from their cultural origins. It is also difficult to show the degree to which religion controls daily life: Christian Western Europe, for example, is now far less dominated by its religion than are the Islamic nations of the Middle East. Similarly, figures for the major faiths' adherents make no distinction between nominal believers enrolled at birth and those for whom religion is a vital part of existence.

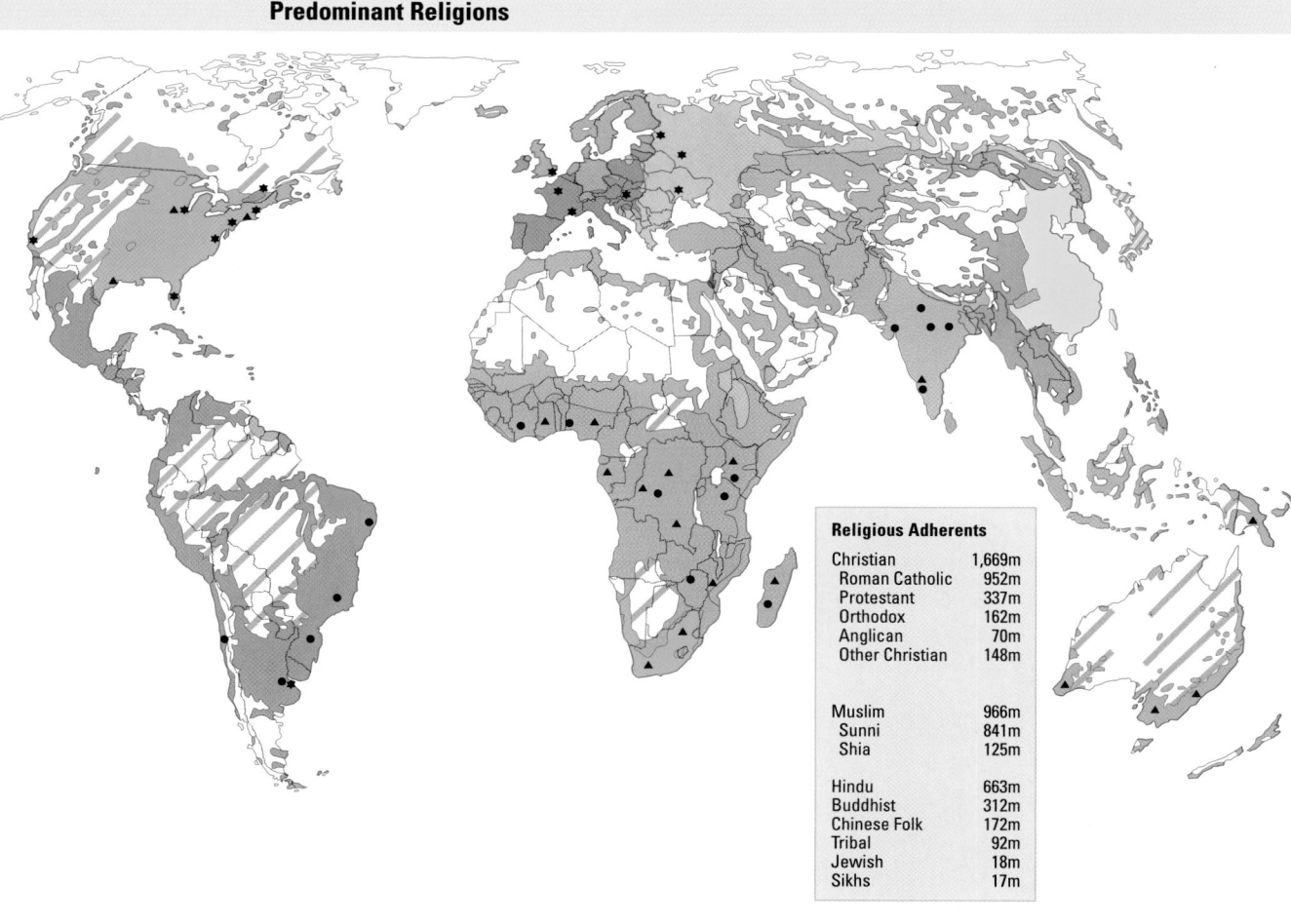

Religious Adherents

Christian	1,669m
Roman Catholic	952m
Protestant	337m
Orthodox	162m
Anglican	70m
Other Christian	148m
Muslim	966m
Sunni	841m
Shia	125m
Hindu	663m
Buddhist	312m
Chinese Folk	172m
Tribal	92m
Jewish	18m
Sikhs	17m

Conflict and Cooperation

For more information:
28 Migration
29 Religion

The 20th century witnessed two world wars, followed by a Cold War which several times threatened to erupt into a third world war, fought with nuclear weapons. The Cold War was marked by a great number of conflicts. Some were colonial wars, as the empires of the first half of the century fell apart, some were border wars, and some were civil wars. All the wars have caused great suffering among civilians, many of whom were forced to join the ranks of the world's refugees.

In the late 1980s, many people hoped that the end of the Cold War, following the collapse of Communist regimes in the former Soviet Union and Eastern Europe, would herald a new era of international stability. Instead, old ethnic and religious antagonisms surfaced in many areas, leading to civil war in such places as Chechenia, in Russia, and the former Yugoslavia. Nationalist rivalries, suppressed under Communist rule, replaced ideological factors as the major cause of conflict.

War is a very human activity, with no real equivalent in any other species. Yet humans also function well when they cooperate. Evolution has made this so. Hunter-gatherers in cooperative bands were far more effective than animals that prowled. Agriculture, urbanization and industrialization all depend on the ability of humans to cooperate.

The creation of the United Nations in 1945 held out hope that the world's nations, tired of war, would have the means to control humanity's aggressive instincts. Although the UN lacks the power to halt conflicts, it has often helped to achieve negotiation. Economic pressures have led to another kind of cooperation, the creation of common markets and economic unions, such as ASEAN in Southeast Asia, the European Union and NAFTA in North America.

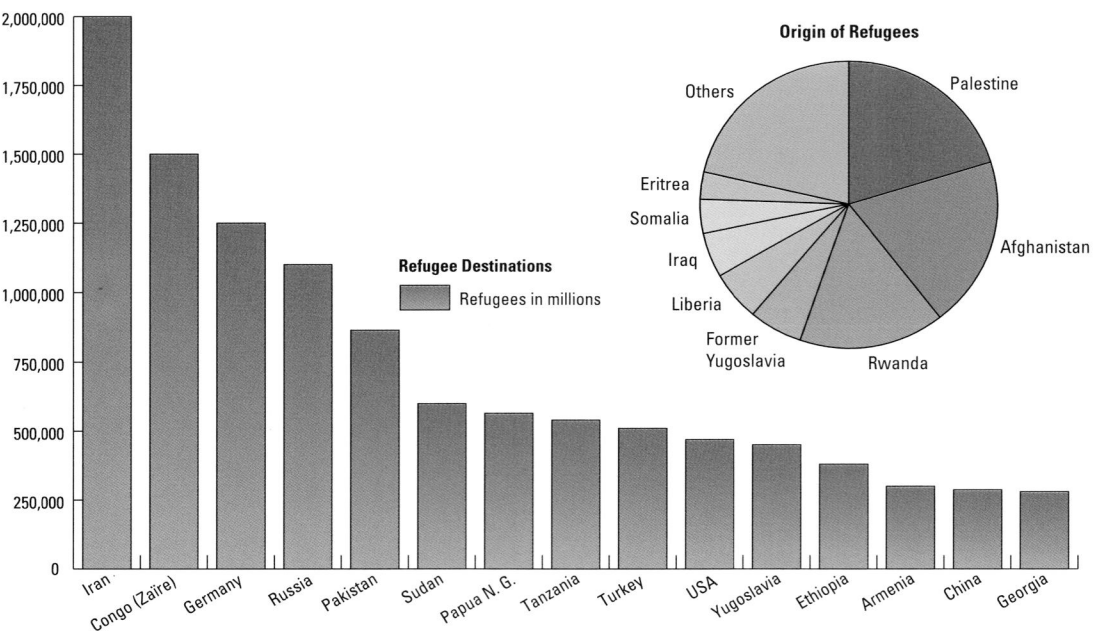

The World's Refugees

Refugees by host nation (bar chart, left) and by nation of origin (pie chart, left) (1995). The source is the United Nations High Commission for Refugees (UNHCR). The 3.2 million Palestinian refugees living in Jordan, Syria, Lebanon, Gaza and the West Bank fall under the mandate of United Nations Relief and Works Agency (UNRWA) and are not included on the bar chart.

The pie chart shows the origins of the world's refugees, while the bar chart below shows their destinations. According to the United Nations High Commission for Refugees (UNHCR) in 1995 there were 14.5 million refugees. However, the UNHCR definition of a refugee, "a person who has left or remains outside their own country because they have a well-founded fear of persecution, or because their safety is threatened by events seriously disturbing public order," does not include people who are in a refugee-like situation but who have not been formally recognized. In 1995, there were a further 3.5 million of these people worldwide and a further 4.5 million people who were internally displaced.

All but a few who cross international boundaries seek asylum in neighboring countries, which are often the least equipped to deal with them. Lacking any rights or power, they frequently become an unwelcome burden to their hosts. Usually, the best any refugee can hope for is rudimentary food and shelter in temporary camps. Many Palestinians have been forced to live in camps since 1948.

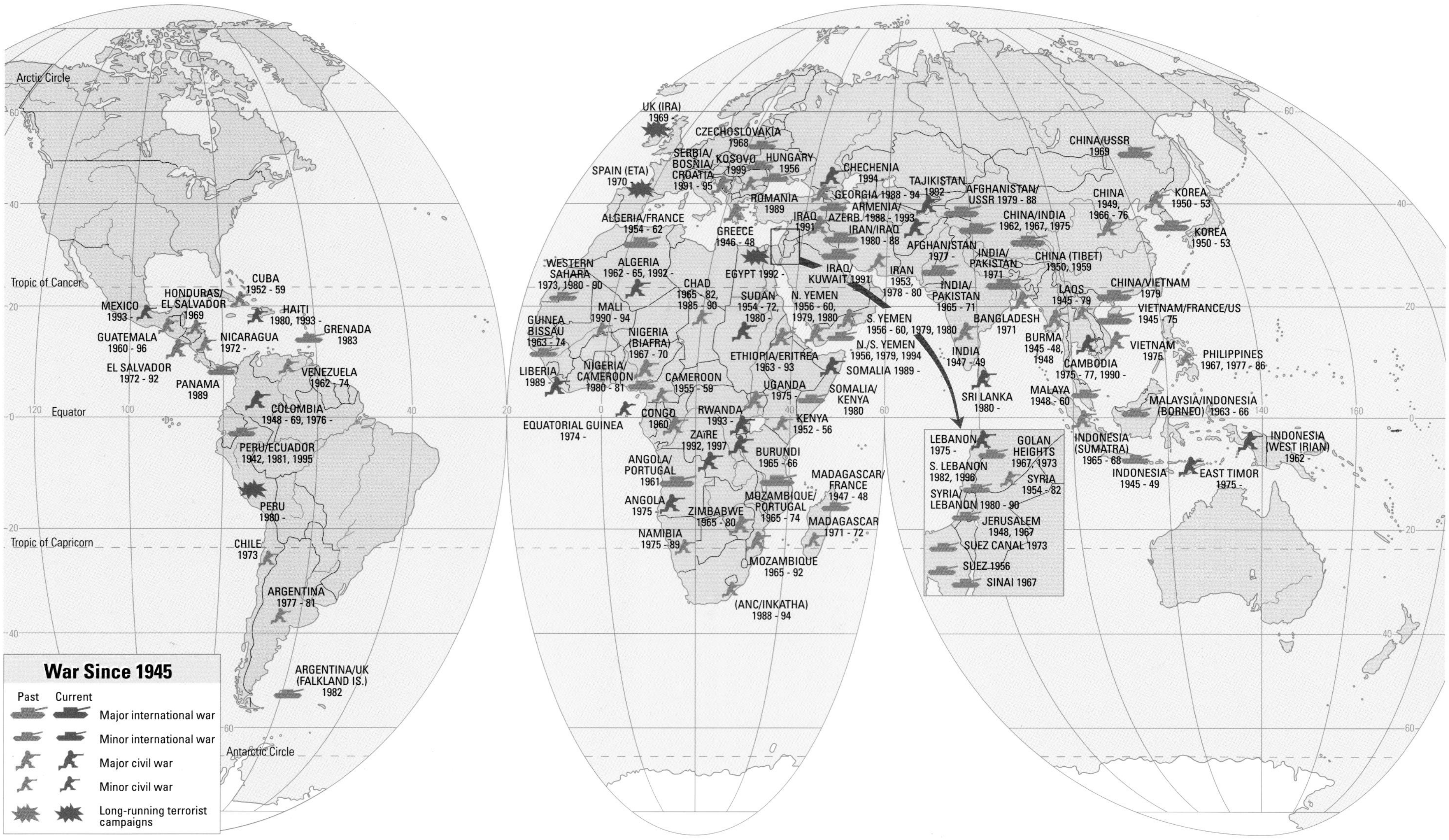

United Nations

The United Nations Organization was born as World War II drew to its conclusion. Six years of strife had strengthened the world's desire for peace, but an effective international organization was needed to help achieve it. That body would replace the League of Nations which, since its inception in 1920, had failed to curb the aggression of at least some of its member nations. At the United Nations Conference on International Organization held in San Francisco, the United Nations Charter was drawn up. Ratified by the Security Council and signed by the 51 original members, it came into effect on October 24, 1945.

The Charter set out the aims of the organization: to maintain peace and security, and develop friendly relations between nations; to achieve international cooperation in solving economic, social, cultural and humanitarian problems; to promote respect for human rights and fundamental freedoms; and to harmonize the activities of nations in order to achieve these common goals.

The United Nations has five principal organs :
The General Assembly
The forum at which member nations discuss moral and political issues affecting world development, peace and security meets annually in September, under a newly-elected President whose tenure lasts one year. Any member can bring business to the agenda, and each member nation has one vote.
The Security Council
A legislative and executive body, the Security Council is the primary instrument for establishing and maintaining international peace by attempting to settle disputes between nations. It has the power to dispatch UN forces, and member nations undertake to provide armed forces, assistance and facilities. The Security Council has ten temporary members elected by the General Assembly for two-year terms, and five permanent members – China, France, Russia, UK and USA.
The Economic and Social Council
By far the largest United Nations executive, the Council operates as a conduit between the General Assembly and the many United Nations agencies it instructs to implement Assembly decisions, and whose work it coordinates. The Council also commissions studies on economic conditions, collects data and makes recommendations to the Assembly.
The Secretariat
This is the staff of the United Nations, and its task is to administer the policies and programs of the UN and its organs, and assist and advise the Head of the Secretariat, the Secretary-General – a full-time, non-political appointment made by the General Assembly.
The Trusteeship Council
This no longer administers any of the original 11 trust territories as they are all now independent.
The International Court of Justice (the World Court)
The World Court is the judicial organ of the United Nations. It deals only with United Nations disputes and all members are subject to its jurisdiction. There are 15 judges, elected for nine-year terms by the General Assembly and the Security Council.

The social and humanitarian operations of the UN include:
United Nations Development Program (UNDP) Plans and funds projects to help developing countries make better use of their resources.
United Nations International Childrens' Fund (UNICEF) Created at the General Assembly's first session in 1945 to help children in the aftermath of World War II, it now provides basic health care and aid worldwide.
Food and Agriculture Organization (FAO) Aims to raise living standards and nutrition levels in rural areas by improving food production and distribution.
United Nations Educational, Scientific and Cultural Organization (UNESCO) Promotes international cooperation through broader and better education.
World Health Organization (WHO) Promotes and provides for better health care, public and environmental health and medical research.

United Nations agencies are involved in many aspects of international trade, safety and security:
International Maritime Organization (IMO) Promotes unity amongst merchant shipping, especially in regard to safety, marine pollution and standardization.
International Labor Organization (ILO) Seeks to improve labor conditions and promote productive employment to raise living standards.
World Meteorological Organization (WMO) Promotes co-operation in weather observation, reporting and forecasting.
World Trade Organization (WTO) On January 1, 1995, the WTO replaced GATT. It advocates a common code of conduct and its aim is the liberalization of world trade.
Disarmament Commission Considers and makes recommendations to the General Assembly on disarmament issues.
International Atomic Energy Agency (IAEA) Fosters development of peaceful uses for nuclear energy and establishes safety standards.

The **World Bank** comprises three United Nations agencies:
International Monetary Fund (IMF) Cultivates international monetary cooperation and expansion of trade.
International Bank for Reconstruction and Development (IBRD) Provides funds and technical assistance to developing countries.
International Finance Corporation (IFC) Encourages the growth of productive private enterprise in less developed countries.

Membership There are seven independent states which are not members of the UN – Kiribati, Nauru, Switzerland, Taiwan, Tonga, Tuvalu and Vatican City. Official languages are Chinese, English, French, Russian, Spanish and Arabic.
Funding The UN budget for 1996–97 was US $2.6 billion. Contributions are assessed by the members' ability to pay, with the maximum 25% of the total, the minimum 0.01%.
Peacekeeping The UN has been involved in 43 peacekeeping operations worldwide since 1948. At the end of 1996 there were 16 areas of UN patrol and 25,649 "blue berets."

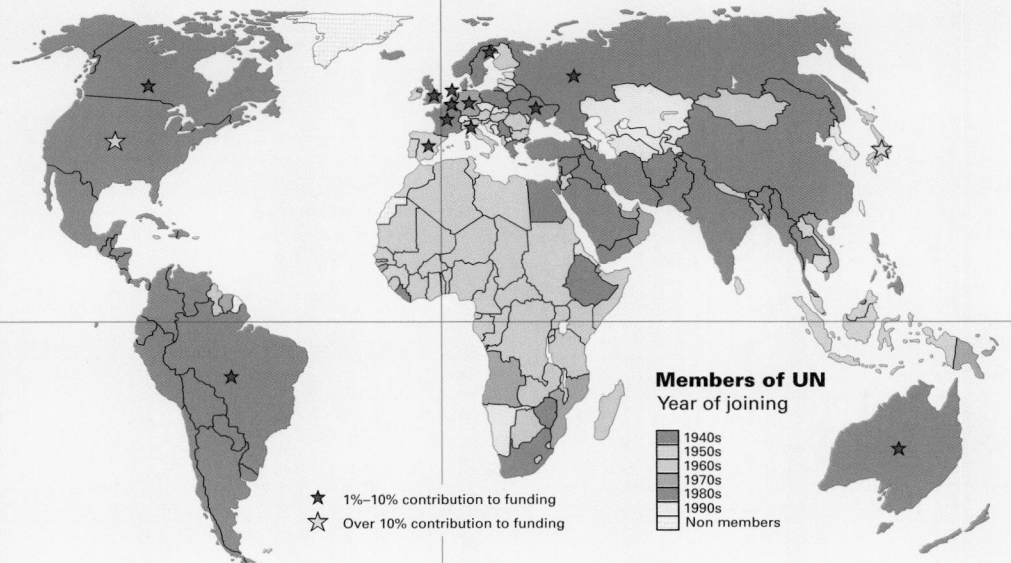

Members of UN
Year of joining
- 1940s
- 1950s
- 1960s
- 1970s
- 1980s
- 1990s
- Non members

★ 1%–10% contribution to funding
☆ Over 10% contribution to funding

Military Spending

Military expenditure as a % of GNP or GDP, ranked selection of countries (1994)

1. Iraq	74.9%	14. Jordan	7.5%
2. North Korea	26.3%	15. Laos	7.4%
3. Angola	23.9%	16. Pakistan	6.0%
4. Oman	18.1%	17. UAE	5.7%
5. Syria	17.9%	18. Seychelles	5.6%
6. Sudan	17.1%	19. Sierra Leone	4.9%
7. Saudi Arabia	14.2%	20. Taiwan	4.8%
8. Yemen	14.1%	21. Liberia	4.8%
9. Russia	12.4%	22. Singapore	4.5%
10. Kuwait	11.1%	23. Sri Lanka	4.5%
11. Mozambique	8.7%	24. USA	4.3%
12. Israel	8.6%	25. Malaysia	4.2%
13. Rwanda	7.6%		

It is worth noting that the total amount of expenditure varies considerably depending on the size of the economy, so that although the percentages show the importance given to military spending within each country, they give no idea as to the total expenditure. In 1997, for example, the USA spent a total of US $271 billion, Russia US $70 billion, and the UK US $36 billion. In 1993, the USA also provided the most military assistance worldwide, providing US $3.4 billion, compared to a total of US $0.9 billion from Western Europe.

The period 1987–94 saw a decline in global military spending which generated what the United Nations Development Program term a "peace dividend" of US $935 billion. Unfortunately, there is no clear link between reduced military spending and enhanced expenditure on human development. Moreover, the poorest regions of the world (notably sub-Saharan Africa) failed to contain their military spending and, in some cases, it increased.

International Organizations

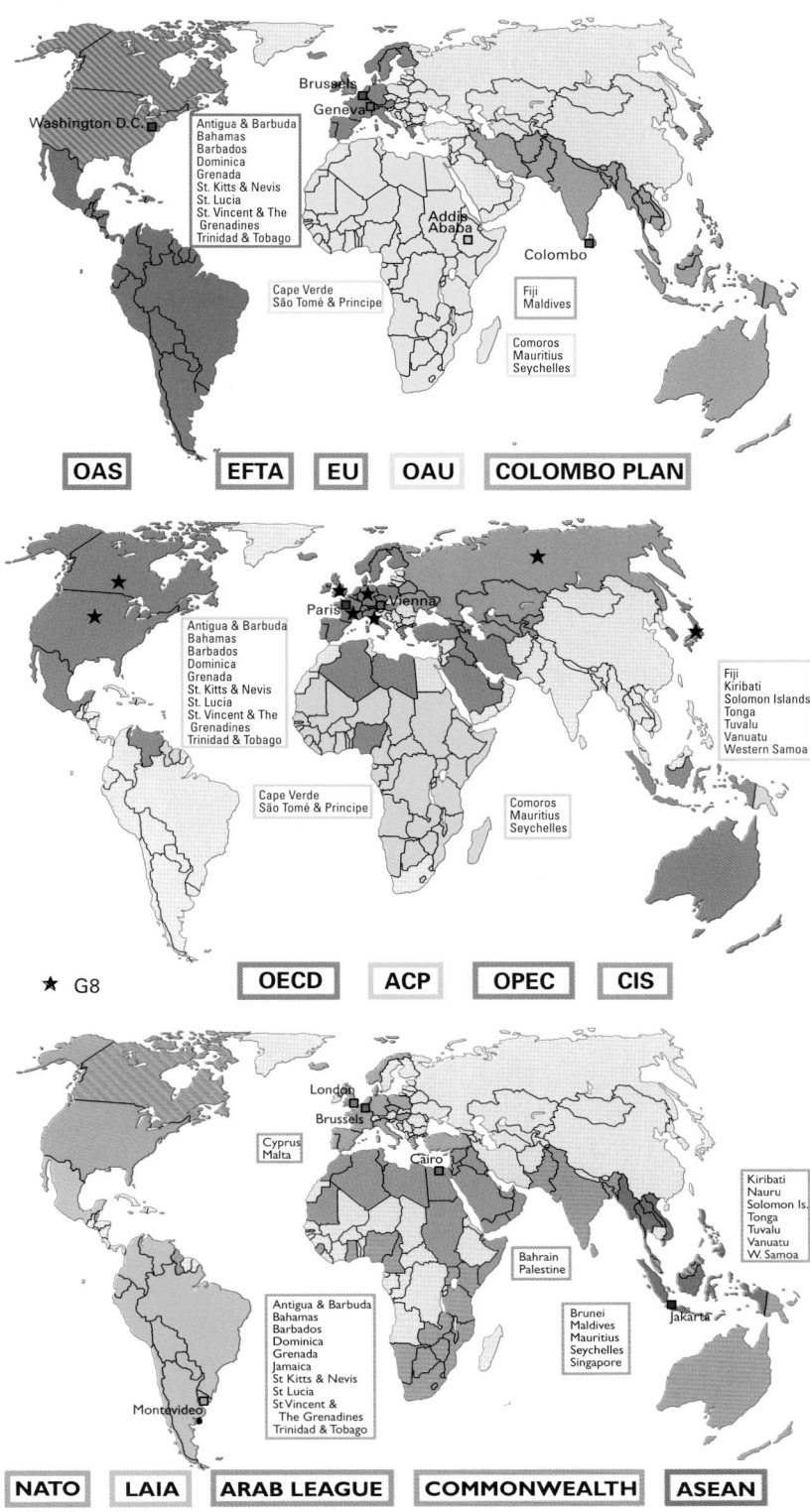

OAS | EFTA | EU | OAU | COLOMBO PLAN

★ G8

OECD | ACP | OPEC | CIS

NATO | LAIA | ARAB LEAGUE | COMMONWEALTH | ASEAN

EU The European Union evolved from the European Community (EC) in 1993. The original body, the European Coal and Steel Community (ECSC), was created in 1951 following the signing of the Treaty of Paris. The 15 members of the EU – Austria, Belgium, Denmark, Finland, France, Germany, Greece, Ireland, Italy, Luxembourg, Netherlands, Portugal, Spain, Sweden and the UK – aim to integrate economies, coordinate social developments and bring about political union. These members, of what is now the world's biggest market, share agricultural and industrial policies and tariffs on trade.
EFTA European Free Trade Association (formed in 1960). Portugal left the original "Seven" in 1989 to join what was then the EC, followed by Austria, Finland and Sweden in 1995. There are now only four members: Iceland, Liechtenstein, Norway, and Switzerland.
ACP African-Caribbean-Pacific (formed in 1963). Members enjoy economic ties with the EU.
NATO North Atlantic Treaty Organization (formed in 1949). It continues despite the winding up of the Warsaw Pact in 1991. Thee Czech Rep., Hungary and Poland were the latest to join in 1999.
OAS Organization of American States (formed in 1948). It aims to promote social and economic cooperation between countries in the developed North America and developing Latin America.
ASEAN Association of Southeast Asian Nations (formed in 1967). Burma and Laos joined in 1997.
OAU Organization of African Unity (1963). Its 53 members represent over 94% of Africa's population. Arabic, English, French, and Portuguese are recognized as working languages.
LAIA The Latin American Integration Association (formed in 1980) superceded the Latin American Free Trade Association formed in 1961. Its aim is to promote freer regional trade.
OECD Organization for Economic Cooperation and Development (formed in 1961). It comprises 29 major free-market economies. The "G8" is its "inner group" of leading industrial nations, comprising Canada, France, Germany, Italy, Japan, Russia, UK and the USA.
COMMONWEALTH The Commonwealth of Nations evolved from the British Empire; it comprises 16 nations recognizing the British monarch as head of state, 32 republics and 5 indigenous monarchies, giving a total of 53. Nigeria was suspended in 1995.
CIS The Commonwealth of Independent States (formed in 1991) comprises the countries of the former Soviet Union except for Estonia, Latvia and Lithuania.
OPEC Organization of Petroleum Exporting Countries (formed in 1960). It controls about three-quarters of the world's oil supply. Gabon formally withdrew from OPEC in August 1996.
ARAB LEAGUE (1945) Aims to promote economic, social, cultural and military cooperation.
COLOMBO PLAN (formed in 1951) Its 26 members aim to promote economic and social development in Asia and the Pacific.

Agriculture

Bad harvests in 1995 caused a drop in world grain reserves to a 20-year low. This revived the ongoing debate as to whether the population explosion will cause major food crises in the 21st century.

Experts estimate that 3.3 billion tons of cereals will be needed to feed the world's population in 25 years' time, as compared with 2 billion tons at present. To expand food production to this extent, some argue, will place great strain on the environment. One suggestion to alleviate the situation is that people in developed countries should eat less meat. This would release more grain, which is used as cattle fodder, to feed people.

Other experts argue that there should be no food crises. World grain production tripled between 1950 and 1990, largely as a result of the Green Revolution, during which genetically improved, high-yield varieties of maize, rice and wheat, the world's three leading staple crops, were developed. These new varieties have helped many developing countries to achieve food surpluses and prevent widespread starvation.

The only region of the world which seems likely to suffer food shortages in the 21st century is sub-Saharan Africa, where in the late 1990s the average daily calorie intake was 6% less than what was needed and where the population is expected to double in 20 years. Improved land management and a huge increase in global trade, especially in food distribution, is necessary if sub-Saharan Africans are not to go hungry.

The development of agriculture more than 10,000 years ago transformed human existence more than any other major advance. By supporting larger populations, it led to the growth of early civilizations and later it sustained people in the industrial cities which sprang up in the 19th century.

Today, agricultural production varies a great deal between the developed world, where it is highly mechanized and employs few people, such as 3% of the workforce in the United States, and the developing world, such as sub-Saharan Africa, where it employs 66% of the workforce. Many Africans are engaged in subsistence farming, providing the basic needs of their families but not contributing to the national economy. Much of Africa also suffers from economic mismanagement, as well as civil war and banditry.

Political problems have also affected food production in other parts of the world. The former USSR had much excellent farmland, but the failure of the collectives and state farms to maintain sufficiently high levels of production helped to bring about the collapse of Communism.

Farmers are under great pressure not only to maintain high levels of production but to increase them. However, the cultivation of marginal areas is one of the prime causes of soil erosion and desertification.

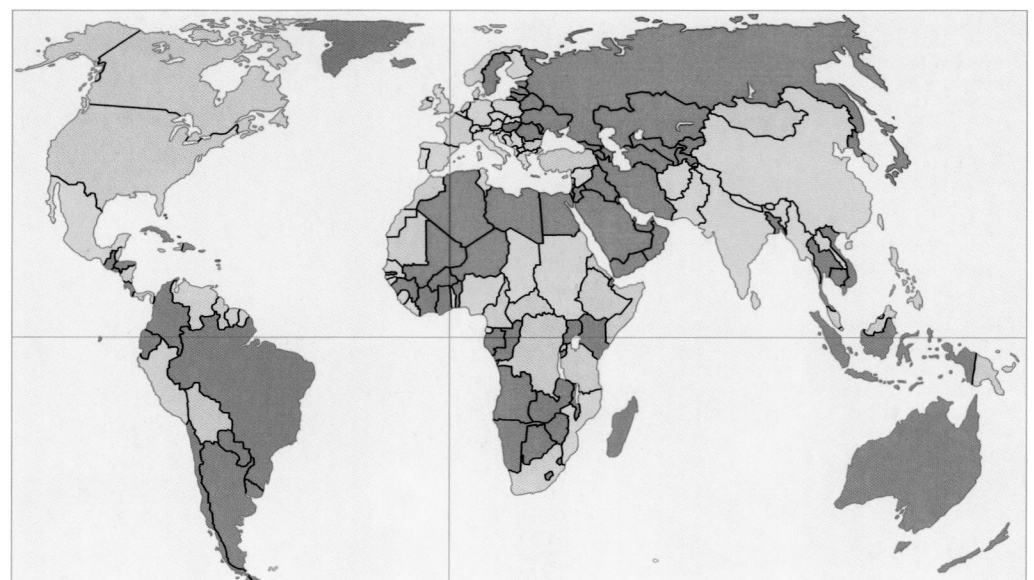

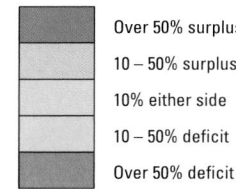

Self-sufficiency in Food

Balance of trade in food products as a percentage of total trade in food products – S.I.T.C. Classes 0, 1 and 4 (latest available year)

- Over 50% surplus
- 10 – 50% surplus
- 10% either side
- 10 – 50% deficit
- Over 50% deficit

Most self-sufficient		Least self-sufficient	
Argentina	95%	Algeria	−98%
Zimbabwe	87%	Djibouti	−97%
Honduras	81%	Yemen	−95%
Malawi	81%	Zambia	−95%
Costa Rica	79%	Japan	−91%
Iceland	78%	Gabon	−90%
Chile	75%	Kuwait	−90%
Uruguay	75%	Brunei	−89%
Ecuador	74%	Burkina Faso	−82%

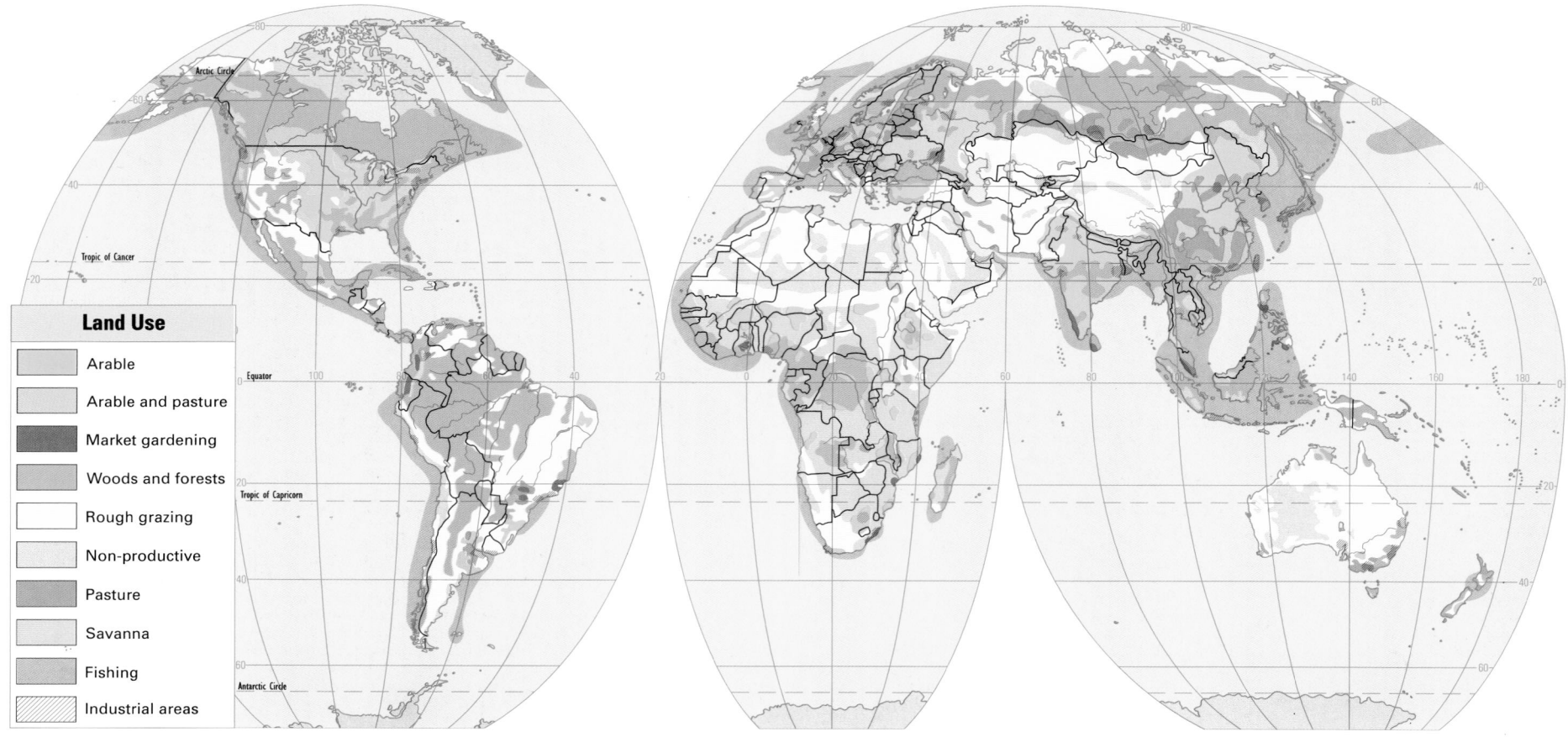

Land Use

- Arable
- Arable and pasture
- Market gardening
- Woods and forests
- Rough grazing
- Non-productive
- Pasture
- Savanna
- Fishing
- Industrial areas

Staple Crops

Wheat: Grown in a range of climates, with most varieties – including the highest-quality bread wheats – requiring temperate conditions. Mainly used in baking, it is also used for pasta and breakfast cereals.

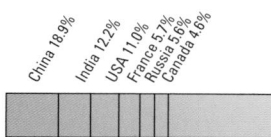

China 18.9% | India 12.2% | USA 11.0% | France 5.7% | Russia 5.6% | Canada 4.6%

World total (1996): 584,874,000 tons

Maize: Originating in the New World and still an important human food in Africa and Latin America, in the developed world it is processed into breakfast cereals, oil, starches and adhesives. It is also used for animal feed.

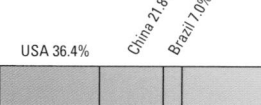

USA 36.4% | China 21.8% | Brazil 7.0%

World total (1996): 576,821,000 tons

Oats: Most widely used to feed livestock, but eaten by humans as oatmeal or porridge. Oats have a beneficial effect on the cardiovascular system, and human consumption is likely to increase.

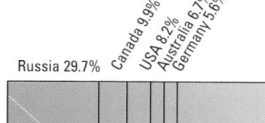

Russia 29.7% | Canada 8.9% | USA 8.2% | Australia 6.7% | Germany 5.6%

World total (1996): 28,794,000 tons

Millet: The name covers a number of small-grained cereals, members of the grass family with a short growing season. Used to produce flour, meal and animal feed, and fermented to make beer, especially in Africa.

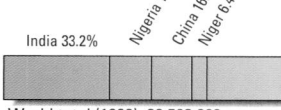

India 33.2% | Nigeria 18.3% | China 16.1% | Niger 6.4%

World total (1996): 29,563,000 tons

Sugars

Sugarcane: Confined to tropical regions, cane sugar accounts for the bulk of international trade in sugar. Most is produced as a foodstuff, but some countries, notably Brazil and South Africa, distill sugarcane to make motor fuels.

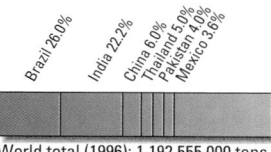

Brazil 26.0% | India 22.2% | China 6.0% | Thailand 5.0% | Pakistan 4.0% | Mexico 3.6%

World total (1996): 1,192,555,000 tons

Cereals are grasses with starchy, edible seeds; every important civilization has depended on them as a source of food. The major cereal grains contain about 10% protein and 75% carbohydrate. Grain contributes more than any other group of foods to the energy and protein content of human diet. Starchy tuber crops or root crops are second in importance after cereals as staple foods; easily cultivated, they provide high yields for little effort.

Rice: Thrives on the high humidity and temperatures of the Far East, where it is the traditional staple food of half the human race. Usually grown standing in water, rice responds well to continuous cultivation, with three or four crops annually.

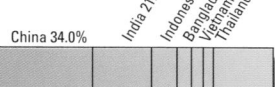

China 34.0% | India 21.7% | Indonesia 9.0% | Bangladesh 4.8% | Vietnam 4.4% | Thailand 3.8%

World total (1996): 562,259,000 tons

Potatoes: The most important of the edible tubers, potatoes grow in well-watered, temperate areas. Weight for weight less nutritious than grain, they are a human staple as well as an important animal feed.

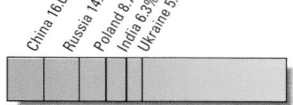

China 16.0% | Russia 14.0% | Poland 8.7% | India 6.3% | Ukraine 5.2%

World total (1996): 294,834,000 tons

Soya: Beans from soya bushes are very high (30–40%) in protein. Most are processed into oil and proprietary protein foods. Consumption since 1950 has tripled, mainly due to the health-conscious developed world.

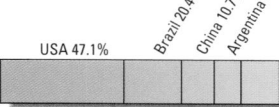

USA 47.1% | Brazil 20.4% | China 10.7% | Argentina 9.6%

World total (1996): 130,302,000 tons

Cassava: A tropical shrub that needs high rainfall (over 125 inches annually) and a 10–30 month growing season to produce its large, edible tubers. Used as flour by humans, as cattle feed and in industrial starches.

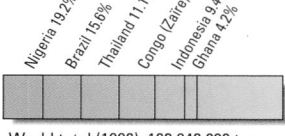

Nigeria 19.2% | Brazil 15.6% | Thailand 11.1% | Congo (Zaire) 10.7% | Indonesia 9.4% | Ghana 4.2%

World total (1996): 162,942,000 tons

Sugar beet: Closely related to the beetroot, sugar beet's yield after processing is indistinguishable from cane sugar. It is replacing sugarcane imports in Europe, to the detriment of the developing countries that rely on it as a major cash crop.

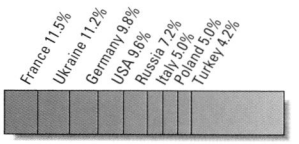

France 11.5% | Ukraine 11.2% | Germany 9.8% | USA 3.6% | Russia 7.2% | Italy 5.0% | Poland 5.0% | Turkey 4.2%

World total (1996): 255,500,000 tons

Food and Population

Comparison of food production and population by continent.

The left column indicates the % of world food production and the right shows population in proportion.

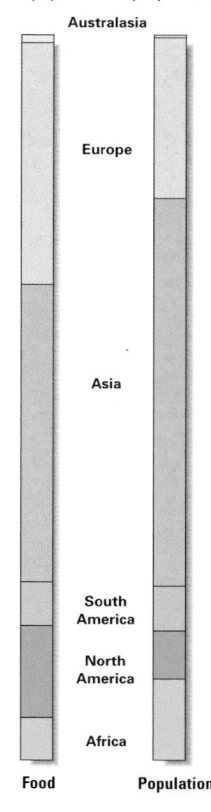

Australasia
Europe
Asia
South America
North America
Africa

Food | Population

Agricultural Population

Percentage of the total population dependent on agriculture for their livelihood (1997)

- Over 75% dependent
- 50 – 75% dependent
- 25 – 50% dependent
- 10 – 25% dependent
- Under 10% dependent

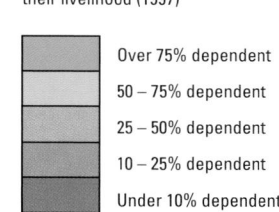

Top 5 countries (1997)		Bottom 5 countries (1997)	
Bhutan	94%	Singapore	0.2%
Nepal	93%	Kuwait	1.0%
Burkina Faso	92%	Brunei	1.0%
Rwanda	91%	Bahrain	1.3%
Burundi	91%	Qatar	1.7%

Animal Products

Traditionally, food animals subsisted on land unsuitable for cultivation, supporting agricultural production with their fertilizing dung. But free-ranging animals grow slowly and yield less meat than those more intensively reared; the demands of urban markets in the developed world have encouraged the growth of factory-like production methods. A large proportion of staple crops, especially cereals, are fed to animals, an inefficient way to produce protein but one likely to continue as long as people value meat and dairy products in their diet.

Cheese: Least perishable of all dairy products, cheese is milk fermented with selected bacterial strains to produce a foodstuff with a potentially immense range of flavors and textures. The vast majority of cheeses are made from cow's milk, although sheep and goat cheeses are highly prized.

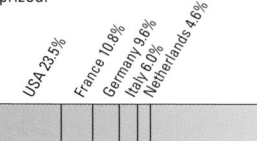

USA 23.5% | France 10.8% | Germany 8.9% | Italy 6.0% | Netherlands 4.5%

World total (1995): 14,754,000 tons

Beef and Veal: Most beef and veal is reared for home markets, and the top five producers are also the biggest consumers. The USA produces nearly a quarter of the world's beef and eats even more.

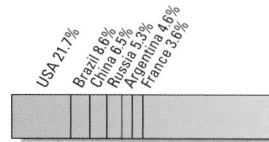

USA 21.7% | Brazil 8.6% | China 6.5% | Russia 5.3% | Argentina 4.6% | France 3.6%

World total (1996): 53,965,000 tons

Milk: Many human groups, including most Asians, find raw milk indigestible after infancy, and it is often only the starting point for other dairy products such as butter, cheese and yoghurt. Most world milk production comes from cows, but sheep's milk and goats' milk are also important.

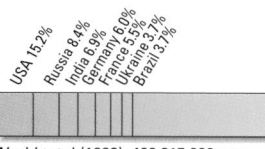

USA 15.2% | Russia 8.4% | India 6.9% | Germany 6.0% | France 5.5% | Ukraine 3.7% | Brazil 3.7%

World total (1996): 466,317,000 tons

Butter: A traditional source of vitamin A as well as calories, butter has lost much popularity in the developed world for health reasons, although it remains a valuable food. Most butter from India, the world's largest producer, is clarified into ghee, which has religious as well as nutritional importance.

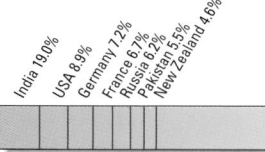

India 19.0% | USA 8.9% | Germany 7.2% | France 6.7% | Russia 6.2% | Pakistan 5.5% | New Zealand 4.6%

World total (1996): 6,565,000 tons

Pork: Although pork is forbidden to many millions, notably Muslims, on religious grounds, more is produced than any other meat in the world, mainly because it is the cheapest. It accounts for about 90% of China's meat output, although per capita meat consumption is relatively low.

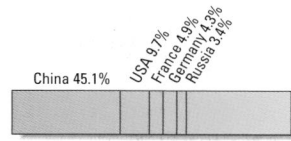

China 45.1% | USA 9.7% | France 4.9% | Germany 4.3% | Russia 3.1%

World total (1996): 85,761,000 tons

Crisis in Africa

Each year 40 million people, almost half of whom are children, die from starvation and related diseases. By the year 2000, an estimated 600 million people worldwide will be suffering from malnutrition. Africa suffers from more natural disasters than any other continent; pests such as locusts destroy crops, and tropical storms and flooding ruin harvests. Famines periodically affect parts of Africa causing widespread hardship, even though enough food is produced worldwide to feed everyone.

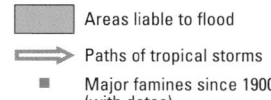

- Areas liable to invasions by locusts
- Areas liable to flood
- Paths of tropical storms
- Major famines since 1900 (with dates)

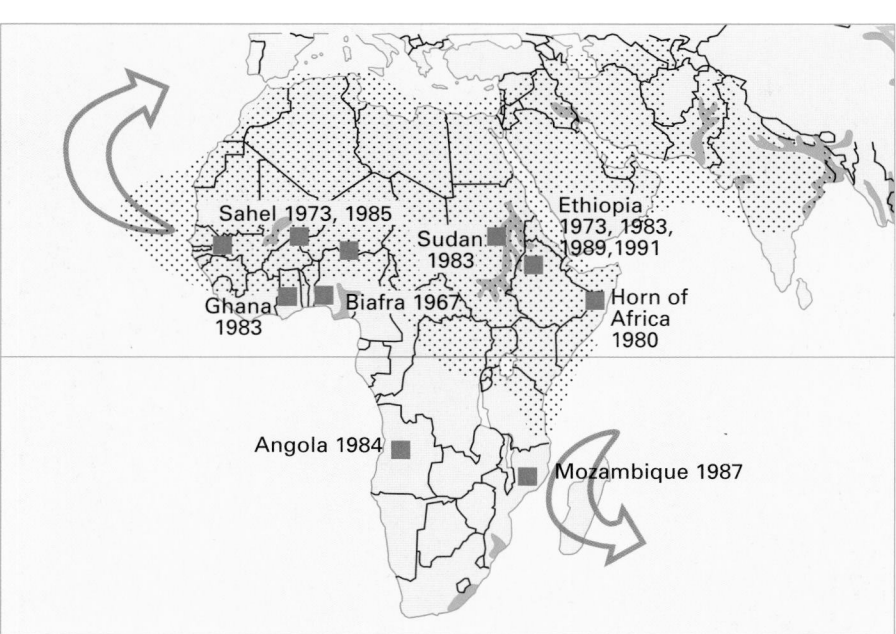

Sahel 1973, 1985
Ethiopia 1973, 1983, 1989, 1991
Sudan 1983
Ghana 1983
Biafra 1967
Horn of Africa 1980
Angola 1984
Mozambique 1987

Energy

Every year, the world's energy consumption is about the equivalent of what would come from burning 8 billion tons of oil (8,000 MtOe) – a twenty-fold increase since 1850. Two-fifths of this total actually comes from burning oil and most of the rest comes from coal and natural gas.

The oil crises in the 1970s precipitated concern over dependence on finite fossil fuels as the primary source of energy, and growing environmental awareness has added impetus to the search for alternative energy resources.

Fossil fuel combustion damages the environment through the release of gases and particulate matter but two other major sources of energy, hydroelectricity and nuclear power, are also controversial. For example, hydroelectricity production involves flooding large areas to create reservoirs, while nuclear power stations, which are costly to build, generate dangerous radioactive wastes, and can lead to disasters on an international scale.

Alternative energy resources may soon provide a much larger proportion of the world's energy consumption, especially in developing countries where millions of people currently have no access to electricity. Experts have predicted that solar and wind energy may have an important future in such countries as China and India, while other areas under development, such as tidal, wave and geothermal power, all have potential in appropriate areas. World Bank experts have calculated that solar power could, in theory, supply between five and ten times the present electricity supply of developing countries.

For more information:
22 Carbon dioxide
   Greenhouse power
   CO₂ producers
   Global warming
23 Water pollution
39 World shipping

Conversions

For historical reasons, oil is still traded in barrels. The weight and volume equivalents shown below are all based on average density "Arabian light" crude oil, and should be considered approximate.

The energy equivalents given for a ton of oil are also somewhat imprecise: oil and coal of different qualities will have varying energy contents, a fact usually reflected in their price on world markets.

1 barrel:
0.15 tons
159 liters
35 Imperial gallons
42 US gallons

1 ton:
7.33 barrels
1185 liters
256 Imperial gallons
261 US gallons

1 ton oil:
1.5 tons hard coal
3.0 tons lignite
12,000 kWh

1 gallon (Imperial):
227,42 inches
1.201 US gallons
4,546 liters

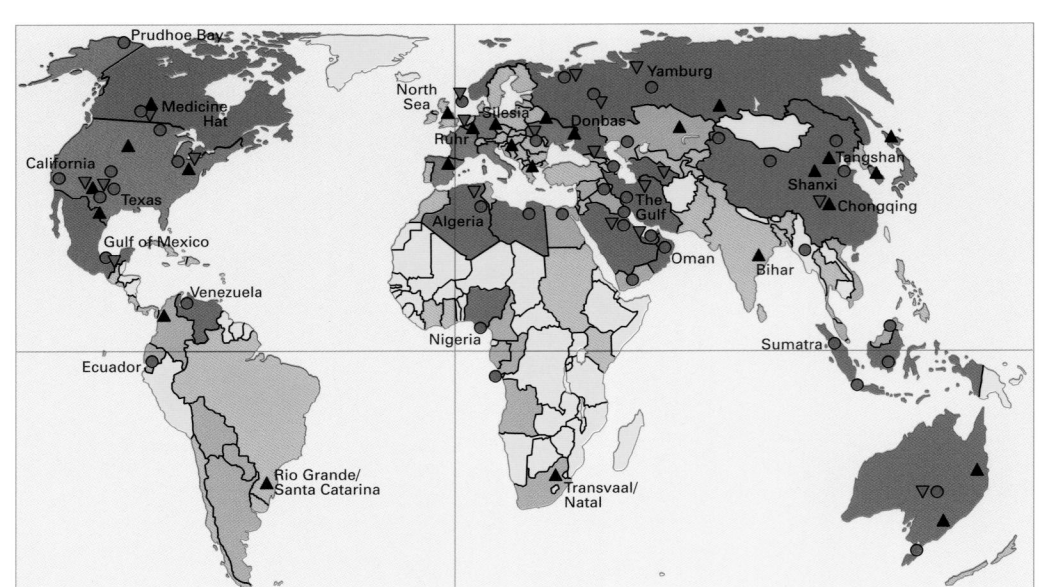

Energy Balance

Difference between energy production and consumption in millions of tons of oil equivalent (MtOe) (latest available year)

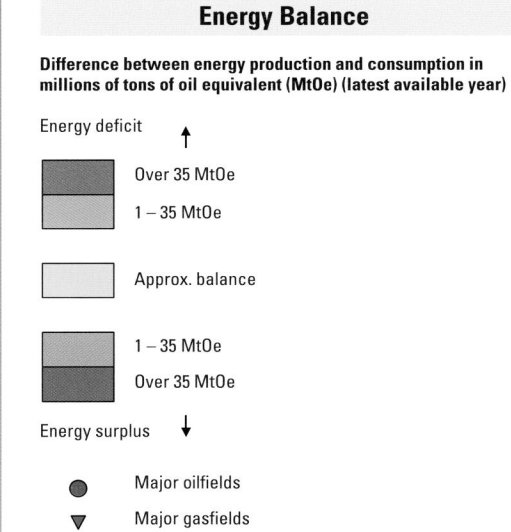

World Energy Consumption

Energy consumed by world regions, measured in million tons of oil equivalent in 1997. Total world consumption was 8,509 MtOe. Only energy from oil, gas, coal, nuclear and hydroelectric sources are included. Excluded are fuels such as wood, peat, animal waste, wind, solar and geothermal which, though important in some countries, are unreliably documented in terms of consumption statistics.

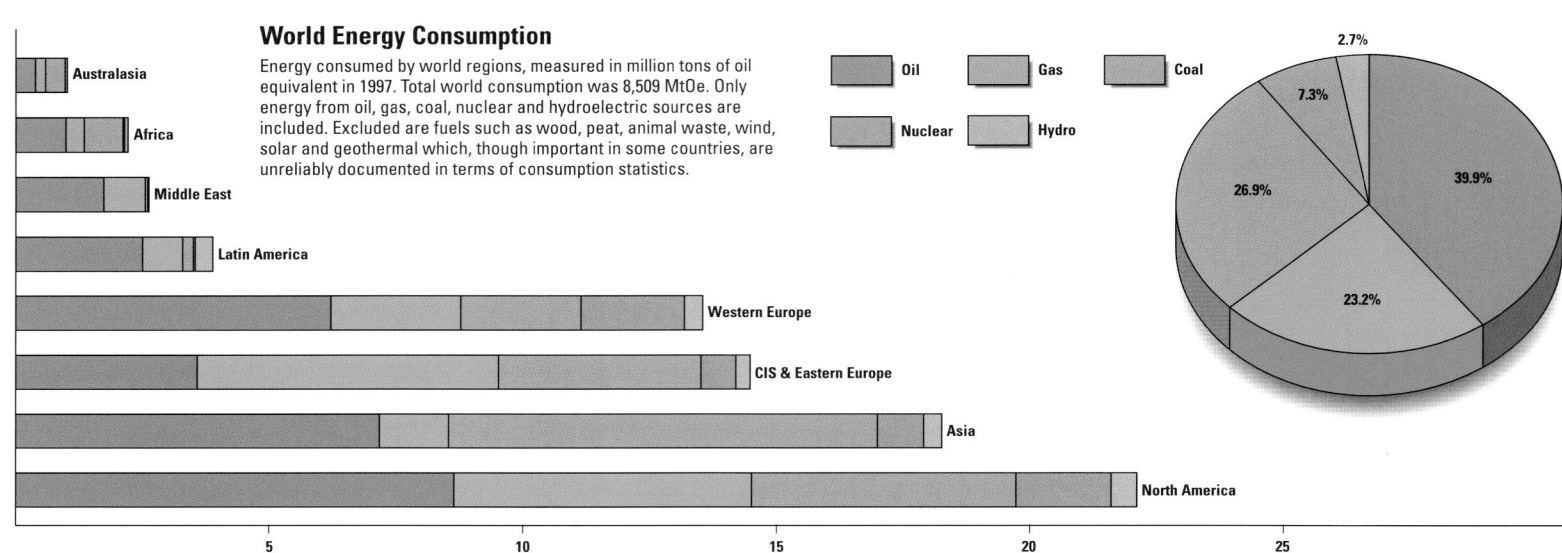

Energy Production

Primary energy production expressed in kilograms of coal equivalent per person (1994)

In developing countries traditional fuels are still very important. These so-called biomass fuels include wood, charcoal and dried dung. The pie chart highlights the importance of biomass in terms of energy consumption in Nigeria. Collecting fuelwood can be a time-consuming task, sometimes taking all day.

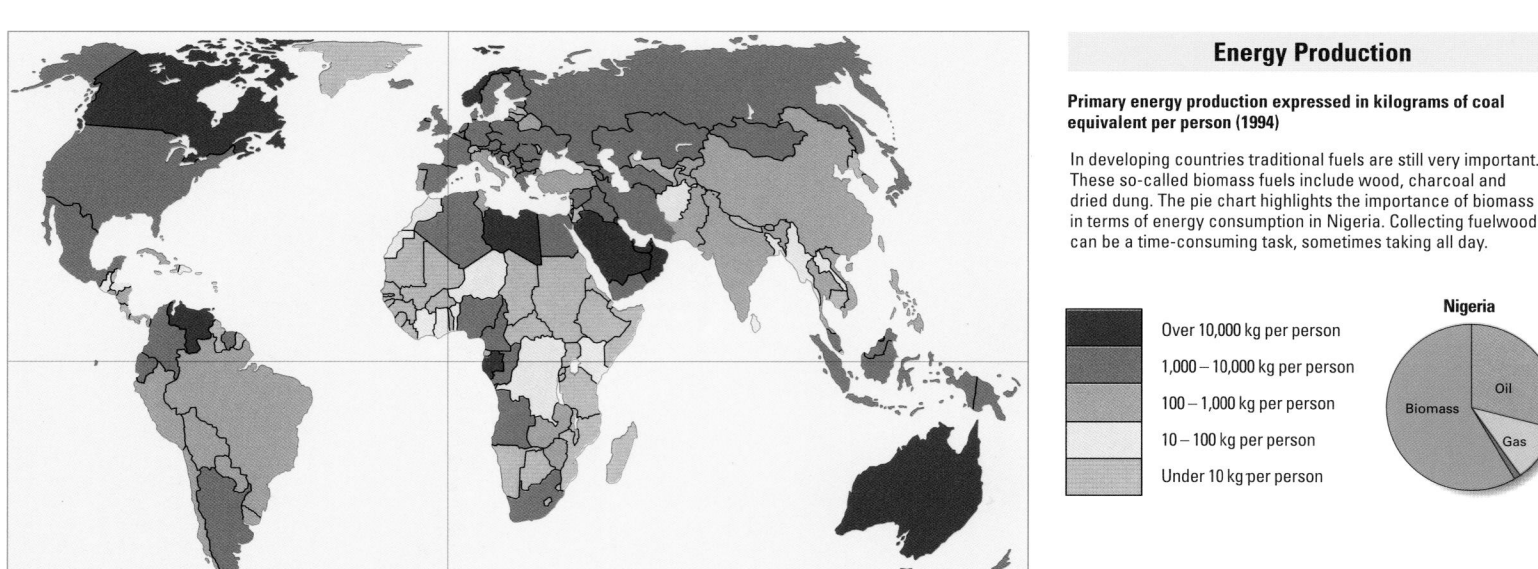

34

Oil Movements

Major world movements of oil in millions of tons (1997)

Middle East to Asia (not Japan)	294.4
Middle East to Japan	218.1
Middle East to Western Europe	187.9
South and Central America to USA	132.1
North Africa to Western Europe	97.9
CIS to Western Europe	90.8
Middle East to USA	86.9
Canada to USA	72.7
West Africa to USA	68.3
Mexico to USA	68.0
West Africa to Western Europe	40.1
Western Europe to USA	32.9
Middle East to Africa	32.0
CIS to Central Europe	31.8
Middle East to South and Central America	27.8
Middle East to Central Europe	19.3

Total world imports ....1,978,900 billion tons

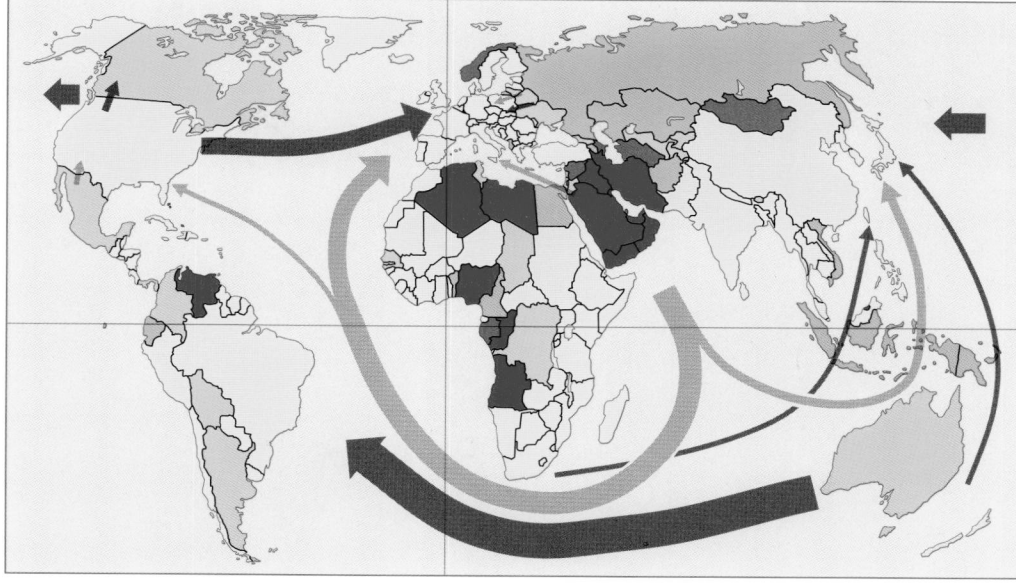

Fuel Exports

Fuels as a percentage of total value of exports (1996)

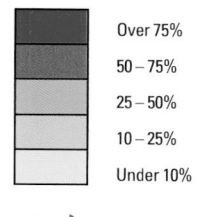

- Over 75%
- 50 – 75%
- 25 – 50%
- 10 – 25%
- Under 10%

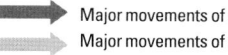

- Major movements of coal
- Major movements of oil

In the 1970s, oil exports became a political issue when OPEC sought to increase the influence of developing countries in world affairs by raising oil prices and restricting production. But its power was short-lived, following a fall in demand for oil in the 1980s, due to an increase in energy efficiency and development of alternative resources.

Coal Reserves

Proved coal reserves in place by region and country, billion tons (1993)

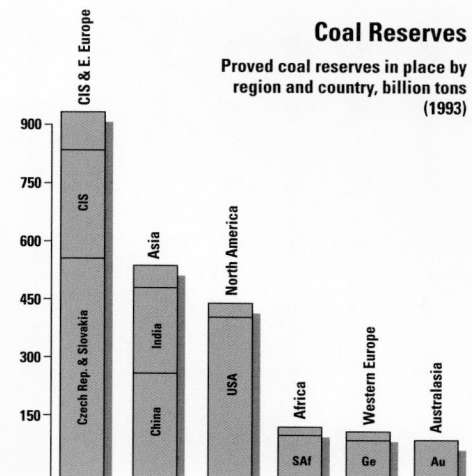

Gas Reserves

Proved recoverable natural gas reserves by region and country, billion tons (1993)

Oil Reserves

Crude oil reserves by region and country, billion tons (1993)

Al: Algeria
Au: Australia
Ca: Canada
Cn: China
Ge: Germany
Iq: Iraq
Ka: Kazakstan
Li: Libya
Ma: Malaysia
Mx: Mexico
Ni: Nigeria
No: Norway
Qa: Qatar
Ru: Russia
SA: Saudi Arabia
SAf: South Africa
Tm: Turkmenistan
Uk: Ukraine
Ve: Venezuela

Nuclear Power

Percentage of electricity generated by nuclear power stations, leading nations (1995)

1.	Lithuania	85%	11.	Spain	33%
2.	France	77%	12.	Finland	30%
3.	Belgium	56%	13.	Germany	29%
4.	Slovak Rep.	49%	14.	Japan	29%
5.	Sweden	48%	15.	UK	27%
6.	Bulgaria	41%	16.	Ukraine	27%
7.	Hungary	41%	17.	Czech Rep.	22%
8.	Switzerland	39%	18.	Canada	19%
9.	Slovenia	38%	19.	USA	18%
10.	South Korea	33%	20.	Russia	12%

Although the 1980s were a bad time for the nuclear power industry (major projects ran over budget and fears of long-term environmental damage were heavily reinforced by the 1986 disaster at Chernobyl), the industry picked up in the early 1990s. Whilst the number of reactors is still increasing, however, orders for new plants have shrunk. In 1997, the Swedish government began to decommission the country's 12 nuclear power plants; a bold environmental decision that could cost US $50 billion.

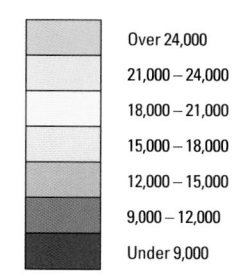

Renewable Energy

Average annual solar irradiance in kWh/ft², with selected major hydroelectric and geothermal power stations

- Over 24,000
- 21,000 – 24,000
- 18,000 – 21,000
- 15,000 – 18,000
- 12,000 – 15,000
- 9,000 – 12,000
- Under 9,000

▲ Hydroelectric plants
● Geothermal plants

Hydroelectricity

Percentage of electricity generated by hydroelectric power stations, leading nations (1995)

1.	Paraguay	99.9%	11.	Rwanda	97.6%
2.	Congo (Zaïre)	99.7%	12.	Malawi	97.6%
3.	Bhutan	99.6%	13.	Cameroon	96.9%
4.	Zambia	99.5%	14.	Nepal	96.7%
5.	Norway	99.4%	15.	Laos	95.3%
6.	Ghana	99.3%	16.	Albania	95.2%
7.	Congo	99.3%	17.	Iceland	94.0%
8.	Uganda	99.1%	18.	Brazil	92.2%
9.	Burundi	98.3%	19.	Honduras	87.6%
10.	Uruguay	98.0%	20.	Tanzania	87.1%

Countries heavily reliant on hydroelectricity are usually small and nonindustrial: a high proportion of hydroelectric power more often reflects a modest energy budget than vast hydroelectric resources. The USA, for instance, produces only 9% of power requirements from hydroelectricity; yet that 9% amounts to more than three times the hydropower generated by the whole of Africa.

Alternative Energy Resources

Solar: Each year the Sun bestows upon the Earth almost a million times as much energy as is locked up in all the planet's oil reserves, but only an insignificant fraction is trapped and used commercially. In a few installations around the world, mirrors focus the Sun's rays on to boilers, whose steam generates electricity by spinning turbines.

Wind: Caused by uneven heating of the Earth, winds are themselves a form of solar energy. Windmills have been used for centuries to turn wind power into mechanical work; recent models, often arranged in banks on wind-swept high ground, usually generate electricity. Figures for wind power worldwide are given in the table, right.

Tidal: The energy from tides is potentially enormous, although only a few installations have so far been built to exploit it. In theory at least, waves and currents could also provide almost unimaginable power, and the thermal differences in the ocean depths are another huge well of potential energy. But work on extracting it is still in the experimental stage.

Geothermal: The Earth's temperature rises by 1°F for every 50 feet descent, with much steeper temperature gradients in geologically active areas. El Salvador, for example, produces 39% of its electricity from geothermal power stations, whilst the USA, the world leader, produced 3,331 megawatts in 1993. Some of the oldest and most successful applications are in Iceland, where 86% of all households are heated by geothermal energy.

Biomass: The oldest of human fuels ranges from animal dung, still burned in cooking fires in much of North Africa and elsewhere, to sugarcane plantations feeding high-technology distilleries to produce ethanol for motor vehicle engines. In Brazil and South Africa, plant ethanol provides up to 25% of motor fuel. Throughout the developing world, most biomass energy comes from firewood: although accurate figures are impossible to obtain, it may yield as much as 10% of the world's total energy consumption.

Wind Power

World wind energy generating capacity, in megawatts

1980	10
1981	25
1982	90
1983	210
1984	600
1985	1,020
1986	1,270
1987	1,450
1988	1,580
1989	1,730
1990	1,930
1991	2,170
1992	2,510
1993	3,050
1994	3,710

Wind power is the fastest growing source of energy worldwide but still provides only 1% of the world's energy. Output grew by 33% in 1995.

Minerals

The use of metals played a vital part in the evolving technologies of early peoples. Copper first came into use around 10,000 years ago, bronze about 5,000 years ago, and iron 3,300 years ago. In the early stages of the Industrial Revolution, the location of coal, iron ore and water power usually determined the location of new industries. But due to continuing improvements in transport, including oil pipelines, industries can now be located almost anywhere.

Minerals are distributed unevenly and some industrial countries, lacking their own mineral resources, import most of the raw materials they need. Some imports come from mineral-rich countries, such as Australia but others come from developing countries, especially in Africa and South America. Most of the developing countries export unprocessed ores, losing out on the much higher revenues gained from exporting metals.

Most minerals come from land deposits, because undersea deposits, with the exception of oil reserves under the continental shelves, have been regarded as inaccessible. But shortages of terrestrial minerals may one day encourage exploitation of the ocean floor.

Mineral Exports

Minerals and metals as a percentage of total exports (latest available year)

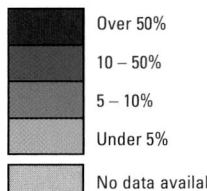

- Over 50%
- 10 – 50%
- 5 – 10%
- Under 5%
- No data available

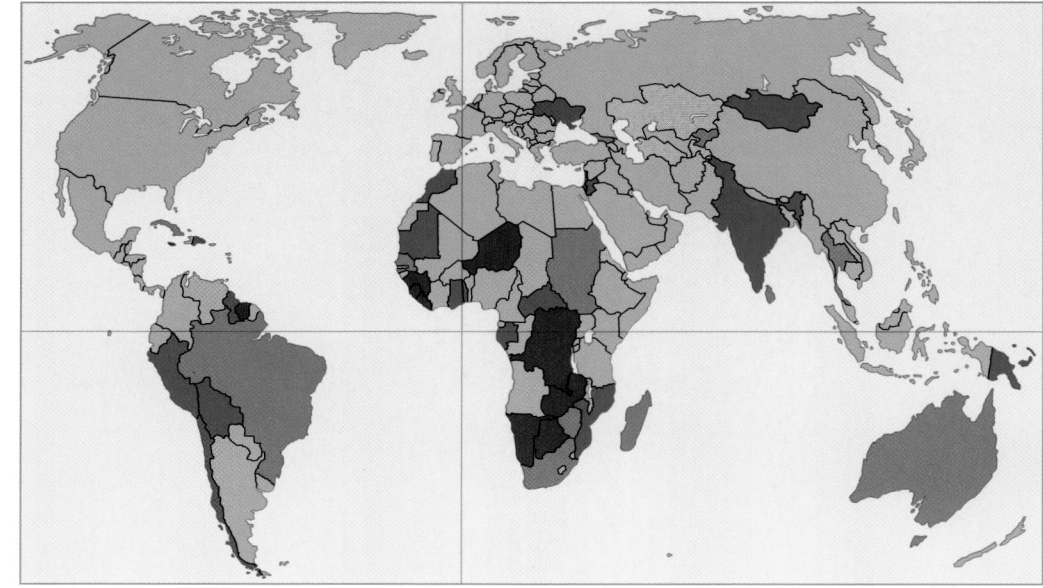

Uranium

In its pure state, uranium is an immensely heavy, white metal; but although spent uranium is employed as projectiles in antimissile cannons, where its mass ensures a lethal punch, its main use is as a fuel in nuclear reactors, and in nuclear weaponry. Uranium is very scarce: the main source is the rare ore pitchblende, which itself contains only 0.2% uranium oxide. Only a minute fraction of that is the radioactive U^{235} isotope, though so-called breeder reactors can transmute the more common U^{238} into highly radioactive plutonium.

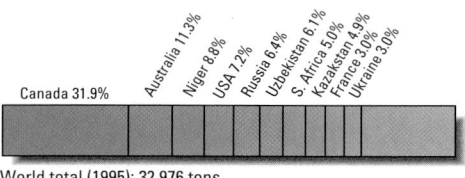

Canada 31.9% — Australia 11.3% — Niger 8.8% — USA 7.2% — Russia 6.4% — Uzbekistan 6.1% — S. Africa 5.0% — Kazakstan 4.5% — France 3.0% — Ukraine 3.0%

World total (1995): 32,976 tons

Metals

* Figures for aluminum are for refined metal; all other figures refer to ore production.

The world's leading producers of aluminum ore (bauxite) in 1995 were as follows:

1. Australia 41.9%
2. Papua New Guinea 14.3%
3. Jamaica 10.8%
4. Brazil 10.1%
5. Russia 6.7%
6. China 5.7%
7. India 5.0%
8. Surinam 2.8%
9. Venezuela 2.6%
10. Greece 1.9%

The figures shown above are in stark contrast to the figures showing aluminum production on the right. Australia, for example, produces 41.9% of the world's bauxite but only 5.9% of the aluminum metal. Papua New Guinea and Jamaica account for 25% of the bauxite mined but have no smelters and export virtually all of it to countries like the USA and Canada.

Diamond

Most of the world's diamond is found in kimberlite, or "blue ground," a basic peridotite rock; erosion may wash the diamond from its kimberlite matrix and deposit it with sand or gravel on river beds. Only a small proportion of the world's diamond, the most flawless, is cut into gemstones – "diamonds"; most is used in industry, where the material's remarkable hardness and abrasion resistance finds a use in cutting tools, drills and dies, as well as in styluses. Australia, not among the top 12 producers at the beginning of the 1980s, had by 1986 become world leader and by 1993 was the source of 40.6% of world production. The other main producers were Congo (Zaïre) (16.3%), Botswana (14.6%), Russia (11.4%) and South Africa (9.7%). Between them, these five nations accounted for over 82% of the world total of 100,850,000 carats.

Aluminum: Produced mainly from its oxide, bauxite, which yields 25% of its weight in aluminum. The cost of refining and production is often too high for producer-countries to bear, so bauxite is largely exported. Lightweight and corrosion resistant, aluminum alloys are widely used in aircraft, vehicles, cans and packaging.

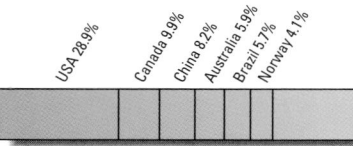

USA 28.9% — Canada 9.9% — China 8.2% — Australia 5.9% — Brazil 5.7% — Norway 4.1%

World total (1995): 22,706,000 tons *

Lead: A soft metal, obtained mainly from galena (lead sulfide), which occurs in veins associated with iron, zinc and silver sulfides. Its use in vehicle batteries accounts for the USA's prime consumer status; lead is also made into sheeting and piping. Its use as an additive to paints and petrol is decreasing.

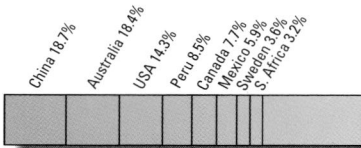

China 18.7% — Australia 18.4% — USA 14.3% — Peru 8.5% — Canada 7.7% — Mexico 5.9% — Sweden 3.6% — S. Africa 3.2%

World total (1995): 2,751,000 tons *

Tin: Soft, pliable and non-toxic, used to coat "tin" (tin-plated steel) cans, in the manufacture of foils and in alloys. The principal tin-bearing mineral is cassiterite (SnO_2), found in ore formed from molten rock. Producers and refiners were hit by a price collapse in 1991.

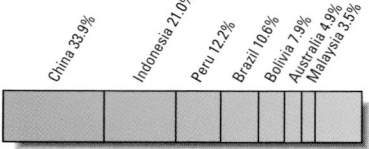

China 33.9% — Indonesia 21.0% — Peru 12.2% — Brazil 10.6% — Bolivia 7.9% — Australia 4.9% — Malaysia 3.5%

World total (1995): 182,518 tons *

Gold: Regarded for centuries as the most valuable metal in the world and used to make coins, gold is still recognized as the monetary standard. A soft metal, it is alloyed to make jewelry; the electronics industry values its corrosion resistance and conductivity.

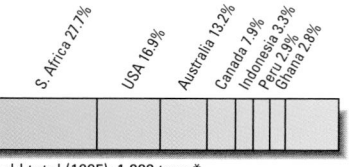

S. Africa 27.7% — USA 16.9% — Australia 13.2% — Canada 7.9% — Indonesia 3.3% — Peru 2.9% — Ghana 2.8%

World total (1995): 1,889 tons *

Copper: Derived from low-yielding sulfide ores, copper is an important export for several developing countries. An excellent conductor of heat and electricity, it forms part of most electrical items, and is used in the manufacture of brass and bronze. Major importers include Japan and Germany.

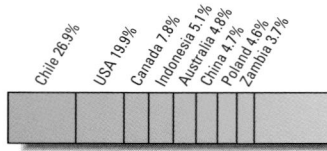

Chile 26.9% — USA 19.9% — Canada 7.8% — Indonesia 5.1% — Australia 4.9% — China 4.7% — Poland 4.6% — Zambia 3.7%

World total (1995): 9,311,000 tons *

Mercury: The only metal that is liquid at normal temperatures, most is derived from its sulfide, cinnabar, found only in small quantities in volcanic areas. Apart from its value in thermometers and other instruments, most mercury production is used in antifungal and antifouling preparations, and to make detonators.

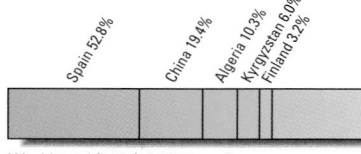

Spain 52.8% — China 19.4% — Algeria 10.3% — Kyrgyzstan 6.0% — Finland 3.2%

World total (1995): 2,837 tons *

Zinc: Often found in association with lead ores, zinc is highly resistant to corrosion, and about 40% of the refined metal is used to plate sheet steel, particularly vehicle bodies – a process known as galvanizing. Zinc is also used in dry batteries, paints and dyes.

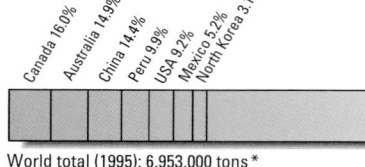

Canada 16.0% — Australia 14.9% — Peru 14.4% — USA 9.9% — China 9.2% — Mexico 5.2% — North Korea 3.1%

World total (1995): 6,953,000 tons *

Silver: Most silver comes from ores mined and processed for other metals (including lead and copper). Pure or alloyed with harder metals, it is used for jewelry and ornaments. Industrial use includes dentistry, electronics, photography and as a chemical catalyst.

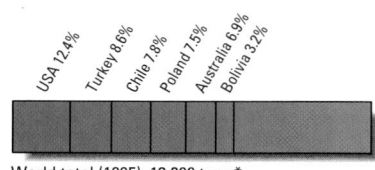

USA 12.4% — Turkey 8.6% — Chile 7.8% — Poland 7.5% — Australia 6.9% — Bolivia 3.2%

World total (1995): 13,266 tons *

Strategic Minerals

Ever since the art of high-temperature smelting was discovered, some time in the second millennium BC, iron has been by far the most important metal known to man. The earliest iron plows transformed primitive agriculture and led to the first human population explosion, while iron weapons – or the lack of them – ensured the rise or fall of entire cultures.

Widely distributed around the world, iron ores usually contain 25–60% iron; blast furnaces process the raw product into pig iron, which is then alloyed with carbon and other minerals to produce steels of various qualities. From the time of the Industrial Revolution, steel has been almost literally the backbone of modern civilization, the prime structural material on which all else is built.

Iron smelting usually developed close to the sources of ore and, later, to the coalfields that fueled the furnaces. Today, most ore comes from a few richly-endowed locations where large-scale mining is possible. Iron and steel plants are generally built at coastal sites so that giant ore carriers, which account for a sizable proportion of the world's merchant fleet, can easily discharge their cargoes.

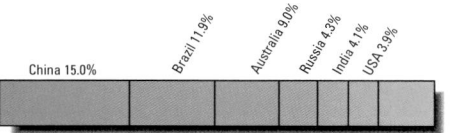

World total production of iron ore (1995): 1,020,000,000 tons

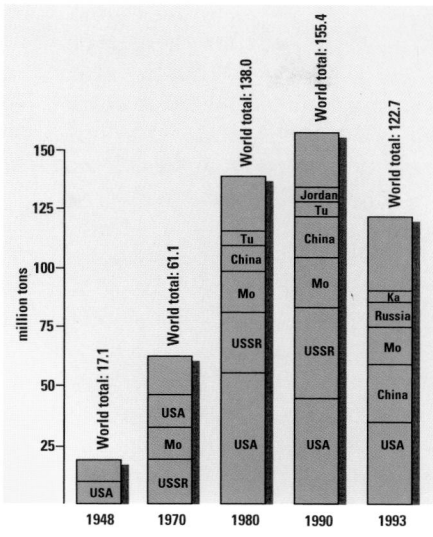

World production of phosphates in millions of tons (1993). Phosphate production is vital to the economies of several small countries. Nauru, for example, is heavily dependent on phosphate exports – the island has one of the world's richest deposits. In 1994, 613,000 tons were mined, employing 1,000 people. In Togo, earnings from phosphate exports have superseded all agricultural exports.

Percentage of total world phosphate production (1994)

1. USA	32.4%		7. Israel	3.1%
2. China	20.2%		8. Brazil	2.6%
3. Morocco	15.4%		9. South Africa	2.0%
4. Russia	6.2%		10. Togo	1.7%
5. Tunisia	4.4%		11. Kazakstan	1.6%
6. Jordan	3.3%		12. Senegal	1.4%

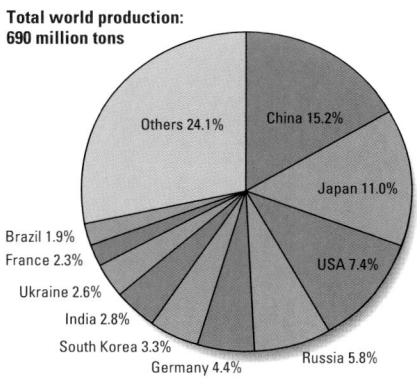

World production of pig iron and ferroalloys (1995). All countries with an annual output of more than 1 million tons are shown

Total world production: 690 million tons

Others 24.1%
China 15.2%
Japan 11.0%
USA 7.4%
Russia 5.8%
Germany 4.4%
South Korea 3.3%
India 2.8%
Ukraine 2.6%
France 2.3%
Brazil 1.9%

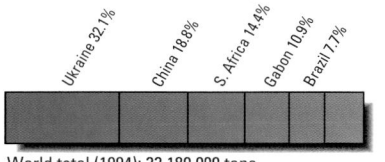

Manganese: In its pure state, manganese is a hard, brittle metal. Alloyed with chrome, iron and nickel, it produces abrasion-resistant steels; manganese-aluminum alloys are light but tough. Found in batteries and inks, manganese is also used in glass production. Manganese ores are frequently found in the same location as sedimentary iron ores. Pyrolusite (MnO_2) and psilomelane are the main economically-exploitable sources.

World total (1994): 22,180,000 tons

Chromium: Most of the world's chromium production is alloyed with iron and other metals to produce steels with various different properties. Combined with iron, nickel, cobalt and tungsten, chromium produces an exceptionally hard steel, resistant to heat; chrome steels are used for many household items where utility must be matched with appearance – cutlery, for example. Chromium is also used in production of refractory bricks, and its salts for tanning and dyeing leather and cloth.

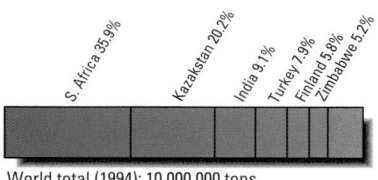

World total (1994): 10,000,000 tons

Nickel: Combined with chrome and iron, nickel produces stainless and high-strength steels; similar alloys go to make magnets and electrical heating elements. Nickel combined with copper is widely used to make coins; cupro-nickel alloy is very resistant to corrosion. Its ores yield only modest quantities of nickel – 0.5% to 3.0% – but also contain copper, iron and small amounts of precious metals. Japan, USA, UK, Germany and France are the principal importers.

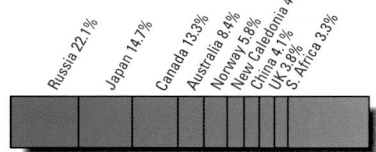

World total (1995): 920,000 tons

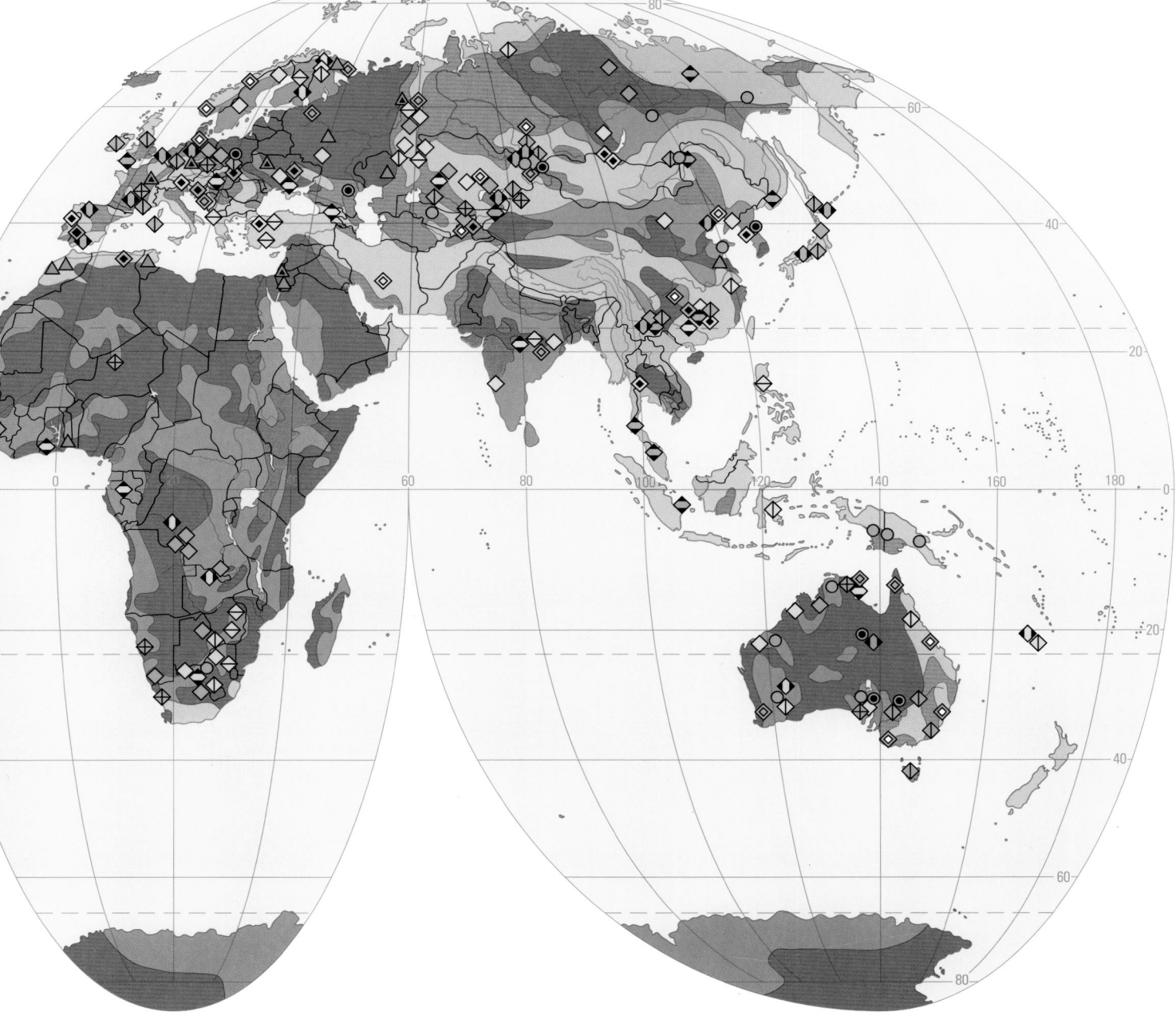

Distribution of Minerals

Structural Regions

- Pre-Cambrian shields
- Sedimentary cover on Pre-Cambrian shields
- Paleozoic (Caledonian and Hercynian) folding
- Sedimentary cover on Paleozoic folding
- Mesozoic folding
- Sedimentary cover on Mesozoic folding
- Cenozoic (Alpine) folding
- Sedimentary cover on Cenozoic folding
- Intensive Mesozoic and Cenozoic vulcanism

Distribution

Iron and ferro-alloys

- Chrome
- Cobalt
- Iron Ore
- Manganese
- Molybdenum
- Nickel Ore
- Tungsten

Non-ferrous metals

- Bauxite (Aluminum)
- Copper
- Lead
- Mercury
- Tin
- Zinc
- Uranium

Precious metals and stones

- Diamonds
- Gold
- Silver

Fertilizers

- Phosphates
- Potash

Manufacturing

The Industrial Revolution which began in Britain in the late 18th century, represented a major technological advance in the evolution of human society. It enabled a group of countries to become prosperous by replacing expensive human labor with increasingly sophisticated machinery. In economic terms, manufacturing is the transformation of raw materials, energy, labor and machines into finished goods, which have a higher value than the various elements used in production.

The economies of countries can be compared by reference to their per capita Gross National Products (or per capita GNPs), namely, the total value of goods and services produced in a country in a year, divided by the population.

The industrialized, or developed, countries accounted for 16% of the world's population in 1997 with an average per capita GNP of US $25,700. On the other hand, developing countries, with comparatively small industrial sectors and low-income economies, accounted for 35% of the world's population, with an average per capita GNP of just $350.

Kenya, with its low-income economy, had a per capita GNP in 1997 of $330. Agriculture employs 77% of the people, industry 8% and services 15%. The major industries are the processing of agricultural products and import substitution (the manufacture of such necessities as cement, footwear and textiles). Heavy industry plays a comparatively small part in the economy. By contrast, Germany, a major industrialized nation, had a per capita GNP in 1997

of $28,260. Agriculture employs only 1% of the population, with 32% in industry, and 67% in services. Germany's industrial sector differs greatly from Kenya's, with an emphasis on the manufacture of vehicles, machinery and chemicals.

Since the 1970s, some former developing countries in Asia have been transformed by rapid industrialization. These "economic tigers," including China, Malaysia, South Korea, Singapore, Taiwan, and Thailand, owe their success to low labor costs and substantial investment in education, together with advances in telecommunications, transport, and computers, which have made technology more readily transferable around the world than ever before. They have also benefited from economic freedom and trade liberalization.

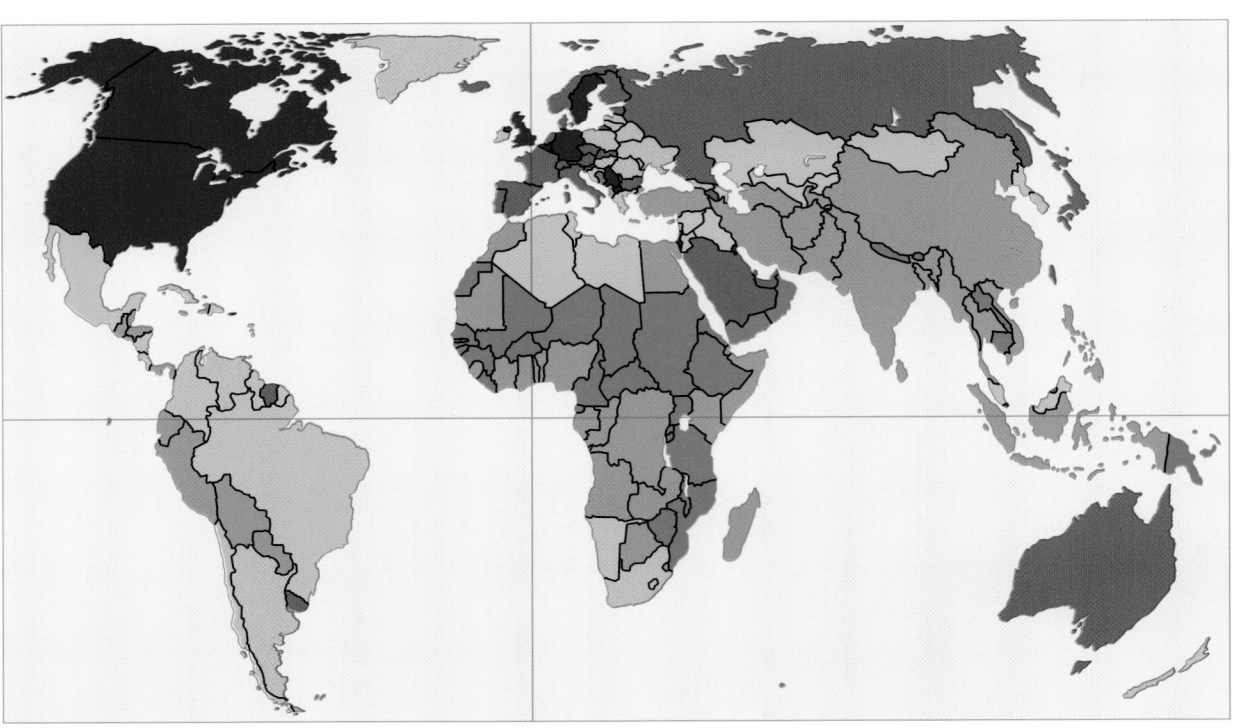

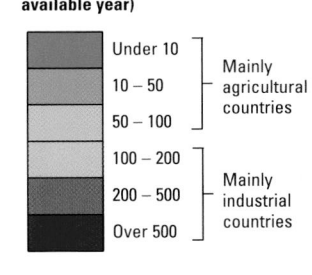

Employment

The number of workers employed in manufacturing for every 100 workers engaged in agriculture (latest available year)

Under 10	}	Mainly agricultural countries
10 – 50		
50 – 100		
100 – 200	}	Mainly industrial countries
200 – 500		
Over 500		

Selected countries (latest available year)

Singapore	8,860
UK	1,270
Belgium	820
Germany	800
Kuwait	767
Bahrain	660
USA	657
Israel	633

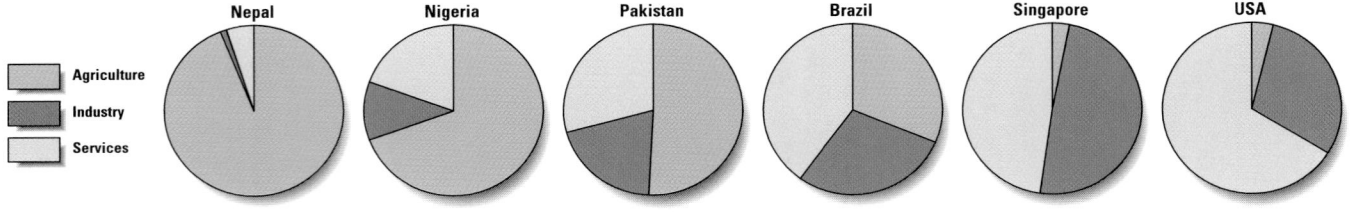

Nepal   Nigeria   Pakistan   Brazil   Singapore   USA

■ Agriculture
■ Industry
□ Services

Division of Employment

Distribution of workers between agriculture, industry and services, selected countries (latest available year)

The six countries selected illustrate the usual stages of economic development, from dependence on agriculture through industrial growth to the expansion of the service sector.

The Work Force

Percentages of men and women between 15 and 64 in employment, selected countries (latest available year)

The figures include employees and the self-employed, who in developing countries are often subsistence farmers. People in full-time education are excluded. Because of the population age structure in developing countries, the employed population has to support a far larger number of non-workers than its industrial equivalent. For example, more than 52% of Kenya's people are under 15, an age group that makes up less than a tenth of the UK population.

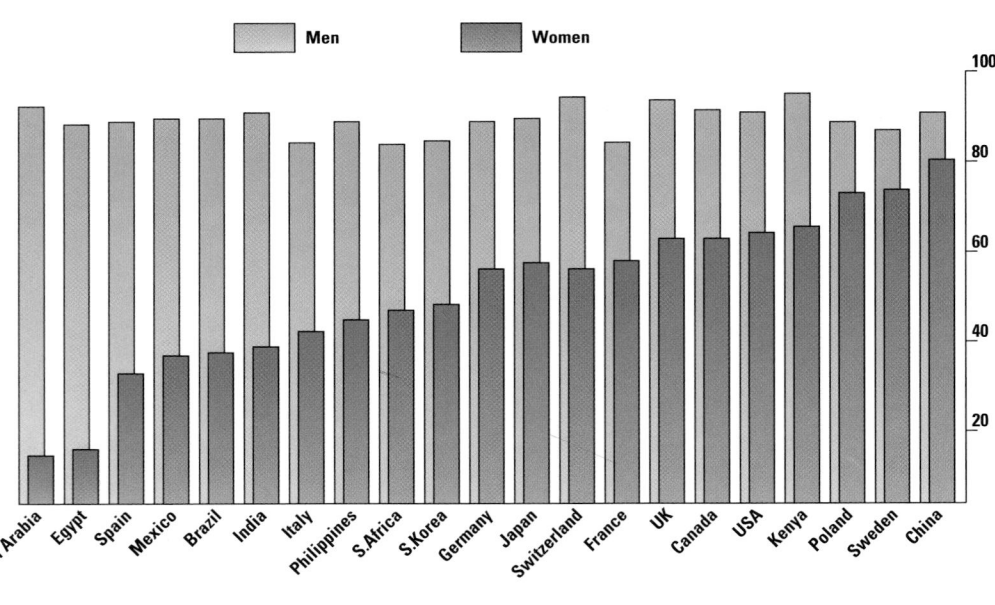

■ Men   ■ Women

Saudi Arabia, Egypt, Spain, Mexico, Brazil, India, Italy, Philippines, S.Africa, S.Korea, Germany, Japan, Switzerland, France, UK, Canada, USA, Kenya, Poland, Sweden, China

Wealth Creation

The Gross National Product (GNP) of the world's largest economies, US $ million (1997)

1.	USA	7,690,100	21.	Austria	225,900
2.	Japan	4,772,300	22.	Indonesia	221,900
3.	Germany	2,319,300	23.	Turkey	199,500
4.	France	1,526,400	24.	Denmark	171,400
5.	UK	1,220,200	25.	Thailand	169,600
6.	Italy	1,155,400	26.	Hong Kong	164,400
7.	China	1,055,400	27.	Norway	158,900
8.	Brazil	773,400	28.	Poland	138,900
9.	Canada	583,900	29.	South Africa	130,200
10.	Spain	570,100	30.	Saudi Arabia	128,900
11.	South Korea	485,200	31.	Greece	126,200
12.	Russia	403,500	32.	Finland	123,800
13.	Netherlands	402,700	33.	Portugal	103,900
14.	Australia	380,000	34.	Singapore	101,800
15.	India	373,900	35.	Malaysia	98,200
16.	Mexico	348,600	36.	Philippines	89,300
17.	Switzerland	313,500	37.	Israel	87,600
18.	Argentina	305,700	38.	Columbia	86,800
19.	Belgium	268,400	39.	Venezuela	78,700
20.	Sweden	232,000	40.	Chile	73,300

Patterns of Production

Breakdown of industrial output by value, selected countries (latest available year)

	Food & agric. products	Textiles & clothing	Machinery & transport	Chemicals	Other
Algeria	26%	20%	11%	1%	41%
Argentina	24%	10%	16%	12%	37%
Australia	18%	7%	21%	8%	45%
Austria	17%	8%	25%	6%	43%
Belgium	19%	8%	23%	13%	36%
Brazil	15%	12%	24%	9%	40%
Burkina Faso	62%	18%	2%	1%	17%
Canada	15%	7%	25%	9%	44%
Denmark	22%	6%	23%	10%	39%
Egypt	20%	27%	13%	10%	31%
Finland	13%	6%	24%	7%	50%
France	18%	7%	33%	9%	33%
Germany	12%	5%	38%	10%	36%
Greece	20%	22%	14%	7%	38%
Hungary	6%	11%	37%	11%	35%
India	11%	16%	26%	15%	32%
Indonesia	23%	11%	10%	10%	47%
Iran	13%	22%	22%	7%	36%
Israel	13%	10%	28%	8%	42%
Ireland	28%	7%	20%	15%	28%
Italy	7%	13%	32%	10%	38%
Japan	10%	6%	38%	10%	37%
Kenya	35%	12%	14%	9%	29%
Malaysia	21%	5%	23%	14%	37%
Mexico	24%	12%	14%	12%	39%
Netherlands	19%	4%	28%	11%	38%
New Zealand	26%	10%	16%	6%	43%
Norway	21%	3%	26%	7%	44%
Pakistan	34%	21%	8%	12%	25%
Philippines	40%	7%	7%	10%	35%
Poland	15%	16%	30%	6%	33%
Portugal	17%	22%	16%	8%	38%
Singapore	6%	5%	46%	8%	36%
South Africa	14%	8%	17%	11%	49%
South Korea	15%	17%	24%	9%	35%
Spain	17%	9%	22%	9%	43%
Sweden	10%	2%	35%	8%	44%
Thailand	30%	17%	14%	6%	33%
Turkey	20%	14%	15%	8%	43%
UK	14%	6%	32%	11%	36%
USA	12%	5%	35%	10%	38%
Venezuela	23%	8%	9%	11%	49%

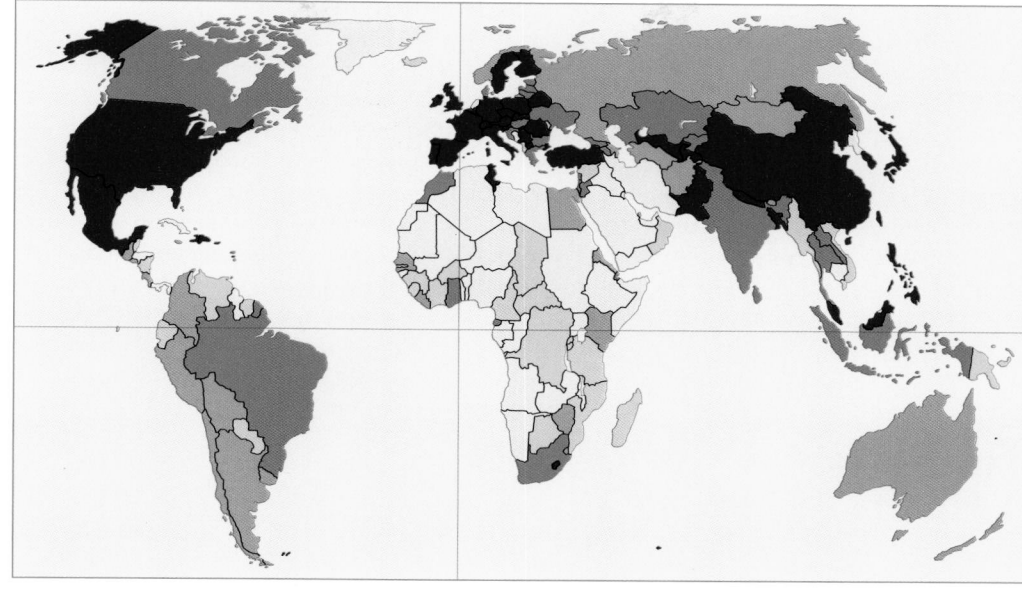

Industry and Trade

Manufactured goods (including machinery and transport) as a percentage of total exports (1996)

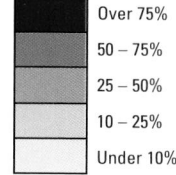

- Over 75%
- 50 – 75%
- 25 – 50%
- 10 – 25%
- Under 10%

The Far East and Southeast Asia (Japan 98%, Macau 96%, Taiwan 95%, Hong Kong [now part of China] 94%, South Korea 94%) are most dominant but many countries in Europe (e.g. Slovenia 93%) are also heavily dependent on manufactured goods.

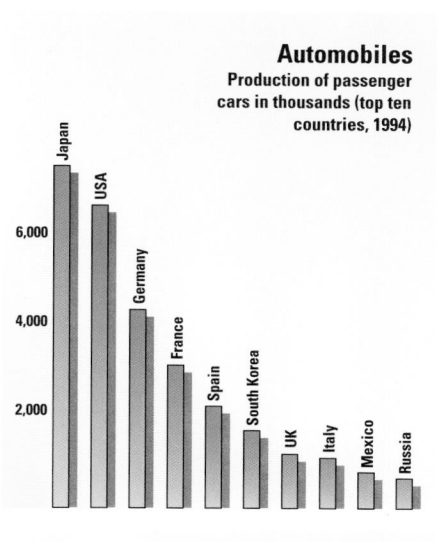

Automobiles
Production of passenger cars in thousands (top ten countries, 1994)

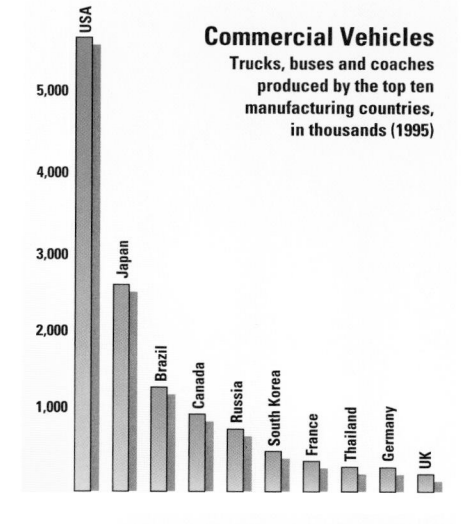

Commercial Vehicles
Trucks, buses and coaches produced by the top ten manufacturing countries, in thousands (1995)

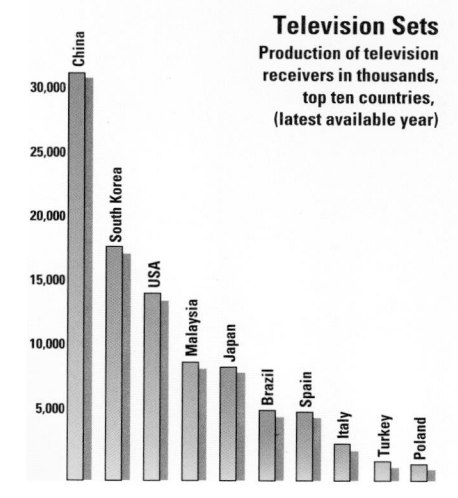

Television Sets
Production of television receivers in thousands, top ten countries, (latest available year)

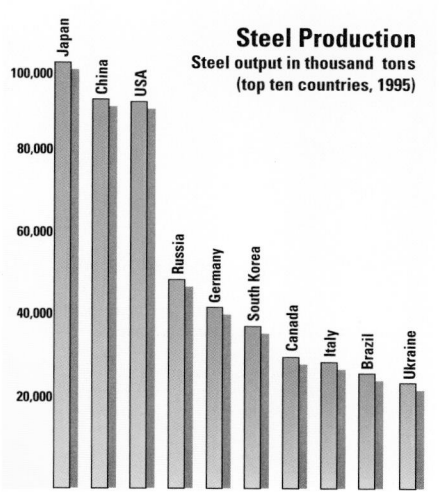

Steel Production
Steel output in thousand tons (top ten countries, 1995)

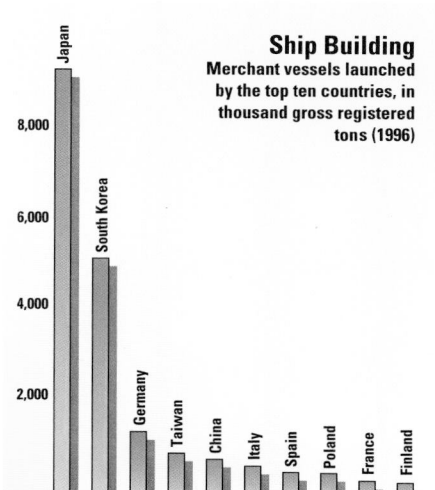

Ship Building
Merchant vessels launched by the top ten countries, in thousand gross registered tons (1996)

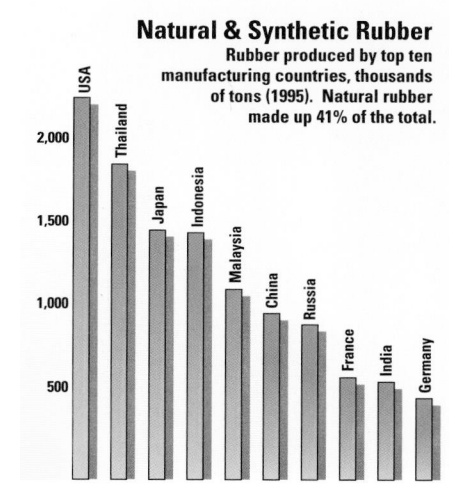

Natural & Synthetic Rubber
Rubber produced by top ten manufacturing countries, thousands of tons (1995). Natural rubber made up 41% of the total.

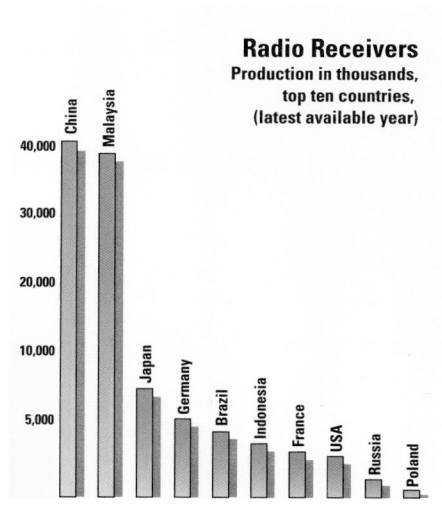

Radio Receivers
Production in thousands, top ten countries, (latest available year)

Industrial Output

Industrial output (mining, manufacturing, construction, energy, and water production), US $ billion (1995)

1.	Japan	1,941	21.	Sweden	73
2.	USA	1,808	22.	Saudi Arabia	67
3.	Germany	780	=	Thailand	67
4.	France	415	24.	Mexico	65
5.	UK	354	25.	Turkey	51
6.	Italy	337	26.	Denmark	50
7.	China	335	27.	Finland	46
8.	Brazil	255	=	Poland	46
9.	South Korea	196	29.	Norway	44
10.	Spain	187	30.	Malaysia	37
11.	Canada	174	=	Portugal	37
12.	Russia	131	32.	Ukraine	34
13.	Netherlands	107	33.	Greece	33
14.	Australia	98	34.	Singapore	30
15.	Switzerland	96	35.	Venezuela	29
16.	India	94	=	Israel	29
17.	Argentina	87	37.	Chile	24
18.	Belgium	83	=	Colombia	24
=	Indonesia	83	=	Hong Kong	24
20.	Austria	79	=	Philippines	24

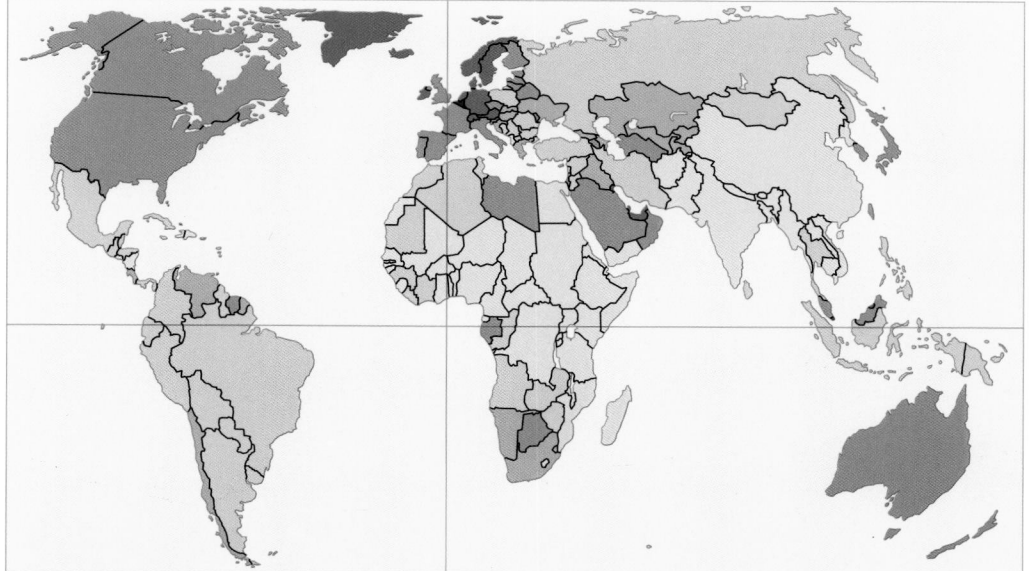

Exports Per Capita

Value of exports in US $, divided by total population (latest available year)

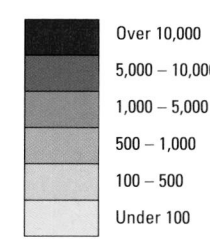

- Over 10,000
- 5,000 – 10,000
- 1,000 – 5,000
- 500 – 1,000
- 100 – 500
- Under 100

[UK 3,135] [USA 1,967]

Highest per capita exports (1993)

Singapore	25,787
Hong Kong	22,339
Benelux	12,295
Brunei	8,778
Netherlands	8,578
Switzerland	8,457

Trade

Trade played a vital role in the growth of early civilizations and it was later a spur to European exploration and colonization. The colonial powers grew rich by exporting cheap manufactures, such as clothing and footwear, while obtaining primary products from their colonies.

From the late 19th century to the early 1950s, as transport technology improved, primary products, especially oil in the later stages of this period, dominated world trade. However, since that time, manufactures have become the chief commodities in world trade, which is dominated by the industrialized countries. Nearly half of all world trade flows between the developed market economies of the European Union, the United States and Japan, although the Asian "tiger economies," notably Singapore, South Korea, Taiwan, Malaysia and Thailand, have increased their share in recent years. Recent predictions suggest that the next "tigers" might include Argentina and Chile in South America, Indonesia, the Philippines and Vietnam in Asia, and the Czech Republic and Poland in Europe.

There is little trade between developing countries, although some mineral- and oil-rich nations obtain a high proportion of their GNP from export sales. Growth in world trade is regarded as a sign of economic health, as is a favorable balance of trade (or trade surplus) in any country.

World Trade

Percentage share of total world exports by value (1996)

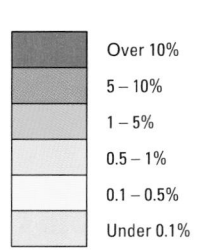

- Over 10%
- 5 – 10%
- 1 – 5%
- 0.5 – 1%
- 0.1 – 0.5%
- Under 0.1%

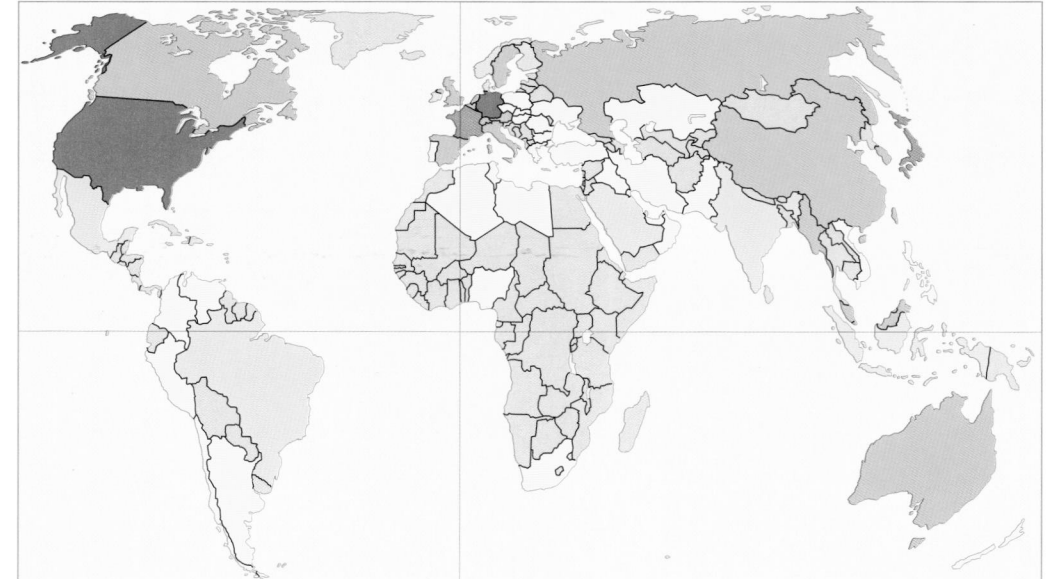

The Main Trading Nations

The imports and exports of the top ten trading nations as a percentage of world trade (1994). Each country's trade in manufactured goods is shown in dark blue. The graph shows that, in 1994, virtually all of Japan's imports and exports were manufactured goods.

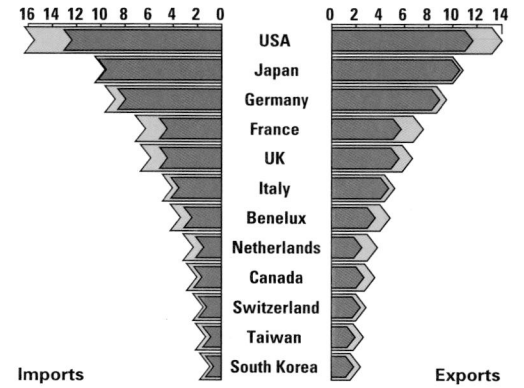

Imports — USA, Japan, Germany, France, UK, Italy, Benelux, Netherlands, Canada, Switzerland, Taiwan, South Korea — Exports

Dependence on Trade

Value of exports as a percentage of Gross Domestic Product (1997)

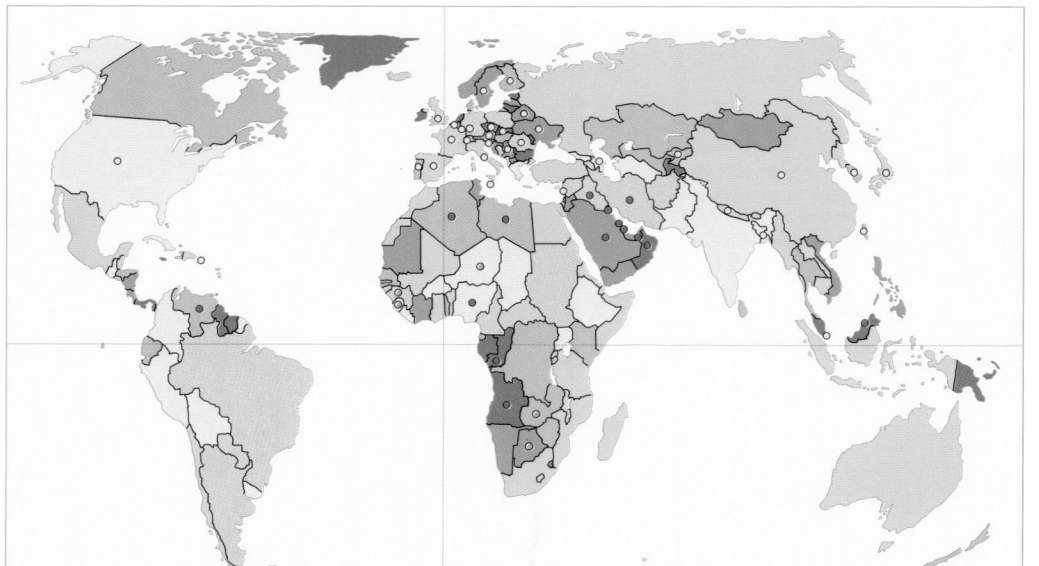

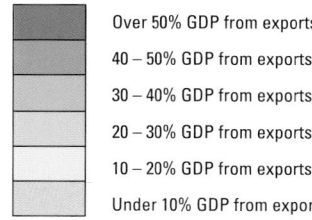

- Over 50% GDP from exports
- 40 – 50% GDP from exports
- 30 – 40% GDP from exports
- 20 – 30% GDP from exports
- 10 – 20% GDP from exports
- Under 10% GDP from exports

- ○ Most dependent on industrial exports (over 75% of total exports)
- ● Most dependent on fuel exports (over 75% of total exports)
- ◍ Most dependent on metal and mineral exports (over 75% of total exports)

Major Exports

Leading manufactured items and their exporters, by percentage of world total in US $ (latest available year)

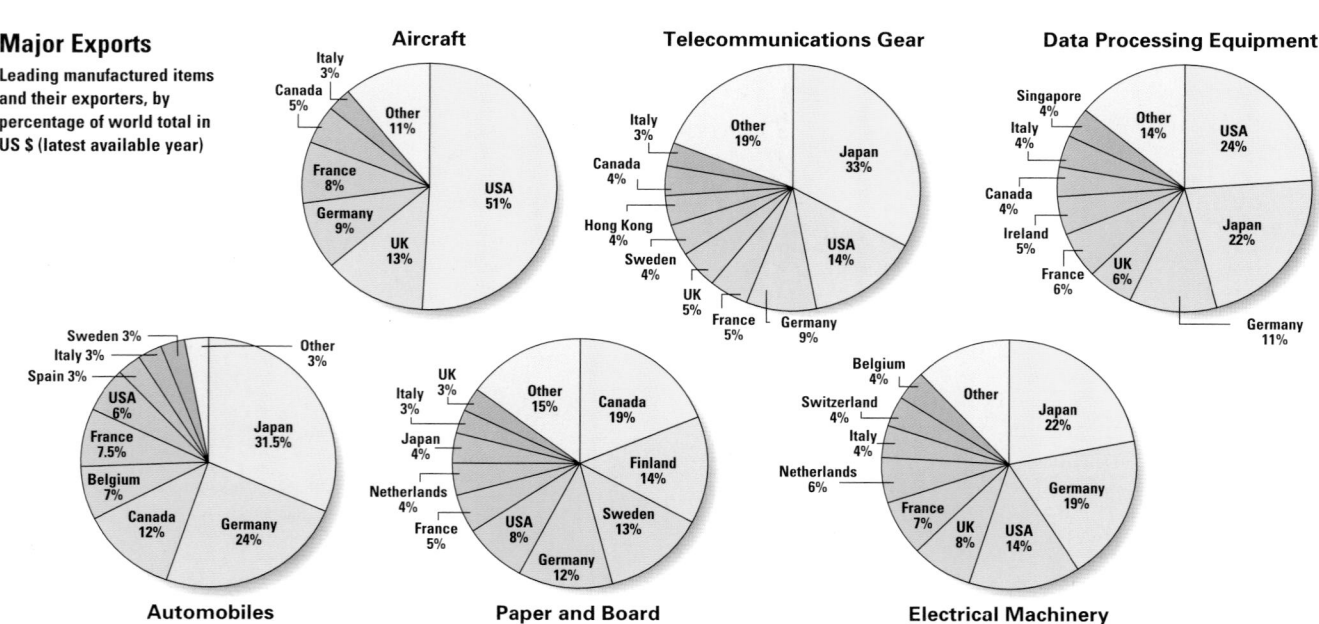

Aircraft
USA 51%, UK 13%, Germany 9%, France 8%, Canada 5%, Italy 3%, Other 11%

Telecommunications Gear
Japan 33%, USA 14%, Germany 9%, France 5%, UK 5%, Sweden 4%, Hong Kong 4%, Canada 4%, Italy 3%, Other 19%

Data Processing Equipment
USA 24%, Japan 22%, Germany 11%, UK 6%, France 6%, Ireland 5%, Canada 4%, Italy 4%, Singapore 4%, Other 14%

Automobiles
Japan 31.5%, Germany 24%, Canada 12%, Belgium 7%, France 7.5%, USA 6%, Spain 3%, Italy 3%, Sweden 3%, Other 3%

Paper and Board
Canada 19%, Finland 14%, Sweden 13%, Germany 12%, USA 8%, France 5%, Netherlands 4%, Japan 4%, Italy 3%, UK 3%, Other 15%

Electrical Machinery
Japan 22%, Germany 19%, USA 14%, UK 8%, France 7%, Netherlands 6%, Italy 4%, Switzerland 4%, Belgium 4%, Other

Traded Products

Top ten manufactures traded, by value in billions of US $ (latest available year)

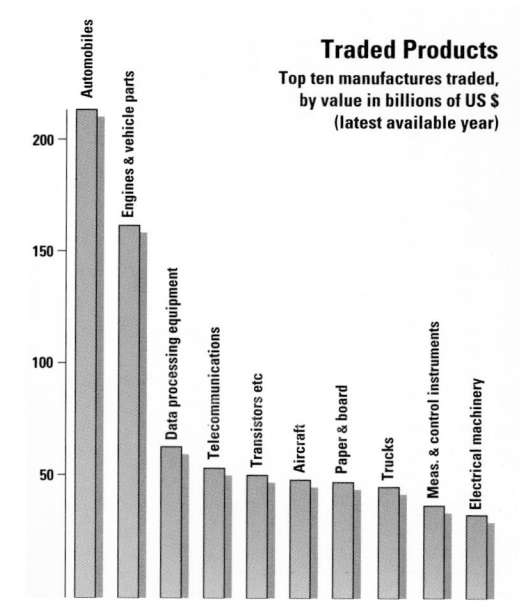

Automobiles, Engines & vehicle parts, Data processing equipment, Telecommunications, Transistors etc, Aircraft, Paper & board, Trucks, Meas. & control instruments, Electrical machinery

CARTOGRAPHY BY PHILIP'S. COPYRIGHT GEORGE PHILIP LTD

World Shipping

While ocean passenger traffic is nowadays relatively modest, sea transport still carries most of the world's trade. Oil and bulk carriers make up the majority of the world fleet, although the general cargo category is the fastest growing. Two innovations have revolutionized sea transport. The first is the development of the roll-on/roll-off (Ro-Ro) method where lorries or even trains loaded with freight are driven straight on to the ship, thus saving time. The second is containerization in which goods are packed into containers (the dimensions of which are fixed) at the factory, driven to the port and loaded on board by specialist machinery.

Almost 30% of world shipping sails under a "flag of convenience," whereby owners take advantage of low taxes by registering their vessels in a foreign country the ships will never see, notably Panama and Liberia.

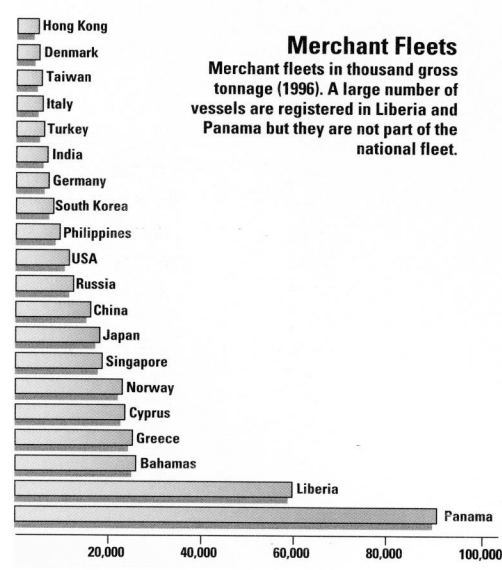

Merchant Fleets

Merchant fleets in thousand gross tonnage (1996). A large number of vessels are registered in Liberia and Panama but they are not part of the national fleet.

Hong Kong
Denmark
Taiwan
Italy
Turkey
India
Germany
South Korea
Philippines
USA
Russia
China
Japan
Singapore
Norway
Cyprus
Greece
Bahamas
Liberia
Panama

20,000　40,000　60,000　80,000　100,000

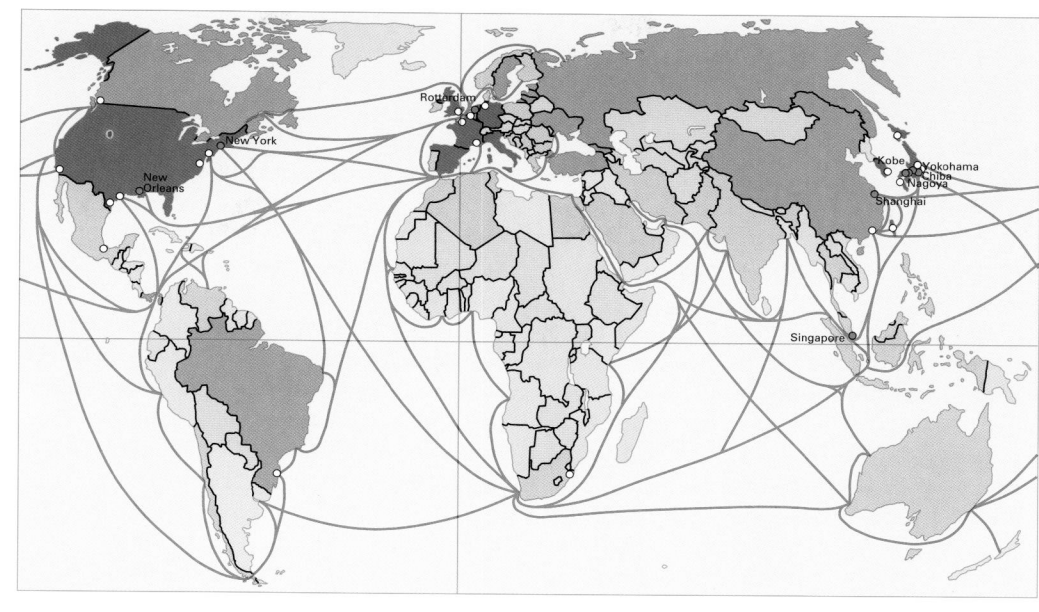

Freight

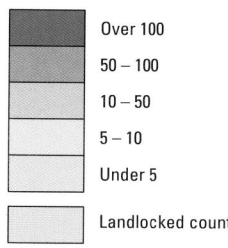

Freight unloaded in millions of tons (latest available year)

Over 100
50 – 100
10 – 50
5 – 10
Under 5
Landlocked countries

Major seaports

Over 100 million tons per year
50 – 100 million tons per year
major shipping routes

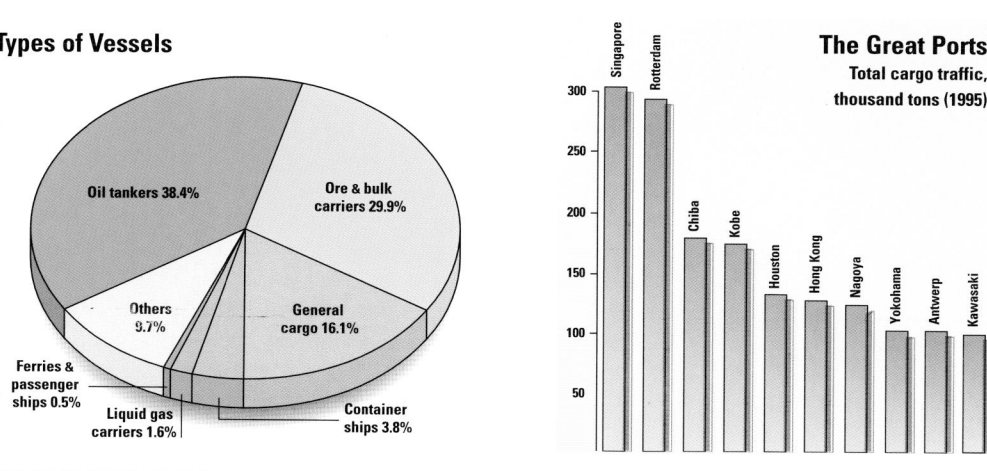

Types of Vessels

Oil tankers 38.4%
Ore & bulk carriers 29.9%
Others 9.7%
General cargo 16.1%
Ferries & passenger ships 0.5%
Liquid gas carriers 1.6%
Container ships 3.8%

The Great Ports

Total cargo traffic, thousand tons (1995)

Singapore
Rotterdam
Chiba
Kobe
Houston
Hong Kong
Nagoya
Yokohama
Antwerp
Kawasaki

300
250
200
150
100
50

Trade in Primary Products

Primary products (excluding fuels, minerals and metals) as a percentage of total export value (latest available year)

Over 75%
50 – 75%
25 – 50%
10 – 25%
Under 10%

Primary products are raw materials or partly processed products which form the basis for manufacturing. They are the necessary requirements of industries and include agricultural products, minerals and timber, as well as many semimanufactured goods such as cotton, which has been spun but not woven, wood pulp or flour. Many developed countries have few natural resources and rely on imports for the majority of their primary products. The countries of Southeast Asia export hardwoods to the rest of the world, whilst many South American countries are heavily dependent on coffee exports.

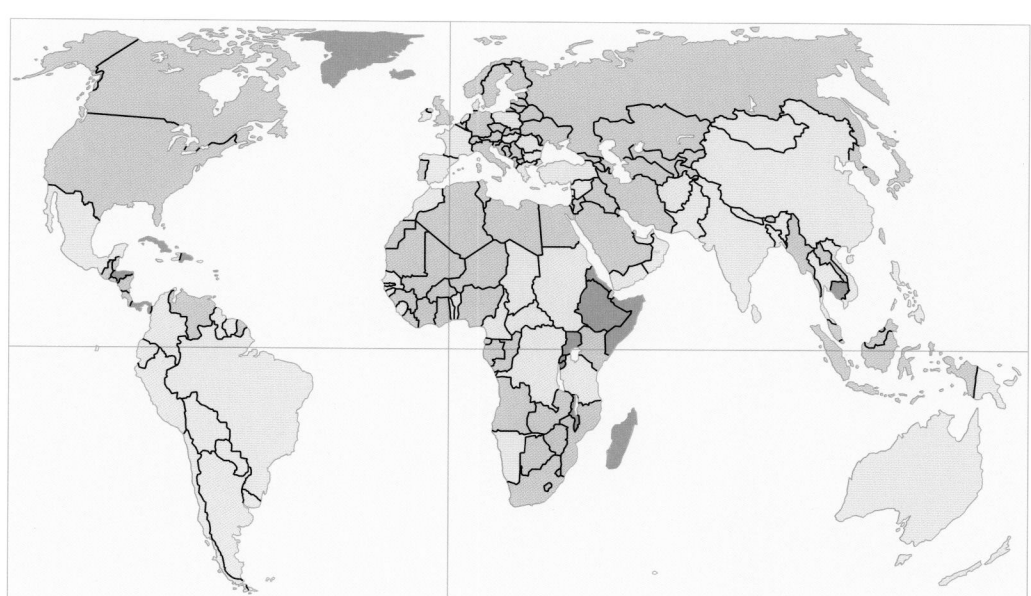

Balance of Trade

Value of exports in proportion to the value of imports (1995)

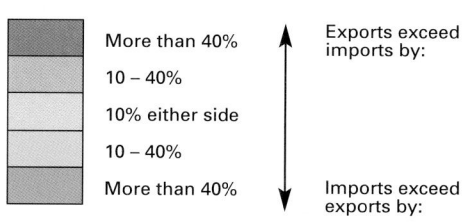

More than 40%
10 – 40%
10% either side
10 – 40%
More than 40%

Exports exceed imports by:

Imports exceed exports by:

The total world trade balance should amount to zero, since exports must equal imports on a global scale. In practice, at least $100 billion in exports go unrecorded, leaving the world with an apparent deficit and many countries in a better position than public accounting reveals. However, a favorable trade balance is not necessarily a sign of prosperity: many poorer countries must maintain a high surplus in order to service debts, and do so by restricting imports below the levels needed to sustain successful economies.

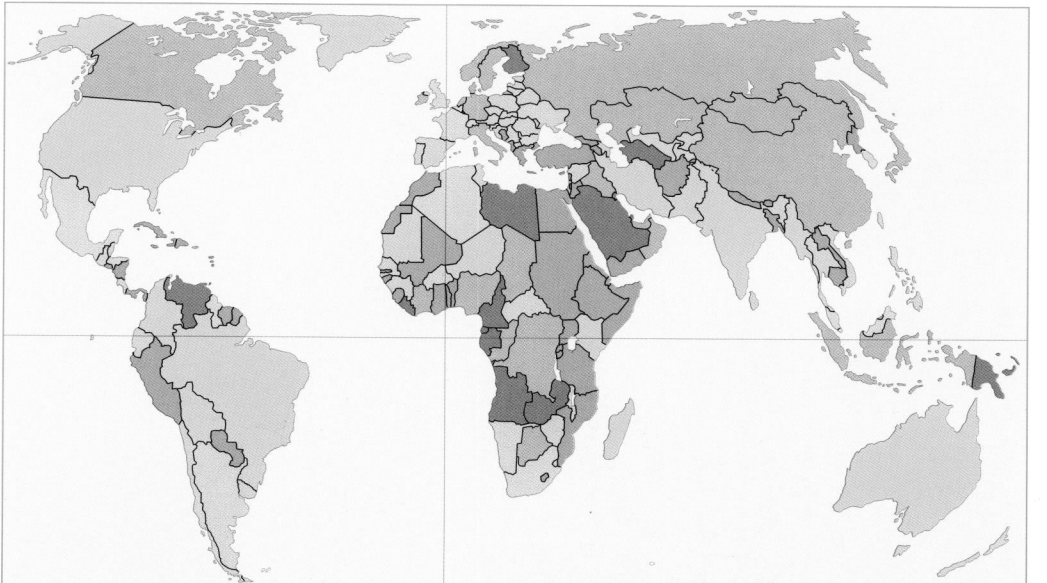

Air Freight

Trends in air freight in million ton-km*, selected countries (1988–92)

20,000
15,000
10,000
5,000

1988　1989　1990　1991　1992

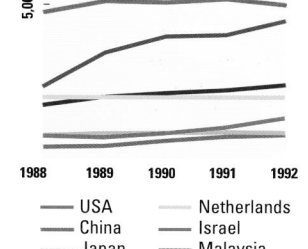

USA
China
Japan
UK
Netherlands
Israel
Malaysia

* Equivalent to million tons of air freight flown over 1 million km [650,000 miles] per year.

Air transport is important to countries of considerable size; where ground terrain is difficult; when crossing short stretches of sea; and where goods are of high value, light in weight or perishable. Recent deregulation of airlines (in the USA since 1978 and the EU in 1993) has led to increased competition and lower fares.

Health

Average life expectancies all over the world have never been higher. They range from an average of 77 years in high-income economies, to 67 years in middle-income economies and 63 in low-income economies. Even in poverty-stricken and strife-torn Burundi and Ethiopia, average life expectancies are around 50 years, as compared with less than 30 years for a citizen of Berlin in 1880.

In global terms, the radical improvements in health have much to do with improvements in agriculture and, hence, nutrition, as well as health education, an increase in sanitation and the quality of drinking water, together with advances in medicine. These radical changes have been responsible for falling death rates and rapid population growth, together with the expectation by most people that improvements in health will continue.

Health standards, life expectancies and causes of death vary considerably between the developed and developing world. The map on this page shows that in most of Africa, Asia and Latin America, the average daily calorie supply per person is so low as to cause malnutrition. (The daily requirement rated adequate by the World Health Organization is between 2,300 and 2,500 calories per person per day.) Malnutrition is a serious condition.

For example, among pregnant women it causes high rates of child mortality.

Deficiency diseases occur when people do not have a balanced diet. Protein deficiency causes stunting and kwashiorkor, which can be fatal, especially among young children, while vitamin deficiencies cause such illnesses as beri beri, pellagra, scurvy and rickets. Iron deficiency causes anemia, while a lack of iodine causes mental retardation. A UN report in the early 1990s reported that iodine deficiency affected 458 million women world-wide, as compared with 238 million men. Women's nutritional problems are especially acute in southern Asia. For example, the UN report stated that 88% of pregnant women in India were anemic, as compared with 15% in developed countries.

Infectious diseases in association, directly or indirectly, with deficient diets, continue to affect people in developing countries, especially the 48 countries in the low human development category, where, in 1990–95, only 32% of the people had access to sanitation and 68% to safe water supplies.

A World Health report in 1996 stated that infectious diseases cause 17 million deaths per year. Most of the victims are young and otherwise fit people in developing countries. The major killers in 1995 were respiratory infections, including pneumonia (which caused

4.4 million deaths), cholera, typhoid, dysentery (3.1 million together), tuberculosis (almost 3 million), malaria (2.1 million), hepatitis B (1.1 million), AIDS and measles (more than 1 million each). Many of these diseases are preventable and, according to the United Nations Children's Fund, an investment of US $25,000 million per year, about half the money spent annually on cigarettes in Europe alone, would save the lives of all the children who currently die from avoidable diseases.

Infectious diseases are much less important as causes of death in developed countries, where cancer and circulatory diseases, such as atherosclerosis and hypertension, which cause strokes and heart attacks, are the most common causes of fatality. Because these diseases tend to kill older people, they are relatively less important in developing countries where people have shorter lifespans.

Harmful habits are also generally practised more by the rich than the poor. For example, smoking is an important cause of death in developed countries, though, curiously, the Japanese, with an average life expectancy of 79 years in 1996, are among the highest tobacco consumers. Similarly, high alcohol consumption, although it has bad effects on health, does not seem to affect longevity. The leading consumers, the French, had a life expectancy of 78 in 1996.

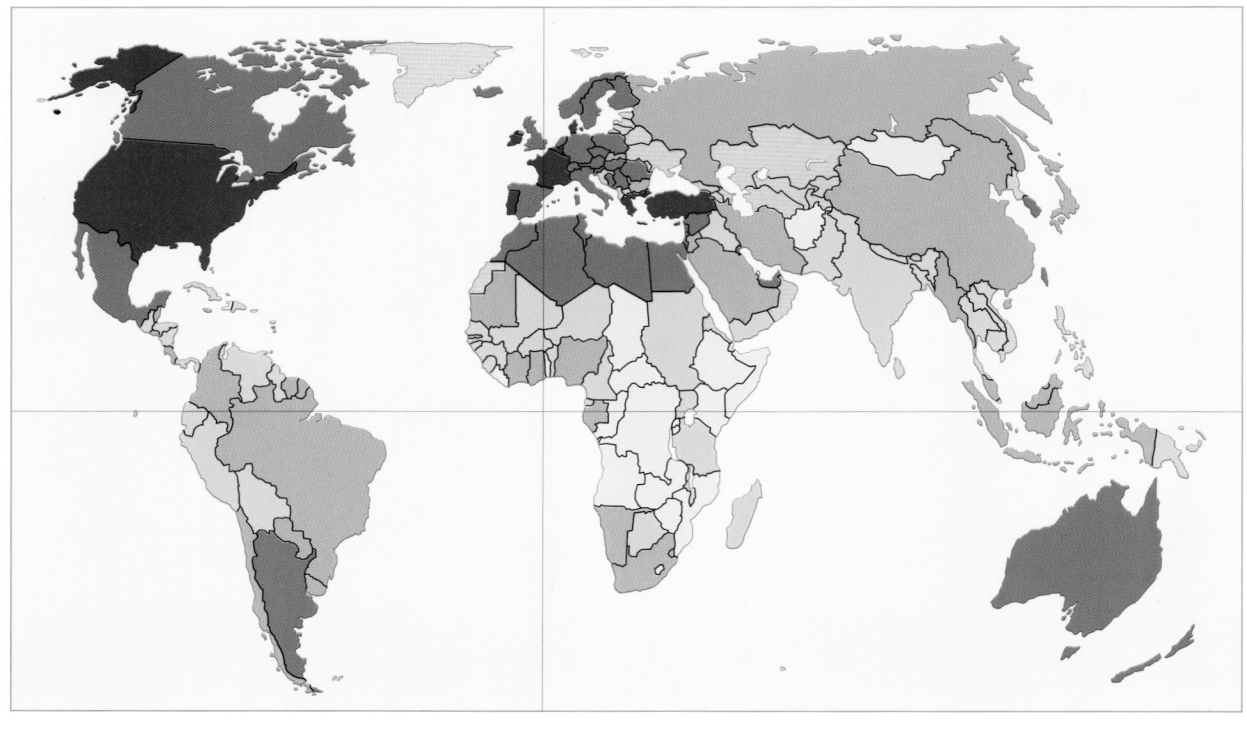

Food Consumption

Average daily food intake in calories per person (1995)

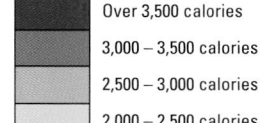

- Over 3,500 calories
- 3,000 – 3,500 calories
- 2,500 – 3,000 calories
- 2,000 – 2,500 calories
- Under 2,000 calories
- No available data

Top 5 countries

Cyprus	3,708 calories
Denmark	3,704 calories
Portugal	3,639 calories
Ireland	3,638 calories
USA	3,603 calories

Bottom 5 countries

Congo (D. Rep.)	1,879 calories
Djibouti	1,831 calories
Togo	1,754 calories
Burundi	1,749 calories
Mozambique	1,678 calories

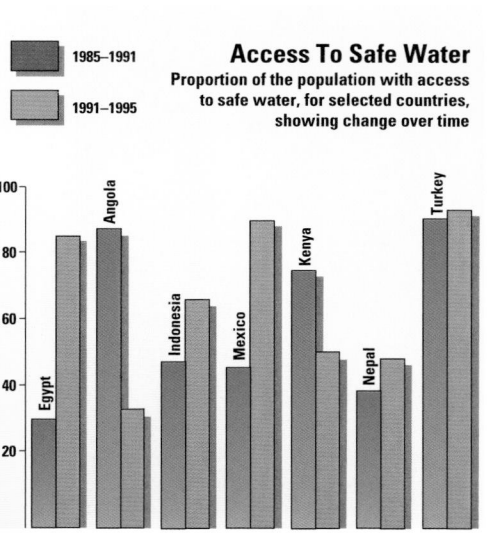

Access To Safe Water
Proportion of the population with access to safe water, for selected countries, showing change over time

1985–1991
1991–1995

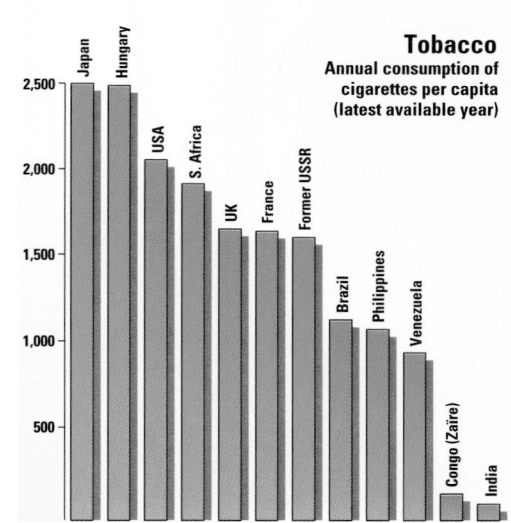

Tobacco
Annual consumption of cigarettes per capita (latest available year)

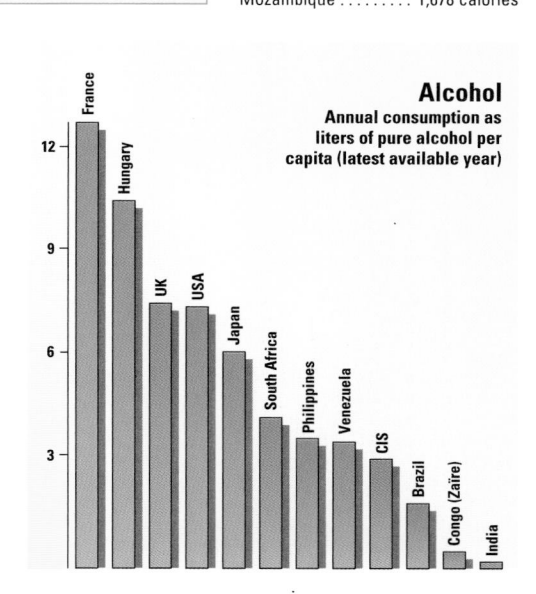

Alcohol
Annual consumption as liters of pure alcohol per capita (latest available year)

Life Expectancy

Years of life expectancy at birth, selected countries (1997)

The chart shows combined data for both sexes. On average, women live longer than men worldwide, even in developing countries with high maternal mortality rates. Overall, life expectancy is steadily rising, though the difference between rich and poor nations remains dramatic.

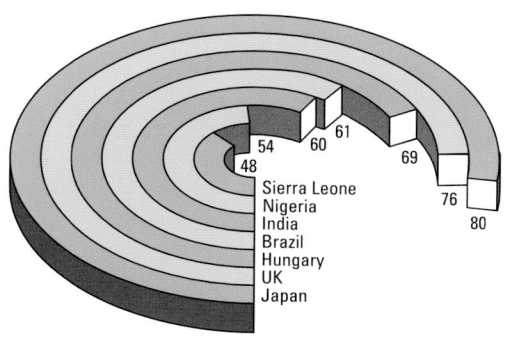

48	Sierra Leone
54	Nigeria
60	India
61	Brazil
69	Hungary
76	UK
80	Japan

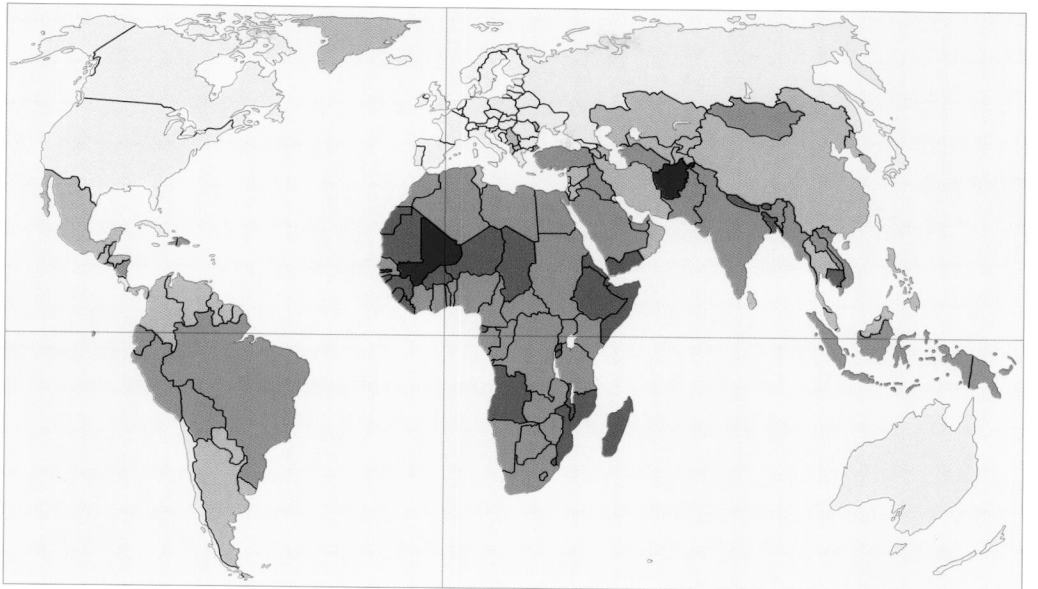

Child Mortality

Number of babies who will die under the age of one, per 1,000 births (average 1990–95)

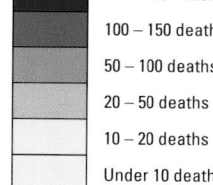

- Over 150 deaths
- 100 – 150 deaths
- 50 – 100 deaths
- 20 – 50 deaths
- 10 – 20 deaths
- Under 10 deaths

Highest child mortality

Afghanistan .... 162 deaths
Mali .... 159 deaths

Lowest child mortality

Iceland .... 5 deaths
Finland .... 5 deaths

[UK 8 deaths] [USA 8 deaths]

Expenditure on Health

Public expenditure on health as a percentage of GNP (1996)

Countries with the highest spending		Countries with the lowest spending	
USA	14.2	Sudan	0.3
Argentina	10.6	Cameroon	1.4
Germany	10.4	Ghana	1.4
Croatia	10.1	Nigeria	1.4
Switzerland	10.0	Indonesia	1.8
France	9.9	Sri Lanka	1.9
Canada	9.6	Eritrea	2.0
Czech Rep.	9.6	Bangladesh	2.4
Australia	8.9	Kenya	2.5

The allocation of limited funds for health care in developing countries is rarely evenly spread – the quality of treatment can vary enormously from place to place within the same country. Urban dwellers tend to have much better access to health provisions than those living in rural areas.

Medical Provision

Doctors per 100,000 population, selected countries (latest available year, 1996)

Although the ratio of people to doctors gives a good approximation of a country's health provision, it is not an absolute indicator. Raw numbers may mask inefficiency and other weaknesses: the high proportion of physicians in Hungary, for example, has not prevented infant mortality rates more than twice as high as in the United Kingdom.

The definition of a doctor also varies from nation to nation. As well as registered medical practitioners, it may include trained medical assistants – an especially important category in developing countries, where they provide many of the same services as fully qualified physicians, including simple operations.

Ghana 4
Indonesia 15
Brazil 147
UK 156
Venezuela 160
Egypt 211
Australia 250
USA 274
France 277
Latvia 303
Hungary 366
Italy 518

| 500 | 400 | 300 | 200 | 100 |

The Aids Crisis

The Acquired Immune Deficiency Syndrome (AIDS) was first identified in 1981 when American doctors found otherwise healthy young men succumbing to rare infections. By 1984 the cause had been traced to the Human Immunodeficiency Virus (HIV) which can remain dormant for many years and perhaps indefinitely: only half of those known to carry the virus in 1981 had developed AIDS ten years later.

In Western countries in the mid-1990s, most AIDS deaths were among male homosexuals or needle-sharing drug-users. However, the disease is spreading fastest among heterosexual men and women, which is its usual vector in the developing world where most of its victims live.

The World Health Organization estimated that 1.3 million people died of AIDS in 1995 and that by the end of the same year 22 million people were HIV-positive. India has the largest number of HIV infections totaling more than 3 million, but two-thirds of all infections are in sub-Saharan Africa (where, unlike the rest of the world, more women are infected than men). It was estimated that 2 million African children would die of AIDS before the year 2000 and some 10 million would be orphaned.

Causes of Death

- Accidents, poisoning & violence
- Respiratory & digestive diseases
- Nervous & circulatory diseases
- Metabolic disorders
- Cancers
- Infectious & parasitic diseases

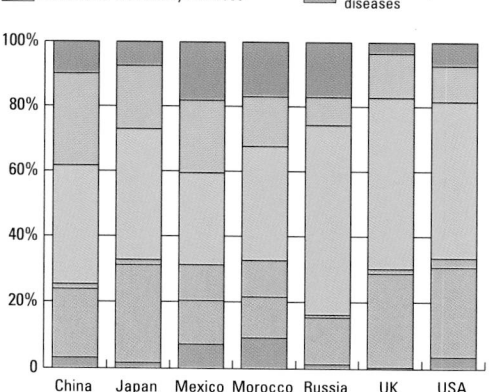

China Japan Mexico Morocco Russia UK USA

Circulatory Disease in Europe

Diseases of the circulatory system per 100,000 people (latest available year 1992–95)

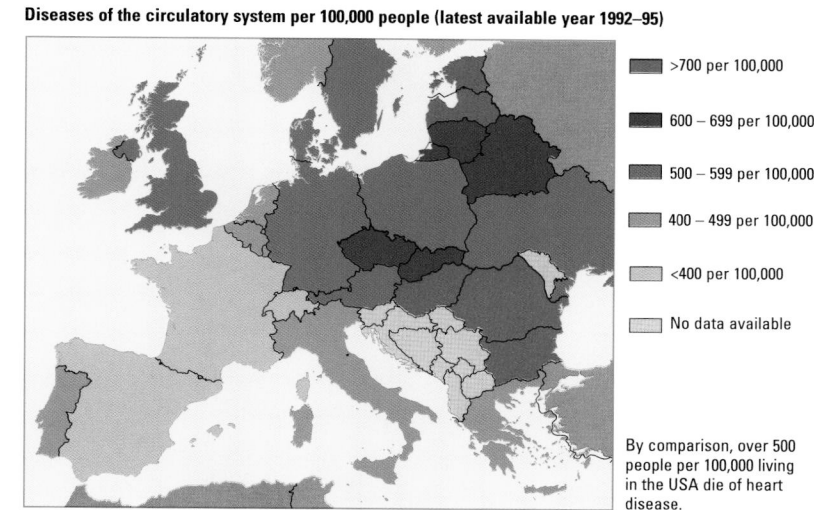

- >700 per 100,000
- 600 – 699 per 100,000
- 500 – 599 per 100,000
- 400 – 499 per 100,000
- <400 per 100,000
- No data available

By comparison, over 500 people per 100,000 living in the USA die of heart disease.

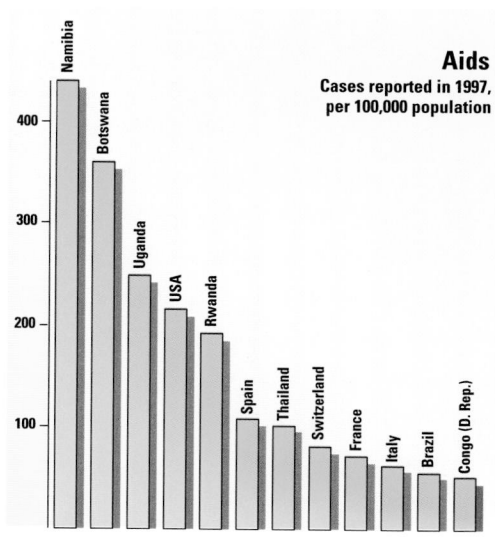

Aids

Cases reported in 1997, per 100,000 population

Namibia, Botswana, Uganda, USA, Rwanda, Spain, Thailand, Switzerland, France, Italy, Brazil, Congo (D. Rep.)

Sanitation

- Urban
- Rural

Percentage of the population with access to sanitation services, selected countries (latest available year)

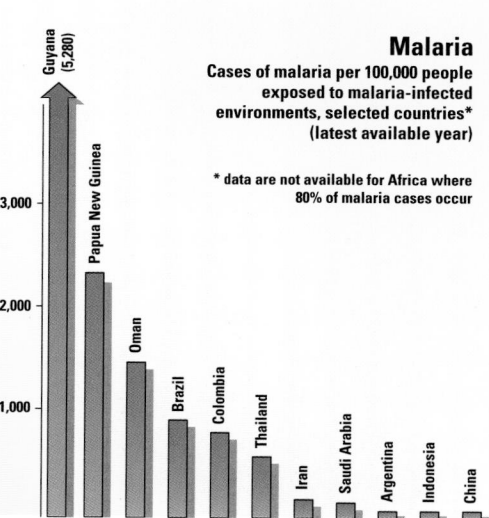

China, Kuwait, Botswana, Zimbabwe, Iran, Syria, Colombia, Mexico, Papua New Guinea, Pakistan, Nepal

Malaria

Cases of malaria per 100,000 people exposed to malaria-infected environments, selected countries* (latest available year)

* data are not available for Africa where 80% of malaria cases occur

Guyana (5,280), Papua New Guinea, Oman, Brazil, Colombia, Thailand, Iran, Saudi Arabia, Argentina, Indonesia, China

Infectious and parasitic diseases, such as malaria, which claimed 2.1 million lives in 1995, remain a scourge in the developing countries. Respiratory infections and injury also claim more lives in developing countries, which lack the drugs and the medical personnel to deal with them. Developing countries lack the basic services taken for granted in developed nations. For example, in sub-Saharan Africa in 1990–95, only 31% of the population had access to sanitation and 45% to safe water, with the situation being worse in rural areas. By contrast, circulatory diseases and cancer are the main causes of death in the rich, industrialized countries. For example, in the UK in the mid-1990s, circulatory diseases, which cause heart attacks and strokes, accounted for nearly half the deaths, with cancer accounting for nearly a quarter.

Wealth

Perhaps the most glaring differences in the world today are those between the rich and the poor. The World Bank divides countries into three main groups based on average economic production expressed in terms of per capita GNP (Gross National Product). They are the low-income economies, including most African countries and much of Asia; the middle-income economies, including most of Latin America and most of the former USSR; and the high-income economies of Canada, the United States, Western Europe, Japan and Australia.

Per capita GNPs are a measure of the total goods and services produced by a country divided by the population, and then converted into US dollars at official exchange rates. They are useful indicators of a country's prosperity, though, like all statistics, they must be treated with care. For example, the prices for goods and services in China are far cheaper than they are in the United States. China's per capita GNP in 1997 was $860 (as compared with $28,740 in the USA) but the PPP (Purchasing-Power Parity) estimate of China's per capita GNP was considerably higher at $3,570. Another problem with per capita GNPs is that they are averages, which often conceal wide internal variations.

The pattern of poverty varies from region to region. In Latin America, much progress has been made through industrialization, though startling inequalities still exist between rich and poor. In Asia, the "tiger economies" have followed Japan's example in pursuing export-led industrial policies, while the success of China's Special Economic Zones, where foreign investment is encouraged, has led to a huge rise in China's per capita GNP, as shown on the map on page 45, bottom right.

Solutions to poverty in Africa are much harder to find because of its high population growth, civil wars, natural disasters and high inflation rates. Although Africa receives more aid than any other continent, aid is only a partial solution. Much aid has been wasted on overambitious projects, in the servicing of huge national debts, or lost by inexperienced or corrupt governments. One initiative in some African countries has been to improve the infrastructure and develop tourism, creating employment and providing much-needed foreign currency. But tourism alone cannot solve the problems of underdevelopment.

The International Monetary Fund and the World Bank argue that real economic progress in Africa will be achieved only when African countries create market-friendly economies that encourage trade through export-led manufacturing, while at the same time strictly controlling public spending on welfare, the civil service and other areas.

Currencies

Currency units of the world's most powerful economies

1. USA: US dollar ($, US $) = 100 cents
2. Japan: Yen (Y, ¥) = 100 sen
3. Germany: Euro; Deutsche Mark (DM)= 100 Pfennig
4. France: Euro; French franc (Fr) = 100 centimes
5. Italy: Euro; Italian lira (L, £, Lit) = 100 centesimi
6. UK: Pound sterling (£) = 100 pence
7. Canada: Canadian dollar (C$, Can$) = 100 cents
8. China: Renminbi yuan (RMBY, $, Y) = 10 jiao = 100 fen
9. Brazil: Cruzeiro real (BRC) = 100 centavos
10. Spain: Euro; Peseta (Pta, Pa) = 100 céntimos
11. India: Indian rupee (Re, Rs) = 100 paisa
12. Australia: Australian dollar ($A) = 100 cents
13. Netherlands: Euro; Guilder, florin (Gld, f) = 100 centimes
14. Switzerland: Swiss franc (SFr, SwF) = 100 centimes
15. South Korea: Won (W) = 100 chon
16. Sweden: Swedish krona (SKr) = 100 öre
17. Mexico: Mexican peso (Mex$) = 100 centavos
18. Belgium: Euro; Belgian franc (BFr) = 100 centimes
19. Austria: Euro; Schilling (S, Sch) = 100 Groschen
20. Finland: Euro; Markka (FMk) = 100 penniä
21. Denmark: Danish krone (DKr) = 100 øre
22. Norway: Norwegian krone (NKr) = 100 øre
23. Saudi Arabia: Riyal (SAR, SRl$) = 100 halalah
24. Indonesia: Rupiah (Rp) = 100 sen
25. South Africa: Rand (R) = 100 cents

Continental Shares

Shares of population and of wealth (GNP) by continent

These generalized continental figures show the startling difference between rich and poor but mask the successes or failures of individual countries. Japan, for example, with less than 4% of Asia's population, produces almost 70% of the continent's output. Within countries, the difference between rich and poor can also be startling. In Brazil, for example, the richest 20% of the population own 60% of the wealth.

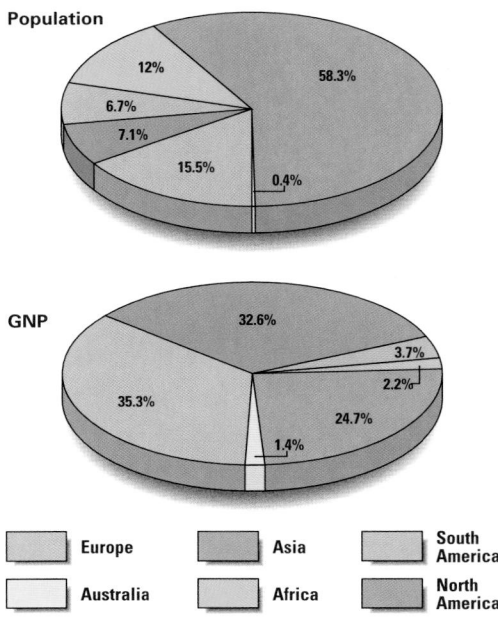

Population

GNP

| Europe | Asia | South America |
| Australia | Africa | North America |

Indicators

The gap between the world's rich and poor is now so great that it is difficult to illustrate on a single graph. Within each income group (as defined by the World Bank), however, comparisons have some meaning; the Chinese, perhaps because of propaganda value, have more TV sets than Indians, whereas Nigerians prefer to spend their money on radios. However, the wealth gap in many developing countries is wide, with a small, rich class and a large, impoverished majority, while many high-income countries contain an underclass of unemployed and homeless people.

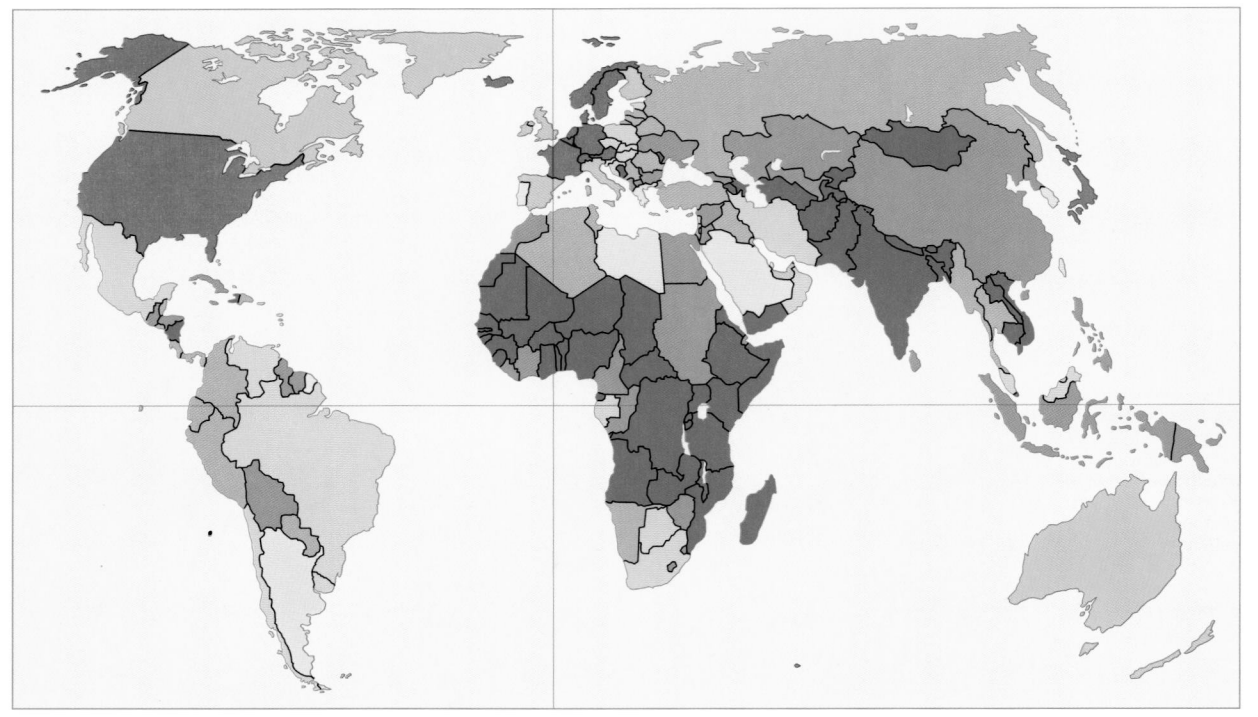

Levels of Income

Gross National Product per capita: the value of total production divided by the population (1997)

- Over 400% of world average
- 200 – 400%
- 100 – 200%
  [World average wealth per person US $6,316]
- 50 – 100%
- 25 – 50%
- 10 – 25%
- Under 10%

Top 5 countries

Luxembourg	$45,360
Switzerland	$44,220
Japan	$37,850
Norway	$36,090
Liechtenstein	$33,000

Bottom 5 countries

Mozambique	$90
Ethiopia	$110
Congo (Dem. Rep.)	$110
Burundi	$180
Sierra Leone	$200

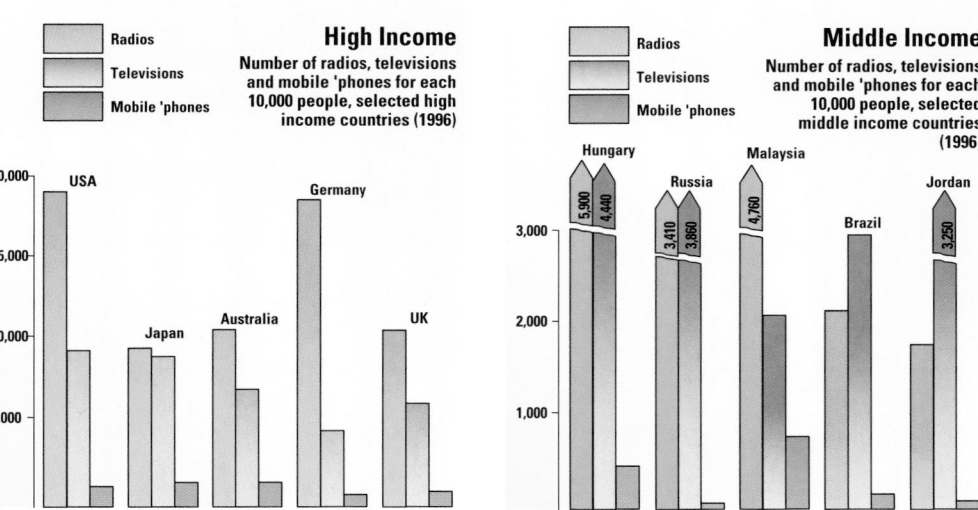

High Income

Number of radios, televisions and mobile 'phones for each 10,000 people, selected high income countries (1996)

Middle Income

Number of radios, televisions and mobile 'phones for each 10,000 people, selected middle income countries (1996)

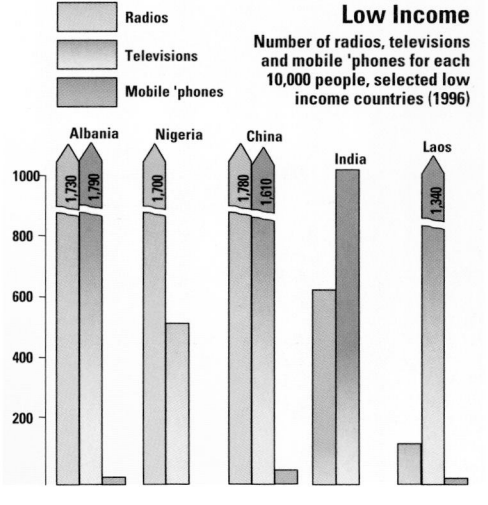

Low Income

Number of radios, televisions and mobile 'phones for each 10,000 people, selected low income countries (1996)

World Tourism

Passenger miles (the number of passengers carried, multiplied by distance flown from airport of origin) (1996)

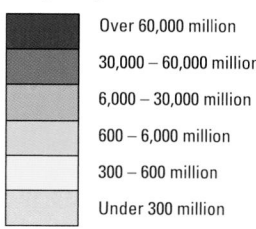

- Over 60,000 million
- 30,000 – 60,000 million
- 6,000 – 30,000 million
- 600 – 6,000 million
- 300 – 600 million
- Under 300 million

Leisure and tourism is the world's second largest industry in terms of revenue generated. Small economies in attractive areas are often completely dominated by tourism: in some Caribbean islands, tourist spending provides over 90% of the total income and is the biggest foreign exchange earner. In cash terms the USA is the world leader: its 1996 earnings exceeded US $75 billion, though that sum amounted to only 0.9% of its total GDP. Of the 49 million visitors to the USA, 34% came from Canada and 25% from Mexico. Germany spends the most on overseas tourism; in 1996 Germany spent over US $50,000 million abroad. The next biggest spenders were the USA, Japan, and the UK.

The world's busiest airport in terms of total number of passengers is Chicago's O'Hare Airport (67.3 million passengers in 1996); the busiest international airport is Heathrow, the largest of London's airports.

Aid Donors

Development aid by donor country, in millions of US $ and as a percentage of donor's GNP (latest available year)

Not all aid is given in cash grants: much is delivered in the form of cheap loans or technical assistance. Since the 1970s, OECD countries belonging to the Development Assistance Committee (DAC) have agreed in principle to give 0.7% of their GNP. Most have failed to meet their commitment. In 1994, three countries exceeded this level. They were Norway (1.05%), the Netherlands (1.03%) and Sweden (0.96%). The countries with the largest aid budgets were Japan (US $13,239 million or 0.29% of GNP) and the United States (US $9,927 million or 0.15% of GNP).

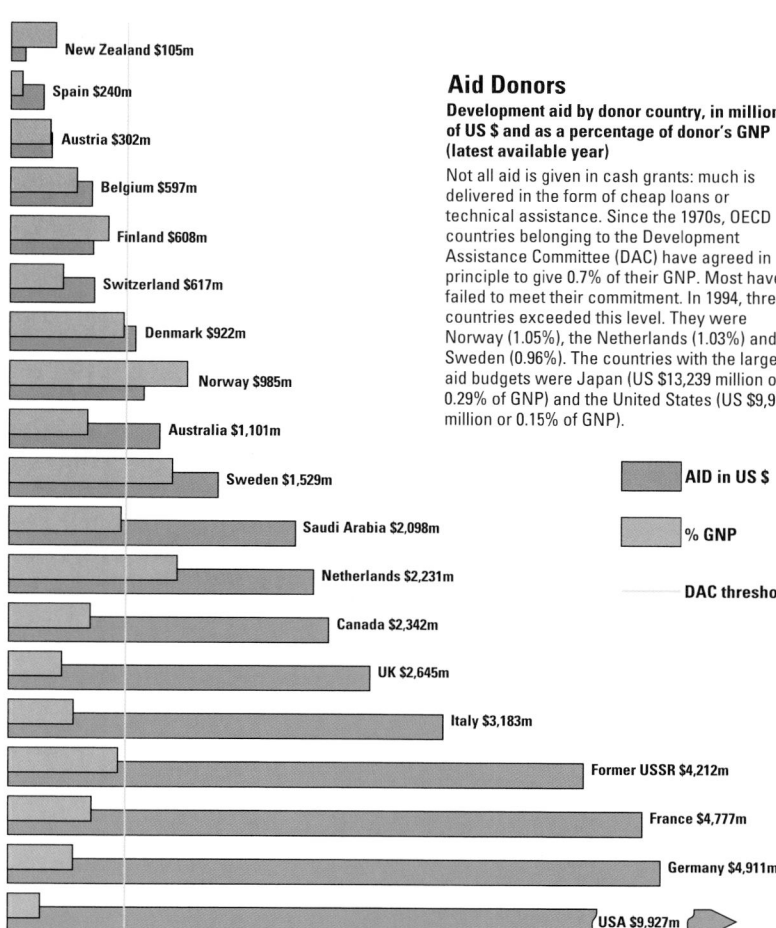

- New Zealand $105m
- Spain $240m
- Austria $302m
- Belgium $597m
- Finland $608m
- Switzerland $617m
- Denmark $922m
- Norway $985m
- Australia $1,101m
- Sweden $1,529m
- Saudi Arabia $2,098m
- Netherlands $2,231m
- Canada $2,342m
- UK $2,645m
- Italy $3,183m
- Former USSR $4,212m
- France $4,777m
- Germany $4,911m
- USA $9,927m
- Japan $13,239m

AID in US $
% GNP
DAC threshold

0.5% 1% 1.5% 2% 2.5%

State Finance

Inflation rates, shown on the map, right, are an index of a country's financial stability and usually of its prosperity. Annual inflation rates above 20% are usually marked by slow or even negative growth of the GNP. Above 50%, it becomes hyperinflation and an economy is reeling. In the late 1980s and early 1990s, many high-income countries had to contend with annual inflation rates of 10% or more, while Japan, the growth leader, had an average inflation rate of 1.3% between 1985 and 1994.

The per capita GNP figures listed below are useful indicators of economic success or failure, but they do not account for living costs. Nor do they reveal the gaps between the rich and poor within countries.

Market-friendly policies, including low taxes and state spending, liberal trade policies and a welcome for foreign investors, are major factors in countries which have enjoyed rapid economic growth since 1980. For example, the setting up of Special Economic Zones in eastern China has led to a spectacular rise in the per capita GNP. Other successful countries include the "tiger economies" of South Korea, Thailand and Singapore, although an Asian market crash in 1997 temporarily halted the dramatic economic expansion in these countries.

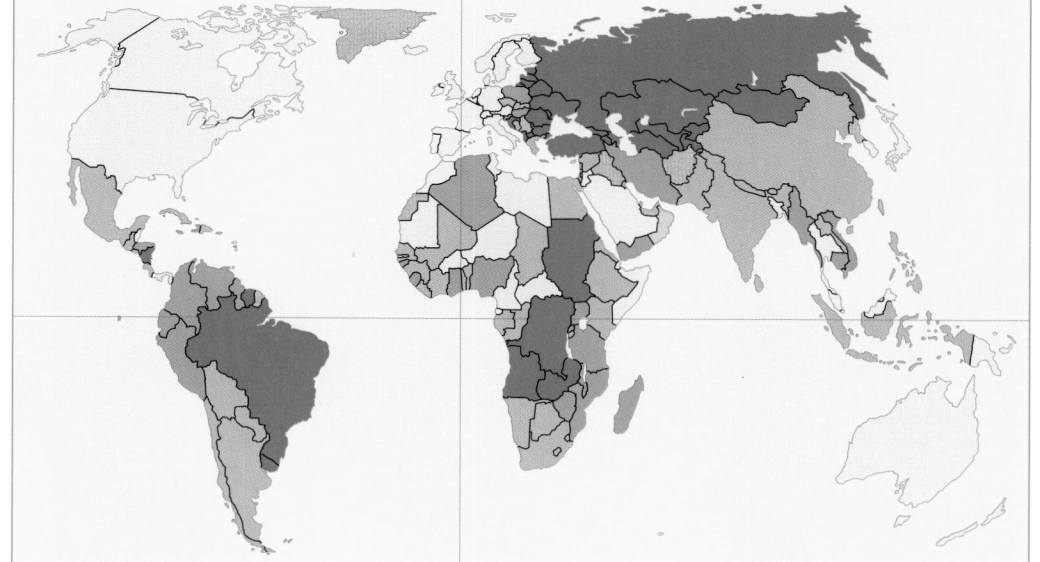

Inflation

Average annual rate of inflation (1990–96)

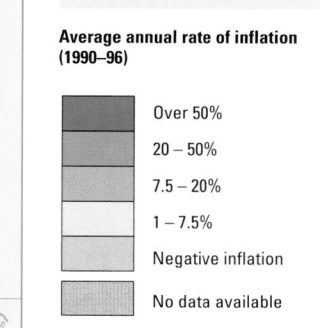

- Over 50%
- 20 – 50%
- 7.5 – 20%
- 1 – 7.5%
- Negative inflation
- No data available

Highest average inflation

Congo (Dem. R.) 2747%
Georgia................................. 2279%
Angola 1103%

Lowest average inflation

Oman .... –3.0%
Bahrain .... –0.5%
Brunei.................................. –0.0%

The Wealth Gap

The world's richest and poorest countries, by Gross National Product per capita in US $ (1997)

1. Luxembourg	45,360	1. Mozambique	90
2. Switzerland	44,220	2. Ethiopia	110
3. Japan	37,850	3. Congo (D. Rep.)	110
4. Norway	36,090	4. Burundi	180
5. Liechtenstein	33,000	5. Sierra Leone	200
6. Singapore	32,940	6. Niger	200
7. Denmark	32,500	7. Rwanda	210
8. Bermuda	31,870	8. Tanzania	210
9. USA	28,740	9. Nepal	210
10. Germany	28,260	10. Malawi	220
11. Austria	27,980	11. Chad	240
12. Iceland	26,580	12. Madagascar	250
13. Belgium	26,420	13. Mali	260
14. Sweden	26,220	14. Yemen	270
15. France	26,050	15. Cambodia	300
16. Netherlands	25,820	16. Bosnia-Herzegovina	300
17. Monaco	25,000	17. Gambia, The	320
18. Hong Kong	22,990	18. Haiti	330
19. Finland	20,580	19. Kenya	330
20. UK	18,700	20. Angola	340

GNP per capita is calculated by dividing a country's Gross National Product by its total population.

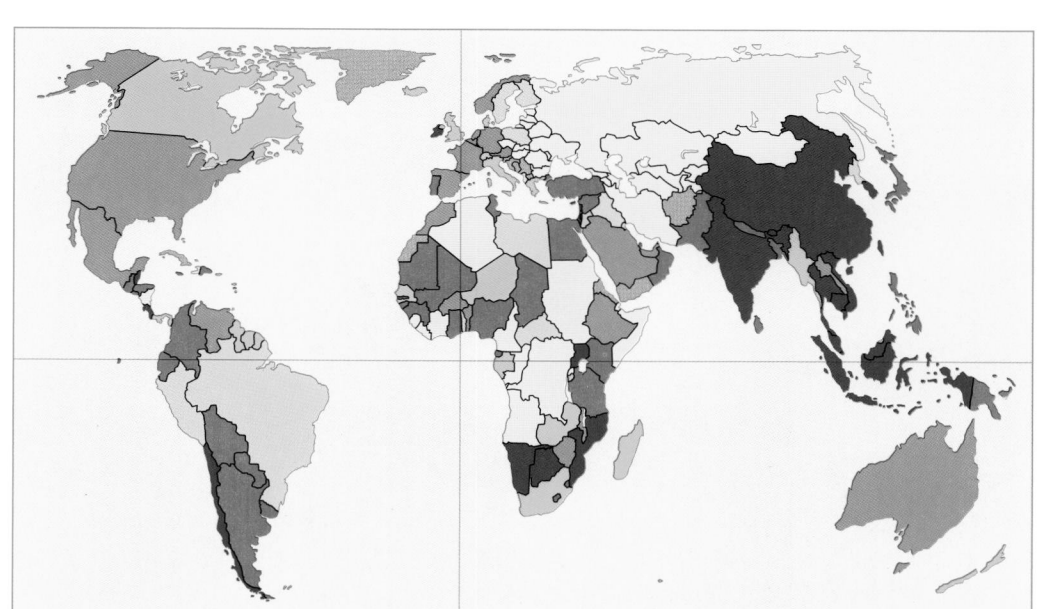

Growth in GNP

GNP per capita annual growth rate (1985–95)

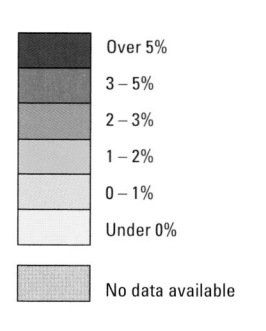

- Over 5%
- 3 – 5%
- 2 – 3%
- 1 – 2%
- 0 – 1%
- Under 0%
- No data available

Countries with highest growth rates

Maldives.................................... 9.9%
Thailand.................................... 9.7%
China.. 9.3%
Botswana.................................... 9.0%
South Korea............................... 8.5%

Standards of Living

Wealth is a basic factor in determining standards of living. Everywhere, the rich have more of everything, including higher average life expectancies, while the poor have to spend most of their income on basic human needs, such as food and clothing. Yet poverty and wealth are relative terms. Slum dwellers living on social security in an industrial society feel their poverty acutely, but they have far more resources than an average African living in a rural area.

In 1990 the United Nations Development Program published its first Human Development Index (HDI), an attempt to construct a comparative scale by which a simplified form of well-being might be measured. The HDI, expressed as a value between 0 and 0.999, combines figures for life expectancy and literacy with a wealth scale, based on Purchasing-Power Parity. The world's countries are divided into three groups, those with a high HDI (0.800 and above); those with a medium HDI (0.500 to 0.799); and those with a low HDI (below 0.500).

National scores for 1993 ranged from 0.951 for Canada to a low of 0.204 in Niger. In fact, of the 48 countries with a low HDI, 37 were from Africa, 10 from Asia, plus Haiti from the Caribbean.

Besides having low per capita GNPs, the average life expectancy in these countries was 56 years, while the adult literacy rate was 49%. By comparison, the average life expectancy at birth in countries in the high HDI group was 74 years, while the literacy rate was 97%.

Comparisons between countries with similar per capita GNPs reveal the effects of government actions. For example, the World Bank classifies both India and China as low-income economies, but India's HDI at 0.436 is much lower than that of China, at 0.609. This reflects not only China's economic progress in the 1980s and 1990s, but also differences in average life expectancies (61 years in India and 69 years in China), and adult literacy rates (51% in India and 80% in China).

Disparities in standards of living exist not only between countries but also between individuals, groups and regions within countries. For example, income distribution figures for 1995 show that, in the United States, the poorest 20% of households received less than 4% of the income.

Other contrasts exist in developing countries between rural communities, where incomes are low and basic services are often in short supply, and urban areas, where even those living in slums are generally better off than their rural neighbors. Other striking differences exist between men and women. For example, while adult literacy rates for men and women living in developed countries are more or less the same, large differences exist in many developing countries. In 1995, in countries in the lowest HDI category, only 37% of women were literate, as compared with 62% of men.

Female education is a factor in population control, especially as women's fertility rates appear to fall in direct proportion to the amount of secondary education they receive. This point was acknowledged in 1994 by the UN Population Fund, which defined four main objectives relating to women and population control. They were: the reduction of maternal, infant and child mortality; better education, especially for girls; universal access to reproductive health services; and gender equality.

Statistical analysis presents many problems of interpretation, especially when trying to define such intangible factors as a sense of well-being. For example, education helps create wealth; but are rich countries wealthy because their people are well-educated, or are they well-educated because they are rich?

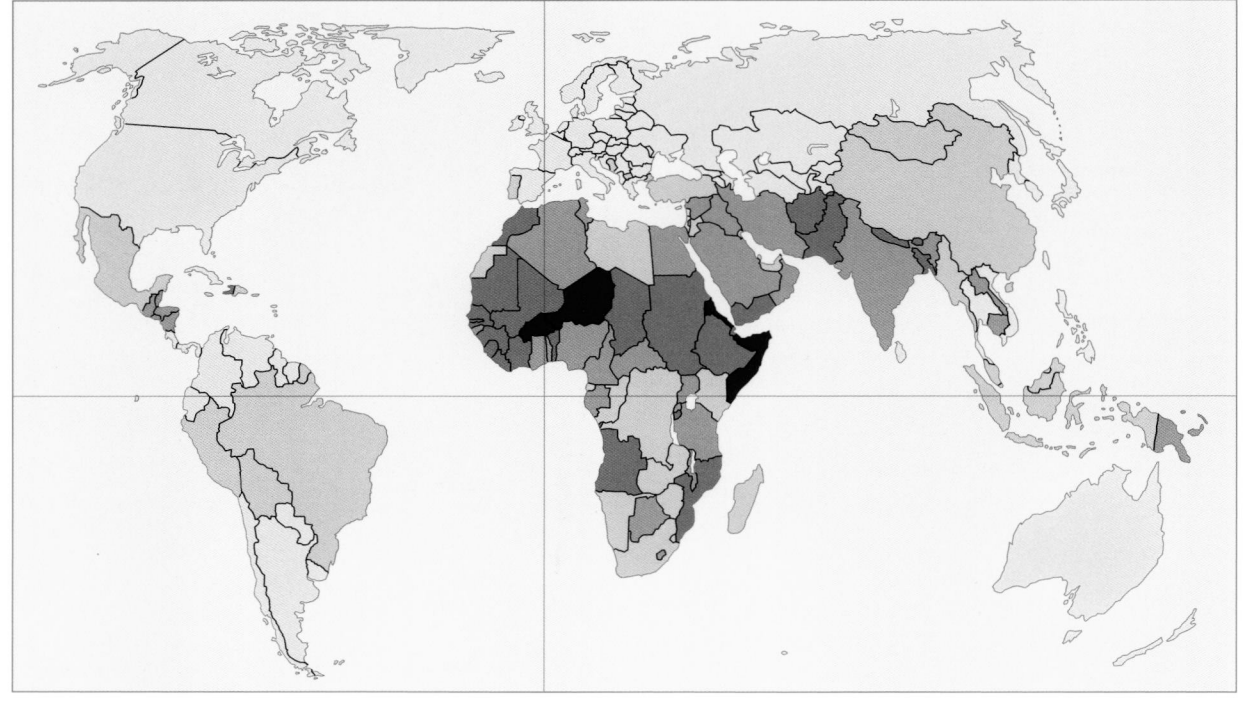

Illiteracy

% of the total population unable to read or write (1996)

- Over 75% illiterate
- 50 – 75% illiterate
- 25 – 50% illiterate
- 10 – 25% illiterate
- Under 10% illiterate

Educational expenditure per person (latest available year)

Top 5 countries

Sweden	$997
Qatar	$989
Canada	$983
Norway	$971
Switzerland	$796

Bottom 5 countries

Chad	$2
Bangladesh	$3
Ethiopia	$3
Nepal	$4
Somalia	$4

[UK $447]

Education

The developing countries made great efforts in the 1970s and 1980s to bring at least a basic education to their people. Primary school enrolments rose above 60% in all but the poorest nations. Figures often include teenagers or young adults, however, and there are still an estimated 300 million children worldwide who receive no schooling at all. A lack of resources has restricted the development of secondary and higher education. Most primary education is free in the poorer countries, but fees are often paid for secondary and higher education, thus heightening the differences between rich and poor.

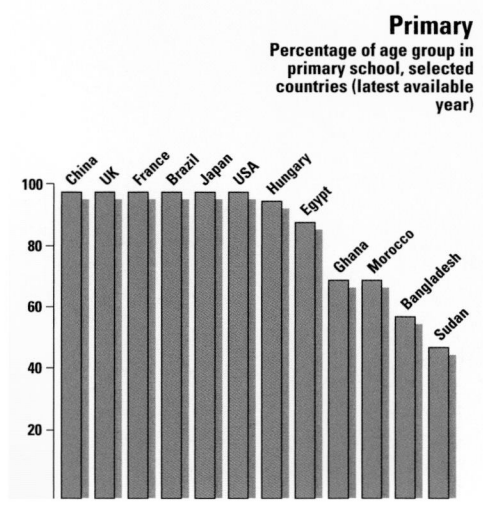

Primary
Percentage of age group in primary school, selected countries (latest available year)

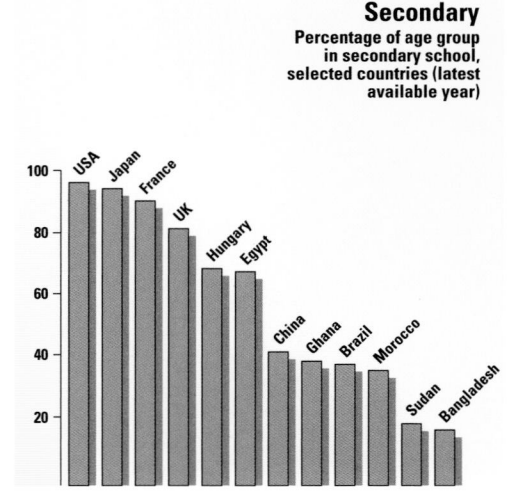

Secondary
Percentage of age group in secondary school, selected countries (latest available year)

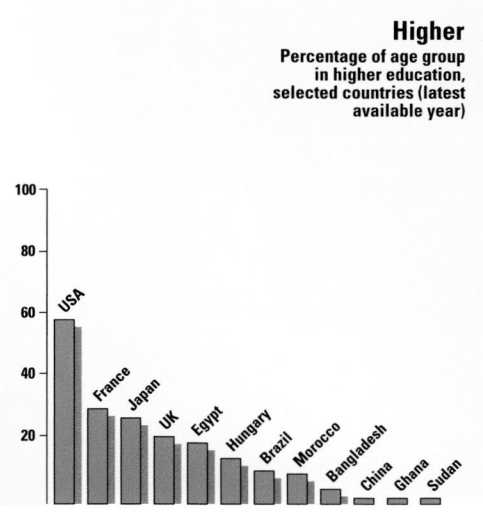

Higher
Percentage of age group in higher education, selected countries (latest available year)

Distribution of Spending

Percentage share of household spending (latest available year)

A high proportion of the average income of households in developing nations is spent on basic needs such as food and clothing. In most Western countries food and clothing account for less than 25% of expenditure.

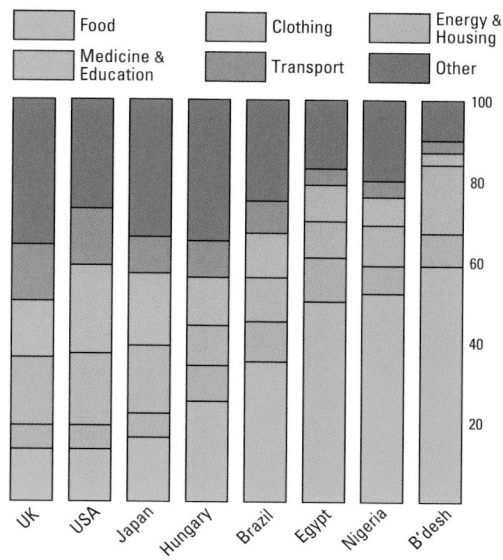

Food
Medicine & Education
Clothing
Transport
Energy & Housing
Other

UK USA Japan Hungary Brazil Egypt Nigeria B'desh

Distribution of Income

Percentage share of household income from poorest fifth to richest fifth, selected countries (latest available year)

The graph below shows that wealth is not distributed evenly throughout the population of the six countries. In every country worldwide the richest 20% of the population have a disproportionately high percentage of the income. This disparity between rich and poor is nowhere more pronounced than in Brazil, where the richest 20% of the population have over 60% of the income. The poorest 20%, on the other hand, have less than 5%.

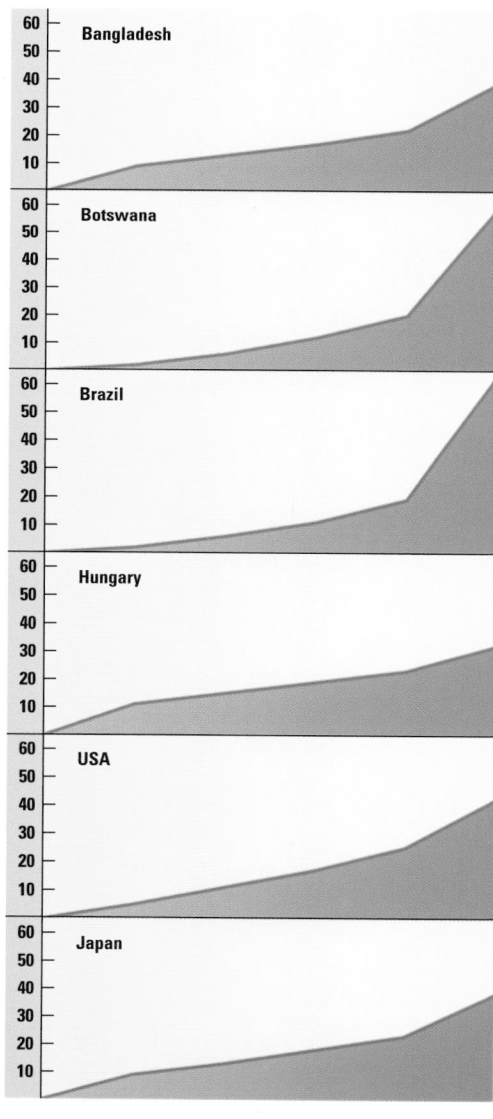

Bangladesh
Botswana
Brazil
Hungary
USA
Japan

Fertility and Education

Fertility rates compared with female education, selected countries (1992–95)

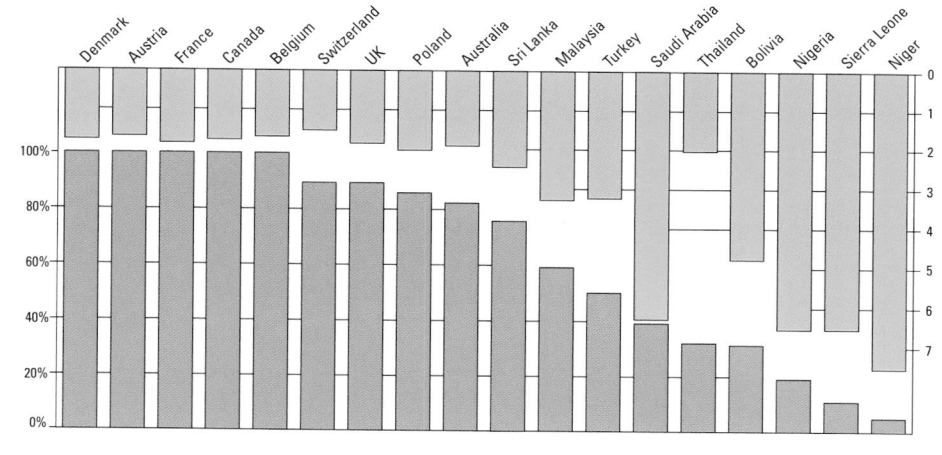

Denmark Austria France Canada Belgium Switzerland UK Poland Australia Sri Lanka Malaysia Turkey Saudi Arabia Thailand Bolivia Nigeria Sierra Leone Niger

Percentage of females aged 12–17 in secondary education

Fertility rate: average number of children borne per woman

Access to secondary education is closely linked to low fertility rates in developed countries. By contrast, in many developing countries, women's lives are dominated by agriculture, or they lack access to secondary and higher education for cultural reasons, as in Muslim countries. Such disparities are reflected in women's parliamentary representation which is only one-seventh that of men, despite the emergence of such figures as Mrs Indira Gandhi, India's former prime minister. Female wages are also, on average, only two-thirds of those of men.

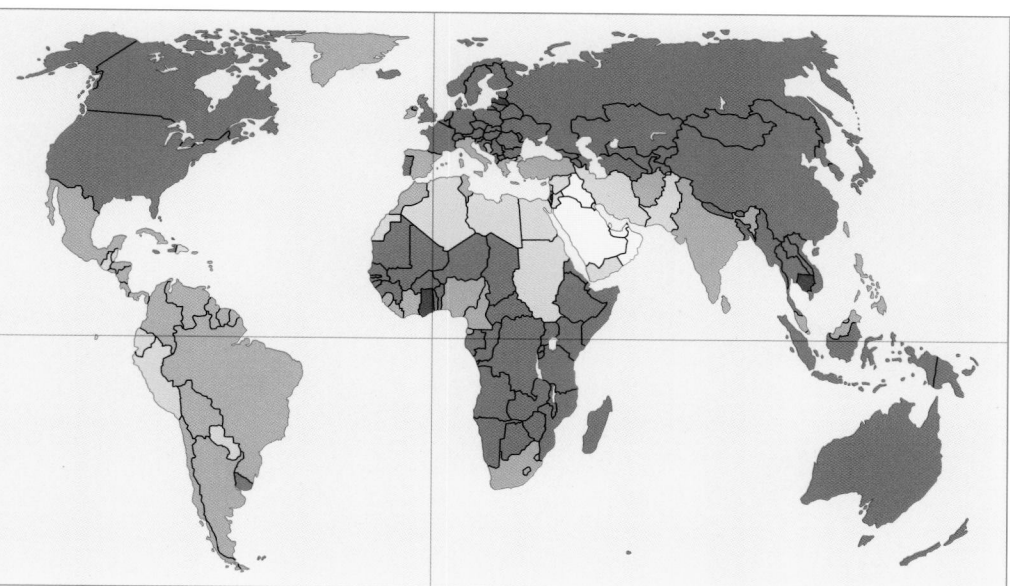

Women at Work

Women in paid employment as a percentage of the total work force (1996)

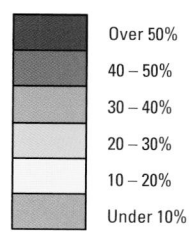

Over 50%
40 – 50%
30 – 40%
20 – 30%
10 – 20%
Under 10%

Most women in work
Cambodia 53%
Ghana 51%
Latvia 50%

Fewest women in work
Iraq... 18%
Oman 15%
Saudi Arabia................................ 14%

Car Ownership

Proportion of the world's vehicles, by region (1996)

0 10% 20% 30% 40%

North America
Western Europe
Asia
E.Europe & CIS
Others

TOTAL = 312 million vehicles

Motor cars per 100 people (1996)
Lebanon 73.1
Brunei 57.5
Italy 56.8
Luxembourg........................ 56.1
USA...................................... 51.8

Standards of Living in the USA by Race, Age and Region

A comparison of measures of income and education, by selected characteristics (1995)

Median income per household (US $), by age and region	Per capita income (US $), by race and Hispanic origin of householder	Percentage of persons aged 25 and over who have completed High School, by race or origin
15–24 years 20,979	ALL RACES 17,227	ALL RACES 1975 .... 62.5
25–34 years 34,701	White 18,304	1995 .... 81.7
35–44 years 43,465	Black 10,982	White 1975 .... 64.5
45–54 years 48,058	Asian & Pacific Is. 16,567	1995 .... 83.0
55–64 years 38,077	Hispanic (any race)............. 9,300	Black 1975 .... 42.5
65 years and over.............. 19,096		1995 .... 73.8
	The poorest 20% of households received just 3.6% of the income, whereas the richest 20% received 48.2%.	Hispanic 1975 .... 37.9
Northeast.......................... 36,111		1995 .... 53.4
Midwest............................. 35,839		
South 30,942		
West 35,979		

Regional Inequality in Italy

Gross Domestic Product (GDP) per capita in Italy, by region (1993)

Over US $20,000
$16,000 – $19,999
$12,000 – $15,999
$8,000 – $11,999
Under $8,000

Average GDP per capita for Italy was $18,878. The per capita GDP, by comparison, for the UK was $17,920; for the USA $25,650; and for the EU $25,900.

The number of inhabitants per doctor, another social indicator, varies from less than 500 in the northwest of Italy to over 800 in the far south, with a national average of 607.

The southern part of Italy, known as the *Mezzogiorno* (or "Land of the midday sun"), has been described as the poorest part of the European Union. It is identifiable on the map, left, as all the regions with a GDP per capita of less than $12,000 (including the two islands of Sicily and Sardinia), plus Abruzzi whose capital is L'Aquila.

The *Mezzogiorno* region suffers from a lack of mineral and energy resources, industry, commerce, services and skilled labour. As a result, standards of living in the region are well below the rest of Italy and Europe. Employment is predominantly agricultural and small-scale.

The north of Italy accounts for 60% of the population but 80% of the GDP, whereas the *Mezzogiorno* accounts for 40% of the population and only 20% of the GDP. Manpower surpluses in the south led to emigration to other parts of Europe and the Americas. It has also led, especially in the last 50 years, to inter-regional migration from the islands and the southern mainland to the north. The main regions attracting migrants were the northwest – the prosperous Liguria–Piedmont–Lombardy triangle with its great industrial cities of Genoa, Milan and Turin – and the Venetia region in the northeast. As a result, the north has experienced much higher population growth rates than the rest of Italy.

In 1996 the Northern League, one of Italy's political parties, exploited the regional differences by declaring the north to be the independent "Republic of Padania." However, only a small minority of northerners supports secession.

Los Angeles, Southern California, USA

CITY
MAPS

Oslo, Copenhagen 2, Helsinki, Stockholm 3, London 4, Paris 5, The Ruhr 6, Berlin,
Hamburg, Munich 7, Madrid, Barcelona, Lisbon, Athens 8, Turin, Milan, Rome,
Naples 9, Prague, Warsaw, Vienna, Budapest 10, Moscow, St Petersburg 11,
Osaka, Hong Kong, Seoul 12, Tokyo 13, Peking, Shanghai, Tientsin, Canton 14,
Bangkok, Manila, Singapore, Jakarta 15, Delhi, Bombay, Calcutta 16,
Istanbul, Tehran, Baghdad, Karachi 17, Lagos, Cairo, Johannesburg 18, Sydney,
Melbourne 19, Montréal, Toronto 20, Boston 21, New York 22, Philadelphia 24,
Washington, Baltimore 25, Chicago 26, San Francisco 27, Los Angeles 28,
Mexico City 29, Havana, Caracas, Lima, Santiago 30, Rio de Janeiro,
São Paulo 31, Buenos Aires 32

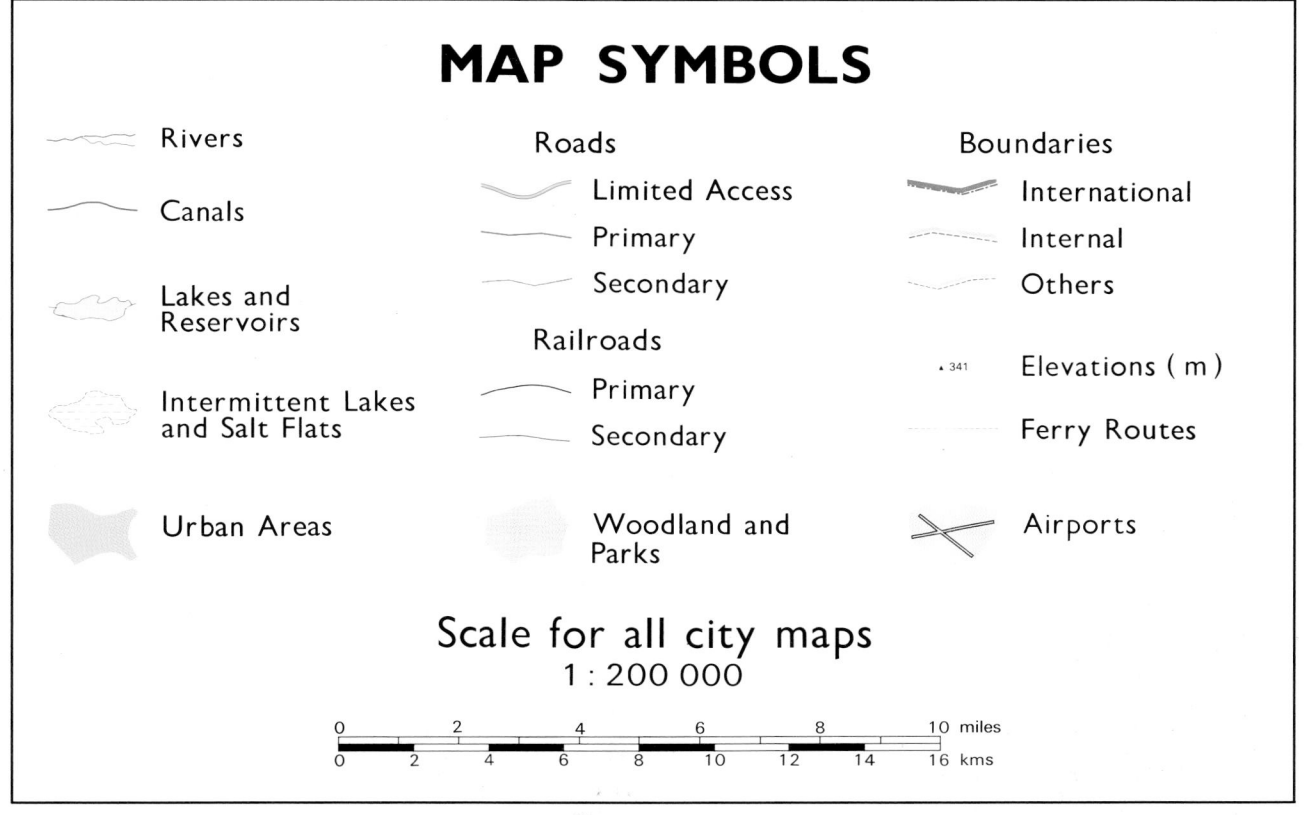

MAP SYMBOLS

Rivers	
Canals	
Lakes and Reservoirs	
Intermittent Lakes and Salt Flats	
Urban Areas	

Roads
- Limited Access
- Primary
- Secondary

Railroads
- Primary
- Secondary

Woodland and Parks

Boundaries
- International
- Internal
- Others

• 341 Elevations (m)

Ferry Routes

Airports

Scale for all city maps
1 : 200 000

0   2   4   6   8   10 miles

0   2   4   6   8   10   12   14   16 kms

1: 200 000

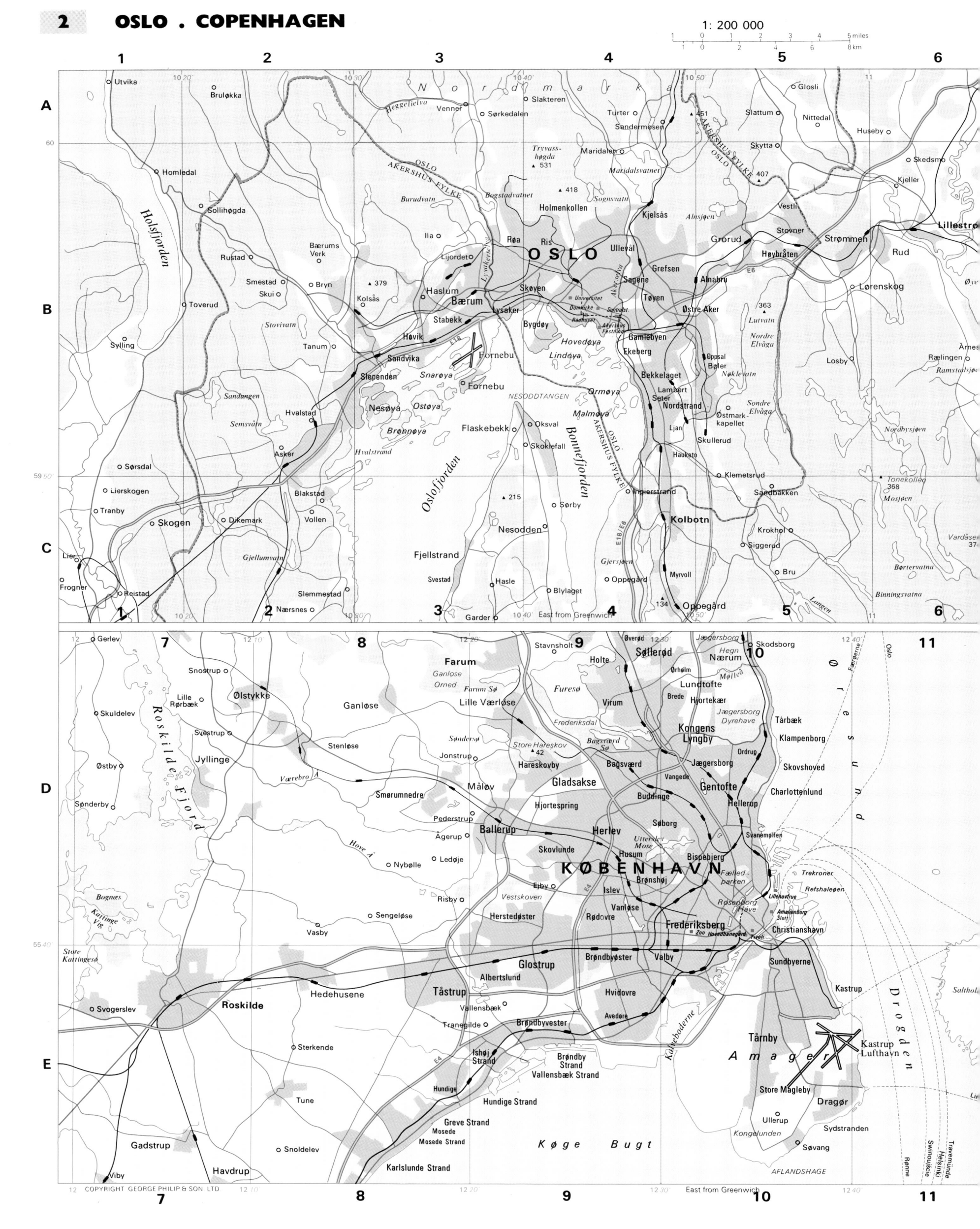

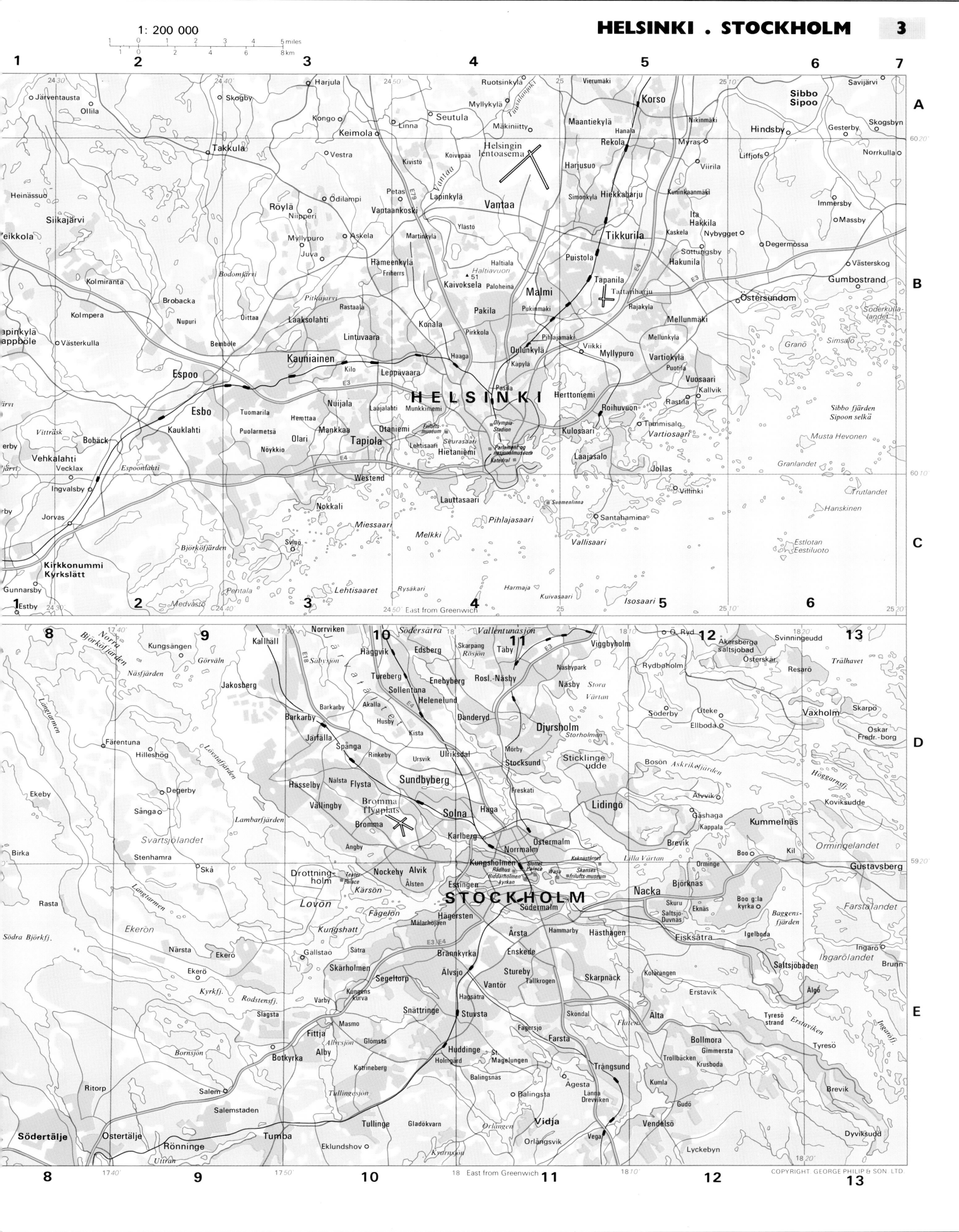

1: 200 000

5 miles
8 km

HELSINKI

STOCKHOLM

1 : 200 000

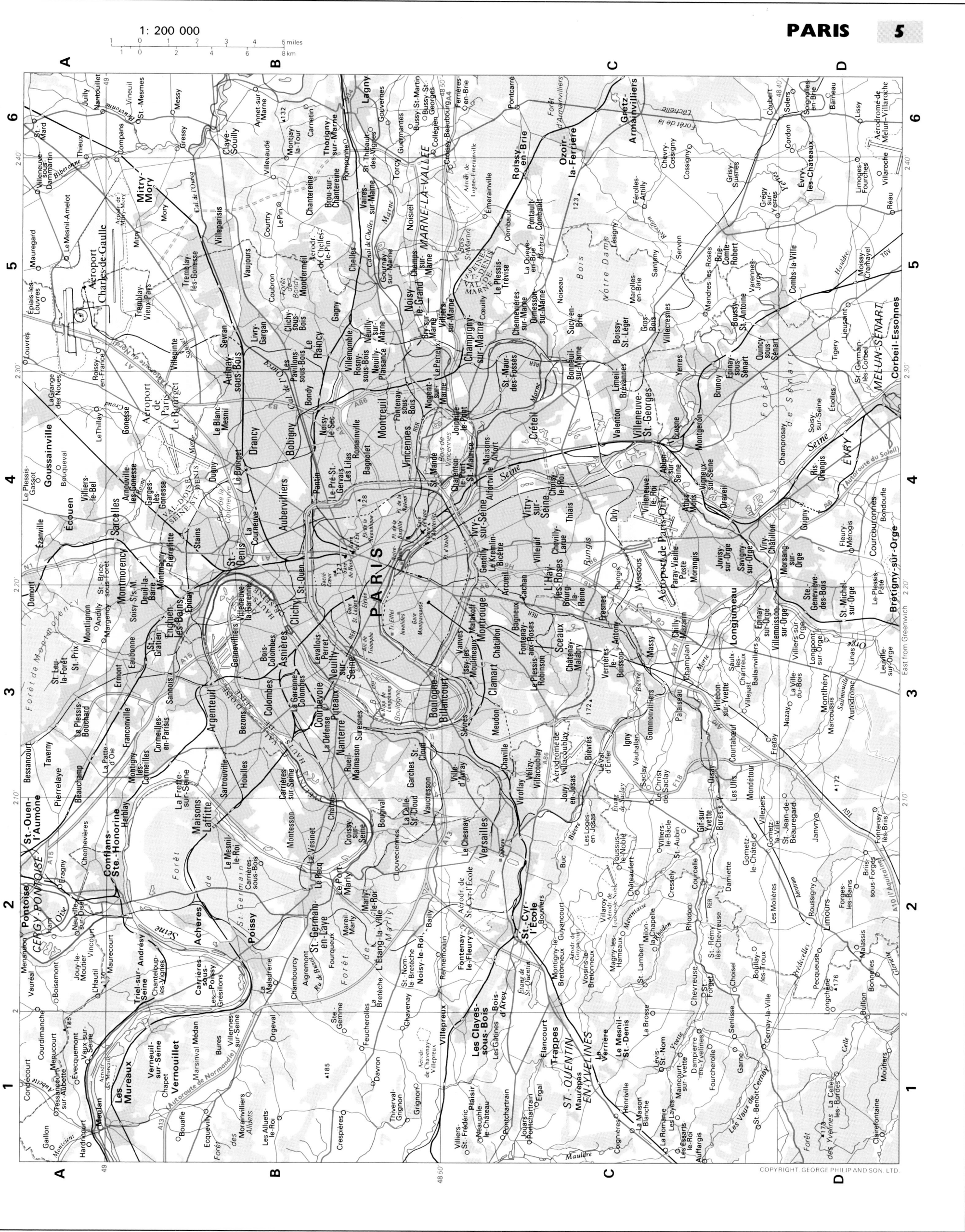

1: 200 000

5 miles
8 km

East from Greenwich

COPYRIGHT GEORGE PHILIP AND SON LTD.

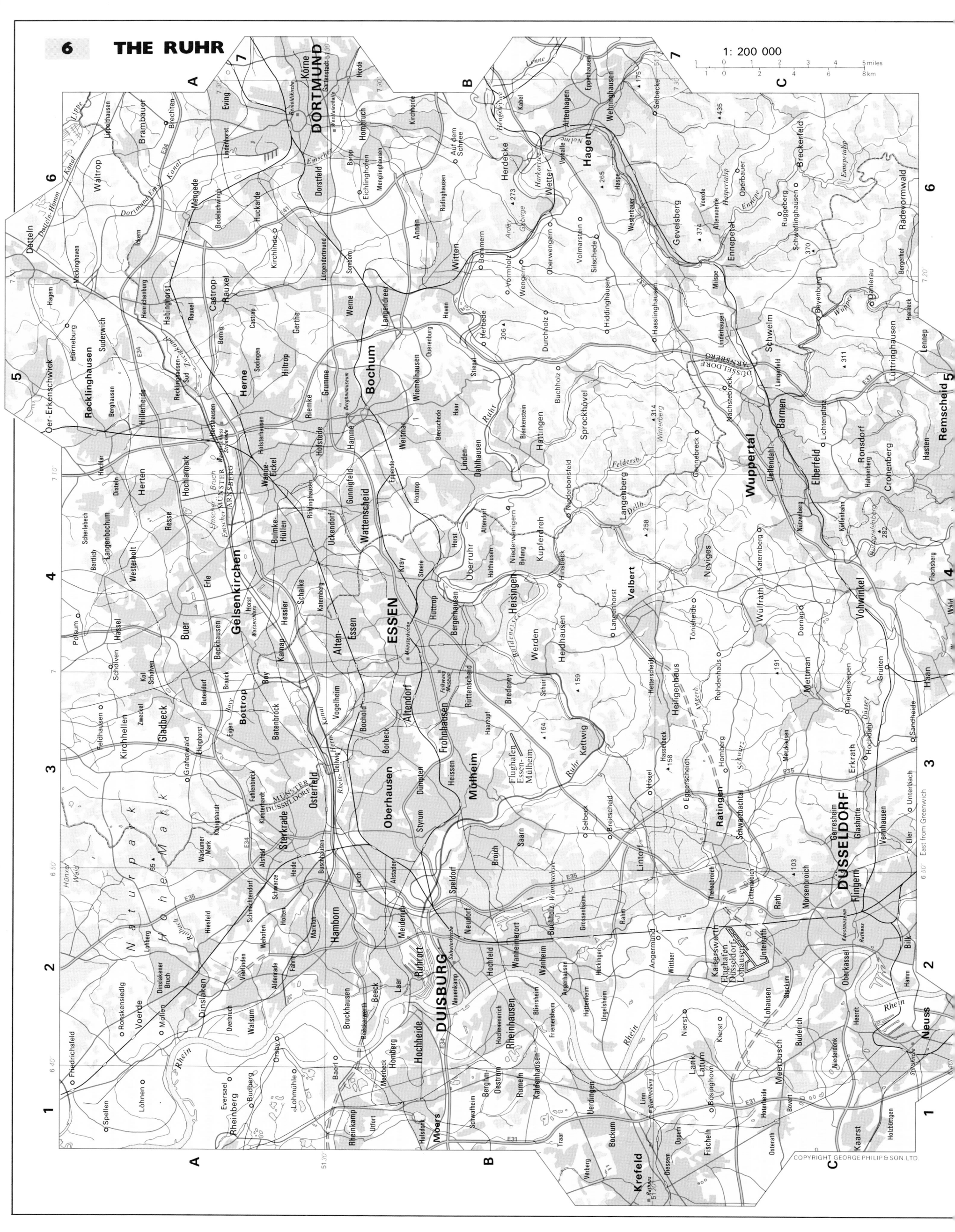

1: 200 000

1 : 200 000

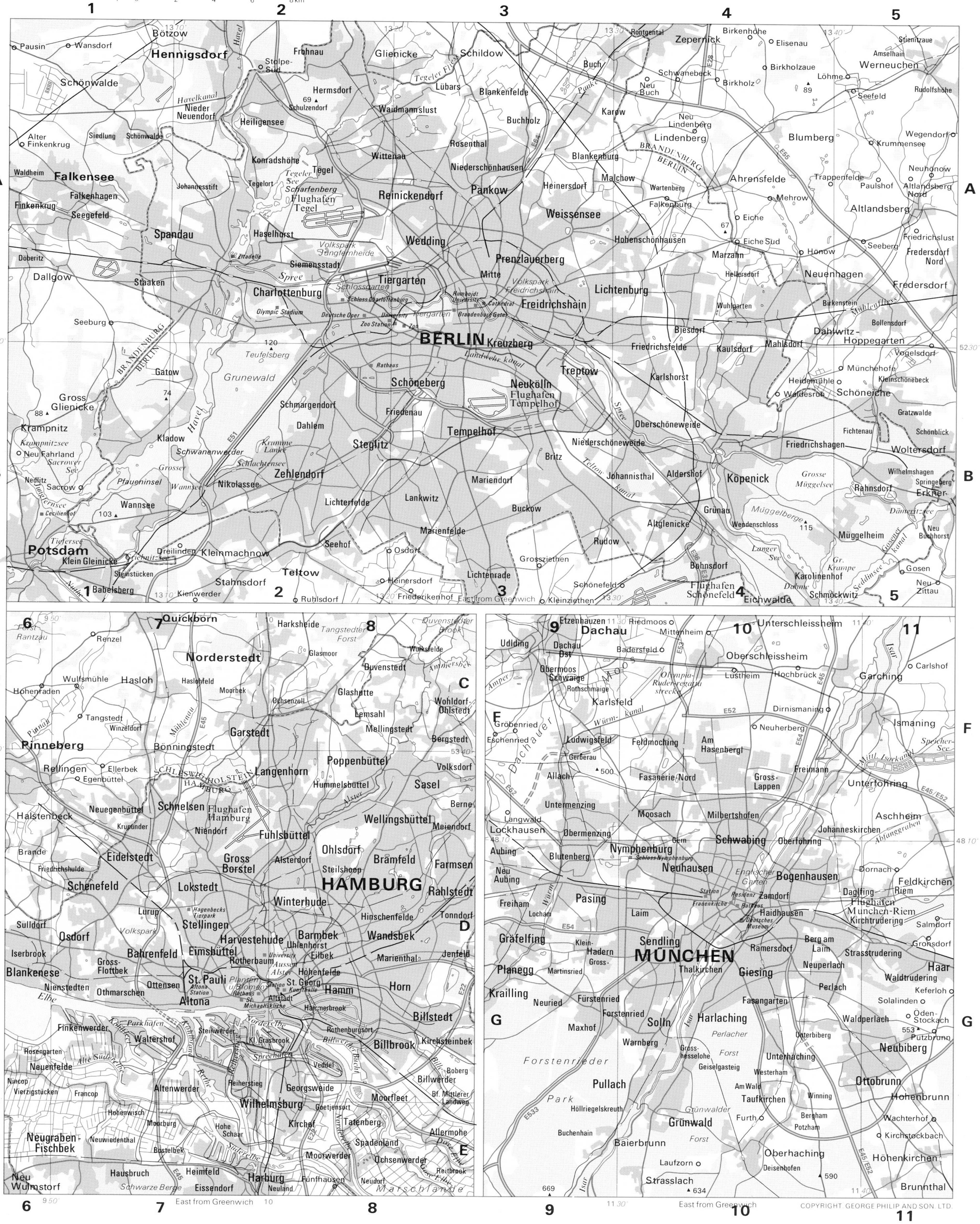

1 0 1 2 3 4 5 miles
1 0 2 4 6 8 km

BERLIN

Pausin · Wansdorf · Bötzow · Hennigsdorf · Frohnau · Glienicke · Schildow · Zepernick · Birkenhöhe · Elisenau · Amselhain · Werneuchen · Steinitzaue

Schönwalde · Stolpe-Süd · Hermsdorf · Lübars · Blankenfelde · Buch · Schwanebeck · Birkholzaue · Löhme · Rudolfshöhe

Alter Finkenkrug · Siedlung Schönwalde · Nieder Neuendorf · Heiligensee · Schulzendorf · Waidmannslust · Buchholz · Neu Buch · Karow · Neu Lindenberg · Birkholz · Seefeld · Wegendorf

Waldheim · Falkensee · Falkenhagen · Johannesstift · Tegelort · Tegel · Scharfenberg · Reinickendorf · Pankow · Heinersdorf · Lindenberg · Blankenburg · Malchow · Ahrensfelde · Trappenfelde · Neuhonow · Altlandsberg Nord

Finkenkrug · Seegefeld · Haselhorst · Flughafen Tegel · Wedding · Prenzlauerberg · Weissensee · Hohenschönhausen · Wartenberg · Mehrow · Eiche · Honow · Seeberg · Friedrichslust · Altlandsberg

Doberitz · Spandau · Siemensstadt · Tiergarten · Mitte · Friedrichshain · Lichtenburg · Falkenburg · Hellersdorf · Marzahn · Neuenhagen · Fredersdorf Nord

Dallgow · Staaken · Charlottenburg · Schloss Charlottenburg · Deutsche Oper · Zoo Station · **BERLIN** · Kreuzberg · Friedrichsfelde · Kaulsdorf · Mahlsdorf · Dahlwitz-Hoppegarten · Fredersdorf

Seeburg · Teufelsberg · Grunewald · Rathaus · Schöneberg · Neukölln · Flughafen Tempelhof · Treptow · Karlshorst · Biesdorf · Birkenstein · Bollensdorf · Vogelsdorf

Gross Glienicke · Gatow · Schmargendorf · Friedenau · Tempelhof · Oberschöneweide · Niederschöneweide · Heidemühle · Münchehofe · Kleinschönebeck · Gratzwalde · Schönblick

Krampnitz · Neu Fahrland · Kladow · Schwanenwerder · Schlachtensee · Dahlem · Steglitz · Britt · Johannisthal · Aldershof · Waldesruh · Schöneiche · Woltersdorf

Sacrow · Pfaueninsel · Nikolassee · Zehlendorf · Lichterfelde · Mariendorf · Grünau · Köpenick · Grosse Müggelsee · Rahnsdorf · Wilhelmshagen · Springeberg · Erkner

Nedlitz · Wannsee · Lankwitz · Buckow · Altglienicke · Wendenschloss · Müggelberge · Müggelheim · Neu Buchhorst · Neu Zittau

Potsdam · Klein Gleinicke · Kleinmachnow · Seehof · Marienfelde · Rudow · Bahnsdorf · Langer See · Karolinenhof · Gosen

Babelsberg · Steinstücken · Stahnsdorf · Teltow · Osdorf · Lichtenrade · Grossziethen · Schönefeld · Flughafen Schönefeld · Eichwalde · Schmöckwitz

Kienwerder · Rubisdorf · Friederikenhof · Heinersdorf · Kleinziethen · Schönefeld

East from Greenwich

HAMBURG

Rantzau · Quickborn · Harksheide · Tangstedter Forst · Duvenstedter Brook

Renzel · Norderstedt · Glasmoor · Wulksfelde · Ammersbek

Hohenraden · Wulfsmühle · Hasloh · Haslohfeld · Moorbek · Buvenstedt · Glashütte · Wohldorf-Ohlstedt

Tangstedt · Winzeldorf · Ochsenzoll · Lemsahl · Mellingstedt · Bergstedt

Pinneberg · Rellingen · Ellerbek · Egenbüttel · Bönningstedt · Garstedt · Langenhorn · Poppenbüttel · Volksdorf

Halstenbeck · Neuegenbüttel · Krupunder · Schnelsen · Flughafen Hamburg · Niendorf · Hummelsbüttel · Sasel · Berne

Brande · Friedrichshulde · Eidelstedt · Gross Borstel · Alsterdorf · Ohlsdorf · Brämfeld · Farmsen · Meiendorf

Sulldorf · Osdorf · Schenefeld · Lokstedt · Steilshoop · Wandsbek · Rahlstedt

Iserbrook · Bahrenfeld · Stellingen · Winterhude · Hinschenfelde · Tonndorf

Blankenese · Gross-Flottbek · Eimsbüttel · Harvestehude · Barmbek · Uhlenhorst · Eilbek · Marienthal · Jenfeld

Nienstedten · Othmarschen · Ottensen · St. Pauli · Altona · Rotherbaum · **HAMBURG** · Hamm · Horn

Finkenwerder · Waltershof · Steinwerder · St. Georg · Hammerbrook · Billstedt · Kirchsteinbek

Rosengarten · Neuenfelde · Parkhafen · Kl. Grasbrook · Rothenburgsort · Veddel · Billwerder · Boberg

Nincop · Vierzigstücken · Francop · Altenwerder · Reiherstieg · Georgswerder · Moorfleet · Billwerder · Bf. Mittlerer Landweg

Neugraben-Fischbek · Neuwiedenthal · Bostelbek · Wilhelmsburg · Kirchel · Tatenberg · Spadenland · Ochsenwerder · Allermöhe · Moorwerder

Neu Wulmstorf · Hausbruch · Heimfeld · Harburg · Neuland · Schwarze Berge · Hohe Schaar · Reitbrook · Marschlande

Eissendorf · Funfhausen · Moorwerder

East from Greenwich

MÜNCHEN

Etzenhausen · Riedmoos · Unterschleissheim · Udlding · Dachau · Mittenheim · Dachau Ost · Badersfeld · Oberschleissheim · Garching · Carlshof

Obermoos · Schwaige · Rothschwaige · Karlsfeld · Olympia-Ruderregatta strecke · Lüstheim · Hochbrück · Dirnismaning

Grobenried · Eschenried · Ludwigsfeld · Feldmoching · Am Hasenbergl · Neuherberg · Ismaning · Speicher See

Gerberau · Allach · Fasanerie Nord · Gross-Lappen · Freimann · Unterföhring

Langwald · Untermenzing · Moosach · Milbertshofen · Aschheim

Lockhausen · Obermenzing · Gern · Schwabing · Oberföhring · Johanneskirchen · Dornach

Aubing · Nymphenburg · Schloss Nymphenburg · Neuhausen · Englischer Garten · Bogenhausen · Daglfing · Feldkirchen

Neu Aubing · Station · Residenz · Zamdorf · Flughafen München-Riem · Riem

Freiham · Pasing · Laim · Haidhausen · Deutsches Museum · Kirchtrudering · Salmdorf

Lochham · Fraunhofer Kirche · Gräfelfing · Klein-Hadern · Gross-Hadern · **MÜNCHEN** · Ramersdorf · Berg am Laim · Strassrudering · Gronsdorf

Planegg · Martinsried · Thalkirchen · Giesing · Neuperlach · Waldtrudering · Haar

Krailling · Neuried · Fürstenried · Sendling · Perlach · Keferloh · Solalinden

Forstenried · Solln · Harlaching · Waldperlach · Oden-Stockach

Maxhof · Warnberg · Grosshesselohe · Perlacher Forst · Unterbiberg · Putzbrunn · Neubiberg

Forstenrieder Park · Pullach · Unterhaching · Westerham · Winning · Ottobrunn · Hohenbrunn

Baierbrunn · Geiselgasteig · Am Wald · Taufkirchen · Bergham · Potzham · Oberhaching · Kirchstockbach

Buchenhain · Höllriegelskreuth · Grünwald · Grünwalder Forst · Furth · Deisenhofen · Hohenkirchen

Laufzorn · Strasslach · Brunnthal

East from Greenwich

1:200 000

5 miles
8 km

Barcelona (top-left)

Mongat
Badalona
San Adrián de Besós
Sta. Coloma de Gramanet
La Puntxola
151
San Joan
303 Poyo
C'an
Betós
Llano de Can Gineu
327
Sta. Eulalia
Vallcarca
La Sagrera
San Andrés
La Llacuna
San Martín
Gracia
Pueblo Nuevo
La Faxonera
Puxet
BARCELONA
Parque de Güell
Templo de la Sagrada Familia
Parque de la Ciudadela
La Fransa
Barceloneta
Moyo Maritimo
Sarriá
Pedralbes
Univers.
Campo F.C. Barcelona
Plaza de Las Arenas
Palacio Nacional
Montaña de Montjuich
Las Corts
Sans
Hostafranchs
Sant Cugat
512
Tibidabo
387
S. Pedro Martir
Vallvidrera
435
San Martín
Santa Cruz de Olorde
Hospitalet
Esplugas
S. Just Desvern
389
Cornellá
Prat de Llobregat
336
Madrona
Papiol
Mollins de Rey
Castelbisbal
S. Feliu de Llobregat
Joan Despí
Lafibera
Gieli
Colonia Güell
2
Palleja
S. Vicenç dels Horts
Santa Coloma de Cervello
Torrellas de Llobregat
Sant Boi de Llobregat
Sant Clemente del Llobregat
Gavá
Viladecans
Aeropuerto de Barcelona-Prat
La Pineda
Gavamar
Laguna de la Ricarda
Laguna del Remola
Río Llobregat

MEDITERRANEAN SEA

Mahón
Palma
Ibiza
Malaga
Cadiz
Islas Canarias
East from Greenwich

Athens (top-right)

Drafi
Pallini
Hristoupoli
Spata
Markopoulo
Kalivia Thorikou
Gerakas
Kitsi
Koropi
Peania
Karellas
Glika Nera
Baráko
230
Kholargós
1026
Évzonos
765
Néa-Ionia
Filothei
Psikhikón
Ampelókipi
Zográfos
Kipséli
Neapolis
University
Kaisariani
Viron
Imittos
Iliódpolis
N. Alexandhria
Voula
Vouliagmeni
Patisia
Galatsion
Attiki
Station
Ay. Paraskevi
Pangrati
Dháfni
Nea Liósia
Filadhelfia
Sepolia
Kolonos
Kolonáki
Ay. Dhimítrios
Petroupolis
Verdi
Peristérion
Aiyáleo
ATHINAI
Távros
Kallithéa
N.Smirni
N. Faliron
P. Faliron
Glifada
Skára-mangás
Dhafni
Khaidhárion
Nikaia
Piraévs
Athinai Ellinikón Airport
Ellinikó
Koridhallós
Néapolis
468
Dhrapetsón
Ay. Gheorghios
Distiria
Ormos Faliron
Saronikós Kólpos
Kithnos
Sifnos
Kórinthos
Aiyína
East from Greenwich

Madrid (bottom-left)

Las Rozas de Madrid
703
Paracuellos del Jarama
Guardias
703
Aeropuerto Transoceánico de Barajas
Barrio de La Estación
San Fernando de Henares
680
Barajas
Ciudad Fin de Semana
Canillejas
674
San Cristobal
Rivas de Jarama
Rivas Vaciamadrid
La Moraleja
Valdebeba
Manoteras
Hortaleza
Canillas
Pueblo Nuevo
Vicálvaro
Fuencarral
Convento de Valverde
Progreso
Ciudad Lineal
Moratalaz
Vallecas
633
Canteras de Vallecas
Cumbres de Vallecas
581
Salmedina
Almenara
Chamartín
MADRID
Estadio Bernabeu
Buenavista
Ventas
El Pardo
Tetuán
Chamberí
University
Colonia Puerta de Hierro
Universidad
Palacio Real
Museo del Prado
Retiro
Mediodia
Palomeras
Mercamadrid
Perales del Rio
Cerro de los Angeles
Hipódromo de la Zarzuela
Chamartín
Plaza Mayor
Puerta Station
Arganzuela
Legazpi
Los Angeles
Avda de Andalucia
Villaverde Bajo
Convento de Santo Cristo
Portillos de las Rozas
Pozuelo de Alarcón
Aravaca
La Estación
Casa de Campo
Latina
Usera
Carabanchel Bajo
Villaverde
Getafe
El Plantío
Manzanares
La Fortuna
Campamento
Carabanchel Alto
Leganés
Majadahonda
Boadilla del Monte
Cuatro Vientos
705
Ventorro
Alcorcón
Móstoles
West from Greenwich

Lisbon (bottom-right)

Alcochete
Lagoa da Pedra
Montijo
Sarilhos Pequeños
Sarilhos Grandes
Moita
Samoueo
Base Aérea
Alhos Vedros
Santo António da Charneca
Rosairinho
Lavradio
Santo André
Baixa da Banheira
S. João da Talha
Sacavém
Beirolas
Matinha
Palhais
LISBOA
Barreiro
Coina
Friélas
163
Apelação
Beato
Xabregas
Sta. Apolónia Station
Cacilhas
Amora
Seixal
Unhos
Moscavide
Aeroporto de Portela
Olivais
Povoa de Santo Adrião
Camarate
Charneca
Ameixoeira
Rossio
Sé
Basílica da Estrela
Almada
Cova da Piedade
Campo Grande
University
Campo Pequeño
Rato
Cacilhas
Amadora
Pontinha
Carnide
Alcántara
Benfica
Monsanto
Parque Florestal
Santo Amaro
Ajuda
Belém
Banatica
125
Odivelas
Paia
Lumiar
Campolide
Lisboa Setúbal
Loures
357
Camaroes
Canecas
Ada Beja
Damaia
Carnaxide
210
Queluz
Trafaria
Caparica
Costa da Caparica
Feijó
Sobreda
Capuchos
283
Belas
Barcarena
Linda-a-Pastora
Caxias
Paço de Arcos
Cruz de Pau
Charneca
320
Tapada
Piedade
Telhal
Agualva-Cacem
Massamá
Venda Seca
Leião
222
Talaide
Rio de Mouro
Sabugo
Oeiras
Terrugem
Bugio
Ota de Sto. António
ATLANTIC OCEAN
West from Greenwich

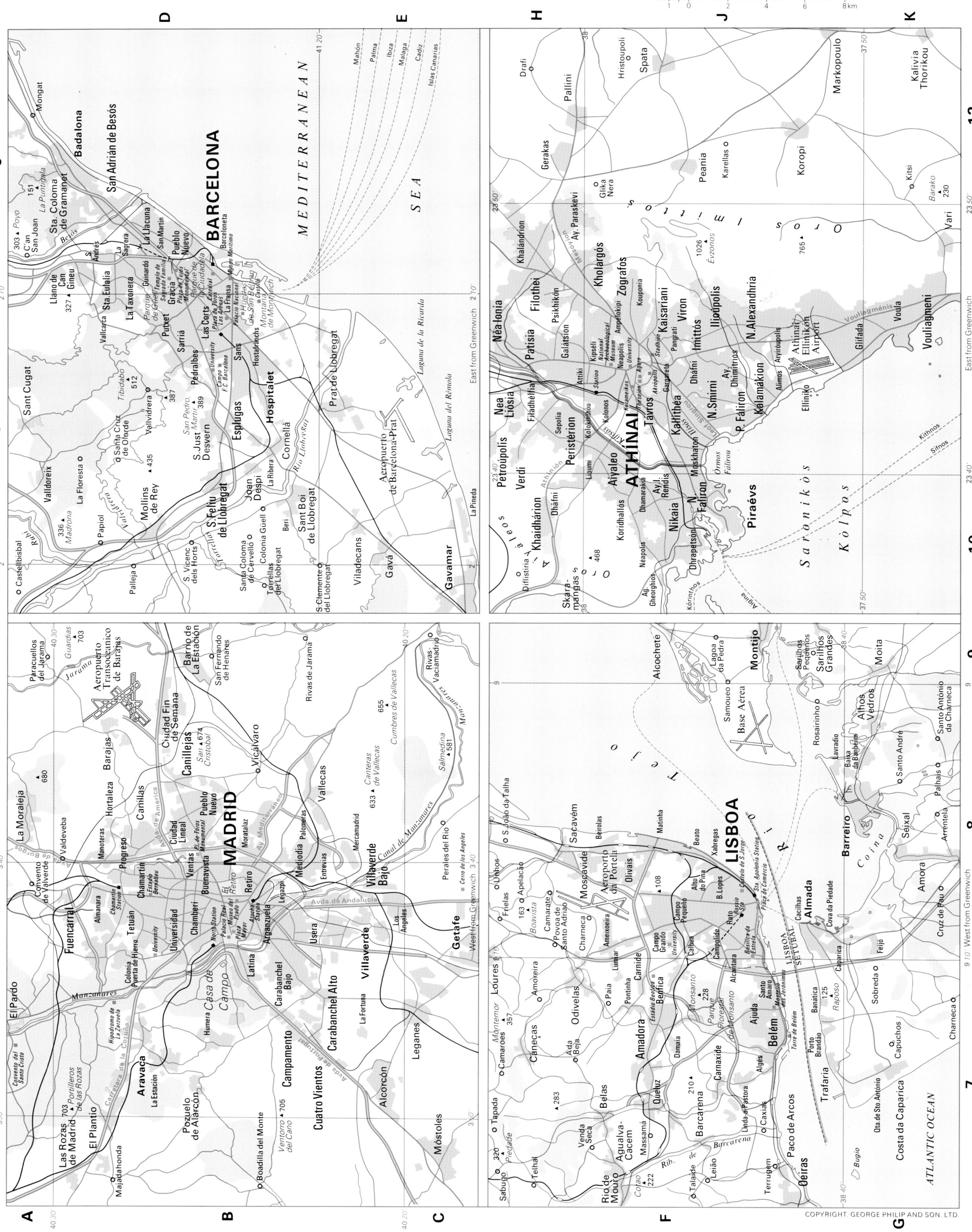

COPYRIGHT. GEORGE PHILIP AND SON LTD.

1: 200 000

0 1 2 3 4 5 miles
0 2 4 6 8 km

MILANO

Monza
Lissone
Desio
Cinisello Bàlsamo
Sesto S. Giovanni
Cologno Monz.
Brughério
Concorezzo
Villasanta
Muggiò
Bovisio
Masciago
Varedo
Cusano Mil.
Paderno Dugnano
Cinisello
Bresso
Cormano
Greco
Lambrate
Crescenzago
Loreto
Stazione Centrale
La Scala
Le Duomo
Città degli Studi
Calvairate
Morivione
Vigentino
Chiaravalle
Gambolòita
Baldinasco
Musocca
S. Siro
Fiera Camp.
Basilica di Sant'Ambrogio
Castello Sforzesco
Cristoforo
Corsico
Baggio
Quinto Rom.
Trenno
Figino
Pero
Settimo Mil.
Monzoro
Assiano
Cusago
Cesano Bosc.
Romano Banco
Trezzano s. Nav.
Quartiere Zingone
Cisliano
S. Pietro Best.
Rosio
Fagnano
Vittuone
Sedriano
Pregnana Mil.
Rho
Vanzago
Pogliano Mil.
Nerviano
Lainate
Caronno Pert.
Pertusella
Garbagnate Mil.
Cesate
Senago
Limbiate
Varedo
Solaro
Ceriano
Bollate
Novate Mil.
Cassina Nuova
Arese
Lucernate
Terrazzano Ospiate
Barbaiana
Passirana
Cornaredo
Bareggio
S. Pietro all'Olmo
Sedriano
Seguro
Vighignolo
Cornaredo
Solaro
Ceriano Laghetto
Cogliate
Ceriano
Mombello
Binzago
Uboldo
Origgio
Gerenzano
Saronno
Cislago

TORINO

Volpiano
Léini
Settimo Tor.
Gassino Torinese
Castiglione Torinese
Cordova
San Mauro Tor.
Superga
Basilica di Superga 670
Rivodora
Pino Torinese
Chieri
Baldissero Tor.
Pavarolo
Cipresso
Mongreno
Pecetto Tor.
Castelvecchio
S. Felice
Pino Torinese
S. Mauro Tor.
Reaglie
S. Margherita
l'Éremo
Colle di Maddalena 715
Cavoretto
Moncalieri
Testona
Trofarello
Nichelino
Mirafiori
Lingotto
Stadio
Gerbido
Beinasco
Borgaretto
Stupinigi
Orbassano
Rivalta di Torino
Bruino
Sangano
Rivoli
Rosta
Alpignano
Caselette
Pianezza
Collegno
Grugliasco
Druento
Venaria
Savonera
Borgaro Torinese
Mappano
Caselle Tor.
Aeroporto di Caselle
Malanghero
S. Francesco al Campo
San Maurizio
Lombardore
Rivarossa
Rivarolo
Balangero
Ciriè
Robassomero
Fiano
Villanova Canavese
Nole
Grosso
Mathi
Lanzo Torinese
Germagnano
Monastero di Lanzo
Balme
Ala di Stura
Usseglio
Viù
Rubiana
Almese
Avigliana
Buttigliera Alta
Rosta
Villardora
Caselette
Pianezza
Mte. Musinè 1150
Cafasse
Monastero di Lanzo
la Cassa
Givoletto
Val della Torre
Brione
Grange
Reano
Trana
Giaveno
Coazze
Valgioie
Sangano
Piossasco
Volvera
Airasca
None
Candiolo
Vinovo
La Loggia
Carignano
Carmagnola

NÁPOLI

Acerra
Caivano
Afragola
Frattamaggiore
Frattaminore
Grumo Nevano
Arzano
Casoria
Casalnuovo di Nap.
S. Pietro a Pat.
Cardito
Crispano
Cercola
Volla
Caravita
Ponticelli
Barra
Pòrtici
S. Giorgio a Crem.
San Giovanni a Ted.
Torre del Greco
Resina
Ercolano
Pòllena
Trócchia
Massa di Somma
S. Sebastiano al Ves.
S. Anastasia
Pomigliano d'Arco
Marigliano
Mariglianella
Brusciano
Castello di Cisterna
Somma Ves.
Ottaviano
S. Giuseppe Vesuviano
Terzigno
Boscoreale
Boscotrecase
Trecase
Torre Annunziata
Pompei
Mte. Somma 1132
Vesùvio 1277
Sciano
Palazzuolo
S. Antimo
Casandrino
Melito di Nap.
Mugnano di Nap.
Villaricca
Calvizzano
Qualiano
Marano di Nap.
Giugliano in Camp.
Quarto
Pianura
Agnano Terme
Campi Flegrei
Pozzuoli
Bagnoli
Coròglio
Posillipo
Soccavo
S. Paolo
Fuorigrotta
Vomero
Capodimonte
Secondigliano
Miano
Museo e Galleria Naz.
Stazione Centrale
Sta. Lucia
Palazzo Reale
Cast. dell'Ovo
Golfo di Nápoli
Sorrento
Capri
Ischia
Prócida

ROMA

CITTÀ DEL VATICANO
S. Pietro
Castel Sant'Angelo
Trastévere
Gianicolense
Monteverde Nuovo
Aurelio
Trionfale
Mte. Mario 139
Foro Italico
Ponte Milvio
Villa Borghese
Villa Ada
Stazione Termini
Università
Tiburtino
Pietralata
Tufello
Mte. Sacro
Prenestino Labicano
Centocelle
Cinecittà
Quadraro
Tuscolano
Appio
Ostiense
E.U.R.
Garbatella
Magliana
Corviale
Valcanuta
Pisana
la Pisana
Casalotti
Primavalle
Torrevecchia
Ottavia
la Giustiniana
Tomba di Nerone
Tor di Quinto
Acqua Acetosa
Aniene
Tor Sapienza
la Rustica
Rebibbia
S. Basilio
Settecamini
Via Nomentana
Via Tiburtina
Via Prenestina
Via Casilina
Via Appia Antica
Via Ardeatina
Via Ostiense
Via del Mare
Via Cristoforo Colombo
Via Aurelia
Via Portuense
Aeroporto Intercontinentale Leonardo da Vinci
Ponte Galéria
Acilia
Vitìnia
Spinaceto
Tévere
Aniene
Aeron. d. Ciampino
Ciampino
Cecchignola
Torricola
Vallerano
G.R.A.

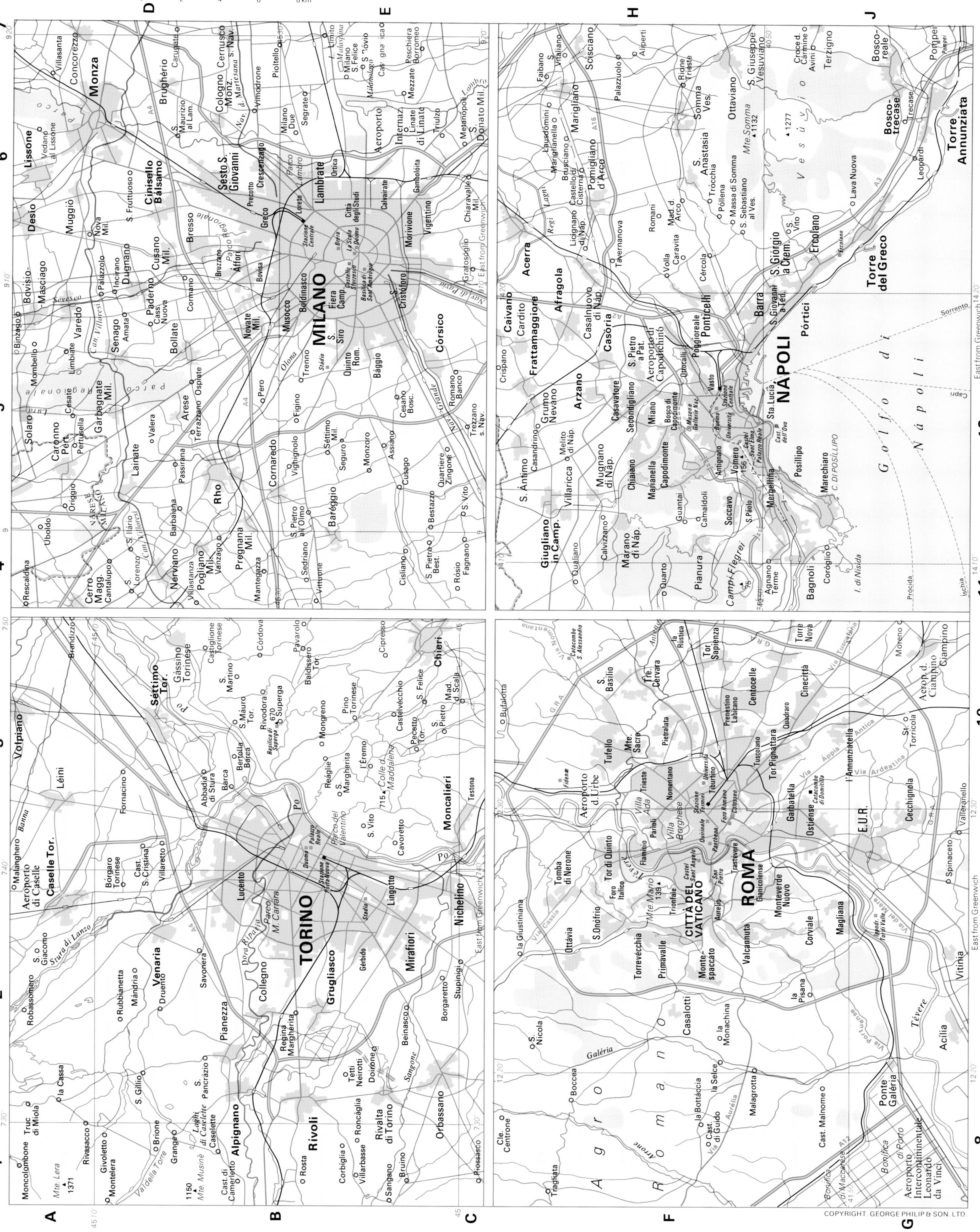

COPYRIGHT GEORGE PHILIP & SON. LTD.

1: 200 000

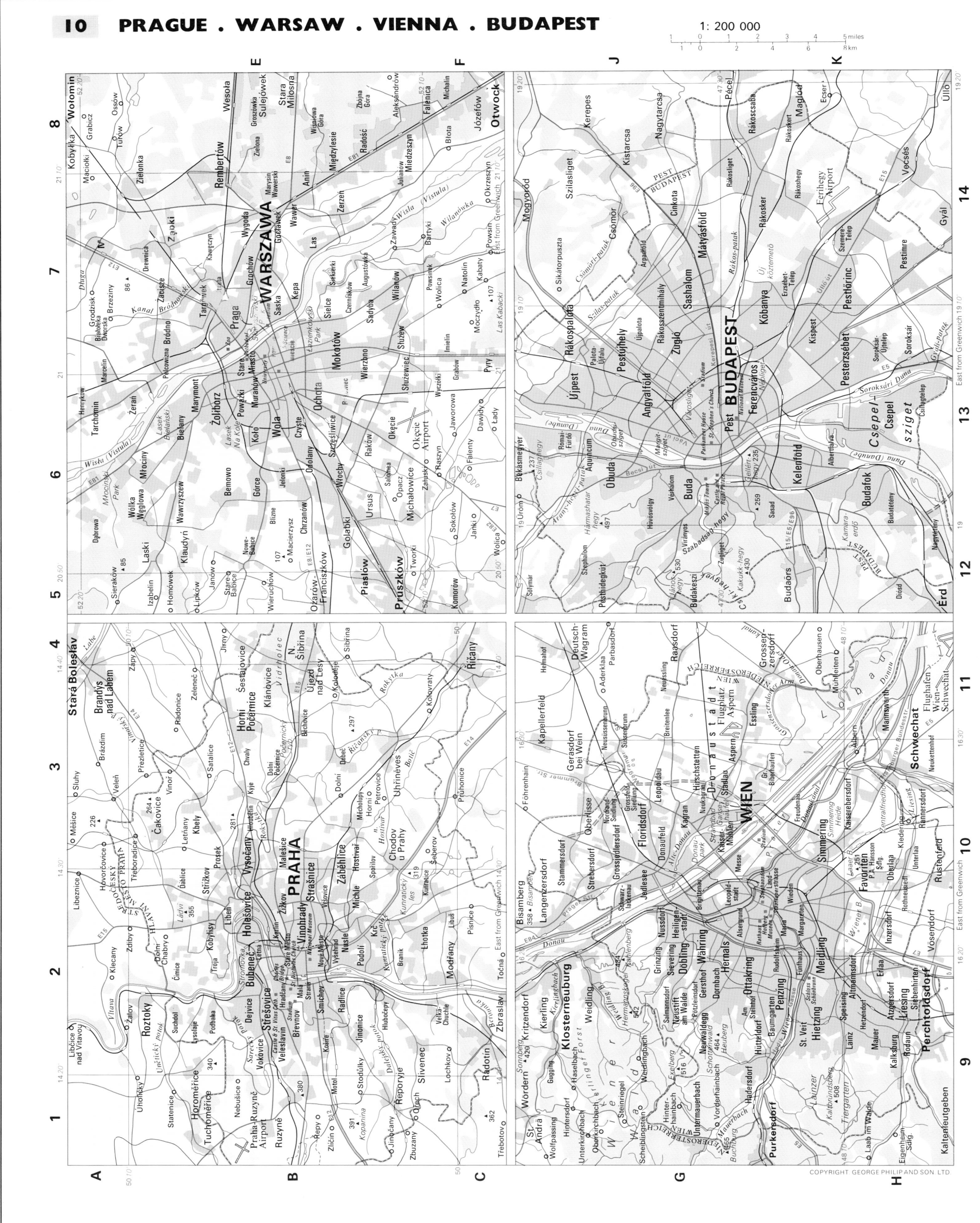

1: 200 000

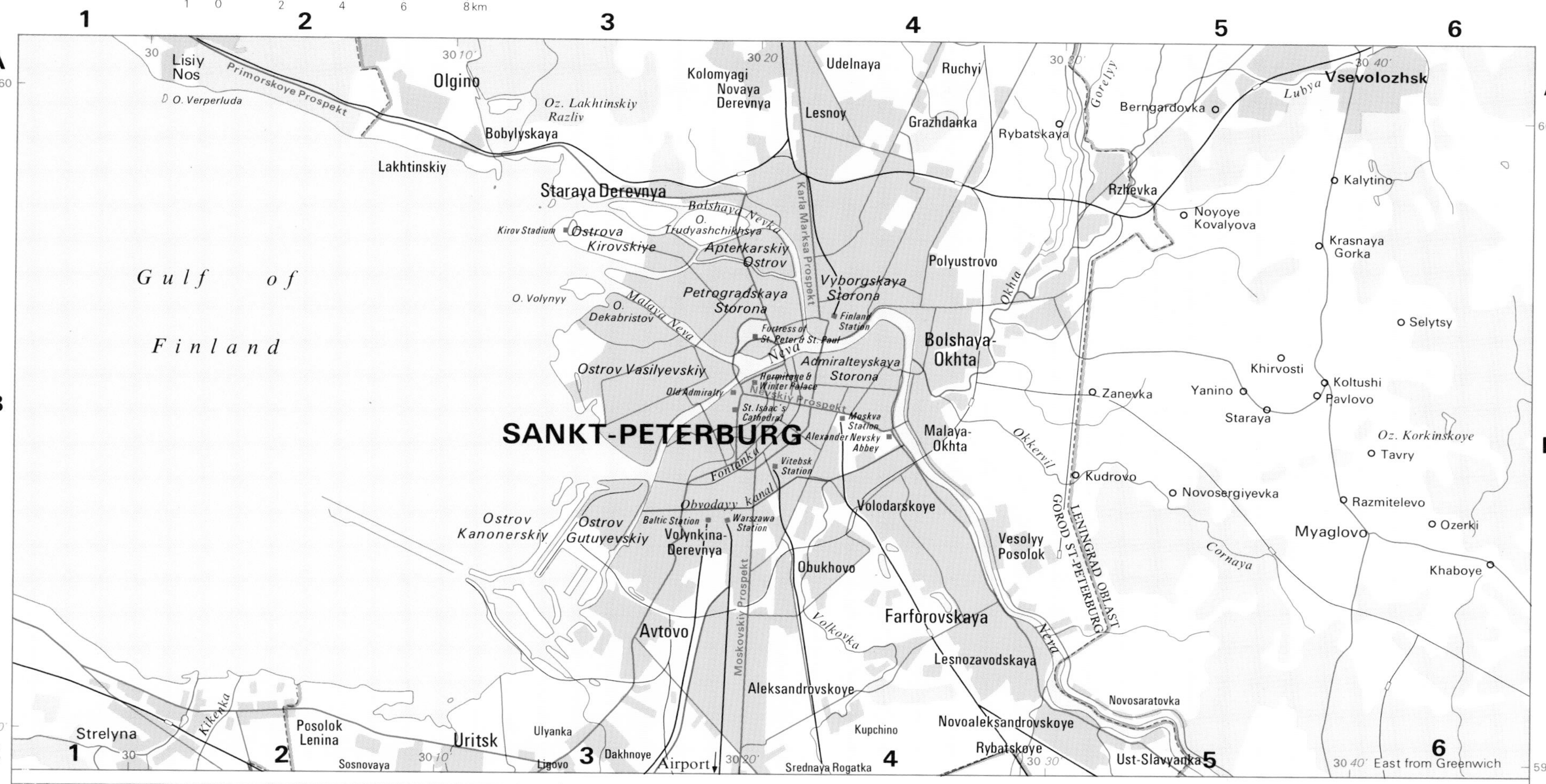

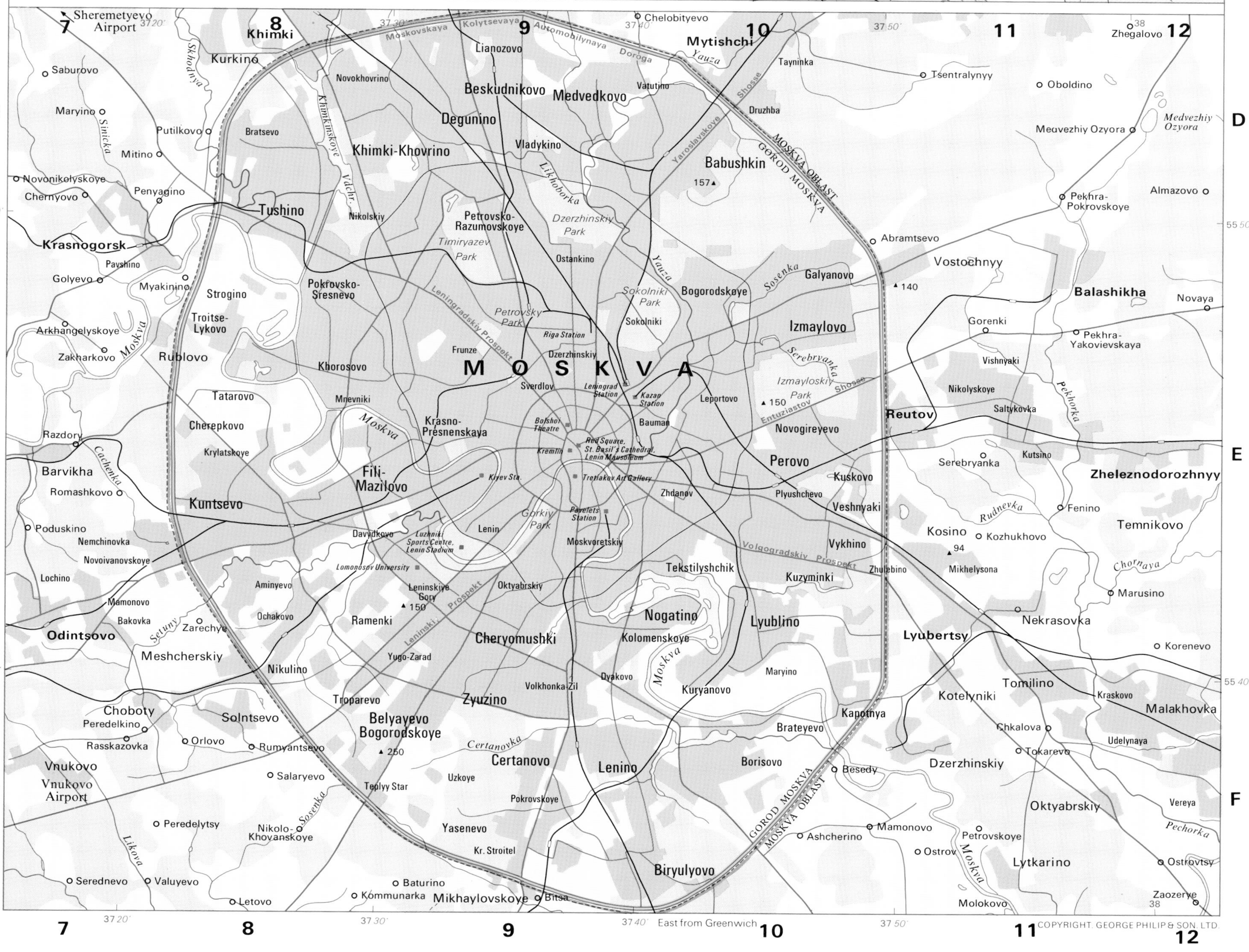

1 0 1 2 3 4 5 miles
1 0 1 2 4 6 8 km

1 2 3 4 5 6

A 60

Lisiy Nos
Olgino
Udelnaya
Ruchyi
Gorelyi
Vsevolozhsk
Lubya
30
30 20
30 50
30 40
O. Verperluda
Primorskoye Prospekt
Kolomyagi
Novaya Derevnya
Lesnoy
Berngardovka
Lakhtinskiy
Bobylyskaya
Oz. Lakhtinskiy Razliv
Grazhdanka
Rybatskaya
Rzhevka
Kalytino
Staraya Derevnya
Bolshaya Nevka
Trudyashchikhsya
Kirov Stadium
Ostrova Kirovskiye
Apterkarskiy Ostrov
Vyborgskaya Storona
Polyustrovo
Noyoye Kovalyova
Krasnaya Gorka
Petrogradskaya Storona
O. Volynyy
O. Dekabristov
Malaya Neva
Selytsy
Fortress of St. Peter & St. Paul
Bolshaya-Okhta
Okhta
Khirvosti
Koltushi

B

Ostrov Vasilyevskiy
Hermitage & Winter Palace
Admiralteyskaya Storona
Admiralty
Zanevka
Yanino
Pavlovo
Old Admiralty
Neva
Moskva Station
Malaya-Okhta
Staraya
Oz. Korkinskoye
St. Isaac's Cathedral
Nevskiy Prospekt
Alexander Nevsky Abbey
Tavry
SANKT-PETERBURG
Fontanka
Vitebsk Station
Kudrovo
Novosergiyevka
Razmitelevo
Fontanka
Obvodyy kanal
Volodarskoye
Ostrov Kanonerskiy
Ostrov Gutuyevskiy
Baltic Station
Warszawa Station
Volynkina-Derevnya
Vesolyy Posolok
Myaglovo
Ozerki
Obukhovo
Khaboye
Moskovskiy Prospekt
Avtovo
Farforovskaya
Cornaya
Volkovka
LENINGRAD OBLAST
GOROD ST-PETERBURG
Lesnozavodskaya
Aleksandrovskoye
Novosaratovka
Strelyna
Posolok Lenina
Uritsk
Ulyanka
Srednyaya Rogatka
Novoaleksandrovskoye
C 59 50
Sosnovaya
Ligovo
Dakhnoye
Airport
Kupchino
Rybatskoye
Ust-Slavyanka
30 10
30 20
30 30
30 40' East from Greenwich
59 50
1 2 3 4 5 6

7 8 9 10 11 12
Sheremetyevo Airport
Khimki
Chelobityevo
Mytishchi
Zhegalovo
37 20'
37 40'
37 50'
38
Saburovo
Kurkino
Moskovskaya
Kolytsevaya
Automobilynaya Doroga
Tayninka
Tsentralynyy
Oboldino
Maryino
Novokhorino
Lianozovo
Vatutino
Yauza
Mitino
Putilkovo
Bratsevo
Beskudnikovo
Medvedkovo
Druzhba
Medvezhiy Ozyora
D 55 50
Novonikolyskoye
Khimki-Khovrino
Degunino
Vladykino
Babushkin
Medvezhiy Ozyora
Almazovo
Chernyovo
Penyagino
Nikolskiy
157
Pekhra-Pokrovskoye
Tushino
Petrovsko-Razumovskoye
Dzerzhinskiy Park
Yauza
Abramtsevo
Vostochnyy
Krasnogorsk
Timiryazev Park
Ostankino
Sokolniki Park
Bogorodskoye
Galyanovo
140
Balashikha
Pavshino
Pokrovsko-Stresnevo
Sokolniki
Serebryanka
Novaya
Golyevo
Myakinino
Strogino
Riga Station
Izmaylovo
Gorenki
Arkhangelyskoye
Troitse-Lykovo
Frunze
Petrovsky Park
Izmaylskiy Park
Vishnyaki
Pekhra-Yakovievskaya
Zakharkovo
Rublovo
Khorosovo
Dzerzhinskiy
Nikolyskoye
E
Razdory
MOSKVA
Sverdlov
Leningrad Station
Kazay Station
Leportovo
150
Entuziastov Shosse
Novogireyevo
Reutov
Barvikha
Cherepkovo
Mnevniki
Krasno-Presnenskaya
Bolshoi Theatre
Red Square, St. Basil's Cathedral
Bauman
Perovo
Kuskovo
Serebryanka
Kutsino
Zheleznodorozhnyy
Romashkovo
Krylatskoye
Kremlin
Lenin Mausoleum
Tretlakov Art Gallery
Plyushchevo
Fenino
Poduskino
Kuntsevo
Kiyev Sta.
Zhdanov
Veshnyaki
Kosino
Kozhukhovo
Temnikovo
Nemchinovka
Fili-Mazilovo
Gorkiy Park
Pavelets Station
Vykhino
Mikhelysona
Novoivanovskoye
Davidkovo
Luzhniki Sports Centre, Lenin Stadium
Lenin
Kuzyminki
94
Marusino
Lochino
Lomonosov University
Moskvoretskiy
Volgogradskiy Prospekt
Nekrasovka
Mamonovo
Bakovka
Aminyevo
Ochakovo
Oktyabrskiy
Tekstilyshchik
Koreneyo
Zarechye
150
Ramenki
Nogatino
Lyublino
Lyubertsy
Tomilino
Odintsovo
Setun
Nikulino
Yugo-Zarad
Cheryomushki
Kolomenskoye
Maryino
Kraskovo
Meshcherskiy
Troparevo
Zyuzino
Volkhonka Zil
Dyakovo
Kuryanovo
Kapotnya
Kotelyniki
Malakhovka
F 55 40'
Choboty
Solntsevo
Rumyantsevo
Belyayevo Bogorodskoye
Certanovka
Lenino
Brateyevo
Chkalova
Udelnaya
Dzerzhinskiy
Peredelkino
Orlovo
Uzkoye
Pokrovskoye
Borisovo
Besedy
Rasskazovka
250
Certanovo
Tokareva
Vnukovo
Salaryevo
Teplyy Star
Yasenevo
Biryulyovo
Petrovskoye
Vereya
Vnukovo Airport
Peredelytsy
Nikolo-Khovanskoye
Kr. Stroitel
Ashcherino
Oktyabrskiy
Serednevo
Valuyevo
Letovo
Baturino
Kommunarka
Mikhaylovskoye
Bitsa
Ostrov
Lytkarino
Ostrovtsy
Molokovo
Zaozerye
7 8 9 10 11 12
37 20'
37 30'
37 40' East from Greenwich
37 50'
38

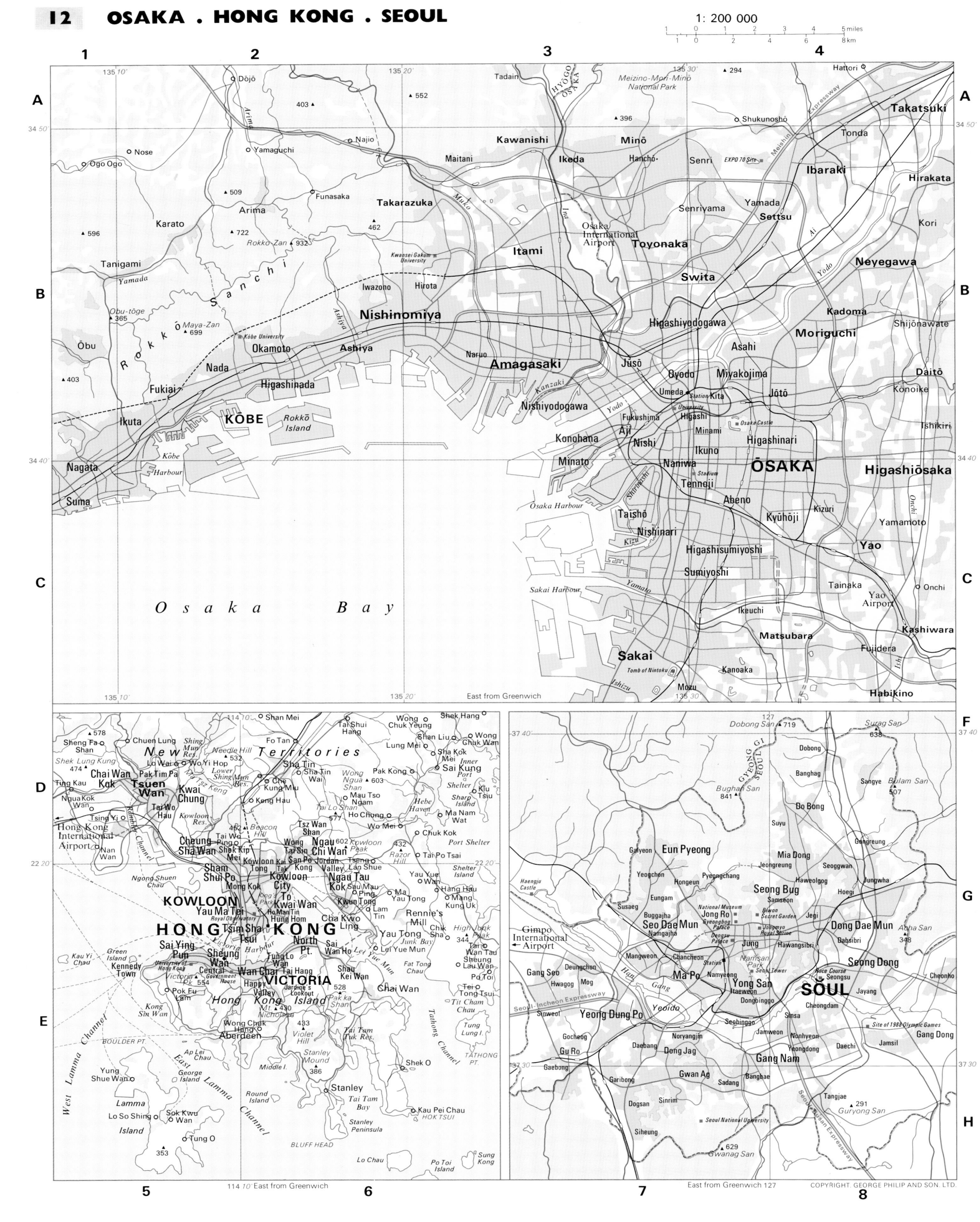

1: 200 000

5 miles
8 km

A

Dōjō
403 ▲
552 ▲
294 ▲
Meizino-Mori-Mino
National Park
Tadain
Shukunoshō
Hattori
Takatsuki
Najio
Yamaguchi
Kawanishi
Ikeda
Minō
Hanchō
Senri
EXPO 70 Site
Tonda
Ibaraki
Hirakata
Karato
Maitani
Senriyama
Yamada
Settsu
Kori
596 ▲
509 ▲
Funasaka
Takarazuka
462 ▲
Itami
Osaka
International
Airport
Toyonaka
Swita
Neyegawa
722 ▲
Rokkō Zan
932 ▲
Kwansei Gakuin
University

B

Obu-tōge
365
Maya-Zan
699 ▲
Kōbe University
Iwazono
Hirota
Nishinomiya
Higashiyodogawa
Kadoma
Moriguchi
Shijōnawate
Ōbu
Okamoto
Ashiya
Naruo
Amagasaki
Jūsō
Asahi
Dāitō
Fukiai
Nada
Higashinada
Kanzaki
Ōyodo
Miyakojima
Kōnoike
403 ▲
Ikuta
Kōbe
University
Umeda
Station Kita
Jōtō
Nishiyodogawa
Yodo
Fukushima
Higashi
Osaka Castle
Ishikiri
Suma
Kōbe
Harbour
Rokkō
Island
Konohana
Aji
Nishi
Minami
Ikuno
Higashinari
Higashiōsaka

C

Nagata
Minato
Naniwa
ŌSAKA
Tennōji
Stadium
Abeno
Kyūhōji
Kizuri
Yamamoto
Osaka Harbour
Taishō
Nishinari
Yao
Kizu
Higashisumiyoshi
Tainaka
Onchi
Sakai Harbour
Yamato
Sumiyoshi
Yao
Airport
Kashiwara
Ikeuchi
Matsubara
Fujidera
Sakai
Tomb of Nintoku
Kanaoka
Ishizu
Mozu
Habikino

Osaka Bay

East from Greenwich

D

Shan Mei
Shek Hang
Dobong San
719
Surag San
638
Chuen Lung
Shing Mun Res.
Fo Tan
Tai Shui Hang
Wong Chuk Yeung
Shan Liu
Lung Mei
Wong Chuk Wan
New
Lo Wai
Wo Yi Hop
532
Sha Tin
Sha Kok Mei
Inner Port
Sai Kung
Dobong
Sheng Fa Shan
578
Territories
Needle Hill
Lower Shing Mun Res.
Sha Tin Wai
Pak Kong
Banghag
Sangye
Bulam San
507
Shek Lung Kung
474
Pak Tim Pa
Chai Wan Kok
Kwai Chung
Tsz Keng
Kung Miu
Wong Ngua Shan
603
Mau Tso Shan
Hebe Haven
Ma Nam Wat
Bughan San
841
Suyu
Do Bong
Tsuen Wan
Tai Wo Hau
Kowloon Res.
Beacon Hill
Tai Lo Shan
577
Ho Chung
Wo Mei
Chuk Kok
Port Shelter

E

Ng ua Kok Wan
Tsing Yi
Cheung Sha Wan
Ping Shek
Wong Tai Sin
Ngau Chi Wan
602
Kowloon Peak
432
Razor Hill
Tai Po Tsai
Shelter Island
Gimpo International Airport
Seo Dae Mun
Namgaiho
Jung
Hong Kong International Airport
Nan Wan
Sham Shui Po
Mong Kok
Tong Tau
Kowloon City
San Po Kong
Kowloon Bay
Kwun Tong
Jordan
Tseng Lan Shue
Yau Yue Wan
Hang Hau
Shelter Island

KOWLOON
Yau Ma Tei
Ho Man Tin
Kwai Wan
Chi Wan
Kok
Ma Ping
Lam Tin
Yau Tong
Mang Kung Uk
Rennie's Mill
Chik Chau
High Junk Peak
344
Tai
Po Toi

HONG KONG
Tsim Sha Tsui
Hung Hom
Cha Kwo Ling
Yau Tong
Lei Yue Mun
Sheung Lau Wan
Po Toi
Sai Ying Pun
Sheung Wan
North Pt.
Sai Wan Ho
Shau Kei Wan
Fat Tong Chau
Tei Tong Tsui

Kennedy Town
VICTORIA
Wan Chai
Tai Hang
528
Tung Lung I.
Happy Valley
Jardine's Lookout
Pak ka Shan
Chai Wan
TATHONG PT.

SOUL area (right):
Haengju Castle
Galyeon
Eun Pyeong
Mia Dong
Seoggwan
Haweolgog
Jungwha
Yeogchon
Hongeun
Pyeongchang
Seong Bug
Samseon
Hoegi
Susaeg
Buggajha
Jong Ro
Gyeongbog Palace
Biwon
Secret Garden
Jegi
National Museum
Changgyeong Palace
Hawangsibri
Dong Dae Mun
348
Abha San
Gang Seo
Deungchon
Hwagog
Mog
Mangweon
Changcheon
Station
Namsan
Park
Seoul Tower
Jung
Namyeong
Yong San
Itaewon
Hawangsibri
Seong Dong
Seongsu
Cheonho
Mt. 430
Nicholson
Wong Chuk Hang
Aberdeen
Violet Hill
Stanley Mound
386
Gu Ro
Yeong Dung Po
Yeoido
Han Gang
Seobinggo
Jamwon
Nonhyeon
Jayang

Hong Kong Island

Ap Lei Chau
George Island
Middle I.
Round Island
Stanley
Tai Tam Bay
Site of 1988 Olympic Games
Gang Nam
Gang Dong

Yung Shue Wan
Lo So Shing
Sok Kwu Wan
Tung O
353
Lamma Island
Stanley Peninsula
BLUFF HEAD
Kau Pei Chau
HOK TSUI
Lo Chau
Po Toi Island
Sung Kong

East from Greenwich

1: 200 000

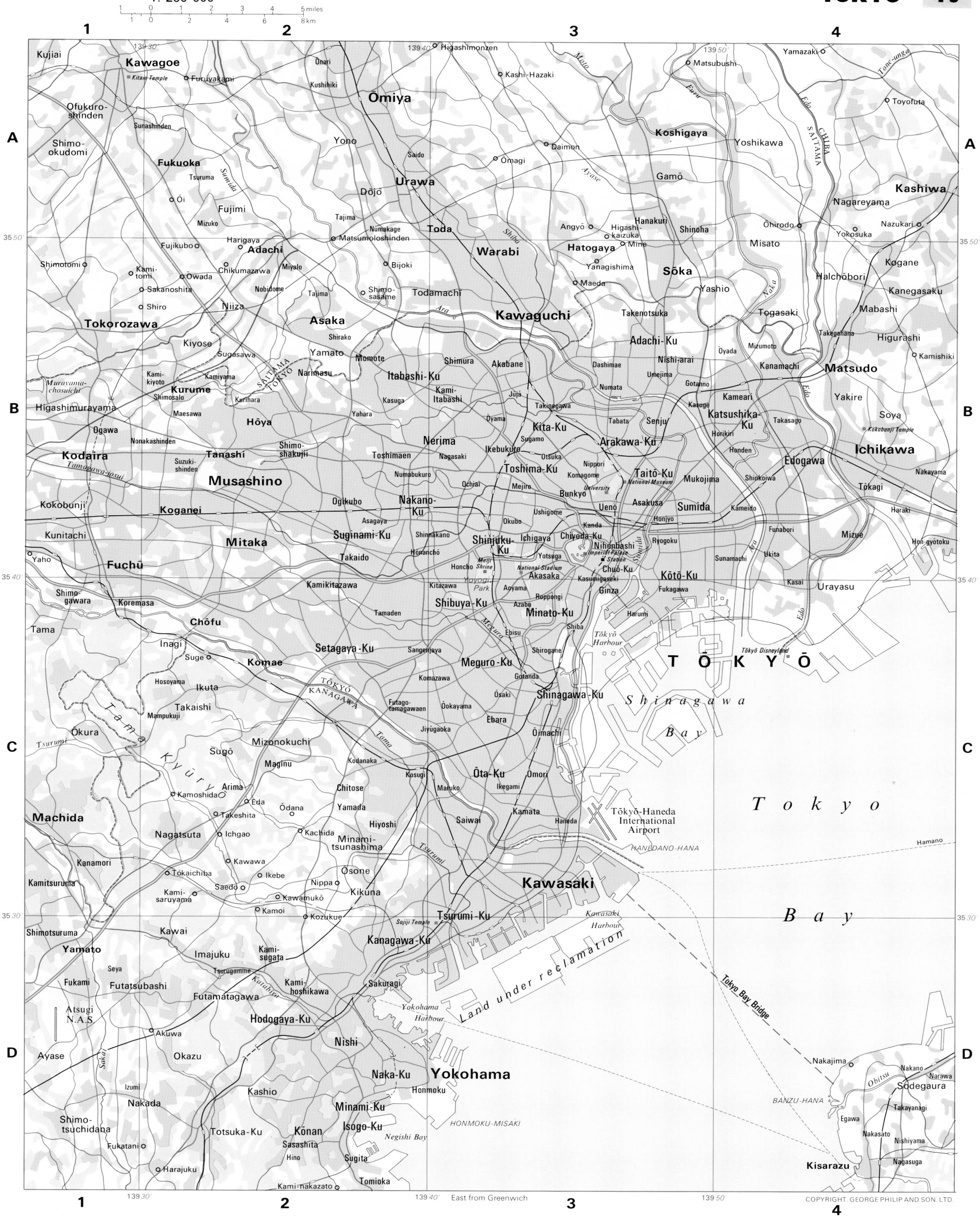

5 miles
8 km

1   2   3   4

Kujiai
Kawagoe
Kitani Temple   Furuyakami
Ōnari
Higashimonzen   Yamazaki
Kashi-Hazaki   Matsubushi
Kushihiki
Ōmiya
Ōfukuro-shinden
Toyofuta
Sunashinden
Yono
Koshigaya
Saido
Daimon
Yoshikawa
Shimo-okudomi
Ōmagi
Gamō
Fukuoka
Urawa
Kashiwa
Tsuruma
Fujimi
Dōjō
Nagareyama
Ōi
Mizuko
Tajima
Hanakuri
Angyō   Higashi-kaizuka   Shinoha
Nazukari
Ōhirodo   Yokosuka
Fujikubo   Harigaya
Adachi
Chikumazawa   Matsumotoshinden
Numakage
Toda
Warabi
Hatogaya
Mine
Maeda
Yanagishima
Misato
Halchōbori
Shimotomi
Kami-tomi
Miyalo
Bijoki
Shimo-sasame
Sōka
Kōgane
Owada
Shiro
Nobidome
Tajima
Todamachi
Yashio
Kanegasaku
Sakanoshita
Kawaguchi
Takenotsuka
Togasaki
Mabashi
Niiza
Asaka
Shirako
Shimura
Akabane
Adachi-Ku
Ōyada
Mizumoto
Takagahana
Higurashi
Tokorozawa
Kiyose
Yamato
Momote
Nishi-arai
Kamishiki
Sugasawa
Kamiyama
Narimasu
Itabashi-Ku
Dashimae   Umejima
Kanamachi
Matsudo
Kami-kiyoto
Kuríhara
Kasuga
Kami-Itabashi
Jūjō
Numata
Gotanno
Yakire
Kurume
Maesawa
Yahara
Takinegawa
Tabata
Senju
Kameari
Soya
Higashimurayama
Hōya
Kita-Ku
Horikiri
Honden
Takasago
Murayama-chosuichi
Ogawa
Nonakashinden
Tanashi
Shimo-shakujii
Nerima
Nagasaki
Ikebukuro
Ōyama
Arakawa-Ku
Kokubunji Temple
Ichikawa
Suzuki-shinden
Toshimaen
Numabukuro
Sugamo
Ōtsuka
Nippori
Katsushika-Ku
Kodaira
Tamagawa-josui
Musashino
Toshima-Ku
Komagome
National Museum
Mukojima
Edogawa
Ōchiai
Mejiro
Shinkoiwa
Nakayama
Kokobunji
Koganei
Ogikubo
Nakano-Ku
Ushigome
Bunkyo
University
Asakusa
Sumida
Kameido
Tōkagi
Asagaya
Shinmakano
Okubo
Kanda
Honjyo
Haraki
Kunitachi
Mitaka
Suginami-Ku
Shinjuku-Ku
Ichigaya
Chiyoda-Ku
Ryogoku
Mizue
Yaho
Takaido
Hōanchō
Yotsuga
Nihonbashi
Station
Sunamachi
Ukita
Hon-gyotoku
Fuchū
Kamikitazawa
Honcho
Meiji Shrine
National Stadium
Imperial Palace
Chūō-Ku
Kōtō-Ku
Shimo-gawara
Koremasa
Yoyogi Park
Akasaka
Kasumigaseki
Ginza
Fukagawa
Kasai
Urayasu
Tama
Tamaden
Shibuya-Ku
Aoyama
Roppongi
Tōkyō Disneyland
Chōfu
Setagaya-Ku
Sangenjaya
Meguro-Ku
Azabu
Minato-Ku
Shiba
Harumi
Inagi
Suge
Komae
Komazawa
Gotanda
Ebisu
Shirogane
Tōkyō Harbour
TŌKYŌ
Hosoyama
Ikuta
Futago-tamagawaen
Ōkayama
Ōsaki
Shinagawa-Ku
Shinagawa
Takaishi
Mampukuji
Jiyūgaoka
Ebara
Bay
Okura
Sugō
Mizonokuchi
Kotanaka
Ōimachi
Tokyo
Magínu
Ōta-Ku
Machida
Arima
Chitose
Yamada
Kamata
Ōmori
Kamoshida
Eda
Ōdana
Ikegami
Bay
Nagatsuta
Ichgao
Takeshita
Hiyoshi
Saiwai
Haneda
Kanamori
Kachida
Tōkyō-Haneda International Airport
Kawawa
Minami-tsunashima
Hamano
Kamitsuruma
Tōkaichiba
Ikebe
Ōsone
HANEDANO-HANA
Kami-saruyama
Saedo
Nippa
Kikuna
Kawasaki
Kamoi
Kawamukō
Kozukue
Sojiji Temple
Tsurumi-Ku
Kawasaki Harbour
Shimotsuruma
Kawai
Kami-sugata
Kanagawa-Ku
Yamato
Imajuku
Tsurugamine
Land under reclamation
Seya
Futatsubashi
Katabira
Kami-hoshikawa
Sakuragi
Tokyo Bay Bridge
Fukami
Futamatagawa
Yokohama Harbour
Atsugi N.A.S
Hodogaya-Ku
Nakajima
Nakano
Narawa
Ayase
Akuwa
Okazu
Nishi
Sōdegaura
Obitsu
Izumi
Naka-Ku
Yokohama
BANZU-HANA
Egawa
Takayanagi
Shimo-tsuchidana
Nakada
Kashio
Honmoku
Minami-Ku
Nakasato
Nishiyama
Fukatani
Kōnan
Isogo-Ku
HONMOKU-MISAKI
Negishi Bay
Sasashita
Hino
Sugita
Kisarazu
Nagasuga
Harajuku
Tomioka
Kami-nakazato

East from Greenwich
COPYRIGHT. GEORGE PHILIP AND SON. LTD.

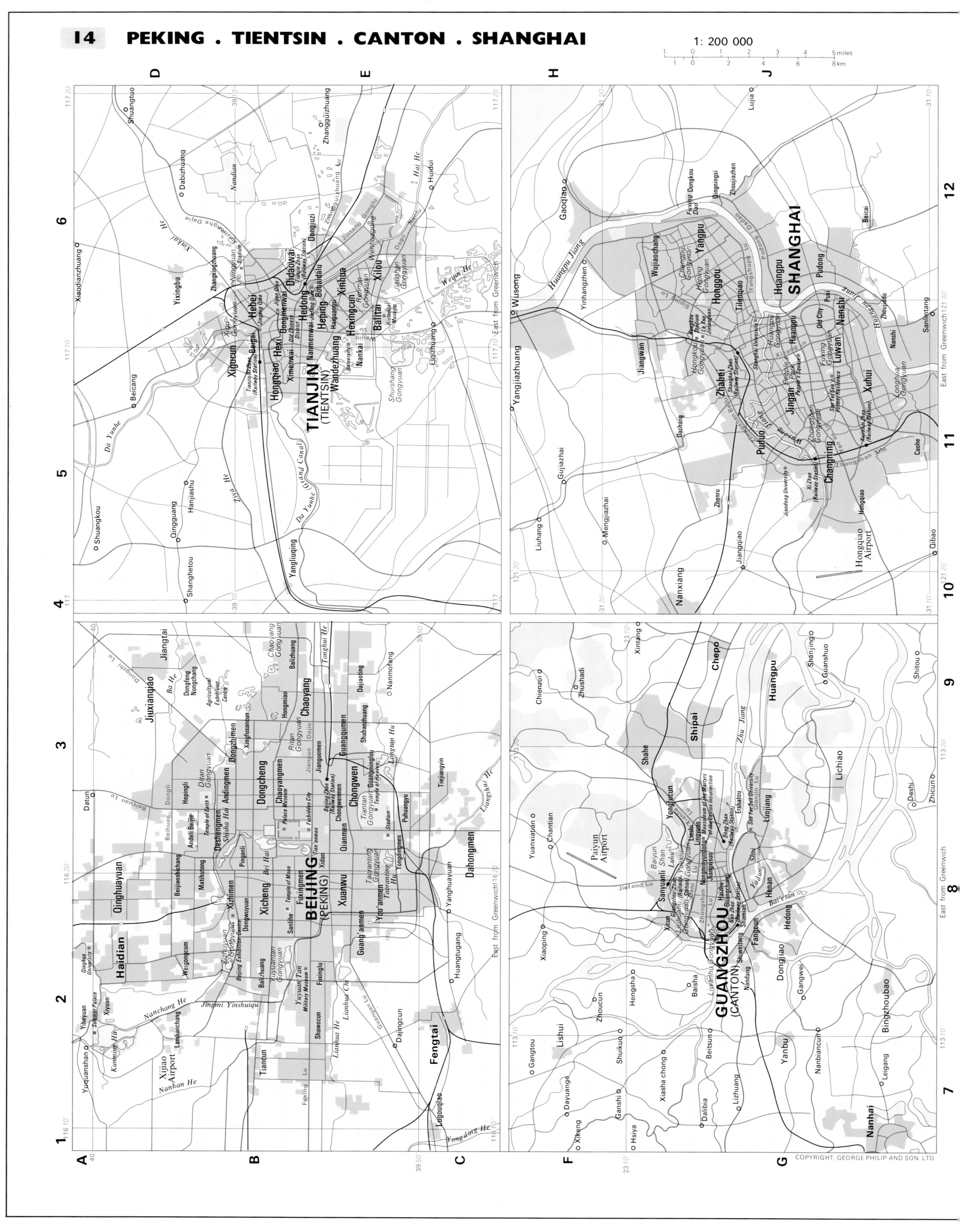

1 : 200 000

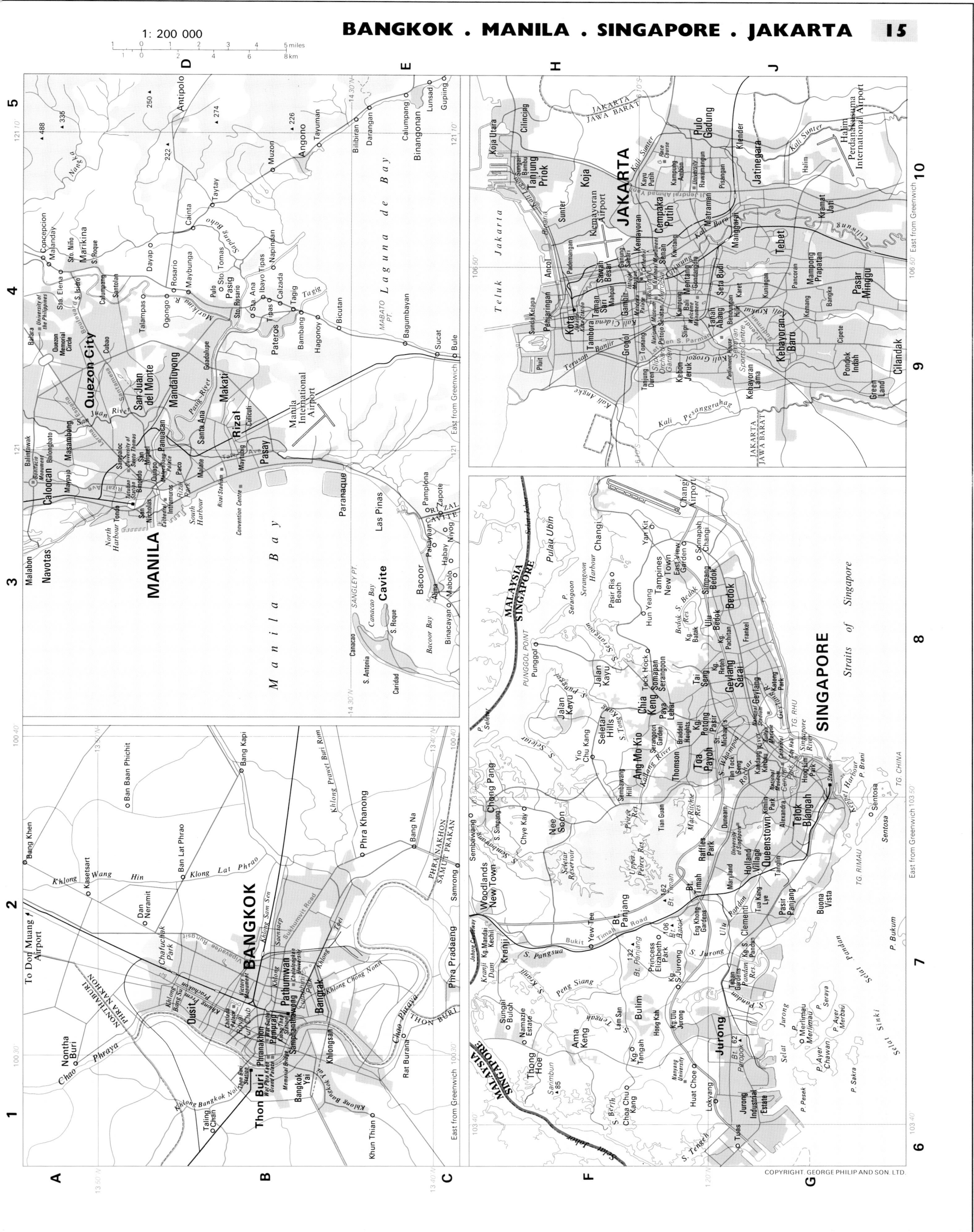

1 : 200 000

1 : 200 000

1   0   1   2   3   4   5 miles
1   0   2   4   6   8 km

Calcutta (grid C–F, 4–6)

Naihati · Madatpur · Gauripur · Panpur · Bhatpara · Bidyadharpur · Mirzapur · Basudebpur · Beraberi · Balagarh · Bandipur · Madhyamgram · Phinga · Dum Dum Int. Airport · Gopalparo · Satgachi · Baguiati · Salt Water · Lake · Atghara · Atghara · Hathara · Naoabad

Chunchura · Bhatpara · Kankinara · Jagatdal · Aipur · Garulia · Ichapur · Barrackpore Airport · Telinipara · Newabganj · Sodpur · Khardah · Panihati · Kamarhati · Nimta · Nimta · CALCUTTA · Tollygunge

Simla · Kamdebpur · Chandannagar · Mankundu · Bhadreswar · Champdani · Baidyabati · Shrirampur · Ballabhpur · Satghara · Rishra · Konnagar · Kotrang · Uttarpara · Bally · Liluah · Bantra · Haora · Sibpur · Kidderpore · Alipore · Ballygunge · Bhawanipore · Russa

Hooghly · Grand Trunk Rd. North · Garden Reach · Behala · Panchur · Mahikpur · Nangi · Baj Baj · Bauria · Chakdaha

Delhi / New Delhi (grid A–B, 1–3)

Sahibabad · Nangloi Jat · Rithala · Puth Kalan · Daulatpur · Loni · Subhepur · Rampur · Jauli · Atzalpur · Bhopura · Shahdara · Maharajpur · Nithari · Atta · Aganpur · Ghazipur · Kondli · Chhlera Bangar

DELHI · NEW DELHI · Delhi Cantonment · Palam Int. Airport · Safdar Jang Airport · Red Fort · Yamuna · Grand Trunk Road · Ring Road · The Ridge · UTTAR PRADESH · DELHI · Agra Canal · Okhla · Kalkaji · Shahpur Jat · Munirka · Mehram Nagar

Bombay (grid G–H, 7–9)

BOMBAY · Bandra · BANDRA POINT · Colaba · COLABA POINT · Santa Cruz · Mahim · Worli · Parel · Byculla · Mazagaon · Girgaum · Malabar Hill · Towers of Silence · Back Bay · Marine Dr. · Gateway of India · Chhatrapati Shivaji Terminus · Victoria Gardens

Salsette Island · Thana Creek · Ghatkopar · Chembur · Kurla · Trombay · Elephanta Island (Gharapuri) · Elephanta Caves · Bombay Harbour · Butcher Island · Cross Island · Oyster Rock · Panvel Creek · Sheva · Uran · Karanja · Dhutumkhar · Salt Pans

ARABIAN SEA · Juhu · Santa Cruz International Airport · Sahar International Airport · Belapurpada · Shahabad

East from Greenwich

COPYRIGHT. GEORGE PHILIP AND SON. LTD.

1: 200 000

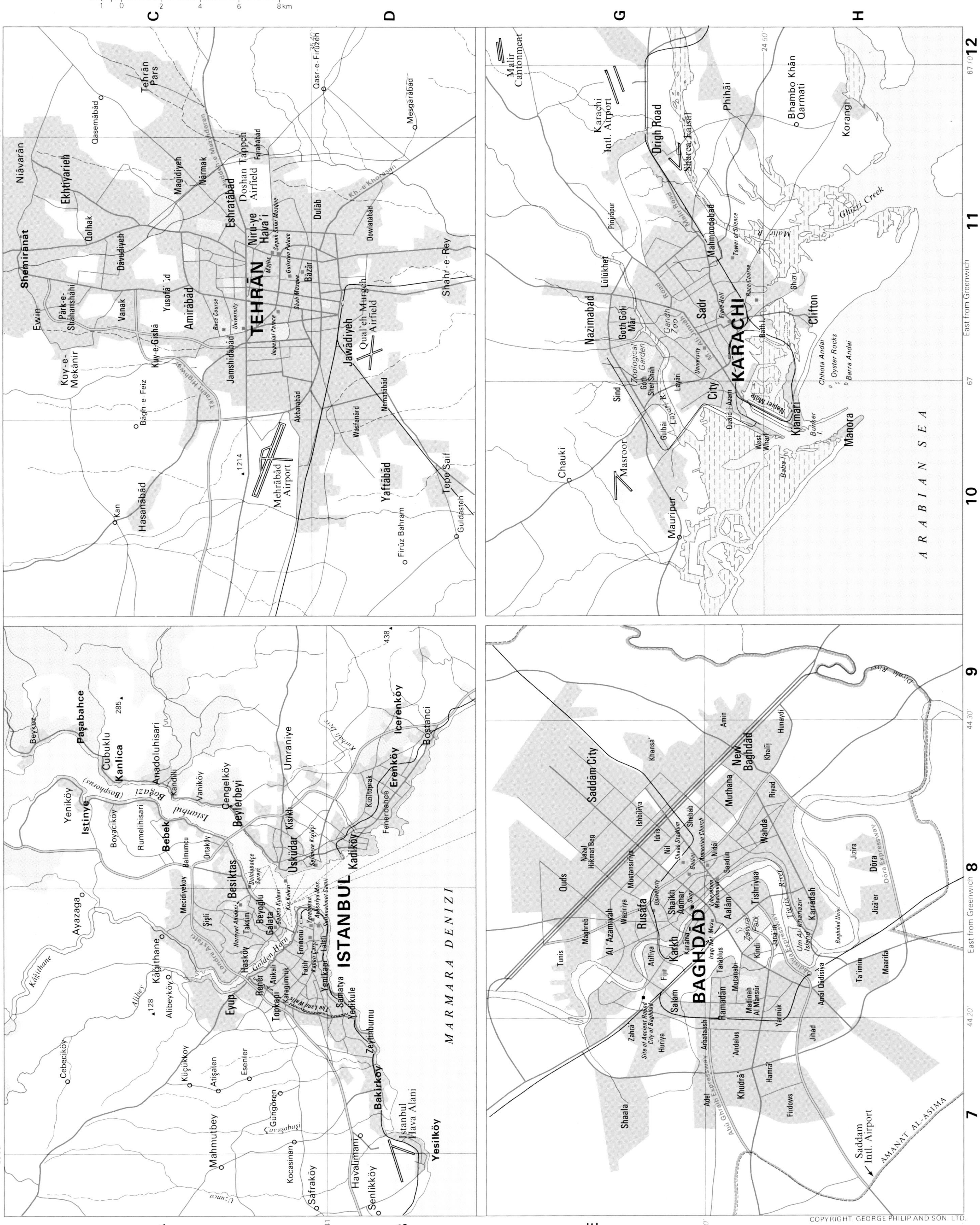

miles / km scale bar

ISTANBUL (map)

Beykoz, Paşabahçe, Çubuklu, Kanlıca, Anadoluhisarı, Kandilli, Vaniköy, Çengelköy, Beylerbeyi, Küçüksu, Yeniköy, İstinye, Boğaziçi (Bosphorus), Rumelihisarı, Boyacıköy, Bebek, Arnavutköy, Ortaköy, Balmumcu, Üsküdar, Kısıklı, Umraniye, Erenköy, İçerenköy, Bostancı, Fenerbahçe, Kızıltoprak, Kadıköy, Haydarpaşa

Beykoz, Mecidiyeköy, Şişli, Beşiktaş, Kağıthane, Hasköy, Beyoğlu, Taksim, Galata, Eminönü, Dolmabahçe Sarayı, Galata Kulesi, Fatih, Aksaray, ISTANBUL, Topkapı, Eyüp, Rami, Zeytinburnu, Yedikule, Silivrikapı, Samatya

Avazaga, Kağıthane, Alibeyköy, Alibeyköy, Küçükköy, Esenler, Güngören, Gaziosmanpaşa, Mahmutbey, Bakırköy, İstanbul Hava Alanı, Yeşilköy, İstanbul Hava Limanı, Havalimanı, Cebeciköy, Küçükköy, Atışalan, Kocasinan, Safraköy, Şenlikköy

MARMARA DENİZİ

TEHRAN (map)

Tehrān Pars, Qasemābād, Niāvarān, Ekhtiyārieh, Uolhak, Dāvūdīyeh, Shemirānāt, Ewin, Park-e-Shāhanshāhī, Kuy-e-Mekānir, Kuy-e-Gishā, Vanak, Amīrābād, Yusofābād, Bāgh-e-Feiz, Jamshīdābād, University, Imperial Palace, TEHRĀN, Magidīyeh, Narmak, Eshratābād, Doshan Tappeh Airfield, Farahābād, Niru-ye Havā'ī, Sepah Shāh Mosque, Golestan Palace, Bāzār, Shāh Mosque, Dulāb, Dowlatābād, Qasr-e-Fīrūzeh, Mesgārābād, Shahr-e-Rey

Hasanābād, Kan, Mehrābād Airport, Akbarābād, Wastanārd, Mehmābād, Jawādīyeh, Qal'eh-Murgh Airfield, Yaftābād, Tepp Saif, Guldasteh, Fīrūz Bahram

BAGHDAD (map)

Saddām City, Khansā, Amin, New Baghdad, Idris, Khalij, Hunaydī, Nazal, Hikmat Beg, Ishbīlīya, Nidāl, Riyad, Jizīra, Dōra, Quds, Nil, Shebāb, Sha'ab Stadium, Baijey, Armenian Church, Shaadūn, Wahda, Jizā'er, Tunis, Mustansirīya, Maghreb, Al 'Azamīyah, Waẓīrīya, RUSĀFA, Shaikh 'Aqmar, Aalām, Tishrīyaa, Baghdad Univ., Atifiya, Fijiir, KARKH, BAGHDAD, Shaikh Omar, Tigris River, Karrādah, Ta'mīm, Salam, Ramadān, Mutaabī, Madinah Al Mansur, Amāl Qadisīya, Maarifa, Zahra, Site of Ancient Ruined City of Baghdad, Huriya, Andalus, Jihād, Yarmūk, Khudrā, Hamrā, Firdows, Shaala, Adel, Saddam Intl. Airport, AMANAT AL-ASIMA, Dijlah River, Dōra Expressway, Abū Ghraib Expressway

KARACHI (map)

Malir Cantonment, Karachi Intl. Airport, Drigh Road, Phihāi, Bhambo Khān Qarmati, Korangī, Ghizri Creek, Pipūrī, Mahmoodabad, Phusī, Lūlūkhet, Tower of Silence, Nazimabad, Goth Goti Mār, Gandhi Zoo, Sadr, Race Course, Ghizri, Clifton, University, Zoological Garden, Goth Sher Shāh, Sind, Liāqūni, Lāyāri, City, KARACHI, Bath I., Chhota Andai, Oyster Rocks, Barra Andai, Chauki, Bunder, Napier Mole, Kiamāri, Masroor, Gulbāi, Lāyāri R., West Wharf, Bāba I., Mauripur, Manora, ARABIAN SEA

East from Greenwich

1 : 200 000

1 0 1 2 3 4 5 miles
1 0 1 2 3 4 6 8 km

Lagos / Cairo panel

Cairo (El Qâhira)

Cairo International Airport
Almaza Airport
Masr el Gedida (Heliopolis)
EL QÂHIRA
Madinet Masr el Qadima (Old Cairo)
EL GIZA
El Giza
Imbâba
El Muski
Citadel
El Matariya
El Zeitûn
El Qubba
El 'Abbasiya
El Bandariya
Shubrâ el Kheima
El Wayli el Kubra
Hilmiya
Bûlâq
'Abdin
Garden City
Presidential Palace
El Zamâlik
El Duqqi
El Awkaf
University
Zoological Gardens
Gezirat edh Dhahab
Madinet el Muqattam
Gebel el Muqattam
Gebel el Ahmar
Gebel et Tura
EL BAHR EL AHMAR
EL QÂHIRA
El Ma'âdi
Tura
Tammûn
El Basâtin
El Talibiya
Saft el Laban
Birak el Kiyam
El Baragil
El Kôm el Ahmar
Minshât el Bekkari
Kafr es Sammân
Zâwiyet Abû Musallam
Shabrâmant
Abû en Numrûs
Tirsa
Nahia
Hakim
Kirdâsa
Bahrig
Ausim
Burtus
Basûs
Gezirat Warrâq Muhammad el Hadri
Warrâq el 'Arab
Warrâq el Hadi
Bahtim
Musturud
Streil
El Qanâtir el Khairiya
Qanal el 'and Illya
Wâdi Digla
Wâdi en Nahdein
Wâdi el Lablâba
Nahr en Nil
Bahr el Lubeini
El Muhît Idkû el Gharbi
Pyramids (Cheops, Khefren, Mykerinos)
Sphinx
Kafr es Sammân
256▲ ▲478 ▲204 ▲193 ▲83

Lagos

LAGOS
Lagos Lagoon
Ikorodu Lagos Municipality
Bight of Benin
Victoria Island
Ikoyi
Lagos Island
Ebute-Metta
Apapa
Iddo
Lagos Harbour
Five Cowrie Creek
Porto Novo Creek
Tarqua Bay
Ebute-Ikorodu
University of Lagos
Oba's Palace
Iddo Station
Lagos State House
National Stadium
Lagos-Ikeja Airport
Ikeja
Mushin
Oshodi
Shogunle
Shomolu
Bariga
Yaba
Ebute-Metta
Surulere
Agege
Idi-Oro
Coker
Ajegunle
Ajara
Ikeja
Badagri
Igbologun
Kirikiri
Amuwo
Okeogbe
Ikuata
Ogogoro
Ipara
Oworonsoki
Oshoro
Moba
Ogoyo
Alaguntan
Iboju
Igbopa
Ogbogbo
Malekete
Ason
Ofin
Ibese
Osorun
Oreta
Erunkan
Onisigun
Ojota
Ogudu
Oke-Afa
Ikotun
Isolo
Isagatedo
Ejigbo
Ewu
Eregun
Idimuo
Arida
Cardoso
Okunola
Olofin
Olsheri-Olofin
Olute
Agboju
Isunba
Imore
Ijesa-Tedo
Ijesa-Osun
Iseri-Osun
Agboyi Creek

Lagos Lagoon
Bight of Benin
East from Greenwich

Johannesburg panel

JOHANNESBURG
Soweto
Germiston
Boksburg
Benoni
Brakpan
Springs
Kwa-Thema
Daveyton
Kempton Park
Modderfontein
Alexandra
Sandton
Sandown
Morningside
Randburg
Roodepoort
Krugersdorp
Discovery
Florida
Meadowlands
Orlando East
Orlando West
Moroka
Nancefield
Alberton
Elsburg
Witfield
Edenvale
Bedford View
Kensington
Rosettenville
Turffontein
Diepkloof
Baragwanath Airport
Johannesburg International Airport
Rand Airport
Jan Smuts Ave
Main Reef Road
New Modder
Springs
Dunswart
Parktown
Parkview
Parktown North
Houghton
Observatory
Mayfair
Westdene
Newlands
Maraisburg
New Canada
Diepkloof Dam
Orlando Dam
Klipspruit
Klip River
Jukskei
Modderfontein
Van Ryn Dam
Geduld Dam
Homestead Lake
Cinderella Dam

East from Greenwich

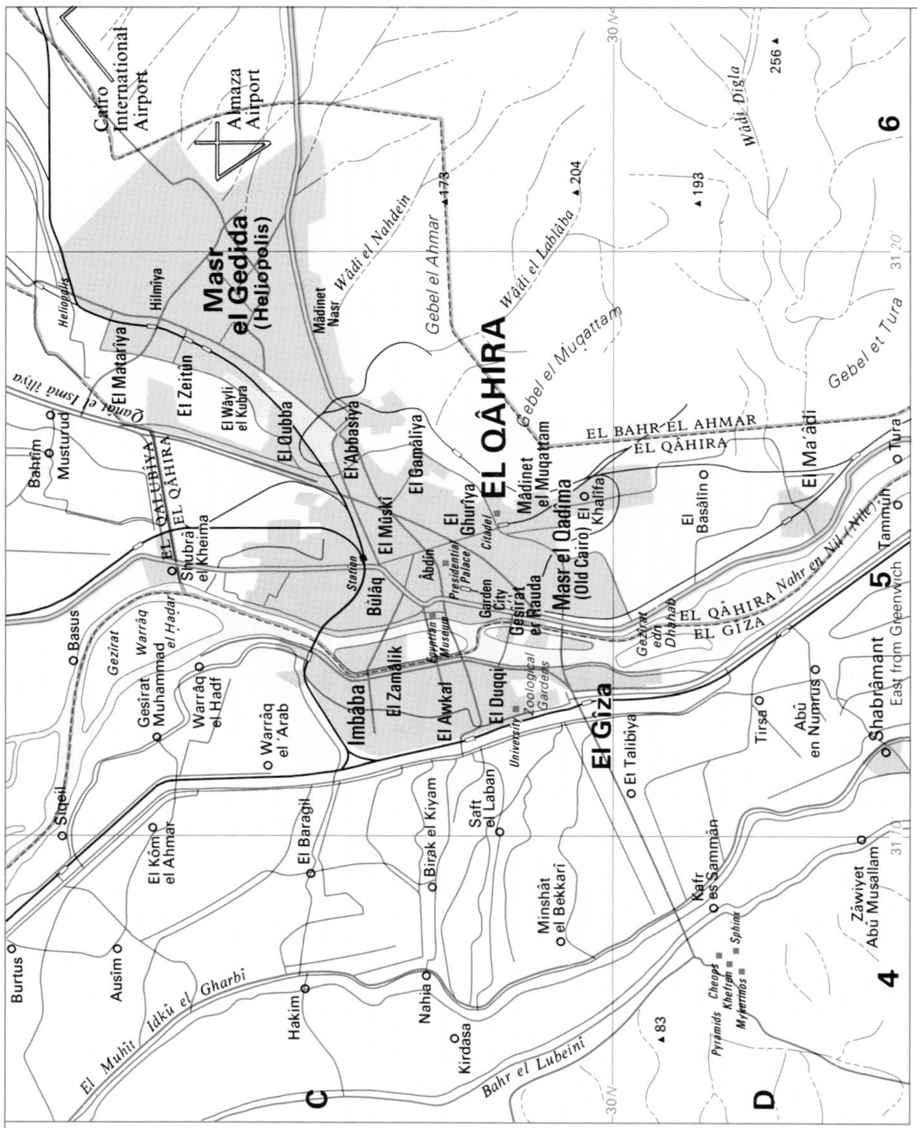

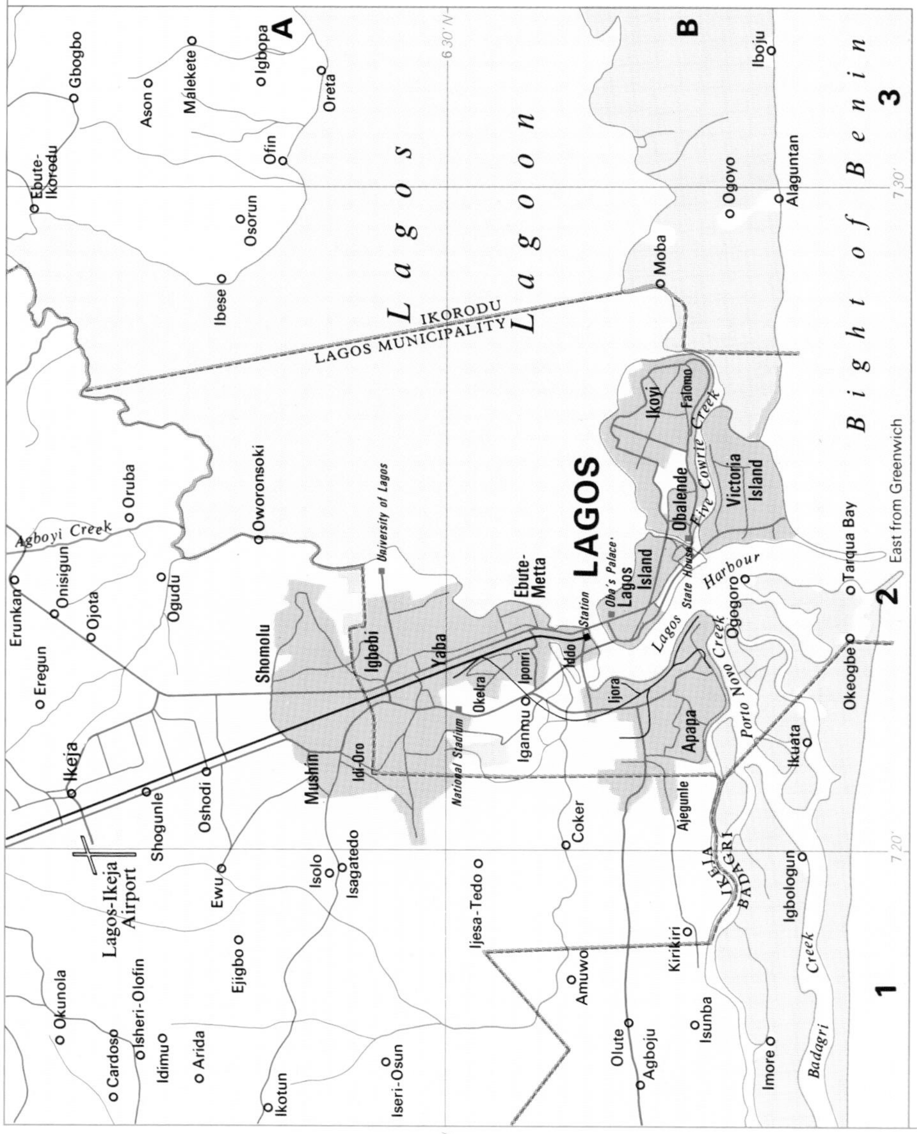

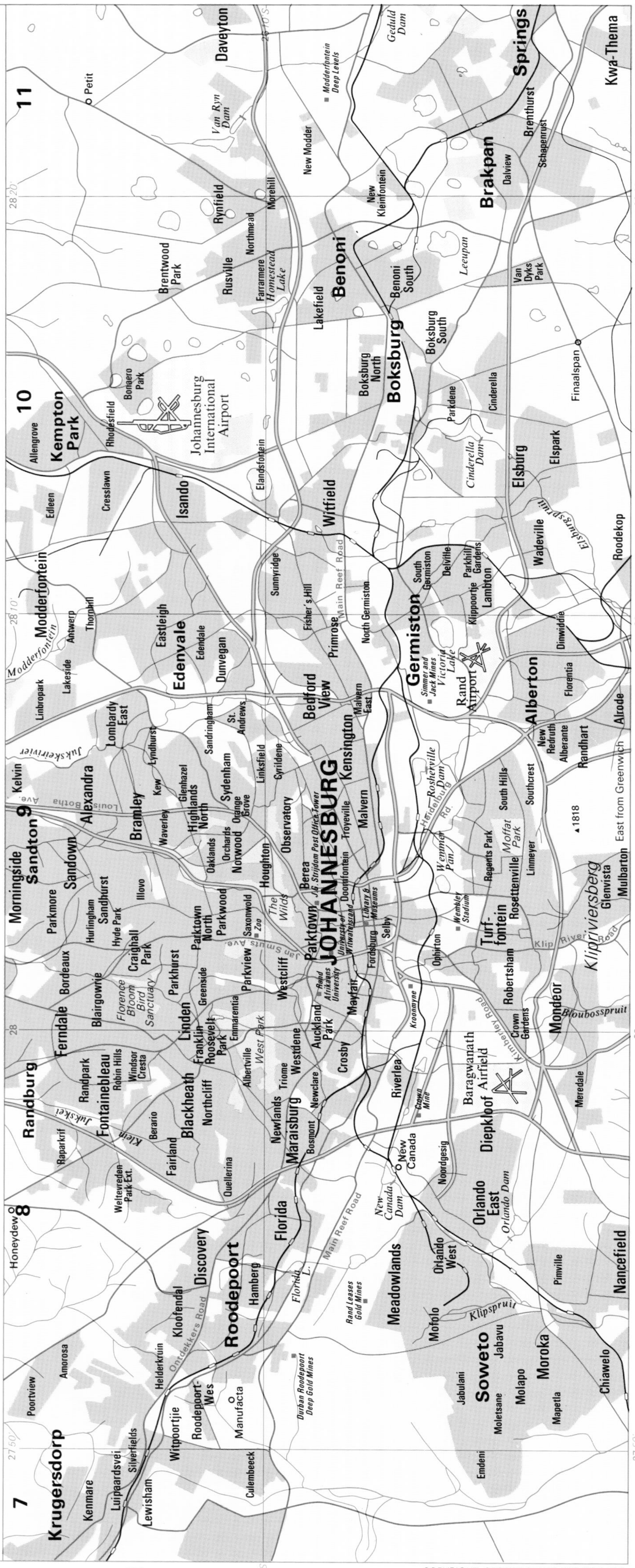

COPYRIGHT. GEORGE PHILIP AND SON. LTD.

1 : 200 000

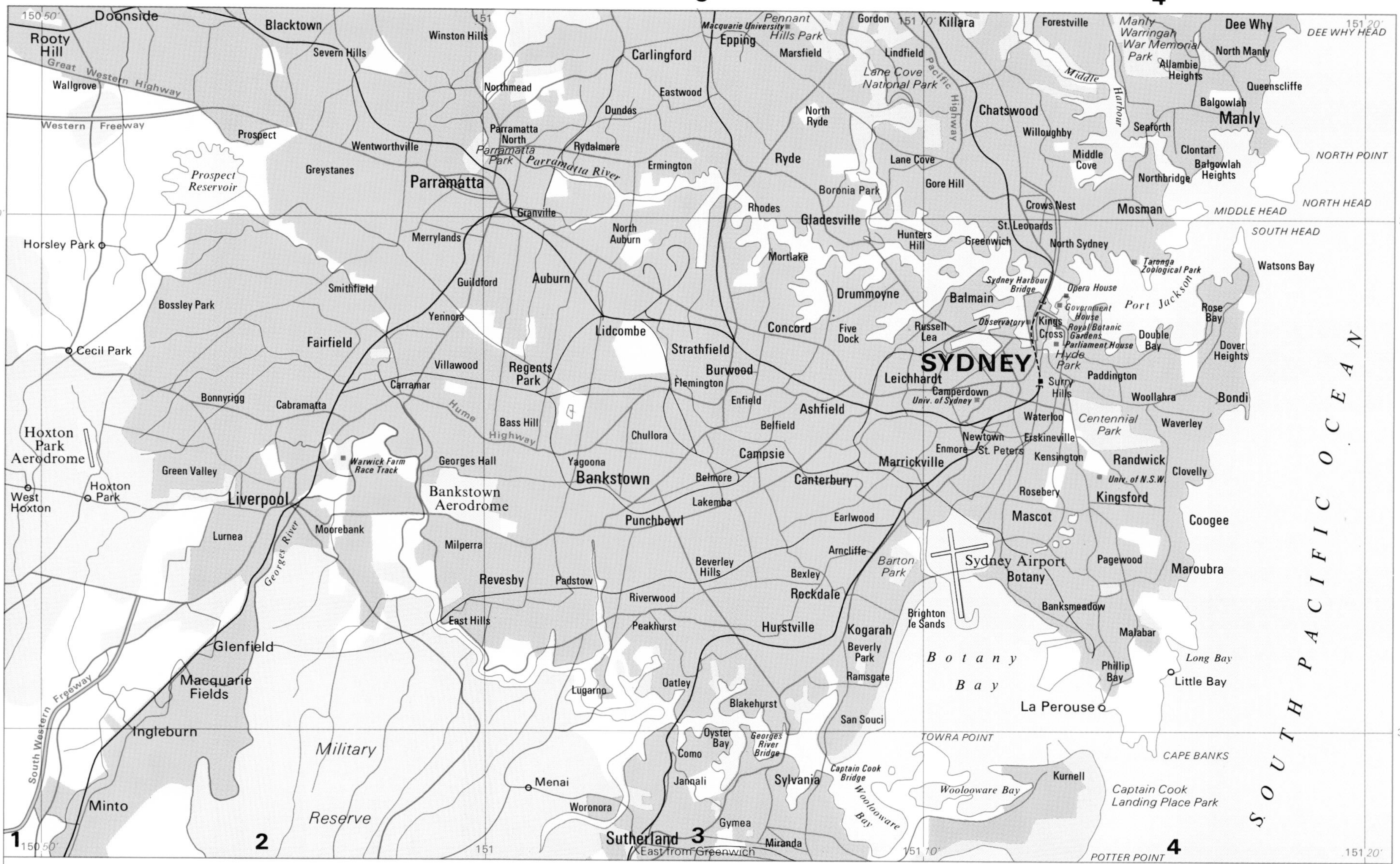

5 miles
8 km

SYDNEY

MELBOURNE

Sydney area

Doonside, Rooty Hill, Blacktown, Winston Hills, Severn Hills, Carlingford, Epping, Marsfield, Macquarie University, Pennant Hills Park, Gordon, Killara, Forestville, Manly Warringah War Memorial Park, Dee Why, DEE WHY HEAD, North Manly, Allambie Heights, Queenscliffe

Wallgrove, Western Freeway, Western Highway, Great Western Highway, Prospect, Wentworthville, Northmead, Parramatta North, Dundes, Eastwood, North Ryde, Lindfield, Lane Cove National Park, Chatswood, Willoughby, Middle Harbour, Seaforth, Balgowlah, Manly, Clontarf, Balgowlah Heights, Northbridge, NORTH POINT

Horsley Park, Greystanes, Parramatta, Parramatta Park, Parramatta River, Ermington, Ryde, Boronia Park, Gore Hill, Crows Nest, Middle Cove, Mosman, MIDDLE HEAD, NORTH HEAD

Prospect Reservoir, Granville, Merrylands, North Auburn, Rhodes, Gladesville, Hunters Hill, Greenwich, St Leonards, North Sydney, Taronga Zoological Park, Port Jackson, SOUTH HEAD

Cecil Park, Bossley Park, Smithfield, Fairfield, Guildford, Yennora, Auburn, Villawood, Lidcombe, Strathfield, Concord, Five Dock, Drummoyne, Balmain, Sydney Harbour Bridge, Observatory, Opera House, Government House, Royal Botanic Gardens, Parliament House, Russell Lea, Watsons Bay, Rose Bay, Double Bay, Dover Heights

SYDNEY, Leichhardt, Camperdown, Univ. of Sydney, Kings Cross, Hyde Park, Surry Hills, Paddington, Woollahra, Bondi

West Hoxton, Hoxton Park Aerodrome, Hoxton Park, Green Valley, Liverpool, Warwick Farm Race Track, Bankstown Aerodrome, Bonnyrigg, Cabramatta, Carramar, Bass Hill, Georges Hall, Chullora, Yagoona, Belmore, Campsie, Canterbury, Marrickville, Enmore, St. Peters, Newtown, Erskineville, Kensington, Randwick, Clovelly, Waverley, Centennial Park, Univ. of N.S.W.

Lurnea, Moorebank, Georges River, Milperra, Revesby, Padstow, Bankstown, Punchbowl, Lakemba, Earlwood, Arncliffe, Waterloo, Mascot, Rosebery, Kingsford, Coogee, Maroubra

Glenfield, Macquarie Fields, South Western Freeway, Ingleburn, Hume Highway, East Hills, Riverwood, Beverley Hills, Bexley, Rockdale, Barton Park, Sydney Airport, Botany, Banksmeadow, Pagewood, Phillip Bay, Long Bay, Little Bay

Minto, Military Reserve, Menai, Woronora, Gymea, Miranda, Como, Jannali, Oyster Bay, Georges River Bridge, Sylvania, San Souci, Brighton le Sands, Kogarah, Hurstville, Beverly Park, Ramsgate, Blakehurst, Captain Cook Bridge, Woolooware Bay, Towra Point, Kurnell, Captain Cook Landing Place Park, CAPE BANKS, La Perouse, Botany Bay

Sutherland, East from Greenwich, POTTER POINT

SOUTH PACIFIC OCEAN

Melbourne area

Westmeadows, Broadmeadows, Epping, Lalor, Mill Park, Plenty, Wattle Glen, Watsons Creek, Little Sugarloaf, Maribyrnong, Melbourne Airport, Tullamarine, Campbellfield, Thomastown, Greensborough, Diamond Creek, Maroonda Ck, Kangaroo Ground, Mt. Lofty

Keilor, Airport West, Glenroy, Fawkner, Bundoora, Bundoora Park, Reservoir, Watsonia, Research, Eltham, Warrandyte, Warrandyte Park, Wonga Park

Brimbank Park, Keilor East, Niddrie, Essendon, Pascoe Vale, Essendon Airport, Preston, Heidelberg West, Latrobe Uni., Macleod, Rosanna, View Bank, Lower Plenty, Banyule Flats Res., Yarra River, Warrandyte South, Chirnside Park, Lilydale

Avondale Heights, Moonee Ponds, Coburg, Thornbury, Heidelberg, Templestowe, Warranwood, Park Orchards, Croydon North, Mooroolbark

Braybrook, Ascot Vale, Brunswick, Northcote, Ivanhoe, Fairfield, Bullen Park, Bulleen, Templestowe Lower, Doncaster East, Doncaster, Donvale

Sunshine, Maidstone, Royal Park Zoo, Flemington Racecourse, Carlton, Melb. Uni., Kew, Balwyn North, Box Hill North, Ringwood, Croydon

Tottenham, Footscray, Yarraville, Richmond, M.C.G., Balwyn, Box Hill, Blackburn, Mitcham, East Ringwood, Kilsyth, Mt. Dandenong

Brooklyn, Newport, Spotswood, Park House, Fitzroy Gdns, Surrey Park, Blackburn Lake, Nunawading, Heathmont, Montrose

Altona North, Williamstown, Port Melbourne, Middle Park, Albert Park, Govt. House, Victorian Lawn Tennis Ass. Courts, Sth. Yarra, Toorak, Canterbury, Surrey Hills, Camberwell, Burwood, Blackburn South, Forest Hill, Vermont, Bayswater, Dongala Forest Res.

Altona, Altona Sports Park, Altona Bay, Hobsons Bay, St. Kilda, Caulfield, Malvern, Armadale, Glen Iris, Ashburton, Burwood East, Vermont Sth., Wantirna, Boronia, The Basin, Olinda

Elwood, Elsternwick, Mt. Waverley, Syndal, Glen Waverley, Ferntree Gully, Sassafras, One Tree Hill, Ferntree Gully N.P., Tremont

Brighton, McKinnon, Bentleigh, Carnegie, Murrumbeena, Glenhuntly, Ormond, Bentleigh East, Chadstone, Ashwood, Jells Park, Knoxfield, Scoresby, Upper Ferntree Gully, Upwey, Belgrave, Tecoma

Oakleigh, Notting Hill, Monash Uni., Mulgrave, Caribbean Gardens, Wheelers Hill, Rowville, Clayton

1: 200 000

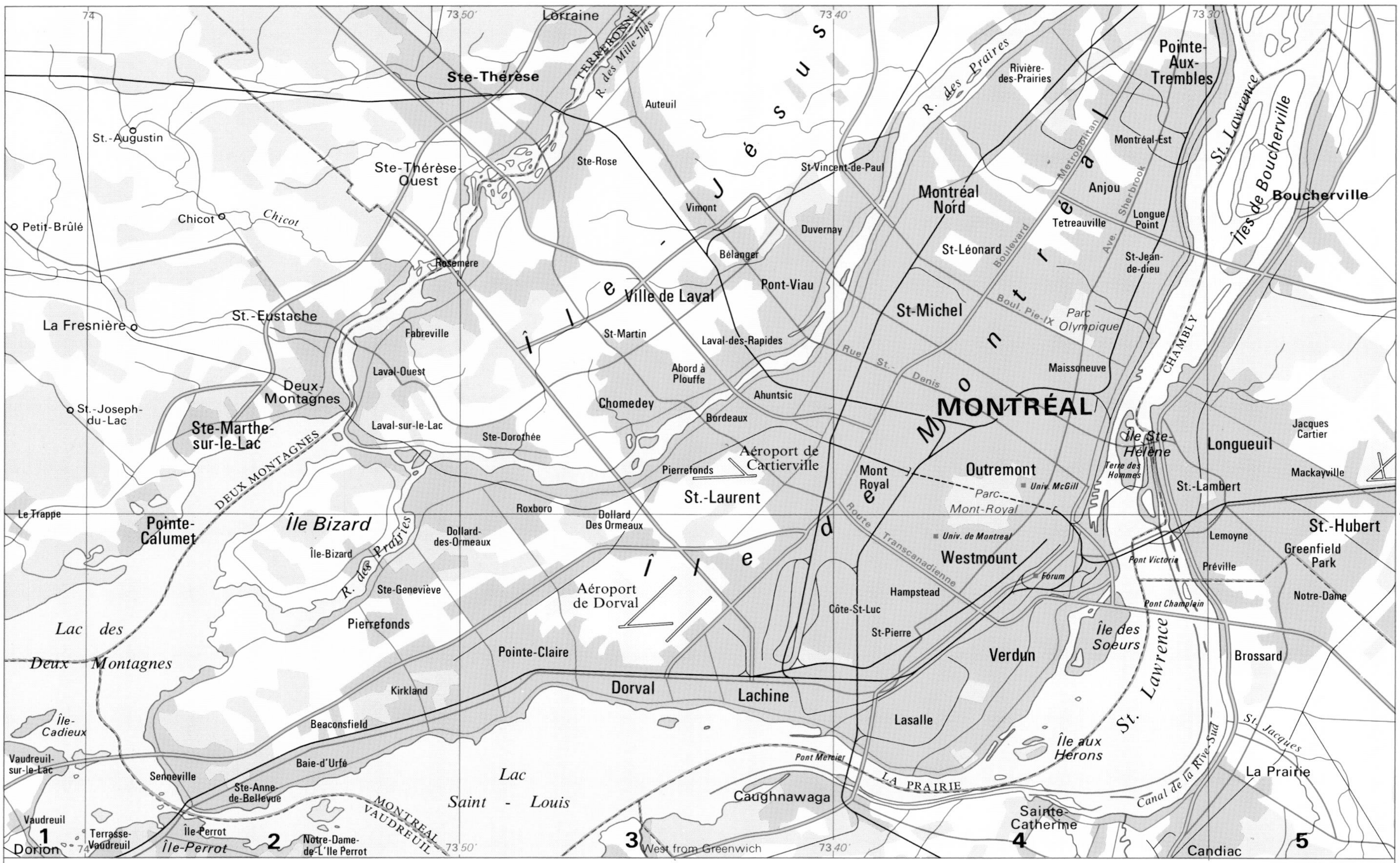

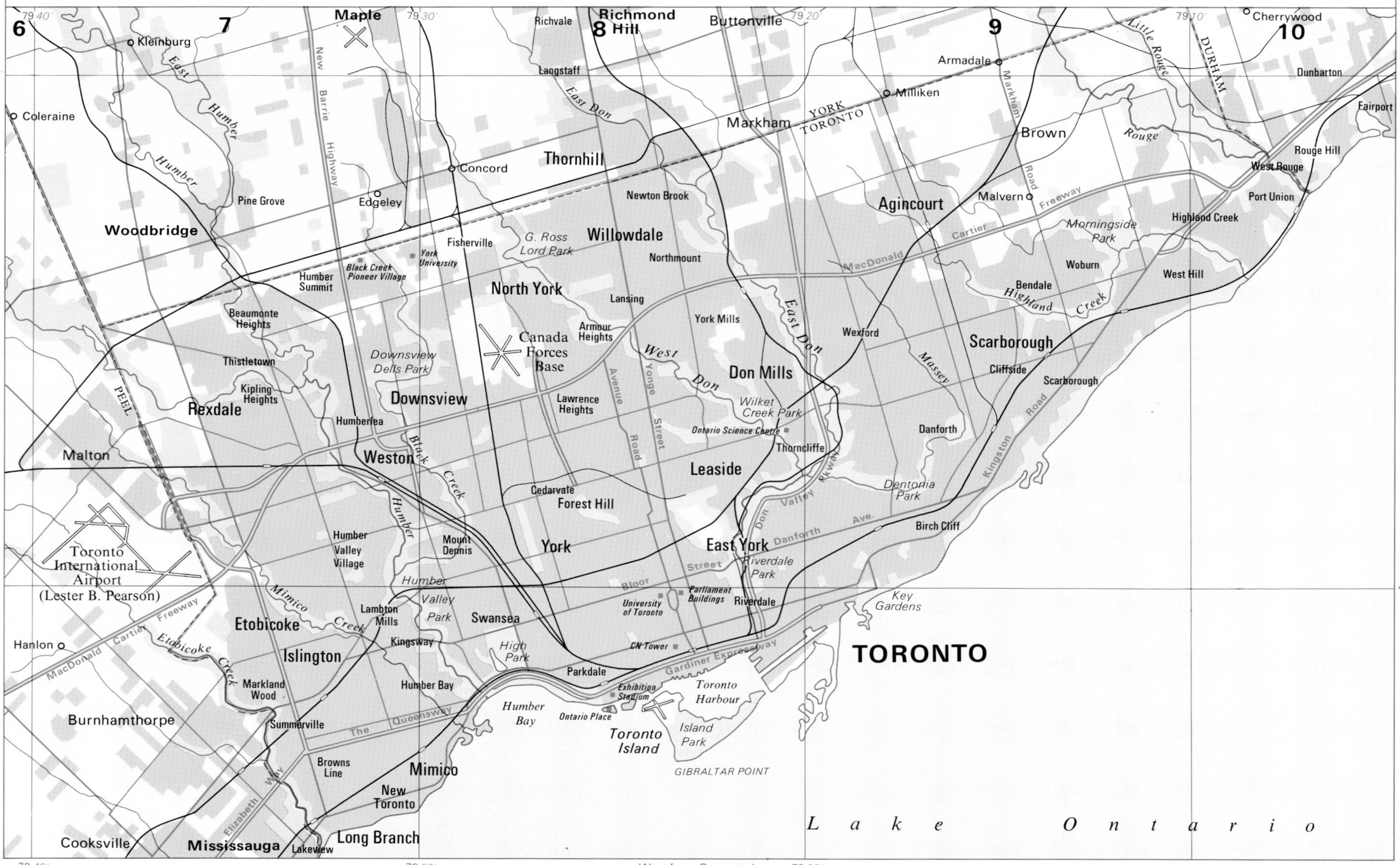

5 miles
8 km

1 **2** **3** **4** **5**

St.-Augustin
Lorraine
Ste-Thérèse
Auteuil
Pointe-Aux-Trembles
Boucherville

A

Petit-Brûlé
Chicot
Chicot
Ste-Thérèse-Ouest
Ste-Rose
St-Vincent-de-Paul
Rivière-des-Prairies
R. des Prairies
St. Lawrence
Îles de Boucherville

Rosemère
Vimont
Montréal-Est
Anjou

La Fresnière
St.-Eustache
Fabreville
St-Martin
Duvernay
Montréal Nord
St-Léonard
St-Jean-de-dieu
Tetreauville
Longue Point
Ave. Sherbrook

Deux-Montagnes
Laval-Ouest
Ville de Laval
Pont-Viau
Laval-des-Rapides
St-Michel
Maissoneuve
CHAMBLY

St.-Joseph-du-Lac
St.-Joseph-du-Lac
Ste-Marthe-sur-le-Lac
Laval-sur-le-Lac
Chomedey
Abord à Plouffe
Ahuntsic
Bordeaux
MONTRÉAL
Longueuil
Jacques Cartier

Le Trappe
Pointe-Calumet
Île Bizard
Île-Bizard
Ste-Geneviève
Roxboro
Dollard Des Ormeaux
Aéroport de Cartierville
St-Laurent
Mont Royal
Outremont
Univ. McGill
Île Ste-Hélène
Terre des Hommes
St-Lambert
Mackayville

Deux Montagnes
R. des Prairies
Dollard-des-Ormeaux
Parc Mont-Royal
Lemoyne
St.-Hubert

Lac des
Pierrefonds
Aéroport de Dorval
Univ. de Montréal
Westmount
Pont Victoria
Préville
Greenfield Park

Deux Montagnes
Pierrefonds
Pointe-Claire
Hampstead
Côte-St-Luc
St-Pierre
Fôrum
Pont Champlain
Notre-Dame

B

Île-Cadieux
Kirkland
Dorval
Lachine
Verdun
Île des Soeurs
St. Lawrence
Brossard

Vaudreuil-sur-le-Lac
Beaconsfield
Lasalle
Île aux Hérons
St. Jacques
La Prairie

Senneville
Baie-d'Urfé
Lac
Pont Mercier
Canal de la Riv.-Sud

Vaudreuil
Terrasse-Vaudreuil
Ste-Anne-de-Bellevue
Saint - Louis
Caughnawaga
LA PRAIRIE
Sainte-Catherine
Candiac

Dorion
Île-Perrot
Notre-Dame-de-L'Île Perrot
West from Greenwich
MONTRÉAL VAUDREUIL

1 **2** **3** **4** **5**

6 **7** **8** **9** **10**

Maple
Richvale
Richmond Hill
Buttonville
Cherrywood

C

Kleinburg
Langstaff
Armadale
Dunbarton

Coleraine
Milliken
Fairport

Humber
Markham
YORK TORONTO
Brown
Rouge
West Rouge
Rouge Hill

Thornhill
Concord
Newton Brook
Agincourt
Malvern
Port Union

Woodbridge
Pine Grove
Edgeley
Fisherville
G. Ross Lord Park
Willowdale
Northmount
MacDonald
Cartier Freeway
Morningside Park
Highland Creek

Humber Summit
Black Creek Pioneer Village
York University
North York
Lansing
Woodbine
West Hill

D

Beaumonte Heights
Canada Forces Base
Armour Heights
York Mills
Wexford
Scarborough
Cliffside
Scarborough

Thistletown
Downsview Dells Park
Lawrence Heights
West Don
Don Mills
Bendale
Woburn

Kipling Heights
Rexdale
Humberlea
Downsview
Wilket Creek Park
Ontario Science Centre
Danforth
Highland Creek
Kingston Road

Malton
Weston
Black Creek
Leaside
Thorncliffe
Dentonia Park
Birch Cliff

Cedarvale
Forest Hill
Don Valley
East York
Riverdale Park

Toronto International Airport (Lester B. Pearson)
Humber Valley Village
Mount Dennis
York
Danforth Ave.
Bloor Street
Key Gardens

Hanlon
Mimico Creek
Lambton Mills
Valley Park
Swansea
University of Toronto
Parliament Buildings
Riverdale

Etobicoke
Kingsway
High Park
CN Tower
TORONTO

E

Burnhamthorpe
Markland Wood
Islington
Humber Bay
Parkdale
Gardiner Expressway
Exhibition Stadium
Toronto Harbour
Toronto Island Park

Summerville
The Queensway
Humber Bay
Ontario Place
Island Park

Browns Line
Mimico
Toronto Island
GIBRALTAR POINT

Cooksville
Mississauga
Lakeview
Long Branch
New Toronto

Lake Ontario

6 **7** West from Greenwich **8** **9** **10**

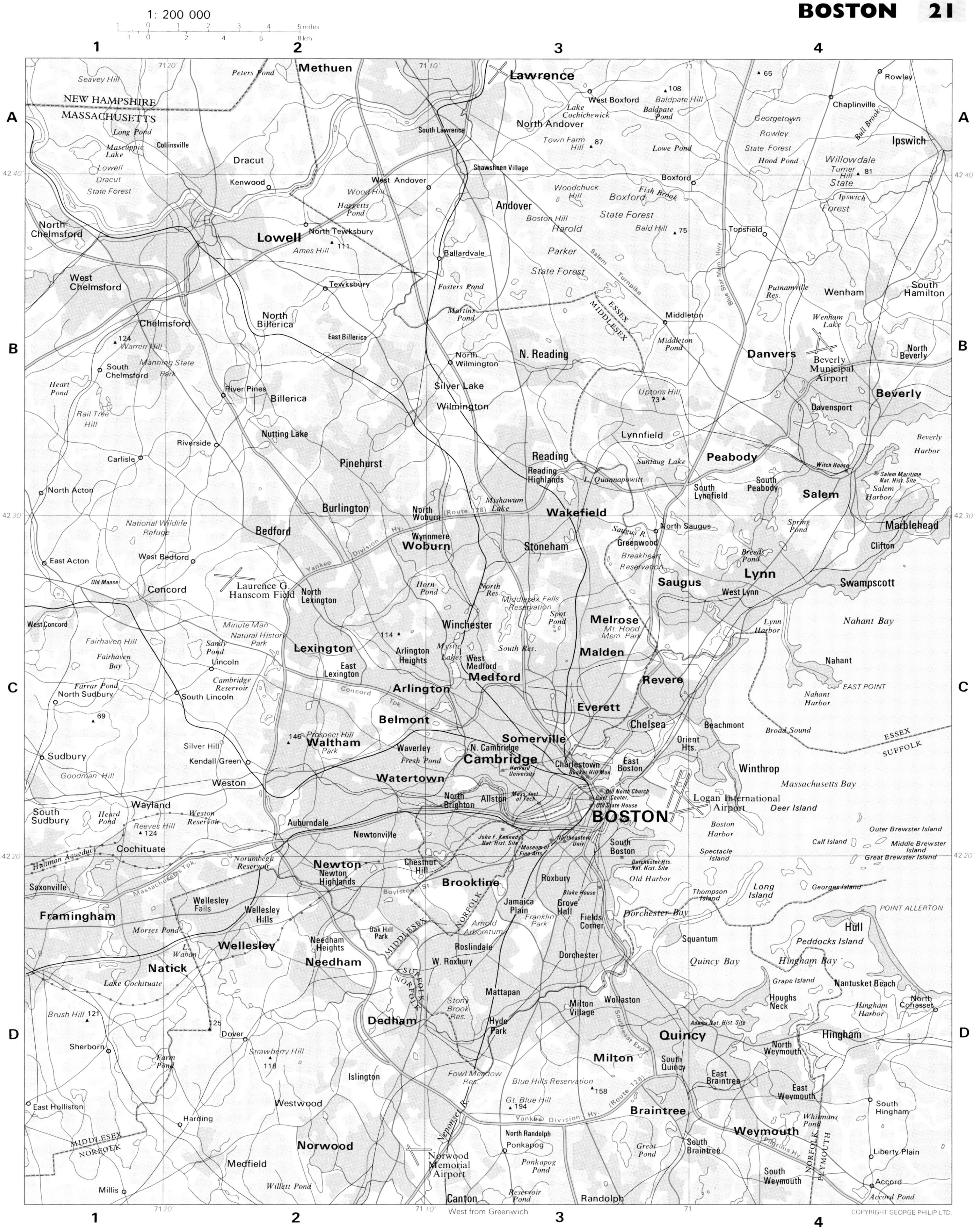

1: 200 000

5 miles
8 km

1   **2**   **3**   **4**

NEW HAMPSHIRE
MASSACHUSETTS

Seavey Hill
Long Pond
Mascuppic Lake
Lowell Dracut State Forest
Collinsville
Peters Pond
Methuen
Lawrence
West Boxford
North Andover
Baldpate Hill
Baldpate Pond
108
65
Chaplinville
Rowley
Ipswich
Bull Brook
Georgetown
Rowley State Forest
Hood Pond
Willowdale State Forest
Turner Hill 81

A

North Chelmsford
West Chelmsford
Dracut
Kenwood
Wood Hill
West Andover
Haggetts Pond
North Tewksbury
Ames Hill 111
Shawsheen Village
Andover
Boston Hill
Woodchuck Hill
Harold
Boxford State Forest
Fish Brook
Town Farm Hill 87
Lowe Pond
Boxford
Bald Hill 75
Topsfield
Ipswich
Putnamville Res.
Wenham
South Hamilton
42 40'

B

Warren Hill 124
South Chelmsford
Manning State Park
Chelmsford
North Billerica
East Billerica
Tewksbury
Fosters Pond
Martins Pond
Ballardvale
Parker State Forest
Salem Turnpike
ESSEX
MIDDLESEX
Middleton
Middleton Pond
Blue Star Mem. Hwy
N. Reading
Uptons Hill 73
Danvers
Beverly Municipal Airport
Davensport
North Beverly
Beverly
Wenham Lake
Beverly Harbor

Heart Pond
Rail Tree Hill
West Chelmsford
River Pines
Billerica
Nutting Lake
Riverside
Carlisle
North Acton
Pinehurst
Burlington
North Wilmington
Silver Lake
Wilmington
Reading
Reading Highlands
L. Quannapowitt
Lynnfield
Suntaug Lake
South Lynnfield
South Peabody
Peabody
Salem
Witch House
Salem Maritime Nat. Hist. Site
Salem Harbor
Beverly Harbor

42 30'

C

East Acton
National Wildlife Refuge
West Bedford
Old Manse
Concord
West Concord
Fairhaven Hill
Fairhaven Bay
Farrar Pond
North Sudbury 69
Sudbury
Goodman Hill
Bedford
Laurence G. Hanscom Field
North Lexington
Minute Man Natural History Park
Sandy Pond
Lincoln
South Lincoln
Cambridge Reservoir
Lexington
East Lexington
114
Arlington Heights
Mystic Lakes
Arlington
Concord Tpk.
Belmont
Prospect Hill 146
Waltham Park
Silver Hill
Kendall Green
Weston
Woburn
North Woburn
Wynnmere
Horn Pond
North Res.
Winchester
West Medford
South Res.
Spot Pond
Middlesex Fells Reservation
Stoneham
Wakefield
North Saugus
Saugus R.
Greenwood
Breakheart Reservation
Melrose
Mt. Hood Mem. Park
Malden
Saugus
West Lynn
Breed Pond
Lynn
Spring Pond
Clifton
Swampscott
Marblehead
Nahant Bay
Lynn Harbor
Nahant
EAST POINT
Nahant Harbor

Revere
Everett
Chelsea
Beachmont
Broad Sound
ESSEX
SUFFOLK

42 30'

D

Sudbury
South Sudbury
Heard Pond
Reeves Hill 124
Wayland
Weston Reservoir
Norumbega Reservoir
Cochituate
Saxonville
Framingham
Natick
Lake Cochituate
Brush Hill 121
Sherborn
Farm Pond
East Holliston
Harding
Millis
Medfield
Norwood
Strawberry Hill 118
Dover 125
MIDDLESEX
NORFOLK
Auburndale
Newtonville
Newton
Newton Highlands
Wellesley Falls
Wellesley Hills
Morses Pond
L. Waban
Wellesley
Needham Heights
Oak Hill Park
Needham
Chestnut Hill
Brookline
Jamaica Plain
Arnold Arboretum
Roslindale
W. Roxbury
NORFOLK
SUFFOLK
Islington
Westwood
Dedham
Hyde Park
Stony Brook Res.
Mattapan
Fowl Meadow Res.
Blue Hills Reservation 158
Gt. Blue Hill 194
Milton
North Randolph
Ponkapog
Ponkapog Pond
Canton
Reservoir Pond
Randolph
Norwood Memorial Airport
Neponset R.
Yankee Division Hy.

North Brighton
Allston
Mass. Inst. of Tech.
Cambridge
Harvard University
Watertown
Waverley
Fresh Pond
N. Cambridge
Somerville
Charlestown
Bunker Hill Mon.
East Boston
Old North Church
East Center
Old State House
BOSTON
Northeastern Univ.
South Boston
John F. Kennedy Nat. Hist. Site
Museum of Fine Arts
Roxbury
Blake House
Grove Hall
Franklin Park
Fields Corner
Dorchester Hts. Nat. Hist. Site
Old Harbor
Dorchester
Wollaston
Milton Village
Quincy
South Quincy
Adams Nat. Hist. Site
East Braintree
North Weymouth
East Weymouth
Weymouth
Whitmans Pond
South Hingham
Liberty Plain
Accord
Accord Pond
South Braintree
Braintree
South Weymouth
Great Pond

Logan International Airport
Deer Island
Orient Hts.
Winthrop
Boston Harbor
Massachusetts Bay
Spectacle Island
Thompson Island
Long Island
Georges Island
Outer Brewster Island
Calf Island
Middle Brewster Island
Great Brewster Island
POINT ALLERTON
Hull
Peddocks Island
Grape Island
Hingham Bay
Quincy Bay
Dorchester Bay
Squantum
Nantasket Beach
North Cohasset
Hingham Harbor
Houghs Neck
Hingham
Pilgrims Hy.
NORFOLK
PLYMOUTH

42 20'

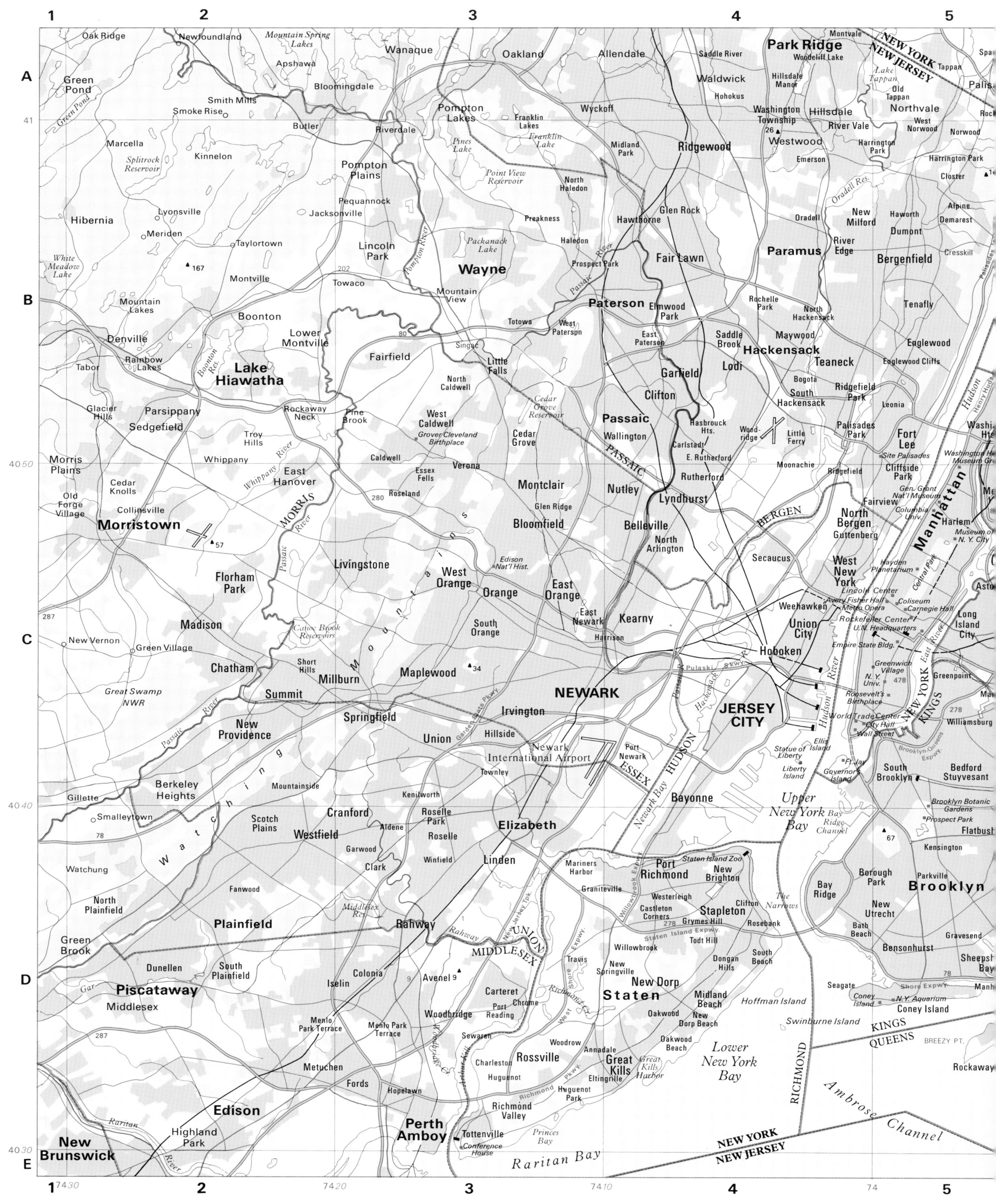

1 **2** **3** **4** **5**

A

Oak Ridge Newfoundland Mountain Spring Lakes Wanaque Oakland Allendale Saddle River **Park Ridge** Montvale Woodcliff Lake **NEW YORK NEW JERSEY** Tappan Spa

Green Pond Apshawa Bloomingdale Pompton Lakes Franklin Lakes Wyckoff Waldwick Hohokus Hillsdale Manor Lake Tappan Pali

Green Pond Smith Mills Smoke Rise Butler Riverdale Pompton Lakes Pines Lake Franklin Lake Midland Park Ridgewood Washington Township 26 Westwood Hillsdale River Vale Old Tappan Northvale West Norwood Norwood

Marcella Kinnelon Pequannock Jacksonville Point View Reservoir North Haledon Preakness Haledon Glen Rock Hawthorne Prospect Park Fair Lawn Oradell New Milford Emerson Harrington Park Harrington Park Closter Alpine

Hibernia Lyonsville Meriden Taylortown 167 Pompton Plains Lincoln Park 202 Wayne Packanack Lake Paterson Elmwood Park Rochelle Park North Hackensack Maywood Paramus River Edge Bergenfield Demarest Cresskill

White Meadow Lake Montville Towaco Mountain View Totowa West Paterson East Paterson Saddle Brook Hackensack Teaneck Englewood Englewood Cliffs Tenafly

B

Mountain Lakes Boonton Lower Montville Fairfield 80 Singac Little Falls Garfield Lodi South Hackensack Bogota Ridgefield Park Leonia Hudson

Denville Rainbow Lakes Lake Hiawatha Rockaway Neck Pine Brook North Caldwell West Caldwell Clifton Passaic Hasbrouck Hts. Carlstadt Wood-ridge Little Ferry Palisades Park Fort Lee Washi.

Glacier Hills Parsippany Sedgefield Troy Hills Whippany Caldwell Grover Cleveland Birthplace Cedar Grove Wallington E. Rutherford Moonachie Ridgefield Cliffside Park Washington Museum

Morris Plains Cedar Knolls Collinsville East Hanover Whippany River 280 Roseland Essex Fells Verona Montclair Nutley Rutherford North Bergen Gen. Grant Nat'l Museum Columbia Univ. Manhattan

Old Forge Village MORRIS Passaic River Glen Ridge Bloomfield Belleville Lyndhurst Bergen Guttenberg Harlem Museum of N.Y. City

Morristown 57 Florham Park Livingstone West Orange Orange East Orange North Arlington Secaucus West New York Hayden Planetarium Central Park Astoria

C

New Vernon Green Village Madison Caties Brook Reservoirs Orange East Newark Kearny Harrison Weehawken Avery Fisher Hall Metro Opera Rockefeller Center U.N. Headquarters Long Island City Coliseum Carnegie Hall

Chatham Short Hills Millburn Maplewood 34 South Orange Union City Lincoln Center Empire State Bldg. 478 Greenpoint

287 Great Swamp NWR Summit Springfield Hoboken Pulaski Skwy Greenwich Village N.Y. Univ. Manh.

New Providence Irvington Hillside NEWARK JERSEY CITY World Trade Center Roosevelt's Birthplace City Hall KINGS Williamsburg 278

Berkeley Heights Mountainside Kenilworth Union Newark International Airport Townley Port Newark Ellis Island Wall Street Brooklyn-Queens Bedford Stuyvesant

Gillette Smalleytown 78 Scotch Plains Cranford Roselle Park Aldene Roselle Elizabeth Statue of Liberty Liberty Island Governor's Island Ft. Jay South Brooklyn

40 40 Watchung Berkeley Heights Westfield Garwood Winfield Linden Bayonne Upper New York Bay Bay Ridge Channel Brooklyn Botanic Gardens Prospect Park 67 Flatbush

D

North Plainfield Clark Mariners Harbor Port Richmond Staten Island Zoo New Brighton The Narrows Borough Park Bay Ridge New Utrecht Brooklyn

Plainfield Fanwood Rahway Graniteville Westerleigh Castleton Corners Clifton Stapleton Rosebank Bath Beach Parkville Kensington

Green Brook Middlesex Res. UNION MIDDLESEX 278 Grymes Hill Todt Hill Bensonhurst Gravesend

Dunellen South Plainfield Iselin Colonia 9 Avenel 9 Woodbridge Willowbrook New Springville Travis New Dorp Dongan Hills South Beach Seagate Coney Island N.Y. Aquarium Sheepshead Bay

Piscataway Middlesex Menlo Park Terrace Menlo Park Terrace Carteret Port Reading Chrome Sewaren Richmond Midland Beach Hoffman Island Coney Island Swinburne Island KINGS QUEENS BREEZY PT.

287 Metuchen Fords Woodbridge Woodrow Rossville Huguenot Annadale Great Kills Oakwood Beach New Dorp Beach Lower New York Bay Rockaway

E

New Brunswick Edison Highland Park Raritan River Hopelawn Perth Amboy Tottenville Conference House Charleston Eltingville Richmond Valley Huguenot Park Great Kills Harbor Princes Bay RICHMOND Ambrose Channel

Garf Great Swamp Raritan Bay NEW YORK NEW JERSEY

1 74 30 **2** 74 20 **3** 74 10 **4** 74 **5**

41

40 50

40 40

40 30

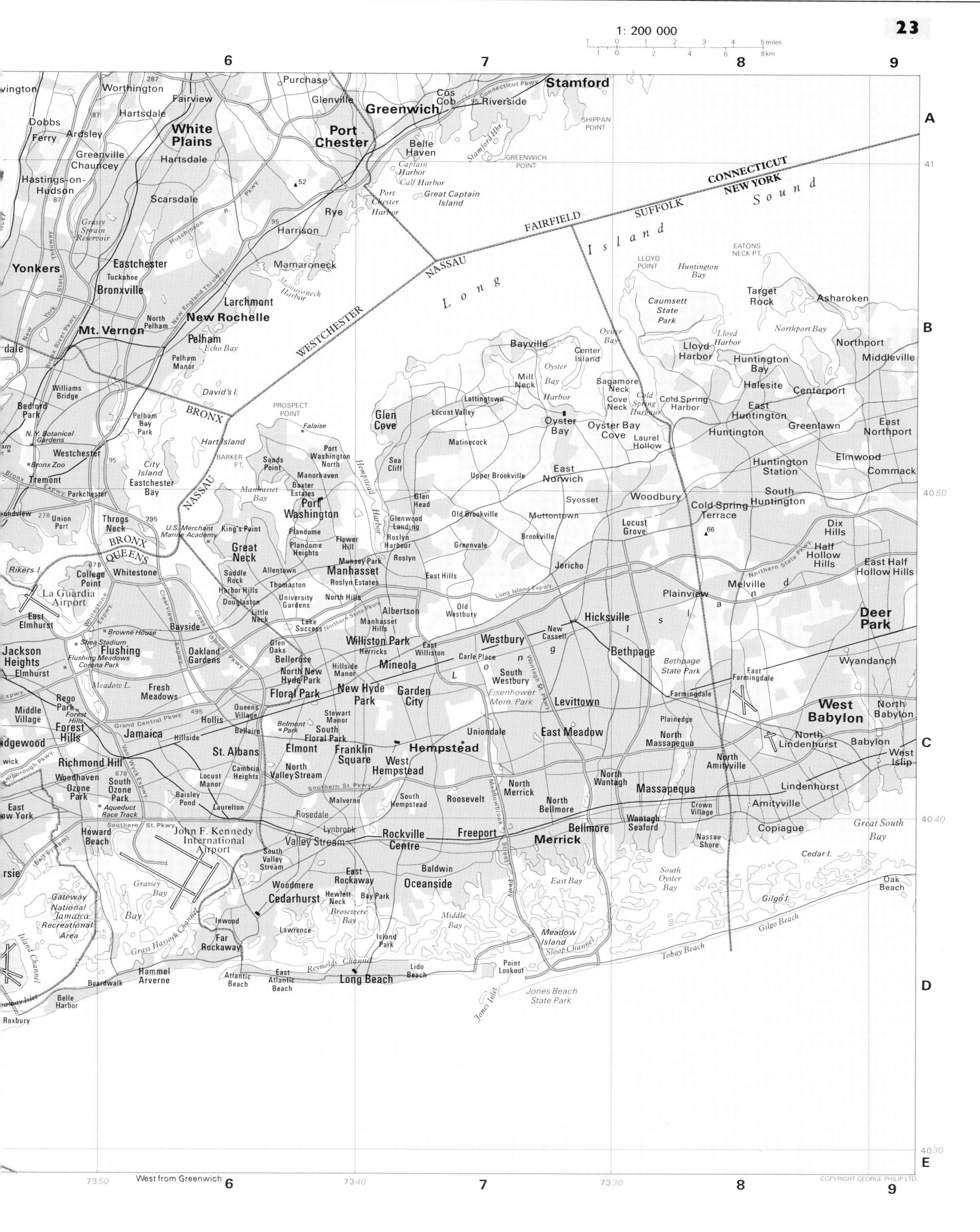

1: 200 000

1 0 1 2 3 4 5 miles
1 0 2 4 6 8 km

West from Greenwich

COPYRIGHT GEORGE PHILIP LTD

1: 200 000

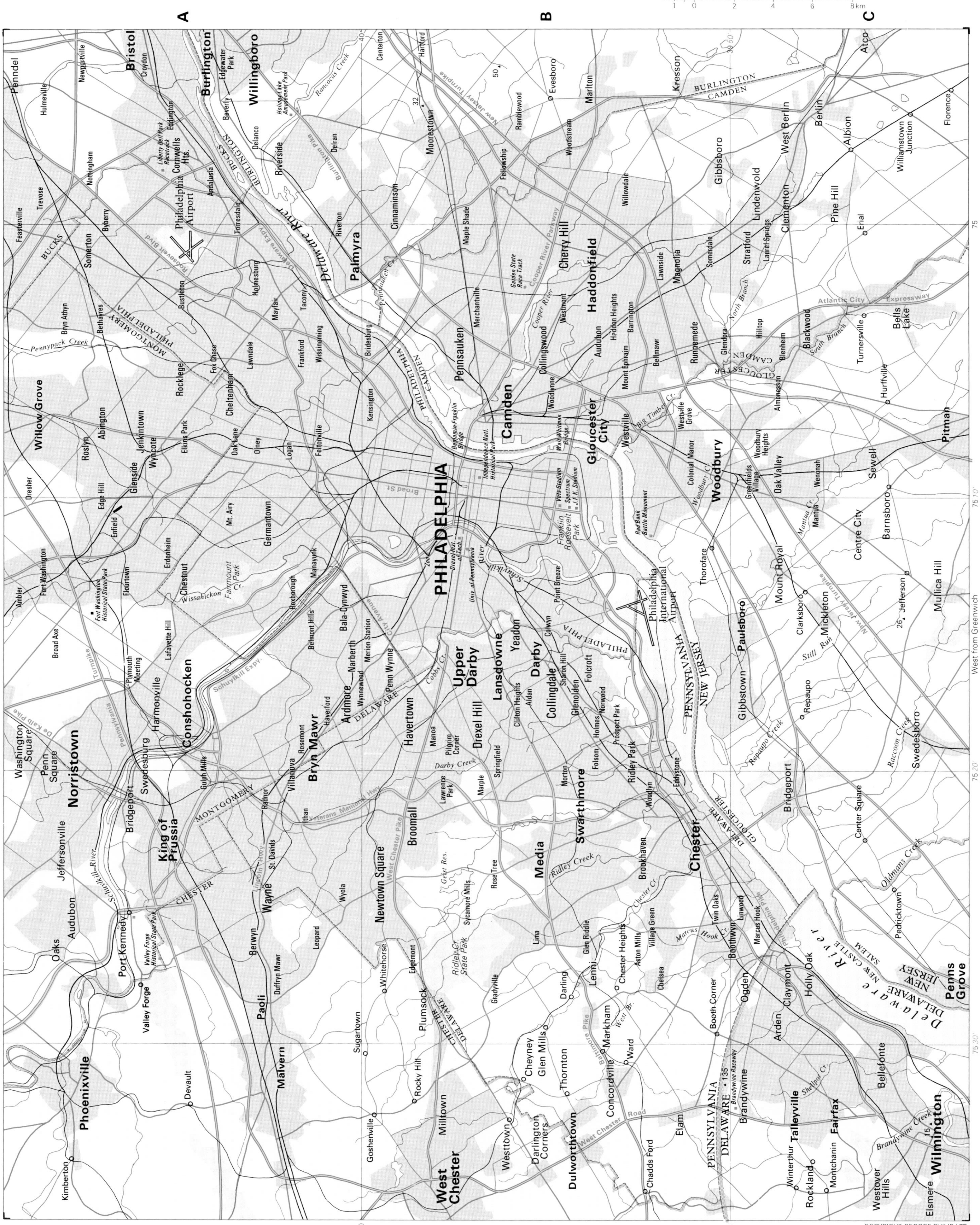

5 miles
8 km

A   B   C

PHILADELPHIA

Camden

Norristown

King of Prussia

Conshohocken

Bryn Mawr

Upper Darby

Haddonfield

Cherry Hill

Pennsauken

Gloucester City

Woodbury

Palmyra

Willingboro

Burlington

Bristol

Willow Grove

Wilmington

West Chester

Media

Swarthmore

Chester

Newtown Square

Phoenixville

Malvern

Paoli

Wayne

Lansdowne

Darby

Yeadon

Havertown

Broomall

Collingdale

Drexel Hill

Ardmore

Penns Grove

Paulsboro

Delaware River

Schuylkill River

Pennypack Creek

Darby Creek

PENNSYLVANIA
NEW JERSEY

DELAWARE
NEW CASTLE · SALEM

MONTGOMERY
PHILADELPHIA

BUCKS

BURLINGTON
CAMDEN

GLOUCESTER
CAMDEN

DELAWARE
CHESTER

Philadelphia Airport

Philadelphia International Airport

West from Greenwich

COPYRIGHT GEORGE PHILIP LTD.

1: 200 000

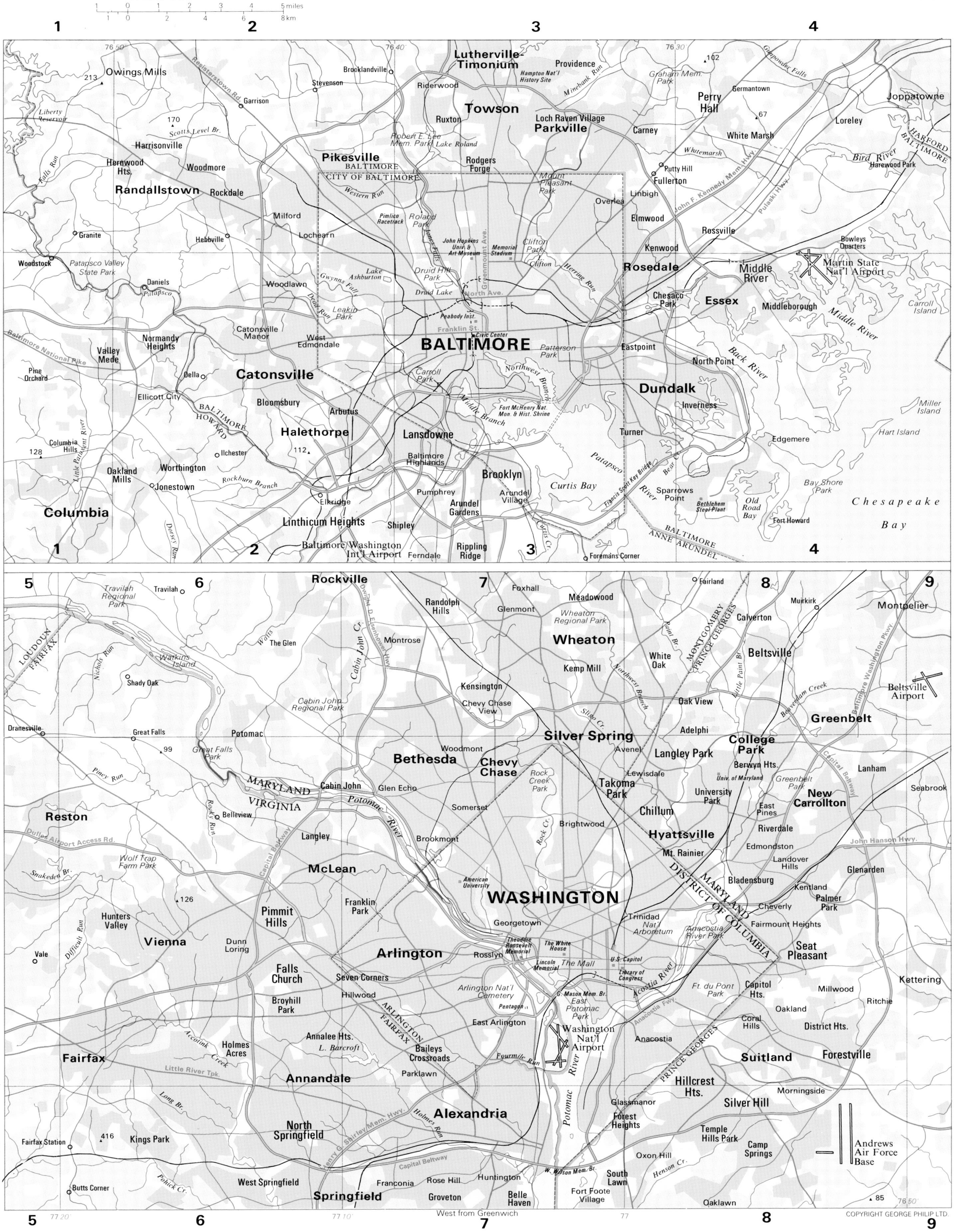

0 1 2 3 4 5 miles
0 2 4 6 8km

1 **2** **3** **4**

76 50   76 40   76 30

213 Owings Mills
Lutherville-Timonium
Brooklandville Providence
Hampton Nat'l History Site
Graham Mem. Park
102
Germantown
Joppatowne
Stevenson
Riderwood
Towson
Minebank Run
Perry Hall
67
Loreley
Garrison
Ruxton
Loch Raven Village
Parkville
Carney
White Marsh
Whitemarsh
HARFORD BALTIMORE

A
170
Scotts Level Br.
Harrisonville
Woodmore
Robert E. Lee Mem. Park/ Lake Roland
Rodgers Forge
Mount Pleasant Park
Putty Hill
Fullerton
Linbigh
John F. Kennedy Mem'l Hwy
Bird River
Harewood Park
Pulaski Hwy
A
Hernwood Hts.
Randallstown
Rockdale
Pikesville
BALTIMORE
CITY OF BALTIMORE
Western Run
Overlea
Elmwood
Kenwood
Rossville
Bowleys Quarters
Carroll Island

39 20
Woodstock
Granite
Milford
Lochearn
Pimlico Racetrack
Roland Park
John Hopkins Univ. & Art Museum
Memorial Stadium
Clifton Park
L. Clifton
Herring Run
Rosedale
Middle River
Martin State Nat'l Airport
39 20
Patapsco Valley State Park
Daniels
Patapsco
Woodlawn
Lake Ashburton
Druid Hill Park
Druid Lake
North Ave.
Chesaco Park
Essex
Middleborough
Carroll Island

B
Normandy Heights
Catonsville Manor
West Edmondale
Peabody Inst.
Franklin St.
Civic Center
Patterson Park
Eastpoint
North Point
Dundalk
Inverness
Miller Island
B
Valley Mede
Pine Orchard
Della
Catonsville
Bloomsbury
Arbutus
Carroll Park
Middle Branch
Fort McHenry Nat. Mon. & Hist. Shrine
Northwest Branch
Turner
Edgemere
Hart Island
Columbia Hills
128
Ellicott City
BALTIMORE HOWARD
Halethorpe
Lansdowne
Baltimore Highlands
Brooklyn
Patapsco River
Francis Scott Key Bridge
Sparrows Point
Bay Shore Park
Oakland Mills
Worthington
Ilchester
112
Rockburn Branch
Pumphrey
Arundel Gardens
Arundel Village
Curtis Bay
Bethlehem Steel Plant
Old Road Bay
Fort Howard
Chesapeake Bay
Columbia
Jonestown
Elkridge
Linthicum Heights
Shipley
Rippling Ridge
Curtis Cr.
BALTIMORE ANNE ARUNDEL
Jonestown

1 **2** Baltimore/Washington Int'l Airport Ferndale **3** Foreman's Corner **4**

5 **6** **7** **8** **9**

Rockville
Foxhall
Meadowood
Fairland
Muirkirk
Montpelier
Travilah Regional Park
Travilah
Randolph Hills
Glenmont
Wheaton Regional Park
Montgomery Prince Georges
Calverton
C
Watts Br.
The Glen
Montrose
Wheaton
White Oak
Point Br.
Beltsville
C
LOUDOUN FAIRFAX
Watkins Island
Cabin John Cr.
Kemp Mill
Northwest Branch
Little Paint Br.
Beltsville Airport
Shady Oak
Cabin John Regional Park
Kensington
Chevy Chase View
Oak View
Greenbelt

39
Dranesville
Great Falls
99
Potomac
Slide Cr.
Silver Spring
Adelphi
College Park
Greenbelt
39
Great Falls Park
Woodmont
Chevy Chase
Rock Creek Park
Avenel
Langley Park
Berwyn Hts.
Lanham
Piney Run
Bethesda
Somerset
Univ. of Maryland
Greenbelt Park
Seabrook
MARYLAND VIRGINIA
Cabin John
Glen Echo
Potomac River
Takoma Park
University Park
East Pines
New Carrollton
Reston
Belleview
Brightwood
Chillum
Riverdale
Dulles Airport Access Rd.
Langley
Brookmont
Rock Cr.
Hyattsville
Edmondston
John Hanson Hwy.

D
Wolf Trap Farm Park
Mt. Rainier
Landover Hills
Glenarden
D
Snakeden Br.
126
McLean
American University
Bladensburg
Cheverly
Kentland
Palmer Park
Hunters Valley
Pimmit Hills
Franklin Park
WASHINGTON
Trinidad Nat'l Arboretum
Anacostia River Park
Fairmount Heights
Vienna
Georgetown
MARYLAND DISTRICT OF COLUMBIA
Seat Pleasant
Vale
Difficult Run
Dunn Loring
Theodore Roosevelt Memorial
The White House
U.S. Capitol
Falls Church
Rosslyn
The Mall
Lincoln Memorial
Library of Congress
Ft. du Pont Park
Capitol Hts.
Millwood
Kettering
Broyhill Park
ARLINGTON FAIRFAX
Hillwood
Arlington Nat'l Cemetery
Pentagon
G. Mason Mem. Br.
East Potomac Park
Oakland
Ritchie
Accotink Creek
Seven Corners
East Arlington
Washington Nat'l Airport
Anacostia
District Hts.
Fairfax
Holmes Acres
Annalee Hts.
L. Barcroft
Baileys Crossroads
Parklawn
Anacostia Fwy
PRINCE GEORGES
Coral Hills
Suitland
Forestville
Little River Tpk.
Annandale
Potomac River
Fourmile Run
Hillcrest Hts.
Morningside
38 50
416
Kings Park
North Springfield
Alexandria
Glassmanor
Forest Heights
Silver Hill
38 50
Fairfax Station
Holmes Run
Capital Beltway
Temple Hills Park
Camp Springs
Andrews Air Force Base
E
Butts Corner
Pohick Cr.
West Springfield
Franconia
Rose Hill
Huntington
W. Wilson Mem. Br.
Oxon Hill
Henson Cr.
85
E
Springfield
Groveton
Belle Haven
Fort Foote Village
South Lawn
Oaklawn
76 50

Henry G. Shirley Mem. Hwy

West from Greenwich

77 20   77 10   77

COPYRIGHT GEORGE PHILIP LTD.

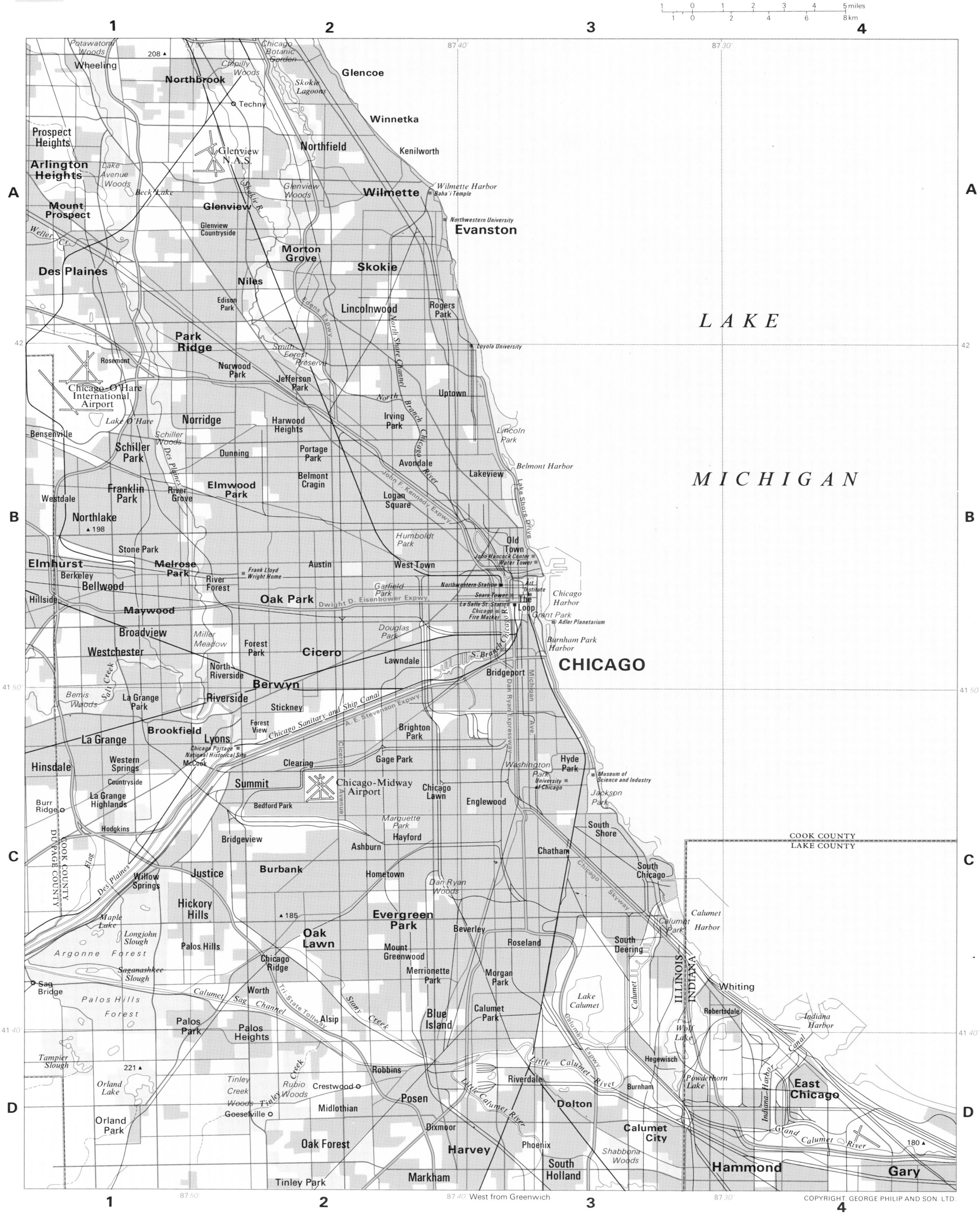

1: 200 000

1 0 1 2 3 4 5 miles
1 0 2 4 6 8 km

1   2   87 40   3   87 30   4

A

Potawatomi Woods
208 ▲
Wheeling
Chililly Woods
Chicago Botanic Garden
Glencoe
Northbrook
Techny
Winnetka
Prospect Heights
Northfield
Kenilworth
Arlington Heights
Glenview N.A.S.
Lake Avenue Woods
Beck Lake
Glenview Woods
Wilmette Harbor
Baha'i Temple
Mount Prospect
Glenview
Wilmette
Glenview Countryside
Northwestern University
Des Plaines
Morton Grove
Evanston
Niles
Skokie
Edison Park
Lincolnwood
Rogers Park

A

LAKE

Park Ridge
Smith Forest Preserve
Loyola University
42
Rosemont
North Shore Channel
Chicago-O'Hare International Airport
Norwood Park
Jefferson Park
Uptown
Lake O'Hare
Norridge
Harwood Heights
North Branch Chicago River
Irving Park
Lincoln Park
Bensenville
Schiller Woods
Dunning
Portage Park
Avondale
Lakeview
Belmont Harbor

MICHIGAN

Des Plaines River
Schiller Park
Elmwood Park
Belmont Cragin
Logan Square
Franklin Park
River Grove
Westdale
Northlake
198 ▲

B

Stone Park
Humboldt Park
Old Town
John Hancock Center
Water Tower
Elmhurst
Melrose Park
Austin
West Town
Berkeley
Frank Lloyd Wright Home
River Forest
Garfield Park
Northwestern Station
Art Institute
Bellwood
Oak Park
Sears Tower
The Loop
Chicago Harbor
Hillside
Dwight D. Eisenhower Expwy
La Salle St. Station
Chicago Fire Marker
Grant Park
Maywood
Adler Planetarium
Douglas Park
Burnham Park Harbor
Broadview
Miller Meadow
Forest Park
Lawndale
CHICAGO
Westchester
Cicero
S. Branch
Bridgeport
North Riverside
Berwyn
41 50
Bemis Woods
La Grange Park
Riverside
Stickney
Chicago Sanitary and Ship Canal
Brighton Park
A. E. Stevenson Expwy
Dan Ryan Expressway
Forest View
La Grange
Brookfield
Lyons
Clearing
Gage Park
Hyde Park
Hinsdale
Chicago Portage National Historical Site
McCook
Washington Park
Museum of Science and Industry
Western Springs
Summit
Chicago-Midway Airport
Chicago Lawn
Englewood
University of Chicago
Jackson Park
Countryside
Bedford Park
Burr Ridge
La Grange Highlands
Hodgkins
Bridgeview
Marquette Park
Hayford
South Shore

C

COOK COUNTY
LAKE COUNTY
DU PAGE COUNTY
Ashburn
Chatham
Flag Creek
Willow Springs
Justice
Burbank
Hometown
Dan Ryan Woods
South Chicago
Des Plaines River
Hickory Hills
185 ▲
Oak Lawn
Evergreen Park
Beverley
Chicago Skyway
Calumet Park
Calumet Harbor
Maple Lake
Longjohn Slough
Palos Hills
Chicago Ridge
Mount Greenwood
Roseland
South Deering
Argonne Forest
Saganashkee Slough
Merrionette Park
Morgan Park
Whiting
ILLINOIS
INDIANA
Calumet
Lake Calumet
Sag Bridge
Worth
Stony Creek
Robertsdale
Palos Hills Forest
Calumet Sag Channel
Alsip
Blue Island
Calumet Park
Wolf Lake
Indiana Harbor
Palos Park
Tri-State Tollway
Little Calumet River
Riverdale
Powderhorn Lake
Palos Heights
Burnham
Tampier Slough
221 ▲
Robbins
Little Calumet River
Hegewisch
East Chicago
Orland Lake
Crestwood
Posen
Dolton
Grand Calumet River
180 ▲

D

Orland Park
Tinley Creek
Rubio Woods
Midlothian
Calumet City
Goeseville
Dixmoor
Phoenix
Shabbona Woods
Oak Forest
Harvey
South Holland
Hammond
Gary
Tinley Park
Markham
87 50 West from Greenwich 87 40 87 30

1   2   3   4

1: 200 000

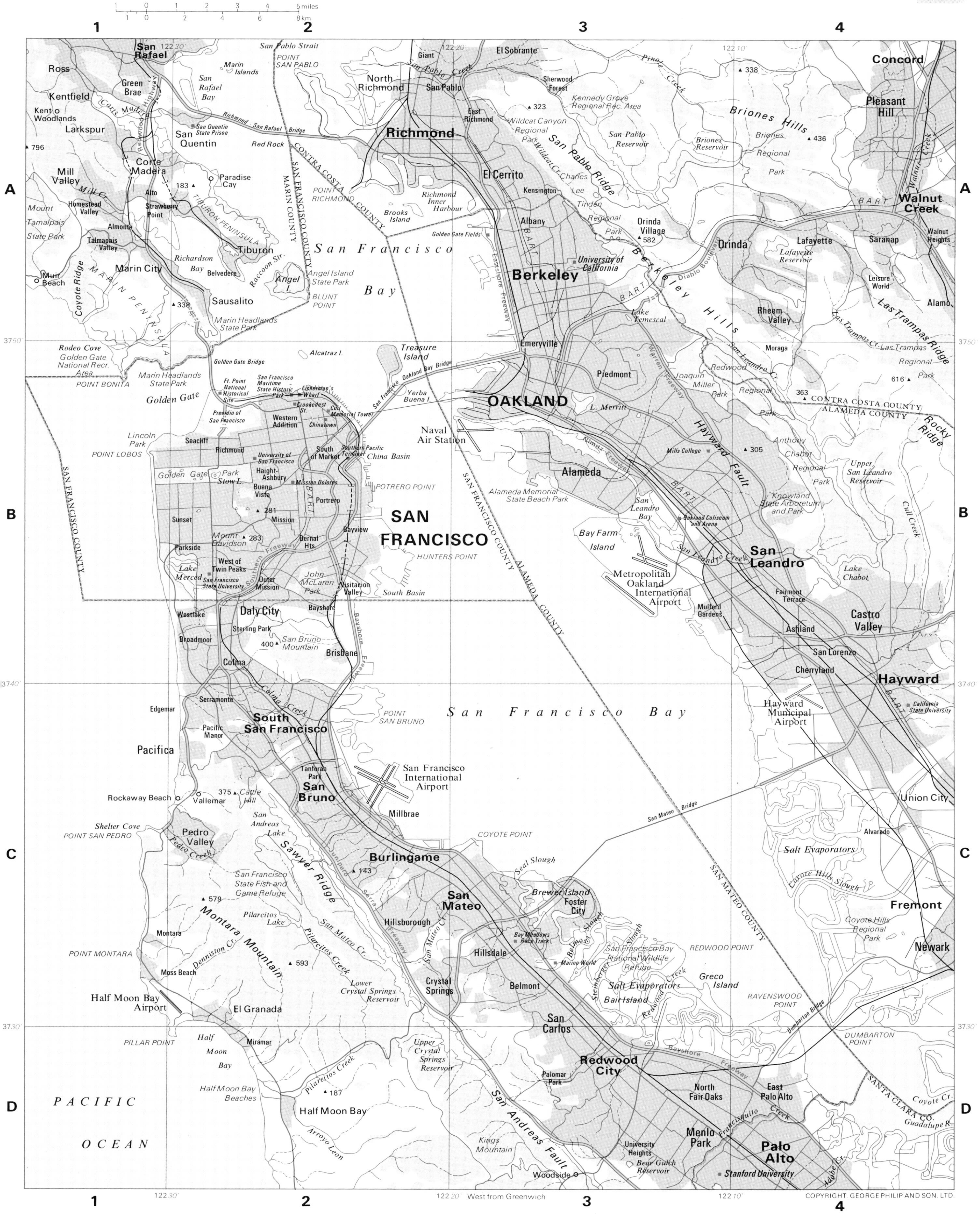

0 1 2 3 4 5 miles
0 2 4 6 8 km
San Rafael
San Pablo Strait
POINT SAN PABLO
Giant
El Sobrante
Concord
Ross
Marin Islands
San Rafael Bay
Green Brae
North Richmond
San Pablo
Sherwood Forest
338
Pinole Creek
Kentfield
Kent Woodlands
Larkspur
Corte Madera Cr.
Redwood Highway
Richmond - San Rafael Bridge
San Quentin State Prison
San Quentin
East Richmond
Richmond
323
Wildcat Canyon Regional Park
Kennedy Grove Regional Rec. Area
Briones Hills
Pleasant Hill
796
Red Rock
San Pablo Ridge
San Pablo Reservoir
Briones Reservoir
Briones Regional Park
436
Mill Valley
Corte Madera
Paradise Cay
183
El Cerrito
Wildcat Cr.
Charles Lee Tinden Regional Park
Walnut Creek
Mount Tamalpais State Park
Homestead Valley
Alto
Strawberry Point
TIBURON PENINSULA
CONTRA COSTA COUNTY
SAN FRANCISCO COUNTY
MARIN COUNTY
POINT RICHMOND
Richmond Inner Harbour
Brooks Island
Kensington
Albany
B.A.R.T.
Orinda Village
582
Almonte
Tamalpais Valley
Tiburon
Golden Gate Fields
University of California
Berkeley
Orinda
Lafayette
Lafayette Reservoir
Saranap
Walnut Heights
Muir Beach
Coyote Ridge
MARIN PENINSULA
Marin City
Richardson Bay
Belvedere
Raccoon Str.
Angel I.
Angel Island State Park
San Francisco Bay
BLUNT POINT
Eastshore Freeway
Diablo Boulevard
Berkeley Hills
Leisure World
Alamo
338
Sausalito
Marin Headlands State Park
Lake Temescal
Rheem Valley
Las Trampas Ridge
Las Trampas Cr.
Rodeo Cove
Golden Gate National Recr. Area
Golden Gate Bridge
Alcatraz I.
Treasure Island
Emeryville
Moraga
San Leandro Cr.
Las Trampas Regional Park
Marin Headlands State Park
POINT BONITA
Ft. Point National Historical Site
San Francisco Maritime State Historic Park
Fisherman's Wharf
Oakland Bay Bridge
Piedmont
Redwood
Joaquin Miller Park
616
Golden Gate
Presidio of San Francisco
Crookedest St.
Coit Memorial Tower
Yerba Buena I.
OAKLAND
L. Merritt
Regional Park
363
CONTRA COSTA COUNTY
ALAMEDA COUNTY
Rocky Ridge
Lincoln Park
Western Addition
Chinatown
Naval Air Station
Warren Freeway
Hayward Fault
Anthony Chabot Regional Park
POINT LOBOS
Seacliff
Richmond
University of San Francisco
South of Market
Southern Pacific Terminal
China Basin
Nimitz Freeway
Mills College
305
Golden Gate Park
Stow L.
Haight-Ashbury
Mission Dolores
POTRERO POINT
Alameda
Upper San Leandro Reservoir
SAN FRANCISCO COUNTY
Buena Vista
Portrero
Alameda Memorial State Beach Park
Knowland State Arboretum and Park
Sunset
281
Mission
SAN FRANCISCO
San Leandro Bay
Oakland Coliseum and Arena
Cull Creek
Mount Davidson
283
Bernal Hts
Bayview
Bay Farm Island
ALAMEDA COUNTY
San Leandro Creek
San Leandro
Parkside
HUNTERS POINT
Lake Chabot
Lake Merced
West of Twin Peaks
Southern Freeway
San Francisco State University
Outer Mission
John McLaren Park
Visitacion Valley
South Basin
Metropolitan Oakland International Airport
Fairmont Terrace
Mulford Gardens
Castro Valley
Westlake
Daly City
Bayshore
Bayshore Freeway
Ashland
Sterling Park
Broadmoor
400
San Bruno Mountain
Brisbane
San Lorenzo
Colma
Cherryland
Hayward
Edgemar
Serramonte
Colma Creek
POINT SAN BRUNO
San Francisco Bay
Hayward Municipal Airport
California State University
South San Francisco
Pacific Manor
Pacifica
Tanforan Park
San Bruno
San Francisco International Airport
Rockaway Beach
Vallemar
375
Cattle Hill
Millbrae
San Mateo Bridge
Union City
Shelter Cove
POINT SAN PEDRO
San Andreas Lake
Pedro Valley
Pedro Creek
Sawyer Ridge
COYOTE POINT
Alvarado
Salt Evaporators
Burlingame
143
Junipero Serra Freeway
Seal Slough
Coyote Hills Slough
San Francisco State Fish and Game Refuge
San Mateo
Brewer Island
Foster City
SAN MATEO COUNTY
579
Montara Mountain
Pilarcitos Lake
San Mateo Cr.
Hillsborough
Fremont
Coyote Hills Regional Park
Montara
Bay Meadows Race Track
Belmont Slough
Steinberger Slough
Hillsdale
San Francisco Bay National Wildlife Refuge
REDWOOD POINT
POINT MONTARA
Denniston Cr.
593
Pilarcitos Creek
Marine World
Newark
Moss Beach
Lower Crystal Springs Reservoir
Crystal Springs
Belmont
Redwood Creek
Greco Island
Salt Evaporators
Bair Island
Half Moon Bay Airport
El Granada
RAVENSWOOD POINT
Dumbarton Bridge
San Carlos
DUMBARTON POINT
PILLAR POINT
Half Moon Bay
Miramar
Upper Crystal Springs Reservoir
Redwood City
Bayshore Freeway
SANTA CLARA CO.
Coyote Cr.
Guadalupe R.
Palomar Park
North Fair Oaks
East Palo Alto
PACIFIC OCEAN
Half Moon Bay Beaches
Pilarcitos Creek
187
Half Moon Bay
San Andreas Fault
Francisquito Creek
Menlo Park
Arroyo Leon
Kings Mountain
University Heights
Bear Gulch Reservoir
Palo Alto
Stanford University
Adobe Cr.
Woodside
122 30′
122 20′
122 10′
37 50′
37 40′
37 30′
West from Greenwich
1 2 3 4
A B C D

1: 200 000

5 miles
8 km

LOS ANGELES

Waterman Mountain

Silver Mountain

San Gabriel River

Angeles *National* *Forest*

Mount Waterman

Strawberry Peak 1879

Josephine Pk.

Mount Disappointment

San Gabriel Peak 1877

Mount Lowe

Mount Markham

Mount Harvard

Mt. Wilson
Mt. Wilson Observatory

Echo Mountain

Mount Lukens

Big Tujunga Canyon

Mount Lukens

Big Tujunga Canyon

617

Highway Highlands

Tujunga

Foothill Fwy.

Sunland

La Crescenta

Montrose

La Cañada

Verdugo Mountains

San Rafael Hills

Flint Peak 575

Rose Bowl

Altadena

Pasadena

California Inst. of Tech

South Pasadena

El Sereno

Sierra Madre

Arcadia

Temple City

Colorado Fwy.

Monrovia

Las Lomas

Duarte

Azusa

Irwindale

Santa Fe Flood Control Basin

San Gabriel River

San Gabriel River Fwy.

Baldwin Park

West Covina

La Puente

Rowland

Fallon

Bassett

Hacienda Hts.

Puente Hills

Hillgrove District

Pomona Fwy.

LOS ANGELES
ORANGE

Sunshine Acres

La Habra

La Habra Heights

Fuller Park

Buena Park

San Bernardino Fwy.

El Monte

South San Gabriel

Rosemead

San Gabriel

Monterey Park

Whittier

Santa Fe Springs

Los Nietos

Norwalk

Artesia

San Gabriel River

Rio Hondo

Pico Rivera

Santa Ana Fwy.

Rosemead Blvd.

Alhambra

California State University

East Los Angeles

Montebello

Commerce

Bell Gardens

Downey

Bellflower

Artesia Fwy.

Clearwater

Hynes

Paramount

North Long Beach

Boyle Heights

Maywood

Huntington Park

Bell

Florence

South Gate

Lynwood

Willowbrook

Compton

Gardena

Redondo Beach Fwy.

Hollydale

Glen Anderson Fwy.

Eagle Rock

Highland Park

Garvanza

San Pascual

Lincoln Heights

Pasadena Fwy.

Dodger Stadium

Civic Center

Glendale

Golden State Fwy.

Los Angeles River

Burbank

N.B.C.

Cahuenga Peak 555

Griffith Park

Hollywood Bowl

Hollywood Fwy.

The Coliseum

Harbour Fwy.

Inglewood

The Forum

Lennox

Hawthorne

Lawndale

San Fernando

San Fernando Airport

Pacoima

Panorama City

Sepulveda

Golden State Fwy.

San Diego Fwy.

Van Nuys Airport

Van Nuys

Reseda

Winnetka

Granada Hills

Northridge

Lower Van Norman Lake

Aliso Canyon Wash

San Fernando Valley

Tarzana

Encino

216

Sherman Oaks

459

Stone Canyon Reservoir

Encino Reservoir

Santa Monica Mts.

648

Santa Ynez Canyon

J. Paul Getty Museum

Will Rogers State Historical Park

Pacific Palisades

Santa Monica

Santa Monica Municipal Airport

Venice

Santa Monica Fwy.

San Diego Fwy.

Culver City

Twentieth Century Fox

Beverly Hills

West Hollywood

Bel Air

Westwood Village

Beverly Glen

Franklin Reservoir

Glen Aire Golf Club

Brentwood Park

Hermosa Beach

Manhattan Beach

El Segundo

Los Angeles Intl. Airport

Santa *Monica* *Bay*

Baldwin Hills

Windsor Hills

Ventura Fwy.

Tujunga Wash

Studio City

Universal City

Cahuenga Blvd.

San Valley

Hollywood-Burbank Airport

Chandler Blvd.

North Hollywood

243

Stonehurst

Lockheed

San Fernando Airport

West from Greenwich

COPYRIGHT GEORGE PHILIP LTD.

A B C
1 2 3 4 5

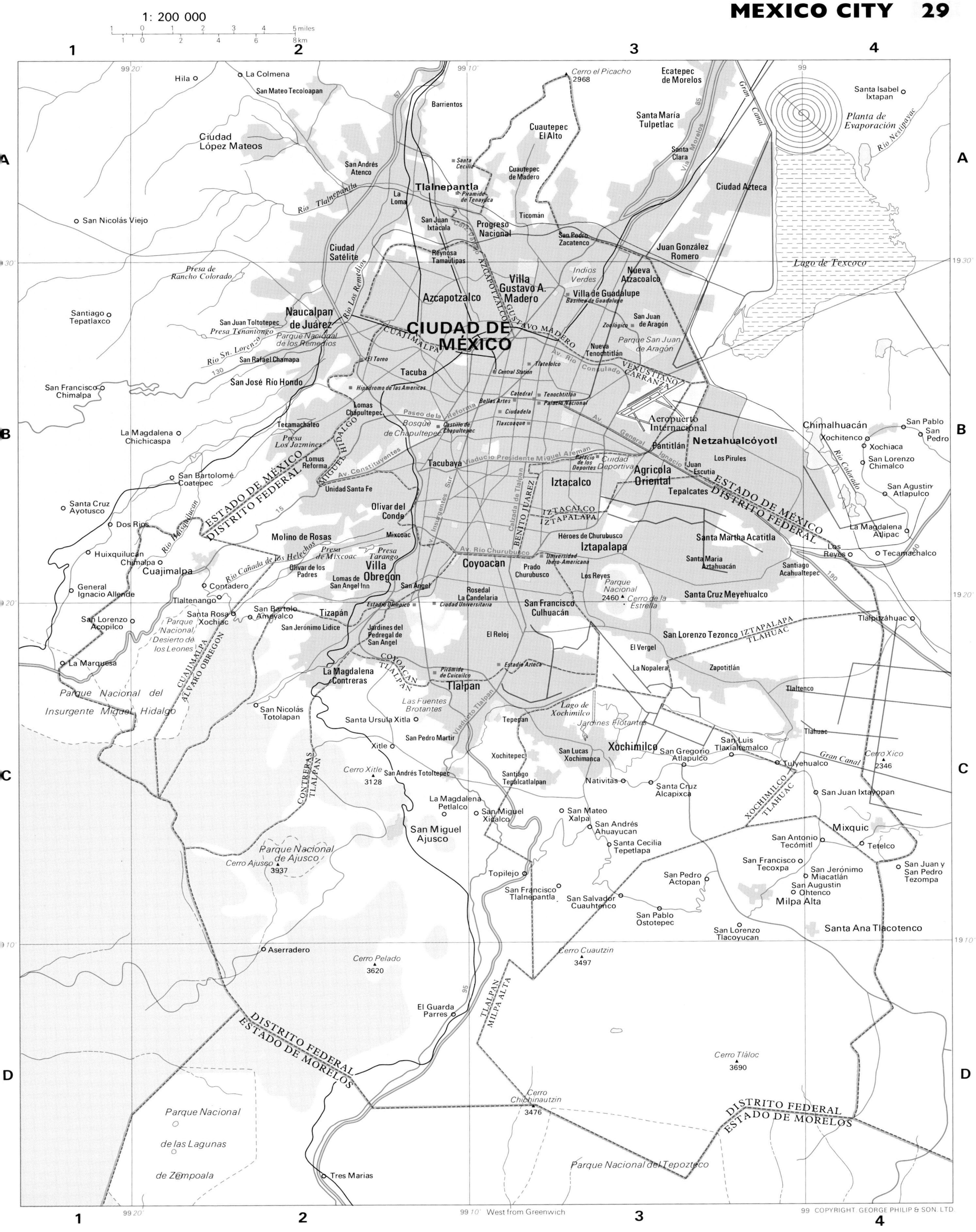

1 : 200 000

5 miles
8 km

CIUDAD DE MÉXICO

Hila
La Colmena
San Mateo Tecoloapan
Barrientos
Ciudad López Mateos
Cerro el Picacho 2968
Ecatepec de Morelos
Santa Isabel Ixtapan
Planta de Evaporación
Rio Nexquipayac
Cuautepec El Alto
Santa María Tulpetlac
San Andrés Atenco
Santa Cecilia
Cuautepec de Madero
Santa Clara
Ciudad Azteca
Tlalnepantla
Pirámide de Tenayuca
La Loma
Ticomán
Ciudad Azteca
San Nicolás Viejo
San Juan Ixtacala
Progreso Nacional
San Pedro Zacatenco
Juan González Romero
Ciudad Satélite
Reynosa Tamaulipas
Villa Gustavo A. Madero
Nueva Atzacoalco
Presa de Rancho Colorado
Rio Los Remedios
Azcapotzalco
Indios Verdes
Villa de Guadalupe
Basílica de Guadalupe
San Juan de Aragón
Santiago Tepatlaxco
Naucalpan de Juárez
San Juan Toltotepec
Presa Tenantongo
Parque Nacional de los Remedios
Zoológico
Parque San Juan de Aragón
Rio Sn. Lorenzo
San Rafael Chamapa
El Toreo
Nueva Tenochtitlán
Av. Rio Consulado
San Francisco Chimalpa
San José Rio Hondo
Tacuba
Hipódromo de las Americas
Central Station
Tlatelolco
Lomas Chapultepec
Paseo de la Reforma
Catedral
Tenochtitlán
Palacio Nacional
Tecamachalco
Bosque de Chapultepec
Castillo de Chapultepec
Bellas Artes
Ciudadela
La Magdalena Chichicaspa
Presa Los Jazmines
Tlacoaque
Chimalhuacán
Xochitenco
Xochiaca
San Pablo San Pedro
Lomas Reforma
Aeropuerto Internacional
Pantitlán
Netzahualcóyotl
San Bartolomé Coatepec
Tacubaya
Viaducto Presidente Miguel Alemán
Palacio de los Deportes
Ciudad Deportiva
Los Pirules
San Lorenzo Chimalco
Santa Cruz Ayotusco
Unidad Santa Fe
Juan Escutia
Agrícola Oriental
San Agustín Atlapulco
Dos Rios
Olivar del Conde
Iztacalco
Tepalcates
La Magdalena Atlipac
Huixquilucan Chimalpa
Mixcoac
Héroes de Churubusco
Tecamachalco
Cuajimalpa
Olivar de los Padres
Villa Obregón
Iztapalapa
Santa Martha Acatitla
Las Reyes
General Ignacio Allende
Contadero
Lomas de San Angel Inn
San Angel
Coyoacan
Universidad Ibero-Americana
Santa María Aztahuacán
Santiago Acahualtepec
Tlaltenango
Prado Churubusco
Los Reyes
Santa Cruz Meyehualco
San Lorenzo Acopilco
Santa Rosa Xochiac
San Bartolo Ameyalco
Tizapán
Estadio Olímpico
Ciudad Universitaria
Rosedal La Candelaria
Parque Nacional 2460
Cerro de la Estrella
San Francisco Culhuacán
Tlalpitzáhuac
Parque Nacional Desierto de los Leones
San Jerónimo Lidice
Jardines del Pedregal de San Angel
El Reloj
San Lorenzo Tezonco
El Vergel
La Marquesa
Estadio Azteca
La Nopalera
Zapotitlán
Tlaltenco
La Magdalena Contreras
Pirámide de Cuicuilco
Tlalpan
Las Fuentes Brotantes
Lago de Xochimilco
Jardines Flotantes
Tlahuac
Cerro Xico 2346
Parque Nacional del Insurgente Miguel Hidalgo
San Nicolás Totolapan
Santa Ursula Xitla
Tepepan
Xochimilco
San Luis Tlaxialtemalco
Tulyehualco
Xitle
San Pedro Martir
Xochitepec
San Lucas Xochimanca
San Gregorio Atlapulco
San Juan Ixtayopan
Cerro Xitle 3128
San Andrés Totoltepec
Santiago Tepalcatlalpan
Nativitas
Santa Cruz Alcapixca
La Magdalena Petlalco
San Miguel Xicalco
San Mateo Xalpa
Mixquic
Tetelco
San Miguel Ajusco
San Andrés Ahuayucan
Santa Cecilia Tepetlapa
San Antonio Tecómitl
San Juan y San Pedro Tezompa
Parque Nacional de Ajusco
Cerro Ajusco 3937
Topilejo
San Pedro Actopan
San Francisco Tecoxpa
San Jerónimo Miacatlán
San Augustín Ohtenco
Milpa Alta
San Francisco Tlalnepantla
San Salvador Cuauhtenco
San Pablo Ostotepec
San Lorenzo Tlacoyucan
Santa Ana Tlacotenco
Aserradero
Cerro Pelado 3620
Cerro Cuautzin 3497
El Guarda Parres
Cerro Tláloc 3690
DISTRITO FEDERAL ESTADO DE MORELOS
Parque Nacional de las Lagunas de Zempoala
Tres Marias
Cerro Chichinautzin 3476
DISTRITO FEDERAL ESTADO DE MORELOS
Parque Nacional del Tepozteco

ESTADO DE MÉXICO
DISTRITO FEDERAL
Lago de Texcoco
Rio Tlalnepantla
Gran Canal
Rio Colorado

1 : 200 000

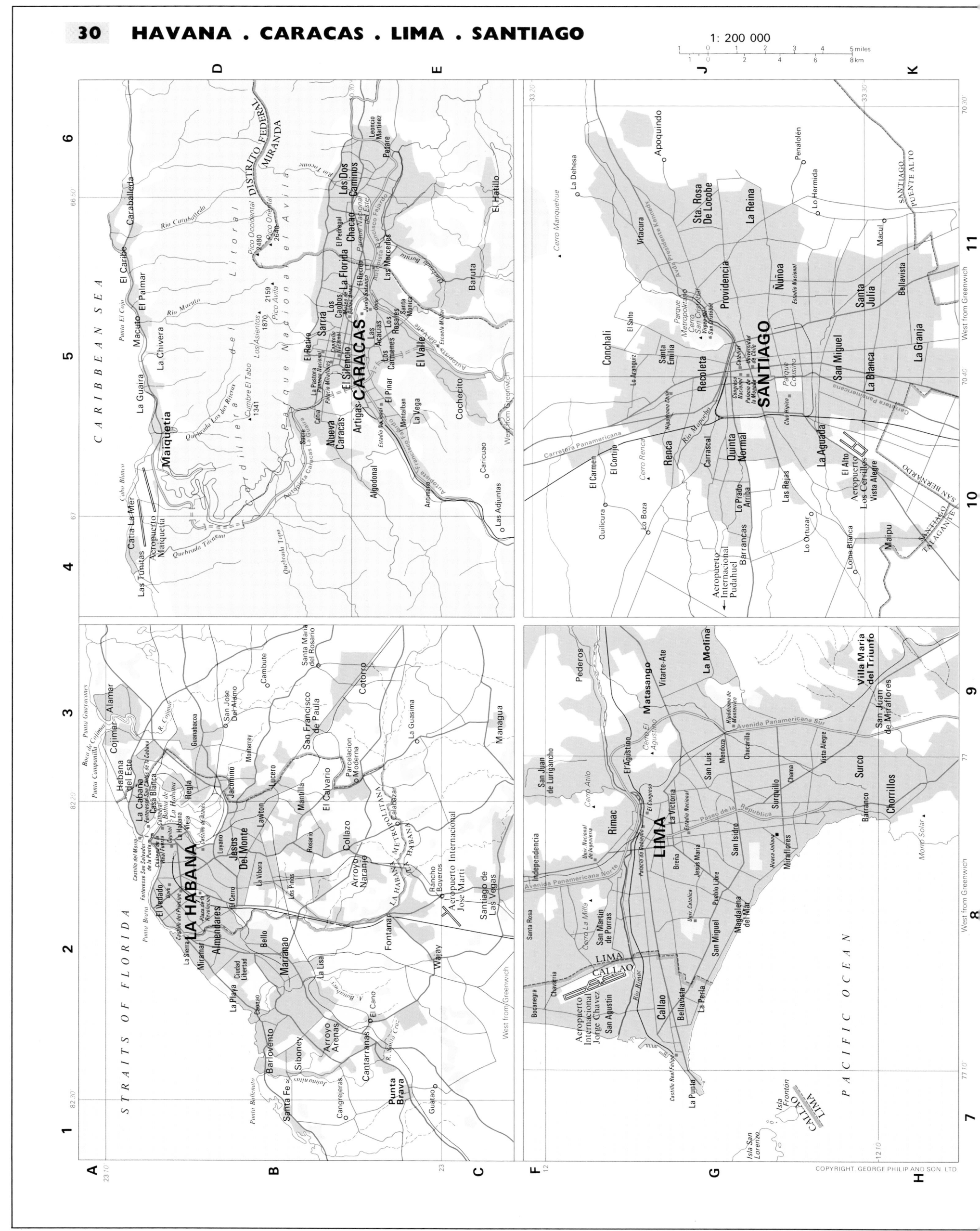

1: 200 000

1 0 1 2 3 4 5 miles
1 0 2 4 6 8 km

1 **2** **3**

Rio de Janeiro (upper map)

Mesquita
Eden
Coelho da Rocha
43°20′
Duque de Caxias
Nilópolis
São João de Meriti
São Mateus
Anchieta
Vigário Geral
Cocota
Ilha do Governador
Jardim Guanabara
Zumbi
Galeão
Canal Imboassú
São Gonçalo
Olinda
Guadelupe
Cordovil
Penha
Aéroporto de Gateão
Ilha dos Tavares
Irajá
Olaria
22°50′
NITEROI RIO DE JANEIRO
Deodoro
Ilha do Engenho
São Gonçalo
Avenida Brasil
Magalhães
Rocha Miranda
Ramos
Bonsucesso
Ilha da Cidade Universitária
Cidade Universitária
Pont Rio - Niteroi
Ilha de Santa Cruz
Barreto
Sete Pontes
Tribobo
Bangu
Realengo
Bastos
Madureira
Inhaúma
Méier
Benfica
Caju
B a i a   d e
Ilha da Conceição
Neves
Baldeador
Padre Miguel
Serra do Bangu
Cascadura
Piedade
Engenho Nôvo
São Cristóvão
Aéroporto de Manguinho
G u a n a b a r a
Armação
Centro
Maria Paula
Pequena Arroio Fundo
Serra do Engenho Velho
Praça Seca
Encantado
Zoological Gardens
Palácio das Exposições
Ilha das Cobras
S. Domingos
Palácio do Govêrno
Niterói
Vila Progresso
Pedra Branca 1025
Taquara
Pechincha
Serra dos Pretos Forros
Vila Isabel
Isabel
Gamboa
Estádio Maracanã
National Museum
Canto do Rio
Enseada de Jurujuba
Vila Progresso
Morro de Sta Bárbara 851
Jacarepaguá
Serra dos Três Rios
Andarai
Rio Comprido
Maracanã
Lapa
Mouton Palace
Cafete
Aéroport Santos Dumont
Naval Academy
Icarai
Badu
Taquara
Pico da Tijuca 1022
Gruta Paulo E. Virginia
Tijuca
RIO DE JANEIRO
Laranjeiras
Museum of the Republic
Morro do Macaco 268
Piratininga
Engenho do Mato
G u a n a b a r a
Flamengo
Botofogo
Urca 404
Sugar Loaf Mt.
L.° de Piratininga
Canto do Pontes
Serra da Carioca
Monumento do Cristo Redentor 740
Corcovado
Jardim Botanical Gardens Botânico
Alto do Bôa Vista
Hipodromo da Gávea
Gávea
Lagoa Rodrigo de Freitas
Ilha de Cotunduba
Itaocaia
Vargem Grande
Copacabana
Ipanema
Itaipu
Lagoa de Tijuca
Pedra da Gávea 845
Niemeyer 535
Leblon
Forte de Copacabana
Ilha do Pai
BR-6
Rio do Cortado
Lagoa de Marapendi
Tijucamar
Gruta da Imprensa
23′
Praia dos Bandeirantes
Ilhas Tijucas
Ilhas Cagarras
A T L A N T I C   O C E A N
West from Greenwich
43°20′ 43°10′

1 **2** **3**

São Paulo (lower map)

4 **5** **6** **7**

Pico de Jaraguá 1133
Jaraguá
Bananal
Cantareira
Horto Florestal
Rib. Piqueri
Vila Galvão
Baquirivú
Pimenta
Congo
Tremembé
Rio Baquirivú-Guaçu
Baquirivú-Guaçu
Rio Tietê
Itaberaba
Piqueri
Rib. Tremembé
Tucuruvi
Guarulhos
Ermelino Matarazzo
Itaquaquecetuba
Pirituba
Imirim
Casa Verde
Parque Edú Chaves
São Miguel Paulista
Itaim
23°30′
Jardim Munhoz
Mutinga
Rio Verde
Jaguara
N. Senhora do O.
Rio Mandaqui
Mandaqui
Santana
Rib. Cabuçú de Baixo
Cangaiba
Bairro do Limoeiro
Vila Nova Curuçá
Tamboré
Rio Tietê
Lapa
Base Aérea de Marte
Vila Maria
Jardim Munhoz
Penha
Vila Ré
Carapicuiba
Quitaúna
Osasco
Jaguaré
Alto da Lapa
Agua Branca
Bom Retiro
Barra Funda
Estação da Luz
Pari
Rio Tietê
Tatuapé
Vila Matilde
Ferraz de Vasconcelos
Vila Dirce
Jardim Osasco
Cidade de Deus
Sumaré
Perdizes
Sta. Eligênia
Estação João Prestes
Belenzinho
Cor. Gamelinha
Arthur Alvim
Itaquera
Bussocaba
Vila Dalva de Baixo
Cidade Universitária
Vila Madalena
Biblioteca Municipal
Consolação
Teatro Municipal
Brás
Água Rasa
Cidade Líder
Guianazes
Aldeia de Carapiculba
Instituto Butantã
Butantã
Cerqueira Cesar
Bela Vista
SÃO PAULO
Parque Don Pedro II
Liberdade
Cambuci
Moóca
Vila Formosa
Roseiras
Granja Viana
Jardim Arpoador
Jardim Ouro Preto
Rio Pequeno
Jaqui Club
Jardim América
Aclimação
Alto da Moóca
Colônia
Cunhas
Vila Ema
Parque S. Lucas
Cidade S. Matheus
Canguera
Cor. do Sapateiro
Jardim Paulista
Vila Mariana
Museu Iparanga
Vila Prudente
Jardim Vera Cruz
Taboão da Serra
Caxingui
Parque Ibirapuera
Ipiranga
Cor. Moinho Velho
Cor. Tamanduatei
Jardim Sapopemba
Campo Belo
Rio Pirajussara
Vila Sonia
Rib. Ubetaba
Ibirapuera
Indianópolis
Sacomã
Vila Barcelona
Rio do Oratorio
Mombaça
Jardim Vista Alegre
Vila Indiana
Vila Iasi
Pirajussara
Vila Andrade
Estádio do Morumbi
Rio Pinheiros
Brooklin
Bosque da Saúde
São Caetano do Sul
Iguassú
Morro Pelado
Embu
Valo Velho
Campo Limpo
Alto da Boa Vista
Rio Aguá Espraiada
S. João Climaco
Utinga
Parque das Nações
Capuava
Jardim S. Francisco
Rib. da Cochoeira
Capelinha
Santo Amaro
Cupecê
Rio Ipiranga
Parque Zoológico do Estado
Rio dos Meninos
Santo André
Mauá
Jardim Zaira
Capão Redondo
Vila Remo
Jurubatuba
Cupecê
Cor. Couros
Santa Tereza
Vila Pires
Jardim Santista
Pilar Velho
Jardim S. Bento
Itupu
Rib. Zuvuvú
Jardim do Mar
Nova Pet.
Bairro da Matriz
Jardim Anchieta
Jardim Petrópolis
Embú-Mirim
Interagos
Piraporinha
Pedreira
Zuvuvús
Diadema
Vila Gonçales
Itapecerica da Serra
M'Boi Mirim
Cidade Ipava
Vila Eldorado
São Bernardo do Campo
Ribeirão Pires
Reservatorio
Represa Billings
de Guarapiranga
West from Greenwich
46°50′ 46°40′ 46°30′

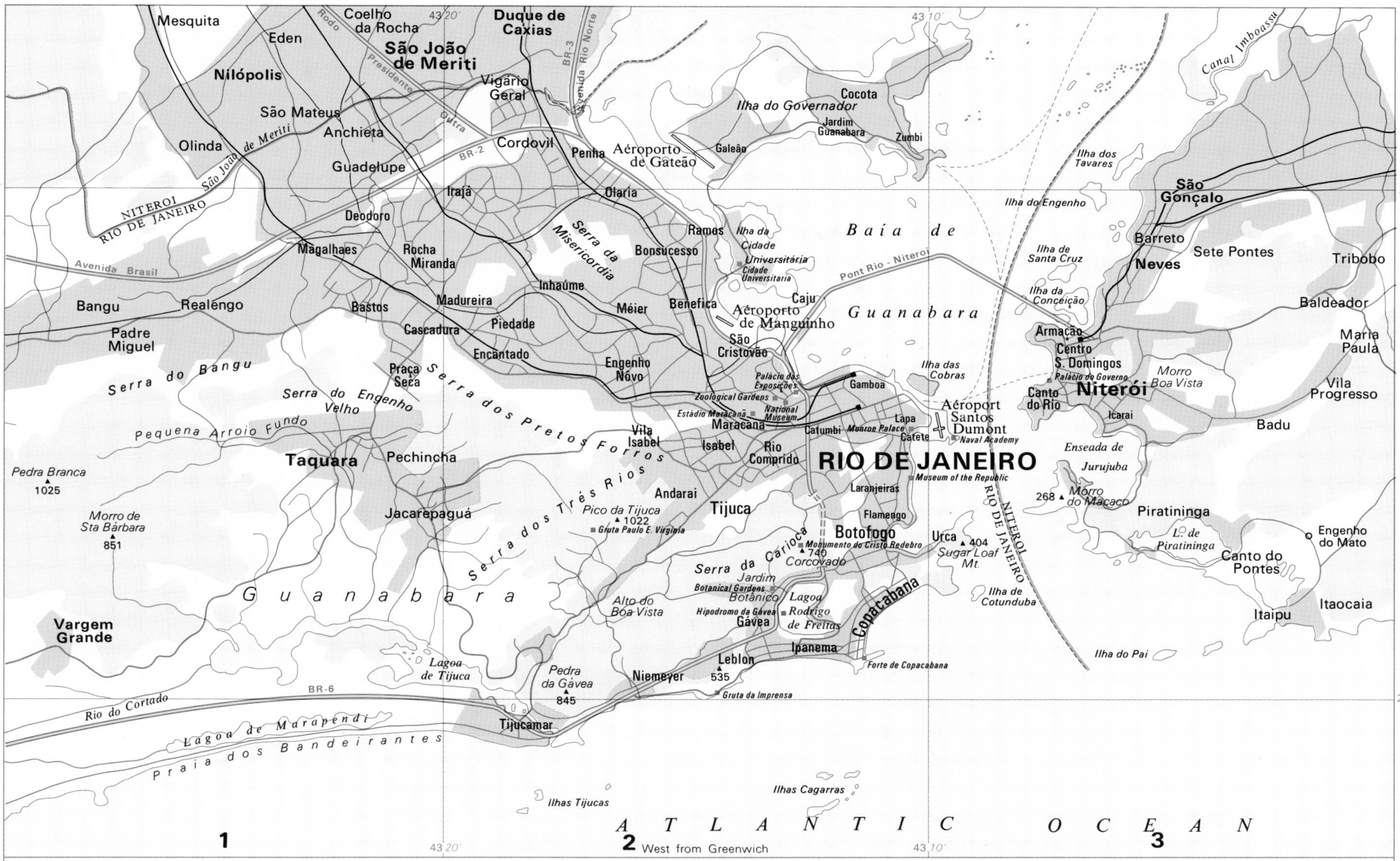

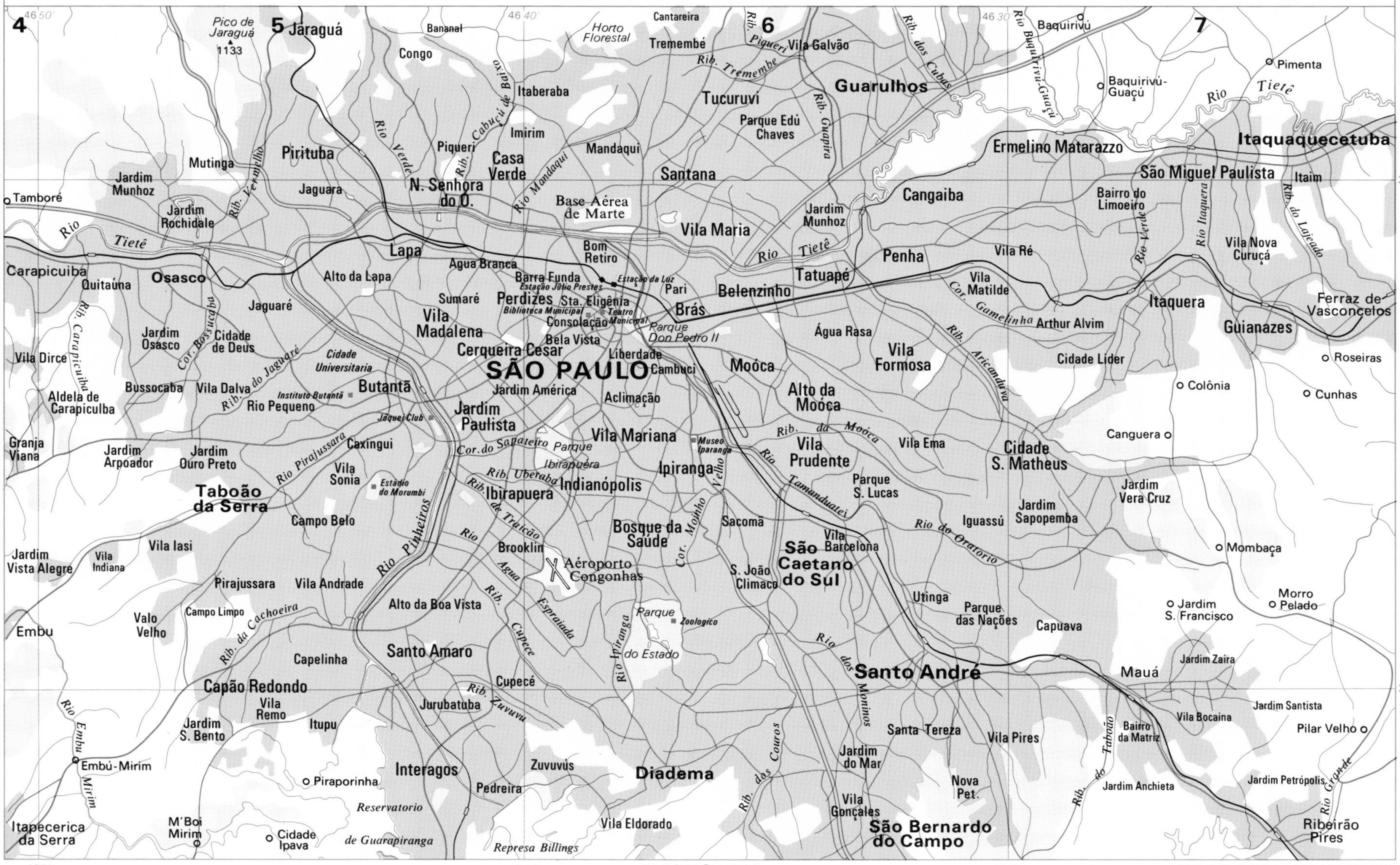

COPYRIGHT GEORGE PHILIP AND SON LTD.

4 **5** **6** **7**

1: 200 000

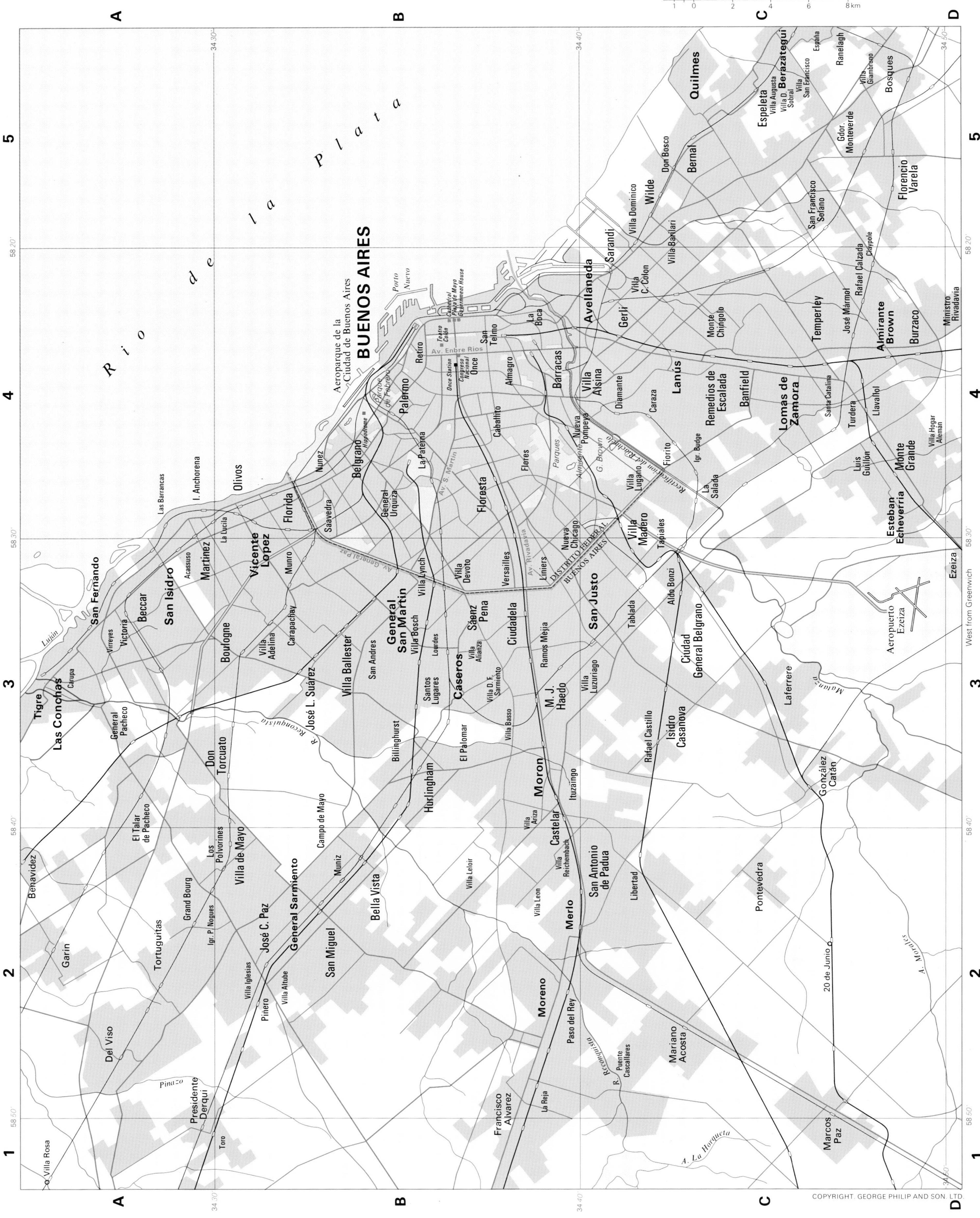

5 miles
8 km

BUENOS AIRES

Rio de la Plata

A B C D

5

4

3

2

1

Quilmes
Berazategui
Espeleta
Villa Augusta
Villa D. Sobral
Villa San Francisco
Ranelagh
Villa Guaminí
Bosques
Gdor. Monteverde
San Francisco Solano
Villa Rafael Calzada
Claypole
Florencio Varela
Don Bosco
Bernal
Wilde
Villa Dominico
Villa C. Colón
Villa Bañari
Sarandi
Avellaneda
Gerli
Monte Chingolo
Temperley
José Mármol
Almirante Brown
Burzaco
Ministro Rivadavia
Lanús
Remedios de Escalada
Banfield
Lomas de Zamora
Caraza
Santa Catalina
Turdera
Llavallol
Villa Alsina
Diamante
Barracas
La Boca
San Telmo
Once
Almagro
Nueva Pompeya
Villa Lugano
Fiorito
Ing. Budge
La Salada
Luis Guillón
Esteban Echeverria
Monte Grande
Villa Hogar Alemán
Ezeiza
Aeropuerto Ezeiza
Palermo
Belgrano
Núñez
Olivos
I. Anchorena
Las Barrancas
Florida
Saavedra
Cabalito
Flores
Floresta
Parques
Versailles
Liniers
Villa Devoto
Villa Lynch
General Urquiza
Villa Madero
Tapiales
San Justo
Tablada
Aldo Bonzi
Ciudad General Belgrano
Laferrere
Rafael Castillo
Isidro Casanova
González Catán
Ramos Mejía
Ciudadela
Sáenz Peña
Caseros
Santos Lugares
Villa Ballester
General San Martín
San Andrés
Villa Bosch
Villa Adelina
Carapachay
Munro
Vicente López
Martínez
San Isidro
Beccar
Boulogne
Villa D. F. Sarmiento
Lourdes
M. J. Haedo
Morón
Castelar
San Antonio de Padua
Villa Luzuriaga
Villa Leon
Villa Lelor
Hurlingham
El Palomar
Villa Basso
Billinghurst
Ituzaingó
Libertad
Merlo
Pontevedra
Mariano Acosta
Paso del Rey
Moreno
San Miguel
Bella Vista
General Sarmiento
Muñiz
José C. Paz
Villa de Mayo
Los Polvorines
Ing. P. Nogués
Grand Bourg
Tortuguitas
Garín
Benavidez
Villa Iglesias
Villa Altube
Piñero
Presidente Derqui
Del Viso
Villa Rosa
Toro
Francisco Alvarez
La Reja
Marcos Paz
20 de Junio
Puente Cascallares
Tigre
Las Conchas
General Pacheco
El Talar de Pacheco
San Fernando
San Andrés
Victoria
Vireyes
La Lucila
Acassuso
Luján
Reconquista
Don Torcuato
José L. Suárez
Campo de Mayo
Aeroparque de la Ciudad de Buenos Aires
Retiro
Porto Nuevo
Teatro Colón
General Paz y de Mayo
Government House
Once Station
Congreso Nacional
Av. Entre Rios
Av. S. Martin
Av. Rivadavia
Av. General Paz
Distrito Federal
Buenos Aires
Nueva Chicago
Rectificación del Riachuelo
G. Brown
R. Matanza
A. Mordillo
A. La Horqueta

West from Greenwich

COPYRIGHT. GEORGE PHILIP AND SON LTD.

INDEX TO CITY MAPS

Place names in this index are given a letter-figure reference to a map square made from the lines of latitude and longitude that appear on the city maps. The full geographic reference is provided in the border of each map.
The letter-figure reference will take the reader directly to the square, and by using the geographical coordinates the place sought can be pinpointed within that square.

The location given is the city or suburban center, and not necessarily the name. Lakes, airports and other features having a large area are given coordinates for their centers. Rivers that enter the sea, lake or main stream within the map area have the coordinates of that entrance.

If the river flows through the map, then the coordinates are given to the name. The same rule applies to canals. A river carries the symbol → after its name.

As an aid to identification, every place name is followed by the city map name or its abbreviation; for example, Oakland in California will be followed by S.F. Some of the place names so described will be completely independent of the main city.

An explanation of the alphabetical order rules is to be found at the beginning of the World Map Index.

ABBREVIATIONS USED IN THE INDEX

Ath. – Athinai (Athens)
B. – Baie, Bahía, Bay, Bucht
B.A. – Buenos Aires
Bagd. – Baghdad
Balt. – Baltimore
Bangk. – Bangkok
Barc. – Barcelona
Beij. – Beijing (Peking)
Berl. – Berlin
Bomb. – Bombay
Bost. – Boston
Bud. – Budapest
C. – Cabo, Cap, Cape
Calc. – Calcutta
Car. – Caracas
Chan. – Channel
Chic. – Chicago
Cr. – Creek
E. – East
El Qâ. – El Qâhira (Cairo)
G. – Golfe, Golfo, Gulf, Guba
Gzh. – Guangzhou (Canton)
H.K. – Hong Kong
Hbg. – Hamburg
Hd. – Head
Hels. – Helsinki
Hts. – Heights
I.(s) – Île, Ilha, Insel, Isla, Island, Isle
Ist. – Istanbul
J. – Jabal, Jebel
Jak. – Jakarta
Jobg. – Johannesburg
K. – Kap, Kapp
Kar. – Karachi
Kep. – Kepulauan
Købn. – København (Copenhagen)
L. – Lac, Lacul, Lago, Lagoa, Lake
L.A. – Los Angeles
La Hab. – La Habana (Havana)
Lisb. – Lisboa (Lisbon)
Lon. – London
Mdrd. – Madrid
Melb. – Melbourne
Méx. – México
Mil. – Milano
Mos. – Moskva (Moscow)
Mt. (e) – Mont, Monte, Monti, Montaña, Mountain
Mtrl. – Montréal
Mün. – München (Munich)
N. – Nord, Norte, North, Northern, Nouveau
Nápl. – Nápoli (Naples)
N.Y. – New York City
Os. – Ostrov
Oz. – Ozero
Pen. – Peninsula, Peninsule
Phil. – Philadelphia
Pk. – Park, Peak
Pra. – Praha (Prague)
Pt. – Point
Pta. – Ponta, Punta
Pte. – Pointe
R. – Rio, River
Ra. (s) – Range(s)
Res. – Reserve, Reservoir
Rio J. – Rio de Janeiro
S. – San, South
S.F. – San Francisco
S. Pau. – São Paulo
Sa. – Serra, Sierra
Sd. – Sound
Shang. – Shanghai
Sing. – Singapore
St. – Saint, Sankt, Sint
St-Pet. – St-Peterburg
Sta. – Santa, Station
Ste. – Sainte
Stgo. – Santiago
Sto. – Santo
Stock. – Stockholm
Str. – Strait, Stretto
Syd. – Sydney
Tehr. – Tehran
Tianj. – Tianjin (Tientsin)
Tori. – Torino (Turin)
Trto. – Toronto
W. – West
Wash. – Washington
Wsaw. – Warszawa (Warsaw)

A

Aalām, *Bagd.* **17 F8** 33 19N 44 23 E
Abada, *Calc.* **16 E5** 22 32N 88 13 E
Abbadia di Stura, *Tori.* **9 B3** 45 7N 7 44 E
Abbey Wood, *Lon.* **4 C5** 51 29N 0 7 E
Abbots Langley, *Lon.* **4 A2** 51 42N 0 25W
Abeno, *Ōsaka* **12 C4** 34 38N 135 31 E
Aberdeen, *H.K.* **12 E6** 22 14N 114 8 E
Abfanggraben, *Mün.* **7 F11** 48 10N 11 41 E
Abington, *Phil.* **24 A4** 40 7N 75 7W
Ablon-sur-Seine, *Paris* **5 C4** 48 43N 2 25 E
Abord à Plouffe, *Mtrl.* **20 A3** 43 32N 73 43W
Abramtsevo, *Mos.* **11 E10** 55 49N 37 49 E
Abridge, *Lon.* **4 B5** 51 38N 0 7 E
Abû en Numrus, *El Qâ.* **18 D5** 29 57N 31 12 E
Acassuso, *B.A.* **32 A3** 34 29 S 58 30W
Accord, *Bost.* **21 D4** 42 10N 70 52W
Accord Pond, *Bost.* **21 D4** 42 10N 70 53W
Accotink Cr. →, *Wash.* **25 D6** 38 51N 77 15W
Acerra, *Nápl.* **9 H13** 40 56N 14 22 E
Acha San, *Sŏul* **12 G8** 37 33N 127 5 E
Acheres, *Paris* **5 B2** 48 57N 2 3 E
Acília, *Rome* **9 G9** 41 47N 12 21 E
Aclimação, *S. Pau.* **31 E6** 23 34 S 46 37W
Acostia →, *Wash.* **25 D8** 38 51N 77 1W
Acton, *Lon.* **4 B3** 51 30N 0 16W
Açúcar, Pão de, *Rio J.* **31 B3** 22 56 S 43 9W
Ada Beja, *Lisb.* **8 F7** 38 47N 9 13W
Adabe Cr. →, *S.F.* **27 D4** 37 26N 122 6W
Adachi, *Tōkyō* **13 B2** 35 49N 139 34 E
Adachi-Ku, *Tōkyō* **13 B3** 35 47N 139 47 E
Adams Nat. Hist. Site, *Bost.* **21 D4** 42 15N 71 0W
Addington, *Lon.* **4 C4** 51 21N 0 1W
Addiscombe, *Lon.* **4 C4** 51 22N 0 4W
Adel, *Bagd.* **17 E7** 33 20N 44 17 E
Adelphi, *Wash.* **25 C8** 39 0N 76 58W
Aderklaa, *Wien* **10 G11** 48 17N 16 32 E
Admiralteyskaya Storona, *St-Pet.* **11 B4** 59 56N 30 20 E
Áffori, *Mil.* **9 D6** 45 31N 9 10 E
Aflandshage, *Købn.* **2 E10** 55 33N 12 35 E
Afragola, *Nápl.* **9 H12** 40 55N 14 18 E
Aganpur, *Delhi* **16 B3** 28 33N 77 20 E
Agboju, *Lagos* **18 B1** 6 27N 7 16 E
Agboyi Cr. →, *Lagos* **18 A2** 6 33N 7 24 E
Ågerup, *Købn.* **2 D8** 55 43N 12 19 E
Ågesta, *Stock.* **3 E11** 59 12N 18 6 E
Agincourt, *Trto.* **20 D9** 43 47N 79 16W
Agnano Terme, *Nápl.* **9 J12** 40 49N 14 10 E
Agora, *Ath.* **8 J11** 37 57N 23 43 E
Agra Canal, *Delhi* **16 B2** 28 33N 77 17 E
Agricola Oriental, *Méx.* **29 B3** 19 23N 99 4W
Agro Romano, *Rome* **9 F8** 41 56N 12 17 E
Agua Branca, *S. Pau.* **31 E5** 23 31 S 46 40W
Agua Espraiada →, *S. Pau.* **31 E6** 23 36 S 46 41W
Água Rasa, *S. Pau.* **31 E6** 23 32 S 46 33W
Agualva-Cacem, *Lisb.* **8 F7** 38 46N 9 15W
Agustino, Cerro El, *Lima* **30 G8** 12 3 S 76 59W
Ahrensfelde, *Berl.* **7 A4** 52 34N 13 34 E
Ahuntsic, *Mtrl.* **20 A3** 43 32N 73 41W
Ai →, *Ōsaka* **12 B4** 34 46N 135 35 E
Aigremont, *Paris* **5 B2** 48 54N 2 1 E
Airport West, *Melb.* **19 E6** 37 42 S 144 52 E
Aiyaleo, *Ath.* **8 J11** 37 59N 23 40 E
Ajegunle, *Lagos* **18 B2** 6 26N 7 20 E
Aji, *Ōsaka* **12 B3** 34 40N 135 27 E
Ajuda, *Lisb.* **8 F7** 38 42N 9 12W
Ajusco, Parque Nacional de, *Méx.* **29 C2** 19 12N 99 15W
Akabane, *Tōkyō* **13 B3** 35 46N 139 42 E
Akalla, *Stock.* **3 D10** 59 24N 17 55 E
Akasaka, *Tōkyō* **13 B3** 35 40N 139 43 E
Akbarābād, *Tehr.* **17 C5** 35 40N 51 20 E
Åkersberga Saltsjobad, *Stock.* **3 D12** 59 26N 18 15 E
Akerselva →, *Oslo* **2 B4** 59 54N 10 45 E
Akrópolis, *Ath.* **8 J11** 37 57N 23 43 E
Akuwa, *Tōkyō* **13 D2** 35 26N 139 30 E
Al 'Azamiyah, *Bagd.* **17 E8** 33 22N 44 22 E
Alaguntan, *Lagos* **18 B2** 6 25N 7 29 E
Alamar, *La Hab.* **30 B3** 23 9N 82 16W
Alameda, *S.F.* **27 B3** 37 46N 122 15W
Alameda Memorial State Beach Park, *S.F.* **27 B3** 37 45N 122 16W
Alamo, *S.F.* **27 A4** 37 51N 122 2W
Albany, *S.F.* **27 A3** 37 53N 122 17W
Alberante, *Jobg.* **18 F9** 26 16 S 28 7 E
Albern, *Wien* **10 H10** 48 9N 16 29 E
Albert Hall, *Lon.* **4 C3** 51 29N 0 10W
Albert Park, *Melb.* **19 F6** 37 51 S 144 58 E
Albertfalva, *Bud.* **10 K13** 47 26N 19 3 E
Alberton, *Jobg.* **18 F9** 26 15 S 28 7 E
Albertslund, *Købn.* **2 E9** 55 39N 12 21 E
Albertson, *N.Y.* **23 C7** 40 46N 73 38W
Albertville, *Jobg.* **18 E8** 26 9 S 27 58 E
Albion, *Phil.* **24 C5** 39 46N 74 57W
Alby, *Stock.* **3 E10** 59 14N 17 51 E
Albysjön, *Stock.* **3 E10** 59 14N 17 52 E
Alcantara, *Lisb.* **8 F7** 38 43N 9 10W
Alcatraz I., *S.F.* **27 B2** 37 49N 122 25W
Alcochete, *Lisb.* **8 F9** 38 45N 8 58W
Alcorcón, *Mdrd.* **8 B2** 40 20N 3 48W
Aldan, *Phil.* **24 B3** 39 55N 75 17W
Aldela de Carapiculba, *S. Pau.* **31 E5** 23 34 S 46 49W
Aldene, *N.Y.* **22 D3** 40 39N 74 17W
Aldenrade, *Ruhr* **6 A2** 51 31N 6 44 E
Alder Planetarium, *Chic.* **26 B3** 41 5N 87 36W
Aldershof, *Berl.* **7 B4** 52 26N 13 33 E
Aldo Bonzi, *B.A.* **32 C3** 34 42 S 58 31W
Aleksandrovskoye, *St-Pet.* **11 B4** 59 51N 30 20 E
Aleksandrów, *Wsaw.* **10 E8** 52 10N 21 14 E
Alexander Nevsky Abbey, *St-Pet.* **11 B4** 59 54N 30 23 E
Alexandra, *Jobg.* **18 E9** 26 6 S 28 5 E
Alexandra, *Sing.* **15 G7** 1 17N 103 49 E
Alexandria, *Wash.* **25 E7** 38 49N 77 5W
Alfortville, *Paris* **5 C4** 48 48N 2 24 E
Algés, *Lisb.* **8 F7** 38 42N 9 13W
Älgo, *Stock.* **3 E13** 59 16N 18 20 E
Algodonal, *Car.* **30 E5** 10 29N 66 58W
Alhambra, *L.A.* **28 B4** 34 5N 118 7W
Alhos Vedros, *Lisb.* **8 G8** 38 39N 9 1W
Alibey →, *Ist.* **17 A2** 41 3N 28 56 E
Alibeyköy, *Ist.* **17 A2** 41 4N 28 56 E
Alima, *Manila* **15 E3** 14 27N 120 55 E
Alimos, *Ath.* **8 J11** 37 52N 23 43 E
Aliperti, *Nápl.* **9 H13** 40 53N 14 28 E
Alipore, *Calc.* **16 E6** 22 31N 88 20 E
Alipur, *Calc.* **16 D5** 22 43N 88 12 E
Aliso Canyon Wash →, *L.A.* **28 A1** 34 15N 118 31W
Allach, *Mün.* **7 F9** 48 11N 11 27 E
Allambie Heights, *Syd.* **19 A4** 33 46 S 151 15 E
Allendale, *N.Y.* **22 A4** 41 1N 74 9W
Allengrove, *Jobg.* **18 E10** 26 5 S 28 14 E
Allentown, *N.Y.* **23 C6** 40 47N 73 43W
Allermohe, *Hbg.* **7 E8** 53 29N 10 7 E
Allerton, Pt., *Bost.* **21 D4** 42 18N 70 52W
Allston, *Bost.* **21 C3** 42 21N 71 7W
Alluets, Forêt des, *Paris* **5 B1** 48 56N 1 55 E
Almada, *Lisb.* **8 F8** 38 41N 9 8W
Almagro, *B.A.* **32 B4** 34 38 S 58 24W
Almanara, *Mdrd.* **8 B2** 40 28N 3 41W
Almaza Airport, *El Qâ.* **18 C6** 30 5N 31 21 E
Almazovo, *Mos.* **11 D12** 55 50N 38 3 E
Almendares, *La Hab.* **30 B2** 23 6N 82 23W
Almendares →, *La Hab.* **30 B2** 23 7N 82 24W
Almirante Brown, *B.A.* **32 C4** 34 48 S 58 23W
Almirante G. Brown, Parques, *B.A.* **32 C4** 34 40 S 58 28W
Almonesson, *Phil.* **24 C4** 39 48N 75 5W
Almonte, *S.F.* **27 A1** 37 53N 122 31W
Alnabru, *Oslo* **2 B5** 59 55N 10 50 E
Alnsjøen, *Oslo* **2 B5** 59 57N 10 51 E
Alperton, *Lon.* **4 B3** 51 32N 0 17W
Alpignano, *Tori.* **9 B1** 45 6N 7 31 E
Alpine, *N.Y.* **22 B5** 40 57N 73 57W
Alpur, *Calc.* **16 C6** 22 50N 88 23 E
Alrode, *Jobg.* **18 F9** 26 17 S 28 7 E
Alsergrund, *Wien* **10 G10** 48 13N 16 21 E
Alsfeld, *Ruhr* **6 A3** 51 31N 6 50 E
Alsip, *Chic.* **26 C2** 41 40N 87 44W
Alstaden, *Ruhr* **6 B2** 51 28N 6 49 E
Ålsten, *Stock.* **3 E10** 59 19N 17 57 E
Alster →, *Hbg.* **7 D8** 53 38N 10 4 E
Alsterdorf, *Hbg.* **7 D8** 53 36N 10 0 E
Älta, *Stock.* **3 E12** 59 15N 18 11 E
Altadena, *L.A.* **28 A4** 34 11N 118 8W
Alte-Donau →, *Wien* **10 G10** 48 14N 16 25 E
Alte Süderelbe, *Hbg.* **7 D7** 53 31N 9 52 E
Alten-Essen, *Ruhr* **6 B4** 51 29N 7 1 E
Altendorf, *Ruhr* **6 B3** 51 27N 6 58 E
Altenhagen, *Ruhr* **6 B6** 51 22N 7 27 E
Altenvoerde, *Ruhr* **6 C6** 51 18N 7 22 E
Altenwerder, *Hbg.* **7 D7** 53 30N 9 55 E
Alter Finkenkrug, *Berl.* **7 A1** 52 35N 13 3 E
Altglenicke, *Berl.* **7 B4** 52 25N 13 32 E
Altlandsberg Nord, *Berl.* **7 A5** 52 34N 13 43 E
Altmannsdorf, *Wien* **10 H9** 48 9N 16 18 E
Alto, *S.F.* **27 A1** 37 54N 122 30W
Alto da Boa Vista, *S. Pau.* **31 E5** 23 38 S 46 42W
Alto da Lapa, *S. Pau.* **31 E5** 23 31 S 46 43W
Alto da Moóca, *S. Pau.* **31 E6** 23 34 S 46 33W
Alto do Pina, *Lisb.* **8 F8** 38 44N 9 7W
Altona, *Hbg.* **7 D7** 53 32N 9 56 E
Altona, *Melb.* **19 F5** 37 51 S 144 49 E
Altona B., *Melb.* **19 F6** 37 52 S 144 51 E
Altona North, *Melb.* **19 F5** 37 50 S 144 49 E
Altona Sports Park, *Melb.* **19 F6** 37 51 S 144 51 E
Altstadt, *Hbg.* **7 D8** 53 32N 10 0 E
Alvarado, *S.F.* **27 C4** 37 35N 122 4W
Alvik, *Stock.* **3 E10** 59 19N 17 58 E
Älvsjo, *Stock.* **3 E11** 59 16N 18 0 E
Älvvik, *Stock.* **3 D12** 59 21N 18 15 E
Am Hasenbergl, *Mün.* **7 F10** 48 12N 11 33 E
Am Steinhof, *Wien* **10 G9** 48 12N 16 17 E
Am Wald, *Mün.* **7 G10** 48 3N 11 36 E
Ama Keng, *Sing.* **15 F7** 1 23N 103 41 E
Amadora, *Lisb.* **8 F7** 38 45N 9 13W
Amagasaki, *Ōsaka* **12 B3** 34 42N 135 23 E
Amager, *Købn.* **2 E10** 55 36N 12 35 E
Amāl Qādisiya, *Bagd.* **17 F8** 33 16N 44 20 E
Amalienborg Slott, *Købn.* **2 D10** 55 41N 12 35 E
Amata, *Mil.* **9 D5** 45 34N 9 8 E
Ambler, *Phil.* **24 A3** 40 9N 75 13W
Ambrose Channel, *N.Y.* **22 D5** 40 31N 73 50W
Ameixoeira, *Lisb.* **8 F8** 38 46N 9 8W
Ames Hill, *Bost.* **21 B2** 42 38N 71 13W
Amin, *Bagd.* **17 F8** 33 19N 44 29 E
Aminyevo, *Mos.* **11 E8** 55 41N 37 25 E
Amirābād, *Tehr.* **17 C5** 35 43N 51 24 E
Amityville, *N.Y.* **23 C8** 40 40N 73 23W
Ammersbek →, *Hbg.* **7 C8** 53 42N 10 7 E
Amora, *Lisb.* **8 G8** 38 37N 9 6W
Amoreira, *Lisb.* **8 F7** 38 48N 9 11W
Amorosa, *Jobg.* **18 E8** 26 5 S 27 52 E
Ampelokipi, *Ath.* **8 J11** 37 58N 23 47 E
Amper →, *Mün.* **7 F9** 48 14N 11 25 E
Amselhain, *Berl.* **7 A5** 52 38N 13 43 E
Amuwo, *Lagos* **18 B1** 6 28N 7 18 E
Anacostia, *Wash.* **25 D8** 38 51N 76 59W
Anacostia River Park, *Wash.* **25 D8** 38 54N 76 57W
Anadoluhisari, *Ist.* **17 A3** 41 4N 29 3 E
Anandanagar, *Calc.* **16 C5** 22 51N 88 16 E
Anchieta, *Rio J.* **31 A1** 22 48 S 43 21W
Ancol, *Jak.* **15 H9** 6 7 S 106 49 E
Andalus, *Bagd.* **17 F7** 33 19N 44 18 E
Andalusia, *Phil.* **24 A5** 40 4N 74 58W
Andarai, *Rio J.* **31 B2** 22 56 S 43 14W
Andeli Beijie, *Beij.* **14 B3** 39 57N 116 21 E
Anderson Cr. →, *Melb.* **19 E8** 37 44 S 145 12 E
Andilly, *Paris* **5 A3** 49 0N 2 17 E
Andingmen, *Beij.* **14 B3** 39 55N 116 23 E
Andover, *Bost.* **21 B3** 42 39N 71 7W
Andrésy, *Paris* **5 B2** 48 58N 2 3 E
Andrews Air Force Base, *Wash.* **25 E8** 38 48N 76 52W
Ang Mo Kio, *Sing.* **15 F8** 1 22N 103 50 E
Ängby, *Stock.* **3 D10** 59 20N 17 53 E
Angel I., *S.F.* **27 A2** 37 52N 122 25W
Angel Island State Park, *S.F.* **27 A2** 37 52N 122 25W
Angerbruch →, *Ruhr* **6 C3** 51 18N 6 59 E
Angerhausen, *Ruhr* **6 B2** 51 22N 6 43 E
Angermund, *Ruhr* **6 C2** 51 19N 6 46 E
Angke, Kali →, *Jak.* **15 H9** 6 6 S 106 46 E
Angono, *Manila* **15 D4** 14 31N 121 8 E
Angyalföld, *Bud.* **10 J13** 47 32N 19 5 E
Angyō, *Tōkyō* **13 A3** 35 50N 139 45 E
Aniene →, *Rome* **9 F10** 41 56N 12 35 E
Anik, *Bomb.* **16 G8** 19 1N 72 53 E
Anin, *Wsaw.* **10 E7** 52 13N 21 9 E
Anjou, *Mtrl.* **20 A4** 43 36N 73 33W
Annadale, *N.Y.* **22 D3** 40 32N 74 10W
Annalee Heights, *Wash.* **25 D6** 38 51N 77 10W
Annandale, *Wash.* **25 D6** 38 50N 77 11W
Annen, *Ruhr* **6 B6** 51 27N 7 22 E
Annet-sur-Marne, *Paris* **5 B6** 48 55N 2 43 E
Anthony Chabot Regional Park, *S.F.* **27 B4** 37 46N 122 7W
Antignano, *Nápl.* **9 H12** 40 51N 14 13 E
Antimano, *Car.* **30 E5** 10 27N 66 59W
Antipolo, *Manila* **15 D5** 14 35N 121 10 E
Antony, *Paris* **5 C3** 48 44N 2 17 E
Antwerp, *Jobg.* **18 E9** 26 5 S 28 9 E
Aoyama, *Tōkyō* **13 C3** 35 39N 139 42 E
Ap Lei Chau, *H.K.* **12 E5** 22 14N 114 9 E
Apapa, *Lagos* **18 B2** 6 26N 7 21 E
Apelacão, *Lisb.* **8 F8** 38 48N 9 7W
Apoquindo, *Stgo* **30 J11** 33 23 S 70 30W
Apshawa, *N.Y.* **22 A2** 41 1N 74 22W
Apterkarskiy Os., *St-Pet.* **11 B4** 59 57N 30 20 E
Aquincum, *Bud.* **10 J13** 47 33N 19 3 E
Ara →, *Tōkyō* **13 B4** 35 41N 139 50 E
Arakawa-Ku, *Tōkyō* **13 B3** 35 44N 139 48 E
Arakpur, *Delhi* **16 B2** 28 35N 77 11 E
Arany-hegyi-patak →, *Bud.* **10 J13** 47 34N 19 4 E
Aravaca, *Mdrd.* **8 B2** 40 27N 3 47W
Arbataash, *Bagd.* **17 E7** 33 20N 44 19 E
Arbutus, *Balt.* **25 B2** 39 15N 76 41W
Arc de Triomphe, *Paris* **5 B3** 48 52N 2 17 E
Arcadia, *L.A.* **28 B4** 34 7N 118 1W
Arceuil, *Paris* **5 C3** 48 48N 2 19 E
Arden, *Phil.* **24 C2** 39 48N 75 29W
Ardey Gebirge, *Ruhr* **6 B6** 51 24N 7 23 E
Ardmore, *Phil.* **24 A3** 40 0N 75 17W
Ardsley, *N.Y.* **23 A5** 41 0N 73 50W
Arese, *Mil.* **9 D5** 45 32N 9 4 E
Arganzuela, *Mdrd.* **8 B2** 40 23N 3 42W
Argenteuil, *Paris* **5 B3** 48 56N 2 15 E
Argonne Forest, *Chic.* **26 C1** 41 42N 87 53W
Ariadana, *Calc.* **16 E6** 22 39N 88 22 E
Aricanduva →, *S. Pau.* **31 E6** 23 31 S 46 33W
Arida, *Lagos* **18 A1** 6 33N 7 16 E
Arima, *Ōsaka* **12 B2** 34 47N 135 15 E
Arima, *Tōkyō* **13 C2** 35 33N 139 33 E
Arima →, *Ōsaka* **12 A2** 34 50N 135 14 E
Arkhangelyskoye, *Mos.* **11 E7** 55 47N 37 17 E
Arkley, *Lon.* **4 B3** 51 38N 0 13W
Arlington, *Bost.* **21 C2** 42 24N 71 10W
Arlington, *Wash.* **25 D7** 38 53N 77 7W
Arlington Heights, *Bost.* **21 C2** 42 25N 71 10W
Arlington Heights, *Chic.* **26 A1** 42 5N 87 55W
Arlington Nat. Cemetery, *Wash.* **25 D7** 38 52N 77 4W
Armação, *Rio J.* **31 B3** 22 52 S 43 6W
Armadale, *Melb.* **19 F7** 37 51 S 145 0 E
Armadale, *Trto.* **20 C9** 43 50N 79 14W
Armainvilliers, Forêt d', *Paris* **5 C6** 48 46N 2 42 E
Armour Heights, *Trto.* **20 D8** 43 45N 79 25W
Arncliffe, *Syd.* **19 B3** 33 56 S 151 8 E
Arnold Arboretum, *Bost.* **21 D3** 42 18N 71 8W
Arnouville-les-Gonesse, *Paris* **5 B4** 48 59N 2 24 E
Arrentela, *Lisb.* **8 G8** 38 37N 9 6W
Arrone →, *Rome* **9 F8** 41 55N 12 16 E
Arroyo Arenas, *La Hab.* **30 B2** 23 3N 82 27W
Arroyo Cr. →, *S.F.* **26 D2** 37 27N 122 25W
Arroyo Naranjo, *La Hab.* **30 B2** 23 2N 82 21W
Årsta, *Stock.* **3 E11** 59 17N 18 3 E
Artesia, *L.A.* **28 C4** 33 51N 118 4W
Arthur Alvim, *S. Pau.* **31 E7** 23 32 S 46 28W
Arthur Kill →, *N.Y.* **22 D3** 40 32N 74 15W
Artigas, *Car.* **30 E5** 10 29N 66 56W
Arundel Gardens, *Balt.* **25 B3** 39 12N 76 37W
Arundel Village, *Balt.* **25 B3** 39 13N 76 35W
Aryiróupolis, *Ath.* **8 J11** 37 52N 23 44 E
Arzano, *Nápl.* **9 H12** 40 54N 14 16 E
Asagaya, *Tōkyō* **13 B2** 35 41N 139 38 E
Asahi, *Ōsaka* **12 B4** 34 43N 135 31 E
Asaka, *Tōkyō* **13 B2** 35 47N 139 35 E
Asakusa, *Tōkyō* **13 B3** 35 42N 139 47 E
Asalatpur, *Delhi* **16 B1** 28 37N 77 4 E
Asati, *Calc.* **16 F5** 22 28N 88 15 E
Aschheim, *Mün.* **7 F11** 48 10N 11 42 E
Ascot Vale, *Melb.* **19 E6** 37 46 S 144 53 E
Aserradero, *Méx.* **29 D2** 19 10N 99 16W
Asharoken, *N.Y.* **23 B8** 40 55N 73 21W
Ashburn, *Chic.* **26 C2** 41 45N 87 43W
Ashburton, *Melb.* **19 F7** 37 51 S 145 4 E

34 Ashburton, L.

Ashburton, L., *Balt.* 25 B2 39 19N 76 40W
Ashchherino, *Mos.* 11 F10 55 36N 37 46 E
Ashfield, *Syd.* 19 B3 33 53 S 151 7 E
Ashford, *Lon.* 4 C2 51 25N 0 26W
Ashiya, *Ōsaka* 12 B2 34 43N 135 18 E
Ashiya →, *Ōsaka* 12 B2 34 42N 135 18 E
Ashland, *S.F.* 27 B4 37 41N 122 7W
Ashstead, *Lon.* 4 D3 51 18N 0 17W
Ashwood, *Melb.* 19 F7 37 52 S 145 5 E
Asker, *Oslo* 2 B2 59 50N 10 25 E
Askisto, *Hels.* 3 B3 60 16N 24 47 E
Askrikefjärden, *Stock.* 3 D12 59 22N 18 13 E
Asnieres, *Paris* 5 B3 48 54N 2 16 E
Ason, *Lagos* 18 A3 6 34N 7 31 E
Aspern, *Wien* 10 G10 48 13N 16 29 E
Aspern, Flugplatz, *Wien* 10 G11 48 13N 16 30 E
Assiano, *Mil.* 9 E5 45 27N 9 3 E
Aston Mills, *Phil.* 24 B2 39 52N 75 26W
Astoria, *N.Y.* 22 C5 40 46N 73 55W
Atares, Castillo de, *La Hab.* 30 B2 23 7N 82 21W
Atco, *Phil.* 24 C5 39 46N 74 53W
Atghara, *Calc.* 16 E6 22 37N 88 26 E
Athens = Athínai, *Ath.* 8 J11 37 58N 23 43 E
Athínai, *Ath.* 8 J11 37 58N 23 43 E
Athinai-Ellinikón Airport, *Ath.* 8 J2 37 51N 23 44 E
Athis-Mons, *Paris* 5 C4 48 42N 2 23 E
Atifīya, *Bagd.* 17 E8 33 21N 44 21 E
Atikali, *Ist.* 17 A2 41 1N 28 56 E
Atilo, Cerro, *Lima* 30 G8 12 2 S 77 2W
Atişalen, *Ist.* 17 A2 41 3N 28 52 E
Atlandsberg, *Berl.* 7 A5 52 33N 13 43 E
Atlantic Beach, *N.Y.* 23 D6 40 35N 73 44W
Atta, *Delhi* 16 B2 28 34N 77 19 E
Attiki, *Ath.* 8 H11 38 0N 23 43 E
Atzalpur, *Delhi* 16 A3 28 43N 77 20 E
Atzgersdorf, *Wien* 10 H9 48 8N 16 18 E
Aubervilliers, *Paris* 5 B4 48 54N 2 22 E
Aubing, *Mün.* 7 G9 48 9N 11 25 E
Auburn, *Syd.* 19 B3 33 51 S 151 1 E
Auburndale, *Bost.* 21 C2 42 20N 71 14W
Auckland Park, *Jobg.* 18 F9 26 11 S 28 0 E
Audubon, *Phil.* 24 A2 40 7N 75 25W
Auf-dem-Schnee, *Ruhr* 6 B6 51 26N 7 25 E
Auffargis, *Paris* 5 C1 48 42N 1 53 E
Augustówka, *Wsaw.* 10 E7 52 11N 21 5 E
Aulnay-sous-Bois, *Paris* 5 B4 48 56N 2 29 E
Aurelio, *Rome* 9 F9 41 54N 12 26 E
Ausîm, *El Qâ.* 18 C4 30 7N 31 8 E
Aussen Alster, *Hbg.* 7 D8 53 33N 10 0 E
Austerlitz, Gare d', *Paris* 5 B4 48 50N 2 22 E
Austin, *Chic.* 26 B2 41 53N 87 45W
Auteuil, *Mtrl.* 20 A3 45 37N 73 44W
Avedøre, *Købn.* 2 E9 55 37N 12 27 E
Aveley, *Lon.* 4 C6 51 29N 0 15 E
Avellaneda, *B.A.* 32 C4 34 40 S 58 22W
Avenel, *N.Y.* 22 D3 40 34N 74 16W
Avenel, *Wash.* 25 D8 38 59N 76 59W
Avila, Parque National el, *Car.* 30 D5 10 31N 66 52W
Avila, Pico, *Car.* 30 D5 10 32N 66 52W
Avini, *Nápl.* 9 J13 40 48N 14 28 E
Avondale, *Chic.* 26 B2 41 56N 87 41W
Avondale Heights, *Melb.* 19 E6 37 45 S 144 52 E
Avtovo, *St-Pet.* 11 B3 59 51N 30 16 E
Ayase, *Tōkyō* 13 D1 35 25N 139 26 E
Ayase →, *Tōkyō* 13 A3 35 52N 139 45 E
Ayazaga, *Ist.* 17 A2 41 6N 28 59 E
Ayer Chawan, P., *Sing.* 15 G7 1 16N 103 41 E
Ayer Merbau, P., *Sing.* 15 G7 1 16N 103 42 E
Ayia Paraskevi, *Ath.* 8 H11 38 1N 23 49 E
Áyios Dhimitrios, *Ath.* 8 J11 37 53N 23 44 E
Áyios Ioánnis Rendis, *Ath.* 8 J10 37 57N 23 39 E
Azabu, *Tōkyō* 13 C3 35 39N 139 43 E
Azadpur, *Delhi* 16 A2 28 42N 77 10 E
Azcapotzalco, *Méx.* 29 B2 19 28N 99 10W
Azteca, Estadia, *Méx.* 29 C3 19 18N 99 9W
Azusa, *L.A.* 28 B5 34 7N 117 54W

B

Ba He →, *Beij.* 14 B3 39 57N 116 27 E
Baba I., *Kar.* 17 H10 24 49N 66 57 E
Babarpur, *Delhi* 16 A2 28 41N 77 16 E
Babelsberg, *Berl.* 7 B1 52 22N 13 7 E
Babushkin, *Mos.* 11 D10 55 51N 37 42 E
Babylon, *N.Y.* 23 C9 40 42N 73 19W
Back →, *Balt.* 25 B4 39 17N 76 27W
Back B., *Bomb.* 16 H7 18 56N 72 48 E
Bacoor, *Manila* 15 E3 14 27N 120 56 E
Bacoor B., *Manila* 15 E3 14 27N 120 54 E
Badagri Cr. →, *Lagos* 18 B1 6 24N 7 17 E
Badahela, *Delhi* 16 B1 28 38N 77 4 E
Badalona, *Barc.* 8 D6 41 26N 2 14 E
Badersfeld, *Mün.* 7 F10 48 15N 11 31 E
Badgers Mt., *Lon.* 4 C5 51 20N 0 8 E
Badi, *Delhi* 16 A1 28 44N 77 8 E
Badinan, *Calc.* 16 C5 22 53N 88 14 E
Badu, *Rio J.* 31 B3 22 54 S 43 3W
Baerl, *Ruhr* 6 B2 51 29N 6 40 E
Bærum, *Oslo* 2 B3 59 54N 10 36 E
Bærums Verk, *Oslo* 2 B2 59 56N 10 28 E
Baggensfjärden, *Stock.* 3 E12 59 18N 18 26 E
Bàggio, *Mil.* 9 E5 45 27N 9 6 E
Bāgh-e-Feiz, *Tehr.* 17 C4 35 44N 51 19 E
Baghdād, *Bagd.* 17 E8 33 20N 44 23 E
Bagmari, *Calc.* 16 E6 22 34N 88 23 E
Bagneux, *Paris* 5 C3 48 47N 2 18 E
Bagnolet, *Paris* 5 B4 48 52N 2 25 E
Bagnoli, *Nápl.* 9 J11 40 48N 14 9 E
Bagraula, *Delhi* 16 B1 28 34N 77 4 E
Bagsværd, *Købn.* 2 D9 55 45N 12 27 E
Bagsværd Sø, *Købn.* 2 D9 55 46N 12 28 E
Baguiati, *Calc.* 16 E6 22 36N 88 25 E
Bagumbayan, *Manila* 15 E4 14 28N 121 3 E
Baha'i Temple, *Chic.* 26 A2 42 4N 87 41W
Bahrenfeld, *Hbg.* 7 D7 53 34N 9 55 E
Bahtîm, *El Qâ.* 18 C5 30 8N 31 16 E
Bahu Bheri, *Calc.* 16 C5 22 50N 88 14 E
Baidyabati, *Calc.* 16 D5 22 46N 88 19 E
Baie-d'Urfé, *Mtrl.* 20 B2 43 25N 73 53W
Baierbrunn, *Mün.* 7 G10 48 1N 11 29 E
Baijala, *Calc.* 16 C5 22 51N 88 16 E
Baileys Crossroads, *Wash.* 25 D7 38 50N 77 6W
Bailly, *Paris* 5 B2 48 50N 2 4 E
Bainchipota, *Calc.* 16 C5 22 51N 88 16 E
Bair I., *S.F.* 27 C3 37 30N 122 13W
Bairro da Matriz, *S. Pau.* 31 F7 23 40 S 46 27W
Bairro do Limoeiro, *S. Pau.* 31 E7 23 30 S 46 27W
Baisha, *Gzh.* 14 G8 23 4N 113 15 E
Baisley Pond, *N.Y.* 23 C6 40 40N 73 47W
Baixa da Banheira, *Lisb.* 8 G8 38 39N 9 2W
Baiyun Shan, *Gzh.* 14 G8 23 8N 113 15 E
Baj Baj, *Calc.* 16 F5 22 28N 88 11 E
Bakirkoy, *Ist.* 17 B2 40 58N 28 52 E
Bakovka, *Mos.* 11 E8 55 40N 37 19 E
Bala-Cynwyd, *Phil.* 24 A3 40 0N 75 15W
Balagarh, *Calc.* 16 D6 22 44N 88 27 E
Balara, *Manila* 15 D4 14 39N 121 3 E
Balarambati, *Calc.* 16 D5 22 48N 88 12 E
Balashikha, *Mos.* 11 E11 55 48N 37 58 E
Bald Hill, *Bost.* 21 B3 42 38N 71 0W
Baldeador, *Rio J.* 31 B3 22 51 S 43 1W
Baldeneysee, *Ruhr* 6 B4 51 24N 7 1 E
Baldissero Torinese, *Tori.* 9 B3 45 4N 7 48 E
Baldpate Hill, *Bost.* 21 A3 42 42N 71 0W
Baldpate Pond, *Bost.* 21 A3 42 41N 71 0W
Baldwin, *N.Y.* 23 D7 40 38N 73 37W
Baldwin Hills, *L.A.* 28 B2 34 0N 118 21W
Baldwin Hills Res., *L.A.* 28 B2 34 0N 118 21W
Baldwin Park, *L.A.* 28 B5 34 5N 117 57W
Bal'etan →, *Gzh.* 14 G8 23 5N 113 14 E
Balgowlah, *Syd.* 19 A4 33 47 S 151 16 E
Balgowlah Heights, *Syd.* 19 A4 33 48 S 151 16 E
Balham, *Lon.* 4 C4 51 26N 0 8W
Balihati, *Calc.* 16 D5 22 44N 88 18 E
Balingsnäs, *Stock.* 3 E11 59 13N 18 0 E
Balingsta, *Stock.* 3 E11 59 12N 18 3 E
Balintawak, *Manila* 15 D3 14 39N 120 59 E
Balitai, *Tianj.* 14 E6 39 5N 117 11 E
Balizhuang, *Beij.* 14 B3 39 53N 116 28 E
Ballabhpur, *Calc.* 16 D6 22 44N 88 20 E
Ballainvilliers, *Paris* 5 C3 48 40N 2 17 E
Ballardvale, *Bost.* 21 B3 42 37N 71 9W
Ballenato, Pta., *La Hab.* 30 B2 23 55N 82 28W
Ballerup, *Købn.* 2 D9 55 43N 12 21 E
Bally, *Calc.* 16 E6 22 38N 88 20 E
Ballygunge, *Calc.* 16 E6 22 31N 88 21 E
Balmain, *Syd.* 19 B4 33 51 S 151 11 E
Balmumcu, *Ist.* 17 A3 41 3N 29 2 E
Balongbato, *Manila* 15 D3 14 39N 120 59 E
Baltikri, *Calc.* 16 E5 22 36N 88 18 E
Baltimore, *Balt.* 25 B3 39 17N 76 37W
Baltimore Highlands, *Balt.* 25 B3 39 14N 76 38W
Baltimore-Washington Int. Airport, *Balt.* 25 B3 39 11N 76 39W
Baluhati, *Calc.* 16 E5 22 39N 88 15 E
Balwyn, *Melb.* 19 E7 37 48 S 145 4 E
Balwyn North, *Melb.* 19 E7 37 47 S 145 4 E
Bambang, *Manila* 15 D4 14 31N 121 4 E
Bamondongri, *Bomb.* 16 H9 18 58N 73 1 E
Ban Baan Phichit, *Bangk.* 15 B2 13 49N 100 37 E
Ban Hugli, *Calc.* 16 E6 22 38N 88 22 E
Ban Lat Phrao, *Bangk.* 15 B2 13 47N 100 35 E
Banabuey →, *La Hab.* 30 B2 23 5N 82 27W
Bananal, *S. Pau.* 31 D5 23 27 S 46 41W
Banática, *Lisb.* 8 F7 38 40N 9 11W
Bandeirantes, Praia dos, *Rio J.* 31 C1 23 0 S 43 23W
Bandipur, *Calc.* 16 D6 22 43N 88 26 E
Bandipur, *Calc.* 16 C4 22 50N 88 9 E
Bandra, *Bomb.* 16 G7 19 3N 72 49 E
Bandra Pt., *Bomb.* 16 G7 19 2N 72 49 E
Banfield, *B.A.* 32 C4 34 44 S 58 24W
Bang Kapi, *Bangk.* 15 B2 13 45N 100 38 E
Bang Khen, *Bangk.* 15 A2 13 52N 100 35 E
Bang Na, *Bangk.* 15 B2 13 40N 100 36 E
Bang Su, Khlong →, *Bangk.* 15 B2 13 47N 100 31 E
Bangbae, *Sŏul* 12 H7 37 29N 126 59 E
Banghag, *Sŏul* 12 G8 37 38N 127 1 E
Bangka, *Jak.* 15 J9 6 15 S 106 48 E
Bangkok, *Bangk.* 15 B2 13 44N 100 30 E
Bangkok Noi, Khlong →, *Bangk.* 15 B1 13 45N 100 29 E
Bangkok Yai, *Bangk.* 15 B1 13 43N 100 29 E
Bangkok Yai, Khlong →, *Bangk.* 15 B1 13 44N 100 29 E
Banglo, *Calc.* 16 E5 22 31N 88 14 E
Bangrak, *Bangk.* 15 B2 13 43N 100 31 E
Bangu, *Rio J.* 31 B1 22 52 S 43 26W
Bangu, Sa. do, *Rio J.* 31 B1 22 53 S 43 24W
Bankipur, *Calc.* 16 D5 22 47N 88 13 E
Bankra, *Calc.* 16 E5 22 36N 88 17 E
Banks, C., *Syd.* 19 C4 34 0 S 151 16 E
Bankstown, *Syd.* 19 B3 33 55 S 151 2 E
Bankstown Aerodrome, *Syd.* 19 B2 33 55 S 150 59 E
Banna →, *Tori.* 9 A3 45 12N 7 42 E
Banstala, *Calc.* 16 E6 22 31N 88 24 E
Banstead, *Lon.* 4 D3 51 18N 0 12W
Bantra, *Calc.* 16 E5 22 35N 88 18 E
Banyule Flats Res., *Melb.* 19 E7 37 44 S 145 5 E
Baquirivú, *S. Pau.* 31 E7 23 26 S 46 28W
Baquirivú-Guaçu, *S. Pau.* 31 D7 23 28 S 46 28W
Bara, *Calc.* 16 D5 22 45N 88 16 E
Baragwanath Airfield, *Jobg.* 18 F8 26 14 S 27 58 E
Barai, *Calc.* 16 C6 22 52N 88 22 E
Barajas, *Mdrd.* 8 B3 40 28N 3 34W
Barajas, Aeropuerto Transoceanico de, *Mdrd.* 8 B3 40 28N 3 33W
Barakpur, *Calc.* 16 D6 22 47N 88 21 E
Baranagar, *Calc.* 16 E6 22 38N 88 22 E
Barbaiana, *Mil.* 9 D5 45 32N 9 1 E
Barca, *Tori.* 9 B3 45 6N 7 43 E
Barcarena, *Lisb.* 8 F7 38 43N 9 16W
Barcarena →, *Lisb.* 8 F7 38 41N 9 16W
Barcelona, *Barc.* 8 D6 41 22N 2 10 E
Barcelona-Prat, Aeropuerta de, *Barc.* 8 E5 41 17N 2 5 E
Barceloneta, *Barc.* 8 D6 41 22N 2 11 E
Barcroft, L., *Wash.* 25 D6 38 50N 77 9W
Baréggio, *Mil.* 9 E5 45 28N 9 0 E
Bariti Bil, *Calc.* 16 D6 22 48N 88 26 E
Barkarby, *Stock.* 3 D10 59 24N 17 52 E
Barker Pt., *N.Y.* 22 B5 40 50N 73 44W
Barking, *Lon.* 4 B5 51 32N 0 5 E
Barkingside, *Lon.* 4 B5 51 35N 0 4 E
Barlovento, *La Hab.* 30 B2 23 5N 82 28W
Barmbek, *Hbg.* 7 D8 53 34N 10 2 E
Barmen, *Ruhr* 6 C5 51 16N 7 12 E
Barneau, *Paris* 5 D6 48 38N 2 43 E
Barnes, *Lon.* 4 C3 51 28N 0 14W
Barnet, *Lon.* 4 B3 51 39N 0 11W
Barnsboro, *Phil.* 24 C4 39 45N 75 9W
Baronia Park, *Syd.* 19 A3 33 49 S 151 8 E
Barop, *Ruhr* 6 B6 51 29N 7 25 E
Barra, *Nápl.* 9 H12 40 50N 14 19 E
Barra Andai, *Kar.* 17 H11 24 47N 66 59 E
Barra Funda, *S. Pau.* 31 E6 23 31 S 46 39W
Barracas, *B.A.* 32 B4 34 39 S 58 23W
Barrackpore Airport, *Calc.* 16 D6 22 46N 88 21 E
Barrancas, *Stgo* 30 J10 33 26 S 70 44W
Barranco, *Lima* 30 G8 12 9 S 77 2W
Barreiro, *Lisb.* 8 G8 38 39N 9 5W
Barreto, *Rio J.* 31 B3 22 50 S 43 6W
Barrientos, *Méx.* 29 A2 19 34N 99 11W
Barrington, *Phil.* 24 B4 39 52N 75 3W
Barrio de La Estación, *Mdrd.* 8 B3 40 26N 3 32W
Bartala, *Calc.* 16 E5 22 32N 88 15 E
Barton Park, *Syd.* 19 B3 33 56 S 151 9 E
Bartyki, *Wsaw.* 10 F7 52 10N 21 6 E
Baru, Kali →, *Jak.* 15 J10 6 12 S 106 51 E
Baruipara, *Calc.* 16 D5 22 45N 88 13 E
Baruta, *Car.* 30 E5 10 26N 66 52W
Barvikha, *Mos.* 11 E7 55 44N 37 16 E
Basai Darapur, *Delhi* 16 B1 28 38N 77 6 E
Bass Hill, *Syd.* 19 B3 33 54 S 151 0 E
Bassett, *L.A.* 28 B5 34 3N 117 59W
Bastille, Place de la, *Paris* 5 B4 48 51N 2 22 E
Bastos, *Rio J.* 31 B1 22 52 S 43 21W
Basudebpur, *Calc.* 16 D6 22 49N 88 24 E
Basus, *El Qâ.* 18 C5 30 7N 31 12 E
Batanagar, *Calc.* 16 E5 22 31N 88 15 E
Batenbrock, *Ruhr* 6 A3 51 31N 6 57 E
Bath Beach, *N.Y.* 22 D4 40 36N 74 0W
Bath I., *Kar.* 17 H11 24 49N 67 1 E
Batok, Bukit, *Sing.* 15 F7 1 21N 103 46 E
Battersea, *Lon.* 4 C4 51 28N 0 9W
Baturino, *Mos.* 11 F9 55 35N 37 30 E
Bauman, *Mos.* 11 E10 55 45N 37 40 E
Baumgarten, *Wien* 10 G9 48 12N 16 17 E
Bauria, *Calc.* 16 E5 22 30N 88 10 E
Baxter Estates, *N.Y.* 23 B6 40 50N 73 42W
Bay Farm I., *S.F.* 27 B3 37 44N 122 14W
Bay Meadows Race Track, *S.F.* 27 C3 37 32N 122 17W
Bay Park, *N.Y.* 23 D7 40 37N 73 39W
Bay Ridge, *N.Y.* 22 D4 40 37N 74 1W
Bay Ridge Channel, *N.Y.* 22 D4 40 39N 74 1W
Bay Shore Park, *Balt.* 25 B4 39 13N 76 25W
Baykoz, *Ist.* 17 A3 41 7N 29 7 E
Bayonne, *N.Y.* 22 C4 40 40N 74 6W
Bayshore, *S.F.* 27 B3 37 42N 122 24W
Bayside, *N.Y.* 23 C6 40 45N 73 46W
Bayswater, *Lon.* 4 B3 51 30N 0 10W
Bayswater, *Melb.* 19 F8 37 50 S 145 17 E
Bayview, *S.F.* 27 B2 37 44N 122 23W
Bayville, *N.Y.* 23 B7 40 54N 73 33W
Bāzār, *Tehr.* 17 C5 35 40N 51 25 E
Beachmont, *Bost.* 21 C4 42 23N 70 59W
Beacon Hill, *H.K.* 12 D6 22 21N 114 10 E
Beaconsfield, *Mtrl.* 20 B2 43 25N 73 53W
Beacontree Heath, *Lon.* 4 B5 51 33N 0 9 E
Beam →, *Lon.* 4 B6 51 30N 0 10 E
Bear Cr. →, *Balt.* 25 B3 39 13N 76 30W
Bear Gulch Res., *S.F.* 27 D3 37 26N 122 13W
Beato, *Lisb.* 8 F8 38 44N 9 5W
Beauchamp, *Paris* 5 A3 49 0N 2 11 E
Beaumonte Heights, *Trto.* 20 D7 43 45N 79 34W
Beaverdam Cr. →, *Wash.* 25 C8 39 0N 76 5W
Bebek, *Ist.* 17 A3 41 4N 29 2 E
Beccar, *B.A.* 32 A3 34 27 S 58 32W
Běchovice, *Pra.* 10 B3 50 4N 14 36 E
Beck L., *Chic.* 26 A1 42 4N 87 52W
Beckenham, *Lon.* 4 C4 51 24N 0 1W
Beckhausen, *Ruhr* 6 A4 51 33N 7 1 E
Beckton, *Lon.* 4 B5 51 30N 0 4 E
Beddington, *Lon.* 4 C4 51 21N 0 8W
Beddington Corner, *Lon.* 4 C4 51 23N 0 9W
Bedford, *Bost.* 21 C2 42 27N 71 15W
Bedford Park, *Chic.* 26 C2 41 46N 87 46W
Bedford Park, *N.Y.* 23 B5 40 52N 73 52W
Bedford Stuyvesant, *N.Y.* 22 C5 40 41N 73 56W
Bedford View, *Jobg.* 18 F9 26 10 S 28 7 E
Bedok, *Sing.* 15 G8 1 19N 103 56 E
Beeck, *Ruhr* 6 B2 51 28N 6 44 E
Beeckerwerth, *Ruhr* 6 B2 51 28N 6 42 E
Behala, *Calc.* 16 E5 22 30N 88 18 E
Bei Hai, *Beij.* 14 B3 39 54N 116 21 E
Beicai, *Shang.* 14 J12 31 11N 121 32 E
Beicang, *Tianj.* 14 D5 39 13N 117 7 E
Beigai, *Tianj.* 14 E6 39 0N 117 16 E
Beijiaoshichang, *Beij.* 14 B3 39 57N 116 19 E
Beijing, *Beij.* 14 B2 39 53N 116 21 E
Beinasco, *Tori.* 9 B2 45 1N 7 34 E
Beirolas, *Lisb.* 8 F8 38 46N 9 5W
Beitsun, *Gzh.* 14 G8 23 7N 113 10 E
Békásmegyer, *Bud.* 10 J13 47 35N 19 3 E
Bekkelaget, *Oslo* 2 B4 59 53N 10 47 E
Bel Air, *L.A.* 28 B2 34 4N 118 27W
Bela Vista, *S. Pau.* 31 E6 23 33 S 46 38W
Bélanger, *Mtrl.* 20 A3 43 35N 73 42W
Belas, *Lisb.* 8 F7 38 46N 9 17W
Belém, *Lisb.* 8 F7 38 41N 9 12W
Belém, Torre de, *Lisb.* 8 F7 38 41N 9 12W
Belenzinho, *S. Pau.* 31 E6 23 32 S 46 34W
Belfield, *Syd.* 19 B3 33 53 S 151 6 E
Belgachi, *Calc.* 16 E6 22 36N 88 23 E
Belgharia, *Calc.* 16 E6 22 39N 88 22 E
Belgrano, *B.A.* 32 B4 34 33 S 58 27W
Belgrave, *Melb.* 19 F9 37 54 S 145 21 E
Bell Gardens, *L.A.* 28 C4 33 58N 118 9W
Bella Vista, *B.A.* 32 B2 34 34 S 58 41W
Bellaire, *N.Y.* 23 C6 40 42N 73 44W
Bellavista, *Lima* 30 G8 12 4 S 77 8W
Bellavista, *Stgo* 30 K11 33 31 S 70 35W
Belle Harbour, *N.Y.* 23 D5 40 34N 73 51W
Belle Haven, *N.Y.* 23 A7 41 0N 73 37W
Belle Haven, *Wash.* 25 D7 38 46N 77 3W
Bellefonte, *Phil.* 24 C1 39 45N 75 33W
Bellerose, *N.Y.* 23 C6 40 43N 73 42W
Belleview, *Wash.* 25 E7 38 46N 77 3W
Belleville, *N.Y.* 22 C4 40 48N 74 8W
Bellflower, *L.A.* 28 C4 33 53N 118 7W
Bellingham, *Lon.* 4 C4 51 25N 0 1W
Bellmawr, *Phil.* 24 B4 39 52N 75 5W
Bellmore, *N.Y.* 23 D7 40 39N 73 31W
Bello, *La Hab.* 30 B3 23 5N 82 24W
Bells Lake, *Phil.* 24 C4 39 45N 75 6W
Bellwood, *Chic.* 26 B1 41 52N 87 53W
Belmont, *Bost.* 21 C2 42 23N 71 10W
Belmont, *Lon.* 4 B3 51 36N 0 18W
Belmont, *S.F.* 27 C3 37 31N 122 17W
Belmont Cragin, *Chic.* 26 B2 41 55N 87 46W
Belmont Harbor, *Chic.* 26 B3 41 56N 87 38W
Belmont Hills, *Phil.* 24 A3 40 1N 75 15W
Belmont Slough, *S.F.* 27 C3 37 32N 122 15W
Belmore, *Syd.* 19 B3 33 55 S 151 5 E
Belopurpada, *Bomb.* 16 G9 19 1N 73 0 E
Beltsville, *Wash.* 25 C8 39 2N 76 54W
Beltsville Airport, *Wash.* 25 C9 39 1N 76 49W
Belur, *Calc.* 16 E6 22 37N 88 21 E
Belvedere, *Lon.* 4 C5 51 29N 0 9 E
Belvedere, *S.F.* 27 A2 37 52N 122 27W
Belyayevo Bogorodskoye, *Mos.* 11 F9 55 39N 37 31 E
Bemböle, *Hels.* 3 B2 60 13N 24 39 E
Bemis Woods, *Chic.* 26 C1 41 49N 87 54W
Bemowo, *Wsaw.* 10 E6 52 15N 20 53 E
Benavidez, *B.A.* 32 A2 34 24 S 58 41W
Bendale, *Trto.* 20 D9 43 45N 79 13W
Bendungan Hilir, *Jak.* 15 J9 6 12 S 106 48 E
Benefica, *Rio J.* 31 B2 22 52 S 43 14W
Benfica, *Lisb.* 8 F8 38 45N 9 11W
Benin B., *Lagos* 18 B2 6 24N 7 28 E
Benjamin Franklin Br., *Phil.* 24 B4 39 57N 75 8W
Benoni, *Jobg.* 18 F10 26 11 S 28 18 E
Benoni South, *Jobg.* 18 F10 26 12 S 28 17 E
Bensenville, *Chic.* 26 B1 41 57N 87 56W
Bensonhurst, *N.Y.* 22 D5 40 35N 73 59W
Bentleigh, *Melb.* 19 F7 37 54 S 145 2 E
Bentleigh East, *Melb.* 19 F7 37 54 S 145 4 E
Beraberi, *Calc.* 16 D6 22 46N 88 27 E
Berario, *Jobg.* 18 E8 26 7 S 27 57 E
Berazategui, *B.A.* 32 C5 34 45 S 58 15W
Berea, *Jobg.* 18 F9 26 10 S 28 3 E
Berg am Laim, *Mün.* 7 G10 48 7N 11 38 E
Bergbaumuseum, *Ruhr* 6 B5 51 29N 7 13 E
Bergenfield, *N.Y.* 22 B5 40 55N 73 59W
Berger, *Oslo* 2 B6 59 56N 11 7 E
Bergerhausen, *Ruhr* 6 B4 51 26N 7 2 E
Bergerhof, *Ruhr* 6 C6 51 12N 7 21 E
Bergham, *Mün.* 7 G10 48 2N 11 37 E
Berghausen, *Ruhr* 6 A5 51 36N 7 12 E
Berghm-Oestrum, *Ruhr* 6 B1 51 25N 6 39 E
Bergstedt, *Hbg.* 7 C8 53 40N 10 7 E
Beri, *Barc.* 8 D5 41 20N 2 1 E
Berih, Sungei →, *Sing.* 15 F7 1 22N 103 40 E
Berkeley, *Chic.* 26 B1 41 53N 87 54W
Berkeley, *S.F.* 27 A3 37 51N 122 16W
Berkeley Heights, *N.Y.* 22 C2 40 40N 74 26W
Berkeley Hills, *S.F.* 27 A3 37 51N 122 11W
Berlin, *Berl.* 7 A3 52 31N 13 23 E
Berlin, *Phil.* 24 C5 39 47N 74 55W
Bermondsey, *Lon.* 4 C4 51 29N 0 3W
Bernabeu, Estadio, *Mdrd.* 8 B2 40 27N 3 41W
Bernal, *B.A.* 32 C5 34 43 S 58 17W
Bernal Heights, *S.F.* 27 B2 37 44N 122 24W
Berne, *Hbg.* 7 D8 53 38N 10 8 E
Berngardovka, *St-Pet.* 11 A5 60 0N 30 33 E
Berthpage, *N.Y.* 23 C8 40 45N 73 29W
Bertlich, *Ruhr* 6 A4 51 36N 7 4 E
Bertolla Barca, *Tori.* 9 B3 45 6N 7 44 E
Berwyn, *Chic.* 26 B2 41 50N 87 47W
Berwyn, *Phil.* 24 A2 40 2N 75 26W
Berwyn Heights, *Wash.* 25 D8 38 59N 76 55W
Besedy, *Mos.* 11 F10 55 38N 37 47 E
Besiktas, *Ist.* 17 A3 41 2N 29 0 E
Beskudnikovo, *Mos.* 11 D9 55 52N 37 34 E
Besós →, *Barc.* 8 D6 41 24N 2 13 E
Bessancourt, *Paris* 5 A3 49 2N 2 12 E
Bestazzo, *Mil.* 9 E5 45 25N 9 0 E
Bethayres, *Phil.* 24 A4 40 7N 75 3W
Bethesda, *Wash.* 25 D7 38 59N 77 6W
Bethlehem Steel Plant, *Balt.* 25 B4 39 13N 76 29W
Bethnal Green, *Lon.* 4 B4 51 31N 0 2W
Bethpage State Park, *N.Y.* 23 C8 40 45N 73 25W
Betor, *Calc.* 16 E5 22 34N 88 17 E
Beuvronne →, *Paris* 5 B6 48 59N 2 40 E
Beverley, *Chic.* 26 C2 41 42N 87 39W
Beverley Hills, *Syd.* 19 B3 33 56 S 151 5 E
Beverley Park, *Syd.* 19 B3 33 58 S 151 8 E
Beverly, *Bost.* 21 B4 42 34N 70 53W
Beverly, *Phil.* 24 A5 40 3N 74 55W
Beverly Glen, *L.A.* 28 B2 34 6N 118 26W
Beverly Harbor, *Bost.* 21 B4 42 32N 70 51W
Beverly Hills, *L.A.* 28 B2 34 5N 118 24W
Beverly Municipal Airport, *Bost.* 21 B4 42 36N 70 55W
Bexley, *Lon.* 4 C5 51 26N 0 8 E
Bexley, *Syd.* 19 B3 33 56 S 151 7 E
Bexleyheath, *Lon.* 4 C5 51 27N 0 8 E
Beyenburg, *Ruhr* 6 C5 51 15N 7 19 E
Beylerbeyi, *Ist.* 17 A3 41 2N 29 2 E
Beyoğlu, *Ist.* 17 A2 41 1N 28 58 E
Bezons, *Paris* 5 B3 48 56N 2 13 E
Bhadrakali, *Calc.* 16 D6 22 40N 88 20 E
Bhadreswar, *Calc.* 16 D5 22 49N 88 22 E
Bhadua, *Calc.* 16 D5 22 40N 88 18 E
Bhalswa, *Delhi* 16 A2 28 44N 77 10 E
Bhambo Khān Qarmati, *Kar.* 17 H11 24 49N 67 7 E
Bhandardaha, *Calc.* 16 E5 22 37N 88 12 E
Bhatpara, *Calc.* 16 C6 22 52N 88 25 E
Bhatpur, *Calc.* 16 D5 22 43N 88 15 E
Bhatsala, *Calc.* 16 E5 22 30N 88 16 E
Bhawanipore, *Calc.* 16 E6 22 32N 88 21 E
Bhopura, *Delhi* 16 A2 28 41N 77 19 E
Białołeka Dworska, *Wsaw.* 10 E7 52 19N 21 1 E
Bickley, *Lon.* 4 C5 51 23N 0 3 E
Bicutan, *Manila* 15 D4 14 30N 121 3 E
Bidyadharpur, *Calc.* 16 C6 22 50N 88 24 E
Bielany, *Wsaw.* 10 E6 52 17N 20 57 E
Biesdorf, *Berl.* 7 A4 52 30N 13 33 E
Bièvre →, *Paris* 5 C2 48 44N 2 9 E
Bièvres, *Paris* 5 C3 48 45N 2 13 E
Big Timber Cr. →, *Phil.* 24 B4 39 52N 75 7W
Big Tujunga Canyon →, *L.A.* 28 A3 34 16N 118 12W
Biggin Hill, *Lon.* 4 D5 51 18N 0 1 E
Bijoki, *Tōkyō* 13 B2 35 49N 139 38 E
Bilibiran, *Manila* 15 E5 14 29N 121 10 E
Bilk, *Ruhr* 6 C2 51 12N 6 46 E
Billbrook, *Hbg.* 7 D8 53 31N 10 4 E
Bille →, *Hbg.* 7 D8 53 32N 10 5 E
Billerica, *Bost.* 21 A2 42 33N 71 16W
Billingshurst, *B.A.* 32 B3 34 34 S 58 37W
Billings, Represa, *S. Pau.* 31 F6 23 42 S 46 39W
Billstedt, *Hbg.* 7 D8 53 32N 10 6 E
Billwerder, *Hbg.* 7 E8 53 30N 10 7 E
Billwerder B., *Hbg.* 7 E8 53 32N 10 3 E
Binacayan, *Manila* 15 E3 14 27N 120 55 E
Binangonan, *Manila* 15 E5 14 28N 121 10 E
Binaria, *Jak.* 15 H10 6 7 S 106 51 E
Bingzhoubao, *Gzh.* 14 G8 23 2N 113 11 E
Binningsvatna, *Oslo* 2 C6 50 46N 11 3 E
Binondo, *Manila* 15 D3 14 36N 120 58 E
Binzago, *Mil.* 9 D5 45 37N 9 8 E
Birak el Kiyam, *El Qâ.* 18 C4 30 2N 31 8 E
Birch Cliff, *Trto.* 20 D9 43 41N 79 16W
Bird →, *Balt.* 25 A4 39 22N 76 22W
Birka, *Stock.* 3 D8 59 20N 17 33 E
Birkenhöhe, *Berl.* 7 A5 52 37N 13 45 E
Birkenstein, *Berl.* 7 A5 52 31N 13 38 E
Birkholz, *Berl.* 7 A4 52 37N 13 33 E
Birkholzaue, *Berl.* 7 A4 52 38N 13 36 E
Biryulyovo, *Mos.* 11 F10 55 35N 37 40 E
Bisamberg, *Wien* 10 G10 48 19N 16 21 E
Bispebjerg, *Købn.* 2 D10 55 42N 12 31 E
Bitsa, *Mos.* 11 F9 55 35N 37 36 E
Biwon Secret Garden, *Sŏul* 12 G7 37 34N 126 59 E
Bizard, Î., *Mtrl.* 20 B2 43 29N 73 53W
Björknas, *Stock.* 3 E12 59 19N 18 20 E
Björkőfjärden, *Hels.* 3 C2 60 7N 24 38 E
Black Cr. →, *Trto.* 20 D8 43 40N 79 30W
Blackburn, *Melb.* 19 E7 37 48 S 145 9 E
Blackburn L., *Melb.* 19 E7 37 49 S 145 9 E
Blackburn South, *Melb.* 19 F7 37 50 S 145 9 E
Blackfen, *Lon.* 4 C5 51 26N 0 6 E
Blackheath, *Jobg.* 18 E8 26 8 S 27 57 E
Blackheath, *Lon.* 4 C4 51 27N 0 0 E
Blackmore, *Lon.* 4 A6 51 41N 0 19 E
Blacktown, *Syd.* 19 A2 33 46 S 150 56 E
Blackwall, *Lon.* 4 B4 51 30N 0 0 E
Blackwood, *Phil.* 24 C4 39 47N 75 4W
Bladensburg, *Wash.* 25 D8 38 55N 76 55W
Blairgowrie, *Jobg.* 18 E9 26 6 S 28 0 E
Blakehurst, *Syd.* 19 B3 33 59 S 151 6 E
Blakstad, *Oslo* 2 C2 50 49N 10 28 E
Blanco, C., *Car.* 30 D5 10 36N 66 59W
Blankenburg, *Berl.* 7 A3 52 35N 13 27 E
Blankenese, *Hbg.* 7 D6 53 33N 9 48 E
Blankenfelde, *Berl.* 7 A3 52 37N 13 23 E
Blankenstein, *Ruhr* 6 B5 51 24N 7 11 E
Blenheim, *Phil.* 24 C4 39 48N 75 4W
Bliersheim, *Ruhr* 6 B2 51 23N 6 42 E
Blind Cr. →, *Melb.* 19 F8 37 53 S 145 12 E
Blizne, *Wsaw.* 10 E6 52 14N 20 52 E
Bloomfield, *N.Y.* 22 C3 40 48N 74 12W
Bloomingdale, *N.Y.* 22 A3 41 0N 74 19W
Bloomsbury, *Balt.* 25 B2 39 15N 76 44W
Błota, *Wsaw.* 10 F8 52 9N 21 11 E
Bloubosspruit →, *Jobg.* 18 F9 26 16 S 28 0 E
Blue Hills Reservation, *Bost.* 21 D3 42 13N 71 5W
Blue Island, *Chic.* 26 C2 41 40N 87 40W
Bluff Hd., *H.K.* 12 E6 22 11N 114 12 E
Blumberg, *Berl.* 7 A4 52 36N 13 39 E
Blunt Pt., *S.F.* 27 A2 37 51N 122 25W
Blutenberg, *Mün.* 7 G9 48 9N 11 27 E
Blylaget, *Oslo* 2 C4 59 46N 10 41 E
Boa Vista, Alto do, *Rio J.* 31 B2 22 58 S 43 16W
Boa Vista, Morro, *Rio J.* 31 B3 22 53 S 43 5W
Boadilla del Monte, *Mdrd.* 8 B1 40 24N 3 52W
Boardwalk, *N.Y.* 23 D6 40 34N 73 49W
Boavista, *Lisb.* 8 F8 38 48N 9 8W
Bobäck, *Hels.* 3 B3 60 10N 24 31 E
Boberg, *Hbg.* 7 D8 53 30N 10 9 E
Bobigny, *Paris* 5 B4 48 54N 2 26 E
Bobylskaya, *St-Pet.* 11 B3 59 59N 30 10 E
Bocanegra, *Lima* 30 F8 11 59 S 77 7W
Boccea, *Rome* 9 F8 41 57N 12 19 E
Bochold, *Ruhr* 6 B3 51 28N 6 57 E
Bochum, *Ruhr* 6 B5 51 28N 7 13 E
Bockum, *Ruhr* 6 B1 51 21N 6 37 E
Bodelschwingh, *Ruhr* 6 A6 51 33N 7 22 E
Bodomjärvi, *Hels.* 3 B3 60 15N 24 40 E
Bogenhausen, *Mün.* 7 G10 48 8N 11 36 E
Bognæs, *Købn.* 2 D7 55 41N 12 1 E
Bogorodskoye, *Mos.* 11 E10 55 48N 37 42 E
Bogota, *N.Y.* 22 B4 40 52N 74 2W
Bogstadvatnet, *Oslo* 2 B3 59 58N 10 37 E
Bohaidalu, *Tianj.* 14 E6 39 7N 117 12 E
Bohnsdorf, *Berl.* 7 B4 52 23N 13 34 E
Bois-Colombes, *Paris* 5 B3 48 55N 2 16 E
Bois-d'Arcy, *Paris* 5 C2 48 48N 2 1 E
Boisement, *Paris* 5 A2 49 1N 2 0 E
Boissy-St-Léger, *Paris* 5 C5 48 44N 2 31 E
Boksburg, *Jobg.* 18 F10 26 12 S 28 15 E
Boksburg North, *Jobg.* 18 F10 26 12 S 28 15 E
Boksburg South, *Jobg.* 18 F10 26 13 S 28 16 E
Boldinasco, *Mil.* 9 E5 45 29N 9 8 E
Bøler, *Oslo* 2 B5 59 53N 10 50 E
Bollate, *Mil.* 9 D5 45 32N 9 7 E
Bollensdorf, *Berl.* 7 A5 52 30N 13 42 E
Bollmora, *Stock.* 3 E12 59 14N 18 14 E
Bolshaya Nevka, *St-Pet.* 11 B3 59 58N 30 18 E
Bolshaya-Okhta, *St-Pet.* 11 B4 59 56N 30 26 E
Bolshoi Theatre, *Mos.* 11 E9 55 45N 37 37 E
Bom Retiro, *S. Pau.* 31 E6 23 31 S 46 38W
Bombay, *Bomb.* 16 H8 18 56N 72 50 E
Bombay Harbour, *Bomb.* 16 H8 18 58N 72 55 E
Bombay Univ., *Bomb.* 16 H7 18 55N 72 49 E
Bommern, *Ruhr* 6 B6 51 25N 7 20 E
Bonaero Park, *Jobg.* 18 E10 26 7 S 28 15 E
Bondi, *Syd.* 19 B4 33 53 S 151 16 E
Bondoufle, *Paris* 5 D4 48 36N 2 22 E
Bondy, *Paris* 5 B4 48 54N 2 28 E
Bondy, Forêt de, *Paris* 5 B5 48 54N 2 33 E
Bonifacio Monument, *Manila* 15 D3 14 38N 120 58 E
Bonifica di Maccarese, *Rome* 9 F8 41 50N 12 15 E
Bonifica di Porto, *Rome* 9 G8 41 48N 12 18 E
Bonita, Pt., *S.F.* 27 B1 37 48N 122 31W
Bonnelles, *Paris* 5 D2 48 37N 2 1 E
Bonneuil-sur-Marne, *Paris* 5 C4 48 46N 2 30 E
Bönningstedt, *Hbg.* 7 C7 53 40N 9 54 E
Bonnyrigg, *Syd.* 19 B2 33 53 S 150 54 E
Bonsari, *Bomb.* 16 G9 19 4N 73 1 E
Bonsucesso, *Rio J.* 31 B2 22 51 S 43 15W
Boo, *Stock.* 3 D12 59 20N 18 16 E
Boonton, *N.Y.* 22 B2 40 54N 74 24W
Boonton Res., *N.Y.* 22 B2 40 53N 74 24W
Booth Corner, *Phil.* 24 B2 39 50N 75 29W
Boothwyn, *Phil.* 24 C2 39 49N 75 26W
Borbeck, *Ruhr* 6 B3 51 28N 6 56 E
Bordeaux, *Jobg.* 18 E9 26 5 S 28 1 E
Bordeaux, *Mtrl.* 20 A3 43 31N 73 43W
Borehamwood, *Lon.* 4 B3 51 39N 0 15W
Borgaretto, *Tori.* 9 B2 45 0N 7 35 E
Borgaro Torinese, *Tori.* 9 B2 45 9N 7 39 E
Borghese, Villa, *Rome* 9 F9 41 54N 12 29 E
Borisovo, *Mos.* 11 F10 55 38N 37 41 E
Borle, *Bomb.* 16 G8 19 2N 72 54 E
Bornig, *Ruhr* 6 A5 51 33N 7 16 E
Bornsjön, *Stock.* 3 E9 59 14N 17 44 E
Boronia, *Melb.* 19 F8 37 51 S 145 17 E
Borough Green, *Lon.* 4 D6 51 17N 0 19 E
Borough Park, *N.Y.* 22 D5 40 38N 73 59W
Børtervatna, *Oslo* 2 C6 50 46N 11 3 E
Boscoreale, *Nápl.* 9 J13 40 46N 14 28 E
Boscotrecase, *Nápl.* 9 J13 40 46N 14 27 E
Bösinghovn, *Ruhr* 6 C1 51 18N 6 38 E
Bosmont, *Jobg.* 18 F8 26 10 S 27 57 E
Bosön, *Stock.* 3 D12 59 22N 18 11 E
Bosporus = Istanbul Boğazi, *Ist.* 17 A3 41 5N 29 3 E
Bosque da Saúde, *S. Pau.* 31 E6 23 36 S 46 37W
Bosques, *B.A.* 32 C5 34 48 S 58 15W
Bossley Park, *Syd.* 19 B2 33 51 S 150 53 E
Bossucaba →, *S. Pau.* 31 E5 23 31 S 46 46W
Bostanci, *Ist.* 17 B3 40 57N 29 5 E
Bostelbek, *Hbg.* 7 E7 53 28N 9 55 E
Boston, *Bost.* 21 C3 42 21N 71 3W
Boston B., *Bost.* 21 C4 42 22N 70 58W
Boston Harbor, *Bost.* 21 C3 42 20N 71 0W
Boston Hill, *Bost.* 21 B4 42 38N 71 5W
Botany, *Syd.* 19 B4 33 56 S 151 12 E
Botany B., *Lon.* 4 A4 51 40N 0 7W
Botany B., *Syd.* 19 B4 33 58 S 151 11 E
Botič →, *Pra.* 10 B3 50 4N 14 26 E
Botkyrka, *Stock.* 3 E9 59 12N 17 49 E
Botofogo, *Rio J.* 31 B2 22 56 S 43 10W
Bottrop, *Ruhr* 6 A3 51 31N 6 57 E
Bötzow, *Berl.* 7 A1 52 39N 13 8 E
Bouafle, *Paris* 5 B1 48 58N 1 54 E
Boucherville, *Mtrl.* 20 A5 43 36N 73 28W
Boucherville, Îs. de, *Mtrl.* 20 A5 43 36N 73 28W
Bougival, *Paris* 5 B2 48 51N 2 8 E
Boulder Pt., *H.K.* 12 E5 22 14N 114 6 E

Choisy-le-Roi 35

Boullay-les-Troux, *Paris* 5 C2 48 40N 2 2 E
Boulogne, *B.A.* 32 B3 34 30 S 58 33W
Boulogne, Bois de, *Paris* 5 B3 48 51N 2 14 E
Boulogne-Billancourt, *Paris* 5 B3 48 50N 2 14 E
Bouqueval, *Paris* 5 A4 49 1N 2 25 E
Bourg-la-Reine, *Paris* 5 C3 48 46N 2 19 E
Boussy-St.-Antoine, *Paris* 5 C5 48 41N 2 33 E
Bouviers, *Paris* 5 C2 48 46N 2 4 E
Bovert, *Ruhr* 6 C1 51 16N 6 37 E
Bovisa, *Mil.* 9 D6 45 30N 9 10 E
Bovísio-Masciago, *Mil.* 9 D5 45 36N 9 8 E
Bow, *Lon.* 4 B4 51 31N 0 1W
Bowleys Quarters, *Balt.* 25 A4 39 20N 76 24W
Box Hill, *Melb.* 19 E7 37 48 S 145 6 E
Boxford State Forest, *Bost.* 21 B3 42 39N 71 2W
Boy, *Ruhr* 6 A3 51 31N 7 0 E
Boyaciköy, *Ist.* 17 A3 41 5N 29 2 E
Boye →, *Ruhr* 6 A3 51 30N 6 59 E
Boyle Heights, *L.A.* 28 B3 34 1N 118 12 E
Braddell Heights, *Sing.* 15 F8 1 20N 103 51 E
Brahmanpur, *Bomb.* 16 G8 19 5N 72 52 E
Braintree, *Bost.* 21 D3 42 12N 71 0W
Brakpan, *Jobg.* 18 F11 26 14 S 28 20 E
Brambauer, *Ruhr* 6 A6 51 35N 7 26 E
Bramfeld, *Hbg.* 7 D8 53 36N 10 5 E
Bramley, *Jobg.* 18 E9 26 7 S 28 4 E
Brande, *Hbg.* 7 D6 53 37N 9 49 E
Brandenburg Gate, *Berl.* 7 A3 52 30N 13 21 E
Brandizzo, *Tori.* 9 A3 45 10N 7 49 E
Brands Hatch, *Lon.* 4 C6 51 21N 0 15 E
Brandýs nad Labem, *Pra.* 10 A3 50 10N 14 39 E
Brandywine, *Phil.* 24 C1 39 49N 75 32W
Brandywine Cr. →, *Phil.* 24 C1 39 43N 75 31W
Brani, P., *Sing.* 15 G8 1 15N 103 50 E
Braník, *Pra.* 10 B2 50 1N 14 25 E
Brännkyrka, *Stock.* 3 E11 59 17N 18 0 E
Brás, *S. Pau.* 31 E6 23 32 S 46 36W
Brateyevo, *Mos.* 11 F10 55 39N 37 45 E
Bratsevo, *Mos.* 11 D8 55 51N 37 24 E
Brauck, *Ruhr* 6 A3 51 32N 7 0 E
Brava, Pta., *La Hab.* 30 B2 23 8N 82 23W
Braybrook, *Melb.* 19 E6 37 46 S 144 51 E
Brázdim, *Pra.* 10 A3 50 10N 14 35 E
Breakheart Reservation, *Bost.* 21 C3 42 28N 71 1W
Brechten, *Ruhr* 6 A6 51 34N 7 27 E
Breckerfeld, *Ruhr* 6 C6 51 15N 7 28 E
Brede, *Købn.* 2 D10 55 47N 12 30 E
Bredeney, *Ruhr* 6 B3 51 24N 6 59 E
Breeds Pond, *Bost.* 21 C4 42 28N 70 58W
Breezy Pt., *N.Y.* 22 D5 40 33N 73 56W
Breitenlee, *Wien* 10 G11 48 15N 16 30 E
Breitscheid, *Ruhr* 6 B3 51 21N 6 51 E
Breña, *Lima* 30 G8 12 3 S 77 3W
Brenschede, *Ruhr* 6 B5 51 26N 7 12 E
Brent, *Lon.* 4 B3 51 33N 0 15W
Brent →, *Lon.* 4 B3 51 30N 0 20W
Brent Res., *Lon.* 4 B3 51 34N 0 14W
Brentford, *Lon.* 4 C3 51 28N 0 18W
Brenthurst, *Jobg.* 18 F11 26 15 S 28 21 E
Brentwood, *Lon.* 4 B6 51 36N 0 18 E
Brentwood Park, *Jobg.* 18 E10 26 7 S 28 17 E
Brentwood Park, *L.A.* 28 B2 34 3N 118 29W
Brera, *Mil.* 9 E6 45 28N 9 11 E
Bresso, *Mil.* 9 D6 45 32N 9 11 E
Brétigny-sur-Orge, *Paris* 5 D3 48 36N 2 18 E
Brevik, *Stock.* 3 D12 59 20N 18 12 E
Břevnov, *Pra.* 10 B2 50 4N 14 22 E
Brewer I., *S.F.* 27 C3 37 33N 122 16W
Bricket Wood, *Lon.* 4 A2 51 42N 0 21W
Bridesburg, *Phil.* 24 B4 39 59N 75 4W
Bridgeport, *Chic.* 26 B3 41 50N 87 38W
Bridgeport, *Phil.* 24 A2 40 6N 75 21W
Bridgeview, *Chic.* 26 C2 41 45N 87 48W
Brie-Comte-Robert, *Paris* 5 C5 48 41N 2 36 E
Brighton, *Melb.* 19 F6 37 55 S 144 59 E
Brighton le Sands, *Syd.* 19 B3 33 57 S 151 9 E
Brighton Park, *Chic.* 26 C2 41 48N 87 41W
Brightwood, *Wash.* 25 D7 38 57N 77 1W
Brigittenau, *Wien* 10 G10 48 14N 16 22 E
Briis-sous-Forges, *Paris* 5 D2 48 37N 2 7 E
Brimbank Park, *Melb.* 19 E6 37 43 S 144 50 E
Brimsdown, *Lon.* 4 B4 51 39N 0 0 E
Brione, *Tori.* 9 B1 45 8N 7 28 E
Briones Hills, *S.F.* 27 A4 37 56N 122 8W
Briones Regional Park, *S.F.* 27 A4 37 55N 122 8W
Briones Res., *S.F.* 27 A4 37 55N 122 11W
Brisbane, *S.F.* 27 B2 37 40N 122 23W
Bristol, *Phil.* 24 A5 40 6N 74 53W
Britz, *Berl.* 7 B3 52 26N 13 27 E
Brixton, *Lon.* 4 C4 51 27N 0 8W
Broad Axe, *Phil.* 24 A3 40 8N 75 14W
Broad Sd., *Bost.* 21 C4 42 23N 70 56W
Broadmeadows, *Melb.* 19 E6 37 40 S 144 55 E
Broadmoor, *S.F.* 27 B2 37 41N 122 29W
Broadview, *Chic.* 26 B1 41 51N 87 52W
Brobacka, *Hels.* 3 B2 60 15N 24 36 E
Brockley, *Lon.* 4 C4 51 27N 0 2W
Bródno, *Wsaw.* 10 E7 52 17N 21 1 E
Bródnowski, Kanal, *Wsaw.* 10 E7 52 17N 21 3 E
Broich, *Ruhr* 6 B3 51 25N 6 50 E
Bromley, *Lon.* 4 C5 51 24N 0 0 E
Bromley-by-Bow, *Lon.* 4 B4 51 31N 0 0 E
Bromley Common, *Lon.* 4 C5 51 22N 0 2 E
Bromma, *Stock.* 3 D10 59 21N 17 55 E
Bromma flygplats, *Stock.* 3 D10 59 21N 17 56 E
Brompton, *Lon.* 4 C3 51 29N 0 10W
Brøndby Strand, *Købn.* 2 E9 55 36N 12 25 E
Brøndbyøster, *Købn.* 2 E9 55 39N 12 26 E
Brøndbyvester, *Købn.* 2 E9 55 37N 12 23 E
Brondesbury, *Lon.* 4 B3 51 32N 0 12W
Brønnøya, *Oslo* 2 B3 59 51N 10 32 E
Brønshøj, *Købn.* 2 D9 55 41N 12 29 E
Bronx Zoo, *N.Y.* 23 B5 40 50N 73 51W
Bronxville, *N.Y.* 23 B6 40 56N 73 49W
Brook Street, *Lon.* 4 B6 51 36N 0 17 E
Brookfield, *Chic.* 26 C1 41 48N 87 50W
Brookhaven, *Phil.* 24 B2 39 52N 75 23W
Brooklandville, *Balt.* 25 A2 39 25N 76 40W
Brooklin, *S. Pau.* 31 E6 23 37 S 46 39W
Brookline, *Bost.* 21 D3 42 19N 71 8W
Brooklyn, *Balt.* 25 B3 39 13N 76 36W
Brooklyn, *Melb.* 19 E5 37 49 S 144 49 E
Brooklyn, *N.Y.* 22 D5 40 37N 73 57W
Brookmont, *Wash.* 25 D7 38 57N 77 7W
Brooks I., *S.F.* 27 A2 37 53N 122 21W
Brookville, *N.Y.* 23 C7 40 48N 73 33W
Broomall, *Phil.* 24 B2 39 58N 75 22W
Brosewere B., *N.Y.* 23 D6 40 37N 73 40W
Brossard, *Mtrl.* 20 B5 43 27N 73 28W
Brou-sur-Chantereine, *Paris* 5 B5 48 53N 2 37 E
Brown, *Trto.* 20 D9 43 48N 79 14W
Browns Line, *Trto.* 20 E7 43 36N 79 32W
Broyhill Park, *Wash.* 25 D6 38 52N 77 12W
Bru, *Oslo* 2 C5 59 47N 10 54 E
Bruckhausen, *Ruhr* 6 B2 51 29N 6 43 E
Brughério, *Mil.* 9 D6 45 33N 9 17 E
Bruino, *Tori.* 9 B1 45 1N 7 27 E
Bruløkka, *Oslo* 2 A2 60 1N 10 22 E
Brunn, *Stock.* 3 E13 59 17N 18 25 E
Brunnthal, *Mün.* 7 G11 48 0N 11 41 E
Brunoy, *Paris* 5 C4 48 41N 2 29 E
Brunswick, *Melb.* 19 E6 37 45 S 144 57 E
Brusciano, *Nápl.* 9 H13 40 55N 14 25 E
Brush Hill, *Bost.* 21 D1 42 15N 71 22W
Bruzzano, *Mil.* 9 D6 45 31N 9 10 E
Bry-sur-Marne, *Paris* 5 B5 48 50N 2 32 E
Bryn, *Oslo* 2 B2 59 55N 10 27 E
Bryn Athyn, *Phil.* 24 A4 40 8N 75 3W
Bryn Mawr, *Phil.* 24 A3 40 1N 75 19W
Brzeziny, *Wsaw.* 10 E7 52 19N 21 2 E
Bubeneč, *Pra.* 10 B2 50 6N 14 24 E
Buc, *Paris* 5 C2 48 46N 2 7 E
Buch, *Berl.* 7 A3 52 38N 13 29 E
Buchburg, *Wien* 10 G9 48 13N 16 11 E
Buchenhain, *Mün.* 7 G9 48 1N 11 29 E
Buchholz, *Berl.* 7 A3 52 36N 13 25 E
Buchholz, *Ruhr* 6 B2 51 23N 6 46 E
Buckhurst Hill, *Lon.* 4 B5 51 37N 0 2 E
Buckingham Palace, *Lon.* 4 B4 51 30N 0 8W
Buckow, *Berl.* 7 B3 52 25N 13 26 E
Buda, *Bud.* 10 J13 47 30N 19 2 E
Budafok, *Bud.* 10 K13 47 25N 19 2 E
Budakeszi, *Bud.* 10 J12 47 30N 18 56 E
Budaörs, *Bud.* 10 K12 47 27N 18 57 E
Budapest, *Bud.* 10 K13 47 29N 19 3 E
Budatétény, *Bud.* 10 K13 47 25N 19 1 E
Budberg, *Ruhr* 6 A1 51 32N 6 38 E
Buddinge, *Købn.* 2 D10 55 44N 12 30 E
Büderich, *Ruhr* 6 C2 51 15N 6 41 E
Buena Park, *L.A.* 28 C4 33 51N 118 1W
Buena Vista, *S.F.* 27 B2 37 45N 122 26W
Buenavista, *Mdrd.* 8 B2 40 25N 3 40W
Buenos Aires, *B.A.* 32 B4 34 36 S 58 22W
Buenos Aires, Aeroparque de la Ciudad de, *B.A.* 32 B4 34 34 S 58 25W
Buer, *Ruhr* 6 A4 51 34N 7 2 E
Bufalotta, *Rome* 9 F10 41 59N 12 33 E
Buggajha, *Sŏul* 12 G7 37 34N 126 55 E
Bughan San, *Sŏul* 12 G7 37 38N 126 58 E
Bugio, *Lisb.* 8 G7 38 39N 9 18W
Bukit Panjang, *Sing.* 15 F7 1 22N 103 45 E
Bukit Timah, *Sing.* 15 F7 1 20N 103 47 E
Bulam San, *Sŏul* 12 G8 37 38N 127 4 E
Bûlâq, *El Qâ.* 18 C5 30 3N 31 14 E
Bule, *Manila* 15 E4 14 26N 121 2 E
Bulim, *Sing.* 15 F7 1 22N 103 43 E
Bull Brook →, *Bost.* 21 A4 42 41N 70 52W
Bulleen, *Melb.* 19 E7 37 46 S 145 4 E
Bullen Park, *Melb.* 19 E7 37 46 S 145 4 E
Bullion, *Paris* 5 D1 48 37N 1 59 E
Bulmke-Hüllen, *Ruhr* 6 A4 51 31N 7 7 E
Bulphan, *Lon.* 4 B7 51 32N 0 21 E
Bundoora, *Melb.* 19 E7 37 41 S 145 3 E
Bundoora Park, *Melb.* 19 E7 37 42 S 145 2 E
Bunker I., *Kar.* 17 H10 24 48N 66 57 E
Bunkyo, *Tōkyō* 13 B3 35 42N 139 45 E
Bunnefjorden, *Oslo* 2 B4 59 50N 10 44 E
Buona Vista, *Sing.* 15 G7 1 16N 103 47 E
Buquirivú-Guaçu →, *S. Pau.* 31 D7 23 28 S 46 28W
Burbank, *Chic.* 26 C2 41 44N 87 46W
Burbank, *L.A.* 28 A3 34 12N 118 18W
Bures, *Paris* 5 B1 48 56N 1 57 E
Bures-sur-Yvette, *Paris* 5 C2 48 41N 2 9 E
Burggrafenberg, *Ruhr* 6 C4 51 13N 7 7 E
Burgh Heath, *Lon.* 4 D3 51 18N 0 13W
Burlingame, *S.F.* 27 C2 37 34N 122 20W
Burlington, *Bost.* 21 B2 42 30N 71 13W
Burlington, *Phil.* 24 A5 40 4N 74 50W
Burnham, *Chic.* 26 D3 41 38N 87 33W
Burnham Park Harbor, *Chic.* 26 B3 41 51N 87 36W
Burnhamthorpe, *Trto.* 20 E7 43 37N 79 35W
Burnt Oak, *Lon.* 4 B3 51 36N 0 15W
Burr Ridge, *Chic.* 26 C1 41 46N 87 54W
Burtus, *El Qâ.* 18 C4 30 8N 31 8 E
Burudvatn, *Oslo* 2 B3 59 58N 10 35 E
Burwood, *Melb.* 19 F7 37 50 S 145 6 E
Burwood, *Syd.* 19 B3 33 52 S 151 6 E
Burwood East, *Melb.* 19 F7 37 51 S 145 8 E
Burzaco, *B.A.* 32 C4 34 49 S 58 23W
Buschhausen, *Ruhr* 6 A3 51 30N 6 50 E
Bush Hill Park, *Lon.* 4 B4 51 38N 0 4W
Bushey, *Lon.* 4 B2 51 38N 0 22W
Bushwick, *N.Y.* 23 C5 40 41N 73 54W
Bushy Cr. →, *Melb.* 19 E8 37 42 S 145 17 E
Bushy Park, *Lon.* 4 C2 51 24N 0 20W
Bussocaba, *S. Pau.* 31 E5 23 34 S 46 47W
Bussy-St.-Georges, *Paris* 5 B6 48 50N 2 41 E
Bussy-St.-Martin, *Paris* 5 B6 48 50N 2 41 E
Bustleton, *Phil.* 24 A4 40 4N 75 2W
Butantã, *S. Pau.* 31 E5 23 34 S 46 42W
Butcher I., *Bomb.* 16 H8 18 57N 72 53 E
Butendorf, *Ruhr* 6 A5 51 33N 6 59 E
Butler, *N.Y.* 22 B2 40 59N 74 20W
Buttonville, *Trto.* 20 C8 43 51N 79 20W
Butts Corner, *Wash.* 25 E6 38 46N 77 19W
Byailla, *Bomb.* 16 H8 18 58N 72 50 E
Byberry, *Phil.* 24 A4 40 6N 74 59W
Byfang, *Ruhr* 6 B4 51 24N 7 5 E
Byfleet, *Lon.* 4 D2 51 19N 0 28W
Bygdøy, *Oslo* 2 B3 59 54N 10 40 E

C

C.N. Tower, *Trto.* 20 E8 43 38N 79 23W
Caballito, *B.A.* 32 B4 34 37 S 58 25W
Cabin John, *Wash.* 25 D6 38 58N 77 10W
Cabin John Cr. →, *Wash.* 25 C7 39 2N 77 8W
Cabin John Regional Park, *Wash.* 25 C6 39 0N 77 10W
Cabramatta, *Syd.* 19 B2 33 53 S 150 56 E
Cabuçú de Baixo →, *S. Pau.* 31 D5 23 30 S 46 40W
Cachan, *Paris* 5 C3 48 47N 2 19 E
Cachenka →, *Mos.* 11 E7 55 46N 37 17 E
Cachoeira →, *S. Pau.* 31 E5 23 38 S 46 43W
Cacilhas, *Lisb.* 8 F8 38 41N 9 8W
Cadieux, Î., *Mtrl.* 20 B1 43 25N 74 1W
Cagarras, Is., *Rio J.* 31 C2 23 1 S 43 12W
Cahuenga Pk., *L.A.* 28 B3 34 8N 118 19 E
Cainta, *Manila* 15 D4 14 34N 121 6 E
Cairo = El Qâhira, *El Qâ.* 18 C5 30 2N 31 13 E
Cairo Int. Airport, *El Qâ.* 18 C6 30 7N 31 23 E
Caivano, *Nápl.* 9 H12 40 57N 14 18 E
Caju, *Rio J.* 31 B2 22 52 S 43 12W
Čakovice, *Pra.* 10 B3 50 9N 14 31 E
Calabazar, *La Hab.* 30 B2 23 1N 82 20W
Calcutta, *Calc.* 16 E6 22 34N 88 21 E
Caldwell, *N.Y.* 22 B3 40 50N 74 19W
Calf Harbour, *N.Y.* 23 B7 40 59N 73 37W
Calf I., *Bost.* 21 C4 42 20N 70 53W
Calhua, *Lisb.* 8 F8 38 44N 9 9W
California, Univ. of, *S.F.* 27 A3 37 52N 122 16W
California Inst. of Tech., *L.A.* 28 B4 34 8N 118 8W
California State Univ., *L.A.* 28 B3 34 4N 118 10W
California State Univ., *S.F.* 27 C4 37 39N 122 6W
Callao, *Lima* 30 G8 12 3 S 77 8W
Caloocan, *Manila* 15 D3 14 39N 120 58 E
Calumet →, *Chic.* 26 C3 41 43N 87 31W
Calumet, L., *Chic.* 26 C3 41 40N 87 35W
Calumet City, *Chic.* 26 D3 41 36N 87 32W
Calumet Harbor, *Chic.* 26 C3 41 43N 87 30W
Calumet Park, *Chic.* 26 C3 41 40N 87 39W
Calumet Sag Channel →, *Chic.* 26 C2 41 40N 87 47W
Calumpang, *Manila* 15 D4 14 37N 121 5 E
Calvairate, *Mil.* 9 E6 45 27N 9 13 E
Calverton, *Wash.* 25 C8 39 3N 76 56W
Calvizzano, *Nápl.* 9 H12 40 54N 14 11 E
Calzada, *Manila* 15 D4 14 32N 121 4 E
Camarate, *Lisb.* 8 F8 38 48N 9 7W
Camaroes, *Lisb.* 8 F7 38 49N 9 14W
Camberwell, *Lon.* 4 C4 51 28N 0 5W
Camberwell, *Melb.* 19 F7 37 50 S 145 5 E
Cambria Heights, *N.Y.* 23 C6 40 41N 73 44W
Cambridge, *Bost.* 21 C3 42 23N 71 7W
Cambridge Res., *Bost.* 21 C2 42 24N 71 16W
Cambuci, *S. Pau.* 31 E6 23 33 S 46 47W
Cambute, *La Hab.* 30 B3 23 5N 82 16W
Camden, *Lon.* 4 B4 51 32N 0 8W
Camden, *Phil.* 24 B4 39 56N 75 7W
Camp Springs, *Wash.* 25 E8 38 48N 76 55W
Campamento, *Mdrd.* 8 B2 40 23N 3 46W
Campanilla, Pta., *La Hab.* 30 A3 23 10N 82 18W
Campbellfield, *Melb.* 19 E6 37 40 S 144 57 E
Camperdown, *Syd.* 19 B4 33 53 S 151 11 E
Campi Flegrei, *Nápl.* 9 H11 40 50N 14 9 E
Campo, Casa de, *Mdrd.* 8 B2 40 25N 3 45W
Campo Belo, *S. Pau.* 31 E5 23 36 S 46 44W
Campo de Mayo, *B.A.* 32 B2 34 32 S 58 40W
Campo Grande, *Lisb.* 8 F8 38 45N 9 9W
Campo Limpo, *S. Pau.* 31 E5 23 38 S 46 46W
Campo Pequeño, *Lisb.* 8 F8 38 44N 9 8W
Campolide, *Lisb.* 8 F8 38 43N 9 9W
Campsie, *Syd.* 19 B3 33 54 S 151 6 E
C'an San Joan, *Barc.* 8 D6 41 28N 2 11 E
Canacao, *Manila* 15 E3 14 29N 120 54 E
Canacao B., *Manila* 15 E3 14 29N 120 54 E
Cañada de los Helechos →, *Méx.* 29 B2 19 21N 99 15W
Canarsie, *N.Y.* 23 D5 40 38N 73 53W
Candiac, *Mtrl.* 20 B5 43 23N 73 29W
Caneças, *Lisb.* 8 F7 38 48N 9 13W
Cangaiba, *S. Pau.* 31 E6 23 30 S 46 31W
Cangrejeras, *La Hab.* 30 B1 23 3N 82 30W
Canguera, *S. Pau.* 31 E7 23 34 S 46 26W
Canillas, *Mdrd.* 8 B3 40 27N 3 38W
Canillejas, *Mdrd.* 8 B3 40 26N 3 36W
Cann Hall, *Lon.* 4 B5 51 33N 0 0 E
Canning Town, *Lon.* 4 B5 51 30N 0 1 E
Canoe Grove Res., *N.J.* 22 C2 40 45N 74 21W
Cantalupo, *Mil.* 9 D4 45 34N 8 58 E
Cantareira, *S. Pau.* 31 D6 23 26 S 46 36W
Cantarranas, *La Hab.* 30 B2 23 2N 82 28W
Canteras de Vallecas, *Mdrd.* 8 B3 40 20N 3 37W
Canterbury, *Melb.* 19 E7 37 49 S 145 4 E
Canterbury, *Syd.* 19 B3 33 55 S 151 7 E
Canto do Rio, *Rio J.* 31 B3 22 54 S 43 7W
Canton, *Bost.* 21 D3 42 10N 71 8W
Caohe, *Shang.* 14 J11 31 10N 121 24 E
Caonao, *La Hab.* 30 B2 23 5N 82 24W
Capão Redondo, *S. Pau.* 31 E5 23 39 S 46 45W
Caparica, *Lisb.* 8 F8 38 40N 9 9W
Caparica, Costa da, *Lisb.* 8 G7 38 38N 9 15W
Capelinha, *S. Pau.* 31 E5 23 39 S 46 44W
Capitol Heights, *Wash.* 25 D8 38 52N 76 55W
Capodichino, Aeroporto di, *Nápl.* 9 H12 40 52N 14 17 E
Capodimonte, *Nápl.* 9 H12 40 52N 14 14 E
Capodimonte, Bosco di, *Nápl.* 9 H12 40 52N 14 15 E
Captain Cook Bridge, *Syd.* 19 C3 34 0 S 151 7 E
Captain Cook Landing Place Park, *Syd.* 19 C4 34 1 S 151 14 E
Captain Harbour, *N.Y.* 23 B7 40 59N 73 37W
Capuava, *S. Pau.* 31 E7 23 38 S 46 28W
Capuchos, *Lisb.* 8 G7 38 38N 9 13W
Caraballeda, *Car.* 30 D5 10 36N 66 50W
Carabanchel Alto, *Mdrd.* 8 B2 40 22N 3 44W
Carabanchel Bajo, *Mdrd.* 8 B2 40 23N 3 44W
Carabatteda →, *Car.* 30 D5 10 37N 66 51W
Caracas, *Car.* 30 E5 10 30N 66 54W
Carapachay, *B.A.* 32 B3 34 31 S 58 32W
Carapicuiba, *S. Pau.* 31 E5 23 31 S 46 49W
Carapicuiba →, *S. Pau.* 31 E5 23 31 S 46 49W
Caravita, *Nápl.* 9 H13 40 52N 14 21 E
Caraza, *B.A.* 32 C4 34 41 S 58 25W
Cardito, *Nápl.* 9 H12 40 56N 14 17 E
Cardoso, *Lagos* 18 A1 6 34N 7 16 E
Caribbean Gardens, *Melb.* 19 F8 37 54 S 145 12 E
Caricuao, *Car.* 30 E5 10 25N 66 58W
Caridad, *Manila* 15 E3 14 28N 120 53 E
Carioca, Sa. da, *Rio J.* 31 B2 22 57 S 43 13W
Carle Place, *N.Y.* 23 C7 40 44N 73 36W
Carlingford, *Syd.* 19 A3 33 46 S 151 3 E
Carlisle, *Bost.* 21 B1 42 31N 71 20W
Carlshof, *Mün.* 7 F11 48 15N 11 41 E
Carlstadt, *N.Y.* 22 B4 40 50N 74 6W
Carlton, *Melb.* 19 E6 37 47 S 144 57 E
Carnaxide, *Lisb.* 8 F7 38 43N 9 14W
Carnegie, *Melb.* 19 F7 37 53 S 145 3 E
Carnegie Hall, *N.Y.* 22 C5 40 45N 73 59W
Carnetin, *Paris* 5 B6 48 54N 2 42 E
Carney, *Balt.* 25 A3 39 23N 76 31W
Carnide, *Lisb.* 8 F8 38 45N 9 10W
Caronno Pert, *Mil.* 9 D5 45 35N 9 2 E
Carramar, *Syd.* 19 B2 33 51 S 150 58 E
Carrascal, *Stgo* 30 J10 33 25 S 70 42W
Carrières-sous-Bois, *Paris* 5 B2 48 55N 2 6 E
Carrières-sous-Poissy, *Paris* 5 B2 48 56N 2 2 E
Carrières-sur-Seine, *Paris* 5 B3 48 55N 2 11 E
Carroll I., *Balt.* 25 B4 39 19N 76 20W
Carroll Park, *Balt.* 25 B3 39 16N 76 38W
Carshalton, *Lon.* 4 C3 51 22N 0 10W
Carshalton on the Hill, *Lon.* 4 C4 51 20N 0 9W
Carteret, *N.Y.* 22 D3 40 34N 74 13W
Cartierville, Aéroport de, *Mtrl.* 20 A3 43 31N 73 42 E
Carugate, *Mil.* 9 D6 45 32N 9 20 E
Carupa, *B.A.* 32 A3 34 25 S 58 33W
Casa Blanca, *La Hab.* 30 B3 23 8N 82 19W
Casa Verde, *S. Pau.* 31 D5 23 29 S 46 40W
Casalnuovo di Nápoli, *Nápl.* 9 H12 40 54N 14 20 E
Casalotti, *Rome* 9 F9 41 54N 12 22 E
Casandrino, *Nápl.* 9 H12 40 56N 14 15 E
Casavatore, *Nápl.* 9 H12 40 53N 14 15 E
Cascadura, *Rio J.* 31 B2 22 52 S 43 19W
Caselette, *Tori.* 9 B1 45 6N 7 28 E
Caselette, Laghi di, *Tori.* 9 B1 45 7N 7 29 E
Caselle Torinese, *Tori.* 9 A3 45 10N 7 38 E
Caseros, *B.A.* 32 B3 34 36 S 58 34W
Casória, *Nápl.* 9 H12 40 54N 14 17 E
Cassignanica, *Mil.* 9 E7 45 27N 9 20 E
Cassiobury Park, *Lon.* 4 B2 51 39N 0 25W
Castel di Camerletto, *Tori.* 9 B1 45 6N 7 27 E
Castel di Guido, *Rome* 9 F8 41 53N 12 17 E
Castel Malnome, *Rome* 9 F8 41 50N 12 19 E
Castel San Cristina, *Tori.* 9 B3 45 8N 7 40 E
Castel Sant'Angelo, *Rome* 9 F9 41 54N 12 27 E
Castelar, *B.A.* 32 B3 34 39 S 58 39W
Castellbisbal, *Barc.* 8 D4 41 28N 1 58 E
Castello di Cisterna, *Nápl.* 9 H13 40 54N 14 24 E
Castelvécchio, *Tori.* 9 B3 45 1N 7 46 E
Castiglione Torinese, *Tori.* 9 B3 45 6N 7 48 E
Castleton Corners, *N.Y.* 22 D4 40 36N 74 8W
Castro Valley, *S.F.* 27 B4 37 41N 122 5W
Castrop, *Ruhr* 6 A5 51 32N 7 18 E
Castrop-Rauxel, *Ruhr* 6 A5 51 33N 7 18 E
Cat Rock Hill, *Bost.* 21 C2 42 23N 71 18W
Caterham, *Lon.* 4 D4 51 16N 0 5W
Catete, *Rio J.* 31 B2 22 54 S 43 10W
Catford, *Lon.* 4 C4 51 26N 0 1W
Catia, *Car.* 30 D5 10 31N 66 56W
Catia La Mer, *Car.* 30 D4 10 36N 67 0W
Catonsville, *Balt.* 25 B2 39 16N 76 43W
Catonsville Manor, *Balt.* 25 B2 39 17N 76 44W
Cattle Hill, *S.F.* 27 C2 37 36N 122 27W
Catumbi, *Rio J.* 31 B2 22 54 S 43 12W
Caughnawaga, *Mtrl.* 20 B3 43 24N 73 40W
Caulfield, *Melb.* 19 F7 37 52 S 145 1 E
Caulfield Racecourse, *Melb.* 19 F7 37 53 S 145 4 E
Caumsett State Park, *N.Y.* 23 B8 40 55N 73 27W
Cavite, *Manila* 15 E3 14 29N 120 54 E
Cavoretto, *Tori.* 9 B3 45 1N 7 41 E
Caxias, *Lisb.* 8 F7 38 42N 9 16W
Caxingui, *S. Pau.* 31 E5 23 35 S 46 43W
Cebeciköy, *Ist.* 17 A2 41 7N 28 53 E
Cecchignola, *Rome* 9 G10 41 48N 12 29 E
Cecil Park, *Syd.* 19 B2 33 52 S 150 51 E
Cecilienhof, *Berl.* 7 B1 52 25N 13 5 E
Cedar Grove, *N.Y.* 22 B3 40 50N 74 13W
Cedar Grove Res., *N.Y.* 22 B3 40 51N 74 12W
Cedar I., *N.Y.* 23 D8 40 38N 73 22W
Cedar Knolls, *N.Y.* 22 C2 40 49N 74 27W
Cedarhurst, *N.Y.* 23 D6 40 37N 73 43W
Cedarvale, *Trto.* 20 D8 43 41N 79 26W
Celle →, *Paris* 5 B1 48 36N 1 59 E
Cempaka Putih, *Jak.* 15 J10 6 10 S 106 51 E
Çengelköy, *Ist.* 17 A3 41 2N 29 3 E
Centennial Park, *Syd.* 19 B4 33 53 S 151 14 E
Center Square, *Phil.* 24 C2 39 46N 75 22W
Centerport, *N.Y.* 23 B8 40 53N 73 22W
Centerton, *Phil.* 24 B5 39 59N 74 53W
Centocelle, *Rome* 9 F10 41 52N 12 34 E
Central Park, *N.Y.* 22 C5 40 47N 73 58W
Central Park, *Sing.* 15 G8 1 17N 103 50 E
Centre City, *Phil.* 24 B4 39 46N 75 11W
Centre I., *N.Y.* 23 B7 40 54N 73 31W
Cércola, *Nápl.* 9 H13 40 51N 14 21 E
Cergy-Pontoise, *Paris* 5 A2 49 1N 2 4 E
Cernay-la-Ville, *Paris* 5 C1 48 40N 1 58 E
Cernusco sul Navíglio, *Mil.* 9 D6 45 31N 9 19 E
Cerqueira Cesar, *S. Pau.* 31 E5 23 33 S 46 40W
Cerro Ajusco, *Méx.* 29 C2 19 12N 99 15W
Cerro de la Estrella, *Méx.* 29 B3 19 20N 99 5W
Cerro de los Angeles, *Mdrd.* 8 C2 40 18N 3 41W
Cerro el Picacho, *Méx.* 29 A3 19 35N 99 6W
Cerro Maggiore, *Mil.* 9 D4 45 35N 8 57 E
Certanovka →, *Mos.* 11 F9 55 38N 37 48 E
Certanovo, *Mos.* 11 F9 55 38N 37 36 E
Cesano Boscone, *Mil.* 9 E5 45 26N 9 5 E
Cesate, *Mil.* 9 D5 45 35N 9 4 E
Cha Kwo Ling, *H.K.* 12 E6 22 18N 114 13 E
Chabot, L., *S.F.* 27 B4 37 43N 122 6W
Chacao, *Car.* 30 D5 10 30N 66 50W
Chacarilla, *Lima* 30 G9 12 6 S 76 59W
Chadds Ford, *Phil.* 24 B1 39 52N 75 35W
Chadstone, *Melb.* 19 F7 37 52 S 145 6 E
Chadwell Heath, *Lon.* 4 B5 51 34N 0 8 E
Chadwell St. Mary, *Lon.* 4 C7 51 29N 0 20 E
Chai Wan, *H.K.* 12 E6 22 16N 114 14 E
Chai Wan Kok, *H.K.* 12 D5 22 22N 114 6 E
Chakdaha, *Calc.* 16 F5 22 28N 88 19 E
Chama, *Lima* 30 G8 12 7 S 77 0W
Chamartín, *Mdrd.* 8 B2 40 27N 3 40W
Chamberí, *Mdrd.* 8 B2 40 26N 3 42W
Chambourcy, *Paris* 5 B2 48 54N 2 2 E
Champdani, *Calc.* 16 D5 22 48N 88 19 E
Champigny-sur-Marne, *Paris* 5 C5 48 49N 2 30 E
Champlain, Pont, *Mtrl.* 20 B4 43 28N 73 31W
Champlan, *Paris* 5 C3 48 42N 2 16 E
Champrosay, *Paris* 5 D4 48 39N 2 28 E
Champs-sur-Marne, *Paris* 5 B5 48 50N 2 34 E
Chamrail, *Calc.* 16 E5 22 38N 88 17 E
Chancheon, *Sŏul* 12 G7 37 33N 126 56 E
Chandernagore, *Calc.* 16 C6 22 51N 88 21 E
Chanditala, *Calc.* 16 D5 22 43N 88 17 E
Changi, *Sing.* 15 F8 1 23N 103 59 E
Changi Airport, *Sing.* 15 F8 1 21N 103 59 E
Changning, *Shang.* 14 J11 31 13N 121 24 E
Changpu Gongyuan, *Shang.* 14 J12 31 17N 121 31 E
Chanteloup-les-Vignes, *Paris* 5 B2 48 58N 2 1 E
Chantereine, *Paris* 5 B5 48 53N 2 37 E
Chantian, *Gzh.* 14 F8 23 12N 113 16 E
Chao Phraya →, *Bangk.* 15 B2 13 40N 100 31 E
Chaoyang, *Beij.* 14 B3 39 53N 116 26 E
Chaoyang Gongyuan, *Beij.* 14 B3 39 54N 116 28 E
Chaoyangmen, *Beij.* 14 B3 39 54N 116 23 E
Chapel End, *Lon.* 4 B4 51 35N 0 1W
Chapet, *Paris* 5 B1 48 58N 1 55 E
Chaplinville, *Bost.* 21 A4 42 42N 70 54W
Chapultepec, Bosque de, *Méx.* 29 B2 19 25N 99 11W
Chapultepec, Castillo de, *Méx.* 29 B2 19 25N 99 10W
Charenton-le-Pont, *Paris* 5 C4 48 49N 2 25 E
Charles-de-Gaulle, Aéroport, *Paris* 5 A5 49 0N 2 33 E
Charles Lee Tinden Regional Park, *S.F.* 27 A3 37 53N 122 14W
Charleston, *N.Y.* 22 D3 40 32N 74 14W
Charlestown, *Bost.* 21 C3 42 22N 71 4W
Charlottenburg, *Berl.* 7 A2 52 31N 13 14 E
Charlottenburg, Schloss, *Berl.* 7 A2 52 31N 13 18 E
Charlottenlund, *Købn.* 2 D10 55 44N 12 35 E
Charlton, *Lon.* 4 C5 51 29N 0 1 E
Charneca, *Lisb.* 8 F8 38 47N 9 8W
Charneca, *Lisb.* 8 G7 38 37N 9 12W
Chase Side, *Lon.* 4 B4 51 39N 0 4W
Châteaufort, *Paris* 5 C2 48 44N 2 5 E
Châtenay-Malabry, *Paris* 5 C3 48 46N 2 16 E
Chatham, *Chic.* 26 C3 41 45N 87 36W
Chatham, *N.Y.* 22 C2 40 44N 74 23W
Châtillon, *Paris* 5 C3 48 48N 2 17 E
Chatou, *Paris* 5 B3 48 53N 2 9 E
Chatpur, *Calc.* 16 E6 22 36N 88 22 E
Chatra, *Calc.* 16 D6 22 45N 88 19 E
Chatswood, *Syd.* 19 A4 33 47 S 151 11 E
Chauki, *Kar.* 17 G10 24 55N 66 56 E
Chavarria, *Lima* 30 G8 12 0 S 77 7W
Chavenay, *Paris* 5 B1 48 51N 1 59 E
Chavenay-Villepreux, Aérodrôme de, *Paris* 5 B1 48 50N 1 58 E
Chaville, *Paris* 5 C3 48 48N 2 11 E
Che Kung Miu, *H.K.* 12 D6 22 22N 114 10 E
Cheam, *Lon.* 4 C3 51 21N 0 12W
Chelles, *Paris* 5 B5 48 53N 2 35 E
Chelles, Canal de, *Paris* 5 B5 48 51N 2 35 E
Chells-le-Pin, Aérodrome, *Paris* 5 B5 48 53N 2 36 E
Chelmsford, *Bost.* 21 B1 42 35N 71 20W
Chelobityevo, *Mos.* 11 D10 55 54N 37 40 E
Chelsea, *Bost.* 21 C3 42 23N 71 1W
Chelsea, *Lon.* 4 C3 51 29N 0 10W
Chelsea, *Phil.* 24 B2 39 51N 75 27W
Chelsfield Village, *Lon.* 4 C6 51 21N 0 8 E
Cheltenham, *Phil.* 24 A4 40 3N 75 6W
Chembur, *Bomb.* 16 G8 19 3N 72 53 E
Chennevières, *Paris* 5 A2 49 0N 2 6 E
Chennevières-sur-Marne, *Paris* 5 C5 48 47N 2 31 E
Cheongdam, *Sŏul* 12 G8 37 31N 127 2 E
Cheonho, *Sŏul* 12 G8 37 32N 127 6 E
Cheops, *El Qâ.* 18 D4 29 58N 31 8 E
Chepo, *Gzh.* 14 G9 23 7N 113 23 E
Cherepkovo, *Mos.* 11 E8 55 45N 37 21 E
Chernyovo, *Mos.* 11 D7 55 50N 37 17 E
Cherry Hill, *Phil.* 24 B4 39 54N 75 1W
Cherry L., *Melb.* 19 F5 37 51 S 144 49 E
Cherryland, *S.F.* 27 B4 37 40N 122 7W
Cherrywood, *Trto.* 20 C10 43 51N 79 8W
Chertsey, *Lon.* 4 C2 51 23N 0 29W
Cheryomushki, *Mos.* 11 E9 55 40N 37 35 E
Chesaco Park, *Balt.* 25 B3 39 18N 76 30W
Chesapeake B., *Balt.* 25 B4 39 12N 76 22W
Cheshunt, *Lon.* 4 A4 51 42N 0 0 E
Chess →, *Lon.* 4 B2 51 38N 0 27W
Chessington, *Lon.* 4 C3 51 21N 0 18W
Chessington Zoo, *Lon.* 4 C3 51 20N 0 19W
Chester, *Phil.* 24 B2 39 50N 75 23W
Chester Cr. →, *Phil.* 24 B2 39 50N 75 21W
Chester Heights, *Phil.* 24 B2 39 53N 75 27W
Chestnut, *Phil.* 24 A3 40 4N 75 13W
Chestnut Hill, *Bost.* 21 D2 42 19N 71 10W
Cheung Sha Wan, *H.K.* 12 D5 22 20N 114 8 E
Cheverly, *Wash.* 25 D8 38 55N 76 54W
Chevilly-Larue, *Paris* 5 C4 48 46N 2 21 E
Chevreuse, *Paris* 5 C1 48 42N 2 2 E
Chevry-Cossigny, *Paris* 5 C5 48 43N 2 39 E
Chevy Chase, *Wash.* 25 D7 38 59N 77 4W
Chevy Chase View, *Wash.* 25 C7 39 0N 77 4W
Cheyney, *Phil.* 24 B1 39 55N 75 31W
Chhalera Bangar, *Delhi* 16 B2 28 33N 77 17 E
Chhinamor, *Calc.* 16 D5 22 48N 88 17 E
Chhota Andai, *Kar.* 17 H11 24 48N 66 59 E
Chia Keng, *Sing.* 15 F8 1 21N 103 52 E
Chiaiano, *Nápl.* 9 H12 40 53N 14 13 E
Chiaravalle Milanese, *Mil.* 9 E6 45 24N 9 16 E
Chiawelo, *Jobg.* 18 F8 26 17 S 27 51 E
Chicago, *Chic.* 26 B3 41 52N 87 38W
Chicago, Univ. of, *Chic.* 26 C3 41 47N 87 35W
Chicago Harbor, *Chic.* 26 B3 41 52N 87 36W
Chicago Lawn, *Chic.* 26 C2 41 47N 87 40W
Chicago-Midway Airport, *Chic.* 26 C2 41 47N 87 45W
Chicago-O'Hare Int. Airport, *Chic.* 26 B1 41 58N 87 53W
Chicago Ridge, *Chic.* 26 C2 41 41N 87 46W
Chicago Sanitary and Ship Canal, *Chic.* 26 C2 41 49N 87 45W
Chichinautzin, Cerro, *Méx.* 29 D3 19 6N 99 8W
Chicot, *Mtrl.* 20 A2 43 35N 73 56W
Chicot →, *Mtrl.* 20 A2 43 34N 73 51W
Chienzui, *Gzh.* 14 F9 23 12N 113 22 E
Chieri, *Tori.* 9 B3 45 0N 7 49 E
Chigwell, *Lon.* 4 B5 51 36N 0 6 E
Chigwell Row, *Lon.* 4 B5 51 37N 0 7 E
Chik Sha, *H.K.* 12 E6 22 17N 114 16 E
Chikumazawa, *Tōkyō* 13 B2 35 49N 139 32 E
Childs Hill, *Lon.* 4 B3 51 33N 0 12W
Chilla Saroda, *Delhi* 16 B2 28 35N 77 18 E
Chillum, *Wash.* 25 D8 38 57N 76 58W
Chilly-Mazarin, *Paris* 5 C3 48 42N 2 17 E
Chimalhuacán, *Méx.* 29 B4 19 25N 89 57 E
Chimalpa, *Méx.* 29 B2 19 21N 99 19W
China, Tg., *Sing.* 15 G8 1 14N 103 50 E
China Basin, *S.F.* 27 B2 37 46N 122 22W
Chingford, *Lon.* 4 B5 51 37N 0 0 E
Chingupota, *Calc.* 16 F5 22 29N 88 14 E
Chipilly Woods, *Chic.* 26 A2 42 8N 87 48W
Chipperfield, *Lon.* 4 A2 51 42N 0 29W
Chipping Ongar, *Lon.* 4 A6 51 41N 0 15 E
Chipstead, *Lon.* 4 D4 51 17N 0 8W
Chirle, *Bomb.* 16 H9 18 55N 73 2 E
Chirnside Park, *Melb.* 19 E8 37 45 S 145 18 E
Chislehurst, *Lon.* 4 C5 51 24N 0 4 E
Chislehurst West, *Lon.* 4 C5 51 25N 0 3 E
Chiswick, *Lon.* 4 C3 51 29N 0 16W
Chiswick House, *Lon.* 4 C3 51 28N 0 15W
Chitlade Palace, *Bangk.* 15 B2 13 45N 100 31 E
Chitose, *Tōkyō* 13 C2 35 38N 139 37 E
Chiyoda-Ku, *Tōkyō* 13 B3 35 41N 139 44 E
Chkalova, *Mos.* 11 F11 55 37N 38 0 E
Choa Chu Kang, *Sing.* 15 F7 1 22N 103 40 E
Choboty, *Mos.* 11 F8 55 39N 37 21 E
Chodov u Prahy, *Pra.* 10 B3 50 1N 14 30 E
Chōfu, *Tōkyō* 13 C2 35 38N 139 32 E
Choisel, *Paris* 5 C1 48 41N 2 1 E
Choisy-le-Roi, *Paris* 5 C4 48 46N 2 24 E

36 Chomedey

Chomedey, *Mtrl.* 20 A3 43 32N 73 45W
Chong Nonsi, Khlong →, *Bangk.* 15 B2 13 42N 100 32 E
Chong Pang, *Sing.* 15 F7 1 26N 103 49 E
Chongwen, *Beij.* 14 B3 39 52N 116 23 E
Chongwenmen, *Beij.* 14 B3 39 52N 116 22 E
Chorleywood, *Lon.* 4 B2 51 39N 0 29W
Chornaya →, *Mos.* 11 E12 55 41N 38 0 E
Chorrillos, *Lima* 30 H8 12 10 S 77 1W
Christianshavn, *Købn.* 2 D10 55 40N 12 35 E
Chrome, *N.Y.* 22 D3 40 34N 74 13W
Chrzanów, *Wsaw.* 10 E6 52 13N 20 53 E
Chuen Lung, *H.K.* 12 D5 22 23N 114 6 E
Chuk Kok, *H.K.* 12 D6 22 20N 114 15 E
Chulalongkon Univ., *Bangk.* 15 B2 13 44N 100 31 E
Chullora, *Syd.* 19 B3 33 54 S 151 5 E
Chunchura, *Calc.* 16 C6 22 53N 88 23 E
Chuō-Ku, *Tōkyō* 13 B3 35 40N 139 46 E
Church End, *Lon.* 4 B3 51 35N 0 11W
Chvaly, *Pra.* 10 B3 50 6N 14 35 E
Chye Kay, *Sing.* 15 F7 1 25N 103 49 E
Ciampino, *Rome* 9 G10 41 47N 12 36 E
Ciampino, Aeroporto di, *Rome* 9 G10 41 47N 12 35 E
Cicero, *Chic.* 26 B2 41 51N 87 44W
Cidade, I. da, *Rio J.* 31 B2 22 51 S 43 13W
Cidade de Deus, *S. Pau.* 31 E5 23 33 S 46 45W
Cidade Ipava, *S. Pau.* 31 F5 23 42 S 46 45W
Cidade Lider, *S. Pau.* 31 E7 23 33 S 46 27W
Cidade São Matheus, *S. Pau.* 31 E7 23 35 S 46 29W
Cidena, Kali →, *Jak.* 15 H9 6 9 S 106 48 E
Cilandak, *Jak.* 15 J9 6 17 S 106 47 E
Cilincing, *Jak.* 15 H10 6 6 S 106 54 E
Ciliwung →, *Jak.* 15 J10 6 6 S 106 47 E
Čimice, *Pra.* 10 B2 50 8N 14 25 E
Cinderella, *Jobg.* 18 F10 26 14 S 28 15 E
Cinderella Dam, *Jobg.* 18 F10 26 14 S 28 14 E
Cinecittà, *Rome* 9 F10 41 51N 12 34 E
Cinisello Bálsamo, *Mil.* 9 D6 45 33N 9 13 E
Cinkota, *Bud.* 10 J14 47 31N 19 14 E
Cinnaminson, *Phil.* 24 B5 39 59N 74 59W
Cipete, *Jak.* 15 J9 6 15 S 106 47 E
Cipresso, *Tori.* 9 B3 45 2N 7 48 E
Cisliano, *Mil.* 9 E4 45 26N 8 59 E
Citta degli Studi, *Mil.* 9 E6 45 28N 9 12 E
Città del Vaticano, *Rome* 9 F9 41 54N 12 26 E
City I., *N.Y.* 23 B6 40 50N 73 47W
Ciudad Azteca, *Méx.* 29 A3 19 32N 99 1W
Ciudad Fin de Semana, *Mdrd.* 8 B3 40 26N 3 34W
Ciudad General Belgrano, *B.A.* 32 C3 34 43 S 58 33W
Ciudad Libertad, *La Hab.* 30 B2 23 5N 82 25W
Ciudad Lineál, *Mdrd.* 8 B3 40 26N 3 38W
Ciudad López Mateos, *Méx.* 29 A2 19 33N 99 16W
Ciudad Satélite, *Méx.* 29 A2 19 30N 99 13W
Ciudad Universitaria, *Méx.* 29 C2 19 9N 99 10W
Ciudadela, *B.A.* 32 B3 34 38 S 58 32W
Ciudadela, Parque de la, *Barc.* 8 D6 41 23N 2 11 E
Clairefontaine, *Paris* 5 D1 48 36N 1 54 E
Clamart, *Paris* 5 C3 48 48N 2 15 E
Clapham, *Lon.* 4 C4 51 27N 0 8W
Clapton, *Lon.* 4 B4 51 33N 0 3W
Clark, *N.Y.* 22 D3 40 38N 74 18W
Clarksboro, *Phil.* 24 C3 39 48N 75 13W
Claye-Souilly, *Paris* 5 B6 48 56N 2 41 E
Claygate, *Lon.* 4 C3 51 21N 0 19W
Clayhall, *Lon.* 4 B5 51 35N 0 3 E
Clayhill, *Lon.* 4 A4 51 40N 0 5W
Claymont, *Phil.* 24 C2 39 48N 75 27W
Claypole, *B.A.* 32 C4 34 48 S 58 20W
Clayton, *Melb.* 19 F7 37 55 S 145 7 E
Clearing, *Chic.* 26 C2 41 47N 87 45W
Clearwater, *L.A.* 28 C3 33 52N 118 10W
Clement, *Sing.* 15 G7 1 18N 103 46 E
Clementon, *Phil.* 24 C5 39 48N 74 59W
Clichy, *Paris* 5 B3 48 54N 2 18 E
Clichy-sous-Bois, *Paris* 5 B5 48 54N 2 32 E
Cliffside, *Trto.* 20 D9 43 44N 79 14W
Cliffside Park, *N.Y.* 22 C5 40 49N 73 59W
Clifton, *Bost.* 21 C4 42 29N 70 52W
Clifton, *Kar.* 17 H11 24 48N 67 1 E
Clifton, *N.Y.* 22 D4 40 37N 74 4W
Clifton, *N.Y.* 22 B4 40 51N 74 7W
Clifton, L., *Balt.* 25 B3 39 19N 76 35W
Clifton Heights, *Phil.* 24 B3 39 55N 75 17W
Clifton Park, *Balt.* 25 A3 39 20N 76 35W
Clontarf, *Syd.* 19 A4 33 48 S 151 16 E
Closter, *N.Y.* 22 B5 40 58N 73 57W
Clovelly, *Syd.* 19 B4 33 54 S 151 15 E
Cobbin's Brook →, *Lon.* 4 A5 51 40N 0 0 E
Cobbs Cr. →, *Phil.* 24 B3 39 58N 75 18W
Cobham, *Lon.* 4 D2 51 19N 0 23W
Cobras, I. das, *Rio J.* 31 B3 22 53 S 43 9W
Coburg, *Melb.* 19 E6 37 44 S 144 56 E
Cochecito, *Car.* 30 E5 10 26N 66 55W
Cochichewick, L., *Bost.* 21 A3 42 42N 71 5W
Cochituate, *Bost.* 21 C1 42 20N 71 21W
Cochituate, L., *Bost.* 21 D1 42 16N 71 21W
Cockfosters, *Lon.* 4 B4 51 39N 0 8W
Cocota, *Rio J.* 31 A2 22 48 S 43 11W
Coelho da Rocha, *Rio J.* 31 A1 22 46 S 43 21W
Cœuilly, *Paris* 5 C5 48 48N 2 32 E
Coignières, *Paris* 5 C1 48 44N 1 55 E
Coina, *Lisb.* 8 G8 38 39N 9 5W
Cojimar, *La Hab.* 30 B3 23 9N 82 17W
Cojimar →, *La Hab.* 30 B3 23 9N 82 17W
Cojimar, Boca de, *La Hab.* 30 A3 23 10N 82 17W
Coker, *Lagos* 18 B2 6 28N 7 20 E
Colaba, *Bomb.* 16 H7 18 53N 72 48 E
Colaba Pt., *Bomb.* 16 H7 18 53N 72 48 E
Cold Spring Harbor, *N.Y.* 23 B8 40 52N 73 27W
Cold Spring Terrace, *N.Y.* 23 C8 40 49N 73 25W
Coleraine, *Trto.* 20 D6 43 49N 79 40W
Colindale, *Lon.* 4 B3 51 35N 0 15W
Collazo, *La Hab.* 30 B2 23 2N 82 21W
College Park, *Wash.* 25 D8 38 59N 76 55W
College Point, *N.Y.* 23 C5 40 47N 73 50W
Collégien, *Paris* 5 B6 48 50N 2 41 E
Collegno, *Tori.* 9 B2 45 5N 7 34 E
Collier Row, *Lon.* 4 B5 51 35N 0 9 E
Colliers Wood, *Lon.* 4 C3 51 24N 0 10W
Collingdale, *Phil.* 24 B3 39 54N 75 17W
Collingswood, *Phil.* 24 B4 39 55N 75 5W
Collinsville, *Bost.* 21 A1 42 40N 71 20W
Collinsville, *N.Y.* 22 C2 40 48N 74 26W
Colma, *S.F.* 27 B2 37 40N 122 27W
Colma Cr. →, *S.F.* 27 C2 37 38N 122 23W
Colney Hatch, *Lon.* 4 B4 51 36N 0 9W
Cologno Monzese, *Mil.* 9 D6 45 31N 9 16 E
Colombes, *Paris* 5 B3 48 55N 2 15 E
Colonia, *N.Y.* 22 D3 40 35N 74 18W
Colônia, *S. Pau.* 31 E7 23 33 S 46 27W
Colonia Güell, *Barc.* 8 D5 41 21N 2 2 E
Colonia Puerta de Hierro, *Mdrd.* 8 B2 40 27N 3 43W
Colonial Manor, *Phil.* 24 B4 39 51N 75 9W
Colorado →, *Méx.* 29 B4 19 23N 89 58 E
Colosseo, *Rome* 9 F9 41 53N 12 29 E
Columbia, *Balt.* 25 B1 39 12N 76 50W
Columbia Hills, *Balt.* 25 B1 39 14N 76 51W
Columbia Univ., *N.Y.* 22 C5 40 48N 73 58W
Colwyn, *Phil.* 24 B3 39 54N 75 14W
Combault, *Paris* 5 C5 48 48N 2 37 E
Combs-la-Ville, *Paris* 5 D5 48 39N 2 33 E
Comércio, Praça do, *Lisb.* 8 F8 38 41N 9 9W
Commack, *N.Y.* 23 B9 40 50N 73 19W
Commerce, *L.A.* 28 B4 34 0N 118 9W
Como, *Syd.* 19 C3 34 0 S 151 4 E
Compans, *Paris* 5 B5 48 59N 2 39 E
Compton, *L.A.* 28 C3 33 53N 118 14W
Conceição, I. da, *Rio J.* 31 B3 22 52 S 43 6W
Concepcion, *Manila* 15 D4 14 39N 121 6 E
Conchali, *Stgo* 30 J11 33 22 S 70 39W
Concord, *Bost.* 21 C1 42 27N 71 20W
Concord, *S.F.* 27 A4 37 58N 122 3W
Concord, *Syd.* 19 B3 33 52 S 151 6 E
Concord, *Trto.* 20 D8 43 48N 79 29W
Concordville, *Phil.* 24 B1 39 53N 75 31W
Concorezzo, *Mil.* 9 D6 45 35N 9 19 E
Condécourt, *Paris* 5 A1 49 2N 1 56 E
Coney Island, *N.Y.* 22 D4 40 34N 74 0W
Conflans-Ste.-Honorine, *Paris* 5 B2 48 59N 2 5 E
Congo, *S. Pau.* 31 D5 23 27 S 46 42W
Congonhas, Aéroporto, *S. Pau.* 31 E6 23 38 S 46 39W
Conshohocken, *Phil.* 24 A3 40 4N 75 18W
Contadero, *Méx.* 29 B2 19 20N 99 17W
Convento de Valverde, *Mdrd.* 8 A2 40 30N 3 40W
Coogee, *Syd.* 19 B4 33 55 S 151 16 E
Cooksville, *Trto.* 20 E7 43 35N 79 38W
Cooper →, *Phil.* 24 B4 39 57N 75 6W
Copacabana, *Rio J.* 31 B2 22 58 S 43 11W
Copenhagen = København, *Købn.* 2 D9 55 40N 12 26 E
Copiague, *N.Y.* 23 D8 40 39N 73 23W
Coral Hills, *Wash.* 25 D8 38 51N 76 55W
Corbeil-Essonnes, *Paris* 5 D4 48 36N 2 29 E
Corbets Tey, *Lon.* 4 B6 51 32N 0 15 E
Corbiglia, *Tori.* 9 B1 45 3N 7 29 E
Corcovado, *Rio J.* 31 B2 22 57 S 43 12W
Cordon, *Paris* 5 D6 48 39N 2 41 E
Córdova, *Tori.* 9 B3 45 5N 7 48 E
Cordovil, *Rio J.* 31 A2 22 49 S 43 18W
Cormano, *Mil.* 9 D6 45 32N 9 10 E
Cormeilles-en-Parisis, *Paris* 5 B3 48 58N 2 11 E
Cornaredo, *Mil.* 9 D5 45 30N 9 1 E
Cornaya →, *St-Pet.* 11 B5 59 53N 30 35 E
Cornellá, *Barc.* 8 D5 41 21N 2 4 E
Cornwells Heights, *Phil.* 24 A5 40 4N 74 57W
Coróglio, *Nápl.* 9 J12 40 48N 14 10 E
Coronation Memorial, *Delhi* 16 A2 28 42N 77 12 E
Córsico, *Mil.* 9 E5 45 25N 9 6 E
Corte Madera, *S.F.* 27 A1 37 55N 122 30W
Corte Madera →, *S.F.* 27 A1 37 55N 122 30W
Corviale, *Rome* 9 F9 41 51N 12 25 E
Cos Cob, *N.Y.* 23 A7 41 1N 73 36W
Cossigny, *Paris* 5 C6 48 43N 2 40 E
Cossipure, *Calc.* 16 E6 22 37N 88 22 E
Cotao, *Lisb.* 8 F7 38 45N 9 17W
Côte St.-Luc, *Mtrl.* 20 B4 43 28N 73 39W
Cotorro, *La Hab.* 30 B3 23 2N 82 15W
Cotunduba, I. de, *Rio J.* 31 B3 22 57 S 43 8W
Coubert, *Paris* 5 C6 48 40N 2 41 E
Coubron, *Paris* 5 B5 48 54N 2 34 E
Coulsdon, *Lon.* 4 D4 51 18N 0 7W
Countryside, *Chic.* 26 C1 41 47N 87 52W
Courbevoie, *Paris* 5 B3 48 53N 2 14 E
Courcouronnes, *Paris* 5 D4 48 37N 2 24 E
Courdimanche, *Paris* 5 A1 49 2N 2 0 E
Courellle, *Paris* 5 C2 48 43N 2 7 E
Couros →, *S. Pau.* 31 F6 23 37 S 46 34W
Courtry, *Paris* 5 B5 48 55N 2 35 E
Cousino, Parque, *Stgo* 30 J11 33 27 S 70 40W
Cove Neck, *N.Y.* 23 B8 40 52N 73 29W
Cowley, *Lon.* 4 B2 51 31N 0 28W
Coyoacan, *Méx.* 29 B3 19 21N 99 9W
Coyote Cr. →, *S.F.* 27 D4 37 28N 122 4W
Coyote Hills Regional Park, *S.F.* 27 C4 37 32N 122 7W
Coyote Hills Slough, *S.F.* 27 C4 37 33N 122 7W
Coyote Pt., *S.F.* 27 C3 37 35N 122 18W
Coyote Ridge, *S.F.* 27 A1 37 51N 122 33W
Craighall Park, *Jobg.* 18 E9 26 7 S 28 1 E
Crane →, *Lon.* 4 C2 51 29N 0 29W
Cranford, *Lon.* 4 C2 51 29N 0 25W
Cranford, *N.Y.* 22 D3 40 39N 74 19W
Cranham, *Lon.* 4 B6 51 33N 0 16 E
Cray →, *Lon.* 4 C5 51 28N 0 8 E
Crayford, *Lon.* 4 C6 51 27N 0 11 E
Creekmouth, *Lon.* 4 B5 51 30N 0 6 E
Crerskill, *N.Y.* 22 B5 40 56N 73 57W
Crescenzago, *Mil.* 9 D6 45 30N 9 14 E
Crespières, *Paris* 5 B1 48 52N 1 55 E
Cressely, *Paris* 5 C2 48 44N 2 6 E
Cresslawn, *Jobg.* 18 E10 26 6 S 28 13 E
Crestwood, *Chic.* 26 D2 41 38N 87 43W
Creteil, *Paris* 5 C4 48 47N 2 27 E
Cricklewood, *Lon.* 4 B3 51 33N 0 13W
Crispano, *Nápl.* 9 H12 40 57N 14 17 E
Cristo Redebro, Monumento do, *Rio J.* 31 B2 22 56 S 43 12W
Crockenhill, *Lon.* 4 C5 51 22N 0 9 E
Croissy-Beaubourg, *Paris* 5 C5 48 49N 2 39 E
Croissy-sur-Seine, *Paris* 5 B2 48 52N 2 8 E
Cronenberg, *Ruhr* 6 C4 51 12N 7 9 E
Crosby, *Jobg.* 18 F8 26 11 S 27 59 E
Crosne, *Paris* 5 C4 48 43N 2 27 E
Cross I., *Bomb.* 16 H8 18 56N 72 51 E
Crouch End, *Lon.* 4 B4 51 34N 0 7W
Croud →, *Paris* 5 B4 48 57N 2 24 E
Crown Gardens, *Jobg.* 18 F9 26 15 S 28 0 E
Crown Mines, *Jobg.* 18 F8 26 12 S 27 57 E
Crown Village, *N.Y.* 23 C8 40 40N 73 26W
Crows Nest, *Syd.* 19 A4 33 49 S 151 12 E
Croxley Green, *Lon.* 4 B2 51 38N 0 26W
Croydon, *Lon.* 4 C4 51 22N 0 5W
Croydon, *Melb.* 19 E8 37 48 S 145 17 E
Croydon, *Phil.* 24 A5 40 5N 74 54W
Croydon North, *Melb.* 19 E8 37 46 S 145 16 E
Cruz de Pau, *Lisb.* 8 G8 38 37N 9 7W
Crystal Palace, *Lon.* 4 C4 51 25N 0 4W
Crystal Springs, *S.F.* 27 C2 37 31N 122 20W
Csepel, *Bud.* 10 K13 47 25N 19 4 E
Csepelsziget, *Bud.* 10 K13 47 25N 19 4 E
Csillaghegy, *Bud.* 10 J13 47 35N 19 2 E
Csillagtelep, *Bud.* 10 K13 47 24N 19 5 E
Cski-hegyek, *Bud.* 10 K12 47 30N 18 57 E
Csömör, *Bud.* 10 J14 47 33N 19 14 E
Cuajimalpa, *Méx.* 29 B2 19 21N 99 17W
Cuatro Vientos, *Mdrd.* 8 B2 40 22N 3 47W
Cuautepec de Madero, *Méx.* 29 A3 19 32N 99 8W
Cuautepec El Alto, *Méx.* 29 A3 19 33N 99 7W
Cuautzin, Cerro, *Méx.* 29 D3 19 10N 99 8W
Cubao, *Manila* 15 D4 14 37N 121 3 E
Cubas →, *S. Pau.* 31 D6 23 28 S 46 31W
Cubuklu, *Ist.* 17 A3 41 5N 29 4 E
Cudham, *Lon.* 4 D5 51 19N 0 4 E
Cuffley, *Lon.* 4 A4 51 42N 0 6W
Cuicuilco, Pirámido de, *Méx.* 29 C2 19 17N 99 10W
Culembeeck, *Jobg.* 18 E7 26 9 S 27 49 E
Culiculi, *Manila* 15 D4 14 33N 121 0 E
Cull Creek, *S.F.* 27 B4 37 45N 122 2W
Culver City, *L.A.* 28 B2 34 1N 118 24W
Culverstone Green, *Lon.* 4 C7 51 20N 0 20 E
Cumbre El Tabo, *Car.* 30 D5 10 33N 66 56W
Cumbres de Vallecas, *Mdrd.* 8 B3 40 20N 3 33W
Cunhas, *S. Pau.* 31 E7 23 34 S 46 23W
Cupecé, *S. Pau.* 31 E5 23 39 S 46 40W
Cupece →, *S. Pau.* 31 E6 23 37 S 46 42W
Curtis B., *Balt.* 25 B3 39 13N 76 34W
Curtis Cr. →, *Balt.* 25 B3 39 12N 76 34W
Cusago, *Mil.* 9 E5 45 26N 9 1 E
Cusano Milanese, *Mil.* 9 D6 45 33N 9 11 E
Çuvuşabaşi →, *Ist.* 17 A2 40 58N 28 51 E
Cyrildene, *Jobg.* 18 F9 26 10 S 28 6 E
Czernrakow, *Wsaw.* 10 E7 52 11N 21 3 E
Czyste, *Wsaw.* 10 E6 52 13N 20 57 E

D

Da Yunhe →, *Tianj.* 14 D5 39 19N 117 10 E
Dabizhuang, *Tianj.* 14 D6 39 11N 117 16 E
Ďablice, *Pra.* 10 B2 50 8N 14 29 E
Dabsibri, *Sŏul* 12 G8 37 33N 127 2 E
Dachang, *Shang.* 14 J11 31 17N 121 24 E
Dachau, *Mün.* 7 F9 48 15N 11 27 E
Dachau-Ost, *Mün.* 7 F9 48 15N 11 27 E
Dachauer Moos, *Mün.* 7 F9 48 13N 11 27 E
Daebang, *Sŏul* 12 G7 37 30N 126 55 E
Daechi, *Sŏul* 12 G8 37 30N 127 2 E
Dagenham, *Lon.* 4 B5 51 32N 0 8 E
Daglfing, *Mün.* 7 G10 48 8N 11 39 E
Dahirpur, *Delhi* 16 A2 28 43N 77 11 E
Dahlem, *Berl.* 7 B2 52 27N 13 16 E
Dahlerau, *Ruhr* 6 C5 51 13N 7 18 E
Dahlwitz-Hoppegarten, *Berl.* 7 A5 52 30N 13 41 E
Dahongmen, *Beij.* 14 C3 39 48N 116 21 E
Daiman, *Tōkyō* 13 A3 35 53N 139 44 E
Daitō, *Ōsaka* 12 B4 34 42N 135 38 E
Dajiaoting, *Beij.* 14 B3 39 51N 116 27 E
Dajingcun, *Beij.* 14 B2 39 50N 116 13 E
Dakhnoye, *St-Pet.* 11 C3 59 49N 30 15 E
Dalar, *Bomb.* 16 G7 19 0N 72 49 E
Dalejsky →, *Pra.* 10 B2 50 2N 14 24 E
Dalibia, *Gzh.* 14 G7 23 2N 113 6 E
Dallgow, *Berl.* 7 A1 52 32N 13 5 E
Dalston, *Lon.* 4 B4 51 32N 0 4W
Dalview, *Jobg.* 18 F11 26 14 S 28 20 E
Daly City, *S.F.* 27 B2 37 42N 122 27W
Damaia, *Lisb.* 8 F7 38 44N 9 12W
Dämeritzsee, *Berl.* 7 B5 52 34N 13 43 E
Damiette, *Paris* 5 C2 48 41N 2 7 E
Dampierre, *Paris* 5 C1 48 42N 1 59 E
Dan Neramit, *Bangk.* 15 B2 13 48N 100 34 E
Dan Ryan Woods, *Chic.* 26 C2 41 44N 87 40W
Dandenong, Mt., *Melb.* 19 E9 37 49 S 145 21 E
Danderyd, *Stock.* 3 D11 59 24N 18 1 E
Danforth, *Trto.* 20 D9 43 43N 79 16W
Daniels, *Balt.* 25 B2 39 19N 76 48W
Danvers, *Bost.* 21 B4 42 34N 70 56W
Dapharpur, *Calc.* 16 E5 22 38N 88 14 E
Darangan, *Manila* 15 E5 14 29N 121 10 E
Darave, *Bomb.* 16 G9 19 1N 73 1 E
Darby, *Phil.* 24 B3 39 55N 75 15W
Darby Cr. →, *Phil.* 24 B3 39 54N 75 15W
Darent →, *Lon.* 4 C6 51 21N 0 12 E
Darling, *Phil.* 24 B2 39 54N 75 28W
Darlington Corners, *Phil.* 24 B1 39 55N 75 34W
Dartford, *Lon.* 4 C6 51 26N 0 13 E
Dashi, *Gzh.* 14 G8 23 1N 113 17 E
Dashimae, *Tōkyō* 13 B3 35 46N 139 46 E
Datteln, *Ruhr* 6 A6 51 39N 7 20 E
Datteln-Hamm Kanal, *Ruhr* 6 A6 51 38N 7 28 E
Datun, *Beij.* 14 A3 40 0N 116 23 E
Dauko, *Calc.* 16 E5 22 31N 88 12 E
Daulatpur, *Delhi* 16 A1 28 44N 77 6 E
Davensport, *Bost.* 21 B4 42 33N 70 54W
Daveyton, *Jobg.* 18 E11 26 9 S 28 24 E
Davidkovo, *Mos.* 11 E8 55 43N 37 29 E
David's I., *N.Y.* 23 B6 40 53N 73 46W
Davidson, Mt., *S.F.* 27 B2 37 44N 122 27W
Davron, *Paris* 5 B1 48 52N 1 56 E
Dāvudiyeh, *Tehr.* 17 C5 35 45N 51 25 E
Dawidy, *Wsaw.* 10 F6 52 8N 20 58 E
Dayap, *Manila* 15 D4 14 35N 121 4 E
Dayuange, *Gzh.* 14 F7 23 11N 113 7 E
Dead Run →, *Balt.* 25 B2 39 18N 76 41W
Dedham, *Bost.* 21 D2 42 15N 71 10W
Dee Why, *Syd.* 19 A4 33 46 S 151 17 E
Deer I., *Bost.* 21 C4 42 21N 70 57W
Deer Park, *N.Y.* 23 C9 40 46N 73 19W
Degerby, *Stock.* 3 D9 59 22N 17 42 E
Degermossa, *Hels.* 3 B6 60 17N 25 12 E
Degunino, *Mos.* 11 D9 55 52N 37 33 E
Deisenhofen, *Mün.* 7 G10 48 0N 11 35 E
Dejvice, *Pra.* 10 B2 50 6N 14 23 E
Dekabristov, Os., *St-Pet.* 11 B3 59 56N 30 15 E
Del Viso, *B.A.* 32 A2 34 27 S 58 47W
Delanco, *Phil.* 24 A5 40 2N 74 57W
Delaware →, *Phil.* 24 A4 40 1N 75 0W
Delbruch, *Ruhr* 6 B4 51 22N 7 8 E
Delhi, *Delhi* 16 B2 28 39N 77 13 E
Delhi Cantonment, *Delhi* 16 B1 28 35N 77 7 E
Delhi Univ., *Delhi* 16 A2 28 41N 77 12 E
Dellwig, *Ruhr* 6 B3 51 29N 6 55 E
Delran, *Phil.* 24 A5 40 0N 74 57W
Delville, *Jobg.* 18 F10 26 11 S 28 13 E
Demarest, *N.Y.* 22 B5 40 57N 73 57W
Denham, *Lon.* 4 B1 51 35N 0 30W
Denham Green, *Lon.* 4 B2 51 34N 0 29W
Denniston Cr. →, *S.F.* 27 C2 37 30N 122 29W
Dentonia Park, *Trto.* 20 D9 43 42N 79 17W
Denville, *N.Y.* 22 B2 40 53N 74 28W
Deodoro, *Rio J.* 31 B1 22 50 S 43 21W
Depgsu Palace, *Sŏul* 12 G7 37 34N 126 58 E
Deptford, *Lon.* 4 C4 51 28N 0 1W
Der Sarai, *Delhi* 16 B2 28 33N 77 10 E
Des Plaines, *Chic.* 26 A1 42 2N 87 54W
Des Plaines →, *Chic.* 26 B1 41 48N 87 49W
Deshengmen, *Beij.* 14 B3 39 56N 116 21 E
Desierto de los Leones, Parque Nacional, *Méx.* 29 C2 19 18N 99 18W
Desio, *Mil.* 9 D6 45 36N 9 12 E
Deuil-la-Barre, *Paris* 5 B3 48 58N 2 19 E
Deulpur, *Calc.* 16 E5 22 36N 88 10 E
Deungchon, *Sŏul* 12 G7 37 33N 126 52 E
Deutsch-Wagram, *Wien* 10 G11 48 17N 16 33 E
Deutsche Oper, *Berl.* 7 A2 52 30N 13 19 E
Deutscher Museum, *Mün.* 7 G10 48 7N 11 35 E
Deux-Montagnes, *Mtrl.* 20 A2 43 32N 73 53W
Deux Montagnes, L. des, *Mtrl.* 20 B2 43 27N 73 59W
Devault, *Phil.* 24 A1 40 4N 75 32W
Dháfni, *Ath.* 8 J11 37 55N 23 44 E
Dhakuria, *Calc.* 16 E6 22 30N 88 22 E
Dhakuria L., *Calc.* 16 E6 22 30N 88 21 E
Dhamarakia, *Ath.* 8 J10 37 58N 23 39 E
Dharava, *Bomb.* 16 G8 19 1N 72 51 E
Dhrapersón, *Ath.* 8 J10 37 56N 23 37 E
Dhutumkhar, *Bomb.* 16 H9 18 54N 73 1 E
Dia Deva, *Bomb.* 16 H8 18 57N 72 53 E
Diadema, *S. Pau.* 31 F6 23 41 S 46 37W
Diamante, *B.A.* 32 C4 34 41 S 58 25W
Diamond Cr. →, *Melb.* 19 E7 37 44 S 145 9 E
Diamond Creek, *Melb.* 19 E8 37 40 S 145 10 E
Didaowai, *Tianj.* 14 E6 39 8N 117 12 E
Diepensiepen, *Ruhr* 6 C3 51 14N 6 58 E
Diepkloof, *Jobg.* 18 F8 26 14 S 27 57 E
Diessem, *Ruhr* 6 C1 51 19N 6 34 E
Difficult Run →, *Wash.* 25 D6 38 55N 77 18W
Digla, W. →, *El Qâ.* 18 D6 29 58N 31 22 E
Digra, *Calc.* 16 D5 22 49N 88 19 E
Dikemark, *Oslo* 2 C2 59 48N 10 22 E
Dilerpur, *Calc.* 16 C5 22 51N 88 10 E
Dinslaken, *Ruhr* 6 A2 51 33N 6 43 E
Dinslakener Bruch, *Ruhr* 6 A2 51 34N 6 44 E
Dinwiddie, *Jobg.* 18 F9 26 16 S 28 9 E
Diósd, *Bud.* 10 K12 47 24N 18 57 E
Dirnismaning, *Mün.* 7 F10 48 13N 11 38 E
Disappointment, Mt., *L.A.* 28 A4 34 15N 118 7W
Discovery, *Jobg.* 18 E8 26 8 S 27 54 E
Disteln, *Ruhr* 6 A4 51 36N 7 9 E
District Heights, *Wash.* 25 D8 38 51N 76 53W
Ditan Gongyuan, *Beij.* 14 B3 39 56N 116 23 E
Dix Hills, *N.Y.* 23 C8 40 48N 73 21W
Dixmoor, *Chic.* 26 D2 41 37N 87 40W
Diyala →, *Bagd.* 17 F9 33 13N 44 30 E
Djakarta = Jakarta, *Jak.* 15 H10 6 9 S 106 52 E
Djursholm, *Stock.* 3 D11 59 24N 18 5 E
Do Bong, *Sŏul* 12 G8 37 37N 127 1 E
Dobbs, *N.Y.* 23 A5 41 1N 73 52W
Döberitz, *Berl.* 7 A1 52 32N 13 3 E
Döbling, *Wien* 10 G10 48 14N 16 20 E
Dobong, *Sŏul* 12 G8 37 39N 127 2 E
Dobong San, *Sŏul* 12 F8 37 40N 127 0 E
Dōbrowa, *Wsaw.* 10 E6 52 19N 20 52 E
Doddinghurst, *Lon.* 4 A6 51 40N 0 18 E
Dodger Stadium, *L.A.* 28 B3 34 4N 118 14W
Dogsan, *Sŏul* 12 H7 37 28N 126 54 E
Doirone, *Tori.* 9 B2 45 3N 7 32 E
Dōjō, *Ōsaka* 12 A2 34 51N 135 14 E
Dōjō, *Tōkyō* 13 A2 35 51N 139 37 E
Dollard-des-Ormeaux, *Mtrl.* 20 B3 43 29N 73 49W
Dollis Hill, *Lon.* 4 B3 51 33N 0 13W
Dolni, *Pra.* 10 B3 50 3N 14 33 E
Dolni Chabry, *Pra.* 10 B2 50 8N 14 26 E
Dolni Počernice, *Pra.* 10 B3 50 5N 14 34 E
Dolton, *Chic.* 26 D3 41 37N 87 35W
Domont, *Paris* 5 A3 49 2N 2 19 E
Don Bosco, *B.A.* 32 C5 34 42 S 58 17W
Don Mills, *Trto.* 20 D8 43 44N 79 21W
Don Pedro II, Parque, *S. Pau.* 31 E6 23 33 S 46 36W
Don Torcuato, *B.A.* 32 A3 34 29 S 58 38W
Donau →, *Bud.* 10 J13 47 33N 19 4 E
Donau-Oder Kanal, *Wien* 10 G11 48 12N 16 32 E
Donaufeld, *Wien* 10 G10 48 15N 16 24 E
Donaukanal, *Wien* 10 G10 48 10N 16 27 E
Donaupark, *Wien* 10 G10 48 14N 16 24 E
Donaustadt, *Wien* 10 G10 48 13N 16 29 E
Doncaster, *Melb.* 19 E7 37 47 S 145 8 E
Doncaster East, *Melb.* 19 E7 37 46 S 145 8 E
Dong Dae Mun, *Sŏul* 12 G8 37 34N 127 2 E
Dong Jag, *Sŏul* 12 G7 37 30N 126 56 E
Dongala Forest Reserve, *Melb.* 19 F9 37 50 S 145 20 E
Dongan Hills, *N.Y.* 22 D4 40 35N 74 5W
Dongbinggo, *Sŏul* 12 G7 37 31N 126 58 E
Dongcheng, *Beij.* 14 B3 39 54N 116 23 E
Dongfeng Nongchang, *Beij.* 14 B3 39 57N 116 28 E
Dongjiao, *Gzh.* 14 G8 23 5N 113 12 E
Dongjuzi, *Tianj.* 14 E6 39 7N 117 14 E
Dongkou, *Shang.* 14 J12 31 17N 121 33 E
Dongmenwai, *Tianj.* 14 E6 39 8N 117 11 E
Dongri, *Bomb.* 16 H8 18 53N 72 57 E
Dongwuyuan, *Beij.* 14 B2 39 55N 116 18 E
Dongzhimen, *Beij.* 14 B3 39 55N 116 24 E
Donvale, *Melb.* 19 E8 37 47 S 145 11 E
Doonside, *Syd.* 19 A2 33 46 S 150 51 E
Doornfontein, *Jobg.* 18 F9 26 11 S 28 3 E
Dōra, *Bagd.* 17 F8 33 15N 44 25 E
Dora Riparia →, *Tori.* 9 B2 45 4N 7 38 E
Dorchester, *Bost.* 21 D3 42 17N 71 4W
Dorchester B., *Bost.* 21 D3 42 18N 71 1W
Dorchester Heights Nat. Hist. Site, *Bost.* 21 D3 42 19N 71 2W
Dorion, *Mtrl.* 20 B1 43 23N 74 1W
Dornach, *Mün.* 7 G11 48 9N 11 41 E
Dornap, *Ruhr* 6 C4 51 15N 7 3 E
Dornbach, *Wien* 10 G9 48 13N 16 18 E
Dorsey Run →, *Balt.* 25 B2 39 11N 76 47W
Dorstfeld, *Ruhr* 6 A6 51 30N 7 24 E
Dortmund, *Ruhr* 6 A6 51 30N 7 28 E
Dorval, *Mtrl.* 20 B3 43 26N 73 45W
Dorval, Aéroport de, *Mtrl.* 20 B3 43 28N 73 44 E
Dos Rios, *Méx.* 29 B1 19 22N 99 20W
Doshan Tappeh Airport, *Tehr.* 17 C5 35 41N 51 28 E
Dotmund-Ems Kanal, *Ruhr* 6 A6 51 35N 7 24 E
Double B., *Syd.* 19 B4 33 52 S 151 15 E
Douglas Park, *Chic.* 26 B2 41 51N 87 42W
Douglaston, *N.Y.* 23 C6 40 46N 73 44W
Dove Elbe →, *Hbg.* 7 E8 53 28N 10 7 E
Dover, *Bost.* 21 D2 42 14N 71 16W
Dover Heights, *Syd.* 19 B4 33 52 S 151 16 E
Dowlatābād, *Tehr.* 17 D5 35 38N 51 27 E
Downe, *Lon.* 4 C5 51 20N 0 3 E
Downey, *L.A.* 28 C4 33 56N 118 9W
Downsview, *Trto.* 20 D7 43 43N 79 30W
Downsview Dells Park, *Trto.* 20 D7 43 44N 79 30W
Dracut, *Bost.* 21 A2 42 40N 71 17W
Dragør, *Købn.* 2 E10 55 35N 12 38 E
Drancy, *Paris* 5 B4 48 55N 2 26 E
Dranesville, *Wash.* 25 C5 39 0N 77 20W
Draveil, *Paris* 5 C4 48 41N 2 23 E
Drayton Green, *Lon.* 4 B3 51 30N 0 19W
Dreilinden, *Berl.* 7 B2 52 24N 13 10 E
Dresher, *Phil.* 24 A4 40 9N 75 9W
Drewnica, *Wsaw.* 10 E7 52 18N 21 6 E
Drexel Hill, *Phil.* 24 B3 39 56N 75 18W
Drexel Inst. of Technology, *Phil.* 24 B3 39 57N 75 11W
Drigh Road, *Kar.* 17 G11 24 52N 67 7 E
Drogden, *Købn.* 2 E11 55 37N 12 42 E
Drottningholm, *Stock.* 3 E10 59 19N 17 53 E
Druento, *Tori.* 9 B2 45 8N 7 34 E
Druid Hill Park, *Balt.* 25 B3 39 19N 76 38W
Druid Lake, *Balt.* 25 B3 39 19N 76 38W
Drummoyne, *Syd.* 19 B3 33 51 S 151 8 E
Druzhba, *Mos.* 11 D10 55 52N 37 44 E
Duarte, *L.A.* 28 B5 34 8N 117 57W
Dubeč, *Pra.* 10 B3 50 3N 14 35 E
Dubi Bheri, *Calc.* 16 C5 22 52N 88 16 E
Duffryn Mawr, *Phil.* 24 A2 40 2N 75 27W
Dugnano, *Mil.* 9 D6 45 33N 9 11 E
Dugny, *Paris* 5 B4 48 57N 2 24 E
Duiha, *Calc.* 16 E5 22 34N 88 15 E
Duisburg, *Ruhr* 6 B2 51 26N 6 45 E
Dulāb, *Tehr.* 17 D5 35 39N 51 27 E
Dulworthtown, *Phil.* 24 B1 39 54N 75 33W
Dum Dum, *Calc.* 16 E6 22 38N 88 25 E
Dum Dum Int. Airport, *Calc.* 16 E6 22 38N 88 26 E
Dumbarton Pt., *S.F.* 27 D4 37 29N 122 6W
Dumjor, *Calc.* 16 E5 22 37N 88 13 E
Dumont, *N.Y.* 22 B5 40 56N 73 59W
Dümpten, *Ruhr* 6 B3 51 27N 6 54 E
Duna →, *Bud.* 10 J13 47 33N 19 4 E
Dunbarton, *Trto.* 20 C10 43 50N 79 6W
Dundalk, *Balt.* 25 B3 39 17N 76 31W
Dundas, *Syd.* 19 A3 33 47 S 151 3 E
Dunearn, *Sing.* 15 G7 1 19N 103 49 E
Dunellen, *N.Y.* 22 D2 40 35N 74 26W
Dunn Loring, *Wash.* 25 D6 38 54N 77 13W
Dunning, *Chic.* 26 B2 41 56N 87 48W
Dunton Green, *Lon.* 4 D6 51 17N 0 11 E
Dunvegan, *Jobg.* 18 E9 26 9 S 28 8 E
Duomo, *Mil.* 9 E6 45 28N 9 11 E
Duomo, *Nápl.* 9 H12 40 51N 14 15 E
Duomo, *Tori.* 9 B3 45 4N 7 45 E
Duque de Caxias, *Rio J.* 31 A2 22 46 S 43 18W
Durban Roodepoort Deep Gold Mines, *Jobg.* 18 F8 26 11 S 27 52 E
Durchholz, *Ruhr* 6 B5 51 23N 7 18 E
Düssel →, *Ruhr* 6 C3 51 13N 6 58 E
Düsseldorf, *Ruhr* 6 C2 51 13N 6 46 E
Düsseldorf-Lohausen, Flughafen, *Ruhr* 6 C2 51 17N 6 45 E
Duvenstedt, *Hbg.* 7 C8 53 42N 10 6 E
Duvenstedter Brook, *Hbg.* 7 C8 53 43N 10 8 E
Duvernay, *Mtrl.* 20 A3 43 35N 73 40W
Dyakovo, *Mos.* 11 E9 55 40N 37 39 E
Dyviksudd, *Stock.* 3 E13 59 11N 18 23 E
Dzerzhinskiy, *Mos.* 11 F11 55 38N 37 51 E
Dzerzhinskiy, *Mos.* 11 E9 55 47N 37 37 E
Dzerzhinskiy Park, *Mos.* 11 E9 55 50N 37 37 E

E

Eagle Rock, *L.A.* 28 B3 34 8N 118 12 E
Ealing, *Lon.* 4 B3 51 30N 0 18W
Earls Court, *Lon.* 4 C3 51 29N 0 11W
Earlsfield, *Lon.* 4 C3 51 26N 0 10W
Earlwood, *Syd.* 19 B3 33 55 S 151 8 E
East Acton, *Bost.* 21 C1 42 28N 71 24W
East Acton, *Lon.* 4 B3 51 30N 0 14W
East Arlington, *Wash.* 25 D7 38 51N 77 4W
East Atlantic Beach, *N.Y.* 23 D6 40 35N 73 43W
East B., *N.Y.* 23 D7 40 38N 73 32W
East Barnet, *Lon.* 4 B4 51 38N 0 9W
East Bedfont, *Lon.* 4 C2 51 26N 0 28W
East Billerica, *Bost.* 21 B2 42 35N 71 13W
East Boston, *Bost.* 21 C3 42 22N 71 1W
East Braintree, *Bost.* 21 D4 42 13N 70 58W
East Chicago, *Chic.* 26 D4 41 38N 87 26W
East Don →, *Trto.* 20 D8 43 48N 79 25W
East Dulwich, *Lon.* 4 C4 51 26N 0 4W
East Elmhurst, *N.Y.* 23 C5 40 45N 73 52W
East Farmingdale, *N.Y.* 23 C8 40 44N 73 25W
East Finchley, *Lon.* 4 B3 51 35N 0 10W
East Half Hollow Hills, *N.Y.* 23 C9 40 47N 73 19W
East Ham, *Lon.* 4 B5 51 32N 0 3 E
East Hanover, *N.Y.* 22 C2 40 49N 74 21W
East Hills, *N.Y.* 23 C7 40 47N 73 37W
East Hills, *Syd.* 19 B2 33 57 S 150 59 E
East Holliston, *Bost.* 21 D1 42 12N 71 25W
East Horsley, *Lon.* 4 D2 51 16N 0 25W
East Humber →, *Trto.* 20 D7 43 47N 79 35W
East Huntington, *N.Y.* 23 B8 40 52N 73 24W
East Lamma Channel, *H.K.* 12 E5 22 13N 114 9 E
East Lexington, *Bost.* 21 C2 42 25N 71 12W
East Los Angeles, *L.A.* 28 B3 34 1N 118 10 E
East Meadow, *N.Y.* 23 C7 40 42N 73 31W
East Molesey, *Lon.* 4 C2 51 24N 0 21W
East New York, *N.Y.* 23 C5 40 40N 73 53W
East Newark, *N.Y.* 22 C3 40 45N 74 10W
East Northport, *N.Y.* 23 B9 40 52N 73 18W
East Norwich, *N.Y.* 23 B7 40 50N 73 31W
East Orange, *N.Y.* 22 C3 40 46N 74 11W
East Palo Alto, *S.F.* 27 D4 37 28N 122 8W
East Paterson, *N.Y.* 22 B4 40 53N 74 8W
East Pines, *Wash.* 25 D8 38 57N 76 54W
East Point, *Bost.* 21 C4 42 25N 70 54W
East Potomac Park, *Wash.* 25 D7 38 52N 77 1W
East Richmond, *S.F.* 27 A3 37 56N 122 19W
East Ringwood, *Melb.* 19 E8 37 48 S 145 15 E
East River →, *N.Y.* 22 C5 40 44N 73 58W
East Rockaway, *N.Y.* 23 D6 40 38N 73 40W
East Rutherford, *N.Y.* 22 B4 40 50N 74 5W
East Sheen, *Lon.* 4 C3 51 27N 0 16W
East View Garden, *Sing.* 15 F8 1 20N 103 57 E
East Weymouth, *Bost.* 21 D4 42 13N 70 55W
East Wickham, *Lon.* 4 C5 51 28N 0 5 E
East Williston, *N.Y.* 23 C7 40 45N 73 37W
East York, *Trto.* 20 D8 43 40N 79 22W
Eastchester, *N.Y.* 23 B6 40 56N 73 49W
Eastchester B., *N.Y.* 23 B6 40 50N 73 47W
Eastcote, *Lon.* 4 B2 51 34N 0 23W
Eastleigh, *Jobg.* 18 E9 26 7 S 28 9 E
Eastpoint, *Balt.* 25 B3 39 17N 76 34W
Eastwood, *Syd.* 19 A3 33 47 S 151 4 E
Eatons Neck Pt., *N.Y.* 23 B8 40 57N 73 24W
Eaubonne, *Paris* 5 B3 48 59N 2 16 E
Ebara, *Tōkyō* 13 C3 35 35N 139 42 E
Ebisu, *Tōkyō* 13 C3 35 38N 139 42 E
Ebute-Ikorodu, *Lagos* 18 A2 6 35N 7 29 E

Gerthe 37

Ebute-Metta, *Lagos* 18 B2 6 28N 7 23 E
Ecatepec de Morelos, *Méx.* 29 A3 19 35N 99 2W
Echo B., *N.Y.* 23 B6 40 54N 73 45W
Echo Mt., *L.A.* 28 A4 34 12N 118 8W
Écouen, *Paris* 5 A4 49 1N 2 22 E
Ecquevilly, *Paris* 5 B1 48 57N 1 55 E
Ecser, *Bud.* 10 K14 47 26N 19 19 E
Eda, *Tōkyō* 13 C2 35 33N 139 33 E
Eddington, *Phil.* 24 A5 40 5N 74 55W
Eddystone, *Phil.* 24 B2 39 51N 75 20W
Eden, *Rio J.* 31 A1 22 47 S 43 23W
Edendale, *Jobg.* 18 E9 26 8 S 28 9 E
Edenvale, *Jobg.* 18 E9 26 8 S 28 9 E
Edgars Cr. →, *Melb.* 19 E6 37 43 S 144 58 E
Edge Hill, *Phil.* 24 A4 40 7N 75 9W
Edgeley, *Trto.* 20 D7 43 47N 79 31W
Edgemar, *S.F.* 27 C2 37 39N 122 29W
Edgemere, *Balt.* 25 B4 39 14N 76 26W
Edgemont, *Phil.* 24 B2 39 58N 75 26W
Edgewater Park, *Phil.* 24 A5 40 3N 74 54W
Edgware, *Lon.* 4 B3 51 36N 0 15W
Edison, *N.Y.* 22 D2 40 31N 74 23W
Edison Park, *Chic.* 26 A2 42 1N 87 48W
Edleen, *Jobg.* 18 E10 26 5 S 28 12 E
Edmondston, *Wash.* 25 D8 38 56N 76 54W
Edo →, *Tōkyō* 13 C4 35 38N 139 52 E
Edogawa, *Tōkyō* 13 B4 35 43N 139 52 E
Edsberg, *Stock.* 3 D10 59 26N 17 57 E
Edwards L., *Melb.* 19 E6 37 42 S 144 59 E
Eestiluoto, *Hels.* 3 C6 60 7N 25 13 E
Egawa, *Tōkyō* 13 D4 35 22N 139 54 E
Egenbüttel, *Hbg.* 7 D7 53 39N 9 51 E
Eggerscheidt, *Ruhr* 6 C3 51 19N 6 53 E
Egham, *Lon.* 4 C1 51 25N 0 30W
Eiche, *Berl.* 7 A4 52 33N 13 35 E
Eiche Sud, *Berl.* 7 A4 52 33N 13 35 E
Eichlinghofen, *Ruhr* 6 B6 51 29N 7 24 E
Eichwalde, *Berl.* 7 B4 52 22N 13 37 E
Eidelstedt, *Hbg.* 7 D7 53 36N 9 54 E
Eiffel, Tour, *Paris* 5 B3 48 51N 2 17 E
Eigen, *Ruhr* 6 A3 51 32N 6 56 E
Eilbek, *Hbg.* 7 D8 53 34N 10 2 E
Eimsbüttel, *Hbg.* 7 D7 53 34N 9 57 E
Eissendorf, *Hbg.* 7 E7 53 27N 9 57 E
Ejby, *Købn.* 2 D9 55 41N 12 24 E
Ejigbo, *Lagos* 18 A1 6 33N 7 18 E
Ekeberg, *Oslo* 2 B4 59 53N 10 46 E
Ekeby, *Stock.* 3 D8 59 21N 17 35 E
Ekerö, *Stock.* 3 E9 59 17N 17 46 E
Ekerön, *Stock.* 3 E9 59 18N 17 41 E
Ekhtiyarieh, *Tehr.* 17 C5 35 46N 51 28 E
Eklundshov, *Stock.* 3 E10 59 11N 17 54 E
Eknäs, *Stock.* 3 E12 59 18N 18 13 E
El 'Abbasiya, *El Qâ.* 18 C5 30 3N 31 16 E
El Agustino, *Lima* 30 G8 12 2 S 77 0W
El Alto, *Stgo* 30 J10 33 29 S 70 42W
El Awkal, *El Qâ.* 18 C5 30 2N 31 12 E
El Baragil, *El Qâ.* 18 C4 30 4N 31 9 E
El Basâlin, *El Qâ.* 18 D5 29 58N 31 16 E
El Calvario, *La Hab.* 30 B3 23 3N 82 19W
El Cano, *La Hab.* 30 B2 23 2N 82 27W
El Caribe, *Car.* 30 D5 10 36N 66 52W
El Carmen, *Stgo* 30 J10 33 22 S 70 43W
El Cerrito, *S.F.* 27 A3 37 54N 122 18W
El Cerro, *La Hab.* 30 B2 23 6N 82 23W
El Cojo, Pta., *Car.* 30 D5 10 36N 66 53W
El Cortijo, *Stgo* 30 J10 33 22 S 70 42W
El Duqqi, *El Qâ.* 18 C5 30 1N 31 12 E
El Gamâlîya, *El Qâ.* 18 C5 30 2N 31 15 E
El Ghurîya, *El Qâ.* 18 C5 30 2N 31 15 E
El Gîza, *El Qâ.* 18 C5 30 0N 31 12 E
El Granada, *S.F.* 27 C2 37 30N 122 27W
El Guarda Parres, *Méx.* 29 D2 19 9N 99 11W
El Hatillo, *Car.* 30 E6 10 25N 66 49W
El Khalîfa, *El Qâ.* 18 C5 30 0N 31 15 E
El Kôm el Ahmar, *El Qâ.* 18 C5 30 6N 31 10 E
El Ma'âdi, *El Qâ.* 18 D5 29 57N 31 15 E
El Matarîya, *El Qâ.* 18 C5 30 7N 31 18 E
El Monte, *L.A.* 28 B4 34 3N 118 1W
El Muhît Idkû el Gharbî →, *El Qâ.* 18 C4 30 6N 31 6 E
El Mûskî, *El Qâ.* 18 C5 30 3N 31 15 E
El Palmar, *Car.* 30 D5 10 36N 66 53W
El Palomar, *B.A.* 32 B3 34 36 S 58 37W
El Pardo, *Mdrd.* 8 A2 40 30N 3 46W
El Pedregal, *Car.* 30 D5 10 30N 66 51W
El Pinar, *Car.* 30 E5 10 28N 66 56W
El Plantio, *Mdrd.* 8 B1 40 28N 3 51W
El Qâhira, *El Qâ.* 18 C5 30 2N 31 13 E
El Qubba, *El Qâ.* 18 C5 30 4N 31 16 E
El Recreo, *Car.* 30 E5 10 29N 66 52W
El Reloj, *Méx.* 29 C3 19 19N 99 9W
El Retiro, *Car.* 30 D5 10 31N 66 54W
El Salto, *Stgo* 30 J11 33 22 S 70 38W
El Segundo, *L.A.* 28 C2 33 55N 118 24W
El Sereno, *L.A.* 28 B3 34 6N 118 10 E
El Silencio, *Car.* 30 D5 10 30N 66 55W
El Sobrante, *S.F.* 27 A3 37 58N 122 17W
El Talar de Pacheco, *B.A.* 32 A3 34 27 S 58 38W
El Talibîya, *El Qâ.* 18 D5 29 59N 31 10 E
El Valle, *Car.* 30 E5 10 29N 66 54W
El Vedado, *La Hab.* 30 B2 23 8N 82 23W
El Vergel, *Méx.* 29 C3 19 18N 99 5W
El Wâyli el Kubra, *El Qâ.* 18 C5 30 5N 31 17 E
El Zamalik, *El Qâ.* 18 C5 30 3N 31 12 E
Elam, *Phil.* 24 B1 39 51N 75 32W
Élancourt, *Paris* 5 C1 48 47N 1 57 E
Elandsfortein, *Jobg.* 18 E10 26 9 S 28 13 E
Elbe →, *Hbg.* 7 D6 53 32N 9 49 E
Elberfeld, *Ruhr* 6 C4 51 15N 7 10 E
Elephanta Caves, *Bomb.* 16 H8 18 57N 72 57 E
Elephanta I., *Bomb.* 16 H8 18 57N 72 56 E
Elisenau, *Berl.* 7 A4 52 38N 13 37 E
Elizabeth, *N.Y.* 22 D3 40 39N 74 13W
Elkins Park, *Phil.* 24 A4 40 4N 75 8W
Elkridge, *Balt.* 25 B2 39 13N 76 42W
Ellboda, *Stock.* 3 D12 59 24N 18 15 E
Eller, *Ruhr* 6 C3 51 12N 6 51 E
Ellerbek, *Hbg.* 7 D7 53 39N 9 52 E
Ellicott City, *Balt.* 25 B2 39 15N 76 49W
Ellinghorst, *Ruhr* 6 A3 51 33N 6 57 E
Ellinikón, *Ath.* 8 J11 37 50N 23 45 E
Ellis I., *N.Y.* 22 C4 40 41N 74 2W
Elm Park, *Lon.* 4 B6 51 32N 0 12 E
Elmers End, *Lon.* 4 C4 51 23N 0 2W
Elmhurst, *Chic.* 26 B1 41 53N 87 55W
Elmhurst, *N.Y.* 23 C5 40 44N 73 53W
Elmont, *N.Y.* 23 C6 40 42N 73 42W
Elmstead, *Lon.* 4 C5 51 24N 0 2 E
Elmwood, *Balt.* 25 A3 39 20N 76 31W
Elmwood, *N.Y.* 23 B8 40 51N 73 20W
Elmwood Park, *Chic.* 26 B2 41 55N 87 48W
Elmwood Park, *N.Y.* 22 B4 40 54N 74 7W
Elsburg, *Jobg.* 18 F10 26 15 S 28 13 E
Elsburgspruit →, *Jobg.* 18 F10 26 16 S 28 12 E
Elsmere, *Phil.* 24 C1 39 44N 75 35W
Elspark, *Jobg.* 18 F10 26 15 S 28 13 E
Elsternwick, *Melb.* 19 F7 37 52 S 145 0 E
Eltham, *Lon.* 4 C5 51 27N 0 3 E
Eltham, *Melb.* 19 E7 37 42 S 145 9 E
Elthorn Heights, *Lon.* 4 B2 51 31N 0 20W
Eltingrille, *N.Y.* 22 D4 40 32N 74 9W
Elwood, *Melb.* 19 F6 37 53 S 144 59 E
Élysée, *Paris* 5 B3 48 52N 2 19 E
Embu, *S. Pau.* 31 E4 23 38 S 46 50W
Embu-Mirim, *S. Pau.* 31 F5 23 41 S 46 49W
Embu Mirim →, *S. Pau.* 31 F5 23 43 S 46 47W
Emdeni, *Jobg.* 18 F7 26 14 S 27 49 E
Émerainville, *Paris* 5 C5 48 48N 2 37 E
Emerson, *N.Y.* 22 B4 40 57N 74 2W
Emerson Park, *Lon.* 4 B6 51 34N 0 13 E
Emeryville, *S.F.* 27 B3 37 49N 122 17W
Eminonu, *Ist.* 17 A2 41 0N 28 57 E
Emmarentia, *Jobg.* 18 E9 26 9 S 28 0 E
Emperor's Palace, *Tōkyō* 13 B3 35 40N 139 45 E
Empire State Building, *N.Y.* 22 C5 40 44N 73 59W
Emscher →, *Ruhr* 6 A6 51 30N 7 26 E
Emscher Bruch, *Ruhr* 6 A4 51 33N 7 8 E
Emscher Zweigkanal, *Ruhr* 6 A4 51 33N 7 9 E
Encantado, *Rio J.* 31 B2 22 53 S 43 19W
Encino, *L.A.* 28 B2 34 9N 118 28W
Encino Res., *L.A.* 28 B1 34 8N 118 30W
Enebyberg, *Stock.* 3 D10 59 25N 17 59 E
Enfield, *Lon.* 4 B4 51 39N 0 4W
Enfield, *Phil.* 24 A3 40 6N 75 11W
Enfield, *Syd.* 19 B3 33 53 S 151 6 E
Enfield Chase, *Lon.* 4 A4 51 40N 0 8W
Enfield Highway, *Lon.* 4 B4 51 39N 0 2W
Enfield Lock, *Lon.* 4 A4 51 40N 0 1W
Enfield Wash, *Lon.* 4 B4 51 39N 0 2W
Eng Khong Gardens, *Sing.* 15 F7 1 20N 103 46 E
Engenho, I. do, *Rio J.* 31 B3 22 50 S 43 6W
Engenho Nôvo, *Rio J.* 31 B2 22 53 S 43 17W
Engenho Velho, Sa. do, *Rio J.* 31 B1 22 54 S 43 21W
Engenno do Mato, *Rio J.* 31 B3 22 56 S 43 2W
Enghein-les-Bains, *Paris* 5 B3 48 58N 2 18 E
Englewood, *Chic.* 26 C3 41 46N 87 38W
Englewood, *N.Y.* 22 B5 40 53N 73 58W
Englewood Cliffs, *N.Y.* 22 B5 40 53N 73 59W
Englischer Garten, *Mün.* 7 G10 48 9N 11 35 E
Enmore, *Syd.* 19 B4 33 54 S 151 10 E
Ennepe →, *Ruhr* 6 C6 51 17N 7 23 E
Ennepetal, *Ruhr* 6 C6 51 17N 7 21 E
Ennepetalsp →, *Ruhr* 6 C6 51 14N 7 24 E
Enskede, *Stock.* 3 E11 59 17N 18 4 E
Entrevias, *Mdrd.* 8 B2 40 22N 3 40W
Épiais-les-Louvres, *Paris* 5 A5 49 1N 2 33 E
Epinay, *Paris* 5 B3 48 57N 2 19 E
Epinay-sous-Sénart, *Paris* 5 C5 48 41N 2 30 E
Epinay-sur-Orge, *Paris* 5 C3 48 40N 2 19 E
Eppende, *Ruhr* 6 B6 51 28N 7 9 E
Eppenhausen, *Ruhr* 6 B6 51 22N 7 29 E
Epping, *Lon.* 4 A5 51 41N 0 6 E
Epping, *Melb.* 19 D7 37 39 S 145 1 E
Epping, *Syd.* 19 A3 33 46 S 151 5 E
Epping Forest, *Lon.* 4 B5 51 39N 0 2 E
Epsom, *Lon.* 4 D3 51 19N 0 15W
Epsom Racecourse, *Lon.* 4 D3 51 18N 0 15W
Éragny, *Paris* 5 A2 49 1N 2 5 E
Ercolano, *Nápl.* 9 J13 40 48N 14 21 E
Érd, *Bud.* 10 K12 47 23N 18 56 E
Erdenheim, *Phil.* 24 A3 40 5N 75 12W
Eregun, *Lagos* 18 A2 6 35N 7 22 E
Erenköy, *Ist.* 17 B3 40 58N 29 3 E
Ergal, *Paris* 5 C1 48 47N 1 55 E
Erial, *Phil.* 24 C4 39 46N 75 0W
Erith, *Lon.* 4 C6 51 28N 0 11 E
Erkner, *Berl.* 7 B5 52 25N 13 44 E
Erkrath, *Ruhr* 6 C3 51 13N 6 54 E
Erlaa, *Wien* 10 H9 48 9N 16 19 E
Erle, *Ruhr* 6 A4 51 33N 7 4 E
Ermelino Matarazzo, *S. Pau.* 31 D7 23 29 S 46 28W
Ermington, *Syd.* 19 A3 33 48 S 151 4 E
Ermont, *Paris* 5 B3 48 59N 2 15 E
Ersébet-Telep, *Bud.* 10 K14 47 27N 19 10 E
Ershatou, *Gzh.* 14 G8 23 6N 113 18 E
Erskineville, *Syd.* 19 B4 33 54 S 151 12 E
Erstavik, *Stock.* 3 E12 59 16N 18 14 E
Erstaviken, *Stock.* 3 E12 59 16N 18 20 E
Erunkan, *Lagos* 18 A2 6 36N 7 23 E
Eschenried, *Mün.* 7 F9 48 13N 11 24 E
Esenler, *Ist.* 17 A2 41 1N 28 52 E
Esher, *Lon.* 4 C2 51 22N 0 20W
Eshratābād, *Tehr.* 17 C5 35 42N 51 27 E
España, *B.A.* 32 C5 34 46 S 58 14W
Espeleta, *B.A.* 32 C5 34 45 S 58 15W
Esplugas, *Barc.* 8 D5 41 22N 2 5 E
Espoo, *Hels.* 3 B2 60 13N 24 38 E
Espoonlahti, *Hels.* 3 B2 60 9N 24 31 E
Esposizione Univ. di Roma (E.U.R.), *Rome* 9 G9 41 49N 12 28 E
Essen, *Ruhr* 6 B4 51 27N 7 0 E
Essen-Mülheim, Flughafen, *Ruhr* 6 B3 51 24N 6 56 E
Essendon, *Melb.* 19 E6 37 44 S 144 55 E
Essendon Airport, *Melb.* 19 E6 37 43 S 144 54 E
Essex, *Balt.* 25 B4 39 18N 76 28W
Essex Falls, *N.Y.* 22 C3 40 49N 74 16W
Essingen, *Stock.* 3 E10 59 19N 17 59 E
Essling, *Wien* 10 G11 48 12N 16 30 E
Est, Gare de l', *Paris* 5 B4 48 52N 2 21 E
Estado, Parque do, *S. Pau.* 31 E6 23 38 S 46 38W
Estby, *Hels.* 3 C1 60 5N 24 27W
Este, Parque Nacional del, *Car.* 30 E5 10 29N 66 50W
Esteban Echeverria, *B.A.* 32 C4 34 48 S 58 29W
Estlotan, *Hels.* 3 B5 60 7N 25 13 E
Estrela, Basilica da, *Lisb.* 8 F8 38 42N 9 9W
Étiolles, *Paris* 5 D4 48 38N 2 28 E
Etobicoke, *Trto.* 20 E7 43 39N 79 34W
Etobicoke Cr. →, *Trto.* 20 E7 43 35N 79 32W
Etzenhauzen, *Mün.* 7 F9 48 16N 11 27 E
Eun Pyeong, *Sŏul* 12 G7 37 36N 126 56 E
Eungam, *Sŏul* 12 G7 37 34N 126 55 E
Evanston, *Chic.* 26 A2 42 3N 87 40W
Évecquemont, *Paris* 5 A1 49 0N 1 56 E
Everett, *Bost.* 21 C3 42 24N 71 3W
Evergreen Park, *Chic.* 26 C2 41 43N 87 42W
Eversael, *Ruhr* 6 A1 51 32N 6 39 E
Evesboro, *Phil.* 24 B5 39 54N 74 56W
Eving, *Ruhr* 6 A6 51 33N 7 28 E
Evry, *Paris* 5 D4 48 38N 2 26 E
Évry-les-Châteaux, *Paris* 5 D5 48 39N 2 38 E
Évzonos, *Ath.* 8 J11 37 55N 23 45 E
Ewin, *Tehr.* 17 C5 35 47N 51 23 E
Ewu, *Lagos* 18 A1 6 33N 7 19 E
Exelberg, *Wien* 10 G9 48 14N 16 15 E
Eynsford, *Lon.* 4 C6 51 21N 0 12 E
Eyup, *Ist.* 17 A2 41 2N 28 55 E
Ez Zeitûn, *El Qâ.* 18 C5 30 6N 31 18 E
Ézanville, *Paris* 5 A4 49 1N 2 21 E
Ezeiza, *B.A.* 32 D3 34 50 S 58 31W
Ezeiza, Aeropuerto, *B.A.* 32 C3 34 48 S 58 32W

F

Fabreville, *Mtrl.* 20 A2 43 33N 73 51W
Fælledparken, *Købn.* 2 D10 55 42N 12 34 E
Fågelön, *Stock.* 3 E10 59 18N 17 55 E
Fagersjo, *Stock.* 3 E11 59 14N 18 4 E
Fagnano, *Mil.* 9 E4 45 24N 8 59 E
Fahrn, *Ruhr* 6 A2 51 30N 6 45 E
Faibano, *Nápl.* 9 H13 40 55N 14 27 E
Fair Lawn, *N.Y.* 22 B4 40 55N 74 7W
Fairfax, *Phil.* 24 C1 39 47N 75 33W
Fairfax, *Wash.* 25 D6 38 50N 77 19W
Fairfax Station, *Wash.* 25 E6 38 48N 77 19W
Fairfield, *Melb.* 19 E7 37 46 S 145 2 E
Fairfield, *N.Y.* 22 B3 40 53N 74 17W
Fairfield, *Syd.* 19 B2 33 52 S 150 56 E
Fairhaven, *Bost.* 21 C1 42 25N 71 21W
Fairhaven Hill, *Bost.* 21 C1 42 26N 71 21W
Fairland, *Jobg.* 18 E8 26 8 S 27 57 E
Fairland, *Wash.* 25 C8 39 4N 76 57W
Fairmont Terrace, *S.F.* 27 B4 37 42N 122 7W
Fairmount Heights, *Wash.* 25 D8 38 54N 76 54W
Fairmount Park, *Phil.* 24 A3 40 3N 75 13W
Fairport, *Trto.* 20 D10 43 49N 79 4W
Fairview, *N.Y.* 22 C5 40 48N 73 59W
Fairview, *N.Y.* 23 A6 41 1N 73 46W
Falenica, *Wsaw.* 10 F8 52 9N 21 12 E
Falenty, *Wsaw.* 10 F6 52 8N 20 55 E
Falkenburg, *Berl.* 7 A4 52 34N 13 32 E
Falkenhagen, *Berl.* 7 A1 52 34N 13 5 E
Falkensee, *Berl.* 7 A1 52 34N 13 4 E
Fallon, *L.A.* 28 C5 33 59N 117 54W
Falls Church, *Wash.* 25 D6 38 53N 77 12W
Falls Run →, *Balt.* 25 A1 39 21N 76 52W
Falomo, *Lagos* 18 B2 6 26N 7 26 E
Fangcun, *Gzh.* 14 G8 23 6N 113 13 E
Fanwood, *N.Y.* 22 D2 40 37N 74 23W
Far Rockaway, *N.Y.* 23 D6 40 36N 73 45W
Farahābād, *Tehr.* 17 C5 35 41N 51 29 E
Färentuna, *Stock.* 3 D8 59 23N 17 39 E
Farforovskaya, *St-Pet.* 11 B4 59 52N 30 27 E
Farm Pond, *Bost.* 21 D2 42 13N 71 20W
Farmingdale, *N.Y.* 23 C8 40 43N 73 27W
Farmsen, *Hbg.* 7 D8 53 36N 10 8 E
Farnborough, *Lon.* 4 C5 51 21N 0 3 E
Farningham, *Lon.* 4 C6 51 23N 0 12 E
Farrar Pond, *Bost.* 21 C1 42 24N 71 21W
Farrarmere, *Jobg.* 18 E10 26 9 S 28 18 E
Farsta, *Stock.* 3 E11 59 14N 18 5 E
Farstalandet, *Stock.* 3 E13 59 18N 18 23 E
Farum, *Købn.* 2 D8 55 48N 12 21 E
Farum Sø, *Købn.* 2 D9 55 48N 12 21 E
Fasanerie-Nord, *Mün.* 7 F10 48 11N 11 32 E
Fasangarten, *Mün.* 7 G10 48 5N 11 36 E
Fat Tau Chau, *H.K.* 12 E6 22 16N 114 16 E
Fatih, *Ist.* 17 A2 41 0N 28 56 E
Favoriten, *Wien* 10 H10 48 9N 16 23 E
Fawkner, *Melb.* 19 E6 37 42 S 144 56 E
Fawkner Park, *Melb.* 19 F6 37 50 S 144 58 E
Feasterville, *Phil.* 24 A4 40 9N 75 0W
Febrero, Parque de, *B.A.* 32 B4 34 36 S 58 25W
Feijó, *Lisb.* 8 G8 38 39N 9 9W
Feldersbruch →, *Ruhr* 6 B5 51 23N 7 4 E
Feldhausen, *Ruhr* 6 A3 51 36N 6 58 E
Feldkirchen, *Mün.* 7 G11 48 8N 11 43 E
Feldmoching, *Mün.* 7 F10 48 14N 11 32 E
Fellowship, *Phil.* 24 B5 39 56N 74 57W
Feltham, *Lon.* 4 C2 51 26N 0 24W
Feltonville, *Phil.* 24 A4 40 1N 75 8W
Fenerbahce, *Ist.* 17 B3 40 58N 29 2 E
Fengtai, *Beij.* 14 C2 39 49N 116 14 E
Fenino, *Mos.* 11 E11 55 43N 37 56 E
Ferencváros, *Bud.* 10 K13 47 29N 19 5 E
Ferihegyi Airport, *Bud.* 10 K14 47 26N 19 14 E
Ferndale, *Balt.* 25 B3 39 11N 76 38W
Ferndale, *Jobg.* 18 E9 26 5 S 28 0 E
Ferntree Gully, *Melb.* 19 F8 37 52 S 145 17 E
Ferntree Gully Nat. Park, *Melb.* 19 F8 37 52 S 145 19 E
Ferny Cr. →, *Melb.* 19 F8 37 54 S 145 16 E
Férolles-Attilly, *Paris* 5 C5 48 44N 2 37 E
Ferraz de Vasconcelos, *S. Pau.* 31 E7 23 32 S 46 22W
Ferrières-en-Brie, *Paris* 5 C6 48 49N 2 42 E
Ferry, *N.Y.* 23 A5 41 0N 73 52W
Fetcham, *Lon.* 4 D2 51 17N 0 21W
Feucherolles, *Paris* 5 B1 48 52N 1 58 E
Fichtenau, *Berl.* 7 B5 52 27N 13 42 E
Fields Corner, *Bost.* 21 D3 42 18N 71 3W
Fiera Camp, *Mil.* 9 E5 45 28N 9 9 E
Figino, *Mil.* 9 E5 45 29N 9 4 E
Fijir, *Bagd.* 17 E8 33 21N 44 21 E
Filadhélfia, *Ath.* 8 H11 38 2N 23 43 E
Fili-Masilovo, *Mos.* 11 E8 55 44N 37 29 E
Filothei, *Ath.* 8 H11 38 2N 23 48 E
Finaalspan, *Jobg.* 18 F10 26 16 S 28 16 E
Finchley, *Lon.* 4 B3 51 36N 0 11W
Finkenkrug, *Berl.* 7 A1 52 33N 13 3 E
Finkenwerder, *Hbg.* 7 D7 53 32N 9 51 E
Finsbury, *Lon.* 4 B4 51 31N 0 5W
Finsbury Park, *Lon.* 4 B4 51 34N 0 6W
Fiorito, *B.A.* 32 C4 34 42 S 58 26W
Firdows, *Bagd.* 17 F7 33 17N 44 17 E
Firōz Bahram, *Tehr.* 17 D4 35 37N 51 14 E
Fischeln, *Ruhr* 6 C1 51 18N 6 35 E
Fish Brook →, *Bost.* 21 B3 42 39N 71 1W
Fishermans Bend, *Melb.* 19 E6 37 49 S 144 55 E
Fisher's Hill, *Jobg.* 18 F10 26 10 S 28 10 E
Fisherville, *Trto.* 20 D8 43 46N 79 28W
Fisksätra, *Stock.* 3 E12 59 17N 18 15 E
Fittja, *Stock.* 3 E10 59 14N 17 51 E
Fitzroy Gardens, *Melb.* 19 F7 37 48 S 144 58 E
Five Cowrie Cr. →, *Lagos* 18 B2 6 26N 7 25 E
Five Dock, *Syd.* 19 B3 33 52 S 151 8 E
Fjellstrand, *Oslo* 2 C3 59 47N 10 36 E
Flachsberg, *Ruhr* 6 C4 51 11N 7 4 E
Flag →, *Chic.* 26 C1 41 43N 87 55W
Flamengo, *Rio J.* 31 B2 22 56 S 43 11W
Flaminio, *Rome* 9 F9 41 55N 12 28 E
Flaskebekk, *Oslo* 2 B3 59 51N 10 39 E
Flatbush, *N.Y.* 22 D5 40 39N 73 56W
Flaten, *Stock.* 3 E11 59 15N 18 9 E
Flemington, *Syd.* 19 B3 33 53 S 151 4 E
Flemington Racecourse, *Melb.* 19 E6 37 47 S 144 54 E
Fleury-Mérogis, *Paris* 5 D4 48 37N 2 21 E
Flingern, *Ruhr* 6 C2 51 13N 6 48 E
Flint Pk., *L.A.* 28 B3 34 9N 118 11 E
Floral Park, *N.Y.* 23 C6 40 43N 73 42W
Florence, *L.A.* 28 C3 33 57N 118 14W
Florence, *Phil.* 24 C5 39 44N 74 55W
Florence Bloom Bird Sanctuary, *Jobg.* 18 E9 26 7 S 28 0 E
Florencio Varela, *B.A.* 32 C5 34 49 S 58 18W
Florentia, *Jobg.* 18 F9 26 16 S 28 8 E
Flores, *B.A.* 32 B4 34 38 S 58 27W
Floresta, *B.A.* 32 B4 34 37 S 58 27W
Florham Park, *N.Y.* 22 C2 40 46N 74 23W
Florida, *B.A.* 32 B4 34 31 S 58 28W
Florida, *Jobg.* 18 F8 26 10 S 27 55 E
Florida L., *Jobg.* 18 F8 26 10 S 27 54 E
Floridsdorf, *Wien* 10 G10 48 15N 16 26 E
Flourtown, *Phil.* 24 A3 40 6N 75 13W
Flower Hill, *N.Y.* 23 C6 40 48N 73 40W
Flushing, *N.Y.* 23 C6 40 45N 73 49W
Flushing Meadows Corona Park, *N.Y.* 23 C5 40 44N 73 50W
Flysta, *Stock.* 3 D10 59 22N 17 54 E
Fo Tan, *H.K.* 12 D6 22 23N 114 11 E
Föhrenhain, *Wien* 10 G10 48 19N 16 26 E
Folcroft, *Phil.* 24 B3 39 53N 75 16W
Folsom, *Phil.* 24 B3 39 53N 75 19W
Fontainebleau, *Jobg.* 18 E8 26 6 S 27 57 E
Fontana, *La Hab.* 30 B2 23 1N 82 24W
Fontanka, *St-Pet.* 11 B3 59 54N 30 16 E
Fontenay-aux-Roses, *Paris* 5 C3 48 47N 2 17 E
Fontenay-le-Fleury, *Paris* 5 C2 48 48N 2 2 E
Fontenay-lès-Briis, *Paris* 5 D2 48 37N 2 9 E
Fontenay-sous-Bois, *Paris* 5 B4 48 51N 2 28 E
Foots Cray, *Lon.* 4 C5 51 24N 0 7 E
Footscray, *Melb.* 19 E6 37 48 S 144 56 E
Forbidden City, *Beij.* 14 B3 39 53N 116 21 E
Fordham Univ., *N.Y.* 23 B5 40 51N 73 51W
Fords, *N.Y.* 22 D3 40 31N 74 19W
Fordsburg, *Jobg.* 18 F9 26 12 S 28 2 E
Foremans Corner, *Balt.* 25 B3 39 11N 76 33W
Forest Gate, *Lon.* 4 B5 51 32N 0 1 E
Forest Heights, *Wash.* 25 E7 38 48N 77 0W
Forest Hill, *Lon.* 4 C4 51 26N 0 2W
Forest Hill, *Melb.* 19 F8 37 50 S 145 10 E
Forest Hill, *Trto.* 20 D8 43 41N 79 25W
Forest Hills, *N.Y.* 23 C5 40 42N 73 51W
Forest Park, *Chic.* 26 B2 41 51N 87 47W
Forest View, *Chic.* 26 C2 41 48N 87 47W
Forestville, *Syd.* 19 A4 33 46 S 151 12 E
Forestville, *Wash.* 25 D8 38 50N 76 52W
Forges-les-Bains, *Paris* 5 D2 48 37N 2 5 E
Fornacino, *Tori.* 9 B3 45 9N 7 44 E
Fornebu, *Oslo* 2 B3 59 53N 10 36 E
Fornebu Airport, *Oslo* 2 B3 59 56N 10 37 E
Foro Italico, *Rome* 9 F9 41 56N 12 26 E
Foro Romano, *Rome* 9 F9 41 53N 12 29 E
Forst Rantzau, *Hbg.* 7 C6 53 43N 9 49 E
Forstenried, *Mün.* 7 G9 48 5N 11 29 E
Forstenrieder Park, *Mün.* 7 G9 48 3N 11 27 E
Fort du Pont Park, *Wash.* 25 D8 38 52N 76 56W
Fort Foote Village, *Wash.* 25 E7 38 46N 77 1W
Fort Howard, *Balt.* 25 B4 39 12N 76 26W
Fort Lee, *N.Y.* 22 B5 40 50N 73 58W
Fort McHenry Nat. Mon., *Balt.* 25 B3 35 15N 76 35W
Fort Washington, *Phil.* 24 A3 40 8N 75 13W
Fort William, *Calc.* 16 E6 22 33N 88 20 E
Foster City, *S.F.* 27 C3 37 33N 122 15W
Fosters Pond, *Bost.* 21 B3 42 36N 71 8W
Fourcherolle, *Paris* 5 C1 48 42N 1 58 E
Fourmile Run →, *Wash.* 25 D7 38 50N 77 2W
Fourqueux, *Paris* 5 B2 48 53N 2 3 E
Fowl Meadow Res., *Bost.* 21 D3 42 13N 71 8W
Fox Chase, *Phil.* 24 A4 40 4N 75 5W
Foxhall, *Wash.* 25 C7 39 4N 77 3W
Framingham, *Bost.* 21 D1 42 18N 71 24W
Francisco Alvarez, *B.A.* 32 B1 34 38 S 58 50W
Francisquito Cr. →, *S.F.* 27 D4 37 27N 122 9W
Franconia, *Wash.* 25 E7 38 47N 77 7W
Franconville, *Paris* 5 B3 48 59N 2 13 E
Francop, *Hbg.* 7 D7 53 30N 9 51 E
Frankel, *Sing.* 15 G8 1 18N 103 55 E
Frankford, *Phil.* 24 A4 40 1N 75 5W
Franklin L., *N.Y.* 22 B3 40 59N 74 13W
Franklin Lakes, *N.Y.* 22 B3 40 59N 74 13W
Franklin Park, *Bost.* 21 D3 42 18N 71 5W
Franklin Park, *Chic.* 26 B1 41 55N 87 52W
Franklin Park, *Wash.* 25 D7 38 55N 77 9W
Franklin Res., *L.A.* 28 B2 34 5N 118 24W
Franklin Roosevelt Park, *Jobg.* 18 E8 26 8 S 27 59 E
Franklin Roosevelt Park, *Phil.* 24 B3 39 54N 75 10W
Franklin Square, *N.Y.* 23 C6 40 42N 73 40W
Frattamaggiore, *Nápl.* 9 H12 40 56N 14 16 E
Frauenkirche, *Mün.* 7 G10 48 8N 11 34 E
Frederiksberg, *Købn.* 2 D10 55 40N 12 33 E
Frederiksdal, *Købn.* 2 D9 55 46N 12 25 E
Fredersdorf, *Berl.* 7 A5 52 31N 13 45 E
Fredersdorf Nord, *Berl.* 7 A5 52 32N 13 44 E
Freeport, *N.Y.* 23 D7 40 39N 73 35W
Freidrichshain, Volkspark, *Berl.* 7 A3 52 31N 13 25 E
Freiham, *Mün.* 7 G9 48 8N 11 23 E
Freimann, *Mün.* 7 F10 48 11N 11 37 E
Fremont, *S.F.* 27 C4 37 33N 122 2W
Fresh Meadows, *N.Y.* 23 C6 40 43N 73 47W
Fresh Pond, *Bost.* 21 C3 42 22N 71 8W
Freskati, *Stock.* 3 D11 59 22N 18 3 E
Fresnes, *Paris* 5 C3 48 45N 2 18 E
Fretay, *Paris* 5 C3 48 40N 2 12 E
Freudenau, *Wien* 10 G10 48 11N 16 25 E
Friedenau, *Berl.* 7 B2 52 28N 13 20 E
Friederikenhof, *Berl.* 7 B3 52 23N 13 25 E
Friedrichsfeld, *Ruhr* 6 A1 51 37N 6 39 E
Friedrichsfelde, *Berl.* 7 B4 52 29N 13 33 E
Friedrichshagen, *Berl.* 7 B4 52 27N 13 37 E
Friedrichshain, *Berl.* 7 A3 52 31N 13 25 E
Friedrichshulde, *Hbg.* 7 D7 53 36N 9 51 E
Friedrichslust, *Berl.* 7 A5 52 33N 13 43 E
Frielas, *Lisb.* 8 F8 38 49N 9 6W
Friemersheim, *Ruhr* 6 B2 51 23N 6 42 E
Friern Barnet, *Lon.* 4 B4 51 37N 0 9W
Friherrs, *Hels.* 3 B3 60 16N 24 49 E
Frogner, *Oslo* 2 A6 60 1N 11 6 E
Frohnau, *Berl.* 7 A2 52 38N 13 16 E
Frohnhausen, *Ruhr* 6 B4 51 26N 6 58 E
Frontón, I., *Lima* 30 G7 12 7 S 77 11W
Frunze, *Mos.* 11 E9 55 43N 37 33 E
Fuchū, *Tōkyō* 13 B1 35 40N 139 29 E
Fuencarral, *Mdrd.* 8 B2 40 29N 3 42W
Fuhlenbrock, *Ruhr* 6 A3 51 32N 6 54 E
Fuhlsbüttel, *Hbg.* 7 D8 53 37N 10 1 E
Fujidera, *Ōsaka* 12 C4 34 34N 135 36 E
Fujikubo, *Tōkyō* 13 B2 35 49N 139 31 E
Fujimi, *Tōkyō* 13 A2 35 51N 139 32 E
Fukagawa, *Tōkyō* 13 C3 35 39N 139 48 E
Fukami, *Tōkyō* 13 D1 35 28N 139 29 E
Fukiai, *Ōsaka* 12 B2 34 42N 135 12 E
Fukuoka, *Tōkyō* 13 A2 35 52N 139 31 E
Fukushima, *Ōsaka* 12 B3 34 41N 135 28 E
Fulatani, *Tōkyō* 13 D1 35 22N 139 30 E
Fulham, *Lon.* 4 C3 51 28N 0 12W
Fuller Park, *L.A.* 28 C5 33 51N 117 56W
Fullerton, *Balt.* 25 A3 39 22N 76 30W
Funabori, *Tōkyō* 13 B4 35 41N 139 52 E
Funasaka, *Ōsaka* 12 B2 34 48N 135 16 E
Fünfhaus, *Wien* 10 G10 48 11N 16 20 E
Fünfhausen, *Hbg.* 7 E8 53 27N 10 2 E
Furesø, *Købn.* 2 D9 55 47N 12 25 E
Fürstenried, *Mün.* 7 G9 48 5N 11 28 E
Furth, *Mün.* 7 G10 48 2N 11 35 E
Furu →, *Tōkyō* 13 A3 35 54N 139 49 E
Furuyakami, *Tōkyō* 13 A2 35 54N 139 31 E
Futago-tamagawaen, *Tōkyō* 13 C2 35 36N 139 39 E
Futamatagawa, *Tōkyō* 13 D2 35 27N 139 31 E
Futatsubashi, *Tōkyō* 13 D1 35 28N 139 29 E
Fuxing Dao, *Shang.* 14 J12 31 16N 121 33 E
Fuxing Gongyuan, *Shang.* 14 J11 31 13N 121 27 E
Fuxinglu, *Beij.* 14 B2 39 52N 116 16 E
Fuxingmen, *Beij.* 14 B2 39 53N 116 19 E

G

Gadstrup, *Købn.* 2 E7 55 34N 12 5 E
Gaebong, *Sŏul* 12 H7 37 29N 126 52 E
Gage Park, *Chic.* 26 C2 41 47N 87 42W
Gagny, *Paris* 5 B5 48 53N 2 32 E
Gaillon, *Paris* 5 A1 49 1N 1 53 E
Galata, *Ist.* 17 A2 41 1N 28 58 E
Galátsion, *Ath.* 8 H11 38 1N 23 45 E
Galeão, *Rio J.* 31 A2 22 49 S 43 14W
Galéria →, *Rome* 9 F9 41 57N 12 20 E
Gallows Corner, *Lon.* 4 B6 51 35N 0 13 E
Gällstaö, *Stock.* 3 E10 59 17N 17 51 E
Galyanovo, *Mos.* 11 E10 55 48N 37 47 E
Galyeon, *Sŏul* 12 G7 37 36N 126 55 E
Gambir, *Jak.* 15 H9 6 9 S 106 48 E
Gamboa, *Rio J.* 31 B2 22 53 S 43 11W
Gamboloita, *Mil.* 9 E6 45 26N 9 13 E
Gamelinha →, *S. Pau.* 31 E6 23 31 S 46 31W
Gamlebyen, *Oslo* 2 B4 59 54N 10 46 E
Gamlebyen, *Shang.* 14 J11 31 13N 121 29 E
Gamō, *Tōkyō* 13 A3 35 52N 139 48 E
Gang Dong, *Sŏul* 12 G8 37 30N 127 5 E
Gang Nam, *Sŏul* 12 G8 37 30N 126 59 E
Gang Sea, *Sŏul* 12 G7 37 32N 126 51 E
Gangadharpur, *Calc.* 16 E5 22 35N 88 11 E
Gangtou, *Gzh.* 14 F7 23 12N 113 8 E
Gangwei, *Gzh.* 14 G8 23 4N 113 11 E
Ganløse, *Købn.* 2 D8 55 47N 12 15 E
Ganløse Orned, *Købn.* 2 D8 55 48N 12 16 E
Ganshi, *Gzh.* 14 F7 23 10N 113 8 E
Gants Hill, *Lon.* 4 B5 51 34N 0 4 E
Gaoqiao, *Shang.* 14 H12 31 21N 121 34 E
Garbagnate Milanese, *Mil.* 9 D5 45 34N 9 4 E
Garbatella, *Rome* 9 F10 41 51N 12 30 E
Garches, *Paris* 5 B3 48 50N 2 11 E
Garching, *Mün.* 7 F11 48 14N 11 39 E
Garden City, *El Qâ.* 18 C5 30 2N 31 14 E
Garden City, *N.Y.* 23 C7 40 43N 73 37W
Garden Reach, *Calc.* 16 E5 22 33N 88 15 E
Gardena, *L.A.* 28 C3 33 53N 118 18W
Garder, *Oslo* 2 C3 59 45N 10 38 E
Garfield, *N.Y.* 22 B4 40 52N 74 7W
Garfield Park, *Chic.* 26 B2 41 52N 87 42W
Gargareta, *Ath.* 8 J11 37 57N 23 43 E
Garges-lès-Gonesse, *Paris* 5 B4 48 58N 2 25 E
Garhi Naraina, *Delhi* 16 B1 28 37N 77 8 E
Garibong, *Sŏul* 12 H7 37 29N 126 54 E
Garin, *B.A.* 32 A2 34 25 S 58 44W
Gariya, *Calc.* 16 F6 22 28N 88 23 E
Garji, *Calc.* 16 C5 22 50N 88 19 E
Garne, *Paris* 5 C1 48 41N 1 58 E
Garrison, *Balt.* 25 A2 39 24N 76 45W
Garstedt, *Hbg.* 7 C7 53 40N 9 59 E
Gartenstadt, *Ruhr* 6 B6 51 30N 7 30 E
Garulia, *Calc.* 16 D6 22 48N 88 22 E
Garvanza, *L.A.* 28 B3 34 6N 118 11 E
Garwood, *N.Y.* 22 D3 40 38N 74 18W
Gary, *Chic.* 26 D4 41 35N 87 20W
Gåshaga, *Stock.* 3 D12 59 21N 18 13 E
Gàssino Torinese, *Tori.* 9 B3 45 7N 7 49 E
Gästerby, *Hels.* 3 C1 60 8N 24 27 E
Gateão, Aéroporto de, *Rio J.* 31 A2 22 49 S 43 15W
Gateway of India, *Bomb.* 16 H8 18 55N 72 50 E
Gatow, *Berl.* 7 B1 52 29N 13 11 E
Gaurhati, *Calc.* 16 D6 22 48N 88 21 E
Gauripur, *Calc.* 16 C6 22 53N 88 25 E
Gavá, *Barc.* 8 E5 41 18N 2 0 E
Gavamar, *Barc.* 8 E4 41 16N 1 58 E
Gavanpada, *Bomb.* 16 H9 18 57N 73 0 E
Gávea, *Rio J.* 31 B2 22 58 S 43 13W
Gávea, Pedra da, *Rio J.* 31 B2 22 59 S 43 18W
Gbogbo, *Lagos* 18 A3 6 35N 7 31 E
Gebel el Ahmar, *El Qâ.* 18 C5 30 2N 31 19 E
Gebel el Muqattam, *El Qâ.* 18 C5 30 1N 31 17 E
Gebel et Tura, *El Qâ.* 18 D5 29 56N 31 15 E
Geduld Dam, *Jobg.* 18 F11 26 12 S 28 24 E
Geiselgasteig, *Mün.* 7 G10 48 3N 11 33 E
Geist Res., *Phil.* 24 B2 39 57N 75 26W
Gellért hegy, *Bud.* 10 K13 47 29N 19 3 E
Gelsenkirchen, *Ruhr* 6 A4 51 32N 7 6 E
General Ignacio Allende, *Méx.* 29 B1 19 20N 99 21W
General Pacheco, *B.A.* 32 A3 34 27 S 58 36W
General San Martin, *B.A.* 32 B3 34 35 S 58 32W
General Sarmiento, *B.A.* 32 B2 34 32 S 58 43W
General Urquiza, *B.A.* 32 B4 34 34 S 58 28W
Gennebreck, *Ruhr* 6 C5 51 18N 7 12 E
Gennevilliers, *Paris* 5 B3 48 56N 2 17 E
Gentilly, *Paris* 5 B4 48 48N 2 21 E
Gentofte, *Købn.* 2 D10 55 44N 12 32 E
Georges →, *Syd.* 19 B2 33 56 S 150 55 E
Georges Hall, *Syd.* 19 B2 33 54 S 150 59 E
Georges I., *Bost.* 21 D4 42 19N 70 55W
Georges River Bridge, *Syd.* 19 C3 34 0 S 151 6 E
Georgetown, *Wash.* 25 D7 38 54N 77 3W
Georgetown Rowley State Forest, *Bost.* 21 A4 42 41N 70 56W
Georgsweide, *Hbg.* 7 D8 53 30N 10 1 E
Gerasdorf bei Wien, *Wien* 10 G10 48 17N 16 28 E
Gerberau, *Mün.* 7 F9 48 12N 11 27 E
Gérbido, *Tori.* 9 B2 45 2N 7 36 E
Gerlev, *Købn.* 2 D7 55 49N 12 0 E
Gerli, *B.A.* 32 C4 34 41 S 58 22W
Germantown, *Balt.* 25 A4 39 24N 76 28W
Germantown, *Phil.* 24 A3 40 3N 75 10W
Germiston, *Jobg.* 18 F9 26 13 S 28 10 E
Gerresheim, *Ruhr* 6 C3 51 14N 6 51 E
Gersthof, *Wien* 10 G9 48 14N 16 18 E
Gerthe, *Ruhr* 6 A5 51 31N 7 16 E

38 Gesîrat el Rauda

Gesîrat el Rauda, *El Qâ.* 18 C5 30 1N 31 13 E
Gesîrat Muhammad, *El Qâ.* 18 C5 30 6N 31 11 E
Gesterby, *Hels.* 3 A6 60 20N 25 17 E
Getafe, *Mdrd.* 8 C2 40 18N 3 43W
Gevelsberg, *Ruhr* 6 C6 51 19N 7 21 E
Geylang, *Sing.* 15 G8 1 18N 103 53 E
Geylang →, *Sing.* 15 G8 1 18N 103 52 E
Geylang Serai, *Sing.* 15 G8 1 19N 103 53 E
Gezîrat edn Dhahab, *El Qâ.* 18 D5 29 59N 31 13 E
Gezîrat Warrâq el Hadar, *El Qâ.* 18 C5 30 6N 31 13 E
Gharapuri, *Bomb.* 16 H8 18 57N 72 57 E
Ghatkopar, *Bomb.* 16 G8 19 4N 72 54 E
Ghazipur, *Delhi* 16 B2 28 37N 77 19 E
Ghizri, *Kar.* 17 H11 24 49N 67 2 E
Ghizri Cr. →, *Kar.* 17 H11 24 47N 67 5 E
Ghonda, *Delhi* 16 A2 28 41N 77 16 E
Ghushuri, *Calc.* 16 E6 22 37N 88 21 E
Gianicolense, *Rome* 9 F9 41 53N 12 28 E
Giant, *S.F.* 27 A2 37 58N 122 20W
Gibbsboro, *Phil.* 24 B5 39 50N 74 57W
Gibbstown, *Phil.* 24 C3 39 49N 75 17W
Gibraltar Pt., *Trto.* 20 E8 43 36N 79 23W
Gidea Park, *Lon.* 4 B6 51 35N 0 11 E
Giesing, *Mün.* 7 G10 48 6N 11 35 E
Gif-sur-Yvette, *Paris* 5 C2 48 42N 2 8 E
Gilgo Beach, *N.Y.* 23 D8 40 36N 73 24W
Gilgo I., *N.Y.* 23 D8 40 37N 73 23W
Gillette, *N.Y.* 22 C2 40 40N 74 29W
Gimmersta, *Stock.* 3 E12 59 14N 18 14 E
Ginza, *Tōkyō* 13 C3 35 39N 139 46 E
Girgaum, *Bomb.* 16 H8 18 57N 72 50 E
Giugliano in Campània, *Nápl.* 9 H12 40 55N 14 12 E
Givoletto, *Tori.* 9 B1 45 9N 7 29 E
Gjellumvatn, *Oslo* 2 C2 59 47N 10 26 E
Gjersjøen, *Oslo* 2 C4 59 47N 10 47 E
Glacier Hills, *N.Y.* 22 B2 40 51N 74 28W
Gladbeck, *Ruhr* 6 A3 51 34N 6 58 E
Gladesville, *Syd.* 19 B3 33 50 S 151 8 E
Gladökvarn, *Stock.* 3 E10 59 11N 17 59 E
Gladsakse, *Købn.* 2 D9 55 45N 12 25 E
Glashutte, *Hbg.* 7 C8 53 41N 10 2 E
Glashütte, *Ruhr* 6 C3 51 13N 6 51 E
Glasmoor, *Hbg.* 7 C8 53 42N 10 1 E
Glassmanor, *Wash.* 25 E7 38 49N 77 0W
Glen Cove, *N.Y.* 23 B7 40 52N 73 38W
Glen Echo, *Wash.* 25 D7 38 58N 77 8W
Glen Hd., *N.Y.* 23 C7 40 49N 73 37W
Glen Iris, *Melb.* 19 F7 37 51 S 145 3 E
Glen Mills, *Phil.* 24 B2 39 55N 75 29W
Glen Oaks, *N.Y.* 23 C6 40 45N 73 43W
Glen Riddle, *Phil.* 24 B2 39 53N 75 26W
Glen Ridge, *N.Y.* 22 C3 40 48N 74 12W
Glen Rock, *N.Y.* 22 B4 40 57N 74 7W
Glen Waverley, *Melb.* 19 F8 37 52 S 145 10 E
Glenardon, *Wash.* 25 D8 38 56N 76 51W
Glencoe, *Chic.* 26 A2 42 7N 87 44W
Glendale, *L.A.* 28 A3 34 9N 118 15W
Glendora, *Phil.* 24 B4 39 50N 75 4W
Glenfield, *Syd.* 19 B2 33 58 S 150 53 E
Glenhazel, *Jobg.* 18 E9 26 8 S 28 6 E
Glenhuntly, *Melb.* 19 F7 37 52 S 145 1 E
Glenmont, *Wash.* 25 C7 39 3N 77 4W
Glenolden, *Phil.* 24 B3 39 54N 75 17W
Glenroy, *Melb.* 19 E6 37 42 S 144 55 E
Glenside, *Phil.* 24 A4 40 6N 75 9W
Glenview, *Chic.* 26 A2 42 3N 87 48W
Glenview Countryside, *Chic.* 26 A2 42 3N 87 49W
Glenview Woods, *Chic.* 26 A2 42 4N 87 46W
Glenville, *N.Y.* 23 A6 41 1N 73 41W
Glenvista, *Jobg.* 18 F9 26 17 S 28 3 E
Glenwood Landing, *N.Y.* 23 C7 40 48N 73 38W
Glienicke, *Berl.* 7 A2 52 38N 13 18 E
Glömsta, *Stock.* 3 E10 59 14N 17 55 E
Glosli, *Oslo* 2 A5 60 1N 10 55 E
Glostrup, *Købn.* 2 E9 55 39N 12 23 E
Gloucester City, *Phil.* 24 B4 39 53N 75 7W
Gocheog, *Sŏul* 12 G7 37 30N 126 52 E
Gocławek, *Wsaw.* 10 E7 52 14N 21 7 E
Goeselville, *Chic.* 26 D2 41 37N 87 46W
Goetjensort, *Hbg.* 7 E8 53 29N 10 2 E
Golabari, *Calc.* 16 E6 22 35N 88 20 E
Golabki, *Wsaw.* 10 E6 52 12N 20 52 E
Golden Gate, *S.F.* 27 B2 37 48N 122 29W
Golden Gate Bridge, *S.F.* 27 B2 37 49N 122 28W
Golden Gate National Recreation Area, *S.F.* 27 B1 37 49N 122 31W
Golden Gate Park, *S.F.* 27 B2 37 46N 122 28W
Golden Horn, *Ist.* 17 A2 41 1N 28 57 E
Golders Green, *Lon.* 4 B3 51 34N 0 11W
Golyevo, *Mos.* 11 E7 55 48N 37 18 E
Gometz-la-Ville, *Paris* 5 C2 48 40N 2 7 E
Gometz-le-Châtel, *Paris* 5 C2 48 40N 2 8 E
Gondangdra, *Jak.* 15 J9 6 11 S 106 49 E
Gonesse, *Paris* 5 B4 48 59N 2 26 E
Gongreung, *Sŏul* 12 G8 37 36N 127 3 E
González Catán, *B.A.* 32 C3 34 46 S 58 38W
Goodman Hill, *Bost.* 21 C1 42 22N 71 23W
Goodmayes, *Lon.* 4 B5 51 33N 0 6 E
Gopalnagar, *Calc.* 16 E6 22 50N 88 13 E
Gopalpur, *Calc.* 16 E6 22 38N 88 26 E
Górce, *Wsaw.* 10 E6 52 15N 20 55 E
Gordon, *Syd.* 19 A3 33 46 S 151 8 E
Gore Hill, *Syd.* 19 A4 33 49 S 151 10 E
Gorelyy →, *St-Pet.* 11 A5 60 1N 30 30 E
Gorenki, *Mos.* 11 E11 55 47N 37 53 E
Gorkiy Park, *Mos.* 11 E9 55 43N 37 36 E
Görväln, *Stock.* 3 D9 59 26N 17 45 E
Gose Elbe →, *Hbg.* 7 E8 53 28N 10 6 E
Gosen, *Berl.* 7 B5 52 23N 13 43 E
Gosener kanal, *Berl.* 7 B5 52 24N 13 42 E
Goshenville, *Phil.* 24 B1 39 59N 75 32W
Gospel Oak, *Lon.* 4 B4 51 32N 0 9W
Gotanda, *Tōkyō* 13 C3 35 37N 139 43 E
Gotanno, *Tōkyō* 13 B3 35 45N 139 49 E
Goth Goli Mār, *Kar.* 17 G11 24 53N 67 1 E
Goth Sher Shāh, *Kar.* 17 G10 24 53N 66 59 E
Gournay-sur-Marne, *Paris* 5 B5 48 51N 2 34 E
Goussainville, *Paris* 5 A4 49 1N 2 27 E
Gouvernes, *Paris* 5 B6 48 51N 2 41 E
Governador, I. do, *Rio J.* 31 A2 22 48 S 43 13W
Governor's I., *N.Y.* 22 C4 40 41N 74 1W
Grabicz, *Wsaw.* 10 E8 52 19N 21 12 E
Grabów, *Wsaw.* 10 F6 52 8N 20 59 E
Gracia, *Barc.* 8 D6 41 24N 2 10 E
Gradyville, *Phil.* 24 B2 39 56N 75 27W
Gräfelfing, *Mün.* 7 G9 48 7N 11 25 E
Grafenwald, *Ruhr* 6 A3 51 34N 6 54 E
Graham Memorial Park, *Balt.* 25 A4 39 25N 76 29W
Gran Canal, *Méx.* 29 A3 19 34N 99 1W
Granada Hills, *L.A.* 28 A1 34 16N 118 30W
Grand Bourg, *B.A.* 32 A2 34 29 S 58 42W
Grand Calumet →, *Chic.* 26 D4 41 37N 87 28W
Grand Union Canal, *Lon.* 4 A2 51 42N 0 26W
Grande →, *S. Pau.* 31 F7 23 43 S 46 24W
Grange, *Tori.* 9 B1 45 7N 7 29 E
Grange Hill, *Lon.* 4 B5 51 36N 0 5 E
Granite, *Balt.* 25 A1 39 20N 76 51W
Graniteville, *N.Y.* 22 D3 40 37N 74 10W
Granja Viana, *S. Pau.* 31 E4 23 35 S 46 50W
Granlandet, *Hels.* 3 B6 60 10N 25 15 E
Granö, *Hels.* 3 B6 60 13N 25 14 E
Grant Park, *Chic.* 26 B3 41 52N 87 37W
Granville, *Syd.* 19 A3 33 49 S 151 1 E
Grape I., *Bost.* 21 D4 42 16N 70 55W
Grass Hassock Channel, *N.Y.* 23 D6 40 36N 73 47W
Grassy B., *N.Y.* 23 D6 40 37N 73 47W
Grassy Sprain Res., *N.Y.* 23 B5 40 58N 73 50W
Gratosóglio, *Mil.* 9 E6 45 24N 9 1 E
Gratzwalde, *Berl.* 7 B5 52 28N 13 42 E
Gravesend, *N.Y.* 22 D5 40 36N 73 56W
Grays, *Lon.* 4 C6 51 28N 0 19 E
Grazhdanka, *St-Pet.* 11 B4 59 59N 30 24 E
Great Blue Hill, *Bost.* 21 D3 42 12N 71 4W
Great Bookham, *Lon.* 4 D2 51 16N 0 21W
Great Brewster I., *Bost.* 21 C4 42 19N 70 53W
Great Captain I., *N.Y.* 23 B7 40 59N 73 37W
Great Falls, *Wash.* 25 C6 38 59N 77 17W
Great Falls Park, *Wash.* 25 D6 38 59N 77 14W
Great Kills, *N.Y.* 22 D4 40 32N 74 9W
Great Kills Harbour, *N.Y.* 22 D4 40 32N 74 8W
Great Neck, *N.Y.* 23 C6 40 48N 73 44W
Great Pond, *Bost.* 21 D3 42 11N 71 2W
Great South B., *N.Y.* 23 D9 40 39N 73 19W
Greco, *Mil.* 9 D6 45 30N 9 12 E
Greco I., *S.F.* 27 C3 37 30N 122 10W
Green Brae, *S.F.* 27 A1 37 57N 122 31W
Green Brook, *N.Y.* 22 D2 40 35N 74 26W
Green I., *H.K.* 12 E5 22 17N 114 6 E
Green Land, *Jak.* 15 J9 6 17 S 106 46 E
Green Pond, *N.Y.* 22 A2 41 1N 74 29W
Green Street, *Lon.* 4 A3 51 40N 0 16W
Green Street Green, *Lon.* 4 C5 51 21N 0 5 E
Green Valley, *Syd.* 19 B2 33 54 S 150 53 E
Green Village, *N.Y.* 22 C2 40 44N 74 27W
Greenbelt, *Wash.* 25 C8 39 0N 76 52W
Greenbelt Park, *Wash.* 25 D8 38 58N 76 53W
Greenfield Park, *Mtrl.* 20 B5 45 29N 73 28W
Greenfields Village, *Phil.* 24 C4 39 49N 75 9W
Greenford, *Lon.* 4 B2 51 31N 0 21W
Greenhithe, *Lon.* 4 C6 51 27N 0 17 E
Greenlawn, *N.Y.* 23 B8 40 52N 73 22W
Greenpoint, *N.Y.* 22 C5 40 43N 73 57W
Greensborough, *Melb.* 19 E7 37 41 S 145 5 E
Greenside, *Jobg.* 18 E9 26 8 S 28 1 E
Greenvale, *N.Y.* 23 C7 40 48N 73 35W
Greenville Chauncey, *N.Y.* 23 B5 40 59N 73 50W
Greenwich, *Lon.* 4 C4 51 28N 0 0 E
Greenwich, *N.Y.* 23 A7 41 1N 73 37W
Greenwich, *Syd.* 19 B4 33 50 S 151 11 E
Greenwich Observatory, *Lon.* 4 C4 51 28N 0 0 E
Greenwich Pt., *N.Y.* 23 A7 41 0N 73 34W
Greenwich Village, *N.Y.* 22 C5 40 44N 73 59W
Greenwood, *Bost.* 21 C3 42 29N 71 2W
Grefsen, *Oslo* 2 B4 59 56N 10 47 E
Grégy-sur-Yerres, *Paris* 5 C5 48 40N 2 37 E
Greiffenburg, *Ruhr* 6 B1 51 20N 6 37 E
Gressy, *Paris* 5 B6 48 58N 2 40 E
Greve Strand, *Købn.* 2 E8 55 34N 12 18 E
Greystanes, *Syd.* 19 A2 33 49 S 150 58 E
Griebnitzsee, *Berl.* 7 B1 52 23N 13 8 E
Griffith Park, *L.A.* 28 B3 34 7N 118 18W
Grignon, *Paris* 5 B1 48 50N 1 56 E
Grigny, *Paris* 5 D4 48 39N 2 23 E
Grinzing, *Wien* 10 G10 48 15N 16 20 E
Grisy-Suisnes, *Paris* 5 C6 48 41N 2 40 E
Gröbenried, *Mün.* 7 F9 48 13N 11 25 E
Grochów, *Wsaw.* 10 E7 52 15N 21 5 E
Grodzisk, *Wsaw.* 10 E7 52 19N 21 4 E
Grogol, *Jak.* 15 H9 6 9 S 106 47 E
Grogol, Kali →, *Jak.* 15 J9 6 11 S 106 47 E
Gronsdorf, *Mün.* 7 G11 48 7N 11 42 E
Grorud, *Oslo* 2 B5 59 57N 10 52 E
Gross Borstel, *Hbg.* 7 D7 53 36N 9 58 E
Gross Flottbek, *Hbg.* 7 D7 53 33N 9 53 E
Gross Glienicke, *Berl.* 7 B1 52 28N 13 6 E
Gross-Hadern, *Mün.* 7 G9 48 6N 11 29 E
Gross-Lappen, *Mün.* 7 F10 48 11N 11 35 E
Gross Krampe, *Berl.* 7 B5 52 23N 13 43 E
Grosse Müggelsee, *Berl.* 7 B4 52 26N 13 38 E
Grossenbaum, *Ruhr* 6 B2 51 22N 6 46 E
Grossenzersdorf, *Wien* 10 G11 48 12N 16 33 E
Grossenzersdorfer Arm →, *Wien* 10 G11 48 12N 16 31 E
Grosser Biberhaufen, *Wien* 10 G10 48 12N 16 28 E
Grosser Wannsee, *Berl.* 7 B2 52 25N 13 10 E
Grossfeld-Siedlung, *Wien* 10 G10 48 16N 16 26 E
Grosshesselohe, *Mün.* 7 G10 48 3N 11 32 E
Grossjedlersdorf, *Wien* 10 G10 48 16N 16 23 E
Grossziethen, *Berl.* 7 B3 52 23N 13 26 E
Groszówka, *Wsaw.* 10 E8 52 14N 21 13 E
Grove Hall, *Bost.* 21 D3 42 18N 71 4W
Grove Park, *Lon.* 4 C5 51 25N 0 1 E
Grove Park, *Lon.* 4 C3 51 28N 0 15W
Groveton, *Wash.* 25 E7 38 46N 77 6W
Grugliasco, *Tori.* 9 B2 45 5N 7 34 E
Gruiten, *Ruhr* 6 C4 51 12N 7 0 E
Grumme, *Ruhr* 6 B5 51 30N 7 15 E
Grumo Nevano, *Nápl.* 9 H12 40 56N 14 15 E
Grünau, *Berl.* 7 B4 52 25N 13 34 E
Grunewald, *Berl.* 7 B2 52 28N 13 15 E
Grünwald, *Mün.* 7 G10 48 2N 11 31 E
Grünwalder Forst, *Mün.* 7 G10 48 2N 11 33 E
Grymes Hill, *N.Y.* 22 D4 40 36N 74 6W
Gu Ro, *Sŏul* 12 G7 37 30N 126 51 E
Guadalupe, *Manila* 15 D4 14 34N 121 2 E
Guadalupe →, *S.F.* 27 D4 37 23N 122 4W
Guadalupe, Basilica de, *Méx.* 29 B3 19 29N 99 7W
Guadelupe, *Rio J.* 31 A2 22 49 S 43 20W
Guanabacoa, *La Hab.* 30 B3 23 7N 82 17W
Guanabara, *Rio J.* 31 B1 22 57 S 43 20W
Guanabara, B. de, *Rio J.* 31 B2 22 52 S 43 10W
Guanabara, Jardim, *Rio J.* 31 A2 22 48 S 43 11W
Guang'anmen, *Beij.* 14 B2 39 51N 116 18 E
Guangminglou, *Beij.* 14 B3 39 51N 116 25 E
Guangqumen, *Beij.* 14 B3 39 52N 116 25 E
Guangzhou, *Gzh.* 14 G8 23 6N 113 13 E
Guanshuo, *Gzh.* 14 G9 23 4N 113 22 E
Guantai, *Nápl.* 9 H12 40 52N 14 11 E
Guapira →, *S. Pau.* 31 D6 23 30 S 46 33W
Guarapiranga, Res. de, *S. Pau.* 31 F5 23 42 S 46 43W
Guardias, *Mdrd.* 8 B3 40 29N 3 31W
Guarulhos, *S. Pau.* 31 D7 23 28 S 46 32W
Guatao, *La Hab.* 30 B2 23 0N 82 29W
Guayacanes, Pta., *La Hab.* 30 A3 23 10N 82 16W
Gubernador Monteverde, *B.A.* 32 C5 34 47 S 58 16W
Gudö, *Stock.* 3 E12 59 12N 18 12 E
Güell, Parque de, *Barc.* 8 D6 41 24N 2 10 E
Guermantes, *Paris* 5 B6 48 51N 2 42 E
Gugging, *Wien* 10 G9 48 18N 16 15 E
Guianazes, *S. Pau.* 31 E7 23 32 S 46 24W
Guildford, *Syd.* 19 B2 33 51 S 150 59 E
Guinardó, *Barc.* 8 D6 41 24N 2 10 E
Gujiazhai, *Shang.* 14 H11 31 21N 121 23 E
Gulbāi, *Kar.* 17 G10 24 52N 66 58 E
Guldasteh, *Tehr.* 17 D4 35 36N 51 15 E
Gulistan Palace, *Tehr.* 17 C5 35 40N 51 24 E
Gulph Mills, *Phil.* 24 A2 40 4N 75 20W
Gumbostrand, *Hels.* 3 B6 60 15N 25 17 E
Güngören, *Ist.* 17 A2 41 1N 28 52 E
Gunnarsby, *Hels.* 3 C1 60 6N 24 28 E
Gunnersbury, *Lon.* 4 C3 51 29N 0 17W
Gunnigfeld, *Ruhr* 6 B4 51 29N 7 8 E
Gunpowder Falls →, *Balt.* 25 A4 39 23N 76 36W
Gunung Sahari, *Jak.* 15 H9 6 9 S 106 49 E
Gupiing, *Manila* 15 E5 14 27N 121 11 E
Guryong San, *Sŏul* 12 H8 37 28N 127 3 E
Gustavsberg, *Stock.* 3 E13 59 19N 18 23 E
Guttenberg, *N.Y.* 22 C4 40 48N 74 0W
Gutuyevskiy, Os., *St-Pet.* 11 B3 59 53N 30 15 E
Guyancourt, *Paris* 5 C2 48 46N 2 4 E
Guyancourt, Aérodrome de, *Paris* 5 C2 48 45N 2 3 E
Gvali-patak →, *Bud.* 10 K13 47 23N 19 7 E
Gwan Ag, *Sŏul* 12 H7 37 29N 126 57 E
Gwanag San, *Sŏul* 12 H7 37 27N 126 58 E
Gwynns Falls →, *Balt.* 25 B2 39 19N 76 42W
Gyál, *Bud.* 10 K14 47 23N 19 13 E
Gyeongbong Palace, *Sŏul* 12 G7 37 34N 126 58 E
Gynea, *Syd.* 19 C3 34 1 S 151 5 E

H

Haaga, *Hels.* 3 B4 60 13N 24 53 E
Haan, *Ruhr* 6 C3 51 11N 6 59 E
Haar, *Mün.* 7 G11 48 6N 11 43 E
Haar, *Ruhr* 6 B5 51 26N 7 13 E
Haarzopf, *Ruhr* 6 B3 51 25N 6 57 E
Habana del Este, *La Hab.* 30 B3 23 9N 82 19W
Habay, *Manila* 15 E3 14 27N 120 56 E
Habikino, *Ōsaka* 12 C4 34 33N 135 36 E
Habinghorst, *Ruhr* 6 A5 51 34N 7 18 E
Hacienda Heights, *L.A.* 28 C5 33 59N 117 59W
Hackbridge, *Lon.* 4 C4 51 23N 0 9W
Hackensack, *N.Y.* 22 B4 40 52N 74 4W
Hackney, *Lon.* 4 B4 51 32N 0 3W
Hackney Wick, *Lon.* 4 B4 51 32N 0 1W
Haddon Heights, *Phil.* 24 B4 39 53N 75 3W
Haddonfield, *Phil.* 24 B4 39 53N 75 3W
Hadersdorf, *Wien* 10 G9 48 12N 16 14 E
Hadley Wood, *Lon.* 4 B3 51 39N 0 10W
Haga, *Stock.* 3 D11 59 21N 18 1 E
Hagem, *Ruhr* 6 A5 51 38N 7 19 E
Hagen, *Ruhr* 6 B6 51 21N 7 27 E
Hägersten, *Stock.* 3 E10 59 18N 17 59 E
Hägetts Pond, *Bost.* 21 B2 42 39N 71 11W
Häggvik, *Stock.* 3 D10 59 26N 17 56 E
Hagonoy, *Manila* 15 D4 14 30N 121 4 E
Hagsätra, *Stock.* 3 E11 59 15N 18 0 E
Hahipur, *Calc.* 16 D5 22 47N 88 10 E
Hahnerberg, *Ruhr* 6 C4 51 12N 7 9 E
Hai He →, *Tianj.* 14 E6 39 4N 117 17 E
Haidarpur, *Delhi* 16 A1 28 43N 77 8 E
Haidhausen, *Mün.* 7 G10 48 7N 11 36 E
Haidian, *Beij.* 14 B2 39 59N 116 18 E
Haight-Ashbury, *S.F.* 27 B2 37 46N 122 26W
Haiguangsi, *Tianj.* 14 E6 39 7N 117 11 E
Hainault, *Lon.* 4 B5 51 36N 0 6 E
Haizhu Guangchang, *Gzh.* 14 G8 23 6N 113 14 E
Hakim, *El Qâ.* 18 C4 30 4N 31 7 E
Hakunila, *Hels.* 3 B5 60 16N 25 6 E
Halchōbori, *Tōkyō* 13 B4 35 48N 139 55 E
Haledon, *N.Y.* 22 B3 40 57N 74 11W
Halesite, *N.Y.* 23 B8 40 53N 73 24W
Halethorpe, *Balt.* 25 B2 39 14N 76 41W
Half Hollow Hills, *N.Y.* 23 C8 40 48N 73 21W
Half Moon B., *S.F.* 26 D2 37 27N 122 25W
Half Moon Bay Airport, *S.F.* 27 C1 37 31N 122 30W
Half Moon Bay Beaches, *S.F.* 26 D2 37 28N 122 28W
Halim, *Jak.* 15 J10 6 15 S 106 53 E
Halim Perdanakusuma Airport, *Jak.* 15 J10 6 16 S 106 53 E
Halstead, *Lon.* 4 D5 51 19N 0 8 E
Halstenbeck, *Hbg.* 7 D7 53 38N 9 50 E
Haltiala, *Hels.* 3 B4 60 16N 24 57 E
Haltiavuori, *Hels.* 3 B4 60 16N 24 56 E
Ham, *Lon.* 4 C3 51 25N 0 18W
Ham, *Paris* 5 A2 49 1N 2 4 E
Hamberg, *Jobg.* 18 E8 26 9 S 27 54 E
Hamborn, *Ruhr* 6 B2 51 29N 6 46 E
Hamburg, *Hbg.* 7 D8 53 33N 10 0 E
Hamburg Flughafen, *Hbg.* 7 D7 53 38N 9 59 E
Hämeenkylä, *Hels.* 3 B3 60 16N 24 48 E
Hamm, *Hbg.* 7 D8 53 33N 10 1 E
Hamm, *Ruhr* 6 C2 51 12N 6 44 E
Hammarby, *Stock.* 3 E11 59 17N 18 5 E
Hamme, *Ruhr* 6 B5 51 29N 7 12 E
Hammel Arverne, *N.Y.* 23 D6 40 35N 73 48W
Hammerbrook, *Hbg.* 7 D8 53 32N 10 1 E
Hammersmith, *Lon.* 4 C3 51 29N 0 14W
Hammond, *Chic.* 26 D4 41 36N 87 29W
Hampstead, *Lon.* 4 B3 51 33N 0 10W
Hampstead, *Mtrl.* 20 B4 45 28N 73 37W
Hampstead Garden Suburb, *Lon.* 4 B3 51 34N 0 11W
Hampstead Heath, *Lon.* 4 B3 51 33N 0 10W
Hampton Court Palace, *Lon.* 4 C2 51 24N 0 20W
Hampton Hill, *Lon.* 4 C2 51 25N 0 21W
Hampton Wick, *Lon.* 4 C3 51 24N 0 18W
Hamrā, *Bagd.* 17 F7 33 18N 44 18 E
Han Gang →, *Sŏul* 12 G7 37 32N 126 55 E
Hanakuri, *Tōkyō* 13 A3 35 50N 139 47 E
Hanala, *Hels.* 3 A5 60 18N 25 4 E
Hancho, *Ōsaka* 12 B3 34 48N 135 28 E
Haneda, *Tōkyō* 13 C3 35 32N 139 44 E
Hang Hau, *H.K.* 12 E6 22 19N 114 16 E
Hanjiashu, *Tianj.* 14 D5 39 11N 117 4 E
Hanlon, *Trto.* 20 E7 43 38N 79 39W
Hansen Flood Control Basin, *L.A.* 28 A2 34 15N 118 23W
Hansia, *Calc.* 16 D6 22 48N 88 25 E
Hanskinen, *Hels.* 3 C6 60 8N 25 15 E
Hanwell, *Lon.* 4 B2 51 30N 0 19W
Hanworth, *Lon.* 4 C2 51 25N 0 22W
Haora, *Calc.* 16 E5 22 34N 88 18 E
Happy Valley, *H.K.* 12 E6 22 16N 114 10 E
Harajuku, *Tōkyō* 13 D2 35 22N 139 30 E
Haraki, *Tōkyō* 13 B4 35 42N 139 56 E
Harat, *Calc.* 16 C5 22 52N 88 11 E
Harbor Hills, *N.Y.* 23 C6 40 46N 73 44W
Harburg, *Hbg.* 7 E7 53 27N 9 59 E
Harding, *Bost.* 21 D2 42 12N 71 19W
Hardricourt, *Paris* 5 A1 49 0N 1 53 E
Harefield, *Lon.* 4 B1 51 36N 0 28W
Hareskovby, *Købn.* 2 D9 55 45N 12 23 E
Harewood Park, *Balt.* 25 A4 39 22N 76 21W
Harigaya, *Tōkyō* 13 B2 35 49N 139 33 E
Haringey, *Lon.* 4 B4 51 34N 0 4W
Haripur, *Calc.* 16 D5 22 42N 88 10 E
Harjula, *Hels.* 3 B6 60 21N 25 14 E
Harjusuo, *Hels.* 3 B5 60 19N 25 0 E
Harkortsee, *Ruhr* 6 B6 51 23N 7 24 E
Harksheide, *Hbg.* 7 C8 53 43N 10 0 E
Harlaching, *Mün.* 7 G10 48 5N 11 33 E
Harlem, *N.Y.* 22 C5 40 48N 73 56W
Harlesden, *Lon.* 4 B3 51 32N 0 14W
Harlington, *Lon.* 4 C2 51 29N 0 25W
Harmaja, *Hels.* 3 C4 60 6N 24 58 E
Harmashatar hegy, *Bud.* 10 J13 47 33N 19 0 E
Harmondsworth, *Lon.* 4 C2 51 29N 0 29W
Harmonville, *Phil.* 24 A3 40 5N 75 18W
Harold Hill, *Lon.* 4 B6 51 36N 0 14 E
Harold Parker State Forest, *Bost.* 21 B3 42 37N 71 4W
Harold Wood, *Lon.* 4 B6 51 35N 0 14 E
Harrington Park, *N.Y.* 22 B5 40 59N 73 59W
Harrison, *N.Y.* 22 C4 40 44N 74 9W
Harrison, *N.Y.* 23 B6 40 57N 73 42W
Harrisonville, *Balt.* 25 A2 39 22N 76 49W
Harrow, *Lon.* 4 B2 51 34N 0 20W
Harrow on the Hill, *Lon.* 4 B2 51 34N 0 21W
Harrow School, *Lon.* 4 B2 51 34N 0 20W
Harrow Weald, *Lon.* 4 B2 51 36N 0 20W
Hart I., *Balt.* 25 B4 39 14N 76 23W
Hart I., *N.Y.* 23 B6 40 51N 73 46W
Hartford, *Phil.* 24 B5 39 58N 74 53W
Hartley, *Lon.* 4 C6 51 22N 0 18 E
Hartsdale, *N.Y.* 23 A6 41 1N 73 48W
Harumi, *Tōkyō* 13 C3 35 38N 139 47 E
Harvard, Mt., *L.A.* 28 A4 34 12N 118 4W
Harvard Univ., *Bost.* 21 C3 42 23N 71 7W
Harvestehude, *Hbg.* 7 D7 53 34N 9 58 E
Harvey, *Chic.* 26 D3 41 36N 87 39W
Harwood Heights, *Chic.* 26 B2 41 57N 87 46W
Hasanābād, *Tehr.* 17 C4 35 44N 51 16 E
Hasbrouck Heights, *N.Y.* 22 B4 40 51N 74 4W
Haselbach, *Wien* 10 G9 48 18N 16 14 E
Haselhorst, *Berl.* 7 A2 52 33N 13 14 E
Hasköy, *Ist.* 17 A2 41 2N 28 57 E
Hasle, *Oslo* 2 C3 59 46N 10 38 E
Hasloh, *Hbg.* 7 C7 53 41N 9 54 E
Haslohfeld, *Hbg.* 7 C7 53 41N 9 56 E
Haslum, *Oslo* 2 B3 59 55N 10 34 E
Haspe, *Ruhr* 6 B6 51 21N 7 25 E
Haspertalsp, *Ruhr* 6 C6 51 17N 7 24 E
Hasselbeck, *Ruhr* 6 C3 51 19N 6 56 E
Hässelby, *Stock.* 3 D10 59 22N 17 50 E
Hasslinghausen, *Ruhr* 6 C5 51 20N 7 16 E
Hasten, *Ruhr* 6 C5 51 11N 7 11 E
Hästhagen, *Stock.* 3 E11 59 18N 18 9 E
Hastings-on-Hudson, *N.Y.* 23 B5 40 59N 73 51W
Hatch End, *Lon.* 4 B2 51 36N 0 22W
Hatiara, *Calc.* 16 E6 22 36N 88 26 E
Hatogaya, *Tōkyō* 13 B3 35 49N 139 44 E
Hattingen, *Ruhr* 6 B5 51 23N 7 11 E
Hatton, *Lon.* 4 C2 51 28N 0 25W
Hattori, *Ōsaka* 12 A4 34 51N 135 26 E
Hauketo, *Oslo* 2 B4 59 50N 10 48 E
Hauldres →, *Paris* 5 D5 48 37N 2 37 E
Hausbruch, *Hbg.* 7 E7 53 28N 9 53 E
Havalimani, *Ist.* 17 B2 40 59N 28 50 E
Havana = La Habana, *La Hab.* 30 B2 23 7N 82 21W
Havdrup, *Købn.* 2 E7 55 33N 12 7 E
Havel →, *Berl.* 7 A2 52 37N 13 11 E
Havelkanal, *Berl.* 7 A2 52 36N 13 10 E
Haverford, *Phil.* 24 A3 40 0N 75 18W
Havering, *Lon.* 4 B6 51 33N 0 12 E
Havering-atte-Bower, *Lon.* 4 B6 51 37N 0 11 E
Havertown, *Phil.* 24 B3 39 58N 75 18W
Hawangsibri, *Sŏul* 12 G8 37 33N 127 1 E
Haweolgog, *Sŏul* 12 G8 37 35N 127 1 E
Haworth, *N.Y.* 22 B5 40 57N 73 59W
Hawthorne, *L.A.* 28 C2 33 54N 118 21W
Hawthorne, *N.Y.* 22 B4 40 57N 74 8W
Hayes, *Lon.* 4 C5 51 22N 0 0 E
Hayes, *Lon.* 4 B2 51 30N 0 25W
Hayes End, *Lon.* 4 B2 51 31N 0 25W
Hayford, *Chic.* 26 C2 41 45N 87 42W
Hayward, *S.F.* 27 C4 37 40N 122 4W
Hayward Fault, *S.F.* 27 B3 37 46N 122 10W
Haywood Municipal Airport, *S.F.* 27 C4 37 39N 122 9W
Headley, *Lon.* 4 D3 51 16N 0 16W
Headstone, *Lon.* 4 B2 51 35N 0 21W
Heard Pond, *Bost.* 21 C1 42 20N 71 23W
Heart Pond, *Bost.* 21 B1 42 33N 71 23W
Heath Park, *Lon.* 4 B6 51 34N 0 12 E
Heathmont, *Melb.* 19 E8 37 49 S 145 14 E
Heathrow Airport, *Lon.* 4 C2 51 28N 0 27W
Hebbville, *Balt.* 25 A2 39 20N 76 45W
Hebe Haven, *H.K.* 12 D6 22 21N 114 15 E
Hebei, *Tianj.* 14 E6 39 9N 117 11 E
Hedehusene, *Købn.* 2 E8 55 39N 12 11 E
Hedong, *Gzh.* 14 G8 23 5N 113 14 E
Hedong, *Tianj.* 14 E6 39 7N 117 11 E
Heerdt, *Ruhr* 6 C2 51 13N 6 42 E
Hegewisch, *Chic.* 26 D3 41 39N 87 32W
Heggelielva →, *Oslo* 2 A3 60 1N 10 36 E
Heide, *Ruhr* 6 B3 51 31N 6 50 E
Heidelberg, *Melb.* 19 E7 37 45 S 145 4 E
Heidelberg West, *Melb.* 19 E7 37 43 S 145 2 E
Heidemühle, *Berl.* 7 B5 52 29N 13 40 E
Heidhausen, *Ruhr* 6 B4 51 22N 7 1 E
Heiligenhaus, *Ruhr* 6 C3 51 19N 6 57 E
Heiligensee, *Berl.* 7 A2 52 36N 13 13 E
Heiligenstadt, *Wien* 10 G10 48 14N 16 21 E
Heimfeld, *Hbg.* 7 E7 53 28N 9 57 E
Heinässuo, *Hels.* 3 B1 60 18N 24 27 E
Heinersdorf, *Berl.* 7 A3 52 34N 13 26 E
Heisingen, *Ruhr* 6 B4 51 24N 7 3 E
Heissen, *Ruhr* 6 B3 51 25N 6 56 E
Helderkruin, *Jobg.* 18 E8 26 7 S 27 51 E
Helenelund, *Stock.* 3 D10 59 24N 17 58 E
Heliopolis, *El Qâ.* 18 C5 30 5N 31 19 E
Hellersdorf, *Berl.* 7 A4 52 32N 13 35 E
Hellerup, *Købn.* 2 D10 55 44N 12 33 E
Helmahof, *Wien* 10 G11 48 18N 16 34 E
Helsingfors = Helsinki, *Hels.* 3 B4 60 10N 24 55 E
Helsinki, *Hels.* 3 B4 60 10N 24 55 E
Helsinki Airport, *Hels.* 3 B4 60 18N 24 58 E
Hempstead, *N.Y.* 23 C7 40 42N 73 37W
Hempstead Harbor, *N.Y.* 23 B7 40 50N 73 39W
Henan, *Gzh.* 14 G8 23 5N 113 14 E
Hendon, *Lon.* 4 B3 51 35N 0 14W
Hengsha, *Gzh.* 14 G8 23 9N 113 12 E
Hengsteysee, *Ruhr* 6 B6 51 24N 7 27 E
Hennigsdorf, *Berl.* 7 A2 52 38N 13 12 E
Henrichenburg, *Ruhr* 6 A5 51 35N 7 19 E
Henriville, *Paris* 5 C1 48 44N 1 56 E
Henrykow, *Wsaw.* 10 E6 52 19N 20 58 E
Henson Cr. →, *Wash.* 25 E8 38 47N 76 58W
Henttaa, *Hels.* 3 B3 60 11N 24 45 E
Heping, *Tianj.* 14 E6 39 7N 117 11 E
Heping Gongyuan, *Shang.* 14 J12 31 16N 121 30 E
Hepingli, *Beij.* 14 B3 39 57N 116 23 E
Herbeck, *Ruhr* 6 C5 51 12N 7 18 E
Herbede, *Ruhr* 6 B5 51 25N 7 16 E
Herblay, *Paris* 5 B2 48 59N 2 9 E
Herdecke, *Ruhr* 6 B6 51 24N 7 26 E
Herlev, *Købn.* 2 D9 55 43N 12 27 E
Hermannskogel, *Wien* 10 G9 48 16N 16 17 E
Hermitage and Winter Palace, *St-Pet.* 11 B3 59 55N 30 19 E
Hermosa Beach, *L.A.* 28 C2 33 51N 118 23W
Hermsdorf, *Berl.* 7 A2 52 37N 13 18 E
Hernals, *Wien* 10 G10 48 13N 16 20 E
Herne, *Ruhr* 6 A5 51 32N 7 13 E
Herne Hill, *Lon.* 4 C4 51 27N 0 6W
Hernwood Heights, *Balt.* 25 A2 39 22N 76 49W
Héroes de Churubusco, *Méx.* 29 B3 19 21N 99 6W
Herongate, *Lon.* 4 B7 51 35N 0 21 E
Herons, Î. aux, *Mtrl.* 20 B4 45 25N 73 34W
Herricks, *N.Y.* 23 C7 40 45N 73 39W
Herring Run →, *Balt.* 25 B3 39 18N 76 30W
Hersham, *Lon.* 4 C2 51 21N 0 22W
Herstedøster, *Købn.* 2 D9 55 40N 12 22 E
Herten, *Ruhr* 6 A4 51 35N 7 8 E
Herttoniemi, *Hels.* 3 B5 60 12N 25 2 E
Hessler, *Ruhr* 6 A4 51 31N 7 3 E
Heston, *Lon.* 4 C2 51 28N 0 22W
Hetterscheidt, *Ruhr* 6 C3 51 20N 6 59 E
Hetzendorf, *Wien* 10 H9 48 9N 16 17 E
Heuberg, *Wien* 10 G9 48 13N 16 16 E
Heven, *Ruhr* 6 B5 51 26N 7 18 E
Hewlett Neck, *N.Y.* 23 D6 40 37N 73 41W
Hexi, *Tianj.* 14 E5 39 8N 117 9 E
Hexingcun, *Tianj.* 14 E6 39 6N 117 10 E
Hextable, *Lon.* 4 C6 51 24N 0 10 E
Heybridge, *Lon.* 4 B7 51 39N 0 22 E
Hibernia, *N.Y.* 22 B2 40 57N 74 29W
Hickory Hills, *Chic.* 26 C2 41 43N 87 49W
Hicksville, *N.Y.* 23 C7 40 46N 73 30W
Hiddinghausen, *Ruhr* 6 B5 51 21N 7 17 E
Hiekkaharju, *Hels.* 3 B5 60 18N 25 2 E
Hiesfeld, *Ruhr* 6 A2 51 33N 6 46 E
Hietaniemi, *Hels.* 3 B4 60 10N 24 54 E
Hietzing, *Wien* 10 G9 48 10N 16 17 E
Higashi, *Ōsaka* 12 B4 34 41N 135 30 E
Higashi-kaizuka, *Tōkyō* 13 A3 35 50N 139 46 E
Higashimonzen, *Tōkyō* 13 A3 35 55N 139 40 E
Higashimurayama, *Tōkyō* 13 B1 35 45N 139 26 E
Higashinada, *Ōsaka* 12 B2 34 42N 135 15 E
Higashinari, *Ōsaka* 12 B4 34 40N 135 32 E
Higashiōsaka, *Ōsaka* 12 C4 34 39N 135 37 E
Higashisumiyoshi, *Ōsaka* 12 C4 34 37N 135 31 E
Higashiyodogawa, *Ōsaka* 12 B3 34 44N 135 28 E
High Beach, *Lon.* 4 B5 51 39N 0 1 E
High Junk Pk., *H.K.* 12 E6 22 17N 114 17 E
High Park, *Trto.* 20 E8 43 38N 79 27W
Higham Hill, *Lon.* 4 B4 51 35N 0 2W
Highbury, *Lon.* 4 B4 51 33N 0 6W
Highgate, *Lon.* 4 B4 51 34N 0 8W
Highland Cr. →, *Trto.* 20 D9 43 45N 79 13W
Highland Creek, *Trto.* 20 D9 43 46N 79 8W
Highland Park, *L.A.* 28 B3 34 7N 118 13W
Highland Park, *N.Y.* 22 D2 40 30N 74 25W
Highlands North, *Jobg.* 18 E9 26 8 S 28 5 E
Highway Highlands, *L.A.* 28 A3 34 14N 118 16W
Higurashi, *Tōkyō* 13 B4 35 47N 139 55 E
Hila, *Méx.* 29 A2 19 35N 99 17W
Hillcrest Heights, *Wash.* 25 E8 38 49N 76 57W
Hillerheide, *Ruhr* 6 A5 51 35N 7 12 E
Hilleshög, *Stock.* 3 D9 59 23N 17 42 E
Hillgrove District, *L.A.* 28 B5 34 1N 117 58W
Hillingdon, *Lon.* 4 B2 51 32N 0 27W
Hillingdon Heath, *Lon.* 4 B2 51 31N 0 26W
Hillsborough, *S.F.* 27 C2 37 32N 122 21W
Hillsdale, *N.Y.* 22 A4 41 0N 74 1W
Hillsdale, *S.F.* 27 C3 37 32N 122 18W
Hillsdale Manor, *N.Y.* 22 A4 41 1N 74 3W
Hillside, *Chic.* 26 B1 41 52N 87 55W
Hillside, *N.Y.* 23 C6 40 42N 73 46W
Hillside Manor, *N.Y.* 23 C6 40 44N 73 40W
Hilltop, *Phil.* 24 C4 39 49N 75 4W
Hillwood, *Wash.* 25 D7 38 52N 77 9W
Hilmîya, *El Qâ.* 18 C5 30 6N 31 19 E
Hiltrop, *Ruhr* 6 A5 51 31N 7 15 E
Hindsby, *Hels.* 3 A6 60 20N 25 13 E
Hingham, *Bost.* 21 D4 42 14N 70 54W
Hingham B., *Bost.* 21 D4 42 17N 70 56W
Hingham Harbor, *Bost.* 21 D4 42 15N 70 53W
Hino, *Tōkyō* 13 D2 35 23N 139 35 E
Hinsbeck, *Ruhr* 6 B4 51 25N 7 4 E
Hinschenfelde, *Hbg.* 7 D8 53 35N 10 5 E
Hinsdale, *Chic.* 26 C1 41 47N 87 55W
Hinterhainbach, *Wien* 10 G9 48 14N 16 13 E
Hintersdorf, *Wien* 10 G9 48 18N 16 13 E
Hirakata, *Ōsaka* 12 A5 34 48N 135 38 E
Hirota, *Ōsaka* 12 B3 34 45N 135 20 E
Hirschstetten, *Wien* 10 G10 48 14N 16 27 E
Hither Green, *Lon.* 4 C4 51 26N 0 0 E
Hiyoshi, *Tōkyō* 13 C2 35 32N 139 38 E
Hjortekær, *Købn.* 2 D10 55 47N 12 32 E
Hjortespring, *Købn.* 2 D9 55 44N 12 25 E
Hlubočepy, *Pra.* 10 B2 50 2N 14 23 E
Ho Chung, *H.K.* 12 D6 22 21N 114 14 E
Ho Man Tin, *H.K.* 12 E6 22 18N 114 11 E
Hoboken, *N.Y.* 22 C4 40 44N 74 3W
Hobsons B., *Melb.* 19 F6 37 51 S 144 55 E
Hochbrück, *Mün.* 7 F10 48 14N 11 37 E
Hochdahl, *Ruhr* 6 C3 51 13N 6 55 E
Hochemmerich, *Ruhr* 6 B2 51 24N 6 41 E
Hochfeld, *Ruhr* 6 B2 51 25N 6 45 E
Hochheide, *Ruhr* 6 B2 51 27N 6 40 E
Hochlar, *Ruhr* 6 A5 51 36N 7 11 E
Hochlarmark, *Ruhr* 6 A4 51 34N 7 11 E
Hodgkins, *Chic.* 26 C1 41 46N 87 53W
Hodogaya-Ku, *Tōkyō* 13 D2 35 26N 139 35 E
Hoegi, *Sŏul* 12 G8 37 35N 127 3 E
Hofberg, *Wien* 10 G10 48 12N 16 21 E
Hoffman I., *N.Y.* 22 D4 40 34N 74 4W
Hofstede, *Ruhr* 6 A5 51 30N 7 11 E
Höggarnsfjärden, *Stock.* 3 D13 59 22N 18 22 E
Hohe Mark, Naturpark, *Ruhr* 6 A2 51 35N 6 49 E
Hohe Schaar, *Hbg.* 7 E7 53 29N 9 58 E
Hohenbrunn, *Mün.* 7 G11 48 2N 11 42 E
Hohenfelde, *Hbg.* 7 D8 53 33N 10 1 E
Hohenkirchen, *Mün.* 7 G11 48 1N 11 42 E
Hohenraden, *Hbg.* 7 C6 53 41N 9 49 E
Hohenschönhausen, *Berl.* 7 A4 52 33N 13 30 E
Hohenwisch, *Hbg.* 7 E7 53 29N 9 53 E

Kennedy Grove Regional Rec. Area 39

Hohokus, N.Y. 22 A4 41 0N 74 5W
Hok Tsui, H.K. 12 E6 22 12N 114 15 E
Holborn, Lon. 4 B4 51 31N 0 7W
Holešovice, Pra. 10 B2 50 6N 14 28 E
Holland Village, Sing. 15 G7 1 18N 103 47 E
Hollis, N.Y. 23 C6 40 42N 73 45W
Höllriegelskreuth, Mün. 7 G9 48 2N 11 30 E
Holly Oak, Phil. 24 C2 39 47N 75 27W
Hollydale, L.A. 28 C4 33 55N 118 10W
Hollywood Bowl, L.A. 28 B2 34 6N 118 21W
Hollywood-Burbank Airport, L.A. 28 A2 34 11N 118 21W
Holmenkollen, Oslo 2 B4 59 57N 10 41 E
Holmes, Phil. 24 B3 39 53N 75 18W
Holmes Acres, Wash. 25 D6 38 51N 77 13W
Holmes Run →, Wash. 25 E7 38 48N 77 6W
Holmesburg, Phil. 24 A4 40 2N 75 2W
Holmgård, Stock. 3 E10 59 14N 18 0 E
Holsfjorden, Oslo 2 B1 59 58N 10 17 E
Holsterhausen, Ruhr 6 A5 51 32N 7 11 E
Holte, Købn. 2 D9 55 48N 12 27 E
Holten, Ruhr 6 A2 51 31N 6 47 E
Holthausen, Ruhr 6 B4 51 25N 7 5 E
Holzbüttgen, Ruhr 6 C1 51 13N 6 37 E
Homberg, Ruhr 6 B2 51 27N 6 41 E
Hombruch, Ruhr 6 B6 51 28N 7 27 E
Homerton, Lon. 4 B4 51 32N 0 2W
Homestead Lake, Jobg. 18 F10 26 10 S 28 17 E
Homestead Valley, S.F. 27 A1 37 53N 122 32W
Hometown, Chic. 26 C2 41 44N 87 42W
Homledal, Oslo 2 B1 59 59N 10 18 E
Homówek, Wsaw. 10 E5 52 17N 20 48 E
Hon-gyōtoku, Tōkyō 13 B4 35 41N 139 57 E
Hōnanchō, Tōkyō 13 B2 35 40N 139 39 E
Honcho, Tōkyō 13 B3 35 40N 139 41 E
Honden, Tōkyō 13 B4 35 43N 139 50 E
Honeydew, Jobg. 18 E8 26 4 S 27 55 E
Hong Kah, Sing. 15 F7 1 21N 103 43 E
Hong Kong, H.K. 12 E5 22 17N 114 11 E
Hong Kong, Univ. of, H.K. 12 E5 22 16N 114 8 E
Hong Kong Airport, H.K. 12 E6 22 19N 114 11 E
Hong Kong I., H.K. 12 E6 22 16N 114 11 E
Hong Lim Park, Sing. 15 G8 1 17N 103 50 E
Hongeun, Sŏul 12 G7 37 35N 126 56 E
Hongqiao, Shang. 14 J11 31 12N 121 22 E
Honggou, Shang. 14 J11 31 16N 121 29 E
Hongkou Gongyuan, Shang. 14 J11 31 17N 121 28 E
Hongmiao, Beij. 14 B3 39 54N 116 26 E
Hongqiao, Tianj. 14 E5 39 8N 117 9 E
Hongqiao Airport, Shang. 14 J10 31 12N 121 19 E
Honjyo, Tōkyō 13 B3 35 41N 139 48 E
Honmoku, Tōkyō 13 D2 35 24N 139 39 E
Hönow, Berl. 7 A4 52 32N 13 38 E
Höntrop, Ruhr 6 B4 51 27N 7 9 E
Hood Pond, Bost. 21 A4 42 40N 70 57W
Hooghly →, Calc. 16 D6 22 41N 88 21 E
Hook, Lon. 4 C3 51 22N 0 17W
Hopelawn, N.Y. 22 D3 40 31N 74 17W
Hörde, Ruhr 6 B7 51 29N 7 30 E
Horikiri, Tōkyō 13 B4 35 44N 139 50 E
Horn, Hbg. 7 D8 53 33N 10 5 E
Horn Pond, Bost. 21 C2 42 28N 71 9W
Hornchurch, Lon. 4 B6 51 33N 0 14 E
Horneburg, Ruhr 6 A5 51 37N 7 17 E
Horni, Pra. 10 B3 50 2N 14 33 E
Horni Počernice, Pra. 10 B3 50 6N 14 36 E
Hornsey, Lon. 4 B4 51 35N 0 7W
Horoměřice, Pra. 10 B1 50 8N 14 20 E
Horsley Park, Syd. 19 B2 33 50 S 150 51 E
Horst, Ruhr 6 B4 51 26N 7 6 E
Horsthausen, Ruhr 6 A5 51 33N 7 12 E
Hortaleza, Mdrd. 8 B3 40 28N 3 38W
Horto Florestal, S. Pau. 31 D6 23 27 S 46 38W
Horton Kirby, Lon. 4 C6 51 23N 0 14 E
Hösel, Ruhr 6 B3 51 20N 6 53 E
Hosoyama, Tōkyō 13 C2 35 36N 139 31 E
Hospitalet, Barc. 8 D5 41 21N 2 6 E
Hostafrancs, Barc. 8 D5 41 21N 2 8 E
Hoterheide, Ruhr 6 C1 51 16N 6 37 E
Houbetin, Pra. 10 B3 50 6N 14 33 E
Houghs Neck, Bost. 21 D4 42 15N 70 57W
Houghton, Jobg. 18 F9 26 10 S 28 3 E
Houilles, Paris 5 B3 48 56N 2 11 E
Hounslow, Lon. 4 C2 51 28N 0 21W
Houses of Parliament, Lon. 4 C4 51 29N 0 7W
Hove Å →, Købn. 2 D8 55 43N 12 7 E
Hovedøya, Oslo 2 B4 59 53N 10 43 E
Høvik, Oslo 2 B3 59 54N 10 34 E
Hovorčovice, Pra. 10 A3 50 10N 14 31 E
Howard Beach, N.Y. 23 D5 40 39N 73 50W
Hoxton Park, Syd. 19 B2 33 55 S 150 51 E
Hoxton Park Aerodrome, Syd. 19 B2 33 54 S 150 50 E
Hōya, Tōkyō 13 B2 35 44N 139 34 E
Høybråten, Oslo 2 B5 59 56N 10 55 E
Hradčany, Pra. 10 B2 50 5N 14 24 E
Hsiya, Gzh. 14 G7 23 9N 113 6 E
Huangpu, Gzh. 14 G9 23 5N 113 23 E
Huangpu, Shang. 14 J12 31 14N 121 30 E
Huangpu Gongyuan, Shang. 14 J11 31 14N 121 29 E
Huangpu Jiang →, Shang. 14 J11 31 11N 121 29 E
Huangtugang, Beij. 14 C2 39 49N 116 15 E
Huat Choe, Sing. 15 F7 1 20N 103 41 E
Huckarde, Ruhr 6 A6 51 32N 7 24 E
Huckingen, Ruhr 6 B2 51 21N 6 44 E
Huddinge, Stock. 3 E11 59 14N 18 0 E
Hudson →, N.Y. 22 B5 40 43N 73 6W
Huertas de San Beltran, Barc. 8 D5 41 22N 2 9 E
Huguenot, N.Y. 22 D3 40 32N 74 13W
Huguenot Park, N.Y. 22 D3 40 31N 74 12W
Huidui, Tianj. 14 E6 39 4N 117 16 E
Huisquilucan →, Méx. 29 B2 19 24N 99 17W
Huixquilucan, Méx. 29 B1 19 21N 99 21W
Hull, Bost. 21 D4 42 18N 70 54W
Hulman Aqueduct, Bost. 21 C1 42 20N 71 23W
Hulmeville, Phil. 24 A5 40 8N 74 55W
Hulsdonk, Ruhr 6 B1 51 27N 6 36 E
Humaljärvi, Hels. 3 B1 60 10N 24 26 E
Humber →, Trto. 20 D7 43 47N 79 38W
Humber B., Trto. 20 E8 43 37N 79 27W
Humber Bay, Trto. 20 E8 43 38N 79 29W
Humber Summit, Trto. 20 D7 43 45N 79 32W
Humber Valley Park, Trto. 20 E8 43 39N 79 29W
Humber Valley Village, Trto. 20 D7 43 40N 79 31W
Humberlea, Trto. 20 D7 43 43N 79 31W
Humboldt Park, Chic. 26 B2 41 54N 87 42W
Humera, Mdrd. 8 B2 40 25N 3 46W
Hummelsbüttel, Hbg. 7 D8 53 39N 10 4 E
Hun Yeang, Sing. 15 F8 1 21N 103 55 E
Hunaydī, Bagd. 17 F8 33 18N 44 29 E
Hundige, Købn. 2 E8 55 35N 12 18 E
Hundige Strand, Købn. 2 E9 55 35N 12 20 E
Hung Hom, H.K. 12 E6 22 18N 114 11 E
Hunters Hill, Syd. 19 B3 33 50 S 151 9 E
Hunters Pt., S.F. 27 B2 37 43N 122 21W
Hunters Valley, Wash. 25 D6 38 54N 77 17W
Huntington, N.Y. 23 B8 40 51N 73 25W
Huntington, Wash. 25 E7 38 47N 77 4W
Huntington B., N.Y. 23 B8 40 54N 73 24W
Huntington Bay, N.Y. 23 B8 40 56N 73 26W
Huntington Park, L.A. 28 C3 33 58N 118 13W
Huntington Station, N.Y. 23 B8 40 50N 73 23W
Hünxer Wald, Ruhr 6 A2 51 37N 6 49 E
Hurffville, Phil. 24 C4 39 45N 75 6W
Hurīya, Bagd. 17 E7 33 21N 44 19 E
Hurlingham, B.A. 32 B3 34 35 S 58 37W
Hurlingham, Jobg. 18 E9 26 6 S 28 2 E
Hurstville, Syd. 19 B3 33 57 S 151 6 E
Husby, Stock. 3 D10 59 24N 17 56 E
Huseby, Oslo 2 A6 60 0N 11 1 E
Hustivař, Pra. 10 B3 50 3N 14 31 E
Husum, Købn. 2 D9 55 42N 12 27 E
Hütteldorf, Wien 10 G9 48 12N 16 15 E
Hüttenheim, Ruhr 6 B2 51 21N 6 43 E
Huttrop, Ruhr 6 B4 51 26N 7 3 E
Hüvösvölgy, Bud. 10 J13 47 32N 19 0 E
Hvalstad, Oslo 2 B2 59 51N 10 27 E
Hvalstrand, Oslo 2 B3 59 50N 10 30 E
Hvidovre, Købn. 2 E9 55 38N 12 27 E
Hwagog, Sŏul 12 G7 37 32N 126 51 E
Hyattsville, Wash. 25 D8 38 57N 76 57W
Hyde Park, Bost. 21 D3 42 15N 71 7W
Hyde Park, Chic. 26 C3 41 47N 87 35W
Hyde Park, Jobg. 18 E9 26 6 S 28 2 E
Hyde Park, Lon. 4 B3 51 30N 0 10W
Hyde Park, Syd. 19 B4 33 52 S 151 12 E
Hynes, L.A. 28 C3 33 52N 118 10W

I

Ibaraki, Ōsaka 12 B4 34 48N 135 34 E
Ibayo Tipas, Manila 15 D4 14 32N 121 4 E
Ibese, Lagos 18 A2 6 33N 7 28 E
Ibirapuera, S. Pau. 31 E5 23 36 S 46 40W
Ibirapuera, Parque, S. Pau. 31 E6 23 35 S 46 38W
Iboju, Lagos 18 B3 6 25N 7 31 E
Icarai, Rio J. 31 B3 22 54 S 43 6W
Icerenköy, Ist. 17 B3 40 58N 29 6 E
Ichapur, Calc. 16 D6 22 48N 88 22 E
Ichgao, Tōkyō 13 C2 35 32N 139 32 E
Ichigaya, Tōkyō 13 B3 35 41N 139 43 E
Ichikawa, Tōkyō 13 B4 35 43N 139 54 E
Ickenham, Lon. 4 B2 51 33N 0 26W
Ickern, Ruhr 6 A6 51 35N 7 21 E
Iddo, Lagos 18 B2 6 28N 7 22 E
Idi-Oro, Lagos 18 A2 6 31N 7 22 E
Idimu, Lagos 18 A1 6 34N 7 17 E
Idrīs, Bagd. 17 E8 33 22N 44 27 E
Iganmu, Lagos 18 B2 6 28N 7 22 E
Igbobi, Lagos 18 A2 6 31N 7 22 E
Igbologun, Lagos 18 B1 6 24N 7 19 E
Igbopa, Lagos 18 A3 6 32N 7 30 E
Igelboda, Stock. 3 E12 59 17N 18 17 E
Igny, Paris 5 C3 48 44N 2 13 E
Iguassú, S. Pau. 31 E6 23 36 S 46 30W
Ijesa-Tedo, Lagos 18 B1 6 29N 7 19 E
Ijora, Lagos 18 B2 6 27N 7 22 E
Ikebe, Tōkyō 13 C2 35 31N 139 34 E
Ikebukuro, Tōkyō 13 B3 35 43N 139 42 E
Ikeda, Ōsaka 12 B3 34 48N 135 25 E
Ikegami, Tōkyō 13 C3 35 33N 139 42 E
Ikeja, Lagos 18 A2 6 35N 7 20 E
Ikeuchi, Ōsaka 12 C4 34 35N 135 32 E
Ikotun, Lagos 18 A1 6 32N 7 16 E
Ikoyi, Lagos 18 B2 6 27N 7 26 E
Ikuata, Lagos 18 B2 6 24N 7 21 E
Ikuno, Ōsaka 12 B4 34 40N 135 30 E
Ikuta, Lagos 18 B2 6 27N 7 21 E
Ikuta, Tōkyō 13 C2 35 36N 139 32 E
Ila, Oslo 2 B3 59 57N 10 35 E
Ilchester, Balt. 25 B2 39 14N 76 46W
Ilford, Lon. 4 B5 51 33N 0 4 E
Ilioúpolis, Ath. 8 J11 37 54N 23 47 E
Illovo, Jobg. 18 E9 26 7 S 28 3 E
Ilsós →, Ath. 8 J11 37 55N 23 41 E
Imajuku, Tōkyō 13 D2 35 28N 139 32 E
Imbâba, El Qâ. 18 C5 30 3N 31 12 E
Imielin, Wsaw. 10 F7 52 9N 21 0 E
Imirim, S. Pau. 31 D6 23 29 S 46 39W
Imittós, Ath. 8 J11 37 55N 23 45 E
Immersby, Hels. 3 B6 60 18N 25 16 E
Imore, Lagos 18 B1 6 25N 7 17 E
Imperial Palace, Tōkyō 13 B3 35 41N 139 45 E
Ina →, Ōsaka 12 B3 34 48N 135 27 E
Inagi, Tōkyō 13 C2 35 38N 139 31 E
Incirano, Mil. 9 D5 45 34N 9 9 E
Independencia, Lima 30 F8 11 59 S 77 3W
Indian Gabe, Delhi 16 B2 28 36N 77 13 E
Indian Museum, Calc. 16 E6 22 33N 88 21 E
Indiana Harbor, Chic. 26 C4 41 40N 87 26W
Indiana Harbor Canal, Chic. 26 D4 41 39N 87 26W
Indianópolis, S. Pau. 31 E6 23 35 S 46 38W
Indios Verdes, Méx. 29 B3 19 29N 99 6W
Ingarö, Stock. 3 E13 59 17N 18 24 E
Ingaröfjärden, Stock. 3 E13 59 15N 18 25 E
Ingarölandet, Stock. 3 E13 59 17N 18 22 E
Ingenieur Budge, B.A. 32 C4 34 43 S 58 27W
Ingierstrand, Oslo 2 C4 59 49N 10 46 E
Ingleburn, Syd. 19 C2 34 0 S 150 52 E
Inglewood, L.A. 28 C3 33 57N 118 19W
Ingrave, Lon. 4 B7 51 35N 0 20 E
Ingvalsby, Hels. 3 C2 60 9N 24 32 E
Inhaúme, Rio J. 31 B2 22 51 S 43 17W
Inner Port Shelter, H.K. 12 D6 22 22N 114 17 E
Interagos, S. Pau. 31 F5 23 41 S 46 42W
Intramuros, Manila 15 D3 14 35N 120 57 E
Invalides, Paris 5 B3 48 51N 2 18 E
Inverness, Balt. 25 B4 39 15N 76 29W
Inwood, N.Y. 23 D6 40 36N 73 45W
Inzersdorf, Wien 10 H10 48 8N 16 21 E
Ipanema, Rio J. 31 B2 22 59 S 43 12W
Ipiranga, S. Pau. 31 E6 23 35 S 46 36W
Ipiranga →, S. Pau. 31 E6 23 37 S 46 37W
Iponri, Lagos 18 B2 6 28N 7 22 E
Ipswich, Bost. 21 A4 42 41N 70 50W
Ipswich →, Bost. 21 A4 42 39N 70 53W
Irajá, Rio J. 31 B2 22 50 S 43 19W
Irving Park, Chic. 26 B2 41 57N 87 42W
Irvington, N.Y. 23 A5 41 2N 73 52W
Irwindale, L.A. 28 B5 34 6N 117 54W
Isabel, Rio J. 31 B2 22 55 S 43 14W
Isagatedo, Lagos 18 A1 6 31N 7 19 E
Isando, Jobg. 18 E10 26 8 S 28 12 E
Isar →, Mün. 7 F11 48 15N 11 40 E
Iselin, N.Y. 22 D3 40 34N 74 19W
Iserbrook, Hbg. 7 D6 53 34N 9 49 E
Iseri-Osun, Lagos 18 A1 6 30N 7 16 E
Ishbīlīya, Bagd. 17 E8 33 21N 44 26 E
Isheri-Olofin, Lagos 18 A1 6 34N 7 16 E
Ishi →, Ōsaka 12 C4 34 34N 135 37 E
Ishikiri, Ōsaka 12 B4 34 40N 135 39 E
Ishizu →, Ōsaka 12 C3 34 33N 135 26 E
Ishøj Strand, Købn. 2 E9 55 36N 12 20 E
Isidro Casanova, B.A. 32 C3 34 42 S 58 36W
Island Channel, N.Y. 23 D5 40 35N 73 52W
Island Park, N.Y. 23 D7 40 36N 73 38W
Island Park, Trto. 20 E8 43 37N 79 22W
Islev, Købn. 2 D9 55 41N 12 27 E
Isleworth, Lon. 4 C3 51 28N 0 19W
Islington, Bost. 21 D2 42 13N 71 13W
Islington, Lon. 4 B4 51 32N 0 6W
Islington, Trto. 20 E7 43 38N 79 30W
Ismaning, Mün. 7 F11 48 13N 11 40 E
Ismayloskiypark, Mos. 11 E10 55 46N 37 46 E
Isogo-Ku, Tōkyō 13 D2 35 23N 139 37 E
Isolo, Lagos 18 A1 6 31N 7 19 E
Isosaari, Hels. 3 C5 60 6N 25 3 E
Issy-les-Moulineaux, Paris 5 C3 48 49N 2 15 E
Istanbul, Ist. 17 B2 41 0N 28 58 E
Istanbul Boğazi, Ist. 17 A3 41 5N 29 3 E
Istanbul Hava Alani, Ist. 17 B2 40 58N 28 50 E
Istead Rise, Lon. 4 C7 51 24N 0 21 E
Istinye, Ist. 17 A3 41 6N 29 3 E
Isunba, Lagos 18 B1 6 25N 7 17 E
Itä Hakkila, Hels. 3 B5 60 17N 25 7 E
Itabashi-Ku, Tōkyō 13 B2 35 46N 139 38 E
Itaberaba, S. Pau. 31 D6 23 28 S 46 39W
Itaeweon, Sŏul 12 G7 37 32N 126 58 E
Itaim, S. Pau. 31 D7 23 29 S 46 23W
Itaipu, Rio J. 31 B3 22 58 S 43 2W
Italie, Place d', Paris 5 C4 48 49N 2 22 E
Itami, Ōsaka 12 B3 34 46N 135 24 E
Itaocaia, Rio J. 31 B3 22 58 S 43 2W
Itapecerica da Serra, S. Pau. 31 F5 23 42 S 46 50W
Itaquaquecetuba, S. Pau. 31 D7 23 29 S 46 23W
Itaquera, S. Pau. 31 E7 23 32 S 46 27W
Itaquera →, S. Pau. 31 E7 23 28 S 46 26W
Ithan, Phil. 24 A2 40 1N 75 21W
Itupu, S. Pau. 31 F5 23 40 S 46 43W
Ituzaingo, B.A. 32 B3 34 39 S 58 38W
Ivanhoe, Melb. 19 E7 37 45 S 145 3 E
Iver, Lon. 4 B1 51 32N 0 30W
Ivry-sur-Seine, Paris 5 C4 48 49N 2 22 E
Iwazono, Ōsaka 12 B2 34 45N 135 18 E
Izabelin, Wsaw. 10 E5 52 17N 20 48 E
Izmaylovo, Mos. 11 E10 55 47N 37 47 E
Iztacalco, Méx. 29 B3 19 23N 99 6W
Iztapalapa, Méx. 29 B3 19 21N 99 6W
Izumi, Tōkyō 13 D1 35 25N 139 29 E

J

J. G. Strijdom Post Office Tower, Jobg. 18 F9 26 11 S 28 2 E
J. Paul Getty Museum, L.A. 28 B1 34 2N 118 33W
Jabavu, Jobg. 18 F8 26 14 S 27 52 E
Jabulani, Jobg. 18 F8 26 14 S 27 51 E
Jacarepaguá, Rio J. 31 B1 22 56 S 43 20W
Jackson Heights, N.Y. 23 C5 40 44N 73 53W
Jackson Park, Chic. 26 C3 41 46N 87 34W
Jacksonville, N.Y. 22 B3 40 57N 74 18W
Jacomino, La Hab. 30 B3 23 6N 82 19W
Jacques Cartier, Mtrl. 20 A5 45 31N 73 27W
Jægersborg, Købn. 2 D10 55 45N 12 31 E
Jægersborg Dyrehave, Købn. 2 D10 55 46N 12 33 E
Jægersborg Hegn, Købn. 2 D10 55 49N 12 33 E
Jafarpur, Calc. 16 D6 22 45N 88 22 E
Jagacha, Calc. 16 E5 22 35N 88 17 E
Jagannathpur, Calc. 16 D5 22 43N 88 18 E
Jagatdal, Calc. 16 C6 22 51N 88 23 E
Jagatmagar, Calc. 16 D5 22 46N 88 13 E
Jagatpur, Delhi 16 A2 28 44N 77 13 E
Jagdishpur, Calc. 16 E5 22 39N 88 17 E
Jaguara, S. Pau. 31 E5 23 30 S 46 45W
Jaguaré, S. Pau. 31 E5 23 32 S 46 45W
Jaguaré →, S. Pau. 31 E5 23 32 S 46 45W
Jahangirpur, Delhi 16 A2 28 43N 77 12 E
Jaimanitas →, La Hab. 30 B2 23 5N 82 29W
Jakarta, Jak. 15 H10 6 9 S 106 52 E
Jakarta, Teluk, Jak. 15 H9 6 5 S 106 50 E
Jakobsberg, Stock. 3 D9 59 25N 17 47 E
Jalan Kayu, Sing. 15 F8 1 24N 103 52 E
Jamaica, N.Y. 23 C6 40 42N 73 48W
Jamaica B., N.Y. 23 D6 40 36N 73 49W
Jamaica Plain, Bost. 21 D3 42 18N 71 6W
Jamshīdābād, Tehr. 17 C5 35 42N 51 22 E
Jamsil, Sŏul 12 G8 37 30N 127 4 E
Jamweon, Sŏul 12 G8 37 30N 127 0 E
Jan Smuts Airport, Jobg. 18 E10 26 7 S 28 14 E
Janai, Calc. 16 D5 22 43N 88 15 E
Janā'in, Bagd. 17 F8 33 18N 44 22 E
Janki, Wsaw. 10 F6 52 8N 20 52 E
Jannali, Syd. 19 C3 34 0 S 151 4 E
Jánoshegy, Bud. 10 J12 47 31N 18 57 E
Janów, Wsaw. 10 E6 52 16N 20 50 E
Janvry, Paris 5 D2 48 38N 2 9 E
Jaraguá, S. Pau. 31 D5 23 27 S 46 44W
Jaraguá, Pico de, S. Pau. 31 D5 23 27 S 46 46W
Jarama →, Mdrd. 8 B3 40 29N 3 32W
Jardim América, S. Pau. 31 E6 23 34 S 46 39W
Jardim Anchieta, S. Pau. 31 F7 23 41 S 46 27W
Jardim Arpoador, S. Pau. 31 E5 23 35 S 46 48W
Jardim do Mar, S. Pau. 31 F6 23 41 S 46 33W
Jardim Munhoz, S. Pau. 31 E6 23 30 S 46 33W
Jardim Osasco, S. Pau. 31 E5 23 33 S 46 47W
Jardim Ouro Preto, S. Pau. 31 E5 23 35 S 46 46W
Jardim Paulista, S. Pau. 31 E6 23 34 S 46 41W
Jardim Petrópolis, S. Pau. 31 E6 23 41 S 46 39W
Jardim Rochidale, S. Pau. 31 E5 23 30 S 46 46W
Jardim Santista, S. Pau. 31 F7 23 40 S 46 24W
Jardim São Bento, S. Pau. 31 F5 23 40 S 46 46W
Jardim São Francisco, S. Pau. 31 E7 23 36 S 46 28W
Jardim Sapopemba, S. Pau. 31 E7 23 36 S 46 29W
Jardim Vera Cruz, S. Pau. 31 E7 23 35 S 46 27W
Jardim Vista Alegre, S. Pau. 31 E5 23 37 S 46 49W
Jardim Zaira, S. Pau. 31 E7 23 39 S 46 25W
Jardines Flotantes, Méx. 29 C3 19 16N 99 6W
Jardine's Lookout, H.K. 12 E6 22 16N 114 11 E
Järfälla, Stock. 3 D10 59 24N 17 50 E
Järvafältet, Stock. 3 D10 59 25N 17 51 E
Järventausta, Hels. 3 A1 60 21N 24 28 E
Jasai, Bomb. 16 H9 18 56N 73 1 E
Jaskhar, Bomb. 16 H8 18 54N 72 59 E
Jatinegara, Jak. 15 J10 6 13 S 106 52 E
Jauli, Delhi 16 A3 28 44N 77 20 E
Jawādiyeh, Tehr. 17 D5 35 39N 51 22 E
Jaworowa, Wsaw. 10 F6 52 9N 20 56 E
Jayang, Sŏul 12 G8 37 32N 127 3 E
Jedlesee, Wien 10 G10 48 15N 16 23 E
Jefferson, Phil. 24 C3 39 45N 75 12W
Jefferson Park, Chic. 26 B2 41 58N 87 46W
Jeffersonville, Phil. 24 A2 40 8N 75 23W
Jegi, Sŏul 12 G8 37 34N 127 1 E
Jells Park, Melb. 19 F8 37 53 S 145 11 E
Jelonki, Wsaw. 10 E6 52 14N 20 54 E
Jenfeld, Hbg. 7 D8 53 34N 10 8 E
Jenkintown, Phil. 24 A4 40 6N 75 8W
Jeongreung, Sŏul 12 G8 37 35N 127 0 E
Jericho, N.Y. 23 C7 40 47N 73 32W
Jerónimes, Mosteiro dos, Lisb. 8 F7 38 41N 9 11W
Jersey City, N.Y. 22 C4 40 42N 74 4W
Jésus, Î., Mtrl. 20 A3 43 36N 73 44W
Jesus Del Monte, La Hab. 30 B2 23 6N 82 21W
Jesús Maria, Lima 30 G8 12 4 S 77 3W
Jhenkari, Calc. 16 D5 22 45N 88 18 E
Jhil Kuranga, Delhi 16 B2 28 39N 77 14 E
Jiangqiao, Shang. 14 J11 31 15N 121 20 E
Jiangtai, Beij. 14 B3 39 57N 116 28 E
Jianguomen, Beij. 14 B3 39 53N 116 24 E
Jiangwan, Shang. 14 J11 31 18N 121 28 E
Jianshan Gongyuan, Tianj. 14 E6 39 5N 117 12 E
Jihād, Bagd. 17 F7 33 17N 44 19 E
Jingan, Shang. 14 J11 31 14N 121 25 E
Jinočany, Pra. 10 B1 50 2N 14 16 E
Jinonice, Pra. 10 B2 50 3N 14 22 E
Jirny, Pra. 10 B4 50 7N 14 41 E
Jiuxianqiao, Beij. 14 B3 39 58N 116 28 E
Jiyūgaoka, Tōkyō 13 C3 35 35N 139 40 E
Jizā'er, Bagd. 17 F8 33 15N 44 23 E
Jizīra, Bagd. 17 F8 33 15N 44 25 E
Joan Despi, Barc. 8 D5 41 22N 2 2 E
Joaquin Miller Park, S.F. 27 B3 37 48N 122 11W
Johannesburg, Jobg. 18 F9 26 11 S 28 2 E
Johanneskirchen, Mün. 7 F10 48 10N 11 38 E
Johannesstift, Berl. 7 A2 52 34N 13 12 E
Johannisthal, Berl. 7 B4 52 26N 13 30 E
John F. Kennedy Int. Airport, N.Y. 23 D6 40 39N 73 45W
John F. Kennedy Nat. Hist. Site, Bost. 21 C3 42 20N 71 7W
John Hancock Center, Chic. 26 B3 41 53N 87 37W
John Hopkins Univ., Balt. 25 B3 39 19N 76 37W
John McLaren Park, S.F. 27 B2 37 43N 122 24W
Joinville-le-Pont, Paris 5 C4 48 49N 2 27 E
Jollas, Hels. 3 B5 60 10N 25 5 E
Jones Beach State Park, N.Y. 23 D7 40 35N 73 32W
Jones Falls →, Balt. 25 B3 39 20N 76 36W
Jones Inlet, N.Y. 23 D7 40 34N 73 34W
Jonestown, Balt. 25 B3 39 17N 76 35W
Jong Ro, Sŏul 12 G7 37 34N 126 58 E
Jongmyo Royal Shrine, Sŏul 12 G7 37 34N 126 59 E
Jonstrup, Købn. 2 D9 55 45N 12 20 E
Joppatowne, Balt. 25 A4 39 24N 76 20W
Jordan Valley, H.K. 12 D6 22 20N 114 12 E
Jorge Chavez, Aeropuerto Int., Lima 30 G8 12 2 S 77 8W
Jorvas, Hels. 3 C2 60 8N 24 30 E
José C. Paz, B.A. 32 B2 34 31 S 58 44W
José L. Suárez, B.A. 32 B3 34 32 S 58 34W
José Mármol, B.A. 32 C4 34 47 S 58 22W
Jose Marti, Aeropuerto Int., La Hab. 30 C2 22 59N 82 22W
Josephine Pk., L.A. 28 A4 34 17N 118 7W
Jōsō, Ōsaka 12 B3 34 42N 135 27 E
Jōtō, Ōsaka 12 B4 34 42N 135 33 E
Jouars-Pontchartrain, Paris 5 C1 48 47N 1 53 E
Jouy-en-Josas, Paris 5 C3 48 46N 2 10 E
Jouy-le-Moutier, Paris 5 A2 49 0N 2 2 E
Józefów, Wsaw. 10 F8 52 8N 21 13 E
Juan Escutia, Méx. 29 B3 19 23N 99 3W
Juan González Romero, Méx. 29 A3 19 30N 99 3W
Juhu, Bomb. 16 G9 19 5N 73 0 E
Juilly, Paris 5 A6 49 0N 2 42 E
Jūjā, Tōkyō 13 B3 35 45N 139 43 E
Jukskeirivier →, Jobg. 18 E9 26 5 S 28 6 E
Julianów, Wsaw. 10 E7 52 22N 21 0 E
Jung, Sŏul 12 G7 37 33N 126 59 E
Jungfernheide, Volkspark, Berl. 7 A2 52 32N 13 18 E
Jungfernsee, Berl. 7 B1 52 25N 13 6 E
Jungwha, Sŏul 12 G8 37 35N 127 3 E
Junk B., H.K. 12 E6 22 17N 114 15 E
Jurong, Sing. 15 G7 1 19N 103 40 E
Jurong, Selat, Sing. 15 G7 1 17N 103 42 E
Jurong, Sungei →, Sing. 15 G7 1 17N 103 45 E
Jurubatuba, S. Pau. 31 F5 23 40 S 46 41W
Jurujuba, Enseada de, Rio J. 31 B3 22 54 S 43 6W
Justice, Chic. 26 C2 41 44N 87 49W
Jusujärvi, Hels. 3 B1 60 12N 24 26 E
Juva, Hels. 3 B1 60 14N 24 27 E
Juvisy-sur-Orge, Paris 5 C4 48 41N 2 21 E
Jwalahari, Delhi 16 B1 28 40N 77 6 E
Jyllinge, Købn. 2 D7 55 45N 12 6 E

K

Kaarst, Ruhr 6 C1 51 13N 6 36 E
Kabaty, Wsaw. 10 F7 52 8N 21 4 E
Kabel, Ruhr 6 A6 51 24N 7 28 E
Kadiköy, Ist. 17 B3 40 59N 29 1 E
Kadoma, Ōsaka 12 B4 34 44N 135 35 E
Kafr es Sammân, El Qâ. 18 D4 29 58N 31 8 E
Kâğithane, Ist. 17 A2 41 4N 28 58 E
Kâğithane →, Ist. 17 A2 41 9N 28 56 E
Kagran, Wien 10 G10 48 14N 16 26 E
Kahlenberg, Wien 10 G9 48 16N 16 19 E
Kai Tak, H.K. 12 D6 22 20N 114 11 E
Kaisariani, Ath. 8 J11 37 57N 23 46 E
Kaiser-Mühlen, Wien 10 G10 48 13N 16 25 E
Kaiserebersdorf, Wien 10 H10 48 9N 16 26 E
Kaiserswerth, Ruhr 6 C2 51 18N 6 44 E
Kaivoksela, Hels. 3 B4 60 15N 24 53 E
Kakukk-hegy, Bud. 10 K12 47 29N 18 57 E
Kalachhara, Calc. 16 D5 22 42N 88 15 E
Kalamákion, Ath. 8 J11 37 52N 23 43 E
Kaldenhausen, Ruhr 6 B1 51 23N 6 39 E
Kalipur, Calc. 16 D5 22 40N 88 17 E
Kalkaji, Delhi 16 B2 28 32N 77 12 E
Kalksburg, Wien 10 H9 48 8N 16 15 E
Kallang →, Sing. 15 F8 1 18N 103 52 E
Kallhäll, Stock. 3 D9 59 26N 17 48 E
Kallithéa, Ath. 8 J11 37 56N 23 41 E
Kallvik, Hels. 3 B5 60 12N 25 8 E
Kaltbründsberg, Wien 10 G9 48 10N 16 13 E
Kaltenleutgeben, Wien 10 H9 48 7N 16 11 E
Kalveboderne, Købn. 2 E10 55 37N 12 31 E
Kalytino, St-Pet. 11 B5 59 59N 30 39 E
Kamaraerdö, Bud. 10 K12 47 26N 18 59 E
Kamarhati, Calc. 16 D6 22 40N 88 23 E
Kamarkunda, Calc. 16 D5 22 49N 88 12 E
Kamata, Tōkyō 13 C3 35 33N 139 43 E
Kamdebpur, Calc. 16 C5 22 53N 88 19 E
Kameari, Tōkyō 13 B4 35 45N 139 50 E
Kameido, Tōkyō 13 B4 35 42N 139 50 E
Kami-hoshikawa, Tōkyō 13 D2 35 27N 139 35 E
Kami-Itabashi, Tōkyō 13 B3 35 45N 139 40 E
Kami-nakazato, Tōkyō 13 D2 35 25N 139 36 E
Kami-saruyama, Tōkyō 13 C2 35 30N 139 31 E
Kami-sugata, Tōkyō 13 D2 35 28N 139 34 E
Kami-tomi, Tōkyō 13 B1 35 48N 139 29 E
Kamikitazawa, Tōkyō 13 C2 35 39N 139 36 E
Kamikiyoto, Tōkyō 13 B2 35 45N 139 30 E
Kamishiki, Tōkyō 13 B4 35 46N 139 57 E
Kamitsuruma, Tōkyō 13 C1 35 30N 139 26 E
Kamiyama, Tōkyō 13 B2 35 46N 139 32 E
Kamoi, Tōkyō 13 D2 35 30N 139 34 E
Kamoshida, Tōkyō 13 C2 35 33N 139 31 E
Kampong Batak, Sing. 15 F8 1 20N 103 54 E
Kampong Mandai Kechil, Sing. 15 F7 1 26N 103 46 E
Kampong Pachitan, Sing. 15 G8 1 19N 103 54 E
Kampong Potong Pasir, Sing. 15 F8 1 20N 103 52 E
Kampong Reteh, Sing. 15 G8 1 19N 103 53 E
Kampong Tengah, Sing. 15 F7 1 22N 103 42 E
Kampong Ulu Jurong, Sing. 15 F7 1 20N 103 42 E
Kampung Ambon, Jak. 15 J10 6 11 S 106 53 E
Kampung Bali, Jak. 15 J9 6 11 S 106 48 E
Kan, Tehr. 17 C4 35 45N 51 16 E
Kanagawa-Ku, Tōkyō 13 D2 35 29N 139 38 E
Kanamachi, Tōkyō 13 B4 35 46N 139 52 E
Kanamori, Tōkyō 13 C1 35 31N 139 27 E
Kanda, Tōkyō 13 B3 35 41N 139 45 E
Kandang Kerbau, Sing. 15 G8 1 18N 103 51 E
Kandilli, Ist. 17 A3 41 4N 29 3 E
Kanegasaku, Tōkyō 13 B4 35 48N 139 56 E
Kangaroo Ground, Melb. 19 E8 37 41 S 145 13 E
Kankinara, Calc. 16 C6 22 51N 88 24 E
Kankurgachi, Calc. 16 E6 22 34N 88 23 E
Kanlica, Ist. 17 A3 41 6N 29 4 E
Kanoaka, Ōsaka 12 C4 34 33N 135 31 E
Kanonerskiy, Os., St-Pet. 11 B3 59 53N 30 13 E
Kanzaki →, Ōsaka 12 B3 34 41N 135 24 E
Kapellerfeld, Wien 10 G10 48 18N 16 29 E
Kapotnya, Mos. 11 F10 55 39N 37 48 E
Käppala, Stock. 3 D12 59 21N 18 13 E
Käpylä, Hels. 3 B4 60 13N 24 57 E
Karachi, Kar. 17 G11 24 50N 67 0 E
Karachi Int. Airport, Kar. 17 G11 24 54N 67 9 E
Karachi Univ., Kar. 17 G11 24 51N 67 0 E
Karagümrük, Ist. 17 A2 41 1N 28 56 E
Karāma, Bagd. 17 E8 33 20N 44 22 E
Karato, Ōsaka 12 B2 34 46N 135 12 E
Karave, Bomb. 16 G9 19 0N 73 0 E
Karet, Jak. 15 J9 6 12 S 106 49 E
Karkar Duman, Delhi 16 B2 28 39N 77 18 E
Karkh, Bagd. 17 E8 33 20N 44 22 E
Karlberg, Stock. 3 D11 59 20N 18 1 E
Karlin, Pra. 10 B2 50 5N 14 26 E
Karlsfeld, Mün. 7 F9 48 13N 11 28 E
Karlshorst, Berl. 7 B4 52 29N 13 31 E
Karlslunde Strand, Købn. 2 E8 55 33N 12 15 E
Karnap, Ruhr 6 A4 51 31N 7 0 E
Karolinenhof, Berl. 7 B4 52 23N 13 38 E
Karow, Berl. 7 A3 52 36N 13 29 E
Karrādah, Bagd. 17 F8 33 17N 44 23 E
Kärsön, Stock. 3 E10 59 19N 17 54 E
Kasai, Tōkyō 13 C4 35 39N 139 52 E
Kasetsart, Bangk. 15 A2 13 50N 100 34 E
Kashi-Hazaki, Tōkyō 13 A3 35 54N 139 42 E
Kashio, Tōkyō 13 D2 35 24N 139 34 E
Kashiwa, Tōkyō 13 A4 35 51N 139 57 E
Kashiwara, Ōsaka 12 C4 34 34N 135 37 E
Kaskela, Hels. 3 B5 60 17N 25 6 E
Kastrup, Købn. 2 E10 55 38N 12 39 E
Kastrup Lufthavn, Købn. 2 E11 55 37N 12 39 E
Kasuga, Tōkyō 13 B2 35 45N 139 38 E
Kasuge, Tōkyō 13 B3 35 45N 139 49 E
Kasumigasek, Tōkyō 13 B3 35 40N 139 45 E
Katabira →, Tōkyō 13 D2 35 27N 139 34 E
Katernberg, Ruhr 6 A4 51 30N 7 3 E
Katong Park, Sing. 15 G8 1 18N 103 54 E
Katrineberg, Stock. 3 E10 59 13N 17 54 E
Katsushika-Ku, Tōkyō 13 B4 35 44N 139 51 E
Kattinge Vig, Købn. 2 D7 55 40N 12 5 E
Kau Pei Chau, H.K. 12 E6 22 12N 114 15 E
Kau Yi Chau, H.K. 12 E5 22 17N 114 4 E
Kauklahti, Hels. 3 B2 60 11N 24 36 E
Kaulsdorf, Berl. 7 B4 52 29N 13 34 E
Kauniainen, Hels. 3 B3 60 13N 24 44 E
Kawagoe, Tōkyō 13 A1 35 54N 139 29 E
Kawaguchi, Tōkyō 13 B3 35 47N 139 43 E
Kawai, Tōkyō 13 D2 35 29N 139 31 E
Kawamukō, Tōkyō 13 C2 35 30N 139 34 E
Kawanishi, Ōsaka 12 A3 34 49N 135 24 E
Kawasaki, Tōkyō 13 C3 35 31N 139 43 E
Kawasaki Harbour, Tōkyō 13 D3 35 30N 139 47 E
Kawawa, Tōkyō 13 C2 35 31N 139 33 E
Kawęczyn, Wsaw. 10 E7 52 16N 21 5 E
Kayu Putih, Jak. 15 J10 6 10 S 106 53 E
Kbely, Pra. 10 B3 50 8N 14 32 E
Kearny, N.Y. 22 C4 40 45N 74 8W
Kebayoran Baru, Jak. 15 J9 6 14 S 106 47 E
Kebayoran Lama, Jak. 15 J9 6 13 S 106 46 E
Kebon Jeruk, Jak. 15 J9 6 11 S 106 46 E
Keferloh, Mün. 7 G11 48 5N 11 43 E
Keilor, Melb. 19 E6 37 42 S 144 50 E
Keilor East, Melb. 19 E6 37 44 S 144 51 E
Keimola, Hels. 3 A3 60 20N 24 49 E
Kelenföld, Bud. 10 K13 47 27N 19 2 E
Kelvedon Hatch, Lon. 4 A6 51 40N 0 16 E
Kelvin, Jobg. 18 E9 26 4 S 28 5 E
Kemang, Jak. 15 J9 6 15 S 106 48 E
Kemayoran, Jak. 15 J10 6 10 S 106 51 E
Kemayoran Airport, Jak. 15 H10 6 8 S 106 50 E
Kemp Mill, Wash. 25 C7 39 0N 77 1W
Kempton Park, Jobg. 18 E10 26 5 S 28 14 E
Kempton Racecourse, Lon. 4 C2 51 24N 0 23W
Kemsing, Lon. 4 D6 51 18N 0 12 E
Kendall Green, Bost. 21 C2 42 22N 71 16W
Kendua, Calc. 16 E5 22 34N 88 10 E
Keng Hau, H.K. 12 D6 22 22N 114 10 E
Kenilworth, Chic. 26 A2 42 5N 87 42W
Kenilworth, N.Y. 22 C3 40 40N 74 16W
Kenley, Lon. 4 D4 51 19N 0 6W
Kenmare, Jobg. 18 E7 26 6 S 27 48 E
Kennedy Grove Regional Rec. Area, S.F. 27 A3 37 56N 122 14W

Midland Park 41

Lille Værløse, Købn. 2 D9 55 47N 12 22 E
Lillehavfrue, Købn. 2 D10 55 42N 12 35 E
Lillestrøm, Oslo 2 B6 59 57N 11 3 E
Liluah, Calc. 16 E5 22 37N 88 19 E
Lilydale, Melb. 19 E9 37 45 S 145 21 E
Lima, Lima 30 G8 12 3 S 77 2W
Lima, Phil. 24 B2 39 55N 75 26W
Limbiate, Mil. 9 D5 45 35N 9 7 E
Limehouse, Lon. 4 B4 51 30N 0 1W
Limeil-Brévannes, Paris 5 C4 48 44N 2 29 E
Limito, Mil. 9 E6 45 28N 9 19 E
Limoges-Fourches, Paris 5 D5 48 37N 2 39 E
Limours, Paris 5 D2 48 38N 2 4 E
Linas, Paris 5 D3 48 37N 2 16 E
Linate, Mil. 9 E6 45 26N 9 16 E
Linate, Aeroporto Internazionale di, Mil. 9 E6 45 26N 9 16 E
Linbigh, Balt. 25 A3 39 21N 76 31W
Linbropark, Jobg. 18 E9 26 5 S 28 7 E
Lincoln, Bost. 21 C2 42 25N 71 18W
Lincoln Center, N.Y. 22 C5 40 46N 43 59W
Lincoln Heights, L.A. 28 B3 34 4N 118 12 E
Lincoln Memorial, Wash. 25 D7 38 53N 77 2W
Lincoln Park, Chic. 26 B3 41 57N 87 38W
Lincoln Park, N.Y. 22 B3 40 56N 74 18W
Lincoln Park, S.F. 27 B1 37 47N 122 30W
Lincolnwood, Chic. 26 A2 42 1N 87 43W
Linda-a-Pastora, Lisb. 8 F7 38 42N 9 15W
Linden, Jobg. 18 E9 26 8 S 28 0 E
Linden, N.Y. 22 D3 40 38N 74 14W
Linden-Dahlhausen, Ruhr 6 B5 51 25N 7 10 E
Lindenberg, Berl. 7 A4 52 36N 13 31 E
Lindenhorst, Ruhr 6 A6 51 33N 7 27 E
Lindenhurst, N.Y. 23 C8 40 40N 73 22W
Lindenwold, Phil. 24 C5 39 49N 74 59W
Linderhausen, Ruhr 6 C5 51 17N 7 17 E
Lindfield, Syd. 19 A3 33 46 S 151 9 E
Lindøya, Oslo 2 B4 59 53N 10 42 E
Lingotto, Tori. 9 B2 45 1N 7 39 E
Liniers, B.A. 32 B3 34 39 S 58 30W
Linksfield, Jobg. 18 E9 26 9 S 28 6 E
Linmeyer, Jobg. 18 F9 26 15 S 28 4 E
Linn, Ruhr 6 B1 51 20N 6 38 E
Linna, Hels. 3 A4 60 20N 24 50 E
Linthicum Heights, Balt. 25 B2 39 12N 76 47W
Lintorf, Ruhr 6 B3 51 20N 6 50 E
Lintuvaara, Hels. 3 B3 60 14N 24 49 E
Linwood, Phil. 24 C2 39 49N 75 25W
Lioúmi, Ath. 8 J11 38 0N 23 40 E
Lipków, Wsaw. 10 E5 52 16N 20 48 E
Lippalthausen, Ruhr 6 A6 51 36N 7 26 E
Liqizhuang, Tianj. 14 E6 39 4N 117 10 E
Lirich, Ruhr 6 B2 51 29N 6 49 E
Lisboa, Lisb. 8 F8 38 42N 9 8W
Lisbon = Lisboa, Lisb. 8 F8 38 42N 9 8W
Lishui, Gzh. 14 F7 23 12N 113 9 E
Lisiy Nos, St-Pet. 11 A2 60 1N 30 0 E
Lissone, Mil. 9 D6 45 36N 9 14 E
Lissy, Paris 5 D6 48 38N 2 42 E
Litoral, Cord. del, Car. 30 D5 10 33N 66 54W
Little B., Syd. 19 B4 33 58 S 151 15 E
Little Calumet →, Chic. 26 D3 41 39N 87 34W
Little Falls, N.Y. 22 B3 40 52N 74 14W
Little Ferry, N.Y. 22 B4 40 50N 74 2W
Little Neck, N.Y. 23 C6 40 46N 73 43W
Little Paint Br. →, Wash. 25 C8 39 0N 76 55W
Little Patuxent →, Balt. 25 B1 39 13N 76 51W
Little Rouge →, Trto. 20 C9 43 45N 79 11W
Little Sugarloaf, Melb. 19 E8 37 40 S 145 18 E
Little Thurrock, Lon. 4 C7 51 29N 0 20 E
Liuhang, Shang. 14 H11 31 21N 121 21 E
Liuhuahu Gongyuan, Gzh. 14 G8 23 8N 113 14 E
Liverpool, Syd. 19 B2 33 55 S 150 55 E
Livingstone, N.Y. 22 C3 40 47N 74 19W
Livry-Gargan, Paris 5 B5 48 55N 2 31 E
Liwanhu Gongyuan, Gzh. 14 G8 23 7N 113 13 E
Lizhuang, Gzh. 14 G7 23 6N 113 7 E
Ljan, Oslo 2 B4 59 51N 10 48 E
Llano de Can Gineu, Barc. 8 D6 41 27N 2 10 E
Llavallol, B.A. 32 C4 34 48 S 58 25W
Llobregat →, Barc. 8 D5 41 19N 2 5 E
Lloyd Harbor, N.Y. 23 B8 40 54N 73 26W
Lloyd Pt., N.Y. 23 B8 40 56N 73 29W
Lo Aranguiz, Stgo 30 J11 33 23 S 70 40W
Lo Boza, Stgo 30 J10 33 23 S 70 43W
Lo Chau, H.K. 12 E6 22 11N 114 15 E
Lo Hermida, Stgo 30 J11 33 28 S 70 33W
Lo Ortuzar, Stgo 30 J10 33 28 S 70 43W
Lo Prado Arriba, Stgo 30 J10 33 26 S 70 42W
Lo So Shing, H.K. 12 E5 22 12N 114 7 E
Lo Wai, H.K. 12 D5 22 22N 114 8 E
Lobau, Wien 10 G11 48 10N 16 31 E
Lobos, Pt., S.F. 27 B1 37 46N 122 30W
Loch Raven Village, Balt. 25 A3 39 23N 76 34W
Locham, Mün. 7 G9 48 7N 11 26 E
Lochearn, Balt. 25 A2 39 20N 76 43W
Lochino, Mos. 11 E7 55 41N 37 17 E
Lochkov, Pra. 10 B2 50 0N 14 21 E
Lockhausen, Mün. 7 F9 48 10N 11 24 E
Locksbottom, Lon. 4 C5 51 21N 0 3 E
Locust Grove, N.Y. 23 C8 40 48N 73 29W
Locust Manor, N.Y. 23 C6 40 41N 73 45W
Locust Valley, N.Y. 23 B7 40 52N 73 36W
Lodi, N.Y. 22 B4 40 52N 74 5W
Lofty, Mt., Melb. 19 E8 37 42 S 145 17 E
Logan, Phil. 24 A4 40 2N 75 8W
Logan Int. Airport, Bost. 21 C4 42 22N 71 0W
Logan Square, Chic. 26 B2 41 55N 87 42W
Lognes-Émerainville, Aérodrome de, Paris 5 C5 48 49N 2 37 E
Lohausen, Ruhr 6 C2 51 16N 6 44 E
Lohberg, Ruhr 6 A2 51 34N 6 45 E
Löhme, Berl. 7 A5 52 37N 13 40 E
Lohmühle, Ruhr 6 A1 51 30N 6 39 E
Löhnen, Ruhr 6 A1 51 35N 6 39 E
Lokstedt, Hbg. 7 D7 53 36N 9 56 E
Lokyang, Sing. 15 G7 1 19N 103 40 E
Lôlôkhet, Kar. 17 G11 24 54N 67 2 E
Loma Blanca, Stgo 30 J10 33 29 S 70 43W
Lomas Chapultepec, Méx. 29 B2 19 25N 99 12W
Lomas de San Angel Inn, Méx. 29 B2 19 20N 99 13W
Lomas de Zamora, B.A. 32 C4 34 45 S 58 24W
Lombardy East, Jobg. 18 E9 26 6 S 28 7 E
Lomonosov Univ., Mos. 11 E9 55 42N 37 31 E
Lomus Reforma, Méx. 29 B2 19 24N 99 14W
London, Lon. 4 B4 51 30N 0 6W
London, City of, Lon. 4 B4 51 30N 0 6W
London, Tower of, Lon. 4 B4 51 30N 0 4W
London Zoo, Lon. 4 B4 51 31N 0 9W
Long B., Syd. 19 B4 33 59 S 151 15 E
Long Beach, N.Y. 23 D7 40 35N 73 40W
Long Branch, Trto. 20 E7 43 35N 79 31W
Long Brook →, Wash. 25 E6 38 49N 77 15W
Long Ditton, Lon. 4 C3 51 22N 0 19W
Long I., Bost. 21 D4 42 19N 70 59W
Long I., N.Y. 23 C7 40 45N 73 30W
Long Island City, N.Y. 22 C5 40 45N 73 56W
Long Island Sd., N.Y. 23 B7 40 57N 73 30W
Long Pond, Bost. 21 A1 42 41N 71 22W
Longchamp, Hippodrôme de, Paris 5 B3 48 51N 2 13 E
Longchêne, Paris 5 D2 48 38N 2 0 E
Longhua Gongyuan, Shang. 14 J11 31 10N 121 26 E
Longjohn Slough, Chic. 26 C1 41 42N 87 52W
Longjumeau, Paris 5 C3 48 41N 2 17 E
Longlands, Lon. 4 C5 51 25N 0 5 E
Longpont-sur-Orge, Paris 5 D3 48 38N 2 17 E
Longtan Hu →, Beij. 14 B3 39 51N 116 24 E
Longue Point, Mtrl. 20 A4 43 35N 73 31W
Longueuil, Mtrl. 20 A5 43 31N 73 29W
Loni, Delhi 16 A2 28 45N 77 17 E
Lord's Cricket Ground, Lon. 4 B3 51 31N 0 10W
Loreley, Balt. 25 A4 39 23N 76 24W
Lørenskog, Oslo 2 B5 59 55N 10 59 E
Loreto, Mil. 9 E6 45 29N 9 12 E
Lorraine, Mtrl. 20 A3 43 39N 73 46W
Los Angeles, L.A. 28 B3 34 3N 118 14 E
Los Angeles, Mdrd. 8 B2 40 20N 3 41W
Los Angeles →, L.A. 28 C3 33 55N 118 10W
Los Angeles Int. Airport, L.A. 28 C2 33 56N 118 23W
Los Asientos, Car. 30 D5 10 32N 66 53W
Los Caobos, Car. 30 D5 10 30N 66 53W
Los Carmenes, Car. 30 E5 10 28N 66 54W
Los Cerrillas, Aeroporto, Stgo 30 J10 33 29 S 70 42W
Los Dos Caminos, Car. 30 D6 10 30N 66 49W
Los Dos Riteras →, Car. 30 D5 10 35N 66 57W
Los Jazmines, Presa, Méx. 29 B2 19 25N 99 15W
Los Nietos, L.A. 28 C4 33 57N 118 4W
Los Pinos, La Hab. 30 B2 23 4N 82 22W
Los Pirules, Méx. 29 B3 19 24N 99 2W
Los Polvorines, B.A. 32 B2 34 30 S 58 41W
Los Remedios →, Méx. 29 B2 19 28N 99 13W
Los Remedios, Parque Nacional de, Méx. 29 B2 19 27N 99 15W
Los Reyes, Méx. 29 B4 19 21N 99 6W
Los Rosales, Car. 30 E5 10 28N 66 53W
Losby, Oslo 2 B5 59 53N 10 59 E
Loughton, Lon. 4 B5 51 38N 0 4 E
Loures, Lisb. 8 F7 38 49N 9 10W
Louveciennes, Paris 5 B2 48 51N 2 8 E
Louvres, Paris 5 A5 49 2N 2 30 E
Lovön, Stock. 3 E10 59 18N 17 51 E
Lövstafjärden, Stock. 3 D9 59 23N 17 46 E
Lowe, Mt., L.A. 28 A4 34 13N 118 5W
Lowe Pond, Bost. 21 A3 42 41N 71 0W
Lowell, Bost. 21 B2 42 38N 71 16W
Lowell Dracut State Forest, Bost. 21 B1 42 39N 71 22W
Lower Crystal Springs Res., S.F. 27 C2 37 31N 122 21W
Lower Edmonton, Lon. 4 B4 51 37N 0 3W
Lower Montville, N.Y. 22 B2 40 53N 74 21W
Lower New York B., N.Y. 22 D4 40 32N 74 5W
Lower Plenty, Melb. 19 E7 37 44 S 145 7 E
Lower Shing Mun Res., H.K. 12 D5 22 22N 114 9 E
Lower Sydenham, Lon. 4 C4 51 25N 0 2W
Lower Van Norman L., L.A. 28 A2 34 17N 118 28W
Lübars, Berl. 7 A3 52 37N 13 21 E
Lubeini, Bahr el →, El Qâ. 18 C4 30 1N 31 5 E
Lubya →, St-Pet. 11 A5 60 1N 30 39 E
Lucento, Tori. 9 B2 45 5N 7 39 E
Lucero, La Hab. 30 B3 23 5N 82 19W
Ludwigsfeld, Mün. 7 F9 48 12N 11 27 E
Lugarno, Syd. 19 B3 33 59 S 151 2 E
Lugouqiao, Beij. 14 C2 39 49N 116 10 E
Luhu, Gzh. 14 G8 23 9N 113 16 E
Luipaardsvlei, Jobg. 18 E7 26 6 S 27 49 E
Luís Guillón, B.A. 32 C4 34 48 S 58 26W
Lujia, Shang. 14 J12 31 15N 121 37 E
Lukens, Mt., L.A. 28 A3 34 16N 118 12W
Lumiar, Lisb. 8 F8 38 4N 9 10W
Lundtofte, Købn. 2 D10 55 47N 12 32 E
Lung Mei, H.K. 12 D6 22 23N 114 15 E
Lunsad, Manila 15 E5 14 27N 121 11 E
Luojiang, Gzh. 14 G8 23 5N 113 17 E
Lura →, Mil. 9 D5 45 34N 9 5 E
Lurnea, Syd. 19 B2 33 56 S 150 54 E
Lurup, Hbg. 7 D7 53 35N 9 54 E
Lustheim, Mün. 7 F10 48 14N 11 34 E
Lütgendortmund, Ruhr 6 A6 51 30N 7 20 E
Lutherville-Timonium, Balt. 25 A3 39 25N 76 36W
Lüttringhausen, Ruhr 6 C5 51 12N 7 14 E
Lutvatn, Oslo 2 B5 59 54N 10 52 E
Luwan, Shang. 14 J11 31 12N 121 27 E
Luyano, La Hab. 30 B2 23 6N 82 21W
Luzhniki Sports Centre, Mos. 11 E9 55 43N 37 31 E
Lyckebyn, Stock. 3 E12 59 11N 18 13 E
Lynbrook, N.Y. 23 D6 40 38N 73 40W
Lyndhurst, Jobg. 18 E9 26 7 S 28 6 E
Lyndhurst, N.Y. 22 C4 40 49N 74 7W
Lynn, Bost. 21 C4 42 28N 70 57W
Lynn Harbor, Bost. 21 C4 42 26N 70 57W
Lynn Woods Res., Bost. 21 C3 42 29N 71 2W
Lynwood, L.A. 28 C3 33 55N 118 11W
Lyon, Gare de, Paris 5 B4 48 50N 2 22 E
Lyons, Chic. 26 C2 41 48N 87 49W
Lyonsville, N.Y. 22 B2 40 57N 74 26W
Lysaker, Oslo 2 B3 59 54N 10 38 E
Lysakerselva →, Oslo 2 B3 59 54N 10 38 E
Lysolaje, Pra. 10 B2 50 8N 14 22 E
Lytkarino, Mos. 11 F11 55 35N 37 55 E
Lyubertsy, Mos. 11 E11 55 40N 37 51 E
Lyublino, Mos. 11 E10 55 41N 37 44 E

M

Ma Nam Wat, H.K. 12 D6 22 21N 114 16 E
Ma Po, Sŏul 12 G7 37 32N 126 56 E
Ma Tsz Keng, H.K. 12 D5 22 22N 114 7 E
Ma Yau Tong, H.K. 12 E6 22 19N 114 14 E
Maantiekylä, Hels. 3 A5 60 20N 25 0 E
Maarifa, Bagd. 17 F8 33 15N 44 21 E
Mabashi, Tōkyō 13 B4 35 48N 139 55 E
Mabato Pt., Manila 15 E4 14 29N 121 3 E
Mabolo, Manila 15 E3 14 26N 120 56 E
Macaco, Morro do, Rio J. 31 B3 22 56 S 43 6W
McCook, Chic. 26 C2 41 47N 87 49W
McGill Univ., Mtrl. 20 A4 43 30N 73 35W
Machida, Tōkyō 13 C1 35 32N 139 26 E
Macierzysz, Wsaw. 10 E6 52 13N 20 50 E
Maciolki, Wsaw. 10 E7 52 19N 21 9 E
Mackayville, Mtrl. 20 A5 43 30N 73 26W
McKinnon, Melb. 19 F7 37 54 S 145 1 E
Mclean, Wash. 25 D6 38 56N 77 10W
Macleod, Melb. 19 E7 37 43 S 145 4 E
Macopocho →, Stgo 30 J10 33 24 S 70 40W
Macquarie Fields, Syd. 19 B2 33 59 S 150 53 E
Macquarie Univ., Syd. 19 A3 33 46 S 151 7 E
MacRitchie Res., Sing. 15 F7 1 20N 103 49 E
Macul, Stgo 30 K11 33 30 S 70 35W
Macuto, Car. 30 D5 10 36N 66 53W
Macuto →, Car. 30 D5 10 36N 66 53W
Madatpur, Calc. 16 C6 22 53N 88 27 E
Maddalena, Colle della, Tori. 9 B3 45 2N 7 43 E
Madhudaha, Calc. 16 E6 22 30N 88 24 E
Madhyamgram, Calc. 16 D6 22 41N 88 26 E
Madīnah Al Mansōr, Bagd. 17 F8 33 18N 44 20 E
Mâdinet el Muqattam, El Qâ. 18 C5 30 1N 31 15 E
Mâdinet Nasr, El Qâ. 18 C5 30 4N 31 18 E
Madipur, Delhi 16 B1 28 40N 77 8 E
Madison, N.Y. 22 C2 40 45N 74 24W
Madonna della Scala, Tori. 9 B3 44 59N 7 46 E
Madonna dell'Arco, Nápl. 9 H13 40 52N 14 23 E
Madrid, Mdrd. 8 B2 40 24N 3 42W
Madrona, Barc. 8 D5 41 27N 2 1 E
Madureira, Rio J. 31 B2 22 52 S 43 19W
Maeda, Tōkyō 13 B3 35 48N 139 45 E
Maesawa, Tōkyō 13 B2 35 44N 139 31 E
Magalhaes, Rio J. 31 B1 22 51 S 43 22W
Magdalena del Mar, Lima 30 G8 12 5 S 77 5W
Magholpur, Delhi 16 A1 28 41N 77 6 E
Maghreb, Bagd. 17 E8 33 23N 44 22 E
Magidiyeh, Tehr. 17 C5 35 43N 51 28 E
Maginu, Tōkyō 13 C2 35 34N 139 34 E
Magliana, Rome 9 F9 41 50N 12 26 E
Maglód, Bud. 10 K14 47 27N 19 18 E
Magnolia, Phil. 24 B4 39 51N 75 1W
Magny-les-Hameaux, Paris 5 C2 48 44N 2 3 E
Maharajpur, Delhi 16 B2 28 39N 77 19 E
Maheshtala, Calc. 16 F5 22 29N 88 15 E
Mahiari, Calc. 16 E5 22 35N 88 14 E
Mahikpur, Calc. 16 E5 22 32N 88 13 E
Mahim, Bomb. 16 G8 19 2N 72 50 E
Mahim B., Bomb. 16 G7 19 2N 72 49 E
Mahishdanga, Calc. 16 C5 22 53N 88 11 E
Mahlsdorf, Berl. 7 A4 52 30N 13 37 E
Mahmoodabad, Kar. 17 G11 24 51N 67 4 E
Mahmutbey, Ist. 17 A1 41 2N 28 49 E
Mahpar, Jak. 15 H9 6 9 S 106 49 E
Mahul, Bomb. 16 G8 19 0N 72 53 E
Maida Vale, Lon. 4 B3 51 31N 0 11W
Maidstone, Melb. 19 E6 37 47 S 144 52 E
Maincourt-sur-Yvette, Paris 5 C1 48 42N 1 58 E
Maipu, Stgo 30 K10 33 30 S 70 45W
Maiquetía, Car. 30 D5 10 35N 66 57W
Maiquetía Aeropuerto, Car. 30 D4 10 36N 67 0W
Maisons-Alfort, Paris 5 C4 48 48N 2 26 E
Maisons-Laffitte, Paris 5 B2 48 57N 2 8 E
Maissoneuve, Mtrl. 20 A4 43 32N 73 33W
Maitani, Ōsaka 12 B3 34 48N 135 22 E
Majadahonda, Mdrd. 8 B1 40 28N 3 52W
Majlis, Tehr. 17 C5 35 41N 51 25 E
Makati, Manila 15 D4 14 33N 121 1 E
Mäkiniitty, Hels. 3 A4 60 20N 24 58 E
Mala Strana, Pra. 10 B2 50 4N 14 24 E
Malabar, Syd. 19 B4 33 58 S 151 14 E
Malabar Hill, Bomb. 16 H7 18 57N 72 48 E
Malabon, Manila 15 D3 14 39N 120 56 E
Malacanang Palace, Manila 15 D3 14 35N 120 59 E
Malagrotta, Rome 9 F9 41 52N 12 20 E
Malakhovka, Mos. 11 F12 55 39N 38 0 E
Malakoff, Paris 5 C3 48 49N 2 18 E
Malakpur, Delhi 16 A2 28 42N 77 12 E
Malanday, Manila 15 D4 14 38N 121 5 E
Malanghero, Tori. 9 A2 45 12N 7 39 E
Mälarhöjaen, Stock. 3 E10 59 18N 17 58 E
Malaspina, L., Mil. 9 E6 45 28N 9 8 E
Malassis, Paris 5 D3 48 37N 2 3 E
Malate, Manila 15 D3 14 34N 120 59 E
Malaya Neva, St-Pet. 11 B3 59 56N 30 16 E
Malaya-Okhta, St-Pet. 11 B4 59 55N 30 25 E
Malchow, Berl. 7 A3 52 34N 13 29 E
Malden, Bost. 21 C3 42 26N 71 3W
Malden, Lon. 4 C3 51 23N 0 15W
Malečice, Pra. 10 B3 50 5N 14 30 E
Malekete, Lagos 18 A3 6 33N 7 32 E
Malir →, Kar. 17 H11 24 49N 67 4 E
Malir Cantonment, Kar. 17 G12 24 58N 67 10 E
Malmi, Hels. 3 B4 60 15N 24 59 E
Malmøya, Oslo 2 B4 59 52N 10 45 E
Målov, Købn. 2 D9 55 44N 12 20 E
Malton, Trto. 20 D7 43 42N 79 38W
Malvern, Jobg. 18 F9 26 11 S 28 5 E
Malvern, Melb. 19 F7 37 50 S 145 2 E
Malvern, Phil. 24 A1 40 2N 75 31W
Malvern, Trto. 20 D9 43 47N 79 13W
Malvern East, Jobg. 18 F9 26 11 S 28 7 E
Malverne, N.Y. 23 C6 40 40N 73 40W
Mamaroneck, N.Y. 23 B6 40 56N 73 44W
Mamaroneck Harbour, N.Y. 23 B6 40 56N 73 42W
Mamonovo, Mos. 11 F10 55 36N 37 49 E
Mamonovo, Mos. 11 E8 55 41N 37 18 E
Mampong Prapatan, Jak. 15 J9 6 15 S 106 49 E
Mampukuji, Tōkyō 13 C2 35 36N 139 31 E
Man Budrukh, Bomb. 16 G8 19 2N 72 55 E
Man Khurd, Bomb. 16 G8 19 3N 72 55 E
Managua, La Hab. 30 C3 22 58N 82 17W
Manayunk, Phil. 24 A3 40 1N 75 12W
Mandaluyong, Manila 15 D4 14 35N 121 1 E
Mandaoli, Delhi 16 B2 28 37N 77 17 E
Mandaqui, S. Pau. 31 D6 23 29 S 46 37W
Mandaqui →, S. Pau. 31 D6 23 30 S 46 40W
Mandres-les-Roses, Paris 5 C5 48 42N 2 32 E
Mandvi, Bomb. 16 H8 18 56N 72 50 E
Mang Kung Uk, H.K. 12 E6 22 18N 114 16 E
Manggarai, Jak. 15 J10 6 12 S 106 50 E
Manguinho, Aéroporto de, Rio J. 31 B2 22 52 S 43 14W
Mangweon, Sŏul 12 G7 37 33N 126 55 E
Manhasset, N.Y. 23 C6 40 47N 73 40W
Manhasset B., N.Y. 23 C6 40 49N 73 43W
Manhasset Hills, N.Y. 23 C7 40 45N 73 40W
Manhattan, N.Y. 22 C5 40 48N 73 57W
Manhattan Beach, L.A. 28 C2 33 53N 118 24W
Manhatten, N.Y. 22 D5 40 34N 73 56W
Manila, Manila 15 D3 14 35N 120 58 E
Manila B., Manila 15 D3 14 32N 120 58 E
Manila Int. Airport, Manila 15 D4 14 31N 121 0 E
Mankkaa, Hels. 3 B3 60 11N 24 47 E
Mankunda, Calc. 16 C6 22 50N 88 22 E
Manly, Syd. 19 A4 33 47 S 151 17 E
Manly Warringah War Memorial Park, Syd. 19 A4 33 46 S 151 15 E
Manning State Park, Bost. 21 B1 42 34N 71 20W
Mannsworth, Wien 10 H11 48 8N 16 30 E
Manoa, Phil. 24 B3 39 58N 75 18W
Manor Park, Lon. 4 B5 51 32N 0 1 E
Manora, Kar. 17 H10 24 47N 66 58 E
Manorhaven, N.Y. 23 B6 40 50N 73 41W
Manoteras, Mdrd. 8 B3 40 28N 3 39W
Manquehue, Cerro, Stgo 30 J11 33 21 S 70 35W
Mantegazza, Mil. 9 D4 45 30N 8 58 E
Mantilla, La Hab. 30 B3 23 4N 82 20W
Mantua, Phil. 24 C3 39 47N 75 10W
Mantua Cr. →, Phil. 24 C3 39 47N 75 13W
Manufacta, Jobg. 18 E8 26 9 S 27 51 E
Manzanares, Canal de, Mdrd. 8 C3 40 19N 3 38W
Mapetla, Jobg. 18 F8 26 16 S 27 51 E
Maple, Trto. 20 C7 43 51N 79 30W
Maple L., Chic. 26 C1 41 43N 87 53W
Maple Shade, Phil. 24 B4 39 57N 75 0W
Maplewood, N.Y. 22 C3 40 43N 74 16W
Maracana, Rio J. 31 B2 22 54 S 43 13W
Maraisburg, Jobg. 18 F8 26 10 S 27 57 E
Marano di Nápoli, Nápl. 9 H12 40 53N 14 11 E
Maraoli, Bomb. 16 G8 19 2N 72 53 E
Marapendi, L. de, Rio J. 31 C1 23 0 S 43 23W
Marblehead, Bost. 21 C4 42 29N 70 51W
Marcelin, Wsaw. 10 E6 52 19N 20 59 E
Marcella, N.Y. 22 B2 40 59N 74 29W
Marcos Paz, B.A. 32 C2 34 46 S 58 49W
Marcoussis, Paris 5 D3 48 38N 2 13 E
Marcus Hook, Phil. 24 C2 39 49N 75 25W
Marcus Hook Cr. →, Phil. 24 B2 39 49N 75 24W
Marechiaro, Nápl. 9 J12 40 48N 14 12 E
Mareil-Marly, Paris 5 B2 48 52N 2 4 E
Margareten, Wien 10 G10 48 11N 16 20 E
Margency, Paris 5 A3 49 0N 2 17 E
Margitsziget, Bud. 10 J13 47 31N 19 2 E
Maria, Wien 10 G10 48 11N 16 21 E
Maria Paula, Rio J. 31 B3 22 53 S 43 1W
Marianao, La Hab. 30 B2 23 4N 82 25W
Marianella, Nápl. 9 H12 40 53N 14 13 E
Mariano Acosta, B.A. 32 C2 34 42 S 58 47W
Mariano J. Haedo, B.A. 32 B3 34 39 S 58 35W
Maridalen, Oslo 2 B4 59 59N 10 45 E
Maridalsvatnet, Oslo 2 B4 59 58N 10 46 E
Mariendorf, Berl. 7 B3 52 26N 13 23 E
Marienfelde, Berl. 7 B3 52 24N 13 23 E
Marienthal, Hbg. 7 D8 53 34N 10 4 E
Mariglianella, Nápl. 9 H13 40 55N 14 26 E
Marigliano, Nápl. 9 H13 40 55N 14 27 E
Marikina, Manila 15 D4 14 38N 121 5 E
Marikina →, Manila 15 D4 14 33N 121 3 E
Marin City, S.F. 27 A1 37 52N 122 30W
Marin Headlands State Park, S.F. 27 A2 37 50N 122 28W
Marin Is., S.F. 27 A2 37 57N 122 27W
Marin Pen., S.F. 27 A1 37 50N 122 30W
Marine World, S.F. 27 C3 37 32N 122 16W
Mariners Harbour, N.Y. 22 D3 40 38N 74 10W
Mario, Mt., Rome 9 F9 41 55N 12 27 E
Markham, Chic. 26 D2 41 35N 87 40W
Markham, Phil. 24 B1 39 53N 75 30W
Markham, Trto. 20 D8 43 49N 79 22W
Markham, Mt., L.A. 28 A4 34 14N 118 6W
Marki, Wsaw. 10 E7 52 19N 21 6 E
Markland Wood, Trto. 20 E7 43 38N 79 34W
Marlton, Phil. 24 B5 39 53N 74 55W
Marly, Forêt de, Paris 5 B2 48 52N 2 2 E
Marly-le-Roi, Paris 5 B2 48 52N 2 5 E
Marne →, Paris 5 C4 48 47N 2 29 E
Marne-la-Vallée, Paris 5 B5 48 50N 2 37 E
Marolles-en-Brie, Paris 5 C5 48 44N 2 33 E
Maroonda Aquaduct, Melb. 19 E7 37 40 S 145 9 E
Maroubra, Syd. 19 B4 33 56 S 151 16 E
Marple, Phil. 24 B2 39 56N 75 21W
Marquette Park, Chic. 26 C2 41 46N 87 42W
Marrickville, Syd. 19 B3 33 54 S 151 9 E
Marschlande, Hbg. 7 E8 53 27N 10 6 E
Marsfield, Syd. 19 A3 33 46 S 151 7 E
Marte, Base Aérea de, S. Pau. 31 E6 23 30 S 46 38W
Martesana, Navíglio della, Mil. 9 D6 45 31N 9 17 E
Martin State Nat. Airport, Balt. 25 B4 39 19N 76 24W
Martinez, B.A. 32 A3 34 29 S 58 31W
Martinkylä, Hels. 3 B4 60 17N 24 51 E
Martins Pond, Bost. 21 B3 42 35N 71 7W
Martinsried, Mün. 7 G9 48 6N 11 27 E
Maruko, Tōkyō 13 C3 35 33N 139 39 E
Marusino, Mos. 11 E11 55 41N 37 58 E
Marxloh, Ruhr 6 A2 51 30N 6 47 E
Maryino, Mos. 11 E10 55 40N 37 45 E
Maryland, Sing. 15 G7 1 19N 103 47 E
Maryland, Univ. of, Wash. 25 D8 39 58N 76 56W
Marylebone, Lon. 4 B4 51 31N 0 9W
Marymont, Wsaw. 10 E6 52 16N 20 58 E
Marysin Wawerski, Wsaw. 10 E7 52 14N 21 9 E
Marzahn, Berl. 7 A4 52 32N 13 34 E
Masambong, Manila 15 D4 14 38N 121 0 E
Mascot, Syd. 19 B4 33 55 S 151 12 E
Mascuppic L., Bost. 21 A1 42 40N 71 23W
Masmo, Stock. 3 E10 59 15N 17 53 E
Maspeth, N.Y. 22 C5 40 43N 73 55W
Masr el Gedida, El Qâ. 18 C5 30 5N 31 19 E
Masr el Qadîma, El Qâ. 18 C5 30 0N 31 14 E
Masroor Airport, Kar. 17 G10 24 53N 66 56 E
Massa di Somma, Nápl. 9 H13 40 50N 14 22 E
Massachusetts B., Bost. 21 C4 42 25N 70 50W
Massachusetts Inst. of Tech., Bost. 21 C3 42 22N 71 6W
Massamá, Lisb. 8 F7 38 45N 9 16W
Massapequa, N.Y. 23 C8 40 40N 73 28W
Massby, Hels. 3 B6 60 17N 25 20 E
Massey →, Trto. 20 D9 43 42N 79 19W
Massy, Paris 5 C3 48 43N 2 16 E
Matarza →, B.A. 32 C3 34 47 S 58 35W
Matasango, Lima 30 G9 12 3 S 76 58W
Mathle, Calc. 16 E5 22 34N 88 13 E
Matihutong, Beij. 14 B3 39 56N 116 19 E
Matinecock, N.Y. 23 B7 40 51N 73 36W
Matinha, Lisb. 8 F8 38 45N 9 5W
Matramam, Jak. 15 J10 6 12 S 106 51 E
Matsubara, Ōsaka 12 C4 34 34N 135 33 E
Matsubushi, Tōkyō 13 A3 35 55N 139 49 E
Matsudo, Tōkyō 13 B4 35 46N 139 54 E
Matsumoloshinden, Tōkyō 13 B2 35 50N 139 36 E
Mattapan, Bost. 21 D3 42 16N 71 6W
Mátyásföld, Bud. 10 J14 47 30N 19 12 E
Mau Tso Ngam, H.K. 12 D6 22 21N 114 15 E
Mauá, S. Pau. 31 E7 23 39 S 46 27W
Mauer, Wien 10 H9 48 9N 16 15 E
Mauerbach →, Wien 10 G9 48 12N 16 13 E
Mauldre, Paris 5 C1 48 49N 1 52 E
Maurecourt, Paris 5 B2 48 59N 2 3 E
Mauregard, Paris 5 A5 49 2N 2 34 E
Maurepas, Paris 5 C1 48 46N 1 55 E
Mauripur, Kar. 17 G10 24 52N 66 55 E
Maxhof, Mün. 7 G9 48 4N 11 29 E
Maya-Zan, Ōsaka 12 B2 34 43N 135 12 E
Maybunga, Manila 15 D4 14 34N 121 4 E
Mayfair, Jobg. 18 F9 26 11 S 28 0 E
Mayfair, Phil. 24 A4 40 2N 75 3W
Maypajo, Manila 15 D3 14 38N 120 58 E
Maytubig, Manila 15 D3 14 33N 120 59 E
Maywood, Chic. 26 B1 41 52N 87 51W
Maywood, L.A. 28 C3 33 59N 118 12W
Maywood, N.Y. 22 B4 40 53N 74 3W
Mazagaon, Bomb. 16 H8 18 57N 72 50 E
M'Boi Mirim, S. Pau. 31 F5 23 42 S 46 46W
Meadow I., N.Y. 23 D7 40 36N 73 32W
Meadow L., N.Y. 23 C5 40 44N 73 50W
Meadowlands, Jobg. 18 F8 26 12 S 27 53 E
Meadowood, Wash. 25 C7 39 4N 77 0W
Měcholupy, Pra. 10 B3 50 3N 14 32 E
Měčice, Pra. 10 A3 50 11N 14 31 E
Mecidiyekoy, Ist. 17 A3 41 4N 29 0 E
Meckinghoven, Ruhr 6 A5 51 37N 7 19 E
Médan, Paris 5 B1 48 57N 1 59 E
Medfield, Bost. 21 D2 42 11N 71 18W
Medford, Bost. 21 C3 42 25N 71 7W
Media, Phil. 24 B2 39 55N 75 23W
Mediodia, Mdrd. 8 B3 40 22N 3 39W
Medvastö, Hels. 3 C2 60 5N 24 38 E
Medvedkovo, Mos. 11 D9 55 52N 37 37 E
Medvezhiy Ozyora, Mos. 11 D11 55 52N 37 59 E
Meerbeck, Ruhr 6 B1 51 28N 6 38 E
Meerbusch, Ruhr 6 C2 51 16N 6 40 E
Meguro →, Tōkyō 13 C3 35 37N 139 45 E
Meguro-Ku, Tōkyō 13 C3 35 37N 139 42 E
Mehpalpur, Delhi 16 B1 28 32N 77 7 E
Mehrābād Airport, Tehr. 17 C4 35 41N 51 18 E
Mehram Nagar, Delhi 16 B1 28 34N 77 8 E
Mehrow, Berl. 7 A4 52 34N 13 37 E
Meiderich, Ruhr 6 B2 51 27N 6 47 E
Meidling, Wien 10 G10 48 10N 16 20 E
Meiendorf, Hbg. 7 D8 53 37N 10 8 E
Méier, Rio J. 31 B2 22 52 S 43 15W
Meiji Shrine, Tōkyō 13 B3 35 41N 139 41 E
Meizino-Mori-Minō National Park, Ōsaka 12 A3 34 51N 135 28 E
Mejiro, Tōkyō 13 B3 35 43N 139 43 E
Melbourne, Melb. 19 E6 37 48 S 144 58 E
Melbourne Airport, Melb. 19 E6 37 40 S 144 50 E
Melbourne Univ., Melb. 19 E6 37 47 S 144 57 E
Melito di Nápoli, Nápl. 9 H12 40 55N 14 13 E
Melkki, Hels. 3 C4 60 8N 24 53 E
Mellingstedt, Hbg. 7 C8 53 40N 10 6 E
Mellunkylä, Hels. 3 B5 60 14N 25 5 E
Mellunmäki, Hels. 3 B5 60 14N 25 6 E
Melrose, Bost. 21 C3 42 27N 71 2W
Melrose, N.Y. 22 C5 40 49N 73 55W
Melrose Park, Chic. 26 B1 41 53N 87 50W
Melun-Sénart, Paris 5 D5 48 3N 2 31 E
Melun-Villaroche, Aérodrome de, Paris 5 D6 48 37N 2 41 E
Melville, N.Y. 23 C8 40 47N 73 24W
Menai, Syd. 19 C3 34 1 S 151 1 E
Menandon, Paris 5 A2 49 2N 2 3 E
Mendoza, Lima 30 G9 12 1 S 76 59W
Mengede, Ruhr 6 A6 51 34N 7 23 E
Mengjiazhai, Shang. 14 J11 31 19N 121 21 E
Menglinghausen, Ruhr 6 B6 51 28N 7 26 E
Menlo Park, S.F. 27 D3 37 27N 122 11W
Menlo Park Terrace, N.Y. 22 D3 40 34N 74 18W
Mentang, Jak. 15 J9 6 11 S 106 49 E
Menucourt, Paris 5 A1 49 1N 1 59 E
Meopham, Lon. 4 C7 51 22N 0 21 E
Mérantaise →, Paris 5 C2 48 42N 2 8 E
Mercamadrid, Mdrd. 8 B3 40 21N 3 39W
Merced, L., S.F. 27 B2 37 43N 122 29W
Merchantville, Phil. 24 B4 39 56N 75 3W
Mercier, Pont, Mtrl. 20 B3 43 24N 73 39W
Merdeka Palace, Jak. 15 J9 6 10 S 106 49 E
Meredale, Jobg. 18 F8 26 17 S 27 58 E
Mergellina, Nápl. 9 J12 40 49N 14 13 E
Meriden, N.Y. 22 B2 40 56N 74 27W
Merion Station, Phil. 24 B3 39 59N 75 15W
Merlimau, Sing. 15 G7 1 17N 103 42 E
Merlimau, P., Sing. 15 G7 1 17N 103 42 E
Merlo, B.A. 32 B2 34 39 S 58 43W
Merri Cr. →, Melb. 19 E6 37 47 S 144 59 E
Merrick, N.Y. 23 D7 40 39N 73 32W
Merrionette Park, Chic. 26 C2 41 41N 87 40W
Merritt, L., S.F. 27 B3 37 48N 122 15W
Merrylands, Syd. 19 B2 33 50 S 150 59 E
Merton, Lon. 4 C3 51 24N 0 11W
Mesgarābād, Tehr. 17 D6 35 27N 51 30 E
Meshcherskiy, Mos. 11 E8 55 40N 37 23 E
Mesquita, Rio J. 31 A1 22 46 S 43 25W
Messe, Wien 10 G10 48 13N 16 24 E
Messy, Paris 5 B6 48 58N 2 42 E
Metanópoli, Mil. 9 E6 45 24N 9 15 E
Methuen, Bost. 21 A2 42 42N 71 12W
Metropolitan Opera, N.Y. 22 C5 40 46N 74 59W
Mettman, Ruhr 6 C3 51 15N 6 58 E
Metuchen, N.Y. 22 D2 40 32N 74 21W
Metzkausen, Ruhr 6 C3 51 16N 6 57 E
Meudon, Paris 5 C3 48 48N 2 14 E
Meulan, Paris 5 A1 49 0N 1 54 E
México, Aeropuerto Int. de, Méx. 29 B3 19 25N 99 4W
México, Ciudad de, Méx. 29 B2 19 25N 99 7W
Mezzate, Mil. 9 E6 45 26N 9 17 E
Mia Dong, Sŏul 12 G8 37 36N 127 0 E
Miano, Nápl. 9 H12 40 53N 14 15 E
Miasto, Wsaw. 10 E6 52 13N 21 0 E
Michalin, Wsaw. 10 F8 52 9N 21 13 E
Michałowice, Wsaw. 10 E6 52 10N 20 52 E
Michle, Pra. 10 B2 50 3N 14 26 E
Mickleton, Phil. 24 C3 39 47N 75 14W
Middle →, Balt. 25 B4 39 19N 76 25W
Middle B., N.Y. 23 D7 40 38N 73 36W
Middle Branch →, Balt. 25 B3 39 15N 76 37W
Middle Brewster I., Bost. 21 C4 42 20N 70 51W
Middle Cove, Syd. 19 A4 33 48 S 151 13 E
Middle Harbour, Syd. 19 A4 33 47 S 151 14 E
Middle Hd., Syd. 19 A4 33 49 S 151 15 E
Middle I., H.K. 12 E6 22 16N 114 10 E
Middle Park, Melb. 19 F6 37 50 S 144 57 E
Middle River, Balt. 25 A4 39 20N 76 26W
Middle Village, N.Y. 23 C5 40 42N 73 52W
Middleborough, Balt. 25 B4 39 18N 76 26W
Middlesex, N.Y. 22 D2 40 34N 74 29W
Middlesex Fells Reservation, Bost. 21 C3 42 27N 71 6W
Middlesex Res., N.Y. 22 D3 40 37N 74 19W
Middleton, Bost. 21 B3 42 35N 71 0W
Middleton Pond, Bost. 21 B3 42 36N 71 1W
Middleville, N.Y. 23 B9 40 54N 73 19W
Midland Beach, N.Y. 22 D4 40 34N 74 5W
Midland Park, N.Y. 22 B4 40 59N 74 9W

42 Midlothian

Midlothian, *Chic.* 26 D2 41 37N 87 43W
Miedzeszyn, *Wsaw.* 10 E8 52 10N 21 11 E
Międzylesie, *Wsaw.* 10 E8 52 12N 21 10 E
Miessaari, *Hels.* 3 C3 60 8N 24 47 E
Mikhaylovskoye, *Mos.* 11 F9 55 35N 37 35 E
Mikhelysona, *Mos.* 11 E11 55 42N 37 52 E
Milano, *Mil.* 9 E5 45 28N 9 10 E
Milano Due, *Mil.* 9 E6 45 29N 9 16 E
Milano San Felice, *Mil.* 9 E6 45 28N 9 18 E
Milanolago, *Mil.* 9 E6 45 27N 9 17 E
Milbertshofen, *Mün.* 7 F10 48 10N 11 34 E
Milburn, *N.Y.* 22 C3 40 43N 74 19W
Milford, *Balt.* 25 A2 39 21N 76 43W
Mill Cr. →, *S.F.* 27 A1 37 53N 122 31W
Mill Hill, *Lon.* 4 B3 51 37N 0 14W
Mill Neck, *N.Y.* 23 B7 40 53N 73 33W
Mill Park, *Melb.* 19 E7 37 40 S 145 3 E
Mill Valley, *S.F.* 27 A1 37 54N 122 33W
Millbrae, *S.F.* 27 C2 37 35N 122 22W
Mille-Iles, R. des →, *Mtrl.* 20 A3 43 39N 73 46W
Miller I., *Balt.* 25 B4 39 15N 76 21W
Miller Meadow, *Chic.* 26 B2 41 51N 87 49W
Milliken, *Trto.* 20 D9 43 49N 79 17W
Millis, *Bost.* 21 D1 42 10N 71 21W
Mills College, *S.F.* 27 B3 37 46N 122 10W
Milltown, *Phil.* 24 B1 39 57N 75 32W
Millwall, *Lon.* 4 C4 51 29N 0 0 E
Millwood, *Wash.* 25 D8 38 52N 76 52W
Milon-la-Chapelle, *Paris* 5 C2 48 43N 2 3 E
Milpa Alta, *Méx.* 29 C3 19 11N 99 0W
Milperra, *Syd.* 19 B2 33 56 S 150 59 E
Milspe, *Ruhr* 6 C5 51 18N 7 19 E
Milton, *Bost.* 21 D3 42 14N 71 2W
Milton Village, *Bost.* 21 D3 42 15N 71 4W
Mimico, *Trto.* 20 E8 43 36N 79 29W
Mimico Cr. →, *Trto.* 20 E7 43 37N 79 33W
Minami, *Ōsaka* 12 B4 34 40N 135 30 E
Minami-Ku, *Tōkyō* 13 D2 35 24N 139 37 E
Minami-tsunashima, *Tōkyō* 13 C2 35 32N 139 37 E
Minato, *Ōsaka* 12 C3 34 39N 135 25 E
Minato-Ku, *Tōkyō* 13 C3 35 39N 139 44 E
Mine, *Tōkyō* 13 B3 35 49N 139 46 E
Minebank Run →, *Balt.* 25 A3 39 24N 76 33W
Mineola, *N.Y.* 23 C7 40 44N 73 38W
Ministro Rivadavia, *B.A.* 32 D4 34 50 S 58 22W
Minō, *Ōsaka* 12 B3 34 49N 135 28 E
Minshât el Bekkarî, *El Qâ.* 18 C4 30 0N 31 8 E
Minto, *Syd.* 19 C2 34 1 S 150 51 E
Minute Man Nat. Hist. Park, *Bost.* 21 C2 42 25N 71 16W
Mirafiori, *Tori.* 9 B2 45 1N 7 36 E
Miraflores, *Lima* 30 G8 12 7 S 77 2W
Miramar, *La Hab.* 30 B2 23 7N 82 25W
Miramar, *S.F.* 27 D2 37 29N 122 27W
Miranda, *Syd.* 19 C3 34 2 S 151 6 E
Mirzapur, *Calc.* 16 D6 22 49N 88 24 E
Misato, *Tōkyō* 13 B4 35 49N 139 51 E
Misericordia, Sa. da, *Rio J.* 31 B2 22 51 S 43 17W
Mishawum L., *Bost.* 21 B3 42 30N 71 8W
Mission, *S.F.* 27 B2 37 44N 122 25W
Mississauga, *Trto.* 20 E7 43 35N 79 34W
Mitaka, *Tōkyō* 13 B2 35 41N 139 34 E
Mitcham, *Lon.* 4 C3 51 23N 0 10W
Mitcham, *Melb.* 19 E8 37 48 S 145 12 E
Mitcham Common, *Lon.* 4 C4 51 23N 0 8W
Mitino, *Mos.* 11 D8 55 51N 37 20 E
Mitry, *Paris* 5 B5 48 59N 2 36 E
Mitry-Mory, *Paris* 5 B5 48 59N 2 38 E
Mitry-Mory, Aérodrome de, *Paris* 5 B5 48 59N 2 37 E
Mitte, *Berl.* 7 A3 52 32N 13 24 E
Mittel Isarkanal, *Mün.* 7 F11 48 12N 11 40 E
Mittenheim, *Mün.* 7 F10 48 15N 11 33 E
Mixcoac, Presa de, *Méx.* 29 B2 19 21N 99 14W
Mixquic, *Méx.* 29 C4 19 13N 98 58W
Miyakojima, *Ōsaka* 12 B4 34 42N 135 31 E
Miyalo, *Tōkyō* 13 B2 35 49N 139 35 E
Mizonokuchi, *Tōkyō* 13 C2 35 35N 139 34 E
Mizue, *Tōkyō* 13 B4 35 41N 139 54 E
Mizuko, *Tōkyō* 13 A2 35 50N 139 32 E
Mizumoto, *Tōkyō* 13 B4 35 46N 139 52 E
Młocinski Park, *Wsaw.* 10 E6 52 19N 20 57 E
Młociny, *Wsaw.* 10 E6 52 18N 20 55 E
Mnevniki, *Mos.* 11 E8 55 45N 37 28 E
Moba, *Lagos* 18 B2 6 26N 7 28 E
Moczydło, *Wsaw.* 10 F7 52 8N 21 2 E
Modderfontein, *Jobg.* 18 E10 26 5 S 28 10 E
Modderfontein →, *Jobg.* 18 E9 26 5 S 28 10 E
Modřany, *Pra.* 10 B2 50 0N 14 24 E
Moers, *Ruhr* 6 B1 51 26N 6 37 E
Moffat Park, *Jobg.* 18 F9 26 15 S 28 4 E
Mofolo, *Jobg.* 18 F8 26 13 S 27 53 E
Mog, *Sŏul* 12 G7 37 32N 126 52 E
Mogyorod, *Bud.* 10 J14 47 35N 19 14 E
Mohili, *Bomb.* 16 G8 19 5N 72 52 E
Moinho Velho →, *S. Pau.* 31 E6 23 35 S 46 35W
Moissy-Cramayel, *Paris* 5 D5 48 37N 2 35 E
Moita, *Lisb.* 8 G9 38 39N 8 59W
Mokotów, *Wsaw.* 10 E7 52 12N 21 0 E
Molapo, *Jobg.* 18 F8 26 15 S 27 51 E
Mole →, *Lon.* 4 D2 51 14N 0 20W
Moletsane, *Jobg.* 18 F8 26 14 S 27 50 E
Molino de Rosas, *Méx.* 29 B2 19 21N 99 14W
Mølleå →, *Købn.* 2 D10 55 48N 12 35 E
Möllen, *Ruhr* 6 A2 51 35N 6 41 E
Mollins de Rey, *Barc.* 8 D5 41 24N 2 1 E
Molokovo, *Mos.* 11 F11 55 35N 37 53 E
Mombaça, *S. Pau.* 31 E7 23 37 S 46 25W
Mombello, *Mil.* 9 D5 45 36N 9 7 E
Momote, *Tōkyō* 13 B2 35 46N 139 37 E
Monash Univ., *Melb.* 19 F7 37 54 S 145 8 E
Monbulk Cr. →, *Melb.* 19 F8 37 55 S 145 12 E
Moncalieri, *Tori.* 9 B3 45 0N 7 41 E
Moncolombone, *Tori.* 9 A1 45 12N 7 28 E
Mondeor, *Jobg.* 18 F9 26 16 S 28 0 E
Moneda, Palacio de la, *Stgo* 30 J11 33 26 S 70 39W
Mong Kok, *H.K.* 12 E6 22 19N 114 10 E
Mongat, *Barc.* 8 D6 41 27N 2 16 E
Mongreno, *Tori.* 9 B3 45 3N 7 45 E
Moninos →, *S. Pau.* 31 F6 23 40 S 46 33W
Monrovia, *L.A.* 28 B4 34 9N 118 1W
Monsanto, *Lisb.* 8 F7 38 44N 9 12W
Monsanto, Parque Florestal de, *Lisb.* 8 F7 38 43N 9 11W
Mont Royal, *Mtrl.* 20 A4 43 30N 73 38W
Mont-Royal, Parc, *Mtrl.* 20 A4 43 30N 73 36W
Montalban, *Car.* 30 E5 10 28N 66 56W
Montana de Montjuich, *Barc.* 8 D5 41 21N 2 9 E
Montara, *S.F.* 27 C2 37 32N 122 30W
Montara, Pt., *S.F.* 27 C1 37 32N 122 31W
Montara Mt., *S.F.* 27 C2 37 32N 122 27W
Montchanin, *Phil.* 24 C1 39 47N 75 35W
Montclair, *N.Y.* 22 C3 40 49N 74 12W
Monte Chingolo, *B.A.* 32 C4 34 43 S 58 22W
Monte Grande, *B.A.* 32 C4 34 48 S 58 27W
Monte Sacro, *Rome* 9 F10 41 56N 12 32 E
Montebello, *L.A.* 28 B4 34 1N 118 8W
Montelera, *Tori.* 9 B1 45 9N 7 26 E
Montemor, *Lisb.* 8 F7 38 49N 9 12W
Monterey Park, *L.A.* 28 B4 34 3N 118 7W
Monterrey, *La Hab.* 30 B3 23 5N 82 18W
Montespaccato, *Rome* 9 F9 41 54N 12 23 E
Montesson, *Paris* 5 B2 48 54N 2 8 E
Monteverde Nuovo, *Rome* 9 F9 41 52N 12 26 E
Montfermeil, *Paris* 5 B5 48 54N 2 33 E
Montgeron, *Paris* 5 C4 48 42N 2 27 E
Montigny-le-Bretonneux, *Paris* 5 C2 48 46N 2 1 E
Montigny-les-Cormeilles, *Paris* 5 B3 48 59N 2 11 E
Montijo, *Lisb.* 8 F9 38 42N 8 58W
Montjay-la-Tour, *Paris* 5 B6 48 54N 2 40 E
Montlhéry, *Paris* 5 D3 48 38N 2 16 E
Montlignon, *Paris* 5 A3 49 0N 2 16 E
Montmagny, *Paris* 5 B4 48 58N 2 21 E
Montmorency, *Paris* 5 B3 48 59N 2 19 E
Montmorency, Forêt de, *Paris* 5 A3 49 2N 2 16 E
Montparnasse, Gare, *Paris* 5 B3 48 50N 2 19 E
Montpelier, *Wash.* 25 C8 39 3N 76 50W
Montréal, *Mtrl.* 20 A4 43 30N 73 33W
Montréal, Î. de, *Mtrl.* 20 A4 43 30N 73 40W
Montréal, Univ. de, *Mtrl.* 20 B4 43 29N 73 37W
Montréal-Est, *Mtrl.* 20 A4 43 37N 73 31W
Montréal Nord, *Mtrl.* 20 A4 43 36N 73 36W
Montreuil, *Paris* 5 B4 48 51N 2 27 E
Montrose, *L.A.* 28 A3 34 12N 118 12W
Montrose, *Melb.* 19 E8 37 49 S 145 19 E
Montrose, *Wash.* 25 C7 39 2N 77 7W
Montrouge, *Paris* 5 C3 48 48N 2 18 E
Montvale, *N.Y.* 22 A4 41 2N 74 1W
Montville, *N.Y.* 22 B2 40 55N 74 23W
Monza, *Mil.* 9 D6 45 35N 9 16 E
Monzoro, *Mil.* 9 E5 45 27N 9 2 E
Moóca, *S. Pau.* 31 E6 23 33 S 46 35W
Moóca →, *S. Pau.* 31 E6 23 35 S 46 35W
Moonachie, *N.Y.* 22 C4 40 50N 74 2W
Moonee Ponds, *Melb.* 19 E6 37 45 S 144 53 E
Moonee Valley Racecourse, *Melb.* 19 E6 37 45 S 144 55 E
Moorbek, *Hbg.* 7 C7 53 41N 9 58 E
Moorburg, *Hbg.* 7 E7 53 29N 9 55 E
Moorebank, *Syd.* 19 B2 33 56 S 150 56 E
Moorestown, *Phil.* 24 B5 39 58N 74 56W
Moorfleet, *Hbg.* 7 D8 53 30N 10 4 E
Mooroolbark, *Melb.* 19 E8 37 46 S 145 19 E
Moorwerder, *Hbg.* 7 E8 53 28N 10 3 E
Moosach, *Mün.* 7 F10 48 10N 11 30 E
Mora, *Bomb.* 16 H8 18 54N 72 55 E
Moraga, *S.F.* 27 B4 37 49N 122 7W
Morainvilliers, *Paris* 5 B1 48 55N 1 56 E
Morales →, *B.A.* 32 C2 34 47 S 58 35W
Morangis, *Paris* 5 C4 48 42N 2 20 E
Moratalaz, *Mdrd.* 8 B3 40 24N 3 39W
Morbras →, *Paris* 5 C5 48 46N 2 30 E
Mörby, *Stock.* 3 D11 59 23N 18 3 E
Morce →, *Paris* 5 B4 48 57N 2 25 E
Morden, *Lon.* 4 C3 51 24N 0 13W
Morehill, *Jobg.* 18 F11 26 10 S 28 20 E
Moreno, *B.A.* 32 B2 34 38 S 58 45W
Moreno, *Rome* 9 G10 41 48N 12 37 E
Morgan Park, *Chic.* 26 C3 41 41N 87 38W
Moriguchi, *Ōsaka* 12 B4 34 43N 135 34 E
Morivione, *Mil.* 9 E6 45 26N 9 12 E
Morningside, *Jobg.* 18 E9 26 4 S 28 3 E
Morningside, *Wash.* 25 E8 38 49N 76 53W
Morningside Park, *Trto.* 20 D9 43 46N 79 12W
Moroka, *Jobg.* 18 F8 26 15 S 27 52 E
Moron, *B.A.* 32 B3 34 39 S 58 37W
Morris Plains, *N.Y.* 22 C2 40 49N 74 29W
Morristown, *N.Y.* 22 C2 40 47N 74 28W
Morro, Castillo del, *La Hab.* 30 B2 23 8N 82 21W
Morro Pelado, *S. Pau.* 31 E7 23 38 S 46 24W
Morro Solar, *Lima* 30 H8 12 11 S 77 1W
Morsang-sur-Orge, *Paris* 5 D4 48 39N 2 21 E
Mörsenbroich, *Ruhr* 6 C2 51 15N 6 48 E
Morses Pond, *Bost.* 21 D2 42 17N 71 19W
Morte →, *Paris* 5 C3 48 40N 2 16 E
Mortlake, *Lon.* 4 C3 51 27N 0 15W
Mortlake, *Syd.* 19 B3 33 50 S 151 6 E
Morton, *Phil.* 24 B2 39 54N 75 20W
Morton Grove, *Chic.* 26 A2 42 2N 87 46W
Mory, *Paris* 5 B5 48 58N 2 37 E
Moscavide, *Lisb.* 8 F8 38 47N 9 6W
Moscow = Moskva, *Mos.* 11 E9 55 45N 37 37 E
Mosede, *Købn.* 2 E8 55 34N 12 17 E
Mosede Strand, *Købn.* 2 E8 55 34N 12 17 E
Mosjøen, *Oslo* 2 C6 50 49N 11 0 E
Moskhaton, *Ath.* 8 J11 37 55N 23 40 E
Moskva, *Mos.* 11 E9 55 45N 37 37 E
Moskvoretskiy, *Mos.* 11 E9 55 42N 37 37 E
Mosman, *Syd.* 19 A4 33 49 S 151 15 E
Moss Beach, *S.F.* 27 C2 37 31N 122 30W
Móstoles, *Mdrd.* 8 C1 40 18N 3 51W
Moto →, *Tōkyō* 13 A3 35 53N 139 45 E
Motol, *Pra.* 10 B1 50 3N 14 19 E
Motspur Park, *Lon.* 4 C3 51 23N 0 14W
Mottingham, *Lon.* 4 C5 51 26N 0 1 E
Mount Airy, *Phil.* 24 A3 40 3N 75 10W
Mount Dennis, *Trto.* 20 D8 43 40N 79 28W
Mount Ephraim, *Phil.* 24 B4 39 52N 75 5W
Mount Greenwood, *Chic.* 26 C2 41 42N 87 42W
Mount Hood Memorial Park, *Bost.* 21 C3 42 26N 71 1W
Mount Pleasant, *Lon.* 4 B2 51 30N 0 22W
Mount Pleasant Park, *Balt.* 25 A3 39 22N 76 34W
Mount Prospect, *Chic.* 26 A1 42 3N 87 54W
Mount Royal, *Phil.* 24 C3 39 48N 75 12W
Mount Tamalpais State Park, *S.F.* 27 A1 37 53N 122 34W
Mount Vernon, *N.Y.* 23 B6 40 54N 73 49W
Mount Waverley, *Melb.* 19 F7 37 52 S 145 7 E
Mount Wilson Observatory, *L.A.* 28 A4 34 13N 118 4W
Mountain Lakes, *N.Y.* 22 B2 40 54N 74 27W
Mountain Spring Ls., *N.Y.* 22 A2 41 2N 74 21W
Mountain View, *N.Y.* 22 B3 40 55N 74 15W
Mountainside, *N.Y.* 22 C2 40 40N 74 21W
Mountnessing, *Lon.* 4 B7 51 39N 0 21 E
Moûtiers, *Paris* 5 D1 48 36N 1 58 E
Mozu, *Ōsaka* 12 C3 34 33N 135 29 E
Müggelberge, *Berl.* 7 B4 52 25N 13 37 E
Müggelheim, *Berl.* 7 B5 52 24N 13 40 E
Muggiò, *Mil.* 9 D6 45 35N 9 13 E
Mugnano di Nápoli, *Nápl.* 9 H12 40 54N 14 12 E
Mühleiten, *Wien* 10 G11 48 10N 16 33 E
Mühlenau →, *Hbg.* 7 C7 53 41N 9 56 E
Mühlenfliess →, *Berl.* 7 A5 52 32N 13 42 E
Muir Beach, *S.F.* 27 A1 37 51N 122 34W
Muirkirk, *Wash.* 25 C8 39 3N 76 53W
Mujahidpur, *Delhi* 16 B2 28 33N 77 14 E
Mukandpur, *Delhi* 16 A2 28 44N 77 10 E
Muko →, *Ōsaka* 12 B3 34 48N 135 22 E
Mukojima, *Tōkyō* 13 B3 35 43N 139 49 E
Mulbarton, *Jobg.* 18 F9 26 17 S 28 3 E
Mulford Gardens, *S.F.* 27 B3 37 42N 122 10W
Mulgrave, *Melb.* 19 F8 37 55 S 145 12 E
Mülheim, *Ruhr* 6 B3 51 25N 6 53 E
Mullica Hill, *Phil.* 24 C3 39 44N 75 13W
Mullum Mullum Cr. →, *Melb.* 19 E8 37 44 S 145 10 E
Münchehofe, *Berl.* 7 B5 52 29N 13 40 E
München, *Mün.* 7 G10 48 8N 11 34 E
Munchen-Riem, Flughafen, *Mün.* 7 G11 48 7N 11 42 E
Munich = München, *Mün.* 7 G10 48 8N 11 34 E
Munirka, *Delhi* 16 B2 28 33N 77 10 E
Muniz, *B.A.* 32 B2 34 33 S 58 41W
Munkkiniemi, *Hels.* 3 B4 60 11N 24 52 E
Munro, *B.A.* 32 B3 34 31 S 58 31W
Munsey Park, *N.Y.* 23 C6 40 47N 73 40W
Münsterkirche, *Ruhr* 6 B4 51 27N 7 0 E
Muranów, *Wsaw.* 10 E6 52 14N 20 58 E
Murayama-chosuichi, *Tōkyō* 13 B1 35 45N 139 26 E
Murrumbeena, *Melb.* 19 F7 37 53 S 145 4 E
Musashino, *Tōkyō* 13 B2 35 42N 139 33 E
Mushin, *Lagos* 18 A2 6 31N 7 21 E
Musinè, Mte., *Tori.* 9 B1 45 7N 7 27 E
Musocco, *Mil.* 9 E5 45 29N 9 8 E
Musta Hevonen, *Hels.* 3 B6 60 11N 25 14 E
Mustafabad, *Delhi* 16 A2 28 43N 77 13 E
Mustansiriya, *Bagd.* 17 E8 33 22N 44 24 E
Musturud, *El Qâ.* 18 C5 30 8N 31 17 E
Muswell Hill, *Lon.* 4 B4 51 35N 0 8W
Mutanabi, *Bagd.* 17 F8 33 19N 44 21 E
Muthana, *Bagd.* 17 F8 33 19N 44 27 E
Mutinga, *S. Pau.* 31 D5 23 29 S 46 46W
Muttontown, *N.Y.* 23 C7 40 49N 73 32W
Muzon, *Manila* 15 D4 14 32N 121 8 E
Myaglovo, *St-Pet.* 11 B5 59 53N 30 39 E
Myakinino, *Mos.* 11 E8 55 48N 37 22 E
Mykerinos, *El Qâ.* 18 D4 29 28N 31 8 E
Myllykylä, *Hels.* 3 A4 60 21N 24 57 E
Myllypuro, *Hels.* 3 B5 60 13N 25 3 E
Myras, *Hels.* 3 B5 60 19N 25 6 E
Myrvoll, *Oslo* 2 C4 59 47N 10 48 E
Mystic Lakes, *Bost.* 21 C3 42 26N 71 8W
Mytishchi, *Mos.* 11 D10 55 53N 37 44 E

N

Nababpur, *Calc.* 16 D5 22 42N 88 12 E
Nações, Parque das, *S. Pau.* 31 E6 23 38 S 46 30W
Nachstebreck, *Ruhr* 6 C5 51 17N 7 14 E
Nacka, *Stock.* 3 E12 59 19N 18 10 E
Nada, *Ōsaka* 12 B2 34 42N 135 13 E
Nærsnes, *Oslo* 2 C2 59 45N 10 27 E
Nærum, *Købn.* 2 D10 55 48N 12 33 E
Nagareyama, *Tōkyō* 13 A4 35 51N 139 54 E
Nagasaki, *Tōkyō* 13 B3 35 43N 139 40 E
Nagasuga, *Tōkyō* 13 D4 35 21N 139 57 E
Nagata, *Ōsaka* 12 C1 34 39N 135 8 E
Nagatsuta, *Tōkyō* 13 C2 35 32N 139 31 E
Nagytarcsa, *Bud.* 10 J14 47 31N 19 17 E
Nagytétény, *Bud.* 10 K12 47 23N 18 59 E
Nahant, *Bost.* 21 C4 42 25N 70 54W
Nahant B., *Bost.* 21 C4 42 26N 70 54W
Nahant Harbor, *Bost.* 21 C4 42 25N 70 55W
Nahdein, W. el →, *El Qâ.* 18 C5 30 3N 31 19 E
Nahia, *El Qâ.* 18 C4 30 2N 31 7 E
Naihati, *Calc.* 16 C6 22 53N 88 25 E
Najafgarh Drain →, *Delhi* 16 B1 28 39N 77 4 E
Najio, *Ōsaka* 12 B2 34 49N 135 18 E
Naka →, *Tōkyō* 13 B4 35 49N 139 52 E
Naka-Ku, *Tōkyō* 13 D2 35 25N 139 38 E
Nakada, *Tōkyō* 13 D2 35 24N 139 30 E
Nakajima, *Tōkyō* 13 D4 35 25N 139 54 E
Nakano, *Tōkyō* 13 D4 35 25N 139 56 E
Nakano-Ku, *Tōkyō* 13 B2 35 42N 139 39 E
Nakasato, *Tōkyō* 13 D4 35 22N 139 55 E
Nakayama, *Tōkyō* 13 B4 35 43N 139 57 E
Nalikul, *Calc.* 16 D5 22 49N 88 10 E
Nalpur, *Calc.* 16 E5 22 31N 88 10 E
Namazie Estate, *Sing.* 15 F7 1 25N 103 42 E
Namgajha, *Sŏul* 12 G7 37 33N 126 55 E
Namsan Park, *Sŏul* 12 G7 37 32N 126 59 E
Namyeong, *Sŏul* 12 G7 37 32N 126 57 E
Nan Wan, *H.K.* 12 D5 22 20N 114 5 E
Nanbiancun, *Gzh.* 14 G7 23 4N 113 10 E
Nancefield, *Jobg.* 18 F8 26 17 S 27 54 E
Nanchang He →, *Beij.* 14 B2 39 58N 116 14 E
Nandaha, *Calc.* 16 D5 22 49N 88 18 E
Nandang, *Gzh.* 14 G8 23 6N 113 12 E
Nandian, *Tianj.* 14 D6 39 10N 117 16 E
Nangal Dewat, *Delhi* 16 B1 28 33N 77 5 E
Nangi, *Calc.* 16 E5 22 30N 88 13 E
Nangka →, *Manila* 15 D4 14 38N 121 8 E
Nangloi, *Delhi* 16 A1 28 41N 77 4 E
Nangloi Jat, *Delhi* 16 A1 28 41N 77 3 E
Nanhai, *Gzh.* 14 G7 23 2N 113 6 E
Nanhan He →, *Beij.* 14 B2 39 57N 116 11 E
Naniwa, *Ōsaka* 12 C3 34 39N 135 29 E
Nankai, *Tianj.* 14 E5 39 7N 117 10 E
Nanmenwai, *Tianj.* 14 E6 39 8N 117 10 E
Nanole, *Bomb.* 16 G8 19 0N 72 55 E
Nanshi, *Shang.* 14 J11 31 12N 121 29 E
Nanterre, *Paris* 5 B3 48 53N 2 12 E
Nantouillet, *Paris* 5 A6 49 0N 2 42 E
Nantusket Beach, *Bost.* 21 D4 42 16N 70 52W
Nanxiang, *Shang.* 14 J10 31 17N 121 18 E
Naoabad, *Calc.* 16 F6 22 28N 88 26 E
Napara, *Calc.* 16 E6 22 38N 88 23 E
Napier Mole, *Kar.* 17 H10 24 49N 66 58 E
Napindan, *Manila* 15 D4 14 32N 121 5 E
Naples = Nápoli, *Nápl.* 9 J12 40 50N 14 14 E
Nápoli, *Nápl.* 9 J12 40 50N 14 14 E
Nápoli, G. di, *Nápl.* 9 J12 40 46N 14 15 E
Naraina, *Delhi* 16 B1 28 36N 77 8 E
Narawa, *Tōkyō* 13 D4 35 25N 139 58 E
Narayanpara, *Calc.* 16 C5 22 53N 88 18 E
Narberth, *Phil.* 24 A3 40 0N 75 16W
Narimasu, *Tōkyō* 13 B2 35 46N 139 35 E
Nārmak, *Tehr.* 17 C5 35 42N 51 28 E
Närsta, *Stock.* 3 E9 59 17N 17 43 E
Naruo, *Ōsaka* 12 B3 34 43N 135 22 E
Näsby, *Stock.* 3 D11 59 25N 18 5 E
Näsbypark, *Stock.* 3 D11 59 25N 18 5 E
Näsfjärden, *Stock.* 3 D9 59 25N 17 41 E
Nassau Shore, *N.Y.* 23 D8 40 39N 73 26W
Natick, *Bost.* 21 D2 42 16N 71 19W
Nation, Place de la, *Paris* 5 B4 48 51N 2 23 E
National Arboretum, *Wash.* 25 D8 39 54N 76 59W
Nativitas, *Méx.* 29 C3 19 15N 99 5W
Natolin, *Wsaw.* 10 F7 52 8N 21 4 E
Naucalpan de Juárez, *Méx.* 29 B2 19 28N 99 14W
Naupada, *Bomb.* 16 G8 19 3N 72 50 E
Navíglio di Pavia, *Mil.* 9 E5 45 24N 9 9 E
Navíglio Grande, *Mil.* 9 E5 45 25N 9 5 E
Navotas, *Manila* 15 D3 14 39N 120 56 E
Nazal Hikmat Beg, *Bagd.* 17 E8 33 23N 44 25 E
Nazimabad, *Kar.* 17 G11 24 54N 67 1 E
Nazukari, *Tōkyō* 13 A4 35 50N 139 57 E
Néa Alexandhria, *Ath.* 8 J11 37 52N 23 46 E
Néa Faliron, *Ath.* 8 J10 37 55N 23 39 E
Néa Ionía, *Ath.* 8 H11 38 3N 23 45 E
Néa Liósia, *Ath.* 8 H11 38 3N 23 43 E
Néa Smirni, *Ath.* 8 J11 37 54N 23 43 E
Neapolis, *Ath.* 8 J11 37 58N 23 45 E
Neasden, *Lon.* 4 B3 51 35N 0 16W
Neauphle-le-Château, *Paris* 5 C1 48 48N 1 53 E
Nebučice, *Pra.* 10 B1 50 6N 14 19 E
Nedlitz, *Berl.* 7 B1 52 25N 13 3 E
Nee Soon, *Sing.* 15 F7 1 24N 103 49 E
Needham, *Bost.* 21 D2 42 16N 71 13W
Needham Heights, *Bost.* 21 D2 42 17N 71 14W
Needle Hill, *H.K.* 12 D5 22 23N 114 9 E
Negishi B., *Tōkyō* 13 D2 35 23N 139 38 E
Nehiti, *Calc.* 16 D5 22 42N 88 16 E
Nekrasovka, *Mos.* 11 E11 55 41N 37 55 E
Nematābād, *Tehr.* 17 D5 35 38N 51 21 E
Nemchinovka, *Mos.* 11 E7 55 42N 37 19 E
Népliget, *Bud.* 10 K13 47 29N 19 7 E
Neponset →, *Bost.* 21 D3 42 12N 71 9W
Nerima, *Tōkyō* 13 B3 35 44N 139 40 E
Nerul, *Bomb.* 16 G9 19 2N 73 0 E
Nerviano, *Mil.* 9 D4 45 32N 8 58 E
Nesodden, *Oslo* 2 C4 59 48N 10 41 E
Nesoddtangen, *Oslo* 2 B4 59 52N 10 41 E
Nesøya, *Oslo* 2 B3 59 52N 10 31 E
Nestipayac →, *Méx.* 29 A4 19 33N 89 57W
Netzahualcóyotl, *Méx.* 29 B3 19 24N 99 2W
Neu Aubing, *Mün.* 7 G9 48 8N 11 25 E
Neu Buch, *Berl.* 7 A4 52 37N 13 31 E
Neu Buchhorst, *Berl.* 7 B5 52 24N 13 44 E
Neu Fahrland, *Berl.* 7 B1 52 26N 13 3 E
Neu Lindenberg, *Berl.* 7 A4 52 36N 13 33 E
Neu Wulmstorf, *Hbg.* 7 E6 53 27N 9 48 E
Neu Zittau, *Berl.* 7 B5 52 23N 13 44 E
Neubiberg, *Mün.* 7 G11 48 4N 11 40 E
Neudorf, *Hbg.* 7 E8 53 27N 10 4 E
Neudorf, *Ruhr* 6 B2 51 25N 6 47 E
Neuegenbüttel, *Hbg.* 7 D7 53 38N 9 54 E
Neuenfelde, *Hbg.* 7 D6 53 31N 9 48 E
Neuenhagen, *Berl.* 7 A4 52 32N 13 38 E
Neuenkamp, *Ruhr* 6 B2 51 26N 6 43 E
Neuessling, *Wien* 10 G11 48 15N 16 32 E
Neugraben-Fischbek, *Hbg.* 7 E6 53 28N 9 49 E
Neuhausen, *Mün.* 7 G10 48 9N 11 32 E
Neuherberg, *Mün.* 7 F10 48 13N 11 35 E
Neuhönow, *Berl.* 7 A5 52 34N 13 44 E
Neuilly-Plaisance, *Paris* 5 B5 48 51N 2 30 E
Neuilly-sur-Marne, *Paris* 5 B5 48 51N 2 31 E
Neuilly-sur-Seine, *Paris* 5 B3 48 53N 2 15 E
Neukagran, *Wien* 10 G10 48 14N 16 27 E
Neukettenhof, *Wien* 10 H10 48 7N 16 28 E
Neukölln, *Berl.* 7 B3 52 28N 13 25 E
Neuland, *Hbg.* 7 E8 53 27N 10 0 E
Neuperlach, *Mün.* 7 G10 48 6N 11 37 E
Neuried, *Mün.* 7 G9 48 5N 11 27 E
Neuss, *Ruhr* 6 C2 51 12N 6 42 E
Neustift am Walde, *Wien* 10 G9 48 14N 16 17 E
Neusüssenbrunn, *Wien* 10 G10 48 16N 16 29 E
Neuville-sur-Oise, *Paris* 5 A2 49 0N 2 3 E
Neuwaldegg, *Wien* 10 G9 48 14N 16 17 E
Neuwiedenthal, *Hbg.* 7 E7 53 28N 9 52 E
Neva →, *St-Pet.* 11 B4 59 56N 30 20 E
Neves, *Rio J.* 31 B3 22 51 S 43 5W
Neviges, *Ruhr* 6 C4 51 18N 7 6 E
New Addington, *Lon.* 4 C4 51 20N 0 0 E
New Ash Green, *Lon.* 4 C6 51 22N 0 18 E
New Baghdād, *Bagd.* 17 F8 33 18N 44 28 E
New Barnet, *Lon.* 4 B3 51 38N 0 10W
New Brighton, *N.Y.* 22 D4 40 38N 74 5W
New Brunswick, *N.Y.* 22 D2 40 30N 74 29W
New Canada, *Jobg.* 18 F8 26 12 S 27 56 E
New Canada Dam, *Jobg.* 18 F8 26 12 S 27 56 E
New Canal →, *Calc.* 16 E6 22 33N 88 25 E
New Carrollton, *Wash.* 25 D8 38 58N 76 52W
New Cassell, *N.Y.* 23 C7 40 45N 73 32W
New Cross, *Lon.* 4 C4 51 28N 0 1W
New Delhi, *Delhi* 16 B2 28 36N 77 11 E
New Dorp, *N.Y.* 22 D4 40 34N 74 7W
New Dorp Beach, *N.Y.* 22 D4 40 33N 74 6W
New Hyde Park, *N.Y.* 23 C7 40 43N 73 39W
New Kleinfontein, *Jobg.* 18 F11 26 11 S 20 20 E
New Malden, *Lon.* 4 C3 51 24N 0 15W
New Milford, *N.Y.* 22 B4 40 56N 74 0W
New Modder, *Jobg.* 18 F11 26 10 S 28 21 E
New Providence, *N.Y.* 22 C2 40 42N 74 23W
New Redruth, *Jobg.* 18 F9 26 15 S 28 7 E
New Rochelle, *N.Y.* 23 B6 40 55N 73 45W
New South Wales, Univ. of, *Syd.* 19 B4 33 55 S 151 14 E
New Southgate, *Lon.* 4 B4 51 37N 0 7W
New Springville, *N.Y.* 22 D4 40 35N 74 9W
New Territories, *H.K.* 12 D5 22 23N 114 10 E
New Toronto, *Trto.* 20 E7 43 35N 79 30W
New Utrecht, *N.Y.* 22 D5 40 36N 73 59W
New Vernon, *N.Y.* 22 C2 40 44N 74 30W
New York Aquarium, *N.Y.* 22 D5 40 33N 73 59W
New York Botanical Gdns., *N.Y.* 23 B5 40 51N 73 51W
New York Univ., *N.Y.* 22 C5 40 43N 74 59W
Newabgarj, *Calc.* 16 D6 22 47N 88 23 E
Newark, *N.Y.* 22 C3 40 43N 74 10W
Newark, *S.F.* 27 C4 37 32N 122 2W
Newark B., *N.Y.* 22 C4 40 40N 74 8W
Newark Int. Airport, *N.Y.* 22 C3 40 41N 74 10W
Newbury Park, *Lon.* 4 B5 51 34N 0 5 E
Newclare, *Jobg.* 18 F8 26 11 S 27 58 E
Newfoundland, *N.Y.* 22 A2 41 2N 74 25W
Newham, *Lon.* 4 B5 51 31N 0 1 E
Newlands, *Jobg.* 18 F8 26 10 S 27 57 E
Newport, *Melb.* 19 F6 37 50 S 144 51 E
Newportville, *Phil.* 24 A5 40 7N 74 53W
Newton, *Bost.* 21 D2 42 19N 71 13W
Newton Brook, *Trto.* 20 D8 43 47N 79 24W
Newton Highlands, *Bost.* 21 D2 42 19N 71 13W
Newtonville, *Bost.* 21 C2 42 20N 71 11W
Newtown, *Syd.* 19 B4 33 54 S 151 11 E
Newtown Square, *Phil.* 24 B2 39 59N 75 24W
Neyegawa, *Ōsaka* 12 B4 34 45N 135 36 E
Ngau Chi Wan, *H.K.* 12 D6 22 20N 114 12 E
Ngau Tau Kok, *H.K.* 12 E6 22 19N 114 12 E
Ngong Shuen Chau, *H.K.* 12 E5 22 19N 114 8 E
Ngua Kok Wan, *H.K.* 12 D5 22 21N 114 5 E
Niāvarān, *Tehr.* 17 C5 35 47N 51 29 E
Nibria, *Calc.* 16 E5 22 36N 88 15 E
Nichelino, *Tori.* 9 C2 44 59N 7 38 E
Nichols Run →, *Wash.* 25 C6 39 2N 77 17W
Nicholson, Mt., *H.K.* 12 E6 22 15N 114 11 E
Nidāl, *Bagd.* 17 F8 33 19N 44 25 E
Niddrie, *Melb.* 19 E6 37 44 S 144 51 E
Nieder Neuendorf, *Berl.* 7 A2 52 36N 13 12 E
Niederbonsfeld, *Ruhr* 6 B4 51 22N 7 8 E
Niederdonk, *Ruhr* 6 C2 51 14N 6 41 E
Niederschöneweide, *Berl.* 7 B3 52 27N 13 30 E
Niederschönhausen, *Berl.* 7 A3 52 35N 13 25 E
Niederwenigern, *Ruhr* 6 B4 51 24N 7 8 E
Niemeyer, *Rio J.* 31 B2 22 59 S 43 16W
Niendorf, *Hbg.* 7 D7 53 37N 9 57 E
Nienstedten, *Hbg.* 7 D7 53 33N 9 51 E
Nierst, *Ruhr* 6 C2 51 19N 6 43 E
Nihonbashi, *Tōkyō* 13 B3 35 41N 139 46 E
Niipperi, *Hels.* 3 B3 60 18N 24 45 E
Niiza, *Tōkyō* 13 B2 35 48N 139 33 E
Nikaia, *Ath.* 8 J10 37 57N 23 38 E
Nikinmäki, *Hels.* 3 A5 60 20N 25 8 E
Nikolassee, *Berl.* 7 B2 52 25N 13 12 E
Nikolo-Khovanskoye, *Mos.* 11 F8 55 36N 37 27 E
Nikolskiy, *Mos.* 11 E8 55 49N 37 29 E
Nikolyskoye, *Mos.* 11 E11 55 46N 37 53 E
Nikulino, *Mos.* 11 E8 55 40N 37 25 E
Nil, *Bagd.* 17 E8 33 21N 44 25 E
Nil, Nahr en →, *El Qâ.* 18 D5 29 57N 31 14 E
Nile = Nil, Nahr en →, *El Qâ.* 18 D5 29 57N 31 14 E
Niles, *Chic.* 26 A2 42 1N 87 48W
Nilganj, *Calc.* 16 D6 22 45N 88 25 E
Nilópolis, *Rio J.* 31 A1 22 47 S 43 23W
Nimta, *Calc.* 16 D6 22 40N 88 24 E
Nincop, *Hbg.* 7 D6 53 30N 9 48 E
Ningyuan, *Tianj.* 14 E6 39 9N 117 12 E
Nippa, *Tōkyō* 13 C2 35 31N 139 36 E
Nippori, *Tōkyō* 13 B3 35 43N 139 45 E
Niru-ye-Hava'i, *Tehr.* 17 C5 35 41N 51 26 E
Nishi, *Ōsaka* 12 B3 34 40N 135 28 E
Nishi, *Tōkyō* 13 D2 35 26N 139 37 E
Nishi-arai, *Tōkyō* 13 B3 35 46N 139 48 E
Nishinari, *Ōsaka* 12 C3 34 37N 135 28 E
Nishinomiya, *Ōsaka* 12 B2 34 44N 135 18 E
Nishiyama, *Tōkyō* 13 D4 35 22N 139 57 E
Nishiyodogawa, *Ōsaka* 12 B3 34 41N 135 24 E
Nisida, I. di, *Nápl.* 9 J11 40 47N 14 10 E
Niterói, *Rio J.* 31 B3 22 53 S 43 7W
Nithari, *Delhi* 16 B3 28 34N 77 20 E
Nittedal, *Oslo* 2 A5 60 0N 10 57 E
Niyog, *Manila* 15 E3 14 27N 120 57 E
Noapara, *Calc.* 16 D6 22 49N 88 22 E
Nobidome, *Tōkyō* 13 B2 35 48N 139 34 E
Nockeby, *Stock.* 3 E10 59 19N 17 56 E
Noel Park, *Lon.* 4 B4 51 35N 0 5W
Nogatino, *Mos.* 11 E10 55 41N 37 41 E
Nogent-sur-Marne, *Paris* 5 B4 48 50N 2 28 E
Noiseau, *Paris* 5 C5 48 46N 2 32 E
Noisiel, *Paris* 5 B5 48 51N 2 37 E
Noisy-le-Grand, *Paris* 5 B5 48 50N 2 33 E
Noisy-le-Roi, *Paris* 5 B2 48 50N 2 3 E
Noisy-le-Sec, *Paris* 5 B4 48 53N 2 27 E
Nokkala, *Hels.* 3 C3 60 8N 24 45 E
Nøklevatn, *Oslo* 2 B5 59 52N 10 52 E
Nolme →, *Ruhr* 6 B6 51 23N 7 26 E
Nomentano, *Rome* 9 F10 41 55N 12 30 E
Nonakashinden, *Tōkyō* 13 B2 35 44N 139 30 E
Nongminyundong Jiangxisuo, *Gzh.* 14 G8 23 7N 113 15 E
Nonhyeon, *Sŏul* 12 G8 37 30N 127 1 E
Nontha Buri, *Bangk.* 15 A1 13 50N 100 29 E
Noordgesig, *Jobg.* 18 F8 26 13 S 27 56 E
Nord, Gare du, *Paris* 5 B4 48 52N 2 21 E
Nordbysjøen, *Oslo* 2 B6 59 51N 11 1 E
Nordereble, *Hbg.* 7 D7 53 32N 9 59 E
Norderelbe →, *Hbg.* 7 E8 53 29N 10 3 E
Norderstedt, *Hbg.* 7 C7 53 42N 9 59 E
Nordmarka, *Oslo* 2 A4 60 1N 10 38 E
Nordrand-Seidlung, *Wien* 10 G10 48 16N 16 26 E
Nordre Elvåga, *Oslo* 2 B5 59 53N 10 54 E
Nordstrand, *Oslo* 2 B4 59 52N 10 48 E
Normandy Heights, *Balt.* 25 B2 39 17N 76 48W
Norra Björköfjärden, *Stock.* 3 D8 59 26N 17 39 E
Norridge, *Chic.* 26 B2 41 57N 87 49W
Norristown, *Phil.* 24 A2 40 7N 75 20W
Norrkula, *Hels.* 3 B6 60 19N 25 20 E
Norrmalm, *Stock.* 3 D11 59 20N 18 3 E
Norrviken, *Stock.* 3 D10 59 27N 17 52 E
North Acton, *Bost.* 21 B1 42 30N 71 23W
North Amityville, *N.Y.* 23 C8 40 41N 73 25W
North Andover, *Bost.* 21 A3 42 41N 71 7W
North Arlington, *N.Y.* 22 C4 40 47N 74 7W
North Auburn, *Syd.* 19 B3 33 50 S 151 3 E
North Babylon, *N.Y.* 23 C9 40 43N 73 19W
North Bellmore, *N.Y.* 23 C7 40 40N 73 32W
North Bergen, *N.Y.* 22 C4 40 48N 74 0W
North Beverly, *Bost.* 21 B4 42 34N 70 51W
North Billerica, *Bost.* 21 B2 42 35N 71 16W
North Branch →, *Phil.* 24 C4 39 50N 75 5W
North Branch Chicago River →, *Chic.* 26 B2 41 53N 87 42W
North Brighton, *Bost.* 21 C3 42 21N 71 8W
North Caldwell, *N.Y.* 22 B3 40 52N 74 15W
North Cambridge, *Bost.* 21 C3 42 23N 71 7W
North Cheam, *Lon.* 4 C3 51 22N 0 11W
North Chelmsford, *Bost.* 21 B1 42 38N 71 23W
North Cohasset, *Bost.* 21 D4 42 15N 70 50W
North Cray, *Lon.* 4 C5 51 25N 0 8 E
North Fair Oaks, *S.F.* 27 D3 37 28N 122 11W
North Finchley, *Lon.* 4 B3 51 36N 0 10W
North Germiston, *Jobg.* 18 F9 26 12 S 28 9 E
North Hackensack, *N.Y.* 22 B4 40 54N 74 2W
North Haledon, *N.Y.* 22 B3 40 58N 74 11W
North Harbour, *Manila* 15 D3 14 37N 120 57 E
North Hd., *Syd.* 19 A4 33 49 S 151 18 E
North Hills, *N.Y.* 23 C6 40 46N 73 40W
North Hollywood, *L.A.* 28 B2 34 9N 118 22W
North Lexington, *Bost.* 21 C2 42 27N 71 14W
North Lindenhurst, *N.Y.* 23 C8 40 42N 73 22W
North Long Beach, *L.A.* 28 C3 33 53N 118 10W
North Manly, *Syd.* 19 A4 33 46 S 151 17 E
North Massapequa, *N.Y.* 23 C8 40 42N 73 27W
North Merrick, *N.Y.* 23 C7 40 41N 73 33W
North New Hyde Park, *N.Y.* 23 C6 40 44N 73 42W
North Pelham, *N.Y.* 23 B6 40 54N 73 46W
North Plainfield, *N.Y.* 22 D2 40 37N 74 27W
North Point, *Balt.* 25 B4 39 16N 76 29W
North Pt., *H.K.* 12 E6 22 17N 114 12 E
North Pt., *Syd.* 19 A4 33 48 S 151 18 E
North Randolph, *Bost.* 21 D3 42 11N 71 5W
North Reading, *Bost.* 21 B3 42 34N 71 5W
North Res., *Bost.* 21 C3 42 27N 71 6W
North Richmond, *S.F.* 27 A2 37 57N 122 22W
North Riverside, *Chic.* 26 B2 41 50N 87 48W
North Ryde, *Syd.* 19 A3 33 47 S 151 7 E
North Saugus, *Bost.* 21 C3 42 29N 71 0W
North Shore Channel →, *Chic.* 26 B2 41 58N 87 42W

Pitampura Kalan 43

North Springfield, *Wash.* **25 E6** 38 48N 77 11W
North Stifford, *Lon.* **4 B6** 51 30N 0 18 E
North Sudbury, *Bost.* **21 C1** 42 24N 71 24W
North Sydney, *Syd.* **19 B4** 33 50 S 151 13 E
North Tewksbury, *Bost.* **21 B2** 42 38N 71 14W
North Valley Stream, *N.Y.* **23 C6** 40 41N 73 42W
North Wantagh, *N.Y.* **23 C7** 40 41N 73 30W
North Weymouth, *Bost.* **21 D4** 42 14N 70 56W
North Wilmington, *Bost.* **21 B3** 42 34N 71 9W
North Woburn, *Bost.* **21 B2** 42 30N 71 10W
North Woolwich, *Lon.* **4 B5** 51 30N 0 3 E
North York, *Trto.* **20 D8** 43 45N 79 27W
Northaw, *Lon.* **4 A4** 51 42N 0 8W
Northbridge, *Syd.* **19 A4** 33 49 S 151 15 E
Northbrook, *Chic.* **26 A1** 42 7N 87 50W
Northcliff, *Jobg.* **18 E8** 26 8 S 27 58 E
Northcote, *Melb.* **19 E7** 37 46 S 145 0 E
Northeastern Univ., *Bost.* **21 C3** 42 20N 71 4W
Northfield, *Chic.* **26 A2** 42 5N 87 45W
Northfleet, *Lon.* **4 C7** 51 26N 0 21 E
Northlake, *Chic.* **26 B1** 41 54N 87 53W
Northmead, *Jobg.* **18 E10** 26 9 S 28 19 E
Northmead, *Syd.* **19 A3** 33 47 S 151 0 E
Northmount, *Trto.* **20 D8** 43 46N 79 23W
Northolt, *Lon.* **4 B2** 51 32N 0 22W
Northport, *N.Y.* **23 B8** 40 54N 73 20W
Northport B., *N.Y.* **23 B8** 40 54N 73 22W
Northridge, *L.A.* **28 A1** 34 14N 118 30W
Northumberland Heath, *Lon.* **4 C6** 51 28N 0 10 E
Northvale, *N.Y.* **22 A5** 41 0N 73 59W
Northwest Branch →, *Balt.* **25 B3** 39 16N 76 35W
Northwest Branch →, *Wash.* **25 C8** 39 2N 76 56W
Northwestern Univ., *Chic.* **26 A2** 42 3N 87 40W
Northwood, *Lon.* **4 B2** 51 36N 0 25W
Norumbega Res., *Bost.* **21 D2** 42 19N 71 17W
Norwalk, *L.A.* **28 C4** 33 53N 118 4W
Norwood, *Bost.* **21 D2** 42 11N 71 13W
Norwood, *Jobg.* **18 E9** 26 9 S 28 4 E
Norwood, *N.Y.* **22 B5** 40 59N 73 57W
Norwood, *Phil.* **24 B3** 39 53N 75 17W
Norwood Memorial Airport, *Bost.* **21 D3** 42 11N 71 9W
Norwood Park, *Chic.* **26 B2** 41 59N 87 48W
Noryangjin, *Sŏul* **12 G7** 37 30N 126 56 E
Nose, *Ōsaka* **12 B2** 34 49N 135 10 E
Nossa Senhora do Ó, *S. Pau.* **31 E5** 23 30 S 46 41W
Notre-Dame, *Mtrl.* **20 B5** 43 28N 73 28W
Notre-Dame, *Paris* **5 B4** 48 51N 2 21 E
Notre-Dame, Bois, *Paris* **5 C5** 48 45N 2 34 E
Notre Dame de L'Île Perrot, *Mtrl.* **20 B2** 43 23N 73 53W
Notting Hill, *Lon.* **4 B3** 51 30N 0 12W
Notting Hill, *Melb.* **19 F7** 37 54 S 145 9 E
Nottingham, *Phil.* **24 A5** 40 7N 74 58W
Nova Milanese, *Mil.* **9 D6** 45 35N 9 12 E
Novate Milanese, *Mil.* **9 D5** 45 30N 9 8 E
Novaya Derevnya, *St-Pet.* **11 A3** 60 0N 30 19 E
Nové Mesto, *Pra.* **10 B2** 50 4N 14 25 E
Novoaleksandrovskoye, *St-Pet.* **11 B4** 59 50N 30 31 E
Novogireyevo, *Mos.* **11 E10** 55 45N 37 46 E
Novoivanovskoye, *Mos.* **11 E7** 55 42N 37 21 E
Novokhovrino, *Mos.* **11 D8** 55 53N 37 27 E
Novonikolyskoye, *Mos.* **11 D7** 55 50N 37 14 E
Novosaratovka, *St-Pet.* **11 B5** 59 50N 30 32 E
Novosergiyevka, *St-Pet.* **11 B5** 59 54N 30 34 E
Nowe-Babice, *Wsaw.* **10 E6** 52 15N 20 51 E
Nöykkiö, *Hels.* **3 B3** 60 10N 24 42 E
Noyoye Kovalyova, *St-Pet.* **11 B5** 59 58N 30 34 E
Nozay, *Paris* **5 D3** 48 39N 2 14 E
Nueva Atzacoalco, *Méx.* **29 B3** 19 29N 99 4W
Nueva Caracas, *Car.* **30 D5** 10 30N 66 57W
Nueva Chicago, *B.A.* **32 B4** 34 39 S 58 29W
Nueva Pompeya, *B.A.* **32 C4** 34 40 S 58 25W
Nueva Tenochtitlán, *Méx.* **29 B3** 19 27N 99 5W
Nuijala, *Hels.* **3 B3** 60 12N 24 46 E
Numabukuro, *Tōkyō* **13 B2** 35 43N 139 39 E
Numakage, *Tōkyō* **13 A2** 35 50N 139 37 E
Numata, *Tōkyō* **13 B3** 35 45N 139 46 E
Nunawading, *Melb.* **19 E8** 37 49 S 145 10 E
Nunez, *B.A.* **32 B4** 34 32 S 58 27W
Nunhead, *Lon.* **4 C4** 51 27N 0 3W
Ñuñoa, *Stgo* **30 J11** 33 27 S 70 35W
Nupuri, *Hels.* **3 B2** 60 14N 24 36 E
Nusle, *Pra.* **10 B2** 50 3N 14 26 E
Nussdorf, *Wien* **10 G10** 48 15N 16 21 E
Nuthe →, *Berl.* **7 B1** 52 22N 13 5 E
Nutley, *N.Y.* **22 C4** 40 49N 74 9W
Nutting L., *Bost.* **21 B2** 42 32N 71 16W
Nützenberg, *Ruhr* **6 C4** 51 15N 7 8 E
Nybølle, *Købn.* **2 D8** 55 42N 12 15 E
Nybygget, *Hels.* **3 B6** 60 17N 25 11 E
Nymphenburg, *Mün.* **7 G10** 48 9N 11 30 E
Nymphenburg, Schloss, *Mün.* **7 G10** 48 9N 11 30 E

O

Oak Beach, *N.Y.* **23 D9** 40 38N 73 19W
Oak Forest, *Chic.* **26 D2** 41 36N 87 44W
Oak Hill Park, *Bost.* **21 D2** 42 17N 71 11W
Oak Lane, *Phil.* **24 A4** 40 3N 75 8W
Oak Lawn, *Chic.* **26 C2** 41 42N 87 45W
Oak Park, *Chic.* **26 B2** 41 52N 87 47W
Oak Ridge, *N.Y.* **22 A2** 41 2N 74 28W
Oak Valley, *Phil.* **24 C4** 39 48N 75 9W
Oak View, *Wash.* **25 C8** 39 1N 76 58W
Oakland, *N.Y.* **22 A3** 41 1N 74 13W
Oakland, *S.F.* **27 B3** 37 48N 122 18W
Oakland, *Wash.* **25 D8** 38 52N 76 54W
Oakland Coliseum, *S.F.* **27 B3** 37 44N 122 11W
Oakland Gardens, *N.Y.* **23 C6** 40 45N 73 46W
Oakland Int. Airport, *S.F.* **27 B3** 37 43N 122 12W
Oakland Mills, *Balt.* **25 B2** 39 13N 76 49W
Oakland Naval Air Station, *S.F.* **27 B3** 37 47N 122 19W
Oaklands, *Jobg.* **18 E9** 26 8 S 28 4 E
Oaklawn, *Wash.* **25 E8** 38 46N 76 56W
Oakleigh, *Melb.* **19 F7** 37 54 S 145 5 E
Oaks, *Phil.* **24 A2** 40 8N 75 26W
Oakwood, *N.Y.* **22 D4** 40 34N 74 7W
Oakwood Beach, *N.Y.* **22 D4** 40 33N 74 7W
Oatley, *Syd.* **19 B3** 33 59 S 151 4 E
Obalende, *Lagos* **18 B2** 6 26N 7 25 E
Oba's Palace, *Lagos* **18 B2** 6 26N 7 22 E
Oberbauer, *Ruhr* **6 C6** 51 17N 7 25 E
Oberföhring, *Mün.* **7 G10** 48 10N 11 37 E
Oberhaching, *Mün.* **7 G10** 48 1N 11 35 E
Oberhausen, *Ruhr* **6 B3** 51 28N 6 54 E
Oberhausen, *Wien* **10 G11** 48 10N 16 34 E
Oberkassel, *Ruhr* **6 C2** 51 14N 6 45 E
Oberkirchbach, *Wien* **10 G9** 48 17N 16 12 E
Oberlaa, *Wien* **10 H10** 48 8N 16 24 E
Oberlisse, *Wien* **10 G10** 48 17N 16 26 E
Obermenzing, *Mün.* **7 F9** 48 10N 11 28 E
Obermoos Schwaige, *Mün.* **7 F9** 48 14N 11 27 E
Oberschleissheim, *Mün.* **7 F10** 48 15N 11 33 E
Oberschöneweide, *Berl.* **7 B4** 52 27N 13 31 E
Oberwengern, *Ruhr* **6 B6** 51 23N 7 22 E
Obitsu →, *Tōkyō* **13 D4** 35 25N 139 56 E
Oboldino, *Mos.* **11 D11** 55 53N 37 56 E
Observatory, *Jobg.* **18 F9** 26 10 S 28 4 E
Ōbu, *Ōsaka* **12 B1** 34 43N 135 8 E
Obu-tōge, *Ōsaka* **12 B1** 34 44N 135 9 E
Óbuda, *Bud.* **10 J13** 47 33N 19 2 E
Obudaisziget, *Bud.* **10 J13** 47 33N 19 3 E
Obukhovo, *St-Pet.* **11 B4** 59 53N 30 22 E
Occidental, Pico, *Car.* **30 D5** 10 32N 66 51W
Oceanside, *N.Y.* **23 D7** 40 38N 73 37W
Ochakovo, *Mos.* **11 E8** 55 41N 37 26 E
Ochiai, *Tōkyō* **13 B3** 35 43N 139 42 E
Ochota, *Wsaw.* **10 E6** 52 13N 20 58 E
Ochsenwerder, *Hbg.* **7 E8** 53 28N 10 4 E
Ochsenzoll, *Hbg.* **7 C8** 53 41N 10 0 E
Odana, *Tōkyō* **13 C2** 35 33N 139 35 E
Oden-Stockach, *Mün.* **7 G11** 48 5N 11 41 E
Odilampi, *Hels.* **3 B3** 60 18N 24 45 E
Odintsovo, *Mos.* **11 E7** 55 40N 37 16 E
Odivelas, *Lisb.* **8 F7** 38 47N 9 10W
Odolany, *Wsaw.* **10 E6** 52 13N 20 55 E
Oeiras, *Lisb.* **8 F7** 38 41N 9 18W
Oella, *Balt.* **25 B2** 39 16N 76 46W
Oer-Erkenschwick, *Ruhr* **6 A5** 51 38N 7 15 E
Oern, *Mün.* **7 G10** 48 10N 11 32 E
Ofin, *Lagos* **18 A3** 6 32N 7 30 E
Ofukuro-shinden, *Tōkyō* **13 A1** 35 53N 139 28 E
Ogawa, *Tōkyō* **13 B1** 35 44N 139 28 E
Ogden, *Phil.* **24 C2** 39 49N 75 27W
Ogikubo, *Tōkyō* **13 B2** 35 42N 139 37 E
Ogo Ogo, *Ōsaka* **12 B1** 34 49N 135 8 E
Ogogoro, *Lagos* **18 B2** 6 25N 7 24 E
Ogongo, *Manila* **15 D4** 14 35N 121 4 E
Ogoyo, *Lagos* **18 B2** 6 25N 7 29 E
Ogudu, *Lagos* **18 A2** 6 34N 7 24 E
O'Hare, L., *Chic.* **26 B1** 41 57N 87 53W
Ōhirodo, *Tōkyō* **13 A4** 35 50N 139 53 E
Ohlsdorf, *Hbg.* **7 D8** 53 37N 10 3 E
Ōi, *Tōkyō* **13 A2** 35 51N 139 31 E
Ōimachi, *Tōkyō* **13 C3** 35 35N 139 43 E
Oise →, *Paris* **5 A2** 49 2N 2 5 E
Oittaa, *Hels.* **3 B3** 60 15N 24 42 E
Ojota, *Lagos* **18 A2** 6 35N 7 23 E
Okamoto, *Ōsaka* **12 B2** 34 43N 135 15 E
Okazu, *Tōkyō* **13 D2** 35 25N 139 31 E
Okęcie, *Wsaw.* **10 E6** 52 11N 20 56 E
Okęcie Airport, *Wsaw.* **10 E6** 52 10N 20 57 E
Okelra, *Lagos* **18 B2** 6 29N 7 22 E
Okeogbe, *Lagos* **18 B2** 6 24N 7 23 E
Okhla, *Delhi* **16 B2** 28 33N 77 16 E
Okhta →, *St-Pet.* **11 B4** 59 56N 30 25 E
Okkervil →, *St-Pet.* **11 B4** 59 56N 30 30 E
Okrzeszyn, *Wsaw.* **10 F7** 52 8N 21 8 E
Oksval, *Oslo* **2 B4** 59 51N 10 40 E
Oktyabrskiy, *Mos.* **11 F11** 55 37N 37 58 E
Oktyabrskiy, *Mos.* **11 E9** 55 41N 37 35 E
Okubo, *Tōkyō* **13 B3** 35 41N 139 42 E
Okunola, *Lagos* **18 A1** 6 35N 7 17 E
Ōkura, *Tōkyō* **13 C1** 35 35N 139 27 E
Olari, *Hels.* **3 B3** 60 10N 24 44 E
Olaria, *Rio J.* **31 B2** 22 50 S 43 16W
Old Brookville, *N.Y.* **23 C7** 40 49N 73 35W
Old Cairo, *El Qâ.* **18 C5** 30 0N 31 14 E
Old Coulsdon, *Lon.* **4 D4** 51 17N 0 6W
Old Forge Village, *N.Y.* **22 C2** 40 48N 74 29W
Old Harbor, *Bost.* **21 D3** 42 19N 71 1W
Old Road B., *Balt.* **25 B4** 39 12N 76 27W
Old Tappan, *N.Y.* **22 A5** 41 0N 73 59W
Old Town, *Chic.* **26 B3** 41 54N 87 37W
Old Westbury, *N.Y.* **23 C7** 40 46N 73 35W
Oldmans Cr. →, *Phil.* **24 C2** 39 47N 75 26W
Olgino, *St-Pet.* **11 A3** 60 0N 30 10 E
Olimpico, Estadio, *Méx.* **29 C2** 19 19N 99 11W
Olinda, *Melb.* **19 F9** 37 51 S 145 21 E
Olinda, *Rio J.* **31 A1** 22 49 S 43 25W
Olivais, *Lisb.* **8 F8** 38 45N 9 7W
Olivar de los Padres, *Méx.* **29 B2** 19 21N 99 14W
Olivar del Conde, *Méx.* **29 B2** 19 22N 99 12W
Olivos, *B.A.* **32 B4** 34 30 S 58 28W
Ollila, *Hels.* **3 A2** 60 20N 24 32 E
Olney, *Phil.* **24 A4** 40 2N 75 8W
Olona →, *Mil.* **9 E5** 45 29N 9 6 E
Ølstykke, *Købn.* **2 D7** 55 47N 12 8 E
Olute, *Lagos* **18 B1** 6 27N 7 17 E
Olympia-Stadion, *Hels.* **3 B4** 60 11N 24 55 E
Olympique Parc, *Mtrl.* **20 A4** 43 33N 73 33W
Ōmagi, *Tōkyō* **13 A3** 35 52N 139 43 E
Ōmiya, *Tōkyō* **13 A2** 35 54N 139 37 E
Ōmori, *Tōkyō* **13 C3** 35 34N 139 43 E
Ōnari, *Tōkyō* **13 A2** 35 55N 139 36 E
Once, *B.A.* **32 B4** 34 37 S 58 24W
Onchi, *Ōsaka* **12 C4** 34 36N 135 38 E
Onchi →, *Ōsaka* **12 C4** 34 38N 135 37 E
One Tree Hill, *Melb.* **19 F8** 37 52 S 145 19 E
Onisigun, *Lagos* **18 A2** 6 35N 7 24 E
Ōokayama, *Tōkyō* **13 C3** 35 36N 139 40 E
Opacz, *Wsaw.* **10 E6** 52 10N 20 53 E
Ophirton, *Jobg.* **18 F9** 26 13 S 28 1 E
Oppegård, *Oslo* **2 C4** 59 45N 10 49 E
Oppsal, *Oslo* **2 B5** 59 53N 10 50 E
Oppum, *Ruhr* **6 C1** 51 19N 6 36 E
Oradell, *N.Y.* **22 B4** 40 57N 74 2W
Oradell Res., *N.Y.* **22 B4** 40 58N 74 0W
Orange, *N.Y.* **22 C3** 40 46N 74 15W
Orange Grove, *Jobg.* **18 E9** 26 9 S 28 5 E
Oratorio →, *S. Pau.* **31 E6** 23 36 S 46 32W
Orbassano, *Tori.* **9 B2** 45 0N 7 31 E
Orchards, *Jobg.* **18 E9** 26 9 S 28 4 E
Ordrup, *Købn.* **2 D10** 55 45N 12 34 E
Orech, *Pra.* **10 B1** 50 1N 14 17 E
Øresund, *Købn.* **2 D11** 55 45N 12 40 E
Oreta, *Lagos* **18 A3** 6 31N 7 31 E
Orge →, *Paris* **5 D3** 48 36N 2 17 E
Orgeval, *Paris* **5 B1** 48 55N 1 58 E
Orhølm, *Købn.* **2 D10** 55 48N 12 30 E
Orient Heights, *Bost.* **21 C4** 42 23N 70 59W
Oriental, Pico, *Car.* **30 D5** 10 32N 66 51W
Origgio, *Mil.* **9 D5** 45 35N 9 1 E
Orinda, *S.F.* **27 A3** 37 52N 122 10W
Orinda Village, *S.F.* **27 A3** 37 53N 122 12W
Orland L., *Chic.* **26 D1** 41 38N 87 52W
Orland Park, *Chic.* **26 D1** 41 37N 87 52W
Orlando Dam, *Jobg.* **18 F8** 26 15 S 27 55 E
Orlando East, *Jobg.* **18 F8** 26 14 S 27 55 E
Orlando West, *Jobg.* **18 F8** 26 13 S 27 54 E
Orlången, *Stock.* **3 E11** 59 11N 18 2 E
Orlångsvik, *Stock.* **3 E11** 59 11N 18 3 E
Orlovo, *Mos.* **11 F8** 55 38N 37 22 E
Orly, *Paris* **5 C4** 48 45N 2 23 E
Ormesson-sur-Marne, *Paris* **5 C5** 48 47N 2 32 E
Orminge, *Stock.* **3 E12** 59 19N 18 14 E
Ormingelandet, *Stock.* **3 D13** 59 20N 18 22 E
Ormond, *Melb.* **19 F7** 37 54 S 145 1 E
Órmos Fálirou, *Ath.* **8 J11** 37 54N 23 40 E
Ormøya, *Oslo* **2 B4** 59 52N 10 45 E
Oros Aiyáleos, *Ath.* **8 J10** 38 0N 23 36 E
Oros Imittoś, *Ath.* **8 J11** 37 53N 23 48 E
Örpadfold, *Bud.* **10 J14** 47 32N 19 12 E
Orpington, *Lon.* **4 C5** 51 22N 0 6 E
Orsay, *Paris* **5 C3** 48 41N 2 11 E
Orsby, *Ruhr* **6 A2** 51 31N 6 41 E
Orsett, *Lon.* **4 B7** 51 30N 0 22 E
Ortaköy, *Ist.* **17 A3** 41 3N 29 1 E
Ortica, *Mil.* **9 E6** 45 28N 9 16 E
Oruba, *Lagos* **18 A2** 6 34N 7 24 E
Ōsaka, *Ōsaka* **12 C4** 34 42N 135 30 E
Ōsaka B., *Ōsaka* **12 C2** 34 35N 135 18 E
Ōsaka Castle, *Ōsaka* **12 B4** 34 41N 135 30 E
Ōsaka Harbour, *Ōsaka* **12 C3** 34 38N 135 25 E
Ōsaka Univ., *Ōsaka* **12 B3** 34 41N 135 29 E
Ōsaki, *Tōkyō* **13 C3** 35 36N 139 42 E
Osasco, *S. Pau.* **31 E5** 23 31 S 46 46W
Osdorf, *Berl.* **7 B3** 52 24N 13 20 E
Osdorf, *Hbg.* **7 D7** 53 34N 9 50 E
Oshodi, *Lagos* **18 A2** 6 33N 7 21 E
Oskar Frederikborg, *Stock.* **3 D13** 59 24N 18 24 E
Oslo, *Oslo* **2 B4** 59 54N 10 43 E
Oslofjorden, *Oslo* **2 C3** 59 40N 10 35 E
Ōsone, *Tōkyō* **13 C2** 35 31N 139 37 E
Osorun, *Lagos* **18 A2** 6 33N 7 29 E
Ospiate, *Mil.* **9 D5** 45 32N 9 6 E
Ossów, *Wsaw.* **10 E8** 52 18N 21 12 E
Ostankino, *Mos.* **11 E9** 55 49N 37 37 E
Østby, *Købn.* **2 D7** 55 45N 12 2 E
Osterath, *Ruhr* **6 C1** 51 16N 6 36 E
Österby, *Hels.* **3 B1** 60 10N 24 25 E
Osterfeld, *Ruhr* **6 A3** 51 30N 6 53 E
Osterley, *Lon.* **4 C2** 51 28N 0 21W
Osterley Park, *Lon.* **4 C2** 51 29N 0 21W
Östermalm, *Stock.* **3 D11** 59 20N 18 4 E
Österskär, *Stock.* **3 D12** 59 26N 18 16 E
Östersundom, *Hels.* **3 B6** 60 15N 25 10 E
Östertälje, *Stock.* **3 E8** 59 11N 17 39 E
Ostiense, *Rome* **9 F9** 41 51N 12 29 E
Østmarkkapellet, *Oslo* **2 B5** 59 52N 10 51 E
Ostøya, *Oslo* **2 B3** 59 52N 10 34 E
Östra Ryd, *Stock.* **3 D12** 59 27N 18 11 E
Østre Aker, *Oslo* **2 B4** 59 54N 10 49 E
Ostrov, *Mos.* **11 F11** 55 36N 37 50 E
Ostrovtsy, *Mos.* **11 F12** 55 36N 38 0 E
Ōta-Ku, *Tōkyō* **13 C3** 35 34N 139 41 E
Otaniemi, *Hels.* **3 B3** 60 11N 24 49 E
Otford, *Lon.* **4 D6** 51 18N 0 11 E
Othmarschen, *Hbg.* **7 D7** 53 33N 9 53 E
Otsuka, *Tōkyō* **13 B3** 35 43N 139 44 E
Ottakring, *Wien* **10 G9** 48 12N 16 18 E
Ottávia, *Rome* **9 F9** 41 57N 12 24 E
Ottaviano, *Nápl.* **9 H13** 40 50N 14 28 E
Ottensen, *Hbg.* **7 D7** 53 33N 9 55 E
Ottobrunn, *Mün.* **7 G11** 48 3N 11 40 E
Ottocalli, *Nápl.* **9 H12** 40 52N 14 17 E
Otwock, *Wsaw.* **10 F8** 52 8N 21 13 E
Ouerenburg, *Ruhr* **6 B5** 51 27N 7 16 E
Ouiapo, *Manila* **15 D3** 14 35N 120 59 E
Oulunkylä, *Hels.* **3 B4** 60 13N 24 58 E
Ourcq, Canal de l', *Paris* **5 B4** 48 54N 2 28 E
Ousit, *Bangk.* **15 B2** 13 47N 100 31 E
Outer Brewster I., *Bost.* **21 C4** 42 20N 70 52W
Outer Mission, *S.F.* **27 B2** 37 43N 122 26W
Outremont, *Mtrl.* **20 A4** 43 31N 73 36W
Overbruch, *Ruhr* **6 A2** 51 32N 6 43 E
Overlea, *Balt.* **25 A3** 39 21N 76 32W
Øverød, *Købn.* **2 D9** 55 48N 12 28 E
Ōwada, *Tōkyō* **13 B2** 35 48N 139 31 E
Owings Mills, *Balt.* **25 A2** 39 25N 76 47W
Oworonsoki, *Lagos* **18 A2** 6 32N 7 24 E
Oxon Hill, *Wash.* **25 E8** 38 48N 76 59W
Oxshott, *Lon.* **4 D2** 51 19N 0 21W
Oyada, *Tōkyō* **13 B4** 35 46N 139 50 E
Ōyama, *Tōkyō* **13 B3** 35 44N 139 42 E
Øyeren, *Oslo* **2 B6** 59 55N 11 6 E
Oyodo, *Ōsaka* **12 B3** 34 42N 135 29 E
Oyster B., *N.Y.* **23 B7** 40 52N 73 31W
Oyster B., *Syd.* **19 C3** 34 0 S 151 5 E
Oyster Bay Cove, *N.Y.* **23 B8** 40 51N 73 29W
Oyster Bay Harbour, *N.Y.* **23 B7** 40 53N 73 32W
Oyster Rock, *Bomb.* **16 H7** 18 54N 72 49 E
Oyster Rocks, *Kar.* **17 H11** 24 48N 66 59 E
Ozarów-Franciszków, *Wsaw.* **10 E5** 52 13N 20 48 E
Ozerki, *St-Pet.* **11 B6** 59 53N 30 42 E
Ozoir-la-Ferrière, *Paris* **5 C6** 48 46N 2 40 E
Ozone Park, *N.Y.* **23 C5** 40 40N 73 50W

P

Pacific Manor, *S.F.* **27 C2** 37 38N 122 27W
Pacific Palisades, *L.A.* **28 B1** 34 2N 118 32W
Pacifica, *S.F.* **27 C2** 37 37N 122 27W
Packanack L., *N.Y.* **22 B3** 40 56N 74 15W
Paco, *Manila* **15 D3** 14 35N 120 59 E
Paco de Arcos, *Lisb.* **8 F7** 38 41N 9 17W
Paddington, *Lon.* **4 B3** 51 30N 0 10W
Paddington, *Syd.* **19 B4** 33 53 S 151 14 E
Pademangan, *Jak.* **15 H9** 6 7 S 106 49 E
Paderno, *Mil.* **9 D5** 45 33N 9 9 E
Padre Miguel, *Rio J.* **31 B1** 22 52 S 43 25W
Padstow, *Syd.* **19 B3** 33 57 S 151 2 E
Pagewood, *Syd.* **19 B4** 33 56 S 151 14 E
Pagote, *Bomb.* **16 H8** 18 53N 72 59 E
Pai, I. do, *Rio J.* **31 B3** 22 59 S 43 5W
Paia, *Lisb.* **8 F7** 38 46N 9 11W
Paikpara, *Calc.* **16 E6** 22 36N 88 23 E
Paint Br. →, *Wash.* **25 C8** 38 57N 76 55W
Paiyun Airport, *Gzh.* **14 F8** 23 10N 113 15 E
Pak ka Shan, *H.K.* **12 E6** 22 16N 114 13 E
Pak Kong, *H.K.* **12 D6** 22 22N 114 15 E
Pak Tim Pa, *H.K.* **12 D5** 22 22N 114 7 E
Pakila, *Hels.* **3 B4** 60 15N 24 55 E
Palace Museum, *Beij.* **14 B3** 39 54N 116 21 E
Palaión Fáliron, *Ath.* **8 J11** 37 53N 23 42 E
Palaiseau, *Paris* **5 C3** 48 42N 2 14 E
Palam, *Delhi* **16 B1** 28 35N 77 4 E
Palam Int. Airport, *Delhi* **16 B1** 28 32N 77 8 E
Palazzo Reale, *Nápl.* **9 H12** 40 50N 14 15 E
Palazzo Reale, *Tori.* **9 B3** 45 4N 7 40 E
Palazzolo, *Mil.* **9 D5** 45 34N 9 9 E
Palazzuolo, *Nápl.* **9 H13** 40 54N 14 28 E
Palermo, *B.A.* **32 B4** 34 35 S 58 24W
Palhais, *Lisb.* **8 G8** 38 37N 9 2W
Palisades, *N.Y.* **22 A5** 41 1N 73 57W
Palisades Park, *N.Y.* **22 B4** 40 50N 74 1W
Palleja, *Barc.* **8 D5** 41 25N 2 0 E
Palmer Park, *Wash.* **25 D8** 38 55N 76 52W
Palmers Green, *Lon.* **4 B4** 51 36N 0 6W
Palmyra, *Phil.* **24 A4** 40 0N 75 1W
Palo Alto, *S.F.* **27 D4** 37 27N 122 8W
Paloheinä, *Hels.* **3 B4** 60 15N 24 56 E
Palomar Park, *S.F.* **27 D3** 37 29N 122 16W
Palomeras, *Mdrd.* **8 B3** 40 22N 3 39W
Palos Heights, *Chic.* **26 D2** 41 39N 87 47W
Palos Hills, *Chic.* **26 C2** 41 42N 87 49W
Palos Hills Forest, *Chic.* **26 C1** 41 40N 87 52W
Palos Park, *Chic.* **26 C1** 41 40N 87 50W
Palota-Újfalu, *Bud.* **10 J13** 47 33N 19 7 E
Palpara, *Calc.* **16 E6** 22 38N 88 22 E
Palta, *Calc.* **16 D6** 22 46N 88 23 E
Pamplona, *Manila* **15 E3** 14 27N 120 58 E
Panayaan, *Manila* **15 E3** 14 27N 120 57 E
Panchghara, *Calc.* **16 D5** 22 44N 88 16 E
Panchur, *Calc.* **16 E5** 22 32N 88 16 E
Pancoran, *Jak.* **15 J9** 6 14 S 106 49 E
Pandan, Selat, *Sing.* **15 G7** 1 16N 103 45 E
Pandan, Sungei →, *Sing.* **15 G7** 1 18N 103 43 E
Pandan Res., *Sing.* **15 G7** 1 18N 103 44 E
Panehpara, *Calc.* **16 E5** 22 34N 88 15 E
Pangrati, *Ath.* **8 J11** 37 56N 23 45 E
Pangsua, Sungei →, *Sing.* **15 F7** 1 25N 103 45 E
Panihati, *Calc.* **16 D6** 22 41N 88 22 E
Panjang, Bukit, *Sing.* **15 F7** 1 22N 103 45 E
Panje, *Bomb.* **16 H8** 18 54N 72 57 E
Panke →, *Berl.* **7 A3** 52 31N 13 22 E
Pankow, *Berl.* **7 A3** 52 34N 13 23 E
Panorama City, *L.A.* **28 A2** 34 13N 118 26W
Panpur, *Calc.* **16 C6** 22 51N 88 26 E
Pantheon, *Rome* **9 F9** 41 53N 12 28 E
Pantin, *Paris* **5 B4** 48 53N 2 24 E
Pantitlán, *Méx.* **29 B3** 19 24N 99 4W
Panuacan, *Manila* **15 D4** 14 35N 121 0 E
Panvel Cr. →, *Bomb.* **16 H9** 18 59N 73 0 E
Paoli, *Phil.* **24 A2** 40 2N 75 28W
Papiol, *Barc.* **8 D5** 41 25N 2 0 E
Paracuellos del Jarama, *Mdrd.* **8 A3** 40 30N 3 31W
Paradise Cay, *S.F.* **27 A2** 37 54N 122 28W
Paramount, *L.A.* **28 C3** 33 53N 118 11W
Paramus, *N.Y.* **22 B4** 40 56N 74 2W
Paranaque, *Manila* **15 D3** 14 30N 120 59 E
Paray-Vieille-Poste, *Paris* **5 C4** 48 42N 2 20 E
Parbasdorf, *Wien* **10 G11** 48 16N 16 35 E
Parbatipur, *Calc.* **16 E5** 22 39N 88 13 E
Parcelacion Moderna, *La Hab.* **30 B3** 23 2N 82 19W
Parco Regionale, *Mil.* **9 D5** 45 35N 9 5 E
Parel, *Bomb.* **16 H7** 18 59N 72 49 E
Pari, *S. Pau.* **31 E6** 23 32 S 46 36W
Parioli, *Rome* **9 F9** 41 55N 12 29 E
Paris, *Paris* **5 B4** 48 53N 2 20 E
Paris-Le Bourget, Aéroport de, *Paris* **5 B4** 48 58N 2 26 E
Paris-Orly, Aéroport de, *Paris* **5 C4** 48 43N 2 22 E
Pārk-e-Shahānshāh, *Tehr.* **17 C5** 35 46N 51 24 E
Park Orchards, *Melb.* **19 E8** 37 46 S 145 13 E
Park Ridge, *Chic.* **26 A1** 42 0N 87 50W
Park Ridge, *N.Y.* **22 A4** 41 2N 74 2W
Park Royal, *Lon.* **4 B3** 51 31N 0 16W
Parkchester, *N.Y.* **23 C5** 40 49N 73 50W
Parkdale, *Trto.* **20 E8** 43 38N 79 25W
Parkdene, *Jobg.* **18 F10** 26 11 S 28 15 E
Parkhafen, *Hbg.* **7 D7** 53 32N 9 54 E
Parkhill Gardens, *Jobg.* **18 F10** 26 14 S 28 11 E
Parkhurst, *Jobg.* **18 E9** 26 8 S 28 1 E
Parklawn, *Wash.* **25 D7** 38 50N 77 7W
Parkmore, *Jobg.* **18 E9** 26 5 S 28 2 E
Parkside, *S.F.* **27 B2** 37 44N 122 29W
Parktown, *Jobg.* **18 F9** 26 10 S 28 2 E
Parktown North, *Jobg.* **18 E9** 26 8 S 28 2 E
Parkview, *Jobg.* **18 E9** 26 9 S 28 1 E
Parkville, *Balt.* **25 A3** 39 23N 76 34W
Parkville, *N.Y.* **22 D5** 40 38N 73 57W
Parkwood, *Jobg.* **18 E9** 26 9 S 28 2 E
Parque Edú Chaves, *S. Pau.* **31 D6** 23 29 S 46 34W
Parramatta, *Syd.* **19 A2** 33 49 S 150 59 E
Parramatta →, *Syd.* **19 A3** 33 49 S 151 3 E
Parramatta North, *Syd.* **19 A3** 33 48 S 151 0 E
Parramatta Park, *Syd.* **19 A3** 33 48 S 151 0 E
Parsippany, *N.Y.* **22 B2** 40 51N 74 26W
Paşabahce, *Ist.* **17 A3** 41 6N 29 5 E
Pasadena, *L.A.* **28 B4** 34 9N 118 8W
Pasar Minggu, *Jak.* **15 J9** 6 16 S 106 49 E
Pasay, *Manila* **15 D3** 14 32N 120 59 E
Pascoe Vale, *Melb.* **19 E6** 37 43 S 144 55 E
Pasig, *Manila* **15 D4** 14 33N 121 4 E
Pasig →, *Manila* **15 D4** 14 31N 121 6 E
Pasila, *Hels.* **3 B4** 60 12N 24 56 E
Pasing, *Mün.* **7 G9** 48 8N 11 28 E
Pasir Panjang, *Sing.* **15 G7** 1 17N 103 46 E
Pasir Ris Beach, *Sing.* **15 F8** 1 22N 103 56 E
Paso del Rey, *B.A.* **32 B2** 34 39 S 58 45W
Passaic, *N.Y.* **22 B4** 40 51N 74 9W
Passaic →, *N.Y.* **22 B3** 40 42N 74 10W
Passirana, *Mil.* **9 D5** 45 32N 9 2 E
Patapsco →, *Balt.* **25 B2** 39 19N 76 49W
Patapsco State Park, *Balt.* **25 B2** 39 18N 76 47W
Pateres, *Manila* **15 D4** 14 32N 121 3 E
Paterson, *N.Y.* **22 B4** 40 54N 74 9W
Pathumwan, *Bangk.* **15 B2** 13 44N 100 31 E
Patipukun, *Calc.* **16 E6** 22 36N 88 24 E
Patisia, *Ath.* **8 H11** 38 2N 23 45 E
Patterson Park, *Balt.* **25 B3** 39 17N 76 34W
Patul, *Calc.* **16 D4** 22 45N 88 9 E
Paulo E. Virginia, Gruta, *Rio J.* **31 B2** 22 56 S 43 16W
Paulsboro, *Phil.* **24 C3** 39 49N 75 14W
Paulshof, *Berl.* **7 A5** 52 34N 13 42 E
Pausin, *Berl.* **7 A1** 52 38N 13 2 E
Pavarolo, *Tori.* **9 B3** 45 4N 7 49 E
Pavlovo, *St-Pet.* **11 B5** 59 55N 30 38 E
Pavne, *Bomb.* **16 G9** 19 5N 73 1 E
Pavshino, *Mos.* **11 E7** 55 49N 37 20 E
Paya Lebar, *Sing.* **15 F8** 1 21N 103 52 E
Paylampur, *Calc.* **16 D5** 22 46N 88 15 E
Peabody, *Bost.* **21 B4** 42 32N 70 57W
Peabody Inst., *Balt.* **25 B3** 39 17N 76 37W
Peakhurst, *Syd.* **19 B3** 33 57 S 151 3 E
Pécel, *Bud.* **10 K14** 47 29N 19 20 E
Pecetto Torinese, *Tori.* **9 B3** 45 1N 7 44 E
Pechincha, *Rio J.* **31 B1** 22 55 S 43 20W
Pechorka →, *Mos.* **11 F12** 55 37N 38 2 E
Peckham, *Lon.* **4 C4** 51 28N 0 3W
Pecqueuse, *Paris* **5 D2** 48 38N 2 3 E
Peddocks I., *Bost.* **21 D4** 42 17N 70 56W
Pederstrup, *Købn.* **2 D9** 55 44N 12 20 E
Pedra Branca, *Rio J.* **31 B1** 22 55 S 43 26W
Pedralbes, *Barc.* **8 D5** 41 23N 2 7 E
Pedregal de San Angel, Jardines del, *Méx.* **29 C2** 19 19N 99 12W
Pedreira, *S. Pau.* **31 F5** 23 41 S 46 40W
Pedreros, *Lima* **30 G8** 12 2 S 76 57W
Pedricktown, *Phil.* **24 C2** 39 45N 75 24W
Pedro Cr. →, *S.F.* **27 C2** 37 35N 122 31W
Pedro Valley, *S.F.* **27 C2** 37 35N 122 29W
Peirce Res., *Sing.* **15 F7** 1 22N 103 49 E
Pekhra-Pokrovskoye, *Mos.* **11 D11** 55 50N 37 56 E
Pekhra-Yakovievskaya, *Mos.* **11 E11** 55 47N 37 57 E
Peking = Beijing, *Beij.* **14 B2** 39 53N 116 21 E
Pelado, Cerro, *Méx.* **29 D2** 19 10N 99 14W
Pelcowizna, *Wsaw.* **10 E7** 52 17N 21 0 E
Pelham, *N.Y.* **23 B6** 40 54N 73 46W
Pelham B. Park, *N.Y.* **23 B6** 40 52N 73 48W
Pelham Manor, *N.Y.* **23 B6** 40 53N 73 46W
Penalolén, *Stgo* **30 J11** 33 28 S 70 30W
Peng Siang →, *Sing.* **15 F7** 1 24N 103 43 E
Penge, *Lon.* **4 C4** 51 24N 0 3W
Penha, *Rio J.* **31 A2** 22 49 S 43 17W
Penha, *S. Pau.* **31 E6** 23 31 S 46 32W
Penjaringan, *Jak.* **15 H9** 6 7 S 106 48 E
Penn Square, *Phil.* **24 A3** 40 8N 75 19W
Penn Wynne, *Phil.* **24 B3** 39 59N 75 16W
Pennant Hills Park, *Syd.* **19 A3** 33 46 S 151 6 E
Penndel, *Phil.* **24 A5** 40 9N 74 54W
Penns Grove, *Phil.* **24 C2** 39 44N 75 27W
Pennsauken, *Phil.* **24 B4** 39 57N 75 5W
Pennsauken Cr. →, *Phil.* **24 B4** 39 59N 75 3W
Pennsylvania, Univ. of, *Phil.* **24 B3** 39 51N 75 11W
Pennypack Cr. →, *Phil.* **24 A4** 40 0N 75 3W
Pentala, *Hels.* **3 C3** 60 6N 24 40 E
Penyagino, *Mos.* **11 D8** 55 50N 37 20 E
Penzing, *Wien* **10 G9** 48 11N 16 18 E
Pequannock, *N.Y.* **22 B3** 40 57N 74 17W
Pequena Arroio Fundo →, *Rio J.* **31 B1** 22 58 S 43 21W
Perales del Rio, *Mdrd.* **8 C3** 40 18N 3 38W
Perchtoldsdorf, *Wien* **10 H9** 48 7N 16 17 E
Perdizes, *S. Pau.* **31 E6** 23 32 S 46 39W
Peredelkino, *Mos.* **11 F8** 55 38N 37 20 E
Peredelytsy, *Mos.* **11 F8** 55 36N 37 21 E
Peristérion, *Ath.* **8 H11** 38 1N 23 42 E
Perivale, *Lon.* **4 B3** 51 31N 0 18W
Perlach, *Mün.* **7 G10** 48 5N 11 37 E
Perlacher Forst, *Mün.* **7 G10** 48 4N 11 34 E
Pero, *Mil.* **9 D5** 45 30N 9 5 E
Peropok, Bukit, *Sing.* **15 G7** 1 19N 103 42 E
Perovo, *Mos.* **11 E10** 55 44N 37 45 E
Perrot, Î., *Mtrl.* **20 B2** 43 23N 73 56W
Perry Hall, *Balt.* **25 A4** 39 24N 76 28W
Perth Amboy, *N.Y.* **22 D3** 40 30N 74 16W
Pertusella, *Mil.* **9 D5** 45 35N 9 3 E
Pesanggrahag, Kali →, *Jak.* **15 J9** 6 10 S 106 44 E
Peschiera Borromeo, *Mil.* **9 E6** 45 26N 9 19 E
Pesek, P., *Sing.* **15 G7** 1 17N 103 41 E
Pest, *Bud.* **10 K13** 47 29N 19 4 E
Pesterzsébet, *Bud.* **10 K13** 47 26N 19 6 E
Pesthidegkút, *Bud.* **10 J12** 47 33N 18 57 E
Pestimre, *Bud.* **10 K14** 47 24N 19 11 E
Pestlörinc, *Bud.* **10 K14** 47 26N 19 11 E
Pestujhely, *Bud.* **10 J13** 47 32N 19 7 E
Petare, *Car.* **30 E6** 10 29N 66 48W
Petas, *Hels.* **3 B4** 60 15N 24 50 E
Peters Pond, *Bost.* **21 A2** 42 43N 71 15W
Petit, *Jobg.* **18 E11** 26 6 S 28 22 E
Petit-Brûlé, *Mtrl.* **20 A1** 43 35N 74 2W
Petojo Selatan, *Jak.* **15 J9** 6 10 S 106 48 E
Petrograd = St. Petersburg, *St-Pet.* **11 B3** 59 55N 30 15 E
Petrogradskaya Storona, *St-Pet.* **11 B4** 59 56N 30 20 E
Petroúpolis, *Ath.* **8 H11** 38 3N 23 40 E
Petrovice, *Pra.* **10 B3** 50 2N 14 33 E
Petrovsko-Rasumovskoye, *Mos.* **11 E9** 55 49N 37 34 E
Petrovskoye, *Mos.* **11 F11** 55 36N 37 53 E
Petrovsky Park, *Mos.* **11 E9** 55 47N 37 34 E
Pfaueninsel, *Berl.* **7 B1** 52 26N 13 7 E
Phihāi, *Kar.* **17 G11** 24 50N 67 8 E
Philadelphia, *Phil.* **24 B3** 39 57N 75 11W
Philadelphia Airport, *Phil.* **24 A5** 40 4N 75 0W
Philadelphia Int. Airport, *Phil.* **24 B3** 39 52N 75 16W
Phillip B., *Syd.* **19 B4** 33 58 S 151 14 E
Phinga, *Calc.* **16 D6** 22 41N 88 25 E
Phoenix, *Chic.* **26 D3** 41 36N 87 37W
Phoenixville, *Phil.* **24 A1** 40 7N 75 31W
Phra Khanong, *Bangk.* **15 B2** 13 40N 100 36 E
Phra Pradaeng, *Bangk.* **15 C2** 13 39N 100 33 E
Phranakhon, *Bangk.* **15 B1** 13 44N 100 29 E
Pianezza, *Tori.* **9 B2** 45 6N 7 32 E
Pianura, *Nápl.* **9 H11** 40 51N 14 10 E
Piaslów, *Wsaw.* **10 E5** 52 11N 20 49 E
Pico Rivera, *L.A.* **28 C4** 33 59N 118 5W
Piedade, *Lisb.* **8 F7** 38 49N 9 16W
Piedade, *Rio J.* **31 B2** 22 52 S 43 18W
Piedade, Cova da, *Lisb.* **8 F8** 38 40N 9 8W
Piedmont, *S.F.* **27 B3** 37 49N 122 14W
Pierrefitte, *Paris* **5 B4** 48 58N 2 21 E
Pierrefonds, *Mtrl.* **20 B2** 43 27N 73 52W
Pierrelaye, *Paris* **5 A2** 49 1N 2 8 E
Pietralata, *Rome* **9 F10** 41 55N 12 33 E
Pihlajamäki, *Hels.* **3 B4** 60 14N 24 58 E
Pihlajasaari, *Hels.* **3 C4** 60 8N 24 55 E
Pikesville, *Balt.* **25 A2** 39 22N 76 42W
Pilar Velho, *S. Pau.* **31 F7** 23 40 S 46 22W
Pilarcitos Cr. →, *S.F.* **27 C2** 37 33N 122 24W
Pilarcitos L., *S.F.* **27 C2** 37 33N 122 25W
Pilgrim Corner, *Phil.* **24 B3** 39 57N 75 19W
Pilgrims Hatch, *Lon.* **4 B6** 51 37N 0 17 E
Pillar Pt., *S.F.* **26 D2** 37 29N 122 30W
Pimenta, *S. Pau.* **31 D7** 23 27 S 46 24W
Pimlico, *Lon.* **4 C4** 51 29N 0 8W
Pimmit Hills, *Wash.* **25 D6** 38 54N 77 12W
Pimville, *Jobg.* **18 F8** 26 16 S 27 54 E
Pinazo →, *B.A.* **32 A2** 34 29 S 58 49W
Pine Brook, *N.Y.* **22 B3** 40 51N 74 18W
Pine Grove, *Trto.* **20 D7** 43 47N 79 34W
Pine Hill, *Phil.* **24 C5** 39 47N 74 59W
Pine Orchard, *Balt.* **25 B1** 39 16N 76 52W
Pinehurst, *Bost.* **21 B2** 42 31N 71 12W
Piñero, *B.A.* **32 B2** 34 31 S 58 46W
Pines Lake, *N.Y.* **22 B3** 40 59N 74 15W
Piney Run →, *Wash.* **25 D6** 38 58N 77 14W
Pinganli, *Beij.* **14 B3** 39 56N 116 20 E
Pinheiros →, *S. Pau.* **31 E5** 23 37 S 46 44W
Pinjrāpur, *Kar.* **17 G11** 24 53N 67 4 E
Pinn →, *Lon.* **4 B2** 51 30N 0 28W
Pinnau →, *Hbg.* **7 C6** 53 40N 9 49 E
Pinneberg, *Hbg.* **7 C6** 53 40N 9 48 E
Pinner, *Lon.* **4 B2** 51 35N 0 22W
Pinner Green, *Lon.* **4 B2** 51 35N 0 23W
Pino Torinese, *Tori.* **9 B3** 45 2N 7 46 E
Pinole Cr. →, *S.F.* **27 A3** 37 58N 122 12W
Pioltello, *Mil.* **9 D6** 45 30N 9 19 E
Piossasco, *Tori.* **9 C1** 44 59N 7 27 E
Piqueri, *S. Pau.* **31 D5** 23 29 S 46 41W
Piqueri →, *S. Pau.* **31 D6** 23 27 S 46 34W
Pira, *Delhi* **16 A1** 28 40N 77 7 E
Piraévs, *Ath.* **8 J10** 37 54N 23 39 E
Pirajussara, *S. Pau.* **31 E5** 23 37 S 46 46W
Pirajussara →, *S. Pau.* **31 E5** 23 33 S 46 42W
Piraporinha, *S. Pau.* **31 F5** 23 41 S 46 44W
Piratininga, *Rio J.* **31 B3** 22 56 S 43 4W
Piratininga, L. de, *Rio J.* **31 B3** 22 56 S 43 4W
Pirituba, *S. Pau.* **31 D5** 23 29 S 46 44W
Pirkkola, *Hels.* **3 B4** 60 14N 24 55 E
Pisangan, *Jak.* **15 J10** 6 12 S 106 52 E
Piscataway, *N.Y.* **22 D2** 40 34N 74 27W
Pisnice, *Pra.* **10 C2** 49 59N 14 28 E
Pitampura Kalan, *Delhi* **16 A1** 28 41N 77 7 E

44 Pitkäjärvi

Pitkäjärvi, *Hels.* **3 B3** 60 15N 24 45 E
Pitman, *Phil.* **24 C4** 39 44N 75 7W
Plainedge, *N.Y.* **23 C8** 40 43N 73 27W
Plainfield, *N.Y.* **22 D2** 40 36N 74 23W
Plainview, *N.Y.* **23 C8** 40 46N 73 27W
Plaisir, *Paris* **5 C1** 48 49N 1 56 E
Plandome, *N.Y.* **23 C6** 40 48N 73 42W
Plandome Heights, *N.Y.* **23 C6** 40 48N 73 42W
Planegg, *Mün.* **7 G9** 48 6N 11 25 E
Plazo Mayor, *Mdrd.* **8 B2** 40 25N 3 43W
Pleasant Hill, *S.F.* **27 A4** 37 56N 122 4W
Plenty, *Melb.* **19 E7** 37 40 S 145 5 E
Pluit, *Jak.* **15 H9** 6 7 S 106 47 E
Plumsock, *Phil.* **24 B2** 39 58N 75 28W
Plumstead, *Lon.* **4 C5** 51 29N 0 5 E
Plymouth Meeting, *Phil.* **24 A3** 40 6N 75 16W
Plyushchevo, *Mos.* **11 E10** 55 44N 37 45 E
Po →, *Tori.* **9 B3** 45 7N 7 46 E
Po Toi, *H.K.* **12 E6** 22 16N 114 17 E
Po Toi I., *H.K.* **12 E6** 22 10N 114 15 E
Podbaba, *Pra.* **10 B2** 50 7N 14 22 E
Podoli, *Pra.* **10 B2** 50 2N 14 25 E
Podra, *Calc.* **16 E5** 22 33N 88 16 E
Poduskino, *Mos.* **11 E7** 55 43N 37 15 E
Poggioreale, *Nápl.* **9 H12** 40 51N 14 17 E
Pogliano Milanese, *Mil.* **9 D4** 45 32N 8 59 E
Pohick Cr. →, *Wash.* **25 E6** 38 47N 77 16W
Point Breeze, *Phil.* **24 B3** 39 54N 75 13W
Point Lookout, *N.Y.* **23 D7** 40 35N 73 34W
Point View Res., *N.Y.* **22 B3** 40 58N 74 14W
Pointe-Aux-Trembles, *Mtrl.* **20 A4** 43 38N 73 30W
Pointe-Calumet, *Mtrl.* **20 B2** 43 29N 73 58W
Pointe-Claire, *Mtrl.* **20 B3** 43 27N 73 48W
Poissy, *Paris* **5 B2** 48 55N 2 2 E
Pok Fu Lam, *H.K.* **12 E5** 22 16N 114 7 E
Pokrovsko-Sresnevo, *Mos.* **11 E8** 55 48N 37 27 E
Pokrovskoye, *Mos.* **11 F9** 55 37N 37 36 E
Póllena, *Nápl.* **9 H13** 40 51N 14 22 E
Polsum, *Ruhr* **6 A4** 51 37N 7 2 E
Polyustrovo, *St-Pet.* **11 B4** 59 57N 30 25 E
Pomigliano d'Arco, *Nápl.* **9 H13** 40 54N 14 23 E
Pompei, *Nápl.* **9 J13** 40 45N 14 29 E
Pomponne, *Paris* **5 B6** 48 52N 2 40 E
Pomprap, *Bangk.* **15 B2** 13 44N 100 30 E
Pompton →, *N.Y.* **22 B3** 40 53N 74 16W
Pompton Lakes, *N.Y.* **22 A3** 41 0N 74 15W
Pompton Plains, *N.Y.* **22 B3** 40 58N 74 18W
Ponders End, *Lon.* **4 B4** 51 38N 0 2W
Pondok Indah, *Jak.* **15 J9** 6 16 S 106 46 E
Ponkapog, *Bost.* **21 D3** 42 11N 71 4W
Ponkapog Pond, *Bost.* **21 D3** 42 11N 71 5W
Pont-Viau, *Mtrl.* **20 A3** 43 34N 73 41W
Pontault-Combault, *Paris* **5 C5** 48 47N 2 36 E
Pontcarré, *Paris* **5 C6** 48 47N 2 42 E
Pontchartrain, *Paris* **5 C1** 48 48N 1 54 E
Ponte Galéria, *Rome* **9 G8** 41 48N 12 19 E
Pontes, Canto do, *Rio J.* **31 B3** 22 56 S 43 3W
Pontevedra, *B.A.* **32 C2** 34 44 S 58 41W
Ponticelli, *Nápl.* **9 H12** 40 51N 14 19 E
Pontinha, *Lisb.* **8 F7** 38 45N 9 11W
Pontoise, *Paris* **5 A2** 49 2N 2 4 E
Poortview, *Jobg.* **18 E8** 26 5 S 27 51 E
Poplar, *Lon.* **4 B4** 51 30N 0 0 E
Poppenbüttel, *Hbg.* **7 D8** 53 39N 10 4 E
Port Chester, *N.Y.* **23 A6** 41 0N 73 40W
Port Chester Harbour, *N.Y.* **23 B7** 40 58N 73 38W
Port Jackson, *Syd.* **19 B4** 33 51 S 151 14 E
Port Kennedy, *Phil.* **24 A2** 40 6N 75 25W
Port Melbourne, *Melb.* **19 F6** 37 50 S 144 54 E
Port Newark, *N.Y.* **22 C4** 40 41N 74 9W
Port Reading, *N.Y.* **22 D3** 40 34N 74 13W
Port Richmond, *N.Y.* **22 D4** 40 38N 74 7W
Port Shelter, *H.K.* **12 D6** 22 20N 114 17 E
Port Union, *Trto.* **20 D10** 43 47N 79 7W
Port Washington, *N.Y.* **23 C6** 40 49N 73 42W
Port Washington North, *N.Y.* **23 B6** 40 50N 73 41W
Portage Park, *Chic.* **26 B2** 41 56N 87 45W
Portela, Aeroporto da, *Lisb.* **8 F8** 38 46N 9 7W
Pórtici, *Nápl.* **9 J12** 40 48N 14 19 E
Porto Brandão, *Lisb.* **8 F7** 38 40N 9 12W
Porto Novo Cr. →, *Lagos* **18 B2** 6 25N 7 22 E
Porto Nuevo, *B.A.* **32 B4** 34 35 S 58 22W
Portrero, *S.F.* **27 B3** 37 46N 122 25W
Posen, *Chic.* **26 D2** 41 38N 87 41W
Posíllipo, *Nápl.* **9 J12** 40 49N 14 13 E
Posíllipo, C. di, *Nápl.* **9 J12** 40 48N 14 12 E
Posolok Lenina, *St-Pet.* **11 C2** 59 50N 30 5 E
Potawatomi Woods, *Chic.* **26 A1** 42 8N 87 53W
Potomac, *Wash.* **25 D6** 38 59N 77 13W
Potomac →, *Wash.* **25 D7** 38 58N 77 9W
Potrero Pt., *S.F.* **27 B2** 37 45N 122 22W
Potsdam, *Berl.* **7 B1** 52 23N 13 3 E
Potter Pt., *Syd.* **19 C4** 34 2 S 151 13 E
Potters Bar, *Lon.* **4 A4** 51 41N 0 10W
Potzham, *Mün.* **7 G10** 48 1N 11 36 E
Pötzleinsdorf, *Wien* **10 G9** 48 14N 16 17 E
Povoa de Santo Adriao, *Lisb.* **8 F8** 38 47N 9 9W
Powderhorn L., *Chic.* **26 D3** 41 38N 87 31W
Powiĉle, *Wsaw.* **10 E7** 52 14N 21 1 E
Powōzki, *Wsaw.* **10 E6** 52 15N 20 58 E
Powsin, *Wsaw.* **10 F7** 52 8N 21 6 E
Powsinek, *Wsaw.* **10 F7** 52 9N 21 6 E
Poyo, *Barc.* **8 D6** 41 28N 2 12 E
Pozuelo de Alarcón, *Mdrd.* **8 B2** 40 25N 3 48W
Praça Seca, *Rio J.* **31 B1** 22 53 S 43 20W
Prado, Museo del, *Mdrd.* **8 B2** 40 25N 3 42W
Prado Churubusco, *Méx.* **29 B3** 19 20N 99 8W
Praga, *Wsaw.* **10 E7** 52 15N 21 2 E
Prague = Praha, *Pra.* **10 B2** 50 4N 14 25 E
Praha, *Pra.* **10 B2** 50 4N 14 25 E
Praha-Ruzyně Airport, *Pra.* **10 B1** 50 6N 14 16 E
Praires, R. des →, *Mtrl.* **20 A4** 43 38N 73 36W
Prat de Llobregat, *Barc.* **8 E5** 41 19N 2 5 E
Prater, *Wien* **10 G10** 48 12N 16 25 E
Pratts Bottom, *Lon.* **4 C5** 51 20N 0 7 E
Prawet Buri Rom, Khlong →, *Bangk.* **15 B2** 13 43N 100 38 E
Preakness, *N.Y.* **22 B3** 40 56N 74 12W
Precotto, *Mil.* **9 D6** 45 30N 9 13 E
Prédecelles →, *Paris* **5 D2** 48 36N 2 7 E
Pregnana Milanese, *Mil.* **9 D4** 45 30N 9 0 E
Prem Prachakan, Khlong →, *Bangk.* **15 B2** 13 46N 100 35 E
Prenestino Labicano, *Rome* **9 F10** 41 53N 12 33 E
Prenzlauerberg, *Berl.* **7 A3** 52 32N 13 24 E
Presidente Derqui, *B.A.* **32 A1** 34 29 S 58 50W
Presidente Outra, Rodo, *Rio J.* **31 A1** 22 47 S 43 21W
Preston, *Melb.* **19 E6** 37 44 S 144 59 E
Pretos Forros, Sa. dos, *Rio J.* **31 B2** 22 54 S 43 17W
Préville, *Mtrl.* **20 B5** 43 28N 73 29W
Přezletice, *Pra.* **10 B3** 50 9N 14 34 E
Primavalle, *Rome* **9 F9** 41 55N 12 25 E
Primrose, *Jobg.* **18 F9** 26 11 S 28 9 E
Princes B., *N.Y.* **22 D3** 40 30N 74 12W
Princess Elizabeth Park, *Sing.* **15 F7** 1 21N 103 45 E
Progreso, *Mdrd.* **8 B3** 40 27N 3 39W
Progreso Nacional, *Méx.* **29 A3** 19 30N 99 9W
Prosek, *Pra.* **10 B3** 50 7N 14 30 E
Prospect, *Syd.* **19 A2** 33 48 S 150 55 E
Prospect Heights, *Chic.* **26 A1** 42 5N 87 55W
Prospect Hill Park, *Bost.* **21 C2** 42 23N 71 13W
Prospect Park, *N.Y.* **22 B3** 40 55N 74 10W
Prospect Park, *Phil.* **24 B3** 39 53N 75 18W
Prospect Pt., *N.Y.* **23 B6** 40 52N 73 42W
Prospect Res., *Syd.* **19 A2** 33 49 S 150 53 E
Providence, *Balt.* **25 A3** 39 25N 76 34W
Providencia, *Stgo* **30 J11** 33 25 S 70 36W
Průhonice, *Pra.* **10 C3** 50 0N 14 33 E
Pruszków, *Wsaw.* **10 E5** 52 10N 20 48 E
Psikhikón, *Ath.* **8 H11** 38 1N 23 46 E
Pudong, *Shang.* **14 J12** 31 13N 121 30 E
Puduo, *Shang.* **14 J11** 31 15N 121 24 E
Pueblo Libre, *Lima* **30 G8** 12 5 S 77 4W
Pueblo Nuevo, *Barc.* **8 D6** 41 23N 2 11 E
Pueblo Nuevo, *Mdrd.* **8 B3** 40 25N 3 37W
Puente Cascallares, *B.A.* **32 C2** 34 41 S 58 48W
Puente Hills, *L.A.* **28 C5** 33 59N 117 59W
Puffing Billy Station, *Melb.* **19 F9** 37 54 S 145 20 E
Puhuangyu, *Beij.* **14 B3** 39 50N 116 22 E
Puistola, *Hels.* **3 B5** 60 16N 25 2 E
Pukinmäki, *Hels.* **3 B4** 60 15N 24 57 E
Pullach, *Mün.* **7 G9** 48 3N 11 31 E
Pulo, *Manila* **15 D4** 14 34N 121 4 E
Pulo Gadung, *Jak.* **15 J10** 6 11 S 106 54 E
Pumphrey, *Balt.* **25 B3** 39 13N 76 39W
Punchbowl, *Syd.* **19 B3** 33 55 S 151 3 E
Punde, *Bomb.* **16 H8** 18 53N 72 57 E
Punggol, *Sing.* **15 F8** 1 23N 103 54 E
Punggol, Sungei →, *Sing.* **15 F8** 1 24N 103 54 E
Punggol Pt., *Sing.* **15 F8** 1 24N 103 54 E
Punta Brava, *La Hab.* **30 B2** 23 1N 82 29W
Puolarmetsä, *Hels.* **3 B3** 60 11N 24 41 E
Puotila, *Hels.* **3 B5** 60 13N 25 6 E
Purchase, *N.Y.* **23 A6** 41 2N 73 43W
Purfleet, *Lon.* **4 C6** 51 29N 0 14 E
Purkersdorf, *Wien* **10 G9** 48 12N 16 11 E
Purley, *Lon.* **4 C4** 51 20N 0 6W
Puteaux, *Paris* **5 B3** 48 53N 2 14 E
Puth Kalan, *Delhi* **16 A1** 28 42N 77 4 E
Putilkovo, *Mos.* **11 D8** 55 51N 37 22 E
Putnamville Res., *Bost.* **21 B4** 42 36N 70 56W
Putney, *Lon.* **4 C3** 51 27N 0 13W
Putty Hill, *Balt.* **25 A3** 39 22N 76 30W
Putxet, *Barc.* **8 D5** 41 24N 2 8 E
Putzbrunn, *Mün.* **7 G11** 48 4N 11 42 E
Pyeongchang, *Sŏul* **12 G7** 37 35N 126 57 E
Pyramids, *El Qâ.* **18 D4** 29 58N 31 7 E
Pyry, *Wsaw.* **10 F6** 52 8N 21 0 E

Q

Qanât el Ismâîlîya, *El Qâ.* **18 C5** 30 7N 31 17 E
Qasemābād, *Tehr.* **17 C6** 35 4N 51 3 E
Qasr-e-Firōzeh, *Tehr.* **17 D6** 35 29N 51 31 E
Qianmen, *Beij.* **14 B3** 39 51N 116 21 E
Qibao, *Shang.* **14 K11** 31 9N 121 20 E
Qingguang, *Tianj.* **14 D5** 39 11N 117 2 E
Qinghua Univ., *Beij.* **14 A2** 40 0N 116 17 E
Qinghuayuan, *Beij.* **14 B2** 39 59N 116 19 E
Qingningsi, *Shang.* **14 J12** 31 16N 121 33 E
Qolhak, *Tehr.* **17 C5** 35 45N 51 26 E
Quadraro, *Rome* **9 F10** 41 51N 12 33 E
Quaid-i-Azam, *Kar.* **17 G10** 24 50N 66 59 E
Qual'eh Murgeh Airport, *Tehr.* **17 D5** 35 38N 51 22 E
Qualiano, *Nápl.* **9 H11** 40 55N 14 9 E
Quannapowitt, L., *Bost.* **21 B3** 42 30N 71 4W
Quartiere Zingone, *Mil.* **9 E5** 45 25N 9 3 E
Quarto, *Nápl.* **9 H11** 40 52N 14 8 E
Quds, *Bagd.* **17 E8** 33 23N 44 24 E
Quebrada Baruta →, *Car.* **30 E5** 10 29N 66 53W
Quebrada Tácagua →, *Car.* **30 D4** 10 36N 67 1W
Quebrada Topo →, *Car.* **30 D4** 10 32N 67 0W
Queen Mary Res., *Lon.* **4 C2** 51 24N 0 27W
Queens Village, *N.Y.* **23 C6** 40 43N 73 44W
Queensbury, *Lon.* **4 B3** 51 35N 0 16W
Queenscliffe, *Syd.* **19 A4** 33 47 S 151 17 E
Queenstown, *Sing.* **15 G7** 1 18N 103 48 E
Quellerina, *Jobg.* **18 E8** 26 9 S 27 56 E
Queluz, *Lisb.* **8 F7** 38 45N 9 14W
Quezon City, *Manila* **15 D4** 14 37N 121 2 E
Quickborn, *Hbg.* **7 C7** 53 43N 9 54 E
Quilicura, *Stgo* **30 J10** 33 22 S 70 43W
Quilmes, *B.A.* **32 C5** 34 43 S 58 15W
Quincy, *Bost.* **21 D3** 42 14N 71 0W
Quincy B., *Bost.* **21 D4** 42 16N 70 59W
Quincy-sous-Sénart, *Paris* **5 C5** 48 40N 2 32 E
Quinta Normal, *Stgo* **30 J10** 33 26 S 70 40W
Quinto Romano, *Mil.* **9 E5** 45 28N 9 7 E
Quirinale, *Rome* **9 F9** 41 53N 12 29 E
Quitaúna, *S. Pau.* **31 E5** 23 31 S 46 48W

R

Raasdorf, *Wien* **10 G11** 48 14N 16 33 E
Raccoon Cr. →, *Phil.* **24 C3** 39 48N 75 21W
Raccoon Str., *S.F.* **27 A2** 37 52N 122 26W
Radevormwald, *Ruhr* **6 C6** 51 12N 7 22 E
Radlett, *Lon.* **4 A3** 51 41N 0 19W
Radlice, *Pra.* **10 B2** 50 3N 14 23 E
Radnor, *Phil.* **24 A2** 40 2N 75 21W
Radonice, *Pra.* **10 B3** 50 8N 14 36 E
Radotin, *Pra.* **10 C2** 49 59N 14 21 E
Rælingen, *Oslo* **2 B6** 59 53N 11 5 E
Rafael Calzada, *B.A.* **32 C4** 34 47 S 58 21W
Rafael Castillo, *B.A.* **32 C3** 34 42 S 58 36W
Raffles Park, *Sing.* **15 G7** 1 19N 103 48 E
Raghunathpur, *Calc.* **16 D5** 22 41N 88 16 E
Rahlstedt, *Hbg.* **7 D8** 53 35N 10 7 E
Rahm, *Ruhr* **6 B2** 51 21N 6 47 E
Rahnsdorf, *Berl.* **7 B5** 52 25N 13 41 E
Rahway, *N.Y.* **22 D3** 40 36N 74 17W
Rail Tree Hill, *Bost.* **21 B1** 42 32N 71 22W
Rainbow Lakes, *N.Y.* **22 B2** 40 53N 74 27W
Rainham, *Lon.* **4 B6** 51 31N 0 11 E
Rainier, Mt., *Wash.* **25 D8** 38 56N 76 57W
Raj Bhawan, *Calc.* **16 E6** 22 33N 88 20 E
Rajakylä, *Hels.* **3 B5** 60 15N 25 5 E
Rajapur, *Calc.* **16 E5** 22 39N 88 11 E
Rajganj, *Calc.* **16 E5** 22 34N 88 14 E
Rajpur, *Delhi* **16 A2** 28 41N 77 12 E
Rákos-patak →, *Bud.* **10 K14** 47 29N 19 12 E
Rákoscsaba, *Bud.* **10 K14** 47 28N 19 17 E
Rákoshegy, *Bud.* **10 K14** 47 27N 19 14 E
Rákosker, *Bud.* **10 K14** 47 28N 19 14 E
Rákoskert, *Bud.* **10 K14** 47 27N 19 18 E
Rákosliget, *Bud.* **10 K14** 47 29N 19 16 E
Rákospalota, *Bud.* **10 J13** 47 34N 19 7 E
Rákosszentmihály, *Bud.* **10 J13** 47 31N 19 8 E
Raków, *Wsaw.* **10 E6** 52 11N 20 56 E
Rakowiec, *Wsaw.* **10 E6** 52 12N 20 58 E
Ramadān, *Bagd.* **17 F8** 33 19N 44 20 E
Ramanathpur, *Calc.* **16 D5** 22 41N 88 14 E
Rambler Channel, *H.K.* **12 D5** 22 21N 114 6 E
Ramblewood, *Phil.* **24 B5** 39 55N 74 56W
Ramenki, *Mos.* **11 E8** 55 41N 37 28 E
Ramersdorf, *Mün.* **7 G10** 48 6N 11 35 E
Ramnathpur, *Calc.* **16 E5** 22 35N 88 18 E
Ramos, *Rio J.* **31 B2** 22 50 S 43 14W
Ramos Mejia, *B.A.* **32 B3** 34 39 S 58 33W
Rampur, *Delhi* **16 A2** 28 44N 77 18 E
Ramsgate, *Syd.* **19 B3** 33 58 S 151 8 E
Ramstadjøen, *Oslo* **2 B6** 59 53N 11 3 E
Rancho Boyeros, *La Hab.* **30 C2** 22 59N 82 22W
Rancho Colorado, Presa de, *Méx.* **29 B2** 19 29N 99 16W
Rancocas Cr. →, *Phil.* **24 A5** 40 2N 74 58W
Rand Afrikaans Univ., *Jobg.* **18 F9** 26 11 S 28 0 E
Rand Airport, *Jobg.* **18 F9** 26 14 S 28 8 E
Randallstown, *Balt.* **25 A2** 39 21N 76 46W
Randburg, *Jobg.* **18 E8** 26 5 S 27 57 E
Randhart, *Jobg.* **18 F9** 26 16 S 28 7 E
Randolph, *Bost.* **21 D3** 42 10N 71 3W
Randolph Hills, *Wash.* **25 C7** 39 3N 77 6W
Randpark, *Jobg.* **18 E8** 26 6 S 27 58 E
Randwick, *Syd.* **19 B4** 33 54 S 151 14 E
Ranelagh, *B.A.* **32 C5** 34 47 S 58 14W
Rannersdorf, *Wien* **10 H10** 48 7N 16 27 E
Raparkrif, *Jobg.* **18 E8** 26 5 S 27 57 E
Raposo, *Lisb.* **8 F7** 38 40N 9 11W
Raritan →, *N.Y.* **22 D2** 40 30N 74 27W
Raritan B., *N.Y.* **22 E3** 40 29N 74 12W
Rasskazovka, *Mos.* **11 F8** 55 38N 37 20 E
Rasta, *Stock.* **3 E8** 59 18N 17 37 E
Rastaala, *Hels.* **3 B3** 60 15N 24 47 E
Rastila, *Hels.* **3 B5** 60 12N 25 7 E
Raszyn, *Wsaw.* **10 F6** 52 9N 20 54 E
Rat Burana, *Bangk.* **15 B2** 13 40N 100 30 E
Ratanpur, *Calc.* **16 D5** 22 49N 88 14 E
Rath, *Ruhr* **6 C2** 51 16N 6 49 E
Ratingen, *Ruhr* **6 C3** 51 18N 6 52 E
Rato, *Lisb.* **8 F8** 38 43N 9 8W
Rauxel, *Ruhr* **6 A5** 51 34N 7 18 E
Ravenswood Pt., *S.F.* **27 C4** 37 30N 122 8W
Rawamangun, *Jak.* **15 J10** 6 11 S 106 52 E
Rayners Lane, *Lon.* **4 B2** 51 34N 0 23W
Raynes Park, *Lon.* **4 C3** 51 24N 0 12W
Raypur, *Calc.* **16 F6** 22 28N 88 22 E
Razdory, *Mos.* **11 E7** 55 44N 37 17 E
Razmitelevo, *St-Pet.* **11 B5** 59 54N 30 39 E
Razor Hill, *H.K.* **12 D6** 22 20N 114 15 E
Reading, *Bost.* **21 B3** 42 31N 71 5W
Reading Highlands, *Bost.* **21 B3** 42 31N 71 5W
Reáglie, *Tori.* **9 B3** 45 3N 7 44 E
Real, Palacio, *Mdrd.* **8 B2** 40 25N 3 43W
Real Felipe, Castillo, *Lima* **30 G8** 12 4 S 77 9W
Real Fuerta, Château de la, *La Hab.* **30 B2** 23 8N 82 20W
Realengo, *Rio J.* **31 B1** 22 52 S 43 24W
Réau, *Paris* **5 D5** 48 36N 2 37 E
Recklinghausen, *Ruhr* **6 A5** 51 37N 7 12 E
Recklinghausen-Süd, *Ruhr* **6 A5** 51 34N 7 14 E
Recoleta, *Stgo* **30 J11** 33 25 S 70 40W
Reconquista →, *B.A.* **32 B3** 34 35 S 58 35W
Red Bank Battle Mon., *Phil.* **24 B3** 39 52N 75 11W
Red Fort, *Delhi* **16 B2** 28 39N 77 14 E
Red Rock, *S.F.* **27 A2** 37 55N 122 25W
Red Square, *Mos.* **11 E9** 55 45N 37 37 E
Redbridge, *Lon.* **4 B5** 51 34N 0 3 E
Redwood City, *S.F.* **27 D3** 37 29N 122 14W
Redwood Cr. →, *S.F.* **27 C3** 37 31N 122 11W
Redwood Pt., *S.F.* **27 C3** 37 32N 122 11W
Redwood Regional Park, *S.F.* **27 B4** 37 48N 122 8W
Reeves Hill, *Bost.* **21 C1** 42 20N 71 20W
Refshaleøen, *Købn.* **2 D10** 55 41N 12 36 E
Regents Park, *Jobg.* **18 F9** 26 14 S 28 3 E
Regents Park, *Lon.* **4 B4** 51 31N 0 9W
Regents Park, *Syd.* **19 B3** 33 52 S 151 1 E
Regi Lagni →, *Nápl.* **9 H13** 40 56N 14 23 E
Regina Margherita, *Tori.* **9 B2** 45 4N 7 34 E
Regla, *La Hab.* **30 B3** 23 7N 82 19W
Rego Park, *N.Y.* **23 C5** 40 43N 73 51W
Reiherstieg, *Hbg.* **7 D7** 53 30N 9 58 E
Reinickendorf, *Berl.* **7 A3** 52 34N 13 22 E
Reinoldikirche, *Ruhr* **6 A6** 51 30N 7 28 E
Reistad, *Oslo* **2 C1** 59 46N 10 16 E
Reitbrook, *Hbg.* **7 E8** 53 28N 10 8 E
Rekola, *Hels.* **3 B5** 60 19N 25 4 E
Rellingen, *Hbg.* **7 D7** 53 39N 9 50 E
Rembertów, *Wsaw.* **10 E7** 52 15N 21 9 E
Remedios de Escalada, *B.A.* **32 C4** 34 43 S 58 24W
Rémola, Laguna del, *Barc.* **8 E5** 41 16N 2 4 E
Remscheid, *Ruhr* **6 C5** 51 11N 7 11 E
Renca, *Stgo* **30 J10** 33 24 S 70 42W
Renca, Cerro, *Stgo* **30 J10** 33 23 S 70 40W
Rener, *Ist.* **17 A2** 41 1N 28 56 E
Renmin Gongyuan, *Tianj.* **14 E6** 39 6N 117 12 E
Rennemoulin, *Paris* **5 B2** 48 50N 2 2 E
Rennie's Mill, *H.K.* **12 E6** 22 18N 114 15 E
Renzel, *Hbg.* **7 C7** 53 43N 9 52 E
Repaupo, *Phil.* **24 C3** 39 48N 75 18W
Repaupo Cr. →, *Phil.* **24 C3** 39 49N 75 20W
Řeporyje, *Pra.* **10 B1** 50 1N 14 18 E
République, Place de la, *Paris* **5 B4** 48 52N 2 22 E
Repy, *Pra.* **10 B1** 50 4N 14 17 E
Resarö, *Stock.* **3 D13** 59 25N 18 20 E
Rescaldna, *Mil.* **9 D4** 45 36N 8 57 E
Research, *Melb.* **19 E8** 37 42 S 145 10 E
Reseda, *L.A.* **28 A1** 34 12N 118 31W
Reservoir, *Melb.* **19 E7** 37 42 S 145 1 E
Reservoir Pond, *Bost.* **21 D3** 42 10N 71 7W
Residenz, *Mün.* **7 G10** 48 8N 11 34 E
Resse, *Ruhr* **6 A4** 51 34N 7 6 E
Reston, *Wash.* **25 D6** 38 57N 77 20W
Retiro, *B.A.* **32 B4** 34 35 S 58 23W
Retiro, *Mdrd.* **8 B2** 40 24N 3 40W
Reutov, *Mos.* **11 E11** 55 45N 37 50 E
Réveillon →, *Paris* **5 C5** 48 42N 2 30 E
Revere, *Bost.* **21 C3** 42 25N 71 0W
Revesby, *Syd.* **19 B3** 33 57 S 151 0 E
Revolucion, Plaza de la, *La Hab.* **30 B2** 23 7N 82 23W
Rexdale, *Trto.* **20 D7** 43 43N 79 35W
Reynolds Channel, *N.Y.* **23 D6** 40 35N 73 41W
Reynosa Tamaulipas, *Méx.* **29 A2** 19 30N 99 10W
Rheem Valley, *S.F.* **27 A4** 37 50N 122 8W
Rhein-Herne Kanal, *Ruhr* **6 B3** 51 29N 6 59 E
Rheinberg, *Ruhr* **6 A1** 51 32N 6 37 E
Rheinhausen, *Ruhr* **6 B2** 51 24N 6 43 E
Rheinkamp, *Ruhr* **6 B1** 51 29N 6 36 E
Rho, *Mil.* **9 D5** 45 31N 9 2 E
Rhodes, *Syd.* **19 A3** 33 49 S 151 6 E
Rhodesfield, *Jobg.* **18 E10** 26 6 S 28 14 E
Rhodon, *Paris* **5 C2** 48 42N 2 3 E
Rhodon →, *Paris* **5 C2** 48 42N 2 4 E
Rhu, Tg., *Sing.* **15 G8** 1 17N 103 51 E
Ribeirão Pires, *S. Pau.* **31 F7** 23 42 S 46 23W
Říčanský →, *Pra.* **10 B3** 50 5N 14 36 E
Říčany, *Pra.* **10 C3** 49 59N 14 39 E
Ricarda, Laguna de la, *Barc.* **8 E5** 41 17N 2 6 E
Richardson B., *S.F.* **27 A2** 37 52N 122 29W
Richmond, *Lon.* **4 C3** 51 27N 0 17W
Richmond, *Melb.* **19 E7** 37 48 S 145 0 E
Richmond, *S.F.* **27 B2** 37 46N 122 27W
Richmond, *S.F.* **27 A2** 37 56N 122 21W
Richmond →, *N.Y.* **22 D3** 40 34N 74 11W
Richmond, Pt., *S.F.* **27 A2** 37 54N 122 23W
Richmond Hill, *N.Y.* **23 C5** 40 41N 73 51W
Richmond Hill, *Trto.* **20 C8** 43 51N 79 24W
Richmond Inner Harbour, *S.F.* **27 A2** 37 54N 122 20W
Richmond Park, *Lon.* **4 C3** 51 26N 0 16W
Richmond Valley, *N.Y.* **22 D3** 40 31N 74 13W
Richvale, *Trto.* **20 C8** 43 51N 79 26W
Rickers I., *N.Y.* **23 C5** 40 47N 73 53W
Rickmansworth, *Lon.* **4 B2** 51 38N 0 28W
Riddel Cr. →, *Melb.* **19 F8** 37 52 S 145 13 E
Riderwood, *Balt.* **25 A3** 39 24N 76 37W
Ridgefield, *N.Y.* **22 C4** 40 49N 74 0W
Ridgefield Park, *N.Y.* **22 B4** 40 52N 74 1W
Ridgewood, *N.Y.* **23 C5** 40 42N 73 53W
Ridley Cr. →, *Phil.* **24 B2** 39 51N 75 20W
Ridley Creek State Park, *Phil.* **24 B2** 39 57N 75 26W
Ridley Park, *Phil.* **24 B3** 39 52N 75 19W
Riedmoos, *Mün.* **7 F10** 48 16N 11 32 E
Riem, *Mün.* **7 G11** 48 8N 11 41 E
Riemke, *Ruhr* **6 A5** 51 30N 7 12 E
Rimac, *Lima* **30 G8** 12 2 S 77 2W
Rimau, Tg., *Sing.* **15 G7** 1 15N 103 48 E
Ringwood, *Melb.* **19 E8** 37 48 S 145 4 E
Rinkeby, *Stock.* **3 D10** 59 23N 17 55 E
Rio Comprido, *Rio J.* **31 B2** 22 55 S 43 12W
Rio de Janeiro, *Rio J.* **31 B2** 22 54 S 43 12W
Rio de Mouro, *Lisb.* **8 F7** 38 46N 9 15W
Rio Hondo →, *L.A.* **28 B4** 34 2N 118 15W
Rio Pequeno, *S. Pau.* **31 E5** 23 34 S 46 44W
Rione Trieste, *Nápl.* **9 H13** 40 52N 14 27 E
Ripley, *Lon.* **4 D2** 51 17N 0 29W
Rippling Ridge, *Balt.* **25 B3** 39 11N 76 37W
Ris, *Oslo* **2 B4** 59 56N 10 41 E
Ris-Orangis, *Paris* **5 D4** 48 38N 2 24 E
Risby, *Købn.* **2 D8** 55 41N 12 19 E
Rishra, *Calc.* **16 D6** 22 42N 88 20 E
Ritan Gongyuan, *Beij.* **14 B3** 39 53N 116 24 E
Ritchie, *Wash.* **25 D8** 38 52N 76 51W
Rithala, *Delhi* **16 A1** 28 43N 77 6 E
Ritorp, *Stock.* **3 E8** 59 12N 17 38 E
Rivalta di Torino, *Tori.* **9 B1** 45 2N 7 31 E
Rivas de Jarama, *Mdrd.* **8 B3** 40 22N 3 31W
Rivas-Vaciamadrio, *Mdrd.* **8 C3** 40 19N 3 30W
Rivasacco, *Tori.* **9 A1** 45 10N 7 29 E
Rive Sud, Canal de la, *Mtrl.* **20 B4** 43 24N 73 31W
River Edge, *N.Y.* **22 B4** 40 56N 74 1W
River Forest, *Chic.* **26 B2** 41 53N 87 49W
River Grove, *Chic.* **26 B1** 41 55N 87 50W
River Pines, *Bost.* **21 B2** 42 33N 71 17W
River Vale, *N.Y.* **22 B4** 40 59N 74 1W
Riverdale, *Chic.* **26 D3** 41 38N 87 37W
Riverdale, *N.Y.* **22 B3** 40 59N 74 17W
Riverdale, *Trto.* **20 E8** 43 39N 79 21W
Riverdale, *Wash.* **25 D8** 38 57N 76 54W
Riverdale Park, *Trto.* **20 D8** 43 40N 79 21W
Riverhead, *Lon.* **4 D6** 51 16N 0 10 E
Riverlea, *Jobg.* **18 F8** 26 12 S 27 58 E
Riverside, *Bost.* **21 B2** 42 32N 71 18W
Riverside, *Chic.* **26 C2** 41 49N 87 49W
Riverside, *N.Y.* **23 B5** 40 54N 73 54W
Riverside, *N.Y.* **23 A7** 41 1N 73 34W
Riverside, *Phil.* **24 A5** 40 2N 74 57W
Riverton, *Phil.* **24 A4** 40 0N 75 0W
Riverwood, *Syd.* **19 B3** 33 57 S 151 3 E
Rivière-des-Praires, *Mtrl.* **20 A4** 43 38N 73 34W
Rivodora, *Tori.* **9 B3** 45 5N 7 47 E
Rivoli, *Tori.* **9 B1** 45 4N 7 30 E
Riyad, *Bagd.* **17 F8** 33 18N 44 27 E
Rizal, *Manila* **15 D4** 14 33N 121 0 E
Rizal Park, *Manila* **15 D3** 14 35N 120 58 E
Rizel Stadium, *Manila* **15 D3** 14 34N 120 59 E
Røa, *Oslo* **2 B3** 59 57N 10 39 E
Robassomero, *Tori.* **9 A2** 45 11N 7 34 E
Robbins, *Chic.* **26 D2** 41 38N 87 42W
Robert E. Lee Memorial Park, *Balt.* **25 A3** 39 23N 76 40 E
Robertsdale, *Chic.* **26 C3** 41 40N 87 30W
Robertsham, *Jobg.* **18 F9** 26 15 S 28 1 E
Robin Hills, *Jobg.* **18 E8** 26 6 S 27 58 E
Rocha Miranda, *Rio J.* **31 B1** 22 51 S 43 20W
Rochar →, *Sing.* **15 G8** 1 18N 103 52 E
Rochelle Park, *N.Y.* **22 B4** 40 54N 74 4W
Rock Cr. →, *Wash.* **25 D7** 38 54N 77 3W
Rock Creek Park, *Wash.* **25 D7** 38 56N 77 2W
Rockaway, *N.Y.* **22 D5** 40 32N 73 56W
Rockaway Beach, *S.F.* **27 C2** 37 36N 122 29W
Rockaway Islet, *N.Y.* **23 D5** 40 34N 73 53W
Rockaway Neck, *N.Y.* **22 B2** 40 51N 74 21W
Rockaway Point, *N.Y.* **23 D5** 40 33N 73 54W
Rockburn Branch →, *Balt.* **25 B2** 39 13N 76 43W
Rockdale, *Balt.* **25 A2** 39 21N 76 46W
Rockdale, *Syd.* **19 B3** 33 57 S 151 8 E
Rockland, *Phil.* **24 C1** 39 47N 75 34W
Rocklege, *Phil.* **24 A4** 40 4N 75 5W
Rockleigh, *N.Y.* **22 A5** 41 0N 73 55W
Rockville, *Wash.* **25 C6** 39 4N 77 10W
Rockville Centre, *N.Y.* **23 D7** 40 39N 73 38W
Rocky Hill, *Phil.* **24 B1** 39 58N 75 32W
Rocky Ridge, *S.F.* **27 B4** 37 47N 122 2W
Rocky Run →, *Wash.* **25 D6** 38 58N 77 14W
Rodaon, *Wien* **10 H9** 48 8N 16 16 E
Rodeo Cove, *S.F.* **27 B1** 37 49N 122 32W
Rodgers Forge, *Balt.* **25 A3** 39 22N 76 37W
Roding →, *Lon.* **4 B5** 51 30N 0 5 E
Rodość, *Wsaw.* **10 E8** 52 11N 21 11 E
Rødovre, *Købn.* **2 D9** 55 40N 12 26 E
Rodrigo de Freitas, L., *Rio J.* **31 B2** 22 58 S 43 12W
Rodstensfjärden, *Stock.* **3 E9** 59 16N 17 48 E
Roehampton, *Lon.* **4 C3** 51 27N 0 15W
Rogers Park, *Chic.* **26 A2** 42 0N 87 40W
Rohdenhaus, *Ruhr* **6 C4** 51 18N 7 0 E
Röhlinghausen, *Ruhr* **6 A4** 51 30N 7 9 E
Roihuvuori, *Hels.* **3 B5** 60 11N 25 2 E
Roissy, *Paris* **5 C5** 48 47N 2 39 E
Roissy-en-France, *Paris* **5 A5** 49 0N 2 30 E
Rokkō Sanchi, *Ōsaka* **12 B2** 34 44N 135 13 E
Rokko-Zan, *Ōsaka* **12 B2** 34 46N 135 16 E
Rokytka →, *Pra.* **10 B3** 50 6N 14 27 E
Roland Lake, *Balt.* **25 A3** 39 23N 76 38W
Roland Park, *Balt.* **25 A3** 39 20N 76 39W
Roma, *Rome* **9 F9** 41 54N 12 28 E
Római-Fürdö, *Bud.* **10 J13** 47 34N 19 4 E
Romainville, *Paris* **5 B4** 48 52N 2 26 E
Romani, *Nápl.* **9 H13** 40 52N 14 22 E
Romano Banco, *Mil.* **9 E5** 45 25N 9 6 E
Romashkovo, *Mos.* **11 E7** 55 43N 37 19 E
Rome = Roma, *Rome* **9 F9** 41 54N 12 28 E
Romford, *Lon.* **4 B6** 51 34N 0 11 E
Roncáglia, *Tori.* **9 B1** 45 2N 7 29 E
Rönninge, *Stock.* **3 E9** 59 12N 17 45 E
Ronsdorf, *Ruhr* **6 C5** 51 13N 7 11 E
Ronskensiedig, *Ruhr* **6 A2** 51 36N 6 41 E
Rontgental, *Berl.* **7 A4** 52 38N 13 31 E
Roodekop, *Jobg.* **18 F10** 26 17 S 28 11 E
Roodepoort, *Jobg.* **18 E8** 26 9 S 27 53 E
Roodepoort-Wes, *Jobg.* **18 E8** 26 8 S 27 51 E
Roosevelt, *N.Y.* **23 C7** 40 40N 73 35W
Rooty Hill, *Syd.* **19 A2** 33 46 S 150 50 E
Roppongi, *Tōkyō* **13 C3** 35 39N 139 44 E
Rosairinho, *Lisb.* **8 F8** 38 40N 9 0W
Rosanna, *Melb.* **19 E7** 37 44 S 145 4 E
Rosario, *La Hab.* **30 B2** 23 3N 82 21W
Rosario, *Manila* **15 D4** 14 35N 121 4 E
Rose B., *Syd.* **19 B4** 33 51 S 151 16 E
Rose Hill, *Wash.* **25 E7** 38 47N 77 6W
Rose Tree, *Phil.* **24 B2** 39 56N 75 23W
Rosebank, *N.Y.* **22 D4** 40 36N 74 4W
Rosebery, *Syd.* **19 B4** 33 55 S 151 12 E
Rosedal La Candelaria, *Méx.* **29 B3** 19 20N 99 10W
Rosedale, *Balt.* **25 B3** 39 19N 76 31W
Rosedale, *N.Y.* **23 D6** 40 39N 73 43W
Roseiras, *S. Pau.* **31 E7** 23 33 S 46 23W
Roseland, *Chic.* **26 C3** 41 42N 87 37W
Roseland, *N.Y.* **22 C3** 40 49N 74 17W
Roselle, *N.Y.* **22 D3** 40 39N 74 15W
Roselle Park, *N.Y.* **22 D3** 40 39N 74 16W
Rosemead, *L.A.* **28 B4** 34 4N 118 4W
Rosemere, *Mtrl.* **20 A2** 43 34N 73 50W
Rosemont, *Chic.* **26 B1** 41 59N 87 52W
Rosemont, *Phil.* **24 A3** 40 1N 75 19W
Rosenborg Have, *Købn.* **2 D10** 55 41N 12 33 E
Rosengarten, *Hbg.* **7 D6** 53 31N 9 49 E
Rosenthal, *Berl.* **7 A3** 52 35N 13 22 E
Rosettenville, *Jobg.* **18 F9** 26 15 S 28 3 E
Rosherville Dam, *Jobg.* **18 F9** 26 13 S 28 6 E
Rósio, *Mil.* **9 E4** 45 25N 8 57 E
Rösjön, *Stock.* **3 D11** 59 26N 18 0 E
Roskilde, *Købn.* **2 E7** 55 38N 12 5 E
Roskilde Fjord, *Købn.* **2 D7** 55 45N 12 4 E
Roslags-Näsby, *Stock.* **3 D11** 59 25N 18 2 E
Roslindale, *Bost.* **21 D3** 42 17N 71 7W
Roslyn, *N.Y.* **23 C7** 40 47N 73 38W
Roslyn, *Phil.* **24 A4** 40 7N 75 8W
Roslyn Estates, *N.Y.* **23 C6** 40 47N 73 40W
Roslyn Harbour, *N.Y.* **23 C7** 40 48N 73 38W
Rosne →, *Paris* **5 B4** 48 58N 2 25 E
Rosny-sous-Bois, *Paris* **5 B5** 48 52N 2 30 E
Ross, *S.F.* **27 A1** 37 57N 122 33W
Rosslyn, *Wash.* **25 D7** 38 53N 77 4W
Rossville, *Balt.* **25 A4** 39 20N 76 28W
Rossville, *N.Y.* **22 D3** 40 32N 74 12W
Rosta, *Tori.* **9 B1** 45 4N 7 27 E
Rotbach →, *Ruhr* **6 A2** 51 34N 6 41 E
Rothenburgsort, *Hbg.* **7 D8** 53 32N 10 2 E
Rotherbaum, *Hbg.* **7 D7** 53 33N 9 58 E
Rotherhithe, *Lon.* **4 C4** 51 29N 0 2W
Rothneusiedl, *Wien* **10 H10** 48 8N 16 23 E
Rothschmaige, *Mün.* **7 F9** 48 14N 11 27 E
Rouge →, *Trto.* **20 D9** 43 47N 79 12W
Rouge Hill, *Trto.* **20 D10** 43 48N 79 6W
Round I., *H.K.* **12 E6** 22 13N 114 11 E
Roundshaw, *Lon.* **4 C4** 51 20N 0 7W
Roussigny, *Paris* **5 D2** 48 38N 2 6 E
Rowland, *L.A.* **28 B5** 34 0N 117 55W
Rowley, *Bost.* **21 A4** 42 43N 70 52W
Rowville, *Melb.* **19 F8** 37 55 S 145 14 E
Roxboro, *Mtrl.* **20 A3** 43 30N 73 48W
Roxborough, *Phil.* **24 A3** 40 1N 75 13W
Roxbury, *Bost.* **21 D3** 42 19N 71 5W
Roxbury, *N.Y.* **23 D5** 40 33N 73 53W
Roxeth, *Lon.* **4 B2** 51 33N 0 20W
Royal Observatory, *H.K.* **12 E6** 22 18N 114 10 E
Royal Park, *Melb.* **19 E6** 37 46 S 144 57 E
Röylä, *Hels.* **3 B3** 60 18N 24 42 E
Royston Park, *Lon.* **4 B2** 51 36N 0 22W
Rozas, Portilleros de las, *Mdrd.* **8 B2** 40 29N 3 49W
Roztoky, *Pra.* **10 B2** 50 9N 14 23 E
Rubbianetta, *Tori.* **9 B2** 45 9N 7 34 E
Rubi →, *Barc.* **8 D5** 41 26N 2 0 E
Rubio Woods, *Chic.* **26 D2** 41 38N 87 45W
Rublovo, *Mos.* **11 E8** 55 47N 37 21 E
Ruchyi, *St-Pet.* **11 A4** 60 0N 30 25 E
Rud, *Oslo* **2 B6** 59 56N 11 0 E
Rüdinghausen, *Ruhr* **6 B6** 51 26N 7 22 E
Rudnevka →, *Mos.* **11 E11** 55 43N 37 56 E
Rudolfsheim, *Wien* **10 G10** 48 12N 16 20 E
Rudolfshöhe, *Berl.* **7 A5** 52 37N 13 44 E
Rudow, *Berl.* **7 B3** 52 24N 13 29 E
Rueil-Malmaison, *Paris* **5 B3** 48 52N 2 11 E
Ruffys Cr. →, *Melb.* **19 E7** 37 45 S 145 7 E
Ruggeberg, *Ruhr* **6 C6** 51 16N 7 23 E
Ruhlsdorf, *Berl.* **7 B2** 52 22N 13 15 E
Ruhr →, *Ruhr* **6 B3** 51 27N 6 56 E
Ruhrort, *Ruhr* **6 B2** 51 27N 6 44 E
Ruislip, *Lon.* **4 B2** 51 34N 0 24W
Rumelihisari, *Ist.* **17 A3** 41 4N 29 2 E
Rumeln, *Ruhr* **6 B1** 51 24N 6 39 E
Rumyantsevo, *Mos.* **11 F8** 55 38N 37 25 E
Rungis, *Paris* **5 C4** 48 44N 2 20 E
Runnemede, *Phil.* **24 B4** 39 50N 75 4W
Ruotsinkylä, *Hels.* **3 A4** 60 21N 24 57 E
Rusāfa, *Bagd.* **17 E8** 33 21N 44 23 E
Rush Green, *Lon.* **4 B6** 51 33N 0 10 E
Russa, *Calc.* **16 F6** 22 29N 88 21 E
Russell Lea, *Syd.* **19 B4** 33 52 S 151 10 E
Rustad, *Oslo* **2 B2** 59 56N 10 24 E
Rustenfeld, *Wien* **10 H10** 48 7N 16 23 E
Rusville, *Jobg.* **18 E10** 26 9 S 28 18 E
Rutherford, *N.Y.* **22 C4** 40 49N 74 6W
Rüttenscheid, *Ruhr* **6 B3** 51 25N 6 58 E
Ruxton, *Balt.* **25 A3** 39 23N 76 38W
Ruzyně, *Pra.* **10 B1** 50 5N 14 17 E
Rybatskaya, *St-Pet.* **11 B4** 59 59N 30 29 E
Rybatskoye, *St-Pet.* **11 B4** 59 50N 30 29 E
Rydalmere, *Syd.* **19 A3** 33 48 S 151 2 E
Rydboholm, *Stock.* **3 D12** 59 26N 18 12 E
Ryde, *Syd.* **19 A3** 33 48 S 151 6 E
Rye, *N.Y.* **23 B6** 40 58N 73 40W
Rynfield, *Jobg.* **18 E10** 26 9 S 28 19 E
Ryogoku, *Tōkyō* **13 B3** 35 40N 139 48 E
Rysäkari, *Hels.* **3 C4** 60 6N 24 50 E
Rzhevka, *St-Pet.* **11 B5** 59 59N 30 31 E

Serangoon Garden **45**

S

Saadōn, *Bagd.* **17 F8** 33 19N 44 25 E
Saarn, *Ruhr* **6 B3** 51 24N 6 51 E
Saavedra, *B.A.* **32 B4** 34 33 S 58 29W
Saboli, *Delhi* **16 A2** 28 42N 77 18 E
Sabugo, *Lisb.* **8 F7** 38 49N 9 17W
Saburovo, *Mos.* **11 D7** 55 53N 37 15 E
Säbysjön, *Stock.* **3 D10** 59 26N 17 52 E
Sabzi Mandi, *Delhi* **16 A2** 28 40N 77 12 E
Sacavém, *Lisb.* **8 F8** 38 47N 9 5W
Saclay, *Paris* **5 C3** 48 43N 2 10 E
Saclay, Étang de, *Paris* **5 C2** 48 44N 2 9 E
Sacoma, *S. Pau.* **31 E6** 23 36 S 46 35W
Sacré-Coeur, *Paris* **5 B4** 48 53N 2 20 E
Sacrow, *Berl.* **7 B1** 52 25N 13 6 E
Sacrower See, *Berl.* **7 B1** 52 26N 13 6 E
Sadang, *Sŏul* **12 H7** 37 29N 126 58 E
Sadar Bazar, *Delhi* **16 B2** 28 39N 77 11 E
Saddām City, *Bagd.* **17 E8** 33 23N 44 27 E
Saddle Brook, *N.Y.* **22 B4** 40 53N 74 5W
Saddle River, *N.Y.* **22 A4** 41 1N 74 6W
Saddle Rock, *N.Y.* **23 C6** 40 47N 73 45W
Sadr, *Kar.* **17 G11** 24 51N 67 2 E
Sadyba, *Wsaw.* **10 E7** 52 11N 21 3 E
Saedo, *Tōkyō* **13 C2** 35 30N 139 33 E
Saensaep, Khlong →, *Bangk.* **15 B2** 13 44N 100 32 E
Sáenz Pena, *B.A.* **32 B3** 34 37 S 58 32W
Safdar Jang Airport, *Delhi* **16 B2** 28 35N 77 12 E
Safdar Jangs Tomb, *Delhi* **16 B2** 28 35N 77 12 E
Safraköy, *Ist.* **17 A1** 41 0N 28 48 E
Saft el Laban, *El Qâ.* **18 C5** 30 1N 31 10 E
Sag Bridge, *Chic.* **26 C1** 41 41N 87 55W
Sagamore Neck, *N.Y.* **23 B8** 40 53N 73 29W
Saganashkee Slough, *Chic.* **26 C1** 41 41N 87 53W
Sagene, *Oslo* **2 B4** 59 55N 10 46 E
Sagrada Família, Temple de, *Barc.* **8 D6** 41 24N 2 10 E
Sahapur, *Calc.* **16 E5** 22 31N 88 11 E
Sahibabad, *Delhi* **16 A1** 28 45N 77 4 E
Sai Kung, *H.K.* **12 D6** 22 22N 114 16 E
Sai Wan Ho, *H.K.* **12 E6** 22 17N 114 12 E
Sai Ying Pun, *H.K.* **12 E5** 22 17N 114 8 E
Saido, *Tōkyō* **13 A2** 35 52N 139 39 E
Sailmouille →, *Paris* **5 D3** 48 37N 2 17 E
St. Albans, *N.Y.* **23 C6** 40 42N 73 44W
St. Andrä, *Wien* **10 G9** 48 19N 16 12 E
St. Andrews, *Jobg.* **18 E9** 26 9 S 28 7 E
St. Aubin, *Paris* **5 C2** 48 44N 2 8 E
St. Augustin, *Mtrl.* **20 A2** 43 37N 73 58W
St. Basil's Cathedral, *Mos.* **11 E9** 55 45N 37 38 E
St.-Benoit, *Paris* **5 C1** 48 40N 1 54 E
St.-Brice-sous-Forêt, *Paris* **5 A4** 49 0N 2 21 E
St.-Cloud, *Paris* **5 B3** 48 50N 2 12 E
St.-Cyr-l'École, *Paris* **5 C2** 48 47N 2 4 E
St.-Cyr-l'École, Aérodrome de, *Paris* **5 C2** 48 48N 2 4 E
St. Davids, *Phil.* **24 A2** 40 2N 75 23W
St.-Denis, *Paris* **5 B4** 48 56N 2 20 E
St. Eustache, *Mtrl.* **20 A2** 43 33N 73 54W
St.-Forget, *Paris* **5 C2** 48 42N 2 0 E
St. Georg, *Hbg.* **7 D8** 53 33N 10 1 E
St.-Germain, Forêt de, *Paris* **5 B2** 48 57N 2 5 E
St. Germain-en-Laye, *Paris* **5 B2** 48 53N 2 4 E
St.-Germain-lès-Corbeil, *Paris* **5 D4** 48 37N 2 29 E
St.-Gratien, *Paris* **5 B3** 48 58N 2 17 E
St. Helier, *Lon.* **4 C3** 51 23N 0 11W
St.-Hubert, *Mtrl.* **20 B5** 43 29N 73 25W
St. Isaac's Cathedral, *St-Pet.* **11 B3** 59 55N 30 19 E
St. Jacques →, *Mtrl.* **20 B5** 43 26N 73 29W
St.-Jean-de-Beauregard, *Paris* **5 D3** 48 39N 2 10 E
St.-Jean-de-dieu, *Mtrl.* **20 A4** 43 34N 73 31W
St. Joseph-du-Lac, *Mtrl.* **20 A1** 43 32N 74 0W
St. Katherine's Dock, *Lon.* **4 B4** 51 30N 0 5W
St. Kilda, *Melb.* **19 F6** 37 51 S 144 58 E
St. Lambert, *Mtrl.* **20 A5** 43 30N 73 29W
St.-Lambert, *Paris* **5 C2** 48 43N 2 1 E
St.-Laurent, *Mtrl.* **20 A3** 43 30N 73 43W
St. Lawrence, *Mtrl.* **20 A5** 43 26N 73 29W
St.-Lazare, Gare, *Paris* **5 B3** 48 52N 2 19 E
St.-Léonard, *Mtrl.* **20 A4** 43 35N 73 34W
St. Leonards, *Syd.* **19 B4** 33 50 S 151 12 E
St. Leu-la-Forêt, *Paris* **5 A3** 49 1N 2 14 E
St.-Louis, L., *Mtrl.* **20 B3** 43 24N 73 48W
St. Magelungen, *Stock.* **3 E11** 59 13N 18 4 E
St.-Mandé, *Paris* **5 B4** 48 50N 2 24 E
St.-Mard, *Paris* **5 A6** 49 2N 2 41 E
St.-Martin, *Mtrl.* **20 A3** 43 33N 73 45W
St.-Martin, Bois, *Paris* **5 C5** 48 48N 2 35 E
St. Mary Cray, *Lon.* **4 C5** 51 23N 0 7 E
St.-Maur-des-Fossés, *Paris* **5 C4** 48 48N 2 29 E
St.-Maurice, *Paris* **5 C4** 48 49N 2 24 E
St.-Mesmes, *Paris* **5 B6** 48 59N 2 41 E
St. Michaeliskirche, *Hbg.* **7 D7** 53 32N 9 59 E
St. Michael's, *Sing.* **15 G8** 1 19N 103 51 E
St.-Michel, *Mtrl.* **20 A4** 43 34N 73 37W
St.-Michel-sur-Orge, *Paris* **5 D3** 48 38N 2 18 E
St. Nikolaus-Kirken, *Pra.* **10 B2** 50 5N 14 23 E
St. Nom-la-Bretèche, *Paris* **5 B2** 48 51N 2 1 E
St.-Ouen, *Paris* **5 B4** 48 56N 2 20 E
St. Ouen-l'Aumône, *Paris* **5 A2** 49 2N 2 6 E
St. Pauli, *Hbg.* **7 D7** 53 33N 9 57 E
St. Pauls Cathedral, *Lon.* **4 B4** 51 30N 0 5W
St. Paul's Cray, *Lon.* **4 C5** 51 23N 0 6 E
St. Petersburg, *St-Pet.* **11 B3** 59 55N 30 15 E
St.-Pierre, *Mtrl.* **20 B4** 43 27N 73 38W
St. Prix, *Paris* **5 A3** 49 0N 2 15 E
St.-Quentin, Étang de, *Paris* **5 C2** 48 47N 2 0 E
St. Quentin-en-Yvelines, *Paris* **5 C1** 48 46N 1 57 E
St.-Rémy-lès-Chevreuse, *Paris* **5 C2** 48 42N 2 4 E
St.-Thibault-des-Vignes, *Paris* **5 B6** 48 52N 2 41 E
St. Veit, *Wien* **10 G9** 48 11N 16 16 E
St.-Vincent-de-Paul, *Mtrl.* **20 A4** 43 36N 73 39W
Ste.-Anne-de-Bellevue, *Mtrl.* **20 B2** 43 24N 73 55W
Ste.-Catherine, *Mtrl.* **20 B4** 43 24N 73 34W
Ste.-Dorothée, *Mtrl.* **20 A3** 43 31N 73 48W
Ste.-Gemme, *Paris* **5 B1** 48 52N 1 59 E
Ste.-Geneviève, *Mtrl.* **20 B2** 43 28N 73 51W
Ste.-Geneviève-des-Bois, *Paris* **5 D3** 48 38N 2 19 E
Ste.-Hélène, Î., *Mtrl.* **20 A4** 43 31N 73 32W
Ste. Marthe-sur-le-Lac, *Mtrl.* **20 A2** 43 31N 73 56W
Ste.-Rose, *Mtrl.* **20 A3** 43 37N 73 46W
Ste. Thérèse, *Mtrl.* **20 A3** 43 38N 73 49W
Ste. Thérèse-Ouest, *Mtrl.* **20 A2** 43 36N 73 50W
Saiwai, *Tōkyō* **13 C3** 35 32N 139 41 E
Sakai, *Ōsaka* **12 C3** 34 34N 135 27 E
Sakai →, *Tōkyō* **13 D1** 35 27N 139 29 E
Sakai Harbour, *Ōsaka* **12 C3** 34 36N 135 26 E
Sakanoshita, *Tōkyō* **13 B2** 35 48N 139 30 E
Sakra, P., *Sing.* **15 G7** 1 15N 103 41 E
Sakuragi, *Tōkyō* **13 D2** 35 28N 139 38 E
Salam, *Bagd.* **17 E8** 33 20N 44 20 E
Salaryevo, *Mos.* **11 F8** 55 37N 37 25 E
Salem, *Bost.* **21 B4** 42 30N 70 54W
Salem, *Stock.* **3 E9** 59 13N 17 46 E
Salem Harbor, *Bost.* **21 B4** 42 30N 70 52W
Salem Maritime Nat. Hist. Site, *Bost.* **21 B4** 42 31N 70 52W
Salemstaden, *Stock.* **3 E9** 59 13N 17 46 E
Salkhia, *Calc.* **16 E6** 22 36N 88 21 E
Salmannsdorf, *Wien* **10 G9** 48 14N 16 14 E
Salmdorf, *Mün.* **7 G11** 48 7N 11 43 E
Salmedina, *Mdrd.* **8 C3** 40 18N 3 35W
Salomea, *Wsaw.* **10 E6** 52 11N 20 55 E
Salsette I., *Bomb.* **16 G8** 19 2N 72 53 E
Salt Cr. →, *Chic.* **26 C1** 41 51N 87 54W
Salt Cr. →, *Melb.* **19 E7** 37 45 S 145 4 E
Salt Water L., *Calc.* **16 E6** 22 33N 88 26 E
Saltholm, *Købn.* **2 E11** 55 38N 12 46 E
Saltsjö-Duvnäs, *Stock.* **3 E12** 59 18N 18 12 E
Saltsjöbaden, *Stock.* **3 E12** 59 16N 18 18 E
Saltykovka, *Mos.* **11 E11** 55 45N 37 54 E
Salvatorkirche, *Ruhr* **6 B2** 51 26N 6 45 E
Sam Sen, Khlong →, *Bangk.* **15 B2** 13 45N 100 33 E
Samatya, *Ist.* **17 B2** 40 59N 28 55 E
Samoueo, *Lisb.* **8 F8** 38 43N 8 59W
Sampaloc, *Manila* **15 D3** 14 36N 120 59 E
Samphanthawong, *Bangk.* **15 B2** 13 44N 100 31 E
Samrong, *Bangk.* **15 C2** 13 39N 100 35 E
Samseon, *Sŏul* **12 G8** 37 34N 127 0 E
San Agustin, *Lima* **30 G8** 12 1 S 77 9W
San Agustin Atlapulco, *Méx.* **29 B4** 19 23N 89 57 E
San Andreas Fault, *S.F.* **27 D3** 37 27N 122 18W
San Andreas L., *S.F.* **27 C2** 37 35N 122 25W
San Andres, *B.A.* **32 B3** 34 34 S 58 33W
San Andrés, *Barc.* **8 D6** 41 26N 2 11 E
San Andrés Ahuayucan, *Méx.* **29 C3** 19 13N 99 7W
San Andrés Atenco, *Méx.* **29 A2** 19 32N 99 13W
San Andrés Totoltepec, *Méx.* **29 C2** 19 15N 99 10W
San Andrián de Besós, *Barc.* **8 D6** 41 25N 2 13 E
San Angel, *Méx.* **29 B2** 19 20N 99 11W
San Antonia, *Manila* **15 E3** 14 29N 120 53 E
San Antonio de Padua, *B.A.* **32 C2** 34 40 S 58 42W
San Augustin Ohtenco, *Méx.* **29 C3** 19 12N 99 0W
San Bartolo Ameyalco, *Méx.* **29 C2** 19 19N 99 16W
San Bartolomé Coatepec, *Méx.* **29 B2** 19 23N 99 18W
San Basilio, *Rome* **9 F10** 41 56N 12 35 E
San Bóvio, *Mil.* **9 E6** 45 27N 9 18 E
San Bruno, *S.F.* **27 C2** 37 36N 122 24W
San Bruno, Pt., *S.F.* **27 C2** 37 39N 122 22W
San Bruno Mt., *S.F.* **27 B2** 37 41N 122 26W
San Carlos, *S.F.* **27 C3** 37 30N 122 16W
San Carlos de la Cabana, Forteresse, *La Hab.* **30 B2** 23 8N 82 20W
San Clemente del Llobregat, *Barc.* **8 E4** 41 19N 1 59 E
San Cristobal, *Mdrd.* **8 B3** 40 25N 3 35W
San Cristobal, Cerro, *Stgo* **30 J11** 33 25 S 70 38W
San Cristoforo, *Mil.* **9 E5** 45 26N 9 9 E
San Donato Milanese, *Mil.* **9 E6** 45 24N 9 16 E
San Felice, *Tori.* **9 B3** 45 1N 7 46 E
San Feliu de Llobregat, *Barc.* **8 D5** 41 22N 2 2 E
San Fernando, *B.A.* **32 A3** 34 26 S 58 32W
San Fernando, *L.A.* **28 A2** 34 17N 118 26W
San Fernando Airport, *L.A.* **28 A2** 34 17N 118 25W
San Fernando de Henares, *Mdrd.* **8 B3** 40 25N 3 31W
San Fernando Valley, *L.A.* **28 A1** 34 12N 118 31W
San Francisco, *S.F.* **27 B2** 37 46N 122 23W
San Francisco, Univ. of, *S.F.* **27 B2** 37 47N 122 27W
San Francisco B., *S.F.* **27 C3** 37 39N 122 14W
San Francisco Chimalpa, *Méx.* **29 B1** 19 26N 99 20W
San Francisco Culhuacán, *Méx.* **29 C3** 19 19N 99 8W
San Francisco de Paula, *La Hab.* **30 B3** 23 3N 82 17W
San Francisco Int. Airport, *S.F.* **27 C2** 37 37N 122 22W
San Francisco Solano, *B.A.* **32 C5** 34 46 S 58 19W
San Francisco State Univ., *S.F.* **27 B2** 37 43N 122 28W
San Francisco Tecoxpa, *Méx.* **29 C3** 19 12N 99 0W
San Francisco Tlalnepantla, *Méx.* **29 C3** 19 12N 99 8W
San Fruttuoso, *Mil.* **9 D6** 45 34N 9 14 E
San Gabriel, *L.A.* **28 B4** 34 5N 118 5W
San Gabriel →, *L.A.* **28 C4** 33 53N 118 6W
San Gabriel Pk., *L.A.* **28 A4** 34 14N 118 5W
San Giacomo, *Tori.* **9 A2** 45 11N 7 36 E
San Gillio, *Tori.* **9 B2** 45 8N 7 32 E
San Giórgio a Crem, *Nápl.* **9 J13** 40 50N 14 20 E
San Giovanni a Teduccio, *Nápl.* **9 J12** 40 49N 14 18 E
San Giuseppe Vesuviano, *Nápl.* **9 H13** 40 50N 14 29 E
San Gregorio Atlapulco, *Méx.* **29 C3** 19 15N 99 4W
San Isidro, *B.A.* **32 A3** 34 28 S 58 30W
San Isidro, *Lima* **30 G8** 12 5 S 77 2W
San Isidro, *Manila* **15 D4** 14 38N 121 5 E
San Jerónimo Lidice, *Méx.* **29 C2** 19 19N 99 14W
San Jerónimo Miacatlán, *Méx.* **29 C4** 19 12N 98 59W
San Jorge, Castelo de, *Lisb.* **8 F8** 38 42N 9 8W
San Jose Del Alamo, *La Hab.* **30 B3** 23 6N 82 17W
San José Rio Hondo, *Méx.* **29 B2** 19 26N 99 14W
San Juan →, *Manila* **15 D4** 14 35N 121 0 E
San Juan de Aragón, *Méx.* **29 B3** 19 28N 99 4W
San Juan de Aragón, Parque, *Méx.* **29 B3** 19 27N 99 4W
San Juan de Lurigancho, *Lima* **30 F8** 11 59 S 77 0W
San Juan de Miraflores, *Lima* **30 H9** 12 10 S 76 58W
San Juan del Monte, *Manila* **15 D4** 14 36N 121 1 E
San Juan Ixtacala, *Méx.* **29 A2** 19 31N 99 10W
San Juan Ixtayopan, *Méx.* **29 C4** 19 14N 98 59W
San Juan Toltotepec, *Méx.* **29 B2** 19 28N 99 15W
San Juan y San Pedro Tezompa, *Méx.* **29 C4** 19 12N 98 57W
San Just Desvern, *Barc.* **8 D5** 41 22N 2 4 E
San Justo, *B.A.* **32 C3** 34 40 S 58 33W
San Leandro, *S.F.* **27 B4** 37 43N 122 9W
San Leandro B., *S.F.* **27 B3** 37 45N 122 13W
San Leandro Cr. →, *S.F.* **27 B3** 37 44N 122 12W
San Lorenzo, *Mil.* **9 D4** 45 34N 8 57 E
San Lorenzo, *S.F.* **27 B4** 37 41N 122 6W
San Lorenzo →, *Méx.* **29 B2** 19 28N 99 17W
San Lorenzo, I., *Lima* **30 G7** 12 6 S 77 12W
San Lorenzo Acopilco, *Méx.* **29 C1** 19 19N 99 20 E
San Lorenzo Chimalco, *Méx.* **29 B4** 19 24N 89 58 E
San Lorenzo Tezonco, *Méx.* **29 C3** 19 19N 99 3W
San Lorenzo Tlacoyucan, *Méx.* **29 C3** 19 10N 99 2W
San Lucas Xochimanca, *Méx.* **29 C3** 19 15N 99 6W
San Luis, *Lima* **30 G8** 12 4 S 77 0W
San Luis Tlaxialtemalco, *Méx.* **29 C3** 19 16N 99 2W
San Marino, *L.A.* **28 B4** 34 7N 118 5W
San Martin, *Barc.* **8 D6** 41 24N 2 11 E
San Martin de Porras, *Lima* **30 G8** 12 1 S 77 5W
San Martino, *Tori.* **9 B3** 45 6N 7 47 E
San Mateo, *S.F.* **27 C3** 37 33N 122 19W
San Mateo Cr. →, *S.F.* **27 C2** 37 31N 122 22W
San Mateo Tecoloapan, *Méx.* **29 A2** 19 35N 99 14W
San Mateo Xalpa, *Méx.* **29 C3** 19 13N 99 8W
San Máuro Torinese, *Tori.* **9 B3** 45 6N 7 45 E
San Miguel, *B.A.* **32 B2** 34 32 S 58 43W
San Miguel, *Lima* **30 G8** 12 5 S 77 6W
San Miguel, *Manila* **15 D3** 14 36N 120 59 E
San Miguel, *Stgo* **30 J11** 33 29 S 70 39W
San Miguel Ajusco, *Méx.* **29 C2** 19 13N 99 11W
San Miguel Xicalco, *Méx.* **29 C3** 19 13N 99 9W
San Nicholas, *Manila* **15 D3** 14 36N 120 57 E
San Nicola, *Rome* **9 F9** 41 58N 12 21 E
San Nicolás Totolapan, *Méx.* **29 C2** 19 16N 99 16W
San Nicolás Viejo, *Méx.* **29 A1** 19 31N 99 21W
San Onófrio, *Rome* **9 F9** 41 57N 12 25 E
San Pablo, *Méx.* **29 B4** 19 25N 89 56 E
San Pablo, *S.F.* **27 A2** 37 57N 122 20W
San Pablo, Pt., *S.F.* **27 A2** 37 57N 122 25W
San Pablo Cr. →, *S.F.* **27 A2** 37 58N 122 22W
San Pablo Ostotepec, *Méx.* **29 C3** 19 11N 99 5W
San Pablo Res., *S.F.* **27 A3** 37 55N 122 14W
San Pablo Ridge, *S.F.* **27 A3** 37 55N 122 15W
San Pablo Str., *S.F.* **27 A2** 37 58N 122 25W
San Pancrázio, *Tori.* **9 B2** 45 6N 7 32 E
San Pedro, *Méx.* **29 B4** 19 24N 89 56 E
San Pedro, Pt., *S.F.* **27 C1** 37 35N 122 31W
San Pedro Actopan, *Méx.* **29 C3** 19 12N 99 4W
San Pedro Martir, *Barc.* **8 D5** 41 23N 2 6 E
San Pedro Martir, *Méx.* **29 C2** 19 16N 99 10W
San Pedro Zacatenco, *Méx.* **29 A3** 19 30N 99 6W
San Pietro, *Rome* **9 F9** 41 53N 12 27 E
San Pietro, *Tori.* **9 B3** 45 1N 7 45 E
San Pietro a Patierno, *Nápl.* **9 H12** 40 53N 14 17 E
San Pietro all'Olmo, *Mil.* **9 E5** 45 29N 9 0 E
San Po Kong, *H.K.* **12 D6** 22 20N 114 11 E
San Quentin, *S.F.* **27 A2** 37 56N 122 27W
San Rafael, *S.F.* **27 A1** 37 58N 122 30W
San Rafael B., *S.F.* **27 A2** 37 57N 122 28W
San Rafael Chamapa, *Méx.* **29 B2** 19 27N 99 15W
San Rafael Hills, *L.A.* **28 A3** 34 10N 118 12W
San Roque, *Manila* **15 D4** 14 37N 121 5 E
San Salvador Cuauhtenco, *Méx.* **29 C3** 19 11N 99 8W
San Salvador de la Punta, Forteresse, *La Hab.* **30 B2** 23 8N 82 21W
San Sebastiano al Vesúvio, *Nápl.* **9 H13** 40 50N 14 22 E
San Siro, *Mil.* **9 E5** 45 28N 9 7 E
San Souci, *Syd.* **19 B3** 33 59 S 151 8 E
San Telmo, *B.A.* **32 B4** 34 37 S 58 23W
San Vicenc dels Horts, *Barc.* **8 D5** 41 23N 2 0 E
San Vitaliano, *Nápl.* **9 H13** 40 55N 14 28 E
San Vito, *Mil.* **9 E5** 45 24N 9 0 E
San Vito, *Nápl.* **9 J13** 40 49N 14 22 E
San Vito, *Tori.* **9 B3** 45 2N 7 41 E
Sandbakken, *Oslo* **2 C5** 59 49N 10 54 E
Sandermosen, *Oslo* **2 A4** 60 0N 10 48 E
Sanderstead, *Lon.* **4 D4** 51 19N 0 4W
Sandheide, *Ruhr* **6 C3** 51 12N 6 56 E
Sandhurst, *Jobg.* **18 E9** 26 6 S 28 3 E
Sandown, *Jobg.* **18 E9** 26 5 S 28 4 E
Sandown Racecourse, *Lon.* **4 C2** 51 22N 0 21W
Sandringham, *Jobg.* **18 E9** 26 8 S 28 6 E
Sands Point, *N.Y.* **23 B6** 40 50N 73 43W
Sandton, *Jobg.* **18 E9** 26 5 S 28 4 E
Sandungen, *Oslo* **2 B2** 59 52N 10 21 E
Sandvika, *Oslo* **2 B3** 59 53N 10 32 E
Sandy Pond, *Bost.* **21 C2** 42 26N 71 18W
Sånga, *Stock.* **3 D9** 59 21N 17 42 E
Sangano, *Tori.* **9 B1** 45 1N 7 26 E
Sangenjaya, *Tōkyō* **13 C2** 35 37N 139 39 E
Sangley Pt., *Manila* **15 E3** 14 29N 120 54 E
Sangone →, *Tori.* **9 B2** 45 1N 7 32 E
Sangye, *Sŏul* **12 G8** 37 38N 127 3 E
Sankrail, *Calc.* **16 E5** 22 33N 88 13 E
Sanlihe, *Beij.* **14 B2** 39 53N 116 18 E
Sanlintang, *Shang.* **14 K11** 31 9N 121 29 E
Sannois, *Paris* **5 B3** 48 58N 2 15 E
Sanpada, *Bomb.* **16 G9** 19 3N 73 0 E
Sans, *Barc.* **8 D5** 41 22N 2 7 E
Sant Ambrogio, Basilica di, *Mil.* **9 E6** 45 27N 9 10 E
Sant Boi de Llobregat, *Barc.* **8 D5** 41 20N 2 2 E
Sant Cugat, *Barc.* **8 D5** 41 28N 2 5 E
Santa Ana, *Manila* **15 D4** 14 34N 121 0 E
Santa Ana Tlacotenco, *Méx.* **29 C4** 19 11N 98 58W
Santa Bárbara, Morro de, *Rio J.* **31 B1** 22 56 S 43 26W
Santa Catalina, *B.A.* **32 C4** 34 47 S 58 24W
Santa Cecilia Tepetlapa, *Méx.* **29 C3** 19 13N 99 5W
Santa Clara, *Méx.* **29 A3** 19 33N 99 3W
Santa Coloma de Cervelló, *Barc.* **8 D5** 41 21N 2 0 E
Santa Coloma de Gramanet, *Barc.* **8 D6** 41 27N 2 12 E
Santa Cruz, *Bomb.* **16 G7** 19 4N 72 51 E
Santa Cruz →, *La Hab.* **30 B2** 23 4N 82 29W
Santa Cruz, Ilhe de, *Rio J.* **31 B3** 22 51 S 43 7W
Santa Cruz Alcapixca, *Méx.* **29 C3** 19 14N 99 4W
Santa Cruz Ayotusco, *Méx.* **29 B1** 19 22N 99 21W
Santa Cruz de Olorde, *Barc.* **8 D5** 41 25N 2 3 E
Santa Cruz Int. Airport, *Bomb.* **16 G8** 19 5N 72 51 E
Santa Cruz Meyehualco, *Méx.* **29 B3** 19 20N 99 2W
Santa Elena, *Manila* **15 D4** 14 38N 121 5 E
Santa Eligênia Consolação, *S. Pau.* **31 E6** 23 32 S 46 38W
Santa Emilia, *Stgo* **30 J11** 33 23 S 70 39W
Santa Eulalia, *Barc.* **8 D6** 41 25N 2 10 E
Santa Fe, *La Hab.* **30 B2** 23 4N 82 30W
Santa Fe Flood Control Basin, *L.A.* **28 B5** 34 7N 117 57W
Santa Fe Springs, *L.A.* **28 C4** 33 56N 118 3W
Santa Isabel Ixtapan, *Méx.* **29 A4** 19 35N 89 57W
Santa Julia, *Stgo* **30 K11** 33 30 S 70 35W
Santa Lucia, *Nápl.* **9 J12** 40 49N 14 15 E
Santa Margherita, *Tori.* **9 B3** 45 3N 7 43 E
Santa Maria Aztahuacán, *Méx.* **29 B3** 19 21N 99 2W
Santa Maria del Rosario, *La Hab.* **30 B3** 23 3N 82 15W
Santa Maria Tulpetlac, *Méx.* **29 A3** 19 34N 99 3W
Santa Martha Acatitla, *Méx.* **29 B3** 19 21N 99 2W
Santa Monica, *Car.* **30 E5** 10 28N 66 53W
Santa Monica, *L.A.* **28 B2** 34 1N 118 29W
Santa Monica B., *L.A.* **28 C1** 33 58N 118 30W
Santa Monica Mt., *L.A.* **28 B2** 34 6N 118 29W
Santa Rosa, *Lima* **30 F8** 11 59 S 77 5W
Santa Rosa De Locobe, *Stgo* **30 J11** 33 25 S 70 33W
Santa Rosa Xochiac, *Méx.* **29 C2** 19 19N 99 17W
Santa Tereza, *S. Pau.* **31 F6** 23 40 S 46 33W
Santa Ursula Xitla, *Méx.* **29 C2** 19 16N 99 11W
Santa Ynez Canyon →, *L.A.* **28 B1** 34 2N 118 33W
Santahamina, *Hels.* **3 C5** 60 8N 25 2 E
Santana, *S. Pau.* **31 D6** 23 29 S 46 36W
Sant'Anastasia, *Nápl.* **9 H13** 40 51N 14 24 E
Sant'Ántimo, *Nápl.* **9 H12** 40 56N 14 14 E
Santeny, *Paris* **5 C5** 48 43N 2 34 E
Santiago, *Stgo* **30 J11** 33 26 S 70 40W
Santiago Acahualtepec, *Méx.* **29 B3** 19 20N 99 0W
Santiago de Las Vegas, *La Hab.* **30 C2** 22 58N 82 22W
Santiago Tepalcatlalpan, *Méx.* **29 C3** 19 14N 99 8W
Santiago Tepatlaxco, *Méx.* **29 B1** 19 28N 99 20W
Sant'Ilário, *Mil.* **9 D4** 45 34N 8 59 E
Santo Amaro, *Lisb.* **8 F7** 38 42N 9 11W
Santo Amaro, *S. Pau.* **31 E5** 23 39 S 46 42W
Santo Andre, *Lisb.* **8 G8** 38 38N 9 3W
Santo André, *S. Pau.* **31 E6** 23 39 S 46 41W
Santo António, Qta. de, *Lisb.* **8 G7** 38 39N 9 15W
Santo António da Charneca, *Lisb.* **8 G8** 38 37N 9 1W
Santo Niño, *Manila* **15 D4** 14 38N 121 5 E
Santo Rosario, *Manila* **15 D4** 14 33N 121 4 E
Santo Thomas, Univ. of, *Manila* **15 D3** 14 36N 120 59 E
Santo Tomas, *Manila* **15 D4** 14 33N 121 4 E
Santolan, *Manila* **15 D4** 14 36N 121 4 E
Santos Dumont, Aéroport, *Rio J.* **31 B3** 22 54 S 43 9W
Santos Lugares, *B.A.* **32 B3** 34 35 S 58 35W
Santoshpur, *Calc.* **16 E5** 22 31N 88 16 E
Santragachi, *Calc.* **16 E5** 22 35N 88 17 E
Sanyuanli, *Gzh.* **14 G8** 23 8N 113 14 E
São Bernardo do Campo, *S. Pau.* **31 F6** 23 42 S 46 32W
São Caetano do Sul, *S. Pau.* **31 E6** 23 37 S 46 34W
São Cristovão, *Rio J.* **31 B2** 22 53 S 43 13W
São Domingos, Centro, *Rio J.* **31 B3** 22 53 S 43 6W
São Gonçalo, *Rio J.* **31 A3** 22 49 S 43 4W
São João Climaco, *S. Pau.* **31 E6** 23 37 S 46 35W
São João da Talha, *Lisb.* **8 F8** 38 49N 9 5W
São João de Meriti, *Rio J.* **31 A1** 22 47 S 43 18W
São Lucas, Parque, *S. Pau.* **31 E6** 23 35 S 45 32W
São Mateus, *Rio J.* **31 A1** 22 48 S 43 22W
São Miguel Paulista, *S. Pau.* **31 D7** 23 29 S 46 26W
São Paulo, *S. Pau.* **31 E6** 23 32 S 46 38W
Sapa, *Calc.* **16 E5** 22 30N 88 15 E
Sapang Baho →, *Manila* **15 D4** 14 33N 121 4 E
Sapateiro →, *S. Pau.* **31 E5** 23 35 S 46 41W
Saranap, *S.F.* **27 A4** 37 52N 122 4W
Sarandi, *B.A.* **32 C4** 34 40 S 58 20W
Saraswati →, *Calc.* **16 D5** 22 46N 88 15 E
Sarcelles, *Paris* **5 B4** 48 59N 2 22 E
Sarecky →, *Pra.* **10 B2** 50 7N 14 23 E
Sarenga, *Calc.* **16 E5** 22 31N 88 12 E
Sarilhos Grandes, *Lisb.* **8 F9** 38 40N 8 58W
Sarilhos Pequenos, *Lisb.* **8 F9** 38 40N 8 58W
Sarimbun, *Sing.* **15 F7** 1 24N 103 40 E
Saronikòs Kòlpos, *Ath.* **8 J10** 37 52N 23 38 E
Sarriá, *Barc.* **8 D5** 41 22N 2 8 E
Sarria, *Car.* **30 D5** 10 30N 66 53W
Sarsol, *Bomb.* **16 G9** 19 2N 73 0 E
Sartrouville, *Paris* **5 B3** 48 56N 2 10 E
Sasad, *Bud.* **10 K13** 47 28N 19 0 E
Sasashita, *Tōkyō* **13 D2** 35 23N 139 35 E
Sasel, *Hbg.* **7 D8** 53 39N 10 7 E
Sashalom, *Bud.* **10 J14** 47 30N 19 10 E
Saska, *Wsaw.* **10 E7** 52 14N 21 3 E
Sassafras, *Melb.* **19 F9** 37 52 S 145 20 E
Satalice, *Pra.* **10 B3** 50 7N 14 34 E
Satgachi, *Calc.* **16 E6** 22 37N 88 25 E
Satghara, *Calc.* **16 D6** 22 43N 88 21 E
Satpukur, *Calc.* **16 E6** 22 37N 88 24 E
Sätra, *Stock.* **3 E10** 59 17N 17 54 E
Satsuna, *Calc.* **16 F5** 22 28N 88 17 E
Sau Mau Ping, *H.K.* **12 E6** 22 19N 114 13 E
Saugus, *Bost.* **21 C3** 42 28N 71 0W
Saugus →, *Bost.* **21 C3** 42 27N 70 58W
Saulx-les-Chartreux, *Paris* **5 C3** 48 41N 2 16 E
Sausalito, *S.F.* **27 A2** 37 51N 122 28W
Sausset →, *Paris* **5 B5** 48 56N 2 28 E
Savigny-sur-Orge, *Paris* **5 C4** 48 40N 2 21 E
Savijärvi, *Hels.* **3 A6** 60 21N 25 19 E
Savonera, *Tori.* **9 B2** 45 7N 7 36 E
Sawah Besar, *Jak.* **15 H9** 6 8 S 106 49 E
Sawyer Ridge, *S.F.* **27 C2** 37 34N 122 24W
Saxonville, *Bost.* **21 D1** 42 19N 71 24W
Saxonwold, *Jobg.* **18 E9** 26 9 S 28 2 E
Scarborough, *Trto.* **20 D9** 43 44N 79 14W
Scarsdale, *N.Y.* **23 B6** 40 58N 73 47W
Sceaux, *Paris* **5 C3** 48 46N 2 17 E
Schalke, *Ruhr* **6 A4** 51 33N 7 4 E
Schapenrust, *Jobg.* **18 F11** 26 15 S 28 21 E
Scharfenberg, *Berl.* **7 A2** 52 35N 13 15 E
Scheiblingstein, *Wien* **10 G9** 48 16N 16 13 E
Schenefeld, *Hbg.* **7 D7** 53 36N 9 52 E
Scherlebech, *Ruhr* **6 A4** 51 37N 7 8 E
Schildow, *Berl.* **7 A3** 52 38N 13 22 E
Schiller Park, *Chic.* **26 B1** 41 56N 87 52W
Schiller Woods, *Chic.* **26 B1** 41 57N 87 51W
Schlachtensee, *Berl.* **7 B2** 52 26N 13 13 E
Schlossgarten, *Berl.* **7 A2** 52 31N 13 18 E
Schmachtendorf, *Ruhr* **6 A2** 51 32N 6 48 E
Schmargendorf, *Berl.* **7 B2** 52 28N 13 17 E
Schmöckwitz, *Berl.* **7 B5** 52 22N 13 38 E
Schnelsen, *Hbg.* **7 D7** 53 38N 9 54 E
Scholven, *Ruhr* **6 A4** 51 36N 7 0 E
Schönblick, *Berl.* **7 B5** 52 27N 13 43 E
Schönbrunn, Schloss, *Wien* **10 G9** 48 10N 16 19 E
Schöneberg, *Berl.* **7 B3** 52 28N 13 20 E
Schönefeld, *Berl.* **7 B4** 52 23N 13 30 E
Schöneiche, *Berl.* **7 B5** 52 28N 13 41 E
Schönwalde, *Berl.* **7 A1** 52 37N 13 7 E
Schottenwald, *Wien* **10 G9** 48 13N 16 16 E
Schuir, *Ruhr* **6 B3** 51 23N 6 59 E
Schulzendorf, *Berl.* **7 A2** 52 36N 13 16 E
Schuylkill →, *Phil.* **24 B3** 39 53N 75 11W
Schwabing, *Mün.* **7 G10** 48 10N 11 35 E
Schwafheim, *Ruhr* **6 B1** 51 25N 6 36 E
Schwanebeck, *Berl.* **7 A4** 52 37N 13 32 E
Schwanenwerder, *Berl.* **7 B2** 52 26N 13 10 E
Schwarz →, *Ruhr* **6 C3** 51 19N 6 44 E
Schwarzbachtal, *Ruhr* **6 C3** 51 17N 6 51 E
Schwarze, *Ruhr* **6 A2** 51 31N 6 48 E
Schwarze Berge, *Hbg.* **7 E7** 53 27N 9 54 E
Schwarzlackenau, *Wien* **10 G10** 48 16N 16 23 E
Schwechat, *Wien* **10 H10** 48 8N 16 28 E
Schweflinghaüsen, *Ruhr* **6 C6** 51 15N 7 24 E
Schwelm, *Ruhr* **6 C5** 51 16N 7 16 E
Scisciano, *Nápl.* **9 H13** 40 54N 14 28 E
Scoresby, *Melb.* **19 F8** 37 54 S 145 14 E
Scotch Plains, *N.Y.* **22 D2** 40 39N 74 22W
Scotts Level Br. →, *Balt.* **25 A2** 39 23N 76 45W
Sea Cliff, *N.Y.* **23 B7** 40 50N 73 38W
Seabrook, *Wash.* **25 D9** 38 58N 76 49W
Seacliff, *S.F.* **27 B2** 37 47N 122 28W
Seaforth, *Syd.* **19 A4** 33 48 S 151 15 E
Seagate, *N.Y.* **22 D4** 40 34N 74 0W
Seal Slough, *S.F.* **27 C3** 37 34N 122 17W
Sears Tower, *Chic.* **26 B3** 41 52N 87 38W
Seat Pleasant, *Wash.* **25 D8** 38 53N 76 53W
Seavey Hill, *Bost.* **21 A1** 42 42N 71 23W
Šeberov, *Pra.* **10 B3** 50 0N 14 30 E
Secaucus, *N.Y.* **22 C4** 40 47N 74 3W
Secondigliano, *Nápl.* **9 H12** 40 53N 14 15 E
Seddinsee, *Berl.* **7 B5** 52 23N 13 41 E
Sedgefield, *N.Y.* **22 B2** 40 51N 74 26W
Sedriano, *Mil.* **9 E4** 45 29N 8 58 E
Seeberg, *Berl.* **7 A5** 52 33N 13 41 E
Seeburg, *Berl.* **7 A1** 52 30N 13 7 E
Seefeld, *Berl.* **7 A5** 52 37N 13 40 E
Seegefeld, *Berl.* **7 A1** 52 33N 13 5 E
Seehof, *Berl.* **7 B2** 52 24N 13 17 E
Segeltorp, *Stock.* **3 E10** 59 16N 17 56 E
Segrate, *Mil.* **9 E6** 45 29N 9 17 E
Seguro, *Mil.* **9 E5** 45 28N 9 3 E
Seine →, *Paris* **5 C4** 48 48N 2 25 E
Seixal, *Lisb.* **8 G8** 38 38N 9 5W
Selbeck, *Ruhr* **6 B3** 51 22N 6 51 E
Selbecke, *Ruhr* **6 C6** 51 20N 7 28 E
Selby, *Jobg.* **18 F9** 26 12 S 28 2 E
Seletar, P., *Sing.* **15 F8** 1 26N 103 51 E
Seletar, Sungei →, *Sing.* **15 F8** 1 25N 103 51 E
Seletar Hills, *Sing.* **15 F8** 1 23N 103 52 E
Seletar Res., *Sing.* **15 F7** 1 24N 103 48 E
Selghar, *Bomb.* **16 H9** 18 57N 73 1 E
Selhurst, *Lon.* **4 C4** 51 23N 0 5W
Selsdon, *Lon.* **4 C4** 51 20N 0 3W
Selytsy, *St-Pet.* **11 B6** 59 56N 30 42 E
Sembawang, *Sing.* **15 F7** 1 26N 103 49 E
Sembawang, Sungei →, *Sing.* **15 F7** 1 26N 103 48 E
Sembawang Hill, *Sing.* **15 F7** 1 22N 103 49 E
Semsvatn, *Oslo* **2 B2** 59 51N 10 25 E
Senago, *Mil.* **9 D5** 45 34N 9 7 E
Senan, *Jak.* **15 J10** 6 10 S 106 50 E
Sénart, Forêt de, *Paris* **5 D4** 48 40N 2 28 E
Senayan Sports Centre, *Jak.* **15 J9** 6 12 S 106 47 E
Sendling, *Mün.* **7 G10** 48 7N 11 31 E
Sengeløse, *Købn.* **2 D8** 55 40N 12 14 E
Senju, *Tōkyō* **13 B3** 35 44N 139 48 E
Senlikköy, *Ist.* **17 B1** 40 58N 28 47 E
Senlisse, *Paris* **5 C1** 48 41N 1 59 E
Senneville, *Mtrl.* **20 B2** 43 24N 73 57W
Senri, *Ōsaka* **12 B4** 34 49N 135 30 E
Senriyama, *Ōsaka* **12 B4** 34 47N 135 30 E
Sentosa, *Sing.* **15 G7** 1 15N 103 49 E
Sentosa, P., *Sing.* **15 G7** 1 15N 103 49 E
Seo Dae Mun, *Sŏul* **12 G7** 37 34N 126 55 E
Seobinngo, *Sŏul* **12 G7** 37 31N 126 58 E
Seoggwan, *Sŏul* **12 G8** 37 35N 127 2 E
Seong Bug, *Sŏul* **12 G8** 37 35N 127 0 E
Seong Dong, *Sŏul* **12 G8** 37 33N 127 3 E
Seongsu, *Sŏul* **12 G8** 37 32N 127 2 E
Seoul = Sŏul, *Sŏul* **12 G8** 37 34N 127 51 E
Seoul National Univ., *Sŏul* **12 H7** 37 28N 126 57 E
Seoul Tower, *Sŏul* **12 G7** 37 32N 126 59 E
Sepah Salar Mosque, *Tehr.* **17 C5** 35 40N 51 25 E
Sepolia, *Ath.* **8 H11** 38 1N 23 42 E
Sepulveda, *L.A.* **28 A2** 34 13N 118 27W
Sepulveda Flood Control Basin, *L.A.* **28 A2** 34 10N 118 28W
Serangoon, P., *Sing.* **15 F8** 1 23N 103 55 E
Serangoon, Sungei →, *Sing.* **15 F8** 1 23N 103 55 E
Serangoon Garden, *Sing.* **15 F8** 1 21N 103 51 E

46 Serangoon Harbour

Serangoon Harbour, *Sing.* 15 F8 1 23N 103 57 E
Seraya, P., *Sing.* 15 G7 1 16N 103 43 E
Serebryanka, *Mos.* 11 E11 55 44N 37 53 E
Serebryanka →, *Mos.* 11 E10 55 47N 37 44 E
Serednevo, *Mos.* 11 F7 55 35N 37 18 E
Serramonte, *S.F.* 27 C2 37 39N 122 28W
Servon, *Paris* 5 C5 48 43N 2 35 E
Šestajovice, *Pra.* 10 B3 50 6N 14 40 E
Sesto San Giovanni, *Mil.* 9 D6 45 31N 9 13 E
Seta Budi, *Jak.* 15 J9 6 12 S 106 49 E
Setagaya-Ku, *Tōkyō* 13 C2 35 37N 139 36 E
Sete Pontes, *Rio J.* 31 B3 22 50 S 43 4W
Seter, *Oslo* 2 B4 59 52N 10 47 E
Séttimo Milanese, *Mil.* 9 E5 45 28N 9 3 E
Séttimo Torinese, *Tori.* 9 B3 45 8N 7 46 E
Settsu, *Ōsaka* 12 B4 34 47N 135 33 E
Setuny →, *Mos.* 11 E8 55 43N 37 21 E
Seurasaari, *Hels.* 3 B4 60 11N 24 53 E
Seutula, *Hels.* 3 A4 60 20N 24 52 E
Seven Corners, *Wash.* 25 D7 38 53N 77 9W
Seven Kings, *Lon.* 4 B5 51 33N 0 5 E
Sevenoaks, *Lon.* 4 D6 51 16N 0 11 E
Severn Hills, *Syd.* 19 A2 33 46 S 150 57 E
Sévesco →, *Mil.* 9 D5 45 35N 9 9 E
Sevran, *Paris* 5 B5 48 56N 2 31 E
Sèvres, *Paris* 5 C3 48 49N 2 13 E
Sewaren, *N.Y.* 22 D3 40 33N 74 15W
Sewell, *Phil.* 24 C4 39 46N 75 8W
Sewri, *Bomb.* 16 H8 18 59N 72 50 E
Seya, *Tōkyō* 13 D1 35 28N 139 28 E
Sforzesso, Castello, *Mil.* 9 E6 45 28N 9 10 E
Sha Kok Mei, *H.K.* 12 D6 22 23N 114 16 E
Sha Tin, *H.K.* 12 D6 22 23N 114 11 E
Sha Tin Wai, *H.K.* 12 D6 22 22N 114 11 E
Shaala, *Bagd.* 17 E7 33 22N 44 16 E
Shabanzhuang, *Beij.* 14 B3 39 51N 116 25 E
Shabbona Woods, *Chic.* 26 D3 41 36N 87 33W
Shabrâmant, *El Qâ.* 18 D5 29 56N 31 11 E
Shadipur, *Delhi* 16 B2 28 38N 77 11 E
Shady Oak, *Wash.* 25 C6 39 1N 77 17W
Shahabad, *Bomb.* 16 G9 19 0N 73 2 E
Shahar, *Bomb.* 16 G8 19 5N 72 52 E
Shahdara, *Delhi* 16 A2 28 40N 77 18 E
Shahe, *Gzh.* 14 G8 23 9N 113 19 E
Shahpur Jel, *Delhi* 16 B2 28 33N 77 12 E
Shahr-e-Rey, *Tehr.* 17 D5 35 36N 51 25 E
Shaikh Aomar, *Bagd.* 17 E8 33 20N 44 23 E
Shakarpor Khas, *Delhi* 16 B2 28 37N 77 14 E
Shakurpur, *Delhi* 16 A1 28 40N 77 8 E
Sham Shui Po, *H.K.* 12 E5 22 19N 114 9 E
Shamepur, *Delhi* 16 A1 28 44N 77 8 E
Shamian, *Gzh.* 14 G8 23 6N 113 13 E
Shamspur, *Delhi* 16 B2 28 36N 77 17 E
Shan Liu, *H.K.* 12 D6 22 23N 114 16 E
Shan Mei, *H.K.* 12 D6 22 24N 114 10 E
Shanghai, *Shang.* 14 J12 31 14N 121 28 E
Shanghetou, *Tianj.* 14 D5 39 11N 117 0 E
Shanjing, *Gzh.* 14 G9 23 4N 113 23 E
Sharea Faisal, *Kar.* 17 G11 24 52N 67 8 E
Sharon Hill, *Phil.* 24 B3 39 54N 75 16W
Sharp I., *H.K.* 12 D6 22 21N 114 17 E
Sharp Park, *S.F.* 27 C2 37 38N 122 29W
Shau Kei Wan, *H.K.* 12 E6 22 16N 114 13 E
Shawocun, *Beij.* 14 B2 39 53N 116 13 E
Shawsheen Village, *Bost.* 21 A3 42 40N 71 7W
Shea Stadium, *N.Y.* 23 C5 40 45N 73 50W
Sheakhala, *Calc.* 16 D5 22 45N 88 10 E
Shebāb, *Bagd.* 17 E8 33 20N 44 26 E
Sheepshead B., *N.Y.* 22 D5 40 35N 73 55W
Shek Hang, *H.K.* 12 D6 22 24N 114 17 E
Shek Kip Mei, *H.K.* 12 D5 22 20N 114 9 E
Shek Lung Kung, *H.K.* 12 D5 22 23N 114 5 E
Shek O, *H.K.* 12 E6 22 13N 114 15 E
Shellpot Cr. →, *Phil.* 24 C1 39 44N 75 30W
Shelter Cove, *S.F.* 27 C1 37 35N 122 30W
Shelter I., *H.K.* 12 E6 22 19N 114 17 E
Shemīrānāt, *Tehr.* 17 C5 35 47N 51 25 E
Shenfield, *Lon.* 4 B6 51 37N 0 19 E
Sheng Fa Shan, *H.K.* 12 D5 22 23N 114 5 E
Shenley, *Lon.* 4 A3 51 41N 0 16W
Shepherds Bush, *Lon.* 4 B3 51 30N 0 13W
Shepperton, *Lon.* 4 C2 51 23N 0 26W
Sherborn, *Bost.* 21 D1 42 14N 71 22W
Sherman Oaks, *L.A.* 28 B2 34 8N 118 29W
Sherwood Forest, *S.F.* 27 A3 37 57N 122 16W
Shet Bandar, *Bomb.* 16 H8 18 57N 72 55 E
Sheung Lau Wan, *H.K.* 12 E6 22 16N 114 16 E
Sheung Wan, *H.K.* 12 E5 22 16N 114 9 E
Sheva, *Bomb.* 16 H8 18 56N 72 57 E
Sheva Nhava, *Bomb.* 16 H8 18 57N 72 57 E
Shiba, *Tōkyō* 13 C3 35 38N 139 45 E
Shiba →, *Tōkyō* 13 A3 35 50N 139 44 E
Shibuya-Ku, *Tōkyō* 13 C3 35 39N 139 41 E
Shijōnawate, *Ōsaka* 12 B4 34 44N 135 37 E
Shimo-okudomi, *Tōkyō* 13 A1 35 52N 139 27 E
Shimo-tsuchidana, *Tōkyō* 13 D1 35 24N 139 27 E
Shimogawara, *Tōkyō* 13 C1 35 39N 139 27 E
Shimosalo, *Tōkyō* 13 B2 35 45N 139 31 E
Shimosasame, *Tōkyō* 13 B2 35 48N 139 37 E
Shimoshakujii, *Tōkyō* 13 B2 35 43N 139 35 E
Shimotomi, *Tōkyō* 13 B1 35 49N 139 27 E
Shimotsuruma, *Tōkyō* 13 D1 35 29N 139 26 E
Shimura, *Tōkyō* 13 B3 35 46N 139 41 E
Shinagawa B., *Tōkyō* 13 C3 35 35N 139 48 E
Shinagawa-Ku, *Tōkyō* 13 C3 35 36N 139 44 E
Shing Mun Res., *H.K.* 12 D5 22 23N 114 8 E
Shinjuku-Ku, *Tōkyō* 13 B3 35 41N 139 42 E
Shinkoiwa, *Tōkyō* 13 B4 35 43N 139 51 E
Shinnakano, *Tōkyō* 13 B3 35 41N 139 40 E
Shinoha, *Tōkyō* 13 A3 35 50N 139 49 E
Shipai, *Gzh.* 14 G9 23 8N 113 20 E
Shipley, *Balt.* 25 B3 39 12N 76 39W
Shippan Pt., *N.Y.* 23 A7 41 1N 73 31W
Shirako, *Tōkyō* 13 B2 35 47N 139 36 E
Shiraone, *Bomb.* 16 G9 19 2N 73 1 E
Shirinashi →, *Ōsaka* 12 C3 34 38N 135 27 E
Shirley, *Lon.* 4 C4 51 22N 0 2W
Shiro, *Tōkyō* 13 B2 35 48N 139 30 E
Shirogane, *Tōkyō* 13 C3 35 37N 139 44 E
Shisha Hai, *Beij.* 14 B3 39 55N 116 21 E
Shitou, *Gzh.* 14 G9 23 1N 113 23 E
Shiweitang, *Gzh.* 14 G8 23 6N 113 12 E
Shogunle, *Lagos* 18 A2 6 34N 7 20 E
Shomolu, *Lagos* 18 A2 6 32N 7 22 E
Shooters Hill, *Lon.* 4 C5 51 28N 0 4 E
Shoreditch, *Lon.* 4 B4 51 31N 0 4W
Shoreham, *Lon.* 4 D6 51 19N 0 10 E
Short Hills, *N.Y.* 22 C2 40 44N 74 21W
Shortlands, *Lon.* 4 C5 51 23N 0 0 E
Shrirampur, *Calc.* 16 D5 22 45N 88 21 E
Shuangkou, *Tianj.* 14 D5 39 14N 117 2 E
Shuangtuo, *Tianj.* 14 D6 39 13N 117 19 E
Shubrâ el Kheima, *El Qâ.* 18 C5 30 6N 31 14 E
Shuikuo, *Gzh.* 14 F8 23 10N 113 10 E
Shuishang Gongyuan, *Tianj.* 14 E5 39 5N 117 9 E
Shukunoshō, *Ōsaka* 12 A4 34 50N 135 31 E
Sibbo, *Hels.* 3 A6 60 21N 25 14 E
Sibbo fjärden, *Hels.* 3 B6 60 11N 25 17 E
Siboney, *La Hab.* 30 B2 23 4N 82 28W
Sibpur, *Calc.* 16 E5 22 34N 88 19 E
Sibřina, *Pra.* 10 B4 50 3N 14 40 E
Sidcup, *Lon.* 4 C5 51 25N 0 6 E
Siebenhirten, *Wien* 10 H9 48 8N 16 17 E
Siedlung, *Berl.* 7 A1 52 35N 13 7 E
Siekierki, *Wsaw.* 10 E7 52 12N 21 4 E
Sielce, *Wsaw.* 10 E7 52 12N 21 2 E
Siemensstadt, *Berl.* 7 A2 52 32N 13 16 E
Sieraków, *Wsaw.* 10 E5 52 19N 20 48 E
Sierra Madre, *L.A.* 28 B4 34 9N 118 3W
Sievering, *Wien* 10 G10 48 15N 16 20 E
Siggerud, *Oslo* 2 C5 59 47N 10 52 E
Siheung, *Sŏul* 12 H7 37 28N 126 54 E
Siikajärvi, *Hels.* 3 B2 60 17N 24 31 E
Sikátorpuszta, *Bud.* 10 J14 47 34N 19 10 E
Silampur, *Delhi* 16 B2 28 39N 77 16 E
Silschede, *Ruhr* 6 B6 51 21N 7 22 E
Silver Hill, *Wash.* 25 E8 38 49N 76 55W
Silver L., *Bost.* 21 B3 42 33N 71 9W
Silver Mt., *L.A.* 28 A5 34 12N 117 55W
Silver Spring, *Wash.* 25 D7 38 59N 77 2W
Silverfields, *Jobg.* 18 E7 26 7 S 27 49 E
Silvertown, *Lon.* 4 C5 51 29N 0 1 E
Simla, *Calc.* 16 E6 22 35N 88 22 E
Simmer and Jack Mines, *Jobg.* 18 F9 26 12 S 28 8 E
Simmering, *Wien* 10 G10 48 10N 16 24 E
Simmering Heide, *Wien* 10 G10 48 10N 16 26 E
Simonkylä, *Hels.* 3 B5 60 18N 25 1 E
Simpang Bedok, *Sing.* 15 G8 1 19N 103 56 E
Simsalö, *Hels.* 3 B6 60 14N 25 17 E
Singao, *N.Y.* 22 B3 40 53N 74 14W
Singapore, *Sing.* 15 G8 1 17N 103 51 E
Singapore →, *Sing.* 15 G8 1 17N 103 51 E
Singapore, Univ. of, *Sing.* 15 G7 1 19N 103 49 E
Singapore Airport, *Sing.* 15 F8 1 21N 103 54 E
Singlewell, *Lon.* 4 C7 51 25N 0 21 E
Singur, *Calc.* 16 D5 22 48N 88 13 E
Sinicka →, *Mos.* 11 D7 55 52N 37 18 E
Sinki, Selat, *Sing.* 15 G7 1 15N 103 42 E
Sinrim, *Sŏul* 12 H7 37 28N 126 56 E
Sinsa, *Sŏul* 12 G8 37 31N 127 0 E
Sinthi, *Calc.* 16 E6 22 37N 88 23 E
Sinweol, *Sŏul* 12 G7 37 31N 126 51 E
Sipoo, *Hels.* 3 A6 60 21N 25 14 E
Sipoon selkä, *Hels.* 3 B6 60 11N 25 17 E
Sipson, *Lon.* 4 C2 51 29N 0 26W
Siqeil, *El Qâ.* 18 C4 30 7N 31 10 E
Şişli, *Ist.* 17 A2 41 3N 28 58 E
Skå, *Stock.* 3 E9 59 19N 17 44 E
Skärholmen, *Stock.* 3 E10 59 16N 17 53 E
Skarpäng, *Stock.* 3 D11 59 26N 18 0 E
Skarpnäck, *Stock.* 3 E11 59 16N 18 7 E
Skarpö, *Stock.* 3 D13 59 24N 18 22 E
Skedsmo, *Oslo* 2 B6 59 59N 11 2 E
Skhodnya →, *Mos.* 11 D8 55 53N 37 23 E
Skodsborg, *Købn.* 2 D10 55 49N 12 34 E
Skogby, *Hels.* 3 A2 60 21N 24 40 E
Skogen, *Oslo* 2 C1 59 48N 10 18 E
Skogsbyn, *Hels.* 3 A6 60 20N 25 18 E
Skokie, *Chic.* 26 A2 42 2N 87 43W
Skokie →, *Chic.* 26 A2 42 3N 87 46W
Skokie Lagoons, *Chic.* 26 A2 42 7N 87 46W
Skoklefall, *Oslo* 2 B4 59 50N 10 40 E
Sköndal, *Stock.* 3 E11 59 15N 18 6 E
Skovlunde, *Købn.* 2 D9 55 42N 12 25 E
Skovshoved, *Købn.* 2 D10 55 45N 12 35 E
Skøyen, *Oslo* 2 B4 59 55N 10 40 E
Skui, *Oslo* 2 B2 59 55N 10 25 E
Skuldelev, *Købn.* 2 D7 55 46N 12 1 E
Skullerud, *Oslo* 2 B5 59 51N 10 50 E
Skuru, *Stock.* 3 E12 59 18N 18 12 E
Skytta, *Oslo* 2 B5 59 59N 10 54 E
Slade Green, *Lon.* 4 C6 51 27N 0 11 E
Slagsta, *Stock.* 3 E9 59 15N 17 48 E
Slakteren, *Oslo* 2 A4 60 1N 10 40 E
Slattum, *Oslo* 2 A5 60 0N 10 55 E
Slemmestad, *Oslo* 2 C2 59 46N 10 29 E
Slependen, *Oslo* 2 B3 59 52N 10 30 E
Sligo Cr. →, *Wash.* 25 C7 39 0N 77 1W
Slipi, *Jak.* 15 J9 6 11 S 106 47 E
Slipi Orchard Garden, *Jak.* 15 J9 6 10 S 106 46 E
Slivenec, *Pra.* 10 B2 50 1N 14 21 E
Slone Canyon Res., *L.A.* 28 B2 34 6N 118 27W
Sloop Channel, *N.Y.* 23 D7 40 36N 73 31W
Sluhy, *Pra.* 10 A3 50 11N 14 33 E
Służew, *Wsaw.* 10 E7 52 10N 21 1 E
Służewiec, *Wsaw.* 10 E7 52 10N 21 0 E
Smalleytown, *N.Y.* 22 D2 40 39N 74 28W
Smestad, *Oslo* 2 B2 59 55N 10 25 E
Smíchov, *Pra.* 10 B2 50 4N 14 23 E
Smith Forest Preserve, *Chic.* 26 B2 41 59N 87 45W
Smith Mills, *N.Y.* 22 A2 41 0N 74 23W
Smithfield, *Syd.* 19 B2 33 51 S 150 56 E
Smoke Rise, *N.Y.* 22 A2 41 0N 74 24W
Smørumnedre, *Købn.* 2 D8 55 44N 12 7 E
Snakeden Br. →, *Wash.* 25 D6 38 58N 77 17W
Snarøya, *Oslo* 2 B3 59 52N 10 33 E
Snättringe, *Stock.* 3 E10 59 15N 17 58 E
Snoldelev, *Købn.* 2 E8 55 33N 12 10 E
Snostrup, *Købn.* 2 D7 55 48N 12 7 E
Søborg, *Købn.* 2 D9 55 43N 12 29 E
Sobreda, *Lisb.* 8 G7 38 39N 9 11W
Soccavo, *Nápl.* 9 H12 40 50N 14 11 E
Sodegaura, *Tōkyō* 13 D4 35 24N 139 57 E
Söderby, *Stock.* 3 D12 59 24N 18 12 E
Söderkullalandet, *Hels.* 3 B6 60 14N 25 19 E
Södermalm, *Stock.* 3 E11 59 18N 18 4 E
Södersätra, *Stock.* 3 D10 59 27N 17 56 E
Södertälje, *Stock.* 3 E8 59 11N 17 36 E
Sodingen, *Ruhr* 6 A5 51 32N 7 15 E
Sodpur, *Calc.* 16 D6 22 42N 88 24 E
Södra Björkfjärden, *Stock.* 3 E8 59 17N 17 34 E
Soeurs, Î. des, *Mtrl.* 20 B4 43 27N 73 32W
Sognsvatn, *Oslo* 2 B4 59 58N 10 43 E
Soignolles-en-Brie, *Paris* 5 D6 48 39N 2 43 E
Soisy-sous-Montmorency, *Paris* 5 B3 48 59N 2 17 E
Soisy-sur-Seine, *Paris* 5 D4 48 39N 2 27 E
Sojiji Temple, *Tōkyō* 13 D3 35 29N 139 40 E
Sok Kwu Wan, *H.K.* 12 E5 22 12N 114 7 E
Sōka, *Tōkyō* 13 B3 35 49N 139 48 E
Sokolniki, *Mos.* 11 E10 55 47N 37 40 E
Sokolniki Park, *Mos.* 11 E10 55 48N 37 40 E
Sokołów, *Wsaw.* 10 F6 52 9N 20 51 E
Solalinden, *Mün.* 7 G11 48 5N 11 42 E
Solaro, *Mil.* 9 D5 45 36N 9 6 E
Solers, *Paris* 5 D6 48 39N 2 43 E
Solingen, *Ruhr* 6 C4 51 10N 7 5 E
Sollentuna, *Stock.* 3 D10 59 25N 17 56 E
Søllerød, *Købn.* 2 D9 55 48N 12 29 E
Sollihøgda, *Oslo* 2 B2 59 58N 10 21 E
Solln, *Mün.* 7 G10 48 4N 11 31 E
Solna, *Stock.* 3 D10 59 21N 17 59 E
Solntsevo, *Mos.* 11 F8 55 39N 37 24 E
Solymár, *Bud.* 10 J12 47 35N 18 56 E
Somapah Changi, *Sing.* 15 F8 1 20N 103 57 E
Somapan Serangoon, *Sing.* 15 F8 1 21N 103 53 E
Somborn, *Ruhr* 6 B6 51 29N 7 20 E
Somerdale, *Phil.* 24 B4 39 50N 75 1W
Somerset, *Wash.* 25 D7 38 57N 77 5W
Somerton, *Phil.* 24 A4 40 7N 75 1W
Somerville, *Bost.* 21 C3 42 22N 71 5W
Somma, Mte., *Nápl.* 9 H13 40 50N 14 25 E
Somma Vesuviana, *Nápl.* 9 H13 40 52N 14 26 E
Sonari, *Bomb.* 16 H8 18 54N 72 59 E
Sønderby, *Købn.* 2 D7 55 44N 12 2 E
Søndersø, *Købn.* 2 D9 55 46N 12 21 E
Sondre Elvåga, *Oslo* 2 B5 59 51N 10 54 E
Sonnberg, *Wien* 10 G9 48 19N 16 15 E
Sørby, *Oslo* 2 C4 59 49N 10 41 E
Sørkedalen, *Oslo* 2 A3 60 1N 10 37 E
Soroksár, *Bud.* 10 K13 47 24N 19 7 E
Soroksár-Újtelep, *Bud.* 10 K13 47 25N 19 7 E
Soroksari Duna →, *Bud.* 10 K13 47 25N 19 5 E
Sørsdal, *Oslo* 2 B1 59 50N 10 16 E
Sosenka →, *Mos.* 11 E10 55 46N 37 42 E
Sosnovaya, *St-Pet.* 11 C2 59 49N 30 8 E
Sottungsby, *Hels.* 3 B5 60 16N 25 8 E
Sŏul, *Sŏul* 12 G8 37 34N 127 51 E
Soundview, *N.Y.* 23 C5 40 49N 73 53W
South Basin, *S.F.* 27 B2 37 42N 122 22W
South Beach, *N.Y.* 22 D4 40 35N 74 4W
South Boston, *Bost.* 21 C3 42 20N 71 2W
South Braintree, *Bost.* 21 D4 42 11N 70 59W
South Branch →, *Phil.* 24 C4 39 50N 75 5W
South Brooklyn, *N.Y.* 22 C5 40 41N 73 59W
South Chelmsford, *Bost.* 21 B1 42 34N 71 22W
South Chicago, *Chic.* 26 C3 41 44N 87 32W
South Darenth, *Lon.* 4 C6 51 23N 0 15 E
South Deering, *Chic.* 26 C3 41 42N 87 33W
South Floral Park, *N.Y.* 23 C6 40 42N 73 41W
South Gate, *L.A.* 28 C3 33 56N 118 12W
South Germiston, *Jobg.* 18 F10 26 11 S 28 13 E
South Hackensack, *N.Y.* 22 B4 40 51N 74 2W
South Hamilton, *Bost.* 21 B4 42 36N 70 52W
South Harbour, *Manila* 15 D3 14 34N 120 58 E
South Harrow, *Lon.* 4 B2 51 33N 0 21W
South Hd., *Syd.* 19 B4 33 50 S 151 16 E
South Hempstead, *N.Y.* 23 C7 40 40N 73 37W
South Hills, *Jobg.* 18 F9 26 14 S 28 5 E
South Hingham, *Bost.* 21 D4 42 12N 70 53W
South Holland, *Chic.* 26 D3 41 36N 87 35W
South Hornchurch, *Lon.* 4 B6 51 32N 0 11 E
South Huntington, *N.Y.* 23 C8 40 49N 73 23W
South Lawn, *Wash.* 25 E7 38 47N 77 0W
South Lawrence, *Bost.* 21 A3 42 41N 71 9W
South Lincoln, *Bost.* 21 C2 42 24N 71 19W
South Lynnfield, *Bost.* 21 B4 42 30N 70 59W
South Norwood, *Lon.* 4 C4 51 23N 0 3W
South Ockendon, *Lon.* 4 B6 51 30N 0 16 E
South of Market, *S.F.* 27 B2 37 46N 122 24W
South Orange, *N.Y.* 22 C3 40 45N 74 14W
South Oxley, *Lon.* 4 B2 51 37N 0 23W
South Oyster B., *N.Y.* 23 D8 40 38N 73 27W
South Ozone Park, *N.Y.* 23 C6 40 41N 73 49W
South Pasadena, *L.A.* 28 B4 34 7N 118 8W
South Peabody, *Bost.* 21 B4 42 30N 70 57W
South Peters, *Syd.* 19 B4 33 54 S 151 11 E
South Plainfield, *N.Y.* 22 D2 40 35N 74 24W
South Quincy, *Bost.* 21 D3 42 13N 71 0W
South Res., *Bost.* 21 C3 42 26N 71 6W
South San Francisco, *S.F.* 27 C2 37 38N 122 26W
South San Gabriel, *L.A.* 28 B4 34 3N 118 6W
South Shore, *Chic.* 26 C3 41 45N 87 34W
South Sudbury, *Bost.* 21 C1 42 21N 71 24W
South Valley Stream, *N.Y.* 23 D6 40 38N 73 43W
South Westbury, *N.Y.* 23 C7 40 44N 73 34W
South Weymouth, *Bost.* 21 D4 42 10N 70 56W
South Wimbledon, *Lon.* 4 C3 51 24N 0 11W
South Yarra, *Melb.* 19 F6 37 50 S 144 59 E
Southall, *Lon.* 4 B2 51 30N 0 22W
Southborough, *Lon.* 4 C5 51 23N 0 3 E
Southcrest, *Jobg.* 18 F9 26 15 S 28 5 E
Southend, *Lon.* 4 C4 51 25N 0 0 E
Southfields, *Lon.* 4 C3 51 26N 0 11W
Southgate, *Lon.* 4 B4 51 38N 0 7W
Southwark, *Lon.* 4 C4 51 29N 0 5W
Søvang, *Købn.* 2 E10 55 34N 12 37 E
Soweto, *Jobg.* 18 F8 26 14 S 27 52 E
Soya, *Tōkyō* 13 B4 35 44N 139 55 E
Spadenland, *Hbg.* 7 E8 53 28N 10 3 E
Spandau, *Berl.* 7 A1 52 33N 13 9 E
Spånga, *Stock.* 3 D10 59 23N 17 53 E
Sparkhill, *N.Y.* 22 A5 41 1N 73 55W
Sparrows Point, *Balt.* 25 B4 39 13N 76 29W
Spectacle I., *Bost.* 21 C4 42 19N 70 59W
Speicher-See, *Mün.* 7 F11 48 12N 11 42 E
Speising, *Wien* 10 H9 48 10N 16 17 E
Speldorf, *Ruhr* 6 B2 51 26N 6 49 E
Spellen, *Ruhr* 6 A1 51 36N 6 36 E
Sphinx, *El Qâ.* 18 D4 29 58N 31 8 E
Spinaceto, *Rome* 9 G9 41 47N 12 27 E
Splitrock Res., *N.Y.* 22 B2 40 58N 74 26W
Spořilov, *Pra.* 10 B3 50 2N 14 29 E
Spot Pond, *Bost.* 21 C3 42 26N 71 4W
Spotswood, *Melb.* 19 F6 37 50 S 144 52 E
Spree →, *Berl.* 7 A2 52 32N 13 12 E
Spreehafen, *Hbg.* 7 D7 53 31N 9 59 E
Spring Pond, *Bost.* 21 C4 42 29N 70 56W
Springeberg, *Berl.* 7 B5 52 26N 13 43 E
Springfield, *N.Y.* 22 C3 40 42N 74 18W
Springfield, *Phil.* 24 B3 39 56N 75 19W
Springfield, *Wash.* 25 E6 38 46N 77 10W
Springs, *Jobg.* 18 F11 26 15 S 28 23 E
Sprockhövel, *Ruhr* 6 B5 51 22N 7 14 E
Squantum, *Bost.* 21 D3 42 17N 71 0W
Squirrel's Heath, *Lon.* 4 B6 51 34N 0 12 E
Srednaya Rogatka, *St-Pet.* 11 C4 59 49N 30 22 E
Sródmieċcie, *Wsaw.* 10 E7 52 13N 21 0 E
Staaken, *Berl.* 7 A1 52 31N 13 8 E
Staatsoper, *Wien* 10 G10 48 12N 16 21 E
Stabekk, *Oslo* 2 B3 59 54N 10 36 E
Stadlau, *Wien* 10 G10 48 13N 16 27 E
Stahnsdorf, *Berl.* 7 B2 52 23N 13 12 E
Staines, *Lon.* 4 C2 51 26N 0 29W
Stains, *Paris* 5 B4 48 57N 2 22 E
Stamford, *N.Y.* 23 A7 41 2N 73 32W
Stamford Harbor, *N.Y.* 23 A7 41 0N 73 34W
Stamford Hill, *Lon.* 4 B4 51 34N 0 4W
Stammersdorf, *Wien* 10 G10 48 18N 16 24 E
Stanford Univ., *S.F.* 27 D4 37 26N 122 10W
Stanley, *H.K.* 12 E6 22 13N 114 12 E
Stanley Mound, *H.K.* 12 E6 22 13N 114 12 E
Stanley Pen., *H.K.* 12 E6 22 12N 114 12 E
Stanmore, *Lon.* 4 B3 51 37N 0 18W
Stansted, *Lon.* 4 C6 51 20N 0 18 E
Stapleford Abbotts, *Lon.* 4 B6 51 37N 0 10 E
Stapleton, *N.Y.* 22 D4 40 36N 74 5W
Stará Boleslav, *Pra.* 10 A3 50 11N 14 39 E
Stara Milosna, *Wsaw.* 10 E8 52 15N 21 12 E
Staraya, *St-Pet.* 11 B5 59 55N 30 37 E
Staraya Derevnya, *St-Pet.* 11 B3 59 58N 30 15 E
Stare, *Wsaw.* 10 E7 52 15N 21 0 E
Stare Babice, *Wsaw.* 10 E5 52 15N 20 49 E
Staré Mesto, *Pra.* 10 B2 50 5N 14 25 E
State House, *Lagos* 18 B2 6 26N 7 24 E
Staten, *N.Y.* 22 D4 40 34N 74 7W
Staten Island Zoo, *N.Y.* 22 D4 40 38N 74 6W
Statenice, *Pra.* 10 B1 50 9N 14 19 E
Stavnsholt, *Købn.* 2 D9 55 48N 12 24 E
Steele, *Ruhr* 6 B4 51 27N 7 4 E
Steele Creek, *Melb.* 19 E6 37 44 S 144 52 E
Steglitz, *Berl.* 7 B2 52 27N 13 19 E
Stehstücken, *Berl.* 7 B1 52 23N 13 7 E
Steilshoop, *Hbg.* 7 D8 53 36N 10 2 E
Steinberger Slough, *S.F.* 27 C3 37 32N 122 13W
Steinriegel, *Wien* 10 G9 48 16N 16 12 E
Steinstücken, *Berl.* 7 B1 52 21N 13 7 E
Steinwerder, *Hbg.* 7 D7 53 32N 9 57 E
Stellingen, *Hbg.* 7 D7 53 35N 9 56 E
Stenhamra, *Stock.* 3 D9 59 20N 17 40 E
Stenløse, *Købn.* 2 D8 55 46N 12 11 E
Stephansdom, *Wien* 10 G10 48 12N 16 21 E
Stepney, *Lon.* 4 B4 51 30N 0 3W
Sterkende, *Købn.* 2 E8 55 36N 12 10 E
Sterkrade, *Ruhr* 6 A3 51 31N 6 52 E
Sterling Park, *S.F.* 27 B2 37 41N 122 27W
Stevenson, *Balt.* 25 A2 39 24N 76 42W
Stewart Manor, *N.Y.* 23 C6 40 43N 73 40W
Sticklinge udde, *Stock.* 3 D11 59 23N 18 6 E
Stickney, *Chic.* 26 C2 41 49N 87 46W
Stienitzaue, *Berl.* 7 A5 52 38N 13 44 E
Stiepel, *Ruhr* 6 B5 51 25N 7 14 E
Stiftskirche, *Ruhr* 6 C2 51 12N 6 41 E
Still Run →, *Phil.* 24 C3 39 47N 75 16W
Stockholm, *Stock.* 3 E11 59 19N 18 4 E
Stocksund, *Stock.* 3 D11 59 23N 18 3 E
Stockum, *Ruhr* 6 C2 51 16N 6 44 E
Stodůlky, *Pra.* 10 B1 50 3N 14 19 E
Stoke D'Abernon, *Lon.* 4 D2 51 19N 0 23W
Stoke Newington, *Lon.* 4 B4 51 33N 0 4W
Stolpe-Süd, *Berl.* 7 A2 52 37N 13 14 E
Stone, *Lon.* 4 C6 51 26N 0 16 E
Stone Grove, *Lon.* 4 B3 51 37N 0 16W
Stone Park, *Chic.* 26 B1 41 53N 87 52W
Stonebridge, *Lon.* 4 B3 51 32N 0 16W
Stoneham, *Bost.* 21 C3 42 29N 71 5W
Stonehurst, *L.A.* 28 A2 34 15N 118 21W
Stony Brook Res., *Bost.* 21 D3 42 15N 71 8W
Stony Cr. →, *Chic.* 26 C2 41 40N 87 45W
Stony Cr. →, *Melb.* 19 E6 37 49 S 144 53 E
Stora Värtan, *Stock.* 3 D11 59 25N 18 7 E
Store Hareskov, *Købn.* 2 D9 55 46N 12 23 E
Store Kattingesø, *Købn.* 2 E7 55 39N 12 0 E
Store Magleby, *Købn.* 2 E10 55 35N 12 35 E
Storholmen, *Stock.* 3 D11 59 23N 18 8 E
Stovivatn, *Oslo* 2 B2 59 54N 10 26 E
Stovner, *Oslo* 2 B5 59 57N 10 55 E
Stow L., *S.F.* 27 B2 37 46N 122 28W
Stračnice, *Pra.* 10 B2 50 4N 14 28 E
Strandbad Gansehäufe, *Wien* 10 G10 48 13N 16 26 E
Strasslach, *Mün.* 7 G10 48 0N 11 30 E
Strasstrudering, *Mün.* 7 G11 48 6N 11 41 E
Stratford, *Lon.* 4 B5 51 33N 0 0 E
Stratford, *Phil.* 24 C4 39 49N 75 0W
Strathfield, *Syd.* 19 B3 33 52 S 151 5 E
Strawberry Hill, *Bost.* 21 D2 42 14N 71 15W
Strawberry Pk., *L.A.* 28 A4 34 16N 118 7W
Strawberry Pt., *S.F.* 27 A1 37 53N 122 30W
Streatham, *Lon.* 4 C4 51 25N 0 7W
Streatham Vale, *Lon.* 4 C4 51 24N 0 8W
Strebersdorf, *Wien* 10 G10 48 17N 16 23 E
Střečovice, *Pra.* 10 B2 50 5N 14 23 E
Strelyna, *St-Pet.* 11 C1 59 49N 30 0 E
Střížkov, *Pra.* 10 B2 50 7N 14 28 E
Strogino, *Mos.* 11 E8 55 48N 37 24 E
Strømmen, *Oslo* 2 B5 59 56N 10 59 E
Stromovka, *Pra.* 10 B2 50 6N 14 25 E
Strunkede Wasserschloss, *Ruhr* 6 A5 51 33N 7 12 E
Studio City, *L.A.* 28 B2 34 8N 118 24W
Stupinigi, *Tori.* 9 C2 44 59N 7 36 E
Stura di Lanzo →, *Tori.* 9 A2 45 11N 7 47 E
Stureby, *Stock.* 3 E11 59 15N 18 4 E
Stuvsta, *Stock.* 3 E11 59 15N 18 0 E
Styrum, *Ruhr* 6 B3 51 27N 6 52 E
Subhepur, *Delhi* 16 A2 28 44N 77 15 E
Sucat, *Manila* 15 E4 14 27N 121 2 E
Success, L., *N.Y.* 23 C6 40 45N 73 42W
Suchdol, *Pra.* 10 B2 50 8N 14 22 E
Sucre, *Car.* 30 D5 10 31N 66 57W
Sucy-en-Brie, *Paris* 5 C5 48 46N 2 31 E
Sudberg, *Ruhr* 6 C4 51 10N 7 6 E
Sudbury, *Bost.* 21 C1 42 22N 71 24W
Suderelbe →, *Hbg.* 7 E7 53 28N 9 58 E
Suderwich, *Ruhr* 6 A5 51 36N 7 16 E
Sugamo, *Tōkyō* 13 B3 35 44N 139 43 E
Sugar Loaf Mt. = Açúcar, Pão de, *Rio J.* 31 B3 22 56 S 43 9W
Sugartown, *Phil.* 24 B1 39 59N 75 30W
Sugasawa, *Tōkyō* 13 B2 35 46N 139 32 E
Suge, *Tōkyō* 13 C2 35 37N 139 32 E
Suginami-Ku, *Tōkyō* 13 B2 35 41N 139 37 E
Sugita, *Tōkyō* 13 D2 35 22N 139 37 E
Sugō, *Tōkyō* 13 C2 35 34N 139 33 E
Suitland, *Wash.* 25 D8 38 50N 76 55W
Sukchar, *Calc.* 16 D6 22 42N 88 22 E
Sulejówek, *Wsaw.* 10 E8 52 14N 21 14 E
Sulldorf, *Hbg.* 7 D6 53 34N 9 49 E
Sultan Mosque, *Sing.* 15 G8 1 18N 103 51 E
Suma, *Ōsaka* 12 C1 34 38N 135 8 E
Sumaré, *S. Pau.* 31 E5 23 32 S 46 41W
Sumida, *Tōkyō* 13 B3 35 42N 139 49 E
Sumida →, *Tōkyō* 13 B3 35 39N 139 45 E
Sumiyoshi, *Ōsaka* 12 C4 34 36N 135 30 E
Summer Palace, *Beij.* 14 B2 39 59N 116 13 E
Summerville, *Trto.* 20 E7 43 37N 79 33W
Summit, *Chic.* 26 C2 41 47N 87 47W
Summit, *N.Y.* 22 C2 40 43N 74 22W
Sun Valley, *L.A.* 28 A2 34 13N 118 21W
Sunamachi, *Tōkyō* 13 B4 35 40N 139 50 E
Sunashinden, *Tōkyō* 13 A2 35 53N 139 30 E
Sunbury, *Lon.* 4 C2 51 25N 0 26W
Sunda Kelapa, *Jak.* 15 H9 6 6 S 106 48 E
Sundbyberg, *Stock.* 3 D10 59 22N 17 57 E
Sundbyerne, *Købn.* 2 E10 55 39N 12 36 E
Sung Kong, *H.K.* 12 E6 22 11N 114 17 E
Sungai Bambu, *Jak.* 15 H10 6 6 S 106 53 E
Sungai Buloh, *Sing.* 15 F7 1 25N 103 42 E
Sungei Simpang, *Sing.* 15 F7 1 26N 103 49 E
Sunland, *L.A.* 28 A3 34 15N 118 18W
Sunnyridge, *Jobg.* 18 F10 26 10 S 28 10 E
Sunset, *S.F.* 27 B2 37 44N 122 29W
Sunshine, *Melb.* 19 E5 37 48 S 144 49 E
Sunshine Acres, *L.A.* 28 C5 33 56N 117 59W
Suntaug L., *Bost.* 21 B3 42 31N 71 0W
Sunter, *Jak.* 15 H10 6 7 S 106 51 E
Sunter, Kali, *Jak.* 15 J10 6 10 S 106 53 E
Suomenlinna, *Hels.* 3 C4 60 9N 24 59 E
Superga, *Tori.* 9 B3 45 4N 7 46 E
Superga, Basilica di, *Tori.* 9 B3 45 5N 7 45 E
Sura, *Calc.* 16 E6 22 33N 88 24 E
Surag San, *Sŏul* 12 F8 37 40N 127 4 E
Surbiton, *Lon.* 4 C3 51 23N 0 17W
Surco, *Lima* 30 G8 12 9 S 77 0W
Suresnes, *Paris* 5 B3 48 52N 2 13 E
Surquillo, *Lima* 30 G8 12 6 S 77 1W
Surrey Hills, *Melb.* 19 F7 37 50 S 145 5 E
Surrey Hills, *Syd.* 19 B4 33 53 S 151 13 E
Surrey Park, *Melb.* 19 E7 37 49 S 145 6 E
Susaeg, *Sŏul* 12 G7 37 34N 126 54 E
Süssenbrunn, *Wien* 10 G10 48 16N 16 29 E
Sutherland, *Syd.* 19 C3 34 2 S 151 3 E
Sutton, *Lon.* 4 C3 51 21N 0 11W
Sutton at Hone, *Lon.* 4 C6 51 24N 0 14 E
Suyu, *Sŏul* 12 G8 37 37N 127 0 E
Suzukishinden, *Tōkyō* 13 B2 35 43N 139 31 E
Svanemøllen, *Købn.* 2 D10 55 43N 12 34 E
Svartsjölandet, *Stock.* 3 D9 59 20N 17 43 E
Sverdlov, *Mos.* 11 E9 55 46N 37 36 E
Svestad, *Oslo* 2 C3 59 46N 10 36 E
Svestrup, *Købn.* 2 D7 55 46N 12 8 E
Svinningeudd, *Stock.* 3 D12 59 26N 18 17 E
Svinö, *Hels.* 3 C3 60 7N 24 44 E
Svogerslev, *Købn.* 2 E7 55 38N 12 0 E
Swampscott, *Bost.* 21 C4 42 28N 70 53W
Swanley, *Lon.* 4 C5 51 23N 0 9 E
Swanscombe, *Lon.* 4 C6 51 26N 0 18 E
Swansea, *Trto.* 20 E8 43 39N 79 27W
Swarthmore, *Phil.* 24 B2 39 54N 75 22W
Swedesboro, *Phil.* 24 C3 39 45N 75 17W
Swedesburg, *Phil.* 24 A3 40 5N 75 19W
Swinburne I., *N.Y.* 22 D4 40 33N 74 3W
Swita, *Ōsaka* 12 B4 34 45N 135 30 E
Syampur, *Calc.* 16 F5 22 28N 88 12 E
Sycamore Mills, *Phil.* 24 B2 39 57N 75 25W
Sydenham, *Jobg.* 18 E9 26 9 S 28 5 E
Sydney, *Syd.* 19 B4 33 52 S 151 12 E
Sydney, Univ. of, *Syd.* 19 B4 33 54 S 151 11 E
Sydney Airport, *Syd.* 19 B4 33 56 S 151 10 E
Sydney Harbour Bridge, *Syd.* 19 B4 33 51 S 151 12 E
Sydstranden, *Købn.* 2 E10 55 34N 12 38 E
Sylling, *Oslo* 2 B1 59 54N 10 16 E
Sylvania, *Syd.* 19 C3 34 0 S 151 7 E
Syndal, *Melb.* 19 F7 37 52 S 145 9 E
Syon House, *Lon.* 4 C3 51 28N 0 18W
Syosset, *N.Y.* 23 C7 40 49N 73 30W
Szabadság-hegy, *Bud.* 10 J12 47 30N 18 59 E
Szczęsliwice, *Wsaw.* 10 E6 52 12N 20 57 E
Szemere-Telep, *Bud.* 10 K14 47 26N 19 13 E
Széphalom, *Bud.* 10 J12 47 34N 18 57 E
Szilasliget, *Bud.* 10 J14 47 34N 19 16 E

T

Tabata, *Tōkyō* 13 B3 35 44N 139 46 E
Tablada, *B.A.* 32 C3 34 41 S 58 32W
Taboão →, *S. Pau.* 31 F7 23 40 S 46 27W
Taboão da Serra, *S. Pau.* 31 E5 23 36 S 46 45W
Tabor, *N.Y.* 22 B2 40 52N 74 28W
Täby, *Stock.* 3 D11 59 26N 18 2 E
Tacony, *Phil.* 24 A4 40 1N 75 2W
Tacuba, *Méx.* 29 B2 19 26N 99 11W
Tacubaya, *Méx.* 29 B2 19 24N 99 10W
Tadain, *Ōsaka* 12 A3 34 51N 135 24 E
Tadworth, *Lon.* 4 D3 51 17N 0 14W
Tagig, *Manila* 15 D4 14 31N 121 4 E
Tagig →, *Manila* 15 D4 14 31N 121 5 E
Tai Hang, *H.K.* 12 E6 22 16N 114 11 E
Tai Lo Shan, *H.K.* 12 D6 22 21N 114 13 E
Tai Po Tsai, *H.K.* 12 D6 22 20N 114 15 E
Tai Seng, *Sing.* 15 F8 1 20N 103 53 E
Tai Shui Hang, *H.K.* 12 D6 22 24N 114 13 E
Tai Tam B., *H.K.* 12 E6 22 12N 114 13 E
Tai Tam Tuk Res., *H.K.* 12 E6 22 14N 114 13 E
Tai Wan Tau, *H.K.* 12 E6 22 17N 114 17 E
Tai Wo Hau, *H.K.* 12 D5 22 21N 114 7 E
Tai Wo Ping, *H.K.* 12 D5 22 20N 114 9 E
Ta'imim, *Bagd.* 17 F8 33 15N 44 21 E
Tainaka, *Ōsaka* 12 C4 34 36N 135 35 E
Taishō, *Ōsaka* 12 C3 34 38N 135 27 E
Taitō-Ku, *Tōkyō* 13 B3 35 43N 139 47 E
Tajima, *Tōkyō* 13 B2 35 48N 139 36 E
Tajpur, *Calc.* 16 D5 22 44N 88 15 E
Takaido, *Tōkyō* 13 B2 35 40N 139 37 E
Takaishi, *Tōkyō* 13 C2 35 36N 139 31 E
Takarazuka, *Ōsaka* 12 B2 34 47N 135 20 E
Takasago, *Tōkyō* 13 B4 35 44N 139 52 E
Takatsuki, *Ōsaka* 12 A4 34 50N 135 37 E
Takayanagi, *Tōkyō* 13 D4 35 23N 139 57 E
Takegahana, *Tōkyō* 13 B4 35 47N 139 54 E
Takenotsuka, *Tōkyō* 13 B3 35 47N 139 47 E
Takeshita, *Tōkyō* 13 C2 35 33N 139 32 E
Takinegawa, *Tōkyō* 13 B3 35 45N 139 44 E
Takkula, *Hels.* 3 B2 60 19N 24 38 E
Takoma Park, *Wash.* 25 D7 38 58N 77 0W
Taksim, *Ist.* 17 A2 41 2N 28 58 E
Talaide, *Lisb.* 8 F7 38 44N 9 18W
Talampas, *Manila* 15 D4 14 36N 121 4 E
Taling Chan, *Bangk.* 15 B1 13 46N 100 27 E
Talleyville, *Phil.* 24 C1 39 48N 75 32W
Tallkrogen, *Stock.* 3 E11 59 16N 18 4 E
Talmapais Valley, *S.F.* 27 A1 37 52N 122 32W
Tama, *Tōkyō* 13 C1 35 38N 139 26 E
Tama →, *Tōkyō* 13 C2 35 32N 139 39 E
Tama Kyźryō, *Tōkyō* 13 C2 35 34N 139 30 E
Tamaden, *Tōkyō* 13 C2 35 39N 139 38 E
Tamagawa-josui →, *Tōkyō* 13 B1 35 41N 139 47 E
Taman Sari, *Jak.* 15 H9 6 8 S 106 48 E
Tamanduatei →, *S. Pau.* 31 E6 23 37 S 46 38W
Tambora, *Jak.* 15 H9 6 8 S 106 47 E
Tamboré, *S. Pau.* 31 E4 23 30 S 46 50W
Tammisalo, *Hels.* 3 B5 60 11N 25 5 E
Tammûh, *El Qâ.* 18 D5 29 55N 31 15 E
Tampier Slough, *Chic.* 26 D1 41 39N 87 54W
Tan Tock Seng, *Sing.* 15 G8 1 19N 103 50 E
Tanah Abang, *Jak.* 15 J9 6 12 S 106 48 E
Tanashi, *Tōkyō* 13 B2 35 43N 139 32 E
Tanforan Park, *S.F.* 27 C2 37 37N 122 24W
Tangjae, *Sŏul* 12 H8 37 29N 127 2 E
Tanglin, *Sing.* 15 G7 1 18N 103 47 E
Tangstedt, *Hbg.* 7 C7 53 40N 9 51 E
Tangstedter Forst, *Hbg.* 7 C8 53 43N 10 3 E
Tanigami, *Ōsaka* 12 B2 34 45N 135 10 E
Tanjung Duren, *Jak.* 15 J9 6 10 S 106 46 E
Tanjung Priok, *Jak.* 15 H10 6 6 S 106 52 E
Tanum, *Oslo* 2 B2 59 53N 10 28 E
Taoranting Gongyuan, *Beij.* 14 B3 39 51N 116 20 E
Taoranting Hu, *Beij.* 14 B3 39 50N 116 20 E
Tapada, *Lisb.* 8 F7 38 49N 9 16W
Tapanila, *Hels.* 3 B5 60 15N 25 2 E
Tapiales, *B.A.* 32 C3 34 42 S 58 30W
Tapiola, *Hels.* 3 B3 60 10N 24 48 E
Tappan, *N.Y.* 22 A5 41 1N 73 57W
Tappan, L., *N.Y.* 22 A5 41 1N 73 59W
Tappeh, *Tehr.* 17 C5 35 41N 51 29 E
Tapsia, *Calc.* 16 E6 22 32N 88 23 E
Taquara, *Rio J.* 31 B1 22 55 S 43 21W
Tara, *Bomb.* 16 G7 19 5N 72 49 E
Tarāblus, *Bagd.* 17 F8 33 19N 44 21 E
Tarango, Presa, *Méx.* 29 B2 19 21N 99 12W
Tårbæk, *Købn.* 2 D10 55 46N 12 35 E
Tarchomin, *Wsaw.* 10 E6 52 19N 20 58 E
Tardeo, *Bomb.* 16 H7 18 57N 72 48 E
Target Rock, *N.Y.* 23 B8 40 55N 73 24W
Targówek, *Wsaw.* 10 E7 52 16N 21 3 E
Tårnby, *Købn.* 2 E10 55 37N 12 35 E

Villecresnes 47

Taronga Zoo. Park, Syd. 19 B4 33 50 S 151 14 E
Tarqua B., Lagos 18 B2 6 24N 7 23 E
Tarzana, L.A. 28 A1 34 10N 118 32W
Tåstrup, København 2 E8 55 39N 12 18 E
Tatarovo, Mos. 11 E8 55 45N 37 24 E
Tatarpur, Delhi 16 B1 28 38N 77 9 E
Tatenberg, Hbg. 7 E8 53 29N 10 3 E
Tathong Channel, H.K. 12 E6 22 15N 114 16 E
Tathong Pt., H.K. 12 E6 22 14N 114 17 E
Tatsfield, Lon. 4 D5 51 17N 0 1 E
Tattariharju, Hels. 3 B5 60 15N 25 2 E
Tatuapé, S. Pau. 31 E6 23 31 S 46 33W
Taufkirchen, Mün. 7 G10 48 2N 11 36 E
Tavares, I. dos, Rio J. 31 A3 22 49 S 43 6W
Tavernanova, Nápl. 9 H13 40 54N 14 21 E
Taverny, Paris 5 A3 49 1N 2 13 E
Távros, Ath. 8 J11 37 57N 23 43 E
Tavry, St-Pet. 11 B6 59 54N 30 40 E
Taylortown, N.Y. 22 B2 40 56N 74 23W
Tayninka, Mos. 11 D10 55 53N 37 45 E
Taytay, Manila 15 D4 14 34N 121 7 E
Tayuman, Manila 15 D4 14 31N 121 9 E
Teaneck, N.Y. 22 B4 40 52N 74 1W
Teatro Colón, B.A. 32 B4 34 36 S 58 23 E
Teban Gardens, Sing. 15 G7 1 19N 103 44 E
Tebet, Jak. 15 J10 6 14 S 106 50 E
Tecamachaleo, Méx. 29 B2 19 25N 99 14W
Techny, Chic. 26 A2 42 6N 87 48W
Teck Hock, Sing. 15 F8 1 21N 103 54 E
Tecoma, Melb. 19 F9 37 54 S 145 20 E
Teddington, Lon. 4 C2 51 25N 0 20W
Tegel, Berl. 7 A2 52 34N 13 16 E
Tegel, Flughafen, Berl. 7 A2 52 35N 13 15 E
Tegeler Fliess →, Berl. 7 A3 52 37N 13 21 E
Tegeler See, Berl. 7 A2 52 34N 13 15 E
Tegelort, Berl. 7 A2 52 34N 13 13 E
Tehar, Delhi 16 B1 28 37N 77 7 E
Tehrān, Tehr. 17 C5 35 41N 51 25 E
Tehrān Pars, Tehr. 17 C6 35 44N 51 32 E
Tei Tong Tsui, H.K. 12 E6 22 16N 114 17 E
Tejo →, Lisb. 8 F8 38 45N 9 3W
Tekstilyshchik, Mos. 11 E10 55 42N 37 41 E
Tela, Delhi 16 A2 28 43N 77 19 E
Telhal, Lisb. 8 F7 38 48N 9 18W
Telinipara, Calc. 16 D6 22 46N 88 23 E
Telok Blangah, Sing. 15 G7 1 17N 103 49 E
Teltow, Berl. 7 B2 52 23N 13 17 E
Teltow kanal, Berl. 7 B3 52 26N 13 29 E
Temescal, L., S.F. 27 A3 37 50N 122 13W
Temnikovo, Mos. 11 E12 55 43N 38 1 E
Tempelhof, Berl. 7 B3 52 27N 13 23 E
Tempelhof, Flughafen, Berl. 7 B3 52 28N 13 27 E
Temperley, B.A. 32 C4 34 46 S 58 22W
Temple City, L.A. 28 B4 34 6N 118 3W
Temple Hills Park, Wash. 25 E8 38 48N 76 56W
Templestowe, Melb. 19 E7 37 45 S 145 8 E
Templestowe Lower, Melb. 19 E7 37 45 S 145 6 E
Tenafly, N.Y. 22 B5 40 54N 73 58W
Tenantongo, Presa, Méx. 29 B2 19 28N 99 15W
Tengah →, Sing. 15 F7 1 23N 103 43 E
Tengeh, Sungei →, Sing. 15 F6 1 20N 103 39 E
Tennoji, Ōsaka 12 C4 34 39N 135 30 E
Tenochtitlán, Méx. 29 B3 19 26N 99 7W
Tepalcates, Méx. 29 B3 19 23N 99 3W
Tepe Saif, Tehr. 17 D4 35 36N 51 17 E
Tepepan, Méx. 29 C3 19 16N 99 9W
Teplyy Star, Mos. 11 F9 55 37N 37 30 E
Tepozteco, Parque Nac. del, Méx. 29 D3 19 3N 99 5W
Terrasse Vaudreuil, Mtrl. 20 B2 43 23N 73 59W
Terrazzano, Mil. 9 D5 45 32N 9 4 E
Terrugem, Lisb. 8 F7 38 41N 9 17W
Terusan Banjir, Jak. 15 H9 6 7 S 106 46 E
Terzigno, Nápl. 9 J13 40 48N 14 29 E
Tessancourt-sur-Aubette, Paris 5 A1 49 1N 1 55 E
Testona, Tori. 9 C3 44 59N 7 42 E
Tetelco, Méx. 29 C4 19 12N 98 57W
Tetreauville, Mtrl. 20 A4 43 35N 73 32W
Tetti Neirotti, Tori. 9 B2 45 3N 7 32 E
Tetuán, Mdrd. 8 B2 40 27N 3 42W
Teufelsberg, Berl. 7 B2 52 29N 13 14 E
Tévere →, Rome 9 F9 41 56N 12 27 E
Tewksbury, Bost. 21 B2 42 37N 71 12W
Texcoco, L. de, Méx. 29 B4 19 30N 89 58 E
Thalkirchen, Mün. 7 G10 48 6N 11 32 E
Thames Ditton, Lon. 4 C2 51 23N 0 20W
Thamesmead, Lon. 4 B5 51 30N 0 7 E
Thana Cr. →, Bomb. 16 G8 19 4N 72 54 E
The Basin, Melb. 19 F8 37 51 S 145 19 E
The Glen, Wash. 25 C6 39 2N 77 12W
The Loop, Chic. 26 B3 41 52N 87 37W
The Narrows, N.Y. 22 D4 40 37N 74 3W
The Ridge, Delhi 16 B2 28 37N 77 10 E
The White House, Wash. 25 D7 38 53N 77 1W
The Wilds, Jobg. 18 F9 26 10 S 28 2 E
Theseión, Ath. 8 J11 37 57N 23 43 E
Theydon Bois, Lon. 4 A5 51 40N 0 6 E
Thiais, Paris 5 C4 48 46N 2 23 E
Thieux, Paris 5 A6 49 0N 2 40 E
Thistletown, Trto. 20 D7 43 44N 79 34W
Thiverval-Grignon, Paris 5 B1 48 51N 1 55 E
Thomaston, N.Y. 23 C6 40 47N 73 43W
Thomastown, Melb. 19 E7 37 40 S 145 2 E
Thompson I., Bost. 21 D4 42 19N 70 59W
Thomson, Sing. 15 F8 1 20N 103 50 E
Thon Buri, Bangk. 15 B1 13 45N 100 29 E
Thong Hoe, Sing. 15 F7 1 25N 103 42 E
Thorigny-sur-Marne, Paris 5 B6 48 53N 2 41 E
Thornbury, Melb. 19 E7 37 44 S 145 1 E
Thorncliffe, Trto. 20 D8 43 42N 79 20W
Thornhill, Jobg. 18 E9 26 6 S 28 9 E
Thornhill, Trto. 20 D8 43 48N 79 25W
Thornton, Phil. 24 B1 39 54N 75 31W
Thornton Heath, Lon. 4 C4 51 23N 0 6W
Thorofare, Phil. 24 B3 39 50N 75 11W
Throgs Neck, N.Y. 23 C6 40 48N 73 49W
Tian Guan, Sing. 15 F7 1 21N 103 49 E
Tian'anmen, Beij. 14 B3 39 53N 116 21 E
Tiancun, Beij. 14 B2 39 54N 116 12 E
Tianjin, Tianj. 14 E5 39 7N 117 12 E
Tiantan Gongyuan, Beij. 14 B3 39 51N 116 22 E
Tiateloco, Méx. 29 B3 19 27N 99 8W
Tibidabo, Barc. 8 D5 41 25N 2 6 E
Tiburon, S.F. 27 A2 37 52N 122 27W
Tiburon Pen., S.F. 27 A2 37 53N 122 28W
Tiburtino, Rome 9 F10 41 53N 12 30 E
Ticomán, Méx. 29 A3 19 31N 99 8W
Tiefenbroich, Ruhr 6 C2 51 18N 6 49 E
Tiefersee, Berl. 7 B1 52 24N 13 5 E
Tiejiangyin, Beij. 14 C3 39 49N 116 23 E
Tientsin = Tianjin, Tianj. 14 E5 39 7N 117 12 E
Tiergarten, Berl. 7 A3 52 31N 13 20 E
Tietê →, S. Pau. 31 D7 23 28 S 46 24W
Tigery, Paris 5 D5 48 38N 2 30 E
Tigre, B.A. 32 A3 34 25 S 58 34W
Tigris →, Bagd. 17 F8 33 17N 44 23 E
Tijuca, Rio J. 31 B2 22 56 S 43 13W
Tijuca, L. de, Rio J. 31 B2 22 59 S 43 20W
Tijuca, Pico da, Rio J. 31 B2 22 56 S 43 15W
Tijucamar, Rio J. 31 C2 23 0 S 43 18W
Tijucas, Is., Rio J. 31 C2 23 1 S 43 17W
Tikkurila, Hels. 3 B5 60 17N 25 2 E
Tilanqiao, Shang. 14 J11 31 15N 121 29 E
Tilbury, Lon. 4 C7 51 27N 0 21 E
Timah, Bukit, Sing. 15 F7 1 21N 103 46 E
Timiryazev Park, Mos. 11 E9 55 49N 37 33 E
Ting Kau, H.K. 12 D5 22 22N 114 4 E
Tinley Cr. →, Chic. 26 D2 41 39N 87 45W
Tinley Creek Woods, Chic. 26 D2 41 38N 87 48W
Tinley Park, Chic. 26 D2 41 35N 87 46W
Tipas, Manila 15 D4 14 32N 121 4 E
Tirsa, El Qâ. 18 D5 29 57N 31 12 E
Tishrīyaa, Bagd. 17 F8 33 18N 44 24 E
Tit Cham Chau, H.K. 12 E6 22 15N 114 17 E
Titagarh, Calc. 16 D6 22 44N 88 22 E
Tivoli, København 2 D10 55 40N 12 35 E
Tizapán, Méx. 29 C2 19 19N 99 13W
Tlalnepantla, Méx. 29 A2 19 32N 99 11W
Tlalnepantla →, Méx. 29 A2 19 30N 99 18W
Tláloc, Cerro, Méx. 29 D3 19 7N 99 3W
Tlalpan, Méx. 29 C2 19 17N 99 10W
Tlalpitzáhuac, Méx. 29 C4 19 19N 98 56W
Tlaltenango, Méx. 29 B2 19 20N 99 17W
Tlaltenco, Méx. 29 C3 19 19N 99 0W
Tlaxcoaque, Méx. 29 B3 19 25N 99 8W
To Kwai Wan, H.K. 12 E6 22 18N 114 11 E
Toa Payoh, Sing. 15 F8 1 20N 103 50 E
Tobay Beach, N.Y. 23 D8 40 36N 73 26W
Točná, Pra. 10 C2 49 58N 14 25 E
Tocome →, Car. 30 D6 10 28N 66 49W
Toda, Tōkyō 13 A3 35 50N 139 40 E
Todamachī, Tōkyō 13 B2 35 48N 139 39 E
Todt Hill, N.Y. 22 D4 40 36N 74 6W
Toei, Khlong →, Bangk. 15 B2 13 43N 100 32 E
Togasaki, Tōkyō 13 B4 35 47N 139 51 E
Tōkagi, Tōkyō 13 B4 35 42N 139 55 E
Tōkaichiba, Tōkyō 13 C2 35 31N 139 30 E
Tokarevo, Mos. 11 F11 55 38N 37 54 E
Tokorozawa, Tōkyō 13 B1 35 47N 139 28 E
Tōkyō, Tōkyō 13 C3 35 43N 139 45 E
Tōkyō B., Tōkyō 13 C4 35 33N 139 53 E
Tōkyō-Haneda Int. Airport, Tōkyō 13 C3 35 33N 139 45 E
Tōkyō Harbour, Tōkyō 13 C3 35 38N 139 46 E
Tokyo Univ., Tōkyō 13 B3 35 42N 139 46 E
Tollygunge, Calc. 16 F6 22 29N 88 21 E
Tolly's Nala, Calc. 16 E6 22 33N 88 19 E
Tolworth, Lon. 4 C3 51 22N 0 17W
Tomang, Jak. 15 J9 6 10 S 106 47 E
Tomba di Nerone, Rome 9 F9 41 58N 12 26 E
Tomilino, Mos. 11 F11 55 39N 37 55 E
Tomioka, Tōkyō 13 D2 35 22N 139 37 E
Tonda, Ōsaka 12 B4 34 49N 135 35 E
Tondo, Manila 15 D3 14 36N 120 57 E
Tone-unga →, Tōkyō 13 A4 35 55N 139 56 E
Tonekollen, Oslo 2 C6 50 49N 11 0 E
Tong Kang, Sungei →, Sing. 15 F8 1 23N 103 53 E
Tonghui He →, Beij. 14 B3 39 53N 116 28 E
Tönisheide, Ruhr 6 C4 51 18N 7 3 E
Tonndorf, Hbg. 7 D8 53 35N 10 8 E
Toorak, Melb. 19 F7 37 50 S 145 1 E
Toot Hill, Lon. 4 A6 51 41N 0 11 E
Topilejo, Méx. 29 C3 19 12N 99 9W
Topkapi, Ist. 17 A2 41 1N 28 55 E
Topsfield, Bost. 21 B4 42 38N 70 57W
Tor di Quinto, Rome 9 F9 41 56N 12 27 E
Tor Pignattara, Rome 9 F10 41 52N 12 31 E
Tor Sapienza, Rome 9 F10 41 53N 12 35 E
Torcy, Paris 5 B5 48 51N 2 39 E
Torino, Tori. 9 B2 45 5N 7 39 E
Toro, B.A. 32 B1 34 30 S 58 50W
Toronto, Trto. 20 E9 43 39N 79 13W
Toronto, Univ. of, Trto. 20 E8 43 39N 79 23W
Toronto Harbour, Trto. 20 E8 43 38N 79 21W
Toronto I., Trto. 20 E8 43 37N 79 23W
Toronto Int. Airport, Trto. 20 D7 43 40N 79 38 E
Torre Annunziata, Nápl. 9 J13 40 45N 14 26 E
Torre Cervara, Rome 9 F10 41 55N 12 35 E
Torre del Greco, Nápl. 9 J13 40 47N 14 21 E
Torre Novo, Rome 9 F10 41 51N 12 36 E
Torrellas →, Barc. 8 D5 41 23N 2 1 E
Torrellas del Llobregat, Barc. 8 D4 41 20N 1 59 E
Torresdale, Phil. 24 A5 40 3N 74 59W
Torrevécchia, Rome 9 F9 41 55N 12 25 E
Tortuguitas, B.A. 32 A2 34 28 S 58 44W
Toshima-Ku, Tōkyō 13 B3 35 43N 139 43 E
Toshimaen, Tōkyō 13 B2 35 43N 139 38 E
Totowa, N.Y. 22 B3 40 54N 74 13W
Totsuka-Ku, Tōkyō 13 D2 35 23N 139 32 E
Tottenham, Lon. 4 B4 51 35N 0 4W
Tottenham, Melb. 19 E6 37 48 S 144 51 E
Tottenville, N.Y. 22 D3 40 30N 74 14W
Totteridge, Lon. 4 B3 51 37N 0 11W
Toussus-le-Noble, Paris 5 C2 48 44N 2 6 E
Toussus-le-Noble, Aérodrome de, Paris 5 C2 48 44N 2 6 E
Toverud, Oslo 2 B2 59 55N 10 20 E
Towaco, N.Y. 22 B3 40 55N 74 18W
Tower Hamlets, Lon. 4 B4 51 31N 0 2W
Town Farm Hill, Bost. 21 A3 42 40N 71 3W
Townley, N.Y. 22 C3 40 41N 74 14W
Towra Pt., Syd. 19 C4 34 0 S 151 10 E
Towson, Balt. 25 A3 39 24N 76 36W
Tøyen, Oslo 2 B4 59 55N 10 47 E
Toyofuta, Tōkyō 13 A4 35 54N 139 55 E
Toyonaka, Ōsaka 12 B3 34 46N 135 28 E
Traar, Ruhr 6 B1 51 22N 6 36 E
Trafaria, Lisb. 8 F7 38 40N 9 13W
Tragliata, Rome 9 F8 41 58N 12 14 E
Traicão →, S. Pau. 31 E6 23 35 S 46 41W
Trälhavet, Stock. 3 D13 59 26N 18 22 E
Tranby, Oslo 2 C1 59 49N 10 14 E
Tranegilde, København 2 E9 55 37N 12 20 E
Trångsund, Stock. 3 E11 59 13N 18 8 E
Trappenfelde, Berl. 7 A4 52 34N 13 39 E
Trappes, Paris 5 C1 48 46N 1 59 E
Trastévere, Rome 9 F9 51 53N 12 28 E
Travilah, Wash. 25 C6 39 4N 77 15W
Travilah Regional Park, Wash. 25 C6 39 4N 77 17W
Travis, N.Y. 22 D3 40 35N 74 11W
Treasure I., S.F. 27 B2 37 49N 122 22W
Třeboradice, Pra. 10 B3 50 9N 14 31 E
Třebotov, Pra. 10 C1 49 58N 14 17 E
Trecase, Nápl. 9 J13 40 46N 14 26 E
Trekroner, København 2 D10 55 42N 12 36 E
Tremblay-lès-Gonesse, Paris 5 B5 48 58N 2 30 E
Tremembé, S. Pau. 31 D6 23 27 S 46 36W
Tremembe →, S. Pau. 31 D6 23 27 S 46 34W
Tremont, Melb. 19 F9 37 53 S 145 20 E
Tremont, N.Y. 23 B5 40 50N 73 52W
Trenno, Mil. 9 E5 45 29N 9 6 E
Treptow, Berl. 7 B3 52 29N 13 27 E
Tres Marias, Méx. 29 D2 19 3N 99 15W
Trés Rios, Sa. dos, Rio J. 31 B2 22 56 S 43 17W
Tretiakov Art Gallery, Mos. 11 E9 55 44N 37 38 E
Trevose, Phil. 24 A5 40 8N 74 59W
Trezzano sul Navíglio, Mil. 9 E5 45 24N 9 4 E
Tribobo, Rio J. 31 B3 22 50 S 43 0W
Triel-sur-Seine, Paris 5 B2 48 58N 2 0 E
Trieste, Rome 9 F10 41 55N 12 30 E
Trinidad, Wash. 25 D8 38 54N 76 59W
Triome, Jobg. 18 F8 26 10 S 27 58 E
Trionfale, Rome 9 F9 41 54N 12 26 E
Triulzo, Mil. 9 E6 45 25N 9 16 E
Trócchia, Nápl. 9 H13 40 51N 14 23 E
Troitse-Lykovo, Mos. 11 E8 55 47N 37 23 E
Troja, Pra. 10 B2 50 7N 14 25 E
Trollbäcken, Stock. 3 E12 59 14N 18 12 E
Trombay, Bomb. 16 G8 19 2N 72 56 E
Troparevo, Mos. 11 F8 55 39N 37 29 E
Trottiscliffe, Lon. 4 D7 51 18N 0 21 E
Troy Hills, N.Y. 22 B2 40 50N 74 23W
Troyeville, Jobg. 18 F9 26 11 S 28 4 E
Truc di Miola, Tori. 9 A2 45 11N 7 30 E
Trudyashchikhsya, Os., St-Pet. 11 B3 59 58N 30 18 E
Trutlandet, Hels. 3 C6 60 9N 25 17 E
Tryvasshøgda, Oslo 2 B4 59 59N 10 40 E
Tseng Lan Shue, H.K. 12 D6 22 20N 114 14 E
Tsentralynyy, Mos. 11 D11 55 53N 37 51 E
Tsim Sha Tsui, H.K. 12 E6 22 17N 114 10 E
Tsing Yi, H.K. 12 D5 22 21N 114 6 E
Tsuen Wan, H.K. 12 D5 22 22N 114 7 E
Tsurugamine, Tōkyō 13 D2 35 28N 139 33 E
Tsuruma, Tōkyō 13 A2 35 52N 139 31 E
Tsurumi →, Tōkyō 13 C3 35 32N 139 40 E
Tsurumi-Ku, Tōkyō 13 D3 35 30N 139 41 E
Tsz Wan Shan, H.K. 12 D6 22 20N 114 11 E
Tua Kang Lye, Sing. 15 G7 1 18N 103 46 E
Tuas, Sing. 15 G6 1 19N 103 39 E
Tuchoměřice, Pra. 10 B1 50 7N 14 16 E
Tuckahoe, N.Y. 23 B6 40 56N 73 49W
Tucuruvi, S. Pau. 31 D6 23 28 S 46 35W
Tufello, Rome 9 F10 41 56N 12 32 E
Tufnell Park, Lon. 4 B4 51 33N 0 8W
Tujunga, L.A. 28 A3 34 15N 118 16W
Tujunga Wash →, L.A. 28 A2 34 12N 118 23W
Tullamarine, Melb. 19 E6 37 41 S 144 50 E
Tullinge, Stock. 3 E10 59 12N 17 54 E
Tullingesjön, Stock. 3 E10 59 12N 17 52 E
Tulse Hill, Lon. 4 C4 51 26N 0 6W
Tulyehualco, Méx. 29 C3 19 15N 99 0W
Tumba, Stock. 3 E9 59 12N 17 49 E
Tune, København 2 E8 55 35N 12 10 E
Tung Lo Wan, H.K. 12 E6 22 17N 114 11 E
Tung Lung I., H.K. 12 E6 22 15N 114 17 E
Tung O, H.K. 12 E5 22 11N 114 8 E
Tunis, Bagd. 17 E8 33 23N 44 21 E
Tuomarila, Hels. 3 B3 60 11N 24 41 E
Tura, El Qâ. 18 D5 29 55N 31 16 E
Turambhe, Bomb. 16 G9 19 4N 73 0 E
Turdera, B.A. 32 C4 34 48 S 58 26W
Tureberg, Stock. 3 D10 59 25N 17 55 E
Turffontein, Jobg. 18 F9 26 14 S 28 2 E
Turin = Torino, Tori. 9 B2 45 5N 7 39 E
Turner, Balt. 25 B3 39 14N 76 31W
Turner Hill, Bost. 21 A4 42 40N 70 53W
Turnersville, Phil. 24 C4 39 46N 75 3W
Turnham Green, Lon. 4 C3 51 29N 0 16W
Turów, Wsaw. 10 E8 52 19N 21 11 E
Turter, Oslo 2 A4 60 0N 10 46 E
Tuscolano, Rome 9 F10 41 52N 12 31 E
Tushino, Mos. 11 D8 55 50N 37 24 E
Tuusulanjoki →, Hels. 3 A4 60 20N 24 54 E
Twickenham, Lon. 4 C2 51 26N 0 20W
Twickenham Rugby Ground, Lon. 4 C2 51 27N 0 20W
Twin Oaks, Phil. 24 B2 39 50N 75 25W
Twórki, Wsaw. 10 E5 52 10N 20 49 E
Tyresö, Stock. 3 E13 59 14N 18 20 E
Tyresö strand, Stock. 3 E12 59 15N 18 17 E

U

Uberaba →, S. Pau. 31 E6 23 35 S 46 41W
Uberruhr, Ruhr 6 B4 51 25N 7 4 E
Ubin, P., Sing. 15 F8 1 24N 103 57 E
Uboldo, Mil. 9 D5 45 36N 9 0 E
Uckendorf, Ruhr 6 B4 51 29N 7 7 E
Udelnaya, St-Pet. 11 A4 60 0N 30 21 E
Udelynaya, Mos. 11 F11 55 38N 37 59 E
Udlding, Mün. 7 F9 48 15N 11 25 E
Uellendahl, Ruhr 6 C5 51 16N 7 10 E
Ueno, Tōkyō 13 B3 35 42N 139 46 E
Uerdingen, Ruhr 6 B1 51 21N 6 38 E
Uhlenhorst, Hbg. 7 D8 53 34N 10 1 E
Úholičky, Pra. 10 B1 50 9N 14 19 E
Uhříněves, Pra. 10 B3 50 2N 14 35 E
Újezd nad Lesy, Pra. 10 B3 50 4N 14 39 E
Újpalota, Bud. 10 J13 47 32N 19 8 E
Újpest, Bud. 10 J13 47 35N 19 4 E
Ukita, Tōkyō 13 B4 35 40N 139 51 E
Ullerup, København 2 E10 55 34N 12 36 E
Ullevål, Oslo 2 B4 59 56N 10 46 E
Üllo, Bud. 10 K14 47 23N 19 20 E
Ulriksdal, Stock. 3 D10 59 23N 17 59 E
Ulu Bedok, Sing. 15 G8 1 19N 103 55 E
Ulu Pandan →, Sing. 15 G7 1 19N 103 45 E
Ulyanka, St-Pet. 11 B3 59 50N 30 14 E
Um Al-Khanazir, Bagd. 17 F8 33 17N 44 22 E
Umeda, Ōsaka 12 B3 34 41N 135 29 E
Umejima, Tōkyō 13 B3 35 46N 139 48 E
Umraniye, Ist. 17 A3 41 1N 29 4 E
Unětický →, Pra. 10 B2 50 9N 14 24 E
Ungelsheim, Ruhr 6 B2 51 21N 6 43 E
Unhos, Lisb. 8 F8 38 49N 9 7W
Unidad Santa Fe, Méx. 29 B2 19 23N 99 13W
Union, N.Y. 22 C3 40 42N 74 16W
Union City, N.Y. 22 C4 40 45N 74 2W
Union City, S.F. 27 C4 37 36N 122 2W
Union Port, N.Y. 23 C5 40 48N 73 51W
Uniondale, N.Y. 23 C7 40 42N 73 35W
United Nations H.Q., N.Y. 22 C5 40 45N 73 59W
Universal City, L.A. 28 B2 34 8N 118 21W
Universidad de Chila, Stgo 30 J11 33 26 S 70 39W
University Gardens, N.Y. 23 C6 40 46N 73 42W
University Heights, S.F. 27 D3 37 26N 122 13W
University Park, Wash. 25 D8 38 58N 76 56W
Unsani, Calc. 16 E5 22 35N 88 15 E
Unterbach, Ruhr 6 C3 51 12N 6 53 E
Unterbiberg, Mün. 7 G10 48 6N 11 38 E
Unterföhring, Mün. 7 F11 48 11N 11 38 E
Unterhaching, Mün. 7 G10 48 3N 11 37 E
Unterkirchbach, Wien 10 G9 48 17N 16 12 E
Unterlaa, Wien 10 H10 48 8N 16 24 E
Untermauerbach, Wien 10 G9 48 14N 16 11 E
Untermenzing, Mün. 7 F9 48 10N 11 28 E
Unterrath, Ruhr 6 C2 51 16N 6 45 E
Unterschleissheim, Mün. 7 F10 48 16N 11 35 E
Upminster, Lon. 4 B6 51 33N 0 14 E
Upper Brookville, N.Y. 23 B7 40 50N 73 35W
Upper Crystal Springs Res., S.F. 26 D2 37 28N 122 20W
Upper Darby, Phil. 24 B3 39 57N 75 16W
Upper Edmonton, Lon. 4 B4 51 36N 0 3W
Upper Elmers End, Lon. 4 C4 51 23N 0 1W
Upper Fern Tree Gully, Melb. 19 F8 37 53 S 145 18 E
Upper New York B., N.Y. 22 D4 40 39N 74 3W
Upper Norwood, Lon. 4 C4 51 24N 0 6W
Upper Peirce Res., Sing. 15 F7 1 22N 103 47 E
Upper San Leandro Res., S.F. 27 B4 37 46N 122 6W
Upper Sydenham, Lon. 4 C4 51 26N 0 4W
Upper Tooting, Lon. 4 C4 51 25N 0 9W
Upton, Lon. 4 B5 51 32N 0 1 E
Uptons Hill, Bost. 21 B3 42 33N 71 0W
Uptown, Chic. 26 B2 41 58N 87 40W
Upwey, Melb. 19 F9 37 53 S 145 20 E
Urawa, Tōkyō 13 A2 35 51N 139 39 E
Urayasu, Tōkyō 13 C4 35 39N 139 53 E
Urbe, Aeroporto d', Rome 9 F10 41 57N 12 30 E
Urca, Rio J. 31 B3 22 56 S 43 9W
Uritsk, St-Pet. 11 C3 59 49N 30 10 E
Üröm, Bud. 10 J13 47 35N 19 1 E
Ursus, Wsaw. 10 E6 52 11N 20 52 E
Ursvik, Stock. 3 D10 59 23N 17 57 E
Usera, Mdrd. 8 B2 40 22N 3 42W
Ushigome, Tōkyō 13 B3 35 42N 139 44 E
Usküdar, Ist. 17 A3 41 1N 29 0 E
Ust-Slavyanka, St-Pet. 11 C5 59 51N 30 32 E
Uteke, Stock. 3 D12 59 24N 18 15 E
Utfort, Ruhr 6 B1 51 28N 6 37 E
Utinga, S. Pau. 31 E6 23 38 S 46 31W
Utrata, Wsaw. 10 E7 52 15N 21 4 E
Uttarpara, Calc. 16 E5 22 39N 88 21 E
Utterslev Mose, København 2 D9 55 42N 12 29 E
Uttran, Stock. 3 E9 59 12N 17 43 E
Utvika, Oslo 2 A1 60 2N 10 15 E
Uxbridge, Lon. 4 B2 51 32N 0 28W
Uzkoye, Mos. 11 F9 55 37N 37 32 E
Uzunca →, Ist. 17 A1 41 54N 28 50 E

V

Vadaul, Bomb. 16 G8 19 2N 72 55 E
Værebro Å →, København 2 D8 55 47N 12 7 E
Vahal, Bomb. 16 H9 18 58N 73 2 E
Vaires-sur-Marne, Paris 5 B5 48 52N 2 38 E
Val della Torre, Tori. 9 B1 45 8N 7 27 E
Valby, København 2 E9 55 39N 12 29 E
Valcannuta, Rome 9 F9 41 52N 12 25 E
Valdeveba, Mdrd. 8 B3 40 29N 3 39W
Vale, Wash. 25 D5 38 55N 77 20W
Valentino, Parco del, Tori. 9 B3 45 3N 7 41 E
Valenton, Paris 5 C4 48 44N 2 27 E
Valera, Mil. 9 D5 45 33N 9 3 E
Vallcarca, Barc. 8 D5 41 25N 2 9 E
Valldoreix, Barc. 8 D5 41 27N 2 3 E
Vallecas, Mdrd. 8 B3 40 22N 3 37W
Vallemar, S.F. 27 C2 37 36N 122 28W
Vallensbæk, København 2 E9 55 38N 12 21 E
Vallensbæk Strand, København 2 E9 55 36N 12 23 E
Vallentunasjön, Stock. 3 D11 59 27N 18 1 E
Valleranello, Rome 9 G9 41 46N 12 29 E
Valley Forge, Phil. 24 A2 40 5N 75 27W
Valley Forge Hist. State Park, Phil. 24 A2 40 5N 75 27W
Valley Mede, Balt. 25 B1 39 16N 76 50W
Valley Stream, N.Y. 23 C6 40 40N 73 43W
Vällingby, Stock. 3 D10 59 21N 17 52 E
Vallisaari, Hels. 3 C5 60 7N 25 0 E
Vallvidrera, Barc. 8 D5 41 24N 2 6 E
Valo Velho, S. Pau. 31 E5 23 38 S 46 47W
Valuyevo, Mos. 11 F8 55 30N 37 21 E
Valvidrera →, Barc. 8 D5 41 25N 2 0 E
Van Dyks Park, Jobg. 18 F10 26 15 S 28 18 E
Van Nuys, L.A. 28 A2 34 11N 118 27W
Van Nuys Airport, L.A. 28 A2 34 12N 118 29W
Van Ryn Dam, Jobg. 18 E11 26 8 S 28 21 E
Vanak, Tehr. 17 C5 35 45N 51 23 E
Vangede, København 2 D10 55 45N 12 30 E
Vaniköy, Ist. 17 A3 41 3N 29 3 E
Vanløse, København 2 D9 55 41N 12 28 E
Vantaa, Hels. 3 B4 60 18N 24 56 E
Vantaa →, Hels. 3 B4 60 13N 24 53 E
Vantaankoski, Hels. 3 B4 60 18N 24 50 E
Vantör, Stock. 3 E11 59 16N 18 2 E
Vanves, Paris 5 C3 48 49N 2 17 E
Vanzago, Mil. 9 D4 45 31N 8 59 E
Värby, Stock. 3 E10 59 15N 17 52 E
Vardåsen, Oslo 2 C6 50 48N 11 6 E
Varedo, Mil. 9 D5 45 35N 9 8 E
Varennes-Jarcy, Paris 5 C5 48 40N 2 33 E
Vargem Grande, Rio J. 31 B1 22 58 S 43 27W
Városliget, Bud. 10 J13 47 30N 19 5 E
Vartiokylä, Hels. 3 B5 60 13N 25 6 E
Vartiosaari, Hels. 3 B5 60 11N 25 5 E
Vasby, København 2 D8 55 40N 12 12 E
Vashi, Bomb. 16 G8 19 4N 72 59 E
Vasilyevskiy, Os., St-Pet. 11 B3 59 55N 30 16 E
Västerkulla, Hels. 3 B2 60 16N 24 31 E
Västerskog, Hels. 3 B6 60 16N 25 17 E
Vasto, Nápl. 9 H12 40 51N 14 16 E
Vatutino, Mos. 11 D10 55 52N 37 40 E
Vaucresson, Paris 5 B2 48 50N 2 9 E
Vaudreuil, Mtrl. 20 B1 43 24N 74 1W
Vaudreuil-sur-le Lac, Mtrl. 20 B1 43 25N 74 1W
Vauhallan, Paris 5 C3 48 44N 2 12 E
Vaujours, Paris 5 B5 48 56N 2 34 E
Vauréal, Paris 5 A2 49 2N 2 1 E
Vaux-sur-Seine, Paris 5 A1 49 0N 1 57 E
Vauxhall, Lon. 4 C4 51 29N 0 7W
Vaxholm, Stock. 3 D13 59 24N 18 20 E
Vecklax, Hels. 3 B2 60 10N 24 31 E
Vecsés, Bud. 10 K14 47 24N 19 16 E
Vedano al Lissone, Mil. 9 D6 45 36N 9 16 E
Veddel, Hbg. 7 D8 53 31N 10 2 E
Vega, Stock. 3 E11 59 11N 18 8 E
Vehkalahti, Hels. 3 B2 60 11N 24 30 E
Veikkola, Hels. 3 B1 60 17N 24 26 E
Velbert, Ruhr 6 B4 51 21N 7 1 E
Veleň, Pra. 10 A3 50 10N 14 33 E
Veleslavin, Pra. 10 B2 50 5N 14 21 E
Vélizy-Villacoublay, Paris 5 C3 48 47N 2 11 E
Velka-Chuchle, Pra. 10 B2 50 0N 14 23 E
Venaria, Tori. 9 B2 45 8N 7 37 E
Venda Seca, Lisb. 8 F7 38 46N 9 15W
Vendelsö, Stock. 3 E12 59 12N 18 11 E
Venice, L.A. 28 C2 33 59N 118 27W
Venner, Oslo 2 A3 60 1N 10 36 E
Vennhausen, Ruhr 6 C3 51 13N 6 51 E
Ventas, Mdrd. 8 B2 40 26N 3 40W
Ventorro del Cano, Mdrd. 8 B2 40 23N 3 49W
Verberg, Ruhr 6 B1 51 21N 6 34 E
Verde →, S. Pau. 31 E7 23 29 S 46 27W
Verdi, Ath. 8 H11 38 2N 23 40 E
Verdugo Mt., L.A. 28 A3 34 12N 118 17W
Verdun, Mtrl. 20 B4 43 27N 73 35W
Vereya, Mos. 11 F12 55 37N 38 2 E
Vérhalom, Bud. 10 J13 47 31N 19 1 E
Vermelho →, S. Pau. 31 E5 23 30 S 46 46W
Vermont, Melb. 19 F8 37 50 S 145 12 E
Vermont South, Melb. 19 F8 37 51 S 145 11 E
Verneuil-sur-Seine, Paris 5 B1 48 58N 1 59 E
Vernouillet, Paris 5 B1 48 58N 1 56 E
Verona, N.Y. 22 C3 40 49N 74 15W
Verperluda, Os., St-Pet. 11 B2 59 59N 30 0 E
Verrières-le-Buisson, Paris 5 C3 48 44N 2 16 E
Versailles, B.A. 32 B3 34 38 S 58 31W
Versailles, Paris 5 C2 48 48N 2 7 E
Veshnyaki, Mos. 11 E10 55 43N 37 48 E
Vesolyy Posolok, St-Pet. 11 B4 59 53N 30 28 E
Vestli, Oslo 2 B5 59 58N 10 55 E
Vestra, Hels. 3 B3 60 19N 24 46 E
Vestskoven, København 2 D9 55 41N 12 23 E
Vesuvio, Nápl. 9 J13 40 49N 14 25 E
Vets Stadium, Phil. 24 B3 39 54N 75 10W
Viby, København 2 E7 55 33N 12 1 E
Vicálvaro, Mdrd. 8 B3 40 24N 3 36W
Vicente Lopez, B.A. 32 B4 34 31 S 58 30W
Victoria, B.A. 32 A3 34 27 S 58 32W
Victoria, H.K. 12 E6 22 17N 114 11 E
Victoria, Pont, Mtrl. 20 B4 43 29N 73 32W
Victoria Gardens, Bomb. 16 H8 18 58N 72 50 E
Victoria Harbour, H.K. 12 E5 22 17N 114 10 E
Victoria Island, Lagos 18 B2 6 25N 7 25 E
Victoria L., Jobg. 18 F9 26 13 S 28 9 E
Victoria Lawn Tennis Courts, Melb. 19 F7 37 50 S 145 1 E
Victoria Park, H.K. 12 E5 22 16N 114 8 E
Vidja, Stock. 3 E11 59 12N 18 4 E
Vidrholec, Pra. 10 B3 50 5N 14 39 E
Vienna = Wien, Wien 10 G10 48 12N 16 22 E
Vienna, Wash. 25 D6 38 54N 77 16W
Vieringhausen, Ruhr 6 C4 51 10N 7 9 E
Vierlinden, Ruhr 6 A2 51 32N 6 45 E
Vierumäki, Hels. 3 A5 60 21N 25 2 E
Vierzigstücken, Hbg. 7 D6 53 30N 9 49 E
View Bank, Melb. 19 E7 37 43 S 145 6 E
Vigário Geral, Rio J. 31 A2 22 48 S 43 18W
Vigentino, Mil. 9 E6 45 26N 9 13 E
Viggbyholm, Stock. 3 D11 59 26N 18 7 E
Vighignolo, Mil. 9 E5 45 29N 9 2 E
Vigneux-sur-Seine, Paris 5 C4 48 42N 2 24 E
Viikki, Hels. 3 B5 60 13N 25 1 E
Viirilä, Hels. 3 B5 60 19N 25 8 E
Vila Andrade, S. Pau. 31 E5 23 37 S 46 44W
Vila Barcelona, S. Pau. 31 E6 23 37 S 46 33W
Vila Bocaina, S. Pau. 31 F7 23 40 S 46 26W
Vila Dalva, S. Pau. 31 E5 23 34 S 46 46W
Vila Dirce, S. Pau. 31 E4 23 33 S 46 50W
Vila Eldorado, S. Pau. 31 F6 23 42 S 46 38W
Vila Ema, S. Pau. 31 E6 23 35 S 46 31W
Vila Formosa, S. Pau. 31 E6 23 36 S 46 44W
Vila Galvão, S. Pau. 31 D6 23 27 S 46 34W
Vila Gonçales, S. Pau. 31 F6 23 42 S 46 33W
Vila Iasi, S. Pau. 31 E5 23 37 S 46 47W
Vila Indiana, S. Pau. 31 E5 23 37 S 46 48W
Vila Isabel, Rio J. 31 B2 22 54 S 43 15W
Vila Madalena, S. Pau. 31 E5 23 32 S 46 41W
Vila Maria, S. Pau. 31 E6 23 31 S 46 36W
Vila Mariana, S. Pau. 31 E6 23 34 S 46 36W
Vila Matilde, S. Pau. 31 E6 23 31 S 46 30W
Vila Nova Curuçá, S. Pau. 31 E7 23 31 S 46 25W
Vila Pires, S. Pau. 31 F6 23 41 S 46 30W
Vila Progresso, Rio J. 31 B3 22 53 S 43 1W
Vila Prudente, S. Pau. 31 E6 23 35 S 46 33W
Vila Ré, S. Pau. 31 E7 23 31 S 46 29W
Vila Remo, S. Pau. 31 F5 23 40 S 46 45W
Vila Sonia, S. Pau. 31 E5 23 35 S 46 43W
Viladecans, Barc. 8 E5 41 18N 2 1 E
Villa Ada, Rome 9 F10 41 55N 12 30 E
Villa Adelina, B.A. 32 B3 34 31 S 58 33W
Villa Alianza, B.A. 32 B3 34 37 S 58 33W
Villa Alsina, B.A. 32 C4 34 40 S 58 24W
Villa Altube, B.A. 32 B2 34 31 S 58 45W
Villa Ariza, B.A. 32 B3 34 38 S 58 39W
Villa Augusta, B.A. 32 C5 34 45 S 58 15W
Villa Ballester, B.A. 32 B3 34 33 S 58 33W
Villa Barilari, B.A. 32 C4 34 42 S 58 20W
Villa Basso, B.A. 32 B3 34 38 S 58 36W
Villa Bosch, B.A. 32 B3 34 35 S 58 33W
Villa C. Colon, B.A. 32 C4 34 41 S 58 21W
Villa D. F. Sarmiento, B.A. 32 B3 34 38 S 58 35W
Villa D. Sobral, B.A. 32 C5 34 45 S 58 15W
Villa de Guadalupe, Méx. 29 B3 19 29N 99 6W
Villa de Mayo, B.A. 32 B2 34 30 S 58 40W
Villa Devoto, B.A. 32 B3 34 36 S 58 31W
Villa Dominico, B.A. 32 C5 34 41 S 58 19W
Villa Giambruno, B.A. 32 C5 34 48 S 58 15W
Villa Gustavo A. Madero, Méx. 29 B3 19 29N 99 8W
Villa Hogar Alemán, B.A. 32 C4 34 49 S 58 26W
Villa Iglesias, B.A. 32 B2 34 30 S 58 45W
Villa Leloir, B.A. 32 B2 34 36 S 58 41W
Villa Leon, B.A. 32 B2 34 38 S 58 41W
Villa Lugano, B.A. 32 C4 34 41 S 58 27W
Villa Luzuriago, B.A. 32 C3 34 40 S 58 34W
Villa Lynch, B.A. 32 B3 34 35 S 58 31W
Villa Madero, B.A. 32 C3 34 41 S 58 30W
Villa Maria del Triunfo, Lima 30 G9 12 9 S 76 57W
Villa Obregon, Méx. 29 B2 19 20N 99 12W
Villa Reichembach, B.A. 32 B2 34 39 S 58 40W
Villa Rosa, B.A. 32 A1 34 25 S 58 5W
Villa San Francisco, B.A. 32 C5 34 46 S 58 15W
Villacoublay, Aérodrome de, Paris 5 C3 48 46N 2 12 E
Village Green, Phil. 24 B2 39 52N 75 26W
Villanova, Phil. 24 A2 40 1N 75 20W
Villarbasse, Tori. 9 B1 45 2N 7 27 E
Villaretto, Tori. 9 B3 45 8N 7 41 E
Villaricca, Nápl. 9 H12 40 55N 14 11 E
Villaroche, Paris 5 D5 48 37N 2 39 E
Villaroy, Paris 5 C2 48 46N 2 5 E
Villasanta, Mil. 9 D6 45 36N 9 18 E
Villastanza, Mil. 9 D4 45 32N 8 57 E
Villaverde, Mdrd. 8 B2 40 21N 3 42W
Villaverde Bajo, Mdrd. 8 B2 40 20N 3 40W
Villawood, Syd. 19 B2 33 52 S 150 58 E
Ville-d'Avray, Paris 5 C3 48 49N 2 11 E
Ville de Laval, Mtrl. 20 A3 43 34N 73 43W
Villebon-sur-Yvette, Paris 5 C3 48 41N 2 14 E
Villecresnes, Paris 5 C5 48 43N 2 31 E

48 Villejuif

Villejuif, *Paris* 5 C4 48 47N 2 21 E
Villejust, *Paris* 5 C3 48 41N 2 15 E
Villemoisson-sur-Orge, *Paris* 5 C3 48 40N 2 19 E
Villemomble, *Paris* 5 B5 48 52N 2 30 E
Villeneuve-la-Garenne, *Paris* 5 B3 48 56N 2 19 E
Villeneuve-le-Roi, *Paris* 5 C4 48 43N 2 24 E
Villeneuve-St.-Georges, *Paris* 5 C4 48 43N 2 27 E
Villeneuve-sous-Dammartin, *Paris* 5 A5 49 2N 2 38 E
Villennes-sur-Seine, *Paris* 5 B1 48 56N 2 0 E
Villeparisis, *Paris* 5 B5 48 56N 2 36 E
Villepinte, *Paris* 5 B5 48 57N 2 30 E
Villepreux, *Paris* 5 C1 48 49N 1 59 E
Villevaudé, *Paris* 5 B5 48 55N 2 39 E
Villeziers, *Paris* 5 C3 48 40N 2 10 E
Villiers-le-Bâcle, *Paris* 5 C2 48 44N 2 8 E
Villiers-le-Bel, *Paris* 5 A4 49 0N 2 23 E
Villiers-St. Frédéric, *Paris* 5 C1 48 49N 1 53 E
Villiers-sur-Marne, *Paris* 5 C5 48 49N 2 32 E
Villiers-sur-Orge, *Paris* 5 D3 48 39N 2 18 E
Villinki, *Hels.* 3 C5 60 9N 25 6 E
Villoresi, Canale, *Mil.* 9 D4 45 33N 8 59 E
Vimodrone, *Mil.* 9 D6 45 30N 9 16 E
Vimont, *Mtrl.* 20 A3 43 36N 73 43W
Vincennes, *Paris* 5 B4 48 51N 2 26 E
Vincennes, Bois de, *Paris* 5 C4 48 49N 2 26 E
Vinohrady, *Pra.* 10 B2 50 4N 14 26 E
Vinoř, *Pra.* 10 B3 50 8N 14 34 E
Vinořský →, *Pra.* 10 A3 50 11N 14 39 E
Violet Hill, *H.K.* 12 E6 22 15N 114 11 E
Virányos, *Bud.* 10 J12 47 31N 18 59 E
Virgeo del San Cristóbal, *Stgo* 30 J11 33 25 S 70 38W
Viroflay, *Paris* 5 C3 48 48N 2 10 E
Viron, *Ath.* 8 J11 37 55N 23 46 E
Virreyes, *B.A.* 32 A3 34 27 S 58 33W
Virum, *Købn.* 2 D9 55 47N 12 27 E
Viry-Châtillon, *Paris* 5 C4 48 40N 2 21 E
Vishnyaki, *Mos.* 11 E11 55 46N 37 53 E
Visitacion Valley, *S.F.* 27 B2 37 42N 122 23W
Vista Alegre, *Lima* 30 G9 12 8 S 76 59W
Vista Alegre, *Stgo* 30 K10 33 30 S 70 43W
Vitacura, *Stgo* 30 J11 33 23 S 70 35W
Vitarte-Ate, *Lima* 30 G9 12 3 S 76 57W
Vitinia, *Rome* 9 G9 41 47N 12 24 E
Vitry-sur-Seine, *Paris* 5 C4 48 47N 2 23 E
Vitträsk, *Hels.* 3 B1 60 11N 24 29 E
Vittuone, *Mil.* 9 E4 45 28N 8 57 E
Vladykino, *Mos.* 11 D9 55 51N 37 35 E
Vltava →, *Pra.* 10 A2 50 10N 14 2 E
Vnukovo, *Mos.* 11 F7 55 37N 37 17 E
Voerde, *Ruhr* 6 C6 51 18N 7 23 E
Voerde, *Ruhr* 6 A2 51 35N 6 42 E
Vogelheim, *Ruhr* 6 B3 51 29N 6 59 E
Vohwinkel, *Ruhr* 6 C4 51 13N 7 4 E
Voisins-le-Bretonneux, *Paris* 5 C2 48 45N 2 3 E
Vokovice, *Pra.* 10 B2 50 5N 14 21 E
Volgelsdorf, *Berl.* 7 B5 52 30N 13 44 E
Volkhonka-Zil, *Mos.* 11 F9 55 39N 37 37 E
Volkovka →, *St-Pet.* 11 B4 59 54N 30 25 E
Volksdorf, *Hbg.* 7 D8 53 39N 10 8 E
Volla, *Nápl.* 9 H13 40 52N 14 20 E
Vollen, *Oslo* 2 C2 59 48N 10 27 E
Volmarstein, *Ruhr* 6 B6 51 22N 7 22 E
Volodarskoye, *St-Pet.* 11 B4 59 54N 30 23 E
Volpiano, *Tori.* 9 A3 45 12N 7 46 E
Volynkina-Derevnya, *St-Pet.* 11 B3 59 53N 30 18 E
Volynyy, Os., *St-Pet.* 11 B3 59 57N 30 14 E
Vōmero, *Nápl.* 9 H12 40 50N 14 13 E
Vorderhainbach, *Wien* 10 G9 48 13N 16 12 E
Vorhalle, *Ruhr* 6 B6 51 23N 7 26 E
Vormholz, *Ruhr* 6 B5 51 24N 7 19 E
Vösendorf, *Wien* 10 H10 48 7N 16 20 E
Vostochnyy, *Mos.* 11 E11 55 49N 37 51 E
Vouliagmeni, *Ath.* 8 K11 37 50N 23 46 E
Vrčovice, *Pra.* 10 B2 50 4N 14 28 E
Vsevolozhsk, *St-Pet.* 11 A5 60 0N 30 39 E
Vuosaari, *Hels.* 3 B5 60 13N 25 8 E
Vyborgskaya Storona, *St-Pet.* 11 B4 59 57N 30 22 E
Vyčehrad, *Pra.* 10 B2 50 3N 14 25 E
Vykhino, *Mos.* 11 E10 55 42N 37 48 E
Vysočany, *Pra.* 10 B2 50 6N 14 29 E

W

Waban, L., *Bost.* 21 D2 42 17N 71 18W
Wachterhof, *Mün.* 7 G11 48 2N 11 42 E
Waddington, *Lon.* 4 D4 51 18N 0 7W
Wadeville, *Jobg.* 18 F10 26 15 S 28 11 E
Wahda, *Bagd.* 17 F8 33 18N 44 26 E
Währing, *Wien* 10 G10 48 14N 16 20 E
Waidmannslust, *Berl.* 7 A3 52 36N 13 20 E
Wajay, *La Hab.* 30 B2 23 0N 82 25W
Wakefield, *Bost.* 21 B3 42 30N 71 5W
Wald, *Ruhr* 6 C4 51 11N 7 3 E
Waldesruh, *Berl.* 7 B4 52 28N 13 37 E
Waldheim, *Berl.* 7 A1 52 34N 13 3 E
Waldperlach, *Mün.* 7 G11 48 4N 11 40 E
Waldtrudering, *Mün.* 7 G11 48 6N 11 42 E
Waldwick, *N.Y.* 22 A4 41 1N 74 5W
Wall Street, *N.Y.* 22 C4 40 42N 74 0W
Wallgrove, *Syd.* 19 A2 33 47 S 150 51 E
Wallington, *Lon.* 4 C4 51 21N 0 8W
Wallington, *N.Y.* 22 B4 40 50N 74 8W
Walnut Cr. →, *S.F.* 27 A4 37 55N 122 3W
Walnut Creek, *S.F.* 27 A4 37 53N 122 3W
Walnut Heights, *S.F.* 27 A4 37 52N 122 2W
Walsum, *Ruhr* 6 A2 51 32N 6 42 E
Walsumer Mark, *Ruhr* 6 A3 51 33N 6 50 E
Walt Whitman Br., *Phil.* 24 B4 39 4N 75 9W
Waltershof, *Hbg.* 7 D7 53 31N 9 54 E
Waltham, *Bost.* 21 C2 42 23N 71 14W
Waltham Abbey, *Lon.* 4 A5 51 41N 0 1 E
Waltham Forest, *Lon.* 4 B4 51 36N 0 0 E
Walthamstow, *Lon.* 4 B4 51 34N 0 1W
Walton on Thames, *Lon.* 4 C2 51 22N 0 23W
Walton on the Hill, *Lon.* 4 D3 51 16N 0 14W
Waltrop, *Ruhr* 6 A6 51 36N 7 25 E
Walworth, *Lon.* 4 C4 51 29N 0 5W
Wambachsee, *Ruhr* 6 B2 51 23N 6 47 E
Wan Chai, *H.K.* 12 E6 22 16N 114 10 E
Wanaque, *N.Y.* 22 A3 41 1N 74 17W
Wandezhuang, *Tianj.* 14 E5 39 6N 117 10 E
Wandle →, *Lon.* 4 C3 51 27N 0 11W
Wandsbek, *Hbg.* 7 D8 53 34N 10 4 E
Wandsworth, *Lon.* 4 C3 51 27N 0 11W
Wang Hin, Khlong →, *Bangk.* 15 A2 13 50N 100 35 E
Wanheim, *Ruhr* 6 B2 51 23N 6 45 E
Wanheimerort, *Ruhr* 6 B2 51 24N 6 45 E
Wanne-Eickel, *Ruhr* 6 A4 51 31N 7 9 E
Wannsee, *Berl.* 7 B1 52 25N 13 9 E
Wansdorf, *Berl.* 7 A1 52 38N 13 5 E
Wanstead, *Lon.* 4 B5 51 34N 0 1 E
Wantagh Seaford, *N.Y.* 23 D8 40 39N 73 28W
Wantirna, *Melb.* 19 F8 37 50 S 145 14 E
Wapping, *Lon.* 4 B4 51 30N 0 3W
Warabi, *Tōkyō* 13 B3 35 49N 139 42 E
Ward, *Phil.* 24 B1 39 52N 75 30W
Warlingham, *Lon.* 4 D4 51 18N 0 2W
Warnberg, *Mün.* 7 G10 48 4N 11 31 E
Warngal Park, *Melb.* 19 E7 37 45 S 145 4 E
Warrandyte, *Melb.* 19 E8 37 43 S 145 13 E
Warrandyte Park, *Melb.* 19 E8 37 44 S 145 14 E
Warrandyte South, *Melb.* 19 E8 37 44 S 145 14 E
Warranwood, *Melb.* 19 E8 37 46 S 145 14 E
Warrâq el 'Arab, *El Qâ.* 18 C5 30 4N 31 11 E
Warrâq el Hadf, *El Qâ.* 18 C5 30 5N 31 12 E
Warren Hill, *Bost.* 21 B1 42 35N 71 21W
Warsaw = Warszawa, *Wsaw.* 10 E7 52 14N 21 0 E
Warszawa, *Wsaw.* 10 E7 52 14N 21 0 E
Wartenberg, *Berl.* 7 A4 52 34N 13 31 E
Warwick Farm Racetrack, *Syd.* 19 B2 33 54 S 150 56 E
Wasa, *Stock.* 3 E11 59 19N 18 5 E
Wasfanārd, *Tehr.* 17 D5 35 38N 51 20 E
Washington, *Wash.* 25 D7 38 53N 77 2W
Washington Heights, *N.Y.* 22 B5 40 51N 73 56W
Washington Memorial Museum, *Phil.* 24 A2 40 5N 75 26W
Washington Nat. Airport, *Wash.* 25 D7 38 51N 77 2W
Washington Park, *Chic.* 26 C3 41 47N 87 36W
Washington Square, *Phil.* 24 A3 40 9N 75 19W
Washington Township, *N.Y.* 22 A4 41 0N 74 3W
Wasserschloss, *Ruhr* 6 A4 51 32N 7 1 E
Watching Mts., *N.Y.* 22 C2 40 43N 74 20W
Watchung, *N.Y.* 22 D2 40 38N 74 29W
Waterloo, *Syd.* 19 B4 33 53 S 151 12 E
Waterman Mt., *L.A.* 28 A5 34 14N 117 56W
Watertown, *Bost.* 21 C2 42 22N 71 10W
Watford, *Lon.* 4 A2 51 40N 0 27W
Watkins Island, *Wash.* 25 C6 39 2N 77 15W
Watsonia, *Melb.* 19 E7 37 43 S 145 6 E
Watsons B., *Syd.* 19 B4 33 50 S 151 18 E
Watsons Creek, *Melb.* 19 E8 37 40 S 145 13 E
Wattenscheid, *Ruhr* 6 B4 51 28N 7 8 E
Wattle Glen, *Melb.* 19 D8 37 39 S 145 11 E
Wattle Park, *Melb.* 19 F7 37 50 S 145 6 E
Watts →, *Wash.* 25 C6 39 2N 77 15W
Waverley, *Bost.* 21 C2 42 23N 71 10W
Waverley, *Jobg.* 18 E9 26 7 S 28 4 E
Waverley, *Syd.* 19 B4 33 53 S 151 15 E
Wawer, *Wsaw.* 10 E7 52 13N 21 8 E
Wawrzyszew, *Wsaw.* 10 E6 52 17N 20 53 E
Wayland, *Bost.* 21 C1 42 21N 71 20W
Wayne, *N.Y.* 22 B3 40 55N 74 15W
Wayne, *Phil.* 24 A2 40 2N 75 24W
Wazirabad, *Delhi* 16 A2 28 43N 77 13 E
Wazīrīya, *Bagd.* 17 E8 33 22N 44 23 E
Wazirpur, *Delhi* 16 A2 28 41N 77 10 E
Weald Park, *Lon.* 4 B6 51 37N 0 16 E
Wedding, *Berl.* 7 A3 52 32N 13 21 E
Weehawken, *N.Y.* 22 C4 40 45N 74 2W
Wegendorf, *Berl.* 7 A5 52 36N 13 45 E
Wehofen, *Ruhr* 6 A2 51 31N 6 46 E
Wehringhausen, *Ruhr* 6 B6 51 21N 7 28 E
Weidling, *Wien* 10 G9 48 17N 16 18 E
Weidling →, *Wien* 10 G9 48 17N 16 19 E
Weidlingbach, *Wien* 10 G9 48 16N 16 15 E
Weigongcum, *Beij.* 14 B2 39 57N 116 16 E
Weijin He →, *Tianj.* 14 E6 39 3N 117 12 E
Weissensee, *Berl.* 7 A3 52 33N 13 27 E
Weitmar, *Ruhr* 6 B5 51 27N 7 11 E
Welcome Monument, *Jak.* 15 J9 6 12N 106 49 E
Weller Creek, *Chic.* 26 A1 42 2N 87 52W
Wellesley, *Bost.* 21 D2 42 17N 71 17W
Wellesley Fells, *Bost.* 21 D2 42 18N 71 18W
Wellesley Hills, *Bost.* 21 D2 42 18N 71 16W
Welling, *Lon.* 4 C5 51 27N 0 6 E
Wellingsbüttel, *Hbg.* 7 D8 53 38N 10 6 E
Weltevreden Park Extension, *Jobg.* 18 E8 26 7 S 27 56 E
Wembley, *Lon.* 4 B3 51 33N 0 17W
Wembley Stadium, *Jobg.* 18 F9 26 13 S 28 1 E
Wembley Stadium, *Lon.* 4 B3 51 33N 0 16W
Wemmer Pan, *Jobg.* 18 F9 26 13 S 28 3 E
Wendenschloss, *Berl.* 7 B4 52 24N 13 35 E
Wengern, *Ruhr* 6 B6 51 24N 7 20 E
Wenham, *Bost.* 21 B4 42 36N 70 53W
Wenham L., *Bost.* 21 B4 42 35N 70 53W
Wenhuagong, *Tianj.* 14 E6 39 5N 117 14 E
Wennington, *Lon.* 4 B6 51 30N 0 12 E
Wenonah, *Phil.* 24 C4 39 47N 75 9W
Wentworthville, *Syd.* 19 A2 33 48 S 150 58 E
Werden, *Ruhr* 6 B4 51 23N 7 1 E
Werne, *Ruhr* 6 B5 51 29N 7 18 E
Werneuchen, *Berl.* 7 A5 52 38N 13 44 E
Wesoła, *Wsaw.* 10 E8 52 15N 21 13 E
West Andover, *Bost.* 21 B2 42 39N 71 10W
West Babylon, *N.Y.* 23 C8 40 43N 73 21W
West Bedford, *Bost.* 21 C2 42 28N 71 18W
West Berlin, *Phil.* 24 C5 39 48N 74 56W
West Boxford, *Bost.* 21 A3 42 42N 71 3W
West Caldwell, *N.Y.* 22 B3 40 51N 74 16W
West Chelmsford, *Bost.* 21 B1 42 36N 71 23W
West Chester, *Phil.* 24 B1 39 57N 75 35W
West Concord, *Bost.* 21 C1 42 27N 71 24W
West Covina, *L.A.* 28 B5 34 4N 117 55W
West Don →, *Trto.* 20 D8 43 44N 79 24W
West Drayton, *Lon.* 4 B2 51 30N 0 28W
West Dulwich, *Lon.* 4 C4 51 26N 0 5W
West Edmondale, *Balt.* 25 B2 39 17N 76 42W
West Ham, *Lon.* 4 B5 51 31N 0 1 E
West Harrow, *Lon.* 4 B2 51 34N 0 21W
West Heath, *Lon.* 4 C5 51 29N 0 7 E
West Hempstead, *N.Y.* 23 C7 40 41N 73 38W
West Hill, *Trto.* 20 D9 43 46N 79 10W
West Hollywood, *L.A.* 28 B2 34 5N 118 21W
West Hoxton, *Syd.* 19 B1 33 55 S 150 49 E
West Islip, *N.Y.* 23 C9 40 41N 73 18W
West Kingsdown, *Lon.* 4 C6 51 20N 0 15 E
West Lamma Channel, *H.K.* 12 E5 22 14N 114 4 E
West Lynn, *Bost.* 21 C4 42 27N 70 58W
West Medford, *Bost.* 21 C3 42 25N 71 7W
West New York, *N.Y.* 22 C4 40 46N 74 1W
West Norwood, *N.Y.* 22 B5 40 59N 73 58W
West of Twin Peaks, *S.F.* 27 B2 37 43N 122 27W
West Orange, *N.Y.* 22 C3 40 46N 74 15W
West Park, *Jobg.* 18 E8 26 9 S 27 59 E
West Paterson, *N.Y.* 22 B3 40 54N 74 11W
West Rouge, *Trto.* 20 D10 43 48N 79 7W
West Roxbury, *Bost.* 21 D3 42 16N 71 9W
West Springfield, *Wash.* 25 E6 38 47N 77 13W
West Thurrock, *Lon.* 4 C6 51 28N 0 16 E
West Town, *Chic.* 26 B2 41 53N 87 42W
West Wharf, *Kar.* 17 H10 24 49N 66 58 E
West Wickham, *Lon.* 4 C4 51 22N 0 0 E
Westbury, *N.Y.* 23 C7 40 45N 73 34W
Westchester, *Chic.* 26 B1 41 51N 87 53W
Westchester, *N.Y.* 23 B5 40 51N 73 51W
Westcliff, *Jobg.* 18 F9 26 10 S 28 1 E
Westdale, *Chic.* 26 B1 41 55N 87 54W
Westdene, *Jobg.* 18 F8 26 10 S 27 59 E
Westend, *Hels.* 3 C3 60 9N 24 48 E
Westerbauer, *Ruhr* 6 B6 51 20N 7 23 E
Westerham, *Lon.* 4 D5 51 16N 0 4 E
Westerham, *Mün.* 7 G10 48 3N 11 36 E
Westerholt, *Ruhr* 6 A4 51 36N 7 5 E
Westerleigh, *N.Y.* 22 D4 40 37N 74 7W
Western Addition, *S.F.* 27 B2 37 47N 122 25W
Western Run →, *Balt.* 25 A2 39 22N 76 39W
Western Springs, *Chic.* 26 C1 41 47N 87 52W
Westfalenhalle, *Ruhr* 6 B6 51 29N 7 27 E
Westfield, *N.Y.* 22 D2 40 39N 74 21W
Westlake, *S.F.* 27 B2 37 42N 122 29W
Westmeadows, *Melb.* 19 D6 37 39 S 144 55 E
Westminster, *Lon.* 4 B4 51 30N 0 7W
Westminster Abbey, *Lon.* 4 C4 51 29N 0 7W
Westmont, *Phil.* 24 B4 39 54N 75 3W
Westmount, *Mtrl.* 20 B4 43 29N 73 35W
Weston, *Bost.* 21 C2 42 22N 71 16W
Weston, *Trto.* 20 D7 43 42N 79 30W
Weston Res., *Bost.* 21 C2 42 20N 71 11W
Westover Hills, *Phil.* 24 C1 39 45N 75 35W
Westtown, *Phil.* 24 B1 39 56N 75 32W
Westville, *Phil.* 24 B4 39 52N 75 7W
Westville Grove, *Phil.* 24 B4 39 51N 75 7W
Westwood, *Bost.* 21 D2 42 12N 71 14W
Westwood, *N.Y.* 22 B4 40 59N 74 3W
Westwood Village, *L.A.* 28 B2 34 3N 118 26W
Wetter, *Ruhr* 6 B6 51 23N 7 23 E
Wexford, *Trto.* 20 D9 43 45N 79 18W
Wey →, *Lon.* 4 D2 51 18N 0 27W
Weybridge, *Lon.* 4 C2 51 22N 0 27W
Weyer, *Ruhr* 6 C4 51 10N 7 1 E
Weymouth, *Bost.* 21 D4 42 12N 70 57W
Whampoa, Sungei →, *Sing.* 15 G8 1 18N 103 52 E
Wheaton, *Wash.* 25 C7 39 2N 77 2W
Wheaton Regional Park, *Wash.* 25 C7 39 3N 77 1W
Wheelers Hill, *Melb.* 19 F8 37 53 S 145 10 E
Wheeling, *Chic.* 26 A1 42 8N 87 54W
Whetstone, *Lon.* 4 B3 51 37N 0 10W
Whippany, *N.Y.* 22 B2 40 49N 74 24W
Whippany →, *N.Y.* 22 B2 40 50N 74 20W
White Marsh, *Balt.* 25 A4 39 23N 76 28W
White Meadow L., *N.Y.* 22 B1 40 55N 74 30W
White Oak, *Wash.* 25 C8 39 2N 76 59W
White Plains, *N.Y.* 23 A6 41 0N 73 46W
Whitechapel, *Lon.* 4 B4 51 31N 0 3W
Whitehorse, *Phil.* 24 B2 39 59N 75 28W
Whiteley Village, *Lon.* 4 C2 51 21N 0 25W
Whitemarsh →, *Balt.* 25 A4 39 22N 76 29W
Whitestone, *N.Y.* 23 C6 40 47N 73 48W
Whiting, *Chic.* 26 C4 41 41N 87 30W
Whitmans Pond, *Bost.* 21 D4 42 12N 70 55W
Whittier, *L.A.* 28 C4 33 58N 118 2W
Whitton, *Lon.* 4 C2 51 27N 0 21W
Whyteleafe, *Lon.* 4 D4 51 18N 0 5W
Wieden, *Wien* 10 G10 48 11N 16 22 E
Wiemelhausen, *Ruhr* 6 B5 51 27N 7 13 E
Wien, *Wien* 10 G10 48 12N 16 22 E
Wien-Schwechat, Flughafen, *Wien* 10 H11 48 6N 16 34 E
Wiener Berg, *Wien* 10 H10 48 9N 16 21 E
Wiener Wald, *Wien* 10 G9 48 16N 16 14 E
Wieruchów, *Wsaw.* 10 E5 52 14N 20 49 E
Wierzbno, *Wsaw.* 10 E7 52 11N 21 1 E
Wilanów, *Wsaw.* 10 E7 52 10N 21 4 E
Wilanówka →, *Wsaw.* 10 F7 52 13N 21 6 E
Wildcat Canyon Regional Park, *S.F.* 27 A3 37 56N 122 17W
Wildcat Cr. →, *S.F.* 27 A3 37 57N 122 15W
Wilde, *B.A.* 32 C5 34 24 S 58 18W
Wilhelmsburg, *Hbg.* 7 E7 53 29N 9 59 E
Wilhelmshagen, *Berl.* 7 B5 52 26N 13 42 E
Wilket Creek Park, *Trto.* 20 D8 43 43N 79 21W
Willesden, *Lon.* 4 B3 51 32N 0 15W
Willesden Green, *Lon.* 4 B3 51 32N 0 13W
Willett Pond, *Bost.* 21 D2 42 10N 71 14W
William Girling Res., *Lon.* 4 B4 51 38N 0 1W
Williams Bridge, *N.Y.* 23 B5 40 52N 73 51W
Williamsburg, *N.Y.* 22 C5 40 42N 73 56W
Williamstown, *Melb.* 19 F6 37 51 S 144 52 E
Williamstown Junction, *Phil.* 24 C5 39 45N 74 56W
Willingboro, *Phil.* 24 A5 40 2N 74 53W
Williston Park, *N.Y.* 23 C7 40 45N 73 38W
Willoughby, *Syd.* 19 A4 33 48 S 151 12 E
Willow Grove, *Phil.* 24 A4 40 8N 75 7W
Willow Springs, *Chic.* 26 C1 41 44N 87 51W
Willowbrook, *L.A.* 28 C3 33 54N 118 13W
Willowbrook, *N.Y.* 22 D4 40 35N 74 8W
Willowdale, *Phil.* 24 B5 39 52N 74 58W
Willowdale, *Trto.* 20 D8 43 46N 79 25W
Willowdale State Forest, *Bost.* 21 B4 42 39N 70 54W
Wilmette, *Chic.* 26 A2 42 4N 87 42W
Wilmette Harbor, *Chic.* 26 A2 42 4N 87 41W
Wilmington, *Bost.* 21 B3 42 33N 71 9W
Wilmington, *Lon.* 4 C6 51 25N 0 12 E
Wilmington, *Phil.* 24 C1 39 44N 75 33W
Wilson, Mt., *L.A.* 28 A4 34 13N 118 4W
Wimbledon, *Lon.* 4 C3 51 25N 0 13W
Wimbledon Common, *Lon.* 4 C3 51 26N 0 14W
Wimbledon Park, *Lon.* 4 C3 51 25N 0 11W
Wimbledon Tennis Ground, *Lon.* 4 C3 51 25N 0 12W
Winchester, *Bost.* 21 C3 42 26N 71 8W
Winchmore Hill, *Lon.* 4 B4 51 38N 0 5W
Windsor Cresta, *Jobg.* 18 E8 26 7 S 27 59 E
Winfield, *N.Y.* 22 D3 40 38N 74 16W
Winnetka, *Chic.* 26 A2 42 6N 87 43W
Winnetka, *L.A.* 28 A1 34 10N 118 32W
Winning, *Mün.* 7 G10 48 2N 11 37 E
Winston Hills, *Syd.* 19 A2 33 46 S 150 57 E
Winterberg, *Ruhr* 6 C5 51 19N 7 12 E
Winterhude, *Hbg.* 7 D8 53 35N 10 0 E
Winterthur, *Phil.* 24 C1 39 48N 75 35W
Winthrop, *Bost.* 21 C4 42 22N 70 58W
Winzeldorf, *Hbg.* 7 C7 53 40N 9 54 E
Wisley Gardens, *Lon.* 4 D2 51 18N 0 28W
Wiśniowa Góra, *Wsaw.* 10 E8 52 13N 21 12 E
Wissahickon Cr. →, *Phil.* 24 A3 40 0N 75 12W
Wissinoming, *Phil.* 24 A4 40 1N 75 4W
Wissous, *Paris* 5 C3 48 44N 2 19 E
Witch House, *Bost.* 21 B4 42 31N 70 54W
Witfield, *Jobg.* 18 F10 26 11 S 28 12 E
Witpoortjie, *Jobg.* 18 E8 26 8 S 27 50 E
Witten, *Ruhr* 6 B6 51 26N 7 20 E
Wittenau, *Berl.* 7 A2 52 35N 13 19 E
Wittlaer, *Ruhr* 6 C2 51 19N 6 44 E
Witwatersrand, Univ. of, *Jobg.* 18 F9 26 11 S 28 1 E
Włochy, *Wsaw.* 10 E6 52 12N 20 54 E
Wo Mei, *H.K.* 12 D6 22 21N 114 15 E
Wo Yi Hop, *H.K.* 12 D5 22 23N 114 8 E
Woburn, *Bost.* 21 C3 42 29N 71 9W
Woburn, *Trto.* 20 D9 43 46N 79 12W
Wohldorf-Ohlstedt, *Hbg.* 7 C8 53 41N 10 7 E
Wola, *Wsaw.* 10 E6 52 14N 20 57 E
Woldingham, *Lon.* 4 D4 51 16N 0 1W
Wolf Lake, *Chic.* 26 D3 41 39N 87 31W
Wolf Trap Farm Park, *Wash.* 25 D6 38 56N 77 17W
Wolfpassing, *Wien* 10 G9 48 18N 16 10 E
Wolica, *Wsaw.* 10 F7 52 9N 21 3 E
Wolica, *Wsaw.* 10 F6 52 7N 20 51 E
Wólka Węglowa, *Wsaw.* 10 E6 52 18N 20 52 E
Wollaston, *Bost.* 21 D3 42 15N 71 2W
Wołomin, *Wsaw.* 10 D8 52 20N 21 12 E
Woltersdorf, *Berl.* 7 B5 52 27N 13 44 E
Wong Chuk Hang, *H.K.* 12 E6 22 15N 114 10 E
Wong Chuk Wan, *H.K.* 12 D6 22 23N 114 17 E
Wong Chuk Yeung, *H.K.* 12 D6 22 24N 114 15 E
Wong Ngua Shan, *H.K.* 12 D6 22 22N 114 14 E
Wong Tai Sin, *H.K.* 12 D6 22 20N 114 11 E
Wonga Park, *Melb.* 19 E8 37 44 S 145 17 E
Wood End, *Lon.* 4 B2 51 33N 0 21W
Wood Green, *Lon.* 4 B4 51 36N 0 6W
Wood Hill, *Bost.* 21 B2 42 39N 71 11W
Woodbridge, *N.Y.* 22 D3 40 33N 74 16W
Woodbridge, *Trto.* 20 D7 43 47N 79 35W
Woodbridge Cr. →, *N.Y.* 22 D3 40 32N 74 15W
Woodbury, *N.Y.* 23 C8 40 49N 73 28W
Woodbury, *Phil.* 24 B4 39 50N 75 9W
Woodbury Cr. →, *Phil.* 24 B4 39 51N 75 11W
Woodbury Heights, *Phil.* 24 C4 39 49N 75 7W
Woodchuck Hill, *Bost.* 21 B3 42 39N 71 4W
Woodcliff Lake, *N.Y.* 22 A4 41 1N 74 2W
Woodford, *Lon.* 4 B5 51 36N 0 1 E
Woodford Bridge, *Lon.* 4 B5 51 36N 0 3 E
Woodford Green, *Lon.* 4 B5 51 36N 0 1 E
Woodford Wells, *Lon.* 4 B5 51 37N 0 1 E
Woodhaven, *N.Y.* 23 C5 40 41N 73 51W
Woodlands, *Sing.* 15 F7 1 26N 103 46 E
Woodlawn, *Balt.* 25 B2 39 19N 76 44W
Woodlyn, *Phil.* 24 B2 39 52N 75 21W
Woodlynne, *Phil.* 24 B4 39 54N 75 6W
Woodmere, *N.Y.* 23 D6 40 38N 73 43W
Woodmont, *Wash.* 25 D7 38 59N 77 5W
Woodmore, *Balt.* 25 A2 39 22N 76 47W
Woodridge, *N.Y.* 22 B4 40 50N 74 4W
Woodrow, *N.Y.* 22 D3 40 32N 74 11W
Woodside, *Lon.* 4 C4 51 23N 0 4W
Woodside, *N.Y.* 23 C5 40 44N 73 54W
Woodside, *S.F.* 27 D3 37 26N 122 16W
Woodstock, *Balt.* 25 B1 39 19N 76 52W
Woodstream, *Phil.* 24 B5 39 54N 74 57W
Woollahra, *Syd.* 19 B4 33 53 S 151 15 E
Woolooware B., *Syd.* 19 C3 34 1 S 151 8 E
Woolwich, *Lon.* 4 C5 51 29N 0 4 E
Wördern, *Wien* 10 G9 48 19N 16 12 E
World Trade Center, *N.Y.* 22 C4 40 42N 74 0W
Worli, *Bomb.* 16 G7 19 1N 72 49 E
Woronora, *Syd.* 19 C3 34 1 S 151 2 E
Worth, *Chic.* 26 C2 41 41N 87 47W
Worthington, *Balt.* 25 B2 39 14N 76 47W
Worthington, *N.Y.* 23 A6 41 2N 73 49W
Wrotham, *Lon.* 4 D6 51 18N 0 18 E
Wrotham Park, *Lon.* 4 A3 51 40N 0 10W
Wuhlgarten, *Berl.* 7 A4 52 31N 13 34 E
Wujiaochang, *Shang.* 14 J12 31 18N 121 31 E
Wülfrath, *Ruhr* 6 C4 51 16N 7 2 E
Wulfsmühle, *Hbg.* 7 C7 53 41N 9 51 E
Wulksfelde, *Hbg.* 7 C8 53 42N 10 6 E
Wupper →, *Ruhr* 6 C5 51 14N 7 18 E
Wuppertal, *Ruhr* 6 C5 51 17N 7 10 E
Würm →, *Mün.* 7 G9 48 8N 11 27 E
Würm-kanal, *Mün.* 7 F9 48 13N 11 29 E
Wusong, *Shang.* 14 H11 31 22N 121 29 E
Wusong Jiang →, *Shang.* 14 J11 31 15N 121 29 E
Wyandanch, *N.Y.* 23 C8 40 44N 73 20W
Wyckoff, *N.Y.* 22 A3 41 0N 74 10W
Wyczółki, *Wsaw.* 10 F6 52 9N 20 59 E
Wygoda, *Wsaw.* 10 E7 52 15N 21 7 E
Wyncote, *Phil.* 24 A4 40 5N 75 8W
Wynnewood, *Phil.* 24 A3 40 0N 75 17W
Wynnmere, *Bost.* 21 C3 42 29N 71 9W
Wyola, *Phil.* 24 A2 40 0N 75 24W

X

Xabregas, *Lisb.* 8 F8 38 43N 9 6W
Xiaodianzhuang, *Tianj.* 14 D6 39 14N 117 14 E
Xiaoping, *Gzh.* 14 F8 23 12N 113 13 E
Xiasha chong, *Gzh.* 14 G7 23 8N 113 9 E
Xicheng, *Beij.* 14 B2 39 54N 116 19 E
Xico, Cerro, *Méx.* 29 C4 19 15N 98 56W
Xicun, *Gzh.* 14 G8 23 8N 113 13 E
Xidan, *Beij.* 14 B3 39 52N 116 20 E
Xigu Gongyuan, *Tianj.* 14 D6 39 10N 117 10 E
Xigucun, *Tianj.* 14 D5 39 10N 117 9 E
Xijiao Airport, *Beij.* 14 B2 39 57N 116 12 E
Xikeng, *Gzh.* 14 F7 23 11N 113 6 E
Xilou, *Tianj.* 14 E6 39 5N 117 12 E
Ximenwai, *Tianj.* 14 E5 39 8N 117 9 E
Xingfusancun, *Beij.* 14 B3 39 55N 116 25 E
Xinhua, *Tianj.* 14 E6 39 6N 117 12 E
Xinkai He →, *Tianj.* 14 D6 39 12N 117 15 E
Xintang, *Gzh.* 14 G9 23 9N 113 24 E
Xitle, *Méx.* 29 C2 19 15N 99 12W
Xitle, Cerro, *Méx.* 29 C2 19 14N 99 12W
Xiyuan, *Beij.* 14 B2 39 59N 116 14 E
Xizhimen, *Beij.* 14 B2 39 55N 116 19 E
Xochiaca, *Méx.* 29 B4 19 24N 89 58 E
Xochimilco, *Méx.* 29 C3 19 15N 99 5W
Xochimilco, L. de, *Méx.* 29 C3 19 16N 99 7W
Xochitenco, *Méx.* 29 B4 19 24N 89 58 E
Xochitepec, *Méx.* 29 C3 19 15N 99 9W
Xuanwu, *Beij.* 14 B2 39 52N 116 19 E
Xuhui, *Shang.* 14 J11 31 11N 121 26 E

Y

Yaba, *Lagos* 18 A2 6 30N 7 22 E
Yadun Shui, *Gzh.* 14 G8 23 5N 113 15 E
Yaftābād, *Tehr.* 17 D4 35 37N 51 17 E
Yagoona, *Syd.* 19 B3 33 54 S 151 2 E
Yahara, *Tōkyō* 13 B2 35 44N 139 37 E
Yaho, *Tōkyō* 13 B1 35 40N 139 26 E
Yakire, *Tōkyō* 13 B4 35 45N 139 54 E
Yamada, *Ōsaka* 12 B4 34 47N 135 32 E
Yamada, *Tōkyō* 13 C2 35 33N 139 37 E
Yamada →, *Ōsaka* 12 B2 34 45N 135 10 E
Yamaguchi, *Ōsaka* 12 B2 34 49N 135 14 E
Yamamoto, *Ōsaka* 12 C4 34 38N 135 37 E
Yamato, *Tōkyō* 13 B2 35 46N 139 36 E
Yamato, *Tōkyō* 13 D1 35 29N 139 27 E
Yamato →, *Ōsaka* 12 C3 34 36N 135 26 E
Yamazaki, *Tōkyō* 13 A4 35 55N 139 53 E
Yamuna →, *Delhi* 16 B2 28 37N 77 15 E
Yan Kit, *Sing.* 15 F8 1 21N 103 58 E
Yanagishima, *Tōkyō* 13 B3 35 49N 139 45 E
Yanbu, *Gzh.* 14 G7 23 5N 113 9 E
Yanghuayuan, *Beij.* 14 C2 39 49N 116 18 E
Yangjiazhuang, *Shang.* 14 H11 31 22N 121 25 E
Yangliuqing, *Tianj.* 14 E5 39 8N 117 0 E
Yangpu, *Shang.* 14 J12 31 16N 121 32 E
Yanino, *St-Pet.* 11 B5 59 55N 30 36 E
Yao, *Ōsaka* 12 C4 34 37N 135 36 E
Yao Airport, *Ōsaka* 12 C4 34 35N 135 36 E
Yarmōk, *Bagd.* 17 F7 33 18N 44 19 E
Yarra →, *Melb.* 19 E6 37 51 S 144 53 E
Yarra Bend Nat. Park, *Melb.* 19 E7 37 47 S 145 0 E
Yarraville, *Melb.* 19 E6 37 48 S 144 53 E
Yasenevo, *Mos.* 11 F9 55 36N 37 21 E
Yashio, *Tōkyō* 13 B3 35 48N 139 49 E
Yau Ma Tei, *H.K.* 12 E5 22 18N 114 10 E
Yau Tong, *H.K.* 12 E6 22 17N 114 14 E
Yau Yue Wan, *H.K.* 12 E6 22 19N 114 15 E
Yauza →, *Mos.* 11 D10 55 54N 37 43 E
Yeading, *Lon.* 4 B2 51 31N 0 23W
Yeadon, *Phil.* 24 B3 39 55N 75 15W
Yedikule, *Ist.* 17 B2 40 59N 28 55 E
Yenikapi, *Ist.* 17 A2 41 0N 28 56 E
Yeniköy, *Ist.* 17 A3 41 6N 29 3 E
Yennora, *Syd.* 19 B2 33 51 S 150 58 E
Yeogchon, *Sŏul* 12 G7 37 35N 126 55 E
Yeoido, *Sŏul* 12 G7 37 31N 126 55 E
Yeong Dung Po, *Sŏul* 12 G7 37 31N 126 54 E
Yeongdong, *Sŏul* 12 G8 37 30N 127 1 E
Yerba Buena I., *S.F.* 27 B2 37 48N 122 21W
Yerres, *Paris* 5 C5 48 43N 2 30 E
Yerres →, *Paris* 5 C5 48 43N 2 26 E
Yesilköy, *Ist.* 17 B2 40 57N 28 50 E
Yew Tee, *Sing.* 15 F7 1 23N 103 45 E
Yiewsley, *Lon.* 4 B2 51 31N 0 27W
Yiheyuan, *Beij.* 14 A2 40 0N 116 14 E
Yinhangzhen, *Shang.* 14 H12 31 20N 121 31 E
Yio Chu Kang, *Sing.* 15 F8 1 23N 103 51 E
Yixingbu, *Tianj.* 14 D6 39 11N 117 12 E
Ylästö, *Hels.* 3 B4 60 17N 24 35 E
Yodo →, *Ōsaka* 12 B4 34 45N 135 35 E
Yokohama, *Tōkyō* 13 D3 35 26N 139 41 E
Yokohama Harbour, *Tōkyō* 13 D2 35 27N 139 39 E
Yokosuka, *Tōkyō* 13 A4 35 50N 139 54 E
Yong San, *Sŏul* 12 G7 37 32N 126 58 E
Yongding He →, *Beij.* 14 C1 39 49N 116 10 E
Yongdingmen, *Beij.* 14 B3 39 50N 116 20 E
Yongfucun, *Gzh.* 14 G8 23 8N 113 17 E
Yonkers, *N.Y.* 23 B5 40 56N 73 52W
Yono, *Tōkyō* 13 A2 35 52N 139 37 E
York, *Trto.* 20 D8 43 40N 79 26W
York Mills, *Trto.* 20 D8 43 45N 79 22W
Yoshikawa, *Tōkyō* 13 A4 35 53N 139 50 E
Yotsuga, *Tōkyō* 13 B3 35 40N 139 44 E
You'anmen, *Beij.* 14 B2 39 51N 116 19 E
Yoyogi Park, *Tōkyō* 13 C3 35 40N 139 41 E
Yuanxiatian, *Gzh.* 14 F8 23 12N 113 17 E
Yuexiu Gongyuan, *Gzh.* 14 G8 23 8N 113 16 E
Yugo-Zarad, *Mos.* 11 E9 55 40N 37 30 E
Yung Shue Wan, *H.K.* 12 E5 22 13N 114 6 E
Yuquanshan, *Beij.* 14 A2 40 0N 116 13 E
Yusofābād, *Tehr.* 17 C5 35 43N 51 24 E
Yuyuan Tan, *Beij.* 14 B2 39 53N 116 16 E
Yuyuantan Gongyuan, *Beij.* 14 B2 39 54N 116 16 E
Yvelines, Forêt des, *Paris* 5 D1 48 38N 1 53 E
Yvette →, *Paris* 5 C1 48 43N 1 57 E

Z

Záběhlice, *Pra.* 10 B2 50 3N 14 29 E
Żacisze, *Wsaw.* 10 E7 52 17N 21 4 E
Zahrā, *Bagd.* 17 E7 33 22N 44 19 E
Zakharkovo, *Mos.* 11 E7 55 46N 37 18 E
Żalov, *Pra.* 10 A2 50 10N 14 22 E
Załuski, *Wsaw.* 10 F6 52 9N 20 55 E
Zamdorf, *Mün.* 7 G10 48 8N 11 35 E
Zanevka, *St-Pet.* 11 B5 59 55N 30 31 E
Zaozerye, *Mos.* 11 F12 55 35N 38 1 E
Zapote, *Manila* 15 E3 14 27N 120 56 E
Zapotitlán, *Méx.* 29 C3 19 18N 99 2W
Zápy, *Pra.* 10 B4 50 9N 14 40 E
Zarechye, *Mos.* 11 E8 55 41N 37 22 E
Zawady, *Wsaw.* 10 E7 52 10N 21 6 E
Zâwiyet Abû Musallam, *El Qâ.* 18 D4 29 56N 31 9 E
Zawrā Park, *Bagd.* 17 F8 33 18N 44 23 E
Zbójna Góra, *Wsaw.* 10 E8 52 11N 21 13 E
Zbraslav, *Pra.* 10 C2 49 58N 14 23 E
Zbuzany, *Pra.* 10 B1 50 1N 14 17 E
Zdiby, *Pra.* 10 B2 50 9N 14 27 E
Zehlendorf, *Berl.* 7 B2 52 26N 13 16 E
Zeleneč, *Pra.* 10 B3 50 8N 14 39 E
Zempoala, Parque Nac. de las Lagunas de, *Méx.* 29 D2 19 5N 99 18W
Zepernick, *Berl.* 7 A4 52 38N 13 33 E
Żerań, *Wsaw.* 10 E6 52 18N 20 58 E
Zerzeń, *Wsaw.* 10 E7 52 12N 21 7 E
Zeytinburnu, *Ist.* 17 B2 40 58N 28 53 E
Zhabei, *Shang.* 14 J11 31 16N 121 26 E
Zhangguizhuang, *Tianj.* 14 E6 39 7N 117 19 E
Zhangxingzhuang, *Tianj.* 14 D6 39 10N 117 12 E
Zhdanov, *Mos.* 11 E10 55 44N 37 41 E
Zhegalovo, *Mos.* 11 D11 55 54N 37 59 E
Zheleznodorozhnyy, *Mos.* 11 E12 55 45N 38 0 E
Zhenru, *Shang.* 14 J11 31 16N 121 22 E
Zhicun, *Gzh.* 14 G8 23 0N 113 18 E
Zhongshan Gongyuan, *Shang.* 14 J11 31 13N 121 24 E
Zhoucun, *Gzh.* 14 F8 23 11N 113 11 E
Zhoujiadu, *Shang.* 14 J11 31 11N 121 29 E
Zhoujiazhen, *Shang.* 14 J12 31 16N 121 33 E
Zhu Jiang →, *Gzh.* 14 G9 23 6N 113 20 E
Zhulebino, *Mos.* 11 E11 55 42N 37 50 E
Zhushadi, *Gzh.* 14 F9 23 11N 113 22 E
Zielona, *Wsaw.* 10 E8 52 14N 21 11 E
Zielonka, *Wsaw.* 10 E7 52 18N 21 9 E
Zitadella, *Berl.* 7 A2 52 31N 13 11 E
Zizhuyuan Gongyuan, *Beij.* 14 B2 39 55N 116 17 E
Żižkov, *Pra.* 10 B2 50 5N 14 28 E
Zličin, *Pra.* 10 B1 50 3N 14 17 E
Zōbki, *Wsaw.* 10 E7 52 17N 21 6 E
Zografos, *Ath.* 8 J11 37 58N 23 47 E
Żoliborz, *Wsaw.* 10 E6 52 16N 20 57 E
Zugliget, *Bud.* 10 K12 47 30N 18 59 E
Zugló, *Bud.* 10 J13 47 31N 19 8 E
Zumbi, *Rio J.* 31 A2 22 49 S 43 10W
Zuvuvu →, *S. Pau.* 31 F5 23 40 S 46 42W
Zuvuvus, *S. Pau.* 31 F6 23 41 S 46 39W
Zweckel, *Ruhr* 6 A3 51 35N 6 57 E
Zyuzino, *Mos.* 11 F9 55 39N 37 34 E

WORLD MAPS

SETTLEMENTS

■ **PARIS**   ▣ **Berne**   ◉ **Livorno**   ◎ **Brugge**   ⊙ **Algeciras**   ○ *Frejus*   ○ *Oberammergau*   ○ *Thira*

Settlement symbols and type styles vary according to the scale of each map and indicate the importance
of towns on the map rather than specific population figures

∴ Ruins or Archæological Sites   ⌣ Wells in Desert

ADMINISTRATION

——— International Boundaries

- - - - International Boundaries
(Undefined or Disputed)

·········· Internal Boundaries

▢ National Parks

Country Names
NICARAGUA

Administrative
Area Names
KENT
CALABRIA

International boundaries show the *de facto* situation where there are rival claims to territory

COMMUNICATIONS

——— Principal Roads

——— Other Roads

→·--← Road Tunnels

⋈ Passes

✈ Airfields

——— Principal Railways

- - - Railways
Under Construction

——— Other Railways

→·--← Railway Tunnels

·········· Principal Canals

PHYSICAL FEATURES

—— Perennial Streams

- - - Intermittent Streams

⬭ Perennial Lakes

⬬ Intermittent Lakes

≋ Swamps and Marshes

▨ Permanent Ice
and Glaciers

▲ 8848 Elevations in metres

▼ 8500 Sea Depths in metres

1134 Height of Lake Surface
Above Sea Level in metres

ELEVATION AND DEPTH TINTS

Height of Land above Sea Level		Land Below Sea Level	Depth of Sea	

in metres   6000 4000 3000 2000 1500 1000 400 200 0

6000 12 000 15 000 18 000 24 000   in feet

in feet   18 000 12 000 9000 6000 4500 3000 1200 600

0 200 2000 4000 5000 6000 8000   in metres

Some of the maps have different contours to highlight and clarify the principal relief features

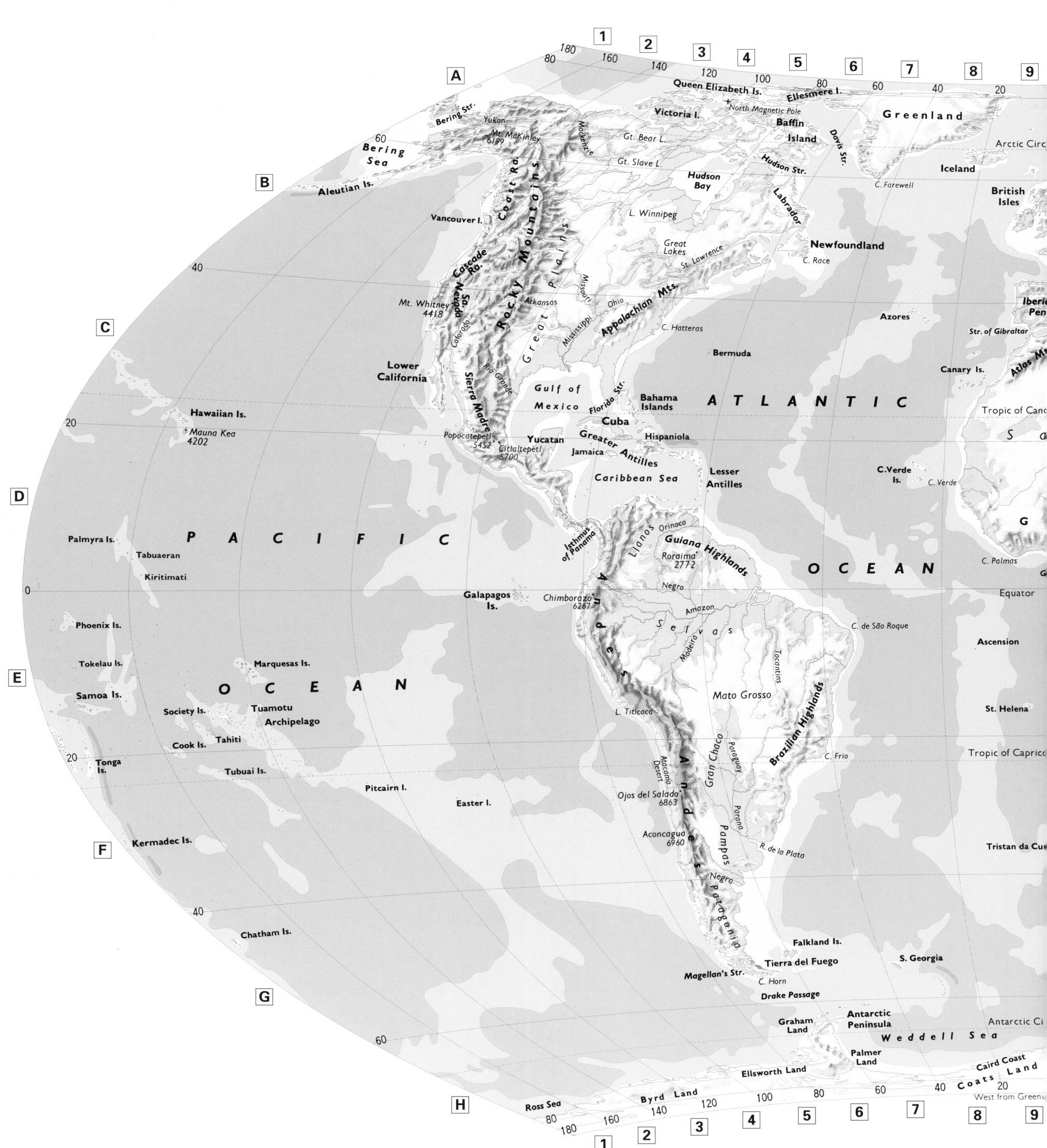

A

1   180   2   160   3   140   4   120   5   100   6   80   7   60   8   40   9   20

Queen Elizabeth Is.
North Magnetic Pole
Ellesmere I.
Greenland
Arctic Circle

Bering Str.
Yukon
Mt. McKinley
6199
Victoria I.
Baffin Island
Davis Str.
Iceland

B

Bering Sea
Mackenzie
Gt. Bear L.
Gt. Slave L.
Hudson Str.
C. Farewell
British Isles

Aleutian Is.
Hudson Bay
Labrador

Vancouver I.
L. Winnipeg
Great Lakes
St. Lawrence
Newfoundland
C. Race

40

C

Coast Ra.
Rocky Mountains
Great Plains
Missouri
Ohio
Appalachian Mts.
Azores
Iberian Pen.

Cascade Ra.
Sa. Nevada
Mt. Whitney
4418
Arkansas
Mississippi
C. Hatteras
Bermuda
Str. of Gibraltar

Colorado
Lower California
Rio Grande
Sierra Madre
Gulf of Mexico
Florida Str.
Bahama Islands
ATLANTIC
Canary Is.
Atlas Mts.

20
Tropic of Cancer

Hawaiian Is.
Mauna Kea
4202
Popocatepetl
5452
Citlaltepetl
5700
Yucatan
Cuba
Greater Antilles
Hispaniola
OCEAN
C. Verde Is.
C. Verde
Sa

D

Jamaica
Caribbean Sea
Lesser Antilles

PACIFIC
Palmyra Is.
Tabuaeran
Isthmus of Panama
Llanos
Orinoco
Guiana Highlands
C. Palmas

Kiritimati
Negro
Roraima
2772

0
Galapagos Is.
Chimborazo
6267
Amazon
Madeira
Equator

Phoenix Is.
Andes
Selvas
C. de São Roque
Ascension

E

Tokelau Is.
Marquesas Is.
Negro
Mato Grosso
St. Helena

Samoa Is.
OCEAN
Society Is.
Tahiti
Tuamotu Archipelago
L. Titicaca
Brazilian Highlands

20
Cook Is.
Tubuai Is.
Gran Chaco
Paraguay
C. Frio
Tropic of Capricorn

Tonga Is.
Pitcairn I.
Easter I.
Atacama Desert
Ojos del Salado
6863
Paraná
Pampas

F

Kermadec Is.
Aconcagua
6960
R. de la Plata
Tristan da Cunha

Andes
Negro
Patagonia

40
Chatham Is.
Falkland Is.

G

Magellan's Str.
Tierra del Fuego
S. Georgia
C. Horn
Drake Passage

Graham Land
Antarctic Peninsula
Antarctic Ci

60
Palmer Land
Weddell Sea

Ellsworth Land
Caird Coast
Coats Land

H
Ross Sea
Byrd Land
West from Green

80   1   180   2   160   140   3   120   100   4   80   5   60   6   40   7   20   8   9

Projection: Hammer Equal Area

3

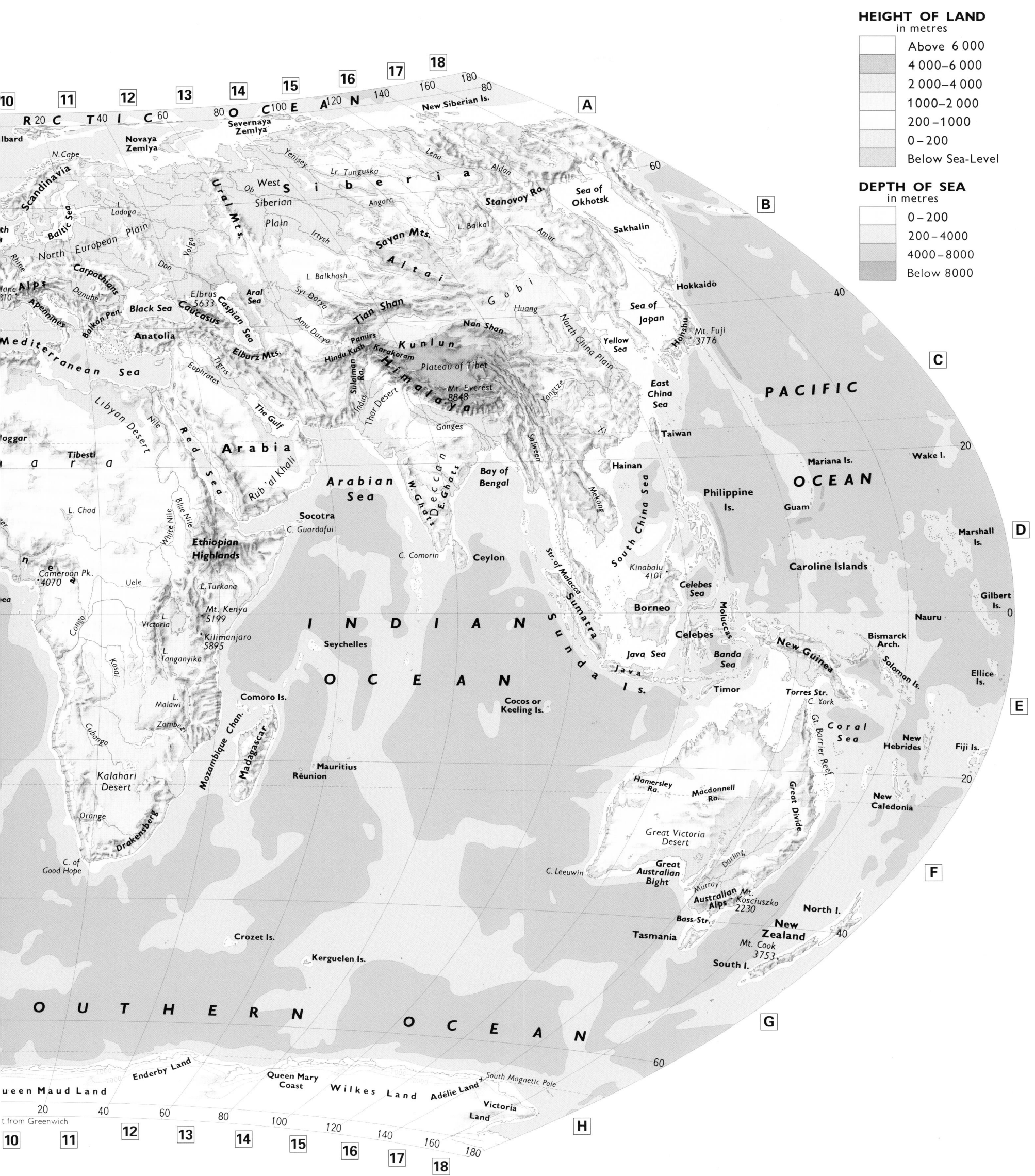

HEIGHT OF LAND
in metres

- Above 6 000
- 4 000–6 000
- 2 000–4 000
- 1000–2 000
- 200–1000
- 0–200
- Below Sea-Level

DEPTH OF SEA
in metres

- 0–200
- 200–4000
- 4000–8000
- Below 8000

A R C T I C   O C E A N

Ibard
N. Cape
Novaya Zemlya
Severnaya Zemlya
New Siberian Is.

Scandinavia
Baltic Sea
L. Ladoga
North European Plain
Ural Mts.
Ob
West Siberian Plain
Yenisey
Lr. Tunguska
Lena
Aldan
Stanovoy Ra.
Sea of Okhotsk

Rhine
Alps
Mont Blanc
4810
Apennines
Carpathians
Danube
Don
Volga
Angara
Irtysh
Soyan Mts.
Altai
L. Baikal
Amur
Sakhalin
Hokkaido

Balkan Pen.
Black Sea
Caucasus
Elbrus 5633
Caspian Sea
Aral Sea
Syr Darya
L. Balkhash
Gobi
Huang
Sea of Japan
Honshu
Mt. Fuji 3776

Anatolia
Elburz Mts.
Amu Darya
Tian Shan
Nan Shan
Kunlun
North China Plain
Yellow Sea
East China Sea

Mediterranean Sea
Tigris
Euphrates
Hindu Kush
Pamirs
Karakoram
Suleiman Ra.
Himalaya
Plateau of Tibet
Mt. Everest 8848
Yangtze
Xi
Taiwan

Libyan Desert
Nile
Red Sea
The Gulf
Arabia
Indus
Thar Desert
Ganges
Salween
Mekong

Sahara
Tibesti
oggar

Arabian Sea
Rub 'al Khali
W. Ghats
Deccan
E. Ghats
Bay of Bengal
Hainan
South China Sea
Philippine Is.
Guam
Mariana Is.
Wake I.

PACIFIC OCEAN

Socotra
C. Guardafui
C. Comorin
Ceylon
Str. of Malacca
Sumatra
Caroline Islands
Marshall Is.

L. Chad
Ethiopian Highlands
L. Turkana
Cameroon Pk. 4070
Uele
Congo

Mt. Kenya 5199
L. Victoria
Kilimanjaro 5895
L. Tanganyika

Sunda Is.
Kinabalu 4101
Borneo
Celebes Sea
Celebes
Moluccas
New Guinea
Bismarck Arch.
Solomon Is.
Gilbert Is.
Nauru
Ellice Is.

Seychelles

I N D I A N   O C E A N

Java Sea
Java
Banda Sea
Timor
Coral Sea
Torres Str.
C. York
New Hebrides
Fiji Is.

Kasai
L. Malawi
Zambezi
Cubango
Comoro Is.
Mozambique Chan.
Madagascar
Mauritius
Réunion
Cocos or Keeling Is.
Gt. Barrier Reef
New Caledonia

Orange
Kalahari Desert
Drakensberg
C. of Good Hope

Crozet Is.
Kerguelen Is.

Hamersley Ra.
Macdonnell Ra.
Great Divide
Great Victoria Desert
Darling
Murray
Australian Alps
Mt. Kosciuszko 2230
Great Australian Bight
C. Leeuwin
North I.
Bass Str.
Tasmania
New Zealand
Mt. Cook 3753
South I.

S O U T H E R N   O C E A N

Queen Maud Land
Enderby Land
Queen Mary Coast
Wilkes Land
Adélie Land
South Magnetic Pole
Victoria Land

t from Greenwich

A B C D E F G H
10 11 12 13 14 15 16 17 18

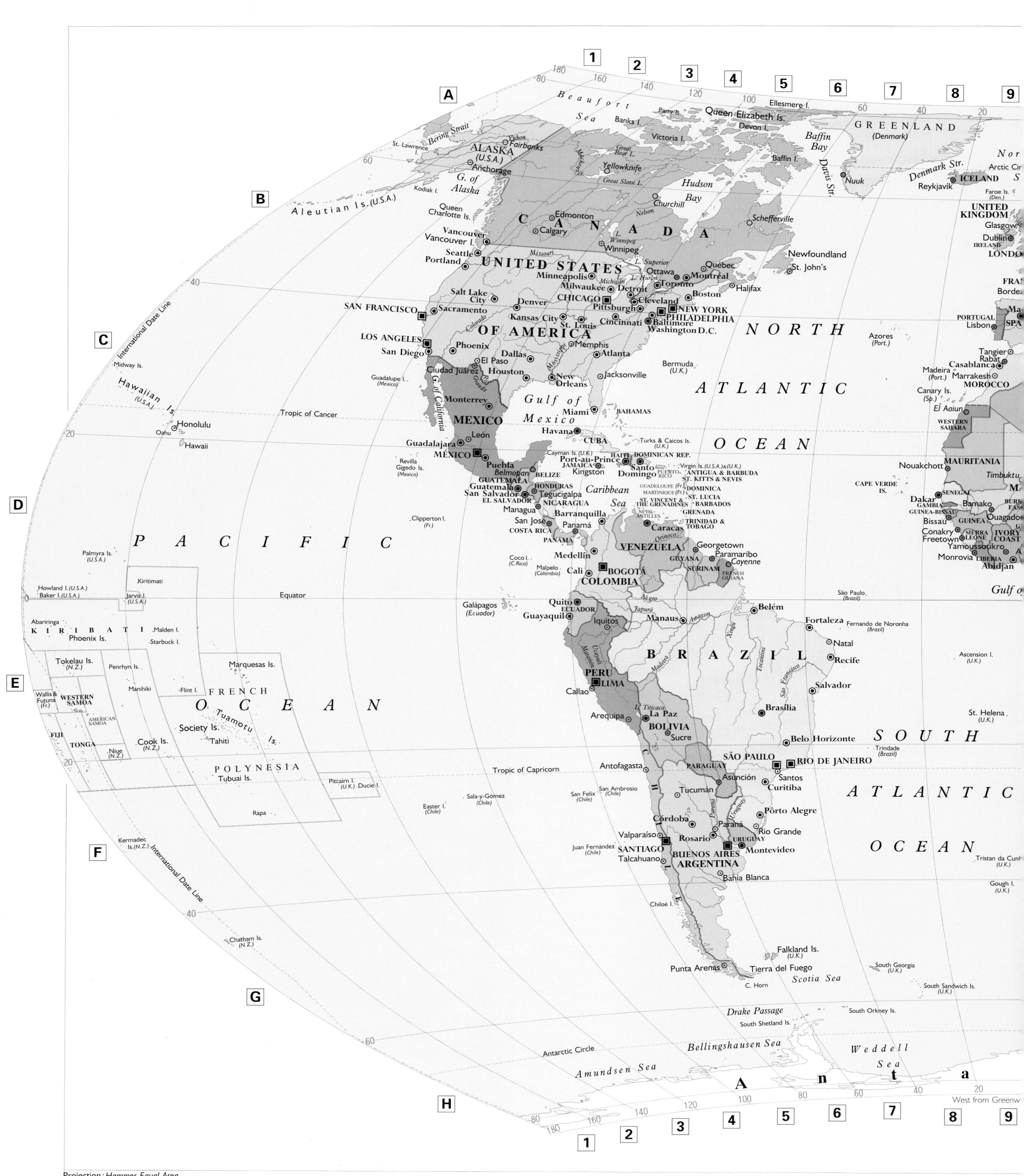

Projection: *Hammer Equal Area*

A
B
C
D
E
F
G
H

10 11 12 13 14 15 16 17 18

ARCTIC OCEAN

Barents Sea *Novaya Zemlya* *Kara Sea* *Severnaya Zemlya* *Laptev Sea* New Siberian Is. *East Siberian Sea* Wrangel I.

Arctic Circle

Murmansk Arkhangelsk Norilsk Salekhard Yenisey Ob Verkhoyansk Lena Yakutsk Magadan Okhotsk *Sea of Okhotsk* Petropavlovsk-Kamchatskiy *Bering Sea* International Date Line

NORWAY Oslo SWEDEN FINLAND Helsinki ST.PETERSBURG EST. Stockholm LATVIA LITH. MOSCOW Perm Yekaterinburg Tomsk Krasnoyarsk *L. Baikal* Irkutsk Ulan Ude Khabarovsk Komsomolsk Sakhalin Sapporo

DENMARK Copenhagen POLAND BELARUS Minsk Kazan *Volga* Samara Chelyabinsk Novosibirsk Barnaul *Irtysh* Ulan Bator Harbin Changchun Vladivostok *Kuril Is.*

amburg Amsterdam NETH. Berlin Prague Warsaw Kiev UKRAINE Volgograd Saratov KAZAKSTAN Astana Qaraghandy *L. Balkhash* MONGOLIA SHENYANG BEIJING TIANJIN Pyŏngyang NORTH KOREA SEOUL JAPAN

BRUSSELS LUX. GERMANY Vienna CZECH SLOVAK REP. AUSTRIA HUNG. ROMANIA Bucharest Odessa Astrakhan *Caspian Sea* *Aral Sea* UZBEKISTAN Almaty Bishkek KYRGYZSTAN Ürümqi CHINA Lanzhou Taiyuan Dalian SOUTH KOREA Osaka Kitakyūshu TŌKYŌ

PARIS FR. SW. SLOV. CROATIA B-H. YUG. BULGARIA Belgrade Black Sea GEORGIA Tbilisi Baku Samarkand Tashkent Dushanbe TAJIKISTAN CHINA Xi'an *Hwang-ho* Nanjing

Milan ITALY Rome ALB. MAC. Sofia ISTANBUL Ankara ARM. AZER. TURKMENISTAN Ashkhabad AFGHANISTAN Kābul Islamabad TIBET Lhasa Chengdu CHONGQING Wuhan SHANGHAI *East China Sea*

Marseilles Sardinia Naples GREECE Athens İzmir TURKEY Yerevan Tabriz Mashhad Esfahān PAKISTAN Lahore NEPAL Katmandu BHU. Kunming GUANGZHOU Fuzhou Taipei TAIWAN

Barcelona *Mediterranean Sea* Sicily MALTA Crete CYPRUS SYRIA Damascus Baghdād IRAQ IRAN Shīrāz DELHI New Delhi Kanpur BANGLA-DESH DACCA Hong Kong *Ryukyu Is.*

Algiers Tunis TUNISIA Tripoli Benghazi Beirut Jerusalem ISR. JORDAN Amman KUWAIT BAHRAIN QATAR Abu Dhabi U.A.E. Muscat INDIA Nagpur CALCUTTA BURMA (MYANMAR) Rangoon Hanoi Hainan *South China Sea* *Tropic of Cancer*

LIBYA EGYPT Aswān *Red Sea* Riyadh SAUDI ARABIA Mecca OMAN *Arabian Sea* Ahmadabad KARACHI MUMBAI (Bombay) Hyderabad CHENNAI (Madras) Andaman Is. (India) THAILAND BANGKOK VIET-NAM Vientiane

NIGER CHAD *L. Chad* SUDAN Omdurmân Khartoum ERITREA Asmara Sana YEMEN Aden *G. of Aden* Socotra (Yemen) Bangalore Colombo SRI LANKA Nicobar Is. (India) CAMBODIA Phnom Penh Ho Chi Minh City MANILA PHILIPPINES

Niamey Kano NIGERIA Abuja Ndjamena CENTRAL AFRICAN REP. Addis Ababa ETHIOPIA DJIBOUTI SOMALI REP. Lakshadweep Is. (India) MALDIVES *Equator* Medan Kuala Lumpur MALAYSIA SINGAPORE Borneo SARAWAK SABAH BRUNEI Yap PALAU FEDERATED STATES OF MICRONESIA *Caroline Is.* Truk Pohnpei MARSHALL IS. Wake I. (U.S.A.) NORTHERN MARIANAS (U.S.A.) GUAM (U.S.A.)

Ibadan Lagos CAMEROON Douala Yaoundé EQUATORIAL GUINEA SÃO TOMÉ & PRÍNCIPE GABON Libreville CONGO DEM.REP.OF THE CONGO (Zaïre) Kisangani UGANDA Kampala KENYA Nairobi Mogadishu SEYCHELLES Amirante Is. Diego Garcia Chagos Arch. (U.K.) INDONESIA Palembang Sumatra Banjarmasin IRIAN JAYA NAURU KIRIBATI Gilbert Is.

Brazzaville Kinshasa Kigali RWANDA BURUNDI Bujumbura Kananga *Kasai* Dodoma TANZANIA Mombasa Zanzibar Dar es Salaam *L. Victoria* *L. Tanganyika* *Congo* INDIAN OCEAN JAKARTA Bandung Java Surabaya Ujung Pandang PAPUA NEW GUINEA New Ireland New Britain SOLOMON IS. Santa Cruz I. TUVALU

Luanda CABINDA (Angola) ANGOLA Benguela Lubumbashi Kananga *L. Tanganyika* COMOROS Mayotte (Fr.) Aldabra Is. Agalega Is. Cocos Is. (Austral.) Christmas I. (Austral.) Timor *Arafura Sea* Port Moresby C. York VANUATU FIJI Suva

ZAMBIA Lusaka MALAWI Lilongwe *Malawi* ZIMBABWE MOZAMBIQUE *Mozambique Channel* MADAGASCAR Antananarivo SEYCHELLES Cargados Carajos Rodriguez MAURITIUS Diego Garcia Darwin AUSTRALIA Alice Springs Cairns Townsville NEW CALEDONIA (Fr.)

NAMIBIA Windhoek BOTSWANA Gaborone Bulawayo Harare SWAZILAND RÉUNION (Fr.) *Tropic of Capricorn* Port Hedland Geraldton Rockhampton Brisbane

Johannesburg Pretoria SOUTH AFRICA LESOTHO Maputo Durban Perth Fremantle Kalgoorlie-Boulder Adelaide *Darling* Newcastle Lord Howe I. (Austral.)

Cape Town C. of Good Hope Port Elizabeth Amsterdam I. (Fr.) St.Paul (Fr.) *Great Australian Bight* Melbourne Canberra Sydney *Tasman Sea* Norfolk I. (Austral.) NORTH I.

PACIFIC OCEAN

Bonin Is. (Japan) Volcano Is. (Japan) Marcus I. (Japan)

Tasmania Hobart NEW ZEALAND Wellington South I. Christchurch

Bouvet I. (Norw.) Prince Edward Is. (S.Africa) Crozet Is. (Fr.) Kerguelen (Fr.) McDonald Is. (Austral.) Heard I. (Austral.) Macquarie I. (Austral.) Campbell I. (N.Z.) Auckland Is. (N.Z.) Antipodes Is. Bounty Is. (N.Z.) Stewart I. Dunedin

SOUTHERN OCEAN

Antarctica

Antarctic Circle

East from Greenwich Ross Sea

10 11 12 13 14 15 16 17 18

Hanoi ● Capital Cities

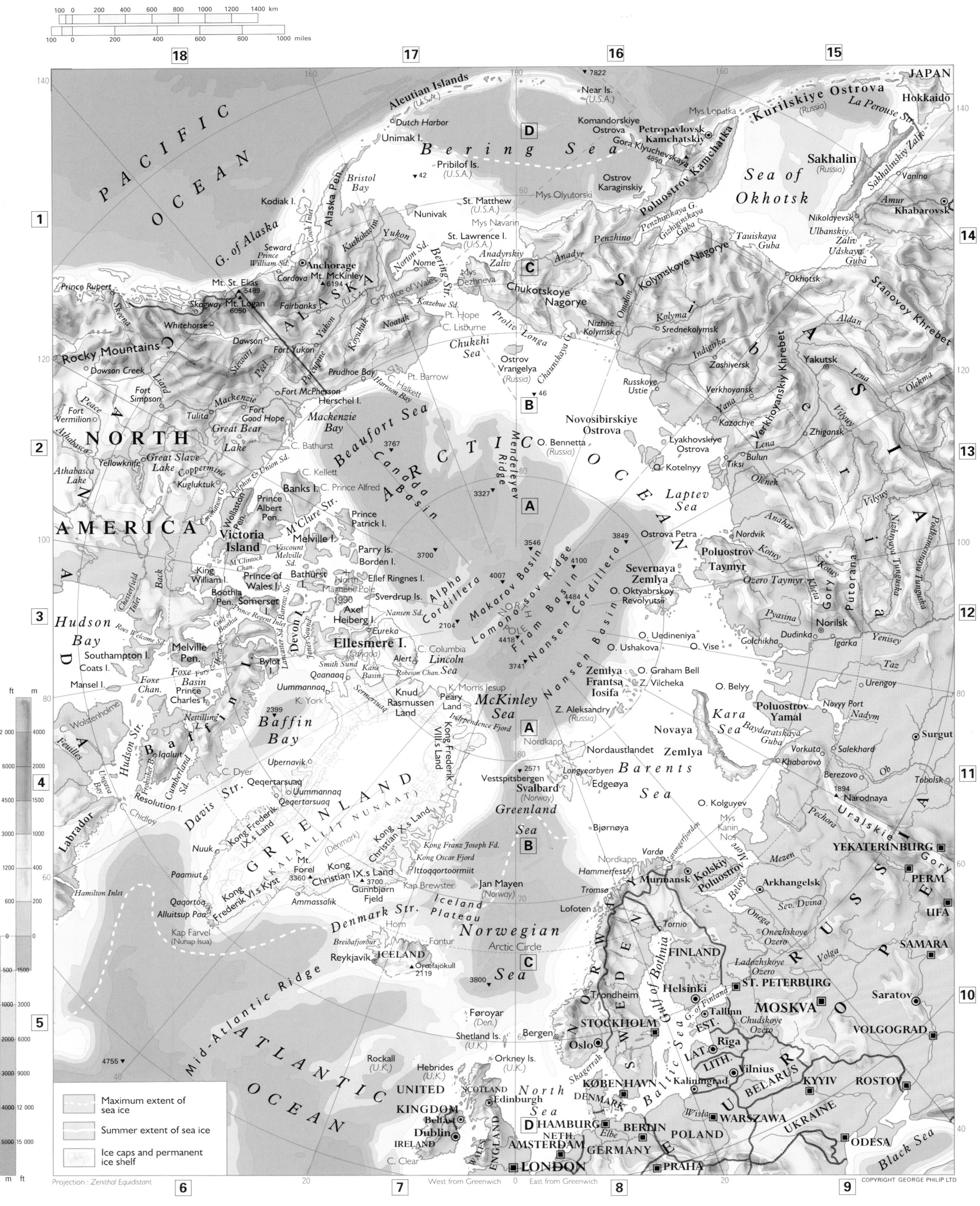

100 0 200 400 600 800 1000 1200 1400 km
100 0 200 400 600 800 1000 miles

18 **17** **16** **15**

JAPAN

PACIFIC OCEAN

Aleutian Islands (U.S.A.)
Near Is. (U.S.A.)
Dutch Harbor
Unimak I.
Bristol Bay
Bering Sea
Komandorskiye Ostrova
Mys Lopatka
Kurilskiye Ostrova (Russia)
La Perouse Str.
Hokkaidō

Kodiak I.
Pribilof Is. (U.S.A.)
St. Matthew (U.S.A.)
Nunivak
St. Lawrence I. (U.S.A.)
Mys Navarin
Anadyrskiy Zaliv
Petropavlovsk Kamchatskiy
Gora Klyuchevskaya
Poluostrov Kamchatka
Ostrov Karaginskiy
Mys Olyutorski
Penzhino
Penzhinskaya G.
Gizhiginskaya Guba
Tauiskaya Guba
Sea of Okhotsk
Sakhalin (Russia)
Sakhalinskiy Zaliv
Vanino
Amur
Khabarovsk

1

Prince Rupert
Seward
Prince William Sd.
Cook Inlet
Anchorage
Mt. McKinley 6194
Cordova
Mt. St. Elias 5489
Skagway Mt. Logan 6050
Whitehorse
Fairbanks
ALASKA (U.S.A.)
Nome
Bering Str.
Mys Dezhneva
Prince of Wales
Kotzebue Sd.
Pt. Hope
C. Lisburne
Chukotskoye Nagorye
Anadyr
Nizhne Kolymsk
Srednekolymsk
Kolyma
Kolymskoye Nagorye
Okhotsk
Nikolayevsk
Ulbanskiy Zaliv
Udskaya Guba
Stanovoy Khrebet
Aldan

Rocky Mountains
Dawson
Fort Yukon
Yukon
Porcupine
Fort McPherson
Prudhoe Bay
Pt. Barrow
Chukchi Sea
Proliv Longa
Ostrov Vrangelya (Russia)
Chaunskaya G.
Russkoye Ustie
Indigirka
Zashiversk
Verkhoyansk
Yana
Kazachye
Zhigansk
Yakutsk
Lena
Vilyuy
Olekma

NORTH AMERICA
Dawson Creek
Peace
Fort Simpson
Fort Good Hope
Tulita
Great Bear Lake
Mackenzie
C. Bathurst
3767
C. Kellett
Beaufort Sea
Canada Basin
ARCTIC OCEAN
Mendeleyev Ridge
O. Bennetta (Russia)
Novosibirskiye Ostrova
Lyakhovskiye Ostrova
Kotelnyy
Tiksi
Bulun
Olenek
Laptev Sea
Verkhoyanskiy Khrebet
Gory Putorana
ASIA

2 **13**

Fort Vermilion
Athabasca
Yellowknife
Great Slave Lake
Coppermine
Kugluktuk
Banks I.
C. Prince Alfred
Prince Patrick I.
Borden I.
3327
3546
4007
Makarov Basin
Lomonosov Ridge
4100
4484
Nansen Cordillera
Ostrova Petra
Severnaya Zemlya
O. Oktyabrskoy Revolyutsii
Poluostrov Taymyr
Ozero Taymyr
Khatanga
Nordvik
Anabar
Nizhnyaya Tunguska
Podkamennaya Tunguska

Athabasca Lake
Wollaston Pen.
Victoria Island
M'Clure Str.
Melville I.
Parry Is.
3700
Prince Patrick I.
Ellef Ringnes I.
Sverdrup Is.
Alpha Cordillera
3849
Fram Basin
Nansen Basin
Severnaya Zemlya
O. Uedineniya
O. Vise
Golchikha
Norilsk
Dudinka
Igarka
Yenisey

3
Hudson Bay
Chesterfield Inlet
Back
King William I.
Boothia Pen.
Somerset I.
Bathurst I.
North Magnetic Pole 1990
Axel Heiberg I.
Nansen Sd.
2104
NORTH POLE
4418
3741
Nansen Basin
O. Ushakova
O. Graham Bell
Zemlya Frantsa Iosifa
O. Belyy
Urengoy
Taz
Pyasina
Ob

Southampton I.
Coats I.
Melville Pen.
Foxe Basin
Prince Charles I.
Prince Albert Pen.
Devon I.
Ellesmere I.
C. Columbia
Alert
Lincoln Sea
Robeson Chan.
Kane Basin
Knud Rasmussen Land
Peary Land
McKinley Sea
Z. Vilcheka
Z. Aleksandry (Russia)
Zemlya Frantsa Iosifa
Novaya Zemlya
Poluostrov Yamal
Novyy Port
Nadym
Vorkuta
Salekhard
Khabarovo

Mansel I.
Foxe Chan.
Baffin Island
Hudson Str.
Baffin Bay
Iqaluit
Qaanaaq
Uummannaq
K. York
2399
Smith Sund
Kong Frederik VIII.s Land
Independence Fjord
Nordkapp
Nordaustlandet
Kara Sea
Baydaratskaya Guba
O. Belyy
Berezovo
Tobolsk

4 **11**

Labrador
C. Chidley
C. Dyer
Upernavik
Uummannaq
Qeqertarsuaq
GREENLAND (KALAALLIT NUNAAT) (Denmark)
Kong Christian X.s Land
2571
Vestspitsbergen
Svalbard (Norway)
Edgeøya
Barents Sea
Longyearbyen
Novaya Zemlya
O. Kolguyev
1894 Narodnaya
Pechora
Uralskie Gory
YEKATERINBURG
PERM

Davis Str.
Nuuk
Paamiut
Kong Frederik VI.s Kyst
Mt. Forel 3360
Kong Christian IX.s Land
Kong Franz Joseph Fd.
Ittoqqortoormiit
Greenland Sea
Bjørnøya
Nordkapp
Mys Kanin Nos
Mezen
More
Vardø
Varangerfjorden

5
Qaqortoq
Alluitsup Paa
Kap Farvel (Nunap Isua)
Breiðafjörður
Ammassalik
3700
Gunnbjørn Fjeld
Kap Brewster
Jan Mayen (Norway)
Denmark Str.
Iceland Plateau
Hammerfest
Tromsø
Murmansk
Arkhangelsk
Kolskiy Poluostrov
Sev. Dvina
Onega
Onezhskoye Ozero
Ladozhskoye Ozero
SAMARA
UFA
Volga
Saratov

4755
Horn
Fontur
2119 Öræfajökull
Reykjavík
ICELAND
Føroyar (Den.)
Norwegian Sea
3800
Arctic Circle
Trondheim
FINLAND
Helsinki
ST. PETERBURG
Chudskoye Ozero
MOSKVA
VOLGOGRAD

10

Shetland Is. (U.K.)
Bergen
Oslo
STOCKHOLM
SWEDEN
NORWAY
Tornio
Gulf of Bothnia
G. of Finland
Tallinn
EST.
Riga
LAT.
LITH.
Vilnius
Kaliningrad
Chudskoye Ozero
ROSTOV

Rockall (U.K.)
Hebrides (U.K.)
Orkney Is. (U.K.)
SCOTLAND
Edinburgh
North Sea
Skagerrak
KØBENHAVN
DENMARK
Baltic Sea
Gdansk
Wisła
WARSZAWA
POLAND
BELARUS
KYYIV
UKRAINE
ODESA
Black Sea

UNITED KINGDOM
Belfast
Dublin
IRELAND
ENGLAND
C. Clear
LONDON
Mid-Atlantic Ridge
ATLANTIC OCEAN
HAMBURG
AMSTERDAM
NETH.
GERMANY
BERLIN
Elbe
PRAHA

Maximum extent of sea ice
Summer extent of sea ice
Ice caps and permanent ice shelf

Projection : Zenithal Equidistant

6 West from Greenwich **7** 0 East from Greenwich **8** **9**

COPYRIGHT GEORGE PHILIP LTD

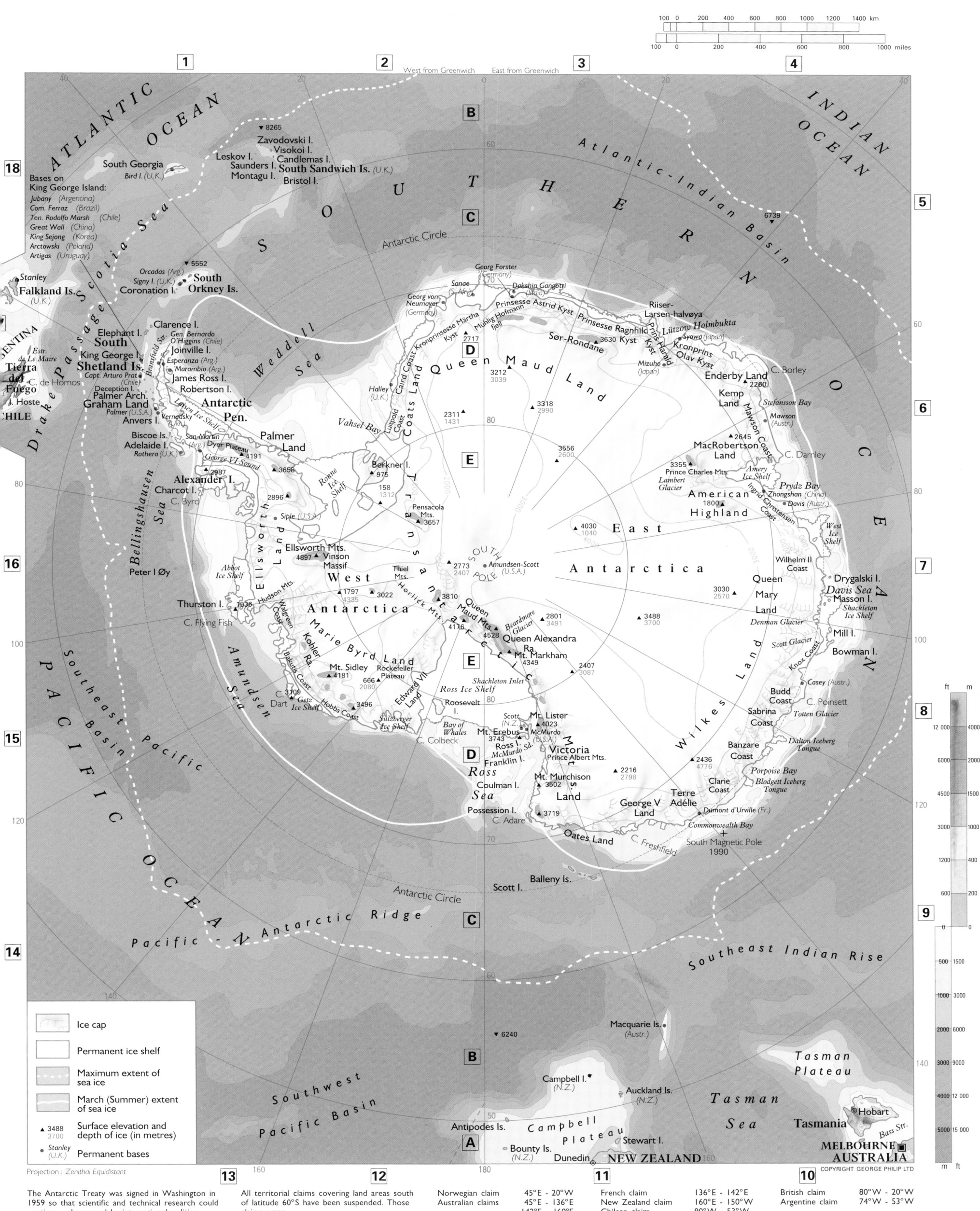

A B C D E F G H

Novaya Zemlya
RUSSIA
Barents Sea
Murmansk
FINLAND
Helsinki
ST-PETERSBURG
Tromsø
Bjørnøya (Norw.)
NORWAY
SWEDEN
G. of Bothnia
Stockholm
Göteborg
Oslo
N.
Lofoten
Trondheim
Bergen
Faroyar (Den.)
Baltic Sea
Gdansk
POLAND
Warszawa
DENMARK
København
Malmö
Hamburg
Berlin
GERMANY
Amsterdam NETH.
Brussel BELG.
CZECH REP. SLOVAK.
Wien AUSTRIA HUNGARY
Zagreb CROATIA
BOS. H.
ITALY
Milano
Roma
Napoli
Adriatic Sea
Sicilia
Tunis
Taràbulus
TUNISIA
Mt. Blanc 4807
SWITZ.
Bern
Rhein
Elbe
North Sea
Glasgow
Liverpool
Dublin
IRELAND
LONDON
UNITED KINGDOM
Celtic Sea
Rockall (U.K.)
Le Havre
PARIS
FRANCE
Loire
Bordeaux
Bay of Biscay
Marseille
Corse
Sardegna
Barcelona
Alger
Madrid
SPAIN
PORTUGAL
Lisboa
Porto
Vigo
A Coruña
C. Fisterra
Douro
Ebro
C. de São Vicente
Str. of Gibraltar
Tanger
Rabat
Casablanca
MOROCCO
Marrakech
Madeira (Port.)
Funchal
Is. Canarias (Sp.)
Las Palmas
Mediterranean Sea
Mt.
MALTA
ALGERIA
Chott Djerid
Chott Melr.
S a h a r a
WESTERN SAHARA
El Aiún
Ras Nouâdhibou
MAURITANIA
Nouakchott
St-Louis
Dakar
C. Vert
SENEGAL
GAMBIA
GUINEA-BISSAU
GUINEA
Conakry
Freetown
SIERRA LEONE
LIBERIA
Monrovia
IVORY COAST
Abidjan
Sekondi-
GHANA
Accra
Bamako
Kayes
MALI
Tombouctou
Ouagadougou
BURKINA FASO
NIGER
Kano
NIGERIA
Lagos
Niger
Benue
BENIN
TOGO
CAMEROON
Douala
Port
CAPE VERDE IS.
São Vicente
Boa Vista
Santiago
Praia

Svalbard (Norw.)
Jan Mayen (Norw.)
Greenland Sea
ICELAND
Reykjavík
Öraefajökull 2119
Norwegian Sea

GREENLAND (Denmark)
Ammassalik
Denmark Strait
Nuuk
K. Farvel

ATLANTIC
NORTH
OCEAN
Azores (Port.)
Ponta Delgada
Sargasso Sea
6551
7292
6995

Queen Elizabeth Islands
Devon I.
Lancaster Sd.
Melville I.
Prince of Wales I.
Victoria I.
Banks I.
Beaufort Sea
C. Bathurst
Great Bear Lake
Boothia Pen.
Baffin I.
Baffin Bay
Davis Strait
Cumberland Sd.
C. Dyer
Frobisher B.
C. Chidley
C. Henrietta Maria
Southampton I.
Foxe Chan.
Melville Pen.
Hudson Str.
Labrador Sea
Hamilton Inlet
Str. of Belle Isle
Newfoundland
Flemish Cap
St. John's
C. Race
Cape Breton I.
Grand Banks
Hudson Bay
Belcher Is.
James Bay
Churchill
Moosonee
Nelson
Albany
CANADA
Regina
Winnipeg
L. Winnipeg
Great Slave Lake
Minneapolis
Omaha
UNITED STATES
Missouri
CHICAGO
L. Superior
L. Michigan
L. Huron
Detroit
L. Erie
Pittsburgh
Ohio
St. Louis
Mississippi
Red
Arkansas
Appalachian Mts.
Tennessee
Alabama
Atlanta
New Orleans
Houston
Galveston
Gulf of Mexico
Tampico
Veracruz
G. de Campeche
MEXICO
Canal de Yucatán
Montréal
Québec
St. Lawrence
Gulf of St. Lawrence
Ottawa
Toronto
L. Ontario
Halifax
Boston
C. Cod
NEW YORK CITY
PHILADELPHIA
Baltimore
Washington D.C.
Chesapeake Bay
C. Hatteras
Charleston
Jacksonville
Miami
Florida Strait
Nassau
BAHAMAS
La Habana
CUBA
Santiago de Cuba
JAMAICA
Kingston
Cayman Trough
HAITI
DOM. REP.
9200
PUERTO RICO (U.S.A.)
Puerto Rico Trench
Leeward Is.
GUADELOUPE (Fr.)
DOMINICA
MARTINIQUE (Fr.)
ST. LUCIA
BARBADOS
Windward Is.
TRINIDAD & TOBAGO
ST. VINCENT
GRENADA
West Indies
Tropic of Cancer
Bermuda (U.K.)
Hamilton
GUATEMALA
BELIZE
G. de Honduras
HONDURAS
EL SALVADOR
NICARAGUA
L. de Nicaragua
COSTA RICA
Panamá
PANAMA
G. del Darién
Curaçao
Is. de Venezuela
Caribbean Sea
Caracas
VENEZUELA
Maracaibo
Sierra Nevada de Santa Marta
Barranquilla
5000
Bogotá
COLOMBIA
Meta
6000
2810
Mt. Roraima
GUYANA
Georgetown
SURINAM
Paramaribo
FRENCH GUIANA
Cayenne
C. Orange
Arctic Circle

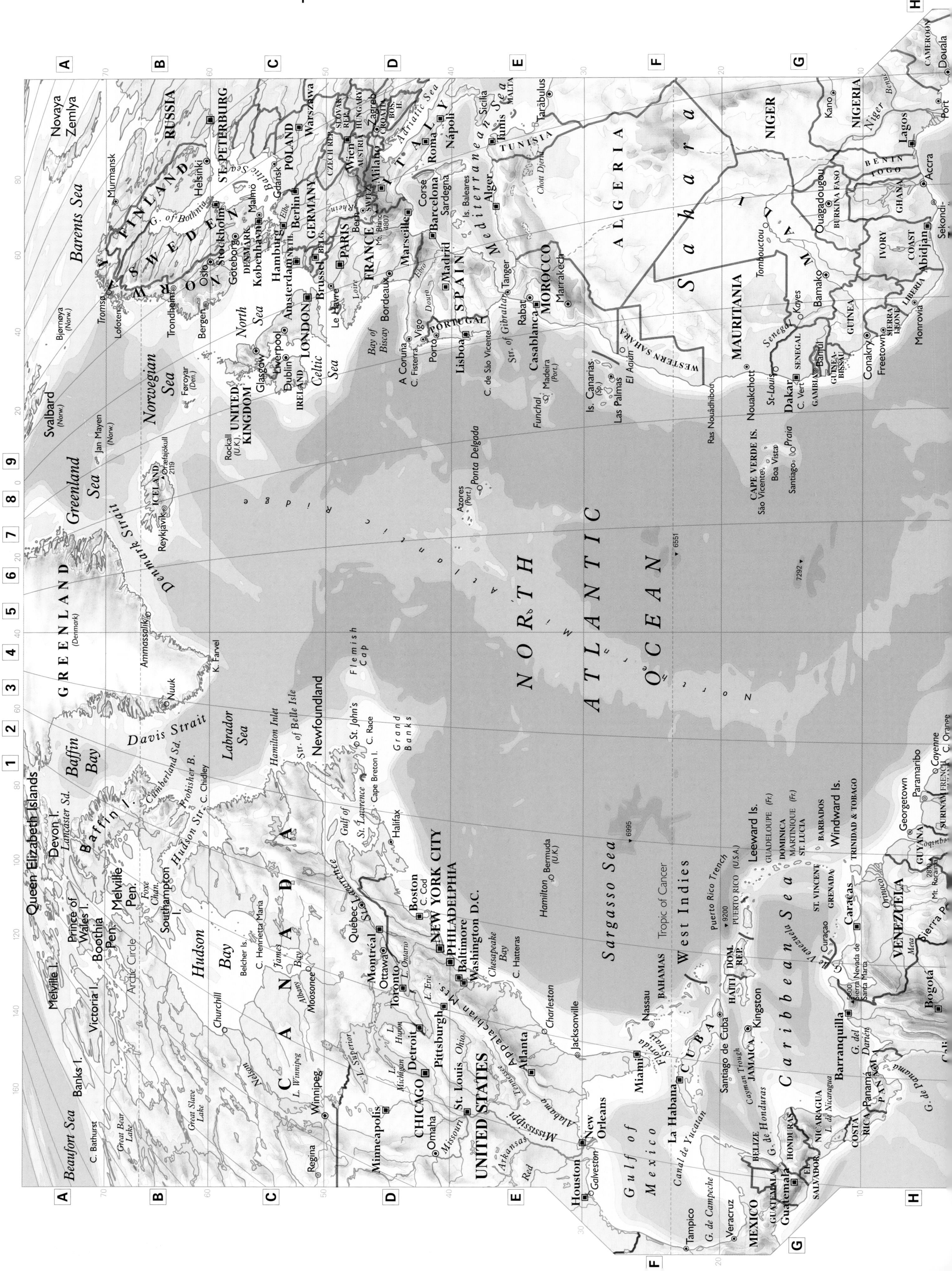

SOUTH ATLANTIC OCEAN
PACIFIC OCEAN
BRAZIL
PERU
BOLIVIA
PARAGUAY
ARGENTINA
CHILE
URUGUAY
ECUADOR
GABON
CONGO
ANGOLA
NAMIBIA
SOUTH AFRICA
SÃO TOMÉ & PRINCIPE
GUINEA
Andes
Pampas
Patagonia
Gran Chaco
Quito
Cotopaxi 5897
Chimborazo 6267
Guayaquil
G. de Guayaquil
Pta. Pariñas
C. de San Francisco
Iquitos
Trujillo
Callao
LIMA
L. Titicaca
Nevada Ancohuma 6550
La Paz
L. de Poopó
Arica
Iquique
Antofagasta
8050
Ojos del Salado 6863
San Miguel de Tucumán
Córdoba
Mt. Aconcagua 6960
Valparaíso
SANTIAGO
Concepción
Santa Fe
Rosario
BUENOS AIRES
Montevideo
Rio de la Plata
Bahía Blanca
G. San Matías
Pen. Valdés
Golfo San Jorge
Puerto Montt
I. de Chiloé
Arch de los Chonos
Pen. de Taitao
G. de Penas
Est. de Magallanes
Punta Arenas
Tierra del Fuego
I. Santa Inés
C. de Hornos
Drake Passage
Falkland Is. (U.K.)
Burdwood Banks
29
Shag Rocks
South Georgia (U.K.)
South Sandwich Trench
8265
South Sandwich Is. (U.K.)
South Orkney Is.
South Shetland Is.
Scotia Sea
Weddell Sea
Antarctic Circle
Antarctic Peninsula
Graham Land
Peter I Øy
Arch. de Juan Fernández (Chile)
San Ambrosio (Chile)
Peru-Chile Trench
Chile Rise
Putumayo
Marañón
Ucayali
Japurá
Negro
Amazonas
Purus
Madeira
Aripuanã
Tapajós
Xingu
Tocantins
Parnaíba
São Francisco
Pilcomayo
Salado
Paraná
Paraguay
Uruguay
Colorado
Chubut
Manaus
Santarém
Belém
São Luís
Fortaleza
Fernando de Noronha
C. de São Roque
Natal
Recife
Maceió
Salvador
Brasília
Goiânia
Belo Horizonte
2890
Serra da Mantiqueira
C. de São Tomé
C. Frio
RIO DE JANEIRO
SÃO PAULO
Santos
Asunción
Curitiba
Pôrto Alegre
L. dos Patos
Equator
São Paulo (Brazil)
Tropic of Capricorn
Trindade (Brazil)
Ascension I. (U.K.)
St. Helena (U.K.)
Tristan de Cunha (U.K.)
Gough I. (U.K.)
Bouvetøya (Norw.)
Mid-Atlantic Ridge
Southern Mid-Atlantic Ridge
Walvis Ridge
Atlantic Indian Ridge
7758
6537
6013
638
892
5457
411
6212
6739
Libreville
C. Lopez
Ogooué
Annobón (São Tomé)
Brazzaville
Pointe Noire
Luanda
Lobito
Benguela
Namibe
C. Fria
Windhoek
Walvis Bay
Lüderitz
Port Nolloth
Orange
Cape Town
C. of Good Hope
J
K
L
M
N
P
Q
1
2
3
4
5
6
7
8
9
0
10
20
30
40
50
60
70
80
100
120
ft
m
12 000
9000
6000
3000
1500
600
200
4000
3000
2000
1000
500
200
0
600
1000 3000
2000 6000
4000 12 000
6000 18 000
8000 24 000
m ft
Projection: Mollweide
West from Greenwich
COPYRIGHT GEORGE PHILIP LTD.

GREENLAND 1:10 000 000

100 0 100 200 300 400 500 km
100 0 50 100 150 200 250 300 350 miles
A
B
C
D
E
F
1
2
3
4
5
6
7
8
9
10
11
12
13
ARCTIC OCEAN
CANADA
Axel Heiberg I.
Ellesmere Island
Alert
Lincoln Sea
Robeson Chan.
Kennedy Kanal
Nares Str.
Smith Sund
Kane Basin
Jones Sd.
Devon Island
Hall Land
Washington Land
Nyeboe Land
Wulff Land
Warming Land
Kap Morris Jesup
1920
Frederick E. Hyde Fjord
Nansen Land
Peary Land
J. P. Koch Fjord
Jørgen Brønlund Fjord
Heilprin Land
Independence Fjord
Station Nord
Nordostrundingen
McKinley Sea
Mylius Erichsen Land
Danmark Fjord
Kronprins Christian Land
Ingolf Fjord
Mallemukfjeld
Knud Rasmussen Land
Inglefield Land
Siorapaluk
Qeqertarsuaq
Qaanaaq (Thule)
Kap Atholl
Uummannaq (Dundas)
Pituffik (Thule Air Base)
Kap York
Lauge Koch Kyst
Melville Bugt
2170
AVANNAARSUA (NORDGRØNLAND)
Lambert Land
Hovgaard Ø
Nioghalvfjerdsfjorden
Norske Øer
GREENLAND SEA
Kong Frederik VIII.s Land
Franske Øer
Germania Land
Danmarkshavn
Store Koldewey
Dove Bugt
Hochstetter Forland
Shannon
Dronning Margrethe II Land
Steenstrup Gletscher
Baffin Bay
Nuussuaq (Kraulshavn)
Zackenberg
Wollaston Forland
Clavering Ø
Ole Rømer Land
Andrée Land
Nationalparken i Nord-og Østgrønland
2935
Kong Christian X.s Land
Kejser Franz Joseph Fd.
2940
Petermann Bjerg
Traill Ø
Mestersvig
Kong Oscar Fjord
Upernavik
Kangersuatsiaq
Upernavik Kujalleq
Clyde River
KITAA (VESTGRØNLAND)
TUNU (ØSTGRØNLAND)
3220
Nunavik
Illorsuit
Maarmorilik
Uummannaq
2092
Ikerasak
Saqqaq
Stauning Alper
Jameson Land
Renland
Illoqqortoormiut (Scoresbysund)
Uunarteq
Milne Land
Ittaajimmiut
Scoresby Sund
Kangikajik (Kap Brewster)
Kap Dalton
Qeqertarsuaq (Disko)
Kangerluk
Qeqertarsuaq (Godhavn)
Disko Bugt
Ilulissat (Jakobshavn)
Qasigiannguit (Christianshåb)
Aasiaat (Egedesminde)
Ikamiut
Kangaatsiaq
GREENLAND (KALAALLIT NUNAAT)
(Denmark)
Kong Christian IX.s Land
Gunnbjørn Fjeld
3700
Blosseville Kyst
Nordre Strømfjord
Sisimiut (Holsteinsborg)
Kangerlussuaq (Søndre Strømfjord)
Hilleq
Søndre Strømfjord
Kangaamiut
Maniitsoq (Sukkertoppen)
Kong Frederik IX.s Land
Kangerdlugssuaq
Denmark Strait
Arctic Circle
Mt. Forel
3360
Kap Gustav Holm
Ikkatteq
Kuummiut
Kulusuk
Isortoq
Tasiilaq (Ammassalik)
Horn
Húnaflói
Eyjafjörður
Akureyri
Neskaupstaður
Ísafjörður
ICELAND
Breidafjörður
Snæfellsnæs
Vatnajökull
2119
Öræfajökull
Faxaflói
Reykjavík
Vestmannaeyjar
Heimaey
Surtsey
Nuuk (Godthåb)
Kapisillit
Kangerluarsoruseq (Færingehavn)
Qeqertarsuatsiaat (Fiskenæsset)
2850
Davis Strait
Kong Frederik VI.s Kyst
Gyldenløve Fjord
Kap Møsting
Kap Moltke
Kap Skjold
Timmiarmiut
Mogens Heinesen Fjord
ATLANTIC OCEAN
Paamiut (Frederikshåb)
Narsalik
Kangilinnguit (Grønnedal)
Arsuk
Ivittuut
Narsarsuaq
Narsaq
Qaqortoq (Julianehåb)
Alluitsup Paa (Sydprøven)
Lindenow Fjord
Nanortalik
Nunap Isua (Kap Farvel)
Prins Christian Sund
Nordaustlandet
Nordkapp
Olgastredet
Spitsbergen
Longyearbyen
Edgeøya
Storfjorden
Barentsburg
Svalbard (Norway)
Sørkapp
Jan Mayen (Norway)
ft m
3000 1000
1200 400
600 200
0 0
200 600
m ft
Projection: Conic
West from Greenwich
50 40 30 20
COPYRIGHT GEORGE PHILIP LTD.

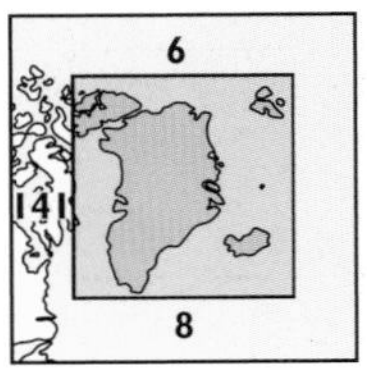

6
4
8

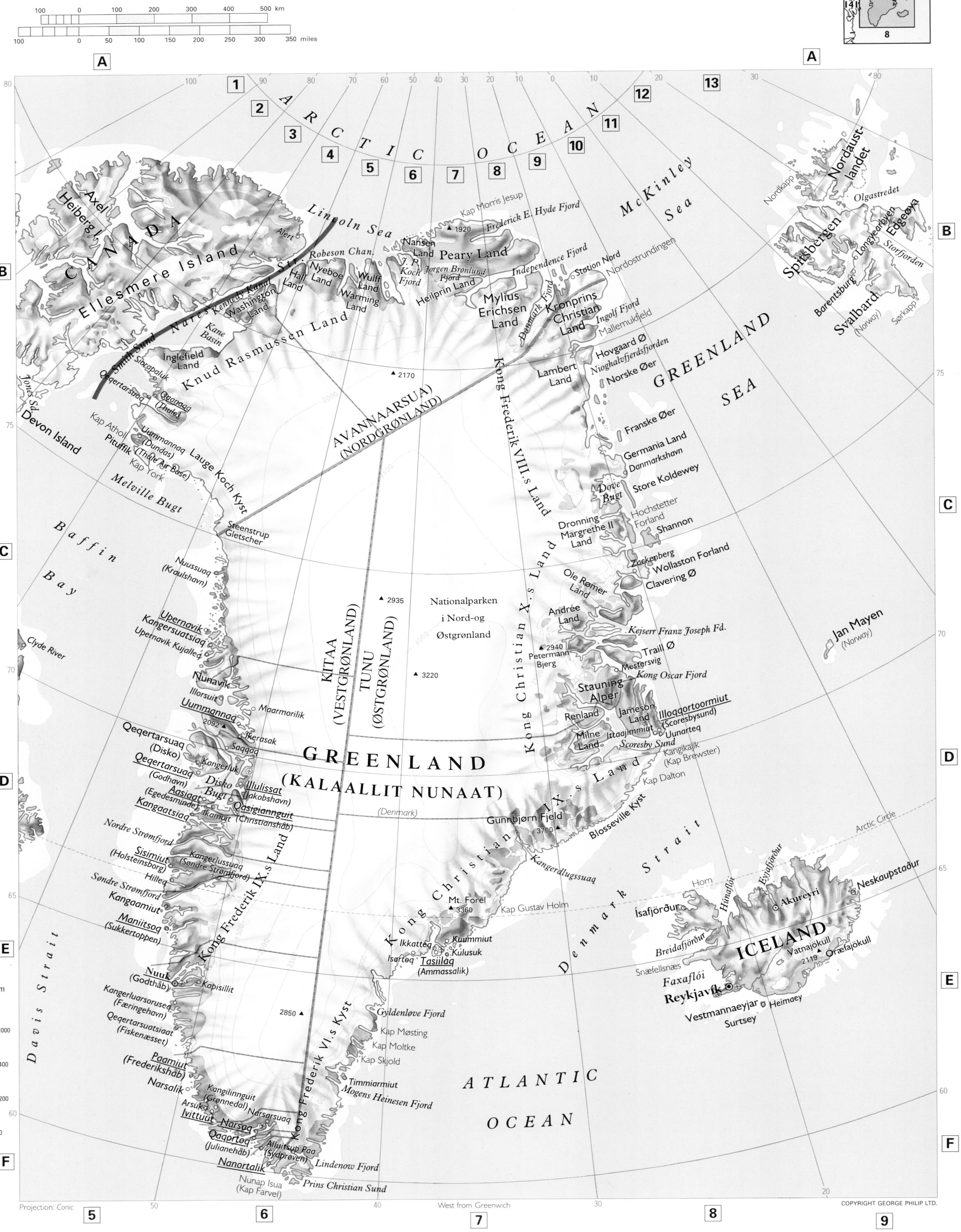

Underlined towns give their name to the administrative area in which they stand.

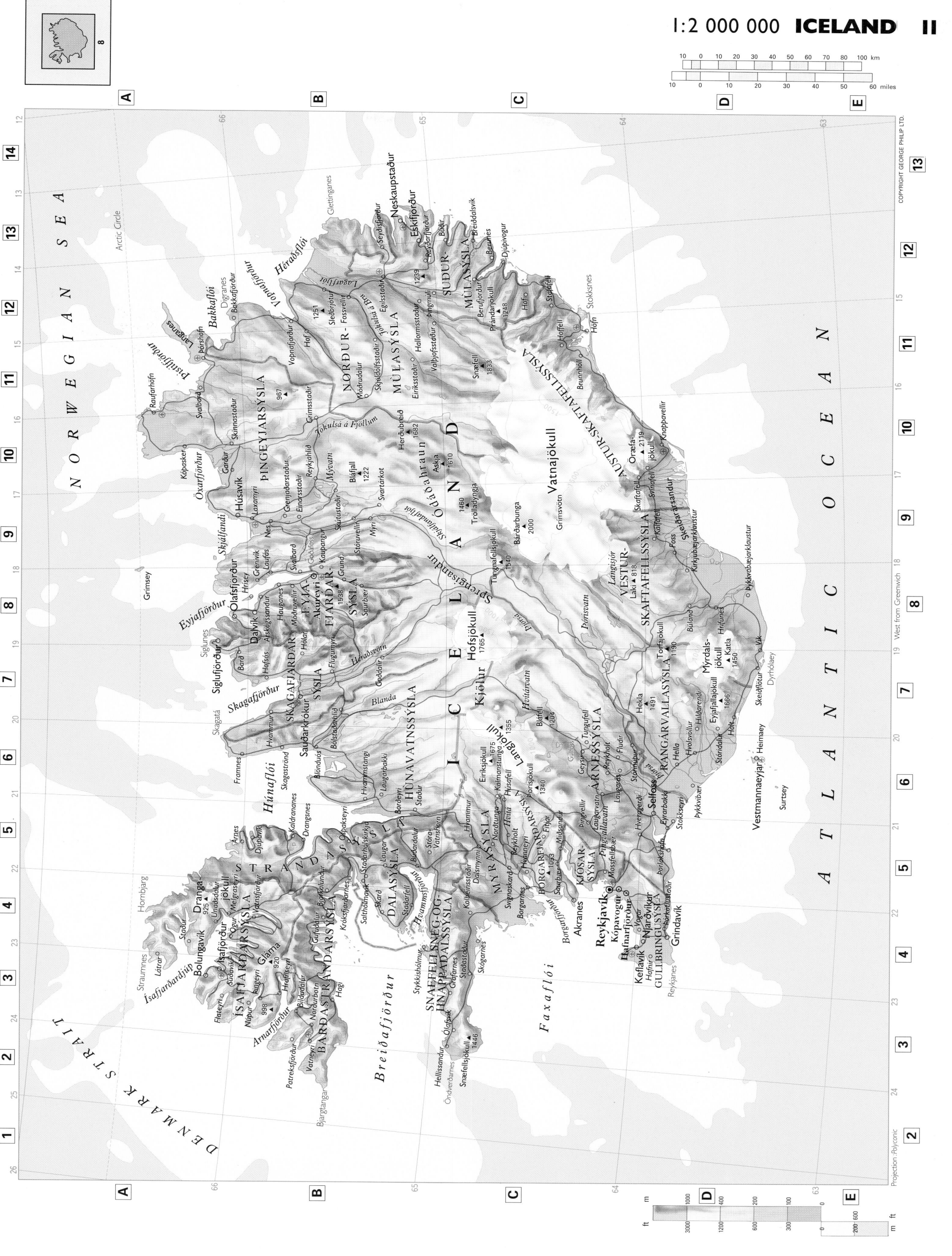

COPYRIGHT GEORGE PHILIP LTD.

10 0 10 20 30 40 50 60 70 80 100 km
10 0 10 20 30 40 50 60 miles

N O R W E G I A N   S E A

A T L A N T I C   O C E A N

DENMARK STRAIT

Arctic Circle

I C E L A N D

Vatnajökull

Hofsjökull

Langjökull

Vestmannaeyjar

Reykjavík

Akureyri

Ísafjörður

Húsavík

Selfoss

Keflavík

Grindavík

Höfn

West from Greenwich

Projection: Polyconic

m ft
3000
1200
600
300
0
1000
400
200
100
0
200 600
ft m

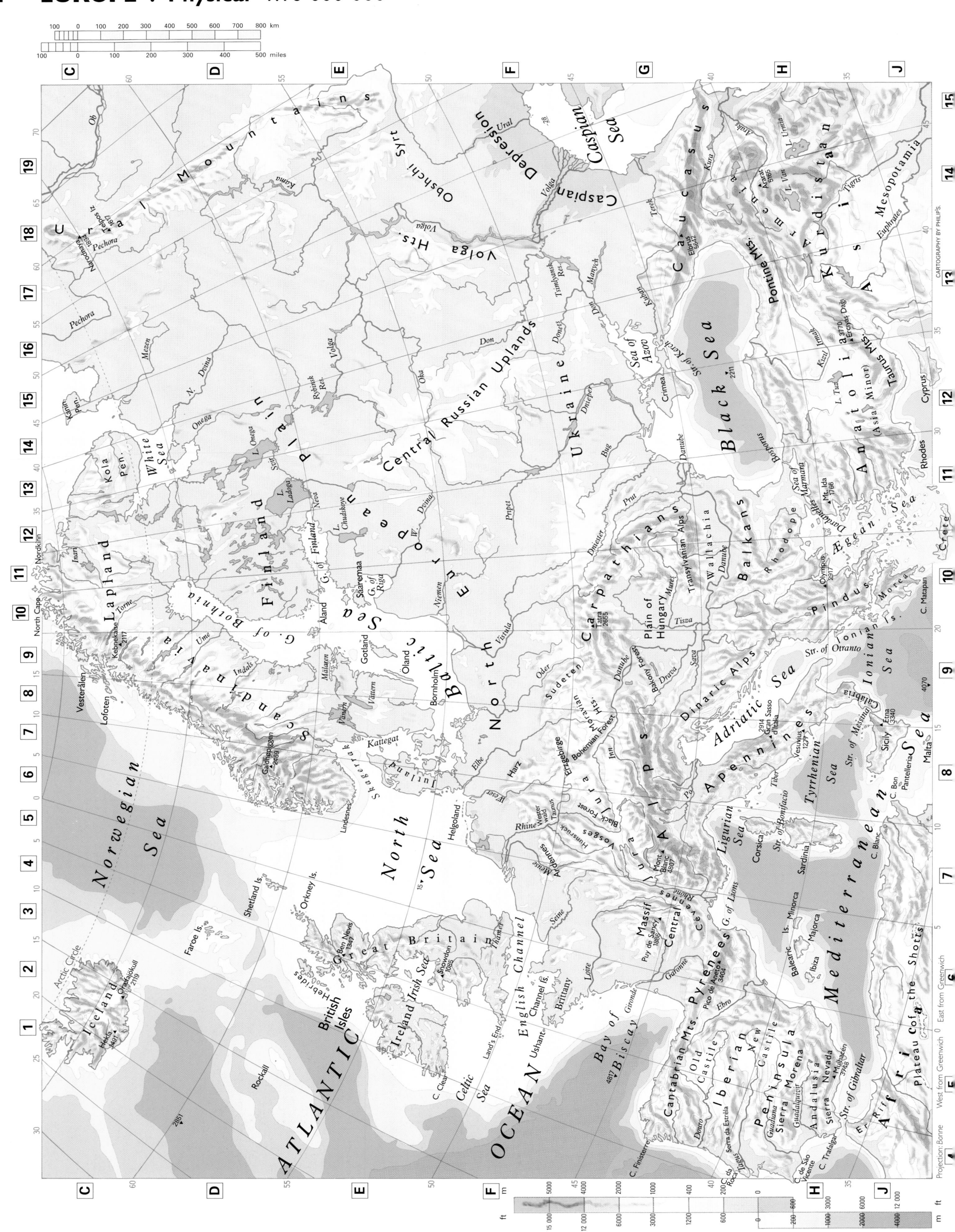

CARTOGRAPHY BY PHILIP'S

Projection: Bonne

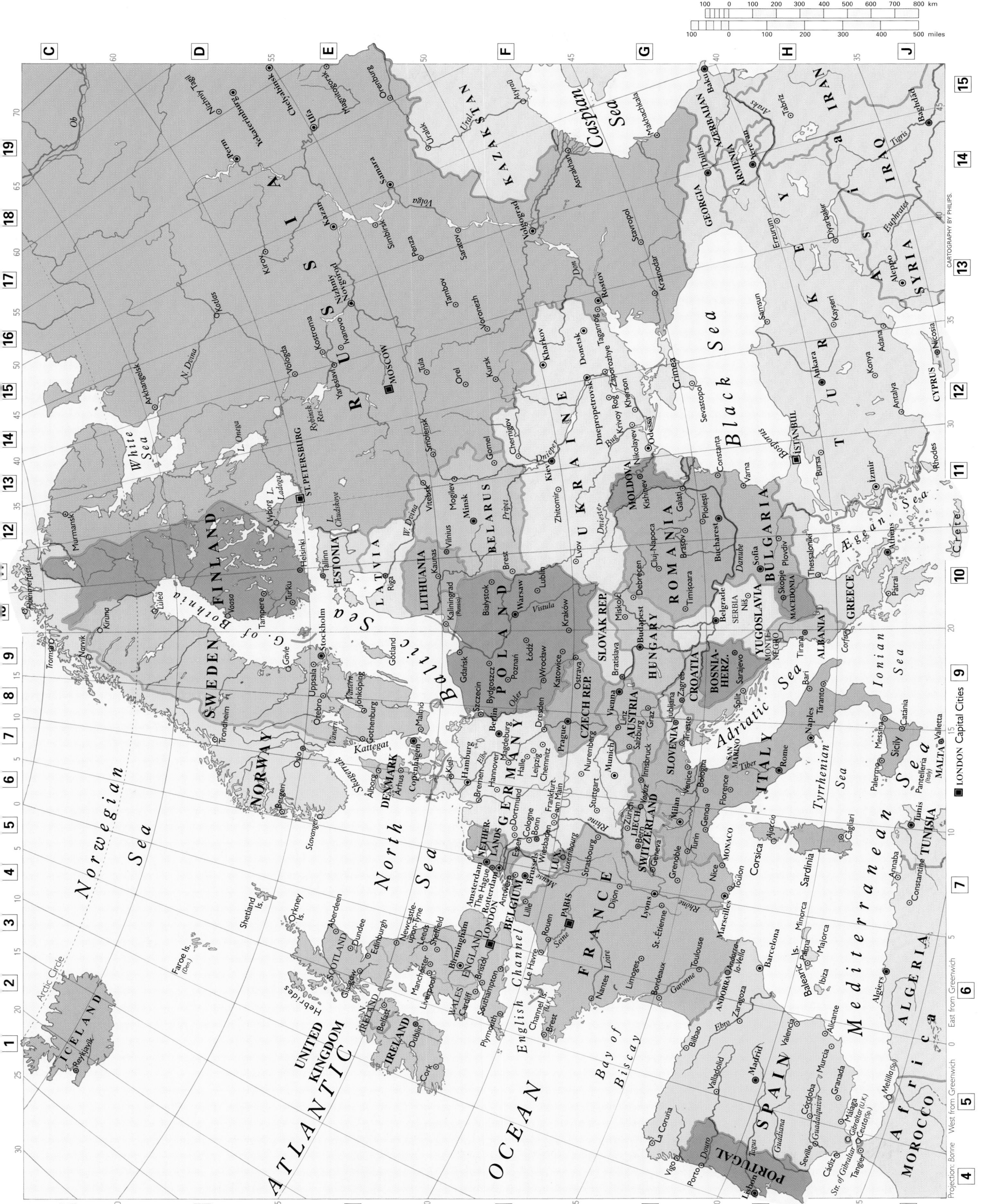

SCANDINAVIA 1:4 000 000

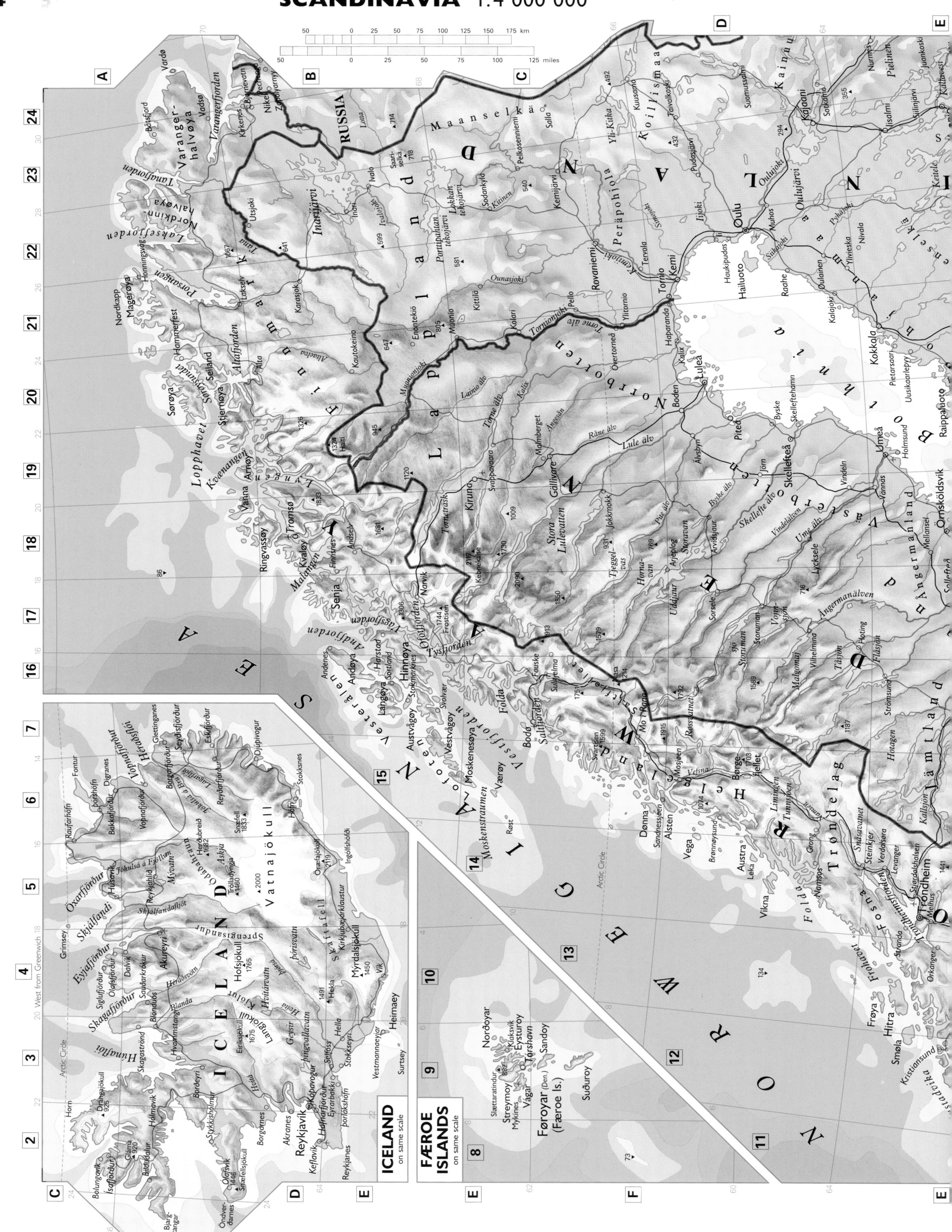

ICELAND
on same scale

FÆROE
ISLANDS
on same scale

Projection: Conical with two standard parallels

East from Greenwich

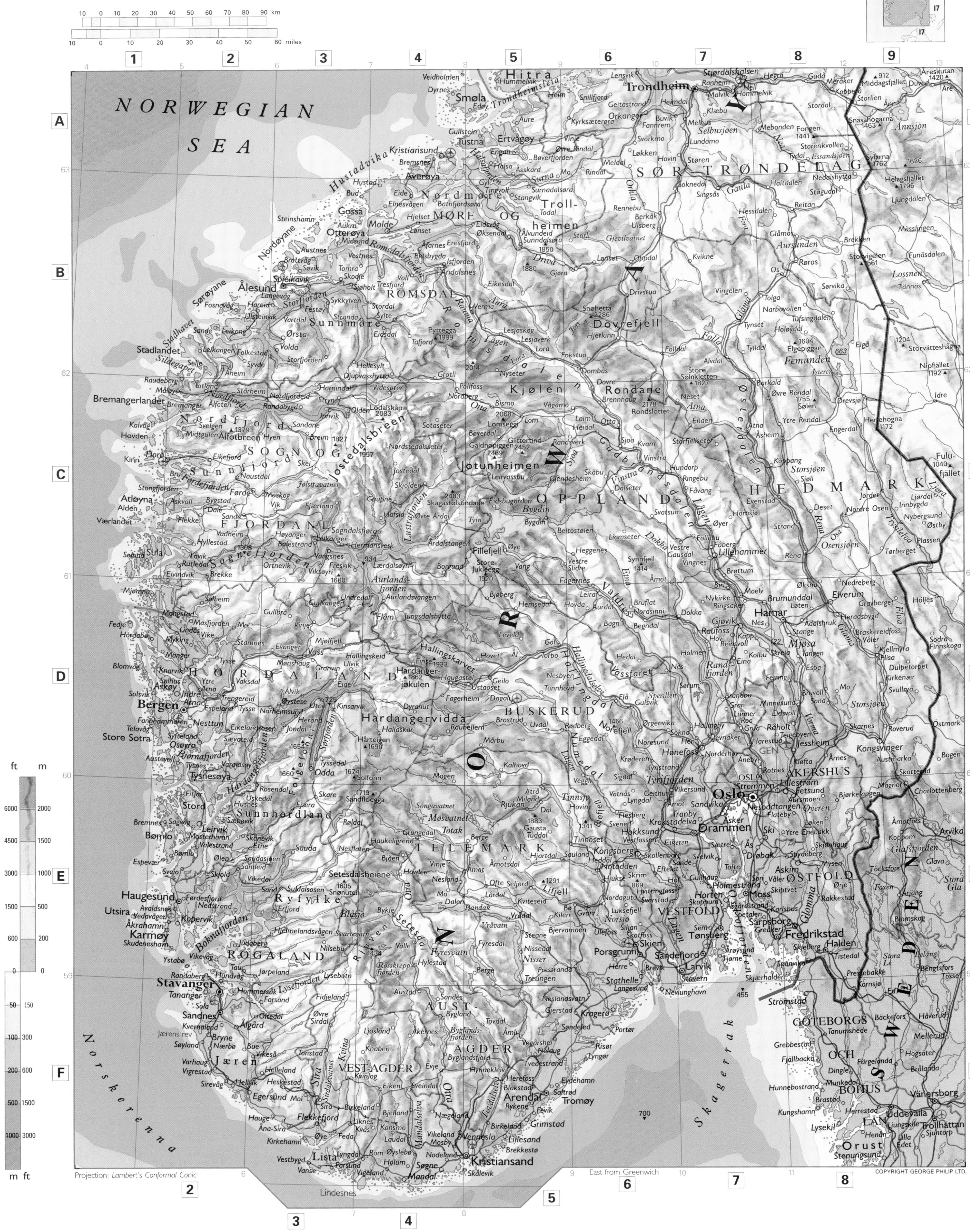

10 0 10 20 30 40 50 60 70 80 90 km

10 0 10 20 30 40 50 60 miles

NORWEGIAN SEA

Trondheim

SØR-TRØNDELAG

MØRE OG ROMSDAL

Ålesund

Molde

Kristiansund

Romsdal

Sunnmøre

Dovrefjell

Snøhetta 2286

HEDMARK

Røros

Nordfjord

SOGN OG FJORDANE

Jostedalsbreen

Jotunheimen

Galdhøpiggen 2469

Glittertind 2452

OPPLAND

Rondane

Lillehammer

Gjøvik

Hamar

Mjøsa

Elverum

Bergen

HORDALAND

Hardangervidda

Hardangerjøkulen

BUSKERUD

Hønefoss

AKERSHUS

Oslo

Drammen

Kongsvinger

Haugesund

Karmøy

ROGALAND

Ryfylke

Sunnhordland

TELEMARK

Skien

Porsgrunn

VESTFOLD

Tønsberg

Sandefjord

Larvik

ØSTFOLD

Sarpsborg

Fredrikstad

Halden

Stavanger

Sandnes

Jæren

VEST-AGDER

AUST-AGDER

Arendal

Kristiansand

Mandal

Lindesnes

SWEDEN

GÖTEBORGS OCH BOHUS LÄN

Uddevalla

Trollhättan

Skagerrak

Norskerenna

ft m

m ft

Projection: Lambert's Conformal Conic

East from Greenwich

COPYRIGHT GEORGE PHILIP LTD.

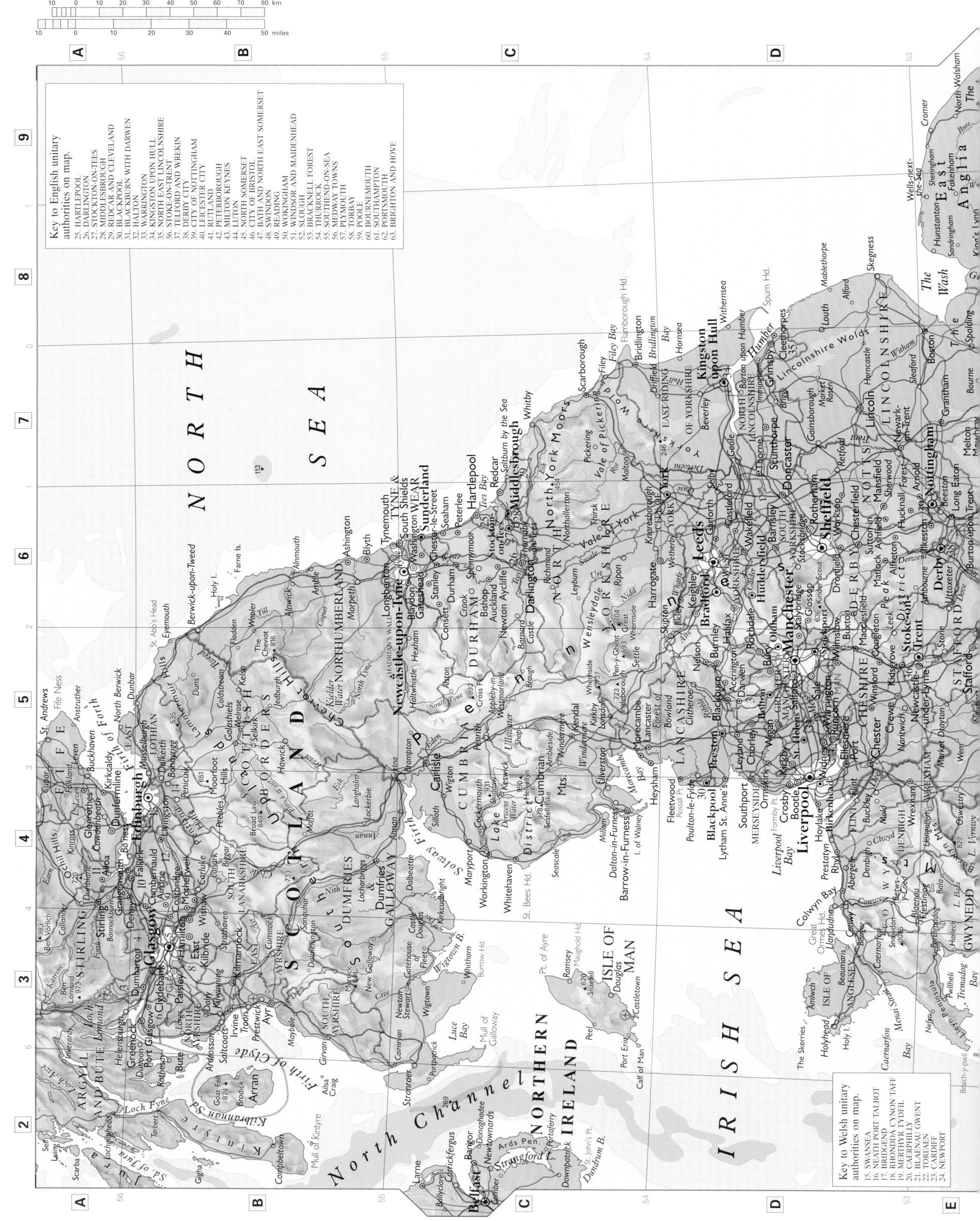

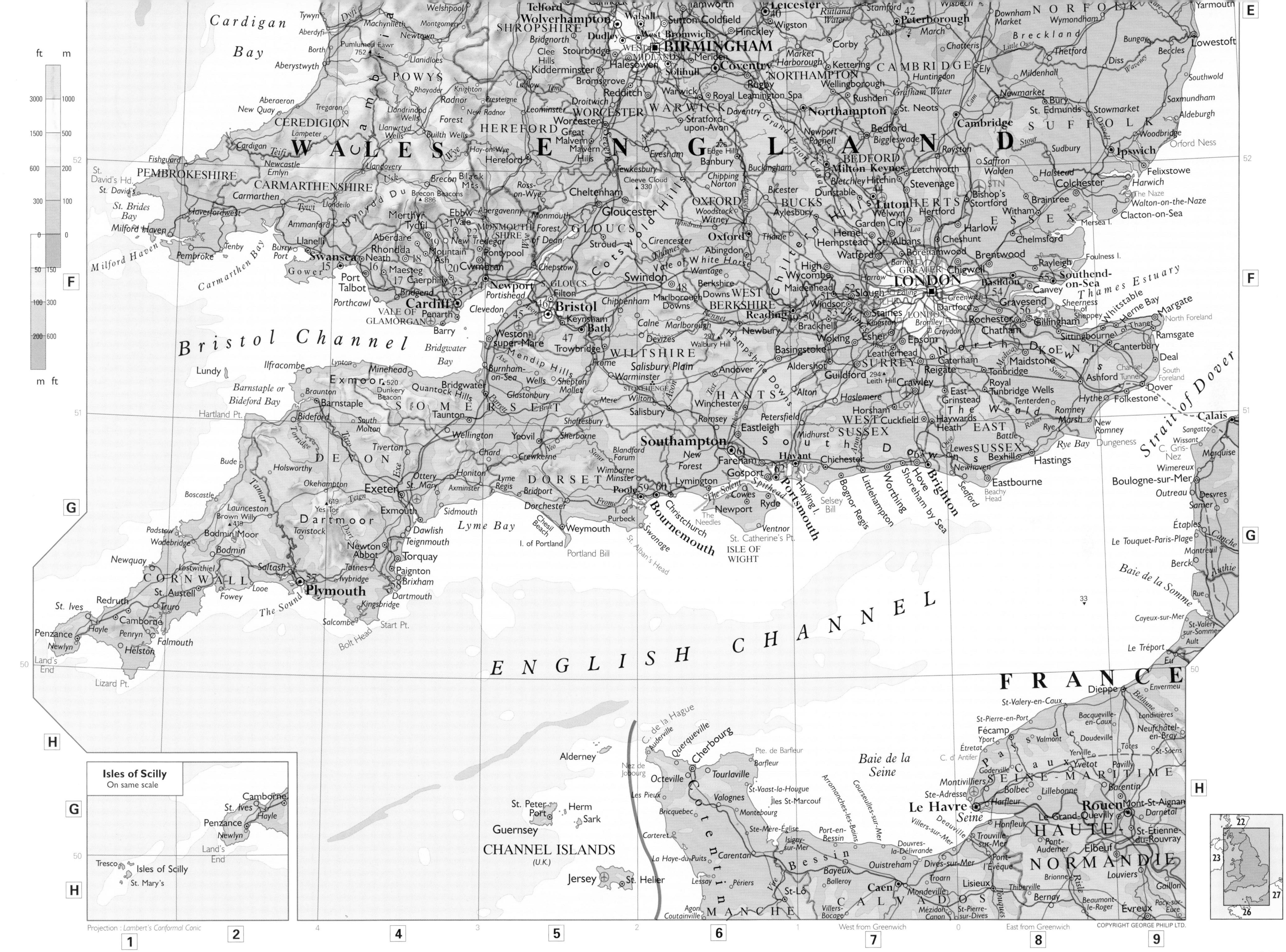

ENGLAND

WALES

FRANCE

HAUTE-NORMANDIE

NORMANDIE

SEINE-MARITIME

CALVADOS

MANCHE

ENGLISH CHANNEL

Bristol Channel

Cardigan Bay

Strait of Dover

English Channel

LONDON

BIRMINGHAM

Plymouth

Bristol

Cardiff

Southampton

Portsmouth

Bournemouth

Brighton

Le Havre

Rouen

Caen

Cherbourg

Calais

Dieppe

Boulogne-sur-Mer

CHANNEL ISLANDS (U.K.)

Jersey

Guernsey

Alderney

Sark

Herm

St. Peter Port

St. Helier

Baie de la Seine

Baie de la Somme

Cotentin

ISLE OF WIGHT

Newport

Cowes

Ryde

CORNWALL

DEVON

DORSET

SOMERSET

WILTSHIRE

HANTS

BERKSHIRE

SURREY

WEST SUSSEX

EAST SUSSEX

KENT

ESSEX

SUFFOLK

NORFOLK

CAMBRIDGE

BEDFORD

BUCKS

OXFORD

GLOUCS

HEREFORD

WORCESTER

WARWICK

NORTHAMPTON

SHROPSHIRE

POWYS

CEREDIGION

CARMARTHENSHIRE

PEMBROKESHIRE

GLAMORGAN

VALE OF GLAMORGAN

Lyme Bay

Isles of Scilly
On same scale
St. Mary's
Tresco
Land's End

Projection: Lambert's Conformal Conic

COPYRIGHT GEORGE PHILIP LTD.

East from Greenwich

West from Greenwich

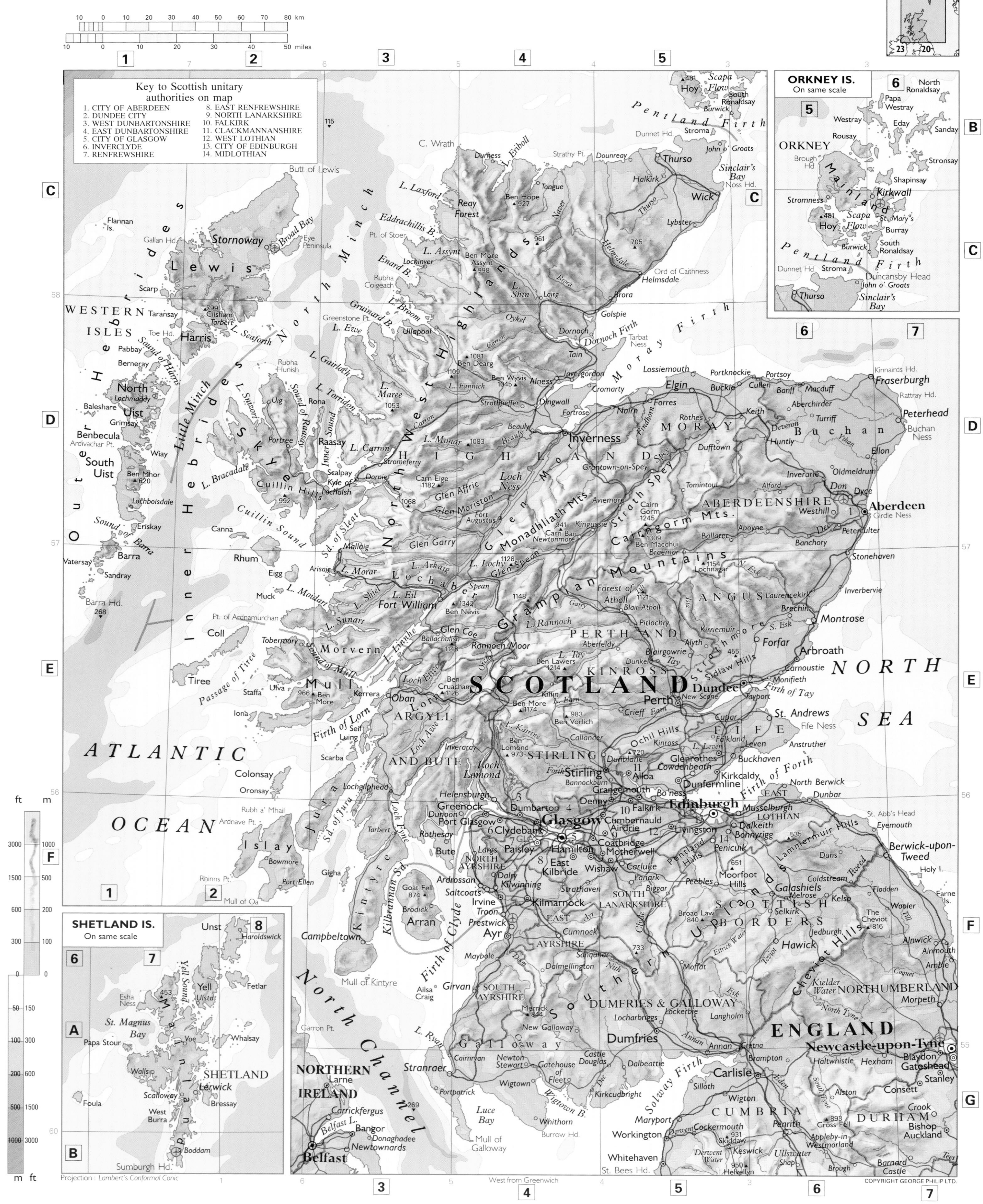

10 0 10 20 30 40 50 60 70 80 km
10 0 10 20 30 40 50 miles

Key to Scottish unitary authorities on map
1. CITY OF ABERDEEN
2. DUNDEE CITY
3. WEST DUNBARTONSHIRE
4. EAST DUNBARTONSHIRE
5. CITY OF GLASGOW
6. INVERCLYDE
7. RENFREWSHIRE
8. EAST RENFREWSHIRE
9. NORTH LANARKSHIRE
10. FALKIRK
11. CLACKMANNANSHIRE
12. WEST LOTHIAN
13. CITY OF EDINBURGH
14. MIDLOTHIAN

ORKNEY IS.
On same scale
ORKNEY
North Ronaldsay
Papa Westray
Westray
Eday
Sanday
Rousay
Stronsay
Mainland
Shapinsay
Brough
Stromness
Kirkwall
Hoy
Scapa Flow
481
St. Mary's
Burray
South Ronaldsay
Burwick
Dunnet Hd. Stroma
Thurso John o' Groats
Duncansby Head
Sinclair's Bay

Butt of Lewis
Flannan Is.
Stornoway
Broad Bay
Eye Peninsula
Gallan Hd.
WESTERN ISLES
Taransay
Scarp
Toe Hd.
Harris
Clisham 799
Tarbert
North Uist
Lochmaddy
Baleshare
Grimsay
Benbecula
Ardivachar Pt.
South Uist
Wiay
Ben Mhor 620
Lochboisdale
Eriskay
Barra
Vatersay
Sandray
Barra Hd. 268

LEWIS
Sound of Harris
North Minch
C. Wrath
Durness
L. Eriboll
Strathy Pt.
Reay Forest
Ben Hope 927
Tongue
L. Laxford
Eddrachillis B.
Pt. of Stoer
L. Assynt
Ben More Assynt 998
Lochinver
Enard B.
Rubha Coigeach
Ullapool
L. Broom
Gruinard B.
Greenstone Pt.
L. Ewe
L. Maree 1053
L. Gairloch
Rubha Hunish
Uig
Portree
Raasay
Rona
Scalpay
Inner Sound
L. Torridon
Stromeferry
Kyle of Lochalsh
Kyleakin
Glenelg
Sd. of Sleat
Mallaig
Arisaig
L. Morar
L. Moidart
Rhum
Eigg
Muck
Canna
Pt. of Ardnamurchan
Coll
Tobermory
Tiree
Staffa
Ulva
Iona
Mull
Ben More 966
Kerrera
Oban
Seil
Luing
Scarba
Colonsay
Oronsay
Islay
Bowmore
Rhinns Pt.
Port Ellen
Mull of Oa
Gigha
Jura
Sd. of Jura
Tarbert
Lochgilphead
Rubh a' Mhail
Ardnave Pt.
Kintyre
Campbeltown
Mull of Kintyre

Dounreay
Thurso
Halkirk
Wick
Dunnet Hd.
John o' Groats
Pentland Firth
Strathy
Lybster
Ord of Caithness
Helmsdale
705
Brora
Golspie
Dornoch
Dornoch Firth
Tarbat Ness
Tain
Invergordon
Cromarty
Moray Firth
Lossiemouth
Elgin
Forres
Nairn
MORAY
Rothes
Keith
Dufftown
Buckie
Portknockie
Cullen
Banff
Macduff
Aberchirder
Turriff
Huntly
Inverurie
Oldmeldrum
BUCHAN
Fraserburgh
Rattray Hd.
Peterhead
Buchan Ness
Ellon
Dyce
ABERDEENSHIRE
Westhill
Aberdeen
Girdle Ness
Alford
Inverbervie
Stonehaven
Banchory
Aboyne
Ballater
Braemar
Ben Macdhui 1309
Cairn Gorm 1245
CAIRNGORM MTS.
Aviemore
Kingussie
Newtonmore
Strath Spey
Grantown-on-Spey
L. Ness
Loch Ness
Fort Augustus
Glen Moriston
Glen Affric
Beauly
Inverness
Dingwall
Strathpeffer
Alness
Ben Wyvis 1045
Carn Eige 1183
MONADHLIATH MTS.
Carn Ban
Laggan
Fort William
Ben Nevis 1344
Glen Spean
L. Lochy 1128
L. Arkaig
LOCHABER
Glen Garry
L. Garry
Spean
Forest of Atholl 1121
Blair Atholl
GRAMPIAN MOUNTAINS
Lochnagar 1154
Mt. Keen
N. Esk
Laurencekirk
ANGUS
Brechin
Montrose
Forfar
Kirriemuir
Arbroath
Carnoustie
Monifieth
Sidlaw Hills
Strathmore
Blairgowrie
Alyth
Aberfeldy
L. Tay
Ben Lawers 1214
Killin
PERTH AND KINROSS
Pitlochry
Rannoch Moor
L. Rannoch
Ben Cruachan 1126
Glen Coe
Ballachulish
L. Linnhe
L. Eil
L. Shiel
Glen Garry
Morvern
Sound of Mull
Lorn
Firth of Lorn
ARGYLL AND BUTE
Inveraray
L. Awe
L. Fyne
Loch Lomond
Ben Lomond 973
L. Katrine
Callander
Crieff
Comrie
Ben Vorlich 983
Ben More 1174
L. Earn
Perth
New Scone
Dundee
Newport
Firth of Tay
Cupar
St. Andrews
Fife Ness
FIFE
Falkland
Glenrothes
Leven
Anstruther
Buckhaven
Kirkcaldy
Ochil Hills
Kinross
L. Leven
Alloa
Cowdenbeath
Dunfermline
Dunblane
Stirling
Bannockburn
STIRLING
Denny
Grangemouth
Bo'ness
Firth of Forth
North Berwick
Dunbar
St. Abb's Head
Eyemouth
EAST LOTHIAN
Musselburgh
EDINBURGH
Livingston
Bathgate
Penicuik
Dalkeith
Bonnyrigg
Lammermuir Hills
Duns
Coldstream
Kelso
Berwick-upon-Tweed
Holy I.
Farne Is.
Bamburgh
Wooler
The Cheviot 816
Jedburgh
Hawick
Cheviot Hills
Alnwick
Ainmouth
Amble
Coquet
NORTHUMBERLAND
Morpeth
Kielder Water
North Tyne
Hexham
Haltwhistle
Carlisle
Brampton
CUMBRIA
Penrith
Appleby-in-Westmorland
Cross Fell 893
Alston
Consett
Stanley
DURHAM
Bishop Auckland
Barnard Castle
Crook
Gateshead
Blaydon
Newcastle-upon-Tyne
Tees
Helvellyn 950
Keswick
Ullswater
Derwent Water
Skiddaw 931
Cockermouth
Workington
Maryport
Wigton
Silloth
Kirkcudbright
Solway Firth
Annan
Dumfries
Lockerbie
Langholm
Moffat
Locharbriggs
DUMFRIES & GALLOWAY
New Galloway
Castle Douglas
Dalbeattie
Gatehouse of Fleet
Newton Stewart
Wigtown
Whithorn
Burrow Hd.
Luce Bay
Mull of Galloway
Stranraer
Cairnryan
Portpatrick
L. Ryan
GALLOWAY
Southern Uplands
Broad Law 840
SCOTTISH BORDERS
Peebles
Moorfoot Hills
Pentland Hills
651
Galashiels
Melrose
Selkirk
Ettrick Water
Tweed
Biggar
Lanark
SOUTH LANARKSHIRE
Carluke
Wishaw
Strathaven
EAST KILBRIDE
Hamilton
Motherwell
Coatbridge
Airdrie
Cumbernauld
Falkirk
Glasgow
Clydebank
Paisley
Greenock
Port Glasgow
Dumbarton
Helensburgh
Rothesay
Bute
Dunoon
Largs
NORTH AYRSHIRE
Ardrossan
Saltcoats
Kilwinning
Irvine
Troon
Prestwick
Ayr
Kilmarnock
EAST AYRSHIRE
Cumnock
Sanquhar
Dalmellington
Maybole
Girvan
SOUTH AYRSHIRE
Ailsa Craig
Arran
Goat Fell 874
Brodick
Lamlash
Kilbrannan Sd.
Firth of Clyde
Merrick 844

ATLANTIC OCEAN
NORTH SEA
NORTH CHANNEL
IRISH SEA
NORTHERN IRELAND
Belfast
Belfast L.
Larne
Carrickfergus
Bangor
Donaghadee
Newtownards
ENGLAND
SCOTLAND

HIGHLAND
NORTHWEST HIGHLANDS
Skye
Cuillin Hills 992
Cuillin Sound
L. Bracadale
Inner Hebrides
Little Minch
Sound of Harris
Outer Hebrides

SHETLAND IS.
On same scale
Unst
Haroldswick
Fetlar
Yell
Yell Sound
Whalsay
St. Magnus Bay
Papa Stour
Walls
Foula
West Burra
Scalloway
Lerwick
Bressay
SHETLAND
Mainland
Esha Ness
Sumburgh Hd.

ft m
3000 1000
1500 500
600 200
300 100
150 50
0 0
m ft

Projection: Lambert's Conformal Conic
West from Greenwich
COPYRIGHT GEORGE PHILIP LTD.

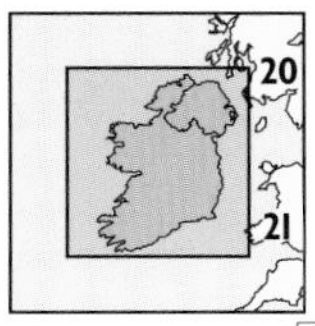

10 0 10 20 30 40 50 60 70 80 km
10 0 10 20 30 40 50 miles

ATLANTIC OCEAN

NORTH CHANNEL

Firth of Clyde

Kintyre
Campbeltown
Mull of Kintyre
Brodick
Arran
Ailsa Craig
Cairnryan
Stranraer
Portpatrick

Mull of Oa
Giants Causeway
Rathlin I.
Fair Hd.
Ballycastle
Garron Pt.
Trostan 554

Malin Hd.
Malin Pen.
Carndonagh
Moville
Portstewart
Portrush
Coleraine
Ballymoney
Limavady
L. Foyle
Garvagh
Mts. of Antrim
Larne
269

Tory I.
Horn Hd.
Sheep Haven
Mulroy B.
Lough Swilly
Fanad Hd.
Inishowen Pen.
Buncrana
LONDONDERRY
Londonderry
Ballymena
ANTRIM
Carrickfergus
Belfast L.
Bangor

Bloody Foreland
Inishfree B.
Aran I.
Gweedore
The Rosses
Errigal 752
683
Rathmelton
Letterkenny
DONEGAL
Derryveagh Mts.
Sawel Mt. 683
Sperrin Mts.
Roe
Magherafelt
Randalstown Ballyclare
NORTHERN
Newtownabbey
Belfast
Donaghadee
Newtownards
Ards Pen.

Crohy Hd.
Gweebarra B.
Dawros Hd.
Glenties
Lavagh More 676
Lifford
Strabane
Sion Mills
Newtownstewart
TYRONE
Omagh
Ulster
Cookstown
Coalisland
Dungannon
Moneymore
Lough Neagh
Antrim
Craigavon
Lisburn
Saintfield
DOWN
Comber
Strangford

Killybegs
Donegal
St. John's Pt.
Donegal Bay
Ballyshannon
Bundoran
Lower L. Erne
Enniskillen
FERMANAGH
Upper L. Erne
IRELAND
Irvinestown
Dromore
Aughnacloy
ARMAGH
Armagh
Middletown
Keady
Portadown
Lurgan
Banbridge
Lagan
Tandragee
Ballynahinch
Downpatrick
Dundrum
Dundrum B.
Ballyquintin Pt.
Portaferry

Rossan Pt.
Line
L. Allen
Clones
MONAGHAN
Monaghan
Belturbet
Finn
Cootehill
Castleblaney
Newry
Mourne Mts.
Slieve Donard 852
577 Slieve Gullion
Warrenpoint
Kilkeel
Greenore
Carlingford L.
St. John's Pt.
Clogher Hd.
Newcastle

Broad Haven
Erris Hd.
Belmullet
Mullet Pen.
Inishkea North
Inishkea South
Blacksod Bay
Downpatrick Hd.
Killala B.
Dromore West
544
Sligo Bay
SLIGO
Sligo
Collooney
Ballymote
L. Arrow
LEITRIM
Leitrim
Annalee
Cavan
Carrickmacross
Kingscourt
Dundalk
Louth
LOUTH
Ardee
Dunleer
Dundalk Bay

Achill Hd.
Achill I.
Corraun Pen.
Clare I.
Clew Bay
Inishturk
Inishbofin
Inishshark
Slyne Hd.
MAYO
Nephin 806
L. Conn
Ballina
Killala
Swinford
Charlestown
Slieve Gamph
Boyle
Carrick-on-Shannon
L. Gowna
ROSCOMMON
CAVAN
Kingscourt
Oldcastle
Ceanannus Mor (Kells)
Blackwater
Clogher Hd.
Drogheda

Croagh Patrick 765
Mweelrea 819
Killary Harbour
Connemara
Clifden
Westport
Newport
Castlebar
Knock
Ballyhaunis
Claremorris
Ballinrobe
Lough Mask
Connacht
Castlerea
Roscommon
Ballaghaderreen
Longford
LONGFORD
Granard
L. Sheelin
Castlepollard
MEATH
An Uaimh (Navan)
Boyne
Balbriggan

Bertraghboy B.
Slyne Hd.
Oughterard
Lough Corrib
GALWAY
Galway
Tuam
Glennamaddy
Athenry
Loughrea
Ballinasloe
Suck
Athlone
WESTMEATH
Moate
Mullingar
Leinster
Clara
Royal Canal
Trim
Athboy
Rush
Lambay I.
Swords
Malahide
Howth Hd.
DUBLIN
Dublin
Dun Laoghaire

Galway Bay
Black Hd.
Aran Is.
Inishmore
Inishmaan
Inisheer
Hags Hd.
Liscannor Bay
Mal Bay
Mutton I.
Ennistimon
CLARE
Tulla
Ennis
Gort
Slieve Aughty 368
Portumna
Shannon
Birr
OFFALY
Tullamore
Daingean
Grand Canal
Portarlington
Kildare
KILDARE
Naas
Maynooth
Bog of Allen
Liffey
Edenderry
Droichead Nua
Monasterevin
Kilcullen
Clondalkin
DUBLIN
Kippure 754
Bray
Greystones
123

Loop Hd.
Kilkee
Kilrush
Shannon Airport
Sixmilebridge
Killaloe
Nenagh
Lough Derg
Roscrea
Templemore
Slieve Bloom
Arderin 528
Mountmellick
Port Laoise
Athy
LAOIS
Durrow
Carlow
CARLOW
Muine Bheag
Tullow
Wicklow Mts.
Lugnaquilla 926
Rathdrum
Wicklow
Wicklow Hd.
WICKLOW
Poulaphouca Res.
Arklow
Mizen Hd.

Mouth of the Shannon
Kerry Hd.
Foynes
LIMERICK
Limerick
Rathkeale
Newcastle West
Listowel
Feale
TIPPERARY
Golden Vale
Tipperary
Cashel
Thurles
Kilkenny
KILKENNY
Callan
Mt. Leinster 796
Bunclody
Gorey
Shillelagh
Cahore Pt.

Smerwick Harbour
Brandon B.
Tralee B.
Tralee
Brandon Mt. 953
Dingle
Slieve Mish 853
Dunmore Hd.
Dingle Bay
Maine
Laune
KERRY
Killarney
Killorglin
Newmarket
Kanturk
Buttevant
Mitchelstown
Galty Mts. 920
Galtymore
Knockmealdown Mts. 795
Caher
Clonmel
Carrick-on-Suir
WEXFORD
New Ross
Enniscorthy
Barrow
Nore
Slievenamon 722
Saltee Is.
Hook Hd.
Wexford Harbour
Rosslare
Greenore Pt.
Wexford
Carnsore Pt.

Great Blasket I.
Inishvickillane
Valencia I.
Puffin I.
Great Skellig
Cahirciveen
Ballinskelligs B.
Scariff I.
Dursey I.
Crow Hd.
Castletown Bearhaven
Bear I.
Bantry Bay
Dunmanus B.
Mizen Hd.
Macgillycuddy's Reeks
Carrauntoohill 1041
L. Leane
Kenmare
Kenmare River
Caha Mts. 686
Glengarriff
Bantry
Dunmanway
Skibbereen
Clonakilty B.
Skull
Long I.
Baltimore
Sherkin I.
Clear I.
C. Clear
Galley Hd.
Boggeragh Mts. 646
Macroom
Blarney
CORK
Cork
Lee
Passage West
Cobh
Crosshaven
Cork Harbour
Kinsale
Old Head of Kinsale
Bandon
Clonakilty
Mallow
Blackwater
Fermoy
Ferntoy
Lismore
WATERFORD
Dungarvan
Comeragh Mts. 792
Tramore
Waterford
Waterford Harbour
Tramore B.
Dungarvan Harbour
Youghal
Youghal B.
Midleton
115

St. David's Hd.
St. David's
St. Brides Bay

IRISH SEA

St. George's Channel

CELTIC SEA

ft   m
1500   500
600   200
300   100
0   0
50   150
100   300
200   600
500   1500
1000   3000
2000   6000
m   ft

Projection : Lambert's Conformal Conic
West from Greenwich
COPYRIGHT GEORGE PHILIP LTD.

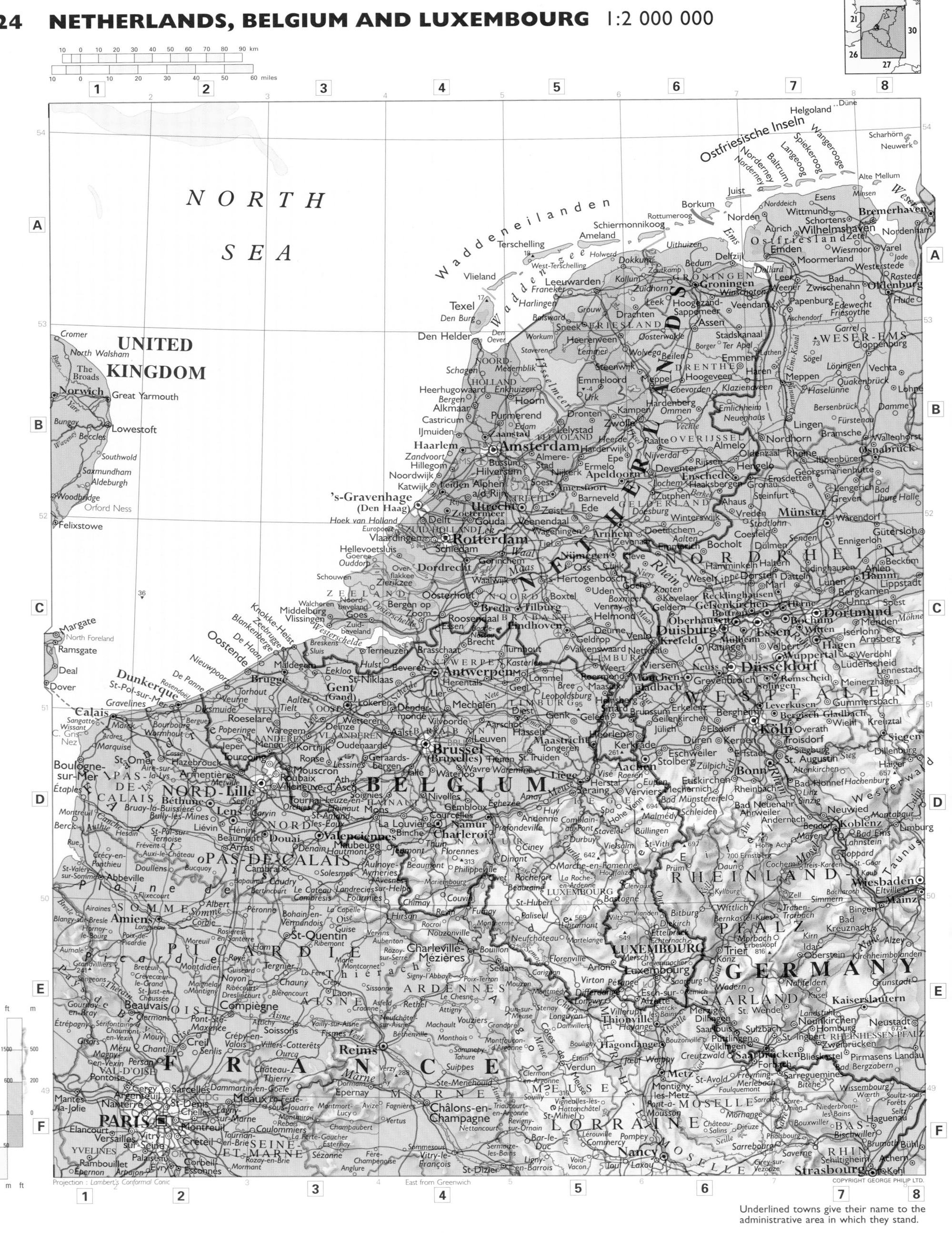

Projection: Lambert's Conformal Conic

East from Greenwich

COPYRIGHT GEORGE PHILIP LTD.

Underlined towns give their name to the administrative area in which they stand.

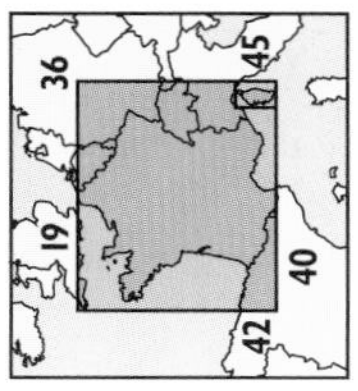

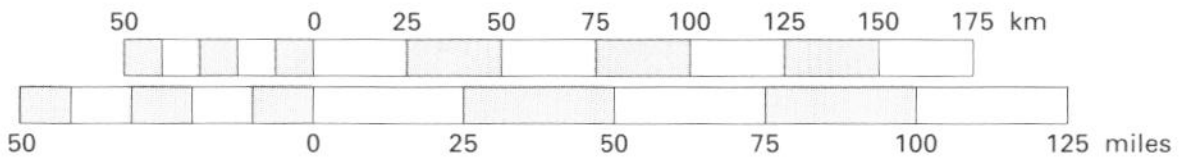

50 0 25 50 75 100 125 150 175 km

50 0 25 50 75 100 125 miles

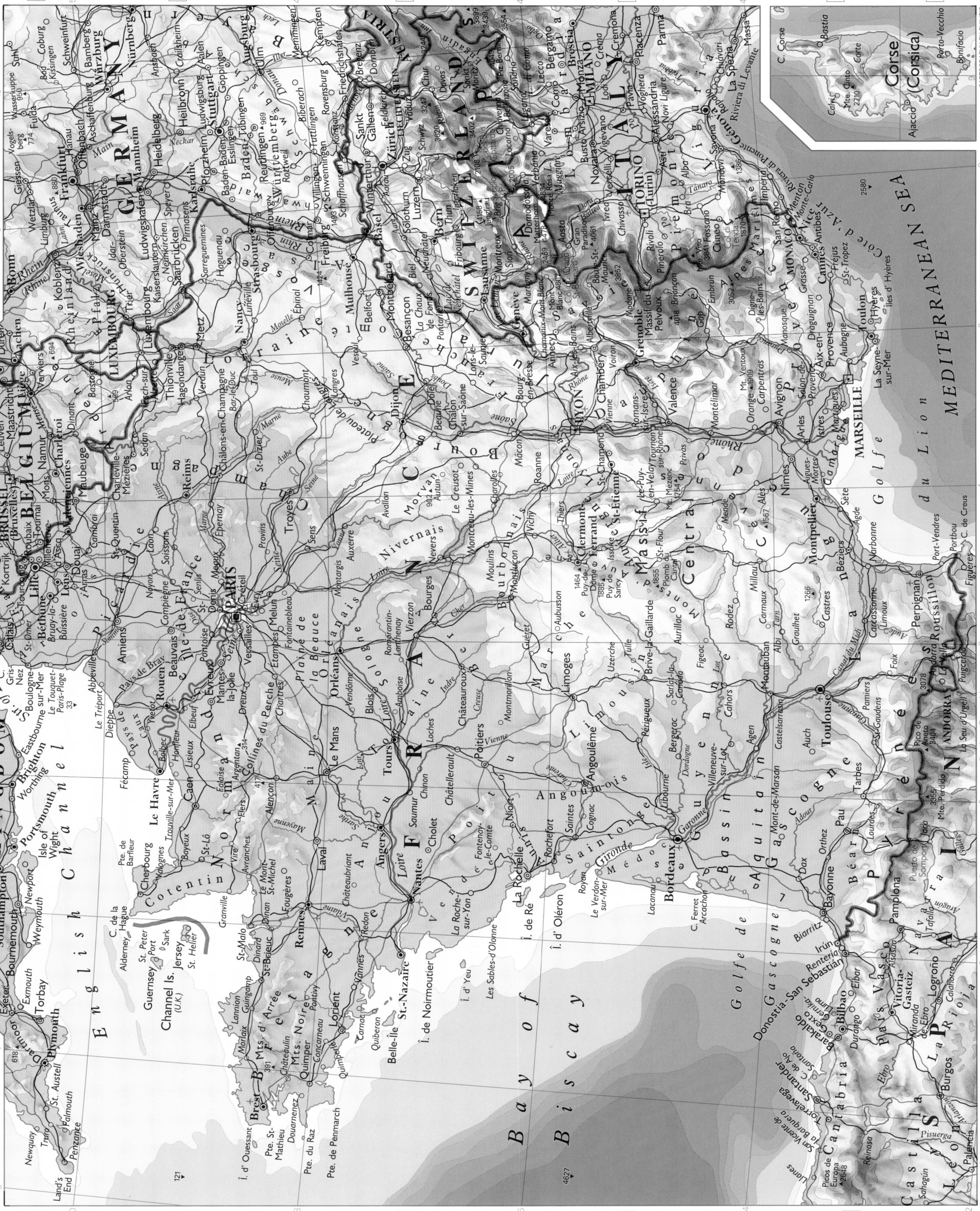

Corse (Corsica)

C. Corse · Bastia · Calvi · Corte · Porto-Vecchio · Bonifacio · Ajaccio · Mte. Cinto 2710

GERMANY

Coburg · Bamberg · Würzburg · Nürnberg · Schweinfurt · Fulda · Frankfurt · Wiesbaden · Mainz · Darmstadt · Mannheim · Heidelberg · Heilbronn · Ludwigsburg · Stuttgart · Karlsruhe · Baden-Baden · Ulm · Augsburg · München · Memmingen · Kempten

AUSTRIA
Bregenz · Feldkirch

SWITZERLAND
Basel · Zürich · Bern · Luzern · Genève · Lausanne · Montreux · Sankt Gallen · Schaffhausen · Solothurn · Neuchâtel · Fribourg · Mont Blanc 4807

ITALY
MILANO · TORINO (Turin) · Cremona · Parma · Piacenza · Bergamo · Brescia · Pavia · Alessandria · Novara · Cuneo · Genova · La Spézia · Riviera di Levante

BELGIUM
BRUSSEL (Bruxelles) · Gent · Antwerpen · Leuven · Namur · Charleroi · Tournai · Mons · Liège

LUXEMBOURG

UNITED KINGDOM
Plymouth · Exeter · Torbay · Newquay · Truro · Penzance · Land's End · Southampton · Portsmouth · Bournemouth · Brighton · Worthing · Isle of Wight · Newport · Eastbourne · Folkestone · Dover · Winchester · Crawley

FRANCE
PARIS · Lille · Calais · Dunkerque · Boulogne-sur-Mer · Amiens · Rouen · Le Havre · Caen · Cherbourg · Brest · Rennes · Nantes · St-Nazaire · Lorient · Quimper · Angers · Le Mans · Tours · Orléans · Chartres · Versailles · Reims · Metz · Nancy · Strasbourg · Mulhouse · Belfort · Besançon · Dijon · Chaumont · Troyes · Auxerre · Bourges · Nevers · Moulins · Vichy · Clermont-Ferrand · LYON · St-Étienne · Grenoble · Chambéry · Annecy · Valence · Avignon · Nîmes · Montpellier · Béziers · Narbonne · Perpignan · MARSEILLE · Toulon · Nice · MONACO · Cannes · Antibes · Grasse · Aix-en-Provence · Arles · Toulouse · Montauban · Albi · Rodez · Aurillac · Limoges · Angoulême · Poitiers · La Rochelle · Niort · Rochefort · Bordeaux · Bergerac · Périgueux · Agen · Pau · Tarbes · Bayonne · Biarritz · Carcassonne · Foix · Andorra

SPAIN
Bilbao · Pamplona · Vitoria-Gasteiz · San Sebastián · Logroño · Burgos · Santander · Palencia

Côte d'Azur

MEDITERRANEAN SEA

Golfe du Lion

Bay of Biscay

Golfe de Gascogne

English Channel

Channel Is. (U.K.) · Guernsey · Jersey · St. Peter Port · St. Helier · Alderney · Sark

m ft — elevation scale

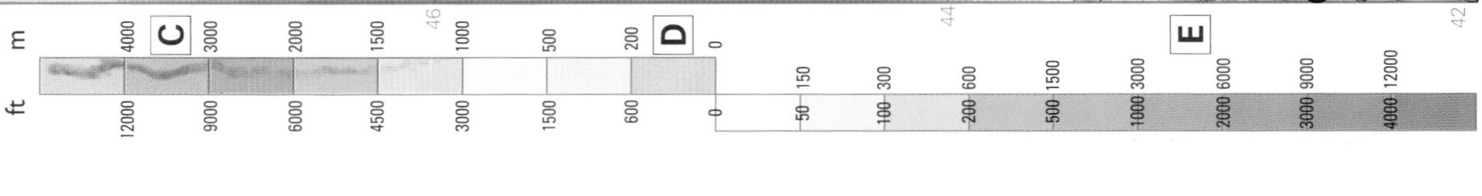

DÉPARTEMENTS IN THE PARIS AREA
1. Ville de Paris   3. Val-de-Marne
2. Seine-St-Denis   4. Hauts-de-Seine

Projection : Lambert's Conformal Conic

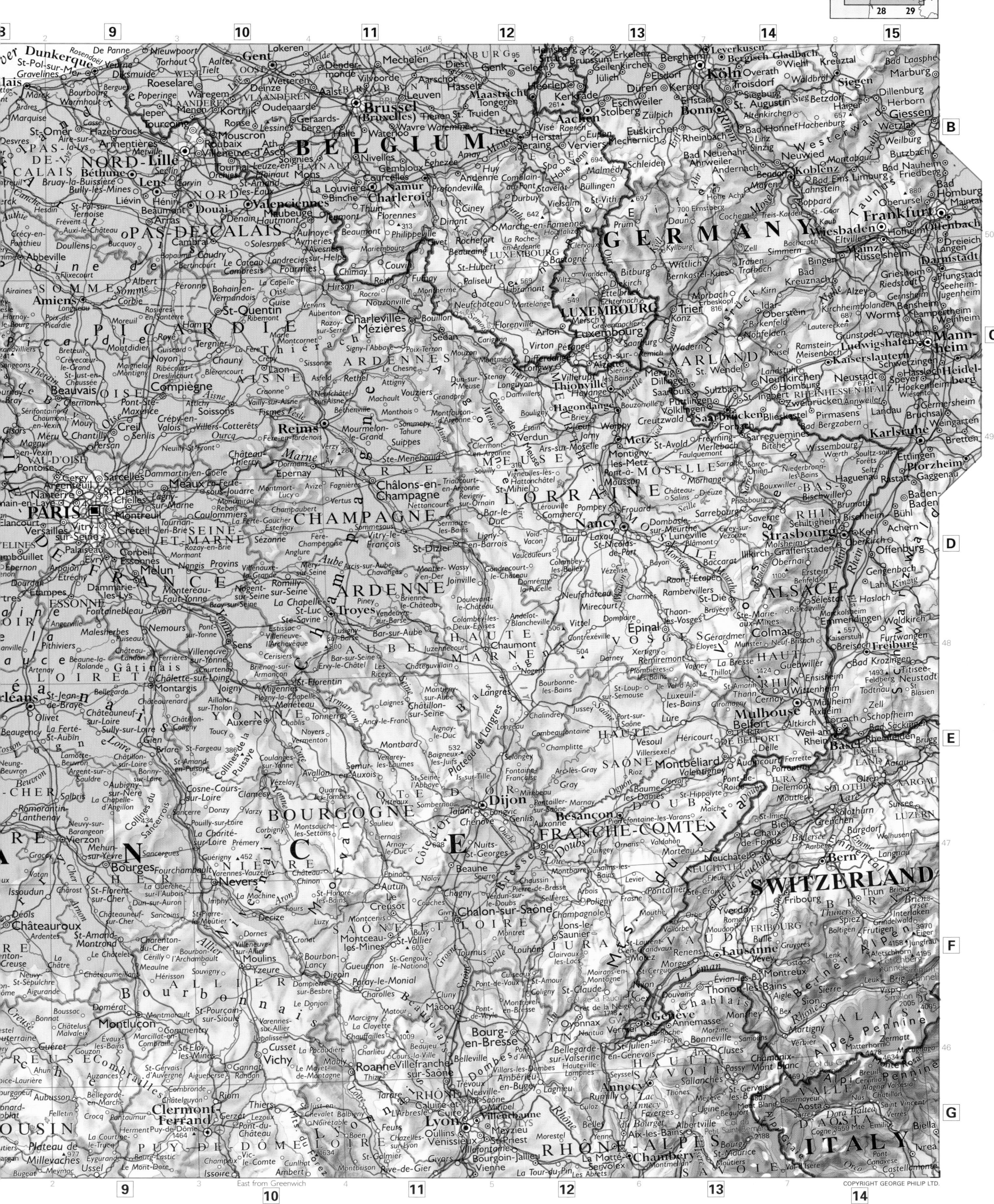

Underlined towns give their name to the administrative area in which they stand.

East from Greenwich

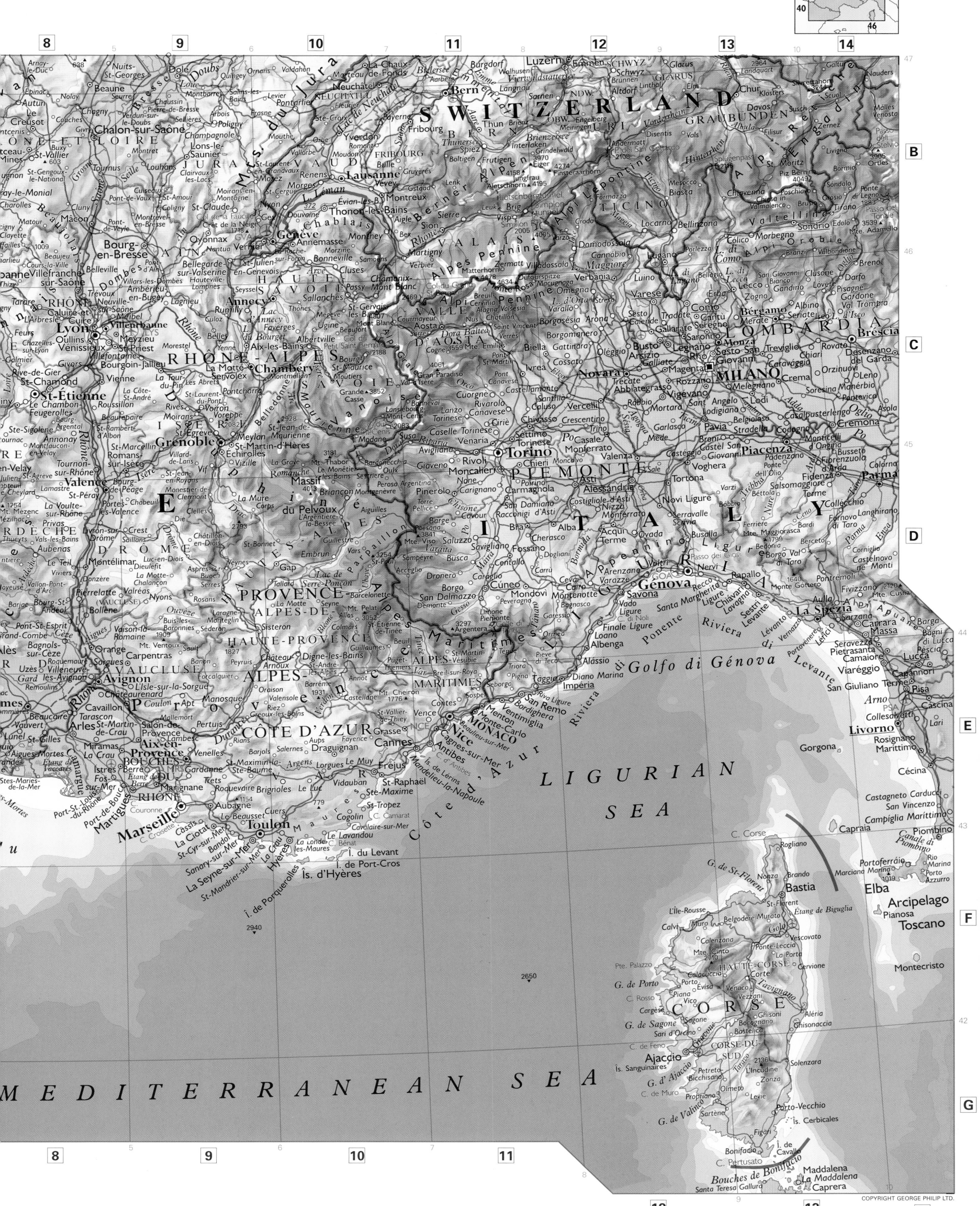

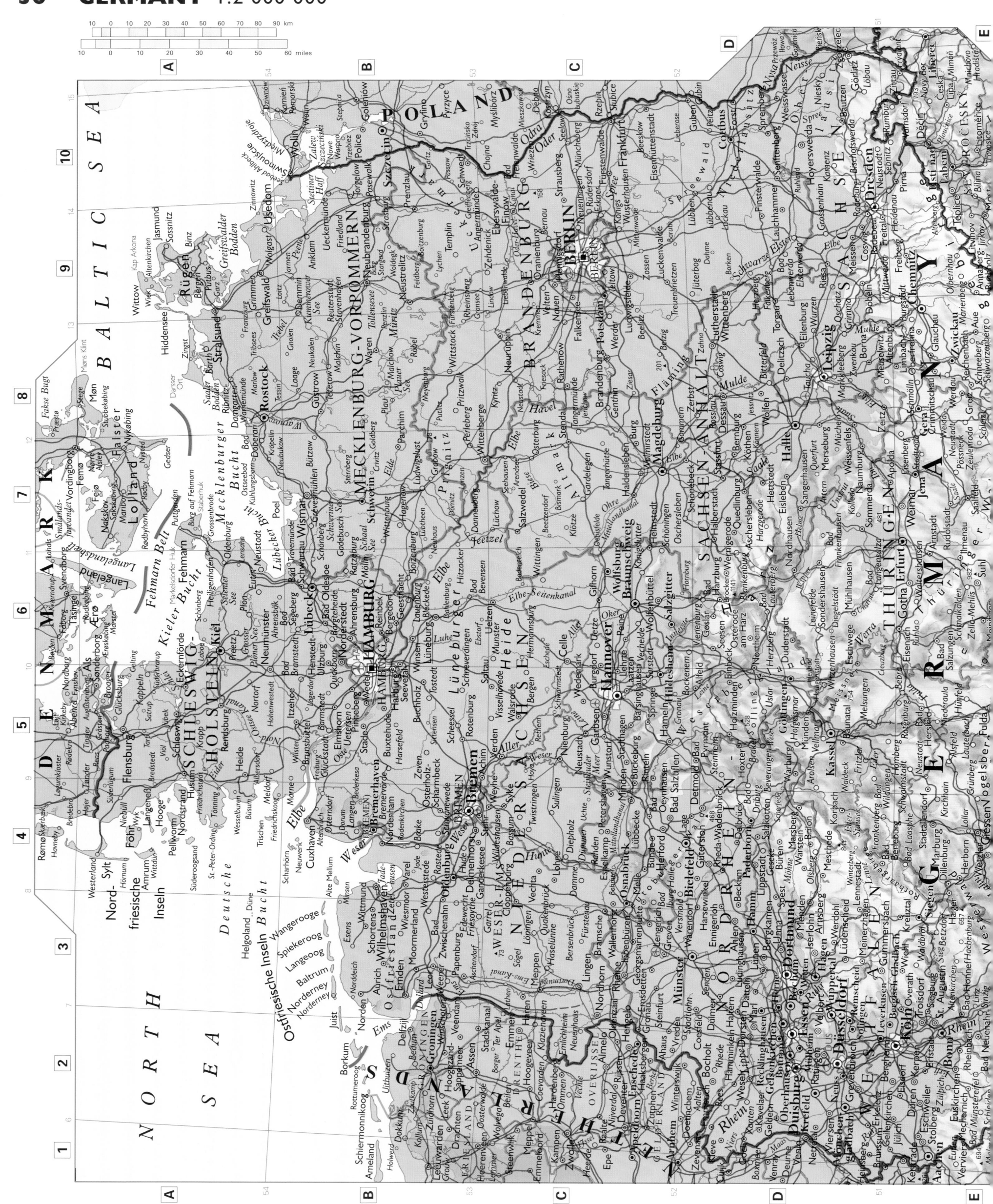

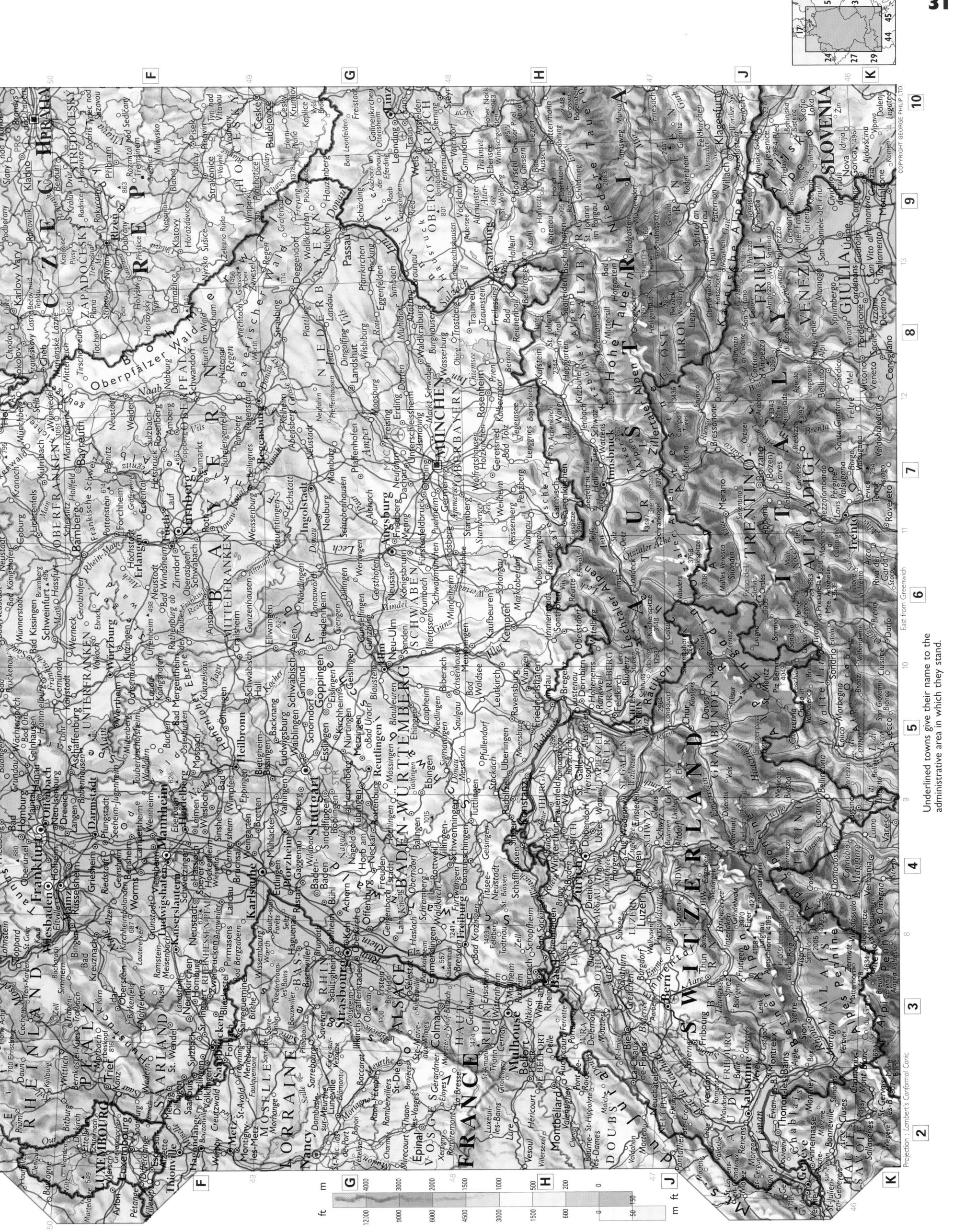

Underlined towns give their name to the
administrative area in which they stand.

COPYRIGHT GEORGE PHILIP LTD.

East from Greenwich

Projection : Lambert's Conformal Conic

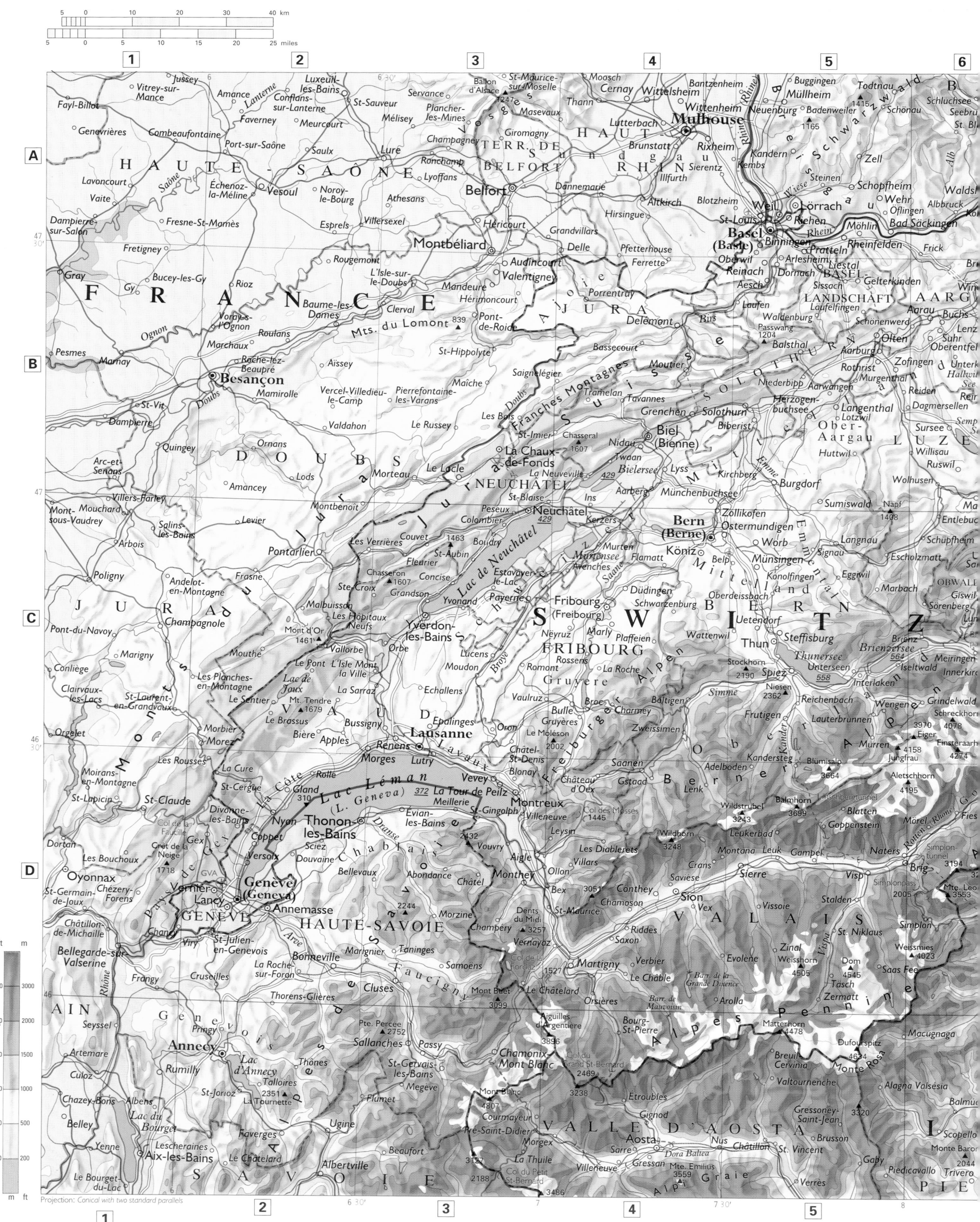

Underlined towns give their name to the administrative area in which they stand.

COPYRIGHT GEORGE PHILIP LTD.

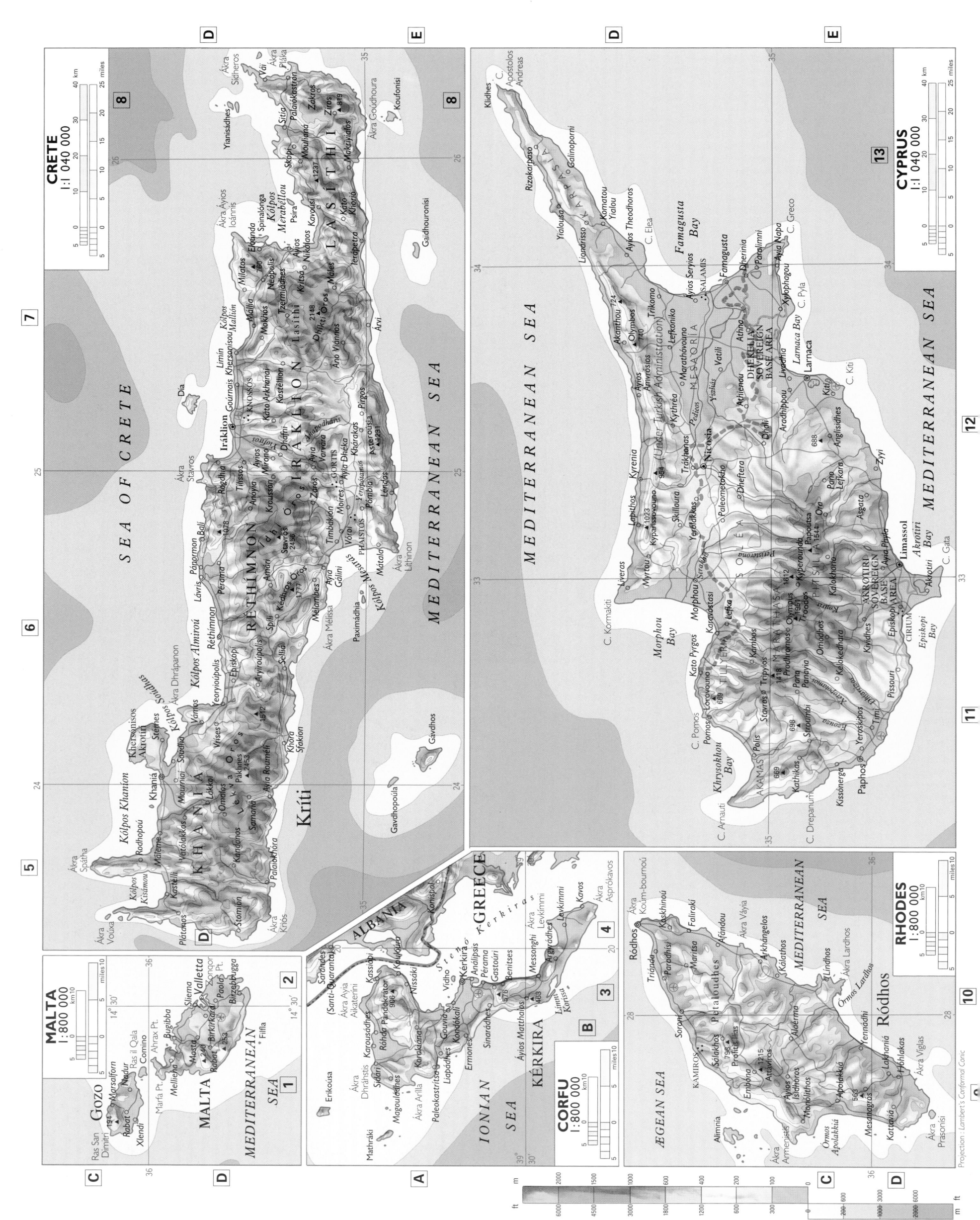

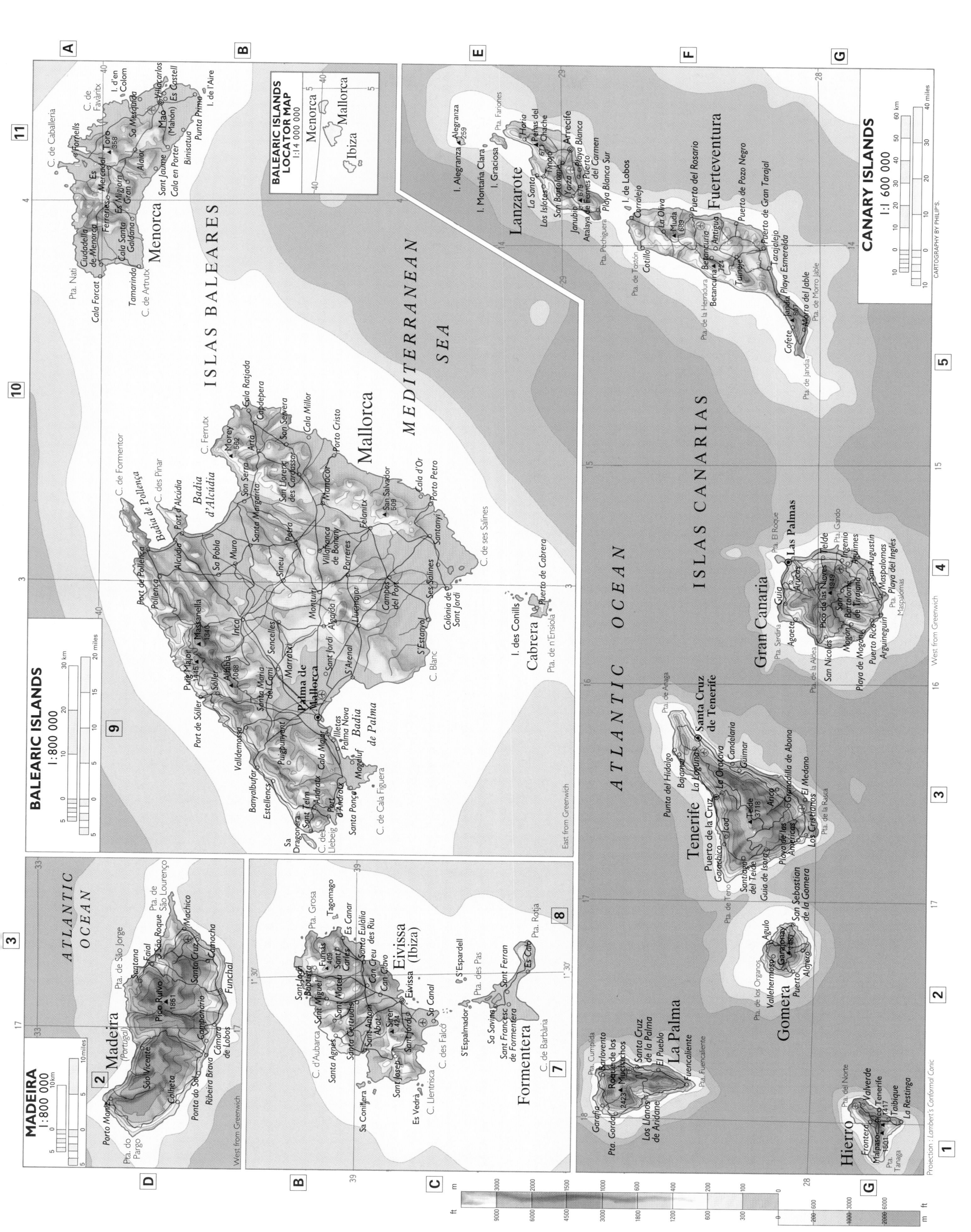

THE BALEARICS, THE CANARIES AND MADEIRA

CANARY ISLANDS 1:1 600 000

CARTOGRAPHY BY PHILIP'S.

BALEARIC ISLANDS LOCATOR MAP 1:14 000 000

Menorca
Mallorca
Ibiza

BALEARIC ISLANDS 1:800 000

MADEIRA 1:800 000

Projection: Lambert's Conformal Conic

ATLANTIC OCEAN

MEDITERRANEAN SEA

ISLAS BALEARES

Menorca

Mallorca

Palma de Mallorca

Cabrera

Eivissa (Ibiza)

Formentera

Madeira (Portugal)

Funchal

ISLAS CANARIAS

Lanzarote

Fuerteventura

Gran Canaria

Las Palmas

Tenerife

Santa Cruz de Tenerife

Gomera

La Palma

Hierro

West from Greenwich

East from Greenwich

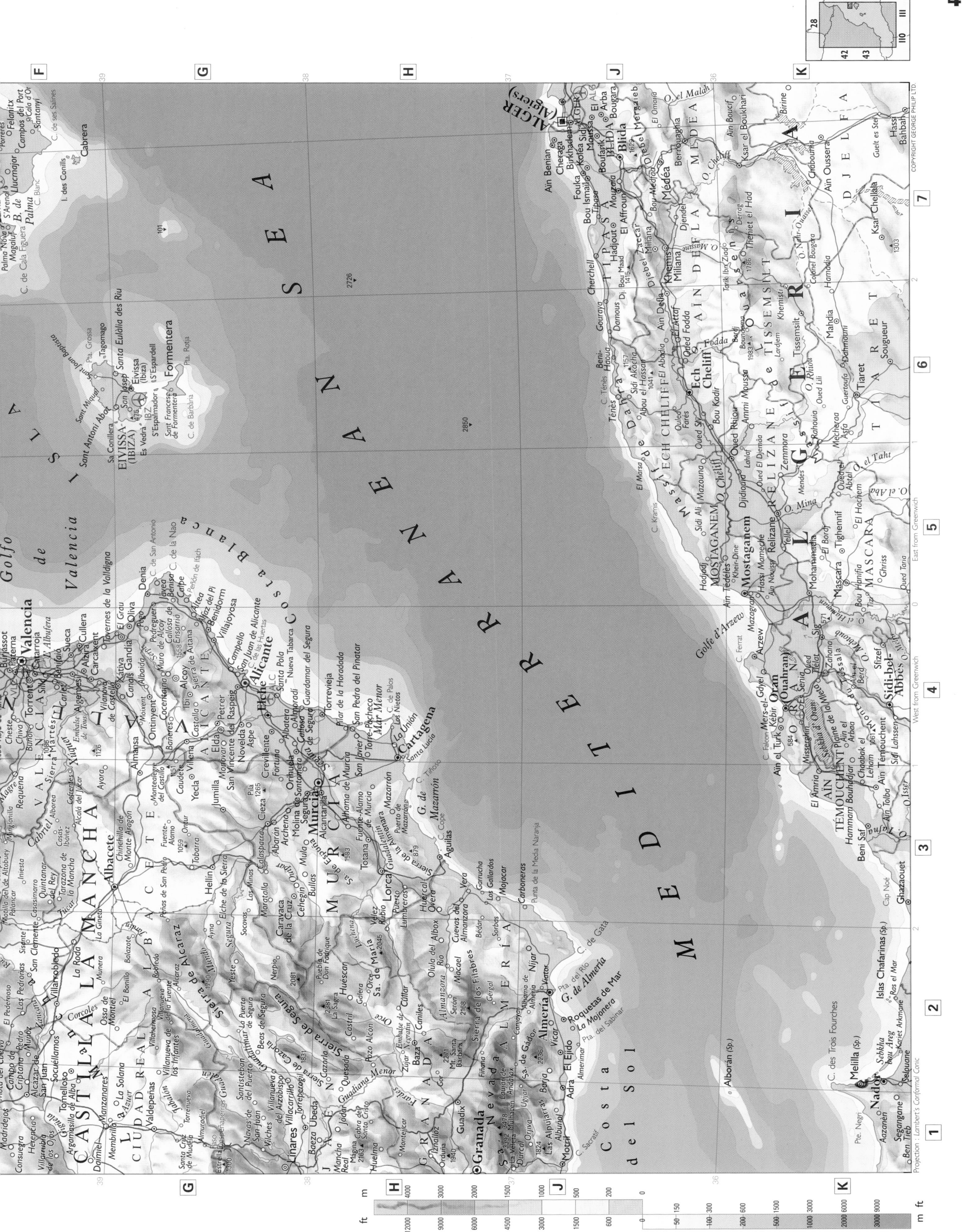

MEDITERRANEAN SEA

ALGER (ALGIERS)

VALENCIA
Valencia
Golfo de Valencia
Costa Blanca
Alicante
Elche
Murcia
Cartagena
Almería
Costa del Sol
Granada
Albacete
CASTILLA-LA MANCHA
CIUDAD REAL
Linares
Nador
Melilla

EIVISSA (IBIZA)
Formentera
Palma

A L G E R I A
Oran
Mostaganem
Blida
Médéa
Mascara
Sidi-bel-Abbès
Tiaret
DJELFA

Projection : Lambert's Conformal Conic

m ft
4000 12000
3000 9000
2000 6000
1500 4500
1000 3000
500 1500
200 600
0 0

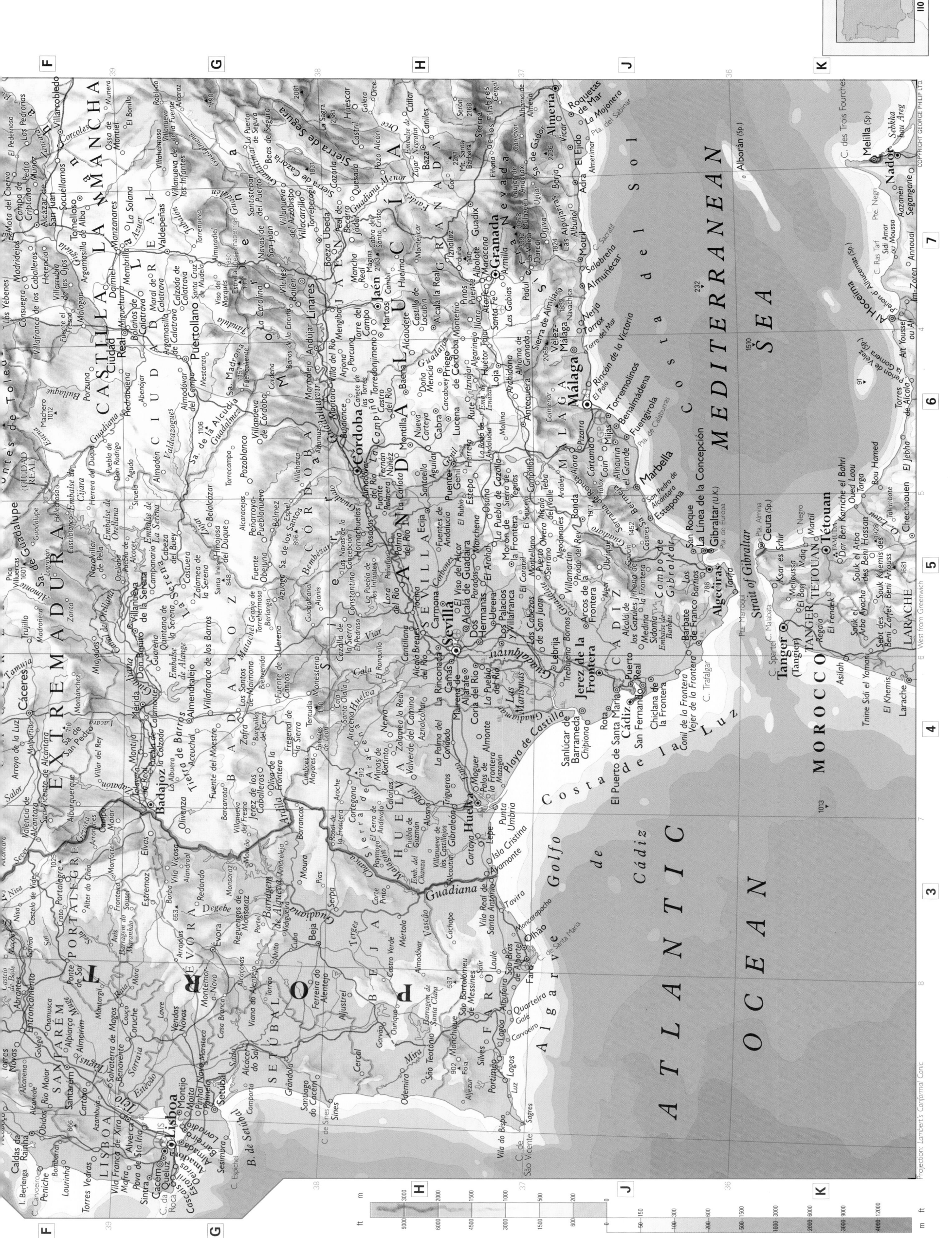

Underlined towns give their name to the
administrative area in which they stand

Administrative divisions in Croatia:

Brodsko-Posavska
Koprivničko-Križevačka
Krapinsko-Zagorska
4. Medimurska
6. Požeško-Slavonska
7. Varaždinska
8. Virovitičko-Podravska
10. Zagrebačka

Inter-entity boundaries as agreed
at the 1995 Dayton Peace Agreement.

COPYRIGHT GEORGE PHILIP LTD.

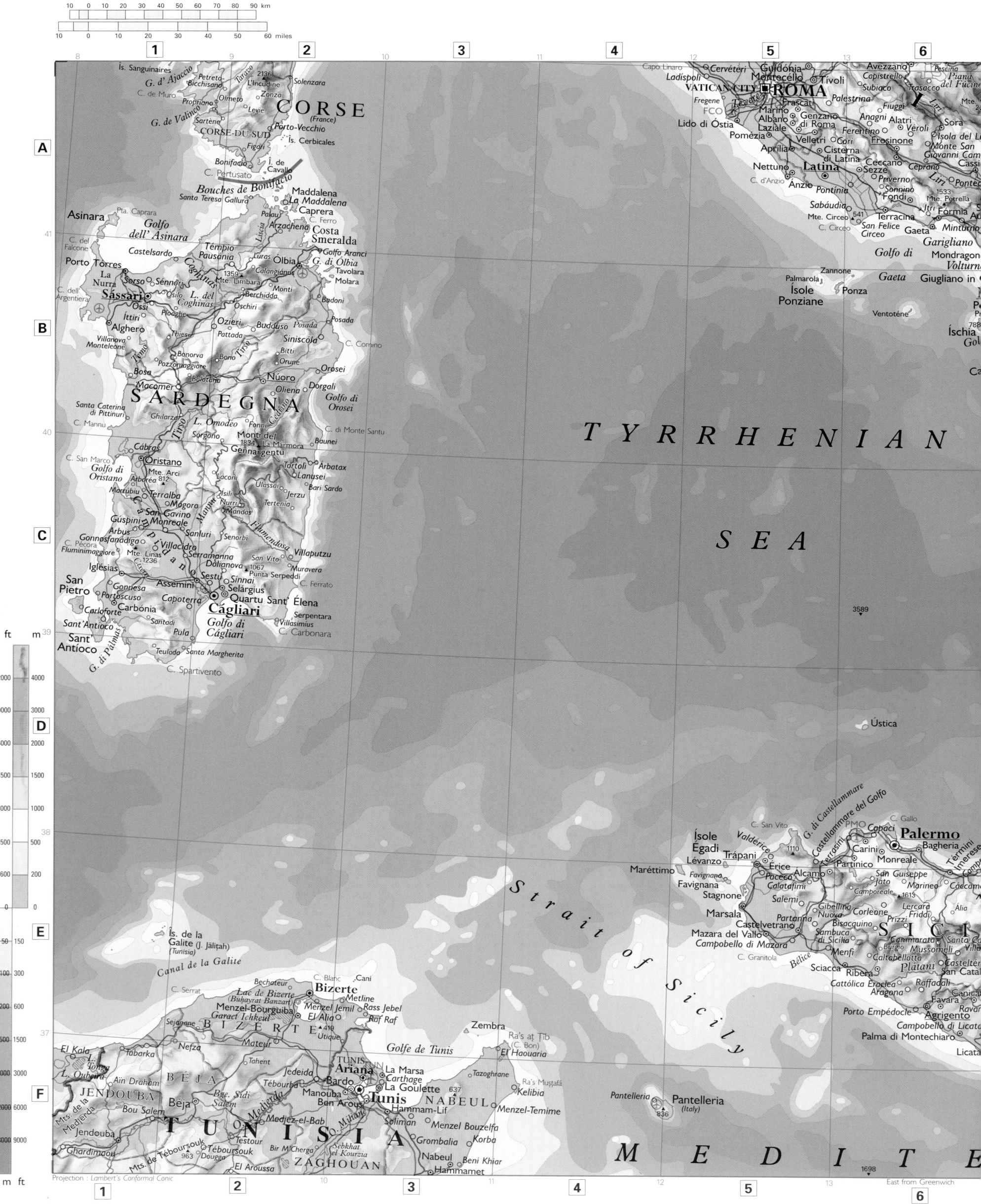

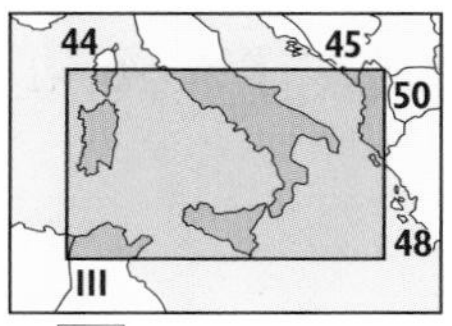

A D R I A T I C   S E A

I O N I A N   S E A

MEDITERRANEAN SEA

(...)RRANEAN SEA

ALBANIA

GREECE

Strait of Otranto

Golfo di Táranto

Golfo di Squillace

Golfo di Sant' Eufémia

Golfo di Policastro

Golfo di Salerno

Str. di Messina

Ísole Eólie

BASILICATA

CALABRIA

Términi

Campomarino L. di Lésina

Montenero di Bisáccia

Guglionesi

Castelmauro

Trivento

Agnone

MOLISE

Isernia

Campobasso

Bojano

Benevento

Caserta

Salerno

Avellino

Potenza

Matera

Bari

Brindisi

Lecce

Táranto

Fóggia

Barletta

Andria

Biscéglie

Molfetta

Trani

Cerignola

Foggia

Manfredónia

Golfo di Manfredónia

Monte Sant' Ángelo

Vieste

Testa del Gargano

Cosenza

Catanzaro

Crotone

Ísola di Capo Rizzuto

C. Colonna

Vibo Valéntia

Reggio di Calábria

Messina

Taormina

Etna

Catánia

Golfo di Catánia

Siracusa

Augusta

Gela

Ragusa

Módica

Noto

Golfo di Noto

Stróngoli

Strómboli

Lípari

Vulcano

Panarea

Salina

Filicudi

Alicudi

Kérkira (Corfu)

Tiranë

Durrës

Vlorë

Sarandë

C. Santa Maria di Léuca

C. Spartivento

C. Passero

C. Murro di Porco

Gallípoli

Otranto

COPYRIGHT GEORGE PHILIP LTD.

Underlined towns give their name to the administrative area in which they stand.

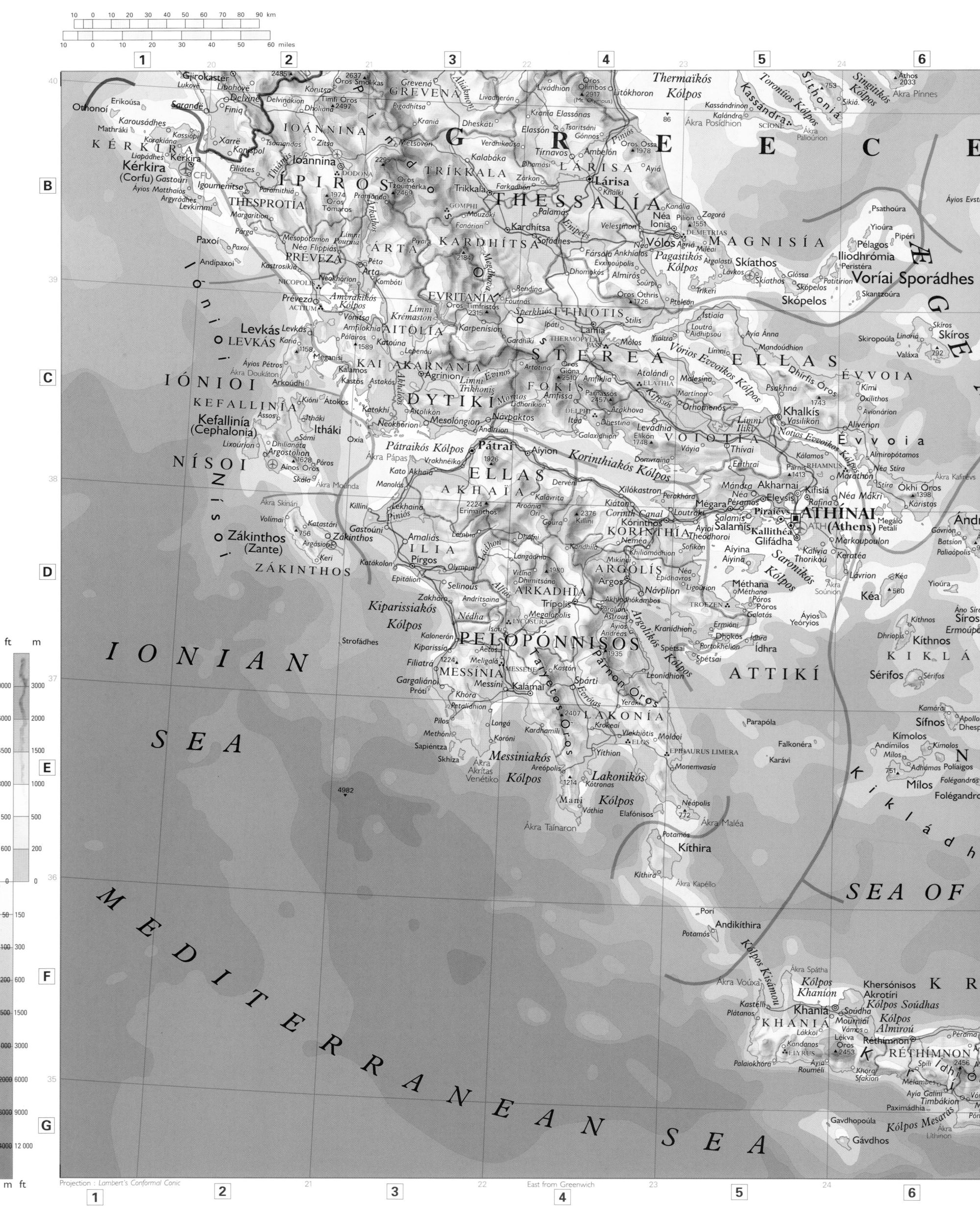

Projection: Lambert's Conformal Conic

East from Greenwich

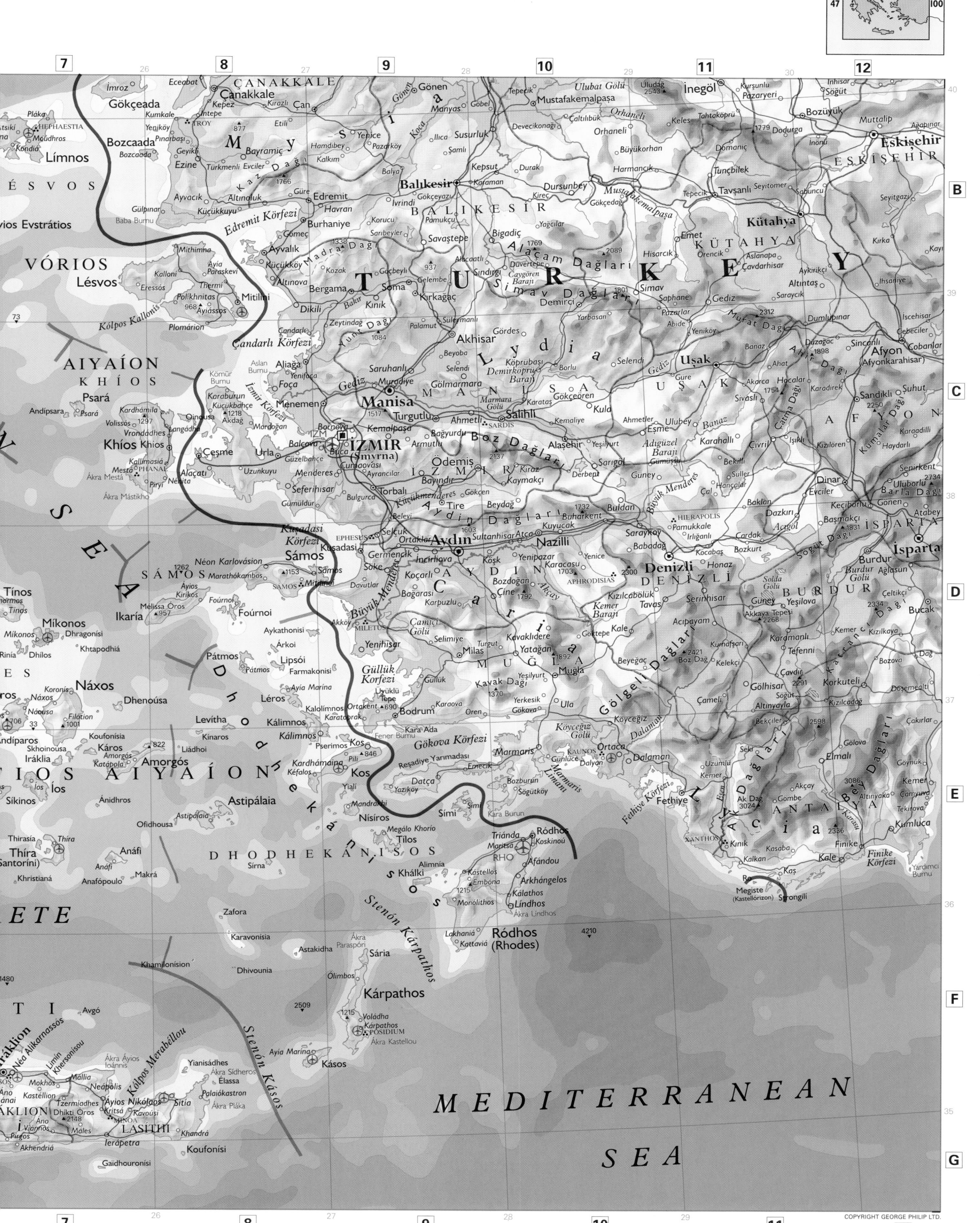

East from Greenwich

Inter-entity boundaries as agreed
at the 1995 Dayton Peace Agreement.

Underlined towns give their name to the administrative area in which they stand.

COPYRIGHT GEORGE PHILIP LTD.

Projection : Lambert's Conformal Conic

Administrative divisions in Croatia:
1. Brodsko-Posavska
2. Koprivničko-Križevačka
4. Medimurska
5. Osječko-Baranjska
6. Požeško-Slavonska
8. Virovitičko-Podravska
9. Vukovarsko-Srijemska

Inter-entity boundaries as agreed
at the 1995 Dayton Peace Agreement.

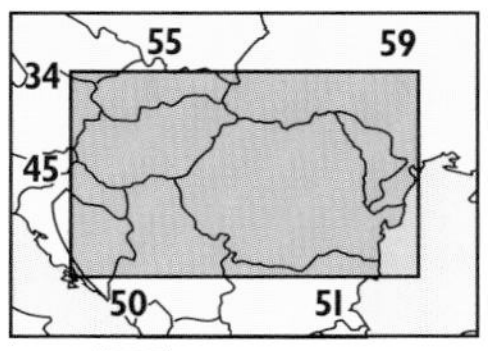

55 59
34
45
50 51

8 9 10 11 12 13 14

UKRAINE

Ivano-Frankivsk
FRANKIVSKA
Kolomyya
CHERNIVETSKA
Chernivtsi
Kamyanets-Podilskyy
VINNYTSKA

KARPATSKA

MOLDOVA

Botoşani
BOTOŞANI
Bălţi
Soroca
Rezina
Râbniţa
Balta

SUCEAVA
Suceava

BISTRIŢA NĂSĂUD
Bistriţa

Iaşi
IAŞI

Orhei
Chişinău (Kishinev)
Tiraspol
Tighina

Cluj-Napoca
CLUJ

MUREŞ
Târgu Mureş

NEAMŢ
Piatra Neamţ

Roman
Vaslui
VASLUI

Bacău
BACĂU

Bârlad
Comrat
ODESKA

HARGHITA

ALBA
Alba-Iulia

Sibiu
SIBIU

COVASNA
Sfântu Gheorghe

VRANCEA
Focşani

Galaţi
GALAŢI

ROMANIA

BRAŞOV
Braşov

PRAHOVA
Ploieşti

BUZĂU
Buzău

BRĂILA
Brăila

Reni
Izmayil
TULCEA
Tulcea

Craiova
DOLJ

VÂLCEA
Râmnicu Vâlcea

ARGEŞ
Piteşti

DÂMBOVIŢA
Târgovişte

Bucureşti

IALOMIŢA
Slobozia

CONSTANŢA
Constanţa

OLT
Slatina

VALAHIA

GIURGIU
Giurgiu

CĂLĂRAŞI
Călăraşi

TELEORMAN
Alexandria

Ruse

Pleven
BULGARIA
Dobrich
DOBRICH

BLACK SEA

Underlined towns give their name to the administrative area in which they stand.

COPYRIGHT GEORGE PHILIP LTD.

8 9 10 11 12 13 14

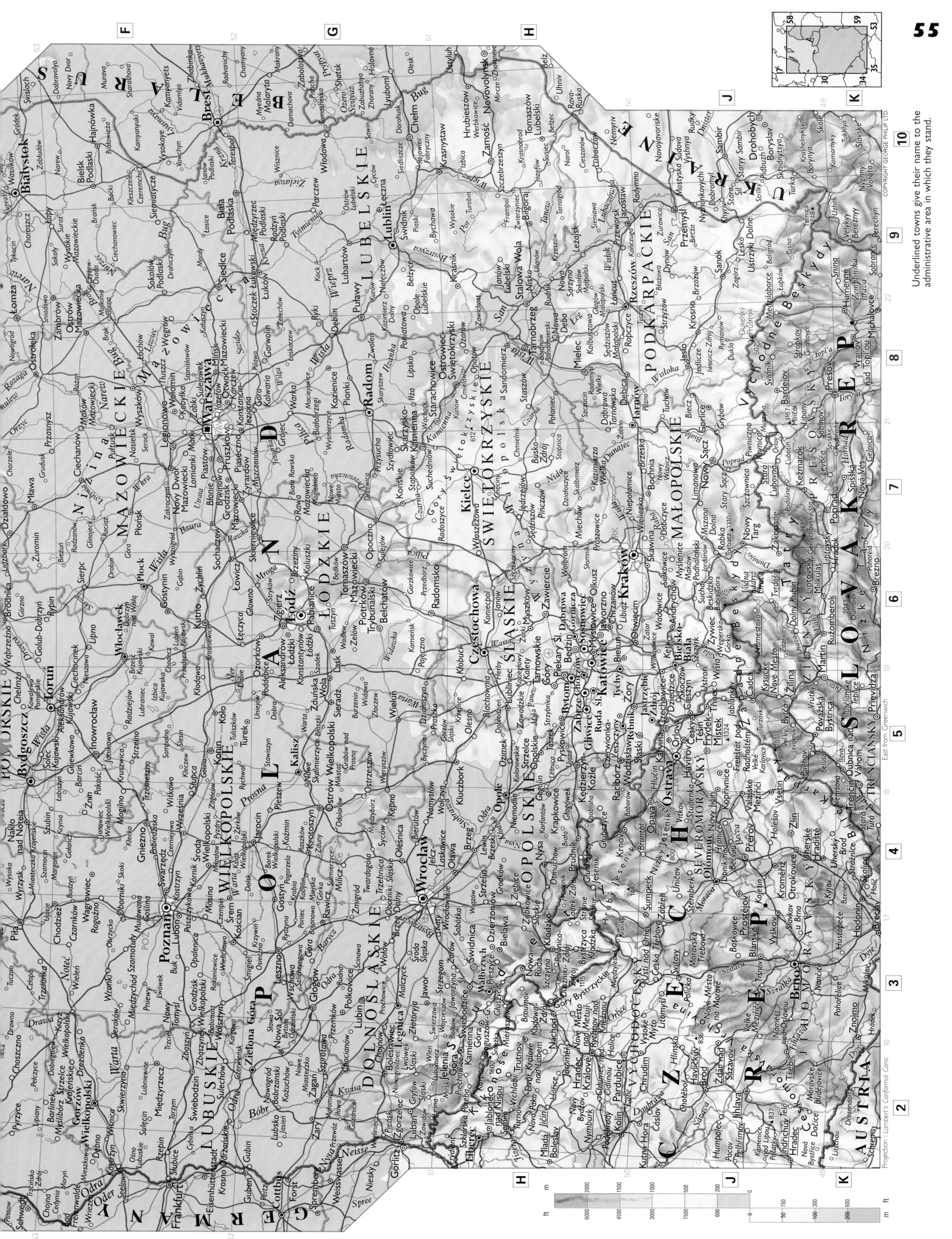

Underlined towns give their name to the administrative area in which they stand.

Projection : Lambert's Conformal Conic

East from Greenwich

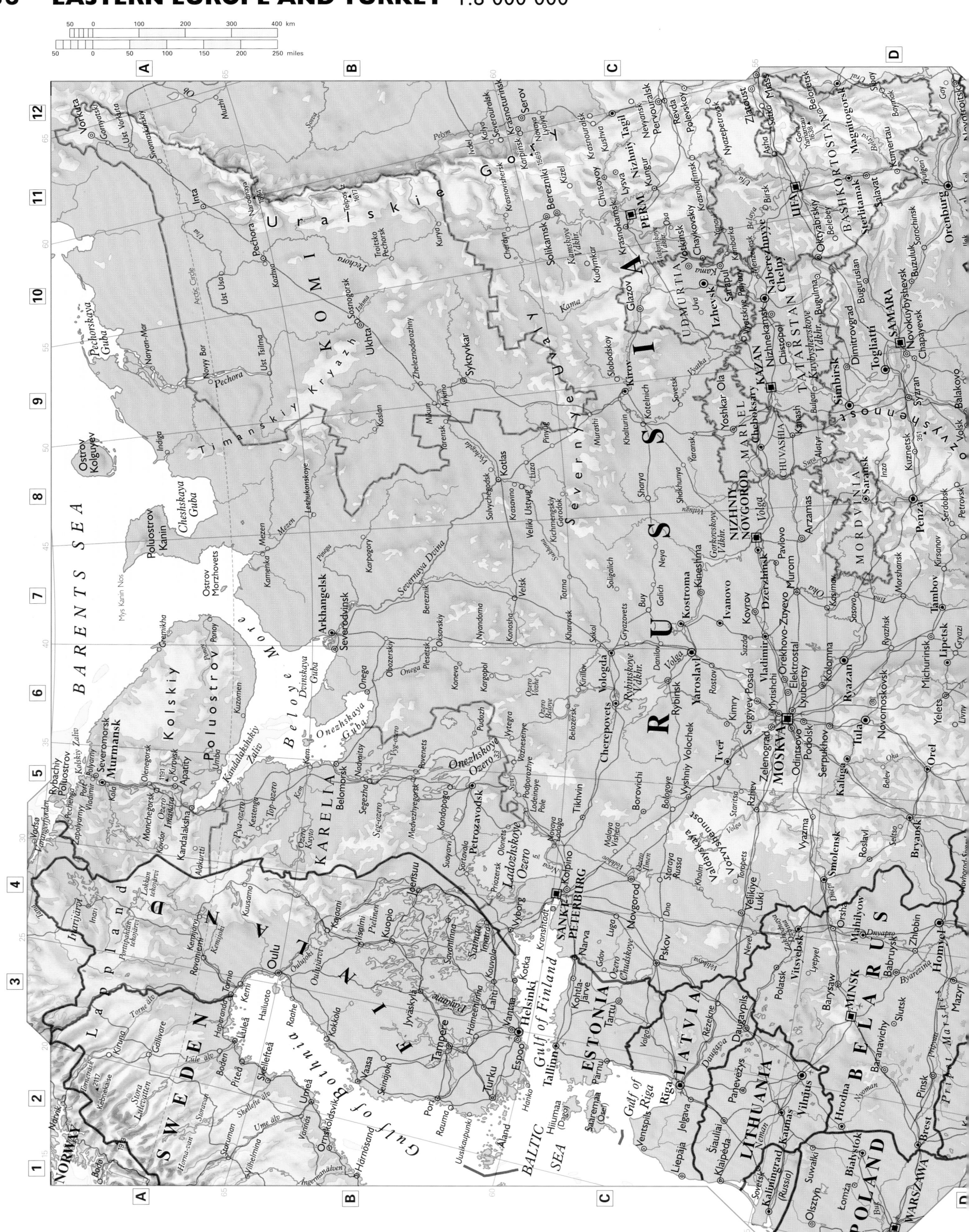

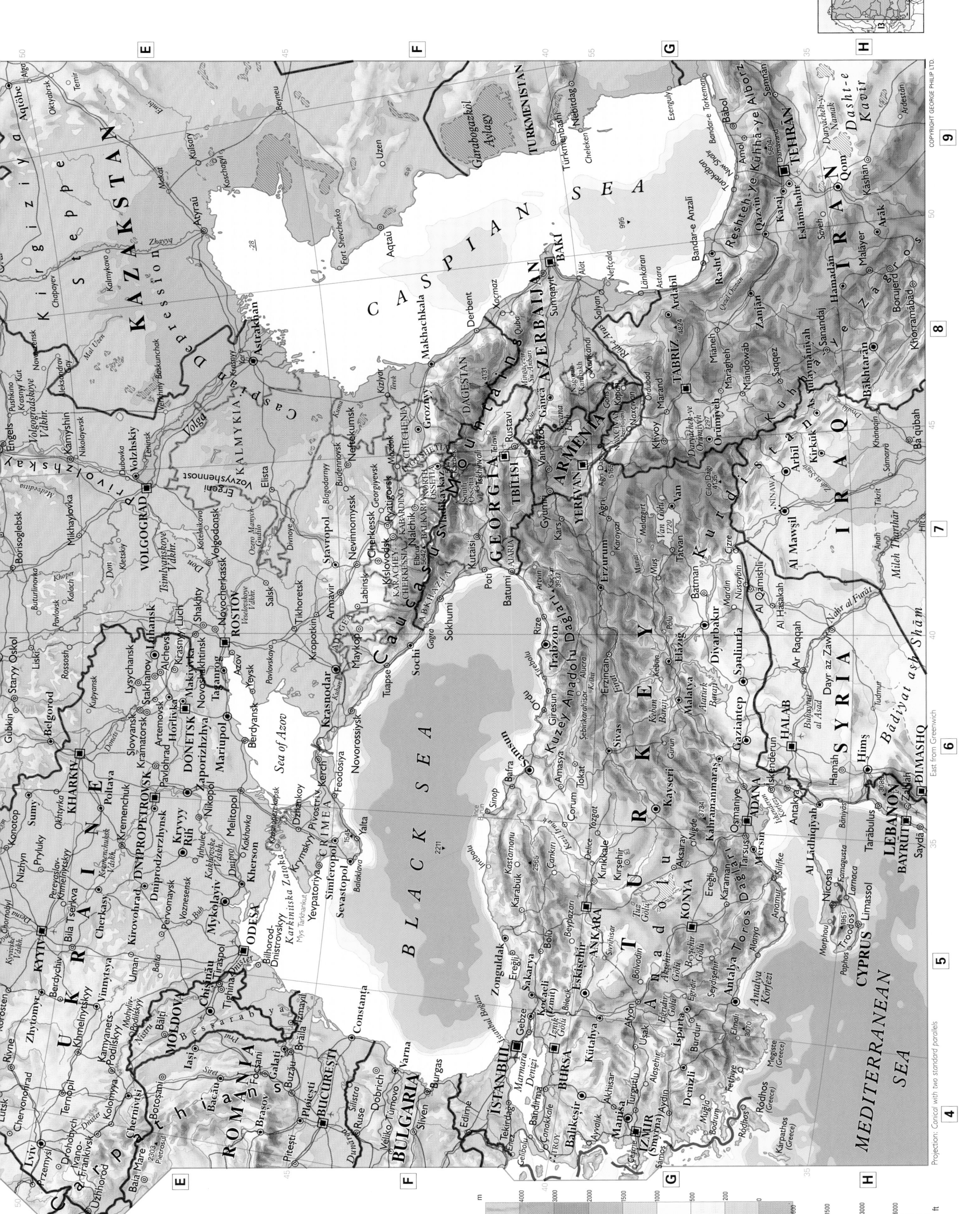

Projection: Conic with two standard parallels

East from Greenwich

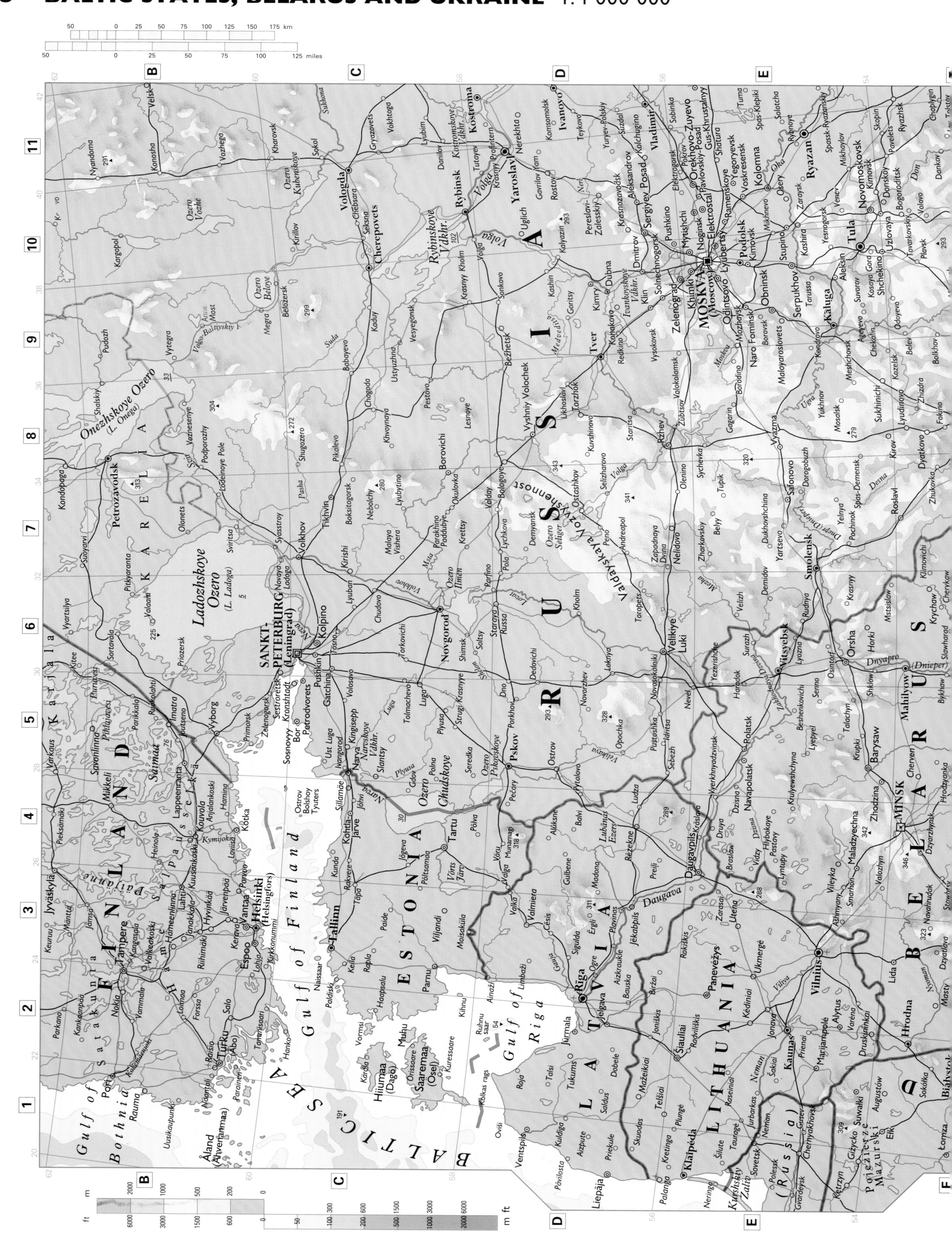

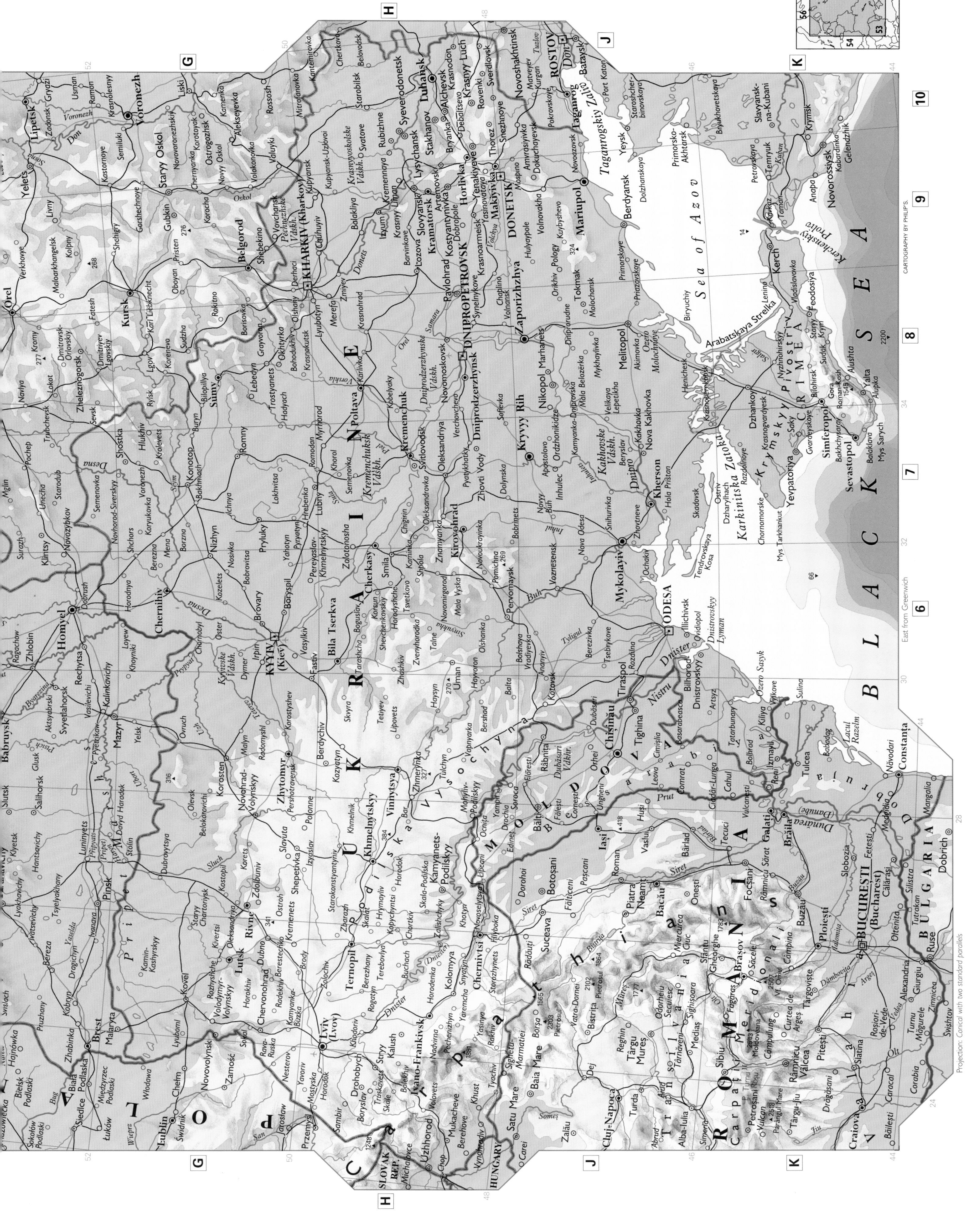

Sea of Azov

BLACK SEA

CRIMEA

ROSTOV
KHARKIV (Kharkov)
DONETSK
DNIPROPETROVSK
KYIV (Kiev)
ODESA
Mykolaviv
Kherson
Zaporizhzhya
Mariupol
Taganrog
Novorossiysk
Simferopol
Sevastopol
Yalta
Poltava
Sumy
Kursk
Belgorod
Voronezh
Lipetsk
Orel
Homyel
Chernihiv
Zhytomyr
Vinnytsya
Khmelnytskyy
Ternopil
Rivne
Lutsk
Lviv (Lvov)
Ivano-Frankivsk
Chernivtsi
Cherkasy
Kirovohrad
Kryvyy Rih
Kremenchuk
Dniprodzerzhynsk
Luhansk
Syeverodonetsk

BUCURESTI (Bucharest)
ROMANIA
MOLDOVA
Chişinău
Constanţa
Galaţi
Braila
Ploieşti
Iaşi
Bacău
Cluj-Napoca
Sibiu
Braşov
Târgu Mures

BULGARIA
Ruse
Dobrich

SLOVAK REP.
HUNGARY

Carpathians
Transilvania

Projection: Conical with two standard parallels
East from Greenwich
CARTOGRAPHY BY PHILIP'S.

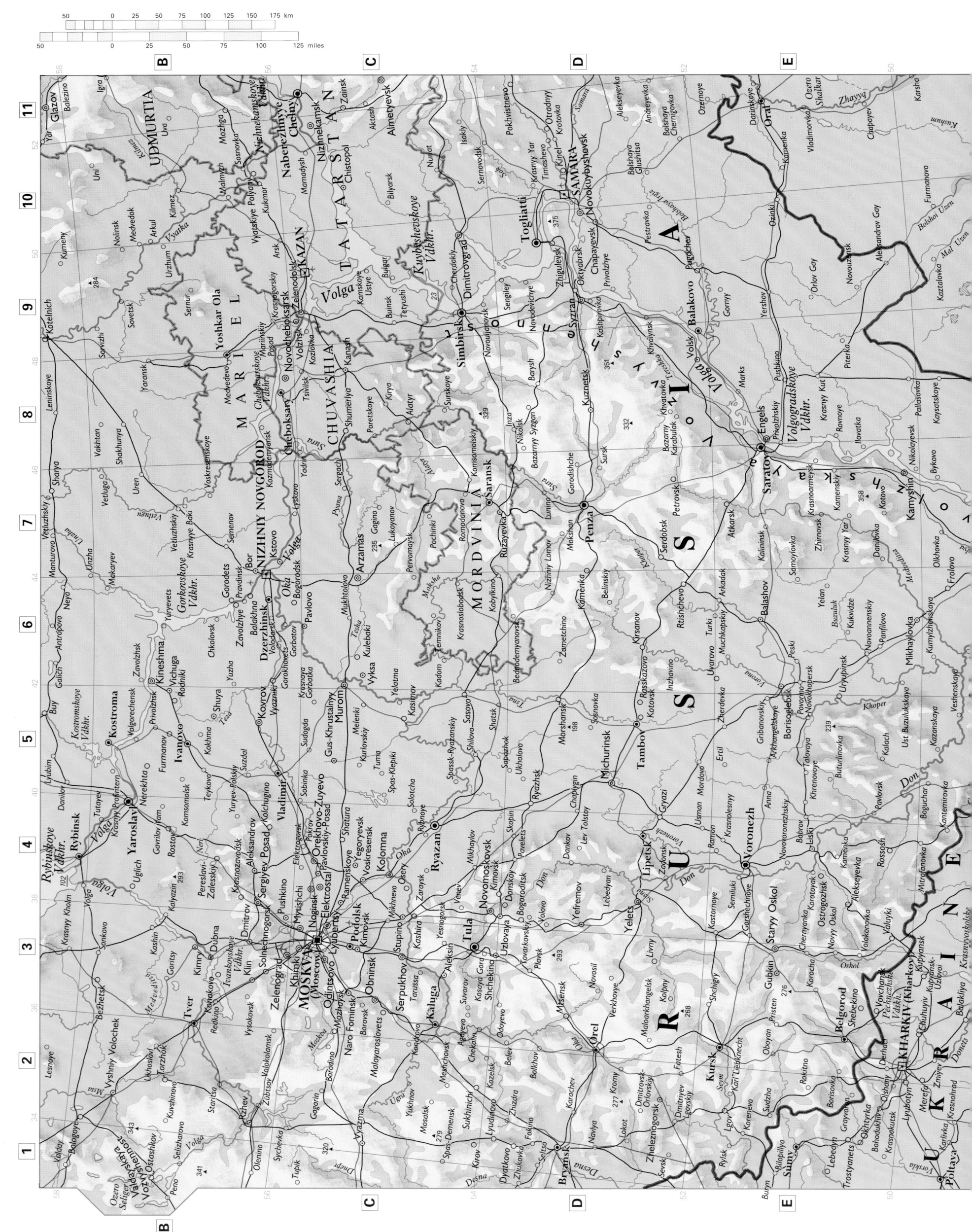

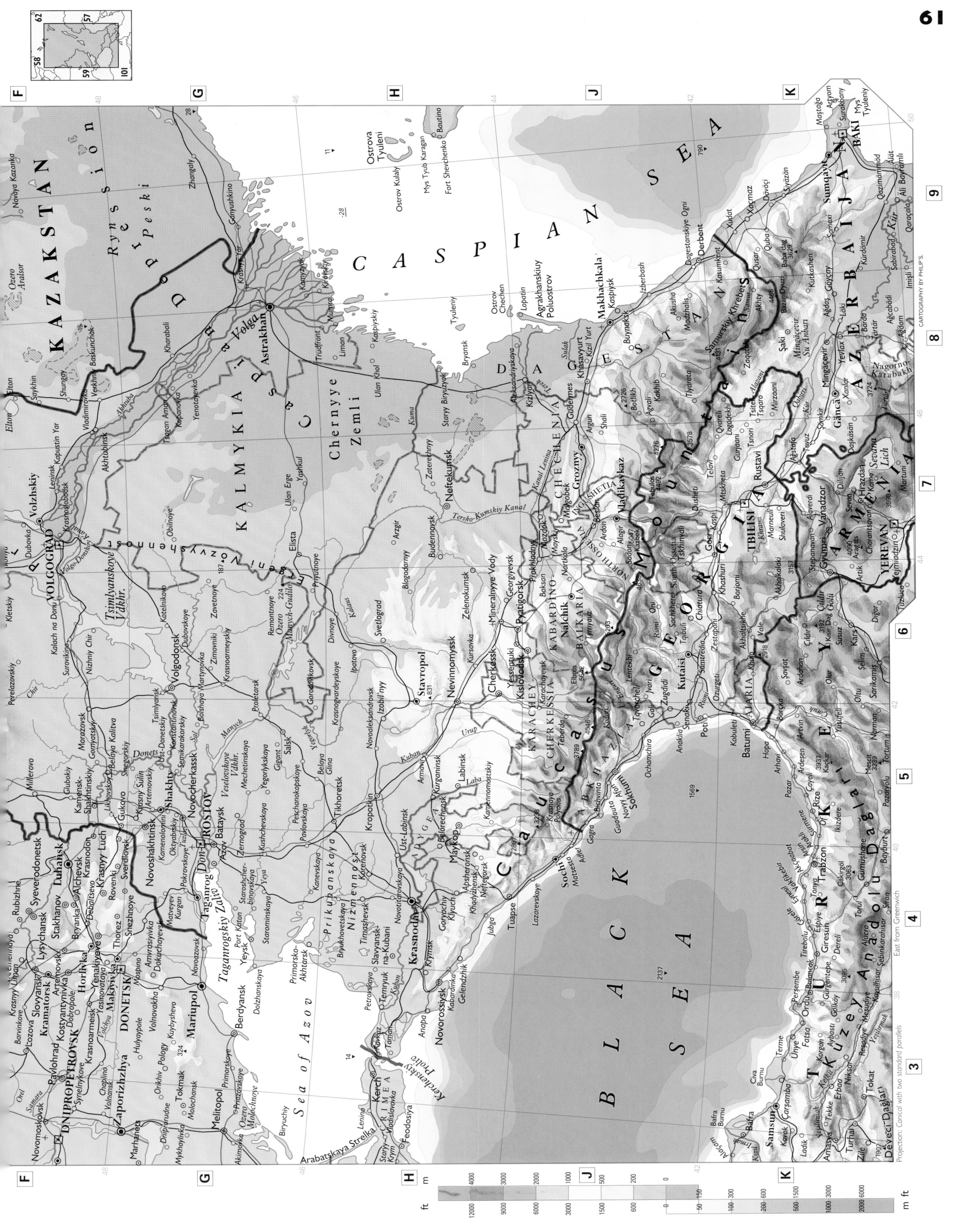

CASPIAN SEA

BLACK SEA

Sea of Azov

KAZAKSTAN

AZERBAIJAN

ARMENIA

GEORGIA

T U R K E Y

Projection: Conical with two standard parallels

CARTOGRAPHY BY PHILIP'S.

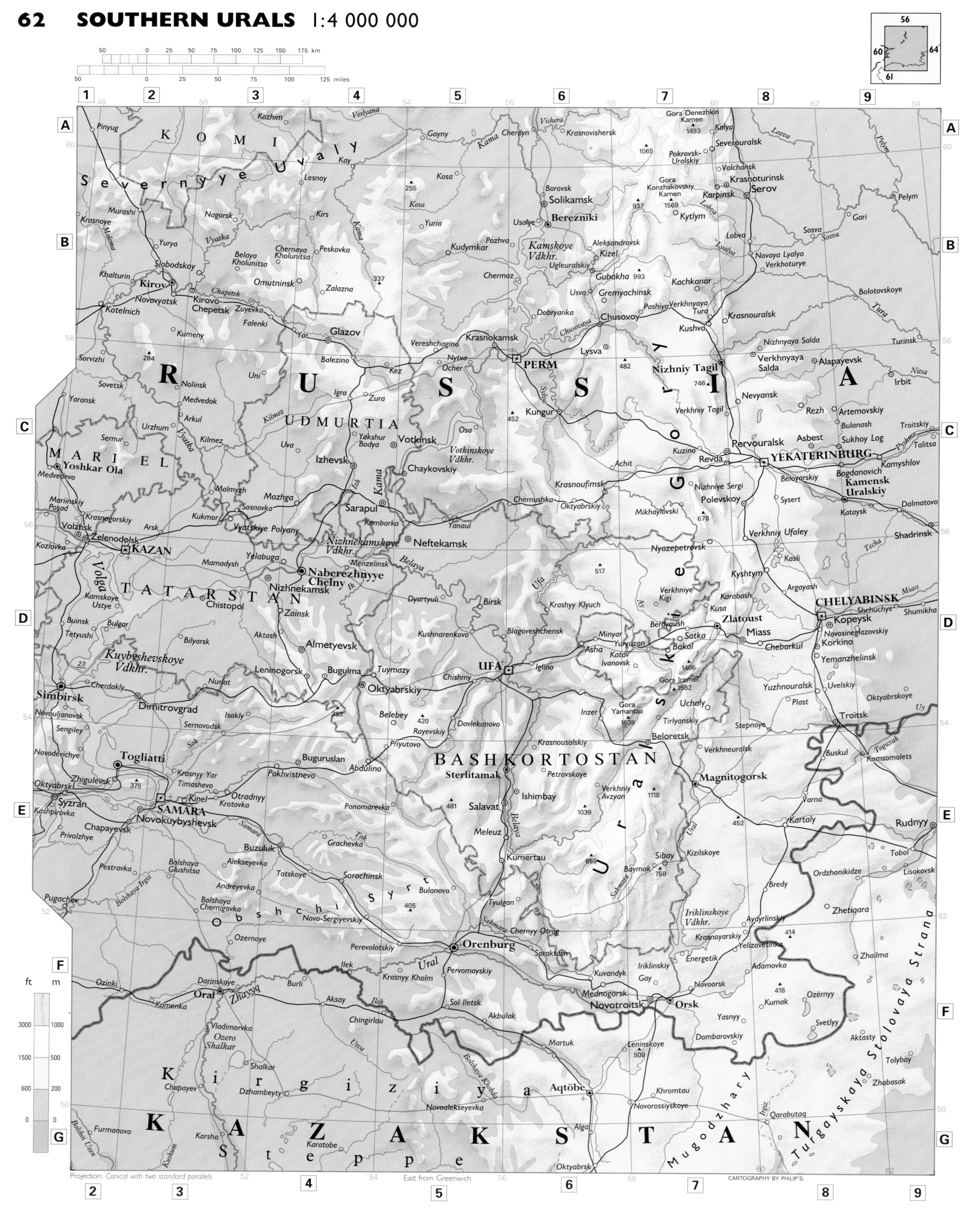

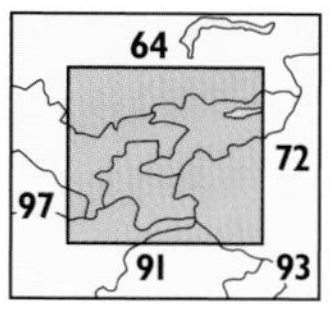

50 0 25 50 75 100 125 150 175 km
50 0 25 50 75 100 125 miles

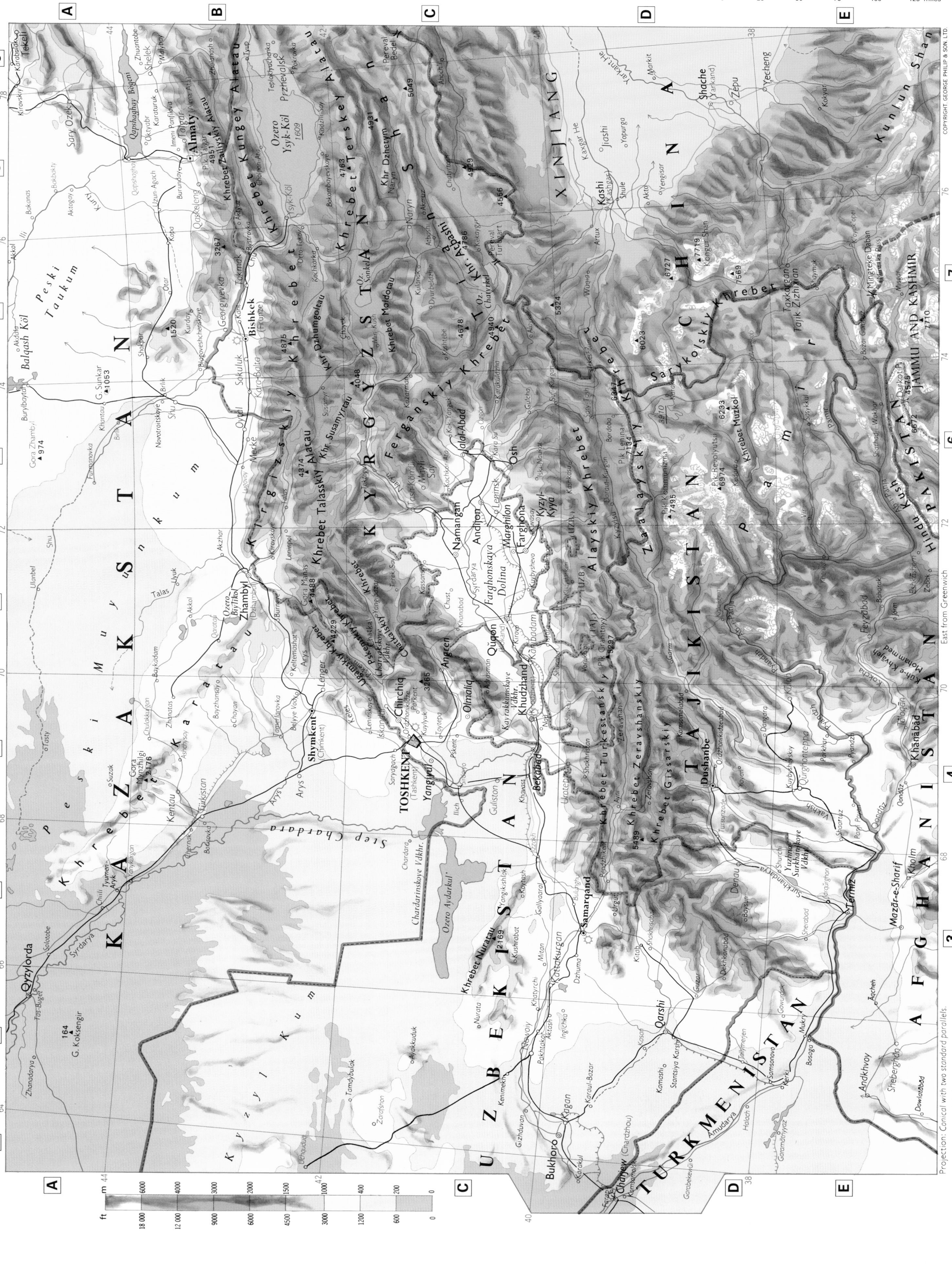

COPYRIGHT GEORGE PHILIP & SON LTD.

East from Greenwich

Projection: Conical with two standard parallels.

K A Z A K S T A N

KYRGYZSTAN

UZBEKISTAN

TAJIKISTAN

TURKMENISTAN

AFGHANISTAN

XINJIANG

C H I N A

JAMMU AND KASHMIR

Peski Taukum

Balqash Köl

Ozero Ysyk-Köl 1609

Almaty

Bishkek (Frunze)

TOSHKENT (Tashkent)

Shymkent (Chimkent)

Chirchiq

Samarqand

Bukhoro

Dushanbe

Termiz

Mazār-e-Sharif

Qarshi

Qyzylorda

Kh, Dzhetym

5049

Kunlun Shan

Hindu Kush

Kara-Kum

Kyzyl Kum

Syrdarya

Amudarya

ft m
18 000 6000
12 000 4000
9000 3000
6000 2000
4500 1500
3000 1000
1200 400
600 200
0 0

RUSSIA
1 Adygea
2 Karachey-Cherkessia
3 Kabardino-Balkaria
4 North Ossetia
5 Ingushetia
6 Chechenia
7 Dagestan
8 Mordvinia
9 Chuvashia
10 Mari El
11 Tatarstan
12 Udmurtia
13 Khakassia
AZERBAIJAN
14 Naxçivan
GEORGIA
15 Ajaria
16 Abkhazia
UKRAINE
17 Crimea

Projection: Conical Orthomorphic with two standard parallels

East from Greenwich

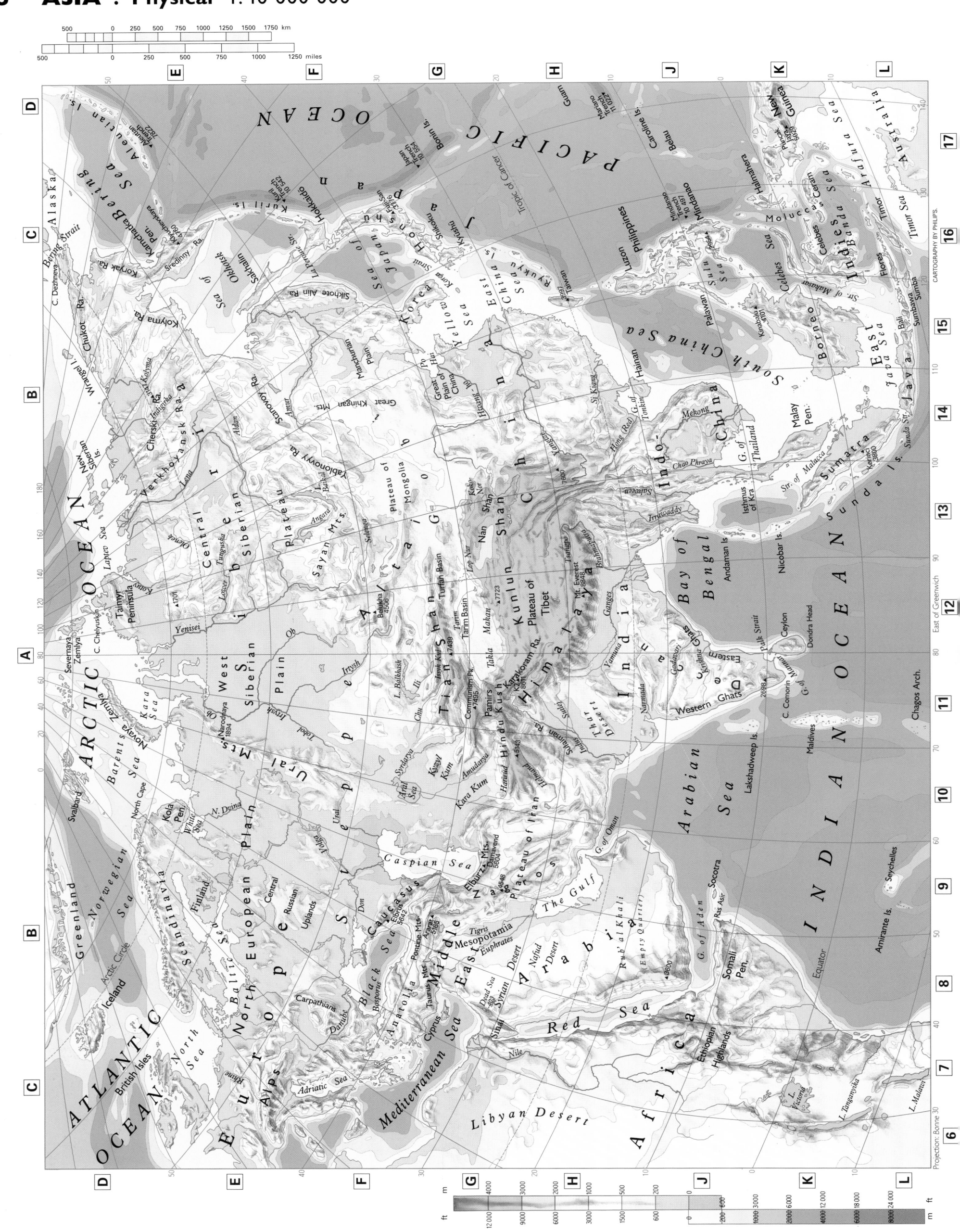

CARTOGRAPHY BY PHILIPS

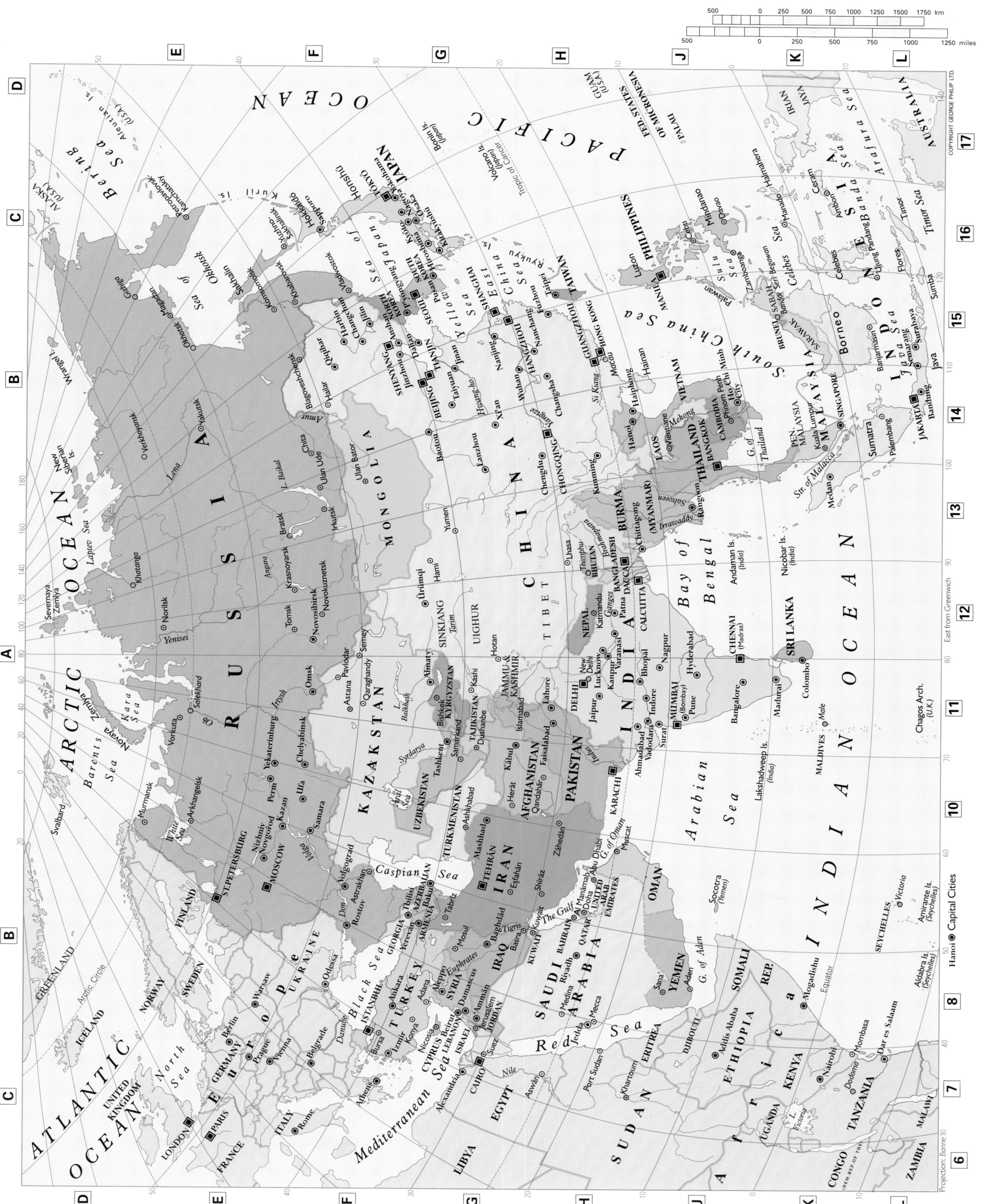

JAPAN 1:4 000 000

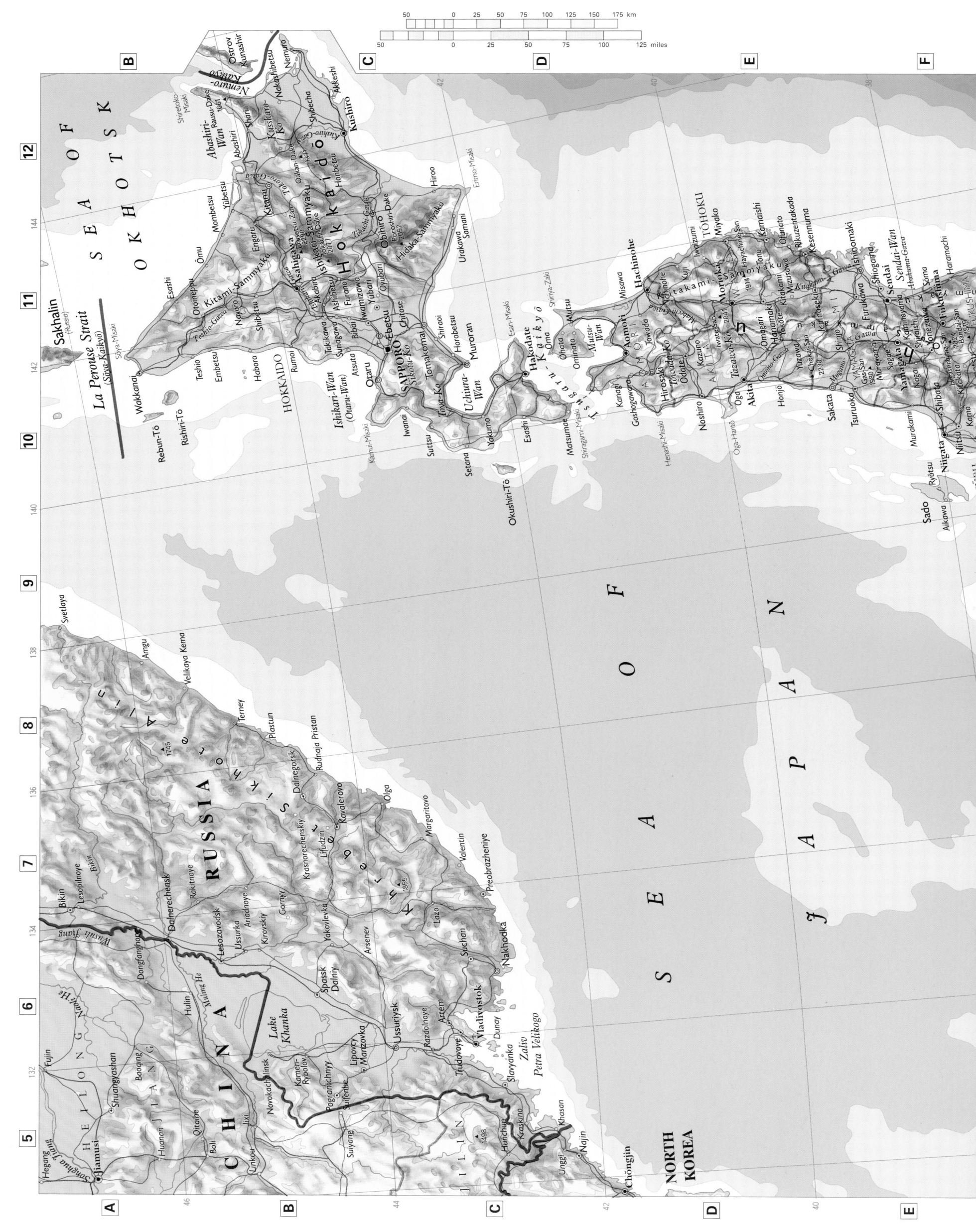

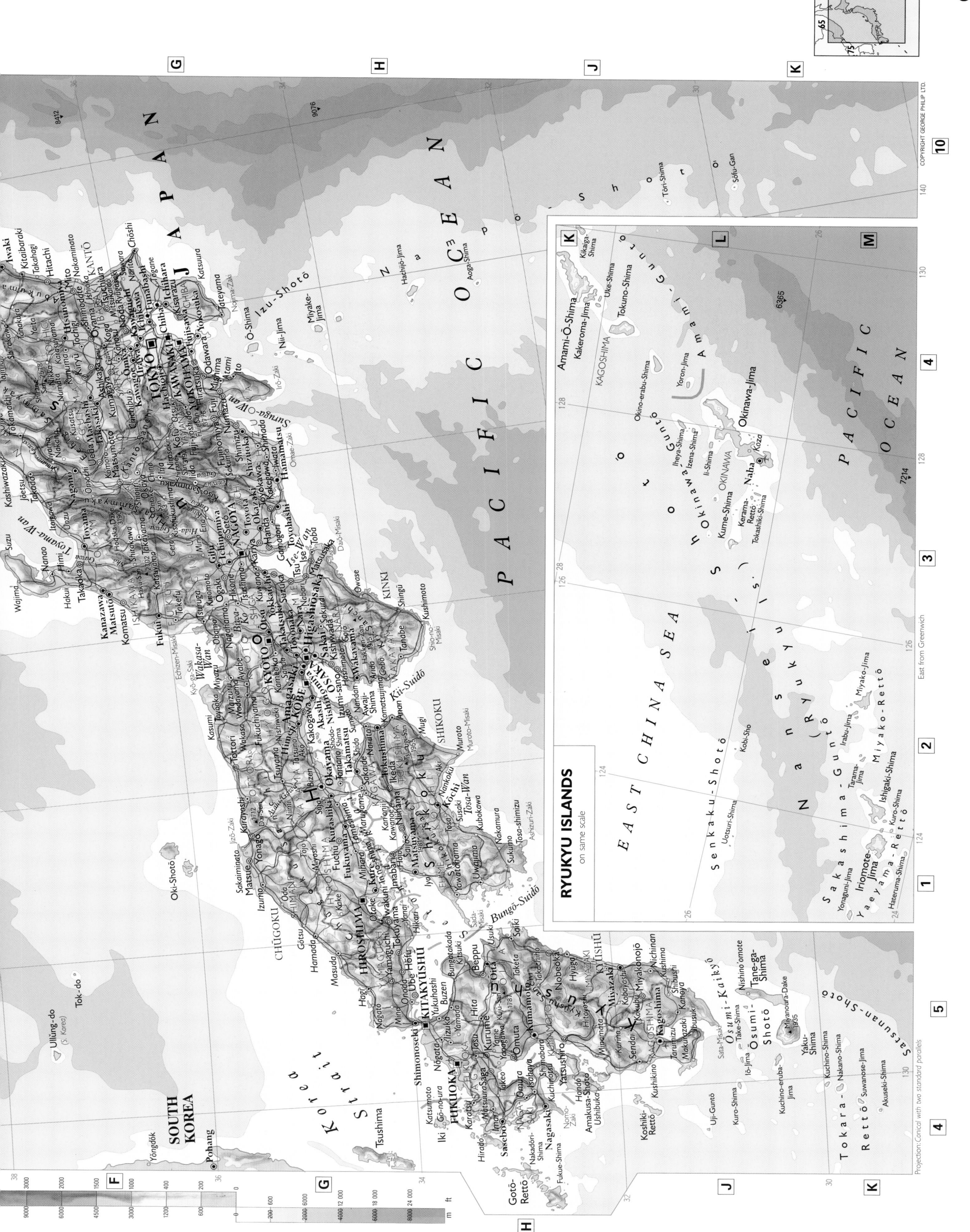

COPYRIGHT GEORGE PHILIP LTD.

RYUKYU ISLANDS
on same scale

Projection: Conical with two standard parallels
East from Greenwich

JAPAN

SOUTH KOREA

PACIFIC OCEAN

EAST CHINA SEA

Nansei Shotō (Ryūkyū)

KANTŌ

TOKYO

YOKOHAMA

KAWASAKI

NAGOYA

KYOTO

OSAKA

KOBE

HIROSHIMA

KITAKYUSHU

FUKUOKA

KUMAMOTO

KAGOSHIMA

NAGASAKI

SHIKOKU

KYUSHU

CHŪGOKU

KINKI

KAGOSHIMA

OKINAWA

Amami-Ō-Shima

Okinawa-Jima

Naha

PACIFIC OCEAN

3000
2000
1500
1000
400
200
m ft
9000
6000
4500
3000
1200
600
0

9000 6000 4500 3000 1500 1200 600 0 200 600 2000 6000 12 000 18 000 24 000 ft

SEA OF JAPAN

SOUTH KOREA

HONS

CHŪGOKU - DISTRICT

Tsushima

Genkai-
Nada

SHIKOKU

SHIKOKU-DISTRICT

KYŪSHŪ

KYŪSHŪ - DISTRICT

Projection:
Lambert's Conformal
Conic

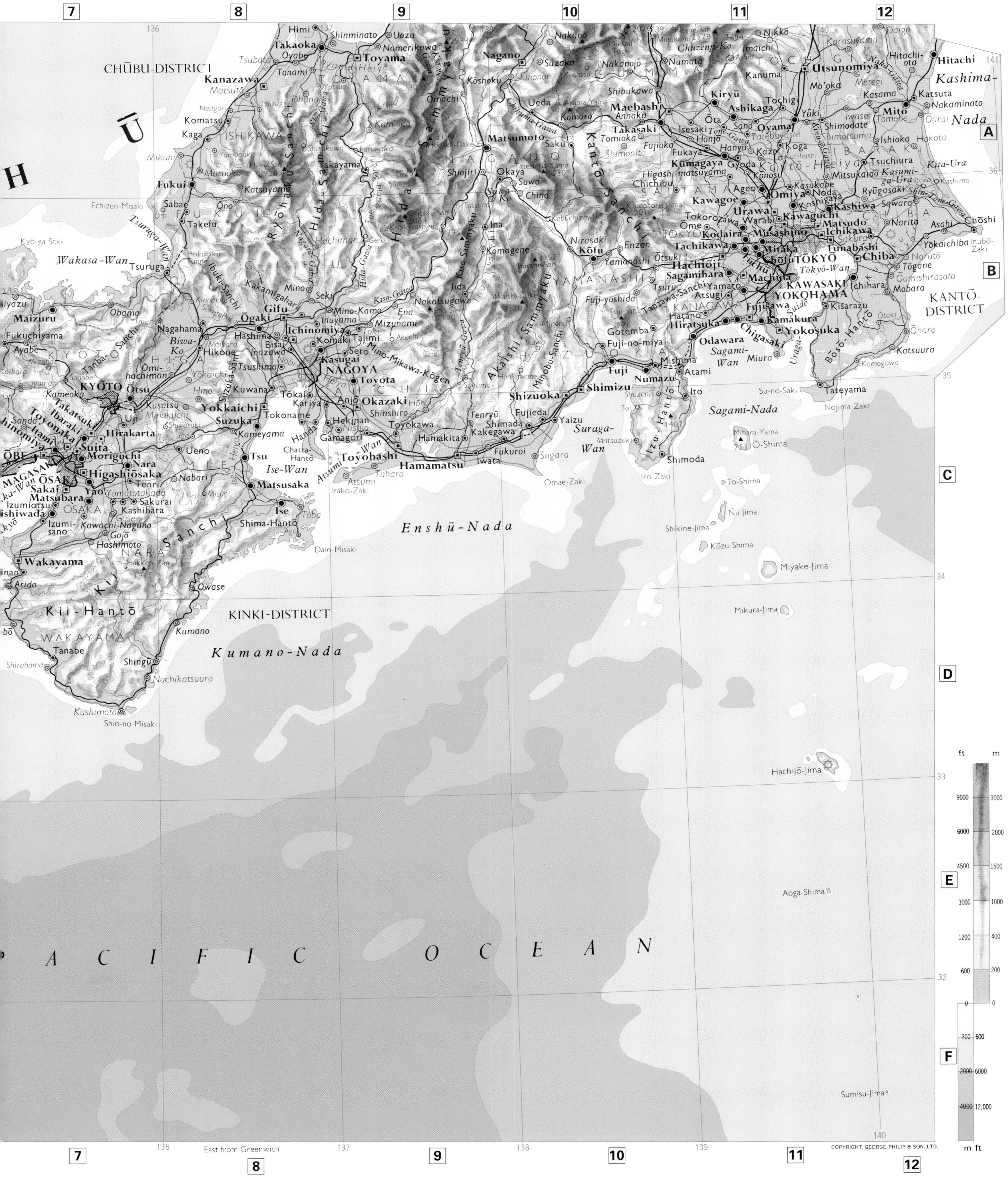

CHŪBU-DISTRICT

Kanazawa
Matsutā

HŪ

Fukui

CHŪBU-DISTRICT

Himi Shinminato Uozu Namerikawa Nakano
Takaoka *Tsubata* Oyabe Tonami **Toyama** Suzaka Nakanojo **Nikko** Imaichi
Nagano Chuzenji-Ko Numata Utsunomiya Kanuma Kasama
Komatsu Jōhana Kōshoku Shinonoi Shibukawa Kiryū Tochigi Mito Katsuta Nakaminato
Kaga Takayama Ōmachi Ueda Komoro Annaka **Maebashi** Ashikaga Yūki Shimodate Ōarai
ISHIKAWA Kamioka **Matsumoto** Saku **Takasaki** Isesaki Honjo Oyama Ishioka
Sabae Ono Katsuyama Shiojiri Okaya Tomioka Shimonita Fukaya Hanyū Kazo Mitsukaido Tsuchiura
Fukui Takefu Suwa Chino Chichibu Kumagaya Gyoda Konosu Kasukabe
Tsuruga Gujō-Hachiman Gero Ina Kōfu Kawagoe Ageo Omiya
FUKUI Ōgaki Gifu Mino-Kamo Nirasaki Enzan Tachikawa **Urawa** Warabi Kawaguchi Matsudo Ichikawa Narita
Gifu Ichinomiya Mizunami YAMANASHI Kōdaira Musashino **TŌKYŌ** Funabashi Chiba Asahi
Seki Komaki Tajimi Ena Yamanashi **Hachiōji** Mitaka Chōshi
NAGOYA **Toyota** Tsuru Fuji-yoshida Sagamihara Yamato Yōkaichiba
Kuwana Tōkai Okazaki Shinshiro Fuji-san Gotemba Atsugi **KAWASAKI**
Yokkaichi Suzuka Kariya Toyokawa Fuji-no-miya **YOKOHAMA** Mobara
Kameyama Handa Hekinan Hamakita Fuji Mishima Odawara Hiratsuka Chigasaki Kamakura Katsuura
Tsu Gamagori **Toyohashi** Shizuoka Shimizu Numazu Atami Yokosuka
Matsusaka Iwata **Hamamatsu** Fukuroi Fujieda Ito Kamogawa
Ise Toyohashi Kakegawa Shimada Yaizu Shimoda Tateyama

Wakasa-Wan *Tsuruga-Wan* *Biwa-Ko* *Ise-Wan* *Suruga-Wan* *Sagami-Wan* *Tōkyō-Wan*

KYŌTO Ōtsu Kusatsu Hikone Nagahama Nara Sakurai
ŌSAKA Suita Moriguchi Higashiōsaka Yao Sakai Matsubara

Wakayama Tanabe Shingū Nachikatsuura Kushimoto
Kii-Hantō *Shio-no-Misaki*
WAKAYAMA

KINKI-DISTRICT

KANTŌ-DISTRICT

Kashima-Nada

Enshū-Nada *Daiō-Misaki* *Omae-Zaki*

Kumano-Nada

Sagami-Nada
Ō-Shima Miyake-Jima Mikura-Jima Hachijō-Jima Aoga-Shima Sumisu-Shima
To-Shima Nii-Jima Kōzu-Shima Shikine-Jima

PACIFIC OCEAN

East from Greenwich

COPYRIGHT GEORGE PHILIP & SON. LTD.

ft m
9000 3000
6000 2000
4500 1500
3000 1000
1200 400
600 200
0 0
200 600
2000 6000
4000 12,000
m ft

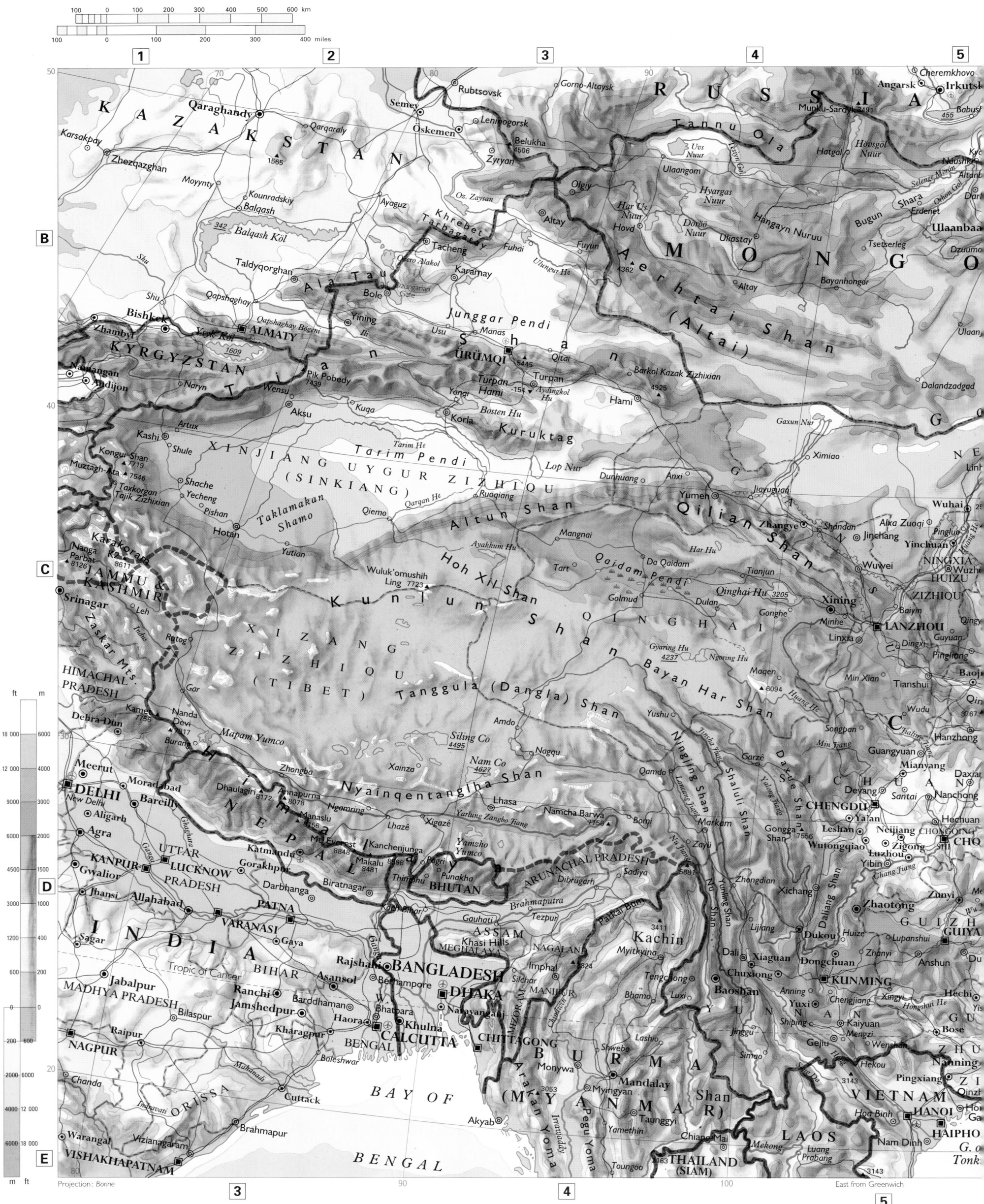

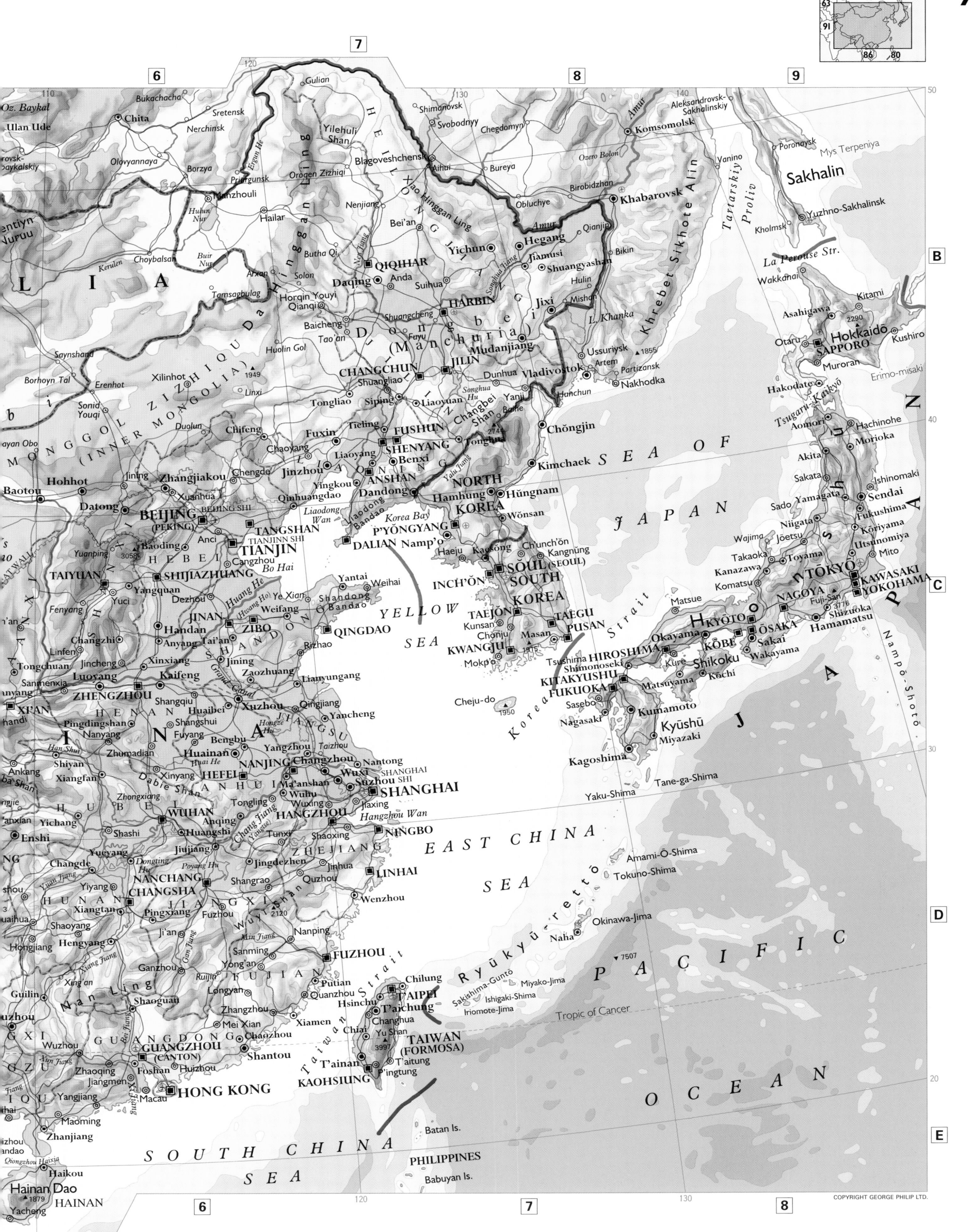

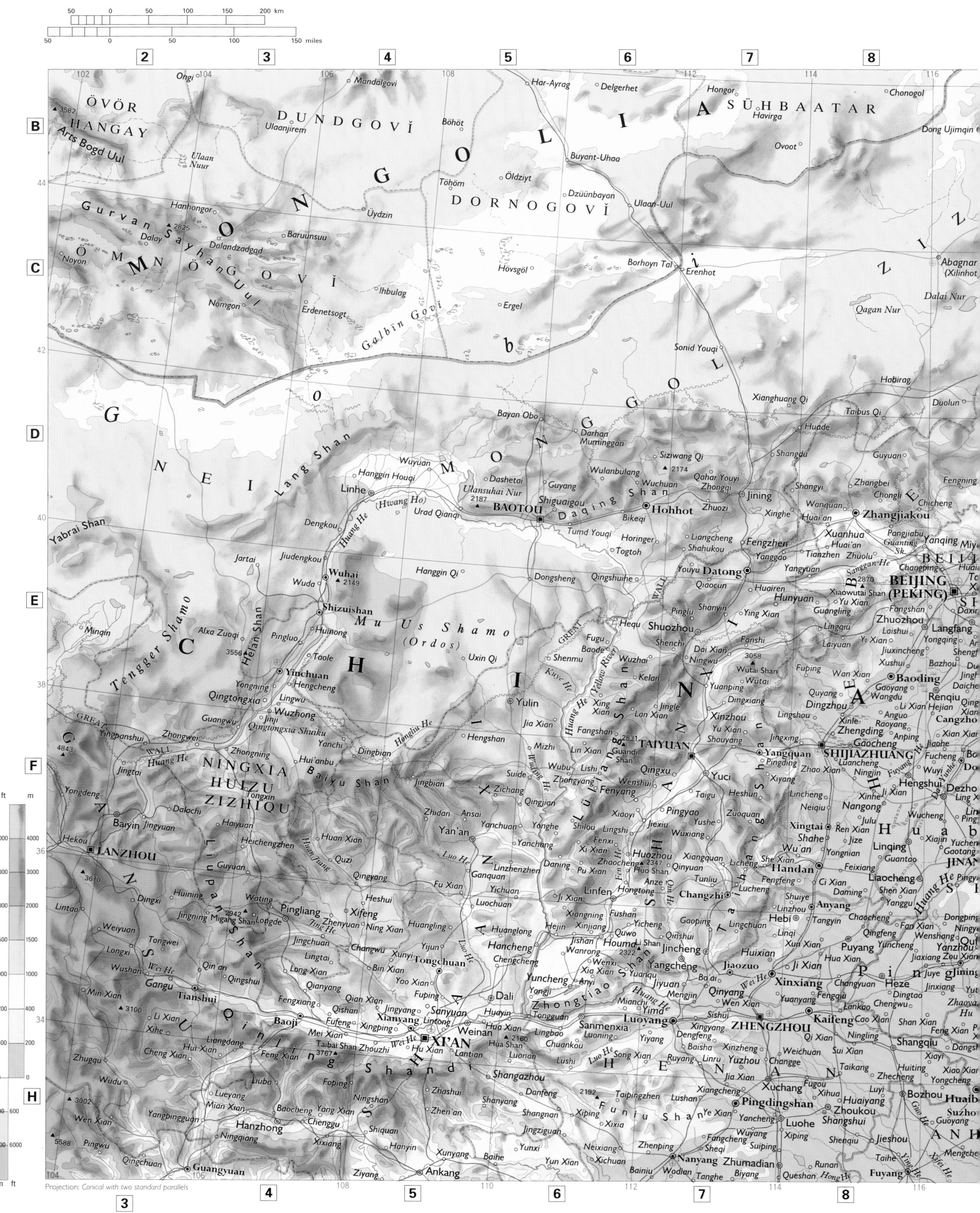

Projection: Conical with two standard parallels

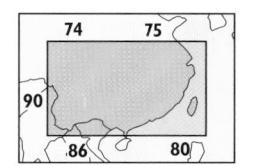

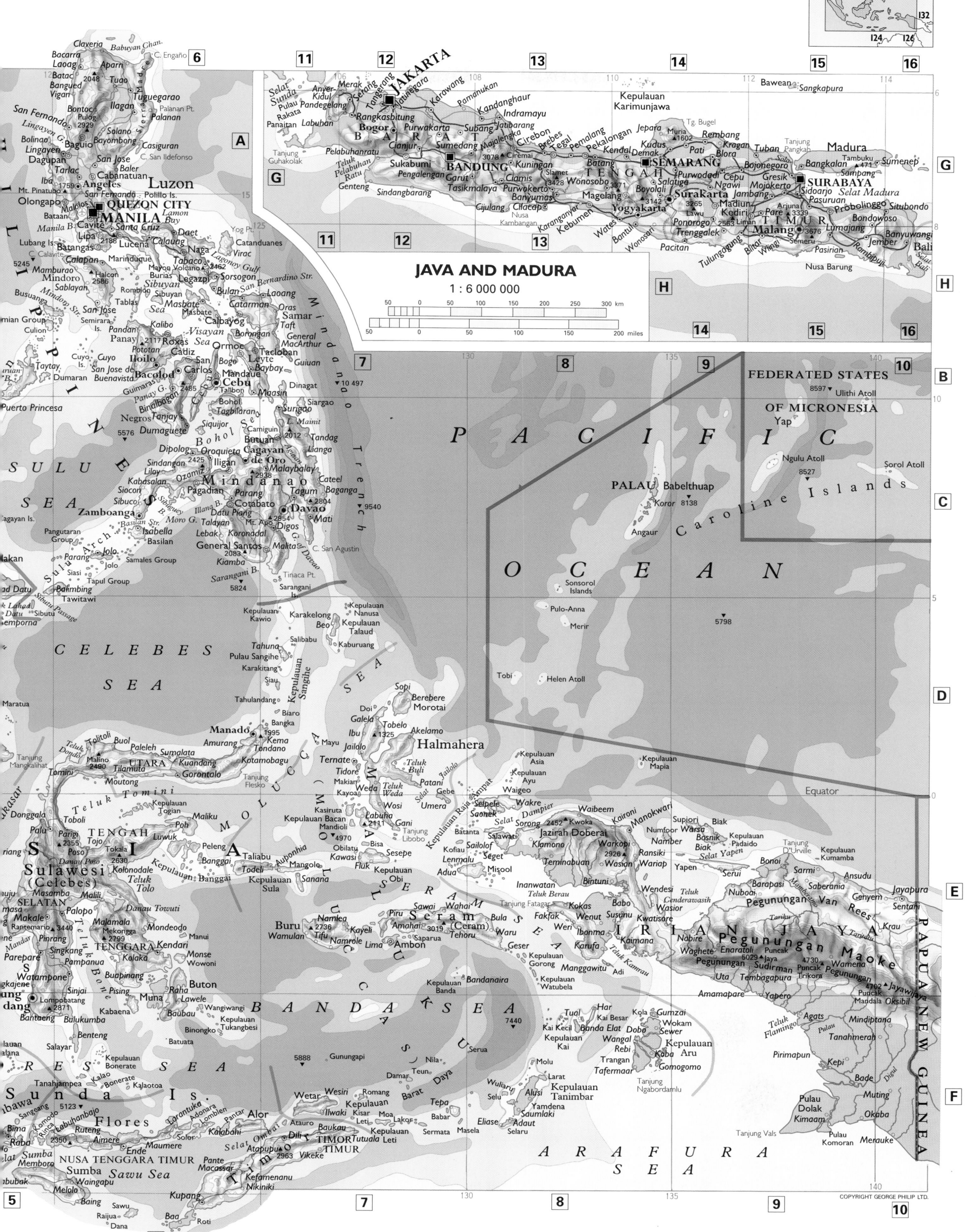

JAVA AND MADURA
1 : 6 000 000

50 0 50 100 150 200 250 300 km

50 0 50 100 150 200 miles

FEDERATED STATES
OF MICRONESIA

PACIFIC

OCEAN

Caroline Islands

CELEBES
SEA

SULU
SEA

MINDANAO

PHILIPPINE

Luzon

QUEZON CITY
MANILA

MOLUCCA SEA

Halmahera

SERAM SEA

BANDA SEA

CERAM SEA

ARAFURA
SEA

IRIAN JAYA

PAPUA NEW GUINEA

Pegunungan Maoke

NUSA TENGGARA TIMUR

Flores

TIMOR

Sawu Sea

SULAWESI
(Celebes)

COPYRIGHT GEORGE PHILIP LTD.

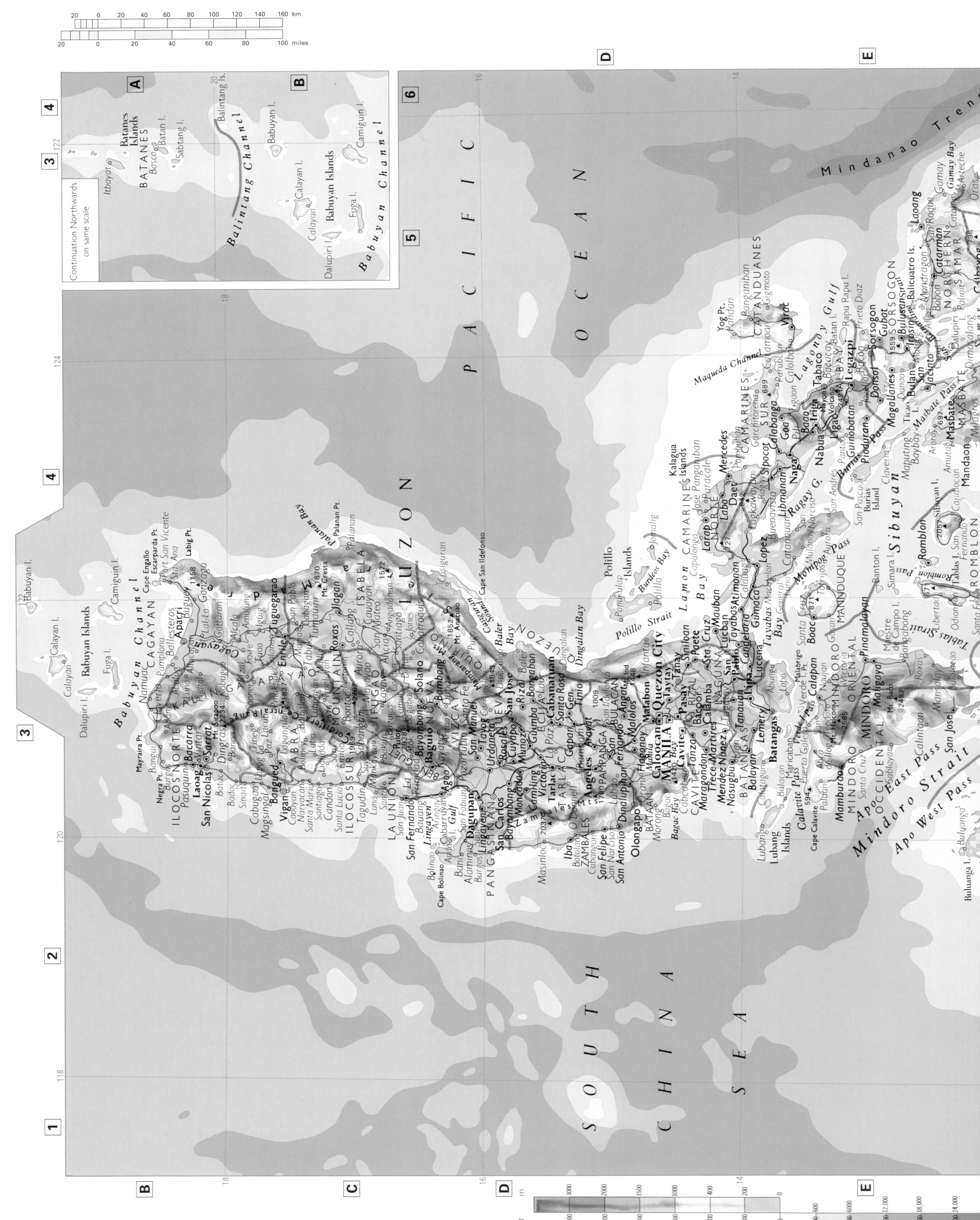

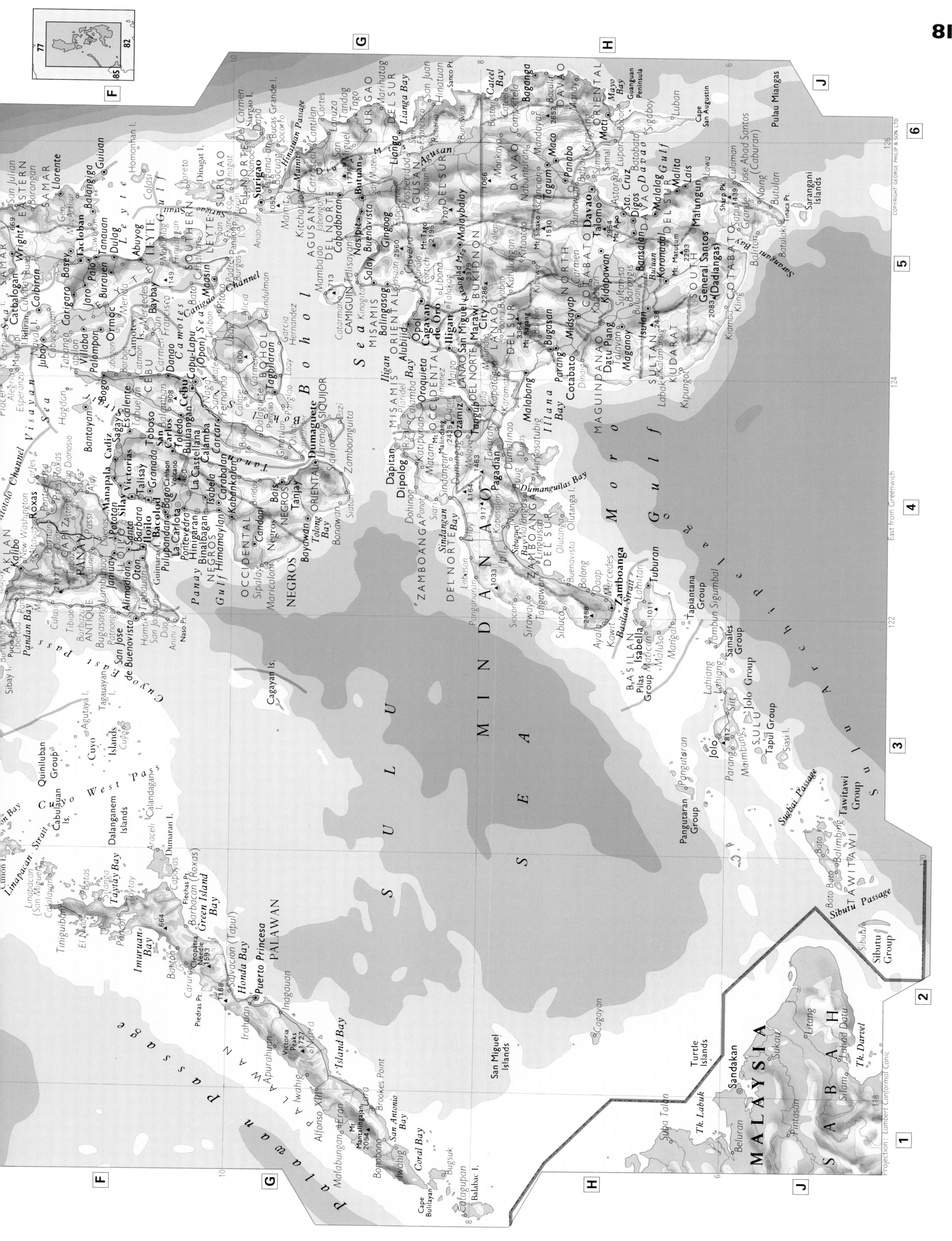

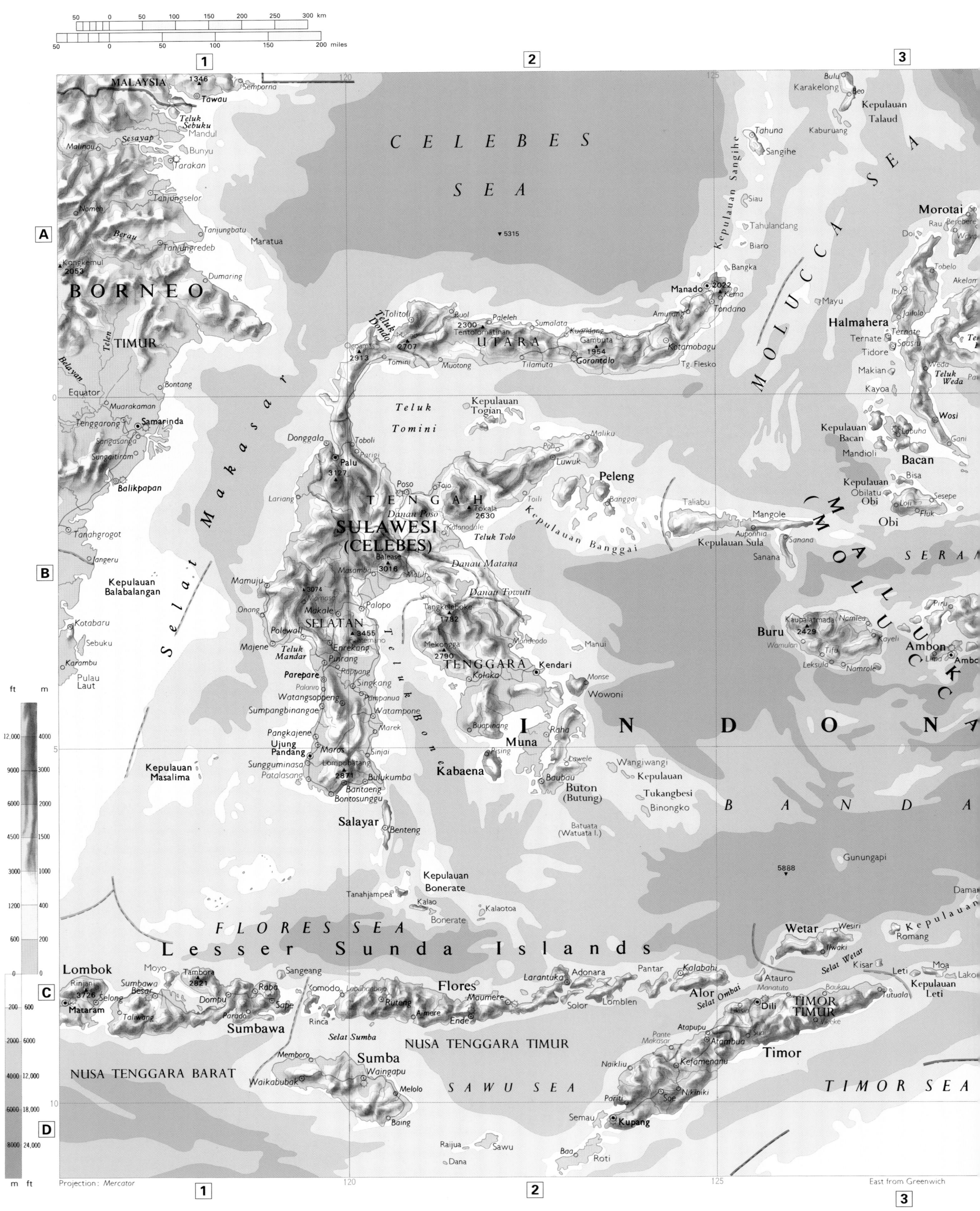

PACIFIC

OCEAN

Tobi

Helen
Atoll

Kepulauan
Asia

Kepulauan
Mapia

Kepulauan
Ayu

Gebe

Umera
Selpele
Kabarai
Wakre
Waigeo
▽4625
Equator   0

Saonek
Kwoka
3000
Waibeem
Kgironi
Manokwari
Warsa
Supion

Gam
Selat Dampier
Jazirah Doberai
(Vogelkop)
Biak
Bosnik
Kepulauan
Padaido

Batanta
Sorong
Klamono
Numfoor

Salawati
Sailolo
Wersar
▲3100
Ransiki
Num
Selat Yapen
Tg. D'Urville
Mataboor
Kepulauan
Kumamba

Seget
Wariap
Yapen
Bonoi
Saberania
Sarmi

Adua
Lermalu
Mogol
Wasian
Serui
Barapasi
Ansudu

Misool
Bira
Bintuni
Teluk
Cenderawasih
Nuboai
Pegunungan Van Rees
Genyem
Jayapura

SEA
Wahai
Tg.
Fatagar
Teluk Berau
Saga
Babo
Wendesi
Wasior
Nabire
Tariku
Taritatu
Krau
Sentani

Binaiya
3019
Bula
Kokas
Susunu
Kwatisore
IRIAN   JAYA
Wamena

Seram
(Ceram)
Haya
Waru
Fakfak
Wefi
Wenut
Ibonma
Kaimana
Enarotali
Woghete
Puncak
Jaya
5029
Pegunungan
Puncak
Trikora
4750
Pegunungan Jayawijaya
Mandala
4702

Geser
Karufa
Teluk
Kamrau
Pegunungan Sudirman
M a o k e

Kepulauan
Gorong
Manggawitu
Adi
Wanapiri
Uta
Yapero

Bandanaira
Kepulauan
Watubela
Wanggar

Kepulauan
Banda
INDONESIA
Agats
Pulau

ESIA
Teluk Flamingo

Kepulauan
Kai
Har
Mindiptana

Kepulauan
Kai Besar
Gymzar
Kola
Doba
Wokam
Pirimapun
Kepi
Tanahmerah

Tual
Kai
Kecil
Sewer
Kepulauan
Aru
Kassue
Digul
Asike

SEA   A   7440
Wangal
Maikoor
Kobroor
Bade
Fly

Daya
Serua
Rebi
Koba
Trangan
Tafermaar
Gomogomo
Muting

Nila
Molu
Larat
Tg. Ngabordamlu
PAPUA NEW GUINEA

Teun
Wuliaru
Selu
Alusi
Muting

Tepa
Saumlaki
Adaut
Yamdena
Pulau
Yos Sudarso
Kimaan
Okaba

Babar
Masela
Selaru
Eliase
Kepulauan Tanimbar
Tg. Vals
Pulau
Komoran
Merauke

ARAFURA   SEA
10

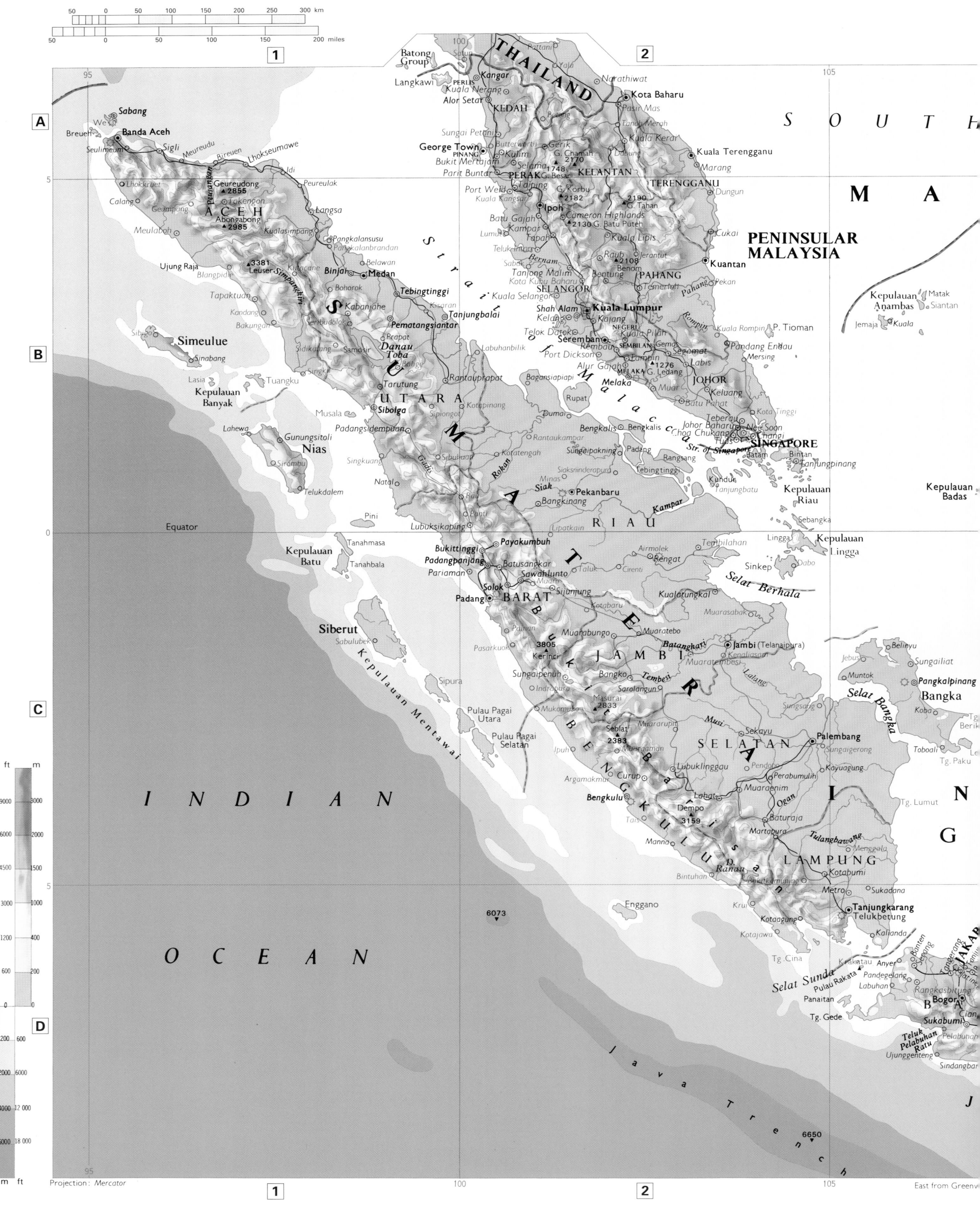

Projection: Mercator

East from Greenwi

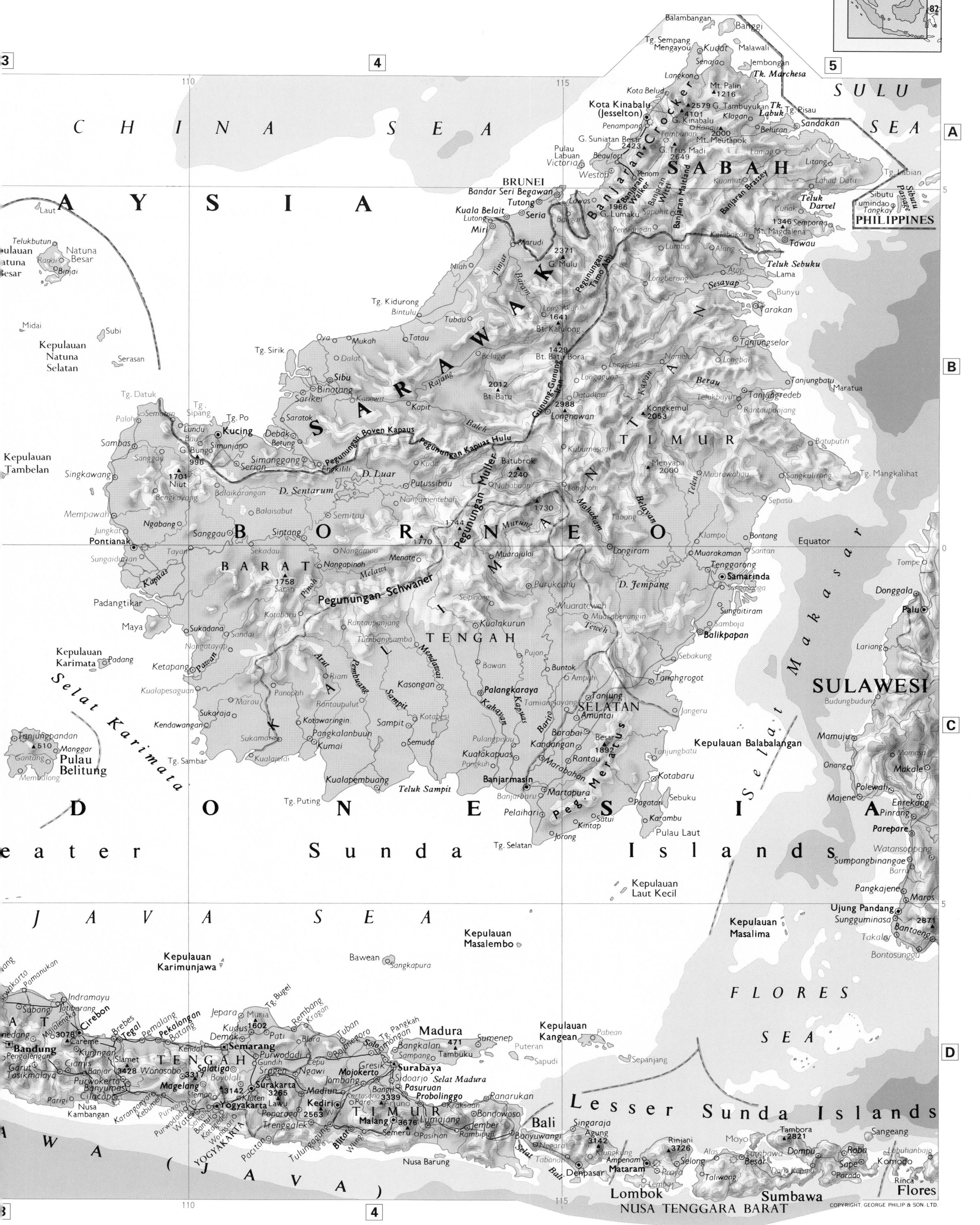

CHINA SEA

SULU SEA

MAYSIA

BRUNEI

SABAH

Balambangan
Banggi
Tg. Sempang
Mengayou
Kudat
Malawali
Senajao
Jembongan
Langkon
Tk. Marchesa
Mt. Palin
1216
Kota Belud
Kota Kinabalu
(Jesselton)
2579 G. Tambuyukan
4101
G. Kinabalu
Klagan
Tg. Pisau
Tk. Labuk
Sandakan
Penampang
Ranggu
2000
Mt. Meutapok
Pulau
Labuan
Victoria
G. Suniatan Besar
2423
G. Trus Madi
2649
Beluran
Beaufort
Tenom
Lahad Datu
Westoh
Kuamut
Litang
Tg. Labian
Bandar Seri Begawan
Tutong
Lawas
Mt. Magdalena
1346
Sempora
Kuala Belait
Seria
G. Lumaku
1966
Pensiangan
Tawau
Miri
1730
Teluk Darvel
Lutong
Banjaran Maitland
PHILIPPINES

Laut
Teluk Sebuku
Telukbutun
Kepulauan
Natuna
Besar
Ranai
Binjai
Marudi
2371
G. Mulu
Pegunungan Tama Abu
Longberang
Sesayap
Lama
Midai
Subi
Serasan
Tg. Kidurong
Niah
Bintulu
Long Akah
1641
Bt. Kalulong
Bunyu
Kepulauan
Natuna
Selatan
Tubau
Tarakan
Oya
Mukah
Tatau
Belaga
Bt. Batu Bora
1429
Longidai
Tanjungselor
Dalat
Kapit
Kayan
Tg. Sirik
Tg. Datuk
Sibu
Sarikei
Kanowit
Rajang
2012
Bt. Batu
Gunung Gunung
Longagung
Berau
Tanjungredeb
Maratua
Paloh
Semitau
Saratok
Baleh
2988
Longnawan
Datadian
Kongkemul
2053
Telukbayur
Tg.
Sipang
Lundu
Debak
Betung
Serian
Enkilili
Kubumesaai
Menyapa
2000
Muarawahau
Tg. Mangkalihat
Kepulauan
Tambelan
Tg. Po
Kucing
Bau
G. Bungo
996
Simunjan
Simanggang
D. Luar
Kuda
Batubrok
2240
Nahabuan
Sangkulirang
Sepasu
Singkawang
1701
Niut
Balaikarangan
D. Sentarum
Putussibau
Longbuan
Teleti
Tabang
Batuputih
Sambas
Sanggau
Balaisabut
Nangamentebah
Muarakaman
Sanggau
1744
Murung
1730
Longiram
Mempawah
Ngabang
Sintang
Nangamau
Seipinang
Santan
Equator
Pontianak
Sekadau
Nangapinoh
Menate
Muarajulai
Tenggarong
Bontang
BARAT
Melawi
Samarinda
Sungaiduran
Tayan
1758
Sarah
Pinoh
Purukcahu
D. Jempang
Sungaitiram
Padangtikar
Pegunungan Schwaner
Rantaupanjang
Muaratewen
Muarakaman
Maya
Sukadana
Kotabaru
Tumbangsamba
Menukung
Kualakurun
Muarabenangin
Samboja
Balikpapan
Nongatayap
Sandai
Kepulauan
Karimata
Padang
Ketapang
Pawan
Arut
Kendang
Pembuang
Bawan
Teweh
Pujon
Sebakung
Tanahgrogot
Kualapesaguan
Riam
Kasongan
Buntok
Ampah
Kualejelai
Marau
Panopah
Rantaupulut
Sampit
Kotabesi
Kahayan
Palangkaraya
Tamianglayang
Jangeru
Tanjung
Selat Makasar
Tanjungpandan
Manggar
Sukaraja
Kotawaringin
Kumai
Semuda
Pulangpisau
SELATAN
Amuntai
Gantung
510
Pulau
Belitung
Kumai
Pangkalanbuun
Sampit
Pangkoh
Kualakapuas
Barabai
Kandangan
1892
Kotabaru
Membalong
Kualapembuang
Tg. Sambar
Teluk Sampit
Banjarmasin
Rantau
Marabahan
Banjarbaru
Martapura
Sebuku
Tg. Puting
Pelaihari
Pagatan
Pulau Laut
Tg. Selatan
Satui
Karambu
Kintap
Jorong

BORNEO

KALIMANTAN

TIMUR

TENGAH

SARAWAK

INDONESIA

SULAWESI

Donggala
Palu
Lariang
Mamuju
Budungbudung
Mamasa
Makale
Onang
Polewali
Majene
Enrekang
Pinrang
Parepare
Watansoppeng
Sumpangbinangae
Barru
Pangkajene
Maros
Ujung Pandang
Sungguminasa
2871
Bantaeng
Takalar
Bontosunggu

Kepulauan Balabalangan

Kepulauan
Masalima

SULA
SEA

Greater Sunda Islands

JAVA SEA

Kepulauan
Masalembo
Bawean
Sangkapura

Kepulauan
Karimunjawa

Kepulauan
Kangean
Pabean
Puteran
Sapudi
Sepanjang

FLORES
SEA

BARAT
3078
Bandung
Indramayu
Subang
Jatibarang
Cirebon
Brebes
Tegal
Pemalang
Pekalongan
Batang
Jepara
Muria
1602
Kudus
Pati
Rembang
Tuban
Lasem
Krogan
Madura
Sumenep
Pamanukan
Kuningan
Careme
Pengalengan
Slamet
Wonosobo
3428
Salatiga
Purwodadi
Gundih
Blora
Cepu
Bojonegoro
Bangkalan
Tambuku
Garut
Tasikmalaya
Banjar
Ciamis
TENGAH
3265
Magelang
Boyolali
Ngawi
Jombang
Gresik
Surabaya
Ponorogo
Pasuruan
Pacitan
Madiun
Kediri
3339
Probolinggo
Panarukan
Bali
LESSER Sunda Islands
Cilacap
Banyumas
Purwokerto
Purworejo
3142
Klaten
YOGYAKARTA
Lawu
Kertosono
Pare
Mojokerto
TIMUR
Malang
3676
Lumajang
Jember
Bondowoso
Rambipuji
Banyuwangi
Singaraja
Moyo
Sangeang
Singapura
Nusa
Kambangan
Wates
Bantul
Wonosari
Trenggalek
Tulungagung
Blitar
Wlingi
Semeru
Opasinan
Rinjani
3726
Agung
3142
Klungkung
Negara
Tambora
2821
Dompu
Roba
Sape
Komodo
YOGYAKARTA
Pacitan
2563
Nusa Barung
Denpasar
Mataram
Ampenam
Selong
Praya
Selat Lombok
Alas
Sumbawa
Besar
Labuhanbajo
Lombok
Sumbawa
Taliwang
Lembar
Pado
Flores
Rinca
NUSA TENGGARA BARAT

JAVA

J A V A   S E A

ater   Sunda   Islands

AWA (JAVA)

COPYRIGHT. GEORGE PHILIP & SON. LTD.

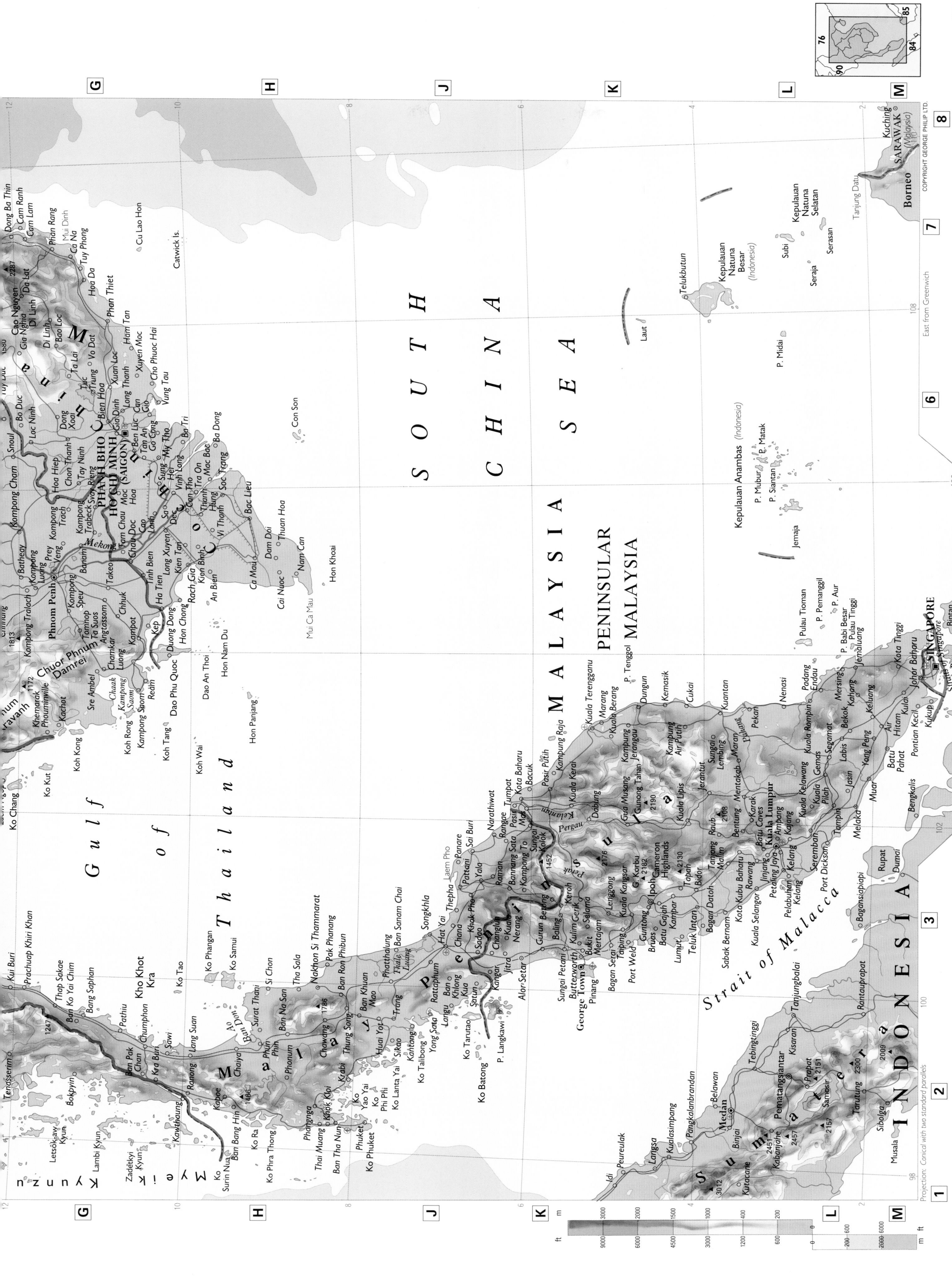

SOUTH CHINA SEA

Gulf of Thailand

Thailand

PENINSULAR MALAYSIA

MALAYSIA

INDONESIA

Strait of Malacca

Sumatera

Borneo

SARAWAK (Malaysia)

Kuching

Tanjung Datu

Kepulauan Natuna Besar (Indonesia)

Kepulauan Natuna Selatan

Subi

Seraja

Serasan

Telukbutun

P. Midai

Laut

P. Mubur   P. Matak

P. Siantan

Kepulauan Anambas (Indonesia)

Jemaja

Con Son

Catwick Is.

Cu Lao Hon

Dong Ba Thin
Cam Ranh
Cam Lam
Phan Rang
Ca Na
Tuy Phong
Mui Dinh
Hoa Da
Phan Thiet
Cao Nguyen 2287
Da Lat
Di Linh
Gia Nghia
Bao Loc
Ta Lai
Ham Tan
Xuan Thanh
Vo Dat
Ho Da

PHANH BHO HO CHI MINH (SAIGON)
Bien Hoa
Thu Duc
Tan An
Go Cong
Ba Tri
Gio Linh
Long Thanh
Vung Tau
Ben Luc
Cho Phuoc Hai
Ba Dong

My Tho
Tan Chau
Chau Doc
Cao Lanh
Can Tho
Vinh Long
Sa Dec
Tra On
Tra Vinh
Soc Trang
Bac Lieu
Ca Mau
Nam Can
Dam Doi
Thanh Hung
Thuan Hoa
Hon Khoai
Mui Ca Mau
Rach Gia
Ha Tien
Kien Bhit
Long Xuyen
Kien Tan
Kien Giang
An Bien
Cai Nuoc

Kompong Cham
Phnom Penh
Kompong Speu
Kompong Trach
Kampot
Kep
Takeo
Prey Veng
Svay Rieng
Trabeck
Bassac
Neak Luong
Mekong

Chuor Phnum Damrei
Khernarak 1172
Kampong Saom
Sre Ambel
Koh Kong
Koh Rong
Koh Tang
Koh Wai
Duong Dong
Dao Phu Quoc
Hon Nam Du
Hon Chong

Ko Chang
Ko Kut
Ko Mak
Ko Phangan
Ko Samui
Ko Tao
Ko Phra Thong
Ko Lanta Yai
Ko Talibong
Ko Tarutao
Ko Batong
Ko Surin Nua
Ko Ra
P. Langkawi

Prachuap Khiri Khan
Kui Buri
Thap Sakae
Bang Saphan
Chumphon
Lang Suan
Kho Khot Kra
Pathiu
Ban Ko Yai Chim
Ban Pak Chan
Kra Buri
1466
Ranong
Kapoe
Takua Pa
Surat Thani
Si Chon
Nakhon Si Thammarat
Pak Phanang
Ban Ron Phibun
Thung Song
Chawang
1786
Ban Na San
Ban Dan
Phunphin
Trang
Kantang
Yong Sata
Langu
Satun
Ban Khuan Mao
Phatthalung
Ban Sanam Chai
Songkhla
Hat Yai
Ranot
Sadao
Laem Pho
Rattaphum
Khlong Ngae
Chana
Thepha
Pattani
Yala
Narathiwat
Rangae
Tumpat
Sungai Kolok
Kota Baharu
Bacuk
Pasir Putih
Kampung Raja
Kuala Terengganu
Marang
Kuala Berang
Dungun
Kemasik
Cukai

Phuket
Ban Tha Nun
Phangnga
Krabi
Phi Phi
Sikao
Thai Muang
Yao Noi
Yao Yai
Tarutao

Tenasserim
Bokpyin
Lenya
Letsók-aw Kyun
Zadetkyi Kyun
Lambi Kyun
Kawthaung
1227

Gunong Tahan 2190
Cameron Highlands 2182
Ipoh
Kuala Lumpur
Kelang
Seremban
Melaka
Muar
Batu Pahat
Pontian Kecil
Kukup
Johor Baharu
SINGAPORE
Singapore
Straits of Singapore
Batam
Bintan
Tanjungpinang
Kota Tinggi
Mersing
Kluang
Keluang
Labis
Segamat
Tampin
Gemas
Kuala Pilah
Kuala Kelawang
Kajang
Petaling Jaya
Batu Caves
Rawang
Kuala Selangor
Port Kelang
Kuala Kubu Bahru
Kuala Lipis
Raub 2108
Bentung
Karak
Mentakab
Temerloh
Maran
Kuantan
Pekan
Padang Endau
Endau
Nenasi
Pulau Tioman
P. Tenggol
P. Pemanggil
P. Aur
P. Babi Besar
Pulau Tinggi
Air Hitam
Yong Peng
Kulai
Kahang
Jemaluang
Kampung Air Putih
Jerantut
Triang
Bahau
Tapah
Bidor
Teluk Intan
Bagan Datoh
Sabak Bernam
Kuala Kangsar
Taiping
Bruas
Lumut
Port Weld
Kampar
Bidor
Kota Bharu

Gerik
Baling
Kroh
Grik
Kulim
Baling
Sungai Petani
Butterworth
George Town
Pinang (Penang)
Bagan Serai
Bukit Mertajam
Kangar
Jitra
Alor Setar
Kuala Nerang
Kuala Ketil
Sadao
Changlun
Narathiwat
Betong
Banang Sata
Raman
Kampong To
Kok Phra
Khok Pho

Pergau
Perak
Kuala Krai
Dabong
Gua Musang
Kuala Lipis
2716
1452

Port Dickson
Kelang
Kuala Selangor
Kota Bahru
Pelabuhan Kelang

Medan
Belawan
Binjai
Pematangsiantar
Prapat
2151
Samosir
Tarutung
2300
2457
2157
Sibolga
Musala
Kabanjiche
2451
3012
Kutacane
Peureulak
Langsa
Idi
Kualasimpang
Pangkalanbrandan
Tebingtinggi
Kisaran
Tanjungbalai
Rantauprapat
Bagansiapiapi
Dumai
Rupat
Bengkalis
2009

Phan Rang
Hoa Da

East from Greenwich

108

106

102

100

98

Projection: Conical with two standard parallels

COPYRIGHT GEORGE PHILIP LTD.

m   ft
3000 9000
2000 6000
1500 4500
1000 3000
600 2000
400 1200
200 600
0 0
200 600
2000 6000
6000 ft
m

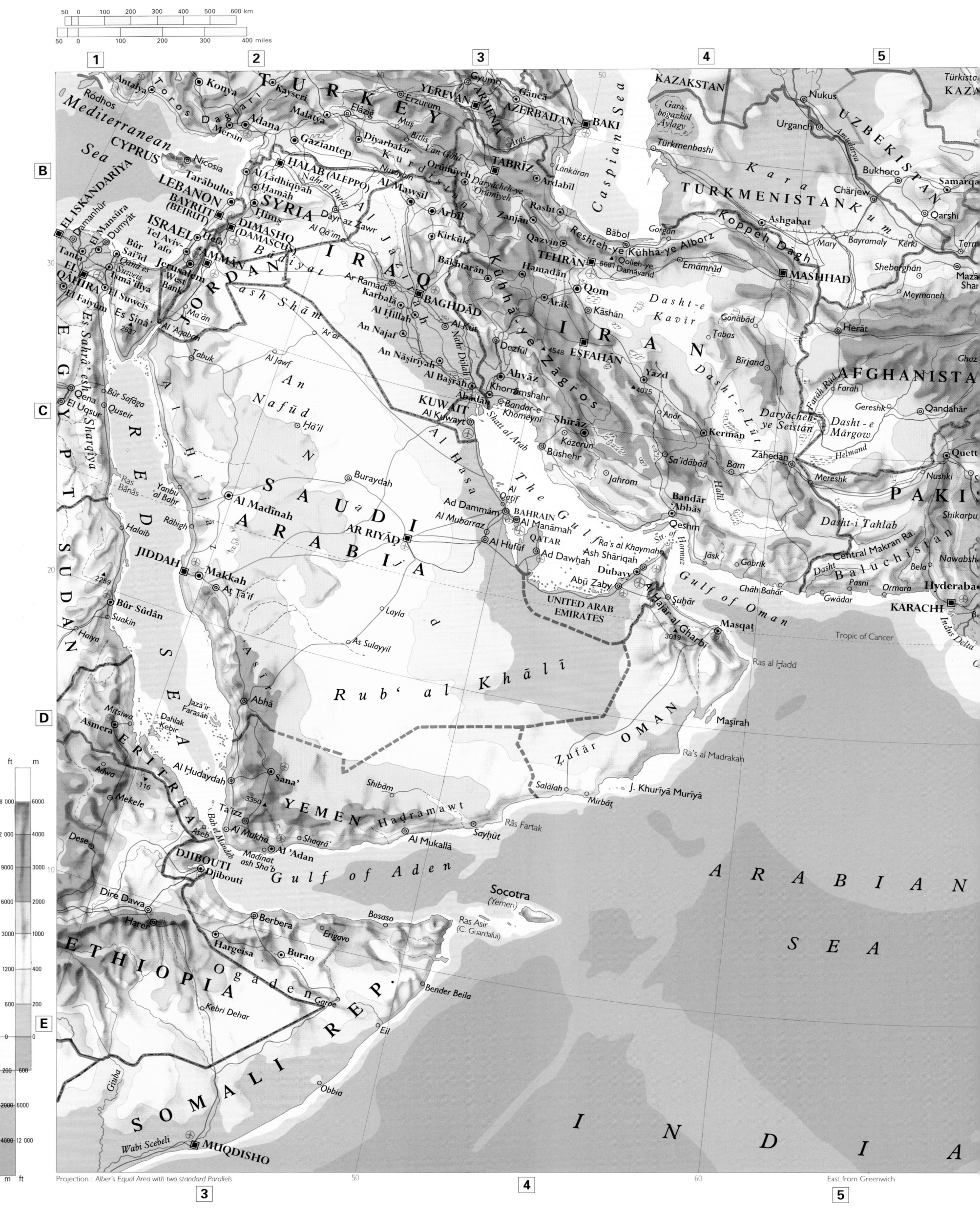

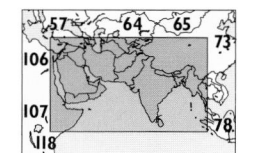

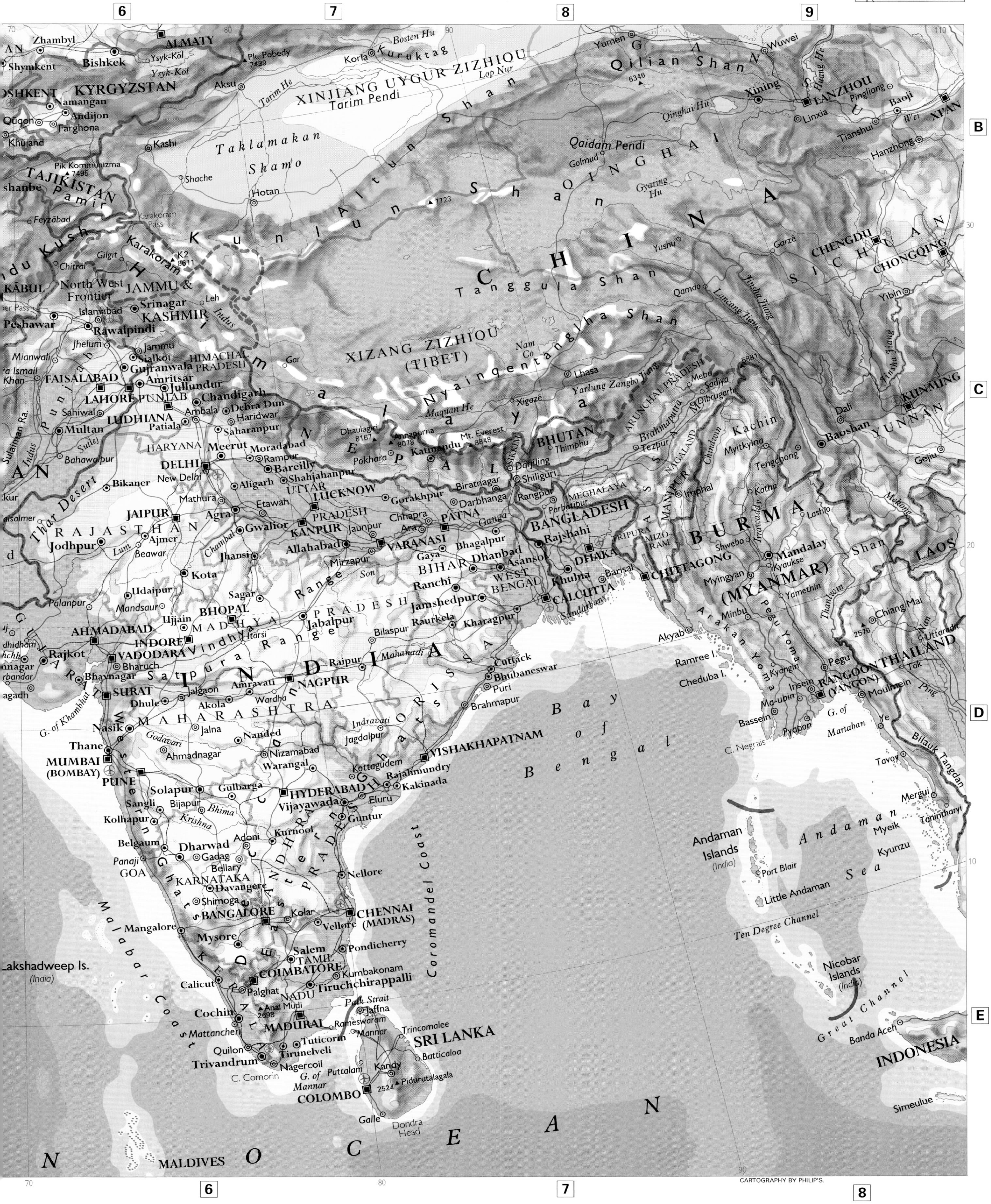

1:4 800 000

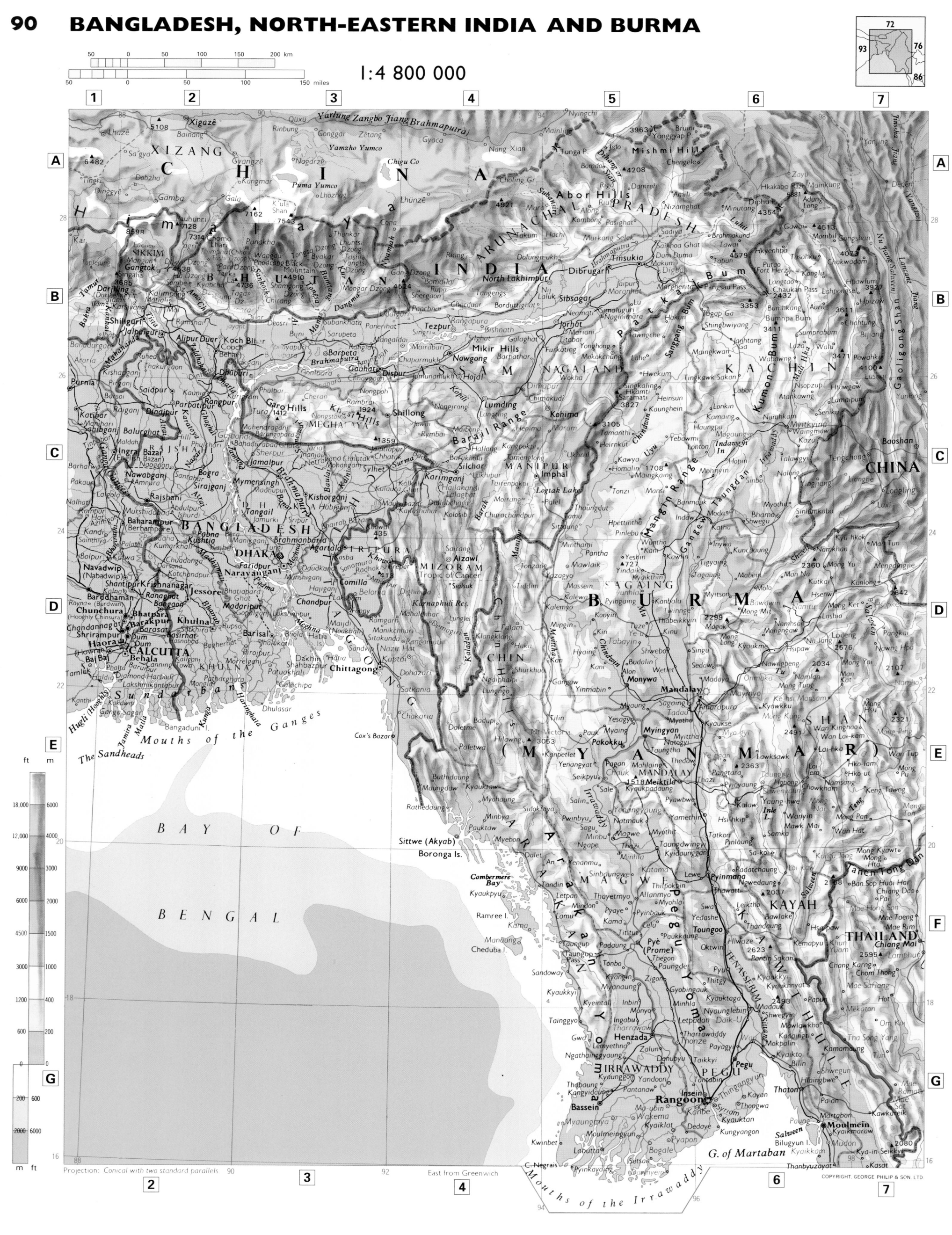

Projection: Conical with two standard parallels

East from Greenwich

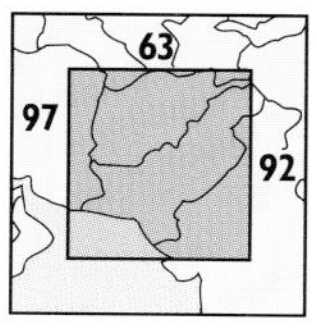

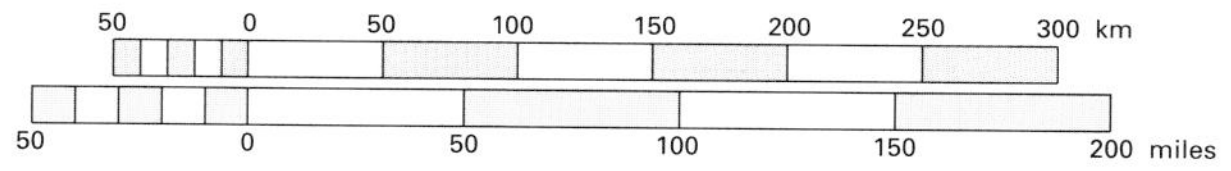

50 0 50 100 150 200 250 300 km
50 0 50 100 150 200 miles

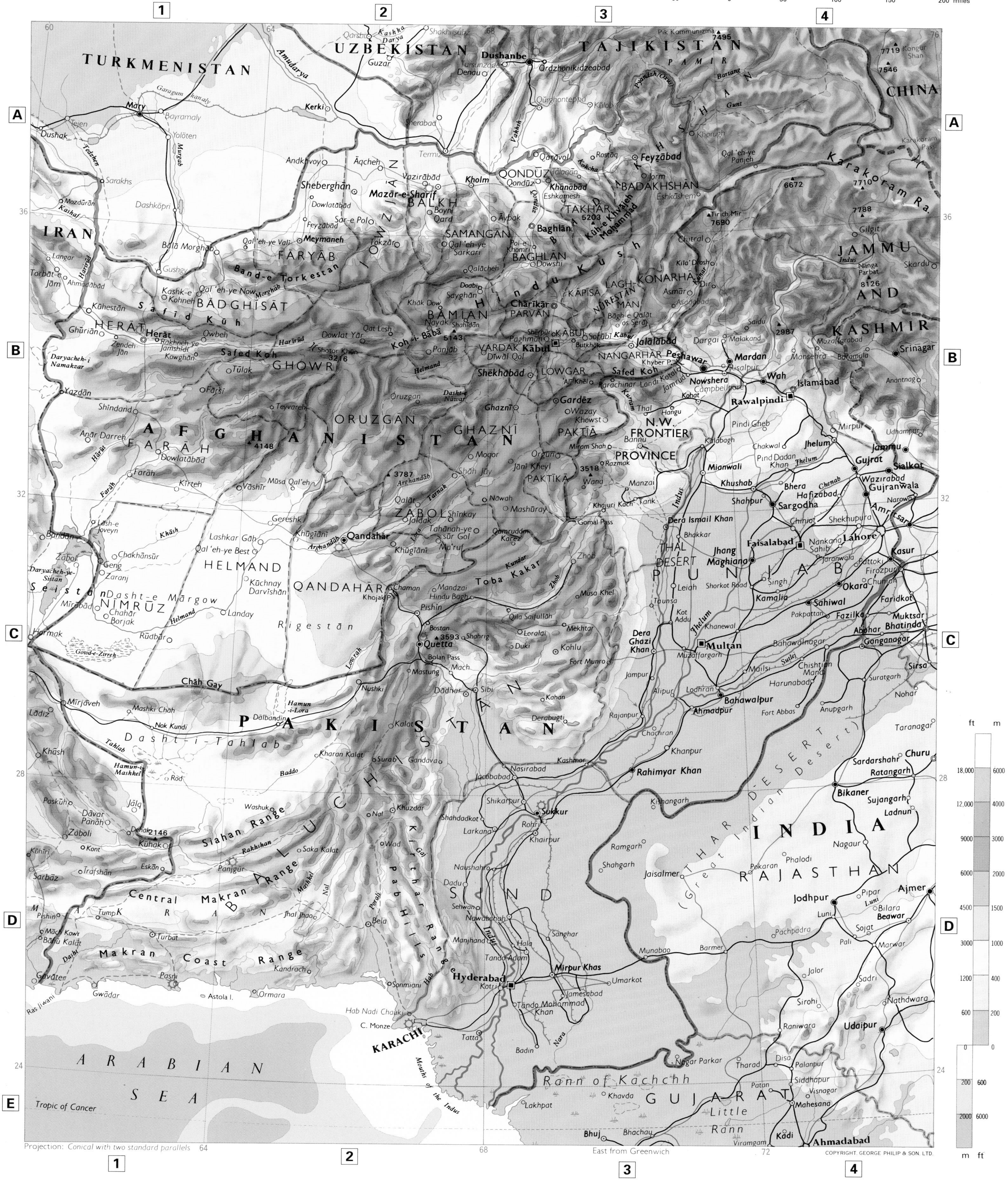

1 2 3 4

TURKMENISTAN

UZBEKISTAN

TAJIKISTAN

CHINA

Mary
Bayramaly
Yolöten
Murgab
Tejen
Dushak
Teджen
Sarakhs
Kaskhi
Mozdūrān
Kuskh

IRAN

Andkhvoy
Āqcheh
Termiz
Sherabad
Kerki
Garagum kanaly
Amudarya
Guzar
Qarshi
Kashka Darya
Shakhrisabz
Dushanbe
Ordzhonikidzeabad
Denau
Qūrghonteppa
Kūlob
Pik Kommunizma 7495
7719 Kongur Shan
7546

QONDUZ
Qonduz
Khanabad
Feyzābād
BADAKHSHAN
Eshkamesh
Eshkāshem
6672
7710
7788
Tirich Mir 7690
Chitral

Sheberghān
MAZĀR-E-SHARIF
BALKH
SAMANGAN
Āybak
Baghlān
BAGHLĀN
Dowshi
TAKHĀR 5203
Kūh-e Khvājeh Moḥammad
Gilgit
Nanga Parbat 8126
Skardu

Meymaneh
FĀRYĀB
Band-e Torkestan
JOWZJĀN
Tokzār
Sar-e Pol
Qal'eh-ye Vali
BĀDGHĪSĀT
Safīd Kūh

JAMMU AND KASHMIR
Srinagar
Anantnag
Muzaffarabad

HERĀT
Herāt
Owbeh
GHOWR
Safed Koh 3276
Dowlat Yār
Shotor Khan
Koh-i-Bābā 5143
BĀMIĀN
Nāyak Shahīdān
PARVĀN
Chārīkar
KĀPISA
LAGH-MĀN
NŪRESTĀN
KONARHA
Asmār
Jalālābād
Peshawar
NANGARHĀR
Mardan
Islamabad
Rawalpindi

AFGHANISTAN

FARĀH
Farāh
ORUZGĀN
4148
GHAZNĪ
Ghaznī
Gardēz
PAKTIĀ
N.W. FRONTIER PROVINCE
Bannu
Kohat
Safed Koh
Khyber P.
3518
Razmak

ZĀBOL
Qalāt
Shinkay
PAKTĪKĀ
Wana
Manzai
Dera Ismail Khan
Mianwali
Khushab
Sargodha
PUNJAB
Faisalabad
Lāhore
Kasur

Qandahār
QANDAHĀR
Chaman
Pishin
Quetta 3593
Bostan
Toba Kakar
Zhob
Bolan Pass
Mastung
Sibi
Kalat

Lashkar Gāh
HELMAND
Gereshk
Rīgestān
Khash

NIMRŪZ
Zaranj
Rūdbar
Chāh Gay
Dasht-i-Tahlab
Dālbandin
Nushki
Kharan Kalat
Surāb
PAKISTAN

B A L U C H I S T A N
Siahan Range
Central Makran Range
Panjgur
Turbat
Kalat
Khuzdar
Kirthar Range
Pab Hills
SIND
Dadu
Sukkur
Larkana
Shikarpur
Jacobabad
Nasirabad

Makran Coast Range
Pasni
Gwādar
Ras Jiwani
Ormara
C. Monze
KARACHI
Hyderabad
Tatta
Mirpur Khas
Umarkot

INDIA
RAJASTHAN
Bikaner
Jodhpur
Jaisalmer
Pokaran
Phalodi
Nagaur
Ajmer
Beawar
Udaipur

(Great Indian Desert)
THAR DESERT
Bahawalpur
Rahimyar Khan
Khanpur
Multan
Bahawalnagar

Rann of Kachchh
GUJARAT
Bhuj
Bhachau
Ahmadabad
Mahesana
Little Rann

ARABIAN SEA
Tropic of Cancer

ft m
18,000 6000
12,000 4000
9000 3000
6000 2000
4500 1500
3000 1000
1200 400
600 200
200 600
2000 6000
m ft

Projection: Conical with two standard parallels

East from Greenwich

COPYRIGHT. GEORGE PHILIP & SON, LTD.

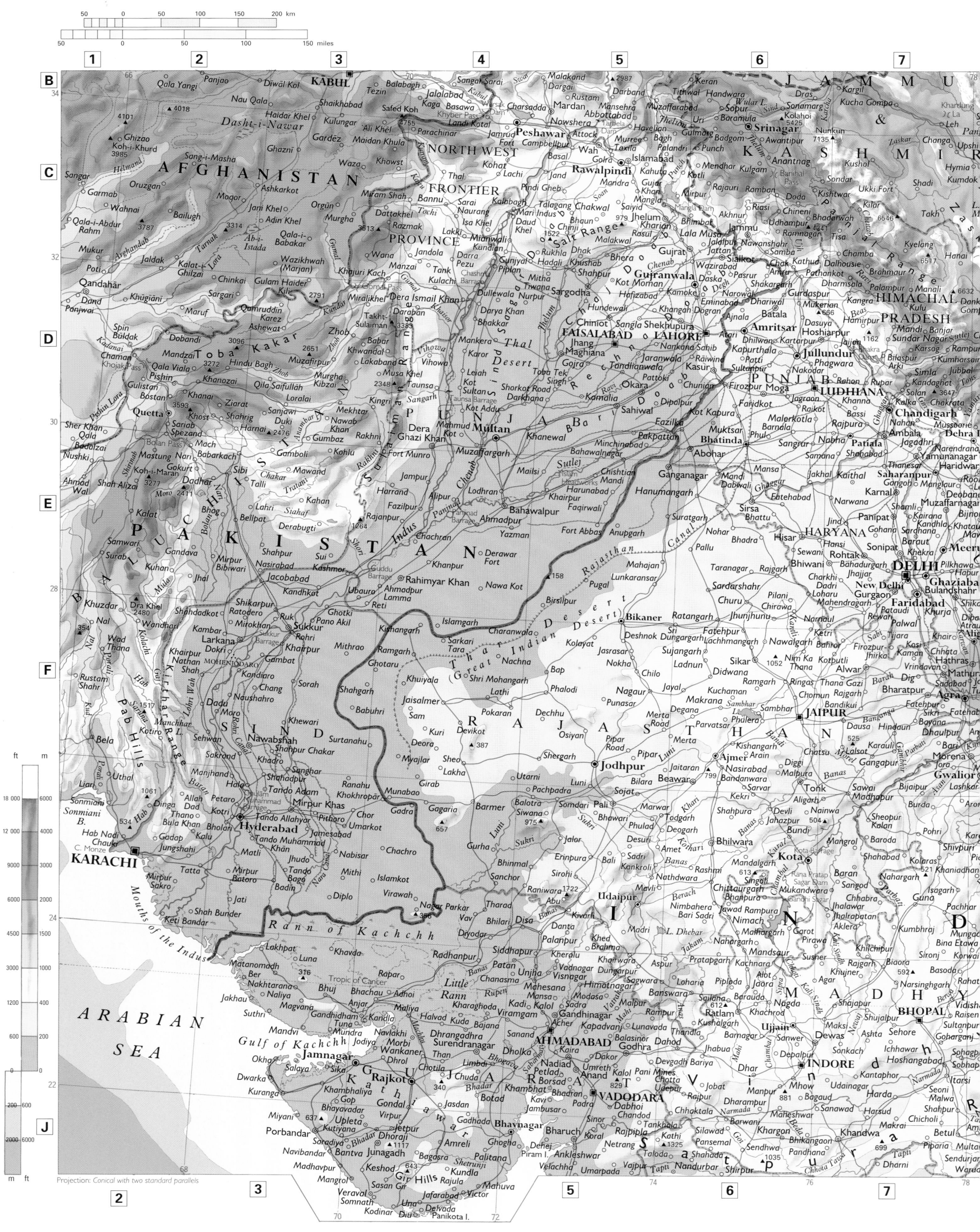

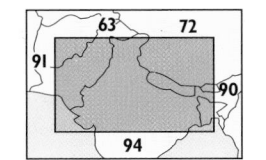

JAMMU AND KASHMIR
On same scale as Main Map

East from Greenwich

COPYRIGHT GEORGE PHILIP LTD.

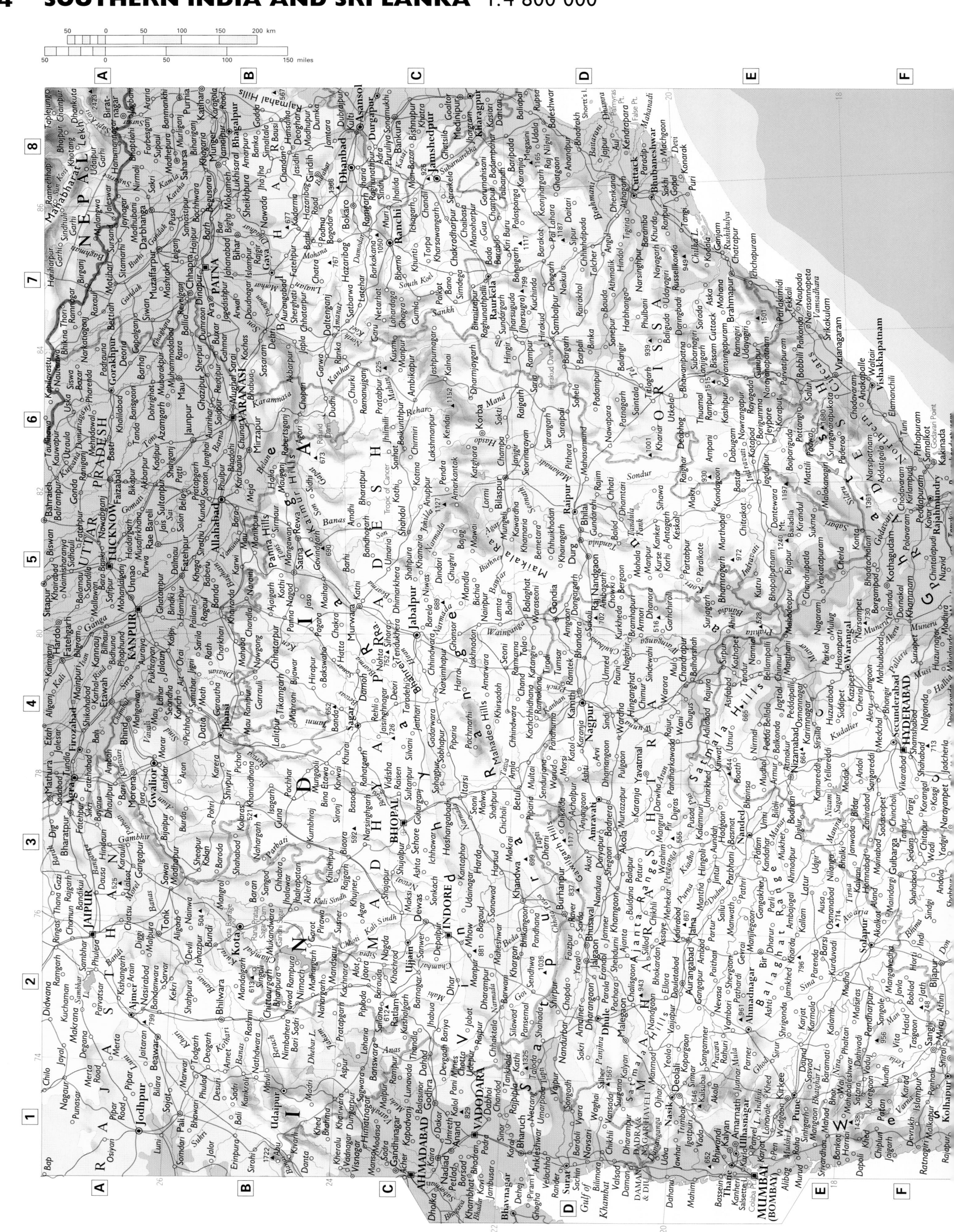

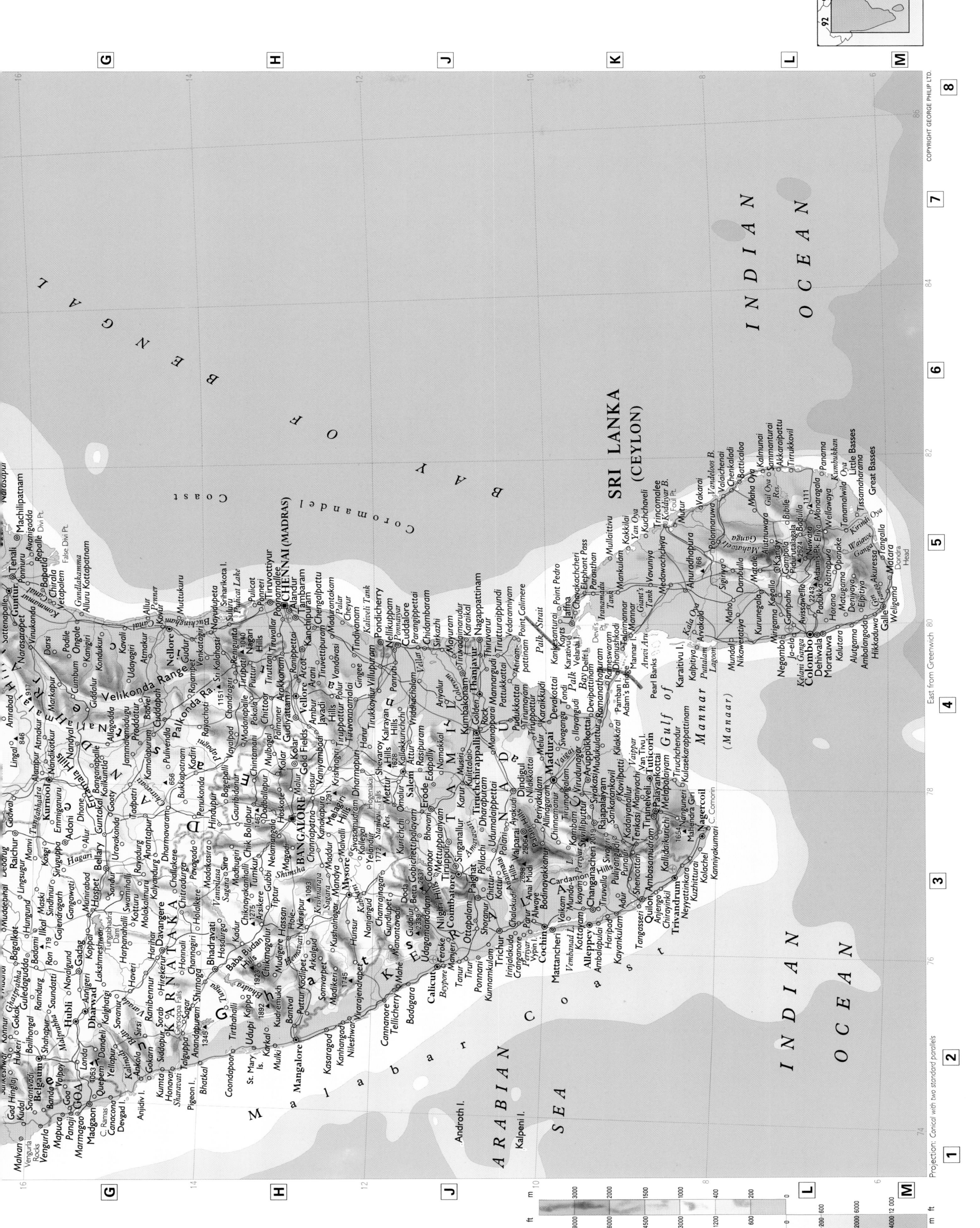

INDIAN

OCEAN

BAY OF BENGAL

Coromandel Coast

CHENNAI (MADRAS)

SRI LANKA
(CEYLON)

INDIAN

OCEAN

ARABIAN

SEA

Malabar Coast

KARNATAKA

BANGALORE

TAMIL NADU

Gulf of Mannar

(Mannaar)

Palk Strait

Projection: Conical with two standard parallels

East from Greenwich

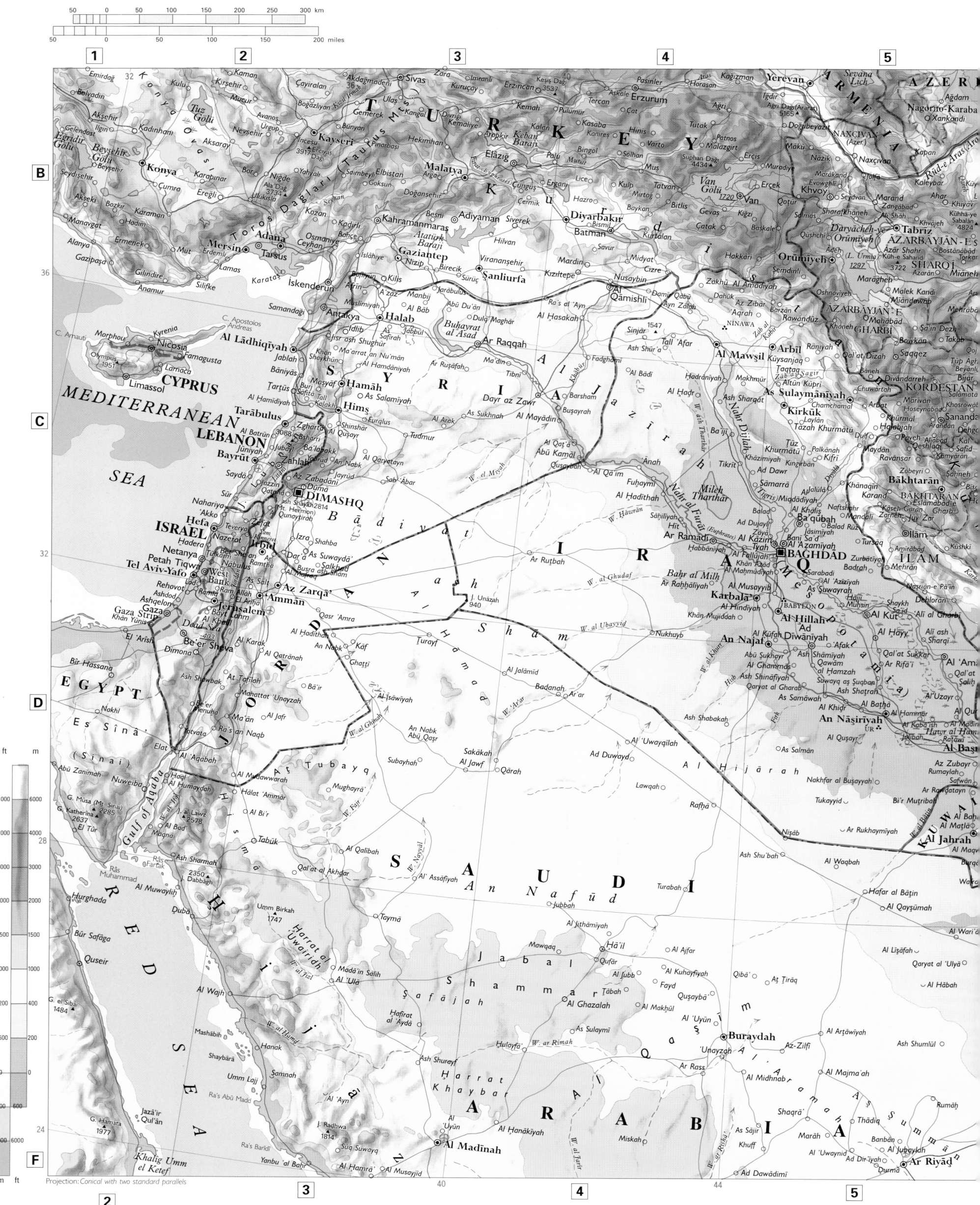

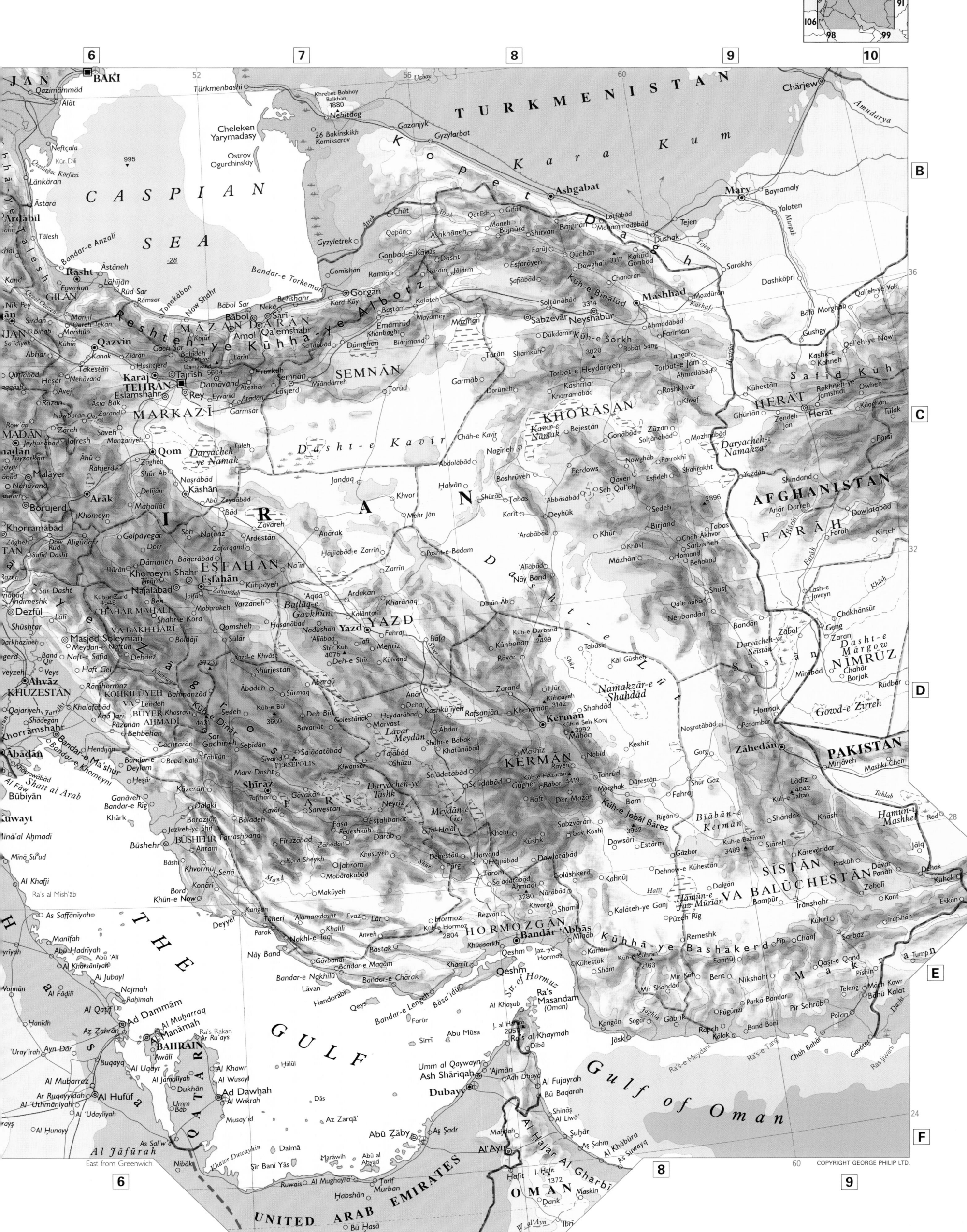

CASPIAN

SEA

TURKMENISTAN

Kopet Dagh

Kara Kum

IRAN

AFGHANISTAN

PAKISTAN

THE GULF

Gulf of Oman

UNITED ARAB EMIRATES

OMAN

QATAR

BAHRAIN

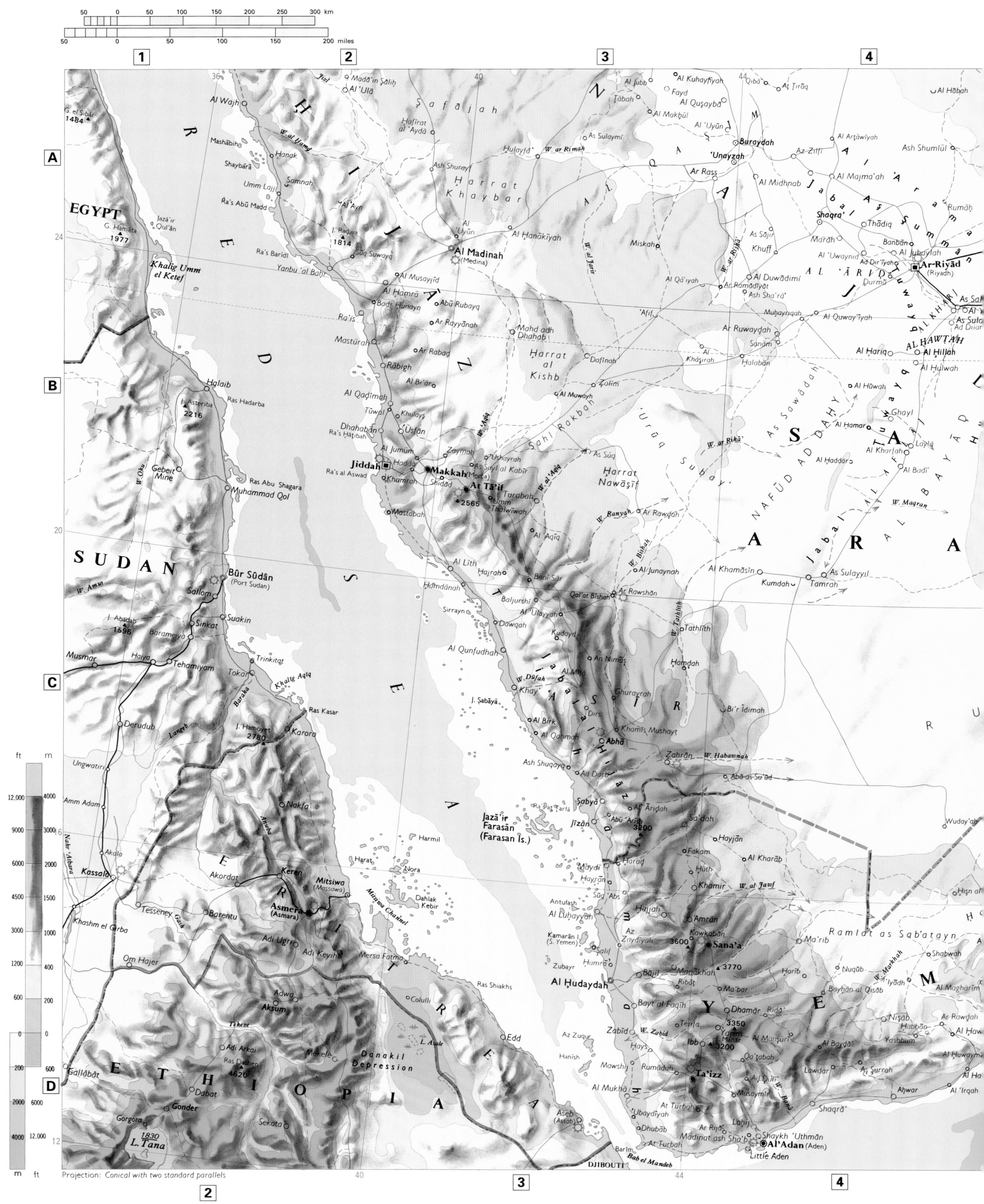

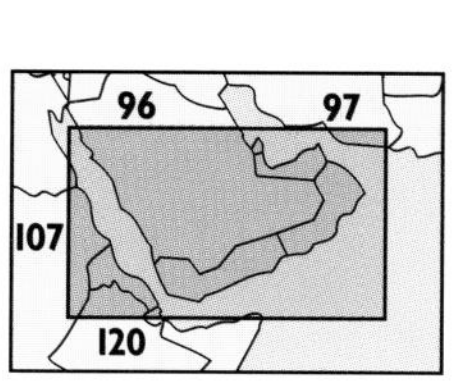

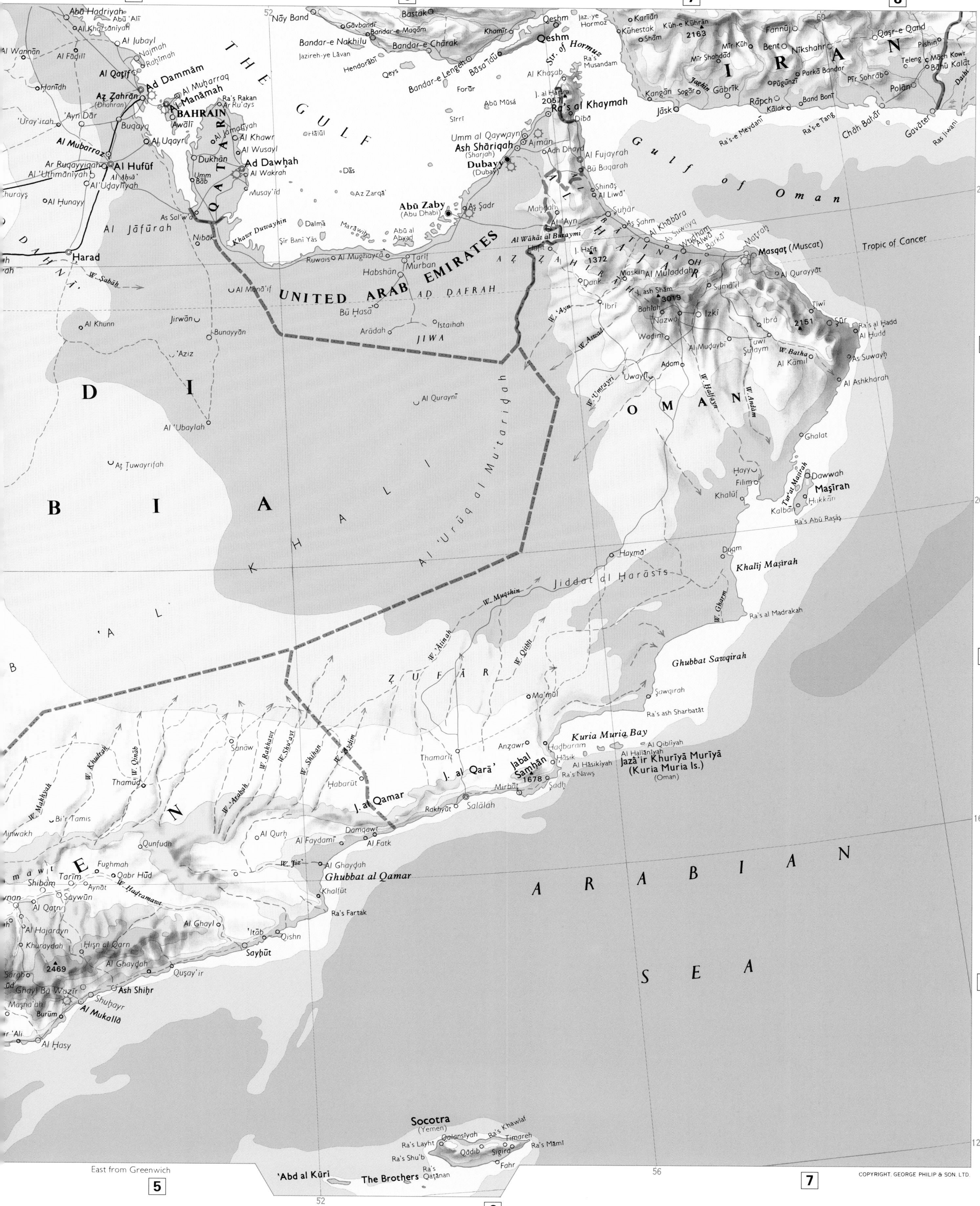

96 97
107
120

5 6 7 8

Nāy Band
Bastak
Bandar-e Nakhilu
Bandar-e Magām
Bandar-e Chārak
Khamīr
Qeshm
Jaz.-ye Hormoz
Kariān
Kūh-e Kūhrān
2163
Fannūj
Mīr Kūh
Bent
Nīkshahr
Qaşr-e Qand
Abū Hadrīyah
Abū 'Alī
Al Khaţşānīyah
Jazīreh-ye Lāvan
Qeys
Bandar-e Lengeh
Bāsa 'īdū
Qeshm
Str. of Hormuz
Kūhestak
Shām
Mīr Shahdād
Jaghīn
Gābrīk
Parka Bandar
Pīr Sohrāb
Polān
Bahū Kalāt
Al Wannān
Al Faḍilī
Al Jubayl
Najmah
Rahīmah
Hendorābī
Forūr
Abū Mūsā
Ra's al Khaymah
Dibā
Ra's Musandam
J. al Ḥarīm
2057
Kangān
Sogar
Jāsk
Ra's-e Meydānī
Ra's-e Tang
Chāh Bahār
Gavāter
Ra's Jīwanī
Al Qaţīf
Ad Dammām
Al Muḥarraq
Ra's Rakan
Ra's Ru'ays
Az Zahrān (Dhahran)
BAHRAIN
AL MANĀMAH
Awālī
Al Khaşab

A

Ḥanīdh
'Uray'irah
'Ayn Dār
Buqayq
Al Mubarraz
Ar Ru'ays
Al Jumaylīyah
Al Khawr
Ash Shāriqah (Sharjah)
Ajmān
Umm al Qaywayn
Adh Dhayd
Al Fujayrah
Bū Baqarah
Shinās
Şuḥār
Gulf of Oman
Ar Ruqayyiqah
Al Hufūf
Al Aḥsā
Al 'Uthmānīyah
Al 'Uqaylīyah
Dukhān
Ad Dawḥah
Umm Sa'īd
Al Wakrah
QATAR
Das
Az Zarqā'
Abū Zaby (Abu Dhabi)
Aş Şadr
Maḥḍah
Al 'Ayn
Al Wāḥāt al Buraymī
Al Liwā'
Al Khābūra
Aş Şuwayq
Wudhām
'Alwa
Maţrah
Masqaţ (Muscat)
Tropic of Cancer
24

Al Hunayy
As Sal'wa
Nibak
Khawr Duwayhin
Şīr Banī Yās
Ruwais
Al Mughayrā
Tarīf
Murban
Abū al Abyaḍ
Marāwiḥ
Dalmā
Hīlī
1372
J. Ḥafīt
Dank
Maskin
Al Muladdaḥ
Sumā'il
Al Quray'yāt
Harad
W. Sabāh
Al Jāfūrah
UNITED ARAB EMIRATES
AD DAFRAH
Ḥabshān
Bū Ḥasa
W. 'Ayn
Ibrī
Nazwā
3019
Izkī
Ibrā
2151
Şūr
Ra's al Ḥadd
Al Ḥudd

B

DAHNĀ
Al Khunn
Jirwān
Bunayyān
'Azīz
Arādah
Istaihah
JIWA
Al Quraynī
W. Amadī
Waḍām
Adam
Al Muḍaybī
Şulaym
W. Baṭḥa
Al Kāmil
As Suwayḥ
Al Ashkharah
D

Aţ Ţuwayrifah
Al 'Ubaylah
KHALI
OMAN
Uwayfī
Uwī
Ghalat
N

B I A
'A L
Ghalat
Ghubbat Sawqirah
Ghalat
Hayy
Filim
Khalūf
Kalbān
Dawwah
Maşīrah
Hikkān
Ra's Abū Raşaş
20

Al Urūq al Mu'tariḍah
Haymā'
Jiddat al Ḥarāsīs
Dūqm
Khalīj Maşīrah

C

W. Muqshin
W. 'Aintah
W. Qiṭbī
W. Ghanm
Ra's al Madrakah
Ghubbat Sawqirah

N
ZUFĀR
Ma'mūl
Şawqirah
Ra's ash Sharbatāt

W. Khudrah
W. Qinab
W. Rakhyūt
W. Shiḥan
W. Ghudūn
W. Ayūnī
Sanāw
Thamarīt
J. al Qarā'
Jabal Samḥān
1678
Ḥāsik
Kuria Muria Bay
Al Qiblīyah
Al Ḥallānīyah
Jazā'ir Khurīyā Murīyā (Kuria Muria Is.) (Oman)

Ainwakh
Bi'r Tamis
Thamūd
Anzawr
Ḥabarūt
Ḥaḍbaram
Mirbāţ
Ra's Nawş
Şadḥ
16

ma...wt
Fughmah
Tarīm
Shibām
Saywūn
Qabr Hūd
W. Ḥaḍramawt
J. al Qamar
Rakhyūt
Salālah
W. Jīz
Al Ghaydah
Damqawt
Al Fatk
Qunfudh
Al Qurh
Al Faydamī
Ghubbat al Qamar
Khalfūt

E
Al Ḥajarayn
Ḥiṣn al Qarn
'Itāb
Qishn
Sayḥūt
Ra's Fartak
ARABIAN

Sārab
Ghayl Bā Wazīr
Al Mukallā
Ghayl
Al Ghaydah
Quşay'ir
2469
Khuraydah
Qaţn
Shuḥayr
Ash Shiḥr
Burūm

SEA

'Ali
Al Ḥasy
Māsī'ah

D

Socotra (Yemen)
Qalansīyah
Ra's Khawlat
Timareh
Ra's Māmī
Ra's Layht
Ra's Shu'b
Qōdib
Sīgīra
Fahr
12

'Abd al Kūri
The Brothers
Ra's Qaţanan

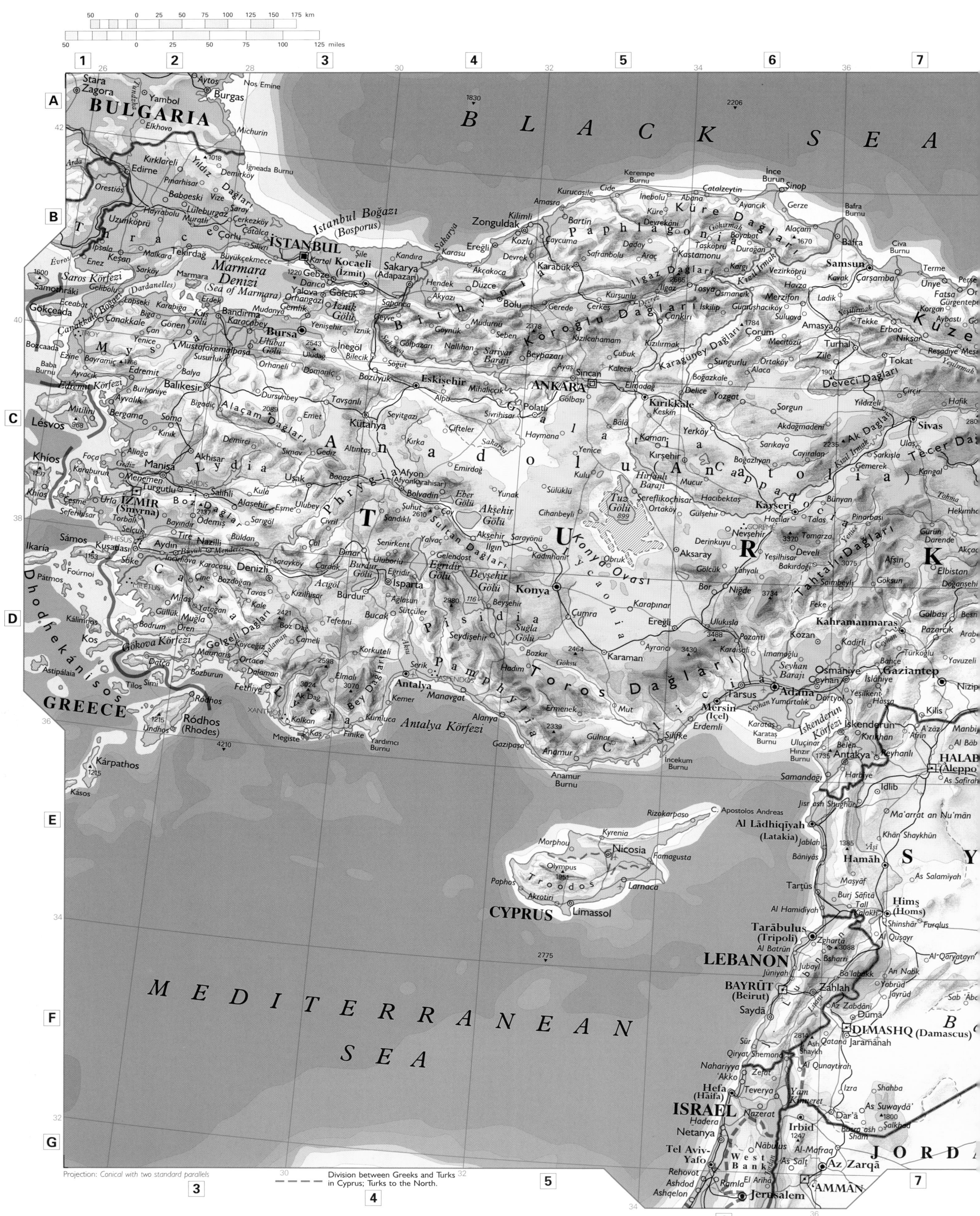

Projection: Conical with two standard parallels

Division between Greeks and Turks in Cyprus; Turks to the North.

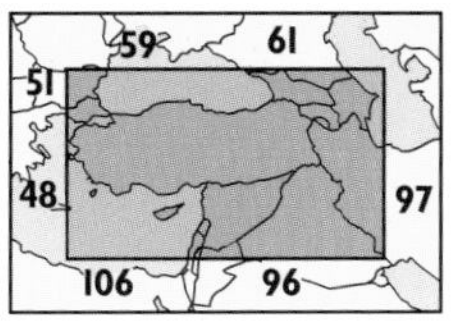

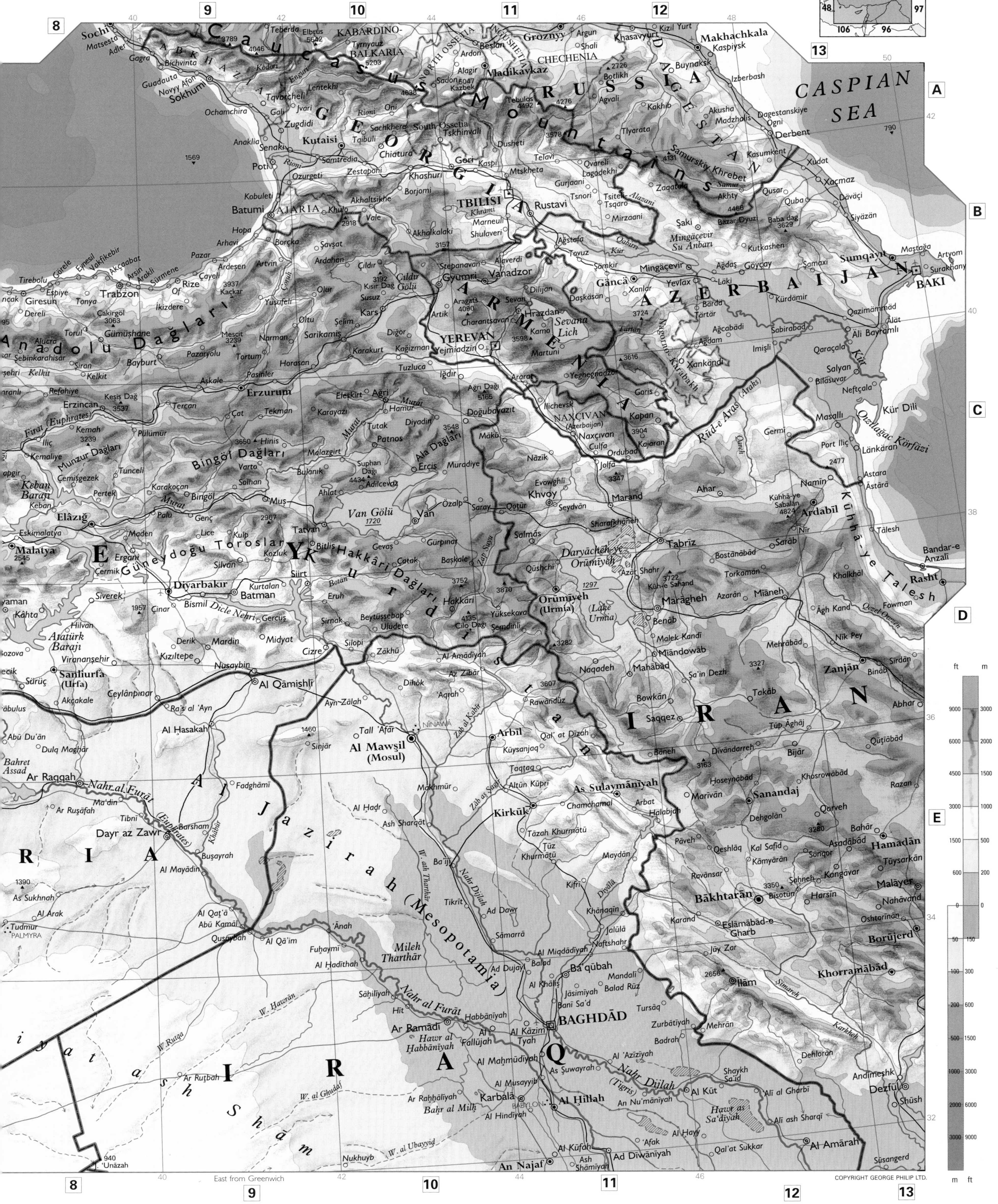

CASPIAN SEA

CAUCASUS Mountains

RUSSIA

GEORGIA
ABKHAZIA
AJARIA
NORTH OSSETIA
SOUTH OSSETIA
KABARDINO-BALKARIA
INGUSHETIA
CHECHENIA
DAGESTAN

ARMENIA

AZERBAIJAN
NAXCIVAN (Azerbaijan)

IRAN

IRAQ

SYRIA

Al Jazirah (Mesopotamia)

Anadolu Dağları

Güneydoğu Toroslar

Kurdistan

Sochi, Matsesta, Adler, Gagra, Bichvinta, Guadauta, Novyy Afon, Sokhumi, Ochamchira, Gali, Zugdidi, Anaklia, Senaki, Poti, Kobuleti, Batumi, Hopa, Arhavi, Pazar, Çayeli, Rize, Of, Sürmene, Trabzon, Akçaabat, Arsin, Tonya, Görele, Tirebolu, Espiye, Giresun, Bulancak

Teberda, Elbrus 5642, Elbrus 4046, 5203, 3789, Kёdori, Lentekhi, Tqvarcheli, Jvari, Oni, Rioni, Sachkhere, Tqibuli, Kutaisi, Samtredia, Chiatura, Khashuri, Gori, Kaspi, Mtskheta, Telavi, Tsiteli, Lagodekhi, TBILISI, Rustavi, Marneuli, Shulaveri, Akhalkalaki, Borjomi, Vale, Akhaltsikhe, Khulo

Vladikavkaz, Alagir, Ardon, Beslan, Nazran, Grozny, Argun, Khasavyurt, Kizil Yurt, Makhachkala, Kaspiysk, Buynaksk, Izberbash, Derbent

Gyumri, Vanadzor, Dilijan, Sevan, Sevana Lich, Aragts 4090, Artik, Charantsvan, Hrazdan, YEREVAN, Yejmiadzin, Martuni, Yeghegnadzor, Goris, Kapan, Kajaran, Jolfa

BAKI, Sumqayit, Maştağa, Artyom, Surakhany, Şamaxı, Gäncä, Mingäçevir, Mingäçevir Su Anbarı, Şäki, Zaqatala, Samur, Akhty, Bazar Dyuz 4466, Baba dağ 3629, Qusar, Quba, Xaçmaz, Xudat, Däväçi, Siyäzän, Xanlar, Yevlax, Barda, Tärtär, Ağdam, Xankändı, Ağcäbädi, Imişli, Sabirabad, Äli Bayramlı, Salyan, Neftçala, Länkäran, Astara

Erzurum, Erzincan, Elâzığ, Malatya, Diyarbakır, Batman, Siirt, Bitlis, Van, Van Gölü 1720, Tatvan, Muş, Bingöl, Ağri, Kars, Sarıkamış, Horasan, Tutak, Patnos, Erciş, Ahlat, Doğubayazıt, Ağri Dağı 5165

Orūmīyeh (Urmia), Daryācheh-ye Orūmīyeh (Lake Urmia), Tabrīz, Marand, Khvoy, Salmās, Mahābād, Miāndowāb, Naqadeh, Bowkān, Saqqez, Sanandaj, Marīvān, Takāb, Zanjān, Ardabīl, Rasht, Bandar-e Anzalī, Āstārā, Hamadān, Malāyer, Nahāvand, Borūjerd, Khorramābād, Bākhtarān, Dezfūl, Andīmeshk, Shūsh

Al Mawşil (Mosul), NĪNAWÁ, Arbīl, Kirkūk, As Sulaymānīyah, Halabjah, Tall 'Afar, Sinjār, Al Hasakah, Ar Raqqah, Dayr az Zawr, Abū Kamāl, Tikrīt, Sāmarrā, BAGHDĀD, Al Fallūjah, Ar Ramādī, Karbalā, An Najaf, Al Hillah, BABYLON, Al Kūt, Al 'Amārah, Ad Dīwānīyah

East from Greenwich

COPYRIGHT GEORGE PHILIP LTD.

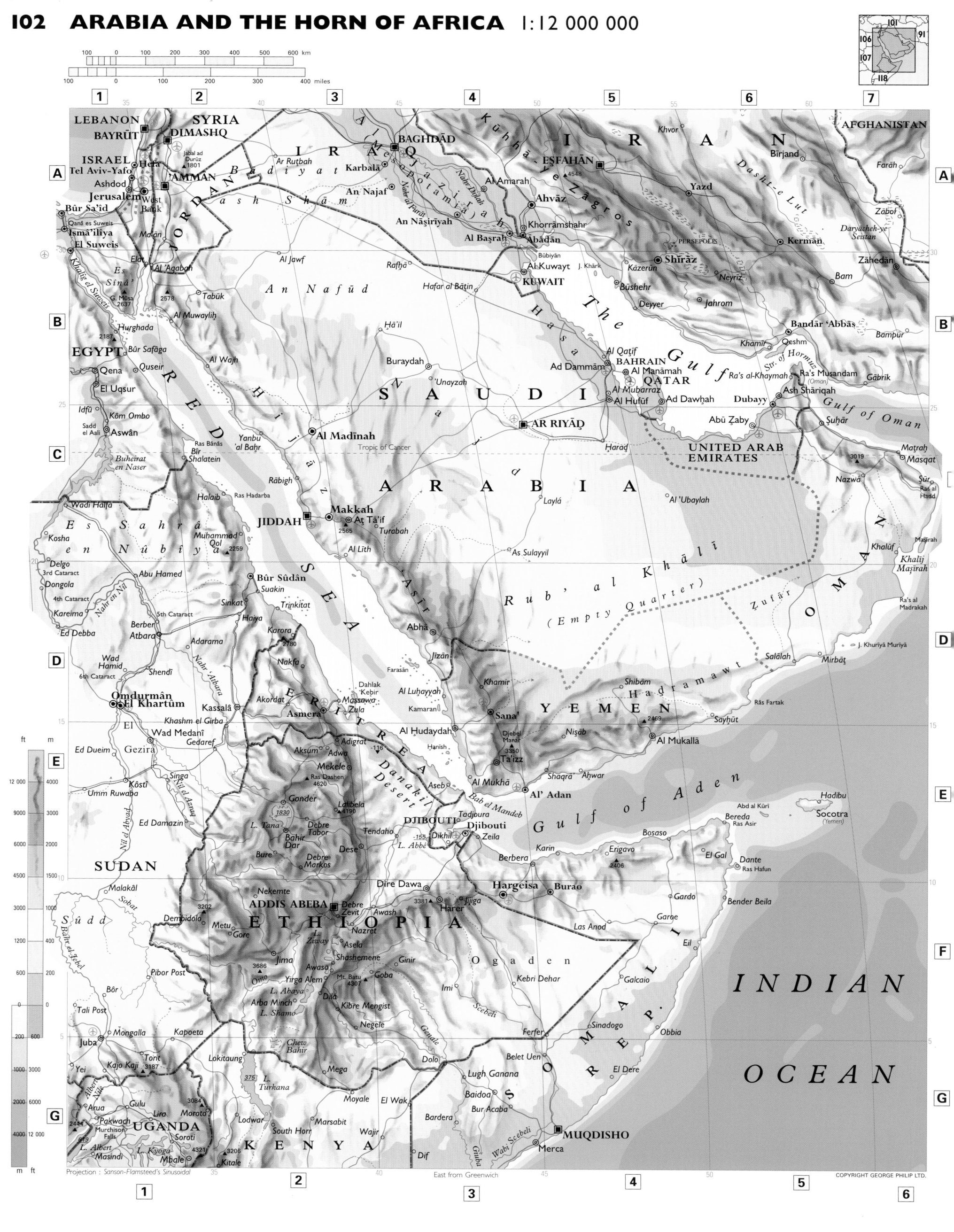

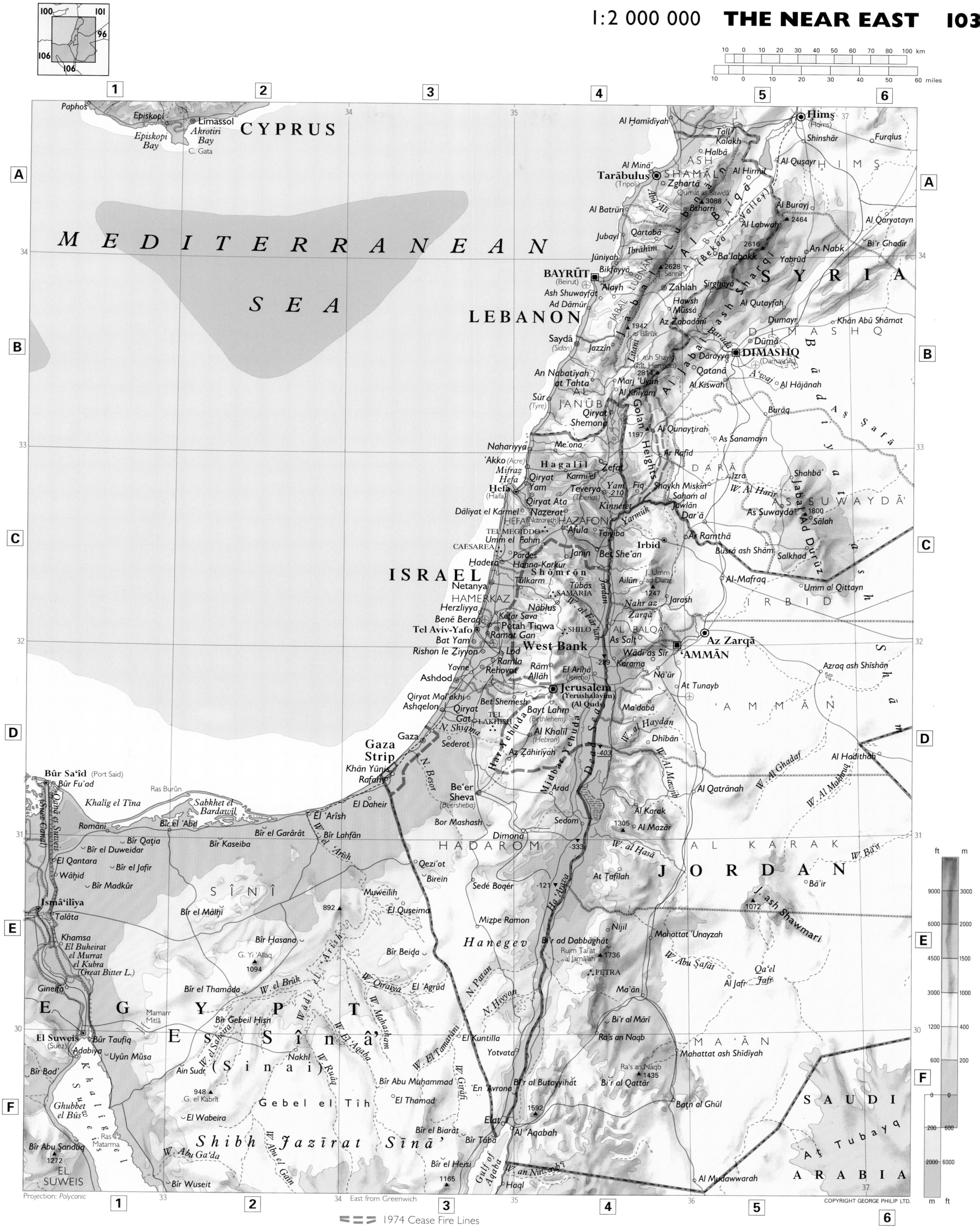

100 101 96
106 106

10 0 10 20 30 40 50 60 70 80 100 km
10 0 10 20 30 40 50 60 miles

1　2　3　4　5　6

A

Paphos
Episkopi
Episkopi Bay
Limassol
Akrotiri Bay
C. Gata
CYPRUS

Al Hamidiyah
Hims (Homs)
Tall Kalakh
Shinshar
Furqlus

ASH SHAMAL
Al Mina'
Tarabulus (Tripoli)
Zgharta
Halba
Al Hirmil
Al Qusayr
Al Burayj
Al Qaryatayn

Qurnat as Sawda' 3088
Bsharri
Al Batrun
2464
Al Labwah
2616
Jubayl
Qartaba
An Nabk
Bi'r Ghadir
Ibrahim
Juniyah
Bikfayya
1942
2628
Sannin
Zahlah
Ba'labakk
Yabrud

B

MEDITERRANEAN

BAYRUT (Beirut)
'Alayh
Sirghaya
Khan Abu Shamat
Ash Shuwayfat
Ad Damur
Hawsh
Mussa
Az Zabadani
Dumayr
DIMASHQ

LEBANON
Sayda (Sidon)
Jazzin
J. ash Shayk (Mt. Hermon) 2814
Duma
Darayya
DIMASHQ (Damascus)
Qatana
A'waj

SEA

An Nabatiyah at Tahta
AL JANUB
Sur (Tyre)
Qiryat Shemona
1197
Al Qunaytirah
Marj 'Uyun
Al Khiyam
Al Kiswah
Al Hajanah
Buraq
SYRIA

DIMASHQ

C

Nahariyya
Me'ona
Zefat
Golan Heights
Ar Rafid
As Sanamayn

'Akko (Acre)
Mifraz Hefa
HAGALIL
Qiryat Yam
Karmi'el
Yam Kinneret 210
Fiq
Shaykh Miskin
Izra
Shahba' 1800
DARA

Hefa (Haifa)
Qiryat Ata
Teverya (Tiberias)
Saham al Jawlan
Dar'a
AS SUWAYDA
Daliyat el Karmel
Nazerat
HAZAFON
Yarmuk
As Suwayda
Salah

TEL MEGIDDO
Umm el Fahm
Afula
Taiyiba
Ar Ramtha
Busra ash Sham
Salkhad
Ad Duruz

CAESAREA
Pardes
Janin
Bet She'an
Ailun
Al-Mafraq

Hadera
Hanna-Karkur
SHOMRON
Tubas
J. Umm ad Daraj
Umm al Qittayn
IRBID

ISRAEL
Tulkarm
SAMARIA
1247
Jarash
HAMERKAZ
Netanya
Nablus
Nahr az Zarqa
Herzliyya
Bene Beraq
Kefar Sava
SHILO
Jerash
Tel Aviv-Yafo
Petah Tiqwa
AL BALQA
Ramat Gan
As Salt
Az Zarqa
Bat Yam
WEST BANK
Wadi as Sir
AMMAN
Rishon le Ziyyon
Lod
Ramla
Ram Allah
289
Karama
Yavne
Rehovot
El Ariha (Jericho)
Na'ur
Azraq ash Shishan

D

Ashdod
Jerusalem (Yerushalayim) (Al Quds)
Ma'daba
'AMMAN
Qiryat Mal'akhi
Bet Shemesh
Bayt Lahm (Bethlehem)
At Tunayb
Ashqelon
Qiryat Gat
TEL LAKHISH
Harē Yehuda
Al Khalil (Hebron)
W. al Haydan
Dhiban
Gaza Strip
Gaza
Sederot
N. Shiqma
Az Zahiriyah
403
W. al Mawjib
Al Hadithah
Khan Yunis
Rafah
N. Besor
Arad
W. al Ghadaf
W. al Makhruq
Bur Sa'id (Port Said)
Bur Fu'ad
Be'er Sheva (Beersheba)
Al Qatranah
Ras Burun
Sabkhet el Bardawil
Bor Mashash
Sedom
Al Karak
Khalig el Tina
El Arish
1305
Al Mazar
W. al Hasa
W. Ba'ir

E

Romani
Bir el 'Abd
El Daheir
Dimona
HADAROM
AL KARAK
Bir Qatia
Bir el Gararat
Bir Lahfan
333
Bir el Duweidar
Bir Kaseiba
Qezi'ot
JORDAN
El Qantara
Wahid
Bir Madkur
SINI
892
Muweilih
At Tafilah
Ba'ir
Isma'iliya
Talata
El Quseima
Sedé Boqer
1072
Khamsa
El Buheirat el Murrat el Kubra (Great Bitter L.)
Bir el Malhi
Mizpe Ramon
121
Nijil
Mahattat 'Unayzah
Bir Hasana
Hanegev
Bi'r ad Dabbaghat
Ruim Tal'at al Jamalah
1736
W. Abu Safat
Qa'el Jafr
Gineifa
Bir Beida
EGYPT
El Agrud
N. Paran
PETRA
Al Jafr

F

El Suweis (Suez)
Bur Taufiq
Adabiya
Uyun Musa
948
G. el Kabrit
ES SINA (Sinai)
El Kuntilla
Ma'an
Bir Bad'
1094
Bir el Thamada
W. el Bruk
El Qusaima
Yotvata
Ra's an Naqb
MA'AN
Mahattat ash Shidiyah
Gineifa
Mamarr Mitla
Bir Gebeil Hisn
Wadi el Sdeira
W. el Agaba
W. Mahashem
'En 'Avrona
Ra's an Naqb
1435
Ghubbet el Bus
Ain Sudr
Nakhl
W. Ruaq
Bir Abu Muhammad
Wadi al Butayyihat
Bi'r al Qattar
1592
SAUDI
Ras Matarma
El Wabeira
Gebel el Tih
El Thamad
Elat
Botn al Ghul
1272
EL SUWEIS
Shibh Jazirat Sina'
Bir el Biarat
Al 'Aqabah
At Tubayq
Bir Abu Sanduq
W. Abu el Gatn
Bir el Hesi
Gulf of Aqaba
Haql
Al Mudawwarah
ARABIA
Bir Wuseit
1165
W. an Nuwaybi'

ft m
9000 3000
6000 2000
4500 1500
3000 1000
1200 400
600 200
0 0
200 600
2000 6000
m ft

Projection: Polyconic
East from Greenwich
COPYRIGHT GEORGE PHILIP LTD.

1974 Cease Fire Lines

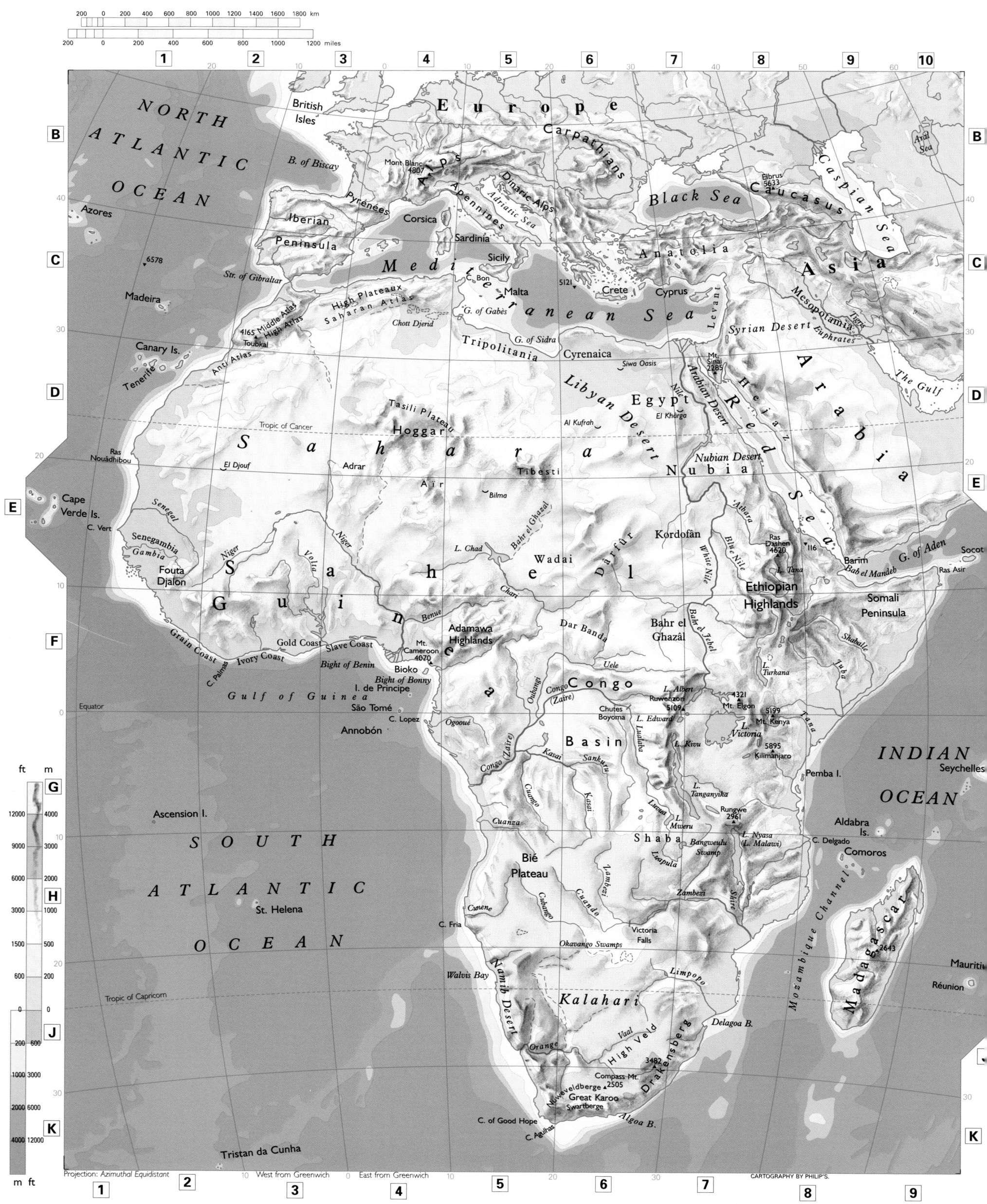

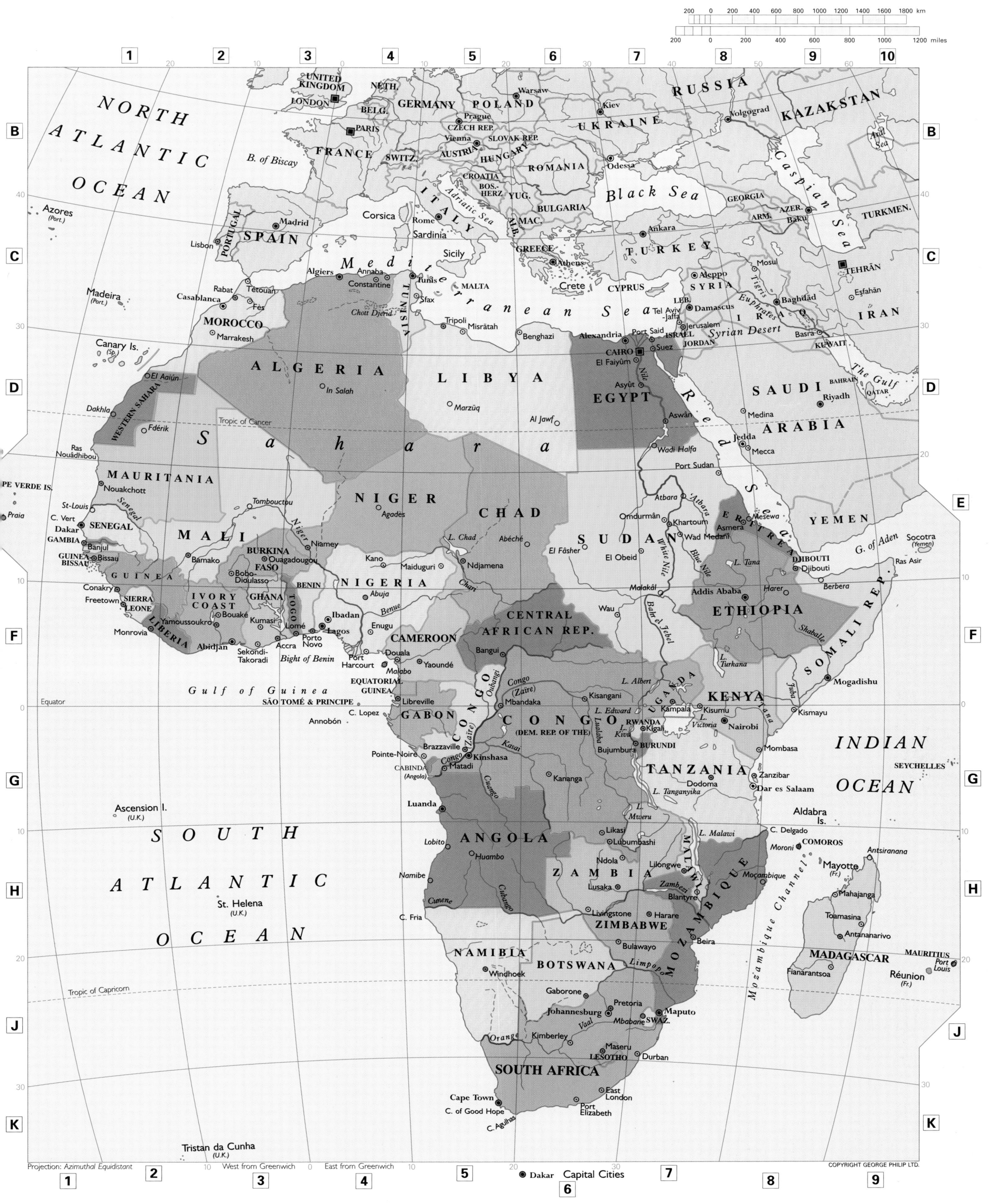

200 0 200 400 600 800 1000 1200 1400 1600 1800 km
200 0 200 400 600 800 1000 1200 miles

1 20 **2** 10 **3** 0 **4** 10 **5** 20 **6** 30 **7** 40 **8** 50 **9** 60 **10**

B ... B

NORTH

ATLANTIC

OCEAN

Azores
(Port.)

40

B. of Biscay

UNITED
KINGDOM
●London

NETH.
BELG.
●PARIS
FRANCE SWITZ.

GERMANY POLAND
Warsaw●
Prague
CZECH REP.
Vienna
AUSTRIA HUNGARY
CROATIA
BOS.-
HERZ. YUG.

●Kiev

RUSSIA

UKRAINE

Odessa●

ROMANIA
BULGARIA

●Volgograd

KAZAKSTAN

Aral
Sea

Black Sea

GEORGIA
ARM. AZER.
●Baku

Caspian Sea

TURKMEN.

C

Madeira
(Port.)

Lisbon●
PORTUGAL

●Madrid
SPAIN

Corsica
Rome●
ITALY
Sardinia
Adriatic Sea
ALB.
MAC.

MALTA

Sicily

GREECE
Athens●
Crete

TURKEY
Ankara●

CYPRUS

Aleppo●
SYRIA
LEB.
●Damascus
ISRAEL
Tel Aviv-
Jaffa
Jerusalem●
JORDAN

Mosul●

Tigris
I R A Q
●Baghdad

Basra●

●Mosul

Euphrates

TEHRĀN■

Eşfahān●

IRAN

C

30

Canary Is.
(Sp.)

Algiers●
Rabat● Tétouan●
Casablanca●
●Fès
MOROCCO
Marrakesh●

Annaba●
Constantine●
TUNIS●
TUNISIA
Sfax●
Chott Djerid

Tripoli●
Misrātah●

Mediterranean Sea

Benghazi●

Alexandria●
Port Said●
CAIRO■
El Faiyûm●
Suez●

SAUDI

BAHRAIN
Medina●
●Riyadh QATAR
Mecca●

The Gulf
●KUWAIT

D

Dakhla

WESTERN SAHARA

Ras
Nouâdhibou

ALGERIA
In Salah●

Marzûq●
Tropic of Cancer
Fdérik●

LIBYA

EGYPT
Asyût●

Aswân●

Red Sea

ARABIA

Jedda●

D

PE VERDE IS.

St-Louis●
C. Vert●
Dakar● SENEGAL
Praia● GAMBIA
Banjul●

MAURITANIA
Nouakchott●

Senegal

Tombouctou●

S a h a r a

NIGER

CHAD

Al Jawf●

SUDAN

Wadi Halfa●

Atbara●
Omdurmân●
Khartoum●
Wad Medani●

Port Sudan●

Atbara
Nile

ERITREA
Mesewa●
Asmera●

Blue Nile
L. Tana

YEMEN

G. of Aden

Socotra
(Yemen)

Ras Asir●

E

GUINEA
BISSAU●Bissau

MALI
Bamako●

Agades●
Niamey●

Niger

Kano●
Maiduguri●
Ndjamena●

L. Chad

Abéché●

El Fâsher●
El Obeid●

White Nile

Addis Ababa●
Harer●
Berbera●

DJIBOUTI
Djibouti●

SOMALI REP.

F

Conakry●
Freetown●
SIERRA
LEONE
Monrovia●
LIBERIA

GUINEA

Bobo-
Dioulasso●
BURKINA
FASO
Ouagadougou●
IVORY
COAST
Yamoussoukro●
Bouaké●
Kumasi●
GHANA
Abidjan●
Accra●
Sekondi-
Takoradi●

BENIN
TOGO
Lomé●
Porto
Novo●
Ibadan●
Lagos●
Enugu●
Port
Harcourt●

NIGERIA
Abuja●
Benue

CAMEROON
Douala●
Yaoundé●
Malabo●

CENTRAL
AFRICAN REP.
Bangui●

Chari

Wau●
Malakâl●
Bahr el Jebel

L. Turkana

ETHIOPIA

Shabelle

Mogadishu●

F

0

Gulf of Guinea

SÃO TOMÉ & PRINCIPE

Bight of Benin

EQUATORIAL
GUINEA
Libreville●
C. Lopez

Annobón●

GABON

Equator

CONGO

Congo (Zaïre)

Mbandaka●

Ubangi
Congo

CONGO
(DEM. REP. OF THE)

Kisangani●

L. Albert

L. Edward

UGANDA
Kampala●
RWANDA
Kigali●
BURUNDI
Bujumbura●

L. Kivu
Lualaba

L. Victoria

Kisumu●
KENYA
Nairobi●

Kismayu●

INDIAN

OCEAN

SEYCHELLES

G

Pointe-Noire●
Brazzaville●
Kinshasa●
CABINDA
(Angola)
Matadi●

Congo (Zaïre)

Kananga●
Kasai
Cuango

TANZANIA
Dodoma●
Dar es Salaam●
Zanzibar●

Mombasa●

L. Tanganyika

G

10

Ascension I.
(U.K.)

Luanda●

SOUTH

Lobito●
Huambo●

ANGOLA

Namibe●

L. Mweru

Likasi●
Lubumbashi●
Ndola●

ZAMBIA
Lusaka●

L. Malawi

Lilongwe●
MALAWI
Blantyre●

Moçambique●

C. Delgado
COMOROS
Moroni●

Mayotte
(Fr.)

Antsiranana●

H

ATLANTIC

St. Helena
(U.K.)

OCEAN

C. Fria

Cunene

Cubango

Livingstone●
ZIMBABWE
Bulawayo●

Harare●
Beira●

MOZAMBIQUE

Zambezi

Mozambique Channel

Mahajanga●
Toamasina●
Antananarivo●

MADAGASCAR

MAURITIUS
Port
Louis●

H

20

NAMIBIA
Windhoek●

BOTSWANA
Gaborone●

Limpopo

Réunion
(Fr.)

J

Tropic of Capricorn

Pretoria●
Johannesburg●
Kimberley●
Vaal
Orange
Maseru●
LESOTHO

Mbabane●
SWAZ.
Maputo●

J

K

Cape Town●
C. of Good Hope
C. Agulhas

SOUTH AFRICA
East
London●
Port
Elizabeth●

Durban●

K

Tristan da Cunha
(U.K.)

Projection: *Azimuthal Equidistant*

1 20 **2** 10 *West from Greenwich* **3** 0 *East from Greenwich* **4** 10 **5** 20 ●Dakar Capital Cities **7** 40 **8** 50 **9**

COPYRIGHT GEORGE PHILIP LTD.

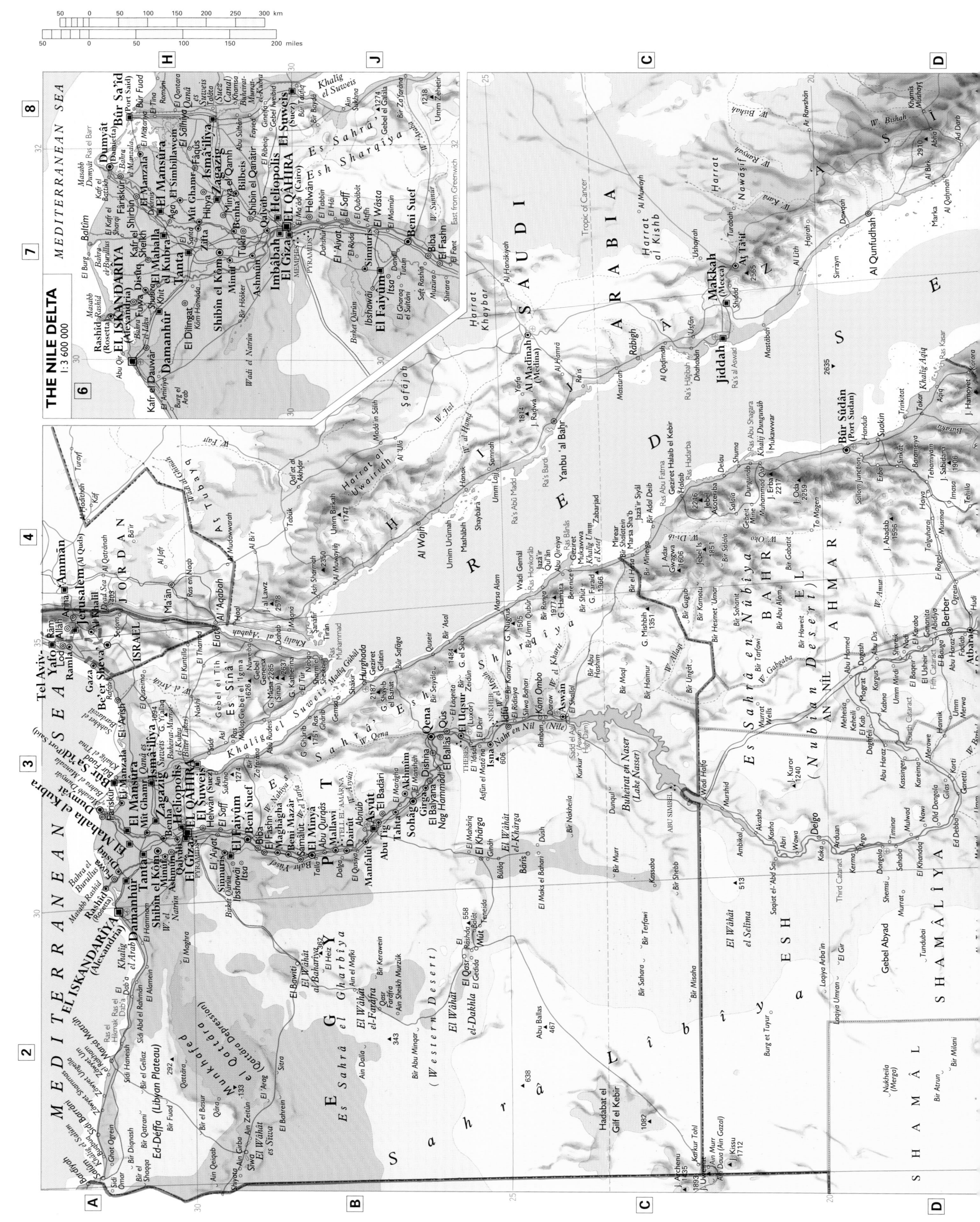

Projection Lambert's Equivalent Azimuthal

East from Greenwich

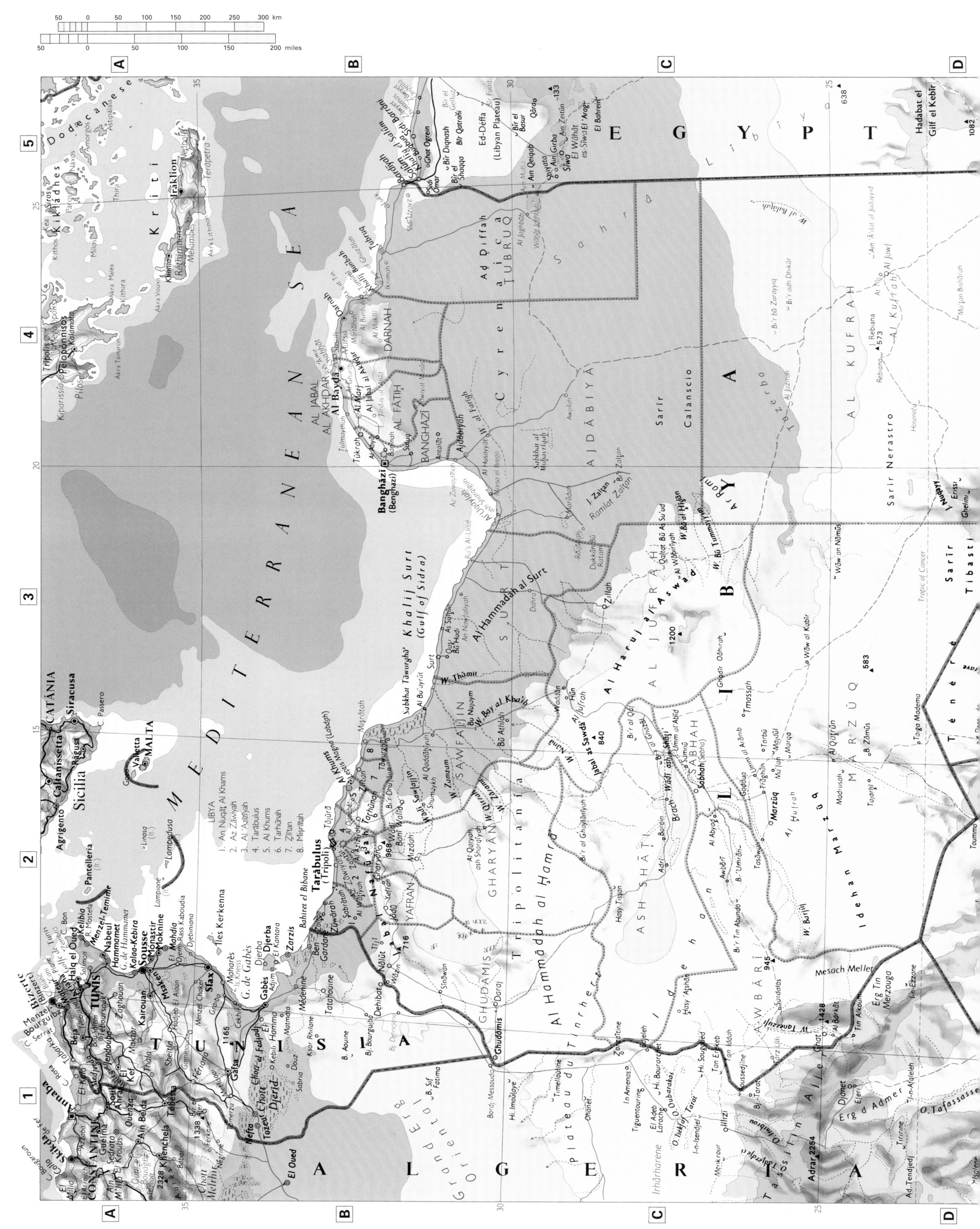

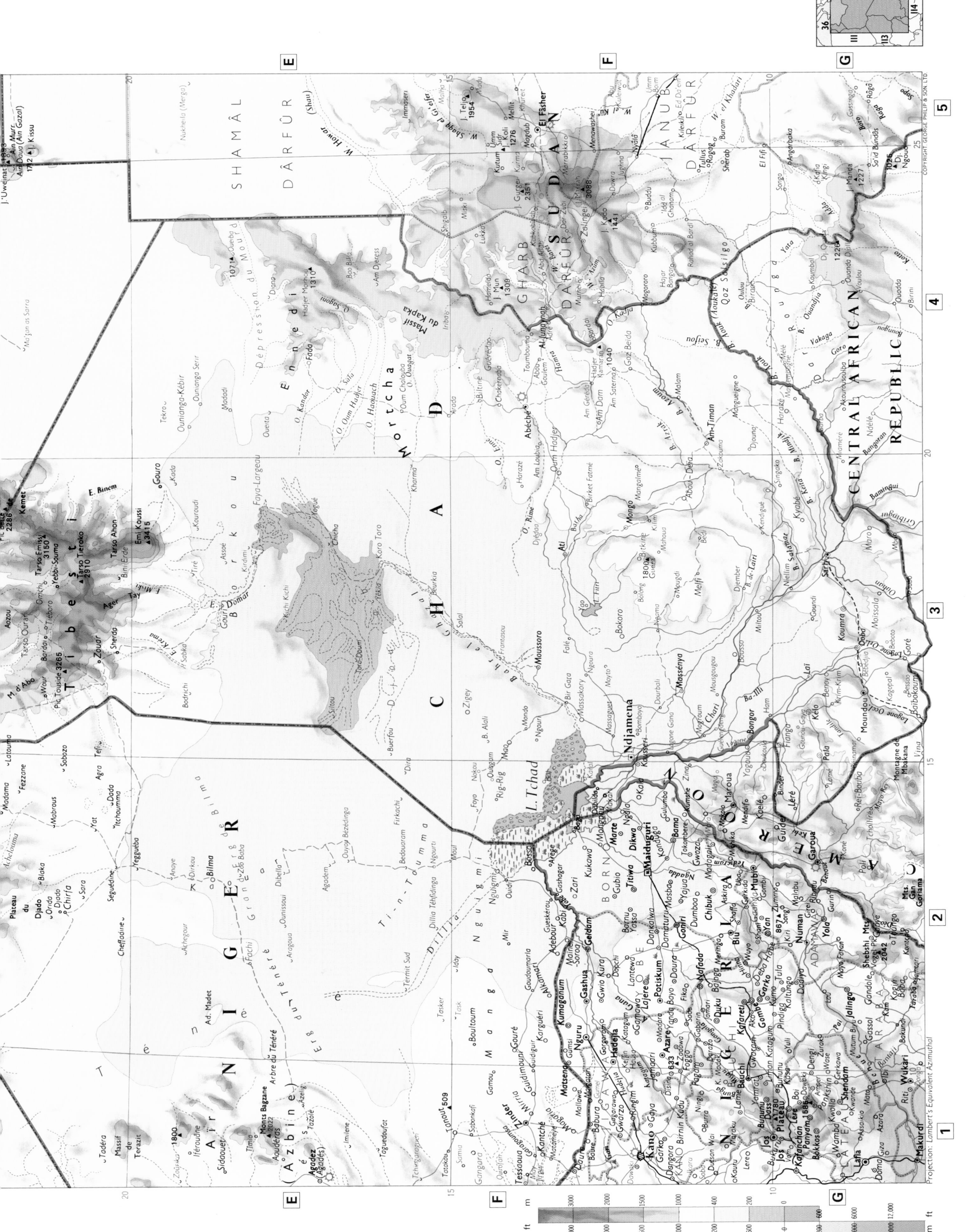

Projection: Lambert's Equivalent Azimuthal

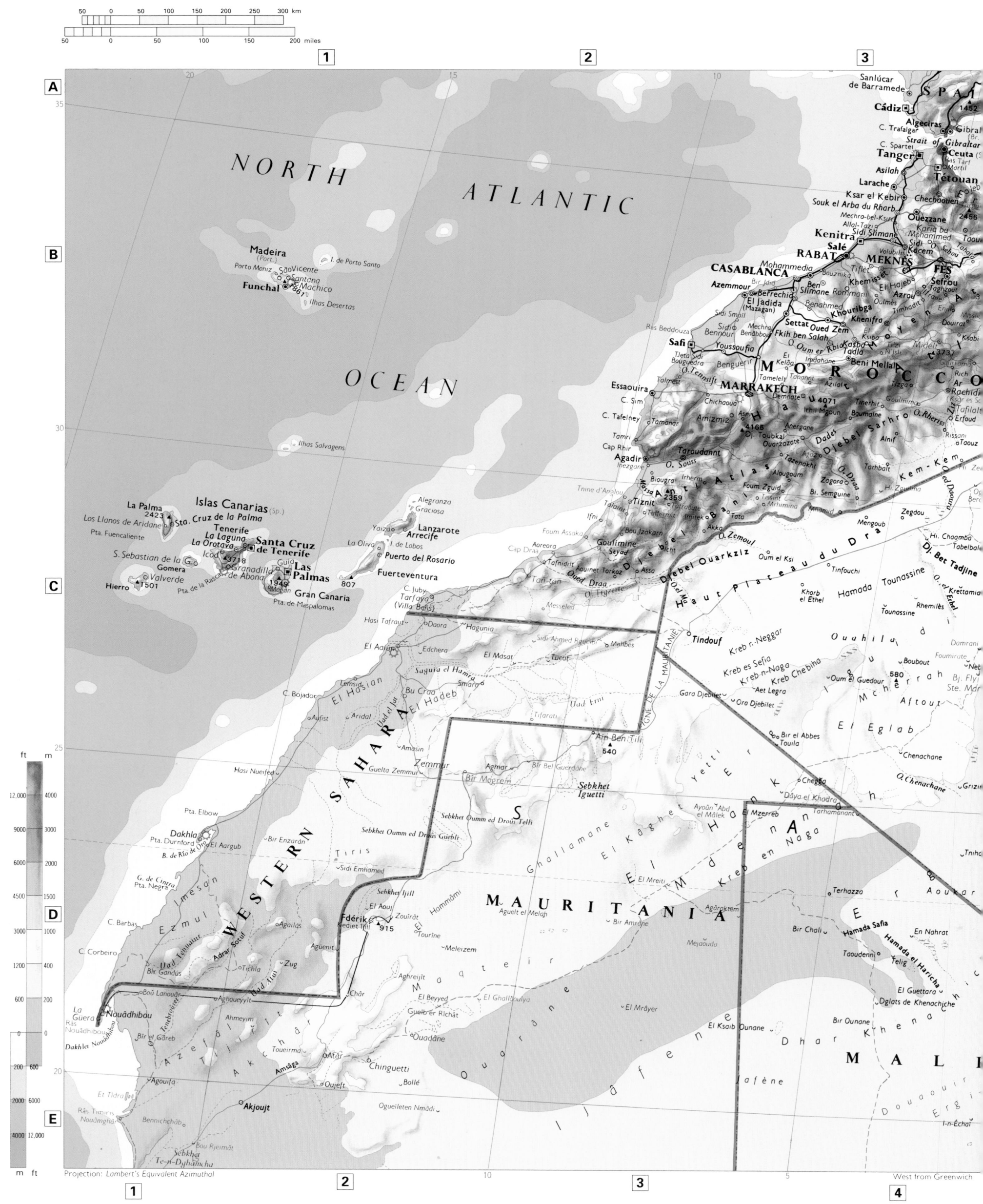

50 0 50 100 150 200 250 300 km
50 0 50 100 150 200 miles

NORTH ATLANTIC OCEAN

Madeira (Port.)
Porto Moniz · SãoVicente · I. de Porto Santo
Santana
Funchal Machico
6861
Ilhas Desertas

Ilhas Salvagens

Islas Canarias (Sp.)
La Palma 2423 ▲ Sta. Cruz de la Palma
Los Llanos de Aridane
Pta. Fuencaliente
Tenerife
La Laguna
Santa Cruz
La Orotava **de Tenerife**
3718
S. Sebastian de la G. Icod Granadilla
Gomera de Abona
Valverde 1949 **Las**
Hierro ▲1501 **Palmas**
Pta. de la Rasca de Abona Mogán
807
Pta. de Maspalomas Gran Canaria

Alegranza
Graciosa
Yaizao **Lanzarote**
Arrecife
La Oliva · I. de Lobos
Puerto del Rosario
C. Juby **Fuerteventura**
Tarfaya
(Villa Bens)

ft m
12,000 4000
9000 3000
6000 2000
4500 1500
3000 1000
1200 400
600 200
0 0
200 600
2000 6000
4000 12,000
m ft

C. Bojador
C. Barbas
C. Corbeiro

WESTERN SAHARA

El Aaiun
El Hasian
Bu Craa El Hadeb
Aridal
Aufist
Amasin
Zemmur
Guelta Zemmur
Hasi Nueifed

Pta. Elbow
Pta. Durnford **Dakhla**
B. de Rio do Oro
Bir Enzaran
Sidi Emhamed
Sebkhet Ijill
El Aouj
Zouirat
Fdérik
Kediet Ijill 915
Guelb er Richat
G. de Cintra
Pta. Negra
Agailas
Aguenit
Agha
Zug
Tichla
Adrar Setuf
C. Barbas
Blc Gandús
Uad Tenuhaiat
Bôu Lanouâr
Aghoueyyit
La Güera
Ras Nouâdhibou **Nouâdhibou**
Dakhlet Nouâdhibou
Bir el Gâreb
Ahmeyim
Akjoujt
Ras Tîmiris
Nouâmghâr
Bennichâb
Bou Rjeimât
Sebkha
Te-n-Dghâmcha

MAURITANIA

Tindouf
Kreb n. Neggar
Kreb es Sefia
Kreb n-Naga
Kreb Chebiha
Aet Legra
Gara Djebilet
Oro Djebilet
Bir el Abbes
Touila
Ain Ben Tili
540
Ayoûn Abd
el Mâlek
El Mzereb
Terhazza
Agâroktém
Bir Amrâne
Aguelt el Melah
Meleizem
Tourine
Char
Agherjit
El Beyyed
El Ghallaoûya
Mejaôudu
Chinguetti
Tafène
El Mrâyer
Ouâdane
Terjit
Atâr
Touejmat
Agouita
Boû Lanouar
Ouadane
Amsâga
Bollé
Oujeft
Et Tidra Ioe
Ogueileten Nmâdi
Akchâr

Oum er Rbia
MOROCCO
CASABLANCA
MARRAKECH
Agadir
C. Sim
C. Tafelney
Tamri
Cap Rhir
Essaouira
Chichaoua
Amizmiz
Taroudannt
Inezgane
O. Souss
Tiznit
Goulimine
Seyad
Tan-tan
Messeled
Haut Plateau du Dra
Ligne de la Mauritanie
Sebkhet Oumm ed Drous Telli
Sebkhet Oumm ed Drous Guebli
Tiris
Hammâmi
Ghallamane
El Kâghe
El Mreiti
Ayoûn
Dâya el Khadra
Tarhamanant
Kreb en Naga
Mâden
Hamada Tounassine
Tounassine
Rhemilès
Mcherrah
Aftout
El Eglab
Chenachane
O. Chenachane
Boubout
580
Bj. Fly
Ste. Mar
Mengoub
Zegdou
Hl. Chaamba
O. Zemoul
Oum el Ksi
Bir el Ksiba
Hamada Safia
En Nahrat
El Guettara
Taoudenni
Telig
Hamada el Haricha
Bir Ounane
El Ksaib Ounane
Dglats de Khenachiche
Bir Chali
Hamada el Haricha
Dhar
Oûarâne
Aoukar
El Hank
Kreb en Naga
Ouahila
Damrani
Foumirute
Net
MALI

West from Greenwich

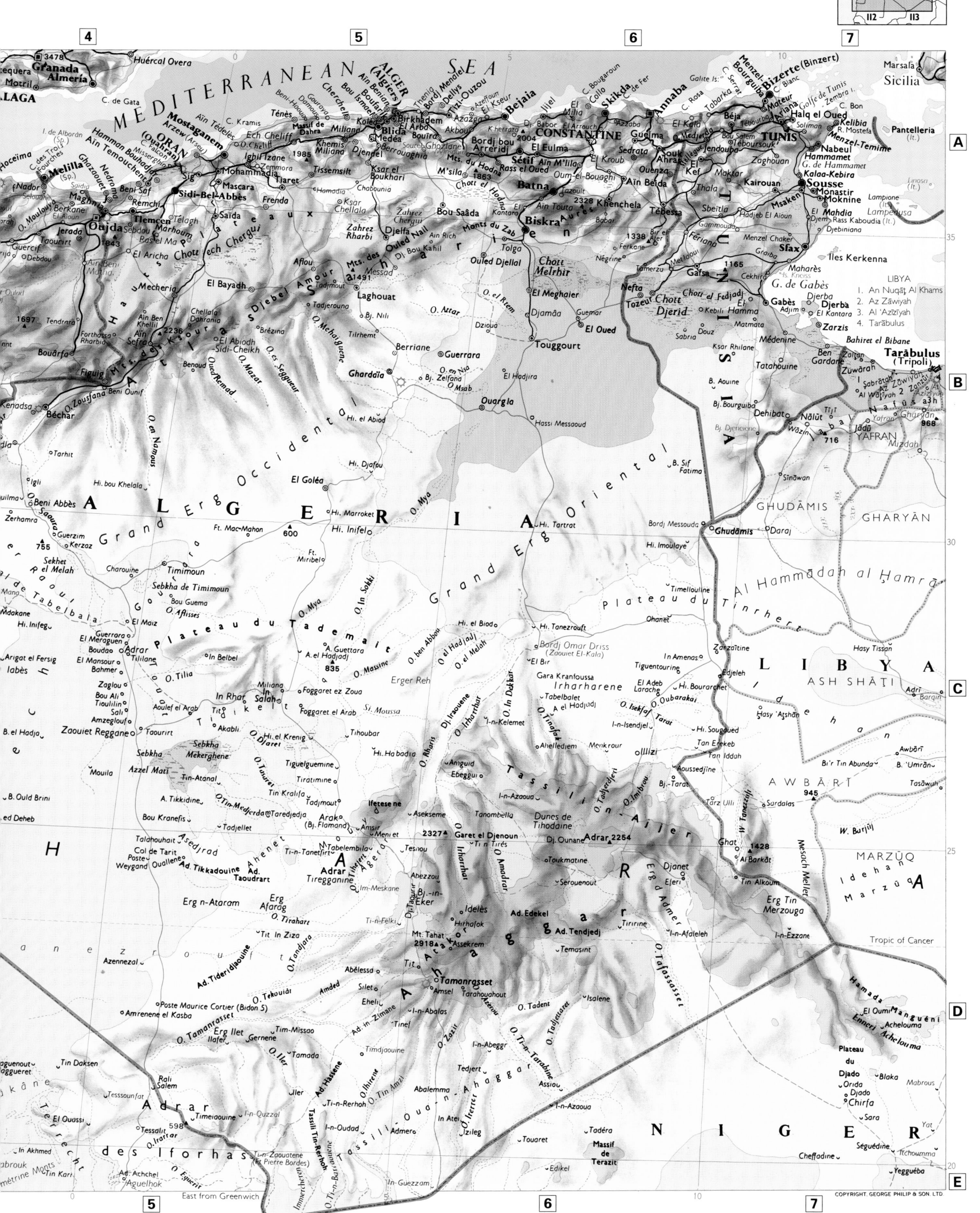

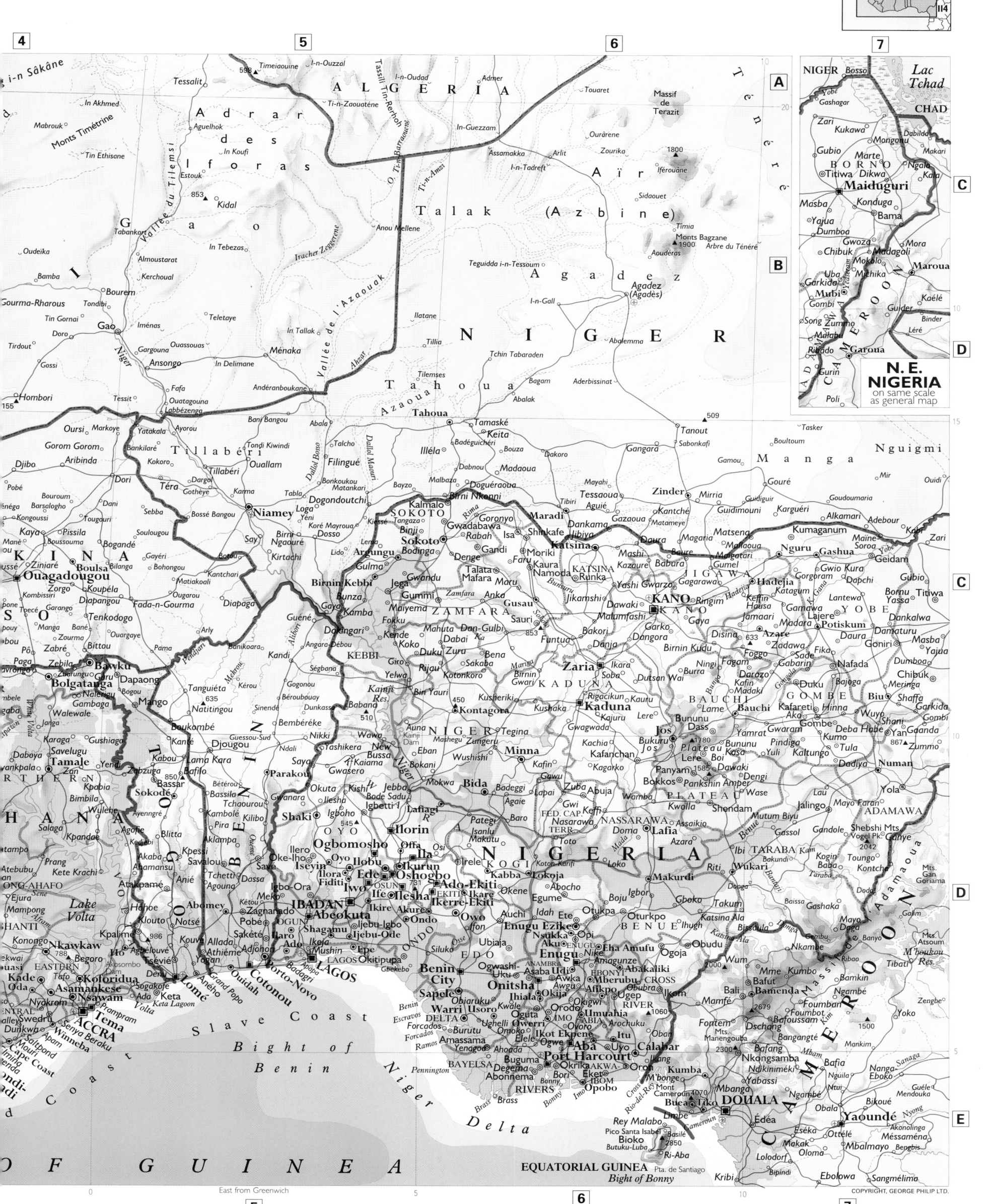

N. E. NIGERIA
on same scale
as general map

COPYRIGHT, GEORGE PHILIP LTD.

East from Greenwich

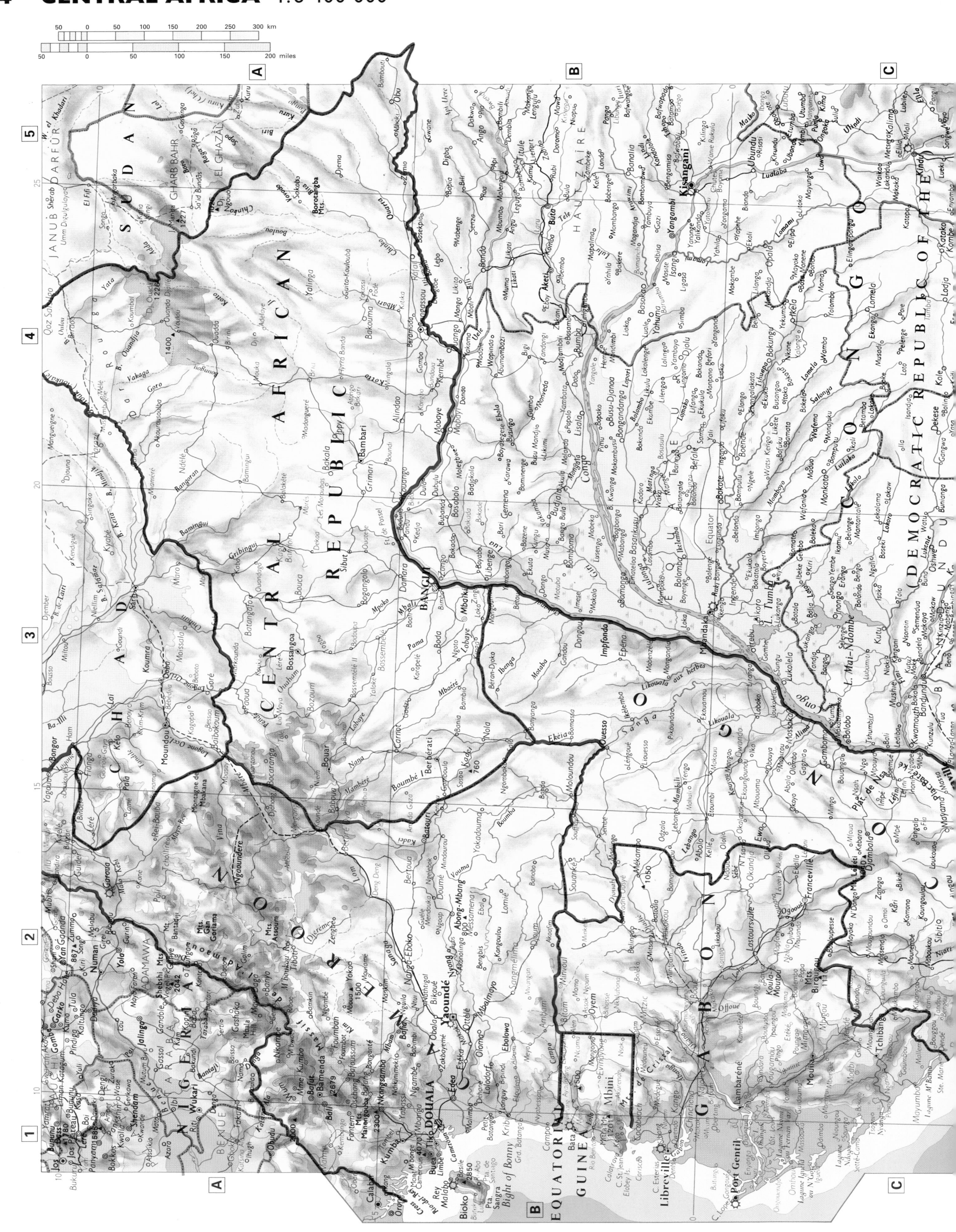

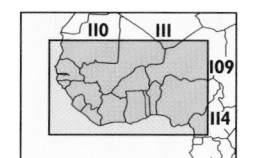

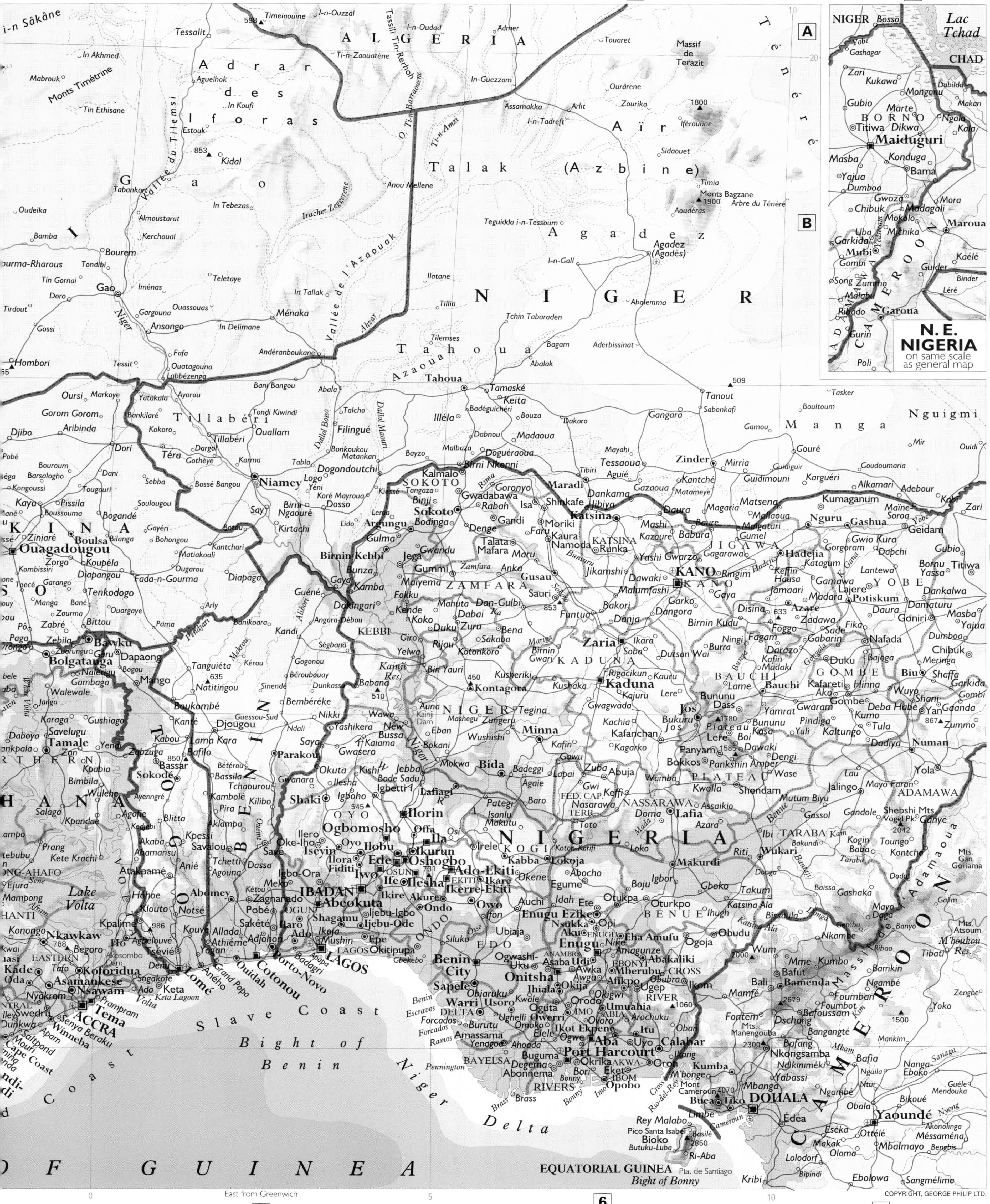

N. E. NIGERIA on same scale as general map

COPYRIGHT, GEORGE PHILIP LTD.

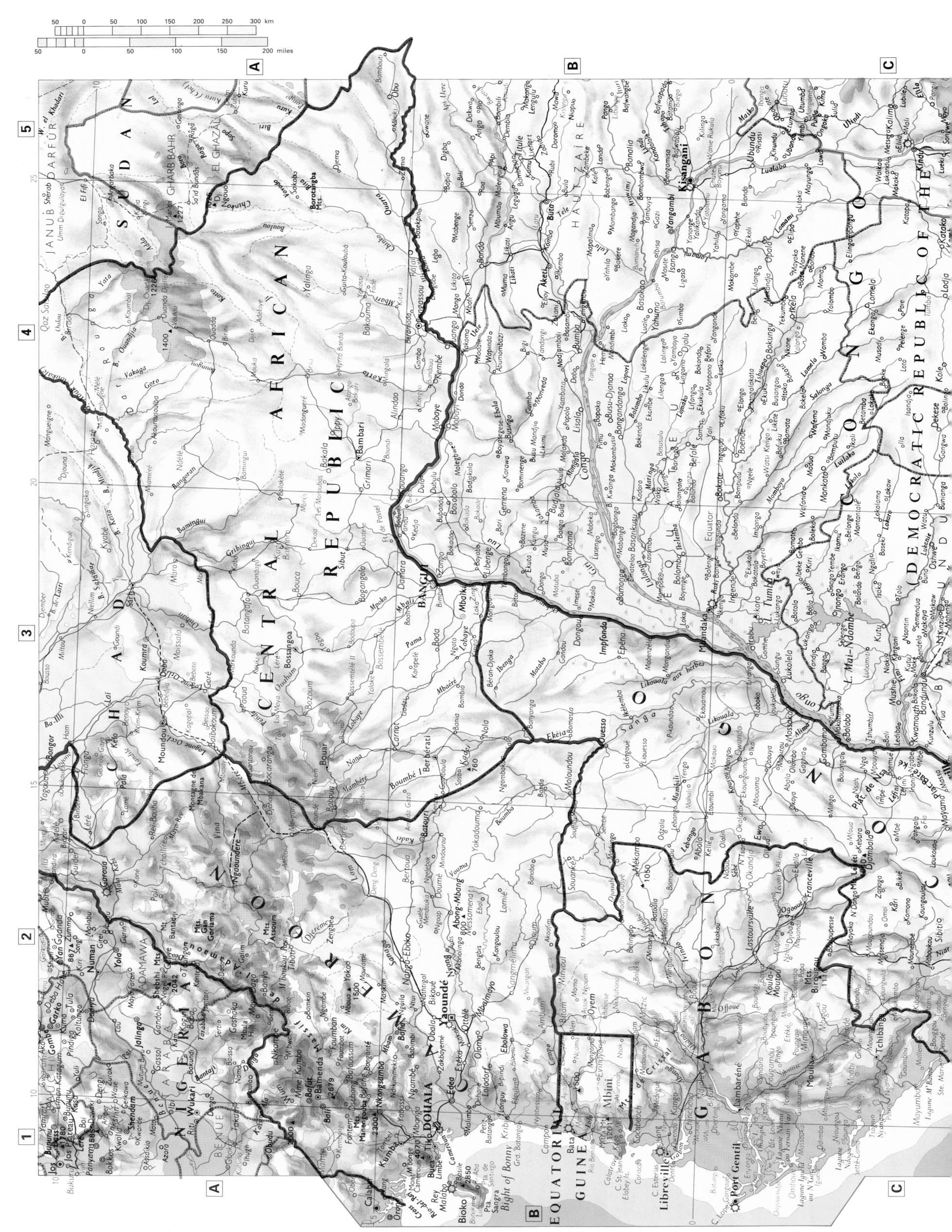

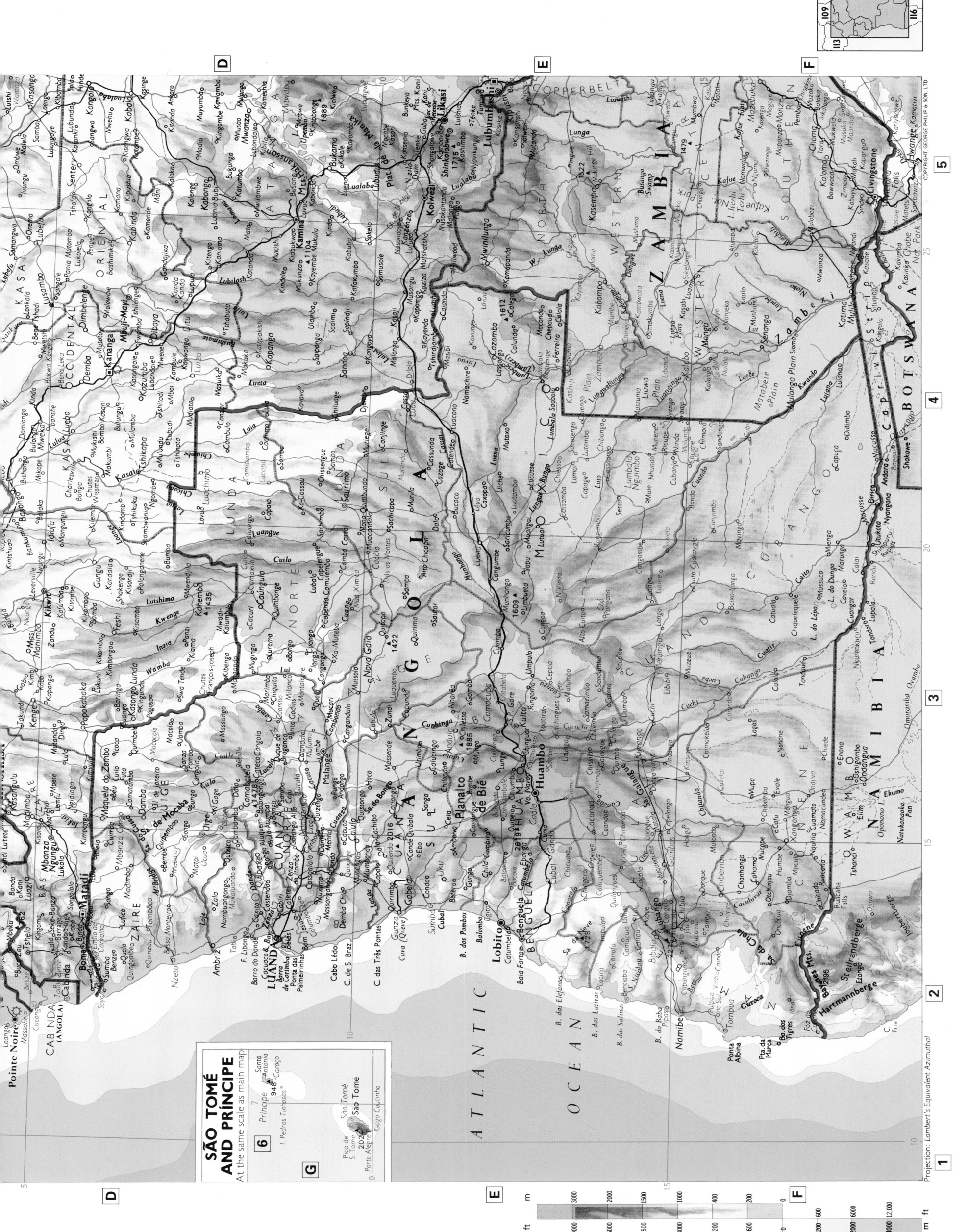

SÃO TOMÉ
AND PRÍNCIPE
At the same scale as main map

Projection: Lambert's Equivalent Azimuthal

COPYRIGHT GEORGE PHILIP & SON, LTD.

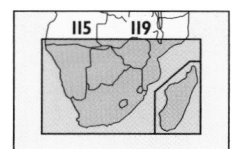

MADAGASCAR

On same scale as General Map

COPYRIGHT GEORGE PHILIP LTD.

MOZAMBIQUE CHANNEL

INDIAN OCEAN

ZIMBABWE

MOZAMBIQUE

MADAGASCAR

ANTANANARIVO

Tropic of Capricorn

East from Greenwich

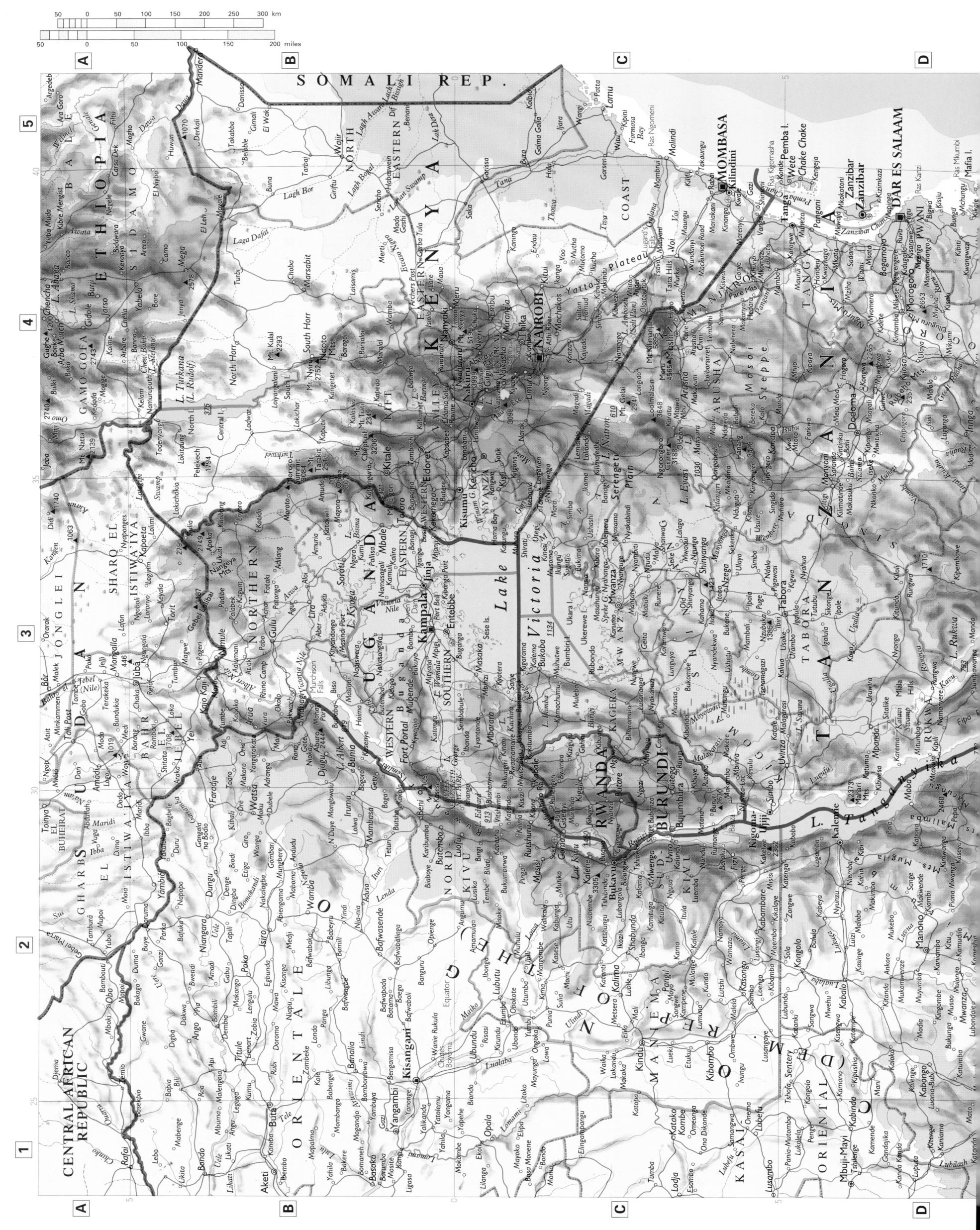

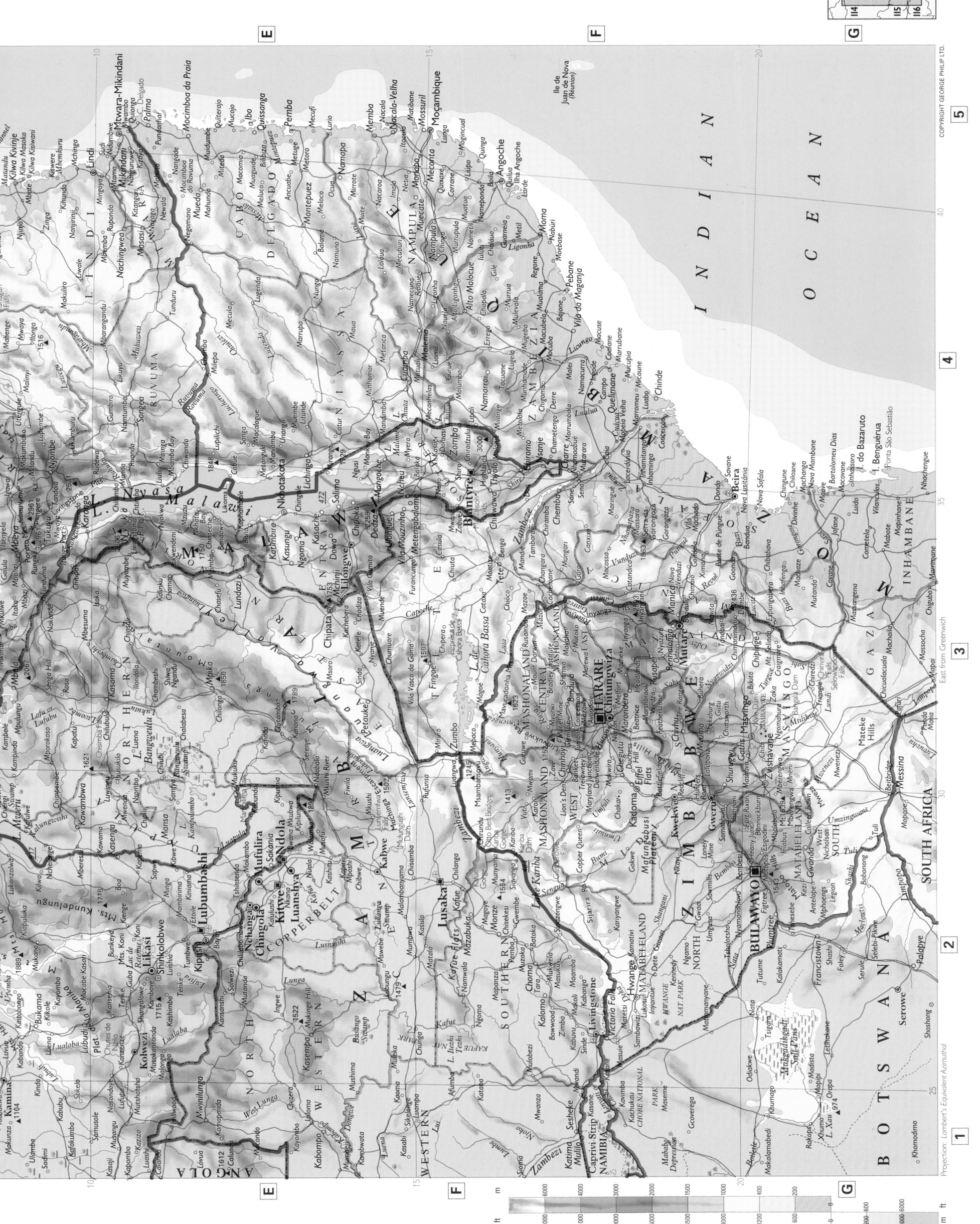

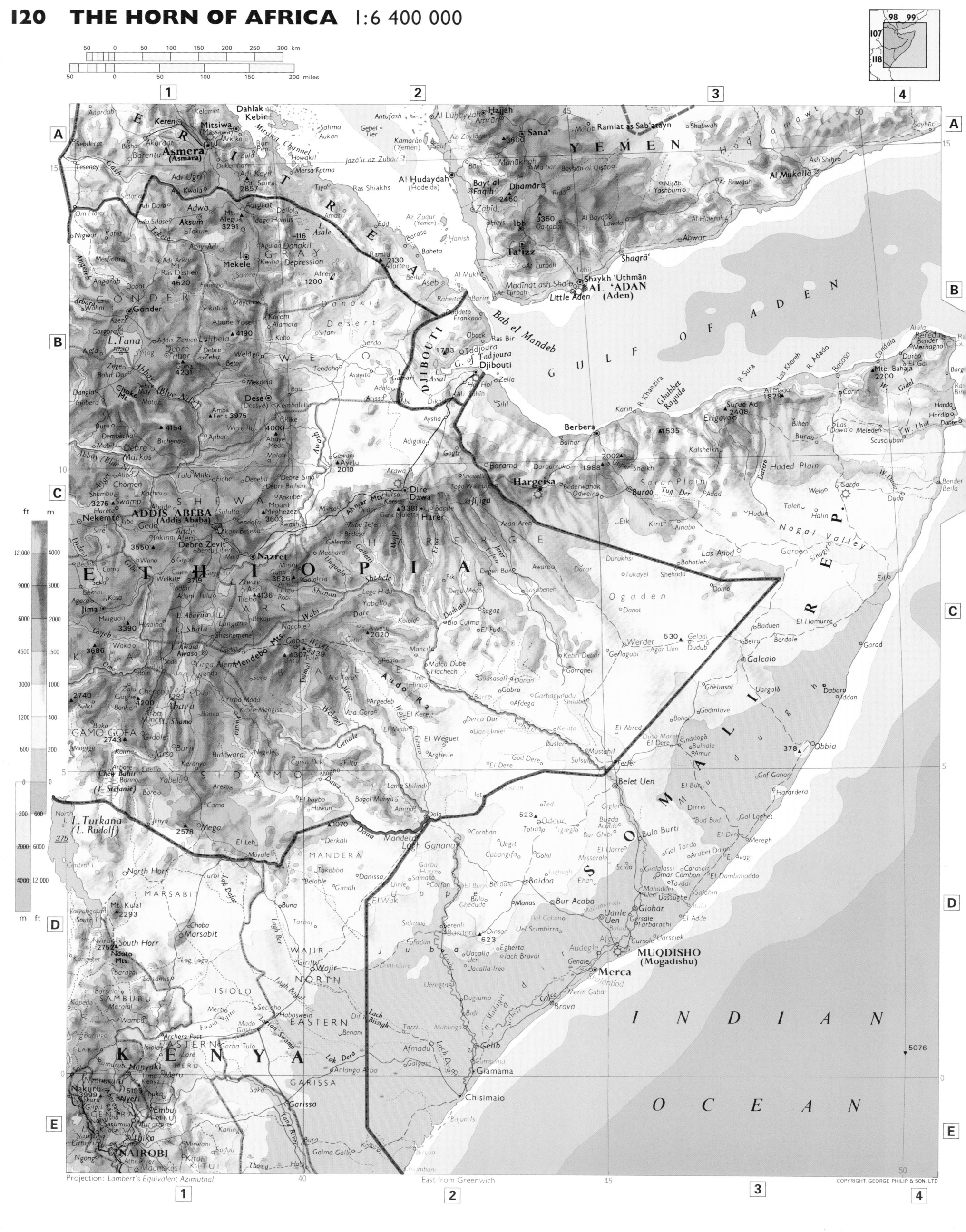

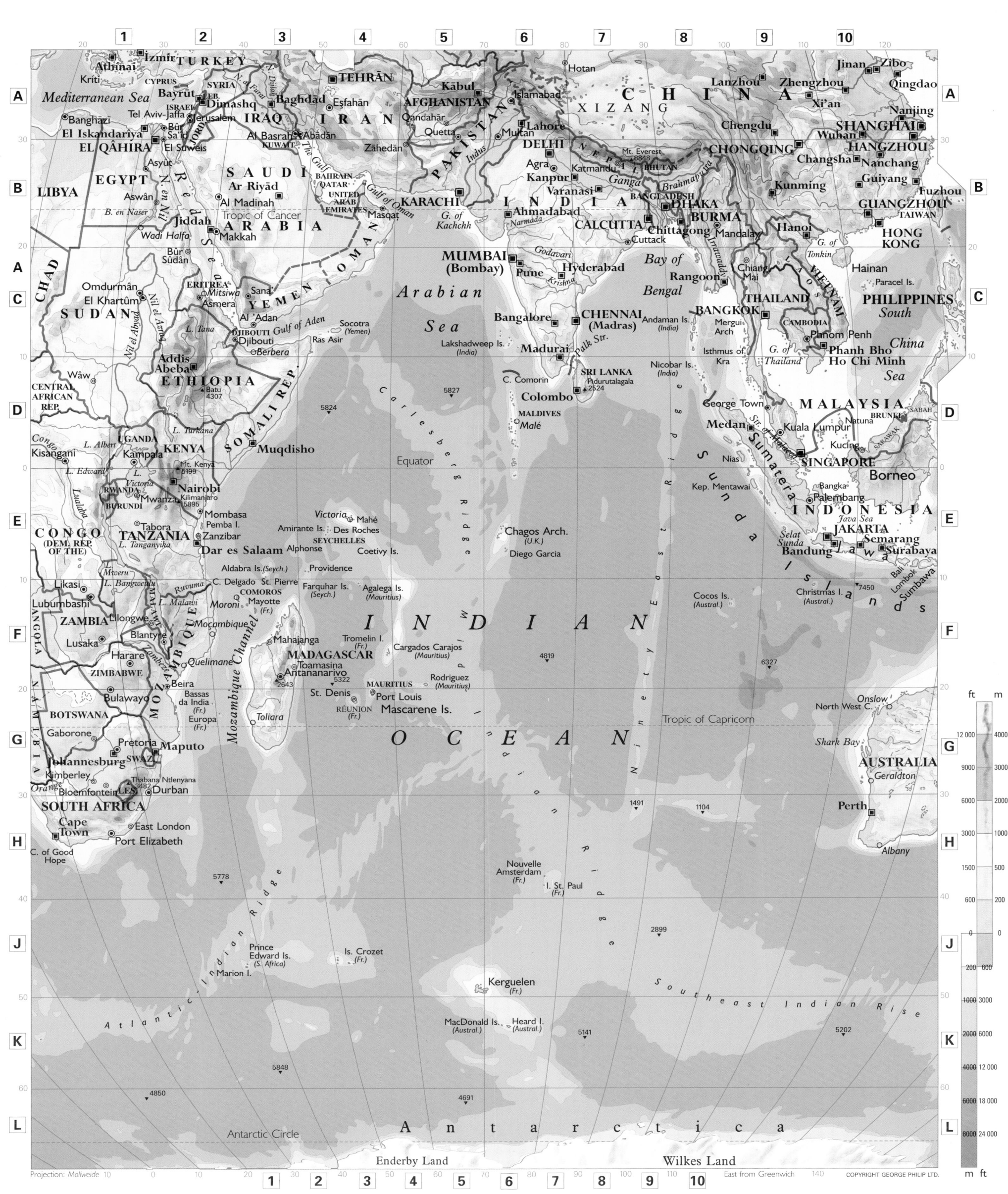

Projection: Lambert's Equivalent Azimuthal

East from Greenwich

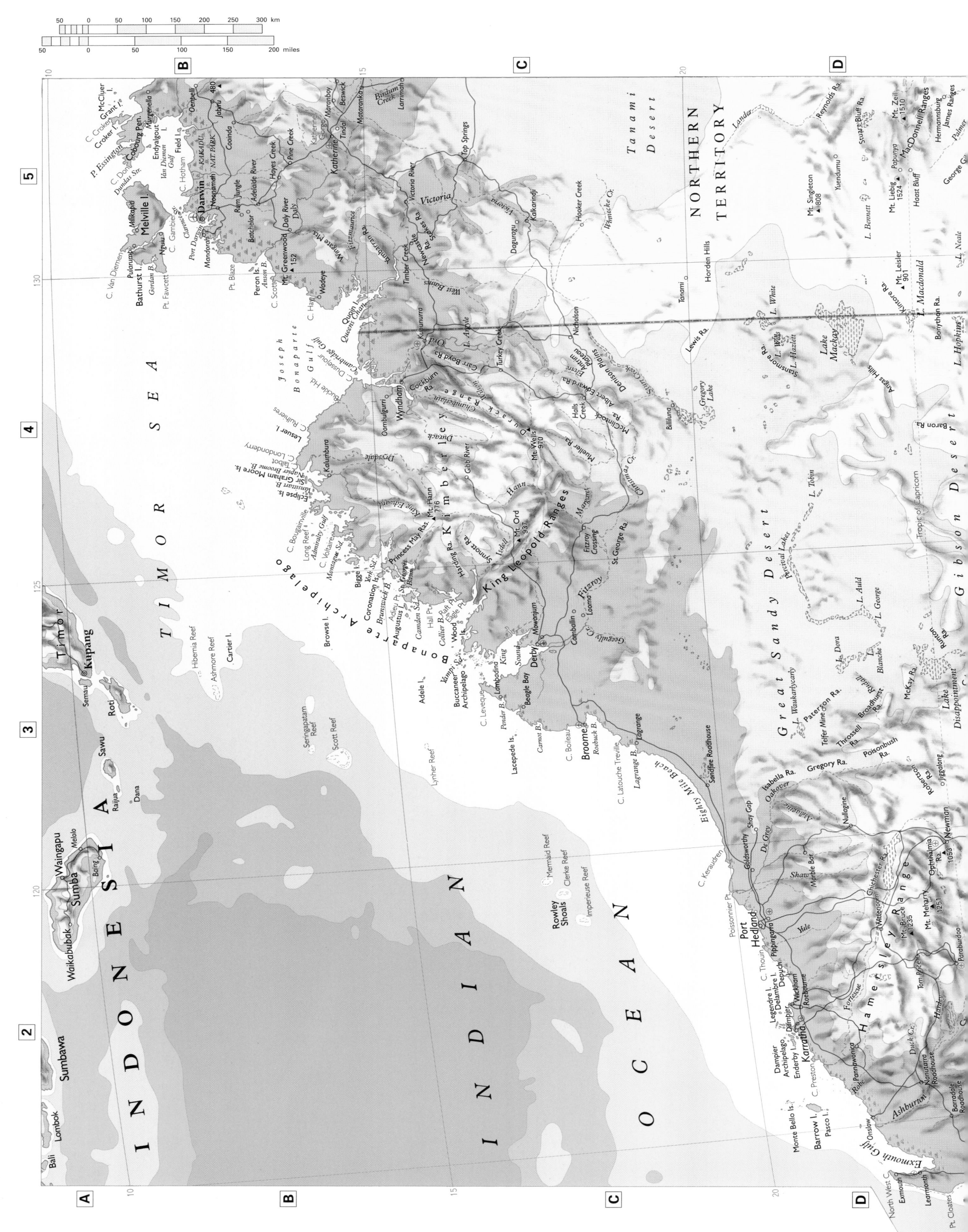

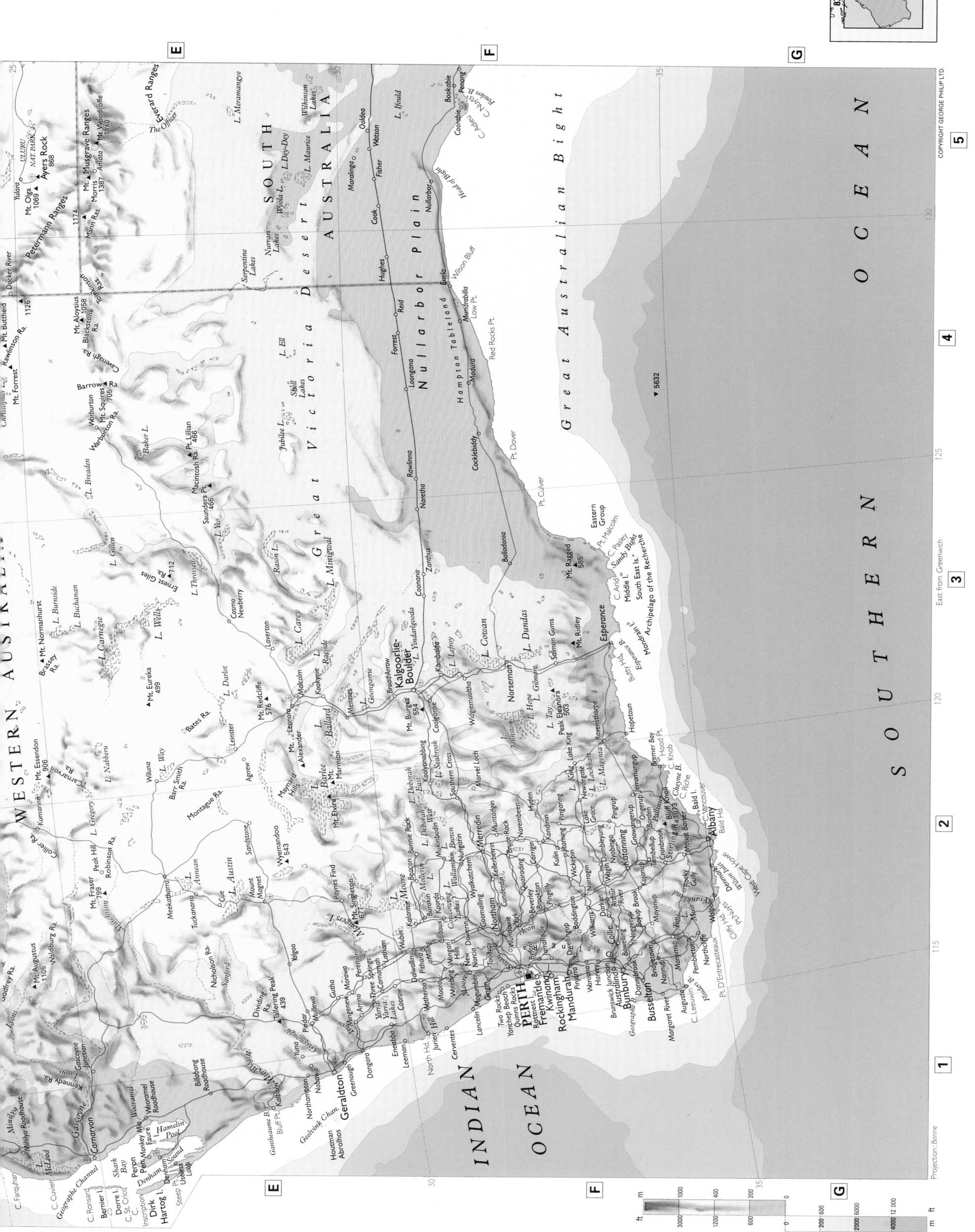

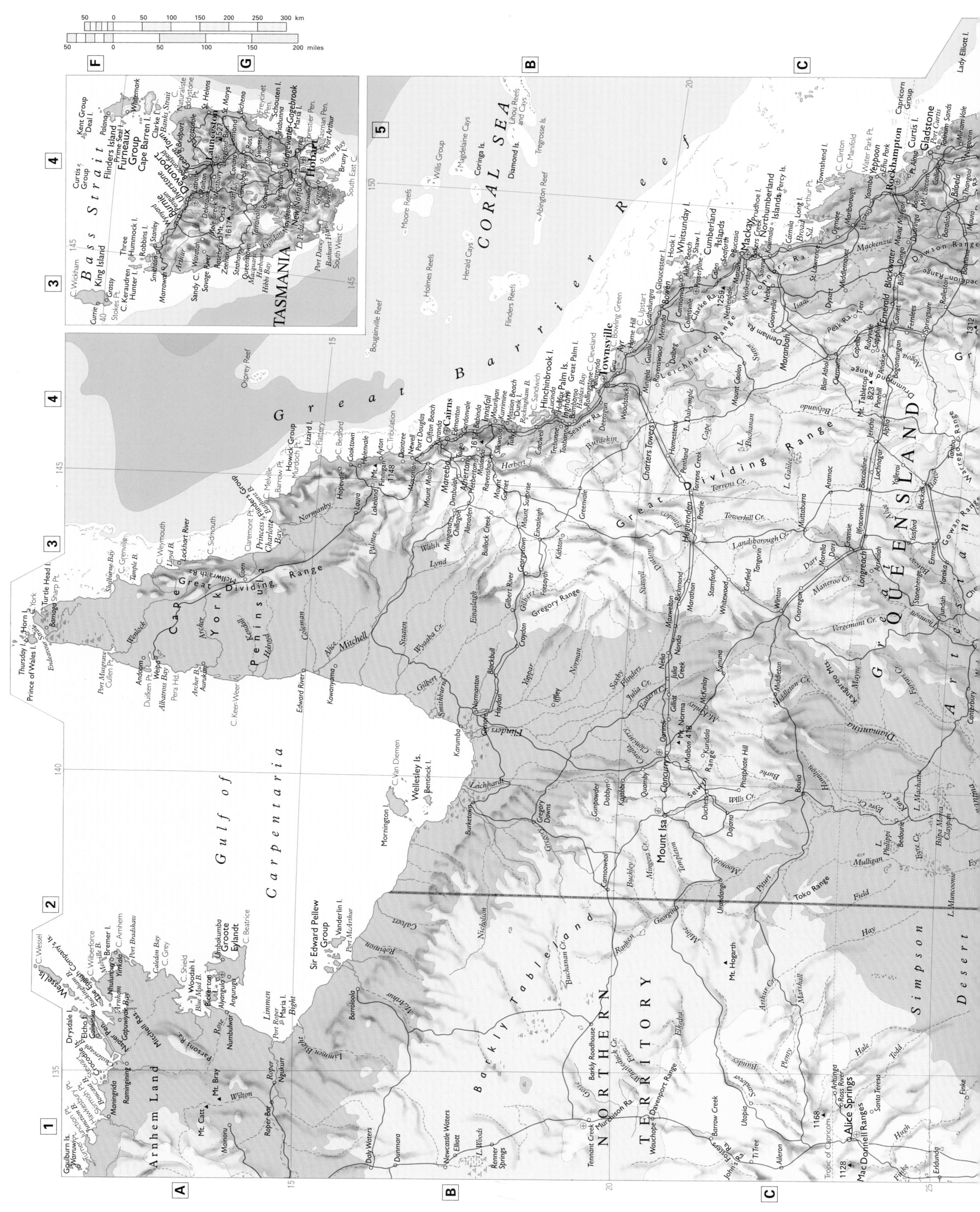

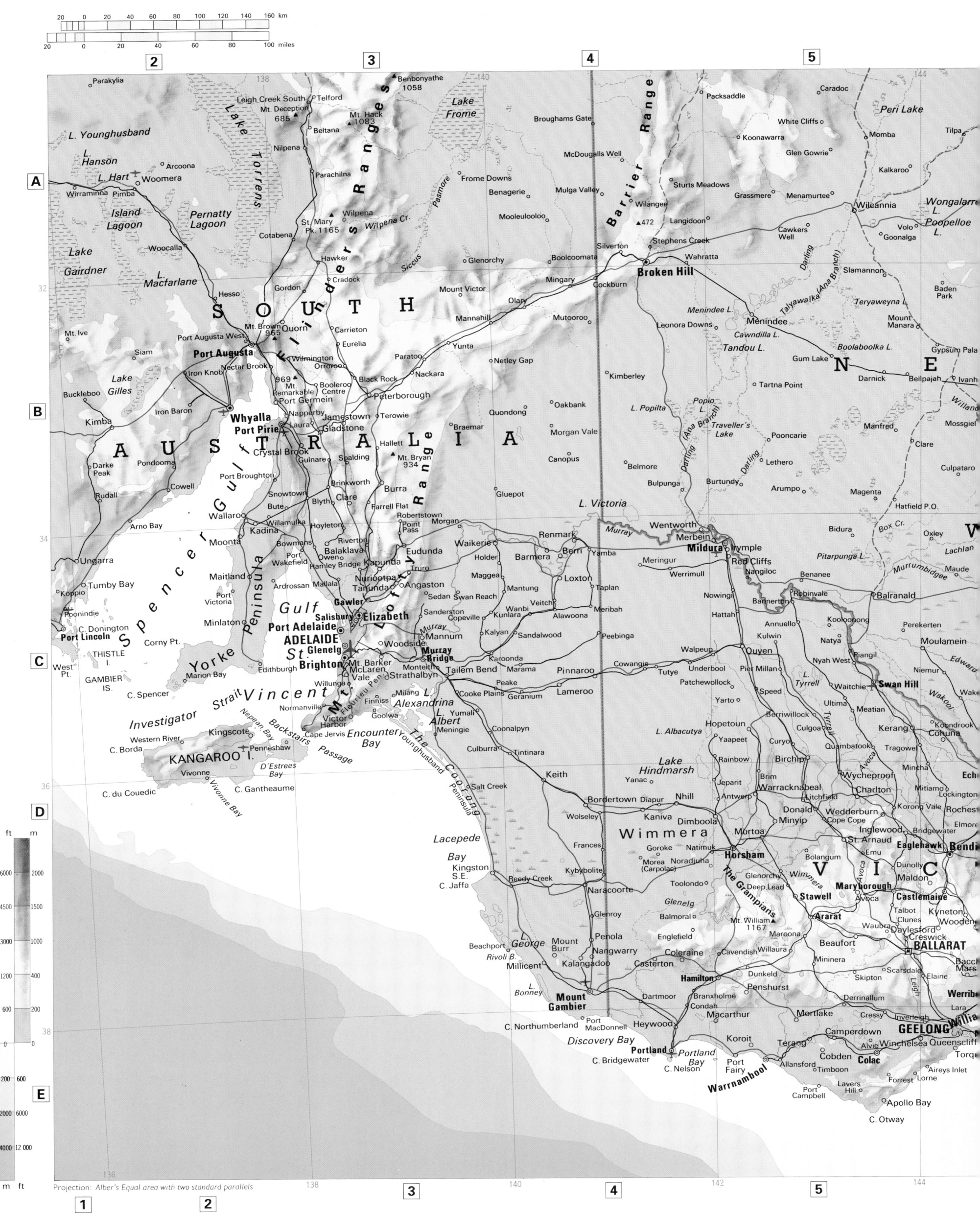

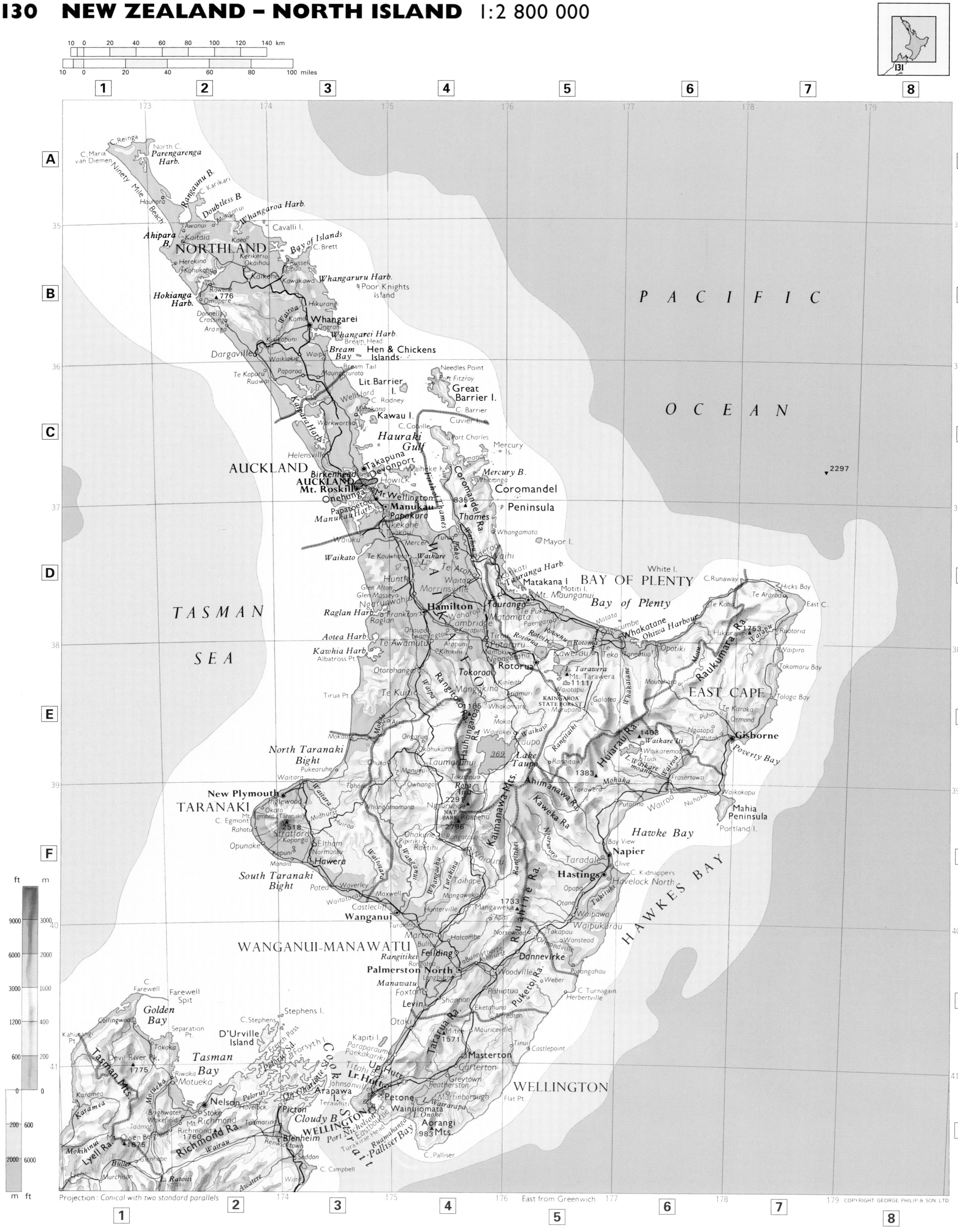

10 0 20 40 60 80 100 120 140 km
10 0 20 40 60 80 100 miles

1 2 3 4 5 6 7 8

173 174 175 176 177 178 179

A

C. Reinga
C. Maria van Diemen
North C.
Parengarenga Harb.
Rangaunu B.
Doubtless B.
C. Karikari
Whangaroa Harb.

35

Ninety Mile Beach
Houhora
Awanui
Kaitaia
Mangonui
Kerikeri
Russell
Cavalli I.
Bay of Islands
C. Brett

NORTHLAND

Ahipara B.
Kaikohe
Kaeo
Okaihau
Herekino
Kohukohu
Kawakawa

B

Hokianga Harb.
Rawene
Omapere
▲776
Waima
Donnelly's Crossing
Aranga
Hikurangi
Whangaruru Harb.
Poor Knights Island

Kamo
Whangarei
Onerahi
Whangarei Harb.
Bream Head

Dargaville
Kaikohe
Waipu
Bream Bay
Hen & Chickens Islands

36

Te Koporu
Ruawai
Paparoa
Bream Tail
Maungaturoto

Needles Point
Port Fitzroy
Great Barrier I.

Matakohe
Lit.Barrier I.
Wellsford
C. Rodney
Cuvier I.
C. Barrier

Warkworth
Kawau I.
C. Colville
Port Charles

PACIFIC

C

Helensville
Hauraki Gulf
Coromandel
Mercury Is.
Port Charles

OCEAN

AUCKLAND
Birkenhead **Takapuna**
Devonport
Howick
Waiheke I.
Coromandel
▽2297

AUCKLAND
Mt. Roskill
Onehunga
Mt. Wellington
835
Coromandel Peninsula

37

Papatoetoe
Manukau
Papakura
Thames
Thames Ra.

Manukau Harb.
Pukekohe
Whangamata

Waiuku
Mercer
Mayor I.

D

Waikato
Te Kauwhata
Waihi
Te Aroha
White I.
C.Runaway
Hicks Bay

Huntly
Morrinsville
Matakana I.
BAY OF PLENTY
Te Araroa
East C.

Glen Alton
Ngaruawahia
Tauranga Harb.
Mt. Maunganui
Bay of Plenty
▲1753

Glen Massey
Hamilton
Cambridge
Te Puke
Whakatane
Ohiwa Harbour
Hikurangi

TASMAN

Raglan
Frankton
Matamata
Tirau
Rotoehu
Kawerau
Teko
Opotiki
Raukumara Ra.
Ruatoria
Waipiro

Raglan Harb.
Aotea Harb.
Te Awamutu
Putaruru
Rotorua
Rotoma
EAST CAPE
Tokomaru Bay
Tolaga Bay

38

Kihikihi
Rotorua
L.Tarawera
Mt. Tarawera
1111
Te Karaka
Ormond

Kawhia Harb.
Albatross Pt.
Otorohanga
Tokoroa
KAINGAROA STATE FOREST
Murupara
Galatea
▲408
Waikare Iti
Gisborne

SEA

Tirua Pt.
Te Kuiti
Mangakino
Tudi
Poverty Bay

North Taranaki Bight
Pukearuhe
Mokau
Ongarue
Whakamaru
Rangataiki
1383
Mahia Peninsula
Portland I.

E

369
Taumarunui
Lake Taupo
Mohaka
Fraserton
Waikokopu

New Plymouth
Inglewood
Okato
Waitara
TARANAKI
Ohakune
Raurimu
Rangataua
Ruapehu
Ahimanawa Mts.
Kaweka Ra.
Hawke Bay

39

C. Egmont
▲2518
Stratford
Kapuni
Normanby
TONGARIRO NAT. PARK
2796
Rangitoto
Bay View
Napier

Rahotu
Opunake
Eltham
Hawera
Waverley
Taihape
Ruahine Ra.
Taradale
C. Kidnappers
Hastings
Havelock North

South Taranaki Bight
Manaia
Patea
Maxwell
Mangaweka
1733
Hunterville
Waipawa
HAWKES BAY

F

Waitotara
Castlecliff
Wanganui
Marton
Bulls
Feilding
Waipukurau

40

WANGANUI-MANAWATU
Rangitikei
Palmerston North
Dannevirke
Woodville
C. Turnagain
Herbertville

G

C. Farewell
Golden Bay
Farewell Spit
Manawatu
Foxton
Levin
Shannon
Pahiatua
Eketahuna
Alfredton

Kahurangi Pt.
Collingwood
C. Stephens
Stephens I.
Otaki
Kapiti I.
Paraparaumu
Paekakariki
Carterton
Castlepoint

Tasman Mts.
Takaka
Separation Pt.
D'Urville Island
French Pass
Mitre 1571
Masterton
Tinui

▲1775
Motueka
Tasman Bay
Up.Hutt
Greytown
Featherston

41

Karamea
Brightwater
Stoke
Nelson
Picton
Lr.Hutt
Petone
Wainuiomata
Palliser Bay

WELLINGTON

Mt. Richmond
Richmond Ra.
WELLINGTON
Port Nicholson
Eastbourne
Aorangi Mts. 983
C. Palliser

H

Mokihinui
Lyell Ra. ▲1875
Murchison
Blenheim
Renwicktown
Seddon
C. Campbell

ft m
9000 3000
6000 2000
3000 1000
1200 400
600 200
0
200 600
2000 6000
m ft

Projection: Conical with two standard parallels
East from Greenwich
COPYRIGHT GEORGE PHILIP & SON LTD.

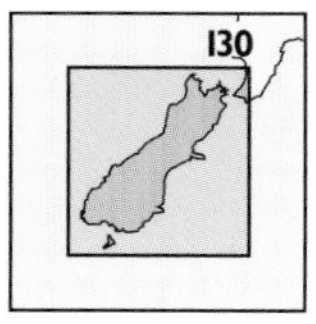

130

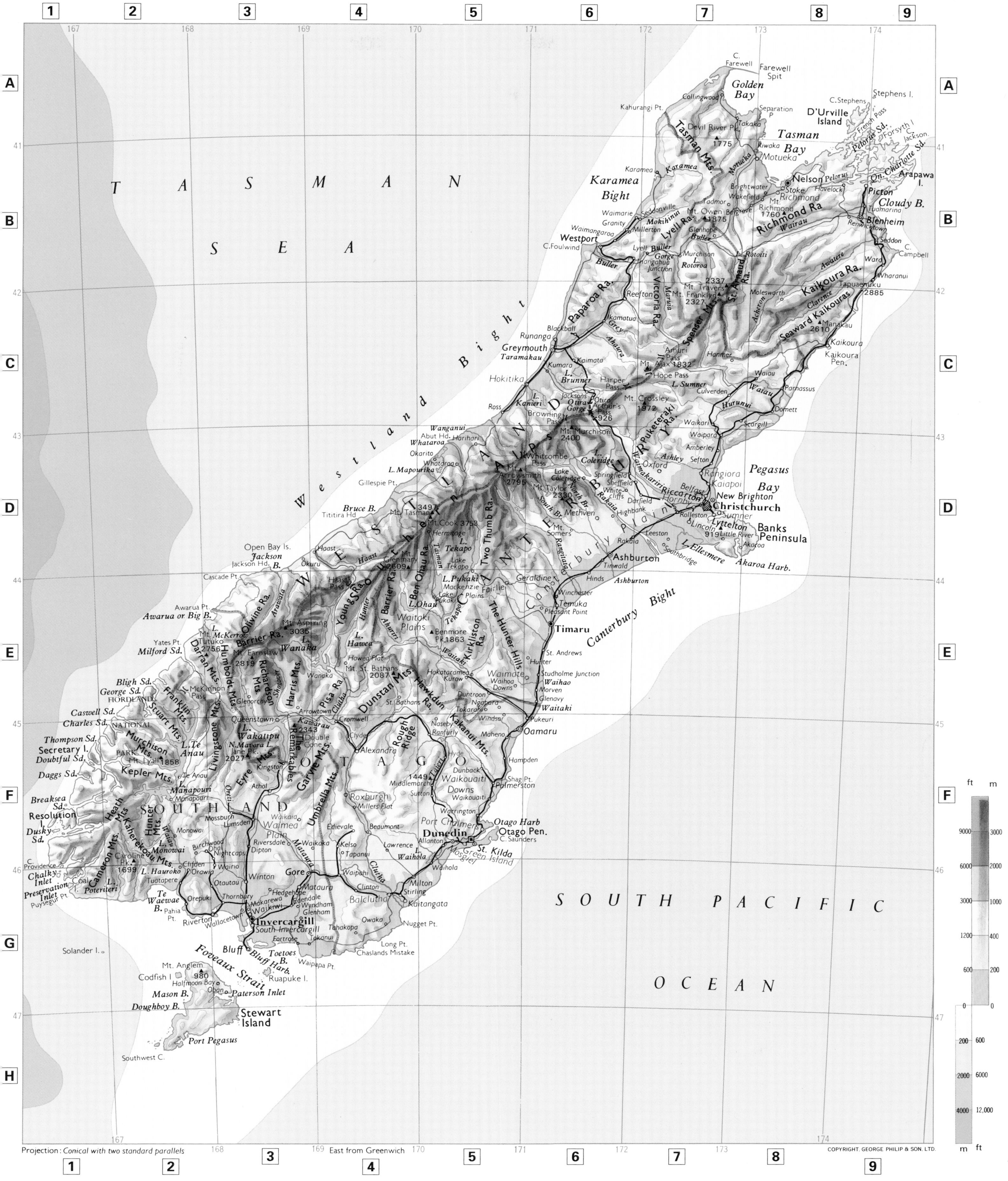

10 0 20 40 60 80 100 120 140 km
10 0 20 40 60 80 100 miles

A B C D E F G H

TASMAN SEA

SOUTH PACIFIC OCEAN

C. Farewell
Farewell Spit
Collingwood
Golden Bay
Separation Pt.
Takaka
C. Stephens
Stephens I.
D'Urville Island
Tasman Bay
Kahurangi Pt.
Devil River Pt.
Riwaka
Motueka
French Pass
Jackson
Pelorus Sd.
Forsyth I.
On. Charlotte Sd.
Arapawa I.
Tasman Mts. 1775
Karamea Bight
Karamea
Nelson
Pelorus
Havelock
Picton
Cloudy B.
Tuamarina
Stoke
Richmond
Waimarie
Seddonville
Granity
Millerton
Waimangaroa
Mokihinui
Mt. Owen 1875
Belgrove
Wakefield
Brightwater
Tadmor
Glenhope
Mt. Richmond 1760
Richmond Ra.
Blenheim
Renwicktown
Seddon
C. Campbell
Ward
Wharanui
Westport
C. Foulwind
Lyell Ra.
Buller Gorge
Inangahua Junction
Murchison
L. Rotoroa
L. Rotoiti
Wairau
Awatere
Kaikoura Ra.
Tapuaenuku 2885
Paparoa Ra.
Reefton
Victoria Ra.
Mt. Travers 2337
Spenser Mts.
Mt. Franklyn 2327
St. Arnaud Ra.
Molesworth
Clarence
Seaward Kaikouras
Manakau 2610
Kaikoura
Kaikoura Pen.
Runanga
Blackball
Grey
Ahaura
Kamatua
Amuri Pass
Hanmer
Waiau
Greymouth
Taramakau
Kumara
Kaimata
L. Brunner
Harper Pass
Hope Pass
L. Sumner
Mt. Ajax 1832
Culverden
Hurunui
Waiau
Parnassus
Hokitika
Kanieri
Jacksons
Otira Gorge
Arthur's Pass
Mt. Crossley 1872
Waikari
Scargill
Domett
Ross
Browning Pass
Mt. Murchison 2400
Waipara
Amberley
Sefton
Rangiora
Kaiapoi
Pegasus Bay
Wanganui
Abut Hd.
Harihari
Whataroa
Okarito
L. Mapourika
Gillespie Pt.
Whitcombe Pass
Lake Coleridge
L. Coleridge
Springfield
Sheffield
White-cliffs
Oxford
Belfast
Hornby
New Brighton
Christchurch
Riccarton
Mt. Arrowsmith 2795
Mt. Taylor
South B.
Rakaia
Darfield
Highbank
Rolleston
Sumner
Lyttelton 919
Lincoln
Banks Peninsula
Little River
Akaroa
Akaroa Harb.
Bruce B.
Tititira Hd.
Mt. Tasman 3497
Mt. Cook 3753
Hermitage
Two Thumb Ra.
Tasman
Methven
Mt. Somers
Teeston
Ellesmere
Southbridge
Open Bay Is.
Jackson
Jackson Hd.
Jackson B.
Okuru
Haast
Glenmary
Mt. Sefton 3050
L. Tekapo
Lake Tekapo
Fairlie
Geraldine
Hinds
Ashburton
Tinwald
Cascade Pt.
Haast Pass
L. Pukaki
Mackenzie Plains
Lake Pukaki
Burkes Pass
Winchester
Temuka
Pleasant Point
Canterbury Bight
Awarua Pt.
Awarua or Big B.
Mt. Aspiring 3035
Barrier Ra.
Benmore Pk. 1863
L. Ohau
Waitaki Plains
The Hunter Hills
Timaru
Yates Pt.
Milford Sd.
Mt. McKerrow 2756
Mt. Tutoko
Darran Mts.
Olivine Ra.
Earnslaw 2819
Richardson Mts.
Harris Mts.
Pisa Ra.
L. Hawea
Mt. St. Bathans 2087
Dunstan Mts.
Hawea Flat
Hawkdun Ra.
Kirkliston Ra.
Kurow
Hakataramea
Waimate
Waihao Downs
St. Andrews
Studholme Junction
Hunter
Bligh Sd.
George Sd.
FIORDLAND
McKinnon Pass
Wanaka
L. Wanaka
Arrowtown
Cromwell
Waitaki
Duntroon
Ngatapa
Tokarahi
Morven
Waihao
Waitaki
Caswell Sd.
Charles Sd.
NATIONAL
Eglinton
Glenorchy
Queenstown
Kawarau
Clyde
Naseby
Kyeburn
Windsor
Pukeuri
Oamaru
Thompson Sd.
Secretary I.
Doubtful Sd.
Daggs Sd.
NATIONAL PARK
Murchison Mts.
Mt. Lyall 1858
L. Te Anau
The Remarkables
Double Cone 2343
Alexandra
Rough Ridge
Ranfurly
Maheno
Hampden
Breaksea Sd.
Resolution I.
Dusky Sd.
Kepler Mts.
Te Anau
L. Manapouri
Mt. Tarn 2027
N. Mavora L.
Eyre Mts.
Garvie Mts.
Kingston
Athol
Roxburgh
Millers Flat
Middlemarch
Sutton
Dunback
Waikouaiti Downs
Waikouaiti
Palmerston
Chalky Inlet
Providence Pt.
Cameron Mts.
Caroline Pk. 1699
L. Poteriteri
Preservation Inlet
Puysegur Pt.
Kaherekoau Mts.
Hunter Mts.
Monowai
L. Monowai
L. Hauroko
Clifden
Orawia
Birchwood
Mossburn
Lumsden
Waimea Plain
Riversdale
Dipton
Waikaka
Umbrella Mts.
Beaumont
Lawrence
Waitahuna
Port Chalmers
Otago Harb.
Otago Pen.
C. Saunders
Dunedin
Allanton
St. Kilda
Green Island
Mosgiel
Te Waewae B.
Pahia Pt.
Monowai
Nightcaps
Otautau
Thornbury
Winton
Hedgehope
Gore
Mataura
Clinton
Kelso
Tapanui
Waipahi
Clinton
Milton
Stirling
Waihola
L. Waihola
Chalky Inlet
Colac
Riverton
Wallacetown
Makarewa
Waikiwi
Wairio
Edendale
Wyndham
Edievale
Balclutha
Kaitangata
Invercargill
South Invercargill
Woodlands
Fortrose
Tahakopa
Owaka
Nugget Pt.
Bluff
Toetoes
Bluff Harb.
Waipapa Pt.
Long Pt.
Chaslands Mistake
Foveaux Strait
Solander I.
Codfish I.
Mt. Anglem 980
Mt. Angle
Halfmoon Bay
Oban
Ruapuke I.
Mason B.
Doughboy B.
Paterson Inlet
Stewart Island
Port Pegasus
Southwest C.

Westland Bight

WESTLAND

CANTERBURY

OTAGO

SOUTHLAND

Canterbury Plains

Pegasus Bay

167 168 169 170 171 172 173 174

41 42 43 44 45 46 47

ft m
9000 3000
6000 2000
3000 1000
1200 400
600 200
0 0
200 600
600 2000
2000 6000
4000 12000
m ft

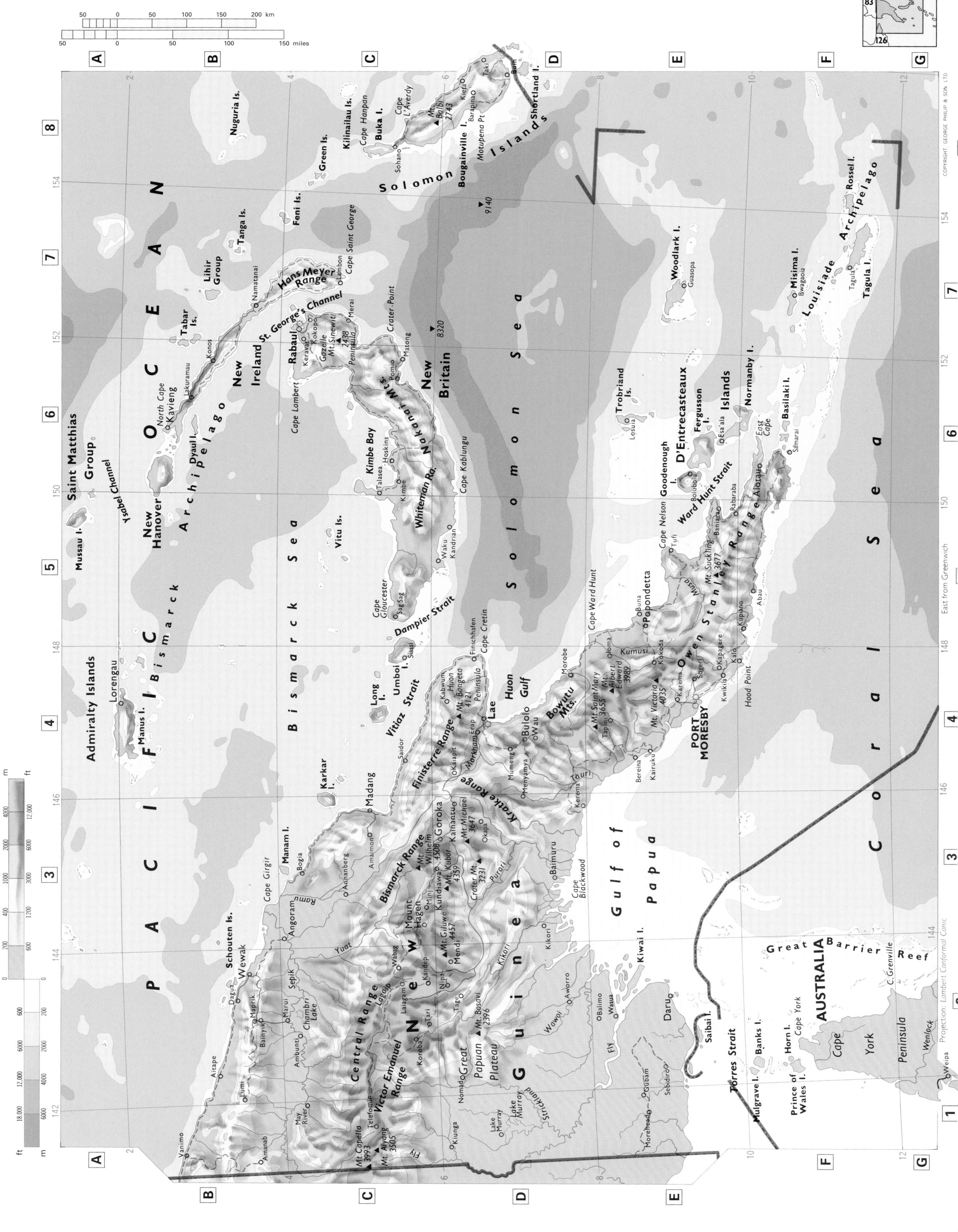

50 0 50 100 150 200 km
50 0 50 100 150 miles

83
126

PACIFIC OCEAN

Saint Matthias Group
Mussau I.
Ysabel Channel
New Hanover
North Cape
Kavieng
Lakuramau
Konos
New Ireland
Dyaul I.
Cape Lambert
Admiralty Islands
Lorengau
Manus I.
Bismarck Archipelago
Bismarck Sea
Schouten Is.
Manam I.
Karkar I.
Madang
Saidor
Finisterre Range
Kratke Range
Bogia
Angoram
Ramu
Sepik
Yuat
Wewak
Dagua
Maprik
Marui
Bainyik
Aitape
Vanimo
Amanab
May River
Telefomin
Mt Capella 3993
Mt Aiyang 3505
Fly
Central Range
Victor Emanuel Range
Ambunti
Chambri Lake
Lumi
NEW GUINEA
Papuan Great Plateau
Nomad
Kiunga
Lake Murray
Strickland
Fly
Morehead
Sebdiro
Daru
Kiwai I.
Gulf of Papua
Cape Blackwood
Kikori
Wabag
Laiagam
Wapenamanda
Mendi
Mt Giluwe 4457
Mt Hagen 4508
Mount Hagen
Bismarck Range
Mt Wilhelm 4508
Kainantu
Goroka
Kundiawa
Mt Michael 3647
Crater Mt. 3231
Mt Kubor 4359
Kerowagi
Tari
Koroba
Kandep
Nipa
Tago
Mendi
Kokori
Baimuru
Kerema
Tauri
Berena
Kairuku
Wau
Bulolo
Bowutu Mts.
Mt Saint Mary 3655
Mt Albert Edward 3990
Owen Stanley Range
Mt Victoria 4035
Mt Suckling 3677
PORT MORESBY
Hood Point
Kupiano
Abau
Kwikila
Amazon Bay
Aroma
Kaiasu
Kwoda
Kokoda
Popondetta
Buna
Cape Nelson
Tufi
Cape Ward Hunt
Oro Bay
D'Entrecasteaux Islands
Goodenough I.
Fergusson I.
Normanby I.
Ferguson I.
Trobriand Is.
Losuia
Kiriwina
Esa'ala
East Cape
Alotau
Basilaki I.
Samarai
Woodlark I.
Guasopa
Misima I.
Bwagaoia
Louisiade Archipelago
Tagula I.
Rossel I.
Coral Sea
AUSTRALIA
Great Barrier Reef
Cape York
York Peninsula
C. Grenville
Weipa
Wenlock
Prince of Wales I.
Horn I.
Banks I.
Mulgrave I.
Saibai I.
Torres Strait

Solomon Islands
Nuguria Is.
Green Is.
Kilinailau Is.
Buka I.
Cape Hanpan
Cape L'Averdy
Kieta
Bougainville I.
Mt Balbi 2743
Sohano
Shortland I.
Buin
Feni Is.
Tanga Is.
Lihir Group
Tabar Is.
Namatanai
Hans Meyer Range
St George's Channel
Cape Saint George
Rabaul
Gazelle Peninsula
Mt Sinewit 2438
Kokopo
Keravat
Merai
Crater Point
Matong
Romo
Talasea
Kimbe Bay
Hoskins
Kimbe
Nakanai Mts.
Whiteman Ra.
New Britain
Cape Kablungu
Cape Gloucester
Sag Sag
Dampier Strait
Vitu Is.
Cape Cretin
Finschhafen
Huon Peninsula
Huon Gulf
Lae
Markham
Erap
Mumeng
Menyamya
Siassi
Umboi I.
Long I.
Vitiaz Strait
Bismarck Sea

8320
9140

Solomon Sea

PAPUA NEW GUINEA
COPYRIGHT GEORGE PHILIP & SON LTD
East from Greenwich
Projection: Lambert Conformal Conic

m   ft
4000 12,000
2000 6000
1000 3000
400 1200
200 600
0   0
200 600
2000 6000
4000 12,000
6000 18,000
m   ft

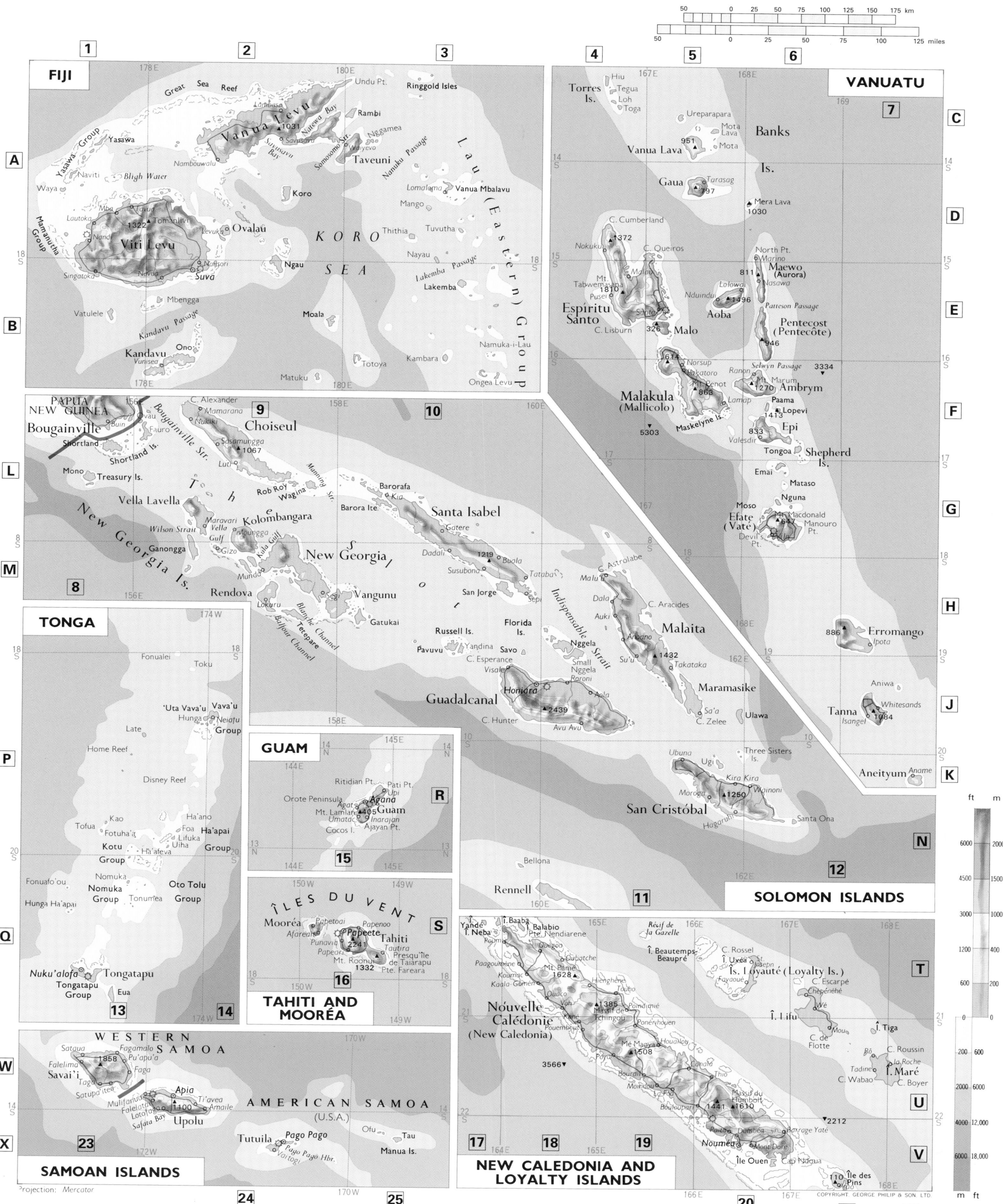

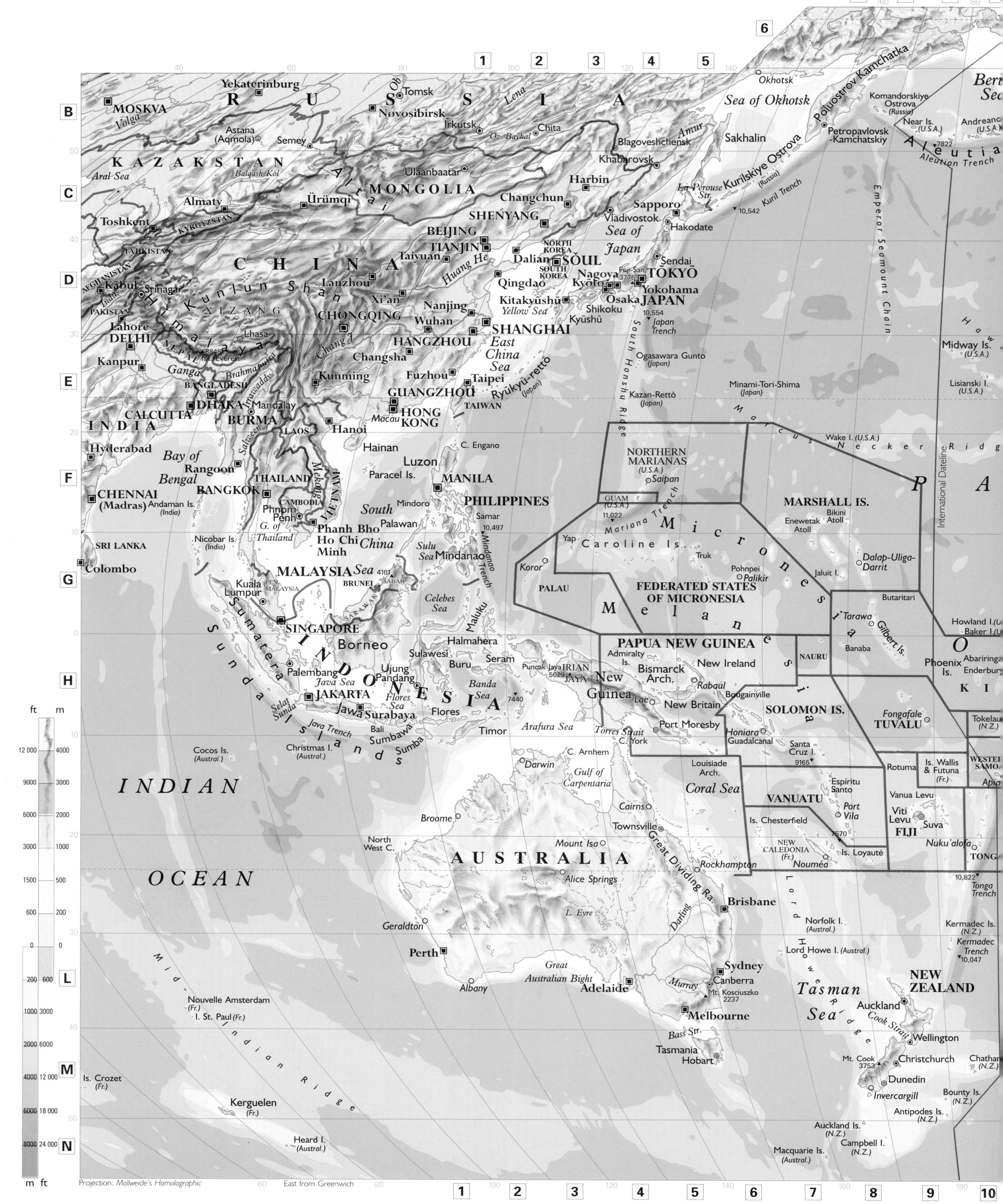

Grid references (top)
6 7 8 9 10
1 2 3 4 5

B
C
D
E
F
G
H
L
M
N

Map labels

Russia / Central Asia
MOSKVA, Volga, Yekaterinburg, Tomsk, Novosibirsk, Irkutsk, Oz. Baykal, Chita, R U S S I A, Lena, Ob, Amur, Blagoveshchensk, Khabarovsk, Sakhalin, Okhotsk, Sea of Okhotsk, Poluostrov Kamchatka, Komandorskiye Ostrova (Russia), Petropavlovsk-Kamchatskiy, Near Is. (U.S.A.), Andreano (U.S.A.), Aleutian, Aleutian Trench, 7822, Bering Sea

KAZAKSTAN, Astana (Aqmola), Semey, Aral Sea, Balqash Köl, Altai, MONGOLIA, Ulaanbaatar, Almaty, Toshkent, KYRGYZSTAN, TAJIKISTAN, AFGHANISTAN, Kabul, PAKISTAN, Srinagar, Lahore, DELHI, Kanpur, Kunlun Shan, XIZANG, Himalaya, NEPAL, Lhasa, Mt. Everest 8848, Ganga, Brahmaputra, INDIA, Hyderabad, CALCUTTA, DHAKA, BANGLADESH, Irrawaddy, Mandalay, BURMA, Rangoon, Bay of Bengal, CHENNAI (Madras), SRI LANKA, Colombo, Andaman Is. (India), Nicobar Is. (India)

China / East Asia
C H I N A, Ürümqi, Lanzhou, Xi'an, CHONGQING, Changsha, Kunming, Taiyuan, BEIJING, TIANJIN, SHENYANG, Changchun, Harbin, Huang He, Chang Jiang, Nanjing, Wuhan, HANGZHOU, SHANGHAI, Yellow Sea, Qingdao, Dalian, NORTH KOREA, SOUTH KOREA, SŎUL, Vladivostok, Hakodate, Sapporo, Sea of Japan, Sendai, TOKYO, Yokohama, JAPAN, Nagoya, Kyoto, Osaka, Fuji-San 3776, Shikoku, Kyūshū, Kitakyushu, Fuzhou, Taipei, TAIWAN, Ryūkyū-rettō (Japan), East China Sea, GUANGZHOU, HONG KONG, Macau, Hainan, Hanoi, LAOS, THAILAND, BANGKOK, VIETNAM, CAMBODIA, Phnom Penh, Phanh Bho Ho Chi Minh, G. of Thailand, Mekong, Salween

Philippines / SE Asia
Luzon, Paracel Is., MANILA, Mindoro, Samar, PHILIPPINES, Palawan, Mindanao, Sulu Sea, South China Sea, 4101, MALAYSIA, Kuala Lumpur, PEN. MALAYSIA, SINGAPORE, BRUNEI, SARAWAK, SABAH, Borneo, Sumatera, Palembang, Ujung Pandang, JAKARTA, Java Sea, Jawa, Surabaya, Bali, Sumbawa, Sumba, Flores, Flores Sea, INDONESIA, Sulawesi, Buru, Seram, Celebes Sea, Maluku, Halmahera, Banda Sea, 7440, Timor, Sunda Islands, Selat Sunda, Java Trench, C. Engano

Australia
Arafura Sea, Torres Strait, C. York, C. Arnhem, Gulf of Carpentaria, Darwin, Broome, North West C., A U S T R A L I A, Mount Isa, Cairns, Townsville, Rockhampton, Alice Springs, L. Eyre, Great Australian Bight, Geraldton, Perth, Albany, Darling, Murray, Great Dividing Ra., Brisbane, Sydney, Canberra, Mt. Kosciuszko 2237, Adelaide, Melbourne, Bass Str., Tasmania, Hobart, Cocos Is. (Austral.), Christmas I. (Austral.)

Oceania
NORTHERN MARIANAS (U.S.A.), Saipan, GUAM (U.S.A.) 11,022, Mariana Trench, Yap, Koror, PALAU, Caroline Is., Micronesia, Truk, FEDERATED STATES OF MICRONESIA, Pohnpei, Palikir, Jaluit I., MARSHALL IS., Bikini Atoll, Enewetak Atoll, Dalap-Uliga-Darrit, Wake I. (U.S.A.), Necker Ridge, Minami-Tori-Shima (Japan), Kazan-Rettō (Japan), Ogasawara Gunto (Japan), South Honshu Ridge, Japan Trench 10,554, Marcus Ridge, Midway Is. (U.S.A.), Lisianski I. (U.S.A.), Emperor Seamount Chain, Kuril Trench 10,542, Kuril'skiye Ostrova (Russia), La Pérouse Str., International Dateline, PAPUA NEW GUINEA, Admiralty Is., Bismarck Arch., New Ireland, New Guinea, IRIAN JAYA, Puncak Jaya 5029, Lae, Rabaul, New Britain, Bougainville, Port Moresby, Louisiade Arch., Coral Sea, SOLOMON IS., Honiara, Guadalcanal, Santa Cruz I. 9165, VANUATU, Espíritu Santo, Port Vila, Is. Chesterfield, NEW CALEDONIA (Fr.), Nouméa, Is. Loyauté, 7670, NAURU, Butaritari, Tarawa, Banaba, Gilbert Is., Melanesia, Rotuma, Is. Wallis & Futuna (Fr.), Vanua Levu, Viti Levu, FIJI, Suva, Nuku'alofa, WESTERN SAMOA, Apia, Fongafale, TUVALU, Tokelau (N.Z.), KIRIBATI, Phoenix Is., Abariringa, Enderbury, Howland I. (U.S.), Baker I. (U.S.), P A C I F I C   O C E A N, Norfolk I. (Austral.), Lord Howe I. (Austral.), Kermadec Is. (N.Z.), Kermadec Trench 10,047, Tonga Trench 10,822, TONGA, Lord Howe Rise, NEW ZEALAND, Auckland, Cook Strait, Wellington, Christchurch, Chatham Is. (N.Z.), Mt. Cook 3753, Dunedin, Invercargill, Bounty Is. (N.Z.), Antipodes Is. (N.Z.), Auckland Is. (N.Z.), Campbell I. (N.Z.), Macquarie Is. (Austral.), Tasman Sea, Tasman Rise

Indian Ocean
INDIAN OCEAN, Mid-Indian Ridge, Nouvelle Amsterdam (Fr.), I. St. Paul (Fr.), Is. Crozet (Fr.), Kerguelen (Fr.), Heard I. (Austral.)

Elevation scale (left)
ft / m
12 000 / 4000
9000 / 3000
6000 / 2000
3000 / 1000
1500 / 500
600 / 200
0 / 0
200 / 600
1000 / 3000
2000 / 6000
4000 / 12 000
6000 / 18 000
8000 / 24 000
m ft

Projection: Mollweide's Homolographic
East from Greenwich

Grid references (bottom)
1 2 3 4 5 6 7 8 9 10

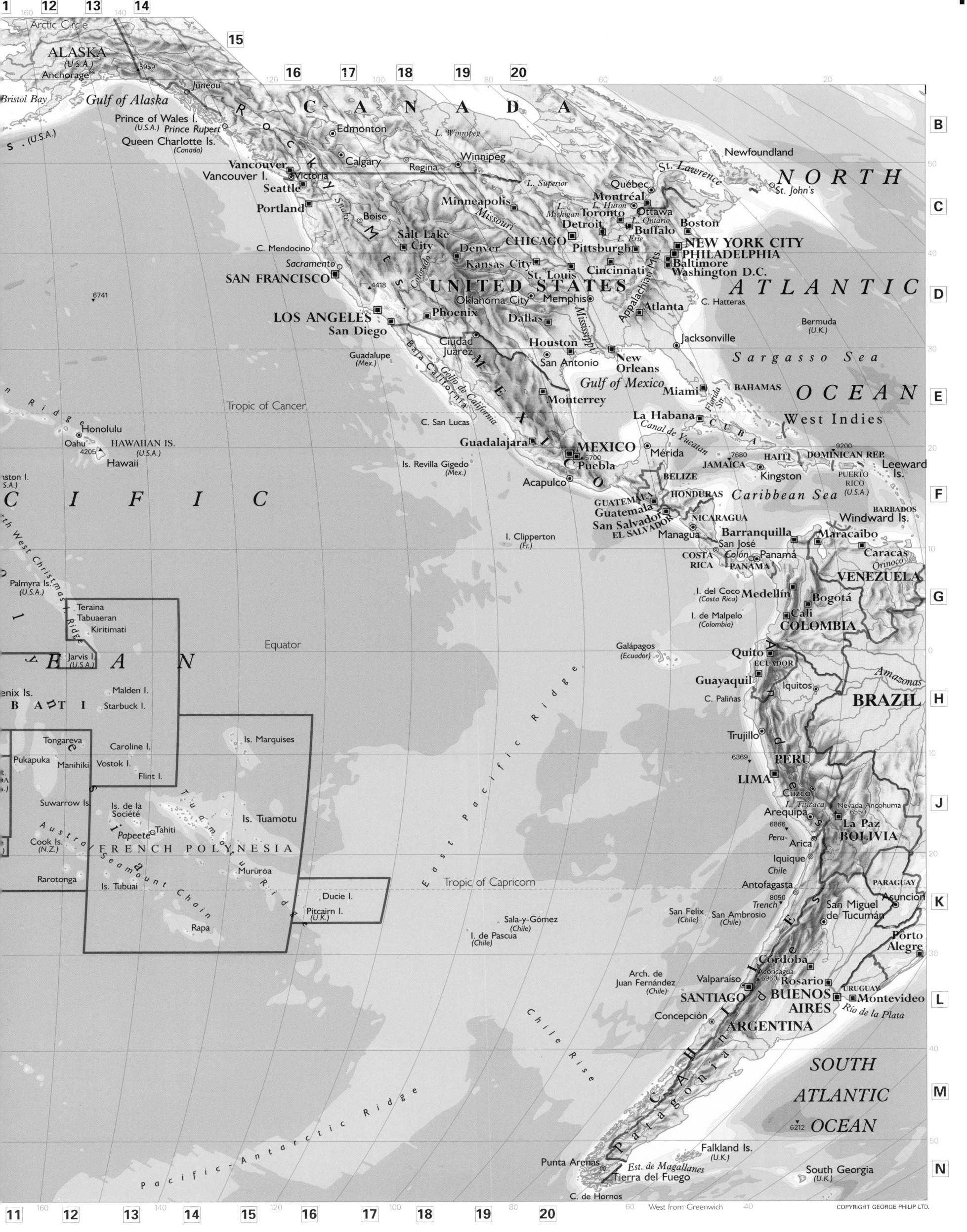

Arctic Circle

ALASKA
(U.S.A.)
Anchorage

Bristol Bay

Gulf of Alaska

Juneau

Prince of Wales I.
(U.S.A.) Prince Rupert
Queen Charlotte Is.
(Canada)

C A N A D A

Edmonton

Calgary

L. Winnipeg

Winnipeg

Newfoundland

N O R T H

Vancouver
Vancouver I.
Victoria
Seattle
Portland

Regina

Boise

St. Lawrence

Québec

St. John's

Minneapolis
Salt Lake
City
Denver
Sacramento

L. Superior

L. Michigan

Montréal
Ottawa
Toronto
Detroit
L. Huron
L. Ontario
L. Erie

Boston

Buffalo

SAN FRANCISCO

CHICAGO
Kansas City

Pittsburgh

Cincinnati

NEW YORK CITY
PHILADELPHIA
Baltimore
Washington D.C.

A T L A N T I C

LOS ANGELES
San Diego

UNITED STATES
Oklahoma City
Phoenix
Dallas

St. Louis
Memphis

Atlanta

C. Hatteras

Colorado

Houston

Ciudad
Juárez

San Antonio

New
Orleans

Jacksonville

Bermuda
(U.K.)

Sargasso Sea

Guadalupe
(Mex.)

Gulf of Mexico
Miami

BAHAMAS

O C E A N

Tropic of Cancer

C. San Lucas

Monterrey

La Habana

CUBA

West Indies

Honolulu
Oahu
HAWAIIAN IS.
(U.S.A.)
Hawaii

Guadalajara

MEXICO
Puebla

Mérida

Canal de Yucatán

HAITI

DOMINICAN REP.

Leeward
Is.

PUERTO
RICO
(U.S.A.)

C I F I C

Is. Revilla Gigedo
(Mex.)

Acapulco

BELIZE

JAMAICA
Kingston

GUATEMALA
Guatemala
San Salvador
EL SALVADOR

HONDURAS
NICARAGUA

Caribbean Sea

BARBADOS
Windward Is.

I. Clipperton
(Fr.)

Managua

Barranquilla

Maracaibo

Caracas

COSTA
RICA

San José
Colón Panamá
PANAMA

VENEZUELA

B A N

Equator

I. del Coco
(Costa Rica)

I. de Malpelo
(Colombia)

Galápagos
(Ecuador)

Medellín

Bogotá
Cali
COLOMBIA

Quito
ECUADOR

Guayaquil
C. Paliñas

Iquitos

Amazonas

BRAZIL

Malden I.
Starbuck I.

Trujillo

Tongareva
Pukapuka
Manihiki

Caroline I.
Vostok I.
Flint I.

Is. Marquises

PERU

Suwarrow Is.

LIMA

Cuzco
L. Titicaca

Nevada Ancohuma
6550

Cook Is.
(N.Z.)

Is. de la
Société
Papeete Tahiti

Is. Tuamotu

Arequipa

Peru-

La Paz
BOLIVIA

Rarotonga

Is. Tubuai

FRENCH POLYNESIA

Muroroa

Arica

Iquique
Chile

Tropic of Capricorn

Antofagasta

PARAGUAY

Ducie I.

San Felix
(Chile)

San Ambrosio
(Chile)

San Miguel
de Tucumán

Asunción

Pitcairn I.
(U.K.)

Sala-y-Gómez
(Chile)

Trench

Rapa

I. de Pascua
(Chile)

Porto
Alegre

Arch. de
Juan Fernández
(Chile)

Córdoba
Aconcagua
Valparaíso
Rosario

URUGUAY

SANTIAGO
BUENOS
AIRES
Concepción
ARGENTINA

Montevideo
Río de la Plata

Chile Rise

SOUTH

ATLANTIC

Pacific-Antarctic Ridge

OCEAN

Punta Arenas
Est. de Magallanes
Tierra del Fuego

Falkland Is.
(U.K.)

South Georgia
(U.K.)

C. de Hornos

West from Greenwich

COPYRIGHT GEORGE PHILIP LTD.

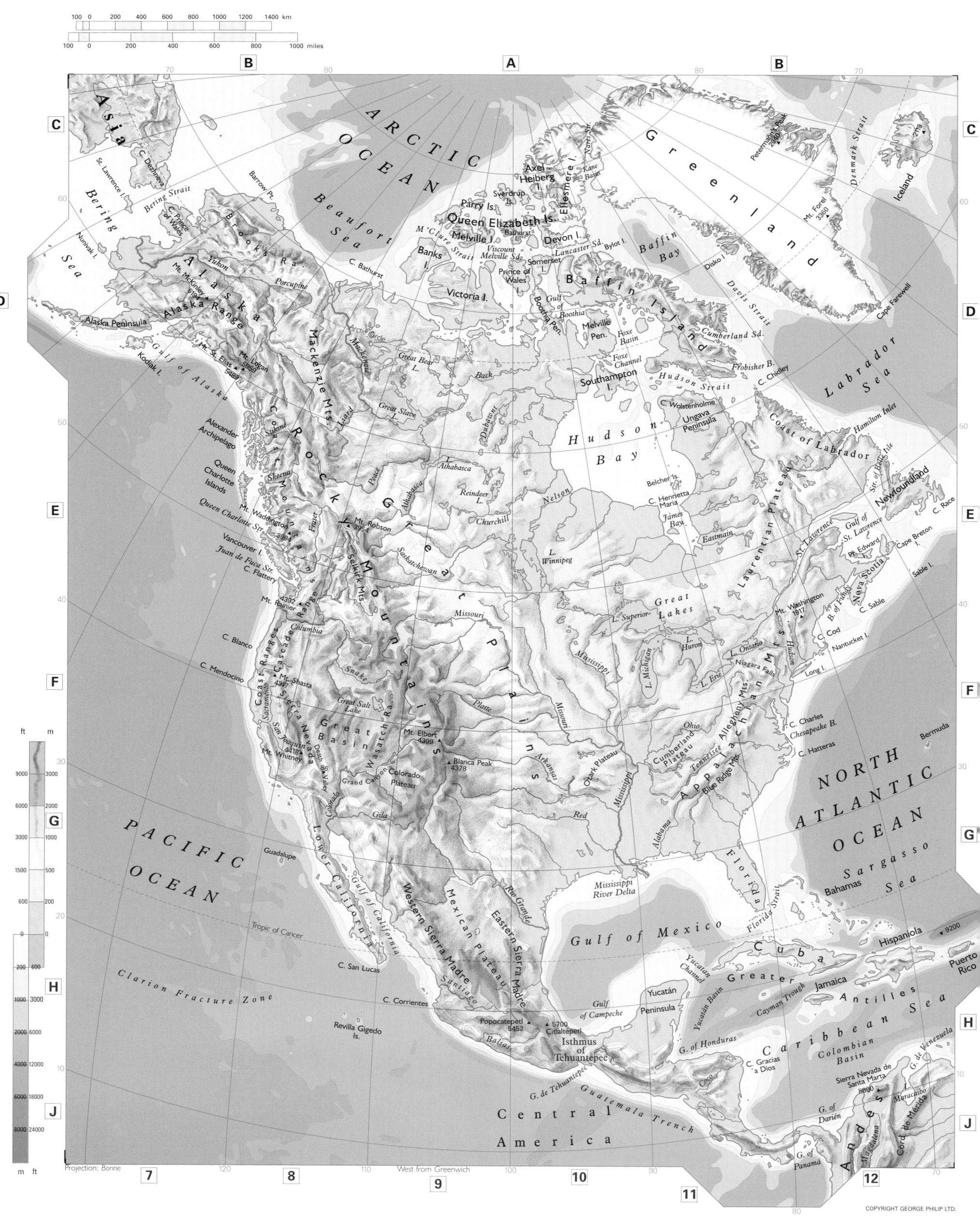

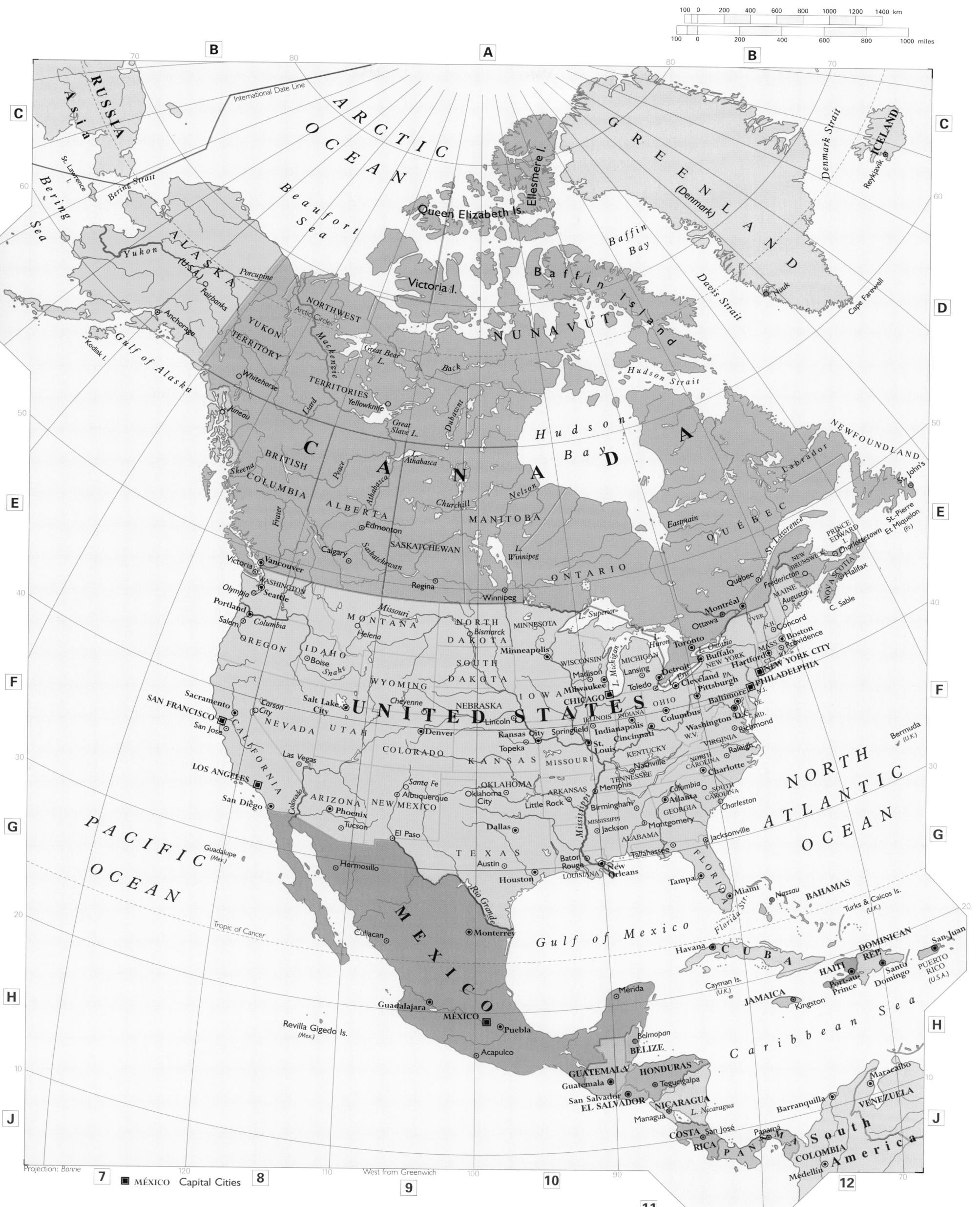

100 0 100 200 300 400 500 600 km
100 0 100 200 300 400 miles

PACIFIC OCEAN

ALASKA
Anchorage
Wasilla
Palmer
Glenallen
Valdez
Cordova
Soldotna
Seward
Kenai
Homer
Cook Inlet

Fairbanks
Delta Junction
Tanana
Tok
Eagle
Dawson
Yukon

ALASKA RANGE
Mt. Sanford 4940
Mt. Lucania 5226
Mt. Logan 5959
Mt. St. Elias 5489
Wrangell Mts.
St. Elias Mts.
Yakutat
Mt. Fairweather 4663

YUKON TERRITORY
Carmacks
Ross River
Whitehorse
Haines Junction
Skagway
Selwyn Mts.
Faro
Teslin
Watson Lake

Chichagof I.
Alexander Archipelago
Sitka
Baranof I.
Juneau
Admiralty I.
Petersburg
Wrangell
Ketchikan
Metlakatla
Prince of Wales I.

3959

Queen Charlotte Is.
Graham I.
Moresby I.
Hecate Str.
Dixon Entrance

BRITISH COLUMBIA
Terrace
Kitimat
Prince Rupert
Bella Coola
Port McNeill
Vancouver I.
Campbell River
Courtenay
Port Alberni
Nanaimo
VANCOUVER
Victoria
Juan de Fuca Str.
C. Flattery

Mackenzie Mountains
Norman Wells
Fort Simpson
Fort Liard
Fort Nelson
Fort St. John
Dawson Creek
Chetwynd
Mackenzie
Williston L.
Prince George
Quesnel
Williams Lake
Rocky Mountains
Mt. Robson 3954
Jasper 1146
Yellowhead Pass
Revelstoke
Kamloops
Merritt
Kelowna
Penticton
Nelson
Cranbrook

NORTHWEST TERRITORIES
Great Bear L.
Echo Bay
Déline
Fort Good Hope
Franklin Mts.
1462
Wrigley
Mackenzie
Fort Providence
Rae
Yellowknife
Great Slave L.
Hay River
Fort Resolution
Pine Point
Fort Smith
Caribou Mts. 1036
High Level
Rainbow Lake

Old Crow
Fort McPherson
Tsiigehtchic
Inuvik
Tuktoyaktuk
Aklavik

Amundsen Gulf
Holman
Paulatuk
Darnley Bay
Horton
Prince Albert Sd.
Dolphin and Union Str.
Coronation Gulf
Kugluktuk
Coppermine
Burnside
Contwoyto L.
Point L.

Banks Island 747

Victoria Island
Prince Albert Pen.
Wollaston Pen.
Baring I.

Viscount Melville Sound
McClintock Channel
Prince of Wales I.
Somerset I.
Franklin Str.
Boothia Peninsula 573
Bathurst Inlet
MacAlpine L.
Queen Maud Gulf
Adelaide Pen.
King William I.
Gjoa Haven
Taloyoak
Chantrey Inlet

Kent Pen.
Ikaluktutiak
Bathurst Inlet

MANITOBA
Thompson
Gillam
Churchill
Gods L.
Norway House
Lake Winnipeg
Grand Rapids
The Pas
Flin Flon
Cedar L.
L. Winnipegosis
Swan River
Dauphin 831
Portage La Prairie
WINNIPEG
Selkirk
Brandon
Virden
Morden
Winkler

SASKATCHEWAN
Uranium City
Lake Athabasca
Fort Chipewyan
Fond-du-Lac
L. Clair
Wollaston L.
Cree L.
Reindeer Lake
Brochet
La Loche
La Ronge
Churchill
Flin Flon
Meadow Lake
Prince Albert
North Battleford
Saskatoon
Melfort
Tisdale
Humboldt
Biggar
Kindersley
Rosetown
Kerrobert
Watrous
Canora
Yorkton
Melville
Regina
Moose Jaw
Swift Current
Medicine Hat
Weyburn
Estevan
Assiniboia

ALBERTA
Fort McMurray
Fort Mackay
Peace River
High Prairie
Slave Lake
Lesser Slave L.
Grande Prairie
Whitecourt
Edson
Edmonton
Wetaskiwin
Lacombe
Red Deer
Camrose
Stettler
Vegreville
Lloydminster
Hanna
Drumheller
Brooks
Calgary
Airdrie
Banff
High River
Fort Macleod
Lethbridge
Cardston

Frobisher L.
Churchill L.

PACIFIC OCEAN

ft m
9000 3000
6000 2000
4500 1500
3000 1000
1200 400
600 200
0 0
200 600
2000 6000
4000 12000
m ft

Projection: Bonne

ALASKA
1:24 000 000
100 0 100 200 300 400 500 600 km
100 0 100 200 300 400 miles

CHUKCHI SEA
Barrow
Prudhoe Bay
Point Hope
Colville
Brooks Range 2699
Kotzebue
Seward Pen.
Fort Yukon
Circle
Dawson
Nome
Norton Sound
Galena
ALASKA (U.S.A.)
Fairbanks
Anderson
Fort Yukon
Mt. McKinley 6194
Tok
Unalakleet
Emmonak
Hooper Bay
Bethel
Nunivak I.
Kuskokwim Bay
Anchorage
Valdez
Kenai
Seward
Homer
Mt. Logan 5959
Whitehorse
Skagway
Juneau
Dillingham 2047
Bristol Bay
Iliamna L.
Kodiak
Kodiak I.
Alexander Archipelago
Sitka
Petersburg
Ketchikan
Prince Rupert
Queen Charlotte Is.
GULF OF ALASKA

RUSSIA
Koryakskoye Nagorye
Anadyr
Uelen
Bering Str.
Providenija
Anadyrski Zaliv
Ugolnyj
Ossora
O. Karaginskij 4079
BERING SEA
St. Lawrence I.
St. Matthew I.
Pribilof Is.

CANADA

ALEUTIAN
Near Is.
Rat Is.
Attu I. 7822
Amchitka I.
Adak I.
Atka I.
Amlia I.
Andreanof Is.
Unalaska
Dutch Harbor
Umnak I.
Unimak I.
Shumagin Is.
Alaska Peninsula

PACIFIC OCEAN
West from Greenwich

WASHINGTON
SEATTLE
Tacoma
Olympia
Everett
Bellingham
Victoria
Aberdeen
Longview
Vancouver
Yakima
Mt. Adams 3751
Spokane
Coeur d'Alene
Sandpoint

MONTANA
Havre
Glasgow
Fort Peck L.
Lewistown
Miles City
Glendive
Milk
Missouri
Yellowstone
Powder

NORTH DAKOTA
Williston
Minot
Devils Lake
Grand Forks
Dickinson
Bismarck
Jamestown
Fargo
Moorhead

SOUTH DAKOTA
Mobridge
Aberdeen
Pierre
Rapid City
Black Hills 2207
Huron
Brookings
Mitchell
Hot Springs
Chadron
Oahe L.
Cheyenne
White
Niobrara

NEBRASKA
Alliance
Scottsbluff
North Platte
Grand Island
Sterling
Chadron

MINNESOTA
Bemidji
Brainerd
Hibbing
Virginia
Duluth
St. Cloud
MINNEAPOLIS
ST. PAUL
Mankato
Rochester
Albert Lea
Austin
WISCONSIN

IOWA
Sioux City
Sioux Falls
Yankton
Fort Dodge
Mason City
Waterloo
Cedar Rapids
Des Moines
Omaha
Council Bluffs
Dubuque
La Crosse

UNITED STATES

Lake Superior
L. of the Woods
Kenora
Dryden
Fort Frances
Thief River Falls
Red L.
Sioux Lookout
Lac Seul
Rainy L.
English River

Gods L.
Island L.
Sandy L.
Trout L.
Red Lake

Cedar Rapids

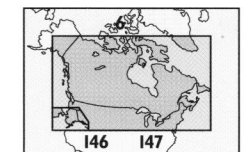

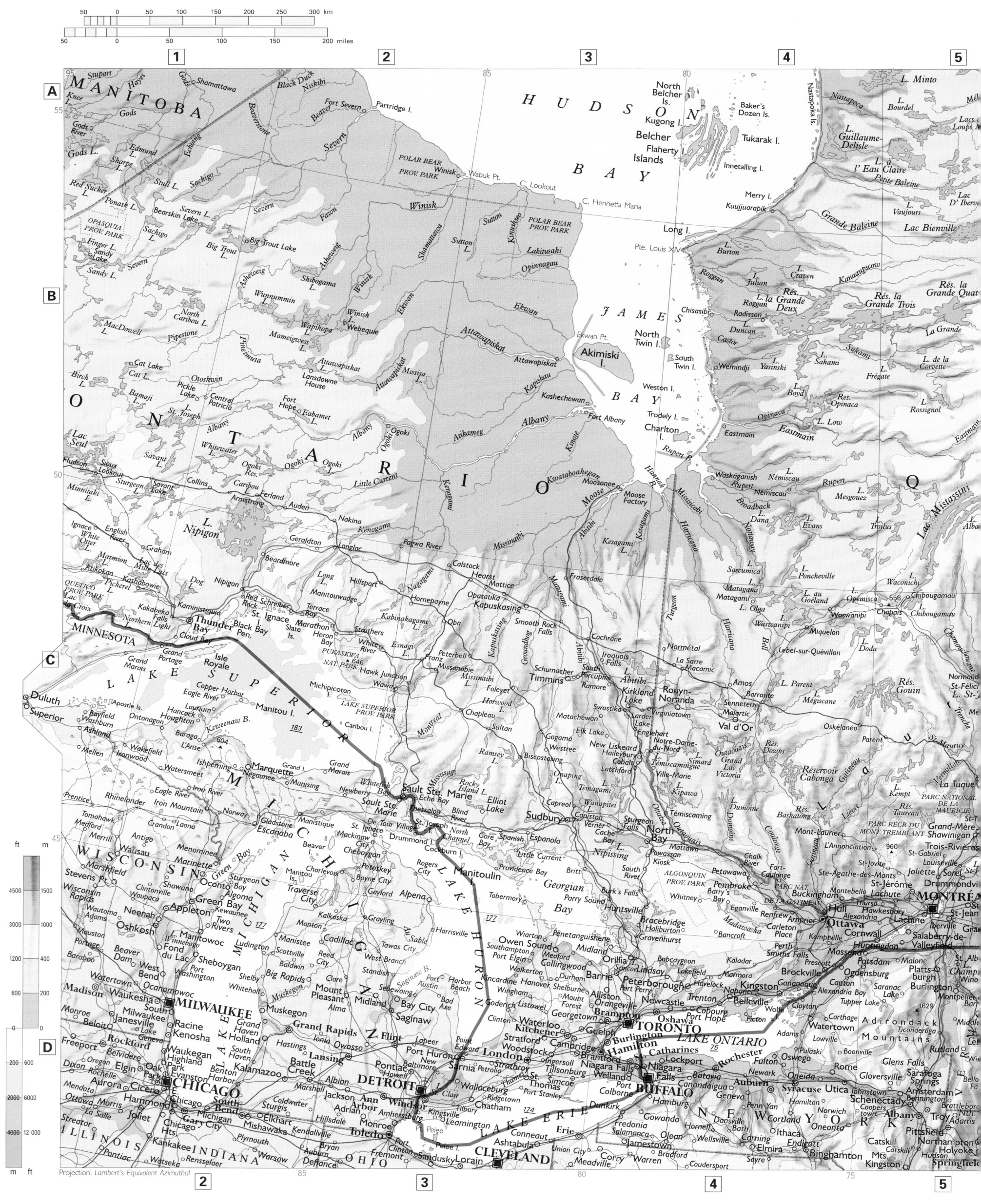

COPYRIGHT GEORGE PHILIP LTD.

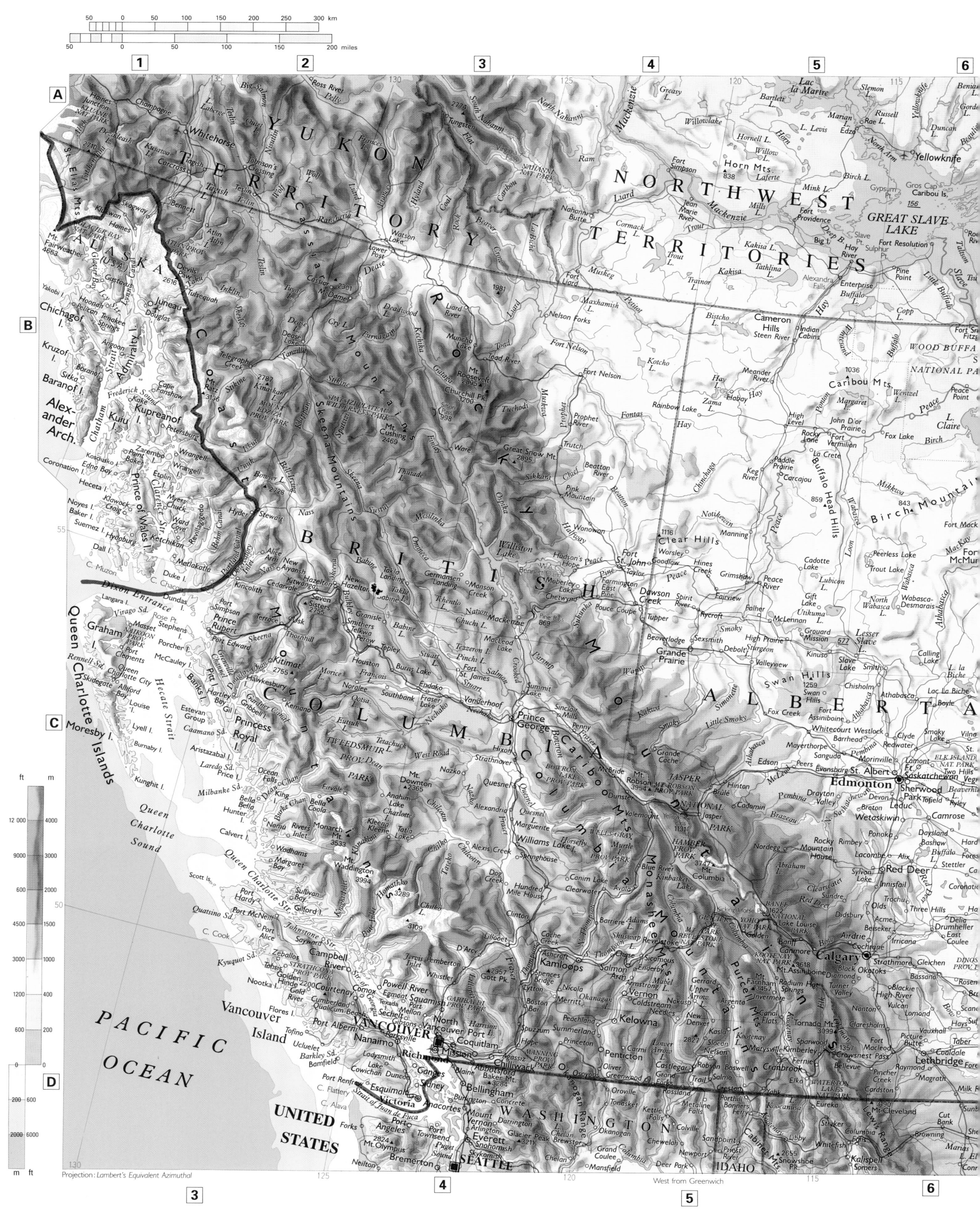

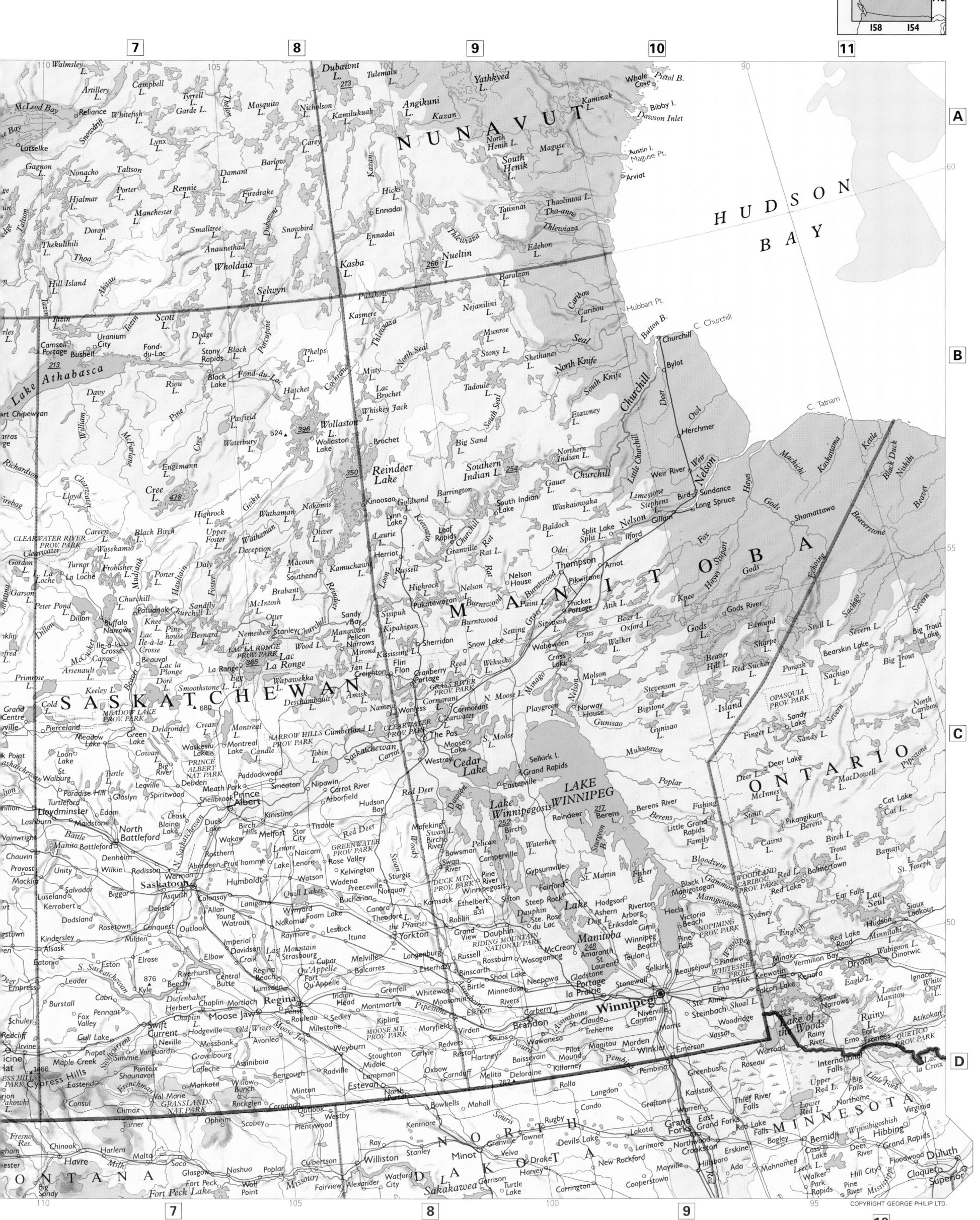

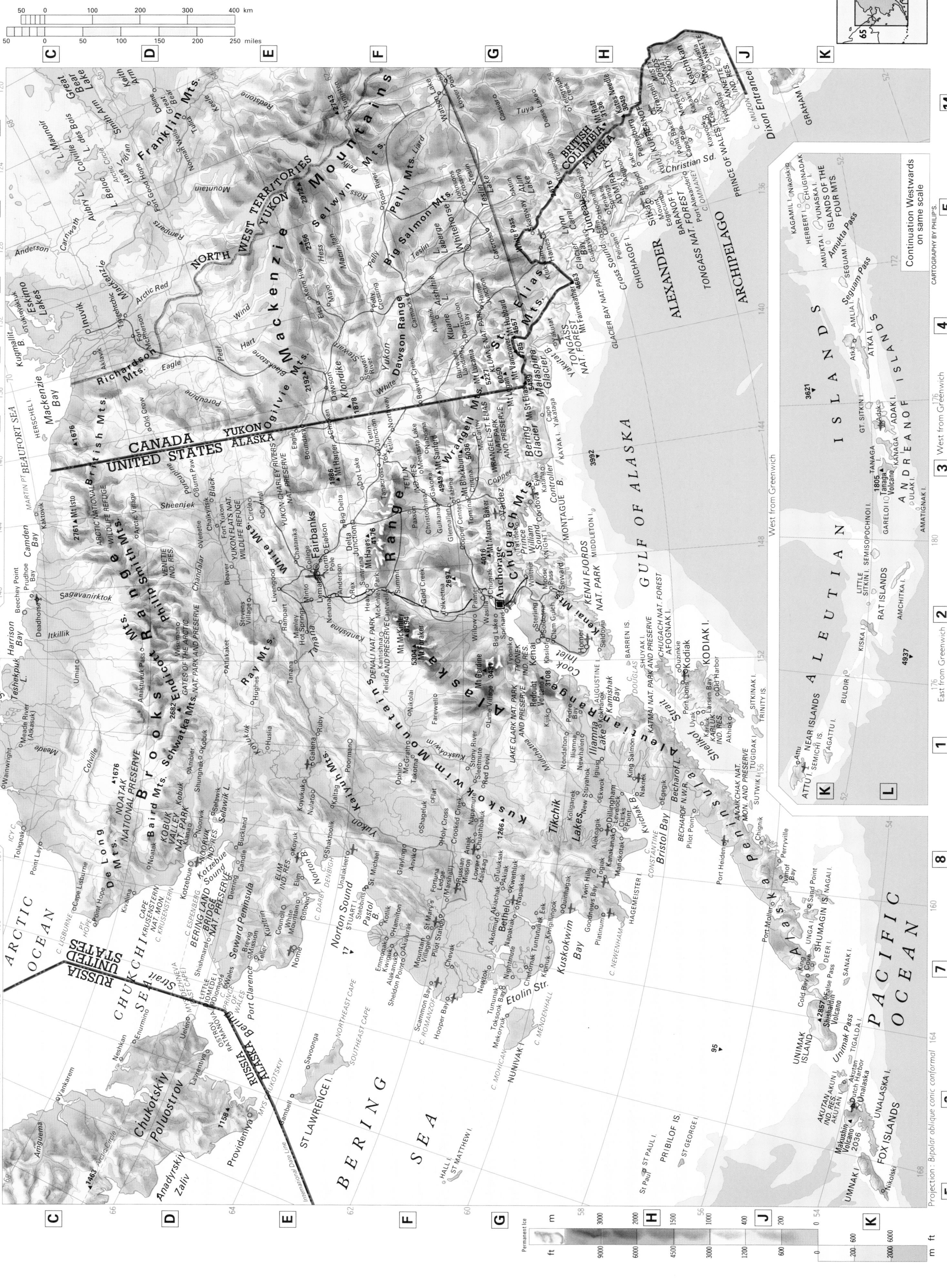

50 0 100 200 300 400 km
50 0 50 100 150 200 250 miles

CANADA
UNITED STATES
YUKON
ALASKA

BRITISH COLUMBIA
ALASKA

NORTH WEST TERRITORIES

Yukon Mountains
Mackenzie Mountains
Selwyn Mts.
Pelly Mts.
Big Salmon Mts.
Franklin Mts.
Richardson Mts.
Ogilvie Mts.
Dawson Range
Wrangell Mts.
St Elias Mts.
Chugach Mts.
Kenai Mts.
Alaska Range
Brooks Range
Endicott Mts.
Philip Smith Mts.
Baird Mts.
Schwatka Mts.
De Long Mts.
Ray Mts.
White Mts.
Kuskokwim Mountains
Kaiyuh Mts.
Aleutian Range

BEAUFORT SEA
ARCTIC OCEAN
CHUKCHI SEA
BERING SEA
GULF OF ALASKA
PACIFIC OCEAN

RUSSIA
UNITED STATES
Chukotskiy Poluostrov
Anadyrskiy Zaliv

Seward Peninsula
Norton Sound
Bristol Bay
Kuskokwim Bay
Cook Inlet
Prince William Sound

Fairbanks
Anchorage
Whitehorse
Juneau
Ketchikan
Barrow
Prudhoe Bay
Nome
Bethel
Kodiak
Valdez

Mt McKinley 6194
Mt Hayes 4176

St Lawrence I.
Nunivak I.
St Matthew I.
Nunivak I.
Kodiak I.
Afognak I.
Prince of Wales
Admiralty I.
Baranof I.
Chichagof I.

ALEXANDER ARCHIPELAGO
Tongass Nat. Forest
Chugach Nat. Forest
Alaska Peninsula
Shumagin Is.
Fox Islands
Unimak Island
Unalaska I.

Denali Nat. Park
Gates of the Arctic Nat. Park and Preserve
Noatak National Preserve
Kobuk Valley Nat. Park
Arctic National Wildlife Refuge
Yukon Flats Nat. Wildlife Refuge
Yukon-Charley Rivers Nat. Preserve
Wrangell-St Elias Nat. Park and Preserve
Kluane Nat. Park
Glacier Bay Nat. Park
Kenai Fjords Nat. Park
Lake Clark Nat. Park and Preserve
Katmai Nat. Park and Preserve
Aniakchak Nat. Mon. and Preserve
Becharof N.W.R.

ALEUTIAN ISLANDS
Continuation Westwards on same scale

NEAR ISLANDS
RAT ISLANDS
ANDREANOF ISLANDS
ISLANDS OF THE FOUR MTS
Attu I.
Kiska I.
Adak I.
Atka I.
Tanaga
Amchitka I.
Amukta Pass
Seguam Pass

West from Greenwich
East from Greenwich

CARTOGRAPHY BY PHILIP'S
Projection: Bipolar oblique conic conformal

Permanent Ice
m
ft
9000 6000 3000 2000 1500 600 200 0
ft
6000 4500 3000 1200 600 0

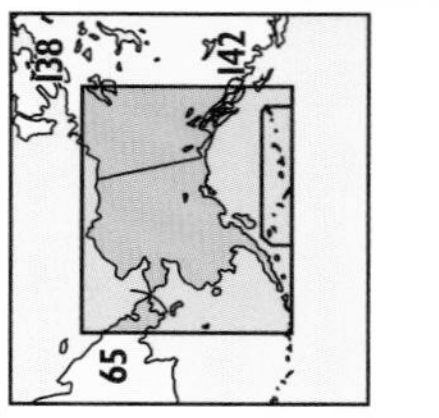

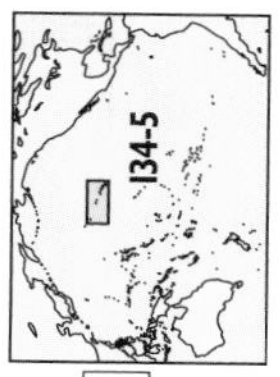

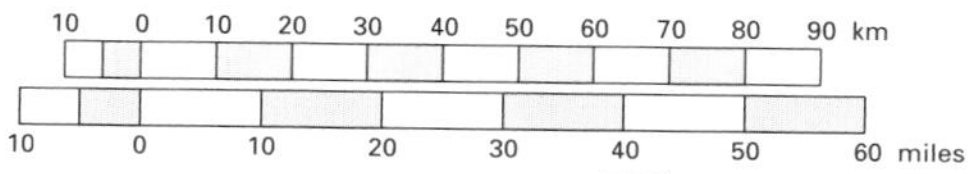

10 0 10 20 30 40 50 60 70 80 90 km

10 0 10 20 30 40 50 60 miles

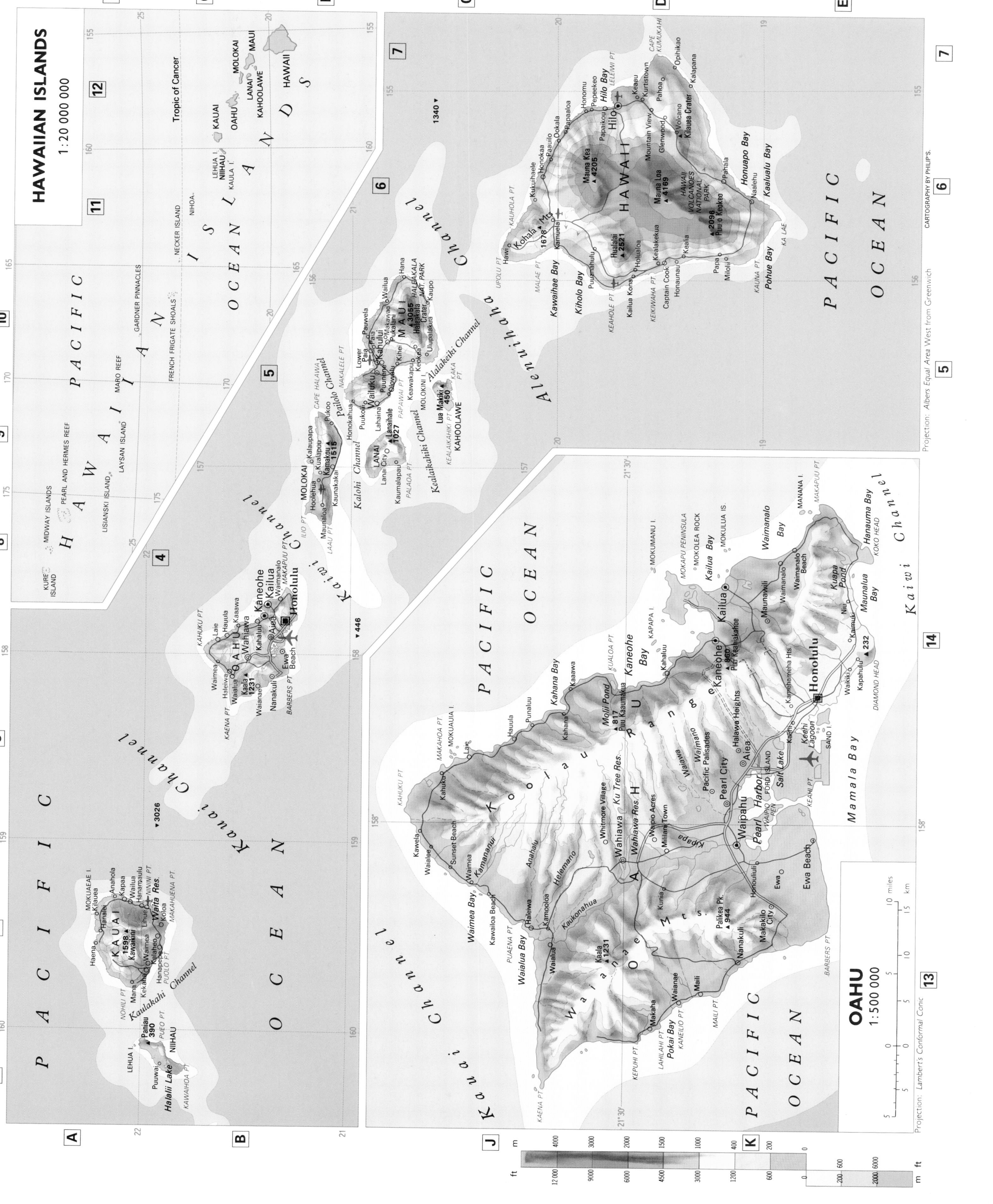

HAWAIIAN ISLANDS
1:20 000 000

Tropic of Cancer

KAUAI
LEHUA I.
NIIHAU
KAULA I.
OAHU
MOLOKAI
MAUI
LANAI
KAHOOLAWE
HAWAII

I S L A N D S

NIHOA

NECKER ISLAND

GARDNER PINNACLES

FRENCH FRIGATE SHOALS

MARO REEF

LAYSAN ISLAND

LISIANSKI ISLAND

PEARL AND HERMES REEF

MIDWAY ISLANDS

KURE ISLAND

H A W A I I A N

P A C I F I C

P A C I F I C   O C E A N

CARTOGRAPHY BY PHILLIPS.

Projection: Albers Equal Area West from Greenwich

Hawaii (island)

Kohala Mts. 1676
CAPE KUMUKAHI
LELEIWI PT.
UPOLU PT.
Hawi
Kukuihaele
Honokaa
Paauhau
Pepeekeo
Honomu
Papaikou
Hilo Bay
Hilo
Keaau
Kurtistown
Pahoa
Kalapana
Volcano
Kilauea Crater
HAWAII VOLCANOES NATIONAL PARK
Mountain View
Glenwood
Ophikao
Pahala
Honuapo Bay
Kaalualu Bay
Naalehu
KA LAE
Waiohinu
Miloli
Papa
Hookena
Honaunau
Captain Cook
Kealakekua
Keahole
Kailua Kona
Puuanahulu
Keauhou
Puuohikao
Pohakuloa
Kamuela
Kawaihae Bay
Kiholo Bay
KEAHOLE PT.
KEIKIWAHA PT.
KAUNA PT.
KALUA PT.
KAILKIWAHA PT.
MALAE PT.
KAUHOLA PT.
Mauna Kea ▲4205
Mauna Loa ▲4169
Hualalai ▲2521
Puu o Keokeo ▲2096
Pohue Bay
Ookala

H A W A I I

1340 ▼

Alenuihaha Channel

P A C I F I C   O C E A N

Maui, Molokai, Lanai, Kahoolawe

M A U I
Hana
Wailua
Pauwela
Paia
Makawao
Pukalani
Hana
HALEAKALA
Haleakala Crater NAT. PARK ▲3055
Kihei
Keokea
Ulupalakua
Keawekapu
Lahaina
Puunene
Kahului
Wailuku
Waiehu
Lower Paia
Puukolii
MOLOKINI I.
Alalakeiki Channel
Kealaikahiki Channel
Kaualapapa
Kalaupapa
CAPE HALAWA
Kualapuu
Kaunakakai
Maunaloa
Hoolehua
Kamakou ▲1515
LAAU PT.
ILIO PT.
M O L O K A I
Pailolo Channel
NAKALELE PT.
PAPAWAI PT.
KEALAIKAHIKI PT.
KAKA PT.
Lua Makika ▲450
K A H O O L A W E
L A N A I
Lanai City
Kaumalapau
PALAOA PT.
Lanaihale ▲1027
Honokahua
Kaunolu
Kaumalapau
Kalohi Channel
KAKA PT.

Oahu (main map)

O A H U
Kaena
KAHUKU PT.
Laie
Kahuku
Haula
Kahana Bay
Kaaawa
Kahana
MOKUAUIA I.
MAKAHOA PT.
Punaluu
Sunset Beach
Waimea Bay
Kawela
Kawailoa Beach
Waialee
Kamananui
Haleiwa
Waialua
Waialua Bay
PUAENA PT.
KAENA PT.
Kaena
Mokuleia
Waialua
Kaala ▲1231
Ku Tree Res.
Whitmore Village
Wahiawa Res.
Wahiawa
Helemano
Kipapa
Waipio
Waimalu
Waimano
Pacific Palisades
Mililani Town
Wapio Acres
Pearl City
Waipahu
Pearl Harbor
FORD ISLAND
Aiea
Halawa Heights
Salt Lake
Keehi Lagoon
SAND I.
Honolulu
Waikiki
Kapahulu
Kaimuki
DIAMOND HEAD
KOKO HEAD
Hanauma Bay
Kuapa Pond
Kahala
Niu
Kuliouou
Maunalua
Maunalua Bay ▲232
Kailua
Kaneohe ▲957 Puu Keahiakahoe
Kaneohe Bay
Kahaluu
Waiahole
Waikane
Kualoa
KUALOA PT.
KAPAPA I.
MOKOLEA ROCK
KUKULUAIA I.
MOKUMANU I.
MOKAPU PENINSULA
ULUPAU HEAD
Kailua
Kailua Bay
Kapaa
Lanikai
Waimanalo
Waimanalo Beach
Waimanalo Bay
MANANA I.
MAKAPUU PT.
KAOHIKAIPU I.
Kaneohe
Koolau Range
K o o l a u   R a n g e
W a i a n a e   M t s.
Makaha
MAKAHA PT.
Makaha
Waianae
KEPUHI PT.
LAHILAHI PT.
Maili
MAILI PT.
Nanakuli
Makakilo City
Kapolei
Ewa
Ewa Beach
Honouliuli
Kunia
Kaukonahua
Palikea Pk. ▲944
Kamaoa
Kaala ▲1231
Maunawili
Puu Kaaumakua ▲801
Molii Pond
WAIAHOLE
KEAHI PT.
KAHO PT.
KUAPA
BARBERS PT.
Barbers Pt.
KANEILIO PT.
Pokai Bay
Kaena
Mamala Bay

P A C I F I C   O C E A N

K a i w i   C h a n n e l

K a u a i   C h a n n e l

OAHU
1:500 000

10 miles
km
5   0   5   10   15   km
5   0   5   10   miles

Projection: Lambert's Conformal Conic

Kauai and Niihau (inset)

K A U A I
MOKUAEAE I.
Haena
Kilauea
Anahola
Hanalei
Kapaa
Wailua
Waimea
Hanamaulu
Lihue
Puhi
Nawiliwili
Kalaheo
Koloa
Kekaha
Mana
Kaumakani
Hanapepe
Kawaikini ▲1598
Waialeale
Waimea Canyon
Waita Res.
NOHILI PT.
PUEO PT.
PUOLO PT.
MAKAHUENA PT.
NIWINI PT.
Kaulakahi Channel
N I I H A U
Puuwai
LEHUA I.
Halalii Lake
Paniau ▲390
KAWAIHOA PT.

3026 ▼

P A C I F I C

K a u a i   C h a n n e l

O C E A N

Kaieie Channel

O A H U
Kahuku
Laie
Hauula
Kaaawa
Kaneohe
Kailua
Waimanalo
Honolulu
Wahiawa
Waianae
Haleiwa
Waimea
Nanakuli
Ewa
Barbers Pt.
Beach
Kaala ▲1231
KAENA PT.
KAHUKU PT.
BARBERS PT.
MAKAPUU PT.
ILIO PT.

446 ▼

Elevation scales

m
4000
3000
2000
1000
400
200
0
ft
12 000
9000
6000
4500
3000
1200
600
0

ft
2000
6000
m
200
600

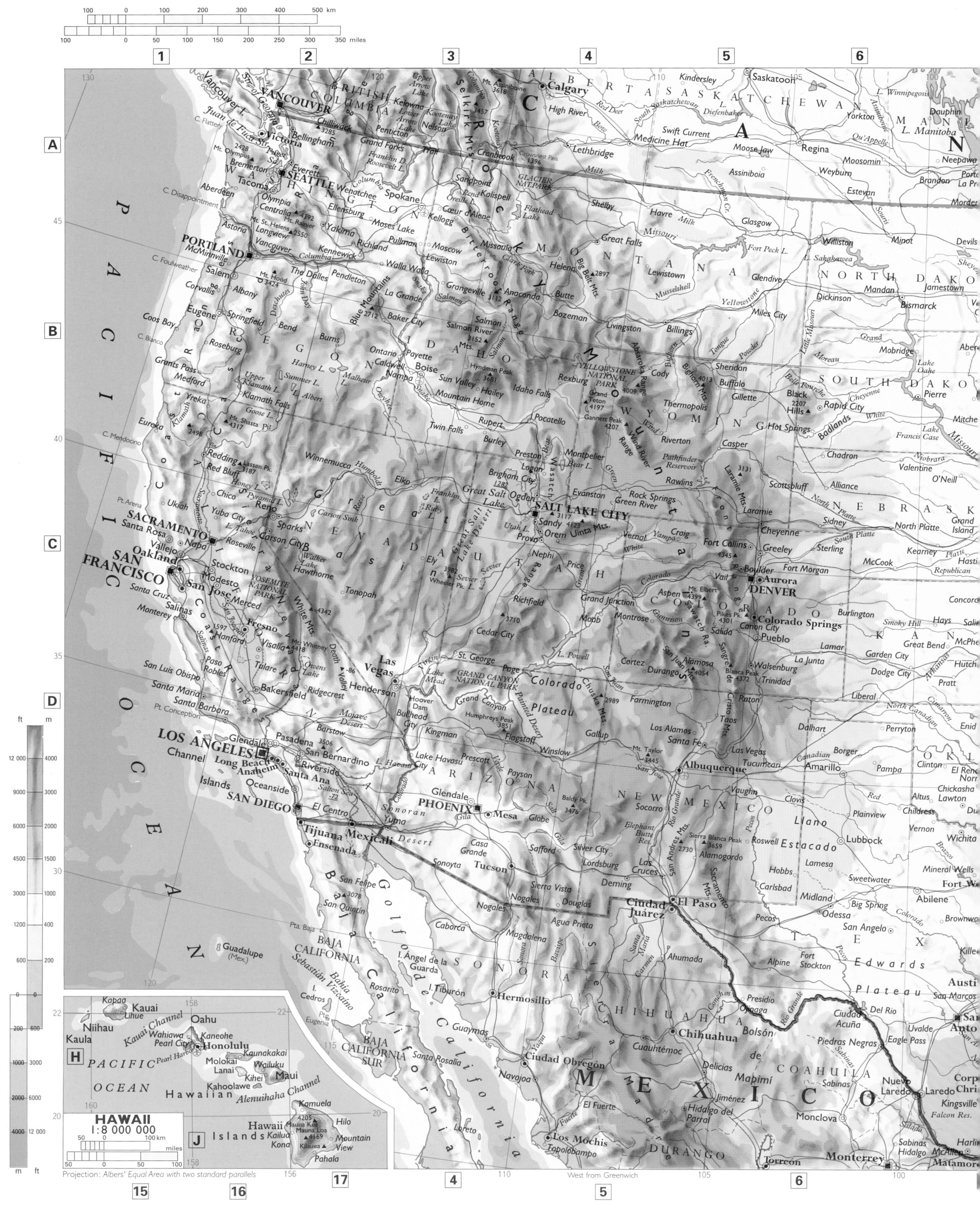

0 50 100 150 200 km
0 50 100 150 miles
QUEBEC
ONTARIO
NEW HAMPSHIRE
VERMONT
MASS.
R.I.
NEW YORK
NEW YORK CITY
NEW JERSEY
PENNSYLVANIA
DELAWARE
MARYLAND
WASHINGTON D.C.
VIRGINIA
WEST VIRGINIA
OHIO
INDIANA
KENTUCKY
MICHIGAN
WISCONSIN
ILLINOIS
LAKE SUPERIOR
LAKE MICHIGAN
LAKE HURON
LAKE ERIE
LAKE ONTARIO
Georgian Bay
Chesapeake Bay
Delaware Bay
Long Island Sound
MONTRÉAL
Québec
Ottawa
TORONTO
BOSTON
HARTFORD
PHILADELPHIA
BALTIMORE
PITTSBURGH
BUFFALO
CLEVELAND
DETROIT
CHICAGO
MILWAUKEE
COLUMBUS
INDIANAPOLIS
CINCINNATI

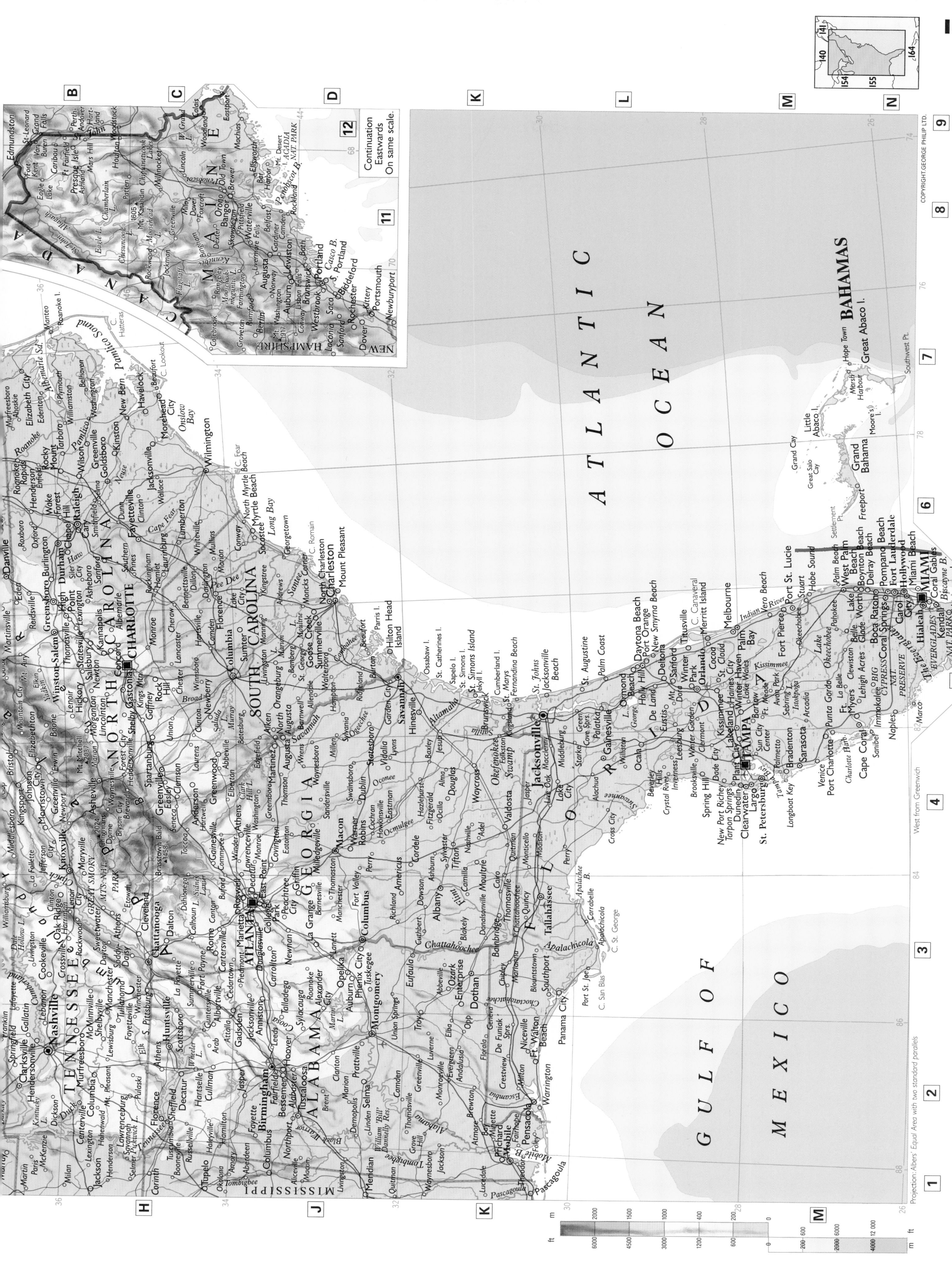

MAINE

ACADIA NAT. PARK

Continuation Eastwards On same scale.

NEW HAMPSHIRE

C A N A D A

TENNESSEE

NORTH CAROLINA

CHARLOTTE

SOUTH CAROLINA

Columbia · Charleston

GEORGIA

ATLANTA · Macon · Savannah

ALABAMA

Birmingham · Montgomery · Mobile

MISSISSIPPI

FLORIDA

Jacksonville · Orlando · TAMPA · St. Petersburg · MIAMI · Fort Lauderdale · Hialeah · Coral Gables · Kendall · Homestead

EVERGLADES NAT. PARK · BIG CYPRESS NAT. PRESERVE

BAHAMAS

Great Abaco I. · Grand Bahama · Freeport

A T L A N T I C   O C E A N

G U L F   O F   M E X I C O

COPYRIGHT GEORGE PHILIP LTD.

Projection: Albers' Equal Area with two standard parallels

West from Greenwich

ft m
6000 2000
4500 1500
3000 1000
1200
600 400
200
0 0
200
600
2000 6000
4000 12 000
m ft

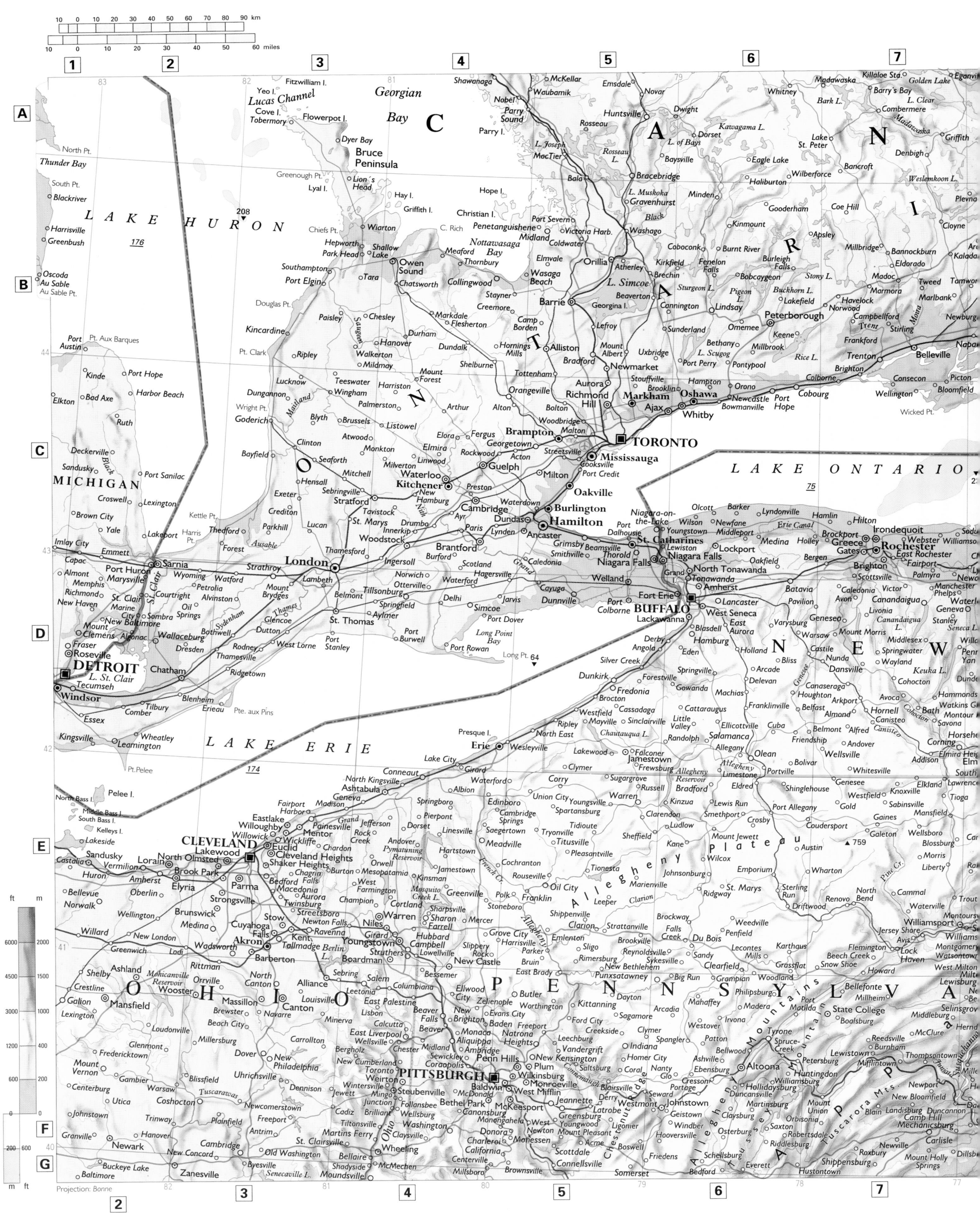

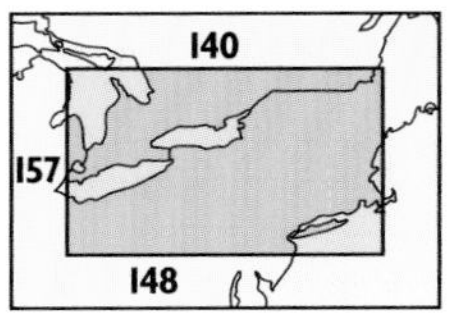

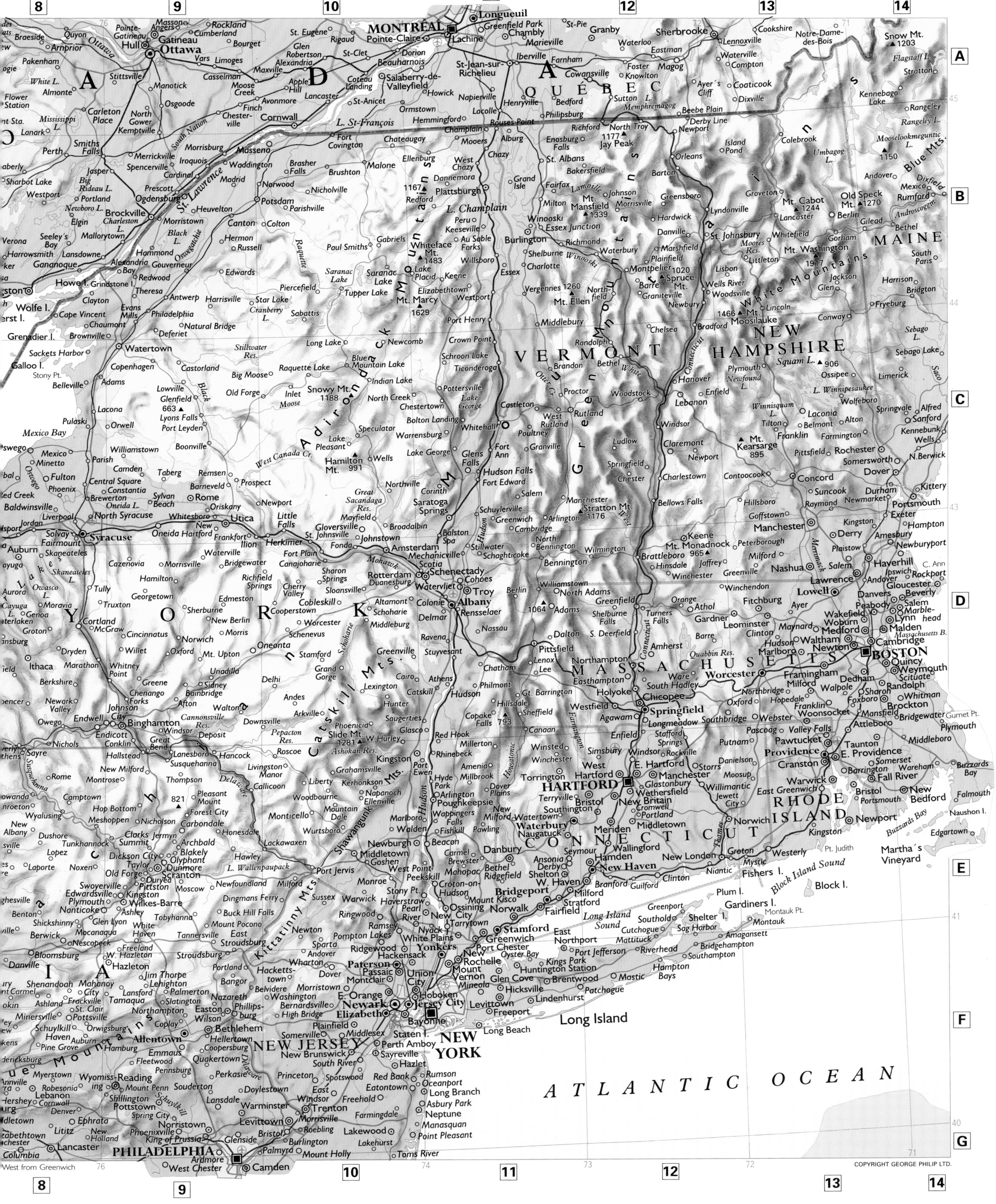

ATLANTIC OCEAN

MONTREAL
OTTAWA
QUÉBEC
NEW YORK
PHILADELPHIA
BOSTON
VERMONT
NEW HAMPSHIRE
MAINE
MASSACHUSETTS
CONNECTICUT
RHODE ISLAND
NEW JERSEY
PENNSYLVANIA
YORK

Long Island
Martha's Vineyard
Block I.
L. Champlain
Lake George

West from Greenwich

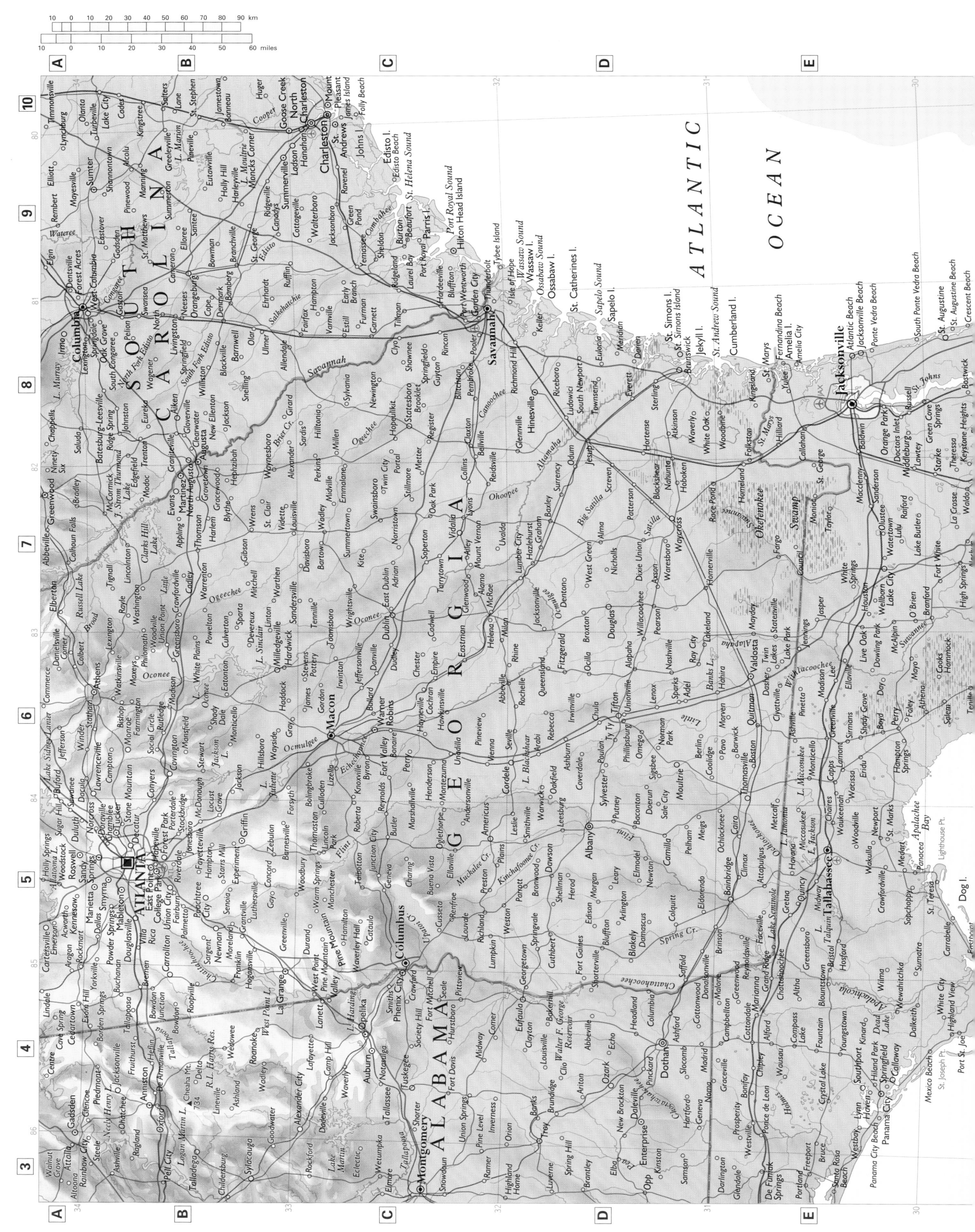

164

Projection: Albers Equal Area

West from Greenwich

COPYRIGHT GEORGE PHILIP LTD

GULF OF MEXICO

FLORIDA

Cities and places (peninsula):

Ormond by the Sea, Ormond Beach, Daytona Beach, Port Orange, New Smyrna Beach, Edgewater, Oak Hill, Titusville, Mims, Cocoa, Rockledge, Cocoa Beach, Satellite Beach, Indian Harbour Beach, Indialantic, Melbourne, Palm Bay, Malabar, Grant, Micco, Sebastian, Wabasso, Gifford, Vero Beach, Indrio, Fort Pierce, St. Lucie, Port St. Lucie, Jensen Beach, Stuart, Port Salerno, Hobe Sound, Jupiter, Juno Beach, Riviera Beach, West Palm Beach, Palm Beach, Lake Park, Lake Clarke Shores, Lantana, Boynton Beach, Delray Beach, Boca Raton, Deerfield Beach, Lighthouse Point, Pompano Beach, Fort Lauderdale, Hollywood, Hallandale, North Miami Beach, Miami Shores, Surfside, Miami Beach, MIAMI, Coral Gables, South Miami, Kendall, Perrine, Cutler Ridge, Goulds, Leisure City, Homestead, Florida City, Biscayne Bay, Elliott Key, Key Largo

Crescent Lake, Crescent City, Pierson, Barberville, De Leon Springs, Lake Helen, DeBary, Deltona, Sanford, Oviedo, Winter Park, Union Park, Orlando, Belle Isle, East Lake, L. Harney, Deer Park, Holopaw, Kenansville, Fellsmere, Blue Cypress Lake, Lakewood Park

Flagler Beach, Bunnell, Korona, Holly Hill, South Daytona, De Land, Orange City, Apopka, Winter Garden, Windermere, Ocoee, Lockhart, Fairview Shores, Pine Hills, Conway, St. Cloud, Kissimmee, Campbell, Davenport, Haines City, Winter Haven, Lake Alfred, Auburndale, Highland City, Bartow, Fort Meade, Frostproof, Avon Park, Sebring, L. Istokpoga, Lake Placid, Venus, Fisheating Ck.

Lake Okeechobee, Okeechobee, Basinger, Brighton, Cornwell, Lorida, Indiantown, Port Mayaca, Canal Point, W. Palm Beach Canal, Pahokee, Belle Glade, South Bay, Clewiston, Moore Haven, Lake Harbor, Miami Canal, Hillsboro Canal, N. New River Canal, Tamiami Canal

Pomona Park, Seville, Lake George, Astor, Silver Springs, Ocala, Belleview, Summerfield, Lady Lake, Leesburg, Tavares, Mount Dora, Eustis, Umatilla, Fruitland Park, Wildwood, Webster, Bushnell, Center Hill, Clermont, Groveland, Mascotte, Loughman, Poinciana, Zephyrhills, Dade City, Lacoochee, Trilby, Plant City, Lakeland, Mulberry, Brandon, Riverview, Gibsonton, Sun City Center, Ruskin, Parrish, Palmetto, Bradenton, Samoset, Oneco, Sarasota, Bee Ridge, Osprey, Nokomis, Venice, Laurel, South Venice, Englewood, Grove City, Rotonda

TAMPA, St. Petersburg, Largo, Clearwater, Dunedin, Palm Harbor, Tarpon Springs, Holiday, New Port Richey, Port Richey, Hudson, Bayonet Point, Spring Hill, Weeki Wachee, Brooksville, Hernando, Inverness, Floral City, Citrus Springs, Dunnellon, Beverly Hills, Homosassa Springs, Crystal River, Bayport, Gowers Corner, Lutz, Oldsmar, Safety Harbor, Seminole, Indian Rocks Beach, Treasure Island, St. Petersburg Beach, Holmes Beach, Longboat Key, Anna Maria, Terra Ceia, Ellenton

Archer, Williston, Bronson, Chiefland, Otter Creek, Cedar Key, Suwannee, Inglis, Yankeetown, Lebanon Station, Morriston, Citra, Reddick, Anthony, Kendrick, Micanopy, McIntosh, Orange Lake, Lochloosa L., Raleigh, Hawthorne, Lochloosa

Southwest coast:
Tice, Fort Myers, North Fort Myers, Cape Coral, San Carlo Park, Fort Myers Beach, Bonita Springs, Estero, Sanibel, Captiva, Pine Island, Bokeelia, St. James City, Boca Grande, Gasparilla I., Punta Gorda, Port Charlotte, Charlotte Harbor, El Jobean, Englewood, Nokomis, Arcadia, Nocatee, Fort Ogden, De Soto City, Gardner, Zolfo Springs, Wauchula, Bowling Green, Ona, Myakka, Verna, Bee Ridge

Naples, Naples Park, North Naples, Marco, Goodland, Cape Romano, Ten Thousand Is., Gullivan Bay, Chokoloskee, Everglades City, Copeland, Ochopee, East Naples, Immokalee, La Belle, Caloosahatchee, Palmdale, Lehigh Acres, Felda, Alva

Interior / labels:
FLORIDA, BIG CYPRESS, BIG CYPRESS NAT. PRESERVE, EVERGLADES NATIONAL PARK, Whitewater Bay, Flamingo, Ponce de Leon Bay, C. Sable, C. Romano

Keys inset:
Florida Keys, Straits of Florida, Key Largo, Tavernier, Islamorada, Layton, Key Colony Beach, Marathon, Big Pine, Summerland Key, Stock Island, Key West, Marquesas Keys, C. Sable, Flamingo, Florida Bay

Panhandle inset (ALABAMA / FLORIDA):
ALABAMA, FLORIDA, GULF OF MEXICO, Apalachicola, Apalachicola Bay, St. Vincent I., C. St. George, Eastpoint, Carrabelle, Apalachee, Wewahitchka, Port St. Joe, St. Joseph Pt., C. San Blas, Highland View, White City, Panama City, Panama City Beach, Callaway, Springfield, Lynn Haven, Youngstown, Southport, Fountain, Ebro, Bristol, Hosford, Bloomington, Blountstown, Altha, Marianna, Cottondale, Alford, Campbellton, Greenwood, Malone, Grand Ridge, Sneads, Chattahoochee, Gretna, Quincy, Havana, Midway, Sumatra, Wilma, Kinard, Compass Lake, Dead Lakes, Wausau, Vernon, Chipley, Bonifay, Westville, Ponce de Leon, De Funiak Springs, Freeport, Portland, Bruce, Santa Rosa Beach, Destin, Fort Walton Beach, Mary Esther, Shalimar, Valparaiso, Niceville, Crestview, Baker, Milligan, Holt, Laurel Hill, Florala, Paxton, Noma, Graceville, Madrid, Geneva, Bonifay, Cottondale, Glendale, Prosperity, Bascom, Kinard, Youngstown

Pensacola, West Pensacola, Warrington, Gulf Breeze, Milton, Pace, Bagdad, Jay, Bay Minette, Atmore, Century, Walnut Hill, McDavid, Molino, Cantonment, Ensley, Myrtle Grove, Perdido Bay, Bay Navarre, Santa Rosa I., Navarre, Riverview, Allentown, Munson, Berrydale, Blackman, Baker, Munson

KEY TO MAP INSETS, Continuation Southwards, Continuation Westwards, FLORIDA

COPYRIGHT GEORGE PHILIP LTD.

Continuation Southwards on same scale

Projection: Albers' Equal Area with two standard parallels

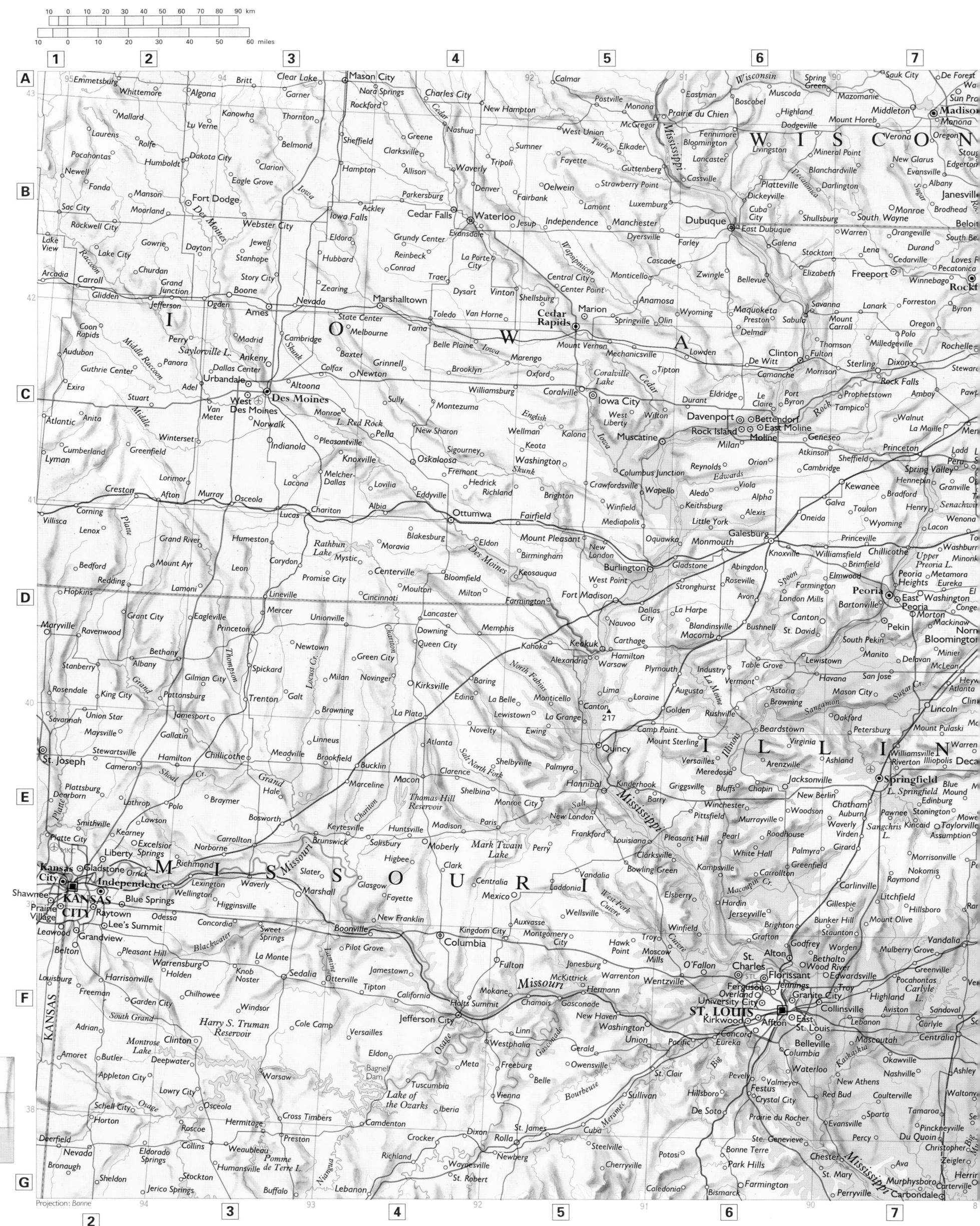

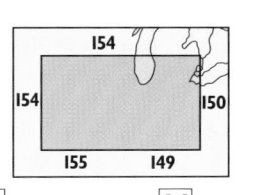

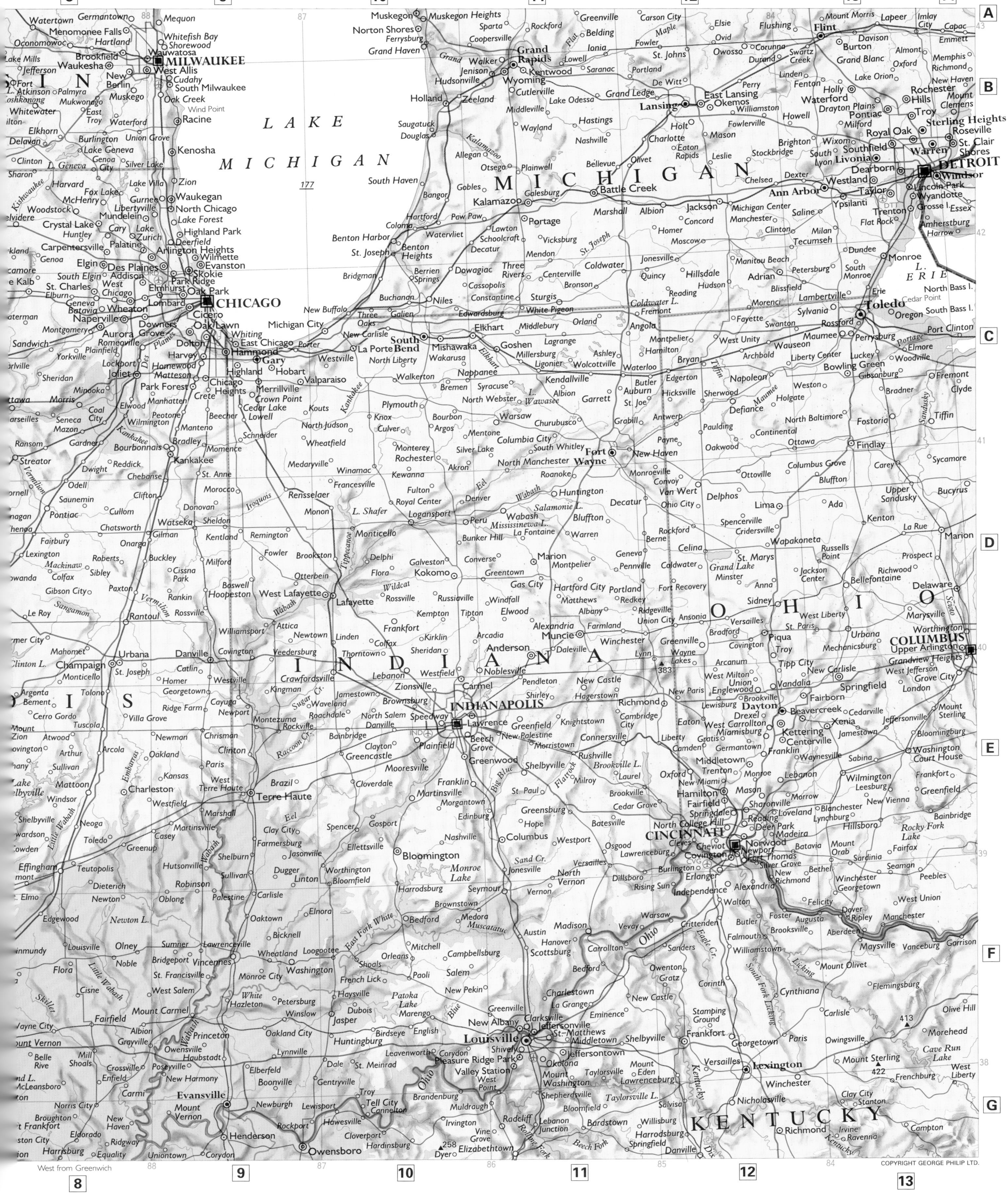

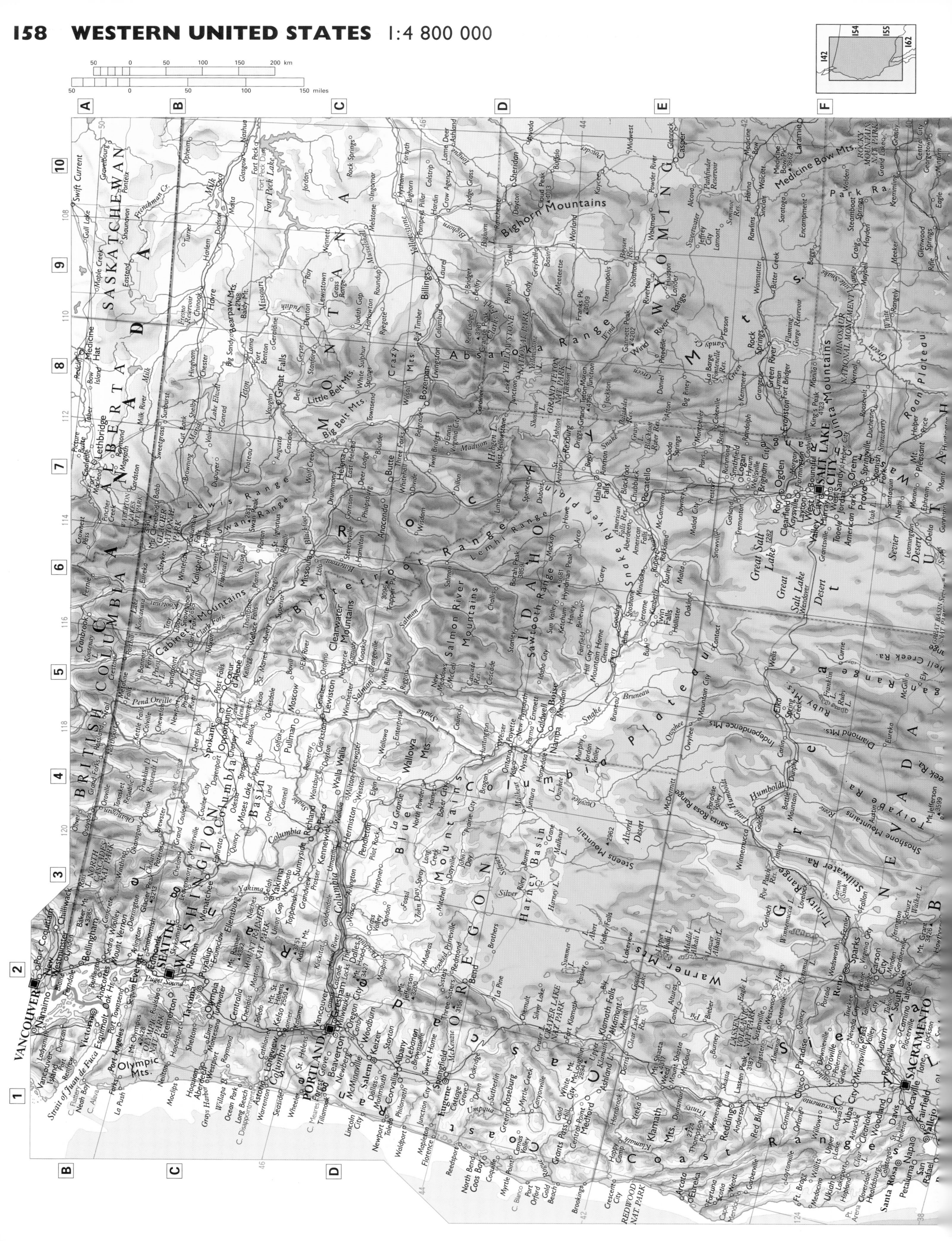

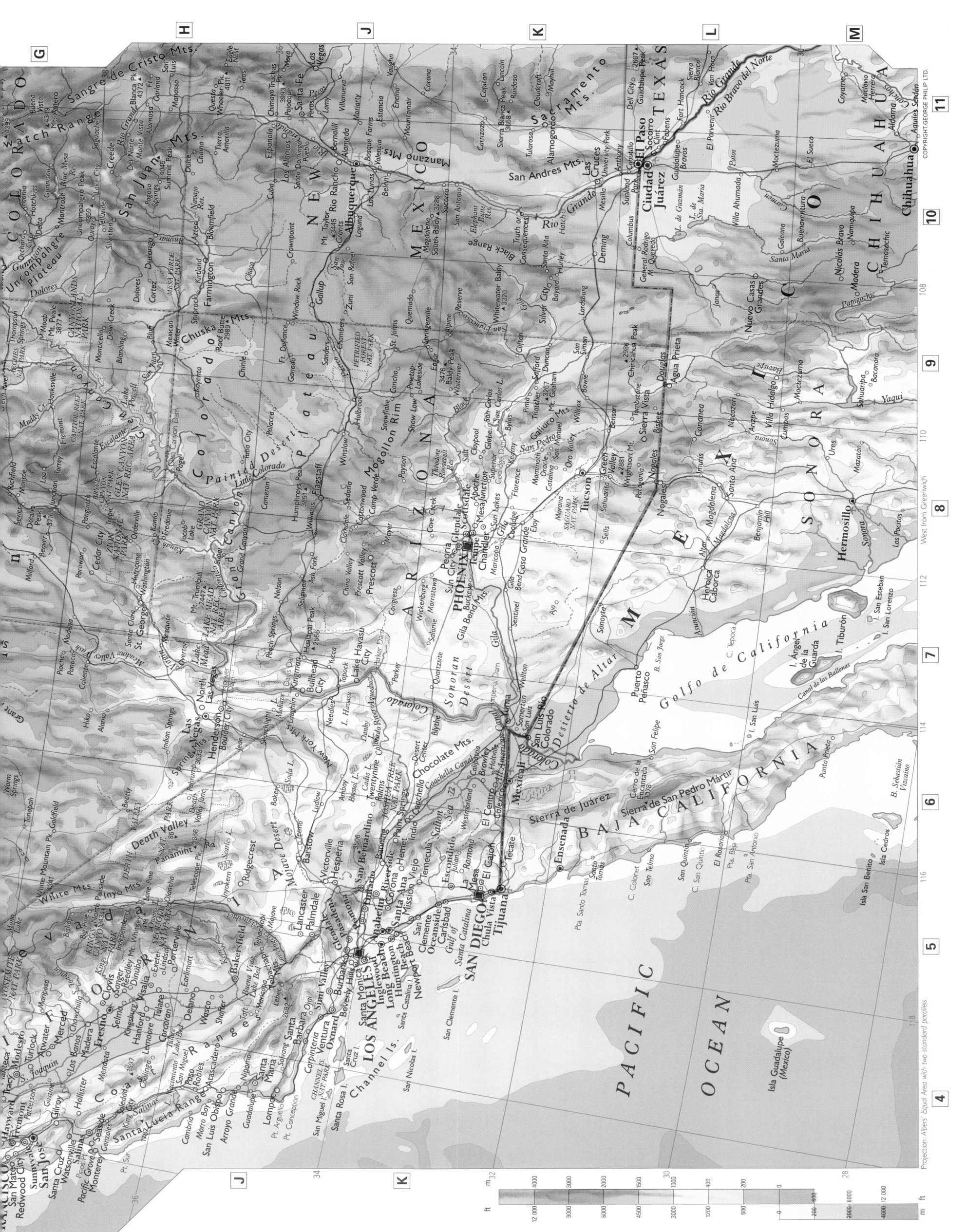

WESTERN WASHINGTON REGION
On same scale

REFERENCE TO NUMBERS

1 Distrito Federal   5 México
2 Aguascalientes   6 Morelos
3 Guanajuato   7 Querétaro
4 Hidalgo   8 Tlaxcala

Projection: Bi-polar oblique Conical Orthomorphic

West from Greenwich

Projection: Conical with two standard parallels

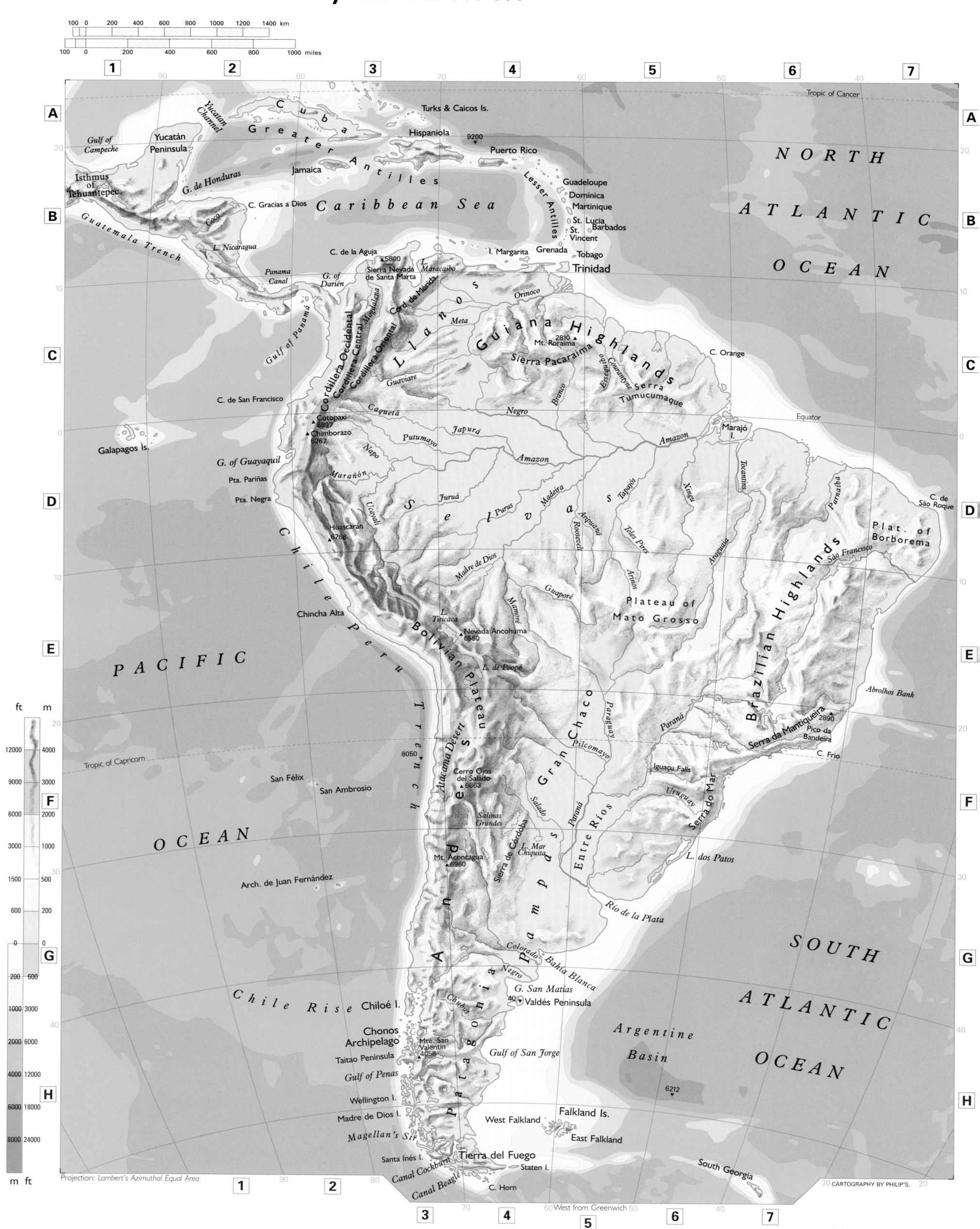

100 0 200 400 600 800 1000 1200 1400 km
100 0 200 400 600 800 1000 miles

Projection: Lambert's Azimuthal Equal Area

CARTOGRAPHY BY PHILIP'S.

ft m
12000 4000
9000 3000
6000 2000
3000 1000
1500 500
600 200
0 0
200 600
1000 3000
2000 6000
4000 12000
6000 18000
8000 24000
m ft

NORTH ATLANTIC OCEAN

Tropic of Cancer

Yucatan Channel
Gulf of Campeche
Yucatán Peninsula
Isthmus of Tehuantepec
G. de Honduras
Guatemala Trench
Coco
L. Nicaragua
C. Gracias a Dios

Cuba
Greater Antilles
Turks & Caicos Is.
Hispaniola
9200
Puerto Rico
Jamaica
Caribbean Sea
Lesser Antilles
Guadeloupe
Dominica
Martinique
St. Lucia
St. Vincent
Barbados
Grenada
Tobago
Trinidad
I. Margarita

Panama Canal
G. of Darién
Gulf of Panamá
C. de la Aguja
Sierra Nevada de Santa Marta 5800
L. Maracaibo
C. de la Vela

Cordillera Occidental
Cordillera Central
Cordillera Oriental
Magdalena
Llanos
Orinoco
Meta
Guayané
Guaviare
Caquetá

Guiana Highlands
Mt. Roraima 2810
Sierra Pacaraima
Serra Tumucumaque
Cuyuní
Essequibo
Negro
Branco
C. Orange

C. de San Francisco
Cotopaxi 4897
Chimborazo 6267
G. of Guayaquil
Pta. Pariñas
Pta. Negra

Galapagos Is.

Napo
Putumayo
Japurá
Marañón
Ucayali
Furuá
Purus
Madeira
Amazon
Equator
Marajó I.
Tocantins

PACIFIC

Huascaran 6768
Chincha Alta
L. Titicaca
Bolivian Plateau
Nevada Ancohuma 6580
Madre de Dios
Mamoré
Guaporé
Roosevelt
Aripuanã
Tapajós
Xingu
Araguaia
São Francisco
Plat. of Borborema
C. de São Roque

Brazilian Highlands
Plateau of Mato Grosso
Telés Pires
Arinos

Chile Peru Trench

Atacama Desert
Andes
8050
Cerro Ojos del Salado 6863
Salinas Grandes
Salado
Gran Chaco
Pilcomayo
Paraguay
Paraná
Iguaçu Falls
Serra da Mantiqueira 2890
Pico da Bandeira
Serra do Mar
C. Frio
Abrolhos Bank

Tropic of Capricorn
San Félix
San Ambrosio

OCEAN

Arch. de Juan Fernández

Mt. Aconcagua 6960
Sierra de Córdoba
L. Mar Chiquita
Uruguay
L. dos Patos

Entre Ríos
Paraná
Río de la Plata

Pampas
Colorado
Negro
Bahía Blanca
G. San Matías
Valdés Peninsula

Chile Rise
Chiloé I.
Chonos Archipelago
Taitao Peninsula
Mte. San Valentin 4058
Gulf of Penas
Wellington I.
Madre de Dios I.

Patagonia

Colorado
G. San Jorge

Argentine Basin

SOUTH ATLANTIC OCEAN

6212

Magellan's Str.
Santa Inés I.
Canal Cockburn
Canal Beagle
Tierra del Fuego
Staten I.
C. Horn
West Falkland
Falkland Is.
East Falkland
South Georgia

West from Greenwich

100 0   200   400   600   800   1000 1200 1400 km

100 0   200   400   600   800   1000 miles

A   Tropic of Cancer   **A**

Havana   BAHAMAS   Turks & Caicos Is.
C U B A   (U.K.)

Virgin Is.   N O R T H

HAITI   San Juan   (U.K.)
DOMINICAN
REP.

MEXICO   JAMAICA   Kingston   Port-au-   PUERTO   ANTIGUA &   A T L A N T I C
Prince   RICO   BARBUDA
(U.S.A.)   ST. KITTS
BELIZE   & NEVIS   Basse-Terre GUADELOUPE
(Fr.)
B   GUATEMALA   HONDURAS   DOMINICA   MARTINIQUE   O C E A N   **B**
Guatemala   Tegucigalpa   Fort-de-France   (Fr.)
C a r i b b e a n   S e a   Castries   ST. LUCIA
San Salvador   NICARAGUA   ST. VINCENT   BARBADOS
EL SALVADOR   Kingstown   Bridgetown
Managua   Aruba   GRENADA   St. George's
COSTA   San José   C. de   Curaçao   Port of
la Aguja   Maracaibo   Caracas   Spain   TRINIDAD &
RICA   Panamá   Barranquilla   TOBAGO
P A N A M A   Cartagena   Barquisimeto   Valencia
Cúcuta   Orinoco
Medellín   Bucaramanga   San Cristóbal VENEZUELA   Ciudad Guayana
C   Georgetown   **C**
Cali   Bogotá   GUYANA   Paramaribo
Magdalena   SURINAM   Cayenne
COLOMBIA   RORAIMA   Essequibo   FRENCH   C. Orange
Branco   GUIANA
AMAPÁ
Quito   Equator
ECUADOR   Napo   Putumayo   Japurá   Marajó
Guayaquil   Marañón   Amazon   Manaus Santarém   I.   Belém
G. of Guayaquil   Iquitos   São Luís
Madeira   PARÁ   Fortaleza
D   Chiclayo   Ucayali   Juruá   Purus   Tapajós   Xingu   MARANHÃO   Teresina   C. de   **D**
AMAZONAS   São Roque
Trujillo   A C R E   CEARÁ   Natal
RIO G.
Chimbote   Pôrto Velho   PIAUÍ   DO NORTE
PERU   RONDÔNIA   B R A Z I L   PERNAMBUCO Campina Grande PARAÍBA
Callao   Lima   Madre de Dios   Recife
E   Cuzco   MATO GROSSO   BAHÍA   ALAGOAS Maceió   **E**
L.   Mamoré   GOIÁS   São Francisco   SERGIPE Aracaju
Titicaca   BOLIVIA   Cuiabá   DIS. FED Brasília   Salvador
Arequipa   La Paz   Cochabamba   Goiânia
Santa Cruz   MATO GROSSO   MINAS GERAIS
Sucre   DO SUL   Ribeirão
Iquique   Paraná   Prêto   Belo   ESPÍRITO
Horizonte SANTO
F   PARAGUAY   Paraná   Juiz   Vitória   **F**
Tropic of Capricorn   de Fora
Antofagasta   Pilcomayo   SÃO PAULO Campinas R. DE J. Campos
Salta   Asunción   PARANÁ   SÃO   Niterói
San Félix   Curitiba   PAULO   RIO DE
(Chile)   Salado   Resistencia   SANTA CATARINA JANEIRO
San Ambrosio   San Miguel   Corrientes   Uruguay
(Chile)   de Tucumán   RIO GRANDE
O C E A N   DO SUL   Pôrto Alegre
Córdoba   Santa Fe   Paraná   Pelotas
G   Arch. de Juan Fernández   San Juan   Rosario   URUGUAY   S O U T H   **G**
(Chile)   Viña del Mar   Montevideo
Valparaíso Mendoza   BUENOS AIRES
SANTIAGO   La Plata   Río de la Plata   A T L A N T I C
Talca   Bahía   Mar del Plata
Concepción   A R G E N T I N A   Blanca
Colorado   O C E A N
Valdivia   Negro   Viedma
Puerto Montt   Chubut
H   West Falkland FALKLAND IS.   **H**
Gulf of Penas   Comodoro Rivadavia   (U.K.)
Gulf of San Jorge   Stanley
East Falkland
Punta Arenas   Magellan's Str.
Tierra del Fuego   South Georgia
C. Horn   (U.K.)

PACIFIC   O C E A N

Projection: Lambert's Azimuthal Equal Area

1   **2**   **3**   **4**   **5**   **6**   **7**

■ LIMA Capital Cities   West from Greenwich

CARTOGRAPHY BY PHILIP'S.

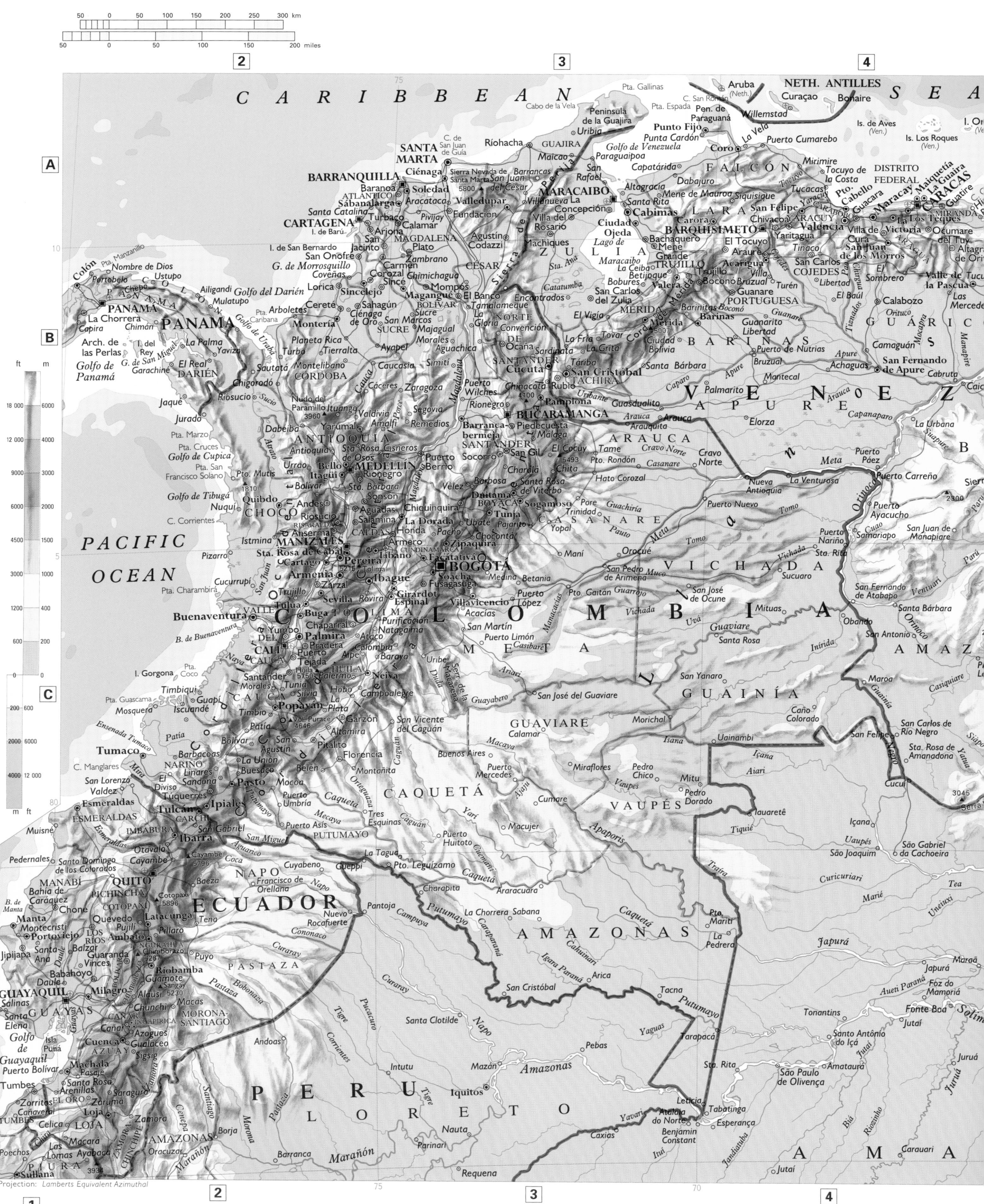

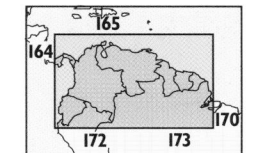

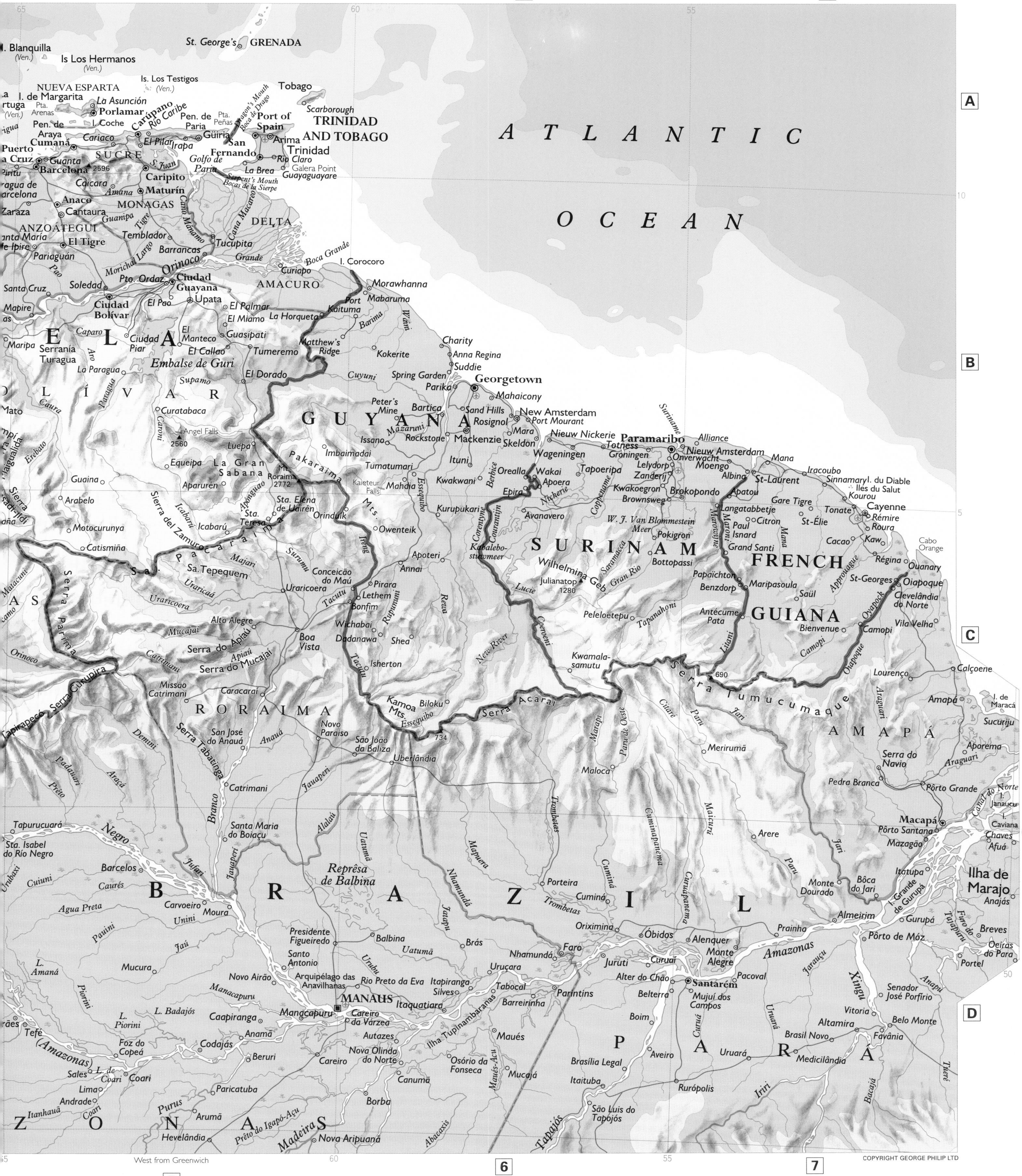

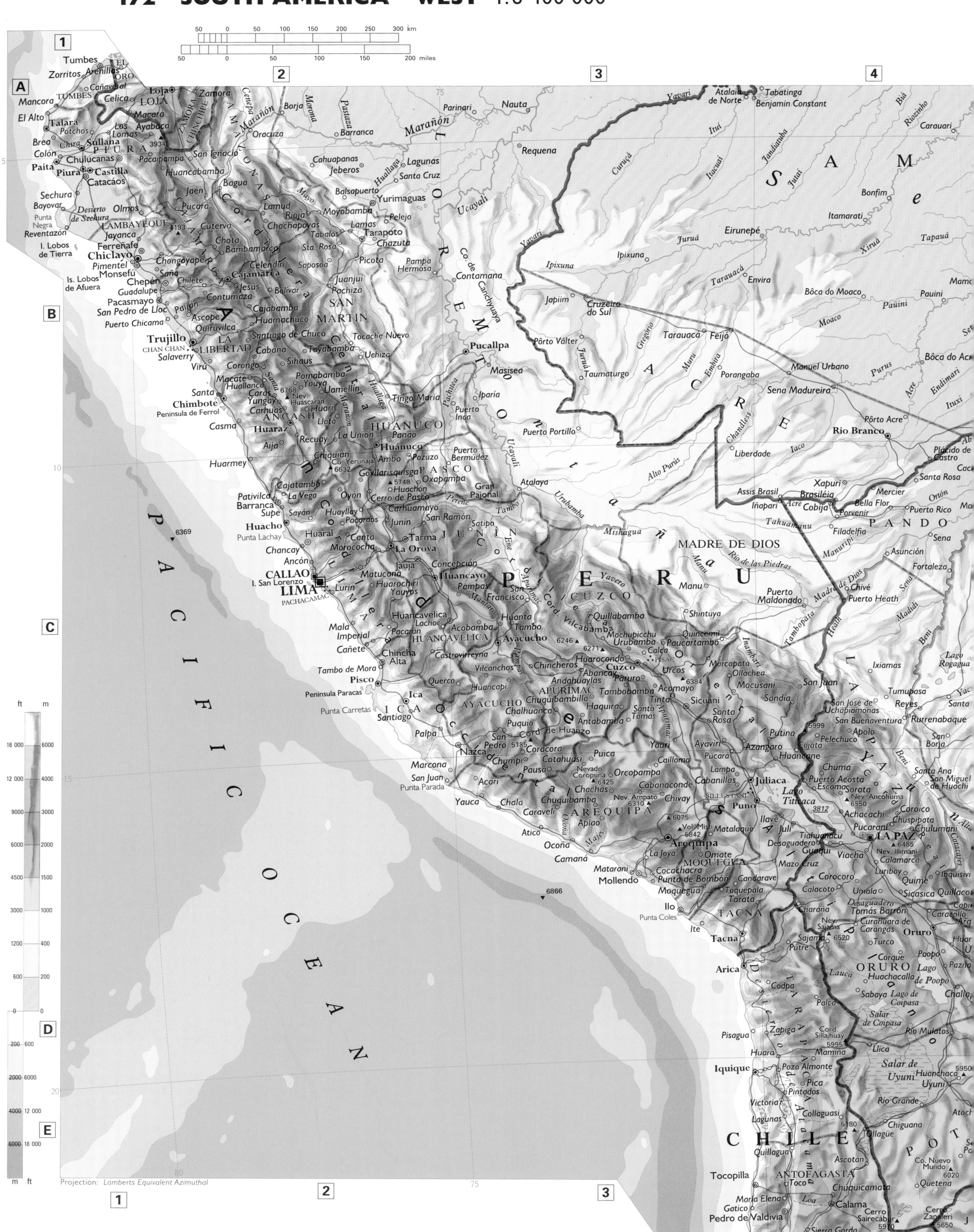

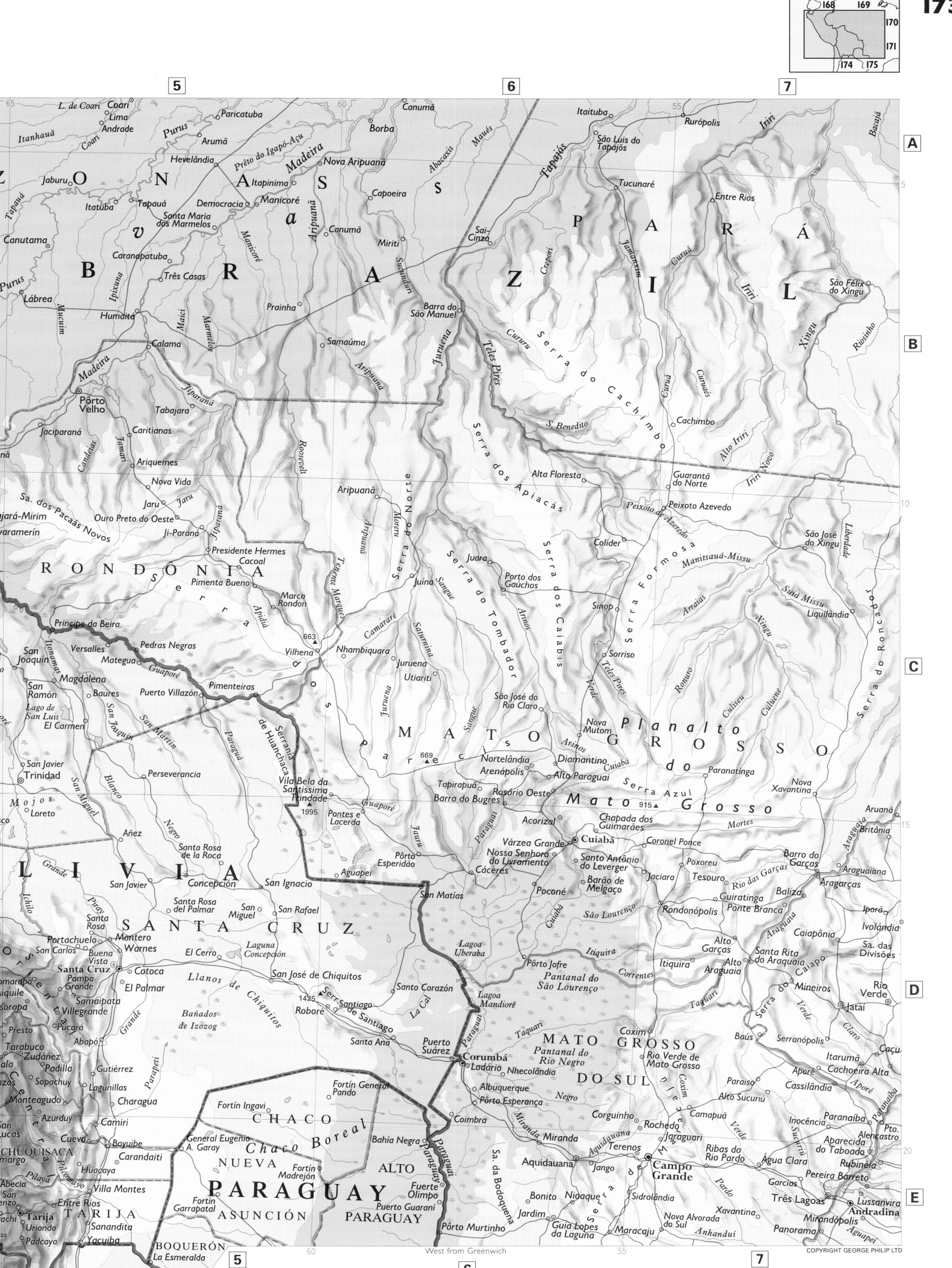

5   6   7

A

B

C

D

E

West from Greenwich

COPYRIGHT GEORGE PHILIP LTD

5   6   7

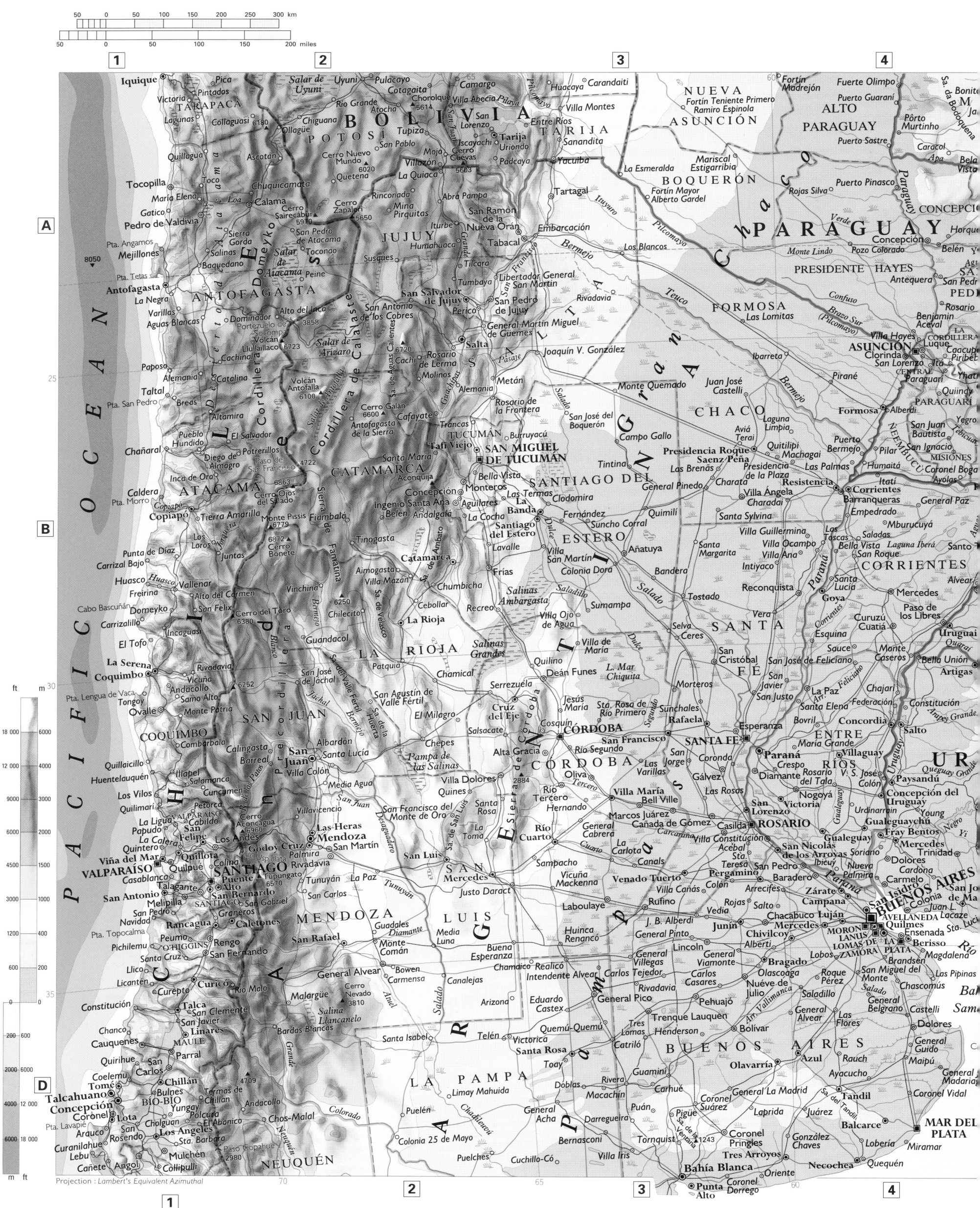

MATO GROSSO DO SUL

Sidrolândia
Nioaque
Lopes
Laguna
Maracaju
Dourados
Nova Alvorada do Sul
Ponta Porã
Pedro Juan Caballero
Amambaí
Mundo Novo
Salto del Guairá
CANINDEYU
Curuguaty
AZÚ
ALTO PARANÁ
el Oviedo
Ciudad del Este
Irala
APÁ
Bernardo de Irigoyen
APUÁ
Paraná
MISIONES
Posadas
Encarnación
Candelaria
Corpus
Obera
Leandro N. Alem
San Javier
Apóstoles
San
Santo Ángelo
Santiago

Três Lagoas
Xavantina
Andradina
Mirassol
Araçatuba
Panorama
Presidente Epitácio
Adamantina
Martinópolis
Presidente Prudente
Rancharia
Assis
Cambará
Londrina
Rolândia
Maringá
Apucarana
Arapongas
Mandaguari

SÃO PAULO
Olímpia
São José do Rio Prêto
Bebedouro
Catanduva
Taquaritinga
Jaboticabal
Ribeirão Prêto
Mocóca
Lins
Novo Horizonte
Bauru
Jaú
Rio Claro
Limeira
Americana
Campinas

BRAZIL
PARANÁ
Londrina
Cândido de Abreu
Ponta Grossa
Curitiba
Antonina
Paranaguá

RIO GRANDE DO SUL
PÔRTO ALEGRE

ATLANTIC

OCEAN

5304

West from Greenwich
COPYRIGHT GEORGE PHILIP LTD

Tropic of Capricorn

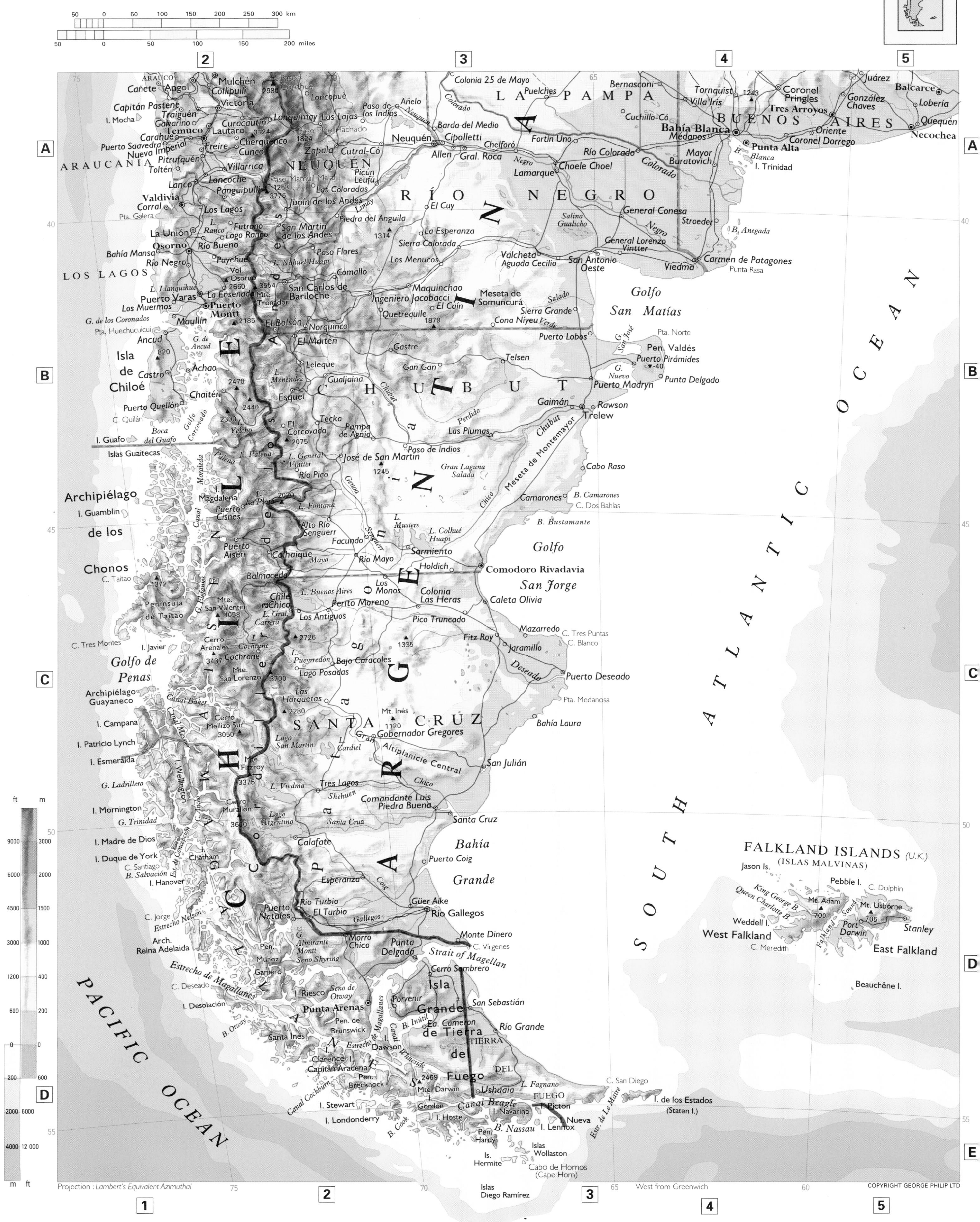

50 0 50 100 150 200 250 300 km
50 0 50 100 150 200 miles
174 175
1 2 3 4 5
A B C D E
LA PAMPA
BUENOS AIRES
NEUQUÉN
RÍO NEGRO
CHUBUT
SANTA CRUZ
TIERRA DEL FUEGO
ARAUCANIA
LOS LAGOS
CHILE
ARGENTINA
Cordillera de los Andes
Patagonia
Colonia 25 de Mayo
Puelches
Bernasconi
Tornquist
Coronel Pringles
Juárez
Balcarce
Lobería
Quequén
Necochea
González Chaves
Tres Arroyos
Villa Iris
Cuchillo-Có
Bahía Blanca
Médanos
Oriente
Coronel Dorrego
Punta Alta
B. Blanca
I. Trinidad
Mayor Buratovich
Río Colorado
Fortín Uno
Choele Choel
Lamarque
General Conesa
Stroeder
B. Anegada
General Lorenzo Vintter
Carmen de Patagones
Viedma
Punta Rasa
San Antonio Oeste
Salina Gualicho
Valcheta
Aguada Cecilio
Golfo San Matías
Sierra Grande
Puerto Lobos
Meseta de Somuncurá
Cona Niyeu
Pta. Norte
G. San José
Pen. Valdés
Puerto Pirámides
Punta Delgado
G. Nuevo
Puerto Madryn
Rawson
Trelew
Gaimán
Telsen
Gan Gan
Gastre
Cabo Raso
B. Camarones
C. Dos Bahías
Camarones
Meseta de Montemayor
B. Bustamante
Golfo San Jorge
Comodoro Rivadavia
Caleta Olivia
Mazarredo
C. Tres Puntas
C. Blanco
Fitz Roy
Jaramillo
Puerto Deseado
Pta. Medanosa
Bahía Laura
San Julián
Santa Cruz
Bahía Grande
Puerto Coig
Güer Aike
Río Gallegos
Monte Dinero
C. Vírgenes
Strait of Magellan
Punta Delgada
Cerro Sombrero
Isla Grande de Tierra del Fuego
San Sebastián
Río Grande
Ea. Cameron
Porvenir
L. Fagnano
Ushuaia
Canal Beagle
I. Picton
I. Nueva
I. Lennox
I. Navarino
B. Nassau
Estr. de Le Maire
I. de los Estados (Staten I.)
C. San Diego
Islas Wollaston
Is. Hermite
Cabo de Hornos (Cape Horn)
Islas Diego Ramírez
Pen. Hardy
I. Hoste
I. Gordon
I. Londonderry
I. Stewart
B. Cook
Canal Cockburn
Mte. Darwin
2469
Pen. Brecknock
Capitán Aracena
Clarence I.
Santa Ines
Dawson
Pen. de Brunswick
Punta Arenas
I. Riesco
Seno de Otway
Seno Skyring
Pen. Muñoz Gamero
G. Almirante Montt
Morro Chico
Puerto Natales
Río Turbio
El Turbio
Esperanza
Calafate
Lago Argentino
Cerro Murallón
3600
Mte. Fitzroy
3375
L. Viedma
Tres Lagos
Comandante Luis Piedra Buena
Gobernador Gregores
Altiplanicie Central
Mt. Inés
1120
L. Cardiel
Lago San Martín
Cerro Mellizo Sur
3050
Las Horquetas
2280
Lago Posadas
L. Pueyrredón
Bajo Caracoles
1335
Pico Truncado
Perito Moreno
Los Antiguos
Chile Chico
L. Buenos Aires
Colonia Las Heras
Los Monos
Holdich
Sarmiento
Río Mayo
Facundo
L. Colhué Huapi
L. Musters
Alto Río Senguerr
Balmaceda
Coihaique
Puerto Aisén
Puerto Cisnes
Magdalena
L. Fontana
L. La Plata
2020
Río Pico
L. General Vintter
José de San Martín
1245
Gran Laguna Salada
Paso de Indios
Las Plumas
El Corcovado
2075
Tecka
Pampa de Agnia
Esquel
Gualjaina
Leleque
El Maitén
El Bolsón
Norquinco
Ingeniero Jacobacci
Maquinchao
El Caín
Quetrequile
1879
Comallo
Paso Flores
San Carlos de Bariloche
L. Nahuel Huapi
San Martín de los Andes
Junín de los Andes
Los Menucos
Sierra Colorada
La Esperanza
1314
Piedra del Anguila
El Cuy
Las Coloradas
Picún Leufú
Zapala
Cutral-Có
Neuquén
Cipolletti
Allen
Gral. Roca
Chelforó
Barda del Medio
Añelo
Paso de los Indios
Loncopué
Las Lajas
Paso Pino Hachado
1824
Paso Copahue
2980
Paso Mamuil Malal
1253
3776
Araucó
Cañete
Angol
Mulchén
Collipulli
Victoria
Traiguén
Capitán Pastene
I. Mocha
Galvarino
Curacautín
Lonquimay
Carahue
Temuco
Lautaro
3124
Puerto Saavedra
Nueva Imperial
Freire
Cunco
Cherquenco
Pitrufquén
Toltén
Villarrica
Loncoche
Lanco
Panguipulli
Valdivia
Corral
Los Lagos
Pta. Galera
La Unión
L. Ranco
Futrono
Lago Ranco
Osorno
Río Bueno
Bahía Mansa
Río Negro
Puyehue
Vol. Osorno
2660
3554
L. Llanquihue
La Ensenada
Mte. Tronador
Puerto Varas
Los Muermos
Puerto Montt
Maullín
2185
G. de los Coronados
Pta. Huechucuicui
Ancud
G. de Ancud
Isla de Chiloé
820
Castro
Achao
2470
Chaitén
2440
Puerto Quellón
C. Quilán
Golfo Corcovado
2300
L. Yelcho
Boca del Guafo
I. Guafo
Islas Guaitecas
Palena
L. Palena
Moraleda
Canal Moraleda
Archipiélago de los Chonos
I. Guamblin
C. Taitao
1372
Península de Taitao
G. Elefantes
Mte. San Valentín
4058
L. Gral. Carrera
2726
Cerro Arenales
3437
Cochrane
L. Cochrane
Mte. San Lorenzo
3700
C. Tres Montes
I. Javier
Golfo de Penas
Archipiélago Guayaneco
Canal Baker
I. Campana
Canal Messier
I. Patricio Lynch
I. Esmeralda
I. Wellington
G. Ladrillero
I. Mornington
G. Trinidad
C. Ancho
I. Madre de Dios
I. Duque de York
Est. de Concepción
Chatham
C. Santiago
B. Salvación
I. Hanover
C. Jorge
Estrecho Nelson
Arch. Reina Adelaida
Estrecho de Magallanes
C. Deseado
I. Desolación
B. Otway
PACIFIC OCEAN
SOUTH ATLANTIC OCEAN
FALKLAND ISLANDS (U.K.) (ISLAS MALVINAS)
Jason Is.
Pebble I.
C. Dolphin
King George B.
Queen Charlotte B.
Mt. Adam
700
Mt. Usborne
705
Falkland Sound
Port Darwin
Stanley
Weddell I.
West Falkland
C. Meredith
East Falkland
Beauchêne I.
ft m
9000 3000
6000 2000
4500 1500
3000 1000
1200 400
600 200
0 0
200 600
2000 6000
4000 12 000
m ft
75 70 65 60
40 45 50 55
Projection : Lambert's Equivalent Azimuthal
West from Greenwich
COPYRIGHT GEORGE PHILIP LTD

INDEX

The index contains the names of all the principal places and features shown on the World Maps. Each name is followed by an additional entry in italics giving the country or region within which it is located. The alphabetical order of names composed of two or more words is governed primarily by the first word and then by the second. This is an example of the rule:

Mīr Kūh, *Iran* **97 E8** 26 22N 58 55E
Mīr Shahdād, *Iran* **97 E8** 26 15N 58 29E
Mira, *Italy* **45 C9** 45 26N 12 8E
Mira por vos Cay, *Bahamas* . **165 B5** 22 9N 74 30W
Mīrābād, *Afghan* **91 C1** 30 25N 61 50E

Physical features composed of a proper name (Erie) and a description (Lake) are positioned alphabetically by the proper name. The description is positioned after the proper name and is usually abbreviated:

Erie, L., *N. Amer.* **150 D4** 42 15N 81 0W

Where a description forms part of a settlement or administrative name however, it is always written in full and put in its true alphabetic position:

Mount Morris, *U.S.A.* **150 D7** 42 44N 77 52W

Names beginning with M' and Mc are indexed as if they were spelled Mac. Names beginning St. are alphabetised under Saint, but Sankt, Sint, Sant', Santa and San are all spelt in full and are alphabetised accordingly. If the same place name occurs two or more times in the index and all are in the same country, each is followed by the name of the administrative subdivision in which it is located. The names are placed in the alphabetical order of the subdivisions. For example:

Jackson, *Ky., U.S.A.* **148 G4** 37 33N 83 23W
Jackson, *Mich., U.S.A.* **157 B12** 42 15N 84 24W
Jackson, *Minn., U.S.A.* **154 D7** 43 37N 95 1W

The number in bold type which follows each name in the index refers to the number of the map page where that feature or place will be found. This is usually the largest scale at which the place or feature appears.

The letter and figure which are in bold type immediately after the page number give the grid square on the map page, within which the feature is situated. The letter represents the latitude and the figure the longitude.

In some cases the feature itself may fall within the specified square, while the name is outside. This is usually the case only with features which are larger than a grid square.

For a more precise location the geographical coordinates which follow the letter/figure references give the latitude and the longitude of each place. The first set of figures represent the latitude which is the distance north or south of the Equator measured as an angle at the centre of the earth. The Equator is latitude 0°, the North Pole is 90°N, and the South Pole 90°S.

The second set of figures represent the longitude, which is the distance East or West of the prime meridian, which runs through Greenwich, England. Longitude is also measured as an angle at the centre of the earth and is given East or West of the prime meridian, from 0° to 180° in either direction.

The unit of measurement for latitude and longitude is the degree, which is subdivided into 60 minutes. Each index entry states the position of a place in degrees and minutes, a space being left between the degrees and the minutes.

The latitude is followed by N(orth) or S(outh) and the longitude by E(ast) or W(est).

Rivers are indexed to their mouths or confluences, and carry the symbol ⇾ after their names. A solid square ■ follows the name of a country, while an open square □ refers to a first order administrative area.

ABBREVIATIONS USED IN THE INDEX

A.C.T. – Australian Capital Territory
Afghan. – Afghanistan
Ala. – Alabama
Alta. – Alberta
Amer. – America(n)
Arch. – Archipelago
Ariz. – Arizona
Ark. – Arkansas
Atl. Oc. – Atlantic Ocean
B. – Baie, Bahía, Bay, Bucht, Bugt
B.C. – British Columbia
Bangla. – Bangladesh
Barr. – Barrage
Bos.-H. – Bosnia-Herzegovina
C. – Cabo, Cap, Cape, Coast
C.A.R. – Central African Republic
C. Prov. – Cape Province
Calif. – California
Cent. – Central
Chan. – Channel
Colo. – Colorado
Conn. – Connecticut
Cord. – Cordillera
Cr. – Creek
Czech. – Czech Republic
D.C. – District of Columbia
Del. – Delaware
Dep. – Dependency
Des. – Desert
Dist. – District
Dj. – Djebel
Domin. – Dominica
Dom. Rep. – Dominican Republic
E. – East

E. Salv. – El Salvador
Eq. Guin. – Equatorial Guinea
Fla. – Florida
Falk. Is. – Falkland Is.
G. – Golfe, Golfo, Gulf, Guba, Gebel
Ga. – Georgia
Gt. – Great, Greater
Guinea-Biss. – Guinea-Bissau
H.K. – Hong Kong
H.P. – Himachal Pradesh
Hants. – Hampshire
Harb. – Harbor, Harbour
Hd. – Head
Hts. – Heights
I.(s). – Île, Ilha, Insel, Isla, Island, Isle
Ill. – Illinois
Ind. – Indiana
Ind. Oc. – Indian Ocean
Ivory C. – Ivory Coast
J. – Jabal, Jebel, Jazira
Junc. – Junction
K. – Kap, Kapp
Kans. – Kansas
Kep. – Kepulauan
Ky. – Kentucky
L. – Lac, Lacul, Lago, Lagoa, Lake, Limni, Loch, Lough
La. – Louisiana
Liech. – Liechtenstein
Lux. – Luxembourg
Mad. P. – Madhya Pradesh
Madag. – Madagascar
Man. – Manitoba
Mass. – Massachusetts

Md. – Maryland
Me. – Maine
Medit. S. – Mediterranean Sea
Mich. – Michigan
Minn. – Minnesota
Miss. – Mississippi
Mo. – Missouri
Mont. – Montana
Mozam. – Mozambique
Mt.(e) – Mont, Monte, Monti, Montaña, Mountain
N. – Nord, Norte, North, Northern, Nouveau
N.B. – New Brunswick
N.C. – North Carolina
N. Cal. – New Caledonia
N. Dak. – North Dakota
N.H. – New Hampshire
N.I. – North Island
N.J. – New Jersey
N. Mex. – New Mexico
N.S. – Nova Scotia
N.S.W. – New South Wales
N.W.T. – North West Territory
N.Y. – New York
N.Z. – New Zealand
Nebr. – Nebraska
Neths. – Netherlands
Nev. – Nevada
Nfld. – Newfoundland
Nic. – Nicaragua
O. – Oued, Ouadi
Occ. – Occidentale
Okla. – Oklahoma
Ont. – Ontario
Or. – Orientale

Oreg. – Oregon
Os. – Ostrov
Oz. – Ozero
P. – Pass, Passo, Pasul, Pulau
P.E.I. – Prince Edward Island
Pa. – Pennsylvania
Pac. Oc. – Pacific Ocean
Papua N.G. – Papua New Guinea
Pass. – Passage
Pen. – Peninsula, Péninsule
Phil. – Philippines
Pk. – Park, Peak
Plat. – Plateau
Prov. – Province, Provincial
Pt. – Point
Pta. – Ponta, Punta
Pte. – Pointe
Qué. – Québec
Queens. – Queensland
R. – Rio, River
R.I. – Rhode Island
Ra.(s). – Range(s)
Raj. – Rajasthan
Reg. – Region
Rep. – Republic
Res. – Reserve, Reservoir
S. – San, South, Sea
Si. Arabia – Saudi Arabia
S.C. – South Carolina
S. Dak. – South Dakota
S.I. – South Island
S. Leone – Sierra Leone
Sa. – Serra, Sierra
Sask. – Saskatchewan
Scot. – Scotland
Sd. – Sound

Sev. – Severnaya
Sib. – Siberia
Sprs. – Springs
St. – Saint
Sta. – Santa, Station
Ste. – Sainte
Sto. – Santo
Str. – Strait, Stretto
Switz. – Switzerland
Tas. – Tasmania
Tenn. – Tennessee
Tex. – Texas
Tg. – Tanjung
Trin. & Tob. – Trinidad & Tobago
U.A.E. – United Arab Emirates
U.K. – United Kingdom
U.S.A. – United States of America
Ut. P. – Uttar Pradesh
Va. – Virginia
Vdkhr. – Vodokhranilishche
Vf. – Virful
Vic. – Victoria
Vol. – Volcano
Vt. – Vermont
W. – Wadi, West
W. Va. – West Virginia
Wash. – Washington
Wis. – Wisconsin
Wlkp. – Wielkopolski
Wyo. – Wyoming
Yorks. – Yorkshire
Yug. – Yugoslavia

A

Al Kāmil 179

Ageo, Japan 71 B11 35 58N 139 36 E
Ager Tay, Chad 109 E3 20 0N 17 41 E
Agerbæk, Denmark 17 J2 55 36N 8 48 E
Agersø, Denmark 17 J5 55 13N 11 12 E
Ageyevo, Russia 58 E9 54 10N 36 27 E
Āgh Kand, Iran 97 B6 37 15N 48 4 E
Aghireşu, Romania 53 D8 46 53N 23 15 E
Aghoueyyît, Mauritania 110 D1 21 10N 15 6W
Aginskoye, Russia 65 D12 51 6N 114 32 E
Ağlasun, Turkey 49 D12 37 39N 30 31 E
Agly →, France 28 F7 42 46N 3 3 E
Agnew, Australia 125 E3 28 1 S 120 31 E
Agnibilékrou, Ivory C. 112 D4 7 10N 3 11W
Agnita, Romania 53 E9 45 59N 24 40 E
Agno, Switz. 33 E7 45 59N 8 53 E
Agnone, Italy 45 G11 41 48N 14 22 E
Ago, Japan 71 C8 34 20N 136 51 E
Agofie, Ghana 113 D5 8 27N 0 15 E
Agogna →, Italy 44 C5 45 4N 8 54 E
Agogo, Sudan 107 F2 7 50N 28 45 E
Agön, Sweden 16 C11 61 34N 17 23 E
Agon Coutainville, France 26 C5 49 2N 1 34W
Agoo, Phil. 80 C3 16 20N 120 22 E
Ágordo, Italy 45 B9 46 18N 12 2 E
Agori, India 93 G10 24 33N 82 57 E
Agouna, Benin 113 D5 7 39N 1 47 E
Agout →, France 28 E5 43 47N 1 41 E
Agra, India 92 F7 27 17N 77 58 E
Agrakhanskiy Poluostrov, Russia 61 J8 43 42N 47 36 E
Agramunt, Spain 40 D6 41 48N 1 6 E
Agreda, Spain 40 D3 41 51N 1 55W
Ağri, Turkey 101 C10 39 44N 43 4 E
Agri →, Italy 47 B9 40 13N 16 44 E
Ağrı Dağı, Turkey 101 C11 39 50N 44 15 E
Ağrı Karakose = Ağrı, Turkey 57 G7 39 44N 43 3 E
Agriá, Greece 48 B5 39 20N 23 1 E
Agrigento, Italy 46 E6 37 19N 13 34 E
Agrínion, Greece 48 C3 38 37N 21 27 E
Agrópoli, Italy 47 B7 40 21N 14 59 E
Ağstafa, Azerbaijan 61 K7 41 7N 45 27 E
Água Branca, Brazil 170 C3 5 50 S 42 40W
Agua Caliente, Baja Calif., Mexico 161 N10 32 29N 116 59W
Agua Caliente, Sinaloa, Mexico 162 B3 26 30N 108 20W
Agua Caliente Springs, U.S.A. 161 N10 32 56N 116 19W
Água Clara, Brazil 173 E7 20 25 S 52 45W
Agua Hechicero, Mexico 161 N10 32 26N 116 14W
Agua Preta →, Brazil 169 D5 1 41 S 63 48W
Agua Prieta, Mexico 162 A3 31 20N 109 32W
Aguachica, Colombia 168 B3 8 19N 73 38W
Aguada Cecilio, Argentina 176 B3 40 51 S 65 51W
Aguadas, Colombia 168 B2 5 40N 75 38W
Aguadilla, Puerto Rico 165 C6 18 26N 67 10W
Aguadulce, Panama 164 E3 8 15N 80 32W
Aguanga, U.S.A. 161 M10 33 27N 116 51W
Aguanish, Canada 141 B7 50 14N 62 2W
Aguanus →, Canada 141 B7 50 13N 62 5W
Aguapeí, Brazil 173 D6 16 12 S 59 43W
Aguapeí →, Brazil 171 F1 21 0 S 51 0W
Aguapey →, Argentina 174 B4 29 7 S 56 36W
Aguaray Guazú →, Paraguay 174 A4 24 47 S 57 19W
Aguarico →, Ecuador 168 D2 0 59 S 75 11W
Aguas →, Spain 40 D4 41 20N 0 30W
Aguas Blancas, Chile 174 A2 24 15 S 69 55W
Aguas Calientes, Sierra de, Argentina 174 B2 25 26 S 66 40W
Águas Formosas, Brazil 171 E3 17 5 S 40 57W
Aguascalientes, Mexico 162 C4 21 53N 102 12W
Aguascalientes □, Mexico 162 C4 22 0N 102 20W
Agudo, Spain 43 G6 38 59N 4 52W
Águeda, Portugal 42 E2 40 34N 8 27W
Agueda →, Spain 42 D4 41 2N 6 56W
Aguelhok, Mali 113 B5 19 29N 0 52 E
Aguié, Niger 113 C6 13 31N 7 46 E
Aguilafuente, Spain 42 D6 41 13N 4 7W
Aguilar, Spain 43 H6 37 31N 4 40W
Aguilar de Campóo, Spain 42 C6 42 47N 4 15W
Aguilares, Argentina 174 B2 27 26 S 65 35W
Aguilas, Spain 41 H3 37 23N 1 35W
Agüimes, Canary Is. 39 G4 27 58N 15 27W
Aguja, C. de la, Colombia 168 A3 11 18N 74 12W
Agulaa, Ethiopia 107 E4 13 40N 39 40 E
Agulhas, C., S. Africa 116 E3 34 52 S 20 0 E
Agulo, Canary Is. 39 F2 28 11N 17 12W
Agung, Indonesia 78 F5 8 20 S 115 28 E
Agur, Uganda 118 B3 2 28N 32 55 E
Agusan →, Phil. 79 C7 9 0N 125 30 E
Agusan del Norte □, Phil. 81 G5 9 20N 125 10 E
Agusan del Sur □, Phil. 81 G5 8 30N 125 30 E
Agustín Codazzi, Colombia 168 A3 10 2N 73 14W
Agutaya I., Phil. 81 F3 11 9N 120 58 E
Ağva, Turkey 51 E13 41 8N 29 51 E
Agvali, Russia 61 J8 42 36N 46 8 E
Aha Mts., Botswana 116 B3 19 45 S 21 0 E
Ahaggar, Algeria 111 D6 23 0N 6 30 E
Ahamansu, Ghana 113 D5 7 38N 0 35 E
Ahar, Iran 101 C12 38 35N 47 0 E
Ahat, Turkey 49 C11 38 39N 29 47 E
Ahaura →, N.Z. 131 C6 42 21 S 171 34 E
Ahaus, Germany 30 C2 52 4N 7 0 E
Åheim, Norway 18 B2 62 2N 5 13 E
Ahelledjem, Algeria 111 C6 26 37N 6 58 E
Ahimanawa Ra., N.Z. 130 F5 39 3 S 176 30 E
Ahipara B., N.Z. 130 B2 35 5 S 173 5 E
Ahir Dağı, Turkey 49 C12 38 45N 30 10 E
Ahiri, India 94 E5 19 30N 80 0 E
Ahlat, Turkey 101 C10 38 45N 42 29 E
Ahlen, Germany 30 D3 51 45N 7 53 E
Ahmad Wal, Pakistan 92 E1 29 18N 65 58 E
Ahmadabad, India 92 H5 23 0N 72 40 E
Aḩmadābād, Khorāsān, Iran 97 C9 35 3N 60 50 E
Aḩmadābād, Khorāsān, Iran 97 C8 35 49N 59 42 E
Aḩmadī, Iran 97 E8 27 56N 56 42 E
Ahmadnagar, India 94 E2 19 7N 74 46 E
Ahmadpur, India 94 E3 18 40N 76 57 E
Ahmadpur, Pakistan 92 E4 29 12N 71 10 E
Ahmadpur Lamma, Pakistan 92 E4 28 19N 70 3 E
Ahmar, Ethiopia 107 F5 9 20N 41 15 E
Ahmedabad = Ahmadabad, India 92 H5 23 0N 72 40 E
Ahmednagar = Ahmadnagar, India 94 E2 19 7N 74 46 E
Ahmetbey, Turkey 51 E11 41 26N 27 34 E
Ahmetler, Turkey 49 C11 38 28N 29 5 E
Ahmetli, Turkey 49 C9 38 32N 27 57 E
Ahoada, Nigeria 113 D6 5 8N 6 36 E
Ahome, Mexico 162 B3 25 55N 109 11W
Ahoskie, U.S.A. 149 G7 36 17N 76 59W
Ahr →, Germany 30 E3 50 32N 7 16 E
Ahram, Iran 97 D6 28 52N 51 16 E
Ahrax Pt., Malta 38 D1 35 59N 14 22 E
Ahrensbök, Germany 30 A6 54 2N 10 35 E
Ahrensburg, Germany 30 B6 53 40N 10 13 E
Āhū, Iran 97 C6 34 33N 50 2 E
Ahuachapán, El Salv. 164 D2 13 54N 89 52W
Ahun, France 27 F9 46 4N 2 5 E
Ahuriri →, N.Z. 131 E5 44 31 S 170 12 E
Åhus, Sweden 17 J8 55 56N 14 18 E
Ahvāz, Iran 97 D6 31 20N 48 40 E
Ahvenanmaa = Åland, Finland 15 F19 60 15N 20 0 E
Aḩwar, Yemen 98 D4 13 30N 46 40 E
Ahzar →, Mali 113 B5 15 30N 3 20 E
Ai →, India 93 F14 26 26N 90 44 E
Ai-Ais, Namibia 116 D2 27 54 S 17 59 E
Aiari →, Brazil 168 C4 1 22N 68 36W
Aichach, Germany 31 G7 48 27N 11 8 E
Aichi □, Japan 71 B9 35 0N 137 15 E
Aiea, U.S.A. 145 K14 21 23N 157 56W
Aigle, Switz. 32 D3 46 18N 6 58 E
Aignay-le-Duc, France 27 E11 47 40N 4 43 E
Aigoual, Mt., France 28 D7 44 8N 3 35 E
Aigre, France 28 C4 45 54N 0 1 E
Aigua, Uruguay 175 C5 34 13 S 54 46W
Aigueperse, France 27 F10 46 3N 3 13 E
Aigues →, France 29 D8 44 7N 4 43 E
Aigues-Mortes, France 29 E8 43 35N 4 12 E
Aigues-Mortes, G. d', France 29 E8 43 31N 4 3 E
Aiguilles, France 29 D10 44 47N 6 51 E
Aiguillon, France 28 D4 44 18N 0 21 E
Aigurande, France 27 F8 46 27N 1 49 E
Aihui, China 73 A7 50 10N 127 30 E
Aija, Peru 172 B2 9 50 S 77 45W
Aikawa, Japan 68 E9 38 2N 138 15 E
Aiken, U.S.A. 152 B8 33 34N 81 43W
Ailao Shan, China 76 F3 24 0N 101 20 E
Aileron, Australia 126 C1 22 39 S 133 20 E
Ailey, U.S.A. 152 C7 32 11N 82 34W
Ailigandi, Panama 168 B2 9 14N 78 1W
Aillant-sur-Tholon, France 27 E10 47 52N 3 20 E
Aillik, Canada 141 A8 55 11N 59 18W
Ailsa Craig, U.K. 22 F3 55 15N 5 6W
'Ailūn, Jordan 103 C4 32 18N 35 47 E
Aim, Russia 65 D14 59 0N 133 55 E
Aimere, Indonesia 79 F6 8 45 S 121 3 E
Aimogasta, Argentina 174 B2 28 33 S 66 50W
Aimorés, Brazil 171 E3 19 30 S 41 4W
Ain □, France 27 F12 46 5N 5 20 E
Ain →, France 29 C9 45 45N 5 11 E
Aïn Beïda, Algeria 111 A6 35 50N 7 29 E
Aïn Ben Khellil, Algeria 111 B4 33 15N 0 49W
Aïn Ben Tili, Mauritania 110 C3 25 59N 9 27W
Aïn Beni Mathar, Morocco 111 B4 34 1N 2 0W
Aïn Benian, Algeria 111 A5 36 48N 2 55 E
Ain Dalla, Egypt 106 B2 27 20N 27 23 E
Ain el Mafki, Egypt 106 B2 27 30N 28 15 E
Ain Girba, Egypt 106 B2 29 20N 25 14 E
Aïn M'lila, Algeria 111 A6 36 2N 6 35 E
Ain Murr, Sudan 106 C2 21 50N 25 9 E
Ain Qeiqab, Egypt 106 B1 29 42N 24 55 E
Aïn-Sefra, Algeria 111 B4 32 47N 0 37W
Ain Sheikh Murzûk, Egypt 106 B2 26 47N 27 45 E
'Ain Sudr, Egypt 103 F2 29 50N 33 6 E
Ain Sukhna, Egypt 106 J8 29 32N 32 20 E
Aïn Tédelès, Algeria 111 A5 36 0N 0 21 E
Aïn-Témouchent, Algeria 111 A4 35 16N 1 8W
Aïn Touta, Algeria 111 A6 35 26N 5 54 E
Ain Zeitûn, Egypt 106 B2 29 10N 25 48 E
Aïn Zorah, Morocco 111 B4 34 37N 3 32W
Ainabo, Somali Rep. 120 C3 9 0N 46 25 E
Ainaži, Latvia 15 H21 57 50N 24 24 E
Aínos Óros, Greece 48 C2 38 10N 20 35 E
Ainsworth, U.S.A. 154 D5 42 33N 99 52W
Aioi, Japan 70 C6 34 48N 134 28 E
Aipe, Colombia 168 C2 3 13N 75 15W
Aiquile, Bolivia 173 D4 18 10 S 65 10W
Aïr, Niger 113 B6 18 30N 8 0 E
Air Force I., Canada 139 B12 67 58N 74 5W
Air Hitam, Malaysia 87 M4 1 55N 103 11 E
Airaines, France 27 C8 49 58N 1 55 E
Airão, Brazil 169 D5 1 56 S 61 22W
Airdrie, Canada 142 C6 51 18N 114 2W
Airdrie, U.K. 22 F5 55 52N 3 57W
Aire →, France 27 C11 49 18N 4 49 E
Aire →, U.K. 20 D7 53 43N 0 55W
Aire, I. de l', Spain 39 B11 39 48N 4 16 E
Aire-sur-la-Lys, France 27 B9 50 37N 2 22 E
Aire-sur-l'Adour, France 28 E3 43 42N 0 15W
Aireys Inlet, Australia 128 E6 38 29 S 144 5 E
Airlie Beach, Australia 126 C4 20 16 S 148 43 E
Airolo, Switz. 33 C7 46 32N 8 37 E
Airvault, France 26 F6 46 50N 0 8W
Aisch →, Germany 31 F6 49 49N 10 58 E
Aisen □, Chile 176 C2 46 30 S 73 0W
Aisne □, France 27 C10 49 42N 3 40 E
Aisne →, France 27 C9 49 26N 2 50 E
Ait, India 93 G8 25 54N 79 14 E
Aitana, Sierra de, Spain 41 G4 38 35N 0 24W
Aitape, Papua N. G. 132 B2 3 11 S 142 22 E
Aitkin, U.S.A. 154 B8 46 32N 93 42W
Aitolía Kai Akarnanía □, Greece 48 C3 38 45N 21 18 E
Aitolikón, Greece 48 C3 38 26N 21 21 E
Aiuaba, Brazil 170 C3 6 38 S 40 7W
Aiud, Romania 53 D8 46 19N 23 44 E
Aix-en-Provence, France 29 E9 43 32N 5 27 E
Aix-la-Chapelle = Aachen, Germany 30 E2 50 45N 6 6 E
Aix-les-Bains, France 29 C9 45 41N 5 53 E
Aixe-sur-Vienne, France 28 C5 45 47N 1 9 E
Aiyang, Mt., Papua N. G. 132 C1 5 10 S 141 20 E
Aíyina, Greece 48 D5 37 45N 23 26 E
Aiyínion, Greece 50 F6 40 28N 22 28 E
Aíyion, Greece 48 C4 38 15N 22 5 E
Aizawl, India 90 D4 23 40N 92 44 E
Aizenay, France 26 F5 46 44N 1 38W
Aizkraukle, Latvia 15 H21 56 36N 25 11 E
Aizpute, Latvia 15 H19 56 43N 21 40 E
Aizuwakamatsu, Japan 68 F9 37 30N 139 56 E
Ajaccio, France 29 G12 41 55N 8 40 E
Ajaccio, G. d', France 29 G12 41 52N 8 40 E
Ajaigarh, India 93 G9 24 52N 80 16 E
Ajaju →, Colombia 168 C3 0 59N 72 20W
Ajalpan, Mexico 163 D5 18 22N 97 15W
Ajanta, India 94 D2 20 28N 75 48 E
Ajanta Ra., India 94 D2 20 28N 75 50 E
Ajari Rep. = Ajaria □, Georgia 61 K6 41 30N 42 0 E
Ajaria □, Georgia 61 K6 41 30N 42 0 E
Ajax, Canada 150 C5 43 50N 79 1W
Ajax, Mt., N.Z. 131 C7 42 35 S 172 5 E
Ajayan Pt., Guam 133 R15 13 15N 144 43 E
Ajdâbiyah, Libya 108 B4 30 54N 20 4 E
Ajdovščina, Slovenia 45 C10 45 54N 13 54 E
Ajibar, Ethiopia 107 E4 10 35N 38 36 E
Ajka, Hungary 52 C2 47 4N 17 31 E
'Ajmān, U.A.E. 97 E7 25 25N 55 30 E
Ajmer, India 92 F6 26 28N 74 37 E
Ajnala, India 92 D6 31 50N 74 48 E
Ajo, U.S.A. 159 K7 32 22N 112 52W
Ajo, C. de, Spain 42 B7 43 31N 3 35W
Ajoie, Switz. 32 B4 47 22N 7 0 E
Ajok, Sudan 107 F2 9 15N 28 28 E
Ajuy, Phil. 81 F4 11 10N 123 1 E
Ak Dağ, Turkey 49 E11 36 30N 29 32 E
Ak Dağları, Muğla, Turkey 49 E11 36 30N 29 30 E
Ak Dağları, Sivas, Turkey 100 C7 39 32N 36 12 E
Akaba, Togo 113 D5 8 10N 1 2 E
Akabira, Japan 68 C11 43 33N 142 5 E
Akabli, Algeria 111 C5 26 49N 1 31 E
Akaishi-Dake, Japan 71 B10 35 27N 138 9 E
Akaishi-Sammyaku, Japan 71 B10 35 25N 138 10 E
Akaki Beseka, Ethiopia 107 F4 8 55N 38 45 E
Akala, Sudan 107 D4 15 39N 36 13 E
Akalkot, India 94 F3 17 32N 76 13 E
Akamas □, Cyprus 38 D11 35 3N 32 18 E
Akanthou, Cyprus 38 D12 35 22N 33 45 E
Akarca, Turkey 49 C11 38 35N 29 35 E
Akaroa, N.Z. 131 D7 43 49 S 172 59 E
Akaroa Harbour, N.Z. 131 D7 43 50 S 172 55 E
Akasha, Sudan 106 C3 21 10N 30 32 E
Akashi, Japan 70 C6 34 45N 134 58 E
Akbarpur, Bihar, India 93 G10 24 39N 83 58 E
Akbarpur, Ut. P., India 93 F10 26 25N 82 32 E
Akbou, Algeria 111 A5 36 31N 4 31 E
Akbulak, Russia 62 F3 51 1N 55 37 E
Akçaabat, Turkey 101 B8 41 1N 39 34 E
Akçadağ, Turkey 100 C7 38 27N 37 43 E
Akçakale, Turkey 101 D8 36 41N 38 56 E
Akçakoca, Turkey 100 B4 41 5N 31 8 E
Akçaova, Turkey 51 E13 41 3N 29 57 E
Akçay, Turkey 49 E11 36 36N 29 45 E
Akçay →, Turkey 49 D10 37 50N 28 15 E
Akchâr, Mauritania 110 D2 20 20N 14 28W
Akdağ, Turkey 49 C8 38 33N 26 30 E
Akdağmadeni, Turkey 100 C6 39 39N 35 53 E
Akdala, Kazakstan 63 A7 45 2N 74 35 E
Akechi, Japan 71 B9 35 18N 137 23 E
Akelamo, Indonesia 79 D7 1 35N 129 40 E
Åkernes, Norway 18 F4 58 45N 7 30 E
Åkers styckebruk, Sweden 16 E11 59 15N 17 5 E
Åkersberga, Sweden 16 E12 59 29N 18 18 E
Akershus □, Norway 18 D8 60 0N 11 10 E
Akeru →, India 94 F5 17 25N 80 5 E
Aketi, Dem. Rep. of the Congo 114 B4 2 38N 23 47 E
Akhaïa □, Greece 48 C3 38 5N 21 45 E
Akhalkalaki, Georgia 61 K6 41 27N 43 25 E
Akhaltsikhe, Georgia 61 K6 41 40N 43 0 E
Akharnaí, Greece 48 C5 38 5N 23 44 E
Akhelóös →, Greece 48 C3 38 19N 21 7 E
Akhendriá, Greece 49 G7 34 59N 25 13 E
Akhiok, U.S.A. 144 H9 56 57N 154 10W
Akhisar, Turkey 49 C9 38 56N 27 48 E
Akhladhókambos, Greece 48 D4 37 31N 22 35 E
Akhmîm, Egypt 106 B3 26 31N 31 47 E
Akhnur, India 93 C6 32 52N 74 45 E
Akhtopol, Bulgaria 51 D11 42 6N 27 56 E
Akhtuba →, Russia 61 G8 47 41N 46 55 E
Akhtubinsk, Russia 61 F8 48 13N 46 7 E
Akhty, Russia 61 K8 41 30N 47 45 E
Akhtyrka = Okhtyrka, Ukraine 59 G8 50 25N 35 0 E
Aki, Japan 70 D5 33 30N 133 54 E
Aki-Nada, Japan 70 C4 34 5N 132 40 E
Akiachak, U.S.A. 144 F7 60 55N 161 26W
Akiéni, Gabon 114 C2 1 11 S 13 53 E
Akimiski I., Canada 140 B3 52 50N 81 30W
Akimovka, Ukraine 59 J8 46 44N 35 0 E
Åkirkeby, Denmark 17 J8 55 4N 14 55 E
Akita, Japan 68 E10 39 45N 140 7 E
Akita □, Japan 68 E10 39 40N 140 30 E
Akjoujt, Mauritania 112 B2 19 45N 14 15W
Akka, Mali 112 B4 15 24N 4 11W
Akka, Morocco 110 C3 29 22N 8 9W
Akkaraipattu, Sri Lanka 95 L5 7 13N 81 51 E
Akkaya Tepesi, Turkey 49 D11 37 25N 29 38 E
Akkeshi, Japan 68 C12 43 2N 144 51 E
'Akko, Israel 103 C4 32 55N 35 4 E
Akkol, Kazakstan 63 B5 43 36N 70 45 E
Akköy, Turkey 49 D9 37 29N 27 15 E
Aklampa, Benin 113 D5 8 15N 2 10 E
Aklan □, Phil. 81 F4 11 50N 122 30 E
Aklavik, Canada 138 B6 68 12N 135 0W
Aklera, India 92 G7 24 26N 76 32 E
Akmenė, Lithuania 54 B9 56 15N 22 45 E
Akmenrags, Latvia 54 B8 56 50N 21 4 E
Akmolinsk = Astana, Kazakstan 64 D8 51 10N 71 30 E
Akmonte = Almonte, Spain 43 H4 37 13N 6 38W
Akmuz, Kyrgyzstan 63 C8 41 15N 76 10 E
Aknoul, Morocco 111 B4 34 40N 3 55W
Akō, Japan 70 C6 34 45N 134 24 E
Ako, Nigeria 113 C7 10 19N 10 48 E
Akôbô, Sudan 107 F3 7 47N 33 1 E
Akobo →, Ethiopia 107 F3 7 48N 33 3 E
Akola, India 94 D3 20 42N 77 2 E
Akola, India 94 E2 19 32N 74 3 E
Akolmiut, U.S.A. 144 F7 60 55N 162 20W
Akonolinga, Cameroon 113 E7 3 50N 12 18 E
Akor, Mali 112 C3 14 59N 6 58W
Akordat, Eritrea 102 D2 15 30N 37 40 E
Akosombo Dam, Ghana 113 D5 6 20N 0 5 E
Akot, India 94 D3 21 10N 77 10 E
Akot, Sudan 107 F3 6 31N 30 9 E
Akoupé, Ivory C. 112 D4 6 23N 3 54W
Akourousoulba, C.A.R. 114 A4 8 58N 20 46 E
Akpatok I., Canada 139 B13 60 25N 68 8W
Åkrahamn, Norway 15 G11 59 15N 5 10 E
Akranes, Iceland 11 C4 64 19N 22 5W
Akreïjit, Mauritania 112 B3 18 19N 9 11W
Akrítas Venétiko, Ákra, Greece 48 E3 36 43N 21 54 E
Akron, Colo., U.S.A. 154 E3 40 10N 103 13W
Akron, Ind., U.S.A. 157 C10 41 2N 86 1W
Akron, Ohio, U.S.A. 150 E3 41 5N 81 31W
Akrotiri, Cyprus 38 E11 34 36N 32 57 E
Akrotíri, Ákra, Greece 51 F9 40 26N 25 27 E
Akrotiri Bay, Cyprus 38 E12 34 35N 33 10 E
Aksai Chin, India 93 B8 35 15N 79 55 E
Aksaray, Turkey 100 C6 38 25N 34 2 E
Aksay, Kazakstan 57 D9 51 11N 53 0 E
Akşehir, Turkey 100 C4 38 18N 31 30 E
Akşehir Gölü, Turkey 100 C4 38 30N 31 25 E
Akstafa = Ağstafa, Azerbaijan 61 K7 41 7N 45 27 E
Aksu, China 72 B3 41 5N 80 10 E
Aksu →, Turkey 100 D4 36 52N 30 57 E
Aksum, Ethiopia 102 E2 14 5N 38 40 E
Aktash, Russia 60 C11 55 2N 52 0 E
Aktash, Uzbekistan 63 D2 39 55N 65 55 E
Aktasty, Kazakstan 62 F8 50 42N 61 42 E
Aktogay, Almaty, Kazakstan 63 A8 44 25N 76 44 E
Aktogay, Semey, Kazakstan 64 E8 46 57N 79 40 E
Aktsyabrski, Belarus 59 F5 52 38N 28 53 E
Aktyubinsk = Aqtöbe, Kazakstan 57 D10 50 17N 57 10 E
Aktyuz, Kyrgyzstan 63 B8 42 54N 76 7 E
Aku, Nigeria 113 D6 6 40N 7 18 E
Akula, Dem. Rep. of the Congo 114 B4 2 22N 20 12 E
Akune, Japan 70 E2 32 1N 130 12 E
Akure, Nigeria 113 D6 7 15N 5 5 E
Akurenan, Eq. Guin. 114 B2 1 2N 10 40 E
Akuressa, Sri Lanka 95 L5 6 5N 80 29 E
Akureyri, Iceland 11 B8 65 40N 18 6W
Akuseki-Shima, Japan 69 K4 29 27N 129 37 E
Akusha, Russia 61 J8 42 18N 47 30 E
Akutan, U.S.A. 144 J6 54 8N 165 46W
Akutan Indian Reservation, U.S.A. 144 J6 54 10N 166 0W
Akwa-Ibom □, Nigeria 113 E6 4 30N 7 30 E
Akyab = Sittwe, Burma 90 E4 20 18N 92 45 E
Akyazı, Turkey 100 B4 40 40N 30 38 E
Akzhar, Kazakstan 63 B5 43 8N 71 37 E
Ål, Norway 18 D5 60 38N 8 33 E
Al Abyār, Libya 108 B4 32 9N 20 29 E
Al 'Adan, Yemen 98 D4 12 45N 45 0 E
Al Aḩsā = Hasa □, Si. Arabia 97 E6 25 50N 49 0 E
Al Ajfar, Si. Arabia 96 E4 27 26N 43 0 E
Al Amādīyah, Iraq 101 D10 37 5N 43 30 E
Al 'Amārah, Iraq 101 G12 31 55N 47 15 E
Al 'Aqabah, Jordan 103 F4 29 31N 35 0 E
Al 'Aqīq, Si. Arabia 98 B3 20 39N 41 25 E
Al Arak, Syria 101 E8 34 38N 38 35 E
Al 'Aramah, Si. Arabia 96 E5 25 30N 46 0 E
Al 'Ariḑah, Si. Arabia 98 C3 17 3N 43 5 E
Al Arṭāwīyah, Si. Arabia 96 E5 26 31N 45 20 E
Al Ashkhara, Oman 99 B7 21 50N 59 30 E
Al 'Āşimah = 'Ammān □, Jordan 103 D5 31 40N 36 30 E
Al 'Assāfīyah, Si. Arabia 96 D3 28 17N 38 59 E
Al 'Ayn, Oman 97 E7 24 15N 55 45 E
Al 'Ayn, Si. Arabia 96 E3 25 4N 38 6 E
Al 'Azamīyah, Iraq 96 C5 33 22N 44 22 E
Al 'Azīzīyah, Iraq 101 F11 32 54N 45 4 E
Al 'Azīzīyah, Libya 108 B2 32 30N 13 1 E
Al Bāb, Syria 100 D7 36 23N 37 29 E
Al Bad', Si. Arabia 96 D2 28 28N 35 1 E
Al Bādī, Iraq 96 C4 35 56N 41 32 E
Al Badī', Si. Arabia 98 B4 22 0N 46 35 E
Al Baḩrah, Kuwait 96 D5 29 40N 47 52 E
Al Baḩral Mayyit = Dead Sea, Asia 103 D4 31 30N 35 30 E
Al Balqā' □, Jordan 103 C4 32 5N 35 45 E
Al Barkāt, Libya 108 D2 24 56N 10 14 E
Al Bārūk, J., Lebanon 103 B4 33 39N 35 40 E
Al Başrah, Iraq 96 D5 30 30N 47 50 E
Al Baṭḩā, Iraq 96 D5 31 6N 45 53 E
Al Batrūn, Lebanon 103 A4 34 15N 35 40 E
Al Bayāḑ, Si. Arabia 98 B4 22 0N 47 0 E
Al Bayḑā, Libya 108 B4 32 50N 21 44 E
Al Bayḑā', Yemen 98 D4 14 5N 45 42 E
Al Bayḑā □, Libya 108 B4 32 0N 21 30 E
Al Bi'ār, Si. Arabia 98 B2 22 39N 39 40 E
Al Biqā, Lebanon 103 A5 34 10N 36 10 E
Al Bi'r, Si. Arabia 96 D3 28 51N 36 16 E
Al Birk, Si. Arabia 98 C3 18 13N 41 33 E
Al Bu'ayrāt al Ḩasūn, Libya 108 B3 31 24N 15 44 E
Al Burayj, Syria 103 A5 34 15N 36 46 E
Al Faḑilī, Si. Arabia 97 E6 26 58N 49 10 E
Al Fallūjah, Iraq 101 F10 33 20N 43 55 E
Al Fatk, Yemen 99 C6 16 31N 52 41 E
Al Fāw, Iraq 97 D6 30 0N 48 30 E
Al Faydamī, Yemen 99 C6 16 25N 52 26 E
Al Fujayrah, U.A.E. 97 E8 25 7N 56 18 E
Al Ghadaf, W. →, Jordan 103 D5 31 26N 36 43 E
Al Ghammās, Iraq 96 D5 31 45N 44 37 E
Al Gharīb, Libya 108 B4 31 25N 21 11 E
Al Ghayḑah, Yemen 99 C6 16 13N 52 11 E
Al Ghayḑah, Yemen 99 D5 14 55N 50 0 E
Al Ghayl, Yemen 99 D5 15 30N 50 54 E
Al Ghazālah, Si. Arabia 96 E4 26 48N 41 19 E
Al Hābah, Si. Arabia 96 E5 27 10N 47 0 E
Al Ḩadd, Oman 99 B7 22 35N 59 48 E
Al Ḩaddār, Si. Arabia 98 B4 21 58N 45 57 E
Al Ḩadīthah, Iraq 101 E10 34 0N 41 13 E
Al Ḩadīthah, Si. Arabia 103 D6 31 28N 37 8 E
Al Ḩaḑr, Iraq 101 E10 35 35N 42 44 E
Al Hājānah, Syria 103 B5 33 20N 36 33 E
Al Hajar al Gharbi, Oman 97 E8 24 10N 56 15 E
Al Hajarayn, Yemen 99 D5 15 29N 48 20 E
Al Hallānīyah, Oman 99 C7 17 30N 56 1 E
Al Hāmad, Si. Arabia 96 D3 31 30N 39 30 E
Al Ḩamar, Si. Arabia 98 B4 22 26N 46 12 E
Al Hamdānīyah, Syria 96 C3 35 25N 36 50 E
Al Ḩamīdīyah, Syria 103 A4 34 42N 35 57 E
Al Hammādah al Ḩamrā', Libya 108 C2 29 30N 12 0 E
Al Ḩammār, Iraq 96 D5 30 57N 46 51 E
Al Ḩamrā', Si. Arabia 96 E3 24 2N 38 55 E
Al Ḩanākīyah, Si. Arabia 96 E4 24 51N 40 31 E
Al Ḩarīq, Si. Arabia 98 B4 23 29N 46 27 E
Al Harīr, W. →, Syria 103 C4 32 44N 35 59 E
Al Harūj al Aswad, Libya 108 C3 27 0N 17 10 E
Al Ḩasā, W. →, Jordan 103 D4 31 4N 35 29 E
Al Ḩasakah, Syria 101 D9 36 35N 40 45 E
Al Hāsikīyah, Oman 99 C6 17 28N 55 36 E
Al Ḩasy, Yemen 99 D5 14 3N 48 40 E
Al Ḩawrah, Yemen 98 D4 13 50N 47 35 E
Al Ḩawṭah, Yemen 98 D4 14 23N 47 24 E
Al Ḩawṭah □, Si. Arabia 98 B4 23 30N 47 0 E
Al Haydān, W. →, Jordan 103 D4 31 29N 35 34 E
Al Ḩayy, Iraq 101 F12 32 5N 46 5 E
Al Ḩijārah, Asia 96 D4 30 0N 44 0 E
Al Ḩillah, Iraq 101 F11 32 30N 44 25 E
Al Ḩillah, Si. Arabia 98 B4 23 35N 46 50 E
Al Hindīyah, Iraq 101 F11 32 30N 44 10 E
Al Hirmil, Lebanon 103 A5 34 26N 36 24 E
Al Hoceïma, Morocco 110 A4 35 8N 3 58W
Al Ḩudaydah, Yemen 98 D3 14 50N 43 0 E
Al Ḩufrah, Libya 108 C2 25 32N 14 1 E
Al Hufūf, Si. Arabia 97 E6 25 25N 49 45 E
Al Ḩulwah, Si. Arabia 98 B4 23 24N 46 48 E
Al Ḩumayḑah, Si. Arabia 96 D2 29 14N 34 56 E
Al Ḩunayy, Si. Arabia 97 E6 25 58N 48 45 E
Al Ḩurayḑah, Yemen 99 D5 15 36N 48 12 E
Al Husayyāt, Libya 108 B4 30 24N 20 37 E
Al Hūwah, Si. Arabia 98 B4 23 2N 45 48 E
Al Ḩuwaymī, Yemen 98 D4 14 5N 47 35 E
Al 'Irqah, Yemen 98 D4 13 39N 47 22 E
Al Īsāwīyah, Si. Arabia 96 D3 30 43N 37 59 E
Al Ittihad = Madīnat ash Sha'b, Yemen 98 D4 12 50N 45 0 E
Al Jafr, Jordan 103 E5 30 18N 36 14 E
Al Jāfūrah, Si. Arabia 97 E7 25 0N 50 15 E
Al Jaghbūb, Libya 108 C4 29 42N 24 38 E
Al Jahrah, Kuwait 96 D5 29 25N 47 40 E
Al Jalāmīd, Si. Arabia 96 D3 31 20N 40 6 E
Al Jamalīyah, Qatar 97 E6 25 37N 51 5 E
Al Janūb □, Lebanon 103 B4 33 20N 35 20 E
Al Jawf, Libya 108 D4 24 10N 23 24 E
Al Jawf, Si. Arabia 96 D3 29 55N 39 40 E
Al Jazirah, Iraq 101 E10 33 30N 44 0 E
Al Jazirah, Libya 108 C4 26 10N 21 20 E
Al Jithāmīyah, Si. Arabia 96 E4 27 41N 41 43 E
Al Jubayl, Si. Arabia 97 E6 27 0N 49 50 E
Al Jubaylah, Si. Arabia 96 E5 24 55N 46 25 E
Al Jubb, Si. Arabia 96 E4 27 11N 42 12 E
Al Jumūm, Si. Arabia 98 B2 21 37N 39 42 E
Al Junaynah, Sudan 109 F4 13 27N 22 45 E
Al Kabā'ish, Iraq 96 D5 30 58N 47 0 E
Al Kāmil, Oman 99 B7 22 13N 59 12 E

Amrenene el Kasba 181

Allatoona L., *U.S.A.* **152 A5** 34 10N 84 44W
Ålleberg, *Sweden* **17 F7** 58 8N 13 36 E
Allegan, *U.S.A.* **157 B11** 42 32N 85 51W
Allegany, *U.S.A.* **150 D6** 42 6N 78 30W
Allegheny →, *U.S.A.* **150 F5** 40 27N 80 1W
Allegheny Mts., *U.S.A.* **148 G6** 38 15N 80 10W
Allegheny Reservoir, *U.S.A.* **150 E6** 41 50N 79 0W
Allègre, *France* **28 C7** 45 12N 3 41 E
Allen, *Argentina* **176 A3** 38 58 S 67 50W
Allen, *Phil.* **80 E5** 12 30N 124 17 E
Allen, Bog of, *Ireland* **23 C5** 53 15N 7 0W
Allen, L., *Ireland* **23 B3** 54 8N 8 4W
Allendale, *U.S.A.* **152 B8** 33 1N 81 18W
Allende, *Mexico* **162 B4** 28 20N 100 50W
Allensbach, *Germany* **33 A8** 47 43N 9 4 E
Allentown, *U.S.A.* **151 F9** 40 37N 75 29W
Allentsteig, *Austria* **34 C8** 48 41N 15 20 E
Alleppey, *India* **95 K3** 9 30N 76 28 E
Allepuz, *Spain* **40 E4** 40 29N 0 44W
Aller →, *Germany* **30 C5** 52 56N 9 12 E
Alliance, *Surinam* **169 B7** 5 50N 54 50W
Alliance, *Nebr., U.S.A.* **154 D3** 42 6N 102 52W
Alliance, *Ohio, U.S.A.* **150 F3** 40 55N 81 6W
Allier ◻, *France* **27 F9** 46 25N 2 40 E
Allier →, *France* **27 F10** 46 57N 3 4 E
Alliford Bay, *Canada* **142 C2** 53 12N 131 58W
Allinagaram, *India* **95 J3** 10 2N 77 30 E
Allinge, *Denmark* **17 J8** 55 17N 14 50 E
Allison, *U.S.A.* **156 B4** 42 45N 92 48W
Alliston, *Canada* **140 D4** 44 9N 79 52W
Alloa, *U.K.* **22 E5** 56 7N 3 47W
Allones, *France* **26 D8** 48 20N 1 40 E
Allora, *Australia* **127 D5** 28 2 S 152 0 E
Allos, *France* **29 D10** 44 15N 6 38 E
Alluitsup Paa, *Greenland* **10 E6** 60 30N 45 35W
Allur, *India* **95 G5** 14 40N 80 4 E
Alluru Kottapatnam, *India* **95 G5** 15 24N 80 7 E
Alma, *Canada* **141 C5** 48 35N 71 40W
Alma, *Ga., U.S.A.* **152 D7** 31 33N 82 28W
Alma, *Kans., U.S.A.* **154 F6** 39 1N 96 17W
Alma, *Mich., U.S.A.* **148 D3** 43 23N 84 39W
Alma, *Nebr., U.S.A.* **154 E5** 40 6N 99 22W
Alma Ata = Almaty, *Kazakstan* **64 E8** 43 15N 76 57 E
Almacelles, *Spain* **40 D5** 41 43N 0 27 E
Almada, *Portugal* **43 G1** 38 40N 9 9W
Almaden, *Australia* **126 B3** 17 22 S 144 40 E
Almadén, *Spain* **43 G6** 38 49N 4 52W
Almalyk = Olmaliq, *Uzbekistan* **63 C4** 40 50N 69 35 E
Almanor, L., *U.S.A.* **158 F3** 40 14N 121 9W
Almansa, *Spain* **41 G3** 38 51N 1 5W
Almanza, *Spain* **42 C5** 42 39N 5 3W
Almanzor, Pico, *Spain* **42 E5** 40 15N 5 18W
Almanzora →, *Spain* **41 H3** 37 14N 1 46W
Almas, *Brazil* **171 D2** 11 33 S 47 9W
Almaş, Munţii, *Romania* **52 F7** 44 49N 22 12 E
Almassora, *Spain* **40 F4** 39 57N 0 3W
Almaty, *Kazakstan* **64 E8** 43 15N 76 57 E
Almazán, *Spain* **40 D2** 41 30N 2 30W
Almeirim, *Brazil* **169 D7** 1 30 S 52 34W
Almeirim, *Portugal* **43 F2** 39 12N 8 37W
Almelo, *Neths.* **24 B6** 52 22N 6 42 E
Almenar de Soria, *Spain* **40 D2** 41 43N 2 12W
Almenara, *Brazil* **171 E3** 16 11 S 40 42W
Almenara, *Spain* **40 F4** 39 46N 0 14W
Almenara, Sierra de la, *Spain* **41 H3** 37 34N 1 32W
Almendra, Embalse de, *Spain* **42 D4** 41 10N 6 5W
Almendralejo, *Spain* **43 G4** 38 41N 6 26W
Almere-Stad, *Neths.* **24 B5** 52 20N 5 15 E
Almería, *Spain* **43 J8** 36 52N 2 27W
Almería ◻, *Spain* **41 H2** 37 20N 2 20W
Almería, G. de, *Spain* **41 J2** 36 41N 2 28W
Almetyevsk, *Russia* **60 C11** 54 53N 52 20 E
Älmhult, *Sweden* **17 H8** 56 33N 14 8 E
Almirante, *Panama* **164 E3** 9 10N 82 30W
Almirante Montt, G., *Chile* **176 D2** 51 52 S 72 50W
Almiropótamos, *Greece* **48 C6** 38 16N 24 11 E
Almirós, *Greece* **48 B4** 39 11N 22 45 E
Almiroú, Kólpos, *Greece* **38 D6** 35 23N 24 20 E
Almodôvar, *Portugal* **43 H2** 37 31N 8 2W
Almodóvar del Campo, *Spain* **43 G6** 38 43N 4 10W
Almodóvar del Río, *Spain* **43 H5** 37 48N 5 1W
Almond, *U.S.A.* **150 D7** 42 19N 77 44W
Almont, *U.S.A.* **150 D1** 42 55N 83 3W
Almonte, *Canada* **151 A8** 45 14N 76 12W
Almonte, *Spain* **43 H4** 37 13N 6 38W
Almora, *India* **93 E8** 29 38N 79 40 E
Almoradí, *Spain* **41 G4** 38 7N 0 46W
Almorox, *Spain* **42 E6** 40 14N 4 24W
Almoustarat, *Mali* **113 B5** 17 35N 0 8 E
Älmsta, *Sweden* **16 E12** 59 58N 18 50 E
Almudévar, *Spain* **40 C4** 42 3N 0 35W
Almuñécar, *Spain* **43 J7** 36 43N 3 41W
Almunge, *Sweden* **16 E12** 59 53N 18 3 E
Almuradiel, *Spain* **43 G7** 38 32N 3 28W
Alness, *U.K.* **22 D4** 57 41N 4 16W
Alnif, *Morocco* **110 B3** 31 10N 5 8W
Alnmouth, *U.K.* **20 B6** 55 24N 1 37W
Alnwick, *U.K.* **20 B6** 55 24N 1 42W
Aloi, *Uganda* **118 B3** 2 16N 33 10 E
Alon, *Burma* **90 D5** 22 12N 95 5 E
Alor, *Indonesia* **79 F6** 8 15 S 124 30 E
Alor Setar, *Malaysia* **78 C2** 6 7N 100 22 E
Álora, *Spain* **43 J6** 36 49N 4 46W
Alosno, *Spain* **43 H3** 37 33N 7 7W
Alot, *India* **92 H6** 23 56N 75 40 E
Alotau, *Papua N. G.* **132 F6** 10 16 S 150 30 E
Alougoum, *Morocco* **110 B3** 30 17N 6 56W
Aloum, *Cameroon* **114 B2** 2 16N 10 34 E
Aloysius, Mt., *Australia* **125 E4** 26 0 S 128 38 E
Alpaugh, *U.S.A.* **160 K7** 35 53N 119 29W
Alpedrinha, *Portugal* **42 E3** 40 6N 7 27W
Alpena, *U.S.A.* **148 C4** 45 4N 83 27W
Alpercatas →, *Brazil* **170 C3** 6 2 S 44 19W
Alpes-de-Haute-Provence ◻, *France* **29 D10** 44 8N 6 10 E
Alpes-Maritimes ◻, *France* **29 E11** 43 55N 7 10 E
Alpha, *Australia* **126 C4** 23 39 S 146 37 E
Alpha, *U.S.A.* **156 C6** 41 12N 90 23W
Alphen aan den Rijn, *Neths.* **24 B4** 52 7N 4 40 E
Alphonse, *Seychelles* **121 E4** 7 0 S 52 45 E
Alpiarça, *Portugal* **43 F2** 39 15N 8 35W
Alpine, *Ariz., U.S.A.* **159 K9** 33 51N 109 9W
Alpine, *Calif., U.S.A.* **161 N10** 32 50N 116 46W
Alpine, *Tex., U.S.A.* **155 K3** 30 22N 103 40W
Alpnach Dorf, *Switz.* **33 C6** 46 57N 8 17 E
Alps, *Europe* **12 F7** 46 30N 9 30 E
Alpu, *Turkey* **100 C4** 39 46N 30 58 E
Alqueta, Barragem do, *Portugal* **43 G3** 38 20N 7 25W
Alrø, *Denmark* **17 J4** 55 52N 10 5 E
Als, *Denmark* **17 K3** 54 59N 9 55 E
Alsace, *France* **27 D14** 48 15N 7 25 E
Alsask, *Canada* **143 C7** 51 21N 109 59W
Alsasua, *Spain* **40 C2** 42 54N 2 10W
Alsek →, *U.S.A.* **142 B1** 59 10N 138 12W
Alsfeld, *Germany* **30 E5** 50 44N 9 16 E
Alsten, *Norway* **14 D15** 65 58N 12 40 E
Alstermo, *Sweden* **17 H9** 56 58N 15 38 E
Alston, *U.K.* **20 C5** 54 49N 2 25W
Alta, *Norway* **14 B20** 69 57N 23 10 E
Alta, Sierra, *Spain* **40 E3** 40 31N 1 30W
Alta Floresta, *Brazil* **173 B6** 9 57 S 55 58W
Alta Gracia, *Argentina* **174 C3** 31 40 S 64 30W
Alta Sierra, *U.S.A.* **161 K8** 35 42N 118 33W
Altaelva →, *Norway* **14 B20** 69 54N 23 17 E
Altafjorden, *Norway* **14 A20** 70 5N 23 5 E
Altagracia, *Venezuela* **168 A3** 10 45N 71 30W
Altagracia de Orituco, *Venezuela* **168 B4** 9 52N 66 23W
Altai = Aerhtai Shan, *Mongolia* **72 B4** 46 40N 92 45 E
Altamachi →, *Bolivia* **172 D4** 16 8 S 66 50W
Altamaha →, *U.S.A.* **152 D8** 31 20N 81 20W
Altamira, *Brazil* **169 D7** 3 12 S 52 10W
Altamira, *Chile* **174 B2** 25 47 S 69 51W
Altamira, *Colombia* **168 C2** 2 3N 75 47W
Altamira, *Mexico* **163 C5** 22 24N 97 55W
Altamira, Cuevas de, *Spain* **42 B6** 43 20N 4 5W
Altamont, *Ill., U.S.A.* **157 E8** 39 4N 88 45W
Altamont, *N.Y., U.S.A.* **151 D10** 42 43N 74 3W
Altamura, *Italy* **47 B9** 40 49N 16 33 E
Altanbulag, *Mongolia* **72 A5** 50 16N 106 30 E
Altar, *Mexico* **162 A2** 30 40N 111 50W
Altar, Desierto de, *Mexico* **162 B2** 30 10N 112 0W
Altata, *Mexico* **162 C3** 24 30N 108 0W
Altavas, *Phil.* **81 F4** 11 32N 122 29 E
Altavista, *U.S.A.* **148 G6** 37 6N 79 17W
Altay, *China* **72 B3** 47 48N 88 10 E
Altdorf, *Switz.* **33 C7** 46 52N 8 36 E
Alte Mellum, *Germany* **30 B4** 53 43N 8 10 E
Altea, *Spain* **41 G4** 38 38N 0 2W
Altenberg, *Germany* **30 E9** 50 45N 13 45 E
Altenbruch, *Germany* **30 B4** 53 49N 8 46 E
Altenburg, *Germany* **30 E8** 50 59N 12 25 E
Altenkirchen, *Mecklenburg-Vorpommern, Germany* **30 A9** 54 38N 13 22 E
Altenkirchen, *Rhld-Pfz., Germany* **30 E3** 50 41N 7 39 E
Altenmarkt, *Austria* **34 D7** 47 43N 14 39 E
Alter do Chão, *Brazil* **169 D6** 2 31 S 54 57W
Alter do Chão, *Portugal* **43 F3** 39 12N 7 40W
Altha, *U.S.A.* **152 E4** 30 34N 85 8W
Altınoluk, *Turkey* **49 B8** 39 34N 26 45 E
Altınova, *Turkey* **49 B8** 39 12N 26 47 E
Altıntaş, *Turkey* **49 B12** 39 4N 30 7 E
Altınyaka, *Turkey* **49 E12** 36 33N 30 20 E
Altınyayla, *Turkey* **49 D11** 37 0N 29 33 E
Altiplano = Bolivian Plateau, *S. Amer.* **166 E4** 20 0 S 67 30W
Altiplano, *Bolivia* **172 D4** 17 0 S 68 0W
Altkirch, *France* **27 E14** 47 37N 7 15 E
Altmark, *Germany* **30 C7** 52 45N 11 30 E
Altmühl →, *Germany* **31 G7** 48 54N 11 52 E
Altmunster, *Austria* **34 D6** 47 54N 13 45 E
Alto Adige = Trentino-Alto Adige ◻, *Italy* **45 B8** 46 30N 11 20 E
Alto Alegre, *Brazil* **169 C5** 2 50N 61 20W
Alto Araguaia, *Brazil* **173 D7** 17 15 S 53 20W
Alto Chicapa, *Angola* **115 E3** 10 52 S 19 17 E
Alto Cuchumatanes = Cuchumatanes, Sierra de los, *Guatemala* **164 C1** 15 35N 91 25W
Alto Cuito, *Angola* **115 E3** 13 27 S 18 49 E
Alto del Carmen, *Chile* **174 B1** 28 46 S 70 30W
Alto del Inca, *Chile* **174 A2** 24 10 S 68 10W
Alto Garças, *Brazil* **173 D7** 16 56 S 53 32W
Alto Iriri →, *Brazil* **173 B7** 8 50 S 53 25W
Alto Ligonha, *Mozam.* **119 F4** 15 30 S 38 11 E
Alto Molocue, *Mozam.* **119 F4** 15 50 S 37 35 E
Alto Paraguai, *Brazil* **173 C6** 14 30 S 56 31W
Alto Paraguay ◻, *Paraguay* **174 A4** 21 0 S 58 30W
Alto Paraiso de Goiás, *Brazil* **171 D2** 14 7 S 47 31W
Alto Paraná ◻, *Paraguay* **175 B5** 25 30 S 54 50W
Alto Parnaíba, *Brazil* **170 C2** 9 6 S 45 57W
Alto Purús →, *Peru* **172 B3** 9 12 S 70 28W
Alto Río Senguerr, *Argentina* **176 C2** 45 2 S 70 50W
Alto Santo, *Brazil* **170 C4** 5 31 S 38 15W
Alto Sucuriú, *Brazil* **173 D7** 19 19 S 52 47W
Alto Turi, *Brazil* **170 B2** 2 54 S 45 38W
Alton, *Canada* **150 C4** 43 54N 80 5W
Alton, *U.K.* **21 F7** 51 9N 0 59W
Alton, *Ill., U.S.A.* **156 F6** 38 53N 90 11W
Alton, *N.H., U.S.A.* **151 C13** 43 27N 71 13W
Altoona, *Ala., U.S.A.* **152 A3** 34 2N 86 20W
Altoona, *Iowa, U.S.A.* **156 C3** 41 39N 93 28W
Altoona, *Pa., U.S.A.* **150 F6** 40 31N 78 24W
Altos, *Brazil* **170 C3** 5 3 S 42 28W
Altötting, *Germany* **31 G8** 48 12N 12 39 E
Altstätten, *Switz.* **33 B9** 47 22N 9 33 E
Altūn Kūprī, *Iraq* **101 E11** 35 45N 44 9 E
Altun Shan, *China* **72 C3** 38 30N 88 0 E
Alturas, *U.S.A.* **158 F3** 41 29N 120 32W
Altus, *U.S.A.* **155 H5** 34 38N 99 20W
Alubijid, *Phil.* **81 G5** 8 35N 124 29 E
Alucra, *Turkey* **101 B8** 40 22N 38 47 E
Aluk, *Sudan* **107 F2** 8 25N 27 30 E
Alūksne, *Latvia* **15 H22** 57 24N 27 3 E
Alùla, *Somali Rep.* **120 B4** 11 50N 50 45 E
Alunda, *Sweden* **16 D12** 60 4N 18 5 E
Alunite, *U.S.A.* **161 K12** 35 59N 114 55W
Aluoro →, *Ethiopia* **107 F3** 8 26N 33 24 E
Alupka, *Ukraine* **59 K8** 44 23N 34 2 E
Alur, *India* **95 E3** 15 24N 77 15 E
Alur Gajah, *Malaysia* **84 B2** 2 23N 102 13 E
Alushta, *Ukraine* **59 K8** 44 40N 34 25 E
Alusi, *Indonesia* **79 F8** 7 35 S 131 40 E
Alustante, *Spain* **40 E3** 40 36N 1 40W
Alutgama, *Sri Lanka* **95 L4** 6 26N 79 59 E
Alutnuwara, *Sri Lanka* **95 L5** 7 19N 80 59 E
Alva, *U.S.A.* **155 G5** 36 48N 98 40W
Alvaiázere, *Portugal* **42 F2** 39 49N 8 23W
Älvängen, *Sweden* **17 G6** 57 58N 12 8 E
Alvarado, *Mexico* **163 D5** 18 40N 95 50W
Alvarado, *U.S.A.* **155 J6** 32 24N 97 13W
Alvarães, *Brazil* **169 D5** 3 12 S 64 50W
Alvaro Obregón, Presa, *Mexico* **162 B3** 27 55N 109 52W
Alvdal, *Norway* **18 B7** 62 6N 10 37 E
Älvdalen, *Sweden* **16 C8** 61 13N 14 4 E
Alvear, *Argentina* **174 B4** 29 5 S 56 30W
Alverca, *Portugal* **43 G1** 38 56N 9 1W
Alvesta, *Sweden* **17 H8** 56 54N 14 35 E
Alvie, *Australia* **128 E5** 38 14 S 143 30 E
Ålvik, *Norway* **18 D3** 60 26N 6 26 E
Alvin, *U.S.A.* **155 L7** 29 26N 95 15W
Alvinston, *Canada* **150 D3** 42 49N 81 52W
Alvito, *Portugal* **43 G3** 38 15N 7 58W
Älvkarleby, *Sweden* **16 D11** 60 34N 17 26 E
Alvorado, *Brazil* **171 D2** 12 28 S 49 6W
Alvord Desert, *U.S.A.* **158 E4** 42 30N 118 25W
Älvros, *Sweden* **16 B8** 62 3N 14 38 E
Älvsborgs län ◻, *Sweden* **17 F6** 58 30N 12 30 E
Älvsbyn, *Sweden* **14 D19** 65 40N 21 0 E
Ålvundeid, *Norway* **18 B5** 62 45N 8 33 E
Alwar, *India* **92 F7** 27 38N 76 34 E
Alwaye, *India* **95 J3** 10 8N 76 24 E
Alxa Zuoqi, *China* **74 E3** 38 50N 105 40 E
Alyangula, *Australia* **126 A2** 13 55 S 136 30 E
Alyata = Älät, *Azerbaijan* **61 L9** 39 58N 49 25 E
Alyth, *U.K.* **22 E5** 56 38N 3 13W
Alytus, *Lithuania* **15 J21** 54 24N 24 3 E
Alzada, *U.S.A.* **154 C2** 45 2N 104 25W
Alzey, *Germany* **31 F4** 49 45N 8 7 E
Alzira, *Spain* **41 F4** 39 9N 0 30W
Am Dam, *Chad* **109 F4** 12 40N 20 35 E
Am Géréda, *Chad* **109 F4** 12 53N 21 14 E
Am-Timan, *Chad* **109 F4** 11 0N 20 10 E
Amada Gaza, *C.A.R.* **114 B3** 4 46N 15 9 E
Amadeus, L., *Australia* **125 D5** 24 54 S 131 0 E
Amadi, *Dem. Rep. of the Congo* **118 B2** 3 40N 26 40 E
Amâdi, *Sudan* **107 F3** 5 29N 30 25 E
Amadjuak L., *Canada* **139 B12** 65 0N 71 8W
Amadora, *Portugal* **43 G1** 38 45N 9 13W
Amagansett, *U.S.A.* **151 F12** 40 59N 72 9W
Amagasaki, *Japan* **71 C7** 34 42N 135 20 E
Amager, *Denmark* **17 J6** 55 37N 12 35 E
Amagi, *Japan* **70 D2** 33 25N 130 39 E
Amagunze, *Nigeria* **113 D6** 6 20N 7 40 E
Amahai, *Indonesia* **79 E7** 3 20 S 128 55 E
Amahai, *Indonesia* **83 B3** 3 20 S 128 55 E
Amaimon, *Papua N. G.* **132 C3** 5 12 S 145 30 E
Amakusa-Nada, *Japan* **70 E2** 32 35N 130 5 E
Amakusa-Shotō, *Japan* **70 E2** 32 15N 130 10 E
Åmål, *Sweden* **16 E6** 59 3N 12 42 E
Amalapuram, *India* **95 F5** 16 35N 81 55 E
Amalfi, *Colombia* **168 B2** 6 55N 75 4W
Amalfi, *Italy* **47 B7** 40 38N 14 36 E
Amaliás, *Greece* **48 D3** 37 47N 21 22 E
Amalner, *India* **94 D2** 21 5N 75 5 E
Amamapare, *Indonesia* **79 E9** 4 53 S 136 38 E
Amambaí, *Brazil* **175 A4** 23 5 S 55 13W
Amambaí →, *Brazil* **175 A5** 23 22 S 53 56W
Amambay ◻, *Paraguay* **175 A4** 23 0 S 56 0W
Amambay, Cordillera de, *S. Amer.* **175 A4** 23 0 S 55 45W
Amami-Guntō, *Japan* **69 L4** 27 16N 129 21 E
Amami-Ō-Shima, *Japan* **69 L4** 28 0N 129 0 E
Amana →, *Venezuela* **169 B5** 9 45N 62 39W
Amaná, L., *Brazil* **169 D5** 2 35 S 64 40W
Amanab, *Papua N. G.* **132 B1** 3 40 S 141 14 E
Amanat →, *India* **93 G11** 24 7N 84 4 E
Amanda Park, *U.S.A.* **160 C3** 47 28N 123 55W
Amangeldy, *Kazakstan* **64 D7** 50 10N 65 10 E
Amantea, *Italy* **47 C9** 39 8N 16 4 E
Amapá, *Brazil* **169 C7** 2 5N 50 50W
Amapá ◻, *Brazil* **169 C7** 1 40N 52 0W
Amapari, *Brazil* **169 C7** 0 37N 51 39W
Amara, *Sudan* **107 E3** 10 25N 34 10 E
Amarante, *Brazil* **170 C3** 6 14 S 42 50W
Amarante, *Portugal* **42 D2** 41 16N 8 5W
Amarante do Maranhão, *Brazil* **170 C2** 5 36 S 46 45W
Amaranth, *Canada* **143 C9** 50 36N 98 43W
Amarapura, *Burma* **90 E6** 21 54N 96 3 E
Amaravati →, *India* **95 J4** 11 0N 78 15 E
Amareleja, *Portugal* **43 G3** 38 12N 7 13W
Amargosa, *Brazil* **171 D4** 13 2 S 39 36W
Amargosa →, *U.S.A.* **161 J10** 36 14N 116 51W
Amargosa Range, *U.S.A.* **161 J10** 36 20N 116 45W
Amári, *Greece* **38 D6** 35 13N 24 40 E
Amarillo, *U.S.A.* **155 H4** 35 13N 101 50W
Amarkantak, *India* **93 H9** 22 40N 81 45 E
Amârna, Tell el', *Sudan* **106 B3** 27 38N 30 52 E
Amarnath, *India* **94 E1** 19 12N 73 22 E
Amaro, Mte., *Italy* **45 F11** 42 5N 14 5 E
Amaro Leite, *Brazil* **171 D2** 13 58 S 49 9W
Amarpur, *India* **93 G12** 25 5N 87 0 E
Amarti, *Eritrea* **107 E5** 14 17N 41 6 E
Amarwara, *India* **93 H8** 22 18N 79 10 E
Amasra, *Turkey* **100 B5** 41 45N 32 23 E
Amassama, *Nigeria* **113 D6** 5 1N 6 2 E
Amasya, *Turkey* **100 B6** 40 40N 35 50 E
Amasya ◻, *Turkey* **57 F6** 40 40N 35 50 E
Amata, *Australia* **125 E5** 26 9 S 131 9 E
Amataurá, *Brazil* **168 D4** 3 29 S 68 6W
Amatikulu, *S. Africa* **117 D5** 29 3 S 31 33 E
Amatitlán, *Guatemala* **164 D1** 14 29N 90 38W
Amatrice, *Italy* **45 F10** 42 38N 13 17 E
Amay, *Belgium* **24 D5** 50 33N 5 19 E
Amazon = Amazonas →, *S. Amer.* **169 D7** 0 5 S 50 0W
Amazonas ◻, *Brazil* **173 B5** 5 0 S 65 0W
Amazonas ◻, *Peru* **172 B2** 5 0 S 78 0W
Amazonas ◻, *Venezuela* **168 C4** 3 30N 66 0W
Amazonas →, *S. Amer.* **169 D7** 0 5 S 50 0W
Amba Ferit, *Ethiopia* **107 E4** 10 55N 38 50 E
Ambad, *India* **94 E2** 19 38N 75 50 E
Ambagarh Chowki, *India* **94 D5** 20 47N 80 43 E
Ambah, *India* **92 F8** 26 43N 78 13 E
Ambahakily, *Madag.* **117 C7** 21 36 S 43 41 E
Ambahita, *Madag.* **117 C8** 24 1 S 45 16 E
Ambajogal, *India* **94 E3** 18 44N 76 23 E
Ambala, *India* **92 D7** 30 23N 76 56 E
Ambalangoda, *Sri Lanka* **95 L5** 6 15N 80 5 E
Ambalapulai, *India* **95 K3** 9 25N 76 25 E
Ambalavao, *Madag.* **117 C8** 21 50 S 46 56 E
Ambam, *Cameroon* **114 B2** 2 20N 11 15 E
Ambanja, *Madag.* **117 A8** 13 40 S 48 27 E
Ambararata, *Madag.* **117 B8** 15 3 S 48 33 E
Ambarchik, *Russia* **65 C17** 69 40N 162 20 E
Ambarijeby, *Madag.* **117 A8** 14 56 S 47 41 E
Ambaro, Helodranon', *Madag.* **117 A8** 13 23 S 48 38 E
Ambasamudram, *India* **95 K3** 8 43N 77 25 E
Ambato, *Ecuador* **168 D2** 1 5 S 78 42W
Ambato, *Madag.* **117 A8** 13 24 S 48 29 E
Ambato, Sierra de, *Argentina* **174 B2** 28 25 S 66 10W
Ambato Boeny, *Madag.* **117 B8** 16 28 S 46 43 E
Ambatofinandrahana, *Madag.* **117 C8** 20 33 S 46 48 E
Ambatolampy, *Madag.* **117 B8** 19 20 S 47 35 E
Ambatomainty, *Madag.* **117 B8** 17 41 S 45 40 E
Ambatomanoina, *Madag.* **117 B8** 18 18 S 47 37 E
Ambatondrazaka, *Madag.* **117 B8** 17 55 S 48 28 E
Ambatosoratra, *Madag.* **117 B8** 17 37 S 48 31 E
Ambelón, *Greece* **48 B4** 39 45N 22 22 E
Ambenja, *Madag.* **117 B8** 15 17 S 46 58 E
Amberg, *Germany* **31 F7** 49 26N 11 52 E
Ambergris Cay, *Belize* **163 D7** 18 0N 88 0W
Ambérieu-en-Bugey, *France* **29 C9** 45 57N 5 20 E
Amberley, *N.Z.* **131 D7** 43 9 S 172 44 E
Ambert, *France* **28 C7** 45 33N 3 44 E
Ambidédi, *Mali* **112 C2** 14 35N 11 47W
Ambikapur, *India* **93 H10** 23 15N 83 15 E
Ambikol, *Sudan* **106 C3** 21 20N 30 50 E
Ambilobé, *Madag.* **117 A8** 13 10 S 49 3 E
Ambinanindrano, *Madag.* **117 C8** 20 5 S 48 23 E
Ambinanitelo, *Madag.* **117 B8** 15 21 S 49 35 E
Ambinda, *Madag.* **117 B8** 16 25 S 45 52 E
Amble, *U.K.* **20 B6** 55 20N 1 36W
Ambler, *U.S.A.* **144 C8** 67 5N 157 52W
Ambleside, *U.K.* **20 C5** 54 26N 2 58W
Ambo, *Peru* **172 C2** 10 5 S 76 10W
Amboahangy, *Madag.* **117 C8** 24 15 S 46 22 E
Ambodifototra, *Madag.* **117 B8** 16 59 S 49 52 E
Ambodilazana, *Madag.* **117 B8** 18 6 S 49 10 E
Ambodiriana, *Madag.* **117 B8** 17 55 S 49 18 E
Ambohidratrimo, *Madag.* **117 B8** 18 50 S 47 26 E
Ambohidray, *Madag.* **117 B8** 18 36 S 48 18 E
Ambohimahamasina, *Madag.* **117 C8** 21 56 S 47 11 E
Ambohimahasoa, *Madag.* **117 C8** 21 7 S 47 13 E
Ambohimanga, *Madag.* **117 C8** 20 52 S 47 36 E
Ambohimitombo, *Madag.* **117 C8** 20 43 S 47 26 E
Ambohitra, *Madag.* **117 A8** 12 30 S 49 10 E
Amboise, *France* **26 E8** 47 24N 1 2 E
Amboiva, *Angola* **115 E2** 11 33 S 14 43 E
Ambon, *Indonesia* **79 E7** 3 35 S 128 20 E
Ambon, *Indonesia* **82 B3** 3 43 S 128 12 E
Ambondro, *Madag.* **117 D8** 25 13 S 45 44 E
Amboseli, L., *Kenya* **118 C4** 2 40 S 37 10 E
Ambositra, *Madag.* **117 C8** 20 31 S 47 25 E
Ambovombe, *Madag.* **117 D8** 25 11 S 46 5 E
Amboy, *Calif., U.S.A.* **161 L11** 34 33N 115 45W
Amboy, *Ill., U.S.A.* **156 C7** 41 44N 89 20W
Amboyna Cay, *S. China Sea* **78 C4** 7 50N 112 50 E
Ambridge, *U.S.A.* **150 F4** 40 36N 80 14W
Ambriz, *Angola* **115 D2** 7 48 S 13 8 E
Ambrym, *Vanuatu* **133 F6** 16 15 S 168 10 E
Ambunti, *Papua N. G.* **132 C2** 4 13 S 142 52 E
Ambur, *India* **95 H4** 12 48N 78 43 E
Amchitka I., *U.S.A.* **138 C1** 51 32N 179 0 E
Amderma, *Russia* **64 C7** 69 45N 61 30 E
Amdhi, *India* **93 H9** 23 51N 81 27 E
Ameca, *Mexico* **162 C4** 20 30N 104 0W
Ameca →, *Mexico* **162 C3** 20 40N 105 15W
Amecameca, *Mexico* **163 D5** 19 7N 98 46W
Ameland, *Neths.* **24 A5** 53 27N 5 45 E
Amélia, *Italy* **45 F9** 42 33N 12 25 E
Amelia City, *U.S.A.* **152 E8** 30 35N 81 28W
Amelia I., *U.S.A.* **152 E8** 30 40N 81 25W
Amendolara, *Italy* **47 C9** 39 57N 16 35 E
Amenia, *U.S.A.* **151 E11** 41 51N 73 33W
American Falls, *U.S.A.* **158 E7** 42 47N 112 51W
American Falls Reservoir, *U.S.A.* **158 E7** 42 47N 112 52W
American Fork, *U.S.A.* **158 F8** 40 23N 111 48W
American Highland, *Antarctica* **7 D6** 73 0 S 75 0 E
American Samoa ■, *Pac. Oc.* **133 X24** 14 20 S 170 40W
Americana, *Brazil* **175 A6** 22 45 S 47 20W
Americus, *U.S.A.* **152 C5** 32 4N 84 14W
Amersfoort, *Neths.* **24 B5** 52 9N 5 23 E
Amersfoort, *S. Africa* **117 D4** 26 59 S 29 53 E
Amery Ice Shelf, *Antarctica* **7 C6** 69 30 S 72 0 E
Ames, *Spain* **42 C2** 42 54N 8 38W
Ames, *U.S.A.* **156 C3** 42 2N 93 37W
Amesbury, *U.S.A.* **151 D14** 42 51N 70 56W
Amet, *India* **92 G5** 25 18N 73 56 E
Amfíklia, *Greece* **48 C4** 38 38N 22 35 E
Amfilokhía, *Greece* **48 C3** 38 52N 21 9 E
Amfípolis, *Greece* **50 F7** 40 48N 23 52 E
Ámfissa, *Greece* **48 C4** 38 32N 22 22 E
Amga, *Russia* **65 C14** 60 50N 132 0 E
Amga →, *Russia* **65 C14** 62 38N 134 32 E
Amgaon, *India* **94 D5** 21 22N 80 22 E
Amgu, *Russia* **65 E14** 45 45N 137 15 E
Amgun →, *Russia* **65 D14** 52 56N 139 38 E
Amherst, *Canada* **141 C7** 45 48N 64 8W
Amherst, *Mass., U.S.A.* **151 D12** 42 23N 72 31W
Amherst, *N.Y., U.S.A.* **150 D6** 42 59N 78 48W
Amherst, *Ohio, U.S.A.* **150 E2** 41 24N 82 14W
Amherst I., *Canada* **151 B8** 44 8N 76 43W
Amherstburg, *Canada* **140 D3** 42 6N 83 6W
Amiata, Mte., *Italy* **45 F8** 42 53N 11 37 E
Amidon, *U.S.A.* **154 B3** 46 29N 103 19W
Amiens, *France* **27 C9** 49 54N 2 16 E
Amili, *India* **90 A5** 28 25N 95 52 E
Amindaion, *Greece* **50 F5** 40 42N 21 42 E
Åminne, *Sweden* **17 G7** 57 7N 14 0 E
Amino, *Ethiopia* **107 G5** 4 25N 41 52 E
Aminuis, *Namibia* **116 C2** 23 43 S 19 21 E
Amīrābād, *Iran* **96 C5** 33 20N 46 16 E
Amirante Is., *Seychelles* **66 K9** 6 0 S 53 0 E
Amisk L., *Canada* **143 C8** 54 35N 102 15W
Amistad, Presa de la, *Mexico* **162 B4** 29 24N 101 0W
Amite, *U.S.A.* **155 K9** 30 44N 90 30W
Amizmiz, *Morocco* **110 B3** 31 12N 8 15W
Amla, *India* **92 J8** 21 56N 78 7 E
Åmli, *Norway* **18 F5** 58 45N 8 32 E
Amlia I., *U.S.A.* **138 C2** 52 4N 173 30W
Amlwch, *U.K.* **20 D3** 53 24N 4 20W
Amm Adam, *Sudan* **107 D4** 16 20N 36 1 E
'Ammān, *Jordan* **103 D4** 31 57N 35 52 E
'Ammān ◻, *Jordan* **103 D5** 31 40N 36 30 E
Ammanford, *U.K.* **21 F4** 51 48N 3 59W
Ammassalik = Tasiilaq, *Greenland* **10 D7** 65 40N 37 20W
Ammerån →, *Sweden* **16 A10** 63 9N 16 13 E
Ammersee, *Germany* **31 G7** 48 0N 11 7 E
Ammon, *U.S.A.* **158 E8** 43 28N 111 58W
Amnat Charoen, *Thailand* **86 E5** 15 51N 104 38 E
Amnura, *Bangla.* **93 G13** 24 37N 88 25 E
Amo Jiang →, *China* **76 F3** 23 0N 101 50 E
Āmol, *Iran* **97 B7** 36 23N 52 20 E
Amoret, *U.S.A.* **156 F2** 38 15N 94 35W
Amorgós, *Greece* **49 E7** 36 50N 25 57 E
Amory, *U.S.A.* **149 J1** 33 59N 88 29W
Amos, *Canada* **140 C4** 48 35N 78 5W
Åmot, *Buskerud, Norway* **15 G13** 59 57N 9 54 E
Åmot, *Oppland, Norway* **18 D7** 61 0N 10 2 E
Åmot, *Telemark, Norway* **18 E5** 59 34N 8 0 E
Åmotfors, *Sweden* **16 E6** 59 47N 12 22 E
Åmotsdal, *Norway* **18 E5** 59 37N 8 26 E
Amour, Djebel, *Algeria* **111 B5** 33 42N 1 37 E
Amoy = Xiamen, *China* **77 E12** 24 25N 118 4 E
Ampanavoana, *Madag.* **117 B9** 15 41 S 50 22 E
Ampang, *Malaysia* **87 L3** 3 8N 101 45 E
Ampangalana, Lakandranon', *Madag.* **117 C8** 22 48 S 47 50 E
Ampani, *India* **94 E6** 19 35N 82 38 E
Ampanihy, *Madag.* **117 C7** 24 40 S 44 45 E
Amparafaravola, *Madag.* **117 B8** 17 35 S 48 13 E
Ampasinambo, *Madag.* **117 C8** 20 31 S 48 0 E
Ampasindava, Helodranon', *Madag.* **117 A8** 13 40 S 48 15 E
Ampasindava, Saikanosy, *Madag.* **117 A8** 13 42 S 47 55 E
Ampato, Nevado, *Peru* **172 D3** 15 40 S 71 56W
Ampenan, *Indonesia* **78 F5** 8 35 S 116 13 E
Amper, *Nigeria* **113 D6** 9 25N 9 40 E
Amper →, *Germany* **31 G7** 48 29N 11 55 E
Ampezzo, *Italy* **45 B9** 46 25N 12 48 E
Ampitsikinana, *Réunion* **117 A8** 12 57 S 49 49 E
Ampombiantambo, *Madag.* **117 A8** 12 42 S 48 57 E
Amposta, *Spain* **40 E5** 40 43N 0 34 E
Ampotaka, *Madag.* **117 D7** 25 3 S 44 41 E
Ampoza, *Madag.* **117 C7** 22 20 S 44 44 E
Amqui, *Canada* **141 C6** 48 28N 67 27W
Amrabad, *India* **95 F4** 16 23N 78 50 E
'Amrān, *Yemen* **98 D3** 15 41N 43 55 E
Amravati, *India* **94 D3** 20 55N 77 45 E
Amreli, *India* **92 J4** 21 35N 71 17 E
Amrenene el Kasba, *Algeria* **111 D5** 22 10N 0 30 E

Arkhángelos 183

Anxi, Fujian, China 77 E12 25 2N 118 12 E
Anxi, Gansu, China 72 B4 40 30N 95 43 E
Anxian, China 76 B5 31 40N 104 25 E
Anxiang, China 77 C9 29 27N 112 11 E
Anxious B., Australia 127 E1 33 24 S 134 45 E
Anyama, Ivory C. 112 D4 5 30N 4 3W
Anyang, China 74 F8 36 5N 114 21 E
Anyer, Indonesia 84 D3 6 4 S 105 53 E
Anyer-Kidul, Indonesia 79 G11 6 4 S 105 53 E
Anyi, Jiangxi, China 77 C10 28 49N 115 25 E
Anyi, Shanxi, China 74 G6 35 2N 111 2 E
Anyuan, China 77 E10 25 9N 115 21 E
Anyue, China 76 B5 30 9N 105 50 E
Anza, U.S.A. 161 M10 33 35N 116 39W
Anzawr, Oman 99 C6 17 28N 52 50 E
Anze, China 74 F7 36 10N 112 12 E
Anzhero-Sudzhensk, Russia 64 D9 56 10N 86 0 E
Ânzio, Italy 46 A5 41 27N 12 37 E
Anzoátegui □, Venezuela 169 B5 9 0N 64 30W
Aoba, Vanuatu 133 E5 15 25 S 167 50 E
Aoga-Shima, Japan 71 E11 32 28N 139 46 E
Aoiz, Spain 40 C3 42 46N 1 22W
Aomen = Macau □, China 77 F9 22 16N 113 35 E
Aomori, Japan 68 D10 40 45N 140 45 E
Aomori □, Japan 68 D10 40 45N 140 40 E
Aonla, India 93 E8 28 16N 79 11 E
Aono-Yama, Japan 70 C3 34 28N 131 48 E
Aorangi Mts., N.Z. 130 H4 41 28 S 175 22 E
Aosta, Italy 44 C4 45 45N 7 20 E
Aotea Harbour, N.Z. 130 D3 38 0 S 174 50 E
Aoudéras, Niger 113 B6 17 45N 8 20 E
Aouinet Torkoz, Morocco 110 C3 28 31N 9 46W
Aouk, Bahr →, C.A.R. 114 A4 8 51N 18 53 E
Aoukar, Mali 110 D4 23 50N 2 45W
Aoukâr, Mauritania 112 B3 17 40N 10 0W
Aoulef el Arab, Algeria 111 C5 26 55N 1 2 E
Aozou, Chad 109 D3 21 45N 17 28 E
Apa →, S. Amer. 174 A4 22 6 S 58 2W
Apache, U.S.A. 155 H5 34 54N 98 22W
Apache Junction, U.S.A. 159 K8 33 25N 111 33W
Apalachee B., U.S.A. 152 E5 30 0N 84 0W
Apalachicola, U.S.A. 152 F5 29 43N 84 59W
Apalachicola →, U.S.A. 152 F5 29 43N 84 58W
Apalachicola B., U.S.A. 152 F3 29 40N 85 0W
Apam, Ghana 113 D4 5 19N 0 42W
Apapa, Nigeria 113 D5 6 25N 3 25 E
Apaporis →, Colombia 168 D4 1 23 S 69 25W
Aparecida do Taboado, Brazil 171 F1 20 5 S 51 5W
Aparri, Phil. 79 A6 18 22N 121 38 E
Aparurén, Venezuela 169 B5 5 6N 62 8W
Apateu, Romania 52 D6 46 36N 21 47 E
Apatin, Serbia, Yug. 52 E4 45 40N 19 0 E
Apatity, Russia 56 A5 67 34N 33 22 E
Apatou, Fr. Guiana 169 B7 5 9N 54 20W
Apatzingán, Mexico 162 D4 19 0N 102 20W
Apayao □, Phil. 80 B3 18 10N 121 10 E
Apeldoorn, Neths. 24 B5 52 13N 5 57 E
Apen, Germany 30 B3 53 13N 7 48 E
Apennines = Appennini, Italy 44 E7 44 0N 10 0 E
Apere →, Bolivia 173 C4 13 44 S 65 18W
Aphrodisias, Turkey 49 D10 37 42N 28 46 E
Apia, W. Samoa 133 W24 13 50 S 171 50W
Apiacás, Serra dos, Brazil 173 B6 9 50 S 57 0W
Apiaí, Brazil 171 F2 24 31 S 48 50W
Apiaú →, Brazil 169 C5 2 39N 61 12W
Apiaú, Serra do, Brazil 169 C5 2 30N 62 0W
Apidiá →, Brazil 173 C5 11 39 S 61 11W
Apies →, S. Africa 117 D4 25 15 S 28 8 E
Apinajé, Brazil 171 D2 11 31 S 48 18W
Apiti, N.Z. 130 F4 39 58 S 175 54 E
Apizaco, Mexico 163 D5 19 26N 98 9W
Aplao, Peru 172 D3 16 0 S 72 40W
Apo, Mt., Phil. 79 C7 6 53N 125 14 E
Apo East Pass, Phil. 80 E3 12 40N 120 40 E
Apo West Pass, Phil. 80 E3 12 31N 120 22 E
Apodi, Brazil 170 C4 5 39 S 37 48W
Apoera, Surinam 169 B6 5 12N 57 10W
Apolakkiá, Greece 38 C9 36 5N 27 48 E
Apolakkiá, Órmos, Greece 38 C9 36 5N 27 45 E
Apolda, Germany 30 D7 51 2N 11 32 E
Apollo Bay, Australia 128 E5 38 45 S 143 40 E
Apollonia = Marsá Susah, Libya 108 B4 32 52N 21 59 E
Apollonia, Greece 48 E6 36 58N 24 43 E
Apolo, Bolivia 172 C4 14 30 S 68 30W
Apónguao →, Venezuela 169 C5 4 48N 61 36W
Apopka, U.S.A. 153 G8 28 40N 81 31W
Apopka L., U.S.A. 153 G8 28 38N 81 38W
Aporé, Brazil 173 D7 18 58 S 52 1W
Aporé →, Brazil 171 E1 19 27 S 50 57W
Aporema, Brazil 171 A1 1 14N 50 49W
Apostle Is., U.S.A. 154 B9 47 0N 90 40W
Apóstoles, Argentina 175 B4 28 0 S 56 0W
Apostolos Andreas, C., Cyprus 38 D13 35 42N 34 35 E
Apostolovo, Ukraine 59 J7 47 39N 33 39 E
Apoteri, Guyana 169 C6 4 2N 58 32W
Appalachian Mts., U.S.A. 148 G6 38 0N 80 0W
Appelbo, Sweden 16 D8 60 29N 14 1 E
Appennini, Italy 44 E7 44 0N 10 0 E
Appennino Ligure, Italy 44 D6 44 30N 9 0 E
Appenzell, Switz. 33 B8 47 20N 9 25 E
Appenzell-Ausser Rhoden □, Switz. 33 B8 47 23N 9 23 E
Appenzell-Inner Rhoden □, Switz. 33 B8 47 20N 9 25 E
Appiano, Italy 45 B8 46 28N 11 15 E
Apple Hill, Canada 151 A10 45 13N 74 46W
Apple Valley, U.S.A. 161 L9 34 32N 117 14W
Appleby-in-Westmorland, U.K. 20 C5 54 35N 2 29W
Apples, Switz. 32 C2 46 33N 6 26 E
Appleton, U.S.A. 148 C1 44 16N 88 25W
Appleton City, U.S.A. 156 F2 38 11N 94 2W
Appling, U.S.A. 152 B7 33 33N 82 19W
Approuague, Fr. Guiana 169 C7 4 20N 52 0W
Aprica, Italy 33 D10 46 9N 10 6 E
Apricena, Italy 45 G12 41 47N 15 27 E
Aprília, Italy 46 A5 41 36N 12 39 E
Apsheronsk, Russia 61 H4 44 28N 39 42 E
Apsley, Canada 150 B6 44 45N 78 6W
Apt, France 29 E9 43 53N 5 24 E
Apuane, Alpi, Italy 44 D7 44 7N 10 14 E
Apuaú, Brazil 169 D5 2 25 S 60 53W
Apucarana, Brazil 175 A5 23 55 S 51 33W
Apulia = Púglia □, Italy 47 A9 41 15N 16 15 E
Apurauan, Phil. 81 G2 9 35N 118 20 E
Apure □, Venezuela 168 B4 7 10N 68 50W
Apure →, Venezuela 168 B4 7 37N 66 25W
Apurímac □, Peru 172 C3 14 0 S 73 0W
Apurimac →, Peru 172 C3 12 17 S 73 56W
Apuseni, Munţii, Romania 52 D7 46 30N 22 45 E
Āqā Jarī, Iran 97 D6 30 42N 49 50 E
Aqaba = Al 'Aqabah, Jordan 103 F4 29 31N 35 0 E
Aqaba, G. of, Red Sea 96 D2 28 15N 33 20 E
'Aqabah, Khalīj al = Aqaba, G. of, Red Sea 96 D2 28 15N 33 20 E
Āqcheh, Afghan. 91 A2 36 56N 66 11 E
'Aqdā, Iran 97 C7 32 26N 53 37 E
Aqîq, Sudan 106 D4 18 14N 38 12 E
Aqîq, Khalîg, Sudan 106 D4 18 20N 38 10 E
'Aqīq, W. al →, Si. Arabia 98 B3 20 16N 41 40 E
Aqmola = Astana, Kazakstan 64 D8 51 10N 71 30 E
Aqrah, Iraq 101 D10 36 46N 43 45 E
Aqtaū, Kazakstan 64 E6 43 39N 51 12 E
Aqtöbe, Kazakstan 57 D10 50 17N 57 10 E
Aquidauana, Brazil 173 E6 20 30 S 55 50W
Aquidauana →, Brazil 173 D6 19 44 S 56 50W
Aquiles Serdán, Mexico 162 B3 28 37N 105 54W
Aquin, Haiti 165 C5 18 16N 73 24W
Aquitaine □, France 28 D3 44 25N 0 30W
Ar Rabaḍ, Si. Arabia 98 B2 23 11N 39 52 E
Ar Rachidiya, Morocco 110 B4 31 58N 4 20W
Ar Rafīd, Syria 103 C4 32 57N 35 52 E
Ar Raḥḥālīyah, Iraq 101 F10 32 44N 43 23 E
Ar Ramādī, Iraq 101 F10 33 25N 43 20 E
Ar Ramādīyāt, Si. Arabia 98 A3 24 18N 43 52 E
Ar Raml, Libya 108 C3 26 45N 19 40 E
Ar Ramthā, Jordan 103 C5 32 34N 36 0 E
Ar Raqqah, Syria 101 E8 35 59N 39 8 E
Ar Rass, Si. Arabia 96 E4 25 50N 43 40 E
Ar Rawḍah, Si. Arabia 98 B3 21 16N 42 50 E
Ar Rawḍah, Yemen 98 D4 14 28N 47 17 E
Ar Rawshān, Si. Arabia 98 B3 20 2N 42 36 E
Ar Rayyānah, Si. Arabia 98 B2 23 32N 39 45 E
Ar Rifā'ī, Iraq 96 D5 31 50N 46 10 E
Ar Rijā', Yemen 98 D4 13 1N 44 35 E
Ar Riyāḍ, Si. Arabia 96 E5 24 41N 46 42 E
Ar Ru'ays, Qatar 97 E6 26 8N 51 12 E
Ar Rukhaymīyah, Iraq 96 D5 29 22N 45 38 E
Ar Ruqayyidah, Si. Arabia 97 E6 25 21N 49 34 E
Ar Ruṣāfah, Syria 101 E8 35 45N 38 49 E
Ar Ruṭbah, Iraq 101 F9 33 0N 40 15 E
Ar Ruwayḍah, Si. Arabia 98 B4 23 40N 44 40 E
Ara, India 93 G11 25 35N 84 32 E
Ara Goro, Ethiopia 107 F5 5 48N 41 18 E
Ara Tera, Ethiopia 107 F5 6 38N 40 57 E
Arab, U.S.A. 149 H2 34 19N 86 30W
'Arab, Bahr el →, Sudan 107 F2 9 0N 29 30 E
Arab, Khalîg el, Egypt 106 A2 30 55N 29 0 E
'Araba, W. →, Egypt 106 J8 29 19N 33 31 E
'Arabābād, Iran 97 C8 33 2N 57 41 E
'Arabah, W. →, Yemen 99 C5 18 5N 51 26 E
Araban, Turkey 100 D7 37 28N 37 44 E
Arabatskaya Strelka, Ukraine 59 K8 45 40N 35 0 E
Arabba, Italy 45 B8 46 30N 11 52 E
Arabelo, Venezuela 169 C5 4 55N 64 13W
Arabi, U.S.A. 152 D6 31 50N 83 44W
Arabia, Asia 66 G8 25 0N 45 0 E
Arabian Desert = Es Sahrâ' Esh Sharqîya, Egypt 106 B3 27 30N 32 30 E
Arabian Gulf = Gulf, The, Asia 97 E6 27 0N 50 0 E
Arabian Sea, Ind. Oc. 66 H10 16 0N 65 0 E
Araç, Turkey 100 B5 41 15N 33 21 E
Aracaju, Brazil 170 D4 10 55 S 37 4W
Aracataca, Colombia 168 A3 10 38N 74 9W
Aracati, Brazil 170 B4 4 30 S 37 44W
Araçatuba, Brazil 175 A5 21 10 S 50 30W
Araceli, Phil. 81 F2 10 33N 119 59 E
Aracena, Spain 43 H4 37 53N 6 38W
Aracena, Sierra de, Spain 43 H4 37 50N 6 50W
Aracides, C., Solomon Is. 133 M11 8 21 S 161 0 E
Aračinovo, Macedonia 50 D5 42 1N 21 34 E
Araçuaí, Brazil 171 E3 16 52 S 42 4W
Araçuaí →, Brazil 171 E3 16 46 S 42 2W
'Arad, Israel 103 D4 31 15N 35 12 E
Arad, Romania 52 D6 46 10N 21 20 E
Arad □, Romania 52 D6 46 20N 22 0 E
Arada, Chad 109 F4 15 0N 20 20 E
Arādān, Iran 97 C7 35 21N 52 30 E
Aradhippou, Cyprus 38 E12 34 57N 33 36 E
Arafura Sea, E. Indies 83 C5 9 0 S 135 0 E
Aragarças, Brazil 173 D7 15 55 S 52 15W
Aragats, Armenia 61 K7 40 30N 44 15 E
Aragon, U.S.A. 152 A4 34 2N 85 3W
Aragón □, Spain 40 D4 41 25N 0 40W
Aragón →, Spain 40 C3 42 13N 1 44W
Aragona, Italy 46 E6 37 24N 13 27 E
Aragua □, Venezuela 168 B4 10 0N 67 10W
Aragua de Barcelona, Venezuela 169 B5 9 28N 64 49W
Araguacema, Brazil 170 C2 8 50 S 49 20W
Araguaçu, Brazil 171 D2 12 49 S 49 51W
Araguaia →, Brazil 170 C2 5 21 S 48 41W
Araguaiana, Brazil 173 D7 15 43 S 51 51W
Araguaína, Brazil 170 C2 7 12 S 48 12W
Araguari, Brazil 171 E2 18 38 S 48 11W
Araguari →, Brazil 169 C8 1 15N 49 55W
Araguatins, Brazil 170 C2 5 38 S 48 7W
Arain, India 92 F6 26 27N 75 2 E
Araioses, Brazil 170 B3 2 53 S 41 55W
Arak, Algeria 111 C5 25 20N 3 45 E
Arāk, Iran 97 C6 34 0N 49 40 E
Araka, Sudan 107 G3 4 20N 30 23 E
Arakan □, Burma 90 F5 19 0N 94 15 E
Arakan Yoma, Burma 90 F5 20 0N 94 40 E
Arákhova, Greece 48 C4 38 28N 22 35 E
Arakkonam, India 95 H4 13 7N 79 43 E
Arakli, Turkey 101 B8 41 6N 40 2 E
Araks = Aras, Rūd-e →, Azerbaijan 61 K9 40 5N 48 29 E
Aral, Kazakstan 64 E7 46 41N 61 45 E
Aral Sea, Asia 64 E7 44 30N 60 0 E
Aral Tengizi = Aral Sea, Asia 64 E7 44 30N 60 0 E
Aralsk = Aral, Kazakstan 64 E7 46 41N 61 45 E
Aralskoye More = Aral Sea, Asia 64 E7 44 30N 60 0 E
Aralsor, Ozero, Kazakstan 61 F9 49 5N 48 12 E
Aramac, Australia 126 C4 22 58 S 145 14 E
Aran →, India 94 E4 19 55N 78 12 E
Aran Areh, Ethiopia 120 C2 9 2N 43 54 E
Aran I., Ireland 23 A3 55 0N 8 30W
Aran Is., Ireland 23 C2 53 6N 9 38W
Aranda de Duero, Spain 42 D7 41 39N 3 42W
Arandān, Iran 96 C5 35 23N 46 55 E
Arandelovac, Serbia, Yug. 50 B4 44 18N 20 34 E
Aranga, N.Z. 130 B2 35 44 S 173 40 E
Arani, Bolivia 173 D4 17 34 S 65 46W
Arani, India 95 H4 12 43N 79 19 E
Aranjuez, Spain 42 E7 40 1N 3 40W
Aranos, Namibia 116 C2 24 9 S 19 7 E
Aransas Pass, U.S.A. 155 M6 27 55N 97 9W
Aranyaprathet, Thailand 78 B2 13 41N 102 30 E
Arao, Japan 70 E2 32 59N 130 25 E
Araouane, Mali 112 B4 18 55N 3 30W
Arapahoe, U.S.A. 154 E5 40 18N 99 54W
Arapari, Brazil 170 C2 5 34 S 49 15W
Arapawa I., N.Z. 131 B9 41 11 S 174 17 E
Arapey Grande →, Uruguay 174 C4 30 55 S 57 49W
Arapgir, Turkey 101 C8 39 5N 38 30 E
Arapiraca, Brazil 170 C4 9 45 S 36 39W
Arapongas, Brazil 175 A5 23 29 S 51 28W
Arapuni, N.Z. 130 E4 38 4 S 175 39 E
Ar'ar, Si. Arabia 96 D4 30 59N 41 2 E
Araracuara, Colombia 168 D3 0 24 S 72 17W
Araranguá, Brazil 175 B6 29 0 S 49 30W
Araraquara, Brazil 171 F2 21 50 S 48 0W
Araras, Brazil 171 F2 22 22 S 47 23W
Ararás, Serra das, Brazil 175 B5 25 0 S 53 10W
Ararat, Armenia 101 C11 39 48N 44 50 E
Ararat, Australia 128 D5 37 16 S 143 0 E
Ararat, Mt. = Ağrı Dağı, Turkey 101 C11 39 50N 44 15 E
Arari, Brazil 170 B3 3 28 S 44 47W
Araria, India 93 F12 26 9N 87 33 E
Araripe, Chapada do, Brazil 170 C3 7 20 S 40 0W
Araripina, Brazil 170 C3 7 33 S 40 34W
Araruama, L. de, Brazil 171 F3 22 53 S 42 12W
Araruna, Brazil 170 C4 6 52 S 35 44W
Aras, Rūd-e →, Azerbaijan 61 K9 40 5N 48 29 E
Aratāne, Mauritania 112 B3 18 24N 8 32W
Araticu, Brazil 170 B2 1 58 S 49 51W
Arauca, Colombia 168 B3 7 0N 70 40W
Arauca □, Colombia 168 B3 6 40N 71 0W
Arauca →, Venezuela 168 B4 7 24N 66 35W
Arauco, Chile 174 D1 37 16 S 73 25W
Araújos, Brazil 171 E2 19 56 S 45 14W
Arauquita, Colombia 168 B3 7 2N 71 25W
Araure, Venezuela 168 B4 9 34N 69 13W
Arawa, Ethiopia 107 F5 9 57N 41 58 E
Arawata →, N.Z. 131 E3 44 0 S 168 40 E
Araxá, Brazil 171 E2 19 35 S 46 55W
Araya, Pen. de, Venezuela 169 A5 10 40N 64 0W
Arayat, Phil. 80 D3 15 10N 120 46 E
Arba Gugu, Ethiopia 107 F5 8 40N 40 15 E
Arba Minch, Ethiopia 102 F2 6 0N 37 30 E
Arbat, Iraq 101 E11 35 25N 45 35 E
Árbatax, Italy 46 C2 39 56N 9 42 E
Arbedo, Switz. 33 D8 46 12N 9 3 E
Arbi, Ethiopia 107 F4 9 4N 35 7 E
Arbīl, Iraq 101 D11 36 15N 44 5 E
Arboga, Sweden 16 E9 59 24N 15 52 E
Arbois, France 27 F12 46 55N 5 46 E
Arboletes, Colombia 168 B2 8 51N 76 26W
Arbon, Switz. 33 A8 47 31N 9 26 E
Arbore, Ethiopia 107 F4 5 3N 36 50 E
Arboréa, Italy 46 C1 39 46N 8 35 E
Arborfield, Canada 143 C8 53 6N 103 39W
Arborg, Canada 143 C9 50 54N 97 13W
Arbre du Ténéré, Niger 113 B7 17 50N 10 4 E
Arbroath, U.K. 22 E6 56 34N 2 35W
Arbuckle, U.S.A. 160 F4 39 1N 122 3W
Arbus, Italy 46 C1 39 30N 8 33 E
Arc →, France 29 C10 45 34N 6 12 E
Arc-lès-Gray, France 27 E12 47 28N 5 34 E
Arcachon, France 28 D2 44 40N 1 10W
Arcachon, Bassin d', France 28 D2 44 42N 1 10W
Arcade, Calif., U.S.A. 161 L8 34 2N 118 15W
Arcade, N.Y., U.S.A. 150 D6 42 32N 78 25W
Arcadia, Fla., U.S.A. 149 M5 27 13N 81 52W
Arcadia, Ind., U.S.A. 157 D10 40 11N 86 1W
Arcadia, Iowa, U.S.A. 156 B1 42 5N 95 3W
Arcadia, La., U.S.A. 155 J8 32 33N 92 55W
Arcadia, Pa., U.S.A. 150 F6 40 47N 78 51W
Arcanum, U.S.A. 157 E12 39 59N 84 33W
Arcata, U.S.A. 158 F1 40 52N 124 5W
Arcévia, Italy 45 E9 43 30N 12 56 E
Archangel = Arkhangelsk, Russia 56 B7 64 38N 40 36 E
Archar, Bulgaria 50 C6 43 50N 22 54 E
Archbald, U.S.A. 151 E9 41 30N 75 32W
Archbold, U.S.A. 157 C12 41 31N 84 18W
Archena, Spain 41 G3 38 9N 1 16W
Archer, U.S.A. 153 F7 29 32N 82 32W
Archer →, Australia 126 A3 13 28 S 141 41 E
Archer B., Australia 126 A3 13 20 S 141 30 E
Archers Post, Kenya 118 B4 0 35N 37 35 E
Arches National Park, U.S.A. 159 G9 38 45N 109 25W
Archidona, Spain 43 H6 37 6N 4 22W
Arci, Mte., Italy 46 C1 39 47N 8 45 E
Arcidosso, Italy 45 F8 42 52N 11 33 E
Arcila = Asilah, Morocco 110 A3 35 29N 6 0W
Arcis-sur-Aube, France 27 D11 48 32N 4 10 E
Arckaringa Cr. →, Australia 127 D2 28 10 S 135 22 E
Arco, Italy 44 C7 45 55N 10 53 E
Arco, U.S.A. 158 E7 43 38N 113 18W
Arcola, U.S.A. 157 E8 39 41N 88 19W
Arcoona, Australia 128 A2 31 2 S 137 1 E
Arcos = Arcos de Jalón, Spain 40 D2 41 12N 2 16W
Arcos de Jalón, Spain 40 D2 41 12N 2 16W
Arcos de la Frontera, Spain 43 J5 36 45N 5 49W
Arcos de Valdevez, Portugal 42 D2 41 55N 8 22W
Arcot, India 95 H4 12 53N 79 20 E
Arcoverde, Brazil 170 C4 8 25 S 37 4W
Arcozelo, Portugal 42 E3 40 32N 7 47W
Arctic Bay, Canada 139 A11 73 1N 85 7W
Arctic Ocean, Arctic 6 B18 78 0N 160 0W
Arctic Red River = Tsiigehtchic, Canada 138 B6 67 15N 134 0W
Arda →, Bulgaria 51 E10 41 40N 26 30 E
Arda →, Italy 44 C7 45 2N 10 2 E
Ardabīl, Iran 97 B6 38 15N 48 18 E
Ardahan, Turkey 101 B10 41 7N 42 41 E
Ardakān = Sepīdān, Iran 97 D7 30 20N 52 5 E
Ardakān, Iran 97 C7 32 19N 53 59 E
Ardala, Sweden 17 F7 58 22N 13 19 E
Ardales, Spain 43 J6 36 53N 4 51W
Årdalstangen, Norway 18 C4 61 14N 7 43 E
Ardèche □, France 29 D8 44 42N 4 16 E
Ardèche →, France 29 D8 44 16N 4 39 E
Ardee, Ireland 23 C5 53 52N 6 33W
Arden, Canada 150 B8 44 43N 76 56W
Arden, Denmark 17 H3 56 46N 9 52 E
Arden, Calif., U.S.A. 160 G5 38 36N 121 33W
Arden, Nev., U.S.A. 161 J11 36 1N 115 14W
Ardenne, Belgium 12 F7 49 50N 5 5 E
Ardennes = Ardenne, Belgium 12 F7 49 50N 5 5 E
Ardennes □, France 27 C11 49 35N 4 40 E
Ardentes, France 27 F8 46 45N 1 50 E
Arderin, Ireland 23 C4 53 2N 7 39W
Ardeşen, Turkey 101 B9 41 12N 41 2 E
Ardestān, Iran 97 C7 33 20N 52 25 E
Ardez, Switz. 33 C10 46 47N 10 12 E
Árdhas →, Greece 51 E10 41 40N 26 30 E
Ardhéa, Greece 48 C4 40 58N 22 3 E
Ardila →, Portugal 43 G3 38 12N 7 28W
Ardino, Bulgaria 51 E9 41 34N 25 9 E
Ardivachar Pt., U.K. 22 D1 57 23N 7 26W
Ardlethan, Australia 129 C7 34 22 S 146 53 E
Ardmore, Okla., U.S.A. 155 H6 34 10N 97 8W
Ardmore, Pa., U.S.A. 151 G9 39 58N 75 18W
Ardnamurchan, Pt. of, U.K. 22 E2 56 43N 6 14W
Ardnave Pt., U.K. 22 F2 55 53N 6 20W
Ardon, Russia 61 J7 43 10N 44 18 E
Ardore, Italy 47 D9 38 11N 16 10 E
Ardres, France 27 B8 50 50N 1 59 E
Ardrossan, Australia 128 C2 34 26 S 137 53 E
Ardrossan, U.K. 22 F4 55 39N 4 49W
Ards Pen., U.K. 23 B6 54 33N 5 34W
Arduan, Sudan 106 D3 19 54N 30 20 E
Ardud, Romania 52 C7 47 37N 22 52 E
Åre, Sweden 16 A7 63 22N 13 15 E
Arecibo, Puerto Rico 165 C6 18 29N 66 43W
Areia Branca, Brazil 170 B4 5 0 S 37 0W
Arena, Pt., U.S.A. 160 G3 38 57N 123 44W
Arenal, Honduras 164 C2 15 21N 86 50W
Arenales, Cerro, Chile 176 C2 47 5 S 73 40W
Arenápolis, Brazil 173 C6 14 26 S 56 49W
Arenas = Las Arenas, Spain 42 B6 43 17N 4 50W
Arenas, Pta., Venezuela 169 A5 10 31N 64 14W
Arenas de San Pedro, Spain 42 E5 40 12N 5 5W
Arendal, Norway 15 G13 58 28N 8 46 E
Arendsee, Germany 30 C7 52 52N 11 27 E
Arenillas, Ecuador 168 D1 3 33 S 80 10W
Arenys de Mar, Spain 40 D7 41 35N 2 33 E
Arenzano, Italy 44 D5 44 24N 8 41 E
Arenzville, U.S.A. 156 E6 39 53N 90 22W
Areópolis, Greece 48 E4 36 40N 22 22 E
Arequipa, Peru 172 D3 16 20 S 71 30W
Arequipa □, Peru 172 D3 16 0 S 72 50W
Arere, Brazil 169 D7 0 16 S 53 52W
Arero, Ethiopia 107 G4 4 41N 38 50 E
Arès, France 28 D2 44 47N 1 8W
Arévalo, Spain 42 D6 41 3N 4 43W
Arezzo, Italy 45 E8 43 25N 11 53 E
Arga, Turkey 96 B3 38 21N 37 59 E
Arga →, Spain 40 C3 42 18N 1 47W
Argalasti, Greece 48 B5 39 13N 23 13 E
Argamakmur, Indonesia 84 C2 3 35 S 102 0 E
Argamasilla de Alba, Spain 43 F7 39 8N 3 5W
Argamasilla de Calatrava, Spain 43 G6 38 44N 4 4W
Arganda, Spain 42 E7 40 19N 3 26W
Arganil, Portugal 42 E2 40 13N 8 3W
Argao, Phil. 81 G4 9 52N 123 36 E
Argayash, Russia 62 D8 55 29N 60 52 E
Argedeb, Ethiopia 107 F5 6 11N 41 13 E
Argelès-Gazost, France 28 E3 43 0N 0 6W
Argelès-sur-Mer, France 28 F7 42 34N 3 1 E
Argens →, France 29 E10 43 24N 6 44 E
Argent-sur-Sauldre, France 27 E9 47 33N 2 25 E
Argenta, Canada 142 C5 50 11N 116 56W
Argenta, Italy 45 D8 44 37N 11 50 E
Argenta, U.S.A. 157 E8 39 59N 88 49W
Argentan, France 26 D6 48 45N 0 1W
Argentário, Mte., Italy 45 F8 42 24N 11 9 E
Argentat, France 28 C5 45 6N 1 56 E
Argentera, Italy 44 D4 44 12N 7 5 E
Argenteuil, France 27 D9 48 57N 2 14 E
Argentia, Canada 141 C9 47 18N 53 58W
Argentiera, C. dell', Italy 46 B1 40 44N 8 8 E
Argentière, Aiguilles d', Switz. 32 E4 45 59N 7 2 E
Argentina ■, S. Amer. 176 B3 35 0 S 66 0W
Argentina Is., Antarctica 7 C17 66 0 S 64 0W
Argentino, L., Argentina 176 D2 50 10 S 73 0W
Argenton-Château, France 26 F6 46 59N 0 27W
Argenton-sur-Creuse, France 27 F8 46 36N 1 30 E
Argeş □, Romania 53 F9 45 0N 24 45 E
Argeş →, Romania 53 F11 44 5N 26 38 E
Arghandab →, Afghan. 91 C2 31 30N 64 15 E
Argheile, Ethiopia 107 F5 5 19N 42 4 E
Argo, Sudan 106 D3 19 28N 30 30 E
Argolikós Kólpos, Greece 48 D4 37 20N 22 52 E
Argolís □, Greece 48 D4 37 38N 22 50 E
Argonne, France 27 C12 49 10N 5 0 E
Árgos, Greece 48 D4 37 40N 22 43 E
Argos, U.S.A. 157 C10 41 14N 86 15W
Árgos Orestikón, Greece 50 F5 40 27N 21 18 E
Argostólion, Greece 48 C2 38 12N 20 33 E
Arguedas, Spain 40 C3 42 11N 1 36W
Arguello, Pt., U.S.A. 161 L6 34 35N 120 39W
Arguineguín, Canary Is. 39 G4 27 46N 15 41W
Argun, Russia 61 J7 43 18N 45 52 E
Argun →, Russia 65 D13 53 20N 121 28 E
Argungu, Nigeria 113 C5 12 40N 4 31 E
Argus Pk., U.S.A. 161 K9 35 52N 117 26W
Argyle, L., Australia 124 C4 16 20 S 128 40 E
Argyll & Bute □, U.K. 22 E3 56 13N 5 28W
Arhavi, Turkey 101 B9 41 21N 41 18 E
Århus, Denmark 17 H4 56 8N 10 11 E
Århus Amtskommune □, Denmark 17 H4 56 15N 10 15 E
Aria, N.Z. 130 E4 38 33 S 175 0 E
Ariadnoye, Russia 68 B7 45 8N 134 25 E
Ariamsvlei, Namibia 116 D2 28 9 S 19 51 E
Ariana, Tunisia 108 A2 36 52N 10 12 E
Ariano Irpino, Italy 47 A8 41 9N 15 5 E
Ariari →, Colombia 168 C3 2 35N 72 47W
Aribinda, Burkina Faso 113 C4 14 17N 0 52W
Arica, Chile 172 D3 18 32 S 70 20W
Arica, Colombia 168 D3 2 0 S 71 50W
Arico, Canary Is. 39 F3 28 9N 16 29W
Arid, C., Australia 125 F3 34 1 S 123 10 E
Arida, Japan 71 C7 34 5N 135 8 E
Ariège □, France 28 F5 42 56N 1 30 E
Ariège →, France 28 E5 43 30N 1 25 E
Arieş →, Romania 53 D8 46 24N 23 20 E
Arihā, Israel 106 A4 31 51N 35 27 E
Arilje, Serbia, Yug. 50 C4 43 44N 20 7 E
Arílla, Ákra, Greece 38 A3 39 43N 19 39 E
Arima, Trin. & Tob. 165 D7 10 38N 61 17W
Aringay, Phil. 80 C3 16 26N 120 21 E
Arinos →, Brazil 173 C6 10 25 S 58 20W
Ario de Rosales, Mexico 162 D4 19 12N 102 0W
Ariogala, Lithuania 54 C10 55 16N 23 28 E
Aripuanã, Brazil 173 B5 9 25 S 60 30W
Aripuanã →, Brazil 173 B5 5 7 S 60 25W
Ariquemes, Brazil 173 B5 9 55 S 63 6W
Arisaig, U.K. 22 E3 56 55N 5 51W
Arîsh, W. el →, Egypt 106 A3 31 9N 33 49 E
Arissa, Ethiopia 107 E5 11 10N 41 35 E
Aristazabal I., Canada 142 C3 52 40N 129 10W
Arita, Japan 70 D1 33 11N 129 54 E
Aritao, Phil. 80 C3 16 18N 121 2 E
Ariton, U.S.A. 152 D4 31 36N 85 43W
Arivonimamo, Madag. 117 B8 19 1 S 47 11 E
Ariyalur, India 95 J4 11 8N 79 8 E
Ariza, Spain 40 D2 41 19N 2 3W
Arizaro, Salar de, Argentina 174 A2 24 40 S 67 50W
Arizona, Argentina 174 D2 35 45 S 65 25W
Arizona □, U.S.A. 159 J8 34 0N 112 0W
Arizpe, Mexico 162 A2 30 20N 110 11W
Årjäng, Sweden 16 E6 59 24N 12 8 E
Arjeplog, Sweden 14 D18 66 3N 18 2 E
Arjona, Colombia 168 A2 10 14N 75 22W
Arjona, Spain 43 H6 37 56N 4 4W
Arjuna, Indonesia 79 G15 7 49 S 112 34 E
Arka, Russia 65 C15 60 15N 142 0 E
Arkadak, Russia 60 E6 51 58N 43 30 E
Arkadelphia, U.S.A. 155 H8 34 7N 93 4W
Arkadhía □, Greece 48 D4 37 30N 22 20 E
Arkaig, L., U.K. 22 E3 56 59N 5 10W
Arkalgud, India 95 H3 12 46N 76 3 E
Arkalyk = Arqalyk, Kazakstan 64 D7 50 13N 66 50 E
Arkansas □, U.S.A. 155 H8 35 0N 92 30W
Arkansas →, U.S.A. 155 J9 33 47N 91 4W
Arkansas City, U.S.A. 155 G6 37 4N 97 2W
Arkaroola, Australia 127 E2 30 20 S 139 22 E
Arkathos →, Greece 48 B3 39 20N 21 4 E
Arkhángelos, Greece 38 C10 36 13N 28 7 E

Azraq ash Shīshān 185

Ath, Belgium 24 D3 50 38N 3 47 E
Athabasca, Canada 142 C6 54 45N 113 20W
Athabasca →, Canada 143 B6 58 40N 110 50W
Athabasca, L., Canada 143 B7 59 15N 109 15W
Athagarh, India 94 D7 20 32N 85 37 E
Athboy, Ireland 23 C5 53 37N 6 56W
Athena, U.S.A. 152 F6 29 59N 83 30W
Athenry, Ireland 23 C3 53 18N 8 44W
Athens = Athínai, Greece 48 D5 37 58N 23 46 E
Athens, Ala., U.S.A. 149 H2 34 48N 86 58W
Athens, Ga., U.S.A. 152 B6 33 57N 83 23W
Athens, N.Y., U.S.A. 151 D11 42 16N 73 49W
Athens, Ohio, U.S.A. 148 F4 39 20N 82 6W
Athens, Pa., U.S.A. 151 E8 41 57N 76 31W
Athens, Tenn., U.S.A. 149 H3 35 27N 84 36W
Athens, Tex., U.S.A. 155 J7 32 12N 95 51W
Atherley, Canada 150 B5 44 37N 79 20W
Atherton, Australia 126 B4 17 17 S 145 30 E
Athiéme, Benin 113 D5 6 37N 1 40 E
Athienou, Cyprus 38 D12 35 3N 33 32 E
Athínai, Greece 48 D5 37 58N 23 46 E
Athlone, Ireland 23 C4 53 25N 7 56W
Athmalik, India 94 D7 20 43N 84 32 E
Athna, Cyprus 38 D12 35 3N 33 47 E
Athni, India 94 F2 16 44N 75 6 E
Athol, N.Z. 131 F3 45 30 S 168 35 E
Athol, U.S.A. 151 D12 42 36N 72 14W
Atholl, Forest of, U.K. 22 E5 56 51N 3 50W
Atholl, Kap, Greenland 10 B4 76 25N 69 30W
Atholville, Canada 141 C6 47 59N 66 43W
Áthos, Greece 51 F8 40 9N 24 22 E
Athy, Ireland 23 C5 53 0N 7 0W
Ati, Chad 109 F3 13 13N 18 20 E
Ati, Sudan 107 E2 13 5N 29 2 E
Atiak, Uganda 118 B3 3 12N 32 2 E
Atiamuri, N.Z. 130 E5 38 24 S 176 5 E
Atico, Peru 172 D3 16 14 S 73 40W
Atienza, Spain 40 D2 41 12N 2 52W
Atiit, Sudan 107 F3 6 10N 30 35 E
Atik L., Canada 143 B9 55 15N 96 0W
Atikameg →, Canada 140 B3 52 30N 82 46W
Atikokan, Canada 140 C1 48 45N 91 37W
Atikonak L., Canada 141 B7 52 40N 64 32W
Atimonan, Phil. 80 D3 14 0N 121 55 E
'Âtinah, W. →, Oman 99 C6 18 23N 53 28 E
Atirampattinam, India 95 J4 10 28N 79 20 E
Atka, Russia 65 C16 60 50N 151 48 E
Atka, U.S.A. 144 K4 52 12N 174 12W
Atka I., U.S.A. 144 K4 52 7N 174 30W
Atkarsk, Russia 60 E7 51 55N 45 2 E
Atkinson, Ga., U.S.A. 152 D8 31 13N 81 47W
Atkinson, Ill., U.S.A. 156 C6 41 25N 90 1W
Atkinson, Nebr., U.S.A. 154 D5 42 32N 98 59W
Atlanta, Ga., U.S.A. 152 B5 33 45N 84 23W
Atlanta, Ill., U.S.A. 156 D7 40 16N 89 14W
Atlanta, Mo., U.S.A. 156 E4 39 54N 92 29W
Atlanta, Tex., U.S.A. 155 J7 33 7N 94 10W
Atlantic, U.S.A. 156 C2 41 24N 95 1W
Atlantic Beach, U.S.A. 152 E8 30 20N 81 24W
Atlantic City, U.S.A. 148 F8 39 21N 74 27W
Atlantic-Indian Ridge, Atl. Oc. 9 P9 53 0 S 10 0 E
Atlantic-Indian Ridge, Ind. Oc. 121 J2 53 0 S 15 0 E
Atlantic Ocean 8 H7 0 0 20 0W
Atlántico □, Colombia 168 A2 10 45N 75 0W
Atlas Mts. = Haut Atlas, Morocco 110 B3 32 30N 5 0W
Atlin, Canada 142 B2 59 31N 133 41W
Atlin, L., Canada 142 B2 59 26N 133 45W
Atlin Prov. Park, Canada 142 B2 59 10N 134 30W
Atløyna, Norway 18 C1 61 21N 4 58 E
Atmakur, India 94 E4 18 45N 78 39 E
Atmakur, India 95 G4 14 37N 79 40 E
Atmakur, India 95 G4 15 53N 78 35 E
Atmore, U.S.A. 149 K2 31 2N 87 29W
Atna, Norway 18 C7 61 44N 10 49 E
Atna →, Norway 18 C7 61 44N 10 49 E
Atō, Japan 70 C3 34 25N 131 40 E
Atocha, Bolivia 172 E4 20 56 S 66 14W
Atok, Phil. 80 C3 16 35N 120 41 E
Atoka, U.S.A. 155 H6 34 23N 96 8W
Átokos, Greece 48 C2 38 28N 20 49 E
Atolia, U.S.A. 161 K9 35 19N 117 37W
Atongo-Bakari, C.A.R. 114 A4 5 49N 21 35 E
Atrå, Norway 18 E5 59 59N 8 45 E
Atrai →, Bangla. 93 G13 24 7N 89 22 E
Atrak = Atrek →, Turkmenistan 97 B8 37 35N 53 58 E
Ätran, Sweden 17 G6 57 7N 12 57 E
Ätran →, Sweden 17 H6 56 53N 12 30 E
Atrato →, Colombia 168 B2 8 17N 76 58W
Atrauli, India 92 E8 28 2N 78 20 E
Atrek →, Turkmenistan 97 B8 37 35N 53 58 E
Atri, Italy 45 F10 42 35N 13 58 E
Atsikí, Greece 49 B7 39 56N 25 13 E
Atsoum, Mts., Cameroon 113 D7 6 41N 12 57 E
Atsugi, Japan 71 B11 35 25N 139 21 E
Atsumi, Japan 71 C9 34 35N 137 4 E
Atsumi-Wan, Japan 71 C9 34 44N 137 13 E
Atsuta, Japan 68 C10 43 24N 141 26 E
Attalla, U.S.A. 152 A3 34 1N 86 6W
Attapu, Laos 78 B3 14 48N 106 50 E
Attapulgus, U.S.A. 152 E5 30 45N 84 29W
Attáviros, Greece 38 C9 36 12N 27 50 E
Attawapiskat, Canada 140 B3 52 56N 82 24W
Attawapiskat →, Canada 140 B3 52 57N 82 18W
Attawapiskat L., Canada 140 B2 52 18N 87 54W
Attersee, Austria 34 D6 47 55N 13 32 E
Attica, Ind., U.S.A. 157 D9 40 18N 87 15W
Attica, Ohio, U.S.A. 150 E2 41 4N 82 53W
Attichy, France 27 C10 49 25N 3 3 E
Attigny, France 27 C11 49 28N 4 35 E
Attikamagen L., Canada 141 B6 55 0N 66 30W
Attikí □, Greece 48 D5 37 10N 23 40 E
Attleboro, U.S.A. 151 E13 41 57N 71 17W
Attock, Pakistan 92 C5 33 52N 72 20 E
Attopeu = Attapu, Laos 78 B3 14 48N 106 50 E
Attu I., U.S.A. 144 K1 52 55N 172 55 E
Attunga, Australia 129 A9 30 55 S 150 50 E
Attur, India 95 J4 11 35N 78 30 E
'Atūd, Yemen 99 D5 14 53N 48 10 E
Atuel →, Argentina 174 D2 36 17 S 66 50W
Åtvidaberg, Sweden 17 F10 58 12N 16 0 E
Atwater, U.S.A. 160 H6 37 21N 120 37W
Atwood, Canada 150 C3 43 40N 81 1W
Atwood, Ill., U.S.A. 157 E8 39 48N 88 28W
Atwood, Kans., U.S.A. 154 F4 39 48N 101 3W
Atyraū, Kazakstan 57 E9 47 5N 52 0 E
Au, Austria 33 B9 47 19N 9 59 E
Au Sable, U.S.A. 150 B1 44 25N 83 20W
Au Sable →, U.S.A. 148 C4 44 25N 83 20W
Au Sable Forks, U.S.A. 151 B11 44 27N 73 41W
Au Sable Pt., U.S.A. 150 B1 44 20N 83 20W
Aubagne, France 29 E9 43 17N 5 37 E
Aubarca, C. d', Spain 39 B7 39 4N 1 22 E
Aube □, France 27 D11 48 15N 4 10 E
Aube →, France 27 D10 48 34N 3 43 E
Aubenas, France 29 D8 44 37N 4 24 E
Aubenton, France 27 C11 49 50N 4 12 E
Auberry, U.S.A. 160 H7 37 7N 119 29W
Aubigny-sur-Nère, France 27 E9 47 30N 2 24 E
Aubin, France 28 D6 44 33N 2 15 E
Aubrac, Mts. d', France 28 D7 44 40N 3 2 E
Auburn, Ala., U.S.A. 152 C4 32 36N 85 29W
Auburn, Calif., U.S.A. 160 G5 38 54N 121 4W
Auburn, Ill., U.S.A. 156 E7 39 36N 89 45W
Auburn, Ind., U.S.A. 157 C11 41 22N 85 4W
Auburn, Maine, U.S.A. 149 C10 44 6N 70 14W
Auburn, N.Y., U.S.A. 151 D8 42 56N 76 34W
Auburn, Nebr., U.S.A. 154 E7 40 23N 95 51W
Auburn, Pa., U.S.A. 151 F8 40 36N 76 6W
Auburn, Wash., U.S.A. 160 C4 47 18N 122 14W
Auburn Ra., Australia 127 D5 25 15 S 150 30 E
Auburndale, U.S.A. 149 L5 28 4N 81 48W
Aubusson, France 28 C6 45 57N 2 11 E
Auce, Latvia 54 B9 56 28N 22 53 E
Auch, France 28 E4 43 39N 0 36 E
Auchi, Nigeria 113 D6 7 6N 6 13 E
Auckland, N.Z. 130 C3 36 52 S 174 46 E
Auckland □, N.Z. 130 E6 36 50 S 175 0 E
Auckland Is., Pac. Oc. 134 N8 50 40 S 166 5 E
Aude □, France 28 E6 43 8N 2 28 E
Aude →, France 28 E7 43 13N 3 14 E
Audegle, Somali Rep. 120 D2 1 59N 44 50 E
Auden, Canada 140 B2 50 14N 87 53W
Auderville, France 26 C5 49 43N 1 57W
Audierne, France 26 D2 48 1N 4 34W
Audincourt, France 27 E13 47 30N 6 50 E
Audo, Ethiopia 107 F5 6 20N 41 50 E
Audubon, U.S.A. 156 C2 41 43N 94 56W
Aue, Germany 30 E8 50 35N 12 41 E
Auerbach, Germany 30 E8 50 30N 12 24 E
Aueti Paraná →, Brazil 168 D4 1 51 S 65 37W
Aufist, W. Sahara 110 C2 25 44N 14 39W
Augathella, Australia 127 D4 25 48 S 146 35 E
Aughnacloy, U.K. 23 B5 54 25N 6 59W
Augrabies Falls, S. Africa 116 D3 28 35 S 20 20 E
Augsburg, Germany 31 G6 48 25N 10 52 E
Augusta, Australia 125 F2 34 19 S 115 9 E
Augusta, Italy 47 E8 37 13N 15 13 E
Augusta, Ark., U.S.A. 155 H9 35 17N 91 22W
Augusta, Ga., U.S.A. 152 B8 33 28N 81 58W
Augusta, Ill., U.S.A. 156 D6 40 14N 90 57W
Augusta, Kans., U.S.A. 155 G6 37 41N 96 59W
Augusta, Ky., U.S.A. 157 F12 38 47N 84 0W
Augusta, Maine, U.S.A. 139 D13 44 19N 69 47W
Augusta, Mont., U.S.A. 158 C7 47 30N 112 24W
Augustenborg, Denmark 17 K3 54 57N 9 53 E
Augustine I., U.S.A. 144 G9 59 22N 153 26W
Augustów, Poland 54 E9 53 51N 23 0 E
Augustus, Mt., Australia 125 D2 24 20 S 116 50 E
Augustus I., Australia 124 C3 15 20 S 124 30 E
Aukan, Eritrea 107 D5 15 29N 40 50 E
Auki, Solomon Is. 133 M11 8 45 S 160 42 E
Aukra, Norway 18 B3 62 47N 6 55 E
Aukum, U.S.A. 160 G6 38 34N 120 43W
Aul, India 94 D8 20 41N 86 39 E
Auld, L., Australia 124 D3 22 25 S 123 50 E
Aulla, Italy 44 D6 44 12N 9 58 E
Aulnay, France 28 B3 46 2N 0 22W
Aulne →, France 26 D2 48 17N 4 16W
Aulnoye-Aymeries, France 27 B10 50 12N 3 50 E
Ault, France 26 B8 50 8N 1 26 E
Ault, U.S.A. 154 E2 40 35N 104 44W
Aulus-les-Bains, France 28 F5 42 49N 1 19 E
Aumale, France 27 C8 49 46N 1 46 E
Aumont-Aubrac, France 28 D7 44 43N 3 17 E
Auna, Nigeria 113 C5 10 9N 4 42 E
Aundah, India 94 E3 19 32N 77 3 E
Aundh, India 94 F2 17 33N 74 23 E
Auning, Denmark 17 H4 56 26N 10 22 E
Aunis, France 28 B3 46 5N 0 50W
Auponhia, Indonesia 79 E7 1 58 S 125 27 E
Aups, France 29 E10 43 37N 6 15 E
Aur, Pulau, Malaysia 87 L5 2 35N 104 10 E
Aura, Burma 90 B6 26 59N 97 57 E
Auraiya, India 93 F8 26 28N 79 33 E
Aurangabad, Bihar, India 93 G11 24 45N 84 18 E
Aurangabad, Maharashtra, India 94 E2 19 50N 75 23 E
Auray, France 26 E4 47 40N 2 59W
Aurdal, Norway 18 D6 60 55N 9 26 E
Aure, Norway 18 A5 63 16N 8 33 E
Aurès, Algeria 111 A6 35 8N 6 30 E
Aurich, Germany 30 B3 53 28N 7 28 E
Aurilândia, Brazil 171 E1 16 44 S 50 28W
Aurillac, France 28 D6 44 55N 2 26 E
Aurlandsfjorden, Norway 18 C4 61 3N 7 1 E
Aurlandsvangen, Norway 18 D4 60 55N 7 12 E
Auronzo di Cadore, Italy 45 B9 46 33N 12 26 E
Aurora = Maéwo, Vanuatu 133 E6 15 10 S 168 10 E
Aurora = San Francisco, Phil. 80 E4 13 21N 122 31 E
Aurora, Canada 150 C5 44 0N 79 28W
Aurora, Isabela, Phil. 80 C3 16 59N 121 38 E
Aurora, Zamboanga del S., Phil. 81 H4 7 57N 123 36 E
Aurora, S. Africa 116 E2 32 40 S 18 29 E
Aurora, Colo., U.S.A. 154 F2 39 44N 104 52W
Aurora, Ill., U.S.A. 157 C8 41 45N 88 19W
Aurora, Mo., U.S.A. 155 G8 36 58N 93 43W
Aurora, N.Y., U.S.A. 151 D8 42 45N 76 42W
Aurora, Nebr., U.S.A. 154 E6 40 52N 98 0W
Aurora, Ohio, U.S.A. 150 E3 41 21N 81 20W
Aurora □, Phil. 80 D3 15 30N 121 30 E
Aursmoen, Norway 18 E8 59 55N 11 26 E
Aursunden, Norway 18 B8 62 40N 11 40 E
Aurukun, Australia 126 A3 13 20 S 141 45 E
Aus, Namibia 116 D2 26 35 S 16 12 E
Ausa, India 94 E3 18 15N 76 30 E
Ausable →, Canada 150 C3 43 19N 81 46W
Auschwitz = Oświęcim, Poland 55 H6 50 2N 19 11 E
Aust-Agder □, Norway 18 F4 58 55N 8 0 E
Austad, Norway 18 F4 58 58N 7 37 E
Austerlitz = Slavkov u Brna, Czech Rep. 35 B9 49 10N 16 52 E
Austevoll, Norway 18 D2 60 5N 5 13 E
Austin, Ind., U.S.A. 157 F11 38 45N 85 49W
Austin, Minn., U.S.A. 154 D8 43 40N 92 58W
Austin, Nev., U.S.A. 158 G5 39 30N 117 4W
Austin, Pa., U.S.A. 150 E6 41 38N 78 6W
Austin, Tex., U.S.A. 155 K6 30 17N 97 45W
Austin, L., Australia 125 E2 27 40 S 118 0 E
Austin I., Canada 143 A10 61 10N 94 0W
Austmarka, Norway 18 D9 60 6N 12 21 E
Austnes, Norway 18 B3 62 38N 6 16 E
Austra, Norway 14 D14 65 8N 11 55 E
Austral Is. = Tubuai Is., Pac. Oc. 135 K13 25 0 S 150 0W
Austral Seamount Chain, Pac. Oc. 135 K13 24 0 S 150 0W
Australia ■, Oceania 134 K5 23 0 S 135 0 E
Australian Alps, Australia 129 D8 36 30 S 148 30 E
Australian Capital Territory □, Australia 127 F4 35 30 S 149 0 E
Australind, Australia 125 F2 33 17 S 115 42 E
Austria ■, Europe 34 E7 47 0N 14 0 E
Austur-Skaftafellssýsla □, Iceland 11 C10 64 15N 16 0W
Austvågøy, Norway 14 B16 68 20N 14 40 E
Autazes, Brazil 169 D6 3 35 S 59 8W
Auterive, France 28 E5 43 21N 1 29 E
Authie →, France 27 B8 50 22N 1 38 E
Authon-du-Perche, France 26 D7 48 12N 0 54 E
Autlán, Mexico 162 D4 19 40N 104 30W
Autun, France 27 F11 46 58N 4 17 E
Auvergne, France 28 C7 45 20N 3 15 E
Auvergne, Mts. d', France 28 C6 45 20N 2 55 E
Auvézère →, France 28 C4 45 12N 0 50 E
Auxerre, France 27 E10 47 48N 3 32 E
Auxi-le-Château, France 27 B9 50 15N 2 8 E
Auxonne, France 27 E12 47 10N 5 20 E
Auxvasse, U.S.A. 156 E5 39 1N 91 54W
Auzances, France 27 F9 46 2N 2 30 E
Ava, Ill., U.S.A. 156 G7 37 53N 89 30W
Ava, Mo., U.S.A. 155 G8 36 57N 92 40W
Avaldsnes, Norway 18 E2 59 21N 5 20 E
Avallon, France 27 E10 47 30N 3 53 E
Avalon, U.S.A. 161 M8 33 21N 118 20W
Avalon Pen., Canada 141 C9 47 30N 53 20W
Avanavero, Surinam 169 C6 4 51N 57 22W
Avanigadda, India 95 G5 16 0N 80 56 E
Avannaarsua □, Greenland 10 B5 80 0N 55 0W
Avanos, Turkey 96 B2 38 43N 34 51 E
Avaré, Brazil 175 A6 23 4 S 48 58W
Ávas, Greece 51 F9 40 57N 25 56 E
Avawatz Mts., U.S.A. 161 K10 35 40N 116 30W
Avdan Dağı, Turkey 51 F13 40 23N 29 46 E
Aveiro, Brazil 169 D6 3 10 S 55 5W
Aveiro, Portugal 42 E2 40 37N 8 38W
Aveiro □, Portugal 42 E2 40 40N 8 35W
Āvej, Iran 97 C6 35 40N 49 15 E
Avellaneda, Argentina 174 C4 34 50 S 58 10W
Avellino, Italy 47 B7 40 54N 14 47 E
Avenal, U.S.A. 160 K6 36 0N 120 8W
Avenches, Switz. 32 C4 46 53N 7 2 E
Averøya, Norway 18 A4 63 0N 7 35 E
Aversa, Italy 47 B7 40 58N 14 12 E
Avery, U.S.A. 158 C6 47 15N 115 49W
Aves, Is. las, Venezuela 165 D6 12 0N 67 30W
Avesnes-sur-Helpe, France 27 B10 50 8N 3 55 E
Avesta, Sweden 16 D10 60 9N 16 10 E
Aveyron □, France 28 D6 44 22N 2 45 E
Aveyron →, France 28 D5 44 5N 1 16 E
Avezzano, Italy 45 F10 42 2N 13 25 E
Avgó, Greece 49 F7 35 33N 25 37 E
Aviá Terai, Argentina 174 B3 26 45 S 60 50W
Aviano, Italy 45 B9 46 4N 12 36 E
Aviemore, U.K. 22 D5 57 12N 3 50W
Avigliana, Italy 44 C4 45 5N 7 23 E
Avigliano, Italy 47 B8 40 44N 15 43 E
Avignon, France 29 E8 43 57N 4 50 E
Ávila, Spain 42 E6 40 39N 4 43W
Ávila □, Spain 42 E6 40 30N 5 0W
Ávila, Sierra de, Spain 42 E5 40 40N 5 15W
Avila Beach, U.S.A. 161 K6 35 11N 120 44W
Avilés, Spain 42 B5 43 35N 5 57W
Avintes, Portugal 42 D2 41 7N 8 33W
Avionárion, Greece 48 C6 38 31N 24 8 E
Avis, Portugal 43 F3 39 4N 7 53W
Avis, U.S.A. 150 E7 41 11N 77 19W
Avisio →, Italy 44 B8 46 7N 11 5 E
Avissawella, Sri Lanka 95 L5 6 56N 80 11 E
Aviston, U.S.A. 156 F7 38 36N 89 36W
Aviz = Avis, Portugal 43 F3 39 4N 7 53W
Avize, France 27 D11 48 59N 4 1 E
Avlum, Denmark 17 H2 56 16N 8 47 E
Avoca, U.S.A. 150 D7 42 25N 77 25W
Avoca →, Australia 128 C5 35 40 S 143 43 E
Avoca →, Ireland 23 D5 52 48N 6 10W
Avola, Canada 142 C5 51 45N 119 19W
Avola, Italy 47 F8 36 56N 15 7 E
Avon, Ill., U.S.A. 156 D6 40 40N 90 26W
Avon, N.Y., U.S.A. 150 D7 42 55N 77 45W
Avon →, Australia 125 F2 31 40 S 116 7 E
Avon →, Bristol, U.K. 21 F5 51 29N 2 41W
Avon →, Dorset, U.K. 21 G6 50 44N 1 46W
Avon →, Warks., U.K. 21 E5 52 0N 2 8W
Avon Park, U.S.A. 153 H8 27 36N 81 31W
Avondale, Zimbabwe 119 F3 17 43 S 30 58 E
Avonlea, Canada 143 D8 50 0N 105 0W
Avonmore, Canada 151 A10 45 10N 74 58W
Avramov, Bulgaria 51 D10 42 45N 26 38 E
Avranches, France 26 D5 48 40N 1 20W
Avre →, France 26 D8 48 47N 1 22 E
Avrig, Romania 53 E9 45 43N 24 21 E
Avrillé, France 26 E6 47 30N 0 35W
Avtovac, Bos.-H. 50 C2 43 9N 18 35 E
Avu Avu, Solomon Is. 133 M11 9 50 S 160 22 E
Awag el Baqar, Sudan 107 E3 10 10N 33 10 E
A'waj →, Syria 103 B5 33 23N 36 20 E
Awaji, Japan 71 C7 34 32N 135 1 E
Awaji-Shima, Japan 70 C6 34 30N 134 50 E
'Awālī, Bahrain 97 E6 26 0N 50 30 E
Awantipur, India 93 C6 33 55N 75 3 E
Awanui, N.Z. 130 B2 35 4 S 173 17 E
Awarja →, India 94 F3 17 5N 76 15 E
Awarua B., N.Z. 131 E3 44 28 S 168 4 E
Awarua Pt., N.Z. 131 E3 44 15 S 168 5 E
Awasa, Ethiopia 102 F2 7 2N 38 28 E
Awasa, L., Ethiopia 107 F4 7 0N 38 30 E
Awash, Ethiopia 102 F3 9 1N 40 10 E
Awash →, Ethiopia 107 E5 11 45N 41 5 E
Awaso, Ghana 112 D4 6 15N 2 22W
Awatere →, N.Z. 131 B9 41 37 S 174 10 E
Awbārī, Libya 108 C2 26 46N 12 57 E
Awbārī □, Libya 108 C2 26 35N 12 46 E
Awe, L., U.K. 22 E3 56 17N 5 16W
Aweil, Sudan 107 F2 8 42N 27 20 E
Awgu, Nigeria 113 D6 6 4N 7 24 E
Awjilah, Libya 108 C4 29 8N 21 7 E
Awka, Nigeria 113 D6 6 12N 7 5 E
Aworro, Papua N. G. 132 D2 7 43 S 143 11 E
Ax-les-Thermes, France 28 F5 42 44N 1 50 E
Axat, France 28 F6 42 48N 2 13 E
Axe →, U.K. 21 F5 50 42N 3 4W
Axel Heiberg I., Canada 136 A10 80 0N 90 0W
Axim, Ghana 112 E4 4 51N 2 15W
Axinim, Brazil 169 D6 4 2 S 59 22W
Axintele, Romania 53 F11 44 37N 26 47 E
Axioma, Brazil 173 B5 6 45 S 64 31W
Axiós →, Greece 50 F6 40 57N 22 35 E
Axminster, U.K. 21 G4 50 46N 3 0W
Axson, U.S.A. 152 D7 31 17N 82 44W
Axvall, Sweden 17 F7 58 23N 13 34 E
Ay, France 27 C11 49 3N 4 1 E
Ay →, Russia 62 C6 56 8N 57 40 E
Ayaantang, Eq. Guin. 114 B2 1 58N 10 24 E
Ayabaca, Peru 172 A2 4 40 S 79 53W
Ayabe, Japan 71 B7 35 20N 135 20 E
Ayacucho, Argentina 174 D4 37 5 S 58 20W
Ayacucho, Peru 172 C3 13 0 S 74 0W
Ayacucho □, Peru 172 C3 14 0 S 74 0W
Ayaguz, Kazakstan 64 E9 48 10N 80 10 E
Ayakkuduk, Uzbekistan 63 C2 41 12N 65 12 E
Ayakudi, India 95 J3 10 28N 77 56 E
Ayala, Phil. 81 H3 6 57N 121 57 E
Ayamé, Ivory C. 112 D4 5 35N 3 9W
Ayamonte, Spain 43 H3 37 12N 7 24W
Ayan, Russia 65 D14 56 30N 138 16 E
Ayancık, Turkey 100 B6 41 57N 34 35 E
Ayapel, Colombia 168 B2 8 19N 75 9W
Ayas, Turkey 100 B5 40 2N 32 21 E
Ayaviri, Peru 172 C3 14 50 S 70 35W
Āybak, Afghan. 91 A3 36 15N 68 5 E
Aybastı, Turkey 100 B7 40 41N 37 23 E
Aydim, W. →, Oman 99 C6 18 8N 53 8 E
Aydın, Turkey 100 D2 37 51N 27 51 E
Aydin □, Turkey 49 D9 37 50N 28 0 E
Aydin Dağları, Turkey 49 D10 38 0N 28 0 E
Aydyrlinskiy, Russia 62 E7 52 3N 59 50 E
Ayelu, Ethiopia 107 E5 10 5N 40 42 E
Ayenngré, Togo 113 D5 8 40N 1 1 E
Ayer, U.S.A. 151 D13 42 34N 71 35W
Ayerbe, Spain 40 C4 42 17N 0 41W
Ayer's Cliff, Canada 151 A12 45 10N 72 3W
Ayers Rock, Australia 125 E5 25 23 S 131 5 E
Ayiá, Greece 48 B4 39 43N 22 45 E
Ayia Aikateríni, Ákra, Greece 38 A3 39 50N 19 50 E
Ayía Ánna, Greece 48 C5 38 52N 23 24 E
Ayia Dhéka, Greece 38 D6 35 3N 24 58 E
Ayia Gálini, Greece 38 D6 35 6N 24 41 E
Ayía Marína, Kásos, Greece 49 F8 35 27N 26 53 E
Ayía Marína, Léros, Greece 49 D8 37 11N 26 48 E
Ayia Napa, Cyprus 38 E13 34 59N 34 0 E
Ayía Paraskeví, Greece 49 B8 39 14N 26 21 E
Ayia Phyla, Cyprus 38 E12 34 43N 33 1 E
Ayía Rouméli, Greece 48 F5 35 14N 23 58 E
Ayia Varvára, Greece 38 D7 35 8N 25 1 E
Ayiássos, Greece 49 B8 39 5N 26 23 E
Áyioi Theódhoroi, Greece 48 D5 37 55N 23 9 E
Áyion Óros □, Greece 51 F8 40 25N 24 6 E
Áyios Amvrósios, Cyprus 38 D12 35 20N 33 35 E
Áyios Andréas, Greece 48 D4 37 21N 22 45 E
Áyios Evstrátios, Greece 48 B6 39 34N 24 58 E
Áyios Ioánnis, Ákra, Greece 38 D7 35 20N 25 40 E
Áyios Isidhoros, Greece 38 C9 36 9N 27 51 E
Áyios Kiríkos, Greece 49 D8 37 34N 26 17 E
Áyios Matthaíos, Greece 38 B3 39 30N 19 47 E
Áyios Mírono, Greece 49 F7 35 15N 25 1 E
Áyios Nikólaos, Greece 38 D7 35 11N 25 41 E
Áyios Pétros, Greece 48 C2 38 38N 20 33 E
Áyios Seryios, Cyprus 38 D12 35 12N 33 53 E
Áyios Theodhoros, Cyprus 38 D13 35 22N 34 1 E
Áyios Yeóryios, Greece 48 D5 37 28N 23 57 E
Áykathonisi, Greece 49 D8 37 28N 27 0 E
Aykino, Russia 56 B8 62 15N 49 56 E
Aykirikçi, Turkey 49 B12 39 8N 30 9 E
Aylesbury, U.K. 21 F7 51 49N 0 49W
Aylmer, Canada 150 D4 42 46N 80 59W
Aylmer, L., Canada 138 B8 64 0N 110 8W
'Ayn, Wādī al, Oman 97 F7 22 15N 55 28 E
'Ayn al Ghazālah, Libya 108 B4 32 10N 23 20 E
Ayn Dār, Si. Arabia 97 E7 25 55N 49 10 E
Ayn Zālah, Iraq 101 D10 36 45N 42 35 E
Ayna, Spain 41 G2 38 34N 2 3W
Aynāt, Yemen 99 C5 16 4N 49 9 E
Ayni, Tajikistan 63 D4 39 23N 68 32 E
Ayod, Sudan 107 F3 8 7N 31 26 E
Ayolas, Paraguay 174 B4 27 10 S 56 59W
Ayom, Sudan 107 F2 7 49N 28 23 E
Ayon, Ostrov, Russia 65 C17 69 50N 169 0 E
Ayora, Spain 41 F3 39 3N 1 3W
Ayorou, Niger 113 C5 14 53N 1 0 E
Ayos, Cameroon 114 B2 3 53N 12 31 E
'Ayoûn el 'Atroûs, Mauritania 112 B3 16 38N 9 37W
Ayr, Australia 126 B4 19 35 S 147 25 E
Ayr, Canada 150 C4 43 17N 80 27W
Ayr, U.K. 22 F4 55 28N 4 38W
Ayr →, U.K. 22 F4 55 28N 4 38W
Ayrancı, Turkey 100 D5 37 21N 33 41 E
Ayrancılar, Turkey 49 C9 38 15N 27 18 E
Ayre, Pt. of, U.K. 20 C3 54 25N 4 21W
Aysha, Ethiopia 107 E5 10 50N 42 23 E
Ayton, Australia 126 B4 15 56 S 145 22 E
Aytos, Bulgaria 51 D11 42 42N 27 16 E
Aytoska Planina, Bulgaria 51 D11 42 45N 27 30 E
Ayu, Kepulauan, Indonesia 79 D8 0 35N 131 5 E
Ayutla, Guatemala 164 D1 14 40N 92 10W
Ayutla, Mexico 163 D5 16 58N 99 17W
Ayvacık, Turkey 100 C2 39 36N 26 24 E
Ayvalık, Turkey 49 B8 39 20N 26 46 E
Az Zabadānī, Syria 103 B5 33 43N 36 5 E
Az Ẓāhirīyah, West Bank 103 D3 31 25N 34 58 E
Az Ẓahrān, Si. Arabia 97 E6 26 10N 50 7 E
Az Zarqā, Jordan 103 C5 32 5N 36 4 E
Az Zarqā', U.A.E. 97 E7 24 53N 53 4 E
Az Zāwiyah, Libya 108 B2 32 52N 12 56 E
Az Zaydīyah, Yemen 98 D3 15 20N 43 1 E
Az Zībār, Iraq 101 D11 36 52N 44 4 E
Az Zilfī, Si. Arabia 96 E5 26 12N 44 52 E
Az Zubayr, Iraq 96 D5 30 26N 47 40 E
Az Zuqur, Yemen 98 D3 14 0N 42 45 E
Az Zuwaytīnah, Libya 108 B4 30 58N 20 7 E
Azambuja, Portugal 43 F2 39 4N 8 51W
Azamgarh, India 93 F10 26 5N 83 13 E
Azangaro, Peru 172 C3 14 55 S 70 13W
Azaoua, Niger 113 B5 15 50N 4 0 E
Azaouad, Mali 112 B4 19 0N 3 0W
Azaouak, Vallée de l', Mali 113 B5 15 50N 3 20 E
Āzār Shahr, Iran 101 D11 37 45N 45 59 E
Azara, Nigeria 113 D6 8 22N 9 12 E
Azarān, Iran 101 D12 37 25N 47 16 E
Azärbayjan = Azerbaijan ■, Asia 61 K9 40 20N 48 0 E
Āzarbāyjān-e Gharbī □, Iran 96 B5 37 0N 44 30 E
Āzarbāyjān-e Sharqī □, Iran 96 B5 37 20N 47 0 E
Azare, Nigeria 113 C7 11 55N 10 10 E
Azay-le-Rideau, France 26 E7 47 16N 0 30 E
A'zāz, Syria 100 D7 36 36N 37 4 E
Azazga, Algeria 111 A5 36 48N 4 22 E
Azbine = Aïr, Niger 113 B6 18 30N 8 0 E
Azefal, Mauritania 110 D2 21 0N 14 45W
Azeffoun, Algeria 111 A5 36 51N 4 26 E
Azemmour, Morocco 110 B3 33 20N 9 20W
Azerbaijan ■, Asia 61 K9 40 20N 48 0 E
Azerbaijchan = Azerbaijan ■, Asia 61 K9 40 20N 48 0 E
Azezo, Ethiopia 107 E4 12 28N 37 15 E
Azimganj, India 93 G13 24 14N 88 16 E
Aznalcóllar, Spain 43 H4 37 32N 6 17W
Azogues, Ecuador 168 D2 2 35 S 78 0W
Azores, Atl. Oc. 8 E6 38 44N 29 0W
Azov, Russia 59 J10 47 3N 39 25 E
Azov, Sea of, Europe 59 J9 46 0N 36 30 E
Azovskoye More = Azov, Sea of, Europe 59 J9 46 0N 36 30 E
Azpeitia, Spain 40 B2 43 12N 2 19W
Azraq ash Shīshān, Jordan 103 D5 31 50N 36 49 E

186 Azrou

Azrou, *Morocco* **110 B3** 33 28N 5 19W
Aztec, *U.S.A.* **159 H10** 36 49N 107 59W
Azúa de Compostela, *Dom. Rep.* **165 C5** 18 25N 70 44W
Azuaga, *Spain* **43 G5** 38 16N 5 39W
Azuara, *Spain* **40 D4** 41 15N 0 53W
Azuay □, *Ecuador* **168 D2** 2 55 S 79 0W
Azuer →, *Spain* **43 F7** 39 8N 3 36W
Azuero, Pen. de, *Panama* **164 E3** 7 30N 80 30W
Azuga, *Romania* **53 E10** 45 27N 25 33 E
Azul, *Argentina* **174 D4** 36 42 S 59 43W
Azul, Serra, *Brazil* **173 C7** 14 50 S 54 50W
Azurduy, *Bolivia* **173 D5** 19 59 S 64 29W
Azusa, *U.S.A.* **161 L9** 34 8N 117 52W
Azzaba, *Algeria* **111 A6** 36 48N 7 6 E
Azzano Décimo, *Italy* **45 C9** 45 52N 12 56 E

B

Ba Don, *Vietnam* **78 A3** 17 45N 106 26 E
Ba Dong, *Vietnam* **87 H6** 9 40N 106 33 E
Ba Ngoi = Cam Lam, *Vietnam* **87 G7** 11 54N 109 10 E
Ba Tri, *Vietnam* **87 G6** 10 2N 106 36 E
Ba Xian = Bazhou, *China* **74 E9** 39 8N 116 22 E
Baa, *Indonesia* **79 F6** 10 50 S 123 0 E
Baaba, I., *N. Cal.* **133 T18** 20 3 S 164 59 E
Baamonde, *Spain* **42 B3** 43 7N 7 44W
Baao, *Phil.* **80 E4** 13 27N 123 22 E
Baar, *Switz.* **33 B7** 47 12N 8 32 E
Baarle-Nassau, *Belgium* **24 C4** 51 27N 4 56 E
Bab el Mandeb, *Red Sea* **98 D3** 12 35N 43 25 E
Baba, *Bulgaria* **50 D7** 42 44N 23 59 E
Baba, B. do, *Angola* **115 E2** 14 50 S 12 14 E
Baba Budan Hills, *India* **95 H2** 13 30N 75 44 E
Baba Burnu, *Turkey* **49 B8** 39 29N 26 2 E
Baba dag, *Azerbaijan* **61 K9** 41 0N 48 19 E
Bābā Kalū, *Iran* **97 D6** 30 7N 50 49 E
Babaçulândia, *Brazil* **170 C2** 7 13 S 47 46W
Babadag, *Romania* **53 F13** 44 53N 28 44 E
Babadağ, *Turkey* **49 D10** 37 49N 28 52 E
Babadayhan, *Turkmenistan* **64 F7** 37 42N 60 23 E
Babaeski, *Turkey* **51 E11** 41 26N 27 6 E
Babahoyo, *Ecuador* **168 D2** 1 40 S 79 30W
Babai = Sarju →, *India* **93 F9** 27 21N 81 23 E
Babak, *Phil.* **81 H5** 7 8N 125 41 E
Babana, *Nigeria* **113 C5** 10 31N 3 46 E
Babanusa, *Sudan* **107 E2** 11 20N 27 48 E
Babar, *Algeria* **111 A6** 35 10N 7 6 E
Babar, *Indonesia* **79 F7** 8 0 S 129 30 E
Babar, *Pakistan* **92 D3** 31 7N 69 32 E
Babarkach, *Pakistan* **92 E3** 29 45N 68 0 E
Babayevo, *Russia* **58 C8** 59 24N 35 55 E
Babb, *U.S.A.* **158 B7** 48 51N 113 27W
Babelthuap, *Pac. Oc.* **79 C8** 7 30N 134 30 E
Babenhausen, *Germany* **31 F4** 49 57N 8 57 E
Băbeni, *Romania* **53 F9** 44 59N 24 11 E
Baberu, *India* **93 G9** 25 33N 80 43 E
Babi Besar, Pulau, *Malaysia* **87 L4** 2 25N 103 59 E
Babia Gora, *Europe* **55 J6** 49 38N 19 38 E
Babian Jiang →, *China* **76 F3** 22 55N 101 47 E
Babile, *Ethiopia* **107 F5** 9 16N 42 11 E
Babimost, *Poland* **55 F2** 52 10N 15 49 E
Babinda, *Australia* **126 B4** 17 20 S 145 56 E
Babine, *Canada* **142 B3** 55 22N 126 37W
Babine →, *Canada* **142 B3** 55 45N 127 44W
Babine L., *Canada* **142 C3** 54 48N 126 0W
Babo, *Indonesia* **79 E8** 2 30 S 133 30 E
Babócsa, *Hungary* **52 D2** 46 2N 17 21 E
Bābol, *Iran* **97 B7** 36 40N 52 50 E
Bābol Sar, *Iran* **97 B7** 36 45N 52 45 E
Baborów, *Poland* **55 H5** 50 7N 18 1 E
Baboua, *C.A.R.* **114 A2** 5 49N 14 58 E
Babruysk, *Belarus* **59 F5** 53 10N 29 15 E
Babson Park, *U.S.A.* **153 H8** 27 49N 81 32W
Babuhri, *India* **92 F3** 26 49N 69 43 E
Babuna, *Macedonia* **50 E5** 41 30N 21 40 E
Babura, *Nigeria* **113 C6** 12 51N 8 59 E
Babusar Pass, *Pakistan* **93 B5** 35 12N 73 59 E
Babušnica, *Serbia, Yug.* **50 C6** 43 7N 22 27 E
Babuyan, *Phil.* **81 F2** 10 0N 118 54 E
Babuyan Chan., *Phil.* **79 A6** 18 40N 121 30 E
Babuyan I., *Phil.* **80 B3** 19 32N 121 57 E
Babuyan Is., *Phil.* **80 B3** 19 10N 121 40 E
Babylon, *Iraq* **101 F11** 32 34N 44 22 E
Bač, *Serbia, Yug.* **52 E4** 45 29N 19 17 E
Bâc →, *Moldova* **53 D14** 46 55N 29 26 E
Bac Can, *Vietnam* **76 F5** 22 8N 105 49 E
Bac Giang, *Vietnam* **76 G6** 21 16N 106 11 E
Bac Lieu, *Vietnam* **78 C3** 9 17N 105 43 E
Bac Ninh, *Vietnam* **76 G6** 21 13N 106 4 E
Bac Phan, *Vietnam* **86 B5** 22 0N 105 0 E
Bac Quang, *Vietnam* **76 F5** 22 30N 104 48 E
Bacabal, *Brazil* **170 B3** 4 15 S 44 45W
Bacacay, *Phil.* **80 E4** 13 18N 123 47 E
Bacajá →, *Brazil* **169 D7** 3 25 S 51 50W
Bacalar, *Mexico* **163 D7** 18 50N 87 27W
Bacan, Kepulauan, *Indonesia* **79 E7** 0 35 S 127 30 E
Bacan, Pulau, *Indonesia* **82 B3** 0 50 S 127 30 E
Bacarra, *Phil.* **79 A6** 18 15N 120 37 E
Bacău, *Romania* **53 D11** 46 35N 26 55 E
Bacău □, *Romania* **53 D11** 46 30N 26 45 E
Baccarat, *France* **27 D13** 48 28N 6 42 E
Bacchus Marsh, *Australia* **128 D6** 37 43 S 144 27 E
Bacerac, *Mexico* **162 A3** 30 18N 108 50W
Băcești, *Romania* **53 D12** 46 50N 27 11 E
Bach, *Austria* **33 B10** 47 16N 10 25 E
Bach Long Vi, Dao, *Vietnam* **86 B6** 20 10N 107 40 E
Bachaquero, *Venezuela* **168 B3** 9 56N 71 8W
Bacharach, *Germany* **31 E3** 50 3N 7 44 E
Bachelina, *Russia* **64 D7** 57 45N 67 20 E
Bachhwara, *India* **93 G11** 25 35N 85 54 E
Bachuma, *Ethiopia* **107 F4** 6 48N 35 53 E
Bačina, *Serbia, Yug.* **50 C5** 43 42N 21 23 E
Back →, *Canada* **138 B9** 65 10N 104 0W
Bačka Palanka, *Serbia, Yug.* **52 E4** 45 17N 19 27 E
Bačka Topola, *Serbia, Yug.* **52 E4** 45 49N 19 39 E
Bäckebo, *Sweden* **17 H10** 56 53N 16 4 E
Bäckefors, *Sweden* **17 F6** 58 48N 12 9 E
Bäckhammar, *Sweden* **16 E8** 59 10N 14 11 E
Bački Petrovac, *Serbia, Yug.* **52 E4** 45 29N 19 32 E
Backnang, *Germany* **31 G5** 48 56N 9 26 E
Backstairs Passage, *Australia* **128 C3** 35 40 S 138 5 E
Baco, Mt., *Phil.* **80 E3** 12 49N 121 10 E
Bacolod, *Phil.* **79 B6** 10 40N 122 57 E
Bacon, *Phil.* **80 E5** 13 3N 124 3 E
Baconton, *U.S.A.* **152 D5** 31 23N 84 10W
Bacoor, *Phil.* **80 D3** 14 28N 120 56 E
Bacqueville-en-Caux, *France* **26 C8** 49 47N 1 0 E
Bács-Kiskun □, *Hungary* **52 D4** 46 43N 19 30 E
Bácsalmás, *Hungary* **52 D4** 46 8N 19 17 E
Bacuag = Placer, *Phil.* **81 G5** 9 36N 125 38 E
Bacuk, *Malaysia* **87 J4** 6 4N 102 25 E
Bād, *Iran* **97 C7** 33 41N 52 1 E
Bad →, *U.S.A.* **154 C4** 44 21N 100 22W
Bad Aussee, *Austria* **34 D6** 47 43N 13 45 E
Bad Axe, *U.S.A.* **150 C2** 43 48N 83 0W
Bad Bergzabern, *Germany* **31 F3** 49 6N 7 59 E
Bad Berleburg, *Germany* **30 D4** 51 2N 8 26 E
Bad Bevensen, *Germany* **30 B6** 53 5N 10 35 E
Bad Bramstedt, *Germany* **30 B5** 53 55N 9 53 E
Bad Brückenau, *Germany* **31 E5** 50 18N 9 47 E
Bad Doberan, *Germany* **30 A7** 54 6N 11 53 E
Bad Driburg, *Germany* **30 D5** 51 43N 9 1 E
Bad Ems, *Germany* **31 E3** 50 20N 7 43 E
Bad Frankenhausen, *Germany* **30 D7** 51 21N 11 5 E
Bad Freienwalde, *Germany* **30 C10** 52 46N 14 1 E
Bad Goisern, *Austria* **34 D6** 47 38N 13 38 E
Bad Harzburg, *Germany* **30 D6** 51 52N 10 34 E
Bad Hersfeld, *Germany* **30 E5** 50 52N 9 42 E
Bad Hofgastein, *Austria* **34 D6** 47 17N 13 6 E
Bad Homburg, *Germany* **31 E4** 50 13N 8 38 E
Bad Honnef, *Germany* **30 E3** 50 38N 7 13 E
Bad Iburg, *Germany* **30 C4** 52 10N 8 3 E
Bad Ischl, *Austria* **34 D6** 47 44N 13 38 E
Bad Kissingen, *Germany* **31 E6** 50 11N 10 4 E
Bad Königshofen, *Germany* **31 E6** 50 17N 10 28 E
Bad Kreuznach, *Germany* **31 F3** 49 50N 7 51 E
Bad Krozingen, *Germany* **31 H3** 47 54N 7 42 E
Bad Laasphe, *Germany* **30 E4** 50 56N 8 25 E
Bad Lands, *U.S.A.* **154 D3** 43 40N 102 10W
Bad Langensalza, *Germany* **30 D6** 51 5N 10 38 E
Bad Lauterberg, *Germany* **30 D6** 51 38N 10 28 E
Bad Leonfelden, *Austria* **34 C7** 48 31N 14 18 E
Bad Liebenwerda, *Germany* **30 D9** 51 31N 13 24 E
Bad Mergentheim, *Germany* **31 F5** 49 28N 9 42 E
Bad Münstereifel, *Germany* **30 E2** 50 33N 6 46 E
Bad Nauheim, *Germany* **31 E4** 50 21N 8 43 E
Bad Neuenahr-Ahrweiler, *Germany* **30 E3** 50 32N 7 5 E
Bad Neustadt, *Germany* **31 E6** 50 18N 10 13 E
Bad Oeynhausen, *Germany* **30 C4** 52 12N 8 46 E
Bad Oldesloe, *Germany* **30 B6** 53 48N 10 22 E
Bad Orb, *Germany* **31 E5** 50 12N 9 22 E
Bad Pyrmont, *Germany* **30 D5** 51 59N 9 16 E
Bad Ragaz, *Switz.* **33 C9** 47 0N 9 30 E
Bad Reichenhall, *Germany* **31 H8** 47 43N 12 54 E
Bad Säckingen, *Germany* **31 H3** 47 33N 7 56 E
Bad Salzuflen, *Germany* **30 C4** 52 5N 8 45 E
Bad Salzungen, *Germany* **30 E6** 50 48N 10 14 E
Bad Schwartau, *Germany* **30 B6** 53 55N 10 41 E
Bad Segeberg, *Germany* **30 B6** 53 56N 10 17 E
Bad St. Leonhard, *Austria* **34 E7** 46 58N 14 47 E
Bad Tölz, *Germany* **31 H7** 47 45N 11 34 E
Bad Urach, *Germany* **31 G5** 48 29N 9 23 E
Bad Vöslau, *Austria* **35 D9** 47 58N 16 12 E
Bad Waldsee, *Germany* **31 H5** 47 55N 9 45 E
Bad Wildungen, *Germany* **30 D5** 51 6N 9 7 E
Bad Wimpfen, *Germany* **31 F5** 49 13N 9 11 E
Bad Windsheim, *Germany* **31 F6** 49 36N 10 25 E
Bad Zwischenahn, *Germany* **30 B4** 53 12N 8 1 E
Bada Barabil, *India* **93 H11** 22 7N 85 24 E
Badagara, *India* **95 J2** 11 35N 75 40 E
Badagri, *Nigeria* **113 D5** 6 25N 2 55 E
Badajós, L., *Brazil* **169 D5** 3 15 S 62 50W
Badajoz, *Spain* **43 G4** 38 50N 6 59W
Badajoz □, *Spain* **43 G4** 38 40N 6 30W
Badakhshān □, *Afghan.* **91 A3** 36 30N 71 0 E
Badalona, *Spain* **40 D7** 41 26N 2 15 E
Badalzai, *Afghan.* **92 E1** 29 50N 65 35 E
Badami, *India* **95 G2** 15 55N 75 41 E
Badampahar, *India* **94 C8** 22 10N 86 10 E
Badanah, *Si. Arabia* **96 D4** 30 58N 41 30 E
Badarinath, *India* **93 D8** 30 45N 79 30 E
Badas, Kepulauan, *Indonesia* **78 D3** 0 45N 107 5 E
Baddo →, *Pakistan* **91 D2** 28 0N 64 20 E
Bade, *Indonesia* **79 F9** 7 10 S 139 35 E
Badeggi, *Nigeria* **113 D6** 9 1N 6 8 E
Badéguichéri, *Niger* **113 C6** 14 30N 5 22 E
Baden, *Austria* **35 C9** 48 1N 16 13 E
Baden, *Switz.* **33 B6** 47 28N 8 18 E
Baden, *U.S.A.* **150 F4** 40 38N 80 14W
Baden-Baden, *Germany* **31 G4** 48 44N 8 13 E
Baden Park, *Australia* **128 B6** 32 8 S 144 12 E
Baden-Württemberg □, *Germany* **31 G4** 48 20N 8 40 E
Badgastein, *Austria* **34 D6** 47 7N 13 9 E
Badger, *Canada* **141 C8** 49 0N 56 4W
Badger, *U.S.A.* **160 J7** 36 38N 119 1W
Bādghīsāt □, *Afghan.* **91 B1** 35 0N 63 0 E
Badgom, *India* **93 B6** 34 1N 74 45 E
Badia Polésine, *Italy* **45 C8** 45 6N 11 29 E
Badian, *Phil.* **81 G4** 9 55N 123 24 E
Badin, *Pakistan* **91 D3** 24 38N 68 54 E
Badjokola, *Dem. Rep. of the Congo* **114 B4** 3 54N 20 17 E
Badlands National Park, *U.S.A.* **154 D3** 43 38N 102 56W
Badnera, *India* **94 D3** 20 48N 77 44 E
Badoc, *Phil.* **80 C3** 17 56N 120 28 E
Badogo, *Mali* **112 C3** 11 2N 8 13W
Badoumbé, *Mali* **112 C2** 13 42N 10 15W
Badr Ḩunayn, *Si. Arabia* **98 B2** 23 44N 38 46 E
Badrah, *Iraq* **101 F11** 33 6N 45 58 E
Badrinath, *India* **93 D8** 30 44N 79 29 E
Baduen, *Somali Rep.* **120 C3** 7 15N 47 40 E
Badulla, *Sri Lanka* **95 L5** 7 1N 81 7 E
Badupi, *Burma* **90 E4** 21 36N 93 27 E
Badvel, *India* **95 G4** 14 45N 79 3 E
Baena, *Spain* **43 H6** 37 37N 4 20W
Baerami Creek, *Australia* **129 B9** 32 27 S 150 27 E
Baeza, *Ecuador* **168 D2** 0 25 S 77 53W
Baeza, *Spain* **43 H7** 37 57N 3 25W
Bafang, *Cameroon* **113 D7** 5 9N 10 11 E
Bafatá, *Guinea-Biss.* **112 C2** 12 8N 14 40W
Baffin B., *Canada* **136 B13** 72 0N 64 0W
Baffin I., *Canada* **139 B12** 68 0N 75 0W
Bafia, *Cameroon* **113 E7** 4 40N 11 10 E
Bafilo, *Togo* **113 D5** 9 22N 1 22 E
Bafing →, *Mali* **112 C2** 13 49N 10 50W
Bafliyūn, *Syria* **96 B3** 36 37N 36 59 E
Bafoulabé, *Mali* **112 C2** 13 50N 10 55W
Bafoussam, *Cameroon* **113 D7** 5 28N 10 25 E
Bāfq, *Iran* **97 D7** 31 40N 55 25 E
Bafra, *Turkey* **100 B6** 41 34N 35 54 E
Bafra Burnu, *Turkey* **100 B7** 41 45N 36 2 E
Bāft, *Iran* **97 D8** 29 15N 56 38 E
Bafut, *Cameroon* **113 D7** 6 6N 10 2 E
Bafwasende, *Dem. Rep. of the Congo* **118 B2** 1 3N 27 5 E
Bagabag, *Phil.* **80 C3** 16 30N 121 15 E
Bagac, *Phil.* **80 D3** 14 36N 120 23 E
Bagac Bay, *Phil.* **80 D3** 14 36N 120 20 E
Bagalkot, *India* **95 F2** 16 10N 75 40 E
Bagam, *Niger* **113 B6** 15 43N 6 35 E
Bagamanoc, *Phil.* **80 E5** 13 57N 124 17 E
Bagamoyo, *Tanzania* **118 D4** 6 28 S 38 55 E
Bagan Datoh, *Malaysia* **87 L3** 3 59N 100 47 E
Bagan Serai, *Malaysia* **87 K3** 5 1N 100 32 E
Baganga, *Phil.* **79 C7** 7 34N 126 33 E
Bagani, *Namibia* **116 B3** 18 7 S 21 41 E
Bagansiapiapi, *Indonesia* **78 D2** 2 12N 100 50 E
Bagasra, *India* **92 J4** 21 30N 71 0 E
Bagata, *Dem. Rep. of the Congo* **114 C3** 3 44 S 17 57 E
Bagaud, *India* **92 H6** 22 19N 75 53 E
Bagawi, *Sudan* **107 E3** 12 20N 34 18 E
Bagbag, *Sudan* **107 D3** 15 23N 31 30 E
Bagdad, *Calif., U.S.A.* **161 L11** 34 35N 115 53W
Bagdad, *Fla., U.S.A.* **153 E2** 30 36N 87 2W
Bagdarin, *Russia* **65 D12** 54 26N 113 36 E
Bagé, *Brazil* **175 C5** 31 20 S 54 15W
Bagenalstown = Muine Bheag, *Ireland* **23 D5** 52 42N 6 58W
Bagepalli, *India* **95 H3** 13 47N 77 47 E
Bagevadi, *India* **94 F2** 16 35N 75 58 E
Baggao, *Phil.* **80 C3** 17 56N 121 46 E
Baggs, *U.S.A.* **158 F10** 41 2N 107 39W
Bagh, *Pakistan* **93 C5** 33 59N 73 45 E
Baghain →, *India* **93 G9** 25 32N 81 1 E
Baghdād, *Iraq* **101 F11** 33 20N 44 30 E
Bagherhat, *Bangla.* **90 D2** 22 40N 89 47 E
Bagheria, *Italy* **46 D6** 38 5N 13 30 E
Baghlān, *Afghan.* **91 A3** 36 12N 69 0 E
Baghlān □, *Afghan.* **91 B3** 36 0N 68 30 E
Bagley, *U.S.A.* **154 B7** 47 32N 95 24W
Bagn, *Norway* **18 D6** 60 49N 9 34 E
Bagnara Cálabra, *Italy* **47 D8** 38 17N 15 48 E
Bagnasco, *Italy* **44 D5** 44 18N 8 2 E
Bagnell Dam, *U.S.A.* **156 F4** 38 14N 92 36W
Bagnères-de-Bigorre, *France* **28 E4** 43 5N 0 9 E
Bagnères-de-Luchon, *France* **28 F4** 42 47N 0 38 E
Bagni di Lucca, *Italy* **44 D7** 44 1N 10 35 E
Bagno di Romagna, *Italy* **45 E8** 43 50N 11 57 E
Bagnoles-de-l'Orne, *France* **26 D6** 48 32N 0 25W
Bagnols-sur-Cèze, *France* **29 D8** 44 10N 4 36 E
Bagnorégio, *Italy* **45 F9** 42 37N 12 5 E
Bago = Pegu, *Burma* **90 G6** 17 20N 96 29 E
Bago, *Phil.* **81 F4** 10 32N 122 50 E
Bagodar, *India* **93 G11** 24 5N 85 52 E
Bagrationovsk, *Russia* **15 J19** 54 23N 20 39 E
Bagrdan, *Serbia, Yug.* **50 B5** 44 5N 21 11 E
Bagua, *Peru* **172 B2** 5 35 S 78 22W
Baguio, *Phil.* **79 A6** 16 26N 120 34 E
Bağyurdu, *Turkey* **49 C9** 38 25N 27 41 E
Bagzane, Monts, *Niger* **113 B6** 17 43N 8 45 E
Bah, *India* **93 F8** 26 53N 78 36 E
Bahabón de Esgueva, *Spain* **42 D7** 41 52N 3 43W
Bahadurabad Ghat, *Bangla.* **90 C2** 25 11N 89 44 E
Bahadurganj, *India* **93 F12** 26 16N 87 49 E
Bahadurgarh, *India* **92 E7** 28 40N 76 57 E
Bahama, Canal Viejo de, *W. Indies* **164 B4** 22 10N 77 30W
Bahamas ■, *N. Amer.* **165 B5** 24 0N 75 0W
Bahār, *Iran* **101 E13** 34 54N 48 26 E
Baharampur, *India* **93 G13** 24 2N 88 27 E
Baharîya, El Wâhât al, *Egypt* **106 B2** 28 0N 28 50 E
Bahawalnagar, *Pakistan* **91 C4** 30 0N 73 15 E
Bahawalpur, *Pakistan* **91 C3** 29 24N 71 40 E
Bahçe, *Turkey* **100 D7** 37 13N 36 34 E
Bahçecik, *Turkey* **51 F13** 40 41N 29 44 E
Baheli, *Phil.* **81 F2** 10 0N 118 47 E
Baheri, *India* **93 E8** 28 45N 79 34 E
Bahgul →, *India* **93 F8** 27 45N 79 36 E
Bahi, *Tanzania* **118 D4** 5 58 S 35 21 E
Bahi Swamp, *Tanzania* **118 D4** 6 10 S 35 0 E
Bahía = Salvador, *Brazil* **171 D4** 13 0 S 38 30W
Bahía □, *Brazil* **171 D3** 12 0 S 42 0W
Bahía, Is. de la, *Honduras* **164 C2** 16 45N 86 15W
Bahía Blanca, *Argentina* **174 D3** 38 35 S 62 13W
Bahía de Caráquez, *Ecuador* **168 D1** 0 40 S 80 27W
Bahía Honda, *Cuba* **164 B3** 22 54N 83 10W
Bahía Laura, *Argentina* **176 C3** 48 10 S 66 30W
Bahía Mansa, *Chile* **176 B2** 40 33 S 73 46W
Bahía Negra, *Paraguay* **173 E6** 20 5 S 58 5W
Bahir Dar, *Ethiopia* **102 E2** 11 37N 37 10 E
Bahlah, *Oman* **99 B7** 22 58N 57 18 E
Bahmanzād, *Iran* **97 D6** 31 15N 51 47 E
Bahmer, *Algeria* **111 C4** 27 32N 0 10W
Bahr el Ahmar □, *Sudan* **106 D4** 20 0N 35 0 E
Bahr el Ghazâl □, *Sudan* **107 F2** 7 0N 28 0 E
Bahr el Jabal □, *Sudan* **107 G3** 4 0N 31 0 E
Bahr Salamat →, *Chad* **109 G3** 9 20N 18 0 E
Bahr Yûsef →, *Egypt* **106 B3** 28 25N 30 35 E
Bahraich, *India* **93 F9** 27 38N 81 37 E
Bahrain ■, *Asia* **97 E6** 26 0N 50 35 E
Bahror, *India* **92 F7** 27 51N 76 20 E
Bāhū Kalāt, *Iran* **97 E9** 25 43N 61 25 E
Bai, *Mali* **112 C4** 13 35N 3 28W
Bai Bung, Mui = Ca Mau, Mui, *Vietnam* **78 C2** 8 38N 104 44 E
Bai Duc, *Vietnam* **86 C5** 18 3N 105 49 E
Bai Thuong, *Vietnam* **86 C5** 19 54N 105 23 E
Baia de Aramă, *Romania* **52 E7** 45 0N 22 50 E
Baia Farta, *Angola* **115 E2** 12 40 S 13 11 E
Baia Mare, *Romania* **53 C8** 47 40N 23 35 E
Baia-Sprie, *Romania* **53 C8** 47 41N 23 43 E
Baião, *Brazil* **170 B2** 2 40 S 49 40W
Baïbokoum, *Chad* **109 G3** 7 46N 15 43 E
Baicheng, *China* **75 B12** 45 38N 122 42 E
Băicoi, *Romania* **53 E10** 45 3N 25 52 E
Baidoa, *Somali Rep.* **120 D2** 3 8N 43 30 E
Baie Comeau, *Canada* **141 C6** 49 12N 68 10W
Baie-St-Paul, *Canada* **141 C5** 47 28N 70 32W
Baie Trinité, *Canada* **141 C6** 49 25N 67 20W
Baie Verte, *Canada* **141 C8** 49 55N 56 12W
Baignes-Ste-Radegonde, *France* **28 C3** 45 23N 0 25W
Baigneux-les-Juifs, *France* **27 E11** 47 31N 4 39 E
Baihar, *India* **93 H9** 22 6N 80 33 E
Baihe, *China* **74 H6** 32 50N 110 5 E
Ba'ījī, *Iraq* **101 E10** 35 0N 43 30 E
Baijnath, *India* **93 E8** 29 55N 79 37 E
Baikal, L. = Baykal, Oz., *Russia* **65 D11** 53 0N 108 0 E
Baikunthpur, *India* **93 H10** 23 15N 82 33 E
Bailadila, Mt., *India* **94 E5** 18 43N 81 15 E
Baile Atha Cliath = Dublin, *Ireland* **23 C5** 53 21N 6 15W
Băile Govora, *Romania* **53 E9** 45 5N 24 11 E
Băile Herculane, *Romania* **52 F7** 44 53N 22 26 E
Băile Olănești, *Romania* **53 E9** 45 12N 24 14 E
Băile Tușnad, *Romania* **53 D10** 46 9N 25 51 E
Bailén, *Spain* **43 G7** 38 8N 3 48W
Băilești, *Romania* **53 F8** 44 1N 23 20 E
Bailhongal, *India* **95 G2** 15 55N 74 53 E
Bailique, Ilha, *Brazil* **170 A2** 1 2N 49 58W
Bailundo, *Angola* **115 E3** 12 10 S 15 50 E
Baima, *China* **76 A3** 33 0N 100 26 E
Baimuru, *Papua N. G.* **132 D3** 7 35 S 144 51 E
Bain-de-Bretagne, *France* **26 E5** 47 50N 1 40W
Bainbridge, *Ga., U.S.A.* **152 E5** 30 55N 84 35W
Bainbridge, *Ind., U.S.A.* **157 E10** 39 46N 86 49W
Bainbridge, *N.Y., U.S.A.* **151 D9** 42 18N 75 29W
Bainbridge, *Ohio, U.S.A.* **157 E13** 39 14N 83 16W
Baing, *Indonesia* **79 F6** 10 14 S 120 34 E
Bainiu, *China* **74 H7** 32 50N 112 15 E
Bainyik, *Papua N. G.* **132 B2** 3 40 S 143 4 E
Baiona, *Spain* **42 C2** 42 6N 8 52W
Bā'ir, *Jordan* **103 E5** 30 45N 36 55 E
Bairin Youqi, *China* **75 C10** 43 30N 118 35 E
Bairin Zuoqi, *China* **75 C10** 43 58N 119 15 E
Bairnsdale, *Australia* **129 D7** 37 48 S 147 36 E
Bais, *Phil.* **81 G4** 9 35N 123 7 E
Baisha, *China* **74 G7** 34 20N 112 32 E
Baissa, *Nigeria* **113 D7** 7 14N 10 38 E
Baitadi, *Nepal* **93 E9** 29 35N 80 25 E
Baitarani →, *India* **94 D8** 20 45N 86 48 E
Baixa Grande, *Brazil* **171 D3** 11 57 S 40 11W
Baixo-Longa, *Angola* **115 F3** 15 41 S 18 45 E
Baiyin, *China* **74 F3** 36 45N 104 14 E
Baiyü, *China* **76 B2** 31 16N 98 50 E
Baiyu Shan, *China* **74 F4** 37 15N 107 30 E
Baiyuda, *Sudan* **106 D3** 17 35N 32 7 E
Baj Baj, *India* **93 H13** 22 30N 88 5 E
Baja, *Hungary* **52 D3** 46 12N 18 59 E
Baja, Pta., *Mexico* **162 B1** 29 50N 116 0W
Baja California, *Mexico* **162 A1** 31 10N 115 12W
Baja California □, *Mexico* **162 B2** 30 0N 115 0W
Baja California Sur □, *Mexico* **162 B2** 25 50N 111 50W
Bajag, *India* **93 H9** 22 40N 81 21 E
Bajamar, *Canary Is.* **39 F3** 28 33N 16 20W
Bajana, *India* **92 H4** 23 7N 71 49 E
Bājgīrān, *Iran* **97 B8** 37 36N 58 24 E
Bājil, *Yemen* **98 D3** 15 4N 43 17 E
Bajimba, Mt., *Australia* **127 D5** 29 17 S 152 6 E
Bajina Bašta, *Serbia, Yug.* **50 C3** 43 58N 19 35 E
Bajmok, *Serbia, Yug.* **52 E4** 45 57N 19 24 E
Bajo Caracoles, *Argentina* **176 C2** 47 27 S 70 56W
Bajo Nuevo, *Caribbean* **164 C4** 15 40N 78 50W
Bajoga, *Nigeria* **113 C7** 10 57N 11 20 E
Bajool, *Australia* **126 C5** 23 40 S 150 35 E
Bak, *Hungary* **52 D1** 46 43N 16 51 E
Bakal, *Russia* **62 D7** 54 56N 58 48 E
Bakala, *C.A.R.* **114 A4** 6 15N 20 20 E
Bakanas, *Kazakstan* **63 A8** 44 50N 76 15 E
Bakar, *Croatia* **45 C11** 45 18N 14 32 E
Bakbakty, *Kazakstan* **63 A8** 44 35N 76 40 E
Bakel, *Senegal* **112 C2** 14 56N 12 20W
Baker, *Calif., U.S.A.* **161 K10** 35 16N 116 4W
Baker, *Fla., U.S.A.* **153 E3** 30 48N 86 41W
Baker, *Mont., U.S.A.* **154 B2** 46 22N 104 17W
Baker, Canal, *Chile* **176 C2** 47 45 S 74 45W
Baker, L., *Canada* **138 B10** 64 0N 96 0W
Baker City, *U.S.A.* **158 D5** 44 47N 117 50W
Baker I., *Pac. Oc.* **134 G10** 0 10N 176 35W
Baker I., *U.S.A.* **142 B2** 55 20N 133 40W
Baker L., *Australia* **125 E4** 26 54 S 126 5 E
Baker Lake, *Canada* **138 B10** 64 20N 96 3W
Baker Mt., *U.S.A.* **158 B3** 48 50N 121 49W
Bakere, *Dem. Rep. of the Congo* **114 B4** 1 36N 23 50 E
Bakerhill, *U.S.A.* **152 D4** 31 47N 85 18W
Bakers Creek, *Australia* **126 C4** 21 13 S 149 7 E
Baker's Dozen Is., *Canada* **140 A4** 56 45N 78 45W
Bakersfield, *Calif., U.S.A.* **161 K8** 35 23N 119 1W
Bakersfield, *Vt., U.S.A.* **151 B12** 44 45N 72 48W
Bakhchysaray, *Ukraine* **59 K7** 44 40N 33 45 E
Bakhmach, *Ukraine* **59 G7** 51 10N 32 45 E
Bākhtarān, *Iran* **101 E12** 34 23N 47 0 E
Bākhtarān □, *Iran* **96 C5** 34 0N 46 30 E
Bakı, *Azerbaijan* **61 K9** 40 29N 49 56 E
Bakır →, *Turkey* **49 C9** 38 55N 27 0 E
Bakırdağı, *Turkey* **100 C6** 38 13N 35 46 E
Bakkafjörður, *Iceland* **11 A12** 66 2N 14 48W
Bakkaflói, *Iceland* **11 A12** 66 10N 14 45W
Baklan, *Turkey* **49 C11** 38 0N 29 36 E
Bako, *Ethiopia* **107 F4** 5 51N 36 23 E
Bako, *Ivory C.* **112 D3** 9 8N 7 40W
Bakony, *Hungary* **52 C2** 47 10N 17 30 E
Bakony Forest = Bakony, *Hungary* **52 C2** 47 10N 17 30 E
Bakori, *Nigeria* **113 C6** 11 34N 7 25 E
Bakouma, *C.A.R.* **114 A4** 5 40N 22 56 E
Bakpakty = Bakbakty, *Kazakstan* **63 A8** 44 35N 76 40 E
Baksan, *Russia* **61 J6** 43 42N 43 32 E
Bakswaho, *India* **93 G8** 24 15N 79 18 E
Baku = Bakı, *Azerbaijan* **61 K9** 40 29N 49 56 E
Bakundi, *Nigeria* **113 D7** 8 2N 10 45 E
Bakutis Coast, *Antarctica* **7 D15** 74 0 S 120 0W
Bakwa-Kenge, *Dem. Rep. of the Congo* **115 C4** 4 51 S 22 4 E
Baky = Bakı, *Azerbaijan* **61 K9** 40 29N 49 56 E
Bala, *Canada* **150 A5** 45 1N 79 37W
Bala, *Senegal* **112 C2** 14 1N 13 8W
Bālā, *Turkey* **100 C5** 39 32N 33 6 E
Bala, *U.K.* **20 E4** 52 54N 3 36W
Bala, L., *U.K.* **20 E4** 52 53N 3 37W
Bālā Morghāb, *Afghan.* **91 B1** 35 35N 63 20 E
Balabac, *Phil.* **81 H1** 7 59N 117 4 E
Balabac I., *Phil.* **78 C5** 8 0N 117 0 E
Balabac I., *Phil.* **81 G1** 8 0N 117 0 E
Balabac Str., *E. Indies* **78 C5** 7 53N 117 5 E
Balabagh, *Afghan.* **92 B4** 34 25N 70 12 E
Ba'labakk, *Lebanon* **103 B5** 34 0N 36 10 E
Balabalangan, Kepulauan, *Indonesia* **78 E5** 2 20 S 117 30 E
Balabio, I., *N. Cal.* **133 T18** 20 7 S 164 11 E
Bălăcița, *Romania* **53 F8** 44 23N 23 8 E
Balad, *Iraq* **101 F11** 34 1N 44 9 E
Balad Rūz, *Iraq* **101 F11** 33 42N 45 5 E
Bālādeh, *Fārs, Iran* **97 D6** 29 17N 51 56 E
Bālādeh, *Māzandaran, Iran* **97 B6** 36 12N 51 48 E
Balaghat, *India* **94 D5** 21 49N 80 12 E
Balaghat Ra., *India* **94 E3** 18 50N 76 30 E
Balaguer, *Spain* **40 D5** 41 50N 0 50 E
Balaka, *Dem. Rep. of the Congo* **115 C3** 4 52 S 19 57 E
Balakété, *C.A.R.* **114 A3** 6 56N 19 54 E
Balakhna, *Russia* **60 B6** 56 25N 43 32 E
Balaklava, *Australia* **128 C3** 34 7 S 138 22 E
Balaklava, *Ukraine* **59 K7** 44 30N 33 30 E
Balakliya, *Ukraine* **59 H9** 49 28N 36 55 E
Balakovo, *Russia* **60 D8** 52 4N 47 55 E
Balamau, *India* **93 F9** 27 10N 80 21 E
Balamban, *Phil.* **81 F4** 10 30N 123 43 E
Balambangan, *Malaysia* **85 A5** 7 17N 116 55 E
Bălan, *Romania* **53 D10** 46 39N 25 49 E
Balancán, *Mexico* **163 D6** 17 48N 91 32W
Balanga, *Phil.* **80 D3** 14 41N 120 32 E
Balangala, *Dem. Rep. of the Congo* **114 B3** 0 30N 19 56 E
Balangiga, *Phil.* **81 F5** 11 7N 125 23 E
Balangir, *India* **94 D6** 20 43N 83 35 E
Balaoan, *Phil.* **80 C3** 16 49N 120 24 E
Balapur, *India* **94 D3** 20 40N 76 45 E
Balashov, *Russia* **60 E6** 51 30N 43 10 E
Balasinor, *India* **92 H5** 22 57N 73 23 E
Balasore = Baleshwar, *India* **94 D8** 21 35N 87 3 E
Balassagyarmat, *Hungary* **52 B4** 48 4N 19 15 E
Balât, *Egypt* **106 B2** 25 36N 29 19 E
Balaton, *Hungary* **52 D2** 46 50N 17 40 E
Balatonboglár, *Hungary* **52 D2** 46 46N 17 40 E
Balatonfüred, *Hungary* **52 D2** 46 58N 17 54 E
Balatonszentgyörgy, *Hungary* **52 D2** 46 41N 17 19 E
Balayan, *Phil.* **80 E3** 13 57N 120 44 E
Balazote, *Spain* **41 G2** 38 54N 2 9W

188 Baran

Baran, *India* 92 G7 25 9N 76 40 E
Baran →, *Pakistan* 92 G3 25 13N 68 17 E
Barañain, *Spain* 40 C3 42 48N 1 40W
Baranavichy, *Belarus* 59 F4 53 10N 26 0 E
Barani, *Burkina Faso* 112 C4 13 9N 3 51W
Baranoa, *Colombia* 168 A3 10 48N 74 55W
Baranof, *U.S.A.* 144 H14 57 5N 134 50W
Baranof I., *U.S.A.* 138 C6 57 0N 135 0W
Baranów Sandomierski, *Poland* 55 H8 50 29N 21 30 E
Baranya □, *Hungary* 52 E3 46 0N 18 15 E
Barão de Cocais, *Brazil* 171 E3 19 56 S 43 28W
Barão de Grajaú, *Brazil* 170 C3 6 45 S 43 1W
Barão de Melgaço, *Mato Grosso, Brazil* 173 D6 16 14 S 55 52W
Barão de Melgaço, *Rondônia, Brazil* 173 C5 11 50 S 60 45W
Baraolt, *Romania* 53 D10 46 5N 25 34 E
Barapasi, *Indonesia* 79 E9 2 15 S 137 5 E
Barapina, *Papua N. G.* 132 D8 6 21 S 155 25 E
Baras, *Phil.* 80 E5 13 40N 124 22 E
Barasat, *India* 93 H13 22 46N 88 31 E
Barat Daya, Kepulauan, *Indonesia* 79 F7 7 30 S 128 0 E
Barataria B., *U.S.A.* 155 L10 29 20N 89 55W
Barauda, *India* 92 H6 23 33N 75 15 E
Baraut, *India* 92 E7 29 13N 77 7 E
Baraya, *Colombia* 168 C2 3 10N 75 4W
Barbacan = Roxas, *Phil.* 81 F2 10 20N 119 21 E
Barbacena, *Brazil* 171 F3 21 15 S 43 56W
Barbacoas, *Colombia* 168 C2 1 45N 78 0W
Barbados ■, *W. Indies* 165 D8 13 10N 59 30W
Barbalha, *Brazil* 170 C4 7 19 S 39 17W
Barban, *Croatia* 45 C11 45 5N 14 2 E
Barbària, C. de, *Spain* 39 C7 38 39N 1 24 E
Barbaros, *Turkey* 51 F11 40 54N 27 27 E
Barbastro, *Spain* 40 C5 42 2N 0 5 E
Barbate = Barbate de Franco, *Spain* 43 J5 36 13N 5 56W
Barbate de Franco, *Spain* 43 J5 36 13N 5 56W
Barbaza, *Phil.* 81 F4 11 12N 122 2 E
Barberino di Mugello, *Italy* 45 E8 44 0N 11 15 E
Barbers Pt., *U.S.A.* 145 K13 21 18N 158 7W
Barberton, *S. Africa* 117 D5 25 42 S 31 2 E
Barberton, *U.S.A.* 150 E3 41 0N 81 39W
Barberville, *U.S.A.* 153 F8 29 11N 81 26W
Barbezieux-St-Hilaire, *France* 28 C3 45 28N 0 9W
Barbosa, *Colombia* 168 B3 5 57N 73 37W
Barbourville, *U.S.A.* 149 G4 36 52N 83 53W
Barbuda, *W. Indies* 165 C7 17 30N 61 40W
Bârca, *Romania* 53 G8 43 59N 23 36 E
Barcaldine, *Australia* 126 C4 23 43 S 145 6 E
Barcarena, *Brazil* 170 B2 1 30 S 48 40W
Barcarrota, *Spain* 43 G4 38 31N 6 51W
Barcellona Pozzo di Gotto, *Italy* 47 D8 38 9N 15 13 E
Barcelona, *Spain* 40 D7 41 21N 2 10 E
Barcelona, *Venezuela* 169 A5 10 10N 64 40W
Barcelona □, *Spain* 40 D7 41 30N 2 0 E
Barcelonette, *France* 29 D10 44 23N 6 40 E
Barcelos, *Brazil* 169 D5 1 0 S 63 0W
Barcin, *Poland* 55 F4 52 52N 17 55 E
Barclayville, *Liberia* 112 E3 4 48N 8 10W
Barcoo →, *Australia* 126 D3 25 30 S 142 50 E
Barcs, *Hungary* 52 E2 45 58N 17 28 E
Barczewo, *Poland* 54 E7 53 50N 20 42 E
Bärdä, *Azerbaijan* 61 K8 40 25N 47 10 E
Barda del Medio, *Argentina* 176 A3 38 45 S 68 11W
Bardaï, *Chad* 109 D3 21 25N 17 0 E
Bardas Blancas, *Argentina* 174 D2 35 49 S 69 45W
Barddhaman, *India* 93 H12 23 14N 87 39 E
Bardejov, *Slovak Rep.* 35 B14 49 18N 21 15 E
Bardera, *Somali Rep.* 120 D2 2 20N 42 27 E
Barð, *Iceland* 11 A7 66 3N 19 8W
Bárðarbunga, *Iceland* 11 C9 64 38N 17 32W
Barðastrandarsýsla □, *Iceland* 11 B3 65 40N 23 0W
Bardi, *Italy* 44 D6 44 38N 9 44 E
Bardīyah, *Libya* 108 B5 31 45N 25 5 E
Bardoli, *India* 94 D1 21 12N 73 5 E
Bardolino, *Italy* 44 C7 45 33N 10 43 E
Bardonécchia, *Italy* 44 C3 45 5N 6 42 E
Bardsey I., *U.K.* 20 E3 52 45N 4 47W
Bardstown, *U.S.A.* 157 G11 37 49N 85 28W
Bareilly, *India* 93 E8 28 22N 79 27 E
Barela, *India* 93 H9 23 6N 80 3 E
Barellan, *Australia* 129 C7 34 16 S 146 24 E
Barentin, *France* 26 C7 49 33N 0 58 E
Barenton, *France* 26 D6 48 38N 0 50W
Barents Sea, *Arctic* 66 B7 73 0N 39 0 E
Barentu, *Eritrea* 107 D4 15 2N 37 35 E
Barfleur, *France* 26 C5 49 40N 1 17W
Barfleur, Pte. de, *France* 26 C5 49 42N 1 16W
Barga, *Italy* 44 D7 44 4N 10 29 E
Bargal, *Somali Rep.* 120 B4 11 25N 51 0 E
Bargara, *Australia* 126 C5 24 50 S 152 25 E
Bargarh, *India* 94 D6 21 20N 83 37 E
Bargas, *Spain* 42 F6 39 56N 4 3W
Bârgăului Bistrița, *Romania* 53 C9 47 13N 24 46 E
Barge, *Italy* 44 D4 44 43N 7 20 E
Bargnop, *Sudan* 107 F2 9 32N 28 25 E
Bargo, *Australia* 129 C9 34 18 S 150 35 E
Bargteheide, *Germany* 30 B6 53 44N 10 14 E
Barguzin, *Russia* 65 D11 53 37N 109 37 E
Barh, *India* 93 G11 25 29N 85 46 E
Barhaj, *India* 93 F10 26 18N 83 44 E
Barham, *Australia* 127 F3 35 36 S 144 8 E
Barharwa, *India* 93 G12 24 52N 87 47 E
Barhi, *India* 93 G11 24 15N 85 25 E
Bari, *Dem. Rep. of the Congo* 114 B3 3 20N 19 25 E
Bari, *India* 92 F7 26 39N 77 39 E
Bari, *Italy* 47 A9 41 8N 16 51 E
Bari Doab, *Pakistan* 92 D5 30 20N 73 0 E
Bari Sadri, *India* 92 G6 24 28N 74 30 E
Bari Sardo, *Italy* 46 C2 39 50N 9 38 E
Barīdī, Ra's, *Si. Arabia* 96 E3 24 17N 37 31 E
Barīm, *Yemen* 98 D3 12 39N 43 25 E
Barima →, *Guyana* 169 B5 8 33N 60 25W
Barinas, *Venezuela* 168 B3 8 36N 70 15W
Barinas □, *Venezuela* 168 B4 8 10N 69 50W
Baring, *U.S.A.* 156 D4 40 15N 92 12W
Baring, C., *Canada* 138 B8 70 0N 117 30W
Baringa, *Dem. Rep. of the Congo* 114 B4 0 45N 20 52 E
Baringo, *Kenya* 118 B4 0 47N 36 16 E
Baringo, L., *Kenya* 118 B4 0 47N 36 16 E
Barinitas, *Venezuela* 168 B3 8 45N 70 25W
Baripada, *India* 94 D8 21 57N 86 45 E
Bariri, *Brazil* 171 F2 22 4 S 48 44W
Bârîs, *Egypt* 106 C3 24 42N 30 31 E
Barisal, *Bangla.* 90 D3 22 45N 90 20 E
Barisan, Bukit, *Indonesia* 78 E2 3 30 S 102 15 E
Barito →, *Indonesia* 78 E4 4 0 S 114 50 E
Barjac, *France* 29 D8 44 20N 4 22 E
Barjols, *France* 29 E10 43 34N 6 2 E
Barjūj, Wadi →, *Libya* 108 C2 25 26N 12 12 E
Bark L., *Canada* 150 A7 45 27N 77 51W
Barka = Baraka →, *Sudan* 106 D4 18 13N 37 35 E
Barkakana, *India* 93 H11 23 37N 85 29 E
Barkald, *Norway* 18 C7 61 59N 10 53 E
Barkam, *China* 76 B4 31 51N 102 28 E
Barker, *U.S.A.* 150 C6 43 20N 78 33W
Barkley, L., *U.S.A.* 149 G2 37 1N 88 14W
Barkley Sound, *Canada* 142 D3 48 50N 125 10W
Barkly East, *S. Africa* 116 E4 30 58 S 27 33 E
Barkly Roadhouse, *Australia* 126 B2 19 52 S 135 50 E
Barkly Tableland, *Australia* 126 B2 17 50 S 136 40 E
Barkly West, *S. Africa* 116 D3 28 5 S 24 31 E
Barkol, Wadi →, *Sudan* 106 D3 17 40N 32 0 E
Barkol Kazak Zizhixian, *China* 72 B4 43 37N 93 2 E
Barla Dağı, *Turkey* 49 C12 38 5N 30 40 E
Bârlad, *Romania* 53 D12 46 15N 27 38 E
Bârlad →, *Romania* 53 E12 45 38N 27 32 E
Barlee, L., *Australia* 125 E2 29 15 S 119 30 E
Barlee, Mt., *Australia* 125 D4 24 38 S 128 13 E
Barletta, *Italy* 47 A9 41 19N 16 17 E
Barlinek, *Poland* 55 F2 53 0N 15 15 E
Barlovento, *Canary Is.* 39 F2 28 48N 17 48W
Barlow L., *Canada* 143 A8 62 0N 103 0W
Barmedman, *Australia* 129 C7 34 9 S 147 21 E
Barmer, *India* 92 G4 25 45N 71 20 E
Barmera, *Australia* 128 C4 34 15 S 140 28 E
Barmouth, *U.K.* 20 E3 52 44N 4 4W
Barmstedt, *Germany* 30 B5 53 47N 9 46 E
Barna →, *India* 93 G10 25 21N 83 3 E
Barnagar, *India* 92 H6 23 7N 75 19 E
Barnala, *India* 92 D6 30 23N 75 33 E
Barnard Castle, *U.K.* 20 C6 54 33N 1 55W
Barnato, *Australia* 129 A6 31 38 S 145 0 E
Barnaul, *Russia* 64 D9 53 20N 83 40 E
Barnesville, *U.S.A.* 152 B5 33 3N 84 9W
Barnet, *U.K.* 21 F7 51 38N 0 9W
Barneveld, *Neths.* 24 B5 52 7N 5 36 E
Barneveld, *U.S.A.* 151 C9 43 16N 75 14W
Barneville-Cartevert, *France* 26 C5 49 23N 1 46W
Barnhart, *U.S.A.* 155 K4 31 8N 101 10W
Barnsley, *U.K.* 20 D6 53 34N 1 27W
Barnstaple, *U.K.* 21 F3 51 5N 4 4W
Barnstaple Bay = Bideford Bay, *U.K.* 21 F3 51 5N 4 20W
Barnsville, *U.S.A.* 154 B6 46 43N 96 28W
Barnwell, *U.S.A.* 152 B8 33 15N 81 23W
Baro, *Nigeria* 113 D6 8 35N 6 18 E
Baro →, *Ethiopia* 107 F3 8 26N 33 13 E
Barobo, *Phil.* 81 G6 8 33N 126 7 E
Baroda = Vadodara, *India* 92 H5 22 20N 73 10 E
Baroda, *India* 92 G7 25 29N 76 35 E
Baroe, *S. Africa* 116 E3 33 13 S 24 33 E
Baron Ra., *Australia* 124 D4 23 30 S 127 45 E
Barong, *China* 76 B2 31 3N 99 20 E
Barora Ite, *Solomon Is.* 133 L10 7 36 S 158 24 E
Barorafa, *Solomon Is.* 133 L10 7 30 S 158 20 E
Barouéli, *Mali* 112 C3 13 4N 6 50W
Barpali, *India* 94 D6 21 11N 83 35 E
Barpathar, *India* 90 B4 26 17N 93 53 E
Barpeta, *India* 90 B3 26 20N 91 10 E
Barqin, *Libya* 108 C2 27 33N 13 34 E
Barques, Pt. Aux, *U.S.A.* 150 B2 44 4N 82 58W
Barquísimeto, *Venezuela* 168 A4 10 4N 69 19W
Barr, Ras el, *Egypt* 106 H7 31 32N 31 50 E
Barr Smith Range, *Australia* 125 E3 27 4 S 120 20 E
Barra, *Brazil* 170 D3 11 5 S 43 10W
Barra, *U.K.* 22 E1 57 0N 7 29W
Barra, Sd. of, *U.K.* 22 D1 57 4N 7 25W
Barra da Estiva, *Brazil* 171 D3 13 38 S 41 19W
Barra de Navidad, *Mexico* 162 D4 19 12N 104 41W
Barra do Bugres, *Brazil* 173 C6 15 0 S 57 11W
Barra do Corda, *Brazil* 170 C2 5 30 S 45 10W
Barra do Dande, *Angola* 115 D2 8 28 S 13 22 E
Barra do Mendes, *Brazil* 171 D3 11 43 S 42 4W
Barra do Piraí, *Brazil* 171 F3 22 30 S 43 50W
Barra Falsa, Pta. da, *Mozam.* 117 C6 22 58 S 35 37 E
Barra Hd., *U.K.* 22 E1 56 47N 7 40W
Barra Mansa, *Brazil* 171 F3 22 35 S 44 12W
Barraba, *Australia* 129 A9 30 21 S 150 35 E
Barracão do Barreto, *Brazil* 173 B6 8 48 S 58 24W
Barrackpur = Barakpur, *India* 93 H13 22 44N 88 30 E
Barradale Roadhouse, *Australia* 124 D1 22 42 S 114 58 E
Barrafranca, *Italy* 47 E7 37 22N 14 12 E
Barraigh = Barra, *U.K.* 22 E1 57 0N 7 29W
Barranca, *Lima, Peru* 172 C2 10 45 S 77 50W
Barranca, *Loreto, Peru* 168 D2 4 50 S 76 50W
Barrancabermeja, *Colombia* 168 B3 7 0N 73 50W
Barrancas, *Colombia* 168 A3 10 57N 72 50W
Barrancas, *Venezuela* 169 B5 8 55N 62 5W
Barrancos, *Portugal* 43 G4 38 10N 6 58W
Barranqueras, *Argentina* 174 B4 27 30 S 59 0W
Barranquilla, *Colombia* 168 A3 11 0N 74 50W
Barras, *Brazil* 170 B3 4 15 S 42 18W
Barras, *Colombia* 168 D3 1 45 S 73 13W
Barraute, *Canada* 140 C4 48 26N 77 38W
Barre, *Mass., U.S.A.* 151 D12 42 25N 72 6W
Barre, *Vt., U.S.A.* 151 B12 44 12N 72 30W
Barreal, *Argentina* 174 C2 31 33 S 69 28W
Barrei, *Ethiopia* 120 C2 6 10N 42 49 E
Barreiras, *Brazil* 171 D3 12 8 S 45 0W
Barreirinha, *Brazil* 169 D6 2 47 S 57 3W
Barreirinhas, *Brazil* 170 B3 2 30 S 42 50W
Barreiro, *Portugal* 43 G1 38 40N 9 6W
Barreiros, *Brazil* 170 C4 8 49 S 35 12W
Barrême, *France* 29 E10 43 57N 6 23 E
Barren, Nosy, *Madag.* 117 B7 18 25 S 43 40 E
Barren Is., *U.S.A.* 144 G9 58 55N 152 15W
Barretos, *Brazil* 171 F2 20 30 S 48 35W
Barrhead, *Canada* 142 C6 54 10N 114 24W
Barrie, *Canada* 140 D4 44 24N 79 40W
Barrier, C., *N.Z.* 130 C4 36 25 S 175 32 E
Barrier Ra., *Australia* 128 A4 31 0 S 141 30 E
Barrier Ra., *Otago, N.Z.* 131 E4 44 15 S 169 32 E
Barrier Ra., *W. Coast, N.Z.* 131 E3 44 30 S 168 30 E
Barrière, *Canada* 142 C4 51 12N 120 7W
Barrineau Park, *U.S.A.* 153 E2 30 42N 87 26W
Barrington, *U.S.A.* 151 E13 41 44N 71 18W
Barrington L., *Canada* 143 B8 56 55N 100 15W
Barrington Tops, *Australia* 129 B9 32 6 S 151 28 E
Barringun, *Australia* 127 D4 29 1 S 145 41 E
Barro do Garças, *Brazil* 173 D7 15 54 S 52 16W
Barron, *U.S.A.* 154 C9 45 24N 91 51W
Barrow, *U.S.A.* 138 A4 71 18N 156 47W
Barrow →, *Ireland* 23 D5 52 25N 6 58W
Barrow Creek, *Australia* 126 C1 21 30 S 133 55 E
Barrow I., *Australia* 124 D2 20 45 S 115 20 E
Barrow-in-Furness, *U.K.* 20 C4 54 7N 3 14W
Barrow Pt., *Australia* 126 A3 14 20 S 144 40 E
Barrow Pt., *U.S.A.* 136 B4 71 24N 156 29W
Barrow Ra., *Australia* 125 E4 26 0 S 127 40 E
Barrow Str., *Canada* 6 B3 74 20N 95 0W
Barruecopardo, *Spain* 42 D4 41 4N 6 40W
Barruelo de Santullán, *Spain* 42 C6 42 54N 4 17W
Barry, *U.K.* 21 F4 51 24N 3 16W
Barry, *U.S.A.* 156 E5 39 42N 91 2W
Barry's Bay, *Canada* 140 C4 45 29N 77 41W
Barsalogho, *Burkina Faso* 113 C4 13 25N 1 3W
Barsat, *Pakistan* 93 A5 36 10N 72 45 E
Barsham, *Syria* 101 E9 35 21N 40 33 E
Barsi, *India* 94 E2 18 10N 75 50 E
Barsinghausen, *Germany* 30 C5 52 18N 9 28 E
Barstow, *U.S.A.* 161 L9 34 54N 117 1W
Barth, *Germany* 30 A8 54 22N 12 42 E
Barthélemy, Col, *Vietnam* 86 C5 19 26N 104 6 E
Bartica, *Guyana* 169 B6 6 25N 58 40W
Bartin, *Turkey* 100 B5 41 38N 32 21 E
Bartle Frere, *Australia* 122 D8 17 27 S 145 50 E
Bartlesville, *U.S.A.* 155 G7 36 45N 95 59W
Bartlett, *U.S.A.* 160 J8 36 29N 118 2W
Bartlett, L., *Canada* 142 A5 63 5N 118 20W
Bartolomeu Dias, *Mozam.* 119 G4 21 10 S 35 8 E
Barton, *Phil.* 81 F2 10 24N 119 8 E
Barton, *U.S.A.* 151 B12 44 45N 72 11W
Barton upon Humber, *U.K.* 20 D7 53 41N 0 25W
Bartonville, *U.S.A.* 156 D7 40 39N 89 39W
Bartoszyce, *Poland* 54 D7 54 15N 20 55 E
Bartow, *Fla., U.S.A.* 149 M5 27 54N 81 50W
Bartow, *Ga., U.S.A.* 152 C7 32 53N 82 29W
Barú, I. de, *Colombia* 168 A2 10 15N 75 35W
Barú, Volcan, *Panama* 164 E3 8 55N 82 35W
Barumba, *Dem. Rep. of the Congo* 118 B1 1 3N 23 37 E
Baruth, *Germany* 30 C9 52 4N 13 30 E
Baruunsuu, *Mongolia* 74 C3 43 43N 105 35 E
Barvinkove, *Ukraine* 59 H9 48 57N 37 0 E
Barwani, *India* 92 H6 22 2N 74 57 E
Barwice, *Poland* 54 E3 53 44N 16 21 E
Barwick, *U.S.A.* 152 E6 30 54N 83 44W
Barycz →, *Poland* 55 G3 51 42N 16 15 E
Barysaw, *Belarus* 58 E5 54 17N 28 28 E
Barysh, *Russia* 60 D8 53 39N 47 8 E
Barzān, *Iraq* 96 B5 36 55N 44 3 E
Bârzava, *Romania* 52 D6 46 7N 21 59 E
Bas-Congo □, *Dem. Rep. of the Congo* 115 D2 5 0 S 15 0 E
Bas-Kouilou, *Congo* 115 C2 4 28 S 11 42 E
Bas-Rhin □, *France* 27 D14 48 40N 7 30 E
Bašaid, *Serbia, Yug.* 52 E5 45 38N 20 25 E
Bāsa'idū, *Iran* 97 E7 26 35N 55 20 E
Basal, *Pakistan* 92 C5 33 33N 72 13 E
Basankusa, *Dem. Rep. of the Congo* 114 B3 1 5N 19 50 E
Basarabeasca, *Moldova* 53 D13 46 21N 28 58 E
Basarabi, *Romania* 53 F13 44 10N 28 26 E
Basauri, *Spain* 40 B2 43 13N 2 53W
Basawa, *Afghan.* 92 B4 34 15N 70 50 E
Basco, *Phil.* 80 A3 20 27N 121 58 E
Bascuñán, C., *Chile* 174 B1 28 52 S 71 35W
Basekpio, *Dem. Rep. of the Congo* 114 B4 4 43N 24 36 E
Basel, *Switz.* 32 A5 47 35N 7 35 E
Basel-Landschaft □, *Switz.* 32 B5 47 26N 7 45 E
Basel-Stadt □, *Switz.* 32 A5 47 35N 7 35 E
Basento →, *Italy* 47 B9 40 20N 16 49 E
Basey, *Phil.* 81 F5 11 17N 125 4 E
Bashākerd, Kūhhā-ye, *Iran* 97 E8 26 42N 58 35 E
Bashaw, *Canada* 142 C6 52 35N 112 58W
Bāshī, *Iran* 97 D6 28 41N 51 4 E
Bashkir Republic = Bashkortostan □, *Russia* 62 E6 54 0N 57 0 E
Bashkortostan □, *Russia* 62 E6 54 0N 57 0 E
Basibasy, *Madag.* 117 C7 22 10 S 43 40 E
Basilaki I., *Papua N. G.* 132 F6 10 35 S 151 0 E
Basilan □, *Phil.* 81 H4 6 33N 122 4 E
Basilan I., *Phil.* 79 C6 6 35N 122 0 E
Basilan Str., *Phil.* 79 C6 6 50N 122 0 E
Basildon, *U.K.* 21 F8 51 34N 0 28 E
Basile, *Eq. Guin.* 114 B1 3 42N 8 48 E
Basilicata □, *Italy* 47 B9 40 30N 16 30 E
Basim = Washim, *India* 94 D3 20 3N 77 0 E
Basin, *U.S.A.* 158 D9 44 23N 108 2W
Basinger, *U.S.A.* 153 H8 27 23N 81 2W
Basingstoke, *U.K.* 21 F6 51 15N 1 5W
Basirhat, *Bangla.* 90 D2 22 40N 88 54 E
Baška, *Croatia* 45 D11 44 58N 14 45 E
Başkale, *Turkey* 101 C10 38 2N 43 59 E
Baskatong, Rés., *Canada* 140 C4 46 46N 75 50W
Basle = Basel, *Switz.* 32 A5 47 35N 7 35 E
Başmakçı, *Turkey* 49 D12 37 54N 30 1 E
Basmat, *India* 94 E3 19 15N 77 12 E
Basoda, *India* 92 H7 23 52N 77 54 E
Basodino, *Switz.* 33 D6 46 25N 8 28 E
Basoka, *Dem. Rep. of the Congo* 114 B4 1 14N 23 36 E
Basongo, *Dem. Rep. of the Congo* 115 C4 4 15 S 20 20 E
Basque, Pays, *France* 28 E2 43 15N 1 20W
Basque Provinces = País Vasco □, *Spain* 40 C2 42 50N 2 45W
Basra = Al Başrah, *Iraq* 96 D5 30 30N 47 50 E
Bass Str., *Australia* 126 F4 39 15 S 146 30 E
Bassano, *Canada* 142 C6 50 48N 112 20W
Bassano del Grappa, *Italy* 45 C8 45 46N 11 44 E
Bassar, *Togo* 113 D5 9 19N 0 57 E
Bassas da India, *Ind. Oc.* 121 G2 22 0 S 39 0 E
Basse-Normandie □, *France* 26 D6 48 45N 0 30W
Basse Santa-Su, *Gambia* 112 C2 13 13N 14 15W
Basse-Terre, *Guadeloupe* 165 C7 16 0N 61 44W
Bassecourt, *Switz.* 32 B4 47 20N 7 15 E
Bassein, *Burma* 90 G5 16 45N 94 30 E
Bassein, *India* 94 E1 19 26N 72 48 E
Basseterre, *St. Kitts & Nevis* 165 C7 17 17N 62 43W
Bassett, *U.S.A.* 154 D5 42 35N 99 32W
Bassi, *India* 92 D7 30 44N 76 21 E
Bassigny, *France* 27 E12 48 0N 5 30 E
Bassikounou, *Mauritania* 112 B3 15 55N 6 1W
Bassila, *Benin* 113 D5 9 1N 1 46 E
Bassum, *Germany* 30 C4 52 50N 8 40 E
Båstad, *Sweden* 17 H6 56 25N 12 51 E
Bastak, *Iran* 97 E7 27 15N 54 25 E
Baştām, *Iran* 97 B7 36 29N 55 4 E
Bastar, *India* 94 E5 19 15N 81 40 E
Bastelica, *France* 29 F13 42 1N 9 3 E
Basti, *India* 93 F10 26 52N 82 55 E
Bastia, *France* 29 F13 42 40N 9 30 E
Bastogne, *Belgium* 24 D5 50 1N 5 43 E
Bastrop, *La., U.S.A.* 155 J9 32 47N 91 55W
Bastrop, *Tex., U.S.A.* 155 K6 30 7N 97 19W
Basud, *Phil.* 80 D4 14 4N 122 58 E
Bat Yam, *Israel* 103 C3 32 2N 34 44 E
Bata, *Eq. Guin.* 114 B1 1 57N 9 50 E
Bata, *Romania* 52 D7 46 1N 22 4 E
Bataan □, *Phil.* 79 B6 14 40N 120 25 E
Batabanó, *Cuba* 164 B3 22 40N 82 20W
Batabanó, G. de, *Cuba* 164 B3 22 30N 82 30W
Batac, *Phil.* 79 A6 18 3N 120 34 E
Batagai, *Russia* 65 C14 67 38N 134 38 E
Batajnica, *Serbia, Yug.* 50 B4 44 54N 20 17 E
Batak, *Bulgaria* 51 E8 41 57N 24 12 E
Batala, *India* 92 D6 31 48N 75 12 E
Batalha, *Portugal* 42 F2 39 40N 8 50W
Batam, *Indonesia* 84 B2 1 5N 104 3 E
Batama, *Dem. Rep. of the Congo* 118 B2 0 58N 26 33 E
Batamay, *Russia* 65 C13 63 30N 129 15 E
Batan I., *Phil.* 80 E4 13 15N 124 0 E
Batan I., *Phil.* 80 A3 20 26N 121 58 E
Batanes □, *Phil.* 80 A3 20 40N 121 55 E
Batanes Is., *Phil.* 80 A3 20 30N 122 0 E
Batang, *China* 76 B2 30 1N 99 0 E
Batang, *Indonesia* 79 G13 6 55 S 109 45 E
Batanga, *Gabon* 114 C1 0 21 S 9 18 E
Batangafo, *C.A.R.* 114 A3 7 25N 18 20 E
Batangas, *Phil.* 79 B6 13 35N 121 10 E
Batangas □, *Phil.* 80 E3 13 40N 121 5 E
Batanghari, *Indonesia* 84 C2 1 36 S 103 37 E
Batanta, *Indonesia* 79 E8 0 55 S 130 40 E
Batataraza, *Phil.* 81 G1 8 40N 117 37 E
Batas I., *Phil.* 81 F2 11 10N 119 36 E
Batatais, *Brazil* 175 A6 20 54 S 47 37W
Batavia, *Ill., U.S.A.* 157 C8 41 51N 88 19W
Batavia, *N.Y., U.S.A.* 150 D6 43 0N 78 11W
Batavia, *Ohio, U.S.A.* 157 E12 39 5N 84 11W
Bataysk, *Russia* 59 J10 47 3N 39 45 E
Batchelor, *Australia* 124 B5 13 4 S 131 1 E
Batdambang, *Cambodia* 78 B2 13 7N 103 12 E
Batéké, Plateau, *Congo* 114 C3 3 30 S 15 45 E
Bateman's B., *Australia* 129 C9 35 40 S 150 12 E
Batemans Bay, *Australia* 129 C9 35 44 S 150 11 E
Bates Ra., *Australia* 125 E3 27 27 S 121 5 E
Batesburg-Leesville, *U.S.A.* 152 B8 33 54N 81 33W
Batesville, *Ark., U.S.A.* 155 H9 35 46N 91 39W
Batesville, *Ind., U.S.A.* 157 E11 39 18N 85 13W
Batesville, *Miss., U.S.A.* 155 H10 34 19N 89 57W
Batesville, *Tex., U.S.A.* 155 L5 28 58N 99 37W
Bath, *Canada* 151 B8 44 11N 76 47W
Bath, *U.K.* 21 F5 51 23N 2 22W
Bath, *Maine, U.S.A.* 149 D11 43 55N 69 49W
Bath, *N.Y., U.S.A.* 150 D7 42 20N 77 19W
Bath, *S.C., U.S.A.* 152 B8 33 31N 81 51W
Bath & North East Somerset □, *U.K.* 21 F5 51 21N 2 27W
Batheay, *Cambodia* 87 G5 11 59N 104 57 E
Bathurst = Banjul, *Gambia* 112 C1 13 28N 16 40W
Bathurst, *Australia* 129 B8 33 25 S 149 31 E
Bathurst, *Canada* 141 C6 47 37N 65 43W
Bathurst, *S. Africa* 116 E4 33 30 S 26 50 E
Bathurst, C., *Canada* 138 A7 70 34N 128 0W
Bathurst B., *Australia* 126 A3 14 16 S 144 25 E
Bathurst Harb., *Australia* 126 G4 43 15 S 146 10 E
Bathurst I., *Australia* 124 B5 11 30 S 130 10 E
Bathurst I., *Canada* 136 B9 76 0N 100 30W
Bathurst Inlet, *Canada* 138 B9 66 50N 108 1W
Bati, *Ethiopia* 107 E5 11 10N 40 0 E
Batie, *Burkina Faso* 112 D4 9 53N 2 53W
Batlow, *Australia* 129 C8 35 31 S 148 9 E
Batman, *Turkey* 101 D9 37 55N 41 5 E
Baţn al Ghūl, *Jordan* 103 F4 29 36N 35 56 E
Batna, *Algeria* 111 A6 35 34N 6 15 E
Batnfjordsøra, *Norway* 18 B4 62 53N 7 42 E
Bato, *Catanduanes, Phil.* 80 E5 13 36N 124 18 E
Bato, *Leyte, Phil.* 81 F5 10 13N 124 48 E
Bato Bato, *Phil.* 81 J2 5 6N 119 49 E
Batoala, *Gabon* 114 B2 0 48N 13 27 E
Batobato = San Isidro, *Phil.* 81 H6 6 50N 126 5 E
Batočina, *Serbia, Yug.* 50 B5 44 7N 21 5 E
Batoka, *Zambia* 119 F2 16 45 S 27 15 E
Baton Rouge, *U.S.A.* 155 K9 30 27N 91 11W
Batong, Ko, *Thailand* 87 J2 6 32N 99 12 E
Bátonyterenye, *Hungary* 52 C4 47 59N 19 50 E
Batopilas, *Mexico* 162 B3 27 0N 107 45W
Batouri, *Cameroon* 114 B2 4 30N 14 25 E
Båtsfjord, *Norway* 14 A23 70 38N 29 39 E
Battambang = Batdambang, *Cambodia* 78 B2 13 7N 103 12 E
Batticaloa, *Sri Lanka* 95 L5 7 43N 81 45 E
Battipáglia, *Italy* 47 B7 40 37N 14 58 E
Battle, *U.K.* 21 G8 50 55N 0 30 E
Battle →, *Canada* 143 C7 52 43N 108 15W
Battle Creek, *U.S.A.* 157 B11 42 19N 85 11W
Battle Ground, *U.S.A.* 160 E4 45 47N 122 32W
Battle Harbour, *Canada* 141 B8 52 16N 55 35W
Battle Lake, *U.S.A.* 154 B7 46 17N 95 43W
Battle Mountain, *U.S.A.* 158 F5 40 38N 116 56W
Battlefields, *Zimbabwe* 119 F2 18 37 S 29 47 E
Battleford, *Canada* 143 C7 52 45N 108 15W
Battonya, *Hungary* 52 D6 46 16N 21 3 E
Batu, *Ethiopia* 102 F2 6 55N 39 45 E
Batu, Bukit, *Malaysia* 85 B4 2 16N 113 43 E
Batu, Kepulauan, *Indonesia* 78 E1 0 30 S 98 25 E
Batu Bora, Bukit, *Malaysia* 85 B4 2 43N 114 43 E
Batu Caves, *Malaysia* 87 L3 3 15N 101 40 E
Batu Gajah, *Malaysia* 87 K3 4 28N 101 3 E
Batu Is. = Batu, Kepulauan, *Indonesia* 78 E1 0 30 S 98 25 E
Batu Pahat, *Malaysia* 78 D2 1 50N 102 56 E
Batu Puteh, Gunong, *Malaysia* 84 B2 4 15N 101 31 E
Batuata, *Indonesia* 79 F6 6 12 S 122 42 E
Batulaki, *Phil.* 81 J5 5 34N 125 19 E
Batumi, *Georgia* 61 K5 41 39N 41 44 E
Baturaja, *Indonesia* 78 E2 4 11 S 104 15 E
Baturité, *Brazil* 170 B4 4 28 S 38 45W
Batusangkar, *Indonesia* 84 C2 0 27 S 100 35 E
Bau, *Malaysia* 78 D4 1 25N 110 9 E
Bauang, *Phil.* 80 C3 16 31N 120 20 E
Baubau, *Indonesia* 79 F6 5 25 S 122 38 E
Bauchi, *Nigeria* 113 C6 10 22N 9 48 E
Bauchi □, *Nigeria* 113 C7 10 30N 10 0 E
Baud, *France* 26 E3 47 52N 3 1W
Bauda, *India* 94 D7 20 50N 84 25 E
Baudette, *U.S.A.* 154 A7 48 43N 94 36W
Bauen, *Switz.* 33 C7 46 56N 8 35 E
Bauer, C., *Australia* 127 E1 32 44 S 134 4 E
Bauhinia, *Australia* 126 C4 24 35 S 149 18 E
Baukau, *Indonesia* 79 F7 8 27 S 126 27 E
Bauko, *Phil.* 80 C3 17 0N 120 52 E
Bauld, C., *Canada* 139 C14 51 38N 55 26W
Bauma, *Switz.* 33 B7 47 23N 8 53 E
Baume-les-Dames, *France* 27 E13 47 22N 6 22 E
Baunatal, *Germany* 30 D5 51 14N 9 24 E
Baunei, *Italy* 46 B2 40 2N 9 40 E
Baure, *Nigeria* 113 C6 12 52N 8 50 E
Baures, *Bolivia* 173 C5 13 35 S 63 35W
Bauru, *Brazil* 175 A6 22 10 S 49 0W
Baús, *Brazil* 173 D7 18 22 S 52 47W
Bausi, *India* 93 G12 24 48N 87 1 E
Bauska, *Latvia* 15 H21 56 24N 24 15 E
Bautino, *Kazakstan* 61 H10 44 35N 50 14 E
Bautzen, *Germany* 30 D10 51 10N 14 26 E
Bauya, *S. Leone* 112 D2 8 12N 12 38W
Bavānāt, *Iran* 97 D7 30 28N 53 27 E
Bavanište, *Serbia, Yug.* 52 F5 44 49N 20 53 E
Bavaria = Bayern □, *Germany* 31 G7 48 50N 12 0 E
Båven, *Sweden* 16 E10 59 0N 16 56 E
Bavispe →, *Mexico* 162 B3 29 30N 109 11W
Bawdwin, *Burma* 90 D6 23 5N 97 20 E
Bawean, *Indonesia* 78 F4 5 46 S 112 35 E
Bawku, *Ghana* 113 C4 11 3N 0 19W

190 Bemarivo

Bemarivo, *Madag.* **117 C7** 21 45 S 44 45 E
Bemarivo →, *Antsiranana, Madag.* **117 A9** 14 9 S 50 9 E
Bemarivo →, *Mahajanga, Madag.* **117 B8** 15 27 S 47 40 E
Bemavo, *Madag.* **117 C8** 21 33 S 45 25 E
Bembe, *Angola* **115 D2** 7 3 S 14 25 E
Bembéréke, *Benin* **113 C5** 10 11N 2 43 E
Bembesi, *Zimbabwe* **119 G2** 20 0 S 28 58 E
Bembesi →, *Zimbabwe* **119 F2** 18 57 S 27 47 E
Bembézar →, *Spain* **43 H5** 37 45N 5 13W
Bembibre, *Spain* **42 C4** 42 37N 6 25W
Bement, *U.S.A.* **157 E8** 39 55N 88 34W
Bemetara, *India* **93 J9** 21 42N 81 32 E
Bemidji, *U.S.A.* **154 B7** 47 28N 94 53W
Bemolanga, *Madag.* **117 B8** 17 44 S 45 6 E
Ben, *Iran* **97 C6** 32 32N 50 45 E
Ben Bullen, *Australia* **129 B9** 33 12 S 150 2 E
Ben Cruachan, *U.K.* **22 E3** 56 26N 5 8W
Ben Dearg, *U.K.* **22 D4** 57 47N 4 56W
Ben Gardane, *Tunisia* **108 B2** 33 11N 11 11 E
Ben Hope, *U.K.* **22 C4** 58 25N 4 36W
Ben Lawers, *U.K.* **22 E4** 56 32N 4 14W
Ben Lomond, *N.S.W., Australia* **127 E5** 30 1 S 151 43 E
Ben Lomond, *Tas., Australia* **126 G4** 41 38 S 147 42 E
Ben Lomond, *U.K.* **22 E4** 56 11N 4 38W
Ben Luc, *Vietnam* **87 G6** 10 39N 106 29 E
Ben Macdhui, *U.K.* **22 D5** 57 4N 3 40W
Ben Mhor, *U.K.* **22 D1** 57 15N 7 18W
Ben More, *Arg. & Bute, U.K.* **22 E2** 56 26N 6 1W
Ben More, *Stirl., U.K.* **22 E4** 56 23N 4 32W
Ben More Assynt, *U.K.* **22 C4** 58 8N 4 52W
Ben Nevis, *U.K.* **22 E3** 56 48N 5 1W
Ben Ohau Ra., *N.Z.* **131 E5** 44 1 S 170 4 E
Ben Quang, *Vietnam* **86 D6** 17 3N 106 55 E
Ben Slimane, *Morocco* **110 B3** 33 38N 7 7W
Ben Vorlich, *U.K.* **22 E4** 56 21N 4 14W
Ben Wyvis, *U.K.* **22 D4** 57 40N 4 35W
Bena, *Nigeria* **113 C6** 11 20N 5 50 E
Bena Dibele, *Dem. Rep. of the Congo* **115 C4** 4 4 S 22 50 E
Bena-Leka, *Dem. Rep. of the Congo* **115 D4** 5 8 S 22 10 E
Bena-Tshadi, *Dem. Rep. of the Congo* **115 C4** 4 40 S 22 49 E
Benāb, *Iran* **101 D12** 37 20N 46 4 E
Benadir, *Somali Rep.* **120 D2** 1 30N 44 30 E
Benagerie, *Australia* **128 A4** 31 25 S 140 22 E
Benahmed, *Morocco* **110 B3** 33 4N 7 9W
Benalla, *Australia* **129 D7** 36 30 S 146 0 E
Benalmádena, *Spain* **43 J6** 36 36N 4 34W
Benambra, Mt., *Australia* **129 D7** 36 31 S 147 34 E
Benares = Varanasi, *India* **93 G10** 25 22N 83 0 E
Bénat, C., *France* **29 E10** 43 5N 6 22 E
Benavente, *Portugal* **43 G2** 38 59N 8 49W
Benavente, *Spain* **42 C5** 42 2N 5 43W
Benavides, *U.S.A.* **155 M5** 27 36N 98 25W
Benavides de Órbigo, *Spain* **42 C5** 42 30N 5 54W
Benbecula, *U.K.* **22 D1** 57 26N 7 21W
Benbonyathe, *Australia* **128 A3** 30 25 S 139 11 E
Bend, *U.S.A.* **158 D3** 44 4N 121 19W
Bendela, *Dem. Rep. of the Congo* **114 C3** 3 18 S 17 36 E
Bendemeer, *Australia* **127 E5** 30 53 S 151 8 E
Bender Beila, *Somali Rep.* **120 C4** 9 30N 50 48 E
Bender Merchagno, *Somali Rep.* **120 B4** 11 41N 50 34 E
Bendery = Tighina, *Moldova* **53 D14** 46 50N 29 30 E
Bendigo, *Australia* **128 D6** 36 40 S 144 15 E
Bendorf, *Germany* **30 E3** 50 25N 7 35 E
Benē Beraq, *Israel* **103 C3** 32 6N 34 51 E
Beneditinos, *Brazil* **170 C3** 5 27 S 42 22W
Benedito Leite, *Brazil* **170 C3** 7 13 S 44 34W
Bénéna, *Mali* **112 C4** 13 9N 4 17W
Benenitra, *Madag.* **117 C8** 23 27 S 45 5 E
Benešov, *Czech Rep.* **34 B7** 49 46N 14 41 E
Benevento, *Italy* **47 A7** 41 8N 14 45 E
Benfeld, *France* **27 D14** 48 22N 7 34 E
Benga, *Mozam.* **119 F3** 16 11 S 33 40 E
Bengal, Bay of, *Ind. Oc.* **66 H12** 15 0N 90 0 E
Bengbis, *Cameroon* **113 E7** 3 27N 12 36 E
Bengbis, *Cameroon* **114 B2** 3 27N 12 36 E
Bengbu, *China* **75 H9** 32 58N 117 20 E
Benghazi = Banghāzī, *Libya* **108 B4** 32 11N 20 3 E
Bengkalis, *Indonesia* **78 D2** 1 30N 102 10 E
Bengkulu, *Indonesia* **78 E2** 3 50 S 102 12 E
Bengkulu □, *Indonesia* **78 E2** 3 48 S 102 16 E
Bengo, *Dem. Rep. of the Congo* **114 C3** 2 11 S 19 5 E
Bengo □, *Angola* **115 D2** 9 0 S 13 10 E
Bengough, *Canada* **143 D7** 49 25N 105 10W
Bengtsfors, *Sweden* **16 E6** 59 2N 12 14 E
Benguela, *Angola* **115 E2** 12 37 S 13 25 E
Benguela □, *Angola* **115 E2** 13 0 S 13 30 E
Benguerir, *Morocco* **110 B3** 32 16N 7 56W
Benguérua, I., *Mozam.* **117 C6** 21 58 S 35 28 E
Benguet □, *Phil.* **80 C3** 16 30N 120 40 E
Benha, *Egypt* **106 H7** 30 26N 31 8 E
Beni, *Dem. Rep. of the Congo* **118 B2** 0 30N 29 27 E
Beni □, *Bolivia* **173 C4** 14 0 S 65 0W
Beni →, *Bolivia* **173 C4** 10 23 S 65 24W
Beni Abbès, *Algeria* **111 B4** 30 5N 2 5W
Beni-Haoua, *Algeria* **111 A5** 36 30N 1 30 E
Beni Mazâr, *Egypt* **106 B3** 28 32N 30 44 E
Beni Mellal, *Morocco* **110 B3** 32 21N 6 21W
Beni Ounif, *Algeria* **111 B4** 32 0N 1 10W
Beni Saf, *Algeria* **111 A4** 35 17N 1 15W
Beni Suef, *Egypt* **106 J7** 29 5N 31 6 E
Beniah L., *Canada* **142 A6** 63 23N 112 17W
Benicarló, *Spain* **40 E5** 40 23N 0 23 E
Benicássim, *Spain* **40 E5** 40 3N 0 4 E
Benicia, *U.S.A.* **160 G4** 38 3N 122 9W
Benidorm, *Spain* **41 G4** 38 33N 0 9W
Benin ■, *Africa* **113 D5** 10 0N 2 0 E
Benin →, *Nigeria* **113 D6** 5 45N 5 4 E
Benin, Bight of, *W. Afr.* **113 E5** 5 0N 3 0 E
Benin City, *Nigeria* **113 D6** 6 20N 5 31 E
Benisa, *Spain* **41 G5** 38 43N 0 3 E
Benitses, *Greece* **38 A3** 39 32N 19 55 E
Benjamin Aceval, *Paraguay* **174 A4** 24 58 S 57 34W
Benjamin Constant, *Brazil* **168 D3** 4 40 S 70 15W
Benjamin Hill, *Mexico* **162 A2** 30 10N 111 10W
Benkelman, *U.S.A.* **154 E4** 40 3N 101 32W
Benkovac, *Croatia* **45 D12** 44 2N 15 37 E
Benmore Pk., *N.Z.* **131 E5** 44 25 S 170 8 E
Bennett, *Canada* **142 B2** 59 56N 134 53W
Bennett, L., *Australia* **124 D5** 22 50 S 131 2 E
Bennetta, Ostrov, *Russia* **65 B15** 76 21N 148 56 E
Bennettsville, *U.S.A.* **149 H6** 34 37N 79 41W
Bennichchãb, *Mauritania* **112 B1** 19 32N 15 12W
Bennington, *N.H., U.S.A.* **151 D11** 43 0N 71 55W
Bennington, *Vt., U.S.A.* **151 D11** 42 53N 73 12W
Beno, *Dem. Rep. of the Congo* **114 C3** 3 41 S 17 49 E
Bénodet, *France* **26 E2** 47 53N 4 7W
Benoni, *S. Africa* **117 D4** 26 11 S 28 18 E
Benoud, *Algeria* **111 B5** 32 20N 0 16 E
Benoy, *Chad* **109 G3** 8 59N 16 19 E
Benque Viejo, *Belize* **163 D7** 17 5N 89 8W
Bensheim, *Germany* **31 F4** 49 40N 8 38 E
Benson, *Ariz., U.S.A.* **159 L8** 31 58N 110 18W
Benson, *Minn., U.S.A.* **154 C7** 45 19N 95 36W
Bent, *Iran* **97 E8** 26 20N 59 31 E
Benteng, *Indonesia* **79 F6** 6 10 S 120 30 E
Bentiaba, *Angola* **115 E2** 14 15 S 12 21 E
Bentinck I., *Australia* **126 B2** 17 3 S 139 35 E
Bentiu, *Sudan* **107 F2** 9 10N 29 55 E
Bento Gonçalves, *Brazil* **175 B5** 29 10 S 51 31W
Benton, *Ark., U.S.A.* **155 H8** 34 34N 92 35W
Benton, *Calif., U.S.A.* **160 H8** 37 48N 118 32W
Benton, *Ill., U.S.A.* **156 G8** 38 0N 88 55W
Benton, *Pa., U.S.A.* **151 E8** 41 12N 76 23W
Benton Harbor, *U.S.A.* **157 B10** 42 6N 86 27W
Benton Heights, *U.S.A.* **157 B10** 42 7N 86 24W
Bentonville, *U.S.A.* **155 G7** 36 22N 94 13W
Bentu Liben, *Ethiopia* **107 F4** 8 32N 38 21 E
Bentung, *Malaysia* **87 L3** 3 31N 101 55 E
Benue □, *Nigeria* **113 D6** 7 20N 8 45 E
Benue →, *Nigeria* **113 D6** 7 48N 6 46 E
Benxi, *China* **75 D12** 41 20N 123 48 E
Benza, *Dem. Rep. of the Congo* **115 D2** 4 49 S 13 17 E
Benzdorp, *Surinam* **169 C7** 3 44N 54 5W
Beo, *Indonesia* **79 D7** 4 25N 126 50 E
Beograd, *Serbia, Yug.* **50 B4** 44 50N 20 37 E
Beoumi, *Ivory C.* **112 D3** 7 45N 5 23W
Bepan Jiang →, *China* **76 E6** 24 55N 106 5 E
Beppu, *Japan* **70 D3** 33 15N 131 30 E
Beppu-Wan, *Japan* **70 D3** 33 18N 131 34 E
Beqaa Valley = Al Biqā, *Lebanon* **103 A5** 34 10N 36 10 E
Ber Mota, *India* **92 H3** 23 27N 68 34 E
Bera, *Bangla.* **90 C2** 24 5N 89 37 E
Berach →, *India* **92 G6** 25 15N 75 2 E
Beraketa, *Madag.* **117 C7** 23 7 S 44 25 E
Béran-Djoko, *Congo* **114 B3** 3 15N 17 0 E
Berane, *Montenegro, Yug.* **50 D3** 42 51N 19 52 E
Berati, *Albania* **50 F3** 40 43N 19 59 E
Berau →, *Indonesia* **85 B5** 2 10N 117 42 E
Berau, Teluk, *Indonesia* **79 E8** 2 30 S 132 30 E
Beravina, *Madag.* **117 B8** 18 10 S 45 14 E
Berber, *Sudan* **106 D3** 18 0N 34 0 E
Berbera, *Somali Rep.* **120 B3** 10 30N 45 2 E
Berbérati, *C.A.R.* **114 B3** 4 15N 15 40 E
Berbice →, *Guyana* **169 B6** 6 20N 57 32W
Berceto, *Italy* **44 D6** 44 31N 9 51 E
Berchidda, *Italy* **46 B2** 40 47N 9 10 E
Berchtesgaden, *Germany* **31 H8** 47 38N 13 0 E
Berck, *France* **27 B8** 50 25N 1 36 E
Berdale, *Somali Rep.* **120 C3** 7 4N 47 51 E
Berdichev = Berdychiv, *Ukraine* **59 H5** 49 57N 28 30 E
Berdsk, *Russia* **64 D9** 54 47N 83 2 E
Berdyansk, *Ukraine* **59 J9** 46 45N 36 50 E
Berdyaush, *Russia* **62 D7** 55 9N 59 9 E
Berdychiv, *Ukraine* **59 H5** 49 57N 28 30 E
Berea, *U.S.A.* **148 G3** 37 34N 84 17W
Berebere, *Indonesia* **79 D7** 2 25N 128 45 E
Bereda, *Somali Rep.* **120 B4** 11 45N 51 0 E
Berehove, *Ukraine* **59 H2** 48 15N 22 35 E
Bereina, *Papua N. G.* **132 E4** 8 39 S 146 30 E
Berekum, *Ghana* **112 D4** 7 29N 2 34W
Berenice, *Egypt* **106 C4** 24 2N 35 25 E
Berens →, *Canada* **143 C9** 52 25N 97 2W
Berens I., *Canada* **143 C9** 52 18N 97 18W
Berens River, *Canada* **143 C9** 52 25N 97 0W
Beresford, *U.S.A.* **154 D6** 43 5N 96 47W
Berestechko, *Ukraine* **59 G3** 50 22N 25 5 E
Bereşti, *Romania* **53 D12** 46 6N 27 50 E
Beretău →, *Romania* **52 C6** 47 10N 21 50 E
Berettyó →, *Hungary* **52 D6** 46 59N 21 7 E
Berettyóújfalu, *Hungary* **52 C6** 47 13N 21 33 E
Berevo, *Mahajanga, Madag.* **117 B7** 17 14 S 44 17 E
Berevo, *Toliara, Madag.* **117 B7** 19 44 S 44 58 E
Bereza, *Belarus* **59 F3** 52 31N 24 51 E
Berezhany, *Ukraine* **59 H3** 49 26N 24 58 E
Berezina = Byarezina →, *Belarus* **59 F6** 52 33N 30 14 E
Berezivka, *Ukraine* **59 J6** 47 14N 30 55 E
Berezna, *Ukraine* **59 G6** 51 35N 31 46 E
Bereznik, *Russia* **56 B7** 62 51N 42 40 E
Berezniki, *Russia* **62 B6** 59 24N 56 46 E
Berezovo, *Russia* **64 C7** 64 0N 65 0 E
Berga, *Spain* **40 C6** 42 6N 1 48 E
Berga, *Sweden* **17 G10** 57 14N 16 3 E
Bergama, *Turkey* **49 B9** 39 8N 27 11 E
Bérgamo, *Italy* **44 C6** 45 41N 9 43 E
Bergaon, *India* **94 D5** 20 41N 80 27 E
Bergara, *Spain* **40 B2** 43 9N 2 28W
Bergby, *Sweden* **16 D11** 60 57N 17 2 E
Bergedorf, *Germany* **30 B6** 53 28N 10 12 E
Bergeforsen, *Sweden* **16 B11** 62 32N 17 23 E
Bergen, *Mecklenburg-Vorpommern, Germany* **30 A9** 54 25N 13 25 E
Bergen, *Niedersachsen, Germany* **30 C5** 52 49N 9 57 E
Bergen, *Neths.* **24 B4** 52 40N 4 43 E
Bergen, *Norway* **15 F11** 60 20N 5 20 E
Bergen, *U.S.A.* **150 C7** 43 5N 77 57W
Bergen op Zoom, *Neths.* **24 C4** 51 28N 4 18 E
Bergerac, *France* **28 D4** 44 51N 0 30 E
Bergheim, *Germany* **30 E2** 50 57N 6 38 E
Bergholz, *U.S.A.* **150 F4** 40 31N 80 53W
Bergisch Gladbach, *Germany* **24 D7** 50 59N 7 8 E
Bergkamen, *Germany* **30 D3** 51 37N 7 38 E
Bergkvara, *Sweden* **17 H10** 56 23N 16 5 E
Bergshamra, *Sweden* **16 E12** 59 38N 18 37 E
Bergsjö, *Sweden* **16 C11** 61 59N 17 3 E
Bergues, *France* **27 B9** 50 58N 2 24 E
Bergviken, *Sweden* **16 C10** 61 15N 16 40 E
Bergville, *S. Africa* **117 D4** 28 52 S 29 18 E
Berhala, Selat, *Indonesia* **78 E2** 1 0 S 104 15 E
Berhampore = Baharampur, *India* **93 G13** 24 2N 88 27 E
Berhampur = Brahmapur, *India* **94 E7** 19 15N 84 54 E
Berheci →, *Romania* **53 E12** 45 58N 27 28 E
Bering Glacier, *U.S.A.* **144 F12** 60 20N 143 30W
Bering Sea, *Pac. Oc.* **138 C1** 58 0N 171 0 E
Bering Strait, *Pac. Oc.* **138 B3** 65 30N 169 0W
Beringen, *Switz.* **33 A7** 47 38N 8 34 E
Beringovskiy, *Russia* **65 C18** 63 3N 179 19 E
Berisso, *Argentina* **174 C4** 34 56 S 57 50W
Berja, *Spain* **43 J8** 36 50N 2 56W
Berkåk, *Norway* **18 B6** 62 50N 10 3 E
Berkane, *Morocco* **111 B4** 34 52N 2 20W
Berkeley, *U.S.A.* **160 H4** 37 52N 122 16W
Berkner I., *Antarctica* **7 D18** 79 30 S 50 0W
Berkovitsa, *Bulgaria* **50 C7** 43 16N 23 8 E
Berkshire, *U.S.A.* **151 D8** 42 19N 76 11W
Berkshire Downs, *U.K.* **21 F6** 51 33N 1 29W
Berlanga, *Spain* **43 G5** 38 17N 5 50W
Berlenga, I., *Portugal* **43 F1** 39 25N 9 30W
Berlin, *Germany* **30 C9** 52 30N 13 25 E
Berlin, *Ga., U.S.A.* **152 D6** 31 4N 83 37W
Berlin, *Md., U.S.A.* **148 F8** 38 20N 75 13W
Berlin, *N.H., U.S.A.* **151 B13** 44 28N 71 11W
Berlin, *N.Y., U.S.A.* **151 D11** 42 42N 73 23W
Berlin, *Wis., U.S.A.* **148 D1** 43 58N 88 57W
Berlin □, *Germany* **30 C9** 52 30N 13 20 E
Berlin L., *U.S.A.* **150 E4** 41 3N 81 0W
Bermeja, Sierra, *Spain* **43 J5** 36 30N 5 11W
Bermejo →, *Formosa, Argentina* **174 B4** 26 51 S 58 23W
Bermejo →, *San Juan, Argentina* **174 C2** 32 30 S 67 30W
Bermen, L., *Canada* **141 B6** 53 35N 68 55W
Bermeo, *Spain* **40 B2** 43 25N 2 47W
Bermillo de Sayago, *Spain* **42 D4** 41 22N 6 8W
Bermuda ■, *Atl. Oc.* **8 E2** 32 45N 65 0W
Bern, *Switz.* **32 C4** 46 57N 7 28 E
Bern □, *Switz.* **32 C5** 46 45N 7 40 E
Bernalda, *Italy* **47 B9** 40 24N 16 41 E
Bernalillo, *U.S.A.* **159 J10** 35 18N 106 33W
Bernam →, *Malaysia* **84 B2** 3 45N 101 5 E
Bernardo de Irigoyen, *Argentina* **175 B5** 26 15 S 53 40W
Bernardo O'Higgins □, *Chile* **174 C1** 34 15 S 70 45W
Bernardsville, *U.S.A.* **151 F10** 40 43N 74 34W
Bernasconi, *Argentina* **174 D3** 37 55 S 63 44W
Bernau, *Bayern, Germany* **31 H8** 47 47N 12 22 E
Bernau, *Brandenburg, Germany* **30 C9** 52 40N 13 35 E
Bernay, *France* **26 C7** 49 5N 0 35 E
Bernburg, *Germany* **30 D7** 51 47N 11 44 E
Berndorf, *Austria* **34 D9** 47 59N 16 1 E
Berne = Bern, *Switz.* **32 C4** 46 57N 7 28 E
Berne = Bern □, *Switz.* **32 C5** 46 45N 7 40 E
Berne, *U.S.A.* **157 D12** 40 39N 84 57W
Berner Alpen, *Switz.* **32 D5** 46 27N 7 35 E
Berneray, *U.K.* **22 D1** 57 43N 7 11W
Bernese Oberland = Oberland, *Switz.* **32 C5** 46 35N 7 38 E
Bernier I., *Australia* **125 D1** 24 50 S 113 12 E
Bernina, Passo del, *Switz.* **33 D10** 46 25N 10 2 E
Bernina, Piz, *Switz.* **33 D9** 46 20N 9 54 E
Bernkastel-Kues, *Germany* **31 F3** 49 55N 7 3 E
Bero →, *Angola* **115 F2** 15 10 S 12 9 E
Beroroha, *Madag.* **117 C8** 21 40 S 45 10 E
Béroubouay, *Benin* **113 C5** 10 34N 2 46 E
Beroun, *Czech Rep.* **34 B7** 49 57N 14 5 E
Berounka →, *Czech Rep.* **34 B7** 50 0N 14 22 E
Berovo, *Macedonia* **50 E6** 41 38N 22 51 E
Berrahal, *Algeria* **111 A6** 36 54N 7 33 E
Berre, Étang de, *France* **29 E9** 43 27N 5 5 E
Berre-l'Étang, *France* **29 E9** 43 27N 5 10 E
Berrechid, *Morocco* **110 B3** 33 18N 7 36W
Berri, *Australia* **128 C4** 34 14 S 140 35 E
Berriane, *Algeria* **111 B5** 32 50N 3 46 E
Berrien Springs, *U.S.A.* **157 C10** 41 57N 86 20W
Berrigan, *Australia* **129 C6** 35 38 S 145 49 E
Berriwillock, *Australia* **128 C5** 35 36 S 142 59 E
Berrouaghia, *Algeria* **111 A5** 36 10N 2 53 E
Berry, *Australia* **129 C9** 34 46 S 150 43 E
Berry, *France* **27 F8** 46 50N 2 0 E
Berry Is., *Bahamas* **164 A4** 25 40N 77 50W
Berrydale, *U.S.A.* **153 E2** 30 53N 87 3W
Berryessa L., *U.S.A.* **160 G4** 38 31N 122 6W
Berryville, *U.S.A.* **155 G8** 36 22N 93 34W
Berseba, *Namibia* **116 D2** 26 0 S 17 46 E
Bersenbrück, *Germany* **30 C3** 52 34N 7 56 E
Bershad, *Ukraine* **59 H5** 48 22N 29 31 E
Berthold, *U.S.A.* **154 A4** 48 19N 101 44W
Berthoud, *U.S.A.* **154 E2** 40 19N 105 5W
Bertincourt, *France* **27 B9** 50 5N 2 58 E
Bertolínia, *Brazil* **170 C3** 7 38 S 43 57W
Bertoua, *Cameroon* **114 B2** 4 30N 13 45 E
Bertraghboy B., *Ireland* **23 C2** 53 22N 9 54W
Berufjörður, *Iceland* **11 C12** 64 48N 14 29W
Berunes, *Iceland* **11 C12** 64 42N 14 16W
Beruri, *Brazil* **169 D5** 3 54 S 61 22W
Berwick, *U.S.A.* **151 E8** 41 3N 76 14W
Berwick-upon-Tweed, *U.K.* **20 B6** 55 46N 2 0W
Berwyn Mts., *U.K.* **20 E4** 52 54N 3 26W
Beryslav, *Ukraine* **59 J7** 46 50N 33 30 E
Berzasca, *Romania* **52 F6** 44 39N 21 58 E
Berzence, *Hungary* **52 D2** 46 12N 17 11 E
Besal, *Pakistan* **93 B5** 35 4N 73 56 E
Besalampy, *Madag.* **117 B7** 16 43 S 44 29 E
Besançon, *France* **27 E13** 47 15N 6 2 E
Besar, *Indonesia* **78 E5** 2 40 S 116 0 E
Besar, Gunong, *Malaysia* **84 A2** 5 10N 101 18 E
Beshenkovichi, *Belarus* **58 E5** 55 2N 29 29 E
Beška, *Serbia, Yug.* **52 E5** 45 8N 20 6 E
Beslan, *Russia* **61 J7** 43 15N 44 28 E
Besna Kobila, *Serbia, Yug.* **50 D6** 42 31N 22 10 E
Besnard L., *Canada* **143 B7** 55 25N 106 0W
Besni, *Turkey* **100 D7** 37 41N 37 52 E
Besor, N. →, *Egypt* **103 D3** 31 28N 34 22 E
Bessa Monteiro, *Angola* **115 D2** 7 7 S 13 44 E
Bessarabiya, *Moldova* **59 J5** 47 0N 28 10 E
Bessarabka = Basarabeasca, *Moldova* **53 D13** 46 21N 28 58 E
Bessèges, *France* **29 D8** 44 18N 4 8 E
Bessemer, *Ala., U.S.A.* **149 J2** 33 24N 86 58W
Bessemer, *Mich., U.S.A.* **154 B9** 46 29N 90 3W
Bessemer, *Pa., U.S.A.* **150 F4** 40 59N 80 30W
Bessin, *France* **26 C6** 49 18N 1 0W
Bessines-sur-Gartempe, *France* **28 B5** 46 6N 1 22 E
Beswick, *Australia* **124 B5** 14 34 S 132 53 E
Bet She'an, *Israel* **103 C4** 32 30N 35 30 E
Bet Shemesh, *Israel* **103 D4** 31 44N 35 0 E
Bet Tadjine, Djebel, *Algeria* **110 C4** 29 0N 3 30W
Betafo, *Madag.* **117 B8** 19 50 S 46 51 E
Betamba, *Dem. Rep. of the Congo* **114 C4** 2 17 S 21 24 E
Betancuria, *Canary Is.* **39 F5** 28 25N 14 3W
Betania, *Colombia* **168 C3** 4 22N 72 54W
Betanzos, *Bolivia* **173 D4** 19 34 S 65 27W
Betanzos, *Spain* **42 B2** 43 15N 8 12W
Bétaré Oya, *Cameroon* **114 A2** 5 40N 14 5 E
Betatao, *Madag.* **117 B8** 18 11 S 47 52 E
Bétera, *Spain* **41 F4** 39 35N 0 28W
Bétérou, *Benin* **113 D5** 9 12N 2 16 E
Bethal, *S. Africa* **117 D4** 26 27 S 29 28 E
Bethalto, *U.S.A.* **156 F6** 38 55N 90 2W
Bethanien, *Namibia* **116 D2** 26 31 S 17 8 E
Bethany, *Canada* **150 B6** 44 11N 78 34W
Bethany, *Ill., U.S.A.* **157 E8** 39 39N 88 45W
Bethany, *Mo., U.S.A.* **156 D2** 40 16N 94 2W
Bethel, *Alaska, U.S.A.* **138 B3** 60 48N 161 45W
Bethel, *Conn., U.S.A.* **151 E11** 41 22N 73 25W
Bethel, *Maine, U.S.A.* **151 B14** 44 25N 70 47W
Bethel, *Ohio, U.S.A.* **157 F12** 38 58N 84 5W
Bethel, *Vt., U.S.A.* **151 C12** 43 50N 72 38W
Bethel Park, *U.S.A.* **150 F4** 40 20N 80 1W
Béthenville, *France* **27 C11** 49 18N 4 23 E
Bethlehem = Bayt Lahm, *West Bank* **103 D4** 31 43N 35 12 E
Bethlehem, *S. Africa* **117 D4** 28 14 S 28 18 E
Bethlehem, *U.S.A.* **151 F9** 40 37N 75 23W
Bethulie, *S. Africa* **116 E4** 30 30 S 25 59 E
Béthune, *France* **27 B9** 50 30N 2 38 E
Béthune →, *France* **26 C8** 49 53N 1 9 E
Bethungra, *Australia* **129 C7** 34 45 S 147 51 E
Betijoque, *Venezuela* **168 B3** 9 23N 70 44W
Betioky, *Madag.* **117 C7** 23 48 S 44 20 E
Betong, *Thailand* **87 K3** 5 45N 101 5 E
Betoota, *Australia* **126 D3** 25 45 S 140 42 E
Betor, *Ethiopia* **107 E4** 11 37N 39 2 E
Bétou, *Congo* **114 B3** 3 2N 18 32 E
Betroka, *Madag.* **117 C8** 23 16 S 46 0 E
Betsiamites, *Canada* **141 C6** 48 56N 68 40W
Betsiamites →, *Canada* **141 C6** 48 56N 68 38W
Betsiboka →, *Madag.* **117 B8** 16 3 S 46 36 E
Bettendorf, *U.S.A.* **156 C6** 41 32N 90 30W
Bettiah, *India* **93 F11** 26 48N 84 33 E
Bettna, *Sweden* **17 F10** 58 55N 16 38 E
Bèttola, *Italy* **44 D6** 44 47N 9 36 E
Betul, *India* **94 D3** 21 58N 77 59 E
Betung, *Malaysia* **78 D4** 1 24N 111 31 E
Betws-y-Coed, *U.K.* **20 D4** 53 5N 3 48W
Betxi, *Spain* **40 F4** 39 56N 0 12W
Betzdorf, *Germany* **30 E3** 50 46N 7 52 E
Béu, *Angola* **115 D3** 6 15 S 15 32 E
Beuil, *France* **29 D10** 44 6N 6 59 E
Beulah, *Mich., U.S.A.* **148 C2** 44 38N 86 6W
Beulah, *N. Dak., U.S.A.* **154 B4** 47 16N 101 47W
Beuvron →, *France* **26 E8** 47 29N 1 15 E
Beveren, *Belgium* **24 C4** 51 12N 4 16 E
Beverley, *Australia* **125 F2** 32 9 S 116 56 E
Beverley, *U.K.* **20 D7** 53 51N 0 26W
Beverley Hills, *U.S.A.* **149 L4** 28 56N 82 28W
Beverly, *U.S.A.* **151 D14** 42 33N 70 53W
Beverly Hills, *U.S.A.* **161 L8** 34 4N 118 25W
Beverungen, *Germany* **30 D5** 51 39N 9 22 E
Bevoalavo, *Madag.* **117 D7** 25 13 S 45 26 E
Bewas →, *India* **93 H8** 23 59N 79 21 E
Bex, *Switz.* **32 D4** 46 15N 7 1 E
Bexhill, *U.K.* **21 G8** 50 51N 0 29 E
Bey Dağları, *Turkey* **49 E12** 36 38N 30 29 E
Beyānlū, *Iran* **96 C5** 36 0N 47 51 E
Beyazköy, *Turkey* **51 E11** 41 21N 27 42 E
Beyçayırı, *Turkey* **51 F10** 40 15N 26 55 E
Beydağ, *Turkey* **49 C10** 38 5N 28 13 E
Beyeğaç, *Turkey* **49 D10** 37 14N 28 53 E
Beyin, *Ghana* **112 D4** 5 1N 2 41W
Beykoz, *Turkey* **51 E13** 41 8N 29 7 E
Beyla, *Guinea* **112 D3** 8 30N 8 38W
Beynat, *France* **28 C5** 45 8N 1 44 E
Beyneu, *Kazakstan* **57 E10** 45 18N 55 9 E
Beyoba, *Turkey* **49 C9** 38 48N 27 47 E
Beyoğlu, *Turkey* **51 E12** 41 2N 29 0 E
Beypazarı, *Turkey* **100 B4** 40 10N 31 56 E
Beypore →, *India* **95 J2** 11 10N 75 47 E
Beyşehir, *Turkey* **100 D4** 37 41N 31 43 E
Beyşehir Gölü, *Turkey* **100 D4** 37 41N 31 33 E
Beytüşşebap, *Turkey* **101 D10** 37 35N 43 10 E
Bezau, *Austria* **33 B9** 47 23N 9 54 E
Bezdan, *Serbia, Yug.* **52 E3** 45 50N 18 57 E
Bezhetsk, *Russia* **58 D9** 57 47N 36 39 E
Béziers, *France* **28 E7** 43 20N 3 12 E
Bezwada = Vijayawada, *India* **94 F5** 16 31N 80 39 E
Bhabua, *India* **93 G10** 25 3N 83 37 E
Bhadar →, *Gujarat, India* **92 H5** 22 17N 72 20 E
Bhadar →, *Gujarat, India* **92 J3** 21 27N 69 47 E
Bhadarwah, *India* **93 C6** 32 58N 75 46 E
Bhadohi, *India* **93 G10** 25 25N 82 34 E
Bhadra, *India* **92 E6** 29 8N 75 14 E
Bhadra →, *India* **95 H2** 14 0N 75 20 E
Bhadrachalam, *India* **94 F5** 17 40N 80 53 E
Bhadrakh, *India* **94 D8** 21 10N 86 30 E
Bhadran, *India* **92 H5** 22 19N 72 6 E
Bhadravati, *India* **95 H2** 13 49N 75 40 E
Bhag, *Pakistan* **92 E2** 29 2N 67 49 E
Bhagalpur, *India* **93 G12** 25 10N 87 0 E
Bhagirathi →, *Ut. P., India* **93 D8** 30 8N 78 35 E
Bhagirathi →, *W. Bengal, India* **93 H13** 23 25N 88 23 E
Bhainsa, *India* **94 E3** 19 10N 77 58 E
Bhairab →, *Bangla.* **90 D2** 22 51N 89 34 E
Bhairab Bazar, *Bangla.* **90 C3** 24 4N 90 58 E
Bhakkar, *Pakistan* **91 C3** 31 40N 71 5 E
Bhakra Dam, *India* **92 D7** 31 30N 76 45 E
Bhalki, *India* **94 E3** 18 2N 77 13 E
Bhamo, *Burma* **90 C6** 24 15N 97 15 E
Bhamragarh, *India* **94 E5** 19 30N 80 40 E
Bhandara, *India* **94 D4** 21 5N 79 42 E
Bhanpura, *India* **92 G6** 24 31N 75 44 E
Bhanrer Ra., *India* **93 H8** 23 40N 79 45 E
Bhaptiahi, *India* **93 F12** 26 19N 86 44 E
Bharat = India ■, *Asia* **67 G11** 20 0N 78 0 E
Bharatpur, *Mad. P., India* **93 H9** 23 44N 81 46 E
Bharatpur, *Raj., India* **92 F7** 27 15N 77 30 E
Bharno, *India* **93 H11** 23 14N 84 53 E
Bharuch, *India* **94 D1** 21 47N 73 0 E
Bhatghar L., *India* **94 E1** 18 10N 73 48 E
Bhatiapara Ghat, *Bangla.* **90 D2** 23 13N 89 42 E
Bhatinda, *India* **92 D6** 30 15N 74 57 E
Bhatkal, *India* **95 H2** 13 58N 74 35 E
Bhatpara, *India* **93 H13** 22 50N 88 25 E
Bhattu, *India* **92 E6** 29 36N 75 19 E
Bhaun, *Pakistan* **92 C5** 32 55N 72 40 E
Bhaunagar = Bhavnagar, *India* **94 D1** 21 45N 72 10 E
Bhavani, *India* **95 J3** 11 27N 77 43 E
Bhavnagar, *India* **94 D1** 21 45N 72 10 E
Bhawanipatna, *India* **94 E5** 19 55N 80 10 E
Bhawari, *India* **92 G5** 25 42N 73 4 E
Bhayavadar, *India* **92 J4** 21 51N 70 15 E
Bhera, *Pakistan* **92 C5** 32 29N 72 57 E
Bhikangaon, *India* **92 J6** 21 52N 75 57 E
Bhilai, *India* **94 D5** 21 13N 81 26 E
Bhilsa = Vidisha, *India* **92 H7** 23 28N 77 53 E
Bhilwara, *India* **92 G6** 25 25N 74 38 E
Bhima →, *India* **94 F3** 16 25N 77 17 E
Bhimavaram, *India* **95 F5** 16 30N 81 30 E
Bhimbar, *Pakistan* **93 C6** 32 59N 74 3 E
Bhind, *India* **93 F8** 26 30N 78 46 E
Bhinga, *India* **93 F9** 27 43N 81 56 E
Bhinmal, *India* **92 G5** 25 0N 72 15 E
Bhiwandi, *India* **94 E1** 19 20N 73 0 E
Bhiwani, *India* **92 E7** 28 50N 76 9 E
Bhogava →, *India* **92 H5** 22 26N 72 20 E
Bhokardan, *India* **94 D2** 20 16N 75 46 E
Bhola, *Bangla.* **90 D3** 22 45N 90 35 E
Bholari, *Pakistan* **92 G3** 25 19N 68 13 E
Bhongir, *India* **94 F4** 17 30N 78 56 E
Bhopal, *India* **92 H7** 23 20N 77 30 E
Bhopalpatnam, *India* **94 E5** 18 52N 80 23 E
Bhor, *India* **94 E1** 18 12N 73 53 E
Bhubaneshwar, *India* **94 D7** 20 15N 85 50 E
Bhuj, *India* **92 H3** 23 15N 69 49 E
Bhusaval, *India* **94 D2** 21 3N 75 46 E
Bhutan ■, *Asia* **90 B3** 27 25N 90 30 E
Biá →, *Brazil* **168 D4** 3 28 S 67 23W
Biafra, B. of = Bonny, Bight of, *Africa* **113 E6** 3 30N 9 20 E
Biak, *Indonesia* **79 E9** 1 10 S 136 6 E
Biała, *Poland* **55 H4** 50 24N 17 40 E
Biała →, *Poland* **55 H7** 50 3N 20 55 E
Biała Piska, *Poland* **54 E9** 53 37N 22 5 E
Biała Podlaska, *Poland* **55 F10** 52 4N 23 6 E

192 Bjerringbro

Bjerringbro, *Denmark* 17 H3 56 23N 9 39 E
Bjervamoen, *Norway* 18 E6 59 17N 9 5 E
Bjøberg, *Norway* 18 D5 60 56N 8 13 E
Björbo, *Sweden* 16 D8 60 27N 14 44 E
Bjørkelangen, *Norway* 18 E8 59 53N 11 34 E
Björklinge, *Sweden* 16 D11 60 2N 17 33 E
Bjørnafjorden, *Norway* 18 D2 60 7N 5 28 E
Björneborg, *Sweden* 16 E8 59 14N 14 16 E
Bjørnevatn, *Norway* 14 B23 69 40N 30 0 E
Bjørnøya, *Arctic* 6 B8 74 30N 19 0 E
Bjurås, *Sweden* 16 D9 60 44N 15 25 E
Bjuv, *Sweden* 17 H6 56 5N 12 55 E
Bla, *Mali* 112 C3 12 56N 5 47W
Blace, *Serbia, Yug.* 50 C5 43 18N 21 17 E
Blachownia, *Poland* 55 H5 50 49N 18 56 E
Black = Da →, *Vietnam* 76 G5 21 15N 105 20 E
Black →, *Canada* 150 B5 44 42N 79 19W
Black →, *Alaska, U.S.A.* 144 C11 66 42N 144 42W
Black →, *Ariz., U.S.A.* 159 K8 33 44N 110 13W
Black →, *Ark., U.S.A.* 155 H9 35 38N 91 20W
Black →, *Mich., U.S.A.* 150 D2 42 59N 82 27W
Black →, *N.Y., U.S.A.* 151 C8 43 59N 76 4W
Black →, *Wis., U.S.A.* 154 D9 43 57N 91 22W
Black Bay Pen., *Canada* 140 C2 48 38N 88 21W
Black Birch L., *Canada* 143 B7 56 53N 107 45W
Black Diamond, *Canada* 142 C6 50 45N 114 14W
Black Duck →, *Canada* 140 A2 56 51N 89 2W
Black Forest = Schwarzwald, *Germany* 31 G4 48 30N 8 20 E
Black Forest, *U.S.A.* 154 F2 39 0N 104 43W
Black Hd., *Ireland* 23 C2 53 9N 9 16W
Black Hills, *U.S.A.* 154 D3 44 0N 103 45W
Black I., *Canada* 143 C9 51 12N 96 30W
Black L., *Canada* 143 B7 59 12N 105 15W
Black L., *Mich., U.S.A.* 148 C3 45 28N 84 16W
Black L., *N.Y., U.S.A.* 151 B9 44 31N 75 36W
Black Lake, *Canada* 143 B7 59 11N 105 20W
Black Mesa, *U.S.A.* 155 G3 36 58N 102 58W
Black Mountain, *Australia* 129 A9 30 18 S 151 39 E
Black Mt. = Mynydd Du, *U.K.* 21 F4 51 52N 3 50W
Black Mts., *U.K.* 21 F4 51 55N 3 7W
Black Range, *U.S.A.* 159 K10 33 15N 107 50W
Black River, *Jamaica* 164 C4 18 0N 77 50W
Black River Falls, *U.S.A.* 154 C9 44 18N 90 51W
Black Rock, *Australia* 128 B3 32 50 S 138 44 E
Black Sea, *Eurasia* 57 F6 43 30N 35 0 E
Black Tickle, *Canada* 141 B8 53 28N 55 45W
Black Volta →, *Africa* 112 D4 8 41N 1 33W
Black Warrior →, *U.S.A.* 149 J2 32 32N 87 51W
Blackall, *Australia* 126 C4 24 25 S 145 45 E
Blackball, *N.Z.* 131 C6 42 22 S 171 26 E
Blackbull, *Australia* 126 B3 17 55 S 141 45 E
Blackburn, *U.K.* 20 D5 53 45N 2 29W
Blackburn with Darwen □, *U.K.* 20 D5 53 45N 2 29W
Blackfoot, *U.S.A.* 158 E7 43 11N 112 21W
Blackfoot →, *U.S.A.* 158 C7 46 52N 113 53W
Blackfoot River Reservoir, *U.S.A.* 158 E8 43 0N 111 43W
Blackie, *Canada* 142 C6 50 36N 113 37W
Blackman, *U.S.A.* 153 E3 30 56N 86 38W
Blackpool, *U.K.* 20 D4 53 49N 3 3W
Blackpool □, *U.K.* 20 D4 53 49N 3 3W
Blackriver, *U.S.A.* 150 B1 44 46N 83 17W
Blacks Harbour, *Canada* 141 C6 45 3N 66 49W
Blacksburg, *U.S.A.* 148 G5 37 14N 80 25W
Blackshear, *U.S.A.* 152 D7 31 18N 82 14W
Blackshear, L., *U.S.A.* 152 D6 31 51N 83 56W
Blacksod B., *Ireland* 23 B1 54 6N 10 0W
Blackstone, *U.S.A.* 148 G7 37 4N 78 0W
Blackstone Ra., *Australia* 125 E4 26 0 S 128 30 E
Blackville, *U.S.A.* 152 B8 33 22N 81 16W
Blackwater, *Australia* 126 C4 23 35 S 148 53 E
Blackwater →, *Meath, Ireland* 23 C4 53 39N 6 41W
Blackwater →, *Waterford, Ireland* 23 D4 52 4N 7 52W
Blackwater →, *U.K.* 23 B5 54 31N 6 35W
Blackwater →, *Fla., U.S.A.* 153 E2 30 36N 87 2W
Blackwater →, *Mo., U.S.A.* 156 F4 38 59N 92 59W
Blackwell, *U.S.A.* 155 G6 36 48N 97 17W
Blackwells Corner, *U.S.A.* 161 K7 35 37N 119 47W
Blackwood, C., *Papua N. G.* 132 D3 7 49 S 144 31 E
Blaenau Ffestiniog, *U.K.* 20 E4 53 0N 3 56W
Blaenau Gwent □, *U.K.* 21 F4 51 48N 3 12W
Bláfell, *Iceland* 11 C7 64 30N 19 51W
Bláfjall, *Iceland* 11 B10 65 26N 16 50W
Blagaj, *Bos.-H.* 50 C1 43 16N 17 55 E
Blagnac, *France* 28 E5 43 37N 1 23 E
Blagodarnoye = Blagodarnyy, *Russia* 61 H6 45 7N 43 37 E
Blagodarnyy, *Russia* 61 H6 45 7N 43 37 E
Blagoevgrad, *Bulgaria* 50 D7 42 2N 23 5 E
Blagoveshchensk, *Amur, Russia* 65 D13 50 20N 127 30 E
Blagoveshchensk, *Bashkortostan, Russia* 62 D5 55 1N 55 59 E
Blagoveshchenskoye, *Kazakstan* 63 B7 43 18N 74 12 E
Blain, *France* 26 E5 47 29N 1 45W
Blain, *U.S.A.* 150 F7 40 20N 77 31W
Blaine, *Minn., U.S.A.* 154 C8 45 10N 93 13W
Blaine, *Wash., U.S.A.* 160 B4 48 59N 122 45W
Blaine Lake, *Canada* 143 C7 52 51N 106 52W
Blair, *U.S.A.* 154 E6 41 33N 96 8W
Blair Athol, *Australia* 126 C4 22 42 S 147 31 E
Blair Atholl, *U.K.* 22 E5 56 46N 3 50W
Blairgowrie, *U.K.* 22 E5 56 35N 3 21W
Blairsden, *U.S.A.* 160 F6 39 47N 120 37W
Blairsville, *U.S.A.* 150 F5 40 26N 79 16W
Blaj, *Romania* 53 D8 46 10N 23 57 E
Blake Pt., *U.S.A.* 154 A10 48 11N 88 25W
Blakely, *Ga., U.S.A.* 152 D5 31 23N 84 56W
Blakely, *Pa., U.S.A.* 151 E9 41 28N 75 37W
Blakesburg, *U.S.A.* 156 D4 40 58N 92 38W
Blakstad, *Norway* 18 F5 58 30N 8 39 E
Blâmont, *France* 27 D13 48 35N 6 50 E
Blanc, C., *Spain* 39 B9 39 21N 2 51 E
Blanc, C., *Tunisia* 108 A1 37 15N 9 56 E
Blanc, Mont, *Alps* 29 C10 45 48N 6 50 E
Blanc-Sablon, *Canada* 141 B8 51 24N 57 12W
Blanca, B., *Argentina* 176 A4 39 10 S 61 30W
Blanca Peak, *U.S.A.* 159 H11 37 35N 105 29W
Blanchardville, *U.S.A.* 156 B7 42 49N 89 52W
Blanche, C., *Australia* 127 E1 33 1 S 134 9 E
Blanche, L., *S. Austral., Australia* 127 D2 29 15 S 139 40 E
Blanche, L., *W. Austral., Australia* 124 D3 22 25 S 123 17 E
Blanche Channel, *Solomon Is.* 133 M9 8 30 S 157 30 E
Blanchester, *U.S.A.* 157 E13 39 17N 83 59W
Blanco, *S. Africa* 116 E3 33 55 S 22 23 E
Blanco, *U.S.A.* 155 K5 30 6N 98 25W
Blanco →, *Argentina* 174 C2 30 20 S 68 42W
Blanco →, *Bolivia* 173 C5 12 30 S 64 18W
Blanco, C., *Costa Rica* 164 E2 9 34N 85 8W
Blanco, C., *U.S.A.* 158 E1 42 51N 124 34W
Blanda →, *Iceland* 11 B6 65 37N 20 9W
Blandford Forum, *U.K.* 21 G5 50 51N 2 9W
Blanding, *U.S.A.* 159 H9 37 37N 109 29W
Blandinsville, *U.S.A.* 156 D6 40 33N 90 52W
Blanes, *Spain* 40 D7 41 40N 2 48 E
Blangy-sur-Bresle, *France* 27 C8 49 55N 1 37 E
Blanice →, *Czech Rep.* 34 B7 49 10N 14 5 E
Blankaholm, *Sweden* 17 G10 57 36N 16 31 E
Blankenberge, *Belgium* 24 C3 51 20N 3 9 E
Blankenburg, *Germany* 30 D6 51 47N 10 57 E
Blanquefort, *France* 28 D3 44 55N 0 38W
Blanquilla, I., *Venezuela* 165 D7 11 51N 64 37W
Blanquilla, I., *Venezuela* 169 A5 11 51N 64 37W
Blanquillo, *Uruguay* 175 C4 32 53 S 55 37W
Blansko, *Czech Rep.* 35 B9 49 22N 16 40 E
Blantyre, *Malawi* 119 F4 15 45 S 35 0 E
Blarney, *Ireland* 23 E3 51 56N 8 33W
Blasdell, *U.S.A.* 150 D6 42 48N 78 50W
Blåsjø, *Norway* 18 E3 59 20N 6 50 E
Błaszki, *Poland* 55 G5 51 38N 18 30 E
Blatná, *Czech Rep.* 34 B6 49 25N 13 52 E
Blato, *Croatia* 45 F13 42 56N 16 48 E
Blatten, *Switz.* 32 D5 46 20N 7 50 E
Blaubeuren, *Germany* 31 G5 48 24N 9 46 E
Blaustein, *Germany* 31 G5 48 25N 9 53 E
Blåvands Huk, *Denmark* 17 J2 55 33N 8 4 E
Blaydon, *U.K.* 20 C6 54 58N 1 42W
Blaye, *France* 28 C3 45 8N 0 40W
Blaye-les-Mines, *France* 28 D6 44 1N 2 8 E
Blayney, *Australia* 129 B8 33 32 S 149 14 E
Blaze, Pt., *Australia* 124 B5 12 56 S 130 11 E
Błażowa, *Poland* 55 J9 49 53N 22 7 E
Bleckede, *Germany* 30 B6 53 17N 10 43 E
Bled, *Slovenia* 45 B11 46 27N 14 7 E
Blefjell, *Norway* 18 E6 59 48N 9 10 E
Bleiburg, *Austria* 34 E7 46 35N 14 49 E
Blejeşti, *Romania* 53 F10 44 19N 25 27 E
Blekinge, *Sweden* 15 H16 56 25N 15 20 E
Blekinge län □, *Sweden* 17 H9 56 20N 15 20 E
Blenheim, *Canada* 150 D3 42 20N 82 0W
Blenheim, *N.Z.* 131 B8 41 38 S 173 57 E
Bléone →, *France* 29 D10 44 5N 6 0 E
Blérancourt, *France* 27 C10 49 31N 3 9 E
Bletchley, *U.K.* 21 F7 51 59N 0 44W
Blida, *Algeria* 111 A5 36 30N 2 49 E
Blidet Amor, *Algeria* 111 B6 32 59N 5 58 E
Blidö, *Sweden* 16 E12 59 37N 18 53 E
Blidsberg, *Sweden* 17 G7 57 56N 13 30 E
Blieskastel, *Germany* 31 F3 49 14N 7 12 E
Bligh Sound, *N.Z.* 131 E2 44 47 S 167 32 E
Bligh Water, *Fiji* 133 A2 17 0 S 178 0 E
Blind River, *Canada* 140 C3 46 10N 82 58W
Blinishti, *Albania* 50 E3 41 52N 19 59 E
Blinnenhorn, *Switz.* 33 D6 46 26N 8 19 E
Bliss, *Idaho, U.S.A.* 158 E6 42 56N 114 57W
Bliss, *N.Y., U.S.A.* 150 D6 42 34N 78 15W
Blissfield, *Mich., U.S.A.* 157 C13 41 50N 83 52W
Blissfield, *Ohio, U.S.A.* 150 F3 40 24N 81 58W
Blitar, *Indonesia* 79 H15 8 5 S 112 11 E
Blitchton, *U.S.A.* 152 C8 32 12N 81 26W
Blitta, *Togo* 113 D5 8 23N 1 6 E
Block I., *U.S.A.* 151 E13 41 11N 71 35W
Block Island Sd., *U.S.A.* 151 E13 41 15N 71 40W
Blodgett Iceberg Tongue, *Antarctica* 7 C9 66 8 S 130 35 E
Bloemfontein, *S. Africa* 116 D4 29 6 S 26 7 E
Bloemhof, *S. Africa* 116 D4 27 38 S 25 32 E
Blois, *France* 26 E8 47 35N 1 20 E
Blomskog, *Sweden* 16 E6 59 16N 12 2 E
Blomstermåla, *Sweden* 17 H10 56 59N 16 21 E
Blomvåg, *Norway* 18 D1 60 32N 4 50 E
Blonay, *Switz.* 32 D3 46 28N 6 54 E
Blönduós, *Iceland* 11 B6 65 40N 20 12W
Błonie, *Poland* 55 F7 52 12N 20 37 E
Bloodvein →, *Canada* 143 C9 51 47N 96 43W
Bloody Foreland, *Ireland* 23 A3 55 10N 8 17W
Bloomer, *U.S.A.* 154 C9 45 6N 91 29W
Bloomfield, *Canada* 150 C7 43 59N 77 14W
Bloomfield, *Ind., U.S.A.* 157 E10 39 1N 86 57W
Bloomfield, *Iowa, U.S.A.* 154 D4 40 45N 92 25W
Bloomfield, *Ky., U.S.A.* 157 G11 37 55N 85 19W
Bloomfield, *N. Mex., U.S.A.* 159 H10 36 43N 107 59W
Bloomfield, *Nebr., U.S.A.* 154 D6 42 36N 97 39W
Bloomingburg, *U.S.A.* 157 E13 39 36N 83 24W
Bloomington, *Ill., U.S.A.* 156 D8 40 28N 89 0W
Bloomington, *Ind., U.S.A.* 157 E10 39 10N 86 32W
Bloomington, *Minn., U.S.A.* 154 C8 44 50N 93 17W
Bloomington, *Wis., U.S.A.* 156 B6 42 53N 90 55W
Bloomsburg, *U.S.A.* 151 F8 41 0N 76 27W
Blora, *Indonesia* 79 G14 6 57 S 111 25 E
Blossburg, *U.S.A.* 150 E7 41 41N 77 4W
Blosseville Kyst, *Greenland* 10 D8 68 50N 26 30W
Blotzheim, *France* 32 A4 47 36N 7 29 E
Blouberg, *S. Africa* 117 C4 23 8 S 28 59 E
Blountstown, *U.S.A.* 152 E4 30 27N 85 3W
Bludenz, *Austria* 34 D2 47 10N 9 50 E
Blue →, *U.S.A.* 157 F10 38 11N 86 19W
Blue Cypress L., *U.S.A.* 153 H9 27 44N 80 45W
Blue Earth, *U.S.A.* 154 D8 43 38N 94 6W
Blue Mesa Reservoir, *U.S.A.* 159 G10 38 28N 107 20W
Blue Mound, *U.S.A.* 156 E7 39 42N 89 7W
Blue Mountain Lake, *U.S.A.* 151 C10 43 52N 74 30W
Blue Mts., *Australia* 129 B9 33 40 S 150 0 E
Blue Mts., *Maine, U.S.A.* 151 B14 44 50N 70 35W
Blue Mts., *Oreg., U.S.A.* 158 D4 45 15N 119 0W
Blue Mts., *Pa., U.S.A.* 151 F8 40 30N 76 30W
Blue Mud B., *Australia* 126 A2 13 30 S 136 0 E
Blue Nile = Nîl el Azraq →, *Sudan* 107 D3 15 38N 32 31 E
Blue Rapids, *U.S.A.* 154 F6 39 41N 96 39W
Blue Ridge Mts., *U.S.A.* 149 G5 36 30N 80 15W
Blue River, *Canada* 142 C5 52 6N 119 18W
Blue Springs, *U.S.A.* 156 E2 39 1N 94 17W
Bluefield, *U.S.A.* 148 G5 37 15N 81 17W
Bluefields, *Nic.* 164 D3 12 20N 83 50W
Blueskin B., *N.Z.* 131 F5 45 44 S 170 38 E
Bluff, *Australia* 126 C4 23 35 S 149 4 E
Bluff, *N.Z.* 131 G3 46 37 S 168 20 E
Bluff, *U.S.A.* 159 H9 37 17N 109 33W
Bluff Harbour, *N.Z.* 131 G3 46 36 S 168 21 E
Bluff Knoll, *Australia* 125 F2 34 24 S 118 15 E
Bluff Pt., *Australia* 125 E1 27 50 S 114 5 E
Bluffs, *U.S.A.* 156 E6 39 45N 90 32W
Bluffton, *Ga., U.S.A.* 152 D5 31 31N 84 52W
Bluffton, *Ind., U.S.A.* 157 D11 40 44N 85 11W
Bluffton, *Ohio, U.S.A.* 157 D13 40 54N 83 54W
Bluffton, *S.C., U.S.A.* 152 C9 32 14N 80 52W
Blumenau, *Brazil* 175 B6 27 0 S 49 0W
Blümisalphorn, *Switz.* 32 D5 46 28N 7 47 E
Blunt, *U.S.A.* 154 C5 44 31N 99 59W
Bly, *U.S.A.* 158 E3 42 24N 121 3W
Blyth, *Canada* 150 C3 43 44N 81 26W
Blyth, *U.K.* 20 B6 55 8N 1 31W
Blythe, *Calif., U.S.A.* 161 M12 33 37N 114 36W
Blythe, *Ga., U.S.A.* 152 B7 33 17N 82 12W
Blytheville, *U.S.A.* 155 H10 35 56N 89 55W
Bø, *Norway* 18 E6 59 25N 9 3 E
Bo, *S. Leone* 112 D2 7 55N 11 50W
Bo Duc, *Vietnam* 87 G6 11 58N 106 50 E
Bo Hai, *China* 75 E10 39 0N 119 0 E
Bō-no-Misaki, *Japan* 70 F2 31 15N 130 13 E
Bo Xian = Bozhou, *China* 74 H8 33 55N 115 41 E
Boa Esperança, *Brazil* 169 C5 3 21N 61 23W
Boa Esperança, Represa, *Brazil* 170 C3 6 50 S 43 50W
Boa Nova, *Brazil* 171 D3 14 22 S 40 10W
Boa Viagem, *Brazil* 170 C4 5 7 S 39 44W
Boa Vista, *Brazil* 169 C5 2 48N 60 30W
Boa Vista, *C. Verde Is.* 8 G6 16 0N 22 50W
Boac, *Phil.* 80 E3 13 27N 121 50 E
Boaco, *Nic.* 164 D2 12 29N 85 35W
Bo'ai, *China* 74 G7 35 10N 113 3 E
Boal, *Spain* 42 B4 43 25N 6 49W
Boali, *C.A.R.* 114 B3 4 48N 18 7 E
Boalsburg, *U.S.A.* 150 F7 40 46N 77 47W
Boane, *Mozam.* 117 D5 26 6 S 32 19 E
Boardman, *U.S.A.* 150 E4 41 2N 80 40W
Boath, *India* 94 E4 19 20N 78 20 E
Bobadah, *Australia* 129 B7 32 19 S 146 41 E
Bobai, *China* 76 F7 22 17N 109 59 E
Bobbili, *India* 94 E6 18 35N 83 30 E
Bóbbio, *Italy* 44 D6 44 46N 9 23 E
Bobcaygeon, *Canada* 140 D4 44 33N 78 33W
Boblad, *India* 94 F2 17 13N 75 26 E
Böblingen, *Germany* 31 G5 48 40N 9 1 E
Bobo-Dioulasso, *Burkina Faso* 112 C4 11 8N 4 13W
Bobolice, *Poland* 54 E3 53 58N 16 37 E
Bobon, *Phil.* 80 E5 12 32N 124 34 E
Bobonaza →, *Ecuador* 168 D2 2 36 S 76 38W
Boboshevo, *Bulgaria* 50 D7 42 9N 23 0 E
Bobov Dol, *Bulgaria* 50 D6 42 20N 23 0 E
Bóbr →, *Poland* 55 F2 52 4N 15 4 E
Bobraomby, Tanjon' i, *Madag.* 117 A8 12 40 S 49 10 E
Bobrinets, *Ukraine* 59 H7 48 4N 32 5 E
Bobrov, *Russia* 60 E5 51 5N 40 2 E
Bobrovitsa, *Ukraine* 59 G6 50 45N 31 23 E
Bobruysk = Babruysk, *Belarus* 59 F5 53 10N 29 15 E
Bobures, *Venezuela* 168 B3 9 15N 71 11W
Boca de Drago, *Venezuela* 169 A5 11 0N 61 50W
Bôca do Acre, *Brazil* 172 B4 8 50 S 67 27W
Bôca do Jari, *Brazil* 169 D7 1 7 S 51 58W
Bôca do Moaco, *Brazil* 172 B4 7 41 S 68 17W
Boca Grande, *U.S.A.* 153 J7 26 45N 82 16W
Boca Grande, *Venezuela* 169 B5 8 40N 60 40W
Boca Raton, *U.S.A.* 149 M5 26 21N 80 5W
Bocaiúva, *Brazil* 171 E3 17 7 S 43 49W
Bocanda, *Ivory C.* 112 D4 7 5N 4 31W
Bocaranga, *C.A.R.* 114 A3 7 0N 15 35 E
Bocas del Toro, *Panama* 164 E3 9 15N 82 20W
Boceguillas, *Spain* 42 D7 41 20N 3 39W
Bochnia, *Poland* 55 J7 49 58N 20 27 E
Bocholt, *Germany* 30 D2 51 50N 6 36 E
Bochum, *Germany* 30 D3 51 28N 7 13 E
Bockenem, *Germany* 30 C6 52 1N 10 8 E
Boćki, *Poland* 55 F10 52 39N 23 3 E
Bocognano, *France* 29 F13 42 5N 9 4 E
Bocoio, *Angola* 115 E2 12 28 S 14 10 E
Boconó, *Venezuela* 168 B3 9 15N 70 16W
Boconó →, *Venezuela* 168 B4 8 43N 69 34W
Bocoyna, *Mexico* 162 B3 27 52N 107 35W
Bocşa, *Romania* 52 E6 45 21N 21 47 E
Boda, *C.A.R.* 114 B3 4 19N 17 26 E
Böda, *Kalmar, Sweden* 17 G11 57 15N 17 3 E
Boda, *Kopparberg, Sweden* 16 C9 61 1N 15 13 E
Boda, *Västernorrland, Sweden* 16 B10 62 52N 16 39 E
Bodafors, *Sweden* 17 G8 57 48N 14 23 E
Bodaybo, *Russia* 65 D12 57 50N 114 0 E
Boddam, *U.K.* 22 B7 59 56N 1 17W
Boddington, *Australia* 125 F2 32 50 S 116 30 E
Bode Sadu, *Nigeria* 113 D5 9 0N 4 47 E
Bodega Bay, *U.S.A.* 160 G3 38 20N 123 3W
Boden, *Sweden* 14 D19 65 50N 21 42 E
Bodensee, *Europe* 33 A8 47 35N 9 25 E
Bodenteich, *Germany* 30 C6 52 50N 10 42 E
Bodhan, *India* 94 E3 18 40N 77 44 E
Bodinayakkanur, *India* 95 J3 10 2N 77 10 E
Bodinga, *Nigeria* 113 C6 12 58N 5 10 E
Bodio, *Switz.* 33 D7 46 23N 8 55 E
Bodmin, *U.K.* 21 G3 50 28N 4 43W
Bodmin Moor, *U.K.* 21 G3 50 33N 4 36W
Bodø, *Norway* 14 C16 67 17N 14 24 E
Bodoquena, Serra da, *Brazil* 173 E6 21 0 S 56 50W
Bodoupa, *C.A.R.* 114 A3 5 43N 17 36 E
Bodrog →, *Hungary* 52 B6 48 11N 21 22 E
Bodrum, *Turkey* 49 D9 37 3N 27 30 E
Boduna, *Dem. Rep. of the Congo* 114 A3 5 5N 19 44 E
Bódva →, *Hungary* 52 B5 48 19N 20 45 E
Boembé, *Congo* 114 C3 2 54 S 15 39 E
Boën, *France* 29 C8 45 44N 4 1 E
Boende, *Dem. Rep. of the Congo* 114 C4 0 24 S 21 12 E
Boerne, *U.S.A.* 155 L5 29 47N 98 44W
Boesmans →, *S. Africa* 116 E4 33 42 S 26 39 E
Boffa, *Guinea* 112 C2 10 16N 14 3W
Bofuku, *Dem. Rep. of the Congo* 114 C4 0 57 S 20 53 E
Bogale, *Burma* 90 G5 16 17N 95 24 E
Bogalusa, *U.S.A.* 155 K10 30 47N 89 52W
Bogan →, *Australia* 129 A7 29 59 S 146 17 E
Bogan Gate, *Australia* 129 B7 33 7 S 147 49 E
Bogandé, *Burkina Faso* 113 C4 13 2N 0 8W
Bogangolo, *C.A.R.* 114 A3 5 34N 18 15 E
Bogantungan, *Australia* 126 C4 23 41 S 147 17 E
Bogata, *U.S.A.* 155 J7 33 28N 95 13W
Bogatić, *Serbia, Yug.* 50 B3 44 51N 19 30 E
Boğazkale, *Turkey* 100 B6 40 2N 34 37 E
Boğazlıyan, *Turkey* 100 C6 39 11N 35 14 E
Bogbonga, *Dem. Rep. of the Congo* 114 B3 1 36N 19 24 E
Bogdanovich, *Russia* 62 C9 56 47N 62 1 E
Bogen, *Sweden* 16 D6 60 4N 12 33 E
Bogense, *Denmark* 17 J4 55 34N 10 5 E
Bogetići, *Montenegro, Yug.* 50 D2 42 41N 18 58 E
Boggabilla, *Australia* 127 D5 28 36 S 150 24 E
Boggabri, *Australia* 129 A9 30 45 S 150 5 E
Boggeragh Mts., *Ireland* 23 D3 52 2N 8 55W
Bogia, *Papua N. G.* 132 C3 4 9 S 145 0 E
Boglan = Solhan, *Turkey* 101 C9 38 57N 41 3 E
Bognor Regis, *U.K.* 21 G7 50 47N 0 40W
Bogo, *Phil.* 79 B6 11 3N 124 0 E
Bogodukhov = Bohodukhiv, *Ukraine* 59 G8 50 9N 35 33 E
Bogol Manya, *Ethiopia* 107 G5 4 34N 41 29 E
Bogong, Mt., *Australia* 129 D7 36 47 S 147 17 E
Bogor, *Indonesia* 79 G12 6 36 S 106 48 E
Bogoroditsk, *Russia* 58 F10 53 47N 38 8 E
Bogorodsk, *Russia* 60 B6 56 4N 43 30 E
Bogoso, *Ghana* 112 D4 5 38N 2 3W
Bogotá, *Colombia* 168 C3 4 34N 74 0W
Bogotol, *Russia* 64 D9 56 15N 89 50 E
Bogou, *Togo* 113 C5 10 40N 0 12 E
Bogra, *Bangla.* 90 C2 24 51N 89 22 E
Boguchany, *Russia* 65 D10 58 40N 97 30 E
Boguchar, *Russia* 60 F5 49 55N 40 32 E
Bogué, *Mauritania* 112 B2 16 45N 14 10W
Boguslav, *Ukraine* 59 H6 49 33N 30 56 E
Boguszów-Gorce, *Poland* 55 H3 50 45N 16 12 E
Bohain-en-Vermandois, *France* 27 C10 49 59N 3 28 E
Bohemian Forest = Böhmerwald, *Germany* 31 F9 49 8N 13 14 E
Bohinjska Bistrica, *Slovenia* 45 B11 46 17N 14 1 E
Böhmerwald, *Germany* 31 F9 49 8N 13 14 E
Bohmte, *Germany* 30 C4 52 22N 8 19 E
Bohodukhiv, *Ukraine* 59 G8 50 9N 35 33 E
Bohol, *Somali Rep.* 120 C3 5 45N 46 9 E
Bohol □, *Phil.* 79 C6 9 50N 124 10 E
Bohol Sea, *Phil.* 79 C6 9 0N 124 0 E
Bohol Str., *Phil.* 81 G4 9 45N 123 40 E
Bohongou, *Burkina Faso* 113 C5 12 30N 0 40 E
Böhönye, *Hungary* 52 D2 46 25N 17 28 E
Bohotleh, *Somali Rep.* 120 C3 8 20N 46 25 E
Bohuslän, *Sweden* 17 F5 58 25N 12 0 E
Boi, *Nigeria* 113 D6 9 35N 9 27 E
Boi, Pta. de, *Brazil* 175 A6 23 55 S 45 15W
Boiaçu, *Brazil* 169 D5 0 27 S 61 46W
Boileau, C., *Australia* 124 C3 17 40 S 122 7 E
Boim, *Brazil* 169 D6 2 49 S 55 10W
Boing'o, *Sudan* 107 F3 9 58N 33 44 E
Boipariguda, *India* 94 E6 18 46N 82 26 E
Boipeba, I. de, *Brazil* 171 D4 13 39 S 38 55W
Boiro, *Spain* 42 C2 42 39N 8 54W
Bois →, *Brazil* 171 E1 18 35 S 50 2W
Boise, *U.S.A.* 158 E5 43 37N 116 13W
Boise City, *U.S.A.* 155 G3 36 44N 102 31W
Boissevain, *Canada* 143 D8 49 15N 100 5W
Bóite →, *Italy* 45 B9 46 5N 12 5 E
Boitzenburg, *Germany* 30 B9 53 16N 13 35 E
Boizenburg, *Germany* 30 B6 53 23N 10 43 E
Bojador C., *W. Sahara* 110 C2 26 0N 14 30W
Bojana →, *Albania* 50 E3 41 52N 19 22 E
Bojano, *Italy* 47 A7 41 29N 14 29 E
Bojanowo, *Poland* 55 G3 51 43N 16 42 E
Bøjden, *Denmark* 17 J4 55 6N 10 7 E
Bojnūrd, *Iran* 97 B8 37 30N 57 20 E
Bojonegoro, *Indonesia* 79 G14 7 11 S 111 54 E
Boju, *Nigeria* 113 D6 7 22N 7 55 E
Boka, *Serbia, Yug.* 52 E5 45 22N 20 52 E
Boka Kotorska, *Montenegro, Yug.* 50 D2 42 23N 18 32 E
Bokada, *Dem. Rep. of the Congo* 114 B3 4 8N 19 23 E
Bokala, *Dem. Rep. of the Congo* 114 C3 3 8 S 17 4 E
Bokala, *Ivory C.* 112 D4 8 31N 4 33W
Bokani, *Nigeria* 113 D6 9 28N 5 10 E
Bokaro, *India* 93 H11 23 46N 85 55 E
Bokatola, *Dem. Rep. of the Congo* 114 C3 0 38 S 18 46 E
Boké, *Guinea* 112 C2 10 56N 14 17W
Bokela, *Dem. Rep. of the Congo* 114 C4 1 10 S 21 59 E
Bokenda, *Dem. Rep. of the Congo* 114 B4 1 16N 21 22 E
Bokhara →, *Australia* 127 D4 29 55 S 146 42 E
Bokkos, *Nigeria* 113 D6 9 17N 9 1 E
Boknafjorden, *Norway* 15 G11 59 14N 5 40 E
Bokode, *Dem. Rep. of the Congo* 114 B3 3 55N 19 30 E
Bokolo, *Gabon* 114 C2 2 40 S 10 10 E
Bokombayevskoye, *Kyrgyzstan* 63 B8 42 10N 76 55 E
Bokondo, *Dem. Rep. of the Congo* 114 B4 0 15N 22 32 E
Bokoro, *Chad* 109 F3 12 25N 17 14 E
Bokota, *Dem. Rep. of the Congo* 114 C4 0 56 S 22 24 E
Bokote, *Dem. Rep. of the Congo* 114 C4 0 12 S 21 8 E
Bokpyin, *Burma* 78 B1 11 18N 98 42 E
Boksitogorsk, *Russia* 58 C7 59 22N 33 50 E
Bokungu, *Dem. Rep. of the Congo* 114 C4 0 35 S 22 50 E
Bol, *Chad* 109 F2 13 30N 14 40 E
Bol, *Croatia* 45 E13 43 18N 16 38 E
Bolama, *Guinea-Biss.* 112 C1 11 30N 15 30W
Bolan →, *Pakistan* 92 E2 28 38N 67 42 E
Bolan Pass, *Pakistan* 91 C2 29 50N 67 20 E
Bolangum, *Australia* 128 D5 36 42 S 142 54 E
Bolaños →, *Mexico* 162 C4 21 14N 104 8W
Bolaños de Calatrava, *Spain* 43 G7 38 54N 3 40W
Bolayır, *Turkey* 51 F10 40 31N 26 45 E
Bolbec, *France* 26 C7 49 30N 0 30 E
Boldājī, *Iran* 97 D6 31 56N 51 3 E
Boldeşti-Scăeni, *Romania* 53 E11 45 3N 26 2 E
Bole, *China* 72 B3 45 11N 81 37 E
Bole, *Ethiopia* 107 F4 6 36N 37 20 E
Bole, *Ghana* 112 D4 9 3N 2 23W
Bolekhiv, *Ukraine* 59 H2 49 0N 23 57 E
Boleko, *Dem. Rep. of the Congo* 114 C3 1 35 S 19 50 E
Bolesławiec, *Poland* 55 G2 51 17N 15 37 E
Bolgatanga, *Ghana* 113 C4 10 44N 0 53W
Bolgrad = Bolhrad, *Ukraine* 59 K5 45 40N 28 32 E
Bolhrad, *Ukraine* 59 K5 45 40N 28 32 E
Bolia, *Dem. Rep. of the Congo* 114 C3 1 36 S 18 22 E
Bolinao, *Phil.* 80 C2 16 23N 119 54 E
Bolinao, C., *Phil.* 80 C2 16 23N 119 55 E
Bolingbroke, *U.S.A.* 152 C6 32 57N 83 48W
Bolingo, *Dem. Rep. of the Congo* 114 C4 3 31 S 21 43 E
Bolintin-Vale, *Romania* 53 F10 44 27N 25 46 E
Bolívar, *Argentina* 174 D3 36 15 S 60 53W
Bolívar, *Antioquía, Colombia* 168 B2 5 50N 76 1W
Bolívar, *Cauca, Colombia* 168 C2 2 0N 77 0W
Bolívar, *Peru* 172 B2 7 18 S 77 48W
Bolivar, *Mo., U.S.A.* 155 G8 37 37N 93 25W
Bolivar, *N.Y., U.S.A.* 150 D6 42 4N 78 10W
Bolivar, *Tenn., U.S.A.* 155 H10 35 12N 89 0W
Bolívar □, *Colombia* 168 B3 9 0N 74 40W
Bolívar □, *Ecuador* 168 D2 1 15 S 79 5W
Bolívar □, *Venezuela* 169 B5 6 20N 63 30W
Bolivia ■, *S. Amer.* 173 D5 17 6 S 64 0W
Bolivian Plateau, *S. Amer.* 166 E4 20 0 S 67 30W
Boljevac, *Serbia, Yug.* 50 C5 43 51N 21 58 E
Bolkhov, *Russia* 58 F9 53 25N 36 0 E
Bolków, *Poland* 55 H3 50 55N 16 6 E
Bollebygd, *Sweden* 17 G6 57 40N 12 35 E
Bollène, *France* 29 D8 44 18N 4 45 E
Bollnäs, *Sweden* 16 C10 61 21N 16 24 E
Bollon, *Australia* 127 D4 28 2 S 147 29 E
Bollstabruk, *Sweden* 16 B11 62 59N 17 40 E
Bolmen, *Sweden* 17 H7 56 55N 13 40 E
Bolobo, *Dem. Rep. of the Congo* 114 C3 2 6 S 16 20 E
Bologna, *Italy* 44 D8 44 29N 11 20 E
Bologoye, *Russia* 58 D8 57 55N 34 5 E
Bolomba, *Dem. Rep. of the Congo* 114 B3 0 35N 19 0 E
Bolombo →, *Dem. Rep. of the Congo* 114 B4 1 32N 21 14 E
Boloncheticul, *Mexico* 163 D7 20 0N 89 49W
Bolondo, *Dem. Rep. of the Congo* 114 C3 2 12 S 18 42 E
Bolong, *Phil.* 81 H4 7 6N 122 14 E
Bolongongo, *Angola* 115 D3 8 28 S 15 16 E

Bowdon 193

Bolótana, Italy 46 B1 40 20N 8 52 E
Bolotovskoye, Russia 62 B9 58 31N 62 28 E
Boloven, Cao Nguyen, Laos 86 E6 15 10N 106 30 E
Bolpur, India 93 H12 23 40N 87 45 E
Bolsena, Italy 45 F8 42 39N 11 59 E
Bolsena, L. di, Italy 45 F8 42 36N 11 56 E
Bolshaya Chernigovka, Russia 60 D10 52 6N 50 52 E
Bolshaya Glushitsa, Russia 60 D10 52 28N 50 30 E
Bolshaya Khobda →, Kazakstan 62 F5 50 56N 54 34 E
Bolshaya Martynovka, Russia 61 G5 47 19N 41 37 E
Bolshaya Vradiyevka, Ukraine 59 J6 47 50N 30 40 E
Bolshevik, Ostrov, Russia 65 B11 78 30N 102 0 E
Bolshoi Kavkas = Caucasus Mountains, Eurasia 61 J7 42 50N 44 0 E
Bolshoy Anyuy →, Russia 65 C17 68 30N 160 49 E
Bolshoy Begichev, Ostrov, Russia 65 B12 74 20N 112 30 E
Bolshoy Lyakhovskiy, Ostrov, Russia 65 B15 73 35N 142 0 E
Bolshoy Tokmak = Tokmak, Ukraine 59 J8 47 16N 35 42 E
Bolshoy Tyuters, Ostrov, Russia 15 G22 59 51N 27 13 E
Bólstaðarhlíð, Iceland 11 B7 65 31N 19 49W
Bolsward, Neths. 24 A5 53 3N 5 32 E
Bolt Head, U.K. 21 G4 50 12N 3 48W
Boltaña, Spain 40 C5 42 28N 0 4 E
Boltigen, Switz. 32 C4 46 38N 7 24 E
Bolton, Canada 150 C5 43 54N 79 45W
Bolton, U.K. 20 D5 53 35N 2 26W
Bolton Landing, U.S.A. 151 C11 43 32N 73 35W
Bolu, Turkey 100 B4 40 45N 31 35 E
Bolubolu, Papua N. G. 132 E6 9 21 S 150 20 E
Bolungavík, Iceland 11 A3 66 9N 23 15W
Boluo, China 77 F10 23 3N 114 21 E
Bolvadin, Turkey 100 C4 38 45N 31 4 E
Bolzano, Italy 45 B8 46 31N 11 22 E
Bom Comércio, Brazil 173 B4 9 45 S 65 54W
Bom Conselho, Brazil 170 C4 9 10 S 36 41W
Bom Despacho, Brazil 171 E2 19 43 S 45 15W
Bom Jesus, Angola 115 D2 9 11 S 13 34 E
Bom Jesus, Brazil 170 C3 9 4 S 44 22W
Bom Jesus da Gurguéia, Serra, Brazil 170 C3 9 0 S 43 0W
Bom Jesus da Lapa, Brazil 171 D3 13 15 S 43 25W
Boma, Dem. Rep. of the Congo 115 D2 5 50 S 13 4 E
Bomaderry, Australia 129 C9 34 52 S 150 37 E
Bomandjokou, Congo 114 B2 0 34N 14 23 E
Bomaneh, Dem. Rep. of the Congo 114 B4 1 18N 23 47 E
Bomassa, Congo 114 B3 2 12N 16 12 E
Bomate, Dem. Rep. of the Congo 114 C3 2 14N 25 15 E
Bombala, Australia 129 D8 36 56 S 149 15 E
Bombarral, Portugal 43 F1 39 15N 9 9W
Bombay = Mumbai, India 94 E1 18 55N 72 50 E
Bombo Kasani, Dem. Rep. of the Congo 115 D4 5 51 S 21 54 E
Bomboma, Dem. Rep. of the Congo 114 B3 2 25N 18 55 E
Bombombwa, Dem. Rep. of the Congo 118 B2 1 40N 25 40 E
Bomi Hills, Liberia 112 D2 7 1N 10 38W
Bomili, Dem. Rep. of the Congo 118 B2 1 45N 27 5 E
Bømlo, Norway 15 G11 59 37N 5 13 E
Bomokandi →, Dem. Rep. of the Congo 118 B2 3 39N 26 8 E
Bomongo, Dem. Rep. of the Congo 114 B3 1 27N 18 21 E
Bomputu, Dem. Rep. of the Congo 114 C4 0 23 S 20 6 E
Bomu →, C.A.R. 114 B4 4 40N 22 30 E
Bon, C., Tunisia 108 A2 37 1N 11 2 E
Bon Sar Pa, Vietnam 86 F6 12 24N 107 35 E
Bonaduz, Switz. 33 C8 46 49N 9 25 E
Bonaigarh, India 93 J11 21 50N 84 57 E
Bonaire, Neth. Ant. 165 D6 12 10N 68 15W
Bonaire, U.S.A. 152 C6 32 33N 83 36W
Bonang, Australia 129 D8 37 11 S 148 41 E
Bonanza, Nic. 164 D3 13 54N 84 35W
Bonaparte Arch., Australia 124 B3 14 0 S 124 30 E
Boñar, Spain 42 C5 42 52N 5 19W
Bonaventure, Canada 141 C6 48 5N 65 32W
Bonavista, Canada 141 C9 48 40N 53 5W
Bonavista, C., Canada 141 C9 48 42N 53 5W
Bonavista B., Canada 141 C9 48 45N 53 25W
Bondeno, Italy 45 D8 44 53N 11 25 E
Bondo, Dem. Rep. of the Congo 114 C4 1 22 S 23 54 E
Bondo, Dem. Rep. of the Congo 118 B1 3 55N 23 53 E
Bondoukou, Ivory C. 112 D4 8 2N 2 47W
Bondowoso, Indonesia 79 G15 7 55 S 113 49 E
Bone, Teluk, Indonesia 79 E6 4 10 S 120 50 E
Bonerate, Indonesia 79 F6 7 25 S 121 5 E
Bonerate, Kepulauan, Indonesia 79 F6 6 30 S 121 10 E
Bo'ness, U.K. 22 E5 56 1N 3 37W
Bonete, Cerro, Argentina 174 B2 27 55 S 68 40W
Bonfim, Brazil 169 C6 3 33N 59 25W
Bong Son = Hoai Nhon, Vietnam 78 B3 14 28N 109 1 E
Bonga, Ethiopia 107 F4 7 15N 36 14 E
Bongabon, Phil. 80 D3 15 38N 121 8 E
Bongabong, Phil. 80 E3 12 45N 121 29 E
Bongandanga, Dem. Rep. of the Congo 114 B4 1 24N 21 3 E
Bongao, Phil. 81 J2 5 2N 119 46 E
Bongo, Dem. Rep. of the Congo 114 C3 1 47 S 17 41 E
Bongo, Sa. de, Angola 115 E3 10 3 S 15 15 E
Bongor, Chad 109 F3 10 35N 15 20 E
Bongouanou, Ivory C. 112 D4 6 42N 4 15W
Bonham, U.S.A. 155 J6 33 35N 96 11W
Boni, Mali 112 B4 15 3N 2 10W
Bonifacio, France 29 G13 41 24N 9 10 E
Bonifacio, Bouches de, Medit. S. 46 A2 41 12N 9 15 E
Bonifay, U.S.A. 152 E4 30 47N 85 41W
Bonin Is. = Ogasawara Gunto, Pac. Oc. 66 G18 27 0N 142 0 E
Bonita Springs, U.S.A. 153 J8 26 21N 81 47W
Bonito, Brazil 173 21 8 S 56 28W
Bonke, Ethiopia 107 F4 6 5N 37 16 E
Bonkoukou, Niger 113 C5 14 0N 3 15 E
Bonn, Germany 30 E3 50 46N 7 6 E
Bonnat, France 27 F8 46 20N 1 54 E
Bonne Terre, U.S.A. 155 G9 37 55N 90 33W
Bonneau, U.S.A. 152 B10 33 16N 79 58W
Bonners Ferry, U.S.A. 158 B5 48 42N 116 19W
Bonnétable, France 26 D7 48 11N 0 25 E
Bonneval, Eure-et-Loir, France 26 D8 48 11N 1 24 E
Bonneval, Savoie, France 29 C11 45 22N 7 3 E
Bonneville, France 27 F13 46 4N 6 24 E
Bonney, L., Australia 128 D4 37 50 S 140 20 E
Bonnie Doon, Australia 129 D6 37 2 S 145 53 E
Bonnie Rock, Australia 125 F2 30 29 S 118 22 E
Bonny, Nigeria 113 E6 4 25N 7 13 E
Bonny →, Nigeria 113 E6 4 20N 7 10 E
Bonny, Bight of, Africa 113 E6 3 30N 9 20 E
Bonny-sur-Loire, France 27 E9 47 33N 2 50 E
Bonnyrigg, U.K. 22 F5 55 53N 3 6W
Bonnyville, Canada 143 C6 54 20N 110 45W
Bono, Italy 46 B2 40 25N 9 2 E
Bonoi, Indonesia 79 E9 1 45 S 137 41 E
Bonorva, Italy 46 B1 40 25N 8 46 E
Bonsall, U.S.A. 161 M9 33 16N 117 14W
Bontang, Indonesia 78 D5 0 10N 117 30 E
Bonthain, Indonesia 82 C1 5 34 S 119 56 E
Bonthe, S. Leone 112 D2 7 30N 12 33W
Bontoc, Phil. 79 A6 17 7N 120 58 E
Bontosunggu, Indonesia 82 C1 5 41 S 119 42 E
Bonyeri, Ghana 112 D4 5 1N 2 46W
Bonyhád, Hungary 52 D3 46 18N 18 32 E
Bonython Ra., Australia 124 D4 23 40 S 128 45 E
Bookabie, Australia 125 F5 31 50 S 132 41 E
Booke, Dem. Rep. of the Congo 114 C4 2 34 S 22 39 E
Booker, U.S.A. 155 G4 36 27N 100 32W
Boola, Guinea 112 D3 8 22N 8 41 E
Boolarra, Australia 129 E7 38 20 S 146 20 E
Boolcoomata, Australia 128 A4 31 57 S 140 33 E
Booleroo Centre, Australia 128 A3 32 53 S 138 21 E
Booligal, Australia 129 B6 33 58 S 144 53 E
Boonah, Australia 127 D5 27 58 S 152 41 E
Boone, Iowa, U.S.A. 156 B3 42 4N 93 53W
Boone, N.C., U.S.A. 149 G5 36 13N 81 41W
Booneville, Ark., U.S.A. 155 H8 35 8N 93 55W
Booneville, Miss., U.S.A. 149 H1 34 39N 88 34W
Boonville, Calif., U.S.A. 160 F3 39 1N 123 22W
Boonville, Ind., U.S.A. 157 F9 38 3N 87 16W
Boonville, Mo., U.S.A. 156 F4 38 58N 92 44W
Boonville, N.Y., U.S.A. 151 C9 43 29N 75 20W
Booral, Australia 129 B9 32 30 S 151 56 E
Boorindal, Australia 127 E4 30 22 S 146 11 E
Booroomugga, Australia 129 A7 31 17 S 146 27 E
Boorowa, Australia 129 C8 34 28 S 148 44 E
Boothia, Gulf of, Canada 139 A11 71 0N 90 0W
Boothia Pen., Canada 138 A10 71 0N 94 0W
Bootle, U.K. 20 D4 53 28N 3 1W
Booué, Gabon 114 C2 0 5 S 11 55 E
Bopako, Dem. Rep. of the Congo 114 B4 1 53N 21 13 E
Boppard, Germany 31 E3 50 13N 7 35 E
Boquerón □, Paraguay 173 E5 23 0 S 60 0W
Boquete, Panama 164 E3 8 46N 82 27W
Boquilla, Presa de la, Mexico 162 B3 27 40N 105 30W
Boquillas del Carmen, Mexico 162 B4 29 17N 102 53W
Bor, Czech Rep. 34 B5 49 41N 12 45 E
Bor, Russia 60 B7 56 28N 43 59 E
Bor, Serbia, Yug. 50 B6 44 5N 22 7 E
Bôr, Sudan 107 F3 6 10N 31 40 E
Bor, Sweden 17 G8 57 9N 14 10 E
Bor, Turkey 100 D6 37 54N 34 32 E
Bor Mashash, Israel 103 D3 31 7N 34 50 E
Borah Peak, U.S.A. 158 D7 44 8N 113 47W
Borama, Somali Rep. 120 C2 9 55N 43 7 E
Borang, Sudan 107 G3 4 50N 30 59 E
Borangapara, India 90 C3 25 14N 90 14 E
Borås, Sweden 17 G6 57 43N 12 56 E
Borāzjān, Iran 97 D6 29 22N 51 10 E
Borba, Brazil 169 D6 4 12 S 59 34W
Borba, Portugal 43 G3 38 50N 7 26W
Borbon, Phil. 81 F5 10 50N 124 2 E
Borborema, Planalto da, Brazil 170 C4 7 0 S 37 0W
Borcea, Romania 53 F12 44 20N 27 45 E
Borçka, Turkey 101 B9 41 25N 41 41 E
Bord Khūn-e Now, Iran 97 D6 28 3N 51 28 E
Borda, C., Australia 128 C2 35 45 S 136 34 E
Bordeaux, France 28 D3 44 50N 0 36W
Borden, Australia 125 F2 34 3 S 118 12 E
Borden, Canada 141 C7 46 18N 63 47W
Borden I., Canada 6 B2 78 30N 111 30W
Borden Pen., Canada 139 A11 73 0N 83 0W
Borden Springs, U.S.A. 152 B4 33 56N 85 28W
Borders = Scottish Borders □, U.K. 22 F6 55 35N 2 50W
Bordertown, Australia 128 D4 36 19 S 140 45 E
Borðeyri, Iceland 11 B5 65 12N 21 6W
Bordighera, Italy 44 E4 43 46N 7 39 E
Bordj bou Arreridj, Algeria 111 A5 36 4N 4 45 E
Bordj Bourguiba, Tunisia 108 B2 32 12N 10 2 E
Bordj Fly Ste. Marie, Algeria 110 C4 27 19N 2 32W
Bordj-in-Eker, Algeria 111 D6 24 9N 5 3 E
Bordj Menaiel, Algeria 111 A5 36 46N 3 43 E
Bordj Messouda, Algeria 111 B6 30 12N 9 25 E
Bordj Nili, Algeria 111 B5 33 28N 3 2 E
Bordj Omar Driss, Algeria 111 C6 28 10N 6 40 E
Bordj Sif Fatima, Algeria 111 B6 31 6N 8 41 E
Bordj-Tarat, Algeria 111 C6 25 55N 9 3 E
Bordj Zelfana, Algeria 111 B5 32 27N 4 15 E
Bordoba, Kyrgyzstan 63 D6 39 31N 73 16 E
Bore, Ethiopia 107 G4 4 39N 37 39 E
Borea Creek, Australia 129 C7 35 5 S 146 35 E
Borehamwood, U.K. 21 F7 51 40N 0 15W
Borek Wielkopolski, Poland 55 G4 51 54N 17 11 E
Boremore, Australia 129 B8 33 15 S 149 0 E
Boren Kapuas, Pegunungan, Malaysia 85 B4 1 25N 113 15 E
Borensberg, Sweden 17 F9 58 34N 15 17 E
Borgå = Porvoo, Finland 15 F21 60 24N 25 40 E
Borgampad, India 94 F5 17 39N 80 52 E
Borgarfjarðarsýsla □, Iceland 11 C5 64 30N 21 30W
Borgarfjörður, Iceland 11 C4 64 30N 22 0W
Borgarfjörður, Iceland 11 B13 65 31N 13 49W
Borgarnes, Iceland 11 C5 64 32N 21 55W
Børgefjellet, Norway 14 D15 65 20N 13 45 E
Borger, Neths. 24 B6 52 54N 6 44 E
Borger, U.S.A. 155 H4 35 39N 101 24W
Borgholm, Sweden 17 H10 56 52N 16 39 E
Bórgia, Italy 47 D9 38 49N 16 30 E
Borgo San Dalmazzo, Italy 44 D4 44 20N 7 30 E
Borgo San Lorenzo, Italy 45 E8 43 57N 11 23 E
Borgo Val di Taro, Italy 44 D6 44 29N 9 46 E
Borgo Valsugana, Italy 45 B8 46 3N 11 27 E
Borgomanero, Italy 44 C5 45 42N 8 28 E
Borgorose, Italy 45 F10 42 11N 13 13 E
Borgosésia, Italy 44 C5 45 43N 8 16 E
Borgund, Norway 18 C4 61 3N 7 48 E
Borhoyn Tal, Mongolia 74 C6 43 50N 111 58 E
Bori, Nigeria 113 E6 4 42N 7 21 E
Borigumma, India 94 E6 19 3N 82 33 E
Borikhane, Laos 86 C4 18 33N 103 43 E
Borisoglebsk, Russia 60 E6 51 27N 42 5 E
Borisov = Barysaw, Belarus 58 E5 54 17N 28 28 E
Borisovka, Kazakstan 63 B4 53 15N 68 10 E
Borisovka, Russia 59 G9 50 36N 36 1 E
Borja, Peru 168 D2 4 20 S 77 40W
Borja, Spain 40 D3 41 48N 1 34W
Borjas Blancas = Les Borges Blanques, Spain 40 D5 41 31N 0 52 E
Borjomi, Georgia 61 K6 41 48N 43 28 E
Borken, Germany 30 D9 51 40N 13 10 E
Børkop, Denmark 17 J3 55 39N 9 39 E
Borkou, Chad 109 E3 18 15N 18 50 E
Borkum, Germany 30 B2 53 34N 6 40 E
Borlänge, Sweden 16 D9 60 29N 15 26 E
Borley, C., Antarctica 7 C5 66 15 S 52 30 E
Borlu, Turkey 49 C10 38 44N 28 27 E
Bormida →, Italy 44 D5 44 23N 8 13 E
Bórmio, Italy 44 B7 46 28N 10 22 E
Borna, Germany 30 D8 51 7N 12 29 E
Borne Sulinowo, Poland 54 E3 53 32N 16 36 E
Borneo, E. Indies 78 D5 1 0N 115 0 E
Bornholm, Denmark 17 J8 55 10N 15 0 E
Bornholms Amtskommune □, Denmark 17 J8 55 5N 15 0 E
Bornholmsgattet, Europe 17 J8 55 15N 14 20 E
Borno, Italy 33 E10 45 56N 10 12 E
Borno □, Nigeria 113 C7 11 30N 13 0 E
Bornos, Spain 43 J5 36 48N 5 42W
Bornova, Turkey 49 C9 38 27N 27 14 E
Bornu Yassa, Nigeria 113 C7 12 14N 12 25 E
Boro →, Sudan 107 F2 8 52N 26 11 E
Borobudur, Indonesia 85 D4 7 36 S 110 13 E
Borodino, Russia 58 E8 55 31N 35 40 E
Borogontsy, Russia 65 C14 62 42N 131 8 E
Boromo, Burkina Faso 112 C4 11 45N 2 58W
Boron, U.S.A. 161 L9 35 0N 117 39W
Borongа Is., Burma 90 F4 19 58N 93 6 E
Borongan, Phil. 79 B7 11 37N 125 26 E
Borotangba Mts., C.A.R. 114 A4 6 30N 25 0 E
Borotou, Ivory C. 112 D3 8 46N 7 30W
Borovan, Bulgaria 50 C7 43 27N 23 45 E
Borovichi, Russia 58 C7 58 25N 33 55 E
Borovsk, Berezniki, Russia 62 B6 59 43N 56 40 E
Borovsk, Moskva, Russia 58 E9 55 12N 36 24 E
Borrby, Sweden 17 J8 55 27N 14 10 E
Borrego Springs, U.S.A. 161 M10 33 15N 116 23W
Borriol, Spain 40 E4 40 4N 0 4W
Borroloola, Australia 126 B2 16 4 S 136 17 E
Borşa, Cluj, Romania 53 D8 46 56N 23 40 E
Borşa, Maramureş, Romania 53 C9 47 41N 24 50 E
Borsad, India 92 H5 22 25N 72 54 E
Borsec, Romania 53 D10 46 57N 25 34 E
Borsod-Abaúj-Zemplén □, Hungary 52 B6 48 20N 21 0 E
Bort-les-Orgues, France 28 C6 45 24N 2 29 E
Borth, U.K. 21 E3 52 29N 4 2W
Börtnan, Sweden 16 B7 62 45N 13 50 E
Borūjerd, Iran 97 C6 33 55N 48 50 E
Boryslav, Ukraine 59 H2 49 18N 23 28 E
Boryspil, Ukraine 59 G6 50 21N 30 59 E
Borzhomi = Borjomi, Georgia 61 K6 41 48N 43 28 E
Borzna, Ukraine 59 G7 51 18N 32 26 E
Borzya, Russia 65 D12 50 24N 116 31 E
Bosa, Italy 46 B1 40 18N 8 30 E
Bosa Monene, Dem. Rep. of the Congo 114 C4 1 16 S 23 40 E
Bosaga, Turkmenistan 63 E2 37 33N 65 41 E
Bosambi, Dem. Rep. of the Congo 114 B4 2 24N 22 39 E
Bosanska Dubica, Bos.-H. 45 C13 45 10N 16 50 E
Bosanska Gradiška, Bos.-H. 52 E2 45 10N 17 15 E
Bosanska Kostajnica, Bos.-H. 45 C13 45 11N 16 33 E
Bosanska Krupa, Bos.-H. 45 D13 44 53N 16 10 E
Bosanski Brod, Bos.-H. 52 E2 45 10N 18 0 E
Bosanski Novi, Bos.-H. 45 C13 45 2N 16 22 E
Bosanski Petrovac, Bos.-H. 45 D13 44 35N 16 21 E
Bosanski Šamac, Bos.-H. 52 E3 45 3N 18 29 E
Bosansko Grahovo, Bos.-H. 45 D13 44 12N 16 26 E
Bosaso, Somali Rep. 120 B3 11 12N 49 18 E
Bosavi, Mt., Papua N. G. 132 D2 6 30 S 142 49 E
Boscastle, U.K. 21 G3 50 41N 4 42W
Boscobel, U.S.A. 156 A6 43 8N 90 42W
Bose, China 76 F6 23 53N 106 35 E
Boseki, Dem. Rep. of the Congo 114 C3 2 34 S 19 38 E
Boshan, China 75 F9 36 28N 117 49 E
Boshof, S. Africa 116 D4 28 31 S 25 13 E
Boshrūyeh, Iran 97 C8 33 50N 57 30 E
Bosilegrad, Serbia, Yug. 50 D6 42 30N 22 27 E
Boskovice, Czech Rep. 35 B9 49 29N 16 40 E
Bosna →, Bos.-H. 52 E3 45 4N 18 29 E
Bosna i Hercegovina = Bosnia-Herzegovina ■, Europe 52 G2 44 0N 18 0 E
Bosnia-Herzegovina ■, Europe 52 G2 44 0N 18 0 E
Bosnik, Indonesia 79 E9 1 5 S 136 10 E
Bōsō-Hantō, Japan 71 B12 35 20N 140 20 E
Bosobolo, Dem. Rep. of the Congo 114 B3 4 15N 19 50 E
Bosporus = İstanbul Boğazı, Turkey 51 E13 41 10N 29 10 E
Bosque Farms, U.S.A. 159 J10 34 53N 106 40W
Bossangoa, C.A.R. 114 A3 6 35N 17 30 E
Bossé Bangou, Niger 113 C5 13 20N 1 18 E
Bossembélé, C.A.R. 114 A3 5 25N 17 40 E
Bossemtélé, C.A.R. 114 A3 5 41N 16 38 E
Bossier City, U.S.A. 155 J8 32 31N 93 44W
Bosso, Niger 113 C7 13 43N 13 19 E
Bosso, Dallol →, Niger 113 C5 12 25N 2 50 E
Bostan, Pakistan 92 D2 30 26N 67 2 E
Bostānābād, Iran 101 D12 37 50N 46 50 E
Bosten Hu, China 72 B3 41 55N 87 40 E
Boston, Phil. 81 H6 7 52N 126 22 E
Boston, U.K. 20 E7 52 59N 0 2W
Boston, Ga., U.S.A. 152 E6 30 47N 83 47W
Boston, Mass., U.S.A. 151 D13 42 22N 71 4W
Boston Bar, Canada 142 D4 49 52N 121 30W
Boston Mts., U.S.A. 155 H8 35 42N 93 15W
Bostwick, U.S.A. 152 F8 29 46N 81 38W
Bosusulu, Dem. Rep. of the Congo 114 B4 0 50N 20 45 E
Bosut →, Croatia 52 E3 45 20N 18 45 E
Boswell, Canada 142 D5 49 28N 116 45W
Boswell, Ind., U.S.A. 157 D9 40 31N 87 23W
Boswell, Pa., U.S.A. 150 F5 40 10N 79 2W
Bosworth, U.S.A. 156 E3 39 28N 93 20W
Botad, India 92 H4 22 15N 71 40 E
Botan →, Turkey 101 D10 37 57N 42 2 E
Botene, Laos 86 D3 17 35N 101 12 E
Botera, Angola 115 E2 11 37 S 14 16 E
Botev, Bulgaria 51 D8 42 44N 24 52 E
Botevgrad, Bulgaria 50 D7 42 55N 23 47 E
Bothaville, S. Africa 116 D4 27 23 S 26 34 E
Bothnia, G. of, Europe 14 E19 63 0N 20 15 E
Bothwell, Australia 126 G4 42 20 S 147 1 E
Bothwell, Canada 150 D3 42 38N 81 52W
Boticas, Portugal 42 D3 41 41N 7 40W
Botletle →, Botswana 116 C3 20 10 S 23 15 E
Botlikh, Russia 61 J8 42 39N 46 11 E
Botna →, Moldova 53 D14 46 45N 29 34 E
Botola, Dem. Rep. of the Congo 114 C3 1 17 S 18 13 E
Botolan, Phil. 80 D3 15 17N 120 1 E
Botoroaga, Romania 53 F10 44 8N 25 32 E
Botoşani, Romania 53 C11 47 42N 26 41 E
Botoşani □, Romania 53 C11 47 50N 26 50 E
Botou, Burkina Faso 113 C5 12 42N 1 59 E
Botricello, Italy 47 D9 38 56N 16 51 E
Botro, Ivory C. 112 D3 7 51N 5 19W
Botswana ■, Africa 116 C3 22 0 S 24 0 E
Bottineau, U.S.A. 154 A4 48 50N 100 27W
Bottnaryd, Sweden 17 G7 57 47N 13 50 E
Bottopassi, Surinam 169 C6 4 14N 55 27W
Bottrop, Germany 24 C6 51 31N 6 58 E
Botucatu, Brazil 175 A6 22 55 S 48 30W
Botwood, Canada 141 C8 49 6N 55 23W
Bou Alam, Algeria 111 B5 33 50N 1 26 E
Bou Ali, Algeria 111 C4 27 11N 0 4W
Bou Djébéha, Mali 112 B4 18 25N 2 45W
Bou Guema, Algeria 111 C5 28 49N 0 19 E
Bou Ismael, Algeria 111 A5 36 38N 2 42 E
Bou Izakarn, Morocco 110 C3 29 12N 9 46W
Boû Lanouâr, Mauritania 110 D1 21 12N 16 34W
Boû Rjeïmât, Mauritania 112 B1 19 4N 15 3W
Bou Saâda, Algeria 111 A5 35 11N 4 9 E
Bou Salem, Tunisia 108 A1 36 45N 9 2 E
Bouaflé, Ivory C. 112 D3 7 1N 5 47W
Bouaké, Ivory C. 112 D3 7 40N 5 2W
Bouanga, Congo 114 C3 2 7 S 16 8 E
Bouar, C.A.R. 114 A3 6 0N 15 40 E
Bouârfa, Morocco 111 B4 32 32N 1 58W
Bouca, C.A.R. 114 A3 6 45N 18 25 E
Boucaut B., Australia 126 A1 12 0 S 134 25 E
Bouches-du-Rhône □, France 29 E9 43 37N 5 2 E
Bouda, Algeria 111 C4 27 50N 0 27W
Boudenib, Morocco 110 B4 31 59N 3 31W
Boudry, Switz. 32 C3 46 57N 6 50 E
Boufarik, Algeria 111 A5 36 34N 2 58 E
Bougainville, C., Australia 124 B4 13 57 S 126 4 E
Bougainville I., Papua N. G. 133 L8 6 0 S 155 0 E
Bougainville Reef, Australia 126 B4 15 30 S 147 5 E
Bougainville Str., Solomon Is. 133 L9 6 40 S 156 10 E
Bougaroun, C., Algeria 111 A6 37 6N 6 30 E
Bougie = Bejaia, Algeria 111 A6 36 42N 5 2 E
Bougouni, Mali 112 C3 11 30N 7 20W
Bouillon, Belgium 24 E5 49 44N 5 3 E
Bouïra, Algeria 111 A5 36 20N 3 59 E
Boukombé, Benin 113 C5 10 13N 1 9 E
Boulal, Mali 112 B3 15 8N 8 21W
Boulazac, France 28 C4 45 10N 0 47 E
Boulder, Colo., U.S.A. 154 E2 40 1N 105 17W
Boulder, Mont., U.S.A. 158 C7 46 14N 112 7W
Boulder City, U.S.A. 161 K12 35 59N 114 50W
Boulder Creek, U.S.A. 160 H4 37 7N 122 7W
Boulder Dam = Hoover Dam, U.S.A. 161 K12 36 1N 114 44W
Boulembo, Gabon 114 C2 1 26 S 12 0 E
Bouli, Mauritania 112 B2 15 17N 12 18W
Boulia, Australia 126 C2 22 52 S 139 51 E
Bouligny, France 27 C12 49 17N 5 45 E
Boulogne →, France 26 E5 47 12N 1 47W
Boulogne-sur-Gesse, France 28 E4 43 18N 0 38 E
Boulogne-sur-Mer, France 27 B8 50 42N 1 36 E
Bouloire, France 26 E7 47 59N 0 45 E
Boulou →, C.A.R. 114 A4 6 45N 24 16 E
Boulouli, Mali 112 B3 15 30N 9 25W
Bouloupari, N. Cal. 133 U20 21 52 S 166 4 E
Bouloupesse, Congo 114 C2 1 58 S 12 40 E
Boulsa, Burkina Faso 113 C4 12 39N 0 34W
Boultoum, Niger 113 C7 14 45N 10 25 E
Boumalne, Morocco 110 B3 31 25N 6 0W
Boumba →, Cameroon 114 B2 2 2N 15 12 E
Boumbé →, C.A.R. 114 B3 4 4N 15 23 E
Boûmdeïd, Mauritania 112 B2 17 25N 9 50W
Boun Neua, Laos 86 B3 21 38N 101 54 E
Boun Tai, Laos 86 B3 21 23N 101 58 E
Bouna, Ivory C. 112 D4 9 10N 3 0W
Boundary Peak, U.S.A. 160 H8 37 51N 118 21W
Boundgi, Gabon 114 C2 1 0S 11 51 E
Boundiali, Ivory C. 112 D3 9 30N 6 20W
Boungou →, C.A.R. 114 A4 8 21N 23 46 E
Bountiful, U.S.A. 158 F8 40 53N 111 53W
Bounty Is., Pac. Oc. 134 M9 48 0 S 178 30 E
Boura, Mali 112 C4 12 25N 4 33W
Bourail, N. Cal. 133 U19 21 34 S 165 30 E
Bourbeuse →, U.S.A. 156 F6 38 24N 90 53W
Bourbon, U.S.A. 157 C10 41 18N 86 7W
Bourbon-Lancy, France 27 F10 46 37N 3 45 E
Bourbon-l'Archambault, France 27 F10 46 36N 3 4 E
Bourbonnais, France 27 F10 46 28N 3 0 E
Bourbonnais, U.S.A. 157 C9 41 9N 87 52W
Bourbonne-les-Bains, France 27 E12 47 54N 5 45 E
Bourbourg, France 27 B9 50 56N 2 12 E
Bourdel L., Canada 140 A5 56 43N 74 10W
Bourem, Mali 113 B4 17 0N 0 24W
Bourg, France 28 C3 45 3N 0 34W
Bourg-Argental, France 29 C8 45 18N 4 32 E
Bourg-de-Péage, France 29 C9 45 2N 5 3 E
Bourg-en-Bresse, France 27 F12 46 13N 5 12 E
Bourg-Lastic, France 28 C6 45 39N 2 35 E
Bourg-Madame, France 28 F5 42 26N 1 55 E
Bourg-St-Andéol, France 29 D8 44 23N 4 39 E
Bourg-St-Maurice, France 29 C10 45 35N 6 46 E
Bourg-St. Pierre, Switz. 32 E4 45 57N 7 12 E
Bourganeuf, France 28 C5 45 57N 1 45 E
Bourges, France 27 E9 47 9N 2 25 E
Bourget, Canada 151 A9 45 26N 75 9W
Bourget, Lac du, France 29 C9 45 44N 5 52 E
Bourgneuf, B. de, France 26 E4 47 3N 2 10W
Bourgneuf-en-Retz, France 26 E5 47 2N 1 58W
Bourgogne, France 27 F11 47 0N 4 50 E
Bourgoin-Jallieu, France 29 C9 45 36N 5 17 E
Bourgueil, France 26 E7 47 17N 0 10 E
Bourke, Australia 127 E4 30 8 S 145 55 E
Bourne, U.K. 20 E7 52 47N 0 22W
Bournemouth, U.K. 21 G6 50 43N 1 52W
Bournemouth □, U.K. 21 G6 50 43N 1 52W
Bouroum, Burkina Faso 113 C4 13 37N 0 39W
Bouse, U.S.A. 161 M13 33 56N 114 0W
Boussac, France 27 F9 46 22N 2 13 E
Boussé, Burkina Faso 113 C4 12 39N 1 53W
Bousso, Chad 109 F3 10 34N 16 52 E
Boussouma, Burkina Faso 113 C4 12 52N 1 13W
Boutilimit, Mauritania 112 B2 17 45N 14 40W
Boutonne →, France 28 C3 45 55N 0 50W
Bouvet I. = Bouvetøya, Antarctica 9 P9 54 26 S 3 24 E
Bouvetøya, Antarctica 9 P9 54 26 S 3 24 E
Bouxwiller, France 27 D14 48 49N 7 27 E
Bouza, Niger 113 C6 14 29N 6 2 E
Bouznika, Morocco 110 B3 33 46N 7 6W
Bouzonville, France 27 C13 49 17N 6 32 E
Bova Marina, Italy 47 E8 37 56N 15 55 E
Bovalino Marina, Italy 47 D9 38 10N 16 10 E
Bovec, Slovenia 45 B10 46 20N 13 33 E
Bøverdal, Norway 18 C5 61 44N 8 20 E
Bøverfjorden, Norway 18 A5 63 1N 8 32 E
Bovill, U.S.A. 158 C5 46 51N 116 24W
Bovino, Italy 47 A8 41 15N 15 20 E
Bovril, Argentina 174 C4 31 21 S 59 26W
Bow →, Canada 142 C6 49 57N 111 41W
Bow Island, Canada 142 D6 49 50N 111 23W
Bowbells, U.S.A. 154 A3 48 48N 102 15W
Bowdle, U.S.A. 154 C5 45 27N 99 39W
Bowdon, U.S.A. 152 B4 33 32N 85 15W

Buriti dos Lopes 195

Brooksville, Ky., U.S.A. 157 F12 38 41N 84 4W
Brookton, Australia 125 F2 32 22S 117 0 E
Brookville, Ind., U.S.A. 157 E12 39 25N 85 1W
Brookville, Ohio, U.S.A. 157 E12 39 50N 84 27W
Brookville, Pa., U.S.A. 150 E5 41 10N 79 5W
Brookville L., U.S.A. 157 E11 39 28N 85 0W
Broom, L., U.K. 22 D3 57 55N 5 15W
Broome, Australia 124 C3 18 0S 122 15 E
Broons, France 26 D4 48 20N 2 16W
Brora, U.K. 22 C5 58 0N 3 52W
Brora →, U.K. 22 C5 58 0N 3 51W
Brørup, Denmark 17 J2 55 29N 9 1 E
Brösarp, Sweden 17 J8 55 43N 14 6 E
Brosna →, Ireland 23 C4 53 14N 7 58W
Broşteni, Mehedinți, Romania 52 F7 44 45N 22 59 E
Broşteni, Suceava, Romania 53 C10 47 14N 25 43 E
Brostrud, Norway 18 D5 60 18N 8 34 E
Brotas de Macaúbas, Brazil 171 D3 12 0S 42 38W
Brothers, U.S.A. 158 E3 43 49N 120 36W
Brøttum, Norway 18 C7 61 2N 10 34 E
Brou, France 26 D8 48 13N 1 11 E
Brouage, France 28 C2 45 52N 1 4W
Brough, U.K. 20 C5 54 32N 2 18W
Brough Hd., U.K. 22 B5 59 8N 3 20W
Broughams Gate, Australia 128 A4 30 51S 140 59 E
Broughton, U.S.A. 157 G8 37 56N 88 27W
Broughton Island = Qikiqtarjuaq, Canada 139 B13 67 33N 63 0W
Broumov, Czech Rep. 35 A9 50 35N 16 20 E
Brovary, Ukraine 59 G6 50 34N 30 48 E
Brovst, Denmark 17 G3 57 6N 9 31 E
Brown, L., Australia 125 F2 31 5S 118 15 E
Brown, Mt., Australia 128 B2 32 30S 138 0 E
Brown, Pt., Australia 127 E1 32 32S 133 50 E
Brown City, U.S.A. 150 C2 43 13N 82 59W
Brown Willy, U.K. 21 G3 50 35N 4 37W
Brownfield, U.S.A. 155 J3 33 11N 102 17W
Browning, Ill., U.S.A. 156 D6 40 8N 90 22W
Browning, Mo., U.S.A. 156 D3 40 3N 93 12W
Browning, Mont., U.S.A. 158 B7 48 34N 113 1W
Browning Pass, N.Z. 131 C6 42 55S 171 22 E
Brownsburg, U.S.A. 157 E10 39 51N 86 24W
Brownstown, U.S.A. 157 F10 38 53N 86 3W
Brownsville, Oreg., U.S.A. 158 D2 44 24N 122 59W
Brownsville, Pa., U.S.A. 150 F5 40 1N 79 53W
Brownsville, Tenn., U.S.A. 155 H10 35 36N 89 16W
Brownsville, Tex., U.S.A. 155 N6 25 54N 97 30W
Brownsweg, Surinam 169 B6 5 5N 55 15W
Brownville, U.S.A. 151 C9 44 0N 75 59W
Brownwood, U.S.A. 155 K5 31 43N 98 59W
Browse I., Australia 124 B3 14 7S 123 33 E
Broxton, U.S.A. 152 D7 31 38N 82 53W
Broye →, Switz. 32 C3 46 52N 6 58 E
Bru, Norway 18 C2 61 32N 5 11 E
Bruas, Malaysia 87 K3 4 30N 100 47 E
Bruay-la-Buissière, France 27 B9 50 29N 2 33 E
Bruce, U.S.A. 152 E4 30 28N 85 58W
Bruce, Mt., Australia 124 D2 22 37S 118 8 E
Bruce B., N.Z. 131 D4 43 35S 169 42 E
Bruce Pen., Canada 150 B3 45 0N 81 30W
Bruce Rock, Australia 125 F2 31 52S 118 8 E
Bruche →, France 27 D14 48 34N 7 43 E
Bruchsal, Germany 31 F4 49 7N 8 35 E
Bruck an der Leitha, Austria 35 C9 48 1N 16 47 E
Bruck an der Mur, Austria 34 D8 47 24N 15 16 E
Brue →, U.K. 21 F5 51 13N 2 59W
Bruflat, Norway 18 D6 60 53N 9 37 E
Bruges = Brugge, Belgium 24 C3 51 13N 3 13 E
Brugg, Switz. 32 B6 47 29N 8 11 E
Brugge, Belgium 24 C3 51 13N 3 13 E
Bruin, U.S.A. 150 E5 41 3N 79 43W
Brûlé, Canada 142 C5 53 15N 117 58W
Brûlon, France 26 E6 47 58N 0 15W
Brumado, Brazil 171 D3 14 14S 41 40W
Brumado →, Brazil 171 D3 14 13S 41 40W
Brumath, France 27 D14 48 43N 7 40 E
Brumunddal, Norway 15 F14 60 53N 10 56 E
Brundidge, U.S.A. 152 D4 31 43N 85 49W
Bruneau, U.S.A. 158 E6 42 53N 115 48W
Bruneau →, U.S.A. 158 E6 42 56N 115 57W
Bruneck = Brunico, Italy 45 B8 46 48N 11 56 E
Brunei = Bandar Seri Begawan, Brunei 78 C4 4 52N 115 0 E
Brunei ■, Asia 78 D4 4 50N 115 0 E
Brunflo, Sweden 16 A8 63 5N 14 50 E
Brunico, Italy 45 B8 46 48N 11 56 E
Brünigpass, Switz. 32 C6 46 46N 8 8 E
Brunna, Sweden 16 E11 59 52N 17 25 E
Brunnen, Switz. 33 C7 46 59N 8 37 E
Brunner, L., N.Z. 131 C6 42 37S 171 27 E
Brunnhóll, Iceland 11 C11 64 17N 15 26W
Brunsbüttel, Germany 30 B5 53 53N 9 6 E
Brunssum, Neths. 24 D5 50 57N 5 59 E
Brunswick = Braunschweig, Germany 30 C6 52 15N 10 31 E
Brunswick, Ga., U.S.A. 152 D8 31 10N 81 30W
Brunswick, Maine, U.S.A. 149 D11 43 55N 69 58W
Brunswick, Md., U.S.A. 148 F7 39 19N 77 38W
Brunswick, Mo., U.S.A. 156 E3 39 26N 93 8W
Brunswick, Ohio, U.S.A. 150 E3 41 14N 81 51W
Brunswick, Pen. de, Chile 176 D2 53 30S 71 30W
Brunswick B., Australia 124 C3 15 15S 124 50 E
Brunswick Junction, Australia 125 F2 33 15S 115 50 E
Bruntál, Czech Rep. 35 B10 49 59N 17 27 E
Bruny I., Australia 126 G4 43 20S 147 15 E
Brus Laguna, Honduras 164 C3 15 47N 84 35W
Brusartsi, Bulgaria 50 C7 43 40N 23 5 E
Brush, U.S.A. 154 E3 40 15N 103 37W
Brushton, U.S.A. 151 B10 44 50N 74 31W
Brusio, Switz. 33 D10 46 14N 10 8 E
Brusque, Brazil 175 B6 27 5S 49 0W
Brussel, Belgium 24 D4 50 51N 4 21 E
Brussels = Brussel, Belgium 24 D4 50 51N 4 21 E
Brussels, Canada 150 C3 43 44N 81 15W
Brusy, Poland 54 E4 53 53N 17 43 E
Bruthen, Australia 129 D7 37 42S 147 50 E
Bruvoll, Norway 18 D8 60 27N 11 29 E
Bruxelles = Brussel, Belgium 24 D4 50 51N 4 21 E
Bruyères, France 27 D13 48 10N 6 40 E
Bruz, France 26 D5 48 1N 1 46W
Brwinów, Poland 55 F7 52 9N 20 40 E
Bryagovo, Bulgaria 51 E9 41 58N 25 8 E
Bryan, Ohio, U.S.A. 157 C12 41 28N 84 33W
Bryan, Tex., U.S.A. 155 K6 30 40N 96 22W
Bryan, Mt., Australia 128 B3 33 30S 139 0 E
Bryanka, Ukraine 59 H10 48 32N 38 45 E
Bryansk, Bryansk, Russia 59 F8 53 13N 34 25 E
Bryansk, Dagestan, Russia 61 H8 44 20N 47 10 E
Bryanskoye = Bryansk, Russia 61 H8 44 20N 47 10 E
Bryce Canyon National Park, U.S.A. 159 H7 37 30N 112 10W
Bryne, Norway 15 G11 58 44N 5 38 E
Bryson City, U.S.A. 149 H4 35 26N 83 27W
Bryukhovetskaya, Russia 59 K10 45 48N 39 0 E
Brza Palanka, Serbia, Yug. 50 B6 44 28N 22 27 E
Brzeg, Poland 55 H4 50 52N 17 30 E
Brzeg Dolny, Poland 55 G3 51 16N 16 41 E
Brześć Kujawski, Poland 55 F5 52 36N 18 55 E
Brzesko, Poland 55 J7 49 59N 20 34 E
Brzeziny, Poland 55 G6 51 49N 19 42 E
Brzozów, Poland 55 J9 49 41N 22 3 E
Bsharri, Lebanon 103 A5 34 15N 36 0 E
Bū Athlah, Libya 108 B3 30 9N 15 39 E
Bū Baqarah, U.A.E. 97 E8 25 35N 56 25 E
Bu Craa, W. Sahara 110 C2 26 45N 12 50W
Bū Ḩasā, U.A.E. 97 F7 23 30N 53 20 E
Bua, Sweden 17 G6 57 14N 12 7 E
Bua Yai, Thailand 86 E4 15 33N 102 26 E
Buad I., Phil. 81 F5 11 40N 124 51 E
Buala, Solomon Is. 133 M10 8 10S 159 35 E
Buapinang, Indonesia 79 E6 4 40S 121 30 E
Buba, Guinea-Biss. 112 C2 11 40N 14 59W
Bubanda, Dem. Rep. of the Congo 114 B3 4 14N 19 38 E
Bubanza, Burundi 118 C2 3 6S 29 23 E
Bubaque, Guinea-Biss. 112 C1 11 16N 15 51W
Bube, Ethiopia 107 F4 8 46N 35 48 E
Būbiyān, Kuwait 97 D6 29 45N 48 15 E
Buca, Turkey 49 C9 38 22N 27 11 E
Bucaco, Angola 115 E4 11 26S 20 10 E
Bucak, Turkey 49 D12 37 28N 30 36 E
Bucaramanga, Colombia 168 B3 7 0N 73 0W
Bucas Grande I., Phil. 81 G5 9 40N 125 57 E
Bucasia, Australia 126 C4 21 2S 149 10 E
Bucay, Phil. 80 C3 17 32N 120 43 E
Buccaneer Arch., Australia 124 C3 16 7S 123 20 E
Buccino, Italy 47 B8 40 38N 15 22 E
Bucecea, Romania 53 C11 47 47N 26 28 E
Bucey-lès-Gy, France 32 B1 47 25N 5 51 E
Buchach, Ukraine 59 H3 49 5N 25 25 E
Buchan, Australia 129 D8 37 30S 148 12 E
Buchan, U.K. 22 D6 57 32N 2 21W
Buchan Ness, U.K. 22 D7 57 29N 1 46W
Buchanan, Canada 143 C8 51 40N 102 45W
Buchanan, Liberia 112 D2 5 57N 10 2W
Buchanan, Ga., U.S.A. 152 B4 33 48N 85 11W
Buchanan, Mich., U.S.A. 157 C10 41 50N 86 22W
Buchanan, L., Queens., Australia 126 C4 21 35S 145 52 E
Buchanan, L., W. Austral., Australia 125 E3 25 33S 123 2 E
Buchanan, L., U.S.A. 155 K5 30 45N 98 25W
Buchanan Cr. →, Australia 126 B2 19 13S 136 33 E
Buchans, Canada 141 C8 48 50N 56 52W
Bucharest = Bucureşti, Romania 53 F11 44 27N 26 10 E
Buchen, Germany 31 F5 49 32N 9 20 E
Buchholz, Germany 30 B5 53 19N 9 52 E
Buchloe, Germany 31 G6 48 1N 10 44 E
Buchon, Pt., U.S.A. 160 K6 35 15N 120 54W
Buchs, Switz. 32 B6 47 23N 8 4 E
Buchs, Switz. 33 B8 47 10N 9 28 E
Buciumi, Romania 52 C8 47 3N 23 4 E
Buck Hill Falls, U.S.A. 151 E9 41 11N 75 16W
Bückeburg, Germany 30 C5 52 16N 9 7 E
Buckeye, U.S.A. 159 K7 33 22N 112 35W
Buckeye Lake, U.S.A. 150 G2 39 55N 82 29W
Buckhannon, U.S.A. 148 F5 39 0N 80 8W
Buckhaven, U.K. 22 E5 56 11N 3 3W
Buckhorn L., Canada 150 B6 44 29N 78 23W
Buckie, U.K. 22 D6 57 41N 2 58W
Buckingham, Canada 140 C4 45 37N 75 24W
Buckingham, U.K. 21 F7 51 59N 0 57W
Buckingham B., Australia 126 A2 12 10S 135 40 E
Buckingham Canal, India 95 H5 14 0N 80 5 E
Buckinghamshire □, U.K. 21 F7 51 53N 0 55W
Buckle Hd., Australia 124 B4 14 26S 127 52 E
Buckleboo, Australia 128 B2 32 54S 136 12 E
Buckley, U.K. 20 D4 53 10N 3 5W
Buckley, U.S.A. 157 D8 40 36N 88 2W
Buckley →, Australia 126 C2 20 10S 138 49 E
Bucklin, Kans., U.S.A. 155 G5 37 33N 99 38W
Bucklin, Mo., U.S.A. 156 E4 39 47N 92 53W
Bucks L., U.S.A. 160 F5 39 54N 121 12W
Buco Zau, Angola 115 C2 4 46S 12 33 E
Bucquoy, France 27 B9 50 9N 2 43 E
Buctouche, Canada 141 C7 46 30N 64 45W
Bucureşti, Romania 53 F11 44 27N 26 10 E
Bucyrus, U.S.A. 157 D14 40 48N 82 59W
Bud, Norway 18 B3 62 55N 6 55 E
Budacu, Vf., Romania 53 C10 47 7N 25 41 E
Budalin, Burma 90 D5 22 20N 95 10 E
Budaörs, Hungary 52 C3 47 27N 18 58 E
Budapest, Hungary 52 C4 47 29N 19 5 E
Budapest □, Hungary 52 C4 47 29N 19 5 E
Budaun, India 93 E8 28 5N 79 10 E
Budd Coast, Antarctica 7 C8 68 0S 112 0 E
Buddabadah, Australia 129 A7 31 56S 147 14 E
Buddusò, Italy 46 B2 40 35N 9 15 E
Bude, U.K. 21 G3 50 49N 4 34W
Budennovsk, Russia 61 H7 44 50N 44 10 E
Budeşti, Romania 53 F11 44 13N 26 30 E
Budge Budge = Baj Baj, India 93 H13 22 30N 88 5 E
Budgewoi, Australia 129 B9 33 13S 151 34 E
Búðardalur, Iceland 11 B5 65 7N 21 46W
Búðir, Iceland 11 C12 64 56N 14 1W
Budia, Spain 40 E2 40 38N 2 46W
Büdingen, Germany 31 E5 50 16N 9 7 E
Budjala, Dem. Rep. of the Congo 114 B3 2 50N 19 40 E
Budoni, Italy 46 B2 40 40N 9 45 E
Búdrio, Italy 45 D8 44 32N 11 32 E
Budva, Montenegro, Yug. 50 D2 42 17N 18 50 E
Budzyń, Poland 55 F3 52 54N 16 59 E
Bue, Norway 18 F2 58 40N 5 58 E
Buea, Cameroon 113 E6 4 10N 9 9 E
Buela, Angola 115 D2 5 54S 14 40 E
Buellton, U.S.A. 161 L6 34 37N 120 12W
Buena Esperanza, Argentina 174 C2 34 45S 65 15W
Buena Park, U.S.A. 161 M9 33 52N 117 59W
Buena Vista, Bolivia 173 D5 17 27S 63 40W
Buena Vista, Colo., U.S.A. 159 G10 38 51N 106 8W
Buena Vista, Ga., U.S.A. 152 C5 32 19N 84 31W
Buena Vista, Va., U.S.A. 148 G6 37 44N 79 21W
Buena Vista Lake Bed, U.S.A. 161 K7 35 12N 119 18W
Buenaventura, Colombia 168 C2 3 53N 77 4W
Buenaventura, Mexico 162 B3 29 50N 107 30W
Buenaventura, B. de, Colombia 168 C2 3 48N 77 17W
Buenavista, Agusan del N., Phil. 81 G5 8 59N 125 24 E
Buenavista, Quezon, Phil. 80 E4 13 35N 122 34 E
Buendía, Embalse de, Spain 40 E2 40 25N 2 43W
Buenópolis, Brazil 171 E3 17 54S 44 11W
Buenos Aires, Argentina 174 C4 34 30S 58 20W
Buenos Aires, Colombia 168 C3 1 36N 73 18W
Buenos Aires, Costa Rica 164 E3 9 10N 83 20W
Buenos Aires □, Argentina 174 D4 36 30S 60 0W
Buenos Aires, L., Chile 176 C2 46 35S 72 30W
Buesaco, Colombia 168 C2 1 23N 77 9W
Buet, Mont, France 32 D3 46 2N 6 52 E
Buffalo, Mo., U.S.A. 155 G8 37 39N 93 6W
Buffalo, N.Y., U.S.A. 150 D6 42 53N 78 53W
Buffalo, Okla., U.S.A. 155 G5 36 50N 99 38W
Buffalo, S. Dak., U.S.A. 154 C3 45 35N 103 33W
Buffalo, Wyo., U.S.A. 158 D10 44 21N 106 42W
Buffalo →, Canada 142 A5 60 5N 115 5W
Buffalo →, S. Africa 117 D5 28 43S 30 37 E
Buffalo Head Hills, Canada 142 B5 57 25N 115 55W
Buffalo L., Alta., Canada 142 C6 52 27N 112 54W
Buffalo L., N.W.T., Canada 142 A5 60 12N 115 25W
Buffalo Narrows, Canada 143 B7 55 51N 108 29W
Buffels →, S. Africa 116 D2 29 36S 17 3 E
Buford, U.S.A. 149 H4 34 10N 84 0W
Bug = Buh →, Ukraine 59 J6 46 59N 31 58 E
Bug →, Poland 55 F8 52 31N 21 5 E
Buga, Colombia 168 C2 4 0N 76 15W
Buganda, Uganda 118 C3 0 0 31 30 E
Buganga, Uganda 118 C3 0 3S 32 0 E
Bugasong, Phil. 81 F4 11 3N 122 4 E
Bugeat, France 28 C5 45 36N 1 55 E
Bugel, Tanjung, Indonesia 79 G14 6 26S 111 3 E
Buggingen, Germany 32 A5 47 51N 7 38 E
Bugibba, Malta 38 D1 35 57N 14 25 E
Bugojno, Bos.-H. 52 F2 44 2N 17 25 E
Bugsuk, Phil. 78 C5 8 15N 117 15 E
Bugsuk I., Phil. 81 G1 8 12N 117 18 E
Buguey, Phil. 80 B3 18 17N 121 50 E
Buguias, Phil. 80 C3 16 43N 120 50 E
Bugulma, Russia 62 D4 54 33N 52 48 E
Buguma, Nigeria 113 E6 4 42N 6 55 E
Bugun Shara, Mongolia 72 B5 49 0N 104 0 E
Buguruslan, Russia 62 E4 53 39N 52 26 E
Buh →, Ukraine 59 J6 46 59N 31 58 E
Buharkent, Turkey 49 D10 37 58N 28 44 E
Buheirat-Murrat-el-Kubra, Egypt 106 H8 30 18N 32 26 E
Buhera, Zimbabwe 117 B5 19 18S 31 29 E
Bühl, Germany 31 G4 48 40N 8 8 E
Buhl, U.S.A. 158 E6 42 36N 114 46W
Buhuşi, Romania 53 D11 46 41N 26 45 E
Builth Wells, U.K. 21 E4 52 9N 3 25W
Buin, Papua N. G. 133 L8 6 48S 155 42 E
Buin, Piz, Switz. 33 C10 46 51N 10 7 E
Buinsk, Russia 60 C9 55 0N 48 18 E
Buíque, Brazil 170 C4 8 37S 37 9W
Buir Nur, Mongolia 73 B6 47 50N 117 42 E
Buis-les-Baronnies, France 29 D9 44 17N 5 16 E
Buitrago = Buitrago del Lozoya, Spain 42 E7 40 58N 3 38W
Buitrago del Lozoya, Spain 42 E7 40 58N 3 38W
Bujalance, Spain 43 H6 37 54N 4 23W
Bujanovac, Serbia, Yug. 50 D5 42 28N 21 44 E
Bujaraloz, Spain 40 D4 41 29N 0 10W
Buje, Croatia 45 C10 45 24N 13 39 E
Bujumbura, Burundi 118 C2 3 16S 29 18 E
Bük, Hungary 52 C1 47 22N 16 45 E
Buk, Poland 55 F3 52 21N 16 30 E
Buka I., Papua N. G. 132 C8 5 10S 154 35 E
Bukachacha, Russia 65 D12 52 55N 116 50 E
Bukama, Dem. Rep. of the Congo 119 D2 9 10S 25 50 E
Bukavu, Dem. Rep. of the Congo 118 C2 2 20S 28 52 E
Bukene, Tanzania 118 C3 4 15S 32 48 E
Bukhara = Bukhoro, Uzbekistan 64 F7 39 48N 64 25 E
Bukhoro, Uzbekistan 64 F7 39 48N 64 25 E
Bukidnon □, Phil. 81 G5 8 0N 125 0 E
Bukima, Tanzania 118 C3 1 50S 33 25 E
Bukit Mertajam, Malaysia 87 K3 5 22N 100 28 E
Bukittinggi, Indonesia 78 E2 0 20S 100 20 E
Bükk, Hungary 52 B5 48 0N 20 30 E
Bukkapatnam, India 95 G3 14 14N 77 46 E
Bukoba, Tanzania 118 C3 1 20S 31 49 E
Bukuru, Nigeria 113 D6 9 42N 8 48 E
Bukuya, Uganda 118 B3 0 40N 31 52 E
Būl, Kuh-e, Iran 97 D7 30 48N 52 45 E
Bula, Guinea-Biss. 112 C1 12 7N 15 43W
Bula, Indonesia 79 E8 3 6S 130 30 E
Bula, Phil. 80 E4 13 28N 123 16 E
Bula-Atumba, Angola 115 D2 8 41S 14 52 E
Bulacan □, Phil. 80 D3 15 0N 121 5 E
Bülach, Switz. 33 A7 47 31N 8 32 E
Bulahdelah, Australia 129 B10 32 23S 152 13 E
Bulalacao, Phil. 80 E3 12 31N 121 26 E
Bulan, Phil. 79 B6 12 40N 123 52 E
Bulan, Phil. 62 C9 57 16N 62 0 E
Bulanash, Russia 101 B8 40 56N 38 14 E
Bulancak, Turkey 11 D8 63 46N 18 30W
Búland, Iceland 92 E7 28 28N 77 51 E
Bulandshahr, India 101 C10 39 4N 42 14 E
Bulanık, Turkey 62 E5 52 27N 55 10 E
Bulanovo, Russia 9 P3 25 10N 30 38 E
Bûlâq, Egypt 119 G2 20 7S 28 32 E
Bulawayo, Zimbabwe 49 C10 38 2N 28 50 E
Buldan, Turkey 94 D3 20 30N 76 18 E
Buldana, India 81 H5 7 33N 124 25 E
Buldon, Phil. 60 C9 54 57N 49 4 E
Bulgar, Russia 51 D9 42 35N 25 30 E
Bulgaria ■, Europe 47 B8 40 4N 15 26 E
Bulgheria, Monte, Italy 49 C9 38 9N 27 9 E
Bulgurca, Turkey 120 C3 5 20N 46 29 E
Bulhale, Somali Rep. 120 B2 10 25N 44 30 E
Bulhar, Somali Rep. 79 D7 1 5N 128 25 E
Buli, Teluk, Indonesia 78 C5 8 20N 117 15 E
Bulilluyan, C., Phil. 107 F4 6 11N 36 31 E
Bulki, Ethiopia 142 B3 55 15N 127 40W
Bulkley →, Canada 155 G8 36 22N 92 35W
Bull Shoals L., U.S.A. 43 G6 38 59N 4 17W
Bullaque →, Spain 152 C6 32 38N 83 30W
Bullard, U.S.A. 41 G3 38 2N 1 40W
Bullas, Spain 32 C4 46 37N 7 3 E
Bulle, Switz. 131 B6 41 44S 171 36 E
Buller →, N.Z. 129 D7 37 10S 146 28 E
Buller, Mt., Australia 131 B7 41 40S 172 10 E
Buller Gorge, N.Z. 161 K12 35 8N 114 32W
Bullhead City, U.S.A. 129 C9 34 15S 150 57 E
Bulli, Australia 24 D6 50 25N 6 16 E
Büllingen, Belgium 126 B3 17 43S 144 31 E
Bullock Creek, Australia 127 D3 28 43S 142 30 E
Bulloo →, Australia 127 D3 28 43S 142 25 E
Bulloo L., Australia 130 G4 40 10S 175 24 E
Bulls, N.Z. 27 B9 50 27N 2 44 E
Bully-les-Mines, France 174 D1 36 42S 72 19W
Bulnes, Chile 120 D3 3 50N 45 33 E
Bulo Burti, Somali Rep. 120 D2 2 52N 43 1 E
Bulo Gheduudo, Somali Rep. 132 D4 7 10S 146 40 E
Bulolo, Papua N. G.
Bulongo, Dem. Rep. of the Congo 115 C4 4 45S 21 30 E
Bulpunga, Australia 128 B4 33 47S 141 45 E
Bulqiza, Albania 50 E4 41 30N 20 21 E
Bulsar = Valsad, India 94 D1 20 40N 72 58 E
Bultfontein, S. Africa 116 D4 28 18S 26 10 E
Buluan, Phil. 81 H5 6 44N 124 47 E
Buluan, L., Phil. 81 H5 6 40N 124 49 E
Bulukumba, Indonesia 79 F6 5 33S 120 11 E
Bulun, Russia 65 B13 70 37N 127 30 E
Bulunghur, Uzbekistan 63 D3 39 46N 67 16 E
Bulungu, Dem. Rep. of the Congo 115 D4 6 4S 21 54 E
Bulusan, Phil. 80 E5 12 45N 124 8 E
Bulusan Vol., Phil. 80 E5 12 46N 124 3 E
Bumba, Dem. Rep. of the Congo 114 B4 2 13N 22 30 E
Bumba, Dem. Rep. of the Congo 115 D3 6 58S 19 19 E
Bumbeşti-Jiu, Romania 53 E8 45 10N 23 24 E
Bumbiri I., Tanzania 118 C3 1 40S 31 55 E
Bumbuna, S. Leone 112 D2 9 2N 11 49W
Bumhkang, Burma 90 B6 26 51N 97 40 E
Bumhpa Bum, Burma 90 B6 26 51N 97 14 E
Bumi →, Zimbabwe 119 F2 17 0S 28 20 E
Bumtang →, Bhutan 90 B3 26 56N 90 53 E
Buna, Dem. Rep. of the Congo 114 C3 3 14S 18 59 E
Buna, Kenya 118 B4 2 58N 39 30 E
Buna, Papua N. G. 132 E5 8 42S 148 27 E
Bunawan, Phil. 81 G5 8 12N 125 57 E
Bunazi, Tanzania 118 C3 1 3S 31 23 E
Bunbah, Khalīj, Libya 108 B4 32 20N 23 15 E
Bunbury, Australia 125 F2 33 20S 115 35 E
Bunclody, Ireland 23 D5 52 39N 6 40W
Buncrana, Ireland 23 A4 55 8N 7 27W
Bunda, Dem. Rep. of the Congo 115 C3 4 58S 14 29 E
Bundaberg, Australia 127 C5 24 54S 152 22 E
Bünde, Germany 30 C4 52 11N 8 35 E
Bundey →, Australia 126 C2 21 46S 135 37 E
Bundi, India 92 G6 25 30N 75 35 E
Bundoran, Ireland 23 B3 54 28N 8 16W
Bundukia, Sudan 107 F3 5 14N 30 55 E
Bundure, Australia 129 C7 35 10S 146 1 E
Bung Kan, Thailand 86 C4 18 23N 103 37 E
Bunga →, Nigeria 113 C6 11 23N 9 56 E
Bungatakada, Japan 70 D3 33 35N 131 25 E
Bungay, U.K. 21 E9 52 27N 1 28 E
Bungendore, Australia 129 C8 35 14S 149 30 E
Bungil Cr. →, Australia 127 D4 27 5S 149 5 E
Bungo, Angola 115 D3 7 26S 15 33 E
Bungo, Gunong, Malaysia 85 B4 1 16N 110 9 E
Bungo-Suidō, Japan 70 E4 33 0N 132 15 E
Bungoma, Kenya 118 B3 0 34N 34 34 E
Bungu, Tanzania 118 D4 7 35S 39 0 E
Bunia, Dem. Rep. of the Congo 118 B3 1 35N 30 20 E
Bunianga, Dem. Rep. of the Congo 114 C4 3 28S 20 11 E
Bunji, Pakistan 93 B6 35 45N 74 40 E
Bunker Hill, Ill., U.S.A. 156 E7 39 3N 89 57W
Bunker Hill, Ind., U.S.A. 157 D10 40 40N 86 6W
Bunkie, U.S.A. 155 K8 30 57N 92 11W
Bunnell, U.S.A. 149 L5 29 28N 81 16W
Bunnythorpe, N.Z. 130 G4 40 16S 175 39 E
Buñol, Spain 41 F4 39 25N 0 47W
Bunsuru, Nigeria 113 C5 13 21N 6 23 E
Buntok, Indonesia 78 E4 1 40S 114 58 E
Bununu Dass, Nigeria 113 C6 10 5N 9 31 E
Bununu Kasa, Nigeria 113 D6 9 51N 9 32 E
Bünyan, Turkey 100 C6 38 51N 35 51 E
Bunyu, Indonesia 78 D5 3 35N 117 50 E
Bunza, Nigeria 113 C5 12 8N 4 0 E
Buol, Indonesia 79 D6 1 15N 121 32 E
Buon Brieng, Vietnam 86 F7 13 9N 108 12 E
Buon Ma Thuot, Vietnam 78 B3 12 40N 108 3 E
Buong Long, Cambodia 86 F6 13 44N 106 59 E
Buorkhaya, Mys, Russia 65 B14 71 50N 132 40 E
Buqayq, Si. Arabia 97 E6 26 0N 49 45 E
Buqbuq, Egypt 106 A2 31 29N 25 29 E
Bur Acaba, Somali Rep. 120 D2 3 12N 44 20 E
Bûr Fuad, Egypt 106 H8 31 15N 32 20 E
Bûr Ghibi, Somali Rep. 120 D3 3 56N 45 7 E
Bûr Safâga, Egypt 96 E2 26 43N 33 57 E
Bûr Sa'îd, Egypt 106 H8 31 16N 32 18 E
Bûr Sûdân, Sudan 106 D4 19 32N 37 9 E
Bûr Taufiq, Egypt 106 J8 29 54N 32 32 E
Bura, Kenya 118 C4 1 4S 39 58 E
Burakin, Australia 125 F2 30 31S 117 10 E
Buram, Sudan 107 E2 10 51N 25 9 E
Buran, Somali Rep. 120 B3 10 14N 48 44 E
Burao, Somali Rep. 120 C3 9 32N 45 32 E
Burāq, Syria 103 B5 33 11N 36 29 E
Burauen, Phil. 81 F5 10 58N 124 53 E
Buraydah, Si. Arabia 96 E5 26 20N 44 8 E
Burbank, U.S.A. 161 L8 34 11N 118 19W
Burcher, Australia 129 B7 33 30S 147 16 E
Burda, India 92 G6 25 50N 77 35 E
Burdekin →, Australia 126 B4 19 38S 147 25 E
Burdeos Bay, Phil. 80 D4 14 44N 122 6 E
Burdur, Turkey 49 D12 37 45N 30 17 E
Burdur □, Turkey 49 D12 37 45N 30 0 E
Burdur Gölü, Turkey 49 D12 37 44N 30 10 E
Burdwan = Barddhaman, India 93 H12 23 14N 87 39 E
Burdwood Banks, Atl. Oc. 9 P3 54 0S 59 0W
Bure, Gojam, Ethiopia 102 E2 10 40N 37 4 E
Bure, Ilubabor, Ethiopia 107 F4 8 19N 35 8 E
Bure →, U.K. 20 E9 52 38N 1 43 E
Büren, Germany 30 D4 51 33N 8 35 E
Bureya →, Russia 65 E13 49 27N 129 30 E
Burford, Canada 150 C4 43 7N 80 27W
Burg, Germany 30 C7 52 16N 11 51 E
Burg auf Fehmarn, Germany 30 A7 54 28N 11 9 E
Burg el Arab, Egypt 106 H6 30 54N 29 32 E
Burg et Tuyur, Sudan 106 C2 20 55N 27 56 E
Burg Stargard, Germany 30 B9 53 29N 13 18 E
Burgas, Bulgaria 51 D11 42 33N 27 29 E
Burgas □, Bulgaria 51 D10 42 30N 26 50 E
Burgaski Zaliv, Bulgaria 51 D11 42 30N 27 39 E
Burgdorf, Germany 30 C6 52 27N 10 1 E
Burgdorf, Switz. 32 B5 47 3N 7 37 E
Burgenland □, Austria 35 D9 47 20N 16 20 E
Burgeo, Canada 141 C8 47 37N 57 38W
Burgersdorp, S. Africa 116 E4 31 0S 26 20 E
Burges, Mt., Australia 125 F3 30 50S 121 5 E
Burghausen, Germany 31 G8 48 9N 12 49 E
Búrgio, Italy 46 E6 37 36N 13 17 E
Bürglen, Switz. 33 C7 46 53N 8 40 E
Burglengenfeld, Germany 31 F8 49 12N 12 2 E
Burgohondo, Spain 42 E6 40 26N 4 47W
Burgos, Ilocos N., Phil. 80 B3 18 31N 120 39 E
Burgos, Pangasinan, Phil. 80 C2 16 4N 119 52 E
Burgos, Spain 42 C7 42 21N 3 41W
Burgos □, Spain 42 C7 42 21N 3 42W
Burgstädt, Germany 30 E8 50 54N 12 49 E
Burgsvik, Sweden 17 G12 57 3N 18 19 E
Burguillos del Cerro, Spain 43 G4 38 23N 6 35W
Burgundy = Bourgogne, France 27 F11 47 0N 4 50 E
Burhaniye, Turkey 49 B8 39 30N 26 58 E
Burhanpur, India 94 D3 21 18N 76 14 E
Burhi Gandak →, India 93 G12 25 20N 86 37 E
Burhner →, India 93 H9 22 43N 80 31 E
Buri Pen., Eritrea 107 D4 15 25N 39 55 E
Burias I., Phil. 79 B6 12 55N 123 5 E
Burias Pass, Phil. 80 E4 13 0N 123 15 E
Burica, Pta., Costa Rica 164 E3 8 3N 82 51W
Burien, U.S.A. 160 C4 47 28N 122 21W
Burigi, L., Tanzania 118 C3 2 2S 31 22 E
Burin, Canada 141 C8 47 1N 55 14W
Buriram, Thailand 78 A2 15 0N 103 0 E
Buriti Alegre, Brazil 171 E2 18 9S 49 3W
Buriti Bravo, Brazil 170 C3 5 50S 43 50W
Buriti dos Lopes, Brazil 170 B3 3 10S 41 52W

Cape Pole 197

Caldwell, Kans., U.S.A. 155 G6 37 2N 97 37W
Caldwell, Tex., U.S.A. 155 K6 30 32N 96 42W
Caledon, S. Africa 116 E2 34 14 S 19 26 E
Caledon →, S. Africa 116 E4 30 31 S 26 5 E
Caledon B., Australia 126 A2 12 45 S 137 0 E
Caledonia, Canada 150 C5 43 7N 79 58W
Caledonia, Mo., U.S.A. 156 G6 37 45N 90 46W
Caledonia, N.Y., U.S.A. 150 D7 42 58N 77 51W
Calella, Spain 40 D7 41 37N 2 40 E
Calemba, Angola 116 B2 16 0 S 15 44 E
Calen, Australia 126 C4 20 56 S 148 48 E
Calenzana, France 29 F12 42 31N 8 51 E
Caleta Olivia, Argentina 176 C3 46 25 S 67 25W
Caletones, Chile 174 C1 34 6 S 70 27W
Calexico, U.S.A. 161 N11 32 40N 115 30W
Calf of Man, U.K. 20 C3 54 3N 4 48W
Calgary, Canada 142 C6 51 0N 114 10W
Calheta, Madeira 39 D2 32 44N 17 11W
Calhoun, U.S.A. 149 H3 34 30N 84 57W
Calhoun Falls, U.S.A. 152 A7 34 6N 82 36W
Cali, Colombia 168 C2 3 25N 76 35W
Calicut, India 95 J2 11 15N 75 43 E
Caliente, U.S.A. 159 H6 37 37N 114 31W
California, Mo., U.S.A. 156 F4 38 38N 92 34W
California, Pa., U.S.A. 150 F5 40 4N 79 54W
California □, U.S.A. 160 H7 37 30N 119 30W
California, Baja, Mexico 162 A1 32 10N 115 12W
California, Baja, T.N. = Baja
California □, Mexico 162 B2 30 0N 115 0W
California, Baja, T.S. = Baja
California Sur □, Mexico 162 B2 25 50N 111 50W
California, G. de, Mexico 162 B2 27 0N 111 0W
California City, U.S.A. 161 K9 35 10N 117 55W
California Hot Springs, U.S.A. 161 K8 35 51N 118 41W
Călimănești, Romania 53 E9 45 14N 24 20 E
Călimani, Munții, Romania 53 C10 47 12N 25 0 E
Calingasta, Argentina 174 C2 31 15 S 69 30W
Calinog, Phil. 81 F4 11 7N 122 32 E
Calintaan, Phil. 80 E3 12 35N 120 57 E
Calipatria, U.S.A. 161 M11 33 8N 115 31W
Calistoga, U.S.A. 160 G4 38 35N 122 35W
Calitri, Italy 47 B8 40 54N 15 26 E
Calitzdorp, S. Africa 116 E3 33 33 S 21 42 E
Callabonna, L., Australia 127 D3 29 40 S 140 5 E
Callac, France 26 D3 48 25N 3 27W
Callahan, U.S.A. 152 E8 30 34N 81 50W
Callan, Ireland 23 D4 52 32N 7 24W
Callander, U.K. 22 E4 56 15N 4 13W
Callao, Peru 172 C2 12 0 S 77 0W
Callaway, U.S.A. 152 E4 30 8N 85 36W
Calles, Mexico 163 C5 23 2N 98 42W
Callicoon, U.S.A. 151 E9 41 46N 75 3W
Calling Lake, Canada 142 B6 55 15N 113 12W
Calliope, Australia 126 C5 24 0 S 151 16 E
Callosa de Ensarriá, Spain 41 G4 38 40N 0 8W
Callosa de Segura, Spain 41 G4 38 7N 0 53W
Calmar, U.S.A. 156 A5 43 11N 91 52W
Calne, U.K. 21 F6 51 26N 2 0W
Calola, Angola 116 B2 16 25 S 17 48 E
Calolbon = San Andres, Phil. 80 E5 13 36N 124 6 E
Calonge, Spain 40 D8 41 52N 3 5 E
Caloocan, Phil. 80 D3 14 39N 120 58 E
Caloosahatchee →, U.S.A. 153 J7 26 31N 82 1W
Calore →, Italy 47 A7 41 11N 14 28 E
Caloundra, Australia 127 D5 26 45 S 153 10 E
Calpe, Spain 41 G5 38 39N 0 3 E
Calpella, U.S.A. 160 F3 39 14N 123 12W
Calpine, U.S.A. 160 F6 39 40N 120 27W
Calstock, Canada 140 C3 49 47N 84 9W
Caltabellotta, Italy 46 E6 37 34N 13 13 E
Caltagirone, Italy 47 E7 37 14N 14 31 E
Caltanissetta, Italy 47 E7 37 29N 14 4 E
Çaltılıbük, Turkey 51 G12 39 57N 28 36 E
Caluango, Angola 115 D3 8 20 S 19 39 E
Calubian, Phil. 81 F5 11 27N 124 26 E
Calucinga, Angola 115 E3 11 18 S 16 12 E
Caluire-et-Cuire, France 27 G11 45 48N 4 52 E
Calulo, Angola 115 E2 10 1 S 14 56 E
Calunda, Angola 115 E4 12 7 S 23 36 E
Caluquembe, Angola 115 E2 13 47 S 14 44 E
Caluso, Italy 44 C4 45 18N 7 53 E
Caluya I., Phil. 81 F3 11 55N 121 34 E
Calvados □, France 26 C6 49 5N 0 15W
Calvert →, Australia 126 B2 16 17 S 137 44 E
Calvert I., Canada 142 C3 51 30N 128 0W
Calvert Ra., Australia 124 D3 24 0 S 122 30 E
Calvi, France 29 F12 42 34N 8 45 E
Calviá, Spain 41 F7 39 34N 2 31 E
Calvillo, Mexico 162 C4 21 51N 102 43W
Calvinia, S. Africa 116 E2 31 28 S 19 45 E
Calvo = Calvo, Mte., Italy 45 G12 41 44N 15 46 E
Calvo, Mte., Italy 45 G12 41 44N 15 46 E
Calwa, U.S.A. 160 J7 36 42N 119 46W
Calzada Almuradiel =
Almuradiel, Spain 43 G7 38 32N 3 28W
Calzada de Calatrava, Spain 43 G7 38 42N 3 46W
Cam →, U.K. 21 E8 52 21N 0 16 E
Cam Lam, Vietnam 87 G7 11 54N 109 10 E
Cam Pha, Vietnam 76 G6 21 7N 107 18 E
Cam Ranh, Vietnam 78 B3 11 54N 109 12 E
Cam Xuyen, Vietnam 86 C6 18 15N 106 0 E
Camabatela, Angola 115 D3 8 20 S 15 26 E
Camacã, Brazil 171 E4 15 24 S 39 30W
Camaçari, Brazil 171 D4 12 41 S 38 18W
Camacha, Madeira 39 D3 32 41N 16 49W
Camacho, Mexico 162 C4 24 25N 102 18W
Camacupa, Angola 115 E3 11 58 S 17 22 E
Camaguán, Venezuela 168 B4 8 6N 67 36W
Camagüey, Cuba 164 B4 21 20N 78 0W
Camaiore, Italy 44 E7 43 56N 10 18 E
Camamu, Brazil 171 D4 13 57 S 39 7W
Camaná, Peru 172 D3 16 30 S 72 50W
Camanche, U.S.A. 156 C6 41 47N 90 15W
Camanche Reservoir, U.S.A. 160 G6 38 14N 121 1W
Camapuã, Brazil 173 19 30 S 54 5W
Camaquã, Brazil 175 C5 30 51 S 51 49W
Camaquã →, Brazil 175 C5 31 17 S 51 47W
Câmara de Lobos, Madeira 39 D3 32 39N 16 59W
Camararé →, Brazil 173 C6 12 15 S 58 55W
Camarat, C., France 29 E10 43 12N 6 41 E
Camarès, France 28 E6 43 49N 2 53 E
Camaret-sur-Mer, France 26 D2 48 16N 4 37W
Camargo, Bolivia 173 E4 20 38 S 65 15W
Camargo, Mexico 163 B5 26 19N 98 50W
Camargue, France 29 E8 43 34N 4 34 E
Camarillo, U.S.A. 161 L7 34 13N 119 2W
Camariñas, Spain 42 B1 43 8N 9 12W
Camarines Norte □, Phil. 80 D4 14 10N 122 45 E
Camarines Sur □, Phil. 80 E4 13 40N 123 20 E
Camarón, C., Honduras 164 C2 16 0N 85 5W
Camarones, Argentina 176 B3 44 50 S 65 40W
Camarones, B., Argentina 176 B3 44 45 S 65 35W
Camas, Spain 43 H4 37 24N 6 2W
Camas, U.S.A. 160 E4 45 35N 122 24W
Camas Valley, U.S.A. 158 E2 43 2N 123 40W
Camatambo, Angola 115 D3 6 31 S 15 21 E
Camaxilo, Angola 115 D3 8 21 S 18 56 E
Camba Cassai, Angola 115 D3 9 47 S 19 9 E
Camballin, Australia 124 C3 17 59 S 124 12 E
Cambamba, Angola 115 D2 8 53 S 14 44 E
Cambará, Brazil 175 A5 23 2 S 50 5W
Cambay = Khambhat, India 92 H5 22 23N 72 33 E
Cambil, Spain 43 H7 37 40N 3 33W
Cambo, Angola 115 D3 10 55 S 20 6 E
Cambo-les-Bains, France 28 E2 43 22N 1 23W
Cambodia ■, Asia 78 B3 12 15N 105 0 E
Camborne, U.K. 21 G2 50 12N 5 19W
Cambrai, France 27 B10 50 11N 3 14 E
Cambre, Spain 42 B2 43 17N 8 20W
Cambria, U.S.A. 160 K5 35 34N 121 5W
Cambrian Mts., U.K. 21 E4 52 3N 3 57W
Cambridge, Canada 140 D3 43 23N 80 15W
Cambridge, Jamaica 164 C4 18 18N 77 54W
Cambridge, N.Z. 130 D4 37 54 S 175 29 E
Cambridge, U.K. 21 E8 52 12N 0 8 E
Cambridge, Ill., U.S.A. 156 C6 41 18N 90 12W
Cambridge, Iowa, U.S.A. 156 C3 41 54N 93 32W
Cambridge, Mass., U.S.A. 151 D13 42 22N 71 6W
Cambridge, Minn., U.S.A. 154 C8 45 34N 93 13W
Cambridge, N.Y., U.S.A. 151 C11 43 2N 73 22W
Cambridge, Nebr., U.S.A. 154 E4 40 17N 100 10W
Cambridge, Ohio, U.S.A. 150 F3 40 2N 81 35W
Cambridge Bay = Ikaluktutiak,
Canada 138 B9 69 10N 105 0W
Cambridge City, U.S.A. 157 E11 39 49N 85 10W
Cambridge G., Australia 124 B4 14 55 S 128 15 E
Cambridge Springs, U.S.A. 150 E4 41 48N 80 4W
Cambridgeshire □, U.K. 21 E7 52 25N 0 7W
Cambrils, Spain 40 D6 41 8N 1 3 E
Cambuci, Brazil 171 F3 21 35 S 41 55W
Cambulo, Angola 115 D4 7 49 S 21 15 E
Cambundi-Catembo, Angola 115 E3 10 10 S 17 35 E
Camden, Australia 129 C9 34 1 S 150 43 E
Camden, Ala., U.S.A. 149 K2 31 59N 87 17W
Camden, Ark., U.S.A. 155 J8 33 35N 92 50W
Camden, Maine, U.S.A. 149 C11 44 13N 69 4W
Camden, N.J., U.S.A. 151 G9 39 56N 75 7W
Camden, N.Y., U.S.A. 151 C9 43 20N 75 45W
Camden, Ohio, U.S.A. 157 E12 39 38N 84 39W
Camden, S.C., U.S.A. 149 H5 34 16N 80 36W
Camden Bay, U.S.A. 144 A11 70 10N 145 15W
Camden Sd., Australia 124 C3 15 27 S 124 25 E
Camdenton, U.S.A. 155 F8 38 1N 92 45W
Çameli, Turkey 49 D11 37 5N 29 24 E
Camenca, Moldova 53 B13 48 3N 28 42 E
Camerino, Italy 45 E10 43 8N 13 4 E
Cameron, Ariz., U.S.A. 159 J8 35 53N 111 25W
Cameron, La., U.S.A. 155 L8 29 48N 93 20W
Cameron, Mo., U.S.A. 156 E2 39 44N 94 14W
Cameron, S.C., U.S.A. 152 B9 33 34N 80 43W
Cameron, Tex., U.S.A. 155 K6 30 51N 96 59W
Cameron Highlands, Malaysia 87 K3 4 27N 101 22 E
Cameron Hills, Canada 142 B5 59 48N 118 0W
Cameron Mts., N.Z. 131 G1 46 1 S 167 0 E
Cameroon ■, Africa 114 A2 6 0N 12 30 E
Camerota, Italy 47 B8 40 2N 15 22 E
Cameroun →, Cameroon 113 E6 4 0N 9 35 E
Cameroun, Mt., Cameroon 113 E6 4 13N 9 10 E
Cametá, Brazil 170 B2 2 12 S 49 30W
Çamiçi Gölü, Turkey 49 D9 37 29N 27 28 E
Camiguin □, Phil. 81 G5 9 11N 124 42 E
Camiguin I., Phil. 79 C6 18 56N 121 55 E
Camiling, Phil. 80 D3 15 42N 120 24 E
Camilla, U.S.A. 152 D5 31 14N 84 12W
Caminha, Portugal 42 D2 41 50N 8 50W
Camino, U.S.A. 160 G6 38 44N 120 41W
Camira Creek, Australia 127 D5 29 15 S 152 58 E
Camiranga, Brazil 170 B2 1 48 S 46 17W
Camiri, Bolivia 173 E5 20 3 S 63 31W
Camissombo, Angola 115 D4 8 7 S 20 38 E
Cammal, U.S.A. 150 E7 41 24N 77 28W
Cammarata, Italy 46 E6 37 38N 13 38 E
Camocim, Brazil 170 B3 2 55 S 40 50W
Camooweal, Australia 126 B2 19 56 S 138 7 E
Camopi, Fr. Guiana 169 C7 3 12N 52 17W
Camopi →, Fr. Guiana 169 C7 3 10N 52 20W
Camotes Is., Phil. 81 F5 10 40N 124 24 E
Camotes Sea, Phil. 81 F5 10 30N 124 15 E
Camp Borden, Canada 150 B5 44 18N 79 56W
Camp Hill, Ala., U.S.A. 152 C4 32 48N 85 39W
Camp Hill, Pa., U.S.A. 150 F8 40 14N 76 55W
Camp Nelson, U.S.A. 161 J8 36 8N 118 39W
Camp Pendleton, U.S.A. 161 M9 33 16N 117 23W
Camp Point, U.S.A. 156 D5 40 3N 91 4W
Camp Verde, U.S.A. 159 J8 34 34N 111 51W
Camp Wood, U.S.A. 155 L5 29 40N 100 1W
Campagna, Italy 47 B8 40 40N 15 6 E
Campana, Argentina 174 C4 34 10 S 58 55W
Campana, I., Chile 176 C1 48 20 S 75 20W
Campanário, Madeira 39 D2 32 39N 17 2W
Campanario, Spain 43 G5 38 52N 5 36W
Campânia □, Italy 47 B7 41 0N 14 30 E
Campbell, S. Africa 116 D3 28 48 S 23 44 E
Campbell, Calif., U.S.A. 160 H5 37 17N 121 57W
Campbell, Ohio, U.S.A. 150 E4 41 5N 80 37W
Campbell, C., N.Z. 131 B9 41 47 S 174 18 E
Campbell I., Pac. Oc. 134 N8 52 30 S 169 0 E
Campbell L., Canada 143 A7 63 14N 106 55W
Campbell River, Canada 142 C3 50 5N 125 20W
Campbell Town, Australia 126 G4 41 52 S 147 30 E
Campbellford, Canada 150 B7 44 18N 77 48W
Campbellpur, Pakistan 92 C5 33 46N 72 26 E
Campbellsburg, U.S.A. 157 F10 38 39N 86 16W
Campbellsville, U.S.A. 148 G3 37 21N 85 20W
Campbellton, Canada 141 C6 47 57N 66 43W
Campbellton, U.S.A. 152 E4 30 57N 85 24W
Campbelltown, Australia 129 C9 34 4 S 150 49 E
Campbeltown, U.K. 22 F3 55 26N 5 36W
Campeche, Mexico 163 D6 19 50N 90 32W
Campeche □, Mexico 163 D6 19 50N 90 32W
Campeche, Golfo de, Mexico 163 D6 19 30N 93 0W
Campello, Spain 41 G4 38 26N 0 24W
Câmpeni, Romania 52 D8 46 22N 23 3 E
Camperdown, Australia 128 E5 38 14 S 143 9 E
Camperville, Canada 143 C8 51 59N 100 9W
Campi Salentina, Italy 47 B11 40 24N 18 1 E
Câmpia Turzii, Romania 53 D8 46 34N 23 53 E
Campidano, Italy 46 C1 39 30N 8 47 E
Campíglia Maríttima, Italy 44 E7 43 4N 10 37 E
Campillo de Altobuey, Spain 41 F3 39 36N 1 49W
Campillos, Spain 43 H6 37 4N 4 51W
Câmpina, Romania 53 E10 45 10N 25 45 E
Campina Grande, Brazil 170 C4 7 20 S 35 47W
Campina Verde, Brazil 171 E2 19 31 S 49 28W
Campinas, Brazil 175 A6 22 50 S 47 0W
Campli, Italy 45 F10 42 43N 13 41 E
Campo, Cameroon 114 B1 2 22N 9 50 E
Campo, Spain 40 C5 42 25N 0 24 E
Campo →, Cameroon 114 B2 2 22N 9 49 E
Campo Belo, Brazil 171 F2 20 52 S 45 16W
Campo de Criptana, Spain 43 F7 39 25N 3 7W
Campo de Diauarum, Brazil 173 C7 11 12 S 53 14W
Campo de Gibraltar, Spain 43 J5 36 15N 5 25W
Campo Flórido, Brazil 171 E2 19 47 S 48 35W
Campo Formoso, Brazil 170 D3 10 30 S 40 20W
Campo Grande, Brazil 173 E7 20 25 S 54 40W
Campo Maíor, Brazil 170 B3 4 50 S 42 12W
Campo Maior, Portugal 43 F3 39 2N 7 7W
Campo Mourão, Brazil 175 A5 24 3 S 52 22W
Campo Tencia, Switz. 33 D7 46 26N 8 43 E
Campo Túres, Italy 45 B8 46 53N 11 55 E
Campoalegre, Colombia 168 C2 2 41N 75 20W
Campobasso, Italy 47 A7 41 34N 14 39 E
Campobello di Licata, Italy 46 E6 37 15N 13 55 E
Campobello di Mazara, Italy 46 E5 37 38N 12 45 E
Campofelice di Roccella, Italy 46 E6 37 59N 13 53 E
Campomarino, Italy 45 G12 41 57N 15 2 E
Camporeale, Italy 46 E6 37 54N 13 6 E
Camporrobles, Spain 40 F3 39 39N 1 24W
Campos, Brazil 171 F3 21 50 S 41 20W
Campos Altos, Brazil 171 E2 19 47 S 46 10W
Campos Belos, Brazil 171 D2 13 10 S 47 3W
Campos del Puerto, Spain 39 B10 39 26N 3 1 E
Campos Novos, Brazil 175 B5 27 21 S 51 50W
Campos Sales, Brazil 170 C3 7 4 S 40 23W
Camprodón, Spain 40 C7 42 19N 2 23 E
Campton, Fla., U.S.A. 153 E3 30 53N 86 31W
Campton, Ga., U.S.A. 152 B6 33 52N 83 43W
Campton, Ky., U.S.A. 157 G13 37 44N 83 33W
Camptonville, U.S.A. 160 F5 39 27N 121 3W
Camptown, U.S.A. 151 E8 41 44N 76 14W
Câmpulung, Argeș, Romania 53 E10 45 17N 25 3 E
Câmpulung, Suceava, Romania 53 C10 47 32N 25 30 E
Câmpuri, Romania 53 D11 46 0N 26 50 E
Campuya →, Peru 168 D3 1 40 S 73 30W
Campville, U.S.A. 152 F7 29 40N 82 7W
Camrose, Canada 142 C6 53 0N 112 50W
Camsell Portage, Canada 143 B7 59 37N 109 15W
Camucuio, Angola 115 E2 14 7 S 13 15 E
Çamyuva, Turkey 49 E12 36 30N 30 30 E
Çan, Turkey 51 F11 40 2N 27 3 E
Can Clavo, Spain 39 C7 38 57N 1 27 E
Can Creu, Spain 39 C7 38 58N 1 28 E
Can Gio, Vietnam 87 G6 10 25N 106 58 E
Can Tho, Vietnam 78 B3 10 2N 105 46 E
Canaan, U.S.A. 151 D11 42 2N 73 20W
Canacona, India 95 G2 15 1N 74 4 E
Canada ■, N. Amer. 138 C10 60 0N 100 0W
Cañada de Gómez, Argentina 174 C3 32 40 S 61 30W
Canadian, U.S.A. 155 H4 35 55N 100 23W
Canadian →, U.S.A. 155 H7 35 28N 95 3W
Canadys, U.S.A. 152 B9 33 3N 80 37W
Canajoharie, U.S.A. 151 D10 42 54N 74 35W
Çanakkale, Turkey 51 F10 40 8N 26 24 E
Çanakkale □, Turkey 51 F10 40 10N 26 25 E
Çanakkale Boğazı, Turkey 51 F10 40 17N 26 32 E
Canal Flats, Canada 142 C5 50 10N 115 48W
Canal Point, U.S.A. 153 J9 26 52N 80 38W
Canala, N. Cal. 133 U19 21 32 S 165 57 E
Canalejas, Argentina 174 D2 35 15 S 66 34W
Canals, Argentina 174 C3 33 35 S 62 53W
Canals, Spain 41 G4 38 58N 0 35W
Canandaigua, U.S.A. 150 D7 42 54N 77 17W
Canandaigua L., U.S.A. 150 D7 42 47N 77 19W
Cananea, Mexico 162 A2 31 0N 110 20W
Cañar, Ecuador 168 D2 2 33 S 78 56W
Cañar □, Ecuador 168 D2 2 30 S 79 0W
Canarias, Is., Atl. Oc. 110 C1 28 30N 16 0W
Canarreos, Arch. de los, Cuba 164 B3 21 35N 81 40W
Canary Is. = Canarias, Is.,
Atl. Oc. 110 C1 28 30N 16 0W
Canaseraga, U.S.A. 150 D7 42 27N 77 45W
Canastra, Serra da, Brazil 171 F2 20 0 S 46 20W
Canatlán, Mexico 162 C4 24 31N 104 47W
Cañaveral, Peru 168 D1 3 56 S 80 39W
Canaveral, C., U.S.A. 149 L5 28 27N 80 32W
Cañaveruelas, Spain 40 E2 40 24N 2 38W
Canavieiras, Brazil 171 E4 15 39 S 39 0W
Canbelego, Australia 129 A7 31 32 S 146 18 E
Canberra, Australia 129 C8 35 15 S 149 8 E
Canby, Calif., U.S.A. 158 F3 41 27N 120 52W
Canby, Minn., U.S.A. 154 C6 44 43N 96 16W
Canby, Oreg., U.S.A. 160 E4 45 16N 122 42W
Cancale, France 26 D5 48 40N 1 50W
Canche →, France 27 B8 50 31N 1 39 E
Canchyuaya, Cordillera de,
Peru 172 B3 7 30 S 74 0W
Cancún, Mexico 163 C7 21 8N 86 44W
Candala, Somali Rep. 120 B3 11 30N 49 58 E
Candanchu, Spain 40 C4 42 47N 0 32W
Candarave, Peru 172 D3 17 15 S 70 13W
Çandarlı, Turkey 49 C8 38 56N 26 56 E
Çandarlı Körfezi, Turkey 49 C8 38 52N 26 55 E
Candas, Spain 42 B5 43 35N 5 45W
Candé, France 26 E5 47 34N 1 2W
Candeias →, Brazil 173 B5 8 39 S 63 31W
Candela, Italy 47 A8 41 8N 15 31 E
Candelaria, Argentina 175 B4 27 29 S 55 44W
Candelaria, Canary Is. 39 F3 28 22N 16 22W
Candelaria, Phil. 80 E3 13 56N 121 25 E
Candeleda, Spain 42 E5 40 10N 5 14W
Candelo, Australia 129 D8 36 47 S 149 43 E
Candia = Iráklion, Greece 38 D7 35 20N 25 12 E
Candia, Sea of = Crete, Sea of,
Greece 49 E7 36 0N 25 0 E
Cândido de Abreu, Brazil 171 F1 24 35 S 51 20W
Cândido Mendes, Brazil 170 B2 1 27 S 45 43W
Candle, U.S.A. 144 D7 65 55N 161 56W
Candle L., Canada 143 C7 53 50N 105 18W
Candlemas I., Antarctica 7 B1 57 3 S 26 40W
Cando, U.S.A. 154 A5 48 32N 99 12W
Candon, Phil. 80 C3 17 12N 120 27 E
Canea = Khaniá, Greece 38 D6 35 30N 24 4 E
Canela, Brazil 170 D2 10 15 S 48 25W
Canelli, Italy 44 D5 44 43N 8 17 E
Canelones, Uruguay 175 C4 34 32 S 56 17W
Canet-Plage, France 28 F7 42 41N 3 2 E
Cañete, Chile 174 D1 37 50 S 73 30W
Cañete, Peru 172 C2 13 8 S 76 30W
Cañete, Spain 40 E3 40 3N 1 54W
Cañete de las Torres, Spain 43 H6 37 53N 4 19W
Cangamba, Angola 115 E3 13 40 S 19 54 E
Cangandala, Angola 115 D3 9 45 S 16 33 E
Cangas, Spain 42 C2 42 16N 8 47W
Cangas de Narcea, Spain 42 B4 43 10N 6 32W
Cangas de Onís, Spain 42 B5 43 21N 5 8W
Cangnan, China 77 D13 27 30N 120 23 E
Cangoa, Angola 115 E3 13 8 S 18 30 E
Cangola, Angola 115 D3 7 58 S 15 53 E
Cangolo, Angola 115 E2 15 0 S 13 52 E
Cangombe, Angola 115 E3 14 24 S 19 59 E
Cangongo, Angola 115 D3 9 24 S 17 30 E
Canguaretama, Brazil 170 C4 6 20 S 35 5W
Canguçu, Brazil 175 C5 31 22 S 52 43W
Canguçu, Serra do, Brazil 175 C5 31 20 S 52 40W
Cangumbe, Angola 115 E3 11 58 S 19 12 E
Cangwu, China 77 F8 23 25N 111 17 E
Cangxi, China 76 B5 31 47N 105 59 E
Cangyuan, China 76 F2 23 12N 99 14 E
Cangzhou, China 74 E9 38 19N 116 52 E
Canhoca, Angola 115 D2 9 15 S 14 41 E
Caniapiscau →, Canada 141 A6 56 40N 69 30W
Caniapiscau Rés. de, Canada 141 B6 54 10N 69 55W
Canicattì, Italy 46 E6 37 21N 13 51 E
Canicattini Bagni, Italy 47 E8 37 2N 15 4 E
Canigao Channel, Phil. 81 F5 10 15N 124 42 E
Caniles, Spain 43 H8 37 26N 2 43W
Canim Lake, Canada 142 C4 51 47N 120 54W
Canindé, Brazil 170 B4 4 22 S 39 19W
Canindé →, Brazil 170 C3 6 15 S 42 52W
Canindeyu □, Paraguay 175 A5 24 10 S 55 0W
Canino, Italy 45 F8 42 28N 11 45 E
Canisteo, U.S.A. 150 D7 42 16N 77 36W
Canisteo →, U.S.A. 150 D7 42 7N 77 8W
Cañitas, Mexico 162 C4 23 36N 102 43W
Cañizal, Spain 42 D5 41 12N 5 22W
Canjáyar, Spain 43 H8 37 1N 2 44W
Canjinge, Angola 115 E4 10 12 S 21 17 E
Çankırı, Turkey 100 B5 40 40N 33 37 E
Cankuzo, Burundi 118 C3 3 10 S 30 31 E
Canlaon, Phil. 81 F4 10 22N 123 12 E
Canlaon Volcano, Phil. 81 F4 10 25N 123 8 E
Canmore, Canada 142 C5 51 7N 115 18W
Cann River, Australia 129 D8 37 35 S 149 7 E
Canna, U.K. 22 D2 57 3N 6 33W
Cannanore, India 95 J2 11 53N 75 27 E
Cannelton, U.S.A. 157 G10 37 55N 86 45W
Cannes, France 29 E11 43 32N 7 1 E
Canning Town = Port Canning,
India 93 H13 22 23N 88 40 E
Cannington, Canada 150 B5 44 20N 79 2W
Cannóbio, Italy 44 B5 46 4N 8 42 E
Cannock, U.K. 21 E5 52 41N 2 1W
Cannon Ball →, U.S.A. 154 B4 46 20N 100 38W
Cannondale Mt., Australia 126 D4 25 13 S 148 57 E
Cannonsville Reservoir, U.S.A. 151 D9 42 4N 75 22W
Cannonvale, Australia 126 C4 20 17 S 148 43 E
Caño Colorado, Colombia 168 C4 2 18N 68 22W
Canoas, Brazil 175 B5 29 56 S 51 11W
Canoe L., Canada 143 B7 55 10N 108 15W
Canon City, U.S.A. 154 F2 38 27N 105 14W
Canoochee →, U.S.A. 152 D8 31 59N 81 19W
Canopus, Australia 128 B4 33 29 S 140 42 E
Canora, Canada 143 C8 51 40N 102 30W
Canosa di Púglia, Italy 47 A9 41 13N 16 4 E
Canowindra, Australia 129 B8 33 35 S 148 38 E
Canso, Canada 141 C7 45 20N 61 0W
Canta, Peru 172 C2 11 29 S 76 37W
Cantabria □, Spain 42 B7 43 10N 4 0W
Cantabria, Sierra de, Spain 40 C2 42 40N 2 30W
Cantabrian Mts. = Cantábrica,
Cordillera, Spain 42 C5 43 0N 5 10W
Cantábrica, Cordillera, Spain 42 C5 43 0N 5 10W
Cantal □, France 28 C6 45 5N 2 45 E
Cantal, Plomb du, France 28 C6 45 3N 2 45 E
Cantanhede, Portugal 42 E2 40 20N 8 36W
Cantaura, Venezuela 169 B5 9 19N 64 21W
Cantavieja, Spain 40 E4 40 31N 0 25W
Čantavir, Serbia, Yug. 52 E4 45 55N 19 46 E
Cantemir, Moldova 53 D13 46 17N 28 14 E
Canterbury, Australia 126 D3 25 23 S 141 53 E
Canterbury, U.K. 21 F9 51 16N 1 6 E
Canterbury □, N.Z. 131 D6 43 45 S 171 19 E
Canterbury Bight, N.Z. 131 E6 44 16 S 171 55 E
Canterbury Plains, N.Z. 131 D6 43 55 S 171 22 E
Cantil, U.S.A. 161 K9 35 18N 117 58W
Cantilan, Phil. 81 G5 9 20N 125 58 E
Cantillana, Spain 43 H5 37 36N 5 50W
Canto do Buriti, Brazil 170 C3 8 7 S 42 58W
Canton = Guangzhou, China 77 F9 23 5N 113 10 E
Canton, Ga., U.S.A. 149 H3 34 14N 84 29W
Canton, Ill., U.S.A. 156 D6 40 33N 90 2W
Canton, Miss., U.S.A. 155 J9 32 37N 90 2W
Canton, Mo., U.S.A. 156 D5 40 8N 91 32W
Canton, N.Y., U.S.A. 151 B9 44 36N 75 10W
Canton, Ohio, U.S.A. 150 F3 40 48N 81 23W
Canton, Pa., U.S.A. 150 E8 41 39N 76 51W
Canton, S. Dak., U.S.A. 154 D6 43 18N 96 35W
Canton L., U.S.A. 155 G5 36 6N 98 35W
Cantonment, U.S.A. 153 E2 30 37N 87 20W
Cantù, Italy 44 C6 45 44N 9 8 E
Cantwell, U.S.A. 144 E10 63 24N 148 57W
Canudos, Brazil 173 B6 7 13 S 58 5W
Canumã, Amazonas, Brazil 169 D6 4 2 S 59 4W
Canumã, Amazonas, Brazil 173 B5 6 8 S 60 10W
Canumã →, Brazil 173 A6 3 55 S 59 10W
Canutama, Brazil 173 B5 6 30 S 64 20W
Canutillo, U.S.A. 159 L10 31 55N 106 36W
Canvey, U.K. 21 F8 51 31N 0 37 E
Canyon, U.S.A. 155 H4 34 59N 101 55W
Canyonlands National Park,
U.S.A. 159 G9 38 15N 110 0W
Canyonville, U.S.A. 158 E2 42 56N 123 17W
Canzar, Angola 115 D4 7 35 S 21 34 E
Cao Bang, Vietnam 76 F6 22 40N 106 15 E
Cao He →, China 75 D13 40 10N 124 32 E
Cao Lanh, Vietnam 87 G5 10 27N 105 38 E
Cao Xian, China 74 G8 34 50N 115 35 E
Caombo, Angola 115 D3 8 42 S 16 33 E
Cáorle, Italy 45 C9 45 36N 12 53 E
Cap-aux-Meules, Canada 141 C7 47 23N 61 52W
Cap-Chat, Canada 141 C6 49 6N 66 40W
Cap-de-la-Madeleine, Canada 140 C5 46 22N 72 31W
Cap-Haïtien, Haiti 165 C5 19 40N 72 20W
Cap I., Phil. 81 J3 5 57N 120 6 E
Capac, U.S.A. 150 C2 43 1N 82 56W
Capáccio, Italy 47 B8 40 25N 15 5 E
Capaci, Italy 46 D6 38 10N 13 14 E
Capaia, Angola 115 D4 8 27 S 20 13 E
Capalonga, Phil. 80 D4 14 20N 122 30 E
Capanaparo →, Venezuela 168 B4 7 1N 67 7W
Capanema, Brazil 170 B2 1 12 S 47 11W
Capangombe, Angola 115 F2 15 6 S 13 8 E
Capánnori, Italy 44 E7 43 50N 10 34 E
Caparo →, Barinas, Venezuela 168 B3 7 46N 70 23W
Caparo →, Bolívar, Venezuela 169 B5 7 30N 64 0W
Capatárida, Venezuela 168 A3 11 11N 70 37W
Capayas, Phil. 81 F2 10 28N 119 39 E
Capbreton, France 28 E2 43 39N 1 26W
Capdenac, France 28 D6 44 34N 2 5 E
Capdepera, Spain 40 F8 39 42N 3 26 E
Cape →, Australia 126 C4 20 59 S 146 51 E
Cape Barren I., Australia 126 G4 40 25 S 148 15 E
Cape Breton Highlands Nat.
Park, Canada 141 C7 46 50N 60 40W
Cape Breton I., Canada 141 C7 46 0N 60 30W
Cape Canaveral, U.S.A. 153 G9 28 24N 80 36W
Cape Charles, U.S.A. 148 G8 37 16N 76 1W
Cape Coast, Ghana 113 D4 5 5N 1 15W
Cape Coral, U.S.A. 149 M5 26 33N 81 57W
Cape Dorset, Canada 139 B12 64 14N 76 32W
Cape Fear →, U.S.A. 149 H6 33 53N 78 1W
Cape Girardeau, U.S.A. 155 G10 37 19N 89 32W
Cape Jervis, Australia 128 C3 35 40 S 138 5 E
Cape May, U.S.A. 148 F8 38 56N 74 56W
Cape May Point, U.S.A. 148 F8 38 56N 74 58W
Cape Pole, U.S.A. 144 J14 55 58N 133 48W

Chandan Chauki 199

Castro Verde, Portugal 43 H2 37 41N 8 4W
Castrojeriz, Spain 42 C6 42 17N 4 9W
Castropol, Spain 42 B4 43 32N 7 0W
Castroreale, Italy 47 D8 38 6N 15 12 E
Castrovíllari, Italy 47 C9 39 49N 16 12 E
Castroville, U.S.A. 160 J5 36 46N 121 45W
Castrovirreyna, Peru 172 C2 13 20 S 75 18W
Castuera, Spain 43 G5 38 43N 5 37W
Caswell Sound, N.Z. 131 E2 44 59 S 167 8 E
Çat, Turkey 101 C9 39 40N 41 3 E
Cat Ba, Dao, Vietnam 86 B6 20 50N 107 0 E
Cat I., Bahamas 165 B4 24 30N 75 30W
Cat L., Canada 140 B1 51 40N 91 50W
Cat Lake, Canada 140 B1 51 40N 91 50W
Čata, Slovak Rep. 35 D11 47 58N 18 38 E
Catabola, Angola 115 E3 12 9 S 17 16 E
Catacamas, Honduras 164 D2 14 54N 85 56W
Catacáos, Peru 172 B1 5 20 S 80 45W
Cataguases, Brazil 171 F3 21 23 S 42 39W
Catagupan, Phil. 81 G1 8 1N 116 58 E
Cataingan, Phil. 80 E4 12 0N 124 0 E
Çatak, Turkey 101 C10 38 1N 43 8 E
Catalão, Brazil 171 E2 18 10 S 47 57W
Çatalca, Turkey 51 E12 41 8N 28 27 E
Catalina, Canada 141 C9 48 31N 53 4W
Catalina, Chile 174 B2 25 13 S 69 43W
Catalina, U.S.A. 159 K8 32 30N 110 50W
Catalonia = Cataluña □, Spain 40 D6 41 40N 1 15 E
Cataluña □, Spain 40 D6 41 40N 1 15 E
Çatalzeytin, Turkey 100 B6 41 57N 34 12 E
Catamarca, Argentina 174 B2 28 30 S 65 50W
Catamarca □, Argentina 174 B2 27 0 S 65 50W
Catanauan, Phil. 80 E4 13 36N 122 19 E
Catanduanes □, Phil. 79 B6 13 50N 124 20 E
Catanduva, Brazil 175 A6 21 5 S 48 58W
Catánia, Italy 47 E8 37 30N 15 6 E
Catánia, G. di, Italy 47 E8 37 24N 15 9 E
Catanzaro, Italy 47 D9 38 54N 16 35 E
Catarman, Camiguin, Phil. 81 G5 9 8N 124 40 E
Catarman, N. Samar, Phil. 79 B6 12 28N 124 35 E
Catatumba →, Venezuela 168 B3 9 21N 71 45W
Cataula, U.S.A. 152 C5 32 39N 84 52W
Catbalogan, Phil. 81 F5 11 46N 124 53 E
Cateco Cangola, Angola 115 D3 8 28 S 15 51 E
Cateel, Phil. 79 C7 7 47N 126 24 E
Cateel Bay, Phil. 81 H6 7 54N 126 25 E
Catembe, Mozam. 117 D5 26 0 S 32 33 E
Catende, Angola 115 E4 11 14 S 21 30 E
Catende, Brazil 170 C4 8 40 S 35 43W
Caterham, U.K. 21 F7 51 15N 0 4W
Catete, Angola 115 D2 9 6 S 13 43 E
Cathcart, Australia 129 D8 36 52 S 149 24 E
Cathcart, S. Africa 116 E4 32 18 S 27 10 E
Cathlamet, U.S.A. 160 D3 46 12N 123 23W
Catio, Guinea-Biss. 112 C1 11 17N 15 15W
Catismiña, Venezuela 169 C5 4 5N 63 40W
Catita, Brazil 170 C3 9 31 S 43 1W
Catlettsburg, U.S.A. 148 F4 38 25N 82 36W
Catlin, U.S.A. 157 D9 40 4N 87 42W
Çatma Dağı, Turkey 49 C11 38 25N 29 50 E
Catmon, Phil. 81 F5 10 43N 124 1 E
Catoche, C., Mexico 163 C7 21 40N 87 8W
Catolé do Rocha, Brazil 170 C4 6 21 S 37 45W
Catota, Angola 115 E3 13 57 S 17 30 E
Cátria, Mte., Italy 45 E9 43 28N 12 42 E
Catriló, Argentina 174 D3 36 26 S 63 24W
Catrimani, Brazil 169 C5 0 27N 61 41W
Catrimani →, Brazil 169 C5 0 28N 61 44W
Catskill, U.S.A. 151 D11 42 14N 73 52W
Catskill Mts., U.S.A. 151 D10 42 10N 74 25W
Catt, Mt., Australia 126 A1 13 49 S 134 23 E
Cattaraugus, U.S.A. 150 D6 42 22N 78 52W
Cattólica, Italy 45 E9 43 58N 12 44 E
Cattólica Eraclea, Italy 46 E6 37 26N 13 24 E
Catu, Brazil 171 D4 12 21 S 38 23W
Catuala, Angola 116 B2 16 25 S 19 2 E
Catuane, Mozam. 117 D5 26 48 S 32 18 E
Catubig, Phil. 80 E5 12 24N 125 3 E
Catumbela, Angola 115 E2 12 25 S 13 34 E
Catumbela →, Angola 115 E2 12 29 S 13 28 E
Catur, Mozam. 119 E4 13 45 S 35 30 E
Catwick Is., Vietnam 87 G7 10 0N 109 0 E
Cauayan, Phil. 80 C3 16 56N 121 46 E
Cauayan, Neg. Occ., Phil. 81 G4 9 58N 122 37 E
Cauca □, Colombia 168 C2 2 30N 76 50W
Cauca →, Colombia 168 B3 8 54N 74 28W
Caucaia, Brazil 170 B4 3 40 S 38 35W
Caucasia, Colombia 168 B2 8 0N 75 12W
Caucasus Mountains, Eurasia 61 J7 42 50N 44 0 E
Caudete, Spain 41 G3 38 42N 1 2W
Caudry, France 27 B10 50 7N 3 22 E
Caulnes, France 26 D4 48 18N 2 10W
Caulónia, Italy 47 D9 38 23N 16 24 E
Caungula, Angola 115 D3 8 26 S 18 38 E
Cauquenes, Chile 174 D1 36 0 S 72 22W
Caura →, Venezuela 169 B5 7 38N 64 53W
Caurés →, Brazil 169 D5 1 21 S 62 20W
Cauresi →, Mozam. 119 F3 17 8 S 33 0 E
Căuşani, Moldova 53 D14 46 38N 29 25 E
Causapscal, Canada 141 C6 48 19N 67 12W
Caussade, France 28 D5 44 10N 1 33 E
Causse-Méjean, France 28 D7 44 18N 3 42 E
Cauterets, France 28 F3 42 52N 0 8W
Caux, Pays de, France 26 C7 49 38N 0 35 E
Cava de' Tirreni, Italy 47 B7 40 42N 14 42 E
Cávado →, Portugal 42 D2 41 32N 8 48W
Cavaillon, France 29 E9 43 50N 5 2 E
Cavalaire-sur-Mer, France 29 E10 43 10N 6 33 E
Cavalcante, Brazil 171 D2 13 48 S 47 30W
Cavalese, Italy 45 B8 46 17N 11 27 E
Cavalier, U.S.A. 154 A6 48 48N 97 37W
Cavalla = Cavally →, Africa 112 E3 4 22N 7 32W
Cavalleria, C. de, Spain 39 A11 40 5N 4 5 E
Cavalli Is., N.Z. 130 B2 35 0 S 173 58 E
Cavallo, I. de, France 29 G13 41 22N 9 16 E
Cavally →, Africa 112 E3 4 22N 7 32W
Cavan, Ireland 23 B4 54 0N 7 22W
Cavan □, Ireland 23 C4 54 1N 7 16W
Cavárzere, Italy 45 C9 45 8N 12 5 E
Çavdarhisar, Turkey 49 B11 39 12N 29 37 E
Çavdır, Turkey 49 D11 37 10N 29 42 E
Cave Creek, U.S.A. 159 K7 33 50N 111 57W
Cave Run L., U.S.A. 157 F13 38 5N 83 25W
Cave Spring, U.S.A. 152 A4 34 6N 85 20W
Cavenagh Ra., Australia 125 E4 26 12 S 127 55 E
Cavendish, Australia 128 D5 37 31 S 142 2 E
Caviana, I., Brazil 169 C7 0 10N 50 10W
Cavite, Phil. 79 B6 14 29N 120 55 E
Cavite □, Phil. 80 D3 14 15N 120 50 E
Cavnic, Romania 53 C8 47 40N 23 52 E
Cavour, Italy 44 D4 44 47N 7 22 E
Cavtat, Croatia 50 D2 42 35N 18 13 E
Cawayan, Phil. 81 F4 11 56N 123 46 E
Cawkers Well, Australia 128 A5 31 41 S 142 57 E
Cawndilla L., Australia 128 B5 32 30 S 142 15 E
Cawnpore = Kanpur, India 93 F9 26 28N 80 20 E
Caxias, Brazil 170 B3 4 55 S 43 20W
Caxias do Sul, Brazil 175 B5 29 10 S 51 10W
Caxito, Angola 115 D2 8 30 S 13 30 E
Caxopa, Angola 115 E4 11 52 S 20 52 E
Çay, Turkey 100 C4 38 35N 31 1 E
Cay Sal Bank, Bahamas 164 B4 23 45N 80 0W
Cayambe, Napo, Ecuador 168 C2 0 2N 77 59W
Cayambe, Quito, Ecuador 168 C2 0 3N 78 8W
Çaycuma, Turkey 100 B5 41 25N 32 4 E
Çayeli, Turkey 101 B9 41 5N 40 45 E
Cayenne, Fr. Guiana 169 B7 5 5N 52 18W
Cayenne □, Fr. Guiana 169 C7 5 0N 53 0W
Caygören Barajı, Turkey 49 B10 39 15N 28 12 E
Cayiralan, Turkey 100 C6 39 17N 35 38 E
Caylus, France 28 D5 44 15N 1 47 E
Cayman Brac, Cayman Is. 164 C4 19 43N 79 49W
Cayman Is. ■, W. Indies 164 C3 19 40N 80 30W
Cayo Romano, Cuba 164 B4 22 0N 78 0W
Cayres, France 28 D7 44 55N 3 48 E
Cayuga, Canada 150 D5 42 59N 79 50W
Cayuga, Ind., U.S.A. 157 E9 39 57N 87 28W
Cayuga, N.Y., U.S.A. 151 D8 42 54N 76 44W
Cayuga L., U.S.A. 151 D8 42 41N 76 41W
Cazage, Angola 115 E4 11 2 S 20 45 E
Cazage, Angola 115 E4 11 2 S 20 45 E
Cazalla de la Sierra, Spain 43 H5 37 56N 5 45W
Căzănești, Romania 53 F12 44 36N 27 3 E
Cazaubon, France 28 E3 43 56N 0 3W
Cazaux et de Sanguinet, Étang de, France 28 D2 44 29N 1 10W
Cazenovia, U.S.A. 151 D9 42 56N 75 51W
Cazères, France 28 E5 43 13N 1 5 E
Cazin, Bos.-H. 45 D12 44 57N 15 57 E
Čazma, Croatia 45 C13 45 45N 16 39 E
Cazombo, Angola 115 E4 11 54 S 22 56 E
Cazorla, Spain 43 H7 37 55N 3 2W
Cazorla, Sierra de, Spain 43 G8 38 5N 2 55W
Cea →, Spain 42 C5 42 0N 5 36W
Ceamurlia de Jos, Romania 53 F13 44 43N 28 47 E
Ceanannus Mor, Ireland 23 C5 53 44N 6 53W
Ceará = Fortaleza, Brazil 170 B4 3 45 S 38 35W
Ceará □, Brazil 170 C4 5 0 S 40 0W
Ceará Mirim, Brazil 170 C4 5 38 S 35 25W
Ceauru, L., Romania 53 F8 44 58N 23 11 E
Cebaco, I. de, Panama 164 E3 7 33N 81 9W
Cebollar, Argentina 174 B2 29 10 S 66 35W
Cebollera, Sierra de, Spain 40 D2 42 0N 2 30W
Cebreros, Spain 42 E6 40 27N 4 28W
Cebu, Phil. 79 B6 10 18N 123 54 E
Cebu □, Phil. 81 F4 10 20N 123 40 E
Čečava, Bos.-H. 52 F2 44 42N 17 44 E
Ceccano, Italy 46 A6 41 34N 13 20 E
Cece, Hungary 52 D3 46 46N 18 39 E
Cechi, Ivory C. 112 D4 6 15N 4 25W
Cecil Plains, Australia 127 D5 27 30 S 151 11 E
Cécina, Italy 44 E7 43 19N 10 31 E
Cécina →, Italy 44 E7 43 18N 10 29 E
Ceclavín, Spain 42 F4 39 50N 6 45W
Cedar →, U.S.A. 156 C5 41 17N 91 21W
Cedar City, U.S.A. 159 H7 37 41N 113 4W
Cedar Creek Reservoir, U.S.A. 155 J6 32 11N 96 4W
Cedar Falls, Iowa, U.S.A. 156 B4 42 32N 92 27W
Cedar Falls, Wash., U.S.A. 160 C5 47 25N 121 45W
Cedar Grove, U.S.A. 157 E12 39 22N 84 56W
Cedar Key, U.S.A. 149 L4 29 8N 83 2W
Cedar L., Canada 143 C9 53 10N 100 0W
Cedar Lake, U.S.A. 157 C9 41 22N 87 26W
Cedar Point, U.S.A. 157 C13 41 44N 83 21W
Cedar Rapids, U.S.A. 156 C5 41 59N 91 40W
Cedartown, U.S.A. 152 A4 34 1N 85 15W
Cedarvale, Canada 142 B3 55 1N 128 22W
Cedarville, S. Africa 117 E4 30 23 S 29 3 E
Cedarville, Ill., U.S.A. 156 B7 42 23N 89 38W
Cedarville, Ohio, U.S.A. 157 E13 39 44N 83 49W
Cedeira, Spain 42 B2 43 39N 8 2W
Cedral, Mexico 162 C4 23 50N 100 42W
Cedrino →, Italy 46 B2 40 11N 9 24 E
Cedro, Brazil 170 C4 6 34 S 39 3W
Cedros, I. de, Mexico 162 B1 28 10N 115 20W
Ceduna, Australia 127 E1 32 7 S 133 46 E
Cedynia, Poland 55 F1 52 53N 14 12 E
Cée, Spain 42 C1 42 57N 9 10W
Cefalù, Italy 47 D7 38 2N 14 1 E
Cega →, Spain 42 D6 41 33N 4 46W
Cegléd, Hungary 52 C4 47 11N 19 47 E
Céglie Messápico, Italy 47 B10 40 39N 17 31 E
Cehegín, Spain 41 G3 38 6N 1 48W
Ceheng, China 76 E5 24 58N 105 48 E
Cehu-Silvaniei, Romania 53 C8 47 24N 23 9 E
Ceica, Romania 52 D7 46 53N 22 10 E
Ceira →, Portugal 42 E2 40 13N 8 16W
Cekhira, Tunisia 108 B2 34 20N 10 5 E
Cela, Angola 115 E3 11 25 S 15 7 E
Čelákovice, Czech Rep. 34 A7 50 10N 14 46 E
Celano, Italy 45 F10 42 5N 13 33 E
Celanova, Spain 42 C3 42 9N 7 58W
Celaya, Mexico 162 C4 20 31N 100 37W
Celebes = Sulawesi □, Indonesia 82 B2 2 0 S 120 0 E
Celebes Sea, Indonesia 79 D6 3 0N 123 0 E
Celendín, Peru 172 B2 6 52 S 78 10W
Čelić, Bos.-H. 52 F3 44 43N 18 49 E
Celica, Ecuador 168 D2 4 7 S 79 59W
Celina, U.S.A. 157 D12 40 33N 84 35W
Celinac, Bos.-H. 52 F2 44 44N 17 22 E
Celje, Slovenia 45 B12 46 16N 15 18 E
Celldömölk, Hungary 52 C2 47 16N 17 10 E
Celle, Germany 30 C6 52 37N 10 4 E
Celorico da Beira, Portugal 42 E3 40 38N 7 24W
Celtic Sea, Atl. Oc. 8 C8 50 9N 9 34W
Çeltikçi, Turkey 49 D12 37 32N 30 29 E
Çemişgezek, Turkey 101 C8 39 3N 38 56 E
Cenderwasih, Teluk, Indonesia 79 E9 3 0 S 135 20 E
Cenepa →, Peru 168 D2 4 40 S 78 10W
Cengong, China 76 D7 27 13N 108 44 E
Ceno →, Italy 44 D7 44 4N 10 5 E
Centallo, Italy 44 D4 44 30N 7 35 E
Centelles, Spain 40 D7 41 50N 2 14 E
Centenário do Sul, Brazil 171 F1 22 48 S 51 36W
Center, N. Dak., U.S.A. 154 B4 47 7N 101 18W
Center, Tex., U.S.A. 155 K7 31 48N 94 11W
Center Hill, U.S.A. 153 G7 28 38N 82 3W
Center Point, U.S.A. 156 B5 42 12N 91 46W
Centerburg, U.S.A. 150 F2 40 18N 82 42W
Centerville, Calif., U.S.A. 160 J7 36 44N 119 30W
Centerville, Iowa, U.S.A. 156 D4 40 44N 92 52W
Centerville, Mich., U.S.A. 157 C11 41 55N 85 32W
Centerville, Ohio, U.S.A. 157 E12 39 38N 84 8W
Centerville, Pa., U.S.A. 150 F5 40 3N 79 59W
Centerville, Tenn., U.S.A. 149 H2 35 47N 87 28W
Centerville, Tex., U.S.A. 155 K7 31 16N 95 59W
Cento, Italy 45 D8 44 43N 11 17 E
Central, Brazil 170 D3 11 8 S 42 8W
Central, U.S.A. 144 D11 65 35N 144 48W
Central □, Ghana 113 D4 5 30N 1 0W
Central □, Kenya 118 C4 0 30 S 37 30 E
Central □, Malawi 119 E3 13 30 S 33 30 E
Central □, Zambia 119 E2 14 25 S 28 50 E
Central, Cordillera, Bolivia 173 D5 18 30 S 64 55W
Central, Cordillera, Colombia 168 C2 5 0N 75 0W
Central, Cordillera, Costa Rica 164 D3 10 10N 84 5W
Central, Cordillera, Dom. Rep. 165 C5 19 15N 71 0W
Central, Cordillera, Peru 172 B2 7 0 S 77 30W
Central, Cordillera, Phil. 80 C3 17 20N 120 57 E
Central African Rep. ■, Africa 114 A4 7 0N 20 0 E
Central America, America 136 H11 12 0N 85 0W
Central Butte, Canada 143 C7 50 48N 106 31W
Central City, Colo., U.S.A. 158 G11 39 48N 105 31W
Central City, Iowa, U.S.A. 156 B5 42 12N 91 32W
Central City, Ky., U.S.A. 148 G2 37 18N 87 7W
Central City, Nebr., U.S.A. 154 E6 41 7N 98 0W
Central I., Kenya 118 B4 3 30N 36 0 E
Central Makran Range, Pakistan 91 D2 26 30N 64 15 E
Central Patricia, Canada 140 B1 51 30N 90 9W
Central Point, U.S.A. 158 E2 42 23N 122 55W
Central Ra., Papua N. G. 132 C2 5 0 S 143 0 E
Central Russian Uplands, Europe 12 E13 54 0N 36 0 E
Central Siberian Plateau, Russia 66 C14 65 0N 105 0 E
Central Square, U.S.A. 151 C8 43 17N 76 9W
Centralia, Ill., U.S.A. 156 F7 38 32N 89 8W
Centralia, Mo., U.S.A. 156 E4 39 13N 92 8W
Centralia, Wash., U.S.A. 160 D4 46 43N 122 58W
Centre, U.S.A. 152 A4 34 9N 85 41W
Century, U.S.A. 153 E2 30 58N 87 16W
Cenxi, China 77 F8 22 57N 110 57 E
Čeotina →, Bos.-H. 50 C2 43 36N 18 50 E
Cephalonia = Kefallinía, Greece 48 C2 38 20N 20 30 E
Čepin, Croatia 52 E3 45 32N 18 34 E
Ceprano, Italy 46 A6 41 33N 13 31 E
Ceptia, Angola 115 E3 12 56 S 17 35 E
Ceptura, Romania 53 E11 45 1N 26 21 E
Cepu, Indonesia 79 G14 7 9 S 111 35 E
Ceram = Seram, Indonesia 79 E7 3 10 S 129 0 E
Ceram Sea = Seram Sea, Indonesia 79 E7 2 30 S 128 30 E
Cerbère, France 28 F7 42 26N 3 10 E
Cerbicales, Is., France 29 G13 41 33N 9 22 E
Cercal, Portugal 43 H2 37 48N 8 40W
Cerdaña, Spain 40 C6 42 22N 1 35 E
Cère →, France 28 D5 44 55N 1 49 E
Cerea, Italy 45 C8 45 12N 11 13 E
Ceredigion □, U.K. 21 E3 52 16N 4 15W
Ceres, Argentina 174 B3 29 55 S 61 55W
Ceres, Brazil 171 E2 15 17 S 49 35W
Ceres, S. Africa 116 E2 33 21 S 19 18 E
Ceres, U.S.A. 160 H6 37 35N 120 57W
Céret, France 28 F6 42 30N 2 42 E
Cereté, Colombia 168 B2 8 53N 75 48W
Cergy, France 27 C9 49 2N 2 4 E
Cerignola, Italy 47 A8 41 17N 15 53 E
Cerigo = Kíthira, Greece 48 E5 36 8N 23 0 E
Cérilly, France 27 F9 46 37N 2 50 E
Cerisiers, France 27 D10 48 8N 3 30 E
Cerizay, France 26 F6 46 50N 0 40W
Çerkeş, Turkey 100 B5 40 49N 32 52 E
Çerkezköy, Turkey 51 E12 41 17N 28 0 E
Cerknica, Slovenia 45 C11 45 48N 14 21 E
Cerkovica, Bulgaria 51 C8 43 41N 24 50 E
Cermerno, Serbia, Yug. 50 C4 43 35N 20 25 E
Çermik, Turkey 101 C8 38 8N 39 26 E
Cerna, Romania 53 E13 45 4N 28 17 E
Cerna →, Romania 53 F8 44 38N 23 58 E
Cernavodă, Romania 53 F13 44 22N 28 3 E
Cernay, France 27 E14 47 44N 7 10 E
Cernik, Croatia 52 E2 45 17N 17 22 E
Cerralvo, I., Mexico 162 C3 24 20N 109 45W
Cërrik, Albania 50 E3 41 2N 19 58 E
Cerritos, Mexico 162 C4 22 27N 100 20W
Cerro Chato, Uruguay 175 C4 33 6 S 55 8W
Cerro Gordo, U.S.A. 157 E8 39 53N 88 44W
Cerro Sombrero, Chile 176 D3 52 45 S 69 15W
Certaldo, Italy 44 E8 43 33N 11 2 E
Cervantes, Phil. 80 C3 17 0N 120 44 E
Cervaro →, Italy 47 A8 41 30N 15 52 E
Cervati, Monte, Italy 47 B8 40 17N 15 29 E
Cerventes, Australia 125 F2 30 31 S 115 3 E
Cervera, Spain 40 D6 41 40N 1 16 E
Cervera de Pisuerga, Spain 42 C6 42 51N 4 30W
Cervera del Río Alhama, Spain 40 C3 42 2N 1 58W
Cervéteri, Italy 45 F9 42 0N 12 6 E
Cérvia, Italy 45 D9 44 15N 12 22 E
Cervignano del Friuli, Italy 45 C10 45 49N 13 20 E
Cervinara, Italy 47 A7 41 1N 14 37 E
Cervione, France 29 F13 42 20N 9 29 E
Cervo, Spain 42 B3 43 40N 7 24W
César □, Colombia 168 B3 9 0N 73 30W
Cesarò, Italy 47 E7 37 50N 14 38 E
Cesena, Italy 45 D9 44 8N 12 15 E
Cesenático, Italy 45 D9 44 12N 12 24 E
Cēsis, Latvia 15 H21 57 18N 25 15 E
Česká Lípa, Czech Rep. 34 A7 50 45N 14 30 E
Česká Třebová, Czech Rep. 35 B9 49 54N 16 27 E
České Budějovice, Czech Rep. 34 C7 48 55N 14 25 E
České Velenice, Czech Rep. 34 C7 48 45N 14 57 E
Českomoravská Vrchovina, Czech Rep. 34 B8 49 30N 15 40 E
Český Brod, Czech Rep. 34 A7 50 4N 14 52 E
Český Krumlov, Czech Rep. 34 C7 48 43N 14 21 E
Český Těšín, Czech Rep. 35 B11 49 45N 18 39 E
Česma →, Croatia 45 C13 45 35N 16 29 E
Çeşme, Turkey 49 C8 38 20N 26 23 E
Cessnock, Australia 129 B9 32 50 S 151 21 E
Cesson-Sévigné, France 26 D5 48 7N 1 36W
Cestas, France 28 D3 44 44N 0 41W
Cestos →, Liberia 112 D3 5 40N 9 10W
Cetate, Romania 52 F8 44 7N 23 2 E
Cetin Grad, Croatia 45 C12 45 9N 15 45 E
Cetina →, Croatia 45 E13 43 26N 16 42 E
Cetinje, Montenegro, Yug. 50 D2 42 23N 18 59 E
Cetraro, Italy 47 C8 39 31N 15 55 E
Ceuta, N. Afr. 110 A3 35 52N 5 18W
Ceva, Italy 44 D5 44 23N 8 2 E
Ceve-i-Ra, Fiji 123 E13 21 46 S 174 31 E
Cévennes, France 28 D7 44 10N 3 50 E
Cevio, Switz. 33 D7 46 19N 8 36 E
Ceyhan, Turkey 100 D6 37 4N 35 47 E
Ceyhan →, Turkey 100 D6 36 38N 35 40 E
Ceylânpınar, Turkey 101 D9 36 50N 40 2 E
Ceylon = Sri Lanka ■, Asia 95 L5 7 30N 80 50 E
Cèze →, France 29 D8 44 6N 4 43 E
Cha-am, Thailand 86 F2 12 48N 99 58 E
Cha Pa, Vietnam 86 A4 22 20N 103 47 E
Chá Pungana, Angola 115 E3 13 44 S 18 39 E
Chabanais, France 28 C4 45 50N 0 48 E
Chabeuil, France 29 D9 44 54N 5 3 E
Chablais, France 27 F13 46 20N 6 36 E
Chablis, France 27 E10 47 47N 3 48 E
Chabounia, Algeria 111 A5 35 30N 2 38 E
Chacabuco, Argentina 174 C3 34 40 S 60 27W
Chachapoyas, Peru 172 B2 6 15 S 77 50W
Chachasp, Peru 172 D3 15 30 S 72 15W
Chachoengsao, Thailand 86 F3 13 42N 101 5 E
Chachro, Pakistan 92 G4 25 5N 70 15 E
Chaco □, Argentina 174 B3 26 30 S 61 0W
Chaco □, Paraguay 174 B4 26 0 S 60 0W
Chaco →, U.S.A. 159 H9 36 46N 108 39W
Chacon, C., U.S.A. 142 C2 54 42N 132 0W
Chad ■, Africa 109 F3 15 0N 17 15 E
Chad, L. = Tchad, L., Chad 109 F2 13 30N 14 30 E
Chadan, Russia 65 D10 51 17N 91 35 E
Chadileuvú →, Argentina 174 D2 37 46 S 66 0W
Chadiza, Zambia 119 E3 14 45 S 32 27 E
Chadron, U.S.A. 154 D3 42 50N 103 0W
Chadyr-Lunga = Ciadâr-Lunga, Moldova 53 D13 46 3N 28 51 E
Chae Hom, Thailand 86 C2 18 43N 99 35 E
Chaem →, Thailand 86 C2 18 11N 98 38 E
Chaeryŏng, N. Korea 75 E13 38 24N 125 36 E
Chagda, Russia 65 D14 58 45N 130 38 E
Chagny, France 27 F11 46 57N 4 45 E
Chagoda, Russia 58 C8 59 10N 35 15 E
Chagos Arch., Ind. Oc. 66 K11 6 0 S 72 0 E
Chagrin Falls, U.S.A. 150 E3 41 26N 81 24W
Chāh Ākhvor, Iran 97 C8 32 41N 59 40 E
Chāh Bahār, Iran 97 E9 25 20N 60 40 E
Chāh-e Kavīr, Iran 97 C8 34 29N 56 52 E
Chāh Gay Hills, Afghan. 91 C1 29 30N 64 0 E
Chahār Borjak, Afghan. 91 C1 30 17N 62 3 E
Chahār Mahāll va Bakhtīarī □, Iran 97 C6 32 0N 49 0 E
Chahtung, Burma 90 B7 26 41N 98 10 E
Chaillé-les-Marais, France 28 B2 46 25N 1 2W
Chainat, Thailand 86 E3 15 11N 100 8 E
Chaires, U.S.A. 152 E5 30 26N 84 7W
Chaitén, Chile 176 B2 42 55 S 72 43W
Chaiya, Thailand 87 H2 9 23N 99 14 E
Chaj Doab, Pakistan 92 C5 32 15N 73 0 E
Chajari, Argentina 174 C4 30 42 S 58 0W
Chak Amru, Pakistan 92 C6 32 22N 75 11 E
Chaka, Sudan 107 G3 4 49N 31 14 E
Chakar →, Pakistan 92 E3 29 29N 68 2 E
Chakari, Zimbabwe 117 B4 18 5 S 29 51 E
Chakaria, Bangla. 90 E4 21 45N 92 5 E
Chake Chake, Tanzania 118 D4 5 15 S 39 45 E
Chakhānsūr, Afghan. 91 C1 31 10N 62 0 E
Chakonipau, L., Canada 141 A6 56 18N 68 30W
Chakradharpur, India 93 H11 22 45N 85 40 E
Chakrata, India 92 D7 30 42N 77 51 E
Chakwadam, Burma 90 B7 27 29N 98 31 E
Chakwal, Pakistan 91 B4 32 56N 72 53 E
Chala, Peru 172 D3 15 48 S 74 20W
Chalais, France 28 C4 45 16N 0 3 E
Chalakudi, India 95 J3 10 18N 76 20 E
Chalchihuites, Mexico 162 C4 23 29N 103 53W
Chalcis = Khalkís, Greece 48 C5 38 27N 23 42 E
Châlette-sur-Loing, France 27 D9 48 1N 2 44 E
Chaleur B., Canada 141 C6 47 55N 65 30W
Chalfant, U.S.A. 160 H8 37 32N 118 21W
Chalhuanca, Peru 172 C3 14 15 S 73 15W
Chalindrey, France 27 E12 47 43N 5 26 E
Chaling, China 77 D9 26 58N 113 30 E
Chalisgaon, India 94 D2 20 30N 75 10 E
Chalk River, Canada 140 C4 46 1N 77 27W
Chalkar = Shalkar, Kazakstan 62 F3 50 40N 51 53 E
Chalkar, Ozero = Shalkar, Ozero, Kazakstan 62 F3 50 35N 51 47 E
Chalky Inlet, N.Z. 131 G1 46 3 S 166 31 E
Chalkyitsik, U.S.A. 144 C12 66 39N 143 43W
Challakere, India 95 G3 14 19N 76 39 E
Challans, France 26 F5 46 50N 1 52W
Challapata, Bolivia 172 D4 18 53 S 66 50W
Challis, U.S.A. 158 D6 44 30N 114 14W
Chalmette, U.S.A. 155 L10 29 56N 89 58W
Chalon-sur-Saône, France 27 F11 46 48N 4 50 E
Chalonnes-sur-Loire, France 26 E6 47 20N 0 45W
Châlons-en-Champagne, France 27 D11 48 58N 4 20 E
Châlus, France 28 C4 45 39N 0 58 E
Chalyaphum, Thailand 78 A2 15 48N 102 2 E
Cham, Germany 31 F8 49 13N 12 39 E
Cham, Switz. 33 B6 47 11N 8 28 E
Cham, Cu Lao, Vietnam 86 E7 15 57N 108 30 E
Chama, U.S.A. 159 H10 36 54N 106 35W
Chamah, Gunong, Malaysia 84 A2 5 13N 101 35 E
Chamaicó, Argentina 174 D3 35 3 S 64 58W
Chaman, Pakistan 91 C2 30 58N 66 25 E
Chamba, India 92 C7 32 35N 76 10 E
Chamba, Tanzania 119 E4 11 37 S 37 0 E
Chambal →, India 93 F8 26 29N 79 15 E
Chamberlain, U.S.A. 154 D5 43 49N 99 20W
Chamberlain →, Australia 124 C4 15 30 S 127 54 E
Chamberlain L., U.S.A. 149 B11 46 14N 69 19W
Chambers, U.S.A. 159 J9 35 11N 109 26W
Chambersburg, U.S.A. 148 F7 39 56N 77 40W
Chambéry, France 29 C9 45 34N 5 55 E
Chamblee, U.S.A. 152 B5 33 53N 84 18W
Chambly, Canada 151 A11 45 27N 73 17W
Chambord, Canada 141 C5 48 25N 72 6W
Chamboulive, France 28 C5 45 26N 1 42 E
Chambri L., Papua N. G. 132 C2 4 15 S 143 10 E
Chamchamal, Iraq 101 E11 35 32N 44 50 E
Chamela, Mexico 162 D3 19 32N 105 5W
Chamical, Argentina 174 C2 30 22 S 66 27W
Chamkar Luong, Cambodia 87 G4 11 0N 103 45 E
Chamois, U.S.A. 156 F5 38 41N 91 46W
Chamoli, India 93 D8 30 24N 79 21 E
Chamonix-Mont Blanc, France 29 C10 45 55N 6 51 E
Chamoson, Switz. 32 D4 46 12N 7 13 E
Chamouchouane →, Canada 140 C5 48 37N 72 20W
Champa, India 93 H10 22 2N 82 43 E
Champagne, Canada 142 A1 60 49N 136 30W
Champagne, France 27 D11 48 40N 4 20 E
Champagnole, France 27 F12 46 45N 5 55 E
Champaign, U.S.A. 157 D8 40 7N 88 15W
Champassak, Laos 86 E5 14 53N 105 52 E
Champaubert, France 27 D10 48 50N 3 45 E
Champawat, India 93 E9 29 20N 80 6 E
Champdeniers-St-Denis, France 28 B3 46 29N 0 25W
Champdoré, L., Canada 141 A6 55 55N 65 49W
Champeix, France 28 C7 45 37N 3 8 E
Champéry, Switz. 32 D3 46 11N 6 52 E
Champion, U.S.A. 150 E4 41 19N 80 51W
Champlain, U.S.A. 151 B11 44 59N 73 27W
Champlain, L., U.S.A. 151 B11 44 40N 73 20W
Champlitte, France 27 E12 47 32N 5 31 E
Champotón, Mexico 163 D6 19 20N 90 50W
Champua, India 93 H11 22 5N 85 40 E
Chamrajnagar, India 95 J3 11 52N 76 52 E
Chamusca, Portugal 43 F2 39 21N 8 29W
Chan Chan, Peru 172 B2 8 7 S 79 0W
Chana, Thailand 87 J3 6 55N 100 44 E
Chañaral, Chile 174 B1 26 23 S 70 40W
Chanārān, Iran 97 B8 36 39N 59 6 E
Chanasma, India 92 H5 23 44N 72 5 E
Chancay, Peru 172 C2 11 32 S 77 25W
Chanco, Chile 174 D1 35 44 S 72 32W
Chancy, Switz. 32 D1 46 8N 5 58 E
Chand, India 93 J8 21 57N 79 7 E
Chandalar →, U.S.A. 144 C11 66 37N 146 0W
Chandan, India 93 G12 24 38N 86 40 E
Chandan Chauki, India 93 E9 28 33N 80 47 E

Cicero 201

Chiang Khong, *Thailand* **76 G3** 20 17N 100 24 E
Chiang Mai, *Thailand* **86 C2** 18 47N 98 59 E
Chiang Rai, *Thailand* **76 H2** 19 52N 99 50 E
Chiang Saen, *Thailand* **76 G3** 20 16N 100 5 E
Chiange, *Angola* **115 F2** 15 35 S 13 40 E
Chiapa →, *Mexico* **163 D6** 16 42N 93 0W
Chiapa de Corzo, *Mexico* **163 D6** 16 42N 93 0W
Chiapas □, *Mexico* **163 D6** 17 0N 92 45W
Chiaramonte Gulfi, *Italy* **47 E7** 37 2N 14 42 E
Chiaravalle, *Italy* **45 E10** 43 36N 13 19 E
Chiaravalle Centrale, *Italy* **47 D9** 38 41N 16 25 E
Chiari, *Italy* **44 C6** 45 32N 9 56 E
Chiasso, *Switz.* **33 E8** 45 50N 9 2 E
Chiatura, *Georgia* **61 J6** 42 15N 43 17 E
Chiautla, *Mexico* **163 D5** 18 18N 98 34W
Chiávari, *Italy* **44 D6** 44 19N 9 19 E
Chiavenna, *Italy* **44 B6** 46 19N 9 24 E
Chiba, *Japan* **71 B12** 35 30N 140 7 E
Chiba □, *Japan* **71 B12** 35 30N 140 20 E
Chibabava, *Mozam.* **117 C5** 20 17 S 33 35 E
Chibango, *Angola* **115 E4** 13 38 S 21 56 E
Chibemba, *Cunene, Angola* **115 F2** 15 48 S 14 8 E
Chibemba, *Huila, Angola* **116 B2** 16 20 S 15 20 E
Chibi, *Zimbabwe* **117 C5** 20 18 S 30 25 E
Chibia, *Angola* **115 F2** 15 10 S 13 42 E
Chibougamau, *Canada* **140 C5** 49 56N 74 24W
Chibougamau, L., *Canada* **140 C5** 49 50N 74 20W
Chibuk, *Nigeria* **113 C7** 10 52N 12 50 E
Chibuto, *Mozam.* **117 C5** 24 40 S 33 33 E
Chic-Chocs, Mts., *Canada* **141 C6** 48 55N 66 0W
Chicacole = Srikakulam, *India* **94 E6** 18 14N 83 58 E
Chicago, *U.S.A.* **157 C9** 41 53N 87 38W
Chicago Heights, *U.S.A.* **157 C9** 41 30N 87 38W
Chicapa →,
Dem. Rep. of the Congo **115 D4** 6 25 S 20 48 E
Chichagof I., *U.S.A.* **138 C6** 57 30N 135 30W
Chichaoua, *Morocco* **110 B3** 31 32N 8 44W
Chichén-Itzá, *Mexico* **163 C7** 20 40N 88 36W
Chicheng, *China* **74 D8** 40 55N 115 55 E
Chichester, *U.K.* **21 G7** 50 50N 0 47W
Chichester Ra., *Australia* **124 D2** 22 12 S 119 15 E
Chichibu, *Japan* **71 A11** 36 5N 139 10 E
Ch'ich'ihaerh = Qiqihar, *China* **65 E13** 47 26N 124 0 E
Chicholi, *India* **92 H8** 22 1N 77 40 E
Chickasha, *U.S.A.* **155 H6** 35 3N 97 58W
Chicken, *U.S.A.* **144 D12** 64 5N 141 56W
Chiclana de la Frontera, *Spain* **43 J4** 36 26N 6 9W
Chiclayo, *Peru* **172 B2** 6 42 S 79 50W
Chico, *U.S.A.* **160 F5** 39 44N 121 50W
Chico →, *Chubut, Argentina* **176 B3** 44 0 S 67 0W
Chico →, *Santa Cruz,*
Argentina **176 C3** 50 0 S 68 30W
Chicomba, *Angola* **115 E2** 14 10 S 14 52 E
Chicomo, *Mozam.* **117 C5** 24 31 S 34 6 E
Chicontepec, *Mexico* **163 C5** 20 58N 98 10W
Chicopee, *U.S.A.* **151 D12** 42 9N 72 37W
Chicoutimi, *Canada* **141 C5** 48 28N 71 5W
Chicualacuala, *Mozam.* **117 C5** 22 6 S 31 42 E
Chicuma, *Angola* **115 E2** 13 26 S 14 50 E
Chidambaram, *India* **95 J4** 11 20N 79 45 E
Chidenguele, *Mozam.* **117 C5** 24 55 S 34 11 E
Chidley, C., *Canada* **139 B13** 60 23N 64 26W
Chiducuane, *Mozam.* **117 C5** 24 35 S 34 25 E
Chiede, *Angola* **116 B2** 17 15 S 16 22 E
Chiefland, *U.S.A.* **153 F7** 29 29N 82 52W
Chiefs Pt., *Canada* **150 B3** 44 41N 81 18W
Chiem Hoa, *Vietnam* **86 A5** 22 12N 105 17 E
Chiemsee, *Germany* **31 H8** 47 53N 12 28 E
Chiengi, *Zambia* **119 D2** 8 45 S 29 10 E
Chiengmai = Chiang Mai,
Thailand **86 C2** 18 47N 98 59 E
Chiengo, *Angola* **115 E4** 13 20 S 21 55 E
Chienti →, *Italy* **45 E10** 43 18N 13 45 E
Chieri, *Italy* **44 C4** 45 1N 7 49 E
Chiers →, *France* **27 C11** 49 39N 4 59 E
Chiesa in Valmalenco, *Italy* **44 B6** 46 16N 9 51 E
Chiese →, *Italy* **44 C7** 45 8N 10 25 E
Chieti, *Italy* **45 F11** 42 21N 14 10 E
Chifeng, *China* **75 C10** 42 18N 118 58 E
Chigasaki, *Japan* **71 B11** 35 19N 139 24 E
Chigirin, *Ukraine* **59 H7** 49 4N 32 38 E
Chignecto B., *Canada* **141 C7** 45 30N 64 40W
Chigorodó, *Colombia* **168 B2** 7 41N 76 42W
Chiguana, *Bolivia* **174 A2** 21 0 S 67 58W
Chigwell, *U.K.* **21 F8** 51 37N 0 5 E
Chiha-ri, *N. Korea* **75 E14** 38 40N 126 30 E
Chihli, G. of = Bo Hai, *China* **75 E10** 39 0N 119 0 E
Chihuahua, *Mexico* **162 B3** 28 40N 106 3W
Chihuahua □, *Mexico* **162 B3** 28 40N 106 3W
Chiili, *Kazakstan* **64 E7** 44 20N 66 15 E
Chik Bollapur, *India* **95 H3** 13 25N 77 45 E
Chikalda, *India* **94 D3** 21 24N 77 19 E
Chikhli, *India* **94 D3** 20 20N 76 18 E
Chikhli, *India* **94 D1** 20 45N 73 4 E
Chikmagalur, *India* **95 H2** 13 15N 75 45 E
Chiknayakanhalli, *India* **95 H3** 13 26N 76 37 E
Chikodi, *India* **95 F2** 16 26N 74 38 E
Chikugo, *Japan* **70 D2** 33 14N 130 28 E
Chikuma-Gawa →, *Japan* **71 A10** 36 59N 138 35 E
Chikwawa, *Malawi* **119 F3** 16 2 S 34 50 E
Chila, *Angola* **115 E2** 12 3 S 14 29 E
Chilac, *Mexico* **163 D5** 18 20N 97 24W
Chilam Chavki, *Pakistan* **93 B6** 35 5N 75 5 E
Chilanga, *Zambia* **119 F2** 15 33 S 28 16 E
Chilapa, *Mexico* **163 D5** 17 40N 99 11W
Chilas, *Pakistan* **93 B6** 35 25N 74 5 E
Chilcotin →, *Canada* **142 C4** 51 44N 122 23W
Childers, *Australia* **127 D5** 25 15 S 152 17 E
Childersburg, *U.S.A.* **152 B3** 33 16N 86 21W
Childress, *U.S.A.* **155 H4** 34 25N 100 13W
Chile ■, *S. Amer.* **176 B2** 35 0 S 72 0W
Chile Chico, *Chile* **176 C2** 46 33 S 71 44W
Chile Rise, *Pac. Oc.* **135 L18** 38 0 S 92 0W
Chilecito, *Argentina* **174 B2** 29 10 S 67 30W
Chilesso, *Angola* **115 E3** 11 35 S 16 34 E
Chilete, *Peru* **172 B2** 7 10 S 78 50W
Chilhowee, *U.S.A.* **156 F3** 38 36N 93 51W
Chilia, Bratul →, *Romania* **53 E14** 45 14N 29 42 E
Chilik = Shelek, *Kazakstan* **63 B9** 43 33N 78 17 E
Chililabombwe, *Zambia* **119 E2** 12 18 S 27 43 E
Chilin = Jilin, *China* **75 C14** 43 44N 126 30 E
Chilka L., *India* **94 E7** 19 40N 85 25 E
Chilko →, *Canada* **142 C4** 52 0N 123 40W
Chilko L., *Canada* **142 C4** 51 20N 124 10W
Chillagoe, *Australia* **126 B3** 17 7 S 144 33 E
Chillán, *Chile* **174 D1** 36 40 S 72 10W
Chillicothe, *Ill., U.S.A.* **156 D7** 40 55N 89 29W
Chillicothe, *Mo., U.S.A.* **156 E3** 39 48N 93 33W
Chillicothe, *Ohio, U.S.A.* **148 F4** 39 20N 82 59W
Chilliwack, *Canada* **142 D4** 49 10N 121 54W
Chilo, *India* **92 F5** 27 25N 73 32 E
Chiloane, I., *Mozam.* **117 C5** 20 40 S 34 55 E
Chiloé, I. de, *Chile* **176 B2** 42 30 S 73 50W
Chilonda, *Angola* **115 E3** 11 19 S 16 12 E
Chilongo, *Angola* **115 E3** 13 55 S 16 35 E
Chilpancingo, *Mexico* **163 D5** 17 30N 99 30W
Chiltern, *Australia* **129 D7** 36 10 S 146 36 E
Chiltern Hills, *U.K.* **21 F7** 51 40N 0 53W
Chilton, *U.S.A.* **148 C1** 44 2N 88 10W
Chiluage, *Angola* **115 D4** 9 30 S 21 50 E
Chilubi, *Zambia* **119 E2** 11 5 S 29 58 E
Chilubula, *Zambia* **119 E3** 10 14 S 30 51 E
Chilumba, *Malawi* **119 E3** 10 28 S 34 12 E
Chilung, *Taiwan* **77 E13** 25 3N 121 45 E
Chilwa, L., *Malawi* **119 F4** 15 15 S 35 40 E
Chimakela, *Angola* **115 F3** 15 24 S 16 58 E
Chimaltitán, *Mexico* **162 C4** 21 46N 103 50W
Chimán, *Panama* **164 E4** 8 45N 78 40W
Chimanimani, *Zimbabwe* **117 B5** 19 48 S 32 52 E
Chimay, *Belgium* **24 D4** 50 3N 4 20 E
Chimayo, *U.S.A.* **159 H11** 36 0N 105 56W
Chimbay, *Uzbekistan* **64 E6** 42 57N 59 47 E
Chimborazo, *Ecuador* **168 D2** 1 29 S 78 55W
Chimborazo □, *Ecuador* **168 D2** 1 0 S 78 40W
Chimbote, *Peru* **172 B2** 9 0 S 78 35W
Chimichagua, *Colombia* **168 B3** 9 15N 73 49W
Chimion, *Uzbekistan* **63 C5** 40 15N 71 32 E
Chimkent = Shymkent,
Kazakstan **64 E7** 42 18N 69 36 E
Chimoio, *Mozam.* **119 F3** 19 4 S 33 30 E
Chimpembe, *Zambia* **119 D2** 9 31 S 29 33 E
Chimur, *India* **94 D4** 20 30N 79 23 E
Chin □, *Burma* **90 D4** 22 0N 93 0 E
Chin Hills, *Burma* **90 D4** 22 30N 93 30 E
Chin Ling Shan = Qinling
Shandi, *China* **74 H5** 33 50N 108 10 E
China, *Mexico* **163 B5** 25 40N 99 20W
China ■, *Asia* **73 C6** 30 0N 110 0 E
China Lake, *U.S.A.* **161 K9** 35 44N 117 37W
Chinacota, *Colombia* **168 B3** 7 37N 72 36W
Chinan = Jinan, *China* **74 F9** 36 38N 117 1 E
Chinandega, *Nic.* **164 D2** 12 35N 87 12W
Chinati Peak, *U.S.A.* **155 L2** 29 57N 104 29W
Chincha Alta, *Peru* **172 C2** 13 25 S 76 7W
Chinchaga →, *Canada* **142 B5** 58 53N 118 20W
Chincheros, *Peru* **172 C3** 13 30 S 73 44W
Chinchilla, *Australia* **127 D5** 26 45 S 150 38 E
Chinchilla de Monte Aragón,
Spain **41 G3** 38 53N 1 40W
Chincholi, *India* **94 E3** 17 28N 77 26 E
Chinchorro, Banco, *Mexico* **163 D7** 18 35N 87 20W
Chinchou = Jinzhou, *China* **75 D11** 41 5N 121 3 E
Chinchoua, *Gabon* **114 B1** 0 1N 9 48 E
Chincoteague, *U.S.A.* **148 G8** 37 56N 75 23W
Chinde, *Mozam.* **119 F4** 18 35 S 36 30 E
Chindo, *S. Korea* **75 G14** 34 28N 126 15 E
Chindwin →, *Burma* **90 E5** 21 26N 95 15 E
Chineni, *India* **93 C6** 33 2N 75 15 E
Chinga, *Mozam.* **119 F4** 15 13 S 38 35 E
Chingirlau, *Kazakstan* **62 F5** 51 7N 54 7 E
Chingola, *Zambia* **119 E2** 12 31 S 27 53 E
Chingole, *Malawi* **119 E3** 13 4 S 34 17 E
Chingoroi, *Angola* **115 E2** 13 37 S 14 1 E
Ch'ingtao = Qingdao, *China* **75 F11** 36 5N 120 20 E
Chinguar, *Angola* **115 E3** 12 25 S 16 45 E
Chinguetti, *Mauritania* **110 D2** 20 25N 12 24W
Chingune, *Mozam.* **117 C5** 20 33 S 34 58 E
Chinhae, *S. Korea* **75 G15** 35 9N 128 47 E
Chinhanguanine, *Mozam.* **117 D5** 25 21 S 32 30 E
Chinhoyi, *Zimbabwe* **119 F3** 17 20 S 30 8 E
Chini, *India* **92 D8** 31 32N 78 15 E
Chiniot, *Pakistan* **91 C4** 31 45N 73 0 E
Chínipas, *Mexico* **162 B3** 27 22N 108 32W
Chinji, *Pakistan* **92 C5** 32 42N 72 22 E
Chinju, *S. Korea* **75 G15** 35 12N 128 2 E
Chinko →, *C.A.R.* **114 B4** 4 50N 23 53 E
Chinle, *U.S.A.* **159 H9** 36 9N 109 33W
Chinmen, *Taiwan* **77 E13** 24 26N 118 19 E
Chinmen Tao, *Taiwan* **77 E12** 24 27N 118 23 E
Chinnamanur, *India* **95 K3** 9 50N 77 24 E
Chinnampo = Namp'o,
N. Korea **75 E13** 38 52N 125 10 E
Chinnur, *India* **94 E4** 18 57N 79 49 E
Chino, *Japan* **71 B10** 35 59N 138 9 E
Chino, *U.S.A.* **161 L9** 34 1N 117 41W
Chino Valley, *U.S.A.* **159 J7** 34 45N 112 27W
Chinon, *France* **26 E7** 47 10N 0 15 E
Chinook, *U.S.A.* **158 B9** 48 35N 109 14W
Chinoya, *Zambia* **115 E4** 13 55 S 23 16 E
Chinsali, *Zambia* **119 E3** 10 30 S 32 2 E
Chintalapudi, *India* **94 F5** 17 4N 80 59 E
Chintamani, *India* **95 H4** 13 26N 78 3 E
Chióggia, *Italy* **45 C9** 45 13N 12 17 E
Chíos = Khíos, *Greece* **49 C8** 38 27N 26 9 E
Chipata, *Zambia* **119 E3** 13 38 S 32 28 E
Chiperceni, *Moldova* **53 C13** 47 31N 28 50 E
Chipindo, *Angola* **115 E3** 13 49 S 15 48 E
Chipinge, *Zimbabwe* **119 G3** 20 13 S 32 28 E
Chipiona, *Spain* **43 J4** 36 44N 6 26W
Chipley, *U.S.A.* **152 E4** 30 47N 85 32W
Chiplun, *India* **94 F1** 17 31N 73 34 E
Chipman, *Canada* **141 C6** 46 6N 65 53W
Chipoka, *Malawi* **119 E3** 13 57 S 34 28 E
Chippenham, *U.K.* **21 F5** 51 27N 2 6W
Chippewa →, *U.S.A.* **154 C8** 44 25N 92 5W
Chippewa Falls, *U.S.A.* **154 C9** 44 56N 91 24W
Chipping Norton, *U.K.* **21 F6** 51 56N 1 32W
Chiprovtsi, *Bulgaria* **50 C6** 43 24N 22 52 E
Chiputneticook Lakes, *U.S.A.* **149 C11** 45 35N 67 35W
Chiquelequele, *Angola* **115 F3** 16 44 S 19 5 E
Chiquián, *Peru* **172 C2** 10 10 S 77 0W
Chiquimula, *Guatemala* **164 D2** 14 51N 89 37W
Chiquinquira, *Colombia* **168 B3** 5 37N 73 50W
Chiquitos, Llanos de, *Bolivia* **173 D5** 18 0 S 61 30W
Chir →, *Russia* **61 F6** 48 30N 43 0 E
Chira →, *Peru* **168 D1** 4 54 S 81 8W
Chirala, *India* **95 G5** 15 50N 80 26 E
Chiramba, *Mozam.* **119 F3** 16 55 S 34 39 E
Chiran, *Japan* **70 F2** 31 22N 130 27 E
Chirawa, *India* **92 E6** 28 14N 75 42 E
Chirayinkil, *India* **95 K3** 8 41N 76 49 E
Chirchiq, *Uzbekistan* **64 E7** 41 29N 69 35 E
Chiredzi, *Zimbabwe* **117 C5** 21 0 S 31 38 E
Chirfa, *Niger* **109 D2** 20 55N 12 22 E
Chirgua →, *Venezuela* **168 B4** 8 54N 67 58W
Chiricahua Peak, *U.S.A.* **159 L9** 31 51N 109 18W
Chiriquí, G. de, *Panama* **164 E3** 8 0N 82 10W
Chiriquí, L. de, *Panama* **164 E3** 9 10N 82 0W
Chirivira Falls, *Zimbabwe* **119 G3** 21 10 S 32 12 E
Chirnogi, *Romania* **53 F11** 44 7N 26 32 E
Chirpan, *Bulgaria* **51 D9** 42 10N 25 19 E
Chirripó Grande, Cerro,
Costa Rica **164 E3** 9 29N 83 29W
Chirundu, *Zimbabwe* **117 B4** 16 3 S 28 50 E
Chisamba, *Zambia* **119 E2** 14 55 S 28 20 E
Chisasibi, *Canada* **140 B4** 53 50N 79 0W
Ch'ishan, *Taiwan* **77 F13** 22 44N 120 31 E
Chishmy, *Russia* **62 D5** 54 35N 55 23 E
Chisholm, *Canada* **142 C6** 54 55N 114 10W
Chisholm, *U.S.A.* **154 B8** 47 29N 92 53W
Chishtian Mandi, *Pakistan* **92 E5** 29 50N 72 55 E
Chishui, *China* **76 C5** 28 30N 105 42 E
Chishui He →, *China* **76 C5** 28 49N 105 50 E
Chisimaio, *Somali Rep.* **120 E2** 0 22 S 42 32 E
Chisimba Falls, *Zambia* **119 E3** 10 12 S 30 56 E
Chişinău, *Moldova* **53 C13** 47 2N 28 50 E
Chişineu Criş, *Romania* **52 D6** 46 32N 21 37 E
Chisone →, *Italy* **44 D4** 44 49N 7 25 E
Chisos Mts., *U.S.A.* **155 L3** 29 5N 103 15W
Chissenguе, *Angola* **115 D4** 9 13 S 20 34 E
Chissilo, *Angola* **115 E3** 13 48 S 16 31 E
Chistochina, *U.S.A.* **144 E11** 62 34N 144 40W
Chistopol, *Russia* **60 C10** 55 25N 50 38 E
Chita, *Colombia* **168 B3** 6 11N 72 28W
Chita, *Russia* **65 D12** 52 0N 113 35 E
Chitado, *Angola* **115 F2** 17 10 S 14 8 E
Chitanda →, *Angola* **115 F3** 16 1 S 15 12 E
Chitapur, *India* **94 F3** 17 10N 77 5 E
Chitembo, *Angola* **115 E3** 13 30 S 16 50 E
Chitipa, *Malawi* **119 D3** 9 41 S 33 19 E
Chitose, *Japan* **68 C10** 42 49N 141 39 E
Chitradurga, *India* **95 G3** 14 14N 76 24 E
Chitrakot, *India* **94 E5** 19 10N 81 40 E
Chitral, *Pakistan* **91 B3** 35 50N 71 56 E
Chitravati →, *India* **95 G4** 14 45N 78 15 E
Chitré, *Panama* **164 E3** 7 59N 80 27W
Chittagong, *Bangla.* **90 D3** 22 19N 91 48 E
Chittagong □, *Bangla.* **90 C3** 24 5N 91 0 E
Chittaurgarh, *India* **92 G6** 24 52N 74 38 E
Chittoor, *India* **95 H4** 13 15N 79 5 E
Chittur, *India* **95 J3** 10 40N 76 45 E
Chitungwiza, *Zimbabwe* **119 F3** 18 0 S 31 6 E
Chiumbe →,
Dem. Rep. of the Congo **115 D4** 6 59 S 21 12 E
Chiumbo, *Angola* **115 E3** 12 29 S 16 8 E
Chiume, *Angola* **115 F4** 15 3 S 21 14 E
Chiuro, *Italy* **33 D9** 46 10N 9 59 E
Chiusi, *Italy* **45 E8** 43 1N 11 57 E
Chiva, *Spain* **41 F4** 39 27N 0 41W
Chivacoa, *Venezuela* **168 A4** 10 10N 68 54W
Chivasso, *Italy* **44 C4** 45 11N 7 53 E
Chivay, *Peru* **172 D3** 15 40 S 71 35W
Chivé, *Bolivia* **172 C4** 12 23 S 68 35W
Chivhu, *Zimbabwe* **119 F3** 19 2 S 30 52 E
Chivilcoy, *Argentina* **174 C4** 34 55 S 60 0W
Chiwanda, *Tanzania* **119 E3** 11 23 S 34 55 E
Chixi, *China* **77 G9** 22 0N 112 58 E
Chizela, *Zambia* **115 E4** 13 8 S 25 0 E
Chizera, *Zambia* **119 E2** 13 10 S 25 0 E
Chkalov = Orenburg, *Russia* **62 F5** 51 45N 55 6 E
Chkolovsk, *Russia* **60 B6** 56 50N 43 10 E
Chloride, *U.S.A.* **161 K12** 35 25N 114 12W
Chlumec nad Cidlinou,
Czech Rep. **34 A8** 50 9N 15 29 E
Chmielnik, *Poland* **55 H7** 50 37N 20 43 E
Cho Bo, *Vietnam* **76 G5** 20 46N 105 10 E
Cho-do, *N. Korea* **75 E13** 38 30N 124 40 E
Cho Phuoc Hai, *Vietnam* **87 G6** 10 26N 107 18 E
Choa Chukang, *Malaysia* **84 B2** 1 22N 103 41 E
Choba, *Kenya* **118 B4** 2 30N 38 5 E
Chobe National Park, *Botswana* **116 B4** 18 0 S 25 0 E
Choch'iwŏn, *S. Korea* **75 F14** 36 37N 127 18 E
Chocianów, *Poland* **55 G2** 51 27N 15 55 E
Chociwel, *Poland* **54 E2** 53 29N 15 21 E
Chocó □, *Colombia* **168 B2** 6 0N 77 0W
Chocolate Mts., *U.S.A.* **161 M11** 33 15N 115 15W
Choconta, *Colombia* **168 B3** 5 9N 73 41W
Choctawhatchee →, *U.S.A.* **152 E3** 30 25N 86 8W
Chodavaram, *Andhra Pradesh,*
India **94 F6** 17 50N 82 57 E
Chodavaram, *Andhra Pradesh,*
India **94 F5** 17 27N 81 46 E
Chodecz, *Poland* **55 F6** 52 24N 19 2 E
Chodov, *Czech Rep.* **34 A5** 50 15N 12 45 E
Chodziez, *Poland* **55 F3** 52 58N 16 58 E
Choele Choel, *Argentina* **176 A3** 39 11 S 65 40W
Chōfu, *Japan* **71 B11** 35 39N 139 33 E
Choiseul, *Solomon Is.* **133 L9** 7 0 S 156 40 E
Choix, *Mexico* **162 B3** 26 40N 108 23W
Chojna, *Poland* **55 F1** 52 58N 14 25 E
Chojnice, *Poland* **54 E4** 53 42N 17 32 E
Chojnów, *Poland* **55 G2** 51 18N 15 58 E
Chōkai-San, *Japan* **68 E10** 39 6N 140 3 E
Choke, *Ethiopia* **107 E4** 11 18N 37 15 E
Choke Canyon L., *U.S.A.* **155 L5** 28 30N 98 20W
Chokurdakh, *Russia* **65 B15** 70 38N 147 55 E
Cholame, *U.S.A.* **160 K6** 35 44N 120 18W
Cholet, *France* **26 E6** 47 4N 0 52W
Cholguan, *Chile* **174 D1** 37 10 S 72 3W
Cholpon-Ata, *Kyrgyzstan* **63 B8** 42 40N 77 6 E
Choluteca, *Honduras* **164 D2** 13 20N 87 14W
Choluteca →, *Honduras* **164 D2** 13 0N 87 20W
Chom Bung, *Thailand* **86 F2** 13 37N 99 36 E
Chom Thong, *Thailand* **86 C2** 18 25N 98 41 E
Choma, *Zambia* **119 F2** 16 48 S 26 59 E
Chomen Swamp, *Ethiopia* **107 F4** 9 20N 37 10 E
Chomun, *India* **92 F6** 27 15N 75 40 E
Chomutov, *Czech Rep.* **34 A6** 50 28N 13 23 E
Chon Buri, *Thailand* **78 B2** 13 21N 101 1 E
Chon Thanh, *Vietnam* **87 G6** 11 24N 106 36 E
Ch'onan, *S. Korea* **75 F14** 36 48N 127 9 E
Chone, *Ecuador* **168 D2** 0 40 S 80 0W
Chong Kai, *Cambodia* **86 F4** 13 57N 103 35 E
Chong Mek, *Thailand* **86 E5** 15 10N 105 27 E
Chongde, *China* **77 B13** 30 32N 120 26 E
Chŏngdo, *S. Korea* **75 G15** 35 38N 128 42 E
Chŏngha, *S. Korea* **75 F15** 36 12N 129 21 E
Chŏngjin, *N. Korea* **75 D15** 41 47N 129 50 E
Chŏngjiu, *S. Korea* **75 F14** 36 39N 127 27 E
Chŏngju, *N. Korea* **75 E13** 39 40N 125 5 E
Chongli, *China* **74 D8** 40 58N 115 15 E
Chongming, *China* **77 B13** 31 38N 121 23 E
Chongming Dao, *China* **77 B13** 31 40N 121 30 E
Chongoyape, *Peru* **172 B2** 6 35 S 79 25W
Chongqing, *Chongqing, China* **76 C6** 29 35N 106 25 E
Chongqing, *Sichuan, China* **76 B4** 30 38N 103 40 E
Chongqing □, *China* **72 C5** 30 0N 108 0 E
Chongqing Shi □, *China* **76 C6** 30 0N 108 0 E
Chongren, *China* **77 D11** 27 46N 116 3 E
Chonguene, *Mozam.* **117 C5** 25 3 S 33 49 E
Chŏngŭp, *S. Korea* **75 G14** 35 35N 126 50 E
Chongyi, *China* **77 E10** 25 45N 114 29 E
Chongzuo, *China* **76 F6** 22 23N 107 20 E
Chŏnju, *S. Korea* **75 G14** 35 50N 127 4 E
Chonos, Arch. de los, *Chile* **176 C2** 45 0 S 75 0W
Chop, *Ukraine* **59 H2** 48 26N 22 12 E
Chopda, *India* **94 D2** 21 20N 75 15 E
Chopim →, *Brazil* **175 B5** 25 35 S 53 5W
Chor, *Pakistan* **92 G3** 25 31N 69 46 E
Chorbat La, *India* **93 B7** 34 42N 76 37 E
Chorley, *U.K.* **20 D5** 53 39N 2 38W
Chornobyl, *Ukraine* **59 G6** 51 20N 30 15 E
Chornomorske, *Ukraine* **59 K7** 45 31N 32 40 E
Chorolque, Cerro, *Bolivia* **174 A2** 20 59 S 66 5W
Choroszcz, *Poland* **55 E9** 53 10N 22 59 E
Chorregon, *Australia* **126 C3** 22 40 S 143 32 E
Chortkiv, *Ukraine* **59 H3** 49 2N 25 46 E
Ch'ŏrwon, *S. Korea* **75 E14** 38 15N 127 10 E
Chorzele, *Poland* **55 E7** 53 15N 20 55 E
Chorzów, *Poland* **55 H5** 50 18N 18 57 E
Chos-Malal, *Argentina* **174 D1** 37 20 S 70 15W
Ch'osan, *N. Korea* **75 D13** 40 50N 125 47 E
Chōshi, *Japan* **71 B12** 35 45N 140 51 E
Choszczno, *Poland* **55 E2** 53 7N 15 25 E
Chota, *Peru* **172 B2** 6 33 S 78 39W
Choteau, *U.S.A.* **158 C7** 47 49N 112 11W
Chotěboř, *Czech Rep.* **34 B8** 49 43N 15 40 E
Chotila, *India* **92 H4** 22 23N 71 15 E
Chotta Udepur, *India* **92 H6** 22 19N 74 1 E
Chowchilla, *U.S.A.* **160 H6** 37 7N 120 16W
Chowkham, *Burma* **90 E6** 20 52N 97 28 E
Choybalsan, *Mongolia* **73 B6** 48 4N 114 30 E
Chrisman, *U.S.A.* **157 E9** 39 48N 87 41W
Christchurch, *N.Z.* **131 D7** 43 33 S 172 47 E
Christchurch, *U.K.* **21 G6** 50 44N 1 47W
Christian I., *Canada* **150 B4** 44 50N 80 12W
Christian Sd., *U.S.A.* **144 J14** 55 56N 134 40W
Christiana, *S. Africa* **116 D4** 27 52 S 25 8 E
Christiansfeld, *Denmark* **17 J3** 55 21N 9 29 E
Christianshåb = Qasigiannguit,
Greenland **10 D5** 68 50N 51 18W
Christiansted, *Virgin Is.* **165 C7** 17 45N 64 42W
Christie B., *Canada* **143 A6** 62 32N 111 10W
Christina →, *Canada* **143 B6** 56 40N 111 3W
Christmas Cr. →, *Australia* **124 C4** 18 29 S 125 23 E
Christmas I. = Kiritimati,
Kiribati **135 G12** 1 58N 157 27W
Christmas I., *Ind. Oc.* **121 F9** 10 30 S 105 40 E
Christopher, *U.S.A.* **156 G7** 37 59N 89 3W
Christopher L., *Australia* **125 D4** 24 49 S 127 42 E
Chrudim, *Czech Rep.* **34 B8** 49 58N 15 43 E
Chrzanów, *Poland* **55 H6** 50 10N 19 21 E
Chtimba, *Malawi* **119 E3** 10 35 S 34 13 E
Chu = Shu, *Kazakstan* **64 E8** 43 36N 73 42 E
Chu = Shu →, *Kazakstan* **63 A3** 45 0N 67 44 E
Chu →, *Vietnam* **86 C5** 19 53N 105 45 E
Chu Lai, *Vietnam* **86 E7** 15 28N 108 45 E
Chuadanga, *Bangla.* **90 D2** 23 38N 88 51 E
Ch'uanchou = Quanzhou,
China **77 E12** 24 55N 118 34 E
Chuankou, *China* **74 G6** 34 20N 110 59 E
Chuathbaluk, *U.S.A.* **144 F8** 61 40N 159 15W
Chubbuck, *U.S.A.* **158 E7** 42 55N 112 28W
Chūbu □, *Japan* **71 A9** 36 45N 137 30 E
Chubut □, *Argentina* **176 B3** 43 30 S 69 0W
Chubut →, *Argentina* **176 B3** 43 20 S 65 5W
Chuchi L., *Canada* **142 B4** 55 12N 124 30W
Chuda, *India* **92 H4** 22 29N 71 41 E
Chudovo, *Russia* **58 C6** 59 10N 31 41 E
Chudskoye, Ozero, *Russia* **15 G22** 58 13N 27 30 E
Chugach National Forest,
U.S.A. **144 G9** 58 15N 152 45W
Chūgoku □, *Japan* **70 C4** 35 0N 133 0 E
Chūgoku-Sanchi, *Japan* **70 C4** 35 0N 133 0 E
Chuguyev = Chuhuyiv, *Ukraine* **59 H9** 49 55N 36 45 E
Chugwater, *U.S.A.* **154 E2** 41 46N 104 50W
Chuhuyiv, *Ukraine* **59 H9** 49 55N 36 45 E
Chukchi Sea, *Russia* **65 C19** 68 0N 175 0W
Chukotskoye Nagorye, *Russia* **65 C18** 68 0N 175 0 E
Chula, *U.S.A.* **152 D6** 31 33N 83 32W
Chula Vista, *U.S.A.* **161 N9** 32 39N 117 5W
Chulakkurgan, *Kazakstan* **63 B4** 43 46N 69 9 E
Chulband →, *India* **94 D4** 20 40N 79 54 E
Chulucanas, *Peru* **172 B1** 5 8 S 80 10W
Chulumani, *Bolivia* **172 D4** 16 24 S 67 31W
Chulym →, *Russia* **64 D9** 57 43N 83 51 E
Chum Phae, *Thailand* **86 D4** 16 40N 102 6 E
Chum Saeng, *Thailand* **86 E3** 15 55N 100 15 E
Chuma, *Bolivia* **172 D4** 15 24 S 68 56W
Chumar, *India* **93 C8** 32 40N 78 35 E
Chumbicha, *Argentina* **174 B2** 29 0 S 66 10W
Chumerna, *Bulgaria* **51 D9** 42 45N 25 55 E
Chumikan, *Russia* **65 D14** 54 40N 135 10 E
Chumphon, *Thailand* **78 B1** 10 35N 99 14 E
Chumpi, *Peru* **172 D3** 15 4 S 73 46W
Chumuare, *Mozam.* **119 E3** 14 31 S 31 50 E
Chumunjin, *S. Korea* **75 F15** 37 55N 128 54 E
Chuna →, *Russia* **65 D10** 57 47N 94 37 E
Chun'an, *China* **77 C12** 29 35N 119 3 E
Ch'unch'ŏn, *S. Korea* **75 F14** 37 58N 127 44 E
Chunchura, *India* **93 H13** 22 53N 88 27 E
Chunga, *Zambia* **119 F2** 15 0 S 26 2 E
Chunggang-ŭp, *N. Korea* **75 D14** 41 48N 126 48 E
Chunghwa, *N. Korea* **75 E13** 38 52N 125 47 E
Ch'ungju, *S. Korea* **75 F14** 36 58N 127 58 E
Chungking = Chongqing, *China* **76 C6** 29 35N 106 25 E
Chungli, *Taiwan* **77 E13** 24 57N 121 13 E
Ch'ungmu, *S. Korea* **75 G15** 34 50N 128 20 E
Chungt'iaoshan = Zhongtiao
Shan, *China* **74 G6** 35 0N 111 10 E
Chungyang Shanmo, *Taiwan* **77 F13** 23 10N 121 0 E
Chunian, *Pakistan* **92 D6** 30 57N 74 0 E
Chunya, *Tanzania* **119 D3** 8 30 S 33 27 E
Chunyang, *China* **75 C15** 43 38N 129 23 E
Chuquibamba, *Peru* **172 D3** 15 47 S 72 44W
Chuquibambilla, *Peru* **172 C3** 14 7 S 72 41W
Chuquicamata, *Chile* **174 A2** 22 15 S 69 0W
Chuquisaca □, *Bolivia* **173 E5** 20 30 S 63 30W
Chur, *Switz.* **33 C9** 46 52N 9 32 E
Churachandpur, *India* **90 C4** 24 20N 93 40 E
Churchill, *Canada* **143 B10** 58 47N 94 11W
Churchill →, *Man., Canada* **143 B10** 58 47N 94 12W
Churchill →, *Nfld., Canada* **141 B7** 53 19N 60 10W
Churchill, C., *Canada* **143 B10** 58 46N 93 12W
Churchill Falls, *Canada* **141 B7** 53 36N 64 19W
Churchill L., *Canada* **143 B7** 55 55N 108 20W
Churchill Pk., *Canada* **142 B3** 58 10N 125 10W
Churdan, *U.S.A.* **156 B2** 42 9N 94 29W
Churfisten, *Switz.* **33 B8** 47 8N 9 17 E
Churki, *India* **93 H10** 23 50N 83 12 E
Churu, *India* **92 E6** 28 20N 74 50 E
Churubusco, *U.S.A.* **157 C11** 41 14N 85 19W
Churún Merú = Angel Falls,
Venezuela **169 B5** 5 57N 62 30W
Churwalden, *Switz.* **33 C9** 46 47N 9 33 E
Chushal, *India* **93 C8** 33 40N 78 40 E
Chuska Mts., *U.S.A.* **159 H9** 36 15N 108 50W
Chusovaya →, *Russia* **62 B6** 58 13N 56 54 E
Chusovoy, *Russia* **62 B6** 58 22N 57 50 E
Chuspipata, *Bolivia* **172 D4** 16 18 S 67 48W
Chust, *Uzbekistan* **63 C5** 41 0N 71 13 E
Chute-aux-Outardes, *Canada* **141 C6** 49 7N 68 24W
Chuuronjang, *N. Korea* **75 D15** 41 35N 129 40 E
Chuvash Republic =
Chuvashia □, *Russia* **60 C8** 55 30N 47 0 E
Chuvashia □, *Russia* **60 C8** 55 30N 47 0 E
Chuwārtah, *Iraq* **96 C5** 35 43N 45 34 E
Chuxiong, *China* **76 E3** 25 2N 101 28 E
Chuy, *Uruguay* **175 C5** 33 41 S 53 27W
Chuzhou, *China* **77 A12** 32 19N 118 20 E
Ci Xian, *China* **74 F8** 36 20N 114 25 E
Ciacova, *Romania* **52 E6** 45 35N 21 10 E
Ciadâr-Lunga, *Moldova* **53 D13** 46 3N 28 51 E
Ciamis, *Indonesia* **79 G13** 7 20 S 108 21 E
Cianjur, *Indonesia* **79 G12** 6 49 S 107 8 E
Cianorte, *Brazil* **175 A5** 23 37 S 52 37W
Cibola, *U.S.A.* **161 M12** 33 17N 114 42W
Cicero, *U.S.A.* **157 C9** 41 51N 87 45W

Cícero Dantas, Brazil .... 170 D4 10 36 S 38 23W
Cidacos →, Spain 40 C3 42 21N 1 38W
Cide, Turkey .... 100 B5 41 53N 33 1 E
Ciechanów, Poland .... 55 F7 52 52N 20 38 E
Ciechanowiec, Poland .... 55 F9 52 40N 22 31 E
Ciechocinek, Poland .... 55 F8 52 53N 18 45 E
Ciego de Avila, Cuba 164 B4 21 50N 78 50W
Ciénaga, Colombia 168 A3 11 1N 74 15W
Ciénaga de Oro, Colombia 168 B2 8 53N 75 37W
Cienfuegos, Cuba 164 B3 22 10N 80 30W
Cierp, France .... 28 F4 42 55N 0 40 E
Cíes, Is., Spain 42 C2 42 12N 8 55W
Cieszanów, Poland .... 55 H10 50 14N 23 8 E
Cieszyn, Poland .... 55 J5 49 45N 18 35 E
Cieza, Spain 41 G3 38 17N 1 23W
Çifteler, Turkey .... 100 C4 39 22N 31 2 E
Cifuentes, Spain 40 E2 40 47N 2 37W
Cihanbeyli, Turkey .... 100 C5 38 40N 32 55 E
Cihuatlán, Mexico 162 D4 19 14N 104 35W
Cijara, Embalse de, Spain 43 F6 39 18N 4 52W
Cijulang, Indonesia .... 79 G13 7 42 S 108 27 E
Cilacap, Indonesia .... 79 G13 7 43 S 109 0 E
Çıldır, Turkey .... 101 B10 41 7N 43 15 E
Çıldır Gölü, Turkey .... 101 B10 41 5N 43 5 E
Cili, China .... 77 C8 29 30N 111 8 E
Cilibia, Romania .... 53 E12 45 1N 27 4 E
Cilicia, Turkey .... 100 D5 36 30N 33 40 E
Cill Chainnigh = Kilkenny, Ireland 23 D4 52 39N 7 15W
Çilo Dağı, Turkey .... 101 D10 37 28N 43 55 E
Cima, U.S.A. 161 K11 35 14N 115 30W
Cimarron, Kans., U.S.A. 155 G4 37 48N 100 21W
Cimarron, N. Mex., U.S.A. 155 G2 36 31N 104 55W
Cimarron →, U.S.A. 155 G6 36 10N 96 17W
Cimişlia, Moldova .... 53 D13 46 34N 28 44 E
Cimone, Mte., Italy .... 44 D7 44 12N 10 42 E
Çinar, Turkey .... 101 D9 37 46N 40 19 E
Çınarcık, Turkey .... 51 F13 40 39N 29 5 E
Cinca →, Spain .... 40 D5 41 26N 0 21 E
Cincar, Bos.-H. .... 52 G2 43 55N 17 5 E
Cincinnati, Iowa, U.S.A. 156 D4 40 38N 92 56W
Cincinnati, Ohio, U.S.A. 157 E12 39 6N 84 31W
Cincinnatus, U.S.A. 151 D9 42 33N 75 54W
Çine, Turkey .... 49 D10 37 37N 28 2 E
Ciney, Belgium .... 24 D5 50 18N 5 5 E
Cíngoli, Italy .... 45 E10 43 23N 13 13 E
Cinigiano, Italy .... 45 F8 42 53N 11 24 E
Cinto, Mte., France .... 29 F12 42 24N 8 54 E
Cintruénigo, Spain 40 C3 42 5N 1 49W
Ciocile, Romania .... 53 F12 44 49N 27 14 E
Ciolănești din Deal, Romania .... 53 F10 44 19N 25 5 E
Ciorani, Romania .... 53 F11 44 48N 26 25 E
Čiovo, Croatia .... 45 E13 43 30N 16 17 E
Cipó, Brazil .... 170 D4 11 6 S 38 31W
Cipolletti, Argentina .... 176 A3 38 56 S 67 59W
Circeo, Italy .... 46 A6 41 14N 13 2 E
Çirçir, Turkey .... 100 C7 40 5N 36 47 E
Circle, Alaska, U.S.A. 138 B5 65 50N 144 4W
Circle, Mont., U.S.A. 154 B2 47 25N 105 35W
Circleville, U.S.A. 148 F4 39 36N 82 57W
Cirebon, Indonesia .... 79 G13 6 45 S 108 32 E
Ciremai, Indonesia .... 79 G13 6 55 S 108 27 E
Cirencester, U.K. 21 F6 51 43N 1 57W
Cireşu, Romania .... 52 F7 44 47N 22 31 E
Cirey-sur-Vezouze, France .... 27 D13 48 35N 6 57 E
Ciriè, Italy .... 44 C4 45 14N 7 36 E
Cirium, Cyprus .... 38 E11 34 40N 32 53 E
Cirò, Italy .... 47 C10 39 23N 17 4 E
Cirò Marina, Italy .... 47 C10 39 22N 17 8 E
Ciron →, France 28 D3 44 36N 0 18W
Cisco, U.S.A. 155 J5 32 23N 98 59W
Cislău, Romania .... 53 E11 45 14N 26 20 E
Cisna, Poland .... 55 J9 49 12N 22 20 E
Cisnădie, Romania .... 53 E9 45 42N 24 9 E
Cisne, U.S.A. 157 F8 38 31N 88 26W
Cisneros, Colombia 168 B2 6 33N 75 4W
Cissna Park, U.S.A. 157 D9 40 34N 87 54W
Cisterna di Latina, Italy .... 46 A5 41 35N 12 49 E
Cisternino, Italy .... 47 B10 40 44N 17 25 E
Cistierna, Spain 42 C5 42 48N 5 7W
Citaré →, Brazil 169 C7 1 11N 54 41W
Citeli-Ckaro = Tsiteli-Tsqaro, Georgia .... 61 K8 41 33N 46 0 E
Citlaltépetl, Mexico 163 D5 19 0N 97 20W
Citra, U.S.A. 153 F7 29 25N 82 7W
Citron, Fr. Guiana 169 C7 4 44N 53 57W
Citrus Heights, U.S.A. 160 G5 38 42N 121 17W
Citrus Springs, U.S.A. 153 F7 29 0N 82 27W
Citrusdal, S. Africa .... 116 E2 32 35 S 19 0 E
Città della Pieve, Italy .... 45 F9 42 57N 12 1 E
Città di Castello, Italy .... 45 E9 43 27N 12 14 E
Città Sant' Angelo, Italy .... 45 F11 42 32N 14 5 E
Cittadella, Italy .... 45 C8 45 39N 11 47 E
Cittaducale, Italy .... 45 F9 42 29N 12 57 E
Cittanova, Italy .... 47 D9 38 21N 16 5 E
Ciuc, Munții, Romania .... 53 D11 46 25N 26 5 E
Ciucaş, Vf., Romania .... 53 E10 45 31N 25 56 E
Ciucea, Romania .... 52 D7 46 57N 22 49 E
Ciuciulea, Moldova .... 53 C12 47 40N 27 29 E
Ciuciuleni, Moldova .... 53 C13 47 21N 28 25 E
Ciudad Altamirano, Mexico 162 D4 18 20N 100 40W
Ciudad Bolívar, Venezuela 169 B5 8 5N 63 36W
Ciudad Camargo, Mexico 162 B3 27 41N 105 10W
Ciudad de Valles, Mexico 163 C5 22 0N 99 0W
Ciudad del Carmen, Mexico 163 D6 18 38N 91 50W
Ciudad del Este, Paraguay .... 175 B5 25 30 S 54 50W
Ciudad Delicias = Delicias, Mexico 162 B3 28 10N 105 30W
Ciudad Guayana, Venezuela 169 B5 8 0N 62 30W
Ciudad Guerrero, Mexico 162 B3 28 33N 107 28W
Ciudad Guzmán, Mexico 162 D4 19 40N 103 30W
Ciudad Juárez, Mexico 162 A3 31 40N 106 28W
Ciudad Madero, Mexico 163 C5 22 19N 97 50W
Ciudad Mante, Mexico 163 C5 22 50N 99 0W
Ciudad Obregón, Mexico 162 B3 27 28N 109 59W
Ciudad Ojeda, Venezuela 168 A3 10 12N 71 19W
Ciudad Piar, Venezuela 169 B5 7 27N 63 19W
Ciudad Real, Spain 43 G7 38 59N 3 55W
Ciudad Real □, Spain 43 G7 38 50N 4 0W
Ciudad Rodrigo, Spain 42 E4 40 35N 6 32W
Ciudad Trujillo = Santo Domingo, Dom. Rep. 165 C6 18 30N 69 59W
Ciudad Victoria, Mexico 163 C5 23 41N 99 9W
Ciudadela, Spain .... 39 B10 40 0N 3 50 E
Ciulnița, Romania .... 53 F12 44 26N 27 22 E
Ciumeghiu, Romania .... 52 D6 46 44N 21 35 E
Ciuperceni, Romania .... 52 F8 44 54N 23 4 E
Civa Burnu, Turkey .... 100 B7 41 21N 36 38 E
Cividale del Friuli, Italy .... 45 C10 46 6N 13 25 E
Cívita Castellana, Italy .... 45 F9 42 17N 12 24 E
Civitanova Marche, Italy .... 45 E10 43 18N 13 44 E
Civitavécchia, Italy .... 45 F8 42 6N 11 48 E
Civray, France .... 28 B4 46 10N 0 17 E
Çivril, Turkey .... 49 C11 38 20N 29 43 E
Çixerri →, Italy .... 46 C1 39 17N 8 59 E
Cixi, China .... 77 B13 30 17N 121 9 E
Cizre, Turkey .... 101 D10 37 19N 42 10 E

Cizur Mayor, Spain 40 C3 42 47N 1 41W
Clackmannanshire □, U.K. 22 E5 56 10N 3 43W
Clacton-on-Sea, U.K. .... 21 F9 51 47N 1 11 E
Clain →, France .... 26 F7 46 47N 0 33 E
Claire, L., Canada 142 B6 58 35N 112 5W
Clairton, U.S.A. 150 F5 40 18N 79 53W
Clairvaux-les-Lacs, France .... 27 F12 46 35N 5 45 E
Claise →, France .... 28 B5 46 56N 0 42 E
Clallam Bay, U.S.A. 160 B2 48 15N 124 16W
Clam Gulch, U.S.A. 144 F10 60 15N 151 23W
Clamecy, France .... 27 E10 47 28N 3 30 E
Clanton, U.S.A. 149 J2 32 51N 86 38W
Clanwilliam, S. Africa .... 116 E2 32 11 S 18 52 E
Clara, Ireland 23 C4 53 21N 7 37W
Claraville, U.S.A. 161 K8 35 24N 118 20W
Clare, Australia .... 128 B3 33 50 S 138 37 E
Clare, U.S.A. 148 D3 43 49N 84 46W
Clare □, Ireland 23 D3 52 45N 9 0W
Clare →, Ireland 23 C2 53 20N 9 2W
Clare I., Ireland 23 C1 53 49N 10 0W
Claremont, Calif., U.S.A. 161 L9 34 6N 117 43W
Claremont, N.H., U.S.A. 151 C12 43 23N 72 20W
Claremont Pt., Australia .... 126 A3 14 1 S 143 41 E
Claremore, U.S.A. 155 G7 36 19N 95 36W
Claremorris, Ireland 23 C3 53 45N 9 0W
Clarence, U.S.A. 156 E4 39 45N 92 16W
Clarence →, Australia .... 127 D5 29 25 S 153 22 E
Clarence →, N.Z. .... 131 C8 42 10 S 173 56 E
Clarence, I., Chile .... 176 D2 54 0 S 72 0W
Clarence, Port, U.S.A. 144 D6 65 15N 166 40W
Clarence I., Antarctica .... 7 C18 61 10 S 54 0W
Clarence Str., Australia .... 124 B5 12 0 S 131 0 E
Clarence Town, Bahamas 165 B5 23 6N 74 59W
Clarendon, Pa., U.S.A. 150 E5 41 47N 79 6W
Clarendon, Tex., U.S.A. 155 H4 34 56N 100 53W
Clarenville, Canada 141 C9 48 10N 54 1W
Claresholm, Canada 142 D6 50 0N 113 33W
Clarie Coast, Antarctica .... 7 C9 68 0 S 135 0 E
Clarinda, U.S.A. 156 E7 40 44N 95 2W
Clarion, Iowa, U.S.A. 156 B3 42 44N 93 44W
Clarion, Pa., U.S.A. 150 E5 41 13N 79 23W
Clarion →, U.S.A. 150 E5 41 7N 79 41W
Clark, Mo., U.S.A. 156 E4 39 17N 92 21W
Clark, S. Dak., U.S.A. 150 B3 44 4N 97 44W
Clark, Pt., Canada 148 B3 44 4N 81 45W
Clark Fork, U.S.A. 154 B5 48 9N 116 11W
Clark Fork →, U.S.A. 159 J7 34 46N 112 3W
Clarkdale, U.S.A. 141 B6 50 12N 66 38W
Clarke City, Canada .... 127 G4 40 32 S 148 10 E
Clarke I., Australia .... 126 C4 20 40 S 148 30 E
Clarke Ra., Australia 158 D9 45 39N 108 43W
Clark's Fork →, U.S.A. 141 D6 43 25N 65 38W
Clark's Harbour, Canada 152 B7 33 40N 82 12W
Clarks Hill L., U.S.A. 144 G8 58 51N 158 33W
Clarks Point, U.S.A. 151 E9 41 30N 75 42W
Clarks Summit, U.S.A. 148 F5 39 17N 80 30W
Clarksburg, U.S.A. 155 H9 34 12N 90 35W
Clarksdale, U.S.A. 155 H8 35 28N 93 28W
Clarksville, Ark., U.S.A. 157 F11 38 17N 85 45W
Clarksville, Ind., U.S.A. 156 B4 42 47N 92 40W
Clarksville, Iowa, U.S.A. 156 E6 39 22N 90 54W
Clarksville, Mo., U.S.A. 149 G2 36 32N 87 21W
Clarksville, Tenn., U.S.A. 155 J7 33 37N 95 3W
Clarksville, Tex., U.S.A. .... 171 E1 19 8 S 50 40W
Claro →, Brazil 160 D3 46 6N 123 12W
Clatskanie, U.S.A. 155 H4 35 7N 101 22W
Claude, U.S.A. .... 79 A6 18 37N 121 4 E
Claveria, Cagayan, Phil. .... 80 E4 12 54N 123 15 E
Claveria, Masbate, Phil. .... 81 G5 8 38N 124 55 E
Claveria, Mis. Or., Phil. 10 C8 74 15N 21 0W
Clavering Ø, Greenland 152 C8 32 10N 81 55W
Claxton, U.S.A. 160 G5 38 17N 121 10W
Clay, U.S.A. 154 F6 39 23N 97 8W
Clay Center, U.S.A. 157 E9 39 17N 87 7W
Clay City, Ind., U.S.A. 157 G13 37 52N 83 55W
Clay City, Ky., U.S.A. 159 K8 33 25N 110 51W
Claypool, U.S.A. 150 F6 40 17N 78 27W
Claysburg, U.S.A. 150 F4 40 7N 80 25W
Claysville, U.S.A. 152 D4 31 53N 85 27W
Clayton, Ala., U.S.A. 157 E10 39 41N 86 31W
Clayton, Ind., U.S.A. 155 G3 36 27N 103 11W
Clayton, N. Mex., U.S.A. 151 B8 44 14N 76 5W
Clayton, N.Y., U.S.A. 23 E2 51 25N 9 32W
Clear, C., Ireland 150 A7 45 26N 77 12W
Clear, L., Canada 142 B5 56 40N 119 30W
Clear Hills, Canada 23 E2 51 26N 9 30W
Clear I., Ireland 160 F4 39 2N 122 47W
Clear L., U.S.A. 156 A3 43 8N 93 23W
Clear Lake, Iowa, U.S.A. 154 C6 44 45N 96 41W
Clear Lake, S. Dak., U.S.A. 158 F3 41 56N 121 5W
Clear Lake Reservoir, U.S.A. 150 F6 41 2N 78 27W
Clearfield, Pa., U.S.A. 158 F8 41 7N 112 2W
Clearfield, Utah, U.S.A. 158 G2 38 57N 122 38W
Clearlake, U.S.A. 160 G4 38 57N 122 38W
Clearlake Highlands, U.S.A. 142 C4 51 38N 120 2W
Clearwater, Canada 149 M4 27 58N 82 48W
Clearwater, U.S.A. 142 C6 52 22N 114 57W
Clearwater →, Alta., Canada 143 B6 56 44N 111 23W
Clearwater →, Alta., Canada 143 C9 53 34N 99 49W
Clearwater L., Canada 158 C6 46 5N 115 20W
Clearwater Mts., U.S.A. 143 C8 54 0N 101 0W
Clearwater Prov. Park, Canada 143 B7 56 55N 109 10W
Clearwater River Prov. Park, Canada 155 J6 32 21N 97 23W
Cleburne, U.S.A. 21 E5 52 26N 2 35W
Clee Hills, U.K. 20 D7 53 33N 0 3W
Cleethorpes, U.K. 21 F6 51 56N 2 0W
Cleeve Cloud, U.K. .... 29 D9 44 50N 5 38 E
Clelles, France 149 H4 34 41N 82 50W
Clemson, U.S.A. .... 81 F2 10 7N 118 58 E
Cleopatra Needle, Phil. .... 124 C2 17 22 S 119 20 E
Clerke Reef, Australia .... 126 C4 22 49 S 147 39 E
Clermont, Australia .... 27 C9 49 23N 2 24 E
Clermont, France 153 G8 28 33N 81 46W
Clermont, U.S.A. .... 27 C12 49 5N 5 4 E
Clermont-en-Argonne, France .... 28 C7 45 46N 3 4 E
Clermont-Ferrand, France .... 28 E7 43 38N 3 26 E
Clermont-l'Hérault, France .... 27 E13 47 25N 6 30 E
Clerval, France .... 24 D6 50 4N 6 2 E
Clervaux, Lux. .... 44 B8 46 22N 11 2 E
Cles, Italy .... 128 E2 33 43 S 136 30 E
Cleve, Australia 21 F5 51 26N 2 52W
Clevedon, U.K. 155 J9 33 45N 90 43W
Cleveland, Miss., U.S.A. 150 E3 41 30N 81 42W
Cleveland, Ohio, U.S.A. 155 G6 36 19N 96 28W
Cleveland, Okla., U.S.A. 149 H3 35 10N 84 53W
Cleveland, Tenn., U.S.A. 155 K7 30 21N 95 5W
Cleveland, Tex., U.S.A. .... 126 B4 19 11 S 147 1 E
Cleveland, C., Australia 158 B7 48 56N 113 51W
Cleveland, Mt., U.S.A. 150 E3 41 30N 81 34W
Cleveland Heights, U.S.A. .... 175 B5 26 24 S 52 23W
Clevelândia, Brazil 169 C7 3 49N 51 52W
Clevelândia do Norte, Brazil 157 E12 39 10N 84 45W
Cleves, U.S.A. 23 C2 53 50N 9 49W
Clew B., Ireland 149 M5 26 45N 80 56W
Clewiston, U.S.A. 23 C1 53 29N 10 1W
Clifden, Ireland

Clifden, N.Z. .... 131 G2 46 1 S 167 42 E
Cliffdell, U.S.A. 160 D5 46 56N 121 5W
Cliffy Hd., Australia .... 125 G2 35 1 S 116 29 E
Clifton, Australia .... 127 D5 27 59 S 151 53 E
Clifton, Ariz., U.S.A. 159 K9 33 3N 109 18W
Clifton, Colo., U.S.A. 159 G9 39 7N 108 25W
Clifton, Ill., U.S.A. 157 D9 40 56N 87 56W
Clifton, Tex., U.S.A. 155 K6 31 47N 97 35W
Clifton Beach, Australia .... 126 B4 16 46 S 145 39 E
Climax, Canada 143 D7 49 10N 108 20W
Climax, U.S.A. 152 E5 30 53N 84 26W
Clinch →, U.S.A. 149 H3 35 53N 84 29W
Clingmans Dome, U.S.A. 149 H4 35 34N 83 30W
Clint, U.S.A. 159 L10 31 35N 106 14W
Clinton, B.C., Canada 142 C4 51 6N 121 35W
Clinton, Ont., Canada 140 D3 43 37N 81 32W
Clinton, N.Z. .... 131 G4 46 12 S 169 23 E
Clinton, Ark., U.S.A. 155 H8 35 36N 92 28W
Clinton, Conn., U.S.A. 151 E12 41 17N 72 32W
Clinton, Ill., U.S.A. 156 D8 40 9N 88 57W
Clinton, Ind., U.S.A. 157 E9 39 40N 87 24W
Clinton, Iowa, U.S.A. 156 C6 41 51N 90 12W
Clinton, Mass., U.S.A. 151 D13 42 25N 71 41W
Clinton, Mich., U.S.A. 157 B13 42 4N 83 58W
Clinton, Miss., U.S.A. 155 J9 32 20N 90 20W
Clinton, Mo., U.S.A. 156 F3 38 22N 93 46W
Clinton, N.C., U.S.A. 149 H6 35 0N 78 22W
Clinton, Okla., U.S.A. 155 H5 35 31N 98 58W
Clinton, S.C., U.S.A. 149 H5 34 29N 81 53W
Clinton, Tenn., U.S.A. 149 G3 36 6N 84 8W
Clinton, Wash., U.S.A. 160 C4 47 59N 122 21W
Clinton, Wis., U.S.A. 157 B8 42 34N 88 52W
Clinton C., U.S.A. .... 126 C5 22 30 S 150 45 E
Clinton Colden L., Canada 138 B9 63 58N 107 27W
Clinton L., U.S.A. 157 D8 40 15N 88 45W
Clintonville, U.S.A. 154 C10 44 37N 88 46W
Clio, U.S.A. 152 D4 31 43N 85 37W
Clipperton, I., Pac. Oc. 135 F17 10 18N 109 13W
Clisham, U.K. 22 D2 57 57N 6 49W
Clisson, France 26 E5 47 5N 1 16W
Clitheroe, U.K. 20 D5 53 53N 2 22W
Clive, N.Z. .... 130 F5 39 36 S 176 58 E
Cliza, Bolivia .... 173 D4 17 36 S 65 56W
Clo-oose, Canada 160 B2 48 39N 124 49W
Cloates, Pt., Australia .... 124 D1 22 43 S 113 40 E
Clocolan, S. Africa .... 117 D4 28 55 S 27 34 E
Clodomira, Argentina .... 174 B3 27 35 S 64 14W
Clogher Hd., Ireland 23 C5 53 48N 6 14W
Clonakilty, Ireland 23 E3 51 37N 8 53W
Clonakilty B., Ireland 23 E3 51 35N 8 51W
Cloncurry, Australia .... 126 C3 20 40 S 140 28 E
Cloncurry →, Australia .... 126 B3 18 37 S 140 40 E
Clondalkin, Ireland 23 C5 53 19N 6 25W
Clones, Ireland 23 B4 54 11N 7 15W
Clonmel, Ireland 23 D4 52 21N 7 42W
Cloppenburg, Germany .... 30 C4 52 51N 8 1 E
Cloquet, U.S.A. 154 B8 46 43N 92 28W
Clorinda, Argentina .... 174 B4 25 16 S 57 45W
Cloud Bay, Canada 140 C2 48 9N 89 17W
Cloud Peak, U.S.A. 158 D10 44 23N 107 11W
Cloudcroft, U.S.A. 159 K11 32 58N 105 45W
Cloudy B., N.Z. .... 131 B9 41 25 S 174 10 E
Cloverdale, Calif., U.S.A. 160 G4 38 48N 123 1W
Cloverdale, Ind., U.S.A. 157 E10 39 31N 86 48W
Cloverport, U.S.A. 157 G10 37 50N 86 38W
Clovis, Calif., U.S.A. 160 J7 36 49N 119 42W
Clovis, N. Mex., U.S.A. 155 H3 34 24N 103 12W
Cloyes-sur-le-Loir, France .... 26 E8 48 0N 1 14 E
Cloyne, Canada 150 B7 44 49N 77 11W
Club Terrace, Australia .... 129 D8 37 35 S 148 58 E
Cluj □, Romania .... 53 D8 46 45N 23 30 E
Cluj-Napoca, Romania .... 53 D8 46 47N 23 38 E
Clunes, Australia .... 128 D5 37 20 S 143 45 E
Cluny, France .... 27 F11 46 26N 4 38 E
Cluses, France .... 27 F13 46 5N 6 35 E
Clusone, Italy .... 44 C6 45 53N 9 57 E
Clutha →, N.Z. .... 131 G4 46 20 S 169 49 E
Clwyd □, U.K. 20 D4 53 19N 3 31W
Clyattville, U.S.A. 152 E6 30 42N 83 19W
Clyde, Canada 142 C6 54 9N 113 39W
Clyde, N.Z. .... 131 G3 45 12 S 169 20 E
Clyde, N.Y., U.S.A. 150 C8 43 5N 76 52W
Clyde, Ohio, U.S.A. 150 E4 41 18N 82 59W
Clyde →, U.K. 22 F4 55 55N 4 30W
Clyde, Firth of, U.K. 22 F3 55 22N 5 1W
Clyde River, Canada 139 A13 70 30N 68 30W
Clydebank, U.K. 22 F4 55 54N 4 23W
Clymer, N.Y., U.S.A. 150 D5 42 1N 79 37W
Clymer, Pa., U.S.A. 150 F5 40 40N 79 1W
Clyo, U.S.A. 152 C8 32 29N 81 16W
Ćmielów, Poland .... 55 H8 50 53N 21 31 E
Côa →, Portugal 42 D3 41 5N 7 6W
Coachella, U.S.A. 161 M10 33 41N 116 10W
Coachella Canal, U.S.A. 161 N12 32 43N 114 57W
Coahoma, U.S.A. 155 J4 32 18N 101 18W
Coahuayana →, Mexico 162 D4 18 41N 103 45W
Coahuila □, Mexico 162 B4 27 0N 103 0W
Coal →, Canada 142 B3 59 39N 126 57W
Coal City, U.S.A. 157 C8 41 17N 88 17W
Coal I., N.Z. .... 131 G1 46 8 S 166 40 E
Coalane, Mozam. .... 119 F4 17 48 S 37 2 E
Coalcomán, Mexico 162 D4 18 40N 103 10W
Coaldale, Canada 142 D6 49 45N 112 35W
Coalgate, U.S.A. 155 H6 34 32N 96 13W
Coalinga, U.S.A. 160 J6 36 9N 120 21W
Coalisland, U.K. 23 B5 54 33N 6 42W
Coalville, U.K. 20 E6 52 44N 1 23W
Coalville, U.S.A. 158 F8 40 55N 111 24W
Coaraci, Brazil .... 171 D4 14 38 S 39 32W
Coari, Brazil .... 169 D5 4 8 S 63 7W
Coari →, Brazil .... 169 D5 4 30 S 63 33W
Coari, L. de, Brazil .... 169 D5 4 15 S 63 22W
Coast □, Kenya .... 118 C4 2 40 S 39 45 E
Coast Mts., Canada 142 C3 55 0N 129 20W
Coast Ranges, U.S.A. 160 G4 39 0N 123 0W
Coatbridge, U.K. 22 F4 55 52N 4 6W
Coatepec, Mexico 163 D5 19 27N 96 58W
Coatepeque, Guatemala 164 D1 14 46N 91 55W
Coatesville, U.S.A. 148 F8 39 59N 75 50W
Coaticook, Canada 141 C5 45 10N 71 46W
Coats I., Canada 139 B11 62 30N 83 0W
Coats Land, Antarctica .... 7 D1 77 0 S 25 0W
Coatzacoalcos, Mexico 163 D6 18 7N 94 25W
Cobadin, Romania .... 53 F13 44 5N 28 13 E
Cobalt, Canada 140 C4 47 25N 79 42W
Cobán, Guatemala 164 D1 15 30N 90 21W
Cobar, Australia .... 127 E4 31 27 S 145 48 E
Cobargo, Australia .... 129 F4 36 20 S 149 55 E
Cobbannah, Australia .... 129 E4 37 35 S 147 9 E
Cobberas, Mt., Australia .... 129 E4 36 50 S 148 12 E
Cóbh, Ireland 23 E3 51 51N 8 17W
Cobija, Bolivia .... 172 C4 11 0 S 68 50W
Cobleskill, U.S.A. 151 D10 42 41N 74 29W
Coboconk, Canada 150 B6 44 39N 78 48W
Cobourg, Canada 140 D4 43 58N 78 10W
Cobourg Pen., Australia .... 124 B5 11 20 S 132 15 E

Cobram, Australia .... 129 C6 35 54 S 145 40 E
Cóbuè, Mozam. .... 119 E3 12 0 S 34 58 E
Coburg, Germany .... 31 E6 50 15N 10 58 E
Coca, Spain 42 D6 41 13N 4 32W
Coca →, Ecuador .... 168 D2 0 29 S 76 58W
Cocachacra, Peru .... 172 D3 17 5 S 71 45W
Cocal, Brazil .... 170 B3 3 28 S 41 34W
Cocanada = Kakinada, India .... 94 F6 16 57N 82 11 E
Cocentaina, Spain 41 G4 38 45N 0 27W
Cochabamba, Bolivia .... 173 D4 17 26 S 66 10W
Coche, I., Venezuela 169 A5 10 47N 63 56W
Cochem, Germany .... 31 E3 50 9N 7 9 E
Cochemane, Mozam. .... 119 F3 17 0 S 32 54 E
Cochin, India .... 95 K3 9 58N 76 22 E
Cochin China, Vietnam .... 83 B3 10 30N 106 0 E
Cochran, U.S.A. 152 C6 32 23N 83 21W
Cochrane, Alta., Canada 142 C6 51 11N 114 30W
Cochrane, Ont., Canada 140 C3 49 0N 81 0W
Cochrane, Chile .... 176 C2 47 15 S 72 33W
Cochrane →, Canada 143 B8 59 0N 103 40W
Cochrane, L., Chile .... 176 C2 47 10 S 72 0W
Cochranton, U.S.A. 150 E4 41 31N 80 3W
Cockburn, Australia .... 128 B4 32 5 S 141 0 E
Cockburn, Canal, Chile .... 176 D2 54 30 S 72 0W
Cockburn I., Canada 140 C3 45 55N 83 22W
Cockburn Ra., Australia .... 124 C4 15 46 S 128 0 E
Cockermouth, U.K. 20 C4 54 40N 3 22W
Cocklebiddy, Australia .... 125 F4 32 0 S 126 3 E
Côco →, Brazil .... 170 C2 9 27 S 50 2W
Coco →, Cent. Amer. 164 D3 15 0N 83 8W
Coco, I. del, Pac. Oc. 135 G19 5 25N 87 55W
Coco, Pta., Colombia 168 C2 2 58N 77 43W
Cocoa, U.S.A. 149 L5 28 21N 80 44W
Cocoa Beach, U.S.A. 153 G9 28 19N 80 37W
Cocobeach, Gabon .... 114 B1 0 59N 9 34 E
Cocora, Romania .... 53 F12 44 45N 27 3 E
Côcos, Brazil .... 171 D3 14 10 S 44 33W
Côcos →, Brazil .... 171 D3 14 24 S 44 48W
Cocos I., Guam .... 133 R15 13 14N 144 39 E
Cocos Is., Ind. Oc. .... 121 F8 12 10 S 96 55 E
Cod, C., U.S.A. 148 D10 42 5N 70 10W
Codajás, Brazil .... 169 D5 3 55 S 62 0W
Codera, C., Venezuela 168 A4 10 35N 66 4W
Codfish I., N.Z. .... 131 G2 46 47 S 167 38 E
Codigoro, Italy .... 45 D9 44 49N 12 8 E
Codlea, Romania .... 53 E10 45 42N 25 27 E
Codó, Brazil .... 170 B3 4 30 S 43 55W
Codogno, Italy .... 44 C6 45 9N 9 42 E
Codpa, Chile .... 172 D4 18 50 S 69 44W
Codróipo, Italy .... 45 C10 45 58N 13 0 E
Codru, Munții, Romania .... 52 D7 46 30N 22 15 E
Cody, U.S.A. 158 D9 44 32N 109 3W
Coe Hill, Canada 150 B7 44 52N 77 50W
Coelemu, Chile .... 174 D1 36 30 S 72 48W
Coelho Neto, Brazil .... 170 B3 4 15 S 43 0W
Coen, Australia .... 126 A3 13 52 S 143 12 E
Coeroeni →, Surinam .... 169 C6 3 17 S 57 31W
Coesfeld, Germany .... 30 D3 51 56N 7 10 E
Coetivy Is., Seychelles .... 121 E4 7 8 S 56 16 E
Cœur d'Alene, U.S.A. 158 C5 47 45N 116 51W
Cœur d'Alene L., U.S.A. 158 C5 47 32N 116 48W
Coevorden, Neths. .... 24 B6 52 40N 6 44 E
Cofete, Canary Is. 39 F5 28 6N 14 23W
Coffeyville, U.S.A. 155 G7 37 2N 95 37W
Coffin B., Australia .... 127 E2 34 38 S 135 28 E
Coffin Bay, Australia .... 127 E2 34 37 S 135 29 E
Coffin Bay Peninsula, Australia .... 127 E2 34 32 S 135 15 E
Coffs Harbour, Australia .... 129 A10 30 16 S 153 5 E
Cofrentes, Spain 41 F3 39 13N 1 5W
Cogalnic →, Moldova .... 53 E14 45 49N 29 40 E
Cogealac, Romania .... 53 F13 44 36N 28 36 E
Coghinas →, Italy .... 46 B1 40 55N 8 48 E
Coghinas, L. del, Italy .... 46 B2 40 46N 9 3 E
Cognac, France 28 C3 45 41N 0 20W
Cogne, Italy .... 44 C4 45 37N 7 21 E
Cogolin, France .... 29 E10 43 15N 6 32 E
Cogolludo, Spain 40 E1 40 59N 3 10W
Cohocton, U.S.A. 150 D7 42 30N 77 30W
Cohocton →, U.S.A. 150 D7 42 9N 77 6W
Cohoes, U.S.A. 151 D11 42 46N 73 42W
Cohuna, Australia .... 128 C6 35 45 S 144 15 E
Coiba, I., Panama 164 E3 7 30N 81 40W
Coig →, Argentina .... 176 D3 51 0 S 69 10W
Coigeach, Rubha, U.K. 22 C3 58 6N 5 26W
Coihaique, Chile .... 176 C2 45 30 S 71 45W
Coimbatore, India .... 95 J3 11 2N 76 59 E
Coimbra, Brazil .... 173 D6 19 55 S 57 48W
Coimbra, Portugal 42 E2 40 15N 8 27W
Coimbra □, Portugal 42 E2 40 12N 8 25W
Coín, Spain 43 J6 36 40N 4 48W
Coipasa, L. de, Bolivia .... 172 D4 19 12 S 68 7W
Coipasa, Salar de, Bolivia .... 172 D4 19 26 S 68 9W
Cojata, Peru .... 172 D4 15 2 S 69 25W
Cojedes □, Venezuela 168 B4 9 20N 68 20W
Cojedes →, Venezuela 168 B4 8 34N 68 5W
Cojimies, Ecuador 168 C1 0 20N 80 0W
Cojocna, Romania .... 53 D8 46 45N 23 50 E
Cojutepeque, El Salv. 164 D2 13 41N 88 54W
Čoka, Serbia, Yug. .... 52 C5 45 57N 20 12 E
Cokeville, U.S.A. 158 E8 42 5N 110 57W
Colac, Australia .... 128 E5 38 21 S 143 35 E
Colachel = Kolachel, India .... 95 K3 8 10N 77 15 E
Colatina, Brazil .... 171 E3 19 32 S 40 37W
Colbeck, C., Antarctica .... 7 D13 77 6 S 157 48W
Colbert, U.S.A. 152 A6 34 3N 83 13W
Colbinabbin, Australia .... 129 D6 36 38 S 144 48 E
Colborne, Canada 150 C7 44 0N 77 53W
Colby, U.S.A. 154 F4 39 24N 101 3W
Colchester, U.K. .... 21 F8 51 54N 0 55 E
Cold Bay, U.S.A. 144 J7 55 12N 162 42W
Cold L., Canada 143 C7 54 33N 110 5W
Coldstream, Canada 142 C5 50 13N 119 11W
Coldstream, U.K. 22 F6 55 39N 2 15W
Coldwater, Canada 150 B5 44 42N 79 40W
Coldwater, Kans., U.S.A. 155 G5 37 16N 99 20W
Coldwater, Mich., U.S.A. 157 C11 41 57N 85 0W
Coldwater, Ohio, U.S.A. 157 D12 40 29N 84 38W
Coldwater →, U.S.A. 155 H9 34 28N 90 12W
Cole Camp, U.S.A. 156 F4 38 28N 93 12W
Coleambally, Australia .... 129 C4 34 49 S 145 52 E
Colebrook, U.S.A. 151 B13 44 54N 71 30W
Coleman, Canada 142 D6 49 40N 114 30W
Coleman, Fla., U.S.A. 153 G7 28 48N 82 4W
Coleman, Tex., U.S.A. 155 K5 31 50N 99 26W
Coleman →, Australia .... 126 B3 15 6 S 141 38 E
Colenso, S. Africa .... 117 D4 28 44 S 29 50 E
Coleraine, Australia .... 128 D4 37 36 S 141 40 E
Coleraine, U.K. 23 A5 55 8N 6 41W
Coleridge, L., N.Z. .... 131 D6 43 17 S 171 30 E
Colesberg, S. Africa .... 116 E4 30 45 S 25 5 E
Coleville, U.S.A. 160 G7 38 34N 119 30W
Colfax, Calif., U.S.A. 160 F6 39 6N 120 57W
Colfax, Ind., U.S.A. 157 D10 40 12N 86 40W
Colfax, Iowa, U.S.A. 156 C3 41 41N 93 14W
Colfax, La., U.S.A. 155 K8 31 31N 92 42W

Cornwall 203

Colfax, *Wash., U.S.A.* **158 C5** 46 53N 117 22W
Colhué Huapi, L., *Argentina* **176 C3** 45 30 S 69 0W
Colibaşi, *Moldova* **53 E13** 45 43N 28 11 E
Colibaşi, *Romania* **53 F9** 44 56N 24 54 E
Cólico, *Italy* **44 B6** 46 8N 9 22 E
Colíder, *Brazil* **173 C6** 10 45 S 55 25W
Coligny, *France* **27 F12** 46 23N 5 21 E
Coligny, *S. Africa* **117 D4** 26 17 S 26 15 E
Colima, *Mexico* **162 D4** 19 14N 103 43W
Colima □, *Mexico* **162 D4** 19 10N 103 40W
Colima, Nevado de, *Mexico* **162 D4** 19 35N 103 45W
Colina, *Chile* **174 C1** 33 13 S 70 45W
Colina do Norte, *Guinea-Biss.* **112 C2** 12 28N 15 0W
Colinas, *Goiás, Brazil* **171 D2** 14 15 S 48 2W
Colinas, *Maranhão, Brazil* **170 C3** 6 0 S 44 10W
Colindres, *Spain* **42 B7** 43 24N 3 27W
Colinton, *Australia* **129 C8** 35 50 S 149 10 E
Coll, *U.K.* **22 E2** 56 39N 6 34W
Collaguasi, *Chile* **174 A2** 21 5 S 68 45W
Collarada, Peña, *Spain* **40 C4** 42 43N 0 29W
Collarenebri, *Australia* **127 D4** 29 33 S 148 34 E
Colle di Val d'Elsa, *Italy* **44 E8** 43 25N 11 7 E
Collécchio, *Italy* **44 D7** 44 45N 10 13 E
Colleen Bawn, *Zimbabwe* **119 G2** 21 0 S 29 12 E
College, *U.S.A.* **144 D11** 64 52N 147 49W
College Park, *U.S.A.* **152 B5** 33 40N 84 27W
College Station, *U.S.A.* **155 K6** 30 37N 96 21W
Collesalvetti, *Italy* **44 E7** 43 34N 10 27 E
Collie, *N.S.W., Australia* **129 A8** 31 41 S 148 18 E
Collie, *W. Austral., Australia* **125 F2** 33 22 S 116 8 E
Collier B., *Australia* **124 C3** 16 10 S 124 15 E
Collier Ra., *Australia* **125 D2** 24 45 S 119 10 E
Collina, Passo di, *Italy* **44 D7** 44 2N 10 56 E
Collingwood, *Canada* **142 B4** 44 29N 80 13W
Collingwood, *N.Z.* **131 A7** 40 41 S 172 40 E
Collins, *Canada* **140 B2** 50 17N 89 27W
Collins, *Ga., U.S.A.* **152 C7** 32 11N 82 7W
Collins, *Mo., U.S.A.* **156 G3** 37 54N 93 37W
Collinsville, *Australia* **126 C4** 20 30 S 147 56 E
Collinsville, *U.S.A.* **156 F7** 38 40N 89 59W
Collipulli, *Chile* **174 D1** 37 55 S 72 30W
Collo, *Algeria* **111 A6** 36 58N 6 37 E
Collooney, *Ireland* **23 B3** 54 11N 8 29W
Colmar, *France* **27 D14** 48 5N 7 20 E
Colmars, *France* **29 D10** 44 11N 6 39 E
Colmenar, *Spain* **43 J6** 36 54N 4 20W
Colmenar de Oreja, *Spain* **42 E7** 40 6N 3 25W
Colmenar Viejo, *Spain* **42 E7** 40 39N 3 47W
Colo —►, *Australia* **129 B9** 33 25 S 150 52 E
Cologne = Köln, *Germany* **30 E2** 50 56N 6 57 E
Colom, I. d'en, *Spain* **39 B11** 39 58N 4 16 E
Coloma, *Calif., U.S.A.* **160 G6** 38 48N 120 53W
Coloma, *Mich., U.S.A.* **157 B10** 42 11N 86 19W
Colomb-Béchar = Béchar,
Algeria **111 B4** 31 38N 2 18W
Colombey-les-Belles, *France* **27 D12** 48 32N 5 54 E
Colombey-les-Deux-Églises,
France **27 D11** 48 13N 4 50 E
Colômbia, *Brazil* **171 F2** 20 10 S 48 40W
Colombia ■, *S. Amer.* **168 C3** 3 45N 73 0W
Colombian Basin, *S. Amer.* **136 H12** 14 0N 76 0W
Colombier, *Switz.* **32 C3** 46 58N 6 53 E
Colombo, *Sri Lanka* **95 L4** 6 56N 79 58 E
Colomiers, *France* **28 E5** 43 36N 1 21 E
Colón, *Buenos Aires, Argentina* **174 C3** 33 53 S 61 7W
Colón, *Entre Ríos, Argentina* **174 C4** 32 12 S 58 10W
Colón, *Cuba* **164 B3** 22 42N 80 54W
Colón, *Panama* **164 E4** 9 20N 79 54W
Colón, *Peru* **172 A1** 5 0 S 81 0W
Colonia 25 de Mayo, *Argentina* **176 A3** 37 48 S 67 41W
Colonia de Sant Jordi, *Spain* **39 B9** 39 19N 2 59 E
Colonia del Sacramento,
Uruguay **174 C4** 34 25 S 57 50W
Colonia Dora, *Argentina* **174 B3** 28 34 S 62 59W
Colonia Las Heras, *Argentina* **176 C3** 46 33 S 68 57W
Colonial Beach, *U.S.A.* **148 F7** 38 15N 76 58W
Colonie, *U.S.A.* **151 D11** 42 43N 73 50W
Colonna, C., *Italy* **47 C10** 39 2N 17 12 E
Colonsay, *Canada* **143 C7** 51 59N 105 52W
Colonsay, *U.K.* **22 E2** 56 5N 6 12W
Colorado □, *U.S.A.* **159 G10** 39 30N 105 30W
Colorado —►, *Argentina* **176 A4** 39 50 S 62 8W
Colorado —►, *N. Amer.* **159 L6** 31 45N 114 40W
Colorado —►, *U.S.A.* **155 L7** 28 36N 95 59W
Colorado City, *U.S.A.* **155 J4** 32 24N 100 52W
Colorado Plateau, *U.S.A.* **159 H8** 37 0N 111 0W
Colorado River Aqueduct,
U.S.A. **161 L12** 34 17N 114 10W
Colorado Springs, *U.S.A.* **154 F2** 38 50N 104 49W
Colorno, *Italy* **44 D7** 44 56N 10 23 E
Colotlán, *Mexico* **162 C4** 22 6N 103 16W
Colquechaca, *Bolivia* **173 D4** 18 40 S 66 1W
Colquitt, *U.S.A.* **152 D5** 31 10N 84 44W
Colstrip, *U.S.A.* **158 D10** 45 53N 106 38W
Colton, *U.S.A.* **151 B10** 44 33N 74 56W
Columbia, *Ala., U.S.A.* **152 D4** 31 18N 85 7W
Columbia, *Ill., U.S.A.* **156 F6** 38 27N 90 12W
Columbia, *Ky., U.S.A.* **148 G3** 37 6N 85 18W
Columbia, *La., U.S.A.* **155 J8** 32 6N 92 5W
Columbia, *Miss., U.S.A.* **155 K10** 31 15N 89 50W
Columbia, *Mo., U.S.A.* **156 F4** 38 57N 92 20W
Columbia, *Pa., U.S.A.* **151 F8** 40 2N 76 30W
Columbia, *S.C., U.S.A.* **152 A8** 34 0N 81 2W
Columbia, *Tenn., U.S.A.* **149 H2** 35 37N 87 2W
Columbia —►, *N. Amer.* **160 D2** 46 15N 124 5W
Columbia, C., *Canada* **6 A4** 83 0N 70 0W
Columbia, District of □, *U.S.A.* **148 F7** 38 55N 77 0W
Columbia, Mt., *Canada* **142 C5** 52 8N 117 20W
Columbia Basin, *U.S.A.* **158 C4** 46 45N 119 5W
Columbia City, *U.S.A.* **157 C11** 41 10N 85 29W
Columbia Falls, *U.S.A.* **158 B6** 48 23N 114 11W
Columbia Mts., *Canada* **142 C5** 52 0N 119 0W
Columbia Plateau, *U.S.A.* **158 D5** 44 0N 117 30W
Columbiana, *U.S.A.* **150 F4** 40 53N 80 42W
Columbretes, Is., *Spain* **40 F5** 39 50N 0 50 E
Columbus, *Ga., U.S.A.* **152 C5** 32 28N 84 59W
Columbus, *Ind., U.S.A.* **157 E11** 39 13N 85 55W
Columbus, *Kans., U.S.A.* **155 G7** 37 10N 94 50W
Columbus, *Miss., U.S.A.* **149 J1** 33 30N 88 25W
Columbus, *Mont., U.S.A.* **158 D9** 45 38N 109 15W
Columbus, *N. Mex., U.S.A.* **159 L10** 31 50N 107 38W
Columbus, *Nebr., U.S.A.* **154 E6** 41 26N 97 22W
Columbus, *Ohio, U.S.A.* **157 E13** 39 58N 83 0W
Columbus, *Tex., U.S.A.* **155 L6** 29 42N 96 33W
Columbus Grove, *U.S.A.* **157 D12** 40 55N 84 4W
Columbus Junction, *U.S.A.* **156 C5** 41 17N 91 22W
Colunga, *Spain* **42 B5** 43 29N 5 16W
Colusa, *U.S.A.* **160 F4** 39 13N 122 1W
Colville, *U.S.A.* **158 B5** 48 33N 117 54W
Colville —►, *U.S.A.* **138 A4** 70 25N 150 30W
Colville, C., *N.Z.* **130 C4** 36 29 S 175 21 E
Colwood, *Canada* **160 B3** 48 26N 123 29W
Colwyn Bay, *U.K.* **20 D4** 53 18N 3 44W
Coma, *Ethiopia* **107 F4** 8 29N 36 53 E
Comácchio, *Italy* **45 D9** 44 42N 12 11 E
Comalcalco, *Mexico* **163 D6** 18 16N 93 13W
Comallo, *Argentina* **176 B2** 41 0 S 70 5W
Comana, *Romania* **53 F11** 44 10N 26 10 E
Comanche, *U.S.A.* **155 K5** 31 54N 98 36W
Comandante Luis Piedrabuena,
Argentina **176 C3** 49 59 S 68 54W
Comăneşti, *Romania* **53 D11** 46 25N 26 26 E
Comarapa, *Bolivia* **173 D5** 17 54 S 64 29W
Comarnic, *Romania* **53 E10** 45 15N 25 38 E
Comayagua, *Honduras* **164 D2** 14 25N 87 37W
Combahee —►, *U.S.A.* **149 J5** 32 30N 80 31W
Combara, *Australia* **129 A8** 31 10 S 148 22 E
Combarbalá, *Chile* **174 C1** 31 11 S 71 2W
Combeaufontaine, *France* **27 E12** 47 38N 5 54 E
Comber, *Canada* **150 D2** 42 14N 82 33W
Comber, *U.K.* **23 B6** 54 33N 5 45W
Combermere, *Canada* **150 A7** 45 22N 77 37W
Combermere Bay, *Burma* **90 F4** 19 37N 93 34 E
Comblain-au-Pont, *Belgium* **24 D5** 50 29N 5 35 E
Combourg, *France* **26 D5** 48 25N 1 46W
Comboyne, *Australia* **129 A10** 31 34 S 152 27 E
Combrailles, *France* **27 F9** 46 8N 2 8 E
Combronde, *France* **28 C7** 45 58N 3 5 E
Comer, *Ala., U.S.A.* **152 C4** 32 2N 85 23W
Comer, *Ga., U.S.A.* **152 A6** 34 4N 83 8W
Comeragh Mts., *Ireland* **23 D4** 52 18N 7 34W
Comet, *Australia* **126 C4** 23 36 S 148 38 E
Comilla, *Bangla.* **90 D3** 23 28N 91 10 E
Comino, *Malta* **38 C1** 36 2N 14 20 E
Comino, C., *Italy* **46 B2** 40 32N 9 49 E
Cómiso, *Italy* **47 F7** 36 56N 14 36 E
Comitán, *Mexico* **163 D6** 16 18N 92 9W
Commentry, *France* **27 F9** 46 20N 2 46 E
Commerce, *Ga., U.S.A.* **149 H4** 34 12N 83 28W
Commerce, *Tex., U.S.A.* **155 J7** 33 15N 95 54W
Commercy, *France* **27 D12** 48 43N 5 34 E
Commewijne □, *Surinam* **169 B7** 5 25N 54 45W
Committee B., *Canada* **139 B11** 68 30N 86 30W
Commonwealth B., *Antarctica* **7 C10** 67 0 S 144 0 E
Commoron Cr. —►, *Australia* **127 D5** 28 22 S 150 8 E
Communism Pk. =
Kommunizma, Pik, *Tajikistan* **64 F8** 39 0N 72 2 E
Como, *Italy* **44 C6** 45 47N 9 5 E
Como, Lago di, *Italy* **44 B6** 46 0N 9 11 E
Comodoro Rivadavia, *Argentina* **176 C3** 45 50 S 67 40W
Comorâşte, *Romania* **52 E6** 45 10N 21 35 E
Comorin, C., *India* **95 K3** 8 3N 77 40 E
Comoro Is. = Comoros ■,
Ind. Oc. **105 H8** 12 10 S 44 15 E
Comoros ■, *Ind. Oc.* **105 H8** 12 10 S 44 15 E
Comox, *Canada* **142 D4** 49 42N 124 55W
Compass Lake, *U.S.A.* **152 E4** 30 36N 85 24W
Compiègne, *France* **27 C9** 49 24N 2 50 E
Comporta, *Portugal* **43 G2** 38 22N 8 46W
Compostela, *Mexico* **162 C4** 21 15N 104 53W
Compostela, *Phil.* **81 H6** 7 40N 126 2 E
Comprida, I., *Brazil* **175 A6** 24 50 S 47 42W
Compton, *Canada* **151 A13** 45 14N 71 49W
Compton, *U.S.A.* **161 M8** 33 54N 118 13W
Comrat, *Moldova* **53 D13** 46 18N 28 40 E
Con Cuong, *Vietnam* **86 C5** 19 2N 104 54 E
Con Son, *Vietnam* **78 C3** 8 41N 106 37 E
Cona Niyeu, *Argentina* **176 B3** 41 58 S 67 0W
Conakry, *Guinea* **112 D2** 9 29N 13 49W
Conara, *Australia* **126 G4** 41 50 S 147 26 E
Conargo, *Australia* **129 C6** 35 16 S 145 10 E
Concarneau, *France* **26 E3** 47 52N 3 56W
Conceição, *Brazil* **170 C4** 7 33 S 38 31W
Conceição, *Mozam.* **119 F4** 18 47 S 36 7 E
Conceição da Barra, *Brazil* **171 E4** 18 35 S 39 45W
Conceição do Araguaia, *Brazil* **170 C2** 8 0 S 49 2W
Conceição do Canindé, *Brazil* **170 C3** 7 54 S 41 34W
Conceicao do Maú, *Brazil* **169 C6** 3 35N 59 53W
Concepción, *Argentina* **174 B2** 27 20 S 65 35W
Concepción, *Bolivia* **173 D5** 16 15 S 62 8W
Concepción, *Chile* **174 D1** 36 50 S 73 0W
Concepción, *Mexico* **163 D6** 18 15N 90 5W
Concepción, *Paraguay* **174 A4** 23 22 S 57 26W
Concepción, *Peru* **172 C2** 11 54 S 75 19W
Concepcion, *Phil.* **80 D3** 15 27N 120 47 E
Concepción □, *Chile* **174 D1** 37 0 S 72 30W
Concepción —►, *Mexico* **162 A2** 30 32N 113 2W
Concepción, Est. de, *Chile* **176 D2** 50 30 S 74 55W
Concepción, L., *Bolivia* **173 D5** 17 20 S 61 20W
Concepción, Punta, *Mexico* **162 B2** 26 55N 111 59W
Concepción del Oro, *Mexico* **162 C4** 24 40N 101 30W
Concepción del Uruguay,
Argentina **174 C4** 32 35 S 58 20W
Conception, Pt., *U.S.A.* **161 L6** 34 27N 120 28W
Conception B., *Canada* **141 C9** 47 45N 53 0W
Conception B., *Namibia* **116 C1** 23 55 S 14 22 E
Conception I., *Bahamas* **165 B4** 23 52N 75 9W
Concession, *Zimbabwe* **119 F3** 17 27 S 30 56 E
Conchas Dam, *U.S.A.* **155 H2** 35 22N 104 11W
Conches-en-Ouche, *France* **26 D7** 48 58N 0 56 E
Concho, *U.S.A.* **159 J9** 34 28N 109 36W
Concho —►, *U.S.A.* **155 K5** 31 34N 99 43W
Conchos —►, *Chihuahua,*
Mexico **162 B4** 29 32N 105 0W
Conchos —►, *Tamaulipas,*
Mexico **163 B5** 25 9N 98 35W
Concise, *Switz.* **32 C3** 46 51N 6 43 E
Concord, *Calif., U.S.A.* **160 H4** 37 59N 122 2W
Concord, *Ga., U.S.A.* **152 B5** 33 5N 84 27W
Concord, *Mich., U.S.A.* **157 B12** 42 11N 84 38W
Concord, *Mo., U.S.A.* **156 F6** 38 32N 90 23W
Concord, *N.C., U.S.A.* **149 H5** 35 25N 80 35W
Concord, *N.H., U.S.A.* **151 C13** 43 12N 71 32W
Concordia, *Argentina* **174 C4** 31 20 S 58 2W
Concórdia, *Brazil* **168 D4** 4 36 S 66 36W
Concordia, *Mexico* **162 C3** 23 18N 106 2W
Concordia, *Kans., U.S.A.* **154 F6** 39 34N 97 40W
Concordia, *Mo., U.S.A.* **156 F3** 38 59N 93 34W
Concrete, *U.S.A.* **158 B3** 48 32N 121 45W
Conda, *Angola* **115 E2** 11 9 S 14 20 E
Condah, *Australia* **128 D4** 37 57 S 141 44 E
Condamine, *Australia* **127 D5** 26 56 S 150 9 E
Condat, *France* **28 C6** 45 21N 2 46 E
Condé, *Angola* **115 E2** 10 50 S 14 37 E
Conde, *Brazil* **171 D4** 11 49 S 37 37W
Conde, *U.S.A.* **154 C5** 45 9N 98 6W
Condé-sur-Noireau, *France* **26 D6** 48 51N 0 33W
Condeúba, *Brazil* **171 D3** 14 52 S 42 0W
Condobolin, *Australia* **127 E4** 33 4 S 147 6 E
Condom, *France* **28 E4** 43 57N 0 22 E
Condon, *U.S.A.* **158 D3** 45 14N 120 11W
Conegliano, *Italy* **45 C9** 45 53N 12 18 E
Conejera, I. = Conills, I. des,
Spain **39 B9** 39 11N 2 58 E
Conejos, *Mexico* **162 B4** 26 14N 103 53W
Confolens, *France* **28 B4** 46 2N 0 40 E
Confuso —►, *Paraguay* **174 B4** 25 9 S 57 34W
Congaree —►, *U.S.A.* **152 B9** 33 44N 80 38W
Congaz, *Moldova* **53 D13** 46 7N 28 36 E
Congerville, *U.S.A.* **156 D7** 40 38N 89 11W
Conghua, *China* **87 F9** 23 36N 113 31 E
Congjiang, *China* **76 E7** 25 43N 108 52 E
Congleton, *U.K.* **20 D5** 53 10N 2 13W
Congo, *Brazil* **170 C4** 7 48 S 36 40W
Congo (Kinshasa) = Congo,
Dem. Rep. of the ■, *Africa* **115 C4** 3 0 S 23 0 E
Congo ■, *Africa* **114 C3** 1 0 S 16 0 E
Congo —►, *Africa* **115 D2** 6 4 S 12 24 E
Congo, Dem. Rep. of the ■,
Africa **115 C4** 3 0 S 23 0 E
Congo Basin, *Africa* **104 G6** 0 10 S 24 30 E
Congonhas, *Brazil* **171 F3** 20 30 S 43 52W
Congress, *U.S.A.* **159 J7** 34 9N 112 51W
Conil = Conil de la Frontera,
Spain **43 J4** 36 17N 6 10W
Conil de la Frontera, *Spain* **43 J4** 36 17N 6 10W
Conills, I. des, *Spain* **39 B9** 39 11N 2 58 E
Coniston, *Canada* **140 C3** 46 29N 80 51W
Conjeeveram = Kanchipuram,
India **95 H4** 12 52N 79 45 E
Conklin, *Canada* **143 B6** 55 38N 111 5W
Conklin, *U.S.A.* **151 D9** 42 2N 75 49W
Conn, L., *Ireland* **23 B2** 54 3N 9 15W
Connacht □, *Ireland* **23 C2** 53 43N 9 12W
Conneaut, *U.S.A.* **150 E4** 41 57N 80 34W
Connecticut □, *U.S.A.* **151 E12** 41 30N 72 45W
Connecticut —►, *U.S.A.* **151 E12** 41 16N 72 20W
Connell, *U.S.A.* **158 C4** 46 40N 118 52W
Connellsville, *U.S.A.* **150 F5** 40 1N 79 35W
Connemara, *Ireland* **23 C2** 53 29N 9 45W
Connemaugh —►, *U.S.A.* **150 F5** 40 28N 79 19W
Conner, *Phil.* **80 C3** 17 48N 121 19 E
Connerré, *France* **26 D7** 48 3N 0 30 E
Connersville, *U.S.A.* **157 E11** 39 39N 85 8W
Connors Ra., *Australia* **126 C4** 21 40 S 149 10 E
Conoble, *Australia* **129 B6** 32 55 S 144 33 E
Cononaco —►, *Ecuador* **168 D2** 1 32 S 75 35W
Conques, *France* **28 D6** 44 36N 2 23 E
Conquest, *Canada* **143 C7** 51 32N 107 14W
Conrad, *Iowa, U.S.A.* **156 B4** 42 14N 92 52W
Conrad, *Mont., U.S.A.* **158 B8** 48 10N 111 57W
Conran, C., *Australia* **129 D8** 37 49 S 148 44 E
Conroe, *U.S.A.* **155 K7** 30 19N 95 27W
Consecon, *Canada* **150 C7** 44 0N 77 31W
Conselheiro Lafaiete, *Brazil* **171 F3** 20 40 S 43 48W
Conselheiro Pena, *Brazil* **171 E3** 19 10 S 41 30W
Conselve, *Italy* **45 C8** 45 14N 11 52 E
Consett, *U.K.* **20 C6** 54 51N 1 50W
Consort, *Canada* **143 C6** 52 1N 110 46W
Constance = Konstanz,
Germany **31 H5** 47 40N 9 10 E
Constance, L. = Bodensee,
Europe **33 A8** 47 35N 9 25 E
Constanţa, *Romania* **53 F13** 44 14N 28 38 E
Constanţa □, *Romania* **53 F13** 44 15N 28 15 E
Constantia, *U.S.A.* **151 C8** 43 15N 76 1W
Constantina, *Spain* **43 H5** 37 51N 5 40W
Constantine, *Algeria* **111 A6** 36 25N 6 42 E
Constantine, *U.S.A.* **157 C11** 41 50N 85 40W
Constantine, C., *U.S.A.* **144 G8** 58 24N 158 54W
Constitución, *Chile* **174 D1** 35 20 S 72 30W
Constitución, *Uruguay* **174 C4** 31 0 S 57 50W
Consuegra, *Spain* **43 F7** 39 28N 3 36W
Consul, *Canada* **143 D7** 49 20N 109 30W
Contact, *U.S.A.* **158 F6** 41 46N 114 45W
Contai, *India* **93 J12** 21 54N 87 46 E
Contamana, *Peru* **172 B3** 7 19 S 74 55W
Contarina, *Italy* **45 C9** 45 1N 12 13 E
Contas —►, *Brazil* **171 D4** 14 17 S 39 1W
Contes, *France* **29 E11** 43 49N 7 19 E
Conthey, *Switz.* **32 D4** 46 14N 7 18 E
Continental, *U.S.A.* **157 C12** 41 6N 84 16W
Contoocook, *U.S.A.* **151 C13** 43 13N 71 45W
Contra Costa, *Mozam.* **117 D5** 25 9 S 33 30 E
Contres, *France* **26 E8** 47 24N 1 26 E
Contrexéville, *France* **27 D12** 48 10N 5 53 E
Controller B., *U.S.A.* **144 F11** 60 7N 144 15W
Contumaza, *Peru* **172 B2** 7 23 S 78 57W
Contwoyto L., *Canada* **138 B8** 65 42N 110 50W
Convención, *Colombia* **168 B3** 8 28N 73 21W
Conversano, *Italy* **47 B10** 40 58N 17 7 E
Converse, *U.S.A.* **157 D11** 40 35N 85 52W
Convoy, *U.S.A.* **157 D12** 40 55N 84 43W
Conway = Conwy, *U.K.* **20 D4** 53 17N 3 50W
Conway = Conwy —►, *U.K.* **20 D4** 53 17N 3 50W
Conway, *Ark., U.S.A.* **155 H8** 35 5N 92 26W
Conway, *N.H., U.S.A.* **151 C13** 43 59N 71 7W
Conway, *S.C., U.S.A.* **149 J6** 33 51N 79 3W
Conway, L., *Australia* **127 D2** 28 17 S 135 35 E
Conwy, *U.K.* **20 D4** 53 17N 3 50W
Conwy □, *U.K.* **20 D4** 53 10N 3 44W
Conwy —►, *U.K.* **20 D4** 53 17N 3 50W
Conyers, *U.S.A.* **152 B5** 33 40N 84 1W
Coober Pedy, *Australia* **127 D1** 29 1 S 134 43 E
Cooch Behar = Koch Bihar,
India **90 B2** 26 22N 89 29 E
Cooinda, *Australia* **124 B5** 13 15 S 130 5 E
Cook, *Australia* **125 F5** 30 37 S 130 25 E
Cook, *U.S.A.* **154 B8** 47 49N 92 39W
Cook, B., *Chile* **176 E2** 55 10 S 70 0W
Cook, C., *Canada* **142 C3** 50 8N 127 55W
Cook, Mt., *N.Z.* **131 D5** 43 36 S 170 9 E
Cook Inlet, *U.S.A.* **138 C4** 60 0N 152 0W
Cook Is., *Pac. Oc.* **135 J12** 17 0 S 160 0W
Cook Strait, *N.Z.* **130 H3** 41 15 S 174 29 E
Cooke Plains, *Australia* **128 C3** 35 23 S 139 34 E
Cookeville, *U.S.A.* **149 G3** 36 10N 85 30W
Cookhouse, *S. Africa* **116 E4** 32 44 S 25 47 E
Cooks Hammock, *U.S.A.* **152 F6** 29 56N 83 17W
Cookshire, *Canada* **151 A13** 45 25N 71 38W
Cookstown, *U.K.* **23 B5** 54 39N 6 45W
Cooksville, *Canada* **150 C5** 43 36N 79 35W
Cooktown, *Australia* **126 B4** 15 30 S 145 16 E
Coolabah, *Australia* **129 A7** 31 1 S 146 43 E
Cooladdi, *Australia* **127 D4** 26 37 S 145 23 E
Coolah, *Australia* **129 A8** 31 48 S 149 41 E
Coolamon, *Australia* **127 E4** 34 46 S 147 8 E
Coolgardie, *Australia* **125 F3** 30 55 S 121 8 E
Coolidge, *Ariz., U.S.A.* **159 K8** 32 59N 111 31W
Coolidge, *Ga., U.S.A.* **152 D6** 31 1N 83 52W
Coolidge Dam, *U.S.A.* **159 K8** 33 0N 110 20W
Cooma, *Australia* **127 F4** 36 12 S 149 8 E
Coon Rapids, *Iowa, U.S.A.* **156 C2** 41 53N 94 41W
Coon Rapids, *Minn., U.S.A.* **154 C8** 45 9N 93 19W
Coonabarabran, *Australia* **129 A8** 31 14 S 149 18 E
Coonalpyn, *Australia* **128 C3** 35 43 S 139 52 E
Coonamble, *Australia* **129 A8** 30 56 S 148 27 E
Coonana, *Australia* **125 F3** 31 0 S 123 0 E
Coondapoor, *India* **95 H2** 13 42N 74 40 E
Cooninie, L., *Australia* **127 D2** 26 4 S 139 59 E
Coonoor, *India* **95 J3** 11 21N 76 45 E
Cooper, *U.S.A.* **155 J7** 33 23N 95 42W
Cooper —►, *U.S.A.* **152 C10** 32 50N 79 56W
Cooper Cr. —►, *N. Terr.,*
Australia **122 C5** 12 7 S 132 41 E
Cooper Cr. —►, *S. Austral.,*
Australia **127 D2** 28 29 S 137 46 E
Cooperstown, *N. Dak., U.S.A.* **154 B5** 47 27N 98 8W
Cooperstown, *N.Y., U.S.A.* **151 D10** 42 42N 74 56W
Coopersville, *U.S.A.* **157 A11** 43 4N 85 57W
Coorabie, *Australia* **125 F5** 31 54 S 132 18 E
Coorow, *Australia* **125 E2** 29 53 S 116 2 E
Cooroy, *Australia* **127 D5** 26 22 S 152 54 E
Coos Bay, *U.S.A.* **158 E1** 43 22N 124 13W
Coosa —►, *U.S.A.* **149 J2** 32 30N 86 16W
Cootamundra, *Australia* **129 C8** 34 36 S 148 1 E
Cootehill, *Ireland* **23 B4** 54 4N 7 5W
Copahue Paso, *Argentina* **174 D1** 37 49 S 71 8W
Copainalá, *Mexico* **163 D6** 17 8N 93 11W
Copake Falls, *U.S.A.* **151 D11** 42 7N 73 31W
Copalnic Mănăştur, *Romania* **53 C8** 47 30N 23 41 E
Copán, *Honduras* **164 D2** 14 50N 89 9W
Copatana, *Brazil* **168 D4** 2 48 S 67 4W
Cope, *Colo., U.S.A.* **154 F3** 39 40N 102 51W
Cope, *S.C., U.S.A.* **152 B8** 33 23N 81 0W
Cope, C., *Spain* **41 H3** 37 26N 1 28W
Cope Cope, *Australia* **128 D5** 36 27 S 143 5 E
Copeland, *U.S.A.* **153 K8** 25 57N 81 22W
Copenhagen = København,
Denmark **17 J6** 55 41N 12 34 E
Copenhagen, *U.S.A.* **151 C9** 43 54N 75 41W
Copertino, *Italy* **47 B11** 40 16N 18 3 E
Copeville, *Australia* **128 C3** 34 47 S 139 51 E
Copiapó, *Chile* **174 B1** 27 30 S 70 20W
Copiapó —►, *Chile* **174 B1** 27 19 S 70 56W
Coplay, *U.S.A.* **151 F9** 40 44N 75 29W
Copley, *Australia* **128 A3** 30 36 S 138 26 E
Copp L., *Canada* **142 A6** 60 14N 114 40W
Copparo, *Italy* **45 D8** 44 54N 11 49 E
Coppename —►, *Surinam* **169 B6** 5 48N 55 55W
Copper Harbor, *U.S.A.* **148 B2** 47 28N 87 53W
Copper Queen, *Zimbabwe* **119 F2** 17 29 S 29 18 E
Copperas Cove, *U.S.A.* **155 K6** 31 8N 97 54W
Copperbelt □, *Zambia* **119 E2** 13 15 S 27 30 E
Coppermine = Kugluktuk,
Canada **138 B8** 67 50N 115 5W
Coppermine —►, *Canada* **138 B8** 67 49N 116 4W
Copperopolis, *U.S.A.* **160 H6** 37 58N 120 38W
Coppet, *Switz.* **32 D2** 46 19N 6 12 E
Copşa Mică, *Romania* **53 D9** 46 7N 24 15 E
Coquet —►, *U.K.* **20 B6** 55 20N 1 32W
Coquilhatville = Mbandaka,
Dem. Rep. of the Congo **114 B3** 0 1N 18 18 E
Coquille, *U.S.A.* **158 E1** 43 11N 124 11W
Coquimbo, *Chile* **174 C1** 30 0 S 71 20W
Coquimbo □, *Chile* **174 C1** 31 0 S 71 0W
Corabia, *Romania* **53 G9** 43 48N 24 30 E
Coração de Jesus, *Brazil* **171 E3** 16 43 S 44 22W
Coracora, *Peru* **172 D3** 15 5 S 73 45W
Coraki, *Australia* **127 D5** 28 59 S 153 17 E
Coral, *U.S.A.* **150 F5** 40 29N 79 10W
Coral Bay, *Phil.* **81 G1** 8 25N 117 20 E
Coral Gables, *U.S.A.* **149 N5** 25 45N 80 16W
Coral Harbour = Salliq,
Canada **139 B11** 64 8N 83 10W
Coral Sea, *Pac. Oc.* **134 J7** 15 0 S 150 0 E
Coral Springs, *U.S.A.* **149 M5** 26 16N 80 13W
Coralville, *U.S.A.* **156 C5** 41 40N 91 35W
Coralville L., *U.S.A.* **156 C5** 41 50N 91 40W
Corantijn —►, *Surinam* **169 B6** 5 50N 57 8W
Coraopolis, *U.S.A.* **150 F4** 40 31N 80 10W
Corato, *Italy* **47 A9** 41 9N 16 25 E
Corbeil-Essonnes, *France* **27 D9** 48 36N 2 26 E
Corbie, *France* **27 C9** 49 54N 2 30 E
Corbières, *France* **28 F6** 42 55N 2 35 E
Corbigny, *France* **27 E10** 47 16N 3 40 E
Corbin, *U.S.A.* **148 G3** 36 57N 84 6W
Corbones —►, *Spain* **43 H5** 37 36N 5 39W
Corbu, *Romania* **53 F13** 44 25N 28 39 E
Corby, *U.K.* **21 E7** 52 30N 0 41W
Corcaigh = Cork, *Ireland* **23 E3** 51 54N 8 29W
Corcoran, *U.S.A.* **160 J7** 36 6N 119 33W
Cordele, *U.S.A.* **152 D6** 31 58N 83 47W
Cordell, *U.S.A.* **155 H5** 35 17N 98 59W
Cordenòns, *Italy* **45 C9** 45 59N 12 42 E
Cordes, *France* **28 D5** 44 5N 1 57 E
Cordisburgo, *Brazil* **171 E3** 19 7 S 44 21W
Córdoba, *Argentina* **174 C3** 31 20 S 64 10W
Córdoba, *Mexico* **163 D5** 18 50N 97 0W
Córdoba, *Spain* **43 H6** 37 50N 4 50W
Córdoba □, *Argentina* **174 C3** 31 22 S 64 15W
Córdoba □, *Colombia* **168 B2** 8 20N 75 40W
Córdoba □, *Spain* **43 G6** 38 5N 5 0W
Córdoba, Sierra de, *Argentina* **174 C3** 31 10 S 64 25W
Cordon, *Phil.* **80 C3** 16 42N 121 32 E
Cordova, *U.S.A.* **138 B5** 60 33N 145 45W
Corella, *Spain* **40 C3** 42 7N 1 48W
Corella —►, *Australia* **126 B3** 19 34 S 140 47 E
Coremas, *Brazil* **170 C4** 7 1 S 37 58W
Corentyne —►, *Guyana* **169 B6** 5 50N 57 8W
Corfield, *Australia* **126 C3** 21 40 S 143 21 E
Corfu = Kérkira, *Greece* **38 A3** 39 38N 19 50 E
Corfu, Str. of, *Greece* **38 A4** 39 34N 20 0 E
Corgo = O Corgo, *Spain* **42 C3** 42 56N 7 25W
Corguinho, *Brazil* **173 D7** 19 53 S 54 52W
Cori, *Italy* **46 A5** 41 39N 12 55 E
Coria, *Spain* **42 F4** 39 58N 6 33W
Coria del Río, *Spain* **43 H4** 37 16N 6 3W
Coricudgy, *Australia* **129 B9** 32 51 S 150 24 E
Corigliano Cálabro, *Italy* **47 C9** 39 36N 16 31 E
Corimba, Barra de, *Angola* **115 D2** 8 52 S 13 9 E
Coringa Is., *Australia* **126 B4** 16 58 S 149 58 E
Corinth = Kórinthos, *Greece* **48 D4** 37 56N 22 55 E
Corinth, *Ky., U.S.A.* **157 F12** 38 30N 84 34W
Corinth, *Miss., U.S.A.* **149 H1** 34 56N 88 31W
Corinth, *N.Y., U.S.A.* **151 C11** 43 14N 73 49W
Corinth, G. of = Korinthiakós
Kólpos, *Greece* **48 C4** 38 16N 22 30 E
Corinth Canal, *Greece* **48 D4** 37 58N 23 0 E
Corinto, *Brazil* **171 E3** 18 20 S 44 30W
Corinto, *Nic.* **164 D2** 12 30N 87 10W
Corisco, *Eq. Guin.* **114 B1** 0 55N 9 18 E
Cork, *Ireland* **23 E3** 51 54N 8 29W
Cork □, *Ireland* **23 E3** 51 57N 8 40W
Cork Harbour, *Ireland* **23 E3** 51 47N 8 16W
Corlay, *France* **26 D3** 48 20N 3 5W
Corleone, *Italy* **46 E6** 37 49N 13 18 E
Corleto Perticara, *Italy* **47 B9** 40 23N 16 2 E
Çorlu, *Turkey* **51 E11** 41 11N 27 49 E
Cormack L., *Canada* **142 A4** 60 56N 121 37W
Cormòns, *Italy* **45 C10** 45 58N 13 28 E
Cormorant, *Canada* **143 C8** 54 14N 100 35W
Cormorant L., *Canada* **143 C8** 54 15N 100 50W
Corn Is. = Maíz, Is. del, *Nic.* **164 D3** 12 15N 83 4W
Cornélio Procópio, *Brazil* **175 A5** 23 7 S 50 40W
Cornell, *U.S.A.* **157 D8** 41 0N 88 44W
Corner Brook, *Canada* **141 C8** 48 57N 57 58W
Corneşti, *Moldova* **53 C13** 47 21N 28 1 E
Corníglio, *Italy* **44 D7** 44 29N 10 5 E
Corning, *Ark., U.S.A.* **155 G9** 36 25N 90 35W
Corning, *Calif., U.S.A.* **158 G2** 39 56N 122 11W
Corning, *Iowa, U.S.A.* **156 D2** 40 59N 94 44W
Corning, *N.Y., U.S.A.* **150 D7** 42 9N 77 3W
Corno Grande, *Italy* **45 F10** 42 28N 13 34 E
Cornwall, *Canada* **140 C5** 45 2N 74 44W
Cornwall, *U.S.A.* **151 F8** 40 17N 76 25W
Cornwall □, *U.K.* **21 G3** 50 26N 4 40W

Danilov 205

Cuernavaca, *Mexico* 163 D5 18 55N 99 15W
Cuero, *U.S.A.* 155 L6 29 6N 97 17W
Cuers, *France* 29 E10 43 14N 6 5 E
Cuevas, Cerro, *Bolivia* 173 E4 22 0 S 65 12W
Cuevas del Almanzora, *Spain* 41 H3 37 18N 1 58W
Cuevo, *Bolivia* 173 E5 20 15 S 63 30W
Cugir, *Romania* 53 E8 45 48N 23 25 E
Cugnaux, *France* 28 E5 43 32N 1 20 E
Cuhai-Bakony →, *Hungary* 52 C2 47 35N 17 54 E
Cuiabá, *Brazil* 173 D6 15 30 S 56 0W
Cuiabá →, *Brazil* 173 D6 17 5 S 56 36W
Cuijk, *Neths.* 24 C5 51 44N 5 50 E
Cuilco, *Guatemala* 164 C1 15 24N 91 58W
Cuillin Hills, *U.K.* 22 D2 57 13N 6 15W
Cuillin Sd., *U.K.* 22 D2 57 4N 6 20W
Cuilo, *Angola* 115 D3 8 12 S 19 28 E
Cuilo-Futa, *Angola* 115 D3 6 28 S 15 51 E
Cuima, *Angola* 115 E3 13 25 S 15 45 E
Cuimba, *Angola* 115 D2 6 10 S 14 41 E
Cuiseaux, *France* 27 F12 46 30N 5 22 E
Cuité, *Brazil* 170 C4 6 29 S 36 9W
Cuito →, *Angola* 116 B3 18 1 S 20 48 E
Cuito Cuanavale, *Angola* 115 F3 15 10 S 19 10 E
Cuitzeo, L. de, *Mexico* 162 D4 19 55N 101 5W
Cuiuni →, *Brazil* 169 D5 0 45 S 63 7W
Cuivre →, *U.S.A.* 156 F6 38 55N 90 44W
Cuivre, West Fork →, *U.S.A.* 156 E6 39 2N 90 58W
Cujmir, *Romania* 52 F7 44 13N 22 57 E
Cukai, *Malaysia* 87 K4 4 13N 103 25 E
Culasi, *Phil.* 81 F4 11 26N 122 3 E
Culbertson, *U.S.A.* 154 A2 48 9N 104 31W
Culburra, *Australia* 128 C3 35 50 S 139 58 E
Culcairn, *Australia* 127 F4 35 41 S 147 3 E
Culebra, Sierra de la, *Spain* 42 D4 41 55N 6 20W
Culfa, *Azerbaijan* 101 C11 38 57N 45 38 E
Culgoa, *Australia* 128 C5 35 44 S 143 6 E
Culgoa →, *Australia* 127 D4 29 56 S 146 20 E
Culiacán, *Mexico* 162 C3 24 50N 107 23W
Culiacán →, *Mexico* 162 C3 24 30N 107 42W
Culion, *Phil.* 79 B6 11 54N 119 58 E
Culion I., *Phil.* 81 F2 11 50N 120 0 E
Culiseu →, *Brazil* 173 C7 12 14 S 53 17W
Cúllar, *Spain* 43 H8 37 35N 2 34W
Cullarin Ra., *Australia* 129 C8 34 30 S 149 30 E
Cullen, *U.K.* 22 D6 57 42N 2 49W
Cullen Pt., *Australia* 126 A3 11 57 S 141 54 E
Cullera, *Spain* 41 F4 39 9N 0 17W
Cullman, *U.S.A.* 149 H2 34 11N 86 51W
Culloden, *U.S.A.* 152 C5 32 52N 84 6W
Cullom, *U.S.A.* 157 D8 40 53N 88 16W
Culo →, *Angola* 115 D3 6 13 S 15 34 E
Culoz, *France* 29 C9 45 47N 5 46 E
Culpataro, *Australia* 128 B6 33 40 S 144 22 E
Culpeper, *U.S.A.* 148 F7 38 30N 78 0W
Culuene →, *Brazil* 173 C7 12 56 S 52 51W
Culver, *U.S.A.* 157 C10 41 13N 86 25W
Culver, Pt., *Australia* 125 F3 32 54 S 124 43 E
Culverden, *N.Z.* 131 C7 42 47 S 172 49 E
Culverton, *U.S.A.* 152 B7 33 19N 82 54W
Cuma, *Angola* 115 E3 12 52 S 15 5 E
Cumaná, *Venezuela* 169 A5 10 30N 64 5W
Cumaovası, *Turkey* 49 C9 38 15N 27 9 E
Cumare, *Colombia* 168 C3 0 49N 72 32W
Cumari, *Brazil* 171 E2 18 16 S 48 11W
Cumberland, *B.C., Canada* 142 D4 49 40N 125 0W
Cumberland, *Ont., Canada* 151 A9 45 29N 75 24W
Cumberland, *Iowa, U.S.A.* 156 C2 41 16N 94 52W
Cumberland, *Md., U.S.A.* 148 F6 39 39N 78 46W
Cumberland →, *U.S.A.* 149 G2 36 15N 87 0W
Cumberland, C., *Vanuatu* 133 D4 14 39 S 166 37 E
Cumberland, L., *U.S.A.* 149 G3 36 57N 84 55W
Cumberland I., *U.S.A.* 152 E8 30 50N 81 25W
Cumberland Is., *Australia* 126 C4 20 35 S 149 10 E
Cumberland L., *Canada* 143 C8 54 3N 102 18W
Cumberland Pen., *Canada* 139 B13 67 0N 64 0W
Cumberland Plateau, *U.S.A.* 149 H3 36 0N 85 0W
Cumberland Sd., *Canada* 139 B13 65 30N 66 0W
Cumbernauld, *U.K.* 22 F5 55 57N 3 58W
Cumbira, *Angola* 115 E3 12 11 S 15 8 E
Cumborah, *Australia* 127 D4 29 40 S 147 45 E
Cumbres Mayores, *Spain* 43 G4 38 4N 6 39W
Cumbria □, *U.K.* 20 C5 54 42N 2 52W
Cumbrian Mts., *U.K.* 20 C5 54 30N 3 0W
Cumbum, *India* 95 G4 15 40N 79 10 E
Cuminá, *Brazil* 169 D6 1 57 S 56 2W
Cuminá →, *Brazil* 169 D6 1 30 S 56 0W
Cuminapanema →, *Brazil* 169 D7 1 9 S 54 54W
Cummings Mt., *U.S.A.* 161 K8 35 2N 118 34W
Cummins, *Australia* 127 E2 34 16 S 135 43 E
Cumnock, *Australia* 129 B8 32 59 S 148 46 E
Cumnock, *U.K.* 22 F4 55 28N 4 17W
Cumpas, *Mexico* 162 B3 30 0N 109 48W
Cumplida, Pta., *Canary Is.* 39 F2 28 50N 17 48W
Çumra, *Turkey* 100 D5 37 34N 32 45 E
Cuncumén, *Chile* 174 C1 31 53 S 70 38W
Cunderdin, *Australia* 125 F2 31 37 S 117 12 E
Cundinamarca □, *Colombia* 168 C3 5 0N 74 0W
Cunene □, *Angola* 115 F3 16 30 S 15 0 E
Cunene →, *Angola* 116 B1 17 20 S 11 50 E
Cúneo, *Italy* 44 D4 44 23N 7 32 E
Çüngüş, *Turkey* 96 B3 38 13N 39 17 E
Cunhinga, *Angola* 115 E3 12 11 S 16 47 E
Cunillera, I. = Sa Conillera, *Spain* 39 C7 38 59N 1 13 E
Cunjamba, *Angola* 115 F4 15 27 S 20 10 E
Cunlhat, *France* 28 C7 45 38N 3 32 E
Cunnamulla, *Australia* 127 D4 28 2 S 145 38 E
Cuorgnè, *Italy* 44 C4 45 23N 7 39 E
Cupar, *Canada* 143 C8 50 57N 104 10W
Cupar, *U.K.* 22 E5 56 19N 3 1W
Cupcini, *Moldova* 53 B12 48 6N 27 23 E
Cupica, G. de, *Colombia* 168 B2 6 25N 77 30W
Ćuprija, *Serbia, Yug.* 50 C5 43 57N 21 26 E
Curaçá, *Brazil* 170 C4 8 59 S 39 54W
Curaçao, *Neth. Ant.* 165 D6 12 10N 69 0W
Curacautín, *Chile* 176 A2 38 26 S 71 53W
Curahuara de Carangas, *Bolivia* 172 D4 17 52 S 68 26W
Curanilahue, *Chile* 174 D1 37 29 S 73 28W
Curaray →, *Peru* 168 D3 2 20 S 74 5W
Curatabaca, *Venezuela* 169 B5 6 19N 62 51W
Cure →, *France* 27 E10 47 40N 3 41 E
Curepto, *Chile* 174 D1 35 8 S 72 1W
Curiapo, *Venezuela* 169 B5 8 33N 61 5W
Curicó, *Chile* 174 C1 34 55 S 71 20W
Curicuriari →, *Brazil* 168 D4 0 14 S 66 48W
Curimatá, *Brazil* 170 D3 10 2 S 44 17W
Curinga, *Italy* 47 D9 38 49N 16 19 E
Curiplaya, *Colombia* 168 C3 0 16N 74 52W
Curitiba, *Brazil* 175 B6 25 20 S 49 10W
Curitibanos, *Brazil* 175 B5 27 18 S 50 36W
Curoca →, *Angola* 115 F2 15 43 S 11 55 E
Currabubula, *Australia* 129 A9 31 16 S 150 44 E
Currais Novos, *Brazil* 170 C4 6 13 S 36 30W
Curralinho, *Brazil* 170 B2 1 45 S 49 46W
Currant, *U.S.A.* 158 G6 38 51N 115 32W
Curranyalpa, *Australia* 129 A6 30 53 S 144 39 E
Curraweena, *Australia* 129 A6 30 47 S 145 54 E
Current →, *U.S.A.* 155 G9 36 15N 90 55W
Currie, *Australia* 126 F3 39 56 S 143 53 E
Currie, *U.S.A.* 158 F6 40 16N 114 45W
Cursole, *Somali Rep.* 120 D3 2 14N 45 25 E
Curtea de Argeş, *Romania* 53 E9 45 12N 24 42 E
Curtici, *Romania* 52 D6 46 21N 21 18 E
Curtis, *U.S.A.* 154 E4 40 38N 100 31W
Curtis Group, *Australia* 126 F4 39 30 S 146 37 E
Curtis I., *Australia* 126 C5 23 35 S 151 10 E
Curuá →, *Pará, Brazil* 169 D7 2 24 S 54 5W
Curuá →, *Pará, Brazil* 173 B7 5 23 S 54 22W
Curuá, I., *Brazil* 170 A1 0 48N 50 10W
Curuaés →, *Brazil* 173 B7 7 30 S 54 45W
Curuaí, *Brazil* 169 D6 2 17 S 55 29W
Curuápanema →, *Brazil* 169 D6 2 25 S 55 2W
Curuçá, *Brazil* 170 B2 0 43 S 47 50W
Curuçá →, *Brazil* 172 B3 4 27 S 71 23W
Curuguaty, *Paraguay* 175 A4 24 31 S 55 42W
Curup, *Indonesia* 78 E2 4 26 S 102 13 E
Curupira, Serra, *S. Amer.* 169 C5 1 25N 64 30W
Cururu →, *Brazil* 173 B6 7 12 S 58 3W
Cururupu, *Brazil* 170 B3 1 50 S 44 50W
Curuzú Cuatiá, *Argentina* 174 B4 29 50 S 58 5W
Curvelo, *Brazil* 171 E3 18 45 S 44 27W
Curyo, *Australia* 128 C5 35 50 S 142 47 E
Cushing, *U.S.A.* 155 H6 35 59N 96 46W
Cushing, Mt., *Canada* 142 B3 57 35N 126 57W
Cusihuiriáchic, *Mexico* 162 B3 28 10N 106 50W
Cusna, Mte., *Italy* 44 D7 44 17N 10 23 E
Cusset, *France* 27 F10 46 8N 3 28 E
Cusseta, *U.S.A.* 152 C5 32 18N 84 47W
Cusso, Sa. do, *Angola* 115 D2 6 30 S 14 58 E
Custer, *U.S.A.* 154 D3 43 46N 103 36W
Cut Bank, *U.S.A.* 158 B7 48 38N 112 20W
Cutchogue, *U.S.A.* 151 E12 41 1N 72 30W
Cutervo, *Peru* 172 B2 6 25 S 78 55W
Cuthbert, *U.S.A.* 152 D5 31 46N 84 48W
Cutler, *U.S.A.* 160 J7 36 31N 119 17W
Cutler Ridge, *U.S.A.* 153 K9 25 35N 80 20W
Cutlerville, *U.S.A.* 157 B11 42 50N 85 40W
Cutral-Có, *Argentina* 176 A3 38 58 S 69 15W
Cutro, *Italy* 47 C9 39 2N 16 59 E
Cuttaburra →, *Australia* 127 D3 29 43 S 144 22 E
Cuttack, *India* 94 D7 20 25N 85 57 E
Cuva →, *Angola* 115 E2 11 42 S 14 52 E
Cuvelai, *Angola* 115 F3 15 44 S 15 50 E
Cuvier, C., *Australia* 125 D1 23 14 S 113 22 E
Cuvier I., *N.Z.* 130 C4 36 27 S 175 50 E
Cuxhaven, *Germany* 30 B4 53 51N 8 41 E
Cuyabeno, *Ecuador* 168 D2 0 16 S 75 53W
Cuyahoga Falls, *U.S.A.* 150 E3 41 8N 81 29W
Cuyapo, *Phil.* 80 D3 15 46N 120 40 E
Cuyo, *Phil.* 79 B6 10 50N 121 5 E
Cuyo East Pass, *Phil.* 81 F3 11 0N 121 28 E
Cuyo I., *Phil.* 81 F3 10 51N 121 2 E
Cuyo Islands, *Phil.* 81 F3 11 4N 120 57 E
Cuyo West Pass, *Phil.* 81 F3 11 0N 120 30 E
Cuyuni →, *Guyana* 169 B6 6 23N 58 41W
Cuzco, *Bolivia* 172 E4 20 0 S 66 50W
Cuzco, *Peru* 172 C3 13 32 S 72 0W
Cuzco □, *Peru* 172 C3 13 31 S 71 59W
Čvrsnica, *Bos.-H.* 52 G2 43 36N 17 35 E
Cwmbran, *U.K.* 21 F4 51 39N 3 2W
Cyangugu, *Rwanda* 118 C2 2 29 S 28 54 E
Cybinka, *Poland* 55 F1 52 12N 14 46 E
Cyclades = Kikládhes, *Greece* 48 E6 37 0N 24 30 E
Cygnet, *Australia* 126 G4 43 8 S 147 1 E
Cynthiana, *U.S.A.* 157 F12 38 23N 84 18W
Cypress Hills, *Canada* 143 D7 49 40N 109 30W
Cypress Hills Prov. Park, *Canada* 143 D7 49 40N 109 30W
Cyprus ■, *Asia* 38 E12 35 0N 33 0 E
Cyrenaica, *Libya* 108 B4 27 0N 23 0 E
Cyrene = Shaḥḥāt, *Libya* 108 B4 32 48N 21 54 E
Czaplinek, *Poland* 54 E3 53 34N 16 14 E
Czar, *Canada* 143 C6 52 27N 110 50W
Czarna →, *Łódzkie, Poland* 55 G6 51 18N 19 55 E
Czarna →, *Świętokrzyskie, Poland* 55 H8 50 28N 21 21 E
Czarna Białostocka, *Poland* 55 E10 53 18N 23 17 E
Czarna Woda, *Poland* 54 E5 53 51N 18 6 E
Czarne, *Poland* 54 E3 53 42N 16 58 E
Czarnków, *Poland* 55 F3 52 55N 16 38 E
Czech Rep. ■, *Europe* 34 B8 50 0N 15 0 E
Czechowice-Dziedzice, *Poland* 55 J5 49 54N 18 59 E
Czempiń, *Poland* 55 F3 52 9N 16 43 E
Czeremcha, *Poland* 55 F10 52 31N 23 21 E
Czerniejewo, *Poland* 55 F4 52 26N 17 30 E
Czersk, *Poland* 54 E4 53 46N 17 58 E
Czerwieńsk, *Poland* 55 F2 52 1N 15 23 E
Czerwionka-Leszczyny, *Poland* 55 H5 50 7N 18 37 E
Częstochowa, *Poland* 55 H6 50 49N 19 7 E
Człopa, *Poland* 55 E3 53 6N 16 6 E
Człuchów, *Poland* 54 E4 53 41N 17 22 E
Czyżew-Osada, *Poland* 55 F9 52 48N 22 19 E

D

Da →, *Vietnam* 76 G5 21 15N 105 20 E
Da Hinggan Ling, *China* 73 B7 48 0N 121 0 E
Da Lat, *Vietnam* 78 B3 11 56N 108 25 E
Da Nang, *Vietnam* 78 A3 16 4N 108 13 E
Da Qaidam, *China* 72 C4 37 50N 95 15 E
Da Yunhe →, *China* 75 G11 34 25N 120 5 E
Da'an, *China* 75 B13 45 30N 124 7 E
Daanbantayan, *Phil.* 81 F5 11 17N 124 2 E
Dab'a, Ras el, *Egypt* 106 H6 31 3N 28 31 E
Daba Shan, *China* 76 B7 32 0N 109 0 E
Dabai, *Nigeria* 113 C6 11 25N 5 15 E
Dabajuro, *Venezuela* 168 A3 11 2N 70 40W
Dabakala, *Ivory C.* 112 D4 8 15N 4 20W
Dabaro, *Somali Rep.* 120 C3 6 21N 48 43 E
Dabas, *Hungary* 52 C4 47 11N 19 19 E
Dabat, *Ethiopia* 107 E4 12 58N 37 41 E
Dabbagh, Jabal, *Si. Arabia* 96 E2 27 52N 35 45 E
Dabeiba, *Colombia* 168 B2 7 1N 76 16W
Dabhoi, *India* 92 H5 22 10N 73 20 E
Dąbie, *Poland* 55 F5 52 5N 18 50 E
Dabie Shan, *China* 77 B10 31 20N 115 20 E
Dabilda, *Cameroon* 113 C7 12 45N 14 35 E
Dabnou, *Niger* 113 C6 14 10N 5 22 E
Dabo = Pasirkuning, *Indonesia* 78 E2 0 30 S 104 33 E
Dabola, *Guinea* 112 C2 10 50N 11 5W
Dabou, *Ivory C.* 112 D4 5 20N 4 23W
Daboya, *Ghana* 113 D4 9 30N 1 20W
Dąbrowa Białostocka, *Poland* 54 E10 53 40N 23 21 E
Dąbrowa Górnicza, *Poland* 55 H6 50 15N 19 10 E
Dąbrowa Tarnowska, *Poland* 55 H7 50 10N 21 0 E
Dabu, *China* 77 E11 24 22N 116 41 E
Dabugam, *India* 94 E6 19 27N 82 26 E
Dabung, *Malaysia* 87 K4 5 23N 102 1 E
Dabus →, *Ethiopia* 107 E4 10 48N 35 10 E
Dacato →, *Ethiopia* 107 F5 7 25N 42 40 E
Dacca = Dhaka, *Bangla.* 90 D3 23 43N 90 26 E
Dacca = Dhaka □, *Bangla.* 90 C3 24 25N 90 25 E
Dachau, *Germany* 31 G7 48 15N 11 26 E
Dachstein, Hoher, *Austria* 34 D6 47 28N 13 35 E
Dačice, *Czech Rep.* 34 B8 49 5N 15 26 E
Dacula, *U.S.A.* 152 B6 33 59N 83 54W
Dadali, *Solomon Is.* 133 M10 8 7 S 159 6 E
Dadanawa, *Guyana* 169 C6 2 50N 59 30W
Daday, *Turkey* 100 B5 41 28N 33 27 E
Dade City, *U.S.A.* 149 L4 28 22N 82 11W
Dades, Oued →, *Morocco* 110 B3 30 58N 6 44W
Dadeville, *U.S.A.* 152 C4 32 50N 85 46W
Dadhar, *Pakistan* 92 E2 29 28N 67 39 E
Dadiya, *Nigeria* 113 D7 9 35N 11 24 E
Dadra & Nagar Haveli □, *India* 94 D1 20 5N 73 0 E
Dadri = Charkhi Dadri, *India* 92 E7 28 37N 76 17 E
Dadu, *Pakistan* 91 D2 26 45N 67 45 E
Dadu He →, *China* 76 C4 29 31N 103 46 E
Daet, *Phil.* 79 B6 14 2N 122 55 E
Dafang, *China* 76 D5 27 9N 105 39 E
Dağ, *Turkey* 49 D12 37 12N 30 31 E
Dagali, *Norway* 18 D5 60 25N 8 28 E
Dagana, *Senegal* 112 B1 16 30N 15 35W
Dagash, *Sudan* 106 D3 19 19N 33 25 E
Dagestan □, *Russia* 61 J8 42 30N 47 0 E
Dagestanskiye Ogni, *Russia* 61 J9 42 6N 48 12 E
Dagg Sd., *N.Z.* 131 F1 45 23 S 166 45 E
Daggett, *U.S.A.* 161 L10 34 52N 116 52W
Daghestan Republic = Dagestan □, *Russia* 61 J8 42 30N 47 0 E
Daghfeli, *Sudan* 106 D3 19 18N 32 40 E
Dağlıq Qarabağ = Nagorno-Karabakh, *Azerbaijan* 101 C12 39 55N 46 45 E
Dagmersellen, *Switz.* 32 B5 47 13N 7 59 E
Dagö = Hiiumaa, *Estonia* 15 G20 58 50N 22 45 E
Dagu, *China* 75 E9 38 59N 117 40 E
Dagua, *Papua N. G.* 132 B2 3 27 S 143 20 E
Daguan, *China* 76 D4 27 43N 103 56 E
Dagupan, *Phil.* 79 A6 16 3N 120 20 E
Daguragu, *Australia* 124 C5 17 33 S 130 30 E
Dahab, *Egypt* 106 B3 28 31N 34 31 E
Dahanu, *India* 94 E1 19 58N 72 44 E
Dahivadi, *India* 94 F2 17 43N 74 33 E
Dahlak Kebir, *Eritrea* 102 D3 15 50N 40 10 E
Dahlenburg, *Germany* 30 B6 53 11N 10 44 E
Dahlonega, *U.S.A.* 149 H4 34 32N 83 59W
Dahme, *Germany* 30 D9 51 52N 13 25 E
Dahod, *India* 92 H6 22 50N 74 15 E
Dahomey = Benin ■, *Africa* 113 D5 10 0N 2 0 E
Dahong Shan, *China* 77 B9 31 25N 113 0 E
Dahra, *Senegal* 112 B1 15 22N 15 30W
Dahra, Massif de, *Algeria* 111 A5 36 7N 1 21 E
Dahshûr, *Egypt* 106 J7 29 45N 31 14 E
Dahūk, *Iraq* 101 D10 36 50N 43 1 E
Daḥy, Nafūd ad, *Si. Arabia* 98 B4 22 0N 45 25 E
Dai Hao, *Vietnam* 86 C6 18 1N 106 25 E
Dai-Sen, *Japan* 70 B5 35 22N 133 32 E
Dai Shan, *China* 77 B14 30 25N 122 10 E
Dai Xian, *China* 74 E7 39 4N 112 58 E
Daicheng, *China* 74 E9 38 42N 116 38 E
Daigo, *Japan* 71 A12 36 46N 140 21 E
Daimanji-San, *Japan* 70 A5 36 14N 133 20 E
Daimiel, *Spain* 43 F7 39 5N 3 35W
Daingean, *Ireland* 23 C4 53 18N 7 17W
Dainkog, *China* 76 A1 32 30N 97 58 E
Daintree, *Australia* 126 B4 16 20 S 145 20 E
Daiō-Misaki, *Japan* 71 C8 34 15N 136 45 E
Dair, J. ed, *Sudan* 107 E3 12 27N 30 42 E
Dairût, *Egypt* 106 B3 27 34N 30 43 E
Daisetsu-Zan, *Japan* 68 C11 43 30N 142 57 E
Daitari, *India* 94 D7 21 10N 85 46 E
Daito, *Japan* 70 B4 35 19N 132 58 E
Dajarra, *Australia* 126 C2 21 42 S 139 30 E
Dajin Chuan →, *China* 76 B3 31 16N 101 59 E
Dak Dam, *Cambodia* 86 F6 12 20N 107 21 E
Dak Nhe, *Vietnam* 86 E6 15 28N 107 48 E
Dak Pek, *Vietnam* 86 E6 15 4N 107 44 E
Dak Song, *Vietnam* 87 F6 12 19N 107 35 E
Dak Sui, *Vietnam* 86 E6 14 55N 107 43 E
Dakar, *Senegal* 112 C1 14 34N 17 29W
Dakhla, *W. Sahara* 110 D1 23 50N 15 53W
Dakhla, El Wâhât el-, *Egypt* 106 B2 25 30N 28 50 E
Dakingari, *Nigeria* 113 C5 11 37N 4 1 E
Dakor, *India* 92 H5 22 45N 73 11 E
Dakoro, *Niger* 113 C6 14 31N 6 46 E
Dakota City, *Iowa, U.S.A.* 156 B2 42 43N 94 12W
Dakota City, *Nebr., U.S.A.* 154 D6 42 25N 96 25W
Đakovica, *Kosovo, Yug.* 50 D4 42 22N 20 26 E
Đakovo, *Croatia* 52 E3 45 19N 18 24 E
Dal, *Norway* 18 E5 59 53N 8 40 E
Dala, *Angola* 115 E4 11 3 S 20 17 E
Dala, *Solomon Is.* 133 M11 8 30 S 160 41 E
Dala-Cachibo, *Angola* 115 E2 10 30 S 14 41 E
Dalaas, *Austria* 33 B10 47 7N 10 0 E
Dalaba, *Guinea* 112 C2 10 47N 12 12W
Dalachi, *China* 74 F3 36 48N 105 0 E
Dalaguete, *Phil.* 81 G4 9 46N 123 32 E
Dalai Nur, *China* 74 C9 43 20N 116 45 E
Dālakī, *Iran* 97 D6 29 26N 51 17 E
Dalälven, *Sweden* 16 D10 60 12N 16 43 E
Dalaman, *Turkey* 49 E10 36 48N 28 47 E
Dalaman →, *Turkey* 49 E10 36 41N 28 43 E
Dalandzadgad, *Mongolia* 74 C3 43 27N 104 30 E
Dalanganem Is., *Phil.* 81 F3 10 40N 120 17 E
Dalap-Uliga-Darrit, *Marshall Is.* 134 G9 7 7N 171 24 E
Dalarna, *Sweden* 16 D8 61 0N 14 0 E
Dalasýsla □, *Iceland* 11 B4 65 15N 22 0W
Dalat, *Malaysia* 85 B4 2 44N 111 56 E
Dālbandīn, *Pakistan* 91 C2 29 0N 64 23 E
Dalbeattie, *U.K.* 22 G5 54 56N 3 50W
Dalbeg, *Australia* 126 C4 20 16 S 147 18 E
Dalbosjön, *Sweden* 17 F6 58 40N 12 45 E
Dalby, *Australia* 127 D5 27 10 S 151 17 E
Dalby, *Sweden* 17 J7 55 40N 13 22 E
Dale, *Norway* 18 C2 61 22N 5 24 E
Dale, *U.S.A.* 157 F10 38 10N 86 59W
Dale City, *U.S.A.* 148 F7 38 38N 77 18W
Dale Hollow L., *U.S.A.* 149 G3 36 32N 85 27W
Dalen, *Norway* 18 E4 59 26N 8 0 E
Dalet, *Burma* 90 F4 19 59N 93 51 E
Daletme, *Burma* 90 E4 21 36N 92 46 E
Daleville, *Ala., U.S.A.* 152 D4 31 19N 85 43W
Daleville, *Ind., U.S.A.* 157 D11 40 7N 85 33W
Dalga, *Egypt* 106 B3 27 39N 30 41 E
Dalgān, *Iran* 97 E8 27 31N 59 19 E
Dalhart, *U.S.A.* 155 G3 36 4N 102 31W
Dalhousie, *Canada* 141 C6 48 5N 66 26W
Dalhousie, *India* 92 C6 32 38N 75 58 E
Dali, *Shaanxi, China* 74 G5 34 48N 109 58 E
Dali, *Yunnan, China* 76 E3 25 40N 100 10 E
Dalian, *China* 75 E11 38 50N 121 40 E
Daliang Shan, *China* 76 D4 28 0N 102 45 E
Daling He →, *China* 75 D11 40 55N 121 40 E
Dāliyat el Karmel, *Israel* 103 C4 32 43N 35 2 E
Dalj, *Croatia* 52 E3 45 29N 18 59 E
Dalkeith, *U.K.* 22 F5 55 54N 3 4W
Dalkeith, *U.S.A.* 152 E4 30 0N 85 9W
Dallas, *Ga., U.S.A.* 152 B5 33 55N 84 51W
Dallas, *Oreg., U.S.A.* 158 D2 44 55N 123 19W
Dallas, *Tex., U.S.A.* 155 J6 32 47N 96 49W
Dallas Center, *U.S.A.* 156 C3 41 41N 93 58W
Dallas City, *U.S.A.* 156 D5 40 38N 91 10W
Dallol, *Ethiopia* 107 E5 14 14N 40 17 E
Dalmā, *U.A.E.* 97 E7 24 30N 52 20 E
Dalmacija, *Croatia* 45 E13 43 20N 17 0 E
Dalmas, L., *Canada* 141 B5 53 30N 71 50W
Dalmatia = Dalmacija, *Croatia* 45 E13 43 20N 17 0 E
Dalmatovo, *Russia* 62 C9 56 16N 62 56 E
Dalmau, *India* 93 F9 26 4N 81 2 E
Dalmellington, *U.K.* 22 F4 55 19N 4 23W
Dalnegorsk, *Russia* 65 E14 44 32N 135 33 E
Dalnerechensk, *Russia* 65 E14 45 50N 133 40 E
Daloa, *Ivory C.* 112 D3 7 0N 6 30W
Dalou Shan, *China* 76 C6 28 15N 107 0 E
Dalry, *U.K.* 22 F4 55 42N 4 43W
Dalrymple, L., *Australia* 126 C4 20 40 S 147 0 E
Dals Långed, *Sweden* 17 F6 58 56N 12 18 E
Dalseter, *Norway* 18 C6 61 28N 9 26 E
Dalsjöfors, *Sweden* 17 G7 57 46N 13 5 E
Dalsland, *Sweden* 17 F6 58 48N 12 15 E
Dalsmynni, *Iceland* 11 C5 64 48N 21 29W
Daltenganj, *India* 93 H11 24 0N 84 4 E
Dalton, *Ga., U.S.A.* 149 H3 34 46N 84 58W
Dalton, *Mass., U.S.A.* 151 D11 42 28N 73 11W
Dalton, *Nebr., U.S.A.* 154 E3 41 25N 102 58W
Dalton, Kap, *Greenland* 10 D8 69 25N 24 3W
Dalton Iceberg Tongue, *Antarctica* 7 C9 66 15 S 121 30 E
Dalton-in-Furness, *U.K.* 20 C4 54 10N 3 11W
Dalupiri I., *Cagayan, Phil.* 80 B3 19 5N 121 12 E
Dalupiri I., *N. Samar, Phil.* 80 E5 12 25N 124 16 E
Dalvík, *Iceland* 11 B8 65 58N 18 32W
Dalwallinu, *Australia* 125 F2 30 17 S 116 40 E
Daly →, *Australia* 124 B5 13 35 S 130 19 E
Daly City, *U.S.A.* 160 H4 37 42N 122 28W
Daly L., *Canada* 143 B7 56 32N 105 39W
Daly River, *Australia* 124 B5 13 46 S 130 42 E
Daly Waters, *Australia* 126 B1 16 15 S 133 24 E
Dalyan, *Turkey* 49 E10 36 50N 28 39 E
Dam Doi, *Vietnam* 87 H5 8 50N 105 12 E
Dam Ha, *Vietnam* 86 B6 21 21N 107 36 E
Daman, *India* 94 D1 20 25N 72 57 E
Daman & Diu □, *India* 94 D1 20 25N 72 58 E
Dāmaneh, *Iran* 97 C6 33 1N 50 29 E
Damanganga →, *India* 94 D1 20 25N 72 56 E
Damanhûr, *Egypt* 106 H7 31 0N 30 30 E
Damant L., *Canada* 143 A7 61 45N 105 5W
Damanzhuang, *China* 74 E9 38 5N 116 35 E
Damar, *Indonesia* 79 F7 7 7 S 128 40 E
Damara, *C.A.R.* 114 B3 4 58N 18 42 E
Damaraland, *Namibia* 116 C2 20 0 S 15 0 E
Damascus = Dimashq, *Syria* 103 B5 33 30N 36 18 E
Damascus, *U.S.A.* 152 D5 31 18N 84 43W
Damaturu, *Nigeria* 113 C7 11 45N 11 55 E
Damāvand, *Iran* 97 C7 35 47N 52 0 E
Damāvand, Qolleh-ye, *Iran* 97 C7 35 56N 52 10 E
Damba, *Angola* 115 D3 6 44 S 15 20 E
Dâmboviţa □, *Romania* 53 F10 45 0N 25 30 E
Dâmboviţa →, *Romania* 53 F11 44 12N 26 26 E
Dâmbovnic →, *Romania* 53 F10 44 28N 25 18 E
Dambulla, *Sri Lanka* 95 L5 7 51N 80 39 E
Dame Marie, *Haiti* 165 C5 18 36N 74 26W
Dāmghān, *Iran* 97 B7 36 10N 54 17 E
Dămienesti, *Romania* 53 D11 46 44N 26 59 E
Damietta = Dumyât, *Egypt* 106 H7 31 24N 31 48 E
Daming, *China* 74 F8 36 15N 115 6 E
Damīr Qābū, *Syria* 96 B4 36 58N 41 51 E
Dammai I., *Phil.* 81 J3 5 47N 120 25 E
Dammam = Ad Dammām, *Si. Arabia* 97 E6 26 20N 50 5 E
Dammarie-les-Lys, *France* 27 D9 48 31N 2 39 E
Dammartin-en-Goële, *France* 27 C9 49 3N 2 41 E
Dammastock, *Switz.* 33 C6 46 38N 8 24 E
Damme, *Germany* 30 C4 52 32N 8 11 E
Damodar →, *India* 93 H12 23 17N 87 35 E
Damoh, *India* 93 H8 23 50N 79 28 E
Damous, *Algeria* 111 A5 36 31N 1 42 E
Dampier, *Australia* 124 D2 20 41 S 116 42 E
Dampier, Selat, *Indonesia* 79 E8 0 40 S 131 0 E
Dampier Arch., *Australia* 124 D2 20 38 S 116 32 E
Dampier Str., *Papua N. G.* 132 C5 5 50 S 148 0 E
Dampierre-sur Salon, *France* 32 A1 47 33N 5 41 E
Damqawt, *Yemen* 99 C6 16 34N 52 50 E
Damrei, Chuor Phnum, *Cambodia* 87 G4 11 30N 103 0 E
Damüls, *Austria* 33 B9 47 17N 9 53 E
Damvillers, *France* 27 C12 49 20N 5 21 E
Dan-Gulbi, *Nigeria* 113 C6 11 40N 6 15 E
Dan Xian, *China* 86 C7 19 31N 109 33 E
Dana, *Indonesia* 79 F6 11 0 S 122 52 E
Dana, L., *Canada* 140 B4 50 53N 77 20W
Dana, Mt., *U.S.A.* 160 H7 37 54N 119 12W
Danakil Depression, *Ethiopia* 102 E3 12 45N 41 0 E
Danakil Desert, *Ethiopia* 107 E5 12 30N 41 30 E
Danané, *Ivory C.* 112 D3 7 16N 8 9W
Danao, *Phil.* 81 F5 10 31N 124 1 E
Danau Poso, *Indonesia* 79 E6 1 52 S 120 35 E
Danba, *China* 76 B3 30 54N 101 48 E
Danbury, *U.S.A.* 151 E11 41 24N 73 28W
Danby L., *U.S.A.* 159 J6 34 13N 115 5W
Dand, *Afghan.* 92 D1 31 28N 65 32 E
Dande →, *Angola* 115 D2 6 15 S 15 34 E
Dandeldhura, *Nepal* 93 E9 29 20N 80 35 E
Dandeli, *India* 95 G2 15 5N 74 30 E
Dandenong, *Australia* 129 E6 38 0 S 145 15 E
Dandîl, *Egypt* 106 J7 29 10N 31 2 E
Dandong, *China* 75 D13 40 10N 124 20 E
Danfeng, *China* 74 H6 33 45N 110 25 E
Dangan Liedao, *China* 77 F10 22 2N 114 8 E
Dangara, *Tajikistan* 63 D4 38 6N 69 22 E
Dange, *Angola* 115 D3 7 56 S 15 3 E
Dangé-St-Roman, *France* 28 B4 46 56N 0 36 E
Dângeni, *Romania* 53 C11 47 51N 26 58 E
Danger Is. = Pukapuka, *Cook Is.* 135 J11 10 53 S 165 49W
Danger Pt., *S. Africa* 116 E2 34 40 S 19 17 E
Dangla, *Ethiopia* 107 E4 11 18N 36 56 E
Dangla Shan = Tanggula Shan, *China* 72 C4 32 40N 92 10 E
Dangora, *Nigeria* 113 C6 11 30N 8 7 E
Dangouadougou, *Burkina Faso* 112 D4 10 9N 4 56W
Dangrek, Phnom, *Thailand* 86 E5 14 15N 105 0 E
Dangriga, *Belize* 163 D7 17 0N 88 13W
Dangshan, *China* 74 G9 34 27N 116 22 E
Dangtu, *China* 77 B12 31 32N 118 25 E
Dangyang, *China* 77 B8 30 52N 111 44 E
Dani, *Burkina Faso* 113 C4 13 43N 0 10W
Daniel, *U.S.A.* 158 E8 42 52N 110 4W
Daniel's Harbour, *Canada* 141 B8 50 13N 57 35W
Danielskuil, *S. Africa* 116 D3 28 11 S 23 33 E
Danielson, *U.S.A.* 151 E13 41 48N 71 53W
Danielsville, *U.S.A.* 152 A6 34 8N 83 13W
Danilov, *Russia* 58 C11 58 16N 40 13 E

Dire Dawa 207

Demchok, *India* **93 C8** 32 42N 79 29 E
Demer →, *Belgium* **24 D4** 50 57N 4 42 E
Demetrias, *Greece* **48 B5** 39 22N 23 1 E
Demidov, *Russia* **58 E6** 55 16N 31 30 E
Deming, *N. Mex., U.S.A.* **159 K10** 32 16N 107 46W
Deming, *Wash., U.S.A.* **160 B4** 48 50N 122 13W
Demini →, *Brazil* **169 D5** 0 46 S 62 56W
Demirci, *Turkey* **49 B10** 39 2N 28 38 E
Demirköprü Barajı, *Turkey* **49 C10** 38 42N 28 25 E
Demirköy, *Turkey* **51 E11** 41 49N 27 45 E
Demmin, *Germany* **30 B9** 53 54N 13 2 E
Demnate, *Morocco* **110 B3** 31 44N 6 59W
Democracia, *Brazil* **173 B5** 5 48 S 61 26W
Demonte, *Italy* **44 D4** 44 19N 7 17 E
Demopolis, *U.S.A.* **149 J2** 32 31N 87 50W
Dempo, *Indonesia* **78 E2** 4 2 S 103 15 E
Demyansk, *Russia* **58 D7** 57 40N 32 27 E
Den Burg, *Neths.* **24 A4** 53 3N 4 47 E
Den Chai, *Thailand* **86 D3** 17 59N 100 4 E
Den Haag = 's-Gravenhage, *Neths.* **24 B4** 52 7N 4 17 E
Den Helder, *Neths.* **24 B4** 52 57N 4 45 E
Den Oever, *Neths.* **24 B5** 52 56N 5 2 E
Denain, *France* **27 B10** 50 20N 3 22 E
Denair, *U.S.A.* **160 H6** 37 32N 120 48W
Denau, *Uzbekistan* **64 F7** 38 16N 67 54 E
Denbigh, *Canada* **150 A7** 45 8N 77 15W
Denbigh, *U.K.* **20 D4** 53 12N 3 25W
Denbigh, C., *U.S.A.* **144 D7** 64 23N 161 32W
Denbighshire □, *U.K.* **20 D4** 53 8N 3 22W
Dendang, *Indonesia* **78 E3** 3 7 S 107 56 E
Dendé, *Gabon* **114 C2** 3 46 S 11 9 E
Dendermonde, *Belgium* **24 C4** 51 2N 4 5 E
Deneba, *Ethiopia* **107 F4** 9 47N 39 10 E
Denezhkin Kamen, Gora, *Russia* **62 A7** 60 25N 59 32 E
Deng Deng, *Cameroon* **114 A2** 5 12N 13 31 E
Dengchuan, *China* **76 E3** 25 59N 100 3 E
Denge, *Nigeria* **113 C6** 12 52N 5 21 E
Dengfeng, *China* **74 G7** 34 25N 113 2 E
Dengi, *Nigeria* **113 D6** 9 25N 9 55 E
Dengkou, *China* **74 D4** 40 18N 106 55 E
Dengzhou, *China* **77 A9** 32 34N 112 4 E
Denham, *Australia* **125 E1** 25 56 S 113 31 E
Denham Ra., *Australia* **126 C4** 21 55 S 147 46 E
Denham Sd., *Australia* **125 E1** 25 45 S 113 15 E
Denholm, *Canada* **143 C7** 52 39N 108 1W
Denia, *Spain* **41 G5** 38 49N 0 8 E
Denial B., *Australia* **127 E1** 32 14 S 133 32 E
Deniliquin, *Australia* **129 C6** 35 30 S 144 58 E
Denis, *Gabon* **114 B1** 0 19N 9 22 E
Denison, *Iowa, U.S.A.* **154 E7** 42 1N 95 21W
Denison, *Tex., U.S.A.* **155 J6** 33 45N 96 33W
Denison Plains, *Australia* **124 C4** 18 35 S 128 0 E
Deniyaya, *Sri Lanka* **95 L5** 6 21N 80 33 E
Denizli, *Turkey* **49 D11** 37 42N 29 2 E
Denizli □, *Turkey* **49 D11** 37 45N 29 5 E
Denman, *Australia* **129 B9** 32 24 S 150 42 E
Denman Glacier, *Antarctica* **7 C7** 66 45 S 99 25 E
Denmark, *Australia* **125 F2** 34 59 S 117 25 E
Denmark, *U.S.A.* **152 B8** 33 19N 81 9W
Denmark ■, *Europe* **17 J3** 55 45N 10 0 E
Denmark Str., *Atl. Oc.* **8 B6** 66 0N 30 0W
Dennison, *U.S.A.* **150 F3** 40 24N 81 19W
Denny, *U.K.* **22 E5** 56 1N 3 55W
Denpasar, *Indonesia* **78 F5** 8 45 S 115 14 E
Denton, *Ga., U.S.A.* **152 D3** 31 44N 82 42W
Denton, *Mont., U.S.A.* **158 C9** 47 19N 109 57W
Denton, *Tex., U.S.A.* **155 J6** 33 13N 97 8W
D'Entrecasteaux, Pt., *Australia* **125 F2** 34 50 S 115 57 E
D'Entrecasteaux Is., *Papua N. G.* **132 E6** 9 0 S 151 0 E
Dents du Midi, *Switz.* **32 D3** 46 10N 6 56 E
Dentsville, *U.S.A.* **152 A9** 34 4N 80 58W
Denu, *Ghana* **113 D5** 6 4N 1 8 E
Denver, *Colo., U.S.A.* **154 F2** 39 44N 104 59W
Denver, *Ind., U.S.A.* **157 D10** 40 52N 86 5W
Denver, *Iowa, U.S.A.* **156 B4** 42 40N 92 20W
Denver, *Pa., U.S.A.* **151 F8** 40 14N 76 8W
Denver City, *U.S.A.* **155 J3** 32 58N 102 50W
Deoband, *India* **92 E7** 29 42N 77 43 E
Deobhog, *India* **94 E6** 19 53N 82 44 E
Deodrug, *India* **95 F3** 16 26N 76 55 E
Deogarh, *India* **92 G5** 25 32N 73 54 E
Deogarh, *India* **94 D7** 21 32N 84 45 E
Deoghar, *India* **93 G12** 24 30N 86 42 E
Deolali, *India* **94 E1** 19 58N 73 50 E
Deoli = Devli, *India* **92 G6** 25 50N 75 20 E
Déols, *France* **27 F8** 46 50N 1 43 E
Deora, *India* **92 F4** 26 22N 70 55 E
Deori, *India* **93 H8** 23 24N 79 1 E
Deoria, *India* **93 F10** 26 31N 83 48 E
Deosai Mts., *Pakistan* **93 B6** 35 40N 75 0 E
Deosri, *India* **93 F14** 26 46N 90 29 E
Depalpur, *India* **92 H6** 22 51N 75 33 E
Deping, *China* **75 F9** 37 25N 116 58 E
Deposit, *U.S.A.* **151 D9** 42 4N 75 25W
Depuch I., *Australia* **124 D2** 20 37 S 117 44 E
Deputatskiy, *Russia* **65 C14** 69 18N 139 54 E
Dêqên, *China* **76 C2** 28 34N 98 51 E
Deqing, *China* **77 F8** 23 8N 111 42 E
Dera Ghazi Khan, *Pakistan* **91 C3** 30 5N 70 43 E
Dera Ismail Khan, *Pakistan* **91 C3** 31 50N 70 50 E
Derabugti, *Pakistan* **92 E3** 29 2N 69 9 E
Derawar Fort, *Pakistan* **92 E4** 28 46N 71 20 E
Derbent, *Russia* **61 J9** 42 5N 48 15 E
Derbent, *Turkey* **49 C10** 38 11N 28 33 E
Derby, *Australia* **124 C3** 17 18 S 123 38 E
Derby, *U.K.* **20 E6** 52 56N 1 28W
Derby, *Conn., U.S.A.* **151 E11** 41 19N 73 5W
Derby, *Kans., U.S.A.* **155 G6** 37 33N 97 16W
Derby, *N.Y., U.S.A.* **150 D6** 42 41N 78 58W
Derby City □, *U.K.* **20 E6** 52 56N 1 28W
Derby Line, *U.S.A.* **151 B12** 45 0N 72 6W
Derbyshire □, *U.K.* **20 D6** 53 11N 1 38W
Derecske, *Hungary* **52 C6** 47 20N 21 33 E
Dereköy, *Turkey* **51 E11** 41 55N 27 21 E
Dereli, *Turkey* **101 B8** 40 44N 38 26 E
Derg →, *U.K.* **23 B4** 54 44N 7 26W
Derg, L., *Ireland* **23 D3** 53 0N 8 20W
Dergachi = Derhaci, *Ukraine* **59 G9** 50 9N 36 11 E
Derhaci, *Ukraine* **59 G9** 50 9N 36 11 E
Derik, *Turkey* **101 D9** 37 21N 40 18 E
Derinkuyu, *Turkey* **100 C6** 38 22N 34 45 E
Dermantsi, *Bulgaria* **51 C8** 43 8N 24 17 E
Dermott, *U.S.A.* **155 J9** 33 32N 91 26W
Dêrong, *China* **76 C2** 28 44N 99 9 E
Derrinallum, *Australia* **128 D5** 37 57 S 143 15 E
Derry = Londonderry, *U.K.* **23 B4** 55 0N 7 20W
Derry = Londonderry □, *U.K.* **23 B4** 55 0N 7 20W
Derry, *N.H., U.S.A.* **151 D13** 42 53N 71 19W
Derry, *Pa., U.S.A.* **150 F5** 40 20N 79 18W
Derryveagh Mts., *Ireland* **23 B3** 54 56N 8 11W
Derudub, *Sudan* **106 D4** 17 31N 36 7 E
Derval, *France* **26 E5** 47 40N 1 41W
Dervéni, *Greece* **48 C4** 38 8N 22 25 E
Derventa, *Bos.-H.* **52 F2** 44 59N 17 55 E
Derwent →, *Cumb., U.K.* **20 C4** 54 39N 3 33W
Derwent →, *Derby, U.K.* **20 E6** 52 57N 1 28W
Derwent →, *N. Yorks., U.K.* **20 D7** 53 45N 0 58W
Derwent Water, *U.K.* **20 C4** 54 35N 3 9W
Des Moines, *Iowa, U.S.A.* **156 C3** 41 35N 93 37W
Des Moines, *N. Mex., U.S.A.* **155 G3** 36 46N 103 50W
Des Moines →, *U.S.A.* **156 D5** 40 23N 91 25W
Des Plaines, *U.S.A.* **157 B9** 42 3N 87 52W
Des Plaines →, *U.S.A.* **157 C8** 41 23N 88 15W
Desa, *Romania* **52 G8** 43 52N 23 2 E
Desaguadero, *Peru* **172 D4** 16 34 S 69 3W
Desaguadero →, *Argentina* **174 C2** 34 30 S 66 46W
Desaguadero →, *Bolivia* **172 D4** 16 35 S 69 5W
Descanso, Pta., *Mexico* **161 N9** 32 21N 117 3W
Descartes, *France* **28 B4** 46 59N 0 42 E
Deschaillons, *Canada* **141 C5** 46 32N 72 7W
Deschambault L., *Canada* **143 C8** 54 50N 103 30W
Deschutes →, *U.S.A.* **158 D3** 45 38N 120 55W
Dese, *Ethiopia* **102 E2** 11 5N 39 40 E
Deseado, C., *Chile* **176 D2** 52 45 S 74 42W
Desenzano del Garda, *Italy* **44 C7** 45 28N 10 32 E
Desert Center, *U.S.A.* **161 M11** 33 43N 115 24W
Desert Hot Springs, *U.S.A.* **161 M10** 33 58N 116 30W
Deset, *Norway* **18 C8** 61 20N 11 26 E
Deshnok, *India* **92 F5** 27 48N 73 21 E
Desna →, *Ukraine* **59 G6** 50 33N 30 32 E
Desnătui →, *Romania* **53 G8** 43 53N 23 35 E
Desolación, I., *Chile* **176 D2** 53 0 S 74 0W
Despeñaperros, Paso, *Spain* **43 G7** 38 24N 3 30W
Despotovac, *Serbia, Yug.* **50 B5** 44 6N 21 30 E
Dessau, *Germany* **30 D8** 51 51N 12 14 E
Dessye = Dese, *Ethiopia* **102 E2** 11 5N 39 40 E
Destin, *U.S.A.* **153 E3** 30 24N 86 30W
D'Estrees B., *Australia* **128 C2** 35 55 S 137 45 E
Desuri, *India* **92 G5** 25 18N 73 35 E
Desvres, *France* **27 B8** 50 40N 1 48 E
Det Udom, *Thailand* **86 E5** 14 54N 105 5 E
Deta, *Romania* **52 E6** 45 24N 21 13 E
Dete, *S. Africa* **116 B4** 18 38 S 26 50 E
Dete, *Zimbabwe* **119 F2** 18 38 S 26 50 E
Đetinja →, *Serbia, Yug.* **50 C4** 43 51N 20 5 E
Detmold, *Germany* **30 D4** 51 56N 8 52 E
Detour, Pt., *U.S.A.* **148 C2** 45 40N 86 40W
Detroit, *U.S.A.* **150 D1** 42 20N 83 3W
Detroit Lakes, *U.S.A.* **154 B7** 46 49N 95 51W
Detva, *Slovak Rep.* **35 C12** 48 34N 19 25 E
Deurne, *Neths.* **24 C5** 51 27N 5 49 E
Deutsche Bucht, *Germany* **30 A4** 54 15N 8 0 E
Deutschlandsberg, *Austria* **34 E8** 46 49N 15 14 E
Deux-Sèvres □, *France* **26 F6** 46 35N 0 20W
Deva, *Romania* **52 E7** 45 53N 22 55 E
Devakottai, *India* **95 K4** 9 55N 78 45 E
Devaprayag, *India* **93 D8** 30 13N 78 35 E
Devarkonda, *India* **94 F4** 16 42N 78 56 E
Dévaványa, *Hungary* **52 C5** 47 2N 20 59 E
Deveci Dağları, *Turkey* **100 B7** 40 6N 36 15 E
Devecikonağı, *Turkey* **51 G12** 39 55N 28 34 E
Devecser, *Hungary* **52 C2** 47 6N 17 26 E
Develi, *Turkey* **100 C6** 38 23N 35 29 E
Deventer, *Neths.* **24 B6** 52 15N 6 10 E
Devereux, *U.S.A.* **152 B6** 33 13N 83 5W
Deveron →, *U.K.* **22 D6** 57 41N 2 32W
Devesel, *Romania* **52 F7** 44 28N 22 41 E
Devgad I., *India* **95 G2** 14 48N 74 5 E
Devgadh Bariya, *India* **92 H5** 22 40N 73 55 E
Devgarh, *India* **95 F1** 16 23N 73 23 E
Devi →, *India* **94 E8** 19 59N 86 24 E
Devikot, *India* **92 F4** 26 42N 71 12 E
Devil River Pk., *N.Z.* **131 A7** 40 56 S 172 37 E
Devils Den, *U.S.A.* **160 K7** 35 46N 119 58W
Devils Lake, *U.S.A.* **154 A5** 48 7N 98 52W
Devils Paw, *Canada* **142 B2** 58 47N 134 0W
Devil's Pt., *Sri Lanka* **95 K5** 9 26N 80 6 E
Devil's Pt., *Vanuatu* **133 G6** 17 44 S 168 11 E
Devils Tower Junction, *U.S.A.* **154 C2** 44 31N 104 57W
Devin, *Bulgaria* **51 E8** 41 44N 24 24 E
Devine, *U.S.A.* **155 L5** 29 8N 98 54W
Devipattinam, *India* **95 K4** 9 29N 78 54 E
Devizes, *U.K.* **21 F6** 51 22N 1 58W
Devli, *India* **92 G6** 25 50N 75 20 E
Devnya, *Bulgaria* **51 C11** 43 13N 27 33 E
Devolii →, *Albania* **50 F4** 40 57N 20 15 E
Devon, *Canada* **142 C6** 53 24N 113 44W
Devon □, *U.K.* **21 G4** 50 50N 3 40W
Devon I., *Canada* **136 B11** 75 10N 85 0W
Devonport, *Australia* **126 G4** 41 10 S 146 22 E
Devonport, *N.Z.* **130 C3** 36 49 S 174 49 E
Devrek, *Turkey* **100 B4** 41 13N 31 57 E
Devrekâni, *Turkey* **100 B5** 41 36N 33 50 E
Devrez →, *Turkey* **100 B6** 41 6N 34 25 E
Devrukh, *India* **94 F1** 17 3N 73 37 E
Dewas, *India* **92 H7** 22 59N 76 3 E
Dewetsdorp, *S. Africa* **116 D4** 29 33 S 26 39 E
Dexing, *China* **77 C11** 28 46N 117 30 E
Dexter, *Maine, U.S.A.* **149 C11** 45 1N 69 18W
Dexter, *Mich., U.S.A.* **157 B13** 42 20N 83 53W
Dexter, *Mo., U.S.A.* **155 G10** 36 48N 89 57W
Dexter, *N. Mex., U.S.A.* **155 J2** 33 12N 104 22W
Dey-Dey, L., *Australia* **125 E5** 29 12 S 131 4 E
Deyang, *China* **76 B5** 31 3N 104 27 E
Deyhūk, *Iran* **97 C8** 33 15N 57 30 E
Deyyer, *Iran* **97 E6** 27 55N 51 55 E
Dezadeash L., *Canada* **142 A1** 60 28N 136 58W
Dezfūl, *Iran* **97 C6** 32 20N 48 30 E
Dezhneva, Mys, *Russia* **65 C19** 66 5N 169 40W
Dezhou, *China* **74 F9** 37 26N 116 18 E
Dhadhar →, *India* **93 G11** 24 56N 85 24 E
Dháfni, *Kríti, Greece* **38 D7** 35 13N 25 3 E
Dháfni, *Pelóponnisos, Greece* **48 D4** 37 48N 22 1 E
Dhahaban, *Si. Arabia* **98 B2** 21 58N 39 3 E
Dhahiriya = Aẓ Ẓāhirīyah, *West Bank* **103 D3** 31 25N 34 58 E
Dhahran = Aẓ Ẓahrān, *Si. Arabia* **97 E6** 26 10N 50 7 E
Dhak, *Pakistan* **92 C5** 32 25N 72 33 E
Dhaka, *Bangla.* **90 D3** 23 43N 90 26 E
Dhaka □, *Bangla.* **90 C3** 24 25N 90 25 E
Dhali, *Cyprus* **38 D12** 35 1N 33 25 E
Dhamangaon, *India* **94 D4** 20 48N 78 9 E
Dhamar, *Yemen* **98 D4** 14 30N 44 20 E
Dhamási, *Greece* **48 B4** 39 43N 22 11 E
Dhampur, *India* **93 E8** 29 19N 78 33 E
Dhamra →, *India* **94 D8** 20 47N 86 58 E
Dhamtari, *India* **94 D5** 20 42N 81 35 E
Dhanbad, *India* **93 H12** 23 50N 86 30 E
Dhankuta, *Nepal* **93 F12** 26 55N 87 40 E
Dhanora, *India* **94 D5** 20 20N 80 22 E
Dhanushkodi, *India* **95 K4** 9 11N 79 24 E
Dhar, *India* **92 H6** 22 35N 75 26 E
Dharampur, *Gujarat, India* **94 D1** 20 32N 73 17 E
Dharampur, *Mad. P., India* **92 H6** 22 13N 75 18 E
Dharamsala = Dharmsala, *India* **92 C7** 32 16N 76 23 E
Dharangaon, *India* **94 D2** 21 1N 75 16 E
Dharapuram, *India* **95 J3** 10 45N 77 34 E
Dhariwal, *India* **92 D6** 31 57N 75 19 E
Dharla →, *Bangla.* **93 G13** 25 46N 89 42 E
Dharmapuri, *India* **95 H4** 12 10N 78 10 E
Dharmavaram, *India* **95 G3** 14 29N 77 44 E
Dharmjaygarh, *India* **93 H10** 22 28N 83 13 E
Dharmsala, *India* **92 C7** 32 16N 76 23 E
Dharni, *India* **92 J7** 21 33N 76 53 E
Dharur, *India* **94 E3** 18 3N 76 8 E
Dharwad, *India* **95 G2** 15 30N 75 4 E
Dhasan →, *India* **93 G8** 25 48N 79 24 E
Dhaulagiri, *Nepal* **93 E10** 28 39N 83 28 E
Dhebar, L., *India* **92 G6** 24 10N 74 0 E
Dheftera, *Cyprus* **38 D12** 35 5N 33 16 E
Dhenkanal, *India* **94 D7** 20 45N 85 35 E
Dhenoúsa, *Greece* **49 D7** 37 8N 25 48 E
Dherinia, *Cyprus* **38 D12** 35 3N 33 57 E
Dheskáti, *Greece* **50 G5** 39 55N 21 49 E
Dhespotikó, *Greece* **48 E6** 36 57N 24 58 E
Dhestina, *Greece* **48 C4** 38 25N 22 31 E
Dhiarrizos →, *Cyprus* **38 E11** 34 41N 32 34 E
Dhībān, *Jordan* **103 D4** 31 30N 35 46 E
Dhidhimótikhon, *Greece* **51 E10** 41 22N 26 29 E
Dhíkti Óros, *Greece* **38 D7** 35 8N 25 30 E
Dhilianáta, *Greece* **48 C2** 38 15N 20 34 E
Dhílos, *Greece* **49 D7** 37 23N 25 15 E
Dhilwan, *India* **92 D6** 31 31N 75 21 E
Dhimarkhera, *India* **93 H9** 23 28N 80 22 E
Dhimitsána, *Greece* **48 D4** 37 36N 22 3 E
Dhírfis = Dhírfis Óros, *Greece* **48 C5** 38 40N 23 54 E
Dhírfis Óros, *Greece* **48 C5** 38 40N 23 54 E
Dhodhekánisos, *Greece* **49 E8** 36 35N 27 0 E
Dhodhekánisos □, *Greece* **49 E8** 36 35N 27 0 E
Dhokós, *Greece* **48 D5** 37 20N 23 20 E
Dholiana, *Greece* **48 B2** 39 54N 20 32 E
Dholka, *India* **92 H5** 22 44N 72 29 E
Dhomokós, *Greece* **48 B4** 39 10N 22 18 E
Dhone, *India* **95 E3** 15 25N 77 53 E
Dhoraji, *India* **92 J4** 21 45N 70 37 E
Dhoxáton, *Greece* **51 E8** 41 9N 24 16 E
Dhragonísi, *Greece* **49 D7** 37 27N 25 29 E
Dhráhstis, Ákra, *Greece* **38 A3** 39 48N 19 40 E
Dhrangadhra, *India* **92 H4** 22 59N 71 31 E
Dhrápanon, Ákra, *Greece* **38 D6** 35 28N 24 14 E
Dhriopís, *Greece* **48 D6** 37 25N 24 26 E
Dhrol, *India* **92 H4** 22 33N 70 25 E
Dhubāb, *Yemen* **98 D3** 12 56N 43 25 E
Dhuburi, *India* **90 B2** 26 2N 89 59 E
Dhulasar, *Bangla.* **90 E3** 21 52N 90 14 E
Dhule, *India* **94 D2** 20 58N 74 50 E
Dhupdhara, *India* **90 B3** 26 10N 91 4 E
Di-ib, W. →, *Sudan* **106 C4** 22 38N 36 6 E
Di Linh, *Vietnam* **87 G7** 11 35N 108 4 E
Di Linh, Cao Nguyen, *Vietnam* **87 G7** 11 30N 108 0 E
Día, *Greece* **38 D7** 35 28N 25 14 E
Diabakania, *Guinea* **112 C2** 10 38N 10 58W
Diable, Île du, *Fr. Guiana* **169 B7** 5 16N 52 34W
Diablo, Mt., *U.S.A.* **160 H5** 37 53N 121 56W
Diablo Range, *U.S.A.* **160 J5** 37 20N 121 25W
Diafarabé, *Mali* **112 C4** 14 9N 4 57W
Diala, *Mali* **112 C3** 14 10N 9 58W
Dialakoro, *Mali* **112 C3** 12 18N 7 54W
Dialakoto, *Senegal* **112 C2** 13 21N 13 19W
Diallassagou, *Mali* **112 C4** 13 47N 3 41W
Diamante, *Argentina* **174 C3** 32 5 S 60 40W
Diamante, *Italy* **47 C8** 39 41N 15 49 E
Diamante →, *Argentina* **174 C2** 34 30 S 66 46W
Diamantina, *Brazil* **171 E3** 18 17 S 43 40W
Diamantina →, *Australia* **127 D2** 26 45 S 139 10 E
Diamantino, *Brazil* **173 C6** 14 30 S 56 30W
Diamond Bar, *U.S.A.* **161 L9** 34 1N 117 48W
Diamond Harbour, *India* **93 H13** 22 11N 88 14 E
Diamond Head, *U.S.A.* **145 K14** 21 16N 157 49W
Diamond Is., *Australia* **126 B5** 17 25 S 151 5 E
Diamond Mts., *U.S.A.* **158 G6** 39 50N 115 30W
Diamond Springs, *U.S.A.* **160 G6** 38 42N 120 49W
Dian Chi, *China* **76 E4** 24 50N 102 43 E
Dianalund, *Denmark* **17 J5** 55 32N 11 30 E
Dianbai, *China* **77 G8** 21 33N 111 0 E
Diancheng, *China* **77 G8** 21 30N 111 4 E
Dianjiang, *China* **76 B6** 30 24N 107 20 E
Diano Marina, *Italy* **44 E5** 43 54N 8 5 E
Dianópolis, *Brazil* **171 D2** 11 38 S 46 50W
Dianra, *Ivory C.* **112 D3** 8 45N 6 14W
Diapaga, *Burkina Faso* **113 C5** 12 5N 1 46 E
Diapangou, *Burkina Faso* **113 C5** 12 5N 0 10 E
Diapur, *Australia* **128 D4** 36 19 S 141 29 E
Diariguila, *Guinea* **112 C2** 10 35N 10 2W
Dībā, *Oman* **97 E8** 25 45N 56 16 E
Dibai, *India* **92 E8** 28 13N 78 15 E
Dibaya, *Dem. Rep. of the Congo* **115 D4** 6 30 S 22 57 E
Dibaya-Lubue, *Dem. Rep. of the Congo* **115 C3** 4 12 S 19 54 E
Dibete, *Botswana* **116 C4** 23 45 S 26 32 E
Dibrugarh, *India* **90 B5** 27 29N 94 55 E
Dickens, *U.S.A.* **155 J4** 33 37N 100 50W
Dickeyville, *U.S.A.* **156 B6** 42 38N 90 36W
Dickinson, *U.S.A.* **154 B3** 46 53N 102 47W
Dickson = Dikson, *Russia* **64 B9** 73 40N 80 5 E
Dickson, *U.S.A.* **149 G2** 36 5N 87 23W
Dickson City, *U.S.A.* **151 E9** 41 29N 75 40W
Dicle Nehri →, *Turkey* **101 D9** 37 44N 41 10 E
Dicomano, *Italy* **45 E8** 43 53N 11 31 E
Didesa, W. →, *Ethiopia* **107 E4** 10 2N 35 32 E
Didi, *Sudan* **107 F3** 6 18N 34 29 E
Didiéni, *Mali* **112 C3** 13 53N 8 6W
Didimbo, *Angola* **115 F4** 17 30 S 21 45 E
Didsbury, *Canada* **142 C6** 51 35N 114 10W
Didwana, *India* **92 F6** 27 23N 74 36 E
Die, *France* **29 D9** 44 47N 5 22 E
Diébougou, *Burkina Faso* **112 C4** 11 0N 3 15W
Diecke, *Guinea* **112 D3** 7 27N 8 54W
Diefenbaker, L., *Canada* **143 C7** 51 0N 106 55W
Diego de Almagro, *Chile* **174 B1** 26 22 S 70 3W
Diego Garcia, *Ind. Oc.* **121 E6** 7 50 S 72 50 E
Diego Ramírez, Islas, *Chile* **176 E3** 56 30 S 68 44W
Diekirch, *Lux.* **24 E6** 49 52N 6 10 E
Diéma, *Mali* **112 C3** 14 32N 9 12W
Diembéring, *Senegal* **112 C1** 12 29N 16 47W
Dien Ban, *Vietnam* **86 E7** 15 53N 108 16 E
Dien Bien, *Vietnam* **76 G4** 21 20N 103 0 E
Dien Khanh, *Vietnam* **87 F7** 12 15N 109 6 E
Diepholz, *Germany* **30 C4** 52 37N 8 22 E
Diepoldsau, *Switz.* **33 B9** 47 23N 9 40 E
Dieppe, *France* **26 C8** 49 54N 1 4 E
Dierks, *U.S.A.* **155 H8** 34 7N 94 1W
Diessenhofen, *Switz.* **33 A7** 47 42N 8 46 E
Diest, *Belgium* **24 D5** 50 58N 5 4 E
Dieterich, *U.S.A.* **157 E8** 39 4N 88 23W
Dietikon, *Switz.* **33 B6** 47 24N 8 24 E
Dieulefit, *France* **29 D9** 44 32N 5 4 E
Dieuze, *France* **27 D13** 48 49N 6 43 E
Dif, *Somali Rep.* **102 G3** 0 59N 0 56 E
Differdange, *Lux.* **24 E5** 49 31N 5 54 E
Diffun, *Phil.* **80 C3** 16 36N 121 33 E
Dig, *India* **92 F7** 27 28N 77 20 E
Digba, *Dem. Rep. of the Congo* **118 B2** 4 25N 25 48 E
Digboi, *India* **90 B5** 27 23N 95 38 E
Digby, *Canada* **141 D6** 44 38N 65 50W
Diggi, *India* **92 F6** 26 22N 75 26 E
Dighinala, *Bangla.* **90 D4** 23 15N 92 5 E
Dighton, *U.S.A.* **154 F4** 38 29N 100 28W
Diglur, *India* **94 E3** 18 34N 77 33 E
Digna, *Mali* **112 C3** 14 48N 8 10W
Digne-les-Bains, *France* **29 D10** 44 5N 6 12 E
Digoin, *France* **27 F11** 46 29N 4 1 E
Digor, *Turkey* **101 B10** 40 22N 43 25 E
Digos, *Phil.* **79 C7** 6 45N 125 20 E
Digranes, *Iceland* **11 A12** 66 4N 14 44W
Digras, *India* **94 D3** 20 6N 77 45 E
Digul →, *Indonesia* **79 F9** 7 7 S 138 42 E
Dijlah, Nahr →, *Asia* **96 D5** 31 0N 47 25 E
Dijon, *France* **27 E12** 47 20N 5 3 E
Dikhil, *Djibouti* **102 E3** 11 8N 42 20 E
Dikili, *Turkey* **49 B8** 39 4N 26 53 E
Dikirnis, *Egypt* **106 H7** 31 6N 31 35 E
Dikkil = Dikhil, *Djibouti* **102 E3** 11 8N 42 20 E
Dikodougou, *Ivory C.* **112 D3** 9 4N 5 45W
Diksmuide, *Belgium* **24 C2** 51 2N 2 52 E
Dikson, *Russia* **64 B9** 73 40N 80 5 E
Dikwa, *Nigeria* **113 C7** 12 4N 13 30 E
Dila, *Ethiopia* **102 F2** 6 21N 38 22 E
Dilasag, *Phil.* **80 [illegible]** 16 25N 122 11 E
Dili, *Indonesia* **79 F7** 8 39 S 125 34 E
Dilijan, *Armenia* **61 K7** 40 46N 44 57 E
Dilizhan = Dilijan, *Armenia* **61 K7** 40 46N 44 57 E
Dilj, *Croatia* **52 E3** 45 29N 18 1 E
Dillenburg, *Germany* **30 E4** 50 43N 8 17 E
Dilley, *U.S.A.* **155 L5** 28 40N 99 10W
Dilling, *Sudan* **107 E2** 12 3N 29 35 E
Dillingen, *Bayern, Germany* **31 G6** 48 36N 10 30 E
Dillingen, *Saarland, Germany* **31 F2** 49 22N 6 43 E
Dillingham, *U.S.A.* **138 C4** 59 3N 158 28W
Dillon, *Canada* **143 B7** 55 56N 108 35W
Dillon, *Mont., U.S.A.* **158 D7** 45 13N 112 38W
Dillon, *S.C., U.S.A.* **149 H6** 34 25N 79 22W
Dillon →, *Canada* **143 B7** 55 56N 108 56W
Dillsboro, *U.S.A.* **157 E11** 39 1N 85 4W
Dillsburg, *U.S.A.* **150 F7** 40 7N 77 2W
Dilly, *Mali* **112 C3** 15 1N 7 40W
Dilolo, *Dem. Rep. of the Congo* **115 E4** 10 28 S 22 18 E
Dimapur, *India* **90 C4** 25 54N 93 45 E
Dimas, *Mexico* **162 C3** 23 43N 106 47W
Dimasalang, *Phil.* **80 E4** 12 12N 123 51 E
Dimashq, *Syria* **103 B5** 33 30N 36 18 E
Dimashq □, *Syria* **103 B5** 33 30N 36 30 E
Dimbaza, *S. Africa* **117 E4** 32 50 S 27 14 E
Dimbelenge, *Dem. Rep. of the Congo* **115 D4** 5 33 S 23 7 E
Dimbokro, *Ivory C.* **112 D4** 6 45N 4 46W
Dimboola, *Australia* **128 D5** 36 28 S 142 7 E
Dîmbovița = Dâmbovița →, *Romania* **53 F11** 44 12N 26 26 E
Dimbulah, *Australia* **126 B4** 17 8 S 145 4 E
Dimitrovgrad, *Bulgaria* **51 D9** 42 5N 25 35 E
Dimitrovgrad, *Russia* **60 C9** 54 14N 49 39 E
Dimitrovgrad, *Serbia, Yug.* **50 C6** 43 2N 22 48 E
Dimitrovo = Pernik, *Bulgaria* **50 D7** 42 35N 23 2 E
Dimmitt, *U.S.A.* **155 H3** 34 33N 102 19W
Dimo, *Sudan* **107 F2** 5 19N 29 10 E
Dimona, *Israel* **103 D4** 31 2N 35 1 E
Dimovo, *Bulgaria* **50 C6** 43 43N 22 50 E
Dinagat, *Phil.* **79 B7** 10 10N 125 40 E
Dinaig, *Phil.* **81 H5** 7 11N 124 10 E
Dinajpur, *Bangla.* **90 C2** 25 33N 88 43 E
Dinalupihan, *Phil.* **80 D3** 14 52N 120 28 E
Dinan, *France* **26 D4** 48 28N 2 2W
Dīnān Āb, *Iran* **97 C8** 32 4N 56 49 E
Dinant, *Belgium* **24 D4** 50 16N 4 55 E
Dinapur, *India* **93 G11** 25 38N 85 5 E
Dinar, *Turkey* **49 C12** 38 5N 30 10 E
Dīnār, Kūh-e, *Iran* **97 D6** 30 42N 51 46 E
Dinara Planina, *Croatia* **45 D13** 44 0N 16 30 E
Dinard, *France* **26 D4** 48 38N 2 6W
Dinaric Alps = Dinara Planina, *Croatia* **45 D13** 44 0N 16 30 E
Dinas, *Phil.* **81 H4** 7 38N 123 20 E
Dindanko, *Mali* **112 C3** 14 8N 9 30W
Dinde, *Angola* **115 E2** 14 17 S 13 42 E
Dinder, Nahr ed →, *Sudan* **107 E3** 14 6N 33 40 E
Dindi →, *India* **95 F4** 16 24N 78 15 E
Dindigul, *India* **95 J4** 10 25N 78 0 E
Dindori, *India* **93 H9** 22 57N 81 5 E
Ding Xian = Dingzhou, *China* **74 E8** 38 30N 114 59 E
Dinga, *Dem. Rep. of the Congo* **115 D3** 5 17 S 16 42 E
Dinga, *Pakistan* **92 G2** 25 26N 67 10 E
Dingalan, *Phil.* **80 D3** 15 18N 121 25 E
Dingalan Bay, *Phil.* **80 D3** 15 18N 121 25 E
Dingbian, *China* **74 F4** 37 35N 107 32 E
Dingelstädt, *Germany* **30 D6** 51 18N 10 19 E
Dingle, *Ireland* **23 D1** 52 9N 10 17W
Dingle, *Sweden* **17 F5** 58 32N 11 35 E
Dingle B., *Ireland* **23 D1** 52 3N 10 20W
Dingmans Ferry, *U.S.A.* **151 E10** 41 13N 74 55W
Dingnan, *China* **77 E10** 24 45N 115 0 E
Dingo, *Australia* **126 C4** 23 38 S 149 19 E
Dingolfing, *Germany* **31 G8** 48 37N 12 30 E
Dingras, *Phil.* **80 B3** 18 6N 120 42 E
Dingtao, *China* **74 G8** 35 5N 115 35 E
Dinguira, *Mali* **112 C2** 14 11N 11 16W
Dinguiraye, *Guinea* **112 C2** 11 18N 10 49W
Dingwall, *U.K.* **22 D4** 57 36N 4 26W
Dingxi, *China* **74 G3** 35 30N 104 33 E
Dingxiang, *China* **74 E7** 38 30N 112 58 E
Dingyuan, *China* **77 A11** 32 32N 117 41 E
Dingzhou, *China* **74 E8** 38 30N 114 59 E
Dinh, Mui, *Vietnam* **78 B3** 11 22N 109 1 E
Dinh Lap, *Vietnam* **76 G6** 21 33N 107 6 E
Dinhata, *India* **90 B2** 26 8N 89 27 E
Dinokwe, *Botswana* **116 C4** 23 29 S 26 37 E
Dinorwic, *Canada* **143 D10** 49 41N 92 30W
Dinosaur National Monument, *U.S.A.* **158 F9** 40 30N 108 45W
Dinosaur Prov. Park, *Canada* **142 C6** 50 47N 111 30W
Dinsor, *Somali Rep.* **120 D2** 2 24N 42 59 E
Dinuba, *U.S.A.* **160 J7** 36 32N 119 23W
Diö, *Sweden* **17 H8** 56 37N 14 15 E
Dioïla, *Mali* **112 C3** 12 23N 6 50W
Dioka, *Mali* **112 C2** 14 50N 10 4W
Diomede, *U.S.A.* **144 D5** 65 47N 169 0W
Diongoï, *Mali* **112 C3** 14 38N 8 34W
Diósgyör, *Hungary* **52 B5** 48 7N 20 43 E
Diosig, *Romania* **52 C7** 47 18N 22 2 E
Diougani, *Mali* **112 C4** 14 19N 2 44W
Diouloulou, *Senegal* **112 C1** 13 5N 16 38W
Dioura, *Mali* **112 C3** 14 59N 5 12W
Diourbel, *Senegal* **112 C1** 14 39N 16 12W
Dipaculao, *Phil.* **80 D3** 15 51N 121 32 E
Dipalpur, *Pakistan* **92 D5** 30 40N 73 39 E
Diphu Pass, *India* **90 A6** 28 9N 97 20 E
Diplo, *Pakistan* **92 G3** 24 35N 69 35 E
Dipolog, *Phil.* **79 C6** 8 36N 123 20 E
Dipton, *N.Z.* **131 F3** 45 54 S 168 22 E
Dir, *Pakistan* **91 B3** 35 8N 71 59 E
Diré, *Mali* **112 B4** 16 20N 3 25W
Dire Dawa, *Ethiopia* **102 F3** 9 35N 41 45 E

Eagle Grove 209

Downing, *U.S.A.* **156 D4** 40 29N 92 22W
Downpatrick, *U.K.* **23 B6** 54 20N 5 43W
Downpatrick Hd., *Ireland* **23 B2** 54 20N 9 21W
Downsville, *U.S.A.* **151 D10** 42 5N 74 50W
Downton, Mt., *Canada* **142 C4** 52 42N 124 52W
Dowsārī, *Iran* **97 D8** 28 25N 57 59 E
Dowshī, *Afghan.* **91 B3** 35 35N 68 43 E
Doyle, *U.S.A.* **160 E6** 40 2N 120 6W
Doylestown, *U.S.A.* **151 F9** 40 21N 75 10W
Dozois, Rés., *Canada* **140 C4** 47 30N 77 5W
Dra Khel, *Pakistan* **92 F2** 27 58N 66 45 E
Draa, C., *Morocco* **110 C2** 28 47N 11 0W
Draa, Oued →, *Morocco* **110 C2** 28 40N 11 10W
Drac →, *France* **29 C9** 45 12N 5 42 E
Dračevo, *Macedonia* **50 E5** 41 56N 21 31 E
Drachten, *Neths.* **24 A6** 53 7N 6 5 E
Drăgănești, *Moldova* **53 C13** 47 43N 28 15 E
Drăgănești-Olt, *Romania* **53 F9** 44 9N 24 32 E
Drăgănești-Vlașca, *Romania* **53 F10** 44 5N 25 33 E
Dragaš, *Kosovo, Yug.* **50 D4** 42 5N 20 41 E
Drăgășani, *Romania* **53 F9** 44 39N 24 17 E
Dragichyn, *Belarus* **59 F3** 52 15N 25 8 E
Dragocvet, *Serbia, Yug.* **50 C5** 43 58N 21 15 E
Dragovishtitsa, *Bulgaria* **50 D6** 42 22N 22 39 E
Draguignan, *France* **29 E10** 43 32N 6 27 E
Drain, *U.S.A.* **158 E2** 43 40N 123 19W
Drake, *U.S.A.* **154 B4** 47 55N 100 23W
Drake Passage, *S. Ocean* **7 B17** 58 0 S 68 0W
Drakensberg, *S. Africa* **117 D4** 31 0 S 28 0 E
Dráma, *Greece* **51 E8** 41 9N 24 10 E
Dráma □, *Greece* **51 E8** 41 20N 24 0 E
Drammen, *Norway* **15 G14** 59 42N 10 12 E
Drangajökull, *Iceland* **11 A4** 66 9N 22 15W
Drangedal, *Norway* **18 E6** 59 6N 9 3 E
Drangsnes, *Iceland* **11 B5** 65 41N 21 27W
Dranov, Ostrov, *Romania* **53 F14** 44 55N 29 30 E
Dras, *India* **93 B6** 34 25N 75 48 E
Drau = Drava →, *Croatia* **52 E3** 45 33N 18 55 E
Drava →, *Croatia* **52 E3** 45 33N 18 55 E
Dravograd, *Slovenia* **45 B12** 46 36N 15 5 E
Drawa →, *Poland* **55 F2** 52 52N 15 59 E
Drawno, *Poland* **55 E2** 53 13N 15 46 E
Drawsko Pomorskie, *Poland* **54 E2** 53 35N 15 50 E
Drayton Plains, *U.S.A.* **157 B13** 42 42N 83 23W
Drayton Valley, *Canada* **142 C6** 53 12N 114 58W
Dreieich, *Germany* **31 E4** 50 1N 8 41 E
Dren, *Kosovo, Yug.* **50 C4** 43 8N 20 46 E
Drenthe □, *Neths.* **24 B6** 52 52N 6 40 E
Drepanum, C., *Cyprus* **38 E11** 34 54N 32 19 E
Dresden, *Canada* **150 D2** 42 35N 82 11W
Dresden, *Germany* **30 D9** 51 3N 13 44 E
Dreux, *France* **26 D8** 48 44N 1 23 E
Drevsjø, *Norway* **18 C9** 61 53N 12 1 E
Drexel, *U.S.A.* **157 E12** 39 45N 84 18W
Drezdenko, *Poland* **55 F2** 52 50N 15 49 E
Driffield, *U.K.* **20 C7** 54 0N 0 26W
Driftwood, *U.S.A.* **150 E6** 41 20N 78 8W
Driggs, *U.S.A.* **158 E8** 43 44N 111 6W
Drin i Zi →, *Albania* **50 E4** 41 37N 20 28 E
Drina →, *Bos.-H.* **50 B3** 44 53N 19 21 E
Drincea →, *Romania* **52 F7** 44 20N 22 55 E
Drini →, *Albania* **50 D3** 42 1N 19 38 E
Drinjača →, *Bos.-H.* **52 F4** 44 15N 19 8 E
Drissa = Vyerkhnyadzvinsk,
Belarus **58 E4** 55 45N 27 58 E
Driva →, *Norway* **18 B6** 62 41N 9 31 E
Drivstua, *Norway* **18 B6** 62 26N 9 47 E
Drniš, *Croatia* **45 E13** 43 51N 16 10 E
Drøbak, *Norway* **15 G14** 59 39N 10 39 E
Drobin, *Poland* **55 F6** 52 42N 19 58 E
Drochia, *Moldova* **53 B12** 48 2N 27 48 E
Drogheda, *Ireland* **23 C5** 53 43N 6 22W
Drogichin = Dragichyn, *Belarus* **59 F3** 52 15N 25 8 E
Drogobych = Drohobych,
Ukraine **59 H2** 49 20N 23 30 E
Drohiczyn, *Poland* **55 F9** 52 24N 22 39 E
Drohobych, *Ukraine* **59 H2** 49 20N 23 30 E
Droichead Atha = Drogheda,
Ireland **23 C5** 53 43N 6 22W
Droichead Nua, *Ireland* **23 C5** 53 11N 6 48W
Droitwich, *U.K.* **21 E5** 52 16N 2 8W
Drôme □, *France* **29 D9** 44 38N 5 15 E
Drôme →, *France* **29 D8** 44 46N 4 46 E
Dromedary, C., *Australia* **129 D9** 36 17 S 150 10 E
Dromore, *U.K.* **23 B4** 54 31N 7 28W
Dromore West, *Ireland* **23 B3** 54 15N 8 52W
Dronero, *Italy* **44 D4** 44 28N 7 22 E
Dronfield, *U.K.* **20 D6** 53 19N 1 27W
Dronne →, *France* **28 C3** 45 2N 0 9W
Dronninglund, *Denmark* **17 G4** 57 10N 10 19 E
Dronten, *Neths.* **24 B5** 52 32N 5 43 E
Dropt →, *France* **28 D3** 44 35N 0 6W
Drosendorf, *Austria* **34 C8** 48 52N 15 37 E
Droué, *France* **26 D8** 48 3N 1 6 E
Drouin, *Australia* **129 E6** 38 10 S 145 53 E
Drumbo, *Canada* **150 C4** 43 16N 80 35W
Drumheller, *Canada* **142 C6** 51 25N 112 40W
Drummond, *U.S.A.* **158 C7** 46 40N 113 9W
Drummond I., *U.S.A.* **148 C4** 46 1N 83 39W
Drummond Pt., *Australia* **127 E2** 34 9 S 135 16 E
Drummond Ra., *Australia* **126 C4** 23 45 S 147 10 E
Drummondville, *Canada* **140 C5** 45 55N 72 25W
Drumright, *U.S.A.* **155 H6** 35 59N 96 36W
Druskininkai, *Lithuania* **15 J20** 54 3N 23 58 E
Drut →, *Belarus* **59 F6** 53 8N 30 5 E
Druya, *Belarus* **58 E4** 55 45N 27 28 E
Druzhba, *Bulgaria* **51 C12** 43 15N 28 1 E
Druzhina, *Russia* **65 C15** 68 14N 145 18 E
Drvar, *Bos.-H.* **45 D13** 44 21N 16 23 E
Drvenik, *Croatia* **45 E13** 43 27N 16 3 E
Drwęca →, *Poland* **55 E5** 53 0N 18 42 E
Dry Tortugas, *U.S.A.* **164 B3** 24 38N 82 55W
Dryanovo, *Bulgaria* **51 D9** 42 59N 25 28 E
Dryden, *Canada* **143 D10** 49 47N 92 50W
Dryden, *U.S.A.* **151 D8** 42 30N 76 18W
Drygalski I., *Antarctica* **7 C7** 66 0 S 92 0 E
Drysdale →, *Australia* **124 B4** 13 59 S 126 51 E
Drysdale I., *Australia* **126 A2** 11 41 S 136 0 E
Drzewica, *Poland* **55 G7** 51 27N 20 29 E
Drzewiczka →, *Poland* **55 G7** 51 36N 20 36 E
Dschang, *Cameroon* **113 D7** 5 32N 10 3 E
Du Bois, *U.S.A.* **150 E6** 41 8N 78 46W
Du Gué →, *Canada* **140 A5** 57 21N 70 45W
Du He, *China* **77 A8** 32 48N 110 40 E
Du Quoin, *U.S.A.* **156 G7** 38 1N 89 14W
Du'an, *China* **76 F7** 23 59N 108 3 E
Duanesburg, *U.S.A.* **151 D10** 42 45N 74 11W
Duaringa, *Australia* **126 C4** 23 42 S 149 42 E
Ḍubā, *Si. Arabia* **96 E2** 27 10N 35 40 E
Dubai = Dubayy, *U.A.E.* **97 E7** 25 18N 55 20 E
Dubăsari, *Moldova* **53 C14** 47 15N 29 10 E
Dubăsari Vdkhr., *Moldova* **53 C13** 47 30N 29 0 E
Dubawnt →, *Canada* **143 A8** 64 33N 100 6W
Dubawnt, L., *Canada* **143 A8** 63 4N 101 42W
Dubayy, *U.A.E.* **97 E7** 25 18N 55 20 E
Dubbo, *Australia* **129 B8** 32 11 S 148 35 E
Dubele,
Dem. Rep. of the Congo **118 B2** 2 56N 29 35 E
Dübendorf, *Switz.* **33 B7** 47 24N 8 37 E
Dubica, *Croatia* **45 C13** 45 11N 16 48 E
Dublin, *Ireland* **23 C5** 53 21N 6 15W
Dublin, *Ga., U.S.A.* **152 C7** 32 32N 82 54W
Dublin, *Tex., U.S.A.* **155 J5** 32 5N 98 21W
Dublin □, *Ireland* **23 C5** 53 24N 6 20W
Dubna, *Russia* **58 D9** 56 44N 37 10 E
Dubnica nad Váhom,
Slovak Rep. **35 C11** 48 58N 18 11 E
Dubno, *Ukraine* **59 G3** 50 25N 25 45 E
Dubois, *Idaho, U.S.A.* **158 D7** 44 10N 112 14W
Dubois, *Ind., U.S.A.* **157 F10** 38 27N 86 48W
Dubossary = Dubăsari,
Moldova **53 C14** 47 15N 29 10 E
Dubossary Vdkhr. = Dubăsari
Vdkhr., *Moldova* **53 C13** 47 30N 29 0 E
Dubovka, *Russia* **61 F7** 49 5N 44 50 E
Dubovskoye, *Russia* **61 G6** 47 28N 42 46 E
Dubrajpur, *India* **93 H12** 23 48N 87 25 E
Dubréka, *Guinea* **112 D2** 9 46N 13 31W
Dubrovitsa = Dubrovytsya,
Ukraine **59 G4** 51 31N 26 35 E
Dubrovnik, *Croatia* **50 D2** 42 39N 18 6 E
Dubrovytsya, *Ukraine* **59 G4** 51 31N 26 35 E
Dubulu,
Dem. Rep. of the Congo **114 B4** 4 18N 20 16 E
Dubuque, *U.S.A.* **156 B6** 42 30N 90 41W
Dubysa →, *Lithuania* **54 C10** 55 5N 23 26 E
Duchang, *China* **77 C11** 29 18N 116 12 E
Duchesne, *U.S.A.* **158 F8** 40 10N 110 24W
Duchess, *Australia* **126 C2** 21 20 S 139 50 E
Ducie I., *Pac. Oc.* **135 K15** 24 40 S 124 48W
Duck →, *U.S.A.* **149 G2** 36 2N 87 52W
Duck Cr. →, *Australia* **124 D2** 22 37 S 116 53 E
Duck Lake, *Canada* **143 C7** 52 50N 106 16W
Duck Mountain Prov. Park,
Canada **143 C8** 51 45N 101 0W
Duckwall, Mt., *U.S.A.* **160 H6** 37 58N 120 7W
Duda →, *Colombia* **168 C3** 2 34N 74 3W
Duderstadt, *Germany* **30 D6** 51 31N 10 15 E
Dudhnai, *India* **90 C3** 25 59N 90 47 E
Düdingen, *Switz.* **32 C4** 46 52N 7 12 E
Dudinka, *Russia* **65 C9** 69 30N 86 13 E
Dudley, *U.K.* **21 E5** 52 31N 2 5W
Dudley, *U.S.A.* **152 C6** 32 32N 83 5W
Dudna →, *India* **94 E3** 19 17N 76 54 E
Dudo, *Somali Rep.* **120 C4** 9 20N 50 12 E
Dudub, *Ethiopia* **120 C3** 6 55N 46 43 E
Dudwa, *India* **93 E9** 28 30N 80 41 E
Duékoué, *Ivory C.* **112 D3** 6 40N 7 15W
Duenas, *Phil.* **81 F4** 11 4N 122 37 E
Dueñas, *Spain* **42 D6** 41 52N 4 33W
Dueré, *Brazil* **171 D2** 11 20 S 49 17W
Duero = Douro →, *Europe* **42 D2** 41 8N 8 40W
Dūfah, W. →, *Si. Arabia* **98 C3** 18 45N 41 49 E
Dufftown, *U.K.* **22 D5** 57 27N 3 8W
Dufourspitz, *Switz.* **32 E5** 45 56N 7 52 E
Dugger, *U.S.A.* **157 E9** 39 4N 87 18W
Dugi Otok, *Croatia* **45 D11** 44 0N 15 3 E
Dugiuma, *Somali Rep.* **120 D2** 1 15N 42 34 E
Dugo Selo, *Croatia* **45 C13** 45 51N 16 18 E
Duifken Pt., *Australia* **126 A3** 12 33 S 141 38 E
Duisburg, *Germany* **30 D2** 51 26N 6 45 E
Duitama, *Colombia* **168 B3** 5 50N 73 2W
Duiwelskloof, *S. Africa* **117 C5** 23 42 S 30 10 E
Dujiangyan, *China* **76 B4** 31 2N 103 38 E
Duk Fadiat, *Sudan* **107 F3** 7 45N 31 25 E
Duk Faiwil, *Sudan* **107 F3** 7 30N 31 29 E
Dukati, *Albania* **50 F3** 40 16N 19 32 E
Dūkdamīn, *Iran* **97 C8** 35 59N 57 43 E
Dukelský Průsmyk, *Slovak Rep.* **35 B14** 49 25N 21 42 E
Dukhān, *Qatar* **97 E6** 25 25N 50 50 E
Dukhovshchina, *Russia* **58 E7** 55 15N 32 27 E
Duki, *Pakistan* **91 C3** 30 14N 68 25 E
Dukla, *Poland* **55 J8** 49 30N 21 35 E
Duku, *Bauchi, Nigeria* **113 C7** 10 43N 10 43 E
Duku, *Sokoto, Nigeria* **113 C5** 11 11N 4 55 E
Dula, *Dem. Rep. of the Congo* **114 B4** 4 40N 20 21 E
Dulag, *Phil.* **81 F5** 10 57N 125 2 E
Dulce, *U.S.A.* **159 H10** 36 56N 107 0W
Dulce →, *Argentina* **174 C3** 30 32 S 62 33W
Dulce, G., *Costa Rica* **164 E3** 8 40N 83 20W
Dulf, *Iraq* **96 C5** 35 7N 45 51 E
Dŭlgopol, *Bulgaria* **51 C11** 43 3N 27 22 E
Dulit, Banjaran, *Malaysia* **78 D4** 3 15N 114 30 E
Duliu, *China* **74 E9** 39 2N 116 55 E
Dullewala, *Pakistan* **92 D4** 31 50N 71 25 E
Dullstroom, *S. Africa* **117 D5** 25 27 S 30 7 E
Dülmen, *Germany* **30 D3** 51 49N 7 17 E
Dulovo, *Bulgaria* **51 C11** 43 48N 27 9 E
Dulpetorpet, *Norway* **18 D9** 60 34N 12 19 E
Dulq Maghār, *Syria* **101 D8** 36 22N 38 39 E
Duluth, *Ga., U.S.A.* **152 A5** 34 0N 84 9W
Duluth, *Minn., U.S.A.* **154 B8** 46 47N 92 6W
Dum Dum, *India* **93 H13** 22 39N 88 33 E
Dūmā, *Syria* **103 B5** 33 34N 36 24 E
Dumaguete, *Phil.* **79 C6** 9 17N 123 15 E
Dumai, *Indonesia* **78 D2** 1 35N 101 28 E
Dumalinao, *Phil.* **81 H4** 7 49N 123 23 E
Dumanguilas Bay, *Phil.* **81 H4** 7 34N 123 4 E
Dumanjug, *Phil.* **81 F4** 10 4N 123 26 E
Dumaran, *Phil.* **79 B5** 10 33N 119 50 E
Dumaran I., *Phil.* **81 F2** 10 33N 119 51 E
Dumarao, *Phil.* **81 F4** 11 16N 122 41 E
Dumas, *Ark., U.S.A.* **155 J9** 33 53N 91 29W
Dumas, *Tex., U.S.A.* **155 H4** 35 52N 101 58W
Ḍumayr, *Syria* **103 B5** 33 39N 36 42 E
Dumbarton, *U.K.* **22 F4** 55 57N 4 33W
Dumbea, *N. Cal.* **133 V20** 22 10 S 166 27 E
Ďumbier, *Slovak Rep.* **35 C12** 48 56N 19 38 E
Dumbleyung, *Australia* **125 F2** 33 17 S 117 42 E
Dumbo, *Angola* **115 E3** 14 6 S 17 24 E
Dumboa, *Nigeria* **113 C7** 11 15N 12 55 E
Dumbrăveni, *Romania* **53 D9** 46 14N 24 34 E
Dumfries, *U.K.* **22 F5** 55 4N 3 37W
Dumfries & Galloway □, *U.K.* **22 F5** 55 9N 3 58W
Dumingag, *Phil.* **81 G4** 8 20N 123 20 E
Dumitrești, *Romania* **53 E11** 45 33N 26 55 E
Dumka, *India* **93 G12** 24 12N 87 15 E
Dumlupınar, *Turkey* **49 C12** 38 53N 30 0 E
Dümmer, *Germany* **30 C4** 52 31N 8 20 E
Dumoine →, *Canada* **140 C4** 46 13N 77 51W
Dumoine, L., *Canada* **140 C4** 46 55N 77 55W
Dumraon, *India* **93 G11** 25 33N 84 8 E
Dumyât, *Egypt* **106 H7** 31 24N 31 48 E
Dumyât, Masabb, *Egypt* **106 H7** 31 28N 31 51 E
Dún Dealgan = Dundalk,
Ireland **23 B5** 54 1N 6 24W
Dun Laoghaire, *Ireland* **23 C5** 53 17N 6 8W
Dun-le-Palestel, *France* **27 F8** 46 18N 1 39 E
Dun-sur-Auron, *France* **27 F9** 46 53N 2 33 E
Dun-sur-Meuse, *France* **27 C12** 49 23N 5 11 E
Duna = Dunărea →, *Europe* **53 E14** 45 20N 29 40 E
Duna →, *Hungary* **52 E3** 45 51N 18 48 E
Duna-völgyi-főcsatorna,
Hungary **52 D4** 46 40N 19 14 E
Dunaföldvár, *Hungary* **52 D3** 46 50N 18 57 E
Dunagiri, *India* **93 D8** 30 31N 79 52 E
Dunaj = Dunărea →, *Europe* **53 E14** 45 20N 29 40 E
Dunaj →, *Slovak Rep.* **35 D11** 47 50N 18 50 E
Dunajec →, *Poland* **55 H7** 50 15N 20 44 E
Dunajská Streda, *Slovak Rep.* **35 C10** 48 0N 17 37 E
Dunakeszi, *Hungary* **52 C4** 47 37N 19 8 E
Dunapataj, *Hungary* **52 D4** 46 39N 19 4 E
Dunărea →, *Europe* **53 E14** 45 20N 29 40 E
Dunaszekcső, *Hungary* **52 D3** 46 6N 18 45 E
Dunaújváros, *Hungary* **52 D3** 46 58N 18 57 E
Dunav = Dunărea →, *Europe* **53 E14** 45 20N 29 40 E
Dunavațu de Jos, *Romania* **53 F14** 44 59N 29 13 E
Dunavtsi, *Bulgaria* **50 C6** 43 57N 22 53 E
Dunay, *Russia* **68 C6** 42 52N 132 22 E
Dunback, *N.Z.* **131 F5** 45 23 S 170 36 E
Dunbar, *U.K.* **22 E6** 56 0N 2 31W
Dunblane, *U.K.* **22 E5** 56 11N 3 58W
Duncan, *Canada* **142 D4** 48 45N 123 40W
Duncan, *Ariz., U.S.A.* **159 K9** 32 43N 109 6W
Duncan, *Okla., U.S.A.* **155 H6** 34 30N 97 57W
Duncan, L., *Canada* **140 B4** 53 29N 77 58W
Duncan L., *Canada* **142 A6** 62 51N 113 58W
Duncan Town, *Bahamas* **164 B4** 22 15N 75 45W
Duncannon, *U.S.A.* **150 F7** 40 23N 77 2W
Duncansby Head, *U.K.* **22 C5** 58 38N 3 1W
Duncansville, *U.S.A.* **150 F6** 40 25N 78 26W
Dundaga, *Latvia* **54 A9** 57 31N 22 21 E
Dundalk, *Canada* **150 B4** 44 10N 80 24W
Dundalk, *Ireland* **23 B5** 54 1N 6 24W
Dundalk, *U.S.A.* **148 F7** 39 16N 76 32W
Dundalk Bay, *Ireland* **23 C5** 53 55N 6 15W
Dundas = Uummannaq,
Greenland **10 B4** 77 0N 69 0W
Dundas, *Canada* **150 C5** 43 17N 79 59W
Dundas, L., *Australia* **125 F3** 32 35 S 121 50 E
Dundas I., *Canada* **142 C2** 54 30N 130 50W
Dundas Str., *Australia* **124 B5** 11 15 S 131 35 E
Dundee, *S. Africa* **117 D5** 28 11 S 30 15 E
Dundee, *U.K.* **22 E6** 56 28N 2 59W
Dundee, *Mich., U.S.A.* **157 C13** 41 57N 83 40W
Dundee, *N.Y., U.S.A.* **150 D8** 42 32N 76 59W
Dundee City □, *U.K.* **22 E6** 56 30N 2 58W
Dundgovĭ □, *Mongolia* **74 B4** 45 10N 106 0 E
Dundrum, *U.K.* **23 B6** 54 16N 5 52W
Dundrum B., *U.K.* **23 B6** 54 13N 5 47W
Dunedin, *N.Z.* **131 F5** 45 50 S 170 33 E
Dunedin, *U.S.A.* **149 L4** 28 1N 82 47W
Dunedoo, *Australia* **127 E4** 32 0 S 149 25 E
Dunfermline, *U.K.* **22 E5** 56 5N 3 27W
Dungannon, *Canada* **150 C3** 43 51N 81 36W
Dungannon, *U.K.* **23 B5** 54 31N 6 46W
Dungarpur, *India* **92 H5** 23 52N 73 45 E
Dungarvan, *Ireland* **23 D4** 52 5N 7 37W
Dungarvan Harbour, *Ireland* **23 D4** 52 4N 7 35W
Dungeness, *U.K.* **21 G8** 50 54N 0 59 E
Dungo, L. do, *Angola* **116 B2** 17 15 S 19 0 E
Dungog, *Australia* **129 B9** 32 22 S 151 46 E
Dungu,
Dem. Rep. of the Congo **118 B2** 3 40N 28 32 E
Dungun, *Malaysia* **87 K4** 4 45N 103 25 E
Dunguna, *Sudan* **106 C4** 21 10N 37 9 E
Dungunâb, Khalij, *Sudan* **106 C4** 21 5N 37 12 E
Dunhua, *China* **75 C15** 43 20N 128 14 E
Dunhuang, *China* **72 B4** 40 8N 94 36 E
Dunk I., *Australia* **126 B4** 17 59 S 146 29 E
Dunkassa, *Benin* **113 C5** 10 21N 3 10 E
Dunkeld, *Queens., Australia* **127 E4** 33 25 S 149 29 E
Dunkeld, *Vic., Australia* **128 D5** 37 40 S 142 22 E
Dunkeld, *U.K.* **22 E5** 56 34N 3 35W
Dunkerque, *France* **27 A9** 51 2N 2 20 E
Dunkery Beacon, *U.K.* **21 F4** 51 9N 3 36W
Dunkirk = Dunkerque, *France* **27 A9** 51 2N 2 20 E
Dunkirk, *U.S.A.* **150 D5** 42 29N 79 20W
Dunkuj, *Sudan* **107 E3** 12 50N 32 49 E
Dunkwa, *Central, Ghana* **112 D4** 6 0N 1 47W
Dunkwa, *Central, Ghana* **113 D4** 5 30N 1 0W
Dúnleary = Dun Laoghaire,
Ireland **23 C5** 53 17N 6 8W
Dunleer, *Ireland* **23 C5** 53 50N 6 24W
Dunmanus B., *Ireland* **23 E2** 51 31N 9 50W
Dunmanway, *Ireland* **23 E2** 51 43N 9 6W
Dunmara, *Australia* **126 B1** 16 42 S 133 25 E
Dunmore, *U.S.A.* **151 E9** 41 25N 75 38W
Dunmore Hd., *Ireland* **23 D1** 52 10N 10 35W
Dunmore Town, *Bahamas* **164 A4** 25 30N 76 39W
Dunn, *U.S.A.* **149 H6** 35 19N 78 37W
Dunnellon, *U.S.A.* **149 L4** 29 3N 82 28W
Dunnet Hd., *U.K.* **22 C5** 58 40N 3 21W
Dunning, *U.S.A.* **154 E4** 41 50N 100 6W
Dunnville, *Canada* **150 D5** 42 54N 79 36W
Dunolly, *Australia* **128 D5** 36 51 S 143 44 E
Dunoon, *U.K.* **22 F4** 55 57N 4 56W
Dunphy, *U.S.A.* **158 F5** 40 42N 116 31W
Dunqul, *Egypt* **106 C3** 23 26N 31 37 E
Duns, *U.K.* **22 F6** 55 47N 2 20W
Dunseith, *U.S.A.* **154 A4** 48 50N 100 3W
Dunsmuir, *U.S.A.* **158 F2** 41 13N 122 16W
Dunstable, *U.K.* **21 F7** 51 53N 0 32W
Dunstan Mts., *N.Z.* **131 E4** 44 53 S 169 35 E
Dunster, *Canada* **142 C5** 53 8N 119 50W
Duntroon, *N.Z.* **131 E5** 44 51 S 170 40 E
Dunvegan L., *Canada* **143 A7** 60 8N 107 10W
Duolun, *China* **74 C9** 42 12N 116 28 E
Duong Dong, *Vietnam* **87 G4** 10 13N 103 58 E
Dupax, *Phil.* **80 C3** 16 17N 121 5 E
Dupree, *U.S.A.* **154 C4** 45 4N 101 35W
Dupuyer, *U.S.A.* **158 B7** 48 13N 112 30W
Duqm, *Oman* **99 C7** 19 39N 57 42 E
Duque de Caxias, *Brazil* **171 F3** 22 45 S 43 19W
Duque de York, I., *Chile* **176 D1** 50 37 S 75 25W
Durack →, *Australia* **124 C4** 15 33 S 127 52 E
Durack Ra., *Australia* **124 C4** 16 50 S 127 40 E
Durağan, *Turkey* **100 B6** 41 25N 35 3 E
Durak, *Turkey* **49 B10** 39 42N 28 17 E
Đurakovac, *Kosovo, Yug.* **50 D4** 42 43N 20 29 E
Durance →, *France* **29 E8** 43 55N 4 45 E
Durand, *Ga., U.S.A.* **152 C5** 32 54N 84 51W
Durand, *Ill., U.S.A.* **156 B7** 42 26N 89 20W
Durand, *Mich., U.S.A.* **157 B13** 42 55N 83 59W
Durand, *Wis., U.S.A.* **154 C9** 44 38N 91 58W
Durango, *Mexico* **162 C4** 24 3N 104 39W
Durango, *U.S.A.* **159 H10** 37 16N 107 53W
Durango □, *Mexico* **162 C4** 25 0N 105 0W
Durankulak, *Bulgaria* **51 C12** 43 41N 28 32 E
Durant, *Iowa, U.S.A.* **156 C6** 41 36N 90 54W
Durant, *Miss., U.S.A.* **155 J10** 33 4N 89 51W
Durant, *Okla., U.S.A.* **155 J6** 33 59N 96 25W
Duratón →, *Spain* **42 D6** 41 37N 4 7W
Durazno, *Uruguay* **174 C4** 33 25 S 56 31W
Durazzo = Durrësi, *Albania* **50 E3** 41 19N 19 28 E
Durban, *France* **28 F6** 42 59N 2 49 E
Durban, *S. Africa* **117 D5** 29 49 S 31 1 E
Durbo, *Somali Rep.* **120 B4** 11 37N 50 20 E
Durbuy, *Belgium* **24 D5** 50 21N 5 28 E
Dúrcal, *Spain* **43 J7** 36 59N 3 34W
Đurđevac, *Croatia* **52 D2** 46 2N 17 3 E
Düren, *Germany* **30 E2** 50 48N 6 29 E
Durg, *India* **94 D5** 21 15N 81 22 E
Durgapur, *India* **93 H12** 23 30N 87 20 E
Durham, *Canada* **140 D3** 44 10N 80 49W
Durham, *U.K.* **20 C6** 54 47N 1 34W
Durham, *Calif., U.S.A.* **160 F5** 39 39N 121 48W
Durham, *N.C., U.S.A.* **149 H6** 35 59N 78 54W
Durham, *N.H., U.S.A.* **151 C14** 43 8N 70 56W
Durham □, *U.K.* **20 C6** 54 42N 1 45W
Durlești, *Moldova* **53 C13** 47 1N 28 46 E
Ḍurmā, *Si. Arabia* **96 E5** 24 37N 46 8 E
Durmitor, *Montenegro, Yug.* **50 C2** 43 10N 19 0 E
Durness, *U.K.* **22 C4** 58 34N 4 45W
Durrësi, *Albania* **50 E3** 41 19N 19 28 E
Durrow, *Ireland* **23 D4** 52 51N 7 24W
Dursey I., *Ireland* **23 E1** 51 36N 10 12W
Dursunbey, *Turkey* **49 B10** 39 35N 28 37 E
Durtal, *France* **26 E6** 47 40N 0 18W
Duru, *Dem. Rep. of the Congo* **118 B2** 4 14N 28 50 E
Duru Gölü, *Turkey* **51 E12** 41 20N 28 35 E
Durusu, *Turkey* **51 E12** 41 17N 28 41 E
Durūz, Jabal ad, *Jordan* **103 C5** 32 35N 36 40 E
D'Urville, Tanjung, *Indonesia* **79 E9** 1 28 S 137 54 E
D'Urville I., *N.Z.* **131 A8** 40 50 S 173 55 E
Duryea, *U.S.A.* **151 E9** 41 20N 75 45W
Dusa Mareb, *Somali Rep.* **120 C3** 5 30N 46 15 E
Dûsh, *Egypt* **106 C3** 24 35N 30 41 E
Dushak, *Turkmenistan* **64 F7** 37 13N 60 1 E
Dushan, *China* **76 E6** 25 48N 107 30 E
Dushanbe, *Tajikistan* **64 F7** 38 33N 68 48 E
Dusheti, *Georgia* **61 J7** 42 10N 44 42 E
Dushore, *U.S.A.* **151 E8** 41 31N 76 24W
Dusky Sd., *N.Z.* **131 F1** 45 47 S 166 30 E
Dussejour, C., *Australia* **124 B4** 14 45 S 128 13 E
Düsseldorf, *Germany* **30 D2** 51 14N 6 47 E
Duszniki-Zdrój, *Poland* **55 H3** 50 24N 16 24 E
Dutch Harbor, *U.S.A.* **138 C3** 53 53N 166 32W
Dutlwe, *Botswana* **116 C3** 23 58 S 23 46 E
Dutsan Wai, *Nigeria* **113 C6** 10 50N 8 10 E
Dutton, *Canada* **150 D3** 42 39N 81 30W
Dutton →, *Australia* **126 C3** 20 44 S 143 10 E
Duved, *Sweden* **16 A6** 63 24N 12 55 E
Düvertepe, *Turkey* **49 B10** 39 14N 28 27 E
Duwayhin, Khawr, *U.A.E.* **97 E6** 24 20N 51 25 E
Duyun, *China* **76 D6** 26 18N 107 29 E
Düzağac, *Turkey* **49 C12** 38 48N 30 10 E
Düzce, *Turkey* **100 B4** 40 50N 31 10 E
Duzdab = Zāhedān, *Iran* **97 D9** 29 30N 60 50 E
Dve Mogili, *Bulgaria* **51 C9** 43 35N 25 55 E
Dvina, Severnaya →, *Russia* **56 B7** 64 32N 40 30 E
Dvinsk = Daugavpils, *Latvia* **15 J22** 55 53N 26 32 E
Dvinskaya Guba, *Russia* **56 B6** 65 0N 39 0 E
Dvor, *Croatia* **45 C13** 45 4N 16 22 E
Dvůr Králové nad Labem,
Czech Rep. **34 A8** 50 27N 15 50 E
Dwarka, *India* **92 H3** 22 18N 69 8 E
Dwellingup, *Australia* **125 F2** 32 43 S 116 4 E
Dwight, *Canada* **150 A5** 45 20N 79 1W
Dwight, *U.S.A.* **157 C8** 41 5N 88 26W
Dyatkovo, *Russia* **58 F8** 53 40N 34 27 E
Dyatlovo = Dzyatlava, *Belarus* **58 F3** 53 28N 25 28 E
Dyce, *U.K.* **22 D6** 57 13N 2 12W
Dyer, *U.S.A.* **157 G10** 37 24N 86 13W
Dyer, C., *Canada* **139 B13** 66 40N 61 0W
Dyer Bay, *Canada* **150 A3** 45 10N 81 20W
Dyer Plateau, *Antarctica* **7 D17** 70 45 S 65 30W
Dyerbeldzhin, *Kyrgyzstan* **63 C7** 41 13N 74 54 E
Dyersburg, *U.S.A.* **155 G10** 36 3N 89 23W
Dyersville, *U.S.A.* **156 B5** 42 29N 91 8W
Dyfi →, *U.K.* **21 E3** 52 32N 4 3W
Dyje →, *Czech Rep.* **35 C9** 48 37N 16 56 E
Dymer, *Ukraine* **59 G6** 50 47N 30 18 E
Dynów, *Poland* **55 J9** 49 50N 22 11 E
Dyranut, *Norway* **18 D4** 60 22N 7 31 E
Dyrhólaey, *Iceland* **11 D7** 63 24N 19 8W
Dyrnes, *Norway* **18 A4** 63 25N 7 52 E
Dysart, *Australia* **126 C4** 22 32 S 148 23 E
Dysart, *U.S.A.* **156 B4** 42 10N 92 18W
Dyurtyuli, *Russia* **62 D5** 55 9N 54 4 E
Dzamin Üüd = Borhoyn Tal,
Mongolia **74 C6** 43 50N 111 58 E
Dzerzhinsk, *Russia* **60 B6** 56 14N 43 30 E
Dzhalal-Abad = Jalal-Abad,
Kyrgyzstan **63 C6** 40 56N 73 0 E
Dzhalinda, *Russia* **65 D13** 53 26N 124 0 E
Dzhambeyty, *Kazakstan* **62 F4** 50 16N 52 35 E
Dzhambul = Zhambyl,
Kazakstan **64 E8** 42 54N 71 22 E
Dzhambul, Gora = Zhambyl,
Gora, *Kazakstan* **63 A6** 44 54N 73 0 E
Dzhankoy, *Ukraine* **59 K8** 45 40N 34 20 E
Dzhanybek, *Kazakstan* **60 F8** 49 25N 46 50 E
Dzharkurgan = Jarqŭrghon,
Uzbekistan **63 E3** 37 31N 67 25 E
Dzharylhach, Ostriv, *Ukraine* **59 J7** 46 2N 32 55 E
Dzhetym, Khrebet, *Kyrgyzstan* **63 C8** 41 30N 77 0 E
Dzhezkazgan = Zhezqazghan,
Kazakstan **64 E7** 47 44N 67 40 E
Dzhizak = Jizzakh, *Uzbekistan* **64 E7** 40 6N 67 50 E
Dzhugdzur, Khrebet, *Russia* **65 D14** 57 30N 138 0 E
Dzhuma, *Uzbekistan* **63 D3** 39 42N 66 40 E
Dzhumgoltau, Khrebet,
Kyrgyzstan **63 B7** 42 15N 74 30 E
Dzhungarskiye Vorota =
Dzungarian Gates, *Asia* **72 B3** 45 0N 82 0 E
Dzhvari = Jvari, *Georgia* **61 J6** 42 42N 42 4 E
Działdowo, *Poland* **55 E7** 53 15N 20 15 E
Działoszyce, *Poland* **55 H7** 50 22N 20 20 E
Działoszyn, *Poland* **55 G5** 51 6N 18 50 E
Dzibilchaltun, *Mexico* **163 C7** 21 5N 89 36W
Dzierzgoń, *Poland* **54 E6** 53 58N 19 20 E
Dzierżoniów, *Poland* **55 H3** 50 45N 16 39 E
Dzilam de Bravo, *Mexico* **163 C7** 21 24N 88 53W
Dzioua, *Algeria* **111 B6** 33 14N 5 14 E
Dzisna, *Belarus* **58 E5** 55 34N 28 12 E
Dzisna →, *Belarus* **58 E5** 55 34N 28 12 E
Dziwnów, *Poland* **54 D1** 54 2N 14 45 E
Dzungaria = Junggar Pendi,
China **72 B3** 44 30N 86 0 E
Dzungarian Gates, *Asia* **72 B3** 45 0N 82 0 E
Dzuumod, *Mongolia* **72 B5** 47 45N 106 58 E
Dzyarzhynsk, *Belarus* **58 F4** 53 40N 27 1 E
Dzyatlava, *Belarus* **58 F3** 53 28N 25 28 E

E

Eabamet L., *Canada* **140 B2** 51 30N 87 46W
Eads, *U.S.A.* **154 F3** 38 29N 102 47W
Eagar, *U.S.A.* **159 J9** 34 6N 109 17W
Eagle, *Alaska, U.S.A.* **138 B5** 64 47N 141 12W
Eagle, *Colo., U.S.A.* **158 G10** 39 39N 106 50W
Eagle →, *Canada* **141 B8** 53 36N 57 26W
Eagle Butte, *U.S.A.* **154 C4** 45 0N 101 10W
Eagle Cr. →, *U.S.A.* **157 F11** 38 36N 85 4W
Eagle Grove, *U.S.A.* **156 B3** 42 40N 93 54W

210 Eagle L.

Eagle L., *Canada* **143 D10** 49 42N 93 13W
Eagle L., *Calif., U.S.A.* **158 F3** 40 39N 120 45W
Eagle L., *Maine, U.S.A.* **149 B11** 46 20N 69 22W
Eagle Lake, *Canada* **150 A6** 45 8N 78 29W
Eagle Lake, *Maine, U.S.A.* **149 B11** 47 3N 68 36W
Eagle Lake, *Tex., U.S.A.* **155 L6** 29 35N 96 20W
Eagle Mountain, *U.S.A.* **161 M11** 33 49N 115 27W
Eagle Nest, *U.S.A.* **159 H11** 36 33N 105 16W
Eagle Pass, *U.S.A.* **155 L4** 28 43N 100 30W
Eagle Pk., *U.S.A.* **160 G7** 38 10N 119 25W
Eagle Pt., *Australia* **124 C3** 16 11 S 124 23 E
Eagle River, *Mich., U.S.A.* **148 B1** 47 24N 88 18W
Eagle River, *Wis., U.S.A.* **154 C10** 45 55N 89 15W
Eaglehawk, *Australia* **127 F3** 36 44 S 144 15 E
Eagles Mere, *U.S.A.* **151 E8** 41 25N 76 33W
Eagleville, *U.S.A.* **156 D3** 40 28N 93 59W
Ealing, *U.K.* **21 F7** 51 31N 0 20W
Ear Falls, *Canada* **143 C10** 50 38N 93 13W
Earle, *U.S.A.* **155 H9** 35 16N 90 28W
Earlimart, *U.S.A.* **161 K7** 35 53N 119 16W
Earlville, *U.S.A.* **157 C8** 41 35N 88 55W
Early Branch, *U.S.A.* **152 C9** 32 45N 80 55W
Earn ⟶, *U.K.* **22 E5** 56 21N 3 18W
Earn, L., *U.K.* **22 E4** 56 23N 4 13W
Earnslaw, Mt., *N.Z.* **131 E3** 44 32 S 168 27 E
Earth, *U.S.A.* **155 H3** 34 14N 102 24W
Easley, *U.S.A.* **149 H4** 34 50N 82 36W
East Anglia, *U.K.* **20 E9** 52 30N 1 0 E
East Angus, *Canada* **141 C5** 45 30N 71 40W
East Aurora, *U.S.A.* **150 D6** 42 46N 78 37W
East Ayrshire □, *U.K.* **22 F4** 55 26N 4 11W
East Beskids = Vychodné Beskydy, *Europe* **35 B15** 49 20N 22 0 E
East Brady, *U.S.A.* **150 F5** 40 59N 79 36W
East C., *N.Z.* **130 D7** 37 42 S 178 35 E
East C., *Papua N. G.* **132 F6** 10 13 S 150 53 E
East Chicago, *U.S.A.* **157 C9** 41 38N 87 27W
East China Sea, *Asia* **73 D7** 30 0N 126 0 E
East Coast Bays, *N.Z.* **130 C3** 36 46 S 174 46 E
East Coulee, *Canada* **142 C6** 51 23N 112 27W
East Dereham, *U.K.* **21 E8** 52 41N 0 57 E
East Dublin, *U.S.A.* **152 C7** 32 32N 82 52W
East Dubuque, *U.S.A.* **156 B6** 42 30N 90 39W
East Dunbartonshire □, *U.K.* **22 F4** 55 57N 4 13W
East Falkland, *Falk. Is.* **176 D5** 51 30 S 58 30W
East Grand Forks, *U.S.A.* **154 B6** 47 56N 97 1W
East Greenwich, *U.S.A.* **151 E13** 41 40N 71 27W
East Grinstead, *U.K.* **21 F8** 51 7N 0 0 E
East Hartford, *U.S.A.* **151 E12** 41 46N 72 39W
East Helena, *U.S.A.* **158 C8** 46 35N 111 56W
East Indies, *Asia* **66 K15** 0 0 120 0 E
East Kilbride, *U.K.* **22 F4** 55 47N 4 11W
East Lansing, *U.S.A.* **157 B12** 42 44N 84 29W
East Liverpool, *U.S.A.* **150 F4** 40 37N 80 35W
East London, *S. Africa* **117 E4** 33 0 S 27 55 E
East Lothian □, *U.K.* **22 F6** 55 58N 2 44W
East Lynne, *Australia* **129 C9** 35 35 S 150 16 E
East Main = Eastmain, *Canada* **140 B4** 52 10N 78 30W
East Moline, *U.S.A.* **156 C6** 41 32N 90 26W
East Naples, *U.S.A.* **153 J8** 26 8N 81 46W
East Northport, *U.S.A.* **151 F11** 40 53N 73 20W
East Orange, *U.S.A.* **151 F10** 40 46N 74 13W
East Pacific Ridge, *Pac. Oc.* **135 J17** 15 0 S 110 0W
East Palatka, *U.S.A.* **152 F8** 29 39N 81 36W
East Palestine, *U.S.A.* **150 F4** 40 50N 80 33W
East Peoria, *U.S.A.* **156 D7** 40 40N 89 34W
East Pine, *Canada* **142 B4** 55 48N 120 12W
East Point, *U.S.A.* **152 B5** 33 41N 84 27W
East Providence, *U.S.A.* **151 E13** 41 49N 71 23W
East Pt., *Canada* **141 C7** 46 27N 61 58W
East Renfrewshire □, *U.K.* **22 F4** 55 46N 4 21W
East Retford = Retford, *U.K.* **20 D7** 53 19N 0 56W
East Riding of Yorkshire □, *U.K.* **20 D7** 53 55N 0 30W
East Rochester, *U.S.A.* **150 C7** 43 7N 77 29W
East St. Louis, *U.S.A.* **156 F6** 38 37N 90 9W
East Schelde = Oosterschelde ⟶, *Neths.* **24 C4** 51 33N 4 0 E
East Siberian Sea, *Russia* **65 B17** 73 0N 160 0 E
East Stroudsburg, *U.S.A.* **151 E9** 41 1N 75 11W
East Sussex □, *U.K.* **21 G8** 50 56N 0 19 E
East Tawas, *U.S.A.* **148 C4** 44 17N 83 29W
East Timor = Timor Timur □, *Indonesia* **79 F7** 9 0 S 125 0 E
East Toorale, *Australia* **127 E4** 30 27 S 145 28 E
East Troy, *U.S.A.* **157 B8** 42 47N 88 24W
East Walker ⟶, *U.S.A.* **160 G7** 38 52N 119 10W
East Windsor, *U.S.A.* **151 F10** 40 17N 74 34W
Eastbourne, *N.Z.* **130 H3** 41 19 S 174 55 E
Eastbourne, *U.K.* **21 G8** 50 46N 0 18 E
Eastend, *Canada* **143 D7** 49 32N 108 50W
Easter I. = Pascua, I. de, *Pac. Oc.* **135 K17** 27 0 S 109 0W
Eastern □, *Ghana* **113 D4** 6 30N 0 30W
Eastern □, *Kenya* **118 C4** 0 0 38 30 E
Eastern □, *Uganda* **118 B3** 1 50N 33 45 E
Eastern Cape □, *S. Africa* **116 E4** 32 0 S 26 0 E
Eastern Cr. ⟶, *Australia* **126 C3** 20 40 S 141 35 E
Eastern Ghats, *India* **95 H4** 14 0N 78 50 E
Eastern Group = Lau Group, *Fiji* **133 A3** 17 0 S 178 30W
Eastern Group, *Australia* **125 F3** 33 30 S 124 30 E
Eastern Province □, *S. Leone* **112 D2** 8 15N 11 0W
Eastern Samar □, *Phil.* **81 F5** 11 40N 125 40 E
Eastern Transvaal = Mpumalanga □, *S. Africa* **117 B5** 26 0 S 30 0 E
Easterville, *Canada* **143 C9** 53 8N 99 49W
Easthampton, *U.S.A.* **151 D12** 42 16N 72 40W
Eastlake, *U.S.A.* **150 E3** 41 40N 81 26W
Eastland, *U.S.A.* **155 J5** 32 24N 98 49W
Eastleigh, *U.K.* **21 G6** 50 58N 1 21W
Eastmain, *Canada* **140 B4** 52 10N 78 30W
Eastmain ⟶, *Canada* **140 B4** 52 27N 78 26W
Eastman, *Canada* **151 A12** 45 18N 72 19W
Eastman, *Ga., U.S.A.* **152 C6** 32 12N 83 11W
Eastman, *Wis., U.S.A.* **156 A5** 43 10N 91 1W
Easton, *Md., U.S.A.* **148 F7** 38 47N 76 5W
Easton, *Pa., U.S.A.* **151 F9** 40 41N 75 13W
Easton, *Wash., U.S.A.* **160 C5** 47 14N 121 11W
Eastover, *U.S.A.* **152 B9** 33 52N 80 41W
Eastpoint, *U.S.A.* **152 F5** 29 44N 84 53W
Eastpointe, *U.S.A.* **150 D2** 42 27N 82 56W
Eastport, *U.S.A.* **149 C12** 44 56N 67 0W
Eastsound, *U.S.A.* **160 B4** 48 42N 122 55W
Eaton, *Colo., U.S.A.* **154 E2** 40 32N 104 42W
Eaton, *Ohio, U.S.A.* **157 E12** 39 45N 84 38W
Eaton Rapids, *U.S.A.* **157 B12** 42 31N 84 39W
Eatonia, *Canada* **143 C7** 51 13N 109 25W
Eatonton, *U.S.A.* **152 B6** 33 20N 83 23W
Eatontown, *U.S.A.* **151 F10** 40 19N 74 4W
Eatonville, *U.S.A.* **160 D4** 46 52N 122 16W
Eau Claire, *Fr. Guiana* **169 C7** 3 30N 53 40W
Eau Claire, *U.S.A.* **154 C9** 44 49N 91 30W
Eau Claire, L. à l', *Canada* **140 A5** 56 10N 74 25W
Eauze, *France* **28 E4** 43 53N 0 7 E
Eban, *Nigeria* **113 D5** 9 40N 4 50 E
Ebanga, *Angola* **115 E2** 12 45 S 14 45 E
Ebangalakata, *Dem. Rep. of the Congo* **114 C4** 0 29 S 21 29 E
Ebbw Vale, *U.K.* **21 F4** 51 46N 3 12W
Ebebiyín, *Eq. Guin.* **114 B2** 2 9N 11 20 E
Ebeggui, *Algeria* **111 C6** 26 2N 6 0 E
Ebel, *Gabon* **114 B2** 0 7N 11 5 E
Ebeltoft, *Denmark* **17 H4** 56 12N 10 41 E
Ebeltoft Vig, *Denmark* **17 H4** 56 10N 10 35 E
Ebensburg, *U.S.A.* **150 F6** 40 29N 78 44W
Ebensee, *Austria* **34 D6** 47 48N 13 46 E
Eber Gölü, *Turkey* **100 C4** 38 38N 31 11 E
Eberbach, *Germany* **31 F4** 49 28N 8 59 E
Eberswalde-Finow, *Germany* **30 C9** 52 50N 13 49 E
Ebetsu, *Japan* **68 C10** 43 7N 141 34 E
Ebian, *China* **76 C4** 29 11N 103 13 E
Ebikon, *Switz.* **33 B6** 47 5N 8 21 E
Ebingen, *Germany* **31 G5** 48 13N 9 1 E
Ebino, *Japan* **70 E2** 32 2N 130 48 E
Ebnat-Kappel, *Switz.* **33 B8** 47 16N 9 7 E
Ebo, *Angola* **115 E2** 11 40 S 14 40 E
Ebola ⟶, *Dem. Rep. of the Congo* **114 B4** 3 20N 20 57 E
Éboli, *Italy* **47 B8** 40 39N 15 2 E
Ebolowa, *Cameroon* **113 E7** 2 55N 11 10 E
Ebonyi □, *Nigeria* **113 D6** 6 20N 8 0 E
Eboy, *Dem. Rep. of the Congo* **114 B4** 2 50N 23 11 E
Ebrach, *Germany* **31 F6** 49 51N 10 29 E
Ébrié, Lagune, *Ivory C.* **112 D4** 5 12N 4 26W
Ebro ⟶, *Spain* **40 E5** 40 43N 0 54 E
Ebro, Embalse del, *Spain* **42 C7** 43 0N 3 58W
Ebstorf, *Germany* **30 B6** 53 2N 10 24 E
Eceabat, *Turkey* **51 F10** 40 11N 26 21 E
Ech Cheliff, *Algeria* **111 A5** 36 10N 1 20 E
Echallens, *Switz.* **32 C3** 46 38N 6 38 E
Echechonnee ⟶, *U.S.A.* **152 C6** 32 39N 83 36W
Echigo-Sammyaku, *Japan* **69 F9** 36 50N 139 50 E
Échirolles, *France* **29 C9** 45 8N 5 44 E
Echizen-Misaki, *Japan* **71 B7** 35 59N 135 57 E
Echmiadzin = Yejmiadzin, *Armenia* **61 K7** 40 12N 44 19 E
Echo, *U.S.A.* **152 D4** 31 29N 85 28W
Echo Bay, *N.W.T., Canada* **138 B8** 66 5N 117 55W
Echo Bay, *Ont., Canada* **140 C3** 46 29N 84 4W
Echoing ⟶, *Canada* **140 B1** 55 51N 92 5W
Echternach, *Lux.* **24 E6** 49 49N 6 25 E
Echuca, *Australia* **129 D6** 36 10 S 144 20 E
Ecija, *Spain* **43 H5** 37 30N 5 10W
Eckental, *Germany* **31 F7** 49 35N 11 12 E
Eckernförde, *Germany* **30 A5** 54 28N 9 50 E
Eclectic, *U.S.A.* **152 C3** 32 38N 86 2W
Eclipse Is., *Australia* **124 B4** 13 54 S 126 19 E
Eclipse Sd., *Canada* **139 A11** 72 38N 79 0W
Écommoy, *France* **26 E7** 47 50N 0 17 E
Ecoporanga, *Brazil* **171 E3** 18 23 S 40 50W
Écouché, *France* **26 D6** 48 42N 0 10W
Ecuador ■, *S. Amer.* **168 D2** 2 0 S 78 0W
Écueillé, *France* **26 E8** 47 5N 1 21 E
Ed, *Sweden* **17 F5** 58 55N 11 55 E
Ed Dabbura, *Sudan* **106 D3** 17 40N 34 15 E
Ed Da'ein, *Sudan* **107 E2** 11 26N 26 9 E
Ed Dâmer, *Sudan* **106 D3** 17 27N 34 0 E
Ed Debba, *Sudan* **106 D3** 18 0N 30 51 E
Ed-Déffa, *Egypt* **106 A2** 30 40N 26 30 E
Ed Deim, *Sudan* **107 E2** 10 10N 28 20 E
Ed Dueim, *Sudan* **107 E3** 14 0N 32 10 E
Edam, *Canada* **143 C7** 53 11N 108 46W
Edam, *Neths.* **24 B5** 52 31N 5 3 E
Edane, *Sweden* **16 E6** 59 38N 12 49 E
Edapally, *India* **95 J4** 11 19N 78 3 E
Eday, *U.K.* **22 B6** 59 11N 2 47W
Edd, *Eritrea* **107 E5** 14 0N 41 38 E
Eddrachillis B., *U.K.* **22 C3** 58 17N 5 14W
Eddystone Pt., *Australia* **126 G4** 40 59 S 148 20 E
Eddyville, *U.S.A.* **156 C4** 41 9N 92 38W
Ede, *Neths.* **24 B5** 52 4N 5 40 E
Ede, *Nigeria* **113 D5** 7 45N 4 29 E
Edéa, *Cameroon* **113 E7** 3 51N 10 9 E
Edebäck, *Sweden* **16 D7** 60 4N 13 32 E
Edehon L., *Canada* **143 A9** 60 25N 97 15W
Edekel, Adrar, *Algeria* **111 D6** 23 56N 6 47 E
Edelény, *Hungary* **52 B5** 48 18N 20 44 E
Eden, *Australia* **129 D8** 37 3 S 149 55 E
Eden, *N.C., U.S.A.* **149 G6** 36 29N 79 53W
Eden, *N.Y., U.S.A.* **150 D6** 42 39N 78 55W
Eden, *Tex., U.S.A.* **155 K5** 31 13N 99 51W
Eden ⟶, *U.K.* **20 C4** 54 57N 3 1W
Edenburg, *S. Africa* **116 D4** 29 43 S 25 58 E
Edendale, *N.Z.* **131 G3** 46 19 S 168 48 E
Edendale, *S. Africa* **117 D5** 29 39 S 30 18 E
Edenderry, *Ireland* **23 C4** 53 21N 7 4W
Edenhope, *Australia* **127 F3** 37 4 S 141 19 E
Edenton, *U.S.A.* **149 G7** 36 4N 76 39W
Edenville, *S. Africa* **117 D4** 27 37 S 27 34 E
Eder ⟶, *Germany* **30 D5** 51 12N 9 28 E
Eder-Stausee, *Germany* **30 D4** 51 10N 8 57 E
Edewecht, *Germany* **30 B3** 53 8N 7 58 E
Edgar, *U.S.A.* **154 E6** 40 22N 97 58W
Edgartown, *U.S.A.* **151 E14** 41 23N 70 31W
Edge Hill, *U.K.* **21 E6** 52 8N 1 26W
Edgecumbe, *N.Z.* **130 D5** 37 59 S 176 47 E
Edgefield, *U.S.A.* **152 B8** 33 47N 81 56W
Edgeley, *U.S.A.* **154 B5** 46 22N 98 43W
Edgemont, *U.S.A.* **154 D3** 43 18N 103 50W
Edgeøya, *Svalbard* **6 B9** 77 45N 22 30 E
Edgerton, *Ohio, U.S.A.* **157 C12** 41 27N 84 45W
Edgerton, *Wis., U.S.A.* **156 B7** 42 50N 89 4W
Edgewater, *U.S.A.* **153 G9** 28 59N 80 54W
Edgewood, *U.S.A.* **157 F8** 38 55N 88 40W
Édhessa, *Greece* **50 F6** 40 48N 22 5 E
Edievale, *N.Z.* **131 F4** 45 49 S 169 22 E
Edina, *Liberia* **112 D2** 6 0N 10 10W
Edina, *U.S.A.* **156 D4** 40 10N 92 11W
Edinboro, *U.S.A.* **150 E4** 41 52N 80 8W
Edinburg, *Ill., U.S.A.* **156 E7** 39 39N 89 23W
Edinburg, *Ind., U.S.A.* **157 E11** 39 21N 85 58W
Edinburg, *Tex., U.S.A.* **155 M5** 26 18N 98 10W
Edinburgh, *U.K.* **22 F5** 55 57N 3 13W
Edinburgh, City of □, *U.K.* **22 F5** 55 57N 3 17W
Edineţ, *Moldova* **53 B12** 48 9N 27 18 E
Edirne, *Turkey* **51 E10** 41 40N 26 34 E
Edirne □, *Turkey* **51 E10** 41 12N 26 30 E
Edison, *Ga., U.S.A.* **152 D5** 31 34N 84 44W
Edison, *Wash., U.S.A.* **160 B4** 48 33N 122 27W
Edisto ⟶, *U.S.A.* **152 C9** 32 29N 80 21W
Edisto Beach, *U.S.A.* **152 C9** 32 29N 80 20W
Edisto I., *U.S.A.* **152 C9** 32 35N 80 20W
Edithburgh, *Australia* **128 C2** 35 5 S 137 43 E
Edjeleh, *Algeria* **111 C6** 28 38N 9 50 E
Edmeston, *U.S.A.* **151 D9** 42 42N 75 15W
Edmond, *U.S.A.* **155 H6** 35 39N 97 29W
Edmonds, *U.S.A.* **160 C4** 47 49N 122 23W
Edmonton, *Australia* **126 B4** 17 2 S 145 46 E
Edmonton, *Canada* **142 C6** 53 30N 113 30W
Edmund L., *Canada* **140 B1** 54 45N 93 17W
Edmundston, *Canada* **141 C6** 47 23N 68 20W
Edna, *U.S.A.* **155 L6** 28 59N 96 39W
Edo □, *Nigeria* **113 D6** 6 30N 6 0 E
Edolo, *Italy* **44 B7** 46 10N 10 21 E
Edøy, *Norway* **18 A5** 63 18N 8 10 E
Edremit, *Turkey* **49 B9** 39 34N 27 0 E
Edremit Körfezi, *Turkey* **49 B8** 39 30N 26 45 E
Edsbro, *Sweden* **16 E12** 59 54N 18 29 E
Edsbyn, *Sweden* **16 C9** 61 23N 15 49 E
Edson, *Canada* **142 C5** 53 35N 116 28W
Eduardo Castex, *Argentina* **174 D3** 35 50 S 64 18W
Edward ⟶, *Australia* **128 C5** 35 5 S 143 30 E
Edward, L., *Africa* **118 C2** 0 25 S 29 40 E
Edward River, *Australia* **126 A3** 14 59 S 141 26 E
Edward VII Land, *Antarctica* **7 E13** 80 0 S 150 0W
Edwards, *Calif., U.S.A.* **161 L9** 34 55N 117 51W
Edwards, *N.Y., U.S.A.* **151 B9** 44 20N 75 15W
Edwards ⟶, *U.S.A.* **156 C6** 41 9N 90 59W
Edwards Air Force Base, *U.S.A.* **161 L9** 34 50N 117 40W
Edwards Plateau, *U.S.A.* **155 K4** 30 45N 101 20W
Edwardsburg, *U.S.A.* **157 C10** 41 48N 86 6W
Edwardsville, *Ill., U.S.A.* **156 F7** 38 49N 89 58W
Edwardsville, *Pa., U.S.A.* **151 E9** 41 15N 75 56W
Edzo, *Canada* **142 A5** 62 49N 116 4W
Eeklo, *Belgium* **24 C3** 51 11N 3 33 E
Eel ⟶, *Ind., U.S.A.* **157 E10** 39 7N 86 57W
Eel ⟶, *Ind., U.S.A.* **157 D10** 40 45N 86 22W
Efate, I., *Vanuatu* **133 G6** 17 40 S 168 25 E
Eferding, *Austria* **34 C7** 48 18N 14 1 E
Eferi, *Algeria* **111 D6** 24 30N 9 28 E
Effingham, *U.S.A.* **157 E8** 39 7N 88 33W
Effretikon, *Switz.* **33 B7** 47 25N 8 42 E
Eforie, *Romania* **53 F13** 44 1N 28 37 E
Efoulen, *Cameroon* **114 B2** 2 46N 10 43 E
Eftelφt, *Norway* **18 E6** 59 33N 9 49 E
Ega ⟶, *Spain* **40 C3** 42 19N 1 55W
Égadi, Ísole, *Italy* **46 E5** 37 55N 12 16 E
Egan Range, *U.S.A.* **158 G6** 39 35N 114 55W
Eganville, *Canada* **140 C4** 45 32N 77 5W
Egedesminde = Aasiaat, *Greenland* **10 D5** 68 43N 52 56W
Egegik, *U.S.A.* **144 G8** 58 13N 157 22W
Eger = Cheb, *Czech Rep.* **34 A5** 50 9N 12 28 E
Eger, *Hungary* **52 C5** 47 53N 20 27 E
Eger ⟶, *Hungary* **52 C5** 47 38N 20 50 E
Egersund, *Norway* **15 G12** 58 26N 6 1 E
Egg, *Austria* **33 B9** 47 26N 9 54 E
Egg, *Switz.* **33 B7** 47 18N 8 41 E
Egg L., *Canada* **143 B7** 55 5N 105 30W
Eggedal, *Norway* **18 D6** 60 14N 9 22 E
Eggenburg, *Austria* **34 C8** 48 38N 15 50 E
Eggenfelden, *Germany* **31 G8** 48 23N 12 46 E
Eggiwil, *Switz.* **32 C5** 46 52N 7 47 E
Egherta, *Somali Rep.* **120 D2** 2 4N 43 11 E
Éghezée, *Belgium* **24 D4** 50 35N 4 55 E
Egilsstaðir, *Iceland* **11 B12** 65 16N 14 25W
Egito, *Angola* **115 E2** 12 4 S 13 58 E
Égletons, *France* **28 C6** 45 24N 2 3 E
Eglisau, *Switz.* **33 A7** 47 35N 8 31 E
Egmont, *Canada* **142 D4** 49 45N 123 56W
Egmont, C., *N.Z.* **130 F2** 39 16 S 173 45 E
Egmont, Mt., *N.Z.* **130 F3** 39 17 S 174 5 E
Egra, *India* **93 J12** 21 54N 87 32 E
Eğridir, *Turkey* **100 D4** 37 52N 30 51 E
Eğridir Gölü, *Turkey* **100 D4** 37 53N 30 50 E
Egtved, *Denmark* **17 J3** 55 38N 9 18 E
Éguas ⟶, *Brazil* **171 D3** 13 26 S 44 14W
Egume, *Nigeria* **113 D6** 7 30N 7 14 E
Éguzon-Chantôme, *France* **27 F8** 46 27N 1 33 E
Egvekinot, *Russia* **65 C19** 66 19N 179 50W
Egyek, *Hungary* **52 C5** 47 39N 20 52 E
Egypt ■, *Africa* **106 B3** 28 0N 31 0 E
Eha Amufu, *Nigeria* **113 D6** 6 30N 7 46 E
Ehime □, *Japan* **70 D4** 33 30N 132 40 E
Ehingen, *Germany* **31 G5** 48 16N 9 43 E
Ehrenberg, *U.S.A.* **161 M12** 33 36N 114 31W
Ehrhardt, *U.S.A.* **152 B8** 33 6N 81 1W
Ehrwald, *Austria* **34 D3** 47 24N 10 56 E
Eibar, *Spain* **40 B2** 43 11N 2 28W
Eichstätt, *Germany* **31 G7** 48 54N 11 11 E
Eide, *Hordaland, Norway* **18 D3** 60 31N 6 44 E
Eide, *Møre og Romsdal, Norway* **18 B4** 62 55N 7 27 E
Eider ⟶, *Germany* **30 A4** 54 19N 8 57 E
Eidsbugarden, *Norway* **18 C5** 61 23N 8 16 E
Eidsbygda, *Norway* **18 B4** 62 36N 7 30 E
Eidsdal, *Norway* **18 B4** 62 16N 7 10 E
Eidsvåg, *Norway* **18 B5** 62 46N 8 2 E
Eidsvold, *Australia* **127 D5** 25 25 S 151 12 E
Eidsvoll, *Norway* **15 F14** 60 19N 11 14 E
Eifel, *Germany* **31 E2** 50 15N 6 50 E
Eiffel Flats, *Zimbabwe* **119 F3** 18 20 S 30 0 E
Eiger, *Switz.* **32 C6** 46 34N 8 1 E
Eiger, *Switz.* **44 B5** 46 34N 8 1 E
Eigg, *U.K.* **22 E2** 56 54N 6 10W
Eighty Mile Beach, *Australia* **124 C3** 19 30 S 120 40 E
Eikefjord, *Norway* **18 C2** 61 35N 5 27 E
Eikelandsosen, *Norway* **18 D2** 60 15N 5 43 E
Eiken, *Norway* **18 F4** 58 29N 7 14 E
Eikeren, *Norway* **18 E6** 59 38N 9 58 E
Eikesdal, *Norway* **18 B5** 62 28N 8 12 E
Eil, *Somali Rep.* **120 C3** 8 0N 49 50 E
Eil, L., *U.K.* **22 E3** 56 51N 5 16W
Eildon, *Australia* **129 D6** 37 14 S 145 55 E
Eildon, L., *Australia* **127 F4** 37 10 S 146 0 E
Eilenburg, *Germany* **30 D8** 51 27N 12 36 E
Ein el Luweiqa, *Sudan* **107 E3** 14 5N 33 50 E
Eina, *Norway* **18 D7** 60 38N 10 35 E
Einarsstaðir, *Iceland* **11 B9** 65 44N 17 24W
Einasleigh, *Australia* **126 B3** 18 32 S 144 5 E
Einasleigh ⟶, *Australia* **126 B3** 17 30 S 142 17 E
Einbeck, *Germany* **30 D5** 51 49N 9 53 E
Eindhoven, *Neths.* **24 C5** 51 26N 5 28 E
Einsiedeln, *Switz.* **33 B7** 47 7N 8 46 E
Eire = Ireland ■, *Europe* **23 C4** 53 50N 7 52W
Eiríksjökull, *Iceland* **11 C6** 64 46N 20 24W
Eiríksstaðir, *Iceland* **11 B11** 65 7N 15 25W
Eirunepé, *Brazil* **172 B4** 6 35 S 69 53W
Eiseb ⟶, *Namibia* **116 C2** 20 33 S 20 59 E
Eisenach, *Germany* **30 E6** 50 58N 10 19 E
Eisenberg, *Germany* **30 E7** 50 58N 11 54 E
Eisenerz, *Austria* **34 D7** 47 32N 14 54 E
Eisenhüttenstadt, *Germany* **30 C10** 52 9N 14 38 E
Eisenkappel, *Austria* **34 E7** 46 29N 14 36 E
Eisenstadt, *Austria* **35 D9** 47 51N 16 31 E
Eisfeld, *Germany* **31 E6** 50 25N 10 54 E
Eisleben, *Germany* **30 D7** 51 32N 11 32 E
Eislingen, *Germany* **31 G5** 48 41N 9 42 E
Eivindvik, *Norway* **18 D2** 60 59N 5 5 E
Eivissa, *Spain* **39 C7** 38 54N 1 26 E
Eixe, Serra do, *Spain* **42 C4** 42 24N 6 54W
Ejea de los Caballeros, *Spain* **40 C3** 42 7N 1 9W
Ejeda, *Madag.* **117 C7** 24 20 S 44 31 E
Ejura, *Ghana* **113 D4** 7 23N 1 15W
Ejutla, *Mexico* **163 D5** 16 34N 96 44W
Ekalaka, *U.S.A.* **154 C2** 45 53N 104 33W
Ekalla, *Gabon* **114 C2** 1 27 S 14 0 E
Ekanga, *Dem. Rep. of the Congo* **114 C4** 2 23 S 23 14 E
Ekawasaki, *Japan* **70 D4** 33 13N 132 46 E
Ekenässjön, *Sweden* **17 G9** 57 28N 15 1 E
Ekerö, *Sweden* **16 E11** 59 16N 17 45 E
Eket, *Nigeria* **113 E6** 4 38N 7 56 E
Eketahuna, *N.Z.* **130 G4** 40 38 S 175 43 E
Ekhínos, *Greece* **51 E9** 41 16N 25 1 E
Ekibastuz, *Kazakstan* **64 D8** 51 50N 75 10 E
Ekiti □, *Nigeria* **113 D6** 7 25N 5 20 E
Ekoli, *Dem. Rep. of the Congo* **118 C1** 0 23 S 24 13 E
Ekoln, *Sweden* **16 E11** 59 45N 17 37 E
Ekouamou, *Congo* **114 B3** 0 8N 16 31 E
Ekoungounou, *Congo* **114 C3** 1 10 S 15 52 E
Ekshärad, *Sweden* **16 D7** 60 10N 13 30 E
Eksjö, *Sweden* **17 G8** 57 40N 14 58 E
Ekukola, *Dem. Rep. of the Congo* **114 C3** 0 31 S 18 56 E
Ekuku, *Dem. Rep. of the Congo* **114 C4** 0 41 S 21 42 E
Ekukula, *Dem. Rep. of the Congo* **114 B4** 0 15N 21 30 E
Ekuma ⟶, *Namibia* **116 B2** 18 40 S 16 2 E
Ekuta, *Dem. Rep. of the Congo* **114 B3** 3 0N 18 50 E
Ekwan ⟶, *Canada* **140 B3** 53 12N 82 15W
Ekwan Pt., *Canada* **140 B3** 53 16N 82 7W
Ekwok, *U.S.A.* **144 G8** 59 22N 157 30W
El Aaiún, *W. Sahara* **110 C2** 27 9N 13 12W
El Aargub, *Mauritania* **110 D1** 23 37N 15 52W
El Abanico, *Chile* **174 D1** 37 20 S 71 31W
El Abbasiya, *Sudan* **107 E3** 12 10N 31 18 E
El Abiodh-Sidi-Cheikh, *Algeria* **111 B5** 32 53N 0 31 E
El Adde, *Somali Rep.* **120 D3** 2 35N 46 9 E
El 'Agrûd, *Egypt* **103 E3** 30 14N 34 24 E
El Aïoun, *Morocco* **111 B4** 34 33N 2 30W
El Ait, *Sudan* **107 E2** 12 22N 27 27 E
El 'Aiyat, *Egypt* **106 J7** 29 36N 31 15 E
El Alamein, *Egypt* **106 A2** 30 48N 28 58 E
El Alto, *Peru* **172 A1** 4 15 S 81 14W
El 'Aqaba, W. ⟶, *Egypt* **103 E2** 30 7N 33 54 E
El 'Arag, *Egypt* **106 B2** 28 40N 26 20 E
El Arahal, *Spain* **43 H5** 37 15N 5 33W
El Aricha, *Algeria* **111 B4** 34 13N 1 10W
El Arīḥā, *West Bank* **103 D4** 31 52N 35 27 E
El 'Arîsh, *Egypt* **103 D2** 31 8N 33 50 E
El 'Arîsh, W. ⟶, *Egypt* **103 D2** 31 8N 33 47 E
El Arrouch, *Algeria* **111 A6** 36 37N 6 53 E
El Asnam = Ech Cheliff, *Algeria* **111 A5** 36 10N 1 20 E
El Astillero, *Spain* **42 B7** 43 24N 3 49W
El Badâri, *Egypt* **106 B3** 27 4N 31 25 E
El Bahrein, *Egypt* **106 B2** 28 30N 26 25 E
El Ballâs, *Egypt* **106 B3** 26 2N 32 43 E
El Balyana, *Egypt* **106 B3** 26 10N 32 3 E
El Banco, *Colombia* **168 B3** 9 0N 73 58W
El Baqeir, *Sudan* **106 D3** 18 40N 33 40 E
El Barco de Ávila, *Spain* **42 E5** 40 21N 5 31W
El Barco de Valdeorras = O Barco, *Spain* **42 C4** 42 23N 6 58W
El Bauga, *Sudan* **106 D3** 18 18N 33 52 E
El Baúl, *Venezuela* **168 B4** 8 57N 68 17W
El Bawiti, *Egypt* **106 B2** 28 25N 28 45 E
El Bayadh, *Algeria* **111 B5** 33 40N 1 1 E
El Bierzo, *Spain* **42 C4** 42 45N 6 30W
El Bluff, *Nic.* **164 D3** 11 59N 83 40W
El Bolsón, *Argentina* **176 B2** 41 55 S 71 30W
El Bonillo, *Spain* **41 G2** 38 57N 2 35W
El Brûk, W. ⟶, *Egypt* **103 E2** 30 15N 33 50 E
El Buheirat □, *Sudan* **107 F3** 7 0N 30 0 E
El Bur, *Somali Rep.* **120 D3** 4 40N 46 37 E
El Burgo de Osma, *Spain* **40 D1** 41 35N 3 4W
El Caín, *Argentina* **176 B3** 41 38 S 68 19W
El Cajon, *U.S.A.* **161 N10** 32 48N 116 58W
El Callao, *Venezuela* **169 B5** 7 18N 61 50W
El Campo, *U.S.A.* **155 L6** 29 12N 96 16W
El Carmen, *Bolivia* **173 C5** 13 40 S 63 55W
El Centro, *U.S.A.* **161 N11** 32 48N 115 34W
El Cerro, *Bolivia* **173 D5** 17 30 S 61 40W
El Cerro de Andévalo, *Spain* **43 H4** 37 45N 6 57W
El Cocuy, *Colombia* **168 B3** 6 25N 72 27W
El Compadre, *Mexico* **161 N10** 32 20N 116 14W
El Corcovado, *Argentina* **176 B2** 43 25 S 71 35W
El Coronil, *Spain* **43 H5** 37 5N 5 38W
El Cuy, *Argentina* **176 A3** 39 55 S 68 25W
El Cuyo, *Mexico* **163 C7** 21 30N 87 40W
El Dab'a, *Egypt* **106 H6** 31 0N 28 27 E
El Daheir, *Egypt* **103 D3** 31 13N 34 10 E
El Dambahaddo, *Somali Rep.* **120 D3** 3 17N 46 40 E
El Dátil, *Mexico* **162 B2** 30 7N 112 15W
El Deir, *Egypt* **106 B3** 25 25N 32 20 E
El Dere, *Ethiopia* **120 C2** 5 6N 43 5 E
El Dere, *Somali Rep.* **120 D3** 3 50N 47 8 E
El Dere, *Somali Rep.* **120 C3** 5 22N 46 11 E
El Descanso, *Mexico* **161 N10** 32 12N 116 58W
El Desemboque, *Mexico* **162 A2** 30 30N 112 57W
El Dilingat, *Egypt* **106 H7** 30 50N 30 31 E
El Diviso, *Colombia* **168 C2** 1 22N 78 14W
El Djem, *Tunisia* **108 A2** 35 18N 10 42 E
El Djouf, *Mauritania* **104 D3** 20 0N 9 0W
El Dorado, *Ark., U.S.A.* **155 J8** 33 12N 92 40W
El Dorado, *Kans., U.S.A.* **155 G6** 37 49N 96 52W
El Dorado, *Venezuela* **169 B5** 6 55N 61 37W
El Eglab, *Algeria* **110 C4** 26 20N 4 30W
El 'Ein, *Sudan* **107 D2** 16 35N 29 22 E
El Ejido, *Spain* **43 J8** 36 47N 2 49W
El Escorial, *Spain* **42 E6** 40 35N 4 7W
El Espinar, *Spain* **42 D6** 41 43N 4 15W
El Eulma, *Algeria* **111 A6** 36 9N 5 42 E
El Faiyûm, *Egypt* **106 J7** 29 19N 30 50 E
El Fâsher, *Sudan* **107 E2** 13 33N 25 26 E
El Fashn, *Egypt* **106 J7** 28 50N 30 54 E
El Ferrol = Ferrol, *Spain* **42 B2** 43 29N 8 15W
El Fifi, *Sudan* **107 E2** 10 4N 25 0 E
El Fud, *Ethiopia* **120 C2** 7 15N 42 52 E
El Fuerte, *Mexico* **162 B3** 26 30N 108 40W
El Ga'a, *Sudan* **107 E2** 14 16N 29 59 E
El Gal, *Somali Rep.* **120 B4** 10 58N 50 20 E
El Garef, *Sudan* **107 E3** 12 3N 34 19 E
El Gebir, *Sudan* **107 E2** 13 40N 29 40 E
El Gedida, *Egypt* **106 B2** 25 40N 28 30 E
El Geneina = Al Junaynah, *Sudan* **109 F4** 13 27N 22 45 E
El Geteina, *Sudan* **107 E3** 14 50N 32 27 E
El Gezira □, *Sudan* **107 E3** 15 0N 33 0 E
El Gir, *Sudan* **106 D2** 19 50N 28 18 E
El Gîza, *Egypt* **106 J7** 30 0N 31 10 E
El Goléa, *Algeria* **111 B5** 30 30N 2 50 E
El Grau, *Spain* **41 G4** 39 0N 0 7W
El Hadeb, *W. Sahara* **110 C2** 25 51N 13 0W
El Hadjira, *Algeria* **111 B6** 32 36N 5 30 E
El Hagiz, *Sudan* **107 D4** 15 15N 35 50 E
El Hâi, *Egypt* **106 J7** 29 39N 31 18 E
El Hajeb, *Morocco* **110 B3** 33 43N 5 13W
El Hammam, *Egypt* **106 A2** 30 52N 29 25 E
El Hammâmi, *Mauritania* **110 D2** 23 3N 11 30W
El Hamurre, *Somali Rep.* **120 C3** 7 13N 48 54 E
El Hank, *Mauritania* **110 D3** 24 30N 7 0W
El Hasian, *W. Sahara* **110 C2** 26 20N 14 0W
El Hawata, *Sudan* **107 E3** 13 25N 34 42 E

Ensenada de los Muertos 211

El Heiz, *Egypt* **106 B2** 27 50N 28 40 E
El Hideib, *Sudan* **107 E3** 13 0N 32 50 E
El Hilla, *Sudan* **107 E2** 13 24N 27 2 E
El 'Idisât, *Egypt* **106 B3** 25 30N 32 35 E
El Iskandarîya, *Egypt* **106 H7** 31 13N 29 58 E
El Jadida, *Morocco* **110 B3** 33 11N 8 17W
El Jardal, *Honduras* **164 D2** 14 54N 88 50W
El Jebelein, *Sudan* **107 E3** 12 40N 32 55 E
El Kab, *Sudan* **106 D3** 19 27N 32 46 E
El Kabrît, G., *Egypt* **103 F2** 29 42N 33 16 E
El Kafr el Sharqi, *Egypt* **106 H7** 31 16N 31 10 E
El Kala, *Algeria* **111 A6** 36 50N 8 30 E
El Kalâa, *Morocco* **110 B3** 32 4N 7 27W
El Kamlin, *Sudan* **107 D3** 15 3N 33 11 E
El Kantara, *Algeria* **111 A6** 35 14N 5 45 E
El Kantara, *Tunisia* **108 B2** 33 45N 10 58 E
El Karaba, *Sudan* **106 D3** 18 32N 33 41 E
El Kef, *Tunisia* **108 A1** 36 12N 8 47 E
El Kere, *Ethiopia* **107 F5** 5 50N 42 5 E
El Khandaq, *Sudan* **106 D3** 18 30N 30 30 E
El Khârga, *Egypt* **106 B3** 25 30N 30 33 E
El Khartûm, *Sudan* **107 D3** 15 31N 32 35 E
El Khartûm □, *Sudan* **107 D3** 16 0N 33 0 E
El Khartûm Bahrî, *Sudan* **107 D3** 15 40N 32 31 E
El Khroub, *Algeria* **111 A6** 36 10N 6 55 E
El Kseur, *Algeria* **111 A5** 36 46N 4 49 E
El Ksiba, *Morocco* **110 B3** 32 45N 6 1W
El Kuntilla, *Egypt* **103 E3** 30 1N 34 45 E
El Laqâwa, *Sudan* **107 E2** 11 25N 29 1 E
El Laqeita, *Egypt* **106 B3** 25 50N 33 15 E
El Leh, *Ethiopia* **107 G4** 3 46N 39 13 E
El Leiya, *Sudan* **107 D4** 16 15N 35 28 E
El Maestrazgo, *Spain* **40 E4** 40 30N 0 25W
El Mafâza, *Sudan* **107 E3** 13 38N 34 30 E
El Maghra, *Egypt* **106 A2** 30 15N 28 55 E
El Mahalla el Kubra, *Egypt* **106 H7** 31 0N 31 0 E
El Mahârîq, *Egypt* **106 B3** 25 35N 30 35 E
El Maîmûn, *Egypt* **106 J7** 29 14N 31 12 E
El Maitén, *Argentina* **176 B2** 42 3 S 71 10W
El Maiz, *Algeria* **111 C4** 28 19N 0 9W
El Maks el Bahari, *Egypt* **106 C3** 24 30N 30 40 E
El Manshâh, *Egypt* **106 B3** 26 26N 31 50 E
El Mansour, *Algeria* **111 C4** 27 47N 0 14W
El Mansûra, *Egypt* **106 H7** 31 0N 31 19 E
El Manteco, *Venezuela* **169 B5** 7 38N 62 45W
El Manzala, *Egypt* **106 H7** 31 10N 31 50 E
El Marâgha, *Egypt* **106 B3** 26 35N 31 10 E
El Masid, *Sudan* **107 D3** 15 15N 33 0 E
El Masnou, *Spain* **40 D7** 41 28N 2 20 E
El Matariya, *Egypt* **106 H8** 31 15N 32 0 E
El Meda, *Ethiopia* **107 F5** 5 39N 41 47 E
El Medano, *Canary Is.* **39 F3** 28 3N 16 32W
El Meghaier, *Algeria* **111 B6** 33 55N 5 58 E
El Meraguen, *Algeria* **111 C4** 28 0N 0 7W
El Metemma, *Sudan* **107 D3** 16 50N 33 10 E
El Miamo, *Venezuela* **169 B5** 7 39N 61 46W
El Milagro, *Argentina* **174 C2** 30 59 S 65 59W
El Milia, *Algeria* **111 A6** 36 51N 6 13 E
El Minyâ, *Egypt* **106 B3** 28 7N 30 33 E
El Monte, *U.S.A.* **161 L8** 34 4N 118 1W
El Montseny, *Spain* **40 D7** 41 55N 2 25 E
El Mreyye, *Mauritania* **112 B3** 18 0N 6 0W
El Nido, *Phil.* **81 F2** 11 10N 119 25 E
El Niybo, *Ethiopia* **107 G4** 4 40N 39 55 E
El Obeid, *Sudan* **107 E3** 13 8N 30 10 E
El Odaiya, *Sudan* **107 E2** 12 8N 28 12 E
El Oro, *Mexico* **163 D4** 19 48N 100 8W
El Oro □, *Ecuador* **168 D2** 3 30 S 79 50W
El Oued, *Algeria* **111 B6** 33 20N 6 58 E
El Palmar, *Bolivia* **173 D5** 17 50 S 63 9W
El Palmar, *Venezuela* **169 B5** 7 58N 61 53W
El Palmito, Presa, *Mexico* **162 B3** 25 40N 105 30W
El Paso, *Ill., U.S.A.* **156 D7** 40 44N 89 1W
El Paso, *Tex., U.S.A.* **159 L10** 31 45N 106 29W
El Paso Robles, *U.S.A.* **160 K6** 35 38N 120 41W
El Pedernoso, *Spain* **41 F2** 39 29N 2 45W
El Pedroso, *Spain* **43 H5** 37 51N 5 45W
El Pilar, *Venezuela* **169 A5** 10 32N 63 9W
El Pobo de Dueñas, *Spain* **40 E3** 40 46N 1 39W
El Portal, *U.S.A.* **160 H7** 37 41N 119 47W
El Porvenir, *Mexico* **162 A3** 31 15N 105 51W
El Prat de Llobregat, *Spain* **40 D7** 41 18N 2 3 E
El Progreso, *Honduras* **164 C2** 15 26N 87 51W
El Pueblito, *Mexico* **162 B3** 29 3N 105 4W
El Pueblo, *Canary Is.* **39 F2** 28 36N 17 47W
El Puente del Arzobispo, *Spain* **42 F5** 39 48N 5 10W
El Puerto de Santa María, *Spain* **43 J4** 36 36N 6 13W
El Qâhira, *Egypt* **106 H7** 30 1N 31 14 E
El Qantara, *Egypt* **103 E1** 30 51N 32 20 E
El Qasr, *Egypt* **106 B2** 25 44N 28 42 E
El Qubâbât, *Egypt* **106 J7** 29 28N 31 16 E
El Quseima, *Egypt* **103 E3** 30 40N 34 15 E
El Qusîya, *Egypt* **106 B3** 27 29N 30 44 E
El Râshda, *Egypt* **106 B2** 25 36N 28 57 E
El Reno, *U.S.A.* **155 H6** 35 32N 97 57W
El Rîdisiya, *Egypt* **106 C3** 24 56N 32 51 E
El Rio, *U.S.A.* **161 L7** 34 14N 119 10W
El Ronquillo, *Spain* **43 H4** 37 44N 6 10W
El Roque, Pta., *Canary Is.* **39 F4** 28 10N 15 25W
El Rosarito, *Mexico* **162 B2** 28 38N 114 4W
El Rubio, *Spain* **43 H5** 37 22N 5 0W
El Saff, *Egypt* **106 J7** 29 34N 31 16 E
El Saheira, W. —►, *Egypt* **103 E2** 30 5N 33 25 E
El Salto, *Mexico* **162 C3** 23 47N 105 22W
El Salvador ■, *Cent. Amer.* **164 D2** 13 50N 89 0W
El Sauce, *Nic.* **164 D2** 13 0N 86 40W
El Saucejo, *Spain* **43 H5** 37 4N 5 6W
El Shallal, *Egypt* **106 C3** 24 0N 32 53 E
El Simbillawein, *Egypt* **106 H7** 30 48N 31 13 E
El Sombrero, *Venezuela* **168 B4** 9 23N 67 3W
El Sueco, *Mexico* **162 B3** 29 54N 106 24W
El Suweis, *Egypt* **106 J8** 29 58N 32 31 E
El Tabbîn, *Egypt* **106 J7** 29 47N 31 18 E
El Tamarâni, W. —►, *Egypt* **103 E3** 30 7N 34 43 E
El Thamad, *Egypt* **103 F3** 29 40N 34 28 E
El Tigre, *Venezuela* **169 B5** 8 44N 64 15W
El Tîh, Gebal, *Egypt* **103 F2** 29 40N 33 50 E
El Tîna, *Egypt* **106 H8** 31 3N 32 22 E
El Tîna, Khalîg, *Egypt* **103 D1** 31 10N 32 40 E
El Tocuyo, *Venezuela* **168 B4** 9 47N 69 48W
El Tofo, *Chile* **174 B1** 29 22 S 71 18W
El Tránsito, *Chile* **174 B1** 28 52 S 70 17W
El Tûr, *Egypt* **96 D2** 28 14N 33 36 E
El Turbio, *Argentina* **176 D2** 51 45 S 72 5W
El Uinle, *Somali Rep.* **120 D2** 3 4N 41 42 E
El Uqsur, *Egypt* **106 B3** 25 41N 32 38 E
El Venado, *Mexico* **162 C4** 22 56N 101 10W
El Vendrell, *Spain* **40 D6** 41 10N 1 30 E
El Vergel, *Mexico* **162 B3** 26 28N 106 22W
El Vigía, *Venezuela* **168 B3** 8 38N 71 39W
El Viso del Alcor, *Spain* **43 H5** 37 23N 5 43W
El Wabeira, *Egypt* **103 F2** 29 34N 33 6 E
El Wak, *Kenya* **118 B5** 2 49N 40 56 E
El Wak, *Somali Rep.* **120 D2** 2 44N 41 1 E
El Waqf, *Egypt* **106 B3** 25 45N 32 15 E
El Weguet, *Ethiopia* **107 F5** 5 28N 42 17 E
El Wuz, *Sudan* **107 D3** 15 5N 30 7 E
Elafónisos, *Greece* **48 E4** 36 29N 22 56 E
Elaine, *Australia* **128 D6** 37 44 S 144 2 E
Elamanchili, *India* **94 F6** 17 33N 82 50 E
Élancourt, *France* **27 D8** 48 47N 1 58 E
Elands, *Australia* **129 A10** 31 37 S 152 20 E
Élassa, *Greece* **49 F8** 35 18N 26 21 E
Elassón, *Greece* **48 B4** 39 53N 22 12 E
Elat, *Israel* **103 F3** 29 30N 34 56 E
Eláthia, *Greece* **48 C4** 38 37N 22 46 E
Elâzığ, *Turkey* **101 C8** 38 37N 39 14 E
Elba, *Italy* **44 F7** 42 46N 10 17 E
Elba, *U.S.A.* **152 D3** 31 25N 86 4W
Elbasani, *Albania* **50 E4** 41 9N 20 9 E
Elbe, *U.S.A.* **160 D4** 46 45N 122 10W
Elbe —►, *Europe* **30 B4** 53 50N 9 0 E
Elbe-Seitenkanal, *Germany* **30 C6** 52 45N 10 32 E
Elberfeld, *U.S.A.* **157 F9** 38 10N 87 27W
Elbert, Mt., *U.S.A.* **159 G10** 39 7N 106 27W
Elberton, *U.S.A.* **152 A7** 34 7N 82 52W
Elbeuf, *France* **26 C8** 49 17N 1 2 E
Elbidtan, *Turkey* **96 B3** 38 13N 37 12 E
Elbing = Elbląg, *Poland* **54 D6** 54 10N 19 25 E
Elbistan, *Turkey* **100 C7** 38 13N 37 15 E
Elbląg, *Poland* **54 D6** 54 10N 19 25 E
Elbow, *Canada* **143 C7** 51 7N 106 35W
Elbrus, *Asia* **61 J6** 43 21N 42 30 E
Elburn, *U.S.A.* **157 C8** 41 54N 88 28W
Elburz Mts. = Alborz, Reshteh-ye Kûhhā-ye, *Iran* **97 C7** 36 0N 52 0 E
Elche, *Spain* **41 G4** 38 15N 0 42W
Elche de la Sierra, *Spain* **41 G2** 38 27N 2 3W
Elcho I., *Australia* **126 A2** 11 55 S 135 45 E
Elda, *Spain* **41 G4** 38 29N 0 47W
Elde —►, *Germany* **30 B7** 53 7N 11 15 E
Eldon, *Iowa, U.S.A.* **156 D4** 40 55N 92 13W
Eldon, *Mo., U.S.A.* **156 F4** 38 21N 92 35W
Eldon, *Wash., U.S.A.* **160 C3** 47 33N 123 3W
Eldora, *U.S.A.* **156 B3** 42 22N 93 5W
Eldorado, *Argentina* **175 B5** 26 28 S 54 43W
Eldorado, *Canada* **150 B7** 44 35N 77 31W
Eldorado, *Mexico* **162 C3** 24 20N 107 22W
Eldorado, *Ill., U.S.A.* **157 G8** 37 49N 88 26W
Eldorado, *Tex., U.S.A.* **155 K4** 30 52N 100 36W
Eldorado Springs, *U.S.A.* **155 G8** 37 52N 94 1W
Eldorendo, *U.S.A.* **152 D5** 31 3N 84 39W
Eldoret, *Kenya* **118 B4** 0 30N 35 17 E
Eldred, *U.S.A.* **150 E6** 41 58N 78 23W
Eldridge, *U.S.A.* **156 C6** 41 39N 90 35W
Elea, C., *Cyprus* **38 D13** 35 19N 34 4 E
Eleanora, Pk., *Australia* **125 F3** 32 57 S 121 9 E
Elefantes —►, *Mozam.* **117 C5** 24 10 S 32 40 E
Elefantes, B. das, *Angola* **115 E2** 13 13 S 12 44 E
Elefantes, G., *Chile* **176 C2** 46 28 S 73 49W
Elektrogorsk, *Russia* **58 E10** 55 56N 38 50 E
Elektrostal, *Russia* **58 E10** 55 41N 38 32 E
Elele, *Nigeria* **113 D6** 5 5N 6 50 E
Elena, *Bulgaria* **51 D9** 42 55N 25 53 E
Elephant Butte Reservoir, *U.S.A.* **159 K10** 33 9N 107 11W
Elephant I., *Antarctica* **7 C18** 61 0 S 55 0W
Elephant Pass, *Sri Lanka* **95 K5** 9 35N 80 25 E
Elesbão Veloso, *Brazil* **170 C3** 6 13 S 42 8W
Eleshnitsa, *Bulgaria* **50 E7** 41 52N 23 36 E
Eleşkirt, *Turkey* **101 C10** 39 50N 42 50 E
Eleuthera, *Bahamas* **164 B4** 25 0N 76 20W
Elevsís, *Greece* **48 C5** 38 4N 23 26 E
Elevtheroúpolis, *Greece* **51 F8** 40 52N 24 20 E
Elgå, *Norway* **18 B8** 62 10N 11 56 E
Elgepiggen, *Norway* **18 B8** 62 10N 11 21 E
Elgg, *Switz.* **33 B7** 47 29N 8 52 E
Elgin, *Canada* **151 B8** 44 36N 76 13W
Elgin, *U.K.* **22 D5** 57 39N 3 19W
Elgin, *Ill., U.S.A.* **157 B8** 42 2N 88 17W
Elgin, *N. Dak., U.S.A.* **154 B4** 46 24N 101 51W
Elgin, *Oreg., U.S.A.* **158 D5** 45 34N 117 55W
Elgin, *S.C., U.S.A.* **152 A9** 34 10N 80 48W
Elgin, *Tex., U.S.A.* **155 K6** 30 21N 97 22W
Elgoibar, *Spain* **40 B2** 43 13N 2 24W
Elgon, Mt., *Africa* **118 B3** 1 10N 34 30 E
Eliase, *Indonesia* **79 F8** 8 21 S 130 48 E
Elikón, *Greece* **48 C4** 38 18N 22 45 E
Elim, *Namibia* **116 B2** 17 48 S 15 31 E
Elim, *S. Africa* **116 E2** 34 35 S 19 45 E
Elim Indian Reservation, *U.S.A.* **144 D7** 64 40N 162 0W
Elin Pelin, *Bulgaria* **50 D7** 42 40N 23 36 E
Elingampangu, *Dem. Rep. of the Congo* **114 C4** 2 0 S 24 4 E
Elipa, *Dem. Rep. of the Congo* **114 C4** 1 3 S 24 20 E
Elisabethville = Lubumbashi, *Dem. Rep. of the Congo* **119 E2** 11 40 S 27 28 E
Eliseu Martins, *Brazil* **170 C3** 8 13 S 43 42W
Elista, *Russia* **61 G7** 46 16N 44 14 E
Elizabeth, *Australia* **128 C3** 34 42 S 138 41 E
Elizabeth, *Ill., U.S.A.* **156 B6** 42 19N 90 13W
Elizabeth, *N.J., U.S.A.* **151 F10** 40 39N 74 13W
Elizabeth, *N.J., U.S.A.* **151 F10** 40 40N 74 13W
Elizabeth City, *U.S.A.* **149 G7** 36 18N 76 14W
Elizabethton, *U.S.A.* **149 G4** 36 21N 82 13W
Elizabethtown, *Ky., U.S.A.* **157 G11** 37 42N 85 52W
Elizabethtown, *N.Y., U.S.A.* **151 B11** 44 13N 73 36W
Elizabethtown, *Pa., U.S.A.* **151 F8** 40 9N 76 36W
Elizondo, *Spain* **40 B3** 43 12N 1 30W
Ełk, *Poland* **54 E9** 53 50N 22 21 E
Elk —►, *Canada* **142 C5** 49 11N 115 14W
Ełk —►, *Poland* **54 E9** 53 41N 22 28 E
Elk —►, *U.S.A.* **149 H2** 34 46N 87 16W
Elk City, *U.S.A.* **155 H5** 35 25N 99 25W
Elk Creek, *U.S.A.* **160 F4** 39 36N 122 32W
Elk Grove, *U.S.A.* **160 G5** 38 25N 121 22W
Elk Island Nat. Park, *Canada* **142 C6** 53 35N 112 59W
Elk Lake, *Canada* **140 C3** 47 40N 80 25W
Elk Point, *Canada* **143 C6** 53 54N 110 55W
Elk River, *Idaho, U.S.A.* **158 C5** 46 47N 116 11W
Elk River, *Minn., U.S.A.* **154 C8** 45 18N 93 35W
Elkader, *U.S.A.* **156 B5** 42 51N 91 24W
Elkedra —►, *Australia* **126 C2** 21 8 S 136 22 E
Elkhart, *Ind., U.S.A.* **157 C11** 41 41N 85 58W
Elkhart, *Kans., U.S.A.* **155 G4** 37 0N 101 54W
Elkhart —►, *U.S.A.* **157 C11** 41 41N 85 58W
Elkhorn, *Canada* **143 D8** 49 59N 101 14W
Elkhorn, *U.S.A.* **157 B8** 42 40N 88 33W
Elkhorn —►, *U.S.A.* **154 E6** 41 8N 96 19W
Elkhovo, *Bulgaria* **51 D10** 42 10N 26 35 E
Elkin, *U.S.A.* **149 G5** 36 15N 80 51W
Elkins, *U.S.A.* **148 F6** 38 55N 79 51W
Elkland, *U.S.A.* **150 E7** 41 59N 77 19W
Elko, *Canada* **142 D5** 49 20N 115 10W
Elko, *U.S.A.* **158 F6** 40 50N 115 46W
Elkton, *U.S.A.* **150 C1** 43 49N 83 11W
Ell, L., *Australia* **125 E4** 29 13 S 127 46 E
Ellaville, *U.S.A.* **152 C5** 32 14N 84 19W
Ellef Ringnes I., *Canada* **6 B2** 78 30N 102 2W
Ellen, Mt., *U.S.A.* **151 B12** 44 9N 72 56W
Ellenburg, *U.S.A.* **151 B11** 44 54N 73 48W
Ellendale, *U.S.A.* **154 B5** 46 0N 98 32W
Ellensburg, *U.S.A.* **158 C3** 46 59N 120 34W
Ellenville, *U.S.A.* **151 E10** 41 43N 74 24W
Ellerston, *Australia* **129 A9** 31 49 S 151 20 E
Ellery, Mt., *Australia* **129 D8** 37 28 S 148 47 E
Ellesmere, L., *N.Z.* **131 H7** 47 47 S 172 28 E
Ellesmere I., *Canada* **136 B11** 79 30N 80 0W
Ellesmere Port, *U.K.* **20 D5** 53 17N 2 54W
Ellettsville, *U.S.A.* **157 E10** 39 14N 86 38W
Ellice Is. = Tuvalu ■, *Pac. Oc.* **134 H9** 8 0 S 178 0 E
Ellicottville, *U.S.A.* **150 D6** 42 17N 78 40W
Elliot, *Australia* **126 B1** 17 33 S 133 32 E
Elliot, *S. Africa* **117 E4** 31 22 S 27 48 E
Elliot Lake, *Canada* **140 C3** 46 25N 82 35W
Elliotdale = Xhora, *S. Africa* **117 E4** 31 55 S 28 38 E
Elliott, *U.S.A.* **152 A9** 34 6N 80 10W
Elliott Key, *U.S.A.* **153 K9** 25 27N 80 12W
Ellis, *U.S.A.* **154 F5** 38 56N 99 34W
Elliston, *Australia* **127 E1** 33 39 S 134 53 E
Ellisville, *U.S.A.* **155 K10** 31 36N 89 12W
Ellon, *U.K.* **22 D6** 57 22N 2 4W
Ellora, *India* **94 D2** 20 1N 75 10 E
Ellore = Eluru, *India* **94 F5** 16 48N 81 8 E
Elloree, *U.S.A.* **152 B9** 33 32N 80 34W
Ellsworth, *Kans., U.S.A.* **154 F5** 38 44N 98 14W
Ellsworth, *Maine, U.S.A.* **149 C11** 44 33N 68 25W
Ellsworth Land, *Antarctica* **7 D16** 76 0 S 89 0W
Ellsworth Mts., *Antarctica* **7 D16** 78 30 S 85 0W
Ellwangen, *Germany* **31 G6** 48 57N 10 9 E
Ellwood City, *U.S.A.* **150 F4** 40 52N 80 17W
Ellzey, *U.S.A.* **153 F7** 29 19N 82 48W
Elm, *Switz.* **33 C8** 46 54N 9 10 E
Elma, *Canada* **143 D9** 49 52N 95 55W
Elma, *U.S.A.* **160 D3** 47 0N 123 25W
Elmadağ, *Turkey* **100 C5** 39 55N 33 14 E
Elmalı, *Turkey* **49 E11** 36 44N 29 56 E
Elmhurst, *U.S.A.* **157 C9** 41 53N 87 56W
Elmina, *Ghana* **113 D4** 5 5N 1 21W
Elmira, *Canada* **150 C4** 43 36N 80 33W
Elmira, *U.S.A.* **150 D8** 42 6N 76 48W
Elmira Heights, *U.S.A.* **150 D8** 42 8N 76 50W
Elmodel, *U.S.A.* **152 D5** 31 21N 84 29W
Elmore, *Australia* **128 D6** 36 30 S 144 37 E
Elmore, *Ala., U.S.A.* **152 C3** 32 32N 86 19W
Elmore, *Calif., U.S.A.* **161 M11** 33 7N 115 49W
Elmore, *Minn., U.S.A.* **157 C13** 41 29N 83 18W
Elmshorn, *Germany* **30 B5** 53 43N 9 40 E
Elmvale, *Canada* **150 B5** 44 35N 79 52W
Elmwood, *U.S.A.* **156 D7** 40 47N 89 58W
Elne, *France* **28 F6** 42 36N 2 58 E
Elnesvågen, *Norway* **18 B4** 62 52N 7 10 E
Elnora, *U.S.A.* **157 F9** 38 53N 87 5W
Elobey Is., *Eq. Guin.* **114 B1** 1 1N 9 29 E
Elongo, *Dem. Rep. of the Congo* **114 C4** 0 19 S 21 39 E
Elora, *Canada* **150 C4** 43 41N 80 26W
Elorza, *Venezuela* **168 B4** 7 3N 69 31W
Elos, *Greece* **48 E4** 36 46N 22 43 E
Eloúnda, *Greece* **38 D7** 35 16N 25 42 E
Eloy, *U.S.A.* **159 K8** 32 45N 111 33W
Éloyes, *France* **27 D13** 48 6N 6 36 E
Elpitiya, *Sri Lanka* **95 L5** 6 17N 80 10 E
Elrose, *Canada* **143 C7** 51 12N 108 0W
Elsberry, *U.S.A.* **156 E6** 39 10N 90 47W
Elsdorf, *Germany* **30 E2** 50 55N 6 34 E
Elsie, *Mich., U.S.A.* **157 A12** 43 5N 84 23W
Elsie, *Oreg., U.S.A.* **160 E3** 45 52N 123 36W
Elsinore = Helsingør, *Denmark* **17 H6** 56 2N 12 35 E
Elsinore, *Australia* **129 A6** 31 35 S 145 11 E
Elster —►, *Germany* **30 D7** 51 25N 11 57 E
Elsterwerda, *Germany* **30 D9** 51 27N 13 31 E
Eltham, *Australia* **129 D6** 37 43 S 145 12 E
Eltham, *N.Z.* **130 F3** 39 26 S 174 19 E
Elton, *Russia* **61 F8** 49 5N 46 52 E
Elton, Ozero, *Russia* **61 F8** 49 5N 46 42 E
Eltville, *Germany* **31 E4** 50 2N 8 7 E
Eluru, *India* **94 F5** 16 48N 81 8 E
Elvas, *Portugal* **43 G3** 38 50N 7 10W
Elven, *France* **26 E4** 47 44N 2 36W
Elverum, *Norway* **15 F14** 60 53N 11 34 E
Elvire —►, *Australia* **124 C4** 17 51 S 128 11 E
Elvire, Mt., *Australia* **125 E2** 29 22 S 119 36 E
Elvo —►, *Italy* **44 C5** 45 23N 8 21 E
Elwell, L., *U.S.A.* **158 B8** 48 22N 111 17W
Elwood, *Ill., U.S.A.* **157 C8** 41 24N 88 7W
Elwood, *Ind., U.S.A.* **157 D11** 40 17N 85 50W
Elwood, *Nebr., U.S.A.* **154 E5** 40 36N 99 52W
Elx = Elche, *Spain* **41 G4** 38 15N 0 42W
Ely, *U.K.* **21 E8** 52 24N 0 16 E
Ely, *Minn., U.S.A.* **154 B9** 47 55N 91 51W
Ely, *Nev., U.S.A.* **158 G6** 39 15N 114 54W
Elyria, *U.S.A.* **150 E2** 41 22N 82 7W
Elyrus, *Greece* **48 F5** 35 15N 23 45 E
Elz —►, *Germany* **31 G3** 48 18N 7 44 E
Emådalen, *Sweden* **16 C8** 61 20N 14 44 E
Emai, *Vanuatu* **133 G6** 17 4 S 168 24 E
Emāmrūd, *Iran* **97 B7** 36 30N 55 0 E
Emån —►, *Sweden* **17 G10** 57 8N 16 30 E
Emateloa, *Dem. Rep. of the Congo* **114 B3** 1 16N 18 42 E
Emba, *Kazakstan* **64 E6** 48 50N 58 8 E
Emba —►, *Kazakstan* **57 E9** 46 55N 53 28 E
Embarcación, *Argentina* **174 A3** 23 10 S 64 0W
Embarras —►, *U.S.A.* **157 F9** 38 39N 87 37W
Embarras Portage, *Canada* **143 B6** 58 27N 111 28W
Embetsu, *Japan* **68 B10** 44 44N 141 47 E
Embi, *Kazakstan* **64 E6** 48 50N 58 8 E
Embi = Emba —►, *Kazakstan* **57 E9** 46 55N 53 28 E
Embira —►, *Brazil* **172 B3** 7 19 S 70 15W
Embóna, *Greece* **38 C9** 36 13N 27 51 E
Embrach, *Switz.* **33 B7** 47 30N 8 36 E
Embrun, *France* **29 D10** 44 34N 6 30 E
Embu, *Kenya* **118 C4** 0 32 S 37 38 E
Emden, *Germany* **30 B3** 53 21N 7 12 E
Emecik, *Turkey* **49 E9** 36 46N 27 49 E
Emerald, *Queens., Australia* **126 C4** 23 32 S 148 10 E
Emerald, *Vic., Australia* **122 E8** 37 56 S 145 29 E
Emerson, *Canada* **143 D9** 49 0N 97 10W
Emerson, *U.S.A.* **152 A5** 34 8N 84 45W
Emet, *Turkey* **49 B11** 39 20N 29 15 E
Emi Koussi, *Chad* **109 E3** 19 45N 18 55 E
Emília-Romagna □, *Italy* **44 D8** 44 45N 11 0 E
Emilius, Mte., *Italy* **44 C4** 45 45N 7 20 E
Eminabad, *Pakistan* **92 C6** 32 2N 74 8 E
Emine, Nos, *Bulgaria* **51 D11** 42 40N 27 56 E
Eminence, *U.S.A.* **157 F11** 38 22N 85 11W
Emirdağ, *Turkey* **100 C4** 39 2N 31 8 E
Emlenton, *U.S.A.* **150 E5** 41 11N 79 43W
Emlichheim, *Germany* **30 C2** 52 37N 6 51 E
Emmaboda, *Sweden* **17 H9** 56 37N 15 32 E
Emmalane, *U.S.A.* **152 C7** 32 46N 82 0W
Emmaus, *S. Africa* **116 D4** 29 2 S 25 15 E
Emmaus, *U.S.A.* **151 F9** 40 32N 75 30W
Emme —►, *Switz.* **32 B5** 47 14N 7 32 E
Emmeloord, *Neths.* **24 B5** 52 44N 5 46 E
Emmen, *Neths.* **24 B6** 52 48N 6 57 E
Emmen, *Switz.* **31 H4** 47 5N 8 18 E
Emmenbrücke, *Switz.* **33 B6** 47 4N 8 16 E
Emmendingen, *Germany* **31 G3** 48 6N 7 51 E
Emmental, *Switz.* **32 C4** 46 55N 7 40 E
Emmerich, *Germany* **30 D2** 51 50N 6 14 E
Emmet, *Australia* **126 C3** 24 45 S 144 30 E
Emmetsburg, *U.S.A.* **156 A2** 43 7N 94 41W
Emmett, *Idaho, U.S.A.* **158 E5** 43 52N 116 30W
Emmett, *Mich., U.S.A.* **150 D2** 42 59N 82 46W
Emmiganuru, *India* **95 E3** 15 44N 77 29 E
Emmonak, *U.S.A.* **144 E6** 62 46N 164 30W
Emo, *Canada* **143 D10** 48 38N 93 50W
Emőd, *Hungary* **52 C5** 47 57N 20 47 E
Emona, *Bulgaria* **51 D11** 42 43N 27 53 E
Empalme, *Mexico* **162 B2** 28 1N 110 49W
Empangeni, *S. Africa* **117 D5** 28 50 S 31 52 E
Empedrado, *Argentina* **174 B4** 28 0 S 58 46W
Emperor Seamount Chain, *Pac. Oc.* **134 D9** 40 0N 170 0 E
Empire, *U.S.A.* **152 C6** 32 21N 83 18W
Empoli, *Italy* **44 E7** 43 43N 10 57 E
Emporia, *Kans., U.S.A.* **154 F6** 38 25N 96 11W
Emporia, *Va., U.S.A.* **149 G7** 36 42N 77 32W
Emporium, *U.S.A.* **150 E6** 41 31N 78 14W
Empress, *Canada* **143 C7** 50 57N 110 0W
Empty Quarter = Rub' al Khālī, *Si. Arabia* **99 C5** 18 0N 48 0 E
Ems —►, *Germany* **30 B3** 53 20N 7 12 E
Emsdale, *Canada* **150 A5** 45 32N 79 19W
Emsdetten, *Germany* **30 C3** 52 10N 7 32 E
Emu, *Australia* **128 D5** 36 44 S 143 26 E
Emu, *China* **75 C15** 43 40N 128 6 E
Emu Park, *Australia* **126 C5** 23 13 S 150 50 E
'En 'Avrona, *Israel* **103 F4** 29 43N 35 0 E
En Nahud, *Sudan* **107 E2** 12 45N 28 25 E
En Nofalab, *Sudan* **107 D3** 15 52N 32 32 E
Ena, *Japan* **71 B9** 35 25N 137 25 E
Ena-San, *Japan* **71 B9** 35 26N 137 36 E
Enambú, *Colombia* **168 C3** 1 1N 70 17W
Enana, *Namibia* **116 B2** 17 30 S 16 23 E
Enånger, *Sweden* **16 C11** 61 30N 17 9 E
Enaratoli, *Indonesia* **79 E9** 3 55 S 136 21 E
Enard B., *U.K.* **22 C3** 58 5N 5 20W
Enare = Inarijärvi, *Finland* **14 B22** 69 0N 28 0 E
Encampment, *U.S.A.* **158 F10** 41 12N 106 47W
Encantadas, Serra, *Brazil* **175 C5** 30 40 S 53 0W
Encarnación, *Paraguay* **175 B4** 27 15 S 55 50W
Encarnación de Diaz, *Mexico* **162 C4** 21 30N 102 13W
Enchi, *Ghana* **112 D4** 5 53N 2 48W
Encinitas, *U.S.A.* **161 M9** 33 3N 117 17W
Encino, *U.S.A.* **159 J11** 34 39N 105 28W
Encontrados, *Venezuela* **168 B3** 9 3N 72 14W
Encounter B., *Australia* **128 C3** 35 45 S 138 45 E
Encruzilhada, *Brazil* **171 E3** 15 31 S 40 54W
Encs, *Hungary* **52 B6** 48 20N 21 8 E
Endako, *Canada* **142 C3** 54 6N 125 2W
Ende, *Indonesia* **79 F6** 8 45 S 121 40 E
Endeavour Str., *Australia* **126 A3** 10 45 S 142 0 E
Endelave, *Denmark* **17 J4** 55 46N 10 18 E
Enden, *Norway* **18 C7** 61 47N 10 15 E
Enderbury I., *Kiribati* **134 H10** 3 8 S 171 5W
Enderby, *Canada* **142 C5** 50 35N 119 10W
Enderby I., *Australia* **124 D2** 20 35 S 116 30 E
Enderby Land, *Antarctica* **7 C5** 66 0 S 53 0 E
Enderlin, *U.S.A.* **154 B6** 46 38N 97 36W
Endicott, *U.S.A.* **151 D8** 42 6N 76 4W
Endimari —►, *Brazil* **172 B4** 8 46 S 66 7W
Endwell, *U.S.A.* **151 D8** 42 6N 76 2W
Endyalgout I., *Australia* **124 B5** 11 40 S 132 35 E
Ene —►, *Peru* **172 C3** 11 10 S 74 18W
Eneabba, *Australia* **125 E2** 29 49 S 115 16 E
Energetik, *Russia* **62 F7** 51 45N 58 45 E
Enewetak Atoll, *Marshall Is.* **134 F8** 11 30N 162 15 E
Enez, *Turkey* **51 F10** 40 45N 26 5 E
Enfield, *Canada* **141 D7** 44 56N 63 32W
Enfield, *Conn., U.S.A.* **151 E12** 41 58N 72 36W
Enfield, *Ill., U.S.A.* **157 F8** 38 6N 88 20W
Enfield, *N.H., U.S.A.* **151 C12** 43 39N 72 9W
Engadin, *Switz.* **31 J6** 46 45N 10 10 E
Engan, *Norway* **18 A5** 63 8N 8 31 E
Engaño, C., *Dom. Rep.* **165 C6** 18 30N 68 20W
Engaño, C., *Phil.* **79 A6** 18 35N 122 23 E
Engaru, *Japan* **68 B11** 44 3N 143 31 E
Engcobo, *S. Africa* **117 E4** 31 37 S 28 0 E
Engelberg, *Switz.* **33 C6** 46 48N 8 26 E
Engels, *Russia* **60 E8** 51 28N 46 6 E
Engemann L., *Canada* **143 B7** 58 0N 106 55W
Engerdal, *Norway* **18 C8** 61 45N 11 58 E
Engershatu, *Eritrea* **107 D4** 16 7N 38 34 E
Enggano, *Indonesia* **78 F2** 5 20 S 102 40 E
Engil, *Morocco* **110 B4** 33 12N 4 32W
Engkilili, *Malaysia* **85 B4** 1 3N 111 42 E
England, *U.S.A.* **155 H9** 34 33N 91 58W
England □, *U.K.* **20 D7** 53 0N 2 0W
Englee, *Canada* **141 B8** 50 45N 56 5W
Englefield, *Australia* **128 D4** 37 21 S 141 48 E
Englehart, *Canada* **140 C4** 47 49N 79 52W
Englewood, *Colo., U.S.A.* **154 F2** 39 39N 104 59W
Englewood, *Fla., U.S.A.* **153 J7** 26 58N 82 21W
Englewood, *Ohio, U.S.A.* **157 E12** 39 53N 84 18W
English, *U.S.A.* **157 F10** 38 20N 86 28W
English —►, *Canada* **143 C10** 50 35N 93 30W
English —►, *U.S.A.* **156 C5** 41 29N 91 32W
English Bazar = Ingraj Bazar, *India* **93 G13** 24 58N 88 10 E
English Channel, *Europe* **21 G6** 50 0N 2 0W
English River, *Canada* **140 C1** 49 14N 91 0W
Engures ezers, *Latvia* **54 A10** 57 16N 23 6 E
Enguri —►, *Georgia* **61 J5** 42 27N 41 38 E
Enid, *U.S.A.* **155 G6** 36 24N 97 53W
Enipévs —►, *Greece* **48 B4** 39 22N 22 17 E
Enkhuizen, *Neths.* **24 B5** 52 42N 5 17 E
Enköping, *Sweden* **16 E11** 59 37N 17 4 E
Enle, *China* **76 F3** 24 0N 101 9 E
Enna, *Italy* **47 E7** 37 34N 14 16 E
Ennadai, *Canada* **143 A8** 61 8N 100 53W
Ennadai L., *Canada* **143 A8** 61 0N 101 0W
Ennedi, *Chad* **109 E4** 17 15N 22 0 E
Enngonia, *Australia* **127 D4** 29 21 S 145 50 E
Ennigerloh, *Germany* **30 D4** 51 50N 8 2 E
Ennis, *Ireland* **23 D3** 52 51N 8 59W
Ennis, *Mont., U.S.A.* **158 D8** 45 21N 111 44W
Ennis, *Tex., U.S.A.* **155 J6** 32 20N 96 38W
Enniscorthy, *Ireland* **23 D5** 52 30N 6 34W
Enniskillen, *U.K.* **23 B4** 54 21N 7 39W
Ennistimon, *Ireland* **23 D2** 52 57N 9 17W
Enns, *Austria* **34 C7** 48 12N 14 28 E
Enns —►, *Austria* **34 C7** 48 14N 14 32 E
Enontekiö, *Finland* **14 B20** 68 23N 23 37 E
Enosburg Falls, *U.S.A.* **151 B12** 44 55N 72 48W
Enping, *China* **77 F9** 22 16N 112 21 E
Enrekang, *Indonesia* **82 B1** 3 34 S 119 47 E
Enrile, *Phil.* **80 C3** 17 34N 121 42 E
Enriquillo, L., *Dom. Rep.* **165 C5** 18 20N 72 5W
Enschede, *Neths.* **24 B6** 52 13N 6 53 E
Ensenada, *Argentina* **174 C4** 34 55 S 57 55W
Ensenada, *Mexico* **162 A1** 31 50N 116 50W
Ensenada de los Muertos, *Mexico* **162 C2** 23 59N 109 50W

Feshi 213

Eysturoy, *Færoe Is.* **14 E9** 62 13N 6 54W
Eyvānkī, *Iran* **97 C6** 35 24N 51 56 E
Ez Zeidab, *Sudan* **106 D3** 17 25N 33 55 E
Ezcaray, *Spain* **40 C1** 42 19N 3 0W
Ežerėlis, *Lithuania* **54 D10** 54 53N 23 37 E
Ezhou, *China* **77 B10** 30 23N 114 50 E
Ezine, *Turkey* **49 B8** 39 48N 26 20 E
Ezmul, *Mauritania* **110 D1** 22 15N 15 40W
Ezouza →, *Cyprus* **38 E11** 34 44N 32 27 E

F

F.Y.R.O.M. = Macedonia ■,
Europe **50 E5** 41 53N 21 40 E
Fabala, *Guinea* **112 D3** 9 44N 9 5W
Fabens, *U.S.A.* **159 L10** 31 30N 106 10W
Fåberg, *Norway* **18 C7** 61 10N 10 25 E
Fabero, *Spain* **42 C4** 42 46N 6 37W
Fåborg, *Denmark* **17 J4** 55 6N 10 15 E
Fabriano, *Italy* **45 E9** 43 20N 12 54 E
Făcăeni, *Romania* **53 F12** 44 32N 27 53 E
Facatativá, *Colombia* **168 C3** 4 49N 74 22W
Faceville, *U.S.A.* **152 E5** 30 45N 84 38W
Fachi, *Niger* **109 E2** 18 6N 11 34 E
Facundo, *Argentina* **176 C3** 45 18 S 69 58W
Fada, *Chad* **109 E4** 17 13N 21 34 E
Fada-n-Gourma, *Burkina Faso* **113 C5** 12 10N 0 30 E
Fadd, *Hungary* **52 D3** 46 28N 18 49 E
Faddeyevskiy, Ostrov, *Russia* **65 B15** 76 0N 144 0 E
Faddor, *Sudan* **107 F3** 8 7N 32 17 E
Fadghāmī, *Syria* **101 E9** 35 53N 40 52 E
Fadlab, *Sudan* **106 D3** 17 42N 34 2 E
Faenza, *Italy* **45 D8** 44 17N 11 53 E
Færingehavn =
Kangerluarsoruseq,
Greenland **10 E5** 63 45N 51 27W
Færoe Is. = Føroyar, *Atl. Oc.* **14 F9** 62 0N 7 0W
Fafa, *Mali* **113 B5** 15 22N 0 48 E
Fafe, *Portugal* **42 D2** 41 27N 8 11W
Faga, *W. Samoa* **133 W23** 13 39 S 172 8W
Fagam, *Nigeria* **113 C7** 11 1N 10 1 E
Fagamalo, *W. Samoa* **133 W23** 13 25 S 172 21W
Făgăraș, *Romania* **53 E9** 45 48N 24 58 E
Făgăraș, Munții, *Romania* **53 E9** 45 40N 24 40 E
Fågelmara, *Sweden* **17 H9** 56 16N 15 58 E
Fagerheim, *Norway* **18 D4** 60 26N 7 46 E
Fagerhult, *Sweden* **17 G9** 57 8N 15 40 E
Fagernes, *Norway* **18 D6** 60 59N 9 14 E
Fagersta, *Sweden* **16 D9** 60 1N 15 46 E
Făget, *Romania* **52 E7** 45 52N 22 10 E
Făget, Munții, *Romania* **53 C8** 47 40N 23 10 E
Fagnano, L., *Argentina* **176 D3** 54 30 S 68 0W
Fagnières, *France* **27 D11** 48 58N 4 20 E
Faguibine, L., *Mali* **112 B4** 16 45N 4 0W
Fahlīān, *Iran* **97 D6** 30 11N 51 28 E
Fahr, *Yemen* **99 D6** 12 26N 54 8 E
Fahraj, *Kermān, Iran* **97 D8** 29 0N 59 0 E
Fahraj, *Yazd, Iran* **97 D7** 31 46N 54 36 E
Fai Tsi Long Archipelago,
Vietnam **76 G6** 21 0N 107 30 E
Faial, *Madeira* **39 D3** 32 47N 16 53W
Faido, *Switz.* **33 D7** 46 29N 8 48 E
Fair Haven, *U.S.A.* **148 D9** 43 36N 73 16W
Fair Hd., *U.K.* **23 A5** 55 14N 6 9W
Fair Oaks, *U.S.A.* **160 G5** 38 39N 121 16W
Fairbank, *U.S.A.* **156 B4** 42 38N 92 3W
Fairbanks, *Alaska, U.S.A.* **138 B5** 64 51N 147 43W
Fairbanks, *Fla., U.S.A.* **152 F7** 29 44N 82 16W
Fairborn, *U.S.A.* **157 E12** 39 49N 84 2W
Fairburn, *U.S.A.* **152 B5** 33 34N 84 35W
Fairbury, *Ill., U.S.A.* **157 D8** 40 45N 88 31W
Fairbury, *Nebr., U.S.A.* **154 E6** 40 8N 97 11W
Fairfax, *Ohio, U.S.A.* **157 E13** 39 5N 83 37W
Fairfax, *S.C., U.S.A.* **152 C8** 32 59N 81 15W
Fairfax, *Vt., U.S.A.* **151 B11** 44 40N 73 1W
Fairfield, *Australia* **129 B9** 33 53 S 150 57 E
Fairfield, *Ala., U.S.A.* **149 J2** 33 29N 86 55W
Fairfield, *Calif., U.S.A.* **160 G4** 38 15N 122 3W
Fairfield, *Conn., U.S.A.* **151 E11** 41 9N 73 16W
Fairfield, *Idaho, U.S.A.* **158 E6** 43 21N 114 44W
Fairfield, *Ill., U.S.A.* **157 F8** 38 23N 88 22W
Fairfield, *Iowa, U.S.A.* **156 D5** 40 56N 91 57W
Fairfield, *Ohio, U.S.A.* **157 E12** 39 21N 84 34W
Fairfield, *Tex., U.S.A.* **155 K7** 31 44N 96 10W
Fairford, *Canada* **143 C9** 51 37N 98 38W
Fairhope, *U.S.A.* **149 K2** 30 31N 87 54W
Fairlie, *N.Z.* **131 E5** 44 5 S 170 49 E
Fairmead, *U.S.A.* **160 H6** 37 5N 120 10W
Fairmont, *Minn., U.S.A.* **154 D7** 43 39N 94 28W
Fairmont, *W. Va., U.S.A.* **148 F5** 39 29N 80 9W
Fairmount, *Calif., U.S.A.* **161 L8** 34 45N 118 26W
Fairmount, *N.Y., U.S.A.* **151 C8** 43 5N 76 12W
Fairplay, *U.S.A.* **159 G11** 39 15N 106 2W
Fairport, *U.S.A.* **150 C7** 43 6N 77 27W
Fairport Harbor, *U.S.A.* **150 E3** 41 45N 81 17W
Fairview, *Canada* **142 B5** 56 5N 118 25W
Fairview, *Mont., U.S.A.* **154 B2** 47 51N 104 3W
Fairview, *Okla., U.S.A.* **155 G5** 36 16N 98 29W
Fairweather, Mt., *U.S.A.* **142 B1** 58 55N 137 32W
Faisalabad, *Pakistan* **91 C4** 31 30N 73 5 E
Faith, *U.S.A.* **154 C3** 45 2N 102 2W
Faizabad, *India* **93 F10** 26 45N 82 10 E
Faizpur, *India* **94 D2** 21 14N 75 49 E
Fajardo, *Puerto Rico* **165 C6** 18 20N 65 39W
Fajr, W. →, *Si. Arabia* **96 D3** 29 10N 38 10 E
Fakam, *Yemen* **98 C3** 16 38N 43 49 E
Fakenham, *U.K.* **20 E8** 52 51N 0 51 E
Fåker, *Sweden* **16 A8** 63 0N 14 34 E
Fakfak, *Indonesia* **79 E8** 3 0 S 132 15 E
Fakiya, *Bulgaria* **51 D11** 42 10N 27 6 E
Fakobli, *Ivory C.* **112 D3** 7 23N 7 23W
Fakse, *Denmark* **17 J6** 55 15N 12 8 E
Fakse Bugt, *Denmark* **17 J6** 55 11N 12 15 E
Fakse Ladeplads, *Denmark* **17 J6** 55 11N 12 9 E
Faku, *China* **75 C12** 42 32N 123 21 E
Falaba, *S. Leone* **112 D2** 9 54N 11 22W
Falaise, *France* **26 D6** 48 54N 0 12W
Falaise, Mui, *Vietnam* **86 C5** 19 6N 105 45 E
Falakrón Óros, *Greece* **50 E7** 41 15N 23 58 E
Falam, *Burma* **90 D4** 23 0N 93 45 E
Falces, *Spain* **40 C3** 42 24N 1 48W
Fălciu, *Romania* **53 D13** 46 17N 28 7 E
Falcó, C. des, *Spain* **39 C7** 38 50N 1 23 E
Falcón □, *Venezuela* **168 A4** 11 0N 69 50W
Falcon, C., *Algeria* **111 A4** 35 50N 0 50W
Falcón, Presa, *Mexico* **163 B5** 26 35N 99 10W
Falcon Lake, *Canada* **143 D9** 49 42N 95 15W
Falcon Reservoir, *U.S.A.* **155 M5** 26 34N 99 10W
Falconara Marittima, *Italy* **45 E10** 43 37N 13 24 E
Falcone, C. del, *Italy* **46 B1** 40 58N 8 12 E
Falconer, *U.S.A.* **150 D5** 42 7N 79 13W
Faléa, *Mali* **112 C2** 12 16N 11 17W
Falealupo, *W. Samoa* **133 W24** 13 55 S 171 59W
Falelima, *W. Samoa* **133 W23** 13 32 S 172 41W
Falémé →, *Senegal* **112 C2** 14 46N 12 14W
Falenki, *Russia* **62 B3** 58 22N 51 35 E
Falerum, *Sweden* **17 F10** 58 8N 16 13 E
Faleshty = Fălești, *Moldova* **53 C12** 47 32N 27 44 E
Fălești, *Moldova* **53 C12** 47 32N 27 44 E
Falfurrias, *U.S.A.* **155 M5** 27 14N 98 9W
Falher, *Canada* **142 B5** 55 44N 117 15W
Faliraki, *Greece* **38 C10** 36 22N 28 12 E
Falkenberg, *Germany* **30 D9** 51 35N 13 14 E
Falkenberg, *Sweden* **17 H6** 56 54N 12 30 E
Falkensee, *Germany* **30 C9** 52 34N 13 4 E
Falkirk, *U.K.* **22 F5** 56 0N 3 47W
Falkirk □, *U.K.* **22 F5** 55 58N 3 49W
Falkland, *U.K.* **22 E5** 56 16N 3 12W
Falkland, East, I., *Falk. Is.* **176 D5** 51 40 S 58 30W
Falkland, West, I., *Falk. Is.* **176 D4** 51 40 S 60 0W
Falkland Is. □, *Atl. Oc.* **176 D5** 51 30 S 59 0W
Falkland Sd., *Falk. Is.* **176 D5** 52 0 S 60 0W
Falkonéra, *Greece* **48 E5** 36 50N 23 52 E
Falköping, *Sweden* **17 F7** 58 12N 13 33 E
Fall River, *U.S.A.* **151 E13** 41 43N 71 10W
Fällanden, *Switz.* **33 B7** 47 22N 8 38 E
Fallbrook, *U.S.A.* **161 M9** 33 23N 117 15W
Fallon, *U.S.A.* **158 G4** 39 28N 118 47W
Falls City, *U.S.A.* **154 E7** 40 3N 95 36W
Falls Creek, *U.S.A.* **150 E6** 41 9N 78 48W
Falmouth, *Jamaica* **164 C4** 18 30N 77 40W
Falmouth, *U.K.* **21 G2** 50 9N 5 5W
Falmouth, *Ky., U.S.A.* **157 F12** 38 41N 84 20W
Falmouth, *Mass., U.S.A.* **151 E14** 41 33N 70 37W
Falsa, Pta., *Mexico* **162 B1** 27 51N 115 3W
False B., *S. Africa* **116 E2** 34 15 S 18 40 E
False Divi Pt., *India* **95 G5** 15 43N 80 50 E
False Pass, *U.S.A.* **144 J7** 54 51N 163 25W
False Pt., *India* **94 D8** 20 18N 86 48 E
Falso, C., *Honduras* **164 C3** 15 12N 83 21W
Falster, *Denmark* **17 K5** 54 45N 11 55 E
Falsterbo, *Sweden* **15 J15** 55 23N 12 50 E
Fălticeni, *Romania* **53 C11** 47 21N 26 20 E
Falun, *Sweden* **16 D9** 60 37N 15 37 E
Famagusta, *Cyprus* **38 D12** 35 8N 33 55 E
Famagusta Bay, *Cyprus* **38 D13** 35 15N 34 0 E
Famatina, Sierra de, *Argentina* **174 B2** 27 30 S 68 0W
Family L., *Canada* **143 C9** 51 54N 95 27W
Famoso, *U.S.A.* **161 K7** 35 37N 119 12W
Fan Xian, *China* **74 G8** 35 55N 115 38 E
Fana, *Mali* **112 C3** 13 0N 6 56W
Fanad Hd., *Ireland* **23 A4** 55 17N 7 38W
Fanahammaren, *Norway* **18 D2** 60 16N 5 20 E
Fanárion, *Greece* **48 B3** 39 24N 21 47 E
Fandriana, *Madag.* **117 C8** 20 14 S 47 21 E
Fang, *Thailand* **76 H2** 19 55N 99 13 E
Fang Xian, *China* **77 A8** 32 3N 110 40 E
Fangaga, *Sudan* **106 D4** 17 40N 37 50 E
Fangak, *Sudan* **107 F3** 9 4N 30 53 E
Fangchang, *China* **77 B12** 31 5N 118 4 E
Fangcheng, *China* **74 H7** 33 18N 112 59 E
Fangchenggang, *China* **76 G7** 21 42N 108 21 E
Fangliao, *Taiwan* **77 F13** 22 22N 120 38 E
Fangshan, *China* **74 E6** 38 3N 111 25 E
Fangzi, *China* **75 F10** 36 33N 119 10 E
Fani i Madh →, *Albania* **50 E4** 41 56N 20 16 E
Fanjakana, *Madag.* **117 C8** 21 10 S 46 53 E
Fanjiatun, *China* **75 C13** 43 40N 125 15 E
Fannich, L., *U.K.* **22 D4** 57 38N 4 59W
Fannrem, *Norway* **18 A6** 63 16N 9 50 E
Fannūj, *Iran* **97 E8** 26 35N 59 38 E
Fanø, *Denmark* **17 J2** 55 25N 8 25 E
Fano, *Italy* **45 E10** 43 50N 13 1 E
Fanshi, *China* **74 E7** 39 12N 113 20 E
Fao = Al Fāw, *Iraq* **97 D6** 30 0N 48 30 E
Faqirwali, *Pakistan* **92 E5** 29 27N 73 0 E
Fâqûs, *Egypt* **106 H7** 30 44N 31 47 E
Fara in Sabina, *Italy* **45 F9** 42 12N 12 43 E
Faradje,
Dem. Rep. of the Congo **118 B2** 3 50N 29 45 E
Farafangana, *Madag.* **117 C8** 22 49 S 47 50 E
Farâfra, El Wâhât el-, *Egypt* **106 B2** 27 15N 28 20 E
Farāh, *Afghan.* **91 B1** 32 20N 62 7 E
Farāh □, *Afghan.* **91 B1** 32 25N 62 10 E
Farahalana, *Madag.* **117 A9** 14 26 S 50 10 E
Faraid, Gebel, *Egypt* **106 C4** 23 33N 35 19 E
Farako, *Ivory C.* **112 D4** 10 45N 6 50W
Faramana, *Burkina Faso* **112 C4** 11 56N 4 45W
Faranah, *Guinea* **112 C2** 10 3N 10 45W
Farap, *Turkmenistan* **63 D1** 39 9N 63 36 E
Farasān, Jazā'ir, *Si. Arabia* **98 C3** 16 45N 41 55 E
Farasan Is. = Farasān, Jazā'ir,
Si. Arabia **98 C3** 16 45N 41 55 E
Faratsiho, *Madag.* **117 B8** 19 24 S 46 57 E
Farbarachi, *Somali Rep.* **120 D3** 2 30N 45 30 E
Fardes →, *Spain* **43 H7** 37 35N 3 0W
Fareham, *U.K.* **21 G6** 50 51N 1 11W
Farewell, C., *N.Z.* **131 A7** 40 29 S 172 43 E
Farewell C. = Nunap Isua,
Greenland **10 F6** 59 48N 43 55W
Farewell Spit, *N.Z.* **131 A8** 40 35 S 173 0 E
Färgelanda, *Sweden* **17 F5** 58 34N 12 0 E
Farghona, *Uzbekistan* **64 E8** 40 23N 71 19 E
Farghonskaya Dolina,
Uzbekistan **63 C5** 40 50N 71 30 E
Fargo, *Ga., U.S.A.* **152 E7** 30 41N 82 34W
Fargo, *N. Dak., U.S.A.* **154 B6** 46 53N 96 48W
Fār'iah, W. al →, *West Bank* **103 C4** 32 12N 35 27 E
Faribault, *U.S.A.* **154 C8** 44 18N 93 16W
Faridabad, *India* **92 E6** 28 26N 77 19 E
Faridkot, *India* **92 D6** 30 44N 74 45 E
Faridpur, *Bangla.* **90 D2** 23 15N 89 55 E
Faridpur, *India* **93 E8** 28 13N 79 33 E
Färila, *Sweden* **16 C9** 61 48N 15 50 E
Farim, *Guinea-Biss.* **112 C1** 12 27N 15 9W
Farīmān, *Iran* **97 C8** 35 40N 59 49 E
Farina, *Australia* **127 E2** 30 3 S 138 15 E
Farinha →, *Brazil* **170 C2** 6 51 S 47 30W
Fariones, Pta., *Canary Is.* **39 E6** 29 13N 13 28W
Fâriskûr, *Egypt* **106 H7** 31 20N 31 43 E
Färjestaden, *Sweden* **17 H10** 56 38N 16 27 E
Farkadhón, *Greece* **48 B4** 39 36N 22 4 E
Farley, *U.S.A.* **156 B6** 42 27N 91 0W
Farmakonisi, *Greece* **49 D9** 37 17N 27 5 E
Farmer City, *U.S.A.* **157 D8** 40 15N 88 39W
Farmersburg, *U.S.A.* **157 E9** 39 15N 87 23W
Farmerville, *U.S.A.* **155 J8** 32 47N 92 24W
Farmingdale, *U.S.A.* **151 F10** 40 12N 74 10W
Farmington, *Canada* **142 B4** 55 54N 120 30W
Farmington, *Calif., U.S.A.* **160 H6** 37 55N 120 59W
Farmington, *Ga., U.S.A.* **152 B6** 33 47N 83 26W
Farmington, *Ill., U.S.A.* **156 D7** 40 42N 90 0W
Farmington, *Iowa, U.S.A.* **156 D5** 40 38N 91 44W
Farmington, *Maine, U.S.A.* **149 C10** 44 40N 70 9W
Farmington, *Mo., U.S.A.* **155 G9** 37 47N 90 25W
Farmington, *N.H., U.S.A.* **151 C13** 43 24N 71 4W
Farmington, *N. Mex., U.S.A.* **159 H9** 36 44N 108 12W
Farmington, *Utah, U.S.A.* **158 F8** 41 0N 111 12W
Farmington →, *U.S.A.* **151 E12** 41 51N 72 38W
Farmland, *U.S.A.* **157 D11** 40 15N 85 5W
Farmville, *U.S.A.* **148 G6** 37 18N 78 24W
Färnäs, *Sweden* **16 D8** 61 0N 14 39 E
Farne Is., *U.K.* **20 B6** 55 38N 1 37W
Farnham, *Canada* **151 A12** 45 17N 72 59W
Farnham, Mt., *Canada* **142 C5** 50 29N 116 30W
Faro, *Brazil* **169 D6** 2 10 S 56 39W
Faro, *Canada* **138 B6** 62 11N 133 22W
Faro, *Portugal* **43 H3** 37 2N 7 55W
Fårö, *Sweden* **15 H18** 57 55N 19 5 E
Faro □, *Portugal* **43 H2** 37 12N 8 10W
Fårösund, *Sweden* **17 G13** 57 52N 19 2 E
Farquhar, C., *Australia* **125 D1** 23 50 S 113 36 E
Farquhar Is., *Seychelles* **121 F4** 11 0 S 52 0 E
Farrars Cr. →, *Australia* **126 D3** 25 35 S 140 43 E
Farrāshband, *Iran* **97 D7** 28 57N 52 5 E
Farrell, *U.S.A.* **150 E4** 41 13N 80 30W
Farrell Flat, *Australia* **128 B3** 33 48 S 138 48 E
Farrokhī, *Iran* **97 C8** 33 50N 59 31 E
Farruch, C. = Ferrutx, C.,
Spain **39 B10** 39 47N 3 21 E
Fārs □, *Iran* **97 D7** 29 30N 55 0 E
Fársala, *Greece* **48 B4** 39 17N 22 23 E
Farsī, *Afghan.* **91 B1** 33 47N 63 15 E
Farsø, *Denmark* **17 H3** 56 46N 9 19 E
Farson, *U.S.A.* **158 E9** 42 6N 109 27W
Farsund, *Norway* **15 G12** 58 5N 6 55 E
Fartak, Râs, *Si. Arabia* **96 D2** 28 5N 34 34 E
Fartak, Ra's, *Yemen* **99 D6** 15 38N 52 15 E
Fărțănești, *Romania* **53 E12** 45 49N 27 59 E
Fartura, Serra da, *Brazil* **175 B5** 26 21 S 52 52W
Faru, *Nigeria* **113 C6** 12 48N 6 12 E
Fārūj, *Iran* **97 B8** 37 14N 58 14 E
Fårup, *Denmark* **17 H3** 56 33N 9 51 E
Farvel, Kap = Nunap Isua,
Greenland **10 F6** 59 48N 43 55W
Farwell, *U.S.A.* **155 H3** 34 23N 103 2W
Fāryāb □, *Afghan.* **91 B2** 36 0N 65 0 E
Fasā, *Iran* **97 D7** 29 0N 53 39 E
Fasano, *Italy* **47 B10** 40 50N 17 22 E
Fashoda, *Sudan* **107 F3** 9 50N 32 2 E
Fassa, *Mali* **112 C3** 13 26N 8 15 E
Fastiv, *Ukraine* **59 G5** 50 7N 29 57 E
Fastov = Fastiv, *Ukraine* **59 G5** 50 7N 29 57 E
Fatagar, Tanjung, *Indonesia* **79 E8** 2 46 S 131 57 E
Fataka, *Solomon Is.* **123 C12** 11 55 S 170 12 E
Fatehabad, *Haryana, India* **92 E6** 29 31N 75 27 E
Fatehabad, *Ut. P., India* **92 F8** 27 1N 78 19 E
Fatehgarh, *India* **93 F8** 27 25N 79 35 E
Fatehpur, *Bihar, India* **93 G11** 24 38N 85 14 E
Fatehpur, *Raj., India* **92 F6** 28 0N 74 40 E
Fatehpur, *Ut. P., India* **93 G9** 25 56N 81 13 E
Fatehpur, *Ut. P., India* **93 F9** 27 10N 81 13 E
Fatehpur Sikri, *India* **92 F6** 27 6N 77 40 E
Fatesh, *Russia* **59 F8** 52 8N 35 57 E
Fathai, *Sudan* **107 F3** 8 5N 31 48 E
Fatick, *Senegal* **112 C1** 14 19N 16 27W
Fatima, *Canada* **141 C7** 47 24N 61 53W
Fátima, *Portugal* **43 F2** 39 37N 8 39W
Fatoya, *Guinea* **112 C3** 11 37N 9 10W
Fatsa, *Turkey* **100 B7** 41 2N 37 31 E
Faucille, Col de la, *France* **27 F13** 46 22N 6 2 E
Faulkton, *U.S.A.* **154 C5** 45 2N 99 8W
Faulquemont, *France* **27 C13** 49 3N 6 36 E
Faure I., *Australia* **125 E1** 25 52 S 113 50 E
Făurei, *Romania* **53 E12** 45 6N 27 19 E
Fauresmith, *S. Africa* **116 D4** 29 44 S 25 17 E
Fauro, *Solomon Is.* **133 L9** 6 55 S 156 7 E
Fauske, *Norway* **14 C16** 67 17N 15 25 E
Fåvang, *Norway* **18 C7** 61 27N 10 11 E
Favânia, *Brazil* **169 D7** 3 7 S 51 48W
Favara, *Italy* **46 E6** 37 19N 13 39 E
Faváritx, C. de, *Spain* **39 B11** 40 0N 4 15 E
Faverges, *France* **29 C10** 45 45N 6 17 E
Favignana, *Italy* **46 E5** 37 56N 12 20 E
Favignana, I., *Italy* **46 E5** 37 56N 12 19 E
Fawcett, Pt., *Australia* **124 B5** 11 46 S 130 2 E
Fawn →, *Canada* **140 A2** 55 20N 87 35W
Fawnskin, *U.S.A.* **161 L10** 34 16N 116 56W
Faxaflói, *Iceland* **11 C3** 64 29N 23 0W
Faxälven →, *Sweden* **16 A10** 63 13N 17 13 E
Faya-Largeau, *Chad* **109 E3** 17 58N 19 6 E
Fayaoué, *Vanuatu* **133 K4** 20 38 S 166 33 E
Fayd, *Si. Arabia* **96 E4** 27 1N 42 52 E
Fayence, *France* **29 E10** 43 38N 6 42 E
Fayette, *Ala., U.S.A.* **149 J2** 33 41N 87 50W
Fayette, *Iowa, U.S.A.* **156 B5** 42 51N 91 48W
Fayette, *Mo., U.S.A.* **156 E4** 39 9N 92 41W
Fayette, *Ohio, U.S.A.* **157 C12** 41 40N 84 20W
Fayetteville, *Ark., U.S.A.* **155 G7** 36 4N 94 10W
Fayetteville, *Ga., U.S.A.* **152 B5** 33 27N 84 27W
Fayetteville, *N.C., U.S.A.* **149 H6** 35 3N 78 53W
Fayetteville, *Tenn., U.S.A.* **149 H2** 35 9N 86 34W
Fayied, *Egypt* **106 H8** 30 18N 32 16 E
Fayón, *Spain* **40 D5** 41 15N 0 20 E
Fazenda Libongo, *Angola* **115 D2** 8 24 S 13 24 E
Fazenda Nova, *Brazil* **171 E1** 16 11 S 50 48W
Fazilka, *India* **92 D6** 30 27N 74 2 E
Fazilpur, *Pakistan* **92 E4** 29 18N 70 29 E
Fdérik, *Mauritania* **110 D2** 22 40N 12 45W
Feale →, *Ireland* **23 D2** 52 27N 9 37W
Fear, C., *U.S.A.* **149 J7** 33 50N 77 58W
Feather →, *U.S.A.* **158 G3** 38 47N 121 36W
Feather Falls, *U.S.A.* **160 F5** 39 36N 121 16W
Featherston, *N.Z.* **130 H4** 41 6 S 175 20 E
Featherstone, *Zimbabwe* **119 F3** 18 42 S 30 55 E
Fécamp, *France* **26 C7** 49 45N 0 22 E
Feda, *Norway* **18 F3** 58 17N 6 50 E
Fedala = Mohammedia,
Morocco **110 B3** 33 44N 7 21W
Federación, *Argentina* **174 C4** 31 0 S 57 55W
Federal Capital Terr. □, *Nigeria* **113 D6** 9 0N 7 10 E
Federal Way, *U.S.A.* **160 C4** 47 18N 122 19W
Fedeshküh, *Iran* **97 D7** 28 49N 53 50 E
Fedjadj, Chott el, *Tunisia* **108 B1** 33 52N 9 14 E
Fedje, *Norway* **18 D1** 60 47N 4 43 E
Fehérgyarmat, *Hungary* **52 C7** 47 58N 22 30 E
Fehmarn, *Germany* **30 A7** 54 27N 11 7 E
Fehmarn Bælt, *Europe* **17 K5** 54 35N 11 20 E
Fehmarn Belt = Fehmarn Bælt,
Europe **17 K5** 54 35N 11 20 E
Fei Xian, *China* **75 G9** 35 18N 117 59 E
Feijó, *Brazil* **172 B3** 8 9 S 70 21W
Feilding, *N.Z.* **130 G4** 40 13 S 175 35 E
Feira de Santana, *Brazil* **171 D4** 12 15 S 38 57W
Feiring, *Norway* **18 D8** 60 30N 11 10 E
Feixi, *China* **77 B11** 31 43N 117 59 E
Feixiang, *China* **74 F8** 36 30N 114 45 E
Fejér □, *Hungary* **52 C3** 47 9N 18 30 E
Fejø, *Denmark* **17 K5** 54 55N 11 30 E
Feke, *Turkey* **100 D6** 37 48N 35 56 E
Fekete →, *Hungary* **52 E3** 45 47N 18 15 E
Felanitx, *Spain* **39 B10** 39 28N 3 9 E
Felda, *U.S.A.* **153 J8** 26 34N 81 26W
Feldbach, *Austria* **34 E8** 46 57N 15 52 E
Feldberg, *Baden-W., Germany* **31 H3** 47 52N 8 0 E
Feldberg,
Mecklenburg-Vorpommern,
Germany **30 B9** 53 20N 13 25 E
Feldkirch, *Austria* **34 D2** 47 15N 9 37 E
Feldkirchen, *Austria* **34 E7** 46 44N 14 6 E
Felicity, *U.S.A.* **157 F12** 38 51N 84 6W
Felipe Carrillo Puerto, *Mexico* **163 D7** 19 38N 88 3W
Felixburg, *Zimbabwe* **117 B5** 19 29 S 30 51 E
Felixlândia, *Brazil* **171 E3** 18 47 S 44 55W
Felixstowe, *U.K.* **21 F9** 51 58N 1 23 E
Felletin, *France* **28 C6** 45 53N 2 11 E
Fellingsbro, *Sweden* **16 E9** 59 26N 15 37 E
Fellsmere, *U.S.A.* **153 H9** 27 46N 80 36W
Felton, *U.S.A.* **160 H4** 37 3N 122 4W
Feltre, *Italy* **45 B8** 46 1N 11 54 E
Femer Bælt = Fehmarn Bælt,
Europe **17 K5** 54 35N 11 20 E
Femø, *Denmark* **17 K5** 54 58N 11 35 E
Femunden, *Norway* **15 E14** 62 10N 11 53 E
Fen He →, *China* **74 G6** 35 36N 110 42 E
Fene, *Spain* **42 B2** 43 27N 8 9W
Fenelon Falls, *Canada* **150 B6** 44 32N 78 45W
Fener Burnu, *Turkey* **49 E9** 36 58N 27 18 E
Feneroa, *Ethiopia* **107 E4** 13 5N 39 3 E
Feng Xian, *Jiangsu, China* **74 G9** 34 43N 116 35 E
Feng Xian, *Shaanxi, China* **74 H4** 33 54N 106 40 E
Fengári, *Greece* **51 F9** 40 25N 25 32 E
Fengcheng, *Jiangxi, China* **77 C10** 28 12N 115 48 E
Fengcheng, *Liaoning, China* **75 D13** 40 28N 124 5 E
Fengfeng, *China* **74 F8** 36 28N 114 8 E
Fenggang, *China* **76 D6** 27 57N 107 47 E
Fenghua, *China* **77 C13** 29 40N 121 25 E
Fenghuang, *China* **76 D7** 27 57N 109 29 E
Fengkai, *China* **77 F8** 23 24N 111 30 E
Fengkang, *Taiwan* **77 F13** 22 12N 120 41 E
Fengle, *China* **77 B9** 31 29N 112 29 E
Fenglin, *Taiwan* **77 F13** 23 45N 121 26 E
Fengning, *China* **74 D9** 41 10N 116 33 E
Fengqing, *China* **76 E2** 24 38N 99 55 E
Fengqiu, *China* **74 G8** 35 2N 114 25 E
Fengrun, *China* **75 E10** 39 48N 118 8 E
Fengshan, *Guangxi Zhuangzu,*
China **76 E7** 24 39N 109 15 E
Fengshan, *Guangxi Zhuangzu,*
China **76 E6** 24 31N 107 3 E
Fengshan, *Taiwan* **77 F13** 22 38N 120 21 E
Fengshun, *China* **77 F11** 23 46N 116 10 E
Fengtai, *Anhui, China* **77 A11** 32 50N 116 40 E
Fengtai, *Beijing, China* **74 E9** 39 50N 116 18 E
Fengxian, *China* **77 B13** 30 55N 121 26 E
Fengxiang, *China* **74 G4** 34 29N 107 25 E
Fengxin, *China* **77 C10** 28 41N 115 18 E
Fengyang, *China* **75 H9** 32 51N 117 29 E
Fengyi, *China* **76 E3** 25 37N 100 20 E
Fengyüan, *Taiwan* **77 E13** 24 15N 120 35 E
Fengzhen, *China* **74 D7** 40 25N 113 2 E
Feni Is., *Papua N. G.* **132 C7** 4 0 S 153 40 E
Fennimore, *U.S.A.* **156 B6** 42 59N 90 39W
Fenny, *Bangla.* **90 D3** 22 55N 91 32 E
Feno, C. de, *France* **29 G12** 41 58N 8 33 E
Fenoarivo, *Fianarantsoa,*
Madag. **117 C8** 21 43 S 46 24 E
Fenoarivo, *Fianarantsoa,*
Madag. **117 C8** 20 52 S 46 53 E
Fenoarivo Afovoany, *Madag.* **117 B8** 18 26 S 46 34 E
Fenoarivo Atsinanana, *Madag.* **117 B8** 17 22 S 49 25 E
Fens, The, *U.K.* **20 E7** 52 38N 0 2W
Fensmark, *Denmark* **17 J5** 55 17N 11 48 E
Fenton, *U.S.A.* **157 B13** 42 48N 83 42W
Fenxi, *China* **74 F6** 36 40N 111 31 E
Fenyang, *China* **74 F6** 37 18N 111 48 E
Fenyi, *China* **77 D10** 27 45N 114 47 E
Feodosiya, *Ukraine* **59 K8** 45 2N 35 16 E
Fer, C. de, *Algeria* **111 A6** 37 3N 7 10 E
Ferdows, *Iran* **97 C8** 33 58N 58 2 E
Fère-Champenoise, *France* **27 D10** 48 45N 3 59 E
Fère-en-Tardenois, *France* **27 C10** 49 10N 3 30 E
Ferentino, *Italy* **45 G10** 41 42N 13 15 E
Ferfer, *Somali Rep.* **120 C3** 5 4N 45 9 E
Fergana = Farghona,
Uzbekistan **64 E8** 40 23N 71 19 E
Ferganskaya Dolina =
Farghonskaya Dolina,
Uzbekistan **63 C5** 40 50N 71 30 E
Ferganskiy Khrebet, *Kyrgyzstan* **63 C6** 41 0N 73 50 E
Fergus, *Canada* **150 C4** 43 43N 80 24W
Fergus Falls, *U.S.A.* **154 B6** 46 17N 96 4W
Ferguson, *U.S.A.* **156 F6** 38 45N 90 18W
Fergusson I., *Papua N. G.* **132 E6** 9 30 S 150 45 E
Fériana, *Tunisia* **108 B1** 34 59N 8 33 E
Feričanci, *Croatia* **52 E2** 45 32N 18 0 E
Ferkane, *Algeria* **111 B6** 34 37N 7 26 E
Ferkéssédougou, *Ivory C.* **112 D3** 9 35N 5 6W
Ferlach, *Austria* **34 E7** 46 32N 14 18 E
Ferland, *Canada* **140 B2** 50 19N 88 27W
Ferlo, Vallée du, *Senegal* **112 B2** 15 15N 14 15W
Fermanagh □, *U.K.* **23 B4** 54 21N 7 40W
Fermo, *Italy* **45 E10** 43 9N 13 43 E
Fermont, *Canada* **141 B6** 52 47N 67 5W
Fermoselle, *Spain* **42 D4** 41 19N 6 27W
Fermoy, *Ireland* **23 D3** 52 9N 8 16W
Fernán Nuñéz, *Spain* **43 H6** 37 40N 4 44W
Fernández, *Argentina* **174 B3** 27 55 S 63 50W
Fernandina Beach, *U.S.A.* **152 E8** 30 40N 81 27W
Fernando de Noronha, *Brazil* **170 B5** 4 0 S 33 10W
Fernando Póo = Bioko,
Eq. Guin. **113 E6** 3 30N 8 40 E
Fernandópolis, *Brazil* **171 F1** 20 16 S 50 14W
Ferndale, *U.S.A.* **160 B4** 48 51N 122 36W
Fernie, *Canada* **142 D5** 49 30N 115 5W
Fernlees, *Australia* **126 C4** 23 51 S 148 7 E
Fernley, *U.S.A.* **158 G4** 39 36N 119 15W
Feroke, *India* **95 J2** 11 9N 75 46 E
Ferozepore = Firozpur, *India* **92 D6** 30 55N 74 40 E
Férrai, *Greece* **51 F10** 40 53N 26 10 E
Ferrandina, *Italy* **47 B9** 40 29N 16 27 E
Ferrara, *Italy* **45 D8** 44 50N 11 35 E
Ferrato, C., *Italy* **46 C2** 39 18N 9 38 E
Ferreira, *Angola* **115 E4** 12 53 S 22 48 E
Ferreira do Alentejo, *Portugal* **43 G2** 38 4N 8 6W
Ferreira Gomes, *Brazil* **170 A1** 0 48N 51 8W
Ferreñafe, *Peru* **172 B2** 6 42 S 79 50W
Ferrerías, *Spain* **39 B11** 39 59N 4 1 E
Ferret, C., *France* **28 D2** 44 38N 1 15W
Ferrette, *France* **27 E14** 47 30N 7 20 E
Ferriday, *U.S.A.* **155 K9** 31 38N 91 33W
Ferriere, *Italy* **44 D6** 44 40N 9 30 E
Ferrières, *France* **27 D9** 48 5N 2 48 E
Ferro, Capo, *Italy* **46 A2** 41 9N 9 31 E
Ferrol, *Spain* **42 B2** 43 29N 8 15W
Ferrol, Pen. de, *Peru* **172 B2** 9 10 S 78 35W
Ferron, *U.S.A.* **159 G8** 39 5N 111 8W
Ferros, *Brazil* **171 E3** 19 14 S 43 2W
Ferrutx, C., *Spain* **39 B10** 39 47N 3 21 E
Ferryland, *Canada* **141 C9** 47 2N 52 53W
Ferrysburg, *U.S.A.* **157 A10** 43 5N 86 13W
Fertile, *U.S.A.* **154 B6** 47 32N 96 17W
Fertőszentmiklós, *Hungary* **52 C1** 47 35N 16 53 E
Fès, *Morocco* **110 B4** 34 0N 5 0W
Feshi, *Dem. Rep. of the Congo* **115 D3** 6 8 S 18 10 E

216 Fushan

Fushan, Shandong, China 75 F11 37 30N 121 15 E
Fushan, Shanxi, China 74 G6 35 58N 111 51 E
Fushë Arrëzi, Albania 50 D4 42 4N 20 2 E
Fushë-Krujë, Albania 50 E3 41 29N 19 43 E
Fushun, Liaoning, China 75 D12 41 50N 123 56 E
Fushun, Sichuan, China 76 C5 29 13N 104 52 E
Fusio, Switz. 33 D7 46 27N 8 40 E
Fusong, China 75 C14 42 20N 127 15 E
Füssen, Germany 31 H6 47 34N 10 42 E
Fusui, China 76 F6 22 40N 107 56 E
Futago-Yama, Japan 70 D3 33 35N 131 36 E
Futog, Yugoslavia 52 E4 45 15N 19 42 E
Futrono, Chile 176 B2 40 8 S 72 24W
Futuna, Wall. & F. Is. 134 J9 14 25 S 178 20 E
Fuwa, Egypt 106 H7 31 12N 30 33 E
Fuxian Hu, China 76 E4 24 30N 102 53 E
Fuxin, China 75 C11 42 5N 121 48 E
Fuyang, Anhui, China 74 H8 33 0N 115 48 E
Fuyang, Zhejiang, China 77 B12 30 5N 119 57 E
Fuyang He →, China 74 E9 38 12N 117 0 E
Fuying Dao, China 77 D13 26 34N 120 9 E
Fuyu, China 75 B13 45 12N 124 43 E
Fuyuan, China 76 E5 25 40N 104 16 E
Füzesgyarmat, Hungary 52 C6 47 6N 21 14 E
Fuzhou, China 77 D12 26 5N 119 16 E
Fylde, U.K. 20 D5 53 50N 2 58W
Fyn, Denmark 17 J4 55 20N 10 30 E
Fyne, L., U.K. 22 F3 55 59N 5 23W
Fyns Amtskommune □, Denmark 17 J4 55 15N 10 30 E
Fynshav, Denmark 17 K3 54 59N 9 59 E
Fyresdal, Norway 18 E5 59 11N 8 5 E
Fyresvatn, Norway 18 E5 59 6N 8 10 E

G

Ga, Ghana 112 D4 9 47N 2 30W
Gaanda, Nigeria 113 C7 10 10N 12 27 E
Gabarin, Nigeria 113 C7 11 8N 10 27 E
Gabas →, France 28 E3 43 46N 0 42W
Gabela, Angola 115 E2 11 0 S 14 24 E
Gabès, Tunisia 108 B2 33 53N 10 2 E
Gabès, G. de, Tunisia 108 B2 34 0N 10 30 E
Gabgaba, W. →, Egypt 106 C3 22 10N 33 5 E
Gabia, Dem. Rep. of the Congo 115 C3 4 37 S 17 14 E
Gąbin, Poland 55 F6 52 23N 19 41 E
Gabon ■, Africa 114 C2 0 10 S 10 0 E
Gabon →, Gabon 114 B1 0 25N 9 20 E
Gaborone, Botswana 116 C4 24 45 S 25 57 E
Gabriels, U.S.A. 151 B10 44 26N 74 12W
Gābrīk, Iran 97 E8 25 44N 58 28 E
Gabro, Ethiopia 120 C2 6 18N 43 16 E
Gabrovo, Bulgaria 51 D9 42 52N 25 19 E
Gacé, France 26 D7 48 49N 0 20 E
Gāch Sār, Iran 97 B6 36 7N 51 19 E
Gachsārān, Iran 97 D6 30 15N 50 45 E
Gacko, Bos.-H. 50 C2 43 10N 18 33 E
Gad Hinglaj, India 95 F2 16 14N 74 21 E
Gadag, India 95 G2 15 30N 75 45 E
Gadamai, Sudan 107 D4 17 11N 36 10 E
Gadap, Pakistan 92 G2 25 5N 67 28 E
Gadarwara, India 93 H8 22 50N 78 50 E
Gadebusch, Germany 30 B7 53 42N 11 7 E
Gadein, Sudan 107 F2 8 10N 28 45 E
Gadhada, India 92 J4 22 0N 71 35 E
Gadmen, Switz. 33 C6 46 45N 8 16 E
Gádor, Sierra de, Spain 43 J8 36 57N 2 45W
Gadra, Pakistan 92 G4 25 40N 70 38 E
Gadsden, Ala., U.S.A. 152 A3 34 1N 86 1W
Gadsden, S.C., U.S.A. 152 B9 33 51N 80 46W
Gadwal, India 95 F3 16 10N 77 50 E
Gadyach = Hadyach, Ukraine 59 G8 50 21N 34 0 E
Gadzi, C.A.R. 114 B3 4 47N 16 42 E
Găeşti, Romania 53 F10 44 48N 25 19 E
Gaeta, Italy 46 A6 41 12N 13 35 E
Gaeta, G. di, Italy 46 A6 41 6N 13 30 E
Gaffney, U.S.A. 149 H5 35 5N 81 39W
Gafsa, Tunisia 108 B1 34 24N 8 43 E
Gagarawa, Nigeria 113 C6 12 25N 9 32 E
Gagaria, India 92 G4 25 43N 70 46 E
Gagarin, Russia 58 E8 55 38N 35 0 E
Gaggenau, Germany 31 G4 48 48N 8 18 E
Gaghamni, Sudan 107 E2 11 41N 28 19 E
Gagino, Russia 60 C7 55 15N 45 1 E
Gagliano del Capo, Italy 47 C11 39 50N 18 22 E
Gagnef, Sweden 16 D9 60 36N 15 5 E
Gagnoa, Ivory C. 112 D3 6 56N 5 16W
Gagnon, Canada 141 B6 51 50N 68 5W
Gagnon, L., Canada 143 A6 62 3N 110 27W
Gago Coutinho, São Tomé & Principe 115 G6 0 1 S 6 32 E
Gagra, Georgia 61 J5 43 20N 40 10 E
Gahini, Rwanda 118 C3 1 50 S 30 30 E
Gahmar, India 93 G10 25 27N 83 49 E
Gai Xian = Gaizhou, China 75 D12 40 22N 122 20 E
Gaibanda, Bangla. 90 C2 25 20N 89 36 E
Gaïdhouronísi, Greece 38 E7 34 53N 25 41 E
Gail, U.S.A. 155 J4 32 46N 101 27W
Gail →, Austria 34 E6 46 36N 13 53 E
Gaillac, France 28 E5 43 54N 1 54 E
Gaillimh = Galway, Ireland 23 C2 53 17N 9 3W
Gaillon, France 26 C8 49 10N 1 20 E
Gaimán, Argentina 176 B3 43 10 S 65 25W
Gaines, U.S.A. 150 E7 41 46N 77 35W
Gainesville, Fla., U.S.A. 153 F7 29 40N 82 20W
Gainesville, Ga., U.S.A. 149 H4 34 18N 83 50W
Gainesville, Mo., U.S.A. 155 G8 36 36N 92 26W
Gainesville, Tex., U.S.A. 155 J6 33 38N 97 8W
Gainsborough, U.K. 20 D7 53 24N 0 46W
Gairdner, L., Australia 128 A2 31 30 S 136 0 E
Gairloch, L., U.K. 22 D3 57 43N 5 45W
Gais, Switz. 33 B8 47 22N 9 27 E
Gaizhou, China 75 D12 40 22N 122 20 E
Gaj, Croatia 52 E2 45 28N 17 3 E
Gaj →, Pakistan 92 F2 26 26N 67 21 E
Gajendragarh, India 95 G2 15 44N 75 59 E
Gakona, U.S.A. 144 E11 62 18N 145 18W
Gakuch, Pakistan 93 A5 36 7N 73 45 E
Gal Laghet, Somali Rep. 120 D3 4 9N 47 10 E
Gal Oya Res., Sri Lanka 95 L5 7 5N 81 30 E
Gal Tardo, Somali Rep. 120 D3 3 34N 45 58 E
Galachipa, Bangla. 90 D3 22 8N 90 26 E
Galala, Gebel el, Egypt 106 J8 29 21N 32 22 E
Galán, Cerro, Argentina 174 B2 25 55 S 66 52W
Galana →, Kenya 118 C5 3 9 S 40 8 E
Galangue, Angola 115 E3 13 42 S 16 9 E
Galangue, Serra, Angola 115 E3 14 18 S 15 52 E
Galanta, Slovak Rep. 35 C10 48 11N 17 45 E
Galapagar, Spain 42 E7 40 36N 3 58W
Galápagos, Pac. Oc. 135 H18 0 0 91 0W
Galashiels, U.K. 22 F6 55 37N 2 49W
Galatás, Greece 48 D5 37 30N 23 26 E
Galatea, N.Z. 130 E5 38 24 S 176 45 E
Galaţi, Romania 53 E13 45 27N 28 2 E
Galaţi □, Romania 53 E12 45 45N 27 30 E
Galatia, Turkey 100 C5 39 30N 33 0 E
Galatina, Italy 47 B11 40 10N 18 10 E
Galátone, Italy 47 B11 40 9N 18 4 E
Galax, U.S.A. 149 G5 36 40N 80 56W
Galaxídhion, Greece 48 C4 38 22N 22 23 E
Galcaio, Somali Rep. 102 F4 6 30N 47 30 E
Galdhøpiggen, Norway 15 F12 61 38N 8 18 E
Galeana, Chihuahua, Mexico 162 A3 30 7N 107 38W
Galeana, Nuevo León, Mexico 162 A3 24 50N 100 4W
Galegu, Sudan 107 E4 12 36N 35 2 E
Galela, Indonesia 79 D7 1 50N 127 49 E
Galena, Alaska, U.S.A. 138 B4 64 44N 156 56W
Galena, Ill., U.S.A. 156 B6 42 25N 90 26W
Galera, Spain 41 H2 37 45N 2 33W
Galera, Pta., Chile 176 A2 39 59 S 73 43W
Galera Point, Trin. & Tob. 165 D7 10 8N 61 0W
Galesburg, Ill., U.S.A. 156 D6 40 57N 90 22W
Galesburg, Mich., U.S.A. 157 B11 42 17N 85 26W
Galeton, U.S.A. 150 E7 41 44N 77 39W
Galga, Ethiopia 107 F4 6 39N 37 47 E
Galgasc, Somali Rep. 120 D2 0 11N 41 38 E
Galheirão →, Brazil 171 D2 12 23 S 45 5W
Galheiros, Brazil 171 D2 13 18 S 46 25W
Gali, Georgia 61 J5 42 37N 41 46 E
Galicea Mare, Romania 53 F8 44 4N 23 19 E
Galich, Russia 60 A6 58 22N 42 24 E
Galiche, Bulgaria 50 C7 43 34N 23 53 E
Galicia □, Spain 42 C3 42 43N 7 45W
Galien, U.S.A. 157 C10 41 48N 86 30W
Galilee = Hagalil, Israel 103 C4 32 53N 35 18 E
Galilee, L., Australia 126 C4 22 20 S 145 50 E
Galilee, Sea of = Yam Kinneret, Israel 103 C4 32 45N 35 35 E
Galim, Cameroon 113 D7 7 6N 12 25 E
Galim, Cameroon 114 A2 7 6N 12 25 E
Galinoporni, Cyprus 38 D13 35 31N 34 18 E
Galion, U.S.A. 150 F2 40 44N 82 47W
Galite, Îs. de la, Tunisia 111 A6 37 30N 8 59 E
Galiuro Mts., U.S.A. 159 K8 32 30N 110 20W
Galiwinku, Australia 126 A2 12 2 S 135 34 E
Gallabat, Sudan 107 E4 12 58N 36 11 E
Gallan Hd., U.K. 22 C1 58 15N 7 2W
Gallarate, Italy 44 C5 45 40N 8 48 E
Gallatin, Mo., U.S.A. 156 E3 39 55N 93 58W
Gallatin, Tenn., U.S.A. 149 G2 36 24N 86 27W
Galle, Sri Lanka 95 L5 6 5N 80 10 E
Gállego →, Spain 40 D4 41 39N 0 51W
Gallegos →, Argentina 176 D3 51 35 S 69 0W
Galletti →, Ethiopia 107 F5 8 46N 41 10 E
Galley Hd., Ireland 23 E3 51 32N 8 55W
Galliate, Italy 44 C5 45 29N 8 42 E
Gallinas, Pta., Colombia 168 A3 12 28N 71 40W
Gallipoli = Gelibolu, Turkey 51 F10 40 28N 26 43 E
Gallípoli, Italy 47 B10 40 3N 17 58 E
Gallipolis, U.S.A. 148 F4 38 49N 82 12W
Gällivare, Sweden 14 C19 67 9N 20 40 E
Gallneukirchen, Austria 34 C7 48 21N 14 25 E
Gällö, Sweden 16 B9 62 55N 15 13 E
Gallo, C., Italy 46 D6 38 13N 13 19 E
Gallocanta, L. de, Spain 40 E3 40 58N 1 30W
Galloo I., U.S.A. 151 C8 43 55N 76 25W
Galloway, U.K. 22 F4 55 1N 4 29W
Galloway, Mull of, U.K. 22 G4 54 39N 4 52W
Gallup, U.S.A. 159 J9 35 32N 108 45W
Gallur, Spain 40 D3 41 52N 1 19W
Gallyaaral, Uzbekistan 63 C3 40 2N 67 35 E
Galong, Australia 129 C8 34 37 S 148 34 E
Galt, Calif., U.S.A. 160 G5 38 15N 121 18W
Galt, Mo., U.S.A. 156 D3 40 8N 93 23W
Galten, Denmark 17 H3 56 9N 9 54 E
Galtür, Austria 34 E3 46 58N 10 11 E
Galty Mts., Ireland 23 D3 52 22N 8 10W
Galtymore, Ireland 23 D3 52 21N 8 11W
Galva, U.S.A. 156 C6 41 10N 90 3W
Galvarino, Chile 176 A2 38 24 S 72 47W
Galve de Sorbe, Spain 40 D1 41 13N 3 10W
Galveston, Ind., U.S.A. 157 D10 40 35N 86 11W
Galveston, Tex., U.S.A. 155 L7 29 18N 94 48W
Galveston B., U.S.A. 155 L7 29 36N 94 50W
Gálvez, Argentina 174 C3 32 0 S 61 14W
Galway, Ireland 23 C2 53 17N 9 3W
Galway □, Ireland 23 C2 53 22N 9 1W
Galway B., Ireland 23 C2 53 13N 9 10W
Gam, Indonesia 83 B4 0 27 S 130 36 E
Gam →, Vietnam 86 B5 21 55N 105 12 E
Gamagori, Japan 71 C9 34 50N 137 14 E
Gamari, L., Ethiopia 107 E5 11 32N 41 40 E
Gamawa, Nigeria 113 C7 12 10N 10 31 E
Gamay, Phil. 80 E5 12 23N 125 18 E
Gamay Bay, Phil. 80 E5 12 21N 125 21 E
Gamba, Angola 115 E3 11 42 S 17 14 E
Gambaga, Ghana 113 C4 10 30N 0 28W
Gambat, Pakistan 92 F3 27 17N 68 26 E
Gambela, Ethiopia 107 F3 8 14N 34 38 E
Gambhir →, India 92 F6 26 58N 77 27 E
Gambia ■, W. Afr. 112 C1 13 25N 16 0W
Gambia →, W. Afr. 112 C1 13 28N 16 34W
Gambier, U.S.A. 150 F2 40 22N 82 23W
Gambier, C., Australia 124 B5 11 56 S 130 57 E
Gambier Is., Australia 128 C2 35 3 S 136 30 E
Gambo, C.A.R. 114 B4 4 39N 22 16 E
Gambo, Canada 141 C9 48 47N 54 13W
Gamboli, Pakistan 92 E3 29 53N 68 24 E
Gamboma, Congo 114 C3 1 55 S 15 52 E
Gamboula, C.A.R. 114 B3 4 8N 15 9 E
Gambuta, Indonesia 82 A2 0 30N 123 20 E
Gamka →, S. Africa 116 E3 33 18 S 21 39 E
Gamkab →, Namibia 116 D2 28 4 S 17 54 E
Gamla Uppsala, Sweden 16 E11 59 54N 17 40 E
Gamlakarleby = Kokkola, Finland 14 E20 63 50N 23 8 E
Gamleby, Sweden 17 G10 57 54N 16 24 E
Gammon →, Canada 143 C9 51 24N 95 44W
Gammouda, Tunisia 108 A1 35 3N 9 39 E
Gamo-Gofa □, Ethiopia 107 F4 5 40N 36 40 E
Gamoda-Saki, Japan 70 D6 33 50N 134 45 E
Gamou, Niger 113 C6 14 20N 9 55 E
Gampaha, Sri Lanka 95 L4 7 5N 79 59 E
Gampel, Switz. 32 D5 46 19N 7 44 E
Gampola, Sri Lanka 95 L5 7 10N 80 34 E
Gams, Switz. 33 B8 47 12N 9 26 E
Gamtoos →, S. Africa 116 E4 33 58 S 25 1 E
Gan, France 28 E3 43 12N 0 27W
Gan Gan, Argentina 176 B3 42 30 S 68 10W
Gan Goriama, Mts., Cameroon 113 D7 7 44N 12 45 E
Gan Jiang →, China 77 C11 29 15N 116 0 E
Ganado, U.S.A. 159 J9 35 43N 109 33W
Gananita, Sudan 106 D3 18 22N 33 50 E
Gananoque, Canada 140 D4 44 20N 76 10W
Ganassi, Phil. 81 H5 7 49N 124 6 E
Ganāveh, Iran 97 D6 29 35N 50 35 E
Gäncä, Azerbaijan 61 K8 40 45N 46 20 E
Gancheng, China 86 C7 18 51N 108 37 E
Gand = Gent, Belgium 24 C3 51 2N 3 42 E
Ganda, Angola 115 E2 13 3 S 14 35 E
Gandajika, Dem. Rep. of the Congo 115 D4 6 46 S 23 58 E
Gandak →, India 93 G11 25 39N 85 13 E
Gandara, Phil. 80 E5 12 1N 124 49 E
Gandava, Pakistan 91 C2 28 32N 67 32 E
Gander, Canada 141 C9 48 58N 54 35W
Gander L., Canada 141 C9 48 58N 54 35W
Ganderkesee, Germany 30 B4 53 2N 8 32 E
Ganderowe Falls, Zimbabwe 119 F2 17 20 S 29 10 E
Gandesa, Spain 40 D5 41 3N 0 26 E
Gandhi Sagar, India 92 G6 24 40N 75 40 E
Gandhinagar, India 92 H5 23 15N 72 45 E
Gandi, Nigeria 113 C6 12 55N 5 49 E
Gandía, Spain 41 G4 38 58N 0 9W
Gandino, Italy 44 C6 45 49N 9 54 E
Gando, Pta., Canary Is. 39 G4 27 55N 15 22W
Gandole, Nigeria 113 D7 8 28N 11 35 E
Gandou, Congo 114 B3 2 25N 17 25 E
Gandu, Brazil 171 D4 13 45 S 39 30W
Gâneb, Mauritania 112 B2 18 29N 10 8W
Ganedidalem = Gani, Indonesia 79 E7 0 48 S 128 14 E
Ganetti, Sudan 106 D3 18 0N 31 10 E
Ganga →, India 93 H14 23 20N 90 30 E
Ganga Sagar, India 93 J13 21 38N 88 5 E
Gangafani, Mali 112 C4 14 20N 2 20W
Gangakher, India 94 E3 18 57N 76 45 E
Gangan →, India 93 E8 28 38N 78 58 E
Ganganagar, India 92 E5 29 56N 73 56 E
Gangapur, India 92 F7 26 32N 76 49 E
Gangapur, India 94 E2 19 41N 75 1 E
Gangara, Niger 113 C6 14 35N 8 29 E
Gangaw, Burma 90 D5 22 5N 94 5 E
Gangawati, India 95 G3 15 30N 76 36 E
Ganges = Ganga →, India 93 H14 23 20N 90 30 E
Ganges, Canada 142 D4 48 51N 123 31W
Ganges, France 28 E7 43 56N 3 42 E
Ganges, Mouths of the, India 93 J14 21 30N 90 0 E
Gånghester, Sweden 17 G7 57 42N 13 1 E
Gangi, Italy 47 E7 37 48N 14 12 E
Gângiova, Romania 53 G8 43 54N 23 50 E
Gangoh, India 92 E7 29 46N 77 18 E
Gangroti, India 93 D8 30 50N 79 10 E
Gangtok, India 90 B2 27 20N 88 37 E
Gangu, China 74 G3 34 40N 105 15 E
Gangwa, Dem. Rep. of the Congo 114 C4 3 30 S 20 54 E
Gangyao, China 75 B14 44 12N 126 37 E
Gani, Indonesia 79 E7 0 48 S 128 14 E
Ganj, India 93 F8 27 45N 78 57 E
Ganjam, India 94 E7 19 23N 85 4 E
Ganluc, China 76 C4 28 58N 102 59 E
Gannat, France 27 F10 46 7N 3 11 E
Gannett Peak, U.S.A. 158 E9 43 11N 109 39W
Ganongga, Solomon Is. 133 M9 8 5 S 156 35 E
Ganquan, China 74 F5 36 20N 109 20 E
Gänserdorf, Austria 35 C9 48 20N 16 43 E
Ganshui, China 76 C6 28 40N 106 40 E
Gansu □, China 74 G3 36 0N 104 0 E
Ganta, Liberia 112 D3 7 15N 8 59W
Gantheaume, C., Australia 128 D2 36 4 S 137 32 E
Gantheaume B., Australia 125 E1 27 40 S 114 10 E
Gantsevichi = Hantsavichy, Belarus 59 F4 52 49N 26 30 E
Ganye, Nigeria 113 D7 8 25N 12 4 E
Ganyem = Genyem, Indonesia 79 E10 2 46 S 140 12 E
Ganyu, China 75 G10 34 50N 119 8 E
Ganyushkino, Kazakstan 61 G9 46 35N 49 20 E
Ganzhou, China 77 E10 25 51N 114 56 E
Gao, Mali 113 B4 16 15N 0 5W
Gao, Mali 113 B5 16 20N 0 10W
Gao Xian, China 76 C5 28 21N 104 32 E
Gao'an, China 77 C10 28 26N 115 17 E
Gaochun, China 77 B12 31 20N 118 49 E
Gaohe, China 77 F9 22 46N 112 57 E
Gaohebu, China 77 B11 30 43N 116 49 E
Gaokeng, China 77 D9 27 40N 113 58 E
Gaolan Dao, China 77 G9 21 55N 113 10 E
Gaoligong Shan, China 76 E2 24 45N 98 45 E
Gaomi, China 75 F10 36 20N 119 42 E
Gaoming, China 77 F9 36 9N 113 1 E
Gaoping, China 74 G7 35 45N 112 55 E
Gaotang, China 74 F9 36 50N 116 15 E
Gaoua, Burkina Faso 112 C4 10 20N 3 8W
Gaoual, Guinea 112 C2 11 45N 13 25W
Gaoxiong = Kaohsiung, Taiwan 77 F13 22 35N 120 16 E
Gaoyang, China 74 E8 38 40N 115 45 E
Gaoyao, China 77 F9 23 3N 112 27 E
Gaoyou, China 77 A12 32 47N 119 26 E
Gaoyou Hu, China 75 H10 32 45N 119 20 E
Gaoyuan, China 75 F9 37 8N 117 58 E
Gaozhou, China 77 G8 21 58N 110 50 E
Gap, France 29 D10 44 33N 6 5 E
Gapan, Phil. 80 D3 15 19N 120 57 E
Gapat →, India 93 G10 24 30N 82 28 E
Gapuwiyak, Australia 126 A2 12 25 S 135 43 E
Gar, China 72 C2 32 10N 79 58 E
Garabekewül, Turkmenistan 63 D2 38 30N 64 8 E
Garabogazköl Aylagy, Turkmenistan 57 F9 41 0N 53 30 E
Garachico, Canary Is. 39 F3 28 22N 16 46W
Garachiné, Panama 164 E4 8 0N 78 12W
Garad, Somali Rep. 120 C3 6 57N 49 24 E
Garafia, Canary Is. 39 F2 28 48N 17 57W
Garah, Australia 127 D4 29 5 S 149 38 E
Garajonay, Canary Is. 39 F2 28 7N 17 14W
Garamätnyyaz, Turkmenistan 63 E2 37 45N 64 34 E
Garango, Burkina Faso 113 C4 11 48N 0 34W
Garanhuns, Brazil 170 C4 8 50 S 36 30W
Garautha, India 93 G8 25 34N 79 18 E
Garawe, Liberia 112 E3 4 35N 8 0W
Garba Harre, Somali Rep. 120 D2 3 19N 42 13 E
Garba Tula, Kenya 118 B4 0 30N 38 32 E
Garbagududu, Ethiopia 120 C2 6 12N 43 50 E
Garberville, U.S.A. 158 F2 40 6N 123 48W
Garbiyang, India 93 D9 30 8N 80 54 E
Garbsen, Germany 30 C5 52 26N 9 31 E
Garça, Brazil 171 F2 22 14 S 49 37W
Garças →, Mato Grosso, Brazil 173 D7 15 54 S 52 16W
Garças →, Pernambuco, Brazil 170 C4 8 43 S 39 41W
Garchitorena, Phil. 80 E4 13 52N 123 40 E
Garcia Hernandez, Phil. 81 G5 9 37N 124 18 E
Garcias, Brazil 173 E7 20 34 S 52 13W
Gard □, France 29 D8 44 2N 4 10 E
Gard →, France 29 E8 43 51N 4 37 E
Garda, L. di, Italy 44 C7 45 40N 10 41 E
Gardanne, France 29 E9 43 27N 5 27 E
Gårdby, Sweden 17 H10 56 36N 16 38 E
Garde L., Canada 143 A7 62 50N 106 13W
Gardelegen, Germany 30 C7 52 32N 11 24 E
Garden City, Ga., U.S.A. 152 C8 32 6N 81 9W
Garden City, Kans., U.S.A. 155 G4 37 58N 100 53W
Garden City, Mo., U.S.A. 156 F2 38 34N 94 12W
Garden City, Tex., U.S.A. 155 K4 31 52N 101 29W
Garden Grove, U.S.A. 161 M9 33 47N 117 55W
Gardēz, Afghan. 91 B3 33 37N 69 9 E
Gardhíki, Greece 48 C3 38 50N 21 55 E
Garður, Iceland 11 A10 66 4N 16 46W
Gardiner, Maine, U.S.A. 149 C11 44 14N 69 47W
Gardiner, Mont., U.S.A. 158 D8 45 2N 110 22W
Gardiners I., U.S.A. 151 E12 41 6N 72 6W
Gardner, Fla., U.S.A. 153 H8 27 21N 81 48W
Gardner, Ill., U.S.A. 157 C8 41 12N 88 17W
Gardner, Mass., U.S.A. 151 D13 42 34N 71 59W
Gardner Canal, Canada 142 C3 53 27N 128 8W
Gardner Pinnacles, U.S.A. 145 G10 25 0N 167 55W
Gardnerville, U.S.A. 160 G7 38 56N 119 45W
Gardno, Jezioro, Poland 54 D4 54 40N 17 7 E
Gardo, Somali Rep. 120 C3 9 30N 49 6 E
Gardone Val Trómpia, Italy 44 C7 45 41N 10 11 E
Gárdony, Hungary 52 C3 47 12N 18 39 E
Gare Tigre, Fr. Guiana 169 C7 4 58N 53 9W
Garešnica, Croatia 45 C13 45 36N 16 56 E
Garéssio, Italy 44 D5 44 12N 8 2 E
Garey, U.S.A. 161 L6 34 53N 120 19W
Garfield, U.S.A. 158 C5 47 1N 117 9W
Garforth, U.K. 20 D6 53 47N 1 24W
Gargaliánoi, Greece 48 D3 37 4N 21 38 E
Gargan, Mt., France 28 C5 45 37N 1 39 E
Gargouna, Mali 113 B5 15 56N 0 13 E
Gargždai, Lithuania 54 C8 55 43N 21 24 E
Garhchiroli, India 94 D5 20 10N 80 0 E
Gari, Russia 62 B9 59 26N 62 21 E
Garibaldi Prov. Park, Canada 142 D4 49 50N 122 40W
Gariep, L., S. Africa 116 E4 30 40 S 25 40 E
Garies, S. Africa 116 E2 30 32 S 17 59 E
Garigliano →, Italy 46 A6 41 13N 13 45 E
Garissa, Kenya 118 C4 0 25 S 39 40 E
Garkida, Nigeria 113 C7 10 27N 12 36 E
Garko, Nigeria 113 C6 11 45N 8 35 E
Garland, Tex., U.S.A. 155 J6 32 55N 96 38W
Garland, Utah, U.S.A. 158 F7 41 47N 112 10W
Garlasco, Italy 44 C5 45 12N 8 55 E
Garliava, Lithuania 54 D10 54 49N 23 52 E
Garlin, France 28 E3 43 33N 0 16W
Garm, Tajikistan 64 F8 39 0N 70 20 E
Garmāb, Iran 97 C8 35 25N 56 45 E
Garmisch-Partenkirchen, Germany 31 H7 47 30N 11 6 E
Garmsār, Iran 97 C7 35 20N 52 25 E
Garner, U.S.A. 156 A3 43 6N 93 36W
Garnett, U.S.A. 154 F7 38 17N 95 14W
Garo Hills, India 93 G14 25 30N 90 30 E
Garoe, Somali Rep. 120 C3 8 25N 48 33 E
Garonne →, France 28 C3 45 2N 0 36W
Garonne, Canal Latéral à la, France 28 D4 44 15N 0 18 E
Garot, India 92 G6 24 19N 75 41 E
Garoua, Cameroon 113 D7 9 19N 13 21 E
Garpenberg, Sweden 16 D10 60 19N 16 12 E
Garphyttan, Sweden 16 E8 59 18N 14 56 E
Garrauli, India 93 G8 25 5N 79 22 E
Garrel, Germany 30 C4 52 57N 8 1 E
Garrett, U.S.A. 157 C11 41 21N 85 8W
Garrigue = Garrigues, France 28 E7 43 40N 3 55 E
Garrigues, France 28 E7 43 40N 3 55 E
Garrison, Ky., U.S.A. 157 F13 38 36N 83 10W
Garrison, Mont., U.S.A. 158 C7 46 31N 112 49W
Garrison, N. Dak., U.S.A. 154 B4 47 40N 101 25W
Garrison Res. = Sakakawea, L., U.S.A. 154 B4 47 30N 101 25W
Garron Pt., U.K. 23 A6 55 3N 5 59W
Garrovillas, Spain 43 F4 39 40N 6 33W
Garrucha, Spain 41 H3 37 11N 1 49W
Garry →, U.K. 22 E5 56 44N 3 47W
Garry, L., Canada 138 B9 65 58N 100 18W
Garsen, Kenya 118 C5 2 20 S 40 5 E
Gärsnäs, Sweden 17 J8 55 32N 14 10 E
Garson L., Canada 143 B6 56 19N 110 2W
Gartempe →, France 28 B4 46 47N 0 49 E
Gartz, Germany 30 B10 53 13N 14 22 E
Garu, Ghana 113 C4 10 55N 0 11W
Garu, India 93 H11 23 40N 84 14 E
Garub, Namibia 116 D2 26 37 S 16 0 E
Garut, Indonesia 79 G12 7 14 S 107 53 E
Garvão, Portugal 43 H2 37 42N 8 21W
Garvie Mts., N.Z. 131 F3 45 30 S 168 50 E
Garwa = Garoua, Cameroon 113 D7 9 19N 13 21 E
Garwa, India 93 G10 24 11N 83 47 E
Garwolin, Poland 55 G8 51 55N 21 38 E
Gary, U.S.A. 157 C9 41 36N 87 20W
Garz, Germany 30 A9 54 19N 13 20 E
Garzê, China 76 B3 31 38N 100 1 E
Garzón, Colombia 168 C2 2 10N 75 40W
Gas City, U.S.A. 157 D11 40 29N 85 37W
Gas-San, Japan 68 E10 38 32N 140 1 E
Gasan, Phil. 80 E3 13 19N 121 51 E
Gasan Kuli = Esenguly, Turkmenistan 64 F6 37 37N 53 59 E
Gaschurn, Austria 33 C10 46 59N 10 2 E
Gascogne, France 28 E4 43 45N 0 20 E
Gascogne, G. de, Europe 28 E2 44 0N 2 0W
Gasconade, U.S.A. 156 F5 38 40N 91 34W
Gasconade →, U.S.A. 156 F5 38 41N 91 33W
Gascony = Gascogne, France 28 E4 43 45N 0 20 E
Gascoyne →, Australia 125 D1 24 52 S 113 37 E
Gascoyne Junction, Australia 125 E2 25 2 S 115 17 E
Gascueña, Spain 40 E2 40 18N 2 31W
Gash, Wadi →, Ethiopia 107 D4 16 48N 35 51 E
Gashagar, Nigeria 113 C7 13 22N 12 47 E
Gashaka, Nigeria 113 D7 7 20N 11 29 E
Gasherbrum, Pakistan 93 B7 35 40N 76 40 E
Gashua, Nigeria 113 C7 12 54N 11 0 E
Gasparilla I., U.S.A. 153 J7 26 46N 82 16W
Gaspé, Canada 141 C7 48 52N 64 30W
Gaspé, C. de, Canada 141 C7 48 48N 64 7W
Gaspé, Pén. de, Canada 141 C6 48 45N 65 40W
Gaspésie, Parc de Conservation de la, Canada 141 C6 48 55N 65 50W
Gassan, Burkina Faso 112 C4 12 49N 3 12W
Gassol, Nigeria 113 D7 8 34N 10 25 E
Gasteiz = Vitoria-Gasteiz, Spain 40 C2 42 50N 2 41W
Gaston, U.S.A. 152 B8 33 49N 81 5W
Gastonia, U.S.A. 149 H5 35 16N 81 11W
Gastoúni, Greece 48 D3 37 51N 21 15 E
Gastoúri, Greece 48 B1 39 34N 19 54 E
Gastre, Argentina 176 B3 42 20 S 69 15W
Gästrikland, Sweden 16 D10 60 45N 16 40 E
Gata, C., Cyprus 38 E12 34 34N 33 2 E
Gata, C. de, Spain 41 J2 36 41N 2 13W
Gata, Sierra de, Spain 42 E4 40 20N 6 45W
Gataga →, Canada 142 B3 58 35N 126 59W
Gătaia, Romania 52 E6 45 26N 21 30 E
Gatchina, Russia 58 C6 59 35N 30 9 E
Gatehouse of Fleet, U.K. 22 G4 54 53N 4 12W
Gates, U.S.A. 150 C7 43 9N 77 42W
Gateshead, U.K. 20 C6 54 57N 1 35W
Gatesville, U.S.A. 155 K6 31 26N 97 45W
Gaths, Zimbabwe 119 G3 20 2 S 30 32 E
Gatico, Chile 174 A1 22 29 S 70 20W
Gâtinais, France 27 D9 48 5N 2 40 E
Gâtine, Hauteurs de, France 28 B3 46 35N 0 45W
Gatineau, Canada 151 A9 45 29N 75 38W
Gatineau →, Canada 140 C4 45 27N 75 42W

Greenfield 219

Gorinchem, Neths. 24 C4 51 50N 4 59 E
Gorinhatã, Brazil 171 E2 19 15 S 49 45W
Goris, Armenia 101 C12 39 31N 46 22 E
Goritsy, Russia 58 D9 57 4N 36 43 E
Gorízia, Italy 45 C10 45 56N 13 37 E
Gorj □, Romania 53 E8 45 5N 23 25 E
Gorki = Horki, Belarus 58 E6 54 17N 30 59 E
Gorki = Nizhniy Novgorod, Russia 60 B7 56 20N 44 0 E
Gorkiy = Nizhniy Novgorod, Russia 60 B7 56 20N 44 0 E
Gorkovskoye Vdkhr., Russia 60 B6 57 2N 43 4 E
Gorlice, Poland 55 J8 49 35N 21 11 E
Görlitz, Germany 30 D10 51 9N 14 58 E
Gorlovka = Horlivka, Ukraine 59 H10 48 19N 38 5 E
Gorman, U.S.A. 161 L8 34 47N 118 51W
Gorna Dzhumayo = Blagoevgrad, Bulgaria 50 D7 42 2N 23 5 E
Gorna Oryakhovitsa, Bulgaria 51 C9 43 7N 25 40 E
Gornja Radgona, Slovenia 45 B13 46 40N 16 2 E
Gornja Tuzla, Bos.-H. 52 F3 44 35N 18 46 E
Gornji Grad, Slovenia 45 B11 46 20N 14 52 E
Gornji Milanovac, Serbia, Yug. 50 B4 44 3N 20 29 E
Gornji Vakuf, Bos.-H. 52 G2 43 57N 17 34 E
Gorno Ablanovo, Bulgaria 51 C9 43 37N 25 43 E
Gorno-Altay □, Russia 64 D9 51 0N 86 0 E
Gorno-Altaysk, Russia 64 D9 51 50N 86 5 E
Gornyatski, Russia 56 A11 67 32N 64 3 E
Gornyatskiy, Russia 61 F5 48 18N 40 56 E
Gornyy, Saratov, Russia 60 E9 51 50N 48 30 E
Gornyy, Sib., Russia 68 B6 44 57N 133 59 E
Goro →, C.A.R. 114 A4 9 14N 21 16 E
Gorodenka = Horodenka, Ukraine 59 H3 48 41N 25 29 E
Gorodets, Russia 60 B6 56 38N 43 28 E
Gorodishche = Horodyshche, Ukraine 59 H6 49 17N 31 27 E
Gorodishche, Russia 60 D7 53 13N 45 40 E
Gorodnya = Horodnya, Ukraine 59 G6 51 55N 31 33 E
Gorodok = Haradok, Belarus 58 E6 55 30N 30 3 E
Gorodok = Horodok, Ukraine 59 H2 49 46N 23 32 E
Gorodovikovsk, Russia 61 G5 46 8N 41 58 E
Goroka, Papua N. G. 132 D3 6 7 S 145 25 E
Goroke, Australia 128 D4 36 43 S 141 29 E
Gorokhov = Horokhiv, Ukraine 59 G3 50 30N 24 45 E
Gorokhovets, Russia 60 B6 56 13N 42 39 E
Gorom Gorom, Burkina Faso 113 C4 14 26N 0 14W
Goromonzi, Zimbabwe 119 F3 17 52 S 31 22 E
Gorong, Kepulauan, Indonesia 79 E8 3 59 S 131 25 E
Gorongose →, Mozam. 117 C5 20 30 S 34 40 E
Gorongoza, Mozam. 119 F3 18 44 S 34 2 E
Gorongoza, Sa. da, Mozam. 119 F3 18 27 S 34 2 E
Gorontalo, Indonesia 79 D6 0 35N 123 5 E
Goronyo, Nigeria 113 C6 13 29N 5 39 E
Górowo Iławeckie, Poland 54 D7 54 17N 20 30 E
Gorron, France 26 D6 48 25N 0 50W
Gorshechnoye, Russia 59 G10 51 31N 38 2 E
Gort, Ireland 23 C3 53 3N 8 49W
Gortis, Greece 38 D6 35 4N 24 58 E
Gorumahisani, India 94 C8 22 20N 86 24 E
Góry Bystrzyckie, Poland 55 H3 50 16N 16 33 E
Goryachiy Klyuch, Russia 61 H4 44 38N 39 8 E
Gorzkowice, Poland 55 G6 51 13N 19 36 E
Górzno, Poland 55 E6 53 12N 19 38 E
Gorzów Śląski, Poland 55 G5 51 3N 18 22 E
Gorzów Wielkopolski, Poland 55 F2 52 43N 15 15 E
Göschenen, Switz. 33 C7 46 40N 8 36 E
Gose, Japan 71 C7 34 27N 135 44 E
Gosford, Australia 129 B9 33 23 S 151 18 E
Goshen, Calif., U.S.A. 160 J7 36 21N 119 25W
Goshen, Ind., U.S.A. 157 C11 41 35N 85 50W
Goshen, N.Y., U.S.A. 151 E10 41 24N 74 20W
Goshogawara, Japan 68 D10 40 48N 140 27 E
Goslar, Germany 30 D6 51 54N 10 25 E
Gospič, Croatia 45 D12 44 35N 15 23 E
Gosport, U.K. 21 G6 50 48N 1 9W
Gosport, U.S.A. 157 E10 39 21N 86 40W
Gossa, Norway 18 B3 62 52N 6 50 E
Gossas, Senegal 112 C1 14 28N 16 0W
Gossau, Switz. 33 B8 47 25N 9 15 E
Gosse →, Australia 126 B1 19 32 S 134 37 E
Gossi, Mali 113 B4 15 48N 1 20W
Gossinga, Sudan 107 F2 8 36N 25 59 E
Gostivar, Macedonia 50 E4 41 48N 20 57 E
Gostyń, Poland 55 G4 51 50N 17 3 E
Gostynin, Poland 55 F6 52 26N 19 29 E
Göta älv →, Sweden 17 G5 57 42N 11 54 E
Göta kanal, Sweden 17 F9 58 30N 15 58 E
Götaland, Sweden 17 G8 57 30N 14 30 E
Göteborg, Sweden 17 G5 57 43N 11 59 E
Göteborgs och Bohus län □, Sweden 17 F5 58 30N 11 30 E
Gotemba, Japan 71 B10 35 18N 138 56 E
Götene, Sweden 17 F7 58 32N 13 30 E
Goteşti, Moldova 53 D13 46 9N 28 10 E
Gotha, Germany 30 E6 50 56N 10 42 E
Gothenburg = Göteborg, Sweden 17 G5 57 43N 11 59 E
Gothenburg, U.S.A. 154 E4 40 56N 100 10W
Gothèye, Niger 113 C5 13 52N 1 34 E
Gotland, Sweden 17 G12 57 30N 18 33 E
Gotlands län □, Sweden 17 G12 57 15N 18 30 E
Gotō-Rettō, Japan 69 H4 32 55N 129 5 E
Gotse Delchev, Bulgaria 50 E7 41 36N 23 46 E
Gotska Sandön, Sweden 15 G18 58 24N 19 15 E
Gōtsu, Japan 70 B4 35 0N 132 14 E
Gott Pk., Canada 142 C4 50 18N 122 16W
Góttero, Monte, Italy 44 D6 44 22N 9 42 E
Göttingen, Germany 30 D5 51 31N 9 55 E
Gottwald = Zmiyev, Ukraine 59 H9 49 39N 36 27 E
Gottwaldov = Zlín, Czech Rep. 35 B10 49 14N 17 40 E
Götzis, Austria 33 B9 47 20N 9 38 E
Goubangzi, China 75 D11 41 20N 121 52 E
Gouda, Neths. 24 B4 52 1N 4 42 E
Goúdhoura, Ákra, Greece 38 E8 34 59N 26 6 E
Goudiry, Senegal 112 C2 14 15N 12 45W
Goudoumaria, Niger 113 C7 13 40N 11 10 E
Gouéké, Guinea 112 D3 8 2N 8 43W
Gough I., Atl. Oc. 9 N8 40 10 S 9 45W
Gouin, Rés., Canada 140 C5 48 35N 74 40W
Gouitafla, Ivory C. 112 D3 7 30N 5 53W
Goulburn, Australia 129 C8 34 44 S 149 44 E
Goulburn Is., Australia 126 A1 11 40 S 133 20 E
Goulds, U.S.A. 153 K9 25 33N 80 23W
Goulia, Ivory C. 112 C3 10 1N 7 11W
Goulimine, Morocco 110 C3 28 56N 10 0W
Goulmina, Morocco 110 B4 31 41N 4 57W
Goumbou, Mali 112 B3 15 2N 7 25W
Gouménissa, Greece 50 F6 40 56N 22 37 E
Goundam, Mali 112 B4 16 27N 3 40W
Gounou-Gaya, Chad 109 G3 9 38N 15 31 E
Goúra, Greece 48 D4 37 56N 22 20 E
Gouraya, Algeria 111 A5 36 31N 1 56 E
Gourbassi, Mali 112 C2 13 24N 11 38W
Gourdon, France 28 D5 44 44N 1 23 E
Gouré, Niger 113 C7 14 0N 10 10 E
Gouri, Chad 109 E3 19 36N 19 36 E
Gourin, France 26 D3 48 8N 3 37W
Gourits →, S. Africa 116 E3 34 21 S 21 52 E
Gourma-Rharous, Mali 113 B4 16 55N 1 50W
Goúrnais, Greece 38 D7 35 19N 25 16 E
Gournay-en-Bray, France 27 C8 49 29N 1 44 E
Gourock Ra., Australia 129 C8 36 0 S 149 25 E
Goursi, Burkina Faso 112 C4 12 42N 2 37W
Gouvêa, Brazil 171 E3 18 27 S 43 44W
Gouverneur, U.S.A. 151 B9 44 20N 75 28W
Gouviá, Greece 38 A3 39 39N 19 50 E
Gouzon, France 27 F9 46 12N 2 14 E
Governador Valadares, Brazil 171 E3 18 15 S 41 57W
Governor Generoso, Phil. 81 H6 6 39N 126 5 E
Governor's Harbour, Bahamas 164 A4 25 10N 76 14W
Govindgarh, India 93 G9 24 23N 81 18 E
Gowan Ra., Australia 126 D4 25 0 S 145 0 E
Gowanda, U.S.A. 150 D6 42 28N 78 56W
Gower, U.K. 21 F3 51 35N 4 10W
Gowna, L., Ireland 23 C4 53 51N 7 34W
Gowrie, U.S.A. 156 B2 42 17N 94 17W
Gowurdak, Turkmenistan 63 E3 37 50N 66 4 E
Goya, Argentina 174 B4 29 10 S 59 10W
Göyçay, Azerbaijan 61 K8 40 42N 47 43 E
Goyder Lagoon, Australia 127 D2 27 3 S 138 58 E
Goyllarisquisga, Peru 172 C2 10 31 S 76 24W
Göynük, Antalya, Turkey 49 E12 36 41N 30 33 E
Göynük, Bolu, Turkey 100 B4 40 24N 30 48 E
Goz Beîda, Chad 109 F4 12 10N 21 20 E
Goz Regeb, Sudan 107 D4 16 3N 35 33 E
Gozdnica, Poland 55 G2 51 28N 15 4 E
Gozo, Malta 38 C1 36 3N 14 13 E
Graaff-Reinet, S. Africa 116 E3 32 13 S 24 32 E
Grabill, U.S.A. 157 C12 41 13N 84 57W
Grabo, Ivory C. 112 D3 4 57N 7 30W
Grabow, Germany 30 B7 53 17N 11 34 E
Grabów nad Prosną, Poland 55 G5 51 31N 18 7 E
Grabs, Switz. 33 B8 47 11N 9 27 E
Gračac, Croatia 45 D12 44 18N 15 57 E
Gračanica, Bos.-H. 52 F3 44 43N 18 18 E
Graçay, France 27 E8 47 10N 1 50 E
Graceville, U.S.A. 152 E4 30 58N 85 31W
Gracewood, U.S.A. 152 B7 33 22N 82 2W
Grachevka, Russia 62 E4 52 55N 52 52 E
Gracias a Dios, C., Honduras 164 D3 15 0N 83 10W
Graciosa, I., Canary Is. 39 E6 29 15N 13 32W
Grad Sofiya □, Bulgaria 50 D7 42 35N 23 20 E
Gradac, Montenegro, Yug. 50 C3 43 23N 19 9 E
Gradačac, Bos.-H. 52 F3 44 52N 18 26 E
Gradaús, Brazil 170 C1 7 43 S 51 11W
Gradaús, Serra dos, Brazil 170 C1 8 0 S 50 45W
Gradeška Planina, Macedonia 50 E6 41 30N 22 15 E
Gradets, Bulgaria 51 D10 42 46N 26 30 E
Gradišče, Slovenia 45 B12 46 37N 15 50 E
Grădiştea de Munte, Romania 53 E8 45 37N 23 13 E
Grado, Italy 45 C10 45 40N 13 23 E
Grado, Spain 42 B4 43 23N 6 4W
Grady, U.S.A. 155 H3 34 49N 103 19W
Graeca, Lacul, Romania 53 F11 44 5N 26 10 E
Grafarnes, Iceland 11 C3 64 55N 23 16W
Grafenau, Germany 31 G9 48 51N 13 22 E
Gräfenberg, Germany 31 F7 49 39N 11 14 E
Grafham Water, U.K. 21 E7 52 19N 0 18W
Grafton, Australia 127 D5 29 38 S 152 58 E
Grafton, Ill., U.S.A. 156 F6 38 58N 90 26W
Grafton, N. Dak., U.S.A. 154 A6 48 25N 97 25W
Grafton, W. Va., U.S.A. 148 F5 39 21N 80 2W
Graham, Canada 140 C1 49 20N 90 30W
Graham, Ga., U.S.A. 152 D7 31 50N 82 30W
Graham, Tex., U.S.A. 155 J5 33 6N 98 35W
Graham, Mt., U.S.A. 159 K9 32 42N 109 52W
Graham Bell, Ostrov = Greem-Bell, Ostrov, Russia 64 A7 81 0N 62 0 E
Graham I., B.C., Canada 142 C2 53 40N 132 30W
Graham I., N.W.T., Canada 138 C6 77 25N 90 30W
Graham Land, Antarctica 7 C17 65 0 S 64 0W
Grahamstown, S. Africa 116 E4 33 19 S 26 31 E
Grahamsville, U.S.A. 151 E10 41 51N 74 33W
Grahovo, Montenegro, Yug. 50 D2 42 40N 18 40 E
Graïba, Tunisia 108 B2 34 30N 10 13 E
Graie, Alpi, Europe 29 C11 45 30N 7 10 E
Grain Coast, W. Afr. 112 E3 4 20N 10 0W
Grajaú, Brazil 170 C2 5 50 S 46 4W
Grajaú →, Brazil 170 B3 3 41 S 44 48W
Grajewo, Poland 54 E9 53 39N 22 30 E
Gramada, Bulgaria 50 C6 43 49N 22 39 E
Gramat, France 28 D5 44 48N 1 43 E
Grammichele, Italy 47 E7 37 13N 14 38 E
Grámmos, Óros, Greece 50 F4 40 18N 20 47 E
Grampian, U.S.A. 150 F6 40 58N 78 37W
Grampian Highlands = Grampian Mts., U.K. 22 E5 56 50N 4 0W
Grampian Mts., U.K. 22 E5 56 50N 4 0W
Grampians, The, Australia 128 D5 37 0 S 142 20 E
Gramsh, Albania 50 F4 40 52N 20 12 E
Gran, Norway 18 D7 60 23N 10 31 E
Gran →, Surinam 169 C6 4 1N 55 30W
Gran Altiplanicie Central, Argentina 176 C3 49 0 S 69 30W
Gran Canaria, Canary Is. 39 G4 27 55N 15 35W
Gran Chaco, S. Amer. 174 B3 25 0 S 61 0W
Gran Laguna Salada, Argentina 176 B3 44 24 S 67 23W
Gran Pajonal, Peru 172 C3 10 45 S 74 30W
Gran Paradiso, Italy 44 C4 45 33N 7 17 E
Gran Sasso d'Itália, Italy 45 F10 42 27N 13 42 E
Granada, Nic. 164 D2 11 58N 86 0W
Granada, Spain 43 H7 37 10N 3 35W
Granada, U.S.A. 155 F3 38 4N 102 19W
Granada □, Spain 43 H7 37 18N 3 0W
Granadilla de Abona, Canary Is. 39 F3 28 7N 16 33W
Granard, Ireland 23 C4 53 47N 7 30W
Granbury, U.S.A. 155 J6 32 27N 97 47W
Granby, Canada 140 C5 45 25N 72 45W
Granby, U.S.A. 158 F11 40 5N 105 56W
Grand →, Canada 150 D5 42 51N 79 34W
Grand →, Mich., U.S.A. 157 A10 43 4N 86 15W
Grand →, Mo., U.S.A. 156 E3 39 23N 93 7W
Grand →, S. Dak., U.S.A. 154 C4 45 40N 100 45W
Grand Bahama, Bahamas 164 A4 26 40N 78 30W
Grand Bank, Canada 141 C8 47 6N 55 48W
Grand Banks, Atl. Oc. 8 D3 45 0N 52 0W
Grand Bassam, Ivory C. 112 D4 5 10N 3 49W
Grand Batanga, Cameroon 114 B1 2 50N 9 55 E
Grand Bérèby, Ivory C. 112 E3 4 38N 6 55W
Grand Blanc, U.S.A. 157 B13 42 56N 83 38W
Grand-Bourg, Guadeloupe 165 C7 15 53N 61 19W
Grand Canal = Yun Ho →, China 75 E9 39 10N 117 10 E
Grand Canyon, U.S.A. 159 H7 36 3N 112 9W
Grand Canyon National Park, U.S.A. 159 H7 36 15N 112 30W
Grand Cayman, Cayman Is. 164 C3 19 20N 81 20W
Grand Centre, Canada 143 C6 54 25N 110 13W
Grand Cess, Liberia 112 E3 4 40N 8 12W
Grand Coulee, U.S.A. 158 C4 47 57N 119 0W
Grand Coulee Dam, U.S.A. 158 C4 47 57N 118 59W
Grand Erg du Bilma, Niger 109 E2 18 30N 14 0 E
Grand Erg Occidental, Algeria 111 B5 30 20N 1 0 E
Grand Erg Oriental, Algeria 111 C6 30 0N 6 30 E
Grand Falls, Canada 141 C6 47 3N 67 44W
Grand Falls-Windsor, Canada 141 C8 48 56N 55 40W
Grand Forks, Canada 142 D5 49 0N 118 30W
Grand Forks, U.S.A. 154 B6 47 55N 97 3W
Grand Gorge, U.S.A. 151 D10 42 21N 74 29W
Grand Haven, U.S.A. 157 A10 43 4N 86 13W
Grand I., Mich., U.S.A. 148 B2 46 31N 86 40W
Grand I., N.Y., U.S.A. 150 D6 43 0N 78 58W
Grand Island, U.S.A. 154 E5 40 55N 98 21W
Grand Isle, La., U.S.A. 155 L9 29 14N 90 0W
Grand Isle, Vt., U.S.A. 151 B11 44 43N 73 18W
Grand Junction, Colo., U.S.A. 159 G9 39 4N 108 33W
Grand Junction, Iowa, U.S.A. 156 B2 42 2N 94 14W
Grand L., N.B., Canada 141 C6 45 57N 66 7W
Grand L., Nfld., Canada 141 C8 49 0N 57 30W
Grand L., Nfld., Canada 141 B7 53 40N 60 30W
Grand L., La., U.S.A. 155 L8 29 55N 92 47W
Grand L., Ohio, U.S.A. 157 D12 40 32N 84 25W
Grand Lahou, Ivory C. 112 D3 5 10N 5 5W
Grand Lake, U.S.A. 158 F11 40 15N 105 49W
Grand Ledge, U.S.A. 157 B12 42 45N 84 45W
Grand-Lieu, L. de, France 26 E5 47 6N 1 40W
Grand Manan I., Canada 141 D6 44 45N 66 52W
Grand Marais, Canada 154 B9 47 45N 90 25W
Grand Marais, U.S.A. 148 B3 46 40N 85 59W
Grand-Mère, Canada 140 C5 46 36N 72 40W
Grand Popo, Benin 113 D5 6 15N 1 57 E
Grand Portage, U.S.A. 154 B10 47 58N 89 41W
Grand Prairie, U.S.A. 155 J6 32 47N 97 0W
Grand Rapids, Canada 143 C9 53 12N 99 19W
Grand Rapids, Mich., U.S.A. 157 B10 42 58N 85 40W
Grand Rapids, Minn., U.S.A. 154 B8 47 14N 93 31W
Grand Ridge, U.S.A. 152 E4 30 43N 85 1W
Grand River, U.S.A. 156 D3 40 49N 93 58W
Grand St-Bernard, Col du, Europe 32 E4 45 50N 7 10 E
Grand Santi, Fr. Guiana 169 C7 4 20N 54 24W
Grand Teton, U.S.A. 158 E8 43 54N 111 50W
Grand Teton National Park, U.S.A. 158 D8 43 50N 110 50W
Grand Union Canal, U.K. 21 E7 52 7N 0 53W
Grand View, Canada 143 C8 51 10N 100 42W
Grandas de Salime, Spain 42 B4 43 13N 6 53W
Grande →, Jujuy, Argentina 174 A2 24 20 S 65 2W
Grande →, Mendoza, Argentina 174 D2 36 52 S 69 45W
Grande →, Bolivia 173 D5 15 51 S 64 39W
Grande →, Bahia, Brazil 170 D3 11 30 S 44 30W
Grande →, Minas Gerais, Brazil 171 F1 20 6 S 51 4W
Grande →, Venezuela 169 B5 8 36N 61 39W
Grande, B., Argentina 176 D3 50 30 S 68 20W
Grande, I., Brazil 171 F3 23 9 S 44 14W
Grande, Rio →, U.S.A. 155 N6 25 58N 97 9W
Grande, Serra, Piauí, Brazil 170 C2 8 0 S 45 10W
Grande, Serra, Tocantins, Brazil 170 D2 11 15 S 46 30W
Grande Baleine, R. de la →, Canada 140 A4 55 16N 77 47W
Grande Cache, Canada 142 C5 53 53N 119 8W
Grande Dixence, Barr. de la, Switz. 32 D4 46 5N 7 23 E
Grande-Entrée, Canada 141 C7 47 30N 61 40W
Grande Prairie, Canada 142 B5 55 10N 118 50W
Grande-Rivière, Canada 141 C7 48 26N 64 30W
Grande-Vallée, Canada 141 C6 49 14N 65 8W
Grandfalls, U.S.A. 155 K3 31 20N 102 51W
Grândola, Portugal 43 G2 38 12N 8 35W
Grandpré, France 27 C11 49 20N 4 50 E
Grandson, Switz. 32 C3 46 49N 6 39 E
Grandview, Mo., U.S.A. 156 F2 38 53N 94 32W
Grandview, Wash., U.S.A. 158 C4 46 15N 119 54W
Grandview Heights, U.S.A. 157 E13 39 58N 83 2W
Grandvilliers, France 27 C8 49 40N 1 57 E
Graneros, Chile 174 C1 34 5 S 70 45W
Grangemouth, U.K. 22 E5 56 1N 3 42W
Granger, U.S.A. 158 F9 41 35N 109 58W
Grängesberg, Sweden 16 D9 60 6N 15 1 E
Grangeville, U.S.A. 158 D5 45 56N 116 7W
Granisle, Canada 142 C3 54 53N 126 13W
Granite City, U.S.A. 156 F6 38 42N 90 9W
Granite Falls, U.S.A. 154 C7 44 49N 95 33W
Granite L., Canada 141 C8 48 8N 57 5W
Granite Mt., U.S.A. 161 M10 33 5N 116 28W
Granite Pk., U.S.A. 158 D9 45 10N 109 48W
Graniteville, S.C., U.S.A. 152 B8 33 34N 81 49W
Graniteville, Vt., U.S.A. 151 B12 44 8N 72 29W
Granitnyy, Pik, Kyrgyzstan 63 D5 39 32N 70 20 E
Granitola, C., Italy 46 E5 37 34N 12 39 E
Granity, N.Z. 131 B6 41 39 S 171 51 E
Granja, Brazil 170 B3 3 7 S 40 50W
Granja de Moreruela, Spain 42 D5 41 48N 5 44W
Granja de Torrehermosa, Spain 43 G5 38 19N 5 35W
Gränna, Sweden 17 F8 58 1N 14 28 E
Granollers, Spain 40 D7 41 39N 2 18 E
Gransee, Germany 30 B9 53 1N 13 8 E
Grant, Fla., U.S.A. 153 H9 27 56N 80 32W
Grant, Nebr., U.S.A. 154 E4 40 53N 101 42W
Grant, Mt., U.S.A. 158 G4 38 34N 118 48W
Grant City, U.S.A. 156 D2 40 29N 94 25W
Grant I., Australia 124 B5 11 10 S 132 52 E
Grant Range, U.S.A. 159 G6 38 30N 115 25W
Grantham, U.K. 20 E7 52 55N 0 38W
Grantown-on-Spey, U.K. 22 D5 57 20N 3 36W
Grants, U.S.A. 159 J10 35 9N 107 52W
Grants Pass, U.S.A. 158 E2 42 26N 123 19W
Grantsville, U.S.A. 158 F7 40 36N 112 28W
Grantville, U.S.A. 152 B5 33 14N 84 50W
Granville, France 26 D5 48 50N 1 35W
Granville, Ill., U.S.A. 156 C7 41 16N 89 14W
Granville, N. Dak., U.S.A. 154 A4 48 16N 100 47W
Granville, N.Y., U.S.A. 151 C11 43 24N 73 16W
Granville, Ohio, U.S.A. 150 F2 40 4N 82 31W
Granville L., Canada 143 B8 56 18N 100 30W
Granvin, Norway 18 D3 60 33N 6 45 E
Graskop, S. Africa 117 C5 24 56 S 30 49 E
Gräsö, Sweden 16 D12 60 28N 18 35 E
Grass →, Canada 143 B9 56 3N 96 33W
Grass Range, U.S.A. 158 C9 47 0N 109 0W
Grass River Prov. Park, Canada 143 C8 54 40N 100 50W
Grass Valley, Calif., U.S.A. 160 F6 39 13N 121 4W
Grass Valley, Oreg., U.S.A. 158 D3 45 22N 120 47W
Grassano, Italy 47 B9 40 38N 16 17 E
Grasse, France 29 E10 43 38N 6 56 E
Grassflat, U.S.A. 150 F6 41 0N 78 6W
Grasslands Nat. Park, Canada 143 D7 49 11N 107 38W
Grassmere, Australia 128 A5 31 24 S 142 38 E
Grassy, Australia 126 G3 40 3 S 144 5 E
Gråsten, Denmark 17 K3 54 55N 9 35 E
Grästorp, Sweden 17 F6 58 20N 12 40 E
Gratis, U.S.A. 157 E12 39 38N 84 32W
Gratkorn, Austria 34 D8 47 8N 15 21 E
Gratz, U.S.A. 157 F12 38 28N 84 57W
Graubünden □, Switz. 33 C9 46 45N 9 30 E
Graulhet, France 28 E5 43 45N 1 59 E
Graus, Spain 40 C5 42 11N 0 20 E
Gravatá, Brazil 170 C4 8 10 S 35 29W
Gravberget, Norway 18 D9 60 53N 12 14 E
Grave, Pte. de, France 28 C2 45 34N 1 4W
Gravelbourg, Canada 143 D7 49 50N 106 35W
Gravelines, France 27 A9 51 1N 2 10 E
's-Gravenhage, Neths. 24 B4 52 7N 4 17 E
Gravenhurst, Canada 140 D4 44 52N 79 20W
Gravesend, Australia 127 D5 29 35 S 150 20 E
Gravesend, U.K. 21 F8 51 26N 0 22 E
Gravina in Púglia, Italy 47 B9 40 49N 16 25 E
Gravois, Pointe-à-, Haiti 165 C5 18 15N 73 56W
Gravone →, France 29 G12 41 58N 8 45 E
Gray, France 27 E12 47 22N 5 35 E
Gray, U.S.A. 152 B6 33 1N 83 32W
Grayling, Alaska, U.S.A. 144 E7 62 57N 160 3W
Grayling, Mich., U.S.A. 148 C3 44 40N 84 43W
Grays Harbor, U.S.A. 158 C1 46 59N 124 1W
Grays L., U.S.A. 158 E8 43 4N 111 26W
Grays River, U.S.A. 160 D3 46 21N 123 37W
Grayville, U.S.A. 157 F9 38 16N 88 0W
Grayvoron, Russia 59 G8 50 29N 35 41 E
Graz, Austria 34 D8 47 4N 15 27 E
Grdelica, Serbia, Yug. 50 D6 42 55N 22 3 E
Greåker, Norway 18 E8 59 16N 11 12 E
Greasy L., Canada 142 A4 62 55N 122 12W
Great Abaco I., Bahamas 164 A4 26 25N 77 10W
Great Artesian Basin, Australia 126 C3 23 0 S 144 0 E
Great Australian Bight, Australia 125 F5 33 30 S 130 0 E
Great Bahama Bank, Bahamas 164 B4 23 15N 78 0W
Great Barrier I., N.Z. 130 C4 36 11 S 175 25 E
Great Barrier Reef, Australia 126 B4 18 0 S 146 50 E
Great Barrington, U.S.A. 151 D11 42 12N 73 22W
Great Basin, U.S.A. 158 G5 40 0N 117 0W
Great Basin Nat. Park, U.S.A. 158 G6 38 55N 114 14W
Great Basses, Sri Lanka 95 L5 6 11N 81 29 E
Great Bear →, Canada 138 B7 65 0N 124 0W
Great Bear L., Canada 138 B7 65 30N 120 0W
Great Belt = Store Bælt, Denmark 17 J4 55 20N 11 0 E
Great Bend, Kans., U.S.A. 154 F5 38 22N 98 46W
Great Bend, Pa., U.S.A. 151 E9 41 58N 75 45W
Great Blasket I., Ireland 23 D1 52 6N 10 32W
Great Britain, Europe 12 E5 54 0N 2 15W
Great Codroy, Canada 141 C8 47 51N 59 16W
Great Dividing Ra., Australia 126 C4 23 0 S 146 0 E
Great Driffield = Driffield, U.K. 20 C7 54 0N 0 26W
Great Exuma I., Bahamas 164 B4 23 30N 75 50W
Great Falls, U.S.A. 158 C8 47 30N 111 17W
Great Fish = Groot Vis →, S. Africa 116 E4 33 28 S 27 5 E
Great Guana Cay, Bahamas 164 B4 24 0N 76 20W
Great Inagua I., Bahamas 165 B5 21 0N 73 20W
Great Indian Desert = Thar Desert, India 92 F5 28 0N 72 0 E
Great Karoo, S. Africa 116 E3 31 55 S 21 0 E
Great Lake, Australia 126 G4 41 50 S 146 40 E
Great Lakes, N. Amer. 136 E11 46 0N 84 0W
Great Malvern, U.K. 21 E5 52 7N 2 18W
Great Miami →, U.S.A. 148 F3 39 20N 84 40W
Great Ormes Head, U.K. 20 D4 53 20N 3 52W
Great Ouse →, U.K. 20 E8 52 48N 0 21 E
Great Palm I., Australia 126 B4 18 45 S 146 40 E
Great Papuan Plateau, Papua N. G. 132 D2 6 30 S 142 25 E
Great Plains, N. Amer. 136 E9 47 0N 105 0W
Great Ruaha →, Tanzania 118 D4 7 56 S 37 52 E
Great Sacandaga Res., U.S.A. 151 C10 43 6N 74 16W
Great Saint Bernard Pass = Grand St-Bernard, Col du, Europe 32 E4 45 50N 7 10 E
Great Salt L., U.S.A. 158 F7 41 15N 112 40W
Great Salt Lake Desert, U.S.A. 158 F7 40 50N 113 30W
Great Salt Plains L., U.S.A. 155 G5 36 45N 98 8W
Great Sandy Desert, Australia 124 D3 21 0 S 124 0 E
Great Sangi = Sangihe, Pulau, Indonesia 79 D7 3 45N 125 30 E
Great Scarcies →, S. Leone 112 D2 9 0N 13 0W
Great Sea Reef, Fiji 133 A2 16 15 S 179 0 E
Great Skellig, Ireland 23 E1 51 47N 10 33W
Great Slave L., Canada 142 A5 61 23N 115 38W
Great Smoky Mts. Nat. Park, U.S.A. 149 H4 35 40N 83 40W
Great Snow Mt., Canada 142 B4 57 26N 124 0W
Great Stour = Stour →, U.K. 21 F9 51 18N 1 22 E
Great Victoria Desert, Australia 125 E4 29 30 S 126 30 E
Great Wall, China 74 E5 38 30N 109 30 E
Great Whernside, U.K. 20 C6 54 10N 1 58W
Great Yarmouth, U.K. 21 E9 52 37N 1 44 E
Greater Antilles, W. Indies 165 C5 17 40N 74 0W
Greater London □, U.K. 21 F7 51 31N 0 6W
Greater Manchester □, U.K. 20 D5 53 30N 2 15W
Greater Sunda Is., Indonesia 78 F4 7 0 S 112 0 E
Grebbestad, Sweden 17 F5 58 42N 11 15 E
Grebenka = Hrebenka, Ukraine 59 G7 50 9N 32 22 E
Greco, C., Cyprus 38 E13 34 57N 34 5 E
Greco, Mte., Italy 45 G10 41 48N 13 58 E
Gredos, Sierra de, Spain 42 E6 40 20N 5 0W
Greece, U.S.A. 150 C7 43 13N 77 41W
Greece ■, Europe 48 B3 40 0N 23 0 E
Greeley, Colo., U.S.A. 154 E2 40 25N 104 42W
Greeley, Nebr., U.S.A. 154 E5 41 33N 98 32W
Greeleyville, U.S.A. 152 B10 33 40N 79 59W
Greem-Bell, Ostrov, Russia 64 A7 81 0N 62 0 E
Green, U.S.A. 158 E2 43 9N 123 22W
Green →, Ky., U.S.A. 148 G2 37 54N 87 30W
Green →, Utah, U.S.A. 159 G9 38 11N 109 53W
Green B., U.S.A. 148 C2 45 0N 87 30W
Green Bay, U.S.A. 148 C2 44 31N 88 0W
Green C., Australia 129 D9 37 13 S 150 1 E
Green City, U.S.A. 156 D4 40 16N 92 57W
Green Cove Springs, U.S.A. 152 F8 29 59N 81 42W
Green Is., Papua N. G. 132 C8 4 35 S 154 10 E
Green Island Bay, Phil. 81 F2 10 12N 119 22 E
Green Lake, Canada 143 C7 54 17N 107 47W
Green Mts., U.S.A. 151 C12 43 45N 72 45W
Green Pond, U.S.A. 152 C9 32 44N 80 37W
Green River, Utah, U.S.A. 159 G8 38 59N 110 10W
Green River, Wyo., U.S.A. 158 F9 41 32N 109 28W
Green Valley, U.S.A. 159 L8 31 52N 110 56W
Greenacres City, U.S.A. 153 J9 26 38N 80 7W
Greenbank, U.S.A. 160 B4 48 6N 122 34W
Greenbush, Mich., U.S.A. 150 B1 44 35N 83 19W
Greenbush, Minn., U.S.A. 154 A6 48 42N 96 11W
Greencastle, U.S.A. 157 E10 39 38N 86 52W
Greene, Iowa, U.S.A. 156 B4 42 54N 92 48W
Greene, N.Y., U.S.A. 151 D9 42 20N 75 46W
Greenfield, Calif., U.S.A. 160 J5 36 19N 121 15W
Greenfield, Calif., U.S.A. 161 K8 35 15N 119 0W
Greenfield, Ill., U.S.A. 156 E6 39 21N 90 12W
Greenfield, Ind., U.S.A. 157 E11 39 47N 85 46W
Greenfield, Iowa, U.S.A. 156 C2 41 18N 94 28W
Greenfield, Mass., U.S.A. 151 D12 42 35N 72 36W
Greenfield, Mo., U.S.A. 155 G8 37 25N 93 51W

220 Greenfield

Greenfield, *Ohio, U.S.A.* **157 E13** 39 21N 83 23W
Greenfield Park, *Canada* **151 A11** 45 29N 73 29W
Greenland ■, *N. Amer.* **10 D6** 66 0N 45 0W
Greenland Sea, *Arctic* **10 B10** 73 0N 10 0W
Greenock, *U.K.* **22 F4** 55 57N 4 46W
Greenore, *Ireland* **23 B5** 54 2N 6 8W
Greenore Pt., *Ireland* **23 D5** 52 14N 6 19W
Greenough, *Australia* **125 E1** 28 58 S 114 43 E
Greenough →, *Australia* **125 E1** 28 51 S 114 38 E
Greenough Pt., *Canada* **150 B3** 44 58N 81 26W
Greenport, *U.S.A.* **151 E12** 41 6N 72 22W
Greensboro, *Fla., U.S.A.* **152 E5** 30 34N 84 45W
Greensboro, *Ga., U.S.A.* **152 B6** 33 35N 83 11W
Greensboro, *N.C., U.S.A.* **149 G6** 36 4N 79 48W
Greensboro, *Vt., U.S.A.* **151 B12** 44 36N 72 18W
Greensburg, *Ind., U.S.A.* **157 E11** 39 20N 85 29W
Greensburg, *Kans., U.S.A.* **155 G5** 37 36N 99 18W
Greensburg, *Pa., U.S.A.* **150 F5** 40 18N 79 33W
Greenstone Pt., *U.K.* **22 D3** 57 55N 5 37W
Greentown, *U.S.A.* **157 D11** 40 29N 85 58W
Greenup, *U.S.A.* **157 E8** 39 15N 88 10W
Greenvale, *Australia* **126 B4** 18 59 S 145 7 E
Greenville, *Liberia* **112 D3** 5 1N 9 6W
Greenville, *Ala., U.S.A.* **149 K2** 31 50N 86 38W
Greenville, *Calif., U.S.A.* **160 E6** 40 8N 120 57W
Greenville, *Fla., U.S.A.* **152 E6** 30 28N 83 38W
Greenville, *Ga., U.S.A.* **152 B5** 33 2N 84 43W
Greenville, *Ill., U.S.A.* **156 F7** 38 53N 89 25W
Greenville, *Ind., U.S.A.* **157 F11** 38 22N 85 59W
Greenville, *Maine, U.S.A.* **149 C11** 45 28N 69 35W
Greenville, *Mich., U.S.A.* **157 A11** 43 11N 85 15W
Greenville, *Miss., U.S.A.* **155 J9** 33 24N 91 4W
Greenville, *Mo., U.S.A.* **155 G9** 37 8N 90 27W
Greenville, *N.C., U.S.A.* **149 H7** 35 37N 77 23W
Greenville, *N.H., U.S.A.* **151 D13** 42 46N 71 49W
Greenville, *N.Y., U.S.A.* **151 D10** 42 25N 74 1W
Greenville, *Ohio, U.S.A.* **157 D12** 40 6N 84 38W
Greenville, *Pa., U.S.A.* **150 E4** 41 24N 80 23W
Greenville, *S.C., U.S.A.* **149 H4** 34 51N 82 24W
Greenville, *Tenn., U.S.A.* **149 G4** 36 13N 82 51W
Greenville, *Tex., U.S.A.* **155 J6** 33 8N 96 7W
Greenwater Lake Prov. Park, *Canada* **143 C8** 52 32N 103 30W
Greenwich, *U.K.* **21 F8** 51 29N 0 1 E
Greenwich, *Conn., U.S.A.* **151 E11** 41 2N 73 38W
Greenwich, *N.Y., U.S.A.* **151 C11** 43 5N 73 30W
Greenwich, *Ohio, U.S.A.* **150 E2** 41 2N 82 31W
Greenwood, *Canada* **142 D5** 49 10N 118 40W
Greenwood, *Ark., U.S.A.* **155 H7** 35 13N 94 16W
Greenwood, *Fla., U.S.A.* **152 E4** 30 52N 85 10W
Greenwood, *Ind., U.S.A.* **157 E10** 39 37N 86 7W
Greenwood, *Miss., U.S.A.* **155 J9** 33 31N 90 11W
Greenwood, *S.C., U.S.A.* **149 H4** 34 12N 82 10W
Greenwood, Mt., *Australia* **124 B5** 13 48 S 130 4 E
Gregbe, *Ivory C.* **112 D3** 6 48N 6 43W
Gregório →, *Brazil* **172 B3** 6 50 S 70 46W
Gregory, *U.S.A.* **154 D5** 43 14N 99 20W
Gregory →, *Australia* **126 B2** 17 53 S 139 17 E
Gregory, L., *S. Austral., Australia* **127 D2** 28 55 S 139 0 E
Gregory, L., *W. Austral., Australia* **125 E2** 25 38 S 119 58 E
Gregory Downs, *Australia* **126 B2** 18 35 S 138 45 E
Gregory L., *Australia* **124 D4** 20 0 S 127 40 E
Gregory Ra., *Queens., Australia* **126 B3** 19 30 S 143 40 E
Gregory Ra., *W. Austral., Australia* **124 D3** 21 20 S 121 12 E
Greiffenberg, *Germany* **30 B9** 53 5N 13 57 E
Greifswald, *Germany* **30 A9** 54 5N 13 23 E
Greifswalder Bodden, *Germany* **30 A9** 54 12N 13 35 E
Grein, *Austria* **34 C7** 48 14N 14 51 E
Greiz, *Germany* **30 E8** 50 39N 12 10 E
Gremikha, *Russia* **56 A6** 67 59N 39 47 E
Gremyachinsk, *Russia* **62 B6** 58 34N 57 51 E
Grenå, *Denmark* **17 H4** 56 25N 10 53 E
Grenada, *U.S.A.* **155 J10** 33 47N 89 49W
Grenada ■, *W. Indies* **165 D7** 12 10N 61 40W
Grenade, *France* **28 E5** 43 47N 1 17 E
Grenadier I., *U.S.A.* **151 B8** 44 3N 76 22W
Grenadines, *W. Indies* **165 D7** 12 40N 61 20W
Grenchen, *Switz.* **32 B4** 47 12N 7 24 E
Grenen, *Denmark* **17 G4** 57 44N 10 40 E
Grenfell, *Australia* **129 B8** 33 52 S 148 8 E
Grenfell, *Canada* **143 C8** 50 30N 102 56W
Grenivík, *Iceland* **11 B8** 65 57N 18 11W
Grenjaðarstaður, *Iceland* **11 B9** 65 49N 17 21W
Grenoble, *France* **29 C9** 45 12N 5 42 E
Grenville, C., *Australia* **126 A3** 12 0 S 143 13 E
Grenville Chan., *Canada* **142 C3** 53 40N 129 46W
Gréoux-les-Bains, *France* **29 E9** 43 45N 5 52 E
Gresham, *U.S.A.* **160 E4** 45 30N 122 26W
Gresik, *Indonesia* **79 G15** 7 13 S 112 38 E
Gressan, *Italy* **32 E4** 45 43N 7 17 E
Gretna, *U.K.* **22 F5** 55 0N 3 3W
Gretna, *U.S.A.* **152 E5** 30 37N 84 40W
Greven, *Germany* **30 C3** 52 6N 7 37 E
Grevená, *Greece* **50 F5** 40 4N 21 25 E
Grevená □, *Greece* **50 F5** 40 2N 21 25 E
Grevenbroich, *Germany* **30 D2** 51 5N 6 35 E
Grevenmacher, *Lux.* **24 E6** 49 41N 6 26 E
Grevesmühlen, *Germany* **30 B7** 53 52N 11 12 E
Grevestrand, *Denmark* **17 J6** 55 36N 12 19 E
Grey →, *Canada* **141 C8** 47 34N 57 6W
Grey →, *N.Z.* **131 C6** 42 27 S 171 12 E
Grey, C., *Australia* **126 A2** 13 0 S 136 35 E
Grey Ra., *Australia* **127 D3** 27 0 S 143 30 E
Greybull, *U.S.A.* **158 D9** 44 30N 108 3W
Greymouth, *N.Z.* **131 C6** 42 29 S 171 13 E
Greystones, *Ireland* **23 C5** 53 9N 6 5W
Greytown, *N.Z.* **130 H4** 41 5 S 175 29 E
Greytown, *S. Africa* **117 D5** 29 1 S 30 36 E
Gribanovskiy, *Russia* **60 E5** 51 28N 41 50 E
Gribbell I., *Canada* **142 C3** 53 23N 129 0W
Gribës, Mal i, *Albania* **50 F3** 40 17N 19 45 E
Gribingui →, *C.A.R.* **114 A3** 8 33N 19 5 E
Gridley, *U.S.A.* **160 F5** 39 22N 121 42W
Griekwastad, *S. Africa* **116 D3** 28 49 S 23 15 E
Griesheim, *Germany* **31 F4** 49 51N 8 33 E
Grieskirchen, *Austria* **34 C6** 48 16N 13 48 E
Griffin, *U.S.A.* **152 B5** 33 15N 84 16W
Griffin, L., *U.S.A.* **153 G8** 28 52N 81 51W
Griffith, *Australia* **129 C7** 34 18 S 146 2 E
Griffith, *Canada* **150 A7** 45 15N 77 10W
Griffith I., *Canada* **150 B4** 44 50N 80 55W
Griggsville, *U.S.A.* **156 E6** 39 43N 90 43W
Grignols, *France* **28 D3** 44 23N 0 2W
Grigoriopol, *Moldova* **53 C14** 47 9N 29 18 E
Grimari, *C.A.R.* **114 A4** 5 43N 20 6 E
Grimaylov = Hrymayliv, *Ukraine* **59 H4** 49 20N 26 5 E
Grimes, *U.S.A.* **160 F5** 39 4N 121 54W
Grimma, *Germany* **30 D8** 51 14N 12 43 E
Grimmen, *Germany* **30 A9** 54 7N 13 3 E
Grimsay, *U.K.* **22 D1** 57 29N 7 14W
Grimsby, *Canada* **150 C5** 43 12N 79 34W
Grimsby, *U.K.* **20 D7** 53 34N 0 5W
Grimselpass, *Switz.* **33 C6** 46 34N 8 23 E
Grímsey, *Iceland* **11 A9** 66 33N 17 58W
Grimshaw, *Canada* **142 B5** 56 10N 117 40W
Grimslöv, *Sweden* **17 H8** 56 44N 14 34 E
Grímsstaðir, *Iceland* **11 B10** 65 39N 16 7W
Grimstad, *Norway* **15 G13** 58 20N 8 35 E
Grímsvötn, *Iceland* **11 C9** 64 26N 17 22W
Grindavík, *Iceland* **11 D4** 63 50N 22 26W
Grindelwald, *Switz.* **32 C6** 46 38N 8 2 E
Grindsted, *Denmark* **17 J2** 55 46N 8 55 E
Grindstone I., *Canada* **151 B8** 44 43N 76 14W
Grindu, *Romania* **53 F11** 44 44N 26 50 E
Grinnell, *U.S.A.* **156 C4** 41 45N 92 43W
Grintavec, *Slovenia* **45 B11** 46 22N 14 32 E
Gris-Nez, C., *France* **27 B8** 50 52N 1 35 E
Grisolles, *France* **28 E5** 43 49N 1 19 E
Grisons = Graubünden □, *Switz.* **33 C9** 46 45N 9 30 E
Grisslehamn, *Sweden* **16 D12** 60 5N 18 49 E
Grmeč Planina, *Bos.-H.* **45 D13** 44 43N 16 16 E
Groais I., *Canada* **141 B8** 50 55N 55 35W
Grobiņa, *Latvia* **54 B8** 56 33N 21 10 E
Groblersdal, *S. Africa* **117 D4** 25 15 S 29 25 E
Grobming, *Austria* **34 D6** 47 27N 13 54 E
Grocka, *Serbia, Yug.* **50 B4** 44 40N 20 42 E
Gródek, *Poland* **55 E10** 53 6N 23 40 E
Grodków, *Poland* **55 H4** 50 43N 17 21 E
Grodno = Hrodna, *Belarus* **58 F2** 53 42N 23 52 E
Grodzisk Mazowiecki, *Poland* **55 F7** 52 7N 20 37 E
Grodzisk Wielkopolski, *Poland* **55 F3** 52 15N 16 22 E
Grodzyanka = Hrodzyanka, *Belarus* **58 F5** 53 31N 28 42 E
Groesbeck, *U.S.A.* **155 K6** 30 48N 96 31W
Groix, *France* **26 E3** 47 38N 3 29W
Groix, Î. de, *France* **26 E3** 47 38N 3 28W
Grójec, *Poland* **55 G7** 51 50N 20 58 E
Gronau, *Niedersachsen, Germany* **30 C5** 52 5N 9 47 E
Gronau, *Nordrhein-Westfalen, Germany* **30 C3** 52 12N 7 2 E
Grong, *Norway* **14 D15** 64 25N 12 8 E
Grönhögen, *Sweden* **17 H10** 56 16N 16 24 E
Groningen, *Neths.* **24 A6** 53 15N 6 35 E
Groningen, *Surinam* **169 B6** 5 48N 55 28W
Groningen □, *Neths.* **24 A6** 53 16N 6 40 E
Grønnedal = Kangilinnguit, *Greenland* **10 E6** 61 20N 47 57W
Groom, *U.S.A.* **155 H4** 35 12N 101 6W
Groot →, *S. Africa* **116 E3** 33 45 S 24 36 E
Groot Berg →, *S. Africa* **116 E2** 32 47 S 18 8 E
Groot-Brakrivier, *S. Africa* **116 E3** 34 2 S 22 18 E
Groot Karasberge, *Namibia* **116 D2** 27 20 S 18 40 E
Groot-Kei →, *S. Africa* **117 E4** 32 41 S 28 22 E
Groot Vis →, *S. Africa* **116 E4** 33 28 S 27 5 E
Grootdrink, *S. Africa* **116 D3** 28 33 S 21 42 E
Groote Eylandt, *Australia* **126 A2** 14 0 S 136 40 E
Grootfontein, *Namibia* **116 B2** 19 31 S 18 6 E
Grootlaagte →, *Africa* **116 C3** 20 55 S 21 27 E
Grootvloer →, *S. Africa* **116 E3** 30 0 S 20 40 E
Gros C., *Canada* **142 A6** 61 59N 113 32W
Gros Morne Nat. Park, *Canada* **141 C8** 49 40N 57 50W
Grósio, *Italy* **44 B7** 46 18N 10 16 E
Grosne →, *France* **27 F11** 46 42N 4 56 E
Grosotto, *Italy* **33 D10** 46 17N 10 15 E
Grossa, Pta., *Spain* **39 B8** 39 6N 1 36 E
Grosse I., *U.S.A.* **157 B13** 42 8N 83 9W
Grossenbrode, *Germany* **30 A7** 54 21N 11 4 E
Grossenhain, *Germany* **30 D9** 51 17N 13 32 E
Grosser Arber, *Germany* **31 F9** 49 6N 13 8 E
Grosser Plöner See, *Germany* **30 A6** 54 10N 10 22 E
Grosseto, *Italy* **45 F8** 42 46N 11 8 E
Grossgerungs, *Austria* **34 C7** 48 34N 14 57 E
Grossglockner, *Austria* **34 D5** 47 5N 12 40 E
Groswater B., *Canada* **141 B8** 54 20N 57 40W
Grotli, *Norway* **18 B4** 62 2N 7 42 E
Groton, *Conn., U.S.A.* **151 E12** 41 21N 72 5W
Groton, *N.Y., U.S.A.* **151 D8** 42 36N 76 22W
Groton, *S. Dak., U.S.A.* **154 C5** 45 27N 98 6W
Grottáglie, *Italy* **47 B10** 40 32N 17 26 E
Grottaminarda, *Italy* **47 A8** 41 4N 15 2 E
Grottammare, *Italy* **45 F10** 42 59N 13 52 E
Grouard Mission, *Canada* **142 B5** 55 33N 116 9W
Grouin, Pte. du, *France* **26 D5** 48 43N 1 51W
Groundhog →, *Canada* **140 C3** 48 45N 82 58W
Grouw, *Neths.* **24 A5** 53 5N 5 51 E
Grove City, *Ohio, U.S.A.* **157 E13** 39 53N 83 6W
Grove City, *Pa., U.S.A.* **150 E4** 41 10N 80 5W
Grove Hill, *U.S.A.* **149 K2** 31 42N 87 47W
Groveland, *Calif., U.S.A.* **160 H6** 37 50N 120 14W
Groveland, *Fla., U.S.A.* **153 G8** 28 34N 81 51W
Grover City, *U.S.A.* **161 K6** 35 7N 120 37W
Groves, *U.S.A.* **155 L8** 29 57N 93 54W
Groveton, *U.S.A.* **151 B13** 44 36N 71 31W
Grovetown, *U.S.A.* **152 B7** 33 27N 82 12W
Grožnjan, *Croatia* **45 C10** 45 22N 13 43 E
Groznyy, *Russia* **61 J7** 43 20N 45 45 E
Grua, *Norway* **18 D7** 60 16N 10 40 E
Grubišno Polje, *Croatia* **52 E2** 45 44N 17 12 E
Grudovo, *Bulgaria* **51 D11** 42 21N 27 10 E
Grudusk, *Poland* **55 E7** 53 3N 20 38 E
Grudziądz, *Poland* **54 E5** 53 30N 18 47 E
Gruinard B., *U.K.* **22 D3** 57 56N 5 35W
Gruissan, *France* **28 E7** 43 8N 3 7 E
Grumo Áppula, *Italy* **47 A9** 41 1N 16 42 E
Grums, *Sweden* **16 E7** 59 22N 13 5 E
Grünberg, *Germany* **30 E4** 50 35N 8 58 E
Grund, *Iceland* **11 B8** 65 31N 18 9W
Gründau, *Germany* **31 E5** 50 10N 9 9 E
Grundy Center, *U.S.A.* **156 B4** 42 22N 92 47W
Grungedal, *Norway* **18 E4** 59 44N 7 43 E
Grünstadt, *Germany* **31 F4** 49 34N 8 9 E
Gruvberget, *Sweden* **16 C10** 61 6N 16 10 E
Gruver, *U.S.A.* **155 G4** 36 16N 101 24W
Gruyères, *Switz.* **32 C4** 46 35N 7 4 E
Gruža, *Serbia, Yug.* **50 C4** 43 54N 20 46 E
Gryazi, *Russia* **59 F10** 52 30N 39 58 E
Gryazovets, *Russia* **58 C11** 58 50N 40 10 E
Grybów, *Poland* **55 J7** 49 36N 20 55 E
Grycksbo, *Sweden* **16 D9** 60 40N 15 29 E
Gryfice, *Poland* **54 E2** 53 55N 15 13 E
Gryfino, *Poland* **55 E1** 53 16N 14 29 E
Gryfów Śląski, *Poland* **55 G2** 51 2N 15 24 E
Grythyttan, *Sweden* **16 E8** 59 41N 14 32 E
Gstaad, *Switz.* **32 D4** 46 28N 7 18 E
Gua Musang, *Malaysia* **87 K3** 4 53N 101 58 E
Guacanayabo, G. de, *Cuba* **164 B4** 20 40N 77 20W
Guacara, *Venezuela* **168 A4** 10 14N 67 53W
Guachípas →, *Argentina* **174 B2** 25 40 S 65 30W
Guachiría →, *Colombia* **168 B3** 5 27N 70 36W
Guadajoz →, *Spain* **43 H6** 37 50N 4 51W
Guadalajara, *Mexico* **162 C4** 20 40N 103 20W
Guadalajara, *Spain* **40 E1** 40 37N 3 12W
Guadalajara □, *Spain* **40 E2** 40 47N 2 30W
Guadalcanal, *Solomon Is.* **133 M11** 9 32 S 160 12 E
Guadalcanal, *Spain* **43 G5** 38 5N 5 52W
Guadalén →, *Spain* **43 G7** 38 5N 3 32W
Guadales, *Argentina* **174 C2** 34 30 S 67 55W
Guadalete →, *Spain* **43 J4** 36 35N 6 13W
Guadalimar →, *Spain* **43 G7** 38 5N 3 28W
Guadalmena →, *Spain* **43 G8** 38 19N 2 56W
Guadalmez →, *Spain* **43 G5** 38 46N 5 4W
Guadalope →, *Spain* **40 D4** 41 15N 0 3W
Guadalquivir →, *Spain* **43 J4** 36 47N 6 22W
Guadalupe = Guadeloupe ■, *W. Indies* **165 C7** 16 20N 61 40W
Guadalupe, *Brazil* **170 C3** 6 44 S 43 47W
Guadalupe, *Mexico* **161 N10** 32 4N 116 32W
Guadalupe, *Spain* **43 F5** 39 27N 5 17W
Guadalupe, *U.S.A.* **161 L6** 34 59N 120 33W
Guadalupe →, *Mexico* **161 N10** 32 6N 116 51W
Guadalupe →, *U.S.A.* **155 L6** 28 27N 96 47W
Guadalupe, Sierra de, *Spain* **43 F5** 39 28N 5 30W
Guadalupe Bravos, *Mexico* **162 A3** 31 20N 106 10W
Guadalupe I., *Pac. Oc.* **136 G8** 29 0N 118 50W
Guadalupe Mts. Nat. Park, *U.S.A.* **155 K2** 32 0N 104 30W
Guadalupe Peak, *U.S.A.* **155 K2** 31 50N 104 52W
Guadalupe y Calvo, *Mexico* **162 B3** 26 6N 106 58W
Guadarrama, Sierra de, *Spain* **42 E7** 41 0N 4 0W
Guadauta, *Georgia* **61 J5** 43 7N 40 32 E
Guadeloupe ■, *W. Indies* **165 C7** 16 20N 61 40W
Guadeloupe Passage, *W. Indies* **165 C7** 16 50N 62 15W
Guadelupe, *Peru* **172 B2** 7 15 S 79 29W
Guadiamar →, *Spain* **43 J4** 36 55N 6 24W
Guadiana →, *Portugal* **43 H3** 37 14N 7 22W
Guadiana Menor →, *Spain* **43 H7** 37 56N 3 15W
Guadiaro →, *Spain* **43 J5** 36 17N 5 17W
Guadiato →, *Spain* **43 H5** 37 48N 5 5W
Guadiela →, *Spain* **40 E2** 40 22N 2 49W
Guadix, *Spain* **43 H7** 37 18N 3 11W
Guafo, Boca del, *Chile* **176 B2** 43 35 S 74 0W
Guafo, I., *Chile* **176 B2** 43 35 S 74 50W
Guainía □, *Colombia* **168 C4** 2 30N 69 0W
Guainía →, *Colombia* **168 C4** 2 1N 67 7W
Guaíra, *Brazil* **175 A5** 24 5 S 54 10W
Guaíra □, *Paraguay* **174 B4** 25 45 S 56 30W
Guaitecas, Is., *Chile* **176 B2** 44 0 S 74 30W
Guajará-Mirim, *Brazil* **173 C4** 10 50 S 65 20W
Guajira □, *Colombia* **168 A3** 11 30N 72 30W
Guajira, Pen. de la, *Colombia* **168 A3** 12 0N 72 0W
Gualaceo, *Ecuador* **168 D2** 2 54 S 78 47W
Gualán, *Guatemala* **164 C2** 15 8N 89 22W
Gualdo Tadino, *Italy* **45 E9** 43 14N 12 47 E
Gualeguay, *Argentina* **174 C4** 33 10 S 59 14W
Gualeguaychú, *Argentina* **174 C4** 33 3 S 59 31W
Gualequay →, *Argentina* **174 C4** 33 19 S 59 39W
Gualicho, Salina, *Argentina* **176 B3** 40 25 S 65 20W
Gualjaina, *Argentina* **176 B2** 42 45 S 70 30W
Guam ■, *Pac. Oc.* **133 R15** 13 27N 144 45 E
Guamá, *Brazil* **170 B2** 1 37 S 47 29W
Guamá →, *Brazil* **170 B2** 1 29 S 48 30W
Guamblin, I., *Chile* **176 B1** 44 50 S 75 0W
Guaminí, *Argentina* **174 D3** 37 1 S 62 28W
Guamote, *Ecuador* **168 D2** 1 56 S 78 43W
Guampí, Sierra de, *Venezuela* **169 B4** 6 0N 65 35W
Guamúchil, *Mexico* **162 B3** 25 25N 108 3W
Guanabacoa, *Cuba* **164 B3** 23 8N 82 18W
Guanacaste, Cordillera del, *Costa Rica* **164 D2** 10 40N 85 4W
Guanaceví, *Mexico* **162 B3** 25 40N 106 0W
Guanahani = San Salvador I., *Bahamas* **165 B5** 24 0N 74 40W
Guanajay, *Cuba* **164 B3** 22 56N 82 42W
Guanajuato, *Mexico* **162 C4** 21 0N 101 20W
Guanajuato □, *Mexico* **162 C4** 20 40N 101 20W
Guanambi, *Brazil* **171 D3** 14 13 S 42 47W
Guanare, *Venezuela* **168 B4** 8 42N 69 12W
Guanare →, *Venezuela* **168 B4** 8 13N 67 46W
Guandacol, *Argentina* **174 B2** 29 30 S 68 40W
Guane, *Cuba* **164 B3** 22 10N 84 7W
Guang'an, *China* **76 B6** 30 28N 106 35 E
Guangchang, *China* **77 D11** 26 50N 116 21 E
Guangde, *China* **77 B12** 30 54N 119 25 E
Guangdong □, *China* **77 F9** 23 0N 113 0 E
Guangfeng, *China* **77 C12** 28 20N 118 15 E
Guanghan, *China* **76 B5** 30 58N 104 17 E
Guangling, *China* **74 E8** 39 47N 114 22 E
Guangnan, *China* **76 E5** 24 5N 105 4 E
Guangning, *China* **77 F9** 23 40N 112 22 E
Guangrao, *China* **75 F10** 37 5N 118 25 E
Guangshui, *China* **77 B9** 31 37N 114 0 E
Guangshun, *China* **76 D6** 26 8N 106 21 E
Guangwu, *China* **74 F3** 37 48N 105 57 E
Guangxi Zhuangzu Zizhiqu □, *China* **76 F7** 24 0N 109 0 E
Guangyuan, *China* **76 A5** 32 26N 105 51 E
Guangze, *China* **77 D11** 27 30N 117 12 E
Guangzhou, *China* **77 F9** 23 5N 113 10 E
Guanhães, *Brazil* **171 E3** 18 47 S 42 57W
Guanipa →, *Venezuela* **169 B5** 9 56N 62 26W
Guanling, *China* **76 E5** 25 56N 105 35 E
Guannan, *China* **75 G10** 34 8N 119 21 E
Guanta, *Venezuela* **169 A5** 10 14N 64 36W
Guantánamo, *Cuba* **165 B4** 20 10N 75 14W
Guantao, *China* **74 F8** 36 42N 115 25 E
Guanyang, *China* **77 E8** 25 30N 111 8 E
Guanyun, *China* **75 G10** 34 20N 119 18 E
Guapí, *Colombia* **168 C2** 2 36N 77 54W
Guápiles, *Costa Rica* **164 D3** 10 10N 83 46W
Guaporé, *Brazil* **175 B5** 28 51 S 51 54W
Guaporé →, *Brazil* **173 C4** 11 55 S 65 4W
Guaqui, *Bolivia* **172 D4** 16 41 S 68 54W
Guara, Sierra de, *Spain* **40 C4** 42 19N 0 15W
Guarabira, *Brazil* **170 C4** 6 51 S 35 29W
Guaranda, *Ecuador* **168 D2** 1 36 S 79 0W
Guarapari, *Brazil* **171 F3** 20 40 S 40 30W
Guarapuava, *Brazil* **171 G1** 25 20 S 51 30W
Guaratinguetá, *Brazil* **175 A6** 22 49 S 45 9W
Guaratuba, *Brazil* **175 B6** 25 53 S 48 38W
Guarda, *Portugal* **42 E3** 40 32N 7 20W
Guarda □, *Portugal* **42 E3** 40 40N 7 20W
Guardafui, C. = Asir, Ras, *Somali Rep.* **120 B4** 11 55N 51 10 E
Guardamar del Segura, *Spain* **41 G4** 38 5N 0 39W
Guardavalle, *Italy* **47 D9** 38 30N 16 30 E
Guárdia Sanframondi, *Italy* **47 A7** 41 15N 14 36 E
Guardiagrele, *Italy* **45 F11** 42 11N 14 13 E
Guardo, *Spain* **42 C6** 42 47N 4 50W
Guareña, *Spain* **43 G4** 38 51N 6 6W
Guareña →, *Spain* **42 D5** 41 29N 5 23W
Guárico □, *Venezuela* **168 B4** 8 40N 66 35W
Guarrojo →, *Colombia* **168 C3** 4 6N 70 42W
Guarujá, *Brazil* **175 A6** 24 2 S 46 25W
Guarus, *Brazil* **171 F3** 21 44 S 41 20W
Guasave, *Mexico* **162 B3** 25 34N 108 27W
Guascama, Pta., *Colombia* **168 C2** 2 32N 78 24W
Guasdualito, *Venezuela* **168 B3** 7 15N 70 44W
Guasipati, *Venezuela* **169 B5** 7 28N 61 54W
Guasopa, *Papua N. G.* **132 E7** 9 12 S 152 56 E
Guastalla, *Italy* **44 D7** 44 55N 10 39 E
Guatemala, *Guatemala* **164 D1** 14 40N 90 22W
Guatemala ■, *Cent. Amer.* **164 C1** 15 40N 90 30W
Guatire, *Venezuela* **168 A4** 10 28N 66 32W
Guaviare □, *Colombia* **168 C3** 2 0N 72 30W
Guaviare →, *Colombia* **168 C4** 4 3N 67 44W
Guaxupé, *Brazil* **175 A6** 21 10 S 47 5W
Guayabero →, *Colombia* **168 C3** 2 36N 72 47W
Guayaguayare, *Trin. & Tob.* **169 A5** 10 12N 61 3W
Guayama, *Puerto Rico* **165 C6** 17 59N 66 7W
Guayaneco, Arch., *Chile* **176 C1** 47 45 S 75 10W
Guayaquil, *Ecuador* **168 D2** 2 15 S 79 52W
Guayaquil, G. de, *Ecuador* **168 D1** 3 10 S 81 0W
Guayaramerín, *Bolivia* **173 C4** 10 48 S 65 23W
Guayas →, *Ecuador* **168 D2** 2 36 S 79 52W
Guaymas, *Mexico* **162 B2** 27 59N 110 54W
Guba, *Dem. Rep. of the Congo* **119 E2** 10 38 S 26 27 E
Guba, *Ethiopia* **107 E4** 11 17N 35 20 E
Gubakha, *Russia* **62 B6** 58 52N 57 36 E
Gûbâl, Madîq, *Egypt* **106 B3** 27 30N 34 0 E
Gubam, *Papua N. G.* **132 E1** 8 39 S 141 53 E
Gubat, *Phil.* **80 E5** 12 55N 124 7 E
Gubbi, *India* **95 H3** 13 19N 76 56 E
Gúbbio, *Italy* **45 E9** 43 21N 12 35 E
Guben, *Germany* **30 D10** 51 57N 14 42 E
Gubin, *Poland* **55 G1** 51 57N 14 43 E
Gubio, *Nigeria* **113 C7** 12 30N 12 42 E
Gubkin, *Russia* **59 G9** 51 17N 37 32 E
Guča, *Serbia, Yug.* **50 C4** 43 46N 20 15 E
Gucheng, *China* **77 A8** 32 20N 111 30 E
Gudå, *Norway* **18 A8** 63 27N 11 36 E
Gudalur, *India* **95 J3** 11 30N 76 29 E
Gudata = Guadauta, *Georgia* **61 J5** 43 7N 40 32 E
Gudbrandsdalen, *Norway* **15 F14** 61 33N 10 10 E
Gudenå →, *Denmark* **17 H4** 56 29N 10 13 E
Gudermes, *Russia* **61 J8** 43 24N 46 5 E
Gudhjem, *Denmark* **17 J8** 55 12N 14 58 E
Gudivada, *India* **95 F5** 16 30N 81 3 E
Gudiyattam, *India* **95 H4** 12 57N 78 55 E
Gudur, *India* **95 G4** 14 12N 79 55 E
Gudvangen, *Norway* **18 D3** 60 52N 6 49 E
Guebwiller, *France* **27 E14** 47 55N 7 12 E
Guecho = Getxo, *Spain* **40 B2** 43 21N 2 59W
Guékédou, *Guinea* **112 D2** 8 40N 10 5W
Guéle Mendouka, *Cameroon* **114 B2** 4 23N 12 55 E
Guelma, *Algeria* **111 A6** 36 25N 7 29 E
Guelph, *Canada* **140 D3** 43 35N 80 20W
Guemar, *Algeria* **111 B6** 33 30N 6 49 E
Guémené-Penfao, *France* **26 E5** 47 38N 1 50W
Guémené-sur-Scorff, *France* **26 D3** 48 4N 3 13W
Guéné, *Benin* **113 C5** 11 44N 3 16 E
Güeppí, *Peru* **168 D2** 0 7 S 75 15W
Guer, *France* **26 E4** 47 54N 2 8W
Güer Aike, *Argentina* **176 D3** 51 39 S 69 35W
Guera Pk., *Chad* **109 F3** 11 55N 18 12 E
Guérande, *France* **26 E4** 47 20N 2 26W
Guercif, *Morocco* **111 B4** 34 14N 3 21W
Guéréda, *Chad* **109 F4** 14 31N 22 5 E
Guéret, *France* **27 F8** 46 11N 1 51 E
Guérigny, *France* **27 E10** 47 6N 3 10 E
Guerneville, *U.S.A.* **160 G4** 38 30N 123 0W
Guernica = Gernika-Lumo, *Spain* **40 B2** 43 19N 2 40W
Guernsey, *U.K.* **21 H5** 49 26N 2 35W
Guernsey, *U.S.A.* **154 D2** 42 19N 104 45W
Guerrara, *Oasis, Algeria* **111 B5** 32 51N 4 22 E
Guerrara, *Saoura, Algeria* **111 C4** 28 5N 0 8W
Guerrero □, *Mexico* **163 D5** 17 30N 100 0W
Guerzim, *Algeria* **111 C4** 29 39N 1 40W
Guessou-Sud, *Benin* **113 C5** 10 3N 2 38 E
Gueugnon, *France* **27 F11** 46 36N 4 4 E
Guéyo, *Ivory C.* **112 D3** 5 25N 6 5W
Gufuðalur, *Iceland* **11 B4** 65 34N 22 25W
Gughe, *Ethiopia* **107 F4** 6 12N 37 30 E
Gūgher, *Iran* **97 D8** 29 28N 56 27 E
Guglionesi, *Italy* **45 G11** 41 55N 14 55 E
Guhakolak, Tanjung, *Indonesia* **79 G11** 6 50 S 105 14 E
Gui Jiang →, *China* **77 F8** 23 30N 111 15 E
Guia, *Canary Is.* **39 F4** 28 8N 15 38W
Guia de Isora, *Canary Is.* **39 F3** 28 12N 16 46W
Guia Lopes da Laguna, *Brazil* **175 A4** 21 26 S 56 7W
Guiana, *S. Amer.* **166 C4** 5 10N 60 40W
Guiana, *Venezuela* **169 B5** 5 9N 63 36W
Guibéroua, *Ivory C.* **112 D3** 6 14N 6 10W
Guichi, *China* **77 B11** 30 39N 117 27 E
Guider, *Cameroon* **113 D7** 9 56N 13 57 E
Guidiguir, *Niger* **113 C6** 13 40N 9 50 E
Guidimouni, *Niger* **113 C6** 13 42N 9 31 E
Guiding, *China* **76 D6** 26 34N 107 11 E
Guidong, *China* **77 D9** 26 7N 113 57 E
Guidónia-Montecélio, *Italy* **45 F9** 42 1N 12 45 E
Guiers, L. de, *Senegal* **112 B1** 16 10N 15 50W
Guigang, *China* **76 F7** 23 8N 109 35 E
Guiglo, *Ivory C.* **112 D3** 6 45N 7 30W
Guihulñgan, *Phil.* **81 F4** 10 7N 123 16 E
Guijá, *Mozam.* **117 C5** 24 27 S 33 0 E
Guijuelo, *Spain* **42 E5** 40 33N 5 40W
Guildford, *U.K.* **21 F7** 51 14N 0 34W
Guilford, *U.S.A.* **151 E12** 41 17N 72 41W
Guilin, *China* **77 E8** 25 18N 110 15 E
Guillaume-Delisle L., *Canada* **140 A4** 56 15N 76 17W
Guillaumes, *France* **29 D10** 44 5N 6 52 E
Guillestre, *France* **29 D10** 44 39N 6 40 E
Guilvinec, *France* **26 E2** 47 48N 4 17W
Güimar, *Canary Is.* **39 F3** 28 18N 16 24W
Guimarães, *Brazil* **170 B3** 2 9 S 44 42W
Guimarães, *Portugal* **42 D2** 41 28N 8 24W
Guimaras □, *Phil.* **79 B6** 10 35N 122 37 E
Guimba, *Phil.* **80 D3** 15 40N 120 46 E
Guinayangan, *Phil.* **80 E4** 13 54N 122 27 E
Guinda, *U.S.A.* **160 G4** 38 50N 122 12W
Guindulman, *Phil.* **81 G5** 9 46N 124 29 E
Guinea, *Africa* **104 F4** 8 0N 8 0 E
Guinea ■, *W. Afr.* **112 C2** 10 20N 11 30W
Guinea, Gulf of, *Atl. Oc.* **113 E5** 3 0N 2 30 E
Guinea-Bissau ■, *Africa* **112 C2** 12 0N 15 0W
Güines, *Cuba* **164 B3** 22 50N 82 0W
Guingamp, *France* **26 D3** 48 34N 3 10W
Guinguinéo, *Senegal* **112 C1** 14 20N 15 57W
Guinobatan, *Phil.* **80 E4** 13 11N 123 36 E
Guipavas, *France* **26 D2** 48 26N 4 29W
Guiping, *China* **77 F8** 23 21N 110 2 E
Guipúzcoa □, *Spain* **40 B2** 43 12N 2 15W
Guir, *Mali* **112 B4** 18 52N 2 52W
Guir, O. →, *Algeria* **111 B4** 31 29N 2 17W
Guiratinga, *Brazil* **173 D7** 16 21 S 53 45W
Guirel, *Mauritania* **112 B3** 15 30N 7 3W
Güiria, *Venezuela* **169 A5** 10 32N 62 18W
Guiscard, *France* **27 C10** 49 40N 3 1 E
Guise, *France* **27 C10** 49 52N 3 35 E
Guita-Koulouba, *C.A.R.* **114 A4** 5 58N 23 21 E
Guitiriz, *Spain* **42 B3** 43 11N 7 50W
Guitri, *Ivory C.* **112 D3** 5 30N 5 14W
Guiuan, *Phil.* **79 B7** 11 5N 125 55 E
Guixi, *China* **77 C11** 28 16N 117 15 E
Guiyang, *Guizhou, China* **76 D6** 26 32N 106 40 E
Guiyang, *Hunan, China* **77 E9** 25 46N 112 42 E
Guizhou □, *China* **76 D6** 27 0N 107 0 E
Gujan-Mestras, *France* **28 D2** 44 38N 1 4W
Gujar Khan, *Pakistan* **92 C5** 33 16N 73 19 E
Gujarat □, *India* **92 H4** 23 20N 71 0 E
Gujiang, *China* **77 D10** 27 11N 114 47 E

Ibshawâi 225

Hovd, *Mongolia* 72 B4 48 2N 91 37 E
Hovda, *Norway* 18 D6 60 53N 9 11 E
Hovden, *Aust-Agder, Norway* 18 E4 59 33N 7 22 E
Hovden, *Sogn og Fjordane, Norway* 18 C1 61 41N 4 52 E
Hove, *U.K.* 21 G7 50 50N 0 10W
Hovet, *Norway* 18 D5 60 38N 8 8 E
Hoveyzeh, *Iran* 97 D6 31 27N 48 4 E
Hovgaard Ø, *Greenland* 10 B9 79 55N 18 50W
Hovin, *Norway* 18 E6 59 51N 9 0 E
Hovmantorp, *Sweden* 17 H9 56 47N 15 7 E
Hövsgöl, *Mongolia* 74 C5 43 37N 109 39 E
Hövsgöl Nuur, *Mongolia* 72 A5 51 0N 100 30 E
Hovsta, *Sweden* 16 E9 59 22N 15 15 E
Howakil, *Eritrea* 107 D5 15 10N 40 16 E
Howar, Wadi →, *Sudan* 107 D2 17 30N 27 8 E
Howard, *Australia* 127 D5 25 16 S 152 32 E
Howard, *Pa., U.S.A.* 150 F7 41 1N 77 40W
Howard, *S. Dak., U.S.A.* 154 C6 44 1N 97 32W
Howe, *U.S.A.* 158 E7 43 48N 113 0W
Howe, C., *Australia* 129 D9 37 30 S 150 0 E
Howe I., *Canada* 151 B8 44 16N 76 17W
Howell, *U.S.A.* 157 B13 42 36N 83 56W
Howick, *Canada* 151 A11 45 11N 73 51W
Howick, *N.Z.* 130 C3 36 54 S 174 56 E
Howick, *S. Africa* 117 D5 29 28 S 30 14 E
Howick Group, *Australia* 126 A4 14 20 S 145 30 E
Howitt, L., *Australia* 127 D2 27 40 S 138 40 E
Howland I., *Pac. Oc.* 134 G10 0 48N 176 38W
Howrah = Haora, *India* 93 H13 22 37N 88 20 E
Howth Hd., *Ireland* 23 C5 53 22N 6 3W
Höxter, *Germany* 30 D5 51 46N 9 22 E
Hoy, *U.K.* 22 C5 58 50N 3 15W
Hoya, *Germany* 30 C5 52 49N 9 8 E
Høyanger, *Norway* 15 F12 61 13N 6 4 E
Hoyerswerda, *Germany* 30 D10 51 26N 14 14 E
Hoylake, *U.K.* 20 D4 53 24N 3 10W
Hoyleton, *Australia* 128 C3 34 2 S 138 34 E
Hoyos, *Spain* 42 E4 40 9N 6 45W
Hpa-an = Pa-an, *Burma* 90 G6 16 51N 97 40 E
Hpawlum, *Burma* 90 B7 27 12N 98 12 E
Hpettintha, *Burma* 90 C5 24 14N 95 23 E
Hpizow, *Burma* 90 B7 26 57N 98 24 E
Hradec Králové, *Czech Rep.* 34 A8 50 15N 15 50 E
Hrádek, *Czech Rep.* 35 C9 48 46N 16 16 E
Hrafnseyri, *Iceland* 11 B3 65 46N 23 28W
Hranice, *Czech Rep.* 35 B10 49 34N 17 45 E
Hrazdan, *Armenia* 61 K7 40 30N 44 46 E
Hrebenka, *Ukraine* 59 G7 50 9N 32 22 E
Hrífunes, *Iceland* 11 D8 63 38N 18 30W
Hrísey, *Iceland* 11 B8 66 0N 18 23W
Hrodna, *Belarus* 58 F2 53 42N 23 52 E
Hrodzyanka, *Belarus* 58 F5 53 31N 28 42 E
Hron →, *Slovak Rep.* 35 D11 47 49N 18 45 E
Hrubieszów, *Poland* 55 H10 50 49N 23 51 E
Hrubý Jeseník, *Czech Rep.* 35 A10 50 5N 17 10 E
Hrvatska = Croatia ■, *Europe* 45 C13 45 20N 16 0 E
Hrymayliv, *Ukraine* 59 H4 49 20N 26 5 E
Hsenwi, *Burma* 90 D6 23 22N 97 55 E
Hsiamen = Xiamen, *China* 77 E12 24 25N 118 4 E
Hsian = Xi'an, *China* 74 G5 34 15N 109 0 E
Hsinchu, *Taiwan* 77 E13 24 48N 120 58 E
Hsinhailien = Lianyungang, *China* 75 G10 34 40N 119 11 E
Hsinying, *Taiwan* 77 F13 23 18N 120 19 E
Hsipaw, *Burma* 90 D6 22 37N 97 18 E
Hsopket, *Burma* 76 F2 23 11N 98 26 E
Hsüchou = Xuzhou, *China* 75 G9 34 18N 117 10 E
Htawgaw, *Burma* 90 C7 25 57N 98 23 E
Hu Xian, *China* 74 G5 34 8N 108 42 E
Hua Hin, *Thailand* 78 B1 12 34N 99 58 E
Hua Xian, *Henan, China* 74 G8 35 30N 114 30 E
Hua Xian, *Shaanxi, China* 74 G5 34 30N 109 48 E
Hua'an, *China* 77 E11 25 1N 117 32 E
Huab →, *Namibia* 116 B2 20 52 S 13 25 E
Huacaya, *Bolivia* 173 E5 20 45 S 63 43W
Huachacalla, *Bolivia* 172 D4 18 45 S 68 17W
Huacheng, *China* 77 E10 24 4N 115 37 E
Huachinera, *Mexico* 162 A3 30 9N 108 55W
Huacho, *Peru* 172 C2 11 10 S 77 35W
Huachón, *Peru* 172 C2 10 35 S 76 0W
Huade, *China* 74 D7 41 55N 113 59 E
Huadian, *China* 75 C14 43 0N 126 40 E
Huadu, *China* 77 F9 23 22N 113 12 E
Huai He →, *China* 77 A12 33 0N 118 30 E
Huai Yot, *Thailand* 87 J2 7 45N 99 37 E
Huai'an, *Hebei, China* 74 D8 40 30N 114 20 E
Huai'an, *Jiangsu, China* 75 H10 33 30N 119 10 E
Huaibei, *China* 74 G9 34 0N 116 48 E
Huaibin, *China* 77 A10 32 32N 115 27 E
Huaide = Gongzhuling, *China* 75 C13 43 30N 124 40 E
Huaidezhen, *China* 75 C13 43 48N 124 50 E
Huaihua, *China* 76 D7 27 32N 109 57 E
Huaiji, *China* 77 F9 23 55N 112 12 E
Huainan, *China* 77 A11 32 38N 116 58 E
Huaining, *China* 77 B11 30 24N 116 40 E
Huairen, *China* 74 E7 39 48N 113 20 E
Huairou, *China* 74 D9 40 20N 116 35 E
Huaiyang, *China* 74 H8 33 40N 114 52 E
Huaiyin, *China* 75 H10 33 30N 119 2 E
Huaiyuan, *Anhui, China* 75 H9 32 55N 117 10 E
Huaiyuan, *Guangxi Zhuangzu, China* 76 E7 24 31N 108 22 E
Huajianzi, *China* 75 D13 41 23N 125 20 E
Huajuapan de Leon, *Mexico* 163 D5 17 50N 97 48W
Hualalai, *U.S.A.* 145 D6 19 42N 155 52W
Hualapai Peak, *U.S.A.* 159 J7 35 5N 113 54W
Hualien, *Taiwan* 77 E13 24 0N 121 30 E
Huallaga →, *Peru* 172 B2 5 15 S 75 30W
Huallanca, *Peru* 172 B2 8 50 S 77 56W
Huamachuco, *Peru* 172 B2 7 50 S 78 5W
Huambo, *Angola* 115 E3 12 42 S 15 54 E
Huambo □, *Angola* 115 E3 13 0 S 16 0 E
Huan Jiang →, *China* 74 G5 34 28N 109 0 E
Huan Xian, *China* 74 F4 36 33N 107 7 E
Huancabamba, *Peru* 172 B2 5 10 S 79 15W
Huancane, *Peru* 172 D4 15 10 S 69 44W
Huancapi, *Peru* 172 C3 13 40 S 74 0W
Huancavelica, *Peru* 172 C2 12 50 S 75 5W
Huancavelica □, *Peru* 172 C3 13 0 S 75 0W
Huancayo, *Peru* 172 C2 12 5 S 75 12W
Huanchaca, *Bolivia* 172 E4 20 15 S 66 40W
Huanchaca, Serranía de, *Bolivia* 173 C5 14 30 S 60 39W
Huang Hai = Yellow Sea, *China* 75 G12 35 0N 123 0 E
Huang He →, *China* 75 F10 37 55N 118 50 E
Huang Xian, *China* 75 F11 37 38N 120 30 E
Huangchuan, *China* 77 A10 32 15N 115 10 E
Huanggang, *China* 77 B10 30 29N 114 52 E
Huangguoshu, *China* 76 E5 26 0N 105 40 E
Huangling, *China* 74 G5 35 34N 109 15 E
Huanglong, *China* 74 G5 35 30N 109 59 E
Huanglongtan, *China* 77 A8 32 40N 110 33 E
Huangmei, *China* 77 B10 30 5N 115 56 E
Huangpi, *China* 77 B10 30 50N 114 22 E
Huangping, *China* 76 D6 26 52N 107 54 E
Huangshan, *China* 77 C12 29 42N 118 25 E
Huangshi, *China* 77 B10 30 10N 115 3 E
Huangsongdian, *China* 75 C14 43 45N 127 25 E
Huangyan, *China* 77 C13 28 38N 121 19 E
Huangyangsi, *China* 77 D8 26 33N 111 39 E
Huaning, *China* 76 E4 24 17N 102 56 E
Huanjiang, *China* 76 E7 24 50N 108 18 E
Huanta, *Peru* 172 C3 12 55 S 74 20W
Huantai, *China* 75 F9 36 58N 117 56 E
Huánuco, *Peru* 172 B2 9 55 S 76 15W
Huánuco □, *Peru* 172 B2 9 55 S 76 14W
Huanuni, *Bolivia* 172 D4 18 16 S 66 51W
Huanzo, Cordillera de, *Peru* 172 C3 14 35 S 73 20W
Huaping, *China* 76 D3 26 46N 101 25 E
Huara, *Chile* 172 D4 19 59 S 69 47W
Huaral, *Peru* 172 C2 11 32 S 77 13W
Huaraz, *Peru* 172 B2 9 30 S 77 32W
Huari, *Peru* 172 B2 9 14 S 77 14W
Huarmey, *Peru* 172 C2 10 5 S 78 5W
Huarochiri, *Peru* 172 C2 12 9 S 76 15W
Huarocondo, *Peru* 172 C3 13 26 S 72 14W
Huarong, *China* 77 C9 29 29N 112 30 E
Huascarán, *Peru* 172 B2 9 8 S 77 36W
Huascarán, Nevado, *Peru* 172 B2 9 7 S 77 37W
Huasco, *Chile* 174 B1 28 30 S 71 15W
Huasco →, *Chile* 174 B1 28 27 S 71 13W
Huasna, *U.S.A.* 161 K6 35 6N 120 24W
Huatabampo, *Mexico* 162 B3 26 50N 109 50W
Huauchinango, *Mexico* 163 C5 20 11N 98 3W
Huautla de Jiménez, *Mexico* 163 D5 18 8N 96 51W
Huaxi, *China* 76 D6 26 25N 106 40 E
Huay Namota, *Mexico* 162 C4 21 56N 104 30W
Huayin, *China* 74 G6 34 35N 110 5 E
Huayllay, *Peru* 172 C2 11 3 S 76 21W
Huayuan, *China* 76 C7 28 37N 109 29 E
Huayuan, *China* 76 B6 30 14N 106 40 E
Huazhou, *China* 77 G8 21 33N 110 33 E
Hubbard, *Iowa, U.S.A.* 156 B3 42 18N 93 18W
Hubbard, *Ohio, U.S.A.* 150 E4 41 9N 80 34W
Hubbard, *Tex., U.S.A.* 155 K6 31 51N 96 48W
Hubbart Pt., *Canada* 143 B10 59 21N 94 41W
Hubei □, *China* 77 B9 31 0N 112 0 E
Hubli, *India* 95 G2 15 22N 75 15 E
Huch'ang, *N. Korea* 75 D14 41 25N 127 2 E
Hucknall, *U.K.* 20 D6 53 3N 1 13W
Huddersfield, *U.K.* 20 D6 53 39N 1 47W
Hude, *Germany* 30 B4 53 7N 8 26 E
Hudi, *Sudan* 106 D3 17 43N 34 18 E
Hudiksvall, *Sweden* 16 C11 61 43N 17 10 E
Hudson, *Canada* 140 B1 50 6N 92 9W
Hudson, *Fla., U.S.A.* 153 G7 28 22N 82 42W
Hudson, *Mass., U.S.A.* 151 D13 42 23N 71 34W
Hudson, *Mich., U.S.A.* 157 C12 41 51N 84 21W
Hudson, *N.Y., U.S.A.* 151 D11 42 15N 73 46W
Hudson, *Wis., U.S.A.* 154 C8 44 58N 92 45W
Hudson, *Wyo., U.S.A.* 158 E9 42 54N 108 35W
Hudson →, *U.S.A.* 151 F10 40 42N 74 2W
Hudson Bay, *N.W.T., Canada* 139 C11 60 0N 86 0W
Hudson Bay, *Sask., Canada* 143 C8 52 51N 102 23W
Hudson Falls, *U.S.A.* 151 C11 43 18N 73 35W
Hudson Mts., *Antarctica* 7 D16 74 32 S 99 20W
Hudson Str., *Canada* 139 B13 62 0N 70 0W
Hudson's Hope, *Canada* 142 B4 56 0N 121 54W
Hudsonville, *U.S.A.* 157 B11 42 52N 85 52W
Hue, *Vietnam* 78 A3 16 30N 107 35 E
Huebra →, *Spain* 42 D4 41 2N 6 48W
Huechucuicui, Pta., *Chile* 176 B2 41 48 S 74 2W
Huedin, *Romania* 52 D8 46 52N 23 2 E
Huehuetenango, *Guatemala* 164 C1 15 20N 91 28W
Huejúcar, *Mexico* 162 C4 22 21N 103 13W
Huélamo, *Spain* 40 E3 40 17N 1 48W
Huelgoat, *France* 26 D3 48 22N 3 46W
Huelma, *Spain* 43 H7 37 39N 3 28W
Huelva, *Spain* 43 H4 37 18N 6 57W
Huelva □, *Spain* 43 H4 37 40N 7 0W
Huelva →, *Spain* 43 H5 37 27N 6 0W
Huentelauquén, *Chile* 174 C1 31 38 S 71 33W
Huércal-Overa, *Spain* 41 H3 37 23N 1 57W
Huerta, Sa. de la, *Argentina* 174 C2 31 10 S 67 30W
Huertas, C. de las, *Spain* 41 G4 38 21N 0 24W
Huerva →, *Spain* 40 D4 41 39N 0 52W
Huesca, *Spain* 40 C4 42 8N 0 25W
Huesca □, *Spain* 40 C5 42 20N 0 1 E
Huéscar, *Spain* 41 H2 37 44N 2 35W
Huetamo, *Mexico* 162 D4 18 36N 100 54W
Huete, *Spain* 40 E2 40 10N 2 43W
Huger, *U.S.A.* 152 B10 33 6N 79 48W
Hugh →, *Australia* 126 D1 25 1 S 134 1 E
Hughenden, *Australia* 126 C3 20 52 S 144 10 E
Hughes, *Australia* 125 F4 30 42 S 129 31 E
Hughesville, *U.S.A.* 151 E8 41 14N 76 44W
Hugli →, *India* 93 J13 21 56N 88 4 E
Hugo, *Colo., U.S.A.* 154 F3 39 8N 103 28W
Hugo, *Okla., U.S.A.* 155 H7 34 1N 95 31W
Hugoton, *U.S.A.* 155 G4 37 11N 101 21W
Hui Xian = Huixian, *China* 74 G7 35 27N 113 12 E
Hui Xian, *China* 74 H4 33 50N 106 4 E
Hui'an, *China* 77 E12 25 1N 118 43 E
Hui'anbu, *China* 74 F4 37 28N 106 38 E
Huiarau Ra., *N.Z.* 130 E5 38 45 S 176 55 E
Huichang, *China* 77 E10 25 32N 115 45 E
Huichapán, *Mexico* 163 C5 20 24N 99 40W
Huidong, *Guangdong, China* 77 F10 22 58N 114 43 E
Huidong, *Sichuan, China* 76 D4 26 34N 102 35 E
Huifa He →, *China* 75 C14 43 0N 127 50 E
Huíla, *Angola* 115 F2 15 4 S 13 32 E
Huila □, *Angola* 115 E2 14 0 S 15 0 E
Huila □, *Colombia* 168 C2 2 30N 75 45W
Huila, Nevado del, *Colombia* 168 C2 3 0N 76 0W
Huilai, *China* 77 F11 23 0N 116 18 E
Huili, *China* 76 D4 26 35N 102 17 E
Huimin, *China* 75 F9 37 27N 117 28 E
Huinan, *China* 75 C14 42 40N 126 2 E
Huinca Renancó, *Argentina* 174 C3 34 51 S 64 22W
Huining, *China* 74 G3 35 38N 105 0 E
Huinong, *China* 74 E4 39 5N 106 35 E
Huiroa, *N.Z.* 130 F3 39 15 S 174 30 E
Huisache, *Mexico* 162 C4 22 55N 100 25W
Huishui, *China* 76 D6 26 7N 106 38 E
Huisne →, *France* 26 E7 47 59N 0 11 E
Huiting, *China* 74 G9 34 5N 116 5 E
Huitong, *China* 76 D7 26 51N 109 45 E
Huixian, *China* 74 G7 35 27N 113 12 E
Huixtla, *Mexico* 163 D6 15 9N 92 28W
Huize, *China* 76 D4 26 24N 103 15 E
Huizhou, *China* 77 F10 23 0N 114 23 E
Hukeri, *India* 95 F2 16 14N 74 36 E
Hukou, *China* 77 C11 29 45N 116 21 E
Hukuntsi, *Botswana* 116 C3 23 58 S 21 45 E
Ḥulayfā', *Si. Arabia* 96 E4 25 58N 40 45 E
Huld = Ulaanjirem, *Mongolia* 74 B3 45 5N 105 30 E
Hulin He →, *China* 75 B12 45 0N 122 10 E
Hull = Kingston upon Hull, *U.K.* 20 D7 53 45N 0 21W
Hull, *Canada* 140 C4 45 25N 75 44W
Hull →, *U.K.* 20 D7 53 44N 0 20W
Hulst, *Neths.* 24 C4 51 17N 4 2 E
Hultsfred, *Sweden* 17 G9 57 30N 15 52 E
Hulun Nur, *China* 73 B6 49 0N 117 30 E
Hulyaypole, *Ukraine* 59 J9 47 45N 36 21 E
Humahuaca, *Argentina* 174 A2 23 10 S 65 25W
Humaitá, *Brazil* 173 B5 7 35 S 63 1W
Humaitá, *Paraguay* 174 B4 27 2 S 58 31W
Humansdorp, *S. Africa* 116 E3 34 2 S 24 46 E
Humansville, *U.S.A.* 156 G3 37 48N 93 35W
Humara, J., *Sudan* 107 D3 16 16N 30 59 E
Humbe, *Angola* 116 B1 16 40 S 14 55 E
Humber →, *U.K.* 20 D7 53 42N 0 27W
Humboldt, *Canada* 143 C7 52 15N 105 9W
Humboldt, *Iowa, U.S.A.* 156 B2 42 44N 94 13W
Humboldt, *Tenn., U.S.A.* 155 H10 35 50N 88 55W
Humboldt →, *U.S.A.* 158 F4 39 59N 118 36W
Humboldt Gletscher, *Greenland* 10 B4 79 30N 62 0W
Humboldt Mts., *N.Z.* 131 E3 44 30 S 168 15 E
Humbolt, Massif du, *N. Cal.* 133 U20 21 53 S 166 25 E
Hume, *U.S.A.* 160 J8 36 48N 118 54W
Hume, L., *Australia* 129 D7 36 0 S 147 5 E
Humenné, *Slovak Rep.* 35 C14 48 55N 21 50 E
Humeston, *U.S.A.* 156 D3 40 52N 93 30W
Hummelsta, *Sweden* 16 E10 59 34N 16 58 E
Hummelvik, *Norway* 18 A5 63 29N 8 19 E
Humpata, *Angola* 115 F2 15 2 S 13 24 E
Humphreys, Mt., *U.S.A.* 160 H8 37 17N 118 40W
Humphreys Peak, *U.S.A.* 159 J8 35 21N 111 41W
Humpolec, *Czech Rep.* 34 B8 49 31N 15 20 E
Humptulips, *U.S.A.* 160 C3 47 14N 123 57W
Humula, *Australia* 129 C7 35 30 S 147 46 E
Hūn, *Libya* 108 C3 29 2N 16 0 E
Hun Jiang →, *China* 75 D13 40 50N 125 38 E
Húnaflói, *Iceland* 11 B6 65 50N 20 50W
Hunan □, *China* 77 D9 27 30N 112 0 E
Húnavatnssýsla □, *Iceland* 11 B6 65 30N 20 25W
Hunchun, *China* 75 C16 42 52N 130 28 E
Hundested, *Denmark* 17 J5 55 58N 11 52 E
Hundewali, *Pakistan* 92 D5 31 55N 72 38 E
Hundorp, *Norway* 18 C6 61 33N 9 59 E
Hundred Mile House, *Canada* 142 C4 51 38N 121 18W
Hundvåg, *Norway* 18 E2 59 0N 5 43 E
Hunedoara, *Romania* 52 E7 45 40N 22 50 E
Hunedoara □, *Romania* 52 E7 45 50N 22 54 E
Hünfeld, *Germany* 30 E5 50 39N 9 46 E
Hung Yen, *Vietnam* 76 G6 20 39N 106 4 E
Hunga, *Tonga* 133 P13 18 41 S 174 7W
Hunga Ha'api, *Tonga* 133 Q13 20 41 S 175 7W
Hungary ■, *Europe* 35 D12 47 20N 19 20 E
Hungary, Plain of, *Europe* 12 F10 47 0N 20 0 E
Hungerford, *Australia* 127 D3 28 58 S 144 24 E
Hŭngnam, *N. Korea* 75 E14 39 49N 127 45 E
Hungt'ou Hsü, *Taiwan* 77 F13 22 0N 121 30 E
Hungund, *India* 95 F3 16 4N 76 3 E
Huni Valley, *Ghana* 112 D4 5 33N 1 56W
Hunneberg, *Sweden* 17 F6 58 18N 12 30 E
Hunnebostrand, *Sweden* 17 F5 58 27N 11 18 E
Hunsberge, *Namibia* 116 D2 27 45 S 17 12 E
Hunsrück, *Germany* 31 F3 49 56N 7 27 E
Hunstanton, *U.K.* 20 E8 52 56N 0 29 E
Hunsur, *India* 95 H3 12 16N 76 16 E
Hunte →, *Germany* 30 B4 53 14N 8 28 E
Hunter, *N.Z.* 131 E6 44 36 S 171 2 E
Hunter, *U.S.A.* 151 D10 42 13N 74 13W
Hunter →, *N.Z.* 131 E4 44 21 S 169 27 E
Hunter, C., *Solomon Is.* 133 M10 9 48 S 159 50 E
Hunter I., *Australia* 126 G3 40 30 S 144 45 E
Hunter I., *Canada* 142 C3 51 55N 128 0W
Hunter Mts., *N.Z.* 131 F2 45 43 S 167 25 E
Hunter Ra., *Australia* 129 B9 32 45 S 150 15 E
Hunters Road, *Zimbabwe* 119 F2 19 9 S 29 49 E
Hunterville, *N.Z.* 130 F4 39 56 S 175 35 E
Huntingburg, *U.S.A.* 157 F10 38 18N 86 57W
Huntingdon, *Canada* 140 C5 45 6N 74 10W
Huntingdon, *U.K.* 21 E7 52 20N 0 11W
Huntingdon, *U.S.A.* 150 F6 40 30N 78 1W
Huntington, *Ind., U.S.A.* 157 D11 40 53N 85 30W
Huntington, *Oreg., U.S.A.* 158 D5 44 21N 117 16W
Huntington, *Utah, U.S.A.* 158 G8 39 20N 110 58W
Huntington, *W. Va., U.S.A.* 148 F4 38 25N 82 27W
Huntington Beach, *U.S.A.* 161 M9 33 40N 118 5W
Huntington Station, *U.S.A.* 151 F11 40 52N 73 26W
Huntley, *U.S.A.* 157 B8 42 10N 88 26W
Huntly, *N.Z.* 130 D4 37 34 S 175 11 E
Huntly, *U.K.* 22 D6 57 27N 2 47W
Huntsville, *Canada* 140 C4 45 20N 79 14W
Huntsville, *Ala., U.S.A.* 149 H2 34 44N 86 35W
Huntsville, *Mo., U.S.A.* 156 E4 39 26N 92 33W
Huntsville, *Tex., U.S.A.* 155 K7 30 43N 95 33W
Hunyani →, *Zimbabwe* 119 F3 15 57 S 30 39 E
Hunyuan, *China* 74 E7 39 42N 113 42 E
Hunza →, *India* 93 B6 35 54N 74 20 E
Huo Xian = Huozhou, *China* 74 F6 36 36N 111 42 E
Huon G., *Papua N. G.* 132 D4 7 0 S 147 30 E
Huon Pen., *Papua N. G.* 132 D4 6 20 S 147 30 E
Huong Hoa, *Vietnam* 86 D6 16 37N 106 45 E
Huong Khe, *Vietnam* 86 C5 18 13N 105 41 E
Huonville, *Australia* 126 G4 43 0 S 147 5 E
Huoqiu, *China* 77 A11 32 20N 116 12 E
Huoshan, *Anhui, China* 77 A12 32 28N 118 30 E
Huoshan, *Anhui, China* 77 B11 31 25N 116 20 E
Huoshao Dao = Lü-Tao, *Taiwan* 77 F13 22 40N 121 30 E
Huozhou, *China* 74 F6 36 36N 111 42 E
Hupeh = Hubei □, *China* 77 B9 31 0N 112 0 E
Ḩūr, *Iran* 97 D8 30 50N 57 7 E
Hurbanovo, *Slovak Rep.* 35 D11 47 51N 18 11 E
Hurd, C., *Canada* 150 A3 45 13N 81 44W
Hure Qi, *China* 75 C11 42 45N 121 45 E
Hurezani, *Romania* 53 F8 44 49N 23 40 E
Hurghada, *Egypt* 106 B3 27 15N 33 50 E
Hurley, *N. Mex., U.S.A.* 159 K9 32 42N 108 8W
Hurley, *Wis., U.S.A.* 154 B9 46 27N 90 11W
Huron, *Calif., U.S.A.* 160 J6 36 12N 120 6W
Huron, *Ohio, U.S.A.* 150 E2 41 24N 82 33W
Huron, *S. Dak., U.S.A.* 154 C5 44 22N 98 13W
Huron, L., *U.S.A.* 150 B2 44 30N 82 40W
Hurricane, *U.S.A.* 159 H7 37 11N 113 17W
Hurso, *Ethiopia* 107 F5 9 35N 41 33 E
Hurstboro, *U.S.A.* 152 C4 32 15N 85 25W
Hurunui →, *N.Z.* 131 C8 42 54 S 173 18 E
Hurup, *Denmark* 17 H2 56 46N 8 25 E
Húsafell, *Iceland* 11 C6 64 42N 20 53W
Húsavík, *Iceland* 11 A9 66 3N 17 21W
Huşi, *Romania* 53 D13 46 41N 28 7 E
Huskvarna, *Sweden* 17 G8 57 47N 14 15 E
Husnes, *Norway* 18 E2 59 52N 5 45 E
Hustad, *Norway* 18 B4 62 57N 7 6 E
Hustadvika, *Norway* 14 E12 63 0N 7 0 E
Hustontown, *U.S.A.* 150 F6 40 3N 78 2W
Hustopeče, *Czech Rep.* 35 C9 48 57N 16 43 E
Husum, *Germany* 30 A5 54 28N 9 4 E
Husum, *Sweden* 16 A13 63 21N 19 12 E
Hutchinson, *Kans., U.S.A.* 155 F6 38 5N 97 56W
Hutchinson, *Minn., U.S.A.* 154 C7 44 54N 94 22W
Ḩūth, *Yemen* 98 C3 16 14N 43 58 E
Hutsonville, *U.S.A.* 157 E9 39 7N 87 40W
Hutte Sauvage, L. de la, *Canada* 141 A7 56 15N 64 45W
Hüttenberg, *Austria* 34 E7 46 56N 14 33 E
Hutton, Mt., *Australia* 127 D4 25 51 S 148 20 E
Huttwil, *Switz.* 32 B5 47 7N 7 50 E
Huwun, *Ethiopia* 107 G5 4 23N 40 6 E
Huy, *Belgium* 24 D5 50 31N 5 15 E
Huzhou, *China* 77 B13 30 51N 120 8 E
Huzurabad, *India* 94 E4 18 12N 79 25 E
Huzurnagar, *India* 94 F4 16 54N 79 53 E
Hvalpsund, *Denmark* 17 H3 56 42N 9 11 E
Hvammsfjörður, *Iceland* 11 B4 65 4N 22 5W
Hvammstangi, *Iceland* 11 B6 65 24N 20 57W
Hvammur, *Mýrasýsla, Iceland* 11 C5 64 50N 21 21W
Hvammur, *Skagafjarðarsýsla, Iceland* 11 B7 65 53N 19 51W
Hvanneyri, *Iceland* 11 C5 64 34N 21 36W
Hvar, *Croatia* 45 E13 43 11N 16 28 E
Hvarski Kanal, *Croatia* 45 E13 43 15N 16 35 E
Hveragerði, *Iceland* 11 C5 64 0N 21 12W
Hvítá →, *Iceland* 11 C5 64 30N 21 58W
Hvítárvatn, *Iceland* 11 C7 64 37N 19 50W
Hvittingfoss, *Norway* 18 E7 59 29N 10 0 E
Hvolsvöllur, *Iceland* 11 D6 63 45N 20 14W
Hwachŏn-chŏsuji, *S. Korea* 75 E14 38 5N 127 50 E
Hwang Ho = Huang He →, *China* 75 F10 37 55N 118 50 E
Hwange, *Zimbabwe* 119 F2 18 18 S 26 30 E
Hwange Nat. Park, *Zimbabwe* 116 B4 19 0 S 26 30 E
Hwekum, *Burma* 90 B5 26 7N 95 22 E
Hyannis, *Mass., U.S.A.* 148 E10 41 39N 70 17W
Hyannis, *Nebr., U.S.A.* 154 E4 42 0N 101 46W
Hyargas Nuur, *Mongolia* 72 B4 49 0N 93 0 E
Hybo, *Sweden* 16 C10 61 49N 16 15 E
Hydaburg, *U.S.A.* 142 B2 55 15N 132 50W
Hyde, *N.Z.* 131 F5 45 18 S 170 16 E
Hyde Park, *Guyana* 169 B6 6 30N 58 16W
Hyde Park, *U.S.A.* 151 E11 41 47N 73 56W
Hyden, *Australia* 125 F2 32 24 S 118 53 E
Hyder, *U.S.A.* 142 B2 55 55N 130 5W
Hyderabad, *India* 94 F4 17 22N 78 29 E
Hyderabad, *Pakistan* 91 D3 25 23N 68 24 E
Hyen, *Norway* 18 C2 61 44N 5 56 E
Hyères, *France* 29 E10 43 8N 6 9 E
Hyères, Îs. d', *France* 29 F10 43 0N 6 20 E
Hyesan, *N. Korea* 75 D15 41 20N 128 10 E
Hyland →, *Canada* 142 B3 59 52N 128 12W
Hylestad, *Norway* 18 E4 59 6N 7 29 E
Hyllestad, *Norway* 18 C2 61 10N 5 17 E
Hyltebruk, *Sweden* 17 H7 56 59N 13 15 E
Hymia, *India* 93 C8 33 40N 78 2 E
Hyndman Peak, *U.S.A.* 158 E6 43 45N 114 8W
Hynnekleiv, *Norway* 18 F5 58 36N 8 25 E
Hyōgo □, *Japan* 72 B4 35 15N 134 50 E
Hyrra Banda, *C.A.R.* 114 A4 5 58N 22 1 E
Hyrum, *U.S.A.* 158 F8 41 38N 111 51W
Hysham, *U.S.A.* 158 C10 46 18N 107 14W
Hythe, *U.K.* 21 F9 51 4N 1 5 E
Hyūga, *Japan* 70 E3 32 25N 131 35 E
Hyvinge = Hyvinkää, *Finland* 15 F21 60 38N 24 50 E
Hyvinkää, *Finland* 15 F21 60 38N 24 50 E

I

I-n-Échaï, *Mali* 110 D4 20 10N 2 5W
I-n-Gall, *Niger* 113 B6 16 51N 7 1 E
I-n-Oudad, *Algeria* 113 A5 20 17N 4 38 E
I-n-Ouzzal, *Algeria* 113 A5 20 40N 2 35 E
I-n-Tadreft, *Niger* 113 B6 19 5N 6 38 E
Iabès, Erg, *Algeria* 111 C4 27 30N 2 2W
Iablaniţa, *Romania* 52 F7 44 57N 22 19 E
Iaco →, *Brazil* 172 B4 9 3 S 68 34W
Iacobeni, *Romania* 53 C10 47 25N 25 20 E
Iaçu, *Brazil* 171 D3 12 45 S 40 13W
Iakora, *Madag.* 117 C8 23 6 S 46 40 E
Ialomiţa □, *Romania* 53 F12 44 30N 27 30 E
Ialomiţa →, *Romania* 53 F12 44 42N 27 51 E
Ialoveni, *Moldova* 53 D13 46 56N 28 47 E
Ialpug →, *Moldova* 53 E13 45 41N 28 35 E
Iamonia L., *U.S.A.* 152 E5 30 38N 84 14W
Ianca, *Romania* 53 E12 45 6N 27 29 E
Iara, *Romania* 53 D8 46 31N 23 35 E
Iarda, *Ethiopia* 107 E4 11 9N 35 53 E
Iargara, *Moldova* 53 D13 46 24N 28 23 E
Iaşi, *Romania* 53 C12 47 10N 27 40 E
Iaşi □, *Romania* 53 C12 47 20N 27 0 E
Íasmos, *Greece* 51 E9 41 8N 25 11 E
Iauaretê, *Colombia* 168 C4 0 36N 69 12W
Ib →, *India* 93 J10 21 34N 83 48 E
Iba, *Phil.* 79 A6 15 22N 120 0 E
Ibadan, *Nigeria* 113 D5 7 22N 3 58 E
Ibagué, *Colombia* 168 C2 4 20N 75 20W
Ibaiti, *Brazil* 171 F1 23 50 S 50 10W
Ibajay, *Phil.* 81 F4 11 49N 122 10 E
Iballja, *Albania* 50 D4 42 12N 20 2 E
Ibăneşti, *Botoşani, Romania* 53 B11 48 4N 26 22 E
Ibăneşti, *Mureş, Romania* 53 D9 46 45N 24 57 E
Ibanshe, *Dem. Rep. of the Congo* 115 C4 4 58 S 21 30 E
Ibar →, *Serbia, Yug.* 50 C4 43 43N 20 45 E
Ibara, *Japan* 70 C5 34 36N 133 28 E
Ibaraki, *Japan* 71 C7 34 49N 135 34 E
Ibaraki □, *Japan* 71 A12 36 10N 140 10 E
Ibarra, *Ecuador* 168 C2 0 21N 78 7W
Ibba, *Sudan* 107 G2 4 49N 29 2 E
Ibba, Bahr el →, *Sudan* 107 F2 5 30N 28 55 E
Ibbenbüren, *Germany* 30 C3 52 16N 7 43 E
Ibeke Gembo, *Dem. Rep. of the Congo* 114 C3 1 24 S 18 51 E
Ibembo, *Dem. Rep. of the Congo* 118 B1 2 35N 23 35 E
Ibenga →, *Congo* 114 B3 2 19N 18 9 E
Ibera, L., *Argentina* 174 B4 28 30 S 57 9W
Iberia, *U.S.A.* 156 F4 38 5N 92 18W
Iberian Peninsula, *Europe* 12 H5 40 0N 5 0W
Iberville, *Canada* 140 C5 45 19N 73 17W
Iberville, Lac d', *Canada* 140 A5 55 55N 73 15W
Ibi, *Nigeria* 113 D6 8 15N 9 44 E
Ibi, *Spain* 41 G4 38 38N 0 34W
Ibiá, *Brazil* 171 E2 19 30 S 46 30W
Ibicaraí, *Brazil* 171 D4 14 51 S 39 36W
Ibicuí, *Brazil* 171 D4 14 51 S 39 59W
Ibicuí →, *Brazil* 175 B4 29 25 S 56 47W
Ibicuy, *Argentina* 174 C4 33 55 S 59 10W
Ibioapaba, Sa. da, *Brazil* 170 B3 4 0 S 41 30W
Ibipetuba, *Brazil* 170 D3 11 0 S 44 32W
Ibitiara, *Brazil* 171 D3 12 39 S 42 13W
Ibiza = Eivissa, *Spain* 39 C7 38 54N 1 26 E
Íblei, Monti, *Italy* 47 E7 37 15N 14 45 E
Ibo, *Mozam.* 119 E5 12 22 S 40 40 E
Ibonma, *Indonesia* 79 E8 3 29 S 133 31 E
Ibotirama, *Brazil* 171 D3 12 13 S 43 12W
Ibrāhīm →, *Lebanon* 103 A4 34 4N 35 38 E
'Ibrī, *Oman* 97 F8 23 14N 56 30 E
İbriktepe, *Turkey* 51 E10 41 0N 26 30 E
Ibshawâi, *Egypt* 106 J7 29 21N 30 40 E

Iyo-mishima 227

Inowrocław, *Poland* **55 F5** 52 50N 18 12 E
Inpundong, *N. Korea* **75 D14** 41 25N 126 34 E
Inquisivi, *Bolivia* **172 D4** 16 50 S 67 10W
Ins, *Switz.* **32 B4** 47 1N 7 7 E
Inscription, C., *Australia* **125 E1** 25 29 S 112 59 E
Insein, *Burma* **90 G6** 16 50N 96 5 E
Insjön, *Sweden* **16 D9** 60 41N 15 6 E
Ińsko, *Poland* **54 E2** 53 25N 15 32 E
Însurăţei, *Romania* **53 F12** 44 50N 27 40 E
Inta, *Russia* **56 A11** 66 5N 60 8 E
Intendente Alvear, *Argentina* **174 D3** 35 12 S 63 32W
İntepe, *Turkey* **49 A8** 40 1N 26 20 E
Interlachen, *U.S.A.* **153 F8** 29 37N 81 53W
Interlaken, *Switz.* **32 C5** 46 41N 7 50 E
Interlaken, *U.S.A.* **151 D8** 42 37N 76 44W
International Falls, *U.S.A.* **154 A8** 48 36N 93 25W
Intiyaco, *Argentina* **174 B3** 28 43 S 60 5W
Întorsura Buzăului, *Romania* **53 E11** 45 41N 26 2 E
Intragna, *Switz.* **33 D7** 46 11N 8 42 E
Intutu, *Peru* **168 D3** 3 32 S 74 48W
Inubō-Zaki, *Japan* **71 B12** 35 42N 140 52 E
Inukjuak, *Canada* **139 C12** 58 25N 78 15W
Inútil, B., *Chile* **176 D2** 53 30 S 70 15W
Inuvik, *Canada* **138 B6** 68 16N 133 40W
Inuyama, *Japan* **71 B8** 35 23N 136 56 E
Inveraray, *U.K.* **22 E3** 56 14N 5 5W
Inverbervie, *U.K.* **22 E6** 56 51N 2 17W
Invercargill, *N.Z.* **131 G3** 46 24 S 168 24 E
Inverclyde □, *U.K.* **22 F4** 55 55N 4 49W
Inverell, *Australia* **127 D5** 29 45 S 151 8 E
Invergordon, *U.K.* **22 D4** 57 41N 4 10W
Inverleigh, *Australia* **128 E6** 38 6 S 144 3 E
Inverloch, *Australia* **127 F4** 38 38 S 145 45 E
Invermere, *Canada* **142 C5** 50 30N 116 2W
Inverness, *Canada* **141 C7** 46 15N 61 19W
Inverness, *U.K.* **22 D4** 57 29N 4 13W
Inverness, *Ala., U.S.A.* **152 C4** 32 1N 85 45W
Inverness, *Fla., U.S.A.* **149 L4** 28 50N 82 20W
Inverurie, *U.K.* **22 D6** 57 17N 2 23W
Investigator Group, *Australia* **127 E1** 34 45 S 134 20 E
Investigator Str., *Australia* **128 C2** 35 30 S 137 0 E
Inya, *Russia* **64 D9** 50 28N 86 37 E
Inyanga, *Zimbabwe* **119 F3** 18 12 S 32 40 E
Inyangani, *Zimbabwe* **119 F3** 18 5 S 32 50 E
Inyantue, *Zimbabwe* **116 B4** 18 33 S 26 39 E
Inyo Mts., *U.S.A.* **160 J9** 36 40N 118 0W
Inyokern, *U.S.A.* **161 K9** 35 39N 117 49W
Inywa, *Burma* **90 D6** 23 56N 96 17 E
Inza, *Russia* **60 D8** 53 55N 46 25 E
Inzer, *Russia* **62 D6** 54 14N 57 34 E
Inzhavino, *Russia* **60 D6** 52 22N 42 30 E
Inzia →, *Dem. Rep. of the Congo* **115 C3** 3 45 S 17 57 E
Iō-Jima, *Japan* **69 J5** 30 48N 130 18 E
Ioánnina, *Greece* **48 B2** 39 42N 20 47 E
Ioánnina □, *Greece* **48 B2** 39 39N 20 57 E
Iola, *U.S.A.* **155 G7** 37 55N 95 24W
Ioma, *Papua N. G.* **132 E4** 8 19 S 147 52 E
Ion Corvin, *Romania* **53 F12** 44 7N 27 50 E
Iôna, *Angola* **115 F2** 16 54 S 12 34 E
Iona, *U.K.* **22 E2** 56 20N 6 25W
Ione, *U.S.A.* **160 G6** 38 21N 120 56W
Iongo, *Angola* **115 D3** 9 11 S 17 45 E
Ionia, *U.S.A.* **157 B11** 42 59N 85 4W
Ionian Is. = Iónioi Nísoi, *Greece* **48 C2** 38 40N 20 0 E
Ionian Sea, *Medit. S.* **12 H9** 37 30N 17 30 E
Iónioi Nísoi, *Greece* **48 C2** 38 40N 20 0 E
Íonioi Nísoi □, *Greece* **48 C2** 38 40N 20 0 E
Íos, *Greece* **49 E7** 36 41N 25 20 E
Iowa □, *U.S.A.* **156 C3** 42 18N 93 30W
Iowa →, *U.S.A.* **156 C5** 41 10N 91 1W
Iowa City, *U.S.A.* **156 C5** 41 40N 91 32W
Iowa Falls, *U.S.A.* **156 B3** 42 31N 93 16W
Iowa Park, *U.S.A.* **155 J5** 33 57N 98 40W
Ipala, *Tanzania* **118 C3** 4 30 S 32 52 E
Ipameri, *Brazil* **171 E2** 17 44 S 48 9W
Ipanema, *Brazil* **171 E3** 19 47 S 41 44W
Iparía, *Peru* **172 B3** 9 17 S 74 29W
Ipáti, *Greece* **48 C4** 38 52N 22 14 E
Ipatinga, *Brazil* **171 E3** 19 32 S 42 30W
Ipatovo, *Russia* **61 H6** 45 45N 42 50 E
Ipel' →, *Europe* **35 D11** 47 48N 18 53 E
Ipiales, *Colombia* **168 C2** 0 50N 77 37W
Ipiaú, *Brazil* **171 D4** 14 8 S 39 44W
Ipil, *Phil.* **81 H4** 7 47N 122 35 E
Ipin = Yibin, *China* **76 C5** 28 45N 104 32 E
Ipirá, *Brazil* **171 D4** 12 10 S 39 44W
Ipiranga, *Brazil* **168 D4** 3 13 S 65 57W
Ípiros □, *Greece* **48 B2** 39 30N 20 30 E
Ipixuna, *Brazil* **172 B3** 7 0 S 71 40W
Ipixuna →, *Amazonas, Brazil* **172 B3** 7 11 S 71 51W
Ipixuna →, *Amazonas, Brazil* **173 B5** 5 45 S 63 2W
Ipoh, *Malaysia* **78 D2** 4 35N 101 5 E
Iporã, *Brazil* **171 E1** 16 28 S 51 7W
Ippy, *C.A.R.* **114 A4** 6 5N 21 7 E
İpsala, *Turkey* **51 F10** 40 55N 26 23 E
Ipsárion, Óros, *Greece* **51 F8** 40 40N 24 40 E
Ipswich, *Australia* **127 D5** 27 35 S 152 40 E
Ipswich, *U.K.* **21 E9** 52 4N 1 10 E
Ipswich, *Mass., U.S.A.* **151 D14** 42 41N 70 50W
Ipswich, *S. Dak., U.S.A.* **154 C5** 45 27N 99 2W
Ipu, *Brazil* **170 B3** 4 23 S 40 44W
Ipueiras, *Brazil* **170 B3** 4 33 S 40 43W
Ipupiara, *Brazil* **171 D3** 11 49 S 42 37W
Iqaluit, *Canada* **139 B13** 63 44N 68 31W
Iquique, *Chile* **172 E3** 20 19 S 70 5W
Iquitos, *Peru* **168 D3** 3 45 S 73 10W
Irabu-Jima, *Japan* **69 M2** 24 50N 125 10 E
Iracoubo, *Fr. Guiana* **169 B7** 5 30N 53 10W
Īrafshān, *Iran* **97 E9** 26 42N 61 56 E
Irahuan, *Phil.* **81 G2** 9 48N 118 41 E
Iráklia, *Kikládhes, Greece* **49 E7** 36 50N 25 28 E
Iráklia, *Sérrai, Greece* **50 E7** 41 10N 23 16 E
Iráklion, *Greece* **38 D7** 35 20N 25 12 E
Iráklion □, *Greece* **38 D7** 35 10N 25 10 E
Irako-Zaki, *Japan* **71 C9** 34 35N 137 1 E
Irala, *Paraguay* **175 B5** 25 55 S 54 35W
Iran ■, *Asia* **97 C7** 33 0N 53 0 E
Iran, Gunung-Gunung, *Malaysia* **78 D4** 2 20N 114 50 E
Iran, Plateau of, *Asia* **66 F9** 32 0N 55 0 E
Iran Ra. = Iran, Gunung-Gunung, *Malaysia* **78 D4** 2 20N 114 50 E
Iranamadu Tank, *Sri Lanka* **95 K5** 9 23N 80 29 E
Īrānshahr, *Iran* **97 E9** 27 15N 60 40 E
Irapa, *Venezuela* **169 A5** 10 34N 62 35W
Irapuato, *Mexico* **162 C4** 20 40N 101 30W
Iraq ■, *Asia* **101 F10** 33 0N 44 0 E
Irarrar, O. →, *Mali* **111 D5** 20 0N 1 30 E
Irati, *Brazil* **175 B5** 25 25 S 50 38W
Irbes saurums, *Latvia* **54 A9** 57 45N 22 5 E
Irbid, *Jordan* **103 C4** 32 35N 35 48 E
Irbid □, *Jordan* **103 C5** 32 15N 36 35 E
Irbit, *Russia* **62 C9** 57 41N 63 3 E
Irebu, *Dem. Rep. of the Congo* **114 C3** 0 40 S 17 46 E
Irecê, *Brazil* **170 D3** 11 18 S 41 52W
Iregua →, *Spain* **40 C7** 42 27N 2 24 E
Ireland ■, *Europe* **23 C4** 53 50N 7 52W
Irele, *Nigeria* **113 D6** 7 40N 5 40 E
Iremel, Gora, *Russia* **62 D7** 54 33N 58 50 E
Ireng →, *Brazil* **169 C6** 3 33N 59 51W
Irgiz, Bolshaya →, *Russia* **60 D9** 52 10N 49 10 E
Irhârharene, *Algeria* **111 C6** 27 37N 7 30 E
Irharrhar, O. →, *Algeria* **111 C6** 28 3N 6 15 E
Irherm, *Morocco* **110 B3** 30 7N 8 18W
Irhil Mgoun, *Morocco* **110 B3** 31 30N 6 28W
Irhyangdong, *N. Korea* **75 D15** 41 15N 129 30 E
Iri, *S. Korea* **75 G14** 35 59N 127 0 E
Irian Jaya □, *Indonesia* **79 E9** 4 0 S 137 0 E
Iriba, *Chad* **109 E4** 15 7N 22 15 E
Irié, *Guinea* **112 D3** 8 15N 9 10W
Iriga, *Phil.* **80 E4** 13 25N 123 25 E
Iriklinskiy, *Russia* **62 F7** 51 39N 58 38 E
Iriklinskoye Vdkhr., *Russia* **62 F7** 52 0N 59 0 E
Iringa, *Tanzania* **118 D4** 7 48 S 35 43 E
Iringa □, *Tanzania* **118 D4** 7 48 S 35 43 E
Irinjalakuda, *India* **95 J3** 10 21N 76 14 E
Iriomote-Jima, *Japan* **69 M1** 24 19N 123 48 E
Iriona, *Honduras* **164 C2** 15 57N 85 11W
Iriri →, *Brazil* **169 D7** 3 52 S 52 37W
Iriri Novo →, *Brazil* **173 B7** 8 46 S 53 22W
Irish Republic ■, *Europe* **23 C3** 53 0N 8 0W
Irish Sea, *U.K.* **20 D3** 53 38N 4 48W
Irkeshtam, *Kyrgyzstan* **63 D6** 39 41N 73 55 E
Irkutsk, *Russia* **65 D11** 52 18N 104 20 E
Irlığanlı, *Turkey* **49 D11** 37 53N 29 12 E
Irma, *Canada* **143 C6** 52 55N 111 14W
Irō-Zaki, *Japan* **71 C10** 34 36N 138 51 E
Iroise, Mer d', *France* **26 D2** 48 15N 4 45W
Iron Baron, *Australia* **128 B2** 32 58 S 137 11 E
Iron Gate = Portile de Fier, *Europe* **52 F7** 44 44N 22 30 E
Iron Knob, *Australia* **128 B2** 32 46 S 137 8 E
Iron Mountain, *U.S.A.* **148 C1** 45 49N 88 4W
Iron River, *U.S.A.* **154 B10** 46 6N 88 39W
Irondequoit, *U.S.A.* **150 C7** 43 13N 77 35W
Ironton, *Mo., U.S.A.* **155 G9** 37 36N 90 38W
Ironton, *Ohio, U.S.A.* **148 F4** 38 32N 82 41W
Ironwood, *U.S.A.* **154 B9** 46 27N 90 9W
Iroquois, *Canada* **151 B9** 44 51N 75 19W
Iroquois →, *U.S.A.* **157 C9** 41 5N 87 49W
Iroquois Falls, *Canada* **140 C3** 48 46N 80 41W
Irosin, *Phil.* **80 E5** 12 42N 124 2 E
Irpin, *Ukraine* **59 G6** 50 30N 30 15 E
Irrara Cr. →, *Australia* **127 D4** 29 35 S 145 31 E
Irrawaddy □, *Burma* **90 G5** 17 0N 95 0 E
Irrawaddy →, *Burma* **90 G5** 15 50N 95 6 E
Irricana, *Canada* **142 C6** 51 19N 113 37W
Irsina, *Italy* **47 B9** 40 45N 16 14 E
Irtysh →, *Russia* **64 C7** 61 4N 68 52 E
Irumu, *Dem. Rep. of the Congo* **118 B2** 1 32N 29 53 E
Irún, *Spain* **40 B3** 43 20N 1 52W
Irunea = Pamplona, *Spain* **40 C3** 42 48N 1 38W
Irurzun, *Spain* **40 C3** 42 55N 1 50W
Irvine, *Canada* **143 D6** 49 57N 110 16W
Irvine, *U.K.* **22 F4** 55 37N 4 41W
Irvine, *Calif., U.S.A.* **161 M9** 33 41N 117 46W
Irvine, *Ky., U.S.A.* **157 G13** 37 42N 83 58W
Irvinestown, *U.K.* **23 B4** 54 28N 7 39W
Irving, *U.S.A.* **155 J6** 32 49N 96 56W
Irvington, *U.S.A.* **157 G10** 37 53N 86 17W
Irvona, *U.S.A.* **150 F6** 40 46N 78 33W
Irwin →, *Australia* **125 E1** 29 15 S 114 54 E
Irwinton, *U.S.A.* **152 C6** 32 49N 83 10W
Irwinville, *U.S.A.* **152 D6** 31 39N 83 23W
Irymple, *Australia* **128 C5** 34 14 S 142 8 E
Is, Jebel, *Sudan* **106 C4** 22 3N 35 28 E
Is-sur-Tille, *France* **27 E12** 47 30N 5 8 E
Isa, *Nigeria* **113 C6** 13 14N 6 24 E
Isa Khel, *Pakistan* **92 C4** 32 41N 71 17 E
Isaac →, *Australia* **126 C4** 22 55 S 149 20 E
Isabel, *U.S.A.* **154 C4** 45 24N 101 26W
Isabela, *Phil.* **79 C6** 6 40N 122 10 E
Isabela, *Phil.* **81 F4** 10 12N 122 59 E
Isabela □, *Phil.* **80 C4** 17 0N 122 0 E
Isabela, I., *Mexico* **162 C3** 21 51N 105 55W
Isabelia, Cord., *Nic.* **164 D2** 13 30N 85 25W
Isabella Ra., *Australia* **124 D3** 21 0 S 121 4 E
Isaccea, *Romania* **53 E13** 45 16N 28 28 E
Ísafjarðardjúp, *Iceland* **11 A3** 66 10N 23 0W
Ísafjarðarsýsla □, *Iceland* **11 B3** 66 0N 23 0W
Ísafjörður, *Iceland* **11 A3** 66 5N 23 9W
Isagarh, *India* **92 G7** 24 48N 77 51 E
Isahaya, *Japan* **70 E2** 32 52N 130 2 E
Isaka, *Dem. Rep. of the Congo* **114 C3** 2 33 S 18 54 E
Isaka, *Tanzania* **118 C3** 3 56 S 32 59 E
Isakly, *Russia* **60 C10** 54 8N 51 32 E
Işalniţa, *Romania* **53 F8** 44 24N 23 44 E
Isan →, *India* **93 F9** 26 51N 80 7 E
Isana = Içana →, *Brazil* **168 C4** 0 26N 67 19W
Isandja, *Dem. Rep. of the Congo* **114 C4** 2 59 S 21 59 E
Isangi, *Dem. Rep. of the Congo* **114 B4** 0 52N 24 10 E
Isanlu Makutu, *Nigeria* **113 D6** 8 20N 5 50 E
Isar →, *Germany* **31 G8** 48 48N 12 57 E
Isarco →, *Italy* **45 B8** 46 27N 11 18 E
Ísari, *Greece* **48 D3** 37 22N 22 0 E
Isarog, Mt., *Phil.* **80 E4** 13 39N 123 23 E
Íscar, *Spain* **42 D6** 41 22N 4 32W
Işcayachi, *Bolivia* **173 E4** 21 31 S 65 3W
İscehisar, *Turkey* **49 C12** 38 51N 30 45 E
Ischgl, *Austria* **33 B10** 47 1N 10 17 E
Íschia, *Italy* **46 B6** 40 44N 13 57 E
Iscuandé, *Colombia* **168 C2** 2 28N 77 59W
Isdell →, *Australia* **124 C3** 16 27 S 124 51 E
Ise, *Japan* **71 C8** 34 25N 136 45 E
Ise-Heiya, *Japan* **71 C8** 34 40N 136 30 E
Ise-Wan, *Japan* **71 C8** 34 43N 136 43 E
Isefjord, *Denmark* **17 J5** 55 53N 11 50 E
Isel →, *Austria* **34 E5** 46 50N 12 47 E
Iseltwald, *Switz.* **32 C5** 46 43N 7 58 E
Isenthal, *Switz.* **33 C7** 46 55N 8 34 E
Iseo, *Italy* **44 C7** 45 39N 10 3 E
Iseo, L. d', *Italy* **44 C7** 45 43N 10 4 E
Iseramagazi, *Tanzania* **118 C3** 4 37 S 32 10 E
Isère □, *France* **29 C9** 45 15N 5 40 E
Isère →, *France* **29 D8** 44 59N 4 51 E
Iserlohn, *Germany* **30 D3** 51 22N 7 41 E
Isérnia, *Italy* **47 A7** 41 36N 14 14 E
Isesaki, *Japan* **71 A11** 36 19N 139 12 E
Iseyin, *Nigeria* **113 D5** 8 0N 3 36 E
Isfahan = Eşfahān, *Iran* **97 C6** 32 39N 51 43 E
Isfara, *Tajikistan* **63 C5** 40 7N 70 38 E
Isfjorden, *Norway* **18 B4** 62 35N 7 49 E
Ishenga Oshwe, *Dem. Rep. of the Congo* **114 C4** 3 57 S 22 33 E
Isherton, *Guyana* **169 C6** 2 20N 59 25W
Ishigaki-Shima, *Japan* **69 M2** 24 20N 124 10 E
Ishikari-Gawa →, *Japan* **68 C10** 43 15N 141 23 E
Ishikari-Sammyaku, *Japan* **68 C11** 43 30N 143 0 E
Ishikari-Wan, *Japan* **68 C10** 43 25N 141 1 E
Ishikawa □, *Japan* **71 A8** 36 30N 136 30 E
Ishim, *Russia* **64 D7** 56 10N 69 30 E
Ishim →, *Russia* **64 D8** 57 45N 71 10 E
Ishimbay, *Russia* **62 E6** 53 28N 56 2 E
Ishinomaki, *Japan* **68 E10** 38 32N 141 20 E
Ishioka, *Japan* **71 A12** 36 11N 140 16 E
Ishizuchi-Yama, *Japan* **70 D5** 33 45N 133 6 E
Ishkashim = Eshkāshem, *Tajikistan* **63 E5** 36 44N 71 37 E
Ishkuman, *Pakistan* **93 A5** 36 30N 73 50 E
Ishmi, *Albania* **50 E3** 41 33N 19 34 E
Ishpeming, *U.S.A.* **148 B2** 46 29N 87 40W
Ishurdi, *Bangla.* **90 C2** 24 9N 89 3 E
Isigny-sur-Mer, *France* **26 C5** 49 19N 1 6W
Isıklar Dağı, *Turkey* **51 F11** 40 45N 27 15 E
Işıklı, *Turkey* **49 C11** 38 19N 29 51 E
Isil Kul, *Russia* **64 D8** 54 55N 71 16 E
Ísili, *Italy* **46 C2** 39 44N 9 6 E
Isiolo, *Kenya* **118 B4** 0 24N 37 33 E
Isiro, *Dem. Rep. of the Congo* **118 B2** 2 53N 27 40 E
Isisford, *Australia* **126 C3** 24 15 S 144 21 E
Iskandar, *Uzbekistan* **63 C4** 41 36N 69 41 E
İskenderun, *Turkey* **100 D7** 36 32N 36 10 E
İskenderun Körfezi, *Turkey* **100 D6** 36 40N 35 50 E
Iski-Naukat, *Kyrgyzstan* **63 C6** 40 16N 72 36 E
İskilip, *Turkey* **100 B6** 40 45N 34 29 E
Iskŭr →, *Bulgaria* **51 C8** 43 45N 24 25 E
Iskŭr, Yazovir, *Bulgaria* **50 D7** 42 23N 23 30 E
Iskut →, *Canada* **142 B2** 56 45N 131 49W
Isla →, *U.K.* **22 E5** 56 32N 3 20W
Isla Cristina, *Spain* **43 H3** 37 13N 7 17W
Isla Vista, *U.S.A.* **161 L7** 34 25N 119 53W
İslâhiye, *Turkey* **100 D7** 37 0N 36 35 E
Islam Headworks, *Pakistan* **92 E5** 29 49N 72 33 E
Islamabad, *Pakistan* **91 B4** 33 40N 73 10 E
Islamgarh, *Pakistan* **92 F4** 27 51N 70 48 E
Islamkot, *Pakistan* **92 G4** 24 42N 70 13 E
Islamorada, *U.S.A.* **153 L9** 24 56N 80 37W
Islampur, *India* **93 G11** 25 9N 85 12 E
Islampur, *India* **94 F2** 17 2N 74 20 E
Island Bay, *Phil.* **81 G2** 9 6N 118 10 E
Island L., *Canada* **143 C10** 53 47N 94 25W
Island Lagoon, *Australia* **128 A2** 31 30 S 136 40 E
Island Pond, *U.S.A.* **151 B13** 44 49N 71 53W
Islands, B. of, *Canada* **141 C8** 49 11N 58 15W
Islands, B. of, *N.Z.* **130 B3** 35 15 S 174 6 E
Islay, *U.K.* **22 F2** 55 46N 6 10W
Isle →, *France* **28 D3** 44 55N 0 15W
Isle aux Morts, *Canada* **141 C8** 47 35N 59 0W
Isle of Hope, *U.S.A.* **152 D8** 31 58N 81 5W
Isle of Wight □, *U.K.* **21 G6** 50 41N 1 17W
Isle Royale, *U.S.A.* **154 B10** 48 0N 88 54W
Isle Royale National Park, *U.S.A.* **154 B10** 48 0N 88 55W
Isleton, *U.S.A.* **160 G5** 38 10N 121 37W
Ismail = Izmayil, *Ukraine* **59 K5** 45 22N 28 46 E
Ismâ'ilîya, *Egypt* **106 H8** 30 37N 32 18 E
Ismaning, *Germany* **31 G7** 48 13N 11 40 E
Isna, *Egypt* **106 B3** 25 17N 32 30 E
Isoanala, *Madag.* **117 C8** 23 50 S 45 44 E
Isogstalo, *India* **93 B8** 34 15N 78 46 E
Ísola del Liri, *Italy* **45 G10** 41 41N 13 34 E
Ísola della Scala, *Italy* **44 C7** 45 16N 11 0 E
Ísola di Capo Rizzuto, *Italy* **47 D10** 38 58N 17 6 E
Isparta, *Turkey* **49 D12** 37 47N 30 30 E
Isperikh, *Bulgaria* **51 C10** 43 43N 26 50 E
Íspica, *Italy* **47 F7** 36 47N 14 55 E
Israel ■, *Asia* **103 D3** 32 0N 34 50 E
Isratu, *Eritrea* **107 D4** 16 20N 39 53 E
Issano, *Guyana* **169 B6** 5 49N 59 26W
Issia, *Ivory C.* **112 D3** 6 33N 6 33W
Issoire, *France* **28 C7** 45 32N 3 15 E
Issoudun, *France* **27 F8** 46 57N 1 59 E
Issyk-Kul = Ysyk-Köl, *Kyrgyzstan* **63 B8** 42 26N 76 12 E
Issyk-Kul, Ozero = Ysyk-Köl, Ozero, *Kyrgyzstan* **64 E8** 42 25N 77 15 E
Ist, *Croatia* **45 D11** 44 17N 14 47 E
Istaihah, *U.A.E.* **99 B6** 23 19N 54 4 E
Istállós-kő, *Hungary* **52 B5** 48 4N 20 26 E
İstanbul, *Turkey* **51 E12** 41 0N 29 0 E
İstanbul □, *Turkey* **51 E12** 41 0N 29 0 E
İstanbul Boğazı, *Turkey* **51 E13** 41 10N 29 10 E
Isteren, *Norway* **18 B8** 61 58N 11 47 E
Istiaía, *Greece* **48 C5** 38 57N 23 9 E
Istmina, *Colombia* **168 B2** 5 10N 76 39W
Isto, Mt., *U.S.A.* **144 B12** 69 12N 143 48W
Istok, *Kosovo, Yug.* **50 D4** 42 45N 20 24 E
Istokpoga, L., *U.S.A.* **149 M5** 27 23N 81 17W
Istra, *Croatia* **45 C10** 45 10N 14 0 E
Istres, *France* **29 E8** 43 31N 4 59 E
Istria = Istra, *Croatia* **45 C10** 45 10N 14 0 E
Isugod, *Phil.* **81 G2** 9 19N 118 5 E
Isulan, *Phil.* **81 H5** 6 30N 124 29 E
Itá, *Paraguay* **174 B4** 25 29 S 57 21W
'Itāb, *Yemen* **99 D5** 15 20N 51 29 E
Itabaiana, *Paraíba, Brazil* **170 C4** 7 18 S 35 19W
Itabaiana, *Sergipe, Brazil* **170 D4** 10 41 S 37 37W
Itabaianinha, *Brazil* **170 D4** 11 16 S 37 47W
Itaberaba, *Brazil* **171 D3** 12 32 S 40 18W
Itaberaí, *Brazil* **171 E2** 16 2 S 49 48W
Itabira, *Brazil* **171 E3** 19 37 S 43 13W
Itabirito, *Brazil* **171 F3** 20 15 S 43 48W
Itaboca, *Brazil* **169 D5** 4 50 S 62 40W
Itabuna, *Brazil* **171 D4** 14 48 S 39 16W
Itacajá, *Brazil* **170 C2** 8 19 S 47 46W
Itacaunas →, *Brazil* **170 C2** 5 21 S 49 8W
Itacuaí →, *Brazil* **172 A3** 4 20 S 70 12W
Itaguaçu, *Brazil* **171 E3** 19 48 S 40 51W
Itaguari →, *Brazil* **171 D3** 14 11 S 44 40W
Itaguatins, *Brazil* **170 C2** 5 47 S 47 29W
Itaim →, *Brazil* **170 C3** 7 2 S 42 2W
Itainópolis, *Brazil* **170 C3** 7 24 S 41 31W
Itaipú, Reprêsa de, *Brazil* **175 B5** 25 30 S 54 30W
Itaituba, *Brazil* **169 D6** 4 10 S 55 50W
Itajaí, *Brazil* **175 B6** 27 50 S 48 39W
Itajubá, *Brazil* **171 F2** 22 24 S 45 30W
Itajuípe, *Brazil* **171 D4** 14 41 S 39 22W
Itaka, *Tanzania* **119 D3** 8 50 S 32 49 E
Itako, *Japan* **71 B12** 35 56N 140 33 E
Italy ■, *Europe* **13 G8** 42 0N 13 0 E
Itamaraju, *Brazil* **171 E4** 17 4 S 39 32W
Itamarati, *Brazil* **172 B4** 6 24 S 68 15W
Itamataré, *Brazil* **170 B2** 2 16 S 46 24W
Itambacuri, *Brazil* **171 E3** 18 1 S 41 42W
Itambé, *Brazil* **171 E3** 15 15 S 40 37W
Itampolo, *Madag.* **117 C7** 24 41 S 43 57 E
Itandrano, *Madag.* **117 C8** 21 47 S 45 17 E
Itanhaém, *Brazil* **171 F2** 24 11 S 46 47W
Itanhauã →, *Brazil* **169 D5** 4 45 S 63 48W
Itanhém, *Brazil* **171 E3** 17 9 S 40 20W
Itano, *Japan* **70 C6** 34 7N 134 28 E
Itapaci, *Brazil* **171 D2** 14 57 S 49 34W
Itapagé, *Brazil* **170 B4** 3 41 S 39 34W
Itaparica, I. de, *Brazil* **171 D4** 12 54 S 38 42W
Itapebi, *Brazil* **171 E4** 15 56 S 39 32W
Itapecuru-Mirim, *Brazil* **170 B3** 3 24 S 44 20W
Itaperuna, *Brazil* **171 F3** 21 10 S 41 54W
Itapetinga, *Brazil* **171 E3** 15 15 S 40 15W
Itapetininga, *Brazil* **175 A6** 23 36 S 48 7W
Itapeva, *Brazil* **175 A6** 23 59 S 48 59W
Itapicuru →, *Bahia, Brazil* **170 D4** 11 47 S 37 32W
Itapicuru →, *Maranhão, Brazil* **170 B3** 2 52 S 44 12W
Itapinima, *Brazil* **173 B5** 5 25 S 60 44W
Itapipoca, *Brazil* **170 B4** 3 30 S 39 35W
Itapiranga, *Brazil* **169 D6** 2 45 S 58 1W
Itapiúna, *Brazil* **170 B4** 4 33 S 38 57W
Itaporanga, *Brazil* **170 C4** 7 18 S 38 0W
Itaporanga, *Brazil* **171 F2** 23 42 S 49 29W
Itapuá □, *Paraguay* **175 B4** 26 40 S 55 40W
Itapuranga, *Brazil* **171 E2** 15 40 S 49 59W
Itaquari, *Brazil* **171 F3** 20 20 S 40 25W
Itaquatiara, *Brazil* **169 D6** 2 58 S 58 30W
Itaquí, *Brazil* **174 B4** 29 8 S 56 30W
Itararé, *Brazil* **175 A6** 24 6 S 49 23W
Itarsi, *India* **92 H7** 22 36N 77 51 E
Itarumã, *Brazil* **171 E1** 18 42 S 51 25W
Itatí, *Argentina* **174 B4** 27 16 S 58 15W
Itatira, *Brazil* **170 B4** 4 30 S 39 37W
Itatuba, *Brazil* **173 B5** 5 46 S 63 20W
Itatupa, *Brazil* **169 D7** 0 37 S 51 12W
Itaueira, *Brazil* **170 C3** 7 36 S 43 2W
Itaueira →, *Brazil* **170 C3** 6 41 S 42 55W
Itaúna, *Brazil* **171 F3** 20 4 S 44 34W
Itbayat, *Phil.* **80 A3** 20 47N 121 51 E
Itbayat I., *Phil.* **80 A3** 20 45N 121 50 E
Itchen →, *U.K.* **21 G6** 50 55N 1 22W
Ite, *Peru* **172 D3** 17 55 S 70 57W
Itéa, *Greece* **48 C4** 38 25N 22 25 E
Itezhi Tezhi, L., *Zambia* **119 F2** 15 30 S 25 30 E
Ithaca = Itháki, *Greece* **48 C2** 38 25N 20 40 E
Ithaca, *U.S.A.* **151 D8** 42 27N 76 30W
Itháki, *Greece* **48 C2** 38 25N 20 40 E
Itinga, *Brazil* **171 E3** 16 36 S 41 47W
Itiquira, *Brazil* **173 D7** 17 12 S 54 7W
Itiquira →, *Brazil* **173 D6** 17 18 S 56 44W
Itiruçu, *Brazil* **171 D3** 13 31 S 40 9W
Itiúba, *Brazil* **170 D4** 10 43 S 39 51W
Itkilik →, *U.S.A.* **144 A10** 70 9N 150 56W
Ito, *Japan* **71 C11** 34 58N 139 5 E
Ito Aba I., *S. China Sea* **78 B4** 10 23N 114 21 E
Itogon, *Phil.* **80 C3** 16 22N 120 41 E
Itoigawa, *Japan* **69 F8** 37 2N 137 51 E
Itoko, *Dem. Rep. of the Congo* **114 C4** 1 0 S 21 48 E
Iton →, *France* **26 C8** 49 9N 1 12 E
Itonamas →, *Bolivia* **173 C5** 12 28 S 64 24W
Itri, *Italy* **46 A6** 41 17N 13 32 E
Itsa, *Egypt* **106 J7** 29 15N 30 47 E
Itsukaichi, *Japan* **70 C4** 34 22N 132 22 E
Itsuki, *Japan* **70 E2** 32 24N 130 50 E
Íttiri, *Italy* **46 B1** 40 36N 8 34 E
Itu, *Brazil* **175 A6** 23 17 S 47 15W
Itu, *Nigeria* **113 D6** 5 10N 7 58 E
Ituaçu, *Brazil* **171 D3** 13 50 S 41 18W
Ituango, *Colombia* **168 B2** 7 4N 75 45W
Ituí →, *Brazil* **168 D3** 4 38 S 70 19W
Ituiutaba, *Brazil* **171 E2** 19 0 S 49 25W
Itumbiara, *Brazil* **171 E2** 18 20 S 49 10W
Ituna, *Canada* **143 C8** 51 10N 103 24W
Itunge Port, *Tanzania* **119 D3** 9 40 S 33 55 E
Ituni, *Guyana* **169 B6** 5 28N 58 15W
Itupiranga, *Brazil* **170 C2** 5 9 S 49 20W
Iturama, *Brazil* **171 E1** 19 44 S 50 11W
Iturbe, *Argentina* **174 A2** 23 0 S 65 25W
Ituri →, *Dem. Rep. of the Congo* **118 B2** 1 40N 27 1 E
Iturup, Ostrov, *Russia* **65 E15** 45 0N 148 0 E
Ituverava, *Brazil* **171 F2** 20 20 S 47 47W
Ituxi →, *Brazil* **173 B5** 7 18 S 64 51W
Ituyuro →, *Argentina* **174 A3** 22 40 S 63 50W
Itzehoe, *Germany* **30 B5** 53 55N 9 31 E
Iuka, *U.S.A.* **157 F8** 38 37N 88 47W
Ivahona, *Madag.* **117 C8** 23 27 S 46 10 E
Ivaí →, *Brazil* **175 A5** 23 18 S 53 42W
Ivalo, *Finland* **14 B22** 68 38N 27 35 E
Ivalojoki →, *Finland* **14 B22** 68 40N 27 40 E
Ivanava, *Belarus* **59 F3** 52 7N 25 29 E
Ivančice, *Czech Rep.* **35 B9** 49 6N 16 23 E
Ivăneşti, *Romania* **53 D12** 46 39N 27 27 E
Ivangorod, *Russia* **58 C5** 59 27N 28 13 E
Ivanhoe, *Australia* **128 B6** 32 56 S 144 20 E
Ivanhoe, *Calif., U.S.A.* **160 J7** 36 23N 119 13W
Ivanhoe, *Minn., U.S.A.* **154 C6** 44 28N 96 15W
Ivanić Grad, *Croatia* **45 C13** 45 41N 16 25 E
Ivanjica, *Serbia, Yug.* **50 C4** 43 35N 20 12 E
Ivanjska, *Bos.-H.* **52 F2** 44 55N 17 4 E
Ivankoyskoye Vdkhr., *Russia* **58 D9** 56 37N 36 32 E
Ivano-Frankivsk, *Ukraine* **59 H3** 48 40N 24 40 E
Ivano-Frankovsk = Ivano-Frankivsk, *Ukraine* **59 H3** 48 40N 24 40 E
Ivanof Bay, *U.S.A.* **144 J8** 55 54N 159 29W
Ivanovo = Ivanava, *Belarus* **59 F3** 52 7N 25 29 E
Ivanovo, *Russia* **58 D11** 57 5N 41 0 E
Ivanšćica, *Croatia* **45 B13** 46 12N 16 13 E
Ivato, *Madag.* **117 C8** 20 37 S 47 10 E
Ivatsevichy, *Belarus* **59 F3** 52 43N 25 21 E
Ivaylovgrad, *Bulgaria* **51 E10** 41 32N 26 8 E
Ivdel, *Russia* **56 B11** 60 42N 60 24 E
Ive, Mt., *Australia* **128 B2** 32 25 S 136 5 E
Ivindo →, *Gabon* **114 C2** 0 9 S 12 9 E
Ivinheima →, *Brazil* **175 A5** 23 14 S 53 42W
Ivinhema, *Brazil* **175 A5** 22 10 S 53 37W
Ivittuut, *Greenland* **10 E6** 61 14N 48 12W
Ivohibe, *Madag.* **117 C8** 22 31 S 46 57 E
Ivolândia, *Brazil* **171 E1** 16 34 S 50 51W
Ivory Coast, *W. Afr.* **112 E4** 4 20N 5 0W
Ivory Coast ■, *Africa* **112 D4** 7 30N 5 0W
Ivösjön, *Sweden* **17 H8** 56 8N 14 25 E
Ivrea, *Italy* **44 C4** 45 28N 7 52 E
İvrindi, *Turkey* **49 B9** 39 34N 27 30 E
Ivujivik, *Canada* **139 B12** 62 24N 77 55W
Ivybridge, *U.K.* **21 G4** 50 23N 3 56W
Iwai-Jima, *Japan* **70 D3** 33 47N 131 58 E
Iwaizumi, *Japan* **68 E10** 39 50N 141 45 E
Iwaki, *Japan* **69 F10** 37 3N 140 55 E
Iwakuni, *Japan* **70 C4** 34 15N 132 8 E
Iwami, *Japan* **70 B6** 35 32N 134 15 E
Iwamizawa, *Japan* **68 C10** 43 12N 141 46 E
Iwanai, *Japan* **68 C10** 42 58N 140 30 E
Iwase, *Japan* **71 A12** 36 21N 140 6 E
Iwata, *Japan* **71 C9** 34 42N 137 51 E
Iwate □, *Japan* **68 E10** 39 30N 141 30 E
Iwate-San, *Japan* **68 E10** 39 51N 141 0 E
Iwo, *Nigeria* **113 D5** 7 39N 4 9 E
Iwonicz-Zdrój, *Poland* **55 J8** 49 37N 21 47 E
Iwungu, *Dem. Rep. of the Congo* **115 D3** 5 16 S 19 17 E
Ixiamas, *Bolivia* **172 C4** 13 50 S 68 5W
Ixopo, *S. Africa* **117 E5** 30 11 S 30 5 E
Ixtepec, *Mexico* **163 D5** 16 32N 95 10W
Ixtlán del Río, *Mexico* **162 C4** 21 5N 104 21W
'Iyādh, *Yemen* **98 D4** 14 59N 46 51 E
Iyal Bakhit, *Sudan* **107 E2** 13 20N 28 39 E
Iyo, *Japan* **70 D4** 33 45N 132 45 E
Iyo-mishima, *Japan* **70 D5** 33 58N 133 30 E

K

232 Karst

Karst = Kras, Croatia 45 C10 45 35N 14 0 E
Kartal, Turkey 51 F13 40 53N 29 11 E
Kartál Óros, Greece 51 E9 41 15N 25 13 E
Kartaly, Russia 62 E8 53 3N 60 40 E
Kartapur, India 92 D6 31 27N 75 32 E
Karthaus, U.S.A. 150 E6 41 8N 78 9W
Kartuzy, Poland 54 D5 54 22N 18 10 E
Karuah, Australia 129 B9 32 37 S 151 56 E
Karufa, Indonesia 79 E8 3 50 S 133 20 E
Karumba, Australia 126 B3 17 31 S 140 50 E
Karumo, Tanzania 118 C3 2 25 S 32 50 E
Karumwa, Tanzania 118 C3 3 12 S 32 38 E
Kārūn →, Iran 97 D6 30 26N 48 10 E
Karungu, Kenya 118 C3 0 50 S 34 10 E
Karup, Denmark 17 H3 56 19N 9 10 E
Karur, India 95 J4 10 59N 78 2 E
Karviná, Czech Rep. 35 B11 49 53N 18 31 E
Karwan →, India 92 F8 27 26N 78 4 E
Karwi, India 93 G9 25 12N 80 57 E
Kaş, Turkey 49 E11 36 11N 29 37 E
Kasaan, U.S.A. 144 J14 55 32N 132 24W
Kasaba, Turkey 49 E11 36 18N 29 44 E
Kasabi, Zambia 115 E4 14 52 S 23 45 E
Kasache, Malawi 119 E3 13 25 S 34 20 E
Kasai, Japan 70 C6 34 55N 134 52 E
Kasai →, Dem. Rep. of the Congo 115 C3 3 30 S 16 10 E
Kasaï-Occidental □, Dem. Rep. of the Congo 115 D4 6 0 S 22 0 E
Kasaï-Oriental □, Dem. Rep. of the Congo 118 D1 5 0 S 24 30 E
Kasaji, Dem. Rep. of the Congo 119 E1 10 25 S 23 27 E
Kasama, Japan 71 A12 36 23N 140 16 E
Kasama, Zambia 119 E3 10 16 S 31 9 E
Kasan, Uzbekistan 63 D2 39 2N 65 35 E
Kasan-dong, N. Korea 75 D14 41 18N 126 55 E
Kasane, Namibia 116 B3 17 34 S 24 50 E
Kasanga, Tanzania 119 D3 8 30 S 31 10 E
Kasangaie, Dem. Rep. of the Congo 115 D4 6 20 S 22 42 E
Kasangulu, Dem. Rep. of the Congo 115 C3 4 33 S 15 15 E
Kasaoka, Japan 70 C5 34 30N 133 30 E
Kasar, Ras, Sudan 106 D4 18 2N 38 36 E
Kasaragod, India 95 H2 12 30N 74 58 E
Kasat, Burma 90 G7 15 56N 98 13 E
Kasba, Bangla. 90 D3 23 45N 91 2 E
Kasba L., Canada 143 A8 60 20N 102 10W
Kasba Tadla, Morocco 110 B3 32 36N 6 17W
Kaseda, Japan 70 F2 31 25N 130 19 E
Kāseh Garān, Iran 96 C5 34 5N 46 2 E
Kasempa, Zambia 119 E2 13 30 S 25 44 E
Kasenga, Dem. Rep. of the Congo 119 E2 10 20 S 28 45 E
Kasese, Uganda 118 B3 0 13N 30 3 E
Kasewa, Zambia 119 E2 14 28 S 28 53 E
Kasganj, India 93 F8 27 48N 78 42 E
Kashabowie, Canada 140 C1 48 40N 90 26W
Kashaf, Iran 97 C9 35 58N 61 7 E
Kāshān, Iran 97 C6 34 5N 51 30 E
Kashechewan, Canada 140 B3 52 18N 81 37W
Kashi, China 72 C2 39 30N 76 2 E
Kashihara, Japan 71 C7 34 27N 135 46 E
Kashiji Plain, Zambia 115 E4 13 12 S 22 20 E
Kashima, Ibaraki, Japan 71 B12 35 58N 140 38 E
Kashima, Saga, Japan 70 D2 33 7N 130 6 E
Kashima-Nada, Japan 71 B12 36 0N 140 45 E
Kashimbo, Dem. Rep. of the Congo 119 E2 11 12 S 26 19 E
Kashin, Russia 58 D9 57 20N 37 36 E
Kashipur, Orissa, India 94 E6 19 16N 83 3 E
Kashipur, Ut. P., India 93 E8 29 15N 79 0 E
Kashira, Russia 58 E10 54 45N 38 10 E
Kashiwa, Japan 71 B11 35 52N 139 59 E
Kashiwazaki, Japan 69 F9 37 22N 138 33 E
Kashk-e Kohneh, Afghan. 91 B1 34 55N 62 30 E
Kashkasu, Kyrgyzstan 63 D6 39 54N 72 44 E
Kashkū'īyeh, Iran 97 D7 30 31N 55 40 E
Kāshmar, Iran 97 C8 35 16N 58 26 E
Kashmir, Asia 93 C7 34 0N 76 0 E
Kashmor, Pakistan 91 C3 28 28N 69 32 E
Kashpirovka, Russia 60 D9 53 0N 48 30 E
Kashun Noerh = Gaxun Nur, China 72 B5 42 22N 100 30 E
Kasiari, India 93 H12 22 8N 87 14 E
Kasilof, U.S.A. 144 F10 60 23N 151 18W
Kasimov, Russia 60 C5 54 55N 41 20 E
Kasinge, Dem. Rep. of the Congo 118 D2 6 15 S 26 58 E
Kasiruta, Indonesia 79 E7 0 25 S 127 12 E
Kaskaskia →, U.S.A. 156 G7 37 58N 89 57W
Kaskattama →, Canada 143 B10 57 3N 90 4W
Kaskelen = Qaskeleng, Kazakstan 63 B8 43 20N 76 35 E
Kaskinen, Finland 15 E19 62 22N 21 15 E
Kasli, Russia 62 D8 55 53N 60 46 E
Kaslo, Canada 142 D5 49 55N 116 55W
Kasmere L., Canada 143 B8 59 34N 101 10W
Kasongan, Indonesia 85 C4 2 0 S 113 23 E
Kasongo, Dem. Rep. of the Congo 118 C2 4 30 S 26 33 E
Kasongo Lunda, Dem. Rep. of the Congo 115 D3 6 35 S 16 49 E
Kásos, Greece 49 F8 35 20N 26 55 E
Kásos, Stenón, Greece 49 F8 35 30N 26 30 E
Kaspi, Georgia 61 K7 41 59N 44 26 E
Kaspichan, Bulgaria 51 C11 43 18N 27 11 E
Kaspiysk, Russia 61 J8 42 52N 47 40 E
Kaspiyskiy, Russia 61 H8 45 22N 47 23 E
Kassab ed Doleib, Sudan 107 E3 13 30N 33 35 E
Kassaba, Egypt 106 C2 22 40N 29 55 E
Kassalâ, Sudan 107 D4 15 30N 36 0 E
Kassalâ □, Sudan 107 D4 15 20N 36 26 E
Kassándra, Greece 50 F7 40 0N 23 30 E
Kassándrinon, Greece 50 F7 40 1N 23 27 E
Kassansay, Uzbekistan 63 C5 41 15N 71 31 E
Kassel, Germany 30 D5 51 18N 9 26 E
Kassinger, Sudan 106 D3 18 46N 31 51 E
Kassiópi, Greece 38 A3 39 48N 19 53 E
Kasson, U.S.A. 154 C8 44 2N 92 45W
Kassue, Indonesia 83 C5 6 58 S 139 21 E
Kastamonu, Turkey 100 B5 41 25N 33 43 E
Kastav, Croatia 45 C11 45 22N 14 20 E
Kastélli, Greece 38 D5 35 29N 23 38 E
Kastéllion, Greece 38 D7 35 12N 25 20 E
Kastellórizon = Megiste, Greece 49 E11 36 8N 29 34 E
Kástellos, Greece 49 E9 36 16N 27 49 E
Kastellou, Ákra, Greece 49 F9 35 30N 27 15 E
Kasterlee, Belgium 24 C4 51 15N 4 59 E
Kastlösa, Sweden 17 H10 56 26N 16 25 E
Kastóri, Greece 48 D4 37 10N 22 17 E
Kastoría, Greece 50 F5 40 30N 21 19 E
Kastoría □, Greece 50 F5 40 30N 21 15 E
Kastorías, Límni, Greece 50 F5 40 30N 21 20 E
Kastornoye, Russia 59 G10 51 55N 38 2 E
Kastós, Greece 48 C2 38 35N 20 55 E
Kastrosikiá, Greece 48 B2 39 6N 20 36 E
Kastsyukovichy, Belarus 58 F7 53 20N 32 4 E
Kasugai, Japan 71 B8 35 12N 136 59 E
Kasukabe, Japan 71 B11 35 58N 139 49 E
Kasulu, Tanzania 118 C3 4 37 S 30 5 E
Kasumi, Japan 70 B6 35 38N 134 38 E
Kasumiga-Ura, Japan 71 B12 36 0N 140 25 E
Kasumkent, Russia 61 K9 41 47N 48 15 E
Kasungu, Malawi 119 E3 13 0 S 33 29 E
Kasur, Pakistan 91 C4 31 5N 74 25 E
Kataba, Zambia 119 F2 16 5 S 25 10 E
Katagum, Nigeria 113 C7 12 18N 10 21 E
Katahdin, Mt., U.S.A. 149 C11 45 54N 68 56W
Katako Kombe, Dem. Rep. of the Congo 118 C1 3 25 S 24 20 E
Katákolon, Greece 48 D3 37 38N 21 19 E
Katale, Tanzania 118 C3 4 52 S 31 7 E
Katamatite, Australia 129 D6 36 6 S 145 41 E
Katanda, Katanga, Dem. Rep. of the Congo 118 D1 7 52 S 24 13 E
Katanda, Nord-Kivu, Dem. Rep. of the Congo 118 C2 0 55 S 29 21 E
Katanga □, Dem. Rep. of the Congo 118 D2 8 0 S 25 0 E
Katangi, India 94 D4 21 56N 79 50 E
Katanning, Australia 125 F2 33 40 S 117 33 E
Katapakishi, Dem. Rep. of the Congo 115 D4 8 15 S 22 49 E
Katastári, Greece 48 D2 37 50N 20 45 E
Katav Ivanovsk, Russia 62 D7 54 45N 58 12 E
Katavi Swamp, Tanzania 118 D3 6 50 S 31 10 E
Kataysk, Russia 62 C9 56 20N 62 30 E
Katchiungo, Angola 115 E3 12 35 S 16 13 E
Kateríni, Greece 50 F6 40 18N 22 37 E
Katghora, India 93 H10 22 30N 82 33 E
Katherîna, Gebel, Egypt 96 D2 28 30N 33 57 E
Katherine, Australia 124 B5 14 27 S 132 20 E
Katherine →, Australia 122 C5 14 40 S 131 42 E
Katherine Gorge, Australia 124 B5 14 18 S 132 28 E
Kathi, India 92 J6 21 47N 74 3 E
Kathiawar, India 92 H4 22 20N 71 0 E
Kathikas, Cyprus 38 E11 34 55N 32 25 E
Kathleen, U.S.A. 153 G7 28 7N 82 2W
Kathua, India 92 C6 32 23N 75 34 E
Kati, Mali 112 C3 12 41N 8 4W
Katihar, India 93 G12 25 34N 87 36 E
Katikati, N.Z. 130 D4 37 32 S 175 57 E
Katima Mulilo, Zambia 116 B3 17 28 S 24 13 E
Katimbira, Malawi 119 E3 12 40 S 34 0 E
Katingan = Mendawai →, Indonesia 78 E4 3 30 S 113 0 E
Katiola, Ivory C. 112 D3 8 10N 5 10W
Katipunan, Phil. 81 G4 8 31N 123 17 E
Katla, Iceland 11 D7 63 36N 19 7W
Katlanovo, Macedonia 50 E5 41 52N 21 40 E
Katmandu, Nepal 93 F11 27 45N 85 20 E
Katni, India 93 H9 23 51N 80 24 E
Káto Akhaía, Greece 48 C3 38 8N 21 33 E
Káto Arkhánai, Greece 38 D7 35 15N 25 10 E
Káto Khorió, Greece 38 D7 35 3N 25 47 E
Káto Pyrgos, Cyprus 38 D11 35 11N 32 41 E
Káto Stavros, Greece 50 F7 40 39N 23 43 E
Katokhí, Greece 48 C3 38 26N 21 15 E
Katol, India 94 D4 21 17N 78 38 E
Katompe, Dem. Rep. of the Congo 118 D2 6 2 S 26 23 E
Katonga →, Uganda 118 B3 0 34N 31 50 E
Katoomba, Australia 129 B9 33 41 S 150 19 E
Katoúna, Greece 48 C3 38 47N 21 7 E
Katowice, Poland 55 H6 50 17N 19 5 E
Katrancı Dağı, Turkey 49 D12 37 27N 30 25 E
Katrine, L., U.K. 22 E4 56 15N 4 30W
Katrineholm, Sweden 17 E10 59 9N 16 12 E
Katsepe, Madag. 117 B8 15 45 S 46 15 E
Katsina, Nigeria 113 C6 13 0N 7 32 E
Katsina □, Nigeria 113 C6 12 30N 7 30 E
Katsina Ala, Nigeria 113 D6 7 10N 9 30 E
Katsina Ala →, Nigeria 113 D6 7 10N 9 20 E
Katsumoto, Japan 70 D1 33 51N 129 42 E
Katsuta, Japan 71 A12 36 25N 140 31 E
Katsuura, Japan 71 B12 35 10N 140 20 E
Katsuyama, Japan 71 A8 36 3N 136 30 E
Kattakurgan, Uzbekistan 63 D3 39 55N 66 15 E
Kattaviá, Greece 38 D9 35 57N 27 46 E
Kattegat, Denmark 17 H5 56 40N 11 20 E
Katthammarsvik, Sweden 17 G12 57 26N 18 51 E
Katul, J., Sudan 107 E2 14 12N 29 25 E
Katumba, Dem. Rep. of the Congo 118 D2 7 40 S 25 17 E
Katungu, Kenya 118 C5 2 55 S 40 3 E
Katwa, India 93 H13 23 30N 88 5 E
Katwijk, Neths. 24 B4 52 12N 4 24 E
Kąty Wrocławskie, Poland 55 G3 51 2N 16 45 E
Kauai, U.S.A. 146 H15 22 3N 159 30W
Kauai Channel, U.S.A. 146 H15 21 45N 158 50W
Kaub, Germany 31 E3 50 5N 7 46 E
Kaufbeuren, Germany 31 H6 47 53N 10 37 E
Kaufman, U.S.A. 155 J6 32 35N 96 19W
Kauhajoki, Finland 15 E20 62 25N 22 10 E
Kauhola Pt., U.S.A. 145 C6 20 15N 155 47W
Kaukauna, U.S.A. 148 C1 44 17N 88 17W
Kaukauveld, Namibia 116 C3 20 0 S 20 15 E
Kaukonahua →, U.S.A. 145 J13 21 35N 158 7W
Kaula I., U.S.A. 145 B1 21 40N 160 33W
Kaulakahi Channel, U.S.A. 145 B2 22 0N 159 55W
Kaumalapau, U.S.A. 145 C5 20 47N 156 59W
Kauna Pt., U.S.A. 145 D6 19 2N 155 53W
Kaunakakai, U.S.A. 145 B4 21 6N 157 1W
Kaunas, Lithuania 15 J20 54 54N 23 54 E
Kaunghein, Burma 90 C5 25 41N 95 26 E
Kaunia, Bangla. 93 G13 25 46N 89 26 E
Kaunos, Turkey 49 E10 36 49N 28 39 E
Kaupalatmada, Mt., Indonesia 82 B3 3 30 S 126 10 E
Kaupangur, Iceland 11 B8 65 38N 18 2W
Kaupo, U.S.A. 145 C5 20 38N 156 8W
Kaura Namoda, Nigeria 113 C6 12 37N 6 33 E
Kauru, Nigeria 113 C6 10 33N 8 12 E
Kautokeino, Norway 14 B20 69 0N 23 4 E
Kauwapur, India 93 F10 27 31N 82 18 E
Kavacha, Russia 65 C17 60 16N 169 51 E
Kavadarci, Macedonia 50 E6 41 26N 22 3 E
Kavaja, Albania 50 E3 41 11N 19 33 E
Kavak, Turkey 100 B7 41 4N 36 3 E
Kavak Dağı, Turkey 49 D10 37 10N 28 2 E
Kavaklı, Turkey 51 E11 41 39N 27 10 E
Kavaklıdere, Turkey 49 D10 37 27N 28 21 E
Kavalerovo, Russia 68 B7 44 15N 135 4 E
Kavali, India 95 G5 14 55N 80 1 E
Kavála, Greece 51 F8 40 57N 24 28 E
Kavála □, Greece 51 E8 41 5N 24 30 E
Kavála Kólpos, Greece 51 F8 40 50N 24 25 E
Kavār, Iran 97 D7 29 11N 52 44 E
Kavarna, Bulgaria 51 C12 43 26N 28 22 E
Kavava, Dem. Rep. of the Congo 115 D4 8 52 S 22 19 E
Kavi, India 92 H5 22 12N 72 38 E
Kavieng, Papua N. G. 132 B6 2 36 S 150 51 E
Kavimba, Botswana 116 B3 18 2 S 24 38 E
Kavīr, Dasht-e, Iran 97 C7 34 30N 55 0 E
Kavkaz, Russia 59 K9 45 20N 36 40 E
Kävlinge, Sweden 17 J7 55 47N 13 9 E
Kavos, Greece 38 B4 39 23N 20 3 E
Kavoúsi, Greece 49 F7 35 7N 25 51 E
Kavungo, Angola 115 E4 11 31 S 23 3 E
Kaw, Fr. Guiana 169 C7 4 30N 52 15W
Kawa, Sudan 107 E3 13 42N 32 34 E
Kawachi-Nagano, Japan 71 C7 34 28N 135 31 E
Kawagama L., Canada 150 A6 45 18N 78 45W
Kawagoe, Japan 71 B11 35 55N 139 29 E
Kawaguchi, Japan 71 B11 35 52N 139 45 E
Kawaihae, U.S.A. 146 H17 20 3N 155 50W
Kawaihae B., U.S.A. 145 D6 20 0N 155 50W
Kawailoa Beach, U.S.A. 145 J13 21 37N 158 5W
Kawakawa, N.Z. 130 B3 35 23 S 174 6 E
Kawambwa, Zambia 119 D2 9 48 S 29 3 E
Kawanoe, Japan 70 C5 34 1N 133 34 E
Kawarau, N.Z. 131 F3 45 3 S 168 45 E
Kawardha, India 93 J9 22 0N 81 17 E
Kawasaki, Japan 71 B11 35 35N 139 42 E
Kawasi, Indonesia 79 E7 1 38 S 127 28 E
Kawau I., N.Z. 130 C3 36 25 S 174 52 E
Kaweka Ra., N.Z. 130 F5 39 17 S 176 19 E
Kawela, U.S.A. 145 J13 21 42N 158 1W
Kawerau, N.Z. 130 E5 38 7 S 176 42 E
Kawhia Harbour, N.Z. 130 E3 38 5 S 174 51 E
Kawio, Kepulauan, Indonesia 79 D7 4 30N 125 30 E
Kawkabān, Yemen 98 D3 15 30N 43 54 E
Kawkareik, Burma 90 G7 16 33N 98 14 E
Kawlin, Burma 90 D5 23 47N 95 41 E
Kawthaung, Burma 87 H2 10 5N 98 36 E
Kawthoolei = Kawthule □, Burma 90 G6 18 0N 97 30 E
Kawthule □, Burma 90 G6 18 0N 97 30 E
Kawya, Burma 90 C5 24 50N 94 58 E
Kaxholmen, Sweden 17 G8 57 51N 14 19 E
Kay, Russia 62 B4 59 57N 52 59 E
Kaya, Burkina Faso 113 C4 13 4N 1 10W
Kayah □, Burma 90 F6 19 15N 97 15 E
Kayalıköy Barajı, Turkey 51 E11 41 50N 27 5 E
Kayan, Burma 90 G6 16 54N 96 34 E
Kayan →, Indonesia 78 D5 2 55N 117 35 E
Kayankulam, India 95 K3 9 10N 76 33 E
Kaycee, U.S.A. 158 E10 43 43N 106 38W
Kayeli, Indonesia 79 E7 3 20 S 127 10 E
Kayenda, Dem. Rep. of the Congo 115 E4 10 48 S 23 6 E
Kayenta, U.S.A. 159 H8 36 44N 110 15W
Kayes, Congo 115 C2 4 25 S 11 41 E
Kayes, Mali 112 C2 14 25N 11 30W
Kayı, Turkey 49 B12 39 12N 30 46 E
Kayima, S. Leone 112 D2 8 54N 11 15W
Kayin = Kawthule □, Burma 90 G6 18 0N 97 30 E
Kaymakçı, Turkey 49 C10 38 10N 28 8 E
Kayoa, Indonesia 79 D7 0 1N 127 28 E
Kayomba, Zambia 119 E1 13 11 S 24 2 E
Kayombo, Zambia 115 E4 13 3 S 23 51 E
Kayrakkumskoye Vdkhr., Tajikistan 63 C4 40 20N 70 0 E
Kaysatskoye, Russia 60 F8 49 47N 46 49 E
Kayseri, Turkey 100 C6 38 45N 35 30 E
Kaysville, U.S.A. 158 F8 41 2N 111 56W
Kayts, Sri Lanka 95 K4 9 42N 79 51 E
Kayuagung, Indonesia 84 C2 3 24 S 104 50 E
Kaz Dağı, Turkey 49 B8 39 42N 26 50 E
Kazachye, Russia 65 B14 70 52N 135 58 E
Kazakstan ■, Asia 64 E7 50 0N 70 0 E
Kazan, Russia 60 C9 55 50N 49 10 E
Kazan →, Canada 143 A9 64 3N 95 35W
Kazan-Rettō, Pac. Oc. 134 E6 25 0N 141 0 E
Kazanlŭk, Bulgaria 51 D9 42 38N 25 20 E
Kazanskaya, Russia 60 F5 49 50N 41 10 E
Kazarman, Kyrgyzstan 63 C6 41 24N 73 59 E
Kazatin = Kozyatyn, Ukraine 59 H5 49 45N 28 50 E
Kazaure, Nigeria 113 C6 12 42N 8 28 E
Kazbek, Russia 61 J7 42 42N 44 30 E
Kāzerūn, Iran 97 D6 29 38N 51 40 E
Kazhim, Russia 62 A3 60 21N 51 33 E
Kazi Magomed = Qazimämmäd, Azerbaijan 61 K9 40 3N 49 0 E
Kazimierz Dolny, Poland 55 G8 51 19N 21 57 E
Kazimierza Wielka, Poland 55 H7 50 15N 20 30 E
Kazincbarcika, Hungary 52 B5 48 17N 20 36 E
Kazipet, India 94 F4 17 58N 79 30 E
Kaziza, Dem. Rep. of the Congo 115 E4 10 42 S 23 52 E
Kazlų Rūda, Lithuania 54 D10 54 46N 23 30 E
Kazo, Japan 71 A11 36 7N 139 36 E
Kaztalovka, Kazakstan 60 F9 49 47N 48 43 E
Kazu, Burma 90 C6 25 27N 97 46 E
Kazumba, Dem. Rep. of the Congo 115 D4 6 25 S 22 5 E
Kazuno, Japan 68 D10 40 10N 140 45 E
Kazym →, Russia 64 C7 63 54N 65 50 E
Kcynia, Poland 55 F4 53 0N 17 30 E
Ke-hsi Mansam, Burma 90 E6 21 56N 97 50 E
Ké-Macina, Mali 112 C3 13 58N 5 22W
Kéa, Greece 48 D6 37 35N 24 22 E
Keady, U.K. 23 B5 54 15N 6 42W
Keahi Pt., U.S.A. 145 K14 21 19N 157 59W
Keahole Pt., U.S.A. 145 D5 19 44N 156 4W
Kealaikahiki Channel, U.S.A. 145 C5 20 35N 156 50W
Kealaikahiki Pt., U.S.A. 145 C5 20 32N 156 42W
Kealakekua, U.S.A. 145 D6 19 31N 155 55W
Kealia, U.S.A. 145 D6 19 24N 155 53W
Kearney, Mo., U.S.A. 156 E2 39 22N 94 22W
Kearney, Nebr., U.S.A. 154 E5 40 42N 99 5W
Kearny, U.S.A. 159 K8 33 3N 110 55W
Kearsarge, Mt., U.S.A. 151 C13 43 22N 71 50W
Keawakapu, U.S.A. 145 C5 20 43N 156 27W
Keban, Turkey 101 C8 38 50N 38 50 E
Keban Baraji, Turkey 101 C8 38 41N 38 33 E
Kebara, Congo 114 C2 2 27 S 14 25 E
Kebbi □, Nigeria 113 C5 11 35N 4 0 E
Kébi, Ivory C. 112 D3 9 18N 6 37W
Kebi, Mayo →, Cameroon 114 A2 9 18N 13 33 E
Kebili, Tunisia 108 B1 33 47N 9 0 E
Kebnekaise, Sweden 14 C18 67 53N 18 33 E
Kebri Dehar, Ethiopia 120 C2 6 45N 44 17 E
Kebumen, Indonesia 79 G13 7 42 S 109 40 E
Kecel, Hungary 52 D4 46 31N 19 16 E
Kechika →, Canada 142 B3 59 41N 127 12W
Keçiborlu, Turkey 49 D12 37 57N 30 18 E
Kecskemét, Hungary 52 D4 46 57N 19 42 E
Kedada, Ethiopia 107 F4 5 25N 35 58 E
Kedah □, Malaysia 84 A2 5 50N 100 40 E
Kėdainiai, Lithuania 15 J21 55 15N 24 2 E
Kedarnath, India 93 D8 30 44N 79 4 E
Kedgwick, Canada 141 C6 47 40N 67 20W
Kédhros Óros, Greece 38 D6 35 11N 24 37 E
Kediri, Indonesia 79 G15 7 51 S 112 1 E
Kedja, Dem. Rep. of the Congo 114 B3 4 50N 19 16 E
Kedjebi, Ghana 113 D5 8 12N 0 25 E
Kédougou, Senegal 112 C2 12 35N 12 10W
Kędzierzyn-Koźle, Poland 55 H5 50 20N 18 12 E
Keehi Lagoon, U.S.A. 145 K14 21 20N 157 54W
Keeler, U.S.A. 160 J9 36 29N 117 52W
Keeley L., Canada 143 C7 54 54N 108 8W
Keeling Is. = Cocos Is., Ind. Oc. 121 F8 12 10 S 96 55 E
Keelung = Chilung, Taiwan 77 E13 25 3N 121 45 E
Keene, Canada 150 B6 44 15N 78 10W
Keene, Calif., U.S.A. 161 K8 35 13N 118 33W
Keene, N.H., U.S.A. 151 D12 42 56N 72 17W
Keene, N.Y., U.S.A. 151 B11 44 16N 73 46W
Keeper Hill, Ireland 23 D3 52 45N 8 16W
Keer-Weer, C., Australia 126 A3 14 0 S 141 32 E
Keeseville, U.S.A. 151 B11 44 29N 73 30W
Keetmanshoop, Namibia 116 D2 26 35 S 18 8 E
Keewatin, Canada 143 D10 49 46N 94 34W
Keewatin →, Canada 143 B8 56 29N 100 46W
Kefa □, Ethiopia 107 F4 6 55N 36 30 E
Kefallinía, Greece 48 C2 38 20N 20 30 E
Kefallinía □, Greece 48 C2 38 20N 20 30 E
Kéfalos, Greece 49 E8 36 45N 26 59 E
Kefamenanu, Indonesia 79 F6 9 28 S 124 29 E
Kefar Sava, Israel 103 C3 32 11N 34 54 E
Keffi, Nigeria 113 D6 8 55N 7 43 E
Keffin Hausa, Nigeria 113 C6 12 13N 9 59 E
Keflavík, Iceland 11 C4 64 2N 22 35W
Keftya, Ethiopia 107 E4 13 54N 37 7 E
Keg River, Canada 142 B5 57 54N 117 55W
Kegalla, Sri Lanka 95 L5 7 15N 80 21 E
Kegaska, Canada 141 B7 50 9N 61 18W
Keheili, Sudan 106 D3 19 25N 32 50 E
Kehl, Germany 31 G3 48 34N 7 50 E
Keighley, U.K. 20 D5 53 52N 1 54W
Keikiwaha Pt., U.S.A. 145 D6 19 31N 155 58W
Keila, Estonia 15 G21 59 18N 24 25 E
Keimoes, S. Africa 116 D3 28 41 S 20 59 E
Keita, Niger 113 C6 14 46N 5 56 E
Keitele, Finland 14 E22 63 10N 26 20 E
Keith, Australia 128 D4 36 6 S 140 20 E
Keith, U.K. 22 D6 57 32N 2 57W
Keithsburg, U.S.A. 156 C6 41 6N 90 56W
Keizer, U.S.A. 158 D2 44 57N 123 1W
Kejimkujik Nat. Park, Canada 141 D6 44 25N 65 25W
Kejser Franz Joseph Fd., Greenland 10 C8 73 30N 24 30W
Kekaha, U.S.A. 145 B2 21 58N 159 43W
Kekaygyr, Kyrgyzstan 63 C7 40 42N 75 32 E
Kekri, India 92 G6 26 0N 75 10 E
Kelam, Ethiopia 107 G4 4 48N 35 58 E
Kelamet, Eritrea 107 D4 16 0N 38 30 E
Kelan, China 74 E6 38 43N 111 31 E
Kelang, Malaysia 78 D2 3 2N 101 26 E
Kelani Ganga →, Sri Lanka 95 L4 6 58N 79 50 E
Kelantan □, Malaysia 84 A2 5 10N 102 0 E
Kelantan →, Malaysia 87 J4 6 13N 102 14 E
Këlcyra, Albania 50 F4 40 20N 20 12 E
Kelekçi, Turkey 49 D11 37 15N 29 20 E
Keles, Turkey 51 G13 39 54N 29 14 E
Keles →, Kazakstan 63 C4 41 1N 68 37 E
Keleti-főcsatorna, Hungary 52 C6 47 45N 21 20 E
Kelheim, Germany 31 G7 48 54N 11 52 E
Kelibia, Tunisia 108 A2 36 50N 11 3 E
Kelkit, Turkey 101 B8 40 7N 39 16 E
Kelkit →, Turkey 100 B7 40 45N 36 32 E
Kellé, Congo 114 C2 0 8 S 14 38 E
Keller, U.S.A. 152 D8 31 50N 81 15W
Kellerberrin, Australia 125 F2 31 36 S 117 38 E
Kellett, C., Canada 6 B1 72 0N 126 0W
Kelleys I., U.S.A. 150 E2 41 36N 82 42W
Kellogg, U.S.A. 158 C5 47 32N 116 7W
Kells = Ceanannus Mor, Ireland 23 C5 53 44N 6 53W
Kelmė, Lithuania 54 C9 55 38N 22 56 E
Kélo, Chad 109 G3 9 10N 15 45 E
Kelokedhara, Cyprus 38 E11 34 48N 32 39 E
Kelowna, Canada 142 D5 49 50N 119 25W
Kelseyville, U.S.A. 160 G4 38 59N 122 50W
Kelso, N.Z. 131 F4 45 54 S 169 15 E
Kelso, U.K. 22 F6 55 36N 2 26W
Kelso, U.S.A. 160 D4 46 9N 122 54W
Keltemashat, Kazakstan 63 B5 42 25N 70 8 E
Keluang, Malaysia 78 D2 2 3N 103 18 E
Kelvington, Canada 143 C8 52 10N 103 30W
Kem, Russia 56 B5 65 0N 34 38 E
Kem →, Russia 56 B5 64 57N 34 41 E
Kem-Kem, Morocco 110 B4 30 40N 4 30W
Kema, Indonesia 79 D7 1 22N 125 8 E
Kemah, Turkey 101 C8 39 32N 39 5 E
Kemaliye, Erzincan, Turkey 101 C8 39 16N 38 29 E
Kemaliye, Manisa, Turkey 49 C10 38 27N 28 25 E
Kemalpaşa, Turkey 49 C9 38 25N 27 27 E
Kemaman, Malaysia 78 D2 4 12N 103 18 E
Kemano, Canada 142 C3 53 35N 128 0W
Kemapyu, Burma 90 F6 18 49N 97 19 E
Kemasik, Malaysia 87 K4 4 25N 103 27 E
Kembé, C.A.R. 114 B4 4 36N 21 54 E
Kembolcha, Ethiopia 107 E4 11 2N 39 42 E
Kemer, Antalya, Turkey 49 E12 36 36N 30 34 E
Kemer, Burdur, Turkey 49 D12 37 21N 30 4 E
Kemer, Muğla, Turkey 49 E11 36 40N 29 22 E
Kemer Barajı, Turkey 49 D10 37 30N 28 37 E
Kemerovo, Russia 64 D9 55 20N 86 5 E
Kemi, Finland 14 D21 65 44N 24 34 E
Kemi älv = Kemijoki →, Finland 14 D21 65 47N 24 32 E
Kemijärvi, Finland 14 C22 66 43N 27 22 E
Kemijoki →, Finland 14 D21 65 47N 24 32 E
Kemmerer, U.S.A. 158 F8 41 48N 110 32W
Kemmuna = Comino, Malta 38 C1 36 2N 14 20 E
Kemp, L., U.S.A. 155 J5 33 46N 99 9W
Kemp Land, Antarctica 7 C5 69 0 S 55 0 E
Kempsey, Australia 129 A10 31 1 S 152 50 E
Kempt, L., Canada 140 C5 47 25N 74 22W
Kempten, Germany 31 H6 47 45N 10 17 E
Kempton, Australia 126 G4 42 31 S 147 12 E
Kempton, U.S.A. 157 D10 40 17N 86 14W
Kemptville, Canada 140 D4 45 0N 75 38W
Ken →, India 93 G9 25 13N 80 27 E
Kenadsa, Algeria 110 B4 31 48N 2 26W
Kenai, U.S.A. 138 B4 60 33N 151 16W
Kenansville, U.S.A. 153 H9 27 53N 80 59W
Kendai, India 93 H10 22 45N 82 37 E
Kendal, Indonesia 79 G14 6 56 S 110 14 E
Kendal, U.K. 20 C5 54 20N 2 44W
Kendall, Australia 129 A10 31 35 S 152 44 E
Kendall, U.S.A. 153 K9 25 41N 80 19W
Kendall →, Australia 126 A3 14 4 S 141 35 E
Kendallville, U.S.A. 157 C11 41 27N 85 16W
Kendari, Indonesia 79 E6 3 50 S 122 30 E
Kendawangan, Indonesia 78 E4 2 32 S 110 17 E
Kende, Nigeria 113 C5 11 30N 4 12 E
Kendrapara, India 94 D8 20 35N 86 30 E
Këndrevicës, Maja e, Albania 50 F3 40 15N 19 52 E
Kendrew, S. Africa 116 E3 32 32 S 24 30 E
Kendrick, U.S.A. 153 F7 29 15N 82 10W
Kene Thao, Laos 86 D3 17 44N 101 10 E
Kenedy, U.S.A. 155 L6 28 49N 97 51W
Kenema, S. Leone 112 D2 7 55N 11 14W
Keng Kok, Laos 86 D5 16 26N 105 12 E

Kildare 233

Keng Tawng, *Burma* **90 E7** 20 45N 98 18 E
Keng Tung, *Burma* **76 G2** 21 0N 99 30 E
Kengani, *Dem. Rep. of the Congo* **114 C3** 2 59 S 17 36 E
Kenge, *Dem. Rep. of the Congo* **115 C3** 4 50 S 17 4 E
Kengeja, *Tanzania* **118 D4** 5 26 S 39 45 E
Kenhardt, *S. Africa* **116 D3** 29 19 S 21 12 E
Kéniéba, *Mali* **112 C2** 12 54N 11 17W
Kenimekh, *Uzbekistan* **63 C2** 40 16N 65 7 E
Kenitra, *Morocco* **110 B3** 34 15N 6 40W
Kenli, *China* **75 F10** 37 30N 118 20 E
Kenmare, *Ireland* **23 E2** 51 53N 9 36W
Kenmare, *U.S.A.* **154 A3** 48 41N 102 5W
Kenmare River, *Ireland* **23 E2** 51 48N 9 51W
Kennebago Lake, *U.S.A.* **151 A14** 45 4N 70 40W
Kennebec, *U.S.A.* **154 D5** 43 54N 99 52W
Kennebec →, *U.S.A.* **149 D11** 43 45N 69 46W
Kennebunk, *U.S.A.* **151 C14** 43 23N 70 33W
Kennedy, *Zimbabwe* **116 B4** 18 52 S 27 10 E
Kennedy Kanal, *Arctic* **10 A4** 80 50N 66 0W
Kennedy Ra., *Australia* **125 D2** 24 45 S 115 10 E
Kenner, *U.S.A.* **155 L9** 29 59N 90 15W
Kennesaw, *U.S.A.* **152 A5** 34 1N 84 37W
Kennet →, *U.K.* **21 F7** 51 27N 0 57W
Kenneth Ra., *Australia* **125 D2** 23 50 S 117 8 E
Kennett, *U.S.A.* **155 G9** 36 14N 90 3W
Kennewick, *U.S.A.* **158 C4** 46 12N 119 7W
Kenogami →, *Canada* **140 B3** 51 6N 84 28W
Kenora, *Canada* **143 D10** 49 47N 94 29W
Kenosha, *U.S.A.* **157 B9** 42 35N 87 49W
Kensington, *Canada* **141 C7** 46 28N 63 34W
Kent, *Ohio, U.S.A.* **150 E3** 41 9N 81 22W
Kent, *Tex., U.S.A.* **155 K2** 31 4N 104 13W
Kent, *Wash., U.S.A.* **160 C4** 47 23N 122 14W
Kent □, *U.K.* **21 F8** 51 12N 0 40 E
Kent Group, *Australia* **126 F4** 39 30 S 147 20 E
Kent Pen., *Canada* **138 B9** 68 30N 107 0W
Kentau, *Kazakstan* **64 E7** 43 32N 68 36 E
Kentland, *U.S.A.* **157 D9** 40 46N 87 27W
Kenton, *U.S.A.* **157 D13** 40 39N 83 37W
Kentucky, *Australia* **129 A9** 30 45 S 151 28 E
Kentucky □, *U.S.A.* **148 G3** 37 0N 84 0W
Kentucky →, *U.S.A.* **157 F11** 38 41N 85 11W
Kentucky L., *U.S.A.* **149 G2** 37 1N 88 16W
Kentville, *Canada* **141 C7** 45 6N 64 29W
Kentwood, *La., U.S.A.* **155 K9** 30 56N 90 31W
Kentwood, *Mich., U.S.A.* **157 B11** 42 52N 85 37W
Kenya ■, *Africa* **118 B4** 1 0N 38 0 E
Kenya, Mt., *Kenya* **118 C4** 0 10 S 37 18 E
Kenzou, *Cameroon* **114 B3** 4 10N 15 2 E
Keo Neua, Deo, *Vietnam* **86 C5** 18 23N 105 10 E
Keokea, *U.S.A.* **145 C5** 20 43N 156 22W
Keokuk, *U.S.A.* **156 D5** 40 24N 91 24W
Keonjhargarh, *India* **93 J11** 21 28N 85 35 E
Keosauqua, *U.S.A.* **156 D5** 40 44N 91 58W
Keota, *U.S.A.* **156 C5** 41 22N 91 57W
Kep, *Cambodia* **87 G5** 10 29N 104 19 E
Kep, *Vietnam* **86 B6** 21 24N 106 16 E
Kepez, *Turkey* **51 F10** 40 5N 26 24 E
Kepi, *Indonesia* **79 F9** 6 32 S 139 19 E
Kępice, *Poland* **54 D3** 54 16N 16 51 E
Kepler Mts., *N.Z.* **131 F2** 45 25 S 167 20 E
Kępno, *Poland* **55 G4** 51 18N 17 58 E
Kepsut, *Turkey* **49 B10** 39 40N 28 9 E
Kepuhi Pt., *U.S.A.* **145 K13** 21 29N 158 14W
Kerala □, *India* **95 J3** 11 0N 76 15 E
Kerama-Rettō, *Japan* **69 L3** 26 5N 127 15 E
Keran, *Pakistan* **93 B5** 34 35N 73 59 E
Kerang, *Australia* **128 C5** 35 40 S 143 55 E
Keranyo, *Ethiopia* **107 F4** 5 3N 38 18 E
Kerao →, *Sudan* **107 E3** 11 0N 32 41 E
Keratéa, *Greece* **48 D5** 37 48N 23 58 E
Keraudren, C., *Australia* **124 C2** 19 58 S 119 45 E
Kerava, *Finland* **15 F21** 60 25N 25 5 E
Keravat, *Papua N. G.* **132 C7** 4 17 S 152 2 E
Kerch, *Ukraine* **59 K9** 45 20N 36 20 E
Kerchenskiy Proliv, *Black Sea* **59 K9** 45 10N 36 30 E
Kerchoual, *Mali* **113 B5** 17 12N 0 20 E
Kerema, *Papua N. G.* **132 D3** 7 58 S 145 50 E
Kerempe Burnu, *Turkey* **100 A5** 42 2N 33 20 E
Keren, *Eritrea* **107 D4** 15 45N 38 28 E
Kerewan, *Gambia* **112 C1** 13 29N 16 10W
Kerguelen, *Ind. Oc.* **121 J5** 49 15 S 69 10 E
Keri, *Greece* **48 D2** 37 40N 20 49 E
Keri Kera, *Sudan* **107 E3** 12 21N 32 42 E
Kericho, *Kenya* **118 C4** 0 22 S 35 15 E
Kerikeri, *N.Z.* **130 B2** 35 12 S 173 59 E
Kerinci, *Indonesia* **78 E2** 1 40 S 101 15 E
Kerkenna, Is., *Tunisia* **108 B2** 34 48N 11 11 E
Kerki, *Turkmenistan* **64 F7** 37 50N 65 12 E
Kerkinítis, Límni, *Greece* **50 E7** 41 12N 23 10 E
Kérkira, *Greece* **38 A3** 39 38N 19 50 E
Kérkira □, *Greece* **48 B1** 39 37N 19 50 E
Kerkrade, *Neths.* **24 D6** 50 53N 6 4 E
Kerma, *Sudan* **106 D3** 19 33N 30 32 E
Kermadec Is., *Pac. Oc.* **134 L10** 30 0 S 178 15W
Kermadec Trench, *Pac. Oc.* **134 L10** 30 30 S 176 0W
Kermān, *Iran* **97 D8** 30 15N 57 1 E
Kerman, *U.S.A.* **160 J6** 36 43N 120 4W
Kermān □, *Iran* **97 D8** 30 0N 57 0 E
Kermān, Bīābān-e, *Iran* **97 D8** 28 45N 59 45 E
Kermānshāh = Bākhtarān, *Iran* **101 E12** 34 23N 47 0 E
Kermen, *Bulgaria* **51 D10** 42 30N 26 16 E
Kermit, *U.S.A.* **155 K3** 31 52N 103 6W
Kern →, *U.S.A.* **161 K7** 35 16N 119 18W
Kernhof, *Austria* **34 D8** 47 49N 15 32 E
Kerns, *Switz.* **33 C6** 46 54N 8 17 E
Kernville, *U.S.A.* **161 K8** 35 45N 118 26W
Keroh, *Malaysia* **87 K3** 5 43N 101 1 E
Kérou, *Benin* **113 C5** 10 50N 2 5 E
Kérouane, *Guinea* **112 D3** 9 15N 9 0W
Kerpen, *Germany* **30 E2** 50 51N 6 41 E
Kerrera, *U.K.* **22 E3** 56 24N 5 33W
Kerrobert, *Canada* **143 C7** 51 56N 109 8W
Kerrville, *U.S.A.* **155 K5** 30 3N 99 8W
Kerry □, *Ireland* **23 D2** 52 7N 9 35W
Kerry Hd., *Ireland* **23 D2** 52 25N 9 56W
Kersa, *Ethiopia* **107 F5** 9 28N 41 48 E
Kertosono, *Indonesia* **85 D4** 7 38 S 112 9 E
Kerulen →, *Asia* **73 B6** 48 48N 117 0 E
Kerzaz, *Algeria* **111 C4** 29 29N 1 37W
Kerzers, *Switz.* **32 C4** 46 59N 7 12 E
Kesagami →, *Canada* **140 B4** 51 40N 79 45W
Kesagami L., *Canada* **140 B3** 50 23N 80 15W
Keşan, *Turkey* **51 F10** 40 49N 26 38 E
Kesch, Piz, *Switz.* **33 C9** 46 38N 9 53 E
Kesennuma, *Japan* **68 E10** 38 54N 141 35 E
Keshit, *Iran* **97 D8** 29 43N 58 17 E
Keşiş Dağ, *Turkey* **101 C8** 39 47N 39 46 E
Keskal, *India* **94 D5** 20 5N 81 35 E
Keskin, *Turkey* **100 C5** 39 40N 33 36 E
Kestell, *S. Africa* **117 D4** 28 17 S 28 42 E
Kestenga, *Russia* **56 A5** 65 50N 31 45 E
Keswick, *U.K.* **20 C4** 54 36N 3 8W
Keszthely, *Hungary* **52 D2** 46 50N 17 15 E
Ket →, *Russia* **64 D9** 58 55N 81 32 E
Keta, *Ghana* **113 D5** 5 49N 1 0 E
Keta Lagoon, *Ghana* **113 D5** 5 55N 1 0 E
Ketapang, *Indonesia* **78 E4** 1 55 S 110 0 E
Ketchikan, *U.S.A.* **142 B2** 55 21N 131 39W
Ketchum, *U.S.A.* **158 E6** 43 41N 114 22W
Kete Krachi, *Ghana* **113 D4** 7 46N 0 1W
Ketef, Khalîg Umm el, *Egypt* **96 F2** 23 40N 35 35 E
Keti Bandar, *Pakistan* **92 G2** 24 8N 67 27 E
Kétou, *Benin* **113 D5** 7 25N 2 45 E
Ketri, *India* **92 E6** 28 1N 75 50 E
Kętrzyn, *Poland* **54 D8** 54 7N 21 22 E
Kettering, *U.K.* **21 E7** 52 24N 0 43W
Kettering, *U.S.A.* **157 E12** 39 41N 84 10W
Kettle →, *Canada* **143 B11** 56 40N 89 34W
Kettle Falls, *U.S.A.* **158 B4** 48 37N 118 3W
Kettle Pt., *Canada* **150 C2** 43 13N 82 1W
Kettleman City, *U.S.A.* **160 J7** 36 1N 119 58W
Kęty, *Poland* **55 J6** 49 51N 19 16 E
Keuka L., *U.S.A.* **150 D7** 42 30N 77 9W
Keuruu, *Finland* **15 E21** 62 16N 24 41 E
Kevelaer, *Germany* **30 D2** 51 36N 6 15 E
Kewanee, *U.S.A.* **156 C7** 41 14N 89 56W
Kewanna, *U.S.A.* **157 C10** 41 1N 86 25W
Kewaunee, *U.S.A.* **148 C2** 44 27N 87 31W
Keweenaw B., *U.S.A.* **148 B1** 47 0N 88 15W
Keweenaw Pen., *U.S.A.* **148 B2** 47 30N 88 0W
Keweenaw Pt., *U.S.A.* **148 B2** 47 25N 87 43W
Key Colony Beach, *U.S.A.* **153 L9** 24 45N 80 57W
Key Largo, *U.S.A.* **153 K9** 25 5N 80 27W
Key West, *U.S.A.* **153 L8** 24 33N 81 48W
Keyala, *Sudan* **107 G3** 4 27N 32 52 E
Keynsham, *U.K.* **21 F5** 51 24N 2 29W
Keyser, *U.S.A.* **148 F6** 39 26N 78 59W
Keytesville, *U.S.A.* **156 E4** 39 26N 92 56W
Kez, *Russia* **62 C4** 57 55N 53 46 E
Kezhma, *Russia* **65 D11** 58 59N 101 9 E
Kezi, *Zimbabwe* **117 C4** 20 58 S 28 32 E
Kežmarok, *Slovak Rep.* **35 B13** 49 10N 20 28 E
Khabarovsk, *Russia* **65 E14** 48 30N 135 5 E
Khabr, *Iran* **97 D8** 28 51N 56 22 E
Khābūr →, *Syria* **101 E9** 35 17N 40 35 E
Khachmas = Xaçmaz, *Azerbaijan* **61 K9** 41 31N 48 42 E
Khachrod, *India* **92 H6** 23 25N 75 20 E
Khadari, W. el →, *Sudan* **107 E2** 10 29N 27 15 E
Khadro, *Pakistan* **92 F3** 26 11N 68 50 E
Khadyzhensk, *Russia* **61 H4** 44 26N 39 32 E
Khadzhilyangar, *India* **93 B8** 35 45N 79 20 E
Khaga, *India* **93 G9** 25 47N 81 7 E
Khagaria, *India* **93 G12** 25 30N 86 32 E
Khaipur, *Pakistan* **92 E5** 29 34N 72 17 E
Khair, *India* **92 F7** 27 57N 77 46 E
Khairabad, *India* **93 F9** 27 33N 80 47 E
Khairagarh, *India* **93 J9** 21 27N 81 2 E
Khairpur, *Pakistan* **91 D3** 27 32N 68 49 E
Khairpur Nathan Shah, *Pakistan* **92 F2** 27 6N 67 44 E
Khairwara, *India* **92 H5** 23 58N 73 38 E
Khaisor →, *Pakistan* **92 D3** 31 17N 68 59 E
Khajuri Kach, *Pakistan* **92 C3** 32 4N 69 51 E
Khāk Dow, *Afghan.* **91 B2** 34 57N 67 16 E
Khakassia □, *Russia* **64 D9** 53 0N 90 0 E
Khakhea, *Botswana* **116 C3** 24 48 S 23 22 E
Khalafābād, *Iran* **97 D6** 30 54N 49 24 E
Khalfallah, *Algeria* **111 B5** 34 20N 0 16 E
Khalfūt, *Yemen* **99 D6** 15 52N 52 10 E
Khalilabad, *India* **93 F10** 26 48N 83 5 E
Khalīlī, *Iran* **97 E7** 27 38N 53 17 E
Khalkhāl, *Iran* **97 B6** 37 37N 48 32 E
Khálki, *Dhodhekánisos, Greece* **49 E9** 36 17N 27 35 E
Khálki, *Thessalía, Greece* **48 B4** 39 36N 22 30 E
Khalkidhikí □, *Greece* **50 F7** 40 25N 23 20 E
Khalkís, *Greece* **48 C5** 38 27N 23 42 E
Khalmer-Sede = Tazovskiy, *Russia* **64 C8** 67 30N 78 44 E
Khalmer Yu, *Russia* **64 C7** 67 58N 65 1 E
Khalturin, *Russia* **62 B2** 58 40N 48 50 E
Khalūf, *Oman* **102 C6** 20 30N 58 13 E
Kham Keut, *Laos* **86 C5** 18 15N 104 43 E
Khamaria, *India* **93 H9** 23 5N 80 48 E
Khambhaliya, *India* **92 H3** 22 14N 69 41 E
Khambhat, *India* **92 H5** 22 23N 72 33 E
Khamgaon, *India* **94 D3** 20 42N 76 37 E
Khamilonísion, *Greece* **49 F8** 35 50N 26 15 E
Khamīr, *Iran* **97 E7** 26 57N 55 36 E
Khamir, *Yemen* **98 C3** 16 2N 44 0 E
Khamīs Mushayṭ, *Si. Arabia* **98 C3** 18 18N 42 44 E
Khammam, *India* **94 F5** 17 11N 80 6 E
Khamsa, *Egypt* **103 E1** 30 27N 32 23 E
Khan →, *Namibia* **116 C2** 22 37 S 14 56 E
Khān Abū Shāmat, *Syria* **103 B5** 33 39N 36 53 E
Khān Azād, *Iraq* **96 C5** 33 7N 44 22 E
Khān Mujiddah, *Iraq* **96 C4** 32 21N 43 48 E
Khān Shaykhūn, *Syria* **100 E7** 35 26N 36 38 E
Khān Yūnis, *Gaza Strip* **103 D3** 31 21N 34 18 E
Khānābād, *Afghan.* **91 A3** 36 45N 69 5 E
Khanabad, *Uzbekistan* **63 C5** 40 59N 70 38 E
Khanai, *Pakistan* **92 D2** 30 30N 67 8 E
Khānaqīn, *Iraq* **101 E11** 34 23N 45 25 E
Khānbāghī, *Iran* **97 B7** 36 10N 55 25 E
Khandrá, *Greece* **49 F8** 35 3N 26 8 E
Khandwa, *India* **94 D3** 21 49N 76 22 E
Khandyga, *Russia* **65 C14** 62 42N 135 35 E
Khāneh, *Iran* **96 B5** 36 41N 45 8 E
Khanewal, *Pakistan* **91 C3** 30 20N 71 55 E
Khangah Dogran, *Pakistan* **92 D5** 31 50N 73 37 E
Khanh Duong, *Vietnam* **86 F7** 12 44N 108 44 E
Khaniá, *Greece* **38 D6** 35 30N 24 4 E
Khaniá □, *Greece* **38 D6** 35 30N 24 0 E
Khaniadhana, *India* **92 G8** 25 1N 78 8 E
Khaníon, Kólpos, *Greece* **38 D5** 35 33N 23 55 E
Khanka, L., *Asia* **65 E14** 45 0N 132 24 E
Khankendy = Xankändi, *Azerbaijan* **101 C12** 39 52N 46 49 E
Khanna, *India* **92 D7** 30 42N 76 16 E
Khanozai, *Pakistan* **92 D2** 30 37N 67 19 E
Khanpur, *Pakistan* **91 C3** 28 42N 70 35 E
Khantau, *Kazakstan* **63 A6** 44 13N 73 48 E
Khanty-Mansiysk, *Russia* **64 C7** 61 0N 69 0 E
Khapalu, *Pakistan* **93 B7** 35 10N 76 20 E
Khapcheranga, *Russia* **65 E12** 49 42N 112 24 E
Kharabali, *Russia* **61 G8** 47 25N 47 15 E
Kharaghoda, *India* **92 H4** 23 11N 71 46 E
Kharagpur, *India* **93 H12** 22 20N 87 25 E
Khárakas, *Greece* **38 D7** 35 1N 25 7 E
Kharan Kalat, *Pakistan* **91 C2** 28 34N 65 21 E
Kharānaq, *Iran* **97 C7** 32 20N 54 45 E
Kharda, *India* **94 E2** 18 40N 75 34 E
Khardung La, *India* **93 B7** 34 20N 77 43 E
Khârga, El Wâhât-el, *Egypt* **106 B3** 25 10N 30 35 E
Khargon, *India* **94 D2** 21 45N 75 40 E
Khari →, *India* **92 G6** 25 54N 74 31 E
Kharian, *Pakistan* **92 C5** 32 49N 73 52 E
Khariar, *India* **94 D6** 20 17N 82 46 E
Kharit, Wadi el →, *Egypt* **106 C3** 24 26N 33 3 E
Khārk, Jazīreh-ye, *Iran* **97 D6** 29 15N 50 28 E
Kharkiv, *Ukraine* **59 H9** 49 58N 36 20 E
Kharkov = Kharkiv, *Ukraine* **59 H9** 49 58N 36 20 E
Kharmanli, *Bulgaria* **51 E9** 41 55N 25 55 E
Kharovsk, *Russia* **58 C11** 59 56N 40 13 E
Kharsawangarh, *India* **93 H11** 22 48N 85 50 E
Kharta, *Turkey* **100 B3** 40 55N 29 7 E
Khartoum = El Khartûm, *Sudan* **107 D3** 15 31N 32 35 E
Khasan, *Russia* **68 C5** 42 25N 130 40 E
Khasavyurt, *Russia* **61 J8** 43 16N 46 40 E
Khāsh, *Iran* **97 D9** 28 15N 61 15 E
Khashm el Girba, *Sudan* **107 E4** 14 59N 35 58 E
Khashum, *Sudan* **107 E2** 12 27N 28 2 E
Khashuri, *Georgia* **61 J6** 42 3N 43 35 E
Khasi Hills, *India* **90 C3** 25 30N 91 30 E
Khaskovo, *Bulgaria* **51 E9** 41 56N 25 30 E
Khaskovo □, *Bulgaria* **51 E9** 42 0N 25 40 E
Khatanga, *Russia* **65 B11** 72 0N 102 20 E
Khatanga →, *Russia* **65 B11** 72 55N 106 0 E
Khatauli, *India* **92 E7** 29 17N 77 43 E
Khatra, *India* **93 H12** 22 59N 86 51 E
Khātūnābād, *Iran* **97 D7** 30 1N 55 25 E
Khatyrchi, *Uzbekistan* **63 C2** 40 2N 65 58 E
Khatyrka, *Russia* **65 C18** 62 3N 175 15 E
Khavast, *Uzbekistan* **63 C4** 40 10N 68 49 E
Khavda, *India* **92 H3** 23 51N 69 43 E
Khawlaf, Ra's, *Yemen* **99 D6** 12 40N 54 7 E
Khay', *Si. Arabia* **98 C3** 18 45N 41 24 E
Khaybar, Harrat, *Si. Arabia* **96 E4** 25 45N 40 0 E
Khaydarken, *Kyrgyzstan* **63 D5** 39 57N 71 20 E
Khāzimiyah, *Iraq* **96 C4** 34 46N 43 37 E
Khazzān Jabal al Awliyā, *Sudan* **107 D3** 15 24N 32 20 E
Khe Bo, *Vietnam* **86 C5** 19 8N 104 41 E
Khe Long, *Vietnam* **86 B5** 21 29N 104 46 E
Khed, *Maharashtra, India* **94 F1** 17 43N 73 27 E
Khed, *Maharashtra, India* **94 E1** 18 51N 73 56 E
Khekra, *India* **92 E7** 28 52N 77 20 E
Khemarak Phouminville, *Cambodia* **87 G4** 11 37N 102 59 E
Khemis Miliana, *Algeria* **111 A5** 36 11N 2 14 E
Khemisset, *Morocco* **110 B3** 33 50N 6 1W
Khemmarat, *Thailand* **78 A3** 16 10N 105 15 E
Khenāmān, *Iran* **97 D8** 30 27N 56 29 E
Khenchela, *Algeria* **111 A6** 35 28N 7 11 E
Khenifra, *Morocco* **110 B3** 32 58N 5 46W
Kherrata, *Algeria* **111 A6** 36 27N 5 13 E
Khersān →, *Iran* **97 D6** 31 33N 50 22 E
Khérson, *Greece* **50 E6** 41 5N 22 47 E
Kherson, *Ukraine* **59 J7** 46 35N 32 35 E
Khersónisos Akrotíri, *Greece* **38 D6** 35 30N 24 10 E
Kheta →, *Russia* **65 B11** 71 54N 102 6 E
Khewari, *Pakistan* **92 F3** 26 36N 68 52 E
Khilchipur, *India* **92 G7** 24 2N 76 34 E
Khiliomódhion, *Greece* **48 D4** 37 48N 22 51 E
Khilok, *Russia* **65 D12** 51 30N 110 45 E
Khimki, *Russia* **58 E9** 55 50N 37 20 E
Khíos, *Greece* **49 C8** 38 27N 26 9 E
Khíos □, *Greece* **49 C8** 38 27N 26 9 E
Khirsadoh, *India* **93 H8** 22 11N 78 47 E
Khiuma = Hiiumaa, *Estonia* **15 G20** 58 50N 22 45 E
Khiva, *Uzbekistan* **64 E7** 41 30N 60 18 E
Khīyāv, *Iran* **96 B5** 38 30N 47 45 E
Khlebarovo, *Bulgaria* **51 C10** 43 37N 26 15 E
Khlong Khlung, *Thailand* **86 D2** 16 12N 99 43 E
Khmelnik, *Ukraine* **59 H4** 49 33N 27 58 E
Khmelnitskiy = Khmelnytskyy, *Ukraine* **59 H4** 49 23N 27 0 E
Khmelnytskyy, *Ukraine* **59 H4** 49 23N 27 0 E
Khmer Rep. = Cambodia ■, *Asia* **78 B3** 12 15N 105 0 E
Khoai, Hon, *Vietnam* **87 H5** 8 26N 104 50 E
Khodoriv, *Ukraine* **59 H3** 49 24N 24 19 E
Khodzent = Khudzhand, *Tajikistan* **64 E7** 40 17N 69 37 E
Khojak Pass, *Afghan.* **91 C2** 30 51N 66 34 E
Khok Kloi, *Thailand* **87 H2** 8 17N 98 19 E
Khok Pho, *Thailand* **87 J3** 6 43N 101 6 E
Kholm, *Afghan.* **91 A2** 36 45N 67 40 E
Kholm, *Russia* **58 D6** 57 10N 31 15 E
Kholmsk, *Russia* **65 E15** 47 40N 142 5 E
Khomas Hochland, *Namibia* **116 C2** 22 40 S 16 0 E
Khombole, *Senegal* **112 C1** 14 43N 16 42W
Khomeyn, *Iran* **97 C6** 33 40N 50 7 E
Khomeynī Shahr, *Iran* **97 C6** 32 41N 51 31 E
Khomodino, *Botswana* **116 C3** 22 46 S 23 52 E
Khon Kaen, *Thailand* **78 A2** 16 30N 102 47 E
Khong →, *Cambodia* **78 B3** 13 32N 105 58 E
Khong Sedone, *Laos* **86 E5** 15 34N 105 49 E
Khonuu, *Russia* **65 C15** 66 30N 143 12 E
Khoper →, *Russia* **60 F6** 49 30N 42 20 E
Khor el 'Atash, *Sudan* **107 E3** 13 20N 34 15 E
Khóra, *Greece* **48 D3** 37 3N 21 42 E
Khóra Sfakíon, *Greece* **38 D6** 35 15N 24 9 E
Khorāsān □, *Iran* **97 C8** 34 0N 58 0 E
Khorat = Nakhon Ratchasima, *Thailand* **78 B2** 14 59N 102 12 E
Khorat, Cao Nguyen, *Thailand* **86 E4** 15 30N 102 50 E
Khorb el Ethel, *Algeria* **110 C3** 28 30N 6 17W
Khorixas, *Namibia* **116 C1** 20 16 S 14 59 E
Khorol, *Ukraine* **59 H7** 49 48N 33 15 E
Khorramābād, *Khorāsān, Iran* **97 C8** 35 6N 57 57 E
Khorramābād, *Lorestān, Iran* **97 C6** 33 30N 48 25 E
Khorrāmshahr, *Iran* **97 D6** 30 29N 48 15 E
Khorugh, *Tajikistan* **64 F8** 37 30N 71 36 E
Khosravī, *Iran* **97 D6** 30 48N 51 28 E
Khosrowābād, *Khuzestān, Iran* **97 D6** 30 10N 48 25 E
Khosrowābād, *Kordestān, Iran* **101 E12** 35 31N 47 38 E
Khost, *Pakistan* **92 D2** 30 13N 67 35 E
Khosūyeh, *Iran* **97 D7** 28 32N 54 26 E
Khotyn, *Ukraine* **59 H4** 48 31N 26 27 E
Khouribga, *Morocco* **110 B3** 32 58N 6 57W
Khowai, *Bangla.* **90 C3** 24 5N 91 40 E
Khowst, *Afghan.* **92 C3** 33 22N 69 58 E
Khoyniki, *Belarus* **59 G5** 51 54N 29 55 E
Khrami →, *Georgia* **61 K7** 41 25N 45 0 E
Khrenovoye, *Russia* **60 E5** 51 4N 40 16 E
Khrisoúpolis, *Greece* **51 F8** 40 58N 24 42 E
Khristianá, *Greece* **49 E7** 36 14N 25 13 E
Khromtau, *Kazakstan* **62 F7** 50 17N 58 27 E
Khrysokhou B., *Cyprus* **38 D11** 35 6N 32 25 E
Khtapodhiá, *Greece* **49 D7** 37 24N 25 34 E
Khu Khan, *Thailand* **78 B2** 14 42N 104 12 E
Khudrah, W. →, *Yemen* **99 C5** 18 10N 50 20 E
Khudzhand, *Tajikistan* **64 E7** 40 17N 69 37 E
Khuff, *Si. Arabia* **96 E5** 24 55N 44 53 E
Khūgīānī, *Qandahar, Afghan.* **91 C2** 31 34N 66 32 E
Khūgīānī, *Qandahar, Afghan.* **91 C2** 31 28N 65 14 E
Khuis, *Botswana* **116 D3** 26 40 S 21 49 E
Khuiyala, *India* **92 F4** 27 9N 70 25 E
Khujner, *India* **92 H7** 23 47N 76 36 E
Khulayş, *Si. Arabia* **98 B2** 22 9N 39 19 E
Khulna, *Bangla.* **90 D2** 22 45N 89 34 E
Khulna □, *Bangla.* **90 D2** 22 25N 89 35 E
Khulo, *Georgia* **61 K6** 41 33N 42 19 E
Khumago, *Botswana* **116 C3** 20 26 S 24 32 E
Khumrah, *Si. Arabia* **98 B2** 21 22N 39 13 E
Khūnsorkh, *Iran* **97 E8** 27 9N 56 7 E
Khunti, *India* **93 H11** 23 5N 85 17 E
Khūr, *Iran* **97 C8** 32 55N 58 18 E
Khurai, *India* **92 G8** 24 3N 78 23 E
Khuraydah, *Yemen* **99 D5** 15 33N 48 18 E
Khurayş, *Si. Arabia* **97 E6** 25 6N 48 2 E
Khurda, *India* **94 D7** 20 11N 85 37 E
Khureit, *Sudan* **107 E2** 13 59N 26 3 E
Khurīyā Murīyā, Jazā 'ir, *Oman* **99 C6** 17 30N 55 58 E
Khurja, *India* **92 E7** 28 15N 77 58 E
Khūrmāl, *Iraq* **96 C5** 35 18N 46 2 E
Khurr, Wādī al, *Iraq* **96 C4** 32 3N 43 52 E
Khūsf, *Iran* **97 C8** 32 46N 58 53 E
Khushab, *Pakistan* **91 B4** 32 20N 72 20 E
Khust, *Ukraine* **59 H2** 48 10N 23 18 E
Khuzdar, *Pakistan* **91 D2** 27 52N 66 30 E
Khūzestān □, *Iran* **97 D6** 31 0N 49 0 E
Khvāf, *Iran* **97 C9** 34 33N 60 8 E
Khvājeh, *Iran* **96 B5** 38 9N 46 35 E
Khvājeh Moḩammad, Kūh-e, *Afghan.* **91 A3** 36 22N 70 17 E
Khvalynsk, *Russia* **60 D9** 52 30N 48 2 E
Khvānsār, *Iran* **97 D7** 29 56N 54 8 E
Khvatovka, *Russia* **60 D8** 52 24N 46 32 E
Khvor, *Iran* **97 C7** 33 45N 55 0 E
Khvorgū, *Iran* **97 E8** 27 34N 56 27 E
Khvormūj, *Iran* **97 D6** 28 40N 51 30 E
Khvoy, *Iran* **101 C11** 38 35N 45 0 E
Khvoynaya, *Russia* **58 C8** 58 58N 34 28 E
Khyber Pass, *Afghan.* **91 B3** 34 10N 71 8 E
Kia, *Solomon Is.* **133 L10** 7 32 S 158 26 E
Kiabukwa, *Dem. Rep. of the Congo* **119 D1** 8 40 S 24 48 E
Kiadho →, *India* **94 E3** 19 37N 77 40 E
Kiama, *Australia* **129 C9** 34 40 S 150 50 E
Kiama, *Dem. Rep. of the Congo* **115 D3** 7 19 S 17 49 E
Kiamba, *Phil.* **79 C6** 6 2N 124 46 E
Kiambi, *Dem. Rep. of the Congo* **118 D2** 7 15 S 28 0 E
Kiambu, *Kenya* **118 C4** 1 8 S 36 50 E
Kiana, *U.S.A.* **144 C7** 66 58N 160 26W
Kiangara, *Madag.* **117 B8** 17 58 S 47 2 E
Kiangsi = Jiangxi □, *China* **77 D11** 27 30N 116 0 E
Kiangsu = Jiangsu □, *China* **75 H11** 33 0N 120 0 E
Kiáton, *Greece* **48 C4** 38 1N 22 45 E
Kibæk, *Denmark* **17 H2** 56 2N 8 51 E
Kibanga Port, *Uganda* **118 B3** 0 10N 32 58 E
Kibangou, *Congo* **114 C2** 3 26 S 12 22 E
Kibara, *Tanzania* **118 C3** 2 8 S 33 30 E
Kibare, Mts., *Dem. Rep. of the Congo* **118 D2** 8 25 S 27 10 E
Kibawe, *Phil.* **81 H5** 7 34N 125 0 E
Kibenga, *Dem. Rep. of the Congo* **115 D3** 7 56 S 17 30 E
Kibombo, *Dem. Rep. of the Congo* **118 C2** 3 57 S 25 53 E
Kibondo, *Tanzania* **118 C3** 3 35 S 30 45 E
Kibre Mengist, *Ethiopia* **102 F2** 5 54N 38 59 E
Kibumbu, *Burundi* **118 C2** 3 32 S 29 45 E
Kibungo, *Rwanda* **118 C3** 2 10 S 30 32 E
Kibuye, *Burundi* **118 C2** 3 39 S 29 59 E
Kibuye, *Rwanda* **118 C2** 2 3 S 29 21 E
Kibwesa, *Tanzania* **118 D2** 6 30 S 29 58 E
Kibwezi, *Kenya* **118 C4** 2 27 S 37 57 E
Kicasalih, *Turkey* **51 E10** 41 23N 26 48 E
Kičevo, *Macedonia* **50 E4** 41 34N 20 59 E
Kichha, *India* **93 E8** 28 53N 79 30 E
Kichha →, *India* **93 E8** 28 41N 79 18 E
Kichmengskiy Gorodok, *Russia* **56 B8** 59 59N 45 48 E
Kicking Horse Pass, *Canada* **142 C5** 51 28N 116 16W
Kidal, *Mali* **113 B5** 18 26N 1 22 E
Kidapawan, *Phil.* **81 H5** 7 1N 125 3 E
Kidderminster, *U.K.* **21 E5** 52 24N 2 15W
Kidete, *Tanzania* **118 D4** 6 25 S 37 17 E
Kidira, *Senegal* **112 C2** 14 28N 12 13W
Kidnappers, C., *N.Z.* **130 F6** 39 38 S 177 5 E
Kidsgrove, *U.K.* **20 D5** 53 5N 2 14W
Kidston, *Australia* **126 B3** 18 52 S 144 8 E
Kidugallo, *Tanzania* **118 D4** 6 49 S 38 15 E
Kidurong, Tanjong, *Malaysia* **85 B4** 3 16N 113 3 E
Kiel, *Germany* **30 A6** 54 19N 10 8 E
Kiel Canal = Nord-Ostsee-Kanal, *Germany* **30 A5** 54 12N 9 32 E
Kielce, *Poland* **55 H7** 50 52N 20 42 E
Kielder Water, *U.K.* **20 B5** 55 11N 2 31W
Kieler Bucht, *Germany* **30 A6** 54 35N 10 25 E
Kiembara, *Burkina Faso* **112 C4** 13 15N 2 44W
Kien Binh, *Vietnam* **87 H5** 9 55N 105 19 E
Kien Tan, *Vietnam* **87 G5** 10 7N 105 17 E
Kienge, *Dem. Rep. of the Congo* **119 E2** 10 30 S 27 30 E
Kiessé, *Niger* **113 C5** 13 29N 4 1 E
Kieta, *Papua N. G.* **132 D8** 6 12 S 155 36 E
Kiev = Kyyiv, *Ukraine* **59 G6** 50 30N 30 28 E
Kifaya, *Guinea* **112 C2** 12 10N 13 4W
Kiffa, *Mauritania* **112 B2** 16 37N 11 24W
Kifisiá, *Greece* **48 C5** 38 4N 23 49 E
Kifissós →, *Greece* **48 C5** 38 35N 23 20 E
Kifrī, *Iraq* **101 E11** 34 45N 45 0 E
Kigali, *Rwanda* **118 C3** 1 59 S 30 4 E
Kigarama, *Tanzania* **118 C3** 1 1 S 31 50 E
Kigelle, *Sudan* **107 F3** 8 40N 34 2 E
Kigoma □, *Tanzania* **118 D3** 5 0 S 30 0 E
Kigoma-Ujiji, *Tanzania* **118 C2** 4 55 S 29 36 E
Kigomasha, Ras, *Tanzania* **118 C4** 4 58 S 38 58 E
Kığzı, *Turkey* **96 B4** 38 18N 43 25 E
Kihei, *U.S.A.* **145 C5** 20 47N 156 28W
Kihikihi, *N.Z.* **130 E4** 38 2 S 175 22 E
Kihnu, *Estonia* **15 G21** 58 9N 24 1 E
Kiholo B., *U.S.A.* **145 D6** 19 50N 155 55W
Kii-Hantō, *Japan* **71 D7** 34 0N 135 45 E
Kii-Sanchi, *Japan* **71 C8** 34 20N 136 0 E
Kii-Suidō, *Japan* **70 D6** 33 40N 134 45 E
Kikaiga-Shima, *Japan* **69 K4** 28 19N 129 59 E
Kikinda, *Serbia, Yug.* **52 E5** 45 50N 20 30 E
Kikládhes, *Greece* **48 E6** 37 0N 24 30 E
Kikládhes □, *Greece* **48 D6** 37 0N 25 0 E
Kikoira, *Australia* **129 B7** 33 39 S 146 40 E
Kikombo, *Dem. Rep. of the Congo* **115 D3** 5 37 S 18 50 E
Kikombo, *Dem. Rep. of the Congo* **115 D3** 5 49 S 17 45 E
Kikongo, *Dem. Rep. of the Congo* **115 C3** 4 16 S 17 17 E
Kikori, *Papua N. G.* **132 D3** 7 25 S 144 15 E
Kikori →, *Papua N. G.* **132 D3** 7 38 S 144 20 E
Kikuchi, *Japan* **70 E2** 32 59N 130 47 E
Kikwit, *Dem. Rep. of the Congo* **115 D3** 5 0 S 18 45 E
Kil, *Sweden* **16 E7** 59 30N 13 20 E
Kila' Drosh, *Pakistan* **91 B3** 35 33N 71 52 E
Kilafors, *Sweden* **16 C10** 61 14N 16 36 E
Kilakkarai, *India* **95 K4** 9 12N 78 47 E
Kilar, *India* **92 C7** 33 6N 76 25 E
Kilauea, *U.S.A.* **146 J14** 22 13N 159 25W
Kilauea Crater, *U.S.A.* **146 J17** 19 25N 155 17W
Kilbrannan Sd., *U.K.* **22 F3** 55 37N 5 26W
Kilchberg, *Switz.* **33 B7** 47 18N 8 33 E
Kilchu, *N. Korea* **75 D15** 40 57N 129 25 E
Kilcoy, *Australia* **127 D5** 26 59 S 152 30 E
Kildare, *Ireland* **23 C5** 53 9N 6 55W

Korsun Shevchenkovskiy 235

Klosi, *Albania* **50 E4** 41 28N 20 10 E
Klosterneuburg, *Austria* **35 C9** 48 18N 16 19 E
Klosters, *Switz.* **33 C9** 46 52N 9 52 E
Kloten, *Switz.* **33 B7** 47 27N 8 35 E
Klötze, *Germany* **30 C7** 52 37N 11 10 E
Klouto, *Togo* **113 D5** 6 57N 0 44 E
Kluane L., *Canada* **138 B6** 61 15N 138 40W
Kluane Nat. Park, *Canada* **142 A1** 60 45N 139 30W
Kluczbork, *Poland* **55 H5** 50 58N 18 12 E
Klukwan, *U.S.A.* **144 G14** 59 24N 135 54W
Klyetsk, *Belarus* **59 F4** 53 5N 26 45 E
Klyuchevskaya, Gora, *Russia* **65 D17** 55 50N 160 30 E
Knaben, *Norway* **18 F4** 58 40N 7 4 E
Knappavellir, *Iceland* **11 D10** 63 54N 16 36W
Knäred, *Sweden* **17 H7** 56 31N 13 19 E
Knaresborough, *U.K.* **20 C6** 54 1N 1 28W
Knarvik, *Norway* **18 D2** 60 32N 5 19 E
Knee L., *Man., Canada* **140 A1** 55 3N 94 45W
Knee L., *Sask., Canada* **143 B7** 55 51N 107 0W
Kneïss, Is., *Tunisia* **108 B2** 34 22N 10 18 E
Knezha, *Bulgaria* **51 C8** 43 30N 24 5 E
Knić, *Serbia, Yug.* **50 C4** 43 53N 20 42 E
Knight I., *U.S.A.* **144 F11** 60 21N 147 45W
Knight Inlet, *Canada* **142 C3** 50 45N 125 40W
Knighton, *U.K.* **21 E4** 52 21N 3 3W
Knights Ferry, *U.S.A.* **160 H6** 37 50N 120 40W
Knights Landing, *U.S.A.* **160 G5** 38 48N 121 43W
Knightstown, *U.S.A.* **157 E11** 39 48N 85 32W
Knin, *Croatia* **45 D13** 44 3N 16 17 E
Knislinge, *Sweden* **17 H8** 56 12N 14 5 E
Knittelfeld, *Austria* **34 D7** 47 13N 14 51 E
Knivsta, *Sweden* **16 E11** 59 43N 17 48 E
Knjaževac, *Serbia, Yug.* **50 C6** 43 35N 22 18 E
Knob, C., *Australia* **125 F2** 34 32 S 119 16 E
Knob Noster, *U.S.A.* **156 F3** 38 46N 93 33W
Knock, *Ireland* **23 C3** 53 48N 8 55W
Knockmealdown Mts., *Ireland* **23 D4** 52 14N 7 56W
Knokke-Heist, *Belgium* **24 C3** 51 21N 3 17 E
Knossós, *Greece* **38 D7** 35 16N 25 10 E
Knowlton, *Canada* **151 A12** 45 13N 72 31W
Knox, *U.S.A.* **157 C10** 41 18N 86 37W
Knox Coast, *Antarctica* **7 C8** 66 30 S 108 0 E
Knoxville, *Ga., U.S.A.* **152 C6** 32 47N 83 59W
Knoxville, *Ill., U.S.A.* **156 D6** 40 55N 90 17W
Knoxville, *Iowa, U.S.A.* **156 C4** 41 19N 93 6W
Knoxville, *Pa., U.S.A.* **150 E7** 41 57N 77 27W
Knoxville, *Tenn., U.S.A.* **149 H4** 35 58N 83 55W
Knud Rasmussen Land, *Greenland* **10 B4** 79 0N 60 0W
Knysna, *S. Africa* **116 E3** 34 2 S 23 2 E
Knyszyn, *Poland* **54 E9** 53 20N 22 56 E
Ko Kha, *Thailand* **86 C2** 18 11N 99 24 E
Kō-Saki, *Japan* **70 C1** 34 5N 129 13 E
Koartac = Quaqtaq, *Canada* **139 B13** 60 55N 69 40W
Koba, *Aru, Indonesia* **79 F8** 6 37 S 134 37 E
Koba, *Bangka, Indonesia* **84 C3** 2 26 S 106 14 E
Kobarid, *Slovenia* **45 B10** 46 15N 13 30 E
Kobayashi, *Japan* **70 F2** 31 56N 130 59 E
Kobdo = Hovd, *Mongolia* **72 B4** 48 2N 91 37 E
Kōbe, *Japan* **71 C7** 34 45N 135 10 E
Kobelyaky, *Ukraine* **59 H8** 49 11N 34 9 E
København, *Denmark* **17 J6** 55 41N 12 34 E
Københavns Amtskommune □, *Denmark* **17 J6** 55 42N 12 21 E
Kobenni, *Mauritania* **112 B3** 15 58N 9 24W
Kōbi-Sho, *Japan* **69 M1** 25 56N 123 41 E
Koblenz, *Germany* **31 E3** 50 21N 7 36 E
Koblenz, *Switz.* **32 A6** 47 37N 8 14 E
Kobo, *Dem. Rep. of the Congo* **115 C3** 4 54 S 17 9 E
Kobo, *Ethiopia* **107 E4** 12 2N 39 56 E
Kobroor, Kepulauan, *Indonesia* **83 C4** 6 10 S 134 30 E
Kobryn, *Belarus* **59 F3** 52 15N 24 22 E
Kobuchizawa, *Japan* **71 B10** 35 52N 138 19 E
Kobuk →, *U.S.A.* **144 C7** 66 54N 160 38W
Kobuleti, *Georgia* **61 K5** 41 55N 41 45 E
Kobylin, *Poland* **55 G4** 51 43N 17 12 E
Kobyłka, *Poland* **55 F8** 52 21N 21 10 E
Kobylkino, *Russia* **60 C6** 54 8N 43 56 E
Koca →, *Turkey* **51 F11** 40 8N 27 57 E
Kocabaş, *Turkey* **49 D11** 37 49N 29 20 E
Kocaeli, *Turkey* **51 F13** 40 45N 29 50 E
Kocaeli □, *Turkey* **51 F13** 40 45N 29 55 E
Kočane, *Serbia, Yug.* **50 C5** 43 12N 21 52 E
Kočani, *Macedonia* **50 E6** 41 55N 22 25 E
Koçarlı, *Turkey* **49 D9** 37 45N 27 43 E
Koceljevo, *Serbia, Yug.* **50 B3** 44 28N 19 50 E
Kočevje, *Slovenia* **45 C11** 45 39N 14 50 E
Koch Bihar, *India* **90 B2** 26 22N 89 29 E
Kochang, *S. Korea* **75 G14** 35 41N 127 55 E
Kochas, *India* **93 G10** 25 15N 83 56 E
Kocher →, *Germany* **31 F5** 49 13N 9 12 E
Kōchi, *Japan* **70 D5** 33 30N 133 35 E
Kōchi □, *Japan* **70 D5** 33 40N 133 30 E
Kōchi-Heiya, *Japan* **70 D5** 33 28N 133 30 E
Kochiu = Gejiu, *China* **76 F4** 23 20N 103 10 E
Kochkor-Ata, *Kyrgyzstan* **63 C6** 41 1N 72 29 E
Kochkorka, *Kyrgyzstan* **63 B7** 42 13N 75 46 E
Kock, *Poland* **55 G9** 51 38N 22 27 E
Kodaira, *Japan* **71 B11** 35 44N 139 29 E
Kodala, *India* **94 E7** 19 38N 84 57 E
Kodarma, *India* **93 G11** 24 28N 85 36 E
Koddiyar B., *Sri Lanka* **95 K5** 8 33N 81 15 E
Kode, *Sweden* **17 G5** 57 57N 11 51 E
Kodi, *Dem. Rep. of the Congo* **114 C4** 3 34 S 22 12 E
Kodiak, *U.S.A.* **138 C4** 57 47N 152 24W
Kodiak I., *U.S.A.* **138 C4** 57 30N 152 45W
Kodinar, *India* **92 J4** 20 46N 70 46 E
Kodlipet, *India* **95 H2** 12 48N 75 53 E
Kodok, *Sudan* **107 F3** 9 53N 32 7 E
Kodori →, *Georgia* **61 J5** 42 47N 41 10 E
Kodoro, *Dem. Rep. of the Congo* **114 B4** 1 16N 20 6 E
Koedoesberge, *S. Africa* **116 E3** 32 40 S 20 11 E
Koes, *Namibia* **116 D2** 26 0 S 19 15 E
Kofçaz, *Turkey* **51 E11** 41 58N 27 12 E
Koffiefontein, *S. Africa* **116 D4** 29 30 S 25 0 E
Kofiau, *Indonesia* **79 E7** 1 11 S 129 50 E
Köflach, *Austria* **34 D8** 47 4N 15 5 E
Koforidua, *Ghana* **113 D4** 6 3N 0 17W
Kōfu, *Japan* **71 B10** 35 40N 138 30 E
Koga, *Japan* **71 A11** 36 11N 139 43 E
Kogaluk →, *Canada* **141 A7** 56 12N 61 44W
Køge, *Denmark* **17 J6** 55 27N 12 11 E
Køge Bugt, *Denmark* **17 J6** 55 30N 12 20 E
Kogi □, *Nigeria* **113 D6** 7 45N 6 45 E
Kogin Baba, *Nigeria* **113 D7** 7 55N 11 35 E
Kogo, *Eq. Guin.* **114 B1** 1 5N 9 42 E
Koh-i-Bābā, *Afghan.* **91 B2** 34 30N 67 0 E
Koh-i-Khurd, *Afghan.* **92 C1** 33 30N 65 59 E
Koh-i-Maran, *Pakistan* **92 E2** 29 18N 66 50 E
Kohala Mts., *U.S.A.* **145 C6** 20 5N 155 45W
Kohat, *Pakistan* **91 B3** 33 40N 71 29 E
Kohima, *India* **90 C5** 25 35N 94 10 E
Kohkīlūyeh va Būyer Aḥmadi □, *Iran* **97 D6** 31 30N 50 30 E
Kohler Ra., *Antarctica* **7 D15** 77 0 S 110 0W
Kohlu, *Pakistan* **92 E3** 29 54N 69 15 E
Kohtla-Järve, *Estonia* **15 G22** 59 20N 27 20 E
Kohukohu, *N.Z.* **130 B2** 35 22 S 173 38 E
Koilkuntla, *India* **95 G4** 15 14N 78 19 E
Koillismaa, *Finland* **14 D23** 65 44N 28 36 E
Koin-dong, *N. Korea* **75 D14** 40 28N 126 18 E
Koinare, *Bulgaria* **51 C8** 43 21N 24 8 E
Koindu, *S. Leone* **112 D2** 8 26N 10 19W
Kojetín, *Czech Rep.* **35 B10** 49 21N 17 20 E
Kojima, *Japan* **70 C5** 34 30N 133 50 E
Kōjo, *Japan* **70 C5** 34 33N 133 55 E
Kojŏ, *N. Korea* **75 E14** 38 58N 127 58 E
Kojonup, *Australia* **125 F2** 33 48 S 117 10 E
Kojūr, *Iran* **97 B6** 36 23N 51 43 E
Kok Yangak, *Kyrgyzstan* **63 C6** 41 2N 73 12 E
Koka, *Sudan* **106 C3** 20 5N 30 35 E
Kokand = Qŭqon, *Uzbekistan* **64 E8** 40 30N 70 57 E
Kokas, *Indonesia* **79 E8** 2 42 S 132 26 E
Kokava, *Slovak Rep.* **35 C12** 48 35N 19 50 E
Kokchetav = Kökshetaū, *Kazakstan* **64 D7** 53 20N 69 25 E
Kokemäenjoki →, *Finland* **15 F19** 61 32N 21 44 E
Kokerite, *Guyana* **169 B6** 7 12N 59 35W
Kokhma, *Russia* **60 B5** 56 57N 41 8 E
Koki, *Senegal* **112 B1** 15 30N 15 59W
Kokiri, *N.Z.* **131 C6** 42 29 S 171 25 E
Kokkilai, *Sri Lanka* **95 K5** 9 0N 80 57 E
Kokkola, *Finland* **14 E20** 63 50N 23 8 E
Koko, *Nigeria* **113 C5** 11 28N 4 29 E
Koko Head, *U.S.A.* **145 K14** 21 16N 157 43W
Kokoda, *Papua N. G.* **132 E4** 8 54 S 147 47 E
Kokolopozo, *Ivory C.* **112 D3** 5 8N 6 5W
Kokomo, *U.S.A.* **157 D10** 40 29N 86 8W
Kokonau, *Indonesia* **83 B5** 4 43 S 136 26 E
Kokopo, *Papua N. G.* **132 C7** 4 22 S 152 19 E
Kokoro, *Niger* **113 C5** 14 12N 0 55 E
Koksan, *N. Korea* **75 E14** 38 46N 126 40 E
Koksengir, Gora, *Kazakstan* **63 A2** 44 21N 65 6 E
Kökshetaū, *Kazakstan* **64 D7** 53 20N 69 25 E
Koksoak →, *Canada* **139 C13** 58 30N 68 10W
Kokstad, *S. Africa* **117 E4** 30 32 S 29 29 E
Kokubu, *Japan* **70 F2** 31 44N 130 46 E
Kola, *Indonesia* **79 F8** 5 35 S 134 30 E
Kola, *Russia* **56 A5** 68 45N 33 8 E
Kola Pen. = Kolskiy Poluostrov, *Russia* **56 A6** 67 30N 38 0 E
Kolachel, *India* **95 K3** 8 10N 77 15 E
Kolachi →, *Pakistan* **92 F2** 27 8N 67 2 E
Kolahoi, *India* **93 B6** 34 12N 75 22 E
Kolahun, *Liberia* **112 D2** 8 15N 10 4W
Kolaka, *Indonesia* **79 E6** 4 3 S 121 46 E
Kolar, *India* **95 H4** 13 12N 78 15 E
Kolar Gold Fields, *India* **95 H4** 12 58N 78 16 E
Kolaras, *India* **92 G6** 25 14N 77 36 E
Kolari, *Finland* **14 C20** 67 20N 23 48 E
Kolárovo, *Slovak Rep.* **35 D10** 47 54N 18 0 E
Kolašin, *Montenegro, Yug.* **50 D3** 42 50N 19 31 E
Kolbäck, *Sweden* **16 E10** 59 34N 16 15 E
Kolbäcksån →, *Sweden* **16 E10** 59 36N 16 16 E
Kolbeinsstaðir, *Iceland* **11 C4** 64 59N 22 16W
Kolbermoor, *Germany* **31 H8** 47 51N 12 4 E
Kolbu, *Norway* **18 D7** 60 39N 10 45 E
Kolbuszowa, *Poland* **55 H8** 50 15N 21 46 E
Kolchugino = Leninsk-Kuznetskiy, *Russia* **64 D9** 54 44N 86 10 E
Kolchugino, *Russia* **58 D10** 56 17N 39 22 E
Kolda, *Senegal* **112 C2** 12 55N 14 57W
Koldegi, *Sudan* **107 E3** 12 3N 30 16 E
Kolding, *Denmark* **17 J3** 55 30N 9 29 E
Kole, *Dem. Rep. of the Congo* **114 C4** 3 16 S 22 42 E
Koléa, *Algeria* **111 A5** 36 38N 2 46 E
Kolepom = Dolak, Pulau, *Indonesia* **79 F9** 8 0 S 138 30 E
Kolguyev, Ostrov, *Russia* **56 A8** 69 20N 48 30 E
Kolhapur, *India* **94 F2** 16 43N 74 15 E
Kolia, *Ivory C.* **112 D3** 9 46N 6 28W
Koliganek, *U.S.A.* **144 G8** 59 48N 157 25W
Kolín, *Czech Rep.* **34 A8** 50 2N 15 9 E
Kolind, *Denmark* **17 H4** 56 21N 10 34 E
Kolkas rags, *Latvia* **15 H20** 57 46N 22 37 E
Kölleda, *Germany* **30 D7** 51 11N 11 15 E
Kollegal, *India* **95 H3** 12 9N 77 9 E
Kolleru L., *India* **94 F5** 16 40N 81 10 E
Kollum, *Neths.* **24 A6** 53 17N 6 10 E
Kolmanskop, *Namibia* **116 D2** 26 45 S 15 14 E
Köln, *Germany* **30 E2** 50 56N 6 57 E
Kolno, *Poland* **54 E8** 53 25N 21 56 E
Koło, *Poland* **55 F5** 52 14N 18 40 E
Koloa, *U.S.A.* **145 B2** 21 55N 159 28W
Kołobrzeg, *Poland* **54 D2** 54 10N 15 35 E
Kolokani, *Mali* **112 C3** 13 35N 7 45W
Koloko, *Burkina Faso* **112 C3** 11 5N 5 19W
Kololo, *Ethiopia* **107 F5** 7 29N 41 58 E
Kolombangara, *Solomon Is.* **133 M9** 8 0 S 157 5 E
Kolomna, *Russia* **58 E10** 55 8N 38 45 E
Kolomyya, *Ukraine* **59 H3** 48 31N 25 2 E
Kolondiéba, *Mali* **112 C3** 11 5N 6 54W
Kolonodale, *Indonesia* **79 E6** 2 3 S 121 25 E
Kolonowskie, *Poland* **55 H5** 50 39N 18 22 E
Kolosib, *India* **90 C4** 24 15N 92 45 E
Kolpashevo, *Russia* **64 D9** 58 20N 83 5 E
Kolpino, *Russia* **58 C6** 59 44N 30 39 E
Kolpny, *Russia* **59 F9** 52 17N 37 1 E
Kolskiy Poluostrov, *Russia* **56 A6** 67 30N 38 0 E
Kolskiy Zaliv, *Russia* **56 A5** 69 23N 34 0 E
Kolsva, *Sweden* **16 E9** 59 36N 15 51 E
Kolubara →, *Serbia, Yug.* **50 B4** 44 35N 20 15 E
Koluszki, *Poland* **55 G6** 51 45N 19 46 E
Kolwezi, *Dem. Rep. of the Congo* **119 E2** 10 40 S 25 25 E
Kolyma →, *Russia* **65 C17** 69 30N 161 0 E
Kolymskoye Nagorye, *Russia* **65 C16** 63 0N 157 0 E
Kôm Hamâda, *Egypt* **106 H7** 30 46N 30 41 E
Kôm Ombo, *Egypt* **106 C3** 24 25N 32 52 E
Komadugu Gana →, *Nigeria* **113 C7** 13 5N 12 24 E
Komagene, *Japan* **71 B9** 35 44N 137 58 E
Komaki, *Japan* **71 B8** 35 17N 136 55 E
Komandorskiye Is. = Komandorskiye Ostrova, *Russia* **65 D17** 55 0N 167 0 E
Komandorskiye Ostrova, *Russia* **65 D17** 55 0N 167 0 E
Komárno, *Slovak Rep.* **35 D11** 47 49N 18 5 E
Komárom, *Hungary* **52 C3** 47 43N 18 7 E
Komárom-Esztergom □, *Hungary* **52 C3** 47 35N 18 20 E
Komatipoort, *S. Africa* **117 D5** 25 25 S 31 55 E
Komatou Yialou, *Cyprus* **38 D13** 35 25N 34 8 E
Komatsu, *Japan* **71 A8** 36 25N 136 30 E
Komatsujima, *Japan* **70 D6** 34 0N 134 35 E
Komba, *Dem. Rep. of the Congo* **114 B4** 2 52N 24 3 E
Kombissiri, *Burkina Faso* **113 C4** 12 4N 1 20W
Kombo, *Gabon* **114 C2** 0 20 S 12 22 E
Kombori, *Burkina Faso* **112 C4** 13 26N 3 56W
Kombóti, *Greece* **48 B3** 39 6N 21 5 E
Komen, *Slovenia* **45 C10** 45 49N 13 45 E
Komenda, *Ghana* **113 D4** 5 4N 1 28W
Komi □, *Russia* **56 B10** 64 0N 55 0 E
Komiža, *Croatia* **45 E13** 43 3N 16 11 E
Komló, *Hungary* **52 D3** 46 15N 18 16 E
Kommamur Canal, *India* **95 G5** 16 0N 80 25 E
Kommunarsk = Alchevsk, *Ukraine* **59 H10** 48 30N 38 45 E
Kommunizma, Pik, *Tajikistan* **64 F8** 39 0N 72 2 E
Komodo, *Indonesia* **79 F5** 8 37 S 119 20 E
Komoé →, *Ivory C.* **112 D4** 5 12N 3 44W
Komono, *Congo* **114 C2** 3 10 S 13 20 E
Komoran, Pulau, *Indonesia* **79 F9** 8 18 S 138 45 E
Komoro, *Japan* **71 A10** 36 19N 138 26 E
Komotini, *Greece* **51 E9** 41 9N 25 26 E
Komovi, *Montenegro, Yug.* **50 D3** 42 41N 19 39 E
Kompasberg, *S. Africa* **116 E3** 31 45 S 24 32 E
Kompong Bang, *Cambodia* **87 F5** 12 24N 104 40 E
Kompong Cham, *Cambodia* **78 B3** 12 0N 105 30 E
Kompong Chhnang = Kampang Chhnang, *Cambodia* **78 B2** 12 20N 104 35 E
Kompong Chikreng, *Cambodia* **86 F5** 13 5N 104 18 E
Kompong Kleang, *Cambodia* **86 F5** 13 6N 104 8 E
Kompong Luong, *Cambodia* **87 G5** 11 49N 104 48 E
Kompong Pranak, *Cambodia* **86 F5** 13 35N 104 55 E
Kompong Som = Kampong Saom, *Cambodia* **78 B2** 10 38N 103 30 E
Kompong Som, Chhung = Kampong Saom, Chaak, *Cambodia* **78 B2** 10 50N 103 32 E
Kompong Speu, *Cambodia* **87 G5** 11 26N 104 32 E
Kompong Sralao, *Cambodia* **86 E5** 14 5N 105 46 E
Kompong Thom, *Cambodia* **78 B2** 12 35N 104 51 E
Kompong Trabeck, *Cambodia* **86 F5** 13 6N 105 14 E
Kompong Trabeck, *Cambodia* **87 G5** 11 9N 105 28 E
Kompong Trach, *Cambodia* **87 G5** 11 25N 105 48 E
Kompong Tralach, *Cambodia* **87 G5** 11 54N 104 47 E
Komrat = Comrat, *Moldova* **53 D13** 46 18N 28 40 E
Komsberg, *S. Africa* **116 E3** 32 40 S 20 45 E
Komsomolabad, *Tajikistan* **63 D4** 38 50N 69 55 E
Komsomolets, *Kazakstan* **62 E9** 53 45N 62 2 E
Komsomolets, Ostrov, *Russia* **65 A10** 80 30N 95 0 E
Komsomolsk, *Amur, Russia* **65 D14** 50 30N 137 0 E
Komsomolsk, *Ivanovo, Russia* **58 D11** 57 2N 40 20 E
Komsomolsk, *Turkmenistan* **63 D1** 39 2N 63 36 E
Komsomolskiy, *Russia* **60 C7** 54 27N 45 33 E
Kömür Burnu, *Turkey* **49 C8** 38 39N 26 12 E
Kon Tum, *Vietnam* **78 B3** 14 24N 108 0 E
Kon Tum, Plateau du, *Vietnam* **86 E7** 14 30N 108 30 E
Kona, *Mali* **112 C4** 14 57N 3 53W
Konakovo, *Russia* **58 D9** 56 40N 36 51 E
Konarak, *India* **94 E8** 19 54N 86 7 E
Konarhā □, *Afghan.* **91 B3** 35 30N 71 3 E
Konārī, *Iran* **97 D6** 28 13N 51 36 E
Konch, *India* **93 G8** 26 0N 79 10 E
Kondagaon, *India* **94 E5** 19 35N 81 35 E
Konde, *Tanzania* **118 C4** 4 57 S 39 45 E
Kondiá, *Greece* **49 B7** 39 49N 25 10 E
Kondinin, *Australia* **125 F2** 32 34 S 118 8 E
Kondo, *Dem. Rep. of the Congo* **115 D2** 5 35 S 13 0 E
Kondoa, *Tanzania* **118 C4** 4 55 S 35 50 E
Kondókali, *Greece* **38 A3** 39 38N 19 51 E
Kondopaga, *Russia* **58 A8** 62 12N 34 17 E
Kondratyevo, *Russia* **65 D10** 57 22N 98 15 E
Kondrovo, *Russia* **58 E8** 54 48N 35 56 E
Konduga, *Nigeria* **113 C7** 11 35N 13 26 E
Kondukur, *India* **95 G4** 15 12N 79 57 E
Koné, *Cameroon* **114 A2** 8 50N 13 17 E
Koné, *N. Cal.* **133 U18** 21 4 S 164 52 E
Köneürgench, *Turkmenistan* **64 E6** 42 19N 59 10 E
Konevo, *Russia* **58 A10** 62 8N 39 20 E
Kong = Khong →, *Cambodia* **78 B3** 13 32N 105 58 E
Kong, *Ivory C.* **112 D4** 8 54N 4 36W
Kong, Koh, *Cambodia* **78 B2** 11 20N 103 0 E
Kong Christian IX Land, *Greenland* **10 D7** 68 0N 36 0W
Kong Christian X Land, *Greenland* **10 C8** 74 0N 29 0W
Kong Frederik IX Land, *Greenland* **10 D5** 67 0N 52 0W
Kong Frederik VI Kyst, *Greenland* **10 E6** 63 0N 43 0W
Kong Frederik VIII Land, *Greenland* **10 B8** 78 30N 26 0W
Kong Oscar Fjord, *Greenland* **10 C8** 72 20N 24 0W
Kongbo, *C.A.R.* **114 B4** 4 44N 21 23 E
Kongeå →, *Denmark* **17 J2** 55 23N 8 39 E
Kongerslev, *Denmark* **17 H4** 56 25N 10 8 E
Kongju, *S. Korea* **75 F14** 36 30N 127 0 E
Kongkemul, *Indonesia* **85 B4** 1 52N 112 11 E
Konglu, *Burma* **90 B6** 27 13N 97 57 E
Kongola, *Namibia* **116 B3** 17 45 S 23 20 E
Kongolo, *Kasai-Or., Dem. Rep. of the Congo* **118 D1** 5 26 S 24 49 E
Kongolo, *Katanga, Dem. Rep. of the Congo* **118 D2** 5 22 S 27 0 E
Kongor, *Sudan* **107 F3** 7 1N 31 27 E
Kongoulou, *Cameroon* **114 B2** 2 59N 11 7 E
Kongoussi, *Burkina Faso* **113 C4** 13 19N 1 32W
Kongsberg, *Norway* **15 G13** 59 39N 9 39 E
Kongsvinger, *Norway* **15 F15** 60 12N 12 2 E
Kongwa, *Tanzania* **118 D4** 6 11 S 36 26 E
Koni, *Dem. Rep. of the Congo* **119 E2** 10 40 S 27 11 E
Koni, Mts., *Dem. Rep. of the Congo* **119 E2** 10 36 S 27 10 E
Koniakari, *Mali* **112 C2** 14 35N 10 50W
Koniecpol, *Poland* **55 H6** 50 46N 19 40 E
Königs Wusterhausen, *Germany* **30 C9** 52 19N 13 38 E
Königsberg = Kaliningrad, *Russia* **15 J19** 54 42N 20 32 E
Königsbrunn, *Germany* **31 G6** 48 16N 10 54 E
Königslutter, *Germany* **30 C6** 52 15N 10 49 E
Konin, *Poland* **55 F5** 52 12N 18 15 E
Konispoli, *Albania* **50 G4** 39 42N 20 10 E
Kónitsa, *Greece* **48 A2** 40 5N 20 48 E
Köniz, *Switz.* **32 C4** 46 56N 7 25 E
Konjic, *Bos.-H.* **52 G2** 43 42N 17 58 E
Konkiep, *Namibia* **116 D2** 26 49 S 17 15 E
Konkouré →, *Guinea* **112 D2** 9 50N 13 42W
Könnern, *Germany* **30 D7** 51 41N 11 47 E
Konnur, *India* **95 F2** 16 14N 74 49 E
Kono, *S. Leone* **112 D2** 8 30N 11 5W
Konolfingen, *Switz.* **32 C5** 46 54N 7 38 E
Konongo, *Ghana* **113 D4** 6 40N 1 15W
Konos, *Papua N. G.* **132 B6** 3 10 S 151 44 E
Konosha, *Russia* **58 B11** 61 0N 40 5 E
Kōnosu, *Japan* **71 A11** 36 3N 139 31 E
Konotop, *Ukraine* **59 G7** 51 12N 33 7 E
Konsankoro, *Guinea* **112 D3** 9 2N 9 0W
Końskie, *Poland* **55 G7** 51 15N 20 23 E
Konsmo, *Norway* **18 F4** 58 16N 7 23 E
Konstancin-Jeziorna, *Poland* **55 F8** 52 5N 21 7 E
Konstantinovka = Kostyantynivka, *Ukraine* **59 H9** 48 32N 37 39 E
Konstantinovsk, *Russia* **61 G5** 47 33N 41 10 E
Konstantynów Łódźki, *Poland* **55 G6** 51 45N 19 20 E
Konstanz, *Germany* **31 H5** 47 40N 9 10 E
Kont, *Iran* **97 E9** 26 55N 61 50 E
Konta, *India* **94 F5** 17 48N 81 23 E
Kontagora, *Nigeria* **113 C6** 10 23N 5 27 E
Kontcha, *Cameroon* **113 D7** 7 59N 12 15 E
Kontcha, *Cameroon* **114 A2** 7 59N 12 15 E
Konya, *Turkey* **100 D5** 37 52N 32 35 E
Konya Ovası, *Turkey* **100 C5** 38 9N 33 5 E
Konyin, *Burma* **90 D5** 22 58N 94 42 E
Konz, *Germany* **31 F2** 49 42N 6 34 E
Konza, *Kenya* **118 C4** 1 45 S 37 7 E
Konzhakovskiy Kamen, Gora, *Russia* **62 B7** 59 38N 59 8 E
Koocanusa, L., *Canada* **158 B6** 49 20N 115 15W
Kookynie, *Australia* **125 E3** 29 17 S 121 22 E
Koolau Range, *U.S.A.* **145 J14** 21 35N 157 50W
Kooloonong, *Australia* **128 C5** 34 48 S 143 10 E
Koolyanobbing, *Australia* **125 F2** 30 48 S 119 36 E
Koondrook, *Australia* **128 C6** 35 33 S 144 8 E
Koonibba, *Australia* **127 E1** 31 54 S 133 25 E
Koorawatha, *Australia* **129 C8** 34 2 S 148 33 E
Koorda, *Australia* **125 F2** 30 48 S 117 35 E
Kooskia, *U.S.A.* **158 C6** 46 9N 115 59W
Kootenay →, *U.S.A.* **142 D5** 49 19N 117 39W
Kootenay L., *Canada* **142 D5** 49 45N 116 50W
Kootenay Nat. Park, *Canada* **142 C5** 51 0N 116 0W
Kootjieskolk, *S. Africa* **116 E3** 31 15 S 20 21 E
Kopa, *Kazakstan* **63 B7** 43 31N 75 50 E
Kopanovka, *Russia* **61 G8** 47 28N 46 50 E
Kopaonik, *Yugoslavia* **50 C4** 43 10N 20 50 E
Kopargaon, *India* **94 E2** 19 51N 74 28 E
Kópasker, *Iceland* **11 A10** 66 18N 16 27W
Kópavogur, *Iceland* **11 C5** 64 6N 21 55W
Koper, *Slovenia* **45 C10** 45 31N 13 44 E
Kopervik, *Norway* **15 G11** 59 17N 5 17 E
Kopet Dagh, *Asia* **97 B8** 38 0N 58 0 E
Kopeysk, *Russia* **62 D8** 55 7N 61 37 E
Kopi, *Australia* **127 E2** 33 24 S 135 40 E
Köping, *Sweden* **16 E10** 59 31N 16 3 E
Köpingsvik, *Sweden* **17 H10** 56 53N 16 43 E
Kopište, *Croatia* **45 F13** 42 48N 16 42 E
Kopliku, *Albania* **50 D3** 42 15N 19 25 E
Köpmanholmen, *Sweden* **16 A12** 63 10N 18 35 E
Koppa, *India* **95 H2** 13 33N 75 21 E
Koppal, *India* **95 G3** 15 23N 76 5 E
Koppang, *Norway* **18 C8** 61 34N 11 3 E
Kopparberg, *Sweden* **16 E9** 59 52N 15 0 E
Kopparbergs län □, *Sweden* **16 C8** 61 0N 14 15 E
Koppeh Dāgh = Kopet Dagh, *Asia* **97 B8** 38 0N 58 0 E
Kopperå, *Norway* **18 A8** 63 24N 11 50 E
Koppies, *S. Africa* **117 D4** 27 20 S 27 30 E
Koppio, *Australia* **128 C1** 34 26 S 135 51 E
Koppom, *Sweden* **16 E6** 59 43N 12 10 E
Koprivlen, *Bulgaria* **50 E7** 41 31N 23 53 E
Koprivnica, *Croatia* **45 B13** 46 12N 16 45 E
Kopřivnice, *Czech Rep.* **35 B11** 49 36N 18 9 E
Koprivshtitsa, *Bulgaria* **51 D8** 42 40N 24 19 E
Köprübaşı, *Turkey* **49 C10** 38 43N 28 23 E
Kopychyntsi, *Ukraine* **59 H3** 49 7N 25 58 E
Korab, *Macedonia* **50 E4** 41 44N 20 40 E
Korakiána, *Greece* **38 A3** 39 42N 19 45 E
Koral, *India* **92 J5** 21 50N 73 12 E
Korangal, *India* **94 E3** 17 6N 77 38 E
Koraput, *India* **94 E6** 18 50N 82 40 E
Korarou, L., *Mali* **112 B4** 15 15N 3 15W
Korba, *India* **93 H10** 22 20N 82 45 E
Korbach, *Germany* **30 D4** 51 16N 8 52 E
Korbu, G., *Malaysia* **87 K3** 4 41N 101 18 E
Korça, *Albania* **50 F4** 40 37N 20 50 E
Korce = Korça, *Albania* **50 F4** 40 37N 20 50 E
Korčula, *Croatia* **45 F13** 42 56N 16 57 E
Korčulanski Kanal, *Croatia* **45 E13** 43 3N 16 40 E
Kord Kūy, *Iran* **97 B7** 36 48N 54 7 E
Kord Sheykh, *Iran* **97 D7** 28 31N 52 53 E
Kordestān □, *Iran* **96 C5** 36 0N 47 0 E
Koré Mayroua, *Niger* **113 C5** 13 18N 3 55 E
Korea, North ■, *Asia* **75 E14** 40 0N 127 0 E
Korea, South ■, *Asia* **75 G15** 36 0N 128 0 E
Korea Bay, *Korea* **75 E13** 39 0N 124 0 E
Korea Strait, *Asia* **75 H15** 34 0N 129 30 E
Koregaon, *India* **94 F2** 17 40N 74 10 E
Korem, *Ethiopia* **107 E4** 12 30N 39 32 E
Korenevo, *Russia* **59 G8** 51 27N 34 55 E
Korenovsk, *Russia* **61 H4** 45 30N 39 22 E
Korets, *Ukraine* **59 G4** 50 40N 27 5 E
Korfantów, *Poland* **55 H4** 50 29N 17 36 E
Korgan, *Turkey* **100 B7** 40 44N 37 13 E
Korgus, *Sudan* **106 D3** 19 16N 33 29 E
Korhogo, *Ivory C.* **112 D3** 9 29N 5 28W
Koribundu, *S. Leone* **112 D2** 7 41N 11 46W
Korienzé, *Mali* **112 B4** 15 22N 3 50W
Korim, *Indonesia* **83 B5** 0 58 S 136 10 E
Korinthía □, *Greece* **48 D4** 37 50N 22 35 E
Korinthiakós Kólpos, *Greece* **48 C4** 38 16N 22 30 E
Kórinthos, *Greece* **48 D4** 37 56N 22 55 E
Korioumé, *Mali* **112 B4** 16 35N 3 0W
Koríssa, Límni, *Greece* **38 B3** 39 27N 19 53 E
Kōriyama, *Japan* **68 F10** 37 24N 140 23 E
Korkino, *Russia* **62 D8** 54 54N 61 23 E
Korkuteli, *Turkey* **49 D12** 37 4N 30 13 E
Korla, *China* **72 B3** 41 45N 86 4 E
Kormakiti, C., *Cyprus* **38 D11** 35 23N 32 56 E
Körmend, *Hungary* **52 C1** 47 5N 16 35 E
Kornat, *Croatia* **45 E12** 43 50N 15 20 E
Korneshty = Corneşti, *Moldova* **53 C13** 47 21N 28 1 E
Korneuburg, *Austria* **35 C9** 48 20N 16 20 E
Kórnik, *Poland* **55 F4** 52 15N 17 6 E
Kornsjø, *Norway* **18 F8** 58 57N 11 39 E
Koro, *Fiji* **133 A2** 17 19 S 179 23 E
Koro, *Ivory C.* **112 D3** 8 32N 7 30W
Koro, *Mali* **112 C4** 14 1N 2 58W
Koro Sea, *Fiji* **133 A3** 17 30 S 179 45W
Koro Toro, *Chad* **109 E3** 16 5N 18 30 E
Koroba, *Papua N. G.* **132 C2** 5 44 S 142 47 E
Korocha, *Russia* **59 G9** 50 54N 37 19 E
Köroğlu Dağları, *Turkey* **100 B5** 40 38N 33 0 E
Korogwe, *Tanzania* **118 D4** 5 5 S 38 25 E
Koroit, *Australia* **128 E5** 38 18 S 142 24 E
Korona, *U.S.A.* **153 F8** 29 25N 81 12W
Koronadal, *Phil.* **79 C6** 6 12N 125 1 E
Korong Vale, *Australia* **128 D5** 36 22 S 143 45 E
Koróni, *Greece* **48 E3** 36 48N 21 57 E
Korónia, Limni, *Greece* **50 F7** 40 47N 23 10 E
Koronís, *Greece* **49 D7** 37 12N 25 35 E
Koronowo, *Poland* **55 E4** 53 19N 17 55 E
Koropelé, *C.A.R.* **114 B3** 4 44N 17 11 E
Koror, *Palau* **79 C8** 7 20N 134 28 E
Körös →, *Hungary* **52 D5** 46 43N 20 12 E
Köröstarcsa, *Hungary* **52 D6** 46 53N 21 3 E
Korosten, *Ukraine* **59 G5** 50 54N 28 36 E
Korostyshev, *Ukraine* **59 G5** 50 19N 29 4 E
Korotoyak, *Russia* **59 G10** 51 1N 39 2 E
Korraraika, Helodranon' i, *Madag.* **117 B7** 17 45 S 43 57 E
Korsakov, *Russia* **65 E15** 46 36N 142 42 E
Korsberga, *Sweden* **17 G9** 57 19N 15 7 E
Korshunovo, *Russia* **65 D12** 58 37N 110 10 E
Korsør, *Denmark* **17 J5** 55 20N 11 9 E
Korsun Shevchenkovskiy, *Ukraine* **59 H6** 49 26N 31 16 E

La Cruz 237

Kūhpāyeh, *Kermān, Iran* **97 D8** 30 35N 57 15 E
Kūhrān, Kūh-e, *Iran* **97 E8** 26 46N 58 12 E
Kui Buri, *Thailand* **87 F2** 12 3N 99 52 E
Kuiseb →, *Namibia* **116 B2** 22 59 S 14 31 E
Kuito, *Angola* **115 E3** 12 22 S 16 55 E
Kuiu I., *U.S.A.* **142 B2** 57 45N 134 10W
Kujang, *N. Korea* **75 E14** 39 57N 126 1 E
Kujawsko-Pomorskie □, *Poland* **54 E5** 53 20N 18 30 E
Kuji, *Japan* **68 D10** 40 11N 141 46 E
Kujū-San, *Japan* **70 D3** 33 5N 131 15 E
Kujukuri-Heiya, *Japan* **71 B12** 35 45N 140 30 E
Kukavica, *Serbia, Yug.* **50 D5** 42 48N 21 57 E
Kukawa, *Nigeria* **113 C7** 12 58N 13 27 E
Kukësi, *Albania* **50 D4** 42 5N 20 27 E
Kukmor, *Russia* **60 B10** 56 11N 50 54 E
Kukuihaele, *U.S.A.* **145 C6** 20 5N 155 35W
Kukup, *Malaysia* **87 M4** 1 20N 103 27 E
Kukvidze, *Russia* **60 E6** 50 40N 43 0 E
Kula, *Bulgaria* **50 C6** 43 52N 22 36 E
Kula, *Serbia, Yug.* **52 E4** 45 37N 19 32 E
Kula, *Turkey* **49 C10** 38 32N 28 40 E
Kula Gulf, *Solomon Is.* **133 M9** 8 5 S 157 18 E
Kulachi, *Pakistan* **92 D4** 31 56N 70 27 E
Kulai, *Malaysia* **87 M4** 1 44N 103 35 E
Kulal, Mt., *Kenya* **118 B4** 2 42N 36 57 E
Kulaly, Ostrov, *Kazakstan* **61 H10** 45 0N 50 0 E
Kulanak, *Kyrgyzstan* **63 C7** 41 22N 75 30 E
Kulasekarappattinam, *India* **95 K4** 8 20N 78 5 E
Kulassein I., *Phil.* **81 H3** 6 25N 120 41 E
Kulautuva, *Lithuania* **54 D10** 54 56N 23 36 E
Kuldīga, *Latvia* **15 H19** 56 58N 21 59 E
Kuldīga □, *Latvia* **54 B8** 56 55N 22 0 E
Kuldja = Yining, *China* **64 E9** 43 58N 81 10 E
Kuldu, *Sudan* **107 E2** 12 50N 28 30 E
Kulebaki, *Russia* **60 C6** 55 22N 42 25 E
Kulen, *Cambodia* **78 B2** 13 50N 104 40 E
Kulen Vakuf, *Bos.-H.* **45 D13** 44 35N 16 2 E
Kulgam, *India* **93 C6** 33 36N 75 2 E
Kulgera, *Australia* **126 D1** 25 50 S 133 18 E
Kulim, *Malaysia* **87 K3** 5 22N 100 34 E
Kulin, *Australia* **125 F2** 32 40 S 118 2 E
Kulittalai, *India* **95 J4** 10 55N 78 25 E
Kullen, *Sweden* **17 H6** 56 18N 12 26 E
Kulmbach, *Germany* **31 E7** 50 6N 11 26 E
Kŭlob, *Tajikistan* **64 F7** 37 55N 69 50 E
Kulp, *Turkey* **101 C9** 38 29N 41 2 E
Kulpawn →, *Ghana* **113 D4** 10 20N 1 5W
Kulsary, *Kazakstan* **57 E9** 46 59N 54 1 E
Kulti, *India* **93 H12** 23 43N 86 50 E
Kulu, *India* **92 D7** 31 58N 77 6 E
Kulu, *Turkey* **100 C5** 39 5N 33 4 E
Kulumbura, *Australia* **124 B4** 13 55 S 126 35 E
Kulunda, *Russia* **64 D8** 52 35N 78 57 E
Kulungar, *Afghan.* **92 C3** 34 0N 69 2 E
Kūlvand, *Iran* **97 D7** 31 21N 54 35 E
Kulwin, *Australia* **128 C5** 35 0 S 142 42 E
Kulyab = Kŭlob, *Tajikistan* **64 F7** 37 55N 69 50 E
Kuma, *Japan* **70 D4** 33 39N 132 54 E
Kuma →, *Russia* **61 H8** 44 55N 47 0 E
Kumafşarı, *Turkey* **49 D11** 37 19N 29 32 E
Kumaganum, *Nigeria* **113 C7** 13 8N 10 38 E
Kumagaya, *Japan* **71 A11** 36 9N 139 22 E
Kumai, *Indonesia* **78 E4** 2 44 S 111 43 E
Kumak, *Russia* **62 F8** 51 10N 60 8 E
Kumalar Dağı, *Turkey* **49 C12** 38 15N 30 20 E
Kumamba, Kepulauan, *Indonesia* **79 E9** 1 36 S 138 45 E
Kumamoto, *Japan* **70 E2** 32 45N 130 45 E
Kumamoto □, *Japan* **70 E2** 32 55N 130 55 E
Kumano, *Japan* **71 D8** 33 54N 136 5 E
Kumano-Nada, *Japan* **71 D8** 33 47N 136 20 E
Kumanovo, *Macedonia* **50 D5** 42 9N 21 42 E
Kumara, *N.Z.* **131 C6** 42 37 S 171 12 E
Kumarina, *Australia* **125 D2** 24 41 S 119 32 E
Kumarkhali, *Bangla.* **90 D2** 23 51N 89 15 E
Kumasi, *Ghana* **112 D4** 6 41N 1 38W
Kumayri = Gyumri, *Armenia* **61 K6** 40 47N 43 50 E
Kumba, *Cameroon* **113 E6** 4 36N 9 24 E
Kumbağ, *Turkey* **51 F11** 40 51N 27 27 E
Kumbakonam, *India* **95 J4** 10 58N 79 25 E
Kumbarilla, *Australia* **127 D5** 27 15 S 150 55 E
Kumbhraj, *India* **92 G7** 24 22N 77 3 E
Kumbia, *Australia* **127 D5** 26 41 S 151 39 E
Kumbo, *Cameroon* **113 D7** 6 15N 10 36 E
Kumbukkan Oya →, *Sri Lanka* **95 L5** 6 35N 81 40 E
Kŭmch'ŏn, *N. Korea* **75 E14** 38 10N 126 29 E
Kumdah, *Si. Arabia* **98 B4** 20 23N 45 5 E
Kumdok, *India* **93 C8** 33 32N 78 10 E
Kume-Shima, *Japan* **69 L3** 26 20N 126 47 E
Kumeny, *Russia* **60 A9** 58 10N 49 47 E
Kumertau, *Russia* **62 E5** 52 45N 55 57 E
Kumharsain, *India* **92 D7** 31 19N 77 27 E
Kŭmhwa, *S. Korea* **75 E14** 38 17N 127 28 E
Kumi, *Uganda* **118 B3** 1 30N 33 58 E
Kumkale, *Turkey* **51 G10** 39 59N 26 11 E
Kumla, *Sweden* **16 E9** 59 8N 15 10 E
Kumluca, *Turkey* **49 E12** 36 22N 30 20 E
Kummerower See, *Germany* **30 B8** 53 49N 12 51 E
Kumo, *Nigeria* **113 C7** 10 1N 11 12 E
Kumon Bum, *Burma* **90 B6** 26 30N 97 15 E
Kumotori-Yama, *Japan* **71 B10** 35 51N 138 57 E
Kumta, *India* **95 G2** 14 29N 74 25 E
Kumusi →, *Papua N. G.* **132 E5** 8 16 S 148 13 E
Kumylzhenskaya, *Russia* **60 F6** 49 51N 42 38 E
Kunágota, *Hungary* **52 D6** 46 26N 21 3 E
Kunak, *Malaysia* **85 B5** 4 41N 118 15 E
Kunama, *Australia* **129 C8** 35 35 S 148 4 E
Kunashir, Ostrov, *Russia* **65 E15** 44 0N 146 0 E
Kunda, *Estonia* **15 G22** 59 30N 26 34 E
Kunda, *India* **93 G9** 25 43N 81 31 E
Kundar →, *Pakistan* **92 D3** 31 56N 69 19 E
Kundian, *Pakistan* **92 C4** 32 27N 71 28 E
Kundiawa, *Papua N. G.* **132 D3** 6 2 S 145 1 E
Kundla, *India* **92 J4** 21 21N 71 25 E
Kundur, *Indonesia* **84 C3** 0 58 S 107 48 E
Kunga →, *Bangla.* **93 J13** 21 46N 89 30 E
Kungälv, *Sweden* **17 G5** 57 53N 11 59 E
Kungey Alatau, Khrebet, *Kyrgyzstan* **63 B8** 42 50N 77 0 E
Kunghit I., *Canada* **142 C2** 52 6N 131 3W
Kungrad = Qŭnghirot, *Uzbekistan* **64 E6** 43 6N 58 54 E
Kungsängen, *Sweden* **16 E11** 59 29N 17 45 E
Kungsbacka, *Sweden* **17 G6** 57 30N 12 5 E
Kungsgården, *Sweden* **16 D10** 60 37N 16 35 E
Kungshamn, *Sweden* **17 F5** 58 22N 11 15 E
Kungsör, *Sweden* **16 E10** 59 25N 16 5 E
Kungu, *Dem. Rep. of the Congo* **114 B3** 2 47N 19 12 E
Kungur, *Russia* **62 C6** 57 25N 56 57 E
Kungyangon, *Burma* **90 G6** 16 27N 96 20 E
Kunhar →, *Pakistan* **93 B5** 34 20N 73 30 E
Kunhegyes, *Hungary* **52 C5** 47 22N 20 36 E
Kunia, *U.S.A.* **145 K13** 21 28N 158 4W
Kunimi-Dake, *Japan* **70 E3** 32 33N 131 1 E
Kuningan, *Indonesia* **79 G13** 6 59 S 108 29 E
Kunisaki, *Japan* **70 D3** 33 33N 131 45 E
Kunlara, *Australia* **128 C3** 34 54 S 139 55 E
Kunlong, *Burma* **90 D7** 23 20N 98 50 E
Kunlun Shan, *Asia* **72 C3** 36 0N 86 30 E
Kunmadaras, *Hungary* **52 C5** 47 28N 20 45 E
Kunming, *China* **76 E4** 25 1N 102 41 E
Kunnamkulam, *India* **95 J3** 10 38N 76 7 E
Kunów, *Poland* **55 H8** 50 57N 21 17 E
Kunsan, *S. Korea* **75 G14** 35 59N 126 45 E
Kunshan, *China* **77 B13** 31 22N 120 58 E
Kunszentmárton, *Hungary* **52 D5** 46 50N 20 20 E
Kunszentmiklós, *Hungary* **52 C4** 47 2N 19 8 E
Kuntaur, *Senegal* **112 C2** 13 40N 14 48W
Kununurra, *Australia* **124 C4** 15 40 S 128 50 E
Kunwari →, *India* **93 F8** 26 26N 79 11 E
Kunya-Urgench = Köneürgench, *Turkmenistan* **64 E6** 42 19N 59 10 E
Künzelsau, *Germany* **31 F5** 49 17N 9 42 E
Kunzulu, *Dem. Rep. of the Congo* **114 C3** 3 28 S 16 12 E
Kuopio, *Finland* **14 E22** 62 53N 27 35 E
Kupa →, *Croatia* **45 C13** 45 28N 16 24 E
Kupang, *Indonesia* **79 F6** 10 19 S 123 39 E
Kupiano, *Papua N. G.* **132 F5** 10 4 S 148 14 E
Kupreanof I., *U.S.A.* **142 B2** 56 50N 133 30W
Kupres, *Bos.-H.* **52 G2** 43 56N 17 15 E
Kupyansk, *Ukraine* **59 H9** 49 52N 37 35 E
Kupyansk-Uzlovoi, *Ukraine* **59 H9** 49 40N 37 43 E
Kuqa, *China* **72 B3** 41 35N 82 30 E
Kür →, *Azerbaijan* **101 C13** 39 29N 49 15 E
Kur →, *Bhutan* **90 B3** 26 50N 91 0 E
Kür Dili, *Azerbaijan* **97 B6** 39 3N 49 13 E
Kura = Kür →, *Azerbaijan* **101 C13** 39 29N 49 15 E
Kurahashi-Jima, *Japan* **70 C4** 34 8N 132 31 E
Kuranda, *Australia* **126 B4** 16 48 S 145 35 E
Kuranga, *India* **92 H3** 22 4N 69 10 E
Kurashiki, *Japan* **70 C5** 34 40N 133 50 E
Kurayoshi, *Japan* **70 B5** 35 26N 133 50 E
Kürdämir, *Azerbaijan* **61 K9** 40 25N 48 3 E
Kurday, *Kazakstan* **63 B7** 43 21N 74 59 E
Kurdistan, *Asia* **101 D10** 37 20N 43 30 E
Kurduvadi, *India* **94 E2** 18 8N 75 29 E
Kŭrdzhali, *Bulgaria* **51 E9** 41 38N 25 21 E
Kure, *Japan* **70 C4** 34 14N 132 32 E
Küre, *Turkey* **100 B5** 41 48N 33 43 E
Küre Dağları, *Turkey* **100 B6** 41 50N 34 10 E
Kure I., *U.S.A.* **145 F8** 28 25N 178 25W
Kuressaare, *Estonia* **15 G20** 58 15N 22 30 E
Kurgan, *Russia* **64 D7** 55 26N 65 18 E
Kurgan-Tyube = Qŭrghonteppa, *Tajikistan* **63 E4** 37 50N 68 47 E
Kurganinsk, *Russia* **61 H5** 44 54N 40 34 E
Kurgannaya = Kurganinsk, *Russia* **61 H5** 44 54N 40 34 E
Kuri, *India* **92 F4** 26 37N 70 43 E
Kuria Maria Is. = Khurīyā Murīyā, Jazā 'ir, *Oman* **99 C6** 17 30N 55 58 E
Kuria Muria B., *Oman* **99 C6** 17 40N 55 45 E
Kurichchi, *India* **95 J3** 11 36N 77 35 E
Kuridala, *Australia* **126 C3** 21 16 S 140 29 E
Kurigram, *Bangla.* **90 C2** 25 49N 89 39 E
Kurihashi, *Japan* **71 A11** 36 8N 139 42 E
Kurikka, *Finland* **15 E20** 62 36N 22 24 E
Kuril Is. = Kurilskiye Ostrova, *Russia* **65 E15** 45 0N 150 0 E
Kuril Trench, *Pac. Oc.* **66 E19** 44 0N 153 0 E
Kurilsk, *Russia* **65 E15** 45 14N 147 53 E
Kurilskiye Ostrova, *Russia* **65 E15** 45 0N 150 0 E
Kurino, *Japan* **70 F2** 31 57N 130 43 E
Kurinskaya Kosa = Kür Dili, *Azerbaijan* **97 B6** 39 3N 49 13 E
Kurkheda, *India* **94 D5** 20 37N 80 12 E
Kurkur, *Egypt* **106 C3** 23 50N 32 0 E
Kurla, *India* **94 E1** 19 5N 72 52 E
Kurlovskiy, *Russia* **60 C5** 55 25N 40 40 E
Kurmuk, *Sudan* **107 E3** 10 33N 34 21 E
Kurnool, *India* **95 G4** 15 45N 78 0 E
Kuro-Shima, *Kagoshima, Japan* **69 J4** 30 50N 129 57 E
Kuro-Shima, *Okinawa, Japan* **69 M2** 24 14N 124 1 E
Kurobe-Gawe →, *Japan* **71 A9** 36 55N 137 25 E
Kurogi, *Japan* **70 D2** 33 12N 130 40 E
Kuror, J., *Sudan* **106 C3** 20 27N 31 30 E
Kurow, *N.Z.* **131 E5** 44 44 S 170 29 E
Kurów, *Poland* **55 G9** 51 23N 22 12 E
Kurrajong, *Australia* **129 B9** 33 33 S 150 42 E
Kurram →, *Pakistan* **91 B3** 32 36N 71 20 E
Kurri Kurri, *Australia* **129 B9** 32 50 S 151 28 E
Kurrimine, *Australia* **126 B4** 17 47 S 146 6 E
Kursavka, *Russia* **61 H6** 44 29N 42 32 E
Kurse Korhi, *India* **94 D5** 20 14N 80 46 E
Kuršėnai, *Lithuania* **54 B9** 56 1N 22 58 E
Kurshskiy Zaliv, *Russia* **15 J19** 55 9N 21 6 E
Kursk, *Russia* **59 G9** 51 42N 36 11 E
Kuršumlija, *Serbia, Yug.* **50 C5** 43 9N 21 19 E
Kuršumlijska Banja, *Serbia, Yug.* **50 C5** 43 3N 21 11 E
Kurşunlu, *Bursa, Turkey* **51 F13** 40 3N 29 40 E
Kurşunlu, *Çankırı, Turkey* **100 B5** 40 51N 33 15 E
Kurtalan, *Turkey* **101 D9** 37 56N 41 44 E
Kurtbey, *Turkey* **51 E10** 41 9N 26 35 E
Kurtistown, *U.S.A.* **145 D6** 19 36N 155 4W
Kurty →, *Kazakstan* **63 A8** 44 16N 76 42 E
Kuru, *Sudan* **107 F2** 7 43N 26 31 E
Kuru, Bahr el →, *Sudan* **107 F2** 8 10N 26 50 E
Kurucaşile, *Turkey* **100 B5** 41 49N 32 42 E
Kuruçay, *Turkey* **96 B3** 39 39N 38 29 E
Kuruktag, *China* **72 B3** 41 0N 89 0 E
Kuruman, *S. Africa* **116 D3** 27 28 S 23 28 E
Kuruman →, *S. Africa* **116 D3** 26 56 S 20 39 E
Kurume, *Japan* **70 D2** 33 15N 130 30 E
Kurun →, *Sudan* **107 F3** 5 30N 34 17 E
Kurunegala, *Sri Lanka* **95 L5** 7 30N 80 23 E
Kurupukari, *Guyana* **169 C6** 4 43N 58 37W
Kurya, *Russia* **56 B10** 61 42N 57 9 E
Kus Gölü, *Turkey* **51 F11** 40 10N 27 55 E
Kusa, *Russia* **62 D7** 55 20N 59 29 E
Kuşadası, *Turkey* **100 D2** 37 52N 27 15 E
Kuşadası Körfezi, *Turkey* **49 D8** 37 56N 27 0 E
Kusatsu, *Gumma, Japan* **71 A10** 36 37N 138 36 E
Kusatsu, *Shiga, Japan* **71 C7** 34 58N 135 57 E
Kusawa L., *Canada* **142 A1** 60 20N 136 13W
Kusel, *Germany* **31 F3** 49 32N 7 24 E
Kushaka, *Nigeria* **113 C6** 10 32N 6 48 E
Kushalgarh, *India* **92 H6** 23 10N 74 27 E
Kushalnagar, *India* **95 H2** 12 14N 75 57 E
Kushchevskaya, *Russia* **61 G4** 46 33N 39 35 E
Kusheriki, *Nigeria* **113 C6** 10 33N 6 28 E
Kushikino, *Japan* **70 F2** 31 44N 130 16 E
Kushima, *Japan* **70 F3** 31 29N 131 14 E
Kushimoto, *Japan* **71 D7** 33 28N 135 47 E
Kushiro, *Japan* **68 C12** 43 0N 144 25 E
Kushiro-Gawa →, *Japan* **68 C12** 42 59N 144 23 E
Kūshk, *Iran* **97 D8** 28 46N 56 51 E
Kushka = Gushgy, *Turkmenistan* **64 F7** 35 20N 62 18 E
Kūshkī, *Iran* **96 C5** 33 31N 47 13 E
Kushnarenkovo, *Russia* **62 D5** 55 6N 55 22 E
Kushol, *India* **93 C7** 33 40N 76 36 E
Kushrabat, *Uzbekistan* **63 C3** 40 18N 66 32 E
Kushtia, *Bangla.* **90 D2** 23 55N 89 5 E
Kushum →, *Kazakstan* **60 F10** 49 20N 50 30 E
Kushva, *Russia* **62 B7** 58 18N 59 45 E
Kuskokwim B., *U.S.A.* **138 C3** 59 45N 162 25W
Kusmi, *India* **93 H10** 23 17N 83 55 E
Küsnacht, *Switz.* **33 B7** 47 19N 8 35 E
Kussharo-Ko, *Japan* **68 C12** 43 38N 144 21 E
Küssnacht, *Switz.* **33 B6** 47 5N 8 26 E
Kustanay = Qostanay, *Kazakstan* **64 D7** 53 10N 63 35 E
Kusu, *Japan* **70 D3** 33 16N 131 9 E
Kut, Ko, *Thailand* **78 B2** 11 40N 102 35 E
Kutacane, *Indonesia* **84 B1** 3 50N 97 50 E
Kütahya, *Turkey* **49 B12** 39 30N 30 2 E
Kütahya □, *Turkey* **49 B11** 39 10N 29 30 E
Kutaisi, *Georgia* **61 J6** 42 19N 42 40 E
Kutaraja = Banda Aceh, *Indonesia* **78 C1** 5 35N 95 20 E
Kutch, Gulf of = Kachchh, Gulf of, *India* **92 H3** 22 50N 69 15 E
Kutch, Rann of = Kachchh, Rann of, *India* **92 H4** 24 0N 70 0 E
Kutina, *Croatia* **45 C13** 45 29N 16 48 E
Kutiyana, *India* **92 J4** 21 36N 70 2 E
Kutjevo, *Croatia* **52 E2** 45 23N 17 55 E
Kutkai, *Burma* **90 D6** 23 27N 97 56 E
Kutkashen, *Azerbaijan* **61 K8** 40 58N 47 47 E
Kutná Hora, *Czech Rep.* **34 B8** 49 57N 15 16 E
Kutno, *Poland* **55 F6** 52 15N 19 23 E
Kutru, *India* **94 E5** 19 5N 80 46 E
Kutse, *Botswana* **116 C3** 21 7 S 22 16 E
Kutu, *Dem. Rep. of the Congo* **114 C3** 2 40 S 18 11 E
Kutu Moke, *Dem. Rep. of the Congo* **114 C3** 3 12 S 17 21 E
Kutum, *Sudan* **107 E1** 14 10N 24 40 E
Kúty, *Slovak Rep.* **35 C10** 48 40N 17 3 E
Kuujjuaq, *Canada* **139 C13** 58 6N 68 15W
Kuujjuarapik, *Canada* **140 A4** 55 20N 77 35W
Kuŭp-tong, *N. Korea* **75 D14** 40 45N 126 1 E
Kuusamo, *Finland* **14 D23** 65 57N 29 8 E
Kuusankoski, *Finland* **15 F22** 60 55N 26 38 E
Kuvandyk, *Russia* **62 F6** 51 28N 57 21 E
Kuvango, *Angola* **115 E3** 14 28 S 16 20 E
Kuvasay, *Uzbekistan* **63 C5** 40 18N 71 59 E
Kuvshinovo, *Russia* **58 D8** 57 2N 34 11 E
Kuwait = Al Kuwayt, *Kuwait* **96 D5** 29 30N 48 0 E
Kuwait ■, *Asia* **96 D5** 29 30N 47 30 E
Kuwana, *Japan* **71 B8** 35 5N 136 43 E
Kuwana →, *India* **93 F10** 26 25N 83 15 E
Kuybyshev = Samara, *Russia* **60 D10** 53 8N 50 6 E
Kuybyshev, *Russia* **64 D8** 55 27N 78 19 E
Kuybyshevo, *Ukraine* **59 J9** 47 25N 36 40 E
Kuybyshevo, *Uzbekistan* **63 C5** 40 20N 71 15 E
Kuybyshevskiy, *Tajikistan* **63 E4** 37 52N 68 44 E
Kuybyshevskoye Vdkhr., *Russia* **60 C9** 55 2N 49 30 E
Kuye He →, *China* **74 E6** 38 23N 110 46 E
Kūyeh, *Iran* **96 B5** 38 45N 47 57 E
Kuylyuk, *Uzbekistan* **63 C4** 41 14N 69 17 E
Kūysanjaq, *Iraq* **101 D11** 36 5N 44 38 E
Kuyto, Ozero, *Russia* **56 B5** 65 6N 31 20 E
Kuyucak, *Turkey* **49 D10** 37 55N 28 28 E
Kuyumba, *Russia* **65 C10** 60 58N 96 59 E
Kuzey Anadolu Dağları, *Turkey* **100 B7** 41 30N 35 0 E
Kuzhitturai, *India* **95 K3** 8 18N 77 11 E
Kuzino, *Russia* **62 C7** 57 1N 59 27 E
Kuzitrin →, *U.S.A.* **144 D6** 65 10N 165 25W
Kuzmin, *Serbia, Yug.* **52 E4** 45 2N 19 25 E
Kuznetsk, *Russia* **60 D8** 53 12N 46 40 E
Kuzomen, *Russia* **56 A6** 66 22N 36 50 E
Kvænangen, *Norway* **14 A19** 70 5N 21 15 E
Kværndrup, *Denmark* **17 J4** 55 10N 10 31 E
Kvaløy, *Norway* **14 B18** 69 40N 18 30 E
Kvam, *Norway* **18 C6** 61 40N 9 42 E
Kvänum, *Sweden* **17 F7** 58 18N 13 11 E
Kvareli = Qvareli, *Georgia* **61 K7** 41 57N 45 47 E
Kvarner, *Croatia* **45 D11** 44 50N 14 10 E
Kvarnerič, *Croatia* **45 D11** 44 43N 14 37 E
Kvås, *Norway* **18 F4** 58 16N 7 14 E
Kvernaland, *Norway* **18 F2** 58 47N 5 45 E
Kvichak B., *U.S.A.* **144 G8** 58 48N 157 30W
Kvicksund, *Sweden* **16 E10** 59 27N 16 19 E
Kvikne, *Norway* **18 B7** 62 35N 10 16 E
Kvillsfors, *Sweden* **17 G9** 57 24N 15 29 E
Kvina →, *Norway* **18 F3** 58 19N 6 55 E
Kvinlog, *Norway* **18 F3** 58 31N 6 55 E
Kvismare kanal, *Sweden* **16 E9** 59 11N 15 35 E
Kvissleby, *Sweden* **16 B11** 62 18N 17 22 E
Kviteseid, *Norway* **18 E5** 59 24N 8 29 E
Kwabhaca, *S. Africa* **117 E4** 30 51 S 29 0 E
Kwakhanai, *Botswana* **116 C3** 21 39 S 21 16 E
Kwakoegron, *Surinam* **169 B6** 5 12N 55 25W
Kwale, *Kenya* **118 C4** 4 15 S 39 31 E
Kwale, *Nigeria* **113 D6** 5 46N 6 26 E
Kwamalasamutu, *Surinam* **169 C6** 2 20N 56 47W
KwaMashu, *S. Africa* **117 D5** 29 45 S 30 58 E
Kwamouth, *Dem. Rep. of the Congo* **114 C3** 3 9 S 16 12 E
Kwando →, *Africa* **116 B3** 18 27 S 23 32 E
Kwangdaeri, *N. Korea* **75 D14** 40 31N 127 32 E
Kwangju, *S. Korea* **75 G14** 35 9N 126 54 E
Kwango →, *Dem. Rep. of the Congo* **114 C3** 3 14 S 17 22 E
Kwangsi-Chuang = Guangxi Zhuangzu Zizhiqu □, *China* **76 F7** 24 0N 109 0 E
Kwangtung = Guangdong □, *China* **77 F9** 23 0N 113 0 E
Kwara □, *Nigeria* **113 D6** 8 45N 4 30 E
Kwataboahegan →, *Canada* **140 B3** 51 9N 80 50W
Kwatisore, *Indonesia* **79 E8** 3 18 S 134 50 E
KwaZulu Natal □, *S. Africa* **117 D5** 29 0 S 30 0 E
Kweichow = Guizhou □, *China* **76 D6** 27 0N 107 0 E
Kwekwe, *Zimbabwe* **119 F2** 18 58 S 29 48 E
Kwenge →, *Dem. Rep. of the Congo* **115 C3** 4 50 S 18 44 E
Kwidzyn, *Poland* **54 E5** 53 44N 18 55 E
Kwiha, *Ethiopia* **107 E4** 13 29N 39 32 E
Kwikila, *Papua N. G.* **132 E4** 9 49 S 147 38 E
Kwilu →, *Dem. Rep. of the Congo* **115 C3** 3 22 S 17 22 E
Kwinana New Town, *Australia* **125 F2** 32 15 S 115 47 E
Kwisa →, *Poland* **55 G2** 51 34N 15 24 E
Kwoka, *Indonesia* **79 E8** 0 31 S 132 27 E
Kwolla, *Nigeria* **113 D6** 9 0N 9 15 E
Kya-in-Seikkyi, *Burma* **90 G7** 16 2N 98 8 E
Kyabé, *Chad* **109 G3** 9 30N 19 0 E
Kyabra Cr. →, *Australia* **127 D3** 25 36 S 142 55 E
Kyabram, *Australia* **127 F4** 36 19 S 145 4 E
Kyaiklat, *Burma* **90 G5** 16 25N 95 40 E
Kyaikmaraw, *Burma* **90 G6** 16 23N 97 44 E
Kyaikthin, *Burma* **90 D5** 23 32N 95 40 E
Kyaikto, *Burma* **86 D1** 17 20N 97 3 E
Kyakhta, *Russia* **65 D11** 50 30N 106 25 E
Kyancutta, *Australia* **127 E2** 33 8 S 135 33 E
Kyangin, *Burma* **90 F5** 18 20N 95 20 E
Kyaukhnyat, *Burma* **90 F6** 18 15N 97 31 E
Kyaukse, *Burma* **90 E6** 21 36N 96 10 E
Kyauktaw, *Burma* **90 E4** 20 51N 92 59 E
Kyawkku, *Burma* **90 E6** 21 48N 96 56 E
Kybartai, *Lithuania* **54 D9** 54 39N 22 45 E
Kyburz, *U.S.A.* **160 G6** 38 47N 120 18W
Kybybolite, *Australia* **128 D4** 36 53 S 140 55 E
Kyeintali, *Burma* **90 G5** 18 0N 94 29 E
Kyelang, *India* **92 C7** 32 35N 77 2 E
Kyenjojo, *Uganda* **118 B3** 0 40N 30 37 E
Kyidaunggan, *Burma* **90 F6** 19 53N 96 12 E
Kyjov, *Czech Rep.* **35 B10** 49 1N 17 7 E
Kyle, *Canada* **143 C7** 50 50N 108 2W
Kyle Dam, *Zimbabwe* **119 G3** 20 15 S 31 0 E
Kyle of Lochalsh, *U.K.* **22 D3** 57 17N 5 44W
Kyll →, *Germany* **31 F2** 49 48N 6 41 E
Kyllburg, *Germany* **31 E2** 50 2N 6 34 E
Kymijoki →, *Finland* **15 F22** 60 30N 26 55 E
Kyneton, *Australia* **128 D6** 37 10 S 144 29 E
Kynuna, *Australia* **126 C3** 21 37 S 141 55 E
Kyō-ga-Saki, *Japan* **71 B7** 35 45N 135 15 E
Kyoga, L., *Uganda* **118 B3** 1 35N 33 0 E
Kyogle, *Australia* **127 D5** 28 40 S 153 0 E
Kyom →, *Sudan* **107 F2** 8 58N 28 13 E
Kyongju, *S. Korea* **75 G15** 35 51N 129 14 E
Kyŏngsŏng, *N. Korea* **75 D15** 41 35N 129 36 E
Kyōto, *Japan* **71 B7** 35 0N 135 45 E
Kyōto □, *Japan* **71 B7** 35 15N 135 45 E
Kyparissovouno, *Cyprus* **38 D12** 35 19N 33 10 E
Kyperounda, *Cyprus* **38 E11** 34 56N 32 58 E
Kyrenia, *Cyprus* **38 D12** 35 20N 33 20 E
Kyrgyzstan ■, *Asia* **64 E8** 42 0N 75 0 E
Kyritz, *Germany* **30 C8** 52 56N 12 24 E
Kyrkhult, *Sweden* **17 H8** 56 22N 14 34 E
Kyrksæterøra, *Norway* **18 A6** 63 18N 9 5 E
Kyrönjoki →, *Finland* **14 E19** 63 14N 21 45 E
Kyshtym, *Russia* **62 D8** 55 42N 60 34 E
Kystatyam, *Russia* **65 C13** 67 20N 123 10 E
Kysucké Nové Mesto, *Slovak Rep.* **35 B11** 49 18N 18 47 E
Kythréa, *Cyprus* **38 D12** 35 15N 33 29 E
Kytlym, *Russia* **62 B7** 59 30N 59 12 E
Kyu-hkok, *Burma* **90 C7** 24 4N 98 4 E
Kyunhla, *Burma* **90 D5** 23 25N 95 15 E
Kyuquot Sound, *Canada* **142 D3** 50 2N 127 22W
Kyurdamir = Kürdämir, *Azerbaijan* **61 K9** 40 25N 48 3 E
Kyūshū, *Japan* **70 E3** 33 0N 131 0 E
Kyūshū □, *Japan* **70 E3** 33 0N 131 0 E
Kyūshū-Sanchi, *Japan* **70 E3** 32 35N 131 17 E
Kyustendil, *Bulgaria* **50 D6** 42 16N 22 41 E
Kyusyur, *Russia* **65 B13** 70 19N 127 30 E
Kywong, *Australia* **129 C7** 34 58 S 146 44 E
Kyyiv, *Ukraine* **59 G6** 50 30N 30 28 E
Kyyivske Vdskh., *Ukraine* **59 G6** 51 0N 30 25 E
Kyzyl, *Russia* **65 D10** 51 50N 94 30 E
Kyzyl Kum, *Uzbekistan* **64 E7** 42 30N 65 0 E
Kyzyl-Kyya, *Kyrgyzstan* **64 E8** 40 16N 72 8 E
Kyzylsu →, *Kyrgyzstan* **63 D6** 38 50N 70 0 E
Kzyl-Orda = Qyzylorda, *Kazakstan* **64 E7** 44 48N 65 28 E

L

La Albuera, *Spain* **43 G4** 38 45N 6 49W
La Alcarria, *Spain* **40 E2** 40 31N 2 45W
La Almarcha, *Spain* **40 F2** 39 41N 2 24W
La Almunia de Doña Godina, *Spain* **40 D3** 41 29N 1 23W
La Asunción, *Venezuela* **169 A5** 11 2N 63 53W
La Baie, *Canada* **141 C5** 48 19N 70 53W
La Banda, *Argentina* **174 B3** 27 45 S 64 10W
La Bañeza, *Spain* **42 C5** 42 17N 5 54W
La Barca, *Mexico* **162 C4** 20 20N 102 40W
La Barge, *U.S.A.* **158 E8** 42 16N 110 12W
La Bastide-Puylaurent, *France* **28 D7** 44 35N 3 55 E
La Baule-Escoubiac, *France* **26 E4** 47 17N 2 24W
La Belle, *Fla., U.S.A.* **149 M5** 26 46N 81 26W
La Belle, *Mo., U.S.A.* **156 D5** 40 7N 91 55W
La Biche →, *Canada* **142 B4** 59 57N 123 50W
La Biche, L., *Canada* **142 C6** 54 50N 112 5W
La Bisbal d'Empordà, *Spain* **40 D8** 41 58N 3 2 E
La Bomba, *Mexico* **162 A1** 31 53N 115 2W
La Brea, *Trin. & Tob.* **169 A5** 10 15N 61 37W
La Bresse, *France* **27 D13** 48 2N 6 53 E
La Bureba, *Spain* **42 C7** 42 36N 3 24W
La Cal →, *Bolivia* **173 D6** 17 27 S 58 15W
La Calera, *Chile* **174 C1** 32 50 S 71 10W
La Campiña, *Spain* **43 H6** 37 45N 4 45W
La Canal = Sa Canal, *Spain* **38 C7** 38 51N 1 23 E
La Cañiza = A Cañiza, *Spain* **42 C2** 42 13N 8 16W
La Canourgue, *France* **28 D7** 44 26N 3 13 E
La Capelle, *France* **27 C10** 49 59N 3 50 E
La Carlota, *Argentina* **174 C3** 33 30 S 63 20W
La Carlota, *Phil.* **81 F4** 10 25N 122 55 E
La Carlota, *Spain* **43 H6** 37 40N 4 56W
La Carolina, *Spain* **43 G7** 38 17N 3 38W
La Castellana, *Phil.* **81 F4** 10 20N 123 3 E
La Cavalerie, *France* **28 D7** 44 1N 3 10 E
La Ceiba, *Honduras* **164 C2** 15 40N 86 50W
La Ceiba, *Venezuela* **168 C3** 9 28N 71 4W
La Chaise-Dieu, *France* **28 C7** 45 18N 3 42 E
La Chapelle d'Angillon, *France* **27 E9** 47 21N 2 25 E
La Chapelle-St-Luc, *France* **27 D11** 48 20N 4 3 E
La Chapelle-sur-Erdre, *France* **26 E5** 47 18N 1 34W
La Charité-sur-Loire, *France* **27 E10** 47 10N 3 1 E
La Chartre-sur-le-Loir, *France* **26 E7** 47 44N 0 34 E
La Châtaigneraie, *France* **28 B3** 46 39N 0 44W
La Châtre, *France* **27 F9** 46 35N 2 0 E
La Chaux-de-Fonds, *Switz.* **32 B3** 47 7N 6 50 E
La Chorrera, *Colombia* **168 D3** 0 44 S 73 1W
La Chorrera, *Panama* **164 E4** 8 53N 79 47W
La Ciotat, *France* **29 E9** 43 10N 5 37 E
La Clayette, *France* **27 F11** 46 17N 4 19 E
La Cocha, *Argentina* **174 B2** 27 50 S 65 40W
La Concepción = Ri-Aba, *Eq. Guin.* **113 E6** 3 28N 8 40 E
La Concepción, *Panama* **164 E3** 8 31N 82 37W
La Concepción, *Venezuela* **168 A3** 10 30N 71 50W
La Concordia, *Mexico* **163 D6** 16 8N 92 38W
La Coruña = A Coruña, *Spain* **42 B2** 43 20N 8 25W
La Coruña □, *Spain* **42 B2** 43 10N 8 30W
La Côte, *Switz.* **32 D2** 46 25N 6 15 E
La Côte-St-André, *France* **29 C9** 45 24N 5 15 E
La Courtine-le-Trucq, *France* **28 C6** 45 41N 2 15 E
La Crau, *Bouches-du-Rhône, France* **29 E8** 43 32N 4 40 E
La Crau, *Var, France* **29 E10** 43 9N 6 4 E
La Crescent, *U.S.A.* **154 D9** 43 50N 91 18W
La Crete, *Canada* **142 B5** 58 11N 116 24W
La Crosse, *Fla., U.S.A.* **152 F7** 29 51N 82 24W
La Crosse, *Kans., U.S.A.* **154 F5** 38 32N 99 18W
La Crosse, *Wis., U.S.A.* **154 D9** 43 48N 91 15W
La Cruz, *Costa Rica* **164 D2** 11 4N 85 39W
La Cruz, *Mexico* **162 C3** 23 55N 106 54W

238 La Désirade

La Désirade, Guadeloupe 165 C7 16 18N 61 3W
La Dorada, Colombia 168 B3 5 30N 74 40W
La Ensenada, Chile 176 B2 41 12S 72 33W
La Escondida, Mexico 162 C5 24 6N 99 55W
La Esmeralda, Paraguay 174 A3 22 16S 62 33W
La Esperanza, Argentina 176 B3 40 26S 68 32W
La Esperanza, Cuba 164 B3 22 46N 83 44W
La Esperanza, Honduras 164 D2 14 15N 88 10W
La Estrada = A Estrada, Spain 42 C2 42 43N 8 27W
La Faouët, France 26 D3 48 2N 3 30W
La Fayette, U.S.A. 149 H3 34 42N 85 17W
La Fé, Cuba 164 B3 22 2N 84 15W
La Fère, France 27 C10 49 39N 3 21 E
La Ferté-Bernard, France 26 D7 48 10N 0 40 E
La Ferté-Gaucher, France 27 D10 48 47N 3 19 E
La Ferté-Macé, France 26 D6 48 35N 0 22W
La Ferté-St-Aubin, France 27 E8 47 42N 1 57 E
La Ferté-sous-Jouarre, France 27 D10 48 56N 3 8 E
La Ferté-Vidame, France 26 D7 48 37N 0 53 E
La Flèche, France 26 E6 47 42N 0 4W
La Foa, N. Cal. 133 U19 21 43S 165 50 E
La Follette, U.S.A. 149 G3 36 23N 84 7W
La Fontaine, U.S.A. 157 D11 40 40N 85 43W
La Fregeneda, Spain 42 E4 40 58N 6 54W
La Fría, Venezuela 168 B3 8 13N 72 15W
La Fuente de San Esteban, Spain 42 E4 40 49N 6 15W
La Gacilly, France 26 E4 47 45N 2 8W
La Gineta, Spain 41 F2 39 8N 2 1W
La Gloria, Colombia 168 B3 8 37N 73 48W
La Gran Sabana, Venezuela 169 B5 5 30N 61 30W
La Grand-Combe, France 29 D8 44 13N 4 2 E
La Grande, U.S.A. 158 D4 45 20N 118 5W
La Grande →, Canada 140 B5 53 50N 79 0W
La Grande Deux, Rés., Canada 140 B4 53 40N 76 55W
La Grande-Motte, France 29 E8 43 23N 4 5 E
La Grande Quatre, Rés., Canada 140 B5 54 0N 73 15W
La Grande Trois, Rés., Canada 140 B4 53 40N 75 10W
La Grange, Calif., U.S.A. 160 H6 37 42N 120 27W
La Grange, Ga., U.S.A. 152 B4 33 2N 85 2W
La Grange, Ky., U.S.A. 148 F3 38 25N 85 23W
La Grange, Ky., U.S.A. 157 F11 38 24N 85 22W
La Grange, Mo., U.S.A. 156 D5 40 3N 91 35W
La Grange, Tex., U.S.A. 155 L6 29 54N 96 52W
La Grave, France 29 C10 45 3N 6 18 E
La Grita, Venezuela 168 B3 8 8N 71 59W
La Guaira, Venezuela 168 A4 10 36N 66 56W
La Guardia = A Guarda, Spain 42 D2 41 56N 8 52W
La Gudiña = A Gudiña, Spain 42 C3 42 4N 7 8W
La Güera, Mauritania 110 D1 20 51N 17 0W
La Guerche-de-Bretagne, France 26 E5 47 57N 1 16W
La Guerche-sur-l'Aubois, France 27 F9 46 58N 2 56 E
La Habana, Cuba 164 B3 23 8N 82 22W
La Harpe, U.S.A. 156 D6 40 35N 90 58W
La Haye-du-Puits, France 26 C5 49 17N 1 33W
La Horqueta, Venezuela 169 B5 7 55N 60 20W
La Horra, Spain 42 D7 41 44N 3 53W
La Independencia, Mexico 163 D6 16 31N 91 47W
La Isabela, Dom. Rep. 165 C5 19 58N 71 2W
La Jonquera, Spain 40 C7 42 25N 2 53 E
La Joya, Peru 172 D3 16 43S 71 52W
La Junta, U.S.A. 155 F3 37 59N 103 33W
La Laguna, Canary Is. 39 F3 28 28N 16 18W
La Libertad, Guatemala 164 C1 16 47N 90 7W
La Libertad, Mexico 162 B2 29 55N 112 41W
La Libertad □, Peru 172 B2 8 0S 78 30W
La Ligua, Chile 174 C1 32 30S 71 16W
La Línea de la Concepción, Spain 43 J5 36 15N 5 23W
La Loche, Canada 143 B7 56 29N 109 26W
La Londe-les-Maures, France 29 E10 43 8N 6 14 E
La Lora, Spain 42 C7 42 45N 4 0W
La Loupe, France 26 D8 48 29N 1 0 E
La Louvière, Belgium 24 D4 50 27N 4 10 E
La Machine, France 27 F10 46 54N 3 27 E
La Maddalena, Italy 46 A2 41 13N 9 24 E
La Malbaie, Canada 141 C5 47 40N 70 10W
La Mancha, Spain 41 F2 39 10N 2 54W
La Mariña, Spain 42 B3 43 30N 7 40W
La Martre, L., Canada 142 A5 63 15N 117 55W
La Mesa, U.S.A. 161 N9 32 46N 117 3W
La Misión, Mexico 162 A1 32 5N 116 50W
La Moille, U.S.A. 156 C7 41 32N 89 17W
La Moine →, U.S.A. 156 E6 39 59N 90 31W
La Monte, U.S.A. 156 F3 38 46N 93 26W
La Mothe-Achard, France 26 F5 46 37N 1 40W
La Motte, France 29 D10 44 20N 6 3 E
La Motte-Chalançon, France 29 D9 44 30N 5 21 E
La Motte-Servolex, France 29 C9 45 35N 5 53 E
La Moure, U.S.A. 154 B5 46 21N 98 18W
La Muela, Spain 40 D3 41 36N 1 7W
La Mure, France 29 D9 44 55N 5 48 E
La Negra, Chile 174 A1 23 46S 70 18W
La Neuveville, Switz. 32 B4 47 4N 7 6 E
La Oliva, Canary Is. 39 F6 28 36N 13 57W
La Oraya, Peru 172 C2 11 32S 75 54W
La Orotava, Canary Is. 39 F3 28 22N 16 31W
La Oroya, Peru 172 C2 11 32S 75 54W
La Pacaudière, France 27 F10 46 11N 3 52 E
La Palma, Canary Is. 39 F2 28 40N 17 50W
La Palma, Panama 164 E4 8 15N 78 0W
La Palma del Condado, Spain 43 H4 37 21N 6 38W
La Paloma, Chile 174 C1 30 35S 71 0W
La Pampa □, Argentina 174 D2 36 50S 66 0W
La Paragua, Venezuela 169 B5 6 50N 63 20W
La Paz, Entre Ríos, Argentina 174 C4 30 50S 59 45W
La Paz, San Luis, Argentina 174 C2 33 30S 67 20W
La Paz, Bolivia 172 D4 16 20S 68 10W
La Paz, Honduras 164 D2 14 20N 87 47W
La Paz, Mexico 162 C2 24 10N 110 20W
La Paz, Phil. 80 D3 15 26N 120 45 E
La Paz, Abra, Phil. 80 C3 17 40N 120 41 E
La Paz □, Bolivia 172 D4 15 30S 68 0W
La Paz Centro, Nic. 164 D2 12 20N 86 41W
La Pedrera, Colombia 168 D4 1 18S 69 43W
La Pérade, Canada 141 C5 46 35N 72 12W
La Perouse Str., Asia 68 B11 45 40N 142 0 E
La Pesca, Mexico 163 C5 23 46N 97 47W
La Piedad, Mexico 162 C4 20 20N 102 1W
La Pine, U.S.A. 158 E3 43 40N 121 30W
La Plata, Argentina 174 D4 35 0S 57 55W
La Plata, Colombia 168 C2 2 23N 75 53W
La Plata, U.S.A. 156 D4 40 2N 92 29W
La Plata, L., Argentina 176 B2 44 55S 71 50W
La Pobla de Lillet, Spain 40 C6 42 16N 1 59 E
La Pocatière, Canada 141 C5 47 22N 70 2W
La Pola de Gordón, Spain 42 C5 42 51N 5 41W
La Porta, France 29 F13 42 25N 9 21 E
La Porte, Ind., U.S.A. 157 C10 41 36N 86 43W
La Porte, Tex., U.S.A. 155 L7 29 39N 95 1W
La Porte City, U.S.A. 156 B4 42 19N 92 12W
La Presanella, Italy 44 B7 46 13N 10 40 E
La Puebla = Sa Pobla, Spain 40 F8 39 46N 3 1 E
La Puebla de Cazalla, Spain 43 H5 37 10N 5 20W
La Puebla de los Infantes, Spain 43 H5 37 47N 5 24W
La Puebla de Montalbán, Spain 42 F6 39 52N 4 22W
La Puebla del Río, Spain 43 H4 37 16N 6 3W
La Puerta de Segura, Spain 43 G8 38 22N 2 45W
La Punt, Switz. 33 C9 46 35N 9 56 E
La Purísima, Mexico 162 B2 26 10N 112 4W
La Push, U.S.A. 160 C2 47 55N 124 38W
La Quiaca, Argentina 174 A2 22 5S 65 35W
La Réole, France 28 D3 44 35N 0 1W
La Restinga, Canary Is. 39 G2 27 38N 17 59W
La Rioja, Argentina 174 B2 29 20S 67 0W
La Rioja □, Argentina 174 B2 29 30S 67 0W
La Rioja □, Spain 40 C2 42 20N 2 20W
La Robla, Spain 42 C5 42 50N 5 41W
La Roche, Switz. 32 C4 46 42N 7 7 E
La Roche-Bernard, France 26 E4 47 31N 2 19W
La Roche-Canillac, France 28 C5 45 12N 1 57 E
La Roche-en-Ardenne, Belgium 24 D5 50 11N 5 35 E
La Roche-sur-Foron, France 27 F13 46 4N 6 19 E
La Roche-sur-Yon, France 26 F5 46 40N 1 25W
La Rochefoucauld, France 28 C4 45 44N 0 24 E
La Rochelle, France 28 B2 46 10N 1 9W
La Roda, Spain 41 F2 39 13N 2 15W
La Roda de Andalucía, Spain 43 H6 37 12N 4 46W
La Romana, Dom. Rep. 165 C6 18 27N 68 57W
La Ronge, Canada 143 B7 55 5N 105 20W
La Rue, U.S.A. 157 D13 40 35N 83 23W
La Rumorosa, Mexico 161 N10 32 33N 116 4W
La Sabina = Sa Savina, Spain 39 C7 38 44N 1 25 E
La Sagra, Spain 41 H2 37 57N 2 35W
La Salle, U.S.A. 156 C7 41 20N 89 6W
La Sanabria, Spain 42 C4 42 0N 6 30W
La Santa, Canary Is. 39 E6 29 5N 13 40W
La Sarraz, Switz. 32 C3 46 38N 6 32 E
La Sarre, Canada 140 C4 48 45N 79 15W
La Scie, Canada 141 C8 49 57N 55 36W
La Selva, Spain 40 C7 42 0N 2 45 E
La Selva Beach, U.S.A. 160 J5 36 56N 121 51W
La Selva del Camp, Spain 40 D6 41 13N 1 8 E
La Serena, Chile 174 B1 29 55S 71 10W
La Serena, Spain 43 G5 38 45N 5 40W
La Seu d'Urgell, Spain 40 C6 42 22N 1 23 E
La Seyne-sur-Mer, France 29 E9 43 7N 5 52 E
La Sila, Italy 47 C9 39 15N 16 35 E
La Solana, Spain 43 G7 38 59N 3 14W
La Soufrière, St. Vincent 165 D7 13 20N 61 11W
La Souterraine, France 27 F8 46 15N 1 30 E
La Spézia, Italy 44 D6 44 7N 9 50 E
La Suze-sur-Sarthe, France 26 E7 47 53N 0 2 E
La Tagua, Colombia 168 C3 0 3N 74 40W
La Teste, France 28 D2 44 37N 1 8W
La Tortuga, Venezuela 165 D6 11 0N 65 22W
La Tour de Peilz, Switz. 32 D3 46 27N 6 52 E
La Tour-du-Pin, France 29 C9 45 33N 5 27 E
La Tournette, France 32 E2 45 35N 6 30 E
La Tranche-sur-Mer, France 26 F5 46 20N 1 27W
La Tremblade, France 28 C2 45 46N 1 8W
La Trinidad, Phil. 80 C3 16 28N 120 35 E
La Tuque, Canada 140 C5 47 30N 72 50W
La Unión, Chile 176 B2 40 10S 73 0W
La Unión, Colombia 168 C2 1 35N 77 5W
La Unión, El Salv. 164 D2 13 20N 87 50W
La Unión, Mexico 162 D4 17 58N 101 49W
La Unión, Peru 172 B2 9 43S 76 45W
La Unión, Spain 41 H4 37 38N 0 53W
La Union □, Phil. 80 C3 16 30N 120 25 E
La Urbana, Venezuela 168 B4 7 8N 66 56W
La Vall d'Uixó, Spain 40 F4 39 49N 0 15W
La Vecilla de Curveño, Spain 42 C5 42 51N 5 27W
La Vega, Dom. Rep. 165 C5 19 20N 70 30W
La Vega, Peru 172 C2 10 41S 77 44W
La Vela de Coro, Venezuela 168 A4 11 27N 69 34W
La Veleta, Spain 43 H7 37 1N 3 22W
La Venta, Mexico 163 D6 18 8N 94 3W
La Ventura, Mexico 162 C4 24 38N 100 54W
La Venturosa, Colombia 168 B4 6 8N 68 48W
La Victoria, Venezuela 168 A4 10 14N 67 20W
La Voulte-sur-Rhône, France 29 D8 44 48N 4 46 E
Laa an der Thaya, Austria 35 C9 48 43N 16 23 E
Laaber, Grosse →, Germany 31 G8 48 55N 12 30 E
Laage, Germany 30 B8 53 55N 12 21 E
Laatzen, Germany 30 C5 52 19N 9 48 E
Laba →, Russia 61 H4 45 11N 39 42 E
Laban, Burma 90 C6 25 52N 96 40 E
Labason, Phil. 81 G4 8 4N 122 31 E
Labastide-Murat, France 28 D5 44 39N 1 33 E
Labastide-Rouairoux, France 28 E6 43 28N 2 39 E
Labbézenga, Mali 113 B5 15 2N 0 48 E
Labdah = Leptis Magna, Libya 108 B2 32 40N 14 12 E
Labe = Elbe →, Europe 30 B4 53 50N 9 0 E
Labé, Guinea 112 C2 11 24N 12 16W
Laberge, L., Canada 142 A1 61 11N 135 12W
Labian, Tanjong, Malaysia 85 A5 5 9N 119 13 E
Labig Pt. = Iligan Pt., Phil. 80 B4 18 25N 122 25 E
Labin, Croatia 45 C11 45 5N 14 8 E
Labinsk, Russia 61 H5 44 40N 40 48 E
Labis, Malaysia 87 L4 2 22N 103 2 E
Łabiszyn, Poland 55 F4 52 57N 17 54 E
Labo, Phil. 80 D4 14 9N 122 51 E
Laboe, Germany 30 A6 54 24N 10 13 E
Laboka, Gabon 114 B2 0 19N 11 32 E
Laborec →, Slovak Rep. 35 C14 48 37N 21 58 E
Labouheyre, France 28 D3 44 13N 0 55W
Laboulaye, Argentina 174 C3 34 10S 63 30W
Labrador, Canada 141 B7 53 20N 61 0W
Labrador City, Canada 141 B6 52 57N 66 55W
Labrador Sea, Atl. Oc. 139 C14 57 0N 54 0W
Lábrea, Brazil 173 B5 7 15S 64 51W
Labrède, France 28 D3 44 41N 0 32W
Labruguière, France 28 E6 43 31N 2 16 E
Labuan, Malaysia 78 C5 5 20N 115 14 E
Labuan, Pulau, Malaysia 78 C5 5 21N 115 13 E
Labuha, Indonesia 79 E7 0 30S 127 30 E
Labuhan, Indonesia 79 G11 6 22S 105 50 E
Labuhanbajo, Indonesia 79 F6 8 28S 120 1 E
Labuk, Telok, Malaysia 78 C5 6 10N 117 50 E
Labutta, Burma 90 G5 16 9N 94 46 E
Labyrinth, L., Australia 127 E2 30 40S 135 11 E
Labytnangi, Russia 64 C7 66 39N 66 21 E
Laç, Albania 50 E3 41 38N 19 43 E
Lac Bouchette, Canada 141 C5 48 16N 72 11W
Lac Édouard, Canada 140 C5 47 40N 72 16W
Lac La Biche, Canada 142 C6 54 45N 111 58W
Lac la Martre = Wha Ti, Canada 138 B8 63 8N 117 16W
Lac La Ronge Prov. Park, Canada 143 B7 55 9N 104 41W
Lac-Mégantic, Canada 141 C5 45 35N 70 53W
Lac Seul, Res., Canada 140 B1 50 25N 92 30W
Lac Thien, Vietnam 86 F7 12 25N 108 11 E
Lacanau, France 28 D2 44 58N 1 5W
Lacanau, Étang de, France 28 D2 44 58N 1 7W
Lacantúm →, Mexico 163 D6 16 36N 90 40W
Lacara →, Spain 43 G4 38 55N 6 25W
Lacaune, France 28 E6 43 43N 2 40 E
Lacaune, Mts. de, France 28 E6 43 43N 2 50 E
Laccadive Is. = Lakshadweep Is., Ind. Oc. 66 H11 10 0N 72 30 E
Lacepede B., Australia 128 D3 36 40S 139 40 E
Lacepede Is., Australia 124 C3 16 55S 122 0 E
Lacerdónia, Mozam. 119 F4 18 3S 35 35 E
Lacey, U.S.A. 160 C4 47 7N 122 49W
Lachay, Pta., Peru 172 C2 11 17S 77 44W
Lachen, India 90 B2 27 46N 88 36 E
Lachen, Switz. 33 B7 47 12N 8 51 E
Lachhmangarh, India 92 F6 27 50N 75 4 E
Lachi, Pakistan 92 C4 33 25N 71 20 E
Lachine, Canada 140 C5 45 30N 73 40W
Lachlan →, Australia 128 C5 34 22S 143 55 E
Lachoc, Peru 172 C2 12 50S 75 6W
Lachute, Canada 140 C5 45 39N 74 21W
Lackawanna, U.S.A. 150 D6 42 50N 78 50W
Lackawaxen, U.S.A. 151 E10 41 29N 74 59W
Lacolle, Canada 151 A11 45 5N 73 22W
Lacombe, Canada 142 C6 52 30N 113 44W
Lacon, U.S.A. 156 C7 41 2N 89 24W
Lacona, Iowa, U.S.A. 156 C3 41 12N 93 23W
Lacona, N.Y., U.S.A. 151 C8 43 39N 76 10W
Láconi, Italy 46 C2 39 54N 9 4 E
Laconia, U.S.A. 151 C13 43 32N 71 28W
Lacoochee, U.S.A. 153 G7 28 28N 82 11W
Lacq, France 28 E3 43 25N 0 35W
Ladakh Ra., India 93 C8 34 0N 78 0 E
Ladário, Brazil 173 D6 19 1S 57 35W
Ladd, U.S.A. 156 C7 41 23N 89 13W
Laddonia, U.S.A. 156 E5 39 15N 91 39W
Lądek-Zdrój, Poland 55 H3 50 21N 16 53 E
Ládhon →, Greece 48 D3 37 40N 21 50 E
Ladik, Turkey 100 B6 40 57N 35 58 E
Ladismith, S. Africa 116 E3 33 28S 21 15 E
Ladíspoli, Italy 45 G9 41 56N 12 5 E
Lādīz, Iran 97 D9 28 55N 61 15 E
Ladnun, India 92 F6 27 38N 74 25 E
Ladoga, L. = Ladozhskoye Ozero, Russia 58 B6 61 15N 30 30 E
Ladozhskoye Ozero, Russia 58 B6 61 15N 30 30 E
Ladrillero, G., Chile 176 C1 49 20S 75 35W
Ladson, U.S.A. 152 C9 32 59N 80 6W
Lady Elliott I., Australia 126 C5 24 7S 152 42 E
Lady Grey, S. Africa 116 E4 30 43S 27 13 E
Lady Lake, U.S.A. 153 G8 28 55N 81 55W
Ladybrand, S. Africa 116 D4 29 9S 27 29 E
Ladysmith, Canada 142 D4 49 0N 123 49W
Ladysmith, S. Africa 117 D4 28 32S 29 46 E
Ladysmith, U.S.A. 154 C9 45 28N 91 12W
Lae, Papua N. G. 132 D4 6 40S 147 2 E
Laem Ngop, Thailand 87 F4 12 10N 102 26 E
Laem Pho, Thailand 87 J3 6 55N 101 19 E
Lærdalsøyri, Norway 18 C4 61 6N 7 28 E
Læsø, Denmark 17 G5 57 15N 11 5 E
Læsø Rende, Denmark 17 G4 57 20N 10 45 E
Lafayette, Ala., U.S.A. 152 C4 32 54N 85 24W
Lafayette, Colo., U.S.A. 154 F2 39 58N 105 12W
Lafayette, Ind., U.S.A. 157 D10 40 25N 86 54W
Lafayette, La., U.S.A. 155 K9 30 14N 92 1W
Lafayette, Tenn., U.S.A. 149 G2 36 31N 86 2W
Laferte →, Canada 142 A5 61 53N 117 44W
Lafia, Nigeria 113 D6 8 30N 8 34 E
Lafiagi, Nigeria 113 D6 8 52N 5 20 E
Lafleche, Canada 143 D7 49 45N 106 40W
Lafon, Sudan 107 F3 5 5N 32 29 E
Lagaip →, Papua N. G. 132 C2 5 4S 142 52 E
Lagan, Sweden 17 H7 56 56N 13 58 E
Lagan →, Sweden 17 H6 56 30N 12 58 E
Lagan →, U.K. 23 B6 54 36N 5 55W
Lagangilang, Phil. 80 C3 17 37N 120 44 E
Lagarfljót →, Iceland 11 B12 65 40N 14 18W
Lagarto, Brazil 170 D4 10 54S 37 41W
Lagawe, Phil. 80 C3 16 49N 121 6 E
Lage, Germany 30 D4 51 59N 8 48 E
Lågen →, Oppland, Norway 15 F14 61 8N 10 25 E
Lågen →, Vestfold, Norway 15 G14 59 3N 10 3 E
Lägerdorf, Germany 30 B5 53 53N 9 34 E
Laghmān □, Afghan. 91 B3 34 20N 70 0 E
Laghouat, Algeria 111 B5 33 50N 2 59 E
Lagnieu, France 29 C9 45 55N 5 20 E
Lagny-sur-Marne, France 27 D9 48 52N 2 44 E
Lago, Italy 47 C9 39 10N 16 9 E
Lago Posadas, Argentina 176 C2 47 30S 71 40W
Lago Ranco, Chile 176 B2 40 19S 72 30W
Lagôa, Portugal 43 H2 37 8N 8 27W
Lagoa Vermelha, Brazil 175 B5 28 13S 51 32W
Lagoaça, Portugal 42 D4 41 11N 6 44W
Lagodekhi, Georgia 61 K8 41 50N 46 22 E
Lagónegro, Italy 47 B8 40 8N 15 45 E
Lagonoy G., Phil. 79 B6 13 35N 123 50 E
Lagos, Angola 115 F3 16 3S 16 35 E
Lagos, Nigeria 113 D5 6 25N 3 27 E
Lagos, Portugal 43 H2 37 5N 8 41W
Lagos □, Nigeria 113 D5 6 28N 3 25 E
Lagos de Moreno, Mexico 162 C4 21 21N 101 55W
Lagrange, Australia 124 C3 18 45S 121 43 E
Lagrange, U.S.A. 157 C11 41 39N 85 25W
Lagrange B., Australia 124 C3 18 38S 121 42 E
Laguardia, Spain 40 C2 42 33N 2 35W
Laguépie, France 28 D5 44 8N 1 57 E
Laguna, Brazil 175 B6 28 30S 48 50W
Laguna, U.S.A. 159 J10 35 2N 107 25W
Laguna □, Phil. 80 D3 14 10N 121 20 E
Laguna Beach, U.S.A. 161 M9 33 33N 117 47W
Laguna de Duera, Spain 42 D6 41 35N 4 43W
Laguna Limpia, Argentina 174 B4 26 32S 59 45W
Lagunas, Chile 174 A2 21 0S 69 45W
Lagunas, Peru 172 B2 5 10S 75 35W
Lagunillas, Bolivia 173 D5 19 38S 63 43W
Lahad Datu, Malaysia 79 C5 5 0N 118 20 E
Lahad Datu, Teluk, Malaysia 79 D5 4 50N 118 20 E
Lahan Sai, Thailand 86 E4 14 25N 102 52 E
Lahanam, Laos 86 D5 16 16N 105 16 E
Lahar, India 93 F8 26 12N 78 57 E
Laharpur, India 93 F9 27 43N 80 56 E
Lahat, Indonesia 78 E2 3 45S 103 30 E
Lahe, Burma 90 B5 26 20N 95 26 E
Lahewa, Indonesia 78 D1 1 22N 97 12 E
Laḥij, Yemen 98 D4 13 4N 44 53 E
Lāhījān, Iran 97 B6 37 10N 50 6 E
Lahilahi Pt., U.S.A. 145 K13 21 28N 158 13W
Lahn →, Germany 31 E3 50 19N 7 37 E
Lahnstein, Germany 31 E3 50 19N 7 37 E
Laholm, Sweden 17 H7 56 30N 13 2 E
Laholmsbukten, Sweden 17 H6 56 30N 12 45 E
Lahore, Pakistan 91 C4 31 32N 74 22 E
Lahpongsel, Burma 90 B7 27 7N 98 25 E
Lahr, Germany 31 G3 48 20N 7 53 E
Lahri, Pakistan 92 E3 29 11N 68 13 E
Lahti, Finland 15 F21 60 58N 25 40 E
Lahtis = Lahti, Finland 15 F21 60 58N 25 40 E
Laï, Chad 109 G3 9 25N 16 18 E
Lai Chau, Vietnam 76 F4 22 5N 103 3 E
Lai-hka, Burma 90 E6 21 16N 97 40 E
Laiagam, Papua N. G. 132 C2 5 33S 143 30 E
Lai'an, China 77 A12 32 28N 118 30 E
Laibin, China 76 F7 23 42N 109 14 E
Laie, U.S.A. 145 J14 21 39N 157 56W
Laifeng, China 76 C7 29 27N 109 20 E
L'Aigle, France 26 D7 48 46N 0 38 E
Laignes, France 27 E11 47 50N 4 20 E
L'Aiguillon-sur-Mer, France 28 B2 46 20N 1 18W
Laila = Laylá, Si. Arabia 98 B4 22 10N 46 40 E
Laingsburg, S. Africa 116 E3 33 9S 20 52 E
Lainio älv →, Sweden 14 C20 67 35N 22 40 E
Lairg, U.K. 22 C4 58 2N 4 24W
Lais, Phil. 81 H5 6 20N 125 39 E
Laishui, China 74 E8 39 23N 115 45 E
Laissac, France 28 D6 44 23N 2 50 E
Láives, Italy 45 B8 46 26N 11 20 E
Laiwu, China 75 F9 36 15N 117 40 E
Laixi, China 75 F11 36 50N 120 31 E
Laiyang, China 75 F11 36 59N 120 45 E
Laiyuan, China 74 E8 39 20N 114 40 E
Laizhou, China 75 F10 37 8N 119 57 E
Laizhou Wan, China 75 F10 37 30N 119 30 E
Laja →, Mexico 162 C4 20 55N 100 46W
Lajere, Nigeria 113 C7 12 10N 11 25 E
Lajes, Rio Grande do N., Brazil 170 C4 5 41S 36 14W
Lajes, Sta. Catarina, Brazil 175 B5 27 48S 50 20W
Lajinha, Brazil 171 F3 20 9S 41 37W
Lajkovac, Serbia, Yug. 50 B4 44 27N 20 14 E
Lajosmizse, Hungary 52 C4 47 3N 19 32 E
Lak Sao, Laos 86 C5 18 11N 104 59 E
Lakaband, Pakistan 92 D3 31 2N 69 15 E
Lakamané, Mali 112 C3 14 35N 9 44W
Lakatoro, Vanuatu 133 F5 16 0S 167 0 E
Lake Alfred, U.S.A. 153 G8 28 6N 81 44W
Lake Alpine, U.S.A. 160 G7 38 29N 120 0W
Lake Andes, U.S.A. 154 D5 43 9N 98 32W
Lake Arthur, U.S.A. 155 K8 30 5N 92 41W
Lake Butler, U.S.A. 152 E7 30 1N 82 21W
Lake Cargelligo, Australia 129 B7 33 15S 146 22 E
Lake Charles, U.S.A. 155 K8 30 14N 93 13W
Lake City, Colo., U.S.A. 159 G10 38 2N 107 19W
Lake City, Fla., U.S.A. 152 E7 30 11N 82 38W
Lake City, Iowa, U.S.A. 156 B2 42 16N 94 44W
Lake City, Mich., U.S.A. 148 C3 44 20N 85 13W
Lake City, Minn., U.S.A. 154 C8 44 27N 92 16W
Lake City, Pa., U.S.A. 150 D4 42 1N 80 21W
Lake City, S.C., U.S.A. 152 B10 33 52N 79 45W
Lake Clarke Shores, U.S.A. 153 J9 26 39N 80 5W
Lake Coleridge, N.Z. 131 D6 43 17S 171 30 E
Lake Cowichan, Canada 142 D4 48 49N 124 3W
Lake District, U.K. 20 C4 54 35N 3 20 E
Lake Elsinore, U.S.A. 161 M9 33 38N 117 20W
Lake Forest, U.S.A. 157 B9 42 15N 87 50W
Lake Geneva, U.S.A. 157 B8 42 36N 88 26W
Lake George, U.S.A. 151 C11 43 26N 73 43W
Lake Grace, Australia 125 F2 33 7S 118 28 E
Lake Harbor, U.S.A. 153 J9 26 42N 80 48W
Lake Harbour = Kimmirut, Canada 139 B13 62 50N 69 50W
Lake Havasu City, U.S.A. 161 L12 34 27N 114 22W
Lake Helen, U.S.A. 153 G8 28 59N 81 14W
Lake Hughes, U.S.A. 161 L8 34 41N 118 26W
Lake Isabella, U.S.A. 161 K8 35 38N 118 28W
Lake Jackson, U.S.A. 155 L7 29 3N 95 27W
Lake Junction, U.S.A. 158 D8 44 35N 110 28W
Lake King, Australia 125 F2 33 5S 119 45 E
Lake Lenore, Canada 143 C8 52 24N 104 59W
Lake Louise, Canada 142 C5 51 30N 116 10W
Lake Mead National Recreation Area, U.S.A. 161 K12 36 15N 114 30W
Lake Mills, Iowa, U.S.A. 154 D8 43 25N 93 32W
Lake Mills, Wis., U.S.A. 157 A8 43 5N 88 55W
Lake Murray, Papua N. G. 132 D1 6 48S 141 29 E
Lake Odessa, U.S.A. 157 B11 42 47N 85 8W
Lake Orion, U.S.A. 157 B13 42 47N 83 14W
Lake Park, Fla., U.S.A. 153 J9 26 48N 80 3W
Lake Park, Ga., U.S.A. 152 E6 30 41N 83 11W
Lake Placid, Fla., U.S.A. 153 H8 27 18N 81 22W
Lake Placid, N.Y., U.S.A. 151 B11 44 17N 73 59W
Lake Pleasant, U.S.A. 151 C10 43 28N 74 25W
Lake Providence, U.S.A. 155 J9 32 48N 91 10W
Lake Pukaki, N.Z. 131 E5 44 11S 170 8 E
Lake St. Peter, Canada 150 A6 45 18N 78 2W
Lake Superior Prov. Park, Canada 140 C3 47 45N 84 45W
Lake Tekapo, N.Z. 131 D5 44 0S 170 30 E
Lake View, U.S.A. 156 B1 42 18N 95 3W
Lake Villa, U.S.A. 157 B8 42 25N 88 5W
Lake Village, U.S.A. 155 J9 33 20N 91 17W
Lake Wales, U.S.A. 149 M5 27 54N 81 35W
Lake Worth, U.S.A. 149 M5 26 37N 80 3W
Lake Zurich, U.S.A. 157 B8 42 12N 88 5W
Lakefield, Canada 140 D4 44 25N 78 16W
Lakehurst, U.S.A. 151 F10 40 1N 74 19W
Lakeland, Australia 126 B3 15 49S 144 57 E
Lakeland, Fla., U.S.A. 149 M5 28 3N 81 57W
Lakeland, Ga., U.S.A. 152 D6 31 2N 83 4W
Lakemba, Fiji 133 B3 18 13S 178 47W
Lakeport, Calif., U.S.A. 160 F4 39 3N 122 55W
Lakeport, Mich., U.S.A. 150 C2 43 7N 82 30W
Lakes Entrance, Australia 129 D8 37 50S 148 0 E
Lakeside, Ariz., U.S.A. 159 J9 34 9N 109 58W
Lakeside, Calif., U.S.A. 161 N10 32 52N 116 55W
Lakeside, Nebr., U.S.A. 154 D3 42 3N 102 26W
Lakeside, Ohio, U.S.A. 150 E2 41 32N 82 46W
Lakeview, U.S.A. 158 E3 42 11N 120 21W
Lakeville, U.S.A. 154 C8 44 39N 93 14W
Lakewood, Colo., U.S.A. 154 F2 39 44N 105 5W
Lakewood, N.J., U.S.A. 151 F10 40 6N 74 13W
Lakewood, N.Y., U.S.A. 150 D5 42 6N 79 19W
Lakewood, Ohio, U.S.A. 150 E3 41 29N 81 48W
Lakewood, Wash., U.S.A. 160 C4 47 11N 122 32W
Lakha, India 92 F4 26 9N 70 54 E
Lakhaniá, Greece 38 D9 35 58N 27 54 E
Lakhimpur, India 93 F9 27 57N 80 46 E
Lakhipur, Assam, India 90 C4 24 48N 93 0 E
Lakhipur, Assam, India 90 B3 26 2N 90 18 E
Lakhnadon, India 93 H8 22 36N 79 36 E
Lakhonpheng, Laos 86 E5 15 54N 105 34 E
Lakhpat, India 92 H3 23 48N 68 47 E
Läki, Azerbaijan 61 K8 40 34N 47 22 E
Laki, Iceland 11 C8 64 4N 18 14W
Lakin, U.S.A. 155 G4 37 57N 101 15W
Lakitusaki →, Canada 140 B3 54 21N 82 25W
Lakki, Pakistan 92 C4 32 36N 70 55 E
Lákkoi, Greece 38 D5 35 24N 23 57 E
Lakonía □, Greece 48 E4 36 55N 22 30 E
Lakonikós Kólpos, Greece 48 E4 36 40N 22 40 E
Lakor, Indonesia 79 F7 8 15S 128 17 E
Lakota, Ivory C. 112 D3 5 50N 5 30W
Lakota, U.S.A. 154 A5 48 2N 98 21W
Laksar, India 92 E8 29 46N 78 3 E
Laksefjorden, Norway 14 A22 70 45N 26 50 E
Lakselv, Norway 14 A21 70 2N 25 0 E
Laksettipet, India 94 E4 18 52N 79 13 E
Lakshadweep Is., Ind. Oc. 66 H11 10 0N 72 30 E
Laksham, Bangla. 90 D3 23 14N 91 8 E
Lakshmanpur, India 93 H10 22 58N 83 3 E
Lakshmeshwar, India 95 G2 15 9N 75 28 E
Lakshmikantapur, India 93 H13 22 5N 88 20 E
Lakshmipur, Bangla. 90 D3 22 58N 90 50 E
Lakuramau, Papua N. G. 132 B6 2 54S 151 15 E

Little Belt Mts. 241

Lewis, U.K. 22 C2 58 9N 6 40W
Lewis →, U.S.A. 160 E4 45 51N 122 48W
Lewis, Butt of, U.K. 22 C2 58 31N 6 16W
Lewis Ra., Australia 124 D4 20 3 S 128 50 E
Lewis Range, U.S.A. 158 C7 48 5N 113 5W
Lewis Run, U.S.A. 150 E6 41 52N 78 40W
Lewisburg, Ohio, U.S.A. 157 E12 39 51N 84 33W
Lewisburg, Pa., U.S.A. 150 F8 40 58N 76 54W
Lewisburg, Tenn., U.S.A. 149 H2 35 27N 86 48W
Lewisburg, W. Va., U.S.A. 148 G5 37 48N 80 27W
Lewisport, U.S.A. 157 G10 37 56N 86 54W
Lewisporte, Canada 141 C8 49 15N 55 3W
Lewiston, Idaho, U.S.A. 158 C5 46 25N 117 1W
Lewiston, Maine, U.S.A. 149 C11 44 6N 70 13W
Lewiston, N.Y., U.S.A. 150 C5 43 11N 79 3W
Lewistown, Ill., U.S.A. 156 D6 40 24N 90 9W
Lewistown, Mo., U.S.A. 156 D5 40 5N 91 49W
Lewistown, Mont., U.S.A. 158 C9 47 4N 109 26W
Lewistown, Pa., U.S.A. 150 F7 40 36N 77 34W
Lexington, Ga., U.S.A. 152 B6 33 52N 83 7W
Lexington, Ill., U.S.A. 154 E10 40 39N 88 47W
Lexington, Ky., U.S.A. 157 F12 38 3N 84 30W
Lexington, Mich., U.S.A. 150 C2 43 16N 82 32W
Lexington, Mo., U.S.A. 156 E3 39 11N 93 52W
Lexington, N.C., U.S.A. 149 H5 35 49N 80 15W
Lexington, N.Y., U.S.A. 151 D10 42 15N 74 22W
Lexington, Nebr., U.S.A. 154 E5 40 47N 99 45W
Lexington, Ohio, U.S.A. 150 F2 40 41N 82 35W
Lexington, S.C., U.S.A. 152 B8 33 59N 81 11W
Lexington, Tenn., U.S.A. 149 H1 35 39N 88 24W
Lexington, Va., U.S.A. 148 G6 37 47N 79 27W
Lexington Park, U.S.A. 148 F7 38 16N 76 27W
Leyburn, U.K. 20 C6 54 19N 1 48W
Leye, China 76 E6 24 48N 106 29 E
Leyland, U.K. 20 D5 53 42N 2 43W
Leyre →, France 28 D2 44 39N 1 1W
Leysin, Switz. 32 D4 46 21N 7 1 E
Leyte, Phil. 81 F5 10 30N 125 0 E
Leyte □, Phil. 79 B6 11 0N 125 0 E
Leyte Gulf, Phil. 81 F5 10 50N 125 25 E
Leżajsk, Poland 55 H9 50 16N 22 25 E
Lezay, France 28 B3 46 15N 0 1W
Lezha, Albania 50 E3 41 47N 19 39 E
Lezhi, China 76 B5 30 19N 104 58 E
Lézignan-Corbières, France 28 E6 43 13N 2 43 E
Lezoux, France 28 C7 45 49N 3 21 E
Lgov, Russia 59 G8 51 42N 35 16 E
Lhasa, China 72 D4 29 25N 90 58 E
Lhazê, China 72 D3 29 5N 87 38 E
Lhokkruet, Indonesia 78 D1 4 55N 95 24 E
Lhokseumawe, Indonesia 78 C1 5 10N 97 10 E
L'Hospitalet de Llobregat, Spain 40 D7 41 21N 2 6 E
Lhuntsi Dzong, India 90 B3 27 39N 91 10 E
Li, Thailand 86 D2 17 48N 98 57 E
Li Shui →, China 77 C9 29 24N 112 1 E
Li Xian, Gansu, China 74 G3 34 10N 105 5 E
Li Xian, Hebei, China 74 E8 38 30N 115 35 E
Li Xian, Hunan, China 77 C8 29 36N 111 42 E
Lia-Moya, C.A.R. 114 A3 6 54N 16 17 E
Liádhoi, Greece 49 E8 36 50N 26 11 E
Lian, Phil. 80 D3 14 3N 120 39 E
Liancheng, China 77 E11 25 42N 116 40 E
Lianga, Phil. 79 C7 8 38N 126 6 E
Lianga Bay, Phil. 81 G6 8 37N 126 12 E
Liangcheng, Nei Mongol Zizhiqu, China 74 D7 40 28N 112 25 E
Liangcheng, Shandong, China 75 G10 35 32N 119 37 E
Liangdang, China 74 H4 33 56N 106 18 E
Lianghe, China 76 E2 24 50N 98 20 E
Lianghekou, China 76 C7 29 11N 108 44 E
Liangping, China 76 B6 30 38N 107 47 E
Liangpran, Indonesia 78 D4 1 4N 114 23 E
Lianhua, China 77 D9 27 3N 113 54 E
Lianjiang, Fujian, China 77 D12 26 12N 119 27 E
Lianjiang, Guangdong, China 77 G8 21 40N 110 20 E
Lianping, China 77 E10 24 26N 114 30 E
Lianshan, China 77 E9 24 38N 112 8 E
Lianshanguan, China 75 D12 40 53N 123 43 E
Lianshui, China 75 H10 33 42N 119 20 E
Lianyuan, China 77 D8 27 40N 111 38 E
Lianyungang, China 75 G10 34 40N 119 11 E
Lianzhou, China 77 E9 24 51N 112 22 E
Liao He →, China 75 D11 41 0N 121 50 E
Liaocheng, China 74 F8 36 28N 115 58 E
Liaodong Bandao, China 75 E12 40 0N 122 30 E
Liaodong Wan, China 75 D11 40 20N 121 10 E
Liaoning □, China 75 D12 41 40N 122 30 E
Liaoyang, China 75 D12 41 15N 122 58 E
Liaoyuan, China 75 C13 42 58N 125 2 E
Liaozhong, China 75 D12 41 23N 122 50 E
Liapádhes, Greece 48 B1 39 42N 19 40 E
Liard →, Canada 142 A4 61 51N 121 18W
Liard River, Canada 142 B3 59 25N 126 5W
Liari, Pakistan 92 G2 25 37N 66 30 E
Lîbano, Colombia 168 C2 4 55N 75 4W
Libau = Liepāja, Latvia 15 H19 56 30N 21 0 E
Libby, U.S.A. 158 B6 48 23N 115 33W
Libenge, Dem. Rep. of the Congo 114 B3 3 40N 18 55 E
Liberal, U.S.A. 155 G4 37 3N 100 55W
Liberdade, Brazil 172 C3 10 5 S 70 20W
Liberdade →, Brazil 173 B7 9 40 S 52 17W
Liberec, Czech Rep. 34 A8 50 47N 15 7 E
Liberia, Costa Rica 164 D2 10 40N 85 30W
Liberia ■, W. Afr. 112 D3 6 30N 9 30W
Libertad, Phil. 81 F3 11 46N 121 55 E
Libertad, Venezuela 168 B4 8 20N 69 37W
Liberty, Ind., U.S.A. 157 E12 39 38N 84 56W
Liberty, Mo., U.S.A. 156 E2 39 15N 94 25W
Liberty, N.Y., U.S.A. 151 E10 41 48N 74 45W
Liberty, Pa., U.S.A. 150 E7 41 34N 77 6W
Liberty, Tex., U.S.A. 155 K7 30 3N 94 48W
Liberty Center, U.S.A. 157 C12 41 27N 84 1W
Libertyville, U.S.A. 157 B9 42 18N 87 57W
Libiąż, Poland 55 H6 50 7N 19 21 E
Lîbîyâ, Angola 115 E3 14 42 S 17 44 E
Lîbîya, Sahrâ', Africa 108 C4 25 0N 25 0 E
Libjo, Phil. 81 F5 10 12N 125 32 E
Libmanan, Phil. 80 E4 13 42N 123 4 E
Libo, China 76 E6 25 22N 107 53 E
Libobo, Tanjung, Indonesia 79 E7 0 54 S 128 28 E
Libode, S. Africa 117 E4 31 33 S 29 2 E
Libohava, Albania 50 F4 40 3N 20 10 E
Libona, Phil. 81 G5 8 20N 124 44 E
Libonda, Zambia 115 E4 14 28 S 23 12 E
Libourne, France 28 D3 44 55N 0 14W
Libramont, Belgium 24 E5 49 55N 5 23 E
Librazhdi, Albania 50 E4 41 12N 20 22 E
Libreville, Gabon 114 B1 0 25N 9 26 E
Libya ■, N. Afr. 108 C3 27 0N 17 0 E
Libyan Desert = Lîbîya, Sahrâ', Africa 108 C4 25 0N 25 0 E
Libyan Plateau = Ed-Déffa, Egypt 106 A2 30 40N 26 30 E
Licantén, Chile 174 D1 35 55 S 72 0W
Licata, Italy 46 E6 37 6N 13 56 E
Lice, Turkey 101 C9 38 27N 40 39 E
Licheng, China 74 F7 36 28N 113 20 E
Lichfield, U.K. 21 E6 52 41N 1 49W
Lichinga, Mozam. 119 E4 13 13 S 35 11 E
Lichtenburg, S. Africa 116 D4 26 8 S 26 8 E
Lichtenfels, Germany 31 E7 50 8N 11 4 E
Lichuan, Hubei, China 76 B7 30 18N 108 57 E
Lichuan, Jiangxi, China 77 D11 27 18N 116 55 E
Licking →, U.S.A. 157 F12 39 6N 84 30W
Licosa, Punta, Italy 47 B7 40 15N 14 54 E
Lida, Belarus 15 K21 53 53N 25 15 E
Liden, Sweden 16 B10 62 42N 16 48 E
Lidhoríkion, Greece 48 C4 38 32N 22 12 E
Lidhult, Sweden 17 H7 56 50N 13 27 E
Lidköping, Sweden 17 F7 58 31N 13 7 E
Lido, Italy 45 C9 45 25N 12 22 E
Lido, Niger 113 C5 12 54N 3 44 E
Lido di Roma = Óstia, Lido di, Italy 45 G9 41 43N 12 17 E
Lidzbark, Poland 55 E6 53 15N 19 49 E
Lidzbark Warmiński, Poland 54 D7 54 7N 20 34 E
Liebenwalde, Germany 30 C9 52 52N 13 24 E
Lieberose, Germany 30 D10 51 59N 14 17 E
Liebig, Mt., Australia 124 D5 23 18 S 131 22 E
Liebling, Romania 52 E6 45 36N 21 20 E
Liechtenstein ■, Europe 33 B9 47 8N 9 35 E
Liège, Belgium 24 D5 50 38N 5 35 E
Liège □, Belgium 24 D5 50 32N 5 35 E
Liegnitz = Legnica, Poland 55 G3 51 12N 16 10 E
Lienart, Dem. Rep. of the Congo 118 B2 3 3N 25 31 E
Lienyünchiangshih = Lianyungang, China 75 G10 34 40N 119 11 E
Lienz, Austria 34 E5 46 50N 12 46 E
Liepāja, Latvia 15 H19 56 30N 21 0 E
Liepāja □, Latvia 54 B8 56 30N 21 30 E
Liepājas ezers, Latvia 54 B8 56 27N 21 3 E
Lier, Belgium 24 C4 51 7N 4 34 E
Liernais, France 27 E11 47 13N 4 16 E
Liestal, Switz. 32 B5 47 29N 7 44 E
Lieşti, Romania 53 E12 45 38N 27 34 E
Liévin, France 27 B9 50 24N 2 47 E
Lièvre →, Canada 140 C4 45 31N 75 26W
Liezen, Austria 34 D7 47 34N 14 15 E
Liffey →, Ireland 23 C5 53 21N 6 13W
Lifford, Ireland 23 B4 54 51N 7 29W
Liffré, France 26 D5 48 12N 1 30W
Lifjell, Norway 18 E5 59 27N 8 45 E
Lifudzin, Russia 68 B7 44 21N 134 58 E
Lifuka, Tonga 133 P13 19 48 S 174 21W
Ligao, Phil. 80 E4 13 14N 123 32 E
Ligasa, Dem. Rep. of the Congo 114 B4 0 44N 23 49 E
Lighthouse Point, U.S.A. 153 J9 26 15N 80 7W
Lighthouse Pt., U.S.A. 152 F5 29 54N 84 21W
Lightning Ridge, Australia 127 D4 29 22 S 148 0 E
Lignano Sabbiadoro, Italy 45 C10 45 42N 13 9 E
Ligny-en-Barrois, France 27 D12 48 36N 5 20 E
Ligonier, Ind., U.S.A. 157 C11 41 28N 85 35W
Ligonier, Pa., U.S.A. 150 F5 40 15N 79 14W
Ligoúrion, Greece 48 D5 37 37N 23 4 E
Ligueil, France 26 E7 47 2N 0 49 E
Liguria □, Italy 44 D5 44 30N 8 50 E
Ligurian Sea, Medit. S. 12 G7 43 20N 9 0 E
Lihir Group, Papua N. G. 132 B7 3 0 S 152 35 E
Lihou Reefs and Cays, Australia 126 B5 17 25 S 151 40 E
Lihue, U.S.A. 146 H15 21 59N 159 23W
Lijiang, China 76 D3 26 55N 100 20 E
Likasi, Dem. Rep. of the Congo 119 E2 10 55 S 26 48 E
Likati, Dem. Rep. of the Congo 114 B4 3 20N 24 0 E
Likati →, Dem. Rep. of the Congo 114 B4 2 53N 24 3 E
Likenäs, Sweden 16 D8 60 37N 13 3 E
Likete, Dem. Rep. of the Congo 114 C4 0 48 S 21 31 E
Likhoslavl, Russia 58 D8 57 12N 35 30 E
Likhovskoy, Russia 59 H11 48 10N 40 10 E
Likimi, Dem. Rep. of the Congo 114 B4 2 44N 20 47 E
Likisia, Indonesia 82 C3 8 36 S 125 19 E
Likita, Dem. Rep. of the Congo 114 B4 4 15N 23 36 E
Liknes, Norway 18 F3 58 19N 6 59 E
Likokou, Gabon 114 C2 0 12 S 12 48 E
Likoma I., Malawi 119 E3 12 3 S 34 45 E
Likouala →, Congo 114 C3 0 2N 14 53 E
Likouala aux Herbes →, Congo 114 C3 0 52 S 17 8 E
Likumburu, Tanzania 119 D4 9 43 S 35 8 E
Lilanga, Dem. Rep. of the Congo 114 C4 0 34 S 23 56 E
L'Île-Bouchard, France 26 E7 47 7N 0 26 E
L'Île-Rousse, France 29 F12 42 38N 8 57 E
Lilenga, Dem. Rep. of the Congo 114 B4 1 4N 22 2 E
Liling, China 77 D9 27 42N 113 29 E
Lilla Edet, Sweden 17 F6 58 9N 12 8 E
Lille, France 27 B10 50 38N 3 3 E
Lille Bælt, Denmark 17 J3 55 20N 9 45 E
Lillebonne, France 26 C7 49 30N 0 32 E
Lillehammer, Norway 15 F14 61 8N 10 30 E
Lillesand, Norway 15 G13 58 15N 8 23 E
Lillestrøm, Norway 18 E8 59 58N 11 5 E
Lillhärdal, Sweden 16 C8 61 51N 14 5 E
Lillian Pt., Australia 125 E4 27 40 S 126 6 E
Lillo, Spain 42 F7 39 45N 3 20W
Lillooet, Canada 142 C4 50 44N 121 57W
Lillooet →, Canada 142 D4 49 15N 121 57W
Lilongwe, Malawi 119 E3 14 0 S 33 48 E
Liloy, Phil. 79 C6 8 4N 122 39 E
Lim →, Bos.-H. 50 C3 43 45N 19 15 E
Lima, Brazil 169 D5 4 36 S 63 40W
Lima, Indonesia 79 E7 3 37 S 128 4 E
Lima, Peru 172 C2 12 0 S 77 0W
Lima, Ill., U.S.A. 156 D5 40 11N 91 23W
Lima, Mont., U.S.A. 158 D7 44 38N 112 36W
Lima, Ohio, U.S.A. 157 D12 40 44N 84 6W
Lima □, Peru 172 C2 12 3 S 77 3W
Lima →, Portugal 42 D2 41 41N 8 50W
Liman, Indonesia 79 G14 7 48 S 111 45 E
Liman, Russia 61 H8 45 45N 47 12 E
Limanowa, Poland 55 J7 49 42N 20 22 E
Limassol, Cyprus 38 E12 34 42N 33 1 E
Limavady, U.K. 23 A5 55 3N 6 56W
Limay →, Argentina 176 A3 39 0 S 68 0W
Limay Mahuida, Argentina 174 D2 37 10 S 66 45W
Limbach-Oberfrohna, Germany 30 E8 50 52N 12 43 E
Limbang, Brunei 78 D5 4 42N 115 6 E
Limbara, Mte., Italy 46 B2 40 51N 9 10 E
Limbaži, Latvia 15 H21 57 31N 24 42 E
Limbdi, India 92 H4 22 34N 71 51 E
Limbe, Cameroon 113 E6 4 1N 9 10 E
Limbri, Australia 129 A9 31 3 S 151 5 E
Limbueta, Angola 115 E3 12 30 S 18 42 E
Limburg, Germany 31 E4 50 22N 8 4 E
Limburg □, Belgium 24 C5 51 2N 5 25 E
Limburg □, Neths. 24 C5 51 20N 5 55 E
Lime Village, U.S.A. 144 F9 61 21N 155 28W
Limedsforsen, Sweden 16 D7 60 52N 13 25 E
Limeira, Brazil 175 A6 22 35 S 47 28W
Limenária, Greece 51 F8 40 38N 24 32 E
Limerick, Ireland 23 D3 52 40N 8 37W
Limerick, U.S.A. 151 C14 43 41N 70 48W
Limerick □, Ireland 23 D3 52 30N 8 50W
Limestone, U.S.A. 150 D6 42 2N 78 38W
Limestone →, Canada 143 B10 56 31N 94 7W
Limfjorden, Denmark 17 H3 56 55N 9 0 E
Limia = Lima →, Portugal 42 D2 41 41N 8 50W
Limín Khersonísou, Greece 49 F7 35 18N 25 21 E
Limingen, Norway 14 D15 64 48N 13 35 E
Limmared, Sweden 17 G7 57 34N 13 20 E
Limmat →, Switz. 33 B6 47 26N 8 20 E
Limmen Bight, Australia 126 A2 14 40 S 135 35 E
Limmen Bight →, Australia 126 B2 15 7 S 135 44 E
Límni, Greece 48 C5 38 43N 23 18 E
Límnos, Greece 49 B7 39 50N 25 5 E
Limoeiro, Brazil 170 C4 7 52 S 35 27W
Limoeiro do Norte, Brazil 170 C4 5 5 S 38 0W
Limoges, Canada 151 A9 45 20N 75 16W
Limoges, France 28 C5 45 50N 1 15 E
Limón, Costa Rica 164 E3 10 0N 83 2W
Limon, U.S.A. 154 F3 39 16N 103 41W
Limone Piemonte, Italy 44 D4 44 12N 7 34 E
Limousin, France 28 C5 45 30N 1 30 E
Limousin, Plateaux du, France 28 C5 45 45N 1 15 E
Limoux, France 28 E6 43 4N 2 12 E
Limpopo →, Africa 117 D5 25 5 S 33 30 E
Limuru, Kenya 118 C4 1 2 S 36 35 E
Lin Xian, China 74 F6 37 57N 110 58 E
Lin'an, China 77 B12 30 15N 119 42 E
Linao Pt., Phil. 81 H4 6 46N 123 58 E
Linapacan, Phil. 81 F2 11 30N 119 52 E
Linapacan I., Phil. 81 F2 11 27N 119 49 E
Linapacan Str., Phil. 81 F2 11 37N 119 56 E
Linares, Chile 174 D1 35 50 S 71 40W
Linares, Colombia 168 C2 1 23N 77 31W
Linares, Mexico 163 C5 24 50N 99 40W
Linares, Spain 43 G7 38 10N 3 40W
Linaro, Capo, Italy 45 F8 42 2N 11 50 E
Línas Mte., Italy 46 C1 39 25N 8 38 E
Lincang, China 76 F3 23 58N 100 1 E
Lincheng, China 74 F8 37 25N 114 30 E
Linchuan, China 77 D11 27 57N 116 15 E
Lincoln, Argentina 174 C3 34 55 S 61 30W
Lincoln, N.Z. 131 D7 43 38 S 172 30 E
Lincoln, U.K. 20 D7 53 14N 0 32W
Lincoln, Calif., U.S.A. 160 G5 38 54N 121 17W
Lincoln, Ill., U.S.A. 156 D7 40 9N 89 22W
Lincoln, Kans., U.S.A. 154 F5 39 3N 98 9W
Lincoln, Maine, U.S.A. 149 C11 45 22N 68 30W
Lincoln, N.H., U.S.A. 151 B13 44 3N 71 40W
Lincoln, N. Mex., U.S.A. 159 K11 33 30N 105 23W
Lincoln, Nebr., U.S.A. 154 E6 40 49N 96 41W
Lincoln City, U.S.A. 158 D1 44 57N 124 1W
Lincoln Hav = Lincoln Sea, Arctic 10 A5 84 0N 55 0W
Lincoln Park, Ga., U.S.A. 152 C5 32 52N 84 20W
Lincoln Park, Mich., U.S.A. 157 B13 42 15N 83 11W
Lincoln Sea, Arctic 10 A5 84 0N 55 0W
Lincolnshire □, U.K. 20 D7 53 14N 0 32W
Lincolnshire Wolds, U.K. 20 D7 53 26N 0 13W
Lincolnton, Ga., U.S.A. 152 B7 33 48N 82 29W
Lincolnton, N.C., U.S.A. 149 H5 35 29N 81 16W
L'Incudine, France 29 G13 41 50N 9 12 E
Lind, U.S.A. 158 C4 46 58N 118 37W
Linda, U.S.A. 160 F5 39 8N 121 34W
Lindale, U.S.A. 152 A4 34 11N 85 11W
Lindås, Norway 18 D2 60 44N 5 9 E
Lindau, Germany 31 H5 47 33N 9 42 E
Linden, Guyana 169 B6 6 0N 58 10W
Linden, Ala., U.S.A. 149 J2 32 18N 87 48W
Linden, Calif., U.S.A. 160 G5 38 1N 121 5W
Linden, Ind., U.S.A. 157 D10 40 11N 86 54W
Linden, Mich., U.S.A. 157 B13 42 49N 83 47W
Linden, Tex., U.S.A. 155 J7 33 1N 94 22W
Lindenhurst, U.S.A. 151 F11 40 41N 73 23W
Lindenow Fjord, Greenland 10 E6 60 30N 43 25W
Lindesberg, Sweden 16 E9 59 36N 15 15 E
Lindesnes, Norway 15 H12 57 58N 7 3 E
Líndhos, Greece 38 C10 36 6N 28 4 E
Líndhos, Ákra, Greece 38 C10 36 4N 28 10 E
Lindi, Tanzania 119 D4 9 58 S 39 38 E
Lindi □, Tanzania 119 D4 9 40 S 38 30 E
Lindi →, Dem. Rep. of the Congo 118 B2 0 33N 25 5 E
Lindö, Sweden 17 F10 58 37N 16 15 E
Lindome, Sweden 17 G6 57 35N 12 5 E
Lindoso, Portugal 42 D2 41 52N 8 11W
Lindow, Germany 30 C8 52 58N 12 59 E
Lindsay, Canada 140 D4 44 22N 78 43W
Lindsay, Calif., U.S.A. 160 J7 36 12N 119 5W
Lindsay, Okla., U.S.A. 155 H6 34 50N 97 38W
Lindsborg, U.S.A. 154 F6 38 35N 97 40W
Lindstad, Sweden 17 H10 56 44N 16 18 E
Linesville, U.S.A. 150 E4 41 39N 80 26W
Lineville, Ala., U.S.A. 152 B4 33 19N 85 45W
Lineville, Iowa, U.S.A. 156 D3 40 35N 93 32W
Linfen, China 74 F6 36 3N 111 30 E
Ling Xian, Hunan, China 77 D9 26 29N 113 48 E
Ling Xian, Shandong, China 74 F9 37 22N 116 30 E
Lingal, India 95 F4 16 17N 78 31 E
Lingao, China 86 C7 19 56N 109 42 E
Lingayen, Phil. 79 A6 16 1N 120 14 E
Lingayen G., Phil. 79 A6 16 10N 120 15 E
Lingbi, China 75 H9 33 33N 117 33 E
Lingbo, Sweden 16 C10 61 3N 16 41 E
Lingchuan, Guangxi Zhuangzu, China 77 E8 25 26N 110 21 E
Lingchuan, Shanxi, China 74 G7 35 45N 113 12 E
Lingen, Germany 30 C3 52 31N 7 19 E
Lingga, Indonesia 78 E2 0 12 S 104 37 E
Lingga, Kepulauan, Indonesia 78 E2 0 10 S 104 30 E
Lingga Arch. = Lingga, Kepulauan, Indonesia 78 E2 0 10 S 104 30 E
Linghem, Sweden 17 F9 58 26N 15 47 E
Lingig, Phil. 81 G6 8 2N 126 24 E
Lingle, U.S.A. 154 D2 42 8N 104 21W
Lingomo, Dem. Rep. of the Congo 114 B4 0 38N 22 3 E
Lingqiu, China 74 E8 39 28N 114 22 E
Lingshan, China 76 F7 22 25N 109 18 E
Lingshi, China 74 F6 36 48N 111 48 E
Lingshou, China 74 E8 38 20N 114 20 E
Lingshui, China 86 C8 18 27N 110 0 E
Lingsugur, India 95 F3 16 10N 76 31 E
Lingtai, China 74 G4 35 0N 107 40 E
Linguère, Senegal 112 B1 15 25N 15 5W
Lingui, China 77 E8 25 12N 110 2 E
Lingunda, Dem. Rep. of the Congo 114 C3 0 49N 21 8 E
Lingwu, China 74 E4 38 6N 106 20 E
Lingyuan, China 75 D10 41 10N 119 15 E
Lingyun, China 76 E6 25 2N 106 35 E
Linhai, China 77 C13 28 50N 121 8 E
Linhares, Brazil 171 E3 19 25 S 40 4W
Linhe, China 74 D4 40 48N 107 20 E
Linjiang, China 75 D14 41 50N 127 0 E
Linköping, Sweden 17 F9 58 28N 15 36 E
Linkou, China 75 B16 45 15N 130 18 E
Linli, China 77 C8 29 27N 111 30 E
Linn, U.S.A. 156 F5 38 29N 91 51W
Linneus, U.S.A. 156 E3 39 53N 93 11W
Linnhe, L., U.K. 22 E3 56 36N 5 25W
Linosa, I., Medit. S. 108 A2 35 51N 12 50 E
Linqi, China 74 G7 35 45N 113 52 E
Linqing, China 74 F8 36 50N 115 42 E
Linqu, China 75 F10 36 25N 118 30 E
Linru, China 74 G7 34 11N 112 52 E
Lins, Brazil 175 A6 21 40 S 49 44W
Linshui, China 76 B6 30 21N 106 57 E
Linta →, Madag. 117 D7 25 2 S 44 5 E
Linth →, Switz. 31 H5 47 7N 9 7 E
Linthal, Switz. 33 C8 46 54N 9 0 E
Linton, Ind., U.S.A. 157 F9 39 2N 87 10W
Linton, N. Dak., U.S.A. 154 B4 46 16N 100 14W
Lintong, China 74 G5 34 20N 109 10 E
Linwood, Canada 150 C4 43 35N 80 43W
Linwu, China 77 E9 25 19N 112 31 E
Linxi, China 75 C10 43 36N 118 2 E
Linxia, China 72 C5 35 36N 103 10 E
Linxiang, China 77 C9 29 28N 113 23 E
Linyanti →, Africa 116 B4 17 50 S 25 5 E
Linyi, China 75 G10 35 5N 118 21 E
Linz, Austria 34 C7 48 18N 14 18 E
Linz, Germany 30 E3 50 34N 7 17 E
Linzhenzhen, China 74 F5 36 30N 109 59 E
Linzi, China 75 F10 36 50N 118 20 E
Lioko, Dem. Rep. of the Congo 114 B4 1 25N 23 7 E
Lioko, Dem. Rep. of the Congo 114 B4 0 2N 22 4 E
Liomseter, Norway 18 C6 61 15N 9 35 E
Lion, G. du, France 28 E7 43 10N 4 0 E
Lionárisso, Cyprus 38 D13 35 28N 34 8 E
Lioni, Italy 47 B8 40 52N 15 11 E
Lions, G. of = Lion, G. du, France 28 E7 43 10N 4 0 E
Lion's Den, Zimbabwe 119 F3 17 15 S 30 5 E
Lion's Head, Canada 150 B3 44 58N 81 15W
Liouesso, Congo 114 B3 1 2N 15 43 E
Liozno = Lyozna, Belarus 58 E6 55 0N 30 50 E
Lipa, Phil. 79 B6 13 57N 121 10 E
Lipali, Mozam. 119 F4 15 50 S 35 50 E
Lipany, Slovak Rep. 35 B13 49 9N 20 58 E
Lípari, Italy 47 D7 38 26N 14 58 E
Lípari, I., Italy 47 D7 38 29N 14 56 E
Lípari, Is. = Eólie, Ís., Italy 47 D7 38 30N 14 57 E
Lipcani, Moldova 53 B11 48 14N 26 48 E
Lipetsk, Russia 59 F10 52 37N 39 35 E
Lipiany, Poland 55 E1 53 2N 14 58 E
Liping, China 76 D7 26 15N 109 7 E
Lipkany = Lipcani, Moldova 53 B11 48 14N 26 48 E
Lipljan, Kosovo, Yug. 50 D5 42 31N 21 7 E
Lipník nad Bečvou, Czech Rep. 35 B10 49 32N 17 36 E
Lipno, Poland 55 F6 52 49N 19 15 E
Lipova, Romania 52 D6 46 8N 21 42 E
Lipovcy Manzovka, Russia 68 B6 44 12N 132 26 E
Lipovets, Ukraine 59 H5 49 12N 29 1 E
Lippe →, Germany 30 D2 51 39N 6 36 E
Lippstadt, Germany 30 D4 51 41N 8 22 E
Lipscomb, U.S.A. 155 G4 36 14N 100 16W
Lipsk, Poland 54 E10 53 44N 23 24 E
Lipsko, Poland 55 G8 51 9N 21 40 E
Lipsói, Greece 49 D8 37 19N 26 50 E
Liptovský Hrádok, Slovak Rep. 35 B12 49 2N 19 44 E
Liptovský Milkuláš, Slovak Rep. 35 B12 49 6N 19 35 E
Liptrap C., Australia 129 E6 38 50 S 145 55 E
Lipu, China 77 E8 24 30N 110 22 E
Lira, Uganda 118 B3 2 17N 32 57 E
Liranga, Congo 114 C3 0 43 S 17 32 E
Liri →, Italy 46 A6 41 25N 13 52 E
Liria = Llíria, Spain 41 F4 39 37N 0 35W
Lisakovsk, Kazakstan 62 E9 52 33N 62 37 E
Lisala, Dem. Rep. of the Congo 114 B4 2 12N 21 38 E
Lisboa, Portugal 43 G1 38 42N 9 10W
Lisboa □, Portugal 43 F1 39 0N 9 12W
Lisbon = Lisboa, Portugal 43 G1 38 42N 9 10W
Lisbon, N. Dak., U.S.A. 154 B6 46 27N 97 41W
Lisbon, N.H., U.S.A. 151 B13 44 13N 71 55W
Lisbon, Ohio, U.S.A. 150 F4 40 46N 80 46W
Lisbon Falls, U.S.A. 149 D10 44 0N 70 4W
Lisburn, U.K. 23 B5 54 31N 6 3W
Liscannor B., Ireland 23 D2 52 55N 9 24W
Liscia →, Italy 46 A2 41 11N 9 9 E
Lishe Jiang →, China 76 E3 24 15N 101 35 E
Lishi, China 74 F6 37 31N 111 8 E
Lishu, China 75 C13 43 20N 124 18 E
Lishui, Jiangsu, China 77 B12 31 38N 119 2 E
Lishui, Zhejiang, China 77 C12 28 28N 119 54 E
Lisianski I., Pac. Oc. 134 E10 26 2N 174 0W
Lisianski I., U.S.A. 145 F9 26 2N 174 0W
Lisichansk = Lysychansk, Ukraine 59 H10 48 55N 38 30 E
Lisieux, France 26 C7 49 10N 0 12 E
Liski, Russia 59 G10 51 3N 39 30 E
L'Isle-Jourdain, Gers, France 28 E5 43 36N 1 5 E
L'Isle-Jourdain, Vienne, France 28 B4 46 13N 0 31 E
L'Isle-Mont-la-Ville, Switz. 32 C2 46 37N 6 25 E
L'Isle-sur-la-Sorgue, France 29 E9 43 54N 5 2 E
Lisle-sur-Tarn, France 28 E5 43 52N 1 49 E
Lismore, Australia 127 D5 28 44 S 153 21 E
Lismore, Ireland 23 D4 52 8N 7 55W
Lista, Norway 15 G12 58 7N 6 39 E
Lister, Mt., Antarctica 7 D11 78 0 S 162 0 E
Liston, Australia 127 D5 28 39 S 152 6 E
Listowel, Canada 140 D3 43 44N 80 58W
Listowel, Ireland 23 D2 52 27N 9 29W
Lit, Sweden 16 A8 63 19N 14 51 E
Lit-et-Mixe, France 28 D2 44 2N 1 15W
Litang, Guangxi Zhuangzu, China 76 F7 23 12N 109 8 E
Litang, Sichuan, China 76 B3 30 1N 100 17 E
Litang, Malaysia 85 A5 5 27N 118 31 E
Litang Qu →, China 76 C3 28 4N 101 32 E
Litani →, Lebanon 103 B4 33 20N 35 15 E
Litchfield, Australia 128 D5 36 18 S 142 52 E
Litchfield, Calif., U.S.A. 160 E6 40 24N 120 23W
Litchfield, Conn., U.S.A. 151 E11 41 45N 73 11W
Litchfield, Ill., U.S.A. 156 E7 39 11N 89 39W
Litchfield, Minn., U.S.A. 154 C7 45 8N 94 32W
Liteni, Romania 53 C11 47 32N 26 32 E
Lithgow, Australia 129 B9 33 25 S 150 8 E
Líthinon, Ákra, Greece 38 E6 34 55N 24 44 E
Lithuania ■, Europe 15 J20 55 30N 24 0 E
Litija, Slovenia 45 B11 46 3N 14 50 E
Lititz, U.S.A. 151 F8 40 9N 76 18W
Litókhoron, Greece 50 F6 40 8N 22 34 E
Litoko, Dem. Rep. of the Congo 114 C4 1 13 S 24 47 E
Litoměřice, Czech Rep. 34 A7 50 33N 14 10 E
Litomyšl, Czech Rep. 35 B9 49 52N 16 20 E
Litschau, Austria 34 C8 48 58N 15 4 E
Little Abaco I., Bahamas 164 A4 26 50N 77 30W
Little Aden, Yemen 98 D4 12 45N 44 52 E
Little Barrier I., N.Z. 130 C4 36 12 S 175 8 E
Little Basses, Sri Lanka 95 L5 6 24N 81 43 E
Little Belt Mts., U.S.A. 158 C8 46 40N 110 45W

Lungwebungu 243

Lorestan □, *Iran* 97 C6 33 30N 48 40 E
Loreto, *Bolivia* 173 D5 15 13 S 64 40W
Loreto, *Brazil* 170 C2 7 5 S 45 10W
Loreto, *Italy* 45 E10 43 26N 13 36 E
Loreto, *Mexico* 162 B2 26 1N 111 21W
Loreto, *Phil.* 81 F5 10 21N 125 34 E
Loreto □, *Peru* 168 D3 5 0 S 75 0W
Lorgues, *France* 29 E10 43 28N 6 22 E
Lorhosso, *Burkina Faso* 112 C4 10 17N 3 38W
Lorica, *Colombia* 168 B2 9 14N 75 49W
Lorient, *France* 26 E3 47 45N 3 23W
Lorimor, *U.S.A.* 156 C2 41 8N 94 3W
Lőrinci, *Hungary* 52 C4 47 44N 19 41 E
Lormi, *India* 93 H9 22 17N 81 41 E
Lorn, *U.K.* 22 E3 56 26N 5 10W
Lorn, Firth of, *U.K.* 22 E3 56 20N 5 40W
Lorne, *Australia* 128 E5 38 33 S 143 59 E
Loronyo, *Sudan* 107 G3 4 38N 32 38 E
Lorovouno, *Cyprus* 38 D11 35 8N 32 36 E
Lörrach, *Germany* 31 H3 47 36N 7 40 E
Lorraine □, *France* 27 D13 48 53N 6 0 E
Los, *Sweden* 16 C9 61 45N 15 10 E
Los, Îles de, *Guinea* 112 D2 9 30N 13 50W
Los Alamos, *Calif., U.S.A.* 161 L6 34 44N 120 17W
Los Alamos, *N. Mex., U.S.A.* 159 J10 35 53N 106 19W
Los Altos, *U.S.A.* 160 H4 37 23N 122 7W
Los Andes, *Chile* 174 C1 32 50 S 70 40W
Los Angeles, *Chile* 174 D1 37 28 S 72 23W
Los Angeles, *U.S.A.* 161 M8 34 4N 118 15W
Los Angeles, Bahia de, *Mexico* 162 B2 28 56N 113 34W
Los Angeles Aqueduct, *U.S.A.* 161 K9 35 22N 118 5W
Los Antiguos, *Argentina* 176 C2 46 35 S 71 40W
Los Banos, *U.S.A.* 160 H6 37 4N 120 51W
Los Barrios, *Spain* 43 J5 36 11N 5 30W
Los Blancos, *Argentina* 174 A3 23 40 S 62 30W
Los Chiles, *Costa Rica* 164 D3 11 2N 84 43W
Los Corrales de Buelna, *Spain* 42 B6 43 16N 4 4W
Los Cristianos, *Canary Is.* 39 F3 28 3N 16 42W
Los Gallardos, *Spain* 41 H3 37 10N 1 57W
Los Gatos, *U.S.A.* 160 H5 37 14N 121 59W
Los Hermanos Is., *Venezuela* 165 D7 11 45N 64 25W
Los Islotes, *Canary Is.* 39 E6 29 4N 13 44W
Los Lagos, *Chile* 176 A2 39 51 S 72 50W
Los Llanos de Aridane, *Canary Is.* 39 F2 28 38N 17 54W
Los Lomas, *Peru* 172 A1 4 40 S 80 10W
Los Loros, *Chile* 174 B1 27 50 S 70 6W
Los Lunas, *U.S.A.* 159 J10 34 48N 106 44W
Los Menucos, *Argentina* 176 B3 40 50 S 68 10W
Los Mochis, *Mexico* 162 B3 25 45N 108 57W
Los Monegros, *Spain* 40 D4 41 29N 0 13W
Los Monos, *Argentina* 176 C3 46 1 S 69 36W
Los Muermos, *Chile* 176 B2 41 24 S 73 29W
Los Nietos, *Spain* 41 H4 37 39N 0 47W
Los Olivos, *U.S.A.* 161 L6 34 40N 120 7W
Los Palacios, *Cuba* 164 B3 22 35N 83 15W
Los Palacios y Villafranca, *Spain* 43 H5 37 10N 5 55W
Los Reyes, *Mexico* 162 D4 19 34N 102 30W
Los Ríos □, *Ecuador* 168 D2 1 30 S 79 25W
Los Roques Is., *Venezuela* 165 D6 11 50N 66 45W
Los Santos de Maimona, *Spain* 43 G4 38 27N 6 22W
Los Teques, *Venezuela* 168 A4 10 21N 67 2W
Los Testigos, Is., *Venezuela* 169 A5 11 23N 63 6W
Los Vilos, *Chile* 174 C1 32 10 S 71 30W
Los Yébenes, *Spain* 43 F7 39 36N 3 55W
Łosice, *Poland* 55 F9 52 13N 22 43 E
Loskop Dam, *S. Africa* 117 D4 25 23 S 29 20 E
Løsning, *Denmark* 17 J3 55 48N 9 42 E
Losombo, *Dem. Rep. of the Congo* 114 B3 1 2N 19 4 E
Losone, *Switz.* 33 D7 46 10N 8 45 E
Lossiemouth, *U.K.* 22 D5 57 42N 3 17W
Lostwithiel, *U.K.* 21 G3 50 24N 4 41W
Losuia, *Papua N. G.* 132 E6 8 30 S 151 4 E
Lot □, *France* 28 D5 44 39N 1 40 E
Lot →, *France* 28 D4 44 18N 0 20 E
Lot-et-Garonne □, *France* 28 D4 44 22N 0 30 E
Lota, *Chile* 174 D1 37 5 S 73 10W
Lotagipi Swamp, *Sudan* 107 G3 4 36N 34 55 E
Løten, *Norway* 18 D8 60 51N 11 21 E
Lotfābād, *Iran* 97 B8 37 32N 59 20 E
Lothair, *S. Africa* 117 D5 26 22 S 30 27 E
Loto, *Dem. Rep. of the Congo* 114 C4 2 48 S 22 30 E
Lotofaga, *W. Samoa* 133 X24 14 1 S 171 30W
Lotoi →, *Dem. Rep. of the Congo* 114 C3 1 35 S 18 30 E
Lotorp, *Sweden* 17 F9 58 44N 15 50 E
Lötschbergtunnel, *Switz.* 32 D5 46 26N 7 43 E
Löttorp, *Sweden* 17 G11 57 10N 17 0 E
Lotung, *Taiwan* 77 E13 24 41N 121 46 E
Lotzwil, *Switz.* 32 B5 47 12N 7 48 E
Loubomo, *Congo* 114 C2 4 9 S 12 47 E
Loudéac, *France* 26 D4 48 11N 2 47W
Loudi, *China* 77 D8 27 42N 111 59 E
Loudima, *Congo* 114 C2 4 6 S 13 5 E
Loudonville, *U.S.A.* 150 F2 40 38N 82 14W
Loudun, *France* 26 E7 47 3N 0 5 E
Loue →, *France* 27 E12 47 1N 5 28 E
Louga, *Senegal* 112 B1 15 45N 16 5W
Loughborough, *U.K.* 20 E6 52 47N 1 11W
Loughman, *U.S.A.* 153 G8 28 14N 81 34W
Loughrea, *Ireland* 23 C3 53 12N 8 33W
Loughros More B., *Ireland* 23 B3 54 48N 8 32W
Louhans, *France* 27 F12 46 38N 5 12 E
Louis Trichardt, *S. Africa* 117 C4 23 1 S 29 43 E
Louis XIV, Pte., *Canada* 140 B4 54 37N 79 45W
Louisa, *U.S.A.* 148 F4 38 7N 82 36W
Louisbourg, *Canada* 141 C8 45 55N 60 0W
Louisburg, *U.S.A.* 156 F2 38 37N 94 41W
Louise I., *Canada* 142 C2 52 55N 131 50W
Louiseville, *Canada* 140 C5 46 20N 72 56W
Louisiade Arch., *Papua N. G.* 132 F7 11 10 S 153 0 E
Louisiana, *U.S.A.* 156 E6 39 27N 91 3W
Louisiana □, *U.S.A.* 155 K9 30 50N 92 0W
Louisville, *Ala., U.S.A.* 152 D4 31 47N 85 33W
Louisville, *Ga., U.S.A.* 152 B7 33 0N 82 25W
Louisville, *Ill., U.S.A.* 157 F8 38 46N 88 30W
Louisville, *Ky., U.S.A.* 157 F11 38 15N 85 46W
Louisville, *Miss., U.S.A.* 155 J10 33 7N 89 3W
Louisville, *Ohio, U.S.A.* 150 F3 40 50N 81 16W
Loukoléla, *Congo* 114 C3 1 4 S 17 10 E
Loukouo, *Congo* 114 C2 3 38 S 14 39 E
Loulay, *France* 28 B3 46 3N 0 30W
Loulé, *Portugal* 43 H3 37 9N 8 0W
Louny, *Czech Rep.* 34 A6 50 20N 13 48 E
Loup City, *U.S.A.* 154 E5 41 17N 98 58W
Loups Marins, Lacs des, *Canada* 140 A5 56 30N 73 45W
Lourdes, *France* 28 E3 43 6N 0 3W
Lourenço, *Brazil* 169 C7 2 30N 51 40W
Lourenço-Marques = Maputo, *Mozam.* 117 D5 25 58 S 32 32 E
Lourinhã, *Portugal* 43 F1 39 14N 9 17W
Lousã, *Portugal* 42 E2 40 7N 8 14W
Louta, *Burkina Faso* 112 C4 13 30N 3 10W
Louth, *Australia* 129 A6 30 30 S 145 8 E
Louth, *Ireland* 23 C5 53 58N 6 32W
Louth, *U.K.* 20 D7 53 22N 0 1W
Louth □, *Ireland* 23 C5 53 56N 6 34W
Loutrá Aidhipsoú, *Greece* 48 C5 38 54N 23 2 E
Loutráki, *Greece* 48 D4 37 58N 22 57 E
Louvain = Leuven, *Belgium* 24 D4 50 52N 4 42 E
Louvale, *U.S.A.* 152 C5 32 10N 84 50W
Louviers, *France* 26 C8 49 12N 1 10 E
Louwsburg, *S. Africa* 117 D5 27 37 S 31 7 E
Lovat →, *Russia* 58 C6 58 14N 31 28 E
Lovćen, *Montenegro, Yug.* 50 D2 42 23N 18 51 E
Lovech, *Bulgaria* 51 C8 43 8N 24 42 E
Lovech □, *Bulgaria* 51 C8 43 15N 24 45 E
Loveland, *Colo., U.S.A.* 154 E2 40 24N 105 5W
Loveland, *Ohio, U.S.A.* 157 E12 39 16N 84 16W
Lovell, *U.S.A.* 158 D9 44 50N 108 24W
Lovelock, *U.S.A.* 158 F4 40 11N 118 28W
Lóvere, *Italy* 44 C7 45 49N 10 4 E
Loves Park, *U.S.A.* 156 B7 42 19N 89 3W
Lövestad, *Sweden* 17 J7 55 40N 13 54 E
Loviisa, *Finland* 15 F22 60 28N 26 12 E
Lovilia, *U.S.A.* 156 C4 41 8N 92 55W
Loving, *U.S.A.* 155 J2 32 17N 104 6W
Lovington, *Ill., U.S.A.* 157 E8 39 43N 88 38W
Lovington, *N. Mex., U.S.A.* 155 J3 32 57N 103 21W
Lovisa = Loviisa, *Finland* 15 F22 60 28N 26 12 E
Lovosice, *Czech Rep.* 34 A7 50 30N 14 2 E
Lovran, *Croatia* 45 C11 45 18N 14 15 E
Lovrin, *Romania* 52 E5 45 58N 20 48 E
Lövstabruk, *Sweden* 16 D11 60 25N 17 53 E
Lövstabukten, *Sweden* 16 D11 60 35N 17 45 E
Lóvua, *Angola* 115 E4 11 33 S 23 33 E
Lovua, *Angola* 115 D4 7 19 S 20 12 E
Lovua →, *Dem. Rep. of the Congo* 115 D4 6 6 S 20 37 E
Low, L., *Canada* 140 B4 52 29N 76 17W
Low Pt., *Australia* 125 F4 32 25 S 127 25 E
Low Tatra = Nízké Tatry, *Slovak Rep.* 35 C12 48 55N 19 30 E
Lowa, *Dem. Rep. of the Congo* 118 C2 1 25 S 25 47 E
Lowa →, *Dem. Rep. of the Congo* 118 C2 1 24 S 25 51 E
Lowden, *U.S.A.* 156 C6 41 52N 90 56W
Lowell, *Ind., U.S.A.* 157 C9 41 18N 87 25W
Lowell, *Mass., U.S.A.* 151 D13 42 38N 71 19W
Lowell, *Mich., U.S.A.* 157 B11 42 56N 85 20W
Lowellville, *U.S.A.* 150 E4 41 2N 80 32W
Löwen →, *Namibia* 116 D2 26 51 S 18 17 E
Lower Alkali L., *U.S.A.* 158 F3 41 16N 120 2W
Lower Arrow L., *Canada* 142 D5 49 40N 118 5W
Lower Austria = Niederösterreich □, *Austria* 34 C8 48 25N 15 40 E
Lower California = Baja California, *Mexico* 162 A1 31 10N 115 12W
Lower Hutt, *N.Z.* 130 H3 41 10 S 174 55 E
Lower Kalskag, *U.S.A.* 144 F7 61 31N 160 22W
Lower Lake, *U.S.A.* 160 G4 38 55N 122 37W
Lower Manitou L., *Canada* 143 D10 49 15N 93 0W
Lower Paia, *U.S.A.* 145 C5 20 55N 156 23W
Lower Post, *Canada* 142 B3 59 58N 128 30W
Lower Red L., *U.S.A.* 154 B7 47 58N 95 0W
Lower Saxony = Niedersachsen □, *Germany* 30 C4 52 50N 9 0 E
Lower Tunguska = Tunguska, Nizhnyaya →, *Russia* 65 C9 65 48N 88 4 E
Lowestoft, *U.K.* 21 E9 52 29N 1 45 E
Łowicz, *Poland* 55 F6 52 6N 19 55 E
Lowry City, *U.S.A.* 156 F3 38 8N 93 44W
Lowville, *U.S.A.* 151 C9 43 47N 75 29W
Loxton, *Australia* 128 C4 34 28 S 140 31 E
Loxton, *S. Africa* 116 E3 31 30 S 22 22 E
Loyalton, *U.S.A.* 160 F6 39 41N 120 14W
Loyalty Is. = Loyauté, Is., *N. Cal.* 133 K4 20 50 S 166 30 E
Loyang = Luoyang, *China* 74 G7 34 40N 112 26 E
Loyauté, Is., *N. Cal.* 133 K4 20 50 S 166 30 E
Loyev = Loyew, *Belarus* 59 G6 51 56N 30 46 E
Loyew, *Belarus* 59 G6 51 56N 30 46 E
Loyoro, *Uganda* 118 B3 3 22N 34 14 E
Lož, *Slovenia* 45 C11 45 43N 14 30 E
Lozère □, *France* 28 D7 44 35N 3 30 E
Loznica, *Serbia, Yug.* 50 B3 44 32N 19 12 E
Lozova, *Ukraine* 59 H9 49 0N 36 20 E
Lozva →, *Russia* 62 B9 59 36N 62 20 E
Lü Shan, *China* 77 C11 29 30N 115 55 E
Lü-Tao, *Taiwan* 77 F13 22 40N 121 30 E
Lu Verne, *U.S.A.* 156 B2 42 55N 94 5W
Lua →, *Dem. Rep. of the Congo* 114 B3 2 46N 18 26 E
Lua Makiki, *U.S.A.* 145 C5 20 33N 156 37W
Luachimo, *Angola* 115 D4 7 23 S 20 48 E
Luacono, *Angola* 115 E4 11 15 S 21 37 E
Luajan →, *India* 93 G11 24 44N 85 1 E
Lualaba →, *Dem. Rep. of the Congo* 118 B2 0 26N 25 20 E
Luale, *Dem. Rep. of the Congo* 114 B4 1 9N 23 5 E
Luampa, *Zambia* 119 F1 15 4 S 24 20 E
Luampa →, *Zambia* 115 F4 14 33 S 24 10 E
Lu'an, *China* 77 B11 31 45N 116 29 E
Luan Chau, *Vietnam* 76 G4 21 38N 103 24 E
Luan He →, *China* 75 E10 39 20N 119 5 E
Luan Xian, *China* 75 E10 39 40N 118 40 E
Luancheng, *Guangxi Zhuangzu, China* 76 F7 22 48N 108 55 E
Luancheng, *Hebei, China* 74 F8 37 53N 114 40 E
Luanco, *Spain* 42 B5 43 37N 5 48W
Luanda, *Angola* 115 D2 8 50 S 13 15 E
Luang, Thale, *Thailand* 78 C2 7 30N 100 15 E
Luang Prabang, *Laos* 76 H4 19 52N 102 10 E
Luanginga →, *Zambia* 115 F4 15 11 S 22 55 E
Luangwa, *Zambia* 119 F3 15 35 S 30 16 E
Luangwa →, *Zambia* 119 E3 14 25 S 30 25 E
Luangwa Valley, *Zambia* 119 E3 13 30 S 31 30 E
Luania-Bubi, *Dem. Rep. of the Congo* 115 D4 7 28 S 24 49 E
Luanne, *China* 75 D9 40 55N 117 40 E
Luanping, *China* 75 D9 40 53N 117 23 E
Luanshya, *Zambia* 119 E2 13 3 S 28 28 E
Luapula □, *Zambia* 119 E2 11 0 S 29 0 E
Luapula →, *Africa* 119 D2 9 26 S 28 33 E
Luarca, *Spain* 42 B4 43 32N 6 32W
Luashi, *Dem. Rep. of the Congo* 119 E1 10 50 S 23 36 E
Luatamba, *Angola* 115 E4 12 6 S 20 19 E
Luatira, *Angola* 115 E3 12 52 S 17 14 E
Luau, *Angola* 115 E4 10 40 S 22 10 E
Luba, *Phil.* 80 C3 17 19N 120 42 E
Lubaczów, *Poland* 55 H10 50 10N 23 8 E
Lubalo, *Angola* 115 D3 9 10 S 19 15 E
Lubamiti, *Dem. Rep. of the Congo* 114 C3 2 28 S 17 47 E
Lubań, *Poland* 55 G2 51 5N 15 15 E
Lubana, Ozero = Lubānas Ezers, *Latvia* 15 H22 56 45N 27 0 E
Lubānas Ezers, *Latvia* 15 H22 56 45N 27 0 E
Lubang, *Phil.* 80 E3 13 52N 120 7 E
Lubang Is., *Phil.* 79 B6 13 50N 120 12 E
Lubango, *Angola* 115 E2 14 55 S 13 30 E
Lubartów, *Poland* 55 G9 51 28N 22 42 E
Lubawa, *Poland* 54 E6 53 30N 19 48 E
Lübbecke, *Germany* 30 C4 52 18N 8 37 E
Lübben, *Germany* 30 D9 51 56N 13 54 E
Lübbenau, *Germany* 30 D9 51 52N 13 57 E
Lubbock, *U.S.A.* 155 J4 33 35N 101 51W
Lübeck, *Germany* 30 B6 53 52N 10 40 E
Lübecker Bucht, *Germany* 30 A6 54 3N 10 54 E
Lubefu, *Dem. Rep. of the Congo* 118 C1 4 47 S 24 27 E
Lubefu →, *Dem. Rep. of the Congo* 118 C1 4 10 S 23 0 E
Lubelskie □, *Poland* 55 G9 51 20N 22 50 E
Lubero = Luofu, *Dem. Rep. of the Congo* 118 C2 0 10 S 29 15 E
Lubersac, *France* 28 C5 45 26N 1 23 E
Lubicon L., *Canada* 142 B5 56 23N 115 56W
Lubień Kujawski, *Poland* 55 F6 52 23N 19 9 E
Lubilash →, *Dem. Rep. of the Congo* 115 D4 6 2 S 23 45 E
Lubin, *Poland* 55 G3 51 24N 16 11 E
Lublin, *Poland* 55 G9 51 12N 22 38 E
Lubliniec, *Poland* 55 H5 50 43N 18 45 E
Lubnān, Jabal, *Lebanon* 103 B4 33 45N 35 40 E
Lubniewice, *Poland* 55 F2 52 31N 15 15 E
Lubny, *Ukraine* 59 G7 50 3N 32 58 E
Lubomierz, *Poland* 55 G2 51 1N 15 31 E
Luboń, *Poland* 55 F3 52 21N 16 51 E
Lubondaie, *Dem. Rep. of the Congo* 115 D4 8 1 S 26 32 E
Lubongola, *Dem. Rep. of the Congo* 118 C2 2 35 S 27 50 E
L'ubotín, *Slovak Rep.* 35 B13 49 17N 20 53 E
Lubraniec, *Poland* 55 F5 52 33N 18 50 E
Lubsko, *Poland* 55 G1 51 45N 14 57 E
Lübtheen, *Germany* 30 B7 53 18N 11 5 E
Lubuagan, *Phil.* 80 C3 17 21N 121 10 E
Lubudi, *Dem. Rep. of the Congo* 115 D4 6 51 S 21 18 E
Lubudi →, *Dem. Rep. of the Congo* 115 C4 4 19 S 20 23 E
Lubudi →, *Dem. Rep. of the Congo* 119 D2 9 0 S 25 35 E
Lubuklinggau, *Indonesia* 78 E2 3 15 S 102 55 E
Lubuksikaping, *Indonesia* 78 D2 0 10N 100 15 E
Lubumbashi, *Dem. Rep. of the Congo* 119 E2 11 40 S 27 28 E
Lubunda, *Dem. Rep. of the Congo* 118 D2 5 12 S 26 41 E
Lubungu, *Zambia* 119 E2 14 35 S 26 24 E
Lubuskie □, *Poland* 55 F2 52 10N 15 20 E
Lubutu, *Dem. Rep. of the Congo* 118 C2 0 45 S 26 30 E
Luc An Chau, *Vietnam* 86 A5 22 6N 104 43 E
Luc-en-Diois, *France* 29 D9 44 36N 5 28 E
Lucala, *Angola* 115 D3 9 7 S 15 58 E
Lucala →, *Angola* 115 D3 9 38 S 14 14 E
Lucan, *Canada* 150 C3 43 11N 81 24W
Lucania, Mt., *Canada* 138 B5 61 1N 140 29W
Lucapa, *Angola* 115 D4 8 25 S 20 45 E
Lucas, *U.S.A.* 156 C3 41 2N 93 29W
Lucas Channel, *Canada* 150 A3 45 21N 81 45W
Lucban, *Phil.* 80 D3 14 6N 121 33 E
Lucca, *Italy* 44 E7 43 50N 10 29 E
Lucé, *France* 26 D8 48 26N 1 27 E
Luce Bay, *U.K.* 22 G4 54 45N 4 48W
Lucea, *Jamaica* 164 C4 18 25N 78 10W
Lucedale, *U.S.A.* 149 K1 30 56N 88 35W
Lucena, *Phil.* 79 B6 13 56N 121 37 E
Lucena, *Spain* 43 H6 37 27N 4 31W
Lučenec, *Slovak Rep.* 35 C12 48 18N 19 42 E
Lucens, *Switz.* 32 C3 46 43N 6 51 E
Lucera, *Italy* 47 A8 41 30N 15 20 E
Lucerne = Luzern, *Switz.* 33 B6 47 3N 8 18 E
Lucerne, *U.S.A.* 160 F4 39 6N 122 48W
Lucerne Valley, *U.S.A.* 161 L10 34 27N 116 57W
Lucero, *Mexico* 162 A3 30 49N 106 30W
Luchena →, *Spain* 41 H3 37 44N 1 50W
Lucheng, *China* 74 F7 36 20N 113 11 E
Lucheringo →, *Mozam.* 119 E4 11 43 S 36 17 E
Lüchow, *Germany* 30 C7 52 58N 11 8 E
Luchuan, *China* 77 F8 22 21N 110 12 E
Lucia, *U.S.A.* 160 J5 36 2N 121 33W
Lucie →, *Surinam* 169 C6 3 35N 57 38W
Lucinda, *Australia* 126 B4 18 32 S 146 20 E
Lucindale, *Australia* 127 F3 36 58 S 140 26 E
Lucira, *Angola* 115 E2 14 0 S 12 35 E
Luciras, B. das, *Angola* 115 E2 13 52 S 12 31 E
Luckau, *Germany* 30 D9 51 50N 13 42 E
Luckenwalde, *Germany* 30 C9 52 5N 13 10 E
Luckey, *U.S.A.* 157 C13 41 27N 83 29W
Luckhoff, *S. Africa* 116 D3 29 44 S 24 43 E
Lucknow, *Canada* 150 C3 43 57N 81 31W
Lucknow, *India* 93 F9 26 50N 81 0 E
Luçon, *France* 28 B2 46 28N 1 10W
Lucusse, *Angola* 115 E4 12 32 S 20 48 E
Lüda = Dalian, *China* 75 E11 38 50N 121 40 E
Luda Kamchiya →, *Bulgaria* 51 C11 43 3N 27 29 E
Ludbreg, *Croatia* 45 B13 46 15N 16 38 E
Lüdenscheid, *Germany* 30 D3 51 13N 7 37 E
Lüderitz, *Namibia* 116 D2 26 41 S 15 8 E
Lüderitzbaai, *Namibia* 116 D2 26 36 S 15 8 E
Ludhiana, *India* 92 D6 30 57N 75 56 E
Ludian, *China* 76 D4 27 10N 103 33 E
Luding Qiao, *China* 76 C4 29 53N 102 12 E
Lüdinghausen, *Germany* 30 D3 51 46N 7 27 E
Ludington, *U.S.A.* 148 D2 43 57N 86 27W
Ludlow, *U.K.* 21 E5 52 22N 2 42W
Ludlow, *Calif., U.S.A.* 161 L10 34 43N 116 10W
Ludlow, *Pa., U.S.A.* 150 E6 41 43N 78 56W
Ludlow, *Vt., U.S.A.* 151 C12 43 24N 72 42W
Ludowici, *U.S.A.* 152 D8 31 43N 81 45W
Luduş, *Romania* 53 D9 46 29N 24 5 E
Ludvika, *Sweden* 16 D9 60 8N 15 14 E
Ludwigsburg, *Germany* 31 G5 48 53N 9 11 E
Ludwigsfelde, *Germany* 30 C9 52 17N 13 17 E
Ludwigshafen, *Germany* 31 F4 49 29N 8 26 E
Ludwigslust, *Germany* 30 B7 53 19N 11 30 E
Ludza, *Latvia* 58 D4 56 32N 27 43 E
Lue, *Australia* 129 B8 32 38 S 149 50 E
Luebo, *Dem. Rep. of the Congo* 115 D4 5 21 S 21 23 E
Lueki, *Dem. Rep. of the Congo* 118 C2 3 20 S 25 48 E
Luena, *Angola* 115 E3 12 13 S 19 51 E
Luena, *Dem. Rep. of the Congo* 119 D2 9 28 S 25 43 E
Luena, *Zambia* 119 E3 10 40 S 30 25 E
Luena →, *Angola* 115 E4 12 30 S 22 34 E
Luena →, *Zambia* 115 E4 14 46 S 23 30 E
Luena Flats, *Zambia* 115 E4 14 47 S 23 17 E
Luepa, *Venezuela* 169 B5 5 43N 61 31W
Lueta →, *Dem. Rep. of the Congo* 115 D4 7 4 S 21 40 E
Luete →, *Zambia* 115 F4 15 46 S 23 10 E
Lüeyang, *China* 74 H4 33 22N 106 10 E
Lufeng, *Guangdong, China* 77 F10 22 57N 115 38 E
Lufeng, *Yunnan, China* 76 E4 25 0N 102 5 E
Lufico, *Angola* 115 D2 6 24 S 13 23 E
Lufira →, *Dem. Rep. of the Congo* 119 D2 9 30 S 27 0 E
Lufkin, *U.S.A.* 155 K7 31 21N 94 44W
Lufupa, *Dem. Rep. of the Congo* 119 E1 10 37 S 24 56 E
Luga, *Russia* 58 C5 58 40N 29 55 E
Luga →, *Russia* 58 C5 59 40N 28 18 E
Lugano, *Switz.* 33 E7 46 1N 8 57 E
Lugano, L. di, *Switz.* 33 E8 46 0N 9 0 E
Lugansk = Luhansk, *Ukraine* 59 H10 48 38N 39 15 E
Lugard's Falls, *Kenya* 118 C4 3 6 S 38 41 E
Lugela, *Mozam.* 119 F4 16 25 S 36 43 E
Lugenda →, *Mozam.* 119 E4 11 25 S 38 33 E
Lugh Ganana, *Somali Rep.* 120 D2 3 48N 42 34 E
Lugnaquilla, *Ireland* 23 D5 52 58N 6 28W
Lugo, *Italy* 45 D8 44 25N 11 54 E
Lugo, *Spain* 42 B3 43 2N 7 35W
Lugo □, *Spain* 42 C3 43 0N 7 30W
Lugoj, *Romania* 52 E6 45 42N 21 57 E
Lugovoy, *Kazakstan* 64 E8 42 55N 72 43 E
Lugus I., *Phil.* 81 J3 5 41N 120 50 E
Luhansk, *Ukraine* 59 H10 48 38N 39 15 E
Luhe, *China* 77 A12 32 19N 118 50 E
Luhe →, *Germany* 30 B6 53 23N 10 13 E
Luhuo, *China* 76 B3 31 21N 100 48 E
Lui →, *Angola* 115 D3 8 21 S 17 33 E
Lui →, *Zambia* 115 F4 16 18 S 23 17 E
Luia, *Angola* 115 D4 8 10 S 21 32 E
Luia →, *Angola* 115 D4 8 32 S 21 47 E
Luiana, *Angola* 116 B3 17 25 S 22 59 E
Luiana →, *Angola* 115 F4 17 24 S 23 3 E
Luilaka →, *Dem. Rep. of the Congo* 114 C4 0 52 S 20 12 E
Luimneach = Limerick, *Ireland* 23 D3 52 40N 8 37W
Luing, *U.K.* 22 E3 56 14N 5 39W
Luino, *Italy* 44 C5 45 59N 8 44 E
Luio →, *Angola* 115 E4 13 17 S 21 37 E
Luís Correia, *Brazil* 170 B3 3 0 S 41 35W
Luís Gonçalves, *Brazil* 170 C1 5 37 S 50 25W
Luitpold Coast, *Antarctica* 7 D1 78 30 S 32 0W
Luiza, *Dem. Rep. of the Congo* 115 D4 7 40 S 22 30 E
Luizi, *Dem. Rep. of the Congo* 118 D2 6 0 S 27 25 E
Luján, *Argentina* 174 C4 34 45 S 59 5W
Lujiang, *China* 77 B11 31 20N 117 15 E
Lukala, *Dem. Rep. of the Congo* 115 D2 5 31 S 14 32 E
Lukang, *Taiwan* 77 E13 24 1N 120 22 E
Lukanga, *Dem. Rep. of the Congo* 114 C3 1 41 S 18 9 E
Lukanga, *Dem. Rep. of the Congo* 114 C3 1 0 S 18 8 E
Lukanga Swamp, *Zambia* 119 E2 14 30 S 27 40 E
Lukavac, *Bos.-H.* 52 F3 44 33N 18 32 E
Lukenie →, *Dem. Rep. of the Congo* 114 C3 3 0 S 18 50 E
Lukhisaral, *India* 93 G12 25 11N 86 5 E
Lŭki, *Bulgaria* 51 E8 41 50N 24 43 E
Lukk, *Libya* 108 B4 32 1N 24 46 E
Lukolela, *Équateur, Dem. Rep. of the Congo* 114 C3 1 10 S 17 12 E
Lukolela, *Kasai-Or., Dem. Rep. of the Congo* 118 D1 5 23 S 24 32 E
Lukosi, *Zimbabwe* 119 F2 18 30 S 26 30 E
Lukovë, *Albania* 50 G3 39 59N 19 54 E
Lukovit, *Bulgaria* 51 C8 43 13N 24 11 E
Łuków, *Poland* 55 G9 51 55N 22 23 E
Lukoyanov, *Russia* 60 C7 55 2N 44 29 E
Luksefjell, *Norway* 18 E6 59 23N 9 34 E
Lukuni, *Dem. Rep. of the Congo* 115 D3 5 50 S 17 16 E
Lula, *Dem. Rep. of the Congo* 115 D3 5 22 S 16 2 E
Lule älv →, *Sweden* 14 D19 65 35N 22 10 E
Luleå, *Sweden* 14 D20 65 35N 22 10 E
Lüleburgaz, *Turkey* 51 E11 41 23N 27 22 E
Luliang, *China* 76 E4 25 0N 103 40 E
Luling, *U.S.A.* 155 L6 29 41N 97 39W
Lulong, *China* 75 E10 39 53N 118 51 E
Lulonga →, *Dem. Rep. of the Congo* 114 B3 1 0N 18 10 E
Lulu, *U.S.A.* 152 E7 30 7N 82 29W
Lulu →, *Dem. Rep. of the Congo* 114 B4 1 18N 23 42 E
Lulua →, *Dem. Rep. of the Congo* 115 C4 4 30 S 20 30 E
Luluabourg = Kananga, *Dem. Rep. of the Congo* 115 D4 5 55 S 22 18 E
Lumai, *Angola* 115 E4 13 13 S 21 25 E
Lumajang, *Indonesia* 79 H15 8 8 S 113 13 E
Lumaku, Gunong, *Malaysia* 85 B5 4 52N 115 38 E
Lumbala →, *Angola* 115 E4 12 39 S 22 35 E
Lumbala Kaquengue, *Angola* 115 E4 12 39 S 22 34 E
Lumbala N'guimbo, *Angola* 115 E4 14 18 S 21 18 E
Lumbe →, *Zambia* 115 F4 16 44 S 23 41 E
Lumber City, *U.S.A.* 152 D7 31 56N 82 41W
Lumberton, *U.S.A.* 149 H6 34 37N 79 0W
Lumbwa, *Kenya* 118 C4 0 12 S 35 28 E
Lumding, *India* 90 C4 25 46N 93 10 E
Lumi, *Papua N. G.* 132 B2 3 30 S 142 2 E
Lumpkin, *U.S.A.* 152 C5 32 3N 84 48W
Lumsden, *Canada* 143 C8 50 39N 104 52W
Lumsden, *N.Z.* 131 F3 45 44 S 168 27 E
Lumut, *Malaysia* 87 K3 4 13N 100 37 E
Lumut, Tanjung, *Indonesia* 78 E3 3 50 S 105 58 E
Luna, *India* 92 H3 23 43N 69 16 E
Luna, *Phil.* 80 B3 18 18N 121 21 E
Lunan, *China* 76 E4 24 40N 103 18 E
Lunavada, *India* 92 H5 23 8N 73 37 E
Lunca, *Romania* 53 C10 47 22N 25 1 E
Lunca Corbului, *Romania* 53 F9 44 42N 24 45 E
Lund, *Sweden* 17 J7 55 44N 13 12 E
Lunda Norte □, *Angola* 115 D3 8 0 S 20 0 E
Lunda Sul □, *Angola* 115 D4 10 0 S 20 0 E
Lundamo, *Norway* 18 A7 63 9N 10 17 E
Lundazi, *Zambia* 119 E3 12 20 S 33 7 E
Lunderskov, *Denmark* 17 J3 55 29N 9 19 E
Lundi →, *Zimbabwe* 119 G3 21 43 S 32 34 E
Lundu, *Malaysia* 78 D3 1 40N 109 50 E
Lundy, *U.K.* 21 F3 51 10N 4 41W
Lune →, *U.K.* 20 C5 54 0N 2 51W
Lüneburg, *Germany* 30 B6 53 15N 10 24 E
Lüneburg Heath = Lüneburger Heide, *Germany* 30 B6 53 10N 10 12 E
Lüneburger Heide, *Germany* 30 B6 53 10N 10 12 E
Lunel, *France* 29 E8 43 39N 4 9 E
Lünen, *Germany* 30 D3 51 36N 7 32 E
Lunenburg, *Canada* 141 D7 44 22N 64 18W
Lunéville, *France* 27 D13 48 36N 6 30 E
Lunga, *Dem. Rep. of the Congo* 115 C4 5 46 S 12 14 E
Lunga →, *Zambia* 119 E2 14 34 S 26 25 E
Lunge, *Angola* 115 E3 12 13 S 16 7 E
Lungern, *Switz.* 32 C6 46 48N 8 10 E
Lungi Airport, *S. Leone* 112 D2 8 40N 13 17W
Lunglei, *India* 90 D4 22 55N 92 45 E
Lungngo, *Burma* 90 E4 21 57N 93 36 E
Lungwebungu →, *Zambia* 115 E4 14 19 S 23 14 E

M

246 Maliqi

Maliqi, Albania 50 F4 40 45N 20 48 E
Malita, Phil. 79 C7 6 19N 125 39 E
Maliwun, Burma 78 B1 10 17N 98 40 E
Maliya, India 92 H4 23 5N 70 46 E
Maljenik, Serbia, Yug. 50 C5 43 54N 21 43 E
Malkapur, India 94 D1 20 53N 73 58 E
Malkara, Turkey 51 F10 40 53N 26 53 E
Małkinia Górna, Poland 55 F9 52 42N 22 5 E
Malko Tŭrnovo, Bulgaria 51 E11 41 59N 27 31 E
Mallacoota, Australia 129 D8 37 40 S 149 40 E
Mallacoota Inlet, Australia 129 D8 37 34 S 149 40 E
Mallaig, U.K. 22 D3 57 0N 5 50W
Mallala, Australia 128 C3 34 26 S 138 30 E
Mallaoua, Niger 113 C6 13 2N 9 36 E
Mallard, U.S.A. 156 B2 42 56N 94 41W
Mallawan, India 93 F9 27 4N 80 12 E
Mallawi, Egypt 106 B3 27 44N 30 44 E
Mallembe, Gabon 114 C2 3 34 S 10 53 E
Mallemort, France 29 E9 43 43N 5 11 E
Málles Venosta, Italy 44 B7 46 41N 10 32 E
Mállia, Greece 38 D7 35 17N 25 32 E
Mallicolo = Malakula, Vanuatu 133 F5 16 15 S 167 30 E
Mallión, Kólpos, Greece 38 D7 35 19N 25 27 E
Mallorca, Spain 39 B10 39 30N 3 0 E
Mallorytown, Canada 151 B9 44 29N 75 53W
Mallow, Ireland 23 D3 52 8N 8 39W
Malmbäck, Sweden 17 G8 57 34N 14 28 E
Malmberget, Sweden 14 C19 67 11N 20 40 E
Malmédy, Belgium 24 D6 50 25N 6 2 E
Malmesbury, S. Africa 116 E2 33 28 S 18 41 E
Malmköping, Sweden 16 E10 59 8N 16 44 E
Malmö, Sweden 17 J6 55 36N 12 59 E
Malmslätt, Sweden 17 F9 58 27N 15 33 E
Malmyzh, Russia 60 B10 56 31N 50 41 E
Malnaş, Romania 53 D10 46 2N 25 49 E
Malo, Vanuatu 133 E5 15 40 S 167 11 E
Malo Konare, Bulgaria 51 D8 42 12N 24 24 E
Maloarkhangelsk, Russia 59 F9 52 28N 36 30 E
Maloca, Brazil 169 C6 0 43N 55 57W
Maloja, Switz. 33 D9 46 25N 9 35 E
Malojapass, Switz. 33 D9 46 23N 9 42 E
Malolos, Phil. 79 B6 14 50N 120 49 E
Malombe L., Malawi 119 E4 14 40 S 35 15 E
Małomice, Poland 55 G2 51 34N 15 29 E
Malomir, Bulgaria 51 D10 42 16N 26 32 E
Malone, Fla., U.S.A. 152 E4 30 57N 85 10W
Malone, N.Y., U.S.A. 151 B10 44 51N 74 18W
Malong, China 76 E4 25 24N 103 34 E
Malonga, Dem. Rep. of the Congo 115 E4 10 24 S 23 10 E
Malonno, Italy 33 D10 46 7N 10 18 E
Małopolskie □, Poland 55 J7 49 50N 20 20 E
Malorad, Bulgaria 50 C7 43 28N 23 41 E
Måløy, Norway 15 F11 61 57N 5 6 E
Maloyaroslovets, Russia 58 E9 55 2N 36 20 E
Malpartida, Spain 43 F4 39 26N 6 30W
Malpaso, Canary Is. 39 G1 27 43N 18 3W
Malpelo, I. de, Colombia 135 G19 4 3N 81 35W
Malpica de Bergantiños, Spain 42 B2 43 19N 8 50W
Malprabha →, India 95 F3 16 20N 76 5 E
Malpur, India 92 H5 23 21N 73 27 E
Malpura, India 92 F6 26 17N 75 23 E
Mals = Málles Venosta, Italy 44 B7 46 41N 10 32 E
Malsiras, India 94 F2 17 52N 74 55 E
Malta, Brazil 170 C4 6 54 S 37 31W
Malta, Idaho, U.S.A. 158 E7 42 18N 113 22W
Malta, Mont., U.S.A. 158 B10 48 21N 107 52W
Malta ■, Europe 38 D2 35 50N 14 30 E
Maltahöhe, Namibia 116 C2 24 55 S 17 0 E
Maltepe, Turkey 51 F13 40 55N 29 8 E
Malters, Switz. 32 B6 47 3N 8 11 E
Malton, Canada 150 C5 43 42N 79 38W
Malton, U.K. 20 C7 54 8N 0 49W
Malu'a, Solomon Is. 133 M11 8 0 S 160 0 E
Maluku, Dem. Rep. of the Congo 114 C3 4 3 S 15 34 E
Maluku, Indonesia 79 E7 1 0 S 127 0 E
Maluku □, Indonesia 79 E7 3 0 S 128 0 E
Maluku Sea = Molucca Sea, Indonesia 79 E6 2 0 S 124 0 E
Malumfashi, Nigeria 113 C6 11 48N 7 39 E
Malundo, Angola 115 E4 14 51 S 22 0 E
Malung, Sweden 16 D7 60 42N 13 44 E
Malungon, Phil. 81 H5 6 16N 125 14 E
Malungsfors, Sweden 16 D7 60 44N 13 33 E
Malur, India 95 H3 13 0N 77 55 E
Maluso, Phil. 81 H3 6 33N 121 53 E
Maluwe, Ghana 112 D4 8 40N 2 17W
Malvaglia, Switz. 33 D7 46 24N 8 59 E
Malvalli, India 95 H3 12 28N 77 8 E
Malvan, India 95 F1 16 2N 73 30 E
Malvern, U.S.A. 155 H8 34 22N 92 49W
Malvern Hills, U.K. 21 E5 52 0N 2 19W
Malvik, Norway 18 A7 63 25N 10 40 E
Malvinas, Is. = Falkland Is. □, Atl. Oc. 176 D5 51 30 S 59 0W
Malý Dunaj →, Slovak Rep. 35 D11 47 45N 18 9 E
Malya, Tanzania 118 C3 3 5 S 33 38 E
Malybay, Kazakstan 63 B9 43 30N 78 25 E
Malyn, Ukraine 59 G5 50 46N 29 3 E
Malyy Lyakhovskiy, Ostrov, Russia 65 B15 74 7N 140 36 E
Mama, Russia 65 D12 58 18N 112 54 E
Mamadysh, Russia 60 C10 55 44N 51 23 E
Mamaku, N.Z. 130 E5 38 5 S 176 8 E
Mamala B., U.S.A. 145 K14 21 15N 157 55W
Mamanguape, Brazil 170 C4 6 50 S 35 4W
Mamarr Mitlā, Egypt 103 E1 30 2N 32 54 E
Mamasa, Indonesia 79 E5 2 55 S 119 20 E
Mambajao, Phil. 81 G5 9 15N 124 43 E
Mambasa, Dem. Rep. of the Congo 118 B2 1 22N 29 3 E
Mamberamo →, Indonesia 79 E9 2 0 S 137 50 E
Mambéré →, C.A.R. 114 B3 3 31N 16 3 E
Mambili →, Congo 114 B3 0 6N 16 5 E
Mambilima Falls, Zambia 119 E2 10 31 S 28 45 E
Mambirima, Dem. Rep. of the Congo 119 E2 11 25 S 27 33 E
Mambo, Tanzania 118 C4 4 52 S 38 22 E
Mambrui, Kenya 118 C5 3 5 S 40 5 E
Mamburao, Phil. 79 B6 13 13N 120 39 E
Mameigwess L., Canada 140 B2 52 35N 87 50W
Mamers, France 26 D7 48 21N 0 22 E
Mamfé, Cameroon 113 D6 5 50N 9 15 E
Māmī, Ra's, Yemen 99 D6 12 32N 54 30 E
Mamiña, Chile 172 E4 20 5 S 69 14W
Mammoth, U.S.A. 159 K8 32 43N 110 39W
Mammoth Cave National Park, U.S.A. 148 G3 37 8N 86 13W
Mamoré →, Bolivia 173 C4 10 23 S 65 53W
Mamou, Guinea 112 C2 10 15N 12 0W
Mampatá, Guinea-Biss. 112 C2 11 54N 14 53W
Mampikony, Madag. 117 B8 16 6 S 47 38 E
Mampoko, Dem. Rep. of the Congo 114 B3 0 51N 18 42 E
Mampong, Ghana 113 D4 7 6N 1 26W
Mamry, Jezioro, Poland 54 D8 54 5N 21 50 E
Mamuil Malal, Paso, S. Amer. 176 A2 39 35 S 71 28W
Mamuju, Indonesia 79 E5 2 41 S 118 50 E
Ma'mūl, Oman 99 C6 18 8N 55 16 E
Mamuno, Botswana 116 C3 22 16 S 20 1 E
Mamuras, Albania 50 E3 41 34N 19 41 E
Man, Ivory C. 112 D3 7 30N 7 40W
Man →, India 94 F2 17 31N 75 32 E
Man, I. of, U.K. 20 C3 54 15N 4 30W
Man-Bazar, India 93 H12 23 4N 86 39 E
Man Na, Burma 90 D6 23 27N 97 19 E
Man Tun, Burma 90 D7 23 52N 98 38 E
Mana, Fr. Guiana 169 B7 5 45N 53 55W
Mana →, Fr. Guiana 169 B7 5 45N 53 55W
Manaar, G. of = Mannar, G. of, Asia 95 K4 8 30N 79 0 E
Manabí □, Ecuador 168 D1 0 40 S 80 5W
Manacacías →, Colombia 168 C3 4 23N 72 4W
Manacapuru, Brazil 169 D5 3 16 S 60 37W
Manacapuru →, Brazil 169 D5 3 18 S 60 37W
Manacor, Spain 39 B10 39 34N 3 13 E
Manado, Indonesia 79 D6 1 29N 124 51 E
Managua, Nic. 164 D2 12 6N 86 20W
Managua, L. de, Nic. 164 D2 12 20N 86 30W
Manaia, N.Z. 130 F3 39 33 S 174 8 E
Manakara, Madag. 117 C8 22 8 S 48 1 E
Manakau Mt., N.Z. 131 C8 42 15 S 173 42 E
Manākhah, Yemen 98 D3 15 5N 43 44 E
Manakino, N.Z. 130 E4 38 22 S 175 47 E
Manali, India 92 C7 32 16N 77 10 E
Manam I., Papua N. G. 132 C3 4 5 S 145 0 E
Manama = Al Manāmah, Bahrain 97 E6 26 10N 50 30 E
Manambao →, Madag. 117 B7 17 35 S 44 0 E
Manambato, Madag. 117 A8 13 43 S 49 7 E
Manambolo →, Madag. 117 B7 19 18 S 44 22 E
Manambolosy, Madag. 117 B8 16 2 S 49 40 E
Mánamo, Caño →, Venezuela 169 B5 9 55N 62 16W
Manana I., U.S.A. 145 K14 21 20N 157 40W
Mananara, Madag. 117 B8 16 10 S 49 46 E
Mananara →, Madag. 117 C8 23 21 S 47 42 E
Mananjary, Madag. 117 C8 21 13 S 48 20 E
Manankoro, Mali 112 C3 10 28N 7 25W
Manantavadi, India 95 J3 11 49N 76 1 E
Manantenina, Madag. 117 C8 24 17 S 47 19 E
Manaos = Manaus, Brazil 169 D6 3 0 S 60 0W
Manapala, Phil. 81 F4 10 58N 123 5 E
Manapire →, Venezuela 168 B4 7 42N 66 7W
Manapouri, N.Z. 131 F2 45 34 S 167 39 E
Manapouri, L., N.Z. 131 F2 45 32 S 167 32 E
Manapparai, India 95 J4 10 36N 78 25 E
Manaqil, Sudan 107 E3 14 15N 32 59 E
Manar →, India 94 E3 18 50N 77 20 E
Manār, Jabal, Yemen 98 D4 14 2N 44 17 E
Manaravolo, Madag. 117 C8 23 59 S 45 39 E
Manas, China 72 B3 44 17N 85 56 E
Manas, Somali Rep. 120 D2 2 57N 43 28 E
Manas, Gora, Kyrgyzstan 63 B5 42 22N 71 2 E
Manaslu, Nepal 93 E11 28 33N 84 33 E
Manasquan, U.S.A. 151 F10 40 8N 74 3W
Manassa, U.S.A. 159 H11 37 11N 105 56W
Manatuto, Indonesia 82 C3 8 30 S 126 1 E
Manaung, Burma 90 F4 18 45N 93 40 E
Manaus, Brazil 169 D6 3 0 S 60 0W
Manavgat, Turkey 100 D4 36 47N 31 26 E
Manawan L., Canada 143 B8 55 24N 103 14W
Manawatu →, N.Z. 130 G4 40 28 S 175 12 E
Manay, Phil. 81 H6 7 17N 126 33 E
Manbij, Syria 100 D7 36 31N 37 57 E
Mancha Real, Spain 43 H7 37 48N 3 39W
Manche □, France 26 C5 49 10N 1 20W
Manchegorsk, Russia 64 C4 67 54N 32 58 E
Manchester, U.K. 20 D5 53 29N 2 12W
Manchester, Calif., U.S.A. 160 G3 38 58N 123 41W
Manchester, Conn., U.S.A. 151 E12 41 47N 72 31W
Manchester, Ga., U.S.A. 152 C5 32 51N 84 37W
Manchester, Iowa, U.S.A. 156 B5 42 29N 91 27W
Manchester, Ky., U.S.A. 148 G4 37 9N 83 46W
Manchester, Mich., U.S.A. 157 B12 42 9N 84 2W
Manchester, N.H., U.S.A. 151 D13 42 59N 71 28W
Manchester, N.Y., U.S.A. 150 D7 42 56N 77 16W
Manchester, Ohio, U.S.A. 157 F13 38 41N 83 36W
Manchester, Pa., U.S.A. 151 F8 40 4N 76 43W
Manchester, Tenn., U.S.A. 149 H2 35 29N 86 5W
Manchester, Vt., U.S.A. 151 C11 43 10N 73 5W
Manchester L., Canada 143 A7 61 28N 107 29W
Manchhar L., Pakistan 92 F2 26 25N 67 39 E
Manchuria = Dongbei, China 75 D13 45 0N 125 0 E
Manchurian Plain, China 66 E16 47 0N 124 0 E
Manciano, Italy 45 F8 42 35N 11 31 E
Mancifa, Ethiopia 107 F5 6 53N 41 50 E
Mancora, Peru 172 A1 4 9 S 81 1W
Mand →, India 93 J10 21 42N 83 15 E
Mand →, Iran 97 D7 28 20N 52 30 E
Manda, Ludewe, Tanzania 119 E3 10 30 S 34 40 E
Manda, Mbeya, Tanzania 118 D3 7 58 S 32 29 E
Manda, Mbeya, Tanzania 119 D3 8 30 S 32 49 E
Mandabé, Madag. 117 C7 21 0 S 44 55 E
Mandaguari, Brazil 175 A5 23 32 S 51 42W
Mandah = Töhöm, Mongolia 74 B5 44 27N 108 2 E
Mandal, Norway 15 G12 58 2N 7 25 E
Mandala, Puncak, Indonesia 79 E10 4 44 S 140 20 E
Mandalay, Burma 90 D6 22 0N 96 4 E
Mandale = Mandalay, Burma 90 D6 22 0N 96 4 E
Mandalgarh, India 92 G6 25 12N 75 6 E
Mandalgovi, Mongolia 74 B4 45 45N 106 10 E
Mandalī, Iraq 101 F11 33 43N 45 28 E
Mandan, U.S.A. 154 B4 46 50N 100 54W
Mandaon, Phil. 80 E4 12 13N 123 17 E
Mandar, Teluk, Indonesia 79 E5 3 35 S 119 15 E
Mándas, Italy 46 C2 39 40N 9 8 E
Mandaue, Phil. 79 B6 10 20N 123 56 E
Mandelieu-la-Napoule, France 29 E10 43 34N 6 57 E
Mandera, Kenya 118 B5 3 55N 41 53 E
Mandi, India 92 D7 31 39N 76 58 E
Mandi Dabwali, India 92 E6 29 58N 74 42 E
Mandiana, Guinea 112 C3 10 37N 8 39W
Mandimba, Mozam. 119 E4 14 20 S 35 40 E
Mandioli, Indonesia 79 E7 0 40 S 127 20 E
Mandioré, L., S. Amer. 173 D6 18 8 S 57 33W
Mandla, India 93 H9 22 39N 80 30 E
Mandø, Denmark 17 J2 55 18N 8 33 E
Mandorah, Australia 124 B5 12 32 S 130 42 E
Mandoto, Madag. 117 B8 19 34 S 46 17 E
Mandoúdhion, Greece 48 C5 38 48N 23 29 E
Mándra, Greece 48 C5 38 4N 23 30 E
Mandra, Pakistan 92 C5 33 23N 73 12 E
Mandrákhi, Greece 49 E9 36 36N 27 11 E
Mandrare →, Madag. 117 D8 25 10 S 46 30 E
Mandritsara, Madag. 117 B8 15 50 S 48 49 E
Mandronarivo, Madag. 117 C8 21 7 S 45 38 E
Mandsaur, India 92 G6 24 3N 75 8 E
Mandurah, Australia 125 F2 32 36 S 115 48 E
Mandúria, Italy 47 B10 40 24N 17 38 E
Mandvi, India 92 H3 22 51N 69 22 E
Mandya, India 95 H3 12 30N 77 0 E
Mandzai, Pakistan 92 D2 30 55N 67 6 E
Mané, Burkina Faso 113 C4 12 59N 1 21W
Maneh, Iran 97 B8 37 39N 57 7 E
Manengouba, Mts., Cameroon 113 E6 5 0N 9 50 E
Maner →, India 94 E4 18 30N 79 40 E
Manera, Madag. 117 C7 22 55 S 44 20 E
Manérbio, Italy 44 C7 45 21N 10 8 E
Maneroo Cr. →, Australia 126 C3 23 21 S 143 53 E
Manfalût, Egypt 106 B3 27 20N 30 52 E
Manfred, Australia 128 B5 33 19 S 143 45 E
Manfredónia, Italy 45 G12 41 38N 15 55 E
Manfredónia, G. di, Italy 45 G13 41 35N 16 5 E
Manga, Brazil 171 D3 14 46 S 43 56W
Manga, Burkina Faso 113 C4 11 40N 1 4W
Manga, Congo 114 C3 0 13 S 16 5 E
Manga, Niger 113 C7 15 0N 11 0 E
Mangabeiras, Chapada das, Brazil 170 D2 10 0 S 46 30W
Mangai, Dem. Rep. of the Congo 115 C3 4 2 S 19 33 E
Mangal, Phil. 81 H3 6 25N 121 58 E
Mangalagiri, India 95 F5 16 26N 80 36 E
Mangaldai, India 90 B4 26 26N 92 2 E
Mangaldan, Phil. 80 C3 16 4N 120 24 E
Mangalia, Romania 53 G13 43 50N 28 35 E
Mangalore, Australia 129 D6 36 56 S 145 10 E
Mangalore, India 95 H2 12 55N 74 47 E
Mangalvedha, India 94 F2 17 31N 75 28 E
Mangan, India 93 F13 27 31N 88 32 E
Mangaon, India 94 E1 18 15N 73 20 E
Mangawan, India 93 G9 24 41N 81 33 E
Mangaweka, N.Z. 130 F4 39 48 S 175 47 E
Mangaweka, Mt., N.Z. 130 F5 39 49 S 176 5 E
Mange, Dem. Rep. of the Congo 114 B4 0 54N 20 30 E
Manger, Norway 18 D2 60 38N 5 3 E
Manggar, Indonesia 78 E3 2 50 S 108 10 E
Manggawitu, Indonesia 79 E8 4 8 S 133 32 E
Mangin Range, Burma 90 C5 24 15N 95 45 E
Mangindrano, Madag. 117 A8 14 17 S 48 58 E
Mangkalihat, Tanjung, Indonesia 79 D5 1 2N 118 59 E
Mangla, Pakistan 92 C5 33 7N 73 39 E
Mangla Dam, Pakistan 93 C5 33 9N 73 44 E
Manglares, C., Colombia 168 C2 1 36N 79 2W
Manglaur, India 92 E7 29 44N 77 49 E
Mangnai, China 72 C4 37 52N 91 43 E
Mango, Togo 113 C5 10 20N 0 30 E
Mangoche, Malawi 119 E4 14 25 S 35 16 E
Mangoky →, Madag. 117 C7 21 29 S 43 41 E
Mangole, Indonesia 79 E6 1 50 S 125 55 E
Mangombe, Dem. Rep. of the Congo 118 C2 1 20 S 26 48 E
Mangonui, N.Z. 130 B2 35 1 S 173 32 E
Mangoro →, Madag. 117 B8 20 0 S 48 45 E
Mangrol, Mad. P., India 92 J4 21 7N 70 7 E
Mangrol, Raj., India 92 G6 25 20N 76 31 E
Mangrul Pir, India 94 D3 20 19N 77 21 E
Mangualde, Portugal 42 E3 40 38N 7 48W
Mangueigne, Chad 109 F4 10 30N 21 15 E
Mangueira, L. da, Brazil 175 C5 33 0 S 52 50W
Manguéni, Hamada, Niger 108 D2 22 35N 12 40 E
Mangum, U.S.A. 155 H5 34 53N 99 30W
Mangungu, Dem. Rep. of the Congo 115 D3 5 16 S 19 36 E
Mangyshlak Poluostrov, Kazakstan 64 E6 44 30N 52 30 E
Manhattan, U.S.A. 154 F6 39 11N 96 35W
Manhatten, U.S.A. 157 C9 41 26N 87 59W
Manhiça, Mozam. 117 D5 25 23 S 32 49 E
Manhuaçu, Brazil 171 F3 20 15 S 42 2W
Manhumirim, Brazil 171 F3 20 22 S 41 57W
Maní, Colombia 168 C3 4 49N 72 17W
Mania →, Madag. 117 B8 19 42 S 45 22 E
Maniago, Italy 45 B9 46 10N 12 43 E
Manica, Mozam. 117 B5 18 58 S 32 59 E
Manica □, Mozam. 117 B5 19 10 S 33 45 E
Manicaland □, Zimbabwe 119 F3 19 0 S 32 30 E
Manicoré, Brazil 173 B5 5 48 S 61 16W
Manicoré →, Brazil 173 B5 5 51 S 61 19W
Manicouagan →, Canada 141 C6 49 30N 68 30W
Manicouagan, Rés., Canada 141 B6 51 5N 68 40W
Maniema □, Dem. Rep. of the Congo 118 C2 3 0 S 26 0 E
Manīfah, Si. Arabia 97 E6 27 44N 49 0 E
Manifold, C., Australia 126 C5 22 41 S 150 50 E
Maniganggo, China 76 B2 31 56N 99 10 E
Manigotagan, Canada 143 C9 51 6N 96 18W
Manigotagan →, Canada 143 C9 51 7N 96 20W
Manihari, India 93 G12 25 21N 87 38 E
Manihiki, Cook Is. 135 J11 10 24 S 161 1W
Maniitsoq, Greenland 10 D5 65 26N 52 55W
Manika, Plateau de la, Dem. Rep. of the Congo 119 E2 10 0 S 25 5 E
Manikganj, Bangla. 90 D3 23 52N 90 0 E
Manikpur, India 93 G9 25 4N 81 7 E
Manila, Phil. 79 B6 14 40N 121 3 E
Manila, U.S.A. 158 F9 40 59N 109 43W
Manila B., Phil. 79 B6 14 40N 120 35 E
Manilla, Australia 129 A9 30 45 S 150 43 E
Manimpé, Mali 112 C3 14 11N 5 28W
Maningrida, Australia 126 A1 12 3 S 134 13 E
Maninian, Ivory C. 112 C3 10 3N 7 52W
Manipur □, India 90 C4 25 0N 94 0 E
Manipur →, Burma 90 D5 23 45N 94 20 E
Manisa, Turkey 49 C9 38 38N 27 30 E
Manisa □, Turkey 49 C9 38 40N 28 0 E
Manistee, U.S.A. 148 C2 44 15N 86 19W
Manistee →, U.S.A. 148 C2 44 15N 86 21W
Manistique, U.S.A. 148 C2 45 57N 86 15W
Manito, U.S.A. 156 D7 40 26N 89 47W
Manito L., Canada 143 C7 52 43N 109 43W
Manitoba □, Canada 143 B9 55 30N 97 0W
Manitoba, L., Canada 143 C9 51 0N 98 45W
Manitou, Canada 143 D9 49 15N 98 32W
Manitou, L., Canada 141 B6 50 55N 65 17W
Manitou Beach, U.S.A. 157 C12 41 58N 84 19W
Manitou Is., U.S.A. 148 C3 45 8N 86 0W
Manitou Springs, U.S.A. 154 F2 38 52N 104 55W
Manitoulin I., Canada 140 C3 45 40N 82 30W
Manitouwadge, Canada 140 C2 49 8N 85 48W
Manitowoc, U.S.A. 148 C2 44 5N 87 40W
Manitsauá-Missu →, Brazil 173 C7 10 58 S 53 20W
Maniyachi, India 95 K3 8 51N 77 55 E
Manizales, Colombia 168 B2 5 5N 75 32W
Manja, Madag. 117 C7 21 26 S 44 20 E
Manjacaze, Mozam. 117 C5 24 45 S 34 0 E
Manjakandriana, Madag. 117 B8 18 55 S 47 47 E
Manjeri, India 95 J3 11 7N 76 11 E
Manjhand, Pakistan 91 D3 25 50N 68 10 E
Manjil, Iran 97 B6 36 46N 49 30 E
Manjimup, Australia 125 F2 34 15 S 116 6 E
Manjlegaon, India 94 E3 19 9N 76 14 E
Manjra →, India 94 E3 18 49N 77 52 E
Mankato, Kans., U.S.A. 154 F5 39 47N 98 13W
Mankato, Minn., U.S.A. 154 C8 44 10N 94 0W
Mankayan, Phil. 80 C3 16 52N 120 47 E
Mankayane, Swaziland 117 D5 26 40 S 31 4 E
Mankera, Pakistan 92 D4 31 23N 71 26 E
Mankim, Cameroon 113 D7 5 6N 12 3 E
Mankim, Cameroon 114 A3 5 6N 12 3 E
Mankono, Ivory C. 112 D3 8 1N 6 10W
Mankota, Canada 143 D7 49 25N 107 5W
Mankulam, Sri Lanka 95 K5 9 8N 80 26 E
Manlay = Üydzin, Mongolia 74 B4 44 9N 107 0 E
Manley Hot Springs, U.S.A. 144 D10 65 0N 150 38W
Manlleu, Spain 40 C7 42 2N 2 17 E
Manly, Australia 129 B9 33 48 S 151 17 E
Manmad, India 94 D2 20 18N 74 28 E
Mann Ranges, Australia 125 E5 26 6 S 130 5 E
Manna, Indonesia 78 E2 4 25 S 102 55 E
Mannahill, Australia 128 B3 32 25 S 140 0 E
Mannar, Sri Lanka 95 K4 9 1N 79 54 E
Mannar, G. of, Asia 95 K4 8 30N 79 0 E
Mannar I., Sri Lanka 95 K4 9 5N 79 45 E
Mannargudi, India 95 J4 10 45N 79 51 E
Männedorf, Switz. 33 B7 47 15N 8 43 E
Mannheim, Germany 31 F4 49 29N 8 29 E
Manning, Canada 142 B5 56 53N 117 39W
Manning, Oreg., U.S.A. 160 E3 45 45N 123 13W
Manning, S.C., U.S.A. 152 B9 33 42N 80 13W
Manning Prov. Park, Canada 142 D4 49 5N 120 45W
Manning Str., Solomon Is. 133 L10 7 30 S 158 0 E
Mannu →, Italy 46 C2 39 16N 9 0 E
Mannu, C., Italy 46 B1 40 3N 8 21 E
Mannum, Australia 128 C3 34 50 S 139 20 E
Mano, S. Leone 112 D2 8 3N 12 2W
Mano →, Liberia 112 D2 6 56N 11 30W
Mano River, Liberia 112 D2 7 20N 11 6W
Manoa, Bolivia 173 B4 9 40 S 65 27W
Manoharpur, India 93 H11 22 23N 85 12 E
Manokotak, U.S.A. 144 G8 58 58N 159 3W
Manokwari, Indonesia 79 E8 0 54 S 134 0 E
Manolás, Greece 48 C3 38 4N 21 21 E
Manolo Fortich, Phil. 81 G5 8 28N 124 50 E
Manombo, Madag. 117 C7 22 57 S 43 28 E
Manono, Dem. Rep. of the Congo 118 D2 7 15 S 27 25 E
Manoppello, Italy 45 F11 42 15N 14 3 E
Manosque, France 29 E9 43 49N 5 47 E
Manotick, Canada 151 A9 45 13N 75 41W
Manouane →, Canada 141 C5 49 30N 71 10W
Manouane, L., Canada 141 B5 50 45N 70 45W
Manouro, Pt., Vanuatu 133 G6 17 41 S 168 36 E
Manp'o, N. Korea 75 D14 41 6N 126 24 E
Manpojin = Manp'o, N. Korea 75 D14 41 6N 126 24 E
Manpur, Mad. P., India 92 H6 22 26N 75 37 E
Manpur, Mad. P., India 93 H10 23 17N 83 35 E
Manpur, Mad. P., India 93 J9 20 22N 80 43 E
Manresa, Spain 40 D6 41 48N 1 50 E
Mansa, Gujarat, India 92 H5 23 27N 72 45 E
Mansa, Punjab, India 92 E6 30 0N 75 27 E
Mansa, Zambia 119 E2 11 13 S 28 55 E
Mansalay, Phil. 80 E3 12 31N 121 26 E
Månsåsen, Sweden 16 A8 63 5N 14 18 E
Mansehra, Pakistan 92 B5 34 20N 73 15 E
Mansel I., Canada 139 B11 62 0N 80 0W
Mansfield, Australia 129 D7 37 4 S 146 6 E
Mansfield, U.K. 20 D6 53 9N 1 11W
Mansfield, Ga., U.S.A. 152 B6 33 31N 83 44W
Mansfield, La., U.S.A. 155 J8 32 2N 93 43W
Mansfield, Mass., U.S.A. 151 D13 42 2N 71 13W
Mansfield, Ohio, U.S.A. 150 F2 40 45N 82 31W
Mansfield, Pa., U.S.A. 150 E7 41 48N 77 5W
Mansfield, Mt., U.S.A. 151 B12 44 33N 72 49W
Mansi, Burma 90 C5 24 48N 95 52 E
Mansidão, Brazil 170 D3 10 43 S 44 2W
Mansilla de las Mulas, Spain 42 C5 42 30N 5 25W
Mansle, France 28 C4 45 52N 0 12 E
Manso →, Brazil 171 D2 13 50 S 47 0W
Mansoa, Guinea-Biss. 112 C1 12 0N 15 20W
Manson, U.S.A. 156 B2 42 32N 94 32W
Manson Creek, Canada 142 B4 55 37N 124 32W
Mansoura, Algeria 111 A5 36 1N 4 31 E
Manta, Ecuador 168 D1 1 0 S 80 40W
Manta, B. de, Ecuador 168 D1 0 54 S 80 44W
Mantalingajan, Mt., Phil. 78 C5 8 55N 117 45 E
Mantantale, Dem. Rep. of the Congo 114 C4 2 10 S 20 11 E
Mantare, Tanzania 118 C3 2 42 S 33 13 E
Mantaro →, Peru 172 C3 12 16 S 73 57W
Manteca, U.S.A. 160 H5 37 48N 121 13W
Mantecal, Venezuela 168 B4 7 34N 69 17W
Mantena, Brazil 171 E3 18 47 S 40 59W
Manteno, U.S.A. 157 C9 41 15N 87 50W
Manteo, U.S.A. 149 H8 35 55N 75 40W
Mantes-la-Jolie, France 27 D8 48 58N 1 41 E
Mantha, India 94 E3 19 40N 76 23 E
Manthani, India 94 E4 18 40N 79 35 E
Manti, U.S.A. 158 G8 39 16N 111 38W
Mantiqueira, Serra da, Brazil 171 F3 22 0 S 44 0W
Manton, U.S.A. 148 C3 44 25N 85 24W
Mantorp, Sweden 17 F9 58 21N 15 20 E
Mántova, Italy 44 C7 45 9N 10 48 E
Mänttä, Finland 15 E21 62 0N 24 40 E
Mantua = Mántova, Italy 44 C7 45 9N 10 48 E
Mantung, Australia 128 C4 34 35 S 140 3 E
Manturovo, Russia 60 A7 58 23N 44 45 E
Manu, Peru 172 C3 12 10 S 70 51W
Manu →, Peru 172 C3 12 16 S 70 55W
Manua Is., Amer. Samoa 133 X25 14 13 S 169 35W
Manuel Alves →, Brazil 171 D2 11 19 S 48 28W
Manuel Alves Grande →, Brazil 170 C2 7 27 S 47 35W
Manuel Urbano, Brazil 172 B4 8 53 S 69 18W
Manui, Indonesia 79 E6 3 35 S 123 5 E
Manukan, Phil. 81 G4 8 32N 123 12 E
Manukau Harbour, N.Z. 130 D3 37 3 S 174 45 E
Manunui, N.Z. 130 E4 38 54 S 175 21 E
Manurewa, N.Z. 130 D3 37 1 S 174 54 E
Manuripi →, Bolivia 172 C4 11 6 S 67 36W
Manus I., Papua N. G. 132 B4 2 0 S 147 0 E
Manvi, India 95 G3 15 57N 76 59 E
Manwath, India 94 E3 19 19N 76 32 E
Many, U.S.A. 155 K8 31 34N 93 29W
Manyara, L., Tanzania 118 C4 3 40 S 35 50 E
Manyas, Turkey 51 F11 40 2N 27 59 E
Manych →, Russia 61 G5 47 13N 40 40 E
Manych-Gudilo, Ozero, Russia 61 G6 46 24N 42 38 E
Manyonga →, Tanzania 118 C3 4 10 S 34 15 E
Manyoni, Tanzania 118 D3 5 45 S 34 55 E
Manzai, Pakistan 91 B3 32 12N 70 15 E
Manzala, Bahra el, Egypt 106 H7 31 10N 31 56 E
Manzanares, Spain 43 F7 39 2N 3 22W
Manzaneda, Spain 42 C3 42 12N 7 15W
Manzanillo, Cuba 164 B4 20 20N 77 31W
Manzanillo, Mexico 162 D4 19 0N 104 20W
Manzanillo, Pta., Panama 164 E4 9 30N 79 40W
Manzano Mts., U.S.A. 159 J10 34 40N 106 20W
Manzarīyeh, Iran 97 C6 34 53N 50 50 E
Manzhouli, China 73 B6 49 35N 117 25 E
Manzini, Swaziland 117 D5 26 30 S 31 25 E
Mao, Chad 109 F3 14 4N 15 19 E
Maó, Spain 39 B11 39 53N 4 16 E
Maoke, Pegunungan, Indonesia 79 E9 3 40 S 137 30 E
Maolin, China 75 C12 43 58N 123 30 E

Masaya 247

Maoming, *China* 77 **G8** 21 50N 110 54 E
Maopi T'ou, *China* 77 **G13** 21 56N 120 43 E
Maouri, Dallol →, *Niger* 113 **C5** 12 5N 3 30 E
Maoxian, *China* 76 **B4** 31 41N 103 49 E
Maoxing, *China* 75 **B13** 45 28N 124 40 E
Mapalma,
Dem. Rep. of the Congo 114 **B4** 2 3N 24 30 E
Mapam Yumco, *China* 72 **C3** 30 45N 81 28 E
Mapastepec, *Mexico* 163 **D6** 15 26N 92 54W
Mapfongui, *Gabon* 114 **C2** 1 15 S 12 59 E
Mapia, Kepulauan, *Indonesia* 79 **D8** 0 50N 134 20 E
Mapimí, *Mexico* 162 **B4** 25 50N 103 50W
Mapimí, Bolsón de, *Mexico* 162 **B4** 27 30N 104 15W
Maping, *China* 77 **B9** 31 34N 113 32 E
Mapinga, *Tanzania* 118 **D4** 6 40 S 39 12 E
Mapinhane, *Mozam.* 117 **C6** 22 20 S 35 0 E
Mapire, *Venezuela* 169 **B5** 7 45N 64 42W
Maple →, *U.S.A.* 157 **B12** 42 59N 84 57W
Maple Creek, *Canada* 143 **D7** 49 55N 109 29W
Maple Valley, *U.S.A.* 160 **C4** 47 25N 122 3W
Mapleton, *U.S.A.* 158 **D2** 44 2N 123 52W
Mapourika, L., *N.Z.* 131 **D5** 43 16 S 170 12 E
Maprik, *Papua N. G.* 132 **B2** 3 44 S 143 3 E
Mapuca, *India* 95 **G1** 15 36N 73 46 E
Mapuera →, *Brazil* 169 **D6** 1 5 S 57 2W
Mapulanguene, *Mozam.* 117 **C5** 24 29 S 32 6 E
Maputo, *Mozam.* 117 **D5** 25 58 S 32 32 E
Maputo □, *Mozam.* 117 **D5** 26 0 S 32 25 E
Maputo, B. de, *Mozam.* 117 **D5** 25 50 S 32 45 E
Maqiaohe, *China* 75 **B16** 44 40N 130 30 E
Maqnā, *Si. Arabia* 96 **D2** 28 25N 34 50 E
Maqran, W. →, *Si. Arabia* 98 **B4** 20 55N 47 12 E
Maqteïr, *Mauritania* 110 **D2** 21 50N 11 40W
Maqueda, *Spain* 42 **E6** 40 4N 4 22W
Maqueda Channel, *Phil.* 80 **E5** 13 42N 124 1 E
Maquela do Zombo, *Angola* 115 **D3** 6 0 S 15 15 E
Maquinchao, *Argentina* 176 **B3** 41 15 S 68 50W
Maquoketa, *U.S.A.* 156 **B6** 42 4N 90 40W
Mar, Serra do, *Brazil* 175 **B6** 25 30 S 49 0W
Mar Chiquita, L., *Argentina* 174 **C3** 30 40 S 62 50W
Mar del Plata, *Argentina* 174 **D4** 38 0 S 57 30W
Mar Menor, *Spain* 41 **H4** 37 40N 0 45W
Mara, *Guyana* 169 **B6** 6 0N 57 36W
Mara, *India* 90 **A5** 28 11N 94 14 E
Mara, *Tanzania* 118 **C3** 1 30 S 34 32 E
Mara □, *Tanzania* 118 **C3** 1 45 S 34 20 E
Maraã, *Brazil* 168 **D4** 1 52 S 65 25W
Marabá, *Brazil* 170 **C2** 5 20 S 49 5W
Maracá, I. de, *Brazil* 169 **C7** 2 10N 50 30W
Maracaibo, *Venezuela* 168 **A3** 10 40N 71 37W
Maracaibo, L. de, *Venezuela* 168 **B3** 9 40N 71 30W
Maracaju, *Brazil* 175 **A4** 21 38 S 55 9W
Maracajú, Serra de, *Brazil* 173 **E6** 23 57 S 55 1W
Maracanã, *Brazil* 170 **B2** 0 46 S 47 27W
Maracás, *Brazil* 171 **D3** 13 26 S 40 18W
Maracay, *Venezuela* 168 **A4** 10 15N 67 28W
Maracena, *Spain* 43 **H7** 37 12N 3 38W
Marādah, *Libya* 108 **C3** 29 15N 19 15 E
Maradi, *Niger* 113 **C6** 13 29N 7 20 E
Marāgheh, *Iran* 101 **D12** 37 30N 46 12 E
Maragogipe, *Brazil* 171 **D4** 12 46 S 38 55W
Marāh, *Si. Arabia* 96 **E5** 25 0N 45 35 E
Marajó, B. de, *Brazil* 170 **B2** 1 0 S 48 30W
Marajó, I. de, *Brazil* 170 **B1** 1 0 S 49 30W
Marākand, *Iran* 96 **B5** 38 51N 45 16 E
Maralal, *Kenya* 118 **B4** 1 0N 36 38 E
Maralinga, *Australia* 125 **F5** 30 13 S 131 32 E
Marama, *Australia* 128 **C4** 35 10 S 140 10 E
Maramag, *Phil.* 81 **H5** 7 46N 125 0 E
Maramaraereğlisi, *Turkey* 51 **F11** 40 57N 27 57 E
Maramasike, *Solomon Is.* 133 **M11** 9 30 S 161 25 E
Marampa, *S. Leone* 112 **D2** 8 45N 12 28W
Maramureş □, *Romania* 53 **C9** 47 45N 24 0 E
Maran, *Malaysia* 87 **L4** 3 35N 102 45 E
Marana, *U.S.A.* 159 **K8** 32 27N 111 13W
Maranboy, *Australia* 124 **B5** 14 40 S 132 39 E
Maranchón, *Spain* 40 **D2** 41 6N 2 15W
Marand, *Iran* 101 **C11** 38 30N 45 45 E
Marang, *Malaysia* 87 **K4** 5 12N 103 13 E
Maranguape, *Brazil* 170 **B4** 3 55 S 38 50W
Maranhão = São Luís, *Brazil* 170 **B3** 2 39 S 44 15W
Maranhão □, *Brazil* 170 **B2** 5 0 S 46 0W
Marano, L. di, *Italy* 45 **C10** 45 44N 13 10 E
Maranoa →, *Australia* 127 **D4** 27 50 S 148 37 E
Marañón →, *Peru* 172 **A3** 4 30 S 73 35W
Marão, *Mozam.* 117 **C5** 24 18 S 34 2 E
Marapi →, *Brazil* 169 **C6** 0 37N 55 58W
Marari, *Brazil* 172 **B4** 5 43 S 67 47W
Maraş = Kahramanmaraş,
Turkey 100 **D7** 37 37N 36 53 E
Mărăşeşti, *Romania* 53 **E12** 45 52N 27 14 E
Maratea, *Italy* 47 **C8** 39 59N 15 43 E
Marateca, *Portugal* 43 **G2** 38 34N 8 40W
Marathasa □, *Cyprus* 38 **E11** 34 59N 32 51 E
Marathókambos, *Greece* 49 **D8** 37 43N 26 42 E
Marathon, *Australia* 126 **C3** 20 51 S 143 32 E
Marathon, *Canada* 140 **C2** 48 44N 86 23W
Marathón, *Greece* 48 **C5** 38 11N 23 58 E
Marathon, *Fla., U.S.A.* 153 **L8** 24 43N 81 5W
Marathon, *N.Y., U.S.A.* 151 **D8** 42 27N 76 2W
Marathon, *Tex., U.S.A.* 155 **K3** 30 12N 103 15W
Marathóvouno, *Cyprus* 38 **D12** 35 13N 33 37 E
Maratua, *Indonesia* 79 **D5** 2 10N 118 35 E
Maraú, *Brazil* 171 **D4** 14 6 S 39 0W
Maravatío, *Mexico* 162 **D4** 19 51N 100 25W
Marawi City, *Phil.* 81 **G5** 8 0N 124 21 E
Marāwih, *U.A.E.* 97 **E7** 24 18N 53 18 E
Marbach, *Switz.* 32 **C5** 46 51N 7 53 E
Marbella, *Spain* 43 **J6** 36 30N 4 57W
Marble Bar, *Australia* 124 **D2** 21 9 S 119 44 E
Marble Falls, *U.S.A.* 155 **K5** 30 35N 98 16W
Marblehead, *U.S.A.* 151 **D14** 42 30N 70 51W
Mårbu, *Norway* 18 **D5** 60 11N 8 9 E
Marburg, *Germany* 30 **E4** 50 47N 8 46 E
Marcal →, *Hungary* 52 **C2** 47 41N 17 40 E
Marcali, *Hungary* 52 **D2** 46 35N 17 25 E
Marcapata, *Peru* 172 **C3** 13 31 S 70 52W
Marcaria, *Italy* 44 **C7** 45 7N 10 32 E
Mărcăuţi, *Moldova* 53 **B12** 48 20N 27 14 E
Marceline, *U.S.A.* 156 **E4** 39 43N 92 57W
March, *U.K.* 21 **E8** 52 33N 0 5 E
Marchal,
Dem. Rep. of the Congo 115 **D2** 5 16 S 14 58 E
Marchand = Rommani,
Morocco 110 **B3** 33 31N 6 40W
Marche, *France* 28 **B5** 46 5N 1 20 E
Marche □, *Italy* 45 **E10** 43 30N 13 15 E
Marche-en-Famenne, *Belgium* 24 **D5** 50 14N 5 19 E
Marchena, *Spain* 43 **H5** 37 18N 5 23W
Marches = Marche □, *Italy* 45 **E10** 43 30N 13 15 E
Marciana Marina, *Italy* 44 **F7** 42 48N 10 12 E
Marcianise, *Italy* 47 **A7** 41 2N 14 17 E
Marcigny, *France* 27 **F11** 46 17N 4 2 E
Marcillat-en-Combraille, *France* 27 **F9** 46 12N 2 38 E
Marck, *France* 27 **B8** 50 57N 1 57 E
Marckolsheim, *France* 27 **D14** 48 10N 7 30 E
Marco, *U.S.A.* 153 **K8** 25 58N 81 44W
Marco Rondon, *Brazil* 173 **C5** 12 0 S 60 56W
Marcona, *Peru* 172 **D2** 15 10 S 75 0W
Marcos Juárez, *Argentina* 174 **C3** 32 42 S 62 5W
Mărculeşti, *Moldova* 53 **C13** 47 52N 28 14 E
Marcus Baker, Mt., *U.S.A.* 144 **F11** 61 26N 147 45W
Marcus I. = Minami-Tori-
Shima, *Pac. Oc.* 134 **E7** 24 20N 153 58 E
Marcus Necker Ridge, *Pac. Oc.* 134 **F9** 20 0N 175 0 E
Marcy, Mt., *U.S.A.* 151 **B11** 44 7N 73 56W
Mardan, *Pakistan* 91 **B4** 34 20N 72 0 E
Mardin, *Turkey* 101 **D9** 37 20N 40 43 E
Mårdsjön, *Sweden* 16 **A9** 63 18N 15 35 E
Maré, I., *N. Cal.* 133 **U22** 21 30 S 168 0 E
Marécchia →, *Italy* 45 **D9** 44 4N 12 34 E
Marechal Deodoro, *Brazil* 170 **C4** 9 43 S 35 54W
Maree, L., *U.K.* 22 **D3** 57 40N 5 26W
Mareeba, *Australia* 126 **B4** 16 59 S 145 28 E
Mareetsane, *S. Africa* 116 **D4** 26 9 S 25 25 E
Marek, *Indonesia* 82 **B2** 4 41 S 120 24 E
Maremma, *Italy* 45 **F8** 42 30N 11 30 E
Maréna, *Mali* 112 **C2** 14 36N 10 45W
Maréna, *Mali* 112 **C3** 13 55N 7 20W
Marengo, *Ind., U.S.A.* 157 **F10** 38 22N 86 21W
Marengo, *Iowa, U.S.A.* 156 **C4** 41 48N 92 4W
Marennes, *France* 28 **C2** 45 49N 1 7W
Marenyi, *Kenya* 118 **C4** 4 22 S 39 8 E
Marerano, *Madag.* 117 **C7** 21 23 S 44 52 E
Marèttimo, *Italy* 46 **E5** 37 58N 12 4 E
Mareuil, *France* 28 **C4** 45 26N 0 29 E
Marfa, *U.S.A.* 155 **K2** 30 19N 104 1W
Marfa Pt., *Malta* 38 **D1** 35 59N 14 19 E
Marganets = Marhanets,
Ukraine 59 **J8** 47 40N 34 40 E
Margaret →, *Australia* 124 **C4** 18 9 S 125 41 E
Margaret Bay, *Canada* 142 **C3** 51 20N 127 35W
Margaret L., *Canada* 142 **B5** 58 56N 115 25W
Margaret River, *Australia* 125 **F2** 33 57 S 115 4 E
Margarita, I. de, *Venezuela* 169 **A5** 11 0N 64 0W
Margarítion, *Greece* 48 **B2** 39 22N 20 26 E
Margaritovo, *Russia* 68 **C7** 43 25N 134 45 E
Margate, *S. Africa* 117 **E5** 30 50 S 30 20 E
Margate, *U.K.* 21 **F9** 51 23N 1 23 E
Margate, *U.S.A.* 153 **J9** 26 15N 80 12W
Margelan = Marghilon,
Uzbekistan 63 **C5** 40 27N 71 42 E
Margeride, Mts. de la, *France* 28 **D7** 44 43N 3 38 E
Margherita, *India* 90 **B5** 27 16N 95 40 E
Margherita di Savóia, *Italy* 47 **A9** 41 22N 16 9 E
Marghilon, *Uzbekistan* 63 **C5** 40 27N 71 42 E
Marghita, *Romania* 52 **C7** 47 22N 22 22 E
Margonin, *Poland* 55 **F4** 52 58N 17 5 E
Margosatubig, *Phil.* 81 **H4** 7 34N 123 10 E
Marguerite, *Canada* 142 **C4** 52 30N 122 25W
Marhanets, *Ukraine* 59 **J8** 47 40N 34 40 E
Marhoum, *Algeria* 111 **B4** 34 27N 0 11W
Mari El □, *Russia* 60 **B8** 56 30N 48 0 E
Mari Indus, *Pakistan* 92 **C4** 32 57N 71 34 E
Mari Republic = Mari El □,
Russia 60 **B8** 56 30N 48 0 E
María, Sa. de, *Spain* 41 **H2** 37 39N 2 14W
Maria Aurora, *Phil.* 80 **D3** 15 48N 121 28 E
María Elena, *Chile* 174 **A2** 22 18 S 69 40W
María Grande, *Argentina* 174 **C4** 31 45 S 59 55W
Maria I., *N. Terr., Australia* 126 **A2** 14 52 S 135 45 E
Maria I., *Tas., Australia* 126 **G4** 42 35 S 148 0 E
Maria van Diemen, C., *N.Z.* 130 **A1** 34 29 S 172 40 E
Mariager, *Denmark* 17 **H3** 56 40N 9 59 E
Mariager Fjord, *Denmark* 17 **H4** 56 42N 10 19 E
Mariakani, *Kenya* 118 **C4** 3 50 S 39 27 E
Marian, *Australia* 126 **C4** 21 9 S 148 57 E
Marian L., *Canada* 142 **A5** 63 0N 116 15W
Mariana Trench, *Pac. Oc.* 66 **H18** 13 0N 145 0 E
Marianao, *Cuba* 164 **B3** 23 8N 82 24W
Mariani, *India* 90 **B5** 26 39N 94 19 E
Marianna, *Ark., U.S.A.* 155 **H9** 34 46N 90 46W
Marianna, *Fla., U.S.A.* 152 **E4** 30 46N 85 14W
Mariannelund, *Sweden* 17 **G9** 57 37N 15 35 E
Mariánské Lázně, *Czech Rep.* 34 **B5** 49 58N 12 41 E
Marias →, *U.S.A.* 158 **C8** 47 56N 110 30W
Mariato, Punta, *Panama* 164 **E3** 7 12N 80 52W
Mariazell, *Austria* 34 **D8** 47 47N 15 19 E
Ma'rib, *Yemen* 98 **D4** 15 25N 45 21 E
Maribo, *Denmark* 17 **K5** 54 48N 11 30 E
Maribor, *Slovenia* 45 **B12** 46 36N 15 40 E
Maricaban I., *Phil.* 80 **E3** 13 39N 120 53 E
Marico →, *Africa* 116 **C4** 23 35 S 26 57 E
Maricopa, *Ariz., U.S.A.* 159 **K7** 33 4N 112 3W
Maricopa, *Calif., U.S.A.* 161 **K7** 35 4N 119 24W
Marīdī, *Sudan* 107 **G2** 4 55N 29 25 E
Maridi, Wadi →, *Sudan* 107 **F2** 6 15N 29 21 E
Marié →, *Brazil* 168 **D4** 0 27 S 66 26W
Marie Byrd Land, *Antarctica* 7 **D14** 79 30 S 125 0W
Marie-Galante, *Guadeloupe* 165 **C7** 15 56N 61 16W
Mariecourt = Kangiqsujuaq,
Canada 139 **B12** 61 30N 72 0W
Mariefred, *Sweden* 16 **E11** 59 15N 17 12 E
Marieholm, *Sweden* 17 **J7** 55 53N 13 10 E
Mariembourg, *Belgium* 24 **D4** 50 6N 4 31 E
Marienbad = Mariánské Lázně,
Czech Rep. 34 **B5** 49 58N 12 41 E
Marienberg, *Germany* 30 **E9** 50 39N 13 9 E
Mariental, *Namibia* 116 **C2** 24 36 S 18 0 E
Marienville, *U.S.A.* 150 **E5** 41 28N 79 8W
Mariestad, *Sweden* 17 **F7** 58 43N 13 50 E
Marietta, *Ga., U.S.A.* 152 **B5** 33 57N 84 33W
Marietta, *Ohio, U.S.A.* 148 **F5** 39 25N 81 27W
Marieville, *Canada* 151 **A11** 45 26N 73 10W
Mariga →, *Nigeria* 113 **C6** 9 40N 5 55 E
Marignane, *France* 29 **E9** 43 25N 5 13 E
Marignier, *France* 32 **D3** 46 6N 6 31 E
Marihatag, *Phil.* 81 **G6** 8 48N 126 18 E
Mariinsk, *Russia* 64 **D9** 56 10N 87 20 E
Mariinskiy Posad, *Russia* 60 **B8** 56 10N 47 45 E
Marijampolė, *Lithuania* 15 **J20** 54 33N 23 19 E
Marijampolės □, *Lithuania* 54 **D10** 54 34N 23 21 E
Marília, *Brazil* 175 **A6** 22 13 S 50 0W
Marimba, *Angola* 115 **D3** 8 28 S 17 8 E
Marín, *Spain* 42 **C2** 42 23N 8 42W
Marina, *U.S.A.* 160 **J5** 36 41N 121 48W
Marinduque, *Phil.* 79 **B6** 13 25N 122 0 E
Marinduque □, *Phil.* 80 **E4** 13 18N 122 0 E
Marine City, *U.S.A.* 150 **D2** 42 43N 82 30W
Marineland, *U.S.A.* 152 **F8** 29 40N 81 13W
Marineo, *Italy* 46 **E6** 37 57N 13 25 E
Marinette, *U.S.A.* 148 **C2** 45 6N 87 38W
Maringá, *Brazil* 175 **A5** 23 26 S 52 2W
Maringa →,
Dem. Rep. of the Congo 114 **B3** 1 14N 19 48 E
Marinha Grande, *Portugal* 42 **F2** 39 45N 8 56W
Marino, *Italy* 45 **G9** 41 46N 12 39 E
Marion, *Ala., U.S.A.* 149 **J2** 32 38N 87 19W
Marion, *Ill., U.S.A.* 155 **G10** 37 44N 88 56W
Marion, *Ind., U.S.A.* 157 **D11** 40 32N 85 40W
Marion, *Iowa, U.S.A.* 156 **B5** 42 2N 91 36W
Marion, *Kans., U.S.A.* 154 **F6** 38 21N 97 1W
Marion, *N.C., U.S.A.* 149 **H5** 35 41N 82 1W
Marion, *Ohio, U.S.A.* 157 **D13** 40 35N 83 8W
Marion, *S.C., U.S.A.* 149 **H6** 34 11N 79 24W
Marion, *Va., U.S.A.* 149 **G5** 36 50N 81 31W
Marion, L., *U.S.A.* 152 **B9** 33 28N 80 10W
Marion Bay, *Australia* 128 **C2** 35 12 S 136 59 E
Marion I., *Ind. Oc.* 121 **J2** 47 0 S 38 0 E
Maripa, *Venezuela* 169 **B4** 7 26N 65 9W
Maripasoula, *Fr. Guiana* 169 **C7** 3 40N 54 4W
Mariposa, *U.S.A.* 160 **H7** 37 29N 119 58W
Mariscal Estigarribia, *Paraguay* 174 **A3** 22 3 S 60 40W
Maritime Alps = Maritimes,
Alpes, *Europe* 29 **D11** 44 10N 7 10 E
Maritimes, Alpes, *Europe* 29 **D11** 44 10N 7 10 E
Maritsa = Évros →, *Bulgaria* 100 **B2** 41 40N 26 34 E
Maritsá, *Greece* 38 **C10** 36 22N 28 8 E
Mariupol, *Ukraine* 59 **J9** 47 5N 37 31 E
Marīvān, *Iran* 101 **E12** 35 30N 46 25 E
Mariveles, *Phil.* 80 **D3** 14 26N 120 29 E
Marj 'Uyūn, *Lebanon* 103 **B4** 33 20N 35 35 E
Mark Twain L., *U.S.A.* 156 **E5** 39 28N 91 55W
Marka, *Si. Arabia* 106 **D5** 18 14N 41 19 E
Markah, W. →, *Yemen* 98 **D4** 14 59N 46 36 E
Markam, *China* 76 **C2** 29 42N 98 38 E
Markapur, *India* 95 **G4** 15 44N 79 19 E
Markaryd, *Sweden* 17 **H7** 56 28N 13 35 E
Markazī □, *Iran* 97 **C6** 35 0N 49 30 E
Markdale, *Canada* 150 **B4** 44 19N 80 39W
Marked Tree, *U.S.A.* 155 **H9** 35 32N 90 25W
Markelsdorfer Huk, *Germany* 30 **A7** 54 33N 11 4 E
Market Drayton, *U.K.* 20 **E5** 52 54N 2 29W
Market Harborough, *U.K.* 21 **E7** 52 29N 0 55W
Market Rasen, *U.K.* 20 **D7** 53 24N 0 20W
Markham, *Canada* 150 **C5** 43 52N 79 16W
Markham →, *Papua N. G.* 132 **D4** 6 41 S 147 2 E
Markham, Mt., *Antarctica* 7 **E11** 83 0 S 164 0 E
Marki, *Poland* 55 **F8** 52 20N 21 2 E
Markkleeberg, *Germany* 30 **D8** 51 16N 12 23 E
Markleeville, *U.S.A.* 160 **G7** 38 42N 119 47W
Markounda, *C.A.R.* 114 **A3** 7 39N 16 55 E
Markoupoulon, *Greece* 48 **D5** 37 53N 23 57 E
Markovac, *Serbia, Yug.* 50 **B5** 44 14N 21 7 E
Markovo, *Russia* 65 **C17** 64 40N 170 24 E
Markoye, *Burkina Faso* 113 **C5** 14 39N 0 2 E
Marks, *Russia* 60 **E8** 51 45N 46 50 E
Marksville, *U.S.A.* 155 **K8** 31 8N 92 4W
Markt Schwaben, *Germany* 31 **G7** 48 11N 11 52 E
Marktoberdorf, *Germany* 31 **H6** 47 45N 10 37 E
Marktredwitz, *Germany* 31 **E8** 50 1N 12 6 E
Marl, *Germany* 30 **D3** 51 39N 7 4 E
Marla, *Australia* 127 **D1** 27 19 S 133 33 E
Marlbank, *Canada* 150 **B7** 44 26N 77 6W
Marlboro, *Mass., U.S.A.* 151 **D13** 42 19N 71 33W
Marlboro, *N.Y., U.S.A.* 151 **E11** 41 36N 73 59W
Marlborough, *Australia* 126 **C4** 22 46 S 149 52 E
Marlborough, *U.K.* 21 **F6** 51 25N 1 43W
Marlborough Downs, *U.K.* 21 **F6** 51 27N 1 53W
Marle, *France* 27 **C10** 49 43N 3 47 E
Marlin, *U.S.A.* 155 **K6** 31 18N 96 54W
Marlow, *Germany* 30 **A8** 54 9N 12 33 E
Marlow, *U.S.A.* 155 **H6** 34 39N 97 58W
Marly, *Switz.* 32 **C4** 46 47N 7 10 E
Marmagao, *India* 95 **G1** 15 25N 73 56 E
Marmande, *France* 28 **D4** 44 30N 0 10 E
Marmara, *Turkey* 51 **F11** 40 35N 27 34 E
Marmara, Sea of = Marmara
Denizi, *Turkey* 51 **F12** 40 45N 28 15 E
Marmara Denizi, *Turkey* 51 **F12** 40 45N 28 15 E
Marmara Gölü, *Turkey* 49 **C10** 38 37N 28 2 E
Marmaris, *Turkey* 49 **E10** 36 50N 28 14 E
Marmaris Limanı, *Turkey* 49 **E10** 36 50N 28 19 E
Marmelos →, *Brazil* 173 **B5** 6 6 S 61 46W
Marmion, Mt., *Australia* 125 **E2** 29 16 S 119 50 E
Marmion L., *Canada* 140 **C1** 48 55N 91 20W
Marmolada, Mte., *Italy* 45 **B8** 46 26N 11 51 E
Marmolejo, *Spain* 43 **G6** 38 3N 4 13W
Marmora, *Canada* 140 **D4** 44 28N 77 41W
Mármora, La, *Italy* 46 **C2** 39 59N 9 20 E
Marnay, *France* 27 **E12** 47 16N 5 48 E
Marne, *Germany* 30 **B5** 53 56N 9 2 E
Marne □, *France* 27 **D11** 48 50N 4 10 E
Marne →, *France* 27 **D9** 48 48N 2 24 E
Marneuli, *Georgia* 61 **K7** 41 30N 44 48 E
Maro, *Chad* 109 **G3** 8 30N 19 0 E
Maro Reef, *U.S.A.* 145 **F9** 25 25N 170 35W
Maroa, *U.S.A.* 156 **D8** 40 2N 88 57W
Maroa, *Venezuela* 168 **C4** 2 43N 67 33W
Maroala, *Madag.* 117 **B8** 15 23 S 47 59 E
Maroantsetra, *Madag.* 117 **B8** 15 26 S 49 44 E
Maroelaboom, *Namibia* 116 **B2** 19 15 S 18 53 E
Marofandilia, *Madag.* 117 **C7** 20 7 S 44 34 E
Marolambo, *Madag.* 117 **C8** 20 2 S 48 7 E
Maromandia, *Madag.* 117 **A8** 14 13 S 48 5 E
Marondera, *Zimbabwe* 119 **F3** 18 5 S 31 42 E
Maroni →, *Fr. Guiana* 169 **B7** 5 30N 54 0W
Marónia, *Greece* 51 **F9** 40 53N 25 30 E
Maronne →, *France* 28 **C5** 45 5N 1 56 E
Maroochydore, *Australia* 127 **D5** 26 29 S 153 5 E
Maroona, *Australia* 128 **D5** 37 27 S 142 54 E
Maros, *Indonesia* 82 **C1** 5 0 S 119 34 E
Maros →, *Hungary* 52 **D5** 46 15N 20 13 E
Marosakoa, *Madag.* 117 **B8** 15 26 S 46 38 E
Maroseranana, *Madag.* 117 **B8** 18 32 S 48 51 E
Maróstica, *Italy* 45 **C8** 45 44N 11 39 E
Marotandrano, *Madag.* 117 **B8** 16 10 S 48 50 E
Marotaolano, *Madag.* 117 **A8** 12 47 S 49 15 E
Maroua, *Cameroon* 113 **C7** 10 40N 14 20 E
Marovato, *Madag.* 117 **B8** 15 48 S 48 5 E
Marovoay, *Madag.* 117 **B8** 16 6 S 46 39 E
Marowijne □, *Surinam* 169 **C7** 4 0N 55 0W
Marowijne →, *Surinam* 169 **B7** 5 45N 53 58W
Marquard, *S. Africa* 116 **D4** 28 40 S 27 28 E
Marquesas Is. = Marquises, Is.,
Pac. Oc. 135 **H14** 9 30 S 140 0W
Marquesas Keys, *U.S.A.* 153 **L7** 24 35N 82 10W
Marquette, *U.S.A.* 148 **B2** 46 33N 87 24W
Marquise, *France* 27 **B8** 50 50N 1 40 E
Marquises, Is., *Pac. Oc.* 135 **H14** 9 30 S 140 0W
Marra, Gebel, *Sudan* 107 **F2** 7 20N 27 35 E
Marra, Pta. da, *Angola* 115 **F2** 16 31 S 11 43 E
Marracuene, *Mozam.* 117 **D5** 25 45 S 32 35 E
Marradi, *Italy* 45 **D8** 44 4N 11 37 E
Marrakech, *Morocco* 110 **B3** 31 9N 8 0W
Marratxi, *Spain* 40 **F7** 39 39N 2 48 E
Marrawah, *Australia* 126 **G3** 40 55 S 144 42 E
Marrecas, Serra das, *Brazil* 170 **C3** 9 0 S 41 0W
Marree, *Australia* 127 **D2** 29 39 S 138 1 E
Marrero, *U.S.A.* 155 **L9** 29 54N 90 6W
Marrimane, *Mozam.* 117 **C5** 22 58 S 33 34 E
Marromeu, *Mozam.* 117 **B6** 18 15 S 36 25 E
Marroquí, Punta, *Spain* 43 **K5** 36 0N 5 37W
Marrowie Cr. →, *Australia* 129 **B6** 33 23 S 145 40 E
Marrubane, *Mozam.* 119 **F4** 18 0 S 37 0 E
Marrúbiu, *Italy* 46 **C1** 39 45N 8 35 E
Marrupa, *Mozam.* 119 **E4** 13 8 S 37 30 E
Mars Hill, *U.S.A.* 149 **B12** 46 31N 67 52W
Marsá 'Alam, *Egypt* 106 **B3** 25 5N 34 54 E
Marsá el Brega, *Libya* 108 **B3** 30 24N 19 37 E
Marsá Matrûh, *Egypt* 106 **A2** 31 19N 27 9 E
Marsá Sha'b, *Sudan* 106 **C4** 22 52N 35 47 E
Marsá Susah, *Libya* 108 **B4** 32 52N 21 59 E
Marsabit, *Kenya* 118 **B4** 2 18N 38 0 E
Marsala, *Italy* 46 **E5** 37 48N 12 26 E
Marsalforn, *Malta* 38 **C1** 36 4N 14 15 E
Mârşani, *Romania* 53 **F9** 44 1N 24 1 E
Marsberg, *Germany* 30 **D4** 51 28N 8 52 E
Marsciano, *Italy* 45 **F9** 42 54N 12 20 E
Marsden, *Australia* 129 **B7** 33 47 S 147 32 E
Marseillan, *France* 28 **E7** 43 23N 3 31 E
Marseille, *France* 29 **E9** 43 18N 5 23 E
Marseilles = Marseille, *France* 29 **E9** 43 18N 5 23 E
Marseilles, *U.S.A.* 157 **C8** 41 20N 88 43W
Marsh I., *U.S.A.* 155 **L9** 29 34N 91 53W
Marshall, *Liberia* 112 **D2** 6 8N 10 22W
Marshall, *Ark., U.S.A.* 155 **H8** 35 55N 92 38W
Marshall, *Ill., U.S.A.* 157 **E9** 39 23N 87 42W
Marshall, *Mich., U.S.A.* 157 **B12** 42 16N 84 58W
Marshall, *Minn., U.S.A.* 154 **C7** 44 25N 95 45W
Marshall, *Mo., U.S.A.* 156 **E3** 39 7N 93 12W
Marshall, *Tex., U.S.A.* 155 **J7** 32 33N 94 23W
Marshall →, *Australia* 126 **C2** 22 59 S 136 59 E
Marshall Is. ■, *Pac. Oc.* 134 **G9** 9 0N 171 0 E
Marshalltown, *U.S.A.* 156 **B4** 42 3N 92 55W
Marshallville, *U.S.A.* 152 **C6** 32 27N 83 56W
Marshbrook, *Zimbabwe* 117 **B5** 18 33 S 31 9 E
Marshfield, *Mo., U.S.A.* 155 **G8** 37 15N 92 54W
Marshfield, *Vt., U.S.A.* 151 **B12** 44 20N 72 20W
Marshfield, *Wis., U.S.A.* 154 **C9** 44 40N 90 10W
Marshūn, *Iran* 97 **B6** 36 19N 49 23 E
Mársico Nuovo, *Italy* 47 **B8** 40 25N 15 44 E
Märsta, *Sweden* 16 **E11** 59 37N 17 52 E
Marstal, *Denmark* 17 **K4** 54 51N 10 30 E
Marstrand, *Sweden* 17 **G5** 57 53N 11 35 E
Mart, *U.S.A.* 155 **K6** 31 33N 96 50W
Marta →, *Italy* 45 **F8** 42 14N 11 42 E
Martaban, *Burma* 90 **G6** 16 30N 97 35 E
Martaban, G. of, *Burma* 90 **G6** 16 5N 96 30 E
Martano, *Italy* 47 **B11** 40 12N 18 18 E
Martapura, *Kalimantan,*
Indonesia 78 **E4** 3 22 S 114 47 E
Martapura, *Sumatera, Indonesia* 78 **E2** 4 19 S 104 22 E
Marte, *Nigeria* 113 **C7** 12 23N 13 46 E
Martel, *France* 28 **D5** 44 57N 1 37 E
Martelange, *Belgium* 24 **E5** 49 49N 5 43 E
Martellago, *Italy* 45 **C9** 45 33N 12 9 E
Martés, Sierra, *Spain* 41 **F4** 39 20N 1 0W
Martfű, *Hungary* 52 **C5** 47 1N 20 17 E
Marthapal, *India* 94 **E5** 19 24N 81 37 E
Martha's Vineyard, *U.S.A.* 151 **E14** 41 25N 70 38W
Martigné-Ferchaud, *France* 26 **E5** 47 50N 1 20W
Martigny, *Switz.* 32 **D4** 46 6N 7 3 E
Martigues, *France* 29 **E9** 43 24N 5 4 E
Martil, *Morocco* 110 **A3** 35 36N 5 15W
Martin, *Slovak Rep.* 35 **B11** 49 6N 18 58 E
Martin, *S. Dak., U.S.A.* 154 **D4** 43 11N 101 44W
Martin, *Tenn., U.S.A.* 155 **G10** 36 21N 88 51W
Martín →, *Spain* 40 **D4** 41 18N 0 19W
Martin, L., *U.S.A.* 152 **C4** 32 41N 85 55W
Martin Pt., *U.S.A.* 144 **A12** 70 8N 143 16W
Martina, *Switz.* 33 **C10** 46 53N 10 28 E
Martina Franca, *Italy* 47 **B10** 40 42N 17 20 E
Martinborough, *N.Z.* 130 **H4** 41 14 S 175 29 E
Martinez, *Calif., U.S.A.* 160 **G4** 38 1N 122 8W
Martinez, *Ga., U.S.A.* 149 **J4** 33 31N 82 4W
Martinho Campos, *Brazil* 171 **E2** 19 20 S 45 13W
Martinique ■, *W. Indies* 165 **D7** 14 40N 61 0W
Martinique Passage, *W. Indies* 165 **C7** 15 15N 61 0W
Martínon, *Greece* 48 **C5** 38 35N 23 12 E
Martinópolis, *Brazil* 175 **A5** 22 11 S 51 12W
Martins Ferry, *U.S.A.* 150 **F4** 40 6N 80 44W
Martinsberg, *Austria* 34 **C8** 48 22N 15 9 E
Martinsburg, *Pa., U.S.A.* 150 **F6** 40 19N 78 20W
Martinsburg, *W. Va., U.S.A.* 148 **F7** 39 27N 77 58W
Martinsicuro, *Italy* 45 **F10** 42 54N 13 54 E
Martinsville, *Ill., U.S.A.* 157 **E9** 39 20N 87 53W
Martinsville, *Ind., U.S.A.* 157 **E10** 39 26N 86 25W
Martinsville, *Va., U.S.A.* 149 **G6** 36 41N 79 52W
Marton, *N.Z.* 130 **G4** 40 4 S 175 23 E
Martorell, *Spain* 40 **D6** 41 28N 1 56 E
Martos, *Spain* 43 **H7** 37 44N 3 58W
Martūbah, *Libya* 108 **B4** 32 35N 22 46 E
Martuk, *Kazakstan* 62 **F6** 50 46N 56 31 E
Martuni, *Armenia* 61 **K7** 40 9N 45 20 E
Maru, *Nigeria* 113 **C6** 12 22N 6 22 E
Marudi, *Malaysia* 78 **D4** 4 11N 114 19 E
Ma'ruf, *Afghan.* 91 **C2** 31 30N 67 6 E
Marugame, *Japan* 70 **C5** 34 15N 133 40 E
Marui, *Papua N. G.* 132 **C2** 4 4 S 143 2 E
Maruia →, *N.Z.* 131 **B7** 41 47 S 172 13 E
Maruim, *Brazil* 170 **D4** 10 45 S 37 5W
Marulan, *Australia* 129 **C9** 34 43 S 150 3 E
Marum, Mt., *Vanuatu* 133 **F6** 16 15 S 168 7 E
Marunga, *Angola* 116 **B3** 17 28 S 20 2 E
Marungu, Mts.,
Dem. Rep. of the Congo 118 **D3** 7 30 S 30 0 E
Maruoka, *Japan* 71 **A8** 36 9N 136 16 E
Marv Dasht, *Iran* 97 **D7** 29 50N 52 40 E
Marvast, *Iran* 97 **D7** 30 30N 54 15 E
Marvejols, *France* 28 **D7** 44 33N 3 19 E
Marvel Loch, *Australia* 125 **F2** 31 28 S 119 29 E
Marwar, *India* 92 **G5** 25 43N 73 45 E
Mary, *Turkmenistan* 64 **F7** 37 40N 61 50 E
Maryborough = Port Laoise,
Ireland 23 **C4** 53 2N 7 18W
Maryborough, *Queens.,*
Australia 127 **D5** 25 31 S 152 37 E
Maryborough, *Vic., Australia* 128 **D5** 37 0 S 143 44 E
Maryfield, *Canada* 143 **D8** 49 50N 101 35W
Maryland □, *U.S.A.* 148 **F7** 39 0N 76 30W
Maryland Junction, *Zimbabwe* 119 **F3** 17 45 S 30 31 E
Maryport, *U.K.* 20 **C4** 54 44N 3 28W
Mary's Harbour, *Canada* 141 **B8** 52 18N 55 51W
Marystown, *Canada* 141 **C8** 47 10N 55 10W
Marysville, *Canada* 142 **D5** 49 35N 116 0W
Marysville, *Calif., U.S.A.* 160 **F5** 39 9N 121 35W
Marysville, *Kans., U.S.A.* 154 **F6** 39 51N 96 39W
Marysville, *Mich., U.S.A.* 150 **D2** 42 54N 82 29W
Marysville, *Ohio, U.S.A.* 157 **D13** 40 14N 83 22W
Marysville, *Wash., U.S.A.* 160 **B4** 48 3N 122 11W
Maryville, *Mo., U.S.A.* 156 **D2** 40 21N 94 52W
Maryville, *Tenn., U.S.A.* 149 **H4** 35 46N 83 58W
Marzo, Punta, *Colombia* 168 **B2** 6 50N 77 42W
Marzūq, *Libya* 108 **C2** 25 53N 13 57 E
Masahunga, *Tanzania* 118 **C3** 2 6 S 33 18 E
Masai Steppe, *Tanzania* 118 **C4** 4 30 S 36 30 E
Masaka, *Uganda* 118 **C3** 0 21 S 31 45 E
Masalembo, Kepulauan,
Indonesia 78 **F4** 5 35 S 114 30 E
Masalima, Kepulauan,
Indonesia 78 **F5** 5 4 S 117 5 E
Masallı, *Azerbaijan* 101 **C13** 39 3N 48 40 E
Masamba, *Indonesia* 79 **E6** 2 30 S 120 15 E
Masan, *S. Korea* 75 **G15** 35 11N 128 32 E
Masandam, Ra's, *Oman* 97 **E8** 26 30N 56 30 E
Masasi, *Tanzania* 119 **E4** 10 45 S 38 52 E
Masaya, *Nic.* 164 **D2** 12 0N 86 7W

248 Masba

Masba, *Nigeria* **113 C7** 11 35N 13 1 E
Masbate, *Phil.* **79 B6** 12 21N 123 36 E
Masbate □, *Phil.* **80 E4** 12 20N 123 30 E
Masbate Pass, *Phil.* **80 E4** 12 30N 123 35 E
Máscali, *Italy* **47 E8** 37 45N 15 12 E
Mascara, *Algeria* **111 A5** 35 26N 0 6 E
Mascarene Is., *Ind. Oc.* **121 G4** 22 0 S 55 0 E
Mascota, *Mexico* **162 C4** 20 30N 104 50W
Mascoutah, *U.S.A.* **156 F7** 38 29N 89 48W
Masela, *Indonesia* **79 F7** 8 9 S 129 51 E
Maseru, *Lesotho* **116 D4** 29 18 S 27 30 E
Masfjorden, *Norway* **18 D2** 60 48N 5 18 E
Mashaba, *Zimbabwe* **119 G3** 20 2 S 30 29 E
Mashābih, *Si. Arabia* **96 E3** 25 35N 36 30 E
Mashan, *China* **76 F7** 23 40N 108 11 E
Mashar, *Sudan* **107 F2** 9 16N 26 51 E
Mashegu, *Nigeria* **113 D6** 10 0N 5 35 E
Masherbrum, *Pakistan* **93 B7** 35 38N 76 18 E
Mashhad, *Iran* **97 B8** 36 20N 59 35 E
Mashi, *Nigeria* **113 C6** 13 0N 7 54 E
Mashiki, *Japan* **70 E2** 32 51N 130 53 E
Mashīz, *Iran* **97 D8** 29 56N 56 37 E
Mashkel, Hamun-i, *Pakistan* **91 C1** 28 20N 62 56 E
Mashki Chāh, *Pakistan* **91 C1** 29 5N 62 30 E
Mashonaland Central □, *Zimbabwe* **117 B5** 17 30 S 31 0 E
Mashonaland East □, *Zimbabwe* **117 B5** 18 0 S 32 0 E
Mashonaland West □, *Zimbabwe* **117 B4** 17 30 S 29 30 E
Mashrakh, *India* **93 F11** 26 7N 84 48 E
Mashtaga = Maştağa, *Azerbaijan* **61 K10** 40 35N 49 57 E
Masi Manimba, *Dem. Rep. of the Congo* **115 C3** 4 40 S 17 54 E
Masibi, *Angola* **115 E4** 11 6 S 22 41 E
Masindi, *Uganda* **118 B3** 1 40N 31 43 E
Masindi Port, *Uganda* **118 B3** 1 43N 32 2 E
Masinloc, *Phil.* **80 D2** 15 32N 119 57 E
Maşīrah, *Oman* **102 C6** 21 0N 58 50 E
Maşīrah, Khalīj, *Oman* **99 B7** 20 10N 58 10 E
Maşīrah, Tur'at, *Oman* **99 B7** 20 30N 58 40 E
Masisea, *Peru* **172 B3** 8 35 S 74 22W
Masisi, *Dem. Rep. of the Congo* **118 C2** 1 23 S 28 49 E
Masjed Soleyman, *Iran* **97 D6** 31 55N 49 18 E
Mask, L., *Ireland* **23 C2** 53 36N 9 22W
Maskelyne Is., *Vanuatu* **133 F5** 16 32 S 167 49 E
Maski, *India* **95 G3** 15 56N 76 46 E
Maskin, *Oman* **97 F8** 23 30N 56 50 E
Maslen Nos, *Bulgaria* **51 D11** 42 18N 27 48 E
Maslinica, *Croatia* **45 E13** 43 24N 16 13 E
Maşna'ah, *Yemen* **99 D5** 14 27N 48 17 E
Masnou = El Masnou, *Spain* **40 D7** 41 28N 2 20 E
Masoala, Tanjon' i, *Madag.* **117 B9** 15 59 S 50 13 E
Masoarivo, *Madag.* **117 B7** 19 3 S 44 19 E
Masohi = Amahai, *Indonesia* **79 E7** 3 20 S 128 55 E
Masomeloka, *Madag.* **117 C8** 20 17 S 48 37 E
Mason, *Mich., U.S.A.* **157 B12** 42 35N 84 27W
Mason, *Nev., U.S.A.* **160 G7** 38 56N 119 8W
Mason, *Ohio, U.S.A.* **157 E12** 39 22N 84 19W
Mason, *Tex., U.S.A.* **155 K5** 30 45N 99 14W
Mason B., *N.Z.* **131 G2** 46 55 S 167 45 E
Mason City, *Ill., U.S.A.* **156 D7** 40 12N 89 42W
Mason City, *Iowa, U.S.A.* **156 A3** 43 9N 93 12W
Maspalomas, *Canary Is.* **39 G4** 27 46N 15 35W
Maspalomas, Pta., *Canary Is.* **39 G4** 27 43N 15 36W
Masqat, *Oman* **99 B7** 23 37N 58 36 E
Massa, *Congo* **114 C3** 3 45 S 15 29 E
Massa, *Italy* **44 D7** 44 1N 10 9 E
Massa, O. ⟶, *Morocco* **110 B3** 30 2N 9 40W
Massa Maríttima, *Italy* **44 E7** 43 3N 10 52 E
Massachusetts □, *U.S.A.* **151 D13** 42 30N 72 0W
Massachusetts B., *U.S.A.* **151 D14** 42 20N 70 50W
Massafra, *Italy* **47 B10** 40 35N 17 7 E
Massaguet, *Chad* **109 F3** 12 28N 15 26 E
Massakory, *Chad* **109 F3** 13 0N 15 49 E
Massanella, *Spain* **39 B9** 39 48N 2 51 E
Massangano, *Angola* **115 D2** 9 40 S 14 13 E
Massangena, *Mozam.* **117 C5** 21 34 S 33 0 E
Massango, *Angola* **115 D3** 8 1 S 16 10 E
Massapê, *Brazil* **170 B3** 3 31 S 40 19W
Massat, *France* **28 F5** 42 53N 1 21 E
Massawa = Mitsiwa, *Eritrea* **102 D2** 15 35N 39 25 E
Massena, *U.S.A.* **151 B10** 44 56N 74 54W
Massénya, *Chad* **109 F3** 11 21N 16 9 E
Masset, *Canada* **142 C2** 54 2N 132 10W
Masseube, *France* **28 E4** 43 25N 0 34 E
Massiac, *France* **28 C7** 45 15N 3 11 E
Massif Central, *France* **28 D7** 44 55N 3 0 E
Massigui, *Mali* **112 C3** 11 48N 6 50W
Massillon, *U.S.A.* **150 F3** 40 48N 81 32W
Massima, *Gabon* **114 C2** 1 27 S 11 33 E
Massinga, *Mozam.* **117 C6** 23 15 S 35 22 E
Massingir, *Mozam.* **117 C5** 23 51 S 32 4 E
Mässlingen, *Sweden* **16 B6** 62 40N 12 50 E
Masson, *Canada* **151 A9** 45 32N 75 25W
Masson I., *Antarctica* **7 C7** 66 10 S 93 20 E
Massouka, *Gabon* **114 C1** 1 37 S 9 56 E
Mastābah, *Si. Arabia* **98 B2** 20 49N 39 26 E
Maştağa, *Azerbaijan* **61 K10** 40 35N 49 57 E
Mastanli = Momchilgrad, *Bulgaria* **51 E9** 41 33N 25 23 E
Masterton, *N.Z.* **130 G4** 40 56 S 175 39 E
Mastic, *U.S.A.* **151 F12** 40 47N 72 54W
Mástikho, Ákra, *Greece* **49 C8** 38 10N 26 2 E
Mastuj, *Pakistan* **93 A5** 36 20N 72 36 E
Mastung, *Pakistan* **91 C2** 29 50N 66 56 E
Mastūrah, *Si. Arabia* **98 B2** 23 7N 38 52 E
Masty, *Belarus* **58 F3** 53 27N 24 38 E
Masuda, *Japan* **70 C3** 34 40N 131 51 E
Masuika, *Dem. Rep. of the Congo* **115 D4** 7 37 S 22 32 E
Masvingo, *Zimbabwe* **119 G3** 20 8 S 30 49 E
Masvingo □, *Zimbabwe* **119 G3** 21 0 S 31 30 E
Maşyāf, *Syria* **100 E7** 35 4N 36 20 E
Maszewo, *Poland* **54 E2** 53 29N 15 3 E
Mata de São João, *Brazil* **171 D4** 12 31 S 38 17W
Mata Utu, *Wall. & F. Is.* **123 C15** 13 17 S 176 8W
Matabele Plain, *Zambia* **115 F4** 16 20 S 23 10 E
Matabeleland North □, *Zimbabwe* **119 F2** 19 0 S 28 0 E
Matabeleland South □, *Zimbabwe* **119 G2** 21 0 S 29 0 E
Mataboor, *Indonesia* **83 B5** 1 41 S 138 3 E
Matachel ⟶, *Spain* **43 G4** 38 50N 6 17W
Matachewan, *Canada* **140 C3** 47 56N 80 39W
Matacuni ⟶, *Venezuela* **169 C4** 3 2N 65 16W
Matadi, *Dem. Rep. of the Congo* **115 D2** 5 52 S 13 31 E
Matagalpa, *Nic.* **164 D2** 13 0N 85 58W
Matagami, *Canada* **140 C4** 49 45N 77 34W
Matagami, L., *Canada* **140 C4** 49 50N 77 40W
Matagorda B., *U.S.A.* **155 L6** 28 40N 96 0W
Matagorda I., *U.S.A.* **155 L6** 28 15N 96 30W
Mataguinao, *Phil.* **80 E5** 12 5N 124 55 E
Matak, *Indonesia* **78 D3** 3 18N 106 16 E
Matakana, *Australia* **129 B6** 32 59 S 145 54 E
Matakana, *N.Z.* **130 C3** 36 21 S 174 43 E
Matakana I., *N.Z.* **130 C3** 36 21 S 174 43 E
Matala, *Angola* **115 E3** 14 46 S 15 4 E
Mátala, *Greece* **38 E6** 34 59N 24 45 E
Matalaque, *Peru* **172 D3** 16 26 S 70 49W
Matale, *Sri Lanka* **95 L5** 7 30N 80 37 E
Matam, *Senegal* **112 B2** 15 34N 13 17W
Matamata, *N.Z.* **130 D4** 37 48 S 175 47 E
Matameye, *Niger* **113 C6** 13 26N 8 28 E
Matamoros, *Campeche, Mexico* **163 D6** 18 50N 90 50W
Matamoros, *Coahuila, Mexico* **162 B4** 25 33N 103 15W
Matamoros, *Tamaulipas, Mexico* **163 B5** 25 50N 97 30W
Ma'ţan as Sarra, *Libya* **109 D4** 21 45N 22 0 E
Matana, Danau, *Indonesia* **82 B2** 2 28 S 121 20 E
Matandu ⟶, *Tanzania* **119 D3** 8 45 S 34 19 E
Matane, *Canada* **141 C6** 48 50N 67 33W
Matang, *China* **76 F5** 23 30N 104 7 E
Matankari, *Niger* **113 C5** 13 46N 4 1 E
Matanomadh, *India* **92 H3** 23 33N 68 57 E
Matanzas, *Cuba* **164 B3** 23 0N 81 40W
Matapa, *Botswana* **116 C3** 23 11 S 24 39 E
Matapan, C. = Taínaron, Ákra, *Greece* **48 E4** 36 22N 22 27 E
Matapédia, *Canada* **141 C6** 48 0N 66 59W
Matara, *Sri Lanka* **95 M5** 5 58N 80 30 E
Mataram, *Indonesia* **78 F5** 8 41 S 116 10 E
Matarani, *Peru* **172 D3** 17 0 S 72 10W
Mataranka, *Australia* **124 B5** 14 55 S 133 4 E
Matarma, Râs, *Egypt* **103 E1** 30 27N 32 44 E
Mataró, *Spain* **40 D7** 41 32N 2 29 E
Matarraña ⟶, *Spain* **40 D5** 41 14N 0 22 E
Mataruška Banja, *Serbia, Yug.* **50 C4** 43 40N 20 40 E
Mataso, *Vanuatu* **133 G6** 17 14 S 168 26 E
Matata, *N.Z.* **130 D5** 37 54 S 176 48 E
Matatiele, *S. Africa* **117 E4** 30 20 S 28 49 E
Mataura, *N.Z.* **131 G3** 46 11 S 168 51 E
Mataura ⟶, *N.Z.* **131 G3** 46 34 S 168 44 E
Mategua, *Bolivia* **173 C5** 13 1 S 62 48W
Matehuala, *Mexico* **162 C4** 23 40N 100 40W
Mateira, *Brazil* **171 E1** 18 54 S 50 30W
Mateke, *Dem. Rep. of the Congo* **114 C3** 4 52 S 24 25 E
Mateke Hills, *Zimbabwe* **119 G3** 21 48 S 31 0 E
Matera, *Italy* **47 B9** 40 40N 16 36 E
Matese, Monti del, *Italy* **47 A7** 41 27N 14 22 E
Mátészalka, *Hungary* **52 C7** 47 58N 22 20 E
Matetsi, *Zimbabwe* **119 F2** 18 12 S 26 0 E
Mateur, *Tunisia* **108 A1** 37 0N 9 40 E
Matfors, *Sweden* **16 B11** 62 21N 17 2 E
Matha, *France* **28 C3** 45 52N 0 20W
Mathis, *U.S.A.* **155 L6** 28 6N 97 50W
Mathoura, *Australia* **129 C6** 35 50 S 144 55 E
Mathráki, *Greece* **38 A3** 39 48N 19 31 E
Mathura, *India* **92 F7** 27 30N 77 40 E
Mati, *Phil.* **79 C7** 6 55N 126 15 E
Mati ⟶, *Albania* **50 E3** 41 40N 19 35 E
Matiakoali, *Burkina Faso* **113 C5** 12 28N 1 2 E
Matiali, *India* **93 F13** 26 56N 88 49 E
Matías Romero, *Mexico* **163 D5** 16 53N 95 2W
Matibane, *Mozam.* **119 E5** 14 49 S 40 45 E
Matima, *Botswana* **116 C3** 20 15 S 24 26 E
Matinhos, *Brazil* **171 G2** 25 49 S 48 32W
Matiri Ra., *N.Z.* **131 B7** 41 38 S 172 20 E
Matjiesfontein, *S. Africa* **116 E3** 33 14 S 20 35 E
Matla ⟶, *India* **93 J13** 21 40N 88 40 E
Matlamanyane, *Botswana* **116 B4** 19 33 S 25 57 E
Matli, *Pakistan* **92 G3** 25 2N 68 39 E
Matlock, *U.K.* **20 D6** 53 9N 1 33W
Matmata, *Tunisia* **108 B1** 33 37N 9 59 E
Matna, *Sudan* **107 E4** 13 49N 35 10 E
Matnog, *Phil.* **80 E5** 12 35N 124 5 E
Mato, *Dem. Rep. of the Congo* **115 D4** 8 1 S 24 24 E
Mato ⟶, *Venezuela* **169 B4** 7 9N 65 7W
Mato, Serrania de, *Venezuela* **168 B4** 6 25N 65 25W
Mato Grosso □, *Brazil* **173 C6** 14 0 S 55 0W
Mato Grosso, Planalto do, *Brazil* **173 C7** 15 0 S 55 0W
Mato Grosso do Sul □, *Brazil* **173 D7** 18 0 S 55 0W
Mato Verde, *Brazil* **171 D1** 11 13 S 50 40W
Matochkin Shar, *Russia* **64 B6** 73 10N 56 40 E
Matong, *Papua N. G.* **132 C6** 5 36 S 151 50 E
Matopo Hills, *Zimbabwe* **119 G2** 20 36 S 28 20 E
Matopos, *Zimbabwe* **119 G2** 20 20 S 28 29 E
Matosinhos, *Portugal* **42 D2** 41 11N 8 42W
Matour, *France* **27 F11** 46 19N 4 29 E
Maţraḩ, *Oman* **99 B7** 23 37N 58 30 E
Matroosberg, *S. Africa* **116 E2** 33 23 S 19 40 E
Matsena, *Nigeria* **113 C7** 13 5N 10 5 E
Matsesta, *Russia* **61 J4** 43 34N 39 51 E
Matsu Tao, *Taiwan* **77 E13** 26 9N 119 56 E
Matsubara, *Japan* **71 C7** 34 33N 135 34 E
Matsudo, *Japan* **71 B11** 35 47N 139 54 E
Matsue, *Japan* **70 B5** 35 25N 133 10 E
Matsumae, *Japan* **68 D10** 41 26N 140 7 E
Matsumoto, *Japan* **71 A9** 36 15N 138 0 E
Matsusaka, *Japan* **71 C8** 34 34N 136 32 E
Matsutō, *Japan* **71 A8** 36 31N 136 34 E
Matsuura, *Japan* **70 D1** 33 20N 129 49 E
Matsuyama, *Japan* **70 D4** 33 45N 132 45 E
Matsuzaki, *Japan* **71 C10** 34 43N 138 50 E
Mattagami ⟶, *Canada* **140 B3** 50 43N 81 29W
Mattancheri, *India* **95 K3** 9 50N 76 15 E
Mattawa, *Canada* **140 C4** 46 20N 78 45W
Matterhorn, *Switz.* **32 E5** 45 58N 7 39 E
Mattersburg, *Austria* **35 D9** 47 44N 16 24 E
Matteson, *U.S.A.* **157 C9** 41 30N 87 42W
Matthew, I., *N. Cal.* **123 E13** 22 29 S 171 15 E
Matthew Town, *Bahamas* **165 B5** 20 57N 73 40W
Matthews, *U.S.A.* **157 D11** 40 23N 85 30W
Matthew's Ridge, *Guyana* **169 B5** 7 37N 60 10W
Mattice, *Canada* **140 C3** 49 40N 83 20W
Mattili, *India* **94 E6** 18 33N 82 12 E
Mattituck, *U.S.A.* **151 F12** 40 59N 72 32W
Mattoon, *U.S.A.* **154 F10** 39 29N 88 23W
Matuba, *Mozam.* **117 C5** 24 28 S 32 49 E
Matucana, *Peru* **172 C2** 11 55 S 76 25W
Matugama, *Sri Lanka* **95 L5** 6 31N 80 7 E
Matuku, *Fiji* **133 B2** 19 10 S 179 44 E
Matūn = Khowst, *Afghan.* **92 C3** 33 22N 69 58 E
Maturín, *Venezuela* **169 B5** 9 45N 63 11W
Matutum, Mt., *Phil.* **81 H5** 6 22N 125 5 E
Matveyev Kurgan, *Russia* **59 J10** 47 35N 38 57 E
Matxitxako, C., *Spain* **40 B2** 43 28N 2 47W
Mau, *Mad. P., India* **93 F8** 26 17N 78 41 E
Mau, *Ut. P., India* **93 G10** 25 56N 83 33 E
Mau, *Ut. P., India* **93 G9** 25 17N 81 23 E
Mau Escarpment, *Kenya* **118 C4** 0 40 S 36 0 E
Mau Ranipur, *India* **93 G8** 25 16N 79 8 E
Mauban, *Phil.* **80 D3** 14 12N 121 44 E
Maubeuge, *France* **27 B10** 50 17N 3 57 E
Maubourguet, *France* **28 E4** 43 29N 0 1 E
Maud, Pt., *Australia* **124 D1** 23 6 S 113 45 E
Maude, *Australia* **128 C6** 34 29 S 144 18 E
Maués, *Brazil* **169 D6** 3 20 S 57 45W
Maués-Acu ⟶, *Brazil* **169 D6** 3 22 S 57 44W
Maughold Hd., *U.K.* **20 C3** 54 18N 4 18W
Mauguio, *France* **28 E7** 43 37N 4 1 E
Maui, *U.S.A.* **146 H16** 20 48N 156 20W
Maulamyaing = Moulmein, *Burma* **90 G6** 16 30N 97 40 E
Maule □, *Chile* **174 D1** 36 5 S 72 30W
Mauléon-Licharre, *France* **28 E3** 43 14N 0 54W
Maullín, *Chile* **176 B2** 41 38 S 73 37W
Maulvibazar, *Bangla.* **90 C3** 24 29N 91 42 E
Maumee, *U.S.A.* **157 C13** 41 34N 83 39W
Maumee ⟶, *U.S.A.* **157 C13** 41 42N 83 28W
Maumere, *Indonesia* **79 F6** 8 38 S 122 13 E
Maumusson, Pertuis de, *France* **28 C2** 45 48N 1 14W
Maun, *Botswana* **116 C3** 20 0 S 23 26 E
Mauna Kea, *U.S.A.* **146 J17** 19 50N 155 28W
Mauna Loa, *U.S.A.* **146 J17** 19 30N 155 35W
Maunaloa, *U.S.A.* **145 B4** 21 8N 157 13W
Maunalua B., *U.S.A.* **145 K14** 21 15N 157 45W
Maunawili, *U.S.A.* **145 K14** 21 23N 157 46W
Maungaturoto, *N.Z.* **130 C3** 36 6 S 174 23 E
Maungdow, *Burma* **90 E4** 20 50N 92 21 E
Maungmagan Is., *Burma* **78 B1** 14 0N 97 30 E
Maupin, *U.S.A.* **158 D3** 45 11N 121 5W
Maure-de-Bretagne, *France* **26 E5** 47 59N 1 58W
Maurepas, L., *U.S.A.* **155 K9** 30 15N 90 30W
Maures, *France* **29 E10** 43 15N 6 15 E
Mauriac, *France* **28 C6** 45 13N 2 19 E
Maurice, L., *Australia* **125 E5** 29 30 S 131 0 E
Mauriceville, *N.Z.* **130 G4** 40 45 S 175 42 E
Mauricie, Parc Nat. de la, *Canada* **140 C5** 46 45N 73 0W
Maurienne, *France* **29 C10** 45 13N 6 30 E
Mauritania ■, *Africa* **110 D3** 20 50N 10 0W
Mauritius ■, *Ind. Oc.* **105 J9** 20 0 S 57 0 E
Mauron, *France* **26 D4** 48 9N 2 18W
Maurs, *France* **28 D6** 44 43N 2 12 E
Mauston, *U.S.A.* **154 D9** 43 48N 90 5W
Mauterndorf, *Austria* **34 D6** 47 9N 13 40 E
Mauthen, *Austria* **34 E6** 46 40N 13 0 E
Mauvezin, *France* **28 E4** 43 44N 0 53 E
Mauvoisin, Barr. de, *Switz.* **32 E4** 45 58N 7 20 E
Mauzé-sur-le-Mignon, *France* **28 B3** 46 12N 0 41W
Mavaca ⟶, *Venezuela* **169 C4** 2 31N 65 11W
Mavinga, *Angola* **115 F4** 15 50 S 20 21 E
Mavli, *India* **92 G5** 24 45N 73 55 E
Mavrova, *Albania* **50 F3** 40 26N 19 32 E
Mavuradonha Mts., *Zimbabwe* **119 F3** 16 30 S 31 30 E
Mawa, *Dem. Rep. of the Congo* **118 B2** 2 45N 26 40 E
Mawai, *India* **93 H9** 22 30N 81 4 E
Mawana, *India* **92 E7** 29 6N 77 58 E
Mawand, *Pakistan* **92 E3** 29 33N 68 38 E
Mawk Mai, *Burma* **90 E6** 20 14N 97 37 E
Mawlaik, *Burma* **90 D5** 23 40N 94 26 E
Mawlamyine = Moulmein, *Burma* **90 G6** 16 30N 97 40 E
Mawlawkho, *Burma* **90 G6** 17 50N 97 38 E
Mawqaq, *Si. Arabia* **96 E4** 27 25N 41 8 E
Mawshij, *Yemen* **98 D3** 13 43N 43 17 E
Mawson Coast, *Antarctica* **7 C6** 68 30 S 63 0 E
Max, *U.S.A.* **154 B4** 47 49N 101 18W
Maxcanú, *Mexico* **163 C6** 20 40N 92 0W
Maxesibeni, *S. Africa* **117 E4** 30 49 S 29 23 E
Maxeys, *U.S.A.* **152 B6** 33 45N 83 11W
Maxhamish L., *Canada* **142 B4** 59 50N 123 17W
Maxixe, *Mozam.* **117 C6** 23 54 S 35 17 E
Maxville, *Canada* **151 A10** 45 17N 74 51W
Maxwell, *N.Z.* **130 F3** 39 51 S 174 49 E
Maxwell, *U.S.A.* **160 F4** 39 17N 122 11W
Maxwelton, *Australia* **126 C3** 20 43 S 142 41 E
May, C., *U.S.A.* **148 F8** 38 56N 74 58W
May Pen, *Jamaica* **164 C4** 17 58N 77 15W
May River, *Papua N. G.* **132 C1** 4 19 S 141 58 E
Maya, *Indonesia* **85 C3** 1 10 S 109 35 E
Maya ⟶, *Russia* **65 D14** 60 28N 134 28 E
Maya Mts., *Belize* **163 D7** 16 30N 89 0W
Mayaguana, *Bahamas* **165 B5** 22 30N 72 44W
Mayagüez, *Puerto Rico* **165 C6** 18 12N 67 9W
Mayahi, *Niger* **113 C6** 13 58N 7 40 E
Mayals = Maials, *Spain* **40 D5** 41 22N 0 30 E
Mayama, *Congo* **114 C2** 3 51 S 14 54 E
Mayāmey, *Iran* **97 B7** 36 24N 55 42 E
Mayang, *China* **76 D7** 27 53N 109 49 E
Mayanup, *Australia* **125 F2** 33 57 S 116 27 E
Mayapan, *Mexico* **163 C7** 20 30N 89 25W
Mayarí, *Cuba* **165 B4** 20 40N 75 41W
Mayavaram = Mayuram, *India* **95 J4** 11 3N 79 42 E
Maybell, *U.S.A.* **158 F9** 40 31N 108 5W
Maybole, *U.K.* **22 F4** 55 21N 4 42W
Maychew, *Ethiopia* **107 E4** 12 50N 39 31 E
Maydān, *Iraq* **101 E11** 34 55N 45 37 E
Maydena, *Australia* **126 G4** 42 45 S 146 30 E
Maydī, *Yemen* **98 C3** 16 19N 42 48 E
Mayen, *Germany* **31 E3** 50 19N 7 13 E
Mayenne, *France* **26 D6** 48 20N 0 38W
Mayenne □, *France* **26 D6** 48 10N 0 40W
Mayenne ⟶, *France* **26 E6** 47 30N 0 32W
Mayer, *U.S.A.* **159 J7** 34 24N 112 14W
Mayerthorpe, *Canada* **142 C5** 53 57N 115 8W
Mayesville, *U.S.A.* **152 A9** 34 0N 80 12W
Mayfield, *Ky., U.S.A.* **149 G1** 36 44N 88 38W
Mayfield, *N.Y., U.S.A.* **151 C10** 43 6N 74 16W
Mayhill, *U.S.A.* **159 K11** 32 53N 105 29W
Maykop, *Russia* **61 H5** 44 35N 40 10 E
Mayli-Say, *Kyrgyzstan* **63 C6** 41 17N 72 24 E
Maymyo, *Burma* **86 A1** 22 2N 96 28 E
Maynard, *Mass., U.S.A.* **151 D13** 42 26N 71 27W
Maynard, *Wash., U.S.A.* **160 C4** 47 59N 122 55W
Maynard Hills, *Australia* **125 E2** 28 28 S 119 49 E
Mayne ⟶, *Australia* **126 C3** 23 40 S 141 55 E
Maynooth, *Ireland* **23 C5** 53 23N 6 34W
Mayo, *Canada* **138 B6** 63 38N 135 57W
Mayo, *U.S.A.* **152 E6** 30 3N 83 10W
Mayo □, *Ireland* **23 C2** 53 53N 9 3W
Mayo ⟶, *Argentina* **176 C3** 45 45 S 69 45W
Mayo ⟶, *Peru* **172 B2** 6 38 S 76 15W
Mayo Bay, *Phil.* **81 H6** 6 56N 126 22 E
Mayo Daga, *Nigeria* **113 D7** 6 59N 11 25 E
Mayo Faran, *Nigeria* **113 D7** 8 57N 12 4 E
Mayoko, *Congo* **114 C2** 2 18 S 12 49 E
Mayoko, *Dem. Rep. of the Congo* **114 C4** 1 6 S 23 50 E
Mayon Volcano, *Phil.* **79 B6** 13 15N 123 41 E
Mayor Buratovich, *Argentina* **176 A4** 39 15 S 62 37W
Mayor I., *N.Z.* **130 D5** 37 16 S 176 17 E
Mayorga, *Spain* **42 C5** 42 10N 5 16W
Mayotte, *Ind. Oc.* **105 H8** 12 50 S 45 10 E
Mayoyao, *Phil.* **80 C3** 16 59N 121 14 E
Mayraira Pt., *Phil.* **80 B3** 18 39N 120 51 E
Mayskiy, *Russia* **61 J7** 43 47N 44 2 E
Maysville, *Ky., U.S.A.* **157 F13** 38 39N 83 46W
Maysville, *Mo., U.S.A.* **156 E2** 39 53N 94 22W
Mayu, *Indonesia* **79 D7** 1 30N 126 30 E
Mayumba, *Gabon* **114 C2** 3 25 S 10 39 E
Mayuram, *India* **95 J4** 11 3N 79 42 E
Mayville, *N. Dak., U.S.A.* **154 B6** 47 30N 97 20W
Mayville, *N.Y., U.S.A.* **150 D5** 42 15N 79 30W
Mayya, *Russia* **65 C14** 61 44N 130 18 E
Mazabuka, *Zambia* **119 F2** 15 52 S 27 44 E
Mazagán = El Jadida, *Morocco* **110 B3** 33 11N 8 17W
Mazagão, *Brazil* **169 D7** 0 7 S 51 16W
Mazamet, *France* **28 E6** 43 30N 2 20 E
Mazán, *Peru* **168 D3** 3 30 S 73 0W
Māzandarān □, *Iran* **97 B7** 36 30N 52 0 E
Mazapil, *Mexico* **162 C4** 24 38N 101 34W
Mazar, O. ⟶, *Algeria* **111 B5** 31 50N 1 36 E
Mazar-e Sharīf, *Afghan.* **91 A2** 36 41N 67 0 E
Mazara del Vallo, *Italy* **46 E5** 37 39N 12 35 E
Mazarredo, *Argentina* **176 C3** 47 10 S 66 50W
Mazarrón, *Spain* **41 H3** 37 38N 1 19W
Mazarrón, G. de, *Spain* **41 H3** 37 27N 1 19W
Mazaruni ⟶, *Guyana* **169 B6** 6 25N 58 35W
Mazatán, *Mexico* **162 B2** 29 0N 110 8W
Mazatenango, *Guatemala* **164 D1** 14 35N 91 30W
Mazatlán, *Mexico* **162 C3** 23 13N 106 25W
Mažeikiai, *Lithuania* **15 H20** 56 20N 22 20 E
Māzhān, *Iran* **97 C8** 32 30N 59 0 E
Mazīnān, *Iran* **97 B8** 36 19N 56 56 E
Mazo Cruz, *Peru* **172 D4** 16 45 S 69 44W
Mazoe, *Mozam.* **119 F3** 16 42 S 33 7 E
Mazoe ⟶, *Mozam.* **119 F3** 16 20 S 33 30 E
Mazomanie, *U.S.A.* **156 A7** 43 11N 89 48W
Mazon, *U.S.A.* **157 C8** 41 14N 88 25W
Mazowe, *Zimbabwe* **119 F3** 17 28 S 30 58 E
Mazowieckie □, *Poland* **55 F8** 52 40N 21 0 E
Mazrûb, *Sudan* **107 E2** 14 0N 29 20 E
Mazu Dao, *China* **77 D12** 26 10N 119 55 E
Mazurian Lakes = Mazurski, Pojezierze, *Poland* **54 E7** 53 50N 21 0 E
Mazurski, Pojezierze, *Poland* **54 E7** 53 50N 21 0 E
Mazyr, *Belarus* **59 F5** 51 59N 29 15 E
Mba, *Fiji* **133 A1** 17 33 S 177 41 E
Mbaba, *Senegal* **112 C1** 14 59N 16 44W
Mbabane, *Swaziland* **117 D5** 26 18 S 31 6 E
Mbaéré ⟶, *C.A.R.* **114 B3** 3 47N 17 31 E
Mbagne, *Mauritania* **112 B2** 16 6N 14 47W
M'bahiakro, *Ivory C.* **112 D4** 7 33N 4 19W
Mbaïki, *C.A.R.* **114 B3** 3 53N 18 1 E
Mbakana, Mt. de, *Cameroon* **114 A3** 7 57N 15 6 E
Mbala, *Zambia* **119 D3** 8 46 S 31 24 E
Mbalabala, *Zimbabwe* **117 C4** 20 27 S 29 3 E
Mbale, *Uganda* **118 B3** 1 8N 34 12 E
Mbali ⟶, *C.A.R.* **114 B3** 4 27N 18 20 E
Mbalmayo, *Cameroon* **113 E7** 3 33N 11 33 E
Mbam ⟶, *Cameroon* **113 E7** 4 25N 11 17 E
Mbamba Bay, *Tanzania* **119 E3** 11 13 S 34 49 E
Mbandaka, *Dem. Rep. of the Congo* **114 B3** 0 1N 18 18 E
Mbanga, *Cameroon* **113 E6** 4 30N 9 33 E
M'Banio, Lagune, *Gabon* **114 C2** 3 35 S 11 0 E
Mbanza Congo, *Angola* **115 D2** 6 18 S 14 16 E
Mbanza Ngungu, *Dem. Rep. of the Congo* **115 D2** 5 12 S 14 53 E
Mbarara, *Uganda* **118 C3** 0 35 S 30 40 E
Mbari ⟶, *C.A.R.* **114 B4** 4 34N 22 43 E
Mbashe ⟶, *S. Africa* **117 E4** 32 15 S 28 54 E
Mbatto, *Ivory C.* **112 D4** 6 28N 4 22W
Mbé, *Congo* **114 C3** 3 14 S 15 50 E
Mbe, *Eq. Guin.* **114 B1** 1 47N 9 56 E
Mbengga, *Fiji* **133 B2** 18 23 S 178 8 E
Mbengué, *Gabon* **114 C2** 2 2 S 11 7 E
Mbengui, *Gabon* **114 C2** 2 3 S 10 4 E
Mbenkuru ⟶, *Tanzania* **119 D4** 9 25 S 39 50 E
Mbéré ⟶, *Cameroon* **114 A3** 7 45N 15 36 E
Mberengwa, *Zimbabwe* **119 G2** 20 29 S 29 57 E
Mberengwa, Mt., *Zimbabwe* **119 G2** 20 37 S 29 55 E
Mberubu, *Nigeria* **113 D6** 6 10N 7 38 E
Mbesuma, *Zambia* **119 E3** 10 0 S 32 2 E
Mbeya, *Tanzania* **119 D3** 8 54 S 33 29 E
Mbeya □, *Tanzania* **118 D3** 8 15 S 33 30 E
Mbigou, *Gabon* **114 C2** 1 53 S 11 56 E
M'bili, *Sudan* **107 F2** 7 35N 28 15 E
Mbinga, *Tanzania* **119 E4** 10 50 S 35 0 E
Mbini □, *Eq. Guin.* **114 B2** 1 30N 10 0 E
Mboi, *Dem. Rep. of the Congo* **115 D4** 6 57 S 21 54 E
Mboki, *C.A.R.* **114 A5** 5 19N 25 58 E
Mboli, *Dem. Rep. of the Congo* **114 B4** 4 8N 23 9 E
M'bonge, *Cameroon* **114 B1** 4 33N 9 5 E
Mboro, *Senegal* **112 B1** 15 9N 16 54W
Mboua, *Cameroon* **114 A2** 4 25N 14 16 E
M'boukou Res., *Cameroon* **113 D7** 6 23N 12 50 E
Mboune, *Senegal* **112 C2** 14 42N 13 34W
Mbouoma, *Congo* **114 C3** 0 52 S 15 4 E
Mbour, *Senegal* **112 C1** 14 22N 16 54W
Mbout, *Mauritania* **112 B2** 16 1N 12 38W
Mbrés, *C.A.R.* **114 A3** 6 40N 19 48 E
M'Bridge ⟶, *Angola* **115 D2** 7 12 S 12 51 E
Mbuji-Mayi, *Dem. Rep. of the Congo* **118 D1** 6 9 S 23 40 E
Mbulu, *Tanzania* **118 C4** 3 45 S 35 30 E
Mbuma, *Dem. Rep. of the Congo* **114 B4** 3 32N 24 50 E
Mburucuyá, *Argentina* **174 B4** 28 1 S 58 14W
M'bwat, *Cameroon* **114 A2** 6 29N 10 45 E
Mcherrah, *Algeria* **110 C4** 27 0N 4 30W
Mchinja, *Tanzania* **119 D4** 9 44 S 39 45 E
Mchinji, *Malawi* **119 E3** 13 47 S 32 58 E
Mdennah, *Mauritania* **110 D3** 24 37N 6 0W
Mead, L., *U.S.A.* **161 J12** 36 1N 114 44W
Meade, *U.S.A.* **155 G4** 37 17N 100 20W
Meade ⟶, *U.S.A.* **144 A9** 70 52N 155 55W
Meade River, *U.S.A.* **144 A8** 70 28N 157 24W
Meadow Lake, *Canada* **143 C7** 54 10N 108 26W
Meadow Lake Prov. Park, *Canada* **143 C7** 54 27N 109 0W
Meadow Valley Wash ⟶, *U.S.A.* **161 J12** 36 40N 114 34W
Meadville, *Mo., U.S.A.* **156 E3** 39 47N 93 18W
Meadville, *Pa., U.S.A.* **150 E4** 41 39N 80 9W
Meaford, *Canada* **140 D3** 44 36N 80 35W
Mealhada, *Portugal* **42 E2** 40 22N 8 27W
Mealy Mts., *Canada* **141 B8** 53 10N 58 0W
Meander River, *Canada* **142 B5** 59 2N 117 42W
Meares, C., *U.S.A.* **158 D2** 45 37N 124 0W
Mearim ⟶, *Brazil* **170 B3** 3 4 S 44 35W
Meath □, *Ireland* **23 C5** 53 40N 6 57W
Meath Park, *Canada* **143 C7** 53 27N 105 22W
Meatian, *Australia* **128 C5** 35 34 S 143 21 E
Meaulne, *France* **27 F9** 46 36N 2 36 E
Meaux, *France* **27 D9** 48 58N 2 50 E
Mebechi-Gawa ⟶, *Japan* **68 D10** 40 31N 141 31 E
Mebonden, *Norway* **18 A8** 63 13N 11 2 E
Mecanhelas, *Mozam.* **119 F4** 15 12 S 35 54 E
Mecaya ⟶, *Colombia* **168 C2** 0 29N 75 11W
Mecca = Makkah, *Si. Arabia* **98 B2** 21 30N 39 54 E
Mecca, *U.S.A.* **161 M10** 33 34N 116 5W
Mechanicsburg, *Ohio, U.S.A.* **157 D13** 40 4N 83 33W
Mechanicsburg, *Pa., U.S.A.* **150 F8** 40 13N 77 1W
Mechanicsville, *U.S.A.* **156 C5** 41 54N 91 16W
Mechanicville, *U.S.A.* **151 D11** 42 54N 73 41W
Mechara, *Ethiopia* **107 F5** 8 36N 40 20 E
Mechelen, *Belgium* **24 C4** 51 2N 4 29 E
Mecheria, *Algeria* **111 B4** 33 35N 0 18W

Moncalieri 251

Miramar, *Mozam.* **117 C6** 23 50 S 35 35 E
Miramas, *France* **29 E8** 43 33N 4 59 E
Mirambeau, *France* **28 C3** 45 23N 0 35W
Miramichi, *Canada* **141 C6** 47 2N 65 28W
Miramichi B., *Canada* **141 C7** 47 15N 65 0W
Miramont-de-Guyenne, *France* **28 D4** 44 37N 0 21 E
Miranda, *Brazil* **173 E6** 20 10 S 56 15W
Miranda □, *Venezuela* **168 A4** 10 15N 66 25W
Miranda →, *Brazil* **173 D6** 19 25 S 57 20W
Miranda de Ebro, *Spain* **40 C2** 42 41N 2 57W
Miranda do Corvo, *Portugal* **42 E2** 40 6N 8 20W
Miranda do Douro, *Portugal* **42 D4** 41 30N 6 16W
Mirande, *France* **28 E4** 43 31N 0 25 E
Mirandela, *Portugal* **42 D3** 41 32N 7 10W
Mirándola, *Italy* **44 D8** 44 53N 11 4 E
Mirandópolis, *Brazil* **175 A5** 21 9 S 51 6W
Mirango, *Malawi* **119 E3** 13 32 S 34 58 E
Mirano, *Italy* **45 C9** 45 30N 12 7 E
Miras, *Albania* **50 F4** 40 30N 20 56 E
Mirassol, *Brazil* **175 A6** 20 46 S 49 28W
Mirbāţ, *Oman* **99 C6** 17 0N 54 45 E
Mirboo North, *Australia* **129 E7** 38 24 S 146 10 E
Mirear, *Egypt* **106 C4** 23 15N 35 41 E
Mirebeau, *Côte-d'Or, France* **27 E12** 47 25N 5 20 E
Mirebeau, *Vienne, France* **26 F7** 46 49N 0 10 E
Mirecourt, *France* **27 D13** 48 20N 6 10 E
Mirgorod = Myrhorod, *Ukraine* **59 H7** 49 58N 33 37 E
Miri, *Malaysia* **78 D4** 4 23N 113 59 E
Mirialguda, *India* **94 F4** 16 52N 79 35 E
Miriam Vale, *Australia* **126 C5** 24 20 S 151 33 E
Miribel, *France* **27 G11** 45 50N 4 57 E
Mirigama, *Sri Lanka* **95 L5** 7 15N 80 8 E
Mirim, L., *S. Amer.* **175 C5** 32 45 S 52 50W
Mirimire, *Venezuela* **168 A4** 11 10N 68 43W
Miriti, *Brazil* **173 B6** 6 15 S 59 0W
Mirnyy, *Russia* **65 C12** 62 33N 113 53 E
Miroč, *Serbia, Yug.* **50 B6** 44 32N 22 16 E
Mirokhan, *Pakistan* **92 F3** 27 46N 68 6 E
Mirond L., *Canada* **143 B8** 55 6N 102 47W
Mirosławiec, *Poland* **54 E3** 53 20N 16 5 E
Mirpur, *Pakistan* **93 C5** 33 32N 73 56 E
Mirpur Batoro, *Pakistan* **92 G3** 24 44N 68 16 E
Mirpur Bibiwari, *Pakistan* **92 E2** 28 33N 67 44 E
Mirpur Khas, *Pakistan* **91 D3** 25 30N 69 0 E
Mirpur Sakro, *Pakistan* **92 G2** 24 33N 67 41 E
Mirria, *Niger* **113 C6** 13 43N 9 7 E
Mirsk, *Poland* **55 H2** 50 58N 15 23 E
Mirtağ, *Turkey* **96 B4** 38 23N 41 56 E
Miryang, *S. Korea* **75 G15** 35 31N 128 44 E
Mirzaani, *Georgia* **61 K8** 41 24N 46 5 E
Mirzapur, *India* **93 G10** 25 10N 82 34 E
Mirzapur-cum-Vindhyachal = Mirzapur, *India* **93 G10** 25 10N 82 34 E
Misamis Occidental □, *Phil.* **81 G5** 8 20N 123 42 E
Misamis Oriental □, *Phil.* **81 G5** 8 45N 125 0 E
Misantla, *Mexico* **163 D5** 19 56N 96 50W
Misawa, *Japan* **68 D10** 40 41N 141 24 E
Miscou I., *Canada* **141 C7** 47 57N 64 31W
Mish'āb, Ra's al, *Si. Arabia* **97 D6** 28 15N 48 43 E
Mishagua →, *Peru* **172 C3** 11 12 S 72 58W
Mishan, *China* **73 B8** 45 37N 131 48 E
Mishawaka, *U.S.A.* **157 C10** 41 40N 86 11W
Mishbih, Gebel, *Egypt* **106 C3** 22 38N 34 44 E
Mishima, *Japan* **71 B10** 35 10N 138 52 E
Mishmi Hills, *India* **90 A5** 29 0N 96 0 E
Misima I., *Papua N. G.* **132 F7** 10 40 S 152 45 E
Misión, *Mexico* **161 N10** 32 6N 116 53W
Misión Fagnano, *Argentina* **176 D3** 54 32 S 67 17W
Misiones □, *Argentina* **175 B5** 27 0 S 55 0W
Misiones □, *Paraguay* **174 B4** 27 0 S 56 0W
Miskah, *Si. Arabia* **96 E4** 24 49N 42 56 E
Miskitos, Cayos, *Nic.* **164 D3** 14 26N 82 50W
Miskolc, *Hungary* **52 B5** 48 7N 20 50 E
Misoke, *Dem. Rep. of the Congo* **118 C2** 0 42 S 28 2 E
Misool, *Indonesia* **79 E8** 1 52 S 130 10 E
Misrātah, *Libya* **108 B3** 32 24N 15 3 E
Misrātah □, *Libya* **108 C3** 33 30N 15 0 E
Missanabie, *Canada* **140 C3** 48 20N 84 6W
Missão Catrimani, *Brazil* **169 C5** 2 48N 62 18W
Missão Velha, *Brazil* **170 C4** 7 15 S 39 10W
Missinaibi →, *Canada* **140 B3** 50 43N 81 29W
Missinaibi L., *Canada* **140 C3** 48 23N 83 40W
Mission, *Canada* **142 D4** 49 10N 122 15W
Mission, *S. Dak., U.S.A.* **154 D4** 43 18N 100 39W
Mission, *Tex., U.S.A.* **155 M5** 26 13N 98 20W
Mission Beach, *Australia* **126 B4** 17 53 S 146 6 E
Mission Viejo, *U.S.A.* **161 M9** 33 36N 117 40W
Missirah, *Senegal* **112 C1** 13 40N 16 30W
Missisa L., *Canada* **140 B2** 52 20N 85 7W
Missisicabi →, *Canada* **140 B4** 51 14N 79 31W
Mississagi →, *Canada* **140 C3** 46 15N 83 9W
Mississauga, *Canada* **150 C5** 43 32N 79 35W
Mississinewa L., *U.S.A.* **157 D10** 40 46N 86 3W
Mississippi □, *U.S.A.* **155 J10** 33 0N 90 0W
Mississippi →, *U.S.A.* **155 L10** 29 9N 89 15W
Mississippi L., *Canada* **151 A8** 45 5N 76 10W
Mississippi River Delta, *U.S.A.* **155 L9** 29 10N 89 15W
Mississippi Sd., *U.S.A.* **155 K10** 30 20N 89 0W
Missoula, *U.S.A.* **158 C7** 46 52N 114 1W
Missour, *Morocco* **110 B4** 33 3N 4 0W
Missouri □, *U.S.A.* **156 E3** 38 25N 92 30W
Missouri →, *U.S.A.* **156 F6** 38 49N 90 7W
Missouri City, *U.S.A.* **155 L7** 29 37N 95 32W
Missouri Valley, *U.S.A.* **154 E7** 41 34N 95 53W
Mist, *U.S.A.* **160 E3** 45 59N 123 15W
Mistassibi →, *Canada* **141 B5** 48 53N 72 13W
Mistassini, *Canada* **141 C5** 48 53N 72 12W
Mistassini →, *Canada* **141 C5** 48 42N 72 20W
Mistassini, L., *Canada* **140 B5** 51 0N 73 30W
Mistastin L., *Canada* **141 A7** 55 57N 63 20W
Mistelbach, *Austria* **35 C9** 48 34N 16 34 E
Misterbianco, *Italy* **47 E8** 37 31N 15 1 E
Misti, Volcán, *Peru* **172 D3** 16 18 S 71 24W
Mistinibi, L., *Canada* **141 A7** 55 56N 64 17W
Mistretta, *Italy* **47 E7** 37 56N 14 22 E
Misty L., *Canada* **143 B8** 58 53N 101 40W
Misugi, *Japan* **71 C8** 34 31N 136 16 E
Misumi, *Japan* **70 E2** 32 37N 130 27 E
Misurata = Misrātah, *Libya* **108 B3** 32 24N 15 3 E
Mît Ghamr, *Egypt* **106 H7** 30 42N 31 12 E
Mitaka, *Japan* **71 B11** 35 40N 139 33 E
Mitan, *Uzbekistan* **63 C3** 40 5N 66 35 E
Mitatib, *Sudan* **107 D4** 15 59N 36 12 E
Mitchell, *Australia* **127 D4** 26 29 S 147 58 E
Mitchell, *Canada* **150 C3** 43 28N 81 12W
Mitchell, *Ga., U.S.A.* **152 B7** 33 13N 82 42W
Mitchell, *Ind., U.S.A.* **157 F10** 38 44N 86 28W
Mitchell, *Nebr., U.S.A.* **154 E3** 41 57N 103 49W
Mitchell, *Oreg., U.S.A.* **158 D3** 44 34N 120 9W
Mitchell, *S. Dak., U.S.A.* **154 D6** 43 43N 98 2W
Mitchell →, *Australia* **126 B3** 15 12 S 141 35 E
Mitchell, Mt., *U.S.A.* **149 H4** 35 46N 82 16W
Mitchell Ranges, *Australia* **126 A2** 12 49 S 135 36 E
Mitchelstown, *Ireland* **23 D3** 52 15N 8 16W
Mitha Tiwana, *Pakistan* **92 C5** 32 13N 72 6 E
Mithi, *Pakistan* **92 G3** 24 44N 69 48 E
Míthimna, *Greece* **49 B8** 39 20N 26 12 E
Mithrao, *Pakistan* **92 F3** 27 28N 69 40 E
Mitiamo, *Australia* **128 D6** 36 12 S 144 15 E
Mitilíni, *Greece* **49 B8** 39 6N 26 35 E
Mitilinoí, *Greece* **49 D8** 37 42N 26 56 E
Mito, *Japan* **71 A12** 36 20N 140 30 E
Mitra Mt., *Eq. Guin.* **114 B1** 1 23N 9 19 E
Mitre, Mt., *N.Z.* **130 G4** 40 50 S 175 30 E
Mitrofanovka, *Russia* **59 H10** 49 58N 39 42 E
Mitrovica = Kosovska Mitrovica, *Kosovo, Yug.* **50 D4** 42 54N 20 52 E
Mitsang, *Gabon* **114 B2** 0 42N 12 33 E
Mitsinjo, *Madag.* **117 B8** 16 1 S 45 52 E
Mitsiwa, *Eritrea* **102 D2** 15 35N 39 25 E
Mitsiwa Channel, *Eritrea* **107 D5** 15 30N 40 0 E
Mitsukaidō, *Japan* **71 A11** 36 1N 139 59 E
Mittagong, *Australia* **129 C9** 34 28 S 150 29 E
Mittelberg, *Austria* **33 C11** 46 57N 10 53 E
Mittelberg, *Austria* **33 B10** 47 20N 10 10 E
Mittelberg, *Germany* **33 A10** 47 38N 10 26 E
Mittelfranken □, *Germany* **31 F6** 49 25N 10 40 E
Mittelland, *Switz.* **32 C4** 46 50N 7 23 E
Mittellandkanal →, *Germany* **30 C4** 52 20N 8 28 E
Mittenwalde, *Germany* **30 C9** 52 16N 13 31 E
Mittersill, *Austria* **34 D5** 47 16N 12 29 E
Mitterteich, *Germany* **31 F8** 49 57N 12 14 E
Mittweida, *Germany* **30 E8** 50 59N 12 59 E
Mitú, *Colombia* **168 C3** 1 15N 70 13W
Mituas, *Colombia* **168 C4** 3 52N 68 49W
Mitumba, *Tanzania* **118 D3** 7 8 S 31 2 E
Mitumba, Mts., *Dem. Rep. of the Congo* **118 D2** 7 0 S 27 30 E
Mitwaba, *Dem. Rep. of the Congo* **119 D2** 8 2 S 27 17 E
Mityana, *Uganda* **118 B3** 0 23N 32 2 E
Mitzic, *Gabon* **114 B2** 0 45N 11 40 E
Miura, *Japan* **71 B11** 35 12N 139 40 E
Mixteco →, *Mexico* **163 D5** 18 11N 98 30W
Miyagi □, *Japan* **68 E10** 38 15N 140 45 E
Miyâh, W. el →, *Egypt* **106 C3** 25 0N 33 23 E
Miyâh, W. el →, *Syria* **96 C3** 34 44N 39 57 E
Miyake-Jima, *Japan* **71 C11** 34 5N 139 30 E
Miyako, *Japan* **68 E10** 39 40N 141 59 E
Miyako-Jima, *Japan* **69 M2** 24 45N 125 20 E
Miyako-Rettō, *Japan* **69 M2** 24 24N 125 0 E
Miyakonojō, *Japan* **69 J5** 31 40N 131 5 E
Miyani, *India* **92 J3** 21 50N 69 26 E
Miyanojō, *Japan* **69 J5** 31 54N 130 27 E
Miyanoura-Dake, *Japan* **69 J5** 30 20N 130 31 E
Miyata, *Japan* **70 D2** 33 49N 130 42 E
Miyazaki, *Japan* **70 F3** 31 56N 131 30 E
Miyazaki □, *Japan* **70 E3** 32 30N 131 30 E
Miyazu, *Japan* **71 B7** 35 35N 135 10 E
Miyet, Bahr el = Dead Sea, *Asia* **103 D4** 31 30N 35 30 E
Miyi, *China* **76 D4** 26 47N 102 9 E
Miyoshi, *Japan* **70 C4** 34 48N 132 51 E
Miyun, *China* **74 D9** 40 28N 116 50 E
Miyun Shuiku, *China* **75 D9** 40 30N 117 0 E
Mizan Teferi, *Ethiopia* **107 F4** 6 57N 35 3 E
Mizdah, *Libya* **108 B2** 31 30N 13 0 E
Mizen Hd., *Cork, Ireland* **23 E2** 51 27N 9 50W
Mizen Hd., *Wick., Ireland* **23 D5** 52 51N 6 4W
Mizhi, *China* **74 F6** 37 47N 110 12 E
Mizil, *Romania* **53 F11** 44 59N 26 29 E
Mizoram □, *India* **90 D4** 23 30N 92 40 E
Mizpe Ramon, *Israel* **103 E3** 30 34N 34 49 E
Mizuho, *Japan* **71 B7** 35 6N 135 17 E
Mizunami, *Japan* **71 B9** 35 22N 137 15 E
Mizusawa, *Japan* **68 E10** 39 8N 141 8 E
Mjällby, *Sweden* **17 H8** 56 3N 14 40 E
Mjöbäck, *Sweden* **17 G6** 57 28N 12 53 E
Mjölby, *Sweden* **17 F9** 58 20N 15 10 E
Mjølfjell, *Norway* **18 D3** 60 41N 6 55 E
Mjømna, *Norway* **18 D1** 60 55N 4 55 E
Mjörn, *Sweden* **17 G6** 57 55N 12 25 E
Mjøsa, *Norway* **15 F14** 60 40N 11 0 E
Mkata, *Tanzania* **118 D4** 5 45 S 38 20 E
Mkokotoni, *Tanzania* **118 D4** 5 55 S 39 15 E
Mkomazi, *Tanzania* **118 C4** 4 40 S 38 7 E
Mkomazi →, *S. Africa* **117 E5** 30 12 S 30 50 E
Mkulwe, *Tanzania* **119 D3** 8 37 S 32 20 E
Mkumbi, Ras, *Tanzania* **118 D4** 7 38 S 39 55 E
Mkushi, *Zambia* **119 E2** 14 25 S 29 15 E
Mkushi River, *Zambia* **119 E2** 13 32 S 29 45 E
Mkuze, *S. Africa* **117 D5** 27 10 S 32 0 E
Mladá Boleslav, *Czech Rep.* **34 A7** 50 27N 14 53 E
Mladenovac, *Serbia, Yug.* **50 B4** 44 28N 20 44 E
Mlala Hills, *Tanzania* **118 D3** 6 50 S 31 40 E
Mlange = Mulanje, *Malawi* **119 F4** 16 2 S 35 33 E
Mlava →, *Serbia, Yug.* **50 B5** 44 45N 21 13 E
Mława, *Poland* **55 E7** 53 9N 20 25 E
Mlinište, *Bos.-H.* **45 D13** 44 15N 16 50 E
Mljet, *Croatia* **45 F14** 42 43N 17 30 E
Mljetski Kanal, *Croatia* **45 F14** 42 48N 17 35 E
Młynary, *Poland* **54 D6** 54 12N 19 46 E
Mmabatho, *S. Africa* **116 D4** 25 49 S 25 30 E
Mme, *Cameroon* **113 D7** 6 18N 10 14 E
Mnichovo Hradiště, *Czech Rep.* **34 A7** 50 32N 14 59 E
Mo, *Hordaland, Norway* **18 D2** 60 49N 5 48 E
Mo, *Møre og Romsdal, Norway* **18 A5** 63 0N 8 59 E
Mo, *Telemark, Norway* **18 E4** 59 28N 7 50 E
Mo i Rana, *Norway* **14 C16** 66 20N 14 7 E
Moa, *Cuba* **165 B4** 20 40N 74 56W
Moa, *Indonesia* **79 F7** 8 0 S 128 0 E
Moa →, *S. Leone* **112 D2** 6 59N 11 36W
Moab, *U.S.A.* **159 G9** 38 35N 109 33W
Moabi, *Gabon* **114 C2** 2 24 S 10 59 E
Moaco →, *Brazil* **172 B4** 7 41 S 68 18W
Moala, *Fiji* **133 B2** 18 36 S 179 53 E
Moama, *Australia* **127 F3** 36 7 S 144 46 E
Moamba, *Mozam.* **117 D5** 25 36 S 32 15 E
Moapa, *U.S.A.* **161 J12** 36 40N 114 37W
Moate, *Ireland* **23 C4** 53 24N 7 44W
Moba, *Dem. Rep. of the Congo* **118 D2** 7 0 S 29 48 E
Mobara, *Japan* **71 B12** 35 25N 140 18 E
Mobārakābād, *Iran* **97 D7** 28 24N 53 20 E
Mobaye, *C.A.R.* **114 B4** 4 25N 21 5 E
Mobayi, *Dem. Rep. of the Congo* **114 B4** 4 15N 21 8 E
Mobeka, *Dem. Rep. of the Congo* **114 B3** 1 52N 19 49 E
Mobenzélé, *Congo* **114 B3** 0 56N 17 50 E
Moberley Lake, *Canada* **142 B4** 55 50N 121 44W
Moberly, *U.S.A.* **156 E4** 39 25N 92 26W
Mobile, *U.S.A.* **149 K1** 30 41N 88 3W
Mobile B., *U.S.A.* **149 K2** 30 30N 88 0W
Mobridge, *U.S.A.* **154 C4** 45 32N 100 26W
Mobutu Sese Seko, L. = Albert L., *Africa* **118 B3** 1 30N 31 0 E
Moc Chau, *Vietnam* **86 B5** 20 50N 104 38 E
Moc Hoa, *Vietnam* **87 G5** 10 46N 105 56 E
Mocabe Kasari, *Dem. Rep. of the Congo* **119 D2** 9 58 S 26 12 E
Mocajuba, *Brazil* **170 B2** 2 35 S 49 30W
Moçambique, *Mozam.* **119 F5** 15 3 S 40 42 E
Moçâmedes = Namibe, *Angola* **115 F2** 15 7 S 12 11 E
Mocanaqua, *U.S.A.* **151 E8** 41 9N 76 8W
Mocapra →, *Venezuela* **168 B4** 7 56N 66 46W
Mocha, I., *Chile* **176 A2** 38 22 S 73 56W
Mochudi, *Botswana* **116 C4** 24 27 S 26 7 E
Mocimboa da Praia, *Mozam.* **119 E5** 11 25 S 40 20 E
Mociu, *Romania* **53 D9** 46 46N 24 3 E
Möckeln, *Sweden* **17 H8** 56 40N 14 15 E
Mockfjärd, *Sweden* **16 D8** 60 30N 14 57 E
Moclips, *U.S.A.* **160 C2** 47 14N 124 13W
Mocoa, *Colombia* **168 C2** 1 7N 76 35W
Mococa, *Brazil* **175 A6** 21 28 S 47 0W
Mocorito, *Mexico* **162 B3** 25 30N 107 53W
Moctezuma, *Mexico* **162 B3** 29 50N 109 0W
Moctezuma →, *Mexico* **163 C5** 21 59N 98 34W
Mocuba, *Mozam.* **119 F4** 16 54 S 36 57 E
Mocúzari, Presa, *Mexico* **162 B3** 27 10N 109 10W
Moda, *Burma* **90 C6** 24 22N 96 29 E
Modane, *France* **29 C10** 45 12N 6 40 E
Modasa, *India* **92 H5** 23 30N 73 21 E
Modder →, *S. Africa* **116 D3** 29 2 S 24 37 E
Modderrivier, *S. Africa* **116 D3** 29 2 S 24 38 E
Módena, *Italy* **44 D7** 44 40N 10 55 E
Modena, *U.S.A.* **159 H7** 37 48N 113 56W
Modesto, *U.S.A.* **160 H6** 37 39N 121 0W
Möðrudalur, *Iceland* **11 B11** 65 22N 15 53W
Möðruvellir, *Iceland* **11 B8** 65 46N 18 15W
Módica, *Italy* **47 F7** 36 52N 14 46 E
Modjamboli, *Dem. Rep. of the Congo* **114 B4** 2 28N 22 6 E
Mödling, *Austria* **35 C9** 48 5N 16 17 E
Modo, *Sudan* **107 F3** 5 31N 30 33 E
Modoc, *U.S.A.* **152 B7** 33 44N 82 13W
Modra, *Slovak Rep.* **35 C10** 48 19N 17 20 E
Modriča, *Bos.-H.* **52 F3** 44 57N 18 17 E
Moe, *Australia* **129 E7** 38 12 S 146 19 E
Moebase, *Mozam.* **119 F4** 17 3 S 38 41 E
Moëlan-sur-Mer, *France* **26 E3** 47 49N 3 38W
Moelv, *Norway* **18 D7** 60 56N 10 43 E
Moengo, *Surinam* **169 B7** 5 45N 54 20W
Moësa →, *Switz.* **33 D8** 46 12N 9 10 E
Moffat, *U.K.* **22 F5** 55 21N 3 27W
Moga, *India* **92 D6** 30 48N 75 8 E
Mogadishu = Muqdisho, *Somali Rep.* **120 D3** 2 2N 45 25 E
Mogador = Essaouira, *Morocco* **110 B3** 31 32N 9 42W
Mogadouro, *Portugal* **42 D4** 41 22N 6 47W
Mogalakwena →, *S. Africa* **117 C4** 22 38 S 28 40 E
Mogami-Gawa →, *Japan* **68 E10** 38 45N 140 0 E
Mogán, *Canary Is.* **39 G4** 27 53N 15 43W
Mogandjo, *Dem. Rep. of the Congo* **114 B4** 1 23N 24 15 E
Mogaung, *Burma* **90 C6** 25 20N 97 0 E
Mogen, *Norway* **18 D4** 60 2N 7 52 E
Mogente = Moixent, *Spain* **41 G4** 38 52N 0 45W
Mogho, *Ethiopia* **107 G5** 4 54N 40 16 E
Mogi das Cruzes, *Brazil* **175 A6** 23 31 S 46 11W
Mogi-Guaçu →, *Brazil* **175 A6** 20 53 S 48 10W
Mogi-Mirim, *Brazil* **175 A6** 22 29 S 47 0W
Mogielnica, *Poland* **55 G7** 51 42N 20 41 E
Mogige, *Ethiopia* **107 F4** 5 24N 36 14 E
Mogilev = Mahilyow, *Belarus* **58 F6** 53 55N 30 18 E
Mogilev-Podolskiy = Mohyliv-Podilskyy, *Ukraine* **59 H4** 48 26N 27 48 E
Mogilno, *Poland* **55 F4** 52 39N 17 55 E
Mogincual, *Mozam.* **119 F5** 15 35 S 40 25 E
Mogliano Véneto, *Italy* **45 C9** 45 33N 12 14 E
Mogocha, *Russia* **65 D12** 53 40N 119 50 E
Mogoi, *Indonesia* **83 B4** 1 55 S 133 10 E
Mogok, *Burma* **90 D6** 23 0N 96 40 E
Mogollon Rim, *U.S.A.* **159 J8** 34 10N 110 50W
Mógoro, *Italy* **46 C1** 39 41N 8 47 E
Mograt, *Sudan* **106 D3** 19 28N 33 16 E
Mogriguy, *Australia* **129 B8** 32 3 S 148 40 E
Moguer, *Spain* **43 H4** 37 15N 6 52W
Mogumber, *Australia* **125 F2** 31 2 S 116 3 E
Mohács, *Hungary* **52 E3** 45 58N 18 41 E
Mohaka →, *N.Z.* **130 F6** 39 7 S 177 12 E
Mohala, *India* **94 D5** 20 35N 80 44 E
Mohales Hoek, *Lesotho* **116 E4** 30 7 S 27 26 E
Mohali, *Congo* **114 B3** 0 15N 15 29 E
Mohall, *U.S.A.* **154 A4** 48 46N 101 31W
Moḩammadābād, *Iran* **97 B8** 37 52N 59 5 E
Mohammadia, *Algeria* **111 A5** 35 33N 0 3 E
Mohammedia, *Morocco* **110 B3** 33 44N 7 21W
Mohana, *India* **94 E7** 19 27N 84 16 E
Mohana →, *India* **93 G11** 24 43N 85 0 E
Mohanlalganj, *India* **93 F9** 26 41N 80 58 E
Mohave, L., *U.S.A.* **161 K12** 35 12N 114 34W
Mohawk →, *U.S.A.* **151 D11** 42 47N 73 41W
Moheda, *Sweden* **17 G8** 57 1N 14 35 E
Mohenjodaro, *Pakistan* **92 F3** 27 19N 68 7 E
Mohicanville Reservoir, *U.S.A.* **150 F3** 40 45N 82 0W
Möhlin, *Switz.* **32 A5** 47 33N 7 51 E
Möhne →, *Germany* **30 D3** 51 29N 7 57 E
Mohnyin, *Burma* **90 C6** 24 47N 96 22 E
Mohoro, *Tanzania* **118 D4** 8 6 S 39 8 E
Mohyliv-Podilskyy, *Ukraine* **59 H4** 48 26N 27 48 E
Moi, *Norway* **18 F3** 58 27N 6 32 E
Moia, *Sudan* **107 F2** 5 3N 28 2 E
Moidart, L., *U.K.* **22 E3** 56 47N 5 52W
Moinabad, *India* **94 F3** 17 44N 77 16 E
Moindou, *N. Cal.* **133 U19** 21 42 S 165 41 E
Moinești, *Romania* **53 D11** 46 28N 26 31 E
Moira →, *Canada* **150 B7** 44 21N 77 24W
Moirans, *France* **29 C9** 45 20N 5 33 E
Moirans-en-Montagne, *France* **27 F12** 46 26N 5 43 E
Moíres, *Greece* **38 D6** 35 4N 24 56 E
Moisaküla, *Estonia* **15 G21** 58 3N 25 12 E
Moisie, *Canada* **141 B6** 50 12N 66 1W
Moisie →, *Canada* **141 B6** 50 14N 66 5W
Moissac, *France* **28 D5** 44 7N 1 5 E
Moïssala, *Chad* **109 G3** 8 21N 17 46 E
Moita, *Portugal* **43 G2** 38 38N 8 58W
Moixent, *Spain* **41 G4** 38 52N 0 45W
Möja, *Sweden* **16 E12** 59 26N 18 55 E
Mojácar, *Spain* **41 H3** 37 6N 1 55W
Mojados, *Spain* **42 D6** 41 26N 4 40W
Mojave, *U.S.A.* **161 K8** 35 3N 118 10W
Mojave Desert, *U.S.A.* **161 L10** 35 0N 116 30W
Mojiang, *China* **76 F3** 23 37N 101 35 E
Mojjo →, *Ethiopia* **107 F5** 7 55N 42 0 E
Mojkovac, *Montenegro, Yug.* **50 D3** 42 58N 19 35 E
Mojo, *Bolivia* **174 A2** 21 48 S 65 33W
Mojo, *Ethiopia* **107 F4** 8 35N 39 5 E
Mojokerto, *Indonesia* **79 G15** 7 28 S 112 26 E
Mojos, Llanos de, *Bolivia* **173 D5** 15 10 S 65 0W
Moju, *Brazil* **170 B2** 1 53 S 48 46W
Moju →, *Brazil* **170 B2** 1 40 S 48 25W
Mokai, *N.Z.* **130 E4** 38 32 S 175 56 E
Mokambo, *Dem. Rep. of the Congo* **119 E2** 12 25 S 28 20 E
Mokameh, *India* **93 G11** 25 24N 85 55 E
Mokane, *U.S.A.* **156 F5** 38 41N 91 53W
Mokapu Peninsula, *U.S.A.* **145 K14** 21 25N 157 45W
Mokau, *N.Z.* **130 E3** 38 42 S 174 39 E
Mokau →, *N.Z.* **130 E3** 38 35 S 174 35 E
Mokelumne →, *U.S.A.* **160 G5** 38 13N 121 28W
Mokelumne Hill, *U.S.A.* **160 G6** 38 18N 120 43W
Mokhós, *Greece* **38 D7** 35 16N 25 27 E
Mokhotlong, *Lesotho* **117 D4** 29 22 S 29 2 E
Mokihinui →, *N.Z.* **131 B6** 41 33 S 171 58 E
Möklinta, *Sweden* **16 D10** 60 4N 16 33 E
Moknine, *Tunisia* **108 A2** 35 35N 10 58 E
Mokolea Rock, *U.S.A.* **145 K14** 21 27N 157 44W
Mokolo, *Cameroon* **113 C7** 10 50N 13 55 E
Mokolo, *Dem. Rep. of the Congo* **114 B3** 1 55N 18 6 E
Mokolo →, *S. Africa* **117 C4** 23 14 S 27 43 E
Mokombe, *Dem. Rep. of the Congo* **114 C4** 0 14 S 23 48 E
Mokpalin, *Burma* **90 G6** 17 26N 96 53 E
Mokp'o, *S. Korea* **75 G14** 34 50N 126 25 E
Mokra Gora, *Yugoslavia* **50 D4** 42 50N 20 30 E
Mokronog, *Slovenia* **45 C12** 45 57N 15 9 E
Moksha →, *Russia* **60 C6** 54 45N 41 53 E
Mokshan, *Russia* **60 D7** 53 25N 44 35 E
Mokuaeae I., *U.S.A.* **145 A2** 22 14N 159 25W
Mokuauia I., *U.S.A.* **145 J14** 21 40N 157 56W
Mokulua Is., *U.S.A.* **145 K14** 21 24N 157 42W
Mokwa, *Nigeria* **113 D6** 9 19N 5 0 E
Mol, *Belgium* **24 C5** 51 11N 5 5 E
Mola di Bari, *Italy* **47 A10** 41 4N 17 5 E
Molakalmuru, *India* **95 G3** 14 55N 76 50 E
Molale, *Ethiopia* **107 E4** 10 10N 39 41 E
Molanda, *Dem. Rep. of the Congo* **114 B4** 2 28N 20 48 E
Moláoi, *Greece* **48 E4** 36 49N 22 56 E
Molara, *Italy* **46 B2** 40 52N 9 43 E
Molat, *Croatia* **45 D11** 44 15N 14 50 E
Molave, *Phil.* **81 G4** 8 5N 123 30 E
Molchanovo, *Russia* **64 D9** 57 40N 83 50 E
Mold, *U.K.* **20 D4** 53 9N 3 8W
Moldava nad Bodvou, *Slovak Rep.* **35 C14** 48 38N 21 0 E
Moldavia = Moldova ■, *Europe* **53 C13** 47 0N 28 0 E
Moldavia, *Romania* **53 D12** 46 30N 27 0 E
Molde, *Norway* **14 E12** 62 45N 7 9 E
Moldotau, Khrebet, *Kyrgyzstan* **63 C7** 41 35N 75 0 E
Moldova ■, *Europe* **53 C13** 47 0N 28 0 E
Moldova Nouă, *Romania* **52 F6** 44 45N 21 41 E
Moldoveana, Vf., *Romania* **53 E9** 45 36N 24 45 E
Moldovița, *Romania* **53 C10** 47 41N 25 32 E
Mole →, *U.K.* **21 F7** 51 24N 0 21W
Mole Creek, *Australia* **126 G4** 41 34 S 146 24 E
Molegbwe, *Dem. Rep. of the Congo* **114 B4** 4 12N 20 53 E
Molepolole, *Botswana* **116 C4** 24 28 S 25 28 E
Molesworth, *N.Z.* **131 C8** 42 5 S 173 16 E
Molfetta, *Italy* **47 A9** 41 12N 16 36 E
Molii Pond, *U.S.A.* **145 J14** 21 31N 157 51W
Molina de Aragón, *Spain* **40 E3** 40 46N 1 52W
Molina de Segura, *Spain* **41 G3** 38 3N 1 12W
Moline, *U.S.A.* **156 C6** 41 30N 90 31W
Molinella, *Italy* **45 D8** 44 37N 11 40 E
Molino, *U.S.A.* **153 E2** 30 43N 87 20W
Molinos, *Argentina* **174 B2** 25 28 S 66 15W
Moliro, *Dem. Rep. of the Congo* **118 D3** 8 12 S 30 30 E
Moliterno, *Italy* **47 B8** 40 14N 15 52 E
Molkom, *Sweden* **16 E7** 59 37N 13 44 E
Mölle, *Sweden* **17 H6** 56 17N 12 31 E
Molledo, *Spain* **42 B6** 43 8N 4 6W
Mollendo, *Peru* **172 D3** 17 0 S 72 0W
Mollerin, L., *Australia* **125 F2** 30 30 S 117 35 E
Mollerussa, *Spain* **40 D5** 41 37N 0 54 E
Mollina, *Spain* **43 H6** 37 8N 4 38W
Mölln, *Germany* **30 B6** 53 39N 10 41 E
Mölltorp, *Sweden* **17 F8** 58 30N 14 26 E
Mölnlycke, *Sweden* **17 G6** 57 40N 12 8 E
Molo, *Burma* **90 D6** 23 22N 96 53 E
Molochansk, *Ukraine* **59 J8** 47 15N 35 35 E
Molochnoye, Ozero, *Ukraine* **59 J8** 46 30N 35 20 E
Molodechno = Maladzyechna, *Belarus* **58 E4** 54 20N 26 50 E
Molokai, *U.S.A.* **146 H16** 21 8N 157 0W
Molokini I., *U.S.A.* **145 C5** 20 38N 156 30W
Moloma →, *Russia* **62 B2** 58 29N 48 33 E
Molong, *Australia* **129 B8** 33 5 S 148 54 E
Molopo →, *Africa* **116 D3** 27 30 S 20 13 E
Mólos, *Greece* **48 C4** 38 47N 22 37 E
Molotov = Perm, *Russia* **62 C6** 58 0N 56 10 E
Moloundou, *Cameroon* **114 B3** 2 8N 15 15 E
Molowaie, *Dem. Rep. of the Congo* **115 D4** 5 47 S 23 18 E
Molsheim, *France* **27 D14** 48 33N 7 29 E
Molson L., *Canada* **143 C9** 54 22N 96 40W
Molteno, *S. Africa* **116 E4** 31 22 S 26 22 E
Moltrásio, *Italy* **33 E8** 45 52N 9 6 E
Molu, *Indonesia* **79 F8** 6 45 S 131 40 E
Molucca Sea, *Indonesia* **79 E6** 2 0 S 124 0 E
Moluccas = Maluku, *Indonesia* **79 E7** 1 0 S 127 0 E
Molundo, *Phil.* **81 H5** 7 57N 124 23 E
Moma, *Dem. Rep. of the Congo* **118 C1** 1 35 S 23 52 E
Moma, *Mozam.* **119 F4** 16 47 S 39 4 E
Momba, *Australia* **128 A5** 30 58 S 143 30 E
Mombaça, *Brazil* **170 C4** 5 43 S 39 45W
Mombango, *Dem. Rep. of the Congo* **114 B4** 1 45N 24 26 E
Mombasa, *Kenya* **118 C4** 4 2 S 39 43 E
Mombetsu, *Japan* **68 B11** 44 21N 143 22 E
Mombil, *Burma* **90 B7** 27 46N 98 6 E
Momboyo →, *Dem. Rep. of the Congo* **114 C3** 0 16 S 19 0 E
Mombuey, *Spain* **42 C4** 42 3N 6 20W
Momchilgrad, *Bulgaria* **51 E9** 41 33N 25 23 E
Momence, *U.S.A.* **157 C9** 41 10N 87 40W
Momi, *Dem. Rep. of the Congo* **118 C2** 1 42 S 27 0 E
Mompog Pass, *Phil.* **80 E4** 13 34N 122 13 E
Mompós, *Colombia* **168 B3** 9 14N 74 26W
Møn, *Denmark* **17 K6** 54 57N 12 20 E
Mona, Canal de la, *W. Indies* **165 C6** 18 30N 67 45W
Mona, Isla, *Puerto Rico* **165 C6** 18 5N 67 54W
Mona, Pta., *Costa Rica* **164 E3** 9 37N 82 36W
Mona Quimbundo, *Angola* **115 D3** 9 55 S 19 58 E
Monaca, *U.S.A.* **150 F4** 40 41N 80 17W
Monaco ■, *Europe* **29 E11** 43 46N 7 23 E
Monadhliath Mts., *U.K.* **22 D4** 57 10N 4 4W
Monadnock, Mt., *U.S.A.* **151 D12** 42 52N 72 7W
Monagas □, *Venezuela* **169 B5** 9 20N 63 0W
Monaghan, *Ireland* **23 B5** 54 15N 6 57W
Monaghan □, *Ireland* **23 B5** 54 11N 6 56W
Monahans, *U.S.A.* **155 K3** 31 36N 102 54W
Monapo, *Mozam.* **119 E5** 14 56 S 40 19 E
Monar, L., *U.K.* **22 D3** 57 26N 5 8W
Monaragala, *Sri Lanka* **95 L5** 6 52N 81 22 E
Monarch Mt., *Canada* **142 C3** 51 55N 125 57W
Monashee Mts., *Canada* **142 C5** 51 0N 118 43W
Monasterevin, *Ireland* **23 C4** 53 8N 7 4W
Monastir = Bitola, *Macedonia* **50 E5** 41 1N 21 20 E
Monastir, *Tunisia* **108 A2** 35 50N 10 49 E
Moncada, *Phil.* **80 D3** 15 44N 120 34 E
Moncalieri, *Italy* **44 D4** 45 0N 7 41 E

Muhos 253

Morioka, Japan 68 E10 39 45N 141 8 E
Moris, Mexico 162 B3 28 8N 108 32W
Morisset, Australia 129 B9 33 6 S 151 30 E
Morlaàs, France 28 E3 43 21N 0 18W
Morlaix, France 26 D3 48 36N 3 52W
Mörlunda, Sweden 17 G9 57 19N 15 52 E
Mormanno, Italy 47 C8 39 53N 15 59 E
Mormant, France 27 D9 48 37N 2 52 E
Mornington, Australia 129 E6 38 15 S 145 5 E
Mornington, I., Chile 176 C1 49 50 S 75 30W
Mornington I., Australia 126 B2 16 30 S 139 30 E
Mórnos →, Greece 48 C3 38 25N 21 50 E
Moro, Pakistan 92 F2 26 40N 68 0 E
Moro, Sudan 107 E3 10 50N 30 9 E
Moro →, Pakistan 92 E2 29 42N 67 22 E
Moro G., Phil. 79 C6 6 30N 123 0 E
Morobe, Papua N. G. 132 D4 7 49 S 147 38 E
Morocco, U.S.A. 157 D9 40 57N 87 27W
Morocco ■, N. Afr. 110 B3 32 0N 5 50W
Morococha, Peru 172 C2 11 40 S 76 5W
Morogoro, Tanzania 118 D4 6 50 S 37 40 E
Morogoro □, Tanzania 118 D4 8 0 S 37 0 E
Moroleón, Mexico 162 C4 20 8N 101 32W
Morombe, Madag. 117 C7 21 45 S 43 22 E
Moron, Argentina 174 C4 34 39 S 58 37W
Morón, Cuba 164 B4 22 8N 78 39W
Morón de Almazán, Spain 40 D2 41 29N 2 27W
Morón de la Frontera, Spain 43 H5 37 6N 5 28W
Morona →, Peru 168 D2 4 40 S 77 10W
Morona-Santiago □, Ecuador 168 D2 2 30 S 78 0W
Morondava, Madag. 117 C7 20 17 S 44 17 E
Morondo, Ivory C. 112 D3 8 57N 6 47W
Morong, Phil. 80 D3 14 41N 120 16 E
Morongo Valley, U.S.A. 161 L10 34 3N 116 37W
Moroni, Comoros Is. 105 H8 11 40 S 43 16 E
Moroni, U.S.A. 158 G8 39 32N 111 35W
Moronou, Ivory C. 112 D4 6 16N 4 59W
Morotai, Indonesia 79 D7 2 10N 128 30 E
Moroto, Uganda 118 B3 2 28N 34 42 E
Moroto Summit, Kenya 118 B3 2 30N 34 43 E
Morozov, Bulgaria 51 D9 42 30N 25 10 E
Morozovsk, Russia 61 F5 48 25N 41 50 E
Morpeth, U.K. 20 B6 55 10N 1 41W
Morphou, Cyprus 38 D11 35 12N 32 59 E
Morphou Bay, Cyprus 38 D11 35 15N 32 50 E
Morrelganj, Bangla. 92 D2 22 28N 89 51 E
Morrilton, U.S.A. 155 H8 35 9N 92 44W
Morrinhos, Ceará, Brazil 170 B3 3 14 S 40 7W
Morrinhos, Minas Gerais, Brazil 171 E2 17 45 S 49 10W
Morrinsville, N.Z. 130 D4 37 40 S 175 32 E
Morris, Canada 143 D9 49 25N 97 22W
Morris, Ill., U.S.A. 154 E10 41 22N 88 26W
Morris, Minn., U.S.A. 154 C7 45 35N 95 55W
Morris, N.Y., U.S.A. 151 D9 42 33N 75 15W
Morris, Pa., U.S.A. 150 E7 41 35N 77 17W
Morris, Mt., Australia 125 E5 26 9 S 131 4 E
Morris Jesup, Kap, Greenland 10 A7 83 40N 34 0W
Morrisburg, Canada 151 B9 44 55N 75 7W
Morrison, U.S.A. 154 C7 41 49N 89 58W
Morrisonville, U.S.A. 156 E7 39 25N 89 27W
Morristown, Ariz., U.S.A. 159 K7 33 51N 112 37W
Morristown, Ind., U.S.A. 157 E11 39 40N 85 42W
Morristown, N.J., U.S.A. 151 F10 40 48N 74 29W
Morristown, N.Y., U.S.A. 151 B9 44 35N 75 39W
Morristown, Tenn., U.S.A. 149 G4 36 13N 83 18W
Morrisville, N.Y., U.S.A. 151 D9 42 53N 75 35W
Morrisville, Pa., U.S.A. 151 F10 40 13N 74 47W
Morrisville, Vt., U.S.A. 151 B12 44 34N 72 36W
Morro, Pta., Chile 174 B1 27 6 S 71 0W
Morro Bay, U.S.A. 160 K6 35 22N 120 51W
Morro Chico, Chile 176 D2 52 2 S 71 26W
Morro del Jable, Canary Is. 39 F5 28 3N 14 23W
Morro do Chapéu, Brazil 171 D3 11 33 S 41 9W
Morro Jable, Pta. de, Canary Is. 39 F5 28 2N 14 20W
Morros, Brazil 170 B3 2 52 S 44 3W
Morrosquillo, G. de, Colombia 164 E4 9 35N 75 40W
Morrow, U.S.A. 157 E12 39 21N 84 8W
Mörrum, Sweden 17 H8 56 12N 14 45 E
Morrumbene, Mozam. 117 C6 23 31 S 35 16 E
Mörrumsån →, Sweden 17 H8 56 10N 14 45 E
Mors, Denmark 17 H2 56 50N 8 45 E
Morshansk, Russia 60 D5 53 28N 41 50 E
Morsi, India 94 D4 21 21N 78 0 E
Mörsil, Sweden 16 A7 63 19N 13 40 E
Mortagne →, France 27 D13 48 33N 6 27 E
Mortagne-au-Perche, France 26 D7 48 31N 0 33 E
Mortagne-sur-Gironde, France 28 C3 45 28N 0 47W
Mortagne-sur-Sèvre, France 26 F6 47 0N 0 59W
Mortain, France 26 D6 48 40N 0 57W
Mortara, Italy 44 C5 45 15N 8 44 E
Mortcha, Chad 109 E4 16 0N 21 10 E
Morteau, France 27 E13 47 3N 6 35 E
Morteros, Argentina 174 C3 30 50 S 62 0W
Mortes, R. das →, Brazil 171 D1 11 45 S 50 44W
Mortlach, Canada 143 C7 50 27N 106 4W
Mortlake, Australia 128 E5 38 5 S 142 50 E
Morton, Ill., U.S.A. 156 D7 40 37N 89 28W
Morton, Tex., U.S.A. 155 J3 33 44N 102 46W
Morton, Wash., U.S.A. 160 D4 46 34N 122 17W
Morundah, Australia 129 C7 34 57 S 146 19 E
Moruya, Australia 129 C9 35 58 S 150 3 E
Morvan, France 27 E11 47 5N 4 3 E
Morven, Australia 127 D4 26 22 S 147 5 E
Morven, N.Z. 131 E6 44 50 S 171 6 E
Morven, U.S.A. 152 E6 30 57N 83 30W
Morvern, U.K. 22 E3 56 38N 5 44W
Morwell, Australia 129 E7 38 10 S 146 22 E
Moryń, Poland 55 F1 52 51N 14 22 E
Morzhovets, Ostrov, Russia 56 A7 66 44N 42 35 E
Morzine, France 27 F13 46 11N 6 42 E
Mosalsk, Russia 58 E8 54 30N 34 55 E
Mosbach, Germany 31 F5 49 21N 9 9 E
Mosby, Norway 18 F4 58 12N 7 55 E
Mošćenice, Croatia 45 C11 45 17N 14 16 E
Mosciano Sant' Ángelo, Italy 45 F10 42 42N 13 52 E
Moscos Is. = Maungmagan Is., Burma 78 B1 14 0N 97 30 E
Moscow = Moskva, Russia 58 E9 55 45N 37 35 E
Moscow, Idaho, U.S.A. 158 C5 46 44N 117 0W
Moscow, Mich., U.S.A. 157 B12 42 3N 84 30W
Moscow, Pa., U.S.A. 151 E9 41 20N 75 31W
Moscow Mills, U.S.A. 156 F6 38 57N 90 55W
Mosel →, Europe 27 B14 50 22N 7 36 E
Moselle = Mosel →, Europe 27 B14 50 22N 7 36 E
Moselle □, France 27 D13 48 59N 6 33 E
Moses Lake, U.S.A. 158 C4 47 8N 119 17W
Mosgiel, N.Z. 131 F5 45 53 S 170 21 E
Moshaweng →, S. Africa 116 D3 26 35 S 22 50 E
Moshi, Tanzania 118 C4 3 22 S 37 18 E
Moshupa, Botswana 116 C4 24 46 S 25 29 E
Mosina, Poland 55 F3 52 15N 16 50 E
Mosite, Dem. Rep. of the Congo 114 B4 0 53N 23 40 E
Mosjøen, Norway 14 D15 65 51N 13 12 E
Moskenesøya, Norway 14 C15 67 58N 13 0 E
Moskenstraumen, Norway 14 C15 67 47N 12 45 E
Moskog, Norway 18 C2 61 26N 6 0 E
Moskva, Russia 58 E9 55 45N 37 35 E
Moskva →, Russia 58 E10 55 5N 38 51 E
Moslavačka Gora, Croatia 45 C13 45 40N 16 37 E
Moso, Vanuatu 133 G6 17 30 S 168 15 E
Mosomane, Botswana 116 C4 24 2 S 26 19 E
Moson-magyaróvár, Hungary 52 C2 47 52N 17 18 E
Mošorin, Serbia, Yug. 52 E5 45 19N 20 4 E
Mospino, Ukraine 59 J9 47 52N 38 0 E
Mosqueiro, Brazil 170 B2 1 10 S 48 28W
Mosquera, Colombia 168 C2 2 35N 78 24W
Mosquero, U.S.A. 155 H3 35 47N 103 58W
Mosqueruela, Spain 40 E4 40 21N 0 27W
Mosquitia, Honduras 164 C3 15 20N 84 10W
Mosquito Coast = Mosquitia, Honduras 164 C3 15 20N 84 10W
Mosquito Creek L., U.S.A. 150 E4 41 18N 80 46W
Mosquito L., Canada 143 A8 62 35N 103 20W
Mosquitos, G. de los, Panama 164 E3 9 15N 81 10W
Moss, Norway 15 G14 59 27N 10 40 E
Moss Vale, Australia 129 C9 34 32 S 150 25 E
Mossaka, Congo 114 C3 1 15 S 16 45 E
Mossâmedes, Brazil 171 E1 16 7 S 50 11W
Mossbank, Canada 143 D7 49 56N 105 56W
Mossburn, N.Z. 131 F3 45 41 S 168 15 E
Mosselbaai, S. Africa 116 E3 34 11 S 22 8 E
Mossendjo, Congo 114 C2 2 55 S 12 42 E
Mosses, Col des, Switz. 32 D4 46 25N 7 7 E
Mossfellsbær, Iceland 11 C5 64 11N 21 45W
Mossgiel, Australia 128 B6 33 15 S 144 5 E
Mössingen, Germany 31 G5 48 24N 9 4 E
Mossman, Australia 126 B4 16 21 S 145 15 E
Mossoró, Brazil 170 C4 5 10 S 37 15W
Mossuril, Mozam. 119 E5 14 58 S 40 42 E
Mossy Head, U.S.A. 153 E3 30 45N 86 19W
Most, Czech Rep. 34 A6 50 31N 13 38 E
Mosta, Malta 38 D1 35 54N 14 24 E
Mostaganem, Algeria 111 A5 35 54N 0 5 E
Mostar, Bos.-H. 52 G2 43 22N 17 50 E
Mostardas, Brazil 175 C5 31 2 S 50 51W
Mostefa, Rass, Tunisia 108 A2 36 55N 11 3 E
Mosterhamn, Norway 18 E2 59 42N 5 21 E
Mostiska = Mostyska, Ukraine 59 H2 49 48N 23 4 E
Móstoles, Spain 42 E7 40 19N 3 53W
Mosty = Masty, Belarus 58 F3 53 27N 24 38 E
Mostyska, Ukraine 59 H2 49 48N 23 4 E
Mosul = Al Mawşil, Iraq 101 D10 36 15N 43 5 E
Mosŭlpo, S. Korea 75 H14 33 20N 126 17 E
Møsvatnet, Norway 18 E5 59 52N 8 5 E
Mota, Ethiopia 107 E4 11 5N 37 52 E
Mota, Vanuatu 133 C5 13 49 S 167 42 E
Mota del Cuervo, Spain 41 F2 39 30N 2 52W
Mota del Marqués, Spain 42 D5 41 38N 5 11W
Mota Lava, Vanuatu 133 C5 13 40 S 167 40 E
Motaba, Congo 114 B3 2 6N 18 2 E
Motagua →, Guatemala 164 C2 15 44N 88 14W
Motala, Sweden 17 F9 58 32N 15 1 E
Motaze, Mozam. 117 C5 24 48 S 32 52 E
Moţca, Romania 53 C11 47 15N 26 37 E
Moth, India 93 G8 25 43N 78 57 E
Motherwell, U.K. 22 F5 55 47N 3 58W
Motihari, India 93 F11 26 30N 84 55 E
Motilla del Palancar, Spain 41 F3 39 34N 1 55W
Motiti I., N.Z. 130 D5 37 38 S 176 25 E
Motnik, Slovenia 45 B11 46 14N 14 54 E
Motocurunya, Venezuela 169 C5 4 24N 64 5W
Motovun, Croatia 45 C10 45 20N 13 50 E
Motozintla de Mendoza, Mexico 163 D6 15 21N 92 14W
Motril, Spain 43 J7 36 31N 3 37W
Motru, Romania 52 F7 44 48N 22 59 E
Motru →, Romania 53 F8 44 32N 23 31 E
Mott, U.S.A. 154 B3 46 23N 102 20W
Móttola, Italy 47 B10 40 38N 17 2 E
Motu, N.Z. 131 E6 38 18 S 177 40 E
Motu →, N.Z. 130 D6 37 51 S 177 35 E
Motuba, Dem. Rep. of the Congo 114 B3 2 20N 18 34 E
Motueka, N.Z. 131 B8 41 7 S 173 1 E
Motueka →, N.Z. 131 B8 41 5 S 173 1 E
Motul, Mexico 163 C7 21 0N 89 20W
Motupena Pt., Papua N. G. 132 D8 6 30 S 155 10 E
Mouanda, Gabon 114 C2 1 28 S 13 7 E
Mouchalagane →, Canada 141 B6 50 56N 68 41W
Moúdhros, Greece 49 B7 39 50N 25 18 E
Mouding, China 76 E3 25 20N 101 28 E
Moudjeria, Mauritania 112 B2 17 50N 12 28W
Moudon, Switz. 32 C3 46 40N 6 49 E
Mougoundou, Congo 114 C2 2 40 S 12 41 E
Mouila, Gabon 114 C2 1 50 S 11 0 E
Mouka, C.A.R. 114 A4 7 16N 21 52 E
Moukambo, Gabon 114 C2 3 5 S 11 38 E
Moulamein, Australia 128 C6 35 3 S 144 1 E
Moulianá, Greece 38 D7 35 10N 25 59 E
Moulins, France 27 F10 46 35N 3 19 E
Moulmein, Burma 90 G6 16 30N 97 40 E
Moulmeingyun, Burma 90 G5 16 23N 95 16 E
Moulouya, O. →, Morocco 111 A4 35 5N 2 25W
Moulton, U.S.A. 156 D4 40 41N 92 41W
Moultrie, Ga., U.S.A. 152 D6 31 11N 83 47W
Moultrie, L., U.S.A. 152 B9 33 20N 80 5W
Mounana, Gabon 114 C2 1 18 S 13 13 E
Mound City, Mo., U.S.A. 154 E7 40 7N 95 14W
Mound City, S. Dak., U.S.A. 154 C4 45 44N 100 4W
Moúnda, Ákra, Greece 48 C2 38 5N 20 45 E
Moundou, Chad 109 G3 8 40N 16 10 E
Moundsville, U.S.A. 150 G4 39 55N 80 44W
Mounembé, Congo 114 C2 3 20 S 12 32 E
Moung, Cambodia 86 F4 12 46N 103 27 E
Moungoudi, Congo 114 C2 2 45 S 11 46 E
Mount Airy, U.S.A. 149 G5 36 31N 80 37W
Mount Albert, Canada 150 B5 44 8N 79 19W
Mount Ayr, U.S.A. 156 D2 40 43N 94 14W
Mount Barker, S. Austral., Australia 128 C3 35 5 S 138 52 E
Mount Barker, W. Austral., Australia 125 F2 34 38 S 117 40 E
Mount Beauty, Australia 129 D7 36 47 S 147 10 E
Mount Brydges, Canada 150 D3 42 54N 81 29W
Mount Burr, Australia 127 F3 37 34 S 140 26 E
Mount Carmel, Ill., U.S.A. 157 F9 38 25N 87 46W
Mount Carmel, Pa., U.S.A. 151 F8 40 47N 76 24W
Mount Carroll, U.S.A. 156 B7 42 6N 89 59W
Mount Charleston, U.S.A. 161 J11 36 16N 115 37W
Mount Clemens, U.S.A. 150 D2 42 35N 82 53W
Mount Coolon, Australia 126 C4 21 25 S 147 25 E
Mount Darwin, Zimbabwe 119 F3 16 47 S 31 38 E
Mount Desert I., U.S.A. 149 C11 44 21N 68 20W
Mount Dora, U.S.A. 149 L5 28 48N 81 38W
Mount Eden, U.S.A. 157 F11 38 3N 85 9W
Mount Edziza Prov. Park, Canada 142 B2 57 30N 130 45W
Mount Fletcher, S. Africa 117 E4 30 40 S 28 30 E
Mount Forest, Canada 140 D3 43 59N 80 43W
Mount Gambier, Australia 128 D4 37 50 S 140 46 E
Mount Garnet, Australia 126 B4 17 37 S 145 6 E
Mount Hagen, Papua N. G. 132 C3 5 52 S 144 16 E
Mount Holly, U.S.A. 151 G10 39 59N 74 47W
Mount Holly Springs, U.S.A. 150 F7 40 7N 77 12W
Mount Hope, N.S.W., Australia 129 B6 32 51 S 145 51 E
Mount Hope, S. Austral., Australia 127 E2 34 7 S 135 23 E
Mount Horeb, U.S.A. 156 B7 43 1N 89 44W
Mount Isa, Australia 126 C2 20 42 S 139 26 E
Mount Jewett, U.S.A. 150 E6 41 44N 78 39W
Mount Kisco, U.S.A. 151 E11 41 12N 73 44W
Mount Laguna, U.S.A. 161 N10 32 52N 116 25W
Mount Larcom, Australia 126 C5 23 48 S 150 59 E
Mount Lofty Ra., Australia 128 C3 34 35 S 139 5 E
Mount Magnet, Australia 125 E2 28 2 S 117 47 E
Mount Manara, Australia 128 B5 32 29 S 143 58 E
Mount Maunganui, N.Z. 130 D5 37 40 S 176 14 E
Mount Molloy, Australia 126 B4 16 42 S 145 20 E
Mount Morgan, Australia 126 C5 23 40 S 150 25 E
Mount Morris, Mich., U.S.A. 157 A13 43 7N 83 42W
Mount Morris, N.Y., U.S.A. 150 D7 42 44N 77 52W
Mount Olive, U.S.A. 156 E7 39 4N 89 44W
Mount Olivet, U.S.A. 157 F12 38 32N 84 2W
Mount Orab, U.S.A. 157 E13 39 2N 83 55W
Mount Pearl, Canada 141 C9 47 31N 52 47W
Mount Penn, U.S.A. 151 F9 40 20N 75 54W
Mount Perry, Australia 127 D5 25 13 S 151 42 E
Mount Pleasant, Iowa, U.S.A. 156 D5 40 58N 91 33W
Mount Pleasant, Mich., U.S.A. 148 D3 43 36N 84 46W
Mount Pleasant, Pa., U.S.A. 150 F5 40 9N 79 33W
Mount Pleasant, S.C., U.S.A. 152 C10 32 47N 79 52W
Mount Pleasant, Tenn., U.S.A. 149 H2 35 32N 87 12W
Mount Pleasant, Tex., U.S.A. 155 J7 33 9N 94 58W
Mount Pleasant, Utah, U.S.A. 158 G8 39 33N 111 27W
Mount Pocono, U.S.A. 151 E9 41 7N 75 22W
Mount Pulaski, U.S.A. 156 D7 40 1N 89 17W
Mount Rainier Nat. Park, U.S.A. 160 D5 46 55N 121 50W
Mount Revelstoke Nat. Park, Canada 142 C5 51 5N 118 30W
Mount Robson Prov. Park, Canada 142 C5 53 0N 119 0W
Mount Roskill, N.Z. 130 C3 36 55 S 174 45 E
Mount Selinda, Zimbabwe 117 C5 20 24 S 32 43 E
Mount Shasta, U.S.A. 158 F2 41 19N 122 19W
Mount Signal, U.S.A. 161 N11 32 39N 115 37W
Mount Somers, N.Z. 131 D6 43 45 S 171 27 E
Mount Sterling, Ill., U.S.A. 156 E6 39 59N 90 45W
Mount Sterling, Ky., U.S.A. 157 F13 38 4N 83 56W
Mount Sterling, Ohio, U.S.A. 157 E13 39 43N 83 16W
Mount Surprise, Australia 126 B3 18 10 S 144 17 E
Mount Union, U.S.A. 150 F7 40 23N 77 53W
Mount Upton, U.S.A. 151 D9 42 26N 75 23W
Mount Vernon, Ga., U.S.A. 152 C7 32 11N 82 36W
Mount Vernon, Ill., U.S.A. 148 F1 38 19N 88 55W
Mount Vernon, Ind., U.S.A. 154 F10 38 17N 88 57W
Mount Vernon, Ind., U.S.A. 157 G9 37 56N 87 54W
Mount Vernon, Iowa, U.S.A. 156 C5 41 55N 91 23W
Mount Vernon, N.Y., U.S.A. 151 F11 40 55N 73 50W
Mount Vernon, Ohio, U.S.A. 150 F2 40 23N 82 29W
Mount Vernon, Wash., U.S.A. 160 B4 48 25N 122 20W
Mount Victor, Australia 128 B3 32 11 S 139 44 E
Mount Washington, U.S.A. 157 F11 38 3N 85 33W
Mount Wellington, N.Z. 130 C3 36 55 S 174 52 E
Mount Zion, U.S.A. 157 E8 39 46N 88 53W
Mountain □, Phil. 80 C3 17 20N 121 10 E
Mountain Ash, U.K. 21 F4 51 40N 3 23W
Mountain Center, U.S.A. 161 M10 33 42N 116 44W
Mountain City, Nev., U.S.A. 158 F6 41 50N 115 58W
Mountain City, Tenn., U.S.A. 149 G5 36 29N 81 48W
Mountain Dale, U.S.A. 151 E10 41 41N 74 32W
Mountain Grove, U.S.A. 155 G8 37 8N 92 16W
Mountain Home, Ark., U.S.A. 155 G8 36 20N 92 23W
Mountain Home, Idaho, U.S.A. 158 E6 43 8N 115 41W
Mountain Iron, U.S.A. 154 B8 47 32N 92 37W
Mountain Pass, U.S.A. 161 K11 35 29N 115 35W
Mountain View, Ark., U.S.A. 155 H8 35 52N 92 7W
Mountain View, Calif., U.S.A. 160 H4 37 23N 122 5W
Mountain View, Hawaii, U.S.A. 145 D6 19 33N 155 7W
Mountainair, U.S.A. 159 J10 34 31N 106 15W
Mountlake Terrace, U.S.A. 160 C4 47 47N 122 19W
Mountmellick, Ireland 23 C4 53 7N 7 20W
Mountrath, Ireland 23 D4 53 0N 7 28W
Moura, Australia 126 C4 24 35 S 149 58 E
Moura, Brazil 169 D5 1 32 S 61 38W
Moura, Portugal 43 G3 38 7N 7 30W
Mourão, Portugal 43 G3 38 22N 7 22W
Mourdi, Dépression du, Chad 109 E4 18 10N 23 0 E
Mourdiah, Mali 112 C3 14 35N 7 25W
Mourenx-Ville-Nouvelle, France 28 E3 43 22N 0 38W
Mouri, Ghana 113 D4 5 6N 1 14W
Mourilyan, Australia 126 B4 17 35 S 146 3 E
Mourmelon-le-Grand, France 27 C11 49 8N 4 22 E
Mourne →, U.K. 23 B4 54 52N 7 26W
Mourne Mts., U.K. 23 B5 54 10N 6 0W
Mourniaí, Greece 38 D6 35 29N 24 1 E
Mournies = Mourniaí, Greece 38 D6 35 29N 24 1 E
Mouscron, Belgium 24 D3 50 45N 3 12 E
Moussoro, Chad 109 F3 13 41N 16 35 E
Mouthe, France 27 F13 46 44N 6 12 E
Moutier, Switz. 32 B4 47 16N 7 21 E
Moûtiers, France 29 C10 45 29N 6 32 E
Moutohara, N.Z. 130 E6 38 27 S 177 32 E
Moutong, Indonesia 79 D6 0 28N 121 13 E
Mouy, France 27 C9 49 18N 2 20 E
Mouyondzi, Congo 114 C2 4 1 S 13 59 E
Mouzáki, Greece 48 B3 39 25N 21 37 E
Mouzon, France 27 C12 49 36N 5 3 E
Movas, Mexico 162 B3 28 10N 109 25W
Moville, Ireland 23 A4 55 11N 7 3W
Mowandjum, Australia 124 C3 17 22 S 123 40 E
Moweaqua, U.S.A. 156 E7 39 38N 89 1W
Moxico □, Angola 115 E4 12 0 S 20 30 E
Moxotó →, Brazil 170 C4 9 19 S 38 14W
Moy →, Ireland 23 B2 54 8N 9 8W
Moyale, Kenya 107 G4 3 30N 39 0 E
Moyamba, S. Leone 112 D2 8 4N 12 30W
Moyen Atlas, Morocco 110 B3 33 0N 5 0W
Moyne, L. le, Canada 141 A6 56 45N 68 47W
Moyo, Indonesia 78 F5 8 10 S 117 40 E
Moyobamba, Peru 172 B2 6 0 S 77 0W
Moyyero →, Russia 65 C11 68 44N 103 42 E
Moyynty, Kazakstan 64 E8 47 10N 73 18 E
Mozambique = Moçambique, Mozam. 119 F5 15 3 S 40 42 E
Mozambique ■, Africa 119 F4 19 0 S 35 0 E
Mozambique Chan., Africa 117 B7 17 30 S 42 30 E
Mozdok, Russia 61 J7 43 45N 44 48 E
Mozdūrān, Iran 97 B9 36 9N 60 35 E
Mozhaysk, Russia 58 E9 55 30N 36 2 E
Mozhga, Russia 60 B11 56 26N 52 15 E
Mozhnābād, Iran 97 C9 34 7N 60 6 E
Mozirje, Slovenia 45 B11 46 22N 14 58 E
Mozyr = Mazyr, Belarus 59 F5 51 59N 29 15 E
Mpanda, Tanzania 118 D3 6 23 S 31 1 E
Mpé, Congo 114 C2 2 58 S 14 38 E
Mpese, Dem. Rep. of the Congo 115 D3 5 16 S 15 38 E
Mpésoba, Mali 112 C3 12 31N 5 39W
Mphoengs, Zimbabwe 117 C4 21 10 S 27 51 E
Mpika, Zambia 119 E3 11 51 S 31 25 E
Mpoko →, C.A.R. 114 B3 4 19N 18 33 E
Mpouya, Congo 114 C3 2 38 S 16 13 E
Mpulungu, Zambia 119 D3 8 51 S 31 5 E
Mpumalanga, S. Africa 117 D5 29 50 S 30 33 E
Mpumalanga □, S. Africa 117 B5 26 0 S 30 0 E
Mpwapwa, Tanzania 118 D4 6 23 S 36 30 E
Mqanduli, S. Africa 117 E4 31 49 S 28 45 E
Mqinvartsveri = Kazbek, Russia 61 J7 42 42N 44 30 E
Mrągowo, Poland 54 E8 53 52N 21 18 E
Mramor, Serbia, Yug. 50 C5 43 20N 21 45 E
Mrimina, Morocco 110 C3 29 50N 7 9W
Mrkonjić Grad, Bos.-H. 52 F2 44 26N 17 4 E
Mrkopalj, Croatia 45 C11 45 21N 14 52 E
Mrocza, Poland 55 E4 53 16N 17 35 E
Msab, Oued en →, Algeria 111 B6 32 15N 5 0 E
Msaken, Tunisia 108 A2 35 49N 10 33 E
Msambansovu, Zimbabwe 119 F3 15 50 S 30 3 E
M'sila, Algeria 111 A5 35 46N 4 30 E
Msoro, Zambia 119 E3 13 35 S 31 50 E
Msta →, Russia 58 C6 58 25N 31 20 E
Mstislavl = Mstsislaw, Belarus 58 E6 54 0N 31 50 E
Mstsislaw, Belarus 58 E6 54 0N 31 50 E
Mszana Dolna, Poland 55 J7 49 41N 20 5 E
Mszczonów, Poland 55 G7 51 58N 20 33 E
Mtama, Tanzania 119 E4 10 17 S 39 21 E
Mtamvuna →, S. Africa 117 E5 31 6 S 30 12 E
Mtilikwe →, Zimbabwe 119 G3 21 9 S 31 30 E
Mtima, Congo 114 C2 3 49 S 12 7 E
Mtsensk, Russia 58 F9 53 17N 36 36 E
Mtskheta, Georgia 61 K7 41 52N 44 45 E
Mtubatuba, S. Africa 117 D5 28 30 S 32 8 E
Mtwalume, S. Africa 117 E5 30 30 S 30 38 E
Mtwara-Mikindani, Tanzania 119 E5 10 20 S 40 20 E
Mu →, Burma 90 E5 21 56N 95 38 E
Mu Gia, Deo, Vietnam 86 D5 17 40N 105 47 E
Mu Us Shamo, China 74 E5 39 0N 109 0 E
Muacandala, Angola 115 E3 10 2 S 19 40 E
Muaná, Brazil 170 B2 1 25 S 49 15W
Muanda, Dem. Rep. of the Congo 115 D2 6 0 S 12 20 E
Muang Chiang Rai = Chiang Rai, Thailand 76 H2 19 52N 99 50 E
Muang Khong, Laos 78 B3 14 7N 105 51 E
Muang Lamphun, Thailand 86 C2 18 40N 99 2 E
Muang Pak Beng, Laos 76 H3 19 54N 101 8 E
Muangai, Angola 115 E3 12 32 S 19 55 E
Muar, Malaysia 78 D2 2 3N 102 34 E
Muarabungo, Indonesia 78 E2 1 28 S 102 52 E
Muaraenim, Indonesia 78 E2 3 40 S 103 50 E
Muarajuloi, Indonesia 78 E4 0 12 S 114 3 E
Muarakaman, Indonesia 78 E5 0 2 S 116 45 E
Muaratebo, Indonesia 78 E2 1 30 S 102 26 E
Muaratembesi, Indonesia 78 E2 1 42 S 103 8 E
Muaratewe, Indonesia 78 E4 0 58 S 114 52 E
Mubarakpur, India 93 F10 26 6N 83 18 E
Mubarraz = Al Mubarraz, Si. Arabia 97 E6 25 30N 49 40 E
Mubende, Uganda 118 B3 0 33N 31 22 E
Mubi, Nigeria 113 C7 10 18N 13 16 E
Mubur, Pulau, Indonesia 87 L6 3 20N 106 12 E
Mucajá, Brazil 169 D6 3 57 S 57 32W
Mucajaí →, Brazil 169 C5 2 25N 60 52W
Mucajaí, Serra do, Brazil 169 C5 2 23N 61 10W
Mucari, Angola 115 D3 9 30 S 16 54 E
Muchachos, Roque de los, Canary Is. 39 F2 28 44N 17 52W
Mücheln, Germany 30 D7 51 17N 11 47 E
Muchinga Mts., Zambia 119 E3 11 30 S 31 30 E
Muchkapskiy, Russia 60 E6 51 52N 42 28 E
Muchuan, China 76 C5 28 57N 103 55 E
Muck, U.K. 22 E2 56 50N 6 15W
Muckadilla, Australia 127 D4 26 35 S 148 23 E
Muckalee Cr. →, U.S.A. 152 D5 31 38N 84 9W
Muco →, Colombia 168 C3 4 15N 70 21W
Mucoma, Angola 115 F2 15 18 S 13 39 E
Muconda, Angola 115 E4 10 31 S 21 15 E
Mucope, Angola 115 F2 16 24 S 14 52 E
Mucugê, Brazil 171 D3 13 0 S 41 23W
Mucuim →, Brazil 173 B5 6 33 S 64 18W
Mucur, Turkey 100 C6 39 3N 34 22 E
Mucura, Brazil 169 D5 2 31 S 62 43W
Mucuri, Brazil 171 E4 18 0 S 39 36W
Mucurici, Brazil 171 E3 18 6 S 40 31W
Mucusso, Angola 116 B3 18 1 S 21 25 E
Muda, Canary Is. 39 F6 28 34N 13 57W
Mudanjiang, China 75 B15 44 38N 129 30 E
Mudanya, Turkey 51 F12 40 25N 28 50 E
Muddebihal, India 95 F3 16 20N 76 8 E
Muddy Cr. →, U.S.A. 159 H8 38 24N 110 42W
Mudgee, Australia 129 B8 32 32 S 149 31 E
Mudhol, Andhra Pradesh, India 94 E3 18 58N 77 55 E
Mudhol, Karnataka, India 95 F2 16 21N 75 17 E
Mudiata, Dem. Rep. of the Congo 115 D4 7 15 S 22 1 E
Mudigere, India 95 H2 13 8N 75 38 E
Mudjatik →, Canada 143 B7 56 1N 107 36W
Mudon, Burma 90 G6 16 15N 97 44 E
Mudugh, Somali Rep. 120 C3 7 0N 47 30 E
Mudukulattur, India 95 K4 9 21N 78 31 E
Mudurnu, Turkey 100 B4 40 27N 31 12 E
Muecate, Mozam. 119 E4 14 55 S 39 40 E
Mueda, Mozam. 119 E4 11 36 S 39 28 E
Mueller Ra., Australia 124 C4 18 18 S 126 46 E
Muende, Mozam. 119 E3 14 28 S 33 0 E
Muerto, Mar, Mexico 163 D6 16 10N 94 10W
Mufu Shan, China 77 C10 29 20N 114 30 E
Mufulira, Zambia 119 E2 12 32 S 28 15 E
Mufuma, Angola 115 D3 9 12 S 16 29 E
Mufumbiro Range, Africa 118 C2 1 25 S 29 30 E
Mugardos, Spain 42 B2 43 27N 8 15W
Muge →, Portugal 43 F2 39 8N 8 44W
Múggia, Italy 45 C10 45 36N 13 46 E
Mughal Sarai, India 93 G10 25 18N 83 7 E
Mughayrā', Si. Arabia 96 D3 29 17N 37 41 E
Mugi, Japan 70 D6 33 40N 134 25 E
Mugia = Muxía, Spain 42 B1 43 3N 9 10W
Mugila, Mts., Dem. Rep. of the Congo 118 D2 7 0 S 28 50 E
Muginga, Angola 115 D3 8 21 S 17 36 E
Muğla, Turkey 49 D10 37 15N 28 22 E
Muğla □, Turkey 49 D10 37 15N 28 0 E
Muglad, Sudan 107 E2 11 1N 27 50 E
Mŭglizh, Bulgaria 51 D9 42 37N 25 32 E
Mugu, Nepal 93 E10 29 45N 82 30 E
Muhammad, Ras, Egypt 96 E2 27 44N 34 16 E
Muhammad Qol, Sudan 106 C4 20 53N 37 9 E
Muhammadabad, India 93 F10 26 4N 83 25 E
Muḩayriqah, Si. Arabia 98 B4 23 59N 45 4 E
Muhesi →, Tanzania 118 D4 7 0 S 35 20 E
Mühlacker, Germany 31 G4 48 57N 8 51 E
Mühldorf, Germany 31 G8 48 14N 12 32 E
Mühlhausen, Germany 30 D6 51 12N 10 27 E
Mühlig Hofmann fjell, Antarctica 7 D3 72 30 S 5 0 E
Mühlviertel, Austria 34 C7 48 30N 14 10 E
Muhos, Finland 14 D22 64 47N 25 59 E

N

Natagaima 255

Naab →, Germany 31 F8 49 1N 12 2 E
Na'am, Sudan 107 F2 9 42N 28 27 E
Na'am →, Sudan 107 F2 6 48N 29 57 E
Naantali, Finland 15 F19 60 29N 22 2 E
Naas, Ireland 23 C5 53 12N 6 40W
Nababeep, S. Africa 116 D2 29 36 S 17 46 E
Nabadwip = Navadwip, India 93 H13 23 34N 88 20 E
Nabari, Japan 71 C8 34 37N 136 5 E
Nabawa, Australia 125 E1 28 30 S 114 48 E
Nabberu, L., Australia 125 E3 25 50 S 120 30 E
Nabburg, Germany 31 F8 49 27N 12 11 E
Naberezhnyye Chelny, Russia 60 C11 55 42N 52 19 E
Nabeul, Tunisia 108 A2 36 30N 10 44 E
Nabha, India 92 D7 30 26N 76 14 E
Nabīd, Iran 97 D8 29 40N 57 38 E
Nabire, Indonesia 79 E9 3 15 S 135 26 E
Nabisar, Pakistan 92 G3 25 8N 69 40 E
Nabisipi →, Canada 141 B7 50 14N 62 13W
Nabiswera, Uganda 118 B3 1 27N 32 15 E
Nablus = Nābulus, West Bank 103 C4 32 14N 35 15 E
Naboomspruit, S. Africa 117 C4 24 32 S 28 40 E
Nabou, Burkina Faso 112 C4 11 25N 2 50W
Nabua, Phil. 80 E4 13 24N 123 22 E
Nābulus, West Bank 103 C4 32 14N 35 15 E
Nabunturan, Phil. 81 H5 7 35N 125 58 E
Nacala, Mozam. 119 E5 14 31 S 40 34 E
Nacala-Velha, Mozam. 119 E5 14 32 S 40 34 E
Nacaome, Honduras 164 D2 13 31N 87 30W
Nacaroa, Mozam. 119 E4 14 22 S 39 56 E
Naches, U.S.A. 158 C3 46 44N 120 42W
Naches →, U.S.A. 160 D6 46 38N 120 31W
Nachicapau, L., Canada 141 A6 56 40N 68 5W
Nachikatsuura, Japan 71 D7 33 33N 135 58 E
Nachingwea, Tanzania 119 E4 10 23 S 38 49 E
Nachna, India 92 F4 27 34N 71 41 E
Náchod, Czech Rep. 34 A9 50 25N 16 8 E
Nacimiento L., U.S.A. 160 K6 35 46N 120 53W
Nackara, Australia 128 B3 32 48 S 139 12 E
Naco, Mexico 162 A3 31 20N 109 56W
Nacogdoches, U.S.A. 155 K7 31 36N 94 39W
Nácori Chico, Mexico 162 B3 29 39N 109 1W
Nacozari, Mexico 162 A3 30 24N 109 39W
Nadi, Sudan 106 D3 18 40N 33 41 E
Nadiad, India 92 H5 22 41N 72 56 E
Nădlac, Romania 52 D5 46 10N 20 50 E
Nador, Morocco 111 A4 35 14N 2 58W
Nadur, Malta 38 C1 36 2N 14 17 E
Nadūshan, Iran 97 C7 32 2N 53 35 E
Nadvirna, Ukraine 59 H3 48 37N 24 30 E
Nadvoitsy, Russia 56 B5 63 52N 34 14 E
Nadvornaya = Nadvirna, Ukraine 59 H3 48 37N 24 30 E
Nadym, Russia 64 C8 65 35N 72 42 E
Nadym →, Russia 64 C8 66 12N 72 0 E
Nærbø, Norway 15 G11 58 40N 5 39 E
Næstved, Denmark 17 J5 55 13N 11 44 E
Nafada, Nigeria 113 C7 11 8N 11 20 E
Näfels, Switz. 33 B8 47 6N 9 4 E
Naft-e Safīd, Iran 97 D6 31 40N 49 17 E
Naftshahr, Iran 101 E11 34 0N 45 30 E
Nafud Desert = An Nafūd, Si. Arabia 96 D4 28 15N 41 0 E
Nafūsah, Jabal, Libya 108 B2 32 12N 12 30 E
Nag Hammâdi, Egypt 106 B3 26 2N 32 18 E
Naga, Camarines S., Phil. 79 B6 13 38N 123 15 E
Naga, Cebu, Phil. 81 F4 10 13N 123 45 E
Naga, Zamboanga del S., Phil. 81 H4 7 46N 122 45 E
Naga, Kreb en, Africa 110 D3 24 12N 6 0W
Naga-Shima, Kagoshima, Japan 70 E2 32 10N 130 9 E
Naga-Shima, Yamaguchi, Japan 70 D4 33 49N 132 5 E
Nagahama, Ehime, Japan 70 D4 33 36N 132 29 E
Nagahama, Shiga, Japan 71 B8 35 23N 136 16 E
Nagai, Japan 68 E10 38 6N 140 2 E
Nagai I., U.S.A. 144 J8 55 5N 160 0W
Nagaland □, India 90 B5 26 0N 94 30 E
Nagambie, Australia 129 D6 36 47 S 145 10 E
Nagano, Japan 71 A10 36 40N 138 10 E
Nagano □, Japan 71 A10 36 15N 138 0 E
Nagaoka, Japan 69 F9 37 27N 138 51 E
Nagappattinam, India 95 J4 10 46N 79 51 E
Nagar →, Bangla. 93 G13 24 27N 89 12 E
Nagar Karnul, India 95 F4 16 29N 78 20 E
Nagar Parkar, Pakistan 92 G4 24 28N 70 46 E
Nagara →, Japan 71 B8 35 40N 136 43 E
Nagaram, India 94 E5 18 21N 80 26 E
Nagari Hills, India 95 H4 13 3N 79 45 E
Nagasaki, Japan 70 E1 32 47N 129 50 E
Nagasaki □, Japan 70 E1 32 50N 129 40 E
Nagato, Japan 70 C3 34 19N 131 5 E
Nagaur, India 92 F5 27 15N 73 45 E
Nagbhir, India 94 D4 20 34N 79 55 E
Nagda, India 92 H6 23 27N 75 25 E
Nagercoil, India 95 K3 8 12N 77 26 E
Nagina, India 93 E8 29 30N 78 30 E
Nagīneh, Iran 97 C8 34 20N 57 15 E
Nagir, Pakistan 93 A6 36 12N 74 42 E
Naglarby, Sweden 16 D9 60 25N 15 34 E
Nagod, India 93 G9 24 34N 80 36 E
Nagold, Germany 31 G4 48 32N 8 43 E
Nagold →, Germany 31 G4 48 52N 8 42 E
Nagoorin, Australia 126 C5 24 17 S 151 15 E
Nagorno-Karabakh, Azerbaijan 101 C12 39 55N 46 45 E
Nagornyy, Russia 65 D13 55 58N 124 57 E
Nagorsk, Russia 58 B3 59 18N 50 48 E
Nagoya, Japan 71 B8 35 10N 136 50 E
Nagpur, India 94 D4 21 8N 79 10 E
Nagua, Dom. Rep. 165 C6 19 23N 69 50W
Nagyatád, Hungary 52 D2 46 14N 17 22 E
Nagyecsed, Hungary 52 C7 47 53N 22 24 E
Nagykálló, Hungary 52 C6 47 53N 21 51 E
Nagykanizsa, Hungary 52 D2 46 28N 17 0 E
Nagykáta, Hungary 52 C4 47 25N 19 45 E
Nagykőrös, Hungary 52 C4 47 5N 19 48 E
Naha, Japan 69 L3 26 13N 127 42 E
Nahan, India 92 D7 30 33N 77 18 E
Nahanni Butte, Canada 142 A4 61 2N 123 31W
Nahanni Nat. Park, Canada 142 A4 61 15N 125 0W
Nahargarh, Mad. P., India 92 G6 24 10N 75 14 E
Nahargarh, Raj., India 92 G7 24 55N 76 50 E
Nahariyya, Israel 100 F6 33 1N 35 5 E
Nahāvand, Iran 97 C6 34 10N 48 22 E
Nahe →, Germany 31 F3 49 58N 7 54 E
Nahîya, W. →, Egypt 106 B3 28 55N 31 0 E
Nahuel Huapi, L., Argentina 176 B2 41 0 S 71 32W
Nahunta, U.S.A. 152 D8 31 12N 81 59W
Naic, Phil. 80 D3 14 19N 120 46 E
Naicá, Mexico 162 B3 27 53N 105 31W
Naicam, Canada 143 C8 52 30N 104 30W
Naikoon Prov. Park, Canada 142 C2 53 55N 131 55W
Naikul, India 94 D7 21 20N 84 58 E
Naila, Germany 31 E7 50 19N 11 42 E
Naimisharanya, India 93 F9 27 21N 80 30 E
Nain, Canada 141 A7 56 34N 61 40W
Nā'īn, Iran 97 C7 32 54N 53 0 E
Naini Tal, India 93 E8 29 30N 79 30 E
Naintré, France 26 F7 46 46N 0 29 E
Nainwa, India 92 G6 25 46N 75 51 E
Naipu, Romania 53 F10 44 12N 25 47 E
Nairn, U.K. 22 D5 57 35N 3 53W
Nairobi, Kenya 118 C4 1 17 S 36 48 E
Naissaar, Estonia 15 G21 59 34N 24 29 E
Naita, Mt., Ethiopia 107 F4 5 30N 35 18 E
Naivasha, Kenya 118 C4 0 40 S 36 30 E
Naivasha, L., Kenya 118 C4 0 48 S 36 20 E
Najac, France 28 D5 44 14N 1 58 E
Najafābād, Iran 97 C6 32 40N 51 15 E
Najd, Si. Arabia 102 B3 26 30N 42 0 E
Nájera, Spain 40 C2 42 26N 2 48W
Najerilla →, Spain 40 C2 42 32N 2 48W
Najibabad, India 92 E8 29 40N 78 20 E
Najin, N. Korea 75 C16 42 12N 130 15 E
Najmah, Si. Arabia 97 E6 26 42N 50 6 E
Naju, S. Korea 75 G14 35 3N 126 43 E
Naka →, Japan 71 A12 36 20N 140 36 E
Nakadōri-Shima, Japan 69 H4 32 57N 129 4 E
Nakalagba, Dem. Rep. of the Congo 118 B2 2 50N 27 58 E
Nakama, Japan 70 D2 33 56N 130 43 E
Nakaminato, Japan 71 A12 36 21N 140 36 E
Nakamura, Japan 70 E4 32 59N 132 56 E
Nakanai Mts., Papua N. G. 132 C6 5 40 S 151 0 E
Nakano, Japan 71 A10 36 45N 138 22 E
Nakano-Shima, Japan 69 K4 29 51N 129 52 E
Nakanojō, Japan 71 A10 36 35N 138 51 E
Nakashibetsu, Japan 68 C12 43 33N 144 59 E
Nakatsu, Japan 70 D3 33 34N 131 15 E
Nakatsugawa, Japan 71 B9 35 29N 137 30 E
Nakfa, Eritrea 102 D2 16 40N 38 32 E
Nakhfar al Buşayyah, Iraq 96 D5 30 0N 46 10 E
Nakhichevan = Naxçıvan, Azerbaijan 101 C11 39 12N 45 15 E
Nakhichevan Republic = Naxçıvan □, Azerbaijan 101 C11 39 25N 45 26 E
Nakhl, Egypt 103 F2 29 55N 33 43 E
Nakhl-e Taqī, Iran 97 E7 27 28N 52 36 E
Nakhodka, Russia 65 E14 42 53N 132 54 E
Nakhon Nayok, Thailand 86 E3 14 12N 101 13 E
Nakhon Pathom, Thailand 86 F3 13 49N 100 3 E
Nakhon Phanom, Thailand 78 A2 17 23N 104 43 E
Nakhon Ratchasima, Thailand 78 B2 14 59N 102 12 E
Nakhon Sawan, Thailand 78 A2 15 35N 100 10 E
Nakhon Si Thammarat, Thailand 78 C2 8 29N 100 0 E
Nakhon Thai, Thailand 86 D3 17 5N 100 44 E
Nakhtarana, India 92 H3 23 20N 69 15 E
Nakina, Canada 140 B2 50 10N 86 40W
Nakło nad Noteią, Poland 55 E4 53 9N 17 38 E
Nako, Burkina Faso 112 C4 10 40N 3 4W
Nakodar, India 92 D6 31 8N 75 31 E
Nakskov, Denmark 17 K5 54 50N 11 8 E
Naktong →, S. Korea 75 G15 35 7N 128 57 E
Nakuru, Kenya 118 C4 0 15 S 36 4 E
Nakuru, L., Kenya 118 C4 0 23 S 36 5 E
Nakusp, Canada 142 C5 50 20N 117 45W
Nal, Pakistan 92 F2 27 40N 66 12 E
Nal →, Pakistan 92 G1 25 20N 65 30 E
Nalázi, Mozam. 117 C5 24 3 S 33 20 E
Nalchik, Russia 61 J6 43 30N 43 33 E
Nałęczów, Poland 55 G9 51 17N 22 9 E
Nalerigu, Ghana 113 C4 10 35N 0 25W
Nalgonda, India 94 F4 17 6N 79 15 E
Nalhati, India 93 G12 24 17N 87 52 E
Naliya, India 92 H3 23 16N 68 50 E
Nallamalai Hills, India 95 G4 15 30N 78 50 E
Nallıhan, Turkey 100 B4 40 11N 31 20 E
Nalolo, Zambia 115 F4 15 33 S 23 7 E
Nalón →, Spain 42 B4 43 32N 6 4W
Nālūt, Libya 108 B2 31 54N 11 0 E
Nam Can, Vietnam 87 H5 8 46N 104 59 E
Nam-ch'on, N. Korea 75 E14 38 15N 126 26 E
Nam Co, China 77 C4 30 30N 90 45 E
Nam Dinh, Vietnam 76 G6 20 25N 106 5 E
Nam Du, Hon, Vietnam 87 H5 9 41N 104 21 E
Nam Ngum Dam, Laos 86 C4 18 35N 102 34 E
Nam-Phan = Cochin China, Vietnam 78 B3 10 30N 106 0 E
Nam Phong, Thailand 86 D4 16 42N 102 52 E
Nam Tha, Laos 76 G3 20 58N 101 30 E
Nam Tok, Thailand 78 B1 14 21N 99 4 E
Namachire, Angola 115 E4 11 26 S 22 43 E
Namacunde, Angola 116 B2 17 18 S 15 50 E
Namacurra, Mozam. 117 B6 17 30 S 36 50 E
Namak, Daryācheh-ye, Iran 97 C7 34 30N 52 0 E
Namak, Kavir-e, Iran 97 C8 34 30N 57 30 E
Namakkal, India 95 J4 11 13N 78 13 E
Namakzār, Daryācheh-ye, Iran 97 C9 34 0N 60 30 E
Namaland, Namibia 116 C2 26 0 S 17 0 E
Namangan, Uzbekistan 64 E8 41 0N 71 40 E
Namapa, Mozam. 119 E4 13 43 S 39 50 E
Namaqualand, S. Africa 116 E2 30 0 S 17 25 E
Namasagali, Uganda 118 B3 1 2N 33 0 E
Namatanai, Papua N. G. 132 B7 3 40 S 152 29 E
Namber, Indonesia 79 E8 1 2 S 134 49 E
Nambour, Australia 127 D5 26 32 S 152 58 E
Nambouwalu, Fiji 133 A2 17 0 S 178 45 E
Nambuangongo, Angola 115 D2 8 1 S 14 12 E
Nambucca Heads, Australia 129 A10 30 37 S 153 0 E
Namcha Barwa, China 72 D4 29 40N 95 10 E
Namche Bazar, Nepal 93 F12 27 51N 86 47 E
Namchonjŏm = Nam-ch'on, N. Korea 75 E14 38 15N 126 26 E
Namecunda, Mozam. 119 E4 14 54 S 37 37 E
Nameh, Indonesia 85 B5 2 34N 116 21 E
Nameponda, Mozam. 119 F4 15 50 S 39 50 E
Namerikawa, Japan 71 A9 36 46N 137 20 E
Náměšť nad Oslavou, Czech Rep. 35 B9 49 12N 16 10 E
Námestovo, Slovak Rep. 35 B12 49 24N 19 25 E
Nametil, Mozam. 119 F4 15 40 S 39 21 E
Namew L., Canada 143 C8 54 14N 101 56W
Namgia, India 93 D8 31 48N 78 40 E
Namhkam, Burma 76 E1 23 50N 97 41 E
Namhsan, Burma 90 D6 22 48N 97 2 E
Namib Desert = Namibwoestyn, Namibia 116 C2 22 30 S 15 0 E
Namibe, Angola 115 F2 15 7 S 12 11 E
Namibe □, Angola 116 B1 16 35 S 12 30 E
Namibia ■, Africa 116 C2 22 0 S 18 9 E
Namibwoestyn, Namibia 116 C2 22 30 S 15 0 E
Namīn, Iran 101 C13 38 25N 48 30 E
Namkhan, Burma 90 D6 23 50N 97 41 E
Namlea, Indonesia 79 E7 3 18 S 127 5 E
Namoi →, Australia 129 A8 30 12 S 149 30 E
Namous, O. en →, Algeria 111 B4 31 0N 0 15W
Nampa, U.S.A. 158 E5 43 34N 116 34W
Nampala, Mali 112 B3 15 20N 5 30W
Namp'o, N. Korea 75 E13 38 52N 125 10 E
Nampō-Shotō, Japan 69 J10 32 0N 140 0 E
Nampula, Mozam. 119 F4 15 6 S 39 15 E
Namrole, Indonesia 79 E7 3 46 S 126 46 E
Namsen →, Norway 14 D14 64 28N 11 37 E
Namsos, Norway 14 D14 64 29N 11 30 E
Namtsy, Russia 65 C13 62 43N 129 37 E
Namtu, Burma 90 D6 23 5N 97 28 E
Namtumbo, Tanzania 119 E4 10 30 S 36 4 E
Namu, Canada 142 C3 51 52N 127 50W
Namumea, Tuvalu 123 B14 5 41 S 176 9 E
Namur, Belgium 24 D4 50 27N 4 52 E
Namur □, Belgium 24 D4 50 17N 5 0 E
Namutoni, Namibia 116 B2 18 49 S 16 55 E
Namwala, Zambia 119 F2 15 44 S 26 30 E
Namwŏn, S. Korea 75 G14 35 23N 127 23 E
Namysłów, Poland 55 G4 51 6N 17 42 E
Nan, Thailand 86 C3 18 48N 100 46 E
Nan →, Thailand 86 E3 15 42N 100 9 E
Nan-ch'ang = Nanchang, China 77 C10 28 42N 115 55 E
Nan Ling, China 77 E8 25 0N 112 30 E
Nan Xian, China 77 C9 29 20N 112 22 E
Nana, C.A.R. 114 A3 5 0N 15 50 E
Nana, Romania 53 F11 44 17N 26 34 E
Nana Kru, Liberia 112 D3 4 55N 8 45W
Nanaimo, Canada 142 D4 49 10N 124 0W
Nanakuli, U.S.A. 145 K13 21 24N 158 9W
Nanam, N. Korea 75 D15 41 44N 129 40 E
Nanan, China 77 E12 24 59N 118 21 E
Nanango, Australia 127 D5 26 40 S 152 0 E
Nan'ao, China 77 F11 23 28N 117 5 E
Nanao, Japan 69 F8 37 0N 137 0 E
Nanbu, China 76 B6 31 18N 106 3 E
Nanchang, Jiangxi, China 77 C10 28 42N 115 55 E
Nanchang, Kiangsi, China 77 C10 28 34N 115 48 E
Nancheng, China 77 D11 27 33N 116 35 E
Nanching = Nanjing, China 77 A12 32 2N 118 47 E
Nanchong, China 76 B6 30 43N 106 2 E
Nanchuan, China 76 C6 29 9N 107 6 E
Nancy, France 27 D13 48 42N 6 12 E
Nanda Devi, India 93 D8 30 23N 79 59 E
Nanda Kot, India 93 D9 30 17N 80 5 E
Nandan, China 76 E6 24 58N 107 29 E
Nandan, Japan 70 C6 34 10N 134 42 E
Nanded, India 94 E3 19 10N 77 20 E
Nandewar Ra., Australia 127 E5 30 15 S 150 35 E
Nandgaon, India 94 D2 20 19N 74 39 E
Nandigama, India 94 F5 16 47N 80 18 E
Nandigram, India 93 H12 22 1N 87 58 E
Nandikotkur, India 95 G4 15 52N 78 18 E
Nandura, India 94 D3 20 52N 76 25 E
Nandurbar, India 94 D2 21 20N 74 15 E
Nandyal, India 95 G4 15 30N 78 30 E
Nanfeng, Guangdong, China 77 F8 23 45N 111 47 E
Nanfeng, Jiangxi, China 77 D11 27 12N 116 28 E
Nanga-Eboko, Cameroon 113 E7 4 41N 12 22 E
Nanga Parbat, Pakistan 93 B6 35 10N 74 35 E
Nangade, Mozam. 119 E4 11 5 S 39 36 E
Nangapinoh, Indonesia 78 E4 0 20 S 111 44 E
Nangarhār □, Afghan. 91 B3 34 20N 70 0 E
Nangatayap, Indonesia 78 E4 1 32 S 110 34 E
Nangeya Mts., Uganda 118 B3 3 30N 33 30 E
Nangis, France 27 D10 48 33N 3 1 E
Nangong, China 77 F8 37 23N 115 22 E
Nangtud, Mt., Phil. 81 F4 11 17N 122 11 E
Nanguneri, India 95 K3 8 29N 77 40 E
Nangwarry, Australia 128 D4 37 33 S 140 48 E
Nanhua, China 76 E3 25 13N 101 21 E
Nanhuang, China 75 F11 36 58N 121 48 E
Nanhui, China 77 B13 31 5N 121 44 E
Nanjangud, India 95 H3 12 6N 76 43 E
Nanjeko, Zambia 119 F1 15 31 S 23 30 E
Nanji Shan, China 77 D13 27 27N 121 4 E
Nanjian, China 76 E3 25 2N 100 25 E
Nanjiang, China 76 A6 32 28N 106 51 E
Nanjing, Fujian, China 77 E11 24 25N 117 20 E
Nanjing, Jiangsu, China 77 A12 32 2N 118 47 E
Nanjirinji, Tanzania 119 D4 9 41 S 39 5 E
Nankana Sahib, Pakistan 92 D5 31 27N 73 38 E
Nankang, China 77 E10 25 40N 114 45 E
Nanking = Nanjing, China 77 A12 32 2N 118 47 E
Nankoku, Japan 70 D5 33 39N 133 44 E
Nanling, China 77 B12 30 55N 118 20 E
Nannial, India 94 E4 19 4N 79 38 E
Nanning, China 76 F7 22 48N 108 20 E
Nannup, Australia 125 F2 33 59 S 115 48 E
Nanortalik, Greenland 10 E6 60 10N 45 17W
Nanpan Jiang →, China 76 E6 25 10N 106 5 E
Nanpara, India 93 F9 27 52N 81 33 E
Nanpi, China 74 E9 38 2N 116 45 E
Nanping, Fujian, China 77 D12 26 38N 118 10 E
Nanping, Henan, China 77 C9 29 55N 112 3 E
Nanri Dao, China 77 E12 25 15N 119 25 E
Nanripe, Mozam. 119 E4 13 52 S 38 52 E
Nansei-Shotō = Ryūkyū-rettō, Japan 69 M3 26 0N 126 0 E
Nansen Land, Greenland 10 A6 83 0N 43 0W
Nansen Sd., Canada 6 A3 81 0N 91 0W
Nanshan I., S. China Sea 78 B5 10 45N 115 49 E
Nansio, Tanzania 118 C3 2 3 S 33 4 E
Nant, France 28 D7 44 1N 3 18 E
Nanterre, France 27 D9 48 53N 2 13 E
Nantes, France 26 E5 47 12N 1 33W
Nantiat, France 28 B5 46 1N 1 11 E
Nanticoke, U.S.A. 151 E8 41 12N 76 0W
Nanton, Canada 142 C6 50 21N 113 46W
Nantong, China 77 A13 32 1N 120 52 E
Nantou, Taiwan 77 F13 23 57N 120 35 E
Nantua, France 29 B9 46 10N 5 35 E
Nantucket I., U.S.A. 148 E10 41 16N 70 5W
Nantwich, U.K. 20 D5 53 4N 2 31W
Nanty Glo, U.S.A. 150 F6 40 28N 78 50W
Nanuku Passage, Fiji 133 A3 16 45 S 179 15W
Nanuque, Brazil 171 E3 17 50 S 40 21W
Nanusa, Kepulauan, Indonesia 79 D7 4 45N 127 1 E
Nanutarra Roadhouse, Australia 124 D2 22 32 S 115 30 E
Nanxi, China 76 C5 28 54N 104 59 E
Nanxiong, China 77 E10 25 6N 114 15 E
Nanyang, China 74 H7 33 11N 112 30 E
Nanyi Hu, China 77 B12 31 5N 119 0 E
Nan'yō, Japan 68 E10 38 3N 140 8 E
Nanyuki, Kenya 118 B4 0 2N 37 4 E
Nanzhang, China 77 B8 31 45N 111 50 E
Nao, C. de la, Spain 41 G5 38 44N 0 14 E
Naococane, L., Canada 141 B5 52 50N 70 45W
Naogaon, Bangla. 90 C2 24 52N 88 52 E
Náousa, Imathía, Greece 50 F6 40 42N 22 9 E
Náousa, Kikládhes, Greece 49 D7 37 7N 25 14 E
Naozhou Dao, China 77 G8 20 55N 110 20 E
Napa, U.S.A. 160 G4 38 18N 122 17W
Napa →, U.S.A. 160 G4 38 10N 122 19W
Napakiak, U.S.A. 144 F7 60 42N 161 57W
Napamute, U.S.A. 144 F8 61 33N 158 42W
Napanee, Canada 140 D4 44 15N 77 0W
Napanoch, U.S.A. 151 E10 41 44N 74 22W
Napaskiak, U.S.A. 144 F7 60 43N 161 55W
Nape, Laos 86 C5 18 18N 105 6 E
Nape Pass = Keo Neua, Deo, Vietnam 86 C5 18 23N 105 10 E
Naperville, U.S.A. 157 C8 41 46N 88 9W
Napf, Switz. 32 B5 47 1N 7 56 E
Napier, N.Z. 130 F5 39 30 S 176 56 E
Napier Broome B., Australia 124 B4 14 2 S 126 37 E
Napier Pen., Australia 126 A2 12 4 S 135 43 E
Napierville, Canada 151 A11 45 11N 73 25W
Naples = Nápoli, Italy 47 B7 40 50N 14 15 E
Naples, U.S.A. 149 M5 26 8N 81 48W
Naples Park, U.S.A. 153 J8 26 17N 81 46W
Napo, China 76 F5 23 22N 105 50 E
Napo □, Ecuador 168 D2 0 30 S 77 0W
Napo →, Peru 168 D3 3 20 S 72 40W
Napoleon, N. Dak., U.S.A. 154 B5 46 30N 99 46W
Napoleon, Ohio, U.S.A. 157 C12 41 23N 84 8W
Nápoli, Italy 47 B7 40 50N 14 15 E
Nápoli, G. di, Italy 47 B7 40 43N 14 10 E
Napopo, Dem. Rep. of the Congo 118 B2 4 15N 28 0 E
Nappanee, U.S.A. 157 C11 41 27N 86 0W
Naqâda, Egypt 106 B3 25 53N 32 42 E
Naqadeh, Iran 101 D11 36 57N 45 23 E
Naqb, Ra's an, Jordan 103 F4 30 0N 35 29 E
Naqqāsh, Iran 97 C6 35 40N 49 6 E
Nara, Japan 71 C7 34 40N 135 49 E
Nara, Mali 112 B3 15 10N 7 20W
Nara □, Japan 71 C7 34 30N 136 0 E
Nara Canal, Pakistan 92 G3 24 30N 69 20 E
Nara Visa, U.S.A. 155 H3 35 37N 103 6W
Naracoorte, Australia 128 D4 36 58 S 140 45 E
Naradhan, Australia 129 B7 33 34 S 146 17 E
Naraini, India 93 G9 25 11N 80 29 E
Narasannapeta, India 94 E7 18 25N 84 3 E
Narasapur, India 95 F5 16 26N 81 40 E
Narasaropet, India 95 F5 16 14N 80 4 E
Narathiwat, Thailand 78 C2 6 30N 101 48 E
Narayanapatnam, India 94 E6 18 53N 83 10 E
Narayanganj, Bangla. 90 D3 23 40N 90 33 E
Narayanpet, India 94 F3 16 45N 77 30 E
Narbonne, France 28 E7 43 11N 3 0 E
Narbuvollen, Norway 18 B8 62 21N 11 27 E
Narcea →, Spain 42 B4 43 33N 6 44W
Nardīn, Iran 97 B7 37 3N 55 59 E
Nardò, Italy 47 B11 40 11N 18 2 E
Narembeen, Australia 125 F2 32 7 S 118 24 E
Narendranagar, India 92 D8 30 10N 78 18 E
Nares Str., Arctic 10 B3 80 0N 70 0W
Naretha, Australia 125 F3 31 0 S 124 45 E
Narew →, Poland 55 F7 52 26N 20 41 E
Nari →, Pakistan 92 F2 28 0N 67 40 E
Narindra, Helodranon' i, Madag. 117 A8 14 55 S 47 30 E
Narino □, Colombia 168 C2 1 30N 78 0W
Narita, Japan 71 B12 35 47N 140 19 E
Närke, Sweden 16 E8 59 10N 15 0 E
Narmada →, India 92 J5 21 38N 72 36 E
Narman, Turkey 101 B9 40 26N 41 57 E
Narmland, Sweden 15 F15 60 0N 13 30 E
Narnaul, India 92 E7 28 5N 76 11 E
Narni, Italy 45 F9 42 30N 12 30 E
Naro, Ghana 112 C4 10 22N 2 27W
Naro Fominsk, Russia 58 E9 55 23N 36 43 E
Narodnaya, Russia 56 A10 65 5N 59 58 E
Narok, Kenya 118 C4 1 55 S 35 52 E
Narón, Spain 42 B2 43 32N 8 9W
Narooma, Australia 129 D9 36 14 S 150 4 E
Narowal, Pakistan 91 B4 32 6N 74 52 E
Narra, Phil. 81 G2 9 18N 118 28 E
Narrabri, Australia 127 E4 30 19 S 149 46 E
Narran →, Australia 127 D4 28 37 S 148 12 E
Narrandera, Australia 129 C7 34 42 S 146 31 E
Narrogin, Australia 125 F2 32 58 S 117 14 E
Narromine, Australia 129 B8 32 12 S 148 12 E
Narrow Hills Prov. Park, Canada 143 C8 54 0N 104 37W
Narsampet, India 94 F4 17 57N 79 58 E
Narsaq, Greenland 10 E6 60 57N 46 4W
Narsimhapur, India 93 H8 22 54N 79 14 E
Narsinghgarh, India 92 H7 23 45N 76 40 E
Narsinghpur, India 94 D7 20 28N 85 5 E
Narsipatnam, India 94 F6 17 40N 82 37 E
Nartes, L. e, Albania 50 F3 40 32N 19 25 E
Nartkala, Russia 61 J6 43 33N 43 51 E
Naruto, Kantō, Japan 70 C6 34 11N 134 37 E
Narutō, Shikoku, Japan 71 B12 35 36N 140 25 E
Naruto-Kaikyō, Japan 70 C6 34 14N 134 39 E
Narva, Estonia 58 C5 59 23N 28 12 E
Narva →, Russia 15 G22 59 27N 28 2 E
Narvacan, Phil. 80 C3 17 25N 120 28 E
Narvik, Norway 14 B17 68 28N 17 26 E
Narvskoye Vdkhr., Russia 58 C5 59 18N 28 14 E
Narwana, India 92 E7 29 39N 76 6 E
Naryan-Mar, Russia 56 A9 67 42N 53 12 E
Narym, Russia 64 D9 59 0N 81 30 E
Naryn, Kyrgyzstan 64 E8 41 26N 75 58 E
Naryn →, Uzbekistan 63 C5 40 52N 71 36 E
Nasa, Norway 14 C16 66 29N 15 23 E
Nasarawa, Nigeria 113 D6 8 32N 7 41 E
Năsăud, Romania 53 C9 47 19N 24 29 E
Nasawa, Vanuatu 133 E6 15 0 S 168 0 E
Naseby, N.Z. 131 F5 45 1 S 170 10 E
Naselle, U.S.A. 160 D3 46 22N 123 49W
Naser, Buheirat en, Egypt 106 C3 23 0N 32 30 E
Nashua, Iowa, U.S.A. 156 B4 42 57N 92 32W
Nashua, Mont., U.S.A. 158 B10 48 8N 106 22W
Nashua, N.H., U.S.A. 151 D13 42 45N 71 28W
Nashville, Ark., U.S.A. 155 J8 33 57N 93 51W
Nashville, Ga., U.S.A. 152 D6 31 12N 83 15W
Nashville, Ill., U.S.A. 156 F7 38 21N 89 23W
Nashville, Ind., U.S.A. 157 E10 39 12N 86 15W
Nashville, Mich., U.S.A. 157 B11 42 36N 85 5W
Nashville, Tenn., U.S.A. 149 G2 36 10N 86 47W
Našice, Croatia 52 E3 45 32N 18 4 E
Nasielsk, Poland 55 F7 52 35N 20 50 E
Nasik, India 94 E1 19 58N 73 50 E
Nasipit, Phil. 81 G5 8 57N 125 19 E
Nasir, Sudan 107 F3 8 36N 33 4 E
Nasirabad, India 92 F6 26 15N 74 45 E
Nasirabad, Pakistan 92 E3 28 23N 68 24 E
Naskaupi →, Canada 141 B7 53 47N 60 51W
Naso, Italy 47 D7 38 7N 14 47 E
Naso Pt., Phil. 81 F3 10 25N 121 57 E
Naşrābād, Iran 97 C6 34 8N 51 26 E
Naşriān-e Pā'īn, Iran 96 C5 32 52N 46 52 E
Nass →, Canada 142 C3 55 0N 129 40W
Nassarawa □, Nigeria 113 D6 8 30N 8 20 E
Nassau, Bahamas 164 A4 25 5N 77 20W
Nassau, U.S.A. 151 D11 42 31N 73 37W
Nassau, B., Chile 176 E3 55 20 S 68 0W
Nasser, L. = Naser, Buheirat en, Egypt 106 C3 23 0N 32 30 E
Nasser City = Kôm Ombo, Egypt 106 C3 24 25N 32 52 E
Nassereith, Austria 33 B11 47 19N 10 50 E
Nassian, Ivory C. 112 D4 8 28N 3 28W
Nässjö, Sweden 17 G8 57 39N 14 42 E
Nastapoka →, Canada 140 A4 56 55N 76 33W
Nastapoka, Is., Canada 140 A4 56 55N 76 50W
Nasugbu, Phil. 80 D3 14 5N 120 38 E
Näsum, Sweden 17 H8 56 10N 14 29 E
Näsviken, Sweden 16 C10 61 46N 16 52 E
Nata, Botswana 116 C4 20 12 S 26 12 E
Nata →, Botswana 116 C4 20 14 S 26 10 E
Natagaima, Colombia 168 C2 3 37N 75 6W

256 Natal

Natal, *Brazil* 170 C4 5 47 S 35 13W
Natal, *Indonesia* 78 D1 0 35N 99 7 E
Natalinci, *Serbia, Yug.* 52 F5 44 15N 20 49 E
Naṭanz, *Iran* 97 C6 33 30N 51 55 E
Natashquan, *Canada* 141 B7 50 14N 61 46W
Natashquan →, *Canada* 141 B7 50 7N 61 50W
Natchez, *U.S.A.* 155 K9 31 34N 91 24W
Natchitoches, *U.S.A.* 155 K8 31 46N 93 5W
Naters, *Switz.* 32 D5 46 19N 7 58 E
Natewa B., *Fiji* 133 A2 16 35 S 179 40 E
Nathalia, *Australia* 129 D6 36 1 S 145 13 E
Nathdwara, *India* 92 G5 24 55N 73 50 E
Nati, Pta., *Spain* 39 A10 40 3N 3 50 E
Natimuk, *Australia* 128 D4 36 42 S 142 0 E
Nation →, *Canada* 142 B4 55 30N 123 32W
National City, *U.S.A.* 161 N9 32 41N 117 6W
Natitingou, *Benin* 113 C5 10 20N 1 26 E
Natividad, I., *Mexico* 162 B1 27 50N 115 10W
Natividade, *Brazil* 171 D2 11 43 S 47 47W
Natkyizin, *Burma* 78 B1 14 57N 97 59 E
Natogyi, *Burma* 90 E5 21 25N 95 39 E
Natonin, *Phil.* 80 C3 17 6N 121 18 E
Natron, L., *Tanzania* 118 C4 2 20 S 36 0 E
Natrona Heights, *U.S.A.* 150 F5 40 37N 79 44W
Natrûn, W. el →, *Egypt* 106 H7 30 25N 30 13 E
Nättraby, *Sweden* 17 H9 56 13N 15 31 E
Natukanaoka Pan, *Namibia* 116 B2 18 40 S 15 45 E
Natuna Besar, Kepulauan, *Indonesia* 78 D3 4 0N 108 15 E
Natuna Is. = Natuna Besar, Kepulauan, *Indonesia* 78 D3 4 0N 108 15 E
Natuna Selatan, Kepulauan, *Indonesia* 78 D3 2 45N 109 0 E
Natural Bridge, *U.S.A.* 151 B9 44 5N 75 30W
Naturaliste, C., *Australia* 126 G4 40 50 S 148 15 E
Natya, *Australia* 128 C5 34 57 S 143 13 E
Nau, *Tajikistan* 63 C4 40 9N 69 22 E
Nau Qala, *Afghan.* 92 B3 34 5N 68 5 E
Naucelle, *France* 28 D6 44 13N 2 20 E
Nauders, *Austria* 34 E3 46 54N 10 30 E
Nauen, *Germany* 30 C8 52 36N 12 52 E
Naugatuck, *U.S.A.* 151 E11 41 30N 73 3W
Naujan, *Phil.* 80 E3 13 20N 121 18 E
Naujoji Akmenė, *Lithuania* 54 B9 56 19N 22 54 E
Naulila, *Angola* 115 F2 17 13 S 14 39 E
Naumburg, *Germany* 30 D7 51 9N 11 47 E
Naupada, *India* 94 E7 18 34N 84 18 E
Nā'ūr at Tunayb, *Jordan* 103 D4 31 48N 35 57 E
Nauru ■, *Pac. Oc.* 134 H8 1 0 S 166 0 E
Naushahra = Nowshera, *Pakistan* 91 B3 34 0N 72 0 E
Naushahro, *Pakistan* 92 F3 26 50N 68 7 E
Naushon I., *U.S.A.* 151 E14 41 29N 70 45W
Nausori, *Fiji* 133 B2 18 2 S 178 32 E
Naustdal, *Norway* 18 C2 61 31N 5 43 E
Nauta, *Peru* 168 D3 4 31 S 73 35W
Nautla, *Mexico* 163 C5 20 20N 96 50W
Nauvoo, *U.S.A.* 156 D5 40 33N 91 23W
Nava, *Mexico* 162 B4 28 25N 100 46W
Nava, *Spain* 42 B5 43 21N 5 31W
Nava del Rey, *Spain* 42 D5 41 22N 5 6W
Navadwip, *India* 93 H13 23 34N 88 20 E
Navahermosa, *Spain* 43 F6 39 41N 4 28W
Navahrudak, *Belarus* 58 F3 53 40N 25 50 E
Navajo Reservoir, *U.S.A.* 159 H10 36 48N 107 36W
Naval, *Phil.* 81 F5 11 34N 124 23 E
Navalcarnero, *Spain* 42 E6 40 17N 4 5W
Navalgund, *India* 95 G2 15 34N 75 22 E
Navalmoral de la Mata, *Spain* 42 F5 39 52N 5 33W
Navalvillar de Pela, *Spain* 43 F5 39 9N 5 24W
Navan = An Uaimh, *Ireland* 23 C5 53 39N 6 41W
Navapolatsk, *Belarus* 58 E5 55 32N 28 37 E
Navarino, I., *Chile* 176 E3 55 0 S 67 40W
Navarra □, *Spain* 40 C3 42 40N 1 40W
Navarre, *Fla., U.S.A.* 153 E3 30 24N 86 52W
Navarre, *Ohio, U.S.A.* 150 F3 40 43N 81 31W
Navarro →, *U.S.A.* 160 F3 39 11N 123 45W
Navas de San Juan, *Spain* 43 G7 38 30N 3 19W
Navasota, *U.S.A.* 155 K6 30 23N 96 5W
Navassa I., *W. Indies* 165 C5 18 30N 75 0W
Nävekvarn, *Sweden* 17 F10 58 38N 16 49 E
Naver →, *U.K.* 22 C4 58 32N 4 14W
Navia, *Spain* 42 B4 43 35N 6 42W
Navia →, *Spain* 42 B4 43 15N 6 50W
Navia de Suarna, *Spain* 42 C3 42 58N 7 3W
Navibandar, *India* 92 J3 21 26N 69 48 E
Navidad, *Chile* 174 C1 33 57 S 71 50W
Naviraí, *Brazil* 175 A5 23 8 S 54 13W
Navlakhi, *India* 92 H4 22 58N 70 28 E
Navlya, *Russia* 59 F8 52 53N 34 30 E
Năvodari, *Romania* 53 F13 44 19N 28 36 E
Navoi = Nawoiy, *Uzbekistan* 64 E7 40 9N 65 22 E
Navojoa, *Mexico* 162 B3 27 0N 109 30W
Navolato, *Mexico* 162 C3 24 47N 107 42W
Návpaktos, *Greece* 48 C3 38 24N 21 50 E
Návplion, *Greece* 48 D4 37 33N 22 50 E
Navrongo, *Ghana* 113 C4 10 51N 1 3W
Navsari, *India* 94 D1 20 57N 72 59 E
Nawa Kot, *Pakistan* 92 E4 28 21N 71 24 E
Nawab Khan, *Pakistan* 92 D3 30 17N 69 12 E
Nawabganj, *Bangla.* 90 C2 24 35N 88 14 E
Nawabganj, *Ut. P., India* 93 F9 26 56N 81 14 E
Nawabganj, *Ut. P., India* 93 E8 28 32N 79 40 E
Nawabshah, *Pakistan* 91 D3 26 15N 68 25 E
Nawada, *India* 93 G11 24 50N 85 33 E
Nāwah, *Afghan.* 91 B2 32 19N 67 53 E
Nawakot, *Nepal* 93 F11 27 55N 85 10 E
Nawalgarh, *India* 92 F6 27 50N 75 15 E
Nawanshahr, *India* 93 C6 32 33N 74 48 E
Nawapara, *India* 94 D6 20 46N 82 33 E
Nawar, Dasht-i-, *Afghan.* 92 C3 33 52N 68 0 E
Nawāṣīf, Harrat, *Si. Arabia* 98 B3 21 20N 42 10 E
Nawi, *Sudan* 106 D3 18 32N 30 50 E
Nawng Hpa, *Burma* 90 D7 22 30N 98 30 E
Nawoiy, *Uzbekistan* 64 E7 40 9N 65 22 E
Nawş, Ra's, *Oman* 99 C6 17 15N 55 16 E
Naxçıvan, *Azerbaijan* 101 C11 39 12N 45 15 E
Naxçıvan □, *Azerbaijan* 101 C11 39 25N 45 26 E
Náxos, *Greece* 49 D7 37 8N 25 25 E
Nay, *France* 28 E3 43 10N 0 18W
Nay, Mui, *Vietnam* 78 B3 12 55N 109 23 E
Nāy Band, *Būshehr, Iran* 97 E7 27 20N 52 40 E
Nāy Band, *Khorāsān, Iran* 97 C8 32 20N 57 34 E
Naya →, *Colombia* 168 C2 3 13N 77 22W
Nayagarh, *India* 94 D7 20 8N 85 6 E
Nayakhan, *Russia* 65 C16 61 56N 159 0 E
Nayarit □, *Mexico* 162 C4 22 0N 105 0W
Nayé, *Senegal* 112 C2 14 28N 12 12W
Nayong, *China* 76 D5 26 50N 105 20 E
Nayoro, *Japan* 68 B11 44 21N 142 28 E
Nayudupeta, *India* 95 H4 13 54N 79 54 E
Nayyāl, W. →, *Si. Arabia* 96 D3 28 35N 39 4 E
Nazaré, *Bahia, Brazil* 171 D4 13 2 S 39 0W
Nazaré, *Pará, Brazil* 173 B7 6 25 S 52 29W
Nazaré, *Tocantins, Brazil* 170 C2 6 23 S 47 40W
Nazaré, *Portugal* 43 F1 39 36N 9 4W
Nazareth = Nazerat, *Israel* 103 C4 32 42N 35 17 E
Nazareth, *U.S.A.* 151 F9 40 44N 75 19W
Nazas, *Mexico* 162 B4 25 10N 104 6W
Nazas →, *Mexico* 162 B4 25 35N 103 25W
Nazca, *Peru* 172 C3 14 50 S 74 57W
Naze, The, *U.K.* 21 F9 51 53N 1 18 E
Nazerat, *Israel* 103 C4 32 42N 35 17 E
Nāzīk, *Iran* 101 C11 39 1N 45 4 E
Nazilli, *Turkey* 49 D10 37 55N 28 15 E
Nazir Hat, *Bangla.* 90 D3 22 35N 91 49 E
Nazko, *Canada* 142 C4 53 1N 123 37W
Nazko →, *Canada* 142 C4 53 7N 123 34W
Nazret, *Ethiopia* 102 F2 8 32N 39 22 E
Nazwá, *Oman* 99 B7 22 56N 57 32 E
Ncama, *Eq. Guin.* 114 B2 1 55N 10 56 E
Nchanga, *Zambia* 119 E2 12 30 S 27 49 E
Ncheu, *Malawi* 119 E3 14 50 S 34 47 E
Ndala, *Tanzania* 118 C3 4 45 S 33 15 E
Ndalatando, *Angola* 115 D2 9 12 S 14 48 E
Ndali, *Benin* 113 D5 9 50N 2 46 E
Ndareda, *Tanzania* 118 C4 4 12 S 35 30 E
Ndélé, *C.A.R.* 114 A4 8 25N 20 36 E
Ndendé, *Gabon* 114 C2 2 22 S 11 23 E
Ndikinimeki, *Cameroon* 114 B2 4 46N 10 50 E
N'Dioum, *Senegal* 112 B2 16 31N 14 39W
Ndjamena, *Chad* 109 F2 12 10N 14 59 E
Ndjolé, *Gabon* 114 C2 0 10 S 10 45 E
Ndogo, Lagune, *Gabon* 114 C2 2 35 S 10 0 E
Ndola, *Zambia* 119 E2 13 0 S 28 34 E
Ndoto Mts., *Kenya* 118 B4 2 0N 37 0 E
Ndoua, C., *N. Cal.* 133 V20 22 24 S 166 56 E
Ndouba, *Congo* 114 C2 0 9 S 14 4 E
Nduguti, *Tanzania* 118 C3 4 18 S 34 41 E
Nduindui, *Vanuatu* 133 E5 15 24 S 167 46 E
Nea →, *Norway* 18 A8 63 15N 11 0 E
Néa Alikarnassós, *Greece* 49 F7 35 18N 25 13 E
Néa Ankhíalos, *Greece* 48 B4 39 16N 22 49 E
Néa Epídhavros, *Greece* 48 D5 37 40N 23 7 E
Néa Flippiás, *Greece* 48 B2 39 12N 20 53 E
Néa Ionia, *Greece* 48 B4 39 21N 22 56 E
Néa Kallikrátia, *Greece* 50 F7 40 21N 23 3 E
Néa Mákri, *Greece* 48 C5 38 5N 23 59 E
Néa Moudhaniá, *Greece* 50 F7 40 15N 23 17 E
Néa Péramos, *Attikí, Greece* 48 C5 38 0N 23 26 E
Néa Péramos, *Kaválla, Greece* 51 F8 40 50N 24 18 E
Néa Víssi, *Greece* 51 E10 41 34N 26 33 E
Néa Zíkhna, *Greece* 50 E7 41 2N 23 49 E
Neagari, *Japan* 71 A8 36 26N 136 25 E
Neagh, Lough, *U.K.* 23 B5 54 37N 6 25W
Neah Bay, *U.S.A.* 160 B2 48 22N 124 37W
Neale, L., *Australia* 124 D5 24 15 S 130 0 E
Neamț □, *Romania* 53 C11 47 0N 26 20 E
Neápolis, *Kozáni, Greece* 50 F5 40 20N 21 24 E
Neápolis, *Kríti, Greece* 38 D7 35 15N 25 37 E
Neápolis, *Lakonía, Greece* 48 E5 36 27N 23 8 E
Near Is., *U.S.A.* 144 K1 52 30N 174 0 E
Neath, *U.K.* 21 F4 51 39N 3 48W
Neath Port Talbot □, *U.K.* 21 F4 51 42N 3 45W
Nebbou, *Burkina Faso* 113 C4 11 9N 1 51W
Nebelat el Hagana, *Sudan* 107 E2 13 13N 29 2 E
Nebine Cr. →, *Australia* 127 D4 29 27 S 146 56 E
Nebitdag, *Turkmenistan* 57 G9 39 30N 54 22 E
Nebo, *Australia* 126 C4 21 42 S 148 42 E
Nebolchy, *Russia* 58 C7 59 8N 33 18 E
Nebraska □, *U.S.A.* 154 E5 41 30N 99 30W
Nebraska City, *U.S.A.* 154 E7 40 41N 95 52W
Nébrodi, Monti, *Italy* 47 E7 37 54N 14 35 E
Necedah, *U.S.A.* 154 C9 44 2N 90 4W
Nechako →, *Canada* 142 C4 53 30N 122 44W
Neches →, *U.S.A.* 155 L8 29 58N 93 51W
Neckar →, *Germany* 31 F4 49 27N 8 29 E
Necker I., *U.S.A.* 145 G11 23 35N 164 42W
Necochea, *Argentina* 174 D4 38 30 S 58 50W
Nectar Brook, *Australia* 128 B2 32 43 S 137 57 E
Neda, *Spain* 42 B2 43 30N 8 9W
Nedalshytta, *Norway* 18 B9 62 59N 12 3 E
Nedelino, *Bulgaria* 51 E9 41 27N 25 3 E
Nedelišće, *Croatia* 45 B13 46 23N 16 22 E
Nédha →, *Greece* 48 D3 37 25N 21 45 E
Nedreberg, *Norway* 18 D8 60 59N 11 41 E
Nedroma, *Algeria* 111 A4 35 1N 1 45W
Nedstrand, *Norway* 18 E2 59 21N 5 49 E
Nee Soon, *Singapore* 84 B2 1 24N 103 49 E
Needles, *Canada* 142 D5 49 53N 118 7W
Needles, *U.S.A.* 161 L12 34 51N 114 37W
Needles, The, *U.K.* 21 G6 50 39N 1 35W
Needles Pt., *N.Z.* 130 C4 36 3 S 175 25 E
Neely Henry L., *U.S.A.* 152 B3 33 55N 86 2W
Ñeembucú □, *Paraguay* 174 B4 27 0 S 58 0W
Neemuch = Nimach, *India* 92 G6 24 30N 74 56 E
Neenah, *U.S.A.* 148 C1 44 11N 88 28W
Neepawa, *Canada* 143 C9 50 15N 99 30W
Neeses, *U.S.A.* 152 B8 33 33N 81 7W
Nefta, *Tunisia* 108 B1 33 53N 7 50 E
Neftah Sidi Boubekeur, *Algeria* 111 A5 35 1N 0 4 E
Neftçala, *Azerbaijan* 97 B6 39 19N 49 12 E
Neftegorsk, *Russia* 61 H4 44 25N 39 45 E
Neftekamsk, *Russia* 62 C5 56 6N 54 17 E
Neftekumsk, *Russia* 61 H7 44 46N 44 50 E
Neftenbach, *Switz.* 33 A7 47 32N 8 41 E
Nefyn, *U.K.* 20 E3 52 56N 4 31W
Négala, *Mali* 112 C3 12 52N 8 30W
Negapatam = Nagappattinam, *India* 95 J4 10 46N 79 51 E
Negaunee, *U.S.A.* 148 B2 46 30N 87 36W
Negele, *Ethiopia* 102 F2 5 20N 39 36 E
Negeri Sembilan □, *Malaysia* 84 B2 2 45N 102 10 E
Negev Desert = Hanegev, *Israel* 103 E4 30 50N 35 0 E
Negoiul, Vf., *Romania* 53 E9 45 38N 24 35 E
Negombo, *Sri Lanka* 95 L4 7 12N 79 50 E
Negotin, *Serbia, Yug.* 50 B6 44 16N 22 37 E
Negotino, *Macedonia* 50 E6 41 29N 22 7 E
Negra, Peña, *Spain* 42 C4 42 11N 6 30W
Negra, Pta., *Mauritania* 110 D1 22 54N 16 18W
Negra, Pta., *Peru* 172 B1 6 6 S 81 10W
Negra Pt., *Phil.* 80 B3 18 40N 120 50 E
Negrais C., *Burma* 90 G5 16 0N 94 12 E
Negrești, *Romania* 53 D12 46 50N 27 30 E
Negrești-Oaș, *Romania* 53 C8 47 52N 23 26 E
Negril, *Jamaica* 164 C4 18 22N 78 20W
Négrine, *Algeria* 111 B6 34 30N 7 30 E
Negro →, *Argentina* 176 B4 41 2 S 62 47W
Negro →, *Bolivia* 173 C5 14 11 S 63 7W
Negro →, *Brazil* 169 D6 3 0 S 60 0W
Negro →, *Uruguay* 175 C4 33 24 S 58 22W
Negros, *Phil.* 79 C6 9 30N 122 40 E
Negros Occidental □, *Phil.* 81 F4 10 0N 122 55 E
Negros Oriental □, *Phil.* 81 G4 9 45N 123 0 E
Negru Vodă, *Romania* 53 G13 43 47N 28 21 E
Neguac, *Canada* 141 C6 47 15N 65 5W
Nehalem →, *U.S.A.* 160 E3 45 40N 123 56W
Nehāvand, *Iran* 97 C6 35 56N 49 31 E
Nehbandān, *Iran* 97 D9 31 35N 60 5 E
Nehoiu, *Romania* 53 E11 45 24N 26 20 E
Nei Mongol Zizhiqu □, *China* 74 D7 42 0N 112 0 E
Neiafu, *Tonga* 133 P14 18 39 S 173 59W
Neijiang, *China* 76 C5 29 35N 104 55 E
Neillsville, *U.S.A.* 154 C9 44 34N 90 36W
Neilrex, *Australia* 129 A8 31 44 S 149 20 E
Neilton, *U.S.A.* 158 C2 47 25N 123 53W
Neiqiu, *China* 74 F8 37 15N 114 30 E
Neiva, *Colombia* 168 C2 2 56N 75 18W
Neixiang, *China* 74 H6 33 10N 111 52 E
Nejanilini L., *Canada* 143 B9 59 33N 97 48W
Nejd = Najd, *Si. Arabia* 102 B3 26 30N 42 0 E
Nejo, *Ethiopia* 107 F4 9 30N 35 28 E
Nekā, *Iran* 97 B7 36 39N 53 19 E
Nekemte, *Ethiopia* 102 F2 9 4N 36 30 E
Nêkheb, *Egypt* 106 B3 25 10N 32 48 E
Neksø, *Denmark* 17 J9 55 4N 15 8 E
Nelamangala, *India* 95 H3 13 6N 77 24 E
Nelas, *Portugal* 42 E3 40 32N 7 52W
Nelaug, *Norway* 18 F5 58 39N 8 40 E
Nelia, *Australia* 126 C3 20 39 S 142 12 E
Nelidovo, *Russia* 58 D7 56 13N 32 49 E
Neligh, *U.S.A.* 154 D5 42 8N 98 2W
Nelkan, *Russia* 65 D14 57 40N 136 4 E
Nellikuppam, *India* 95 J4 11 46N 79 43 E
Nellore, *India* 95 G4 14 27N 79 59 E
Nelson, *Canada* 142 D5 49 30N 117 20W
Nelson, *N.Z.* 131 B8 41 18 S 173 16 E
Nelson, *U.K.* 20 D5 53 50N 2 13W
Nelson, *Ariz., U.S.A.* 159 J7 35 31N 113 19W
Nelson, *Nev., U.S.A.* 161 K12 35 42N 114 50W
Nelson →, *Canada* 143 C9 54 33N 98 2W
Nelson, C., *Australia* 128 E4 38 26 S 141 32 E
Nelson, C., *Papua N. G.* 132 E5 9 0 S 149 20 E
Nelson, Estrecho, *Chile* 176 D2 51 30 S 75 0W
Nelson Bay, *Australia* 127 E5 32 43 S 152 9 E
Nelson Forks, *Canada* 142 B4 59 30N 124 0W
Nelson House, *Canada* 143 B9 55 47N 98 51W
Nelson L., *Canada* 143 B8 55 48N 100 7W
Nelspoort, *S. Africa* 116 E3 32 7 S 23 0 E
Nelspruit, *S. Africa* 117 D5 25 29 S 30 59 E
Néma, *Mauritania* 112 B3 16 40N 7 15W
Neman, *Russia* 15 J20 55 2N 22 2 E
Neman →, *Lithuania* 15 J20 55 25N 21 10 E
Neméa, *Greece* 48 D4 37 49N 22 40 E
Nemeiben L., *Canada* 143 B7 55 20N 105 20W
Nemërçkës, Mal, *Albania* 50 F4 40 15N 20 15 E
Nemira, Vf., *Romania* 53 D11 46 17N 26 19 E
Némiscau, *Canada* 140 B4 51 18N 76 54W
Némiscau, L., *Canada* 140 B4 51 25N 76 40W
Nemours, *France* 27 D9 48 16N 2 40 E
Nemšová, *Slovak Rep.* 35 C11 48 58N 18 7 E
Nemunas = Neman →, *Lithuania* 15 J20 55 25N 21 10 E
Nemuro, *Japan* 68 C12 43 20N 145 35 E
Nemuro-Kaikyō, *Japan* 68 C12 43 30N 145 30 E
Nen Jiang →, *China* 75 B13 45 28N 124 30 E
Nenagh, *Ireland* 23 D3 52 52N 8 11W
Nenasi, *Malaysia* 87 L4 3 9N 103 23 E
Nendiarene, Pte., *N. Cal.* 133 T18 20 14 S 164 19 E
Nene →, *U.K.* 21 E8 52 49N 0 11 E
Nénita, *Greece* 49 C8 38 14N 26 6 E
Nenjiang, *China* 73 B7 49 10N 125 10 E
Neno, *Malawi* 119 F3 15 25 S 34 40 E
Nenzing, *Austria* 33 B9 47 11N 9 42 E
Neodesha, *U.S.A.* 155 G7 37 25N 95 41W
Neoga, *U.S.A.* 157 E8 39 19N 88 27W
Neokhórion, *Aitolía kai Akarnanía, Greece* 48 C3 38 25N 21 17 E
Neokhórion, *Árta, Greece* 48 B2 39 4N 21 0 E
Néon Karlovásion, *Greece* 49 D8 37 45N 26 42 E
Néon Petrítsi, *Greece* 50 E7 41 16N 23 15 E
Neópolis, *Brazil* 170 D4 10 18 S 36 35W
Neosho, *U.S.A.* 155 G7 36 52N 94 22W
Neosho →, *U.S.A.* 155 H7 36 48N 95 18W
Nepal ■, *Asia* 93 F11 28 0N 84 30 E
Nepalganj, *Nepal* 93 E9 28 5N 81 40 E
Nepalganj Road, *India* 93 E9 28 1N 81 41 E
Nephi, *U.S.A.* 158 G8 39 43N 111 50W
Nephin, *Ireland* 23 B2 54 1N 9 22W
Nepi, *Italy* 45 F9 42 14N 12 21 E
Nepomuk, *Czech Rep.* 34 B6 49 29N 13 35 E
Neptune, *U.S.A.* 151 F10 40 13N 74 2W
Nera →, *Italy* 45 F9 42 26N 12 24 E
Nera →, *Romania* 52 F6 44 48N 21 25 E
Nérac, *France* 28 D4 44 8N 0 21 E
Nerang, *Australia* 127 D5 27 58 S 153 20 E
Nerastro, Sarîr, *Libya* 108 D4 24 20N 20 37 E
Neratovice, *Czech Rep.* 34 A7 50 16N 14 31 E
Nerchinsk, *Russia* 65 D12 52 0N 116 39 E
Nereju, *Romania* 53 E11 45 43N 26 43 E
Nerekhta, *Russia* 58 D11 57 26N 40 38 E
Néret, L., *Canada* 141 B5 54 45N 70 44W
Neretvanski Kanal, *Croatia* 45 E14 43 7N 17 10 E
Neringa, *Lithuania* 15 J19 55 20N 21 5 E
Nerja, *Spain* 43 J7 36 43N 3 55W
Nerl →, *Russia* 58 D11 56 11N 40 34 E
Nerpio, *Spain* 41 G2 38 11N 2 16W
Nerva, *Spain* 43 H4 37 42N 6 30W
Nervi, *Italy* 44 D6 44 23N 9 2 E
Neryungri, *Russia* 65 D13 57 38N 124 28 E
Nes, *Iceland* 11 B9 65 53N 17 24W
Nes, *Norway* 18 D6 60 34N 9 59 E
Nesbyen, *Norway* 18 D6 60 34N 9 35 E
Nescopeck, *U.S.A.* 151 E8 41 3N 76 12W
Nesebŭr, *Bulgaria* 51 D11 42 41N 27 46 E
Neset, *Norway* 18 C7 61 53N 10 7 E
Nesflaten, *Norway* 18 E3 59 38N 6 48 E
Neskaupstaður, *Iceland* 11 B13 65 9N 13 42W
Nesland, *Norway* 18 E4 59 31N 7 59 E
Neslandsvatn, *Norway* 18 F6 58 57N 9 10 E
Nesoddtangen, *Norway* 18 E7 59 48N 10 40 E
Ness, L., *U.K.* 22 D4 57 15N 4 32W
Ness City, *U.S.A.* 154 F5 38 27N 99 54W
Nesslau, *Switz.* 33 B8 47 14N 9 13 E
Nesterov, *Poland* 59 G2 50 4N 23 58 E
Nestórion, *Greece* 50 F5 40 24N 21 5 E
Néstos →, *Greece* 51 E8 41 20N 24 35 E
Nesttun, *Norway* 18 D2 60 19N 5 20 E
Nesvady, *Slovak Rep.* 35 D11 47 56N 18 7 E
Nesvizh = Nyasvizh, *Belarus* 59 F4 53 14N 26 38 E
Netanya, *Israel* 103 C3 32 20N 34 51 E
Netarhat, *India* 93 H11 23 29N 84 16 E
Nete →, *Belgium* 24 C4 51 7N 4 14 E
Netherdale, *Australia* 126 C4 21 10 S 148 33 E
Netherlands ■, *Europe* 24 C5 52 0N 5 30 E
Netherlands Antilles ■, *W. Indies* 168 A4 12 15N 69 0W
Netley Gap, *Australia* 128 B3 32 43 S 139 59 E
Neto →, *Italy* 47 C10 39 12N 17 9 E
Netrakona, *Bangla.* 90 C3 24 53N 90 47 E
Netrang, *India* 92 J5 21 39N 73 21 E
Netstal, *Switz.* 33 B8 47 3N 9 3 E
Nettancourt, *France* 27 D11 48 51N 4 57 E
Nettetal, *Germany* 30 D2 51 19N 6 12 E
Nettilling L., *Canada* 139 B12 66 30N 71 0W
Nettuno, *Italy* 46 A5 41 27N 12 39 E
Netzahualcoyotl, Presa, *Mexico* 163 D6 17 10N 93 30W
Neu-Isenburg, *Germany* 31 E4 50 3N 8 42 E
Neu-Ulm, *Germany* 31 G6 48 22N 10 0 E
Neubrandenburg, *Germany* 30 B9 53 33N 13 15 E
Neubukow, *Germany* 30 A7 54 2N 11 39 E
Neuburg, *Germany* 31 G7 48 44N 11 11 E
Neuchâtel, *Switz.* 32 C3 47 0N 6 55 E
Neuchâtel □, *Switz.* 32 C3 47 0N 6 55 E
Neuchâtel, Lac de, *Switz.* 32 C3 46 53N 6 50 E
Neudau, *Austria* 34 D9 47 11N 16 6 E
Neuenegg, *Switz.* 32 C4 46 54N 7 18 E
Neuenhagen, *Germany* 30 C9 52 30N 13 38 E
Neuenhaus, *Germany* 30 C2 52 30N 6 58 E
Neuenhof, *Switz.* 33 B6 47 27N 8 19 E
Neuf-Brisach, *France* 27 D14 48 1N 7 30 E
Neufahrn, *Bayern, Germany* 31 G8 48 41N 12 11 E
Neufahrn, *Bayern, Germany* 31 G7 48 18N 11 40 E
Neufchâteau, *Belgium* 24 E5 49 50N 5 25 E
Neufchâteau, *France* 27 D12 48 21N 5 40 E
Neufchâtel-en-Bray, *France* 26 C8 49 44N 1 26 E
Neufchâtel-sur-Aisne, *France* 27 C11 49 26N 4 1 E
Neuhaus, *Germany* 30 B6 53 17N 10 56 E
Neuhausen, *Switz.* 33 A7 47 41N 8 37 E
Neuillé-Pont-Pierre, *France* 26 E7 47 33N 0 33 E
Neuilly-St-Front, *France* 27 C10 49 10N 3 15 E
Neukalen, *Germany* 30 B8 53 49N 12 46 E
Neumarkt, *Germany* 31 F7 49 26N 11 27 E
Neumünster, *Germany* 30 A5 54 4N 9 58 E
Neung-sur-Beuvron, *France* 27 E8 47 30N 1 50 E
Neunkirch, *Switz.* 33 A7 47 42N 8 30 E
Neunkirchen, *Austria* 34 D9 47 43N 16 4 E
Neunkirchen, *Germany* 31 F3 49 20N 7 9 E
Neuquén, *Argentina* 176 A3 38 55 S 68 0W
Neuquén □, *Argentina* 174 D2 38 0 S 69 50W
Neuquén →, *Argentina* 176 A3 38 59 S 68 0W
Neuruppin, *Germany* 30 C8 52 55N 12 48 E
Neusäss, *Germany* 31 G6 48 24N 10 50 E
Neuse →, *U.S.A.* 149 H7 35 6N 76 29W
Neusiedl, *Austria* 35 D9 47 57N 16 50 E
Neusiedler See, *Austria* 35 D9 47 50N 16 47 E
Neuss, *Germany* 30 D2 51 11N 6 42 E
Neussargues-Moissac, *France* 28 C7 45 9N 3 0 E
Neustadt, *Bayern, Germany* 31 F8 49 44N 12 10 E
Neustadt, *Bayern, Germany* 31 G7 48 48N 11 46 E
Neustadt, *Bayern, Germany* 31 F6 49 34N 10 37 E
Neustadt, *Bayern, Germany* 31 E7 50 19N 11 7 E
Neustadt, *Brandenburg, Germany* 30 C8 52 50N 12 27 E
Neustadt, *Hessen, Germany* 30 E5 50 51N 9 9 E
Neustadt, *Niedersachsen, Germany* 30 C5 52 30N 9 30 E
Neustadt, *Rhld-Pfz., Germany* 31 F4 49 21N 8 10 E
Neustadt, *Sachsen, Germany* 30 D10 51 2N 14 12 E
Neustadt, *Schleswig-Holstein, Germany* 30 A6 54 6N 10 49 E
Neustadt, *Thüringen, Germany* 30 E7 50 45N 11 43 E
Neustrelitz, *Germany* 30 B9 53 21N 13 4 E
Neuvic, *France* 28 C6 45 23N 2 16 E
Neuville-sur-Saône, *France* 29 C8 45 52N 4 51 E
Neuvy-le-Roi, *France* 26 E7 47 36N 0 36 E
Neuvy-St-Sépulchre, *France* 27 F8 46 35N 1 48 E
Neuvy-sur-Barangeon, *France* 27 E9 47 20N 2 15 E
Neuwerk, *Germany* 30 B4 53 55N 8 30 E
Neuwied, *Germany* 30 E3 50 26N 7 29 E
Neva →, *Russia* 58 C6 59 50N 30 30 E
Nevada, *Iowa, U.S.A.* 156 B3 42 1N 93 27W
Nevada, *Mo., U.S.A.* 155 G7 37 51N 94 22W
Nevada □, *U.S.A.* 158 G5 39 0N 117 0W
Nevada, Sierra, *Spain* 43 H7 37 3N 3 15W
Nevada, Sierra, *U.S.A.* 158 G3 39 0N 120 30W
Nevada City, *U.S.A.* 160 F6 39 16N 121 1W
Nevado, Cerro, *Argentina* 174 D2 35 30 S 68 32W
Nevasa, *India* 94 E2 19 34N 75 0 E
Neve, Sa. da, *Angola* 115 E2 13 43 S 13 10 E
Nevel, *Russia* 58 D5 56 0N 29 55 E
Nevers, *France* 27 F10 47 0N 3 9 E
Nevertire, *Australia* 129 A7 31 50 S 147 44 E
Nevesinje, *Bos.-H.* 50 C2 43 14N 18 6 E
Neville, *Canada* 143 D7 49 58N 107 39W
Nevinnomyssk, *Russia* 61 H6 44 40N 42 0 E
Nevis, *W. Indies* 165 C7 17 0N 62 30W
Nevlunghavn, *Norway* 18 F6 58 58N 9 53 E
Nevrokop = Gotse Delchev, *Bulgaria* 50 E7 41 36N 23 46 E
Nevşehir, *Turkey* 100 C6 38 33N 34 40 E
Nevyansk, *Russia* 62 C8 57 30N 60 13 E
New →, *Guyana* 169 C6 3 20N 57 37W
New →, *U.S.A.* 148 F5 38 10N 81 12W
New Aiyansh, *Canada* 142 B3 55 12N 129 4W
New Albany, *Ind., U.S.A.* 157 F11 38 18N 85 49W
New Albany, *Miss., U.S.A.* 155 H10 34 29N 89 0W
New Albany, *Pa., U.S.A.* 151 E8 41 36N 76 27W
New Amsterdam, *Guyana* 169 B6 6 15N 57 36W
New Angledool, *Australia* 127 D4 29 5 S 147 55 E
New Athens, *U.S.A.* 156 F7 38 19N 89 53W
New Baltimore, *U.S.A.* 150 D2 42 41N 82 44W
New Bedford, *U.S.A.* 151 E14 41 38N 70 56W
New Berlin, *Ill., U.S.A.* 156 E7 39 44N 89 55W
New Berlin, *N.Y., U.S.A.* 151 D9 42 37N 75 20W
New Berlin, *Pa., U.S.A.* 150 F8 40 50N 76 57W
New Berlin, *Wis., U.S.A.* 157 B8 42 59N 88 6W
New Bern, *U.S.A.* 149 H7 35 7N 77 3W
New Bethlehem, *U.S.A.* 150 F5 41 0N 79 20W
New Bloomfield, *U.S.A.* 150 F7 40 25N 77 11W
New Boston, *U.S.A.* 155 J7 33 28N 94 25W
New Braunfels, *U.S.A.* 155 L5 29 42N 98 8W
New Brighton, *N.Z.* 131 D7 43 29 S 172 43 E
New Brighton, *U.S.A.* 150 F4 40 42N 80 19W
New Britain, *Papua N. G.* 132 C6 5 50 S 150 20 E
New Britain, *U.S.A.* 151 E12 41 40N 72 47W
New Brockton, *U.S.A.* 152 D4 31 23N 85 56W
New Brunswick, *U.S.A.* 151 F10 40 30N 74 27W
New Brunswick □, *Canada* 141 C6 46 50N 66 30W
New Buffalo, *U.S.A.* 157 C10 41 47N 86 45W
New Bussa, *Nigeria* 113 D5 9 53N 4 31 E
New Caledonia ■, *Pac. Oc.* 133 U19 21 0 S 165 0 E
New Carlisle, *Ind., U.S.A.* 157 C10 41 45N 86 32W
New Carlisle, *Ohio, U.S.A.* 157 E12 39 56N 84 2W
New Castile = Castilla-La Mancha □, *Spain* 12 H5 39 30N 3 30W
New Castle, *Ind., U.S.A.* 157 E11 39 55N 85 22W
New Castle, *Ky., U.S.A.* 157 F11 38 26N 85 10W
New Castle, *Pa., U.S.A.* 150 F4 41 0N 80 21W
New City, *U.S.A.* 151 E11 41 9N 73 59W
New Concord, *U.S.A.* 150 G3 39 59N 81 54W
New Cumberland, *U.S.A.* 150 F4 40 30N 80 36W
New Cuyama, *U.S.A.* 161 L7 34 57N 119 38W
New Delhi, *India* 92 E7 28 37N 77 13 E
New Denver, *Canada* 142 D5 50 0N 117 25W
New Don Pedro Reservoir, *U.S.A.* 160 H6 37 43N 120 24W
New Ellenton, *U.S.A.* 152 B8 33 28N 81 41W
New England, *U.S.A.* 154 B3 46 32N 102 52W
New England Ra., *Australia* 127 E5 30 20 S 151 45 E
New Forest, *U.K.* 21 G6 50 53N 1 34W
New Franklin, *U.S.A.* 156 E4 39 1N 92 44W
New Galloway, *U.K.* 22 F4 55 5N 4 9W
New Georgia Is., *Solomon Is.* 133 M9 8 15 S 157 30 E
New Glarus, *U.S.A.* 156 B7 42 49N 89 38W

Ochamchira 259

Nova Sofala, *Mozam.* **117 C5** 20 7 S 34 42 E
Nova Varoš, *Serbia, Yug.* **50 C3** 43 29N 19 48 E
Nova Venécia, *Brazil* **171 E3** 18 45 S 40 24W
Nova Vida, *Brazil* **173 C5** 10 11 S 62 47W
Nova Zagora, *Bulgaria* **51 D10** 42 32N 26 1 E
Novaci, *Macedonia* **50 E5** 41 5N 21 29 E
Novaci, *Romania* **53 E8** 45 10N 23 42 E
Novaféltria, *Italy* **45 E9** 43 53N 12 17 E
Novaleksandrovskaya =
Novoaleksandrovsk, *Russia* **61 H5** 45 29N 41 17 E
Novannenskiy =
Novoannenskiy, *Russia* **60 E6** 50 32N 42 39 E
Novar, *Canada* **150 A5** 45 27N 79 15W
Novara, *Italy* **44 C5** 45 28N 8 38 E
Novato, *U.S.A.* **160 G4** 38 6N 122 35W
Novaya Kakhovka = Nova
Kakhovka, *Ukraine* **59 J7** 46 42N 33 27 E
Novaya Kazanka, *Kazakstan* **61 F9** 48 56N 49 36 E
Novaya Ladoga, *Russia* **58 B7** 60 7N 32 16 E
Novaya Lyalya, *Russia* **62 B8** 59 4N 60 45 E
Novaya Sibir, Ostrov, *Russia* **65 B16** 75 10N 150 0 E
Novaya Zemlya, *Russia* **64 B6** 75 0N 56 0 E
Nové Město, *Slovak Rep.* **35 C10** 48 45N 17 50 E
Nové Město na Moravě,
Czech Rep. **34 B9** 49 34N 16 5 E
Nové Město nad Metují,
Czech Rep. **35 A9** 50 20N 16 10 E
Nové Zámky, *Slovak Rep.* **35 C11** 48 2N 18 8 E
Novelda, *Spain* **41 G4** 38 24N 0 45W
Novellara, *Italy* **44 D7** 44 51N 10 44 E
Novelty, *U.S.A.* **156 D4** 40 1N 92 12W
Noventa Vicentina, *Italy* **45 C8** 45 17N 11 32 E
Novgorod, *Russia* **58 C6** 58 30N 31 25 E
Novgorod-Severskiy =
Novhorod-Siverskyy, *Ukraine* **59 G7** 52 2N 33 10 E
Novhorod-Siverskyy, *Ukraine* **59 G7** 52 2N 33 10 E
Novi Bečej, *Serbia, Yug.* **52 E5** 45 36N 20 10 E
Novi Iskar, *Bulgaria* **50 D7** 42 48N 23 21 E
Novi Kneževac, *Serbia, Yug.* **52 D5** 46 4N 20 8 E
Novi Lígure, *Italy* **44 D5** 44 46N 8 47 E
Novi Pazar, *Bulgaria* **51 C11** 43 25N 27 15 E
Novi Pazar, *Serbia, Yug.* **50 C4** 43 12N 20 28 E
Novi Sad, *Serbia, Yug.* **52 E4** 45 18N 19 52 E
Novi Slankamen, *Serbia, Yug.* **52 E5** 45 8N 20 15 E
Novi Travnik, *Bos.-H.* **52 F2** 44 10N 17 40 E
Novi Vinodolski, *Croatia* **45 C11** 45 10N 14 48 E
Novigrad, *Istra, Croatia* **45 C10** 45 19N 13 33 E
Novigrad, *Zadar, Croatia* **45 D12** 44 10N 15 32 E
Novigradsko More, *Croatia* **45 D12** 44 12N 15 33 E
Novinger, *U.S.A.* **156 D4** 40 14N 92 43W
Novo Acôrdo, *Brazil* **170 D2** 10 10 S 46 48W
Novo Airão, *Brazil* **169 D5** 2 10 S 60 59W
Novo Aripuanã, *Brazil* **169 E5** 5 8 S 60 22W
Nôvo Cruzeiro, *Brazil* **171 E3** 17 29 S 41 53W
Nôvo Hamburgo, *Brazil* **175 B5** 29 37 S 51 7W
Novo Horizonte, *Brazil* **171 F2** 21 25 S 49 10W
Novo Mesto, *Slovenia* **45 C12** 45 47N 15 12 E
Novo Miloševo, *Serbia, Yug.* **52 E5** 45 42N 20 20 E
Novo Paraiso, *Brazil* **169 C5** 1 17N 60 28W
Novo Remanso, *Brazil* **170 C3** 9 41 S 42 4W
Novo-Sergiyevskiy, *Russia* **62 E4** 52 5N 53 38 E
Novoaleksandrovsk, *Russia* **61 H5** 45 29N 41 17 E
Novoalekseyevka, *Kazakstan* **62 F5** 50 8N 55 39 E
Novoannenskiy, *Russia* **60 E6** 50 32N 42 39 E
Novoataysk, *Russia* **64 D9** 53 30N 84 0 E
Novoazovsk, *Ukraine* **59 J10** 47 15N 38 4 E
Novocheboksarsk, *Russia* **60 B8** 56 5N 47 27 E
Novocherkassk, *Russia* **61 G5** 47 27N 40 15 E
Novodevichye, *Russia* **60 D9** 53 37N 48 50 E
Novogrudok = Navahrudak,
Belarus **58 F3** 53 40N 25 50 E
Novohrad-Volynskyy, *Ukraine* **59 G4** 50 34N 27 35 E
Novokachalinsk, *Russia* **68 B6** 45 5N 132 0 E
Novokazalinsk = Zhangaqazaly,
Kazakstan **64 E7** 45 48N 62 6 E
Novokhopersk, *Russia* **60 E5** 51 5N 41 39 E
Novokuybyshevsk, *Russia* **60 D9** 53 7N 49 58 E
Novokuznetsk, *Russia* **64 D9** 53 45N 87 10 E
Novomirgorod, *Ukraine* **59 H6** 48 45N 31 33 E
Novomoskovsk, *Russia* **58 E10** 54 5N 38 15 E
Novomoskovsk, *Ukraine* **59 H8** 48 33N 35 17 E
Novoorsk, *Russia* **62 F7** 51 21N 59 2 E
Novopolotsk = Navapolatsk,
Belarus **58 E5** 55 32N 28 37 E
Novorossiysk, *Russia* **59 K9** 44 43N 37 46 E
Novorossiyskoye, *Kazakstan* **62 F7** 50 13N 58 0 E
Novorybnoye, *Russia* **65 B11** 72 50N 105 50 E
Novorzhev, *Russia* **58 D5** 57 3N 29 25 E
Novosej, *Albania* **50 E4** 41 56N 20 35 E
Novoselytsya, *Ukraine* **59 H4** 48 14N 26 15 E
Novoshakhtinsk, *Russia* **59 J10** 47 46N 39 58 E
Novosibirsk, *Russia* **64 D9** 55 0N 83 5 E
Novosibirskiye Ostrova, *Russia* **65 B15** 75 0N 142 0 E
Novosil, *Russia* **59 F9** 52 59N 37 2 E
Novosineglazovskiy, *Russia* **62 D8** 55 2N 61 21 E
Novosokolniki, *Russia* **58 D6** 56 20N 30 2 E
Novotitarovskaya, *Russia* **61 H4** 45 17N 39 2 E
Novotroitsk, *Russia* **62 F7** 51 10N 58 15 E
Novotroitskoye, *Kazakstan* **63 B6** 43 42N 73 46 E
Novoukrayinka, *Ukraine* **59 H6** 48 25N 31 30 E
Novouljanovsk, *Russia* **60 C9** 54 8N 48 24 E
Novouzensk, *Russia* **60 E9** 50 32N 48 17 E
Novovolynsk, *Ukraine* **59 G3** 50 45N 24 4 E
Novovoronezhskiy, *Russia* **59 G10** 51 19N 39 13 E
Novovyatsk, *Russia* **62 B2** 58 24N 49 45 E
Novozybkov, *Russia* **59 F6** 52 30N 32 0 E
Novska, *Croatia* **45 C14** 45 19N 17 0 E
Novvy Urengoy, *Russia* **64 C8** 65 48N 76 52 E
Nový Bor, *Czech Rep.* **34 A7** 50 46N 14 35 E
Novy Bug = Novyy Buh,
Ukraine **59 J7** 47 34N 32 29 E
Nový Bydžov, *Czech Rep.* **34 A8** 50 14N 15 29 E
Novy Dwór Mazowiecki,
Poland **55 F7** 52 26N 20 44 E
Nový Jičín, *Czech Rep.* **35 B11** 49 30N 18 2 E
Novyy Afon, *Georgia* **61 J5** 43 7N 40 50 E
Novyy Bor, *Russia* **56 A9** 66 43N 52 19 E
Novyy Buh, *Ukraine* **59 J7** 47 34N 32 29 E
Novyy Oskol, *Russia* **59 G9** 50 44N 37 55 E
Novyy Port, *Russia* **64 C8** 67 40N 72 30 E
Now Shahr, *Iran* **97 B6** 36 40N 51 30 E
Nowa Deba, *Poland* **55 H8** 50 26N 21 41 E
Nowa Nowa, *Australia* **129 D8** 37 44 S 148 3 E
Nowa Ruda, *Poland* **55 H3** 50 35N 16 30 E
Nowa Sarzyna, *Poland* **55 H9** 50 21N 22 21 E
Nowa Sól, *Poland* **55 G2** 51 48N 15 44 E
Nowata, *U.S.A.* **155 G7** 36 42N 95 38W
Nowbarān, *Iran* **97 C6** 35 8N 49 42 E
Nowe, *Poland* **54 E5** 53 41N 18 44 E
Nowe Miasteczko, *Poland* **55 G2** 51 42N 15 42 E
Nowe Miasto, *Poland* **55 G7** 51 38N 20 34 E
Nowe Miasto Lubawskie,
Poland **54 E6** 53 27N 19 33 E
Nowe Skalmierzyce, *Poland* **55 G4** 51 43N 18 0 E
Nowe Warpno, *Poland* **54 E1** 53 42N 14 18 E
Nowendoc, *Australia* **129 A9** 31 32 S 151 44 E
Nowghāb, *Iran* **97 C8** 33 53N 59 4 E
Nowgong, *Assam, India* **90 B4** 26 20N 92 50 E
Nowgong, *Mad. P., India* **93 G8** 25 4N 79 27 E
Nowingi, *Australia* **128 C5** 34 33 S 142 15 E
Nowogard, *Poland* **54 E2** 53 41N 15 10 E
Nowogród, *Poland* **55 E8** 53 14N 21 53 E
Nowogród Bobrzanski, *Poland* **55 G2** 51 48N 15 15 E
Nowogrodziec, *Poland* **55 G2** 51 12N 15 24 E
Nowra-Bomaderry, *Australia* **129 C9** 34 53 S 150 35 E
Nowrangapur, *India* **94 E6** 19 14N 82 33 E
Nowshera, *Pakistan* **91 B3** 34 0N 72 0 E
Nowy Dwór Gdański, *Poland* **54 D6** 54 13N 19 7 E
Nowy Sącz, *Poland* **55 J7** 49 40N 20 41 E
Nowy Staw, *Poland* **54 D6** 54 13N 19 2 E
Nowy Targ, *Poland* **55 J7** 49 29N 20 2 E
Nowy Tomyśl, *Poland* **55 F3** 52 19N 16 10 E
Nowy Wiśnicz, *Poland* **55 J7** 49 55N 20 28 E
Noxen, *U.S.A.* **151 E8** 41 25N 76 4W
Noxon, *U.S.A.* **158 C6** 48 0N 115 43W
Noyabr'sk, *Russia* **64 C8** 64 34N 76 21 E
Noyant, *France* **26 E7** 47 30N 0 6 E
Noyers, *France* **27 E10** 47 40N 4 0 E
Noyon, *France* **27 C9** 49 34N 2 59 E
Noyon, *Mongolia* **74 C2** 43 2N 102 4 E
Nozay, *France* **26 E5** 47 34N 1 38W
Nqutu, *S. Africa* **117 D5** 28 13 S 30 32 E
Nsa, O. en →, *Algeria* **111 B6** 32 28N 5 24 E
Nsa, Plateau de, *Congo* **114 C3** 2 26 S 15 20 E
Nsah, *Congo* **114 C3** 2 22 S 15 19 E
Nsanje, *Malawi* **119 F4** 16 55 S 35 12 E
Nsawam, *Ghana* **113 D4** 5 50N 0 24W
Nsok, *Eq. Guin.* **114 B2** 1 10N 11 19 E
Nsomba, *Zambia* **119 E2** 10 45 S 29 51 E
Nsontin,
Dem. Rep. of the Congo **114 C3** 3 7 S 17 56 E
Nsopzup, *Burma* **90 C6** 25 51N 97 30 E
Nsukka, *Nigeria* **113 D6** 6 51N 7 29 E
Ntoum, *Gabon* **114 B1** 0 22N 9 47 E
N'Tsama, *Congo* **114 C2** 0 53 S 14 44 E
Ntui, *Cameroon* **114 B2** 4 27N 11 38 E
Nu Jiang →, *China* **76 E2** 29 58N 97 25 E
Nu Shan, *China* **76 E2** 26 0N 99 20 E
Nuba Mts. = Nubah, Jibalan,
Sudan **107 E3** 12 0N 31 0 E
Nubah, Jibalan, *Sudan* **107 E3** 12 0N 31 0 E
Nubia, *Africa* **104 D7** 21 0N 32 0 E
Nubian Desert = Nûbîya, Es
Sahrâ en, *Sudan* **106 C3** 21 30N 33 30 E
Nûbîya, Es Sahrâ en, *Sudan* **106 C3** 21 30N 33 30 E
Nubledo, *Spain* **42 B5** 43 31N 5 52W
Nuboai, *Indonesia* **79 E9** 2 10 S 136 30 E
Nubra →, *India* **93 B7** 34 35N 77 35 E
Nucet, *Romania* **52 D7** 46 28N 22 35 E
Nueces →, *U.S.A.* **155 M6** 27 51N 97 30W
Nueltin L., *Canada* **143 A9** 60 30N 99 30W
Nueva, I., *Chile* **176 E3** 55 13 S 66 30W
Nueva Antioquia, *Colombia* **168 B4** 6 5N 69 26W
Nueva Asunción □, *Paraguay* **174 A3** 21 0 S 61 0W
Nueva Carteya, *Spain* **43 H6** 37 35N 4 28W
Nueva Ecija □, *Phil.* **80 D3** 15 35N 121 0 E
Nueva Esparta □, *Venezuela* **169 A5** 11 0N 64 0W
Nueva Gerona, *Cuba* **166 B3** 21 53N 82 49W
Nueva Imperial, *Chile* **176 A2** 38 45 S 72 58W
Nueva Palmira, *Uruguay* **174 C4** 33 52 S 58 20W
Nueva Rosita, *Mexico* **162 B4** 28 0N 101 11W
Nueva San Salvador, *El Salv.* **164 D2** 13 40N 89 18W
Nueva Tabarca, *Spain* **41 G4** 38 17N 0 30W
Nueva Vizcaya □, *Phil.* **80 C3** 16 20N 121 20 E
Nuéve de Julio, *Argentina* **174 D3** 35 30 S 61 0W
Nuevitas, *Cuba* **166 B4** 21 30N 77 20W
Nuevo, G., *Argentina* **176 B4** 43 0 S 64 30W
Nuevo Casas Grandes, *Mexico* **162 A3** 30 22N 108 0W
Nuevo Guerrero, *Mexico* **163 B5** 26 34N 99 15W
Nuevo Laredo, *Mexico* **163 B5** 27 30N 99 30W
Nuevo León □, *Mexico* **162 C5** 25 0N 100 0W
Nuevo Mundo, Cerro, *Bolivia* **172 E4** 21 55 S 66 53W
Nuevo Rocafuerte, *Ecuador* **168 D2** 0 55 S 75 27W
Nugget Pt., *N.Z.* **131 G4** 46 27 S 169 50 E
Nugrus, Gebel, *Egypt* **106 C3** 24 47N 34 35 E
Nuhaka, *N.Z.* **130 F6** 39 3 S 177 45 E
Nuits-St-Georges, *France* **27 E11** 47 10N 4 56 E
Nukey Bluff, *Australia* **127 E2** 32 26 S 135 29 E
Nukheila, *Sudan* **106 D2** 19 1N 26 21 E
Nukhuyb, *Iraq* **101 F10** 32 4N 42 3 E
Nuku'alofa, *Tonga* **133 Q14** 21 10 S 174 0W
Nukulaelae, *Tuvalu* **123 B14** 9 23 S 179 52 E
Nukus, *Uzbekistan* **64 E6** 42 27N 59 41 E
Nules, *Spain* **40 F4** 39 51N 0 9W
Nullagine, *Australia* **124 D3** 21 53 S 120 7 E
Nullagine →, *Australia* **124 D3** 21 20 S 120 20 E
Nullarbor, *Australia* **125 F5** 31 28 S 130 55 E
Nullarbor Plain, *Australia* **125 F4** 31 10 S 129 0 E
Numalla, L., *Australia* **127 D3** 28 43 S 144 20 E
Numan, *Nigeria* **113 D7** 9 29N 12 3 E
Numata, *Japan* **71 A11** 36 45N 139 4 E
Numatinna →, *Sudan* **107 F2** 7 38N 27 20 E
Numazu, *Japan* **71 B10** 35 7N 138 51 E
Numbulwar, *Australia* **126 A2** 14 15 S 135 45 E
Numedal, *Norway* **18 D6** 60 6N 9 6 E
Numfoor, *Indonesia* **79 E8** 1 0 S 134 50 E
Numurkah, *Australia* **129 D6** 36 5 S 145 26 E
Nunaksaluk I., *Canada* **141 A7** 55 49N 60 20W
Nunap Isua, *Greenland* **10 F6** 59 48N 43 55W
Nunavut □, *Canada* **139 B11** 66 0N 85 0W
Nunda, *U.S.A.* **150 D7** 42 35N 77 56W
Nungarin, *Australia* **125 F2** 31 12 S 118 6 E
Nungo, *Mozam.* **119 E4** 13 23 S 37 43 E
Nungwe, *Tanzania* **118 C3** 2 48 S 32 2 E
Nunivak I., *U.S.A.* **138 B3** 60 10N 166 30W
Nunkun, *India* **93 C7** 33 57N 76 2 E
Nùoro, *Italy* **46 B2** 40 20N 9 20 E
Núpur, *Iceland* **11 B3** 65 56N 23 46W
Nuqayy, Jabal, *Libya* **108 D3** 23 11N 19 30 E
Nuqūb, *Yemen* **98 D4** 14 59N 45 48 E
Nuquí, *Colombia* **168 B2** 5 42N 77 17W
Nūrābād, *Iran* **97 E8** 27 47N 57 12 E
Nurata, *Uzbekistan* **63 C2** 40 33N 65 41 E
Nuratau, Khrebet, *Uzbekistan* **63 C3** 40 40N 66 30 E
Nure →, *Italy* **44 C6** 45 3N 9 49 E
Nuremberg = Nürnberg,
Germany **31 F7** 49 27N 11 3 E
Nūrestān, *Afghan.* **91 B3** 35 30N 70 45 E
Nuri, *Mexico* **162 B3** 28 2N 109 22W
Nuriootpa, *Australia* **128 C3** 34 27 S 139 0 E
Nurlat, *Russia* **60 C10** 54 29N 50 45 E
Nurmes, *Finland* **14 E23** 63 33N 29 10 E
Nürnberg, *Germany* **31 F7** 49 27N 11 3 E
Nurpur, *Pakistan* **92 D4** 31 53N 71 54 E
Nurra, La, *Italy* **46 B1** 40 45N 8 15 E
Nurran, L. = Terewah, L.,
Australia **127 D4** 29 52 S 147 35 E
Nurrari Lakes, *Australia* **125 E5** 29 1 S 130 5 E
Nurri, *Italy* **46 C2** 39 43N 9 14 E
Nürtingen, *Germany* **31 G5** 48 37N 9 19 E
Nurzec →, *Poland* **55 F9** 52 37N 22 25 E
Nus, *Italy* **44 C4** 45 45N 7 28 E
Nusa Barung, *Indonesia* **79 H15** 8 30 S 113 30 E
Nusa Kambangan, *Indonesia* **79 G13** 7 40 S 108 10 E
Nusa Tenggara Barat □,
Indonesia **78 F5** 8 50 S 117 30 E
Nusa Tenggara Timur □,
Indonesia **79 F6** 9 30 S 122 0 E
Nusaybin, *Turkey* **101 D9** 37 3N 41 10 E
Nushki, *Pakistan* **91 C2** 29 35N 66 0 E
Nuuk, *Greenland* **10 E5** 64 10N 51 35W
Nuussauq, *Greenland* **10 C5** 74 8N 57 3W
Nuwakot, *Nepal* **93 E10** 28 10N 83 55 E
Nuwara Eliya, *Sri Lanka* **95 L5** 6 58N 80 48 E
Nuweiba', *Egypt* **96 D2** 28 59N 34 39 E
Nuwerus, *S. Africa* **116 E2** 31 8 S 18 24 E
Nuweveldberge, *S. Africa* **116 E3** 32 10 S 21 45 E
Nuyts, C., *Australia* **125 F5** 32 2 S 132 21 E
Nuyts, Pt., *Australia* **125 G2** 35 4 S 116 38 E
Nuyts Arch., *Australia* **127 E1** 32 35 S 133 20 E
Nuzvid, *India* **94 F5** 16 47N 80 53 E
N'Vinda, *Angola* **115 E3** 13 8 S 19 2 E
Nxau-Nxau, *Botswana* **116 B3** 18 57 S 21 4 E
Nyaake, *Liberia* **112 E3** 4 52N 7 37W
Nyabessan, *Cameroon* **114 B2** 2 28N 10 24 E
Nyabing, *Australia* **125 F2** 33 33 S 118 9 E
Nyack, *U.S.A.* **151 E11** 41 5N 73 55W
Nyagan, *Russia* **64 C7** 62 30N 65 38 E
Nyah West, *Australia* **128 C5** 35 16 S 143 21 E
Nyahanga, *Tanzania* **118 C3** 2 20 S 33 37 E
Nyahua, *Tanzania* **118 D3** 5 25 S 33 23 E
Nyahururu, *Kenya* **118 B4** 0 2N 36 27 E
Nyainqentanglha Shan, *China* **72 D4** 30 0N 90 0 E
Nyakanazi, *Tanzania* **118 C3** 3 2 S 31 10 E
Nyakrom, *Ghana* **113 D4** 5 40N 0 50W
Nyâlâ, *Sudan* **107 E1** 12 2N 24 58 E
Nyamandhlovu, *Zimbabwe* **119 F2** 19 55 S 28 16 E
Nyambiti, *Tanzania* **118 C3** 2 48 S 33 27 E
Nyamlell, *Sudan* **107 F2** 9 7N 26 59 E
Nyamwaga, *Tanzania* **118 C3** 1 27 S 34 33 E
Nyandekwa, *Tanzania* **118 C3** 3 57 S 32 32 E
Nyanding →, *Sudan* **107 F3** 8 40N 32 41 E
Nyandoma, *Russia* **58 B11** 61 40N 40 12 E
Nyanga →, *Gabon* **114 C2** 2 58 S 10 15 E
Nyangana, *Namibia* **116 B3** 18 0 S 20 40 E
Nyanguge, *Tanzania* **118 C3** 2 30 S 33 12 E
Nyankpala, *Ghana* **113 D4** 9 21N 0 58W
Nyanza, *Rwanda* **118 C2** 2 20 S 29 42 E
Nyanza □, *Kenya* **118 C3** 0 10 S 34 15 E
Nyanza-Lac, *Burundi* **118 C2** 4 21 S 29 36 E
Nyaponges, *Sudan* **107 F3** 5 5N 33 45 E
Nyasa, L., *Africa* **119 E3** 12 30 S 34 30 E
Nyasvizh, *Belarus* **59 F4** 53 14N 26 38 E
Nyaunglebin, *Burma* **90 G6** 17 52N 96 42 E
Nyazepetrovsk, *Russia* **62 C7** 56 3N 59 36 E
Nyazura, *Zimbabwe* **119 F3** 18 40 S 32 16 E
Nyazwidzi →, *Zimbabwe* **119 G3** 20 0 S 31 17 E
Nybergsund, *Norway* **18 C9** 61 15N 12 19 E
Nyborg, *Denmark* **17 J4** 55 18N 10 47 E
Nybro, *Sweden* **17 H9** 56 44N 15 55 E
Nyda, *Russia* **64 C8** 66 40N 72 58 E
Nyeboe Land, *Greenland* **10 A5** 82 0N 57 0W
Nyengo Swamp, *Zambia* **115 E4** 14 51 S 22 7 E
Nyeri, *Kenya* **118 C4** 0 23 S 36 56 E
Nyerol, *Sudan* **107 F3** 8 41N 32 1 E
Nyhammar, *Sweden* **16 D8** 60 17N 14 58 E
Nyinahin, *Ghana* **112 D4** 6 43N 2 3W
Nyíradony, *Hungary* **52 C6** 47 41N 21 55 E
Nyirbátor, *Hungary* **52 C7** 47 49N 22 9 E
Nyíregyháza, *Hungary* **52 C6** 47 58N 21 47 E
Nykirke, *Norway* **18 D7** 60 54N 10 19 E
Nykøbing, *Storstrøm, Denmark* **17 K5** 54 56N 11 52 E
Nykøbing, *Vestsjælland,*
Denmark **17 J5** 55 55N 11 40 E
Nykøbing, *Viborg, Denmark* **17 H2** 56 48N 8 51 E
Nyköping, *Sweden* **17 F11** 58 45N 17 1 E
Nykroppa, *Sweden* **16 E8** 59 37N 14 18 E
Nykvarn, *Sweden* **16 E11** 59 11N 17 25 E
Nyland, *Sweden* **16 A11** 63 1N 17 45 E
Nylstroom, *S. Africa* **117 C4** 24 42 S 28 22 E
Nymagee, *Australia* **129 B7** 32 7 S 146 20 E
Nymburk, *Czech Rep.* **34 A8** 50 10N 15 1 E
Nynäshamn, *Sweden* **17 F11** 58 54N 17 57 E
Nyngan, *Australia* **127 E4** 31 30 S 147 8 E
Nyoma Rap, *India* **93 C8** 33 10N 78 40 E
Nyoman = Neman →,
Lithuania **15 J20** 55 25N 21 10 E
Nyon, *Switz.* **32 D2** 46 23N 6 14 E
Nyong →, *Cameroon* **113 E6** 3 17N 9 54 E
Nyons, *France* **29 D9** 44 22N 5 10 E
Nyora, *Australia* **129 E6** 38 20 S 145 41 E
Nyou, *Burkina Faso* **113 C4** 12 42N 2 1W
Nýrsko, *Czech Rep.* **34 B6** 49 18N 13 9 E
Nysa, *Poland* **55 H4** 50 30N 17 22 E
Nysa →, *Europe* **30 C10** 52 4N 14 46 E
Nysa Kłodzka →, *Poland* **55 H4** 50 49N 17 40 E
Nysäter, *Sweden* **16 E6** 59 17N 12 47 E
Nyseter, *Norway* **18 B5** 62 2N 8 20 E
Nyssa, *U.S.A.* **158 E5** 43 53N 117 0W
Nysted, *Denmark* **17 K5** 54 40N 11 44 E
Nytva, *Russia* **62 C5** 57 56N 55 20 E
Nyūgawa, *Japan* **70 D5** 33 56N 133 5 E
Nyunzu,
Dem. Rep. of the Congo **118 D2** 5 57 S 27 58 E
Nyurba, *Russia* **65 C12** 63 17N 118 28 E
Nyzhnohirskyy, *Ukraine* **59 K8** 45 27N 34 38 E
Nzébéla, *Guinea* **112 D3** 8 9N 9 7W
Nzega, *Tanzania* **118 C3** 4 10 S 33 12 E
Nzérékoré, *Guinea* **112 D3** 7 49N 8 48W
Nzeto, *Angola* **115 D2** 7 10 S 12 52 E
Nzilo, Chutes de,
Dem. Rep. of the Congo **119 E2** 10 18 S 25 27 E
Nzo →, *Ivory C.* **112 D3** 6 15N 7 3W
Nzubuka, *Tanzania* **118 C3** 4 45 S 32 50 E

O

O Barco, *Spain* **42 C4** 42 23N 6 58W
O Carballiño, *Spain* **42 C2** 42 26N 8 5W
O Corgo, *Spain* **42 C3** 42 56N 7 25W
O Pino, *Spain* **42 C2** 42 56N 8 20W
O Porriño, *Spain* **42 C2** 42 10N 8 37W
Ō-Shima, *Fukuoka, Japan* **70 D2** 33 54N 130 25 E
Ō-Shima, *Nagasaki, Japan* **70 C1** 34 29N 129 33 E
Ō-Shima, *Shizuoka, Japan* **71 C11** 34 44N 139 24 E
Oa, Mull of, *U.K.* **22 F2** 55 35N 6 20W
Oacoma, *U.S.A.* **154 D5** 43 48N 99 24W
Oahe, L., *U.S.A.* **154 C4** 44 27N 100 24W
Oahe Dam, *U.S.A.* **154 C4** 44 27N 100 24W
Oahu, *U.S.A.* **146 H16** 21 28N 157 58W
Oak Creek, *U.S.A.* **157 B9** 42 52N 87 55W
Oak Harbor, *U.S.A.* **160 B4** 48 18N 122 39W
Oak Hill, *Fla., U.S.A.* **153 G9** 28 52N 80 51W
Oak Hill, *W. Va., U.S.A.* **148 G5** 37 59N 81 9W
Oak Lawn, *U.S.A.* **157 C9** 41 43N 87 44W
Oak Park, *Ga., U.S.A.* **152 C7** 32 22N 82 19W
Oak Park, *Ill., U.S.A.* **157 C9** 41 53N 87 47W
Oak Ridge, *U.S.A.* **149 G3** 36 1N 84 16W
Oak View, *U.S.A.* **161 L7** 34 24N 119 18W
Oakan-Dake, *Japan* **68 C12** 43 27N 144 10 E
Oakbank, *Australia* **128 B4** 33 4 S 140 33 E
Oakdale, *Calif., U.S.A.* **160 H6** 37 46N 120 51W
Oakdale, *La., U.S.A.* **155 K8** 30 49N 92 40W
Oakes, *U.S.A.* **154 B5** 46 8N 98 6W
Oakesdale, *U.S.A.* **158 C5** 47 8N 117 15W
Oakey, *Australia* **127 D5** 27 25 S 151 43 E
Oakfield, *Ga., U.S.A.* **152 D6** 31 47N 83 58W
Oakfield, *N.Y., U.S.A.* **150 C6** 43 4N 78 16W
Oakford, *U.S.A.* **156 D7** 40 6N 89 58W
Oakham, *U.K.* **21 E7** 52 40N 0 43W
Oakhurst, *U.S.A.* **160 H7** 37 19N 119 40W
Oakland, *Calif., U.S.A.* **160 H4** 37 49N 122 16W
Oakland, *Ill., U.S.A.* **157 E8** 39 39N 88 2W
Oakland City, *U.S.A.* **157 F9** 38 20N 87 21W
Oaklands, *Australia* **129 C7** 35 34 S 146 10 E
Oakley, *Idaho, U.S.A.* **158 E7** 42 15N 113 53W
Oakley, *Kans., U.S.A.* **154 F4** 39 8N 100 51W
Oakley Creek, *Australia* **129 A8** 31 37 S 149 46 E
Oakover →, *Australia* **124 D3** 21 0 S 120 40 E
Oakridge, *U.S.A.* **158 E2** 43 45N 122 28W
Oaktown, *U.S.A.* **157 F9** 38 52N 87 27W
Oakville, *Canada* **150 C5** 43 27N 79 41W
Oakville, *U.S.A.* **160 D3** 46 51N 123 14W
Oakwood, *U.S.A.* **157 C12** 41 6N 84 23W
Oamaru, *N.Z.* **131 F5** 45 5 S 170 59 E
Ōamishirasato, *Japan* **71 B12** 35 31N 140 18 E
Oancea, *Romania* **53 E12** 45 21N 27 42 E
Oarai, *Japan* **71 A12** 36 21N 140 34 E
Oasis, *Calif., U.S.A.* **161 M10** 33 28N 116 6W
Oasis, *Nev., U.S.A.* **160 H9** 37 29N 117 55W
Oates Land, *Antarctica* **7 C11** 69 0 S 160 0 E
Oatlands, *Australia* **126 G4** 42 17 S 147 21 E
Oatman, *U.S.A.* **161 K12** 35 1N 114 19W
Oaxaca, *Mexico* **163 D5** 17 2N 96 40W
Oaxaca □, *Mexico* **163 D5** 17 0N 97 0W
Ob →, *Russia* **64 C7** 66 45N 69 30 E
Oba, *Canada* **140 C3** 49 4N 84 7W
Obala, *Cameroon* **113 E7** 4 9N 11 32 E
Obama, *Fukui, Japan* **71 B7** 35 30N 135 45 E
Obama, *Nagasaki, Japan* **70 E2** 32 43N 130 13 E
Oban, *Nigeria* **113 D6** 5 17N 8 33 E
Oban, *U.K.* **22 E3** 56 25N 5 29W
Obbia, *Somali Rep.* **120 C3** 5 25N 48 30 E
Ober-Aargau, *Switz.* **32 B5** 47 10N 7 45 E
Ober-engadin, *Switz.* **33 C9** 46 35N 9 55 E
Obera, *Argentina* **175 B4** 27 21 S 55 2W
Oberalppass, *Switz.* **33 C7** 46 39N 8 35 E
Oberalpstock, *Switz.* **33 C7** 46 45N 8 47 E
Oberammergau, *Germany* **31 H7** 47 36N 11 4 E
Oberasbach, *Germany* **31 F6** 49 25N 10 57 E
Oberbayern □, *Germany* **31 G7** 48 5N 11 50 E
Oberdiessbach, *Switz.* **32 C5** 46 51N 7 40 E
Oberdrauburg, *Austria* **34 E5** 46 44N 12 58 E
Oberentfelden, *Switz.* **32 B6** 47 21N 8 2 E
Oberfranken □, *Germany* **31 E7** 50 10N 11 20 E
Oberhausen, *Germany* **30 D2** 51 28N 6 51 E
Oberkirch, *Germany* **31 G4** 48 31N 8 4 E
Oberland, *Switz.* **32 C5** 46 35N 7 38 E
Oberlausitz, *Germany* **30 D10** 51 16N 14 24 E
Oberlin, *Kans., U.S.A.* **154 F4** 39 49N 100 32W
Oberlin, *La., U.S.A.* **155 K8** 30 37N 92 46W
Oberlin, *Ohio, U.S.A.* **150 E2** 41 18N 82 13W
Obernai, *France* **27 D14** 48 28N 7 30 E
Oberndorf, *Germany* **31 G4** 48 17N 8 34 E
Oberon, *Australia* **129 B8** 33 45 S 149 52 E
Oberösterreich □, *Austria* **34 C7** 48 10N 14 0 E
Oberpfalz □, *Germany* **31 F8** 49 20N 12 10 E
Oberpfälzer Wald, *Germany* **31 F8** 49 30N 12 30 E
Oberriet, *Switz.* **33 B9** 47 19N 9 34 E
Obersiggenthal, *Switz.* **33 B6** 47 29N 8 18 E
Oberstdorf, *Germany* **31 H6** 47 24N 10 15 E
Oberting, *Gabon* **114 C1** 0 22 S 9 46 E
Oberursel, *Germany* **31 E4** 50 11N 8 35 E
Oberwart, *Austria* **35 D9** 47 17N 16 12 E
Oberwil, *Switz.* **32 A5** 47 32N 7 33 E
Obi, Kepulauan, *Indonesia* **79 E7** 1 23 S 127 45 E
Obi Is. = Obi, Kepulauan,
Indonesia **79 E7** 1 23 S 127 45 E
Obiaruku, *Nigeria* **113 D6** 5 51N 6 9 E
Óbidos, *Brazil* **169 D6** 1 50 S 55 30W
Óbidos, *Portugal* **43 F1** 39 19N 9 10W
Obihiro, *Japan* **68 C11** 42 56N 143 12 E
Obilatu, *Indonesia* **79 E7** 1 25 S 127 20 E
Obilnoye, *Russia* **61 G7** 47 32N 44 30 E
Obing, *Germany* **31 G8** 48 0N 12 24 E
Objat, *France* **28 C5** 45 16N 1 24 E
Oblong, *U.S.A.* **157 F9** 39 0N 87 55W
Obluchye, *Russia* **65 E14** 49 1N 131 4 E
Obninsk, *Russia* **58 E9** 55 8N 36 37 E
Obo, *C.A.R.* **118 A2** 5 20N 26 32 E
Oboa, Mt., *Uganda* **118 B3** 1 45N 34 45 E
Obock, *Djibouti* **107 E5** 12 0N 43 20 E
Oborniki, *Poland* **55 F3** 52 39N 16 50 E
Oborniki Śląskie, *Poland* **55 G3** 51 17N 16 53 E
Obouya, *Congo* **114 C3** 0 56 S 15 43 E
Oboyan, *Russia* **59 G9** 51 15N 36 21 E
Obozerskaya = Obozerskiy,
Russia **56 B7** 63 34N 40 21 E
Obozerskiy, *Russia* **56 B7** 63 34N 40 21 E
Obrenovac, *Serbia, Yug.* **50 B4** 44 40N 20 11 E
O'Brien, *U.S.A.* **152 E7** 30 2N 82 57W
Obrovac, *Croatia* **45 D12** 44 11N 15 41 E
Obruk, *Turkey* **100 C5** 38 7N 33 12 E
Obrzycko, *Poland* **55 F3** 52 42N 16 32 E
Observatory Inlet, *Canada* **142 B3** 55 10N 129 54W
Obshchi Syrt, *Russia* **62 E4** 52 0N 53 0 E
Obskaya Guba, *Russia* **64 C8** 69 0N 73 0 E
Obuasi, *Ghana* **113 D4** 6 17N 1 40W
Obubra, *Nigeria* **113 D6** 6 8N 8 20 E
Obudu, *Nigeria* **113 D6** 6 38N 9 5 E
Obwalden □, *Switz.* **32 C6** 46 55N 8 15 E
Obzor, *Bulgaria* **51 D11** 42 50N 27 52 E
Ocala, *U.S.A.* **149 L4** 29 11N 82 8W
Ocamo →, *Venezuela* **169 C4** 2 48N 65 14W
Ocampo, *Chihuahua, Mexico* **162 B3** 28 9N 108 24W
Ocampo, *Tamaulipas, Mexico* **163 C5** 22 50N 99 20W
Ocaña, *Colombia* **168 B3** 8 15N 73 20W
Ocaña, *Spain* **42 F7** 39 55N 3 30W
Oconomowoc, *U.S.A.* **154 D10** 43 7N 88 30W
Occidental, Cordillera,
Colombia **168 C3** 5 0N 76 0W
Occidental, Cordillera, *Peru* **172 C3** 14 0 S 74 0W
Ocean City, *Md., U.S.A.* **148 F8** 38 20N 75 5W
Ocean City, *N.J., U.S.A.* **148 F8** 39 17N 74 35W
Ocean City, *Wash., U.S.A.* **160 C2** 47 4N 124 10W
Ocean Falls, *Canada* **142 C3** 52 18N 127 48W
Ocean I. = Banaba, *Kiribati* **134 H8** 0 45 S 169 50 E
Ocean Park, *U.S.A.* **160 D2** 46 30N 124 3W
Oceano, *U.S.A.* **161 K6** 35 6N 120 37W
Oceanport, *U.S.A.* **151 F10** 40 19N 74 3W
Oceanside, *U.S.A.* **161 M9** 33 12N 117 23W
Ochagavía, *Spain* **40 C3** 42 55N 1 5W
Ochakiv, *Ukraine* **59 J6** 46 37N 31 33 E
Ochamchira, *Georgia* **61 J5** 42 46N 41 32 E

Ostrožac 261

One Tree, Australia 127 E3 34 11 S 144 43 E
Oneco, U.S.A. 153 H7 27 25N 82 31W
Onega, Russia 56 B6 64 0N 38 10 E
Onega →, Russia 56 B6 63 58N 38 2 E
Onega, G. of = Onezhskaya Guba, Russia 56 B6 64 24N 36 38 E
Onega, L. = Onezhskoye Ozero, Russia 58 B8 61 44N 35 22 E
Onehunga, N.Z. 130 C3 36 55 S 174 48 E
Oneida, Ill., U.S.A. 156 C6 41 4N 90 13W
Oneida, N.Y., U.S.A. 151 C9 43 6N 75 39W
Oneida L., U.S.A. 151 C9 43 12N 75 54W
O'Neill, U.S.A. 154 D5 42 27N 98 39W
Onekotan, Ostrov, Russia 65 E16 49 25N 154 45 E
Onema, Dem. Rep. of the Congo 118 C1 4 35 S 24 30 E
Oneonta, U.S.A. 151 D9 42 27N 75 4W
Onerahi, N.Z. 130 B3 35 45 S 174 22 E
Oneşti, Romania 53 D11 46 17N 26 47 E
Onezhskaya Guba, Russia 56 B6 64 24N 36 38 E
Onezhskoye Ozero, Russia 58 B8 61 44N 35 22 E
Ongarue, N.Z. 130 E4 38 42 S 175 19 E
Ongea Levu, Fiji 133 B3 19 8 S 178 24W
Ongers →, S. Africa 116 E3 31 4 S 23 13 E
Ongerup, Australia 125 F2 33 58 S 118 28 E
Ongjin, N. Korea 75 F13 37 56N 125 21 E
Ongkharak, Thailand 86 E3 14 8N 101 1 E
Ongniud Qi, China 75 C10 43 0N 118 38 E
Ongoka, Dem. Rep. of the Congo 118 C2 1 20 S 26 0 E
Ongole, India 95 G5 15 33N 80 2 E
Ongon = Havirga, Mongolia 74 B7 45 41N 113 5 E
Ongouendjo, Gabon 114 C1 1 23 S 9 5 E
Oni, Georgia 61 J6 42 33N 43 26 E
Onida, U.S.A. 154 C4 44 42N 100 4W
Onilahy →, Madag. 117 C7 23 34 S 43 45 E
Onitsha, Nigeria 113 D6 6 6N 6 42 E
Onmaka, Burma 90 D6 22 17N 96 41 E
Ono, Fiji 133 B2 18 55 S 178 29 E
Ono, Fukui, Japan 71 B8 35 59N 136 29 E
Ono, Hyōgo, Japan 70 C6 34 51N 134 56 E
Onoda, Japan 70 C3 34 2N 131 25 E
Onoke, L., N.Z. 130 H4 41 22 S 175 8 E
Onomichi, Japan 70 C5 34 25N 133 12 E
Onpyŏng-ni, S. Korea 75 H14 33 25N 126 55 E
Ons, I. de, Spain 42 C2 42 23N 8 55W
Onslow, Australia 124 D2 21 40 S 115 12 E
Onslow B., U.S.A. 149 H7 34 20N 77 15W
Ontake-San, Japan 71 B9 35 53N 137 29 E
Ontario, Calif., U.S.A. 161 L9 34 4N 117 39W
Ontario, Oreg., U.S.A. 158 D5 44 2N 116 58W
Ontario □, Canada 140 B2 48 0N 83 0W
Ontario, L., N. Amer. 140 D4 43 20N 78 0W
Ontinyent, Spain 41 G4 38 50N 0 35W
Ontonagon, U.S.A. 154 B10 46 52N 89 19W
Ontur, Spain 41 G3 38 38N 1 29W
Onverwacht, Surinam 169 B6 5 35N 55 11W
Onyx, U.S.A. 161 K8 35 41N 118 14W
Oodnadatta, Australia 127 D2 27 33 S 135 30 E
Ooldea, Australia 125 F5 30 27 S 131 50 E
Oombulgurri, Australia 124 C4 15 15 S 127 45 E
Oorindi, Australia 126 C3 20 40 S 141 1 E
Oost-Vlaanderen □, Belgium 24 C3 51 5N 3 50 E
Oostende, Belgium 24 C2 51 15N 2 54 E
Oosterhout, Neths. 24 C4 51 39N 4 47 E
Oosterschelde →, Neths. 24 C4 51 33N 4 0 E
Oosterwolde, Neths. 24 B6 53 0N 6 17 E
Ootacamund = Udagamandalam, India 95 J3 11 30N 76 44 E
Ootha, Australia 129 B7 33 6 S 147 29 E
Ootsa L., Canada 142 C3 53 50N 126 2W
Opaka, Bulgaria 51 C10 43 28N 26 10 E
Opala, Dem. Rep. of the Congo 118 C1 0 40 S 24 20 E
Opalenica, Poland 55 F3 52 18N 16 24 E
Opan, Bulgaria 51 D9 42 13N 25 41 E
Opanake, Sri Lanka 95 L5 6 35N 80 40 E
Opapa, N.Z. 130 F5 39 47 S 176 42 E
Opasatika, Canada 140 C3 49 30N 82 50W
Opasquia Prov. Park, Canada 140 B1 53 33N 93 5W
Opatija, Croatia 45 C11 45 21N 14 17 E
Opatów, Poland 55 H8 50 50N 21 27 E
Opava, Czech Rep. 35 B10 49 57N 17 58 E
Opelika, U.S.A. 152 C4 32 39N 85 23W
Opelousas, U.S.A. 155 K8 30 32N 92 5W
Opémisca, L., Canada 140 C5 49 56N 74 52W
Open Bay Is., N.Z. 131 D3 43 51 S 168 51 E
Opheim, U.S.A. 158 B10 48 51N 106 24W
Ophthalmia Ra., Australia 124 D2 23 15 S 119 30 E
Opi, Nigeria 113 D6 6 36N 7 28 E
Opihikao, U.S.A. 145 D7 19 26N 154 53W
Opinaca →, Canada 140 B4 52 15N 78 2W
Opinaca, Rés., Canada 140 B4 52 39N 76 20W
Opinnagau →, Canada 140 B3 54 12N 82 25W
Opiscoteo, L., Canada 141 B6 53 10N 68 10W
Opobo, Nigeria 113 E6 4 35N 7 34 E
Opochka, Russia 58 D5 56 42N 28 45 E
Opoczno, Poland 55 G7 51 22N 20 18 E
Opol, Phil. 81 G5 8 31N 124 34 E
Opole, Poland 55 H4 50 42N 17 58 E
Opole Lubelskie, Poland 55 G8 51 9N 21 58 E
Opolskie □, Poland 55 H5 50 30N 18 0 E
Opon = Lapu-Lapu, Phil. 81 F4 10 20N 123 55 E
Opononо L., Namibia 116 B2 18 8 S 15 45 E
Oporto = Porto, Portugal 42 D2 41 8N 8 40W
Opotiki, N.Z. 130 E6 38 1 S 177 19 E
Opp, U.S.A. 152 D3 31 17N 86 16W
Oppdal, Norway 15 E13 62 35N 9 41 E
Óppido Mamertina, Italy 47 D8 38 16N 15 59 E
Oppland □, Norway 18 C6 61 15N 9 40 E
Opportunity, U.S.A. 158 C5 47 39N 117 15W
Oprişor, Romania 52 F8 44 17N 23 5 E
Oprtalj, Croatia 45 C10 45 23N 13 50 E
Opua, N.Z. 130 B3 35 19 S 174 9 E
Opunake, N.Z. 130 F2 39 26 S 173 52 E
Opuwo, Namibia 116 B1 18 3 S 13 45 E
Opuzen, Croatia 45 E14 43 1N 17 34 E
Oquawka, U.S.A. 156 D6 40 56N 90 57W
Ora, Cyprus 38 E12 34 51N 33 12 E
Oracle, U.S.A. 159 K8 32 37N 110 46W
Oracuzar, Peru 168 D2 4 42 S 78 6W
Oradea, Romania 52 C6 47 2N 21 58 E
Öræfajökull, Iceland 11 C10 64 2N 16 39W
Orahovac, Kosovo, Yug. 50 D4 42 24N 20 40 E
Orahovica, Croatia 52 E2 45 35N 17 52 E
Orai, India 93 G8 25 58N 79 30 E
Oraison, France 29 E9 43 55N 5 55 E
Oral = Zhayyq →, Kazakstan 57 E9 47 0N 51 48 E
Oral, Kazakstan 60 E10 51 20N 51 20 E
Oran, Algeria 111 A4 35 45N 0 39W
Orange, Australia 129 B8 33 15 S 149 7 E
Orange, France 29 D8 44 8N 4 47 E
Orange, Calif., U.S.A. 161 M9 33 47N 117 51W
Orange, Mass., U.S.A. 151 D12 42 35N 72 19W
Orange, Tex., U.S.A. 155 K8 30 6N 93 44W
Orange, Va., U.S.A. 148 F6 38 15N 78 7W
Orange →, S. Africa 116 D2 28 41 S 16 28 E
Orange, C., Brazil 169 C7 4 20N 51 30W
Orange City, U.S.A. 153 G8 28 57N 81 18W
Orange Cove, U.S.A. 160 J7 36 38N 119 19W
Orange Free State = Free State □, S. Africa 116 D4 28 30 S 27 0 E
Orange Grove, U.S.A. 155 M6 27 58N 97 56W
Orange L., U.S.A. 153 F7 29 25N 82 13W
Orange Park, U.S.A. 152 E8 30 10N 81 42W
Orange Walk, Belize 163 D7 18 6N 88 33W
Orangeburg, U.S.A. 152 B9 33 30N 80 52W
Orangeville, Canada 140 D3 43 55N 80 5W
Orangeville, U.S.A. 156 B7 42 28N 89 39W
Orango, Guinea-Biss. 112 C1 11 5N 16 0W
Orani, Phil. 80 D3 14 49N 120 32 E
Oranienburg, Germany 30 C9 52 45N 13 14 E
Oranje = Orange →, S. Africa 116 D2 28 41 S 16 28 E
Oranje Vrystaat = Free State □, S. Africa 116 D4 28 30 S 27 0 E
Oranjemund, Namibia 116 D2 28 38 S 16 29 E
Oranjerivier, S. Africa 116 D3 29 40 S 24 12 E
Orarak, Sudan 107 F3 6 15N 32 23 E
Oras, Phil. 79 B7 12 9N 125 28 E
Orašje, Bos.-H. 52 E3 45 1N 18 42 E
Orăştie, Romania 53 E8 45 50N 23 10 E
Oraşul Stalin = Braşov, Romania 53 E10 45 38N 25 35 E
Orava →, Slovak Rep. 35 B12 49 5N 19 8 E
Orava, Vodna nádrž, Slovak Rep. 35 B12 49 25N 19 35 E
Oraviţa, Romania 52 E6 45 2N 21 43 E
Orawia, N.Z. 131 G2 46 1 S 167 50 E
Orb →, France 28 E7 43 15N 3 18 E
Orba →, Italy 44 D5 44 53N 8 37 E
Ørbæk, Denmark 17 J4 55 17N 10 39 E
Orbe, Switz. 32 C3 46 43N 6 32 E
Orbec, France 26 C7 49 1N 0 23 E
Orbetello, Italy 45 F8 42 27N 11 13 E
Órbigo →, Spain 42 C5 42 5N 5 42W
Orbisonia, U.S.A. 150 F7 40 15N 77 54W
Orbost, Australia 129 D8 37 40 S 148 29 E
Örbyhus, Sweden 16 D11 60 15N 17 43 E
Orcas I., U.S.A. 160 B4 48 42N 122 56W
Orce, Spain 41 H2 37 44N 2 28W
Orce →, Spain 41 H2 37 44N 2 28W
Orchard City, U.S.A. 159 G10 38 50N 107 58W
Orchies, France 27 B10 50 28N 3 14 E
Orchila, I., Venezuela 165 D6 11 48N 66 10W
Órcia →, Italy 45 F8 42 58N 11 21 E
Orco →, Italy 44 C4 45 10N 7 52 E
Orcopampa, Peru 172 D3 15 20 S 72 23W
Orcutt, U.S.A. 161 L6 34 52N 120 27W
Ord, U.S.A. 154 E5 41 36N 98 56W
Ord →, Australia 124 C4 15 33 S 128 15 E
Ord, Mt., Australia 124 C4 17 20 S 125 34 E
Ordenes = Ordes, Spain 42 B2 43 5N 8 29W
Orderville, U.S.A. 159 H7 37 17N 112 38W
Ordes, Spain 42 B2 43 5N 8 29W
Ording = St-Peter-Ording, Germany 30 A4 54 20N 8 36 E
Ordos = Mu Us Shamo, China 74 E5 39 0N 109 0 E
Ordu, Turkey 100 B7 40 55N 37 53 E
Ordubad, Azerbaijan 101 C12 38 54N 46 1 E
Orduña, Álava, Spain 40 C2 42 58N 2 58W
Orduña, Granada, Spain 43 H7 37 20N 3 30W
Ordway, U.S.A. 154 F3 38 13N 103 46W
Ordzhonikidze = Vladikavkaz, Russia 61 J7 43 0N 44 35 E
Ordzhonikidze, Kazakstan 62 E8 52 27N 61 39 E
Ordzhonikidze, Ukraine 59 J8 47 39N 34 3 E
Ordzhonikidze, Uzbekistan 63 C4 41 21N 69 22 E
Ordzhonikidzeabad, Tajikistan 63 D4 38 34N 69 1 E
Ore, Dem. Rep. of the Congo 118 B2 3 17N 29 30 E
Ore Mts. = Erzgebirge, Germany 30 E8 50 27N 12 55 E
Orealla, Guyana 169 B6 5 15N 57 23W
Orebić, Croatia 45 F14 43 0N 17 11 E
Örebro, Sweden 16 E9 59 20N 15 18 E
Örebro län □, Sweden 16 E8 59 27N 15 0 E
Oregon, Ill., U.S.A. 156 B7 42 1N 89 20W
Oregon, Ohio, U.S.A. 157 C13 41 38N 83 25W
Oregon, Wis., U.S.A. 156 B7 42 56N 89 23W
Oregon □, U.S.A. 158 E3 44 0N 121 0W
Oregon City, U.S.A. 160 E4 45 21N 122 36W
Öregrund, Sweden 16 D12 60 21N 18 30 E
Öregrundsgrepen, Sweden 16 D12 60 25N 18 15 E
Orekhov = Orikhiv, Ukraine 59 J8 47 30N 35 48 E
Orekhovo-Zuyevo, Russia 58 E10 55 50N 38 55 E
Orel, Russia 59 F9 52 57N 36 3 E
Orel →, Ukraine 59 H8 48 30N 34 39 E
Orellana, Spain 43 F5 39 1N 5 32W
Orellana, Canal de, Spain 43 F5 39 2N 6 0W
Orellana, Embalse de, Spain 43 F5 39 5N 5 10W
Orem, U.S.A. 158 F8 40 19N 111 42W
Ören, Turkey 49 D9 37 3N 27 57 E
Orenburg, Russia 62 F5 51 45N 55 6 E
Örencik, Turkey 49 B11 39 16N 29 33 E
Orense = Ourense, Spain 42 C3 42 19N 7 55W
Orense □, Spain 42 C3 42 15N 7 51W
Orepuki, N.Z. 131 G2 46 19 S 167 46 E
Orestiás, Greece 51 E10 41 30N 26 33 E
Orestos Pereyra, Mexico 162 B3 26 31N 105 40W
Øresund, Europe 17 J6 55 45N 12 45 E
Oreti →, N.Z. 131 G3 46 28 S 168 14 E
Orford Ness, U.K. 21 E9 52 5N 1 35 E
Organà = Organyà, Spain 40 C6 42 13N 1 20 E
Organos, Pta. de los, Canary Is. 39 F2 28 12N 17 17W
Organyà, Spain 40 C6 42 13N 1 20 E
Orgaz, Spain 43 F7 39 39N 3 53W
Ørgenvika, Norway 18 D6 60 17N 9 42 E
Orgeyev = Orhei, Moldova 53 C13 47 24N 28 50 E
Orgūn, Afghan. 91 B3 32 55N 69 12 E
Orhaneli, Turkey 51 G12 39 54N 28 59 E
Orhaneli →, Turkey 51 G12 39 50N 28 55 E
Orhangazi, Turkey 51 F13 40 29N 29 18 E
Orhei, Moldova 53 C13 47 24N 28 50 E
Orhon Gol →, Mongolia 72 A5 50 21N 106 0 E
Ória, Italy 47 B10 40 30N 17 38 E
Oriental, Cordillera, Bolivia 173 D4 17 0 S 66 0W
Oriental, Cordillera, Colombia 168 B3 6 0N 73 0W
Orientale □, Dem. Rep. of the Congo 118 B2 2 20N 26 0 E
Oriente, Argentina 174 D3 38 44 S 60 37W
Orihuela, Spain 41 G4 38 7N 0 55W
Orihuela del Tremedal, Spain 40 E3 40 33N 1 39W
Orikhiv, Ukraine 59 J8 47 30N 35 48 E
Oriku, Albania 50 F3 40 20N 19 26 E
Orillia, Canada 140 D4 44 40N 79 24W
Orinduik, Guyana 169 C5 4 40N 60 3W
Orinoco →, Venezuela 169 B5 9 15N 61 30W
Orion, Canada 143 D6 49 27N 110 49W
Orion, Ala., U.S.A. 152 D4 31 58N 86 0W
Orion, Ill., U.S.A. 156 C6 41 21N 90 23W
Oriskany, U.S.A. 151 C9 43 10N 75 20W
Orissa □, India 94 E7 20 0N 84 0 E
Orissaare, Estonia 15 G20 58 34N 23 5 E
Oristano, Italy 46 C1 39 54N 8 36 E
Oristano, G. di, Italy 46 C1 39 50N 8 29 E
Orituco →, Venezuela 168 B4 8 45N 67 27W
Oriximina, Brazil 169 D6 1 45 S 55 52W
Orizaba, Mexico 163 D5 18 51N 97 6W
Orizare, Bulgaria 51 D11 42 44N 27 39 E
Orizona, Brazil 171 E2 17 3 S 48 18W
Ørje, Norway 18 E8 59 29N 11 39 E
Orjen, Bos.-H. 50 D2 42 35N 18 34 E
Orjiva, Spain 43 J7 36 53N 3 24W
Orkanger, Norway 14 E13 63 18N 9 52 E
Örkelljunga, Sweden 17 H7 56 17N 13 17 E
Örken, Sweden 17 G9 57 6N 15 1 E
Örkény, Hungary 52 C4 47 9N 19 26 E
Orkla →, Norway 14 E13 63 18N 9 51 E
Orkney, S. Africa 116 D4 26 58 S 26 40 E
Orkney □, U.K. 22 B5 59 2N 3 13W
Orkney Is., U.K. 22 B6 59 0N 3 0W
Orland, Calif., U.S.A. 160 F4 39 45N 122 12W
Orland, Ind., U.S.A. 157 C11 41 47N 85 12W
Orlando, U.S.A. 149 L5 28 33N 81 23W
Orlando, C. d', Italy 47 D7 38 10N 14 43 E
Orléanais, France 27 E9 48 0N 2 0 E
Orléans, France 27 E8 47 54N 1 52 E
Orleans, Ind., U.S.A. 157 F10 38 40N 86 27W
Orleans, Vt., U.S.A. 151 B12 44 49N 72 12W
Orléans, I. d', Canada 141 C5 46 54N 70 58W
Orlice →, Czech Rep. 34 A8 50 13N 15 50 E
Orlov, Slovak Rep. 35 B13 49 17N 20 51 E
Orlov Gay, Russia 60 E9 50 56N 48 19 E
Orlová, Czech Rep. 35 B11 49 51N 18 26 E
Orlovat, Serbia, Yug. 52 E5 45 14N 20 33 E
Ormara, Pakistan 91 D2 25 16N 64 33 E
Ormea, Italy 44 D4 44 9N 7 54 E
Ormília, Greece 50 F7 40 16N 23 39 E
Ormoc, Phil. 79 B6 11 0N 124 37 E
Ormond, N.Z. 130 E6 38 33 S 177 56 E
Ormond Beach, U.S.A. 149 L5 29 17N 81 3W
Ormond by the Sea, U.S.A. 153 F8 29 21N 81 4W
Ormondville, N.Z. 130 G5 40 5 S 176 19 E
Ormož, Slovenia 45 B13 46 25N 16 10 E
Ormskirk, U.K. 20 D5 53 35N 2 54W
Ormstown, Canada 151 A11 45 8N 74 0W
Ornans, France 27 E13 47 7N 6 10 E
Ornavasso, Italy 33 E6 45 58N 8 24 E
Orne □, France 26 D7 48 40N 0 5 E
Orne →, France 26 C6 49 18N 0 15W
Orneta, Poland 54 D7 54 8N 20 9 E
Ornö, Sweden 16 E12 59 4N 18 24 E
Örnsköldsvik, Sweden 16 A12 63 17N 18 40 E
Oro, N. Korea 75 D14 40 1N 127 27 E
Oro →, Mexico 162 B3 25 35N 105 2W
Oro Grande, U.S.A. 161 L9 34 36N 117 20W
Oro Valley, U.S.A. 159 K8 32 26N 110 58W
Orobie, Alpi, Italy 44 B6 46 7N 10 0 E
Orocué, Colombia 168 C3 4 48N 71 20W
Orodara, Burkina Faso 112 C4 11 0N 4 55W
Orodo, Nigeria 113 D6 5 34N 7 4 E
Orofino, U.S.A. 158 C5 46 29N 116 15W
Orol Dengizi = Aral Sea, Asia 64 E7 44 30N 60 0 E
Oromocto, Canada 141 C6 45 54N 66 29W
Oron, Nigeria 113 E6 4 48N 8 14 E
Oron, Switz. 32 C3 46 34N 6 50 E
Orono, Canada 150 C6 43 59N 78 37W
Orono, U.S.A. 149 C11 44 53N 68 40W
Oronsay, U.K. 22 E2 56 1N 6 15W
Oropesa, Spain 42 F5 39 57N 5 10W
Oroqen Zizhiqi, China 73 A7 50 34N 123 43 E
Oroquieta, Phil. 81 G4 8 32N 123 44 E
Orós, Brazil 170 C4 6 15 S 38 55W
Orosei, Italy 46 B2 40 23N 9 42 E
Orosei, G. di, Italy 46 B2 40 15N 9 44 E
Orosháza, Hungary 52 D5 46 32N 20 42 E
Oroszlány, Hungary 52 C3 47 29N 18 19 E
Orote Pen., Guam 133 R15 13 26N 144 38 E
Orotukan, Russia 65 C16 62 16N 151 42 E
Oroville, Calif., U.S.A. 160 F5 39 31N 121 33W
Oroville, Wash., U.S.A. 158 B4 48 56N 119 26W
Oroville, L., U.S.A. 160 F5 39 33N 121 29W
Orrefors, Sweden 17 H9 56 50N 15 45 E
Orrick, U.S.A. 156 E2 39 13N 94 7W
Orroroo, Australia 128 B3 32 43 S 138 38 E
Orrviken, Sweden 16 A8 63 6N 14 26 E
Orrville, U.S.A. 150 F3 40 50N 81 46W
Orsa, Sweden 16 C8 61 7N 14 37 E
Orsara di Pùglia, Italy 47 A8 41 17N 15 16 E
Orsasjön, Sweden 16 C8 61 7N 14 37 E
Orsha, Belarus 58 E6 54 30N 30 25 E
Orsières, Switz. 32 D4 46 2N 7 9 E
Örsjö, Sweden 17 H9 56 42N 15 45 E
Orsk, Russia 62 F7 51 12N 58 34 E
Orşova, Romania 52 F7 44 41N 22 25 E
Ørsta, Norway 18 B3 62 13N 6 8 E
Ørsted, Denmark 17 H4 56 30N 10 20 E
Örsundsbro, Sweden 16 E11 59 44N 17 18 E
Orta, L. d', Italy 44 C5 45 49N 8 24 E
Orta Nova, Italy 47 A8 41 19N 15 42 E
Ortaca, Turkey 49 E10 36 49N 28 45 E
Ortakent, Turkey 49 D9 37 5N 27 21 E
Ortaklar, Turkey 49 D9 37 53N 27 30 E
Ortaköy, Çorum, Turkey 100 B6 40 16N 35 15 E
Ortaköy, Niğde, Turkey 100 C6 38 44N 34 3 E
Orte, Italy 45 F9 42 27N 12 23 E
Ortegal, C., Spain 42 B3 43 43N 7 52W
Orteguaza →, Colombia 168 C2 0 43N 75 16W
Orthez, France 28 E3 43 29N 0 48W
Ortigueira, Spain 42 B3 43 40N 7 50W
Orting, U.S.A. 160 C4 47 6N 122 12W
Ortisei, Italy 45 B8 46 34N 11 40 E
Ortles, Italy 44 B7 46 31N 10 33 E
Ortnevik, Norway 18 C3 61 6N 6 7 E
Orto, Tokay, Kyrgyzstan 63 B8 42 20N 76 1 E
Ortón →, Bolivia 172 C4 10 50 S 67 0W
Ortona, Italy 45 F11 42 21N 14 24 E
Ortonville, U.S.A. 154 C6 45 19N 96 27W
Orūmīyeh, Iran 101 D11 37 40N 45 0 E
Orūmīyeh, Daryācheh-ye, Iran 101 D11 37 50N 45 30 E
Orune, Italy 46 B2 40 24N 9 22 E
Oruro, Bolivia 172 D4 18 0 S 67 9W
Oruro □, Bolivia 172 D4 18 40 S 67 30W
Orust, Sweden 17 F5 58 10N 11 40 E
Oruzgān □, Afghan. 91 B2 33 30N 66 0 E
Orvault, France 26 E5 47 17N 1 38W
Orvieto, Italy 45 F9 42 43N 12 7 E
Orwell, N.Y., U.S.A. 151 C9 43 35N 75 50W
Orwell, Ohio, U.S.A. 150 E4 41 32N 80 52W
Orwell →, U.K. 21 F9 51 59N 1 18 E
Orwigsburg, U.S.A. 151 F8 40 38N 76 6W
Oryakhovo, Bulgaria 50 C7 43 40N 23 57 E
Orzinuovi, Italy 44 C6 45 24N 9 55 E
Orzyc →, Poland 55 F8 52 46N 21 14 E
Orzysz, Poland 54 E8 53 50N 21 58 E
Os, Norway 18 B8 62 30N 11 14 E
Osa, Russia 62 C5 57 17N 55 26 E
Osa →, Norway 18 C8 61 18N 11 46 E
Osa →, Poland 54 E5 53 33N 18 46 E
Osa, Pen. de, Costa Rica 164 E3 8 0N 84 0W
Osage, U.S.A. 154 D8 43 17N 92 49W
Osage →, U.S.A. 156 F5 38 35N 91 57W
Osage City, U.S.A. 154 F7 38 38N 95 50W
Ōsaka, Japan 71 C7 34 40N 135 30 E
Ōsaka □, Japan 71 C7 34 30N 135 30 E
Ōsaka-Wan, Japan 71 C7 34 30N 135 18 E
Osan, S. Korea 75 F14 37 11N 127 4 E
Osawatomie, U.S.A. 154 F7 38 31N 94 57W
Osborne, U.S.A. 154 F5 39 26N 98 42W
Osby, Sweden 17 H7 56 23N 13 59 E
Osceola, Ark., U.S.A. 155 H10 35 42N 89 58W
Osceola, Iowa, U.S.A. 156 C3 41 2N 93 46W
Osceola, Mo., U.S.A. 156 F3 38 3N 93 42W
Oschatz, Germany 30 D9 51 17N 13 6 E
Oschersleben, Germany 30 C7 52 2N 11 14 E
Óschiri, Italy 46 B2 40 43N 9 6 E
Oscoda, U.S.A. 150 B1 44 26N 83 20W
Osečina, Serbia, Yug. 50 B3 44 23N 19 34 E
Ösel = Saaremaa, Estonia 15 G20 58 30N 22 30 E
Osensjøen, Norway 18 C8 61 13N 11 50 E
Osery, Russia 58 E10 54 52N 38 28 E
Osgood, U.S.A. 157 E11 39 8N 85 18W
Osgoode, Canada 151 A9 45 8N 75 36W
Osh, Kyrgyzstan 64 E8 40 37N 72 49 E
Oshawa, Canada 140 D4 43 50N 78 50W
Oshigambo, Namibia 116 B2 17 45 S 16 5 E
Oshima, Japan 70 D4 33 55N 132 14 E
Oshkosh, Nebr., U.S.A. 154 E3 41 24N 102 21W
Oshkosh, Wis., U.S.A. 154 C10 44 1N 88 33W
Oshmyany = Ashmyany, Belarus 15 J21 54 26N 25 52 E
Oshnovīyeh, Iran 96 B5 37 2N 45 6 E
Oshogbo, Nigeria 113 D5 7 48N 4 37 E
Oshtorīnān, Iran 97 C6 34 1N 48 38 E
Oshwe, Dem. Rep. of the Congo 114 C3 3 25 S 19 28 E
Osi, Nigeria 113 D6 8 5N 5 14 E
Osieczna, Poland 55 G3 51 55N 16 40 E
Osijek, Croatia 52 E3 45 34N 18 41 E
Ósilo, Italy 46 B1 40 45N 8 40 E
Ósimo, Italy 45 E10 43 29N 13 30 E
Osintorf, Belarus 58 E6 54 40N 30 39 E
Osipenko = Berdyansk, Ukraine 59 J9 46 45N 36 50 E
Osipovichi = Asipovichy, Belarus 58 F5 53 19N 28 33 E
Osiyan, India 92 F5 26 43N 72 55 E
Osizweni, S. Africa 117 D5 27 49 S 30 7 E
Oskaloosa, U.S.A. 156 C4 41 18N 92 39W
Oskarshamn, Sweden 17 G10 57 15N 16 27 E
Oskarström, Sweden 17 H6 56 48N 12 58 E
Oskélanéo, Canada 140 C4 48 5N 75 15W
Öskemen, Kazakstan 64 E9 50 0N 82 36 E
Oskol →, Ukraine 59 H9 49 6N 37 25 E
Oslo, Norway 15 G14 59 55N 10 45 E
Oslo □, Norway 18 D7 59 54N 10 43 E
Oslob, Phil. 81 G4 9 31N 123 26 E
Oslofjorden, Norway 15 G14 59 20N 10 35 E
Osmanabad, India 94 E3 18 5N 76 10 E
Osmancık, Turkey 100 B6 40 58N 34 47 E
Osmaniye, Turkey 100 D7 37 5N 36 10 E
Osmanlı, Turkey 51 E10 41 35N 26 51 E
Osmannagar, India 94 E4 18 32N 79 20 E
Ösmo, Sweden 16 F11 58 58N 17 55 E
Osnabrück, Germany 30 C4 52 17N 8 3 E
Ośno Lubuskie, Poland 55 F1 52 28N 14 51 E
Osoblaha, Czech Rep. 35 A10 50 17N 17 44 E
Osogovska Planina, Macedonia 50 D6 42 10N 22 30 E
Osor, Italy 45 D11 44 42N 14 24 E
Osorio, Brazil 175 B5 29 53 S 50 17W
Osório da Fonseca, Brazil 169 D6 3 52 S 58 14W
Osorno, Chile 176 B2 40 25 S 73 0W
Osorno, Spain 42 C6 42 24N 4 22W
Osorno □, Chile 176 B2 40 34 S 73 9W
Osorno, Vol., Chile 176 B2 41 0 S 72 30W
Osoyoos, Canada 142 D5 49 0N 119 30W
Osøyro, Norway 18 D2 60 9N 5 30 E
Ospakseyri, Iceland 11 B5 65 27N 21 26W
Ospika →, Canada 142 B4 56 20N 124 0W
Osprey, U.S.A. 153 H7 27 12N 82 29W
Osprey Reef, Australia 126 A4 13 52 S 146 36 E
Oss, Neths. 24 C5 51 46N 5 32 E
Ossa, Mt., Australia 126 G4 41 52 S 146 3 E
Óssa, Óros, Greece 48 B4 39 47N 22 42 E
Ossa de Montiel, Spain 43 G2 38 58N 2 45W
Ossabaw I., U.S.A. 152 D8 31 50N 81 5W
Ossabaw Sd., U.S.A. 152 D8 31 50N 81 6W
Osse →, France 28 D4 44 7N 0 17 E
Osse →, Nigeria 113 D6 6 10N 5 20 E
Ossi, Italy 46 B1 40 40N 8 35 E
Ossining, U.S.A. 151 E11 41 10N 73 55W
Ossipee, U.S.A. 151 C13 43 41N 71 7W
Ossokmanuan L., Canada 141 B7 53 25N 65 0W
Ossora, Russia 65 D17 59 20N 163 13 E
Ostashkov, Russia 58 D7 57 4N 33 2 E
Östavall, Sweden 16 B9 62 26N 15 29 E
Østby, Norway 18 C8 61 15N 12 33 E
Oste →, Germany 30 B5 53 49N 9 2 E
Ostend = Oostende, Belgium 24 C2 51 15N 2 54 E
Oster, Ukraine 59 G6 50 57N 30 53 E
Osterburg, Germany 30 C7 52 47N 11 45 E
Osterburg, U.S.A. 150 F6 40 16N 78 31W
Osterburken, Germany 31 F5 49 25N 9 26 E
Österbybruk, Sweden 16 D11 60 13N 17 55 E
Österbymo, Sweden 17 G9 57 49N 15 15 E
Österdalälven, Sweden 16 C7 61 30N 13 45 E
Østerdalen, Norway 15 F14 61 40N 10 50 E
Österfärnebo, Sweden 16 D10 60 19N 16 48 E
Österforse, Sweden 16 A11 63 9N 17 3 E
Östergötlands län □, Sweden 17 F9 58 35N 15 45 E
Osterholz-Scharmbeck, Germany 30 B4 53 13N 8 47 E
Østerild, Denmark 17 G2 57 2N 8 51 E
Ostermundigen, Switz. 32 C4 46 58N 7 27 E
Osterode, Germany 30 D6 51 43N 10 15 E
Östersund, Sweden 16 A8 63 10N 14 38 E
Östervåla, Sweden 16 D11 60 11N 17 11 E
Østfold □, Norway 18 E8 59 25N 11 25 E
Ostfriesische Inseln, Germany 30 B3 53 42N 7 0 E
Ostfriesland, Germany 30 B3 53 20N 7 30 E
Östhammar, Sweden 16 D12 60 16N 18 22 E
Óstia, Lido di, Italy 45 G9 41 43N 12 17 E
Ostíglia, Italy 45 C8 45 4N 11 8 E
Östmark, Sweden 16 D6 60 17N 12 45 E
Östra Husby, Sweden 17 F10 58 35N 16 33 E
Ostrava, Czech Rep. 35 B11 49 51N 18 18 E
Ostróda, Poland 54 E6 53 42N 19 58 E
Ostrogozhsk, Russia 59 G10 50 55N 39 7 E
Ostroh, Ukraine 59 G4 50 20N 26 30 E
Ostrołęka, Poland 55 E8 53 4N 21 32 E
Ostrov, Bulgaria 51 C8 43 40N 24 9 E
Ostrov, Czech Rep. 34 A5 50 18N 12 57 E
Ostrov, Romania 53 F12 44 6N 27 24 E
Ostrov, Russia 58 D5 57 25N 28 20 E
Ostrów Lubelski, Poland 55 G9 51 29N 22 51 E
Ostrów Mazowiecka, Poland 55 F8 52 50N 21 51 E
Ostrów Wielkopolski, Poland 55 G4 51 36N 17 44 E
Ostrowiec-Świętokrzyski, Poland 55 H8 50 55N 21 22 E
Ostrožac, Bos.-H. 52 G2 43 43N 17 49 E

262 Ostrzeszów

Ostrzeszów, *Poland* **55 G4** 51 25N 17 52 E
Ostseebad Kühlungsborn, *Germany* **30 A7** 54 8N 11 44 E
Osttirol □, *Austria* **34 E5** 46 50N 12 30 E
Ostuni, *Italy* **47 B10** 40 44N 17 35 E
Osŭm →, *Bulgaria* **51 C8** 43 40N 24 50 E
Osumi →, *Albania* **50 F4** 40 40N 20 10 E
Ōsumi-Hantō, *Japan* **70 F2** 31 20N 130 55 E
Ōsumi-Kaikyō, *Japan* **69 J5** 30 55N 131 0 E
Ōsumi-Shotō, *Japan* **69 J5** 30 30N 130 0 E
Osun □, *Nigeria* **113 D5** 7 30N 4 30 E
Osuna, *Spain* **43 H5** 37 14N 5 8W
Oswegatchie →, *U.S.A.* **151 B9** 44 42N 75 30W
Oswego, *U.S.A.* **151 C8** 43 27N 76 31W
Oswego →, *U.S.A.* **151 C8** 43 27N 76 30W
Oswestry, *U.K.* **20 E4** 52 52N 3 3W
Oświęcim, *Poland* **55 H6** 50 2N 19 11 E
Ōta, *Japan* **71 A11** 36 18N 139 22 E
Ota-Gawa →, *Japan* **70 C4** 34 21N 132 18 E
Otaci, *Moldova* **53 B12** 48 27N 27 47 E
Otago □, *N.Z.* **131 E4** 45 15 S 170 0 E
Otago Harbour, *N.Z.* **131 F5** 45 47 S 170 42 E
Otago Pen., *N.Z.* **131 F5** 45 48 S 170 39 E
Otahuhu, *N.Z.* **130 C3** 36 56 S 174 51 E
Ōtake, *Japan* **70 C4** 34 12N 132 13 E
Ōtaki, *Japan* **71 B12** 35 17N 140 15 E
Otaki, *N.Z.* **130 G4** 40 45 S 175 10 E
Otane, *N.Z.* **130 F5** 39 54 S 176 39 E
Otar, *Kazakstan* **63 B7** 43 32N 75 12 E
Otaru, *Japan* **68 C10** 43 10N 141 0 E
Otaru-Wan = Ishikari-Wan, *Japan* **68 C10** 43 25N 141 1 E
Otautau, *N.Z.* **131 G3** 46 9 S 168 1 E
Otava →, *Czech Rep.* **34 B7** 49 26N 14 12 E
Otavalo, *Ecuador* **168 C2** 0 13N 78 20W
Otavi, *Namibia* **116 B2** 19 40 S 17 24 E
Otchinjau, *Angola* **116 B1** 16 30 S 13 56 E
Otelec, *Romania* **52 E5** 45 36N 20 50 E
Otelnuk L., *Canada* **141 A6** 56 9N 68 12W
Oțelu Roșu, *Romania* **52 E7** 45 32N 22 22 E
Otero de Rey = Outeiro de Rei, *Spain* **42 B3** 43 6N 7 36W
Othello, *U.S.A.* **158 C4** 46 50N 119 10W
Othonoí, *Greece* **48 B1** 39 52N 19 22 E
Óthris, Óros, *Greece* **48 B4** 39 2N 22 37 E
Otira, *N.Z.* **131 C6** 42 49 S 171 35 E
Otira Gorge, *N.Z.* **131 C6** 42 53 S 171 33 E
Otjiwarongo, *Namibia* **116 C2** 20 30 S 16 33 E
Otmuchów, *Poland* **55 H4** 50 28N 17 10 E
Oto Tolu Group, *Tonga* **133 Q13** 20 21 S 174 32W
Otočac, *Croatia* **45 D12** 44 53N 15 12 E
Otoineppu, *Japan* **68 B11** 44 44N 142 16 E
Otok, *Croatia* **45 E13** 43 42N 16 44 E
Oton, *Phil.* **81 F4** 10 42N 122 29 E
Otorohanga, *N.Z.* **130 E4** 38 12 S 175 14 E
Otoskwin →, *Canada* **140 B2** 52 13N 88 6W
Ōtoyo, *Japan* **70 D5** 33 43N 133 45 E
Otra →, *Norway* **15 G13** 58 9N 8 1 E
Otradnyy, *Russia* **60 D10** 53 22N 51 21 E
Otranto, *Italy* **47 B11** 40 9N 18 28 E
Otranto, C. d', *Italy* **47 B11** 40 7N 18 30 E
Otranto, Str. of, *Italy* **47 B11** 40 15N 18 40 E
Otrokovice, *Czech Rep.* **35 B10** 49 12N 17 32 E
Otse, *S. Africa* **116 D4** 25 2 S 25 45 E
Otsego, *U.S.A.* **157 B11** 42 27N 85 42W
Ōtsu, *Japan* **71 B7** 35 0N 135 50 E
Ōtsuki, *Japan* **71 B10** 35 36N 138 57 E
Otta, *Norway* **18 C6** 61 46N 9 32 E
Otta →, *Norway* **18 C6** 61 46N 9 31 E
Ottapalam, *India* **95 J3** 10 46N 76 23 E
Ottawa = Outaouais →, *Canada* **140 C5** 45 27N 74 8W
Ottawa, *Canada* **140 C4** 45 27N 75 42W
Ottawa, *Ill., U.S.A.* **154 E10** 41 21N 88 51W
Ottawa, *Kans., U.S.A.* **154 F7** 38 37N 95 16W
Ottawa, *Ohio, U.S.A.* **157 C12** 41 1N 84 3W
Ottawa Is., *Canada* **139 C11** 59 35N 80 10W
Ottélé, *Cameroon* **113 E7** 3 38N 11 19 E
Ottensheim, *Austria* **34 C7** 48 21N 14 12 E
Otter Cr. →, *U.S.A.* **151 B11** 44 13N 73 17W
Otter Creek, *U.S.A.* **153 F7** 29 19N 82 46W
Otter L., *Canada* **143 B8** 55 35N 104 39W
Otterbein, *U.S.A.* **157 D9** 40 29N 87 6W
Otterndorf, *Germany* **30 B4** 53 48N 8 53 E
Otterøya, *Norway* **18 B3** 62 45N 6 50 E
Otterup, *Denmark* **17 J4** 55 30N 10 22 E
Otterville, *Canada* **150 D4** 42 55N 80 36W
Otterville, *U.S.A.* **156 F4** 38 42N 93 0W
Ottery St. Mary, *U.K.* **21 G4** 50 44N 3 17W
Otto Beit Bridge, *Zimbabwe* **119 F2** 15 59 S 28 56 E
Ottosdal, *S. Africa* **116 D4** 26 46 S 25 59 E
Ottoville, *U.S.A.* **157 D12** 40 57N 84 22W
Ottumwa, *U.S.A.* **156 D4** 41 1N 92 25W
Otu, *Nigeria* **113 D5** 8 14N 3 22 E
Otukpa, *Nigeria* **113 D6** 7 9N 7 41 E
Oturkpo, *Nigeria* **113 D6** 7 16N 8 8 E
Otway, B., *Chile* **176 D2** 53 30 S 74 0W
Otway, C., *Australia* **128 E5** 38 52 S 143 30 E
Otway, Seno de, *Chile* **176 D2** 53 0 S 71 30W
Otwock, *Poland* **55 F8** 52 5N 21 20 E
Ötztaler Ache →, *Austria* **34 D3** 47 14N 10 50 E
Ötztaler Alpen, *Austria* **34 E3** 46 56N 11 0 E
Ou →, *Laos* **86 B4** 20 4N 102 13 E
Ou Neua, *Laos* **76 F3** 22 18N 101 48 E
Ou-Sammyaku, *Japan* **68 E10** 39 20N 140 35 E
Ouachita →, *U.S.A.* **155 K9** 31 38N 91 49W
Ouachita, L., *U.S.A.* **155 H8** 34 34N 93 12W
Ouachita Mts., *U.S.A.* **155 H7** 34 40N 94 25W
Ouaco, *N. Cal.* **133 T18** 20 50 S 164 29 E
Ouadâne, *Mauritania* **110 D2** 20 50N 11 40W
Ouadda, *C.A.R.* **114 A4** 8 15N 22 20 E
Ouagadougou, *Burkina Faso* **113 C4** 12 25N 1 30W
Ouagam, *Chad* **109 F2** 14 22N 14 42 E
Ouaham →, *C.A.R.* **114 A3** 6 35N 12 15 E
Ouahigouya, *Burkina Faso* **112 C4** 13 31N 2 25W
Ouahila, *Algeria* **110 C3** 27 50N 5 0W
Ouahran = Oran, *Algeria* **111 A4** 35 45N 0 39W
Oualâta, *Mauritania* **112 B3** 17 20N 6 55W
Ouallam, *Niger* **113 C5** 14 23N 2 10 E
Ouallene, *Algeria* **111 D5** 24 41N 1 11 E
Ouanary, *Fr. Guiana* **169 C7** 4 13N 51 40W
Ouanda Djallé, *C.A.R.* **114 A4** 8 55N 22 53 E
Ouandago, *C.A.R.* **114 A3** 7 13N 18 50 E
Ouandjia, Bahr →, *C.A.R.* **114 A4** 9 35N 21 43 E
Ouango, *C.A.R.* **114 B4** 4 19N 22 30 E
Ouantonou, *C.A.R.* **114 A3** 7 19N 15 18 E
Ouarâne, *Mauritania* **110 D2** 21 0N 10 30W
Ouargaye, *Burkina Faso* **113 C5** 11 40N 0 5 E
Ouargla, *Algeria* **111 B6** 31 59N 5 16 E
Ouarkoye, *Burkina Faso* **112 C4** 12 5N 3 40W
Ouarkziz, Djebel, *Algeria* **110 C3** 28 50N 8 0W
Ouarra →, *C.A.R.* **114 A4** 5 5N 24 26 E
Ouarzazate, *Morocco* **110 B3** 30 55N 6 50W
Ouassouas, *Mali* **113 B5** 16 10N 1 23 E
Ouatagouna, *Mali* **113 B5** 15 11N 0 43 E
Ouatere, *C.A.R.* **114 A3** 5 30N 19 8 E
Oubangi →, *Dem. Rep. of the Congo* **114 C3** 0 30 S 17 50 E
Oubarakai, O. →, *Algeria* **111 C6** 27 20N 9 0 E
Oubatche, *N. Cal.* **133 T18** 20 26 S 164 39 E
Ouche →, *France* **27 E12** 47 6N 5 16 E
Ouddorp, *Neths.* **24 C3** 51 50N 3 57 E
Oude Rijn →, *Neths.* **24 B4** 52 12N 4 24 E
Oudeïka, *Mali* **113 B4** 17 30N 1 40W
Oudenaarde, *Belgium* **24 D3** 50 50N 3 37 E
Oudon →, *France* **26 E6** 47 41N 0 53W
Oudtshoorn, *S. Africa* **116 E3** 33 35 S 22 14 E
Oued Zem, *Morocco* **110 B3** 32 52N 6 34W
Ouégoa, *N. Cal.* **133 T18** 20 20 S 164 26 E
Ouellé, *Ivory C.* **112 D4** 7 26N 4 1W
Ouéme →, *Benin* **113 D5** 6 30N 2 30 E
Ouen, I., *N. Cal.* **133 V20** 22 26 S 166 49 E
Ouenza, *Algeria* **111 A6** 35 57N 8 4 E
Ouessa, *Burkina Faso* **112 C4** 11 4N 2 47W
Ouessant, Î. d', *France* **26 D1** 48 28N 5 6W
Ouesso, *Congo* **114 B3** 1 37N 16 5 E
Ouest, Pte. de l', *Canada* **141 C7** 49 52N 64 40W
Ouezzane, *Morocco* **110 B3** 34 51N 5 35W
Ougarou, *Burkina Faso* **113 C5** 12 10N 0 58 E
Oughterard, *Ireland* **23 C2** 53 26N 9 18W
Ouidah, *Benin* **113 D5** 6 25N 2 0 E
Ouidi, *Niger* **113 C7** 14 10N 13 0 E
Ouissongo, *Angola* **115 E3** 7 40 S 15 41 E
Ouistreham, *France* **26 C6** 49 17N 0 18W
Oujda, *Morocco* **111 B4** 34 41N 1 55W
Oujeft, *Mauritania* **110 D2** 20 2N 13 0W
Oulainen, *Finland* **14 D21** 64 17N 24 47 E
Ould Yenjé, *Mauritania* **112 B2** 15 38N 12 16W
Ouled Djellal, *Algeria* **111 B6** 34 28N 5 2 E
Ouled Naïl, Mts. des, *Algeria* **111 B5** 34 30N 3 30 E
Ouli, *Cameroon* **114 A2** 5 12N 14 33 E
Oullins, *France* **29 C8** 45 43N 4 49 E
Oulmès, *Morocco* **110 B3** 33 17N 6 0W
Oulou, Bahr →, *C.A.R.* **114 A4** 9 48N 21 32 E
Oulu, *Finland* **14 D21** 65 1N 25 29 E
Oulujärvi, *Finland* **14 D22** 64 25N 27 15 E
Oulujoki →, *Finland* **14 D21** 65 1N 25 30 E
Oulx, *Italy* **44 C3** 45 2N 6 50 E
Oum Chalouba, *Chad* **109 E4** 15 48N 20 46 E
Oum-el-Bouaghi, *Algeria* **111 A6** 35 55N 7 6 E
Oum-el-Ksi, *Algeria* **110 C3** 29 4N 6 59W
Oum-er-Rbia, O. →, *Morocco* **110 B3** 33 19N 8 21W
Oum Hadjer, *Chad* **109 F3** 13 18N 19 41 E
Oumé, *Ivory C.* **112 D3** 6 21N 5 27W
Ounane, Dj., *Algeria* **111 C6** 25 4N 7 19 E
Ounasjoki →, *Finland* **14 C21** 66 31N 25 40 E
Ounguati, *Namibia* **116 C2** 22 0 S 15 46 E
Ounianga-Kébir, *Chad* **109 E4** 19 4N 20 29 E
Ounianga Sérir, *Chad* **109 E4** 18 54N 20 51 E
Our →, *Lux.* **24 E6** 49 55N 6 5 E
Ouranópolis, *Greece* **50 F7** 40 20N 23 59 E
Ourârene, *Niger* **113 B6** 19 30N 7 10 E
Ouray, *U.S.A.* **159 G10** 38 1N 107 40W
Ourcq →, *France* **27 C10** 49 1N 3 1 E
Ourém, *Brazil* **170 B2** 1 33 S 47 6W
Ourense, *Spain* **42 C3** 42 19N 7 55W
Ouricuri, *Brazil* **170 C3** 7 53 S 40 5W
Ourinhos, *Brazil* **175 A6** 23 0 S 49 54W
Ourique, *Portugal* **43 H2** 37 38N 8 16W
Ouro Fino, *Brazil* **175 A6** 22 16 S 46 25W
Ouro-Ndia, *Mali* **112 B4** 15 8N 4 35W
Ouro Prêto, *Brazil* **171 F3** 20 20 S 43 30W
Ouro Prêto do Oeste, *Brazil* **173 C5** 10 40 S 62 18W
Ouro Sogui, *Senegal* **112 B2** 15 36N 13 19W
Oursi, *Burkina Faso* **113 C4** 14 41N 0 27W
Ourthe →, *Belgium* **24 D5** 50 29N 5 35 E
Ouse →, *E. Susx., U.K.* **21 G8** 50 47N 0 4 E
Ouse →, *N. Yorks., U.K.* **20 D7** 53 44N 0 55W
Oust, *France* **28 F5** 42 52N 1 13 E
Oust →, *France* **26 E4** 47 35N 2 6W
Outaouais →, *Canada* **140 C5** 45 27N 74 8W
Outardes →, *Canada* **141 C6** 49 24N 69 30W
Outat Oulad el Haj, *Morocco* **111 B4** 33 22N 3 42W
Outeiro de Rei, *Spain* **42 B3** 43 6N 7 36W
Outer Hebrides, *U.K.* **22 D1** 57 30N 7 40W
Outes = Serra de Outes, *Spain* **42 C2** 42 52N 8 55W
Outjo, *Namibia* **116 C2** 20 5 S 16 7 E
Outlook, *Canada* **143 C7** 51 30N 107 0W
Outokumpu, *Finland* **14 E23** 62 43N 29 1 E
Outreau, *France* **27 B8** 50 40N 1 36 E
Ouvèze →, *France* **29 E8** 43 59N 4 51 E
Ouyen, *Australia* **128 C5** 35 1 S 142 22 E
Ouzinkie, *U.S.A.* **144 H9** 57 56N 152 30W
Ouzouer-le-Marché, *France* **27 E8** 47 54N 1 32 E
Ovada, *Italy* **44 D5** 44 38N 8 38 E
Ovalau, *Fiji* **133 A2** 17 40 S 178 48 E
Ovalle, *Chile* **174 C1** 30 33 S 71 18W
Ovamboland, *Namibia* **116 B2** 18 30 S 16 0 E
Ovar, *Portugal* **42 E2** 40 51N 8 40W
Ovens, *Australia* **129 D7** 36 35 S 146 46 E
Overath, *Germany* **30 E3** 50 56N 7 17 E
Overflakkee, *Neths.* **24 C4** 51 44N 4 10 E
Overijssel □, *Neths.* **24 B6** 52 25N 6 35 E
Overland, *U.S.A.* **156 F6** 38 41N 90 22W
Overland Park, *U.S.A.* **154 F7** 38 55N 94 50W
Overton, *U.S.A.* **161 J12** 36 33N 114 27W
Övertorneå, *Sweden* **14 C20** 66 23N 23 38 E
Överum, *Sweden* **17 F10** 58 0N 16 20 E
Ovid, *Mich., U.S.A.* **157 A12** 43 1N 84 22W
Ovid, *N.Y., U.S.A.* **151 D8** 42 41N 76 49W
Ovidiopol, *Ukraine* **59 J6** 46 15N 30 30 E
Ovidiu, *Romania* **53 F13** 44 16N 28 34 E
Oviedo, *Spain* **42 B5** 43 25N 5 50W
Oviedo, *U.S.A.* **153 G8** 28 40N 81 13W
Oviksfjällen, *Sweden* **16 A7** 63 0N 13 49 E
Oviši, *Latvia* **15 H19** 57 33N 21 44 E
Ovoot, *Mongolia* **74 B7** 45 21N 113 45 E
Övör Hangay □, *Mongolia* **74 B2** 45 0N 102 30 E
Ovoro, *Nigeria* **113 D6** 5 26N 7 16 E
Øvre Årdal, *Norway* **15 F12** 61 19N 7 48 E
Övre Fryken, *Sweden* **16 E7** 60 0N 13 7 E
Øvre Rendal, *Norway* **18 C8** 61 54N 11 4 E
Øvre Rindal, *Norway* **18 A6** 63 6N 9 10 E
Øvre Sirdal, *Norway* **18 F3** 58 48N 6 43 E
Ovruch, *Ukraine* **59 G5** 51 25N 28 45 E
Owaka, *N.Z.* **131 G4** 46 27 S 169 40 E
Owambo = Ovamboland, *Namibia* **116 B2** 18 30 S 16 0 E
Owando, *Congo* **114 C3** 0 29 S 15 55 E
Owasco L., *U.S.A.* **151 D8** 42 50N 76 31W
Owase, *Japan* **71 C8** 34 7N 136 12 E
Owatonna, *U.S.A.* **154 C8** 44 5N 93 14W
Owbeh, *Afghan.* **91 B1** 34 28N 63 10 E
Owego, *U.S.A.* **151 D8** 42 6N 76 16W
Owen, *Australia* **128 C3** 34 15 S 138 32 E
Owen Falls Dam, *Uganda* **118 B3** 0 30N 33 5 E
Owen Mt., *N.Z.* **131 B7** 41 35 S 172 33 E
Owen Sound, *Canada* **140 D3** 44 35N 80 55W
Owen Stanley Ra., *Papua N. G.* **132 E4** 8 30 S 147 0 E
Owendo, *Gabon* **114 B1** 0 17N 9 30 E
Owens →, *U.S.A.* **160 J9** 36 32N 117 59W
Owens L., *U.S.A.* **161 J9** 36 26N 117 57W
Owensboro, *U.S.A.* **157 G9** 37 46N 87 7W
Owensville, *Ind., U.S.A.* **157 F9** 38 16N 87 41W
Owensville, *Mo., U.S.A.* **156 F5** 38 21N 91 30W
Owenteik, *Guyana* **169 C6** 4 27N 59 35W
Owenton, *U.S.A.* **157 F12** 38 32N 84 50W
Owerri, *Nigeria* **113 D6** 5 29N 7 0 E
Owhango, *N.Z.* **130 F4** 39 0 S 175 23 E
Owingsville, *U.S.A.* **157 F13** 38 9N 83 46W
Owl →, *Canada* **143 B10** 57 51N 92 44W
Owo, *Nigeria* **113 D6** 7 10N 5 39 E
Owosso, *U.S.A.* **157 B12** 43 0N 84 10W
Owyhee, *U.S.A.* **158 F5** 41 57N 116 6W
Owyhee →, *U.S.A.* **158 E5** 43 49N 117 2W
Owyhee, L., *U.S.A.* **158 E5** 43 38N 117 14W
Ox Mts. = Slieve Gamph, *Ireland* **23 B3** 54 6N 9 0W
Oxapampa, *Peru* **172 C2** 10 33 S 75 26W
Öxarfjörður, *Iceland* **11 A10** 66 15N 16 45W
Oxbow, *Canada* **143 D8** 49 14N 102 10W
Oxelösund, *Sweden* **17 F11** 58 43N 17 5 E
Oxford, *N.Z.* **131 D7** 43 18 S 172 11 E
Oxford, *U.K.* **21 F6** 51 46N 1 15W
Oxford, *Ala., U.S.A.* **152 B4** 33 36N 85 51W
Oxford, *Iowa, U.S.A.* **156 C5** 41 43N 91 47W
Oxford, *Mass., U.S.A.* **151 D13** 42 7N 71 52W
Oxford, *Mich., U.S.A.* **157 B13** 42 49N 83 16W
Oxford, *Miss., U.S.A.* **155 H10** 34 22N 89 31W
Oxford, *N.C., U.S.A.* **149 G6** 36 19N 78 35W
Oxford, *N.Y., U.S.A.* **151 D9** 42 27N 75 36W
Oxford, *Ohio, U.S.A.* **157 E12** 39 31N 84 45W
Oxford L., *Canada* **143 C9** 54 51N 95 37W
Oxfordshire □, *U.K.* **21 F6** 51 48N 1 16W
Oxía, *Greece* **48 C3** 38 16N 21 5 E
Oxie, *Sweden* **17 J7** 55 33N 13 6 E
Oxílithos, *Greece* **48 C6** 38 35N 24 7 E
Oxley, *Australia* **128 C6** 34 11 S 144 6 E
Oxnard, *U.S.A.* **161 L7** 34 12N 119 11W
Oxsjövålen, *Sweden* **16 B7** 62 34N 13 57 E
Oxus = Amudarya →, *Uzbekistan* **64 E6** 43 58N 59 34 E
Oya, *Malaysia* **78 D4** 2 55N 111 55 E
Oyabe, *Japan* **71 A8** 36 47N 136 56 E
Oyama, *Japan* **71 A11** 36 18N 139 48 E
Oyana, *Japan* **70 E2** 32 32N 130 30 E
Oyapock →, *Fr. Guiana* **169 C7** 4 8N 51 40W
Øye, *Norway* **18 F3** 58 16N 6 49 E
Oyem, *Gabon* **114 B2** 1 34N 11 31 E
Oyen, *Canada* **143 C6** 51 22N 110 28W
Øyer, *Norway* **18 C7** 61 16N 10 25 E
Øyeren, *Norway* **18 E8** 59 50N 11 15 E
Oykel →, *U.K.* **22 D4** 57 56N 4 26W
Oymyakon, *Russia* **65 C15** 63 25N 142 44 E
Oyo, *Nigeria* **113 D5** 7 46N 3 56 E
Oyo □, *Nigeria* **113 D5** 8 15N 3 30 E
Oyón, *Peru* **172 C2** 10 37 S 76 47W
Oyonnax, *France* **27 F12** 46 16N 5 40 E
Øyslebø, *Norway* **18 F4** 58 9N 7 34 E
Oyster Bay, *U.S.A.* **151 F11** 40 52N 73 32W
Øystese, *Norway* **18 D3** 60 22N 6 9 E
Oytal, *Kazakstan* **63 B6** 42 54N 73 17 E
Ōyübari, *Japan* **68 C11** 43 1N 142 5 E
Özalp, *Turkey* **101 C10** 38 39N 43 59 E
Ozamiz, *Phil.* **79 C6** 8 15N 123 50 E
Ozark, *Ala., U.S.A.* **152 D4** 31 28N 85 39W
Ozark, *Ark., U.S.A.* **155 H8** 35 29N 93 50W
Ozark, *Mo., U.S.A.* **155 G8** 37 1N 93 12W
Ozark Plateau, *U.S.A.* **155 G9** 37 20N 91 40W
Ozarks, L. of the, *U.S.A.* **156 F4** 38 12N 92 38W
Ożarów, *Poland* **55 H8** 50 53N 21 40 E
Ózd, *Hungary* **52 B5** 48 14N 20 15 E
Ozernoye, *Russia* **60 E10** 51 46N 51 28 E
Ozërnyy, *Russia* **62 F8** 51 8N 60 50 E
Ozette L., *U.S.A.* **160 B2** 48 6N 124 38W
Özgön, *Kyrgyzstan* **63 C6** 40 46N 73 18 E
Ozieri, *Italy* **46 B2** 40 35N 9 0 E
Ozimek, *Poland* **55 H5** 50 41N 18 11 E
Ozinki, *Russia* **60 E9** 51 12N 49 44 E
Ozona, *U.S.A.* **155 K4** 30 43N 101 12W
Ozorków, *Poland* **55 G6** 51 57N 19 16 E
Ozren, *Bos.-H.* **52 G3** 43 55N 18 29 E
Ozu, *Ehime, Japan* **70 D4** 33 30N 132 33 E
Ozu, *Kumamoto, Japan* **70 E2** 32 52N 130 52 E
Ozuluama, *Mexico* **163 C5** 21 40N 97 50W
Ozun, *Romania* **53 E10** 45 47N 25 50 E
Ozurgeti, *Georgia* **61 K5** 41 55N 42 0 E

P

Pa, *Burkina Faso* **112 C4** 11 33N 3 19W
Pa-an, *Burma* **90 G6** 16 51N 97 40 E
Pa Mong Dam, *Thailand* **86 D4** 18 0N 102 22 E
Pa Sak →, *Thailand* **78 B2** 15 30N 101 0 E
Paagoumène, *N. Cal.* **133 T18** 20 29 S 164 11 E
Paama, *Vanuatu* **133 F6** 16 28 S 168 14 E
Paamiut, *Greenland* **10 E6** 62 0N 49 43W
Paar →, *Germany* **31 G7** 48 46N 11 36 E
Paarl, *S. Africa* **116 E2** 33 45 S 18 56 E
Paauilo, *U.S.A.* **146 H17** 20 2N 155 22W
Pab Hills, *Pakistan* **91 D2** 26 30N 66 45 E
Pabbay, *U.K.* **22 D1** 57 46N 7 14W
Pabianice, *Poland* **55 G6** 51 40N 19 20 E
Pabna, *Bangla.* **90 C2** 24 1N 89 18 E
Pabo, *Uganda* **118 B3** 3 1N 32 10 E
Pacaás Novos, Serra dos, *Brazil* **173 C5** 10 45 S 64 15W
Pacaipampa, *Peru* **172 B2** 5 35 S 79 39W
Pacaja →, *Brazil* **170 B1** 1 56 S 50 50W
Pacajus, *Brazil* **170 B4** 4 10 S 38 31W
Pacaraima, Sa., *S. Amer.* **169 C5** 4 0N 62 30W
Pacarán, *Peru* **172 C2** 12 50 S 76 3W
Pacaraos, *Peru* **172 C2** 11 12 S 76 42W
Pacasmayo, *Peru* **172 B2** 7 20 S 79 35W
Pace, *U.S.A.* **153 E2** 30 36N 87 10W
Paceco, *Italy* **46 E5** 37 59N 12 33 E
Pachacamac, *Peru* **172 C2** 12 14 S 77 53W
Pachhar, *India* **92 G7** 24 40N 77 42 E
Pachino, *Italy* **47 F8** 36 43N 15 5 E
Pachitea →, *Peru* **172 B3** 8 46 S 74 33W
Pachiza, *Peru* **172 B2** 7 16 S 76 46W
Pachmarhi, *India* **93 H8** 22 28N 78 26 E
Pacho, *Colombia* **168 B3** 5 8N 74 10W
Pachora, *India* **94 D2** 20 38N 75 29 E
Pachuca, *Mexico* **163 C5** 20 10N 98 40W
Pacific, *Canada* **142 C3** 54 48N 128 28W
Pacific, *U.S.A.* **156 F6** 38 29N 90 45W
Pacific-Antarctic Ridge, *Pac. Oc.* **135 M16** 43 0 S 115 0W
Pacific Grove, *U.S.A.* **160 J5** 36 38N 121 56W
Pacific Ocean, *Pac. Oc.* **80 D5** 10 0N 140 0W
Pacific Palisades, *U.S.A.* **145 K14** 21 25N 157 58W
Pacific Rim Nat. Park, *Canada* **160 B2** 48 40N 124 45W
Pacifica, *U.S.A.* **160 H4** 37 36N 122 30W
Pacitan, *Indonesia* **79 H14** 8 12 S 111 7 E
Packsaddle, *Australia* **128 A4** 30 36 S 141 58 E
Packwood, *U.S.A.* **160 D5** 46 36N 121 40W
Pacov, *Czech Rep.* **34 B8** 49 27N 15 0 E
Pacoval, *Brazil* **169 D7** 2 40 S 54 11W
Pacuí →, *Brazil* **171 E2** 16 46 S 45 1W
Pacy-sur-Eure, *France* **26 C8** 49 1N 1 23 E
Padaido, Kepulauan, *Indonesia* **79 E9** 1 5 S 138 0 E
Padampur, *India* **94 D6** 20 59N 83 4 E
Padang, *Indonesia* **78 E2** 1 0 S 100 20 E
Padang Endau, *Malaysia* **87 L4** 2 40N 103 38 E
Padangpanjang, *Indonesia* **78 E2** 0 40 S 100 20 E
Padangsidempuan, *Indonesia* **78 D1** 1 30N 99 15 E
Padangtikar, *Indonesia* **85 C3** 0 44 S 109 15 E
Padatchuang, *Burma* **90 F5** 19 46N 94 48 E
Padauari →, *Brazil* **169 D5** 0 15 S 64 5W
Padborg, *Denmark* **17 K3** 54 49N 9 21 E
Padcaya, *Bolivia* **173 E5** 21 52 S 64 48W
Paddle Prairie, *Canada* **142 B5** 57 57N 117 29W
Paddockwood, *Canada* **143 C7** 53 30N 105 30W
Paderborn, *Germany* **30 D4** 51 42N 8 45 E
Paderoo, *India* **94 E6** 18 5N 82 40 E
Padeș, Vf., *Romania* **52 E7** 45 40N 22 22 E
Padilla, *Bolivia* **173 D5** 19 19 S 64 20W
Padina, *Romania* **53 F12** 44 50N 27 8 E
Padma, *India* **93 G11** 24 12N 85 22 E
Padma →, *Bangla.* **90 D3** 23 22N 90 32 E
Pádova, *Italy* **45 C8** 45 25N 11 53 E
Padra, *India* **92 H5** 22 15N 73 7 E
Padrauna, *India* **93 F10** 26 54N 83 59 E
Padre Burgos, *Phil.* **81 F5** 10 1N 125 0 E
Padre I., *U.S.A.* **155 M6** 27 10N 97 25W
Padrón, *Spain* **42 C2** 42 41N 8 39W
Padstow, *U.K.* **21 G3** 50 33N 4 58W
Padua = Pádova, *Italy* **45 C8** 45 25N 11 53 E
Paducah, *Ky., U.S.A.* **148 G1** 37 5N 88 37W
Paducah, *Tex., U.S.A.* **155 H4** 34 1N 100 18W
Padukka, *Sri Lanka* **95 L5** 6 50N 80 5 E
Padul, *Spain* **43 H7** 37 1N 3 38W
Padwa, *India* **94 E6** 18 27N 82 47 E
Paekakariki, *N.Z.* **130 G3** 40 59 S 174 58 E
Paengaroa, *N.Z.* **130 D5** 37 49 S 176 29 E
Paengnyŏng-do, *S. Korea* **75 F13** 37 57N 124 40 E
Paeroa, *N.Z.* **130 D4** 37 23 S 175 41 E
Paesana, *Italy* **44 D4** 44 41N 7 16 E
Paete, *Phil.* **80 D3** 14 23N 121 29 E
Pafúri, *Mozam.* **117 C5** 22 28 S 31 17 E
Pag, *Croatia* **45 D12** 44 25N 15 3 E
Paga, *Gabon* **114 C2** 0 45 S 10 21 E
Paga, *Ghana* **113 C4** 11 1N 1 8W
Pagadian, *Phil.* **79 C6** 7 55N 123 30 E
Pagai Selatan, Pulau, *Indonesia* **78 E2** 3 0 S 100 15 E
Pagai Utara, Pulau, *Indonesia* **78 E2** 2 35 S 100 0 E
Pagalu = Annobón, *Atl. Oc.* **105 G4** 1 25 S 5 36 E
Pagalungan, *Phil.* **81 H5** 7 4N 124 41 E
Pagara, *India* **93 G9** 24 22N 80 1 E
Pagastikós Kólpos, *Greece* **48 B5** 39 15N 23 0 E
Pagatan, *Indonesia* **78 E5** 3 33 S 115 59 E
Page, *U.S.A.* **159 H8** 36 57N 111 27W
Pagėgiai, *Lithuania* **54 C8** 55 9N 21 54 E
Pago Pago, *Amer. Samoa* **133 X24** 14 16 S 170 43W
Pagosa Springs, *U.S.A.* **159 H10** 37 16N 107 1W
Pagudpud, *Phil.* **80 B3** 18 34N 120 47 E
Pagwa River, *Canada* **140 B2** 50 2N 85 14W
Pahala, *U.S.A.* **146 J17** 19 12N 155 29W
Pahang □, *Malaysia* **84 B2** 3 30N 102 45 E
Pahang →, *Malaysia* **87 L4** 3 30N 103 9 E
Pahia Pt., *N.Z.* **131 G2** 46 20 S 167 41 E
Pahiatua, *N.Z.* **130 G4** 40 27 S 175 50 E
Pahokee, *U.S.A.* **149 M5** 26 50N 80 40W
Pahrump, *U.S.A.* **161 J11** 36 12N 115 59W
Pahute Mesa, *U.S.A.* **160 H10** 37 20N 116 45W
Pai, *Thailand* **86 C2** 19 19N 98 27 E
Paia, *U.S.A.* **146 H16** 20 54N 156 22W
Paicines, *U.S.A.* **160 J5** 36 44N 121 17W
Paide, *Estonia* **15 G21** 58 57N 25 31 E
Paignton, *U.K.* **21 G4** 50 26N 3 35W
Paiho, *Taiwan* **77 F13** 23 21N 120 25 E
Paiján, *Peru* **172 B2** 7 42 S 79 20W
Päijänne, *Finland* **15 F21** 61 30N 25 30 E
Pailani, *India* **93 G9** 25 45N 80 26 E
Pailin, *Cambodia* **86 F4** 12 46N 102 36 E
Paimpol, *France* **26 D3** 48 48N 3 4W
Painan, *Indonesia* **78 E2** 1 21 S 100 34 E
Painesville, *U.S.A.* **150 E3** 41 43N 81 15W
Paint Hills = Wemindji, *Canada* **140 B4** 53 0N 78 49W
Paint L., *Canada* **143 B9** 55 28N 97 57W
Painted Desert, *U.S.A.* **159 J8** 36 0N 111 0W
Paintsville, *U.S.A.* **148 G4** 37 49N 82 48W
País Vasco □, *Spain* **40 C2** 42 50N 2 45W
Paisley, *Canada* **150 B3** 44 18N 81 16W
Paisley, *U.K.* **22 F4** 55 50N 4 25W
Paisley, *U.S.A.* **158 E3** 42 42N 120 32W
Paita, *N. Cal.* **133 V20** 22 8 S 166 22 E
Paita, *Peru* **172 B1** 5 11 S 81 9W
Paithan, *India* **94 E2** 19 29N 75 23 E
Paiva →, *Portugal* **42 D2** 41 4N 8 16W
Paizhou, *China* **77 B9** 30 12N 113 55 E
Pajares, *Spain* **42 B5** 43 1N 5 46W
Pajares, Puerto de, *Spain* **42 C5** 42 58N 5 46W
Pajarito, *Colombia* **168 B3** 5 17N 72 43W
Pajęczno, *Poland* **55 G5** 51 10N 19 0 E
Pak Lay, *Laos* **86 C3** 18 15N 101 27 E
Pak Phanang, *Thailand* **78 C2** 8 21N 100 12 E
Pak Sane, *Laos* **86 C4** 18 22N 103 39 E
Pak Song, *Laos* **86 E6** 15 11N 106 14 E
Pak Suong, *Laos* **76 H4** 19 58N 102 15 E
Pakala, *India* **95 H4** 13 29N 79 8 E
Pakaraima Mts., *Guyana* **169 B5** 6 0N 60 0W
Pakaur, *India* **93 G12** 24 38N 87 51 E
Pakenham, *Australia* **129 E6** 38 6 S 145 30 E
Pakenham, *Canada* **151 A8** 45 18N 76 18W
Pákhnes, *Greece* **38 D6** 35 16N 24 4 E
Pakhtakor, *Uzbekistan* **63 C2** 40 2N 65 46 E
Pakhuis, *S. Africa* **116 E2** 32 9 S 19 5 E
Pakistan ■, *Asia* **91 C3** 30 0N 70 0 E
Pakkading, *Laos* **86 C4** 18 19N 103 59 E
Pakokku, *Burma* **90 E5** 21 20N 95 0 E
Pakość, *Poland* **55 F5** 52 48N 18 6 E
Pakowki L., *Canada* **143 D6** 49 20N 111 0W
Pakpattan, *Pakistan* **91 C4** 30 25N 73 27 E
Pakrac, *Croatia* **52 E2** 45 27N 17 12 E
Pakruojis, *Lithuania* **54 C10** 55 58N 23 52 E
Paks, *Hungary* **52 D3** 46 38N 18 55 E
Paktīā □, *Afghan.* **91 B3** 33 0N 69 15 E
Paktīkā □, *Afghan.* **91 B3** 32 30N 69 0 E
Pakwach, *Uganda* **118 B3** 2 28N 31 27 E
Pakxe, *Laos* **78 A3** 15 5N 105 52 E
Pal Lahara, *India* **93 J11** 21 27N 85 11 E
Pala, *Chad* **109 G3** 9 25N 15 5 E
Pala, *Dem. Rep. of the Congo* **118 D2** 6 45 S 29 30 E
Pala, *U.S.A.* **161 M9** 33 22N 117 5W
Palabek, *Uganda* **118 B3** 3 22N 32 33 E
Palacios, *U.S.A.* **155 L6** 28 42N 96 13W
Palafrugell, *Spain* **40 D8** 41 55N 3 10 E
Palagiano, *Italy* **47 B10** 40 35N 17 2 E
Palagonía, *Italy* **47 E7** 37 19N 14 45 E
Palagruža, *Croatia* **45 F13** 42 24N 16 15 E
Palaiókastron, *Greece* **38 D8** 35 12N 26 15 E
Palaiokhóra, *Greece* **38 D5** 35 16N 23 39 E
Pálairos, *Greece* **48 C2** 38 45N 20 51 E

Parma 263

Palaiseau, *France* **27 D9** 48 43N 2 15 E
Palakol, *India* **95 F5** 16 31N 81 46 E
Palam, *India* **94 E3** 19 0N 77 0 E
Palamás, *Greece* **48 B4** 39 26N 22 4 E
Palamòs, *Spain* **40 D8** 41 50N 3 10 E
Palampur, *India* **92 C7** 32 10N 76 30 E
Palamut, *Turkey* **49 C9** 38 59N 27 41 E
Palana, *Australia* **126 F4** 39 45 S 147 55 E
Palana, *Russia* **65 D16** 59 10N 159 59 E
Palanan, *Phil.* **79 A6** 17 8N 122 29 E
Palanan Bay, *Phil.* **80 C4** 17 9N 122 27 E
Palanan Pt., *Phil.* **79 A6** 17 17N 122 30 E
Palandri, *Pakistan* **93 C5** 33 42N 73 40 E
Palanga, *Lithuania* **15 J19** 55 58N 21 3 E
Palanganene,
Dem. Rep. of the Congo **115 D3** 6 32 S 18 52 E
Palangkaraya, *Indonesia* **78 E4** 2 16 S 113 56 E
Palani, *India* **95 J3** 10 30N 77 30 E
Palani Hills, *India* **95 J3** 10 14N 77 33 E
Palanpur, *India* **92 G5** 24 10N 72 25 E
Palanro, *Indonesia* **82 B1** 3 21 S 119 23 E
Palaoa Pt., *U.S.A.* **145 C5** 20 44N 156 58W
Palapag, *Phil.* **80 E5** 12 33N 125 7 E
Palapye, *Botswana* **116 C4** 22 30 S 27 7 E
Palar →, *India* **95 H5** 12 27N 80 13 E
Palas, *Pakistan* **93 B5** 35 4N 73 14 E
Palas de Rei, *Spain* **42 C3** 42 52N 7 52W
Palashi, *India* **93 H13** 23 47N 88 15 E
Palasponga, *India* **93 J11** 21 47N 85 34 E
Palatine, *U.S.A.* **157 B8** 42 7N 88 3W
Palatka, *Russia* **65 C16** 60 6N 150 54 E
Palatka, *U.S.A.* **152 F8** 29 39N 81 38W
Palau, *Italy* **46 A2** 41 11N 9 23 E
Palau ■, *Pac. Oc.* **66 J17** 7 30N 134 30 E
Palauk, *Burma* **86 F2** 13 10N 98 40 E
Palawan, *Phil.* **78 C5** 9 30N 118 30 E
Palawan □, *Phil.* **81 G2** 10 0N 119 0 E
Palawan Passage, *Phil.* **81 G2** 10 0N 118 0 E
Palayan, *Phil.* **80 D3** 15 36N 121 8 E
Palayankottai, *India* **95 K3** 8 45N 77 45 E
Palazzo, Pte., *France* **29 F12** 42 28N 8 30 E
Palazzo San Gervásio, *Italy* **47 B8** 40 56N 15 59 E
Palazzolo Acréide, *Italy* **47 E7** 37 4N 14 54 E
Palca, *Chile* **172 D4** 19 7 S 69 9W
Paldiski, *Estonia* **15 G21** 59 23N 24 9 E
Pale, *Bos.-H.* **52 G3** 43 50N 18 38 E
Palel, *India* **90 C5** 24 27N 94 2 E
Paleleh, *Indonesia* **79 D6** 1 10N 121 50 E
Palembang, *Indonesia* **78 E2** 3 0 S 104 50 E
Palena →, *Chile* **176 B2** 43 50 S 73 50W
Palena, L., *Chile* **176 B2** 43 55 S 71 40W
Palencia, *Spain* **42 C6** 42 1N 4 34W
Palencia □, *Spain* **42 C6** 42 31N 4 33W
Palenque, *Mexico* **163 D6** 17 31N 91 58W
Paleokastrítsa, *Greece* **38 A3** 39 40N 19 41 E
Paleometokho, *Cyprus* **38 D12** 35 7N 33 11 E
Palermo, *Colombia* **168 C2** 2 54N 75 26W
Palermo, *Italy* **46 D6** 38 7N 13 22 E
Palermo, *U.S.A.* **158 G3** 39 26N 121 33W
Palestine, *Asia* **103 D4** 32 0N 35 0 E
Palestine, *Ill., U.S.A.* **157 F9** 39 0N 87 37W
Palestine, *Tex., U.S.A.* **155 K7** 31 46N 95 38W
Palestrina, *Italy* **45 G9** 41 50N 12 53 E
Paletwa, *Burma* **90 E4** 21 10N 92 50 E
Palghat, *India* **95 J3** 10 46N 76 42 E
Palgrave, Mt., *Australia* **124 D2** 23 22 S 115 58 E
Pali, *India* **92 G5** 25 50N 73 20 E
Palikea Pk., *U.S.A.* **145 K13** 21 26N 158 6W
Palikir, *Micronesia* **134 G7** 6 55N 158 9 E
Palimbang, *Phil.* **81 H5** 6 12N 124 12 E
Palin, Mt., *Malaysia* **85 A5** 6 10N 117 10 E
Palinuro, *Italy* **47 B8** 40 2N 15 17 E
Palinuro, C., *Italy* **47 B8** 40 2N 15 16 E
Palioúrion, Ákra, *Greece* **50 G7** 39 57N 23 45 E
Palisades Reservoir, *U.S.A.* **158 E8** 43 20N 111 12W
Paliseul, *Belgium* **24 E5** 49 54N 5 8 E
Palitana, *India* **92 J4** 21 32N 71 49 E
Palizada, *Mexico* **163 D6** 18 18N 92 8W
Palk Bay, *Asia* **95 K4** 9 30N 79 15 E
Palk Strait, *Asia* **95 K4** 10 0N 79 45 E
Palkānah, *Iraq* **96 C5** 35 49N 44 26 E
Palkonda, *India* **94 E6** 18 36N 83 48 E
Palkonda Ra., *India* **95 H4** 13 50N 79 20 E
Palkot, *India* **93 H11** 22 53N 84 39 E
Palla Road = Dinokwe,
Botswana **116 C4** 23 29 S 26 37 E
Pallanza = Verbánia, *Italy* **44 C5** 45 56N 8 33 E
Pallarenda, *Australia* **126 B4** 19 12 S 146 46 E
Pallasovka, *Russia* **60 E8** 50 4N 47 0 E
Palleru →, *India* **94 F5** 16 45N 80 2 E
Pallës, Bishti i, *Albania* **50 E3** 41 24N 19 24 E
Pallinup →, *Australia* **125 F2** 34 27 S 118 50 E
Pallisa, *Uganda* **118 B3** 1 12N 33 43 E
Palliser, C., *N.Z.* **130 H4** 41 37 S 175 14 E
Palliser B., *N.Z.* **130 H4** 41 26 S 175 5 E
Pallu, *India* **92 E6** 28 59N 74 14 E
Palm Bay, *U.S.A.* **149 L5** 28 2N 80 35W
Palm Beach, *U.S.A.* **149 M6** 26 43N 80 2W
Palm Coast, *U.S.A.* **149 L5** 29 32N 81 10W
Palm Desert, *U.S.A.* **161 M10** 33 43N 116 22W
Palm Harbor, *U.S.A.* **153 G7** 28 5N 82 47W
Palm Is., *Australia* **126 B4** 18 40 S 146 35 E
Palm Springs, *U.S.A.* **161 M10** 33 50N 116 33W
Palma, *Mozam.* **119 E5** 10 46 S 40 29 E
Palma →, *Brazil* **171 D2** 12 33 S 47 52W
Palma, B. de, *Spain* **39 B9** 39 30N 2 39 E
Palma de Mallorca, *Spain* **39 B9** 39 35N 2 39 E
Palma del Río, *Spain* **43 H5** 37 43N 5 17W
Palma di Montechiaro, *Italy* **46 E6** 37 11N 13 46 E
Palma Soriano, *Cuba* **164 B4** 20 15N 76 0W
Palmaner, *India* **95 H4** 13 12N 78 45 E
Palmares, *Brazil* **170 C4** 8 41 S 35 28W
Palmarito, *Venezuela* **168 B3** 7 37N 70 10W
Palmarola, *Italy* **46 B5** 40 56N 12 51 E
Palmas, *Brazil* **175 B5** 26 29 S 52 0W
Palmas, C., *Liberia* **112 E3** 4 27N 7 46W
Pálmas, G. di, *Italy* **46 D1** 39 0N 8 30 E
Palmas de Monte Alto, *Brazil* **171 D3** 14 16 S 43 10W
Palmdale, *Calif., U.S.A.* **161 L8** 34 35N 118 7W
Palmdale, *Fla., U.S.A.* **153 J8** 26 57N 81 19W
Palmeira, *Brazil* **171 G2** 25 25 S 50 0W
Palmeira das Missões, *Brazil* **175 B5** 27 55 S 53 17W
Palmeira dos Índios, *Brazil* **170 C4** 9 25 S 36 37W
Palmeirais, *Brazil* **170 C3** 6 0 S 43 0W
Palmeiras, *Brazil* **171 D3** 12 31 S 41 34W
Palmeiras →, *Brazil* **171 D2** 12 22 S 47 8W
Palmeirinhas, Pta. das, *Angola* **115 D2** 9 2 S 12 57 E
Palmela, *Portugal* **43 G2** 38 32N 8 57W
Palmelo, *Brazil* **171 E2** 17 20 S 48 27W
Palmer, *U.S.A.* **138 B5** 61 36N 149 7W
Palmer →, *Australia* **126 B3** 16 0 S 142 26 E
Palmer Arch., *Antarctica* **7 C17** 64 15 S 65 0W
Palmer Lake, *U.S.A.* **154 F2** 39 7N 104 55W
Palmer Land, *Antarctica* **7 D18** 73 0 S 63 0W
Palmerston, *Canada* **150 C4** 43 50N 80 51W
Palmerston, *N.Z.* **131 F5** 45 29 S 170 43 E
Palmerston North, *N.Z.* **130 G4** 40 21 S 175 39 E
Palmerton, *U.S.A.* **151 F9** 40 48N 75 37W
Palmetto, *Fla., U.S.A.* **149 M4** 27 31N 82 34W
Palmetto, *Ga., U.S.A.* **152 B5** 33 31N 84 40W
Palmi, *Italy* **47 D8** 38 21N 15 51 E
Palmira, *Argentina* **174 C2** 32 59 S 68 34W
Palmira, *Colombia* **168 C2** 3 32N 76 16W
Palmyra = Tudmur, *Syria* **101 E8** 34 36N 38 15 E
Palmyra, *Ill., U.S.A.* **156 E7** 39 26N 90 0W
Palmyra, *Mo., U.S.A.* **156 E5** 39 48N 91 32W
Palmyra, *N.J., U.S.A.* **151 F9** 40 1N 75 1W
Palmyra, *N.Y., U.S.A.* **150 C7** 43 5N 77 18W
Palmyra, *Pa., U.S.A.* **151 F8** 40 18N 76 36W
Palmyra, *Wis., U.S.A.* **157 B8** 42 52N 88 36W
Palmyra Is., *Pac. Oc.* **135 G11** 5 52N 162 5W
Palmyras Pt., *India* **94 D8** 20 46N 87 1 E
Palo, *Phil.* **81 F5** 11 10N 124 59 E
Palo Alto, *U.S.A.* **160 H4** 37 27N 122 10W
Palo Verde, *U.S.A.* **161 M12** 33 26N 114 44W
Paloich, *Sudan* **107 E3** 10 28N 32 32 E
Palompon, *Phil.* **81 F5** 11 3N 124 23 E
Palopo, *Indonesia* **79 E6** 3 0 S 120 16 E
Palos, C. de, *Spain* **41 H4** 37 38N 0 40W
Palos de la Frontera, *Spain* **43 H4** 37 14N 6 53W
Palos Verdes, *U.S.A.* **161 M8** 33 48N 118 23W
Palos Verdes, Pt., *U.S.A.* **161 M8** 33 43N 118 26W
Palpa, *Peru* **172 C2** 14 30 S 75 15W
Pålsboda, *Sweden* **16 E9** 59 3N 15 22 E
Palu, *Indonesia* **79 E5** 1 0 S 119 52 E
Palu, *Turkey* **101 C9** 38 45N 40 0 E
Paluan, *Phil.* **80 E3** 13 26N 120 29 E
Paluke, *Liberia* **112 D3** 5 2N 8 5W
Paluzza, *Italy* **45 B10** 46 32N 13 1 E
Palwal, *India* **92 E7** 28 8N 77 19 E
Pama, *Burkina Faso* **113 C5** 11 19N 0 44 E
Pama →, *C.A.R.* **114 B3** 4 23N 18 43 E
Pamanukan, *Indonesia* **79 G12** 6 16 S 107 49 E
Pamban I., *India* **95 K4** 9 15N 79 20 E
Pamekasan, *Indonesia* **85 D4** 7 10 S 113 28 E
Pamiers, *France* **28 E5** 43 7N 1 39 E
Pamir, *Tajikistan* **64 F8** 37 40N 73 0 E
Pamir →, *Tajikistan* **63 E6** 37 1N 72 41 E
Pamlico →, *U.S.A.* **149 H7** 35 20N 76 28W
Pamlico Sd., *U.S.A.* **149 H8** 35 20N 76 0W
Pampa, *U.S.A.* **155 H4** 35 32N 100 58W
Pampa de Agma, *Argentina* **176 B3** 43 45 S 69 40W
Pampa de las Salinas, *Argentina* **174 C2** 32 1 S 66 58W
Pampa Grande, *Bolivia* **173 D5** 18 5 S 64 6W
Pampa Hermosa, *Peru* **172 B2** 7 7 S 75 4W
Pampanga □, *Phil.* **80 D3** 15 4N 120 40 E
Pampanua, *Indonesia* **79 E6** 4 16 S 120 8 E
Pampas, *Argentina* **174 D3** 35 0 S 63 0W
Pampas, *Peru* **172 C3** 12 20 S 74 50W
Pampas →, *Peru* **172 C3** 13 24 S 73 12W
Pamphylia, *Turkey* **100 D4** 37 0N 31 20 E
Pamplona, *Colombia* **168 B3** 7 23N 72 39W
Pamplona, *Phil.* **80 B3** 18 31N 121 20 E
Pamplona, *Spain* **40 C3** 42 48N 1 38W
Pampoenpoort, *S. Africa* **116 E3** 31 3 S 22 40 E
Pamukçu, *Turkey* **49 B9** 39 30N 27 54 E
Pamukkale, *Turkey* **49 D11** 37 55N 29 8 E
Pan Xian, *China* **76 E5** 25 46N 104 38 E
Pana, *U.S.A.* **156 E7** 39 23N 89 5W
Panabo, *Phil.* **81 H5** 7 19N 125 42 E
Panaca, *U.S.A.* **159 H6** 37 47N 114 23W
Panacea, *U.S.A.* **152 E5** 30 2N 84 23W
Panagyurishte, *Bulgaria* **51 D8** 42 30N 24 15 E
Panaitan, *Indonesia* **79 G11** 6 36 S 105 12 E
Panaji, *India* **95 G1** 15 25N 73 50 E
Panamá, *Panama* **164 E4** 9 0N 79 25W
Panama, *Sri Lanka* **95 L5** 6 45N 81 48 E
Panama ■, *Cent. Amer.* **164 E4** 8 48N 79 55W
Panamá, G. de, *Panama* **164 E4** 8 4N 79 20W
Panama Canal, *Panama* **164 E4** 9 10N 79 37W
Panama City, *U.S.A.* **152 E4** 30 10N 85 40W
Panama City Beach, *U.S.A.* **152 E4** 30 11N 85 48W
Panamint Range, *U.S.A.* **161 J9** 36 20N 117 20W
Panamint Springs, *U.S.A.* **161 J9** 36 20N 117 28W
Panão, *Peru* **172 B2** 9 55 S 75 55W
Panaon I., *Phil.* **81 F5** 10 3N 125 13 E
Panare, *Thailand* **87 J3** 6 51N 101 30 E
Panarea, *Italy* **47 D8** 38 38N 15 4 E
Panaro →, *Italy* **45 D8** 44 55N 11 25 E
Panarukan, *Indonesia* **85 D4** 7 42 S 113 56 E
Panay, *Phil.* **79 B6** 11 10N 122 30 E
Panay, G., *Phil.* **79 B6** 11 0N 122 30 E
Pančevo, *Serbia, Yug.* **52 F5** 44 52N 20 41 E
Panch'iao, *Taiwan* **77 E13** 25 1N 121 27 E
Panciu, *Romania* **53 E12** 45 54N 27 8 E
Pancol, *Phil.* **81 F2** 10 52N 119 25 E
Pancorbo, Desfiladero, *Spain* **42 C7** 42 32N 3 5W
Pâncota, *Romania* **52 D6** 46 20N 21 45 E
Panda, *Mozam.* **117 C5** 24 2 S 34 45 E
Pandan, *Antique, Phil.* **79 B6** 11 45N 122 10 E
Pandan, *Catanduanes, Phil.* **80 D5** 14 3N 124 10 E
Pandan Bay, *Phil.* **81 F4** 11 43N 122 0 E
Pandegelang, *Indonesia* **79 G12** 6 25 S 106 5 E
Pandhana, *India* **92 J7** 21 42N 76 13 E
Pandharkawada, *India* **94 D4** 20 1N 78 32 E
Pandharpur, *India* **94 F2** 17 41N 75 20 E
Pandhurna, *India* **94 D4** 21 36N 78 35 E
Pando, *Uruguay* **175 C4** 34 44 S 56 0W
Pando □, *Bolivia* **172 C4** 11 20 S 67 40W
Pando, L. = Hope, L.,
Australia **127 D2** 28 24 S 139 18 E
Pandokrátor, *Greece* **38 A3** 39 45N 19 50 E
Pandora, *Costa Rica* **164 E3** 9 43N 83 3W
Pandrup, *Denmark* **17 G3** 57 14N 9 40 E
Pandu, *Dem. Rep. of the Congo* **114 B3** 4 59N 19 16 E
Panevėžys, *Lithuania* **15 J21** 55 42N 24 25 E
Panfilov, *Kazakstan* **64 E8** 44 10N 80 0 E
Panfilovo, *Russia* **60 E6** 50 25N 42 46 E
Panga, *Dem. Rep. of the Congo* **118 B2** 1 52N 26 18 E
Pangaíon Óros, *Greece* **51 F8** 40 50N 24 0 E
Pangala, *Congo* **114 C2** 3 16 S 14 34 E
Pangalanes, Canal des =
Ampangalana, Lakandranon',
Madag. **117 C8** 22 48 S 47 50 E
Pangani, *Tanzania* **118 D4** 5 25 S 38 58 E
Pangani →, *Tanzania* **118 D4** 5 26 S 38 58 E
Pangantocan, *Phil.* **81 H5** 7 50N 124 49 E
Pangasinan □, *Phil.* **80 D3** 15 55N 120 20 E
Pangfou = Bengbu, *China* **75 H9** 32 58N 117 20 E
Pangil, *Dem. Rep. of the Congo* **118 C2** 3 10 S 26 35 E
Pangkah, Tanjung, *Indonesia* **79 G15** 6 51 S 112 33 E
Pangkai, *Burma* **90 D7** 22 40N 98 40 E
Pangkajene, *Indonesia* **79 E5** 4 46 S 119 34 E
Pangkalanbrandan, *Indonesia* **78 D1** 4 1N 98 20 E
Pangkalanbuun, *Indonesia* **78 E4** 2 41 S 111 37 E
Pangkalansusu, *Indonesia* **84 B1** 4 2N 98 13 E
Pangkalpinang, *Indonesia* **78 E3** 2 0 S 106 0 E
Pangkoh, *Indonesia* **85 C4** 3 5 S 114 8 E
Panglao, *Phil.* **81 G4** 9 35N 123 45 E
Panglao I., *Phil.* **81 G4** 9 35N 123 48 E
Pangnirtung, *Canada* **139 B13** 66 8N 65 54W
Pango Alucuem, *Angola* **115 D2** 8 43 S 14 33 E
Pangong Tso, *India* **92 B8** 34 40N 78 40 E
Pangrango, *Indonesia* **84 D3** 6 46 S 107 1 E
Pangsau Pass, *Burma* **90 B6** 27 15N 96 10 E
Pangtara, *Burma* **90 E6** 20 57N 96 40 E
Panguipulli, *Chile* **176 A2** 39 38 S 72 20W
Panguitch, *U.S.A.* **159 H7** 37 50N 112 26W
Pangutaran, *Phil.* **81 H3** 6 18N 120 35 E
Pangutaran Group, *Phil.* **79 C6** 6 18N 120 34 E
Panhala, *India* **94 F2** 16 49N 74 7 E
Panhandle, *U.S.A.* **155 H4** 35 21N 101 23W
Pani Mines, *India* **92 H5** 22 29N 73 50 E
Pania-Mutombo,
Dem. Rep. of the Congo **118 D1** 5 11 S 23 51 E
Paniau, *U.S.A.* **145 B1** 21 56N 160 5W
Panié, Mt., *N. Cal.* **133 T18** 20 36 S 164 46 E
Panikota I., *India* **92 J4** 20 46N 71 21 E
Panipat, *India* **92 E7** 29 25N 77 2 E
Panitan, *Phil.* **81 F4** 11 28N 122 46 E
Panjal Range, *India* **92 C7** 32 30N 76 50 E
Panjang, Hon, *Vietnam* **87 H4** 9 20N 103 28 E
Panjgur, *Pakistan* **91 D2** 27 0N 64 5 E
Panjhra →, *India* **94 D2** 21 13N 74 57 E
Panji Poyon, *Tajikistan* **63 E4** 37 12N 68 35 E
Panjim = Panaji, *India* **95 G1** 15 25N 73 50 E
Panjin, *China* **75 D12** 41 3N 122 2 E
Panjnad →, *Pakistan* **92 E4** 28 57N 70 30 E
Panjwai, *Afghan.* **92 D1** 31 26N 65 27 E
Pankshin, *Nigeria* **113 D6** 9 16N 9 25 E
Panmunjŏm, *N. Korea* **75 F14** 37 59N 126 38 E
Panna, *India* **93 G9** 24 40N 80 15 E
Panna Hills, *India* **93 G9** 24 40N 81 15 E
Pannawonica, *Australia* **124 D2** 21 39 S 116 19 E
Pano Akil, *Pakistan* **92 F3** 27 51N 69 7 E
Pano Lefkara, *Cyprus* **38 E12** 34 53N 33 20 E
Pano Panayia, *Cyprus* **38 E11** 34 55N 32 38 E
Panora, *U.S.A.* **156 C2** 41 42N 94 22W
Panorama, *Brazil* **175 A5** 21 21 S 51 51W
Pánormon, *Greece* **38 D6** 35 25N 24 41 E
Panruti, *India* **95 J4** 11 46N 79 35 E
Pansemal, *India* **92 J6** 21 39N 74 42 E
Panshan = Panjin, *China* **75 D12** 41 3N 122 2 E
Panshi, *China* **75 C14** 42 58N 126 5 E
Pantar, *Indonesia* **79 F6** 8 28 S 124 10 E
Pante Macassar, *Indonesia* **79 F6** 9 30 S 123 58 E
Pantelleria, *Italy* **46 F4** 36 50N 11 57 E
Pantha, *Burma* **90 D5** 23 55N 94 35 E
Pantin Sakan, *Burma* **90 F6** 18 38N 97 33 E
Pantoja, *Peru* **168 D2** 0 58 S 75 10W
Pantón, *Spain* **42 C3** 42 31N 7 37W
Pantukan, *Phil.* **81 H5** 7 9N 125 54 E
Panu, *Dem. Rep. of the Congo* **114 C3** 3 50 S 19 10 E
Pánuco, *Mexico* **163 C5** 22 0N 98 15W
Panukulan, *Phil.* **80 D3** 14 56N 121 49 E
Panvel, *India* **94 E1** 18 59N 73 4 E
Panyam, *Nigeria* **113 D6** 9 27N 9 8 E
Panyu, *China* **77 F9** 22 51N 113 20 E
Panzhihua, *China* **76 D3** 26 33N 101 44 E
Panzi, *Dem. Rep. of the Congo* **115 D3** 7 17 S 18 1 E
Pao →, *Anzoátegui, Venezuela* **169 B5** 8 6N 64 17W
Pao →, *Apure, Venezuela* **168 B4** 8 33N 68 1W
Páola, *Italy* **47 C9** 39 21N 16 2 E
Paola, *Malta* **38 D2** 35 52N 14 30 E
Paola, *U.S.A.* **154 F7** 38 35N 94 53W
Paoli, *U.S.A.* **157 F10** 38 33N 86 28W
Paonia, *U.S.A.* **159 G10** 38 52N 107 36W
Paoting = Baoding, *China* **74 E8** 38 50N 115 28 E
Paot'ou = Baotou, *China* **74 D6** 40 32N 110 2 E
Paoua, *C.A.R.* **114 A3** 7 9N 16 20 E
Pápa, *Hungary* **52 C2** 47 22N 17 30 E
Papa, *U.S.A.* **145 D6** 19 13N 155 52W
Papa Stour, *U.K.* **22 A7** 60 20N 1 42W
Papa Westray, *U.K.* **22 B6** 59 20N 2 55W
Papaaloa, *U.S.A.* **145 D6** 19 59N 155 13W
Papagayo →, *Mexico* **163 D5** 16 36N 99 43W
Papagayo, G. de, *Costa Rica* **164 D2** 10 30N 85 50W
Papagni →, *India* **95 G3** 15 35N 77 45 E
Papaïchton, *Fr. Guiana* **169 C7** 3 48N 54 10W
Papakura, *N.Z.* **130 D3** 37 4 S 174 59 E
Papantla, *Mexico* **163 C5** 20 30N 97 30W
Papar, *Malaysia* **78 C5** 5 45N 116 0 E
Paparoa, *N.Z.* **130 C3** 36 6 S 174 16 E
Paparoa Nat. Park, *N.Z.* **131 C6** 42 7 S 171 26 E
Paparoa Ra., *N.Z.* **131 C6** 42 5 S 171 35 E
Pápas, Ákra, *Greece* **48 C3** 38 13N 21 20 E
Papatoetoe, *N.Z.* **130 C3** 36 59 S 174 51 E
Papawai Pt., *U.S.A.* **145 C5** 20 47N 156 32W
Papeete, *Tahiti* **133 S16** 17 32 S 149 34W
Papenburg, *Germany* **30 B3** 53 5N 7 23 E
Paphlagonia, *Turkey* **100 B5** 41 30N 33 0 E
Paphos, *Cyprus* **38 E11** 34 46N 32 25 E
Papien Chiang = Da →,
Vietnam **76 G5** 21 15N 105 20 E
Papigochic →, *Mexico* **162 B3** 29 9N 109 40W
Paposo, *Chile* **174 B1** 25 0 S 70 30W
Papoutsa, *Cyprus* **38 E12** 34 54N 33 4 E
Papua, G. of, *Papua N. G.* **132 E3** 9 0 S 144 50 E
Papua New Guinea ■, *Oceania* **132 D3** 8 0 S 145 0 E
Papudo, *Chile* **174 C1** 32 29 S 71 27W
Papuk, *Croatia* **52 E2** 45 30N 17 30 E
Papun, *Burma* **90 F6** 18 2N 97 30 E
Papunya, *Australia* **124 D5** 23 15 S 131 54 E
Pará = Belém, *Brazil* **170 B2** 1 20 S 48 30W
Pará □, *Brazil* **173 A7** 3 20 S 52 0W
Pará □, *Surinam* **169 B6** 5 20N 55 5W
Paraburdoo, *Australia* **124 D2** 23 14 S 117 32 E
Paracale, *Phil.* **80 D4** 14 17N 122 48 E
Paracas, Pen., *Peru* **172 C2** 13 53 S 76 20W
Paracatu, *Brazil* **171 E2** 17 10 S 46 50W
Paracatu →, *Brazil* **171 E2** 16 30 S 45 4W
Paracel Is., *S. China Sea* **78 A4** 15 50N 112 0 E
Parachilna, *Australia* **128 A3** 31 10 S 138 21 E
Parachinar, *Pakistan* **91 B3** 33 55N 70 5 E
Paraćin, *Serbia, Yug.* **50 C5** 43 54N 21 27 E
Paracuru, *Brazil* **170 B4** 3 24 S 39 4W
Parada, Punta, *Peru* **172 D2** 15 22 S 75 11W
Paradas, *Spain* **43 H5** 37 18N 5 29W
Paradela, *Spain* **42 C3** 42 44N 7 37W
Paradhísi, *Greece* **38 C10** 36 18N 28 7 E
Paradip, *India* **94 D8** 20 15N 86 35 E
Paradise, *Calif., U.S.A.* **160 F5** 39 46N 121 37W
Paradise, *Nev., U.S.A.* **161 J11** 36 9N 115 10W
Paradise →, *Canada* **141 B8** 53 27N 57 19W
Paradise Hill, *Canada* **143 C7** 53 32N 109 28W
Paradise River, *Canada* **141 B8** 53 27N 57 17W
Paradise Valley, *U.S.A.* **158 F5** 41 30N 117 32W
Parado, *Indonesia* **79 F5** 8 42 S 118 30 E
Paragould, *U.S.A.* **155 G9** 36 3N 90 29W
Paraguá →, *Bolivia* **173 C5** 13 34 S 61 53W
Paragua →, *Venezuela* **169 B5** 6 55N 62 55W
Paraguaçu →, *Brazil* **171 D4** 12 45 S 38 54W
Paraguaçu Paulista, *Brazil* **175 A5** 22 22 S 50 35W
Paraguaipoa, *Venezuela* **168 A3** 11 21N 71 57W
Paraguaná, Pen. de, *Venezuela* **168 A3** 12 0N 70 0W
Paraguarí, *Paraguay* **174 B4** 25 36 S 57 0W
Paraguarí □, *Paraguay* **174 B4** 26 0 S 57 10W
Paraguay ■, *S. Amer.* **174 A4** 23 0 S 57 0W
Paraguay →, *Paraguay* **174 B4** 27 18 S 58 38W
Paraíba = João Pessoa, *Brazil* **170 C5** 7 10 S 34 52W
Paraíba □, *Brazil* **170 C4** 7 0 S 36 0W
Paraíba do Sul →, *Brazil* **171 F3** 21 37 S 41 3W
Parainen, *Finland* **15 F20** 60 18N 22 18 E
Paraiso, *Brazil* **173** 19 3 S 52 59W
Paraiso, *Mexico* **163 D6** 18 24N 93 14W
Parak, *Iran* **97 E7** 27 38N 52 25 E
Parakhino Paddubye, *Russia* **58 C7** 58 26N 33 10 E
Parakou, *Benin* **113 D5** 9 25N 2 40 E
Parakylia, *Australia* **128 A2** 30 24 S 136 25 E
Paralimni, *Cyprus* **38 D12** 35 2N 33 58 E
Parálion-Astrous, *Greece* **48 D4** 37 25N 22 45 E
Paralkote, *India* **94 E5** 19 47N 80 41 E
Paramaribo, *Surinam* **169 B6** 5 50N 55 10W
Parambu, *Brazil* **170 C3** 6 13 S 40 43W
Paramillo, Nudo del, *Colombia* **168 B2** 7 4N 75 55W
Paramirim, *Brazil* **171 D3** 13 26 S 42 15W
Paramirim →, *Brazil* **171 D3** 11 34 S 43 18W
Paramithiá, *Greece* **48 B2** 39 30N 20 35 E
Paramushir, Ostrov, *Russia* **65 D16** 50 24N 156 0 E
Paran →, *Israel* **103 E4** 30 20N 35 10 E
Paraná, *Argentina* **174 C3** 31 45 S 60 30W
Paranã, *Brazil* **171 D2** 12 30 S 47 48W
Paraná □, *Brazil* **175 A5** 24 30 S 51 0W
Paraná →, *Argentina* **174 C4** 33 43 S 59 15W
Paranã →, *Brazil* **171 D2** 12 30 S 48 14W
Paranaguá, *Brazil* **175 B6** 25 30 S 48 30W
Paranaíba, *Brazil* **173 D7** 19 40 S 51 11W
Paranaíba →, *Brazil* **171 F1** 20 6 S 51 4W
Paranapanema →, *Brazil* **175 A5** 22 40 S 53 9W
Paranapiacaba, Serra do, *Brazil* **175 A6** 24 31 S 48 35W
Paranas, *Phil.* **81 F5** 11 42N 125 2 E
Paranavaí, *Brazil* **175 A5** 23 4 S 52 56W
Parang, *Maguindanao, Phil.* **79 C6** 7 23N 124 16 E
Parang, *Sulu, Phil.* **79 C6** 5 55N 120 54 E
Parangaba, *Brazil* **170 B4** 3 45 S 38 33W
Parangippettai, *India* **95 J4** 11 30N 79 38 E
Parângul Mare, Vf., *Romania* **53 E8** 45 20N 23 37 E
Paranthan, *Sri Lanka* **95 K5** 9 26N 80 24 E
Paraparauma, *N.Z.* **130 G4** 40 57 S 175 3 E
Parapetí →, *Bolivia* **173 D5** 18 58 S 62 21W
Parapóla, *Greece* **48 E5** 36 55N 23 27 E
Paraspóri, Ákra, *Greece* **49 F9** 35 55N 27 15 E
Paratinga, *Brazil* **171 D3** 12 40 S 43 10W
Paratoo, *Australia* **128 B3** 32 42 S 139 20 E
Paraúna, *Brazil* **171 E1** 16 55 S 50 26W
Paray-le-Monial, *France* **27 F11** 46 27N 4 7 E
Parbati →, *Mad. P., India* **92 G7** 25 50N 76 30 E
Parbati →, *Raj., India* **92 F7** 26 54N 77 53 E
Parbatipur, *Bangla.* **90 C2** 25 39N 88 55 E
Parbhani, *India* **94 E3** 19 8N 76 52 E
Parchim, *Germany* **30 B7** 53 26N 11 52 E
Parczew, *Poland* **55 G9** 51 40N 22 52 E
Pardes Hanna-Karkur, *Israel* **103 C3** 32 28N 34 57 E
Pardilla, *Spain* **42 D7** 41 33N 3 43W
Pardo →, *Bahia, Brazil* **171 E4** 15 40 S 39 0W
Pardo →, *Mato Grosso, Brazil* **175 A5** 21 46 S 52 9W
Pardo →, *Minas Gerais, Brazil* **171 E3** 15 48 S 44 48W
Pardo →, *São Paulo, Brazil* **171 F2** 20 10 S 48 38W
Pardubice, *Czech Rep.* **34 A8** 50 3N 15 45 E
Pare, *Indonesia* **79 G15** 7 43 S 112 12 E
Pare Mts., *Tanzania* **118 C4** 4 0 S 37 45 E
Parecis, Serra dos, *Brazil* **173 C6** 13 0 S 60 0W
Paredes de Nava, *Spain* **42 C6** 42 9N 4 42W
Parelhas, *Brazil* **170 C4** 6 41 S 36 39W
Paren, *Russia* **65 C17** 62 30N 163 15 E
Parenda, *India* **94 E2** 18 16N 75 28 E
Parengarenga Harbour, *N.Z.* **130 A1** 34 31 S 173 0 E
Parent, *Canada* **140 C5** 47 55N 74 35W
Parent, L., *Canada* **140 C4** 48 31N 77 1W
Parentis-en-Born, *France* **28 D2** 44 21N 1 4W
Parepare, *Indonesia* **79 E5** 4 0 S 119 40 E
Parfino, *Russia* **58 D6** 57 59N 31 34 E
Párga, *Greece* **48 B2** 39 15N 20 29 E
Pargi, *India* **94 E3** 17 11N 77 53 E
Pargo, Pta. do, *Madeira* **39 D2** 32 49N 17 17W
Paria, G. de, *Venezuela* **169 A5** 10 20N 62 0W
Paria, Pen. de, *Venezuela* **169 A5** 10 50N 62 30W
Pariaguán, *Venezuela* **169 B5** 8 51N 64 34W
Pariaman, *Indonesia* **84 C2** 0 47 S 100 11 E
Paricatuba, *Brazil* **169 D5** 4 26 S 61 53W
Paricutín, Cerro, *Mexico* **162 D4** 19 28N 102 15W
Parigi, *Java, Indonesia* **85 D3** 7 42 S 108 29 E
Parigi, *Sulawesi, Indonesia* **79 E6** 0 50 S 120 5 E
Parika, *Guyana* **169 B6** 6 50N 58 20W
Parikkala, *Finland* **58 B5** 61 33N 29 31 E
Parima, Serra, *Brazil* **169 C5** 2 30N 64 0W
Parinari, *Peru* **172 A3** 4 35 S 74 25W
Pariñas, Pta., *S. Amer.* **166 D2** 4 30 S 82 0W
Parincea, *Romania* **53 D12** 46 27N 27 9 E
Parintins, *Brazil* **169 D6** 2 40 S 56 50W
Paris, *Canada* **150 C4** 43 12N 80 25W
Paris, *France* **27 D9** 48 50N 2 20 E
Paris, *Idaho, U.S.A.* **158 E8** 42 14N 111 24W
Paris, *Ill., U.S.A.* **157 E9** 39 36N 87 42W
Paris, *Ky., U.S.A.* **157 F12** 38 13N 84 15W
Paris, *Mo., U.S.A.* **156 E5** 39 29N 92 0W
Paris, *Tenn., U.S.A.* **149 G1** 36 18N 88 19W
Paris, *Tex., U.S.A.* **155 J7** 33 40N 95 33W
Paris, Ville de □, *France* **27 D9** 48 50N 2 20 E
Parish, *U.S.A.* **151 C8** 43 25N 76 8W
Parishville, *U.S.A.* **151 B10** 44 38N 74 49W
Pariti, *Indonesia* **82 D2** 10 15 S 123 45 E
Park, *U.S.A.* **160 B4** 48 45N 122 18W
Park City, *U.S.A.* **155 G6** 37 48N 97 20W
Park Falls, *U.S.A.* **154 C9** 45 56N 90 27W
Park Forest, *U.S.A.* **157 C9** 41 29N 87 40W
Park Head, *Canada* **150 B3** 44 36N 81 9W
Park Hills, *U.S.A.* **156 G6** 37 51N 90 31W
Park Range, *U.S.A.* **158 G10** 40 0N 106 30W
Park Rapids, *U.S.A.* **154 B7** 46 55N 95 4W
Park Ridge, *U.S.A.* **157 B9** 42 2N 87 51W
Park River, *U.S.A.* **154 A6** 48 24N 97 45W
Park Rynie, *S. Africa* **117 E5** 30 25 S 30 45 E
Parkā Bandar, *Iran* **97 E8** 25 55N 59 35 E
Parkal, *India* **94 E4** 18 12N 79 43 E
Parkano, *Finland* **15 E20** 62 1N 23 0 E
Parkent, *Uzbekistan* **63 C4** 41 18N 69 40 E
Parker, *Ariz., U.S.A.* **161 L12** 34 9N 114 17W
Parker, *Pa., U.S.A.* **150 E5** 41 5N 79 41W
Parker Dam, *U.S.A.* **161 L12** 34 18N 114 8W
Parkersburg, *Iowa, U.S.A.* **156 B4** 42 35N 92 47W
Parkersburg, *W. Va., U.S.A.* **148 F5** 39 16N 81 34W
Parkes, *Australia* **129 B8** 33 9 S 148 11 E
Parkfield, *U.S.A.* **160 K6** 35 54N 120 26W
Parkhar, *Tajikistan* **63 E4** 37 30N 69 34 E
Parkhill, *Canada* **150 C3** 43 15N 81 38W
Parkland, *U.S.A.* **160 C4** 47 9N 122 26W
Parkston, *U.S.A.* **154 D6** 43 24N 97 59W
Parksville, *Canada* **142 D4** 49 20N 124 21W
Parla, *Spain* **42 E7** 40 14N 3 46W
Parlakimidi, *India* **94 E7** 18 45N 84 5 E
Parli, *India* **94 E3** 18 50N 76 35 E
Pârlița, *Moldova* **53 C12** 47 19N 27 52 E
Parma, *Italy* **44 D7** 44 48N 10 20 E
Parma, *Idaho, U.S.A.* **158 E5** 43 47N 116 57W
Parma, *Ohio, U.S.A.* **150 E3** 41 23N 81 43W

Pigeon I. 265

Pengshan, *China* **76 B4** 30 14N 103 58 E
Pengshui, *China* **76 C7** 29 17N 108 12 E
Penguin, *Australia* **126 G4** 41 8 S 146 6 E
Pengxi, *China* **76 B5** 30 44N 105 45 E
Pengze, *China* **77 C11** 29 52N 116 32 E
Penhalonga, *Zimbabwe* **119 F3** 18 52 S 32 40 E
Peniche, *Portugal* **43 F1** 39 19N 9 22W
Penicuik, *U.K.* **22 F5** 55 50N 3 13W
Penida, *Indonesia* **78 F5** 8 45 S 115 30 E
Peninnes, Alpes = Pennine, Alpi, *Alps* **31 J3** 46 4N 7 30 E
Peninsular Malaysia □, *Malaysia* **78 D2** 4 0N 102 0 E
Peñíscola, *Spain* **40 E5** 40 22N 0 24 E
Penitente, Serra do, *Brazil* **170 C2** 8 45 S 46 20W
Penkridge, *U.K.* **20 E5** 52 44N 2 6W
Penmarch, *France* **26 E2** 47 49N 4 21W
Penmarch, Pte. de, *France* **26 E2** 47 48N 4 22W
Penn Hills, *U.S.A.* **150 F5** 40 28N 79 52W
Penn Yan, *U.S.A.* **150 D7** 42 40N 77 3W
Penna, Punta della, *Italy* **45 F11** 42 10N 14 43 E
Pennant, *Canada* **143 C7** 50 32N 108 14W
Penne, *Italy* **45 F10** 42 27N 13 55 E
Penner →, *India* **95 G5** 14 35N 80 10 E
Penneshaw, *Australia* **128 C2** 35 44 S 137 56 E
Pennine, Alpi, *Alps* **31 J3** 46 4N 7 30 E
Pennines, *U.K.* **20 C5** 54 45N 2 27W
Pennington, *U.S.A.* **160 F5** 39 15N 121 47W
Pennington →, *Nigeria* **113 E6** 4 45N 5 35 E
Pennino, Mte., *Italy* **45 E9** 43 6N 12 53 E
Pennsburg, *U.S.A.* **151 F9** 40 23N 75 29W
Pennsylvania □, *U.S.A.* **148 E7** 40 45N 77 30W
Pennville, *U.S.A.* **157 D11** 40 30N 85 9W
Penny, *Canada* **142 C4** 53 51N 121 20W
Peno, *Russia* **58 D7** 57 2N 32 49 E
Penobscot →, *U.S.A.* **149 C11** 44 30N 68 48W
Penobscot B., *U.S.A.* **149 C11** 44 35N 68 50W
Penola, *Australia* **128 D4** 37 25 S 140 48 E
Penong, *Australia* **125 F5** 31 56 S 133 1 E
Penonomé, *Panama* **164 E3** 8 31N 80 21W
Penot, Mt., *Vanuatu* **133 F5** 16 20 S 167 31 E
Penrith, *Australia* **129 B9** 33 43 S 150 38 E
Penrith, *U.K.* **20 C5** 54 40N 2 45W
Penryn, *U.K.* **21 G2** 50 9N 5 7W
Pensacola, *U.S.A.* **149 K2** 30 25N 87 13W
Pensacola Mts., *Antarctica* **7 E1** 84 0 S 40 0W
Pense, *Canada* **143 C8** 50 25N 104 59W
Penshurst, *Australia* **128 D5** 37 49 S 142 20 E
Pensiangan, *Malaysia* **85 B5** 4 33N 116 19 E
Pentecost = Pentecôte, *Vanuatu* **133 E6** 15 42 S 168 10 E
Pentecoste, *Brazil* **170 B4** 3 48 S 39 17W
Pentecôte, *Vanuatu* **133 E6** 15 42 S 168 10 E
Penticton, *Canada* **142 D5** 49 30N 119 38W
Pentland, *Australia* **126 C4** 20 32 S 145 25 E
Pentland Firth, *U.K.* **22 C5** 58 43N 3 10W
Pentland Hills, *U.K.* **22 F5** 55 48N 3 25W
Penukonda, *India* **95 G3** 14 5N 77 38 E
Penza, *Russia* **60 D7** 53 15N 45 5 E
Penzance, *U.K.* **21 G2** 50 7N 5 33W
Penzberg, *Germany* **31 H7** 47 45N 11 22 E
Penzhino, *Russia* **65 C17** 63 30N 167 55 E
Penzhinskaya Guba, *Russia* **65 C17** 61 30N 163 0 E
Penzhou, *China* **76 B4** 31 4N 103 32 E
Penzlin, *Germany* **30 B9** 53 30N 13 5 E
Peoria, *Ariz., U.S.A.* **159 K7** 33 35N 112 14W
Peoria, *Ill., U.S.A.* **156 D7** 40 42N 89 36W
Peoria Heights, *U.S.A.* **156 D7** 40 45N 89 35W
Peotone, *U.S.A.* **157 C9** 41 20N 87 48W
Pepacton Reservoir, *U.S.A.* **151 D10** 42 5N 74 58W
Pepani →, *S. Africa* **116 D3** 25 49 S 22 47 E
Pepeekeo, *U.S.A.* **145 D6** 19 51N 155 6W
Pepel, *S. Leone* **112 D2** 8 40N 13 5W
Peqini, *Albania* **50 E3** 41 3N 19 44 E
Pera Hd., *Australia* **126 A3** 12 55 S 141 37 E
Perabumulih, *Indonesia* **78 E2** 3 27 S 104 15 E
Perak □, *Malaysia* **84 A2** 5 0N 101 0 E
Perak →, *Malaysia* **87 K3** 4 0N 100 50 E
Perakhóra, *Greece* **48 C4** 38 2N 22 56 E
Perales de Alfambra, *Spain* **40 E4** 40 38N 1 0W
Perales del Puerto, *Spain* **42 E4** 40 10N 6 40W
Pérama, *Kérkira, Greece* **38 A3** 39 34N 19 54 E
Pérama, *Kríti, Greece* **38 D6** 35 20N 24 40 E
Peräpohjola, *Finland* **14 C22** 66 16N 26 10 E
Perast, *Montenegro, Yug.* **50 D2** 42 31N 18 47 E
Percé, *Canada* **141 C7** 48 31N 64 13W
Perche, *France* **26 D8** 48 31N 1 1 E
Perchtoldsdorf, *Austria* **35 C9** 48 7N 16 16 E
Percival Lakes, *Australia* **124 D4** 21 25 S 125 0 E
Percy, *France* **26 D5** 48 55N 1 11W
Percy, *U.S.A.* **156 F7** 38 5N 89 41W
Percy Is., *Australia* **126 C5** 21 39 S 150 16 E
Perdido →, *Argentina* **176 B3** 42 55 S 67 0W
Perdido, Mte., *Spain* **40 C5** 42 40N 0 5 E
Perdu, Mt. = Perdido, Mte., *Spain* **40 C5** 42 40N 0 5 E
Pereira, *Colombia* **168 C2** 4 49N 75 43W
Perekerten, *Australia* **128 C5** 34 55 S 143 40 E
Perelazovskiy, *Russia* **61 F6** 49 8N 42 35 E
Perené →, *Peru* **172 C3** 11 9 S 74 14W
Perenjori, *Australia* **125 E2** 29 26 S 116 16 E
Peresecina, *Moldova* **53 C13** 47 16N 28 46 E
Pereslavl-Zalesskiy, *Russia* **58 D10** 56 45N 38 50 E
Peretu, *Romania* **53 F10** 44 3N 25 5 E
Pereval = Turugart, Pereval, *Kyrgyzstan* **63 C7** 40 32N 75 24 E
Perevolotskiy, *Russia* **62 F5** 51 51N 54 12 E
Pereyaslav-Khmelnytskyy, *Ukraine* **59 G6** 50 3N 31 28 E
Pérez, I., *Mexico* **163 C7** 22 24N 89 42W
Perg, *Austria* **34 C7** 48 15N 14 38 E
Pergamino, *Argentina* **174 C3** 33 52 S 60 30W
Pergau →, *Malaysia* **87 K3** 5 23N 102 2 E
Pérgine Valsugana, *Italy* **45 B8** 46 4N 11 14 E
Pérgola, *Italy* **45 E9** 43 34N 12 50 E
Perham, *U.S.A.* **154 B7** 46 36N 95 34W
Perhentian, Kepulauan, *Malaysia* **78 C2** 5 54N 102 42 E
Peri L., *Australia* **128 A5** 30 45 S 143 35 E
Periam, *Romania* **52 D5** 46 2N 20 52 E
Péribonca →, *Canada* **141 C5** 48 45N 72 5W
Péribonca, L., *Canada* **141 B5** 50 1N 71 10W
Perico, *Argentina* **174 A2** 24 20 S 65 5W
Pericos, *Mexico* **162 B3** 25 3N 107 42W
Périers, *France* **26 C5** 49 11N 1 25W
Périgord, *France* **28 D4** 45 0N 0 40 E
Périgueux, *France* **28 C4** 45 10N 0 42 E
Perijá, Sierra de, *Colombia* **168 B3** 9 30N 73 3W
Peristéra, *Greece* **48 B5** 39 15N 23 58 E
Peristerona →, *Cyprus* **38 D12** 35 8N 33 5 E
Perito Moreno, *Argentina* **176 C2** 46 36 S 70 56W
Peritoró, *Brazil* **170 B3** 4 20 S 44 18W
Perivol = Dragovishtitsa, *Bulgaria* **50 D6** 42 22N 22 39 E
Periyakulam, *India* **95 J3** 10 5N 77 30 E
Periyar →, *India* **95 J3** 10 15N 76 10 E
Periyar, L., *India* **95 K3** 9 25N 77 10 E
Perkasie, *U.S.A.* **151 F9** 40 22N 75 18W
Perković, *Croatia* **45 E13** 43 41N 16 10 E
Perlas, Arch. de las, *Panama* **164 E4** 8 41N 79 7W
Perlas, Punta de, *Nic.* **164 D3** 12 30N 83 30W
Perleberg, *Germany* **30 B7** 53 5N 11 52 E
Perlez, *Serbia, Yug.* **52 E5** 45 11N 20 22 E
Perlis □, *Malaysia* **84 A2** 6 30N 100 15 E
Perm, *Russia* **62 C6** 58 0N 56 10 E
Përmeti, *Albania* **50 F4** 40 15N 20 21 E
Pernambuco = Recife, *Brazil* **170 C5** 8 0 S 35 0W
Pernambuco □, *Brazil* **170 C4** 8 0 S 37 0W
Pernatty Lagoon, *Australia* **128 A2** 31 30 S 137 12 E
Pernik, *Bulgaria* **50 D7** 42 35N 23 2 E
Peron Is., *Australia* **124 B5** 13 9 S 130 4 E
Peron Pen., *Australia* **125 E1** 26 0 S 113 10 E
Péronne, *France* **27 C9** 49 55N 2 57 E
Perosa Argentina, *Italy* **44 D4** 44 58N 7 10 E
Perow, *Canada* **142 C3** 54 35N 126 10W
Perpendicular Pt., *Australia* **127 E5** 31 37 S 152 52 E
Perpignan, *France* **28 F6** 42 42N 2 53 E
Perrine, *U.S.A.* **153 K9** 25 36N 80 21W
Perris, *U.S.A.* **161 M9** 33 47N 117 14W
Perros-Guirec, *France* **26 D3** 48 49N 3 28W
Perry, *Fla., U.S.A.* **152 E6** 30 7N 83 35W
Perry, *Ga., U.S.A.* **152 C6** 32 28N 83 44W
Perry, *Iowa, U.S.A.* **156 C2** 41 51N 94 6W
Perry, *Mich., U.S.A.* **157 B12** 42 50N 84 13W
Perry, *Mo., U.S.A.* **156 E5** 39 26N 91 40W
Perry, *Okla., U.S.A.* **155 G6** 36 17N 97 14W
Perrysburg, *U.S.A.* **157 C13** 41 34N 83 38W
Perryton, *U.S.A.* **155 G4** 36 24N 100 48W
Perryville, *U.S.A.* **155 G10** 37 43N 89 52W
Persan, *France* **27 C9** 49 9N 2 16 E
Persberg, *Sweden* **16 E8** 59 47N 14 15 E
Perşembe, *Turkey* **100 B7** 41 5N 37 46 E
Persepolis, *Iran* **97 D7** 29 55N 52 50 E
Perseverancia, *Bolivia* **173 C5** 14 44 S 62 48W
Pershotravensk, *Ukraine* **59 G4** 50 13N 27 40 E
Persia = Iran ■, *Asia* **97 C7** 33 0N 53 0 E
Persian Gulf = Gulf, The, *Asia* **97 E6** 27 0N 50 0 E
Perstorp, *Sweden* **17 H7** 56 10N 13 25 E
Pertek, *Turkey* **101 C8** 38 51N 39 19 E
Perth, *Australia* **125 F2** 31 57 S 115 52 E
Perth, *Canada* **140 D4** 44 55N 76 15W
Perth, *U.K.* **22 E5** 56 24N 3 26W
Perth & Kinross □, *U.K.* **22 E5** 56 45N 3 55W
Perth Amboy, *U.S.A.* **151 F10** 40 31N 74 16W
Perth-Andover, *Canada* **141 C6** 46 44N 67 42W
Pertuis, *France* **29 E9** 43 42N 5 30 E
Pertusato, C., *France* **29 G13** 41 22N 9 11 E
Peru, *Ill., U.S.A.* **156 C7** 41 20N 89 8W
Peru, *Ind., U.S.A.* **157 D10** 40 45N 86 4W
Peru, *N.Y., U.S.A.* **151 B11** 44 35N 73 32W
Peru ■, *S. Amer.* **168 D2** 4 0 S 75 0W
Peru-Chile Trench, *Pac. Oc.* **135 K20** 20 0 S 72 0W
Perúgia, *Italy* **45 E9** 43 7N 12 23 E
Perušić, *Croatia* **45 D12** 44 40N 15 22 E
Pervomaysk, *Russia* **60 C6** 54 56N 43 58 E
Pervomaysk, *Ukraine* **59 H6** 48 10N 30 46 E
Pervomayskiy, *Russia* **62 F5** 51 32N 55 2 E
Pervouralsk, *Russia* **62 C7** 56 59N 59 59 E
Pésaro, *Italy* **45 E9** 43 54N 12 55 E
Pescadores = Penghu, *Taiwan* **77 F12** 23 34N 119 30 E
Pescara, *Italy* **45 F11** 42 28N 14 13 E
Pescara →, *Italy* **45 F11** 42 28N 14 13 E
Peschanokopskoye, *Russia* **61 G5** 46 14N 41 4 E
Péscia, *Italy* **44 E7** 43 54N 10 41 E
Pescina, *Italy* **45 F10** 42 2N 13 39 E
Peseux, *Switz.* **32 C3** 46 59N 6 53 E
Peshawar, *Pakistan* **91 B3** 34 2N 71 37 E
Peshkopi, *Albania* **50 E4** 41 41N 20 25 E
Peshtera, *Bulgaria* **51 D8** 42 2N 24 18 E
Peshtigo, *U.S.A.* **148 C2** 45 4N 87 46W
Peski, *Russia* **60 E6** 51 14N 42 29 E
Peskovka, *Russia* **62 B4** 59 4N 52 20 E
Pêso da Régua, *Portugal* **42 D3** 41 10N 7 47W
Pesqueira, *Brazil* **170 C4** 8 20 S 36 42W
Pessac, *France* **28 D3** 44 48N 0 37W
Pest □, *Hungary* **52 C4** 47 29N 19 5 E
Pestovo, *Russia* **58 C8** 58 33N 35 42 E
Pestravka, *Russia* **60 D9** 52 28N 49 57 E
Péta, *Greece* **48 B3** 39 10N 21 2 E
Petah Tiqwa, *Israel* **103 C3** 32 6N 34 53 E
Petalídhion, *Greece* **48 E3** 36 57N 21 55 E
Petaling Jaya, *Malaysia* **87 L3** 3 4N 101 42 E
Petaloudhes, *Greece* **38 C10** 36 18N 28 5 E
Petaluma, *U.S.A.* **160 G4** 38 14N 122 39W
Pétange, *Lux.* **24 E5** 49 33N 5 55 E
Petaro, *Pakistan* **92 G3** 25 31N 68 18 E
Petatlán, *Mexico* **162 D4** 17 31N 101 16W
Petauke, *Zambia* **119 E3** 14 14 S 31 20 E
Petawawa, *Canada* **140 C4** 45 54N 77 17W
Petén Itzá, L., *Guatemala* **164 C2** 16 58N 89 50W
Peter I.s Øy, *Antarctica* **7 C16** 69 0 S 91 0W
Peter Pond L., *Canada* **143 B7** 55 55N 108 44W
Peterbell, *Canada* **140 C3** 48 36N 83 21W
Peterborough, *Australia* **128 B3** 32 58 S 138 51 E
Peterborough, *Canada* **140 D4** 44 20N 78 20W
Peterborough, *U.K.* **21 E7** 52 35N 0 15W
Peterborough, *U.S.A.* **151 D13** 42 53N 71 57W
Peterborough □, *U.K.* **21 E7** 52 35N 0 15W
Peterculter, *U.K.* **22 D6** 57 6N 2 16W
Peterhead, *U.K.* **22 D7** 57 31N 1 48W
Peterlee, *U.K.* **20 C6** 54 47N 1 20W
Petermann Bjerg, *Greenland* **10 C8** 73 7N 28 25W
Petermann Gletscher, *Greenland* **10 A4** 80 30N 60 0W
Petermann Ranges, *Australia* **124 E5** 26 0 S 130 30 E
Peter's Mine, *Guyana* **169 B6** 6 14N 59 20W
Petersburg, *Alaska, U.S.A.* **138 C6** 56 48N 132 58W
Petersburg, *Ill., U.S.A.* **156 D7** 40 1N 89 51W
Petersburg, *Ind., U.S.A.* **157 F9** 38 30N 87 17W
Petersburg, *Mich., U.S.A.* **157 C13** 41 54N 83 43W
Petersburg, *Pa., U.S.A.* **150 F6** 40 34N 78 3W
Petersburg, *Va., U.S.A.* **148 G7** 37 14N 77 24W
Petersburg, *W. Va., U.S.A.* **148 F6** 39 1N 79 5W
Petersfield, *U.K.* **21 F7** 51 1N 0 56W
Petershagen, *Germany* **30 C4** 52 23N 8 58 E
Petília Policastro, *Italy* **47 C9** 39 7N 16 48 E
Petit Batanga, *Cameroon* **114 B1** 3 15N 9 54 E
Petit Goâve, *Haiti* **165 C5** 18 27N 72 51W
Petit Jardin, *Canada* **141 C8** 48 28N 59 14W
Petit Lac Manicouagan, *Canada* **141 B6** 51 25N 67 40W
Petit-Mécatina →, *Canada* **141 B8** 50 40N 59 30W
Petit-Mécatina, I. du, *Canada* **141 B8** 50 30N 59 25W
Petit Saint Bernard, Col du, *Italy* **29 C10** 45 40N 6 52 E
Petitcodiac, *Canada* **141 C6** 45 57N 65 11W
Petite Baleine →, *Canada* **140 A4** 56 0N 76 45W
Petite Saguenay, *Canada* **141 C5** 48 15N 70 4W
Petitot →, *Canada* **142 A4** 60 14N 123 29W
Petitsikapau L., *Canada* **141 B6** 54 37N 66 25W
Petlad, *India* **92 H5** 22 30N 72 45 E
Peto, *Mexico* **163 C7** 20 10N 88 53W
Petone, *N.Z.* **130 H3** 41 13 S 174 53 E
Petorca, *Chile* **174 C1** 32 15 S 70 56W
Petoskey, *U.S.A.* **148 C3** 45 22N 84 57W
Petra, *Jordan* **103 E4** 30 20N 35 22 E
Petra, *Spain* **39 B10** 39 37N 3 6 E
Petra, Ostrova, *Russia* **6 B13** 76 15N 118 30 E
Petra Velikogo, Zaliv, *Russia* **68 C6** 42 40N 132 0 E
Petrel = Petrer, *Spain* **41 G4** 38 30N 0 46W
Petrella, Monte, *Italy* **46 A6** 41 18N 13 40 E
Petrer, *Spain* **41 G4** 38 30N 0 46W
Petreto-Bicchisano, *France* **29 G12** 41 47N 8 58 E
Petrich, *Bulgaria* **50 E7** 41 24N 23 13 E
Petrified Forest National Park, *U.S.A.* **159 J9** 35 0N 109 30W
Petrijanec, *Croatia* **45 B13** 46 23N 16 17 E
Petrikov = Pyetrikaw, *Belarus* **59 F5** 52 11N 28 29 E
Petrila, *Romania* **53 E8** 45 29N 23 29 E
Petrinja, *Croatia* **45 C13** 45 28N 16 18 E
Petrodvorets, *Russia* **58 C5** 59 52N 29 54 E
Petrograd = Sankt-Peterburg, *Russia* **58 C6** 59 55N 30 20 E
Petrolândia, *Brazil* **170 C4** 9 5 S 38 20W
Petrolia, *Canada* **140 D3** 42 54N 82 9W
Petrolina, *Brazil* **170 C3** 9 24 S 40 30W
Petropavl, *Kazakstan* **64 D7** 54 53N 69 13 E
Petropavlovsk = Petropavl, *Kazakstan* **64 D7** 54 53N 69 13 E
Petropavlovsk-Kamchatskiy, *Russia* **65 D16** 53 3N 158 43 E
Petropavlovskiy = Akhtubinsk, *Russia* **61 F8** 48 13N 46 7 E
Petrópolis, *Brazil* **171 F3** 22 33 S 43 9W
Petroşani, *Romania* **53 E8** 45 28N 23 20 E
Petrova Gora, *Croatia* **45 C12** 45 15N 15 45 E
Petrovac, *Montenegro, Yug.* **50 D2** 42 13N 18 57 E
Petrovac, *Serbia, Yug.* **50 B5** 44 22N 21 26 E
Petrovaradin, *Serbia, Yug.* **52 E4** 45 16N 19 55 E
Petrovsk, *Russia* **60 D7** 52 22N 45 19 E
Petrovsk-Zabaykalskiy, *Russia* **65 D11** 51 20N 108 55 E
Petrovskaya, *Russia* **59 K9** 45 25N 37 58 E
Petrovskoye = Svetlograd, *Russia* **61 H6** 45 25N 42 58 E
Petrovskoye, *Russia* **62 E6** 53 37N 56 23 E
Petrozavodsk, *Russia* **58 B8** 61 41N 34 20 E
Petrus Steyn, *S. Africa* **117 D4** 27 38 S 28 8 E
Petrusburg, *S. Africa* **116 D4** 29 4 S 25 26 E
Petttits, *Australia* **129 C8** 34 56 S 148 10 E
Petzeck, *Austria* **34 E5** 46 57N 12 48 E
Peumo, *Chile* **174 C1** 34 21 S 71 12W
Peureulak, *Indonesia* **78 D1** 4 48N 97 45 E
Peusangan →, *Indonesia* **84 A1** 5 16N 96 51 E
Pevek, *Russia* **65 C18** 69 41N 171 19 E
Pevely, *U.S.A.* **156 F6** 38 17N 90 24W
Peveragno, *Italy* **44 D4** 44 20N 7 37 E
Peyrehorade, *France* **28 E2** 43 34N 1 7W
Peyruis, *France* **29 D9** 44 1N 5 56 E
Pézenas, *France* **28 E7** 43 28N 3 24 E
Pezinok, *Slovak Rep.* **35 C10** 48 17N 17 17 E
Pfaffenhofen, *Germany* **31 G7** 48 31N 11 31 E
Pfäffikon, *Switz.* **33 B7** 47 13N 8 46 E
Pfäffikon, *Switz.* **33 B7** 47 22N 8 47 E
Pfarrkirchen, *Germany* **31 G8** 48 25N 12 56 E
Pfeffenhausen, *Germany* **31 G7** 48 39N 11 58 E
Pforzheim, *Germany* **31 G4** 48 52N 8 41 E
Pfullendorf, *Germany* **31 H5** 47 55N 9 15 E
Pfungstadt, *Germany* **31 F4** 49 48N 8 35 E
Phaistós, *Greece* **38 D6** 35 2N 24 50 E
Phala, *Botswana* **116 C4** 23 45 S 26 50 E
Phalera = Phulera, *India* **92 F6** 26 52N 75 16 E
Phalodi, *India* **92 F5** 27 12N 72 24 E
Phalsbourg, *France* **27 D14** 48 46N 7 15 E
Phaltan, *India* **94 F2** 17 59N 74 26 E
Phan, *Thailand* **86 C2** 19 28N 99 43 E
Phan Rang, *Vietnam* **78 B3** 11 34N 109 0 E
Phan Ri = Hoa Da, *Vietnam* **87 G7** 11 16N 108 40 E
Phan Thiet, *Vietnam* **78 B3** 11 1N 108 9 E
Phanae, *Greece* **49 C7** 38 8N 25 57 E
Phanat Nikhom, *Thailand* **86 F3** 13 27N 101 11 E
Phangan, Ko, *Thailand* **78 C2** 9 45N 100 0 E
Phangnga, *Thailand* **78 C1** 8 28N 98 30 E
Phanh Bho Ho Chi Minh, *Vietnam* **78 B3** 10 58N 106 40 E
Phanom Sarakham, *Thailand* **86 F3** 13 45N 101 21 E
Phaphund, *India* **93 F8** 26 36N 79 28 E
Pharenda, *India* **93 F10** 27 5N 83 17 E
Pharr, *U.S.A.* **155 M5** 26 12N 98 11W
Phatthalung, *Thailand* **78 C2** 7 39N 100 6 E
Phayao, *Thailand* **86 C2** 19 11N 99 55 E
Phelps, *U.S.A.* **150 D7** 42 58N 77 3W
Phelps L., *Canada* **143 B8** 59 15N 103 15W
Phenix City, *U.S.A.* **149 J3** 32 28N 85 0W
Phet Buri, *Thailand* **78 B1** 13 1N 99 55 E
Phetchabun, *Thailand* **78 A2** 16 25N 101 8 E
Phetchabun, Thiu Khao, *Thailand* **86 E3** 16 0N 101 20 E
Phetchaburi = Phet Buri, *Thailand* **78 B1** 13 1N 99 55 E
Phi Phi, Ko, *Thailand* **87 J2** 7 45N 98 46 E
Phiafay, *Laos* **86 E6** 14 48N 106 0 E
Phibun Mangsahan, *Thailand* **86 E5** 15 14N 105 14 E
Phichai, *Thailand* **86 D3** 17 22N 100 10 E
Phichit, *Thailand* **86 D3** 16 26N 100 22 E
Philadelphia, *Miss., U.S.A.* **155 J10** 32 46N 89 7W
Philadelphia, *N.Y., U.S.A.* **151 B9** 44 9N 75 43W
Philadelphia, *Pa., U.S.A.* **151 G9** 39 57N 75 10W
Philip, *U.S.A.* **154 C4** 44 2N 101 40W
Philip Smith Mts., *U.S.A.* **144 C11** 68 0N 148 0W
Philippeville, *Belgium* **24 D4** 50 12N 4 33 E
Philippi, *Greece* **51 E8** 41 1N 24 16 E
Philippi, *U.S.A.* **148 F5** 39 9N 80 3W
Philippi L., *Australia* **126 C2** 24 20 S 138 55 E
Philippines ■, *Asia* **79 B6** 12 0N 123 0 E
Philippolis, *S. Africa* **116 E4** 30 15 S 25 16 E
Philippopolis = Plovdiv, *Bulgaria* **51 D8** 42 8N 24 44 E
Philipsburg, *Canada* **151 A11** 45 2N 73 5W
Philipsburg, *Mont., U.S.A.* **158 C7** 46 20N 113 18W
Philipsburg, *Pa., U.S.A.* **150 F6** 40 54N 78 13W
Philipstown = Daingean, *Ireland* **23 C4** 53 18N 7 17W
Philipstown, *S. Africa* **116 E3** 30 28 S 24 30 E
Phillip I., *Australia* **129 E6** 38 30 S 145 12 E
Phillips, *U.S.A.* **154 C9** 45 42N 90 24W
Phillipsburg, *Ga., U.S.A.* **152 D6** 31 25N 83 30W
Phillipsburg, *Kans., U.S.A.* **154 F5** 39 45N 99 19W
Phillipsburg, *N.J., U.S.A.* **151 F9** 40 42N 75 12W
Philmont, *U.S.A.* **151 D11** 42 15N 73 39W
Philomath, *Ga., U.S.A.* **152 B7** 33 44N 82 59W
Philomath, *Oreg., U.S.A.* **158 D2** 44 32N 123 22W
Phimai, *Thailand* **86 E4** 15 13N 102 30 E
Phitsanulok, *Thailand* **78 A2** 16 50N 100 12 E
Phnom Dangrek, *Thailand* **78 B2** 14 20N 104 0 E
Phnom Penh, *Cambodia* **78 B2** 11 33N 104 55 E
Phnum Penh = Phnom Penh, *Cambodia* **78 B2** 11 33N 104 55 E
Phoenicia, *U.S.A.* **151 D10** 42 5N 74 14W
Phoenix, *Ariz., U.S.A.* **159 K7** 33 27N 112 4W
Phoenix, *N.Y., U.S.A.* **151 C8** 43 14N 76 18W
Phoenix Is., *Kiribati* **134 H10** 3 30 S 172 0W
Phoenixville, *U.S.A.* **151 F9** 40 8N 75 31W
Phon, *Thailand* **86 E4** 15 49N 102 36 E
Phon Tiou, *Laos* **86 D5** 17 53N 104 37 E
Phong →, *Thailand* **78 A2** 16 23N 102 56 E
Phong Saly, *Laos* **86 B4** 21 42N 102 9 E
Phong Tho, *Vietnam* **86 A4** 22 32N 103 21 E
Phonhong, *Laos* **86 C4** 18 30N 102 25 E
Phonum, *Thailand* **87 H2** 8 49N 98 48 E
Phosphate Hill, *Australia* **126 C2** 21 53 S 139 58 E
Photharam, *Thailand* **86 F2** 13 41N 99 51 E
Phra Nakhon Si Ayutthaya, *Thailand* **78 B2** 14 25N 100 30 E
Phra Thong, Ko, *Thailand* **87 H2** 9 5N 98 17 E
Phrae, *Thailand* **86 C3** 18 7N 100 9 E
Phrom Phiram, *Thailand* **86 D3** 17 2N 100 12 E
Phrygia, *Turkey* **100 C4** 38 40N 30 0 E
Phu Dien, *Vietnam* **86 C5** 18 58N 105 31 E
Phu Loi, *Laos* **86 B4** 20 14N 103 14 E
Phu Ly, *Vietnam* **76 G5** 20 35N 105 50 E
Phu Quoc, Dao, *Vietnam* **78 B2** 10 20N 104 0 E
Phu Tho, *Vietnam* **76 G5** 21 24N 105 13 E
Phuc Yen, *Vietnam* **76 G5** 21 16N 105 45 E
Phuket, *Thailand* **78 C1** 7 52N 98 22 E
Phuket, Ko, *Thailand* **87 J2** 8 0N 98 22 E
Phul, *India* **92 D6** 30 19N 75 14 E
Phulad, *India* **92 G5** 25 38N 73 49 E
Phulbani, *India* **94 D7** 20 28N 84 14 E
Phulbari, *India* **90 C3** 25 55N 90 2 E
Phulchari, *Bangla.* **93 G13** 25 11N 89 37 E
Phulera, *India* **92 F6** 26 52N 75 16 E
Phulpur, *India* **93 G10** 25 31N 82 49 E
Phun Phin, *Thailand* **87 H2** 9 7N 99 12 E
Piacá, *Brazil* **170 C2** 7 42 S 47 18W
Piacenza, *Italy* **44 C6** 45 1N 9 40 E
Piaçubaçu, *Brazil* **170 D4** 10 24 S 36 25W
Piako →, *N.Z.* **130 D4** 37 12 S 175 30 E
Pian Cr. →, *Australia* **127 E4** 30 2 S 148 12 E
Piana, *France* **29 F12** 42 15N 8 34 E
Pianella, *Italy* **45 F11** 42 24N 14 2 E
Piangil, *Australia* **128 C5** 35 5 S 143 20 E
Pianosa, *Puglia, Italy* **45 F12** 42 12N 15 44 E
Pianosa, *Toscana, Italy* **44 F7** 42 35N 10 5 E
Piapot, *Canada* **143 D7** 49 59N 109 8W
Pias, *Portugal* **43 G3** 38 1N 7 29W
Piaseczno, *Poland* **55 F8** 52 5N 21 2 E
Piaski, *Poland* **55 G9** 51 8N 22 52 E
Piastów, *Poland* **55 F7** 52 12N 20 48 E
Piatã, *Brazil* **171 D3** 13 9 S 41 48W
Piatra, *Romania* **53 G10** 43 51N 25 9 E
Piatra Neamţ, *Romania* **53 D11** 46 56N 26 21 E
Piatra Olt, *Romania* **53 F9** 44 22N 24 16 E
Piauí □, *Brazil* **170 C3** 7 0 S 43 0W
Piaui →, *Brazil* **170 C3** 6 38 S 42 42W
Piave →, *Italy* **45 C9** 45 32N 12 44 E
Piazza Ármerina, *Italy* **47 E7** 37 21N 14 20 E
Pibor →, *Sudan* **107 F3** 7 35N 33 0 E
Pibor Post, *Sudan* **107 F3** 6 47N 33 3 E
Pica, *Chile* **172 E4** 20 35 S 69 25W
Picardie, *France* **27 C10** 49 50N 3 0 E
Picardie, Plaine de, *France* **27 C9** 50 0N 2 0 E
Picardy = Picardie, *France* **27 C10** 49 50N 3 0 E
Picayune, *U.S.A.* **155 K10** 30 32N 89 41W
Picerno, *Italy* **47 B8** 40 38N 15 38 E
Pichhor, *India* **93 G8** 25 58N 78 20 E
Pichilemu, *Chile* **174 C1** 34 22 S 72 0W
Pichincha, □, *Ecuador* **168 D2** 0 10 S 78 40W
Pichor, *India* **92 G8** 25 11N 78 11 E
Pickerel L., *Canada* **140 C1** 48 40N 91 25W
Pickering, *U.K.* **20 C7** 54 15N 0 46W
Pickering, Vale of, *U.K.* **20 C7** 54 14N 0 45W
Pickle Lake, *Canada* **140 B1** 51 30N 90 12W
Pickwick L., *U.S.A.* **149 H1** 35 4N 88 15W
Pico Truncado, *Argentina* **176 C3** 46 40 S 68 0W
Picos, *Brazil* **170 C3** 7 5 S 41 28W
Picota, *Peru* **172 B2** 6 54 S 76 24W
Picton, *Australia* **129 C9** 34 12 S 150 34 E
Picton, *Canada* **140 D4** 44 1N 77 9W
Picton, *N.Z.* **131 B9** 41 18 S 174 3 E
Picton, I., *Chile* **176 E3** 55 2 S 66 57W
Pictou, *Canada* **141 C7** 45 41N 62 42W
Picture Butte, *Canada* **142 D6** 49 55N 112 45W
Picuí, *Brazil* **170 C4** 6 31 S 36 21W
Picún Leufú, *Argentina* **176 A3** 39 30 S 69 5W
Pidurutalagala, *Sri Lanka* **95 L5** 7 10N 80 50 E
Piechowice, *Poland* **55 H2** 50 51N 15 36 E
Piedecuesta, *Colombia* **168 B3** 6 59N 73 3W
Piedmont = Piemonte □, *Italy* **44 D5** 45 0N 8 0 E
Piedmont, *Ala., U.S.A.* **152 B4** 33 55N 85 37W
Piedmont, *S.C., U.S.A.* **147 D10** 34 0N 81 30W
Piedmonte Matese, *Italy* **47 A7** 41 22N 14 22 E
Piedra →, *Spain* **40 D3** 41 18N 1 47W
Piedra del Anguila, *Argentina* **176 B2** 40 2 S 70 4W
Piedra Lais, *Venezuela* **168 C4** 3 10N 65 50W
Piedrabuena, *Spain* **43 G6** 39 0N 4 10W
Piedrahita, *Spain* **42 E5** 40 28N 5 23W
Piedralaves, *Spain* **42 E6** 40 19N 4 42W
Piedras, R. de las →, *Peru* **172 C4** 12 30 S 69 15W
Piedras Blancas, *Spain* **42 B5** 43 33N 5 58W
Piedras Negras, *Mexico* **162 B4** 28 42N 100 31W
Piedras Pt., *Phil.* **81 F2** 10 11N 118 48 E
Piekary Śląskie, *Poland* **55 H5** 50 24N 18 57 E
Pieksämäki, *Finland* **15 E22** 62 18N 27 10 E
Piemonte □, *Italy* **44 D5** 45 0N 8 0 E
Pienaarsrivier, *S. Africa* **117 D4** 25 15 S 28 18 E
Pieniężno, *Poland* **54 D7** 54 14N 20 8 E
Pieńsk, *Poland* **55 G2** 51 16N 15 2 E
Pier Millan, *Australia* **128 C5** 35 14 S 142 40 E
Piercefield, *U.S.A.* **151 B10** 44 13N 74 35W
Pierceland, *Canada* **143 C7** 54 20N 109 46W
Piería □, *Greece* **50 F6** 40 13N 22 25 E
Pierpont, *U.S.A.* **150 E4** 41 45N 80 34W
Pierre, *U.S.A.* **154 C4** 44 22N 100 21W
Pierre-Buffière, *France* **28 C5** 45 41N 1 22 E
Pierre-de-Bresse, *France* **27 F12** 46 54N 5 13 E
Pierrefontaine-les-Varans, *France* **27 E13** 47 14N 6 32 E
Pierrefort, *France* **28 D6** 44 55N 2 50 E
Pierrelatte, *France* **29 D8** 44 23N 4 43 E
Pierson, *U.S.A.* **153 F8** 29 14N 81 28W
Piešťany, *Slovak Rep.* **35 C10** 48 38N 17 55 E
Piesting →, *Austria* **35 C9** 48 6N 16 40 E
Pieszyce, *Poland* **55 H3** 50 43N 16 33 E
Piet Retief, *S. Africa* **117 D5** 27 1 S 30 50 E
Pietarsaari, *Finland* **14 E20** 63 40N 22 43 E
Pietermaritzburg, *S. Africa* **117 D5** 29 35 S 30 25 E
Pietersburg, *S. Africa* **117 C4** 23 54 S 29 25 E
Pietragalla, *Italy* **47 B8** 40 45N 15 53 E
Pietrasanta, *Italy* **44 E7** 43 57N 10 14 E
Pietroşiţa, *Romania* **53 E10** 45 11N 25 26 E
Pietrosul, Vf., *Maramureş, Romania* **53 C9** 47 35N 24 43 E
Pietrosul, Vf., *Suceava, Romania* **53 C10** 47 12N 25 18 E
Pieve di Cadore, *Italy* **45 B9** 46 26N 12 22 E
Pieve di Teco, *Italy* **44 D4** 44 3N 7 56 E
Pievepélago, *Italy* **44 D7** 44 12N 10 37 E
Pigadhítsa, *Greece* **50 G5** 39 59N 21 23 E
Pigeon I., *India* **95 G2** 14 2N 74 20 E

Portal 267

Podgorica, *Montenegro, Yug.* . **50 D3** 42 30N 19 19 E
Podgorie, *Albania* . . . . . **50 F4** 40 49N 20 48 E
Podile, *India* . . . . . **95 G4** 15 37N 79 37 E
Podilska Vysochyna, *Ukraine* . **59 H4** 49 0N 28 0 E
Podkarpackie □, *Poland* . . . . **55 H9** 50 0N 22 10 E
Podkova, *Bulgaria* . . . . . **51 E9** 41 24N 25 24 E
Podlapača, *Croatia* . . . . . **45 D12** 44 37N 15 47 E
Podlaskie □, *Poland* . . . . . **55 E10** 53 10N 23 0 E
Podoleni, *Romania* . . . . . **53 D11** 46 46N 26 39 E
Podolínec, *Slovak Rep.* . . . . **35 B13** 49 16N 20 31 E
Podolsk, *Russia* . . . . . **58 E9** 55 25N 37 30 E
Podor, *Senegal* **112 B1** 16 40N 15 2W
Podporozhye, *Russia* . . . . . **58 B8** 60 55N 34 2 E
Podu Iloaiei, *Romania* . . . . **53 C12** 47 13N 27 16 E
Podu Turcului, *Romania* . . . . **53 D12** 46 11N 27 25 E
Podujevo, *Kosovo, Yug.* . . . . **50 D5** 42 54N 21 10 E
Poechos, *Peru* . . . . . **168 D1** 4 41 S 80 34W
Poel, *Germany* . . . . . **30 B6** 54 0N 11 25 E
Pofadder, *S. Africa* . . . . . **116 D2** 29 10 S 19 22 E
Poggiardo, *Italy* . . . . . **47 B11** 40 3N 18 23 E
Poggibonsi, *Italy* . . . . . **44 E8** 43 28N 11 9 E
Póggio Mirteto, *Italy* . . . . **45 F9** 42 16N 12 41 E
Pogoanele, *Romania* . . . . . **53 F12** 44 55N 27 0 E
Pogorzela, *Poland* . . . . . **55 G4** 51 50N 17 12 E
Pogoso,
Dem. Rep. of the Congo . . . . **115 D3** 6 46 S 17 12 E
Pogradeci, *Albania* . . . . . **50 F4** 40 54N 20 37 E
Pogranitšnyi, *Russia* . . . . . **68 B5** 44 25N 131 24 E
Poh, *Indonesia* . . . . . **79 E6** 0 46 S 122 51 E
P'ohang, *S. Korea* . . . . . **75 F15** 36 1N 129 23 E
Pohjanmaa, *Finland* . . . . . **14 E20** 62 58N 22 50 E
Pohnpei, *Micronesia* . . . . . **134 G7** 6 55N 158 10 E
Pohorelá, *Slovak Rep.* . . . . **35 C13** 48 50N 20 2 E
Pohořelice, *Czech Rep.* . . . . **35 C9** 48 59N 16 31 E
Pohorje, *Slovenia* . . . . . **45 B12** 46 30N 15 20 E
Pohri, *India* . . . . . **92 G6** 25 32N 77 22 E
Pohue B., *U.S.A.* **145 E6** 19 0N 155 48W
Poiana Mare, *Romania* . . . . **52 G8** 43 57N 23 5 E
Poiana Ruscăi, Munţii,
Romania . . . . . **52 E7** 45 45N 22 25 E
Poiana Stampei, *Romania* . . . **53 C10** 47 19N 25 8 E
Poindimié, *N. Cal.* . . . . . **133 T19** 20 56 S 165 20 E
Poinsett, C., *Antarctica* . . . . **7 C8** 65 42 S 113 18 E
Point Arena, *U.S.A.* **160 G3** 38 55N 123 41W
Point Baker, *U.S.A.* **142 B2** 56 21N 133 37W
Point Calimere, *India* . . . . . **95 J4** 10 17N 79 49 E
Point Edward, *Canada* **140 D3** 43 0N 82 30W
Point Hope, *U.S.A.* **138 B3** 68 21N 166 47W
Point L., *Canada* **138 B8** 65 15N 113 4W
Point Pass, *Australia* . . . . . **128 C3** 34 5 S 139 5 E
Point Pedro, *Sri Lanka* . . . . **95 K5** 9 50N 80 15 E
Point Pleasant, *N.J., U.S.A.* . . **151 F10** 40 5N 74 4W
Point Pleasant, *W. Va., U.S.A.* . **148 F4** 38 51N 82 8W
Pointe-à-Pitre, *Guadeloupe* . . . **165 C7** 16 10N 61 30W
Pointe-Claire, *Canada* **151 A11** 45 26N 73 50W
Pointe-Gatineau, *Canada* **151 A9** 45 28N 75 42W
Pointe-Noire, *Congo* . . . . . **115 C2** 4 48 S 11 53 E
Poio, *Spain* **42 C2** 42 28N 8 41W
Poirino, *Italy* . . . . . **44 D4** 44 56N 7 48 E
Poisonbush Ra., *Australia* . . . **124 D3** 22 30 S 121 30 E
Poissonnier Pt., *Australia* . . . **124 C2** 19 57 S 119 10 E
Poitiers, *France* . . . . . **26 F7** 46 35N 0 20 E
Poitou, *France* **28 B3** 46 40N 0 10W
Poitou-Charentes □, *France* . . **28 B4** 46 10N 0 15 E
Poix-de-Picardie, *France* . . . . **27 C8** 49 47N 1 58 E
Poix-Terron, *France* . . . . . **27 C11** 49 38N 4 38 E
Pojoaque, *U.S.A.* **159 J11** 35 54N 106 1W
Pokai B., *U.S.A.* **145 K13** 21 27N 158 12W
Pokataroo, *Australia* . . . . . **127 D4** 29 30 S 148 36 E
Pokhara, *Nepal* . . . . . **93 E10** 28 14N 83 58 E
Pokhvistnevo, *Russia* . . . . . **60 D11** 53 36N 52 0 E
Pokigron, *Surinam* **169 C6** 4 30N 55 22W
Poko, *Dem. Rep. of the Congo* . **118 B2** 3 7N 26 52 E
Poko, *Sudan* . . . . . **107 F3** 5 41N 31 55 E
Pokrov, *Russia* . . . . . **58 E10** 55 55N 39 7 E
Pokrovka, *Kyrgyzstan* . . . . . **63 B9** 42 20N 78 0 E
Pokrovsk = Engels, *Russia* . . . **60 E8** 51 28N 46 6 E
Pokrovsk, *Russia* . . . . . **65 C13** 61 29N 129 0 E
Pokrovsk-Uralskiy, *Russia* . . . **62 A7** 60 10N 59 49 E
Pokrovskoye, *Russia* . . . . . **59 J10** 47 25N 38 54 E
Pola = Pula, *Croatia* . . . . . **45 D10** 44 54N 13 57 E
Pola, *Russia* . . . . . **58 D7** 57 55N 32 0 E
Pola de Allande, *Spain* **42 B4** 43 16N 6 37W
Pola de Lena, *Spain* **42 B5** 43 10N 5 49W
Pola de Siero, *Spain* **42 B5** 43 24N 5 39W
Pola de Somiedo, *Spain* **42 B4** 43 5N 6 15W
Polacca, *U.S.A.* **159 J8** 35 50N 110 23W
Polan, *Iran* . . . . . **97 E9** 25 30N 61 10 E
Poland ■, *Europe* . . . . . **55 G3** 52 0N 20 0 E
Polanica-Zdrój, *Poland* . . . . **55 H3** 50 24N 16 32 E
Połaniec, *Poland* . . . . . **55 H8** 50 26N 21 17 E
Polanów, *Poland* . . . . . **54 D3** 54 7N 16 41 E
Polar Bear Prov. Park, *Canada* . **140 A2** 55 0N 83 45W
Polatlı, *Turkey* . . . . . **100 C5** 39 36N 32 9 E
Polatsk, *Belarus* . . . . . **58 E5** 55 30N 28 50 E
Polavaram, *India* . . . . . **94 F5** 17 15N 81 38 E
Polcura, *Chile* . . . . . **174 D1** 37 17 S 71 43W
Połczyn-Zdrój, *Poland* . . . . . **54 E3** 53 47N 16 5 E
Polessk, *Russia* . . . . . **15 J19** 54 50N 21 8 E
Polesye = Pripet Marshes,
Europe . . . . . **59 F5** 52 10N 28 10 E
Polevskoy, *Russia* . . . . . **62 C8** 56 26N 60 11 E
Polgar, *Hungary* . . . . . **52 C6** 47 54N 21 6 E
Pŏlgyo-ri, *S. Korea* . . . . . **75 G14** 34 51N 127 21 E
Poli, *Cameroon* . . . . . **114 A2** 8 34N 13 15 E
Políaigos, *Greece* . . . . . **48 E6** 36 45N 24 38 E
Policastro, G. di, *Italy* . . . . **47 C8** 40 0N 15 35 E
Police, *Poland* . . . . . **54 E1** 53 33N 14 33 E
Polička, *Czech Rep.* . . . . . **35 B9** 49 43N 16 15 E
Policoro, *Italy* . . . . . **47 B9** 40 13N 16 41 E
Polignano a Mare, *Italy* . . . . **47 A9** 41 0N 17 13 E
Poligny, *France* . . . . . **27 F12** 46 50N 5 42 E
Políkhnitas, *Greece* . . . . . **49 B8** 39 6N 26 10 E
Polillo, *Phil.* . . . . . **80 D3** 14 43N 121 56 E
Polillo Is., *Phil.* . . . . . **79 B6** 14 56N 122 0 E
Polillo Strait, *Phil.* . . . . . **80 D3** 14 44N 121 51 E
Polis, *Cyprus* . . . . . **38 D11** 35 2N 32 26 E
Polístena, *Italy* . . . . . **47 D9** 38 24N 16 4 E
Políyiros, *Greece* . . . . . **50 F7** 40 23N 23 25 E
Polk, *U.S.A.* **150 E5** 41 22N 79 56W
Polkowice, *Poland* . . . . . **55 G3** 51 29N 16 3 E
Polla, *Italy* . . . . . **47 B8** 40 31N 15 29 E
Pollachi, *India* . . . . . **95 J3** 10 35N 77 0 E
Pollença, *Spain* . . . . . **39 B10** 39 54N 3 1 E
Pollença, B. de, *Spain* . . . . . **39 B10** 39 53N 3 8 E
Pollfoss, *Norway* . . . . . **18 C4** 61 58N 7 54 E
Póllica, *Italy* . . . . . **47 B8** 40 11N 15 3 E
Pollino, Mte., *Italy* . . . . . **47 C9** 39 55N 16 11 E
Polna, *Russia* . . . . . **58 C5** 58 31N 28 5 E
Polnovat, *Russia* . . . . . **64 C7** 63 50N 65 54 E
Polo, *Ill., U.S.A.* **156 C7** 41 59N 89 35W
Polo, *Mo., U.S.A.* **156 E2** 39 33N 94 3W
Pology, *Ukraine* . . . . . **59 J9** 47 29N 36 15 E
Polonnaruwa, *Sri Lanka* . . . . **95 L5** 7 56N 81 0 E
Polonne, *Ukraine* . . . . . **59 G4** 50 6N 27 30 E
Polonnoye = Polonne, *Ukraine* . **59 G4** 50 6N 27 30 E
Polski Trŭmbesh, *Bulgaria* . . . **51 C9** 43 20N 25 38 E
Polsko Kosovo, *Bulgaria* . . . . **51 C9** 43 23N 25 38 E
Polson, *U.S.A.* **158 C6** 47 41N 114 9W
Poltár, *Slovak Rep.* . . . . . **35 C12** 48 26N 19 48 E
Poltava, *Ukraine* . . . . . **59 H8** 49 35N 34 35 E
Põltsamaa, *Estonia* . . . . . **15 G21** 58 41N 25 58 E
Polunochnoye, *Russia* . . . . . **64 C7** 60 52N 60 25 E
Polur, *India* . . . . . **95 H4** 12 32N 79 11 E
Põlva, *Estonia* . . . . . **15 G22** 58 3N 27 3 E
Polyarny, *Russia* . . . . . **56 A5** 69 8N 33 20 E
Polynesia, *Pac. Oc.* . . . . . **135 J11** 10 0 S 162 0W
Polynésie française = French
Polynesia ■, *Pac. Oc.* . . . . **135 K13** 20 0 S 145 0W
Pomabamba, *Peru* . . . . . **172 B2** 8 50 S 77 28W
Pomarance, *Italy* . . . . . **44 E7** 43 18N 10 52 E
Pomaro, *Mexico* **162 D4** 18 20N 103 18W
Pombal, *Brazil* . . . . . **170 C4** 6 45 S 37 50W
Pombal, *Portugal* **42 F2** 39 55N 8 40W
Pómbia, *Greece* . . . . . **38 E6** 35 0N 24 51 E
Pombos, B. dos, *Angola* . . . . **115 E2** 11 40 S 13 47 E
Pomene, *Mozam.* . . . . . **117 C6** 22 53 S 35 33 E
Pomeroy, *Ohio, U.S.A.* **148 F4** 39 2N 82 2W
Pomeroy, *Wash., U.S.A.* **158 C5** 46 28N 117 36W
Pomézia, *Italy* . . . . . **46 A5** 41 40N 12 30 E
Pomichna, *Ukraine* . . . . . **59 H6** 48 13N 31 36 E
Pomio, *Papua N. G.* . . . . . **132 C6** 5 32 S 151 33 E
Pomme de Terre L., *U.S.A.* . . **156 G3** 37 54N 93 19W
Pomona, *Australia* . . . . . **127 D5** 26 22 S 152 52 E
Pomona, *U.S.A.* **161 L9** 34 4N 117 45W
Pomona Park, *U.S.A.* **153 F8** 29 30N 81 36W
Pomorie, *Bulgaria* . . . . . **51 D11** 42 32N 27 41 E
Pomorskie □, *Poland* . . . . . **54 D5** 54 30N 18 0 E
Pomorskie, Pojezierze, *Poland* . **54 E3** 53 40N 16 37 E
Pomos, *Cyprus* . . . . . **38 D11** 35 9N 32 33 E
Pomos, C., *Cyprus* . . . . . **38 D11** 35 10N 32 33 E
Pompano Beach, *U.S.A.* **149 M5** 26 14N 80 8W
Pompei, *Italy* . . . . . **47 B7** 40 45N 14 30 E
Pompey, *France* . . . . . **27 D13** 48 46N 6 6 E
Pompeys Pillar, *U.S.A.* **158 D10** 45 59N 107 57W
Pompton Lakes, *U.S.A.* **151 F10** 41 0N 74 17W
Ponape = Pohnpei, *Micronesia* . **134 G7** 6 55N 158 10 E
Ponask L., *Canada* **140 B1** 54 0N 92 41W
Ponca, *U.S.A.* **154 D6** 42 34N 96 43W
Ponca City, *U.S.A.* **155 G6** 36 42N 97 5W
Ponce, *Puerto Rico* **165 C6** 18 1N 66 37W
Ponce de Leon, *U.S.A.* **152 E4** 30 44N 85 56W
Ponce de Leon B., *U.S.A.* **153 K8** 25 15N 81 10W
Ponchatoula, *U.S.A.* **155 K9** 30 26N 90 26W
Poncheville, L., *Canada* **140 B4** 50 10N 76 55W
Pond, *U.S.A.* **161 K7** 35 43N 119 20W
Pond Inlet, *Canada* **139 A12** 72 40N 77 0W
Pondicherry, *India* . . . . . **95 J4** 11 59N 79 50 E
Pondooma, *Australia* . . . . . **128 B2** 33 29 S 136 59 E
Ponds, I. of, *Canada* **141 B8** 53 27N 55 52W
Ponérihouen, *N. Cal.* . . . . . **133 U19** 21 5 S 165 24 E
Ponferrada, *Spain* **42 C4** 42 32N 6 35W
Pongo, Wadi ⟶, *Sudan* . . . . **107 F2** 8 42N 27 40 E
Poniatowa, *Poland* . . . . . **55 G9** 51 11N 22 3 E
Poniec, *Poland* . . . . . **55 G3** 51 48N 16 50 E
Ponikva, *Slovenia* . . . . . **45 B12** 46 16N 15 26 E
Ponnaiyar ⟶, *India* . . . . . **95 J4** 11 50N 79 45 E
Ponnani, *India* . . . . . **95 J2** 10 45N 75 59 E
Ponneri, *India* . . . . . **95 H5** 13 20N 80 15 E
Ponnuru, *India* . . . . . **95 F5** 16 5N 80 34 E
Ponoka, *Canada* **142 C6** 52 42N 113 40W
Ponomarevka, *Russia* . . . . . **62 E5** 53 19N 54 8 E
Ponorogo, *Indonesia* . . . . . **79 G14** 7 52 S 111 27 E
Ponot, *Phil.* . . . . . **81 G4** 8 25N 123 0 E
Ponoy, *Russia* . . . . . **56 A7** 67 0N 41 13 E
Ponoy ⟶, *Russia* . . . . . **56 A7** 66 59N 41 17 E
Pons = Ponts, *Spain* . . . . . **40 D6** 41 55N 1 12 E
Pons, *France* **28 C3** 45 35N 0 34W
Ponsul ⟶, *Portugal* **42 F3** 39 40N 7 31W
Pont-à-Mousson, *France* . . . . **27 D13** 48 54N 6 1 E
Pont-Audemer, *France* . . . . . **26 C7** 49 21N 0 30 E
Pont-Aven, *France* **26 E3** 47 51N 3 47W
Pont Canavese, *Italy* . . . . . **44 C4** 45 25N 7 36 E
Pont-d'Ain, *France* . . . . . **27 F12** 46 3N 5 21 E
Pont-de-Roide, *France* . . . . . **27 E13** 47 23N 6 45 E
Pont-de-Salars, *France* . . . . . **28 D6** 44 18N 2 44 E
Pont-de-Vaux, *France* . . . . . **27 F11** 46 26N 4 56 E
Pont-de-Veyle, *France* . . . . . **27 F11** 46 17N 4 53 E
Pont-du-Château, *France* . . . . **27 G10** 45 47N 3 15 E
Pont-l'Abbé, *France* **26 E2** 47 52N 4 15W
Pont-l'Évêque, *France* . . . . . **26 C7** 49 18N 0 11 E
Pont-St-Esprit, *France* . . . . . **29 D8** 44 16N 4 40 E
Pont-St-Martin, *Italy* . . . . . **44 C4** 45 36N 7 48 E
Pont-Ste-Maxence, *France* . . . **27 C9** 49 18N 2 35 E
Pont-sur-Yonne, *France* . . . . **27 D10** 48 18N 3 10 E
Ponta de Pedras, *Brazil* . . . . **170 B2** 1 23 S 48 52W
Ponta Delgada, *Azores* **8 E6** 37 44N 25 40W
Ponta do Sol, *Madeira* **39 D2** 32 42N 17 7W
Ponta Grossa, *Brazil* . . . . . **175 B5** 25 7 S 50 10W
Ponta Pora, *Brazil* . . . . . **175 A4** 22 20 S 55 35W
Pontacq, *France* **28 E3** 43 11N 0 8W
Pontailler-sur-Saône, *France* . . **27 E12** 47 13N 5 25 E
Pontal ⟶, *Brazil* . . . . . **170 C3** 9 8 S 40 12W
Pontalina, *Brazil* . . . . . **171 E2** 17 31 S 49 27W
Pontarlier, *France* . . . . . **27 F13** 46 54N 6 20 E
Pontassieve, *Italy* . . . . . **45 E8** 43 46N 11 26 E
Pontaumur, *France* . . . . . **28 C6** 45 52N 2 40 E
Pontcharra, *France* . . . . . **29 C10** 45 26N 6 1 E
Pontchartrain L., *U.S.A.* **155 K10** 30 5N 90 5W
Pontchâteau, *France* **26 E4** 47 25N 2 5W
Ponte Alta, Serra do, *Brazil* . . **171 E2** 19 42 S 47 40W
Ponte Alta do Norte, *Brazil* . . **170 D2** 10 45 S 47 34W
Ponte Branca, *Brazil* . . . . . **173 D7** 16 27 S 52 40W
Ponte da Barca, *Portugal* **42 D2** 41 48N 8 25W
Ponte de Sor, *Portugal* **43 F2** 39 17N 8 1W
Ponte dell'Ólio, *Italy* . . . . . **44 D6** 44 52N 9 39 E
Ponte di Legno, *Italy* . . . . . **44 B7** 46 16N 10 31 E
Ponte do Lima, *Portugal* **42 D2** 41 46N 8 35W
Ponte do Pungué, *Mozam.* . . . . **119 F3** 19 30 S 34 33 E
Ponte-Leccia, *France* . . . . . **29 F13** 42 28N 9 13 E
Ponte nelle Alpi, *Italy* . . . . . **45 B9** 46 11N 12 16 E
Ponte Nova, *Brazil* . . . . . **171 F3** 20 25 S 42 54W
Ponte Tresa, *Italy* . . . . . **33 E7** 45 58N 8 51 E
Ponte Vedra Beach, *U.S.A.* . . . **152 E8** 30 15N 81 23W
Ponteareas, *Spain* **42 C2** 42 10N 8 28W
Pontebba, *Italy* . . . . . **45 B10** 46 30N 13 18 E
Ponteceso, *Spain* **42 B2** 43 15N 8 54W
Pontecorvo, *Italy* . . . . . **46 A6** 41 27N 13 40 E
Pontedeume, *Spain* **42 B2** 43 24N 8 10W
Ponteix, *Canada* **143 D7** 49 46N 107 29W
Pontes e Lacerda, *Brazil* . . . . **173 D6** 15 12 S 59 22W
Pontevedra, *Capiz, Phil.* . . . . **81 F4** 11 29N 122 50 E
Pontevedra, *Neg. Occ., Phil.* . . **81 F4** 10 22N 122 52 E
Pontevedra, *Spain* **42 C2** 42 26N 8 40W
Pontevedra □, *Spain* **42 C2** 42 25N 8 39W
Pontevedra, R. de ⟶, *Spain* . **42 C2** 42 22N 8 45W
Pontevico, *Italy* . . . . . **44 C7** 45 16N 10 5 E
Pontiac, *Ill., U.S.A.* **154 E10** 40 53N 88 38W
Pontiac, *Mich., U.S.A.* **157 B13** 42 38N 83 18W
Pontian Kecil, *Malaysia* . . . . **87 M4** 1 29N 103 23 E
Pontianak, *Indonesia* . . . . . **78 E3** 0 3 S 109 15 E
Pontine Is. = Ponziane, Ísole,
Italy . . . . . **46 B5** 40 55N 12 57 E
Pontine Mts. = Kuzey Anadolu
Dağları, *Turkey* . . . . . **100 B7** 41 30N 35 0 E
Pontínia, *Italy* . . . . . **46 A6** 41 25N 13 2 E
Pontivy, *France* **26 D4** 48 5N 2 58W
Pontoise, *France* . . . . . **27 C9** 49 3N 2 5 E
Ponton ⟶, *Canada* **142 B5** 58 27N 116 11W
Pontorson, *France* **26 D5** 48 34N 1 30W
Pontrémoli, *Italy* . . . . . **44 D6** 44 22N 9 53 E
Pontresina, *Switz.* . . . . . **33 D9** 46 29N 9 48 E
Pontrieux, *France* **26 D3** 48 42N 3 10W
Ponts, *Spain* . . . . . **40 D6** 41 55N 1 12 E
Pontypool, *Canada* **150 B6** 44 6N 78 38W
Pontypool, *U.K.* **21 F4** 51 42N 3 2W
Ponza, *Italy* . . . . . **46 B5** 40 54N 12 58 E
Ponziane, Ísole, *Italy* . . . . . **46 B5** 40 55N 12 57 E
Poochera, *Australia* . . . . . **127 E1** 32 43 S 134 51 E
Poole, *U.K.* **21 G6** 50 43N 1 59W
Poole □, *U.K.* **21 G6** 50 43N 1 59W
Pooler, *U.S.A.* **152 C8** 32 7N 81 15W
Poona = Pune, *India* . . . . . **94 E1** 18 29N 73 57 E
Poonamallee, *India* . . . . . **95 H5** 13 3N 80 10 E
Pooncarie, *Australia* . . . . . **128 B5** 33 22 S 142 31 E
Poonindie, *Australia* . . . . . **128 C1** 34 34 S 135 54 E
Poopelloe L., *Australia* . . . . **128 A5** 31 40 S 144 0 E
Poopó, *Bolivia* . . . . . **172 D4** 18 23 S 66 59W
Poopó, L. de, *Bolivia* . . . . . **172 D4** 18 30 S 67 35W
Poor Knights Is., *N.Z.* . . . . . **130 B3** 35 29 S 174 43 E
Popa, *Gabon* . . . . . **114 C2** 1 35 S 12 32 E
Popayán, *Colombia* **168 C2** 2 27N 76 36W
Poperinge, *Belgium* . . . . . **24 D2** 50 51N 2 42 E
Popilta L., *Australia* . . . . . **128 B4** 33 10 S 141 42 E
Popina, *Bulgaria* . . . . . **51 B10** 44 7N 26 57 E
Popio L., *Australia* . . . . . **128 B4** 33 10 S 141 52 E
Poplar, *U.S.A.* **154 A2** 48 7N 105 12W
Poplar ⟶, *Canada* **143 C9** 53 0N 97 19W
Poplar Bluff, *U.S.A.* **155 G9** 36 46N 90 24W
Poplarville, *U.S.A.* **155 K10** 30 51N 89 32W
Popocatépetl, Volcán, *Mexico* . **163 D5** 19 2N 98 38W
Popokabaka,
Dem. Rep. of the Congo . . . . **115 D3** 5 41 S 16 40 E
Pópoli, *Italy* . . . . . **45 F10** 42 10N 13 50 E
Popolo,
Dem. Rep. of the Congo . . . . **114 B4** 2 22N 21 8 E
Popondetta, *Papua N. G.* . . . . **132 E5** 8 48 S 148 17 E
Popovača, *Croatia* . . . . . **45 C13** 45 30N 16 41 E
Popovo, *Bulgaria* . . . . . **51 C10** 43 21N 26 18 E
Poppberg, *Germany* . . . . . **31 F7** 49 26N 11 37 E
Poppi, *Italy* . . . . . **45 E8** 43 43N 11 46 E
Poprad, *Slovak Rep.* . . . . . **35 B13** 49 3N 20 18 E
Poprad ⟶, *Slovak Rep.* . . . . **35 B13** 49 38N 20 42 E
Poradaha, *Bangla.* . . . . . **90 D2** 23 51N 89 1 E
Porali ⟶, *Pakistan* . . . . . **91 D2** 25 58N 66 26 E
Porangaba, *Brazil* . . . . . **172 B3** 8 48 S 70 36W
Porangahau, *N.Z.* . . . . . **130 G5** 40 17 S 176 37 E
Porangatu, *Brazil* . . . . . **171 D2** 13 26 S 49 10W
Porce ⟶, *Colombia* **168 B3** 7 28N 74 53W
Porcher I., *Canada* **142 C2** 53 50N 130 30W
Porco, *Bolivia* . . . . . **173 D4** 19 50 S 65 59W
Porcos ⟶, *Brazil* . . . . . **171 D2** 12 42 S 45 7W
Porcuna, *Spain* **43 H6** 37 52N 4 11W
Porcupine ⟶, *Canada* **143 B8** 59 11N 104 46W
Porcupine ⟶, *U.S.A.* **138 B5** 66 34N 145 19W
Pordenone, *Italy* . . . . . **45 C9** 45 57N 12 39 E
Pordim, *Bulgaria* . . . . . **51 C8** 43 23N 24 51 E
Pore, *Colombia* **168 B3** 5 43N 72 0W
Poreč, *Croatia* . . . . . **45 C10** 45 14N 13 36 E
Porecatu, *Brazil* . . . . . **171 F1** 22 43 S 51 24W
Poretskoye, *Russia* . . . . . **60 C8** 55 9N 46 21 E
Pori, *Finland* . . . . . **15 F19** 61 29N 21 48 E
Porí, *Greece* . . . . . **48 F5** 35 58N 23 13 E
Porkhov, *Russia* . . . . . **58 D5** 57 45N 29 38 E
Porlamar, *Venezuela* **169 A5** 10 57N 63 51W
Porlezza, *Italy* . . . . . **44 B6** 46 2N 9 7 E
Porma ⟶, *Spain* **42 C5** 42 49N 5 28W
Pornic, *France* **26 E4** 47 7N 2 5W
Poronaysk, *Russia* . . . . . **65 E15** 49 13N 143 0 E
Póros, *Greece* . . . . . **48 D5** 37 30N 23 30 E
Poroshiri-Dake, *Japan* . . . . . **68 C11** 42 41N 142 52 E
Poroszló, *Hungary* . . . . . **52 C5** 47 39N 20 40 E
Poroto Mts., *Tanzania* . . . . . **119 D3** 9 0 S 33 30 E
Porpoise B., *Antarctica* . . . . **7 C9** 66 0 S 127 0 E
Porquerolles, Î. de, *France* . . . **29 F10** 43 0N 6 13 E
Porrentruy, *Switz.* . . . . . **32 B4** 47 25N 7 6 E
Porreres, *Spain* . . . . . **39 B10** 39 31N 3 2 E
Porsangen, *Norway* . . . . . **14 A21** 70 40N 25 40 E
Porsgrunn, *Norway* . . . . . **15 G13** 59 10N 9 40 E
Port Adelaide, *Australia* . . . . **128 C3** 34 46 S 138 30 E
Port Alberni, *Canada* **142 D4** 49 14N 124 50W
Port Albert, *Australia* . . . . . **129 E7** 38 42 S 146 42 E
Port Alfred, *S. Africa* . . . . . **116 E4** 33 36 S 26 55 E
Port Alice, *Canada* **142 C3** 50 20N 127 25W
Port Allegany, *U.S.A.* **150 E6** 41 48N 78 17W
Port Allen, *U.S.A.* **155 K9** 30 27N 91 12W
Port Alma, *Australia* . . . . . **126 C5** 23 38 S 150 53 E
Port Angeles, *U.S.A.* **160 B3** 48 7N 123 27W
Port Antonio, *Jamaica* **164 C4** 18 10N 76 30W
Port Aransas, *U.S.A.* **155 M6** 27 50N 97 4W
Port Arthur = Lüshun, *China* . . **75 E11** 38 45N 121 15 E
Port Arthur, *Australia* . . . . . **126 G4** 43 7 S 147 50 E
Port Arthur, *U.S.A.* **155 L8** 29 54N 93 56W
Port au Choix, *Canada* **141 B8** 50 43N 57 22W
Port au Port B., *Canada* **141 C8** 48 40N 58 50W
Port-au-Prince, *Haiti* **165 C5** 18 40N 72 20W
Port Augusta, *Australia* . . . . **128 B2** 32 30 S 137 50 E
Port Augusta West, *Australia* . **128 B2** 32 29 S 137 29 E
Port Austin, *U.S.A.* **150 B2** 44 3N 83 1W
Port Bell, *Uganda* . . . . . **118 B3** 0 18N 32 35 E
Port Bergé Vaovao, *Madag.* . . . **117 B8** 15 33 S 47 40 E
Port Blandford, *Canada* **141 C9** 48 20N 54 10W
Port-Bouët, *Ivory C.* **112 D4** 5 16N 3 57W
Port Bradshaw, *Australia* . . . . **126 A2** 12 30 S 137 20 E
Port Broughton, *Australia* . . . **128 B2** 33 37 S 137 56 E
Port Burwell, *Canada* **150 D4** 42 40N 80 48W
Port Byron, *U.S.A.* **156 C6** 41 37N 90 19W
Port Campbell, *Australia* . . . . **128 E5** 38 37 S 143 1 E
Port Canning, *India* . . . . . **93 H13** 22 23N 88 40 E
Port-Cartier, *Canada* **141 B6** 50 2N 66 50W
Port Chalmers, *N.Z.* . . . . . **131 F5** 45 49 S 170 30 E
Port Charles, *N.Z.* . . . . . **130 C4** 36 33 S 175 30 E
Port Charlotte, *U.S.A.* **153 J7** 26 59N 82 6W
Port Chester, *U.S.A.* **151 F11** 41 0N 73 40W
Port Clements, *Canada* **142 C2** 53 40N 132 10W
Port Clinton, *U.S.A.* **157 C14** 41 31N 82 56W
Port Colborne, *Canada* **140 D4** 42 50N 79 10W
Port Coquitlam, *Canada* **142 D4** 49 15N 122 45W
Port Credit, *Canada* **150 C5** 43 33N 79 35W
Port Curtis, *Australia* . . . . . **126 C5** 23 57 S 151 20 E
Port d'Alcúdia, *Spain* . . . . . **39 B10** 39 50N 3 7 E
Port Dalhousie, *Canada* **150 C5** 43 13N 79 16W
Port Darwin, *Australia* . . . . . **124 B5** 12 24 S 130 45 E
Port Darwin, *Falk. Is.* . . . . . **176 D5** 51 50 S 59 0W
Port Davey, *Australia* . . . . . **126 G4** 43 16 S 145 55 E
Port-de-Bouc, *France* . . . . . **29 E8** 43 24N 4 59 E
Port-de-Paix, *Haiti* **165 C5** 19 50N 72 50W
Port de Pollença, *Spain* . . . . **39 B10** 39 54N 3 4 E
Port de Sóller, *Spain* . . . . . **39 B9** 39 48N 2 42 E
Port Dickson, *Malaysia* . . . . . **78 D2** 2 30N 101 49 E
Port Douglas, *Australia* . . . . **126 B4** 16 30 S 145 30 E
Port Dover, *Canada* **150 D4** 42 47N 80 12W
Port Edward, *Canada* **142 C2** 54 12N 130 10W
Port Elgin, *Canada* **140 D3** 44 25N 81 25W
Port Elizabeth, *S. Africa* . . . . **116 E4** 33 58 S 25 40 E
Port Ellen, *U.K.* **22 F2** 55 38N 6 11W
Port-en-Bessin, *France* **26 C6** 49 21N 0 45W
Port Erin, *U.K.* **20 C3** 54 5N 4 45W
Port Essington, *Australia* . . . . **124 B5** 11 15 S 132 10 E
Port Etienne = Nouâdhibou,
Mauritania **110 D1** 20 54N 17 0W
Port Ewen, *U.S.A.* **151 E11** 41 54N 73 59W
Port Fairy, *Australia* . . . . . **128 E5** 38 22 S 142 12 E
Port Fitzroy, *N.Z.* . . . . . **130 C4** 36 8 S 175 20 E
Port Fouâd = Bûr Fuad, *Egypt* . **106 H8** 31 15N 32 20 E
Port Gamble, *U.S.A.* **160 C4** 47 51N 122 35W
Port-Gentil, *Gabon* . . . . . **114 C1** 0 40 S 8 50 E
Port Germein, *Australia* . . . . **127 E2** 33 1 S 138 1 E
Port Gibson, *U.S.A.* **155 K9** 31 58N 90 59W
Port Glasgow, *U.K.* **22 F4** 55 56N 4 41W
Port Harcourt, *Nigeria* . . . . . **113 E6** 4 40N 7 10 E
Port Hardy, *Canada* **142 C3** 50 41N 127 30W
Port Harrison = Inukjuak,
Canada **139 C12** 58 25N 78 15W
Port Hawkesbury, *Canada* **141 C7** 45 36N 61 22W
Port Hedland, *Australia* . . . . **124 D2** 20 25 S 118 35 E
Port Henry, *U.S.A.* **151 B11** 44 3N 73 28W
Port Hood, *Canada* **141 C7** 46 0N 61 32W
Port Hope, *Canada* **140 D4** 43 56N 78 20W
Port Hope, *U.S.A.* **150 C2** 43 57N 82 43W
Port Hope Simpson, *Canada* . . **141 B8** 52 33N 56 18W
Port Hueneme, *U.S.A.* **161 L7** 34 7N 119 12W
Port Huron, *U.S.A.* **150 D2** 42 58N 82 26W
Port Iliç, *Azerbaijan* . . . . . **101 C13** 38 53N 48 47 E
Port Jefferson, *U.S.A.* **151 F11** 40 57N 73 3W
Port Jervis, *U.S.A.* **151 E10** 41 22N 74 41W
Port-Joinville, *France* **26 F4** 46 45N 2 23W
Port Katon, *Russia* . . . . . **59 J10** 46 52N 38 46 E
Port Kelang = Pelabuhan
Kelang, *Malaysia* . . . . . **78 D2** 3 0N 101 23 E
Port Kembla, *Australia* . . . . . **129 C9** 34 52 S 150 49 E
Port Kenny, *Australia* . . . . . **127 E1** 33 10 S 134 41 E
Port-la-Nouvelle, *France* . . . . **28 E7** 43 1N 3 3 E
Port Lairge = Waterford,
Ireland **23 D4** 52 15N 7 8W
Port Laoise, *Ireland* **23 C4** 53 2N 7 18W
Port Lavaca, *U.S.A.* **155 L6** 28 37N 96 38W
Port Leyden, *U.S.A.* **151 C9** 43 35N 75 21W
Port Lincoln, *Australia* . . . . . **128 C1** 34 42 S 135 52 E
Port Lions, *U.S.A.* **144 H9** 57 52N 152 53W
Port Loko, *S. Leone* **112 D2** 8 48N 12 46W
Port Louis, *France* **26 E3** 47 42N 3 22W
Port Louis, *Mauritius* . . . . . **105 H9** 20 10 S 57 30 E
Port Lyautey = Kenitra,
Morocco **110 B3** 34 15N 6 40W
Port MacDonnell, *Australia* . . . **128 E4** 38 5 S 140 48 E
Port McNeill, *Canada* **142 C3** 50 35N 127 6W
Port Macquarie, *Australia* . . . . **129 A10** 31 25 S 152 25 E
Port Maria, *Jamaica* **164 C4** 18 25N 76 55W
Port Matilda, *U.S.A.* **150 F6** 40 48N 78 3W
Port Mayaca, *U.S.A.* **153 J9** 26 59N 80 36W
Port Mellon, *Canada* **142 D4** 49 32N 123 31W
Port-Menier, *Canada* **141 C7** 49 51N 64 15W
Port Moller, *U.S.A.* **144 J7** 55 59N 160 34W
Port Moody, *Canada* **160 A4** 49 17N 122 51W
Port Morant, *Jamaica* **164 C4** 17 54N 76 19W
Port Moresby, *Papua N. G.* . . . **132 E4** 9 24 S 147 8 E
Port Mourant, *Guyana* **169 B6** 6 15N 57 20W
Port Musgrave, *Australia* . . . . **126 A3** 11 55 S 141 50 E
Port-Navalo, *France* **26 E4** 47 34N 2 54W
Port Neches, *U.S.A.* **155 L8** 30 0N 93 59W
Port Nicholson, *N.Z.* . . . . . **130 H3** 41 20 S 174 52 E
Port Nolloth, *S. Africa* . . . . . **116 D2** 29 17 S 16 52 E
Port Nouveau-Québec =
Kangiqsualujjuaq, *Canada* . . **139 C13** 58 30N 65 59W
Port of Spain, *Trin. & Tob.* . . . **165 D7** 10 40N 61 31W
Port Orange, *U.S.A.* **153 F9** 29 9N 80 59W
Port Orchard, *U.S.A.* **160 C4** 47 32N 122 38W
Port Orford, *U.S.A.* **158 E1** 42 45N 124 30W
Port Pegasus, *N.Z.* . . . . . **131 H2** 47 12 S 167 41 E
Port Perry, *Canada* **140 D4** 44 6N 78 56W
Port Phillip B., *Australia* . . . . **127 F3** 38 10 S 144 50 E
Port Pirie, *Australia* . . . . . **128 B3** 33 10 S 138 1 E
Port Radium = Echo Bay,
Canada **138 B8** 66 5N 117 55W
Port Renfrew, *Canada* **142 D4** 48 30N 124 20W
Port Roper, *Australia* . . . . . **126 A2** 14 45 S 135 25 E
Port Rowan, *Canada* **150 D4** 42 40N 80 30W
Port Royal Sd., *U.S.A.* **152 C9** 32 15N 80 40W
Port Safaga = Bûr Safâga,
Egypt . . . . . **96 E2** 26 43N 33 57 E
Port Said = Bûr Sa'îd, *Egypt* . . **106 H8** 31 16N 32 18 E
Port St. Joe, *U.S.A.* **152 F4** 29 49N 85 18W
Port St. Johns = Umzimvubu,
S. Africa . . . . . **117 E4** 31 38 S 29 33 E
Port-St-Louis-du-Rhône, *France* **29 E8** 43 23N 4 49 E
Port St. Lucie, *U.S.A.* **149 M5** 27 20N 80 20W
Port-Ste-Marie, *France* . . . . . **28 D4** 44 15N 0 25 E
Port Salerno, *U.S.A.* **153 H9** 27 9N 80 12W
Port Sanilac, *U.S.A.* **150 C2** 43 26N 82 33W
Port Severn, *Canada* **150 B5** 44 48N 79 43W
Port Shepstone, *S. Africa* . . . . **117 E5** 30 44 S 30 28 E
Port Simpson, *Canada* **142 C2** 54 30N 130 20W
Port Stanley = Stanley,
Falk. Is. . . . . . **176 D5** 51 40 S 59 51W
Port Stanley, *Canada* **140 D3** 42 40N 81 10W
Port Sudan = Bûr Sûdân,
Sudan . . . . . **106 D4** 19 32N 37 9 E
Port Sulphur, *U.S.A.* **155 L10** 29 29N 89 42W
Port-sur-Saône, *France* . . . . . **27 E13** 47 42N 6 2 E
Port Talbot, *U.K.* **21 F4** 51 35N 3 47W
Port Taufiq = Bûr Taufiq,
Egypt . . . . . **106 J8** 29 54N 32 32 E
Port Townsend, *U.S.A.* **160 B4** 48 7N 122 45W
Port-Vendres, *France* . . . . . **28 F7** 42 32N 3 8 E
Port Victoria, *Australia* . . . . **128 C2** 34 30 S 137 29 E
Port Vila, *Vanuatu* . . . . . **134 J8** 17 45 S 168 18 E
Port Vladimir, *Russia* . . . . . **56 A5** 69 25N 33 6 E
Port Wakefield, *Australia* . . . . **128 C3** 34 12 S 138 10 E
Port Washington, *U.S.A.* **148 D2** 43 23N 87 53W
Port Weld = Kuala Sepetang,
Malaysia . . . . . **78 D2** 4 49N 100 28 E
Port Wentworth, *U.S.A.* **152 C8** 32 9N 81 10W
Portachuelo, *Bolivia* . . . . . **173 D5** 17 10 S 63 20W
Portadown, *U.K.* **23 B5** 54 25N 6 27W
Portaferry, *U.K.* **23 B6** 54 23N 5 33W
Portage, *Mich., U.S.A.* **157 B11** 42 12N 85 35W
Portage, *Pa., U.S.A.* **150 F6** 40 23N 78 41W
Portage, *Wis., U.S.A.* **154 D10** 43 33N 89 28W
Portage ⟶, *U.S.A.* **157 C14** 41 31N 83 5W
Portage La Prairie, *Canada* . . . **143 D9** 49 58N 98 18W
Portageville, *U.S.A.* **155 G10** 36 26N 89 42W
Portal, *U.S.A.* **152 C8** 32 33N 81 56W

268 Portalegre

Portalegre, *Portugal* **43 F3** 39 19N 7 25W
Portalegre □, *Portugal* **43 F3** 39 20N 7 40W
Portales, *U.S.A.* **155 H3** 34 11N 103 20W
Portarlington, *Ireland* **23 C4** 53 9N 7 14W
Portbou, *Spain* **40 C8** 42 25N 3 9 E
Porteira, *Brazil* **169 D6** 1 5 S 57 4W
Porteirinha, *Brazil* **171 E3** 15 44 S 43 2W
Portel, *Brazil* **170 B1** 1 57 S 50 49W
Portel, *Portugal* **43 G3** 38 19N 7 41W
Porter, *U.S.A.* **157 C9** 41 36N 87 4W
Porter L., *N.W.T., Canada* **143 A7** 61 41N 108 5W
Porter L., *Sask., Canada* **143 B7** 56 20N 107 20W
Porterville, *S. Africa* **116 E2** 33 0 S 19 0 E
Porterville, *U.S.A.* **160 J8** 36 4N 119 1W
Portes-lès-Valence, *France* **29 D8** 44 52N 4 54 E
Porthcawl, *U.K.* **21 F4** 51 29N 3 42W
Porthill, *U.S.A.* **158 B5** 48 59N 116 30W
Porthmadog, *U.K.* **20 E3** 52 55N 4 8W
Portile de Fier, *Europe* **52 F7** 44 44N 22 30 E
Portimão, *Portugal* **43 H2** 37 8N 8 32W
Portishead, *U.K.* **21 F5** 51 29N 2 46W
Portiţei, Gura, *Romania* **53 F14** 44 41N 29 0 E
Portknockie, *U.K.* **22 D6** 57 42N 2 51W
Portland, *N.S.W., Australia* **129 B8** 33 20 S 150 0 E
Portland, *Vic., Australia* **128 E4** 38 20 S 141 35 E
Portland, *Canada* **151 B8** 44 42N 76 12W
Portland, *Conn., U.S.A.* **151 E12** 41 34N 72 38W
Portland, *Fla., U.S.A.* **152 E3** 30 31N 86 12W
Portland, *Ind., U.S.A.* **157 D12** 40 26N 84 59W
Portland, *Maine, U.S.A.* **139 D12** 43 39N 70 16W
Portland, *Mich., U.S.A.* **157 B12** 42 52N 84 54W
Portland, *Oreg., U.S.A.* **160 E4** 45 32N 122 37W
Portland, *Pa., U.S.A.* **151 F9** 40 55N 75 6W
Portland, *Tex., U.S.A.* **155 M6** 27 53N 97 20W
Portland, I. of, *U.K.* **21 G5** 50 33N 2 26W
Portland B., *Australia* **128 E4** 38 15 S 141 45 E
Portland Bill, *U.K.* **21 G5** 50 31N 2 28W
Portland Canal, *U.S.A.* **142 B2** 55 56N 130 0W
Portland I., *N.Z.* **130 F6** 39 20 S 177 51 E
Portmadoc = Porthmadog, *U.K.* **20 E3** 52 55N 4 8W
Pôrto, *Brazil* **170 B3** 3 54 S 42 42W
Porto, *France* **29 F12** 42 16N 8 42 E
Porto, *Portugal* **42 D2** 41 8N 8 40W
Porto □, *Portugal* **42 D2** 41 8N 8 20W
Porto, G. de, *France* **29 F12** 42 17N 8 34 E
Pôrto Acre, *Brazil* **172 B4** 9 34 S 67 31W
Pôrto Alegre, *Pará, Brazil* **169 D7** 4 22 S 52 44W
Pôrto Alegre, *Rio Grande do S., Brazil* **175 C5** 30 5 S 51 10W
Porto Alegre, *São Tomé & Principe* **115 G6** 0 2N 6 32 E
Porto Amboim = Gunza, *Angola* **115 E2** 10 50 S 13 50 E
Porto Azzurro, *Italy* **44 F7** 42 46N 10 24 E
Pôrto Cajueiro, *Brazil* **173 C6** 11 3 S 55 53W
Porto Cristo, *Spain* **39 B10** 39 33N 3 20 E
Pôrto da Fôlha, *Brazil* **170 C4** 9 55 S 37 17W
Pôrto de Móz, *Brazil* **169 D7** 1 41 S 52 13W
Pôrto de Pedras, *Brazil* **170 C4** 9 10 S 35 17W
Pôrto des Meinacos, *Brazil* **173 C7** 12 33 S 53 7W
Porto dos Gaúchos, *Brazil* **173 C6** 11 32 S 57 16W
Porto Empédocle, *Italy* **46 E6** 37 17N 13 32 E
Pôrto Esperança, *Brazil* **173 D6** 19 37 S 57 29W
Pôrto Esperidão, *Brazil* **173 D6** 15 51 S 58 28W
Pôrto Franco, *Brazil* **170 C2** 6 20 S 47 24W
Pôrto Grande, *Brazil* **169 C7** 0 42N 51 24W
Pôrto Jofre, *Brazil* **173 D6** 17 20 S 56 48W
Pórto Lágos, *Greece* **51 E9** 41 1N 25 6 E
Porto Mendes, *Brazil* **175 A5** 24 30 S 54 15W
Porto Moniz, *Madeira* **39 D2** 32 52N 17 11W
Pôrto Murtinho, *Brazil* **173 E6** 21 45 S 57 55W
Pôrto Nacional, *Brazil* **170 D2** 10 40 S 48 30W
Porto-Novo, *Benin* **113 D5** 6 23N 2 42 E
Porto Petro, *Spain* **39 B10** 39 22N 3 13 E
Porto San Giórgio, *Italy* **45 E10** 43 11N 13 48 E
Porto Sant' Elpídio, *Italy* **45 E10** 43 15N 13 43 E
Pôrto Santana, *Brazil* **169 D7** 0 3 S 51 11W
Porto Santo Stéfano, *Italy* **44 F8** 42 26N 11 7 E
Pôrto São José, *Brazil* **175 A5** 22 43 S 53 10W
Pôrto Seguro, *Brazil* **171 E4** 16 26 S 39 5W
Porto Tolle, *Italy* **45 D9** 44 56N 12 22 E
Porto Tórres, *Italy* **46 B1** 40 50N 8 24 E
Pôrto União, *Brazil* **175 B5** 26 10 S 51 10W
Pôrto Válter, *Brazil* **172 B3** 8 15 S 72 40W
Porto-Vecchio, *France* **29 G13** 41 35N 9 16 E
Pôrto Velho, *Brazil* **173 B5** 8 46 S 63 54W
Portobelo, *Panama* **164 E4** 9 35N 79 42W
Portoferráio, *Italy* **44 F7** 42 48N 10 20 E
Portogruaro, *Italy* **45 C9** 45 47N 12 50 E
Portola, *U.S.A.* **160 F6** 39 49N 120 28W
Portomaggiore, *Italy* **45 D8** 44 42N 11 48 E
Portør, *Norway* **18 F6** 58 48N 9 28 E
Portoscuso, *Italy* **46 C1** 39 12N 8 24 E
Portovénere, *Italy* **44 D6** 44 3N 9 51 E
Portoviejo, *Ecuador* **168 D1** 1 7 S 80 28W
Portpatrick, *U.K.* **22 G3** 54 51N 5 7W
Portree, *U.K.* **22 D2** 57 25N 6 12W
Portrush, *U.K.* **23 A5** 55 12N 6 40W
Portsmouth, *Domin.* **165 C7** 15 34N 61 27W
Portsmouth, *U.K.* **21 G6** 50 48N 1 6W
Portsmouth, *N.H., U.S.A.* **149 D10** 43 5N 70 45W
Portsmouth, *Ohio, U.S.A.* **148 F4** 38 44N 82 57W
Portsmouth, *R.I., U.S.A.* **151 E13** 41 36N 71 15W
Portsmouth, *Va., U.S.A.* **148 G7** 36 50N 76 18W
Portsmouth □, *U.K.* **21 G6** 50 48N 1 6W
Portsoy, *U.K.* **22 D6** 57 41N 2 41W
Portstewart, *U.K.* **23 A5** 55 11N 6 43W
Porttipahtan tekojärvi, *Finland* **14 B22** 68 5N 26 40 E
Portugal ■, *Europe* **42 F3** 40 0N 8 0W
Portugalete, *Spain* **40 B1** 43 19N 3 4W
Portuguesa □, *Venezuela* **168 B4** 9 10N 69 15W
Portumna, *Ireland* **23 C3** 53 6N 8 14W
Portville, *U.S.A.* **150 D6** 42 3N 78 20W
Porvenir, *Bolivia* **172 C4** 11 10 S 68 50W
Porvenir, *Chile* **176 D2** 53 10 S 70 16W
Porvoo, *Finland* **15 F21** 60 24N 25 40 E
Porzuna, *Spain* **43 F6** 39 9N 4 9W
Posada, *Italy* **46 B2** 40 38N 9 43 E
Posada →, *Italy* **46 B2** 40 39N 9 45 E
Posadas, *Argentina* **175 B4** 27 30 S 55 50W
Posadas, *Spain* **43 H5** 37 47N 5 11W
Poschiavo, *Switz.* **33 D10** 46 19N 10 4 E
Posets, *Spain* **40 C5** 42 39N 0 25 E
Poseyville, *U.S.A.* **157 F9** 38 10N 87 47W
Poshan = Boshan, *China* **75 F9** 36 28N 117 49 E
Posht-e-Badam, *Iran* **97 C7** 33 2N 55 23 E
Posídhion, Ákra, *Greece* **50 G7** 39 57N 23 30 E
Posidium, *Greece* **49 F9** 35 30N 27 10 E
Poso, *Indonesia* **79 E6** 1 20 S 120 55 E
Poso, Danau, *Indonesia* **82 B2** 1 52 S 120 35 E
Posoegroenoe, *Surinam* **169 C6** 4 23N 55 43W
Posong, *S. Korea* **75 G14** 34 46N 127 5 E
Posse, *Brazil* **171 D2** 14 4 S 46 18W
Possel, *C.A.R.* **114 A3** 5 5N 19 10 E
Possession I., *Antarctica* **7 D11** 72 4 S 172 0 E
Pössneck, *Germany* **30 E7** 50 42N 11 35 E
Possum Kingdom L., *U.S.A.* **155 J5** 32 52N 98 26W
Post, *U.S.A.* **155 J4** 33 12N 101 23W
Post Falls, *U.S.A.* **158 C5** 47 43N 116 57W
Postavy = Pastavy, *Belarus* **15 J22** 55 4N 26 50 E
Poste-de-la-Baleine = Kuujjuarapik, *Canada* **140 A4** 55 20N 77 35W
Poste Maurice Cortier, *Algeria* **111 D5** 22 14N 1 2 E
Postmasburg, *S. Africa* **116 D3** 28 18 S 23 5 E
Postojna, *Slovenia* **45 C11** 45 46N 14 12 E
Poston, *U.S.A.* **161 M12** 34 0N 114 24W
Postville, *Canada* **141 B8** 54 54N 59 47W
Postville, *U.S.A.* **156 A5** 43 5N 91 34W
Potamós, *Andikíthira, Greece* **48 F5** 35 52N 23 15 E
Potamós, *Kíthira, Greece* **48 E4** 36 15N 22 58 E
Potchefstroom, *S. Africa* **116 D4** 26 41 S 27 7 E
Potcoava, *Romania* **53 F9** 44 30N 24 39 E
Poté, *Brazil* **171 E3** 17 49 S 41 49W
Poteau, *U.S.A.* **155 H7** 35 3N 94 37W
Poteet, *U.S.A.* **155 L5** 29 2N 98 35W
Potenza, *Italy* **47 B8** 40 38N 15 48 E
Potenza →, *Italy* **45 E10** 43 25N 13 40 E
Potenza Picena, *Italy* **45 E10** 43 22N 13 37 E
Poteriteri, L., *N.Z.* **131 G2** 46 5 S 167 10 E
Potgietersrus, *S. Africa* **117 C4** 24 10 S 28 55 E
Poti, *Georgia* **61 J5** 42 10N 41 38 E
Potiraguá, *Brazil* **171 E4** 15 36 S 39 53W
Potiskum, *Nigeria* **113 C7** 11 39N 11 2 E
Potlogi, *Romania* **53 F10** 44 34N 25 34 E
Potomac →, *U.S.A.* **148 G7** 38 0N 76 23W
Potosí, *Bolivia* **173 D4** 19 38 S 65 50W
Potosi, *U.S.A.* **156 G6** 37 56N 90 47W
Potosí □, *Bolivia* **172 E4** 20 31 S 67 0W
Potosi Mt., *U.S.A.* **161 K11** 35 57N 115 29W
Pototan, *Phil.* **79 B6** 10 54N 122 38 E
Potrerillos, *Chile* **174 B2** 26 30 S 69 30W
Potsdam, *Germany* **30 C9** 52 25N 13 4 E
Potsdam, *U.S.A.* **151 B10** 44 40N 74 59W
Pottangi, *India* **94 E6** 18 34N 82 58 E
Pottenstein, *Germany* **31 F7** 49 46N 11 24 E
Pottersville, *U.S.A.* **151 C11** 43 43N 73 50W
Pottery Hill = Abu Ballas, *Egypt* **106 C2** 24 26N 27 36 E
Pottstown, *U.S.A.* **151 F9** 40 15N 75 39W
Pottsville, *U.S.A.* **151 F8** 40 41N 76 12W
P'otzu, *Taiwan* **77 F13** 23 30N 120 25 E
Pouancé, *France* **26 E5** 47 44N 1 10W
Pouce Coupé, *Canada* **142 B4** 55 40N 120 10W
Pouembout, *N. Cal.* **133 U18** 21 8 S 164 53 E
Poughkeepsie, *U.S.A.* **151 E11** 41 42N 73 56W
Pouilly-sur-Loire, *France* **27 E9** 47 17N 2 57 E
Poulan, *U.S.A.* **152 D6** 31 31N 83 47W
Poulaphouca Res., *Ireland* **23 C5** 53 8N 6 30W
Poulsbo, *U.S.A.* **160 C4** 47 44N 122 39W
Poultney, *U.S.A.* **151 C11** 43 31N 73 14W
Poulton-le-Fylde, *U.K.* **20 D5** 53 51N 2 58W
Poum, *N. Cal.* **133 T18** 20 14 S 164 2 E
Pounga-Nganda, *Gabon* **114 C2** 2 58 S 10 51 E
Pouso Alegre, *Mato Grosso, Brazil* **173 C6** 11 46 S 57 16W
Pouso Alegre, *Minas Gerais, Brazil* **175 A6** 22 14 S 45 57W
Pout, *Senegal* **112 C1** 14 45N 17 0W
Pouthisat, *Cambodia* **78 B2** 12 34N 103 50 E
Pouzauges, *France* **26 F6** 46 47N 0 50W
Pova de Sta. Iria, *Portugal* **43 G1** 38 51N 9 4W
Považská Bystrica, *Slovak Rep.* **35 B11** 49 8N 18 27 E
Povenets, *Russia* **56 B5** 62 50N 34 50 E
Poverty B., *N.Z.* **130 E7** 38 43 S 178 2 E
Povlen, *Serbia, Yug.* **50 B3** 44 9N 19 44 E
Póvoa de Lanhosa, *Portugal* **42 D2** 41 33N 8 15W
Póvoa de Varzim, *Portugal* **42 D2** 41 25N 8 46W
Povorino, *Russia* **60 E6** 51 12N 42 5 E
Povungnituk = Puvirnituq, *Canada* **139 B12** 60 2N 77 10W
Powassan, *Canada* **140 C4** 46 5N 79 25W
Poway, *U.S.A.* **161 N9** 32 58N 117 2W
Powder →, *U.S.A.* **154 B2** 46 45N 105 26W
Powder River, *U.S.A.* **158 E10** 43 2N 106 59W
Powder Springs, *U.S.A.* **152 B5** 33 52N 84 41W
Powell, *U.S.A.* **158 D9** 44 45N 108 46W
Powell, L., *U.S.A.* **159 H8** 36 57N 111 29W
Powell River, *Canada* **142 D4** 49 50N 124 35W
Powelton, *U.S.A.* **152 B7** 33 26N 82 52W
Powers, *U.S.A.* **148 C2** 45 41N 87 32W
Powys □, *U.K.* **21 E4** 52 20N 3 20W
Poxoreu, *Brazil* **173 D7** 15 50 S 54 23W
Poya, *N. Cal.* **133 U19** 21 19 S 165 7 E
Poyang Hu, *China* **77 C11** 29 5N 116 20 E
Poyarkovo, *Russia* **65 E13** 49 36N 128 41 E
Poysdorf, *Austria* **35 C9** 48 40N 16 37 E
Poza de la Sal, *Spain* **42 C7** 42 35N 3 31W
Poza Rica, *Mexico* **163 C5** 20 33N 97 27W
Pozanti, *Turkey* **100 D6** 37 25N 34 50 E
Požarevac, *Serbia, Yug.* **50 B5** 44 35N 21 18 E
Pozazal, Puerto, *Spain* **42 C6** 42 56N 4 10W
Požega, *Croatia* **52 E2** 45 20N 17 40 E
Požega, *Serbia, Yug.* **50 C4** 43 53N 20 2 E
Pozhva, *Russia* **62 B6** 59 5N 56 5 E
Poznań, *Poland* **55 F3** 52 25N 16 55 E
Pozo, *U.S.A.* **161 K6** 35 20N 120 24W
Pozo Alcón, *Spain* **43 H8** 37 42N 2 56W
Pozo Almonte, *Chile* **172 E4** 20 10 S 69 50W
Pozo Colorado, *Paraguay* **174 A4** 23 30 S 58 45W
Pozoblanco, *Spain* **43 G6** 38 23N 4 51W
Pozorrubio, *Phil.* **80 C3** 16 7N 120 33 E
Pozuzo, *Peru* **172 C2** 10 5 S 75 35W
Pozzallo, *Italy* **47 F7** 36 43N 14 51 E
Pozzomaggiore, *Italy* **46 B1** 40 24N 8 39 E
Pozzuoli, *Italy* **47 B7** 40 49N 14 7 E
Pra →, *Ghana* **113 D4** 5 1N 1 37W
Prabuty, *Poland* **54 E6** 53 47N 19 15 E
Prača, *Bos.-H.* **52 G3** 43 47N 18 43 E
Prachatice, *Czech Rep.* **34 B6** 49 1N 14 0 E
Prachin Buri, *Thailand* **86 E3** 14 0N 101 25 E
Prachuap Khiri Khan, *Thailand* **78 B1** 11 49N 99 48 E
Pradelles, *France* **28 D7** 44 46N 3 52 E
Pradera, *Colombia* **168 C2** 3 25N 76 15W
Prades, *France* **28 F6** 42 38N 2 23 E
Prado, *Brazil* **171 E4** 17 20 S 39 13W
Prado del Rey, *Spain* **43 J5** 36 48N 5 33W
Præstø, *Denmark* **17 J6** 55 8N 12 2 E
Pragersko, *Slovenia* **45 B12** 46 27N 15 42 E
Prague = Praha, *Czech Rep.* **34 A7** 50 5N 14 22 E
Praha, *Czech Rep.* **34 A7** 50 5N 14 22 E
Prahecq, *France* **28 B3** 46 19N 0 26W
Prahita →, *India* **94 E4** 19 0N 79 55 E
Prahova □, *Romania* **53 E10** 45 10N 26 0 E
Prahova →, *Romania* **53 F10** 44 50N 25 50 E
Prahovo, *Serbia, Yug.* **50 B6** 44 18N 22 39 E
Praia, *C. Verde Is.* **8 G6** 14 55N 23 30W
Práia a Mare, *Italy* **47 C8** 39 50N 15 45 E
Praid, *Romania* **53 D10** 46 32N 25 10 E
Prainha, *Amazonas, Brazil* **173 B5** 7 10 S 60 30W
Prainha, *Pará, Brazil* **169 D7** 1 45 S 53 30W
Prairie, *Australia* **126 C3** 20 50 S 144 35 E
Prairie City, *U.S.A.* **158 D4** 44 28N 118 43W
Prairie Dog Town Fork →, *U.S.A.* **155 H5** 34 30N 99 23W
Prairie du Chien, *U.S.A.* **156 A5** 43 3N 91 9W
Prairie du Rocher, *U.S.A.* **156 F6** 38 5N 90 6W
Prairie Village, *U.S.A.* **156 F2** 38 58N 94 38W
Prairies, L. of the, *Canada* **143 C8** 51 16N 101 32W
Pramánda, *Greece* **48 B3** 39 32N 21 8 E
Prampram, *Ghana* **113 D5** 5 43N 0 8 E
Pran Buri, *Thailand* **86 F2** 12 23N 99 55 E
Prándarjökull, *Iceland* **11 C12** 64 40N 14 55W
Prang, *Ghana* **113 D4** 8 1N 0 56W
Prapat, *Indonesia* **78 D1** 2 41N 98 58 E
Prasonísi, Ákra, *Greece* **38 D9** 35 42N 27 46 E
Prästmon, *Sweden* **16 A11** 63 5N 17 45 E
Praszka, *Poland* **55 G5** 51 5N 18 31 E
Prata, *Brazil* **171 E2** 19 25 S 48 54W
Pratabpur, *India* **93 H10** 23 28N 83 15 E
Pratapgarh, *Raj., India* **92 G6** 24 2N 74 40 E
Pratapgarh, *Ut. P., India* **93 G9** 25 56N 81 59 E
Prätigau, *Switz.* **33 C9** 46 56N 9 44 E
Prato, *Italy* **44 E8** 43 53N 11 6 E
Prato allo Stelvio, *Italy* **33 C11** 46 37N 10 35 E
Prátola Peligna, *Italy* **45 F10** 42 6N 13 52 E
Prats-de-Mollo-la-Preste, *France* **28 F6** 42 25N 2 27 E
Pratt, *U.S.A.* **155 G5** 37 39N 98 44W
Pratteln, *Switz.* **32 A5** 47 31N 7 41 E
Prattville, *U.S.A.* **149 J2** 32 28N 86 29W
Pravara →, *India* **94 E2** 19 35N 74 45 E
Pravdinsk, *Russia* **60 B6** 56 29N 43 28 E
Pravets, *Bulgaria* **50 D7** 42 53N 23 55 E
Pravia, *Spain* **42 B4** 43 30N 6 12W
Praya, *Indonesia* **78 F5** 8 39 S 116 17 E
Pré-en-Pail, *France* **26 D6** 48 28N 0 12W
Precordillera, *Argentina* **174 C2** 30 0 S 69 1W
Predáppio, *Italy* **45 D8** 44 6N 11 59 E
Predazzo, *Italy* **45 B8** 46 19N 11 36 E
Predeal, *Romania* **53 E10** 45 30N 25 34 E
Predejane, *Serbia, Yug.* **50 D6** 42 51N 22 9 E
Preeceville, *Canada* **143 C8** 51 57N 102 40W
Preetz, *Germany* **30 A6** 54 14N 10 18 E
Pregrada, *Croatia* **45 B12** 46 11N 15 45 E
Preiļi, *Latvia* **15 H22** 56 18N 26 43 E
Preko, *Croatia* **45 D12** 44 7N 15 10 E
Prelog, *Croatia* **45 B13** 46 18N 16 32 E
Prémery, *France* **27 E10** 47 10N 3 18 E
Prémia, *Italy* **33 D6** 46 17N 8 20 E
Premià de Mar, *Spain* **40 D7** 41 29N 2 22 E
Premont, *U.S.A.* **155 M5** 27 22N 98 7W
Premuda, *Croatia* **45 D11** 44 20N 14 36 E
Prenjasi, *Albania* **50 E4** 41 4N 20 32 E
Prentice, *U.S.A.* **154 C9** 45 33N 90 17W
Prenzlau, *Germany* **30 B9** 53 19N 13 50 E
Preobrazheniye, *Russia* **68 C6** 42 54N 133 54 E
Přerov, *Czech Rep.* **35 B10** 49 28N 17 27 E
Prescott, *Canada* **140 D4** 44 45N 75 30W
Prescott, *Ariz., U.S.A.* **159 J7** 34 33N 112 28W
Prescott, *Ark., U.S.A.* **155 J8** 33 48N 93 23W
Prescott Valley, *U.S.A.* **159 J7** 34 40N 112 18W
Preservation Inlet, *N.Z.* **131 G1** 46 8 S 166 35 E
Preševo, *Serbia, Yug.* **50 D5** 42 19N 21 39 E
Presho, *U.S.A.* **154 D4** 43 54N 100 3W
Presicce, *Italy* **47 C11** 39 54N 18 16 E
Presidencia de la Plaza, *Argentina* **174 B4** 27 0 S 59 50W
Presidencia Roque Saenz Peña, *Argentina* **174 B3** 26 45 S 60 30W
Presidente Dutra, *Brazil* **170 C3** 5 15 S 44 30W
Presidente Epitácio, *Brazil* **171 F1** 21 56 S 52 6W
Presidente Figueiredo, *Brazil* **169 D5** 1 57 S 60 2W
Presidente Hayes □, *Paraguay* **174 A4** 24 0 S 59 0W
Presidente Hermes, *Brazil* **173 C5** 11 17 S 61 55W
Presidente Prudente, *Brazil* **175 A5** 22 5 S 51 25W
Presidio, *Mexico* **162 B4** 29 29N 104 23W
Presidio, *U.S.A.* **155 L2** 29 34N 104 22W
Preslav, *Bulgaria* **51 C10** 43 10N 26 52 E
Preslavska Planina, *Bulgaria* **51 C10** 43 10N 26 45 E
Prešov, *Slovak Rep.* **35 B14** 49 0N 21 15 E
Prešovský □, *Slovak Rep.* **35 B13** 49 10N 21 0 E
Prespa, *Bulgaria* **51 E8** 41 44N 24 55 E
Prespa, L. = Prespansko Jezero, *Macedonia* **50 F5** 40 55N 21 0 E
Prespansko Jezero, *Macedonia* **50 F5** 40 55N 21 0 E
Presque I., *U.S.A.* **150 D4** 42 9N 80 6W
Presque Isle, *U.S.A.* **149 B12** 46 41N 68 1W
Prestatyn, *U.K.* **20 D4** 53 20N 3 24W
Prestea, *Ghana* **112 D4** 5 22N 2 7W
Presteigne, *U.K.* **21 E5** 52 17N 3 0W
Přeštice, *Czech Rep.* **34 B6** 49 34N 13 20 E
Presto, *Bolivia* **173 D5** 18 55 S 64 56W
Preston, *Canada* **150 C4** 43 23N 80 21W
Preston, *U.K.* **20 D5** 53 46N 2 42W
Preston, *Ga., U.S.A.* **152 C5** 32 4N 84 32W
Preston, *Idaho, U.S.A.* **158 E8** 42 6N 111 53W
Preston, *Iowa, U.S.A.* **156 B6** 42 3N 90 24W
Preston, *Minn., U.S.A.* **154 D8** 43 40N 92 5W
Preston, *Mo., U.S.A.* **156 G3** 37 56N 93 13W
Preston, C., *Australia* **124 D2** 20 51 S 116 12 E
Prestonburg, *U.S.A.* **148 G4** 37 39N 82 46W
Prestranda, *Norway* **18 E6** 59 6N 9 4 E
Prestwick, *U.K.* **22 F4** 55 29N 4 37W
Prêto →, *Amazonas, Brazil* **169 D5** 0 8 S 64 6W
Prêto →, *Bahia, Brazil* **170 D3** 11 21 S 43 52W
Prêto do Igapó-Açu →, *Brazil* **169 D6** 4 26 S 59 48W
Pretoria, *S. Africa* **117 D4** 25 44 S 28 12 E
Preuilly-sur-Claise, *France* **26 F7** 46 51N 0 56 E
Préveza, *Greece* **48 C2** 38 57N 20 47 E
Préveza □, *Greece* **48 B2** 39 10N 20 40 E
Prey Veng, *Cambodia* **78 B3** 11 35N 105 29 E
Priazovskoye, *Ukraine* **59 J8** 46 44N 35 40 E
Pribilof Is., *U.S.A.* **144 H5** 57 0N 170 0W
Priboj, *Serbia, Yug.* **50 C3** 43 35N 19 32 E
Příbram, *Czech Rep.* **34 B7** 49 41N 14 2 E
Price, *U.S.A.* **158 G8** 39 36N 110 49W
Price I., *Canada* **142 C3** 52 23N 128 41W
Prichard, *U.S.A.* **149 K1** 30 44N 88 5W
Priego, *Spain* **40 E2** 40 26N 2 21W
Priego de Córdoba, *Spain* **43 H6** 37 27N 4 12W
Priekule, *Latvia* **15 H19** 56 26N 21 35 E
Prien, *Germany* **31 H8** 47 51N 12 20 E
Prienai, *Lithuania* **15 J20** 54 38N 23 57 E
Prieska, *S. Africa* **116 D3** 29 40 S 22 42 E
Priest L., *U.S.A.* **158 B5** 48 35N 116 52W
Priest River, *U.S.A.* **158 B5** 48 10N 116 54W
Priest Valley, *U.S.A.* **160 J6** 36 10N 120 39W
Prieto Diaz, *Phil.* **80 E5** 13 2N 124 12 E
Prievidza, *Slovak Rep.* **35 C11** 48 46N 18 36 E
Prignitz, *Germany* **30 B7** 53 6N 11 45 E
Prijedor, *Bos.-H.* **45 D13** 44 58N 16 41 E
Prijepolje, *Serbia, Yug.* **50 C3** 43 27N 19 40 E
Prikaspiyskaya Nizmennost = Caspian Depression, *Eurasia* **61 G9** 47 0N 48 0 E
Prikro, *Ivory C.* **112 D4** 7 40N 3 59W
Prikubanskaya Nizmennost, *Russia* **61 H4** 45 39N 38 33 E
Prilep, *Macedonia* **50 E5** 41 21N 21 32 E
Priluki = Pryluky, *Ukraine* **59 G7** 50 30N 32 24 E
Prime Seal I., *Australia* **126 G4** 40 3 S 147 43 E
Primeira Cruz, *Brazil* **170 B3** 2 30 S 43 26W
Primorsk, *Russia* **58 B5** 60 22N 28 37 E
Primorsko, *Bulgaria* **51 D11** 42 15N 27 44 E
Primorsko-Akhtarsk, *Russia* **59 J10** 46 2N 38 10 E
Primorskoye, *Ukraine* **59 J9** 46 48N 36 20 E
Primrose L., *Canada* **143 C7** 54 55N 109 45W
Prince Albert, *Canada* **143 C7** 53 15N 105 50W
Prince Albert, *S. Africa* **116 E3** 33 12 S 22 2 E
Prince Albert Mts., *Antarctica* **7 D11** 76 0 S 161 30 E
Prince Albert Nat. Park, *Canada* **143 C7** 54 0N 106 25W
Prince Albert Pen., *Canada* **138 A8** 72 30N 116 0W
Prince Albert Sd., *Canada* **138 A8** 70 25N 115 0W
Prince Alfred, C., *Canada* **6 B1** 74 20N 124 40W
Prince Charles I., *Canada* **139 B12** 67 47N 76 12W
Prince Charles Mts., *Antarctica* **7 D6** 72 0 S 67 0 E
Prince Edward I. □, *Canada* **141 C7** 46 20N 63 20W
Prince Edward Is., *Ind. Oc.* **121 J2** 46 35 S 38 0 E
Prince Edward Pt., *Canada* **150 C8** 43 56N 76 52W
Prince George, *Canada* **142 C4** 53 55N 122 50W
Prince of Wales, C., *U.S.A.* **136 C3** 65 36N 168 5W
Prince of Wales I., *Australia* **132 F2** 10 40 S 142 10 E
Prince of Wales I., *Canada* **138 A10** 73 0N 99 0W
Prince of Wales I., *U.S.A.* **138 C6** 55 47N 132 50W
Prince Patrick I., *Canada* **6 B2** 77 0N 120 0W
Prince Regent Inlet, *Canada* **6 B3** 73 0N 90 0W
Prince Rupert, *Canada* **142 C2** 54 20N 130 20W
Princesa Isabel, *Brazil* **170 C4** 7 44 S 38 0W
Princess Charlotte B., *Australia* **126 A3** 14 25 S 144 0 E
Princess May Ranges, *Australia* **124 C4** 15 30 S 125 30 E
Princess Royal I., *Canada* **142 C3** 53 0N 128 40W
Princeton, *Canada* **142 D4** 49 27N 120 30W
Princeton, *Calif., U.S.A.* **160 F4** 39 24N 122 1W
Princeton, *Ill., U.S.A.* **156 C7** 41 23N 89 28W
Princeton, *Ind., U.S.A.* **157 F9** 38 21N 87 34W
Princeton, *Ky., U.S.A.* **148 G2** 37 7N 87 53W
Princeton, *Mo., U.S.A.* **156 D3** 40 24N 93 35W
Princeton, *N.J., U.S.A.* **151 F10** 40 21N 74 39W
Princeton, *W. Va., U.S.A.* **148 G5** 37 22N 81 6W
Princeville, *U.S.A.* **156 D7** 40 56N 89 46W
Príncipe, *São Tomé & Principe* **115 G6** 1 37N 7 25 E
Principe, I. de, *Atl. Oc.* **104 F4** 1 37N 7 27 E
Principe da Beira, *Brazil* **173 C5** 12 20 S 64 30W
Prineville, *U.S.A.* **158 D3** 44 18N 120 51W
Prins Christian Sund, *Greenland* **10 E6** 60 4N 43 10W
Prins Harald Kyst, *Antarctica* **7 D4** 70 0 S 35 1 E
Prinsesse Astrid Kyst, *Antarctica* **7 D3** 70 45 S 12 30 E
Prinsesse Ragnhild Kyst, *Antarctica* **7 D4** 70 15 S 27 30 E
Prinzapolca, *Nic.* **164 D3** 13 20N 83 35W
Prior, C., *Spain* **42 B2** 43 34N 8 17W
Priozersk, *Russia* **58 B6** 61 2N 30 7 E
Pripet = Prypyat →, *Europe* **59 G6** 51 20N 30 15 E
Pripet Marshes, *Europe* **59 F5** 52 10N 28 10 E
Pripyat Marshes = Pripet Marshes, *Europe* **59 F5** 52 10N 28 10 E
Pripyats = Prypyat →, *Europe* **59 G6** 51 20N 30 15 E
Prislop, Pasul, *Romania* **53 C9** 47 37N 24 48 E
Pristen, *Russia* **59 G9** 51 15N 36 44 E
Priština, *Kosovo, Yug.* **50 D5** 42 40N 21 13 E
Pritzwalk, *Germany* **30 B8** 53 9N 12 10 E
Privas, *France* **29 D8** 44 45N 4 37 E
Priverno, *Italy* **46 A6** 41 28N 13 11 E
Privolzhsk, *Russia* **60 B5** 57 23N 41 16 E
Privolzhskaya Vozvyshennost, *Russia* **60 E7** 51 0N 46 0 E
Privolzhskiy, *Russia* **60 E8** 51 25N 46 3 E
Privolzhye, *Russia* **60 D9** 52 52N 48 33 E
Priyutnoye, *Russia* **61 G6** 46 12N 43 40 E
Priyutovo, *Russia* **62 E4** 53 55N 53 59 E
Prizren, *Kosovo, Yug.* **50 D4** 42 13N 20 45 E
Prizzi, *Italy* **46 E6** 37 43N 13 26 E
Prnjavor, *Bos.-H.* **52 F2** 44 52N 17 43 E
Probolinggo, *Indonesia* **79 G15** 7 46 S 113 13 E
Prochowice, *Poland* **55 G3** 51 17N 16 20 E
Proctor, *U.S.A.* **151 C11** 43 40N 73 2W
Proddatur, *India* **95 G4** 14 45N 78 30 E
Prodhromos, *Cyprus* **38 E11** 34 57N 32 50 E
Proença-a-Nova, *Portugal* **42 F3** 39 45N 7 54W
Profítis Ilías, *Greece* **38 C9** 36 17N 27 56 E
Profondeville, *Belgium* **24 D4** 50 23N 4 52 E
Progreso, *Coahuila, Mexico* **162 B4** 27 28N 101 4W
Progreso, *Yucatán, Mexico* **163 C7** 21 20N 89 40W
Prokhladnyy, *Russia* **61 J7** 43 50N 44 2 E
Prokletije, *Albania* **50 D3** 42 30N 19 45 E
Prokopyevsk, *Russia* **64 D9** 54 0N 86 45 E
Prokuplje, *Serbia, Yug.* **50 C5** 43 16N 21 36 E
Proletarsk, *Russia* **61 G5** 46 42N 41 50 E
Proletarskaya = Proletarsk, *Russia* **61 G5** 46 42N 41 50 E
Prome = Pyè, *Burma* **90 F5** 18 49N 95 13 E
Promise City, *U.S.A.* **156 D3** 40 45N 93 9W
Prophet →, *Canada* **142 B4** 58 48N 122 40W
Prophet River, *Canada* **142 B4** 58 6N 122 43W
Prophetstown, *U.S.A.* **156 C7** 41 40N 89 56W
Propriá, *Brazil* **170 D4** 10 13 S 36 51W
Propriano, *France* **29 G12** 41 41N 8 52 E
Proserpine, *Australia* **126 C4** 20 21 S 148 36 E
Prosna →, *Poland* **55 F4** 52 6N 17 44 E
Prospect, *N.Y., U.S.A.* **151 C9** 43 18N 75 9W
Prospect, *Ohio, U.S.A.* **157 D13** 40 27N 83 11W
Prosperidad, *Phil.* **81 G5** 8 34N 125 52 E
Prosser, *U.S.A.* **158 C4** 46 12N 119 46W
Prostějov, *Czech Rep.* **35 B10** 49 30N 17 9 E
Prostki, *Poland* **54 E9** 53 42N 22 25 E
Proston, *Australia* **127 D5** 26 8 S 151 32 E
Proszowice, *Poland* **55 H7** 50 13N 20 16 E
Próti, *Greece* **48 D3** 37 5N 21 32 E
Provadiya, *Bulgaria* **51 C11** 43 12N 27 30 E
Provence, *France* **29 E9** 43 40N 5 46 E
Provence-Alpes-Côte d'Azur □, *France* **29 D10** 44 0N 6 15 E
Providence, *Seychelles* **121 E4** 9 14 S 51 2 E
Providence, *Ky., U.S.A.* **148 G2** 37 24N 87 46W
Providence, *R.I., U.S.A.* **151 E13** 41 49N 71 24W
Providence Bay, *Canada* **140 C3** 45 41N 82 15W
Providence C., *N.Z.* **131 F1** 45 59 S 166 29 E
Providence Mts., *U.S.A.* **161 K11** 35 10N 115 15W
Providencia, I. de, *Colombia* **164 D3** 13 25N 81 26W
Provideniya, *Russia* **65 C19** 64 23N 173 18W
Provins, *France* **27 D10** 48 33N 3 15 E
Provo, *U.S.A.* **158 F8** 40 14N 111 39W
Provost, *Canada* **143 C6** 52 25N 110 20W
Prozor, *Bos.-H.* **52 G2** 43 50N 17 34 E
Prudentópolis, *Brazil* **171 G1** 25 12 S 50 57W
Prudhoe Bay, *U.S.A.* **138 A5** 70 18N 148 22W
Prudhoe I., *Australia* **126 C4** 21 19 S 149 41 E
Prud'homme, *Canada* **143 C7** 52 20N 105 54W
Prudnik, *Poland* **55 H4** 50 20N 17 38 E
Prüm, *Germany* **31 E2** 50 12N 6 25 E
Prundu, *Romania* **53 F11** 44 6N 26 14 E
Pruszcz Gdański, *Poland* **54 D5** 54 17N 18 40 E
Pruszków, *Poland* **55 F7** 52 9N 20 49 E

Réthímnon 271

Ramona, *U.S.A.* **161 M10** 33 2N 116 52W
Ramonville-St-Agne, *France* **28 E5** 43 33N 1 28 E
Ramore, *Canada* **140 C3** 48 30N 80 25W
Ramos →, *Nigeria* **113 D6** 5 8N 5 22 E
Ramotswa, *Botswana* **116 C4** 24 50 S 25 52 E
Rampur, *H.P., India* **92 D7** 31 26N 77 43 E
Rampur, *Mad. P., India* **92 H5** 23 25N 73 53 E
Rampur, *Orissa, India* **94 D6** 21 48N 83 58 E
Rampur, *Ut. P., India* **93 E8** 28 50N 79 5 E
Rampur Hat, *India* **93 G12** 24 10N 87 50 E
Rampura, *India* **92 G6** 24 30N 75 27 E
Ramrama Tola, *India* **93 J8** 21 52N 79 55 E
Rāmsar, *Iran* **97 B6** 36 53N 50 41 E
Ramsey, *U.K.* **20 C3** 54 20N 4 22W
Ramsey, *Ill., U.S.A.* **156 E7** 39 8N 89 7W
Ramsey, *N.J., U.S.A.* **151 E10** 41 4N 74 9W
Ramsey L., *Canada* **140 C3** 47 13N 82 15W
Ramsgate, *U.K.* **21 F9** 51 20N 1 25 E
Ramshai, *India* **90 B2** 26 44N 88 51 E
Ramsjö, *Sweden* **16 B9** 62 11N 15 37 E
Ramstein, *Germany* **31 F3** 49 27N 7 32 E
Ramtek, *India* **94 D4** 21 20N 79 15 E
Ramu →, *Papua N. G.* **132 C3** 4 0 S 144 41 E
Ramvik, *Sweden* **16 B11** 62 49N 17 51 E
Rana Pratap Sagar Dam, *India* **92 G6** 24 58N 75 38 E
Ranaghat, *India* **93 H13** 23 15N 88 35 E
Ranahu, *Pakistan* **92 G3** 25 55N 69 45 E
Ranau, *Malaysia* **78 C5** 6 2N 116 40 E
Rancagua, *Chile* **174 C1** 34 10 S 70 50W
Rance →, *France* **26 D5** 48 34N 1 59W
Rancharia, *Brazil* **171 F1** 22 15 S 50 55W
Rancheria →, *Canada* **142 A3** 60 13N 129 7W
Ranchester, *U.S.A.* **158 D10** 44 54N 107 10W
Ranchi, *India* **93 H11** 23 19N 85 27 E
Rancho Cucamonga, *U.S.A.* **161 L9** 34 10N 117 30W
Ranco, L., *Chile* **176 B2** 40 15 S 72 25W
Rand, *Australia* **129 C7** 35 33 S 146 32 E
Randaberg, *Norway* **18 E2** 59 1N 5 36 E
Randabygd, *Norway* **18 C3** 61 51N 6 20 E
Randalstown, *U.K.* **23 B5** 54 45N 6 19W
Randan, *France* **27 F10** 46 2N 3 21 E
Randazzo, *Italy* **47 E7** 37 53N 14 57 E
Rander, *India* **94 D1** 21 14N 72 47 E
Randers, *Denmark* **17 H4** 56 29N 10 1 E
Randers Fjord, *Denmark* **17 H4** 56 37N 10 20 E
Randfontein, *S. Africa* **117 D4** 26 8 S 27 45 E
Randle, *U.S.A.* **160 D5** 46 32N 121 57W
Randolph, *Mass., U.S.A.* **151 D13** 42 10N 71 2W
Randolph, *N.Y., U.S.A.* **150 D6** 42 10N 78 59W
Randolph, *Utah, U.S.A.* **158 F8** 41 40N 111 11W
Randolph, *Vt., U.S.A.* **151 C12** 43 55N 72 40W
Randsburg, *U.S.A.* **161 K9** 35 22N 117 39W
Randsfjorden, *Norway* **18 D7** 60 25N 10 24 E
Randsverk, *Norway* **18 C6** 61 44N 9 3 E
Råne älv →, *Sweden* **14 D20** 65 50N 22 20 E
Ranfurly, *N.Z.* **131 F5** 45 7 S 170 6 E
Rangae, *Thailand* **87 J3** 6 19N 101 44 E
Rangamati, *Bangla.* **90 D4** 22 38N 92 12 E
Rangárvallasýsla □, *Iceland* **11 D7** 63 55N 20 0W
Rangataua, *N.Z.* **130 F4** 39 26 S 175 28 E
Rangaunu B., *N.Z.* **130 A2** 34 51 S 173 15 E
Rangeley, *U.S.A.* **151 B14** 44 58N 70 39W
Rangeley L., *U.S.A.* **151 B14** 44 55N 70 43W
Rangely, *U.S.A.* **158 F9** 40 5N 108 48W
Ranger, *U.S.A.* **155 J5** 32 28N 98 41W
Rangia, *India* **90 B3** 26 28N 91 38 E
Rangiora, *N.Z.* **131 D7** 43 19 S 172 36 E
Rangitaiki, *N.Z.* **130 E5** 38 52 S 176 24 E
Rangitaiki →, *N.Z.* **130 D5** 37 54 S 176 49 E
Rangitata →, *N.Z.* **131 D6** 43 45 S 171 15 E
Rangitikei →, *N.Z.* **130 G4** 40 17 S 175 15 E
Rangitoto Ra., *N.Z.* **130 E4** 38 25 S 175 35 E
Rangkasbitung, *Indonesia* **79 G12** 6 21 S 106 15 E
Rangoon, *Burma* **90 G6** 16 45N 96 20 E
Rangpur, *Bangla.* **90 C2** 25 42N 89 22 E
Rangsang, *Indonesia* **84 B2** 1 20N 103 30 E
Rangsit, *Thailand* **86 F3** 13 59N 100 37 E
Ranheim, *Norway* **18 A7** 63 26N 10 32 E
Ranibennur, *India* **95 G2** 14 35N 75 30 E
Raniganj, *India* **93 F9** 27 3N 82 13 E
Ranikhet, *India* **93 E8** 29 39N 79 25 E
Ranippettai, *India* **95 H4** 12 56N 79 23 E
Rāniyah, *Iraq* **96 B5** 36 15N 44 53 E
Ranka, *India* **93 H10** 23 59N 83 47 E
Ranken →, *Australia* **126 C2** 20 31 S 137 36 E
Rankin, *Ill., U.S.A.* **157 D9** 40 28N 87 54W
Rankin, *Tex., U.S.A.* **155 K4** 31 13N 101 56W
Rankin Inlet, *Canada* **138 B10** 62 30N 93 0W
Rankins Springs, *Australia* **129 B7** 33 49 S 146 14 E
Rankweil, *Austria* **34 D2** 47 17N 9 39 E
Rannoch, L., *U.K.* **22 E4** 56 41N 4 20W
Rannoch Moor, *U.K.* **22 E4** 56 38N 4 48W
Ranobe, Helodranon' i, *Madag.* **117 C7** 23 3 S 43 33 E
Ranohira, *Madag.* **117 C8** 22 29 S 45 24 E
Ranomafana, *Toamasina, Madag.* **117 B8** 18 57 S 48 50 E
Ranomafana, *Toliara, Madag.* **117 C8** 24 34 S 47 0 E
Ranomena, *Madag.* **117 C8** 23 25 S 47 17 E
Ranong, *Thailand* **78 C1** 9 56N 98 40 E
Ranotsara Nord, *Madag.* **117 C8** 22 48 S 46 36 E
Ranpur, *India* **94 D7** 20 5N 85 20 E
Rānsa, *Iran* **97 C6** 33 39N 48 18 E
Ransiki, *Indonesia* **79 E8** 1 30 S 134 10 E
Ransom, *U.S.A.* **157 C8** 41 9N 88 39W
Rantabe, *Madag.* **117 B8** 15 42 S 49 39 E
Rantau, *Indonesia* **85 C5** 2 56 S 115 9 E
Rantauprapat, *Indonesia* **78 D1** 2 15N 99 50 E
Rantemario, *Indonesia* **79 E5** 3 15 S 119 57 E
Rantoul, *U.S.A.* **157 D8** 40 19N 88 9W
Ranum, *Denmark* **17 H3** 56 54N 9 14 E
Ranyah, W. →, *Si. Arabia* **106 C5** 21 18N 43 20 E
Ranyah, W. →, *Si. Arabia* **98 B3** 21 18N 43 20 E
Raon l'Étape, *France* **27 D13** 48 24N 6 50 E
Raoping, *China* **77 F11** 23 42N 117 1 E
Raoui, Erg er, *Algeria* **111 C4** 29 0N 2 0W
Raoyang, *China* **74 E8** 38 15N 115 45 E
Rapa, *Pac. Oc.* **135 K13** 27 35 S 144 20W
Rapallo, *Italy* **44 D6** 44 21N 9 14 E
Rapar, *India* **92 H4** 23 34N 70 38 E
Rāpch, *Iran* **97 E8** 25 40N 59 15 E
Raper, C., *Canada* **139 B13** 69 44N 67 6W
Rapid City, *U.S.A.* **154 D3** 44 5N 103 14W
Rapid River, *U.S.A.* **148 C2** 45 55N 86 58W
Rapla, *Estonia* **15 G21** 59 1N 24 52 E
Rapperswil, *Switz.* **33 B7** 47 14N 8 45 E
Rapti →, *India* **93 F10** 26 18N 83 41 E
Rapu Rapu I., *Phil.* **80 E5** 13 12N 124 9 E
Raqaba ez Zarqa →, *Sudan* **107 F2** 9 14N 29 44 E
Raquette →, *U.S.A.* **151 B10** 45 0N 74 42W
Raquette Lake, *U.S.A.* **151 C10** 43 49N 74 40W
Rarotonga, *Cook Is.* **135 K12** 21 30 S 160 0W
Ra's al 'Ayn, *Syria* **101 D9** 36 45N 40 12 E
Ra's al Khaymah, *U.A.E.* **97 E7** 25 50N 55 59 E
Ra's al-Unuf, *Libya* **108 B3** 30 46N 18 11 E
Ras el Ma, *Algeria* **111 B4** 34 26N 0 50W
Râs el Mâ, *Mali* **112 B4** 16 35N 4 30W
Ras Ghârib, *Egypt* **106 B3** 28 6N 33 18 E
Ras Mallap, *Egypt* **106 B3** 29 18N 32 50 E
Rasa, Punta, *Argentina* **176 B4** 40 50 S 62 15W
Rasca, Pta. de la, *Canary Is.* **39 G3** 27 59N 16 41W
Răşcani, *Moldova* **53 C12** 47 58N 27 33 E
Raseiniai, *Lithuania* **15 J20** 55 25N 23 5 E
Rashad, *Sudan* **107 E3** 11 55N 31 0 E
Rashîd, *Egypt* **106 H7** 31 21N 30 22 E
Rashîd, Masabb, *Egypt* **106 H7** 31 22N 30 17 E
Rashmi, *India* **92 G6** 25 4N 74 22 E
Rasht, *Iran* **97 B6** 37 20N 49 40 E
Rasi Salai, *Thailand* **86 E5** 15 20N 104 9 E
Rasipuram, *India* **95 J4** 11 30N 78 15 E
Raška, *Serbia, Yug.* **50 C4** 43 19N 20 39 E
Râsnov, *Romania* **53 E10** 45 35N 25 27 E
Rason L., *Australia* **125 E3** 28 45 S 124 25 E
Raşova, *Romania* **53 F12** 44 15N 27 55 E
Rasovo, *Bulgaria* **50 C7** 43 42N 23 17 E
Rasra, *India* **93 G10** 25 50N 83 50 E
Rass el Oued, *Algeria* **111 A6** 35 57N 5 2 E
Rasskazovo, *Russia* **60 D5** 52 35N 41 50 E
Rast, *Romania* **53 G8** 43 53N 23 16 E
Rastatt, *Germany* **31 G4** 48 50N 8 11 E
Rastede, *Germany* **30 B4** 53 15N 8 12 E
Răstoliţa, *Romania* **53 D9** 46 59N 24 58 E
Rasul, *Pakistan* **92 C5** 32 42N 73 34 E
Raszków, *Poland* **55 G4** 51 43N 17 40 E
Rat Buri, *Thailand* **86 F2** 13 30N 99 54 E
Rat Islands, *U.S.A.* **138 C1** 52 0N 178 0 E
Rat L., *Canada* **143 B9** 56 10N 99 40W
Ratangarh, *India* **92 E6** 28 5N 74 35 E
Rätansbyn, *Sweden* **16 B8** 62 29N 14 33 E
Raţāwī, *Iraq* **96 D5** 30 38N 47 13 E
Ratcatchers L., *Australia* **128 B5** 32 38 S 143 10 E
Rath, *India* **93 G8** 25 36N 79 37 E
Rath Luirc, *Ireland* **23 D3** 52 21N 8 40W
Rathbun L., *U.S.A.* **156 D4** 40 49N 92 53W
Rathdrum, *Ireland* **23 D5** 52 56N 6 14W
Rathedaung, *Burma* **90 E4** 20 29N 92 45 E
Rathenow, *Germany* **30 C8** 52 37N 12 19 E
Rathkeale, *Ireland* **23 D3** 52 32N 8 56W
Rathlin I., *U.K.* **23 A5** 55 18N 6 14W
Rathmelton, *Ireland* **23 A4** 55 2N 7 38W
Ratibor = Racibórz, *Poland* **55 H5** 50 7N 18 18 E
Rätikon, *Austria* **33 B9** 47 0N 9 55 E
Ratingen, *Germany* **30 D2** 51 18N 6 52 E
Ratlam, *India* **92 H6** 23 20N 75 0 E
Ratnagiri, *India* **94 F1** 16 57N 73 18 E
Ratnapura, *Sri Lanka* **95 L5** 6 40N 80 20 E
Ratodero, *Pakistan* **92 F3** 27 48N 68 18 E
Raton, *U.S.A.* **155 G2** 36 54N 104 24W
Rattaphum, *Thailand* **87 J3** 7 8N 100 16 E
Ratten, *Austria* **34 D8** 47 28N 15 44 E
Rattray Hd., *U.K.* **22 D7** 57 38N 1 50W
Rättvik, *Sweden* **16 D9** 60 52N 15 7 E
Ratz, Mt., *Canada* **142 B2** 57 23N 132 12W
Ratzeburg, *Germany* **30 B6** 53 40N 10 46 E
Raub, *Malaysia* **87 L3** 3 47N 101 52 E
Rauch, *Argentina* **174 D4** 36 45 S 59 5W
Raudales de Malpaso, *Mexico* **163 D6** 17 30N 23 30W
Raudeberg, *Norway* **18 C2** 61 59N 5 7 E
Raufarhöfn, *Iceland* **11 A11** 66 27N 15 57W
Raufoss, *Norway* **15 F14** 60 44N 10 37 E
Rauhellern, *Norway* **18 D4** 60 15N 7 50 E
Raukumara Ra., *N.Z.* **130 E6** 38 5 S 177 55 E
Raul Soares, *Brazil* **171 F3** 20 5 S 42 22W
Rauma, *Finland* **15 F19** 61 10N 21 30 E
Rauma →, *Norway* **18 B4** 62 34N 7 43 E
Raurkela, *India* **93 H11** 22 14N 84 50 E
Rausu-Dake, *Japan* **68 B12** 44 4N 145 7 E
Răut →, *Moldova* **53 C14** 47 15N 29 9 E
Rava-Ruska, *Poland* **59 G2** 50 15N 23 42 E
Rava Russkaya = Rava-Ruska, *Poland* **59 G2** 50 15N 23 42 E
Ravalli, *U.S.A.* **158 C6** 47 17N 114 11W
Ravānsar, *Iran* **101 E12** 34 43N 46 40 E
Ravanusa, *Italy* **46 E6** 37 16N 13 58 E
Rāvar, *Iran* **97 D8** 31 20N 56 51 E
Ravena, *U.S.A.* **151 D11** 42 28N 73 49W
Ravenel, *U.S.A.* **152 C9** 32 46N 80 15W
Ravenna, *Italy* **45 D9** 44 25N 12 12 E
Ravenna, *Ky., U.S.A.* **157 G13** 37 42N 83 55W
Ravenna, *Nebr., U.S.A.* **154 E5** 41 1N 98 55W
Ravenna, *Ohio, U.S.A.* **150 E3** 41 9N 81 15W
Ravensburg, *Germany* **31 H5** 47 46N 9 36 E
Ravenshoe, *Australia* **126 B4** 17 37 S 145 29 E
Ravensthorpe, *Australia* **125 F3** 33 35 S 120 2 E
Ravenswood, *Australia* **126 C4** 20 6 S 146 54 E
Ravenswood, *U.S.A.* **148 F5** 38 57N 81 46W
Ravensworth, *Australia* **129 B9** 32 26 S 151 4 E
Ravenwood, *U.S.A.* **156 D2** 40 22N 94 41W
Raver, *India* **94 D3** 21 15N 76 2 E
Ravi →, *Pakistan* **92 D4** 30 35N 71 49 E
Ravna Gora, *Croatia* **45 C11** 45 24N 14 50 E
Ravna Reka, *Serbia, Yug.* **50 B5** 44 1N 21 35 E
Ravne na Koroškem, *Slovenia* **45 B11** 46 36N 14 59 E
Rawa Mazowiecka, *Poland* **55 G7** 51 46N 20 12 E
Rawalpindi, *Pakistan* **91 B4** 33 38N 73 8 E
Rawāndūz, *Iraq* **101 D11** 36 40N 44 30 E
Rawang, *Malaysia* **87 L3** 3 20N 101 35 E
Rawene, *N.Z.* **130 B2** 35 25 S 173 32 E
Rawicz, *Poland* **55 G3** 51 36N 16 52 E
Rawka →, *Poland* **55 F7** 52 9N 20 8 E
Rawlinna, *Australia* **125 F4** 30 58 S 125 28 E
Rawlins, *U.S.A.* **158 F10** 41 47N 107 14W
Rawlinson Ra., *Australia* **125 D4** 24 40 S 128 30 E
Rawson, *Argentina* **176 B3** 43 15 S 65 5W
Raxaul, *India* **93 F11** 26 59N 84 51 E
Ray, *U.S.A.* **154 A3** 48 21N 103 10W
Ray, C., *Canada* **141 C8** 47 33N 59 15W
Ray City, *U.S.A.* **152 D6** 31 5N 83 11W
Rayachoti, *India* **95 G4** 14 4N 78 50 E
Rayadurg, *India* **95 G3** 14 40N 76 50 E
Rayagada, *India* **94 E6** 19 15N 83 20 E
Raychikhinsk, *Russia* **65 E13** 49 46N 129 25 E
Rāyen, *Iran* **97 D8** 29 34N 57 26 E
Rayevskiy, *Russia* **62 D5** 54 4N 54 56 E
Rayle, *U.S.A.* **152 B7** 33 48N 82 54W
Rayleigh, *U.K.* **21 F8** 51 36N 0 37 E
Raymond, *Canada* **142 D6** 49 30N 112 35W
Raymond, *Calif., U.S.A.* **160 H7** 37 13N 119 54W
Raymond, *Ill., U.S.A.* **156 E7** 39 19N 89 34W
Raymond, *N.H., U.S.A.* **151 C13** 43 2N 71 11W
Raymond, *Wash., U.S.A.* **160 D3** 46 41N 123 44W
Raymond Terrace, *Australia* **129 B9** 32 45 S 151 44 E
Raymondville, *U.S.A.* **155 M6** 26 29N 97 47W
Raymore, *Canada* **143 C8** 51 25N 104 31W
Rayón, *Mexico* **162 B2** 29 43N 110 35W
Rayong, *Thailand* **78 B2** 12 40N 101 20 E
Raytown, *U.S.A.* **156 E2** 39 1N 94 28W
Rayville, *U.S.A.* **155 J9** 32 29N 91 46W
Raz, Pte. du, *France* **26 D2** 48 2N 4 47W
Razan, *Iran* **97 C6** 35 23N 49 2 E
Ražana, *Serbia, Yug.* **50 B3** 44 6N 19 55 E
Ražanj, *Serbia, Yug.* **50 C5** 43 40N 21 31 E
Razdelna, *Bulgaria* **51 C11** 43 13N 27 41 E
Razdel'naya = Rozdilna, *Ukraine* **59 J6** 46 50N 30 2 E
Razdolnoye, *Russia* **68 C5** 43 30N 131 52 E
Razdolnoye, *Ukraine* **59 K7** 45 46N 33 29 E
Razeh, *Iran* **97 C6** 32 47N 48 9 E
Razgrad, *Bulgaria* **51 C10** 43 33N 26 34 E
Razim, Lacul, *Romania* **53 F14** 44 50N 29 0 E
Razlog, *Bulgaria* **50 E7** 41 53N 23 28 E
Razmak, *Pakistan* **91 B3** 32 45N 69 50 E
Ré, Î. de, *France* **28 B2** 46 12N 1 30W
Reading, *U.K.* **21 F7** 51 27N 0 58W
Reading, *Mich., U.S.A.* **157 C12** 41 50N 84 45W
Reading, *Ohio, U.S.A.* **157 E12** 39 13N 84 26W
Reading, *Pa., U.S.A.* **151 F9** 40 20N 75 56W
Reading □, *U.K.* **21 F7** 51 27N 0 58W
Real, Cordillera, *Bolivia* **172 D4** 17 0 S 67 10W
Realicó, *Argentina* **174 D3** 35 0 S 64 15W
Réalmont, *France* **28 E6** 43 48N 2 10 E
Realp, *Switz.* **33 C6** 46 36N 8 30 E
Ream, *Cambodia* **87 G4** 10 34N 103 39 E
Reata, *Mexico* **162 B4** 26 8N 101 5W
Reay Forest, *U.K.* **22 C4** 58 22N 4 55W
Rebais, *France* **27 D10** 48 50N 3 10 E
Rebi, *Indonesia* **79 F8** 6 23 S 134 7 E
Rebiana, *Libya* **108 D4** 24 12N 22 10 E
Rebun-Tō, *Japan* **68 B10** 45 23N 141 2 E
Recanati, *Italy* **45 E10** 43 24N 13 32 E
Recaş, *Romania* **52 E6** 45 46N 21 30 E
Recco, *Italy* **44 D6** 44 22N 9 9 E
Recherche, Arch. of the, *Australia* **125 F3** 34 15 S 122 50 E
Rechna Doab, *Pakistan* **92 D5** 31 35N 73 30 E
Rechytsa, *Belarus* **59 F6** 52 21N 30 24 E
Recife, *Brazil* **170 C5** 8 0 S 35 0W
Recklinghausen, *Germany* **24 C7** 51 37N 7 12 E
Reconquista, *Argentina* **174 B4** 29 10 S 59 45W
Recreio, *Brazil* **173 B6** 8 0 S 58 25W
Recreo, *Argentina* **174 B2** 29 25 S 65 10W
Recuay, *Peru* **172 B2** 9 43 S 77 28W
Recz, *Poland* **55 E2** 53 16N 15 31 E
Red →, *La., U.S.A.* **155 K9** 31 1N 91 45W
Red →, *N. Dak., U.S.A.* **138 C10** 49 0N 97 15W
Red Bank, *U.S.A.* **151 F10** 40 21N 74 5W
Red Bay, *Canada* **141 B8** 51 44N 56 25W
Red Bluff, *U.S.A.* **158 F2** 40 11N 122 15W
Red Bluff L., *U.S.A.* **155 K3** 31 54N 103 55W
Red Bud, *U.S.A.* **156 F7** 38 13N 89 59W
Red Cliffs, *Australia* **128 C5** 34 19 S 142 11 E
Red Cloud, *U.S.A.* **154 E5** 40 5N 98 32W
Red Creek, *U.S.A.* **151 C8** 43 14N 76 45W
Red Deer, *Canada* **142 C6** 52 20N 113 50W
Red Deer →, *Alta., Canada* **143 C7** 50 58N 110 0W
Red Deer →, *Man., Canada* **143 C8** 52 53N 101 1W
Red Deer L., *Canada* **143 C8** 52 55N 101 20W
Red Devil, *U.S.A.* **144 F8** 61 46N 157 19W
Red Hook, *U.S.A.* **151 E11** 41 55N 73 53W
Red Indian L., *Canada* **141 C8** 48 35N 57 0W
Red L., *Canada* **143 C10** 51 3N 93 49W
Red Lake, *Canada* **143 C10** 51 3N 93 49W
Red Lake Falls, *U.S.A.* **154 B6** 47 53N 96 16W
Red Lake Road, *Canada* **143 C10** 49 59N 93 25W
Red Lodge, *U.S.A.* **158 D9** 45 11N 109 15W
Red Mountain, *U.S.A.* **161 K9** 35 37N 117 38W
Red Oak, *U.S.A.* **154 E7** 41 1N 95 14W
Red Rock, *Canada* **140 C2** 48 55N 88 15W
Red Rock, L., *U.S.A.* **156 C3** 41 22N 92 59W
Red Rocks Pt., *Australia* **125 F4** 32 13 S 127 32 E
Red Sea, *Asia* **102 C2** 25 0N 36 0 E
Red Slate Mt., *U.S.A.* **160 H8** 37 31N 118 52W
Red Sucker L., *Canada* **140 B1** 54 9N 93 40W
Red Tower Pass = Turnu Roşu, P., *Romania* **53 E9** 45 33N 24 17 E
Red Wing, *U.S.A.* **154 C8** 44 34N 92 31W
Reda, *Poland* **54 D5** 54 40N 18 19 E
Redang, *Malaysia* **78 C2** 5 49N 103 2 E
Redange, *Lux.* **24 E5** 49 46N 5 52 E
Redcar, *U.K.* **20 C6** 54 37N 1 4W
Redcar & Cleveland □, *U.K.* **20 C7** 54 29N 1 0W
Redcliff, *Canada* **143 C6** 50 10N 110 50W
Redcliffe, *Australia* **127 D5** 27 12 S 153 0 E
Redcliffe, Mt., *Australia* **125 E3** 28 30 S 121 30 E
Reddersburg, *S. Africa* **116 D4** 29 41 S 26 10 E
Reddick, *Fla., U.S.A.* **153 F7** 29 22N 82 12W
Reddick, *Ill., U.S.A.* **157 C8** 41 6N 88 15W
Redding, *Calif., U.S.A.* **158 F2** 40 35N 122 24W
Redding, *Iowa, U.S.A.* **156 D2** 40 36N 94 23W
Redditch, *U.K.* **21 E6** 52 18N 1 55W
Redenção, *Brazil* **170 B4** 4 13 S 38 43W
Redfield, *U.S.A.* **154 C5** 44 53N 98 31W
Redford, *U.S.A.* **151 B11** 44 38N 73 48W
Redkey, *U.S.A.* **157 D11** 40 21N 85 9W
Redkino, *Russia* **58 D9** 56 39N 36 16 E
Redlands, *U.S.A.* **161 M9** 34 4N 117 11W
Redmond, *Oreg., U.S.A.* **158 D3** 44 17N 121 11W
Redmond, *Wash., U.S.A.* **160 C4** 47 41N 122 7W
Redon, *France* **26 E4** 47 40N 2 6W
Redonda, *Antigua* **165 C7** 16 58N 62 19W
Redondela, *Spain* **42 C2** 42 15N 8 38W
Redondo, *Portugal* **43 G3** 38 39N 7 37W
Redondo Beach, *U.S.A.* **161 M8** 33 50N 118 23W
Redoubt Volcano, *U.S.A.* **144 F9** 60 29N 152 45W
Redruth, *U.K.* **21 G2** 50 14N 5 14W
Redvers, *Canada* **143 D8** 49 35N 101 40W
Redwater, *Canada* **142 C6** 53 55N 113 6W
Redwood, *U.S.A.* **151 B9** 44 18N 75 48W
Redwood City, *U.S.A.* **160 H4** 37 30N 122 15W
Redwood Falls, *U.S.A.* **154 C7** 44 32N 95 7W
Redwood National Park, *U.S.A.* **158 F1** 41 40N 124 5W
Ree, L., *Ireland* **23 C3** 53 35N 8 0W
Reed, L., *Canada* **143 C8** 54 38N 100 30W
Reed City, *U.S.A.* **148 D3** 43 53N 85 31W
Reedley, *U.S.A.* **160 J7** 36 36N 119 27W
Reedsburg, *U.S.A.* **154 D9** 43 32N 90 0W
Reedsport, *U.S.A.* **158 E1** 43 42N 124 6W
Reedsville, *U.S.A.* **150 F7** 40 39N 77 35W
Reedy Creek, *Australia* **128 D4** 36 58 S 140 2 E
Reefton, *Australia* **129 C7** 34 15 S 147 27 E
Reefton, *N.Z.* **131 C6** 42 6 S 171 51 E
Rees, *Germany* **30 D2** 51 46N 6 24 E
Reese →, *U.S.A.* **158 F5** 40 48N 117 4W
Refahiye, *Turkey* **101 C8** 39 54N 38 47 E
Reftele, *Sweden* **17 G7** 57 11N 13 35 E
Refugio, *U.S.A.* **155 L6** 28 18N 97 17W
Rega →, *Poland* **54 D2** 54 10N 15 18 E
Regalbuto, *Italy* **47 E7** 37 39N 14 38 E
Regen, *Germany* **31 G9** 48 58N 13 8 E
Regen →, *Germany* **31 F8** 49 1N 12 6 E
Regeneração, *Brazil* **170 C3** 6 15 S 42 41W
Regensburg, *Germany* **31 F8** 49 1N 12 6 E
Regensdorf, *Switz.* **33 B6** 47 26N 8 28 E
Regenstauf, *Germany* **31 F8** 49 7N 12 8 E
Reggello, *Italy* **45 E8** 43 41N 11 32 E
Réggio di Calábria, *Italy* **47 D8** 38 6N 15 39 E
Réggio nell'Emília, *Italy* **44 D7** 44 43N 10 36 E
Reghin, *Romania* **53 D9** 46 46N 24 42 E
Regina, *Canada* **143 C8** 50 27N 104 35W
Régina, *Fr. Guiana* **169 C7** 4 19N 52 8W
Regina Beach, *Canada* **143 C8** 50 47N 105 0W
Register, *U.S.A.* **152 C8** 32 22N 81 53W
Registro, *Brazil* **175 A6** 24 29 S 47 49W
Reguengos de Monsaraz, *Portugal* **43 G3** 38 25N 7 32W
Rehar →, *India* **93 H10** 23 55N 82 40 E
Rehli, *India* **93 H8** 23 38N 79 5 E
Rehoboth, *Namibia* **116 C2** 23 15 S 17 4 E
Rehovot, *Israel* **103 D3** 31 54N 34 48 E
Reichenbach, *Germany* **30 E8** 50 37N 12 17 E
Reichenbach, *Switz.* **32 C5** 46 38N 7 42 E
Reid, *Australia* **125 F4** 30 49 S 128 26 E
Reiden, *Switz.* **32 B5** 47 14N 7 59 E
Reidsville, *Ga., U.S.A.* **152 C7** 32 6N 82 7W
Reidsville, *N.C., U.S.A.* **149 G6** 36 21N 79 40W
Reigate, *U.K.* **21 F7** 51 14N 0 12W
Reillo, *Spain* **40 F3** 39 54N 1 53W
Reims, *France* **27 C11** 49 15N 4 1 E
Reina Adelaida, Arch., *Chile* **176 D2** 52 20 S 74 0W
Reinach, *Aargau, Switz.* **32 B6** 47 14N 8 11 E
Reinach, *Basel, Switz.* **32 B5** 47 29N 7 35 E
Reinbeck, *U.S.A.* **156 B4** 42 19N 92 36W
Reinbek, *Germany* **30 B6** 53 30N 10 16 E
Reindeer →, *Canada* **143 B8** 55 36N 103 11W
Reindeer I., *Canada* **143 C9** 52 30N 98 0W
Reindeer L., *Canada* **143 B8** 57 15N 102 15W
Reinga, C., *N.Z.* **130 A1** 34 25 S 172 43 E
Reinosa, *Spain* **42 B6** 43 2N 4 15W
Reinsvoll, *Norway* **18 D7** 60 40N 10 38 E
Reitan, *Norway* **18 B8** 62 49N 11 22 E
Reitz, *S. Africa* **117 D4** 27 48 S 28 29 E
Reivilo, *S. Africa* **116 D3** 27 36 S 24 8 E
Rejaf, *Sudan* **107 G3** 4 45N 31 35 E
Rejmyre, *Sweden* **17 F9** 58 50N 15 55 E
Rejowiec Fabryczny, *Poland* **55 G10** 51 5N 23 17 E
Reka →, *Slovenia* **45 C11** 45 40N 14 0 E
Rekovac, *Serbia, Yug.* **50 C5** 43 51N 21 3 E
Reliance, *Canada* **143 A7** 63 0N 109 20W
Remad, Oued →, *Algeria* **111 B4** 33 28N 1 20W
Rémalard, *France* **26 D7** 48 26N 0 47 E
Remarkable, Mt., *Australia* **128 B3** 32 48 S 138 10 E
Rembang, *Indonesia* **79 G14** 6 42 S 111 21 E
Rembau, *Malaysia* **84 B2** 2 35N 102 6 E
Rembert, *U.S.A.* **152 A9** 34 6N 80 32W
Remchi, *Algeria* **111 A4** 35 2N 1 26W
Remedios, *Colombia* **168 B3** 7 2N 74 41W
Remedios, *Panama* **164 E3** 8 15N 81 50W
Remeshk, *Iran* **97 E8** 26 55N 58 50 E
Remetea, *Romania* **53 D10** 46 45N 25 29 E
Remich, *Lux.* **24 E6** 49 32N 6 22 E
Remington, *U.S.A.* **157 D9** 40 46N 87 9W
Rémire, *Fr. Guiana* **169 C7** 4 53N 52 17W
Remiremont, *France* **27 D13** 48 2N 6 36 E
Remo, *Ethiopia* **107 F5** 6 48N 41 20 E
Remontnoye, *Russia* **61 G6** 46 34N 43 37 E
Remoulins, *France* **29 E8** 43 55N 4 35 E
Remscheid, *Germany* **24 C7** 51 11N 7 12 E
Ren Xian, *China* **74 F8** 37 8N 114 40 E
Rena, *Norway* **18 C8** 61 8N 11 20 E
Rena →, *Norway* **18 C8** 61 8N 11 23 E
Renascença, *Brazil* **168 D4** 3 50 S 66 21W
Rend Lake, *U.S.A.* **156 F8** 38 2N 88 58W
Rende, *Italy* **47 C9** 39 20N 16 11 E
Rendína, *Greece* **48 B3** 39 4N 21 58 E
Rendova, *Solomon Is.* **133 M9** 8 33 S 157 17 E
Rendsburg, *Germany* **30 A5** 54 17N 9 39 E
Renens, *Switz.* **32 C3** 46 32N 6 35 E
Renfrew, *Canada* **140 C4** 45 30N 76 40W
Renfrewshire □, *U.K.* **22 F4** 55 49N 4 38W
Renfroe, *U.S.A.* **152 C5** 32 14N 84 43W
Rengat, *Indonesia* **78 E2** 0 30 S 102 45 E
Rengo, *Chile* **174 C1** 34 24 S 70 50W
Renhua, *China* **77 E9** 25 5N 113 40 E
Renhuai, *China* **76 D6** 27 48N 106 24 E
Reni, *Ukraine* **59 K5** 45 28N 28 15 E
Renigunta, *India* **95 H4** 13 38N 79 30 E
Renk, *Sudan* **107 E3** 11 50N 32 50 E
Renland, *Greenland* **10 C8** 71 10N 26 30W
Renmark, *Australia* **128 C4** 34 11 S 140 43 E
Rennebu, *Norway* **18 B6** 62 52N 9 49 E
Rennell, *Solomon Is.* **133 N11** 11 40 S 160 10 E
Rennell Sd., *Canada* **142 C2** 53 23N 132 35W
Renner Springs, *Australia* **126 B1** 18 20 S 133 47 E
Rennes, *France* **26 D5** 48 7N 1 41W
Rennie L., *Canada* **143 A7** 61 32N 105 35W
Reno, *U.S.A.* **160 F7** 39 31N 119 48W
Reno →, *Italy* **45 D9** 44 38N 12 16 E
Renovo, *U.S.A.* **150 E7** 41 20N 77 45W
Renqiu, *China* **74 E9** 38 43N 116 5 E
Rens, *Denmark* **17 K3** 54 54N 9 5 E
Renshou, *China* **76 C5** 30 3N 104 9 E
Rensselaer, *Ind., U.S.A.* **157 D9** 40 57N 87 9W
Rensselaer, *N.Y., U.S.A.* **151 D11** 42 38N 73 45W
Rentería, *Spain* **40 B3** 43 19N 1 54W
Renton, *U.S.A.* **160 C4** 47 29N 122 12W
Renwick, *N.Z.* **131 B8** 41 30 S 173 51 E
Réo, *Burkina Faso* **112 C4** 12 28N 2 35W
Reocín, *Spain* **42 B6** 43 21N 4 5W
Reotipur, *India* **93 G10** 25 33N 83 45 E
Repalle, *India* **95 F5** 16 2N 80 45 E
Répcelak, *Hungary* **52 C2** 47 24N 17 1 E
Republic, *Mo., U.S.A.* **155 G8** 37 7N 93 29W
Republic, *Wash., U.S.A.* **158 B4** 48 39N 118 44W
Republican →, *U.S.A.* **154 F6** 39 4N 96 48W
Republiek, *Surinam* **169 B6** 5 30N 55 13W
Repulse Bay, *Canada* **139 B11** 66 30N 86 30W
Requena, *Peru* **172 B3** 5 5 S 73 52W
Requena, *Spain* **41 F3** 39 30N 1 4W
Réquista, *France* **28 D6** 44 1N 2 32 E
Reşadiye = Datça, *Turkey* **49 E9** 36 46N 27 40 E
Reşadiye, *Turkey* **100 B7** 40 23N 37 20 E
Reşadiye Yarımadası, *Turkey* **49 E9** 36 40N 27 45 E
Resavica, *Serbia, Yug.* **50 B5** 44 4N 21 31 E
Resen, *Macedonia* **50 E5** 41 5N 21 0 E
Reserve, *U.S.A.* **159 K9** 33 43N 108 45W
Resht = Rasht, *Iran* **97 B6** 37 20N 49 40 E
Résia, *Italy* **33 C11** 46 50N 10 31 E
Resistencia, *Argentina* **174 B4** 27 30 S 59 0W
Reşiţa, *Romania* **52 E6** 45 18N 21 53 E
Resko, *Poland* **54 E2** 53 47N 15 25 E
Resolution I., *Canada* **139 B13** 61 30N 65 0W
Resolution I., *N.Z.* **131 F1** 45 40 S 166 40 E
Resplandes, *Brazil* **170 C2** 6 17 S 45 13W
Resplendor, *Brazil* **171 E3** 19 20 S 41 15W
Ressano Garcia, *Mozam.* **117 D5** 25 25 S 32 0 E
Reston, *Canada* **143 D8** 49 33N 101 6W
Reszel, *Poland* **54 D8** 54 4N 21 10 E
Retalhuleu, *Guatemala* **164 D1** 14 33N 91 46W
Retenue, L. de, *Dem. Rep. of the Congo* **119 E2** 11 0 S 27 0 E
Retezat, Munţii, *Romania* **52 E8** 45 25N 23 0 E
Retford, *U.K.* **20 D7** 53 19N 0 56W
Rethel, *France* **27 C11** 49 30N 4 20 E
Rethem, *Germany* **30 C5** 52 47N 9 22 E
Réthímnon, *Greece* **38 D6** 35 18N 24 30 E

272 Réthímnon

Réthímnon □, Greece 38 D6 35 23N 24 28 E
Reti, Pakistan 92 E3 28 5N 69 48 E
Retiche, Alpi, Switz. 33 D10 46 30N 10 0 E
Retiers, France 26 E5 47 55N 1 23W
Retortillo, Spain 42 E4 40 48N 6 21W
Retournac, France 29 C8 45 12N 4 2 E
Rétság, Hungary 52 C4 47 58N 19 10 E
Rettenberg, Germany 33 A10 47 35N 10 18 E
Réunion ■, Ind. Oc. 105 J9 21 0S 56 0 E
Reus, Spain 40 D6 41 10N 1 5 E
Reuss →, Switz. 33 B6 47 16N 8 24 E
Reuterstadt Stavenhagen, Germany 30 B8 53 42N 12 54 E
Reutlingen, Germany 31 G5 48 29N 9 12 E
Reutte, Austria 34 D3 47 29N 10 42 E
Reval = Tallinn, Estonia 15 G21 59 22N 24 48 E
Revda, Russia 62 C7 56 48N 59 57 E
Revel, France 28 E6 43 28N 2 1 E
Revelganj, India 93 G11 25 50N 84 40 E
Revelstoke, Canada 142 C5 51 0N 118 10W
Reventazón, Peru 172 B1 6 10 S 80 58W
Revigny-sur-Ornain, France 27 D11 48 49N 4 59 E
Revillagigedo, Is. de, Pac. Oc. 162 D2 18 40N 112 0W
Revin, France 27 C11 49 55N 4 39 E
Revolyutsii, Pik, Tajikistan 63 D6 38 31N 72 21 E
Revúca, Slovak Rep. 35 C13 48 41N 20 7 E
Revuè →, Mozam. 119 F3 19 50 S 34 0 E
Rewa, India 93 G9 24 33N 81 25 E
Rewa →, Guyana 169 C6 3 19N 58 42W
Rewari, India 92 E7 28 15N 76 40 E
Rexburg, U.S.A. 158 E8 43 49N 111 47W
Rey, Iran 97 C6 35 35N 51 25 E
Rey, I. del, Panama 164 E4 8 20N 78 30W
Rey, Mayo →, Cameroon 114 A2 8 47N 14 1 E
Rey, Rio-del- →, Cameroon 114 B1 4 31N 8 45 E
Rey Bouba, Cameroon 114 A2 8 40N 14 15 E
Rey Malabo, Eq. Guin. 113 E6 3 45N 8 50 E
Reyðarfjörður, Iceland 11 B12 65 2N 14 13W
Reyes, Bolivia 172 C4 14 19 S 67 23W
Reyes, Pt., U.S.A. 160 H3 38 0N 123 0W
Reyhanlı, Turkey 100 D7 36 16N 36 35 E
Reykholt, Iceland 11 C6 64 10N 20 25W
Reykholt, Iceland 11 C5 64 40N 21 18W
Reykjahlíð, Iceland 11 B10 65 40N 16 55W
Reykjanes, Iceland 11 D4 63 48N 22 40W
Reykjavík, Iceland 11 C5 64 10N 21 57W
Reynolds, Ga., U.S.A. 152 C5 32 33N 84 6W
Reynolds, Ill., U.S.A. 156 C6 41 20N 90 40W
Reynolds Ra., Australia 124 D5 22 30 S 133 0 E
Reynoldsville, Ga., U.S.A. 152 E5 30 51N 84 47W
Reynoldsville, Pa., U.S.A. 150 E6 41 5N 78 58W
Reynosa, Mexico 163 B5 26 5N 98 18W
Rēzekne, Latvia 15 H22 56 30N 27 17 E
Rezh, Russia 62 C8 57 23N 61 24 E
Rezina, Moldova 53 C13 47 45N 28 58 E
Rezovo, Bulgaria 51 D12 42 0N 28 0 E
Rezvān, Iran 97 E8 27 34N 56 6 E
Rgotina, Serbia, Yug. 50 B6 44 1N 22 17 E
Rhamnus, Greece 48 C6 38 12N 24 3 E
Rharis, O. →, Algeria 111 C6 26 0N 5 4 E
Rhayader, U.K. 21 E4 52 18N 3 29W
Rheda-Wiedenbrück, Germany 30 D4 51 50N 8 20 E
Rhede, Germany 30 D2 51 50N 6 42 E
Rhein →, Europe 24 C6 51 52N 6 2 E
Rhein-Main-Donau-Kanal, Germany 31 F7 49 1N 11 27 E
Rheinbach, Germany 30 E2 50 38N 6 57 E
Rheine, Germany 30 C3 52 17N 7 26 E
Rheineck, Switz. 33 B9 47 28N 9 31 E
Rheinfelden, Germany 31 H3 47 33N 7 47 E
Rheinfelden, Switz. 32 A5 47 32N 7 47 E
Rheinhessen-Pfalz □, Germany 31 F3 49 20N 8 0 E
Rheinland-Pfalz □, Germany 31 E2 50 0N 7 0 E
Rheinsberg, Germany 30 B8 53 6N 12 54 E
Rheinwaldhorn, Switz. 33 D8 46 30N 9 3 E
Rheriss, Oued →, Morocco 110 B4 30 50N 4 34W
Rhin = Rhein →, Europe 24 C6 51 52N 6 2 E
Rhine = Rhein →, Europe 24 C6 51 52N 6 2 E
Rhine, U.S.A. 152 D6 31 59N 83 12W
Rhinebeck, U.S.A. 151 E11 41 56N 73 55W
Rhineland-Palatinate = Rheinland-Pfalz □, Germany 31 E2 50 0N 7 0 E
Rhinelander, U.S.A. 154 C10 45 38N 89 25W
Rhinns Pt., U.K. 22 F2 55 40N 6 29W
Rhino Camp, Uganda 118 B3 3 0N 31 22 E
Rhir, Cap, Morocco 110 B3 30 38N 9 54W
Rho, Italy 44 C6 45 32N 9 2 E
Rhode Island □, U.S.A. 151 E13 41 40N 71 30W
Rhodes = Ródhos, Greece 38 C10 36 15N 28 10 E
Rhodesia = Zimbabwe ■, Africa 119 F3 19 0 S 30 0 E
Rhodope Mts. = Rhodopi Planina, Bulgaria 51 E8 41 40N 24 20 E
Rhodopi Planina, Bulgaria 51 E8 41 40N 24 20 E
Rhön, Germany 30 E5 50 24N 9 58 E
Rhondda, U.K. 21 F4 51 39N 3 31W
Rhondda Cynon Taff □, U.K. 21 F4 51 42N 3 27W
Rhône □, France 29 C8 45 54N 4 35 E
Rhône →, France 29 E8 43 28N 4 42 E
Rhône-Alpes □, France 29 C9 45 40N 6 0 E
Rhum, U.K. 22 E2 57 0N 6 20W
Rhyl, U.K. 20 D4 53 20N 3 29W
Ri-Aba, Eq. Guin. 113 E6 3 28N 8 40 E
Riachão, Brazil 170 C2 7 20 S 46 37W
Riacho de Santana, Brazil 171 D3 13 37 S 42 57W
Rialma, Brazil 171 E2 15 18 S 49 34W
Riang, India 90 B4 27 31N 92 56 E
Riangnom, Sudan 107 F3 9 55N 30 1 E
Riaño, Spain 42 C6 42 59N 4 59W
Rians, France 29 E9 43 37N 5 44 E
Riansáres →, Spain 43 F7 39 32N 3 18W
Riasi, India 93 C6 33 10N 74 50 E
Riau □, Indonesia 78 D2 0 0 102 35 E
Riau, Kepulauan, Indonesia 78 D2 0 30N 104 20 E
Riau Arch. = Riau, Kepulauan, Indonesia 78 D2 0 30N 104 20 E
Riaza, Spain 42 D7 41 18N 3 30W
Riaza →, Spain 42 D7 41 42N 3 55W
Riba de Saelices, Spain 40 E2 40 55N 2 17W
Riba-Roja de Turia, Spain 41 F4 39 33N 0 34W
Ribadavia, Spain 42 C2 42 17N 8 8W
Ribadeo, Spain 42 B3 43 35N 7 5W
Ribadesella, Spain 42 B5 43 30N 5 7W
Ribado, Nigeria 113 D7 9 16N 12 47 E
Ribamar, Brazil 170 B3 2 33 S 44 3W
Ribao, Cameroon 113 D7 6 32N 11 30 E
Ribao, Cameroon 114 A2 6 32N 11 30 E
Ribas = Ribes de Freser, Spain 40 C7 42 19N 2 15 E
Ribas do Rio Pardo, Brazil 173 E7 20 27 S 53 46W
Ribāţ, Yemen 98 D4 14 18N 44 15 E
Ribble →, U.K. 20 D5 53 52N 2 25W
Ribe, Denmark 17 J2 55 19N 8 44 E
Ribe Amtskommune □, Denmark 17 J2 55 35N 8 45 E
Ribeauvillé, France 27 D14 48 10N 7 20 E
Ribécourt-Dreslincourt, France 27 C9 49 30N 2 55 E
Ribeira = Santa Uxía, Spain 42 C2 42 36N 8 58W
Ribeira Brava, Madeira 39 D2 32 41N 17 4W
Ribeira do Pombal, Brazil 170 D4 10 50 S 38 32W
Ribeirão, Brazil 170 C4 8 31 S 35 23W
Ribeirão Prêto, Brazil 175 A6 21 10 S 47 50W
Ribeiro Gonçalves, Brazil 170 C2 7 32 S 45 14W
Ribemont, France 27 C10 49 47N 3 27 E
Ribera, Italy 46 E6 37 30N 13 16 E
Ribérac, France 28 C4 45 15N 0 20 E
Riberalta, Bolivia 173 C4 11 0 S 66 0W
Ribes de Freser, Spain 40 C7 42 19N 2 15 E
Ribnica, Slovenia 45 C11 45 45N 14 45 E
Ribnitz-Damgarten, Germany 34 B7 50 0N 14 40 E
Ričany, Czech Rep. 30 A8 54 15N 12 27 E
Riccarton, N.Z. 131 D7 43 32 S 172 37 E
Ríccia, Italy 47 A7 41 30N 14 50 E
Riccione, Italy 45 E9 43 59N 12 39 E
Rice, U.S.A. 161 L12 34 5N 114 51W
Rice L., Canada 150 B6 44 12N 78 10W
Rice Lake, U.S.A. 154 C9 45 30N 91 44W
Riceboro, U.S.A. 152 D8 31 44N 81 26W
Rich, Morocco 110 B4 32 16N 4 30W
Rich, C., Canada 150 B4 44 43N 80 38W
Richard Toll, Senegal 112 B1 16 25N 15 42W
Richards Bay, S. Africa 117 D5 28 48 S 32 6 E
Richardson →, Canada 143 B6 58 25N 111 14W
Richardson Lakes, U.S.A. 148 C10 44 46N 70 58W
Richardson Mts., N.Z. 131 E3 44 49 S 168 34 E
Richardson Springs, U.S.A. 160 F5 39 51N 121 46W
Riche, C., Australia 125 F2 34 36 S 118 47 E
Richelieu, France 26 E7 47 1N 0 20 E
Richey, U.S.A. 154 B2 47 39N 105 4W
Richfield, U.S.A. 159 G8 38 46N 112 5W
Richfield Springs, U.S.A. 151 D10 42 51N 74 59W
Richford, U.S.A. 151 B12 45 0N 72 40W
Richibucto, Canada 141 C7 46 42N 64 54W
Richland, Ga., U.S.A. 152 C5 32 5N 84 40W
Richland, Iowa, U.S.A. 156 C5 41 13N 92 0W
Richland, Mo., U.S.A. 156 G4 37 51N 92 26W
Richland, Wash., U.S.A. 158 C4 46 17N 119 18W
Richland Center, U.S.A. 154 D9 43 21N 90 23W
Richlands, U.S.A. 148 G5 37 6N 81 48W
Richmond, N.S.W., Australia 129 B9 33 35 S 150 42 E
Richmond, Queens., Australia 126 C3 20 43 S 143 8 E
Richmond, N.Z. 131 B8 41 20 S 173 12 E
Richmond, U.K. 20 C6 54 25N 1 43W
Richmond, Calif., U.S.A. 160 H4 37 56N 122 21W
Richmond, Ind., U.S.A. 157 E12 39 50N 84 53W
Richmond, Ky., U.S.A. 157 G12 37 45N 84 18W
Richmond, Mich., U.S.A. 150 D2 42 49N 82 45W
Richmond, Mo., U.S.A. 156 E3 39 17N 93 58W
Richmond, Tex., U.S.A. 155 L7 29 35N 95 46W
Richmond, Utah, U.S.A. 158 F8 41 56N 111 48W
Richmond, Va., U.S.A. 148 G7 37 33N 77 27W
Richmond, Vt., U.S.A. 151 B12 44 24N 72 59W
Richmond, Mt., N.Z. 131 B8 41 32 S 173 22 E
Richmond Hill, Canada 150 C5 43 52N 79 27W
Richmond Hill, U.S.A. 152 D8 31 56N 81 18W
Richmond Ra., Australia 127 D5 29 0 S 152 45 E
Richmond Ra., N.Z. 131 B8 41 32 S 173 22 E
Richtersveil, Switz. 33 B7 47 13N 8 43 E
Richwood, Ohio, U.S.A. 157 D13 40 26N 83 18W
Richwood, W. Va., U.S.A. 148 F5 38 14N 80 32W
Ricla, Spain 40 D3 41 31N 1 24W
Ricupe, Angola 115 E4 14 37 S 21 25 E
Ridā', Yemen 98 D4 14 25N 44 50 E
Ridder = Leninogorsk, Kazakstan 64 D9 50 20N 83 30 E
Riddes, Switz. 32 D4 46 11N 7 14 E
Riddlesburg, U.S.A. 150 F6 40 9N 78 15W
Ridge Farm, U.S.A. 157 E9 39 54N 87 39W
Ridge Spring, U.S.A. 153 B8 33 51N 81 40W
Ridgecrest, U.S.A. 161 K9 35 38N 117 40W
Ridgefield, Conn., U.S.A. 151 E11 41 17N 73 30W
Ridgefield, Wash., U.S.A. 160 E4 45 49N 122 45W
Ridgeland, U.S.A. 152 C9 32 29N 80 59W
Ridgetown, Canada 140 D3 42 26N 81 52W
Ridgeville, Ind., U.S.A. 157 D11 40 18N 85 2W
Ridgeville, S.C., U.S.A. 152 B9 33 6N 80 19W
Ridgewood, U.S.A. 151 F10 40 59N 74 7W
Ridgway, Ill., U.S.A. 157 G8 37 48N 88 16W
Ridgway, Pa., U.S.A. 150 E6 41 25N 78 44W
Riding Mountain Nat. Park, Canada 143 C9 50 50N 100 0W
Ridley, Mt., Australia 125 F3 33 12 S 122 7 E
Riebeek-Oos, S. Africa 116 E4 33 10 S 26 10 E
Ried, Austria 34 C6 48 14N 13 30 E
Riedlingen, Germany 31 G5 48 9N 9 28 E
Riedstadt, Germany 31 F4 49 45N 8 30 E
Riehen, Switz. 32 A5 47 37N 7 38 E
Rienza →, Italy 45 B8 46 49N 11 47 E
Riesa, Germany 30 D9 51 17N 13 17 E
Riesco, I., Chile 176 D2 52 55 S 72 40W
Riesi, Italy 47 E7 37 17N 14 5 E
Riet →, S. Africa 116 D3 29 0 S 23 54 E
Rietavas, Lithuania 54 C8 55 44N 21 56 E
Rietbron, S. Africa 116 E3 32 54 S 23 10 E
Rietfontein, Namibia 116 C3 21 58 S 20 58 E
Rieti, Italy 45 F9 42 24N 12 51 E
Rieupeyroux, France 28 D6 44 19N 2 12 E
Riez, France 29 E10 43 49N 6 6 E
Riffe L., U.S.A. 160 D4 46 32N 122 26W
Rifle, U.S.A. 158 G10 39 32N 107 47W
Rift Valley □, Kenya 118 B4 0 20N 36 0 E
Rig Rig, Chad 109 F2 14 13N 14 25 E
Rīga, Latvia 15 H21 56 53N 24 8 E
Riga, G. of, Latvia 15 H20 57 40N 23 45 E
Rigacikun, Nigeria 113 C6 10 40N 7 28 E
Rīgān, Iran 97 D8 28 37N 58 58 E
Rīgas Jūras Līcis = Riga, G. of, Latvia 15 H20 57 40N 23 45 E
Rigaud, Canada 151 A10 45 29N 74 18W
Rigby, U.S.A. 158 E8 43 40N 111 55W
Rīgestān □, Afghan. 91 C2 30 15N 65 0 E
Riggins, U.S.A. 158 D5 45 25N 116 19W
Rignac, France 28 D6 44 25N 2 16 E
Rigolet, Canada 141 B8 54 10N 58 23W
Rihand Dam, India 93 G10 24 9N 83 2 E
Riihimäki, Finland 15 F21 60 45N 24 48 E
Riiser-Larsen-halvøya, Antarctica 7 C4 68 0 S 35 0 E
Rijau, Nigeria 113 C6 11 8N 5 17 E
Rijeka, Croatia 45 C11 45 20N 14 21 E
Rijeka Crnojevića, Montenegro, Yug. 50 D3 42 24N 19 1 E
Rijssen, Neths. 24 B6 52 19N 6 31 E
Rikā', W. ar →, Si. Arabia 98 B4 22 25N 44 50 E
Rike, Ethiopia 107 E4 10 50N 39 53 E
Rikuzentakada, Japan 68 E10 39 0N 141 40 E
Rila, Bulgaria 50 D7 42 7N 23 7 E
Rila Planina, Bulgaria 50 D7 42 10N 23 20 E
Riley, U.S.A. 158 E4 43 32N 119 28W
Rima →, Nigeria 113 C6 13 4N 5 10 E
Rimah, Wadi ar →, Si. Arabia 96 E4 26 5N 41 30 E
Rimavská Sobota, Slovak Rep. 35 C13 48 22N 20 2 E
Rimbey, Canada 142 C6 52 35N 114 15W
Rimbo, Sweden 16 E12 59 44N 18 21 E
Rimersburg, U.S.A. 150 E5 41 3N 79 30W
Rimforsa, Sweden 17 F9 58 6N 15 43 E
Rimi, Nigeria 113 C6 12 58N 7 43 E
Rímini, Italy 45 D9 44 3N 12 33 E
Rimouski, Canada 141 C6 48 27N 68 30W
Rimrock, U.S.A. 160 D5 46 38N 121 10W
Rinca, Indonesia 79 F1 8 45 S 119 35 E
Rincon, U.S.A. 152 C8 32 18N 81 14W
Rincón de la Victoria, Spain 43 J6 36 43N 4 18W
Rincón de Romos, Mexico 162 C4 22 14N 102 18W
Rinconada, Argentina 174 A2 22 26 S 66 10W
Rind →, India 93 G9 25 53N 80 33 E
Rindal, Norway 18 A6 63 3N 9 13 E
Ringarum, Sweden 17 F10 58 21N 16 26 E
Ringas, India 92 F6 27 21N 75 34 E
Ringe, Denmark 17 J4 55 13N 10 28 E
Ringebu, Norway 18 C7 61 32N 10 7 E
Ringgold Is., Fiji 133 A3 16 15 S 179 25W
Ringim, Nigeria 113 C6 12 13N 9 10 E
Ringkøbing, Denmark 17 H2 56 5N 8 15 E
Ringkøbing Amtskommune □, Denmark 17 H2 56 10N 8 45 E
Ringkøbing Fjord, Denmark 17 H2 56 0N 8 15 E
Ringoma, Angola 115 E3 12 25 S 17 32 E
Ringsaker, Norway 18 D7 60 54N 10 45 E
Ringsjön, Sweden 17 J7 55 55N 13 30 E
Ringsted, Denmark 17 J5 55 25N 11 46 E
Ringvassøy, Norway 14 B18 69 56N 19 15 E
Ringwood, U.S.A. 151 E10 41 7N 74 15W
Rinía, Greece 49 D7 37 23N 25 13 E
Rinjani, Indonesia 78 F5 8 24 S 116 28 E
Rinteln, Germany 30 C5 52 10N 9 8 E
Río, Punta del, Spain 41 J2 36 49N 2 24W
Rio Benito, Eq. Guin. 114 B1 1 35N 9 37 E
Rio Branco, Brazil 172 B4 9 58 S 67 49W
Río Branco, Uruguay 175 C5 32 40 S 53 40W
Río Bravo del Norte →, Mexico 163 B5 25 57N 97 9W
Rio Brilhante, Brazil 175 A5 21 48 S 54 33W
Río Bueno, Chile 176 B2 40 19 S 72 58W
Río Caribe, Venezuela 169 A5 10 42N 63 7W
Río Chico, Venezuela 168 A4 10 19N 65 59W
Rio Claro, Brazil 175 A6 22 19 S 47 35W
Rio Claro, Trin. & Tob. 165 D7 10 20N 61 25W
Río Colorado, Argentina 176 A4 39 0 S 64 0W
Río Cuarto, Argentina 174 C3 33 10 S 64 25W
Rio das Pedras, Mozam. 117 C6 23 8 S 35 28 E
Rio de Contas, Brazil 171 D3 13 36 S 41 48W
Rio de Janeiro, Brazil 171 F3 23 0 S 43 12W
Rio de Janeiro □, Brazil 171 F3 22 50 S 43 0W
Rio do Prado, Brazil 171 E3 16 35 S 40 34W
Rio do Sul, Brazil 175 B6 27 13 S 49 37W
Río Gallegos, Argentina 176 D3 51 35 S 69 15W
Rio Grande = Grande, Rio →, U.S.A. 155 N6 25 58N 97 9W
Río Grande, Argentina 176 D3 53 50 S 67 45W
Río Grande, Bolivia 172 E4 20 51 S 67 17W
Rio Grande, Brazil 175 C5 32 0 S 52 20W
Río Grande, Mexico 162 C4 23 50N 103 2W
Río Grande, Nic. 164 D3 12 54N 83 33W
Rio Grande City, U.S.A. 155 M5 26 23N 98 49W
Río Grande de Santiago →, Mexico 162 C3 21 36N 105 26W
Rio Grande do Norte □, Brazil 170 C4 5 40 S 36 0W
Rio Grande do Sul □, Brazil 175 C5 30 0 S 53 0W
Río Hato, Panama 164 E3 8 22N 80 10W
Rio Lagartos, Mexico 163 C7 21 36N 88 10W
Rio Largo, Brazil 170 C4 9 28 S 35 50W
Rio Maior, Portugal 43 F2 39 19N 8 57W
Rio Marina, Italy 44 F7 42 49N 10 25 E
Río Mayo, Argentina 176 C2 45 40 S 70 15W
Río Mulatos, Bolivia 172 D4 19 40 S 66 50W
Río Muni = Mbini □, Eq. Guin. 114 B2 1 30N 10 0 E
Rio Negro, Brazil 175 B6 26 0 S 49 55W
Río Negro, Chile 176 B2 40 47 S 73 14W
Rio Negro, Pantanal do, Brazil 173 D6 19 0 S 56 0W
Rio Pardo, Brazil 175 C5 30 0 S 52 30W
Río Pico, Argentina 176 B2 44 0 S 70 22W
Rio Preto da Eva, Brazil 169 D6 2 46 S 59 41W
Rio Rancho, U.S.A. 159 J10 35 14N 106 38W
Rio Real, Brazil 171 D4 11 28 S 37 56W
Río Segundo, Argentina 174 C3 31 40 S 63 59W
Río Tercero, Argentina 174 C3 32 15 S 64 8W
Rio Tinto, Brazil 170 C4 6 48 S 35 5W
Rio Tinto, Portugal 42 D2 41 11N 8 34W
Río Turbio, Argentina 176 D2 51 32 S 72 18W
Rio Verde, Brazil 171 E1 17 50 S 51 0W
Río Verde, Mexico 163 C5 21 56N 99 59W
Rio Verde de Mato Grosso, Brazil 173 D7 18 56 S 54 52W
Rio Vista, U.S.A. 160 G5 38 10N 121 42W
Ríobamba, Ecuador 168 D2 1 50 S 78 45W
Ríohacha, Colombia 168 A3 11 33N 72 55W
Rioja, Peru 172 B2 6 11 S 77 5W
Riom, France 28 C7 45 54N 3 7 E
Riom-ès-Montagnes, France 28 C6 45 17N 2 39 E
Rion-des-Landes, France 28 E3 43 55N 0 56W
Rionegro, Colombia 168 B3 7 15N 73 50W
Rionegro, Colombia 168 B2 6 9N 75 22W
Rionero in Vúlture, Italy 47 B8 40 55N 15 40 E
Rioni →, Georgia 61 J5 42 5N 41 50 E
Riós, Spain 42 D3 41 58N 7 16W
Riosinho →, Brazil 173 B7 7 7 S 51 39W
Ríosucio, Caldas, Colombia 168 B2 5 30N 75 40W
Ríosucio, Choco, Colombia 168 B2 7 27N 77 7W
Riou L., Canada 143 B7 59 7N 106 25W
Rioz, France 27 E13 47 26N 6 5 E
Rozinho →, Brazil 168 D4 2 55 S 67 7W
Ripatransone, Italy 45 F10 42 59N 13 46 E
Ripley, Canada 150 B3 44 4N 81 35W
Ripley, Calif., U.S.A. 161 M12 33 32N 114 39W
Ripley, N.Y., U.S.A. 150 D5 42 16N 79 43W
Ripley, Ohio, U.S.A. 157 F13 38 45N 83 51W
Ripley, Tenn., U.S.A. 155 H10 35 45N 89 32W
Ripley, W. Va., U.S.A. 148 F5 38 49N 81 43W
Ripoll, Spain 40 C7 42 15N 2 13 E
Ripon, U.K. 20 C6 54 9N 1 31W
Ripon, Calif., U.S.A. 160 H5 37 44N 121 7W
Ripon, Wis., U.S.A. 148 D1 43 51N 88 50W
Riposto, Italy 47 E8 37 44N 15 12 E
Risan, Montenegro, Yug. 50 D2 42 32N 18 42 E
Risaralda □, Colombia 168 B2 5 0N 76 10W
Riscle, France 28 E3 43 39N 0 5W
Rishā', W. ar →, Si. Arabia 96 E5 25 33N 44 5 E
Rishiri-Tō, Japan 68 B10 45 11N 141 15 E
Rishon le Ẕiyyon, Israel 103 D3 31 58N 34 48 E
Rising Sun, U.S.A. 157 F12 38 57N 84 51W
Risle →, France 26 C7 49 26N 0 23 E
Rison, U.S.A. 155 J8 33 58N 92 11W
Risør, Norway 15 G13 58 43N 9 13 E
Rissani, Morocco 110 B4 31 18N 4 12W
Rita Blanca Cr. →, U.S.A. 155 H3 35 40N 102 29W
Riti, Nigeria 113 D6 7 57N 9 41 E
Ritidian Pt., Guam 133 R15 13 39N 144 51 E
Ritter, Mt., U.S.A. 160 H7 37 41N 119 12W
Rittman, U.S.A. 150 F3 40 58N 81 47W
Ritzville, U.S.A. 158 C4 47 8N 118 23W
Riu, India 90 A5 28 19N 95 3 E
Riva del Garda, Italy 44 C7 45 53N 10 50 E
Riva Lígure, Italy 44 E4 43 50N 7 50 E
Rivadavia, Buenos Aires, Argentina 174 D3 35 29 S 62 59W
Rivadavia, Mendoza, Argentina 174 C2 33 13 S 68 30W
Rivadavia, Salta, Argentina 174 A3 24 5 S 62 54W
Rivadavia, Chile 174 B1 29 57 S 70 35W
Rivarolo Canavese, Italy 44 C4 45 19N 7 43 E
Rivas, Nic. 164 D2 11 30N 85 50W
Rive-de-Gier, France 29 C8 45 32N 4 37 E
River Cess, Liberia 112 D3 5 30N 9 32W
River Jordan, Canada 160 B2 48 26N 124 3W
Rivera, Argentina 174 D3 37 12 S 63 14W
Rivera, Uruguay 175 C4 31 0 S 55 50W
Riverbank, U.S.A. 160 H6 37 44N 120 56W
Riverdale, Calif., U.S.A. 160 J7 36 26N 119 52W
Riverdale, Ga., U.S.A. 152 B5 33 34N 84 25W
Riverhead, U.S.A. 151 F12 40 55N 72 40W
Riverhurst, Canada 143 C7 50 55N 106 50W
Rivers, Canada 143 C8 50 2N 100 14W
Rivers □, Nigeria 113 E6 4 30N 7 10 E
Rivers Inlet, Canada 142 C3 51 42N 127 15W
Riversdale, N.Z. 131 F3 45 54 S 168 44 E
Riversdale, S. Africa 116 E3 34 7 S 21 15 E
Riverside, U.S.A. 161 M9 33 59N 117 22W
Riverton, Australia 128 C3 34 10 S 138 46 E
Riverton, Canada 143 C9 51 1N 97 0W
Riverton, N.Z. 131 G2 46 21 S 168 0 E
Riverton, Ill., U.S.A. 156 E7 39 51N 89 33W
Riverton, Wyo., U.S.A. 158 E9 43 2N 108 23W
Riverton Heights, U.S.A. 160 C4 47 28N 122 17W
Riverview, U.S.A. 153 H7 27 52N 82 20W
Rives, France 29 C9 45 21N 5 31 E
Rivesaltes, France 28 F6 42 47N 2 50 E
Riviera, U.S.A. 161 K12 35 4N 114 35W
Riviera Beach, U.S.A. 153 J9 26 47N 80 3W
Riviera di Levante, Italy 44 D6 44 15N 9 30 E
Riviera di Ponente, Italy 44 D5 44 10N 8 20 E
Rivière-au-Renard, Canada 141 C7 48 59N 64 23W
Rivière-du-Loup, Canada 141 C6 47 50N 69 30W
Rivière-Pentecôte, Canada 141 C6 49 57N 67 1W
Rivière-Pilote, Martinique 165 D7 14 26N 60 53W
Rivière St. Paul, Canada 141 B8 51 28N 57 45W
Rivne, Ukraine 59 G4 50 40N 26 10 E
Rívoli, Italy 44 C4 45 3N 7 31 E
Rivoli B., Australia 128 D4 37 32 S 140 3 E
Riwaka, N.Z. 131 B7 41 5 S 172 59 E
Rixheim, France 27 E14 47 40N 7 24 E
Riyadh = Ar Riyāḍ, Si. Arabia 96 E5 24 41N 46 42 E
Rizal, Cagayan, Phil. 80 C3 17 51N 121 21 E
Rizal, Nueva Ecija, Phil. 80 D3 15 43N 121 6 E
Rizal, Zamboanga del N., Phil. 81 G4 8 35N 123 26 E
Rize, Turkey 101 B9 41 0N 40 30 E
Rizhao, China 75 G10 35 25N 119 30 E
Rizokarpaso, Cyprus 38 D13 35 36N 34 23 E
Rizzuto, C., Italy 47 D10 38 53N 17 5 E
Rjukan, Norway 15 G13 59 54N 8 33 E
Rjuven, Norway 18 E4 59 9N 7 8 E
Ro, Greece 49 E11 36 9N 29 33 E
Rô, N. Cal. 133 U21 21 22 S 167 50 E
Roa, Dem. Rep. of the Congo 114 B4 3 49N 24 56 E
Roa, Norway 18 D7 60 17N 10 37 E
Roa, Spain 42 D7 41 41N 3 56W
Roachdale, U.S.A. 157 E10 39 51N 86 48W
Road Town, Virgin Is. 165 C7 18 27N 64 37W
Roan Plateau, U.S.A. 158 G9 39 20N 109 20W
Roanne, France 27 F11 46 3N 4 4 E
Roanoke, Ala., U.S.A. 152 B4 33 9N 85 22W
Roanoke, Ind., U.S.A. 157 D11 40 58N 85 22W
Roanoke, Va., U.S.A. 148 G6 37 16N 79 56W
Roanoke →, U.S.A. 149 H7 35 57N 76 42W
Roanoke I., U.S.A. 149 H8 35 55N 75 40W
Roanoke Rapids, U.S.A. 149 G7 36 28N 77 40W
Roatán, Honduras 164 C2 16 18N 86 35W
Rob Roy, Solomon Is. 133 L9 7 23 S 157 36 E
Robāt Sang, Iran 97 C8 35 35N 59 10 E
Robbins I., Australia 126 G4 40 42 S 145 0 E
Róbbio, Italy 44 C5 45 17N 8 35 E
Robe, Australia 128 D3 37 11 S 139 45 E
Robe →, Australia 124 D2 21 42 S 116 15 E
Röbel, Germany 30 B8 53 22N 12 35 E
Robert Lee, U.S.A. 155 K4 31 54N 100 29W
Roberta, U.S.A. 152 C5 32 43N 84 1W
Roberts, U.S.A. 157 D8 40 37N 88 11W
Robertsdale, U.S.A. 150 F6 40 11N 78 6W
Robertsganj, India 93 G10 24 44N 83 4 E
Robertson, Australia 129 C9 34 37 S 150 36 E
Robertson, S. Africa 116 E2 33 46 S 19 50 E
Robertson I., Antarctica 7 C18 65 15 S 59 30W
Robertson Ra., Australia 124 D3 23 15 S 121 0 E
Robertsport, Liberia 112 D2 6 45N 11 26W
Robertstown, Australia 128 B3 33 58 S 139 5 E
Roberval, Canada 141 C5 48 32N 72 15W
Robeson Chan., Greenland 10 A4 82 0N 61 30W
Robesonia, U.S.A. 151 F8 40 21N 76 8W
Robi, Ethiopia 107 F4 7 52N 39 38 E
Robinson, U.S.A. 157 F9 39 0N 87 44W
Robinson →, Australia 126 B2 16 3 S 137 16 E
Robinson Ra., Australia 125 E2 25 40 S 119 0 E
Robinvale, Australia 128 C5 34 40 S 142 45 E
Robledo, Spain 41 G2 38 46N 2 26W
Roblin, Canada 143 C8 51 14N 101 21W
Roboré, Bolivia 173 D6 18 10 S 59 45W
Robson, Canada 142 D5 49 20N 117 41W
Robson, Mt., Canada 142 C5 53 10N 119 10W
Robstown, U.S.A. 155 M6 27 47N 97 40W
Roca, C. da, Portugal 43 G1 38 40N 9 31W
Roca Partida, I., Mexico 162 D2 19 1N 112 2W
Rocamadour, France 28 D5 44 48N 1 37 E
Rocca San Casciano, Italy 45 D8 44 3N 11 50 E
Roccadáspide, Italy 47 B8 40 27N 15 10 E
Roccastrada, Italy 45 F8 43 0N 11 10 E
Roccella Iónica, Italy 47 D9 38 19N 16 24 E
Rocha, Uruguay 175 C5 34 30 S 54 25W
Rochdale, U.K. 20 D5 53 38N 2 9W
Rochechouart, France 28 C4 45 50N 0 49 E
Rochedo, Brazil 173 D7 19 57 S 54 52W
Rochefort, Belgium 24 D5 50 9N 5 12 E
Rochefort, France 28 C3 45 56N 0 57W
Rochefort-en-Terre, France 26 E4 47 42N 2 22W
Rochelle, Ga., U.S.A. 152 D6 31 57N 83 27W
Rochelle, Ill., U.S.A. 156 C7 41 56N 89 4W
Rocher River, Canada 142 A6 61 23N 112 44W
Rocherservière, France 26 F5 46 57N 1 30W
Rochester, Australia 128 D6 36 22 S 144 41 E
Rochester, U.K. 21 F8 51 23N 0 31 E
Rochester, Ind., U.S.A. 157 C10 41 4N 86 13W
Rochester, Minn., U.S.A. 154 C8 44 1N 92 28W
Rochester, N.H., U.S.A. 151 C14 43 18N 70 59W
Rochester, N.Y., U.S.A. 150 C7 43 10N 77 37W
Rochester Hills, U.S.A. 157 B13 42 41N 83 9W
Rociu, Romania 53 F10 44 43N 25 2 E
Rock →, Canada 142 A3 60 7N 127 7W
Rock →, U.S.A. 156 C6 41 29N 90 37W
Rock Creek, U.S.A. 150 E4 41 40N 80 52W
Rock Falls, U.S.A. 156 C7 41 47N 89 41W

Ruhuhu 273

Rock Flat, Australia 129 D8 36 21 S 149 13 E
Rock Hill, U.S.A. 149 H5 34 56N 81 1W
Rock Island, U.S.A. 156 C6 41 30N 90 34W
Rock Rapids, U.S.A. 154 D6 43 26N 96 10W
Rock Sound, Bahamas 164 B4 24 54N 76 12W
Rock Springs, Mont., U.S.A. 158 C10 46 49N 106 15W
Rock Springs, Wyo., U.S.A. 158 F9 41 35N 109 14W
Rock Valley, U.S.A. 154 D6 43 12N 96 18W
Rockall, Atl. Oc. 8 C7 57 37N 13 42W
Rockdale, Tex., U.S.A. 155 K6 30 39N 97 0W
Rockdale, Wash., U.S.A. 160 C5 47 22N 121 28W
Rockefeller Plateau, Antarctica 7 E14 80 0 S 140 0W
Rockford, Ala., U.S.A. 152 C3 32 53N 86 13W
Rockford, Ill., U.S.A. 156 B7 42 16N 89 6W
Rockford, Iowa, U.S.A. 156 A4 43 3N 92 57W
Rockford, Mich., U.S.A. 157 A11 43 7N 85 34W
Rockford, Ohio, U.S.A. 157 D12 40 41N 84 39W
Rockglen, Canada 143 D7 49 11N 105 57W
Rockhampton, Australia 126 C5 23 22 S 150 32 E
Rockingham, Australia 125 F2 32 15 S 115 38 E
Rockingham, U.S.A. 149 H6 34 57N 79 46W
Rockingham B., Australia 126 B4 18 5 S 146 10 E
Rocklake, U.S.A. 154 A5 48 47N 99 15W
Rockland, Canada 151 A9 45 33N 75 17W
Rockland, Idaho, U.S.A. 158 E7 42 34N 112 53W
Rockland, Maine, U.S.A. 149 C11 44 6N 69 7W
Rockland, Mich., U.S.A. 154 B10 46 44N 89 11W
Rockledge, U.S.A. 153 G9 28 20N 80 43W
Rocklin, U.S.A. 160 G5 38 48N 121 14W
Rockmart, U.S.A. 149 H3 34 0N 85 3W
Rockport, Ind., U.S.A. 157 G9 37 53N 87 3W
Rockport, Mass., U.S.A. 151 D14 42 39N 70 37W
Rockport, Mo., U.S.A. 154 E7 40 25N 95 31W
Rockport, Tex., U.S.A. 155 L6 28 2N 97 3W
Rocksprings, U.S.A. 155 K4 30 1N 100 13W
Rockstone, Guyana 169 B6 5 59N 58 33W
Rockville, Conn., U.S.A. 151 E12 41 52N 72 28W
Rockville, Ind., U.S.A. 157 E9 39 46N 87 14W
Rockville, Md., U.S.A. 148 F7 39 5N 77 9W
Rockwall, U.S.A. 155 J6 32 56N 96 28W
Rockwell City, U.S.A. 156 B2 42 24N 94 38W
Rockwood, Canada 150 C4 43 37N 80 8W
Rockwood, Maine, U.S.A. 149 C11 45 41N 69 45W
Rockwood, Tenn., U.S.A. 149 H3 35 52N 84 41W
Rocky Ford, U.S.A. 154 F3 38 3N 103 43W
Rocky Fork Lake, U.S.A. 157 E13 39 12N 83 23W
Rocky Gully, Australia 125 F2 34 30 S 116 57 E
Rocky Harbour, Canada 141 C8 49 36N 57 55W
Rocky Island L., Canada 140 C3 46 55N 83 0W
Rocky Lane, Canada 142 B5 58 31N 116 22W
Rocky Mount, U.S.A. 149 H7 35 57N 77 48W
Rocky Mountain House, Canada 142 C6 52 22N 114 55W
Rocky Mountain National Park, U.S.A. 158 F11 40 25N 105 45W
Rocky Mts., N. Amer. 158 G10 49 0N 115 0W
Rocky Point, Namibia 116 B2 19 3 S 12 30 E
Rocroi, France 27 C11 49 55N 4 30 E
Rod, Pakistan 91 C1 28 10N 63 5 E
Rødberg, Norway 18 D5 60 17N 8 56 E
Rødby, Denmark 17 K5 54 41N 11 23 E
Rødbyhavn, Denmark 17 K5 54 39N 11 22 E
Roddickton, Canada 141 B8 50 51N 56 8W
Rødding, Denmark 17 J3 55 23N 9 3 E
Rödeby, Sweden 17 H9 56 15N 15 37 E
Rødekro, Denmark 17 J3 55 4N 9 20 E
Rodenkirchen, Germany 30 B4 53 23N 8 26 E
Rodez, France 28 D6 44 21N 2 33 E
Rodholívas, Greece 44 D6 40 55N 24 0 E
Rodhópi □, Greece 51 E9 41 5N 25 30 E
Rodhopoú, Greece 38 D5 35 34N 23 45 E
Ródhos, Greece 38 C10 36 15N 28 10 E
Rodi Gargánico, Italy 45 G12 41 55N 15 53 E
Rodna, Romania 53 C9 47 25N 24 50 E
Rodnei, Munţii, Romania 53 C9 47 35N 24 35 E
Rodney, Canada 150 D3 42 34N 81 41W
Rodney, C., N.Z. 130 C3 36 17 S 174 50 E
Rodniki, Russia 60 B5 57 7N 41 47 E
Rodonit, Kepi i, Albania 50 E3 41 35N 19 27 E
Rodriguez, Ind. Oc. 121 F5 19 45 S 63 20 E
Roe →, U.K. 23 A5 55 6N 6 59W
Roebling, U.S.A. 151 F10 40 7N 74 47W
Roebourne, Australia 124 D2 20 44 S 117 9 E
Roebuck B., Australia 124 C3 18 5 S 122 20 E
Roermond, Neths. 24 C6 51 12N 6 0 E
Roes Welcome Sd., Canada 139 B11 65 0N 87 0W
Roeselare, Belgium 24 D3 50 57N 3 7 E
Rogachev = Ragachow, Belarus 59 F6 53 8N 30 5 E
Rogačica, Serbia, Yug. 50 B3 44 4N 19 40 E
Rogagua, L., Bolivia 172 C4 13 43 S 66 50W
Rogaland □, Norway 18 E3 59 12N 6 20 E
Rogaška Slatina, Slovenia 45 B12 46 15N 15 42 E
Rogatec, Slovenia 45 B12 46 15N 15 46 E
Rogatica, Bos.-H. 52 G4 43 47N 19 0 E
Rogatyn, Ukraine 59 H3 49 24N 24 36 E
Rogdhia, Greece 38 D7 35 22N 25 1 E
Rogers, U.S.A. 155 G7 36 20N 94 7W
Rogers City, U.S.A. 148 C4 45 25N 83 49W
Rogersville, Canada 141 C6 46 44N 65 26W
Roggan →, Canada 140 B4 54 24N 79 25W
Roggan L., Canada 140 B4 54 8N 77 50W
Roggeveldberge, S. Africa 116 E3 32 10 S 20 10 E
Roggiano Gravina, Italy 47 C9 39 37N 16 9 E
Rogliano, France 29 F13 42 57N 9 30 E
Rogliano, Italy 47 C9 39 10N 16 19 E
Rogoaguado, L., Bolivia 173 C4 13 0 S 65 30W
Rogoźno, Poland 55 F3 52 45N 16 59 E
Rogue →, U.S.A. 158 E1 42 26N 124 26W
Roha, India 94 E1 18 26N 73 7 E
Rohan, France 26 D4 48 4N 2 45W
Róhda, Greece 38 A3 39 48N 19 46 E
Rohnert Park, U.S.A. 160 G4 38 16N 122 40W
Rohri, Pakistan 91 D3 27 45N 68 51 E
Rohri Canal, Pakistan 92 F3 26 15N 68 27 E
Rohtak, India 92 E7 28 55N 76 43 E
Roi Et, Thailand 78 A2 16 4N 103 40 E
Roja, Latvia 15 H20 57 29N 22 43 E
Rojas, Argentina 174 C3 34 10 S 60 45W
Rojişte, Romania 53 F8 44 4N 23 56 E
Rojo, C., Mexico 163 C5 21 33N 97 20W
Rokan →, Indonesia 78 D2 2 0N 100 50 E
Rokel →, S. Leone 112 D2 8 30N 12 48W
Rokiškis, Lithuania 15 J21 55 55N 25 35 E
Rokitno, Russia 59 G8 50 57N 35 56 E
Rokycany, Czech Rep. 34 B6 49 43N 13 35 E
Rolândia, Brazil 175 A5 23 18 S 51 23W
Røldal, Norway 18 E3 59 47N 6 50 E
Rolfe, U.S.A. 156 B2 42 49N 94 31W
Rolla, U.S.A. 155 G9 37 57N 91 46W
Rollands Plains, Australia 129 A10 31 17 S 152 42 E
Rolle, Switz. 32 D2 46 28N 6 20 E
Rolleston, Australia 126 C4 24 28 S 148 35 E
Rolleston, N.Z. 131 D7 43 35 S 172 24 E
Rolling Fork →, U.S.A. 157 G11 37 55N 85 50W
Rollingstone, Australia 126 B4 19 2 S 146 24 E
Rom, Norway 18 F4 58 8N 7 5 E
Rom, Sudan 107 F3 9 54N 32 16 E
Roma, Australia 127 D4 26 32 S 148 49 E
Roma, Italy 45 G9 41 54N 12 29 E
Roma, Sweden 17 G12 57 32N 18 26 E
Roma, U.S.A. 155 M5 26 25N 99 1W
Romain C., U.S.A. 149 J6 33 0N 79 22W
Romaine, Canada 141 B7 50 13N 60 40W
Romaine →, Canada 141 B7 50 18N 63 47W
Roman, Bulgaria 50 C7 43 8N 23 57 E
Roman, Romania 53 D11 46 57N 26 55 E
Roman-Kosh, Gora, Ukraine 59 K8 44 37N 34 15 E
Romanche →, France 29 C9 45 5N 5 43 E
Romang, Indonesia 79 F7 7 30 S 127 20 E
Românî, Egypt 103 E1 30 59N 32 38 E
Romania ■, Europe 53 D10 46 0N 25 0 E
Romanija, Bos.-H. 52 G3 43 50N 18 45 E
Romano, C., U.S.A. 153 K8 25 51N 81 41W
Romano, Cayo, Cuba 164 B4 22 0N 77 30W
Romanovka = Basarabeasca, Moldova 53 D13 46 21N 28 58 E
Romans-sur-Isère, France 29 C9 45 3N 5 3 E
Romanshorn, Switz. 33 A8 47 33N 9 22 E
Rombari, Sudan 107 G3 4 33N 31 2 E
Romblon, Phil. 79 B6 12 33N 122 17 E
Romblon □, Phil. 80 E4 12 30N 122 15 E
Romblon Pass, Phil. 80 E4 12 27N 122 12 E
Rome = Roma, Italy 45 G9 41 54N 12 29 E
Rome, Ga., U.S.A. 149 H3 34 15N 85 10W
Rome, N.Y., U.S.A. 151 C9 43 13N 75 27W
Rome, Pa., U.S.A. 151 E8 41 51N 76 21W
Romeoville, U.S.A. 157 C8 41 39N 88 3W
Rometta, Italy 47 D8 38 10N 15 25 E
Romilly-sur-Seine, France 27 D10 48 31N 3 44 E
Rommani, Morocco 110 B3 33 31N 6 40W
Romney, U.S.A. 148 F6 39 21N 78 45W
Romney Marsh, U.K. 21 F8 51 2N 0 54 E
Romny, Ukraine 59 G7 50 48N 33 28 E
Rømø, Denmark 17 J2 55 10N 8 30 E
Romodan, Ukraine 59 G7 49 55N 33 15 E
Romodanovo, Russia 60 C7 54 26N 45 23 E
Romont, Switz. 32 C3 46 42N 6 54 E
Romorantin-Lanthenay, France 27 E8 47 21N 1 45 E
Rompin →, Malaysia 84 B2 2 49N 103 29 E
Romsdalen, Norway 15 E12 62 25N 7 52 E
Romsdalsfjorden, Norway 18 B4 62 38N 7 20 E
Romsey, U.K. 21 G6 51 0N 1 29W
Ron, India 95 G2 15 40N 75 44 E
Ron, Vietnam 86 D6 17 53N 106 27 E
Rona, U.K. 22 D3 57 34N 5 59W
Ronan, U.S.A. 158 C6 47 32N 114 6W
Roncador, Cayos, Caribbean 164 D3 13 32N 80 4W
Roncador, Serra do, Brazil 171 D1 12 30 S 52 30W
Ronciglione, Italy 45 F9 42 17N 12 13 E
Ronco →, Italy 45 D9 44 24N 12 12 E
Ronda, Spain 43 J5 36 46N 5 12W
Ronda, Serranía de, Spain 43 J5 36 44N 5 3W
Rondane, Norway 15 F13 61 57N 9 50 E
Rondón, Colombia 168 B3 6 17N 71 6W
Rondônia, Brazil 173 C5 10 52 S 61 57W
Rondônia □, Brazil 173 C5 11 0 S 63 0W
Rondonópolis, Brazil 173 D7 16 28 S 54 38W
Rondslottet, Norway 18 C6 61 55N 9 45 E
Rong, Koh, Cambodia 87 G4 10 45N 103 15 E
Rong Jiang →, China 76 E7 24 35N 109 20 E
Rong Xian, Guangxi Zhuangzu, China 77 F8 22 50N 110 31 E
Rong Xian, Sichuan, China 76 C5 29 23N 104 22 E
Rong'an, China 76 E7 25 14N 109 22 E
Rongchang, China 76 C5 29 20N 105 32 E
Ronge, L. la, Canada 143 B7 55 6N 105 17W
Rongjiang, China 76 E7 25 57N 108 28 E
Rongotea, N.Z. 130 G4 40 19 S 175 25 E
Rongshui, China 76 E7 25 5N 109 12 E
Rønne, Denmark 17 J8 55 6N 14 43 E
Ronne Ice Shelf, Antarctica 7 D18 78 0 S 60 0W
Ronneby, Sweden 17 H9 56 12N 15 17 E
Ronnebyån →, Sweden 17 H9 56 11N 15 18 E
Rönneshytta, Sweden 17 F9 58 56N 15 2 E
Ronsard, C., Australia 125 D1 24 46 S 113 10 E
Ronse, Belgium 24 D3 50 45N 3 35 E
Ronuro →, Brazil 173 C7 11 56 S 53 33W
Roodepoort, S. Africa 117 D4 26 11 S 27 54 E
Roodhouse, U.S.A. 156 E6 39 29N 90 24W
Roof Butte, U.S.A. 159 H9 36 28N 109 5W
Rooiboklaagte →, Namibia 116 C3 20 50 S 21 0 E
Roopville, U.S.A. 152 B4 33 27N 85 8W
Roorkee, India 92 E7 29 52N 77 59 E
Roosendaal, Neths. 24 C4 51 32N 4 29 E
Roosevelt, U.S.A. 158 F8 40 18N 109 59W
Roosevelt →, Brazil 173 B5 7 35 S 60 20W
Roosevelt, Mt., Canada 142 B3 58 26N 125 20W
Roosevelt I., Antarctica 7 D12 79 30 S 162 0W
Root, Switz. 33 B6 47 5N 8 23 E
Ropczyce, Poland 55 H8 50 4N 21 38 E
Roper →, Australia 126 A2 14 43 S 135 27 E
Roper Bar, Australia 126 A1 14 44 S 134 44 E
Roque Pérez, Argentina 174 D4 35 25 S 59 24W
Roquefort, France 28 D3 44 2N 0 20W
Roquemaure, France 29 D8 44 3N 4 48 E
Roquetas de Mar, Spain 41 J2 36 46N 2 36W
Roquetes, Spain 40 E5 40 50N 0 30 E
Roquevaire, France 29 E9 43 20N 5 36 E
Roraima □, Brazil 169 C5 2 0N 61 30W
Roraima, Mt., Venezuela 169 B5 5 10N 60 40W
Røros, Norway 15 E14 62 35N 11 23 E
Rorschach, Switz. 33 B8 47 28N 9 28 E
Rosa, Zambia 119 D3 9 33 S 31 15 E
Rosa, C., Algeria 111 A6 37 0N 8 16 E
Rosa, L., Bahamas 165 B5 21 0N 73 30W
Rosa, Monte, Europe 32 E5 45 57N 7 53 E
Rosa, Monte, Italy 44 C4 45 55N 7 53 E
Rosal de la Frontera, Spain 43 H3 37 59N 7 13W
Rosales, Phil. 80 D3 15 54N 120 38 E
Rosalia, U.S.A. 158 C5 47 14N 117 22W
Rosamond, U.S.A. 161 L8 34 52N 118 10W
Rosans, France 29 D9 44 24N 5 29 E
Rosario, Argentina 174 C3 33 0 S 60 40W
Rosário, Brazil 170 B3 3 0 S 44 15W
Rosario, Baja Calif., Mexico 162 B1 30 0N 115 50W
Rosario, Sinaloa, Mexico 162 C3 23 0N 105 52W
Rosario, Paraguay 174 A4 24 30 S 57 35W
Rosario, Phil. 81 G5 8 24N 125 59 E
Rosario, Villa del, Venezuela 168 A3 10 19N 72 19W
Rosario de la Frontera, Argentina 174 B3 25 50 S 65 0W
Rosario de Lerma, Argentina 174 A2 24 59 S 65 35W
Rosario del Tala, Argentina 174 C4 32 20 S 59 10W
Rosário do Sul, Brazil 175 C5 30 15 S 54 55W
Rosário Oeste, Brazil 173 C6 14 50 S 56 25W
Rosarito, Mexico 161 N9 32 18N 117 4W
Rosarno, Italy 47 D8 38 29N 15 59 E
Rosas = Roses, Spain 40 C8 42 19N 3 10 E
Roscoe, Miss., U.S.A. 156 G3 37 58N 93 48W
Roscoe, N.Y., U.S.A. 151 E10 41 56N 74 55W
Roscoff, France 26 D3 48 44N 3 58W
Roscommon, Ireland 23 C3 53 38N 8 11W
Roscommon □, Ireland 23 C3 53 49N 8 23W
Roscrea, Ireland 23 D4 52 57N 7 49W
Rose →, Australia 126 A2 14 16 S 135 45 E
Rose Blanche, Canada 141 C8 47 38N 58 45W
Rose Pt., Canada 142 C2 54 11N 131 39W
Rose Valley, Canada 143 C8 52 19N 103 49W
Roseau, Domin. 165 C7 15 20N 61 24W
Roseau, U.S.A. 154 A7 48 51N 95 46W
Rosebery, Australia 126 G4 41 46 S 145 33 E
Rosebud, S. Dak., U.S.A. 154 D4 43 14N 100 51W
Rosebud, Tex., U.S.A. 155 K6 31 4N 96 59W
Roseburg, U.S.A. 158 E2 43 13N 123 20W
Rosedale, U.S.A. 155 J9 33 51N 91 2W
Roseland, U.S.A. 160 G4 38 25N 122 43W
Rosemary, Canada 142 C6 50 46N 112 5W
Rosenberg, U.S.A. 155 L7 29 34N 95 49W
Rosendaël, France 27 A9 51 3N 2 24 E
Rosendal, Norway 18 E3 59 59N 6 0 E
Rosendale, U.S.A. 156 D2 40 4N 94 51W
Rosenheim, Germany 31 H8 47 51N 12 7 E
Roses, Spain 40 C8 42 19N 3 10 E
Roses, G. de, Spain 40 C8 42 10N 3 15 E
Roseto degli Abruzzi, Italy 45 F11 42 41N 14 1 E
Rosetown, Canada 143 C7 51 35N 107 59W
Rosetta = Rashîd, Egypt 106 H7 31 21N 30 22 E
Roseville, Calif., U.S.A. 160 G5 38 45N 121 17W
Roseville, Ill., U.S.A. 156 D6 40 44N 90 40W
Roseville, Mich., U.S.A. 150 D2 42 30N 82 56W
Rosewood, N.S.W., Australia 129 C7 35 38 S 147 52 E
Rosewood, Queens., Australia 127 D5 27 38 S 152 36 E
Roshkhvār, Iran 97 C8 34 58N 59 37 E
Rosières-en-Santerre, France 27 C9 49 49N 2 42 E
Rosignano Maríttimo, Italy 44 E7 43 24N 10 28 E
Rosignol, Guyana 169 B6 6 15N 57 30W
Roşiori de Vede, Romania 53 F10 44 9N 25 0 E
Rositsa, Bulgaria 51 C11 43 57N 27 57 E
Rositsa →, Bulgaria 51 C9 43 10N 25 30 E
Roskilde, Denmark 17 J6 55 38N 12 3 E
Roskilde Amtskommune □, Denmark 17 J6 55 35N 12 5 E
Roskovec, Albania 50 F3 40 44N 19 43 E
Roslavl, Russia 58 F7 53 57N 32 55 E
Roslyn, Australia 129 C8 34 29 S 149 37 E
Rosmaninhal, Portugal 42 F3 39 44N 7 5W
Rosmead, S. Africa 116 E4 31 29 S 25 8 E
Røsnæs, Denmark 17 J4 55 44N 10 55 E
Rosolini, Italy 47 F7 36 49N 14 57 E
Rosporden, France 26 E3 47 57N 3 50W
Ross, Australia 126 G4 42 2 S 147 30 E
Ross, N.Z. 131 C5 42 53 S 170 49 E
Ross Béthio, Mauritania 112 B1 16 15N 16 8W
Ross I., Antarctica 7 D11 77 30 S 168 0 E
Ross Ice Shelf, Antarctica 7 E12 80 0 S 180 0 E
Ross L., U.S.A. 158 B3 48 44N 121 4W
Ross-on-Wye, U.K. 21 F5 51 54N 2 34W
Ross River, Australia 126 C1 23 44 S 134 30 E
Ross River, Canada 142 A2 62 30N 131 30W
Ross Sea, Antarctica 7 D11 74 0 S 178 0 E
Rossa, Switz. 33 D8 46 23N 9 8 E
Rossall Pt., U.K. 20 D4 53 55N 3 3W
Rossan Pt., Ireland 23 B3 54 42N 8 47W
Rossano, Italy 47 C9 39 36N 16 39 E
Rossburn, Canada 143 C8 50 40N 100 49W
Rosseau, Canada 150 A5 45 16N 79 39W
Rosseau L., Canada 150 A5 45 10N 79 35W
Rossel, C., Vanuatu 133 L4 20 23 S 166 36 E
Rossens, Switz. 32 C4 46 43N 7 7 E
Rosses, The, Ireland 23 A3 55 2N 8 20W
Rossford, U.S.A. 157 C13 41 36N 83 34W
Rossignol, L., Canada 140 B5 52 43N 73 40W
Rossignol Res., Canada 141 D6 44 12N 65 10W
Rosskreppfjorden, Norway 18 E4 59 4N 7 10 E
Rossland, Canada 142 D5 49 6N 117 50W
Rosslare, Ireland 23 D5 52 17N 6 24W
Rosslau, Germany 30 D8 51 52N 12 15 E
Rosso, Mauritania 112 B1 16 40N 15 45W
Rosso, C., France 29 F12 42 13N 8 32 E
Rossosh, Russia 59 G10 50 15N 39 28 E
Røssvatnet, Norway 14 D16 65 45N 14 5 E
Rossville, Ill., U.S.A. 157 D9 40 23N 87 40W
Rossville, Ind., U.S.A. 157 D10 40 25N 86 36W
Røst, Norway 14 C15 67 32N 12 0 E
Rostāq, Afghan. 91 A3 37 7N 69 49 E
Rosthern, Canada 143 C7 52 40N 106 20W
Rostock, Germany 30 A8 54 5N 12 8 E
Rostov, Don, Russia 59 J10 47 15N 39 45 E
Rostov, Yaroslavl, Russia 58 D10 57 14N 39 25 E
Rostrenen, France 26 D3 48 14N 3 21W
Roswell, Ga., U.S.A. 152 A5 34 2N 84 22W
Roswell, N. Mex., U.S.A. 155 J2 33 24N 104 32W
Rota, Spain 43 J4 36 37N 6 20W
Rotan, U.S.A. 155 J4 32 51N 100 28W
Rote Wand, Austria 33 B9 47 11N 9 59 E
Rotenburg, Hessen, Germany 30 E5 50 59N 9 44 E
Rotenburg, Niedersachsen, Germany 30 B5 53 6N 9 25 E
Roth, Germany 31 F7 49 15N 11 5 E
Rothaargebirge, Germany 30 D4 51 2N 8 13 E
Rothenburg, Switz. 33 B6 47 6N 8 16 E
Rothenburg ob der Tauber, Germany 31 F6 49 23N 10 11 E
Rother →, U.K. 21 G8 50 59N 0 45 E
Rotherham, U.K. 20 D6 53 26N 1 20W
Rothes, U.K. 22 D5 57 32N 3 13W
Rothesay, Canada 141 C6 45 23N 66 0W
Rothesay, U.K. 22 F3 55 50N 5 3W
Rothrist, Switz. 32 B5 47 18N 7 54 E
Roti, Indonesia 79 F6 10 50 S 123 0 E
Rotja, Pta., Spain 41 G6 38 38N 1 35 E
Rotnes, Norway 18 D7 60 3N 10 51 E
Roto, Australia 129 B6 33 0 S 145 30 E
Roto Aira L., N.Z. 130 F4 39 3 S 175 45 E
Rotoehu L., N.Z. 130 E5 38 1 S 176 32 E
Rotoiti, L., N.Z. 130 E5 38 2 S 176 26 E
Rotoiti L., N.Z. 131 B7 41 51 S 172 49 E
Rotoma L., N.Z. 130 E5 38 2 S 176 35 E
Rotoroa, L., N.Z. 131 B7 41 55 S 172 39 E
Rotorua, N.Z. 130 E5 38 9 S 176 16 E
Rotorua, L., N.Z. 130 E5 38 5 S 176 18 E
Rott →, Germany 31 G9 48 27N 13 25 E
Rotten →, Switz. 32 D5 46 18N 7 36 E
Rottenburg, Germany 31 G4 48 28N 8 55 E
Rottenmann, Austria 34 D7 47 31N 14 22 E
Rotterdam, Neths. 24 C4 51 55N 4 30 E
Rotterdam, U.S.A. 151 D10 42 48N 74 1W
Rottne, Sweden 17 G8 57 1N 14 54 E
Rottnest I., Australia 125 F2 32 0 S 115 27 E
Rottumeroog, Neths. 24 A6 53 33N 6 34 E
Rottweil, Germany 31 G4 48 9N 8 37 E
Rotuma, Fiji 134 J9 12 25 S 177 5 E
Roubaix, France 27 B10 50 40N 3 10 E
Roudnice nad Labem, Czech Rep. 34 A7 50 25N 14 15 E
Rouen, France 26 C8 49 27N 1 4 E
Rouergue, France 28 D5 44 15N 2 0 E
Rough Ridge, N.Z. 131 F4 45 10 S 169 55 E
Rouillac, France 28 C3 45 47N 0 4W
Rouleau, Canada 143 C8 50 10N 104 56W
Round Mountain, U.S.A. 158 G5 38 43N 117 4W
Round Mt., Australia 127 E5 30 26 S 152 16 E
Round Rock, U.S.A. 155 K6 30 31N 97 41W
Roundup, U.S.A. 158 C9 46 27N 108 33W
Roura, Fr. Guiana 169 C7 4 44N 52 20W
Rousay, U.K. 22 B5 59 10N 3 2W
Rouses Point, U.S.A. 151 B11 44 59N 73 22W
Rouseville, U.S.A. 150 E5 41 28N 79 42W
Roussillon, Isère, France 29 C8 45 24N 4 49 E
Roussillon, Pyrénées-Or., France 28 F6 42 30N 2 35 E
Roussin, C., N. Cal. 133 U21 21 20 S 167 59 E
Rouxville, S. Africa 116 E4 30 25 S 26 50 E
Rouyn-Noranda, Canada 140 C4 48 20N 79 0W
Rovaniemi, Finland 14 C21 66 29N 25 41 E
Rovato, Italy 44 C7 45 34N 10 0 E
Rovenki, Ukraine 59 H10 48 5N 39 21 E
Rovereto, Italy 44 C8 45 53N 11 3 E
Roverud, Norway 18 D9 60 15N 12 3 E
Rovigo, Italy 45 C8 45 4N 11 47 E
Rovinj, Croatia 45 C10 45 5N 13 40 E
Rovira, Colombia 168 C2 4 15N 75 20W
Rovno = Rivne, Ukraine 59 G4 50 40N 26 10 E
Rovnoye, Russia 60 E8 50 52N 46 3 E
Rovuma = Ruvuma →, Tanzania 119 E5 10 29 S 40 28 E
Row'ān, Iran 97 C6 35 8N 48 51 E
Rowena, Australia 127 D4 29 48 S 148 55 E
Rowes, Australia 129 D8 37 0 S 149 6 E
Rowley Shoals, Australia 124 C2 17 30 S 119 0 E
Roxa, Guinea-Biss. 112 C1 11 15N 15 45W
Roxas, Phil. 81 F2 10 20N 119 21 E
Roxas, Capiz, Phil. 79 B6 11 36N 122 49 E
Roxas, Isabela, Phil. 80 C3 17 8N 121 36 E
Roxas, Mind. Or., Phil. 80 E3 12 35N 121 31 E
Roxboro, U.S.A. 149 G6 36 24N 78 59W
Roxburgh, N.Z. 131 F4 45 33 S 169 19 E
Roxbury, U.S.A. 150 F7 40 6N 77 39W
Roxen, Sweden 17 F9 58 30N 15 40 E
Roy, Mont., U.S.A. 158 C9 47 20N 108 58W
Roy, N. Mex., U.S.A. 155 H2 35 57N 104 12W
Roy, Utah, U.S.A. 158 F7 41 10N 112 2W
Royal Canal, Ireland 23 C4 53 30N 7 13W
Royal Center, U.S.A. 157 D10 40 52N 86 30W
Royal Leamington Spa, U.K. 21 E6 52 18N 1 31W
Royal Oak, U.S.A. 157 B13 42 30N 83 9W
Royal Tunbridge Wells, U.K. 21 F8 51 7N 0 16 E
Royalla, Australia 129 C8 35 30 S 149 9 E
Royan, France 28 C2 45 37N 1 2W
Roye, France 27 C9 49 42N 2 48 E
Royston, U.K. 21 E7 52 3N 0 0W
Rožaj, Montenegro, Yug. 50 D4 42 50N 20 11 E
Różan, Poland 55 F8 52 52N 21 25 E
Rozay-en-Brie, France 27 D9 48 41N 2 58 E
Rozdilna, Ukraine 59 J6 46 50N 30 2 E
Rozhyshche, Ukraine 59 G3 50 54N 25 15 E
Rožmitál pod Třemšínem, Czech Rep. 34 B6 49 36N 13 53 E
Rožňava, Slovak Rep. 35 C13 48 37N 20 35 E
Rozogi, Poland 54 E8 53 28N 21 19 E
Rozoy-sur-Serre, France 27 C11 49 40N 4 8 E
Rozzano, Italy 44 C6 45 22N 9 10 E
Rrësheni, Albania 50 E3 41 47N 19 49 E
Rrogozhino, Albania 50 E3 41 4N 19 50 E
Rtanj, Serbia, Yug. 50 C5 43 45N 21 50 E
Rtishchevo, Russia 60 D6 52 18N 43 46 E
Rúa = A Rúa, Spain 42 C3 42 24N 7 6W
Ruacaná, Angola 116 B1 17 20 S 14 12 E
Ruahine Ra., N.Z. 130 F5 39 55 S 176 2 E
Ruamahanga →, N.Z. 130 H4 41 24 S 175 8 E
Ruapehu, N.Z. 130 F4 39 17 S 175 35 E
Ruapuke I., N.Z. 131 G3 46 46 S 168 31 E
Ruâq, W. →, Egypt 103 F2 30 0N 33 49 E
Ruatoria, N.Z. 130 D7 37 55 S 178 20 E
Ruawai, N.Z. 130 C2 36 8 S 173 59 E
Rub' al Khālī, Si. Arabia 99 C5 18 0N 48 0 E
Rubeho Mts., Tanzania 118 D4 6 50 S 36 25 E
Rubezhnoye = Rubizhne, Ukraine 59 H10 49 6N 38 25 E
Rubh a' Mhail, U.K. 22 F2 55 56N 6 8W
Rubha Hunish, U.K. 22 D2 57 42N 6 20W
Rubha Robhanais = Lewis, Butt of, U.K. 22 C2 58 31N 6 16W
Rubi, Spain 40 D7 41 29N 2 2 E
Rubiataba, Brazil 171 E2 15 8 S 49 48W
Rubicon →, U.S.A. 160 G5 38 53N 121 4W
Rubicone →, Italy 45 D9 44 8N 12 28 E
Rubik, Albania 50 E3 41 46N 19 47 E
Rubinéia, Brazil 171 F1 20 13 S 51 2W
Rubino, Ivory C. 112 D4 6 4N 4 18W
Rubio, Venezuela 168 B3 7 43N 72 22W
Rubizhne, Ukraine 59 H10 49 6N 38 25 E
Rubtsovsk, Russia 64 D9 51 30N 81 10 E
Ruby L., U.S.A. 158 F6 40 10N 115 28W
Ruby Mts., U.S.A. 158 F6 40 30N 115 20W
Rubyvale, Australia 126 C4 23 25 S 147 42 E
Rucheng, China 77 E9 25 33N 113 38 E
Ruciane-Nida, Poland 54 E8 53 40N 21 32 E
Rūd Sar, Iran 97 B6 37 8N 50 18 E
Ruda, Sweden 17 G10 57 6N 16 7 E
Ruda Śląska, Poland 55 H5 50 16N 18 50 E
Rudall, Australia 128 B2 33 43 S 136 17 E
Rudall →, Australia 124 D3 22 34 S 122 13 E
Rūdbār, Afghan. 91 C1 30 9N 62 36 E
Rüdersdorf, Germany 30 C9 52 27N 13 47 E
Rudewa, Tanzania 119 E3 10 7 S 34 40 E
Rudkøbing, Denmark 17 K4 54 56N 10 41 E
Rudna, Poland 55 G3 51 30N 16 17 E
Rudnik, Bulgaria 51 D11 42 36N 27 30 E
Rudnik, Poland 55 H9 50 26N 22 15 E
Rudnik, Serbia, Yug. 50 B4 44 7N 20 35 E
Rudnya, Russia 58 E6 54 55N 31 7 E
Rudnyy, Kazakstan 62 E9 52 57N 63 7 E
Rudo, Bos.-H. 52 G4 43 41N 19 23 E
Rudolfa, Ostrov, Russia 64 A6 81 45N 58 30 E
Rudolstadt, Germany 30 E7 50 44N 11 19 E
Rudong, China 77 A13 32 20N 121 12 E
Rudozem, Bulgaria 51 E8 41 29N 24 51 E
Rudyard, U.S.A. 148 B3 46 14N 84 36W
Rue, France 27 B8 50 15N 1 40 E
Rufa'a, Sudan 107 E3 14 44N 33 22 E
Rufflin, U.S.A. 152 B9 33 0N 80 49W
Rufiji →, Tanzania 118 D4 7 50 S 39 15 E
Rufino, Argentina 174 C3 34 20 S 62 50W
Rufisque, Senegal 112 C1 14 40N 17 15W
Rufunsa, Zambia 119 F2 15 4 S 29 34 E
Rugao, China 77 A13 32 23N 120 31 E
Rugby, U.K. 21 E6 52 23N 1 16W
Rugby, U.S.A. 154 A5 48 22N 100 0W
Rügen, Germany 30 A9 54 22N 13 24 E
Rugles, France 26 D7 48 50N 0 40 E
Ruhea, Bangla. 90 B2 26 10N 88 25 E
Ruhengeri, Rwanda 118 C2 1 30 S 29 36 E
Ruhla, Germany 30 E6 50 53N 10 21 E
Ruhland, Germany 30 D9 51 27N 13 51 E
Ruhnu, Estonia 15 H20 57 48N 23 15 E
Ruhr →, Germany 30 D2 51 27N 6 43 E
Ruhuhu →, Tanzania 119 E3 10 31 S 34 34 E

S

Salisbury 275

St. Croix →, *U.S.A.* 154 C8 44 45N 92 48W
St. Croix Falls, *U.S.A.* 154 C8 45 24N 92 38W
St-Cyprien, *France* 28 F7 42 37N 3 2 E
St-Cyr-sur-Mer, *France* 29 E9 43 11N 5 43 E
St. David, *U.S.A.* 156 D6 40 30N 90 3W
St. David's, *Canada* 141 C8 48 12N 58 52W
St. David's, *U.K.* 21 F2 51 53N 5 16W
St. David's Head, *U.K.* 21 F2 51 54N 5 19W
St-Denis, *France* 27 D9 48 56N 2 22 E
St-Denis, *Réunion* 121 G4 20 52 S 55 27 E
St-Dié, *France* 27 D13 48 17N 6 56 E
St-Dizier, *France* 27 D11 48 38N 4 56 E
St-Égrève, *France* 29 C9 45 14N 5 41 E
St. Elias, Mt., *U.S.A.* 138 B5 60 18N 140 56W
St. Elias Mts., *Canada* 142 A1 60 33N 139 28W
St. Elias Mts., *U.S.A.* 144 G13 60 0N 138 0W
St.-Élie, *Fr. Guiana* 169 C7 4 49N 53 17W
St. Elmo, *U.S.A.* 157 E8 39 2N 88 51W
St-Eloy-les-Mines, *France* 27 F9 46 10N 2 51 E
St-Émilion, *France* 28 D3 44 53N 0 9W
St-Étienne, *France* 29 C8 45 27N 4 22 E
St-Étienne-de-Tinée, *France* 29 D10 44 16N 6 56 E
St-Étienne-du-Rouvray, *France* 26 C8 49 23N 1 6 E
St. Eugène, *Canada* 151 A10 45 30N 74 28W
St. Eustatius, *W. Indies* 165 C7 17 20N 63 0W
St-Fargeau, *France* 27 E10 47 39N 3 4 E
St-Félicien, *Canada* 140 C5 48 40N 72 25W
St-Florent, *France* 29 F13 42 41N 9 18 E
St-Florent, G. de, *France* 29 F13 42 47N 9 12 E
St-Florent-sur-Cher, *France* 27 F9 46 59N 2 15 E
St-Florentin, *France* 27 E10 48 0N 3 45 E
St-Flour, *France* 28 C7 45 2N 3 6 E
St. Francis, *U.S.A.* 154 F4 39 47N 101 48W
St. Francis →, *U.S.A.* 155 H9 34 38N 90 36W
St. Francis, C., *S. Africa* 116 E3 34 14 S 24 49 E
St. Francisville, *Ill., U.S.A.* 157 F9 38 36N 87 39W
St. Francisville, *La., U.S.A.* 155 K9 30 47N 91 23W
St-François, L., *Canada* 151 A10 45 10N 74 22W
St-Fulgent, *France* 26 F5 46 50N 1 10W
St-Gabriel, *Canada* 140 C5 46 17N 73 24W
St. Gallen = Sankt Gallen, *Switz.* 33 B8 47 26N 9 22 E
St. Gallenkirch, *Austria* 33 B9 47 1N 9 58 E
St-Galmier, *France* 27 G11 45 35N 4 19 E
St-Gaudens, *France* 28 E4 43 6N 0 44 E
St-Gaultier, *France* 26 F8 46 39N 1 26 E
St-Gengoux-le-National, *France* 27 F11 46 37N 4 40 E
St-Geniez-d'Olt, *France* 28 D6 44 27N 2 58 E
St. George, *Australia* 127 D4 28 1 S 148 30 E
St. George, *Canada* 141 C6 45 11N 66 50W
St. George, *Ga., U.S.A.* 152 E7 30 31N 82 2W
St. George, *S.C., U.S.A.* 152 B9 33 11N 80 35W
St. George, *Utah, U.S.A.* 159 H7 37 6N 113 35W
St. George, C., *Canada* 141 C8 48 30N 59 16W
St. George, C., *Papua N. G.* 132 C7 4 49 S 152 53 E
St. George, C., *U.S.A.* 149 L3 29 40N 85 5W
St. George I., *Alaska, U.S.A.* 144 H5 56 35N 169 35W
St. George I., *Fla., U.S.A.* 152 F5 29 35N 84 55W
St. George Ra., *Australia* 124 C4 18 40 S 125 0 E
St. George's, *Canada* 141 C8 48 26N 58 31W
St-Georges, *Canada* 141 C5 46 8N 70 40W
St-Georges, *Fr. Guiana* 169 C7 4 0N 52 0W
St. George's, *Grenada* 165 D7 12 5N 61 43W
St. George's B., *Canada* 141 C8 48 24N 58 53W
St. Georges Basin, *N.S.W., Australia* 127 F5 35 7 S 150 36 E
St. Georges Basin, *W. Austral., Australia* 124 C4 15 23 S 125 2 E
St. George's Channel, *Europe* 23 E6 52 0N 6 0W
St. George's Channel, *Papua N. G.* 132 C7 4 10 S 152 20 E
St. Georges Hd., *Australia* 129 C9 35 12 S 150 42 E
St-Georges-lès-Baillargeaux, *France* 28 B4 46 41N 0 22 E
St-Germain-de-Calberte, *France* 28 D7 44 13N 3 48 E
St-Germain-en-Laye, *France* 27 D9 48 54N 2 6 E
St-Germain-Lembron, *France* 28 C7 45 27N 3 14 E
St-Gervais-d'Auvergne, *France* 27 F9 46 4N 2 50 E
St-Gervais-les-Bains, *France* 29 C10 45 53N 6 42 E
St-Gildas, Pte. de, *France* 26 E4 47 8N 2 14W
St-Gilles, *France* 29 E8 43 40N 4 26 E
St-Gingolph, *Switz.* 32 D3 46 24N 6 48 E
St-Girons, *Ariège, France* 28 F5 42 59N 1 8 E
St-Girons, *Landes, France* 28 E2 43 56N 1 18W
St. Gotthard P. = San Gottardo, P. del, *Switz.* 33 C7 46 33N 8 33 E
St. Helena, *U.S.A.* 158 G2 38 30N 122 28W
St. Helena ■, *Atl. Oc.* 9 K8 15 55 S 5 44W
St. Helena, Mt., *U.S.A.* 160 G4 38 40N 122 36W
St. Helena B., *S. Africa* 116 E2 32 40 S 18 10 E
St. Helena Sd., *U.S.A.* 152 C9 32 15N 80 25W
St. Helens, *Australia* 126 G4 41 20 S 148 15 E
St. Helens, *U.K.* 20 D5 53 27N 2 44W
St. Helens, *U.S.A.* 160 E4 45 52N 122 48W
St. Helens, Mt., *U.S.A.* 160 D4 46 12N 122 12W
St. Helier, *U.K.* 21 H5 49 10N 2 7W
St-Herblain, *France* 26 E5 47 13N 1 40W
St-Hilaire-du-Harcouët, *France* 26 D5 48 35N 1 5W
St-Hippolyte, *France* 27 E13 47 19N 6 50 E
St-Hippolyte-du-Fort, *France* 28 E7 43 58N 3 52 E
St-Honoré-les-Bains, *France* 27 F10 46 54N 3 50 E
St-Hubert, *Belgium* 24 D5 50 2N 5 23 E
St-Hyacinthe, *Canada* 140 C5 45 40N 72 58W
St. Ignace, *U.S.A.* 148 C3 45 52N 84 44W
St. Ignace I., *Canada* 140 C2 48 45N 88 0W
St. Ignatius, *U.S.A.* 158 C6 47 19N 114 6W
St-Imier, *Switz.* 32 B3 47 9N 6 58 E
St. Ives, *U.K.* 21 G2 50 12N 5 30W
St-James, *France* 26 D5 48 31N 1 20W
St. James, *Minn., U.S.A.* 154 D7 43 59N 94 38W
St. James, *Mo., U.S.A.* 156 G5 38 0N 91 37W
St-Jean →, *Canada* 141 B7 50 17N 64 20W
St-Jean, L., *Canada* 141 C5 48 40N 72 0W
St-Jean-d'Angély, *France* 28 C3 45 57N 0 31W
St-Jean-de-Braye, *France* 27 E8 47 53N 1 58 E
St-Jean-de-Luz, *France* 28 E2 43 23N 1 39W
St-Jean-de-Maurienne, *France* 29 C10 45 16N 6 21 E
St-Jean-de-Monts, *France* 26 F4 46 47N 2 4W
St-Jean-du-Gard, *France* 28 D7 44 7N 3 52 E
St-Jean-en-Royans, *France* 29 C9 45 1N 5 18 E
St-Jean-Pied-de-Port, *France* 28 E2 43 10N 1 14W
St-Jean-Port-Joli, *Canada* 141 C5 47 15N 70 13W
St-Jean-sur-Richelieu, *Canada* 151 A11 45 20N 73 20W
St-Jérôme, *Canada* 140 C5 45 47N 74 0W
St. Joe, *U.S.A.* 157 C12 41 19N 84 54W
St. John, *Canada* 141 C6 45 20N 66 8W
St. John, *U.S.A.* 155 G5 38 0N 98 46W
St. John →, *Liberia* 112 D2 6 40N 9 10W
St. John →, *U.S.A.* 149 C12 45 12N 66 5W
St. John, C., *Canada* 141 C8 50 0N 55 32W
St. John's, *Antigua* 165 C7 17 6N 61 51W
St. John's, *Canada* 141 C9 47 35N 52 40W
St. Johns, *Ariz., U.S.A.* 159 J9 34 30N 109 22W
St. Johns, *Mich., U.S.A.* 157 B12 43 0N 84 33W
St. Johns →, *U.S.A.* 152 E8 30 24N 81 24W
St. John's Pt., *Ireland* 23 B3 54 34N 8 27W
St. Johnsbury, *U.S.A.* 151 B12 44 25N 72 1W
St. Johnsville, *U.S.A.* 151 D10 43 0N 74 43W
St-Joseph, *N. Cal.* 133 K4 20 27 S 166 36 E
St. Joseph, *Ill., U.S.A.* 157 D8 40 7N 88 2W
St. Joseph, *La., U.S.A.* 155 K9 31 55N 91 14W
St. Joseph, *Mich., U.S.A.* 157 B10 42 6N 86 29W
St. Joseph, *Mo., U.S.A.* 156 E2 39 46N 94 50W
St. Joseph →, *U.S.A.* 157 B10 42 7N 86 29W
St. Joseph, I., *Canada* 140 C3 46 12N 83 58W
St. Joseph, L., *Canada* 140 B1 51 10N 90 35W
St. Joseph Pt., *U.S.A.* 152 F4 29 52N 85 24W
St-Jovite, *Canada* 140 C5 46 8N 74 38W
St-Juéry, *France* 28 E6 43 57N 2 12 E
St-Julien-Chapteuil, *France* 29 C8 45 2N 4 4 E
St-Julien-de-Vouvantes, *France* 26 E5 47 38N 1 13W
St-Julien-en-Genevois, *France* 27 F13 46 9N 6 5 E
St-Junien, *France* 28 C4 45 53N 0 55 E
St-Just-en-Chaussée, *France* 27 C9 49 30N 2 25 E
St-Just-en-Chevalet, *France* 28 C7 45 55N 3 50 E
St. Kilda, *N.Z.* 131 F5 45 53 S 170 31 E
St. Kitts & Nevis ■, *W. Indies* 165 C7 17 20N 62 40W
St. Laurent, *Canada* 143 C9 50 25N 97 58W
St-Laurent, *Fr. Guiana* 169 B7 5 29N 54 3W
St-Laurent-de-la-Salanque, *France* 28 F6 42 46N 2 59 E
St-Laurent-du-Pont, *France* 29 C9 45 23N 5 45 E
St-Laurent-en-Grandvaux, *France* 27 F12 46 35N 5 58 E
St-Laurent-et-Benon, *France* 28 C3 45 8N 0 49W
St. Lawrence, *Australia* 126 C4 22 16 S 149 31 E
St. Lawrence, *Canada* 141 C8 46 54N 55 23W
St. Lawrence →, *Canada* 141 C6 49 30N 66 0W
St. Lawrence, Gulf of, *Canada* 141 C7 48 25N 62 0W
St. Lawrence I., *U.S.A.* 138 B3 63 30N 170 30W
St. Leonard, *Canada* 141 C6 47 12N 67 58W
St-Léonard-de-Noblat, *France* 28 C5 45 49N 1 29 E
St. Leonhard im Pitztal, *Austria* 33 B11 47 4N 10 51 E
St. Lewis →, *Canada* 141 B8 52 26N 56 11W
St-Lô, *France* 26 C5 49 7N 1 5W
St-Louis, *France* 27 E14 47 30N 7 34 E
St. Louis, *Gabon* 114 C2 1 9S 10 1 E
St. Louis, *Senegal* 112 B1 16 8N 16 27W
St. Louis, *U.S.A.* 156 F6 38 37N 90 12W
St. Louis →, *U.S.A.* 154 B8 47 15N 92 45W
St-Loup-sur-Semouse, *France* 27 E13 47 53N 6 16 E
St. Lucia ■, *W. Indies* 165 D7 14 0N 60 50W
St. Lucia, L., *S. Africa* 117 D5 28 5 S 32 30 E
St. Lucia Channel, *W. Indies* 165 D7 14 15N 61 0W
St. Lucie, *U.S.A.* 153 H9 27 29N 80 20W
St. Lucie Canal, *U.S.A.* 153 H9 27 10N 80 18W
St. Maarten, *W. Indies* 165 C7 18 0N 63 5W
St. Magnus B., *U.K.* 22 A7 60 25N 1 35W
St-Maixent-l'École, *France* 28 B3 46 24N 0 12W
St-Malo, *France* 26 D4 48 39N 2 1W
St-Malo, G. de, *France* 26 D4 48 50N 2 30W
St-Mandrier-sur-Mer, *France* 29 E9 43 4N 5 57 E
St-Marc, *Haiti* 165 C5 19 10N 72 41W
St-Marcellin, *France* 29 C9 45 9N 5 20 E
St-Marcouf, Îs., *France* 26 C5 49 30N 1 10W
St. Maries, *U.S.A.* 158 C5 47 19N 116 35W
St. Marks, *U.S.A.* 152 E5 30 9N 84 12W
St-Martin, *W. Indies* 165 C7 18 0N 63 0W
St. Martin, L., *Canada* 143 C9 51 40N 98 30W
St-Martin-de-Crau, *France* 29 E8 43 38N 4 48 E
St-Martin-de-Ré, *France* 28 B2 46 12N 1 21W
St-Martin-d'Hères, *France* 29 C9 45 9N 5 45 E
St-Martin-Vésubie, *France* 29 D11 44 4N 7 15 E
St-Martory, *France* 28 E4 43 9N 0 56 E
St. Mary, *U.S.A.* 156 G7 37 53N 89 57W
St. Mary, Mt., *Papua N. G.* 132 E4 8 8 S 147 2 E
St. Mary Is., *India* 95 H2 13 20N 74 35 E
St. Mary Pk., *Australia* 128 A3 31 32 S 138 34 E
St. Marys, *Australia* 126 G4 41 35 S 148 11 E
St. Marys, *Canada* 150 C3 43 20N 81 10W
St. Mary's, *Corn., U.K.* 21 H1 49 55N 6 18W
St. Mary's, *Orkney, U.K.* 22 C6 58 54N 2 54W
St. Mary's, *Alaska, U.S.A.* 144 E7 62 4N 163 10W
St. Marys, *Ga., U.S.A.* 152 E8 30 44N 81 33W
St. Marys, *Ohio, U.S.A.* 157 D12 40 33N 84 24W
St. Marys, *Pa., U.S.A.* 150 E6 41 26N 78 34W
St. Marys →, *U.S.A.* 152 E8 30 43N 81 27W
St. Mary's, C., *Canada* 141 C9 46 50N 54 12W
St. Mary's B., *Canada* 141 C9 46 50N 53 50W
St. Marys Bay, *Canada* 141 D6 44 25N 66 10W
St-Mathieu, Pte., *France* 26 D2 48 20N 4 45W
St. Matthew I., *U.S.A.* 144 F4 60 24N 172 42W
St. Matthews, *Ky., U.S.A.* 157 F11 38 15N 85 39W
St. Matthews, *S.C., U.S.A.* 152 B9 33 40N 80 46W
St. Matthews, I. = Zadetkyi Kyun, *Burma* 78 C1 10 0N 98 25 E
St. Matthias Group, *Papua N. G.* 132 A5 1 30 S 150 0 E
St-Maurice, *Switz.* 32 D4 46 13N 7 0 E
St-Maurice →, *Canada* 140 C5 46 21N 72 31W
St-Maximin-la-Ste-Baume, *France* 29 E9 43 27N 5 52 E
St-Médard-en-Jalles, *France* 28 D3 44 53N 0 43W
St-Méen-le-Grand, *France* 26 D4 48 11N 2 12W
St. Meinrad, *U.S.A.* 157 F10 38 10N 86 49W
St-Mihiel, *France* 27 D12 48 54N 5 32 E
St. Moritz, *Switz.* 31 J5 46 30N 9 51 E
St-Nazaire, *France* 26 E4 47 17N 2 12W
St. Neots, *U.K.* 21 E7 52 14N 0 15W
St-Nicolas-de-Port, *France* 27 D13 48 38N 6 18 E
St. Niklaas, *Belgium* 24 C4 51 10N 4 8 E
St. Niklaus, *Switz.* 32 D5 46 10N 7 49 E
St-Omer, *France* 27 B9 50 45N 2 15 E
St-Palais-sur-Mer, *France* 28 C2 45 38N 1 5W
St-Pamphile, *Canada* 141 C6 46 58N 69 48W
St-Pardoux-la-Rivière, *France* 28 C4 45 29N 0 45 E
St. Paris, *U.S.A.* 157 D13 40 8N 83 58W
St. Pascal, *Canada* 141 C6 47 32N 69 48W
St. Paul, *Canada* 142 C6 54 0N 111 17W
St-Paul, *France* 29 D10 44 31N 6 45 E
St. Paul, *Alaska, U.S.A.* 144 H5 57 7N 170 17W
St. Paul, *Ind., U.S.A.* 157 E11 39 26N 85 38W
St. Paul, *Minn., U.S.A.* 154 C8 44 57N 93 6W
St. Paul, *Nebr., U.S.A.* 154 E5 41 13N 98 27W
St-Paul →, *Canada* 141 B8 51 27N 57 42W
St. Paul →, *Liberia* 112 D2 6 25N 10 48W
St. Paul, I., *Ind. Oc.* 121 H6 38 55 S 77 34 E
St-Paul-de-Fenouillet, *France* 28 F6 42 48N 2 30 E
St. Paul I., *Canada* 141 C7 47 12N 60 9W
St. Paul I., *U.S.A.* 144 H5 57 10N 170 15W
St-Paul-lès-Dax, *France* 28 E2 43 44N 1 3W
St-Péray, *France* 29 D8 44 57N 4 50 E
St. Peter, *U.S.A.* 154 C8 44 20N 93 57W
St-Peter-Ording, *Germany* 30 A4 54 20N 8 36 E
St. Peter Port, *U.K.* 21 H5 49 26N 2 33W
St. Peters, *N.S., Canada* 141 C7 45 40N 60 53W
St. Peters, *P.E.I., Canada* 141 C7 46 25N 62 35W
St. Petersburg = Sankt-Peterburg, *Russia* 58 C6 59 55N 30 20 E
St. Petersburg, *U.S.A.* 149 M4 27 46N 82 39W
St. Petersburg Beach, *U.S.A.* 153 H7 27 45N 82 45W
St-Philbert-de-Grand-Lieu, *France* 26 E5 47 2N 1 39W
St-Pie, *Canada* 151 A12 45 30N 72 54W
St-Pierre, *St- P. & M.* 141 C8 46 46N 56 12W
St. Pierre, *Seychelles* 121 E3 9 20 S 46 0 E
St-Pierre, L., *Canada* 140 C5 46 12N 72 52W
St-Pierre-d'Oléron, *France* 28 C2 45 57N 1 19W
St-Pierre-en-Port, *France* 26 C7 49 48N 0 30 E
St-Pierre et Miquelon □, *St- P. & M.* 141 C8 46 55N 56 10W
St-Pierre-le-Moûtier, *France* 27 F10 46 47N 3 7 E
St-Pierre-sur-Dives, *France* 26 C6 49 2N 0 1W
St-Pol-de-Léon, *France* 26 D3 48 41N 4 0W
St-Pol-sur-Mer, *France* 27 A9 51 1N 2 20 E
St-Pol-sur-Ternoise, *France* 27 B9 50 23N 2 20 E
St-Pons, *France* 28 E6 43 30N 2 45 E
St-Pourçain-sur-Sioule, *France* 27 F10 46 18N 3 18 E
St-Priest, *France* 29 C8 45 42N 4 57 E
St-Quay-Portrieux, *France* 26 D4 48 39N 2 51W
St. Quentin, *Canada* 141 C6 47 30N 67 23W
St-Quentin, *France* 27 C10 49 50N 3 16 E
St-Rambert-d'Albon, *France* 29 C8 45 17N 4 49 E
St-Raphaël, *France* 29 E10 43 25N 6 46 E
St. Regis, *U.S.A.* 158 C6 47 18N 115 6W
St-Renan, *France* 26 D2 48 26N 4 37W
St. Robert, *U.S.A.* 156 G4 37 48N 92 9W
St-Saëns, *France* 26 C8 49 41N 1 16 E
St-Savin, *France* 28 B4 46 34N 0 53 E
St-Savinien, *France* 28 C3 45 53N 0 42W
St. Sebastien, Tanjon' i, *Madag.* 117 A8 12 26 S 48 44 E
St-Seine-l'Abbaye, *France* 27 E11 47 26N 4 47 E
St-Sernin-sur-Rance, *France* 28 E6 43 54N 2 35 E
St-Sever, *France* 28 E3 43 45N 0 35W
St-Siméon, *Canada* 141 C6 47 51N 69 54W
St. Simons I., *U.S.A.* 152 D8 31 12N 81 15W
St. Simons Island, *U.S.A.* 149 K5 31 9N 81 22W
St. Stephen, *Canada* 141 C6 45 16N 67 17W
St. Stephen, *U.S.A.* 152 B10 33 24N 79 55W
St-Sulpice, *France* 28 E5 43 46N 1 41 E
St-Sulpice-Laurière, *France* 28 B5 46 3N 1 29 E
St-Sulpice-les-Feuilles, *France* 28 B5 46 19N 1 21 E
St-Syprien = St-Cyprien, *France* 28 F7 42 37N 3 2 E
St-Thégonnec, *France* 26 D3 48 31N 3 57W
St. Thomas, *Canada* 140 D3 42 45N 81 10W
St. Thomas I., *Virgin Is.* 165 C7 18 20N 64 55W
St-Tite, *Canada* 140 C5 46 45N 72 34W
St-Tropez, *France* 29 E10 43 17N 6 38 E
St. Troud = St. Truiden, *Belgium* 24 D5 50 48N 5 10 E
St. Truiden, *Belgium* 24 D5 50 48N 5 10 E
St-Vaast-la-Hougue, *France* 26 C5 49 35N 1 17W
St-Valery-en-Caux, *France* 26 C7 49 52N 0 43 E
St-Valéry-sur-Somme, *France* 27 B8 50 11N 1 38 E
St-Vallier, *France* 27 F11 46 38N 4 22 E
St-Vallier-de-Thiey, *France* 29 E10 43 42N 6 51 E
St-Varent, *France* 26 F6 46 53N 0 13W
St-Vaury, *France* 28 B5 46 12N 1 46 E
St. Vincent = São Vicente, *C. Verde Is.* 8 G6 18 0N 26 1W
St. Vincent, *Italy* 44 C4 45 45N 7 39 E
St. Vincent, G., *Australia* 128 C3 35 0 S 138 0 E
St. Vincent & the Grenadines ■, *W. Indies* 165 D7 13 0N 61 10W
St-Vincent-de-Tyrosse, *France* 28 E2 43 39N 1 19W
St. Vincent Passage, *W. Indies* 165 D7 13 30N 61 0W
St-Vith, *Belgium* 24 D6 50 17N 6 9 E
St-Vivien-de-Médoc, *France* 28 C2 45 25N 1 2W
St. Walburg, *Canada* 143 C7 53 39N 109 12W
St-Yrieix-la-Perche, *France* 28 C5 45 31N 1 12 E
Saintala, *India* 94 D6 20 26N 83 20 E
Ste-Adresse, *France* 26 C7 49 31N 0 5 E
Ste-Agathe-des-Monts, *Canada* 140 C5 46 3N 74 17W
Ste-Anne, L., *Canada* 141 B6 50 0N 67 42W
Ste-Anne-des-Monts, *Canada* 141 C6 49 8N 66 30W
Ste-Croix, *Switz.* 32 C3 46 49N 6 34 E
Ste-Enimie, *France* 28 D7 44 22N 3 26 E
Ste-Foy-la-Grande, *France* 28 D4 44 50N 0 13 E
Ste. Genevieve, *U.S.A.* 156 G6 37 59N 90 2W
Ste-Hermine, *France* 28 B2 46 32N 1 4W
Ste-Livrade-sur-Lot, *France* 28 D4 44 24N 0 36 E
Ste-Marguerite →, *Canada* 141 B6 50 9N 66 36W
Ste. Marie, *Gabon* 114 C2 3 48 S 11 1 E
Ste-Marie, *Martinique* 165 D7 14 48N 61 1W
Ste-Marie-aux-Mines, *France* 27 D14 48 15N 7 12 E
Ste-Marie de la Madeleine, *Canada* 141 C5 46 26N 71 0W
Ste-Maure-de-Touraine, *France* 26 E7 47 7N 0 37 E
Ste-Maxime, *France* 29 E10 43 19N 6 39 E
Ste-Menehould, *France* 27 C11 49 5N 4 54 E
Ste-Mère-Église, *France* 26 C5 49 24N 1 19W
Ste-Rose, *Guadeloupe* 165 C7 16 20N 61 45W
Ste. Rose du Lac, *Canada* 143 C9 51 4N 99 30W
Ste-Savine, *France* 27 D11 48 18N 4 3 E
Ste-Sigolène, *France* 29 C8 45 15N 4 14 E
Saintes, *France* 28 C3 45 45N 0 37W
Saintes, I. des, *Guadeloupe* 165 C7 15 50N 61 35W
Stes-Maries-de-la-Mer, *France* 29 E8 43 26N 4 26 E
Saintfield, *U.K.* 23 B6 54 28N 5 49W
Saintonge, *France* 28 C3 45 40N 0 50W
Saipan, *Pac. Oc.* 134 F6 15 12N 145 45 E
Sairecábur, Cerro, *Bolivia* 174 A2 22 43 S 67 54W
Saitama □, *Japan* 71 A11 36 25N 139 30 E
Saiteli = Kadınhanı, *Turkey* 100 C5 38 14N 32 13 E
Saiți, *Moldova* 53 D14 46 30N 29 24 E
Saito, *Japan* 70 E3 32 3N 131 24 E
Saiyid, *Pakistan* 92 C5 33 7N 73 2 E
Sajama, *Bolivia* 172 D4 18 7S 69 0W
Sajama, Nevado, *Bolivia* 172 D4 18 6 S 68 54W
Sajan, *Serbia, Yug.* 52 E5 45 50N 20 20 E
Sajó →, *Hungary* 52 C6 47 56N 21 7 E
Sajószentpéter, *Hungary* 52 B5 48 12N 20 44 E
Sajum, *India* 93 C8 33 20N 79 0 E
Sak →, *S. Africa* 116 E3 30 52 S 20 25 E
Sakaba, *Nigeria* 113 C6 11 4N 5 35 E
Sakai, *Japan* 71 C7 34 30N 135 30 E
Sakaide, *Japan* 70 C5 34 15N 133 50 E
Sakaiminato, *Japan* 70 B5 35 38N 133 11 E
Sakākah, *Si. Arabia* 96 D4 30 0N 40 8 E
Sakakawea, L., *U.S.A.* 154 B4 47 30N 101 25W
Sakami →, *Canada* 140 B4 53 40N 76 40W
Sakami, L., *Canada* 140 B4 53 15N 77 0W
Sâkâne, 'Erg i-n, *Mali* 113 A4 20 30N 1 30W
Sakania, *Dem. Rep. of the Congo* 119 E2 12 43 S 28 30 E
Sakaraha, *Madag.* 117 C7 22 55 S 44 32 E
Sakarya, *Turkey* 100 B4 40 48N 30 25 E
Sakarya →, *Turkey* 100 B4 41 7N 30 39 E
Sakashima-Guntō, *Japan* 69 M2 24 46N 124 0 E
Sakassou, *Ivory C.* 112 D3 7 29N 5 19W
Sakata, *Japan* 68 E9 38 55N 139 50 E
Sakchu, *N. Korea* 75 D13 40 23N 125 2 E
Sakeny →, *Madag.* 117 C8 20 0 S 45 25 E
Sakété, *Benin* 113 D5 6 40N 2 45 E
Sakha □, *Russia* 65 C13 66 0N 130 0 E
Sakhalin, *Russia* 65 D15 51 0N 143 0 E
Sakhalinskiy Zaliv, *Russia* 65 D15 54 0N 141 0 E
Sakhi Gopal, *India* 94 E7 19 58N 85 50 E
Şaki, *Azerbaijan* 61 K8 41 10N 47 5 E
Šakiai, *Lithuania* 15 J20 54 59N 23 2 E
Sakmara →, *Russia* 62 F5 51 46N 55 1 E
Sakoli, *India* 94 D4 21 5N 79 59 E
Sakon Nakhon, *Thailand* 78 A2 17 10N 104 9 E
Sakrand, *Pakistan* 92 F3 26 10N 68 15 E
Sakri, *India* 93 F12 26 13N 86 5 E
Sakri, *India* 94 D2 21 2N 74 20 E
Sakrivier, *S. Africa* 116 E3 30 54 S 20 28 E
Sakskøbing, *Denmark* 17 K5 54 49N 11 39 E
Sakti, *India* 93 H10 22 2N 82 58 E
Saku, *Japan* 71 A10 36 17N 138 31 E
Sakuma, *Japan* 71 B9 35 3N 137 49 E
Sakura, *Japan* 71 B12 35 43N 140 14 E
Sakurai, *Japan* 71 C7 34 30N 135 51 E
Saky, *Ukraine* 59 K7 45 9N 33 34 E
Sal →, *Russia* 61 G5 47 31N 40 45 E
Sala, *Eritrea* 107 D4 16 53N 37 36 E
Šaľa, *Slovak Rep.* 35 C10 48 10N 17 50 E
Sala, *Sweden* 16 E10 59 58N 16 35 E
Sala →, *Eritrea* 107 D4 16 53N 37 36 E
Sala Consilina, *Italy* 47 B8 40 23N 15 36 E
Sala-y-Gómez, *Pac. Oc.* 135 K17 26 28 S 105 28W
Salaberry-de-Valleyfield, *Canada* 140 C5 45 15N 74 8W
Saladas, *Argentina* 174 B4 28 15 S 58 40W
Saladillo, *Argentina* 174 D4 35 40 S 59 55W
Salado →, *Buenos Aires, Argentina* 174 D4 35 44 S 57 22W
Salado →, *La Pampa, Argentina* 176 A3 37 30 S 67 0W
Salado →, *Río Negro, Argentina* 176 B3 41 34 S 65 3W
Salado →, *Santa Fe, Argentina* 174 C3 31 40 S 60 41W
Salado →, *Mexico* 155 M5 26 52N 99 19W
Salaga, *Ghana* 113 D4 8 31N 0 31W
Sālah, *Syria* 103 C5 32 40N 36 45 E
Sălaj □, *Romania* 52 C8 47 15N 23 0 E
Sálakhos, *Greece* 38 C9 36 17N 27 57 E
Salala, *Liberia* 112 D2 6 42N 10 7W
Salala, *Sudan* 106 C4 21 17N 36 16 E
Salālah, *Oman* 99 C6 16 56N 53 59 E
Salamanca, *Chile* 174 C1 31 46 S 70 59W
Salamanca, *Spain* 42 E5 40 58N 5 39W
Salamanca, *U.S.A.* 150 D6 42 10N 78 43W
Salamanca □, *Spain* 42 E5 40 57N 5 40W
Salāmatābād, *Iran* 96 C5 35 39N 47 50 E
Salamina, *Colombia* 168 B2 5 25N 75 29W
Salamis, *Cyprus* 38 D12 35 11N 33 54 E
Salamís, *Greece* 48 D5 37 56N 23 30 E
Salamonie L., *U.S.A.* 157 D11 40 46N 85 37W
Salar de Atacama, *Chile* 174 A2 23 30 S 68 25W
Salar de Uyuni, *Bolivia* 172 E4 20 30 S 67 45W
Sălard, *Romania* 52 C7 47 12N 22 3 E
Salaş, *Spain* 42 B4 43 25N 6 15W
Salas de los Infantes, *Spain* 40 C2 42 2N 3 17W
Salatiga, *Indonesia* 79 G14 7 19 S 110 30 E
Salavat, *Russia* 62 E5 53 21N 55 55 E
Salaverry, *Peru* 172 B2 8 15 S 79 0W
Salawati, *Indonesia* 79 E8 1 7 S 130 52 E
Salay, *Phil.* 81 G5 8 52N 124 47 E
Salaya, *India* 92 H3 22 19N 69 35 E
Salayar, *Indonesia* 79 F6 6 7 S 120 30 E
Salazar →, *Spain* 40 C3 42 40N 1 20W
Salbris, *France* 27 E9 47 25N 2 3 E
Salcedo, *Phil.* 81 F5 11 9N 125 40 E
Salcia, *Romania* 53 G9 43 56N 24 55 E
Sălciua, *Romania* 53 D8 46 24N 23 26 E
Salcombe, *U.K.* 21 G4 50 14N 3 47W
Saldaña, *Spain* 42 C6 42 32N 4 48W
Saldanha, *S. Africa* 116 E2 33 0 S 17 58 E
Saldanha B., *S. Africa* 116 E2 33 6 S 18 0 E
Saldus, *Latvia* 15 H20 56 38N 22 30 E
Saldus □, *Latvia* 54 B9 56 45N 22 30 E
Sale, *Australia* 129 E7 38 6 S 147 6 E
Sale, *Italy* 44 D5 44 59N 8 48 E
Salé, *Morocco* 110 B3 34 3N 6 48W
Sale, *U.K.* 20 D5 53 26N 2 19W
Sale City, *U.S.A.* 152 D5 31 16N 84 1W
Salekhard, *Russia* 64 C7 66 30N 66 35 E
Salem, *India* 95 J4 11 40N 78 11 E
Salem, *Fla., U.S.A.* 152 F6 29 53N 83 25W
Salem, *Ill., U.S.A.* 156 F8 38 38N 88 57W
Salem, *Ind., U.S.A.* 157 F10 38 36N 86 6W
Salem, *Mass., U.S.A.* 151 D14 42 31N 70 53W
Salem, *Mo., U.S.A.* 155 G9 37 39N 91 32W
Salem, *N.H., U.S.A.* 151 D13 42 45N 71 12W
Salem, *N.J., U.S.A.* 148 F8 39 34N 75 28W
Salem, *N.Y., U.S.A.* 151 C11 43 10N 73 20W
Salem, *Ohio, U.S.A.* 150 F4 40 54N 80 52W
Salem, *Oreg., U.S.A.* 158 D2 44 56N 123 2W
Salem, *S. Dak., U.S.A.* 154 D6 43 44N 97 23W
Salem, *Va., U.S.A.* 148 G5 37 18N 80 3W
Salemi, *Italy* 46 E5 37 49N 12 48 E
Sälen, *Sweden* 16 C7 61 15N 13 22 E
Salernes, *France* 29 E10 43 34N 6 15 E
Salerno, *Italy* 47 B7 40 41N 14 47 E
Salerno, G. di, *Italy* 47 B7 40 32N 14 42 E
Sales, *Brazil* 169 D5 4 2S 63 40W
Salford, *U.K.* 20 D5 53 30N 2 18W
Salgir →, *Ukraine* 59 K8 45 38N 35 1 E
Salgótarján, *Hungary* 52 B4 48 5N 19 47 E
Salgueiro, *Brazil* 170 C4 8 4 S 39 6W
Salher, *India* 94 D1 20 40N 73 55 E
Salhus, *Norway* 18 D2 60 30N 5 15 E
Salibabu, *Indonesia* 79 D7 3 51N 126 40 E
Salida, *U.S.A.* 146 C5 38 32N 106 0W
Salies-de-Béarn, *France* 28 E3 43 28N 0 56W
Şalif, *Yemen* 98 D3 15 18N 42 41 E
Salihli, *Turkey* 100 C3 38 28N 28 8 E
Salihorsk, *Belarus* 59 F4 52 51N 27 27 E
Salin, *Burma* 90 E5 20 35N 94 40 E
Salina, *Italy* 47 D7 38 34N 14 50 E
Salina, *Kans., U.S.A.* 154 F6 38 50N 97 37W
Salina, *Utah, U.S.A.* 159 G8 38 58N 111 51W
Salina Cruz, *Mexico* 163 D5 16 10N 95 10W
Salinas, *Brazil* 171 E3 16 10 S 42 10W
Salinas, *Chile* 174 A2 23 31 S 69 29W
Salinas, *Ecuador* 168 D1 2 10 S 80 58W
Salinas, *U.S.A.* 160 J5 36 40N 121 39W
Salinas →, *Guatemala* 163 D6 16 28N 90 31W
Salinas →, *U.S.A.* 160 J5 36 45N 121 48W
Salinas, B. das, *Angola* 115 E2 14 11 S 12 21 E
Salinas, B. de, *Nic.* 164 D2 11 4N 85 45W
Salinas, Pampa de las, *Argentina* 174 C2 31 58 S 66 42W
Salinas Ambargasta, *Argentina* 174 B3 29 0 S 65 0W
Salinas de Hidalgo, *Mexico* 162 C4 22 30N 101 40W
Salinas Grandes, *Argentina* 174 C3 30 0 S 65 0W
Saline, *U.S.A.* 157 B13 42 10N 83 47W
Saline →, *Ark., U.S.A.* 155 J8 33 10N 92 8W
Saline →, *Kans., U.S.A.* 154 F6 38 52N 97 30W
Salines, *Spain* 39 B10 39 21N 3 3 E
Salines, C. de ses, *Spain* 39 B10 39 16N 3 4 E
Salinópolis, *Brazil* 170 B2 0 40 S 47 20W
Salins-les-Bains, *France* 27 F12 46 58N 5 52 E
Salir, *Portugal* 43 H2 37 14N 8 2W
Salisbury = Harare, *Zimbabwe* 119 F3 17 43 S 31 2 E
Salisbury, *Australia* 128 C3 34 46 S 138 40 E
Salisbury, *U.K.* 21 F6 51 4N 1 47W

Selenica 279

Satna, India 93 G9 24 35N 80 50 E
Šator, Bos.-H. 45 D13 44 11N 16 37 E
Sátoraljaújhely, Hungary 52 B6 48 25N 21 41 E
Satpura Ra., India 94 D3 21 25N 76 10 E
Satrup, Germany 30 A5 54 41N 9 36 E
Satsuma-Hantō, Japan 70 F2 31 25N 130 25 E
Satsuna-Shotō, Japan 69 K5 30 0N 130 0 E
Sattahip, Thailand 78 B2 12 41N 100 54 E
Sattenapalle, India 95 F5 16 25N 80 6 E
Satu Mare, Romania 52 C7 47 46N 22 55 E
Satu Mare □, Romania 52 C8 47 45N 23 0 E
Satui, Indonesia 78 E5 3 50 S 115 27 E
Satun, Thailand 78 C2 6 43N 100 2 E
Satupe'itea, W. Samoa 133 W23 13 45 S 172 18W
Saturnina →, Brazil 173 C6 12 15 S 58 10W
Sauce, Argentina 174 C4 30 5 S 58 46W
Sauceda, Mexico 162 B4 25 55N 101 18W
Saucillo, Mexico 162 B3 28 1N 105 17W
Sauda, Norway 15 G12 59 40N 6 20 E
Saudasjøen, Norway 18 E3 59 38N 6 17 E
Saúde, Brazil 170 D3 10 56 S 40 24W
Sauðarkrókur, Iceland 11 B7 65 45N 19 40W
Saudi Arabia ■, Asia 96 B3 26 0N 44 0 E
Saugatuck, U.S.A. 157 B10 42 40N 86 12W
Saugeen →, Canada 150 B3 44 30N 81 22W
Saugerties, U.S.A. 151 D11 42 5N 73 57W
Saugues, France 28 D7 44 58N 3 32 E
Saugus, U.S.A. 161 L8 34 25N 118 32W
Saujon, France 28 C3 45 41N 0 55W
Sauk Centre, U.S.A. 154 C7 45 44N 94 57W
Sauk City, U.S.A. 156 A7 43 17N 89 43W
Sauk Rapids, U.S.A. 154 C7 45 35N 94 10W
Saül, Fr. Guiana 169 C7 3 37N 53 12W
Sauland, Norway 18 E5 59 37N 8 56 E
Saulgau, Germany 31 G5 48 1N 9 29 E
Saulieu, France 27 E11 47 17N 4 14 E
Sault, France 29 D9 44 6N 5 24 E
Sault Ste. Marie, Canada 140 C3 46 30N 84 20W
Sault Ste. Marie, U.S.A. 139 D11 46 30N 84 21W
Saumlaki, Indonesia 79 F8 7 55 S 131 20 E
Saumur, France 26 E6 47 15N 0 5W
Saundatti, India 95 G2 15 47N 75 7 E
Saunders C., N.Z. 131 F5 45 53 S 170 45 E
Saunders I., Antarctica 7 B1 57 48 S 26 28W
Saunders Point, Australia 125 E4 27 52 S 125 38 E
Saunemin, U.S.A. 157 D8 40 54N 88 24W
Saupite, Angola 115 E3 13 54 S 17 43 E
Saurbær, Borgarfjarðarsýsla, Iceland 11 C5 64 24N 21 35W
Saurbær, Eyjafjarðarsýsla, Iceland 11 B8 65 27N 18 13W
Sauri, Nigeria 113 C6 11 42N 6 44 E
Saurimo, Angola 115 D4 9 40 S 20 12 E
Sausalito, U.S.A. 160 H4 37 51N 122 29W
Sautatá, Colombia 168 B2 7 50N 77 4W
Sauveterre-de-Béarn, France 28 E3 43 24N 0 57W
Sauzé-Vaussais, France 28 B4 46 8N 0 8 E
Savá, Honduras 164 C2 15 32N 86 15W
Sava, Italy 47 B10 40 24N 17 33 E
Sava →, Serbia, Yug. 52 F5 44 50N 20 26 E
Savage, U.S.A. 154 B2 47 27N 104 21W
Savage I. = Niue, Cook Is. 135 J11 19 2 S 169 54W
Savage River, Australia 126 G4 41 31 S 145 14 E
Savai'i, W. Samoa 133 W23 13 28 S 172 24W
Savalou, Benin 113 D5 7 57N 1 58 E
Savane, Mozam. 119 F4 19 37 S 35 8 E
Savanna, U.S.A. 156 B6 42 5N 90 8W
Savanna-la-Mar, Jamaica 164 C4 18 10N 78 10W
Savannah, Ga., U.S.A. 152 C8 32 5N 81 6W
Savannah, Mo., U.S.A. 156 E2 39 56N 94 50W
Savannah, Tenn., U.S.A. 149 H1 35 14N 88 15W
Savannah →, U.S.A. 152 C9 32 2N 80 53W
Savannah Beach = Tybee Island, U.S.A. 152 C9 32 1N 80 51W
Savannakhet, Laos 78 A2 16 30N 104 49 E
Savant L., Canada 140 B1 50 16N 90 44W
Savant Lake, Canada 140 B1 50 14N 90 40W
Savantvadi, India 95 G1 15 55N 73 54 E
Savanur, India 95 G2 14 59N 75 21 E
Săvârşin, Romania 52 D7 46 1N 22 14 E
Savaştepe, Turkey 49 B9 39 22N 27 42 E
Savda, India 94 D2 21 9N 75 56 E
Savé, Benin 113 D5 8 2N 2 29 E
Save →, France 28 E5 43 47N 1 17 E
Save →, Mozam. 117 C5 21 16 S 34 0 E
Sāveh, Iran 97 C6 35 2N 50 20 E
Savelugu, Ghana 113 D4 9 38N 0 54W
Savenay, France 26 E5 47 20N 1 55W
Săveni, Romania 53 C11 47 57N 26 52 E
Saverdun, France 28 E5 43 14N 1 34 E
Saverne, France 27 D14 48 43N 7 20 E
Savièse, Switz. 32 D4 46 17N 7 22 E
Savigliano, Italy 44 D4 44 38N 7 40 E
Savigny-sur-Braye, France 26 E7 47 53N 0 49 E
Sávio →, Italy 45 D9 44 19N 12 20 E
Šavnik, Montenegro, Yug. 50 D3 42 59N 19 10 E
Savo, Finland 14 E22 62 45N 27 30 E
Savo, Solomon Is. 133 M10 9 8 S 159 48 E
Savognin, Switz. 33 C9 46 36N 9 37 E
Savoie □, France 29 C10 45 26N 6 25 E
Savona, Italy 44 D5 44 17N 8 30 E
Savona, U.S.A. 150 D7 42 17N 77 13W
Savonlinna, Finland 58 B5 61 52N 28 53 E
Savoonga, U.S.A. 144 E5 63 42N 170 29W
Savoy = Savoie □, France 29 C10 45 26N 6 25 E
Şavşat, Turkey 101 B10 41 15N 42 20 E
Sävsjö, Sweden 17 G8 57 20N 14 40 E
Savur, Turkey 96 B4 37 34N 40 53 E
Savusavu, Fiji 133 A2 16 34 S 179 15 E
Savusavu B., Fiji 133 A2 16 45 S 179 15 E
Sawahlunto, Indonesia 78 E2 0 40 S 100 52 E
Sawai, Indonesia 79 E7 3 0 S 129 5 E
Sawai Madhopur, India 92 G7 26 0N 76 25 E
Sawang Daen Din, Thailand 86 D4 17 28N 103 28 E
Sawankhalok, Thailand 78 A1 17 19N 99 50 E
Sawara, Japan 71 B12 35 55N 140 30 E
Sawatch Range, U.S.A. 159 G10 38 30N 106 30W
Sawdā, Jabal as, Libya 108 C3 28 51N 15 12 E
Sawel Mt., U.K. 23 B4 54 50N 7 2W
Sawfajjin, W. →, Libya 108 B2 31 41N 14 44 E
Sawi, Thailand 87 G2 10 14N 99 5 E
Sawla, Ghana 112 D4 9 17N 2 25W
Sawmills, Zimbabwe 119 F2 19 30 S 28 2 E
Şawqirah, Oman 99 C7 18 7N 56 32 E
Şawqirah, Ghubbat, Oman 99 C7 18 35N 57 0 E
Sawtooth Range, U.S.A. 158 E6 44 3N 114 58W
Sawu, Indonesia 79 F6 10 35 S 121 50 E
Sawu Sea, Indonesia 79 F6 9 30 S 121 50 E
Saxby →, Australia 126 B3 18 25 S 140 53 E
Saxmundham, U.K. 21 E9 52 13N 1 30 E
Saxon, Switz. 32 D4 46 9N 7 11 E
Saxony = Sachsen □, Germany 30 E9 50 55N 13 10 E
Saxony, Lower = Niedersachsen □, Germany 30 C4 52 50N 9 0 E
Saxton, U.S.A. 150 F6 40 13N 78 15W
Say, Mali 112 C4 13 50N 4 57W
Say, Niger 113 C5 13 8N 2 22 E
Saya, Nigeria 113 D5 9 30N 3 18 E
Sayabec, Canada 141 C6 48 35N 67 41W
Sayaboury, Laos 86 C3 19 15N 101 45 E
Sayán, Peru 172 C2 11 8 S 77 12W
Sayan, Vostochnyy, Russia 65 D10 54 0N 96 0 E
Sayan, Zapadnyy, Russia 65 D10 52 30N 94 0 E
Saydā, Lebanon 103 B4 33 35N 35 25 E
Sayghān, Afghan. 91 B2 35 10N 67 55 E
Sayhandulaan = Oldziyt, Mongolia 74 B5 44 40N 109 1 E
Sayḩūt, Yemen 99 D5 15 12N 51 10 E
Saykhin, Kazakstan 61 F8 48 50N 46 47 E
Saylorville L., U.S.A. 156 C3 41 48N 93 46W
Saynshand, Mongolia 73 B6 44 55N 110 11 E
Sayō, Japan 70 C6 34 59N 134 22 E
Sayre, Okla., U.S.A. 155 H5 35 18N 99 38W
Sayre, Pa., U.S.A. 151 E8 41 59N 76 32W
Sayreville, U.S.A. 151 F10 40 28N 74 22W
Sayula, Mexico 162 D4 19 50N 103 40W
Sayward, Canada 142 C3 50 21N 125 55W
Saywūn, Yemen 99 D5 15 56N 48 47 E
Sazanit, Albania 50 F3 40 30N 19 20 E
Sázava →, Czech Rep. 34 B7 49 53N 14 24 E
Sazin, Pakistan 93 B5 35 35N 73 30 E
Sazlika →, Bulgaria 51 E9 41 59N 25 50 E
Sbeïtla, Tunisia 108 A1 35 12N 9 7 E
Scaër, France 26 D3 48 2N 3 42W
Scafell Pike, U.K. 20 C4 54 27N 3 14W
Scalea, Italy 47 C8 39 49N 15 47 E
Scalloway, U.K. 22 A7 60 9N 1 17W
Scalpay, U.K. 22 D3 57 18N 6 0W
Scandia, Canada 142 C6 50 20N 112 0W
Scandiano, Italy 44 D7 44 36N 10 43 E
Scandicci, Italy 45 E8 43 45N 11 11 E
Scandinavia, Europe 12 C8 64 0N 12 0 E
Scansano, Italy 45 F8 42 41N 11 20 E
Scapa Flow, U.K. 22 C5 58 53N 3 3W
Scappoose, U.S.A. 160 E4 45 45N 122 53W
Scarámia, Capo, Italy 47 F7 36 47N 14 29 E
Scarba, U.K. 22 E3 56 11N 5 43W
Scarborough, Trin. & Tob. 165 D7 11 11N 60 42W
Scarborough, U.K. 20 C7 54 17N 0 24W
Scargill, N.Z. 131 C7 42 56 S 172 58 E
Scariff I., Ireland 23 E1 51 44N 10 15W
Scarp, U.K. 22 C1 58 1N 7 8W
Scarsdale, Australia 128 D5 37 41 S 143 39 E
Scebeli, Wabi →, Somali Rep. 120 D2 2 0N 44 0 E
Šćedro, Croatia 45 E13 43 6N 16 43 E
Schaal See, Germany 30 B6 53 36N 10 55 E
Schaan, Liech. 33 B9 47 10N 9 31 E
Schaffhausen, Switz. 33 A7 47 42N 8 39 E
Schaffhausen □, Switz. 33 A7 47 42N 8 36 E
Schagen, Neths. 24 B4 52 49N 4 48 E
Schaghticoke, U.S.A. 151 D11 42 54N 73 35W
Schangnau, Switz. 32 C5 46 50N 7 47 E
Schänis, Switz. 33 B8 47 10N 9 3 E
Schärding, Austria 34 C6 48 27N 13 27 E
Scharhörn, Germany 30 B4 53 57N 8 24 E
Scheessel, Germany 30 B5 53 10N 9 29 E
Schefferville, Canada 141 B6 54 48N 66 50W
Scheibbs, Austria 34 C8 48 1N 15 9 E
Schelde →, Belgium 24 C4 51 15N 4 16 E
Schell City, U.S.A. 156 F2 38 1N 94 7W
Schell Creek Ra., U.S.A. 158 G6 39 15N 114 30W
Schellsburg, U.S.A. 150 F6 40 3N 78 39W
Schenectady, U.S.A. 151 D11 42 49N 73 57W
Schenevus, U.S.A. 151 D10 42 33N 74 50W
Scherfede, Germany 30 D5 51 32N 9 2 E
Schesaplana, Switz. 33 B9 47 5N 9 43 E
Schesslitz, Germany 31 F7 49 58N 11 1 E
Schiedam, Neths. 24 C4 51 55N 4 25 E
Schiermonnikoog, Neths. 24 A6 53 30N 6 15 E
Schiers, Switz. 33 C9 46 58N 9 41 E
Schiltigheim, France 27 D14 48 35N 7 45 E
Schio, Italy 45 C8 45 43N 11 21 E
Schladming, Austria 34 D6 47 23N 13 41 E
Schlanders = Silandro, Italy 44 B7 46 38N 10 46 E
Schlei →, Germany 30 A5 54 40N 10 0 E
Schleiden, Germany 30 E2 50 31N 6 28 E
Schleiz, Germany 30 E7 50 35N 11 49 E
Schleswig, Germany 30 A5 54 31N 9 34 E
Schleswig-Holstein □, Germany 30 A5 54 30N 9 30 E
Schlieren, Switz. 33 B6 47 26N 8 27 E
Schlüchtern, Germany 31 E5 50 20N 9 32 E
Schmalkalden, Germany 30 E6 50 44N 10 26 E
Schmölln, Germany 30 E8 50 54N 12 19 E
Schneeberg, Austria 34 D8 47 47N 15 48 E
Schneeberg, Germany 30 E8 50 35N 12 38 E
Schneider, U.S.A. 157 C9 41 13N 87 28W
Schneverdingen, Germany 30 B5 53 7N 9 48 E
Schoharie, U.S.A. 151 D10 42 40N 74 19W
Schoharie →, U.S.A. 151 D10 42 57N 74 18W
Scholls, U.S.A. 160 E4 45 24N 122 56W
Schönberg, Mecklenburg-Vorpommern, Germany 30 B6 53 52N 10 56 E
Schönberg, Schleswig-Holstein, Germany 30 A6 54 23N 10 21 E
Schönebeck, Germany 30 C7 52 2N 11 44 E
Schönenwerd, Switz. 32 B6 47 23N 8 0 E
Schongau, Germany 31 H6 47 48N 10 53 E
Schöningen, Germany 30 C6 52 8N 10 56 E
Schoolcraft, U.S.A. 157 B11 42 7N 85 38W
Schopfheim, Germany 31 H3 47 38N 7 50 E
Schorndorf, Germany 31 G5 48 47N 9 32 E
Schortens, Germany 30 B3 53 31N 7 56 E
Schouten I., Australia 126 G4 42 20 S 148 20 E
Schouten Is. = Supiori, Indonesia 79 E9 1 0 S 136 0 E
Schouwen, Neths. 24 C3 51 43N 3 45 E
Schramberg, Germany 31 G4 48 13N 8 22 E
Schrankogel, Austria 34 D4 47 3N 11 7 E
Schreckhorn, Switz. 32 C6 46 36N 8 7 E
Schreiber, Canada 140 C2 48 45N 87 20W
Schrems, Austria 34 C8 48 47N 15 4 E
Schrobenhausen, Germany 31 G7 48 34N 11 16 E
Schröcken, Austria 33 B10 47 17N 10 5 E
Schroffenstein, Namibia 116 D2 27 11 S 18 42 E
Schroon Lake, U.S.A. 151 C11 43 50N 73 46W
Schruns, Austria 34 D2 47 5N 9 56 E
Schuler, Canada 143 C6 50 20N 110 6W
Schuls, Switz. 33 C10 46 48N 10 18 E
Schumacher, Canada 140 C3 48 30N 81 16W
Schüpfen, Switz. 32 B4 47 2N 7 24 E
Schüpfheim, Switz. 32 C6 46 57N 8 2 E
Schurz, U.S.A. 158 G4 38 57N 118 49W
Schuyler, U.S.A. 154 E6 41 27N 97 4W
Schuylerville, U.S.A. 151 C11 43 6N 73 35W
Schuylkill →, U.S.A. 151 G9 39 53N 75 12W
Schuylkill Haven, U.S.A. 151 F8 40 37N 76 11W
Schwabach, Germany 31 F7 49 19N 11 2 E
Schwaben □, Germany 31 G6 48 15N 10 30 E
Schwäbisch Gmünd, Germany 31 G5 48 48N 9 47 E
Schwäbisch Hall, Germany 31 F5 49 6N 9 44 E
Schwäbische Alb, Germany 31 G5 48 20N 9 30 E
Schwabmünchen, Germany 31 G6 48 10N 10 46 E
Schwalmstadt, Germany 30 E5 50 55N 9 10 E
Schwanden, Switz. 33 C8 46 58N 9 5 E
Schwandorf, Germany 31 F8 49 20N 12 7 E
Schwaner, Pegunungan, Indonesia 78 E4 1 0 S 112 30 E
Schwanewede, Germany 30 B4 53 14N 8 35 E
Schwarmstedt, Germany 30 C5 52 39N 9 38 E
Schwarze Elster →, Germany 30 D8 51 48N 12 50 E
Schwarzenberg, Germany 30 E8 50 32N 12 47 E
Schwarzenburg, Switz. 32 C4 46 49N 7 20 E
Schwarzrand, Namibia 116 D2 25 37 S 16 50 E
Schwarzwald, Germany 31 G4 48 30N 8 20 E
Schwatka Mts., U.S.A. 144 C8 67 20N 156 30W
Schwaz, Austria 34 D4 47 20N 11 44 E
Schwechat, Austria 35 C9 48 8N 16 28 E
Schwedt, Germany 30 B10 53 3N 14 16 E
Schweinfurt, Germany 31 E6 50 3N 10 14 E
Schweizer Mittelland, Switz. 32 C4 47 0N 7 15 E
Schweizer-Reneke, S. Africa 116 D4 27 11 S 25 18 E
Schwenningen = Villingen-Schwenningen, Germany 31 G4 48 3N 8 26 E
Schwerin, Germany 30 B7 53 36N 11 22 E
Schweriner See, Germany 30 B7 53 43N 11 28 E
Schwetzingen, Germany 31 F4 49 23N 8 35 E
Schwyz, Switz. 33 B7 47 2N 8 39 E
Schwyz □, Switz. 33 B7 47 2N 8 39 E
Sciacca, Italy 46 E6 37 31N 13 3 E
Sciao, Somali Rep. 120 D3 3 26N 45 21 E
Scicli, Italy 47 F7 36 47N 14 42 E
Scilla, Italy 47 D8 38 15N 15 43 E
Scilly, Isles of, U.K. 21 H1 49 56N 6 22W
Ścinawa, Poland 55 G3 51 25N 16 26 E
Scione, Greece 50 G7 39 57N 23 36 E
Scioto →, U.S.A. 157 D13 38 44N 83 1W
Scituate, U.S.A. 151 D14 42 12N 70 44W
Scobey, U.S.A. 154 A2 48 47N 105 25W
Scone, Australia 129 B9 32 5 S 150 52 E
Scordia, Italy 47 E7 37 18N 14 51 E
Scoresby Sund, Greenland 10 C8 70 28N 21 46W
Scoresbysund = Illoqqortoormiit, Greenland 10 C8 70 20N 23 0W
Scorniceşti, Romania 53 F9 44 34N 24 33 E
Scotia, Calif., U.S.A. 158 F1 40 29N 124 6W
Scotia, N.Y., U.S.A. 151 D11 42 50N 73 58W
Scotia Sea, Antarctica 9 P4 56 5 S 56 0W
Scotland, Canada 150 C4 43 1N 80 22W
Scotland □, U.K. 22 E5 57 0N 4 0W
Scott, C., Australia 124 B4 13 30 S 129 49 E
Scott City, U.S.A. 154 F4 38 29N 100 54W
Scott Glacier, Antarctica 7 C8 66 15 S 100 5 E
Scott I., Antarctica 7 C11 67 0 S 179 0 E
Scott Is., Canada 142 C3 50 48N 128 40W
Scott L., Canada 143 B7 59 55N 106 18W
Scott Reef, Australia 124 B3 14 0 S 121 50 E
Scottburgh, S. Africa 117 E5 30 15 S 30 47 E
Scottdale, U.S.A. 150 F5 40 6N 79 35W
Scottish Borders □, U.K. 22 F6 55 35N 2 50W
Scottsbluff, U.S.A. 154 E3 41 52N 103 40W
Scottsboro, U.S.A. 149 H3 34 40N 86 2W
Scottsburg, U.S.A. 157 F11 38 41N 85 47W
Scottsdale, Australia 126 G4 41 9 S 147 31 E
Scottsdale, U.S.A. 159 K7 33 29N 111 56W
Scottsville, Ky., U.S.A. 149 G2 36 45N 86 11W
Scottsville, N.Y., U.S.A. 150 C7 43 2N 77 47W
Scottville, U.S.A. 148 D2 43 58N 86 17W
Scranton, U.S.A. 151 E9 41 25N 75 40W
Screven, U.S.A. 152 D7 31 29N 82 1W
Scugog, L., Canada 150 B6 44 10N 78 55W
Sculeni, Moldova 53 C12 47 20N 27 37 E
Scunthorpe, U.K. 20 D7 53 36N 0 39W
Scuol Schuls, Switz. 33 C10 46 48N 10 17 E
Scusciuban, Somali Rep. 120 B4 10 18N 50 12 E
Scutari = Üsküdar, Turkey 51 F13 41 0N 29 5 E
Seabra, Brazil 171 D3 12 25 S 41 46W
Seabrook, L., Australia 125 F2 30 55 S 119 40 E
Seaford, U.K. 21 G8 50 47N 0 7 E
Seaford, U.S.A. 148 F8 38 39N 75 37W
Seaforth, Australia 126 C4 20 55 S 148 57 E
Seaforth, Canada 150 C3 43 35N 81 25W
Seaforth, L., U.K. 22 D2 57 52N 6 36W
Seagraves, U.S.A. 155 J3 32 57N 102 34W
Seaham, U.K. 20 C6 54 50N 1 20W
Seal →, Canada 143 B10 59 4N 94 48W
Seal L., Canada 141 B7 54 20N 61 30W
Seale, U.S.A. 152 C4 32 18N 85 10W
Sealy, U.S.A. 155 L6 29 47N 96 9W
Seaman, U.S.A. 157 F13 38 57N 83 34W
Searchlight, U.S.A. 161 K12 35 28N 114 55W
Searcy, U.S.A. 155 H9 35 15N 91 44W
Searles L., U.S.A. 161 K9 35 44N 117 21W
Seascale, U.K. 20 C4 54 24N 3 29W
Seaside, Calif., U.S.A. 160 J5 36 37N 121 50W
Seaside, Oreg., U.S.A. 160 E3 46 0N 123 56W
Seaspray, Australia 129 E7 38 25 S 147 15 E
Seattle, U.S.A. 160 C4 47 36N 122 20W
Seaview Ra., Australia 126 B4 18 40 S 145 45 E
Seaward Kaikouras, N.Z. 131 C8 42 10 S 173 44 E
Sebago L., U.S.A. 151 C14 43 52N 70 34W
Sebago Lake, U.S.A. 151 C14 43 51N 70 34W
Sebangka, Indonesia 84 B2 0 7N 104 36 E
Sebastian, U.S.A. 153 H9 27 49N 80 28W
Sebastián Vizcaíno, B., Mexico 162 B2 28 0N 114 30W
Sebastopol = Sevastopol, Ukraine 59 K7 44 35N 33 30 E
Sebastopol, U.S.A. 160 G4 38 24N 122 49W
Sebba, Burkina Faso 113 C5 13 35N 0 32 E
Sebderat, Eritrea 107 D4 15 26N 36 42 E
Sebdou, Algeria 111 B4 34 38N 1 19W
Sébé →, Gabon 114 C2 1 2 S 13 6 E
Sébékoro, Mali 112 C3 12 58N 9 0W
Seben, Turkey 100 B4 40 24N 31 34 E
Sebeş, Romania 53 E8 45 58N 23 34 E
Sebeşului, Munţii, Romania 53 E8 45 36N 23 40 E
Sebewaing, U.S.A. 148 D4 43 44N 83 27W
Sebezh, Russia 58 D5 56 14N 28 22 E
Sebha = Sabhah, Libya 108 C2 27 9N 14 29 E
Sébi, Mali 112 B4 15 50N 4 12W
Şebinkarahisar, Turkey 101 B8 40 22N 38 28 E
Sebiş, Romania 52 D7 46 23N 22 13 E
Sebkra Azzel Mati, Algeria 111 C5 26 10N 0 43 E
Sebkra Mekerghene, Algeria 111 C5 26 21N 1 30 E
Seblat, Indonesia 84 C2 3 14 S 101 38 E
Sebnitz, Germany 30 E10 50 58N 14 15 E
Sebou, Oued →, Morocco 110 B3 34 16N 6 40W
Sebring, Fla., U.S.A. 149 M5 27 30N 81 27W
Sebring, Ohio, U.S.A. 150 F3 40 55N 81 2W
Sebringville, Canada 150 C3 43 24N 81 4W
Sebta = Ceuta, N. Afr. 110 A3 35 52N 5 18W
Sebuku, Indonesia 78 E5 3 30 S 116 25 E
Sebuku, Teluk, Malaysia 78 D5 4 0N 118 10 E
Sečanj, Serbia, Yug. 52 E5 45 25N 20 47 E
Secchia →, Italy 44 C8 45 4N 11 0 E
Sechelt, Canada 142 D4 49 25N 123 42W
Sechura, Peru 172 B1 5 39 S 80 50W
Sechura, Desierto de, Peru 172 B1 6 0 S 80 30W
Seclin, France 27 B10 50 33N 3 2 E
Secondigny, France 26 F6 46 37N 0 26W
Sečovce, Slovak Rep. 35 C14 48 42N 21 40 E
Secretary I., N.Z. 131 F1 45 15 S 166 56 E
Secunderabad, India 94 F4 17 28N 78 30 E
Sécure →, Bolivia 173 D5 15 10 S 64 52W
Security-Widefield, U.S.A. 154 F2 38 45N 104 45W
Sedalia, U.S.A. 156 F3 38 42N 93 14W
Sedam, India 94 E3 17 11N 77 17 E
Sedan, Australia 128 C3 34 34 S 139 19 E
Sedan, France 27 C11 49 43N 4 57 E
Sedan, U.S.A. 155 G6 37 8N 96 11W
Sedano, Spain 42 C7 42 43N 3 49W
Seddon, N.Z. 131 B9 41 40 S 174 7 E
Seddonville, N.Z. 131 B7 41 33 S 172 1 E
Sedé Boqér, Israel 103 E3 30 52N 34 47 E
Sedeh, Fārs, Iran 97 D7 30 45N 52 11 E
Sedeh, Khorāsān, Iran 97 C8 33 20N 59 14 E
Séderon, France 29 D9 44 12N 5 32 E
Sederot, Israel 103 D3 31 32N 34 37 E
Sédhiou, Senegal 112 C1 12 44N 15 30W
Sedico, Italy 45 B9 46 8N 12 6 E
Sedlčany, Czech Rep. 34 B7 49 40N 14 25 E
Sedley, Canada 143 C8 50 10N 104 0W
Sedona, U.S.A. 159 J8 34 52N 111 46W
Sedova, Pik, Russia 64 B6 73 29N 54 58 E
Sedrata, Algeria 111 A6 36 7N 7 31 E
Sedro Woolley, U.S.A. 160 B4 48 30N 122 14W
Šedrun, Switz. 33 C7 46 36N 8 47 E
Šeduva, Lithuania 54 C10 55 45N 23 45 E
Sędziszów, Poland 55 H7 50 35N 20 4 E
Sędziszów Małapolski, Poland 55 H8 50 5N 21 45 E
Seebad Ahlbeck, Germany 30 B10 53 56N 14 10 E
Seefeld in Tirol, Austria 34 D4 47 19N 11 13 E
Seehausen, Germany 30 C7 52 54N 11 45 E
Seeheim, Namibia 116 D2 26 50 S 17 45 E
Seeheim-Jugenheim, Germany 31 F4 49 49N 8 40 E
Seeis, Namibia 116 C2 22 29 S 17 39 E
Seekoei →, S. Africa 116 E4 30 18 S 25 1 E
Seeley's Bay, Canada 151 B8 44 29N 76 14W
Seelow, Germany 30 C10 52 32N 14 23 E
Sées, France 26 D7 48 38N 0 10 E
Seesen, Germany 30 D6 51 54N 10 10 E
Seevetal, Germany 30 B6 53 26N 10 1 E
Sefadu, S. Leone 112 D2 8 35N 10 58W
Seferihisar, Turkey 49 C8 38 10N 26 50 E
Séfeto, Mali 112 C3 14 8N 9 49W
Sefrou, Morocco 110 B4 33 52N 4 52W
Sefton, N.Z. 131 D7 43 15 S 172 41 E
Sefuri-San, Japan 70 D2 33 28N 130 18 E
Sefwi Bekwai, Ghana 112 D4 6 10N 2 25W
Seg-ozero, Russia 56 B5 63 20N 33 46 E
Segag, Ethiopia 120 C2 7 39N 42 50 E
Segamat, Malaysia 78 D2 2 30N 102 50 E
Şegarcea, Romania 53 F8 44 6N 23 43 E
Ségbana, Benin 113 C5 10 55N 3 42 E
Segbwema, S. Leone 112 D2 8 0N 11 0W
Seget, Indonesia 79 E8 1 24 S 130 58 E
Segezha, Russia 56 B5 63 44N 34 19 E
Segguer, O. →, Algeria 111 B5 32 14N 1 48 E
Segonzac, France 28 C3 45 36N 0 14W
Segorbe, Spain 40 F4 39 50N 0 30W
Ségou, Mali 112 C3 13 30N 6 16W
Segovia = Coco →, Cent. Amer. 164 D3 15 0N 83 8W
Segovia, Colombia 168 B3 7 7N 74 42W
Segovia, Spain 42 E6 40 57N 4 10W
Segovia □, Spain 42 E6 40 55N 4 10W
Segré, France 26 E6 47 40N 0 52W
Segre →, Spain 40 D5 41 40N 0 43 E
Séguéla, Ivory C. 112 D3 7 55N 6 40W
Séguénéga, Burkina Faso 113 C4 13 25N 1 58W
Seguin, U.S.A. 155 L6 29 34N 97 58W
Segundo →, Argentina 174 C3 30 53 S 62 44W
Segura →, Spain 41 G4 38 3N 0 44W
Segura, Sierra de, Spain 41 G2 38 5N 2 45W
Seh Konj, Kūh-e, Iran 97 D8 30 6N 57 30 E
Seh Qal'eh, Iran 97 C8 33 40N 58 24 E
Sehitwa, Botswana 116 C3 20 30 S 22 30 E
Sehore, India 92 H7 23 10N 77 5 E
Sehwan, Pakistan 91 D2 26 28N 67 53 E
Şeica Mare, Romania 53 D9 46 1N 24 7 E
Seikpyu, Burma 90 E5 20 54N 94 48 E
Seil, U.K. 22 E3 56 18N 5 38W
Seiland, Norway 14 A20 70 25N 23 15 E
Seilhac, France 28 C5 45 22N 1 43 E
Seiling, U.S.A. 155 G5 36 9N 98 56W
Seille →, Moselle, France 27 C13 49 7N 6 11 E
Seille →, Saône-et-Loire, France 27 F11 46 31N 4 57 E
Sein, Î. de, France 26 D2 48 2N 4 52W
Seinäjoki, Finland 15 E20 62 40N 22 51 E
Seine →, France 26 C7 49 26N 0 26 E
Seine, B. de la, France 26 C6 49 40N 0 40W
Seine-et-Marne □, France 27 D10 48 45N 3 0 E
Seine-Maritime □, France 26 C7 49 40N 1 0 E
Seine-St-Denis □, France 27 D9 48 58N 2 24 E
Seini, Romania 53 C8 47 44N 23 21 E
Seirijai, Lithuania 54 D10 54 14N 23 49 E
Sejerø, Denmark 17 J5 55 54N 11 9 E
Sejerø Bugt, Denmark 17 J5 55 53N 11 15 E
Sejny, Poland 54 D10 54 6N 23 21 E
Seka, Ethiopia 107 F4 8 10N 36 52 E
Sekayu, Indonesia 84 C2 2 51 S 103 51 E
Seke, Tanzania 118 C3 3 20 S 33 31 E
Seke-Banza, Dem. Rep. of the Congo 115 D2 5 20 S 13 16 E
Sekenke, Tanzania 118 C3 4 18 S 34 11 E
Seki, Japan 71 B8 35 29N 136 55 E
Seki, Turkey 49 E11 36 48N 29 33 E
Sekigahara, Japan 71 B8 35 22N 136 28 E
Sekondi-Takoradi, Ghana 112 E4 4 58N 1 45W
Sekota, Ethiopia 107 E4 12 40N 39 2 E
Seksna, Russia 56 C10 59 13N 38 30 E
Sekuma, Botswana 116 C3 24 36 S 23 50 E
Selah, U.S.A. 158 C3 46 39N 120 32W
Selama, Malaysia 87 K3 5 12N 100 42 E
Selangor □, Malaysia 87 L3 3 10N 101 30 E
Selárgius, Italy 46 C2 39 16N 9 10 E
Selaru, Indonesia 79 F8 8 9 S 131 0 E
Selawik L., U.S.A. 144 C7 66 30N 160 45W
Selb, Germany 31 E8 50 10N 12 7 E
Selbusjøen, Norway 18 A7 63 15N 10 50 E
Selby, U.K. 20 D6 53 47N 1 5W
Selby, U.S.A. 154 C4 45 31N 100 2W
Selca, Croatia 45 E13 43 20N 16 50 E
Selçuk, Turkey 49 D9 37 56N 27 22 E
Selden, U.S.A. 154 F4 39 33N 100 34W
Sele →, Italy 47 B7 40 29N 14 56 E
Selebi-Pikwe, Botswana 117 C4 21 58 S 27 48 E
Selemdzha →, Russia 65 D13 51 42N 128 53 E
Selendi, Manisa, Turkey 49 C10 38 43N 28 50 E
Selendi, Manisa, Turkey 49 C9 38 45N 28 0 E
Selenga = Selenge Mörön →, Asia 72 A5 52 16N 106 16 E
Selenge, Dem. Rep. of the Congo 114 C3 1 58 S 18 11 E
Selenge Mörön →, Asia 72 A5 52 16N 106 16 E
Selenica, Albania 50 F3 40 33N 19 39 E

280 Selenter See

Selenter See, Germany 30 A6 54 18N 10 26 E
Sélestat, France 27 D14 48 16N 7 26 E
Seletan, Tanjung, Indonesia 78 E4 4 10 S 114 40 E
Selevac, Serbia, Yug. 50 B4 44 28N 20 52 E
Selfoss, Iceland 11 D6 63 56N 21 0W
Sélibabi, Mauritania 112 B2 15 10N 12 15W
Seliger, Ozero, Russia 58 D7 57 15N 33 0 E
Seligman, U.S.A. 159 J7 35 20N 112 53W
Şelim, Turkey 101 B10 40 30N 42 46 E
Selîma, El Wâhât el, Sudan 106 C2 21 22N 29 19 E
Selimiye, Turkey 49 D9 37 24N 27 40 E
Selinda Spillway →, Botswana 116 B3 18 35 S 23 10 E
Selinoús, Greece 48 D3 37 35N 21 37 E
Selinsgrove, U.S.A. 150 F8 40 48N 76 52W
Selizharovo, Russia 58 D7 56 51N 33 27 E
Selje, Norway 18 B2 62 3N 5 22 E
Seljord, Norway 18 E5 59 30N 8 40 E
Selkirk, Canada 143 C9 50 10N 96 55W
Selkirk, U.K. 22 F6 55 33N 2 50W
Selkirk I., Canada 143 C9 53 20N 99 6W
Selkirk Mts., Canada 138 C8 51 15N 117 40W
Sellama, Sudan 107 E2 12 51N 29 46 E
Selliá, Greece 38 D6 35 12N 24 23 E
Sellières, France 27 F12 46 50N 5 32 E
Sells, U.S.A. 159 L8 31 55N 111 53W
Sellye, Hungary 52 E2 45 52N 17 51 E
Selma, Ala., U.S.A. 149 J2 32 25N 87 1W
Selma, Calif., U.S.A. 160 J7 36 34N 119 37W
Selma, N.C., U.S.A. 149 H6 35 32N 78 17W
Selmer, U.S.A. 149 H1 35 10N 88 36W
Selong, Indonesia 85 D5 8 39 S 116 32 E
Selongey, France 27 E12 47 36N 5 11 E
Selowandoma Falls, Zimbabwe 119 G3 21 15 S 31 50 E
Selpele, Indonesia 79 E8 0 1 S 130 5 E
Selsey Bill, U.K. 21 G7 50 43N 0 47W
Seltso, Russia 58 F8 53 22N 34 4 E
Seltz, France 27 D15 48 54N 8 4 E
Selu, Indonesia 79 F8 7 32 S 130 55 E
Sélune →, France 26 D5 48 38N 1 22W
Selva = La Selva del Camp, Spain 40 D6 41 13N 1 8 E
Selva, Argentina 172 B3 29 50 S 62 0W
Selvas, Brazil 172 B4 6 30 S 67 0W
Selwyn L., Canada 143 B8 60 0N 104 30W
Selwyn Mts., Canada 138 B6 63 0N 130 0W
Selwyn Passage, Vanuatu 133 F6 16 3 S 168 12 E
Selwyn Ra., Australia 126 C3 21 10 S 140 0 E
Sem, Norway 18 E7 59 14N 10 17 E
Semani →, Albania 50 F3 40 47N 19 30 E
Semara, W. Sahara 110 C2 26 48N 11 41W
Semarang, Indonesia 79 G14 7 0 S 110 26 E
Sematan, Malaysia 85 B3 1 48N 109 46 E
Semau, Indonesia 82 D2 10 13 S 123 22 E
Sembabule, Uganda 118 C3 0 4 S 31 25 E
Sembé, Congo 114 B2 1 39N 14 36 E
Şemdinli, Turkey 101 D11 37 18N 44 35 E
Sémé, Senegal 112 B2 15 4N 13 41W
Semeih, Sudan 107 E3 12 43N 30 53 E
Semendua, Dem. Rep. of the Congo 114 C3 3 10 S 18 6 E
Semenov, Russia 60 B7 56 43N 44 30 E
Semenovka, Chernihiv, Ukraine 59 F7 52 8N 32 36 E
Semenovka, Kremenchuk, Ukraine 59 H7 49 37N 33 10 E
Semeru, Indonesia 79 H15 8 4 S 112 55 E
Semey, Kazakstan 64 D9 50 30N 80 10 E
Semichi Is., U.S.A. 144 K1 52 42N 174 0 E
Semikarakorskiy, Russia 61 G5 47 31N 40 48 E
Semiluki, Russia 59 G10 51 41N 39 2 E
Seminoe Reservoir, U.S.A. 158 F10 42 9N 106 55W
Seminole, Fla., U.S.A. 153 H7 27 50N 82 47W
Seminole, Okla., U.S.A. 155 H6 35 14N 96 41W
Seminole, Tex., U.S.A. 155 J3 32 43N 102 39W
Seminole, L., U.S.A. 152 E5 30 43N 84 52W
Seminole Draw →, U.S.A. 155 J3 32 27N 102 20W
Semipalatinsk = Semey, Kazakstan 64 D9 50 30N 80 10 E
Semirara I., Phil. 80 E3 12 4N 121 23 E
Semirara Is., Phil. 79 B6 12 0N 121 20 E
Semitau, Indonesia 78 D4 0 29N 111 57 E
Semiyarka, Kazakstan 64 D8 50 55N 78 23 E
Semiyarskoye = Semiyarka, Kazakstan 64 D8 50 55N 78 23 E
Semmering P., Austria 34 D8 47 41N 15 45 E
Semnān, Iran 97 C7 35 40N 53 23 E
Semnān □, Iran 97 C7 36 0N 54 0 E
Sempang Mengayou, Tanjong, Malaysia 85 A5 7 0N 116 40 E
Semporna, Malaysia 79 D5 4 30N 118 33 E
Semuda, Indonesia 78 E4 2 51 S 112 58 E
Semur-en-Auxois, France 27 E11 47 30N 4 20 E
Sen →, Cambodia 78 B3 13 45N 105 12 E
Sena, Bolivia 172 C4 11 32 S 67 11W
Senā, Iran 97 D6 28 27N 51 36 E
Sena, Mozam. 119 F4 17 25 S 35 0 E
Sena →, Bolivia 172 C4 11 31 S 67 11W
Sena Madureira, Brazil 172 B4 9 5 S 68 45W
Senachwine L., U.S.A. 156 C7 41 10N 89 18W
Senador José Porfírio, Brazil 169 D7 2 35 S 51 55W
Senador Pompeu, Brazil 170 C4 5 40 S 39 20W
Senaja, Malaysia 85 A5 6 45N 117 3 E
Senaki, Georgia 61 J6 42 15N 42 7 E
Senanga, Zambia 115 F4 16 7 S 23 16 E
Senatobia, U.S.A. 155 H10 34 37N 89 58W
Sencelles, Spain 39 B9 39 39N 2 54 E
Sendafa, Ethiopia 107 F4 9 11N 39 3 E
Sendai, Kagoshima, Japan 70 F2 31 50N 130 20 E
Sendai, Miyagi, Japan 68 E10 38 15N 140 53 E
Sendai-Wan, Japan 68 E10 38 15N 141 0 E
Senden, Bayern, Germany 31 G6 48 19N 10 4 E
Senden, Nordrhein-Westfalen, Germany 30 D3 51 52N 7 22 E
Sendhwa, India 92 J6 21 41N 75 6 E
Sendurjana, India 94 D4 21 32N 78 17 E
Sene →, Ghana 113 D4 7 30N 0 33W
Senec, Slovak Rep. 35 C10 48 12N 17 23 E
Seneca, Ill., U.S.A. 157 C8 41 19N 88 37W
Seneca, S.C., U.S.A. 149 H4 34 41N 82 57W
Seneca Falls, U.S.A. 151 D8 42 55N 76 48W
Seneca L., U.S.A. 150 D8 42 40N 76 54W
Senecaville L., U.S.A. 150 G3 39 55N 81 25W
Senegal ■, W. Afr. 112 C2 14 30N 14 30W
Sénégal →, W. Afr. 112 B1 15 48N 16 32W
Senegambia, Africa 104 E2 12 45N 12 0W
Senekal, S. Africa 117 D4 28 20 S 27 36 E
Senftenberg, Germany 30 D10 51 32N 14 0 E
Senga Hill, Zambia 119 D3 9 19 S 31 11 E
Senge Khambab = Indus →, Pakistan 91 D2 24 20N 67 47 E
Sengiley, Russia 60 D9 53 58N 48 46 E
Sengua →, Zimbabwe 119 F2 17 7 S 28 5 E
Senguerr →, Argentina 176 C3 45 35 S 68 50W
Senhor-do-Bonfim, Brazil 170 D3 10 30 S 40 10W
Senica, Slovak Rep. 35 C10 48 41N 17 25 E
Senigállia, Italy 45 E10 43 43N 13 13 E
Seniku, Burma 90 C6 25 32N 97 48 E
Senio →, Italy 45 D9 44 35N 12 15 E
Senirkent, Turkey 49 C12 38 6N 30 33 E
Senise, Italy 47 B9 40 9N 16 17 E
Senj, Croatia 45 D11 45 0N 14 58 E
Senja, Norway 14 B17 69 25N 17 30 E
Senkaku-Shotō, Japan 69 L1 25 45N 124 0 E
Senlis, France 27 C9 49 13N 2 35 E
Senmonorom, Cambodia 78 B3 12 27N 107 12 E
Sennâr, Sudan 107 E3 13 30N 33 35 E
Sennar □, Sudan 107 E3 13 0N 34 0 E
Senneterre, Canada 140 C4 48 25N 77 15W
Senno, Belarus 58 E5 54 45N 29 43 E
Sénnori, Italy 46 B1 40 47N 8 35 E
Seno, Laos 86 D5 16 35N 104 50 E
Senoia, U.S.A. 152 B5 33 18N 84 33W
Senonches, France 26 D8 48 34N 1 2 E
Senorbì, Italy 46 C2 39 32N 9 8 E
Senožeče, Slovenia 45 C11 45 43N 14 3 E
Sens, France 27 D10 48 11N 3 15 E
Senta, Serbia, Yug. 52 E5 45 55N 20 3 E
Sentani, Indonesia 79 E10 2 36 S 140 37 E
Sentery, Dem. Rep. of the Congo 118 D2 5 17 S 25 42 E
Sentinel, U.S.A. 159 K7 32 52N 113 13W
Šentjur, Slovenia 45 B12 46 14N 15 24 E
Sentolo, Indonesia 85 D4 7 55 S 110 13 E
Senya Beraku, Ghana 113 D4 5 28N 0 31W
Seo de Urgel = La Seu d'Urgell, Spain 40 C6 42 22N 1 23 E
Seohara, India 93 E8 29 15N 78 33 E
Seonath →, India 93 J10 21 44N 82 28 E
Seondha, India 93 F8 26 9N 78 48 E
Seoni, India 93 H8 22 5N 79 30 E
Seoni Malwa, India 92 H8 22 27N 77 28 E
Seoriuarayan, India 94 D6 21 45N 82 34 E
Seoul = Sŏul, S. Korea 75 F14 37 31N 126 58 E
Separation Pt., N.Z. 131 A7 40 47 S 172 59 E
Sepatini →, Brazil 172 B4 7 36 S 65 24W
Sepīdān, Iran 97 D7 30 20N 52 5 E
Sepik →, Papua N. G. 132 B3 3 49 S 144 30 E
Sepo-ri, N. Korea 75 E14 38 57N 127 25 E
Sępólno Krajeńskie, Poland 54 E4 53 26N 17 30 E
Sepone, Laos 86 D6 16 45N 106 13 E
Sepopol, Poland 54 D8 54 16N 21 2 E
Sept-Îles, Canada 141 B6 50 13N 66 22W
Septemvri, Bulgaria 53 D8 42 13N 24 6 E
Sepúlveda, Spain 42 D7 41 18N 3 45W
Sequeros, Spain 42 E4 40 31N 6 2W
Sequim, U.S.A. 160 B3 48 5N 123 6W
Sequoia National Park, U.S.A. 160 J8 36 30N 118 30W
Serafimovich, Russia 60 F6 49 36N 42 43 E
Seraing, Belgium 24 D5 50 35N 5 32 E
Seraja, Indonesia 87 L7 2 41N 108 35 E
Serakhis →, Cyprus 38 D11 35 13N 32 55 E
Seram, Indonesia 79 E7 3 10 S 129 0 E
Seram Laut, Kepulauan, Indonesia 83 B4 4 5 S 131 25 E
Seram Sea, Indonesia 79 E7 2 30 S 128 30 E
Seranantsara, Madag. 117 B8 18 30 S 49 5 E
Serang, Indonesia 79 G12 6 8 S 106 10 E
Serasan, Indonesia 78 D3 2 29N 109 4 E
Seravezza, Italy 44 E7 43 59N 10 13 E
Şerbettar, Turkey 51 E10 41 27N 26 46 E
Serbia □, Yugoslavia 52 G5 43 30N 21 0 E
Şercaia, Romania 53 E10 45 49N 25 9 E
Serdo, Ethiopia 107 E5 11 56N 41 14 E
Serdobsk, Russia 60 D7 52 28N 44 10 E
Sered', Slovak Rep. 35 C10 48 17N 17 44 E
Seredka, Russia 58 C5 58 12N 28 10 E
Şereflikoçhisar, Turkey 100 C5 38 56N 33 32 E
Seregno, Italy 44 C6 45 39N 9 12 E
Seremban, Malaysia 78 D2 2 43N 101 53 E
Serengeti Plain, Tanzania 118 C4 2 40 S 35 0 E
Serenje, Zambia 119 E3 13 14 S 30 15 E
Sereth = Siret →, Romania 53 E12 45 24N 28 1 E
Sergach, Russia 60 C7 55 30N 45 30 E
Sergen, Turkey 51 E11 41 41N 27 42 E
Sergino, Russia 64 C7 62 25N 65 12 E
Sergipe □, Brazil 170 D4 10 30 S 37 30W
Sergiyev Posad, Russia 58 D10 56 20N 38 10 E
Seria, Brunei 78 D4 4 37N 114 23 E
Serian, Malaysia 78 D4 1 10N 110 31 E
Seriate, Italy 44 C6 45 41N 9 43 E
Seribu, Kepulauan, Indonesia 78 F3 5 36 S 106 33 E
Sérifontaine, France 27 C8 49 20N 1 45 E
Sérifos, Greece 48 D6 37 9N 24 30 E
Sérignan, France 27 E7 43 17N 3 17 E
Sérigny →, Canada 141 A6 56 47N 66 0W
Serik, Turkey 100 D4 36 55N 31 7 E
Seringapatam Reef, Australia 124 B3 13 38 S 122 5 E
Serinhisar, Turkey 49 D11 37 36N 29 18 E
Sermaize-les-Bains, France 27 D11 48 47N 4 54 E
Sermata, Indonesia 79 F7 8 15 S 128 50 E
Sérmide, Italy 45 D8 45 0N 11 18 E
Sernovodsk, Russia 60 D10 53 54N 51 16 E
Sernur, Russia 60 B9 56 52N 49 2 E
Serock, Poland 55 F8 52 31N 21 4 E
Serón, Spain 41 H2 37 20N 2 29W
Serós, Spain 40 D5 41 27N 0 24 E
Serov, Russia 62 B8 59 29N 60 35 E
Serowe, Botswana 116 C4 22 25 S 26 43 E
Serpa, Portugal 43 H3 37 57N 7 38W
Serpeddí, Punta, Italy 46 C2 39 22N 9 18 E
Serpentara, Italy 46 C2 39 8N 9 36 E
Serpentine Lakes, Australia 125 E4 28 30 S 129 10 E
Serpis →, Spain 41 G4 38 59N 0 9W
Serpukhov, Russia 58 E9 54 55N 37 28 E
Serra de Outes, Spain 42 C2 42 52N 8 55W
Serra do Navio, Brazil 169 C7 0 59N 52 3W
Serra do Salitre, Brazil 171 E2 19 6 S 46 41W
Serra San Bruno, Italy 47 D9 38 35N 16 20 E
Serra Talhada, Brazil 170 C4 7 59 S 38 18W
Serradilla, Spain 42 F4 39 50N 6 9W
Sérrai, Greece 50 E7 41 5N 23 31 E
Sérrai □, Greece 50 E7 41 5N 23 37 E
Serramanna, Italy 46 C1 39 25N 8 55 E
Serranópolis, Brazil 173 18 16 S 52 0W
Serrat, C., Tunisia 108 A1 37 14N 9 10 E
Serravalle, Italy 33 E6 45 41N 8 18 E
Serravalle Scrívia, Italy 44 D5 44 43N 8 51 E
Serre-Ponçon, L. de, France 29 D10 44 22N 6 20 E
Serres, France 29 D9 44 26N 5 43 E
Serrezuela, Argentina 174 C2 30 40 S 65 20W
Serrinha, Brazil 171 D4 11 39 S 39 0W
Serrita, Brazil 170 C4 7 56 S 39 19W
Sersale, Italy 47 C9 39 1N 16 43 E
Sertã, Portugal 42 F2 39 48N 8 6W
Sertânia, Brazil 170 C4 8 5 S 37 20W
Sertanópolis, Brazil 175 A5 23 4 S 51 2W
Sêrtar, China 76 A3 32 20N 100 41 E
Sertig, Switz. 33 C9 46 44N 9 52 E
Serua, Indonesia 79 F8 6 18 S 130 1 E
Serui, Indonesia 79 E9 1 53 S 136 10 E
Serule, Botswana 116 C4 21 57 S 27 20 E
Sérvia, Greece 50 F6 40 11N 22 0 E
Serzedelo, Portugal 42 D2 41 24N 8 14W
Sesayap →, Indonesia 85 B5 3 36N 117 15 E
Sese Is., Uganda 118 C3 0 20 S 32 20 E
Sesepe, Indonesia 79 E7 1 30 S 127 59 E
Sesfontein, Namibia 116 B1 19 7 S 13 39 E
Sesheke, Zambia 116 B3 17 29 S 24 13 E
Sésia →, Italy 44 C5 45 5N 8 37 E
Sesimbra, Portugal 43 G1 38 28N 9 6W
S'Espalmador, Spain 39 C7 38 47N 1 26 E
S'Espardell, Spain 39 C7 38 48N 1 29 E
Sessa, Angola 115 E4 13 56 S 20 38 E
Sessa Aurunca, Italy 46 A6 41 14N 13 56 E
Sesser, U.S.A. 156 F7 38 5N 89 1W
S'Estanyol, Spain 39 B9 39 22N 2 54 E
Sestao, Spain 40 B2 43 18N 3 0W
Sesto Calende, Italy 44 C5 45 44N 8 37 E
Sesto San Giovanni, Italy 44 C6 45 32N 9 14 E
Sestri Levante, Italy 44 D6 44 16N 9 24 E
Sestriere, Italy 44 D3 44 57N 6 53 E
Sestroretsk, Russia 58 B6 60 5N 29 58 E
Sestrunj, Croatia 45 D11 44 10N 15 0 E
Sestu, Italy 46 C2 39 18N 9 5 E
Sesvenna, Switz. 33 C10 46 42N 10 25 E
Setaka, Japan 70 D2 33 9N 130 28 E
Setana, Japan 68 C9 42 26N 139 51 E
Sète, France 28 E7 43 25N 3 42 E
Sete Lagôas, Brazil 171 E3 19 27 S 44 16W
Setesdalsheiene, Norway 18 E3 59 28N 7 10 E
Sétif, Algeria 111 A6 36 9N 5 26 E
Seto, Japan 71 B9 35 14N 137 6 E
Setonaikai, Japan 70 C5 34 20N 133 30 E
Setsan, Burma 90 G5 16 3N 95 23 E
Settat, Morocco 110 B3 33 0N 7 40W
Setté-Cama, Gabon 114 C1 2 32 S 9 45 E
Séttimo Torinese, Italy 44 C4 45 9N 7 46 E
Setting L., Canada 143 C9 55 0N 98 38W
Settle, U.K. 20 C5 54 5N 2 16W
Settlement Pt., Bahamas 149 M6 26 40N 79 0W
Settlers, S. Africa 117 C4 25 2 S 28 30 E
Setúbal, Portugal 43 G2 38 30N 8 58W
Setúbal □, Portugal 43 G2 38 25N 8 35W
Setúbal, B. de, Portugal 43 G2 38 40N 8 56W
Seu d'Urgell, Spain 28 C3 45 42N 0 32W
Seugne →, France 26 C3 48 20N 92 30W
Seul, Lac, Canada 138 C10 50 20N 92 30W
Seulimeum, Indonesia 84 A1 5 27N 95 15 E
Seurre, France 27 F12 47 0N 5 8 E
Seuzach, Switz. 33 A7 47 32N 8 49 E
Sevan, Armenia 61 K7 40 33N 44 56 E
Sevan, Ozero = Sevana Lich, Armenia 61 K7 40 30N 45 20 E
Sevana Lich, Armenia 61 K7 40 30N 45 20 E
Sevastopol, Ukraine 59 K7 44 35N 33 30 E
Sevelen, Switz. 33 B8 47 7N 9 28 E
Seven Sisters, Canada 142 C3 54 56N 128 10W
Sever →, Spain 43 F3 39 40N 7 32W
Sévérac-le-Château, France 28 D7 44 20N 3 5 E
Severn →, Canada 140 A2 56 2N 87 36W
Severn →, U.K. 21 F5 51 35N 2 40W
Severn L., Canada 140 B1 53 54N 90 48W
Severnaya Zemlya, Russia 65 B10 79 0N 100 0 E
Severnyye Uvaly, Russia 62 B2 60 0N 50 0 E
Severo-Kurilsk, Russia 65 D16 50 40N 156 8 E
Severo-Yeniseyskiy, Russia 65 C10 60 22N 93 1 E
Severočeský □, Czech Rep. 34 A7 50 30N 14 0 E
Severodonetsk = Syeverodonetsk, Ukraine 59 H10 48 58N 38 35 E
Severodvinsk, Russia 56 B6 64 27N 39 58 E
Severomoravský □, Czech Rep. 35 B10 49 38N 17 40 E
Severomorsk, Russia 56 A5 69 5N 33 27 E
Severouralsk, Russia 62 A7 60 9N 59 57 E
Sevier, U.S.A. 159 G7 38 39N 112 11W
Sevier →, U.S.A. 159 G7 39 4N 113 6W
Sevier Desert, U.S.A. 158 G7 39 40N 112 45W
Sevier L., U.S.A. 158 G7 38 54N 113 9W
Sevilla, Colombia 168 C2 4 16N 75 57W
Sevilla, Spain 43 H5 37 23N 5 58W
Sevilla □, Spain 43 H5 37 25N 5 30W
Seville = Sevilla, Spain 43 H5 37 23N 5 58W
Seville, Fla., U.S.A. 153 F8 29 19N 81 30W
Seville, Ga., U.S.A. 152 D6 31 58N 83 36W
Sevlievo, Bulgaria 51 C9 43 2N 25 6 E
Sevnica, Slovenia 45 B12 46 2N 15 19 E
Sèvre-Nantaise →, France 26 E5 47 12N 1 33W
Sèvre-Niortaise →, France 28 B3 46 28N 0 50W
Sevsk, Russia 59 F8 52 10N 34 30 E
Sewa →, S. Leone 112 D2 7 20N 12 10W
Sewani, India 92 E6 28 58N 75 39 E
Seward, Alaska, U.S.A. 138 B5 60 7N 149 27W
Seward, Nebr., U.S.A. 154 E6 40 55N 97 6W
Seward, Pa., U.S.A. 150 F5 40 25N 79 1W
Seward Peninsula, U.S.A. 144 D6 65 30N 166 0W
Sewell, Chile 174 C1 34 10 S 70 23W
Sewer, Indonesia 79 F8 5 53 S 134 40 E
Sewickley, U.S.A. 150 F4 40 32N 80 12W
Sexsmith, Canada 142 B5 55 21N 118 47W
Seychelles ■, Ind. Oc. 66 K9 5 0 S 56 0 E
Seyðisfjörður, Iceland 11 B13 65 16N 13 57W
Seydişehir, Turkey 100 D4 37 25N 31 51 E
Seydvān, Iran 101 C11 38 34N 45 2 E
Seyhan →, Turkey 100 D6 36 43N 34 53 E
Seyhan Barajı, Turkey 100 D6 37 2N 35 18 E
Seyitgazi, Turkey 49 B12 39 27N 30 43 E
Seyitömer, Turkey 49 B11 39 34N 29 52 E
Seym →, Ukraine 59 G7 51 27N 32 34 E
Seymen, Turkey 51 E11 41 6N 27 57 E
Seymour, Australia 129 D6 37 0 S 145 10 E
Seymour, S. Africa 117 E4 32 33 S 26 46 E
Seymour, Conn., U.S.A. 151 E11 41 24N 73 4W
Seymour, Ind., U.S.A. 157 F11 38 58N 85 53W
Seymour, Tex., U.S.A. 155 J5 33 35N 99 16W
Seyne, France 29 D10 44 21N 6 22 E
Seyssel, France 29 C9 45 57N 5 50 E
Sežana, Slovenia 45 C10 45 43N 13 41 E
Sézanne, France 27 D10 48 40N 3 40 E
Sezze, Italy 46 A6 41 30N 13 3 E
Sfântu Gheorghe, Covasna, Romania 53 E10 45 52N 25 48 E
Sfântu Gheorghe, Tulcea, Romania 53 F14 44 53N 29 36 E
Sfântu Gheorghe, Braţul →, Romania 53 F14 44 51N 29 36 E
Sfax, Tunisia 108 B2 34 49N 10 48 E
Sha Xi →, China 77 D12 26 35N 118 0 E
Sha Xian, China 77 D11 26 23N 117 45 E
Shaanxi □, China 74 G5 35 0N 109 0 E
Shaartuz, Tajikistan 63 E4 37 16N 68 8 E
Shaba = Katanga □, Dem. Rep. of the Congo 118 D2 8 0 S 25 0 E
Shabla, Bulgaria 51 C12 43 31N 28 32 E
Shabogamo L., Canada 141 B6 53 15N 66 30W
Shabunda, Dem. Rep. of the Congo 118 C2 2 40 S 27 16 E
Shabwah, Yemen 98 D4 15 22N 47 1 E
Shache, China 72 C2 38 20N 77 10 E
Shackleton Ice Shelf, Antarctica 7 C8 66 0 S 100 0 E
Shackleton Inlet, Antarctica 7 E11 83 0 S 160 0 E
Shādegān, Iran 97 D6 30 40N 48 38 E
Shadi, China 77 D10 26 7N 114 47 E
Shadi, India 93 C7 33 24N 77 14 E
Shadrinsk, Russia 62 C9 56 5N 63 32 E
Shady Dale, U.S.A. 152 B6 33 24N 83 36W
Shady Grove, U.S.A. 152 E6 30 17N 83 38W
Shadyside, U.S.A. 150 G4 39 58N 80 45W
Shafer, L., U.S.A. 157 D10 40 46N 86 46W
Shaffa, Nigeria 113 C7 10 30N 12 6 E
Shafter, U.S.A. 161 K7 35 30N 119 16W
Shaftesbury, U.K. 21 F5 51 0N 2 11W
Shag Pt., N.Z. 131 F5 45 29 S 170 52 E
Shag Rocks, Atl. Oc. 9 P4 53 0 S 41 0W
Shagamu, Nigeria 113 D5 6 51N 3 39 E
Shageluk, U.S.A. 144 E8 62 41N 159 34W
Shagram, Pakistan 93 A5 36 24N 72 20 E
Shah Alam, Malaysia 84 B2 3 5N 101 30 E
Shah Alizai, Pakistan 92 E2 29 25N 66 33 E
Shah Bunder, Pakistan 92 G2 24 13N 67 56 E
Shāh Jūy, Afghan. 91 B2 32 31N 67 25 E
Shahabad, Andhra Pradesh, India 94 F4 17 10N 78 7 E
Shahabad, Karnataka, India 94 F3 17 10N 76 54 E
Shahabad, Punjab, India 92 D7 30 10N 76 55 E
Shahabad, Raj., India 92 G7 25 15N 77 11 E
Shahabad, Ut. P., India 93 F8 27 36N 79 56 E
Shahada, India 94 D2 21 33N 74 30 E
Shahadpur, Pakistan 92 G3 25 55N 68 35 E
Shahapur, India 95 G2 15 50N 74 34 E
Shahba, Syria 103 C5 32 52N 36 38 E
Shahdād, Iran 97 D8 30 30N 57 40 E
Shahdād, Namakzār-e, Iran 97 D8 30 20N 58 20 E
Shahdadkot, Pakistan 91 D2 27 50N 67 55 E
Shahdol, India 93 H9 23 19N 81 26 E
Shahe, China 74 F8 37 0N 114 32 E
Shahganj, India 93 F10 26 3N 82 44 E
Shaḥḥāt, Libya 108 B4 32 48N 21 54 E
Shahīdān, Afghan. 91 A2 36 42N 67 49 E
Shahjahanpur, India 93 F8 27 54N 79 57 E
Shahpur, Karnataka, India 94 F3 16 40N 76 48 E
Shahpur, Mad. P., India 92 H7 22 12N 77 58 E
Shahpur, Baluchistan, Pakistan 92 E3 28 46N 68 27 E
Shahpur, Punjab, Pakistan 92 C5 32 17N 72 26 E
Shahpur Chakar, Pakistan 92 F3 26 9N 68 39 E
Shahpura, Mad. P., India 93 H9 23 10N 80 45 E
Shahpura, Raj., India 92 G6 25 38N 74 56 E
Shahr-e Bābak, Iran 97 D7 30 7N 55 9 E
Shahr-e Kord, Iran 97 C6 32 15N 50 55 E
Shāhrakht, Iran 97 C9 33 38N 60 16 E
Shahrig, Pakistan 91 C2 30 15N 67 40 E
Shahukou, China 74 D7 40 20N 112 18 E
Shaikhabad, Afghan. 92 B3 34 2N 68 45 E
Shajapur, India 92 H7 23 27N 76 21 E
Shakargarh, Pakistan 92 C6 32 17N 75 10 E
Shakawe, Botswana 116 B3 18 28 S 21 49 E
Shakenge, Dem. Rep. of the Congo 115 D3 6 14 S 18 41 E
Shaker Heights, U.S.A. 150 E3 41 29N 81 32W
Shakhrisabz, Uzbekistan 63 D3 39 3N 66 50 E
Shakhristan, Tajikistan 63 D4 39 47N 68 49 E
Shakhty, Russia 61 G5 47 40N 40 16 E
Shakhunya, Russia 60 B8 57 40N 46 46 E
Shaki, Nigeria 113 D5 8 41N 3 21 E
Shâkir, Egypt 106 B3 27 30N 33 59 E
Shaktoolik, U.S.A. 144 D7 64 20N 161 9W
Shala, L., Ethiopia 107 F4 7 30N 38 30 E
Shali, Russia 61 J7 43 9N 45 55 E
Shalkar, Kazakstan 62 F3 50 40N 51 53 E
Shalkar, Ozero, Kazakstan 62 F3 50 35N 51 47 E
Shallow Lake, Canada 150 B3 44 36N 81 5W
Shalqar, Kazakstan 64 E6 47 48N 59 39 E
Shalskiy, Russia 58 B8 61 48N 35 58 E
Shaluli Shan, China 76 B2 30 40N 99 55 E
Shām, Iran 97 E8 26 39N 57 21 E
Shām, Bādiyat ash, Asia 96 C3 32 0N 40 0 E
Shām, J. ash, Oman 99 B7 23 10N 57 5 E
Shamâl Bahr el Ghazal □, Sudan 107 F2 8 0N 27 30 E
Shamâl Dârfûr □, Sudan 107 E2 15 0N 25 0 E
Shamâl Kordofân □, Sudan 107 E3 15 0N 30 0 E
Shamattawa, Canada 140 A1 55 51N 92 5W
Shamattawa →, Canada 140 A2 55 1N 85 23W
Shambe, Sudan 107 F3 7 8N 30 46 E
Shambu, Ethiopia 107 F4 9 32N 37 3 E
Shamgong Dzong, Bhutan 90 B3 27 13N 90 35 E
Shamīl, Iran 97 E8 27 30N 56 55 E
Shamkhor = Şämkir, Azerbaijan 61 K8 40 50N 46 0 E
Shāmkūh, Iran 97 C8 35 47N 57 50 E
Shamli, India 92 E7 29 32N 77 18 E
Shammar, Jabal, Si. Arabia 96 E4 27 40N 41 0 E
Shamo = Gobi, Asia 74 C6 44 0N 110 0 E
Shamo, L., Ethiopia 102 F2 5 45N 37 30 E
Shamokin, U.S.A. 151 F8 40 47N 76 34W
Shamrock, U.S.A. 155 H4 35 13N 100 15W
Shamshabad, India 94 F4 17 15N 78 25 E
Shamva, Zimbabwe 119 F3 17 20 S 31 32 E
Shan □, Burma 90 E7 21 30N 98 30 E
Shan Xian, China 74 G9 34 50N 116 5 E
Shanan →, Ethiopia 107 F5 8 0N 40 20 E
Shanchengzhen, China 75 C13 42 20N 125 20 E
Shāndak, Iran 97 D9 28 28N 60 27 E
Shandon, U.S.A. 160 K6 35 39N 120 23W
Shandong □, China 75 G10 36 0N 118 0 E
Shandong Bandao, China 75 F11 37 0N 121 0 E
Shang Xian = Shangzhou, China 74 H5 33 50N 109 58 E
Shangalowe, Dem. Rep. of the Congo 119 E2 10 50 S 26 30 E
Shangani, Zimbabwe 117 B4 19 41 S 29 20 E
Shangani →, Zimbabwe 119 F2 18 41 S 27 10 E
Shangbancheng, China 75 D10 40 50N 118 1 E
Shangcheng, China 77 B10 31 47N 115 26 E
Shangchuan Dao, China 77 G9 21 40N 112 50 E
Shangdu, China 74 D7 41 30N 113 30 E
Shanggao, China 77 C10 28 17N 114 55 E
Shanghai, China 77 B13 31 15N 121 26 E
Shanghai □, China 77 B13 31 0N 121 30 E
Shanghai Shi □, China 77 B13 31 0N 121 30 E
Shanghang, China 77 E11 25 2N 116 23 E
Shanghe, China 75 F9 37 20N 117 10 E
Shanglin, China 76 F7 23 27N 108 33 E
Shangnan, China 74 H6 33 32N 110 50 E
Shangqiu, China 74 G8 34 26N 115 36 E
Shangrao, China 77 C11 28 25N 117 59 E
Shangshui, China 74 H8 33 42N 114 35 E
Shangsi, China 76 F6 22 8N 107 58 E
Shangyou, China 77 E10 25 48N 114 32 E
Shangyu, China 77 B13 30 3N 120 52 E
Shangzhi, China 75 B14 45 22N 127 56 E
Shangzhou, China 74 H5 33 50N 109 58 E
Shanhetun, China 75 B14 44 33N 127 15 E
Shani, Nigeria 113 C7 10 14N 12 2 E
Shannon, Greenland 10 B9 75 10N 18 30W
Shannon, N.Z. 130 G4 40 33 S 175 25 E
Shannon →, Ireland 23 D2 52 35N 9 30W
Shannon, Mouth of the, Ireland 23 D2 52 30N 9 55W
Shannon Airport, Ireland 23 D3 52 42N 8 57W
Shannontown, U.S.A. 152 B9 33 53N 80 21W

Shansi = Shanxi □, *China* **74 F7** 37 0N 112 0 E
Shantar, Ostrov Bolshoy, *Russia* **65 D14** 55 9N 137 40 E
Shantipur, *India* **93 H13** 23 17N 88 25 E
Shantou, *China* **77 F11** 23 18N 116 40 E
Shantung = Shandong □, *China* **75 G10** 36 0N 118 0 E
Shanwei, *China* **77 F10** 22 48N 115 22 E
Shanxi □, *China* **74 F7** 37 0N 112 0 E
Shanyang, *China* **74 H5** 33 31N 109 55 E
Shanyin, *China* **74 E7** 39 25N 112 56 E
Shaodong, *China* **77 D8** 27 15N 111 43 E
Shaoguan, *China* **77 E9** 24 48N 113 35 E
Shaoshan, *China* **77 D9** 27 55N 112 33 E
Shaowu, *China* **77 D11** 27 22N 117 28 E
Shaoxing, *China* **77 C13** 30 0N 120 35 E
Shaoyang, *Hunan, China* **77 D8** 26 59N 111 20 E
Shaoyang, *Hunan, China* **77 D8** 27 14N 111 25 E
Shap, *U.K.* **20 C5** 54 32N 2 40W
Shapinsay, *U.K.* **22 B6** 59 3N 2 51W
Shaqq el Gi'eifer →, *Sudan* **107 D2** 15 16N 26 0 E
Shaqra', *Si. Arabia* **96 E5** 25 15N 45 16 E
Shaqrā', *Yemen* **98 D4** 13 22N 45 44 E
Sharafa, *Sudan* **107 E2** 11 59N 27 7 E
Sharafkhāneh, *Iran* **101 C11** 38 11N 45 29 E
Sharavati →, *India* **95 G2** 14 20N 74 25 E
Sharbatāt, Ra's ash, *Oman* **99 C7** 17 56N 56 21 E
Sharbot Lake, *Canada* **151 B8** 44 46N 76 41W
Shari, *Japan* **68 C12** 43 55N 144 40 E
Sharjah = Ash Shāriqah, *U.A.E.* **97 E7** 25 23N 55 26 E
Shark B., *Australia* **125 E1** 25 30 S 113 32 E
Sharm el Sheikh, *Egypt* **106 B3** 27 53N 34 18 E
Sharon, *Mass., U.S.A.* **151 D13** 42 7N 71 11W
Sharon, *Pa., U.S.A.* **150 E4** 41 14N 80 31W
Sharon, *Wis., U.S.A.* **157 B8** 42 30N 88 44W
Sharon Springs, *Kans., U.S.A.* **154 F4** 38 54N 101 45W
Sharon Springs, *N.Y., U.S.A.* **151 D10** 42 48N 74 37W
Sharonville, *U.S.A.* **157 E12** 39 16N 84 25W
Sharp Pk., *Phil.* **81 J5** 5 58N 125 31 E
Sharp Pt., *Australia* **126 A3** 10 58 S 142 43 E
Sharpe L., *Canada* **140 B1** 54 24N 93 40W
Sharpes, *U.S.A.* **153 G9** 28 26N 80 46W
Sharpsville, *U.S.A.* **150 E4** 41 15N 80 29W
Sharq el Istiwa'iya □, *Sudan* **107 G3** 5 0N 33 0 E
Sharya, *Russia* **60 A7** 58 22N 45 20 E
Shasha, *Ethiopia* **107 F4** 6 29N 35 59 E
Shashemene, *Ethiopia* **102 F2** 7 13N 38 33 E
Shashi, *Botswana* **117 C4** 21 15 S 27 27 E
Shashi, *China* **77 B9** 30 25N 112 14 E
Shashi →, *Africa* **119 G2** 21 14 S 29 20 E
Shasta, Mt., *U.S.A.* **158 F2** 41 25N 122 12W
Shasta L., *U.S.A.* **158 F2** 40 43N 122 25W
Shatawi, *Sudan* **107 E3** 14 39N 32 6 E
Shatsk, *Russia* **60 C5** 54 5N 41 45 E
Shatt al'Arab →, *Iraq* **97 D6** 29 57N 48 34 E
Shatura, *Russia* **58 E10** 55 33N 39 21 E
Shaumyani = Shulaveri, *Georgia* **61 K7** 41 22N 44 45 E
Shaunavon, *Canada* **143 D7** 49 35N 108 25W
Shaver L., *U.S.A.* **160 H7** 37 9N 119 18W
Shaw →, *Australia* **124 D2** 20 21 S 119 17 E
Shaw I., *Australia* **126 C4** 20 30 S 149 2 E
Shawanaga, *Canada* **150 A4** 45 31N 80 17W
Shawangunk Mts., *U.S.A.* **151 E10** 41 35N 74 30W
Shawano, *U.S.A.* **148 C1** 44 47N 88 36W
Shawinigan, *Canada* **140 C5** 46 35N 72 50W
Shawnee, *Ga., U.S.A.* **152 C8** 32 29N 81 25W
Shawnee, *Kans., U.S.A.* **156 E2** 39 1N 94 43W
Shawnee, *Okla., U.S.A.* **155 H6** 35 20N 96 55W
Shay Gap, *Australia* **124 D3** 20 30 S 120 10 E
Shayang, *China* **77 B9** 30 42N 112 29 E
Shaybārā, *Si. Arabia* **96 E3** 25 26N 36 47 E
Shayib el Banat, Gebel, *Egypt* **106 B3** 26 59N 33 29 E
Shaykh, J. ash, *Lebanon* **103 B4** 33 25N 35 50 E
Shaykh Miskīn, *Syria* **103 C5** 32 49N 36 9 E
Shaykh Sa'īd, *Iraq* **101 F12** 32 34N 46 17 E
Shaykh 'Uthmān, *Yemen* **98 D4** 12 52N 44 59 E
Shaymak, *Tajikistan* **63 E7** 37 33N 74 50 E
Shchekino, *Russia* **58 E9** 54 1N 37 34 E
Shcherbakov = Rybinsk, *Russia* **58 C10** 58 5N 38 50 E
Shchigry, *Russia* **59 G9** 51 55N 36 58 E
Shchors, *Ukraine* **59 G6** 51 48N 31 56 E
Shchuchinsk, *Kazakstan* **64 D8** 52 56N 70 12 E
Shchuchye, *Russia* **62 D9** 55 12N 62 46 E
She Xian, *Anhui, China* **77 C12** 29 50N 118 25 E
She Xian, *Hebei, China* **74 F7** 36 30N 113 40 E
Shea, *Guyana* **169 C6** 2 48N 59 4W
Shebekino, *Russia* **59 G9** 50 28N 36 54 E
Shebele = Scebeli, Wabi →, *Somali Rep.* **120 D2** 2 0N 44 0 E
Sheberghān, *Afghan.* **63 E2** 36 40N 65 45 E
Sheboygan, *U.S.A.* **148 D2** 43 46N 87 45W
Shebshi Mts., *Nigeria* **113 D7** 8 30N 12 0 E
Shediac, *Canada* **141 C7** 46 14N 64 32W
Sheelin, L., *Ireland* **23 C4** 53 48N 7 20W
Sheenjek →, *U.S.A.* **144 C11** 66 45N 144 33W
Sheep Haven, *Ireland* **23 A4** 55 11N 7 52W
Sheerness, *U.K.* **21 F8** 51 26N 0 47 E
Sheet Harbour, *Canada* **141 D7** 44 56N 62 31W
Sheffield, *N.Z.* **131 D7** 43 23 S 172 1 E
Sheffield, *U.K.* **20 D6** 53 23N 1 28W
Sheffield, *Ala., U.S.A.* **149 H2** 34 46N 87 41W
Sheffield, *Ill., U.S.A.* **156 C7** 41 21N 89 44W
Sheffield, *Iowa, U.S.A.* **156 B3** 42 54N 93 13W
Sheffield, *Mass., U.S.A.* **151 D11** 42 5N 73 21W
Sheffield, *Pa., U.S.A.* **150 E5** 41 42N 79 3W
Shegaon, *India* **94 D3** 20 48N 76 47 E
Shehojele, *Ethiopia* **107 E4** 10 40N 35 9 E
Shehong, *China* **76 B5** 30 54N 105 18 E
Shehuen →, *Argentina* **176 C3** 49 35 S 69 34W
Sheikh Idris, *Sudan* **107 E3** 11 43N 33 30 E
Sheikhpura, *India* **93 G11** 25 9N 85 53 E
Shek Hasan, *Ethiopia* **107 E4** 12 5N 35 58 E
Shekhupura, *Pakistan* **91 C4** 31 42N 73 58 E
Sheki = Şaki, *Azerbaijan* **61 K8** 41 10N 47 5 E
Shelbina, *U.S.A.* **156 E4** 39 47N 92 2W
Shelburn, *U.S.A.* **157 E9** 39 11N 87 24W
Shelburne, *N.S., Canada* **141 D6** 43 47N 65 20W
Shelburne, *Ont., Canada* **140 D3** 44 4N 80 15W
Shelburne, *U.S.A.* **151 B11** 44 23N 73 14W
Shelburne B., *Australia* **126 A3** 11 50 S 142 50 E
Shelburne Falls, *U.S.A.* **151 D12** 42 36N 72 45W
Shelby, *Mich., U.S.A.* **148 D2** 43 37N 86 22W
Shelby, *Miss., U.S.A.* **155 J9** 33 57N 90 46W
Shelby, *Mont., U.S.A.* **158 B8** 48 30N 111 51W
Shelby, *N.C., U.S.A.* **149 H5** 35 17N 81 32W
Shelby, *Ohio, U.S.A.* **150 F2** 40 53N 82 40W
Shelbyville, *Ill., U.S.A.* **154 F10** 39 24N 88 48W
Shelbyville, *Ind., U.S.A.* **157 E11** 39 31N 85 47W
Shelbyville, *Ky., U.S.A.* **157 F11** 38 13N 85 14W
Shelbyville, *Mo., U.S.A.* **156 E4** 39 48N 92 2W
Shelbyville, *Tenn., U.S.A.* **149 H2** 35 29N 86 28W
Shelbyville, L., *U.S.A.* **157 E8** 39 26N 88 46W
Sheldon, *Ill., U.S.A.* **157 D9** 40 46N 87 34W
Sheldon, *Iowa, U.S.A.* **154 D7** 43 11N 95 51W
Sheldon, *Mo., U.S.A.* **156 G2** 37 40N 94 18W
Sheldon, *S.C., U.S.A.* **152 C9** 32 36N 80 48W
Sheldrake, *Canada* **141 B7** 50 20N 64 51W
Shelek, *Kazakstan* **63 B9** 43 33N 78 17 E
Shelengo, Khawr →, *Sudan* **107 E2** 10 33N 28 40 E
Shelikhova, Zaliv, *Russia* **65 D16** 59 30N 157 0 E
Shell Lakes, *Australia* **125 E4** 29 20 S 127 30 E
Shellbrook, *Canada* **143 C7** 53 13N 106 24W
Shellharbour, *Australia* **129 C9** 34 31 S 150 51 E
Shellman, *U.S.A.* **152 D5** 31 46N 84 37W
Shellsburg, *U.S.A.* **156 B5** 42 6N 91 52W
Shelon →, *Russia* **58 C6** 58 13N 30 47 E
Shelter I, *U.S.A.* **151 E12** 41 5N 72 21W
Shelton, *Conn., U.S.A.* **151 E11** 41 19N 73 5W
Shelton, *Wash., U.S.A.* **160 C3** 47 13N 123 6W
Shemakha = Şamaxi, *Azerbaijan* **61 K9** 40 38N 48 37 E
Shemsi, *Sudan* **106 D2** 19 2N 29 57 E
Shen Xian, *China* **74 F8** 36 15N 115 40 E
Shenandoah, *Iowa, U.S.A.* **154 E7** 40 46N 95 22W
Shenandoah, *Pa., U.S.A.* **151 F8** 40 49N 76 12W
Shenandoah, *Va., U.S.A.* **148 F6** 38 29N 78 37W
Shenandoah →, *U.S.A.* **148 F7** 39 19N 77 44W
Shenandoah National Park, *U.S.A.* **148 F6** 38 35N 78 22W
Shenchi, *China* **74 E7** 39 8N 112 10 E
Shencottah, *India* **95 K3** 8 59N 77 18 E
Shendam, *Nigeria* **113 D6** 8 49N 9 30 E
Shendî, *Sudan* **107 D3** 16 46N 33 22 E
Shendurni, *India* **94 D2** 20 39N 75 36 E
Shenge, *S. Leone* **112 D2** 7 54N 12 55W
Shengfang, *China* **74 E9** 39 3N 116 42 E
Shëngjergji, *Albania* **50 E4** 41 17N 20 10 E
Shëngjin, *Albania* **50 E3** 41 50N 19 35 E
Shengzhou, *China* **77 C13** 29 35N 120 50 E
Shenjingzi, *China* **75 B13** 44 40N 124 30 E
Shenmëria, *Albania* **50 D4** 42 7N 20 13 E
Shenmu, *China* **74 E6** 38 50N 110 29 E
Shennongjia, *China* **77 B8** 31 43N 110 44 E
Shenqiu, *China* **74 H8** 33 25N 115 5 E
Shensi = Shaanxi □, *China* **74 G5** 35 0N 109 0 E
Shenyang, *China* **75 D12** 41 48N 123 27 E
Shenzhen, *China* **77 F10** 22 27N 114 10 E
Sheo, *India* **92 F4** 26 11N 71 15 E
Shepetivka, *Ukraine* **59 G4** 50 10N 27 10 E
Shepetovka = Shepetivka, *Ukraine* **59 G4** 50 10N 27 10 E
Shepherd Is., *Vanuatu* **133 F6** 16 55 S 168 36 E
Shepherdsville, *U.S.A.* **157 G11** 37 59N 85 43W
Shepparton, *Australia* **129 D6** 36 23 S 145 26 E
Sheppey, I. of, *U.K.* **21 F8** 51 25N 0 48 E
Shepton Mallet, *U.K.* **21 F5** 51 11N 2 33W
Sheqi, *China* **74 H7** 33 12N 112 57 E
Sher Qila, *Pakistan* **93 A6** 36 7N 74 2 E
Sherab, *Sudan* **107 E1** 10 44N 24 41 E
Sherabad, *Uzbekistan* **63 E3** 37 40N 67 1 E
Sherborne, *U.K.* **21 G5** 50 57N 2 31W
Sherbro →, *S. Leone* **112 D2** 7 45N 12 55W
Sherbro I., *S. Leone* **112 D2** 7 30N 12 40W
Sherbrooke, *N.S., Canada* **141 C7** 45 8N 61 59W
Sherbrooke, *Qué., Canada* **141 C5** 45 28N 71 57W
Sherburne, *U.S.A.* **151 D9** 42 41N 75 30W
Sherda, *Chad* **109 D3** 20 7N 16 46 E
Shereik, *Sudan* **106 D3** 18 44N 33 47 E
Shergarh, *India* **92 F5** 26 20N 72 18 E
Sherghati, *India* **93 G11** 24 34N 84 47 E
Sheridan, *Ark., U.S.A.* **155 H8** 34 19N 92 24W
Sheridan, *Ill., U.S.A.* **157 C8** 41 32N 88 41W
Sheridan, *Ind., U.S.A.* **157 D10** 40 8N 86 13W
Sheridan, *Wyo., U.S.A.* **158 D10** 44 48N 106 58W
Sheringham, *U.K.* **20 E9** 52 56N 1 13 E
Sherkin I., *Ireland* **23 E2** 51 28N 9 26W
Sherkot, *India* **93 E8** 29 22N 78 35 E
Sherman, *U.S.A.* **155 J6** 33 40N 96 35W
Shērpūr, *Afghan.* **91 B3** 34 32N 69 10 E
Sherpur, *Bangla.* **90 C3** 25 0N 90 0 E
Sherpur, *India* **93 G10** 25 34N 83 47 E
Sherridon, *Canada* **143 B8** 55 8N 101 5W
Sherwood, *U.S.A.* **157 C12** 41 17N 84 33W
Sherwood Forest, *U.K.* **20 D6** 53 6N 1 7W
Sherwood Park, *Canada* **142 C6** 53 31N 113 19W
Sheslay →, *Canada* **142 B2** 58 48N 132 5W
Shethanei L., *Canada* **143 B9** 58 48N 97 50W
Shetland □, *U.K.* **22 A7** 60 30N 1 30W
Shetland Is., *U.K.* **22 A7** 60 30N 1 30W
Shetrunji →, *India* **92 J5** 21 19N 72 7 E
Shevaroy Hills, *India* **95 J4** 11 58N 78 12 E
Shevgaon, *India* **94 E2** 19 21N 75 14 E
Shewa □, *Ethiopia* **107 F4** 9 33N 38 10 E
Shewa Gimira, *Ethiopia* **107 F4** 7 4N 35 51 E
Sheyenne →, *U.S.A.* **154 B6** 47 2N 96 50W
Shibām, *Yemen* **99 D5** 16 0N 48 36 E
Shibata, *Japan* **68 F9** 37 57N 139 20 E
Shibecha, *Japan* **68 C12** 43 17N 144 36 E
Shibetsu, *Japan* **68 B11** 44 10N 142 23 E
Shibîn el Kôm, *Egypt* **106 H7** 30 31N 30 55 E
Shibîn el Qanâtir, *Egypt* **106 H7** 30 19N 31 19 E
Shibing, *China* **76 D7** 27 2N 108 7 E
Shibogama L., *Canada* **140 B2** 53 35N 88 15W
Shibukawa, *Japan* **71 A10** 36 29N 139 0 E
Shibushi, *Japan* **70 F3** 31 25N 131 8 E
Shibushi-Wan, *Japan* **70 F3** 31 24N 131 8 E
Shicheng, *China* **77 D11** 26 22N 116 20 E
Shickshinny, *U.S.A.* **151 E8** 41 9N 76 9W
Shickshock Mts. = Chic-Chocs, Mts., *Canada* **141 C6** 48 55N 66 0W
Shidād, *Si. Arabia* **98 B3** 21 19N 40 3 E
Shidao, *China* **75 F12** 36 50N 122 25 E
Shidian, *China* **76 E2** 24 40N 99 5 E
Shido, *Japan* **70 C6** 34 19N 134 10 E
Shiel, L., *U.K.* **22 E3** 56 48N 5 34W
Shield, C., *Australia* **126 A2** 13 20 S 136 20 E
Shifang, *China* **76 B5** 31 8N 104 10 E
Shiga □, *Japan* **71 B8** 35 20N 136 0 E
Shigaib, *Sudan* **109 E4** 15 5N 23 35 E
Shigaraki, *Japan* **71 C8** 34 57N 136 2 E
Shigu, *China* **76 D2** 26 51N 99 56 E
Shiguaigou, *China* **74 D6** 40 52N 110 15 E
Shihan, W. →, *Yemen* **99 C5** 17 24N 51 26 E
Shihchiachuangi = Shijiazhuang, *China* **74 E8** 38 2N 114 28 E
Shiiba, *Japan* **70 E3** 32 29N 131 4 E
Shijaku, *Albania* **50 E3** 41 21N 19 33 E
Shijiazhuang, *China* **74 E8** 38 2N 114 28 E
Shijiu Hu, *China* **77 B12** 31 25N 118 50 E
Shikarpur, *India* **92 E8** 28 17N 78 7 E
Shikarpur, *Pakistan* **91 D3** 27 57N 68 39 E
Shikine-Jima, *Japan* **71 C11** 34 19N 139 13 E
Shikohabad, *India* **93 F8** 27 6N 78 36 E
Shikoku, *Japan* **70 D5** 33 30N 133 30 E
Shikoku □, *Japan* **70 D5** 33 30N 133 30 E
Shikoku-Sanchi, *Japan* **70 D5** 33 30N 133 30 E
Shiliguri, *India* **90 B2** 26 45N 88 25 E
Shilka, *Russia* **65 D12** 52 0N 115 55 E
Shilka →, *Russia* **65 D13** 53 20N 121 26 E
Shillelagh, *Ireland* **23 D5** 52 45N 6 32W
Shillington, *U.S.A.* **151 F9** 40 18N 75 58W
Shillong, *India* **90 C3** 25 35N 91 53 E
Shilo, *West Bank* **103 C4** 32 4N 35 18 E
Shilong, *China* **77 F9** 23 5N 113 52 E
Shilou, *China* **74 F6** 37 0N 110 48 E
Shilovo, *Russia* **60 C5** 54 25N 40 57 E
Shima-Hantō, *Japan* **71 C8** 34 22N 136 45 E
Shimabara, *Japan* **70 E2** 32 48N 130 20 E
Shimada, *Japan* **71 C10** 34 49N 138 10 E
Shimane □, *Japan* **70 C4** 35 0N 132 30 E
Shimane-Hantō, *Japan* **70 B5** 35 30N 133 0 E
Shimanovsk, *Russia* **65 D13** 52 15N 127 30 E
Shimen, *China* **77 C8** 29 35N 111 20 E
Shimenjie, *China* **77 C11** 29 29N 116 48 E
Shimian, *China* **76 C4** 29 17N 102 23 E
Shimizu, *Japan* **71 C10** 35 0N 138 30 E
Shimo-Jima, *Japan* **70 E2** 32 15N 130 7 E
Shimo-Koshiki-Jima, *Japan* **70 F1** 31 40N 129 43 E
Shimoda, *Japan* **71 C10** 34 40N 138 57 E
Shimodate, *Japan* **71 A11** 36 20N 139 55 E
Shimoga, *India* **95 H2** 13 57N 75 32 E
Shimoni, *Kenya* **118 C4** 4 38 S 39 20 E
Shimonita, *Japan* **71 A10** 36 13N 138 47 E
Shimonoseki, *Japan* **70 D2** 33 58N 130 55 E
Shimotsuma, *Japan* **71 A11** 36 11N 139 58 E
Shimpuru Rapids, *Angola* **116 B2** 17 45 S 19 55 E
Shimsha →, *India* **95 H3** 13 15N 77 10 E
Shimsk, *Russia* **58 C6** 58 15N 30 50 E
Shin, L., *U.K.* **22 C4** 58 5N 4 30W
Shin-Tone →, *Japan* **71 B12** 35 44N 140 51 E
Shinan, *China* **76 F7** 22 44N 109 53 E
Shinano-Gawa →, *Japan* **69 F9** 36 50N 138 30 E
Shināş, *Oman* **97 E8** 24 46N 56 28 E
Shīndand, *Afghan.* **91 B1** 33 12N 62 8 E
Shingbwiyang, *Burma* **90 B6** 26 41N 96 13 E
Shinglehouse, *U.S.A.* **150 E6** 41 58N 78 12W
Shingū, *Japan* **71 D7** 33 40N 135 55 E
Shingwidzi, *S. Africa* **117 C5** 23 5 S 31 25 E
Shinji, *Japan* **70 B4** 35 24N 132 54 E
Shinji Ko, *Japan* **70 B4** 35 26N 132 57 E
Shinjō, *Japan* **68 E10** 38 46N 140 18 E
Shinkafe, *Nigeria* **113 C6** 13 8N 6 29 E
Shīnkay, *Afghan.* **91 C2** 31 57N 67 26 E
Shinminato, *Japan* **71 A9** 36 47N 137 4 E
Shinonoi, *Japan* **71 A10** 36 35N 138 9 E
Shinshār, *Syria* **103 A5** 34 36N 36 43 E
Shinshiro, *Japan* **71 C9** 34 54N 137 30 E
Shintuya, *Peru* **172 C3** 12 41 S 71 15W
Shinyanga, *Tanzania* **118 C3** 3 45 S 33 27 E
Shinyanga □, *Tanzania* **118 C3** 3 50 S 34 0 E
Shio-no-Misaki, *Japan* **71 D7** 33 25N 135 45 E
Shiogama, *Japan* **68 E10** 38 19N 141 1 E
Shiojiri, *Japan* **71 A9** 36 6N 137 58 E
Shipchenski Prokhod, *Bulgaria* **51 D9** 42 45N 25 15 E
Shiping, *China* **76 F4** 23 45N 102 23 E
Shippegan, *Canada* **141 C7** 47 45N 64 45W
Shippensburg, *U.S.A.* **150 F7** 40 3N 77 31W
Shippenville, *U.S.A.* **150 E5** 41 15N 79 28W
Shiprock, *U.S.A.* **159 H9** 36 47N 108 41W
Shiqian, *China* **76 D7** 27 32N 108 13 E
Shiqma, N. →, *Israel* **103 D3** 31 37N 34 30 E
Shiquan, *China* **74 H5** 33 5N 108 15 E
Shiquan He = Indus →, *Pakistan* **91 D2** 24 20N 67 47 E
Shīr Kūh, *Iran* **97 D7** 31 39N 54 3 E
Shirabad = Sherabad, *Uzbekistan* **63 E3** 37 40N 67 1 E
Shiragami-Misaki, *Japan* **68 D10** 41 24N 140 12 E
Shirahama, *Japan* **71 D7** 33 41N 135 20 E
Shirakawa, *Fukushima, Japan* **69 F10** 37 7N 140 13 E
Shirakawa, *Gifu, Japan* **71 A8** 36 17N 136 56 E
Shirane-San, *Gumma, Japan* **71 A11** 36 48N 139 22 E
Shirane-San, *Yamanashi, Japan* **71 B10** 35 42N 138 9 E
Shiraoi, *Japan* **68 C10** 42 33N 141 21 E
Shīrāz, *Iran* **97 D7** 29 42N 52 30 E
Shirbīn, *Egypt* **106 H7** 31 11N 31 32 E
Shire →, *Africa* **119 F4** 17 42 S 35 19 E
Shiretoko-Misaki, *Japan* **68 B12** 44 21N 145 20 E
Shirinab →, *Pakistan* **92 D2** 30 15N 66 28 E
Shiriya-Zaki, *Japan* **68 D10** 41 25N 141 30 E
Shirley, *U.S.A.* **157 E11** 39 53N 85 35W
Shiroishi, *Japan* **68 F10** 38 0N 140 37 E
Shirol, *India* **94 F2** 16 47N 74 41 E
Shirpur, *India* **94 D2** 21 21N 74 57 E
Shīrvān, *Iran* **97 B8** 37 30N 57 50 E
Shirwa, L. = Chilwa, L., *Malawi* **119 F4** 15 15 S 35 40 E
Shishaldin Volcano, *U.S.A.* **144 J7** 54 45N 163 58W
Shishi, *China* **77 E12** 24 44N 118 37 E
Shishou, *China* **77 C9** 29 38N 112 22 E
Shitai, *China* **77 B11** 30 12N 117 25 E
Shively, *U.S.A.* **157 F11** 38 12N 85 49W
Shivpuri, *India* **92 G7** 25 26N 77 42 E
Shixian, *China* **75 C15** 43 5N 129 50 E
Shixing, *China* **77 E10** 24 46N 114 5 E
Shiyan, *China* **77 A8** 32 35N 110 45 E
Shiyata, *Egypt* **106 B2** 29 25N 25 7 E
Shizhu, *China* **76 C7** 29 58N 108 7 E
Shizong, *China* **76 E5** 24 50N 104 0 E
Shizuishan, *China* **74 E4** 39 15N 106 50 E
Shizuoka, *Japan* **71 C10** 34 57N 138 24 E
Shizuoka □, *Japan* **71 B10** 35 15N 138 40 E
Shklov = Shklow, *Belarus* **58 E6** 54 16N 30 15 E
Shklow, *Belarus* **58 E6** 54 16N 30 15 E
Shkoder = Shkodra, *Albania* **50 D3** 42 4N 19 32 E
Shkodra, *Albania* **50 D3** 42 4N 19 32 E
Shkumbini →, *Albania* **50 E3** 41 2N 19 31 E
Shmidta, Ostrov, *Russia* **65 A10** 81 0N 91 0 E
Shō-Gawa →, *Japan* **71 A9** 36 47N 137 4 E
Shoal Cr. →, *U.S.A.* **156 E3** 39 44N 93 32W
Shoal L., *Canada* **143 D9** 49 33N 95 1W
Shoal Lake, *Canada* **143 C8** 50 30N 100 35W
Shoals, *U.S.A.* **157 F10** 38 40N 86 47W
Shōbara, *Japan* **70 C5** 34 51N 133 1 E
Shōdo-Shima, *Japan* **70 C6** 34 30N 134 15 E
Shokpar, *Kazakstan* **63 B7** 43 49N 74 21 E
Sholapur = Solapur, *India* **94 F2** 17 43N 75 56 E
Shologontsy, *Russia* **65 C12** 66 13N 114 0 E
Shōmrōn, *West Bank* **103 C4** 32 15N 35 13 E
Shoranur, *India* **95 J3** 10 46N 76 19 E
Shorapur, *India* **95 F3** 16 31N 76 48 E
Shoreham by Sea, *U.K.* **21 G7** 50 50N 0 16W
Shorewood, *U.S.A.* **157 A9** 43 5N 87 54W
Shori →, *Pakistan* **92 E3** 28 29N 69 44 E
Shorkot Road, *Pakistan* **92 D5** 30 47N 72 15 E
Shorter, *U.S.A.* **152 C4** 32 24N 85 57W
Shorterville, *U.S.A.* **152 D4** 31 34N 85 6W
Shortland I., *Solomon Is.* **133 L8** 7 0 S 155 45 E
Shortt's I., *India* **94 D8** 20 47N 87 4 E
Shoshone, *Calif., U.S.A.* **161 K10** 35 58N 116 16W
Shoshone, *Idaho, U.S.A.* **158 E6** 42 56N 114 25W
Shoshone L., *U.S.A.* **158 D8** 44 22N 110 43W
Shoshone Mts., *U.S.A.* **158 G5** 39 20N 117 25W
Shoshong, *Botswana* **116 C4** 22 56 S 26 31 E
Shoshoni, *U.S.A.* **158 E9** 43 14N 108 7W
Shostka, *Ukraine* **59 G7** 51 57N 33 32 E
Shou Xian, *China* **77 A11** 32 37N 116 42 E
Shouchang, *China* **77 C12** 29 18N 119 12 E
Shouguang, *China* **75 F10** 37 52N 118 45 E
Shouning, *China* **77 D12** 27 27N 119 31 E
Shouyang, *China* **74 F7** 37 54N 113 8 E
Show Low, *U.S.A.* **159 J9** 34 15N 110 2W
Shpola, *Ukraine* **59 H6** 49 1N 31 30 E
Shreveport, *U.S.A.* **155 J8** 32 31N 93 45W
Shrewsbury, *U.K.* **21 E5** 52 43N 2 45W
Shri Mohangarh, *India* **92 F4** 27 17N 71 18 E
Shrigonda, *India* **94 E2** 18 37N 74 41 E
Shrirampur, *India* **93 H13** 22 44N 88 21 E
Shropshire □, *U.K.* **21 E5** 52 36N 2 45W
Shu, *Kazakstan* **64 E8** 43 36N 73 42 E
Shu →, *Kazakstan* **63 A3** 45 0N 67 44 E
Shuangbai, *China* **76 E3** 24 42N 101 38 E
Shuangcheng, *China* **75 B14** 45 20N 126 15 E
Shuangfeng, *China* **77 D9** 27 29N 112 11 E
Shuanggou, *China* **75 G9** 34 2N 117 30 E
Shuangjiang, *China* **76 F2** 23 26N 99 58 E
Shuangliao, *China* **75 C12** 43 29N 123 30 E
Shuangshanzi, *China* **75 D10** 40 20N 119 8 E
Shuangyang, *China* **75 C13** 43 28N 125 40 E
Shuangyashan, *China* **73 B8** 46 28N 131 5 E
Shu'b, Ra's, *Yemen* **99 D6** 12 30N 53 25 E
Shubra Khit, *Egypt* **106 H7** 31 2N 30 42 E
Shucheng, *China* **77 B11** 31 28N 116 57 E
Shugozero, *Russia* **58 C8** 59 54N 34 10 E
Shuguri Falls, *Tanzania* **119 D4** 8 33 S 37 22 E
Shuḩayr, *Yemen* **99 D5** 14 41N 49 23 E
Shuiji, *China* **77 D12** 27 13N 118 20 E
Shuiye, *China* **74 F8** 36 7N 114 8 E
Shujalpur, *India* **92 H7** 23 18N 76 46 E
Shukpa Kunzang, *India* **93 B8** 34 22N 78 22 E
Shulan, *China* **75 B14** 44 28N 127 0 E
Shulaveri, *Georgia* **61 K7** 41 22N 44 45 E
Shule, *China* **72 C2** 39 25N 76 3 E
Shullsburg, *U.S.A.* **156 B6** 42 35N 90 13W
Shumagin Is., *U.S.A.* **138 C4** 55 7N 160 30W
Shumen, *Bulgaria* **51 C10** 43 18N 26 55 E
Shumerlya, *Russia* **60 C8** 55 30N 46 25 E
Shumikha, *Russia* **62 D9** 55 10N 63 15 E
Shunchang, *China* **77 D11** 26 54N 117 48 E
Shunde, *China* **77 F9** 22 42N 113 14 E
Shungay, *Kazakstan* **61 F8** 48 30N 46 45 E
Shuo Xian = Shuozhou, *China* **74 E7** 39 20N 112 33 E
Shuozhou, *China* **74 E7** 39 20N 112 33 E
Shūr →, *Fārs, Iran* **97 D7** 28 30N 55 0 E
Shūr →, *Kermān, Iran* **97 D8** 30 52N 57 37 E
Shūr →, *Yazd, Iran* **97 D7** 31 45N 55 15 E
Shūr Āb, *Iran* **97 C6** 34 23N 51 11 E
Shūr Gaz, *Iran* **97 D8** 29 10N 59 20 E
Shūrāb, *Iran* **97 C8** 33 43N 56 29 E
Shurab, *Tajikistan* **63 C5** 40 3N 70 33 E
Shurchi, *Uzbekistan* **63 E3** 37 59N 67 47 E
Shūrjestān, *Iran* **97 D7** 31 24N 52 25 E
Shurkhua, *Burma* **90 D4** 22 15N 93 38 E
Shurugwi, *Zimbabwe* **119 F3** 19 40 S 30 0 E
Shūsf, *Iran* **97 D9** 31 50N 60 5 E
Shūsh, *Iran* **101 F13** 32 11N 48 15 E
Shūshtar, *Iran* **97 D6** 32 0N 48 50 E
Shuswap L., *Canada* **142 C5** 50 55N 119 3W
Shuya, *Russia* **60 B5** 56 50N 41 28 E
Shuyang, *China* **75 G10** 34 10N 118 42 E
Shuzenji, *Japan* **71 C10** 34 58N 138 56 E
Shūzū, *Iran* **97 D7** 29 52N 54 30 E
Shwebo, *Burma* **90 D5** 22 30N 95 45 E
Shwegu, *Burma* **90 C6** 24 15N 96 26 E
Shwegun, *Burma* **90 G6** 17 9N 97 39 E
Shwenyaung, *Burma* **90 E6** 20 46N 96 57 E
Shymkent, *Kazakstan* **64 E7** 42 18N 69 36 E
Shyok, *India* **93 B8** 34 13N 78 12 E
Shyok →, *Pakistan* **93 B6** 35 13N 75 53 E
Si Chon, *Thailand* **87 H2** 9 0N 99 54 E
Si Kiang = Xi Jiang →, *China* **77 F9** 22 5N 113 20 E
Si-ngan = Xi'an, *China* **74 G5** 34 15N 109 0 E
Si Prachan, *Thailand* **86 E3** 14 37N 100 9 E
Si Racha, *Thailand* **86 F3** 13 10N 100 48 E
Si Xian, *China* **75 H9** 33 30N 117 50 E
Siahaf →, *Pakistan* **92 E3** 29 3N 68 57 E
Siahan Range, *Pakistan* **91 D2** 27 30N 64 40 E
Siak →, *Indonesia* **84 B2** 1 13N 102 9 E
Siaksriindrapura, *Indonesia* **78 D2** 0 51N 102 0 E
Sialkot, *Pakistan* **91 B4** 32 32N 74 30 E
Sialsuk, *India* **90 D4** 23 24N 92 45 E
Siam = Thailand ■, *Asia* **78 A2** 16 0N 102 0 E
Siam, *Australia* **128 B2** 32 35 S 136 41 E
Sian = Xi'an, *China* **74 G5** 34 15N 109 0 E
Sianów, *Poland* **54 D3** 54 13N 16 18 E
Siantan, *Indonesia* **78 D3** 3 10N 106 15 E
Siàpo →, *Venezuela* **168 C4** 2 7N 66 28W
Sīāreh, *Iran* **97 D9** 28 5N 60 14 E
Siargao I., *Phil.* **79 C7** 9 52N 126 3 E
Siari, *Pakistan* **93 B7** 34 55N 76 40 E
Siasi, *Phil.* **79 C6** 5 34N 120 50 E
Siasi I., *Phil.* **81 J3** 5 33N 120 51 E
Siassi, *Papua N. G.* **132 C4** 5 40 S 147 51 E
Siátista, *Greece* **50 F5** 40 15N 21 33 E
Siaton, *Phil.* **81 G4** 9 4N 123 2 E
Siau, *Indonesia* **79 D7** 2 50N 125 25 E
Šiauliai, *Lithuania* **15 J20** 55 56N 23 15 E
Šiauliai □, *Lithuania* **54 C10** 55 56N 23 19 E
Siazan = Siyäzän, *Azerbaijan* **61 K9** 41 3N 49 10 E
Sibâi, Gebel el, *Egypt* **96 E2** 25 45N 34 10 E
Sibang, *Gabon* **114 B1** 0 25N 9 31 E
Sibay, *Russia* **62 E7** 52 42N 58 39 E
Sibay I., *Phil.* **81 F3** 11 51N 121 29 E
Sibayi, L., *S. Africa* **117 D5** 27 20 S 32 45 E
Sibdu, *Sudan* **107 E2** 10 57N 26 17 E
Šibenik, *Croatia* **45 E12** 43 48N 15 54 E
Siberia, *Russia* **66 C13** 60 0N 100 0 E
Siberut, *Indonesia* **78 E1** 1 30 S 99 0 E
Sibi, *Pakistan* **91 C2** 29 30N 67 54 E
Sibil = Oksibil, *Indonesia* **79 E10** 4 59 S 140 35 E
Sibiti, *Congo* **114 C2** 3 38 S 13 19 E
Sibiu, *Romania* **53 E9** 45 45N 24 9 E
Sibiu □, *Romania* **53 E9** 45 50N 24 15 E
Sibley, *Ill., U.S.A.* **157 D8** 40 35N 88 23W
Sibley, *Iowa, U.S.A.* **154 D7** 43 24N 95 45W
Sibolga, *Indonesia* **78 D1** 1 42N 98 45 E
Sibsagar, *India* **90 B5** 27 0N 94 36 E
Sibu, *Malaysia* **78 D4** 2 18N 111 49 E
Sibuco, *Phil.* **79 C6** 7 20N 122 10 E
Sibuguey B., *Phil.* **79 C6** 7 50N 122 45 E
Sibut, *C.A.R.* **114 A3** 5 46N 19 10 E
Sibutu, *Phil.* **79 D5** 4 45N 119 30 E
Sibutu Group, *Phil.* **81 J2** 4 45N 119 20 E
Sibutu Passage, *E. Indies* **79 D5** 4 50N 120 0 E
Sibuyan I., *Phil.* **79 B6** 12 25N 122 40 E
Sibuyan Sea, *Phil.* **79 B6** 12 30N 122 20 E
Sic, *Romania* **53 D8** 46 56N 23 53 E
Sicamous, *Canada* **142 C5** 50 49N 119 0W
Sicapoo, Mt., *Phil.* **80 B3** 18 1N 120 56 E
Sicasica, *Bolivia* **172 D4** 17 22 S 67 45W
Siccus →, *Australia* **127 E2** 31 26 S 139 30 E
Sichuan □, *China* **76 B5** 30 30N 103 0 E
Sichuan Pendi, *China* **76 B5** 31 0N 105 0 E
Sicilia, *Italy* **47 E7** 37 30N 14 30 E
Sicilia □, *Italy* **47 E7** 37 45N 14 15 E
Sicily = Sicilia, *Italy* **47 E7** 37 30N 14 30 E
Sicuani, *Peru* **172 C3** 14 21 S 71 10W
Šid, *Serbia, Yug.* **52 E4** 45 8N 19 14 E

Solvychegodsk 283

Skalat, *Ukraine* **59 H3** 49 23N 25 55 E
Skálavík, *Iceland* **11 A3** 66 11N 23 29W
Skalbmierz, *Poland* **55 H7** 50 20N 20 25 E
Skälderviken, *Sweden* **17 H6** 56 22N 12 30 E
Skålevik, *Norway* **18 F5** 58 5N 8 1 E
Skalica, *Slovak Rep.* **35 C10** 48 50N 17 15 E
Skallingen, *Denmark* **17 J2** 55 32N 8 13 E
Skalni Dol = Kamenyak, *Bulgaria* **51 C10** 43 24N 26 57 E
Skanderborg, *Denmark* **17 H3** 56 2N 9 55 E
Skåne, *Sweden* **17 J7** 55 59N 13 30 E
Skåne län □, *Sweden* **17 H7** 56 15N 14 0 E
Skaneateles, *U.S.A.* **151 D8** 42 57N 76 26W
Skaneateles L., *U.S.A.* **151 D8** 42 51N 76 22W
Skånevik, *Norway* **18 E2** 59 43N 5 53 E
Skänninge, *Sweden* **17 F9** 58 24N 15 5 E
Skanör med Falsterbo, *Sweden* **17 J6** 55 24N 12 50 E
Skantzoúra, *Greece* **48 B6** 39 5N 24 6 E
Skara, *Sweden* **17 F7** 58 25N 13 30 E
Skaraborgs län □, *Sweden* **17 F7** 58 20N 13 30 E
Skärblacka, *Sweden* **17 F9** 58 35N 15 54 E
Skarð, *Iceland* **11 B4** 65 17N 22 19W
Skardu, *Pakistan* **93 B6** 35 20N 75 44 E
Skare, *Norway* **18 E3** 59 55N 6 36 E
Skåre, *Sweden* **16 E7** 59 26N 13 26 E
Skärhamn, *Sweden* **17 G5** 57 59N 11 34 E
Skarnes, *Norway* **18 D8** 60 15N 11 41 E
Skarszewy, *Poland* **54 D5** 54 4N 18 25 E
Skaryszew, *Poland* **55 G8** 51 19N 21 15 E
Skarżysko-Kamienna, *Poland* **55 G7** 51 7N 20 52 E
Skattkärr, *Sweden* **16 E7** 59 25N 13 40 E
Skattungbyn, *Sweden* **16 C8** 61 10N 14 56 E
Skawina, *Poland* **55 J6** 49 59N 19 50 E
Skebobruk, *Sweden* **16 E12** 59 58N 18 36 E
Skeena →, *Canada* **142 C2** 54 9N 130 5W
Skeena Mts., *Canada* **142 B3** 56 40N 128 30W
Skegness, *U.K.* **20 D8** 53 9N 0 20 E
Skei, *Norway* **18 C3** 61 34N 6 28 E
Skeiðarársandur, *Iceland* **11 D9** 63 54N 17 14W
Skeiðflötur, *Iceland* **11 D7** 63 26N 19 11W
Skeldon, *Guyana* **169 B6** 5 55N 57 20W
Skeleton Coast Park, *Namibia* **116 C1** 20 0 S 13 20 E
Skellefte älv →, *Sweden* **14 D19** 64 45N 21 10 E
Skellefteå, *Sweden* **14 D19** 64 45N 20 50 E
Skelleftehamn, *Sweden* **14 D19** 64 40N 21 9 E
Skender Vakuf, *Bos.-H.* **52 F2** 44 29N 17 22 E
Skerries, The, *U.K.* **20 D3** 53 25N 4 36W
Skhíza, *Greece* **48 E3** 36 41N 21 40 E
Skhoinoúsa, *Greece* **49 E7** 36 53N 25 31 E
Ski, *Norway* **15 G14** 59 43N 10 52 E
Skíathos, *Greece* **48 B5** 39 12N 23 30 E
Skibbereen, *Ireland* **23 E2** 51 33N 9 16W
Skiddaw, *U.K.* **20 C4** 54 39N 3 9W
Skidegate, *Canada* **142 C2** 53 15N 132 1W
Skídhra, *Greece* **50 F6** 40 46N 22 10 E
Skien, *Norway* **15 G13** 59 12N 9 35 E
Skierniewice, *Poland* **55 G7** 51 58N 20 10 E
Skikda, *Algeria* **111 A6** 36 50N 6 58 E
Skillet →, *U.S.A.* **157 F8** 38 5N 88 5W
Skillingaryd, *Sweden* **17 G8** 57 27N 14 5 E
Skillinge, *Sweden* **17 J8** 55 30N 14 16 E
Skilloura, *Cyprus* **38 D12** 35 14N 33 10 E
Skinári, Ákra, *Greece* **48 D2** 37 56N 20 40 E
Skinnastaður, *Iceland* **11 A10** 66 4N 16 27W
Skinnskatteberg, *Sweden* **16 E9** 59 50N 15 42 E
Skipton, *Australia* **128 D5** 37 39 S 143 40 E
Skipton, *U.K.* **20 D5** 53 58N 2 3W
Skiptvet, *Norway* **18 E8** 59 28N 11 11 E
Skirmish Pt., *Australia* **126 A1** 11 59 S 134 17 E
Skiropoúla, *Greece* **48 C6** 38 50N 24 21 E
Skíros, *Greece* **48 C6** 38 55N 24 34 E
Skivarp, *Sweden* **17 J7** 55 26N 13 34 E
Skive, *Denmark* **17 H3** 56 33N 9 2 E
Skjærhalden, *Norway* **18 E8** 59 2N 11 2 E
Skjálfandafljót →, *Iceland* **11 B9** 65 59N 17 25W
Skjálfandi, *Iceland* **11 A9** 66 5N 17 30W
Skjeberg, *Norway* **18 E8** 59 12N 11 12 E
Skjern, *Denmark* **17 J2** 55 57N 8 30 E
Skjold, *Norway* **18 E2** 59 31N 5 34 E
Skjolden, *Norway* **18 C4** 61 29N 7 36 E
Skjöldólfsstaðir, *Iceland* **11 B11** 65 19N 15 7W
Skjønhaug, *Norway* **18 E8** 59 39N 11 19 E
Skoczów, *Poland* **55 J5** 49 49N 18 45 E
Skodje, *Norway* **18 B3** 62 30N 6 43 E
Škofja Loka, *Slovenia* **45 B11** 46 9N 14 19 E
Skógar, *Iceland* **11 D7** 63 32N 19 28W
Skógarnes, *Iceland* **11 C4** 64 46N 22 34W
Skoghall, *Sweden* **16 E7** 59 20N 13 30 E
Skogstorp, *Sweden* **16 E10** 59 19N 16 29 E
Skoki, *Poland* **55 F4** 52 40N 17 11 E
Skokie, *U.S.A.* **157 B9** 42 3N 87 45W
Skole, *Ukraine* **59 H2** 49 3N 23 30 E
Skollenborg, *Norway* **18 E6** 59 38N 9 43 E
Skópelos, *Greece* **48 B5** 39 9N 23 47 E
Skopí, *Greece* **38 D8** 35 11N 26 2 E
Skopin, *Russia* **58 F10** 53 55N 39 32 E
Skopje, *Macedonia* **50 D5** 42 1N 21 26 E
Skoppum, *Norway* **18 E7** 59 23N 10 26 E
Skórcz, *Poland* **54 E5** 53 47N 18 30 E
Skørping, *Denmark* **17 H3** 56 50N 9 53 E
Skotfoss, *Norway* **18 E6** 59 12N 9 30 E
Skotterud, *Norway* **18 D9** 60 0N 12 7 E
Skövde, *Sweden* **17 F7** 58 24N 13 50 E
Skovorodino, *Russia* **65 D13** 54 0N 124 0 E
Skowhegan, *U.S.A.* **149 C11** 44 46N 69 43W
Skradin, *Croatia* **45 E12** 43 52N 15 53 E
Skrea, *Sweden* **17 H6** 56 53N 12 34 E
Skreia, *Norway* **18 D7** 60 40N 10 56 E
Skrim, *Norway* **18 E6** 59 31N 9 38 E
Skrunda, *Latvia* **54 B9** 56 41N 22 1 E
Skrwa →, *Poland* **55 F6** 52 35N 19 32 E
Skudeneshavn, *Norway* **18 E2** 59 10N 5 10 E
Skull, *Ireland* **23 E2** 51 32N 9 34W
Skultorp, *Sweden* **17 F7** 58 24N 13 51 E
Skultuna, *Sweden* **16 E10** 59 43N 16 25 E
Skunk →, *U.S.A.* **156 D5** 40 42N 91 7W
Skuodas, *Lithuania* **15 H19** 56 16N 21 33 E
Skurup, *Sweden* **17 J7** 55 28N 13 30 E
Skutskär, *Sweden* **16 D11** 60 37N 17 25 E
Skútustaðir, *Iceland* **11 B9** 65 34N 17 2W
Skvyra, *Ukraine* **59 H5** 49 44N 29 40 E
Skwierzyna, *Poland* **55 F2** 52 33N 15 30 E
Skye, *U.K.* **22 D2** 57 15N 6 10W
Skykomish, *U.S.A.* **158 C3** 47 42N 121 22W
Skyring, Seno, *Chile* **176 D3** 52 35 S 72 0W
Skyros = Skíros, *Greece* **48 C6** 38 55N 24 34 E
Skyttorp, *Sweden* **16 D11** 60 5N 17 44 E
Slættaratindur, *Færoe Is.* **14 E9** 62 18N 7 1W
Slagelse, *Denmark* **17 J5** 55 23N 11 19 E
Slamannon, *Australia* **128 B5** 32 1 S 143 41 E
Slamet, *Indonesia* **79 G13** 7 16 S 109 8 E
Slaney →, *Ireland* **23 D5** 52 26N 6 33W
Slangberge, *S. Africa* **116 E3** 31 32 S 20 48 E
Slănic, *Romania* **53 E10** 45 14N 25 58 E
Slano, *Croatia* **50 D1** 42 48N 17 53 E
Slantsy, *Russia* **58 C5** 59 7N 28 5 E
Slaný, *Czech Rep.* **34 A7** 50 13N 14 6 E
Śląskie □, *Poland* **55 H6** 50 30N 19 0 E
Slätbaken, *Sweden* **17 F10** 58 25N 16 45 E
Slate Is., *Canada* **140 C2** 48 40N 87 0W
Slater, *U.S.A.* **156 E3** 39 13N 93 4W
Slatina, *Croatia* **52 E2** 45 42N 17 45 E
Slatina, *Romania* **53 F9** 44 28N 24 22 E
Slatina Timiş, *Romania* **52 E7** 45 15N 22 17 E
Slatington, *U.S.A.* **151 F9** 40 45N 75 37W
Slaton, *U.S.A.* **155 J4** 33 26N 101 39W
Slave →, *Canada* **142 A6** 61 18N 113 39W
Slave Coast, *W. Afr.* **113 D5** 6 0N 2 30 E
Slave Lake, *Canada* **142 B6** 55 17N 114 43W
Slave Pt., *Canada* **142 A5** 61 11N 115 56W
Slavgorod, *Russia* **64 D8** 53 1N 78 37 E
Slavinja, *Serbia, Yug.* **50 C6** 43 9N 22 50 E
Slavkov u Brna, *Czech Rep.* **35 B9** 49 10N 16 52 E
Slavonija, *Europe* **52 E2** 45 20N 17 40 E
Slavonski Brod, *Croatia* **52 E3** 45 11N 18 1 E
Slavuta, *Ukraine* **59 G4** 50 15N 27 2 E
Slavyanka, *Russia* **68 C5** 42 53N 131 21 E
Slavyanovo, *Bulgaria* **51 C8** 43 28N 24 52 E
Slavyansk = Slovyansk, *Ukraine* **59 H9** 48 55N 37 36 E
Slavyansk-na-Kubani, *Russia* **59 K10** 45 15N 38 11 E
Sława, *Poland* **55 G3** 51 52N 16 2 E
Slawharad, *Belarus* **58 F6** 53 27N 31 0 E
Sławno, *Poland* **54 D3** 54 20N 16 41 E
Sławoborze, *Poland* **54 E2** 53 55N 15 42 E
Sleaford, *U.K.* **20 D7** 53 0N 0 24W
Sleaford B., *Australia* **127 E2** 34 55 S 135 45 E
Sleat, Sd. of, *U.K.* **22 D3** 57 5N 5 47W
Sleðbrjótur, *Iceland* **11 B12** 65 34N 14 30W
Sleeper Is., *Canada* **139 C11** 58 30N 81 0W
Sleepy Eye, *U.S.A.* **154 C7** 44 18N 94 43W
Sleetmute, *U.S.A.* **144 F8** 61 42N 157 10W
Sleman, *Indonesia* **85 D4** 7 40 S 110 20 E
Slemon L., *Canada* **142 A5** 63 13N 116 4W
Ślesin, *Poland* **55 F5** 52 22N 18 14 E
Slide Mt., *U.S.A.* **151 E10** 42 0N 74 25W
Slidell, *U.S.A.* **155 K10** 30 17N 89 47W
Sliema, *Malta* **38 D2** 35 54N 14 30 E
Slieve Aughty, *Ireland* **23 C3** 53 4N 8 30W
Slieve Bloom, *Ireland* **23 C4** 53 4N 7 40W
Slieve Donard, *U.K.* **23 B6** 54 11N 5 55W
Slieve Gamph, *Ireland* **23 B3** 54 6N 9 0W
Slieve Gullion, *U.K.* **23 B5** 54 7N 6 26W
Slieve Mish, *Ireland* **23 D2** 52 12N 9 50W
Slievenamon, *Ireland* **23 D4** 52 25N 7 34W
Sligeach = Sligo, *Ireland* **23 B3** 54 16N 8 28W
Sligo, *Ireland* **23 B3** 54 16N 8 28W
Sligo, *U.S.A.* **150 E5** 41 6N 79 29W
Sligo □, *Ireland* **23 B3** 54 8N 8 42W
Sligo B., *Ireland* **23 B3** 54 18N 8 40W
Slippery Rock, *U.S.A.* **150 E4** 41 3N 80 3W
Slite, *Sweden* **17 G12** 57 42N 18 48 E
Sliven, *Bulgaria* **51 D10** 42 42N 26 19 E
Slivnitsa, *Bulgaria* **50 D7** 42 50N 23 2 E
Sljeme, *Croatia* **45 C12** 45 57N 15 58 E
Sloan, *U.S.A.* **161 K11** 35 57N 115 13W
Sloansville, *U.S.A.* **151 D10** 42 45N 74 22W
Slobodskoy, *Russia* **62 B3** 58 40N 50 6 E
Slobozia, *Moldova* **53 D14** 46 45N 29 42 E
Slobozia, *Argeş, Romania* **53 F10** 44 30N 25 14 E
Slobozia, *Ialomiţa, Romania* **53 F12** 44 34N 27 23 E
Slocan, *Canada* **142 D5** 49 48N 117 28W
Slocomb, *U.S.A.* **152 D4** 31 7N 85 36W
Słomniki, *Poland* **55 H7** 50 16N 20 4 E
Slonim, *Belarus* **59 F3** 53 4N 25 19 E
Slough, *U.K.* **21 F7** 51 30N 0 36W
Slough □, *U.K.* **21 F7** 51 30N 0 36W
Sloughhouse, *U.S.A.* **160 G5** 38 26N 121 12W
Slovak Rep. ■, *Europe* **35 C13** 48 30N 20 0 E
Slovakia = Slovak Rep. ■, *Europe* **35 C13** 48 30N 20 0 E
Slovakian Ore Mts. = Slovenské Rudohorie, *Slovak Rep.* **35 C12** 48 45N 20 0 E
Slovenia ■, *Europe* **45 C11** 45 58N 14 30 E
Slovenija = Slovenia ■, *Europe* **45 C11** 45 58N 14 30 E
Slovenj Gradec, *Slovenia* **45 B12** 46 31N 15 5 E
Slovenska Bistrica, *Slovenia* **45 B12** 46 24N 15 35 E
Slovenske Konjice, *Slovenia* **45 B12** 46 20N 15 28 E
Slovenské Rudohorie, *Slovak Rep.* **35 C12** 48 45N 20 0 E
Slovyansk, *Ukraine* **59 H9** 48 55N 37 36 E
Słubice, *Poland* **55 F1** 52 22N 14 35 E
Sluch →, *Ukraine* **59 G4** 51 37N 26 38 E
Sluis, *Neths.* **24 C3** 51 18N 3 23 E
Slŭnchev Bryag, *Bulgaria* **51 D11** 42 40N 27 41 E
Slunj, *Croatia* **45 C12** 45 6N 15 33 E
Słupca, *Poland* **55 F4** 52 15N 17 52 E
Słupia →, *Poland* **54 D3** 54 35N 16 51 E
Słupsk, *Poland* **54 D4** 54 30N 17 3 E
Slurry, *S. Africa* **116 D4** 25 49 S 25 42 E
Slutsk, *Belarus* **59 F4** 53 2N 27 31 E
Slyne Hd., *Ireland* **23 C1** 53 25N 10 10W
Slyudyanka, *Russia* **65 D11** 51 40N 103 40 E
Småland, *Sweden* **17 G9** 57 15N 15 25 E
Smålandsfarvandet, *Denmark* **17 J5** 55 10N 11 20 E
Smålandsstenar, *Sweden* **17 G7** 57 10N 13 25 E
Small Nggela, *Solomon Is.* **133 M11** 9 0 S 160 0 E
Smalltree L., *Canada* **143 A8** 61 0N 105 0W
Smallwood Res., *Canada* **141 B7** 54 0N 64 0W
Smarhon, *Belarus* **58 E4** 54 20N 26 24 E
Smarje, *Slovenia* **45 B12** 46 15N 15 34 E
Smartt Syndicate Dam, *S. Africa* **116 E3** 30 45 S 23 10 E
Smartville, *U.S.A.* **160 F5** 39 13N 121 18W
Smeaton, *Canada* **143 C8** 53 30N 104 49W
Smedby, *Sweden* **17 H10** 56 41N 16 13 E
Smederevo, *Serbia, Yug.* **50 B4** 44 40N 20 57 E
Smederevska Palanka, *Serbia, Yug.* **50 B4** 44 22N 20 58 E
Smedjebacken, *Sweden* **16 D9** 60 8N 15 25 E
Smela = Smila, *Ukraine* **59 H6** 49 15N 31 58 E
Smerwick Harbour, *Ireland* **23 D1** 52 12N 10 23W
Smethport, *U.S.A.* **150 E6** 41 49N 78 27W
Smidovich, *Russia* **65 E14** 48 36N 133 49 E
Śmigiel, *Poland* **55 F3** 52 1N 16 32 E
Smila, *Ukraine* **59 H6** 49 15N 31 58 E
Smilyan, *Bulgaria* **51 E8** 41 29N 24 46 E
Smith, *Canada* **142 B6** 55 10N 114 0W
Smith B., *U.S.A.* **144 A9** 70 30N 154 20W
Smith Center, *U.S.A.* **154 F5** 39 47N 98 47W
Smith Sund, *Greenland* **10 B3** 78 30N 74 0W
Smithburne →, *Australia* **126 B3** 17 3 S 140 57 E
Smithers, *Canada* **142 C3** 54 45N 127 10W
Smithfield, *S. Africa* **117 E4** 30 9 S 26 30 E
Smithfield, *N.C., U.S.A.* **149 H6** 35 31N 78 21W
Smithfield, *Utah, U.S.A.* **158 F8** 41 50N 111 50W
Smiths, *U.S.A.* **152 C4** 32 32N 85 6W
Smiths Falls, *Canada* **140 D4** 44 55N 76 0W
Smithton, *Australia* **126 G4** 40 53 S 145 6 E
Smithtown, *Australia* **129 A10** 30 58 S 152 48 E
Smithville, *Canada* **150 C5** 43 6N 79 33W
Smithville, *Ga., U.S.A.* **152 D5** 31 54N 84 15W
Smithville, *Mo., U.S.A.* **156 E2** 39 23N 94 35W
Smithville, *Tex., U.S.A.* **155 K6** 30 1N 97 10W
Smoky →, *Canada* **142 B5** 56 10N 117 21W
Smoky Bay, *Australia* **127 E1** 32 22 S 134 13 E
Smoky Hill →, *U.S.A.* **154 F6** 39 4N 96 48W
Smoky Hills, *U.S.A.* **154 F5** 39 15N 99 30W
Smoky Lake, *Canada* **142 C6** 54 10N 112 30W
Smøla, *Norway* **14 E13** 63 23N 8 3 E
Smolensk, *Russia* **58 E7** 54 45N 32 5 E
Smolikas, Óros, *Greece* **50 F4** 40 9N 20 58 E
Smolník, *Slovak Rep.* **35 C13** 48 43N 20 44 E
Smolyan, *Bulgaria* **51 E8** 41 36N 24 38 E
Smooth Rock Falls, *Canada* **140 C3** 49 17N 81 37W
Smoothstone L., *Canada* **143 C7** 54 40N 106 50W
Smorgon = Smarhon, *Belarus* **58 E4** 54 20N 26 24 E
Smulţi, *Romania* **53 E12** 45 57N 27 44 E
Smyadovo, *Bulgaria* **51 C11** 43 2N 27 1 E
Smygehamn, *Sweden* **17 J7** 55 21N 13 22 E
Smyrna = İzmir, *Turkey* **49 C9** 38 25N 27 8 E
Smyrna, *Del., U.S.A.* **148 F8** 39 18N 75 36W
Smyrna, *Ga., U.S.A.* **152 B5** 33 53N 84 31W
Snæfell, *Iceland* **11 C11** 64 48N 15 34W
Snaefell, *U.K.* **20 C3** 54 16N 4 27W
Snæfellsjökull, *Iceland* **11 C3** 64 49N 23 46W
Snæfellsnessýsla □, *Iceland* **11 C3** 65 0N 23 0W
Snake →, *U.S.A.* **158 C4** 46 12N 119 2W
Snake I., *Australia* **129 E7** 38 47 S 146 33 E
Snake Range, *U.S.A.* **158 G6** 39 0N 114 20W
Snake River Plain, *U.S.A.* **158 E7** 42 50N 114 0W
Snasahögarna, *Sweden* **16 A6** 63 13N 12 21 E
Snåsavatnet, *Norway* **14 D14** 64 12N 12 0 E
Snedsted, *Denmark* **17 H2** 56 55N 8 32 E
Sneek, *Neths.* **24 A5** 53 2N 5 40 E
Sneeuberge, *S. Africa* **116 E3** 31 46 S 24 20 E
Snejbjerg, *Denmark* **17 H2** 56 8N 8 54 E
Snelling, *Calif., U.S.A.* **160 H6** 37 31N 120 26W
Snelling, *S.C., U.S.A.* **152 B8** 33 15N 81 27W
Snezhnoye, *Ukraine* **59 J10** 48 0N 38 58 E
Snežnik, *Slovenia* **45 C11** 45 36N 14 35 E
Śniadowo, *Poland* **55 E8** 53 2N 22 0 E
Sniardwy, Jezioro, *Poland* **54 E8** 53 48N 21 50 E
Śnieżka, *Europe* **34 A8** 50 44N 15 44 E
Snigirevka = Snihurivka, *Ukraine* **59 J7** 47 2N 32 49 E
Snihurivka, *Ukraine* **59 J7** 47 2N 32 49 E
Snillfjord, *Norway* **18 A6** 63 24N 9 30 E
Snina, *Slovak Rep.* **35 C15** 48 58N 22 9 E
Snizort, L., *U.K.* **22 D2** 57 33N 6 28W
Snøhetta, *Norway* **15 E13** 62 19N 9 16 E
Snohomish, *U.S.A.* **160 C4** 47 55N 122 6W
Snønuten, *Norway* **18 E3** 59 31N 6 52 E
Snoul, *Cambodia* **87 F6** 12 4N 106 26 E
Snow Hill, *U.S.A.* **148 F8** 38 11N 75 24W
Snow Lake, *Canada* **143 C8** 54 52N 100 3W
Snow Mt., *Calif., U.S.A.* **160 F4** 39 23N 122 45W
Snow Mt., *Maine, U.S.A.* **151 A14** 45 18N 70 48W
Snow Shoe, *U.S.A.* **150 E7** 41 2N 77 57W
Snowbird L., *Canada* **143 A8** 60 45N 103 0W
Snowdon, *U.K.* **20 D3** 53 4N 4 5W
Snowdoun, *U.S.A.* **152 C3** 32 15N 86 18W
Snowdrift →, *Canada* **143 A6** 62 24N 110 44W
Snowflake, *U.S.A.* **159 J8** 34 30N 110 5W
Snowshoe Pk., *U.S.A.* **158 B6** 48 13N 115 41W
Snowtown, *Australia* **128 B3** 33 46 S 138 14 E
Snowville, *U.S.A.* **158 F7** 41 58N 112 43W
Snowy →, *Australia* **129 D8** 37 46 S 148 30 E
Snowy Mt., *U.S.A.* **151 C10** 43 42N 74 23W
Snowy Mts., *Australia* **129 D8** 36 30 S 148 20 E
Snug Corner, *Bahamas* **165 B5** 22 33N 73 52W
Snyatyn, *Ukraine* **59 H3** 48 27N 25 38 E
Snyder, *Okla., U.S.A.* **155 H5** 34 40N 98 57W
Snyder, *Tex., U.S.A.* **155 J4** 32 44N 100 55W
Soacha, *Colombia* **168 C3** 4 35N 74 13W
Soahanina, *Madag.* **117 B7** 18 42 S 44 13 E
Soalala, *Madag.* **117 B8** 16 6 S 45 20 E
Soaloka, *Madag.* **117 B8** 18 32 S 45 15 E
Soamanonga, *Madag.* **117 C7** 23 52 S 44 47 E
Soan →, *Pakistan* **92 C4** 33 1N 71 44 E
Soanierana-Ivongo, *Madag.* **117 B8** 16 55 S 49 35 E
Soanindraniny, *Madag.* **117 B8** 19 54 S 47 14 E
Şoarş, *Romania* **53 E9** 45 56N 24 55 E
Soavina, *Madag.* **117 C8** 20 23 S 46 56 E
Soavinandriana, *Madag.* **117 B8** 19 9 S 46 45 E
Soba, *Nigeria* **113 C6** 10 58N 8 4 E
Sobat, Nahr →, *Sudan* **107 F3** 9 22N 31 33 E
Soběslav, *Czech Rep.* **34 B7** 49 16N 14 45 E
Sobhapur, *India* **92 H8** 22 47N 78 17 E
Sobinka, *Russia* **58 E11** 56 0N 40 0 E
Sobo-Yama, *Japan* **70 E3** 32 51N 131 22 E
Sobótka, *Poland* **55 H3** 50 54N 16 44 E
Sobra, *Croatia* **45 F14** 42 44N 17 34 E
Sobradinho, Reprêsa de, *Brazil* **170 C3** 9 30 S 42 0 E
Sobral, *Brazil* **170 B3** 3 50 S 40 20W
Sobrance, *Slovak Rep.* **35 C15** 48 45N 22 11 E
Sobreira Formosa, *Portugal* **42 F3** 39 46N 7 51W
Soc Giang, *Vietnam* **76 F6** 22 54N 106 1 E
Soc Trang, *Vietnam* **78 C3** 9 37N 105 50 E
Soča →, *Europe* **34 E6** 46 20N 13 40 E
Socastee, *U.S.A.* **149 J6** 33 41N 79 1W
Sochaczew, *Poland* **55 F7** 52 15N 20 13 E
Soch'e = Shache, *China* **72 C2** 38 20N 77 10 E
Sochi, *Russia* **61 J4** 43 35N 39 40 E
Social Circle, *U.S.A.* **152 B6** 33 39N 83 43W
Société, Is. de la, *Pac. Oc.* **135 J12** 17 0 S 151 0W
Society Hill, *U.S.A.* **152 C4** 32 26N 85 27W
Society Is. = Société, Is. de la, *Pac. Oc.* **135 J12** 17 0 S 151 0W
Socompa, Portezuelo de, *Chile* **174 A2** 24 27 S 68 18W
Socorro, *Colombia* **168 B3** 6 29N 73 16W
Socorro, *Phil.* **81 G5** 9 37N 125 58 E
Socorro, *N. Mex., U.S.A.* **159 J10** 34 4N 106 54W
Socorro, *Tex., U.S.A.* **159 L10** 31 39N 106 18W
Socorro, I., *Mexico* **162 D2** 18 45N 110 58W
Socotra, *Ind. Oc.* **99 D6** 12 30N 54 0 E
Socovos, *Spain* **41 G3** 38 20N 1 58W
Socuéllamos, *Spain* **41 F2** 39 16N 2 47W
Soda L., *U.S.A.* **159 J5** 35 10N 116 4W
Soda Plains, *India* **93 B8** 35 30N 79 0 E
Soda Springs, *U.S.A.* **158 E8** 42 39N 111 36W
Sodankylä, *Finland* **14 C22** 67 29N 26 40 E
Soddy-Daisy, *U.S.A.* **149 H3** 35 17N 85 10W
Söderala, *Sweden* **16 C10** 61 17N 16 55 E
Söderbärke, *Sweden* **16 D9** 60 5N 15 33 E
Söderfors, *Sweden* **16 D11** 60 23N 17 25 E
Söderhamn, *Sweden* **16 C11** 61 18N 17 10 E
Söderköping, *Sweden* **17 F10** 58 31N 16 20 E
Södermanland, *Sweden* **15 G17** 58 56N 16 55 E
Södermanlands län □, *Sweden* **16 E10** 59 10N 16 30 E
Södertälje, *Sweden* **16 E11** 59 12N 17 39 E
Sodiri, *Sudan* **107 E2** 14 27N 29 0 E
Sodo, *Ethiopia* **107 F4** 7 0N 37 41 E
Södra Dellen, *Sweden* **16 C10** 61 48N 16 43 E
Södra Finnskoga, *Sweden* **16 D6** 60 42N 12 34 E
Södra Sandby, *Sweden* **17 J7** 55 43N 13 21 E
Södra Ulvön, *Sweden* **16 B12** 62 59N 18 38 E
Södra Vi, *Sweden* **17 G9** 57 45N 15 45 E
Sodražica, *Slovenia* **45 C11** 45 45N 14 39 E
Sodus, *U.S.A.* **150 C7** 43 14N 77 4W
Soe, *Indonesia* **82 C2** 9 52 S 124 17 E
Soekmekaar, *S. Africa* **117 C4** 23 30 S 29 55 E
Soest, *Germany* **30 D4** 51 34N 8 7 E
Soest, *Neths.* **24 B5** 52 9N 5 19 E
Sofádhes, *Greece* **48 B4** 39 20N 22 4 E
Sofala □, *Mozam.* **117 B5** 19 30 S 34 30 E
Sofara, *Mali* **112 C4** 13 59N 4 9W
Sofia = Sofiya, *Bulgaria* **50 D7** 42 45N 23 20 E
Sofia →, *Madag.* **117 B8** 15 27 S 47 23 E
Sofievka, *Ukraine* **59 H7** 48 6N 33 55 E
Sofikón, *Greece* **48 D5** 37 47N 23 3 E
Sofiya, *Bulgaria* **50 D7** 42 45N 23 20 E
Sofiya □, *Bulgaria* **50 D7** 42 15N 23 20 E
Sōfu-Gan, *Japan* **69 K10** 29 49N 140 21 E
Sogakofe, *Ghana* **113 D5** 6 2N 0 39 E
Sogamoso, *Colombia* **168 B3** 5 43N 72 56W
Sogār, *Iran* **97 E8** 25 53N 58 6 E
Sögel, *Germany* **30 C3** 52 50N 7 31 E
Sogeri, *Papua N. G.* **132 E4** 9 26 S 147 35 E
Sogn og Fjordane □, *Norway* **18 C3** 61 40N 6 45 E
Sogndalsfjøra, *Norway* **15 F12** 61 14N 7 5 E
Søgne, *Norway* **15 G12** 58 5N 7 48 E
Sognefjorden, *Norway* **15 F11** 61 10N 5 50 E
Sogod, *Phil.* **81 F5** 10 28N 124 59 E
Söğüt, *Bilecik, Turkey* **49 A12** 40 2N 30 11 E
Söğüt, *Burdur, Turkey* **49 D11** 37 2N 29 50 E
Sögüt Dağı, *Turkey* **49 D11** 37 50N 29 55 E
Sögütköy, *Turkey* **49 E10** 36 40N 28 8 E
Sŏgwipo, *S. Korea* **75 H14** 33 13N 126 34 E
Soh, *Iran* **97 C6** 33 26N 51 27 E
Sohâg, *Egypt* **106 B3** 26 33N 31 43 E
Sohagpur, *India* **92 H8** 22 42N 78 12 E
Sohano, *Papua N. G.* **132 C8** 5 22 S 154 37 E
Sohela, *India* **94 D6** 21 18N 83 24 E
Sŏhori, *N. Korea* **75 D15** 40 7N 128 23 E
Soignies, *Belgium* **24 D4** 50 35N 4 5 E
Soin, *Burkina Faso* **112 C4** 12 47N 3 50W
Soira, *Eritrea* **107 E4** 14 45N 39 30 E
Soissons, *France* **27 C10** 49 25N 3 19 E
Sōja, *Japan* **70 C5** 34 40N 133 45 E
Sojat, *India* **92 G5** 25 55N 73 45 E
Sok →, *Russia* **60 D10** 53 24N 50 8 E
Sokal, *Ukraine* **59 G3** 50 31N 24 15 E
Söke, *Turkey* **49 D9** 37 48N 27 28 E
Sokelo, *Dem. Rep. of the Congo* **119 D1** 9 55 S 24 36 E
Sokhós, *Greece* **50 F7** 40 48N 23 22 E
Sokhumi, *Georgia* **61 J5** 43 0N 41 0 E
Sokki, Oued In →, *Algeria* **111 C5** 29 30N 3 42 E
Sokna, *Norway* **18 D6** 60 16N 9 58 E
Soknedal, *Norway* **18 B7** 62 57N 10 13 E
Soko Banja, *Serbia, Yug.* **50 C5** 43 40N 21 51 E
Sokodé, *Togo* **113 D5** 9 0N 1 11 E
Sokol, *Russia* **58 C11** 59 30N 40 5 E
Sokolac, *Bos.-H.* **52 G3** 43 56N 18 48 E
Sokółka, *Poland* **54 E10** 53 25N 23 30 E
Sokolo, *Mali* **112 C3** 10 52N 6 59W
Sokolo, *Mali* **112 C3** 14 53N 6 8W
Sokolov, *Czech Rep.* **34 A5** 50 12N 12 40 E
Sokołów Małpolski, *Poland* **55 H9** 50 12N 22 7 E
Sokolów Podlaski, *Poland* **55 F9** 52 25N 22 15 E
Sokoły, *Poland* **55 F9** 52 59N 22 42 E
Sokoto, *Nigeria* **113 C6** 13 2N 5 16 E
Sokoto □, *Nigeria* **113 C6** 12 30N 6 0 E
Sokoto →, *Nigeria* **113 C5** 11 20N 4 10 E
Sokuluk, *Kyrgyzstan* **63 B7** 42 52N 74 18 E
Sol Iletsk, *Russia* **62 F5** 51 10N 55 0 E
Sola, *Norway* **18 F2** 58 53N 5 36 E
Sola →, *Poland* **55 H6** 50 4N 19 15 E
Solai, *Kenya* **118 B4** 0 2N 36 12 E
Solan, *India* **92 D7** 30 55N 77 7 E
Solana, *Phil.* **80 C3** 17 39N 121 41 E
Solander I., *N.Z.* **131 G1** 46 34 S 166 54 E
Solano, *Phil.* **79 A6** 16 31N 121 15 E
Solapur, *India* **94 F2** 17 43N 75 56 E
Solca, *Romania* **53 C10** 47 40N 25 50 E
Solda Gölü, *Turkey* **49 D11** 37 33N 29 42 E
Soldăneşti, *Moldova* **53 C13** 47 49N 28 48 E
Soldotna, *U.S.A.* **144 F10** 60 29N 151 3W
Soléa □, *Cyprus* **38 D12** 35 5N 33 4 E
Solec Kujawski, *Poland* **55 E5** 53 5N 18 14 E
Soledad, *Colombia* **168 A3** 10 55N 74 46W
Soledad, *U.S.A.* **160 J5** 36 26N 121 20W
Soledad, *Venezuela* **169 B5** 8 10N 63 34W
Sølen, *Norway* **18 C8** 61 53N 11 31 E
Solent, The, *U.K.* **21 G6** 50 45N 1 25W
Solenzara, *France* **29 G13** 41 53N 9 23 E
Solesmes, *France* **27 B10** 50 10N 3 30 E
Solfonn, *Norway* **15 F12** 60 2N 6 57 E
Solhan, *Turkey* **101 C9** 38 57N 41 3 E
Sølheim, *Norway* **18 D2** 60 53N 5 27 E
Soligalich, *Russia* **56 C7** 59 5N 42 10 E
Soligorsk = Salihorsk, *Belarus* **59 F4** 52 51N 27 27 E
Solihull, *U.K.* **21 E6** 52 26N 1 47W
Solikamsk, *Russia* **62 B6** 59 38N 56 50 E
Solila, *Madag.* **117 C8** 21 25 S 46 37 E
Solimões = Amazonas →, *S. Amer.* **169 D7** 0 5 S 50 0W
Solin, *Croatia* **45 E13** 43 33N 16 30 E
Solingen, *Germany* **30 D3** 51 10N 7 5 E
Sollebrunn, *Sweden* **17 F6** 58 8N 12 32 E
Sollefteå, *Sweden* **16 A11** 63 12N 17 20 E
Sollentuna, *Sweden* **16 E11** 59 26N 17 56 E
Sóller, *Spain* **39 B9** 39 46N 2 43 E
Sollerön, *Sweden* **16 D8** 60 55N 14 37 E
Solling, *Germany* **30 D5** 51 42N 9 38 E
Solnechnogorsk, *Russia* **58 D9** 56 10N 36 57 E
Solo →, *Indonesia* **79 G15** 6 47 S 112 22 E
Solofra, *Italy* **47 B7** 40 50N 14 51 E
Sologne, *France* **27 E8** 47 40N 1 45 E
Solok, *Indonesia* **78 E2** 0 45 S 100 40 E
Sololá, *Guatemala* **164 D1** 14 49N 91 10W
Solomon, N. Fork →, *U.S.A.* **154 F5** 39 29N 98 26W
Solomon, S. Fork →, *U.S.A.* **154 F5** 39 25N 99 12W
Solomon Is. ■, *Pac. Oc.* **133 L8** 6 0 S 155 0 E
Solomon Sea, *Papua N. G.* **132 D6** 7 0 S 150 0 E
Solon, *China* **73 B7** 46 32N 121 10 E
Solon Springs, *U.S.A.* **154 B9** 46 22N 91 49W
Solonópole, *Brazil* **170 C4** 5 44 S 39 1W
Solor, *Indonesia* **79 F6** 8 27 S 123 0 E
Solotcha, *Russia* **58 E10** 54 48N 39 53 E
Solothurn, *Switz.* **32 B5** 47 13N 7 32 E
Solothurn □, *Switz.* **32 B5** 47 18N 7 40 E
Solotobe, *Kazakstan* **63 A3** 44 37N 66 3 E
Solsona, *Spain* **40 C6** 42 0N 1 31 E
Solsvik, *Norway* **18 D1** 60 26N 4 58 E
Solt, *Hungary* **52 D4** 46 45N 19 1 E
Šolta, *Croatia* **45 E13** 43 24N 16 15 E
Solţānābād, *Khorāsān, Iran* **97 C8** 34 13N 59 58 E
Solţānābād, *Khorāsān, Iran* **97 B8** 36 29N 58 5 E
Soltau, *Germany* **30 C5** 52 59N 9 50 E
Soltsy, *Russia* **58 C6** 58 10N 30 30 E
Solund, *Norway* **18 C1** 61 5N 4 50 E
Solunska Glava, *Macedonia* **50 E5** 41 44N 21 31 E
Solvang, *U.S.A.* **161 L6** 34 36N 120 8W
Solvay, *U.S.A.* **151 C8** 43 3N 76 13W
Sölvesborg, *Sweden* **17 H8** 56 5N 14 35 E
Solvychegodsk, *Russia* **56 B8** 61 21N 46 56 E

Strathnaver 285

Spring Garden, *U.S.A.* **160 F6** 39 52N 120 47W
Spring Green, *U.S.A.* **156 A6** 43 11N 90 4W
Spring Hill, *Australia* **129 B8** 33 23 S 149 9 E
Spring Hill, *Ala., U.S.A.* **152 D4** 31 42N 85 58W
Spring Hill, *Fla., U.S.A.* **153 G7** 28 27N 82 41W
Spring Mts., *U.S.A.* **159 H6** 36 0N 115 45W
Spring Valley, *Calif., U.S.A.* **161 N10** 32 45N 117 5W
Spring Valley, *Ill., U.S.A.* **156 C7** 41 20N 89 12W
Springbok, *S. Africa* **116 D2** 29 42 S 17 54 E
Springboro, *U.S.A.* **150 E4** 41 48N 80 22W
Springdale, *Canada* **141 C8** 49 30N 56 6W
Springdale, *Ark., U.S.A.* **155 G7** 36 11N 94 8W
Springdale, *Ohio, U.S.A.* **157 E12** 39 17N 84 29W
Springe, *Germany* **30 C5** 52 13N 9 33 E
Springer, *U.S.A.* **155 G2** 36 22N 104 36W
Springerville, *U.S.A.* **159 J9** 34 8N 109 17W
Springfield, *Canada* **150 D4** 42 50N 80 56W
Springfield, *N.Z.* **131 D6** 43 19 S 171 56 E
Springfield, *Colo., U.S.A.* **155 G3** 37 24N 102 37W
Springfield, *Fla., U.S.A.* **152 E4** 30 10N 85 37W
Springfield, *Ga., U.S.A.* **152 C8** 32 22N 81 18W
Springfield, *Ill., U.S.A.* **156 E7** 39 48N 89 39W
Springfield, *Ky., U.S.A.* **157 G11** 37 41N 85 13W
Springfield, *Mass., U.S.A.* **151 D12** 42 6N 72 35W
Springfield, *Mo., U.S.A.* **155 G8** 37 13N 93 17W
Springfield, *Ohio, U.S.A.* **157 E13** 39 55N 83 49W
Springfield, *Oreg., U.S.A.* **158 D2** 44 3N 123 1W
Springfield, *S.C., U.S.A.* **152 B8** 33 30N 81 17W
Springfield, *Tenn., U.S.A.* **149 G2** 36 31N 86 53W
Springfield, *Vt., U.S.A.* **151 C12** 43 18N 72 29W
Springfield, L., *U.S.A.* **156 E7** 39 46N 89 36W
Springfontein, *S. Africa* **116 E4** 30 15 S 25 40 E
Springhill, *Canada* **141 C7** 45 40N 64 4W
Springhill, *U.S.A.* **155 J8** 33 0N 93 28W
Springhouse, *Canada* **142 C4** 51 56N 122 7W
Springhurst, *Australia* **129 D7** 36 10 S 146 31 E
Springs, *S. Africa* **117 D4** 26 13 S 28 25 E
Springsure, *Australia* **126 C4** 24 8 S 148 6 E
Springvale, *Ga., U.S.A.* **152 D5** 31 50N 84 53W
Springvale, *Maine, U.S.A.* **151 C14** 43 28N 70 48W
Springville, *Calif., U.S.A.* **160 J8** 36 8N 118 49W
Springville, *Iowa, U.S.A.* **156 B5** 42 3N 91 27W
Springville, *N.Y., U.S.A.* **150 D6** 42 31N 78 40W
Springville, *Utah, U.S.A.* **158 F8** 40 10N 111 37W
Springwater, *U.S.A.* **150 D7** 42 38N 77 35W
Spruce-Creek, *U.S.A.* **150 F6** 40 36N 78 9W
Spruce Mt., *U.S.A.* **151 B12** 44 12N 72 19W
Spur, *U.S.A.* **155 J4** 33 28N 100 52W
Spurn Hd., *U.K.* **20 D8** 53 35N 0 8 E
Spuž, *Montenegro, Yug.* **50 D3** 42 32N 19 10 E
Spuzzum, *Canada* **142 D4** 49 37N 121 23W
Spydeberg, *Norway* **18 E8** 59 36N 11 5 E
Squam L., *U.S.A.* **151 C13** 43 45N 71 32W
Squamish, *Canada* **142 D4** 49 45N 123 10W
Square Islands, *Canada* **141 B8** 52 47N 55 47W
Squillace, G. di, *Italy* **47 D9** 38 45N 16 50 E
Squinzano, *Italy* **47 B11** 40 26N 18 2 E
Squires, Mt., *Australia* **125 E4** 26 14 S 127 28 E
Sragen, *Indonesia* **85 D4** 7 26 S 111 2 E
Srbac, *Bos.-H.* **52 E2** 45 7N 17 30 E
Srbica, *Kosovo, Yug.* **50 D4** 42 45N 20 47 E
Srbija = Serbia □, *Yugoslavia* **50 C5** 43 30N 21 0 E
Srbobran, *Serbia, Yug.* **52 E4** 45 32N 19 48 E
Sre Ambel, *Cambodia* **78 B2** 11 8N 103 46 E
Sre Khtum, *Cambodia* **87 F6** 12 10N 106 52 E
Sre Umbell = Sre Ambel, *Cambodia* **78 B2** 11 8N 103 46 E
Srebrenica, *Bos.-H.* **52 F4** 44 6N 19 18 E
Sredinny Ra. = Sredinnyy Khrebet, *Russia* **65 D16** 57 0N 160 0 E
Sredinnyy Khrebet, *Russia* **65 D16** 57 0N 160 0 E
Središče, *Slovenia* **45 B13** 46 24N 16 17 E
Sredna Gora, *Bulgaria* **51 D8** 42 40N 24 20 E
Srednekolymsk, *Russia* **65 C16** 67 27N 153 40 E
Sredni Rodopi, *Bulgaria* **51 E8** 41 40N 24 45 E
Srednogorie, *Bulgaria* **51 D8** 42 43N 24 10 E
Śrem, *Poland* **55 F4** 52 6N 17 2 E
Sremska Mitrovica, *Serbia, Yug.* **52 F4** 44 59N 19 38 E
Sremski Karlovci, *Serbia, Yug.* **52 E4** 45 12N 19 56 E
Srepok →, *Cambodia* **78 B3** 13 33N 106 16 E
Sretensk, *Russia* **65 D12** 52 10N 117 40 E
Sri Kalahasti, *India* **95 H4** 13 45N 79 44 E
Sri Lanka ■, *Asia* **95 L5** 7 30N 80 50 E
Sriharikota I., *India* **95 H5** 13 40N 80 20 E
Srikakulam, *India* **94 E6** 18 14N 83 58 E
Srinagar, *India* **93 B6** 34 5N 74 50 E
Sripur, *Bangla.* **90 C3** 24 14N 90 30 E
Srivardhan, *India* **94 E1** 18 4N 73 3 E
Srivilliputtur, *India* **95 K3** 9 31N 77 40 E
Šroda Śląska, *Poland* **55 G3** 51 10N 16 36 E
Šroda Wielkopolski, *Poland* **55 F4** 52 15N 17 19 E
Srpska Crnja, *Serbia, Yug.* **52 E5** 45 38N 20 44 E
Srpski Itebej, *Serbia, Yug.* **52 E5** 45 35N 20 44 E
Srungavarapukota, *India* **94 E6** 18 7N 83 10 E
Staaten →, *Australia* **126 B3** 16 24 S 141 17 E
Staberhuk, *Germany* **30 A7** 54 23N 11 18 E
Stade, *Germany* **30 B5** 53 35N 9 29 E
Staðarfell, *Iceland* **11 B4** 65 7N 22 12W
Staðarhólskirkja, *Iceland* **11 B5** 65 23N 21 58W
Staðastaður, *Iceland* **11 C3** 64 49N 23 1W
Stadhavet, *Norway* **18 B2** 62 13N 5 0 E
Staður, *Húnavatnssýsla, Iceland* **11 B5** 65 9N 21 3W
Staður, *Ísafjarðarsýsla, Iceland* **11 A4** 66 15N 22 50W
Stadlandet, *Norway* **18 B2** 62 10N 5 10 E
Stadskanaal, *Neths.* **24 A6** 53 4N 6 55 E
Stadtallendorf, *Germany* **30 E5** 50 48N 9 1 E
Stadthagen, *Germany* **30 C5** 52 19N 9 13 E
Stadtlohn, *Germany* **30 D2** 51 59N 6 55 E
Stadtroda, *Germany* **30 E7** 50 52N 11 44 E
Stäfa, *Switz.* **33 B7** 47 14N 8 45 E
Stafafell, *Iceland* **11 C12** 64 25N 14 52W
Staffa, *U.K.* **22 E2** 56 27N 6 21W
Staffanstorp, *Sweden* **17 J7** 55 39N 13 13 E
Stafford, *U.K.* **20 E5** 52 49N 2 7W
Stafford, *U.S.A.* **155 G5** 37 58N 98 36W
Stafford, L., *U.S.A.* **153 F7** 29 20N 82 29W
Stafford Springs, *U.S.A.* **151 E12** 41 57N 72 18W
Staffordshire □, *U.K.* **20 E5** 52 53N 2 10W
Stagnone, *Italy* **46 E5** 37 53N 12 26 E
Staines, *U.K.* **21 F7** 51 26N 0 29W
Stainz, *Austria* **34 E8** 46 53N 15 17 E
Stakhanov, *Ukraine* **59 H10** 48 35N 38 40 E
Stalać, *Serbia, Yug.* **50 C5** 43 43N 21 28 E
Stalden, *Switz.* **32 D5** 46 14N 7 52 E
Stalingrad = Volgograd, *Russia* **61 F7** 48 40N 44 25 E
Staliniri = Tskhinvali, *Georgia* **61 J7** 42 14N 44 1 E
Stalino = Donetsk, *Ukraine* **59 J9** 48 0N 37 45 E
Stalinogorsk = Novomoskovsk, *Russia* **58 E10** 54 5N 38 15 E
Stalis, *Greece* **38 D7** 35 17N 25 25 E
Stallarholmen, *Sweden* **16 E11** 59 22N 17 12 E
Ställdalen, *Sweden* **16 E8** 59 56N 14 56 E
Stalowa Wola, *Poland* **55 H9** 50 34N 22 3 E
Stalybridge, *U.K.* **20 D5** 53 28N 2 3W
Stamford, *Australia* **126 C3** 21 15 S 143 46 E
Stamford, *U.K.* **21 E7** 52 39N 0 29W
Stamford, *Conn., U.S.A.* **151 E11** 41 3N 73 32W
Stamford, *N.Y., U.S.A.* **151 D10** 42 25N 74 38W
Stamford, *Tex., U.S.A.* **155 J5** 32 57N 99 48W
Stamnes, *Norway* **18 D2** 60 40N 5 45 E
Stamping Ground, *U.S.A.* **157 F12** 38 16N 84 41W
Stampriet, *Namibia* **116 C2** 24 20 S 18 28 E
Stamps, *U.S.A.* **155 J8** 33 22N 93 30W
Stanberry, *U.S.A.* **156 D2** 40 13N 94 35W
Stančevo = Kalipetrovo, *Bulgaria* **51 B11** 44 5N 27 14 E
Standerton, *S. Africa* **117 D4** 26 55 S 29 7 E
Standish, *U.S.A.* **148 D4** 43 59N 83 57W
Stanford, *S. Africa* **116 E2** 34 26 S 19 29 E
Stanford, *U.S.A.* **158 C8** 47 9N 110 13W
Stånga, *Sweden* **17 G12** 57 17N 18 29 E
Stange, *Norway* **18 D8** 60 43N 11 5 E
Stanger, *S. Africa* **117 D5** 29 27 S 31 14 E
Stangvik, *Norway* **18 B5** 62 55N 8 28 E
Stanhope, *Australia* **129 D6** 36 27 S 144 59 E
Stanhope, *U.S.A.* **156 B3** 42 17N 93 48W
Stanišić, *Serbia, Yug.* **52 E4** 45 56N 19 10 E
Stanislaus →, *U.S.A.* **160 H5** 37 40N 121 14W
Stanislav = Ivano-Frankivsk, *Ukraine* **59 H3** 48 40N 24 40 E
Stanisławów, *Poland* **55 F8** 52 18N 21 33 E
Stanley, *Australia* **126 G4** 40 46 S 145 19 E
Stanley, *Canada* **143 B8** 55 24N 104 22W
Stanley, *Falk. Is.* **176 D5** 51 40 S 59 51W
Stanley, *U.K.* **20 C6** 54 53N 1 41W
Stanley, *Idaho, U.S.A.* **158 D6** 44 13N 114 56W
Stanley, *N. Dak., U.S.A.* **154 A3** 48 19N 102 23W
Stanley, *N.Y., U.S.A.* **150 D7** 42 48N 77 6W
Stanley Res., *India* **95 J3** 11 50N 77 40 E
Stanovoy Khrebet, *Russia* **65 D13** 55 0N 130 0 E
Stanovoy Ra. = Stanovoy Khrebet, *Russia* **65 D13** 55 0N 130 0 E
Stans, *Switz.* **33 C6** 46 58N 8 21 E
Stansmore Ra., *Australia* **124 D4** 21 23 S 128 33 E
Stanthorpe, *Australia* **127 D5** 28 36 S 151 59 E
Stanton, *Ky., U.S.A.* **157 G13** 37 54N 83 52W
Stanton, *Tex., U.S.A.* **155 J4** 32 8N 101 48W
Stantsiya Karshi, *Uzbekistan* **63 D2** 38 49N 65 47 E
Stanwood, *U.S.A.* **160 B4** 48 15N 122 23W
Staples, *U.S.A.* **154 B7** 46 21N 94 48W
Stąporków, *Poland* **55 G7** 51 9N 20 31 E
Star City, *Canada* **143 C8** 52 50N 104 20W
Star Lake, *U.S.A.* **151 B9** 44 10N 75 2W
Stará L'ubovňa, *Slovak Rep.* **35 B13** 49 18N 20 42 E
Stara Moravica, *Serbia, Yug.* **52 E4** 45 50N 19 30 E
Stara Pazova, *Serbia, Yug.* **52 F5** 44 58N 20 10 E
Stara Planina, *Bulgaria* **50 C7** 43 15N 23 0 E
Stará Turá, *Slovak Rep.* **35 C10** 48 47N 17 42 E
Stara Zagora, *Bulgaria* **51 D9** 42 26N 25 39 E
Starachowice, *Poland* **55 G8** 51 3N 21 2 E
Staraya Russa, *Russia* **58 D6** 57 58N 31 23 E
Starbuck I., *Kiribati* **135 H12** 5 37 S 155 55W
Starchiojd, *Romania* **53 E11** 45 19N 26 11 E
Stargard Szczeciński, *Poland* **54 E2** 53 20N 15 0 E
Stårheim, *Norway* **18 C2** 61 56N 5 40 E
Stari Bar, *Montenegro, Yug.* **50 D3** 42 7N 19 10 E
Stari Trg, *Slovenia* **45 C12** 45 29N 15 7 E
Staritsa, *Russia* **58 D8** 56 33N 34 55 E
Starke, *U.S.A.* **152 F7** 29 57N 82 7W
Starnberg, *Germany* **31 H7** 48 0N 11 21 E
Starnberger See, *Germany* **31 H7** 47 54N 11 19 E
Starobilsk, *Ukraine* **59 H10** 49 16N 39 0 E
Starodub, *Russia* **59 F7** 52 30N 32 50 E
Starogard Gdański, *Poland* **54 E5** 53 59N 18 30 E
Starokonstantinov = Starokonstyantyniv, *Ukraine* **59 H4** 49 48N 27 10 E
Starokonstyantyniv, *Ukraine* **59 H4** 49 48N 27 10 E
Starominskaya, *Russia* **59 J10** 46 33N 39 0 E
Staroshcherbinovskaya, *Russia* **59 J10** 46 40N 38 53 E
Starrs Mill, *U.S.A.* **152 B5** 33 19N 84 31W
Start Pt., *U.K.* **21 G4** 50 13N 3 39W
Stary Sącz, *Poland* **55 J7** 49 33N 20 35 E
Staryy Biryuzyak, *Russia* **61 H8** 44 46N 46 50 E
Staryy Chartoriysk, *Ukraine* **59 G3** 51 15N 25 54 E
Staryy Krym, *Ukraine* **59 K8** 45 3N 35 8 E
Staryy Oskol, *Russia* **59 G9** 51 19N 37 55 E
Stassfurt, *Germany* **30 D7** 51 51N 11 35 E
Staszów, *Poland* **55 H8** 50 33N 21 10 E
State Center, *U.S.A.* **156 B3** 42 1N 93 10W
State College, *U.S.A.* **150 F7** 40 48N 77 52W
Stateline, *U.S.A.* **160 G7** 38 57N 119 56W
Staten, I. = Estados, I. de Los, *Argentina* **176 D4** 54 40 S 64 30W
Staten I., *U.S.A.* **151 F10** 40 35N 74 9W
Statenville, *U.S.A.* **152 E6** 30 42N 83 2W
Statesboro, *U.S.A.* **152 C8** 32 27N 81 47W
Statesville, *U.S.A.* **149 H5** 35 47N 80 53W
Statham, *U.S.A.* **152 B6** 33 58N 83 35W
Stathelle, *Norway* **18 E6** 59 3N 9 41 E
Stauffer, *U.S.A.* **161 L7** 34 45N 119 3W
Staunton, *Ill., U.S.A.* **156 F7** 39 1N 89 47W
Staunton, *Va., U.S.A.* **148 F6** 38 9N 79 4W
Stavanger, *Norway* **15 G11** 58 57N 5 40 E
Staveley, *N.Z.* **131 D6** 43 40 S 171 32 E
Stavelot, *Belgium* **24 D5** 50 23N 5 55 E
Stavern, *Norway* **15 G14** 59 0N 10 1 E
Stavoren, *Neths.* **24 B5** 52 53N 5 22 E
Stavropol, *Russia* **61 H6** 45 5N 42 0 E
Stavros, *Cyprus* **38 D11** 35 1N 32 38 E
Stavrós, *Greece* **38 D6** 35 12N 24 45 E
Stavrós, Ákra, *Greece* **38 D6** 35 26N 24 58 E
Stavroúpolis, *Greece* **51 E8** 41 12N 24 45 E
Stawell, *Australia* **128 D5** 37 5 S 142 47 E
Stawell →, *Australia* **126 C3** 20 20 S 142 55 E
Stawiski, *Poland* **54 E9** 53 22N 22 9 E
Stawiszyn, *Poland* **55 G5** 51 56N 18 4 E
Stayner, *Canada* **150 B4** 44 25N 80 5W
Stayton, *U.S.A.* **158 D2** 44 48N 122 48W
Steamboat Springs, *U.S.A.* **158 F10** 40 29N 106 50W
Steane, *Norway* **18 E5** 59 16N 8 33 E
Stebbins, *U.S.A.* **144 E7** 63 31N 162 17W
Stebleva, *Albania* **50 E4** 41 23N 20 33 E
Steckborn, *Switz.* **33 A7** 47 44N 8 59 E
Steele, *Ala., U.S.A.* **152 B3** 33 56N 86 12W
Steele, *N. Dak., U.S.A.* **154 B5** 46 51N 99 55W
Steelton, *U.S.A.* **150 F8** 40 14N 76 50W
Steelville, *U.S.A.* **156 G5** 37 58N 91 22W
Steen River, *Canada* **142 B5** 59 40N 117 12W
Steenkool = Bintuni, *Indonesia* **79 E8** 2 7 S 133 32 E
Steens Mt., *U.S.A.* **158 E4** 42 35N 118 40W
Steenstrup Gletscher, *Greenland* **10 B5** 75 15N 57 0W
Steenwijk, *Neths.* **24 B6** 52 47N 6 7 E
Steep Pt., *Australia* **125 E1** 26 8 S 113 8 E
Steep Rock, *Canada* **143 C9** 51 30N 98 48W
Ştefan Vodă, *Moldova* **53 D14** 46 27N 29 42 E
Ştefăneşti, *Romania* **53 C12** 47 44N 27 15 E
Stefanie L. = Chew Bahir, *Ethiopia* **102 G2** 4 40N 36 50 E
Stefansson Bay, *Antarctica* **7 C5** 67 20 S 59 8 E
Steffisburg, *Switz.* **32 C5** 46 47N 7 38 E
Stege, *Denmark* **17 K6** 54 59N 12 18 E
Ştei, *Romania* **52 D7** 46 32N 22 27 E
Steiermark □, *Austria* **34 D8** 47 26N 15 0 E
Steigerwald, *Germany* **31 F6** 49 44N 10 26 E
Steilacoom, *U.S.A.* **160 C4** 47 10N 122 36W
Steilrandberge, *Namibia* **116 B1** 17 45 S 13 20 E
Stein am Rhein, *Switz.* **33 A7** 47 39N 8 51 E
Steinbach, *Canada* **143 D9** 49 32N 96 40W
Steinfurt, *Germany* **30 C3** 52 9N 7 20 E
Steinhatchee, *U.S.A.* **152 F6** 29 40N 83 23W
Steinhausen, *Namibia* **116 C2** 21 49 S 18 20 E
Steinheim, *Germany* **30 D5** 51 51N 9 5 E
Steinhuder Meer, *Germany* **30 C5** 52 29N 9 21 E
Steinkjer, *Norway* **14 D14** 64 1N 11 31 E
Steinkopf, *S. Africa* **116 D2** 29 18 S 17 43 E
Steinshamn, *Norway* **18 B3** 62 47N 6 28 E
Stellarton, *Canada* **141 C7** 45 32N 62 30W
Stellenbosch, *S. Africa* **116 E2** 33 58 S 18 50 E
Stelvio, Paso dello, *Italy* **33 C10** 46 32N 10 27 E
Stenay, *France* **27 C12** 49 29N 5 12 E
Stendal, *Germany* **30 C7** 52 36N 11 53 E
Stende, *Latvia* **54 A9** 57 11N 22 33 E
Stenhamra, *Sweden* **16 E11** 59 20N 17 41 E
Stenstorp, *Sweden* **17 F7** 58 17N 13 45 E
Stenungsund, *Sweden* **17 F5** 58 6N 11 50 E
Steornabhaigh = Stornoway, *U.K.* **22 C2** 58 13N 6 23W
Stepanakert = Xankändi, *Azerbaijan* **101 C12** 39 52N 46 49 E
Stepanavan, *Armenia* **61 K7** 41 1N 44 23 E
Stephens, C., *N.Z.* **131 A8** 40 42 S 173 58 E
Stephens Creek, *Australia* **128 A4** 31 50 S 141 30 E
Stephens I., *Canada* **142 C2** 54 10N 130 45W
Stephens I., *N.Z.* **131 A9** 40 40 S 174 1 E
Stephens L., *Canada* **143 B9** 56 32N 95 0W
Stephenville, *Canada* **141 C8** 48 31N 58 35W
Stephenville, *U.S.A.* **155 J5** 32 13N 98 12W
Stepnica, *Poland* **54 E1** 53 38N 14 36 E
Stepnoi = Elista, *Russia* **61 G7** 46 16N 44 14 E
Stepnoye, *Russia* **62 D8** 54 4N 60 26 E
Steppe, *Asia* **66 D9** 50 0N 50 0 E
Stereá Ellas □, *Greece* **48 C4** 38 50N 23 0 E
Sterkstroom, *S. Africa* **116 E4** 31 32 S 26 32 E
Sterling, *Alaska, U.S.A.* **144 F10** 60 32N 150 46W
Sterling, *Colo., U.S.A.* **154 E3** 40 37N 103 13W
Sterling, *Ga., U.S.A.* **152 D8** 31 16N 81 34W
Sterling, *Ill., U.S.A.* **156 C7** 41 48N 89 42W
Sterling, *Kans., U.S.A.* **154 F5** 38 13N 98 12W
Sterling City, *U.S.A.* **155 K4** 31 51N 101 0W
Sterling Heights, *U.S.A.* **157 B13** 42 35N 83 0W
Sterling Run, *U.S.A.* **150 E6** 41 25N 78 12W
Sterlitamak, *Russia* **62 E6** 53 40N 56 0 E
Šternberg, *Germany* **30 B7** 53 42N 11 50 E
Šternberk, *Czech Rep.* **35 B10** 49 45N 17 15 E
Stérnes, *Greece* **38 D6** 35 30N 24 9 E
Sterzing = Vipiteno, *Italy* **45 B8** 46 54N 11 26 E
Stettin = Szczecin, *Poland* **54 E1** 53 27N 14 27 E
Stettiner Haff, *Germany* **30 B10** 53 47N 14 15 E
Stettler, *Canada* **142 C6** 52 19N 112 40W
Steubenville, *U.S.A.* **150 F4** 40 22N 80 37W
Stevenage, *U.K.* **21 F7** 51 55N 0 13W
Stevens Point, *U.S.A.* **154 C10** 44 31N 89 34W
Stevens Pottery, *U.S.A.* **152 C6** 32 57N 83 17W
Stevenson, *U.S.A.* **160 E5** 45 42N 121 53W
Stevenson L., *Canada* **143 C9** 53 55N 96 0W
Stevensville, *U.S.A.* **158 C6** 46 30N 114 5W
Stevns Klint, *Denmark* **17 J6** 55 17N 12 28 E
Steward, *U.S.A.* **156 C7** 41 51N 89 1W
Stewardson, *U.S.A.* **157 E8** 39 16N 88 38W
Stewart, *B.C., Canada* **142 B3** 55 56N 129 57W
Stewart, *N.W.T., Canada* **138 B6** 63 19N 139 26W
Stewart, *Ga., U.S.A.* **152 B5** 33 25N 83 52W
Stewart, *Nev., U.S.A.* **160 F7** 39 5N 119 46W
Stewart, C., *Australia* **126 A1** 11 57 S 134 56 E
Stewart, I., *Chile* **176 D2** 54 50 S 71 15W
Stewart I., *N.Z.* **131 G2** 46 58 S 167 54 E
Stewarts Point, *U.S.A.* **160 G3** 38 39N 123 24W
Stewartsville, *U.S.A.* **156 E2** 39 45N 94 30W
Stewartville, *U.S.A.* **154 D8** 43 51N 92 29W
Stewiacke, *Canada* **141 C7** 45 9N 63 22W
Steynsburg, *S. Africa* **116 E4** 31 15 S 25 49 E
Steyr, *Austria* **34 C7** 48 3N 14 25 E
Steyr →, *Austria* **34 C7** 48 3N 14 25 E
Steytlerville, *S. Africa* **116 E3** 33 17 S 24 19 E
Stia, *Italy* **45 E8** 43 48N 11 42 E
Stigler, *U.S.A.* **155 H7** 35 15N 95 8W
Stigliano, *Italy* **47 B9** 40 24N 16 14 E
Stigtomta, *Sweden* **17 F10** 58 47N 16 48 E
Stikine →, *Canada* **142 B2** 56 40N 132 30W
Stilfontein, *S. Africa* **116 D4** 26 51 S 26 50 E
Stilís, *Greece* **48 C4** 38 55N 22 47 E
Stillmore, *U.S.A.* **152 C7** 32 27N 82 13W
Stillwater, *N.Z.* **131 C6** 42 27 S 171 20 E
Stillwater, *Minn., U.S.A.* **154 C8** 45 3N 92 49W
Stillwater, *N.Y., U.S.A.* **151 D11** 42 55N 73 41W
Stillwater, *Okla., U.S.A.* **155 G6** 36 7N 97 4W
Stillwater Range, *U.S.A.* **158 G4** 39 50N 118 5W
Stillwater Reservoir, *U.S.A.* **151 C9** 43 54N 75 3W
Stilo, Pta., *Italy* **47 D9** 38 25N 16 35 E
Stilwell, *U.S.A.* **155 H7** 35 49N 94 38W
Štip, *Macedonia* **50 E6** 41 42N 22 10 E
Stira, *Greece* **48 C6** 38 9N 24 14 E
Stirling, *Canada* **150 B7** 44 18N 77 33W
Stirling, *N.Z.* **131 G4** 46 14 S 169 49 E
Stirling, *U.K.* **22 E5** 56 8N 3 57W
Stirling □, *U.K.* **22 E4** 56 12N 4 18W
Stirling Ra., *Australia* **125 F2** 34 23 S 118 0 E
Stittsville, *Canada* **151 A9** 45 15N 75 55W
Stjernøya, *Norway* **14 A20** 70 20N 22 40 E
Stjørdalshalsen, *Norway* **14 E14** 63 29N 10 51 E
Stock Island, *U.S.A.* **153 L8** 24 32N 81 34W
Stockach, *Germany* **31 H5** 47 50N 9 1 E
Stockaryd, *Sweden* **17 G8** 57 19N 14 36 E
Stockbridge, *Ga., U.S.A.* **152 B5** 33 33N 84 14W
Stockbridge, *Mich., U.S.A.* **157 B12** 42 27N 84 11W
Stockerau, *Austria* **35 C9** 48 24N 16 12 E
Stockholm, *Sweden* **16 E12** 59 20N 18 3 E
Stockholms län □, *Sweden* **16 E12** 59 30N 18 20 E
Stockhorn, *Switz.* **32 C5** 46 42N 7 33 E
Stockport, *U.K.* **20 D5** 53 25N 2 9W
Stocksbridge, *U.K.* **20 D6** 53 29N 1 35W
Stockton, *Australia* **129 B9** 32 50 S 151 47 E
Stockton, *Calif., U.S.A.* **160 H5** 37 58N 121 17W
Stockton, *Ill., U.S.A.* **156 B6** 42 21N 90 1W
Stockton, *Kans., U.S.A.* **154 F5** 39 26N 99 16W
Stockton, *Mo., U.S.A.* **155 G8** 37 42N 93 48W
Stockton-on-Tees, *U.K.* **20 C6** 54 35N 1 19W
Stockton-on-Tees □, *U.K.* **20 C6** 54 35N 1 19W
Stockton Plateau, *U.S.A.* **155 K3** 30 30N 102 30W
Stoczek Łukowski, *Poland* **55 G8** 51 58N 21 58 E
Stöde, *Sweden* **16 B10** 62 28N 16 35 E
Stoeng Treng, *Cambodia* **78 B3** 13 31N 105 58 E
Stoer, Pt. of, *U.K.* **22 C3** 58 16N 5 23W
Stogovo, *Macedonia* **50 E4** 41 31N 20 38 E
Stoholm, *Denmark* **17 H3** 56 29N 9 8 E
Stoke, *N.Z.* **131 B8** 41 19 S 173 14 E
Stoke-on-Trent, *U.K.* **20 D5** 53 1N 2 11W
Stoke-on-Trent □, *U.K.* **20 D5** 53 1N 2 11W
Stokes Pt., *Australia* **126 G3** 40 10 S 143 56 E
Stokes Ra., *Australia* **124 C5** 15 50 S 130 50 E
Stokkseyri, *Iceland* **11 D5** 63 50N 21 2W
Stokksnes, *Iceland* **11 C12** 64 14N 14 58W
Stokmarknes, *Norway* **14 B16** 68 34N 14 54 E
Stolac, *Bos.-H.* **50 C1** 43 5N 17 59 E
Stolberg, *Germany* **30 E2** 50 47N 6 13 E
Stolbovoy, Ostrov, *Russia* **65 D17** 74 44N 135 14 E
Stolbtsy = Stowbtsy, *Belarus* **58 F4** 53 30N 26 43 E
Stolin, *Belarus* **59 G4** 51 53N 26 50 E
Stöllet, *Sweden* **16 D7** 60 26N 13 15 E
Stolnici, *Romania* **53 F9** 44 31N 24 48 E
Stomíon, *Greece* **38 D5** 35 21N 23 32 E
Ston, *Croatia* **45 F14** 42 51N 17 43 E
Stone, *U.K.* **20 E5** 52 55N 2 9W
Stone Mountain, *U.S.A.* **152 B5** 33 49N 84 10W
Stoneboro, *U.S.A.* **150 E4** 41 20N 80 7W
Stonehaven, *U.K.* **22 E6** 56 59N 2 12W
Stonehenge, *Australia* **126 C3** 24 22 S 143 17 E
Stonehenge, *U.K.* **21 F6** 51 9N 1 45W
Stonewall, *Canada* **143 C9** 50 10N 97 19W
Stongfjorden, *Norway* **18 C2** 61 26N 5 10 E
Stonington, *U.S.A.* **156 E7** 39 44N 89 12W
Stony L., *Man., Canada* **143 B9** 58 51N 98 40W
Stony L., *Ont., Canada* **150 B6** 44 30N 78 5W
Stony Point, *U.S.A.* **151 E11** 41 14N 73 59W
Stony Pt., *U.S.A.* **151 C8** 43 50N 76 18W
Stony Rapids, *Canada* **143 B7** 59 16N 105 50W
Stony Tunguska = Tunguska, Podkamennaya →, *Russia* **65 C10** 61 50N 90 13 E
Stonyford, *U.S.A.* **160 F4** 39 23N 122 33W
Stopnica, *Poland* **55 H7** 50 27N 20 57 E
Storå, *Sweden* **16 E9** 59 42N 15 6 E
Storå →, *Denmark* **17 H2** 56 20N 8 19 E
Stora Gla, *Sweden* **16 E6** 59 30N 12 30 E
Stora Le, *Sweden* **16 E5** 59 5N 11 55 E
Stora Lulevatten, *Sweden* **14 C18** 67 10N 19 30 E
Stóra-Vatnshorn, *Iceland* **11 B5** 65 4N 21 33W
Storavan, *Sweden* **14 D18** 65 45N 18 10 E
Stord, *Norway* **15 G11** 59 52N 5 23 E
Stordal, *Norway* **18 B4** 62 23N 7 0 E
Store Bælt, *Denmark* **17 J4** 55 20N 11 0 E
Store Creek, *Australia* **129 B8** 32 54 S 149 6 E
Store Heddinge, *Denmark* **17 J6** 55 18N 12 23 E
Store Jukleggi, *Norway* **18 C5** 61 3N 8 12 E
Store Koldewey, *Greenland* **10 B9** 76 30N 19 0W
Store Sølnkletten, *Norway* **18 C7** 61 59N 10 16 E
Store Sotra, *Norway* **18 D1** 60 18N 5 4 E
Storebro, *Sweden* **17 G9** 57 35N 15 52 E
Støren, *Norway* **18 A7** 63 3N 10 18 E
Storerikvollen, *Norway* **18 A8** 63 7N 11 58 E
Storfjellseter, *Norway* **18 C7** 61 40N 10 30 E
Storfjorden, *Møre og Romsdal, Norway* **18 B3** 62 8N 6 33 E
Storfjorden, *Møre og Romsdal, Norway* **18 B3** 62 28N 6 35 E
Storfors, *Sweden* **16 E8** 59 32N 14 17 E
Stóridalur, *Iceland* **11 D7** 63 38N 19 57W
Stórinúpur, *Iceland* **11 C6** 64 3N 20 10W
Storli, *Norway* **18 B6** 62 42N 9 5 E
Storlien, *Sweden* **16 A6** 63 20N 12 5 E
Storm B., *Australia* **126 G4** 43 10 S 147 30 E
Storm Lake, *U.S.A.* **154 D7** 42 39N 95 13W
Stormberge, *S. Africa* **116 E4** 31 16 S 26 17 E
Stormsrivier, *S. Africa* **116 E3** 33 59 S 23 52 E
Stornoway, *U.K.* **22 C2** 58 13N 6 23W
Storo, *Italy* **44 C7** 45 51N 10 35 E
Storozhinets = Storozhynets, *Ukraine* **59 H3** 48 14N 25 45 E
Storozhynets, *Ukraine* **59 H3** 48 14N 25 45 E
Storrs, *U.S.A.* **151 E12** 41 49N 72 15W
Storsjøen, *Hedmark, Norway* **18 D8** 60 20N 11 40 E
Storsjøen, *Hedmark, Norway* **18 C8** 61 30N 11 14 E
Storsjön, *Gävleborg, Sweden* **16 D10** 60 35N 16 45 E
Storsjön, *Jämtland, Sweden* **16 B7** 62 48N 13 7 E
Storsjön, *Jämtland, Sweden* **16 A8** 63 9N 14 30 E
Storstrøms Amtskommune □, *Denmark* **17 J5** 54 50N 11 45 E
Storuman, *Sweden* **14 D17** 65 5N 17 10 E
Storuman, sjö, *Sweden* **14 D17** 65 13N 16 50 E
Stóruvellir, *Iceland* **11 B9** 65 30N 17 29W
Storvätteshågna, *Sweden* **16 B6** 62 6N 12 30 E
Storvigelen, *Norway* **18 B9** 62 32N 12 2 E
Storvik, *Sweden* **16 D10** 60 35N 16 33 E
Storvreta, *Sweden* **16 E11** 59 58N 17 44 E
Story City, *U.S.A.* **156 B3** 42 11N 93 36W
Stouffville, *Canada* **150 C5** 43 58N 79 15W
Stoughton, *Canada* **143 D8** 49 40N 103 0W
Stoughton, *U.S.A.* **156 B8** 42 55N 89 13W
Stour →, *Dorset, U.K.* **21 G6** 50 43N 1 47W
Stour →, *Kent, U.K.* **21 F9** 51 18N 1 22 E
Stour →, *Suffolk, U.K.* **21 F9** 51 57N 1 4 E
Stourbridge, *U.K.* **21 E5** 52 28N 2 8W
Stout L., *Canada* **143 C10** 52 0N 94 40W
Stove Pipe Wells Village, *U.S.A.* **161 J9** 36 35N 117 11W
Støvring, *Denmark* **17 H3** 56 54N 9 50 E
Stow, *U.S.A.* **150 E3** 41 10N 81 27W
Stowbtsy, *Belarus* **58 F4** 53 30N 26 43 E
Stowmarket, *U.K.* **21 E9** 52 12N 1 0 E
Strabane, *U.K.* **23 B4** 54 50N 7 27W
Stracin, *Macedonia* **50 D6** 42 13N 22 2 E
Stradella, *Italy* **44 C6** 45 5N 9 18 E
Strahan, *Australia* **126 G4** 42 9 S 145 20 E
Strajitsa, *Bulgaria* **51 C9** 43 14N 25 58 E
Strakonice, *Czech Rep.* **34 B6** 49 15N 13 53 E
Straldzha, *Bulgaria* **51 D10** 42 35N 26 40 E
Stralsund, *Germany* **30 A9** 54 18N 13 4 E
Strand, *Norway* **18 C8** 61 17N 11 17 E
Strand, *S. Africa* **116 E2** 34 9 S 18 48 E
Stranda, *Møre og Romsdal, Norway* **15 E12** 62 19N 6 58 E
Stranda, *Nord-Trøndelag, Norway* **14 E14** 63 33N 10 14 E
Strandasýsla □, *Iceland* **11 B5** 65 45N 21 45W
Strandby, *Denmark* **17 G4** 57 30N 10 29 E
Strangford L., *U.K.* **23 B6** 54 30N 5 37W
Strängnäs, *Sweden* **16 E11** 59 23N 17 2 E
Stranraer, *U.K.* **22 G3** 54 54N 5 1W
Strasbourg, *Canada* **143 C8** 51 4N 104 55W
Strasbourg, *France* **27 D14** 48 35N 7 42 E
Strasburg, *Germany* **30 B9** 53 30N 13 43 E
Străşeni, *Moldova* **53 C13** 47 8N 28 36 E
Strässa, *Sweden* **16 E9** 59 44N 15 12 E
Stratford, *N.S.W., Australia* **129 B9** 32 7 S 151 55 E
Stratford, *Vic., Australia* **129 D7** 37 59 S 147 7 E
Stratford, *Canada* **140 D3** 43 23N 81 0W
Stratford, *N.Z.* **130 F3** 39 20 S 174 19 E
Stratford, *Calif., U.S.A.* **160 J7** 36 11N 119 49W
Stratford, *Conn., U.S.A.* **151 E11** 41 12N 73 8W
Stratford, *Tex., U.S.A.* **155 G3** 36 20N 102 4W
Stratford-upon-Avon, *U.K.* **21 E6** 52 12N 1 42W
Strath Spey, *U.K.* **22 D5** 57 9N 3 49W
Strathalbyn, *Australia* **128 C3** 35 13 S 138 53 E
Strathaven, *U.K.* **22 F4** 55 40N 4 5W
Strathcona Prov. Park, *Canada* **142 D3** 49 38N 125 40W
Strathmore, *Canada* **142 C6** 51 5N 113 18W
Strathmore, *U.K.* **22 E5** 56 37N 3 7W
Strathmore, *U.S.A.* **160 J7** 36 9N 119 4W
Strathnaver, *Canada* **142 C4** 53 20N 122 33W

Tajimi 287

Susak, *Croatia* **45 D11** 44 30N 14 18 E
Susaki, *Japan* **70 D5** 33 22N 133 17 E
Susamyr, *Kyrgyzstan* **63 B6** 42 12N 73 58 E
Susamyrtau, Khrebet, *Kyrgyzstan* **63 B6** 42 8N 73 15 E
Sūsangerd, *Iran* **97 D6** 31 35N 48 6 E
Susanville, *U.S.A.* **158 F3** 40 25N 120 39W
Susch, *Switz.* **33 C10** 46 46N 10 5 E
Suşehri, *Turkey* **101 B8** 40 10N 38 6 E
Sušice, *Czech Rep.* **34 B6** 49 17N 13 30 E
Susleni, *Moldova* **53 C13** 47 25N 28 59 E
Susner, *India* **92 H7** 23 57N 76 5 E
Susong, *China* **77 B11** 30 10N 116 5 E
Susquehanna, *U.S.A.* **151 E9** 41 57N 75 36W
Susquehanna →, *U.S.A.* **151 G8** 39 33N 76 5W
Susques, *Argentina* **174 A2** 23 35 S 66 25W
Sussex, *Canada* **141 C6** 45 45N 65 37W
Sussex, *U.S.A.* **151 E10** 41 13N 74 37W
Sussex, E. □, *U.K.* **21 G8** 51 0N 0 20 E
Sussex, W. □, *U.K.* **21 G7** 51 0N 0 30W
Sustut →, *Canada* **142 B3** 56 20N 127 30W
Susubona, *Solomon Is.* **133 M10** 8 19 S 159 27 E
Susuman, *Russia* **65 C15** 62 47N 148 10 E
Susunu, *Indonesia* **79 E8** 3 20 S 133 25 E
Susurluk, *Turkey* **49 B10** 39 54N 28 8 E
Susuz, *Turkey* **101 B10** 40 46N 43 8 E
Susz, *Poland* **54 E6** 53 44N 19 20 E
Sütçüler, *Turkey* **100 D4** 37 29N 30 57 E
Şuţeşti, *Romania* **53 E12** 45 13N 27 27 E
Sutherland, *Australia* **129 C9** 34 2 S 151 4 E
Sutherland, *S. Africa* **116 E3** 32 24 S 20 40 E
Sutherland, *U.S.A.* **154 E4** 41 10N 101 8W
Sutherland Falls, *N.Z.* **131 E2** 44 48 S 167 46 E
Sutherlin, *U.S.A.* **158 E2** 43 23N 123 19W
Suthri, *India* **92 H3** 23 3N 68 55 E
Sutlej →, *Pakistan* **91 C3** 29 23N 71 3 E
Sutter, *U.S.A.* **160 F5** 39 10N 121 45W
Sutter Creek, *U.S.A.* **160 G6** 38 24N 120 48W
Sutton, *Canada* **151 A12** 45 6N 72 37W
Sutton, *N.Z.* **131 F5** 45 34 S 170 8 E
Sutton, *Nebr., U.S.A.* **154 E6** 40 36N 97 52W
Sutton, *W. Va., U.S.A.* **148 F5** 38 40N 80 43W
Sutton →, *Canada* **140 A3** 55 15N 83 45W
Sutton Coldfield, *U.K.* **21 E6** 52 35N 1 49W
Sutton in Ashfield, *U.K.* **20 D6** 53 8N 1 16W
Sutton L., *Canada* **140 B3** 54 15N 84 42W
Suttor →, *Australia* **126 C4** 21 36 S 147 2 E
Suttsu, *Japan* **68 C10** 42 48N 140 14 E
Su'u, *Solomon Is.* **133 M11** 9 11 S 160 56 E
Suva, *Fiji* **133 B2** 18 6 S 178 30 E
Suva Gora, *Macedonia* **50 E5** 41 45N 21 3 E
Suva Planina, *Serbia, Yug.* **50 C6** 43 10N 22 5 E
Suva Reka, *Kosovo, Yug.* **50 D4** 42 21N 20 50 E
Suvorov, *Russia* **58 E9** 54 7N 36 30 E
Suvorov Is. = Suwarrow Is., *Cook Is.* **135 J11** 15 0 S 163 0W
Suvorovo, *Bulgaria* **51 C11** 43 20N 27 35 E
Suwa, *Japan* **71 A10** 36 2N 138 8 E
Suwa-Ko, *Japan* **71 A10** 36 3N 138 5 E
Suwałki, *Poland* **54 D9** 54 8N 22 59 E
Suwanee, *U.S.A.* **152 A5** 34 3N 84 4W
Suwannaphum, *Thailand* **86 E4** 15 33N 103 47 E
Suwannee, *U.S.A.* **153 F6** 29 20N 83 9W
Suwannee →, *U.S.A.* **149 L4** 29 17N 83 10W
Suwannee Sd., *U.S.A.* **153 F6** 29 20N 83 15W
Suwanose-Jima, *Japan* **69 K4** 29 38N 129 43 E
Suwarrow Is., *Cook Is.* **135 J11** 15 0 S 163 0W
Suwayq aş Şuqban, *Iraq* **96 D5** 31 32N 46 7 E
Suweis, Khalîg el, *Egypt* **106 J8** 28 40N 33 0 E
Suweis, Qanâ es, *Egypt* **106 H8** 31 0N 32 20 E
Suwŏn, *S. Korea* **75 F14** 37 17N 127 1 E
Suzak, *Kazakstan* **63 A4** 44 9N 68 27 E
Suzaka, *Japan* **71 A10** 36 39N 138 19 E
Suzdal, *Russia* **58 D11** 56 29N 40 26 E
Suzhou, *Anhui, China* **74 H9** 33 41N 116 59 E
Suzhou, *Jiangsu, China* **77 B13** 31 19N 120 38 E
Suzu, *Japan* **69 F8** 37 25N 137 17 E
Suzu-Misaki, *Japan* **69 F8** 37 31N 137 21 E
Suzuka, *Japan* **71 C8** 34 55N 136 36 E
Suzuka-San, *Japan* **71 B8** 35 5N 136 30 E
Suzzara, *Italy* **44 D7** 44 59N 10 45 E
Svalbard, *Arctic* **6 B8** 78 0N 17 0 E
Svalbarð, *Norðurðingeyjarsýsla, Iceland* **11 A11** 66 12N 15 43W
Svalbarð, *Suður-þingeyjarsýsla, Iceland* **11 B8** 65 45N 18 5W
Svalöv, *Sweden* **17 J7** 55 57N 13 8 E
Svaneke, *Denmark* **17 J9** 55 8N 15 8 E
Svängsta, *Sweden* **17 H8** 56 16N 14 47 E
Svanskog, *Sweden* **16 E6** 59 11N 12 33 E
Svappavaara, *Sweden* **14 C19** 67 40N 21 3 E
Svärdsjö, *Sweden* **16 D9** 60 45N 15 54 E
Svarstad, *Norway* **18 E6** 59 27N 9 56 E
Svartå, *Sweden* **16 E8** 59 8N 14 32 E
Svartárkot, *Iceland* **11 B9** 65 20N 17 15W
Svartevatn, *Norway* **18 E3** 59 10N 6 56 E
Svartisen, *Norway* **14 C15** 66 40N 13 50 E
Svartvik, *Sweden* **16 B11** 62 19N 17 24 E
Svatove, *Ukraine* **59 H10** 49 22N 38 15 E
Svatovo = Svatove, *Ukraine* **59 H10** 49 22N 38 15 E
Svatsum, *Norway* **18 C6** 61 20N 9 50 E
Svay Chek, *Cambodia* **86 F4** 13 48N 102 58 E
Svay Rieng, *Cambodia* **78 B3** 11 9N 105 45 E
Svealand □, *Sweden* **16 D9** 60 20N 15 0 E
Svedala, *Sweden* **17 J7** 55 30N 13 15 E
Sveg, *Sweden* **16 B8** 62 2N 14 21 E
Sveindal, *Norway* **18 F4** 58 29N 7 30 E
Sveinseyri, *Iceland* **11 B3** 65 38N 23 51W
Sveio, *Norway* **18 E2** 59 33N 5 23 E
Svelgen, *Norway* **18 C2** 61 46N 5 17 E
Svelvik, *Norway* **18 E7** 59 37N 10 24 E
Svendborg, *Denmark* **17 J4** 55 4N 10 35 E
Svene, *Norway* **18 E6** 59 45N 9 31 E
Svenljunga, *Sweden* **17 G7** 57 29N 13 5 E
Svenstavik, *Sweden* **16 B8** 62 45N 14 26 E
Svenstrup, *Denmark* **17 H3** 56 58N 9 50 E
Sverdlovsk = Yekaterinburg, *Russia* **62 C8** 56 50N 60 30 E
Sverdlovsk, *Ukraine* **59 H10** 48 5N 39 47 E
Sverdrup Is., *Canada* **136 B10** 79 0N 97 0W
Svetac, *Croatia* **45 E12** 43 3N 15 43 E
Sveti Nikola, Prokhad, *Europe* **50 C6** 43 27N 22 6 E
Sveti Nikole, *Macedonia* **50 E5** 41 51N 21 56 E
Sveti Rok, *Croatia* **45 D12** 44 22N 15 39 E
Svetlaya, *Russia* **68 A9** 46 33N 138 18 E
Svetlogorsk = Svyetlahorsk, *Belarus* **59 F5** 52 38N 29 46 E
Svetlograd, *Russia* **61 H6** 45 25N 42 58 E
Svetlovodsk = Svitlovodsk, *Ukraine* **59 H7** 49 2N 33 13 E
Svetlyy, *Russia* **62 F8** 50 48N 60 51 E
Svidník, *Slovak Rep.* **35 B14** 49 20N 21 37 E
Svignaskarð, *Iceland* **11 C5** 64 40N 21 42W
Svilaja Planina, *Croatia* **45 E13** 43 49N 16 31 E
Svilajnac, *Serbia, Yug.* **50 B5** 44 15N 21 11 E
Svilengrad, *Bulgaria* **51 E10** 41 49N 26 12 E
Svinafell, *Iceland* **11 D10** 63 59N 16 51W
Svir →, *Russia* **58 B7** 60 30N 32 48 E
Sviritsa, *Russia* **58 B7** 60 29N 32 51 E
Svishtov, *Bulgaria* **51 C9** 43 36N 25 23 E
Svislach, *Belarus* **59 F3** 53 3N 24 2 E
Svitava →, *Czech Rep.* **35 B9** 49 11N 16 37 E
Svitavy, *Czech Rep.* **35 B9** 49 47N 16 28 E
Svitlovodsk, *Ukraine* **59 H7** 49 2N 33 13 E
Svobodnyy, *Russia* **65 D13** 51 20N 128 0 E
Svoge, *Bulgaria* **50 D7** 42 59N 23 23 E
Svolvær, *Norway* **14 B16** 68 15N 14 34 E
Svorkmo, *Norway* **18 A6** 63 10N 9 46 E
Svratka →, *Czech Rep.* **35 B9** 49 11N 16 38 E
Svrljig, *Serbia, Yug.* **50 C6** 43 25N 22 6 E
Svullrya, *Norway* **18 D9** 60 25N 12 23 E
Svyetlahorsk, *Belarus* **59 F5** 52 38N 29 46 E
Swa, *Burma* **90 F6** 19 15N 96 17 E
Swa Tende, *Dem. Rep. of the Congo* **115 D3** 7 9S 17 7 E
Swabian Alps = Schwäbische Alb, *Germany* **31 G5** 48 20N 9 30 E
Swainsboro, *U.S.A.* **152 C7** 32 36N 82 20W
Swakop →, *Namibia* **116 C2** 22 38 S 14 36 E
Swakopmund, *Namibia* **116 C1** 22 37 S 14 30 E
Swale →, *U.K.* **20 C6** 54 5N 1 20W
Swamihalli, *India* **95 G3** 14 52N 76 38 E
Swan →, *Australia* **125 F2** 32 3 S 115 45 E
Swan →, *Canada* **143 C8** 52 30N 100 45W
Swan Hill, *Australia* **128 C5** 35 20 S 143 33 E
Swan Hills, *Canada* **142 C5** 54 43N 115 24W
Swan Is., *W. Indies* **164 C3** 17 22N 83 57W
Swan L., *Canada* **143 C8** 52 30N 100 40W
Swan Peak, *U.S.A.* **158 C7** 47 43N 113 38W
Swan Ra., *U.S.A.* **158 C7** 48 0N 113 45W
Swan Reach, *Australia* **128 C3** 34 35 S 139 37 E
Swan River, *Canada* **143 C8** 52 10N 101 16W
Swanage, *U.K.* **21 G6** 50 36N 1 58W
Swansea, *N.S.W., Australia* **129 B9** 33 3 S 151 35 E
Swansea, *Tas., Australia* **126 G4** 42 8 S 148 4 E
Swansea, *Canada* **150 C5** 43 38N 79 28W
Swansea, *U.K.* **21 F4** 51 37N 3 57W
Swansea, *U.S.A.* **152 B8** 33 44N 81 6W
Swansea □, *U.K.* **21 F3** 51 38N 4 3W
Swanton, *U.S.A.* **157 C13** 41 35N 83 53W
Swar →, *Pakistan* **93 B5** 34 40N 72 5 E
Swartberge, *S. Africa* **116 E3** 33 20 S 22 0 E
Swartmodder, *S. Africa* **116 D3** 28 1 S 20 32 E
Swartnossob →, *Namibia* **116 C2** 23 8 S 18 42 E
Swartruggens, *S. Africa* **116 D4** 25 39 S 26 42 E
Swarzędz, *Poland* **55 F4** 52 25N 17 4 E
Swastika, *Canada* **140 C3** 48 7N 80 6W
Swatow = Shantou, *China* **77 F11** 23 18N 116 40 E
Swaziland ■, *Africa* **117 D5** 26 30 S 31 30 E
Sweden ■, *Europe* **15 G16** 57 0N 15 0 E
Swedru, *Ghana* **113 D4** 5 32N 0 41W
Sweet Home, *U.S.A.* **158 D2** 44 24N 122 44W
Sweet Springs, *U.S.A.* **156 F3** 38 58N 93 25W
Sweetgrass, *U.S.A.* **158 B8** 48 59N 111 58W
Sweetwater, *Nev., U.S.A.* **160 G7** 38 27N 119 9W
Sweetwater, *Tenn., U.S.A.* **149 H3** 35 36N 84 28W
Sweetwater, *Tex., U.S.A.* **155 J4** 32 28N 100 25W
Sweetwater →, *U.S.A.* **158 E10** 42 31N 107 2W
Swellendam, *S. Africa* **116 E3** 34 1 S 20 26 E
Swider →, *Poland* **55 F8** 52 6N 21 14 E
Świdnica, *Poland* **55 H3** 50 50N 16 30 E
Świdnik, *Poland* **55 G9** 51 13N 22 39 E
Świdwin, *Poland* **54 E2** 53 47N 15 49 E
Świebodzice, *Poland* **55 H3** 50 51N 16 20 E
Świebodzin, *Poland* **55 F2** 52 15N 15 31 E
Świecie, *Poland* **54 E5** 53 25N 18 30 E
Świerzawa, *Poland* **55 G2** 51 1N 15 54 E
Świętokrzyskie □, *Poland* **55 H7** 50 45N 20 45 E
Świętokrzyskie, Góry, *Poland* **55 H7** 51 0N 20 30 E
Swift Current, *Canada* **143 C7** 50 20N 107 45W
Swiftcurrent →, *Canada* **143 C7** 50 38N 107 44W
Swilly, L., *Ireland* **23 A4** 55 12N 7 33W
Swindon, *U.K.* **21 F6** 51 34N 1 46W
Swindon □, *U.K.* **21 F6** 51 34N 1 46W
Swinemünde = Świnoujście, *Poland* **54 E1** 53 54N 14 16 E
Swinford, *Ireland* **23 C3** 53 57N 8 58W
Świnoujście, *Poland* **54 E1** 53 54N 14 16 E
Switzerland ■, *Europe* **32 D6** 46 30N 8 0 E
Swords, *Ireland* **23 C5** 53 28N 6 13W
Swoyerville, *U.S.A.* **151 E9** 41 18N 75 53W
Syasstroy, *Russia* **58 B7** 60 9N 32 33 E
Sycamore, *Ill., U.S.A.* **157 C8** 41 59N 88 41W
Sycamore, *Ohio, U.S.A.* **157 D13** 40 57N 83 10W
Sychevka, *Russia* **58 E8** 55 59N 34 16 E
Syców, *Poland* **55 G4** 51 19N 17 40 E
Sydenham →, *Canada* **150 D2** 42 33N 82 25W
Sydney, *Australia* **129 B9** 33 53 S 151 10 E
Sydney, *Canada* **141 C7** 46 7N 60 7W
Sydney L., *Canada* **143 C10** 50 41N 94 25W
Sydney Mines, *Canada* **141 C7** 46 18N 60 15W
Sydprøven = Alluitsup Paa, *Greenland* **10 E6** 60 30N 45 35W
Sydra, G. of = Surt, Khalīj, *Libya* **108 B3** 31 40N 18 30 E
Syeverodonetsk, *Ukraine* **59 H10** 48 58N 38 35 E
Syfteland, *Norway* **18 D2** 60 14N 5 27 E
Syke, *Germany* **30 C4** 52 55N 8 50 E
Sykesville, *U.S.A.* **150 E6** 41 3N 78 50W
Sykkylven, *Norway* **18 B3** 62 23N 6 35 E
Syktyvkar, *Russia* **56 B9** 61 45N 50 40 E
Sylacauga, *U.S.A.* **152 B3** 33 10N 86 15W
Sylarna, *Sweden* **14 E15** 63 2N 12 13 E
Sylhet, *Bangla.* **90 C3** 24 54N 91 52 E
Sylt, *Germany* **30 A4** 54 54N 8 22 E
Sylte, *Norway* **18 B4** 62 18N 7 17 E
Sylva →, *Russia* **62 B6** 58 0N 56 54 E
Sylvan Beach, *U.S.A.* **151 C9** 43 12N 75 44W
Sylvan Lake, *Canada* **142 C6** 52 20N 114 3W
Sylvania, *Ga., U.S.A.* **152 C8** 32 45N 81 38W
Sylvania, *Ohio, U.S.A.* **157 C13** 41 43N 83 42W
Sylvester, *U.S.A.* **152 D6** 31 32N 83 50W
Sym, *Russia* **64 C9** 60 20N 88 18 E
Symón, *Mexico* **162 C4** 24 42N 102 35W
Synelnykove, *Ukraine* **59 H8** 48 25N 35 30 E
Synnfjell, *Norway* **18 C6** 61 5N 9 46 E
Synnott Ra., *Australia* **124 C4** 16 30 S 125 20 E
Syracuse, *Ind., U.S.A.* **157 C11** 41 26N 85 45W
Syracuse, *Kans., U.S.A.* **155 G4** 37 59N 101 45W
Syracuse, *N.Y., U.S.A.* **151 C8** 43 3N 76 9W
Syracuse, *Nebr., U.S.A.* **154 E6** 40 39N 96 11W
Syrdarya = Sirdaryo, *Uzbekistan* **63 C4** 40 50N 68 40 E
Syrdarya →, *Kazakstan* **64 E7** 46 3N 61 0 E
Syria ■, *Asia* **101 E8** 35 0N 38 0 E
Syriam, *Burma* **90 G6** 16 44N 96 19 E
Syrian Desert = Shām, Bādiyat ash, *Asia* **96 C3** 32 0N 40 0 E
Sysert, *Russia* **62 C8** 56 29N 60 49 E
Sysslebäck, *Sweden* **16 D6** 60 44N 12 52 E
Syvde, *Norway* **18 B2** 62 5N 5 44 E
Syzran, *Russia* **60 D9** 53 12N 48 30 E
Szabolcs-Szatmár-Bereg □, *Hungary* **52 B6** 48 2N 21 45 E
Szadek, *Poland* **55 G5** 51 41N 18 59 E
Szamocin, *Poland* **55 E4** 53 2N 17 7 E
Szamos →, *Hungary* **52 B7** 48 7N 22 20 E
Szamotuły, *Poland* **55 F3** 52 37N 16 33 E
Száraz →, *Hungary* **52 D6** 46 10N 21 15 E
Szarvas, *Hungary* **52 D5** 46 50N 20 38 E
Százhalombatta, *Hungary* **52 C3** 47 20N 18 58 E
Szczawnica, *Poland* **55 J7** 49 26N 20 30 E
Szczebrzeszyn, *Poland* **55 H9** 50 42N 22 59 E
Szczecin, *Poland* **54 E1** 53 27N 14 27 E
Szczecinek, *Poland* **54 E3** 53 43N 16 41 E
Szczeciński, Zalew = Stettiner Haff, *Germany* **30 B10** 53 47N 14 15 E
Szczekociny, *Poland* **55 H6** 50 38N 19 48 E
Szczucin, *Poland* **55 H8** 50 18N 21 4 E
Szczuczyn, *Poland* **54 E9** 53 36N 22 19 E
Szczyrk, *Poland* **55 J6** 49 43N 19 2 E
Szczytna, *Poland* **55 H3** 50 25N 16 28 E
Szczytno, *Poland* **54 E7** 53 33N 21 0 E
Szechwan = Sichuan □, *China* **76 B5** 30 30N 103 0 E
Szécsény, *Hungary* **52 B4** 48 7N 19 30 E
Szeged, *Hungary* **52 D5** 46 16N 20 10 E
Szeghalom, *Hungary* **52 C6** 47 1N 21 10 E
Székesfehérvár, *Hungary* **52 C3** 47 15N 18 25 E
Szekszárd, *Hungary* **52 D3** 46 22N 18 42 E
Szendrő, *Hungary* **52 B5** 48 24N 20 41 E
Szentendre, *Hungary* **52 C4** 47 39N 19 4 E
Szentes, *Hungary* **52 D5** 46 39N 20 21 E
Szentgotthárd, *Hungary* **52 D1** 46 58N 16 19 E
Szentlőrinc, *Hungary* **52 D3** 46 3N 18 1 E
Szerencs, *Hungary* **52 B6** 48 10N 21 12 E
Szigetszentmiklós, *Hungary* **52 C4** 47 21N 19 3 E
Szigetvár, *Hungary* **52 D2** 46 3N 17 46 E
Szikszó, *Hungary* **52 B5** 48 12N 20 56 E
Szklarska Poreba, *Poland* **55 H2** 50 50N 15 33 E
Szkwa →, *Poland* **55 E8** 53 11N 21 43 E
Szlichtyngowa, *Poland* **55 G3** 51 42N 16 15 E
Szob, *Hungary* **52 C3** 47 48N 18 53 E
Szolnok, *Hungary* **52 C5** 47 10N 20 15 E
Szombathely, *Hungary* **52 C1** 47 14N 16 38 E
Szprotawa, *Poland* **55 G2** 51 33N 15 35 E
Sztum, *Poland* **54 E6** 53 55N 19 1 E
Sztutowo, *Poland* **54 D6** 54 20N 19 15 E
Szubin, *Poland* **55 E4** 53 1N 17 45 E
Szydłowiec, *Poland* **55 G7** 51 15N 20 51 E
Szypliszki, *Poland* **54 D10** 54 17N 23 2 E

T

Ta Khli Khok, *Thailand* **86 E3** 15 18N 100 20 E
Ta Lai, *Vietnam* **87 G6** 11 24N 107 23 E
Tab, *Hungary* **52 D3** 46 44N 18 2 E
Tabacal, *Argentina* **174 A3** 23 15 S 64 15W
Tabaco, *Phil.* **79 B6** 13 22N 123 44 E
Tabagné, *Ivory C.* **112 D4** 7 59N 3 4W
Ţābah, *Si. Arabia* **96 E4** 26 55N 42 38 E
Tabajara, *Brazil* **173 B5** 8 56 S 62 8W
Tabalos, *Peru* **172 B2** 6 26 S 76 37W
Tabankort, *Niger* **113 B5** 17 44N 0 20 E
Tabar Is., *Papua N. G.* **132 B7** 2 50 S 152 0 E
Tabarka, *Tunisia* **108 A1** 36 56N 8 46 E
Ţabas, *Khorāsān, Iran* **97 C9** 32 48N 60 12 E
Ţabas, *Khorāsān, Iran* **97 C8** 33 35N 56 55 E
Tabasará, Serranía de, *Panama* **164 E3** 8 35N 81 40W
Tabasco □, *Mexico* **163 D6** 17 45N 93 30W
Tabāsīn, *Iran* **97 D8** 31 12N 57 54 E
Tabatinga, *Brazil* **172 A4** 4 16 S 69 56W
Tabatinga, Serra da, *Brazil* **170 D3** 10 30 S 44 0W
Tabayin, *Burma* **90 D5** 22 42N 95 20 E
Tabelbala, Kahal de, *Algeria* **111 C4** 28 47N 2 0W
Taber, *Canada* **142 D6** 49 47N 112 8W
Taberg, *Sweden* **17 G8** 57 40N 14 5 E
Taberg, *U.S.A.* **151 C9** 43 18N 75 37W
Tabi, *Angola* **115 D2** 8 10 S 13 18 E
Tabira, *Brazil* **170 C4** 7 35 S 37 33W
Tabla, *Niger* **113 C5** 13 46N 3 1 E
Tablas I., *Phil.* **79 B6** 12 25N 122 2 E
Tablas Strait, *Phil.* **80 E3** 12 40N 121 48 E
Table B. = Tafelbaai, *S. Africa* **116 E2** 33 35 S 18 25 E
Table B., *Canada* **141 B8** 53 40N 56 25W
Table Grove, *U.S.A.* **156 D6** 40 20N 90 27W
Table Mt., *S. Africa* **116 E2** 34 0 S 18 22 E
Table Rock L., *U.S.A.* **155 G8** 36 36N 93 19W
Tabletop, Mt., *Australia* **126 C4** 23 24 S 147 11 E
Tabocal, *Brazil* **169 D6** 2 42 S 57 40W
Tábor, *Czech Rep.* **34 B7** 49 25N 14 39 E
Tabora, *Tanzania* **118 D3** 5 2 S 32 50 E
Tabora □, *Tanzania* **118 D3** 5 0 S 33 0 E
Tabou, *Ivory C.* **112 E3** 4 30N 7 20W
Tabrīz, *Iran* **101 C12** 38 7N 46 20 E
Tabuaeran, *Pac. Oc.* **135 G12** 3 51N 159 22W
Tabuenca, *Spain* **40 D3** 41 42N 1 33W
Tabuk, *Phil.* **80 C3** 17 24N 121 25 E
Tabūk, *Si. Arabia* **96 D3** 28 23N 36 36 E
Tabwemasana, Mt., *Vanuatu* **133 E4** 15 20 S 166 44 E
Täby, *Sweden* **16 E12** 59 28N 18 4 E
Tacámbaro de Codallos, *Mexico* **162 D4** 19 14N 101 28W
Tacariqua, Laguna de, *Venezuela* **168 A4** 10 15N 65 50W
Tacheng, *China* **72 B3** 46 40N 82 58 E
Tach'i, *Taiwan* **77 E13** 24 46N 121 0 E
Tachia, *Taiwan* **77 E13** 24 25N 120 28 E
Tachibana-Wan, *Japan* **70 E2** 32 45N 130 7 E
Tachikawa, *Japan* **71 B11** 35 42N 139 25 E
Tach'ing Shan = Daqing Shan, *China* **74 D6** 40 40N 111 0 E
Táchira □, *Venezuela* **168 B3** 8 7N 72 15W
Tachov, *Czech Rep.* **34 B5** 49 47N 12 39 E
Tácina →, *Italy* **47 D9** 38 57N 16 55 E
Tacloban, *Phil.* **79 B6** 11 15N 124 58 E
Tacna, *Peru* **172 D3** 18 0 S 70 20W
Tacna □, *Peru* **172 D3** 17 40 S 70 20W
Tacoma, *U.S.A.* **160 C4** 47 14N 122 26W
Tacuarembó, *Uruguay* **175 C4** 31 45 S 56 0W
Tacurong, *Phil.* **81 H5** 6 40N 124 41 E
Tacutu →, *Brazil* **169 C5** 3 1N 60 29W
Tademaït, Plateau du, *Algeria* **111 C5** 28 30N 2 30 E
Tadent, O. →, *Algeria* **111 D6** 22 25N 6 40 E
Tadio, L., *Ivory C.* **112 D3** 5 10N 5 15W
Tadjerdjeri, O. →, *Algeria* **111 C6** 26 0N 8 0 E
Tadjerouna, *Algeria* **111 B5** 33 31N 2 3 E
Tadjettaret, O. →, *Algeria* **111 D6** 21 20N 7 22 E
Tadjmout, *Oasis, Algeria* **111 B5** 33 52N 2 30 E
Tadjmout, *Saoura, Algeria* **111 C5** 25 37N 3 48 E
Tadjoura, *Djibouti* **102 E3** 11 50N 42 55 E
Tadjoura, Golfe de, *Djibouti* **107 E5** 11 50N 43 0 E
Tadmor, *N.Z.* **131 B7** 41 27 S 172 45 E
Tadotsu, *Japan* **70 C5** 34 16N 133 45 E
Tadoule, L., *Canada* **143 B9** 58 36N 98 20W
Tadoussac, *Canada* **141 C6** 48 11N 69 42W
Tadpatri, *India* **95 G4** 14 55N 78 1 E
Tadzhikistan = Tajikistan ■, *Asia* **64 F8** 38 30N 70 0 E
Taechŏn-ni, *S. Korea* **75 F14** 36 21N 126 36 E
Taegu, *S. Korea* **75 G15** 35 50N 128 37 E
Taegwan, *N. Korea* **75 D13** 40 13N 125 12 E
Taejŏn, *S. Korea* **75 F14** 36 20N 127 28 E
Tafalla, *Spain* **40 C3** 42 30N 1 41W
Tafar, *Sudan* **107 F2** 6 52N 28 15 E
Tafassasset, O. →, *Algeria* **111 D6** 22 0N 9 57 E
Tafelbaai, *S. Africa* **116 E2** 33 35 S 18 25 E
Tafelney, C., *Morocco* **110 B3** 31 3N 9 51W
Tafermaar, *Indonesia* **79 F8** 6 47 S 134 10 E
Taffermit, *Morocco* **110 C3** 29 37N 9 15W
Tafí Viejo, *Argentina* **174 B2** 26 43 S 65 17W
Tafīhān, *Iran* **97 D7** 29 25N 52 39 E
Tafiré, *Ivory C.* **112 D3** 9 4N 5 4W
Tafjord, *Norway* **18 B4** 62 14N 7 24 E
Tafnidilt, *Morocco* **110 C2** 28 47N 10 58W
Tafo, *Ghana* **113 D4** 6 15N 0 20W
Tafraoute, *Morocco* **110 C3** 29 50N 8 58W
Tafresh, *Iran* **97 C6** 34 45N 49 57 E
Taft, *Iran* **97 D7** 31 45N 54 14 E
Taft, *Phil.* **79 B7** 11 57N 125 30 E
Taft, *U.S.A.* **161 K7** 35 8N 119 28W
Taftān, Kūh-e, *Iran* **97 D9** 28 40N 61 0 E
Taga, *W. Samoa* **133 W23** 13 46 S 172 28W
Taga Dzong, *Bhutan* **90 B2** 27 5N 89 55 E
Tagana-an, *Phil.* **81 G5** 9 42N 125 35 E
Taganrog, *Russia* **59 J10** 47 12N 38 50 E
Taganrogskiy Zaliv, *Russia* **59 J10** 47 0N 38 30 E
Tagânt, *Mauritania* **112 B2** 18 20N 11 0W
Tagap Ga, *Burma* **90 B6** 26 56N 96 13 E
Tagatay, *Phil.* **80 D3** 14 6N 120 56 E
Tagauayan I., *Phil.* **81 F3** 10 58N 121 13 E
Tagbilaran, *Phil.* **79 C6** 9 39N 123 51 E
Tage, *Papua N. G.* **132 D2** 6 19 S 143 20 E
Tággia, *Italy* **44 E4** 43 52N 7 51 E
Taghzout, *Morocco* **110 B4** 33 30N 4 49W
Tagish, *Canada* **142 A2** 60 19N 134 16W
Tagish L., *Canada* **142 A2** 60 10N 134 20W
Tagkawayan, *Phil.* **80 E4** 13 58N 122 32 E
Tagliacozzo, *Italy* **45 F10** 42 4N 13 14 E
Tagliamento →, *Italy* **45 C10** 45 38N 13 6 E
Táglio di Po, *Italy* **45 D9** 45 0N 12 12 E
Tagna, *Colombia* **168 D3** 2 24 S 70 37W
Tago, *Phil.* **81 G6** 9 2N 126 13 E
Tago, Mt., *Phil.* **81 G5** 8 23N 125 5 E
Tagomago, *Spain* **39 B8** 39 2N 1 39 E
Tagourăret, *Mauritania* **112 B3** 17 45N 7 45W
Taguatinga, *Brazil* **171 D3** 12 16 S 42 26W
Tagudin, *Phil.* **80 C3** 16 56N 120 27 E
Tagula, *Papua N. G.* **132 F7** 11 22 S 153 15 E
Tagula I., *Papua N. G.* **132 F7** 11 30 S 153 30 E
Tagum, *Phil.* **79 C7** 7 33N 125 53 E
Tagus = Tejo →, *Europe* **43 F2** 38 40N 9 24W
Tahakopa, *N.Z.* **131 G4** 46 30 S 169 23 E
Tahala, *Morocco* **110 B4** 34 0N 4 28W
Tahan, Gunong, *Malaysia* **87 K4** 4 34N 102 17 E
Tahānah-ye sūr Gol, *Afghan.* **91 C2** 31 43N 67 53 E
Tahara, *Japan* **71 C9** 34 40N 137 16 E
Tahat, *Algeria* **111 D6** 23 18N 5 33 E
Tāherī, *Iran* **97 E7** 27 43N 52 20 E
Tahiti, *Pac. Oc.* **135 J13** 17 37 S 149 27W
Tahlequah, *U.S.A.* **155 H7** 35 55N 94 58W
Tahoe, L., *U.S.A.* **160 G6** 39 6N 120 2W
Tahoe City, *U.S.A.* **160 F6** 39 10N 120 9W
Tahoka, *U.S.A.* **155 J4** 33 10N 101 48W
Taholah, *U.S.A.* **160 C2** 47 21N 124 17W
Tahora, *N.Z.* **130 F3** 39 2 S 174 49 E
Tahoua, *Niger* **113 C6** 14 57N 5 16 E
Tahrūd, *Iran* **97 D8** 29 26N 57 49 E
Tahsis, *Canada* **142 D3** 49 55N 126 40W
Tahta, *Egypt* **106 B3** 26 44N 31 32 E
Tahtaköprü, *Turkey* **51 G13** 39 57N 29 39 E
Tahtalı Dağları, *Turkey* **100 C7** 38 20N 36 0 E
Tahuamanu →, *Bolivia* **172 C4** 11 6 S 67 36W
Tahulandang, *Indonesia* **79 D7** 2 27N 125 23 E
Tahuna, *Indonesia* **79 D7** 3 38N 125 30 E
Taï, *Ivory C.* **112 D3** 5 55N 7 30W
Tai Hu, *China* **77 B12** 31 5N 120 10 E
Tai Shan, *China* **75 F9** 36 25N 117 20 E
Tai'an, *China* **75 F9** 36 12N 117 8 E
Taibei = T'aipei, *Taiwan* **77 E13** 25 2N 121 30 E
Taibique, *Canary Is.* **39 G2** 27 42N 17 58W
Taibus Qi, *China* **74 D8** 41 54N 115 22 E
Taicang, *China* **77 B13** 31 30N 121 5 E
T'aichung, *Taiwan* **77 E13** 24 9N 120 37 E
Taieri →, *N.Z.* **131 G5** 46 3 S 170 12 E
Taiga Madema, *Libya* **108 D3** 23 46N 15 25 E
Taigu, *China* **74 F7** 37 28N 112 30 E
Taihang Shan, *China* **74 G7** 36 0N 113 30 E
Taihape, *N.Z.* **130 F4** 39 41 S 175 48 E
Taihe, *Anhui, China* **74 H8** 33 20N 115 42 E
Taihe, *Jiangxi, China* **77 D10** 26 47N 114 52 E
Taihu, *China* **77 B11** 30 22N 116 20 E
Taijiang, *China* **76 D7** 26 39N 108 21 E
Taikang, *China* **74 G8** 34 5N 114 50 E
Taikkyi, *Burma* **90 G6** 17 20N 96 0 E
Tailem Bend, *Australia* **128 C3** 35 12 S 139 29 E
Tailfingen, *Germany* **31 G5** 48 15N 9 1 E
Tailuko, *Taiwan* **77 E13** 24 9N 121 37 E
Taimyr Peninsula = Taymyr, Poluostrov, *Russia* **65 B11** 75 0N 100 0 E
Tain, *U.K.* **22 D4** 57 49N 4 4W
T'ainan, *Taiwan* **77 F13** 23 0N 120 10 E
Taínaron, Ákra, *Greece* **48 E4** 36 22N 22 27 E
Taingyo, *Burma* **90 G5** 17 49N 94 29 E
Taining, *China* **77 D11** 26 54N 117 9 E
Taiobeiras, *Brazil* **171 E3** 15 49 S 42 14W
T'aipei, *Taiwan* **77 E13** 25 2N 121 30 E
Taiping, *China* **77 B12** 30 15N 118 6 E
Taiping, *Malaysia* **78 D2** 4 51N 100 44 E
Taipingzhen, *China* **74 H6** 33 35N 111 42 E
Taipu, *Brazil* **170 C4** 5 37 S 35 36W
Tairbeart = Tarbert, *U.K.* **22 D2** 57 54N 6 49W
Taisha, *Japan* **70 B4** 35 24N 132 40 E
Taishan, *China* **77 F9** 22 14N 112 41 E
Taishun, *China* **77 D12** 27 30N 119 42 E
Taita Hills, *Kenya* **118 C4** 3 25 S 38 15 E
Taitao, C., *Chile* **176 C1** 45 53 S 75 5W
Taitao, Pen. de, *Chile* **176 C2** 46 30 S 75 0W
T'aitung, *Taiwan* **77 F13** 22 43N 121 4 E
Taivalkoski, *Finland* **14 D23** 65 33N 28 12 E
Taiwan ■, *Asia* **77 F13** 23 30N 121 0 E
Taiwan Strait, *Asia* **77 E12** 24 40N 120 0 E
Taixing, *China* **77 A13** 32 11N 120 0 E
Taiyara, *Sudan* **107 E3** 13 12N 30 47 E
Taïyetos Óros, *Greece* **48 D4** 37 0N 22 23 E
Taiyiba, *Israel* **103 C4** 32 36N 35 27 E
Taiyuan, *China* **74 F7** 37 52N 112 33 E
Taizhong = T'aichung, *Taiwan* **77 E13** 24 9N 120 37 E
Taizhou, *China* **77 A12** 32 28N 119 55 E
Taizhou Liedao, *China* **77 C13** 28 30N 121 55 E
Ta'izz, *Yemen* **98 D4** 13 35N 44 2 E
Tājābād, *Iran* **97 D7** 30 2N 54 24 E
Tajapuru, Furo do, *Brazil* **170 B1** 1 50 S 50 25W
Tajarḥī, *Libya* **108 D2** 24 21N 14 28 E
Tajikistan ■, *Asia* **64 F8** 38 30N 70 0 E
Tajima, *Japan* **69 F8** 37 12N 139 46 E
Tajimi, *Japan* **71 B9** 35 19N 137 8 E

Tajo = Tejo →, *Europe* **43 F2** 38 40N 9 24W
Tajrīsh, *Iran* **97 C6** 35 48N 51 25 E
Tājūrā, *Libya* **108 B2** 32 51N 13 21 E
Tak, *Thailand* **78 A1** 16 52N 99 8 E
Takāb, *Iran* **101 D12** 36 24N 47 7 E
Takachiho, *Japan* **70 E3** 32 42N 131 18 E
Takachu, *Botswana* **116 C3** 22 37 S 21 58 E
Takada, *Japan* **69 F9** 37 7N 138 15 E
Takahagi, *Japan* **69 F10** 36 43N 140 45 E
Takahashi, *Japan* **70 C5** 34 51N 133 39 E
Takaka, *N.Z.* **131 A7** 40 51 S 172 50 E
Takamatsu, *Japan* **70 C6** 34 20N 134 5 E
Takanabe, *Japan* **70 E3** 32 8N 131 30 E
Takaoka, *Japan* **71 A8** 36 47N 137 0 E
Takapau, *N.Z.* **130 G5** 40 2 S 176 21 E
Takapuna, *N.Z.* **130 C3** 36 47 S 174 47 E
Takasago, *Japan* **70 C6** 34 45N 134 48 E
Takasaki, *Japan* **71 A10** 36 20N 139 0 E
Takase, *Japan* **70 C5** 34 7N 133 48 E
Takatsuki, *Japan* **71 C7** 34 51N 135 37 E
Takaungu, *Kenya* **118 C4** 3 38 S 39 52 E
Takawa, *Japan* **70 D2** 33 38N 130 51 E
Takayama, *Japan* **71 A9** 36 18N 137 11 E
Takayama-Bonchi, *Japan* **71 B9** 36 0N 137 18 E
Take-Shima, *Japan* **69 J5** 30 49N 130 26 E
Takefu, *Japan* **71 B8** 35 50N 136 10 E
Takehara, *Japan* **70 C4** 34 21N 132 55 E
Takengon, *Indonesia* **78 D1** 4 45N 96 50 E
Takeo, *Japan* **70 D2** 33 12N 130 1 E
Tåkern, *Sweden* **17 F8** 58 22N 14 45 E
Tākestān, *Iran* **97 C6** 36 0N 49 40 E
Taketa, *Japan* **70 E3** 32 58N 131 24 E
Takev, *Cambodia* **78 B2** 10 59N 104 47 E
Takh, *India* **93 C7** 33 6N 77 32 E
Takhār □, *Afghan.* **91 A3** 36 40N 70 0 E
Takht-Sulaiman, *Pakistan* **92 D3** 31 40N 69 58 E
Taki, *Papua N. G.* **132 D8** 6 29 S 155 52 E
Takikawa, *Japan* **68 C10** 43 33N 141 54 E
Takla L., *Canada* **142 B3** 55 15N 125 45W
Takla Landing, *Canada* **142 B3** 55 30N 125 50W
Takla Makan = Taklamakan Shamo, *China* **72 C3** 38 0N 83 0 E
Taklamakan Shamo, *China* **72 C3** 38 0N 83 0 E
Takotna, *U.S.A.* **144 E8** 62 59N 156 4W
Taku, *Japan* **70 D2** 33 18N 130 3 E
Taku →, *Canada* **142 B2** 58 30N 133 50W
Takum, *Nigeria* **113 D6** 7 18N 9 36 E
Takuma, *Japan* **70 C5** 34 13N 133 40 E
Takundi, *Dem. Rep. of the Congo* **115 C3** 4 45 S 16 34 E
Takutu →, *Guyana* **169 C5** 3 1N 60 29W
Tal Halāl, *Iran* **97 D7** 28 54N 55 1 E
Tala, *Uruguay* **175 C4** 34 21 S 55 46W
Talachyn, *Belarus* **58 E5** 54 25N 29 42 E
Talacogan, *Phil.* **81 G5** 8 32N 125 39 E
Talagang, *Pakistan* **92 C5** 32 55N 72 25 E
Talagante, *Chile* **174 C1** 33 40 S 70 50W
Talaimannar, *Sri Lanka* **95 K4** 9 6N 79 43 E
Talaïnt, *Morocco* **110 C3** 29 41N 9 40W
Talak, *Niger* **113 B6** 18 0N 5 0 E
Talakag, *Phil.* **81 G5** 8 16N 124 37 E
Talamanca, Cordillera de, *Cent. Amer.* **164 E3** 9 20N 83 20W
Talant, *France* **27 E11** 47 19N 4 58 E
Talara, *Peru* **172 A1** 4 38 S 81 18W
Talas, *Kyrgyzstan* **64 E8** 42 30N 72 13 E
Talas, *Turkey* **100 C6** 38 41N 35 33 E
Talas →, *Kazakstan* **63 B5** 44 0N 70 20 E
Talasea, *Papua N. G.* **132 C6** 5 20 S 150 2 E
Talasskiy Alatau, Khrebet, *Kyrgyzstan* **63 B6** 42 15N 72 0 E
Talâta, *Egypt* **103 E1** 30 36N 32 20 E
Talata Mafara, *Nigeria* **113 C6** 12 38N 6 4 E
Talaud, Kepulauan, *Indonesia* **79 D7** 4 30N 127 10 E
Talaud Is. = Talaud, Kepulauan, *Indonesia* **79 D7** 4 30N 127 10 E
Talavera de la Reina, *Spain* **42 F6** 39 55N 4 46W
Talavera la Real, *Spain* **43 G4** 38 53N 6 46W
Talawgyi, *Burma* **90 C6** 25 4N 97 19 E
Talayan, *Phil.* **79 C6** 6 52N 124 24 E
Talayuela, *Spain* **42 F5** 39 59N 5 36W
Talbandh, *India* **93 H12** 22 3N 86 20 E
Talbert, Sillon de, *France* **26 D3** 48 53N 3 5W
Talbot, C., *Australia* **124 B4** 13 48 S 126 43 E
Talbotton, *U.S.A.* **152 C5** 32 41N 84 32W
Talbragar →, *Australia* **129 B8** 32 12 S 148 37 E
Talca, *Chile* **174 D1** 35 28 S 71 40W
Talcahuano, *Chile* **174 D1** 36 40 S 73 10W
Talcher, *India* **94 D7** 21 0N 85 18 E
Talcho, *Niger* **113 C5** 14 44N 3 28 E
Taldy Kurgan = Taldyqorghan, *Kazakstan* **64 E8** 45 10N 78 45 E
Taldyqorghan, *Kazakstan* **64 E8** 45 10N 78 45 E
Tālesh, *Iran* **97 B6** 37 58N 48 58 E
Tālesh, Kūhhā-ye, *Iran* **97 B6** 37 42N 48 55 E
Talgar, *Kazakstan* **63 B8** 43 19N 77 15 E
Talgar, Pik, *Kazakstan* **63 B8** 43 5N 77 20 E
Talguharai, *Sudan* **106 D4** 18 19N 35 56 E
Talguppa, *India* **95 G2** 14 13N 74 56 E
Tali Post, *Sudan* **107 F3** 5 55N 30 44 E
Taliabu, *Indonesia* **79 E6** 1 50 S 125 0 E
Talibon, *Phil.* **79 B6** 10 9N 124 20 E
Talibong, Ko, *Thailand* **87 J2** 7 15N 99 23 E
Talihina, *U.S.A.* **155 H7** 34 45N 95 3W
Talikota, *India* **95 F3** 16 29N 76 17 E
Talimardzhan = Tallymerjen, *Turkmenistan* **63 D2** 38 23N 65 37 E
Talipao, *Phil.* **81 J3** 5 59N 121 7 E
Talisay, *Phil.* **81 F4** 10 44N 122 58 E
Talisayan, *Phil.* **81 G5** 9 0N 124 55 E
Talitsa, *Russia* **62 C9** 57 0N 63 43 E
Taliwang, *Indonesia* **78 F5** 8 50 S 116 55 E
Tall 'Afar, *Iraq* **101 D10** 36 22N 42 27 E
Tall Kalakh, *Syria* **103 A5** 34 41N 36 15 E
Talla, *Egypt* **106 B3** 28 5N 30 43 E
Talladega, *U.S.A.* **152 B3** 33 26N 86 6W
Tallahassee, *U.S.A.* **152 E5** 30 27N 84 17W
Tallangatta, *Australia* **129 D7** 36 15 S 147 19 E
Tallapoosa, *U.S.A.* **152 B4** 33 45N 85 17W
Tallapoosa →, *U.S.A.* **152 C3** 32 30N 86 16W
Tallard, *France* **29 D10** 44 28N 6 3 E
Tallarook, *Australia* **129 D6** 37 5 S 145 6 E
Tallassee, *U.S.A.* **152 C4** 32 32N 85 54W
Tallawang, *Australia* **129 B8** 32 12 S 149 28 E
Tällberg, *Sweden* **16 D9** 60 51N 15 2 E
Tallering Pk., *Australia* **125 E2** 28 6 S 115 37 E
Talli, *Pakistan* **92 E3** 29 32N 68 8 E
Tallinn, *Estonia* **15 G21** 59 22N 24 48 E
Tallmadge, *U.S.A.* **150 E3** 41 6N 81 27W
Tallulah, *U.S.A.* **155 J9** 32 25N 91 11W
Tallymerjen, *Turkmenistan* **63 D2** 38 23N 65 37 E
Tălmaciu, *Romania* **53 E9** 45 38N 24 19 E
Talmest, *Morocco* **110 B3** 31 48N 9 21W
Talmont-St-Hilaire, *France* **28 B2** 46 27N 1 37W
Talne, *Ukraine* **59 H6** 48 50N 30 44 E
Talnoye = Talne, *Ukraine* **59 H6** 48 50N 30 44 E
Taloda, *India* **94 D2** 21 34N 74 11 E
Talodi, *Sudan* **107 E3** 10 35N 30 22 E
Tāloqān, *Afghan.* **91 A3** 36 44N 69 33 E
Talovaya, *Russia* **60 E5** 51 6N 40 45 E
Taloyoak, *Canada* **138 B10** 69 32N 93 32W
Talpa de Allende, *Mexico* **162 C4** 20 23N 104 51W
Talquin, L., *U.S.A.* **152 E5** 30 23N 84 39W
Talsi, *Latvia* **15 H20** 57 10N 22 30 E
Talsi □, *Latvia* **54 A9** 57 20N 22 40 E
Talsinnt, *Morocco* **111 B4** 32 33N 3 27W
Taltal, *Chile* **174 B1** 25 23 S 70 33W
Taltson →, *Canada* **142 A6** 61 24N 112 46W
Talwood, *Australia* **127 D4** 28 29 S 149 29 E
Talyawalka →, *Australia* **128 B5** 32 28 S 142 22 E
Tam Chau, *Vietnam* **87 G5** 10 48N 105 12 E
Tam Ky, *Vietnam* **86 E7** 15 34N 108 29 E
Tam Quan, *Vietnam* **86 E7** 14 35N 109 3 E
Tama, *U.S.A.* **156 C4** 41 58N 92 35W
Tamalameque, *Colombia* **168 B3** 8 52N 73 49W
Tamale, *Ghana* **113 D4** 9 22N 0 50W
Taman, *Russia* **59 K9** 45 14N 36 41 E
Tamana, *Japan* **70 E2** 32 58N 130 32 E
Tamana, *Kiribati* **123 A13** 2 30 S 175 59 E
Tamanar, *Morocco* **110 B3** 31 1N 9 46W
Tamani, *Mali* **112 C3** 13 20N 6 50W
Tamano, *Japan* **70 C5** 34 29N 133 59 E
Tamanrasset, *Algeria* **111 D6** 22 50N 5 30 E
Tamanrasset, O. →, *Algeria* **111 D5** 22 0N 2 0 E
Tamanthi, *Burma* **90 C5** 25 19N 95 17 E
Tamaqua, *U.S.A.* **151 F9** 40 48N 75 58W
Tamar →, *U.K.* **21 G3** 50 27N 4 15W
Támara, *Colombia* **168 B3** 5 50N 72 10W
Tamarac, *U.S.A.* **153 J9** 26 12N 80 10W
Tamarang, *Australia* **129 A9** 31 27 S 150 5 E
Tamarinda, *Spain* **39 B10** 39 55N 3 49 E
Tamarite de Litera, *Spain* **40 D5** 41 52N 0 25 E
Tamaroa, *U.S.A.* **156 F7** 38 8N 89 14W
Tamashima, *Japan* **70 C5** 34 32N 133 40 E
Tamási, *Hungary* **52 D3** 46 40N 18 18 E
Tamaské, *Niger* **113 C6** 14 49N 5 43 E
Tamaulipas □, *Mexico* **163 C5** 24 0N 99 0W
Tamaulipas, Sierra de, *Mexico* **163 C5** 23 30N 98 20W
Tamazula, *Mexico* **162 C3** 24 55N 106 58W
Tamazunchale, *Mexico* **163 C5** 21 16N 98 47W
Tamba-Dabatou, *Guinea* **112 C2** 11 50N 10 40W
Tambacounda, *Senegal* **112 C2** 13 45N 13 40W
Tambaram, *India* **95 H5** 12 55N 80 7 E
Tambelan, Kepulauan, *Indonesia* **78 D3** 1 0N 107 30 E
Tambellup, *Australia* **125 F2** 34 4 S 117 37 E
Tambo, *Australia* **126 C4** 24 54 S 146 14 E
Tambo, *Peru* **172 C3** 12 57 S 74 1W
Tambo →, *Peru* **172 C3** 10 42 S 73 47W
Tambo de Mora, *Peru* **172 C2** 13 30 S 76 8W
Tambobamba, *Peru* **172 C3** 13 54 S 72 8W
Tambohorano, *Madag.* **117 B7** 17 30 S 43 58 E
Tambopata →, *Peru* **172 C4** 13 21 S 69 36W
Tambora, *Indonesia* **78 F5** 8 12 S 118 5 E
Tamboritha, Mt., *Australia* **129 D7** 37 31 S 146 40 E
Tambov, *Russia* **60 D5** 52 45N 41 28 E
Tambre →, *Spain* **42 C2** 42 49N 8 53W
Tambuku, *Indonesia* **79 G15** 7 8 S 113 40 E
Tamburâ, *Sudan* **107 F2** 5 40N 27 25 E
Tambuyukan, Gunong, *Malaysia* **85 A5** 6 13N 116 39 E
Tâmchekket, *Mauritania* **112 B2** 17 25N 10 40W
Tamdybulak, *Uzbekistan* **63 C2** 41 46N 64 36 E
Tame, *Colombia* **168 B3** 6 28N 71 44W
Tâmega →, *Portugal* **42 D2** 41 5N 8 21W
Tamelelt, *Morocco* **110 B3** 31 50N 7 32W
Tamenglong, *India* **90 C4** 25 0N 93 35 E
Tamerlanovka, *Kazakstan* **63 B4** 42 36N 69 17 E
Tamerza, *Tunisia* **108 B1** 34 23N 7 58 E
Tamgué, Massif du, *Guinea* **112 C2** 12 0N 12 18W
Tamiahua, L. de, *Mexico* **163 C5** 21 30N 97 30W
Tamiami Canal, *U.S.A.* **153 K8** 25 50N 81 0W
Tamil Nadu □, *India* **95 J3** 11 0N 77 0 E
Tamis →, *Serbia, Yug.* **52 F5** 44 51N 20 39 E
Tamluk, *India* **93 H12** 22 18N 87 58 E
Tammerfors = Tampere, *Finland* **15 F20** 61 30N 23 50 E
Tammisaari, *Finland* **15 F20** 60 0N 23 26 E
Tämnaren, *Sweden* **16 D11** 60 10N 17 25 E
Tamo Abu, Pegunungan, *Malaysia* **78 D5** 3 10N 115 5 E
Tampa, *Angola* **115 F2** 15 30 S 13 27 E
Tampa, *U.S.A.* **149 M4** 27 57N 82 27W
Tampa B., *U.S.A.* **149 M4** 27 50N 82 30W
Tamparan, *Phil.* **81 H5** 7 53N 124 20 E
Tampere, *Finland* **15 F20** 61 30N 23 50 E
Tampico, *Mexico* **163 C5** 22 20N 97 50W
Tampico, *U.S.A.* **156 C7** 41 38N 89 47W
Tampin, *Malaysia* **87 L4** 2 28N 102 13 E
Tamrah, *Si. Arabia* **98 B4** 20 24N 45 25 E
Tamri, *Morocco* **110 B3** 30 49N 9 50W
Tamrida = Qādib, *Yemen* **99 D6** 12 37N 53 57 E
Tamsweg, *Austria* **34 D6** 47 7N 13 49 E
Tamuja →, *Spain* **43 F4** 39 38N 6 29W
Tamworth, *Australia* **129 A9** 31 7 S 150 58 E
Tamworth, *Canada* **150 B8** 44 29N 77 0W
Tamworth, *U.K.* **21 E6** 52 39N 1 41W
Tamyang, *S. Korea* **75 G14** 35 19N 126 59 E
Tan An, *Vietnam* **87 G6** 10 32N 106 25 E
Tan-Tan, *Morocco* **110 C2** 28 29N 11 1W
Tana →, *Kenya* **118 C5** 2 32 S 40 31 E
Tana →, *Norway* **14 A23** 70 30N 28 14 E
Tana, L., *Ethiopia* **102 E2** 13 5N 37 30 E
Tana River, *Kenya* **118 C4** 2 0 S 39 30 E
Tanabe, *Japan* **71 D7** 33 44N 135 22 E
Tanabi, *Brazil* **171 F2** 20 37 S 49 37W
Tanacross, *U.S.A.* **144 E12** 63 23N 143 21W
Tanafjorden, *Norway* **14 A23** 70 45N 28 25 E
Tanaga, Pta., *Canary Is.* **39 G1** 27 42N 18 10W
Tanaga I., *U.S.A.* **144 L3** 51 48N 177 53W
Tanaga Volcano, *U.S.A.* **144 L3** 51 53N 178 8W
Tanah Merah, *Malaysia* **84 A2** 5 48N 102 9 E
Tanahbala, *Indonesia* **78 E1** 0 30 S 98 30 E
Tanahgrogot, *Indonesia* **78 E5** 1 55 S 116 15 E
Tanahjampea, *Indonesia* **79 F6** 7 10 S 120 35 E
Tanahmasa, *Indonesia* **78 E1** 0 12 S 98 39 E
Tanahmerah, *Indonesia* **79 F10** 6 5 S 140 16 E
Tanakpur, *India* **93 E9** 29 5N 80 7 E
Tanakura, *Japan* **69 F10** 37 10N 140 20 E
Tanamalwila, *Sri Lanka* **95 L5** 6 26N 81 8 E
Tanami, *Australia* **124 C4** 19 59 S 129 43 E
Tanami Desert, *Australia* **124 C5** 18 50 S 132 0 E
Tanana →, *U.S.A.* **138 B4** 65 10N 151 58W
Tananarive = Antananarivo, *Madag.* **117 B8** 18 55 S 47 31 E
Tananger, *Norway* **18 F2** 58 57N 5 37 E
Tanannt, *Morocco* **110 B3** 31 54N 6 56W
Tánaro →, *Italy* **44 D5** 44 55N 8 40 E
Tanauan, *Phil.* **80 D3** 14 5N 121 10 E
Tanay, *Phil.* **80 D3** 14 30N 121 17 E
Tanba-Sanchi, *Japan* **71 B7** 35 7N 135 48 E
Tancheng, *China* **75 G10** 34 25N 118 20 E
Tanch'ŏn, *N. Korea* **75 D15** 40 27N 128 54 E
Tanda, *Ut. P., India* **93 F10** 26 33N 82 35 E
Tanda, *Ut. P., India* **93 E8** 28 57N 78 56 E
Tanda, *Ivory C.* **112 D4** 7 48N 3 10W
Tandag, *Phil.* **79 C7** 9 4N 126 9 E
Tandaia, *Tanzania* **119 D3** 9 25 S 34 15 E
Tăndărei, *Romania* **53 F12** 44 39N 27 40 E
Tandaué, *Angola* **116 B2** 16 58 S 18 5 E
Tandil, *Argentina* **174 D4** 37 15 S 59 6W
Tandil, Sa. del, *Argentina* **174 D4** 37 30 S 59 0W
Tandlianwala, *Pakistan* **92 D5** 31 3N 73 9 E
Tando Adam, *Pakistan* **91 D3** 25 45N 68 40 E
Tando Allahyar, *Pakistan* **92 G3** 25 28N 68 43 E
Tando Bago, *Pakistan* **92 G3** 24 47N 68 58 E
Tando Mohommed Khan, *Pakistan* **92 G3** 25 8N 68 32 E
Tando-Zinze, *Angola* **115 D2** 5 22 S 12 30 E
Tandou-Bengou, *Congo* **114 C2** 3 50 S 11 44 E
Tandou L., *Australia* **128 B5** 32 40 S 142 5 E
Tandragee, *U.K.* **23 B5** 54 21N 6 24W
Tandsjöborg, *Sweden* **16 C8** 61 42N 14 43 E
Tandubas, *Phil.* **81 J3** 5 8N 120 20 E
Tandula →, *India* **94 D5** 21 6N 81 14 E
Tandula Tank, *India* **94 D5** 20 40N 81 12 E
Tandur, *India* **94 E4** 19 11N 79 30 E
Tandur, *India* **94 E3** 17 14N 77 35 E
Tane-ga-Shima, *Japan* **69 J5** 30 30N 131 0 E
Taneatua, *N.Z.* **130 E6** 38 4 S 177 1 E
Tanen Tong Dan, *Burma* **86 D2** 16 30N 98 30 E
Tanew →, *Poland* **55 H9** 50 29N 22 16 E
Tanezrouft, *Algeria* **111 D5** 23 9N 0 11 E
Tang, Koh, *Cambodia* **87 G4** 10 16N 103 7 E
Tang, Ra's-e, *Iran* **97 E8** 25 21N 59 52 E
Tang Krasang, *Cambodia* **86 F5** 12 34N 105 3 E
Tanga, *Tanzania* **118 D4** 5 5 S 39 2 E
Tanga □, *Tanzania* **118 D4** 5 20 S 38 0 E
Tanga Is., *Papua N. G.* **132 B7** 3 20 S 153 15 E
Tangail, *Bangla.* **90 C2** 24 15N 89 55 E
Tangalla, *Sri Lanka* **95 L5** 6 1N 80 48 E
Tanganyika, L., *Africa* **118 D3** 6 40 S 30 0 E
Tangasseri, *India* **95 K3** 8 53N 76 35 E
Tangaza, *Nigeria* **113 C5** 13 19N 4 55 E
Tangen, *Norway* **18 D8** 60 37N 11 15 E
Tanger = Tangier, *Morocco* **110 A3** 35 50N 5 49W
Tangerang, *Indonesia* **79 G12** 6 11 S 106 37 E
Tangerhütte, *Germany* **30 C7** 52 26N 11 48 E
Tangermünde, *Germany* **30 C7** 52 33N 11 58 E
Tanggu, *China* **75 E9** 39 2N 117 40 E
Tanggula Shan, *China* **72 C4** 32 40N 92 10 E
Tanghe, *China* **74 H7** 32 47N 112 50 E
Tangi, *India* **94 E7** 19 56N 85 24 E
Tangier, *Morocco* **110 A3** 35 50N 5 49W
Tangkeleboke, *Indonesia* **82 B2** 3 10 S 121 30 E
Tangorin, *Australia* **126 C3** 21 47 S 144 12 E
Tangorombohitr'i Makay, *Madag.* **117 C8** 21 0 S 45 15 E
Tangshan, *China* **75 E10** 39 38N 118 10 E
Tangtou, *China* **75 G10** 35 28N 118 30 E
Tangub, *Phil.* **81 G4** 8 3N 123 44 E
Tanguiéta, *Benin* **113 C5** 10 35N 1 21 E
Tangxi, *China* **77 C12** 29 3N 119 25 E
Tangyan He →, *China* **76 C7** 28 54N 108 19 E
Tanimbar, Kepulauan, *Indonesia* **79 F8** 7 30 S 131 30 E
Tanimbar Is. = Tanimbar, Kepulauan, *Indonesia* **79 F8** 7 30 S 131 30 E
Taninthari = Tenasserim □, *Burma* **86 F2** 14 0N 98 30 E
Taniyama, *Japan* **70 F2** 31 31N 130 31 E
Tanjay, *Phil.* **79 C6** 9 30N 123 5 E
Tanjong Malim, *Malaysia* **87 L3** 3 42N 101 31 E
Tanjore = Thanjavur, *India* **95 J4** 10 48N 79 12 E
Tanjung, *Indonesia* **78 E5** 2 10 S 115 25 E
Tanjungbalai, *Indonesia* **78 D1** 2 55N 99 44 E
Tanjungbatu, *Indonesia* **78 D5** 2 23N 118 3 E
Tanjungkarang Telukbetung, *Indonesia* **78 F3** 5 20 S 105 10 E
Tanjungpandan, *Indonesia* **78 E3** 2 43 S 107 38 E
Tanjungpinang, *Indonesia* **78 D2** 1 5N 104 30 E
Tanjungpriok, *Indonesia* **84 D3** 6 8 S 106 55 E
Tanjungredeb, *Indonesia* **78 D5** 2 9N 117 29 E
Tanjungselor, *Indonesia* **78 D5** 2 55N 117 25 E
Tank, *Pakistan* **91 B3** 32 14N 70 25 E
Tankhala, *India* **92 J5** 21 58N 73 47 E
Tanna, *Vanuatu* **133 J7** 19 30 S 169 20 E
Tännäs, *Sweden* **16 B6** 62 26N 12 42 E
Tannersville, *U.S.A.* **151 E9** 41 3N 75 18W
Tannis Bugt, *Denmark* **17 G4** 57 40N 10 15 E
Tannu-Ola, *Russia* **65 D10** 51 0N 94 0 E
Tannum Sands, *Australia* **126 C5** 23 57 S 151 22 E
Tano →, *Ghana* **112 D4** 5 7N 2 56W
Tanon Str., *Phil.* **81 F4** 10 20N 123 30 E
Tanout, *Niger* **113 C6** 14 50N 8 55 E
Tanquinho, *Brazil* **171 D4** 11 58 S 39 6W
Tanshui, *Taiwan* **77 E13** 25 10N 121 28 E
Tansilla, *Burkina Faso* **112 C4** 12 25N 4 23W
Tanta, *Egypt* **106 H7** 30 45N 30 57 E
Tantoyuca, *Mexico* **163 C5** 21 21N 98 10W
Tantung = Dandong, *China* **75 D13** 40 10N 124 20 E
Tanuku, *India* **94 F5** 16 45N 81 44 E
Tanumshede, *Sweden* **17 F5** 58 42N 11 20 E
Tanunda, *Australia* **128 C3** 34 30 S 139 0 E
Tanur, *India* **95 J2** 11 1N 75 52 E
Tanus, *France* **28 D6** 44 8N 2 19 E
Tanzania ■, *Africa* **118 D3** 6 0 S 34 0 E
Tanzawa-Sanchi, *Japan* **71 B11** 35 27N 139 0 E
Tanzilla →, *Canada* **142 B2** 58 8N 130 43W
Tao, Ko, *Thailand* **87 G2** 10 5N 99 52 E
Tao'an = Taonan, *China* **75 B12** 45 22N 122 40 E
Tao'er He →, *China* **75 B13** 45 45N 124 5 E
Taohua Dao, *China* **77 C14** 29 50N 122 20 E
Taolanaro, *Madag.* **117 D8** 25 2 S 47 0 E
Taole, *China* **74 E4** 38 48N 106 40 E
Taonan, *China* **75 B12** 45 22N 122 40 E
Taormina, *Italy* **47 E8** 37 51N 15 17 E
Taos, *U.S.A.* **159 H11** 36 24N 105 35W
Taoudenni, *Mali* **110 D4** 22 40N 3 55W
Taoudrart, Adrar, *Algeria* **111 D5** 24 25N 2 24 E
Taounate, *Morocco* **110 B4** 34 25N 4 41W
Taourirt, *Algeria* **111 C5** 26 37N 0 20 E
Taourirt, *Morocco* **111 B4** 34 25N 2 53W
Taouz, *Morocco* **110 B4** 30 53N 4 0W
Taoyuan, *China* **77 C8** 28 55N 111 16 E
T'aoyüan, *Taiwan* **77 E13** 25 0N 121 4 E
Tapa, *Estonia* **15 G21** 59 15N 25 50 E
Tapa Shan = Daba Shan, *China* **76 B7** 32 0N 109 0 E
Tapachula, *Mexico* **163 E6** 14 54N 92 17W
Tapah, *Malaysia* **87 K3** 4 12N 101 15 E
Tapajós →, *Brazil* **169 D7** 2 24 S 54 41W
Tapaktuan, *Indonesia* **78 D1** 3 15N 97 10 E
Tapanahoni →, *Surinam* **169 C7** 4 20N 54 25W
Tapanui, *N.Z.* **131 F4** 45 56 S 169 18 E
Tapauá, *Brazil* **173 B5** 5 40 S 64 20W
Tapauá →, *Brazil* **173 B5** 5 40 S 64 21W
Tapaz, *Phil.* **81 F4** 11 16N 122 32 E
Tapes, *Brazil* **175 C5** 30 40 S 51 23W
Tapeta, *Liberia* **112 D3** 6 29N 8 52W
Taphan Hin, *Thailand* **86 D3** 16 13N 100 26 E
Tapia de Casariego, *Spain* **42 B4** 43 34N 6 56W
Tapiantana Group, *Phil.* **81 H4** 6 20N 122 0 E
Tapilon = Daanbantayan, *Phil.* **81 F5** 11 17N 124 2 E
Tapini, *Papua N. G.* **132 E4** 8 19 S 147 0 E
Tapiraí, *Brazil* **171 E2** 19 52 S 46 1W
Tapirapé →, *Brazil* **170 D1** 10 41 S 50 38W
Tapirapecó, Serra, *Venezuela* **169 C5** 1 10N 65 0W
Tapirapuã, *Brazil* **173 C6** 14 51 S 57 45W
Taplan, *Australia* **128 C4** 34 33 S 140 52 E
Tapoeripa, *Surinam* **169 B6** 5 22N 56 34W
Tapolca, *Hungary* **52 D2** 46 53N 17 29 E
Tapuaenuku, Mt., *N.Z.* **131 B8** 42 0 S 173 39 E
Tapul, *Phil.* **81 J3** 5 42N 120 55 E
Tapul Group, *Phil.* **79 C6** 5 35N 120 50 E
Tapul I., *Phil.* **81 J3** 5 43N 120 55 E
Tapun, *India* **90 B6** 27 35N 96 22 E
Tapurucuará, *Brazil* **169 D4** 0 24 S 65 2W
Ţaqţaq, *Iraq* **101 E11** 35 53N 44 35 E
Taquara, *Brazil* **175 B5** 29 36 S 50 46W
Taquari →, *Brazil* **173 D6** 19 15 S 57 17W
Taquaritinga, *Brazil* **171 F2** 21 24 S 48 30W
Tara, *Australia* **127 D5** 27 17 S 150 31 E
Tara, *Canada* **150 B3** 44 28N 81 9W
Tara, *Japan* **70 D2** 33 2N 130 11 E
Tara, *Russia* **64 D8** 56 55N 74 24 E
Tara, *Zambia* **119 F2** 16 58 S 26 45 E
Tara →, *Montenegro, Yug.* **50 C2** 43 21N 18 51 E
Tara-Dake, *Japan* **70 E2** 32 58N 130 6 E
Taraba □, *Nigeria* **113 D7** 8 0N 10 30 E
Taraba →, *Nigeria* **113 D7** 8 30N 10 15 E
Tarabagatay, Khrebet, *Kazakstan* **64 E9** 48 0N 83 0 E
Tarabuco, *Bolivia* **173 D5** 19 10 S 64 57W
Tarābulus, *Lebanon* **103 A4** 34 31N 35 50 E
Tarābulus, *Libya* **108 B2** 32 49N 13 7 E
Taraclia, *Moldova* **53 D14** 46 34N 29 7 E
Taraclia, *Moldova* **53 E13** 45 54N 28 40 E
Taradale, *N.Z.* **130 F5** 39 33 S 176 53 E
Taradehi, *India* **93 H8** 23 18N 79 21 E
Tarahouahout, *Algeria* **111 D6** 22 41N 5 59 E
Tarajalejo, *Canary Is.* **39 F5** 28 12N 14 7W
Tarakan, *Indonesia* **78 D5** 3 20N 117 35 E
Tarakit, Mt., *Kenya* **118 B4** 2 2N 35 10 E
Taralga, *Australia* **129 C8** 34 26 S 149 52 E
Tarama-Jima, *Japan* **69 M2** 24 39N 124 42 E
Taramakau →, *N.Z.* **131 C6** 42 34 S 171 8 E
Taran, Mys, *Russia* **15 J18** 54 56N 19 59 E
Tarana, *Australia* **129 B8** 33 31 S 149 52 E
Taranagar, *India* **92 E6** 28 43N 74 50 E
Taranaki □, *N.Z.* **130 F3** 39 25 S 174 30 E
Tarancón, *Spain* **40 E1** 40 1N 3 1W
Taransay, *U.K.* **22 D1** 57 54N 7 0W
Táranto, *Italy* **47 B10** 40 28N 17 14 E
Táranto, G. di, *Italy* **47 B10** 40 8N 17 20 E
Tarapacá, *Colombia* **168 D4** 2 56 S 69 46W
Tarapacá □, *Chile* **174 A2** 20 45 S 69 30W
Tarapoto, *Peru* **172 B2** 6 30 S 76 20W
Taraquá, *Brazil* **168 C4** 0 6N 68 28W
Tarare, *France* **29 C8** 45 54N 4 26 E
Tararua Ra., *N.Z.* **130 G4** 40 45 S 175 25 E
Tarascon, *France* **29 E8** 43 48N 4 39 E
Tarascon-sur-Ariège, *France* **28 F5** 42 50N 1 36 E
Tarashcha, *Ukraine* **59 H6** 49 30N 30 31 E
Tarata, *Peru* **172 D3** 17 27 S 70 2W
Tarauacá, *Brazil* **172 B3** 8 6 S 70 48W
Tarauacá →, *Brazil* **172 B4** 6 42 S 69 48W
Taravo →, *France* **29 G12** 41 42N 8 49 E
Tarawa, *Kiribati* **134 G9** 1 30N 173 0 E
Tarawera, *N.Z.* **130 F5** 39 2 S 176 36 E
Tarawera L., *N.Z.* **130 E5** 38 13 S 176 27 E
Tarawera Mt., *N.Z.* **130 E5** 38 14 S 176 32 E
Tarazona, *Spain* **40 D3** 41 55N 1 43W
Tarazona de la Mancha, *Spain* **41 F3** 39 16N 1 55W
Tarbat Ness, *U.K.* **22 D5** 57 52N 3 47W
Tarbela Dam, *Pakistan* **92 B5** 34 8N 72 52 E
Tarbert, *Arg. & Bute, U.K.* **22 F3** 55 52N 5 25W
Tarbert, *W. Isles, U.K.* **22 D2** 57 54N 6 49W
Tarbes, *France* **28 E4** 43 15N 0 3 E
Tarboro, *U.S.A.* **149 H7** 35 54N 77 32W
Tarbū, *Libya* **108 C3** 26 0N 15 5 E
Tărcău, Munţii, *Romania* **53 D11** 46 39N 26 7 E
Tarcento, *Italy* **45 B10** 46 13N 13 13 E
Tarcoola, *Australia* **127 E1** 30 44 S 134 36 E
Tarcoon, *Australia* **127 E4** 30 15 S 146 43 E
Tardets-Sorholus, *France* **28 E3** 43 8N 0 52W
Tardoire →, *France* **28 C4** 45 52N 0 14 E
Taree, *Australia* **129 A10** 31 50 S 152 30 E
Tarf, Ras, *Morocco* **110 A3** 35 40N 5 11W
Ţarfā, Ra's aţ, *Si. Arabia* **98 C3** 17 2N 42 22 E
Tarfa, W. el →, *Egypt* **106 B3** 28 25N 30 50 E
Tarfaya, *Morocco* **110 C2** 27 55N 12 55W
Târgovişte, *Romania* **53 F10** 44 55N 25 27 E
Târgu Bujor, *Romania* **53 E12** 45 52N 27 54 E
Târgu Cărbuneşti, *Romania* **53 F8** 44 57N 23 31 E
Târgu Frumos, *Romania* **53 C12** 47 12N 27 2 E
Târgu-Jiu, *Romania* **53 E8** 45 5N 23 19 E
Târgu Lăpuş, *Romania* **53 C8** 47 27N 23 52 E
Târgu Mureş, *Romania* **53 D9** 46 31N 24 38 E
Târgu Neamţ, *Romania* **53 C11** 47 12N 26 25 E
Târgu Ocna, *Romania* **53 D11** 46 16N 26 39 E
Târgu Secuiesc, *Romania* **53 E11** 46 0N 26 10 E
Targuist, *Morocco* **110 B4** 34 59N 4 14W
Târguşor, *Romania* **53 F13** 44 27N 28 25 E
Tărhăus, Vf., *Romania* **53 D11** 46 40N 26 8 E
Tarhbalt, *Morocco* **110 B3** 30 39N 5 20W
Tarhit, *Algeria* **111 B4** 30 58N 2 0W
Tarhūnah, *Libya* **108 B2** 32 27N 13 36 E
Tari, *Papua N. G.* **132 C2** 5 54 S 142 59 E
Táriba, *Venezuela* **168 B3** 7 49N 72 13W
Ţarif, *U.A.E.* **97 E7** 24 3N 53 46 E
Tarifa, *Spain* **43 J5** 36 1N 5 36W
Tarija, *Bolivia* **174 A3** 21 30 S 64 40W
Tarija □, *Bolivia* **174 A3** 21 30 S 63 30W
Tariku →, *Indonesia* **79 E9** 2 55 S 138 26 E
Tarīm, *Yemen* **99 C5** 16 3N 49 0 E
Tarim Basin = Tarim Pendi, *China* **72 B3** 40 0N 84 0 E
Tarim He →, *China* **72 C3** 39 30N 88 30 E
Tarim Pendi, *China* **72 B3** 40 0N 84 0 E
Taringo Downs, *Australia* **129 B6** 32 13 S 145 33 E
Taritatu →, *Indonesia* **79 E9** 2 54 S 138 27 E
Tarka →, *S. Africa* **116 E4** 32 10 S 26 0 E
Tarkastad, *S. Africa* **116 E4** 32 0 S 26 16 E
Tarkhankut, Mys, *Ukraine* **59 K7** 45 25N 32 30 E
Tarko Sale, *Russia* **64 C8** 64 55N 77 50 E
Tarkwa, *Ghana* **112 D4** 5 20N 2 0W
Tarlac, *Phil.* **79 A6** 15 29N 120 35 E
Tarlac □, *Phil.* **80 D3** 15 30N 120 30 E
Tarm, *Denmark* **17 J2** 55 56N 8 31 E
Tarma, *Peru* **172 C2** 11 25 S 75 45W
Tarn □, *France* **28 E6** 43 49N 2 8 E
Tarn →, *France* **28 D5** 44 5N 1 6 E
Tarn-et-Garonne □, *France* **28 D5** 44 8N 1 20 E
Tarna →, *Hungary* **52 C4** 47 31N 19 59 E
Târnava Mare →, *Romania* **53 D8** 46 10N 23 43 E
Târnava Mică →, *Romania* **53 D8** 46 9N 23 55 E
Târnăveni, *Romania* **53 D9** 46 19N 24 13 E
Tarnica, *Poland* **55 J9** 49 4N 22 44 E

Termez 289

Tarnobrzeg, *Poland* **55 H8** 50 35N 21 41 E
Tarnogród, *Poland* **55 H9** 50 22N 22 45 E
Tarnos, *France* **28 E2** 43 32N 1 28W
Târnova, *Moldova* **53 B12** 48 10N 27 40 E
Târnova, *Romania* **52 E6** 45 23N 21 59 E
Tarnów, *Poland* **55 H8** 50 3N 21 0 E
Tarnowskie Góry, *Poland* **55 H5** 50 27N 18 54 E
Tärnsjö, *Sweden* **16 D10** 60 9N 16 56 E
Táro →, *Italy* **44 C7** 45 2N 10 15 E
Ţārom, *Iran* **97 D7** 28 11N 55 46 E
Taroom, *Australia* **127 D4** 25 36 S 149 48 E
Taroudannt, *Morocco* **110 B3** 30 30N 8 52W
Tarp, *Germany* **30 A5** 54 39N 9 24 E
Tarpon Springs, *U.S.A.* **149 L4** 28 9N 82 45W
Tarquínia, *Italy* **45 F8** 42 15N 11 45 E
Tarragona, *Spain* **40 D6** 41 5N 1 17 E
Tarragona □, *Spain* **40 D6** 41 5N 1 0 E
Tarraleah, *Australia* **126 G4** 42 17 S 146 26 E
Tarrasa = Terrassa, *Spain* **40 D7** 41 34N 2 1 E
Tàrrega, *Spain* **40 D6** 41 39N 1 9 E
Tarrytown, *Ga., U.S.A.* **152 C7** 32 19N 82 34W
Tarrytown, *N.Y., U.S.A.* **151 E11** 41 4N 73 52W
Tårs, *Denmark* **17 G4** 57 23N 10 7 E
Tarshiha = Me'ona, *Israel* **103 B4** 33 1N 35 15 E
Tarso Emissi, *Chad* **109 D3** 21 27N 18 36 E
Tarso Ourari, *Chad* **109 D3** 21 27N 17 27 E
Tarsus, *Turkey* **100 D6** 36 58N 34 55 E
Tartagal, *Argentina* **174 A3** 22 30 S 63 50W
Tärtär, *Azerbaijan* **61 K8** 40 20N 46 58 E
Tärtär →, *Azerbaijan* **61 K8** 40 26N 47 20 E
Tartas, *France* **28 E3** 43 50N 0 49W
Tartu, *Estonia* **15 G22** 58 20N 26 44 E
Ţarţūs, *Syria* **100 E6** 34 55N 35 55 E
Tarumirim, *Brazil* **171 E3** 19 16 S 41 59W
Tarumizu, *Japan* **70 F2** 31 29N 130 42 E
Tarussa, *Russia* **58 E9** 54 44N 37 10 E
Tarutao, Ko, *Thailand* **78 C1** 6 33N 99 40 E
Tarutung, *Indonesia* **78 D1** 2 0N 98 54 E
Tarvísio, *Italy* **45 B10** 46 30N 13 35 E
Tarz Ulli, *Libya* **108 C2** 25 32N 10 8 E
Tas-Buget, *Kazakstan* **63 A2** 44 46N 65 33 E
Tasahku, *Burma* **90 B6** 27 33N 97 52 E
Tasāwah, *Libya* **108 C2** 26 0N 13 30 E
Täsch, *Switz.* **32 D5** 46 4N 7 46 E
Taseko →, *Canada* **142 C4** 52 8N 123 45W
Tasgaon, *India* **94 F2** 17 2N 74 39 E
Tash-Kömür, *Kyrgyzstan* **64 E8** 41 40N 72 10 E
Tash-Kumyr = Tash-Kömür, *Kyrgyzstan* **64 E8** 41 40N 72 10 E
Tashauz = Dashhowuz, *Turkmenistan* **64 E6** 41 49N 59 58 E
Tashi Chho Dzong = Thimphu, *Bhutan* **90 B2** 27 31N 89 45 E
Ţashk, Daryācheh-ye, *Iran* **97 D7** 29 45N 53 35 E
Tashkent = Toshkent, *Uzbekistan* **64 E7** 41 20N 69 10 E
Tashtagol, *Russia* **64 D9** 52 47N 87 53 E
Tasiilaq, *Greenland* **10 D7** 65 40N 37 20W
Tasikmalaya, *Indonesia* **79 G13** 7 18 S 108 12 E
Tåsinge, *Denmark* **17 J4** 55 0N 10 35 E
Tåsjön, *Sweden* **14 D16** 64 15N 15 40 E
Taskan, *Russia* **65 C16** 62 59N 150 20 E
Tasker, *Niger* **113 C7** 15 8N 10 40 E
Taşköprü, *Turkey* **100 B6** 41 30N 34 15 E
Taşlâc, *Moldova* **53 C14** 47 4N 29 24 E
Tasman →, *N.Z.* **131 D5** 43 48 S 170 8 E
Tasman, Mt., *N.Z.* **131 D5** 43 34 S 170 12 E
Tasman B., *N.Z.* **131 A8** 40 59 S 173 25 E
Tasman Mts., *N.Z.* **131 B7** 41 3 S 172 25 E
Tasman Pen., *Australia* **126 G4** 43 10 S 148 0 E
Tasman Sea, *Pac. Oc.* **134 L8** 36 0 S 160 0 E
Tasmania □, *Australia* **126 G4** 42 0 S 146 30 E
Tăşnad, *Romania* **52 C7** 47 30N 22 33 E
Tassili n'Ajjer, *Algeria* **111 C6** 25 47N 8 1 E
Tassili-Oua-n-Ahaggar, *Algeria* **111 D6** 20 41N 5 30 E
Tassili Tin-Rerhoh, *Algeria* **111 D5** 20 5N 3 55 E
Tasty, *Kazakstan* **63 A4** 44 47N 69 7 E
Tata, *Hungary* **52 C3** 47 37N 18 19 E
Tata, *Morocco* **110 C3** 29 46N 7 56W
Tatabánya, *Hungary* **52 C3** 47 32N 18 25 E
Tataouine, *Tunisia* **108 B2** 32 57N 10 29 E
Tatar Republic = Tatarstan □, *Russia* **60 C10** 55 30N 51 30 E
Tatarbunary, *Ukraine* **59 K5** 45 50N 29 39 E
Tatarsk, *Russia* **64 D8** 55 14N 76 0 E
Tatarstan □, *Russia* **60 C10** 55 30N 51 30 E
Tatau, *Malaysia* **85 B4** 2 53N 112 51 E
Tatebayashi, *Japan* **71 A11** 36 15N 139 32 E
Tateshina-Yama, *Japan* **71 A10** 36 8N 138 11 E
Tateyama, *Japan* **71 C11** 35 0N 139 50 E
Tathlina L., *Canada* **142 A5** 60 33N 117 39W
Tathlīth, *Si. Arabia* **98 C3** 19 32N 43 30 E
Tathlīth, W. →, *Si. Arabia* **98 B4** 20 35N 44 20 E
Tathra, *Australia* **129 D8** 36 44 S 149 59 E
Tati →, *India* **94 D1** 21 8N 72 41 E
Tatinnai L., *Canada* **143 A9** 60 55N 97 40W
Tatitlek, *U.S.A.* **144 F11** 60 52N 146 41W
Tatla L., *Canada* **142 C4** 52 0N 124 20W
Tatlısu, *Turkey* **51 F11** 40 24N 27 55 E
Tatnam, C., *Canada* **143 B10** 57 16N 91 0W
Tatra = Tatry, *Slovak Rep.* **35 B13** 49 20N 20 0 E
Tatry, *Slovak Rep.* **35 B13** 49 20N 20 0 E
Tatshenshini →, *Canada* **142 B1** 59 28N 137 45W
Tatsuno, *Japan* **70 C6** 34 52N 134 33 E
Tatta, *Pakistan* **91 D2** 24 42N 67 55 E
Tatuī, *Brazil* **175 A6** 23 25 S 47 53W
Tatum, *U.S.A.* **155 J3** 33 16N 103 19W
Tat'ung = Datong, *China* **74 D7** 40 6N 113 18 E
Tatura, *Australia* **129 D6** 36 29 S 145 16 E
Tatvan, *Turkey* **101 C10** 38 31N 42 15 E
Tau, *Amer. Samoa* **133 X25** 14 15 S 169 30W
Tau, *Norway* **18 E2** 59 3N 5 55 E
Tauá, *Brazil* **170 C3** 6 1 S 40 26W
Taubaté, *Brazil* **175 A6** 23 0 S 45 36W
Tauberbischofsheim, *Germany* **31 F5** 49 37N 9 39 E
Taucha, *Germany* **30 D8** 51 23N 12 29 E
Tauern-tunnel, *Austria* **34 D6** 47 0N 13 12 E
Taufikia, *Sudan* **107 F3** 9 24N 31 37 E
Taulé, *France* **26 D3** 48 37N 3 55W
Taumarunui, *N.Z.* **130 E4** 38 53 S 175 15 E
Taumaturgo, *Brazil* **172 B3** 8 54 S 72 51W
Taung, *S. Africa* **116 D3** 27 33 S 24 47 E
Taungdwingyi, *Burma* **90 E5** 20 1N 95 40 E
Taunggyi, *Burma* **90 E6** 20 50N 97 0 E
Taungtha, *Burma* **90 E5** 21 12N 95 25 E
Taungup, *Burma* **90 F5** 18 51N 94 14 E
Taungup Pass, *Burma* **90 F5** 18 40N 94 45 E
Taunsa, *Pakistan* **92 D4** 30 42N 70 39 E
Taunsa Barrage, *Pakistan* **92 D4** 30 42N 70 50 E
Taunton, *U.K.* **21 F4** 51 1N 3 5W
Taunton, *U.S.A.* **151 E13** 41 54N 71 6W
Taunus, *Germany* **31 E4** 50 13N 8 34 E
Taupo, *N.Z.* **130 E5** 38 41 S 176 7 E
Taupo, L., *N.Z.* **130 E4** 38 46 S 175 55 E
Tauragė, *Lithuania* **15 J20** 55 14N 22 16 E
Tauragė □, *Lithuania* **54 C9** 55 15N 22 17 E
Tauranga, *N.Z.* **130 D5** 37 42 S 176 11 E
Tauranga Harb., *N.Z.* **130 D5** 37 30 S 176 5 E
Taureau, Rés., *Canada* **140 C5** 46 46N 73 50W
Tauri →, *Papua N. G.* **132 E4** 8 8 S 146 8 E
Taurianova, *Italy* **47 D9** 38 21N 16 1 E
Taurus Mts. = Toros Dağları, *Turkey* **100 D5** 37 0N 32 30 E
Tauste, *Spain* **40 D3** 41 58N 1 18W
Tauz = Tovuz, *Azerbaijan* **61 K7** 41 0N 45 40 E
Tavaar, *Somali Rep.* **120 D3** 3 6N 46 1 E
Tavannes, *Switz.* **32 B4** 47 13N 7 12 E
Tavares, *U.S.A.* **153 G8** 28 48N 81 44W
Tavas, *Turkey* **49 D11** 37 34N 29 4 E
Tavda, *Russia* **64 D7** 58 7N 65 8 E
Tavda →, *Russia* **64 D7** 57 47N 67 18 E
Tavernes de la Valldigna, *Spain* **41 F4** 39 5N 0 13W
Tavernier, *U.S.A.* **153 K9** 25 1N 80 31W
Taveta, *Tanzania* **118 C4** 3 23 S 37 37 E
Taveuni, *Fiji* **133 A3** 16 51 S 179 58W
Taviano, *Italy* **47 C11** 39 59N 18 5 E
Tavignano →, *France* **29 F13** 42 7N 9 33 E
Tavira, *Portugal* **43 H3** 37 8N 7 40W
Tavistock, *Canada* **150 C4** 43 19N 80 50W
Tavistock, *U.K.* **21 G3** 50 33N 4 9W
Tavolara, *Italy* **46 B2** 40 54N 9 42 E
Távora →, *Portugal* **42 D3** 41 8N 7 35W
Tavoy = Dawei, *Burma* **78 B1** 14 2N 98 12 E
Tavşanlı, *Turkey* **49 B11** 39 32N 29 30 E
Taw →, *U.K.* **21 F3** 51 4N 4 4W
Tawa →, *India* **92 H8** 22 48N 77 48 E
Tawas City, *U.S.A.* **148 C4** 44 16N 83 31W
Tawau, *Malaysia* **78 D5** 4 20N 117 55 E
Taweisha, *Sudan* **107 E2** 12 19N 26 40 E
Ţawī Şulaym, *Oman* **99 B7** 22 33N 58 40 E
Tawi-Tawi □, *Phil.* **81 J3** 5 0N 120 0 E
Tawitawi, *Phil.* **79 B6** 5 10N 120 0 E
Tawitawi Group, *Phil.* **81 J3** 5 10N 120 15 E
Tawngche, *Burma* **90 B5** 26 34N 95 38 E
Tawu, *Taiwan* **77 F13** 22 30N 120 50 E
Tāwurgha', *Libya* **108 B3** 32 1N 15 2 E
Taxco de Alarcón, *Mexico* **163 D5** 18 33N 99 36W
Taxila, *Pakistan* **92 C5** 33 42N 72 52 E
Tay →, *U.K.* **22 E5** 56 37N 3 38W
Tay, Firth of, *U.K.* **22 E5** 56 25N 3 8W
Tay, L., *Australia* **125 F3** 32 55 S 120 48 E
Tay, L., *U.K.* **22 E4** 56 32N 4 8W
Tay Ninh, *Vietnam* **87 G6** 11 20N 106 5 E
Tayabamba, *Peru* **172 B2** 8 15 S 77 16W
Tayabas, *Phil.* **80 D3** 14 1N 121 35 E
Tayabas Bay, *Phil.* **80 E3** 13 45N 121 45 E
Taylakova, *Russia* **64 D8** 59 13N 74 0 E
Taylakovy = Taylakova, *Russia* **64 D8** 59 13N 74 0 E
Taylor, *Canada* **142 B4** 56 13N 120 40W
Taylor, *Fla., U.S.A.* **152 E7** 30 26N 82 18W
Taylor, *Mich., U.S.A.* **157 B13** 42 14N 83 16W
Taylor, *Nebr., U.S.A.* **154 E5** 41 46N 99 23W
Taylor, *Pa., U.S.A.* **151 E9** 41 23N 75 43W
Taylor, *Tex., U.S.A.* **155 K6** 30 34N 97 25W
Taylor, Mt., *N.Z.* **131 D6** 43 30 S 171 20 E
Taylor, Mt., *U.S.A.* **159 J10** 35 14N 107 37W
Taylorsville, *U.S.A.* **157 F11** 38 2N 85 21W
Taylorsville L., *U.S.A.* **157 G11** 38 0N 85 15W
Taylorville, *U.S.A.* **156 E7** 39 33N 89 18W
Taymā, *Si. Arabia* **96 E3** 27 35N 38 45 E
Taymyr, Oz., *Russia* **65 B11** 74 20N 102 0 E
Taymyr, Poluostrov, *Russia* **65 B11** 75 0N 100 0 E
Tayport, *U.K.* **22 E6** 56 27N 2 52W
Tayshet, *Russia* **65 D10** 55 58N 98 1 E
Taytay, *Phil.* **79 B5** 10 45N 119 30 E
Taytay Bay, *Phil.* **81 F2** 10 55N 119 35 E
Tayug, *Phil.* **80 C3** 16 2N 120 45 E
Taz →, *Russia* **64 C8** 67 32N 78 40 E
Taza, *Morocco* **110 B4** 34 16N 4 6W
Tāzah Khurmātū, *Iraq* **101 E11** 35 18N 44 20 E
Tazawa-Ko, *Japan* **68 E10** 39 43N 140 40 E
Taze, *Burma* **90 D5** 22 57N 95 24 E
Tazenakht, *Morocco* **110 B3** 30 35N 7 12W
Tazerbo, *Libya* **108 C4** 25 45N 21 0 E
Tazin, *Canada* **143 B7** 59 48N 109 55W
Tazin L., *Canada* **143 B7** 59 44N 108 42W
Tazlina, *U.S.A.* **144 E11** 62 4N 146 27W
Tazoult, *Algeria* **111 A6** 35 29N 6 11 E
Tazovskiy, *Russia* **64 C8** 67 30N 78 44 E
Tbilisi, *Georgia* **61 K7** 41 43N 44 50 E
Tchad = Chad ■, *Africa* **109 F3** 15 0N 17 15 E
Tchad, L., *Chad* **109 F2** 13 30N 14 30 E
Tchaourou, *Benin* **113 D5** 8 58N 2 40 E
Tch'eng-tou = Chengdu, *China* **76 B5** 30 38N 104 2 E
Tchentlo L., *Canada* **142 B4** 55 15N 125 0W
Tchetti, *Benin* **113 D5** 7 50N 1 40 E
Tchibanga, *Gabon* **114 C2** 2 45 S 11 0 E
Tchien, *Liberia* **112 D3** 5 59N 8 15W
Tchin Tabaraden, *Niger* **113 B6** 15 58N 5 56 E
Tchingou, Massif de, *N. Cal.* **133 T19** 20 54 S 165 0 E
Tchollíré, *Cameroon* **114 A2** 8 24N 14 10 E
Tch'ong-k'ing = Chongqing, *China* **76 C6** 29 35N 106 25 E
Tczew, *Poland* **54 D5** 54 8N 18 50 E
Te Anau, *N.Z.* **131 F2** 45 25 S 167 43 E
Te Anau, L., *N.Z.* **131 F2** 45 15 S 167 45 E
Te Araroa, *N.Z.* **130 D7** 37 39 S 178 25 E
Te Aroha, *N.Z.* **130 D4** 37 32 S 175 44 E
Te Awamutu, *N.Z.* **130 E4** 38 1 S 175 20 E
Te Kaha, *N.Z.* **130 D6** 37 44 S 177 52 E
Te Karaka, *N.Z.* **130 E6** 38 26 S 177 53 E
Te Kauwhata, *N.Z.* **130 D4** 37 25 S 175 9 E
Te Kopuru, *N.Z.* **130 C2** 36 2 S 173 56 E
Te Kuiti, *N.Z.* **130 E4** 38 20 S 175 11 E
Te-n-Dghâmcha, Sebkhet, *Mauritania* **112 B1** 18 30N 15 55W
Te Puke, *N.Z.* **130 D5** 37 46 S 176 22 E
Te Teko, *N.Z.* **130 E5** 38 2 S 176 48 E
Te Waewae B., *N.Z.* **131 G2** 46 13 S 167 33 E
Tea →, *Brazil* **168 D4** 0 30 S 65 9W
Teaca, *Romania* **53 D9** 46 55N 24 30 E
Teague, *U.S.A.* **155 K6** 31 38N 96 17W
Teano, *Italy* **47 A7** 41 15N 14 4 E
Teapa, *Mexico* **163 D6** 18 35N 92 56W
Teba, *Spain* **43 J6** 36 59N 4 55W
Tebakang, *Malaysia* **78 D4** 1 6N 110 30 E
Teberau, *Malaysia* **84 B2** 1 32N 103 45 E
Teberda, *Russia* **61 J5** 43 30N 41 46 E
Tébessa, *Algeria* **111 A6** 35 22N 8 8 E
Tebicuary →, *Paraguay* **174 B4** 26 36 S 58 16W
Tebingtinggi, *Indonesia* **78 D1** 3 20N 99 9 E
Tebintingii, *Indonesia* **78 E2** 1 0N 102 45 E
Tébourba, *Tunisia* **108 A1** 36 49N 9 51 E
Téboursouk, *Tunisia* **108 A1** 36 29N 9 10 E
Tebulos, *Georgia* **61 J7** 42 36N 45 17 E
Tecate, *Mexico* **161 N10** 32 34N 116 38W
Tecer Dağları, *Turkey* **100 C7** 39 27N 37 27 E
Tech →, *France* **28 F7** 42 36N 3 3 E
Techa →, *Russia* **62 C9** 56 13N 62 58 E
Techiman, *Ghana* **112 D4** 7 35N 1 58W
Techirghiol, *Romania* **53 F13** 44 4N 28 32 E
Tecka, *Argentina* **176 B2** 43 29 S 70 48W
Tecomán, *Mexico* **162 D4** 18 55N 103 53W
Tecopa, *U.S.A.* **161 K10** 35 51N 116 13W
Tecoripa, *Mexico* **162 B3** 28 37N 109 57W
Tecuala, *Mexico* **162 C3** 22 23N 105 27W
Tecuci, *Romania* **53 E12** 45 51N 27 27 E
Tecumseh, *Canada* **150 D2** 42 19N 82 54W
Tecumseh, *Mich., U.S.A.* **157 B13** 42 0N 83 57W
Tecumseh, *Okla., U.S.A.* **155 H6** 35 15N 96 56W
Ted, *Somali Rep.* **120 D2** 4 24N 43 55 E
Tedzhen = Tejen, *Turkmenistan* **64 F7** 37 23N 60 31 E
Tees →, *U.K.* **20 C6** 54 37N 1 10W
Tees B., *U.K.* **20 C6** 54 40N 1 9W
Teeswater, *Canada* **150 C3** 43 59N 81 17W
Tefé, *Brazil* **169 D5** 3 25 S 64 50W
Tefé →, *Brazil* **169 D5** 3 35 S 64 47W
Tefenni, *Turkey* **49 D11** 37 18N 29 45 E
Tegal, *Indonesia* **79 G13** 6 52 S 109 8 E
Tegernsee, *Germany* **31 H7** 47 43N 11 46 E
Teggiano, *Italy* **47 B8** 40 23N 15 32 E
Tegid, L. = Bala, L., *U.K.* **20 E4** 52 53N 3 37W
Tegina, *Nigeria* **113 C6** 10 5N 6 11 E
Téglio, *Italy* **33 D10** 46 10N 10 4 E
Tegua, *Vanuatu* **133 C4** 13 15 S 166 37 E
Tegucigalpa, *Honduras* **164 D2** 14 5N 87 14W
Teguidda i-n-Tessoum, *Niger* **113 B6** 17 25N 6 37 E
Tehachapi, *U.S.A.* **161 K8** 35 8N 118 27W
Tehachapi Mts., *U.S.A.* **161 L8** 35 0N 118 30W
Tehamiyam, *Sudan* **106 D4** 18 20N 36 32 E
Tehilla, *Sudan* **106 D4** 17 42N 36 6 E
Téhini, *Ivory C.* **112 D4** 9 39N 3 40W
Tehoru, *Indonesia* **79 E7** 3 19 S 129 37 E
Tehrān, *Iran* **97 C6** 35 44N 51 30 E
Tehri, *India* **93 D8** 30 23N 78 29 E
Tehuacán, *Mexico* **163 D5** 18 30N 97 30W
Tehuantepec, *Mexico* **163 D5** 16 21N 95 13W
Tehuantepec, G. de, *Mexico* **163 D5** 15 50N 95 12W
Tehuantepec, Istmo de, *Mexico* **163 D6** 17 0N 94 30W
Teide, *Canary Is.* **39 F3** 28 15N 16 38W
Teifi →, *U.K.* **21 E3** 52 5N 4 41W
Teigebyen, *Norway* **18 D8** 60 12N 11 0 E
Teign →, *U.K.* **21 G4** 50 32N 3 32W
Teignmouth, *U.K.* **21 G4** 50 33N 3 31W
Teiuş, *Romania* **53 D8** 46 12N 23 40 E
Teixeira, *Brazil* **170 C4** 7 13 S 37 15W
Teixeira Pinto, *Guinea-Biss.* **112 C1** 12 3N 16 0W
Tejam, *India* **93 E9** 29 57N 80 11 E
Tejen, *Turkmenistan* **64 F7** 37 23N 60 31 E
Tejen →, *Turkmenistan* **97 B9** 37 24N 60 38 E
Tejo →, *Europe* **43 F2** 38 40N 9 24W
Tejon Pass, *U.S.A.* **161 L8** 34 49N 118 53W
Tekamah, *U.S.A.* **154 E6** 41 47N 96 13W
Tekapo →, *N.Z.* **131 E5** 44 13 S 170 21 E
Tekapo, L., *N.Z.* **131 D5** 43 53 S 170 33 E
Tekax, *Mexico* **163 C7** 20 11N 89 18W
Teke, *Turkey* **51 E13** 41 4N 29 39 E
Tekeli, *Kazakstan* **64 E8** 44 50N 79 0 E
Tekeze →, *Ethiopia* **107 E4** 14 20N 35 50 E
Tekija, *Serbia, Yug.* **50 B6** 44 42N 22 26 E
Tekirdağ, *Turkey* **51 F11** 40 58N 27 30 E
Tekirdağ □, *Turkey* **51 E11** 41 0N 27 0 E
Tekirova, *Turkey* **49 E12** 36 30N 30 32 E
Tekkali, *India* **94 E7** 18 37N 84 15 E
Tekke, *Turkey* **100 B7** 40 42N 36 12 E
Tekman, *Turkey* **101 C9** 39 38N 41 29 E
Tekoa, *U.S.A.* **158 C5** 47 14N 117 4W
Tekouiât, O. →, *Algeria* **111 D5** 22 25N 2 35 E
Tel →, *India* **94 D6** 20 50N 83 54 E
Tel Aviv-Yafo, *Israel* **103 C3** 32 4N 34 48 E
Tel Lakhish, *Israel* **103 D3** 31 34N 34 51 E
Tel Megiddo, *Israel* **103 C4** 32 35N 35 11 E
Tela, *Honduras* **164 C2** 15 40N 87 28W
Télagh, *Algeria* **111 B4** 34 51N 0 32W
Telanaipura = Jambi, *Indonesia* **78 E2** 1 38 S 103 30 E
Telavåg, *Norway* **18 D1** 60 15N 4 58 E
Telavi, *Georgia* **61 J7** 42 0N 45 30 E
Telč, *Czech Rep.* **34 B8** 49 11N 15 28 E
Telciu, *Romania* **53 C9** 47 25N 24 24 E
Telde, *Canary Is.* **39 G4** 27 59N 15 25W
Tele →, *Dem. Rep. of the Congo* **114 B4** 2 48N 23 54 E
Telefomin, *Papua N. G.* **132 C1** 5 10 S 141 31 E
Telegraph Creek, *Canada* **142 B2** 58 0N 131 10W
Telekhany = Tsyelyakhany, *Belarus* **59 F3** 52 30N 25 46 E
Telemark, *Norway* **15 G12** 59 15N 7 40 E
Telemark □, *Norway* **18 E5** 59 25N 8 30 E
Telén, *Argentina* **174 D2** 36 15 S 65 31W
Telen →, *Indonesia* **85 C5** 0 10 S 117 20 E
Teleneşti, *Moldova* **53 C13** 47 30N 28 22 E
Teleng, *Iran* **97 E9** 25 47N 61 3 E
Teleño, *Spain* **42 C4** 42 23N 6 22W
Teleorman □, *Romania* **53 G10** 44 0N 25 0 E
Teleorman →, *Romania* **53 G10** 43 52N 25 26 E
Teles Pires →, *Brazil* **173 B6** 7 21 S 58 3W
Telescope Pk., *U.S.A.* **161 J9** 36 10N 117 5W
Teletaye, *Mali* **113 B5** 16 31N 1 30 E
Telfer Mine, *Australia* **124 C3** 21 40 S 122 12 E
Telford, *U.K.* **21 E5** 52 40N 2 27W
Telford and Wrekin □, *U.K.* **20 E5** 52 45N 2 27W
Telfs, *Austria* **34 D4** 47 19N 11 4 E
Telida, *U.S.A.* **144 E9** 63 23N 153 16W
Télimélé, *Guinea* **112 C2** 10 54N 13 2W
Teljo, J., *Sudan* **107 E2** 14 42N 25 26 E
Telkwa, *Canada* **142 C3** 54 41N 127 5W
Tell City, *U.S.A.* **157 G10** 37 57N 86 46W
Tellicherry, *India* **95 J2** 11 45N 75 30 E
Telluride, *U.S.A.* **159 H10** 37 56N 107 49W
Telok Datok, *Malaysia* **84 B2** 2 49N 101 31 E
Teloloapán, *Mexico* **163 D5** 18 21N 99 51W
Telpos Iz, *Russia* **56 B10** 63 16N 59 13 E
Telsen, *Argentina* **176 B3** 42 30 S 66 50W
Telšiai, *Lithuania* **15 H20** 55 59N 22 14 E
Telšiai □, *Lithuania* **54 C9** 55 59N 22 15 E
Teltow, *Germany* **30 C9** 52 24N 13 15 E
Teluk Anson = Teluk Intan, *Malaysia* **78 D2** 4 3N 101 0 E
Teluk Betung = Tanjungkarang Telukbetung, *Indonesia* **78 F3** 5 20 S 105 10 E
Teluk Cenderawasih, *Indonesia* **83 B5** 2 30 S 135 20 E
Teluk Darvel, *Malaysia* **81 J2** 4 45N 118 30 E
Teluk Intan, *Malaysia* **78 D2** 4 3N 101 0 E
Telukbutun, *Indonesia* **78 D3** 4 13N 108 12 E
Telukdalem, *Indonesia* **78 D1** 0 33N 97 50 E
Tema, *Ghana* **113 D5** 5 41N 0 0 E
Temanggung, *Indonesia* **85 D4** 7 18 S 110 10 E
Temax, *Mexico* **163 C7** 21 10N 88 50W
Temba, *S. Africa* **117 D4** 25 20 S 28 17 E
Tembagapura, *Indonesia* **79 E9** 4 20 S 137 0 E
Tembe, *Dem. Rep. of the Congo* **118 C2** 0 16 S 28 14 E
Tembesi, *Indonesia* **84 C2** 1 43 S 103 6 E
Tembilahan, *Indonesia* **84 C2** 0 19 S 103 9 E
Temblador, *Venezuela* **169 B5** 8 59N 62 44W
Tembleque, *Spain* **42 F7** 39 41N 3 30W
Temblor Range, *U.S.A.* **161 K7** 35 20N 119 50W
Teme →, *U.K.* **21 E5** 52 11N 2 13W
Temecula, *U.S.A.* **161 M9** 33 30N 117 9W
Temerloh, *Malaysia* **78 D2** 3 27N 102 25 E
Teminabuan, *Indonesia* **79 E8** 1 26 S 132 1 E
Temir, *Kazakstan* **57 E10** 49 1N 57 14 E
Temirtau, *Kazakstan* **64 D8** 50 5N 72 56 E
Temirtau, *Russia* **64 D9** 53 10N 87 30 E
Temiscamie →, *Canada* **141 B5** 50 59N 73 5W
Témiscaming, *Canada* **140 C4** 46 44N 79 5W
Témiscamingue, L., *Canada* **140 C4** 47 10N 79 25W
Temnikov, *Russia* **60 C6** 54 40N 43 11 E
Temo →, *Italy* **46 B1** 40 17N 8 28 E
Temora, *Australia* **129 C7** 34 30 S 147 30 E
Temosachic, *Mexico* **162 B3** 28 58N 107 50W
Tempe, *U.S.A.* **159 K8** 33 25N 111 56W
Témpio Pausánia, *Italy* **46 B2** 40 54N 9 6 E
Tempiute, *U.S.A.* **160 H11** 37 39N 115 38W
Temple, *U.S.A.* **155 K6** 31 6N 97 21W
Temple B., *Australia* **126 A3** 12 15 S 143 3 E
Temple Terrace, *U.S.A.* **153 G7** 28 2N 82 23W
Templemore, *Ireland* **23 D4** 52 47N 7 51W
Templeton, *U.S.A.* **160 K6** 35 33N 120 42W
Templeton →, *Australia* **126 C2** 21 0 S 138 40 E
Templin, *Germany* **30 B9** 53 7N 13 28 E
Tempoal, *Mexico* **163 C5** 21 31N 98 23W
Temryuk, *Russia* **59 K9** 45 15N 37 24 E
Temska →, *Serbia, Yug.* **50 C6** 43 17N 22 33 E
Temuco, *Chile* **176 A2** 38 45 S 72 40W
Temuka, *N.Z.* **131 E6** 44 14 S 171 17 E
Ten Thousand Is., *U.S.A.* **153 K8** 25 55N 81 45W
Tena, *Ecuador* **168 D2** 0 59 S 77 49W
Tenabo, *Mexico* **163 C6** 20 2N 90 12W
Tenaha, *U.S.A.* **155 K7** 31 57N 94 15W
Tenakee Springs, *U.S.A.* **144 H14** 57 47N 135 13W
Tenali, *India* **95 F5** 16 15N 80 35 E
Tenancingo, *Mexico* **163 D5** 19 0N 99 33W
Tenango, *Mexico* **163 D5** 19 7N 99 33W
Tenasserim, *Burma* **78 B1** 12 6N 99 3 E
Tenasserim □, *Burma* **86 F2** 14 0N 98 30 E
Tenby, *U.K.* **21 F3** 51 40N 4 42W
Tenda, Colle di, *France* **29 D11** 44 7N 7 36 E
Tendaho, *Ethiopia* **102 E3** 11 48N 40 54 E
Tende, *France* **29 D11** 44 5N 7 35 E
Tendelti, *Sudan* **107 E3** 13 1N 31 55 E
Tendjedi, Adrar, *Algeria* **111 D6** 23 41N 7 32 E
Tendrara, *Morocco* **111 B4** 33 3N 1 58W
Tendre, Mt., *Switz.* **32 C2** 46 35N 6 18 E
Tendrovskaya Kosa, *Ukraine* **59 J6** 46 16N 31 35 E
Tendukhera, *India* **93 H8** 23 24N 79 33 E
Teneida, *Egypt* **106 B2** 25 30N 29 19 E
Tenenkou, *Mali* **112 C4** 14 28N 4 55W
Tenente Marques →, *Brazil* **173 C6** 11 10 S 59 56W
Ténéré, *Niger* **113 B7** 19 0N 10 30 E
Ténéré, Erg du, *Niger* **109 E2** 17 35N 10 55 E
Tenerife, *Canary Is.* **110 C1** 28 15N 16 35W
Tenerife, Pico, *Canary Is.* **39 G1** 27 43N 18 1W
Ténès, *Algeria* **111 A5** 36 31N 1 14 E
Teng Xian, *Guangxi Zhuangzu, China* **77 F8** 23 21N 110 56 E
Teng Xian, *Shandong, China* **75 G9** 35 5N 117 10 E
Tengah □, *Indonesia* **79 E6** 2 0 S 122 0 E
Tengah, Kepulauan, *Indonesia* **78 F5** 7 5 S 118 15 E
Tengchong, *China* **76 E2** 25 0N 98 28 E
Tengchowfu = Penglai, *China* **75 F11** 37 48N 120 42 E
Tenggara □, *Indonesia* **79 E6** 3 0 S 122 0 E
Tenggarong, *Indonesia* **78 E5** 0 24 S 116 58 E
Tenggol, Pulau, *Malaysia* **78 D2** 4 48N 103 41 E
Tengiz, Ozero, *Kazakstan* **64 D7** 50 30N 69 0 E
Tenhult, *Sweden* **17 G8** 57 41N 14 20 E
Tenigerbad, *Switz.* **33 C7** 46 42N 8 57 E
Tenino, *U.S.A.* **160 D4** 46 51N 122 51W
Tenkasi, *India* **95 K3** 8 55N 77 20 E
Tenke, *Katanga, Dem. Rep. of the Congo* **119 E2** 11 22 S 26 40 E
Tenke, *Katanga, Dem. Rep. of the Congo* **119 E2** 10 32 S 26 7 E
Tenkodogo, *Burkina Faso* **113 C4** 11 54N 0 19W
Tenna →, *Italy* **45 E10** 43 14N 13 47 E
Tennant Creek, *Australia* **126 B1** 19 30 S 134 15 E
Tennessee □, *U.S.A.* **149 H2** 36 0N 86 30W
Tennessee →, *U.S.A.* **148 G1** 37 4N 88 34W
Tennille, *U.S.A.* **152 C7** 32 56N 82 48W
Tennsift, Oued →, *Morocco* **110 B3** 32 3N 9 28W
Teno, Pta. de, *Canary Is.* **39 F3** 28 21N 16 55W
Tenom, *Malaysia* **78 C5** 5 4N 115 57 E
Tenosique, *Mexico* **163 D6** 17 30N 91 24W
Tenri, *Japan* **71 C7** 34 39N 135 49 E
Tenryū, *Japan* **71 C9** 34 52N 137 49 E
Tenryū-Gawa →, *Japan* **71 B9** 35 39N 137 48 E
Tentelomatinan, *Indonesia* **82 A2** 0 56N 121 48 E
Tenterden, *U.K.* **21 F8** 51 4N 0 42 E
Tenterfield, *Australia* **127 D5** 29 0 S 152 0 E
Teo, *Spain* **42 C2** 42 45N 8 30W
Teófilo Otoni, *Brazil* **171 E3** 17 50 S 41 30W
Tepa, *Indonesia* **79 F7** 7 52 S 129 31 E
Tepalcatepec →, *Mexico* **162 D4** 18 35N 101 59W
Tepecik, *Bursa, Turkey* **51 F12** 40 7N 28 25 E
Tepecik, *Kütahya, Turkey* **49 B11** 39 32N 29 28 E
Tepehuanes, *Mexico* **162 B3** 25 21N 105 44W
Tepelena, *Albania* **50 F4** 40 17N 20 2 E
Tepequem, Serra, *Brazil* **169 C5** 3 45N 61 45W
Tepetongo, *Mexico* **162 C4** 22 28N 103 9W
Tepic, *Mexico* **162 C4** 21 30N 104 54W
Teplá, *Czech Rep.* **34 B5** 49 59N 12 52 E
Teplice, *Czech Rep.* **34 A6** 50 40N 13 48 E
Teploklyuchenka, *Kyrgyzstan* **63 B9** 42 30N 78 30 E
Tepoca, C., *Mexico* **162 A2** 30 20N 112 25W
Tequila, *Mexico* **162 C4** 20 54N 103 47W
Ter →, *Spain* **40 C8** 42 2N 3 12 E
Ter Apel, *Neths.* **24 B7** 52 53N 7 5 E
Téra, *Niger* **113 C5** 14 0N 0 45 E
Tera →, *Spain* **42 D5** 41 54N 5 44W
Teraina, *Kiribati* **135 G11** 4 43N 160 25W
Terakeka, *Sudan* **107 F3** 5 26N 31 45 E
Téramo, *Italy* **45 F10** 42 39N 13 42 E
Terang, *Australia* **128 E5** 38 15 S 142 55 E
Terawhiti, C., *N.Z.* **130 H3** 41 16 S 174 38 E
Terazit, Massif de, *Niger* **113 A6** 20 2N 8 30 E
Tercan, *Turkey* **101 C9** 39 47N 40 23 E
Tercero →, *Argentina* **174 C3** 32 58 S 61 47W
Terdal, *India* **94 F2** 16 33N 75 3 E
Terebovlya, *Ukraine* **59 H3** 49 18N 25 44 E
Teregova, *Romania* **52 E7** 45 10N 22 16 E
Tereida, *Sudan* **107 E3** 10 35N 31 17 E
Terek →, *Russia* **61 J8** 44 0N 47 30 E
Terek-Say, *Kyrgyzstan* **63 C5** 41 30N 71 11 E
Terengganu □, *Malaysia* **84 B2** 4 55N 103 0 E
Terenos, *Brazil* **173 E7** 20 26 S 54 50W
Tereshka →, *Russia* **60 E8** 51 48N 46 26 E
Teresina, *Brazil* **170 C3** 5 9 S 42 45W
Teresinha, *Brazil* **169 C7** 0 58N 52 2W
Terespol, *Poland* **55 F10** 52 5N 23 37 E
Terewah, L., *Australia* **127 D4** 29 52 S 147 35 E
Terges →, *Portugal* **43 H3** 37 49N 7 41W
Tergnier, *France* **27 C10** 49 40N 3 17 E
Terhazza, *Mali* **110 D3** 23 38N 5 22W
Teridgerie Cr. →, *Australia* **127 E4** 30 25 S 148 50 E
Terifa, *Yemen* **98 D3** 14 24N 43 48 E
Terlizzi, *Italy* **47 A9** 41 8N 16 32 E
Terme, *Turkey* **100 B7** 41 11N 37 0 E
Termez = Termiz, *Uzbekistan* **64 F7** 37 15N 67 15 E

Tongyu 291

Tílissos, *Greece* 38 D7 35 20N 25 1 E
Till →, *U.K.* 20 B5 55 41N 2 13W
Tillabéri, *Niger* 113 C5 14 28N 1 28 E
Tillamook, *U.S.A.* 158 D2 45 27N 123 51W
Tillberga, *Sweden* 16 E10 59 40N 16 39 E
Tillia, *Niger* 113 B5 16 8N 4 47 E
Tillman, *U.S.A.* 152 C8 32 28N 81 6W
Tillsonburg, *Canada* 140 D3 42 53N 80 44W
Tillyeria □, *Cyprus* 38 D11 35 6N 32 40 E
Tilogne, *Senegal* 112 B2 16 0N 13 40W
Tílos, *Greece* 49 E9 36 27N 27 27 E
Tilpa, *Australia* 127 E3 30 57 S 144 24 E
Tilrhemt, *Algeria* 111 B5 33 9N 3 22 E
Tilsit = Sovetsk, *Russia* 15 J19 55 6N 21 50 E
Tilt →, *U.K.* 22 E5 56 46N 3 51W
Tilton, *U.S.A.* 151 C13 43 27N 71 36W
Tiltonsville, *U.S.A.* 150 F4 40 10N 80 41W
Tim, *Denmark* 17 H2 56 12N 8 19 E
Timagami, L., *Canada* 140 C3 47 0N 80 10W
Timanskiy Kryazh, *Russia* 56 A9 65 58N 50 5 E
Timareh, *Yemen* 99 D6 12 37N 54 17 E
Timaru, *N.Z.* 131 E6 44 23 S 171 14 E
Timashevo, *Russia* 60 D10 53 22N 51 9 E
Timashevsk, *Russia* 61 H4 45 35N 39 0 E
Timau, *Kenya* 118 B4 0 4N 37 15 E
Timbákion, *Greece* 38 D6 35 4N 24 45 E
Timbaúba, *Brazil* 170 C4 7 31 S 35 19W
Timbedgha, *Mauritania* 112 B3 16 17N 8 16W
Timber Creek, *Australia* 124 C5 15 40 S 130 29 E
Timber Lake, *U.S.A.* 154 C4 45 26N 101 5W
Timber Mt., *U.S.A.* 160 H10 37 6N 116 28W
Timbío, *Colombia* 168 C2 2 20N 76 40W
Timbiqui, *Colombia* 168 C2 2 46N 77 42W
Timbo, *Guinea* 112 C2 10 35N 11 50W
Timbo, *Liberia* 112 D3 5 35N 9 45W
Timboon, *Australia* 128 E5 38 30 S 142 58 E
Timbuktu = Tombouctou, *Mali* 112 B4 16 50N 3 0W
Timeiaouine, *Algeria* 113 A5 20 27N 1 50 E
Timellouline, *Algeria* 111 C6 29 22N 8 55 E
Timétrine, Mts., *Mali* 113 B4 19 25N 1 0W
Timfi Óros, *Greece* 48 B2 39 59N 20 45 E
Timfristós, Óros, *Greece* 48 C3 38 57N 21 50 E
Timhadit, *Morocco* 110 B3 33 15N 5 4W
Timi, *Cyprus* 38 E11 34 44N 32 31 E
Tîmia, *Niger* 113 B6 18 4N 8 40 E
Timimoun, *Algeria* 111 C5 29 14N 0 16 E
Timirist, Râs, *Mauritania* 112 B1 19 21N 16 30W
Timiş = Tamis →, *Serbia, Yug.* 52 F5 44 51N 20 39 E
Timiş □, *Romania* 52 E6 45 40N 21 30 E
Timişoara, *Romania* 52 E6 45 43N 21 15 E
Timmersdala, *Sweden* 17 F7 58 32N 13 46 E
Timmins, *Canada* 140 C3 48 28N 81 25W
Timmonsville, *U.S.A.* 152 A10 34 8N 79 57W
Timok →, *Serbia, Yug.* 50 B6 44 10N 22 40 E
Timon, *Brazil* 170 C3 5 8 S 42 52W
Timor, *Indonesia* 79 F7 9 0 S 125 0 E
Timor Sea, *Ind. Oc.* 124 B4 12 0 S 127 0 E
Timor Timur □, *Indonesia* 79 F7 9 0 S 125 0 E
Timrå, *Sweden* 16 B11 62 29N 17 18 E
Tin Alkoum, *Algeria* 111 D7 24 42N 10 17 E
Tin Can Bay, *Australia* 127 D5 25 56 S 153 0 E
Tin Ethisane, *Mali* 113 B4 19 3N 0 52W
Tin Gornai, *Mali* 113 B4 16 38N 0 38W
Tin Mt., *U.S.A.* 160 J9 36 50N 117 10W
Tina →, *S. Africa* 117 E4 31 18 S 29 13 E
Tîna, Khalîg el, *Egypt* 106 A3 31 20N 32 42 E
Tinaca Pt., *Phil.* 79 C7 5 30N 125 25 E
Tinaco, *Venezuela* 168 B4 9 42N 68 26W
Tinafak, O. →, *Algeria* 111 C6 27 10N 7 0 E
Tinajo, *Canary Is.* 39 E6 29 4N 13 42W
Tinca, *Romania* 52 D6 46 46N 21 58 E
Tindal, *Australia* 124 B5 14 31 S 132 22 E
Tindivanam, *India* 95 H4 12 15N 79 41 E
Tindouf, *Algeria* 110 C3 27 42N 8 10W
Tinée →, *France* 29 E11 43 55N 7 11 E
Tineo, *Spain* 42 B4 43 21N 6 27W
Tinerhir, *Morocco* 110 B3 31 29N 5 31W
Tinfouchi, *Algeria* 110 C3 28 52N 5 49W
Ting Jiang →, *China* 77 E11 24 45N 116 35 E
Tinggi, Pulau, *Malaysia* 87 L5 2 18N 104 7 E
Tingkawk Sakan, *Burma* 90 B6 26 4N 96 44 E
Tinglayan, *Phil.* 80 C3 17 15N 121 9 E
Tinglev, *Denmark* 17 K3 54 57N 9 13 E
Tingo Maria, *Peru* 172 B2 9 10 S 75 54W
Tingrela, *Ivory C.* 112 C3 10 27N 6 25W
Tingsryd, *Sweden* 17 H9 56 31N 15 0 E
Tingstäde, *Sweden* 17 G12 57 44N 18 37 E
Tingvoll, *Norway* 18 B5 62 55N 8 12 E
Tinh Bien, *Vietnam* 87 G5 10 36N 104 57 E
Tinharé, I. de, *Brazil* 171 D4 13 30 S 38 58W
Tiniguiban, *Phil.* 81 F2 11 22N 119 30 E
Tinjar →, *Malaysia* 85 B4 4 4N 114 18 E
Tinn = Atrå, *Norway* 18 E5 59 59N 8 45 E
Tinnevelly = Tirunelveli, *India* 95 K3 8 45N 77 45 E
Tinnoset, *Norway* 18 E6 59 43N 9 3 E
Tinnsjø, *Norway* 18 E5 59 55N 8 54 E
Tinogasta, *Argentina* 174 B2 28 5 S 67 32W
Tínos, *Greece* 49 D7 37 33N 25 8 E
Tiñoso, C., *Spain* 41 H3 37 32N 1 6W
Tinpahar, *India* 93 G12 24 59N 87 44 E
Tinsukia, *India* 90 B5 27 29N 95 20 E
Tinta, *Peru* 172 C3 14 3 S 71 20W
Tintina, *Argentina* 174 B3 27 2 S 62 45W
Tintinara, *Australia* 128 C4 35 48 S 140 2 E
Tintioulé, *Guinea* 112 C3 10 13N 9 12W
Tinto →, *Spain* 43 H4 37 12N 6 55W
Tinui, *N.Z.* 130 G5 40 52 S 176 5 E
Tinwald, *N.Z.* 131 D6 43 55 S 171 43 E
Tioga, *N. Dak., U.S.A.* 154 A3 48 23N 102 56W
Tioga, *Pa., U.S.A.* 150 E7 41 55N 77 8W
Tioman, Pulau, *Malaysia* 78 D2 2 50N 104 10 E
Tione di Trento, *Italy* 44 B7 46 2N 10 43 E
Tionesta, *U.S.A.* 150 E5 41 30N 79 28W
Tior, *Sudan* 107 F3 6 26N 31 11 E
Tioulilin, *Algeria* 111 C4 27 1N 0 2W
Tipp City, *U.S.A.* 157 E12 39 58N 84 11W
Tippecanoe →, *U.S.A.* 157 D10 40 30N 86 45W
Tipperary, *Ireland* 23 D3 52 28N 8 10W
Tipperary □, *Ireland* 23 D4 52 37N 7 55W
Tipton, *Calif., U.S.A.* 160 J7 36 4N 119 19W
Tipton, *Ind., U.S.A.* 157 D10 40 17N 86 2W
Tipton, *Iowa, U.S.A.* 156 C5 41 46N 91 8W
Tipton, *Mo., U.S.A.* 156 F4 38 39N 92 47W
Tipton Mt., *U.S.A.* 161 K12 35 32N 114 12W
Tiptonville, *U.S.A.* 155 G10 36 23N 89 29W
Tiptur, *India* 95 H3 13 15N 76 26 E
Tiquié →, *Brazil* 168 C4 0 5N 68 25W
Tiracambu, Serra do, *Brazil* 170 B2 3 15 S 46 30W
Tīrān, *Iran* 97 C6 32 45N 51 8 E
Tīrān, *Si. Arabia* 106 B3 27 57N 34 32 E
Tirana, *Albania* 50 E3 41 18N 19 49 E
Tiranë = Tirana, *Albania* 50 E3 41 18N 19 49 E
Tirano, *Italy* 44 B7 46 13N 10 10 E
Tiraspol, *Moldova* 53 D14 46 55N 29 35 E
Tiratimine, *Algeria* 111 C5 25 56N 3 37 E
Tirau, *N.Z.* 130 D4 37 58 S 175 46 E
Tirdout, *Mali* 113 B4 16 7N 1 5W
Tire, *Turkey* 49 C9 38 5N 27 45 E
Tirebolu, *Turkey* 101 B8 40 58N 38 45 E
Tiree, *U.K.* 22 E2 56 31N 6 55W
Tiree, Passage of, *U.K.* 22 E2 56 30N 6 30W
Tîrgovişte = Târgovişte, *Romania* 53 F10 44 55N 25 27 E
Tîrgu-Jiu = Târgu-Jiu, *Romania* 53 E8 45 5N 23 19 E
Tîrgu Mureş = Târgu Mureş, *Romania* 53 D9 46 31N 24 38 E
Tirich Mir, *Pakistan* 91 A3 36 15N 71 55 E
Tiriolo, *Italy* 47 D9 38 57N 16 30 E
Tiririca, Serra da, *Brazil* 171 E2 17 6 S 47 6W
Tiriro, *Guinea* 112 C3 10 27N 8 40W
Tiris, *W. Sahara* 110 D2 23 10N 13 20W
Tirlyanskiy, *Russia* 62 D7 54 14N 58 35 E
Tirna →, *India* 94 E3 18 4N 76 57 E
Tírnavos, *Greece* 48 B4 39 45N 22 18 E
Tirodi, *India* 94 D4 21 40N 79 44 E
Tirol □, *Austria* 34 D3 47 3N 10 43 E
Tiros, *Brazil* 171 E2 19 0 S 45 58W
Tirrukkovil, *Sri Lanka* 95 L5 7 7N 81 51 E
Tirschenreuth, *Germany* 31 F8 49 53N 12 19 E
Tirso →, *Italy* 46 C1 39 53N 8 32 E
Tirstrup, *Denmark* 17 H4 56 18N 10 42 E
Tirthahalli, *India* 95 H2 13 42N 75 14 E
Tirua, Pt., *N.Z.* 130 E3 38 25 S 174 40 E
Tiruchchendur, *India* 95 K4 8 30N 78 11 E
Tiruchchirappalli, *India* 95 J4 10 45N 78 45 E
Tirukkoyilur, *India* 95 J4 11 57N 79 12 E
Tirumangalam, *India* 95 K3 9 49N 77 58 E
Tirumayam, *India* 95 J4 10 14N 78 45 E
Tirunelveli, *India* 95 K3 8 45N 77 45 E
Tirupati, *India* 95 H4 13 39N 79 25 E
Tiruppattur, *India* 95 J4 10 8N 78 37 E
Tiruppattur, *India* 95 H4 12 30N 78 30 E
Tiruppur, *India* 95 J3 11 5N 77 22 E
Tirur, *India* 95 J2 10 54N 75 55 E
Tiruttani, *India* 95 H4 13 11N 79 58 E
Tirutturaippundi, *India* 95 J4 10 32N 79 41 E
Tiruvadaimarudur, *India* 95 J4 11 2N 79 27 E
Tiruvalla, *India* 95 K3 9 23N 76 34 E
Tiruvallar, *India* 95 H4 13 9N 79 57 E
Tiruvannamalai, *India* 95 H4 12 15N 79 5 E
Tiruvettipuram, *India* 95 H4 12 39N 79 33 E
Tiruvottiyur, *India* 95 H5 13 10N 80 22 E
Tisa, *India* 92 C7 32 50N 76 9 E
Tisa →, *Serbia, Yug.* 52 E5 45 15N 20 17 E
Tisdale, *Canada* 143 C8 52 50N 104 0W
Tishomingo, *U.S.A.* 155 H6 34 14N 96 41W
Tisjön, *Sweden* 16 D7 60 56N 13 0 E
Tisnaren, *Sweden* 17 F9 58 58N 15 56 E
Tišnov, *Czech Rep.* 35 B9 49 21N 16 25 E
Tisovec, *Slovak Rep.* 35 C12 48 41N 19 56 E
Tissamaharama, *Sri Lanka* 95 L5 6 17N 81 17 E
Tissemsilt, *Algeria* 111 A5 35 35N 1 50 E
Tissint, *Morocco* 110 C3 29 57N 7 16W
Tista →, *India* 90 C2 25 23N 89 43 E
Tistedal, *Norway* 18 E8 59 8N 11 27 E
Tisza = Tisa →, *Serbia, Yug.* 52 E5 45 15N 20 17 E
Tiszaföldvár, *Hungary* 52 D5 46 58N 20 14 E
Tiszafüred, *Hungary* 52 C5 47 38N 20 50 E
Tiszalök, *Hungary* 52 B6 48 1N 21 20 E
Tiszavasvári, *Hungary* 52 C6 47 58N 21 18 E
Tit, *Ahaggar, Algeria* 111 D6 23 0N 5 10 E
Tit, *Tademait, Algeria* 111 C5 27 0N 1 29 E
Tit-Ary, *Russia* 65 B13 71 55N 127 2 E
Titaguas, *Spain* 40 F3 39 53N 1 6W
Titahi Bay, *N.Z.* 130 H3 41 6 S 174 50 E
Titao, *Burkina Faso* 113 C4 13 45N 2 5W
Titel, *Serbia, Yug.* 52 E5 45 10N 20 18 E
Tithwal, *Pakistan* 93 B5 34 21N 73 50 E
Titicaca, L., *S. Amer.* 172 D4 15 30 S 69 30W
Titisee, *Germany* 31 H4 47 54N 8 10 E
Titiira Hd., *N.Z.* 131 D4 43 36 S 169 25 E
Titiwa, *Nigeria* 113 C7 12 14N 12 53 E
Titlagarh, *India* 94 D6 20 15N 83 11 E
Titlis, *Switz.* 33 C6 46 46N 8 27 E
Tito, *Italy* 47 B8 40 35N 15 40 E
Titograd = Podgorica, *Montenegro, Yug.* 50 D3 42 30N 19 19 E
Titova Korenica, *Croatia* 45 D12 44 45N 15 41 E
Titu, *Romania* 53 F10 44 39N 25 32 E
Titule, *Dem. Rep. of the Congo* 118 B2 3 15N 25 31 E
Titusville, *Fla., U.S.A.* 149 L5 28 37N 80 49W
Titusville, *Pa., U.S.A.* 150 E5 41 38N 79 41W
Tivaouane, *Senegal* 112 C1 14 56N 16 45W
Tivat, *Montenegro, Yug.* 50 D2 42 28N 18 43 E
Tiverton, *U.K.* 21 G4 50 54N 3 29W
Tívoli, *Italy* 45 G9 41 58N 12 45 E
Tiwī, *Oman* 99 B7 22 45N 59 12 E
Tiyo, *Eritrea* 107 E5 14 41N 40 15 E
Tizga, *Morocco* 110 B3 32 1N 5 9W
Ti'zi N'Isli, *Morocco* 110 B3 32 28N 5 47W
Tizi-Ouzou, *Algeria* 111 A5 36 42N 4 3 E
Tizimín, *Mexico* 163 C7 21 0N 88 1W
Tiznados →, *Venezuela* 168 B4 8 16N 67 47W
Tiznit, *Morocco* 110 C3 29 48N 9 45W
Tjæreborg, *Denmark* 17 J2 55 28N 8 36 E
Tjällmo, *Sweden* 17 F9 58 43N 15 20 E
Tjeggelvas, *Sweden* 14 C17 66 37N 17 45 E
Tjirebon = Cirebon, *Indonesia* 79 G13 6 45 S 108 32 E
Tjøme, *Norway* 18 E7 59 8N 10 26 E
Tjörn, *Sweden* 17 F5 58 0N 11 35 E
Tkibuli = Tqibuli, *Georgia* 61 J6 42 26N 43 0 E
Tkvarcheli = Tqvarcheli, *Georgia* 61 J5 42 47N 41 42 E
Tlacotalpan, *Mexico* 163 D5 18 37N 95 40W
Tlahualilo, *Mexico* 162 B4 26 20N 103 30W
Tlaquepaque, *Mexico* 162 C4 20 39N 103 19W
Tlaxcala, *Mexico* 163 D5 19 20N 98 14W
Tlaxcala □, *Mexico* 163 D5 19 30N 98 20W
Tlaxiaco, *Mexico* 163 D5 17 18N 97 40W
Tlemcen, *Algeria* 111 B4 34 52N 1 21W
Tleta Sidi Bouguedra, *Morocco* 110 B3 32 16N 9 59W
Tłuszcz, *Poland* 55 F8 52 25N 21 25 E
Tlyarata, *Russia* 61 J8 42 9N 46 26 E
Tmassah, *Libya* 108 C3 26 19N 15 51 E
Tnine d'Anglou, *Morocco* 110 C3 29 50N 9 50W
To Bong, *Vietnam* 86 F7 12 45N 109 16 E
To-Shima, *Japan* 71 C11 34 31N 139 17 E
Toad →, *Canada* 142 B4 59 25N 124 57W
Toad River, *Canada* 142 B3 58 51N 125 14W
Toamasina, *Madag.* 117 B8 18 10 S 49 25 E
Toamasina □, *Madag.* 117 B8 18 0 S 49 0 E
Toay, *Argentina* 174 D3 36 43 S 64 38W
Toba, *China* 76 B1 31 19N 97 42 E
Toba, *Japan* 71 C8 34 30N 136 51 E
Toba, Danau, *Indonesia* 78 D1 2 30N 97 30 E
Toba Kakar, *Pakistan* 91 C3 31 30N 69 0 E
Toba Tek Singh, *Pakistan* 92 D5 30 55N 72 25 E
Tobago, *W. Indies* 165 D7 11 10N 60 30W
Tobarra, *Spain* 41 G3 38 37N 1 44W
Tobelo, *Indonesia* 79 D7 1 45N 127 56 E
Tobermory, *Canada* 140 C3 45 12N 81 40W
Tobermory, *U.K.* 22 E2 56 38N 6 5W
Tobi, *Pac. Oc.* 79 D8 2 40N 131 10 E
Tobias Fornier, *Phil.* 81 F3 10 30N 121 57 E
Tobin, *U.S.A.* 160 F5 39 55N 121 19W
Tobin, L., *Australia* 124 D4 21 45 S 125 49 E
Tobin L., *Canada* 143 C8 53 35N 103 30W
Toblach = Dobbiaco, *Italy* 45 B9 46 44N 12 14 E
Toboali, *Indonesia* 78 E3 3 0 S 106 25 E
Tobol, *Kazakstan* 62 E9 52 40N 62 39 E
Tobol →, *Russia* 64 D7 58 10N 68 12 E
Toboli, *Indonesia* 79 E6 0 38 S 120 5 E
Tobolsk, *Russia* 64 D7 58 15N 68 10 E
Tobor, *Senegal* 112 C1 12 40N 16 15W
Toboso, *Phil.* 81 F4 10 43N 123 31 E
Tobruk = Tubruq, *Libya* 108 B4 32 7N 23 55 E
Tobyhanna, *U.S.A.* 151 E9 41 11N 75 25W
Tobyl = Tobol →, *Russia* 64 D7 58 10N 68 12 E
Tocache Nuevo, *Peru* 172 B2 8 9 S 76 26W
Tocantínia, *Brazil* 170 C2 9 33 S 48 22W
Tocantinópolis, *Brazil* 170 C2 6 20 S 47 25W
Tocantins □, *Brazil* 170 D2 10 0 S 48 0W
Tocantins →, *Brazil* 170 B2 1 45 S 49 10W
Toccoa, *U.S.A.* 149 H4 34 35N 83 19W
Toce →, *Italy* 44 C5 45 56N 8 29 E
Tochi →, *Pakistan* 92 C4 32 49N 70 41 E
Tochigi, *Japan* 71 A11 36 25N 139 45 E
Tochigi □, *Japan* 71 A11 36 45N 139 45 E
Tocina, *Spain* 43 H5 37 37N 5 44W
Töcksfors, *Sweden* 16 E5 59 31N 11 52 E
Toco, *Chile* 172 E4 22 5 S 69 35W
Toconao, *Chile* 174 A2 23 11 S 68 1W
Tocopilla, *Chile* 174 A1 22 5 S 70 10W
Tocumwal, *Australia* 129 C6 35 51 S 145 31 E
Tocuyo →, *Venezuela* 168 A4 11 3N 68 23W
Tocuyo de la Costa, *Venezuela* 168 A4 11 2N 68 23W
Todal, *Norway* 18 B5 62 49N 8 44 E
Todd →, *Australia* 126 C2 24 52 S 135 48 E
Todeli, *Indonesia* 79 E6 1 38 S 124 34 E
Todenyang, *Kenya* 118 B4 4 35N 35 56 E
Todgarh, *India* 92 G5 25 42N 73 58 E
Todi, *Italy* 45 F9 42 47N 12 24 E
Tödi, *Switz.* 33 C7 46 48N 8 55 E
Todos os Santos, B. de, *Brazil* 171 D4 12 48 S 38 38W
Todos Santos, *Mexico* 162 C2 23 27N 110 13W
Todtnau, *Germany* 31 H3 47 49N 7 56 E
Toe Hd., *U.K.* 22 D1 57 50N 7 8W
Toecé, *Burkina Faso* 113 C4 11 50N 1 16W
Toetoes B., *N.Z.* 131 G3 46 42 S 168 41 E
Tofield, *Canada* 142 C6 53 25N 112 40W
Tofino, *Canada* 142 D3 49 11N 125 55W
Tofte, *Norway* 18 E7 59 33N 10 34 E
Tofua, *Tonga* 133 P13 19 45 S 175 5W
Toga, *Vanuatu* 133 C4 13 26 S 166 42 E
Tōgane, *Japan* 71 B12 35 33N 140 22 E
Togba, *Mauritania* 112 B2 17 26N 10 12W
Togbo, *C.A.R.* 114 A3 6 0N 17 27 E
Toggenburg, *Switz.* 33 B8 47 16N 9 9 E
Togiak, *U.S.A.* 144 G7 59 4N 160 24W
Togian, Kepulauan, *Indonesia* 79 E6 0 20 S 121 50 E
Togliatti, *Russia* 60 D9 53 32N 49 24 E
Togo ■, *W. Afr.* 113 D5 8 30N 1 35 E
Togtoh, *China* 74 D6 40 15N 111 10 E
Toguzak →, *Kazakstan* 62 D9 54 3N 62 44 E
Tohma →, *Turkey* 100 C7 38 29N 38 23 E
Tōhoku □, *Japan* 68 E10 39 50N 141 45 E
Töhöm, *Mongolia* 74 B5 44 27N 108 2 E
Tohopekaliga, East Lake, *U.S.A.* 153 G8 28 18N 81 15W
Tohopekaliga, L., *U.S.A.* 153 G8 28 12N 81 24W
Toi, *Japan* 71 C10 34 54N 138 47 E
Toinya, *Sudan* 107 F2 6 17N 29 46 E
Toiyabe Range, *U.S.A.* 158 G5 39 30N 117 0W
Tojikiston = Tajikistan ■, *Asia* 64 F8 38 30N 70 0 E
Tojo, *Indonesia* 79 E6 1 20 S 121 15 E
Tōjō, *Japan* 70 C5 34 53N 133 16 E
Tok, *U.S.A.* 144 E12 63 20N 142 59W
Tok →, *Russia* 62 E4 52 46N 52 22 E
Tok-do, *Japan* 69 F5 37 15N 131 52 E
Toka, *Guyana* 169 C6 3 58N 59 17W
Tokaanu, *N.Z.* 130 E4 38 58 S 175 46 E
Tokachi-Dake, *Japan* 68 C11 43 17N 142 5 E
Tokachi-Gawa →, *Japan* 68 C11 42 44N 143 42 E
Tokai, *Japan* 71 B8 35 2N 136 55 E
Tokaj, *Hungary* 52 B6 48 8N 21 27 E
Tokala, *Indonesia* 79 E6 1 30 S 121 40 E
Tōkamachi, *Japan* 69 F9 37 8N 138 43 E
Tokanui, *N.Z.* 131 G3 46 34 S 168 56 E
Tokar, *Sudan* 106 D4 18 27N 37 56 E
Tokara-Rettō, *Japan* 69 K4 29 37N 129 43 E
Tokarahi, *N.Z.* 131 E5 44 56 S 170 39 E
Tokashiki-Shima, *Japan* 69 L3 26 11N 127 21 E
Tokat, *Turkey* 100 B7 40 22N 36 35 E
Tokat □, *Turkey* 57 F6 40 15N 36 30 E
Tŏkch'ŏn, *N. Korea* 75 E14 39 45N 126 18 E
Tokeland, *U.S.A.* 160 D3 46 42N 123 59W
Tokelau Is., *Pac. Oc.* 134 H10 9 0 S 171 45W
Toki, *Japan* 71 B9 35 18N 137 8 E
Tokmak, *Kyrgyzstan* 64 E8 42 49N 75 15 E
Tokmak, *Ukraine* 59 J8 47 16N 35 42 E
Toko Ra., *Australia* 126 C2 23 5 S 138 20 E
Tokomaru Bay, *N.Z.* 130 E7 38 8 S 178 22 E
Tokoname, *Japan* 71 C8 34 53N 136 51 E
Tokoro-Gawa →, *Japan* 68 B12 44 7N 144 5 E
Tokoroa, *N.Z.* 130 E4 38 13 S 175 50 E
Tokorozawa, *Japan* 71 B11 35 47N 139 28 E
Toksook Bay, *U.S.A.* 144 F6 60 32N 165 0W
Toktogul, *Kyrgyzstan* 63 C6 41 50N 72 50 E
Toku, *Tonga* 133 P13 18 10 S 174 11W
Tokuji, *Japan* 70 C3 34 11N 131 42 E
Tokuno-Shima, *Japan* 69 L4 27 56N 128 55 E
Tokushima, *Japan* 70 C6 34 4N 134 34 E
Tokushima □, *Japan* 70 D6 33 55N 134 0 E
Tokuyama, *Japan* 70 C3 34 3N 131 50 E
Tōkyō, *Japan* 71 B11 35 45N 139 45 E
Tōkyō □, *Japan* 71 B11 35 40N 139 30 E
Tōkyō-Wan, *Japan* 71 B11 35 25N 139 47 E
Tokzār, *Afghan.* 91 B2 35 52N 66 26 E
Tolaga Bay, *N.Z.* 130 E7 38 21 S 178 20 E
Tolbukhin = Dobrich, *Bulgaria* 51 C11 43 37N 27 49 E
Tolé, *C.A.R.* 114 A3 6 34N 16 1 E
Toledo, *Brazil* 175 A5 24 44 S 53 45W
Toledo, *Phil.* 81 F4 10 23N 123 38 E
Toledo, *Spain* 42 F6 39 50N 4 2W
Toledo, *Ill., U.S.A.* 157 E8 39 16N 88 15W
Toledo, *Iowa, U.S.A.* 156 C4 42 0N 92 35W
Toledo, *Ohio, U.S.A.* 157 C13 41 39N 83 33W
Toledo, *Oreg., U.S.A.* 158 D2 44 37N 123 56W
Toledo, *Wash., U.S.A.* 158 C2 46 26N 122 51W
Toledo, Montes de, *Spain* 43 F6 39 33N 4 20W
Toledo Bend Reservoir, *U.S.A.* 155 K8 31 11N 93 34W
Tolentino, *Italy* 45 E10 43 12N 13 17 E
Tolfa, *Italy* 45 F8 42 9N 11 56 E
Tolga, *Algeria* 111 B6 34 40N 5 22 E
Tolga, *Australia* 126 B4 17 15 S 145 29 E
Tolga, *Norway* 18 B8 62 26N 11 1 E
Toliara, *Madag.* 117 C7 23 21 S 43 40 E
Toliara □, *Madag.* 117 C8 21 0 S 45 0 E
Tolima, *Colombia* 168 C2 4 40N 75 19W
Tolima □, *Colombia* 168 C2 3 45N 75 15W
Tolitoli, *Indonesia* 79 D6 1 5N 120 50 E
Tolkmicko, *Poland* 54 D6 54 19N 19 31 E
Tollarp, *Sweden* 17 J7 55 55N 13 58 E
Tollensesee, *Germany* 30 B9 53 30N 13 13 E
Tollhouse, *U.S.A.* 160 H7 37 1N 119 24W
Tolmachevo, *Russia* 58 C5 58 56N 29 51 E
Tolmezzo, *Italy* 45 B10 46 24N 13 1 E
Tolmin, *Slovenia* 45 B10 46 11N 13 45 E
Tolna, *Hungary* 52 D3 46 25N 18 48 E
Tolna □, *Hungary* 52 D3 46 30N 18 30 E
Tolo, *Dem. Rep. of the Congo* 114 C3 2 55 S 18 34 E
Tolo, Teluk, *Indonesia* 79 E6 2 20 S 122 10 E
Tolochin = Talachyn, *Belarus* 58 E5 54 25N 29 42 E
Tolong Bay, *Phil.* 81 G4 9 20N 122 49 E
Tolono, *U.S.A.* 157 E8 39 59N 88 16W
Tolosa, *Spain* 40 B2 43 8N 2 5W
Tolox, *Spain* 43 J6 36 41N 4 54W
Toltén, *Chile* 176 A2 39 13 S 74 14W
Toluca, *Mexico* 163 D5 19 20N 99 40W
Toluca, *U.S.A.* 156 C7 41 0N 89 9W
Tolybay, *Kazakstan* 62 F9 50 31N 62 19 E
Tom Burke, *S. Africa* 117 C4 23 5 S 28 0 E
Tom Price, *Australia* 124 D2 22 40 S 117 48 E
Toma, *Burkina Faso* 112 C4 12 45N 2 53W
Tomah, *U.S.A.* 154 D9 43 59N 90 30W
Tomahawk, *U.S.A.* 154 C10 45 28N 89 44W
Tomai, *Moldova* 53 D13 46 34N 28 19 E
Tomakomai, *Japan* 68 C10 42 38N 141 36 E
Tomales, *U.S.A.* 160 G4 38 15N 122 53W
Tomales B., *U.S.A.* 160 G3 38 15N 123 58W
Tomanlivi, *Fiji* 133 A2 17 37 S 178 1 E
Tomar, *Portugal* 43 F2 39 36N 8 25W
Tómaros, Óros, *Greece* 48 B2 39 29N 20 48 E
Tomarza, *Turkey* 100 C6 38 27N 35 48 E
Tomás Barrón, *Bolivia* 172 D4 17 35 S 67 31W
Tomaszów Lubelski, *Poland* 55 H10 50 27N 23 25 E
Tomaszów Mazowiecki, *Poland* 55 G7 51 30N 20 2 E
Tomatlán, *Mexico* 162 D3 19 56N 105 15W
Tombadonkéa, *Guinea* 112 C2 11 0N 14 25W
Tombador, Serra do, *Brazil* 173 C6 12 0 S 58 0W
Tombe, *Sudan* 107 F3 5 53N 31 40 E
Tombel, *Cameroon* 114 B1 4 45N 9 40 E
Tombigbee →, *U.S.A.* 149 K2 31 8N 87 57W
Tombôco, *Angola* 115 D2 6 48 S 13 18 E
Tombouctou, *Mali* 112 B4 16 50N 3 0W
Tombstone, *U.S.A.* 159 L8 31 43N 110 4W
Tombua, *Angola* 116 B1 15 55 S 11 55 E
Tomé, *Chile* 174 D1 36 36 S 72 57W
Tomé-Açu, *Brazil* 170 B2 2 25 S 48 9W
Tomelilla, *Sweden* 17 J7 55 33N 13 58 E
Tomelloso, *Spain* 43 F7 39 10N 3 2W
Tomingley, *Australia* 129 B8 32 26 S 148 16 E
Tomini, *Indonesia* 79 D6 0 30N 120 30 E
Tomini, Teluk, *Indonesia* 79 E6 0 10 S 122 0 E
Tominian, *Mali* 112 C4 13 17N 4 35W
Tomiño, *Spain* 42 D2 41 59N 8 46W
Tomintoul, *U.K.* 22 D5 57 15N 3 23W
Tomislavgrad, *Bos.-H.* 52 G2 43 42N 17 13 E
Tomkinson Ranges, *Australia* 125 E4 26 11 S 129 5 E
Tommot, *Russia* 65 D13 59 4N 126 20 E
Tomnop Ta Suos, *Cambodia* 87 G5 11 20N 104 15 E
Tomo, *Colombia* 168 C4 2 38N 67 32W
Tomo, *Japan* 70 C5 34 23N 133 23 E
Tomo →, *Colombia* 168 B4 5 20N 67 48W
Tomobe, *Japan* 71 A12 36 20N 140 20 E
Tomra, *Norway* 18 B3 62 34N 6 56 E
Toms Place, *U.S.A.* 160 H8 37 34N 118 41W
Toms River, *U.S.A.* 151 G10 39 58N 74 12W
Tomsk, *Russia* 64 D9 56 30N 85 5 E
Tomtabacken, *Sweden* 17 G8 57 30N 14 30 E
Tona, *Spain* 40 D7 41 51N 2 14 E
Tonalá, *Mexico* 163 D6 16 8N 93 41W
Tonale, Passo del, *Italy* 44 B7 46 16N 10 35 E
Tonami, *Japan* 71 A8 36 40N 136 58 E
Tonantins, *Brazil* 168 D4 2 45 S 67 45W
Tonasket, *U.S.A.* 158 B4 48 42N 119 26W
Tonate, *Fr. Guiana* 169 C7 5 0N 52 28W
Tonawanda, *U.S.A.* 150 D6 43 1N 78 53W
Tonbridge, *U.K.* 21 F8 51 11N 0 17 E
Tondano, *Indonesia* 79 D6 1 35N 124 54 E
Tondela, *Portugal* 42 E2 40 31N 8 5W
Tønder, *Denmark* 17 K2 54 58N 8 50 E
Tondi, *India* 95 K4 9 45N 79 4 E
Tondi Kiwindi, *Niger* 113 C5 14 28N 2 2 E
Tondibi, *Mali* 113 B4 16 39N 0 14W
Tondoro, *Namibia* 116 B2 17 45 S 18 50 E
Tone →, *Australia* 125 F2 34 25 S 116 25 E
Tone-Gawa →, *Japan* 69 F9 35 44N 140 51 E
Tonekābon, *Iran* 97 B6 36 45N 51 12 E
Tong Xian, *China* 74 E9 39 55N 116 35 E
Tōngâ, *Sudan* 107 F3 9 28N 31 3 E
Tonga ■, *Pac. Oc.* 133 P13 19 50 S 174 30W
Tonga Trench, *Pac. Oc.* 134 J10 18 0 S 173 0W
Tongaat, *S. Africa* 117 D5 29 33 S 31 9 E
Tongala, *Australia* 129 D6 36 14 S 144 56 E
Tong'an, *China* 77 E12 24 37N 118 8 E
Tongareva, *Cook Is.* 135 H12 9 0 S 158 0W
Tongass National Forest, *U.S.A.* 144 H14 56 30N 134 0W
Tongatapu, *Tonga* 133 Q14 21 10 S 174 0W
Tongatapu Group, *Tonga* 133 Q13 21 0 S 175 0W
Tongbai, *China* 77 A9 32 20N 113 23 E
Tongcheng, *Anhui, China* 77 B11 31 4N 116 56 E
Tongcheng, *Hubei, China* 77 C9 29 15N 113 50 E
Tongchŏn-ni, *N. Korea* 75 E14 39 50N 127 25 E
Tongchuan, *China* 74 G5 35 6N 109 3 E
Tongdao, *China* 76 D7 26 10N 109 42 E
Tongeren, *Belgium* 24 D5 50 47N 5 28 E
Tonggu, *China* 77 C10 28 31N 114 20 E
Tongguan, *China* 74 G6 34 40N 110 25 E
Tonghai, *China* 76 E4 24 10N 102 53 E
Tonghua, *China* 75 D13 41 42N 125 58 E
Tongjiang, *China* 76 B6 31 58N 107 11 E
Tongjosŏn Man, *N. Korea* 75 E15 39 30N 128 0 E
Tongkil, *Phil.* 81 H3 6 3N 121 50 E
Tongking, G. of = Tonkin, G. of, *Asia* 72 E5 20 0N 108 0 E
Tongliang, *China* 76 C6 29 50N 106 3 E
Tongliao, *China* 75 C12 43 38N 122 18 E
Tongling, *China* 77 B11 30 55N 117 48 E
Tonglu, *China* 77 C12 29 45N 119 37 E
Tongnae, *S. Korea* 75 G15 35 12N 129 5 E
Tongnan = Anyue, *China* 76 B5 30 9N 105 50 E
Tongoa, *Vanuatu* 133 F6 16 54 S 168 34 E
Tongobory, *Madag.* 117 C7 23 32 S 44 20 E
Tongoy, *Chile* 174 C1 30 16 S 71 31W
Tongquil I., *Phil.* 81 H3 6 2N 121 51 E
Tongren, *China* 76 D7 27 43N 109 11 E
Tongres = Tongeren, *Belgium* 24 D5 50 47N 5 28 E
Tongsa Dzong, *Bhutan* 90 B3 27 31N 90 31 E
Tongue, *U.K.* 22 C4 58 29N 4 25W
Tongue →, *U.S.A.* 154 B2 46 25N 105 52W
Tongwei, *China* 74 G3 35 0N 105 5 E
Tongxiang, *China* 77 B13 30 39N 120 34 E
Tongxin, *China* 74 F3 36 59N 105 58 E
Tongyang, *N. Korea* 75 E14 39 9N 126 53 E
Tongyu, *China* 75 B12 44 45N 123 4 E

Vang Vieng 295

Urabá, G. de, *Colombia* **168 B2** 8 25N 76 53W
Urad Qianqi, *China* **74 D5** 40 40N 108 30 E
Uraga-Suidō, *Japan* **71 B11** 35 13N 139 45 E
Urakawa, *Japan* **68 C11** 42 9N 142 47 E
Ural = Zhayyq →, *Kazakstan* **57 E9** 47 0N 51 48 E
Ural, *Australia* **129 B7** 33 21 S 146 12 E
Ural Mts. = Uralskie Gory, *Eurasia* **62 C7** 60 0N 59 0 E
Uralla, *Australia* **129 A9** 30 37 S 151 29 E
Uralsk = Oral, *Kazakstan* **60 E10** 51 20N 51 20 E
Uralskie Gory, *Eurasia* **62 C7** 60 0N 59 0 E
Urambo, *Tanzania* **118 D3** 5 4 S 32 0 E
Urana, *Australia* **129 C7** 35 15 S 146 21 E
Urandangi, *Australia* **126 C2** 21 32 S 138 14 E
Uranium City, *Canada* **143 B7** 59 34N 108 37W
Uraricaá →, *Brazil* **169 C5** 3 20N 61 56W
Uraricoera, *Brazil* **169 C5** 3 27N 60 59W
Uraricoera →, *Brazil* **169 C5** 3 2N 60 30W
Uravakonda, *India* **95 G3** 14 57N 77 12 E
Urawa, *Japan* **71 B11** 35 50N 139 40 E
Uray, *Russia* **64 C7** 60 5N 65 15 E
'Uray'irah, *Si. Arabia* **97 E6** 25 57N 48 53 E
Urbana, *Ill., U.S.A.* **157 D8** 40 7N 88 12W
Urbana, *Ohio, U.S.A.* **157 D13** 40 7N 83 45W
Urbandale, *U.S.A.* **156 C3** 41 38N 93 43W
Urbánia, *Italy* **45 E9** 43 40N 12 31 E
Urbano Santos, *Brazil* **170 B3** 3 12 S 43 23W
Urbel →, *Spain* **42 C7** 42 21N 3 40W
Urbino, *Italy* **45 E9** 43 43N 12 38 E
Urbión, Picos de, *Spain* **40 C2** 42 1N 2 52W
Urcos, *Peru* **172 C3** 13 40 S 71 38W
Urdaneta, *Phil.* **80 D3** 15 59N 120 34 E
Urdinarrain, *Argentina* **174 C4** 32 37 S 58 52W
Urdos, *France* **28 F3** 42 51N 0 35W
Urdzhar, *Kazakstan* **64 E9** 47 5N 81 38 E
Ure →, *U.K.* **20 C6** 54 5N 1 20W
Uren, *Russia* **60 B7** 57 35N 45 55 E
Ureparapara, *Vanuatu* **133 C5** 13 32 S 167 20 E
Ures, *Mexico* **162 B2** 29 30N 110 30W
Ureshino, *Japan* **70 D1** 33 6N 129 59 E
Urfa = Sanliurfa, *Turkey* **101 D8** 37 12N 38 50 E
Urganch, *Uzbekistan* **64 E7** 41 40N 60 41 E
Urgench = Urganch, *Uzbekistan* **64 E7** 41 40N 60 41 E
Ürgüp, *Turkey* **96 B2** 38 38N 34 56 E
Urgut, *Uzbekistan* **63 D3** 39 23N 67 15 E
Uri, *India* **93 B6** 34 8N 74 2 E
Uri □, *Switz.* **33 C7** 46 43N 8 35 E
Uribante →, *Venezuela* **168 B3** 7 25N 71 50W
Uribe, *Colombia* **168 C3** 3 13N 74 24W
Uribia, *Colombia* **168 A3** 11 43N 72 16W
Uricani, *Romania* **52 E8** 45 20N 23 9 E
Urimba, *Angola* **115 E3** 10 56 S 16 32 E
Uriondo, *Bolivia* **174 A3** 21 41 S 64 41W
Urique, *Mexico* **162 B3** 27 13N 107 55W
Urique →, *Mexico* **162 B3** 26 29N 107 58W
Urirotstock, *Switz.* **33 C7** 46 52N 8 32 E
Urk, *Neths.* **24 B5** 52 39N 5 36 E
Urla, *Turkey* **49 C8** 38 20N 26 47 E
Urlați, *Romania* **53 F11** 44 59N 26 15 E
Urmia = Orūmīyeh, *Iran* **101 D11** 37 40N 45 0 E
Urmia, L. = Orūmīyeh, Daryācheh-ye, *Iran* **101 D11** 37 50N 45 30 E
Urnäsch, *Switz.* **33 B8** 47 19N 9 17 E
Urner Alpen, *Switz.* **33 C7** 46 45N 8 45 E
Uroševac, *Kosovo, Yug.* **50 D5** 42 23N 21 10 E
Uroteppa, *Tajikistan* **63 D4** 39 55N 69 1 E
Urrao, *Colombia* **168 B2** 6 20N 76 11W
Urshult, *Sweden* **17 H8** 56 31N 14 50 E
Uruaçu, *Brazil* **171 D2** 14 30 S 49 10W
Uruana, *Brazil* **171 E2** 15 30 S 49 41W
Uruapan, *Mexico* **162 D4** 19 30N 102 0W
Uruará, *Brazil* **169 D7** 3 42 S 53 51W
Uruará →, *Brazil* **169 D7** 2 6 S 53 38W
Urubamba, *Peru* **172 C3** 13 20 S 72 10W
Urubamba →, *Peru* **172 C3** 10 43 S 73 48W
Urubaxi →, *Brazil* **169 D5** 0 31 S 64 50W
Urubu →, *Brazil* **169 D6** 2 55 S 58 25W
Uruçara, *Brazil* **169 D6** 2 32 S 57 45W
Uruçuí, *Brazil* **170 C3** 7 20 S 44 28W
Uruçuí, Serra do, *Brazil* **170 C3** 9 0 S 44 45W
Uruçuí Prêto →, *Brazil* **170 C3** 7 20 S 44 38W
Urucuia →, *Brazil* **171 E2** 16 8 S 45 5W
Urucurituba, *Brazil* **169 D6** 2 41 S 57 40W
Uruguai →, *Brazil* **175 B5** 26 0 S 53 30W
Uruguaiana, *Brazil* **174 B4** 29 50 S 57 0W
Uruguay ■, *S. Amer.* **174 C4** 32 30 S 56 30W
Uruguay →, *S. Amer.* **174 C4** 34 12 S 58 18W
Urumchi = Ürümqi, *China* **64 E9** 43 45N 87 45 E
Ürümqi, *China* **64 E9** 43 45N 87 45 E
Urup →, *Russia* **61 H5** 45 0N 41 10 E
Urup, Ostrov, *Russia* **65 E16** 46 0N 151 0 E
Urutaí, *Brazil* **171 E2** 17 28 S 48 12W
Uryupinsk, *Russia* **60 E5** 50 45N 41 58 E
Urzhum, *Russia* **60 B9** 57 10N 49 56 E
Urziceni, *Romania* **53 F11** 44 40N 26 42 E
Usa, *Japan* **70 D3** 33 31N 131 21 E
Usa →, *Russia* **56 A10** 66 16N 59 49 E
Uşak, *Turkey* **49 C11** 38 43N 29 28 E
Uşak □, *Turkey* **49 C11** 38 30N 29 0 E
Usakos, *Namibia* **116 C2** 21 54 S 15 31 E
Usborne, Mt., *Falk. Is.* **176 D5** 51 42 S 58 50W
Ušće, *Serbia, Yug.* **50 C4** 43 30N 20 39 E
Usedom, *Germany* **30 B10** 53 55N 14 2 E
Useless Loop, *Australia* **125 E1** 26 8 S 113 23 E
'Usfān, *Si. Arabia* **98 B2** 21 58N 39 27 E
Ush-Tobe, *Kazakstan* **64 E8** 45 16N 78 0 E
Ushakova, Ostrov, *Russia* **6 A12** 82 0N 80 0 E
Ushant = Ouessant, Î. d', *France* **26 D1** 48 28N 5 6W
Ushashi, *Tanzania* **118 C3** 1 59 S 33 57 E
Ushat, *Sudan* **107 F2** 7 59N 29 28 E
'Ushayrah, *Si. Arabia* **106 C5** 21 46N 40 42 E
Ushibuka, *Japan* **70 E2** 32 11N 130 1 E
Ushuaia, *Argentina* **176 D3** 54 50 S 68 23W
Ushumun, *Russia* **65 D13** 52 47N 126 32 E
Usk, *Canada* **142 C3** 54 38N 128 26W
Usk →, *U.K.* **21 F5** 51 33N 2 58W
Uska, *India* **93 F10** 27 12N 83 7 E
Uskedal, *Norway* **18 E2** 59 56N 5 53 E
Üsküdar, *Turkey* **51 F13** 41 0N 29 5 E
Uslar, *Germany* **30 D5** 51 39N 9 38 E
Usman, *Russia* **59 F10** 52 5N 39 48 E
Usoke, *Tanzania* **118 D3** 5 8 S 32 24 E
Usolye, *Russia* **62 B6** 59 28N 56 31 E
Usolye Sibirskoye, *Russia* **65 D11** 52 48N 103 40 E
Usoro, *Nigeria* **113 D6** 5 33N 6 11 E
Uspallata, P. de, *Argentina* **174 C2** 32 37 S 69 22W
Uspenskiy, *Kazakstan* **64 E8** 48 41N 72 43 E
Ussel, *France* **28 C6** 45 32N 2 18 E
Usson-du-Poitou, *France* **28 B4** 46 16N 0 31 E
Ussuri →, *Asia* **68 A7** 48 27N 135 0 E
Ussuriysk, *Russia* **65 E14** 43 48N 131 59 E
Ussurka, *Russia* **68 B6** 45 12N 133 31 E
Ust-Aldan = Batamay, *Russia* **65 C13** 63 30N 129 15 E
Ust-Amginskoye = Khandyga, *Russia* **65 C14** 62 42N 135 35 E
Ust-Bolsheretsk, *Russia* **65 D16** 52 50N 156 15 E
Ust-Buzulukskaya, *Russia* **60 E6** 50 8N 42 11 E
Ust-Chaun, *Russia* **65 C18** 68 47N 170 30 E
Ust-Donetskiy, *Russia* **61 G5** 47 35N 40 55 E
Ust-Ilimpeya = Yukta, *Russia* **65 C11** 63 26N 105 42 E
Ust-Ilimsk, *Russia* **65 D11** 58 3N 102 39 E
Ust-Ishim, *Russia* **64 D8** 57 45N 71 10 E
Ust-Kamchatsk, *Russia* **65 D17** 56 10N 162 28 E
Ust-Kamenogorsk = Öskemen, *Kazakstan* **64 E9** 50 0N 82 36 E
Ust-Khayryuzovo, *Russia* **65 D16** 57 15N 156 45 E
Ust-Kut, *Russia* **65 D11** 56 50N 105 42 E
Ust-Kuyga, *Russia* **65 B14** 70 1N 135 43 E
Ust-Labinsk, *Russia* **61 H4** 45 15N 39 41 E
Ust-Luga, *Russia* **58 C5** 59 35N 28 20 E
Ust-Maya, *Russia* **65 C14** 60 30N 134 28 E
Ust-Mil, *Russia* **65 D14** 59 40N 133 11 E
Ust-Nera, *Russia* **65 C15** 64 35N 143 15 E
Ust-Nyukzha, *Russia* **65 D13** 56 34N 121 37 E
Ust-Olenek, *Russia* **65 B12** 73 0N 120 5 E
Ust-Omchug, *Russia* **65 C15** 61 9N 149 38 E
Ust-Port, *Russia* **64 C9** 69 40N 84 26 E
Ust-Tsilma, *Russia* **56 A9** 65 28N 52 11 E
Ust Urt = Ustyurt Plateau, *Asia* **64 E6** 44 0N 55 0 E
Ust-Usa, *Russia* **56 A10** 66 2N 56 57 E
Ust-Vorkuta, *Russia* **56 A11** 67 24N 64 0 E
Ustaoset, *Norway* **18 D5** 60 30N 8 2 E
Ustaritz, *France* **28 E2** 43 24N 1 27W
Uster, *Switz.* **33 B7** 47 22N 8 43 E
Ústí nad Labem, *Czech Rep.* **34 A7** 50 41N 14 3 E
Ústí nad Orlicí, *Czech Rep.* **35 B9** 49 58N 16 24 E
Ústica, *Italy* **46 D6** 38 42N 13 11 E
Ustinov = Izhevsk, *Russia* **62 C4** 56 51N 53 14 E
Ustka, *Poland* **54 D3** 54 35N 16 55 E
Ustroń, *Poland* **55 J5** 49 43N 18 48 E
Ustrzyki Dolne, *Poland* **55 J9** 49 27N 22 40 E
Ustupo, *Panama* **168 B2** 9 27N 78 34W
Ustyurt Plateau, *Asia* **64 E6** 44 0N 55 0 E
Ustyuzhna, *Russia* **58 C9** 58 50N 36 32 E
Usu, *China* **72 B3** 44 27N 84 40 E
Usuki, *Japan* **70 D3** 33 8N 131 49 E
Usulután, *El Salv.* **164 D2** 13 25N 88 28W
Usumacinta →, *Mexico* **163 D6** 17 0N 91 0W
Usumbura = Bujumbura, *Burundi* **118 C2** 3 16 S 29 18 E
Usure, *Tanzania* **118 C3** 4 40 S 34 22 E
Usutuo →, *Mozam.* **117 D5** 26 48 S 32 7 E
Usva, *Russia* **62 B6** 58 41N 57 37 E
Uta, *Indonesia* **79 E9** 4 33 S 136 0 E
'Uta Vava'u, *Tonga* **133 P14** 18 36 S 174 0W
Utah □, *U.S.A.* **158 G8** 39 20N 111 30W
Utah L., *U.S.A.* **158 F8** 40 10N 111 58W
Utansjö, *Sweden* **16 B11** 62 46N 17 55 E
Utarni, *India* **92 F4** 26 5N 71 58 E
Utatlan, *Guatemala* **164 C1** 15 2N 91 11W
Ute Creek →, *U.S.A.* **155 H3** 35 21N 103 50W
Utebo, *Spain* **40 D3** 41 43N 1 0W
Utena, *Lithuania* **15 J21** 55 27N 25 40 E
Utete, *Tanzania* **118 D4** 8 0 S 38 45 E
Uthai Thani, *Thailand* **86 E3** 15 22N 100 3 E
Uthal, *Pakistan* **92 G2** 25 44N 66 40 E
Utiariti, *Brazil* **173 C6** 13 0 S 58 10W
Utica, *N.Y., U.S.A.* **151 C9** 43 6N 75 14W
Utica, *Ohio, U.S.A.* **150 F2** 40 14N 82 27W
Utiel, *Spain* **41 F3** 39 37N 1 11W
Utikuma L., *Canada* **142 B5** 55 50N 115 30W
Utinga, *Brazil* **171 D3** 12 6 S 41 5W
Utkela, *India* **94 D6** 20 6N 83 10 E
Utne, *Norway* **18 D3** 60 25N 6 37 E
Utnur, *India* **94 E4** 19 22N 78 46 E
Uto, *Japan* **70 E2** 32 41N 130 40 E
Utö, *Sweden* **16 F12** 58 56N 18 16 E
Utopia, *Australia* **126 C1** 22 14 S 134 33 E
Utraula, *India* **93 F10** 27 19N 82 25 E
Utrecht, *Neths.* **24 B5** 52 5N 5 8 E
Utrecht, *S. Africa* **117 D5** 27 38 S 30 20 E
Utrecht □, *Neths.* **24 B5** 52 6N 5 7 E
Utrera, *Spain* **43 H5** 37 12N 5 48W
Utsira, *Norway* **18 E1** 59 19N 4 53 E
Utsjoki, *Finland* **14 B22** 69 51N 26 59 E
Utsunomiya, *Japan* **71 A11** 36 30N 139 50 E
Uttar Pradesh □, *India* **93 F9** 27 0N 80 0 E
Uttaradit, *Thailand* **78 A2** 17 36N 100 5 E
Uttoxeter, *U.K.* **20 E6** 52 54N 1 52W
Utva →, *Kazakstan* **62 F4** 51 28N 52 40 E
Uummannaq, *Greenland* **10 B4** 77 0N 69 0W
Uummannarsuaq = Nunap Isua, *Greenland* **10 F6** 59 48N 43 55W
Uusikaarlepyy, *Finland* **14 E20** 63 32N 22 31 E
Uusikaupunki, *Finland* **15 F19** 60 47N 21 25 E
Uva, *Russia* **60 B11** 56 59N 52 13 E
Uvá →, *Colombia* **168 C3** 3 41N 70 3W
Uvac →, *Serbia, Yug.* **50 C3** 43 35N 19 30 E
Uvalda, *U.S.A.* **152 C7** 32 2N 82 31W
Uvalde, *U.S.A.* **155 L5** 29 13N 99 47W
Uvarovo, *Russia* **60 E6** 51 59N 42 14 E
Uvat, *Russia* **64 D7** 59 5N 68 50 E
Uvdal, *Norway* **18 D5** 60 17N 8 48 E
Uvelskiy, *Russia* **62 D8** 54 26N 61 22 E
Uvinza, *Tanzania* **118 D3** 5 5 S 30 24 E
Uvira, *Dem. Rep. of the Congo* **118 C2** 3 22 S 29 3 E
Uvs Nuur, *Mongolia* **72 A4** 50 20N 92 30 E
Uwa, *Japan* **70 D4** 33 22N 132 31 E
'Uwairidh, Harrat al, *Si. Arabia* **96 E3** 26 50N 38 0 E
Uwajima, *Japan* **70 D4** 33 10N 132 35 E
'Uwayfī, *Oman* **99 B7** 22 15N 56 59 E
Uweinat, Jebel, *Sudan* **106 C1** 21 54N 24 58 E
Uxbridge, *Canada* **150 B5** 44 6N 79 7W
Uxin Qi, *China* **74 E5** 38 50N 109 5 E
Uxmal, *Mexico* **163 C7** 20 22N 89 46W
Uyak, *U.S.A.* **144 H9** 57 38N 154 0W
Üydzin, *Mongolia* **74 B4** 44 9N 107 0 E
Uyo, *Nigeria* **113 D6** 5 1N 7 53 E
Uyu →, *Burma* **90 C5** 24 51N 94 57 E
Uyuk, *Kazakstan* **63 B5** 43 36N 71 16 E
Üyüklü Tepe, *Turkey* **49 D9** 37 5N 27 21 E
Uyûn Mûsa, *Egypt* **103 F1** 29 53N 32 40 E
Uyuni, *Bolivia* **172 E4** 20 28 S 66 47W
Uzbekistan ■, *Asia* **64 E7** 41 30N 65 0 E
Uzen, *Kazakstan* **57 F9** 43 29N 52 54 E
Uzen, Bolshoi →, *Kazakstan* **61 F9** 49 6N 49 56 E
Uzen, Mal →, *Kazakstan* **61 F9** 49 4N 49 44 E
Uzerche, *France* **28 C5** 45 25N 1 34 E
Uzès, *France* **29 D8** 44 1N 4 26 E
Uzgen = Özgön, *Kyrgyzstan* **63 C6** 40 46N 73 18 E
Uzh →, *Ukraine* **59 G6** 51 15N 30 12 E
Uzhgorod = Uzhhorod, *Ukraine* **59 H2** 48 36N 22 18 E
Uzhhorod, *Ukraine* **59 H2** 48 36N 22 18 E
Užice, *Serbia, Yug.* **50 C3** 43 55N 19 50 E
Uzlovaya, *Russia* **58 F10** 54 0N 38 5 E
Üzümlü, *Turkey* **49 E11** 36 44N 29 14 E
Uzun-Agach, *Kazakstan* **63 B8** 43 35N 76 20 E
Uzunköprü, *Turkey* **51 E10** 41 16N 26 43 E
Uzunkuyu, *Turkey* **49 C8** 38 17N 26 33 E
Uzwil, *Switz.* **33 B8** 47 26N 9 9 E

V

Va. Nova, *Angola* **115 E3** 12 38 S 16 3 E
Vaal →, *S. Africa* **116 D3** 29 4 S 23 38 E
Vaal Dam, *S. Africa* **117 D4** 27 0 S 28 14 E
Vaalwater, *S. Africa* **117 C4** 24 15 S 28 8 E
Vaasa, *Finland* **14 E19** 63 6N 21 38 E
Vabre, *France* **28 E6** 43 42N 2 24 E
Vác, *Hungary* **52 C4** 47 49N 19 10 E
Vacaria, *Brazil* **175 B5** 28 31 S 50 52W
Vacaville, *U.S.A.* **160 G5** 38 21N 121 59W
Vaccarès, Étang de, *France* **29 E8** 43 32N 4 34 E
Vach = Vakh →, *Russia* **64 C8** 60 45N 76 45 E
Vache, Î. à, *Haiti* **165 C5** 18 2N 73 35W
Väckelsång, *Sweden* **17 H8** 56 37N 14 58 E
Vada, *India* **94 E1** 19 39N 73 8 E
Väddö, *Sweden* **16 D12** 60 0N 18 50 E
Väderstad, *Sweden* **17 F8** 58 19N 14 55 E
Vadheim, *Norway* **18 C2** 61 13N 5 49 E
Vadnagar, *India* **92 H5** 23 47N 72 40 E
Vado Lígure, *Italy* **44 D5** 44 17N 8 26 E
Vadodara, *India* **92 H5** 22 20N 73 10 E
Vadret, Piz, *Switz.* **33 C9** 46 51N 9 58 E
Vadsø, *Norway* **14 A23** 70 3N 29 50 E
Vadstena, *Sweden* **17 F8** 58 28N 14 54 E
Vaduj, *India* **94 F2** 17 36N 74 27 E
Vaduz, *Liech.* **33 B9** 47 8N 9 31 E
Værlandet, *Norway* **18 C1** 61 18N 4 44 E
Værøy, *Norway* **14 C15** 67 40N 12 40 E
Vågåmo, *Norway* **18 C6** 61 52N 9 6 E
Vágar, *Færoe Is.* **14 E9** 62 5N 7 15W
Vaggeryd, *Sweden* **17 G8** 57 30N 14 10 E
Vagney, *France* **27 D13** 48 1N 6 43 E
Vagnhärad, *Sweden* **17 F11** 58 57N 17 33 E
Vagos, *Portugal* **42 E2** 40 33N 8 42W
Vågsfjorden, *Norway* **14 B17** 68 50N 16 50 E
Váh →, *Slovak Rep.* **35 D11** 47 43N 18 7 E
Vahsel B., *Antarctica* **7 D1** 75 0 S 35 0W
Váï, *Greece* **38 D8** 35 15N 26 18 E
Vaigach, *Russia* **64 B6** 70 10N 59 0 E
Vaigai →, *India* **95 K4** 9 15N 79 10 E
Vaiges, *France* **26 D6** 48 2N 0 30W
Vaihingen, *Germany* **31 G4** 48 54N 8 57 E
Vaijapur, *India* **94 E2** 19 58N 74 45 E
Vaikam, *India* **95 K3** 9 45N 76 25 E
Vail, *U.S.A.* **146 C5** 39 40N 106 20W
Vailly-sur-Aisne, *France* **27 C10** 49 24N 3 31 E
Vaippar →, *India* **95 K4** 9 0N 78 25 E
Vaisali →, *India* **93 F8** 26 28N 78 53 E
Vaison-la-Romaine, *France* **29 D9** 44 14N 5 4 E
Vajpur, *India* **94 D1** 21 24N 73 17 E
Vakaga →, *C.A.R.* **114 A4** 9 48N 21 32 E
Vakarai, *Sri Lanka* **95 K5** 8 8N 81 26 E
Vakarel, *Bulgaria* **50 D7** 42 35N 23 40 E
Vakfikebir, *Turkey* **101 B8** 41 2N 39 17 E
Vakh →, *Russia* **64 C8** 60 45N 76 45 E
Vakhsh →, *Tajikistan* **63 E4** 37 6N 68 18 E
Vakhtan, *Russia* **60 B8** 57 53N 46 47 E
Vaksdal, *Norway* **18 D2** 60 29N 5 45 E
Vál, *Hungary* **52 C3** 47 22N 18 40 E
Val-de-Marne □, *France* **27 D9** 48 45N 2 28 E
Val-d'Isère, *France* **29 C10** 45 27N 6 59 E
Val-d'Oise □, *France* **27 C9** 49 5N 2 10 E
Val-d'Or, *Canada* **140 C4** 48 7N 77 47W
Val Marie, *Canada* **143 D7** 49 15N 107 45W
Valaam, *Russia* **58 B6** 61 22N 30 57 E
Valadares, *Portugal* **42 D2** 41 5N 8 38W
Valahia, *Romania* **53 F9** 44 35N 25 0 E
Valaichenai, *Sri Lanka* **95 L5** 7 54N 81 32 E
Valais □, *Switz.* **32 D5** 46 12N 7 45 E
Valais, Alpes du, *Switz.* **32 D5** 46 5N 7 35 E
Valandovo, *Macedonia* **50 E6** 41 19N 22 34 E
Valašské Meziříčí, *Czech Rep.* **35 B10** 49 29N 17 59 E
Valáxa, *Greece* **48 C6** 38 50N 24 29 E
Vålberg, *Sweden* **16 E7** 59 23N 13 11 E
Valbo, *Sweden* **16 D10** 60 40N 17 0 E
Valbondione, *Italy* **44 B7** 46 2N 10 1 E
Vălcani, *Romania* **52 D5** 46 0N 20 26 E
Vâlcea □, *Romania* **53 F9** 45 0N 24 10 E
Valcheta, *Argentina* **176 B3** 40 40 S 66 8W
Valdagno, *Italy* **45 C8** 45 39N 11 18 E
Valdahon, *France* **27 E13** 47 8N 6 21 E
Valday, *Russia* **58 D7** 57 58N 33 9 E
Valdayskaya Vozvyshennost, *Russia* **58 D7** 57 0N 33 30 E
Valdeazogues →, *Spain* **43 G6** 38 45N 4 55W
Valdecañas, Embalse de, *Spain* **42 F5** 39 45N 5 25W
Valdemarsvik, *Sweden* **17 F10** 58 14N 16 40 E
Valdemoro, *Spain* **42 E7** 40 12N 3 40W
Valdepeñas, *Spain* **43 G7** 38 43N 3 25W
Valderaduey →, *Spain* **42 D5** 41 31N 5 42W
Valdérice, *Italy* **46 D5** 38 4N 12 37 E
Valderrobres, *Spain* **40 E5** 40 53N 0 9 E
Valdés, Pen., *Argentina* **176 B4** 42 30 S 63 45W
Valdez, *Ecuador* **168 C2** 1 15N 79 0W
Valdez, *U.S.A.* **138 B5** 61 7N 146 16W
Valdivia, *Chile* **176 A2** 39 50 S 73 14W
Valdivia, *Colombia* **168 B2** 7 11N 75 27W
Valdobbiádene, *Italy* **45 C8** 45 54N 12 0 E
Valdosta, *U.S.A.* **152 E6** 30 50N 83 17W
Valdoviño, *Spain* **42 B2** 43 36N 8 8W
Valdres, *Norway* **15 F13** 61 5N 9 5 E
Vale, *Georgia* **61 K6** 41 30N 42 58 E
Vale, *U.S.A.* **158 E5** 43 59N 117 15W
Vale of Glamorgan □, *U.K.* **21 F4** 51 28N 3 25W
Valea lui Mihai, *Romania* **52 C7** 47 32N 22 11 E
Valea Mărului, *Romania* **53 E12** 45 49N 27 42 E
Valemount, *Canada* **142 C5** 52 50N 119 15W
Valença, *Brazil* **171 D4** 13 20 S 39 5W
Valença, *Portugal* **42 C2** 42 1N 8 34W
Valença do Piauí, *Brazil* **170 C3** 6 20 S 41 45W
Valençay, *France* **27 E8** 47 9N 1 34 E
Valence = Valence d'Agen, *France* **28 D4** 44 6N 0 53 E
Valence, *France* **29 D8** 44 57N 4 54 E
Valence d'Agen, *France* **28 D4** 44 6N 0 53 E
Valencia, *Phil.* **81 H5** 7 57N 125 3 E
Valencia, *Spain* **41 F4** 39 27N 0 23W
Valencia, *U.S.A.* **159 J10** 34 48N 106 43W
Valencia, *Venezuela* **168 A4** 10 11N 68 0W
Valencia □, *Spain* **41 F4** 39 20N 0 40W
Valencia, G. de, *Spain* **41 F5** 39 30N 0 20 E
Valencia de Alcántara, *Spain* **43 F3** 39 25N 7 14W
Valencia de Don Juan, *Spain* **42 C5** 42 17N 5 31W
Valencia I., *Ireland* **23 E1** 51 54N 10 22W
Valenciennes, *France* **27 B10** 50 20N 3 34 E
Văleni, *Romania* **53 F9** 44 15N 24 45 E
Vălenii de Munte, *Romania* **53 E11** 45 11N 26 2 E
Valensole, *France* **29 E9** 43 50N 5 59 E
Valentigney, *France* **27 E13** 47 27N 6 51 E
Valentim, Sa. do, *Brazil* **170 C3** 6 0 S 43 30W
Valentin, *Russia* **68 C7** 43 8N 134 17 E
Valentine, *U.S.A.* **155 K2** 30 35N 104 30W
Valenza, *Italy* **44 C5** 45 1N 8 38 E
Våler, *Hedmark, Norway* **18 D8** 60 41N 11 50 E
Våler, *Østfold, Norway* **18 E7** 59 29N 10 51 E
Valera, *Venezuela* **168 B3** 9 19N 70 37W
Valestrand, *Norway* **18 E2** 59 40N 5 26 E
Valga, *Estonia* **15 H22** 57 47N 26 2 E
Valguarnera Caropepe, *Italy* **47 E7** 37 30N 14 23 E
Valier, *U.S.A.* **158 B7** 48 18N 112 16W
Valinco, G. de, *France* **29 G12** 41 40N 8 52 E
Valjevo, *Serbia, Yug.* **50 B3** 44 18N 19 53 E
Valka, *Latvia* **15 H21** 57 42N 25 57 E
Valkeakoski, *Finland* **15 F20** 61 16N 24 2 E
Valkenswaard, *Neths.* **24 C5** 51 21N 5 29 E
Vall de Uxó = La Vall d'Uixó, *Spain* **40 F4** 39 49N 0 15W
Valla, *Sweden* **16 E10** 59 2N 16 20 E
Valladolid, *Mexico* **163 C7** 20 40N 88 11W
Valladolid, *Spain* **42 D6** 41 38N 4 43W
Valladolid □, *Spain* **42 D6** 41 38N 4 43W
Vallata, *Italy* **47 A8** 41 2N 15 15 E
Valldemossa, *Spain* **39 B9** 39 43N 2 37 E
Valle, *Norway* **18 E4** 59 13N 7 33 E
Valle d'Aosta □, *Italy* **44 C4** 45 45N 7 15 E
Valle de Arán, *Spain* **40 C5** 42 50N 0 55 E
Valle de la Pascua, *Venezuela* **168 B4** 9 13N 66 0W
Valle de las Palmas, *Mexico* **161 N10** 32 20N 116 43W
Valle de Santiago, *Mexico* **162 C4** 20 25N 101 15W
Valle de Suchil, *Mexico* **162 C4** 23 38N 103 55W
Valle de Zaragoza, *Mexico* **162 B3** 27 28N 105 49W
Valle del Cauca □, *Colombia* **168 C2** 3 45N 76 30W
Valle Fértil, Sierra del, *Argentina* **174 C2** 30 20 S 68 0W
Valle Hermoso, *Mexico* **163 B5** 25 35N 97 40W
Valledupar, *Colombia* **168 A3** 10 29N 73 15W
Vallehermoso, *Canary Is.* **39 F2** 28 10N 17 15W
Vallejo, *U.S.A.* **160 G4** 38 7N 122 14W
Vallenar, *Chile* **174 B1** 28 30 S 70 50W
Vallentuna, *Sweden* **16 E12** 59 32N 18 5 E
Valleraugue, *France* **28 D7** 44 6N 3 39 E
Vallet, *France* **26 E5** 47 10N 1 15W
Valletta, *Malta* **108 A2** 35 54N 14 31 E
Valley Center, *U.S.A.* **161 M9** 33 13N 117 2W
Valley City, *U.S.A.* **154 B6** 46 55N 98 0W
Valley Falls, *Oreg., U.S.A.* **158 E3** 42 29N 120 17W
Valley Falls, *R.I., U.S.A.* **151 E13** 41 54N 71 24W
Valley Springs, *U.S.A.* **160 G6** 38 12N 120 50W
Valley Station, *U.S.A.* **157 F11** 38 6N 85 52W
Valley View, *U.S.A.* **151 F8** 40 39N 76 33W
Valley Wells, *U.S.A.* **161 K11** 35 27N 115 46W
Valleyview, *Canada* **142 B5** 55 5N 117 17W
Valli di Comácchio, *Italy* **45 D9** 44 40N 12 15 E
Vallimanca, Arroyo, *Argentina* **174 D4** 35 40 S 59 10W
Vallo della Lucánia, *Italy* **47 B8** 40 14N 15 16 E
Vallon-Pont-d'Arc, *France* **29 D8** 44 24N 4 24 E
Vallorbe, *Switz.* **32 C2** 46 42N 6 20 E
Valls, *Spain* **40 D6** 41 18N 1 15 E
Valmaseda = Balmaseda, *Spain* **40 B1** 43 11N 3 12W
Valmeyer, *U.S.A.* **156 F6** 38 18N 90 19W
Valmiera, *Latvia* **15 H21** 57 37N 25 29 E
Valnera, *Spain* **42 B7** 43 9N 3 40W
Valognes, *France* **26 C5** 49 30N 1 28W
Valona = Vlóra, *Albania* **50 F3** 40 32N 19 28 E
Valongo, *Portugal* **42 D2** 41 8N 8 30W
Valozhyn, *Belarus* **58 E4** 54 3N 26 30 E
Valpaços, *Portugal* **42 D3** 41 36N 7 17W
Valparai, *India* **95 J3** 10 22N 76 58 E
Valparaíso, *Chile* **174 C1** 33 2 S 71 40W
Valparaíso, *Mexico* **162 C4** 22 50N 103 32W
Valparaiso, *Fla., U.S.A.* **153 E3** 30 29N 86 30W
Valparaiso, *Ind., U.S.A.* **157 C9** 41 28N 87 4W
Valparaíso □, *Chile* **174 C1** 33 2 S 71 40W
Valpovo, *Croatia* **52 E3** 45 39N 18 25 E
Valpoy, *India* **95 G2** 15 32N 74 8 E
Valréas, *France* **29 D9** 44 24N 5 0 E
Vals, *Switz.* **33 C8** 46 39N 9 11 E
Vals →, *S. Africa* **116 D4** 27 23 S 26 30 E
Vals, Tanjung, *Indonesia* **79 F9** 8 26 S 137 25 E
Vals-les-Bains, *France* **29 D8** 44 42N 4 24 E
Valsad, *India* **94 D1** 20 40N 72 58 E
Valtellina, *Italy* **44 B6** 46 11N 9 55 E
Valþjofsstaður, *Iceland* **11 B12** 65 1N 14 59W
Valuyki, *Russia* **59 G10** 50 10N 38 5 E
Valverde, *Canary Is.* **39 G2** 27 48N 17 55W
Valverde del Camino, *Spain* **43 H4** 37 35N 6 47W
Valverde del Fresno, *Spain* **42 E4** 40 15N 6 51W
Vama, *Romania* **53 C10** 47 34N 25 42 E
Vambori, *India* **94 E2** 19 17N 74 44 E
Vamdrup, *Denmark* **17 J3** 55 25N 9 17 E
Våmhus, *Sweden* **16 C8** 61 7N 14 29 E
Vammala, *Finland* **15 F20** 61 20N 22 54 E
Vámos, *Greece* **38 D6** 35 24N 24 13 E
Vamsadhara →, *India* **94 E7** 18 21N 84 8 E
Van, *Turkey* **101 C10** 38 30N 43 20 E
Van, L. = Van Gölü, *Turkey* **101 C10** 38 30N 43 0 E
Van Alstyne, *U.S.A.* **155 J6** 33 25N 96 35W
Van Blommestein Meer, *Surinam* **169 C6** 4 45N 55 5W
Van Buren, *Canada* **141 C6** 47 10N 67 55W
Van Buren, *Ark., U.S.A.* **155 H7** 35 26N 94 21W
Van Buren, *Maine, U.S.A.* **149 B11** 47 10N 67 58W
Van Buren, *Mo., U.S.A.* **155 G9** 37 0N 91 1W
Van Canh, *Vietnam* **86 F7** 13 37N 109 0 E
Van Diemen, C., *N. Terr., Australia* **124 B5** 11 9 S 130 24 E
Van Diemen, C., *Queens., Australia* **126 B2** 16 30 S 139 46 E
Van Diemen G., *Australia* **124 B5** 11 45 S 132 0 E
Van Gölü, *Turkey* **101 C10** 38 30N 43 0 E
Van Horn, *U.S.A.* **155 K2** 31 3N 104 50W
Van Horne, *U.S.A.* **156 B4** 42 1N 92 4W
Van Meter, *U.S.A.* **156 C3** 41 32N 93 57W
Van Ninh, *Vietnam* **86 F7** 12 42N 109 14 E
Van Rees, Pegunungan, *Indonesia* **79 E9** 2 35 S 138 15 E
Van Tivu, *India* **95 K4** 8 51N 78 15 E
Van Wert, *U.S.A.* **157 D12** 40 52N 84 35W
Van Yen, *Vietnam* **76 G5** 21 4N 104 42 E
Vanadzor, *Armenia* **61 K7** 40 48N 44 30 E
Vanavara, *Russia* **65 C11** 60 22N 102 16 E
Vanceburg, *U.S.A.* **157 F13** 38 36N 83 19W
Vancouver, *Canada* **142 D4** 49 15N 123 10W
Vancouver, *U.S.A.* **160 E4** 45 38N 122 40W
Vancouver, C., *Australia* **125 G2** 35 2 S 118 11 E
Vancouver, Mt., *U.S.A.* **144 F13** 60 20N 139 41W
Vancouver I., *Canada* **142 D3** 49 50N 126 0W
Vandalia, *Ill., U.S.A.* **156 F7** 38 58N 89 6W
Vandalia, *Mo., U.S.A.* **156 E5** 39 19N 91 29W
Vandalia, *Ohio, U.S.A.* **157 E12** 39 54N 84 12W
Vandavasi, *India* **95 H4** 12 30N 79 30 E
Vandeloos B., *Sri Lanka* **95 L5** 8 0N 81 45 E
Vandenburg, *U.S.A.* **161 L6** 34 35N 120 33W
Vanderbijlpark, *S. Africa* **117 D4** 26 42 S 27 54 E
Vandergrift, *U.S.A.* **150 F5** 40 36N 79 34W
Vanderhoof, *Canada* **142 C4** 54 0N 124 0W
Vanderkloof Dam, *S. Africa* **116 E3** 30 4 S 24 40 E
Vanderlin I., *Australia* **126 B2** 15 44 S 137 2 E
Vänern, *Sweden* **17 F7** 58 47N 13 30 E
Vänersborg, *Sweden* **17 F6** 58 26N 12 19 E
Vang, *Norway* **18 C5** 61 7N 8 34 E
Vang Vieng, *Laos* **86 C4** 18 58N 102 32 E

Victoria, *Tarlac, Phil.* .... 80 D3 15 35N 120 41 E
Victoria, *Romania* .... 53 E9 45 44N 24 41 E
Victoria, *Seychelles* .... 121 E4 5 0 S 55 40 E
Victoria, *Kans., U.S.A.* 154 F5 38 52N 99 9W
Victoria, *Tex., U.S.A.* 155 L6 28 48N 97 0W
Victoria □, *Australia* .... 128 D6 37 0 S 144 0 E
Victoria ~, *Australia* .... 124 C4 15 10 S 129 40 E
Victoria, Grand L., *Canada* .. 140 C4 47 31N 77 30W
Victoria, L., *Africa* .... 118 C3 1 0 S 33 0 E
Victoria, L., *Australia* .... 128 B4 33 57 S 141 15 E
Victoria, Mt., *Burma* .... 90 E4 21 15N 93 55 E
Victoria, Mt., *Papua N. G.* .. 132 E4 8 55 S 147 32 E
Victoria Beach, *Canada* 143 C9 50 40N 96 35W
Victoria de Durango =
  Durango, *Mexico* 162 C4 24 3N 104 39W
Victoria de las Tunas, *Cuba* . 164 B4 20 58N 76 59W
Victoria Falls, *Zimbabwe* ... 119 F2 17 58 S 25 52 E
Victoria Harbour, *Canada* ... 150 B5 44 45N 79 45W
Victoria I., *Canada* 138 A8 71 0N 111 0W
Victoria L., *Canada* 141 C8 48 20N 57 27W
Victoria Ld., *Antarctica* ..... 7 D11 75 0 S 160 0 E
Victoria Nile ~, *Uganda* .... 118 B3 2 14N 31 26 E
Victoria Peaks, *Phil.* .... 81 G2 9 22N 118 20 E
Victoria Ra., *N.Z.* .... 131 C7 42 12 S 172 7 E
Victoria River, *Australia* .... 124 C5 16 25 S 131 0 E
Victoria Str., *Canada* 138 B9 69 30N 100 0W
Victoria West, *S. Africa* ..... 116 E3 31 25 S 23 4 E
Victorias, *Phil.* .... 81 F4 10 54N 123 5 E
Victoriaville, *Canada* 141 C5 46 4N 71 56W
Victorica, *Argentina* .... 174 D2 36 20 S 65 30W
Victorville, *U.S.A.* 161 L9 34 32N 117 18W
Vicuña, *Chile* .... 174 C1 30 0 S 70 50W
Vicuña Mackenna, *Argentina* 174 C3 33 53 S 64 25W
Vidal, *U.S.A.* 161 L12 34 7N 114 31W
Vidal Junction, *U.S.A.* 161 L12 34 11N 114 34W
Vidalia, *U.S.A.* 152 C7 32 13N 82 25W
Vidauban, *France* .... 29 E10 43 25N 6 27 E
Videbæk, *Denmark* .... 17 H2 56 6N 8 38 E
Videle, *Romania* .... 53 F10 44 17N 25 31 E
Videseter, *Norway* .... 18 C4 61 57N 7 14 E
Vidette, *U.S.A.* 152 B7 33 2N 82 15W
Vídho, *Greece* .... 38 A3 39 38N 19 55 E
Vidigueira, *Portugal* 43 G3 38 12N 7 48W
Vidin, *Bulgaria* .... 50 C6 43 59N 22 50 E
Vidio, C., *Spain* 42 B4 43 35N 6 14W
Vidisha, *India* .... 92 H7 23 28N 77 53 E
Vidra, *Romania* .... 53 E11 45 56N 26 55 E
Vidusa, *Bos.-H.* .... 50 D2 42 55N 18 21 E
Vidzy, *Belarus* .... 15 J22 55 23N 26 37 E
Viechtach, *Germany* .... 31 F8 49 4N 12 53 E
Viedma, *Argentina* .... 176 B4 40 50 S 63 0W
Viedma, L., *Argentina* ...... 176 C2 49 30 S 72 30W
Vieira do Minho, *Portugal* ... 42 D2 41 38N 8 8W
Vielha, *Spain* .... 40 C5 42 43N 0 44 E
Viella = Vielha, *Spain* ...... 40 C5 42 43N 0 44 E
Vielsalm, *Belgium* .... 24 D5 50 17N 5 54 E
Vienenburg, *Germany* ...... 30 D6 51 57N 10 34 E
Vieng Pou Kha, *Laos* .... 76 G3 20 41N 101 4 E
Vienna = Wien, *Austria* .... 35 C9 48 12N 16 22 E
Vienna, *Ga., U.S.A.* 152 C6 32 6N 83 47W
Vienna, *Ill., U.S.A.* 155 G10 37 25N 88 54W
Vienna, *Mo., U.S.A.* 156 F5 38 11N 91 57W
Vienne, *France* .... 29 C8 45 31N 4 53 E
Vienne □, *France* .... 28 B4 46 30N 0 42 E
Vienne ~, *France* .... 26 E7 47 13N 0 5 E
Vientiane, *Laos* .... 86 D4 17 58N 102 36 E
Vientos, Paso de los, *Caribbean* 165 C5 20 0N 74 0W
Viernheim, *Germany* .... 31 F4 49 31N 8 35 E
Viersen, *Germany* .... 30 D2 51 15N 6 23 E
Vierwaldstättersee, *Switz.* .. 33 C7 47 0N 8 30 E
Vierzon, *France* .... 27 E9 47 13N 2 5 E
Vieste, *Italy* .... 45 G13 41 53N 16 10 E
Vietnam ■, *Asia* .... 86 A3 19 0N 106 0 E
Vieux-Boucau-les-Bains, *France* 28 E2 43 48N 1 23W
Vif, *France* .... 29 C9 45 5N 5 41 E
Viga, *Phil.* .... 80 E5 13 52N 124 18 E
Vigan, *Phil.* .... 79 A6 17 35N 120 28 E
Vigévano, *Italy* .... 44 C5 45 19N 8 51 E
Vigia, *Brazil* .... 170 B2 0 50 S 48 5W
Vigía Chico, *Mexico* 163 D7 19 46N 87 35W
Víglas, Ákra, *Greece* .... 38 D9 35 54N 27 51 E
Vignemale, *France* .... 28 F3 42 47N 0 10 E
Vigneulles-lès-Hattonchâtel,
  France .... 27 D12 48 59N 5 43 E
Vignola, *Italy* .... 44 B4 44 29N 11 1 E
Vigo, *Spain* 42 C2 42 12N 8 41W
Vigo, Ría de, *Spain* 42 C2 42 15N 8 45W
Vigrestad, *Norway* .... 18 F2 58 34N 5 42 E
Vigsø Bugt, *Denmark* .... 17 G2 57 8N 8 47 E
Vihiers, *France* 26 E6 47 10N 0 30W
Vihowa, *Pakistan* .... 92 D4 31 8N 70 30 E
Vihowa ~, *Pakistan* .... 92 D4 31 8N 70 41 E
Vijayadurg, *India* .... 94 F1 16 30N 73 25 E
Vijayawada, *India* .... 94 F5 16 31N 80 39 E
Vík, *Iceland* 11 D7 63 25N 19 1W
Vik, *Norway* .... 18 C3 61 21N 6 6 E
Vika, *Sweden* .... 16 D8 60 57N 14 28 E
Vikarabad, *India* .... 94 E3 17 20N 77 54 E
Vikarbyn, *Sweden* .... 16 D9 60 55N 15 1 E
Vike, *Norway* .... 18 D2 60 42N 5 35 E
Vikedal, *Norway* .... 18 E2 59 30N 5 55 E
Vikeke, *Indonesia* .... 79 F7 8 52 S 126 23 E
Vikeland, *Norway* .... 18 F4 58 5N 7 18 E
Viken, *Skåne, Sweden* ...... 17 H6 56 9N 12 34 E
Viken, *Skaraborg, Sweden* .. 17 F8 58 39N 14 20 E
Vikersund, *Norway* .... 18 E6 59 58N 9 59 E
Vikeså, *Norway* .... 18 F3 58 38N 6 3 E
Vikevåg, *Norway* .... 18 E2 59 5N 5 41 E
Viking, *Canada* 142 C6 53 7N 111 50W
Vikmanshyttan, *Sweden* .... 16 D9 60 18N 15 50 E
Vikna, *Norway* .... 14 D14 64 55N 10 58 E
Viksøyri, *Norway* .... 18 C3 61 4N 6 34 E
Vila Bela da Santissima
  Trindade, *Brazil* .... 173 C6 15 0 S 59 57W
Vila da Maganja, *Mozam.* ... 119 F4 17 18 S 37 30 E
Vila de João Belo = Xai-Xai,
  Mozam. .... 117 D5 25 6 S 33 31 E
Vila de Rei, *Portugal* 42 F2 39 41N 8 9W
Vila do Bispo, *Portugal* 43 H2 37 5N 8 53W
Vila do Conde, *Portugal* 42 D2 41 21N 8 45W
Vila Franca de Xira, *Portugal* . 43 G2 38 57N 8 59W
Vila Gamito, *Mozam.* .... 119 E3 14 12 S 33 0 E
Vila Gomes da Costa, *Mozam.* 117 C5 24 20 S 33 37 E
Vila Machado, *Mozam.* ..... 119 F3 19 15 S 34 14 E
  .... 119 E3 14 48 S 34 25 E
Vila Nova de Famalicão,
  Portugal 42 D2 41 25N 8 32W
Vila Nova de Fos Côa, *Portugal* 42 D3 41 5N 7 9W
Vila Nova de Foz Côa = Vila
  Nova de Fos Côa, *Portugal* 42 D3 41 5N 7 9W
Vila Nova de Gaia, *Portugal* . 42 D2 41 4N 8 40W
Vila Nova de Ourém, *Portugal* 42 F2 39 40N 8 35W
Vila Pouca de Aguiar, *Portugal* 42 D3 41 30N 7 38W
Vila Real, *Portugal* 42 D3 41 17N 7 48W
Vila Real □, *Portugal* 42 D3 41 30N 7 35W
Vila-real de los Infantes, *Spain* 40 F4 39 55N 0 3W
Vila Real de Santo António,
  Portugal 43 H3 37 10N 7 28W

Vila Vasco da Gama, *Mozam.* . 119 E3 14 54 S 32 14 E
Vila Velha, *Amapá, Brazil* 169 C7 3 13N 51 13W
Vila Velha, *Espírito Santo,*
  Brazil .... 171 F3 20 20 S 40 17W
Vila Viçosa, *Portugal* 43 G3 38 45N 7 27W
Vilafranca del Maestrat, *Spain* 40 E4 40 26N 0 16W
Vilafranca del Penedès, *Spain* . 40 D6 41 21N 1 40 E
Vilagarcía de Arousa, *Spain* . 42 C2 42 34N 8 46W
Vilaine ~, *France* 26 E4 47 30N 2 27W
Vilanandro, Tanjona, *Madag.* . 117 B7 16 11 S 44 27 E
Vilanculos, *Mozam.* .... 117 C6 22 1 S 35 17 E
Vilanova de Castelló, *Spain* . 41 F4 39 5N 0 31W
Vilanova i la Geltrú, *Spain* ... 40 D6 41 13N 1 40 E
Vilar Formoso, *Portugal* 42 E4 40 38N 6 45W
Vilaseca, *Spain* .... 40 D6 41 7N 1 9 E
Vilaseca-Salou = Vilaseca,
  Spain .... 40 D6 41 7N 1 9 E
Vilbjerg, *Denmark* .... 17 H2 56 12N 8 46 E
Vilcabamba, Cordillera, *Peru* . 172 C3 13 0 S 73 0W
Vilcanchos, *Peru* .... 172 C3 13 40 S 74 25W
Vilches, *Spain* 43 G7 38 12N 3 30W
Vileyka, *Belarus* .... 58 E4 54 30N 26 53 E
Vilhelmina, *Sweden* .... 14 D17 64 35N 16 39 E
Vilhena, *Brazil* .... 173 C5 12 40 S 60 5W
Viliga, *Russia* .... 65 C16 61 36N 156 56 E
Viliya ~, *Lithuania* .... 15 J21 55 8N 24 16 E
Viljandi, *Estonia* .... 15 G21 58 28N 25 30 E
Vilkaviškis, *Lithuania* ...... 54 D10 54 39N 23 2 E
Vilkija, *Lithuania* .... 54 C10 55 3N 23 35 E
Vilkitskogo, Proliv, *Russia* .. 65 B11 78 0N 103 0 E
Vilkovo = Vylkove, *Ukraine* . 59 K5 45 28N 29 32 E
Villa Abecia, *Bolivia* .... 174 A2 21 0 S 68 18W
Villa Ahumada, *Mexico* 162 A3 30 38N 106 30W
Villa Ana, *Argentina* .... 174 B4 28 28 S 59 40W
Villa Ángela, *Argentina* .... 174 B3 27 34 S 60 45W
Villa Bella, *Bolivia* .... 173 C4 10 25 S 65 22W
Villa Bens = Tarfaya, *Morocco* 110 C2 27 55N 12 55W
Villa Bruzual, *Venezuela* 168 C4 9 20N 69 6W
Villa Cañás, *Argentina* ...... 174 C3 34 0 S 61 35W
Villa Cisneros = Dakhla,
  W. Sahara 110 D1 23 50N 15 53W
Villa Colón, *Argentina* ...... 174 C2 31 38 S 68 20W
Villa Constitución, *Argentina* . 174 C3 33 15 S 60 20W
Villa de Cura, *Venezuela* 168 A4 10 2N 67 29W
Villa de María, *Argentina* ... 174 B3 29 55 S 63 43W
Villa del Rio, *Spain* 43 H6 37 59N 4 17W
Villa del Rosario, *Venezuela* . 168 A3 10 19N 72 19W
Villa Dolores, *Argentina* .... 174 C2 31 58 S 65 15W
Villa Frontera, *Mexico* 162 B4 26 56N 101 27W
Villa Grove, *U.S.A.* 157 E8 39 52N 88 10W
Villa Guillermina, *Argentina* . 174 B4 28 15 S 59 29W
Villa Hayes, *Paraguay* ...... 174 B4 25 5 S 57 20W
Villa Iris, *Argentina* .... 174 D3 38 12 S 63 12W
Villa Juárez, *Mexico* 162 B4 27 37N 100 44W
Villa María, *Argentina* ...... 174 C3 32 20 S 63 10W
Villa Mazán, *Argentina* ..... 174 B2 28 40 S 66 30W
Villa Minozzo, *Italy* .... 44 D7 44 22N 10 28 E
Villa Montes, *Bolivia* .... 174 A3 21 10 S 63 30W
Villa Ocampo, *Argentina* .... 174 B4 28 30 S 59 20W
Villa Ocampo, *Mexico* 162 B3 26 29N 105 30W
Villa Ojo de Agua, *Argentina* . 174 B3 29 30 S 63 44W
Villa Rica, *U.S.A.* 152 B3 33 44N 84 55W
Villa San Giovanni, *Italy* .... 47 D8 38 13N 15 38 E
Villa San José, *Argentina* ... 174 C4 32 12 S 58 15W
Villa San Martín, *Argentina* . 174 B3 28 15 S 64 9W
Villa Santina, *Italy* .... 45 B9 46 24N 12 55 E
Villa Unión, *Mexico* 162 C3 23 12N 106 14W
Villaba, *Phil.* .... 81 F5 11 13N 124 24 E
Villablino, *Spain* 42 C4 42 57N 6 19W
Villacarlos, *Spain* .... 39 B11 39 53N 4 17 E
Villacarriedo, *Spain* 42 B7 43 14N 3 48W
Villacarrillo, *Spain* 43 G7 38 7N 3 3W
Villacastín, *Spain* 42 E6 40 46N 4 25W
Villach, *Austria* .... 34 E6 46 37N 13 51 E
Villacidro, *Italy* .... 46 C1 39 27N 8 44 E
Villada, *Spain* 42 C6 42 15N 4 59W
Villadiego, *Spain* 42 C6 42 31N 4 1W
Villadóssola, *Italy* .... 44 B5 46 4N 8 16 E
Villafeliche, *Spain* 40 D3 41 10N 1 30W
Villafranca, *Spain* 41 C2 42 17N 1 46W
Villafranca de los Barros, *Spain* 43 G4 38 35N 6 18W
Villafranca de los Caballeros,
  Baleares, Spain .... 39 B10 39 34N 3 25 E
Villafranca de los Caballeros,
  Toledo, Spain 43 F7 39 26N 3 21W
Villafranca del Cid = Vilafranca
  del Maestrat, *Spain* 40 E4 40 26N 0 16W
Villafranca del Panadés =
  Vilafranca del Penedès, *Spain* 40 D6 41 21N 1 40 E
Villafranca di Verona, *Italy* .. 44 C7 45 21N 10 50 E
Villafranca Tirrena, *Italy* .... 47 D8 38 20N 15 25 E
Villagrán, *Mexico* 163 C5 24 29N 99 29W
Villaguay, *Argentina* .... 174 C4 32 0 S 59 0W
Villaharta, *Spain* 43 G6 38 9N 4 54W
Villahermosa, *Mexico* 163 D6 17 59N 92 55W
Villahermosa, *Spain* 41 G2 38 46N 2 52W
Villaines-la-Juhel, *France* ... 26 D6 48 21N 0 20W
Villajoyosa, *Spain* 41 G4 38 30N 0 12W
Villalba, *Spain* 42 B3 43 26N 7 40W
Villalba de Guardo, *Spain* ... 42 C6 42 42N 4 49W
Villalón de Campos, *Spain* .. 42 C5 42 5N 5 4W
Villalpando, *Spain* 42 D5 41 51N 5 25W
Villaluenga, *Spain* 42 E7 40 2N 3 54W
Villamanán, *Spain* 42 C5 42 19N 5 35W
Villamartín, *Spain* 43 J5 36 52N 5 38W
Villamayor de Santiago, *Spain* 42 F7 39 50N 2 59W
Villamblard, *France* .... 28 C4 45 2N 0 32 E
Villanova Monteleone, *Italy* .. 46 B1 40 30N 8 28 E
Villanueva, *Colombia* 168 A3 10 37N 72 59W
Villanueva, *U.S.A.* 155 H2 35 16N 105 22W
Villanueva de Castellón =
  Vilanova de Castelló, *Spain* 41 F4 39 5N 0 31W
Villanueva de Córdoba, *Spain* 43 G6 38 20N 4 38W
Villanueva de la Fuente, *Spain* 41 G2 38 42N 2 42W
Villanueva de la Serena, *Spain* 43 G5 38 59N 5 50W
Villanueva de la Sierra, *Spain* 42 E4 40 12N 6 24W
Villanueva de los Castillejos,
  Spain 43 H3 37 30N 7 15W
Villanueva de los Infantes,
  Spain 43 G7 38 44N 3 1W
Villanueva del Arzobispo, *Spain* 41 G2 38 10N 3 0W
Villanueva del Fresno, *Spain* . 43 G3 38 23N 7 10W
Villanueva y Geltrú = Vilanova
  i la Geltrú, *Spain* .... 40 D6 41 13N 1 40 E
Villaputzu, *Italy* .... 46 C2 39 26N 9 34 E
Villaquilambre, *Spain* 42 C5 42 37N 5 33W
Villar del Arzobispo, *Spain* .. 40 F4 39 44N 0 50W
Villar del Rey, *Spain* 43 F4 39 7N 6 50W
Villarcayo, *Spain* 42 C6 42 56N 3 34W
Villarramiel, *Spain* 42 C6 42 2N 4 55W
Villarreal = Vila-real de los
  Infantes, *Spain* 40 F4 39 55N 0 3W
Villarrica, *Chile* .... 176 A2 39 15 S 72 15W
Villarrica, *Paraguay* .... 174 B4 25 40 S 56 30W
Villarrobledo, *Spain* 41 F2 39 18N 2 36W
Villarroya de la Sierra, *Spain* . 40 D3 41 27N 1 46W
Villarrubia de los Ojos, *Spain* . 43 F7 39 14N 3 36W

Villars-les-Dombes, *France* ... 27 F12 46 0N 5 3 E
Villasayas, *Spain* 40 D2 41 24N 2 39W
Villaseco de los Gamitos =
  Villaseco de los Gamitos,
  Spain 42 D4 41 2N 6 7W
Villaseco de los Gamitos, *Spain* 42 D4 41 2N 6 7W
Villasimíus, *Italy* .... 46 C2 39 8N 9 31 E
Villastar, *Spain* 40 E3 40 17N 1 9W
Villatobas, *Spain* 42 F7 39 54N 3 20W
Villavicencio, *Argentina* .... 174 C2 32 28 S 69 0W
Villavicencio, *Colombia* 168 C3 4 9N 73 37W
Villaviciosa, *Spain* 42 B5 43 32N 5 27W
Villazón, *Bolivia* .... 174 A2 22 0 S 65 35W
Ville-Marie, *Canada* 140 C4 47 20N 79 30W
Ville Platte, *U.S.A.* 155 K8 30 41N 92 17W
Villedieu-les-Poêles, *France* . 26 D5 48 50N 1 13W
Villefort, *France* .... 28 D7 44 28N 3 56 E
Villefranche-de-Lauragais,
  France .... 28 E5 43 25N 1 44 E
Villefranche-de-Rouergue,
  France .... 28 D6 44 21N 2 2 E
Villefranche-du-Périgord,
  France .... 28 D5 44 38N 1 5 E
Villefranche-sur-Saône, *France* 29 C8 45 59N 4 43 E
Villegrande, *Bolivia* .... 173 D5 18 30 S 64 10W
Villel, *Spain* 40 E3 40 14N 1 12W
Villemur-sur-Tarn, *France* .. 28 E5 43 51N 1 31 E
Villena, *Spain* 41 G4 38 39N 0 52W
Villenauxe-la-Grande, *France* . 27 D10 48 35N 3 33 E
Villenave-d'Ornon, *France* . 28 D3 44 46N 0 33W
Villeneuve, *France* .... 32 D3 46 24N 6 56 E
Villeneuve-d'Ascq, *France* .. 27 B10 50 38N 3 9 E
Villeneuve-l'Archevêque,
  France .... 27 D10 48 14N 3 32 E
Villeneuve-lès-Avignon, *France* 29 E8 43 58N 4 49 E
Villeneuve-sur-Allier, *France* . 27 F10 46 40N 3 13 E
Villeneuve-sur-Lot, *France* .. 28 D4 44 24N 0 42 E
Villeneuve-sur-Yonne, *France* 27 D10 48 5N 3 18 E
Villeréal, *France* .... 28 D4 44 38N 0 45 E
Villers-Bocage, *France* 26 C6 49 3N 0 40W
Villers-Cotterêts, *France* ... 27 C10 49 15N 3 4 E
Villers-sur-Mer, *France* 26 C6 49 21N 0 2W
Villersexel, *France* .... 27 E13 47 33N 6 26 E
Villerupt, *France* .... 27 C12 49 28N 5 55 E
Villeurbanne, *France* .... 29 C8 45 46N 4 55 E
Villiers, *S. Africa* .... 117 D4 27 2 S 28 36 E
Villingen-Schwenningen,
  Germany .... 31 G4 48 3N 8 26 E
Villisca, *U.S.A.* 156 D2 40 56N 94 59W
Villupuram, *India* .... 95 J4 11 59N 79 31 E
Vilna, *Canada* 142 C6 54 7N 111 55W
Vilnius, *Lithuania* .... 15 J21 54 38N 25 19 E
Vils, *Austria* .... 34 D3 47 33N 10 38 E
Vils ~, *Bayern, Germany* ... 31 G9 48 37N 13 11 E
Vils ~, *Bayern, Germany* ... 31 F7 49 10N 11 57 E
Vilsbiburg, *Germany* .... 31 G8 48 26N 12 23 E
Vilshofen, *Germany* .... 31 G9 48 37N 13 11 E
Vilusi, *Montenegro, Yug.* ... 50 D2 42 44N 18 34 E
Vilvoorde, *Belgium* .... 24 D4 50 56N 4 26 E
Vilyuy ~, *Russia* .... 65 C13 64 24N 126 26 E
Vilyuysk, *Russia* .... 65 C13 63 40N 121 35 E
Vimianzo, *Spain* 42 B1 43 7N 9 2W
Vimioso, *Portugal* 42 D4 41 35N 6 31W
Vimmerby, *Sweden* .... 17 G9 57 40N 15 55 E
Vimoutiers, *France* .... 26 D7 48 57N 0 10 E
Vimperk, *Czech Rep.* ...... 34 B6 49 3N 13 46 E
Vina, *Cameroon* .... 114 A3 7 45N 15 36 E
Viña del Mar, *Chile* .... 174 C1 33 0 S 71 30W
Vinaroz, *Spain* .... 40 E5 40 30N 0 27 E
Vincennes, *U.S.A.* 157 F9 38 41N 87 32W
Vincent, *U.S.A.* 161 L8 34 33N 118 11W
Vinces, *Ecuador* .... 168 D2 1 32 S 79 45W
Vinchina, *Argentina* .... 174 B2 28 45 S 68 15W
Vindelälven ~, *Sweden* .... 14 E18 63 55N 19 50 E
Vindeln, *Sweden* .... 14 D18 64 12N 19 43 E
Vinderup, *Denmark* .... 17 H2 56 29N 8 45 E
Vindhya Ra., *India* .... 92 H7 22 50N 77 0 E
Vine Grove, *U.S.A.* 157 G11 37 49N 85 59W
Vineland, *U.S.A.* 148 F8 39 29N 75 2W
Vineuil, *France* .... 26 47 35N 1 22 E
Vinga, *Romania* .... 52 B6 46 1N 21 14 E
Vingåker, *Sweden* .... 16 E9 59 2N 15 52 E
Vingelen, *Norway* .... 18 B7 62 5N 10 52 E
Vingnes, *Norway* .... 18 C7 61 7N 10 26 E
Vinh, *Vietnam* .... 86 C5 18 45N 105 38 E
Vinh Linh, *Vietnam* .... 86 D6 17 4N 107 2 E
Vinh Long, *Vietnam* .... 87 G5 10 16N 105 57 E
Vinh Yen, *Vietnam* .... 76 G5 21 21N 105 35 E
Vinhais, *Portugal* 42 D3 41 50N 7 5W
Vinica, *Croatia* .... 45 B13 46 20N 16 9 E
Vinica, *Macedonia* .... 50 E6 41 53N 22 32 E
Vinica, *Slovenia* .... 45 C12 45 28N 15 16 E
Vinita, *U.S.A.* 155 G7 36 39N 95 9W
Vinje, *Hordaland, Norway* .. 18 D3 60 48N 6 30 E
Vinje, *Sør-Trøndelag, Norway* 18 A5 63 12N 9 0 E
Vinje, *Telemark, Norway* ... 18 E4 59 37N 7 51 E
Vinkovci, *Croatia* .... 52 B3 45 19N 18 48 E
Vinnitsa = Vinnytsya, *Ukraine* 59 H5 49 15N 28 30 E
Vinnytsya, *Ukraine* .... 59 H5 49 15N 28 30 E
Vinslöv, *Sweden* .... 17 H7 56 7N 13 55 E
Vinstra, *Norway* .... 18 C6 61 37N 9 44 E
Vinstra ~, *Norway* .... 18 C6 61 37N 9 44 E
Vintar, *Phil.* .... 80 B3 18 14N 120 39 E
Vintjärn, *Sweden* .... 16 D10 60 50N 16 4 E
Vinton, *Calif., U.S.A.* 160 F6 39 48N 120 10W
Vinton, *Iowa, U.S.A.* 156 D4 42 10N 92 1W
Vinton, *La., U.S.A.* 155 K8 30 11N 93 35W
Vințu de Jos, *Romania* ... 53 D8 45 0N 23 30 E
Vinukonda, *India* .... 95 F4 16 5N 79 45 E
Viöl, *Germany* .... 30 A5 54 34N 9 11 E
Viola, *U.S.A.* 156 C6 41 12N 90 35W
Violet Town, *Australia* ..... 129 D6 36 38 S 145 42 E
Vipava, *Slovenia* .... 45 C10 45 51N 13 58 E
Vipiteno, *Italy* .... 45 B8 46 54N 11 26 E
Vir, *Croatia* .... 45 D12 44 17N 15 3 E
Vir, *Tajikistan* .... 63 F3 37 45N 72 5 E
Vira, *Switz.* .... 33 D7 46 8N 8 50 E
Virac, *Phil.* .... 79 B6 13 30N 124 20 E
Virachei, *Cambodia* .... 86 F6 13 59N 106 49 E
Virago Sd., *Canada* 142 C2 54 0N 132 30W
Virajpet = Virarajendrapet,
  India .... 95 H2 12 10N 75 50 E
Viramgam, *India* .... 92 H5 23 5N 72 0 E
Viranşehir, *Turkey* .... 101 D8 37 13N 39 45 E
Virarajendrapet, *India* ..... 95 H2 12 10N 75 50 E
Virawah, *Pakistan* .... 92 G4 24 31N 70 46 E
Virbalis, *Lithuania* .... 54 D9 54 39N 22 49 E
Virden, *Canada* 143 D8 49 50N 100 56W
Virden, *U.S.A.* 156 F7 39 30N 89 46W
Vire, *France* 26 D6 48 50N 0 53W
Vire ~, *France* 26 C5 49 20N 1 7W
Virei, *Angola* .... 115 F2 15 43 S 12 52 E
Virgem da Lapa, *Brazil* ..... 171 E3 16 49 S 42 21W
Virgenes, C., *Argentina* .... 176 D3 52 19 S 68 21W
Virgin ~, *U.S.A.* 159 H6 36 28N 114 21W
Virgin Gorda, *Virgin Is.* 165 C7 18 30N 64 26W
Virgin Is. (British) ■, *W. Indies* 165 C7 18 30N 64 30W
Virgin Is. (U.S.) ■, *W. Indies* . 165 C7 18 20N 65 0W

Virginia, *S. Africa* .... 116 D4 28 8 S 26 55 E
Virginia, *Ill., U.S.A.* 156 E6 39 57N 90 13W
Virginia, *Minn., U.S.A.* 154 B8 47 31N 92 32W
Virginia □, *U.S.A.* 148 G7 37 30N 78 45W
Virginia Beach, *U.S.A.* 148 G8 36 51N 75 59W
Virginia City, *Mont., U.S.A.* . 158 D8 45 18N 111 56W
Virginia City, *Nev., U.S.A.* .. 160 F7 39 19N 119 39W
Virginia Falls, *Canada* 142 A3 61 38N 125 42W
Virginiatown, *Canada* 140 C4 48 9N 79 36W
Virje, *Croatia* .... 45 B13 46 4N 16 59 E
Viroqua, *U.S.A.* 154 D9 43 34N 90 53W
Virovitica, *Croatia* .... 52 B2 45 51N 17 21 E
Virpazar, *Montenegro, Yug.* . 50 D3 42 14N 19 6 E
Virpur, *India* .... 92 J3 21 51N 70 42 E
Virserum, *Sweden* .... 17 G9 57 20N 15 35 E
Virton, *Belgium* .... 24 E5 49 35N 5 32 E
Virú, *Peru* .... 172 B2 8 25 S 78 38W
Virudunagar, *India* .... 95 K3 9 30N 77 58 E
Vis, *Croatia* .... 45 E13 43 4N 16 10 E
Visalia, *U.S.A.* 160 J7 36 20N 119 18W
Visayan Sea, *Phil.* .... 79 B6 11 30N 123 30 E
Visby, *Sweden* .... 17 G12 57 37N 18 18 E
Viscount Melville Sd., *Canada* 136 B9 74 10N 108 0W
Visé, *Belgium* .... 24 D5 50 44N 5 41 E
Višegrad, *Bos.-H.* .... 52 G4 43 47N 19 17 E
Viseu, *Brazil* .... 170 B2 1 10 S 46 5W
Viseu, *Portugal* 42 E3 40 40N 7 55W
Viseu □, *Portugal* 42 E3 40 40N 7 55W
Viseu de Sus, *Romania* ..... 53 C9 47 45N 24 25 E
Vishakhapatnam, *India* .... 94 F6 17 45N 83 20 E
Vishera ~, *Russia* .... 62 A6 59 55N 56 25 E
Višina, *Romania* .... 53 G9 43 52N 24 27 E
Vişineşti, *Moldova* .... 53 D13 46 20N 28 27 E
Visingsö, *Sweden* .... 17 F8 58 2N 14 20 E
Viskafors, *Sweden* .... 17 G6 57 37N 12 50 E
Viskan ~, *Sweden* .... 17 H6 57 14N 12 12 E
Viški Kanal, *Croatia* .... 45 E13 43 4N 16 5 E
Vislanda, *Sweden* .... 17 H8 56 46N 14 30 E
Visnagar, *India* .... 92 H5 23 45N 72 32 E
Višnja Gora, *Slovenia* ...... 45 C11 45 58N 14 45 E
Viso, Mte., *Italy* .... 44 D4 44 38N 7 5 E
Viso del Marqués, *Spain* 43 G7 38 32N 3 34W
Visoko, *Bos.-H.* .... 52 G3 43 58N 18 10 E
Visokoi I., *Antarctica* ...... 7 B1 56 43 S 27 15W
Visp, *Switz.* .... 32 D5 46 17N 7 52 E
Vispa ~, *Switz.* .... 32 D5 46 9N 7 48 E
Vissefjärda, *Sweden* .... 17 H9 56 32N 15 35 E
Visselhövde, *Germany* ..... 30 C5 52 59N 9 34 E
Vissenbjerg, *Denmark* ..... 17 J4 55 23N 10 7 E
Vissoie, *Switz.* .... 32 D5 46 13N 7 36 E
Vista, *U.S.A.* 161 M9 33 12N 117 14W
Vistonikos, Ormos = Vistonís,
  Límni, *Greece* .... 51 E9 41 0N 25 7 E
Vistonís, Límni, *Greece* .... 51 E9 41 0N 25 7 E
Vistula = Wisła ~, *Poland* .. 54 D5 54 22N 18 55 E
Vit ~, *Bulgaria* .... 51 C8 43 30N 24 30 E
Vita, *India* .... 94 F2 17 17N 74 33 E
Vitanje, *Slovenia* .... 45 B12 46 25N 15 18 E
Vitebsk = Vitsyebsk, *Belarus* 58 E6 55 10N 30 15 E
Viterbo, *Italy* .... 45 F9 42 25N 12 6 E
Vitez, *Bos.-H.* .... 52 F2 44 10N 17 48 E
Viti Levu, *Fiji* .... 133 A1 17 30 S 177 30 E
Vitigudino, *Spain* 42 D4 41 1N 6 26W
Vitim, *Russia* .... 65 D12 59 28N 112 34 E
Vitim ~, *Russia* .... 65 D12 59 26N 112 34 E
Vitina, *Bos.-H.* .... 45 E14 43 17N 17 24 E
Vitina, *Greece* .... 48 D4 37 40N 22 10 E
Vítkov, *Czech Rep.* .... 35 B10 49 46N 17 45 E
Vitória, *Brazil* .... 169 D7 2 54 S 52 1W
Vitória, *Brazil* .... 171 F3 20 48 S 40 22W
Vitória da Conquista, *Brazil* . 171 D3 14 51 S 40 51W
Vitória de São Antão, *Brazil* . 170 C4 8 10 S 35 20W
Vitória-Gasteiz, *Spain* 40 C2 42 50N 2 41W
Vitorino Freire, *Brazil* ...... 170 B2 4 5 S 45 10W
Vitré, *France* 26 D5 48 8N 1 12W
Vitry-le-François, *France* ... 27 D11 48 43N 4 33 E
Vitry-sur-Seine, *France* .... 27 D9 48 47N 2 24 E
Vitsand, *Sweden* .... 16 D7 60 20N 13 0 E
Vitsi, Óros, *Greece* .... 50 F5 40 40N 21 25 E
Vitsyebsk, *Belarus* .... 58 E6 55 10N 30 15 E
Vittangi, *Sweden* .... 17 H7 56 58N 13 57 E
Vitteaux, *France* .... 27 E11 47 24N 4 30 E
Vittel, *France* .... 27 D12 48 12N 5 57 E
Vittória, *Italy* .... 47 F7 36 57N 14 32 E
Vittório Véneto, *Italy* ...... 45 C9 45 59N 12 18 E
Vittsjö, *Sweden* .... 17 H7 56 20N 13 40 E
Vitu Is., *Papua N. G.* ...... 132 C5 4 50 S 149 25 E
Vitznau, *Switz.* .... 33 B6 47 1N 8 29 E
Vivaio, *Switz.* 42 B3 43 39N 7 38W
Vivero, *U.S.A.* 155 J8 32 53N 93 59W
Viviers, *France* .... 29 D8 44 30N 4 40 E
Vivonne, *Australia* .... 128 C2 35 59 S 137 9 E
Vivonne B., *Australia* ...... 128 C2 35 59 S 137 9 E
Vivonne, *France* .... 28 B4 46 25N 0 15 E
Vizcaíno, Desierto de, *Mexico* 162 B2 27 40N 113 50W
Vizcaíno, Sierra, *Mexico* ... 162 B2 27 30N 114 0W
Vizcaya □, *Spain* 40 B2 43 15N 2 45W
Vize, *Turkey* .... 51 E11 41 34N 27 45 E
Vizianagaram, *India* .... 94 E6 18 6N 83 30 E
Vizille, *France* .... 29 C9 45 5N 5 46 E
Viziñada, *Croatia* .... 45 C10 45 20N 13 46 E
Viziru, *Romania* .... 53 E12 45 0N 27 43 E
Vizzini, *Italy* .... 47 F7 37 10N 14 45 E
Vjosa ~, *Albania* .... 50 F3 40 37N 19 24 E
Vlaardingen, *Neths.* .... 24 C3 51 55N 4 21 E
Vlădeasa, Vf., *Romania* .... 52 D7 46 47N 22 50 E
Vladičin Han, *Serbia, Yug.* .. 50 D6 42 42N 22 1 E
Vladikavkaz, *Russia* .... 61 J7 43 0N 44 35 E
Vladimir, *Russia* .... 58 D11 56 15N 40 30 E
Vladimir Volynskiy =
  Volodymyr-Volynskyy,
  Ukraine .... 59 G3 50 50N 24 18 E
Vladimirci, *Serbia, Yug.* .... 50 B3 44 36N 19 50 E
Vladimirovac, *Serbia, Yug.* .. 52 E5 45 1N 20 53 E
Vladimirovo, *Bulgaria* ..... 50 C7 43 32N 23 22 E
Vladimivo, *Kazakstan* ...... 60 E10 50 51N 51 8 E
Vladislavovka, *Ukraine* .... 59 K8 45 12N 35 29 E
Vladivostok, *Russia* .... 65 E14 43 10N 131 53 E
Vlăhiţa, *Romania* .... 53 D10 46 21N 25 32 E
Vlasenica, *Bos.-H.* .... 52 F3 44 11N 18 59 E
Vlašić, *Bos.-H.* .... 52 F2 44 19N 17 37 E
Vlašim, *Czech Rep.* .... 34 B7 49 40N 14 53 E
Vlasinsko Jezero, *Serbia, Yug.* 50 D6 42 42N 22 22 E
Vlasotince, *Serbia, Yug.* .... 50 D6 42 59N 22 7 E
Vlieland, *Neths.* .... 24 A5 53 16N 4 55 E
Vlissingen, *Neths.* .... 24 C2 51 26N 3 34 E
Vlóra, *Albania* .... 50 F3 40 32N 19 28 E
Vlorës, Gjiri i, *Albania* ..... 50 F3 40 29N 19 27 E
Vltava ~, *Czech Rep.* ...... 34 A7 50 21N 14 30 E
Vo Dat, *Vietnam* .... 87 G6 11 9N 107 31 E
Vobarno, *Italy* .... 44 C7 45 38N 10 30 E
Vočin, *Croatia* .... 52 B2 45 37N 17 38 E
Vöcklabruck, *Austria* ...... 34 C6 48 1N 13 39 E
Vodice, *Croatia* .... 45 E12 43 47N 15 47 E

Wendesi 299

Walters, *U.S.A.* **155 H5** 34 22N 98 19W
Waltershausen, *Germany* **30 E6** 50 54N 10 33 E
Waltham, *U.S.A.* **151 D13** 42 23N 71 14W
Waltman, *U.S.A.* **158 E10** 43 4N 107 12W
Walton, *Ky., U.S.A.* **157 F12** 38 52N 84 37W
Walton, *N.Y., U.S.A.* **151 D9** 42 10N 75 8W
Walton-on-the-Naze, *U.K.* **21 F9** 51 51N 1 17 E
Waltonville, *U.S.A.* **156 F7** 38 13N 89 2W
Walu, *Burma* **90 B7** 26 28N 98 2 E
Walvis Bay, *Namibia* **116 C1** 23 0 S 14 28 E
Walvis Ridge, *Atl. Oc.* **9 L9** 26 0 S 5 0 E
Walvisbaai = Walvis Bay, *Namibia* **116 C1** 23 0 S 14 28 E
Walwa, *Australia* **129 C7** 35 59 S 147 44 E
Wamba, *Dem. Rep. of the Congo* **114 C4** 1 37 S 22 30 E
Wamba, *Dem. Rep. of the Congo* **118 B2** 2 10N 27 57 E
Wamba, *Kenya* **118 B4** 0 58N 37 19 E
Wamba, *Nigeria* **113 D6** 8 57N 8 42 E
Wamba →, *Dem. Rep. of the Congo* **115 C3** 3 56 S 17 12 E
Wamego, *U.S.A.* **154 F6** 39 12N 96 18W
Wamena, *Indonesia* **79 E9** 4 4 S 138 57 E
Wamsutter, *U.S.A.* **158 F9** 41 40N 107 58W
Wamulan, *Indonesia* **79 E7** 3 27 S 126 7 E
Wan Hat, *Burma* **90 E6** 20 14N 97 53 E
Wan Kinghao, *Burma* **90 E7** 21 34N 98 17 E
Wan Lai-kam, *Burma* **90 E7** 21 21N 98 22 E
Wan Tup, *Burma* **90 E7** 21 13N 98 42 E
Wan Xian, *China* **74 E8** 38 47N 115 7 E
Wana, *Pakistan* **91 B3** 32 20N 69 32 E
Wanaaring, *Australia* **127 D3** 29 38 S 144 9 E
Wanaka, *N.Z.* **131 E4** 44 42 S 169 9 E
Wanaka L., *N.Z.* **131 E4** 44 33 S 169 7 E
Wan'an, *China* **77 D10** 26 26N 114 49 E
Wanapiri, *Indonesia* **83 B5** 4 30 S 135 59 E
Wanapitei L., *Canada* **140 C3** 46 45N 80 40W
Wanbi, *Australia* **128 C4** 34 46 S 140 17 E
Wandaik, *Guyana* **169 C6** 4 27N 59 35W
Wandandian, *Australia* **129 C9** 35 6 S 150 30 E
Wandel Sea = McKinley Sea, *Arctic* **10 A11** 82 0N 0 0 E
Wandérama, *Ivory C.* **112 D4** 8 37N 4 25W
Wanderer, *Zimbabwe* **119 F3** 19 36 S 30 1 E
Wandhari, *Pakistan* **92 F2** 27 42N 66 48 E
Wanding, *China* **76 E2** 24 5N 98 4 E
Wandoan, *Australia* **127 D4** 26 5 S 149 55 E
Wanfu, *China* **75 D12** 40 8N 122 38 E
Wang →, *Thailand* **78 A1** 17 8N 99 2 E
Wang Kai, *Sudan* **107 F2** 9 3N 29 23 E
Wang Noi, *Thailand* **86 E3** 14 13N 100 44 E
Wang Saphung, *Thailand* **86 D3** 17 18N 101 46 E
Wang Thong, *Thailand* **86 D3** 16 50N 100 26 E
Wanga, *Dem. Rep. of the Congo* **118 B2** 2 58N 29 12 E
Wangal, *Indonesia* **79 F8** 6 8 S 134 9 E
Wanganella, *Australia* **129 C6** 35 6 S 144 49 E
Wanganui, *N.Z.* **130 F4** 39 56 S 175 3 E
Wanganui →, *W. Coast, N.Z.* **131 D5** 43 3 S 170 26 E
Wanganui →, *Wanganui-Manawatu, N.Z.* **130 F4** 39 55 S 175 4 E
Wangaratta, *Australia* **129 D7** 36 21 S 146 19 E
Wangary, *Australia* **127 E2** 34 35 S 135 29 E
Wangcang, *China* **76 A6** 32 18N 106 20 E
Wangcheng, *China* **77 C9** 28 22N 112 49 E
Wangdu, *China* **74 E8** 38 40N 115 7 E
Wangdu Phodrang, *Bhutan* **90 B2** 27 28N 89 54 E
Wangen, *Germany* **31 H5** 47 41N 9 50 E
Wangerooge, *Germany* **30 B3** 53 47N 7 54 E
Wangi, *Kenya* **118 C5** 1 58 S 40 58 E
Wängi, *Switz.* **33 B7** 47 30N 8 57 E
Wangiwangi, *Indonesia* **79 F6** 5 22 S 123 37 E
Wangjiang, *China* **77 B11** 30 10N 116 42 E
Wangmo, *China* **76 E6** 25 11N 106 5 E
Wangolodougou, *Ivory C.* **112 D3** 9 55N 5 10W
Wangqing, *China* **75 C15** 43 12N 129 42 E
Wani, *India* **94 D4** 20 5N 78 55 E
Wankaner, *India* **92 H4** 22 35N 71 0 E
Wanless, *Canada* **143 C8** 54 11N 101 21W
Wannian, *China* **77 C11** 28 42N 117 4 E
Wanning, *Taiwan* **86 C8** 23 15N 121 17 E
Wanon Niwat, *Thailand* **86 D4** 17 38N 103 46 E
Wanquan, *China* **74 D8** 40 50N 114 40 E
Wanrong, *China* **74 G6** 35 25N 110 50 E
Wanshan, *China* **76 D7** 27 30N 109 12 E
Wanshengchang, *China* **76 C6** 28 57N 106 53 E
Wanstead, *N.Z.* **130 G5** 40 8 S 176 30 E
Wantage, *U.K.* **21 F6** 51 35N 1 25W
Wanyin, *Burma* **90 E6** 20 23N 97 15 E
Wanyuan, *China* **76 A7** 32 4N 108 3 E
Wanzai, *China* **77 C10** 28 7N 114 30 E
Wapakoneta, *U.S.A.* **157 D12** 40 34N 84 12W
Wapato, *U.S.A.* **158 C3** 46 27N 120 25W
Wapawekka L., *Canada* **143 C8** 54 55N 104 40W
Wapello, *U.S.A.* **156 C5** 41 11N 91 11W
Wapikopa L., *Canada* **140 B2** 52 56N 87 53W
Wapinda, *Dem. Rep. of the Congo* **114 B4** 3 41N 22 48 E
Wapiti →, *Canada* **142 B5** 55 5N 118 18W
Wappingers Falls, *U.S.A.* **151 E11** 41 36N 73 55W
Wapsipinicon →, *U.S.A.* **156 C6** 41 44N 90 19W
Warab □, *Sudan* **107 F2** 7 30N 28 30 E
Warabi, *Japan* **71 B11** 35 49N 139 41 E
Warangal, *India* **94 F4** 17 58N 79 35 E
Waraseoni, *India* **93 J9** 21 45N 80 2 E
Waratah, *Australia* **126 G4** 41 30 S 145 30 E
Waratah B., *Australia* **127 F4** 38 54 S 146 5 E
Warburg, *Germany* **30 D5** 51 28N 9 11 E
Warburton, *Vic., Australia* **129 D6** 37 47 S 145 42 E
Warburton, *W. Austral., Australia* **125 E4** 26 8 S 126 35 E
Warburton Ra., *Australia* **125 E4** 25 55 S 126 28 E
Ward, *N.Z.* **131 B9** 41 49 S 174 11 E
Ward →, *Australia* **127 D4** 26 28 S 146 6 E
Ward Hunt, C., *Papua N. G.* **132 E5** 8 2 S 148 10 E
Ward Hunt Str., *Papua N. G.* **132 E6** 9 30 S 150 0 E
Ward Mt., *U.S.A.* **160 H8** 37 12N 118 54W
Warden, *S. Africa* **117 D4** 27 50 S 29 0 E
Wardha, *India* **94 D4** 20 45N 78 39 E
Wards River, *Australia* **129 B9** 32 11 S 151 56 E
Ware, *Canada* **142 B3** 57 26N 125 41W
Ware, *U.S.A.* **151 D12** 42 16N 72 14W
Waregem, *Belgium* **24 D3** 50 53N 3 27 E
Wareham, *U.S.A.* **151 E14** 41 46N 70 43W
Waremme, *Belgium* **24 D5** 50 43N 5 15 E
Waren, *Germany* **30 B8** 53 31N 12 40 E
Warendorf, *Germany* **30 D4** 51 57N 8 1 E
Waresboro, *U.S.A.* **152 D7** 31 15N 82 29W
Warialda, *Australia* **127 D5** 29 29 S 150 33 E
Wariap, *Indonesia* **79 E8** 1 30 S 134 5 E
Warin Chamrap, *Thailand* **86 E5** 15 12N 104 53 E
Warka, *Poland* **55 G8** 51 47N 21 12 E
Warkopi, *Indonesia* **79 E8** 1 12 S 134 9 E
Warkworth, *N.Z.* **130 C3** 36 24 S 174 41 E
Warm Springs, *Ga., U.S.A.* **152 C5** 32 53N 84 41W
Warm Springs, *Nev., U.S.A.* **159 G5** 38 10N 116 20W
Warman, *Canada* **143 C7** 52 19N 106 30W
Warmbad, *Namibia* **116 D2** 28 25 S 18 42 E
Warmbad, *S. Africa* **117 C4** 24 51 S 28 19 E
Warmińsko-Mazurskie □, *Poland* **54 D8** 54 0N 21 0 E
Warminster, *U.K.* **21 F5** 51 12N 2 10W
Warminster, *U.S.A.* **151 F9** 40 12N 75 6W
Warnemünde, *Germany* **30 A8** 54 10N 12 4 E
Warner Mts., *U.S.A.* **158 F3** 41 40N 120 15W
Warner Robins, *U.S.A.* **152 C6** 32 37N 83 36W
Warnes, *Bolivia* **173 D5** 17 30 S 63 10W
Warnow →, *Germany* **30 A8** 54 6N 12 9 E
Waroona, *Australia* **125 F2** 32 50 S 115 58 E
Warora, *India* **94 D4** 20 14N 79 1 E
Warracknabeal, *Australia* **128 D5** 36 9 S 142 26 E
Warragul, *Australia* **129 E6** 38 10 S 145 58 E
Warrego →, *Australia* **127 E4** 30 24 S 145 21 E
Warrego Ra., *Australia* **126 C4** 24 58 S 146 0 E
Warren, *Australia* **129 A7** 31 42 S 147 51 E
Warren, *Ark., U.S.A.* **155 J8** 33 37N 92 4W
Warren, *Ill., U.S.A.* **156 B7** 42 29N 90 0W
Warren, *Ind., U.S.A.* **157 D11** 40 41N 85 26W
Warren, *Mich., U.S.A.* **157 B13** 42 30N 83 0W
Warren, *Minn., U.S.A.* **154 A6** 48 12N 96 46W
Warren, *Ohio, U.S.A.* **150 E4** 41 14N 80 49W
Warren, *Pa., U.S.A.* **150 E5** 41 51N 79 9W
Warrenpoint, *U.K.* **23 B5** 54 6N 6 15W
Warrensburg, *Ill., U.S.A.* **156 E7** 39 56N 89 4W
Warrensburg, *Mo., U.S.A.* **156 F3** 38 46N 93 44W
Warrensburg, *N.Y., U.S.A.* **151 C11** 43 29N 73 46W
Warrenton, *S. Africa* **116 D3** 28 9 S 24 47 E
Warrenton, *Ga., U.S.A.* **152 B7** 33 24N 82 40W
Warrenton, *Mo., U.S.A.* **156 F5** 38 49N 91 9W
Warrenton, *Oreg., U.S.A.* **160 D3** 46 10N 123 56W
Warrenville = Gloverville, *U.S.A.* **152 B8** 33 32N 81 48W
Warri, *Nigeria* **113 D6** 5 30N 5 41 E
Warrina, *Australia* **127 D2** 28 12 S 135 50 E
Warrington, *N.Z.* **131 F5** 45 43 S 170 35 E
Warrington, *U.K.* **20 D5** 53 24N 2 35W
Warrington, *U.S.A.* **149 K2** 30 23N 87 17W
Warrington □, *U.K.* **20 D5** 53 24N 2 35W
Warrnambool, *Australia* **128 E5** 38 25 S 142 30 E
Warroad, *U.S.A.* **154 A7** 48 54N 95 19W
Warruwi, *Australia* **126 A1** 11 36 S 133 20 E
Warsa, *Indonesia* **79 E9** 0 47 S 135 55 E
Warsak Dam, *Pakistan* **92 B4** 34 11N 71 19 E
Warsaw = Warszawa, *Poland* **55 F8** 52 13N 21 0 E
Warsaw, *Ill., U.S.A.* **156 D5** 40 22N 91 26W
Warsaw, *Ind., U.S.A.* **157 C11** 41 14N 85 51W
Warsaw, *Ky., U.S.A.* **157 F12** 38 47N 84 54W
Warsaw, *Mo., U.S.A.* **156 F3** 38 15N 93 23W
Warsaw, *N.Y., U.S.A.* **150 D6** 42 45N 78 8W
Warsaw, *Ohio, U.S.A.* **150 F3** 40 20N 82 0W
Warstein, *Germany* **30 D4** 51 26N 8 22 E
Warszawa, *Poland* **55 F8** 52 13N 21 0 E
Warta, *Poland* **55 G5** 51 43N 18 38 E
Warta →, *Poland* **55 F1** 52 35N 14 39 E
Warth, *Austria* **33 B10** 47 15N 10 11 E
Warthe = Warta →, *Poland* **55 F1** 52 35N 14 39 E
Warthen, *U.S.A.* **152 B7** 33 6N 82 48W
Waru, *Indonesia* **79 E8** 3 30 S 130 36 E
Warud, *India* **94 D4** 21 30N 78 16 E
Warwick, *Australia* **127 D5** 28 10 S 152 1 E
Warwick, *U.K.* **21 E6** 52 18N 1 35W
Warwick, *Ga., U.S.A.* **152 D6** 31 50N 83 57W
Warwick, *N.Y., U.S.A.* **151 E10** 41 16N 74 22W
Warwick, *R.I., U.S.A.* **151 E13** 41 42N 71 28W
Warwickshire □, *U.K.* **21 E6** 52 14N 1 38W
Wasaga Beach, *Canada* **150 B4** 44 31N 80 1W
Wasagaming, *Canada* **143 C9** 50 39N 99 58W
Wasatch Ra., *U.S.A.* **158 F8** 40 30N 111 15W
Wasbank, *S. Africa* **117 D5** 28 15 S 30 9 E
Wasco, *Calif., U.S.A.* **161 K7** 35 36N 119 20W
Wasco, *Oreg., U.S.A.* **158 D3** 45 36N 120 42W
Wase, *Nigeria* **113 D6** 9 4N 9 54 E
Waseca, *U.S.A.* **154 C8** 44 5N 93 30W
Wasekamio L., *Canada* **143 B7** 56 45N 108 45W
Wash, The, *U.K.* **20 E8** 52 58N 0 20 E
Washago, *Canada* **150 B5** 44 45N 79 20W
Washburn, *Ill., U.S.A.* **156 D7** 40 55N 89 17W
Washburn, *N. Dak., U.S.A.* **154 B4** 47 17N 101 2W
Washburn, *Wis., U.S.A.* **154 B9** 46 40N 90 54W
Washim, *India* **94 D3** 20 3N 77 0 E
Washington, *U.K.* **20 C6** 54 55N 1 30W
Washington, *D.C., U.S.A.* **148 F7** 38 54N 77 2W
Washington, *Ga., U.S.A.* **152 B7** 33 44N 82 44W
Washington, *Ill., U.S.A.* **156 D7** 40 42N 89 24W
Washington, *Ind., U.S.A.* **157 F9** 38 40N 87 10W
Washington, *Iowa, U.S.A.* **156 C5** 41 18N 91 42W
Washington, *Mo., U.S.A.* **156 F5** 38 33N 91 1W
Washington, *N.C., U.S.A.* **149 H7** 35 33N 77 3W
Washington, *N.J., U.S.A.* **151 F10** 40 46N 74 59W
Washington, *Pa., U.S.A.* **150 F4** 40 10N 80 15W
Washington, *Utah, U.S.A.* **159 H7** 37 8N 113 31W
Washington □, *U.S.A.* **158 C3** 47 30N 120 30W
Washington, Mt., *U.S.A.* **151 B13** 44 16N 71 18W
Washington Court House, *U.S.A.* **157 E13** 39 32N 83 26W
Washington I., *U.S.A.* **148 C2** 45 23N 86 54W
Washington Land, *Greenland* **10 A4** 80 30N 66 0W
Washougal, *U.S.A.* **160 E4** 45 35N 122 21W
Washuk, *Pakistan* **91 D2** 27 42N 64 45 E
Wasian, *Indonesia* **79 E8** 1 47 S 133 19 E
Wasilków, *Poland* **55 E10** 53 12N 23 13 E
Wasilla, *U.S.A.* **144 F10** 61 35N 149 26W
Wasior, *Indonesia* **79 E8** 2 43 S 134 30 E
Waskaganish, *Canada* **140 B4** 51 30N 78 40W
Waskaiowaka, L., *Canada* **143 B9** 56 33N 96 23W
Waskesiu Lake, *Canada* **143 C7** 53 55N 106 5W
Wassaw I., *U.S.A.* **152 D9** 31 53N 80 58W
Wassaw Sd., *U.S.A.* **152 D9** 31 55N 80 55W
Wassen, *Switz.* **33 C7** 46 42N 8 36 E
Wasserauen, *Switz.* **33 B8** 47 17N 9 26 E
Wasserburg, *Germany* **31 G8** 48 3N 12 14 E
Wasserkuppe, *Germany* **30 E5** 50 29N 9 55 E
Wassy, *France* **27 D11** 48 30N 4 58 E
Waswanipi, *Canada* **140 C4** 49 40N 76 29W
Waswanipi, L., *Canada* **140 C4** 49 35N 76 40W
Watampone, *Indonesia* **79 E6** 4 29 S 120 25 E
Watansoppeng, *Indonesia* **82 B1** 4 10 S 119 56 E
Water Park Pt., *Australia* **126 C5** 22 56 S 150 47 E
Water Valley, *U.S.A.* **155 H10** 34 10N 89 38W
Waterberge, *S. Africa* **117 C4** 24 10 S 28 0 E
Waterbury, *Conn., U.S.A.* **151 E11** 41 33N 73 3W
Waterbury, *Vt., U.S.A.* **151 B12** 44 20N 72 46W
Waterbury L., *Canada* **143 B8** 58 10N 104 22W
Waterdown, *Canada* **150 C5** 43 20N 79 53W
Wateree →, *U.S.A.* **152 B9** 33 45N 80 37W
Waterford, *Canada* **150 D4** 42 56N 80 17W
Waterford, *Ireland* **23 D4** 52 15N 7 8W
Waterford, *Calif., U.S.A.* **160 H6** 37 38N 120 46W
Waterford, *Mich., U.S.A.* **157 B13** 42 45N 83 32W
Waterford, *Pa., U.S.A.* **150 E5** 41 57N 79 59W
Waterford, *Wis., U.S.A.* **157 B8** 42 46N 88 13W
Waterford □, *Ireland* **23 D4** 52 10N 7 40W
Waterford Harbour, *Ireland* **23 D5** 52 8N 6 58W
Waterhen L., *Canada* **143 C9** 52 10N 99 40W
Waterloo, *Belgium* **24 D4** 50 43N 4 25 E
Waterloo, *Ont., Canada* **140 D3** 43 30N 80 32W
Waterloo, *Qué., Canada* **151 A12** 45 22N 72 32W
Waterloo, *S. Leone* **112 D2** 8 26N 13 8W
Waterloo, *Ill., U.S.A.* **156 F6** 38 20N 90 9W
Waterloo, *Ind., U.S.A.* **157 C11** 41 26N 85 1W
Waterloo, *Iowa, U.S.A.* **156 B4** 42 30N 92 21W
Waterloo, *N.Y., U.S.A.* **150 D8** 42 54N 76 52W
Waterloo, *Wis., U.S.A.* **156 A8** 43 11N 88 59W
Waterman, *U.S.A.* **157 C8** 41 46N 88 47W
Watersmeet, *U.S.A.* **154 B10** 46 16N 89 11W
Waterton Lakes Nat. Park, *U.S.A.* **158 B7** 48 45N 115 0W
Watertown, *Conn., U.S.A.* **151 E11** 41 36N 73 7W
Watertown, *Fla., U.S.A.* **152 E7** 30 11N 82 36W
Watertown, *N.Y., U.S.A.* **151 C9** 43 59N 75 55W
Watertown, *S. Dak., U.S.A.* **154 C6** 44 54N 97 7W
Watertown, *Wis., U.S.A.* **154 D10** 43 12N 88 43W
Waterval-Boven, *S. Africa* **117 D5** 25 40 S 30 18 E
Waterville, *Canada* **151 A13** 45 16N 71 54W
Waterville, *Maine, U.S.A.* **149 C11** 44 33N 69 38W
Waterville, *N.Y., U.S.A.* **151 D9** 42 56N 75 23W
Waterville, *Pa., U.S.A.* **150 E7** 41 19N 77 21W
Waterville, *Wash., U.S.A.* **158 C3** 47 39N 120 4W
Watervliet, *Mich., U.S.A.* **157 B10** 42 11N 86 18W
Watervliet, *N.Y., U.S.A.* **151 D11** 42 44N 73 42W
Wates, *Indonesia* **79 G14** 7 51 S 110 10 E
Watford, *Canada* **150 D3** 42 57N 81 53W
Watford, *U.K.* **21 F7** 51 40N 0 24W
Watford City, *U.S.A.* **154 B3** 47 48N 103 17W
Wathaman →, *Canada* **143 B8** 57 16N 102 59W
Wathaman L., *Canada* **143 B8** 56 58N 103 44W
Watheroo, *Australia* **125 F2** 30 15 S 116 0 E
Wating, *China* **74 G4** 35 40N 106 38 E
Watkins Glen, *U.S.A.* **150 D8** 42 23N 76 52W
Watkinsville, *U.S.A.* **152 B6** 33 52N 83 25W
Watling I. = San Salvador I., *Bahamas* **165 B5** 24 0N 74 40W
Watonga, *U.S.A.* **155 H5** 35 51N 98 25W
Watrous, *Canada* **143 C7** 51 40N 105 25W
Watrous, *U.S.A.* **155 H2** 35 48N 104 59W
Watsa, *Dem. Rep. of the Congo* **118 B2** 3 4N 29 30 E
Watseka, *U.S.A.* **157 D9** 40 47N 87 44W
Watsi Kenga, *Dem. Rep. of the Congo* **114 C4** 0 49 S 20 34 E
Watson, *Australia* **125 F5** 30 29 S 131 31 E
Watson, *Canada* **143 C8** 52 10N 104 30W
Watson Lake, *Canada* **142 A3** 60 6N 128 49W
Watsontown, *U.S.A.* **150 E8** 41 5N 76 52W
Watsonville, *U.S.A.* **160 J5** 36 55N 121 45W
Wattenwil, *Switz.* **32 C5** 46 46N 7 31 E
Wattiwarriganna Cr. →, *Australia* **127 D2** 28 57 S 136 10 E
Wattwil, *Switz.* **33 B8** 47 18N 9 6 E
Watu, *Dem. Rep. of the Congo* **114 C4** 3 18 S 20 3 E
Watuata = Batuata, *Indonesia* **79 F6** 6 12 S 122 42 E
Watubela, Kepulauan, *Indonesia* **79 E8** 4 28 S 131 35 E
Watubela Is. = Watubela, Kepulauan, *Indonesia* **79 E8** 4 28 S 131 35 E
Wau = Wâw, *Sudan* **107 F2** 7 45N 28 1 E
Wau, *Papua N. G.* **132 D4** 7 21 S 146 47 E
Waubamik, *Canada* **150 A4** 45 27N 80 1W
Waubay, *U.S.A.* **154 C6** 45 20N 97 18W
Waubra, *Australia* **128 D5** 37 21 S 143 39 E
Wauchope, *N.S.W., Australia* **129 A10** 31 28 S 152 45 E
Wauchope, *N. Terr., Australia* **126 C1** 20 36 S 134 15 E
Wauchula, *U.S.A.* **149 M5** 27 33N 81 49W
Waukarlycarly, L., *Australia* **124 D3** 21 18 S 121 56 E
Waukeenah, *U.S.A.* **152 E6** 30 25N 83 57W
Waukegan, *U.S.A.* **157 B9** 42 22N 87 50W
Waukesha, *U.S.A.* **154 D10** 43 1N 88 14W
Waukon, *U.S.A.* **154 D9** 43 16N 91 29W
Waupaca, *U.S.A.* **154 C10** 44 21N 89 5W
Waupun, *U.S.A.* **154 D10** 43 38N 88 44W
Waurika, *U.S.A.* **155 H6** 34 10N 98 0W
Wausau, *Fla., U.S.A.* **152 E4** 30 38N 85 35W
Wausau, *Wis., U.S.A.* **154 C10** 44 58N 89 38W
Wauseon, *U.S.A.* **157 C12** 41 33N 84 8W
Wautoma, *U.S.A.* **154 C10** 44 4N 89 18W
Wauwatosa, *U.S.A.* **157 A9** 43 3N 88 0W
Waveland, *U.S.A.* **157 E9** 39 53N 87 3W
Waveney →, *U.K.* **21 E9** 52 35N 1 39 E
Waverley, *N.Z.* **130 F3** 39 46 S 174 37 E
Waverley Hall, *U.S.A.* **152 C5** 32 41N 84 44W
Waverly, *Ala., U.S.A.* **152 C4** 32 44N 85 35W
Waverly, *Fla., U.S.A.* **153 H8** 27 59N 81 37W
Waverly, *Ga., U.S.A.* **152 D8** 31 6N 81 43W
Waverly, *Ill., U.S.A.* **156 E7** 39 36N 89 57W
Waverly, *Iowa, U.S.A.* **156 B4** 42 44N 92 29W
Waverly, *Mo., U.S.A.* **156 E3** 39 13N 93 31W
Waverly, *N.Y., U.S.A.* **151 E8** 42 1N 76 32W
Wavre, *Belgium* **24 D4** 50 43N 4 38 E
Wâw, *Sudan* **107 F2** 7 45N 28 1 E
Wâw al Kabîr, *Libya* **108 C3** 25 20N 16 43 E
Wâw an Nāmūs, *Libya* **108 D3** 24 55N 17 46 E
Wawa, *Canada* **140 C3** 47 59N 84 47W
Wawa, *Nigeria* **113 D5** 9 54N 4 27 E
Wawa, *Sudan* **106 C3** 20 30N 30 22 E
Wawanesa, *Canada* **143 D9** 49 36N 99 40W
Wawasee, L., *U.S.A.* **157 C11** 41 24N 85 42W
Wawoi →, *Papua N. G.* **132 D2** 7 48 S 143 16 E
Wawona, *U.S.A.* **160 H7** 37 32N 119 39W
Waxahachie, *U.S.A.* **155 J6** 32 24N 96 51W
Way, L., *Australia* **125 E3** 26 45 S 120 16 E
Wayabula Rau, *Indonesia* **79 D7** 2 29N 128 17 E
Wayang, *Indonesia* **82 A3** 7 52 S 131 47 E
Waycross, *U.S.A.* **152 D7** 31 13N 82 21W
Wayi, *Sudan* **107 F3** 5 8N 30 10 E
Wayland, *Mich., U.S.A.* **157 B11** 42 40N 85 39W
Wayland, *N.Y., U.S.A.* **150 D7** 42 34N 77 35W
Wayne, *Nebr., U.S.A.* **154 D6** 42 14N 97 1W
Wayne, *W. Va., U.S.A.* **148 F4** 38 13N 82 27W
Wayne City, *U.S.A.* **157 F8** 38 21N 88 35W
Wayne Lakes, *U.S.A.* **157 D12** 40 1N 84 40W
Waynesboro, *Ga., U.S.A.* **152 B7** 33 6N 82 1W
Waynesboro, *Miss., U.S.A.* **149 K1** 31 40N 88 39W
Waynesboro, *Pa., U.S.A.* **148 F7** 39 45N 77 35W
Waynesboro, *Va., U.S.A.* **148 F6** 38 4N 78 53W
Waynesburg, *U.S.A.* **148 F5** 39 54N 80 11W
Waynesville, *Mo., U.S.A.* **156 G4** 37 50N 92 12W
Waynesville, *N.C., U.S.A.* **149 H4** 35 28N 82 58W
Waynesville, *Ohio, U.S.A.* **157 E12** 39 32N 84 5W
Waynoka, *U.S.A.* **155 G5** 36 35N 98 53W
Wayside, *U.S.A.* **152 B6** 33 4N 83 37W
Wazay, *Afghan.* **91 B3** 33 22N 69 26 E
Wāzin, *Libya* **108 B2** 31 58N 10 40 E
Wazirabad, *Pakistan* **92 C6** 32 30N 74 8 E
Wda →, *Poland* **54 E5** 53 25N 18 29 E
We, *Indonesia* **78 C1** 5 51N 95 18 E
Weald, The, *U.K.* **21 F8** 51 4N 0 20 E
Wear →, *U.K.* **20 C6** 54 55N 1 23W
Weatherford, *Okla., U.S.A.* **155 H5** 35 32N 98 43W
Weatherford, *Tex., U.S.A.* **155 J6** 32 46N 97 48W
Weaubleau, *U.S.A.* **156 G3** 37 54N 93 32W
Weaverville, *U.S.A.* **158 F2** 40 44N 122 56W
Webb City, *U.S.A.* **155 G7** 37 9N 94 28W
Webequie, *Canada* **140 B2** 52 59N 87 21W
Weber, *N.Z.* **130 G5** 40 24 S 176 20 E
Webo = Nyaake, *Liberia* **112 E3** 4 52N 7 37W
Webster, *Mass., U.S.A.* **151 D13** 42 3N 71 53W
Webster, *N.Y., U.S.A.* **150 C7** 43 13N 77 26W
Webster, *S. Dak., U.S.A.* **154 C6** 45 20N 97 31W
Webster City, *U.S.A.* **156 B3** 42 28N 93 49W
Webster Springs, *U.S.A.* **148 F5** 38 29N 80 25W
Weda, *Indonesia* **79 D7** 0 21N 127 50 E
Weda, Teluk, *Indonesia* **79 D7** 0 30N 127 50 E
Weddell I., *Falk. Is.* **176 D4** 51 50 S 61 0W
Weddell Sea, *Antarctica* **7 D1** 72 30 S 40 0W
Wedderburn, *Australia* **128 D5** 36 26 S 143 33 E
Wedel, *Germany* **30 B5** 53 34N 9 42 E
Wedemark, *Germany* **30 C5** 52 32N 9 43 E
Wedgeport, *Canada* **141 D6** 43 44N 65 59W
Wedowee, *U.S.A.* **152 B4** 33 19N 85 29W
Wedza, *Zimbabwe* **119 F3** 18 40 S 31 33 E
Wee Elwah, *Australia* **129 B6** 33 2 S 145 14 E
Wee Waa, *Australia* **127 E4** 30 11 S 149 26 E
Weed, *U.S.A.* **158 F2** 41 25N 122 23W
Weed Heights, *U.S.A.* **160 G7** 38 59N 119 13W
Weedsport, *U.S.A.* **151 C8** 43 3N 76 35W
Weedville, *U.S.A.* **150 E6** 41 17N 78 30W
Weenen, *S. Africa* **117 D5** 28 48 S 30 7 E
Weener, *Germany* **30 B3** 53 9N 7 20 E
Weert, *Neths.* **24 C5** 51 15N 5 43 E
Weggis, *Switz.* **33 B6** 47 2N 8 26 E
Węgierska-Górka, *Poland* **55 J6** 49 36N 19 7 E
Węgliniec, *Poland* **55 G2** 51 18N 15 10 E
Węgorzewo, *Poland* **54 D8** 54 13N 21 43 E
Węgorzyno, *Poland* **54 E2** 53 32N 15 33 E
Węgrów, *Poland* **55 F9** 52 24N 22 0 E
Wehda □, *Sudan* **107 F3** 8 30N 30 0 E
Wei He →, *Hebei, China* **74 F8** 36 10N 115 45 E
Wei He →, *Shaanxi, China* **74 G6** 34 38N 110 15 E
Weichang, *China* **75 D9** 41 58N 117 49 E
Weichuan, *China* **74 G7** 34 20N 113 59 E
Weida, *Germany* **30 E8** 50 46N 12 2 E
Weiden, *Germany* **31 F8** 49 41N 12 10 E
Weifang, *China* **75 F10** 36 44N 119 7 E
Weihai, *China* **75 F12** 37 30N 122 6 E
Weil, *Germany* **31 H3** 47 35N 7 37 E
Weilburg, *Germany* **30 E4** 50 28N 8 17 E
Weilheim, *Germany* **31 H7** 47 50N 11 9 E
Weimar, *Germany* **30 E7** 50 58N 11 19 E
Weinan, *China* **74 G5** 34 31N 109 29 E
Weinfelden, *Switz.* **33 A8** 47 34N 9 6 E
Weingarten, *Germany* **31 F4** 49 3N 8 31 E
Weinheim, *Germany* **31 F4** 49 32N 8 39 E
Weining, *China* **76 D5** 26 50N 104 17 E
Weipa, *Australia* **126 A3** 12 40 S 141 50 E
Weir →, *Australia* **127 D4** 28 20 S 149 50 E
Weir →, *Canada* **143 B10** 56 54N 93 21W
Weir, L., *U.S.A.* **153 F8** 29 0N 81 57W
Weir River, *Canada* **143 B10** 56 49N 94 6W
Weirsdale, *U.S.A.* **153 G8** 28 59N 81 55W
Weirton, *U.S.A.* **150 F4** 40 24N 80 35W
Weiser, *U.S.A.* **158 D5** 44 10N 117 0W
Weishan, *Shandong, China* **75 G9** 34 47N 117 5 E
Weishan, *Yunnan, China* **76 E3** 25 12N 100 20 E
Weissenbach, *Austria* **33 B11** 47 26N 10 39 E
Weissenburg, *Germany* **31 F6** 49 2N 10 58 E
Weissenfels, *Germany* **30 D7** 51 11N 12 0 E
Weisshorn, *Switz.* **32 D5** 46 7N 7 43 E
Weisskugel, *Austria* **33 C11** 46 48N 10 44 E
Weissmies, *Switz.* **32 D6** 46 8N 8 1 E
Weisstannen, *Switz.* **33 C8** 46 59N 9 22 E
Weisswasser, *Germany* **30 D10** 51 30N 14 36 E
Weitra, *Austria* **34 C7** 48 41N 14 54 E
Weixi, *China* **76 D2** 27 10N 99 10 E
Weixin, *China* **76 D5** 27 48N 105 3 E
Weiyuan, *China* **74 G3** 35 7N 104 10 E
Weiz, *Austria* **34 D8** 47 13N 15 39 E
Weizhou Dao, *China* **76 G7** 21 0N 109 5 E
Wejherowo, *Poland* **54 D5** 54 35N 18 12 E
Wekusko L., *Canada* **143 C9** 54 40N 99 50W
Welch, *U.S.A.* **148 G5** 37 26N 81 35W
Weldya, *Ethiopia* **107 E4** 11 50N 39 34 E
Welega □, *Ethiopia* **107 F3** 9 25N 34 20 E
Weligama, *Sri Lanka* **95 M5** 5 58N 80 25 E
Welkite, *Ethiopia* **107 F4** 8 15N 37 42 E
Welkom, *S. Africa* **116 D4** 28 0 S 26 46 E
Welland, *Canada* **140 D4** 43 0N 79 15W
Welland →, *U.K.* **21 E7** 52 51N 0 5W
Wellawaya, *Sri Lanka* **95 L5** 6 44N 81 6 E
Wellesley Is., *Australia* **126 B2** 16 42 S 139 30 E
Wellingborough, *U.K.* **21 E7** 52 19N 0 41W
Wellington, *Australia* **129 B8** 32 35 S 148 59 E
Wellington, *Canada* **150 C7** 43 57N 77 20W
Wellington, *N.Z.* **130 H3** 41 19 S 174 46 E
Wellington, *S. Africa* **116 E2** 33 38 S 19 1 E
Wellington, *Somst., U.K.* **21 G4** 50 58N 3 13W
Wellington, *Telford & Wrekin, U.K.* **21 E5** 52 42N 2 30W
Wellington, *Colo., U.S.A.* **154 E2** 40 42N 105 0W
Wellington, *Kans., U.S.A.* **155 G6** 37 16N 97 24W
Wellington, *Mo., U.S.A.* **156 E3** 39 8N 93 59W
Wellington, *Nev., U.S.A.* **160 G7** 38 45N 119 23W
Wellington, *Ohio, U.S.A.* **150 E2** 41 10N 82 13W
Wellington, *Tex., U.S.A.* **155 H4** 34 51N 100 13W
Wellington □, *N.Z.* **130 G4** 41 0 S 175 30 E
Wellington, I., *Chile* **176 C2** 49 30 S 75 0W
Wellington, L., *Australia* **129 E7** 38 6 S 147 20 E
Wellman, *U.S.A.* **156 C5** 41 28N 91 50W
Wells, *U.K.* **21 F5** 51 13N 2 39W
Wells, *Maine, U.S.A.* **151 C14** 43 20N 70 35W
Wells, *N.Y., U.S.A.* **151 C10** 43 24N 74 17W
Wells, *Nev., U.S.A.* **158 F6** 41 7N 114 58W
Wells, L., *Australia* **125 E3** 26 44 S 123 15 E
Wells, Mt., *Australia* **124 C4** 17 25 S 127 8 E
Wells Gray Prov. Park, *Canada* **142 C4** 52 30N 120 15W
Wells-next-the-Sea, *U.K.* **20 E8** 52 57N 0 51 E
Wells River, *U.S.A.* **151 B12** 44 9N 72 4W
Wellsboro, *U.S.A.* **150 E7** 41 45N 77 18W
Wellsburg, *U.S.A.* **150 F4** 40 16N 80 37W
Wellsford, *N.Z.* **130 C3** 36 16 S 174 32 E
Wellsville, *Mo., U.S.A.* **156 E5** 39 4N 91 34W
Wellsville, *N.Y., U.S.A.* **150 D7** 42 7N 77 57W
Wellsville, *Ohio, U.S.A.* **150 F4** 40 36N 80 39W
Wellsville, *Utah, U.S.A.* **158 F8** 41 38N 111 56W
Wellton, *U.S.A.* **159 K6** 32 40N 114 8W
Welmel, Wabi →, *Ethiopia* **107 F5** 5 38N 40 47 E
Welo, *Somali Rep.* **120 C3** 9 25N 48 55 E
Welo □, *Ethiopia* **107 E4** 11 50N 39 48 E
Wels, *Austria* **34 C7** 48 9N 14 1 E
Welshpool, *U.K.* **21 E4** 52 39N 3 8W
Welwyn Garden City, *U.K.* **21 F7** 51 48N 0 12W
Wem, *U.K.* **20 E5** 52 52N 2 44W
Wembere →, *Tanzania* **118 C3** 4 10 S 34 15 E
Wemindji, *Canada* **140 B4** 53 0N 78 49W
Wen Xian, *China* **74 G7** 34 55N 113 5 E
Wenatchee, *U.S.A.* **158 C3** 47 25N 120 19W
Wenchang, *China* **86 C8** 19 38N 110 42 E
Wencheng, *China* **77 D13** 27 46N 120 4 E
Wenchi, *Ghana* **112 D4** 7 46N 2 8W
Wenchow = Wenzhou, *China* **77 D13** 28 0N 120 38 E
Wenchuan, *China* **76 B4** 31 22N 103 35 E
Wenden, *U.S.A.* **161 M13** 33 49N 113 33W
Wendeng, *China* **75 F12** 37 15N 122 5 E
Wendesi, *Indonesia* **79 E8** 2 30 S 134 17 E

Xiapu 301

Wilson Bluff, *Australia* 125 F4 31 41 S 129 0 E
Wilson Inlet, *Australia* 125 G2 35 0 S 117 22 E
Wilson Str., *Solomon Is.* 133 M9 8 0 S 156 39 E
Wilsons Promontory, *Australia* 129 E7 38 55 S 146 25 E
Wilster, *Germany* 30 B5 53 55N 9 23 E
Wilton, *Iowa, U.S.A.* 156 C5 41 34N 91 4W
Wilton, *N. Dak., U.S.A.* 154 B4 47 10N 100 47W
Wilton →, *Australia* 126 A1 14 45 S 134 33 E
Wiltshire □, *U.K.* 21 F6 51 18N 1 53W
Wiltz, *Lux.* 24 E5 49 57N 5 55 E
Wiluna, *Australia* 125 E3 26 36 S 120 14 E
Wimborne Minster, *U.K.* 21 G6 50 48N 1 59W
Wimereux, *France* 27 B8 50 45N 1 37 E
Wimmera →, *Australia* 128 D4 36 8 S 141 56 E
Winam G., *Kenya* 118 C3 0 20 S 34 15 E
Winamac, *U.S.A.* 157 C10 41 3N 86 36W
Winburg, *S. Africa* 116 D4 28 30 S 27 2 E
Winchelsea, *Australia* 128 E6 38 10 S 144 1 E
Winchendon, *U.S.A.* 151 D12 42 41N 72 3W
Winchester, *N.Z.* 131 E6 44 11 S 171 17 E
Winchester, *U.K.* 21 F6 51 4N 1 18W
Winchester, *Conn., U.S.A.* 151 E11 41 53N 73 9W
Winchester, *Idaho, U.S.A.* 158 C5 46 14N 116 38W
Winchester, *Ill., U.S.A.* 156 E6 39 38N 90 27W
Winchester, *Ind., U.S.A.* 157 D12 40 10N 84 59W
Winchester, *Ky., U.S.A.* 157 G12 38 0N 84 11W
Winchester, *N.H., U.S.A.* 151 D12 42 46N 72 23W
Winchester, *Nev., U.S.A.* 161 J11 36 6N 115 10W
Winchester, *Ohio, U.S.A.* 157 F13 38 57N 83 40W
Winchester, *Tenn., U.S.A.* 149 H2 35 11N 86 7W
Winchester, *Va., U.S.A.* 148 F6 39 11N 78 10W
Wind →, *U.S.A.* 158 E9 43 12N 108 12W
Wind Point, *U.S.A.* 157 B9 42 47N 87 46W
Wind River Range, *U.S.A.* 158 E9 43 0N 109 30W
Windau = Ventspils, *Latvia* 15 H19 57 25N 21 32 E
Windber, *U.S.A.* 150 F6 40 14N 78 50W
Winder, *U.S.A.* 152 A6 34 0N 83 45W
Windermere, *U.K.* 20 C5 54 23N 2 55W
Windfall, *U.S.A.* 157 D11 40 22N 85 57W
Windhoek, *Namibia* 116 C2 22 35 S 17 4 E
Windisch, *Switz.* 32 B6 47 28N 8 14 E
Windischgarsten, *Austria* 34 D7 47 42N 14 21 E
Windom, *U.S.A.* 154 D7 43 52N 95 7W
Windorah, *Australia* 126 D3 25 24 S 142 36 E
Window Rock, *U.S.A.* 159 J9 35 41N 109 3W
Windrush →, *U.K.* 21 F6 51 43N 1 24W
Windsor, *Australia* 129 B9 33 37 S 150 50 E
Windsor, *N.S., Canada* 141 D7 44 59N 64 5W
Windsor, *Ont., Canada* 140 D3 42 18N 83 0W
Windsor, *N.Z.* 131 E5 44 59 S 170 49 E
Windsor, *U.K.* 21 F7 51 29N 0 36W
Windsor, *Colo., U.S.A.* 154 E2 40 29N 104 54W
Windsor, *Conn., U.S.A.* 151 E12 41 50N 72 39W
Windsor, *Ill., U.S.A.* 157 E8 39 26N 88 36W
Windsor, *Mo., U.S.A.* 156 F3 38 32N 93 31W
Windsor, *N.Y., U.S.A.* 151 D9 42 5N 75 37W
Windsor, *Vt., U.S.A.* 151 C12 43 29N 72 24W
Windsor & Maidenhead □, *U.K.* 21 F7 51 29N 0 40W
Windsorton, *S. Africa* 116 D3 28 16 S 24 44 E
Windward Is., *W. Indies* 165 D7 13 0N 61 0W
Windward Passage = Vientos, Paso de los, *Caribbean* 165 C5 20 0N 74 0W
Winefred L., *Canada* 143 B6 55 30N 110 30W
Winejok, *Sudan* 107 F2 9 1N 27 30 E
Winfield, *Iowa, U.S.A.* 156 C5 41 7N 91 26W
Winfield, *Kans., U.S.A.* 155 G6 37 15N 96 59W
Winfield, *Mo., U.S.A.* 156 F6 39 0N 90 44W
Wingate Mts., *Australia* 124 B5 14 25 S 130 40 E
Wingen, *Australia* 129 A9 31 54 S 150 54 E
Wingham, *Australia* 129 A10 31 48 S 152 22 E
Wingham, *Canada* 140 D3 43 55N 81 20W
Winisk, *Canada* 140 A2 55 20N 85 15W
Winisk →, *Canada* 140 A2 55 17N 85 5W
Winisk L., *Canada* 140 B2 52 55N 87 22W
Wink, *U.S.A.* 155 K3 31 45N 103 9W
Winkler, *Canada* 143 D9 49 10N 97 56W
Winklern, *Austria* 34 E5 46 52N 12 52 E
Winlock, *U.S.A.* 160 D4 46 30N 122 56W
Winneba, *Ghana* 113 D4 5 25N 0 36W
Winnebago, *U.S.A.* 156 B7 42 16N 89 15W
Winnebago, L., *U.S.A.* 148 D1 44 0N 88 26W
Winnecke Cr. →, *Australia* 124 C5 18 35 S 131 34 E
Winnemucca, *U.S.A.* 158 F5 40 58N 117 44W
Winnemucca L., *U.S.A.* 158 F4 40 7N 119 21W
Winnett, *U.S.A.* 158 C9 47 0N 108 21W
Winnfield, *U.S.A.* 155 K8 31 56N 92 38W
Winnibigoshish, L., *U.S.A.* 154 B7 47 27N 94 13W
Winnipeg, *Canada* 143 D9 49 54N 97 9W
Winnipeg →, *Canada* 143 C9 50 38N 96 19W
Winnipeg, L., *Canada* 143 C9 52 0N 97 0W
Winnipeg Beach, *Canada* 143 C9 50 30N 96 58W
Winnipegosis, *Canada* 143 C9 51 39N 99 55W
Winnipegosis L., *Canada* 143 C9 52 30N 100 0W
Winnipesaukee, L., *U.S.A.* 151 C13 43 38N 71 21W
Winnisquam L., *U.S.A.* 151 C13 43 33N 71 31W
Winnsboro, *La., U.S.A.* 155 J9 32 10N 91 43W
Winnsboro, *S.C., U.S.A.* 149 H5 34 23N 81 5W
Winnsboro, *Tex., U.S.A.* 155 J7 32 58N 95 17W
Winokapau, L., *Canada* 141 B7 53 15N 62 50W
Winona, *Minn., U.S.A.* 154 C9 44 3N 91 39W
Winona, *Miss., U.S.A.* 155 J10 33 29N 89 44W
Winooski, *U.S.A.* 151 B11 44 29N 73 11W
Winooski →, *U.S.A.* 151 B11 44 32N 73 17W
Winschoten, *Neths.* 24 A7 53 9N 7 3 E
Winsen, *Germany* 30 B6 53 22N 10 13 E
Winsford, *U.K.* 20 D5 53 12N 2 31W
Winslow, *Ariz., U.S.A.* 159 J8 35 2N 110 42W
Winslow, *Ind., U.S.A.* 157 F9 38 23N 87 13W
Winslow, *Wash., U.S.A.* 160 C4 47 38N 122 31W
Winsted, *U.S.A.* 151 E11 41 55N 73 4W
Winston-Salem, *U.S.A.* 149 G5 36 6N 80 15W
Winter Garden, *U.S.A.* 149 L5 28 34N 81 35W
Winter Haven, *U.S.A.* 149 M5 28 1N 81 44W
Winter Park, *U.S.A.* 149 L5 28 36N 81 20W
Winterberg, *Germany* 30 D4 51 11N 8 33 E
Winterhaven, *U.S.A.* 161 N12 32 47N 114 39W
Winters, *U.S.A.* 160 G5 38 32N 121 58W
Winterset, *U.S.A.* 156 C3 41 20N 94 1W
Wintersville, *U.S.A.* 150 F4 40 23N 80 42W
Winterswijk, *Neths.* 24 C6 51 58N 6 43 E
Winterthur, *Switz.* 33 B7 47 30N 8 44 E
Winthrop, *U.S.A.* 158 B3 48 28N 120 10W
Winton, *Australia* 126 C3 22 24 S 143 3 E
Winton, *N.Z.* 131 G3 46 8 S 168 20 E
Wipper →, *Germany* 30 D7 51 16N 11 12 E
Wirraminna, *Australia* 128 A2 31 12 S 136 13 E
Wirrulla, *Australia* 127 E1 32 24 S 134 31 E
Wisbech, *U.K.* 21 E8 52 41N 0 9 E
Wisconsin □, *U.S.A.* 156 B7 44 45N 89 30W
Wisconsin →, *U.S.A.* 156 A5 43 0N 91 15W
Wisconsin Rapids, *U.S.A.* 154 C10 44 23N 89 49W
Wisdom, *U.S.A.* 158 D7 45 37N 113 27W
Wishaw, *U.K.* 22 F5 55 46N 3 54W
Wishek, *U.S.A.* 154 B5 46 16N 99 33W
Wisła, *Poland* 55 J5 49 38N 18 53 E
Wisła →, *Poland* 54 D5 54 22N 18 55 E
Wisłok →, *Poland* 55 H9 50 13N 22 32 E
Wisłoka →, *Poland* 55 H8 50 27N 21 23 E
Wismar, *Germany* 30 B7 53 54N 11 29 E
Wismar, *Guyana* 169 B6 5 59N 58 18W
Wisner, *U.S.A.* 154 E6 41 59N 96 55W
Wissant, *France* 27 B8 50 52N 1 40 E
Wissembourg, *France* 27 C14 49 2N 7 57 E
Wisznice, *Poland* 55 G10 51 48N 23 13 E
Witbank, *S. Africa* 117 D4 25 51 S 29 14 E
Witdraai, *S. Africa* 116 D3 26 58 S 20 48 E
Witham, *U.K.* 21 F8 51 48N 0 40 E
Witham →, *U.K.* 20 E7 52 59N 0 2W
Withernsea, *U.K.* 20 D8 53 44N 0 1 E
Withlacoochee →, *Fla., U.S.A.* 152 E6 30 24N 83 10W
Withlacoochee →, *Fla., U.S.A.* 153 G7 29 0N 82 45W
Witkowo, *Poland* 55 F4 52 26N 17 45 E
Witney, *U.K.* 21 F6 51 48N 1 28W
Witnica, *Poland* 55 F1 52 40N 14 54 E
Witnossob →, *Namibia* 116 D3 23 55 S 18 45 E
Wittdün, *Germany* 30 A4 54 38N 8 23 E
Witten, *Germany* 30 D3 51 26N 7 20 E
Wittenberge, *Germany* 30 B7 53 0N 11 45 E
Wittenburg, *Germany* 30 B7 53 31N 11 4 E
Wittenheim, *France* 27 E14 47 44N 7 20 E
Wittenoom, *Australia* 124 D2 22 15 S 118 20 E
Witti, Banjaran, *Malaysia* 85 A5 5 11N 116 29 E
Wittingen, *Germany* 30 C6 52 44N 10 44 E
Wittlich, *Germany* 31 F2 49 59N 6 53 E
Wittmund, *Germany* 30 B3 53 34N 7 46 E
Wittow, *Germany* 30 A9 54 38N 13 20 E
Wittstock, *Germany* 30 B8 53 10N 12 28 E
Witvlei, *Namibia* 116 C2 22 23 S 18 32 E
Witzenhausen, *Germany* 30 D5 51 20N 9 51 E
Wixom, *U.S.A.* 157 B13 42 32N 83 32W
Wkra →, *Poland* 55 F7 52 27N 20 44 E
Władysławowo, *Poland* 54 D5 54 48N 18 25 E
Wleń, *Poland* 55 G2 51 2N 15 39 E
Wlingi, *Indonesia* 79 H15 8 5 S 112 25 E
Włocławek, *Poland* 55 F6 52 40N 19 3 E
Włodawa, *Poland* 55 G10 51 33N 23 31 E
Włoszczowa, *Poland* 55 H6 50 50N 19 55 E
Woburn, *U.S.A.* 151 D13 42 29N 71 9W
Wodian, *China* 74 H7 32 50N 112 35 E
Wodonga, *Australia* 129 D7 36 5 S 146 50 E
Wodzisław Śląski, *Poland* 55 H5 50 1N 18 26 E
Wœrth, *France* 27 D14 48 57N 7 45 E
Wohlen, *Switz.* 33 B6 47 21N 8 17 E
Woinbogoin, *China* 76 A2 32 51N 98 39 E
Woippy, *France* 27 C13 49 10N 6 8 E
Wojcieszow, *Poland* 55 H2 50 58N 15 55 E
Wokam, *Indonesia* 79 F8 5 45 S 134 28 E
Wokha, *India* 90 B5 26 6N 94 16 E
Woking, *U.K.* 21 F7 51 19N 0 34W
Wokingham □, *U.K.* 21 F7 51 25N 0 51W
Wolbrom, *Poland* 55 H6 50 24N 19 45 E
Wolcottville, *U.S.A.* 157 C11 41 32N 85 22W
Wołczyn, *Poland* 55 G5 51 1N 18 3 E
Woldegk, *Germany* 30 B9 53 27N 13 34 E
Wolf →, *Canada* 142 A2 60 17N 132 33W
Wolf Creek, *U.S.A.* 158 C7 47 0N 112 4W
Wolf L., *Canada* 142 A2 60 24N 131 40W
Wolf Point, *U.S.A.* 154 A2 48 5N 105 39W
Wolfe I., *Canada* 140 D4 44 7N 76 20W
Wolfeboro, *U.S.A.* 151 C13 43 35N 71 13W
Wolfen, *Germany* 30 D8 51 39N 12 15 E
Wolfenbüttel, *Germany* 30 C6 52 10N 10 33 E
Wolfratshausen, *Germany* 31 H7 47 54N 11 24 E
Wolfsberg, *Austria* 34 E7 46 50N 14 52 E
Wolfsburg, *Germany* 30 C6 52 27N 10 48 E
Wolfurt, *Austria* 33 B9 47 28N 9 45 E
Wolgast, *Germany* 30 A9 54 3N 13 44 E
Wolhusen, *Switz.* 32 B6 47 4N 8 4 E
Wolin, *Poland* 54 E1 53 50N 14 37 E
Wollaston, Is., *Chile* 176 E3 55 40 S 67 30W
Wollaston Forland, *Greenland* 10 C9 74 25N 19 40W
Wollaston L., *Canada* 143 B8 58 7N 103 10W
Wollaston Lake, *Canada* 143 B8 58 3N 103 33W
Wollaston Pen., *Canada* 138 B8 69 30N 115 0W
Wollongong, *Australia* 129 C9 34 25 S 150 54 E
Wolmaransstad, *S. Africa* 116 D4 27 12 S 25 59 E
Wolmirstedt, *Germany* 30 C7 52 14N 11 37 E
Wołomin, *Poland* 55 F8 52 19N 21 15 E
Wołów, *Poland* 55 G3 51 20N 16 38 E
Wolseley, *Australia* 128 D4 36 23 S 140 54 E
Wolseley, *S. Africa* 116 E2 33 26 S 19 7 E
Wolsey, *U.S.A.* 154 C5 44 24N 98 28W
Wolstenholme, C., *Canada* 136 C12 62 35N 77 30W
Wolsztyn, *Poland* 55 F3 52 8N 16 5 E
Wolvega, *Neths.* 24 B6 52 52N 6 0 E
Wolverhampton, *U.K.* 21 E5 52 35N 2 7W
Wonboyn, *Australia* 129 D8 37 15 S 149 55 E
Wondai, *Australia* 127 D5 26 20 S 151 49 E
Wongalarroo L., *Australia* 128 A6 31 32 S 144 0 E
Wongan Hills, *Australia* 125 F2 30 51 S 116 37 E
Wŏnju, *S. Korea* 75 F14 37 22N 127 58 E
Wonosari, *Indonesia* 79 G14 7 58 S 110 36 E
Wonosobo, *Indonesia* 79 G13 7 22 S 109 54 E
Wonowon, *Canada* 142 B4 56 44N 121 48W
Wŏnsan, *N. Korea* 75 E14 39 11N 127 27 E
Wonthaggi, *Australia* 129 E6 38 37 S 145 37 E
Woocalla, *Australia* 128 A2 31 42 S 137 12 E
Wood Buffalo Nat. Park, *Canada* 142 B6 59 0N 113 41W
Wood Is., *Australia* 124 C3 16 24 S 123 19 E
Wood L., *Canada* 143 B8 55 17N 103 17W
Wood River, *U.S.A.* 156 F6 38 52N 90 5W
Woodah I., *Australia* 126 A2 13 27 S 136 10 E
Woodbine, *U.S.A.* 152 E8 30 58N 81 44W
Woodbourne, *U.S.A.* 151 E10 41 46N 74 36W
Woodbridge, *Canada* 150 C5 43 47N 79 36W
Woodbridge, *U.K.* 21 E9 52 6N 1 20 E
Woodburn, *U.S.A.* 158 D2 45 9N 122 51W
Woodbury, *U.S.A.* 152 C5 32 59N 84 35W
Woodenbong, *Australia* 127 D5 28 24 S 152 39 E
Woodend, *Australia* 128 D6 37 20 S 144 33 E
Woodford, *Australia* 127 D5 26 58 S 152 47 E
Woodfords, *U.S.A.* 160 G7 38 47N 119 50W
Woodlake, *U.S.A.* 160 J7 36 25N 119 6W
Woodland, *Calif., U.S.A.* 160 G5 38 41N 121 46W
Woodland, *Maine, U.S.A.* 149 C12 45 9N 67 25W
Woodland, *Pa., U.S.A.* 150 F6 40 59N 78 21W
Woodland, *Wash., U.S.A.* 160 E4 45 54N 122 45W
Woodland Caribou Prov. Park, *Canada* 143 C10 51 0N 94 45W
Woodlark I., *Papua N. G.* 132 E7 9 10 S 152 50 E
Woodridge, *Canada* 143 D9 49 20N 96 9W
Woodroffe, Mt., *Australia* 125 E5 26 20 S 131 45 E
Woods, L., *Australia* 126 B1 17 50 S 133 30 E
Woods, L. of the, *Canada* 143 D10 49 15N 94 45W
Woodside, *S. Austral., Australia* 128 C3 34 58 S 138 52 E
Woodside, *Vic., Australia* 129 E7 38 31 S 146 52 E
Woodson, *U.S.A.* 156 E6 39 37N 90 14W
Woodstock, *N.S.W., Australia* 129 B8 33 45 S 148 53 E
Woodstock, *Queens., Australia* 126 B4 19 35 S 146 50 E
Woodstock, *N.B., Canada* 141 C6 46 11N 67 37W
Woodstock, *Ont., Canada* 140 D3 43 10N 80 45W
Woodstock, *U.K.* 21 F6 51 51N 1 20W
Woodstock, *Ga., U.S.A.* 152 A5 34 6N 84 31W
Woodstock, *Ill., U.S.A.* 154 D10 42 19N 88 27W
Woodstock, *Vt., U.S.A.* 151 C12 43 37N 72 31W
Woodsville, *U.S.A.* 151 B13 44 9N 72 2W
Woodville, *N.Z.* 130 G4 40 20 S 175 53 E
Woodville, *Fla., U.S.A.* 152 E5 30 19N 84 15W
Woodville, *Ga., U.S.A.* 152 B6 33 40N 83 7W
Woodville, *Miss., U.S.A.* 155 K9 31 6N 91 18W
Woodville, *Ohio, U.S.A.* 157 C13 41 27N 83 22W
Woodville, *Tex., U.S.A.* 155 K7 30 47N 94 25W
Woodward, *U.S.A.* 155 G5 36 26N 99 24W
Woody, *U.S.A.* 161 K8 35 42N 118 50W
Woody →, *Canada* 143 C8 52 31N 100 51W
Woolamai, C., *Australia* 129 E6 38 30 S 145 23 E
Wooler, *U.K.* 20 B5 55 33N 2 1W
Woolgoolga, *Australia* 127 E5 30 6 S 153 11 E
Woomera, *Australia* 128 A2 31 5 S 136 50 E
Woonona, *Australia* 129 C9 34 21 S 150 54 E
Woonsocket, *R.I., U.S.A.* 151 E13 42 0N 71 31W
Woonsocket, *S. Dak., U.S.A.* 154 C5 44 3N 98 17W
Wooramel →, *Australia* 125 E1 25 47 S 114 10 E
Wooramel Roadhouse, *Australia* 125 E1 25 45 S 114 17 E
Wooster, *U.S.A.* 150 F3 40 48N 81 56W
Worb, *Switz.* 32 C5 46 56N 7 33 E
Worcester, *S. Africa* 116 E2 33 39 S 19 27 E
Worcester, *U.K.* 21 E5 52 11N 2 12W
Worcester, *Mass., U.S.A.* 151 D13 42 16N 71 48W
Worcester, *N.Y., U.S.A.* 151 D10 42 36N 74 45W
Worcestershire □, *U.K.* 21 E5 52 13N 2 10W
Worden, *U.S.A.* 156 F7 38 56N 89 50W
Wörgl, *Austria* 34 D5 47 29N 12 3 E
Workington, *U.K.* 20 C4 54 39N 3 33W
Worksop, *U.K.* 20 D6 53 18N 1 7W
Workum, *Neths.* 24 B5 52 59N 5 26 E
Worland, *U.S.A.* 158 D10 44 1N 107 57W
Wormhout, *France* 27 B9 50 52N 2 28 E
Worms, *Germany* 31 F4 49 37N 8 21 E
Worsley, *Canada* 142 B5 56 31N 119 8W
Wörth, *Germany* 31 F8 49 1N 12 24 E
Wortham, *U.S.A.* 155 K6 31 47N 96 28W
Wörther See, *Austria* 34 E7 46 37N 14 10 E
Worthing, *U.K.* 21 G7 50 49N 0 21W
Worthington, *Ind., U.S.A.* 157 E10 39 7N 86 59W
Worthington, *Minn., U.S.A.* 154 D7 43 37N 95 36W
Worthington, *Ohio, U.S.A.* 157 D13 40 5N 83 1W
Worthington, *Pa., U.S.A.* 150 F5 40 50N 79 38W
Wosi, *Indonesia* 79 E7 0 15 S 128 0 E
Wou-han = Wuhan, *China* 77 B10 30 31N 114 18 E
Wour, *Chad* 109 D3 21 14N 16 0 E
Wousi = Wuxi, *China* 77 B13 31 33N 120 18 E
Wowoni, *Indonesia* 79 E6 4 5 S 123 5 E
Woy Woy, *Australia* 129 B9 33 30 S 151 19 E
Wrangel I. = Vrangelya, Ostrov, *Russia* 65 B19 71 0N 180 0 E
Wrangell, *U.S.A.* 142 B2 56 28N 132 23W
Wrangell Mts., *U.S.A.* 138 B5 61 30N 142 0W
Wrath, C., *U.K.* 22 C3 58 38N 5 1W
Wray, *U.S.A.* 154 E3 40 5N 102 13W
Wrekin, The, *U.K.* 21 E5 52 41N 2 32W
Wrens, *U.S.A.* 152 B7 33 12N 82 23W
Wrexham, *U.K.* 20 D4 53 3N 3 0W
Wrexham □, *U.K.* 20 D5 53 1N 2 58W
Wriezen, *Germany* 30 C10 52 42N 14 7 E
Wright = Paranas, *Phil.* 81 F5 11 42N 125 2 E
Wright, *U.S.A.* 154 D2 43 47N 105 30W
Wright Pt., *Canada* 150 C3 43 48N 81 44W
Wrightson Mt., *U.S.A.* 159 L8 31 42N 110 51W
Wrightsville, *U.S.A.* 152 C7 32 44N 82 43W
Wrightwood, *U.S.A.* 161 L9 34 21N 117 38W
Wrigley, *Canada* 138 B7 63 16N 123 37W
Wrocław, *Poland* 55 G4 51 5N 17 5 E
Wronki, *Poland* 55 F3 52 41N 16 21 E
Września, *Poland* 55 F4 52 21N 17 36 E
Wschowa, *Poland* 55 G3 51 48N 16 20 E
Wu Jiang →, *China* 76 C6 29 40N 107 20 E
Wu'an, *China* 74 F8 36 40N 114 15 E
Wubin, *Australia* 125 F2 30 6 S 116 37 E
Wubu, *China* 74 F6 37 28N 110 42 E
Wuchang, *China* 75 B14 44 55N 127 5 E
Wucheng, *China* 74 F9 37 12N 116 20 E
Wuchuan, *Guangdong, China* 77 G8 21 33N 110 43 E
Wuchuan, *Guizhou, China* 76 C7 28 25N 108 3 E
Wuchuan, *Nei Mongol Zizhiqu, China* 74 D6 41 5N 111 28 E
Wuday'ah, *Si. Arabia* 98 C4 17 2N 47 7 E
Wudi, *China* 75 F9 37 40N 117 35 E
Wuding, *China* 76 E4 25 24N 102 21 E
Wuding He →, *China* 74 F6 37 2N 110 23 E
Wudinna, *Australia* 127 E2 33 0 S 135 22 E
Wudu, *China* 74 H3 33 22N 104 54 E
Wufeng, *China* 77 B8 30 12N 110 42 E
Wugang, *China* 77 D8 26 44N 110 35 E
Wugong Shan, *China* 77 D9 27 30N 114 0 E
Wuhan, *China* 77 B10 30 31N 114 18 E
Wuhe, *China* 75 H9 33 10N 117 50 E
Wuhsi = Wuxi, *China* 77 B13 31 33N 120 18 E
Wuhu, *China* 77 B12 31 22N 118 21 E
Wujiang, *China* 77 B13 31 10N 120 38 E
Wukari, *Nigeria* 113 D6 7 51N 9 42 E
Wulajie, *China* 75 B14 44 6N 126 33 E
Wulanbulang, *China* 74 D6 41 5N 110 55 E
Wular L., *India* 93 B6 34 20N 74 30 E
Wulehe, *Ghana* 113 D5 8 39N 0 0 E
Wulff Land, *Greenland* 10 A6 82 0N 49 0W
Wulian, *China* 75 G10 35 40N 119 12 E
Wuliang Shan, *China* 76 E3 24 30N 100 40 E
Wuliaru, *Indonesia* 79 F8 7 27 S 131 0 E
Wuling Shan, *China* 76 C7 30 0N 110 0 E
Wulong, *China* 76 C6 29 22N 107 43 E
Wuluk'omushih Ling, *China* 72 C3 36 25N 87 25 E
Wulumuchi = Ürümqi, *China* 64 E9 43 45N 87 45 E
Wum, *Cameroon* 113 D7 6 24N 10 2 E
Wuming, *China* 76 F7 23 12N 108 18 E
Wun Rog, *Sudan* 107 F2 9 0N 28 20 E
Wundowie, *Australia* 125 F2 31 47 S 116 23 E
Wuning, *China* 77 C10 29 17N 115 5 E
Wunna →, *India* 94 D4 20 18N 78 48 E
Wunnummin L., *Canada* 140 B2 52 55N 89 10W
Wunsiedel, *Germany* 31 E8 50 2N 12 0 E
Wunstorf, *Germany* 30 C5 52 25N 9 26 E
Wuntho, *Burma* 90 D5 23 55N 95 45 E
Wuping, *China* 77 E11 25 5N 116 5 E
Wuppertal, *Germany* 30 D3 51 16N 7 12 E
Wuppertal, *S. Africa* 116 E2 32 13 S 19 12 E
Wuqing, *China* 75 E9 39 23N 117 4 E
Würenlingen, *Switz.* 33 A6 47 32N 8 16 E
Wurtsboro, *U.S.A.* 151 E10 41 35N 74 29W
Würzburg, *Germany* 31 F5 49 46N 9 55 E
Wurzen, *Germany* 30 D8 51 21N 12 44 E
Wushan, *China* 74 G3 34 43N 104 53 E
Wushishi, *Nigeria* 113 D6 9 46N 6 7 E
Wusuli Jiang = Ussuri →, *Asia* 68 A7 48 27N 135 0 E
Wutach →, *Germany* 31 H4 47 37N 8 15 E
Wutai, *China* 74 E7 38 40N 113 12 E
Wuting = Huimin, *China* 75 F9 37 27N 117 28 E
Wutong, *China* 77 E8 25 24N 110 4 E
Wutonghaolai, *China* 75 C11 42 50N 120 5 E
Wutongqiao, *China* 76 C4 29 22N 103 50 E
Wuwei, *Anhui, China* 77 B11 31 18N 117 54 E
Wuwei, *Gansu, China* 72 C5 37 57N 102 34 E
Wuxi, *Jiangsu, China* 77 B13 31 33N 120 18 E
Wuxi, *Sichuan, China* 76 B7 31 23N 109 35 E
Wuxiang, *China* 74 F7 36 49N 112 50 E
Wuxuan, *China* 76 F7 23 34N 109 38 E
Wuxue, *China* 77 C10 29 52N 115 30 E
Wuyang, *China* 74 H7 33 25N 113 35 E
Wuyi, *Hebei, China* 74 F8 37 46N 115 56 E
Wuyi, *Zhejiang, China* 77 C12 28 52N 119 50 E
Wuyi Shan, *China* 77 D11 27 0N 117 0 E
Wuyishan, *China* 77 D12 27 45N 118 0 E
Wuyo, *Nigeria* 113 C7 10 23N 11 50 E
Wuyuan, *Jiangxi, China* 77 C11 29 15N 117 50 E
Wuyuan, *Nei Mongol Zizhiqu, China* 74 D5 41 2N 108 20 E
Wuzhai, *China* 74 E6 38 54N 111 48 E
Wuzhi Shan, *China* 86 C7 18 45N 109 45 E
Wuzhong, *China* 74 E4 38 2N 106 12 E
Wuzhou, *China* 77 F8 23 30N 111 18 E
Wyaaba Cr. →, *Australia* 126 B3 16 27 S 141 35 E
Wyalkatchem, *Australia* 125 F2 31 8 S 117 22 E
Wyalusing, *U.S.A.* 151 E8 41 40N 76 16W
Wyandotte, *U.S.A.* 157 B13 42 12N 83 9W
Wyandra, *Australia* 127 D4 27 12 S 145 56 E
Wyangala Res., *Australia* 129 B8 33 54 S 149 0 E
Wyara, L., *Australia* 127 D3 28 42 S 144 14 E
Wycheproof, *Australia* 128 D5 36 5 S 143 17 E
Wye →, *U.K.* 21 F5 51 38N 2 40W
Wyemandoo, *Australia* 125 E2 28 28 S 118 29 E
Wyk, *Germany* 30 A4 54 41N 8 33 E
Wymondham, *U.K.* 21 E9 52 35N 1 7 E
Wymore, *U.S.A.* 154 E6 40 7N 96 40W
Wyndham, *Australia* 124 C4 15 33 S 128 3 E
Wyndham, *N.Z.* 131 G3 46 20 S 168 51 E
Wynne, *U.S.A.* 155 H9 35 14N 90 47W
Wynyard, *Australia* 126 G4 41 5 S 145 44 E
Wynyard, *Canada* 143 C8 51 45N 104 10W
Wyola L., *Australia* 125 E5 29 8 S 130 17 E
Wyoming, *Canada* 150 D2 42 57N 82 7W
Wyoming, *Ill., U.S.A.* 156 C7 41 4N 89 47W
Wyoming, *Iowa, U.S.A.* 156 B6 42 4N 91 0W
Wyoming, *Mich., U.S.A.* 157 B11 42 54N 85 42W
Wyoming □, *U.S.A.* 158 E10 43 0N 107 30W
Wyomissing, *U.S.A.* 151 F9 40 20N 75 59W
Wyong, *Australia* 129 B9 33 14 S 151 24 E
Wyrzysk, *Poland* 55 E4 53 10N 17 17 E
Wyśmierzyce, *Poland* 55 G7 51 37N 20 50 E
Wysoka, *Poland* 55 E4 53 13N 17 2 E
Wysokie, *Poland* 55 H9 50 55N 22 40 E
Wysokie Mazowieckie, *Poland* 55 F9 52 55N 22 30 E
Wyszków, *Poland* 55 F8 52 36N 21 25 E
Wyszogród, *Poland* 55 F7 52 23N 20 9 E
Wytheville, *U.S.A.* 148 G5 36 57N 81 5W
Wyżyna Małopolska, *Poland* 55 H7 50 45N 20 0 E

X

Xa-Cassau, *Angola* 115 D4 9 5 S 20 15 E
Xa-Muteba, *Angola* 115 D3 9 34 S 17 50 E
Xaçmaz, *Azerbaijan* 61 K9 41 31N 48 42 E
Xai-Xai, *Mozam.* 117 D5 25 6 S 33 31 E
Xainza, *China* 72 C3 30 58N 88 35 E
Xambioá, *Brazil* 170 C2 6 25 S 48 40W
Xangongo, *Angola* 116 B2 16 45 S 15 5 E
Xankändi, *Azerbaijan* 101 C12 39 52N 46 49 E
Xanlar, *Azerbaijan* 61 K8 40 37N 46 12 E
Xanten, *Germany* 30 D2 51 39N 6 26 E
Xánthi, *Greece* 51 E8 41 10N 24 58 E
Xánthi □, *Greece* 51 E8 41 10N 24 58 E
Xanthos, *Turkey* 49 E11 36 19N 29 18 E
Xanxerê, *Brazil* 175 B5 26 53 S 52 23W
Xapuri, *Brazil* 172 C4 10 35 S 68 35W
Xar Moron He →, *China* 75 C11 43 25N 120 35 E
Xarrë, *Albania* 50 G4 39 44N 20 3 E
Xátiva, *Spain* 41 G4 38 59N 0 32W
Xau, L., *Botswana* 116 C3 21 15 S 24 44 E
Xavantina, *Brazil* 175 A5 21 15 S 52 48W
Xenia, *U.S.A.* 157 E13 39 41N 83 56W
Xeropotamos →, *Cyprus* 38 E11 34 42N 32 33 E
Xertigny, *France* 27 D13 48 3N 6 24 E
Xhora, *S. Africa* 117 E4 31 55 S 28 38 E
Xhumo, *Botswana* 116 C3 21 7 S 24 35 E
Xi Jiang →, *China* 77 F9 22 5N 113 20 E
Xi Xian, *Henan, China* 77 A10 32 20N 114 43 E
Xi Xian, *Shanxi, China* 74 F6 36 41N 110 58 E
Xia Xian, *China* 74 G6 35 8N 111 12 E
Xiachengzi, *China* 75 B16 44 40N 130 18 E
Xiachuan Dao, *China* 77 G9 21 40N 112 40 E
Xiaguan, *China* 72 D5 25 32N 100 16 E
Xiajiang, *China* 77 D10 27 30N 115 10 E
Xiajin, *China* 74 F9 36 56N 116 0 E
Xiamen, *China* 77 E12 24 25N 118 4 E
Xi'an, *China* 74 G5 34 15N 109 0 E
Xian Xian, *China* 74 E9 38 12N 116 6 E
Xianfeng, *China* 76 C7 29 40N 109 8 E
Xiang Jiang →, *China* 77 C9 28 55N 112 50 E
Xiangcheng, *Henan, China* 74 H8 33 29N 114 52 E
Xiangcheng, *Henan, China* 74 H7 33 50N 113 27 E
Xiangcheng, *Sichuan, China* 76 C2 28 53N 99 47 E
Xiangdu, *China* 76 F6 23 13N 106 58 E
Xiangfan, *China* 77 A9 32 2N 112 8 E
Xianggang = Hong Kong □, *China* 77 F10 22 11N 114 14 E
Xianghuang Qi, *China* 74 C7 42 2N 113 50 E
Xiangning, *China* 74 G6 35 58N 110 50 E
Xiangquan, *China* 74 F7 36 30N 113 1 E
Xiangquan He = Sutlej →, *Pakistan* 91 C3 29 23N 71 3 E
Xiangshan, *China* 77 C13 29 29N 121 51 E
Xiangshui, *China* 75 G10 34 12N 119 33 E
Xiangtan, *China* 77 D9 27 51N 112 54 E
Xiangxiang, *China* 77 D9 27 43N 112 28 E
Xiangyin, *China* 77 C9 28 38N 112 54 E
Xiangyun, *China* 76 E3 25 34N 100 35 E
Xiangzhou, *China* 76 F7 23 58N 109 40 E
Xianju, *China* 77 C13 28 51N 120 44 E
Xianning, *China* 77 C10 29 51N 114 16 E
Xianshui He →, *China* 76 B3 30 10N 100 59 E
Xiantao, *China* 77 B9 30 25N 113 25 E
Xianyang, *China* 74 G5 34 20N 108 40 E
Xianyou, *China* 77 E12 25 22N 118 38 E
Xiao Hinggan Ling, *China* 73 B7 49 0N 127 0 E
Xiao Xian, *China* 74 G9 34 15N 116 55 E
Xiaofeng, *China* 77 B12 30 35N 119 32 E
Xiaogan, *China* 77 B9 30 52N 113 55 E
Xiaojin, *China* 76 B4 30 59N 102 21 E
Xiaolan, *China* 77 F9 22 38N 113 13 E
Xiaoshan, *China* 77 B13 30 12N 120 18 E
Xiaoyi, *China* 74 F6 37 8N 111 48 E
Xiapu, *China* 77 D12 26 54N 119 59 E

302 Xiawa

Xiawa, *China* **75 C11** 42 35N 120 38 E
Xiayi, *China* **74 G9** 34 15N 116 10 E
Xichang, *China* **76 D4** 27 51N 102 19 E
Xichong, *China* **76 B5** 30 57N 105 54 E
Xichou, *China* **76 E5** 23 25N 104 42 E
Xichuan, *China* **74 H6** 33 0N 111 30 E
Xide, *China* **76 C4** 28 8N 102 19 E
Xiemahe, *China* **77 B8** 31 38N 111 12 E
Xieng Khouang, *Laos* **86 C4** 19 17N 103 25 E
Xifei He →, *China* **74 H9** 32 45N 116 40 E
Xifeng, *Gansu, China* **74 G4** 35 40N 107 40 E
Xifeng, *Guizhou, China* **76 D6** 27 7N 106 42 E
Xifeng, *Liaoning, China* **75 C13** 42 42N 124 45 E
Xifengzhen = Xifeng, *China* **74 G4** 35 40N 107 40 E
Xigazê, *China* **72 D3** 29 5N 88 45 E
Xihe, *China* **74 G3** 34 2N 105 20 E
Xihua, *China* **74 H8** 33 45N 114 30 E
Xilaganí, *Greece* **51 F9** 40 58N 25 28 E
Xiliao He →, *China* **75 C12** 43 32N 123 35 E
Xilin, *China* **76 E5** 24 30N 105 6 E
Xilókastron, *Greece* **48 C4** 38 5N 22 38 E
Xime, *Guinea-Biss.* **112 C2** 11 59N 14 57W
Ximeng, *China* **76 F2** 22 50N 99 27 E
Xin Jiang →, *China* **77 C11** 28 45N 116 35 E
Xin Xian = Xinzhou, *China* **74 E7** 38 22N 112 46 E
Xinavane, *Mozam.* **117 D5** 25 2 S 32 47 E
Xinbin, *China* **75 D13** 41 40N 125 2 E
Xincai, *China* **77 A10** 32 43N 114 58 E
Xinchang, *China* **77 C13** 29 28N 120 52 E
Xincheng, *Guangxi Zhuangzu, China* **76 E7** 24 5N 108 39 E
Xincheng, *Jiangxi, China* **77 D10** 26 48N 114 6 E
Xindu, *China* **76 B5** 30 50N 104 10 E
Xinfeng, *Guangdong, China* **77 E10** 24 5N 114 16 E
Xinfeng, *Jiangxi, China* **77 D11** 27 7N 116 11 E
Xinfeng, *Jiangxi, China* **77 E10** 25 27N 114 58 E
Xinfengjiang Skuiku, *China* **77 F10** 23 52N 114 30 E
Xing Xian, *China* **74 E6** 38 27N 111 7 E
Xing'an, *Guangxi Zhuangzu, China* **77 E8** 25 38N 110 40 E
Xingan, *Jiangxi, China* **77 D10** 27 46N 115 20 E
Xingcheng, *China* **75 D11** 40 40N 120 45 E
Xingguo, *China* **77 D10** 26 21N 115 21 E
Xinghe, *China* **74 D7** 40 55N 113 55 E
Xinghua, *China* **75 H10** 32 58N 119 48 E
Xinghua Wan, *China* **77 E12** 25 15N 119 20 E
Xinglong, *China* **75 D9** 40 25N 117 30 E
Xingning, *China* **77 E10** 24 3N 115 42 E
Xingping, *China* **74 G5** 34 20N 108 28 E
Xingren, *China* **76 E5** 25 24N 105 11 E
Xingshan, *China* **77 B8** 31 15N 110 45 E
Xingtai, *China* **74 F8** 37 3N 114 32 E
Xingu →, *Brazil* **169 D7** 1 30 S 51 53W
Xingwen, *China* **76 C5** 28 22N 104 50 E
Xingyang, *China* **74 G7** 34 45N 112 52 E
Xinhe, *China* **74 F8** 37 30N 115 15 E
Xinhua, *China* **77 D8** 27 42N 111 13 E
Xinhuang, *China* **76 D7** 27 21N 109 12 E
Xinhui, *China* **77 F9** 22 25N 113 0 E
Xining, *China* **72 C5** 36 34N 101 40 E
Xinjian, *China* **77 C10** 28 37N 115 46 E
Xinjiang, *China* **74 G6** 35 34N 111 11 E
Xinjiang Uygur Zizhiqu □, *China* **72 C3** 42 0N 86 0 E
Xinjie, *China* **76 D3** 26 48N 101 15 E
Xinjin = Pulandian, *China* **75 E11** 39 25N 121 58 E
Xinjin, *China* **76 B4** 30 24N 103 47 E
Xinkai He →, *China* **75 C12** 43 32N 123 35 E
Xinle, *China* **74 E8** 38 25N 114 40 E
Xinlitun, *China* **75 D12** 42 0N 122 8 E
Xinlong, *China* **76 B3** 30 57N 100 12 E
Xinmin, *China* **75 D12** 41 59N 122 50 E
Xinning, *China* **77 D8** 26 28N 110 50 E
Xinping, *China* **76 E3** 24 5N 101 59 E
Xinshao, *China* **77 D8** 27 21N 111 26 E
Xintai, *China* **75 G9** 35 55N 117 45 E
Xintian, *China* **77 E9** 25 55N 112 13 E
Xinxian, *China* **77 B10** 31 36N 113 51 E
Xinxiang, *China* **74 G7** 35 18N 113 50 E
Xinxing, *China* **77 F9** 22 35N 112 15 E
Xinyang, *China* **77 A10** 32 6N 114 3 E
Xinye, *China* **77 A9** 32 30N 112 21 E
Xinyi, *China* **77 F8** 22 25N 111 0 E
Xinyu, *China* **77 D10** 27 49N 114 58 E
Xinzhan, *China* **75 C14** 43 50N 127 18 E
Xinzheng, *China* **74 G7** 34 20N 113 45 E
Xinzhou, *Hubei, China* **77 B10** 30 50N 114 48 E
Xinzhou, *Shanxi, China* **74 E7** 38 22N 112 46 E
Xinzo de Limia, *Spain* **42 C3** 42 3N 7 47W
Xiongyuecheng, *China* **75 D12** 40 12N 122 5 E
Xiping, *Henan, China* **74 H8** 33 22N 114 5 E
Xiping, *Henan, China* **74 H6** 33 25N 111 8 E
Xiping, *Zhejiang, China* **77 C12** 28 16N 119 29 E
Xique-Xique, *Brazil* **170 D3** 10 50 S 42 40W
Xiruá →, *Brazil* **172 B4** 6 3 S 67 50W
Xisha Qundao = Paracel Is., *S. China Sea* **78 A4** 15 50N 112 0 E
Xishui, *Guizhou, China* **76 C6** 28 19N 106 9 E
Xishui, *Hubei, China* **77 B10** 30 30N 115 15 E
Xitole, *Guinea-Biss.* **112 C2** 11 43N 14 50W
Xiu Shui →, *China* **77 C10** 29 13N 116 0 E
Xiuning, *China* **77 C12** 29 45N 118 10 E
Xiuren, *China* **77 E8** 24 27N 110 12 E
Xiushan, *China* **76 C7** 28 25N 108 57 E
Xiushui, *China* **77 C10** 29 2N 114 33 E
Xiuwen, *China* **76 D6** 26 49N 106 32 E
Xiuyan, *China* **75 D12** 40 18N 123 11 E
Xixia, *China* **74 H6** 33 25N 111 29 E
Xixiang, *China* **74 H4** 33 0N 107 44 E
Xiyang, *China* **74 F7** 37 38N 113 38 E
Xizang Zizhiqu □, *China* **72 C3** 32 0N 88 0 E
Xlendi, *Malta* **38 C1** 36 1N 14 12 E
Xu Jiang →, *China* **77 D11** 28 0N 116 25 E
Xuan Loc, *Vietnam* **87 G6** 10 56N 107 14 E
Xuan'en, *China* **76 C7** 30 0N 109 30 E
Xuanhan, *China* **76 B6** 31 18N 107 38 E
Xuanhua, *China* **74 D8** 40 40N 115 2 E
Xuanwei, *China* **76 C5** 26 15N 103 59 E
Xuanzhou, *China* **77 B12** 30 56N 118 43 E
Xuchang, *China* **74 G7** 34 2N 113 48 E
Xudat, *Azerbaijan* **61 K9** 41 38N 48 41 E
Xuefeng Shan, *China* **77 D8** 27 5N 110 35 E
Xuejiaping, *China* **77 B8** 31 39N 110 16 E
Xun Jiang →, *China* **77 F8** 23 35N 111 30 E
Xun Xian, *China* **74 G8** 35 42N 114 33 E
Xundian, *China* **76 E4** 25 36N 103 15 E
Xunwu, *China* **77 E10** 24 54N 115 37 E
Xunyang, *China* **74 H5** 32 48N 109 22 E
Xunyi, *China* **74 G5** 35 8N 108 20 E
Xupu, *China* **77 D8** 27 53N 110 32 E
Xúquer →, *Spain* **41 F4** 39 5N 0 10W
Xushui, *China* **74 E8** 39 2N 115 40 E
Xuwen, *China* **77 G8** 20 20N 110 10 E
Xuyen Moc, *Vietnam* **87 G6** 10 34N 107 25 E
Xuyong, *China* **76 C5** 28 10N 105 22 E
Xuzhou, *China* **75 G9** 34 18N 117 10 E
Xylophagou, *Cyprus* **38 E12** 34 54N 33 51 E

Y

Ya Xian, *China* **86 C7** 18 14N 109 29 E
Yaamba, *Australia* **126 C5** 23 8 S 150 22 E
Ya'an, *China* **76 C4** 29 58N 103 5 E
Yaapeet, *Australia* **128 C5** 35 45 S 142 3 E
Yabassi, *Cameroon* **113 E6** 4 30N 9 57 E
Yabba North, *Australia* **129 D6** 36 13 S 145 42 E
Yabelo, *Ethiopia* **107 G4** 4 50N 38 8 E
Yablanitsa, *Bulgaria* **51 C8** 43 2N 24 5 E
Yablonovy Ra. = Yablonovyy Khrebet, *Russia* **65 D12** 53 0N 114 0 E
Yablonovyy Khrebet, *Russia* **65 D12** 53 0N 114 0 E
Yabrai Shan, *China* **74 E2** 39 40N 103 0 E
Yabrūd, *Syria* **103 B5** 33 58N 36 39 E
Yacheng, *China* **73 E5** 18 22N 109 6 E
Yacuiba, *Bolivia* **174 A3** 22 0 S 63 43W
Yacuma →, *Bolivia* **173 C4** 13 38 S 65 23W
Yadgir, *India* **94 F3** 16 45N 77 5 E
Yadkin →, *U.S.A.* **149 H5** 35 29N 80 9W
Yadrin, *Russia* **60 C8** 55 57N 46 12 E
Yaeyama-Rettō, *Japan* **69 M1** 24 30N 123 40 E
Yagaba, *Ghana* **113 C4** 10 14N 1 20W
Yağcılar, *Turkey* **49 B10** 39 25N 28 23 E
Yagodnoye, *Russia* **65 C15** 62 33N 149 40 E
Yagoua, *Cameroon* **114 A3** 10 20N 15 13 E
Yaguas →, *Peru* **168 D3** 2 45 S 70 10W
Yahila, *Dem. Rep. of the Congo* **114 B4** 1 48N 23 37 E
Yahila, *Dem. Rep. of the Congo* **118 B1** 0 13N 24 28 E
Yahk, *Canada* **142 D5** 49 6N 116 10W
Yahotyn, *Ukraine* **59 G6** 50 17N 31 46 E
Yahuma, *Dem. Rep. of the Congo* **114 B4** 1 0N 23 10 E
Yahyalı, *Turkey* **100 C6** 38 5N 35 2 E
Yaita, *Japan* **69 F9** 36 48N 139 56 E
Yaiza, *Canary Is.* **39 F6** 28 57N 13 46W
Yaizu, *Japan* **71 C10** 34 52N 138 20 E
Yajiang, *China* **76 B3** 30 2N 100 57 E
Yajua, *Nigeria* **113 C7** 11 27N 12 49 E
Yakage, *Japan* **70 C5** 34 37N 133 35 E
Yakamba, *Dem. Rep. of the Congo* **114 B3** 2 42N 19 38 E
Yakima, *U.S.A.* **158 C3** 46 36N 120 31W
Yakima →, *U.S.A.* **158 C3** 47 0N 120 30W
Yako, *Burkina Faso* **112 C4** 12 59N 2 15W
Yakobi I., *U.S.A.* **142 B1** 58 0N 136 30W
Yakoma, *Dem. Rep. of the Congo* **114 B4** 4 5N 22 27 E
Yakoruda, *Bulgaria* **50 D7** 42 1N 23 39 E
Yakossi, *C.A.R.* **114 A4** 5 37N 23 19 E
Yakovlevka, *Russia* **68 B6** 44 26N 133 28 E
Yakshur Bodya, *Russia* **62 C4** 57 11N 53 7 E
Yaku-Shima, *Japan* **69 J5** 30 20N 130 30 E
Yakumo, *Japan* **68 C10** 42 15N 140 16 E
Yakutat, *U.S.A.* **138 C6** 59 33N 139 44W
Yakutat B., *U.S.A.* **144 G12** 59 45N 140 45W
Yakutia = Sakha □, *Russia* **65 C13** 66 0N 130 0 E
Yakutsk, *Russia* **65 C13** 62 5N 129 50 E
Yala, *Thailand* **78 C2** 6 33N 101 18 E
Yale, *U.S.A.* **150 C2** 43 8N 82 48W
Yalgoo, *Australia* **125 E2** 28 16 S 116 39 E
Yali, *Dem. Rep. of the Congo* **114 B4** 0 4N 21 3 E
Yaligimba, *Dem. Rep. of the Congo* **114 B4** 2 13N 22 56 E
Yalikanda, *Dem. Rep. of the Congo* **114 B4** 0 23N 24 47 E
Yalinga, *C.A.R.* **114 A4** 6 33N 23 10 E
Yalkubul, Punta, *Mexico* **163 C7** 21 32N 88 37W
Yalleroi, *Australia* **126 C4** 24 3 S 145 42 E
Yalobusha →, *U.S.A.* **155 J9** 33 33N 90 10W
Yaloké, *C.A.R.* **114 A3** 5 19N 17 5 E
Yalong Jiang →, *China* **76 D3** 26 40N 101 55 E
Yalova, *Turkey* **51 F13** 40 41N 29 15 E
Yalta, *Ukraine* **59 K8** 44 30N 34 10 E
Yalu Jiang →, *China* **75 E13** 40 0N 124 22 E
Yalvaç, *Turkey* **100 C4** 38 17N 31 10 E
Yam Ha Melah = Dead Sea, *Asia* **103 D4** 31 30N 35 30 E
Yam Kinneret, *Israel* **103 C4** 32 45N 35 35 E
Yamada, *Japan* **70 D2** 33 33N 130 49 E
Yamaga, *Japan* **70 D2** 33 1N 130 41 E
Yamagata, *Japan* **68 E10** 38 15N 140 15 E
Yamagata □, *Japan* **68 E10** 38 30N 140 0 E
Yamagawa, *Japan* **70 F2** 31 12N 130 39 E
Yamaguchi, *Japan* **70 C3** 34 10N 131 32 E
Yamaguchi □, *Japan* **70 C3** 34 20N 131 40 E
Yamal, Poluostrov, *Russia* **64 B8** 71 0N 70 0 E
Yamal Pen. = Yamal, Poluostrov, *Russia* **64 B8** 71 0N 70 0 E
Yamanaka, *Japan* **71 A8** 36 15N 136 22 E
Yamanashi □, *Japan* **71 B10** 35 40N 138 40 E
Yamantau, Gora, *Russia* **62 D7** 54 15N 58 6 E
Yamato, *Japan* **71 B11** 35 27N 139 25 E
Yamatotakada, *Japan* **71 C7** 34 31N 135 45 E
Yamazaki, *Japan* **70 B6** 35 0N 134 32 E
Yamba, *N.S.W., Australia* **127 D5** 29 26 S 153 23 E
Yamba, *S. Austral., Australia* **128 C4** 34 10 S 140 52 E
Yambarran Ra., *Australia* **124 C5** 15 10 S 130 25 E
Yambata, *Dem. Rep. of the Congo* **114 B4** 2 26N 21 58 E
Yambéring, *Guinea* **112 C2** 11 50N 12 18 E
Yâmbiô, *Sudan* **107 G2** 4 35N 28 16 E
Yambol, *Bulgaria* **51 D10** 42 30N 26 30 E
Yamboyo, *Dem. Rep. of the Congo* **114 B4** 0 40N 22 18 E
Yambuya, *Dem. Rep. of the Congo* **114 B4** 1 17N 24 34 E
Yamdena, *Indonesia* **79 F8** 7 45 S 131 20 E
Yame, *Japan* **70 D2** 33 13N 130 35 E
Yamethin, *Burma* **90 E6** 20 29N 96 18 E
Yamma-Yamma, L., *Australia* **127 D3** 26 16 S 141 20 E
Yamoussoukro, *Ivory C.* **112 D3** 6 49N 5 17W
Yampa →, *U.S.A.* **158 F9** 40 32N 108 59W
Yampi Sd., *Australia* **124 C3** 16 8 S 123 38 E
Yampil, *Moldova* **59 H5** 48 15N 28 15 E
Yampol = Yampil, *Moldova* **59 H5** 48 15N 28 15 E
Yamrat, *Nigeria* **113 C6** 10 11N 9 55 E
Yamrukchal = Botev, *Bulgaria* **51 D8** 42 44N 24 52 E
Yamuna →, *India* **93 G9** 25 30N 81 53 E
Yamunanagar, *India* **92 D7** 30 7N 77 17 E
Yamzho Yumco, *China* **72 D4** 28 48N 90 35 E
Yan, *Nigeria* **113 C7** 10 5N 12 11 E
Yan Oya →, *Sri Lanka* **95 K5** 9 0N 81 10 E
Yana →, *Russia* **65 B14** 71 30N 136 0 E
Yanac, *Australia* **128 D4** 36 8 S 141 25 E
Yanagawa, *Japan* **70 D2** 33 10N 130 24 E
Yanahara, *Japan* **70 C6** 34 58N 134 2 E
Yanai, *Japan* **70 D4** 33 58N 132 7 E
Yan'an, *China* **74 F5** 36 35N 109 26 E
Yanaul, *Russia* **62 C5** 56 25N 55 0 E
Yanbian, *China* **76 D3** 26 47N 101 31 E
Yanbu 'al Bahr, *Si. Arabia* **96 F3** 24 0N 38 5 E
Yanchang, *China* **74 F6** 36 43N 110 1 E
Yancheng, *Henan, China* **74 H8** 33 35N 114 0 E
Yancheng, *Jiangsu, China* **75 H11** 33 23N 120 8 E
Yanchep Beach, *Australia* **125 F2** 31 33 S 115 37 E
Yanchi, *China* **74 F4** 37 48N 107 20 E
Yanchuan, *China* **74 F6** 36 51N 110 10 E
Yanco, *Australia* **129 C7** 34 38 S 146 27 E
Yanco Cr. →, *Australia* **129 C6** 35 14 S 145 35 E
Yandé, I., *N. Cal.* **133 T17** 20 3 S 163 49 E
Yandina, *Solomon Is.* **133 M10** 9 7 S 159 13 E
Yandja, *Dem. Rep. of the Congo* **114 C3** 1 41 S 17 43 E
Yandongi, *Dem. Rep. of the Congo* **114 B4** 2 51N 22 16 E
Yandoon, *Burma* **90 G5** 17 0N 95 40 E
Yanfeng, *China* **76 E3** 25 52N 101 8 E
Yanfolila, *Mali* **112 C3** 11 11N 8 9W
Yang Xian, *China* **74 H4** 33 15N 107 30 E
Yang-Yang, *Senegal* **112 B1** 15 30N 15 20W
Yangambi, *Dem. Rep. of the Congo* **114 B4** 0 47N 24 24 E
Yangbi, *China* **76 E2** 25 41N 99 58 E
Yangcheng, *China* **74 G7** 35 28N 112 22 E
Yangch'ü = Taiyuan, *China* **74 F7** 37 52N 112 33 E
Yangchun, *China* **77 F8** 22 11N 111 48 E
Yanggao, *China* **74 D7** 40 21N 113 55 E
Yanggu, *China* **74 F8** 36 8N 115 43 E
Yangibazar, *Kyrgyzstan* **63 C5** 41 40N 70 53 E
Yangikishlak, *Uzbekistan* **63 C3** 40 25N 67 10 E
Yangiyul, *Uzbekistan* **63 C4** 41 0N 69 3 E
Yangjiang, *China* **77 G8** 21 50N 111 59 E
Yangliuqing, *China* **75 E9** 39 2N 117 5 E
Yangon = Rangoon, *Burma* **90 G6** 16 45N 96 20 E
Yangonde, *Dem. Rep. of the Congo* **114 B4** 0 3N 22 43 E
Yangping, *China* **77 B8** 31 12N 111 25 E
Yangpingguan, *China* **74 H4** 32 58N 106 5 E
Yangquan, *China* **74 F7** 37 58N 113 31 E
Yangshan, *China* **77 E9** 24 30N 112 40 E
Yangshuo, *China* **77 E8** 24 48N 110 29 E
Yangtse = Chang Jiang →, *China* **77 B13** 31 48N 121 10 E
Yangtze Kiang = Chang Jiang →, *China* **77 B13** 31 48N 121 10 E
Yangxin, *China* **77 C10** 29 50N 115 12 E
Yangyang, *S. Korea* **75 E15** 38 4N 128 38 E
Yangyuan, *China* **74 D8** 40 1N 114 10 E
Yangzhong, *China* **77 A12** 32 22N 119 22 E
Yangzhou, *China* **77 A12** 32 21N 119 26 E
Yanhe, *China* **76 C7** 28 31N 108 29 E
Yanji, *China* **75 C15** 42 59N 129 30 E
Yanjin, *China* **76 C5** 28 5N 104 18 E
Yanjing, *China* **76 C2** 29 7N 98 33 E
Yankton, *U.S.A.* **154 D6** 42 53N 97 23W
Yanonge, *Dem. Rep. of the Congo* **118 B1** 0 35N 24 38 E
Yanqi, *China* **72 B3** 42 5N 86 35 E
Yanqing, *China* **74 D8** 40 30N 115 58 E
Yanshan, *Hebei, China* **75 E9** 38 4N 117 22 E
Yanshan, *Jiangxi, China* **77 C11** 28 15N 117 41 E
Yanshan, *Yunnan, China* **76 F5** 23 35N 104 20 E
Yanshou, *China* **75 B15** 45 28N 128 22 E
Yantabulla, *Australia* **127 D4** 29 21 S 145 0 E
Yantai, *China* **75 F11** 37 34N 121 22 E
Yanting, *China* **76 B5** 31 11N 105 24 E
Yantra →, *Bulgaria* **51 C9** 43 40N 25 37 E
Yanwa, *China* **76 D2** 27 35N 98 55 E
Yanykurgan, *Kazakstan* **63 B3** 43 50N 68 48 E
Yanyuan, *China* **76 D3** 27 25N 101 30 E
Yanzhou, *China* **74 G9** 35 35N 116 49 E
Yao, *Chad* **109 F3** 12 56N 17 33 E
Yao, *Japan* **71 C7** 34 32N 135 36 E
Yao Xian, *China* **74 G5** 34 55N 108 59 E
Yao Yai, Ko, *Thailand* **87 J2** 8 0N 98 35 E
Yao'an, *China* **76 E3** 25 31N 101 18 E
Yaodu, *China* **76 A5** 32 45N 105 22 E
Yaoundé, *Cameroon* **113 E7** 3 50N 11 35 E
Yaowan, *China* **75 G10** 34 15N 118 3 E
Yap I., *Pac. Oc.* **134 G5** 9 30N 138 10 E
Yapehe, *Dem. Rep. of the Congo* **114 C4** 0 13 S 24 28 E
Yapen, *Indonesia* **79 E9** 1 50 S 136 0 E
Yapen, Selat, *Indonesia* **79 E9** 1 20 S 136 10 E
Yapero, *Indonesia* **79 E9** 4 59 S 137 11 E
Yappar →, *Australia* **126 B3** 18 22 S 141 16 E
Yaqui →, *Mexico* **162 B2** 27 37N 110 39W
Yar, *Russia* **62 B4** 58 14N 52 5 E
Yar-Sale, *Russia* **64 C8** 66 50N 70 50 E
Yaracuy □, *Venezuela* **168 A4** 10 20N 68 45W
Yaracuy →, *Venezuela* **168 A4** 10 33N 68 15W
Yaraka, *Australia* **126 C3** 24 53 S 144 3 E
Yaransk, *Russia* **60 B8** 57 22N 47 49 E
Yarbasan, *Turkey* **49 C10** 38 59N 28 49 E
Yardımcı Burnu, *Turkey* **49 E12** 36 13N 30 25 E
Yare →, *U.K.* **21 E9** 52 35N 1 38 E
Yaremcha, *Ukraine* **59 H3** 48 27N 24 33 E
Yarensk, *Russia* **56 B8** 62 11N 49 15 E
Yarfa, *Si. Arabia* **106 C4** 24 37N 38 35 E
Yarí →, *Colombia* **168 D3** 0 20 S 72 20W
Yaritagua, *Venezuela* **168 A4** 10 5N 69 8W
Yarkand = Shache, *China* **72 C2** 38 20N 77 10 E
Yarker, *Canada* **151 B8** 44 23N 76 46W
Yarkhun →, *Pakistan* **93 A5** 36 17N 72 30 E
Yarmouth, *Canada* **141 D6** 43 50N 66 7W
Yarmūk →, *Syria* **103 C4** 32 42N 35 40 E
Yaroslavl, *Russia* **58 D10** 57 35N 39 55 E
Yarqa, W. →, *Egypt* **103 F2** 30 0N 33 49 E
Yarra Yarra Lakes, *Australia* **125 E2** 29 40 S 115 45 E
Yarram, *Australia* **129 E7** 38 29 S 146 39 E
Yarraman, *Australia* **127 D5** 26 50 S 152 0 E
Yarras, *Australia* **129 A10** 31 25 S 152 20 E
Yarrawonga, *Australia* **129 D6** 36 0 S 146 0 E
Yarto, *Australia* **128 C5** 35 28 S 142 16 E
Yartsevo, *Sib., Russia* **65 C10** 60 20N 90 0 E
Yartsevo, *Smolensk, Russia* **58 E7** 55 6N 32 43 E
Yarumal, *Colombia* **168 B2** 6 58N 75 24W
Yasa, *Dem. Rep. of the Congo* **114 C4** 3 50 S 21 25 E
Yasawa, *Fiji* **133 A1** 16 47 S 177 31 E
Yasawa Group, *Fiji* **133 A1** 17 0 S 177 23 E
Yaselda, *Belarus* **59 F4** 52 7N 26 28 E
Yashbum, *Yemen* **98 D4** 14 19N 46 56 E
Yashi, *Nigeria* **113 C6** 12 23N 7 54 E
Yashikera, *Nigeria* **113 D5** 9 44N 3 29 E
Yashiro-Jima, *Japan* **70 D4** 33 55N 132 15 E
Yashkul, *Russia* **61 G7** 46 11N 45 21 E
Yasin, *Pakistan* **93 A5** 36 24N 73 23 E
Yasinovataya, *Ukraine* **59 H9** 48 7N 37 57 E
Yasinski, L., *Canada* **140 B4** 53 16N 77 35W
Yasinya, *Ukraine* **59 H3** 48 16N 24 21 E
Yasnyy, *Russia* **62 F7** 51 1N 59 58 E
Yasothon, *Thailand* **86 E5** 15 50N 104 10 E
Yass, *Australia* **129 C8** 34 49 S 148 54 E
Yasugi, *Japan* **70 B5** 35 26N 133 15 E
Yata →, *Bolivia* **173 C4** 10 29 S 65 26W
Yata →, *C.A.R.* **114 A4** 10 23N 22 45 E
Yatağan, *Turkey* **49 D10** 37 20N 28 10 E
Yatakala, *Niger* **113 C5** 14 50N 0 22 E
Yates Center, *U.S.A.* **155 G7** 37 53N 95 44W
Yates Pt., *N.Z.* **131 E2** 44 29 S 167 49 E
Yathkyed L., *Canada* **143 A9** 62 40N 98 0W
Yathong, *Australia* **129 B6** 32 37 S 145 33 E
Yatolemu, *Dem. Rep. of the Congo* **114 B4** 0 25N 24 35 E
Yatsuo, *Japan* **71 A9** 36 34N 137 8 E
Yatsushiro, *Japan* **70 E2** 32 30N 130 40 E
Yatsushiro-Kai, *Japan* **70 E2** 32 30N 130 25 E
Yatta Plateau, *Kenya* **118 C4** 2 0 S 38 0 E
Yatua →, *Venezuela* **168 C4** 1 30N 66 30W
Yauca, *Peru* **172 D3** 15 39 S 74 35W
Yauri, *Peru* **172 C3** 14 47 S 71 25W
Yauya, *Peru* **172 B2** 8 59 S 77 17W
Yauyos, *Peru* **172 C2** 12 19 S 75 50W
Yaval, *India* **94 D2** 21 10N 75 42 E
Yavan, *Tajikistan* **63 D4** 38 19N 69 2 E
Yavari →, *Peru* **172 A3** 4 21 S 70 2W
Yávaros, *Mexico* **162 B3** 26 42N 109 31W
Yavatmal, *India* **94 D4** 20 20N 78 15 E
Yavero →, *Peru* **172 C3** 12 6 S 72 57W
Yavne, *Israel* **103 D3** 31 52N 34 45 E
Yavoriv, *Ukraine* **59 H2** 49 55N 23 20 E
Yavorov = Yavoriv, *Ukraine* **59 H2** 49 55N 23 20 E
Yavuzeli, *Turkey* **100 D7** 37 18N 37 24 E
Yawatahama, *Japan* **70 D4** 33 27N 132 24 E
Yawri B., *S. Leone* **112 D2** 8 22N 13 0W
Yaxi, *China* **76 D6** 27 33N 106 41 E
Yazagyo, *Burma* **90 D5** 23 30N 94 6 E
Yazd, *Iran* **97 D7** 31 55N 54 27 E
Yazd □, *Iran* **97 D7** 32 0N 55 0 E
Yazd-e Khvāst, *Iran* **97 D7** 31 31N 52 7 E
Yazdān, *Iran* **91 B1** 33 30N 60 50 E
Yazıköy, *Turkey* **49 E9** 36 40N 27 20 E
Yazman, *Pakistan* **92 E4** 29 8N 71 45 E
Yazoo →, *U.S.A.* **155 J9** 32 22N 90 54W
Yazoo City, *U.S.A.* **155 J9** 32 51N 90 25W
Ybbs, *Austria* **34 C8** 48 12N 15 4 E
Yding Skovhøj, *Denmark* **17 J3** 55 59N 9 46 E
Ydrim, *Yemen* **98 D4** 14 20N 44 22 E
Ye Xian = Laizhou, *China* **75 F10** 37 8N 119 57 E
Ye Xian, *China* **74 H7** 33 35N 113 25 E
Yea, *Australia* **129 D6** 37 14 S 145 26 E
Yearinan, *Australia* **129 A8** 31 10 S 149 11 E
Yebbi-Souma, *Chad* **109 D3** 21 7N 17 54 E
Yebyu, *Burma* **86 E2** 14 15N 98 13 E
Yechŏn, *S. Korea* **75 F15** 36 39N 128 27 E
Yecla, *Spain* **41 G3** 38 35N 1 5W
Yécora, *Mexico* **162 B3** 28 20N 108 58W
Yedashe, *Burma* **90 F6** 19 10N 96 20 E
Yedintsy = Edineț, *Moldova* **53 B12** 48 9N 27 18 E
Yedseram →, *Nigeria* **113 C7** 12 30N 14 5 E
Yefremov, *Russia* **58 F10** 53 8N 38 3 E
Yeghegnadzor, *Armenia* **101 C11** 39 44N 45 19 E
Yegorlyk →, *Russia* **61 G5** 46 35N 41 57 E
Yegorlykskaya, *Russia* **61 G5** 46 35N 40 35 E
Yegoryevsk, *Russia* **58 E10** 55 27N 38 55 E
Yegros, *Paraguay* **174 B4** 26 20 S 56 25W
Yehuda, Midbar, *Israel* **103 D4** 31 35N 35 15 E
Yei, *Sudan* **107 G3** 4 9N 30 40 E
Yei, Nahr →, *Sudan* **107 F3** 6 15N 30 13 E
Yejmiadzin, *Armenia* **61 K7** 40 12N 44 19 E
Yekaterinburg, *Russia* **62 C8** 56 50N 60 30 E
Yekaterinodar = Krasnodar, *Russia* **61 H4** 45 5N 39 0 E
Yekumbe, *Dem. Rep. of the Congo* **114 C4** 1 2 S 23 27 E
Yelabuga, *Russia* **60 C11** 55 45N 52 4 E
Yelan, *Russia* **60 E6** 50 55N 43 43 E
Yelandur, *India* **95 H3** 12 6N 77 0 E
Yelarbon, *Australia* **127 D5** 28 33 S 150 38 E
Yelatma, *Russia* **60 C5** 55 0N 41 45 E
Yelcho, L., *Chile* **176 B2** 43 18 S 72 18W
Yelets, *Russia* **59 F10** 52 40N 38 30 E
Yélimané, *Mali* **112 B2** 15 9N 10 34W
Yelizavetgrad = Kirovohrad, *Ukraine* **59 H7** 48 35N 32 20 E
Yelizavetinka, *Russia* **62 F7** 51 46N 59 45 E
Yell, *U.K.* **22 A7** 60 35N 1 5W
Yell Sd., *U.K.* **22 A7** 60 33N 1 15W
Yellamanchilli = Elamanchili, *India* **94 F6** 17 33N 82 50 E
Yellandu, *India* **94 F5** 17 39N 80 23 E
Yellapur, *India* **95 G2** 14 58N 74 43 E
Yellareddi, *India* **94 E4** 18 12N 78 2 E
Yellow →, *U.S.A.* **153 E3** 30 30N 87 0W
Yellow Sea, *China* **75 G12** 35 0N 123 0 E
Yellowhead Pass, *Canada* **142 C5** 52 53N 118 25W
Yellowknife, *Canada* **142 A6** 62 27N 114 29W
Yellowknife →, *Canada* **142 A6** 62 31N 114 19W
Yellowstone →, *U.S.A.* **154 B3** 47 59N 103 59W
Yellowstone L., *U.S.A.* **158 D8** 44 27N 110 22W
Yellowstone National Park, *U.S.A.* **158 D9** 44 40N 110 30W
Yelnya, *Russia* **58 E7** 54 35N 33 15 E
Yelsk, *Belarus* **59 G5** 51 50N 29 10 E
Yelwa, *Nigeria* **113 C5** 10 49N 4 41 E
Yemanzhelinsk, *Russia* **62 D8** 54 58N 61 18 E
Yemassee, *U.S.A.* **152 C9** 32 41N 80 51W
Yembongo, *Dem. Rep. of the Congo* **114 B3** 3 12N 19 2 E
Yemen ■, *Asia* **98 D4** 15 0N 44 0 E
Yen Bai, *Vietnam* **76 G5** 21 42N 104 52 E
Yenagoa, *Nigeria* **113 E6** 4 58N 6 16 E
Yenakiyeve, *Ukraine* **59 H10** 48 15N 38 15 E
Yenakiyevo = Yenakiyeve, *Ukraine* **59 H10** 48 15N 38 15 E
Yenangyaung, *Burma* **90 E5** 20 30N 95 0 E
Yenanma, *Burma* **90 F5** 19 46N 94 49 E
Yenbo = Yanbu 'al Bahr, *Si. Arabia* **96 F3** 24 0N 38 5 E
Yenda, *Australia* **129 C7** 34 13 S 146 14 E
Yende Millimou, *Guinea* **112 D2** 8 55N 10 10W
Yendéré, *Burkina Faso* **112 C4** 10 12N 4 59W
Yendi, *Ghana* **113 D4** 9 29N 0 1W
Yengo, *Congo* **114 B3** 0 22N 15 29 E
Yéni, *Niger* **113 C5** 13 30N 3 1 E
Yenice, *Ankara, Turkey* **100 C5** 39 14N 32 42 E
Yenice, *Aydın, Turkey* **49 D10** 37 49N 28 35 E
Yenice, *Çanakkale, Turkey* **49 B9** 39 55N 27 17 E
Yenice, *Edirne, Turkey* **51 F10** 40 42N 26 9 E
Yenice →, *Turkey* **100 D6** 37 37N 35 33 E
Yenifoça, *Turkey* **49 C8** 38 44N 26 51 E
Yenihisar, *Turkey* **49 D9** 37 22N 27 16 E
Yeniköy, *Bursa, Turkey* **51 F13** 40 31N 29 22 E
Yeniköy, *Çanakkale, Turkey* **49 B8** 39 55N 26 10 E
Yeniköy, *Kütahya, Turkey* **49 C11** 38 52N 29 17 E
Yenipazar, *Turkey* **49 D10** 37 49N 28 11 E
Yenisaía, *Greece* **51 E8** 41 1N 24 57 E
Yenişehir, *Turkey* **51 F13** 40 16N 29 38 E
Yenisey →, *Russia* **64 B9** 71 50N 82 40 E
Yeniseysk, *Russia* **65 D10** 58 27N 92 13 E
Yeniseyskiy Zaliv, *Russia* **64 B9** 72 20N 81 0 E
Yennádhi, *Greece* **38 C9** 36 2N 27 56 E
Yenne, *France* **29 C9** 45 43N 5 44 E
Yenotayevka, *Russia* **61 G8** 47 15N 47 0 E
Yenyuka, *Russia* **65 D13** 57 57N 121 15 E
Yeo →, *U.K.* **21 G5** 51 2N 2 49W
Yeo, L., *Australia* **125 E3** 28 0 S 124 30 E
Yeo I., *Canada* **150 A3** 45 24N 81 48W

Zamora 303

Yeola, India 94 D2 20 2N 74 30 E
Yeoryioúpolis, Greece 38 D6 35 20N 24 15 E
Yeoval, Australia 129 B8 32 47 S 148 40 E
Yeovil, U.K. 21 G5 50 57N 2 38W
Yepes, Spain 42 F7 39 55N 3 39W
Yeppoon, Australia 126 C5 23 5 S 150 47 E
Yeráki, Greece 48 D4 37 0N 22 42 E
Yerbent, Turkmenistan 64 F6 39 30N 58 50 E
Yerbogachen, Russia 65 C11 61 16N 108 0 E
Yerevan, Armenia 61 K7 40 10N 44 31 E
Yerington, U.S.A. 158 G4 38 59N 119 10W
Yerkesik, Turkey 49 D10 37 7N 28 19 E
Yerköy, Turkey 100 C6 39 38N 34 28 E
Yerla →, India 94 F2 16 50N 74 30 E
Yermak, Kazakstan 64 D8 52 2N 76 55 E
Yermo, U.S.A. 161 L10 34 54N 116 50W
Yerólakkos, Cyprus 38 D12 35 11N 33 15 E
Yeropol, Russia 65 C17 65 15N 168 40 E
Yeropótamos →, Greece 38 D6 35 3N 24 50 E
Yeroskipos, Cyprus 38 E11 34 46N 32 28 E
Yershov, Russia 60 E9 51 23N 48 27 E
Yeruanaja, Cerro, Peru 172 C2 10 16 S 76 55W
Yerushalayim = Jerusalem, Israel 103 D4 31 47N 35 10 E
Yerville, France 26 C7 49 40N 0 53 E
Yes Tor, U.K. 21 G4 50 41N 4 0W
Yesagyo, Burma 78 E5 21 38N 95 14 E
Yesan, S. Korea 75 F14 36 41N 126 51 E
Yeşilhisar, Turkey 100 C6 38 20N 35 5 E
Yeşilırmak →, Turkey 100 B7 41 22N 36 37 E
Yeşilkent, Turkey 100 D7 36 57N 36 12 E
Yeşilköy, Turkey 51 F12 40 57N 28 49 E
Yeşilova, Turkey 49 D11 37 31N 29 46 E
Yeşilyurt, Manisa, Turkey 49 C10 38 22N 28 40 E
Yeşilyurt, Muğla, Turkey 49 D10 37 10N 28 20 E
Yesnogorsk, Russia 58 E9 54 32N 37 38 E
Yeso, U.S.A. 155 H2 34 26N 104 37W
Yessentuki, Russia 61 H6 44 5N 42 53 E
Yessey, Russia 65 C11 68 29N 102 10 E
Yeste, Spain 41 G2 38 22N 2 19W
Yetman, Australia 127 D5 28 56 S 150 48 E
Yeu, Î. d', France 26 F4 46 42N 2 20W
Yevlakh = Yevlax, Azerbaijan 61 K8 40 39N 47 7 E
Yevlax, Azerbaijan 61 K8 40 39N 47 7 E
Yevpatoriya, Ukraine 59 K7 45 15N 33 20 E
Yeya →, Russia 59 J10 46 40N 38 40 E
Yeysk, Russia 59 J10 46 40N 38 12 E
Yezd = Yazd, Iran 97 D7 31 55N 54 27 E
Yezerishche, Belarus 58 E5 55 50N 29 59 E
Yhati, Paraguay 174 B4 25 45 S 56 35W
Yhú, Paraguay 175 B4 25 0 S 56 0W
Yi →, Uruguay 174 C4 33 7 S 57 8W
Yi 'Allaq, G., Egypt 103 E2 30 22N 33 32 E
Yi He →, China 75 G10 34 10N 118 8 E
Yi Xian, Anhui, China 77 C11 29 55N 117 57 E
Yi Xian, Hebei, China 74 E8 39 20N 115 30 E
Yi Xian, Liaoning, China 75 D11 41 30N 121 22 E
Yialí, Greece 49 E9 36 41N 27 11 E
Yialiás →, Cyprus 38 D12 35 9N 33 44 E
Yi'allaq, G., Egypt 106 A3 30 21N 33 31 E
Yialousa, Cyprus 38 D13 35 32N 34 10 E
Yiáltra, Greece 48 C4 38 51N 22 59 E
Yianisádhes, Greece 38 D8 35 20N 26 10 E
Yiannitsa, Greece 50 F6 40 46N 22 24 E
Yibin, China 76 C5 28 45N 104 32 E
Yichang, China 77 B8 30 40N 111 20 E
Yicheng, Henan, China 77 B9 31 41N 112 12 E
Yicheng, Shanxi, China 74 G6 35 42N 111 40 E
Yichuan, China 74 F6 36 2N 110 10 E
Yichun, Heilongjiang, China 73 B7 47 44N 128 52 E
Yichun, Jiangxi, China 77 D10 27 48N 114 22 E
Yidu, China 75 F10 36 43N 118 28 E
Yidun, China 76 B2 30 22N 99 21 E
Yifag, Ethiopia 107 E4 12 4N 37 46 E
Yifeng, China 77 C10 28 22N 114 45 E
Yihuang, China 77 D11 27 30N 116 12 E
Yijun, China 74 G5 35 28N 109 8 E
Yıldız Dağları, Turkey 51 E11 41 48N 27 36 E
Yıldızeli, Turkey 100 C7 39 51N 36 36 E
Yilehuli Shan, China 73 A7 51 20N 124 20 E
Yiliang, Yunnan, China 76 D5 27 38N 104 2 E
Yiliang, Yunnan, China 76 E4 24 56N 103 11 E
Yilong, China 76 B6 31 34N 106 23 E
Yimen, China 76 E4 24 40N 102 10 E
Yimianpo, China 75 B15 45 7N 128 2 E
Yinchuan, China 74 E4 38 30N 106 15 E
Yindarlgooda, L., Australia 125 F3 30 40 S 121 52 E
Ying He →, China 74 H9 32 30N 116 30 E
Ying Xian, China 74 E7 39 32N 113 10 E
Yingcheng, China 77 B9 30 56N 113 35 E
Yingde, China 77 E9 24 10N 113 25 E
Yingjiang, China 76 E1 24 41N 97 55 E
Yingjing, China 76 C4 29 41N 102 52 E
Yingkou, China 75 D12 40 37N 122 18 E
Yingshan, Henan, China 77 B9 31 35N 113 50 E
Yingshan, Hubei, China 77 B10 30 41N 115 32 E
Yingshan, Sichuan, China 76 B6 31 4N 106 35 E
Yingshang, China 77 A11 32 38N 116 12 E
Yingtan, China 77 C11 28 12N 117 0 E
Yining, China 64 E9 43 58N 81 10 E
Yinjiang, China 76 C7 28 1N 108 21 E
Yiofiros →, Greece 38 D7 35 20N 25 6 E
Yioúra, Nótios Aiyaíon, Greece 48 D6 37 32N 24 40 E
Yioúra, Thessalía, Greece 48 B6 39 23N 24 10 E
Yipinglang, China 76 E3 25 10N 101 52 E
Yirba Muda, Ethiopia 107 F4 6 12N 38 42 E
Yirga Alem, Ethiopia 102 F2 6 48N 38 22 E
Yirol, Sudan 107 F3 6 33N 30 30 E
Yirrkala, Australia 126 A2 12 14 S 136 56 E
Yishan, China 76 E7 24 28N 108 38 E
Yishui, China 75 G10 35 47N 118 30 E
Yíthion, Greece 48 E4 36 46N 22 34 E
Yitong, China 75 C13 43 13N 125 20 E
Yiwu, China 77 C13 29 20N 120 3 E
Yixing, China 77 B12 31 21N 119 48 E
Yiyang, Henan, China 74 G7 34 27N 112 10 E
Yiyang, Hunan, China 77 C9 28 35N 112 18 E
Yiyang, Jiangxi, China 77 C11 28 22N 117 20 E
Yizhang, China 77 E9 25 27N 112 57 E
Yizheng, China 77 A12 32 18N 119 10 E
Yli-Kitka, Finland 14 C23 66 8N 28 30 E
Ylitornio, Finland 14 C20 66 19N 23 39 E
Ylivieska, Finland 14 D21 64 4N 24 28 E
Yngaren, Sweden 17 F10 58 50N 16 35 E
Yoakum, U.S.A. 155 L6 29 17N 97 9W
Yobe □, Nigeria 113 C7 12 0N 11 30 E
Yobuko, Japan 70 D1 33 32N 129 54 E
Yog Pt., Phil. 79 B6 14 6N 124 12 E
Yogan, Togo 113 D5 6 23N 1 30 E
Yoğuntaş, Turkey 51 E11 41 50N 27 4 E
Yogyakarta, Indonesia 79 G14 7 49 S 110 22 E
Yogyakarta □, Indonesia 85 D4 7 48 S 110 22 E
Yoho Nat. Park, Canada 142 C5 51 25N 116 30W
Yojoa, L. de, Honduras 164 D2 14 53N 88 0W
Yŏju, S. Korea 75 F14 37 20N 127 35 E
Yokadouma, Cameroon 114 B2 3 26N 14 55 E
Yōkaichiba, Japan 71 B12 35 42N 140 33 E
Yokkaichi, Japan 71 C8 34 55N 136 38 E
Yoko, Cameroon 113 D7 5 32N 12 20 E
Yokohama, Japan 71 B11 35 27N 139 28 E
Yokosuka, Japan 71 B11 35 20N 139 40 E
Yokote, Japan 68 E10 39 20N 140 30 E
Yola, Nigeria 113 D7 9 10N 12 29 E
Yolaina, Cordillera de, Nic. 164 D3 11 30N 84 0W
Yolombo, Dem. Rep. of the Congo 114 C4 1 36 S 23 12 E
Yoloten, Turkmenistan 97 B9 37 18N 62 21 E
Yom →, Thailand 78 A2 15 35N 100 1 E
Yombi, Gabon 114 C2 1 26 S 10 37 E
Yonago, Japan 70 B5 35 25N 133 19 E
Yonaguni-Jima, Japan 69 M1 24 27N 123 0 E
Yŏnan, N. Korea 75 F14 37 55N 126 11 E
Yonezawa, Japan 68 F10 37 57N 140 4 E
Yong Peng, Malaysia 87 L4 2 0N 103 3 E
Yong Sata, Thailand 87 J2 7 8N 99 41 E
Yongama, Dem. Rep. of the Congo 114 B4 0 2N 24 35 E
Yongamp'o, N. Korea 75 E13 39 56N 124 23 E
Yong'an, China 77 E11 25 59N 117 25 E
Yongcheng, China 74 H9 33 55N 116 20 E
Yŏngch'ŏn, S. Korea 75 G15 35 58N 128 56 E
Yongchuan, China 76 C5 29 17N 105 55 E
Yongchun, China 77 E12 25 16N 118 20 E
Yongde, China 76 E2 24 5N 99 25 E
Yongdeng, China 74 F2 36 38N 103 25 E
Yongding, China 77 E11 24 43N 116 45 E
Yŏngdŏk, S. Korea 75 F15 36 24N 129 22 E
Yŏngdŭngpo, S. Korea 75 F14 37 31N 126 54 E
Yongfeng, China 77 D10 27 20N 115 22 E
Yongfu, China 76 E7 24 59N 109 59 E
Yonghe, China 74 F6 36 46N 110 38 E
Yŏnghŭng, N. Korea 75 E14 39 31N 127 18 E
Yongji, China 74 G6 34 52N 110 28 E
Yongjia, China 77 C13 28 10N 120 45 E
Yŏngju, S. Korea 75 F15 36 50N 128 40 E
Yongkang, Yunnan, China 76 E2 24 9N 99 20 E
Yongkang, Zhejiang, China 77 C13 28 55N 120 2 E
Yongnian, China 74 F8 36 47N 114 29 E
Yongning, Guangxi Zhuangzu, China 76 F7 22 44N 108 28 E
Yongning, Ningxia Huizu, China 74 E4 38 15N 106 14 E
Yongping, China 76 E2 25 27N 99 38 E
Yongqing, China 74 E9 39 25N 116 28 E
Yongren, China 76 D3 26 4N 101 40 E
Yongshan, China 76 C4 28 11N 103 35 E
Yongsheng, China 76 D3 26 38N 100 46 E
Yongshun, China 76 C7 29 2N 109 51 E
Yongtai, China 77 E12 25 49N 118 58 E
Yŏngwŏl, S. Korea 75 F15 37 11N 128 28 E
Yongxing = Jinggangshan, China 77 D10 26 58N 114 15 E
Yongxing, China 77 D9 26 9N 113 8 E
Yongxiu, China 77 C10 29 2N 115 42 E
Yongzhou, China 77 D8 26 17N 111 37 E
Yonibana, S. Leone 112 D2 8 30N 12 19W
Yonkers, U.S.A. 151 F11 40 56N 73 54W
Yonne □, France 27 E10 47 50N 3 40 E
Yonne →, France 27 D9 48 23N 2 58 E
Yopal, Colombia 168 B3 5 21N 72 23W
York, Australia 125 F2 31 52 S 116 47 E
York, U.K. 20 D6 53 58N 1 6W
York, Ala., U.S.A. 155 J10 32 29N 88 18W
York, Nebr., U.S.A. 154 E6 40 52N 97 36W
York, Pa., U.S.A. 148 F7 39 58N 76 44W
York, C., Australia 126 A3 10 42 S 142 31 E
York, City of □, U.K. 20 D6 53 58N 1 6W
York, Kap, Greenland 10 B4 75 55N 66 25W
York, Vale of, U.K. 20 C6 54 15N 1 25W
York Haven, U.S.A. 150 F8 40 7N 76 46W
York Sd., Australia 124 C4 15 0 S 125 5 E
Yorke Pen., Australia 128 C2 34 50 S 137 40 E
Yorketown, Australia 127 F2 35 0 S 137 33 E
Yorkshire Wolds, U.K. 20 C7 54 8N 0 31W
Yorkton, Canada 143 C8 51 11N 102 28W
Yorkville, Calif., U.S.A. 160 G3 38 52N 123 13W
Yorkville, Ga., U.S.A. 152 B5 33 55N 84 58W
Yorkville, Ill., U.S.A. 157 C8 41 38N 88 27W
Yoro, Honduras 164 C2 15 9N 87 7W
Yoron-Jima, Japan 69 L4 27 2N 128 26 E
Yorosso, Mali 112 C4 12 17N 4 55W
Yos Sudarso, Pulau = Dolak, Pulau, Indonesia 79 F9 8 0 S 138 30 E
Yosemite National Park, U.S.A. 160 H7 37 45N 119 40W
Yosemite Village, U.S.A. 160 H7 37 45N 119 35W
Yoshii, Japan 70 D1 33 16N 129 46 E
Yoshimatsu, Japan 70 E2 32 0N 130 47 E
Yoshkar Ola, Russia 60 B8 56 38N 47 55 E
Yŏsu, S. Korea 75 G14 34 47N 127 45 E
Yotala, Bolivia 173 D4 19 10 S 65 17W
Yotvata, Israel 103 F4 29 55N 35 2 E
You Jiang →, China 76 F6 22 50N 108 6 E
You Xian, China 77 D9 27 1N 113 17 E
Youbou, Canada 160 B2 48 53N 124 13W
Youghal, Ireland 23 E4 51 56N 7 52W
Youghal B., Ireland 23 E4 51 55N 7 49W
Youkounkoun, Guinea 112 C2 12 35N 13 11W
Young, Australia 129 C8 34 19 S 148 18 E
Young, Canada 143 C7 51 47N 105 45W
Young, Uruguay 174 C4 32 44 S 57 36W
Young Ra., N.Z. 131 E4 44 10 S 169 30 E
Younghusband, L., Australia 128 A2 30 50 S 136 5 E
Younghusband Pen., Australia 128 D3 36 0 S 139 25 E
Youngstown, Canada 143 C6 51 35N 111 10W
Youngstown, Fla., U.S.A. 152 E4 30 22N 85 26W
Youngstown, N.Y., U.S.A. 150 C5 43 15N 79 3W
Youngstown, Ohio, U.S.A. 150 E4 41 6N 80 39W
Youngsville, U.S.A. 150 E5 41 51N 79 19W
Youngwood, U.S.A. 150 F5 40 14N 79 34W
Youssoufia, Morocco 110 B3 32 16N 8 31W
Youxi, China 77 D12 26 10N 118 13 E
Youyang, China 76 C7 28 47N 108 42 E
Youyu, China 74 D7 40 10N 112 20 E
Yowrie, Australia 129 D8 36 17 S 149 46 E
Yozgat, Turkey 100 C6 39 51N 34 47 E
Ypané →, Paraguay 174 A4 23 29 S 57 19W
Yport, France 26 C7 49 45N 0 15 E
Ypres = Ieper, Belgium 24 D2 50 51N 2 53 E
Ypsilanti, U.S.A. 157 B13 42 14N 83 37W
Yreka, U.S.A. 158 F2 41 44N 122 38W
Ysabel Chan., Papua N. G. 132 B5 2 0 S 150 0 E
Yssingeaux, France 29 C8 45 9N 4 8 E
Ystabø, Norway 18 E2 59 3N 5 23 E
Ystad, Sweden 17 J7 55 26N 13 50 E
Ysyk-Köl, Kyrgyzstan 63 B8 42 26N 76 12 E
Ysyk-Köl, Ozero, Kyrgyzstan 64 E8 42 25N 77 15 E
Ythan →, U.K. 22 D7 57 19N 1 59W
Ytre Arna, Norway 18 D2 60 27N 5 25 E
Ytre Enebakk, Norway 18 E8 59 44N 11 0 E
Ytre Rendal, Norway 18 C8 61 46N 11 8 E
Ytterhogdal, Sweden 16 B8 62 12N 14 56 E
Ytyk Kyuyel, Russia 65 C14 62 30N 133 45 E
Yu Jiang →, China 76 F7 23 22N 110 3 E
Yu Xian = Yuzhou, China 74 G7 34 10N 113 28 E
Yu Xian, Hebei, China 74 E8 39 50N 114 35 E
Yu Xian, Shanxi, China 74 E7 38 5N 113 20 E
Yuan Jiang →, Hunan, China 77 C8 28 55N 111 50 E
Yuan Jiang →, Yunnan, China 76 F4 22 20N 103 59 E
Yuan'an, China 77 B8 31 3N 111 34 E
Yuanjiang, Hunan, China 77 C9 28 47N 112 21 E
Yuanjiang, Yunnan, China 76 F4 23 32N 102 0 E
Yüanli, Taiwan 77 E13 24 27N 120 39 E
Yüanlin, Taiwan 77 F13 23 58N 120 30 E
Yuanling, China 77 C8 28 29N 110 22 E
Yuanmou, China 76 E3 25 42N 101 53 E
Yuanqu, China 74 G6 35 18N 111 40 E
Yuanyang, Henan, China 74 G7 35 3N 113 58 E
Yuanyang, Yunnan, China 76 F4 23 10N 102 43 E
Yuat →, Papua N. G. 132 C2 4 10 S 143 52 E
Yuba →, U.S.A. 160 F5 39 8N 121 36W
Yuba City, U.S.A. 160 F5 39 8N 121 37W
Yūbari, Japan 68 C10 43 4N 141 59 E
Yubdo, Ethiopia 107 F4 8 58N 35 24 E
Yūbetsu, Japan 68 B11 44 13N 143 50 E
Yubo, Sudan 107 F2 5 23N 27 25 E
Yucatán □, Mexico 163 C7 21 30N 86 30W
Yucatán, Canal de, Caribbean 164 B2 22 0N 86 30W
Yucatán, Península de, Mexico 136 H11 19 30N 89 0W
Yucatán Basin, Cent. Amer. 136 H11 19 0N 86 0W
Yucatan Str. = Yucatán, Canal de, Caribbean 164 B2 22 0N 86 30W
Yucca, U.S.A. 161 L12 34 52N 114 9W
Yucca Valley, U.S.A. 161 L10 34 8N 116 27W
Yucheng, China 74 F9 36 55N 116 32 E
Yuci, China 74 F7 37 42N 112 46 E
Yudu, China 77 E10 25 59N 115 30 E
Yuechi, China 76 B6 30 34N 106 25 E
Yuendumu, Australia 124 D5 22 16 S 131 49 E
Yueqing, China 77 C13 28 9N 120 59 E
Yueqing Wan, China 77 D13 28 5N 121 20 E
Yuexi, Anhui, China 77 B11 30 50N 116 20 E
Yuexi, Sichuan, China 76 C4 28 37N 102 26 E
Yueyang, China 77 C9 29 21N 113 5 E
Yufu-Dake, Japan 70 D3 33 17N 131 33 E
Yugan, China 77 C11 28 43N 116 37 E
Yugoslavia ■, Europe 50 C4 43 20N 20 0 E
Yuhuan, China 77 C13 28 9N 121 12 E
Yühuan Dao, China 77 C13 28 5N 121 15 E
Yujiang, China 77 C11 28 10N 116 43 E
Yukhnov, Russia 58 E8 54 44N 35 15 E
Yūki, Japan 71 A11 36 18N 139 53 E
Yukon →, U.S.A. 138 B3 62 32N 163 54W
Yukon Territory □, Canada 138 B6 63 0N 135 0W
Yüksekova, Turkey 101 D11 37 34N 44 16 E
Yukta, Russia 65 C11 63 26N 105 42 E
Yukuhashi, Japan 70 D2 33 44N 130 59 E
Yulara, Australia 125 E5 25 10 S 130 55 E
Yule →, Australia 124 D2 20 41 S 118 17 E
Yuleba, Australia 127 D4 26 37 S 149 24 E
Yulee, U.S.A. 152 E8 30 38N 81 36W
Yuli, Nigeria 113 D7 9 44N 10 12 E
Yuli, Taiwan 77 F13 23 20N 121 18 E
Yulin, Guangxi Zhuangzu, China 77 F8 22 40N 110 8 E
Yülin, Hainan, China 87 C7 18 10N 109 31 E
Yulin, Shaanxi, China 74 E5 38 20N 109 30 E
Yuma, Ariz., U.S.A. 161 N12 32 43N 114 37W
Yuma, Colo., U.S.A. 154 E3 40 8N 102 43W
Yuma, B. de, Dom. Rep. 165 C6 18 20N 68 35W
Yumali, Australia 128 C3 35 32 S 139 45 E
Yumbe, Uganda 118 B3 3 28N 31 15 E
Yumbi, Dem. Rep. of the Congo 114 C3 1 53 S 16 34 E
Yumbi, Dem. Rep. of the Congo 118 C2 1 12 S 26 15 E
Yumbo, Colombia 168 C2 3 35N 76 28W
Yumen, China 72 C4 39 50N 97 30 E
Yumurtalık, Turkey 100 D6 36 45N 35 43 E
Yun Gui Gaoyuan, China 76 E3 26 0N 104 0 E
Yun Ho →, China 75 E9 39 10N 117 10 E
Yun Ling, China 76 D2 27 0N 99 20 E
Yun Xian, Hubei, China 77 A8 32 50N 110 46 E
Yun Xian, Yunnan, China 76 E3 24 27N 100 8 E
Yuna, Australia 125 E2 28 20 S 115 0 E
Yunak, Turkey 100 C4 38 49N 31 43 E
Yunan, China 77 F8 23 12N 111 30 E
Yuncheng, Henan, China 74 G8 35 36N 115 57 E
Yuncheng, Shanxi, China 74 G6 35 2N 111 0 E
Yunfu, China 77 F9 22 50N 112 5 E
Yungas, Bolivia 173 D4 17 0 S 66 0W
Yungay, Chile 174 D1 37 10 S 72 5W
Yungay, Peru 172 B2 9 2 S 77 45W
Yunhe, China 77 C12 28 8N 119 33 E
Yunkai Dashan, China 77 F8 22 30N 111 0 E
Yunlin, Taiwan 77 F13 23 42N 120 30 E
Yunlong, China 76 E2 25 57N 99 13 E
Yunmeng, China 77 B9 31 2N 113 43 E
Yunnan □, China 76 E4 25 0N 102 0 E
Yunomae, Japan 70 E2 32 12N 130 59 E
Yunotso, Japan 70 B4 35 5N 132 21 E
Yunquera de Henares, Spain 40 E1 40 47N 3 11W
Yunt Dağı, Turkey 49 C9 38 56N 27 13 E
Yunta, Australia 128 B3 32 34 S 139 36 E
Yunxi, China 74 H6 33 0N 110 22 E
Yunxiao, China 77 F11 23 59N 117 18 E
Yuping, China 76 D7 27 13N 108 56 E
Yupukarri, Guyana 169 C6 3 45N 59 20W
Yupyongdong, N. Korea 75 D15 41 49N 128 53 E
Yuqing, China 76 D6 27 13N 107 53 E
Yurga, Russia 64 D9 55 42N 84 51 E
Yurimaguas, Peru 172 B2 5 55 S 76 7W
Yurla, Russia 62 B5 59 22N 54 21 E
Yurya, Russia 62 B2 59 1N 49 13 E
Yuryev-Polskiy, Russia 58 D10 56 30N 39 40 E
Yuryevets, Russia 60 B6 57 25N 43 2 E
Yuryung Kaya, Russia 65 B12 72 48N 113 23 E
Yuryuzan, Russia 62 D7 54 57N 58 26 E
Yuscarán, Honduras 164 D2 13 58N 86 45W
Yushan, China 77 C12 28 42N 118 10 E
Yushanzhen, China 76 C7 29 28N 108 22 E
Yushe, China 74 F7 37 4N 112 58 E
Yushu, Jilin, China 75 B14 44 43N 126 38 E
Yushu, Qinghai, China 72 C4 33 5N 96 55 E
Yusufeli, Turkey 101 B9 40 50N 41 33 E
Yutai, China 74 G9 35 0N 116 45 E
Yutian, China 75 E9 39 53N 117 45 E
Yuxarı Qarabağ = Nagorno-Karabakh, Azerbaijan 101 C12 39 55N 46 45 E
Yuxi, China 76 E4 24 30N 102 35 E
Yuyao, China 77 B13 30 3N 121 10 E
Yuzawa, Japan 68 E10 39 10N 140 30 E
Yuzha, Russia 60 B6 56 34N 42 1 E
Yuzhno-Sakhalinsk, Russia 65 E15 46 58N 142 45 E
Yuzhno-Surkhanskoye Vdkhr., Uzbekistan 63 E3 37 53N 67 42 E
Yuzhnouralsk, Russia 62 D8 54 26N 61 15 E
Yuzhou, China 74 G7 34 10N 113 28 E
Yvelines □, France 27 D8 48 40N 1 45 E
Yverdon-les-Bains, Switz. 32 C3 46 47N 6 39 E
Yvetot, France 26 C7 49 37N 0 44 E
Yvonand, Switz. 32 C3 46 48N 6 44 E
Yzeure, France 27 F10 46 33N 3 22 E

Z

Zaalayskiy Khrebet, Asia 63 D6 39 20N 73 0 E
Zaanstad, Neths. 24 B4 52 27N 4 50 E
Zab, Monts du, Algeria 111 B6 34 55N 5 0 E
Zāb al Kabīr →, Iraq 101 D10 36 1N 43 24 E
Zāb aş Şagīr →, Iraq 101 E10 35 17N 43 29 E
Žabalj, Serbia, Yug. 52 E5 45 21N 20 5 E
Žabari, Serbia, Yug. 50 B5 44 22N 21 15 E
Zabarjad, Egypt 106 C4 23 40N 36 12 E
Zabaykalsk, Russia 65 E12 49 40N 117 25 E
Zabid, Yemen 98 D3 14 0N 43 10 E
Zabīd, W. →, Yemen 98 D3 14 7N 43 6 E
Zabki, Poland 55 F8 52 17N 21 7 E
Ząbkowice Śląskie, Poland 55 H3 50 35N 16 50 E
Žabljak, Montenegro, Yug. 50 C3 43 18N 19 5 E
Żabłudów, Poland 55 F9 53 0N 23 19 E
Žabno, Poland 55 H7 50 9N 20 53 E
Zābol, Iran 97 D9 31 0N 61 32 E
Zābol □, Afghan. 91 B2 32 0N 67 0 E
Zābolī, Iran 97 E9 27 10N 61 35 E
Zabré, Burkina Faso 113 C4 11 12N 0 36W
Zábřeh, Czech Rep. 35 B9 49 53N 16 52 E
Zabrze, Poland 55 H5 50 18N 18 50 E
Zabzuga, Ghana 113 D5 9 20N 0 30 E
Zacapa, Guatemala 164 D2 14 59N 89 31W
Zacapu, Mexico 162 D4 19 50N 101 43W
Zacatecas, Mexico 162 C4 22 49N 102 34W
Zacatecas □, Mexico 162 C4 23 30N 103 0W
Zacatecoluca, El Salv. 164 D2 13 29N 88 51W
Zachary, U.S.A. 155 K9 30 39N 91 9W
Zachodnio-Pomorskie □, Poland 54 E2 53 40N 15 50 E
Zacoalco, Mexico 162 C4 20 14N 103 33W
Zacualtipán, Mexico 163 C5 20 39N 98 36W
Zadar, Croatia 45 D12 44 8N 15 14 E
Zadawa, Nigeria 113 C7 11 33N 10 19 E
Zadetkyi Kyun, Burma 78 C1 10 0N 98 25 E
Zadonsk, Russia 59 F10 52 25N 38 56 E
Zafarqand, Iran 97 C7 33 11N 52 29 E
Zafora, Greece 49 E8 36 5N 26 24 E
Zafra, Spain 43 G4 38 26N 6 30W
Żagań, Poland 55 G2 51 39N 15 22 E
Žagarė, Lithuania 54 B10 56 21N 23 15 E
Zagazig, Egypt 106 H7 30 40N 31 30 E
Zāgheh, Iran 97 C6 33 30N 48 42 E
Zaghouan, Tunisia 108 A2 36 23N 10 10 E
Zaglivérion, Greece 50 F7 40 36N 23 15 E
Zaglou, Algeria 111 C4 27 17N 0 3W
Zagnanado, Benin 113 D5 7 18N 2 28 E
Zagorá, Greece 48 B5 39 27N 23 6 E
Zagora, Morocco 110 B3 30 22N 5 51W
Zagorje, Slovenia 45 B11 46 8N 15 0 E
Zagórów, Poland 55 F4 52 10N 17 54 E
Zagorsk = Sergiyev Posad, Russia 58 D10 56 20N 38 10 E
Zagórz, Poland 55 J9 49 30N 22 14 E
Zagreb, Croatia 45 C12 45 50N 15 58 E
Zāgros, Kūhhā-ye, Iran 97 C6 33 45N 48 5 E
Zagros Mts. = Zāgros, Kūhhā-ye, Iran 97 C6 33 45N 48 5 E
Žagubica, Serbia, Yug. 50 B5 44 15N 21 47 E
Zaguinaso, Ivory C. 112 C3 10 1N 6 14W
Zagyva →, Hungary 52 C5 47 5N 20 4 E
Zāhedān, Fārs, Iran 97 D7 28 46N 53 52 E
Zāhedān, Sīstān va Balūchestān, Iran 97 D9 29 30N 60 50 E
Zahirabad, India 94 F3 17 43N 77 37 E
Zahlah, Lebanon 103 B4 33 52N 35 50 E
Zahna, Germany 30 D8 51 55N 12 49 E
Záhony, Hungary 52 B7 48 25N 22 11 E
Zahrez Chergui, Algeria 111 A5 35 11N 3 11 E
Zahrez Rharbi, Algeria 111 B5 34 50N 2 55 E
Zailiyskiy Alatau, Khrebet, Kazakstan 63 B8 43 5N 77 0 E
Zainsk, Russia 60 C11 55 18N 52 4 E
Zaïre = Congo →, Africa 115 D2 6 4 S 12 24 E
Zaire □, Angola 115 D2 7 0 S 14 0 E
Zaječar, Serbia, Yug. 50 C6 43 53N 22 18 E
Zaka, Zimbabwe 117 C5 20 20 S 31 29 E
Zakamensk, Russia 65 D11 50 23N 103 17 E
Zakani, Dem. Rep. of the Congo 114 B4 2 33N 23 16 E
Zakataly = Zaqatala, Azerbaijan 61 K8 41 38N 46 35 E
Zakbayemé, Cameroon 114 B2 4 2N 10 34 E
Zakháro, Greece 48 D3 37 30N 21 39 E
Zakhodnaya Dzvina = Daugava →, Latvia 15 H21 57 4N 24 3 E
Zākhū, Iraq 101 D10 37 10N 42 50 E
Zákinthos, Greece 48 D2 37 47N 20 57 E
Zákinthos □, Greece 48 D2 37 47N 20 57 E
Zakopane, Poland 55 J6 49 18N 19 57 E
Zakroczym, Poland 55 F7 52 26N 20 38 E
Zákros, Greece 38 D8 35 6N 26 10 E
Zala, Angola 115 D2 7 52 S 13 42 E
Zala, Ethiopia 107 F4 6 28N 37 13 E
Zala □, Hungary 52 D1 46 42N 16 50 E
Zala →, Hungary 52 D2 46 43N 17 16 E
Zalaegerszeg, Hungary 52 D1 46 53N 16 47 E
Zalakomár, Hungary 52 D2 46 33N 17 10 E
Zalalövő, Hungary 52 D1 46 51N 16 35 E
Zalamea de la Serena, Spain 43 G5 38 40N 5 38W
Zalamea la Real, Spain 43 H4 37 41N 6 38W
Zalău, Romania 52 C8 47 12N 23 3 E
Zalazna, Russia 62 B4 58 39N 52 31 E
Žalec, Slovenia 45 B12 46 16N 15 10 E
Zaleshchiki = Zalishchyky, Ukraine 59 H3 48 45N 25 45 E
Zalew Wiślany, Poland 54 D6 54 20N 19 50 E
Zalewo, Poland 54 E6 53 50N 19 41 E
Zalim, Si. Arabia 98 B3 22 43N 42 10 E
Zalingei, Sudan 109 F4 12 51N 23 29 E
Zalishchyky, Ukraine 59 H3 48 45N 25 45 E
Zaltan, Jabal, Libya 108 C3 28 46N 19 45 E
Zama L., Canada 142 B5 58 45N 119 5W
Zamaro →, Ecuador 168 D2 2 59N 78 13W
Zambales □, Phil. 80 D3 15 20N 120 10 E
Zambales Mts., Phil. 80 D3 15 45N 120 5 E
Zambeke, Dem. Rep. of the Congo 118 B2 2 8N 25 17 E
Zambeze →, Africa 119 F4 18 35 S 36 20 E
Zambezi = Zambeze →, Africa 119 F4 18 35 S 36 20 E
Zambezi, Zambia 115 E4 13 30 S 23 15 E
Zambezia □, Mozam. 119 F4 16 15 S 37 30 E
Zambia ■, Africa 119 F2 15 0 S 28 0 E
Zamboanga, Phil. 79 C6 6 59N 122 3 E
Zamboanga del Norte □, Phil. 81 H4 8 0N 123 0 E
Zamboanga del Sur □, Phil. 81 H4 7 40N 123 0 E
Zambrano, Colombia 168 B3 9 45N 74 49W
Zambrów, Poland 55 F9 52 59N 22 14 E
Zametchino, Russia 60 D6 53 30N 42 30 E
Zamfara □, Nigeria 113 C6 12 10N 6 0 E
Zamfara →, Nigeria 113 C5 12 5N 4 2 E
Zamora, Ecuador 168 D2 4 4 S 78 58W

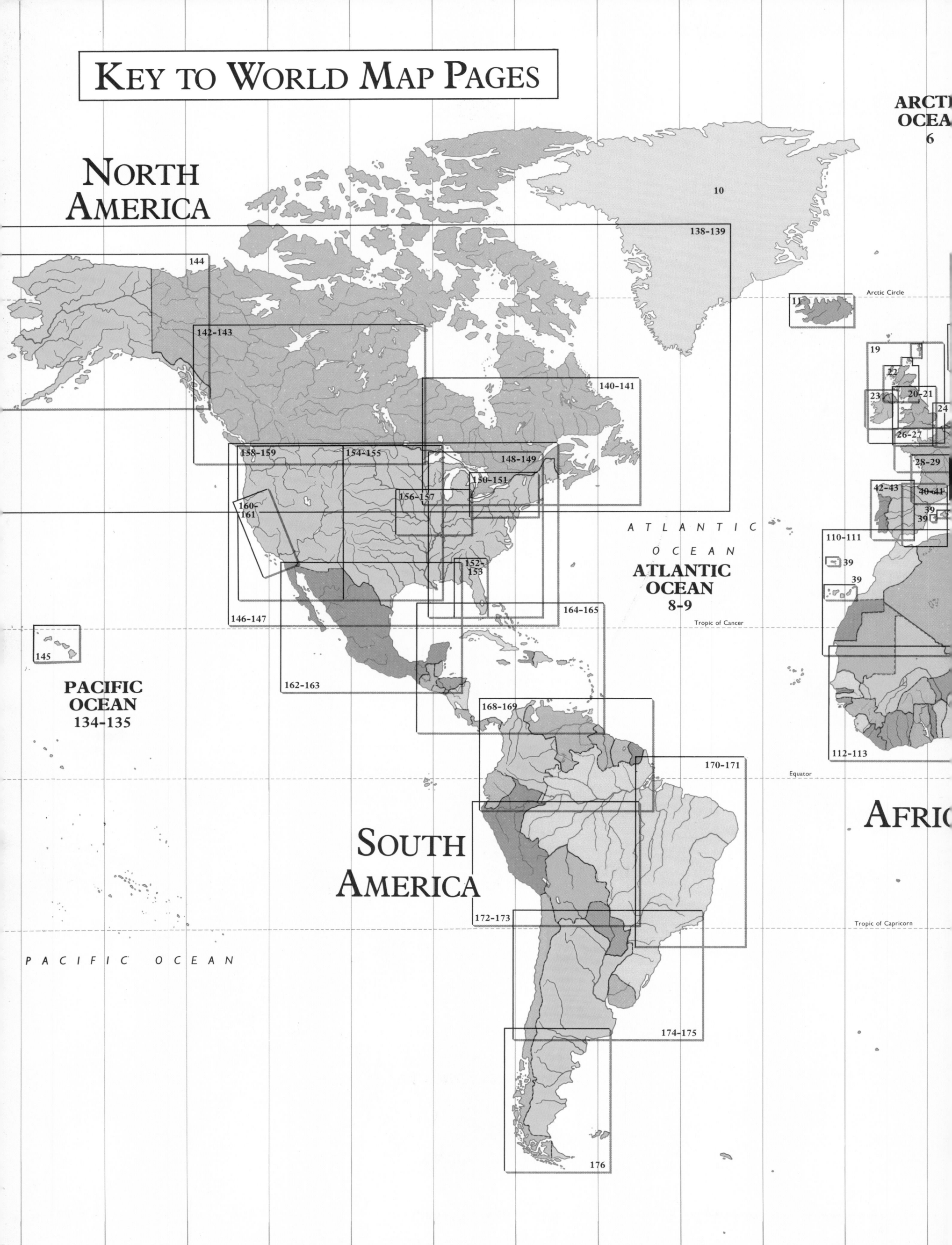

KEY TO WORLD MAP PAGES

NORTH
AMERICA

ARCTIC
OCEAN
6

10

138-139

144

142-143

Arctic Circle

11

19

140-141

22

23   20-21

24

158-159   154-155   148-149   26-27

150-151   28-29

156-157   42-43   40-41

160-161   39   39

ATLANTIC   110-111

OCEAN   39

ATLANTIC   39
OCEAN
8-9

152-153

146-147   Tropic of Cancer

162-163   164-165   112-113

PACIFIC
OCEAN   145
134-135   168-169

170-171   Equator

AFRIC

SOUTH
AMERICA   172-173   Tropic of Capricorn

PACIFIC   OCEAN   174-175

176